Marshall, Dexter.

Presented by his mother
1879.

Julia D. Stowman
Inherited
from Marshall.
1886.

NEW YORK.
Harper & Brothers.

THE

WORKS

OF

WILLIAM SHAKSPEARE.

VOL. I.

NEW-YORK.
Harper & Brothers.

THE

DRAMATIC WORKS AND POEMS

OF

WILLIAM SHAKSPEARE,

WITH

NOTES,

ORIGINAL AND SELECTED, AND INTRODUCTORY REMARKS TO EACH PLAY

BY

SAMUEL WELLER SINGER, F.S.A.

AND

A LIFE OF THE POET,

BY

CHARLES SYMMONS, D.D.

IN TWO VOLUMES.

I.

NEW YORK:
HARPER & BROTHERS, PUBLISHERS,
329 & 331 PEARL STREET,
FRANKLIN SQUARE.
1871.

EDITOR'S PREFACE.

CAN it be wondered at (says Mr. Gifford) that Shakspeare should swell into twenty or even twice twenty volumes, when the latest editor (like the wind Cecias) constantly draws round him the floating errors of all his predecessors ?' Upwards of twenty years ago, when the evil was not so great as it has since become, Steevens confessed that there was an 'exuberance of comment,' arising from the 'ambition in each little Hercules to set up pillars ascertaining how far he had travelled through the dreary wilds of black letter;' so that there was some danger of readers being 'frighted away from Shakspeare, as the soldiers of Cato deserted their comrade when he became bloated with poison—crescens fugere cadaver.' He saw with a prophetic eye that the evil must cure itself, and that the time would arrive when some of this ivy must be removed, which only served to 'hide the princely trunk, and suck the verdure out of it.'

This expurgatory task has been more than once undertaken, but has never hitherto, it is believed, been executed entirely to the satisfaction of the admirers of our great Poet: and the work has even now devolved upon one who, though not wholly unprepared for it by previous studies, has perhaps manifested his presumption in undertaking it 'with weak and unexamined shoulders.' He does not, however, shrink from a comparison with the labours of his predecessors, but would rather solicit that equitable mode of being judged; and will patiently, and with all becoming submission to the decision of a competent tribunal, abide the result.

As a new candidate for public favour, it may be expected that the Editor should explain the ground of his pretensions. The object then of the present publication is to afford the general reader a correct edition of Shakspeare, accompanied by an abridged commentary, in which all superfluous and refuted explanations and conjectures, and all the controversies and squabbles of contending critics should be omitted; and such elucidations only of obsolete words and obscure phrases, and such critical illustrations of the text as might be deemed most generally useful be retained. To effect this it has been necessary, for the sake of compression, to condense in some cases several pages of excursive discussion into a few lines, and often to blend together the information conveyed in the notes of several commentators into one. When these explanations are mere transcripts or abridgments of the labours of his predecessors, and are unaccompanied by any observation of his own, it will of course be understood that the Editor intends to imply by silent 'acquiescence that he has nothing better to propose.' Fortune, however, seems to have been propitious to his labours, for he flatters himself that he has been enabled in many instances to present the reader with more satisfactory explanations of difficult passages, and with more exact definitions of obsolete words and phrases, than are to be found in the notes to the variorum editions.

The causes which have operated to overwhelm the pages of Shaskpeare with superfluous notes are many; but Steevens, though eminently fitted for the task he undertook, was chiefly instrumental in increasing the evil. He has indeed been happily designated 'the Puck of commentators;' he frequently wrote notes, not with the view of illustrating the Poet, but for the purpose of misleading Malone, and of enjoying the pleasure of turning against him that playful ridicule which he knew so well how to direct. Steevens, like Malone, began his career as an Editor of Shakspeare with scrupulous attention to the old copies, but when he once came to entertain some jealousy of Malone's intrusion into his province, he all at once shifted his ground, and adopted maxims entirely opposed to those which guided his rival editor. Upon a recent perusal of a considerable portion of the correspondence between them, one letter seemed to display the circumstances which led to the interruption of their intimacy in so clear a light, and to explain the causes which have so unnecessarily swelled the comments on Shakspeare, that it has been thought not unworthy of the reader's attention. The letter has no date:—

'Sir,—I am at present so much harassed with private business that it is not in my power to afford you the long and regular answer which your letter deserves. Permit me, however, to desert order and propriety, replying to your last sentence first.—I assure you that I only erased the word *friend* because, considering how much controversy was to follow, that distinction seemed to be out of its place, and appeared to carry with it somewhat of a burlesque air. Such was my single motive for the change, and I hope you will do me the honour to believe I had no other design in it.

'As it is some time since my opinions have had the good fortune to coincide with yours in the least matter of consequence, I begin to think so indifferently of my own judgment, that I am ready to give it up without reluctance on the present occasion.—You are at liberty to leave out whatever parts of my note you please. However we may privately disagree, there is no reason why we should make sport for the world, for such is the only effect of public controversies; neither should I have leisure at present to pursue such an undertaking. I only meant to do justice to myself; and as I had no opportunity of replying to your reiterated contradictions in their natural order, on account of your perpetual additions to them; I thought myself under the necessity of observing, that I ought not to be suspected of being impotently silent in regard to objections which I had never read till it was too late for any replication on my side to be made. You rely much on the authority of an editor; but till I am convinced that volunteers are to be treated with less indulgence than other soldiers, I shall still think I have some right at least to be disgusted especially after I had been permitted to observe that truth, not victory, was the object of our critical warfare.

'As for the note at the conclusion of The Puritan, since it gives so much offence, (an offence as undesigned as unforeseen,) I will change a part of it, and subjoin reasons for my dissent both from you and Mr. Tyrwhitt. You cannot surely suspect me of having wished to commence hostilities with either of you; but you have made a very singular comment on this remark indeed. Because I have said I could overturn some of both your arguments on other occasions with ease, you are willing to infer that I meant all of them. Let me ask, for instance sake, what would become of his "undertakers," &c. were I to advance all I could on that subject. I will not offend you by naming any particular position of your own which could with success be disputed. I cannot, however, help adding, that had I followed every sentence of your attempt to ascertain the order of the plays, with a contradiction sedulous and unremitted as that with which you have pursued my Observations on Shakspeare's Will and his Sonnets, you at least would not have found your undertaking a very comfortable one. I was then an editor, and indulged you with even a printed foul copy of your work, which you enlarged as long as you thought fit.—The arrival of people on business prevents me from adding more than that I hope to be still indulged with the correction of my own notes on the Y[orkshire] T[ragedy]. I expect almost every one of them to be disputed, but assure you that I will not add a single word by way of reply. I have not returned you so complete an answer as I would have done had I been at leisure. You have, however, the real sentiments of your most humble servant, G. STEEVENS.'

The temper in which this letter was written is obvious. Steevens was at the time assisting Malone in preparing his Supplement to Shakspeare, and had previously made a liberal present to him of his valuable collection of old plays; he afterwards called himself 'a dowager editor,' and said he would never more trouble himself about Shakspeare. This is gathered from a memorandum by Malone, but Steevens does in effect say in one of his letters; adding, 'Nor will such assistance as I may be able to furnish ever go towards any future *gratuitous* publication of the same author: ingratitude and impertinence from several booksellers have been my reward for conducting two laborious editions, both of which, except a few copies, are already sold.'

In another letter, in reply to a remonstrance about the suspension of his visits to Malone, Steevens says:—'I will confess to you without reserve the cause why I have not made even my business submit to my desire of seeing you. I readily allow that any distinct and subjoined reply to my remarks on your notes is fair; but to change (in consequence of private conversation) the notes that drew from me those remarks, is to turn my own weapons against me. Surely, therefore, it is unnecessary to let me continue building when you are previously determined to destroy my very foundations. As I observed to you yesterday, the result of this proceeding would be, that such of my strictures as might be just on the first copies of your notes, must often prove no better than idle cavils, when applied to the second and amended editions of them. I know not that any editor has insisted on the very extensive privileges which you have continued to claim. In some parts of my Dissertation on Pericles, I am almost reduced to combat with shadows. We had resolved (as I once imagined) to proceed without reserve on either side through the whole of that controversy, but finally you acquainted me with your resolution (in right of editorship) to have the last word. However, for the future, I beg I may be led to trouble you only with observations relative to notes which are *fixed* ones. I had that advantage over my predecessors, and you have enjoyed the same over me; but I never yet possessed the means of obviating objections before they could be effectually made,' &c.

Here then is the secret developed of the subsequent, unceasing, and unrelenting opposition with which Steevens opposed Malone's notes: their controversies served not 'to make sport for the world,' but to annoy the admirers of Shakspeare, by overloading his page with frivolous contention. Steevens had undoubtedly, as he says of himself on another occasion—

'Fallen in the plash his wickedness had made;'

and in some instances contested the force and propriety of his own remarks when applied by Malone to parallel passages; or, as Malone observes: 'They are very good remarks, so far forth as they are his; but when used by me are good for nothing, and the disputed passages become printers' blunders, or Hemingisms and Condelisms.' Hence his unremitted censure of the first folio copy, and support of the readings of the second folio, which Malone treats as of no authority;—his affected contempt for the Poems of Shakspeare, &c.

Mr. Boswell has judiciously characterized Steevens:—'With great diligence, an extensive acquaintance with early literature, and a remarkably retentive memory: he was besides, as Mr. Gifford has justly observed, "a wit and a scholar." But his wit and the sprightliness of his style were too often employed to bewilder and mislead us. His consciousness of his own satirical powers made him much too fond of exercising them at the expense of truth and justice. He was infected to a lamentable degree with the jealousy of authorship; and while his approbation was readily bestowed upon those whose competition he thought he had no reason to dread, he was fretfully impatient of a brother near the throne: his clear understanding would generally have enabled him to discover what was right; but the spirit of contradiction could at any time induce him to maintain what was wrong. It would be impossible, indeed, to explain how any one, possessed of his taste and discernment, could have brought himself to advocate so many indefensible opinions, without entering into a long and ungracious history of the motives by which he was influenced.'

Malone was certainly not so happily gifted, though Mr. Boswell's partiality in delineating his friend, presents us with the picture of an amiable and accomplished gentleman and scholar. There seems to have been a want of grasp in his mind to make proper use of the accumulated materials which his unwearied industry in his favourite pursuit had placed within his reach: his notes on Shakspeare are often tediously circumlocutory and ineffectual: neither does he seem to have been deficient in that jealousy of rivalship, or that pertinacious adherence to his own opinions, which have been attributed to his competitor.

It is superfluous here to enlarge on this topic, for the merits and defects of Johnson, Steevens, and Malone, as commentators on Shakspeare, and the characters of those who preceded them, the reader will find sketched with a masterly pen in the Biographical Preface of Dr. Symmons, which accompanies this edition. The vindication of Shakspeare from idle calumny and ill founded critical animadversion, could not have been placed in better hands than in those of the vindicator of Milton; and his eloquent Essay must afford pleasure to every lover of our immortal Bard. It should be observed that the Editor, in his adoption of readings, differs in opinion on some points from his able coadjutor, with whom he has not the honour of a personal acquaintance. It is to be regretted that no part of the work was communicated to Dr. Symmons until nearly the whole of the Plays were printed; or the Editor and the Public would doubtless have benefited by his animadversions and suggestions in its progress through the press. The reader will not therefore be surprised at the preliminary censure of some readings which are still retained in the text.

Dr. Johnson's far famed Preface—which has so long hung as a dead weight upon the reputation of our great Poet, and which has been justly said to look like 'a laborious attempt to bury the characteristic merits of his author under a load of cumbrous phraseology, and to weigh his excellencies and defects in equal scales stuffed full of swelling figures and sonorous epithets,'—will, for obvious reasons, form no part of this publication. His brie strictures at the end of each play have been retained in compliance with custom, but not without an occasional note of dissent. We may suppose that Johnson himself did not estimate these observations very highly, for he tells us that 'in the plays which are condemned there may be much to be praised, and in those which are praised much to be condemned!' Far be it from us to undervalue or speak slightingly of our great moralist; but his most strenuous admirers must acknowledge that the construction of his mind incapacitated him from forming a true judgment of the creations of one who was 'of imagination all compact,' no less than his physical defects prevented him from relishing the beautiful and harmonious in nature and art.

'Quid valet ad surdas si cantet Phemius aures?
Quid cæcum Thamyram picta tabella juvat?'

It has been the studious endeavour of the Editor to avoid those splenetic and insulting reflections upon the errors of the commentators, where it has been his good fortune to detect them, which have been sometimes too captiously indulged in by labourers in this field of verbal criticism. Indeed it would ill become him to speak contemptuously of those who, with all their defects, have deserved the gratitude of the age; for it is chiefly owing to the labours of Tyrwhitt, Warton, Percy, Steevens, Farmer, and their successors, that attention has been drawn to the mine of wealth which our early literature affords; and no one will affect to deny that a recurrence to it has not been attended with beneficial effects, if it has not raised us in the moral scale of nations.

The plan pursued in the selection, abridgment, and concentration of the notes of others, precluded the necessity of affixing the names of the commentators from whom the information was borrowed; and, excepting in a few cases of controversial discussion, and of some critical observations, authorities are not given. The very curious and valuable Illustrations of Shakspeare by Mr. Douce have been laid under frequent contribution; the obligation has not always been expressed; and it is therefore here acknowledged with thankfulness.

It will be seen that the Editor has not thought, with some of his predecessors, that the text of Shakspeare was 'fixed' in any particular edition beyond the hope or probability of future amendment.' He has rather coincided with the opinion of Mr. Gifford, 'that those would deserve well of the public who should bring back some readings which Steevens discarded, and reject others which he has adopted.'

The text of the present edition is formed upon those of Steevens and Malone, occasionally compared with the early editions; and the satisfaction arising from a rejection of modern unwarranted deviations from the old copies has not unfrequently been the reward of this labour.

The preliminary remarks to each play are augmented with extracts from the more recent writers upon Shakspeare, and generally contain brief critical observations which are in many instances opposed to the dictum of Dr. Johnson. Some of these are extracted from the Lectures on the Drama, by the distinguished German critic, A. W. Schleghel, a writer to whom the nation is deeply indebted, for having pointed out the characteristic excellencies of the great Poet of nature, in an eloquent and philosophical spirit of criticism; which, though it may sometimes be thought a little tinctured with mystical enthusiasm, has dealt out to Shakspeare his due meed of praise; and has, no doubt, tended to dissipate the prejudices of some neighbouring nations who have been too long wilfully blind to his merits.

Mr. Gifford, as it appears, once proposed to favour the public with an edition of Shakspeare: how admirably that excellent critic would have performed the task the world need not now be told. The Editor, who has been frequently indebted to the remarks on the language of our great Poet which occur in the notes to the works of Ben Jonson and Massinger, may be permitted to anticipate the public regret that these humble labours were not presented by that more skilful hand. As it is, he must console himself with having used his best endeavour to accomplish the task which he was solicited to undertake; had his power equalled his desire to render it useful and acceptable, the work would have been more worthy of the public favour, and of the Poet whom he and all unite in idolizing—

'——— The bard of every age and clime,
Of genius fruitful and of soul sublime,
Who, from the flowing mint of fancy, pours
No spurious metal, fused from common ores,
But gold, to matchless purity refin'd,
And stamp'd with all the godhead in his mind;
He whom I feel, but want the power to paint'

JUVENAL, SAT. VII. *Mr. Gifford's Translation.*

MICKLEHAM,
Dec. 3, 1825.

THE LIFE

OF

WILLIAM SHAKSPEARE,

WITH SOME

REMARKS UPON HIS DRAMATIC WRITINGS.

WHEREVER any extraordinary display of human intellect has been made, there will human curiosity, at one period or the other, be busy to obtain some personal acquaintance with the distinguished mortal whom Heaven had been pleased to endow with a larger portion of its own ethereal energy. If the favoured man walked on the high places of the world; if he were conversant with courts; if he directed the movements of armies or of states, and thus held in his hand the fortunes and the lives of multitudes of his fellow-creatures, the interest, which he excites, will be immediate and strong: he stands on an eminence where he is the mark of many eyes; and dark and unlettered indeed must be the age in which the incidents of his eventful life will not be noted, and the record of them be preserved for the instruction or the entertainment of unborn generations. But if his course were through the vale of life: if he were unmingled with the factions and the contests of the great: if the powers of his mind were devoted to the silent pursuits of literature—to the converse of philosophy and the Muse, the possessor of the ethereal treasure may excite little of the attention of his contemporaries; may walk quietly, with a veil over his glories, to the grave; and, in other times, when the expansion of his intellectual greatness has filled the eyes of the world, it may be too late to inquire for his history as a man. The bright track of his genius indelibly remains; but the trace of his mortal footstep is soon obliterated for ever. Homer is now only a name—a solitary name, which assures us, that, at some unascertained period in the annals of mankind, a mighty mind was indulged to a human being, and gave its wonderful productions to the perpetual admiration of men, as they spring in succession in the path of time. Of Homer himself we actually know nothing; and we see only an arm of immense power thrust forth from a mass of impenetrable darkness, and holding up the hero of his song to the applauses of never-dying fame. But it may be supposed that the revolution of, perhaps, thirty centuries has collected the cloud which thus withdraws the father of poesy from our sight. Little more than two centuries has elapsed since William Shakspeare conversed with our tongue, and trod the selfsame soil with ourselves; and if it were not for the records kept by our Church in its registers of births, marriages, and burials, we should at this moment be as personally ignorant of the "sweet swan of Avon" as we are of the old minstrel and rhapsodist of Meles. That William Shakspeare was born in Stratford upon Avon; that he married and had three children; that he wrote a certain number of dramas; that he died before he had attained to old age, and was buried in his native town, are positively the only facts, in the personal history of this extraordinary man, of which we are certainly possessed; and, if we should be solicitous to fill up this bare and most unsatisfactory outline, we must have recourse to the vague reports of unsubstantial tradition, or to the still more shadowy inferences of lawless and vagabond conjecture. Of this remarkable ignorance of one of the most richly endowed with intellect of the human species, who ran his mortal race in our own country, and who stands separated from us by no very great intervention of time, the causes may not be difficult to be ascertained. William Shakspeare was an actor and a writer of plays; in neither of which characters, however he might excel in them, could he be lifted high in the estimation of his contemporaries. He was honoured, indeed, with the friendship of nobles, and the patronage of monarchs. his theatre was frequented by the wits of the metropolis; and he associated with the most intellectual of his times. But the spirit of the age was against him; and, in opposition to it, he could not become the subject of any general or comprehensive interest. The nation, in short, knew little and cared less about him. During his life, and for some years after his death, inferior dramatists outran him in the race of popularity; and then the flood of puritan fanaticism swept him and the stage together into temporary oblivion. On the restoration of the monarchy and the theatre, the school of France perverted our taste, and it was not till the last century was somewhat advanced that William Shakspeare arose again, as it were, from the tomb, in all his proper majesty of light. He then became the subject of solicitous and learned inquiry: but inquiry was then too late; and all that it could recover, from the ravage of time, were only a few human fragments, which could scarcely be united into a man. To these causes of our personal ignorance of the great bard of England, must be added his own strange indifference to the celebrity of genius. When he had produced his admirable works, ignorant or heedless of their value, he abandoned them with perfect indifference to oblivion or to fame. It surpassed his thought that he could grow into the admiration of the world; and, without any reference to the curiosity of future ages, in which he could not conceive himself to possess an interest, he was contented to die in the arms of obscurity, as an unlaurelled burgher of a provincial town. To this combination of causes are we to attribute the scantiness of our materials for the Life of William Shakspeare. His works are in myriads of hands: he constitutes the delight of myriads of readers: his renown is coextensive with the civilization of man; and, striding across the ocean from Europe, it occupies the wide region of transatlantic empire: but he is himself only a shadow which disappoints our grasp; an undefined form which is rather intimated than discovered to the keenest searchings of our eye. Of the little however, questionable or certain, which can be told of him, we must now proceed to make the best use in our power, to write what by courtesy may be called his life; and we have only to lament that the result of our labour must greatly disappoint the curiosity which has been excited by the grandeur of his reputation. The slight narrative of Rowe, founded on the information obtained, in the beginning of the last century, by the inquiries of Betterton, the famous actor, will necessarily supply us with the greater part of the materials with which we are to work.

William Shakspeare, or Shakspere, (for the floating orthography of the name is properly attached to the one or the other of these varieties,) was baptized in the church of Stratford upon Avon, as is ascertained by the parish register, on the 26th of April, 1564; and he is said to have been born on the 23d of the same month, the day consecrated to the tutelar saint of England. His parents, John and Mary Shakspeare, were not of equal ranks in the community; for the former was only a respectable tradesman, whose ancestors cannot be traced into gentility, whilst the latter belonged to an ancient and opulent house in the county of Warwick, being the youngest daughter of Robert Arden of Wilmecote. The family of the Ardens (or Arderaes, as it is written in all the old deeds,) was of considerable antiquity and importance, some of them having served as high sheriffs of their county, and two of them (Sir John Arden and his nephew, the grandfather of Mrs. Shakspeare,) having enjoyed each a station of honour in the personal establishment of Henry VII. The younger of these Ardens was made, by his sovereign, keeper of the park of Aldercar, and bailiff of the lordship of Codnore. He obtained, also, from the crown, a valuable grant in the lease of the manor of Yoxsal, in Staffordshire, consisting of more than 4,600 acres, at a rent of 42*l.* Mary Arden did not come dowerless to her plebeian husband, for she brought to him a small freehold estate called Asbies, and the sum of 6*l.* 13*s.* 4*d.* in money. The freehold consisted of a house and fifty-four acres of land; and, as far as it appears, it was the first piece of landed property which was ever possessed by the Shakspeares. Of this marriage the offspring was four sons and four daughters; of whom Joan (or, according to the orthography of that time, Jone,) and Margaret, the eldest of the children died, one in infancy and one at a somewhat more advanced age; and Gilbert, whose birth immediately succeeded to that of our Poet, is supposed by some not to have reached his maturity, and by others, to have attained to considerable longevity. Joan, the eldest of the four remaining children, and named after her deceased sister, married William Hart, a hatter in her native town; and Edmund, the youngest of the family, adopting the profession of an actor, resided in St. Saviour's parish in London; and was buried in St. Saviour's Church, on the last day of December, 1607, in his twenty-eighth year. Of Anne and Richard, whose births intervened between those of Joan and Edmund, the parish register tells the whole history, when it records that the former was buried on the 4th of April, 1579, in the eighth year of her age, and the latter on the 4th of February, 1612-13, when he had nearly completed his thirty-ninth.

In consequence of a document, discovered in the year 1770, in the house in which, if tradition is to be trusted, our Poet was born, some persons having concluded that John Shakspeare was a Roman Catholic, though he had risen, by the regular gradation of office, to the chief dignity of the corporation of Stratford, that of high bailiff; and, during the whole of this period, had unquestionably conformed to the rites of the Church of England. The asserted fact seemed not to be very probable; and the document in question, which, drawn up in a testamentary form and regularly attested, zealously professes the Roman faith of him in whose name it speaks, having been subjected to a rigid examination by Malone, has been pronounced to be spurious. The trade of John Shakspeare, as well as his religious faith, has recently been made the subject of controversy. According to the testimony of Rowe, grounded on the tradition of Stratford, the father of our Poet was a dealer in wool, or, in the provincial vocabulary of his country, a wool-driver; and such he has been deemed by all the biographers of his son, till the fact was thrown into doubt by the result of the inquisitiveness of Malone. Finding, in an old and obscure MS. purporting to record the proceedings of the bailiff's court in Stratford, our John Shakspeare designated as a glover, Malone exults over the ignorance of poor Rowe, and assumes no small degree of merit to himself as the discoverer of a long sought and a most important historic truth. If he had recollected the remark of the clown in the Twelfth Night,* that "a sentence is but a cheverel glove to a good wit. How quickly the wrong side may be turned outwards!" he would, doubtless, have pressed the observation into his service, and brought it as an irresistible attestation of the veracity of his old MS.

Whatever may have been the trade of John Shakspeare, whether that of wool-merchant or of glover, it seems, with the little fortune of his wife, to have placed him in a state of easy competence. In 1569 or 1570, in consequence partly of his alliance with the Ardens, and partly of his attainment of the prime municipal honours of his town, he obtained a concession of arms from the herald's office, a grant, which placed him and his family on the file of the gentry of England; and, in 1574, he purchased two houses, with gardens and orchards annexed to them, in Henley Street, in Stratford. But before the year 1578, his prosperity, from causes not now ascertainable, had certainly declined; for in that year, as we find from the records of his borough, he was excused, in condescension to his poverty, from the moiety of a very moderate assessment of six shillings and eight pence, made by the members of the corporation on themselves; at the same time that he was altogether exempted from his contribution to the relief of the poor. During the remaining years of his life, his fortunes appear not to have recovered themselves; for he ceased to attend the meetings of the corporation hall, where he had once presided; and, in 1586, another person was substituted as alderman in his place, in consequence of his magisterial inefficiency. He died in the September of 1601, when his illustrious son had already attained to high celebrity; and his wife, Mary Shakspeare, surviving him for seven years, deceased in the September of 1608, the burial of the former being registered on the eighth and that of the latter on the ninth of this month, in each of these respective years.

On the 30th of June, 1564, when our Poet had not yet been three months in this breathing world, his native Stratford was visited by the plague; and, during the six succeeding months, the ravaging disease is calculated to have swept to the grave more than a seventh part of the whole population of the place. But the favoured infant reposed in security in his cradle, and breathed health amid an atmosphere of pestilence. The Genius of England may be supposed to have held the arm of the destroyer, and not to have permitted it to fall on the consecrated dwelling of his and Nature's darling. The disease, indeed, did not overstep his charmed threshold; for the name of Shakspeare is not to be found in the register of deaths throughout that period of accelerated mortality. That he survived this desolating calamity of his townsmen, is all that we know of William Shakspeare from the day of his birth till he was sent, as we are informed by Rowe, to the free-school of Stratford; and was stationed there in the course of his education, till, in consequence of the straitened circumstances of his father, he was recalled to the paternal roof. As we are not told at what age he was sent to school, we cannot form any estimate of the time during which he remained there. But if he was placed under his

* Act iii. sc. i

master when he was six years old, he might have continued in a state of instruction for seven or even for eight years; a term sufficiently long for any boy, not an absolute blockhead, to acquire something more than the mere elements of the classical languages. We are too ignorant, however, of dates in these instances to speak with any confidence on the subject; and we can only assert that seven or eight of the fourteen years, which intervened between the birth of our Poet in 1564 and the known period of his father's diminished fortune in 1578, might very properly have been given to the advantages of the free-school. But now the important question is to be asked—What were the attainments of our young Shakspeare at this seat of youthful instruction? Did he return to his father's house in a state of utter ignorance of classic literature? or was he as far advanced in his school-studies as boys of his age (which I take to be thirteen or fourteen) usually are in the common progress of our public and more reputable schools? That his scholastic attainments did not rise to the point of learning, seems to have been the general opinion of his contemporaries; and to this opinion I am willing to assent. But I cannot persuade myself that he was entirely unacquainted with the classic tongues; or that, as Farmer and his followers labour to convince us, he could receive the instructions, even for three or four years, of a school of any character, and could then depart without any knowledge beyond that of the Latin accidence. The most accomplished scholar may read with pleasure the poetic versions of the classic poets; and the less advanced proficient may consult his indolence by applying to the page of a translation of a prose classic, when accuracy of quotation may not be required: and on evidences of this nature is supported the charge which has been brought, and which is now generally admitted, against our immortal bard, of more than school-boy ignorance. He might, indeed, from necessity apply to North for the interpretation of Plutarch; but he read Golding's Ovid only, as I am satisfied, for the entertainment of its English poetry. Ben Jonson, who must have been intimately conversant with his friend's classic acquisitions, tells us expressly that, "He had small Latin and less Greek." But, according to the usual plan of instruction in our schools, he must have traversed a considerable extent of the language of Rome, before he could touch even the confines of that of Greece. He must in short have read Ovid's Metamorphoses, and a part at least of Virgil, before he could open the grammar of the more ancient, and copious, and complex dialect. This I conceive to be a fair statement of the case in the question respecting Shakspeare's learning. Beyond controversy he was not a scholar; but he had not profited so little by the hours, which he had passed in school, as not to be able to understand the more easy Roman authors without the assistance of a translation. If he himself had been asked, on the subject, he might have parodied his own Falstaff and have answered, "Indeed I am not a Scaliger or a Budæus, but yet no blockhead, friend." I believe also that he was not wholly unacquainted with the popular languages of France and Italy. He had abundant leisure to acquire them; and the activity and the curiosity of his mind were sufficiently strong to urge him to their acquisition. But to discuss this much agitated question would lead me beyond the limits which are prescribed to me; and, contenting myself with declaring that, in my opinion, both parties are wrong, both they who contend for our Poet's learning, and they who place his illiteracy on a level with that of John Taylor, the celebrated water-poet, I must resume my humble and most deficient narrative. The classical studies of William Shakspeare, whatever progress he may or may not have made in them, were now suspended; and he was replaced in his father's house, when he had attained his thirteenth or fourteenth year, to assist with his hand in the maintenance of the family. Whether he continued in this situation whilst he remained in his single state, has not been told to us, and cannot therefore at this period be known. But in the absence of information, conjecture will be busy; and will soon cover the bare desert with unprofitable vegetation. Whilst Malone surmises that the young Poet passed the interval, till his marriage, or a large portion of it, in the office of an attorney, Aubrey stations him during the same term at the head of a country school. But the surmises of Malone are not universally happy; and to the assertions of Aubrey* I am not disposed to attach more credit than was attached to them by Anthony Wood, who knew the old gossip and was competent to appreciate his character. It is more probable that the necessity, which brought young Shakspeare from his school, retained him with his father's occupation at home, till the acquisition of a wife made it convenient for him to remove to a separate habitation. It is reasonable to conclude that a mind like his, ardent, excursive, and "all compact of imagination," would not be satisfied with entire inactivity; but would obtain knowledge where it could, if not from the stores of the ancients, from those at least which were supplied to him by the writers of his own country.

In 1582, before he had completed his eighteenth year, he married Anne Hathaway, the daughter, as Rowe informs us, of a substantial yeoman in the neighbourhood of Stratford. We are unacquainted with the precise period of their marriage, and with the church in which it was solemnized, for in the register of Stratford there is no record of the event; and we are made certain of the year, in which it occurred, only by the baptism of Susanna, the first produce of the union, on the 26th of May, 1583. As young Shakspeare neither increased his fortune by this match, though he probably received some money with his wife, nor raised himself by it in the community, we may conclude that he was induced to it by inclination, and the impulse of love. But the youthful poet's dream of happiness does not seem to have been realized by the result. The bride was eight years older than the bridegroom; and whatever charms she might possess to fascinate the eyes of her boy-lover, she probably was deficient in those powers which are requisite to impose a durable fetter on the heart, and to hold "in sweet captivity" a mind of the very highest order. No charge is intimated against the lady: but she is left in Stratford by her husband during his long residence in the metropolis; and on his death, she is found to be only slightly, and, as it were, casually remembered in his will. Her second pregnancy, which was productive of twins, (Hamnet and Judith, baptized on the 2d of February, 1584–5,) terminated her pride as a mother; and we know nothing more respecting her than that, surviving her illustrious consort by rather more than seven years, she was buried on the 8th of August, 1623, being, as we are told by the inscription on her tomb, of the age of sixty-seven. Respecting the habits of life, or the occupation of our young Poet by which he obtained his subsistence, or even the place of his residence, subsequently to his marriage, not a floating syllable has been wafted to us by tradition for the gratification of our curiosity; and the history of this great man is a perfect blank till the occurrence of an event, which drove him from his native town, and gave his wonderful intellect to break out in its full lustre on the world. From the frequent allusions in his writings to the elegant sport of falconry, it has been suggested that this, possibly, might be one of his favourite amusements: and nothing can be more probable, from the active season

* What credit can be due to this Mr. Aubrey, who picked up information on the highway and scattered it every where as authentic? who whipped Milton at Cambridge in violation of the university statutes; and who, making our young Shakspeare a butcher's boy, could embrue his hands in the blood of calves, and represent him as exulting in poetry over the convulsions of the dying animals?

of his life, and his fixed habitation in the country, than his strong and eager passion for all the pleasures of the field. As a sportsman, in his rank of life, he would naturally become a poacher; and then it is highly probable that he would fall into the acquaintance of poachers; and, associating with them in his idler hours, would occasionally be one of their fellow-marauders on the manors of their rich neighbours. In one of these licentious excursions on the grounds of Sir Thomas Lucy of Charlecote, in the immediate vicinity of Stratford, for the purpose, as it is said, of stealing his deer, our young bard was detected; and, having farther irritated the knight by affixing a satirical ballad on him to the gates of Charlecote, he was compelled to fly before the enmity of his powerful adversary, and to seek an asylum in the capital. Malone,* who is prone to doubt, wishes to question the truth of this whole narrative, and to ascribe the flight of young Shakspeare from his native country to the embarrassment of his circumstances, and the persecution of his creditors. But the story of the deer-stealing rests upon the uniform tradition of Stratford, and is confirmed by the character of Sir T. Lucy, who is known to have been a rigid preserver of his game, by the enmity displayed against his memory by Shakspeare in his succeeding life; and by a part of the offensive ballad† itself, preserved by a Mr. Jones of Tarbick, a village near to Stratford, who obtained it from those who must have been acquainted with the fact, and who could not be biased by any interest or passion to falsify or misstate it. Besides the objector, in this instance, seems not to be aware that it was easier to escape from the resentment of an offended proprietor of game, than from the avarice of a creditor: that whilst the former might be satisfied with the removal of the delinquent to a situation where he could no longer infest his parks or his warrens, the latter would pursue his debtor wherever bailiffs could find and writs could attach him. On every account, therefore, I believe the tradition, recorded by Rowe, that our Poet retired from Stratford before the exasperated power of Sir T. Lucy, and found a refuge in London, not possibly beyond the reach of the arm, but beyond the hostile purposes of his provincial antagonist.

The time of this eventful flight of the great bard of England cannot now be accurately determined: but we may somewhat confidently place it between the years 1585 and 1588; for in the former of these we may conclude him to have been present with his family at the baptism of his twins, Hamnet and Judith; and than the latter of them we cannot well assign a later date for his arrival in London, since we know‡ that before 1592 he had not only written two long poems, the Venus and Adonis, and the Rape of Lucrece, but had acquired no small degree of celebrity as an actor and as a dramatic writer.

At this agitating crisis of his life, the situation of young Shakspeare was certainly, in its obvious aspect, severe and even terrific. Without friends to protect or assist him, he was driven, under the frown of exasperated power, from his profession; from his native fields; from the companions of his childhood and his youth; from his wife and his infant offspring. The world was spread before him, like a dark ocean, in which no fortunate isle could be seen to glitter amid the gloomy and sullen tide. But he was blessed with youth and health; his conscience was unwounded, for the adventure for which he suffered, was regarded, in the estimation of his times, as a mere boy's frolick, of not greater guilt than the robbing of an orchard; and his mind, rich beyond example in the gold of heaven, could throw lustre over the black waste before him, and could people it with a beautiful creation of her own. We may imagine him, then, departing from his home, not indeed like the great Roman captive as he is described by the poet—

> Fertur pudicæ conjugis osculum,
> Parvosque natos, ut capitis minor,
> Ab se removisse, et virilem
> Torvus humi posuisse, vultum, &c.

but touched with some feelings of natural sorrow, yet with an unfaltering step, and with hope vigourous at his heart. It was impossible that he should despair; and if he indulged in sanguine expectation, the event proved him not to be a visionary. In the course of a few years, the exile of Stratford became the associate of wits, the friend of nobles, the favourite of monarchs; and in a period which still left him not in sight of old age, he returned to his birth-place in affluence, with honour, and with the plaudits of the judicious and the noble resounding in his ears.

His immediate refuge in the metropolis was the stage; to which his access, as it appears, was easy. Stratford was fond of theatrical representations, which it accommodated with its town or guildhall; and had frequently been visited by companies of players when our Poet was of an age, not only to enjoy their performances, but to form an acquaintance with their members. Thomas Greene, who was one of their distinguished actors, has been considered by some writers as a kinsman of our author's; and though he, possibly, may have been confounded by them with another Thomas Greene, a barrister, who was unquestionably connected with the Shakspeares, he was certainly a fellow townsman of our fugitive bard's; whilst Heminge and Burbage, two of the leaders of the company in question, belonged either to Stratford or to its immediate neighbourhood. With the door of the theatre thus open to him, and under the impulse of his own natural bias, (for however in after life he may have lamented his degradation as a professional actor, it must be concluded that he now felt a strong attachment to the stage,) it is not wonderful that young Shakspeare should solicit this asylum in his distress; or that he should be kindly received by men who knew him, and some of whom were connected, if not with his family, at least with his native town. The company, to which he united himself, was the Earl of Leicester's or the Queen's; which had obtained the royal license in 1574. The place of its performances, when our Poet became enrolled among its members, was the Globe on the Bankside; and its managers subsequently purchased the theatre of Blackfriars, (the oldest theatre in London,) which they had previously rented for some years; and at these two theatres, the first of which was open in the centre for summer representations, and the last covered for those of winter, were acted all the dramatic productions of Shakspeare. That he was at first received into the company in a very subordinate situation, may be regarded not merely as probable, but as certain: that he ever carried a link to light the frequenters of the theatre, or ever held their horses, must be rejected as an absurd tale, fabricated, no doubt, by the lovers of the marvellous, who were solicitous to obtain a contrast in the humility of his first to the pride of his subsequent fortunes. The mean and servile occupation, thus assigned to him, was incompatible with his circumstances, even in their present afflicted state: and his relations and connec-

* Malone was much addicted to doubt. Knowing, perhaps, that, on all the chief topics of the Grecian schools of philosophy, the great mind of Cicero faltered in doubt, our commentator and critic wished, possibly, to establish his claim to a superiority of intellect by the same academic withholding of assent. He ought, however, to have been aware that scepticism, which is sometimes the misfortune of wise men, is generally the affectation of fools.

† The first stanza of this ballad, which is admitted to be genuine, may properly be preserved as a curiosity. But as it is to be found in every life of our author, with the exception of Rowe's, I shall refer my readers, to whom it could not be gratifying, to some other page for it than my own.

‡ From Robert Greene's posthumous work, written in 1592, and Chettle's Kind Hart's Dream, published very soon afterwards

tions, though far from wealthy, were yet too remote from absolute poverty, to permit him to act for a moment in such a degrading situation. He was certainly, therefore, immediately admitted within the theatre; but in what rank or character cannot now be known. This fact, however, soon became of very little consequence; for he speedily raised himself into consideration among his new fellows by the exertions of his pen, if not by his proficiency as an actor. When he began his career as a dramatic writer; or to what degree of excellence he attained in his personation of dramatic characters, are questions which have been frequently agitated without any satisfactory result. By two publications, which appeared toward the end of 1592, we know, or at least we are induced strongly to infer, that at that period, either as the corrector of old or as the writer of original dramas, he had supplied the stage with a copiousness of materials. We learn also from the same documents that, in his profession of actor, he trod the boards not without the acquisition of applause. The two publications, to which I allude, are Robert Greene's "Groatsworth of Wit bought with a Million of Repentance," and Henry Chettle's "Kind Hart's Dream." In the former of these works, which was published by Chettle subsequently to the unhappy author's decease, the writer, addressing his fellow dramatists, Marlowe, Peele, and Lodge, says, "Yes! trust them not," (the managers of the theatre;) "for there is an upstart crow, beautified with our feathers, that, with his tiger's heart wrapped in a player's hide, supposes he is as well able to bombast out a blank verse as the best of you; and, being an absolute Johannes Factotum, is in his own conceit the only Shake-scene in a country." As it could not be doubtful against whom this attack was directed, we cannot wonder that Shakspeare should be hurt by it: or that he should expostulate on the occasion rather warmly with Chettle as the editor of the offensive matter. In consequence, as it is probable, of this expression of resentment on the part of Shakspeare, a pamphlet from the pen of Chettle called "Kind Hart's Dream" issued from the press before the close of the same year (1592,) which had witnessed the publication of Greene's posthumous work. In this pamphlet, Chettle acknowledges his concern for having edited any thing which had given pain to Shakspeare, of whose character and accomplishments he avows a very favourable opinion. Marlowe, as well as Shakspeare, appears to have been offended by some passages in this production of poor Greene's: and to both of these great dramatic poets Chettle refers in the short citation which we shall now make from his page: "With neither of them that take offence was I acquainted, and with one of them" (concluded to be Marlowe, whose moral character was unhappily not good) "I care not if I never be. The other," (who must necessarily be Shakspeare,) "whom at that time I did not so much spare as since I wish I had; for that, as I have moderated the hate of living authors, and might have used my own discretion, (especially in such a case, the author being dead,) that I did not I am as sorry as if the original fault had been my fault: because myself have seen his demeanor no less civil than he is excellent in the quality he professes. Besides divers of worship have reported his uprightness of dealing, which argues his honesty; and his facetious grace in writing, that approves his art." Shakspeare was now twenty-eight years of age; and this testimony of a contemporary, who was acquainted with him, and was himself an actor, in favour of his moral and his professional excellence, must be admitted as of considerable value. It is evident that he had now written for the stage; and before he entered upon dramatic composition, we are certain that he had completed, though he had not published his two long and laboured poems of Venus and Adonis, and the Rape of Lucrece. We cannot, therefore, date his arrival in the capital later than 1588, or, perhaps, than 1587; and the four or five years which interposed between his departure from Stratford and his becoming the object of Greene's malignant attack, constituted a busy and an important period of his life. Within this term he had conciliated the friendship of the young Thomas Wriothesly, the liberal, the high souled, the romantic Earl of Southampton: a friendship which adhered to him throughout his life; and he had risen to that celebrity, as a poet and a dramatist, which placed him with the first wits of the age, and subsequently lifted him to the notice and the favour of Elizabeth and James, as they successively sate upon the throne of England.

At the point of time which our narrative has now reached, we cannot accurately determine what dramatic pieces had been composed by him: but we are assured that they were of sufficient excellence to excite the envy and the consequent hostility of those who, before his rising, had been the luminaries of the stage. It would be gratifying to curiosity if the feat were possible, to adjust with any precision the order in which his wonderful productions issued from his brain. But the attempt has more than once been made, and never yet with entire success. We know only that his connection with the stage continued for about twenty years, (though the duration even of this term cannot be settled with precision,) and that, within this period he composed either partially, as working on the ground of others, or educing them altogether from his own fertility, thirty-five or (if that wretched thing, Pericles, in consequence of Dryden's testimony in favour of its authenticity, and of a few touches of THE GOLDEN PEN being discoverable in its last scenes, must be added to the number) thirty-six dramas; and that of these it is probable that such as were founded on the works of preceding authors were the first essays of his dramatic talent; and such as were more perfectly his own, and are of the first sparkle of excellence, were among the last. While I should not hesitate, therefore, to station "Pericles," the three parts of "Henry VI.," (for I cannot see any reason for throwing the first of these parts from the protection of our author's name,) "Love's Labour Lost," "The Comedy of Errors," "The Taming of the Shrew," "King John," and "Richard II.," among his earliest productions, I should, with equal confidence, arrange "Macbeth," "Lear," "Othello," "Twelfth Night," and "The Tempest," with his latest, assigning them to that season of his life, when his mind exulted in the conscious plenitude of power. Whatever might be the order of succession in which this illustrious family of genius sprang into existence, they soon attracted notice, and speedily compelled the homage of respect from those who were the most eminent for their learning, their talents, or their rank. Jonson, Selden, Beaumont, Fletcher, and Donne, were the associates and the intimates of our Poet: the Earl of Southampton was his especial friend: the Earls of Pembroke and of Montgomery were avowedly his admirers and patrons: Queen Elizabeth distinguished him with her favour; and her successor, James, with his own hand, honoured the great dramatist with a letter of thanks for the compliment paid in Macbeth to the royal family of the Stuarts.*

The circumstance which first brought the two lords of the stage, Shakspeare and Jonson, into that embrace of friendship which continued indissoluble, as there is reason to believe, during the permission of mortality, is reported to have been the kind assistance given by the former to the latter, when he was offering one of his plays (Every Man in his Humour) for the benefit of representation. The manuscript, as it is said, was on the point of being rejected and returned with a rude answer, when Shakspeare, fortunately glancing his eye over its pages, immediately discovered its

* The existence of this royal letter of thanks is asserted on the authority of Sheffield Duke of Buckingham, who saw it in the possession of Davenant. The cause of the thanks is assigned on the most probable conjecture

merit, and, with his influence, obtained its introduction on the stage. To this story some specious objections have been raised; and there cannot be any necessity for contending for it, as no lucky accident can be required to account for the inducement of amity between two men of high genius, each treading the same broad path to fame and fortune, yet each with a character so peculiarly his own, that he might attain his object without wounding the pride or invading the interests of the other. It has been generally believed that the intellectual superiority of Shakspeare excited the envy and the consequent enmity of Jonson. It is well that of these asserted facts no evidences can be adduced. The friendship of these great men seems to have been unbroken during the life of Shakspeare; and, on his death, Jonson made an offering to his memory of high, just, and appropriate panegyric. He places him above not only the modern but the Greek dramatists; and he professes for him admiration short only of idolatry. They who can discover any penuriousness of praise in the surviving poet must be gifted with a very *peculiar* vision of mind. With the flowers, which he strewed upon the grave of his friend, there certainly was not blended one poisonous or bitter leaf. If, therefore, he was, as he is represented to have been by an impartial and able judge, (Drummond of Hawthornden,) "a great lover and praiser of himself; a contemner and scorner of others; jealous of every word and action of those about him," &c. &c., how can we otherwise account for the uninterrupted harmony of his intercourse with our bard than by supposing that the frailties of his nature were overruled by that pre-eminence of mental power in his friend which precluded competition; and by his friend's sweetness of temper and gentleness of manners, which repressed every feeling of hostility. Between Shakspeare and Thomas Wriothesly, the munificent and the noble Earl of Southampton, distinguished in history by his inviolable attachment to the rash and the unfortunate Essex, the friendship was permanent and ardent. At its commencement, in 1593, when Shakspeare was twenty-nine years of age, Southampton was not more than nineteen; and, with the love of general literature, he was particularly attached to the exhibitions of the theatre. His attention was first drawn to Shakspeare by the poet's dedication to him of the "Venus and Adonis," that "first heir," as the dedicator calls it, "of his invention;" and the acquaintance, once begun between characters and hearts like theirs, would soon mature into intimacy and friendship. In the following year (1594) Shakspeare's second poem, "The Rape of Lucrece," was addressed by him to his noble patron in a strain of less distant timidity; and we may infer from it that the poet had then obtained a portion of the favour which he sought. That his fortunes were essentially promoted by the munificent patronage of Southampton cannot reasonably be doubted. We are told by Sir William Davenant, who surely possessed the means of knowing the fact, that the peer gave at one time to his favoured dramatist the magnificent present of a thousand pounds. This is rejected by Malone as an extravagant exaggeration; and because the donation is said to have been made for the purpose of enabling the poet to complete a purchase which he had then in contemplation; and because no purchase of an adequate magnitude seems to have been accomplished by him, the critic treats the whole story with contempt; and is desirous of substituting a dedication fee of one hundred pounds for the more princely liberality which is attested by Davenant. But surely a purchase might be within the view of Shakspeare, and eventually not be effected; and then of course the thousand pounds in question would be added to his personal property; where it would just complete the income on which he is reported to have retired from the stage. As to the incredibility of the gift in consequence of its value, have we not witnessed a gift, made in the present day, by a noble of the land to a mere actor, of ten times the nominal and twice the effective value of this proud bounty of the great Earl of Southampton's* to one of the master spirits of the human race? †

Of the degree of patronage and kindness extended to Shakspeare by the Earls of Pembroke and Montgomery, we are altogether ignorant: but we know, from the dedication of his works to them by Heminge and Condell, that they had distinguished themselves as his admirers and friends. That he numbered many more of the nobility of his day among the homagers of his transcendent genius, we may consider as a specious probability. But we must not indulge in conjectures, when we can gratify ourselves with the reports of tradition, approaching very nearly to certainties. Elizabeth, as it is confidently said, honoured our illustrious dramatist with her especial notice and regard. She was unquestionably fond of theatric exhibitions; and, with her literary mind and her discriminating eye, it is impossible that she should overlook; and that, not overlooking, she should not appreciate the man, whose genius formed the prime glory of her reign. It is affirmed that, delighted with the character of Falstaff as drawn in the two parts of Henry IV., she expressed a wish to see the gross and dissolute knight under the influence of love; and that the result of our Poet's compliance, with the desire of his royal mistress, was "The Merry Wives of Windsor."‡ Favoured, however, as our Poet seems to have been by Elizabeth, and notwithstanding the fine incense which he offered to her vanity, it does not appear that he profited in any degree by her bounty. She could distinguish and could smile upon genius: but unless it were immediately serviceable to her personal or her political interests, she had not the soul to reward it. However inferior to her in the arts of government and in some of the great characters of mind might be her Scottish successor, he resembled her in his love of letters, and in his own cultivation of learning. He was a scholar, and even a poet: his attachment to the general cause of literature was strong; and his love of the drama and the theatre was particularly warm. Before his accession to the English throne he had written, as we have before noticed, a letter, with his own hand, to Shakspeare,

* As the patron and the friend of Shakspeare, Thomas Wriothesly, Earl of Southampton, is entitled to our especial attention and respect. But I cannot admit his eventful history into the text, without breaking the unity of my biographical narrative; and to speak of him within the compass of a note will be only to inform my readers, that he was born on the 6th of October, 1573 that he was engaged in the mad attempts of his friend, the Earl of Essex, against the government of Elizabeth: that, in consequence, he was confined during her life by that Queen, who was so lenient as to be satisfied with the blood of one of the friends: that, immediately on her death, he was liberated by her successor, not disposed to adopt the enmities of the murderess of his mother: that he was promoted to honours by the new sovereign; and that, finally, being sent with a military command to the Low Countries, he caught a fever from his son, Lord Wriothesly; and, surviving him only five days, concluded his active and honourable career of life at Bergen-op-zoom, on the 10th of November, 1624. It may be added, that, impoverished by his liberalities, he left his widow in such circumstances as to call for the assistance of the crown.

† The late Duke of Northumberland made a present to John Kemble of 10,000*l*.

‡ Animated as this comedy is with much distinct delineation of character, it cannot be pronounced to be unworthy of its great author. But it evinces the difficulty of writing upon a prescribed subject, and of working with effect under the control of another mind. As he sported in the scenes of Henry IV., Falstaff was insusceptible of love: and the egregious dupe of Windsor, ducked and cudgelled as he was, cannot be the wit of Eastcheap, or the guest of Shallow, or the military commander on the field of Shrewsbury. But even the genius of Shakspeare could not effect impossibilities. He did what he could to revive his own Falstaff: but the life which he reinfused into his creature was not the vigorous vitality of Nature; and he placed him in a scene where he could not subsist.

acknowledging, as it is supposed, the compliment paid to him in the noble scenes of Macbeth; and scarcely had the crown of England fallen upon his head, when he granted his royal patent to our Poet and his company of the Globe; and thus raised them from being the Lord Chamberlain's servants to be the servants of the King. The patent is dated on the 19th of May, 1603, and the name of William Shakspeare stands second on the list of the patentees. As the demise of Elizabeth had occurred on the 24th of the preceding March, this early attention of James to the company of the Globe may be regarded as highly complimentary to Shakspeare's theatre, and as strongly demonstrative of the new sovereign's partiality for the drama. But James' patronage of our Poet was not in any other way beneficial to his fortunes. If Elizabeth were too parsimonious for an effective patron, by his profusion on his pleasures and his favourites, James soon became too needy to possess the means of bounty for the reward of talents and of learning. Honour, in short, was all that Shakspeare gained by the favour of two successive sovereigns, each of them versed in literature, each of them fond of the drama, and each of them capable of appreciating the transcendency of his genius.

It would be especially gratifying to us to exhibit to our readers some portion at least of the personal history of this illustrious man during his long residence in the capital;—to announce the names and characters of his associates, a few of which only we can obtain from Fuller; to delineate his habits of life; to record his convivial wit; to commemorate the books which he read; and to number his compositions as they dropped in succession from his pen. But no power of this nature is indulged to us. All that active and efficient portion of his mortal existence, which constituted considerably more than a third part of it, is an unknown region, not to be penetrated by our most zealous and intelligent researches. It may be regarded by us as a kind of central Africa, which our reason assures us to be glowing with fertility and alive with population; but which is abandoned in our maps, from the ignorance of our geographers, to the death of barrenness, and the silence of sandy desolation. By the Stratford register we can ascertain that his only son, Hamnet, was buried, in the twelfth year of his age, on the 11th of August, 1596; and that, after an interval of nearly eleven years, his eldest daughter, Susanna, was married to John Hall, a physician, on the 5th of June, 1607. With the exception of two or three purchases made by him at Stratford, one of them being that of New Place, which he repaired and ornamented for his future residence, the two entries which we have now extracted from the register, are positively all that we can relate with confidence of our great poet and his family, during the long term of his connection with the theatre and the metropolis. We may fairly conclude, indeed, that he was present at each of the domestic events, recorded by the register: that he attended his son to the grave, and his daughter to the altar. We may believe also, from its great probability, even to the testimony of Aubrey, that he paid an annual visit to his native town; whence his family were never removed, and which he seems always to have contemplated as the resting place of his declining age. He probably had nothing more than a lodging in London, and this he might occasionally change: but in 1596 he is said to have lived somewhere near to the Bear-Garden, in Southwark.

In 1606, James procured from the continent a large importation of mulberry trees, with a view to the establishment of the silk manufactory in his dominions; and, either in this year or in the following, Shakspeare enriched his garden at New Place with one of these exotic, and at that time, very rare trees. This plant of his hand took root, and flourished till the year 1752, when it was destroyed by the barbarous axe of one Francis Gastrell, a clergyman, into whose worse than Gothic hands New Place had most unfortunately fallen.

As we are not told the precise time, when Shakspeare retired from the stage and the metropolis to enjoy the tranquillity of life in his native town, we cannot pretend to determine it. As he is said, however, to have passed some years in his establishment at New Place, we may conclude that his removal took place either in 1612 or in 1613, when he was yet in the vigour of life, being not more than forty-eight or forty-nine years old. He had ceased, as it is probable, to tread the stage as an actor at an earlier period; for in the list of actors, prefixed to the Volpone of B. Jonson, performed at the Globe theatre, and published in 1605, the name of William Shakspeare is not to be found. However versed he might be in the science of acting, (and that he was versed in it we are assured by his directions to the players in Hamlet,) and, however well he might acquit himself in some of the subordinate characters of the drama, it does not appear that he ever rose to the higher honours of his profession. But if they were above his attainment, they seem not to have been the objects of his ambition; for by one of his sonnets* we find that he lamented the fortune which had devoted him to the stage, and that he considered himself as degraded by such a public exhibition. The time was not yet come when actors were to be the companions of princes: when their lives, as of illustrious men, were to be written; and when statues were to be erected to them by public contribution!

The amount of the fortune, on which Shakspeare retired from the busy world, has been the subject of some discussion. By Gildon, who forbears to state his authority, this fortune is valued at 300*l.* a year; and by Malone, who, calculating our Poet's real property from authentic documents, assigns a random value to his personal, it is reduced to 200*l.* Of these two valuations of Shakspeare's property, we conceive that Gildon's approaches the more nearly to the truth: for if to Malone's conjectural estimate of the personal property, of which he professes to be wholly ignorant, be added the thousand pounds, given by Southampton, (an act of munificence of which we entertain not a doubt,) the precise total, as money then bore an interest of 10*l.* per cent., of the three hundred pounds a year will be made up. On the smallest of these incomes, however, when money was at least five times its present value, might our Poet possess the comforts and the liberalities of life: and in the society of his family, and of the neighbouring gentry, conciliated by the amiableness of his manners and the pleasantness of his conversation, he seems to have passed his few remaining days in the enjoyment of tranquillity and respect. So exquisite, indeed, appears to have been his relish of the quiet, which was his portion within the walls of New Place, that it induced a complete oblivion of all that had engaged his attention, and had aggrandized his name in the preceding scenes of his life. Without any regard to his literary fame, either present or to come, he saw with perfect unconcern some of his immortal works brought, mutilated and deformed, in surreptitious copies, before the world; and others of them, with an equal indifference to their fate, he permitted to remain in their unrevised or interpolated MSS. in the hands of the theatric prompter. There is not, probably, in the whole compass of literary history, such another instance of a proud superiority to what has been called by a rival genius,

"The last infirmity of noble minds,"

as that which was now exhibited by our illustrious dramatist and poet. He seemed

"As if *he* could not or *he* would not find,
How much *his* worth transcended all *his* kind.†"

* See Sonnet cxi.

† Epitaph on a Fair Maiden Lady, by Dryden.

With a privilege, rarely indulged even to the sons of genius, he had produced his admirable works without any throes or labour of the mind: they had obtained for him all that he had asked from them,—the patronage of the great, the applause of the witty, and a competency of fortune adequate to the moderation of his desires. Having fulfilled, or, possibly, exceeded his expectations, they had discharged their duty; and he threw them altogether from his thought; and whether it were their destiny to emerge into renown, or to perish in the drawer of a manager; to be brought to light in a state of integrity, or to *revisit the glimpses of the moon with a thousand mortal murders on their head*, engaged no part of his solicitude or interest. They had given to him the means of easy life, and he sought from them nothing more. This insensibility in our Author to the offspring of his brain may be the subject of our wonder or admiration: but its consequences have been calamitous to those who in after times have hung with delight over his pages. On the intellect and the temper of these ill-fated mortals it has inflicted a heavy load of punishment in the dullness and the arrogance of commentators and illustrators—in the conceit and petulance of Theobald; the imbecility of Capell; the pert and tasteless dogmatism of Steevens; the ponderous littleness of Malone and of Drake. Some superior men, it is true, have enlisted themselves in the cause of Shakspeare. Rowe, Pope, Warburton, Hanmer, and Johnson have successively been his editors; and have professed to give his scenes in their original purity to the world. But from some cause or other, which it is not our present business to explore, each of these editors, in his turn, has disappointed the just expectations of the public; and, with an inversion of Nature's general rule, the little men have finally prevailed against the great. The blockheads have hooted the wits from the field; and, attaching themselves to the mighty body of Shakspeare, like barnacles to the hull of a proud man of war, they are prepared to plough with him the vast ocean of time; and thus, by the only means in their power, to snatch themselves from that oblivion to which Nature had devoted them. It would be unjust, however, to defraud these gentlemen of their proper praise. They have read for men of talents; and, by their gross labour in the mine, they have accumulated materials to be arranged and polished by the hand of the finer artist. Some apology may be necessary for this short digression from the more immediate subject of my biography. But the three or four years, which were passed by Shakspeare in the peaceful retirement of New Place are not distinguished by any traditionary anecdote deserving of our record; and the chasm may not improperly be supplied with whatever stands in contiguity with it. I should pass in silence, as too trifling for notice, the story of our Poet's extempore and jocular epitaph on John Combe, a rich townsman of Stratford, and a noted money-lender, if my readers would not object to me that I had omitted an anecdote which had been honoured with a place in every preceding biography of my author. As the circumstance is related by Rowe, "In a pleasant conversation among their common friends, Mr. Combe told Shakspeare, in a laughing manner, that he fancied he intended to write his epitaph if he happened to outlive him: and, since he could not know what might be said of him when he was dead, he desired it might be done immediately: upon which Shakspeare gave him these four verses:

> Ten in the hundred lies here ingraved:
> 'Tis a hundred to ten his soul is not saved.
> If any man ask, who lies in this tomb:
> Ho! Ho! quoth the devil, 'tis my John a Combe.

But the sharpness of the satire is said to have stung the man so severely that he never forgave it." By Aubrey the story is differently told; and the lines in question, with some alterations, which evidently make them worse, are said to have been written after Combe's death. Steevens and Malone discredit the whole tale. The two first lines, as given to us by Rowe, are unquestionably not Shakspeare's; and that any lasting enmity subsisted between these two burghers of Stratford is disproved by the respective wills of the parties, John Combe bequeathing five pounds to our Poet, and our Poet leaving his sword to John Combe's nephew and residuary legatee, John Combe himself being at that time deceased. With the two commentators above mentioned, I am inclined, therefore, on the whole, to reject the story as a fabrication; though I cannot, with Steevens, convict the lines of malignity; or think, with him and with Malone, that the character of Shakspeare, on the supposition of his being their author, could require any laboured vindication to clear it from stain. In the anecdote, as related by Rowe, I can see nothing but a whimsical sally, breaking from the mind of one friend, and of a nature to excite a good-humoured smile on the cheek of the other. In Aubrey's hands, the transaction assumes a somewhat darker complexion; and the worse verses, as written after the death of their subject, may justly be branded as malevolent, and as discovering enmity in the heart of their writer. But I have dwelt too long upon a topic which, in truth, is undeserving of a syllable; and if I were to linger on it any longer, for the purpose of exhibiting Malone's reasons for his preference of Aubrey's copy of the epitaph to Rowe's, and his discovery of the propriety and beauty of the single Ho in the last line of Aubrey's, as Ho is the abbreviation of Hobgoblin, one of the names of Robin Good-fellow, the fairy servant of Oberon, my readers would have just cause to complain of me, as sporting with their time and their patience.

On the 9th of July, 1614, Stratford was ravaged by a fire, which destroyed fifty-four dwelling-houses besides barns and out-offices. It abstained, however, from the property of Shakspeare; and he had only to commiserate the losses of his neighbours.

With his various powers of pleasing; his wit and his humour; the gentleness of his manners; the flow of his spirits and his fancy; the variety of anecdote with which his mind must have been stored; his knowledge of the world, and his intimacy with man, in every gradation of the society, from the prompter of a playhouse to the peer and the sovereign, Shakspeare must have been a delightful—nay, a fascinating companion; and his acquaintance must necessarily have been courted by all the prime inhabitants of Stratford and its vicinity. But over this, as over the preceding periods of his life, brood silence and oblivion; and in our total ignorance of his intimacies and friendships, we must apply to our imagination to furnish out his convivial board where intellect presided, and delight, with admiration, gave the applause.

On the 2d of February, 1615-16, he married his youngest daughter, Judith, then in the thirty-first year of her age, to Thomas Quiney, a vintner in Stratford; and on the 25th of the succeeding month he executed his will. He was then, as it would appear, in the full vigour and enjoyment of life; and we are not informed that his constitution had been previously weakened by the attack of any malady. But his days, or rather his hours, were now all numbered; for he breathed his last on the 23d of the ensuing April, on that anniversary of his birth which completed his fifty-second year. It would be gratifying to our curiosity to know something of the disease, which thus prematurely terminated the life of this illustrious man: but the secret is withheld from us; and it would be idle to endeavour to obtain it. We may be certain that Dr. Hall, who was a physician of considerable eminence, attended his father-in-law in his last illness; and Dr. Hall kept a register of all the remarkable cases, with their symptoms and treatment, which in the course of his practice had fallen under his observation. This curious MS., which had escaped the enmity of time, was obtained by Malone: but the recorded cases in it most unfortunately began with the year 1617; and the preceding part of the register, which most probably had been in existence, could no where be found. The mortal complaint, therefore, of William Shakspeare is likely to remain for ever unknown; and as darkness had closed upon his path through life, so darkness now gathered round his bed of death, awfully to cover it from the eyes of succeeding generations.

On the 25th of April, 1616, two days after his decease, he was buried in the chancel of the church of Stratford; and at some period within the seven subsequent years, (for in 1623 it is noticed in the verses of Leonard Digges,) a monument was raised to his memory either by the respect of his townsmen, or by the piety of his relations. It represents the Poet with a countenance of thought, resting on a cushion and in the act of writing. It is placed under an arch, between two Corinthian columns of black marble, the capitals and bases of which are gilt. The face is said, but, as far as I can find, not on any adequate authority, to have been modelled from the face of the deceased; and the whole was painted, to bring the imitation nearer to nature. The face and the hands wore the carnation of life: the eyes were light hazel: the hair and beard were auburn: a black gown, without sleeves, hung loosely over a scarlet doublet. The cushion in its upper part was green: in its lower, crimson; and the tassels were of gold colour. This certainly was not in the high classical taste; though we may learn from Pausanias that statues in Greece were sometimes coloured after life; but as it was the work of contemporary hands, and was intended, by those who knew the Poet, to convey to posterity some resemblance of his lineaments and dress, it was a monument of rare value; and the tastelessness of Malone, who caused all its tints to be obliterated with a daubing of white lead, cannot be sufficiently ridiculed and condemned. Its material is a species of free-stone; and as the chisel of the sculptor was most probably under the guidance of Doctor Hall, it bore some promise of likeness to the mighty dead. Immediately below the cushion is the following distich:—

Judicio Pylium; genio Socratem; arte Maronem
Terra tegit; populus mœret; Olympus habet.

On a tablet underneath are inscribed these lines:—

Stay, passenger, why dost thou go so fast?
Read, if thou can'st, whom envious death has placed
Within this monument—Shakspeare; with whom
Quick Nature died; whose name doth deck the tomb
Far more than cost: since all that he hath writ
Leaves living art but page to serve his wit:

and the flat stone, covering the grave, holds out, in very irregular characters, a supplication to the reader, with the promise of a blessing and the menace of a curse:

Good Friend! for Jesus' sake forbear
To dig the dust inclosed here.
Blest be the man that spares these stones;
And cursed be he that moves my bones.

The last of these inscriptions may have been written by Shakspeare himself under the apprehension of his bones being tumbled, with those of many of his townsmen, into the charnel-house of the parish. But his dust has continued unviolated, and is likely to remain in its holy repose till the last awful scene of our perishable globe. It were to be wished that the two preceding inscriptions were more worthy, than they are, of the tomb to which they are attached. It would be gratifying if we could give any faith to the tradition, which asserts that the bust of this monument was sculptured from a cast moulded on the face of the departed poet; for then we might assure ourselves that we possess one authentic resemblance of this pre-eminently intellectual mortal. But the cast, if taken, must have been taken immediately after his death; and we know neither at whose expense the monument was constructed, nor by whose hand it was executed; nor at what precise time it was erected. It may have been wrought by the artist, acting under the recollections of the Shakspeare family into some likeness of the great townsman of Stratford; and on this probability, we may contemplate it with no inconsiderable interest. I cannot, however, persuade myself that the likeness could have been strong. The forehead, indeed, is sufficiently spacious and intellectual: but there is a disproportionate length in the under part of the face: the mouth is weak; and the whole countenance is heavy and inert. Not having seen the monument itself, I can speak of it only from its numerous copies by the graver; and by these it is possible that I may be deceived. But if we cannot rely on the Stratford bust for a resemblance of our immortal dramatist, where are we to look with any hope of finding a trace of his features? It is highly probable that no portrait of him was painted during his life; and it is certain that no portrait of him, with an incontestible claim to genuineness, is at present in existence. The fairest title to authenticity seems to be assignable to that which is called the Chandos portrait; and is now in the collection of the Duke of Buckingham, at Stowe. The possession of this picture can be distinctly traced up to Betterton and Davenant. Through the hands of successive purchasers, it became the property of Mr. Robert Keck. On the marriage of the heiress of the Keck family, it passed to Mr. Nicholl, of Colney-Hatch, in Middlesex: on the union of this gentleman's daughter with the Duke of Chandos, it found a place in that nobleman's collection; and, finally, by the marriage of the present Duke of Buckingham with the Lady Anne Elizabeth Brydges, the heiress of the house of Chandos, it has settled in the gallery of Stowe. This was pronounced by the late Earl of Orford, (Horace Walpole,) as we are informed by Mr. Granger, to be the only original picture of Shakspeare. But two others, if not more, contend with it for the palm of originality; one, which in consequence of its having been in the possession of Mr. Felton, of Drayton, in the county of Salop, from whom it was purchased by the Boydells, has been called the Felton Shakspeare; and one, a miniature, which, by some connection, as I believe, with the family of its proprietors, found its way into the cabinet of the late Sir James Lamb, more generally, perhaps, known by his original name of James Bland Burgess. The first of these pictures was reported to have been found at the Boar's Head in Eastcheap, one of the favourite haunts, as it was erroneously called, of Shakspeare and his companions; and the second by a tradition, in the family of Somervile the poet, is affirmed to have been drawn from Shakspeare, who sate for it at the pressing instance of a Somervile, one of his most intimate friends. But the genuineness of neither of these pictures can be supported under a rigid investigation; and their pretensions must yield to those of another rival portrait of our Poet, which was once in the possession of Mr. Jennens, of Gopsal in Leicestershire, and is now the property of that liberal and literary nobleman, the Duke of Somerset. For the authenticity of this portrait, attributed to the pencil of Cornelius Jansenn, Mr. Boaden* contends with much zeal and ingenuity. Knowing that some of the family of Lord Southampton, Shakspeare's especial friend and patron, had been painted by Jansenn, Mr. Boaden speciously infers that, at the Earl's request, his favourite dramatist had, likewise, allowed his face to this painter's imitation; and that the Gopsal portrait, the result of the artist's skill on this occasion, had obtained a distinguished place in the picture-gallery of the noble Earl. This, however, is only unsupported assertion, and the mere idleness of conjecture. It is not pretended to be ascertained that the Gopsal portrait was ever in the possession of Shak-

* An Inquiry into the Authenticity of Pictures and Prints offered as Portraits of Shakspeare, p. 67—80

speare s illustrious friend; and its transfers, during the hundred and thirty-seven years, which interposed between the death of Southampton, in 1624, and the time of its emerging from darkness at Gopsal, in 1761, are not made the subjects even of a random guess. On such evidence, therefore, if evidence it can be called, it is impossible for us to receive, with Mr. Boaden, the Gopsal picture as a genuine portrait of Shakspeare. We are now assured that it was from the Chandos portrait Sir Godfrey Kneller copied the painting which he presented to Dryden, a poet inferior only to him whose portrait constituted the gift. The beautiful verses, with which the poet requited the kind attention of the painter, are very generally known: but many may require to be informed that the present, made on this occasion by the great master of the pencil to the greater master of the pen, is still in existence, preserved no doubt by the respect felt to be due to the united names of Kneller, Dryden, and Shakspeare; and is now in the collection of Earl Fitzwilliam at Wentworth Castle.* The original painting, from which Droeshout drew the copy for his engraving, prefixed to the first folio edition of our Poet's dramas, has not yet been discovered; and I feel persuaded that no original painting ever existed for his imitation; but that the artist worked in this instance from his own recollection, assisted probably by the suggestions of the Poet's theatric friends. We are, indeed, strongly of opinion that Shakspeare, remarkable, as he seems to have been, for a lowly estimate of himself, and for a carelessness of all personal distinction, would not readily submit his face to be a painter's study, to the loss of hours, which he might more usefully or more pleasurably assign to reading, to composition, or to conviviality. If any sketch of his features was made during his life, it was most probably taken by some rapid and unprofessional pencil, when the Poet was unaware of it; or, taken by surprise, and exposed by it to no inconvenience, was not disposed to resist it. We are convinced that no authentic portrait of this great man has yet been produced, or is likely to be discovered; and that we must not therefore hope to be gratified with any thing which we can contemplate with confidence as a faithful representation of his countenance. The head of the statue, executed by Scheemaker, and erected, in 1741, to the honour of our poet in Westminster Abbey, was sculptured after a mezzotinto, scraped by Simon nearly twenty years before, and said to be copied from an original portrait, by Zoust. But as this artist was not known by any of his productions in England till the year 1657, no original portrait of Shakspeare could be drawn by his pencil; and, consequently, the marble chiselled by Scheemaker, under the direction of Lord Burlington, Pope, and Mead, cannot lay any claim to an authorized resemblance to the man, for whom it was wrought. We must be satisfied, therefore, with knowing, on the authority of Aubrey, that our Poet "was a handsome, well-shaped man;" and our imagination must supply the expansion of his forehead, the sparkle and flash of his eyes, the sense and good-temper playing round his mouth; the intellectuality and the benevolence mantling over his whole countenance.

It is well that we are better acquainted with the rectitude of his morals, than with the symmetry of his features. To the integrity of his heart; the gentleness and benignity of his manners, we have the positive testimony of Chettle and Ben Jonson; the former of whom seems to have been drawn, by our Poet's good and amiable qualities, from the faction of his dramatic enemies; and the latter, in his love and admiration of the man, to have lost all his natural jealousy of the successful competitor for the poetic palm. I have already cited Chettle: let me now cite Jonson, from whose pages much more of a similar nature might be adduced. "I loved," he says in his 'Discoveries,' "I loved the man, and do honour his memory, on this side idolatry, as much as any. He was, indeed, honest, of an open and free nature; had an excellent fancy, brave notions and gentle expressions," &c. &c. When Jonson apostrophizes his deceased friend, he calls him, "My gentle Shakspeare," and the title of "the sweet swan of Avon," so generally given to him, after the example of Jonson, by his contemporaries, seems to have been given with reference as much to the suavity of his temper as to the harmony of his verse. In their dedication of his works to the Earls of Pembroke and Montgomery, his fellows, Heminge and Condell, profess that their great object in their publication was "only to keep the memory of so worthy a friend and fellow alive as was our Shakspeare:" and their preface to the public appears evidently to have been dictated by their personal and affectionate attachment to their departed friend. If we wish for any further evidence in the support of the moral character of Shakspeare, we may find it in the friendship of Southampton; we may extract it from the pages of his immortal works. Dr. Johnson, in his much over-praised Preface, seems to have taken a view, very different from ours, of the morality of our author's scenes. He says, "His (Shakspeare's) first defect is that to which may be imputed most of the evil in books or in men. He sacrifices virtue to convenience; and is so much more careful to please than to instruct, that he seems to write without any moral purpose. From his writings, indeed, a system of moral duty may be selected," (indeed!) "but his precepts and axioms drop casually from him:" (Would the preface-writer have wished the dramatist to give a connected treatise on ethics like the offices of Cicero?) "he makes no just distribution of good or evil, nor is always careful to show in the virtuous a disapprobation of the wicked: he carries his persons indifferently through right and wrong; and at the close dismisses them without further care, and leaves their examples to operate by chance. This fault the barbarity of the age cannot extenuate; for it is always a writer's duty to make the world better, and justice is a virtue independent on time or place." Why this commonplace on justice should be compelled into the station in which we here most strangely find it, I cannot for my life conjecture. But absurd as it is made by its association in this place, it may not form an improper conclusion to a paragraph which means little, and which, intending censure, confers dramatic praise on a dramatic writer. It is evident, however that Dr. Johnson, though he says that a system of moral duty may be selected from Shakspeare's writings, wished to inculcate that his scenes were not of a moral tendency. On this topic, the first and the greater Jonson seems to have entertained very different sentiments—

——"Look, how the father's face

(says this great man)

Lives in his issue; even so the race
Of Shakspeare's mind and manners, brightly shines
In his well-torned and truefiled lines"

We think, indeed, that his scenes are rich in sterling morality, and that they must have been the effusions of a moral mind. The only criminatior of his morals must be drawn from a few of his sonnets; and from a story first suggested by Anthony Wood, and afterwards told by Oldys on the authority of Betterton and Pope. From the Sonnets* we can collect nothing more than that their writer was blindly attached to an unprincipled woman, who preferred a young and beautiful friend of his to himself. But the story told by Oldys presents some

* I derive my knowledge on this topic from Malone; for till I saw the fact asserted in his page, I was not aware that the picture in question had been preserved amid the wreck of poor Dryden's property. On the authority also of Malone and of Mr. Boaden, I speak of Sir Godfrey's present to Dryden as of a copy from the Chandos portrait

* See Son 141, 144, 147, 151, 152

thing to us of a more tangible nature; and as it possesses some intrinsic merit as a story, and rests, as to its principal facts, on the authority of Wood, who was a native of Oxford and a veracious man, we shall not hesitate, after the example of most of the recent biographers of our Poet, to relate it, and in the very words of Oldys. "If tradition may be trusted, Shakspeare often baited at the Crown Inn or Tavern in Oxford, on his journey to and from London. The landlady was a beautiful woman and of a sprightly wit; and her husband, Mr. John Davenant, (afterwards mayor of that city,) a grave, melancholy man, who, as well as his wife, used much to delight in Shakspeare's pleasant company. Their son, young Will Davenant (afterwards Sir William Davenant) was then a little schoolboy, in the town, of about seven or eight years old; and so fond also of Shakspeare that, whenever he heard of his arrival, he would fly from school to see him. One day, an old townsman, observing the boy running homeward almost out of breath, asked him whither he was posting in that heat and hurry. He answered, to see his *god*-father, Shakspeare. There is a good boy, said the other; but have a care that you don't take God's name in vain! This story Mr. Pope told me at the Earl of Oxford's table, upon occasion of some discourse which arose about Shakspeare's monument, then newly erected in Westminster Abbey."

On these two instances of his frailty, under the influence of the tender passion, one of them supported by his own evidence, and one resting on authority which seems to be not justly questionable, depend all the charges which can be brought against the strict personal morality of Shakspeare. In these days of peculiarly sensitive virtue, he would not possibly be admitted into the party of the saints: but, in the age in which he lived, these errors of his human weakness did not diminish the respect, commanded by the probity of his heart; or the love, conciliated by the benignity of his manners; or the admiration exacted by the triumph of his genius. I blush with indignation when I relate that an offence, of a much more foul and atrocious nature, has been suggested against him by a critic* of the present day, on the pretended testimony of a large number of his sonnets. But his own proud character, which raised him high in the estimation of his contemporaries, sufficiently vindicates him from this abominable imputation. It is admitted that one hundred and twenty of these little poems are addressed to a male, and that in the language of many of them love is too strongly and warmly identified with friendship. But in the days of Shakspeare love and friendship were almost synonymous terms. In the Merchant of Venice,† Lorenzo speaking of Antonio to Portia, says,

> "But if you knew to whom you show this honour,
> How true a gentleman you send relief to;
> How *dear a lover* of my lord, your husband," &c.

and Portia, in her reply calls Antonio "*the bosom lover* of her lord." Drayton, in a letter to his friend, Drummond of Hawthornden, tells him that Mr. Joseph Davies *is in love with him;* and Ben Jonson concludes a letter to Dr. Donne by professing himself as ever *his true lover.* Many more instances of the same perverted language might be educed from the writings of that gross and indelicate age; and I have not a doubt that Shakspeare, without exposing himself to the hazard of suspicion, employed this authorized dialect of his time to give the greater glow to these addresses to his young friend. But who was this young friend? The question has frequently been asked; and never once been even speciously answered. I would as readily believe, with the late Mr. G. Chalmers, that this object of our author's poetic ardour, was Queen Elizabeth, changed for the particular purpose, like the Iphis of the Roman poet, into a man, as I would be induced to think, with the writer "On Shakspeare and his Times," that these familiar and fervent addresses were made to the proud and the lofty Southampton. Neither can I persuade myself, with Malone, that the friend and the mistress are the mere creatures of our Poet's imagination, raised for the sport of his muse, and without "a local habitation or a name." They were, unquestionably, realities: but who they were must for ever remain buried in inscrutable mystery. That those addressed to his male friend are not open to the infamous interpretation, affixed to them by the monthly critic, may be proved, as I persuade myself, to demonstration. The odious vice to which we allude, was always in England held in merited detestation; and would our Poet consent to be the publisher of his own shame? to become a sort of outcast from society? to be made

> "A fixed figure for the hand of time
> To point his slow, unmoving finger at?"

If the sonnets in question were not actually published by him, he refrained to guard them from manuscript distribution; and they soon, as might be expected, found their way to the press; whence they were rapidly circulated, to the honour of his poetry and not to the discredit of his morals. So pure was he from the disgusting vice, imputed to him, for the first time, in the nineteenth century, that he alludes to it only once (if my recollection be at all accurate) in all his voluminous works; and that is where the foul-mouthed Thersites, in Troilus and Cressida,* calls Patroclus "Achilles's masculine whore." Under all the circumstances of the case, therefore, that these sonnets should be the effusions of sexual love is incredible, inconceivable, impossible; and we must turn away from the injurious suggestion with honest abhorrence and disdain.

The Will of Shakspeare, giving to his youngest daughter, Judith, not more than three hundred pounds, and a piece of plate, which probably was valuable, as it is called by the testator, "My broad silver and gilt bowl," assigns almost the whole of his property to his eldest daughter, Susanna Hall, and her husband; whom he appoints to be his executors. The cause of this evident partiality in the father appears to be discoverable in the higher mental accomplishments of the elder daughter; who is reported to have resembled him in her intellectual endowments, and to have been eminently distinguished by the piety and the Christian benevolence which actuated her conduct. Having survived her estimable husband fourteen years, she died on the 11th of July, 1649; and the inscription on her tomb, preserved by Dugdale, commemorates her intellectual superiority, and the influence of religion upon her heart. This inscription, which we shall transcribe, bears witness also, as we must observe, to the piety of her illustrious father.

> Witty above her sex; but that's not all:
> Wise to salvation was good Mistress Hall.
> Something of Shakspeare was in *that;* but *this*
> *Wholly of him*, with whom she's now in bliss
> Then, passenger, hast ne'er a tear
>   To weep with her, that wept with all?
> That wept, yet set herself to cheer
>   Them up with comforts cordial.
> Her love shall live, her mercy spread,
> When thou hast ne'er a tear to shed.

As Shakspeare's last will and testament will be printed at the end of this biography, we may refer our readers to that document for all the minor legacies which it bequeaths; and may pass immediately to an account of our great Poet's family, as far as it can be given from records which are authentic. Judith, his younger daughter, bore to her husband, Thomas Quiney, three sons; Shakspeare, who died in his infancy, Richard and Thomas, who deceased, the first in his 21st year, the last in his 19th,

* See Monthly Review for Dec. 1824; article, Skottowe's Life of Shakspeare.

† Act iii sc 4

* Act v sc 1

unmarried and before their mother; who, having reached her 77th year, expired in February, 1661-2 —being buried on the 9th of that month. She appears either not to have received any education, or not to have profited by the lessons of her teachers, for to a deed, still in existence, she affixes her mark.

We have already mentioned the dates of the birth, marriage, and death of Susanna Hall. She left only one daughter, Elizabeth, who was baptized on the 21st of February, 1607-8, eight years before her grandfather's decease, and was married on the 22d of April, 1626, to Mr. Thomas Nash, a country gentleman, as it appears, of independent fortune. Two years after the death of Mr. Nash, who was buried on the 5th of April, 1647, she married on the 5th of June, 1649, at Billesley in Warwickshire, Sir John Barnard, Knight, of Abington, a small village in the vicinity of Northampton. She died, and was buried at Abington, on the 17th of February, 1669-70; and, as she left no issue by either of her husbands, her death terminated the lineal descendants of Shakspeare. His collateral kindred have been indulged with a much longer period of duration; the descendants of his sister, Joan, having continued in a regular succession of generations even to our days; whilst none of them, with a single exception, have broken from that rank in the community in which their ancestors, William Hart and Joan Shakspeare united their unostentatious fortunes in the year 1599. The single exception to which we allude is that of Charles Hart, believed, for good reasons, to be the son of William the eldest son of William and Joan Hart, and, consequently, the grand-nephew of our Poet. At the early age of seventeen, Charles Hart, as lieutenant in Prince Rupert's regiment, fought at the battle of Edgehill: and, subsequently betaking himself to the stage, he became the most renowned tragic actor of his time. "What Mr. Hart delivers," says Rymer, (I adopt the citation from the page of Malone,) "every one takes upon content: their eyes are prepossessed and charmed by his action before aught of the poet's can approach their ears; and to the most wretched of characters he gives a lustre and brilliancy, which dazzles the sight that the deformities in the poetry cannot be perceived." "Were I a poet," (says another contemporary writer,) "nay a Fletcher or a Shakspeare, I would quit my own title to immortality so that one actor might never die. This I may modestly say of him (nor is it my particular opinion, but the sense of all mankind) that the best tragedies on the English stage have received their lustre from Mr. Hart's performance: that he has left such an impression behind him, that no less than the interval of an age can make them appear again with half their majesty from any second hand." This was a brilliant eruption from the family of Shakspeare; but as it was the first so it appears to have been the last; and the Harts have ever since, as far at least as it is known to us, "pursued the noiseless tenor of their way," within the precincts of their native town on the banks of the soft-flowing Avon.*

Whatever is in any degree associated with the personal history of Shakspeare is weighty with general interest. The circumstance of his birth can impart consequence even to a provincial town; and we are not unconcerned in the past or the present fortunes of the place, over which hovers the glory of his name. But the house, in which he passed the last three or four years of his life, and in which he terminated his mortal labours, is still more engaging to our imaginations, as it is more closely and personally connected with him. Its history, therefore, must not be omitted by us; and if in some respects, we should differ in it from the narrative of Malone, we shall not be without reasons sufficient to justify the deviations in which we indulge. New Place, then, which was not thus first named by Shakspeare, was built in the reign of Henry VII., by Sir Hugh Clopton, Kt., the younger son of an old family resident near Stratford, who had filled in succession the offices of Sheriff and of Lord Mayor of London. In 1563 it was sold by one of the Clopton family to William Bott; and by him it was again sold in 1570 to William Underhill, (the purchaser and the seller being both of the rank of esquires) from whom it was bought by our Poet in 1597. By him it was bequeathed to his daughter, Susanna Hall; from whom it descended to her only child, Lady Barnard. In the June of 1643, this Lady, with her first husband Mr. Nash, entertained, for nearly three weeks, at New Place, Henrietta Maria, the queen of Charles I., when, escorted by Prince Rupert and a large body of troops, she was on her progress to meet her royal consort, and to proceed with him to Oxford. On the death of Lady Barnard without children, New Place was sold, in 1675,† to Sir Edward Walker, Kt., Garter King at Arms; by whom it was left to his only child, Barbara, married to Sir John Clopton, Kt., of Clopton in the parish of Stratford. On his demise, it became the property of a younger son of his, Sir Hugh Clopton, Kt., (this family of the Cloptons seems to have been peculiarly prolific in the breed of knights,) by whom it was repaired and decorated at a very large expense. Malone affirms that it was pulled down by him, and its place supplied by a more sumptuous edifice. If this statement were correct, the crime of its subsequent destroyer would be greatly extenuated; and the hand which had wielded the axe against the hallowed mulberry tree, would be absolved from the second act, imputed to it, of sacrilegious violence. But Malone's acccount is, unquestionably, erroneous. In the May of 1742, Sir Hugh entertained Garrick, Macklin, and Delany under the shade of the Shakspearian mulberry. On the demise of Sir Hugh‡ in the December of 1751, New Place was sold by his son-in-law and executor, Henry Talbot, the Lord Chancellor Talbot's brother, to the Rev. Francis Gastrell, Vicar of Frodsham in Cheshire; by whom, on some quarrel with the magistrates on the subject of the parochial assessments, it was razed to the ground, and its site abandoned to vacancy. On this completion of his outrages§ against the memory of Shakspeare, which his unlucky possession of wealth enabled him to

* By intelligence, on the accuracy of which I can rely, and which has only just reached me, from the birthplace of Shakspeare, I learn that the family of the Harts, after a course of lineal descents during the revolution of two hundred and twenty-six years, is now on the verge of extinction; an aged woman, who retains *in single blessedness* her maiden name of Hart, being at this time (Nov. 1825) its sole surviving representative. For some years she occupied the house of her ancestors, in which Shakspeare is reported to have first seen the light; and here she obtained a comfortable subsistence by showing the antiquities of the venerated mansion to the numerous strangers who were attracted to it. Being dispossessed of this residence by the rapaciousness of its proprietor, she settled herself in a dwelling nearly opposite to it. Here she still lives, and continues to exhibit some relics, not reputed to be genuine, of the mighty bard, with whom her maternal ancestor was nourished in the same womb. She regards herself also as a dramatic poet; and, in support of her pretensions, she produces the rude sketch of a play, uninformed, as it is said, with any of the vitality of genius. For this information I am indebted to Mr. Charles Fellows, of Nottingham; who with the characteristic kindness of his most estimable family, sought for the intelligence which was required by me, and obtained it.

† Malone gives a different account of some of the transfers of New Place. According to him, it passed by sale, on the death of Lady Barnard, to Edward Nash, the cousin-german of that Lady's first husband; and, by him, was bequeathed to his daughter Mary, the wife of Sir Reginald Foster; from whom it was bought by Sir John Clopton, who gave it by deed to his youngest son, Sir Hugh. But the deed, which conveyed New Place to Sir Edward Walker, is still in existence; and has been published by R. B. Wheeler, the historian of Stratford.

‡ Sir Hugh Clopton was knighted by George I. He was a barrister at law; and died in the December of 1751, at the advanced age of eighty.—*Malone*

§ Our days, also, have witnessed a similar profanation of the relics of genius; not, indeed, of genius

commit, Francis Gastrell departed from Stratford, hooted out of the town, and pursued by the execrations of its inhabitants. The fate of New Place has been rather remarkable. After the demolition of the house by Gastrell, the ground, which it had occupied, was thrown into the contiguous garden, and was sold by the widow of the clerical barbarian. Having remained during a certain period, as a portion of a garden, a house was again erected on it; and, in consequence also of some dispute about the parish assessments, that house, like its predecessor, was pulled down; and its site was finally abandoned to Nature, for the production of her fruits and her flowers: and thither may we imagine the little Elves and Fairies frequently to resort, to trace the footsteps of their beloved poet, now obliterated from the vision of man; to throw a finer perfume on the violet; to unfold the first rose of the year, and to tinge its cheek with a richer blush; and, in their dances beneath the full-orbed moon, to chant their harmonies, too subtle for the gross ear of mortality, to the fondly cherished memory of their darling, THE SWEET SWAN OF AVON.

Of the personal history of William Shakspeare, as far as it can be drawn, even in shadowy existence, from the obscurity which invests it, and of whatever stands in immediate connection with it, we have now exhibited all that we can collect; and we are not conscious of having omitted a single circumstance of any moment, or worthy of the attention of our readers. We might, indeed, with old Fuller, speak of our Poet's *wit-combats*, as Fuller calls them, at the Mermaid, with Ben Jonson: but then we have not one anecdote on record of either of these intellectual gladiators to produce, for not a sparkle of our Shakspeare's convivial wit has travelled down to our eyes; and it would be neither instructive nor pleasant to see him represented as a light skiff, skirmishing with a huge galleon, and either evading or pressing attack as prudence suggested, or the alertness of his movements emboldened him to attempt. The lover of heraldry may, perhaps, censure us for neglecting to give the blazon of Shakspeare's arms, for which, as it appears, two patents were issued from the herald's office, one in 1569 or 1570, and one in 1599; and by him, who will insist on the transcription of every word which has been imputed on any authority to the pen of Shakspeare, we may be blamed for passing over in silence two very indifferent epitaphs, which have been charged on him. We will now, therefore, give the arms which were accorded to him; and we will, also, copy the two epitaphs in question. We may then, without any further impediment, proceed to the more agreeable portion of our labours,—the notice of our author's works.

The armorial bearings of the Shakspeare family are, or rather were,—Or, on a bend sable, a tilting spear of the first, point upwards, headed argent. Crest, A falcon displayed, argent, supporting a spear in pale, or.

In a MS. volume of poems, by William Herrick and others, preserved in the Bodleian, is the following epitaph, attributed, certainly not on its internal evidence, to our Poet. Its subject was, probably the member of a family with the surname of James which once existed in Stratford.

> When God was pleased, the world unwilling yet,
> Elias James to nature paid his debt,
> And here reposeth; as he lived he died;
> The saying in him strongly verified,—
> Such life, such death: then, the known truth to tell,
> He lived a godly life and died as well.
>
> WM. SHAKSPEARE

Among the monuments in Tonge Church, in the county of Salop, is one raised to the memory of Sir Thomas Stanley, Knt., who is thought by Malone to have died about the year 1600. With the prose inscription on this tomb, transcribed by Sir W. Dugdale, are the verses which I am about to copy, said by Dugdale to have been made by William Shakspeare, the late famous tragedian.

ON THE EAST END OF THE TOMB.

> Ask who lies here, but do not weep:
> He is not dead, he doth but sleep.
> This stony register is for his bones:
> His fame is more perpetual than these stones:
> And his own goodness with himself being gone,
> Shall live when earthly monument is none

ON THE WEST END.

> Not monumental stone preserves our fame:
> Nor sky-aspiring pyramids our name.
> The memory of him for whom this stands,
> Shall outlive marble and defacer's hands.
> When all to time's consumption shall be given,
> Stanley, for whom this stands, shall stand in heaven

As the great works of Shakspeare have engaged the attention of an active and a learned century since they were edited by Rowe, little that is new on the subject of them can be expected from a pen of the present day. It is necessary, however, that we should notice them, lest our readers should be compelled to seek in another page than ours for the common information which they might conceive themselves to be entitled to expect from us.

Fourteen of his plays were published separately, in quarto copies, during our Poet's life; and, seven years after his death, a complete edition of them was given to the public in folio by his theatric fellows, Heminge and Condell. Of those productions of his, which were circulated by the press while he was yet living, and were all surreptitious, our great author seems to have been as utterly regardless as he necessarily was of those which appeared when he was mouldering in his grave.* We have already

---

equally hallowed with that of which we have been speaking, for Nature has not yet produced a second Shakspeare; but of genius, which had conversed with the immortal Muses, which had once been the delight of the good and the terror of the bad. I allude to the violation of Pope's charming retreat, on the banks of the Thames, by a capricious and tasteless woman, who has endeavoured to blot out every memorial of the great and moral poet from that spot, which his occupation had made classic, and dear to the heart of his country. In the mutability of all human things, and the inevitable shiftings of property, "From you to me, from me to Peter Walter," these lamentable desecrations, which mortify our pride and wound our sensibilities, will of necessity sometimes occur. The site of the Tusculan of Cicero may become the haunt of banditti, or be disgraced with the walls of a monastery. The residences of a Shakspeare and a Pope may be devastated and defiled by a Parson Gastrell and a Baroness Howe. We can only sigh over the ruin when its deformity strikes upon our eyes, and execrate the hands by which it has been savagely accomplished.

* In his essay on the chronological order of Shakspeare's plays, Malone concludes very properly from the title-page of the earliest edition of Hamlet, which he believed then to be extant, that this edition (published in 1604) had been preceded by another of a less correct and less perfect character. A copy of the elder edition, in question, has lately been discovered; and is, indeed, far more remote from perfection than its sucessor, which was collated by Malone. It obviously appears to have been printed from the rude draught of the drama, as it was sketched by the Poet from the first suggestions of his mind. But how this rude and imperfect draught could fall into the hands of its publisher, is a question not easily to be answered. Such, however, is the authority to be attached to all the early quartos. They were obtained by every indirect mean; and the first incorrect MS., blotted again and again by the pens of ignorant transcribers, and multiplied by the press, was suffered, by the apathy of its illustrious author, to be circulated, without check, among the multitude. Hence the grossest anomalies of grammar have been considered, by his far-famed restorers, as belonging to the dialect of Shakspeare; and the most egregious infractions of rhythm, as the tones of his *honey-tongued* muse. The variations of the copy of Hamlet immediately before us, which was published in 1603, from the perfect drama as it subsequently issued from the press, are far too numerous to be noticed in this place, if indeed this place could properly be assigned to such a purpose. I may, however, just mention that Corambis and Montano are

observed on the extraordinary,—nay wonderful indifference of this illustrious man toward the offspring of his fancy; and we make it again the subject of our remark solely for the purpose of illustrating the cause of those numerous and pernicious errors which deform all the early editions of his plays. He must have known that many of these, his intellectual children, were walking through the community in a state of gross disease, with their limbs spotted, as it were, with the leprosy or the plague. But he looked on them without one parental feeling, and stretched not out his hand for their relief. They had broken from the confinement of the players, to whose keeping he had consigned them; and it was their business and not his to reclaim them. As for the rest of his intellectual progeny, they were where he had placed them; and he was utterly unconcerned about their future fate. How fraught and glowing with the principle of life must have been their nature to enable them to subsist, and to force themselves into immortality under so many circumstances of evil!

The copies of the plays, published antecedently to his death, were transcribed either by memory from their recitation on the stage; or from the separate parts, written out for the study of the particular actors, and to be pieced together by the skill of the editor; or, lastly, if stolen or bribed access could be obtained to it, from the prompter's book itself. From any of these sources of acquisition the copy would necessarily be polluted with very flagrant errors; and from every edition, through which it ran, it would naturally contract more pollution and a deeper stain. Such of the first copies as were fortunately transcribed from the prompter's book, would probably be in a state of greater relative correctness: but they are all, in different degrees, deformed with inaccuracies; and not one of them can claim the right to be followed as an authority. What Steevens and Malone call the restoring of Shakspeare's text, by reducing it to the reading of these early quartos, is frequently the restoring of it to error and to nonsense, from which it had luckily been reclaimed by the felicity of conjectural criticism. One instance immediately occurs to me, to support what I have affirmed; and it may be adduced instead of a score, which might be easily found, of these vaunted *restorations.*

In that fine scene between John and Hubert, where the monarch endeavours to work up his agent to the royal purposes of murder, the former says,

—————If thou couldst
Hear me without thine ears, and make reply
Without a tongue, using conceit alone, &c. &c.

Then in despite of *brooded*, watchful day,
I would into thy bosom pour my thoughts, &c. &c.

The passage thus stood in one of these old copies of *authority:* but Pope, not able to discover any meaning in the epithet, *brooded*, most happily substituted "broad-eyed" in its stead. As the compound was poetic and Shakspearian (for Shakspeare has dull-eyed and fire-eyed,) and was also most peculiarly suited to the place which it was to fill, the substitution for a while was permitted to remain; till Steevens, discovering the reading of the old copy, restored *brooded* to the station whence it had been felicitously expelled, and abandoned the line once more to the nonsense of the first editor.

In 1623, the first complete edition of our author's dramatic works was published in folio by his comrades of the theatre, Heminge and Condell; and in this we might expect a text tolerably incorrupt, if not perfectly pure. The editors denounced the copies which had preceded their edition as "stolen and surreptitious copies, maimed and deformed by the frauds and stealths of injurious impostors, that exposed them; even those are now offered to your view cured and perfect of their limbs; and all the rest absolute in their numbers as he conceived them." But notwithstanding these professions, and their honest resentment against impostors and surreptitious copies, the labours of these sole possessors of Shakspeare's MSS. did not obtain the credit which they arrogated; and they are charged with printing from those very quartos, on which they had heaped so much well-merited abuse. They printed, as there cannot be a doubt, from their prompter's book, (for by what temptation could they be enticed beyond it?) but then, from the same book, were transcribed many, perhaps, of the surreptitious quartos; and it is not wonderful that transcripts of the same page should be precisely alike. These editors, however, of the first folio, have incurred the heavy displeasure of some of our modern critics, who are zealous on all occasions to depreciate their work. Wherever they differ from the first quartos, which, for the reason that I have assigned, they must in general very closely resemble, Malone is ready to decide against them, and to defer to the earlier edition. But it is against the editor of the second folio, published in 1632, that he points the full storm of his indignation. He charges this luckless wight, whoever he may be, with utter ignorance of the language of Shakspeare's time, and of the fabric of Shakspeare's verse; and he considers him and Pope as the grand corrupters of Shakspeare's text. Without reflecting that to be ignorant of the language of Shakspeare's time was, in the case of this hapless editor, to be ignorant of his own, for he who published in 1632 could hardly speak with a tongue different from his who died only sixteen years before, Malone indulges in an elaborate display of the unhappy man's ignorance, and of his presumptuous alterations. He (the editor of the second folio) did not know that the double negative was the customary and authorized dialect of the age of Queen Elizabeth; (God help him, poor man! for if he were forty years old when he edited Shakspeare, he must have received the first rudiments of his education in the reign of the maiden queen;) and thus egregiously ignorant (ignorant, by the bye, where Shakspeare himself was ignorant, for his Twelfth Night,* the clown says, "If *your four negatives* make *your two affirmatives*—why then the worse for my friends and the better for my foes," &c.) but thus egregiously ignorant, instead of

"Nor to her bed *no* homage do I owe."

this editor has stupidly printed,

"Nor to her bed *a* homage do I owe."

Again, in "As you Like It," for "I cannot go no further," this blockhead of an editor has substituted "I can go no further." In "Much Ado about Nothing," for

"There will she hide her
To listen our purpose."

this corrupting editor has presumed to relieve the halting metre by printing,—

"There will she hide her
To listen *to* our purpose."

In these instances, I feel convinced that the editor is right, and consequently that the critic is the blockhead who is wrong. In what follows also, I am decidedly of opinion that the scale inclines in favour of the former of these deadly opposites. The double comparative is common in the plays of Shakspeare, says Malone:—true, as I am willing to allow; but always, as I am persuaded, in consequence of the illiteracy or the carelessness of the first transcriber: for why should Shakspeare write more anomalous English than Spenser, Daniel, Hooker, and Bacon? or why in his plays should he be guilty of barba-

the names given in this copy to the Polonius and Reynaldo of the more perfect editions; and the young lord, Osrick, is called in it only a braggart gentleman.

* Act v. sc. I

risms with which those poems of his,* that were printed under his own immediate eye, are altogether unstained? But, establishing the double comparative as one of the peculiar anomalies of Shakspeare's grammar, Malone proceeds to arraign the unfortunate editor as a criminal, for substituting, in a passage of Coriolanus, *more worthy* for *more worthier;* in Othello—for, "opinion, a sovereign mistress, throws *a more safer* voice on you," "opinion, &c. throws *a more safe* voice on you;" and, in Hamlet, instead of "Your wisdom should show itself *more richer* to signify this to the doctor," "Your wisdom should show itself *more rich* to signify this to the doctor." Need I express my conviction that in these passages the editor has corrected the text into what actually fell from Shakspeare's pen? Can it be doubted also that the editor is accurate in his printing of the following passage in "A Midsummer Night's Dream?" As adopted by Malone it stands.

"So will I grow, so live, so die, my lord,
Ere I will yield my virgin patent up
Unto his lordship, whose unwished yoke
My soul consents not to give sovereignty."

i. e., says the critic, to give sovereignty *to*, &c.—To be sure—and, without the insertion, in this instance, of the preposition, the sentence would be nonsense. As it is published by the editor, it is,—

"So will I grow, so live, so die, my lord,
Ere I will yield my virgin patent up
Unto his lordship, *to* whose *unwish'd* yoke
My soul consents not to give sovereignty."

Having now sufficiently demonstrated the editor's ignorance of Shakspeare's language, let us proceed with his critic to ascertain his ignorance of Shakspeare's metre and rhythm. In "The Winter's Tale,"† says Malone, we find,

"What wheels, racks, fires; what flaying, boiling
In leads and oils!"

Not knowing that 'fires' was used as a dissyllable, the editor added the word burning, at the end of the line (I wish that he had inserted it before 'boiling')—

"What wheels, racks, fires; what flaying, boiling, burning."

It is possible that fires may be used by Shakspeare as a dissyllable, though I cannot easily persuade myself that, otherwise than as a monosyllable, it would satisfy an ear, attuned as was his, to the finest harmonies of verse; yet it may be employed as a dissyllable by the rapid and careless bard; and I am ready to allow that the defective verse was not happily supplied, in that place at least, with the word, burning, yet I certainly believe that Shakspeare did not leave the line in question as Malone has adopted it, and that some word has been omitted by the carelessness of the first transcriber. In the next instance, from Julius Cæsar, I feel assured that the editor is right, as his supplement is as beneficial to the sense, as it is necessary to the rhythm. Malone's line is,

"And with the brands fire the traitors' houses:"

the editor's

"And with the brands fire *all* the traitors' houses."

The next charge, brought against the editor, may be still more easily repelled. In a noted passage of Macbeth—

"I would while it was smiling in my face
Have pluck'd my nipple from its boneless gums,
And dash'd the brains out, had I so sworn
As you have done to this."

"Not perceiving," says Malone, "that 'sworn' was used as a dissyllable," (the devil it was?) "He (the editor) reads 'had I *but* so sworn,'"—much as we think, to the advantage of the sense as well as of the metre; and supplying, as we conceive, the very word which Shakspeare had written, and the carelessness of the transcriber omitted. 'Charms' our Poet sometimes uses, according to Malone, as a word of two syllables."—No! impossible! Our Poet might, occasionally, be guilty of an imperfect verse, or the omission of his transcriber might furnish him with one: but never could he use "charms" as a word of two syllables. We feel, therefore, obliged by the editor's supplying an imperfect line in "The Tempest," with the very personal pronoun which, it is our persuasion, was at first inserted by Shakspeare. In the most modern editions, the line in question stands—"Cursed be I that did so! all the charms," &c. but the second folio reads with unquestionable propriety, "Cursed be I that *I* did so! all the charms," &c. As 'hour' has the same prolonged sound with fire, sire, &c. and as it is possible, though, with reference to the fine ear of Shakspeare, I think most improbable, that it might sometimes be made to occupy the place of two syllables, I shall pass over the instance from "Richard II." in which Malone triumphs, though without cause, over his adversary; as I shall also pass over that from "All's Well that End's Well," in which a defective line has been happily supplied by our editor, in consequence of his not knowing that 'sire' was employed as a dissyllable. In the first part of "Henry VI." "Rescued is Orleans from the English," is prolonged by the editor with a syllable which he deemed necessary because he was ignorant that the word, 'English,' was used as a trisyllable. According to him the line is—"Rescued is Orleans from the English *wolves*." We rejoice at this result of the editor's ignorance; and we wish to know who is there who can believe that 'English' was pronounced, by Shakspeare or his contemporaries, as *Engerlish*, or even as *Engleish*, with three syllables? Again, not knowing that 'Charles' was used as a word of two syllables, (and he was sufficiently near to the time of Shakspeare to know his pronunciation of such a common word: but the blockhead could not be taught the most common things,) this provoking editor instead of

"Orleans the bastard, Charles, Burgundy."

has printed,

"Orleans the bastard, Charles, *and* Burgundy."

In the next instance, I must confess myself to be ignorant of Malone's meaning. "Astræa being used," he says "as a word of *three* syllables," (I conclude that he intended to say, as a word of *four* syllables, the diphthong being dialytically separated into its component parts, and the word written and pronounced Astraea,) for "Divinest creature, Astræa's daughter," the editor has given "Divinest creature, *bright* Astræa's daughter."—Shameless interpolation! Not aware that 'sure' is used as a dissyllable, this grand corrupter of Shakspeare's text has substituted, "Gloster, we'll meet to thy *dear* cost, be sure," for "Gloster, we'll meet to thy cost, be sure."—Once more, and to conclude an examination which I could extend to a much greate

---

* In his "Venus and Adonis," and his "Rape of Lucrece," printed under his immediate inspection; and in his 154 Sonnets, printed from correct MSS., and no doubt with his knowledge, are not to be found any of these barbarous anomalies. "The Passionate Pilgrim," and "The Lover's Complaint," are, also, free from them. *Worser* and *lesser* may sometimes occur in these poems: but the last of these improprieties will occasionally find a place in the page of modern composition. In the "Rape of Lucrece," the only anomaly of the double negative, which I have been able to discover, is the following:—

"She touch'd no unknown baits, *nor* fear'd *no* hooks."

and the same impropriety may be found in three or four instances in the Sonnets. *And* substituted for *nor* would restore these few passages to perfect grammar.

† Act iii. sc. 2

length in favour of this much-injured editor, but which I feel to be now becoming tedious, for,

> "And so to arms, victorious father,"

as the line is sanctioned by Malone, 'arms,' being used, as he asserts, for a dissyllable, (arms a dissyllable!) the second folio presents us with—

> "And so to arms, victorious, *noble* father."

I have said enough to convince my readers of the falsity of the charges of stupidity and gross ignorance, brought by Malone against the editor of the second folio edition of our Poet's dramatic works. I am far from assuming to vindicate this editor from the commission of many flagrant errors: but he is frequently right, and was unquestionably conversant, let Malone assert what he pleases, with his author's language and metre. It was not, therefore, without cause, that Steevens held his labours in much estimation. Malone was an invaluable collector of facts: his industry was indefatigable: his researches were deep: his pursuit of truth was sincere and ardent: but he wanted the talents and the taste of a critic; and of all the editors, by whom Shakspeare has suffered, I must consider him as the most pernicious. Neither the indulged fancy of Pope, nor the fondness for innovation in Hanmer, nor the arrogant and headlong self-confidence of Warburton has inflicted such cruel wounds on the text of Shakspeare, as the assuming dulness of Malone. Barbarism and broken rhythm dog him at the heels wherever he treads.

In praise of the third and the fourth folio editions of our author's dramas, printed respectively in 1664 and 1685, nothing can be advanced. Each of these editions implicitly followed its immediate predecessor, and, adopting all its errors, increased them to a frightful accumulation with its own. With the text of Shakspeare in this disorder, the public of Britain remained satisfied during many years. From the period of his death he had not enforced that popularity to which his title was undeniable. Great, though inferior, men, Jonson, Fletcher, Massinger, Shirley, Ford, &c. got possession of the stage, and retained it till it ceased to exist under the puritan domination. On the restoration of the monarchy in 1660, the theatre indeed was again opened; but, under the influence of the vicious taste of the new monarch, it was surrendered to a new school (the French school) of the drama; and its mastery was held by Dryden, with many subordinates, during a long succession of years. Throughout this whole period, Shakspeare was nearly forgotten by his ungrateful or blinded countrymen. His splendour, it is true, was gleaming above the horizon; and his glory, resting in purple and gold upon the hill-summits, obtained the homage of a select band of his worshippers: but it was still hidden from the eyes of the multitude; and it was long before it gained its "meridian tower," whence it was to throw its "glittering shafts" over a large portion of the earth. At length, about the commencement of the last century, Britain began to open her eyes to the excellency of her illustrious son, THE GREAT POET OF NATURE, and to discover a solicitude for the integrity of his works. A new and a more perfect edition of them became the demand of the public; and, to answer it, an edition, under the superintendence of Rowe, made its appearance in 1709. Rowe, however, either forgetting or shrinking from the high and laborious duties, which he had undertaken, selected, most unfortunately, for his model, the last and the worst of the folio editions; and, without collating either of the first two folios or any of the earlier quartos, he gave to the disappointed public a transcript much too exact of the impure text which lay opened before him. Some of its grosser errors, however, he corrected; and he prefixed to his edition a short memoir of the life of his author; which, meagre and weakly written as it is, still constitutes the most authentic biography that we possess of our mighty bard.

On the failure of this edition, after the pause of a few years, another was projected; and that it might be more adequate to the claims of Shakspeare and of Britain, the conduct of it was placed, in homage to his just celebrity, in the hands of Pope. Pope showed himself more conscious of the nature of his task, and more faithful in his execution of it than his predecessor. He disclosed to the public the very faulty state of his author's text, and suggested the proper means of restoring it: he collated many of the earlier editions, and he cleared the page of Shakspeare from many of its deformities: but his collations were not sufficiently extensive; and he indulged, perhaps, somewhat too much in conjectural emendation. This exposed him to the attacks of the petty and minute critics; and, the success of his work falling short of his expectations, he is said to have contracted that enmity to verbal criticism, which actuated him during the remaining days of his life. His edition was published in the year 1725. Before this was undertaken, Theobald, a man of no great abilities and of little learning, had projected the restoration of Shakspeare; but his labours had been suspended, or their result had been withheld from the press, till the issue of Pope's attempt was ascertained by its accomplishment, and publication. The Shakspeare of Theobald's editing was not given to the world before the year 1733; when it obtained more of the public regard than its illustrious predecessor, in consequence of its being drawn from a somewhat wider field of collation; and of its less frequent and presumptuous admission of conjecture. Theobald, indeed, did not wholly abstain from conjecture: but the palm of conjectural criticism was placed much too high for the reach of his hand.

To Theobald, as an editor of Shakspeare, succeeded Sir Thomas Hanmer, who, in 1744, published a superb edition of the great dramatist from the press of Oxford. But Hanmer, building his work on that of Pope, and indulging in the wildest and most wanton innovations, deprived his edition of all pretensions to authenticity, and, consequently, to merit.

The bow of Ulysses was next seized by a mighty hand—by the hand of Warburton; whose Shakspeare was published in 1747. It failed of success; for, conceiving that the editor intended to make his author his showman to exhibit his erudition and intellectual power, the public quickly neglected his work; and it soon disappeared from circulation, though some of its proffered substitutions must be allowed to be happy, and some of its explanations to be just.

After an interval of eighteen years, Shakspeare obtained once more an editor of great name, and seemingly in every way accomplished to assert the rights of his author. In 1765 Doctor Samuel Johnson presented the world with his long-promised edition of our dramatist: and the public expectation, which had been highly raised, was again doomed to be disappointed. Johnson had a powerful intellect, and was perfectly conversant with human life: but he was not sufficiently versed in black-letter lore; and, deficient in poetic taste, he was unable to accompany our great bard in the higher flights of his imagination. The public in general were not satisfied with his commentary on his text: but to his preface they gave the most unlimited applause. The array and glitter of its words; the regular and pompous march of its periods, with its pervading affectation of deep thought and of sententious remark, seem to have fascinated the popular mind; and to have withdrawn from the common observation its occasional poverty of meaning; the inconsistency of its praise and censure; the falsity in some instances of its critical remarks; and its defects now and then even with respect to composition. It has, however, its merits, and Heaven forbid that I should not be just to them. It gives a right view of the difficulties to be encountered by the editor of Shakspeare: it speaks modestly of himself, and candidly of those who had preceded him in the path which he was treading:

it assigns to Pope, Hanmer, and Warburton, those victims to the rage of the minute critics, their due proportion of praise: it is honourably just, in short, to all, who come within the scope of its observations, with the exception of the editor's great author alone. To him also the editor gives abundant praise; but against it he arrays such a frightful host of censure as to command the field; and to leave us to wonder at our admiration of an object so little worthy of it, though he has been followed by the admiration of more than two entire centuries. But Johnson was of a detracting and derogating spirit. He looked at mediocrity with kindness: but of proud superiority he was impatient; and he always seemed pleased to bring down the man of the ethereal soul to the mortal of mere clay. His maxim seems evidently to have been that, which was recommended by the Roman poet to his countrymen,—

"Parcere subjectis et debellare superbos"

in the pre-eminence of intellect, when it was immediately in his view, there was something which excited his spleen; and he exulted in its abasement. In his page, "Shakspeare, in his comic scenes, is seldom successful when he engages his characters in reciprocations of smartness and contests of sarcasm: their jests are commonly gross, and their pleasantry licentious. In tragedy, his performance seems to be constantly worse as his labour is more. The effusions of passion, which exigence forces out, are, *for the most part*, striking and energetic: but whenever he solicits his invention or strains his faculties, the offspring of his throes is tumour, meanness, tediousness, and obscurity! In narration he affects a disproportionate pomp of diction, and a wearisome train of circumlocution, &c. &c. His declamations or set speeches are commonly cold and weak, for *his power was the power of Nature!* when he endeavoured, like other tragic writers, to catch opportunities of amplification; and, instead of inquiring what the occasion demanded, to show how much his stores of knowledge could supply, he seldom escapes without the pity or resentment of his reader?" "But the admirers of this great poet have never less reason to indulge their hopes of supreme excellence, than when he seems fully resolved to sink them in dejection, and mollify them with tender emotions by the fall of greatness, the danger of innocence, or the crosses of love. He is not long soft and pathetic without some idle conceit or contemptible equivocation. He no sooner moves than he counteracts himself; and terror and pity, as they are rising in the mind, are checked and blasted with sudden frigidity!" The egregious editor and critic then proceeds to confound his author with his last and most serious charge, that of an irreclaimable attachment to the offence of verbal conceit. This charge the editor illustrates and enforces, to excite our attention and to make an irresistible assault on our assent, with a variety of figurative and magnificent allusion. First, "a quibble is to Shakspeare, what luminous vapours (a Will o' the wisp) are to travellers: he follows it at all adventures: it is sure to lead him out of his way, and sure to ingulf him in the mire. It has some malignant power over his mind, and its fascinations are irresistible," &c. It then becomes a partridge or a pheasant; for "whatever be the dignity or the profundity of his disquisition, &c. &c. let but a quibble *spring up before him* and he leaves his work unfinished." It next is the golden apple of Atalanta:—"A quibble is to Shakspeare the golden apple for which he will always turn aside from his career, or stoop from his elevation. A quibble, poor and barren as it is, gave him such delight that he was content to purchase it at the sacrifice of reason, propriety, and truth;" and, lastly, the meteor, the bird of game, and the golden apple are converted into the renowned queen of Egypt: for "a quibble is to him (Shakspeare) the fatal Cleopatra, for which he lost the world, and was content to lose it!" Shakspeare lost the world! He won it in an age of intellectual giants—the Anakims of mind were then in the land, and in what succeeding period has he lost it? But, not to take advantage of an idle frolic of the editor's imagination, can the things be which he asserts? Can the author, whom he thus degrades, be the man, whom the greater Jonson, of James's reign, hails as, "The pride, the joy, the wonder of the age!" No! it is impossible! and if we come to a close examination of what our preface writer has here alleged against his author, of which I have transcribed only a part, we shall find that one half of it is false, and one, some thing very like nonsense, disguised in a garb of tinsel embroidery, and covered, as it moves statelily along, with a cloud of words:—

Infert se septus nebula, mirabile dictu,
Per medios, miscetque viris neque cernitur ulli

To discover the falsity or the inanity of the ideas, which strut in our editor's sentences against the fame of his author, we have only to strip them of the diction which envelopes them; and then, with a Shakspeare in our hands, to confront them, in their nakedness, with the truth as it is manifested in his page. But we have deviated from our straight path to regard our editor as a critic in his preface, when we ought, perhaps, to consider him only in his notes, as a commentator to explain the obscurities; or, as an experimentalist to assay the errors of his author's text. As an unfolder of intricate and perplexed passages, Johnson must be allowed to excel. His explanations are always perspicuous; and his proffered amendments of a corrupt text are sometimes successful. But the expectations of the world had been too highly raised to be satisfied with his performance; and it was only to the most exceptionable part of it, the mighty preface, that they gave their unmingled applause. In the year following the publication of Johnson's edition, in 1766, George Steevens made his first appearance as a commentator on Shakspeare; and he showed himself to be deeply conversant with that antiquarian reading, of which his predecessor had been too ignorant. In 1768, an edition of Shakspeare was given to the public by Capell; a man fondly attached to his author, but much too weak for the weighty task which he undertook. He had devoted a large portion of his life to the collection of his materials: he was an industrious collator, and all the merit, which he possesses, must be derived from the extent and the fidelity of his collations. In 1773 was published an edition of our dramatist by the associated labours of Johnson and Steevens; and this edition, in which were united the native powers of the former, with the activity, the sagacity, and the antiquarian learning of the latter, still forms the standard edition for the publishers of our Poet. In 1790 Malone entered the lists against them as a competitor for the editorial palm. After this publication, Malone seems to have devoted the remaining years of his life to the studies requisite for the illustration of his author; and at his death he bequeathed the voluminous papers, which he had prepared, to his and my friend, James Boswell, the younger son of the biographer of Johnson; and by him these papers were published in twenty octavo volumes, just before the close of his own valuable life. That the fund of Shakspearian information has been enlarged by this publication, cannot reasonably be doubted: that the text of Shakspeare has been injured by it, may confidently be asserted. As my opinion of Malone, as an annotator on Shakspeare, has been already expressed, it would be superfluous to repeat it. His stores of antiquarian knowledge were at least equal to those of Steevens: but he was not equally endowed by Nature with that popular commentator: Malone's intellect was unquestionably of a subordinate class. He could collect and amass; but he could not combine and arrange. Like a weak soldier under heavy armour, he is oppressed by his means of safety and triumph. He sinks beneath his knowledge, and cannot profitably use it. The weakness of his judgment deprived the result of his industry of its proper effect. He acts on a right principle of criticism: but, ignorant of its right application, he employs it for the purposes of error. He was not, in short, formed of the costly materials of a critic; and no labour, against the inhibition of Nature, could fashion him into a critic. His page is pregnant with information: but it is thrown into so many involutions and tangles, that it is lighter labour to work it out of the original quarry than to select it amid the confusion in which it is thus brought to your hand. If any copy of indisputable authority had been in existence, Malone would have produced a fac-simile of it, and would thus, indeed, have been an admirable editor of his author, for not a preposition, a copulative, a particle, a comma to be found in his original, would have been out of its place in his transcript. But no such authentic copy of Shakspeare could be discovered; and something more than diligence and accuracy was required in his editor: and to nothing more than diligence and accuracy could Malone's very humble and circumscribed abilities aspire. Attaching, therefore, fictitious authority to some of the earlier copies, he followed them with conscientious precision; and, disclaiming all emendatory criticism, he rejoiced in his fidelity to the errors of the first careless or illiterate transcriber. He closed the long file of the editors of Shakspeare. But although no formal editor or commentator has hitherto appeared to supply the place left vacant by Malone, yet does the importance of our bard continue to excite the man of talents to write in his cause, and to refresh the wreath of fame, which has hung for two centuries on his tomb. On this occasion I must adduce the name of Skottowe, a gentleman who has recently gratified the public with a life of Shakspeare, involving a variety of matter respecting him, in a style eminent for its compression and its neatness. To Mr. Skottowe I must acknowledge my especial obligations, for not infrequently relieving me from the prolixities and the perplexities of Malone; and sometimes for giving to me information in a compendious and lucid form, like a jewel set in the rich simplicity of gold.

When I speak of Malone as the last of the editors of Shakspeare, I speak, of course, with reference to the time at which I am writing, when no later editor has shown himself to the world. But when I am placed before the awful tribunal of the Public, a new Editor of our great dramatist will stand by my side: who, whilst I can be only a suppliant for pardon, may justly be a candidate for praise. With Mr. Singer, the editor in question, I am personally unacquainted; and till a period, long subsequent to my completion of the little task which I had undertaken, I had not seen a line of his Shakspearian illustrations. But, deeming it right to obtain some knowledge of the gentleman, who was bound on the same voyage of adventure, in the same vessel with myself, I have since read the far greater part of his commentary on my author; and it would be unjust in me not to say, that I have found much in it to applaud, and very litttle to censure. Mr. Singer's antiquarian learning is accurate and extensive: his critical sagacity is considerable; and his judgment generally approves itself to be correct. He enters on the field with the strength of a giant; but with the diffidence and the humility of a child. We sometimes wish, indeed, that his humility had been less: for he is apt to defer to inferior men, and to be satisfied with following when he is privileged to lead. His explanations of his author are frequently happy; and sometimes they illustrate a passage, which had been left in unregarded darkness by the commentators who had preceded him. The sole fault of these explanatory notes (if such indeed can be deemed a fault) is their redundancy; and their recurrence in cases were their aid seems to be unnecessary. Mr. Singer and I may occasionally differ in our opinions respecting the text, which he has adopted: but, in these instances of our dissent, it is fully as probable that I may be wrong as he. I feel, in short, confident, on the whole, that Mr. Singer is now advancing, not to claim, (for *to claim* is inconsistent with his modesty,) but to obtain a high place among the editors of Shakspeare; and to have his name enrolled with the names of those who have been the chief benefactors of the reader of our transcendent Poet.

We have now seen, from the first editorial attempt of Rowe, a whole century excited by the greatness of one man, and sending forth its most ambitious spirits, from the man of genius down to the literary mechanic, to tend on him as the vassals of his royalty, and to illustrate his magnificence to the world. Has this excitement had an adequate cause? or has it been only the frenzy of the times, or a sort of meteorous exhalation from an idle and over-exuberant soil? Let us examine our great poet, and dramatist, with the eye of impartial criticism; and then let the result of our examination form the reply to these interrogatories of doubt.

Shakspeare took his stories from any quarter, whence they were offered to him; from Italian novels; from histories; from old story-books; from old plays; and even from old ballads. In one instance, and in one alone, no prototype has been found for his fiction; and the whole of "The Tempest," from its first moving point to the plenitude of its existence, must be admitted to be the offspring of his wonderful imagination.* But whence soever he drew the first suggestion of his story, or whatever might be its original substance, he soon converts it into an image of ivory and gold, like that of the Minerva of Phidias; and then, beyond the efficacy of the sculptor's art, he breathes into it the breath of life. This, indeed, is spoken only of his tragedies and comedies: for his histories, as they were first called, or historical dramas, are transcripts from the page of Hall or Hollingshead; and, in some instances, are his workings on old plays, and belong to him no otherwise than as he imparted to them the powerful delineation of character, or enriched them with some exquisite scenes. These pieces, however, which affect not the combination of a fable; but, wrought upon the page of the chronicler or of the elder dramatist, follow the current of events, as it flows on in historic succession, must be made the first subjects of our remarks; and we will then pass to those dramas, which are more properly and strictly his own. To these historical plays, then, whatever may be their original materials, the power of the Poet has communicated irresistible attraction; not, as Samuel Johnson would wish us to believe, "by being not long soft or pathetic without some idle conceit or contemptible equivocation:" not "by checking and blasting terror and pity, as they are rising in the mind, with sudden frigidity," but by the strongest exertions of the highest poetry; and by commanding, with the royalty of genius, every avenue to the human heart. For the truth of what we assert, we will make our appeal to the frantic and soul-piercing lamentations of Constance in "King John;" to the scene between that monarch and Hubert; and between Hubert and young Arthur; to the subsequent scene between Hubert and his murderous sovereign, when the effects of the reported death of Arthur on the populace are described, and the murderer quarrels with his agent; to the scene, finally, in which the king dies, and which concludes the play.

For the evidence of the power of our great Poet we might appeal also to many scenes and descriptions even in "Richard II.;" though of all his historical dramas this, perhaps, is the least instinct

* This, perhaps, may be affirmed also of "A Midsummer Night's Dream."

with animation, and the least attractive with dramatic interest. Of "Richard II." we may say with Mr. Skottowe, that, "though it is an exquisite poem, it is an indifferent play." But in the drama which, in its historic order, succeeds to it, we receive an ample compensation for any failure of the dramatist in "Richard II." In every page of "Henry IV.," both the serious and the comic, Shakspeare "is himself again;" and our fancy is either elevated or amused without the interruption of a single discordant or uncharacteristic sentiment. Worcester, indeed, says,

"And 'tis no little reason bids us speed
To save our heads by raising of a head,"

and is thus guilty of a quibble; an offence of which the Prince, on two occasions, shows himself to be capable; once when he sees Falstaff apparently dead on the field of Shrewsbury; and once when, on his accession to the throne, he appoints his father's Chief Justice to a continuance in his high office: and these, as I believe, are the sole instances of our Poet's dalliance with his Cleopatra, for whose love he was content to lose the world, throughout the whole of the serious parts of this long and admirable drama.

The succeeding play of "Henry V." bears noble testimony to the poetic and the dramatic supremacy of Shakspeare: to the former, more especially in its three fine choruses, one of them serving as the prologue to the play, one opening the third act, and one describing the night preceeding the battle of Agincourt: to the latter, in every speech of the King's, and in the far greater part of the remaining dialogue, whether it be comic or tragic. "Henry V.," however, is sullied with some weak and silly scenes; and, on the whole, is certainly inferior in dramatic attraction to its illustrious predecessor. But it is a very fine production, and far—far above the reach of any other English writer, who has been devoted to the service of the stage.

Of "Henry VI.," *that drum and trumpet thing*, as it has happily been called by a man of genius,* who ranged himself with the advocates of Shakspeare, I shall not take any notice on the present occasion, as the three parts of this dramatized history are nothing more than three old plays, corrected by the hand of Shakspeare, and here and there illustrious with the fire-drops which fell from his pen. Though we consider them, therefore, as possessing much attraction, and as disclosing Shakspeare in their outbreaks of fine writing, and in their strong characteristic portriature, we shall now pass them by to proceed without delay to their dramatic successor, "Richard III." Of "Richard II.," fine as it occasionally is in poetry, and rich in sentiment and pathos, we have remarked that, with reference to the other productions of its great author, it was low in the scale of merit. In "Richard II." he found an insufficient and an unawakening subject for his genius, and it acted drowsily, and as if it were half asleep: but in the third Richard there was abundant excitement for all its powers; and the victim of Tudor malignity and calumny rushes from the scene of our mighty dramatist in all the black efficiency of the demoniac tyrant. Besides Sir Thomas More's history of Richard of Gloster, our Poet had the assistance, as it seems, of a play upon the same subject, which had been popular before he began his career upon the stage. Adhering servilely neither to the historian nor to the old dramatist, Shakspeare contented himself with selecting from each of them such parts as were suited to his purpose; and with the materials thus obtained, compounded with others supplied by his own invention, he has produced a drama, which cannot be read in the closet, or seen in its representation on the stage without the strongest agitation of the mind. The character of Richard is drawn with inimitable effect; and in the minor parts of the execution of the drama, there is nothing among all the creations of poetry more splendid and terrific than the dream of Clarence. But this noble effort of the tragic power is not altogether faultless. Some of its scenes, as not promoting the action of the drama, are superfluous and even tedious; and the violation of history, for the purpose of introducing the deposed queen, Margaret, upon the stage, may reasonably be censured. I am not certain, however, that I should be satisfied to resign her on the requisition of truth. Her curses are thrilling, and their fulfilment is awful. Shakspeare, as it may be remarked, has accumulated uncommitted crimes on the head of the devoted Richard. By the historian, this monarch is cleared of the deaths of Clarence and of Anne, his wife: to the latter of whom he is said to have approved himself an affectionate husband; whilst the murder of Clarence is imputed to the intrigues of the relations of his sister-in-law, the queen. His hand certainly did not shed the blood of the pious Henry; and even his assassination of the two illegitimate sons of his brother, Edward, is supported by very questionable evidence, for there is reason to think that the eldest of these young princes walked at his uncle's coronation; and that the youngest escaped to meet his death, under the name of Perkin Warbeck, from the hand of the first Tudor. But the scene of Shakspeare has stamped deeper and more indelible deformity on the memory of the last sovereign of the house of York, than all the sycophants of the Tudors had been able to impress; or than all that the impartiality, and the acute research of the modern historian have ever had the power to erase. We are certain that Richard possessed a lawful title to the throne which he filled: that he was a wise and patriotic sovereign: that his death was a calamity to his country, which it surrendered to a race of usurpers and tyrants, who trampled on its liberties, and stained its soil with much innocent and rich blood:—to that cold-blooded murderer and extortioner, Henry VII.—to that monster of cruelty and lust, his ferocious son: to the sanguinary and ruthless bigot, Mary: to the despotic and unamiable Elizabeth; the murderess of a suppliant queen, of kindred blood, who had fled to her for protection. Such was the result of Bosworth's field, preceded, as it was on the stage of Shakspeare, by visions of bliss to Richmond, and by visions of terror to Richard. But Shakspeare wrote with all the prejudices of a partisan of the Tudors: and at a time also when it was still expedient to flatter that detestable family.

His next task was one of yet greater difficulty:—to smooth down the rugged features of the eighth Henry, and to plant a wreath on the brutal and blood-stained brow of the odious father of Elizabeth. This task he has admirably executed, and without offering much violation to the truth of history. He has judiciously limited his scene to that period of the tyrant's reign in which the more disgusting deformities of his character had not yet been revealed—to the death of Catharine, the fall of Wolsey, and the birth of Elizabeth: and the crowned savage appears to us only as the generous, the munificent, the magnanimous monarch, striking down the proud, and supporting with a strong arm the humble and the oppressed. But the whole pathos and power of the scene are devoted to Catharine and Wolsey. On these two characters the dramatist has expended all his force; and our pity is inseparably attached to them to the last moment of their lives. They expire, indeed, bedewed with our tears. Of this, the last of Shakspeare's dramatic histories, it may be remarked that it is written in a style different from that of its predecessors: that it is less interspersed with comic scenes; that in its serious parts its diction is more stately and formal; more elevated and figurative: that its figures are longer and more consistently sustained. that it is more rich in theatric exhibition, or in the spectacle, as Aristotle calls it, and by whom it is

* The late Mr. Maurice Morgann; who wrote an eloquent essay on the dramatic character of Falstaff.

regarded as a component part of the drama. To any attentive reader these distinguishing characters of the dramatic history of Henry VIII. must be sufficiently obvious; and we can only wonder that the same mind should produce such fine pieces as those of "Henry IV.," "Richard III.," and "Henry VIII.," each written with a pen appropriate to itself, and the last with a pen not employed in any other instance.

If we were to pause in this stage of our progress, we might confidently affirm that we had suggested to the minds of our readers such a mass of poetic and dramatic genius as would be sufficient to excite the general interest of an intellectual and literary people. But we are yet only in the vestibule which opens into the magnificence of the palace, where Shakspeare is seated on the throne of his greatness. The plays, which we have hitherto been considering, are constructed, for the most part, with materials not his own, supplied either by the ancient chronicler, or by some preceding dramatist; and are wrought up without any reference to that essential portion of a drama, a plot or fable. But when he is disengaged from the incumbrances to which he had submitted in his histories, he assumes the full character of the more perfect dramatist; and discovers that art, for which, equally with the powers of his imagination, he was celebrated by Ben Jonson. In some of his plays, indeed, we acknowledge the looseness with which his fable is combined, and the careless hurry with which he accelerates its close: but in the greater triumphs of his genius, we find the fable artificially planned and solidly constructed. In "The Merchant of Venice," in "Romeo and Juliet," in "Lear," in "Othello," and, above all, in that intellectual wonder, "The Tempest," we may observe the fable managed with the hand of a master, and contributing its effect, with the characters and the dialogue, to amuse, to agitate, or to surprise. In that beautiful pastoral drama, "As You Like It," the sudden disappearance of old Adam from the scene has been a subject of regret to more than one of the commentators: and Samuel Johnson wishes that the dialogue between the hermit, as he calls him, and the usurping duke, the result of which was the conversion of the latter, had not been omitted on the stage. But old Adam had fulfilled the purposes of his dramatic existence, and it was, therefore, properly closed. He had discovered his honest attachment to his young master, and had experienced his young master's gratitude. He was brought into a place of safety; and his fortunes were now blended with those of the princely exiles of the forest. There was no further part for him to act; and he passed naturally from the stage, no longer the object of our hopes or our fears. On the subject of S. Johnson's wish respecting the dialogue between *the old religious man* and the guilty duke, we may shortly remark, that nothing could have been more undramatic than the intervention of such a scene of dry and didactic morality, at such a crisis of the drama, when the minds of the audience were heated, and hurrying to its approaching close. Like Felix in the sacred history, the royal criminal might have trembled at the lecture of the holy man: but the audience, probably, would have been irritated or asleep. No! Shakspeare was not so ignorant of his art as to require to be instructed in it by the author of Irene.

But it was in the portraiture of the human mind: in the specific delineation of intellectual and moral man, that the genius of Shakspeare was pre-eminently conspicuous. The curious inquisition of his eye into the characters, which were passing beneath its glance, cannot be made too much the subject of our admiration and wonder. He saw them not only under their broad distinctions, when they became obvious to the common observer; but he beheld them in their nicer tints and shadings, by which they are diversified, though the tone of their general colouring may be the same.

——"facies non omnibus una,
Nec diversa tamen."

To illustrate what I mean, let us contemplate Portia, Desdemona, Imogen, Rosalind, Beatrice, Cordelia, and Ophelia. They are equally amiable and affectionate women; equally faithful and attached as wives, as friends, as daughters: two of them, also, are noted for the poignancy and sparkle of their wit: and yet can it be said that any one of them can be mistaken for the other; or that a single speech can with propriety be transferred from the lips of her to whom it has been assigned by her dramatic creator? They are all known to us as the children of one family, with a general resemblance, and an individual discrimination. Benedict and Mercutio are both young men of high birth; of known valour; of playful wit, delighting itself in pleasantry and frolic: yet are they not distinguished beyond the possibility of their being confounded? So intimately conversant is our great dramatist with the varieties of human nature, that he scatters character, as a king on his accession scatters gold, among the populace; and there is not one, perhaps, of his subordinate agents, who has not his peculiar features and a complexion of his own. So mighty is our Poet as a dramatic creator, that characters of the most opposite description are thrown in equal perfection and with equal facility from his hand. The executive decision of Richard; the meditative inefficiency of Hamlet; the melancholy of Jaques, which draws subjects of moral reflection from every object around him; and the hilarity of Mercutio, which forsakes him not in the very act of dying; the great soul of Macbeth, maddened and bursting under accumulated guilt; and "the unimitated and inimitable Falstaff," (as he is called by S. Johnson, in the single outbreak of enthusiasm extorted from him by the wonders of Shakspeare's page) revelling in the tavern at Eastcheap, or jesting on the field of Shrewsbury, are all the creatures of one plastic intellect, and are absolute and entire in their kind. Malignity and revenge constitute the foundation on which are constructed the two very dissimilar characters of Shylock and Iago. But there is something terrific and even awful in the inexorability of the Jew, whilst there is nothing but meanness in the artifices of the Venetian standard-bearer. They are both men of vigorous and acute understandings: we hate them both; but our hatred of the former is mingled with involuntary respect; of the latter our detestation is made more intensely strong by its association with contempt.

In his representation of madness, Shakspeare must be regarded as inimitably excellent; and the picture of this last degradation of humanity, with nature always for his model, is diversified by him at his pleasure. Even over the wreck of the human mind he throws the variegated robe of character. How different is the genuine insanity of Lear from the assumed insanity of Edgar, with which it is immediately confronted; and how distinct, again, are both of these from the disorder which prevails in the brain of the lost and the tender Ophelia.

In one illustrious effort of his dramatic power, our Poet has had the confidence to produce two delineations of the same perversion of the human heart, and to present them, at once similar and dissimilar, to the examination of our wondering eyes. In Timon and Apemantus is exhibited the same deformity of misanthropy: but in the former it springs from the corruption of a noble mind, stricken and laid prostrate by the ingratitude of his species: in the latter, it is a noisome weed, germinating from a bitter root, and cherished by perverse cultivation into branching malignity. In each of them, as the vice has a different parentage, so has it a diversified aspect.

With such an intimacy with all the fine and subtle workings of Nature in her action on the human heart, it is not wonderful that our great dramatist should possess an absolute control over the passions; and should be able to unlock the cell of each of them as the impulse of his fancy may direct. When we follow Macbeth to the chamber of Duncan: when we stand with him by the enchanted caldron; or see him, under the infliction of conscience, glaring at the spectre of the *blood-boltered* Banquo in the possession of the royal chair, horror is by our side, thrilling in our veins, and bristling in our hair. When we attend the Danish prince to his midnight conference with the shade of his murdered father, and hear the ineffable accents of the dead, willing, but prohibited, "to tell the secrets of his prison-house," we are appalled, and our faculties are suspended in terror. When we see the faithful and the lovely Juliet awaking in the house of darkness and corruption with the corpse of her husband on her bosom: when we behold the innocent Desdemona dying by the hand, to which she was the most fondly attached; and charging on herself, with her latest breath, the guilt of her murderer: when we witness the wretchedness of Lear, contending with the midnight storm, and strewing his white locks on the blast; or carrying in his withered arms the body of his Cordelia murdered in his cause, is it possible that the tear of pity should not start from our eyes and trickle down our cheeks? In the forest of Arden, as we ramble with its accidental inmates, our spirits are soothed into cheerfulness, and are, occasionally, elevated into gaiety. In the tavern at Eastcheap, with the witty and debauched knight, we meet with "Laughter holding both his sides;" and we surrender ourselves, willingly and delighted, to the inebriation of his influence. We could dwell for a long summer's day amid the fertility of these charming topics, if we were not called from them to a higher region of poetic enjoyment, possessed by the genius of Shakspeare alone, where he reigns sole lord, and where his subjects are the wondrous progeny of his own creative imagination. From whatever quarter of the world, eastern or northern, England may have originally derived her elves and her fairies, Shakspeare undoubtedly formed these little beings, as they flutter in his scenes, from an idea of his own; and they came from his hand, beneficent and friendly to man; immortal and invulnerable; of such corporeal minuteness as to lie in the bell of a cowslip; and yet of such power as to disorder the seasons; as

> ———————"to bedim
> The noontide sun; call forth the mutinous winds:
> And 'twixt the green sea and the azured vault,
> Set roaring war."

To this little ethereal people our Poet has assigned manners and occupations in perfect consistency with their nature; and has sent them forth, in the richest array of fancy, to gambol before us, to astonish and delight us. They resemble nothing upon earth: but if they could exist with man, they would act and speak as they act and speak, with the inspiration of our Poet, in "The Tempest," and "A Midsummer Night's Dream." In contrast with his Ariel, "a spirit too delicate," as the servant of a witch, "to act her earthy and abhorred commands:" but ready, under the control of his philosophic master,

> "To answer his best pleasure, be it to fly,
> To swim; to dive into the fire; to ride
> On the curl'd clouds;"

in contrast with this aerial being, the imagination of Shakspeare has formed a monster, the offspring of a hag and a demon; and has introduced him into the scene with a mind and a character appropriately and strictly his own. As the drama, into which are introduced these two beings, beyond the action of Nature, as it is discoverable on this earth, one of them rising above, and one sinking beneath the level of humanity, may be received as the proudest evidence, which has hitherto been produced, of the extent and vigour of man's imagination: so it bids fair to stand unrivalled amid all the loftiest aspirations of the human mind in the ages which are yet to come. The great Milton's imagination alone can be placed in competition with that of Shakspeare; and even Milton's must yield the palm to that which is displayed in "A Midsummer Night's Dream," and in the almost divine "Tempest."

But having sported a while with the fairies,

> ———— "as on the sands with printless feet
> They chase the ebbing Neptune,"

or

> ——————— "in the spiced Indian air,
> They dance their ringlets to the whistling wind,"

the mighty Poet turns from their bowers, "over-canopied with luscious woodbine," and plants us on "the blasted heath," trodden by the weird sisters, the Fates of the north; or leads us to the dreadful cave, where they are preparing their infernal caldron, and singing round it the incantations of hell. What a change, from all that is fascinating, to all that is the most appalling to the fancy; and yet each of these scenes is the product of the same astonishing intellect, delighting at one time to lull us on beds of roses, with the spirit of Orpheus, and at another to curdle our blood by throwing at us the viper lock of Alecto. But to show his supreme command of the super-human world, our royal Poet touches the sepulchre with his magic rod, and the sepulchre opens "its pond'rous and marble jaws," and gives its dead to "revisit the glimpses of the moon." The belief that the dead, on some awful occasions, were permitted to assume the semblance of those bodies, in which they had walked upon earth; or that the world of spirits was sometimes disclosed to the eye of mortality, has prevailed in every age of mankind, in the most enlightened as well as in the most dark. When philosophy had attained its widest extent of power, and had enlarged and refined the intellect, not only of its parent Greece, but of its pupil Rome, a spectre is recorded to have shaken the firmness of Dion, the scholar and the friend of Plato; and another to have assayed the constancy of the philosophic and the virtuous Brutus. In the superstitious age of our Elizabeth and of her Scottish successor, the belief in the existence of ghosts and apparitions was nearly universal; and when Shakspeare produced upon his stage the shade of the Danish sovereign, there was not, perhaps, a heart, amid the crowded audience, which did not palpitate with fear. But in any age, however little tainted it might be with superstitious credulity, would the ghost of royal Denmark excite an agitating interest, with such awful solemnity is he introduced, so sublimely terrible is his tale of woe, and such are the effects of his appearance on the persons of the drama, who are its immediate witnesses. We catch, indeed, the terrors of Horatio and the young prince; and if the illusion be not so strong as to seize in the first instance on our own minds, it acts on them in its result from theirs. The melancholy, which previously preyed on the spirits of the youthful Hamlet, was certainly heightened into insanity by this ghostly conference; and from this dreadful moment his madness is partly assumed, and partly unaffected. It is certain that no spectre, ever brought upon the stage, can be compared with this phantom, created by the power of Shakspeare. The apparition of the host, in "The Lover's Progress," by Fletcher, is too contemptible to be mentioned on this occasion: the spirit of Almanzor's mother, in "The Conquest of Granada," by Dryden, is not of a higher class; and even the ghost of Darius, in "The Persians," of the mighty and sublime Æschylus, shrinks into insignificance before this of the murdered Majesty of Denmark. For his success, indeed, in this instance, Shakspeare is greatly indebted to the superior awfulness of his religion; and the use which he has made of the Romish purgatory must be regarded as supremely felicitous. When the imagination of Shakspeare sported without control amid these creations of its own, it unquestionably lifted him high above any competition. As he plays with the fairies in their bowers of eglantine and woodbine; or directs the operations in the magic cave; or calls the dead man from the "cold obstruction" of the tomb, "to make night hideous," he may challenge the poets of every age, from that of Homer to the present, and be fearless of the event. But either from his ignorance of them, which is not easily credible, or from his disregard to them, or rather, perhaps, from his desire to escape from their yoke, he violates without remorse the dramatic unities of time and place, contenting himself to preserve the unity of action or design, without which, indeed, nothing worthy of the name of composition can exist. And who steps forward, in this instance of his licentious liberty, as the champion of Shakspeare, but that very critic who brings such charges against him as a poet and a dramatist, that, if they were capable of being substantiated, would overturn him from his lofty pedestal; and would prove the object of our homage, during two centuries, to be a little deformed image, which we had with the most silly idolatry mistaken for a god? But Johnson's defence of Shakspeare seems to be as weak as his attack; though in either case the want of power in the warrior is concealed under the glare of his ostentatious arms. It is unquestionable that, since the days of the patrician of Argos, recorded by Horace,* who would sit for hours in the vacant theatre, and give his applause to actors who were not there, no man, unattended by a keeper, ever mistook the wooden and narrow platform of a stage for the fields of Philippi or Agincourt; or the painted canvass, shifting under his eye, for the palace of the Ptolemies or the Cæsars; or the walk, which had brought him from his own house to the theatre, for a voyage across the Mediterranean to Alexandria; or the men and women, with whom he had probably conversed in the common intercourse of life, for old Romans and Grecians. Such a power of illusion, quite incompatible with any degree of sanity of mind, has never been challenged by any critic, as attached to poetry and the stage; and it is adduced, in his accustomed style of argument, by Johnson, only for the purpose of confounding his adversaries with absurdity, or of baffling them with ridicule. But there is a power of illusion, belonging to genuine poetry, which, without overthrowing the reason, can seize upon the imagination, and make it subservient to its purposes. This is asserted by Horace in that often cited passage:

> "Ille per extentum funem mihi posse videtur
> Ire poeta, meum qui pectus inaniter angit,
> Irritat, mulcet falsis terroribus implet
> Ut magus; et modo me Thebis modo ponit Athenis."

Assisted by the scenery, the dresses of the actors, and their fine adaptation of the voice and countenance to the design of the poet, this illusion becomes so strong as intimately to blend us with the fictitious personages whom we see before us. We know, indeed, that we are seated upon benches, and are spectators only of a poetic fiction: but the power, which mingles us with the agents upon the stage, is of such a nature that we feel, as it were, one interest with them: we resent the injuries which they suffer, we rejoice at the good fortune which betides them: the pulses of our hearts beat in harmony with theirs; and as the tear gushes from their eyes, it swells and overflows in ours. To account for this influence of poetic imitation, for this contagion of represented passion belongs to the metaphysician, the sole business of the critic is to remark and to reason from the fact. It is unquestionable that our imaginations are, to a certain extent, under the control of authentic poetry, and especially of that poetry which employs the scenic imitation for its instrument. The stream of passion, like a stream of electricity, rushes from the actor to us, and we are as unable as we are unwilling to resist it. Now it is this feeling, which constitutes the poetic probability of what we see and hear, and which may be violated by an injudicious and lawless shifting of the scene. If our passions be interested by an action passing at a place called Rome, it must shock and chill them to have our attentions hurried suddenly, without any reason for the discontinuance of the action, to a place called Alexandria, separated by the intervention of a thousand miles. Let us suppose, then, that in the fulness of the scenic excitement, a friend at our elbow, with the impassible fibre of a Johnson, were to shake us and to say, "What! are you mad? Know you not where you are? in Drury Lane theatre? within a few hundred yards of your own chambers in Lincoln's Inn, and neither at Rome nor at Alexandria? and perceive you not that the old man whom you see there on his knee, with his hands clenched, and his eyes raised in imprecation to heaven, is our old friend, Garrick, who is reciting with much propriety some verses made by a man, long since in his grave? Yes! Garrick, with whom you conversed not many hours ago; and who, a few hours hence, will be talking with his friends, over a comfortable supper, of the effects of his present mimickry?" If we should be thus addressed, (and a sudden shifting of the scene may produce an equal dissipation of the illusion which delights us,) should we be thankful to our wise friend for thus informing our understanding by the interruption of our feelings? Should we not rather exclaim with the Argive noble of Horace, when purged by hellebore into his senses,

> ——— "Pol me occidisti———
> ——— cui sic extorta voluptas
> Et demptus per vim mentis gratissimus error."

With the illusion of the poetic or dramatic imitation, established as an unquestionable truth in our minds, let us now turn and consider the dramatic unities in their origin and effect. The unity of action, indeed, may be thrown altogether from our notice; for, universally acknowledged to be essentially necessary to the drama, and constituting what may be called its living principle, it has escaped from violation even by our lawless Poet himself. The drama, as we know, in Greece, derived its origin from the choral odes, which were sung at certain seasons before the altar of Bacchus. To these, in the first instance, was added a dialogue of two persons; and, the number of speakers being subsequently increased, a regular dramatic fable was, at length, constructed, and the dialogue usurped the prime honours of the performance. But the chorus, though degraded, could not be expelled from the scene, which was once entirely its own; and, consecrated by the regard of the people, it was forced upon the acceptance of the dramatist, to act with it in the best manner that he could. It was stationed, therefore, permanently on the stage, and made to occupy its place with the agents who were to conduct the action of the fable. From the circumstance of its being stationary on the stage, it secured the strict observance of the unity of place: for with a stage, which was never vacant, and consequently with only one scene, the Grecian dramatist could not remove his agents whithersoever he pleased, in accommodation to his immediate convenience; but on the spot, where the scene opened, he was constrained to retain them till the action of the drama was closed, and what could not consistently be acted was necessarily consigned to narration. This was a heavy servitude to the dramatist; but it had its compensations in uninterrupted feeling, and in the greater conservation of probability. To the unity of time, as time is more pliant to the imagination than place, the Grecian dramatist seems to have paid little if any regard. In the Agamemnon of Æschylus, the fire signals have only just announced to Mycenæ the fall of Troy, when the herald arrives with the tidings of the victorious

———* Fuit haud ignobilis Argis, &c. Epis. lib. ii. Ep. ii 1. 128

king's approach; who must thus have passed from Phrygia to the Peloponnesus, obstructed also as his passage was by a tempest, with the celerity nearly of a ray of light; and in the Trachiniæ of Sophocles, a journey of about one hundred and twenty miles is accomplished during the recitation of a hundred verses. The transgression of the unity of time was not, perhaps, much the subject of the auditor's calculation, or in any degree of his concern. With his mind intent on the still occupied stage and the unchanging scene, he was ready to welcome the occurrence of any new event, or to listen with pleasure to any new narration of facts beyond the stage, without pausing to investigate the poet's due apportionment of time. If the scene had been shifted, the feelings of the spectator would have been outraged by such an infringement of the unity of place. When the arbitrary separation of the drama into acts was accomplished by the Roman dramatists, the observance of the unity of place became more easy, though still it was not to be abandoned. An act constitutes a portion of the action of a drama, at the close of which the stage is vacated and the curtain drops. If, during the act, the scene be shifted, the unity of place is broken; the probability of the dramatic imitation is diminished, and our feelings are certainly offended: but in the interval between act and act, the scene may be removed to any place where it may suit the convenience of the poet to plant it, to Venice or to Cyprus; and any lapse of time may, readily and without absurdity, be imagined to intervene. The action of the drama must necessarily be maintained one and entire, and then, with the scene stationary during the act, all the dramatic unities will be sufficiently, if not rigidly, preserved. As we know nothing of the tragic writers of Rome, all their works having perished, with the exception of those of Seneca, from which not any thing of value can be learned, we cannot decide whether or not they availed themselves of the liberty which they had obtained by this division of their plays into acts; and that their plays were divided into acts, like those of the Roman comic writers, we are assured by Horace when he tells the Pisos—

> "Neve minor, neu sit quinto productior actu
> Fabula, &c."*

But if they did not assert the liberty, which they had gained by thus breaking the continued representation of the Grecian theatre, they had themselves only to blame; for they certainly possessed the means of effectively preserving all the power of the unities at a very small expense of difficulty and labour. It is for his inattention to the integrity of the scene during the continuance of each single act that I conceive Shakspeare to be principally censurable; and the variety, to which we are instructed to look as the consequence of his lawlessness in this instance, to be an insufficient compensation for the outrage of probability, for the frequent violation of our feelings, and for the vicious example with which he has corrupted the good taste, and has diminished the efficiency of the English stage. A recent commentator, however, has discovered, and he seems to applaud himself on the felicitous discovery, that our great bard has been faithful to one unity of the drama, though he has treated the others with disregard—that he has been faithful to the unity of feeling—to the unity of feeling! What! when he transports us from the revels and the wit of Falstaff to the council chamber of the politic Bolingbroke, to the military array of the young Percy, to the field of Shrewsbury, to the castle of the plaintiff Northumberland. The tragedies of Rowe, and the comedies of Congreve may vaunt of their unity of feeling: but that mixed species of drama, in which Shakspeare delights, will admit the praise of any other unity in preference to that of feeling.

* De Arte Poetica, l. 189.

If the limits prescribed to me on the present occasion would admit of such a disquisition, I would submit to my readers an analysis of one of our Poet's finest plays, that I might distinctly show how much he has lost by his neglect of the dramatic unities; and how much more effectually he might have wrought for his purpose if he had not disdained or been too idle to solicit their assistance. In two lines of supreme fustian and nonsense, Johnson says of him,

> "Existence saw him spurn her bounded reign,
> And panting time toil'd after him in vain."

If he spurn'd the reign of existence, he must have plunged into some illimitable void, if there be such, in the infinity of space; and what is the idea intended to be conveyed by "Panting time toiling after him in vain," I will confess that I do not precisely comprehend. I conclude, however, that of these lines the first refers to the super-human creatures of the dramatist's invention, to his fairies, his magicians, and his ghosts: and these, indeed, are proud evidences of his imaginative powers; and that the second, in the ludicrous image, which it presents, of old Time, panting and toiling in vain to catch the active and runaway Poet, must allude to the contempt occasionally discovered by our lawless bard for probability and the limitation of time; and this, of which any scribbler may be guilty, is, in truth, the most effective dispraise. But it is more wonderful that Shakspeare, who may be regarded as the father of the English drama, accomplished so much for its perfection, than that he failed to accomplish more.

We have now considered this extraordinary man as the giver of a poetic soul to historic narration, as the framer of a dramatic fable, and excelling equally in the sublime, the pathetic, and the ludicrous; as luxuriating by himself, in a sort of inaccessible glory, in a world of his own imagination; as neglecting the dramatic unities, either from ignorance of their effect, or from an indolent dislike of their restraint. We have made, in short, a cursory survey of his excellencies and his defects. His diction only now remains to be the subject of our attention; and in this subordinate portion of the drama, we shall find him to be as superior to competition as he is in the characteristic and the imaginative. His diction is an instrument, which is admirably adapted to all his purposes. In his tragic strains, it sounds every note of the gamut; and is either sublime or tender, vehement or pathetic, with the passion of which it is the organ: in description it is picturesque, animated, and glowing; and every where its numbers are so harmonious, so varied, almost to infinity, in their cadence and their pauses, that they give to the ear a perpetual feast, in which there is no satiety. As the diction of Shakspeare rises in his higher scenes, without effort or tumour, to the sublime of poetry, so does it fall, in his comic, with facility and grace, into the humility of prose. It has been charged with being harsh and ungrammatical. I believe it to be harsh and unrhythmical (I confine the remark, of course, to the verse portion of it) only when it has been deformed by the perverse industry of tasteless commentators, referring us to incorrect transcriptions for authorities; and to the same cause may be ascribed, as I am satisfied, many, if not all, of its grosser grammatical errors. It will not, indeed, in every instance, as we are willing to allow, abide the rigid analysis of grammar; for it sometimes impresses the idea forcibly and distinctly on the mind without the aid of regular grammar, and without discovering the means by which the exploit has been achieved. As one example of this power of Shakspeare's diction, among many of a similar nature which might be adduced, we will transcribe the often-cited answer of Claudio to his sister, in "Measure for Measure," respecting the unknown terrors of death. The expressions in Italics convey their meaning with great accuracy to the hear er's or the reader's mind; but, if submitted to the philosophical grammarian's examination, they will not easily stand under it; and they may puzzle us to account for their effect in the communication of the poet's ideas.

> 'Ay, but to die, and go we know not where:
> To *lie in cold obstruction*, and to rot:
> *This sensible warm motion to become*
> *A kneaded clod*, and the delighted spirit
> To bathe in fiery floods; or to reside
> In thrilling regions of thick-ribbed ice:
> To be imprison'd in the viewless winds;
> And blown with restless violence about
> The pendent world: or to be worse than worst
> Of those that lawless and uncertain thoughts
> Imagine howlings!——'tis too horrible!
> The weariest and most loathed worldly life,
> That age, ache, penury, imprisonment
> Can lay on nature, is a paradise
> To what we fear of death."

This entire passage, terminating at "howling," is deficient in grammatical correctness, for it contains an antecedent not succeeded by a consequent: but is there a reader of taste who would wish it to be any thing but what it is? As for those barbarisms of the double negative and the double comparative, which Malone is studious to recall from the old copies into Shakspeare's text, I have already declared my conviction that they are falsely charged upon Shakspeare. They are not to be found in those effusions of his muse which issued from the press under his own immediate inspection; and they must assuredly be considered as the illiterate errors of an illiterate transcriber.

I could now easily, and the task would be delightful to me, produce examples, from the page of Shakspeare, of all the excellencies which I have attributed to his diction; of its sublimity, its force, its tenderness, tis pathos, its picturesque character, its sweet and ever varying harmony. But I have already very far transgressed the limits prescribed to me in my volume; and I must restrain myself. When, therefore, I have cited, at the close of what I am now writing, the description by Jaques, in "As you Like it," of the seven ages of man, as an evidence of Shakspeare's power to touch the most familiar topics into poetry, as the Phrygian monarch could touch the basest substances into gold, I shall conclude this long and, as I fear, this fatiguing treatise on Shakspeare and his works, by asking if he be not a mighty genius, sufficiently illustrious and commanding to call forth the choice spirits of a learned and intellectual century to assert his greatness, and to march in his triumph to fame?

> Yes, master of the human heart! we own
> Thy sovereign sway; and bow before thy throne:
> Where, richly deck'd with laurels never sere,
> It stands aloft, and baffles Time's career.
> There warbles Poesy her sweetest song:
> There the wild Passions wait, thy vassal throng.
> There Love, there Hate, there Joy in turn presides;
> And rosy Laughter *holding both his sides.*
> At thy command the varied tumult rolls.
> Now Pity melts, now Terror chills our souls.
> Now, as thou wavest the wizard-rod, are seen
> The Fays and Elves quick glancing o'er the green:
> And, as the moon her perfect orb displays,
> The little people sparkle in her rays.
> There, mid the lightning's blaze, and whirlwind's howl,
> On the scath'd heath the fatal sisters scowl:
> Or, as hell's caldron bubbles o'er the flame,
> Prepare to do *a deed without a name.*
> These are thy wonders, Nature's darling birth!
> And Fame exulting bears thy name o'er earth.
> There, where Rome's eagle never stoop'd for blood,
> By hallow'd Ganges and Missouri's flood:
> Where the bright eyelids of the Morn unclose;
> And where Day's steeds in golden stalls repose;
> Thy peaceful triumphs spread; and mock the pride
> Of Pella's Youth, and Julius slaughter-dyed.
> In ages far remote, when Albion's state
> Hath touch'd the mortal limit, marked by Fate:
> When Arts and Science fly her naked shore:
> And the world's Empress shall be great no more:
> Then Australasia shall thy sway prolong;
> And her rich cities echo with thy song.
> There myriads still shall laugh, or drop the tear,
> At Falstaff's humour, or the woes of Lear:
> Man, wave-like, following man, thy powers admire,
> And thou, my *Shakspeare*, reign till time expire.

C. S

Newstead Abbey,
Aug. 4th, 1825.

SHAKSPEARE'S WILL.

FROM THE ORIGINAL IN THE OFFICE OF THE PREROGATIVE COURT OF CANTERBURY.

Vicesimo quinto die Martii, Anno Regni Domini nostri Jacobi nunc Regis Angliæ, &c. decimo quarto, et Scotiæ quadragesimo nono. Anno Domini 1616.

In the name of God, Amen. I William Shakspeare of Stratford upon Avon, in the county of Warwick, gent. in perfect health and memory (God be praised!) do make and ordain this my last will and testament in manner and form following: that is to say:

First, I commend my soul into the hands of God my creator, hoping, and assuredly believing, through the only merits of Jesus Christ my Saviour, to be made partaker of life everlasting; and my body to the earth whereof it is made.

Item, I give and bequeath unto my daughter Judith, one hundred and fifty pounds of lawful English money, to be paid unto her in manner and form following; that is to say, one hundred pounds in discharge of her marriage portion within one year after my decease, with consideration after the rate of two shillings in the pound for so long a time as the same shall be unpaid unto her after my decease; and the fifty pounds residue thereof, upon her surrendering of, or giving of such sufficient security as the overseers of this my will shall like of, to surrender or grant, all her estate and right that shall descend or come unto her after my decease, or that she now hath, of, in, or to, one copyhold tenement, with the appurtenances, lying and being in Stratford upon Avon aforesaid, in the said county of Warwick, being parcel or holden of the manor of Rowington, unto my daughter Susanna Hall, and her heirs for ever.

Item, I give and bequeath unto my said daughter Judith one hundred and fifty pounds more, if she, or any issue of her body, be living at the end of three years next ensuing the day of the date of this my will, during which time my executors to pay her consideration from my decease according to the rate aforesaid: and if she die within the said term without issue of her body, then my will is, and I do give and bequeath one hundred pounds thereof to my niece Elizabeth Hall, and the fifty pounds to be set forth by my executors during the life of my sister Joan Hart, and the use and profit thereof coming, shall be paid to my said sister Joan, and after her decease the said fifty pounds shall remain amongst the children of my said sister, equally to be divided amongst them; but if my said daughter Judith be living at the end of the said three years, or any issue of her body, then my will is, and so I devise and bequeath the said hundred and fifty pounds to be set out by my executors and overseers for the best benefit of her and her issue, and the stock not to be paid unto her so long as she shall be married and covert baron; but my will is, that she shall have the consideration yearly paid unto her during her life, and after her decease the said stock and consideration to be paid to her children, if she have any, and if not, to her executors and assigns, she living the said term after my decease: provided that if such husband as she shall at the end of the said three years be married unto, or at any [time] after, do sufficiently assure unto her, and the issue of her body, lands answerable to the portion by this my will given unto her, and to be adjudged so by my executors and overseers, then my will is, that the said hundred and fifty pounds shall be paid to such husband as shall make such assurance, to his own use.

Item, I give and bequeath unto my said sister Joan twenty pounds, and all my wearing apparel, to be paid and delivered within one year after my decease; and I do will and devise unto her the house, with the appurtenances, in Stratford, wherein she dwelleth, for her natural life, under the yearly rent of twelve-pence.

Item, I give and bequeath unto her three sons, William Hart, —— Hart, and Michael Hart, five pounds apiece, to be paid within one year after my decease.

Item, I give and bequeath unto the said Elizabeth Hall all my plate (except my broad silver and gilt bowl,) that I now have at the date of this my will.

Item, I give and bequeath the poor of Stratford aforesaid ten pounds; to Mr. Thomas Combe my sword; to Thomas Russel, esq. five pounds; and to Francis Collins of the borough of Warwick, in the county of Warwick, gent. thirteen pounds six shillings and eight-pence, to be paid within one year after my decease.

Item, I give and bequeath to Hamlet [*Hamnet*] Sadler twenty-six shillings eight-pence, to buy him a ring; to William Reynolds, gent. twenty-six shillings eight-pence, to buy him a ring; to my godson William Walker, twenty shillings in gold; to Anthony Nash, gent. twenty-six shillings eight-pence; and to Mr. John Nash, twenty-six shillings eight-pence; and to my fellows, John Hemynge, Richard Burbage, and Henry Cundell, twenty-six shillings eight-pence apiece, to buy them rings.

Item, I give, will, bequeath, and devise, unto my daughter Susanna Hall, for better enabling of her to perform this my will, and towards the performance thereof, all that capital messuage or tenement, with the appurtenances, in Stratford aforesaid, called The New Place, wherein I now dwell, and two messuages or tenements, with the appurtenances, situate, lying, and being in Henley-street, within the borough of Stratford aforesaid; and all my barns, stables, orchards, gardens, lands, tenements, and hereditaments whatsoever, situate, lying, and being, or to be had, received, perceived, or taken, within the towns, hamlets, villages, fields, and grounds of Stratford upon Avon, Old Stratford, Bishopton, and Welcombe, or in any of them, in the said county of Warwick; and also all that messuage or tenement, with the appurtenances, wherein one John Robinson dwelleth, situate, lying, and being, in the Blackfriars in London, near the Wardrobe: and all other my lands, tenements, and hereditaments whatsoever: to have and to hold all and singular the said premises, with their appurtenances, unto the said Susanna Hall, for and during the term of her natural life; and after her decease to the first son of her body lawfully issuing, and to the heirs males of the body of the said first son lawfully issuing; and for default of such issue, to the second son of her body lawfully issuing, and to the heirs males of the body of the said second son lawfully issuing; and for default of such heirs, to the third son of the body of the said Susanna lawfully issuing, and to the heirs males of the body of the said third son lawfully issuing; and for default of such issue, the same so to be and remain to the fourth, fifth, sixth, and seventh sons of her body, lawfully issuing one after another, and to the heirs males of the bodies of the said fourth, fifth, sixth, and seventh sons lawfully issuing, in such manner as it is before limited to be and remain to the first, second, and third sons of her body, and to their heirs males; and for default of such issue, the said premises to be and remain to my said niece Hall, and the heirs males of her body lawfully issuing; and for default of such issue, to my daughter Judith, and the heirs males of her body lawfully issuing; and for default of such issue, to the right heirs of me the said William Shakspeare for ever.

Item, I give unto my wife my second best bed, with the furniture.

Item, I give and bequeath to my said daughter Judith my broad silver gilt bowl. All the rest of my goods, chattles, leases, plate, jewels, and household stuff whatsoever, after my debts and legacies paid, and my funeral expenses discharged, I give devise, and bequeath to my son-in-law, John Hall, gent. and my daughter Susanna his wife, whom I ordain and make executors of this my last will and testament. And I do entreat and appoint the said Thomas Russell, esq. and Francis Collins, gent. to be overseers hereof. And do revoke all former wills, and publish this to be my last will and testament. In witness whereof I have hereunto put my hand, the day and year first above written.

By me WILLIAM SHAKSPEARE

Witness to the publishing hereof,

Fra. Collyns,
Julius Shaw,
John Robinson,
Hamnet Sadler,
Robert Whatcott.

Probatum fuit testamentum suprascriptum apud London, coram Magistro William Byrde, Legum Doctore, &c. vicesimo secundo die mensis Junii, Anno Domini 1616; *juramento Johannis Hall unius ex. cui, &c. de bene, &c. jurat. reservata potestate, &c. Susannæ Hall, alt. ex. &c. eam cum venerit, &c. petitur, &c.*

TO

THE MEMORY

OF MY BELOVED

MR. WILLIAM SHAKSPEARE,

AND WHAT HE HATH LEFT US.

To draw no envy, Shakspeare, on thy name,
Am I thus ample to thy book and fame:
While I confess thy writings to be such,
As neither man nor Muse can praise too much.
'Tis true, and all men's suffrage. But these ways
Were not the paths I meant unto thy praise,
For silliest ignorance on these may light,
Which, when it sounds at best, but echoes right;
Or blind affection, which doth ne'er advance
The truth, but gropes, and urgeth all by chance;
Or crafty malice might pretend this praise,
And think to ruin, where it seem'd to raise.
These are, as some infamous bawd or whore
Should praise a matron. What could hurt her more?
But thou art proof against them, and indeed
Above th' ill fortune of them, or the need.
I therefore will begin. Soul of the age,
Th' applause! delight! the wonder of our stage!
My Shakspeare, rise! I will not lodge thee by
Chaucer, or Spenser, or bid Beaumont lie
A little further, to make thee a room:
Thou art a monument without a tomb,
And art alive still, while thy book doth live,
And we have wits to read, and praise to give.
That I not mix thee so, my brain excuses,
I mean with great, but disproportion'd muses:
For if I thought my judgment were of years,
I should commit thee surely with thy peers,
And tell how far thou didst our Lily outshine,
Or sporting Kid, or Marlow's mighty line.
And though thou hadst small Latin and less Greek,
From thence to honour thee, I will not seek

For names; but call forth thund'ring Eschylus,
Euripides, and Sophocles to us,
Pacuvius, Accius, him of Cordova dead,
To live again, to hear thy buskin tread,
And shake a stage: or when thy socks were on,
Leave thee alone for the comparison
Of all, that insolent Greece, or haughty Rome
Sent forth, or since did from their ashes come.
Triumph, my Britain, thou hast one to show,
To whom all scenes of Europe homage owe.
He was not of an age, but for all time!
And all the Muses still were in their prime,
When, like Apollo, he came forth to warm
Our ears, or like a Mercury to charm!
Nature herself was proud of his designs,
And joy'd to wear the dressing of his lines!
Which were so richly spun, and woven so fit,
As since, she will vouchsafe no other wit.
The merry Greek, tart Aristophanes,
Neat Terence, witty Plautus, now not please;
But antiquated and deserted lie,
As they were not of Nature's family.
Yet must I not give Nature all: thy art,
My gentle Shakspeare, must enjoy a part.
For though the poet's matter nature be,
His art doth give the fashion. And that he
Who casts to write a living line, must sweat,
(Such as thine are) and strike the second heat
Upon the Muse's anvil; turn the same,
And himself with it, that he thinks to frame;
Or for the laurel, he may gain a scorn,
For a good poet's made, as well as born.
And such wert thou. Look how the father's face
Lives in his issue: even so the race
Of Shakspeare's mind and manners brightly shines
In his well-turned, and true filed lines:
In each of which he seems to shake a lance,
As brandish'd at the eyes of ignorance.
Sweet Swan of Avon! what a sight it were,
To see thee in our water yet appear,
And make those slights upon the banks of Thames,
That so did take Eliza, and our James!
But stay, I see thee in the hemisphere
Advanc'd, and made a constellation there!
Shine forth thou star of poets, and with rage,
Or influence, chide, or cheer the drooping stage,
Which, since thy flight from hence, hath mourn'd like night,
And despairs day, but for thy volumes' light.

BEN JONSON.

ON

WORTHY MASTER SHAKSPEARE,

AND HIS POEMS.

A MIND reflecting ages past, whose clear
And equal surface can make things appear,
Distant a thousand years, and represent
Them in their lively colours, just extent:
To outrun hasty time, retrieve the fates,
Rowl back the heavens, blow ope the iron gates
Of death and Lethe, where confused lie
Great heaps of ruinous mortality:
In that deep dusky dungeon, to discern
A royal ghost from churls; by art to learn
The physiognomy of shades, and give
Them sudden birth, wond'ring how oft they live;
What story coldly tells, what poets feign
At second hand, and picture without brain,
Senseless and soulless shews: To give a stage,—
Ample, and true with life,—voice, action, age,
As Plato's year, and new scene of the world,
Them unto us, or us to them had hurl'd:
To raise our ancient sovereigns from their herse,
Make kings his subjects; by exchanging verse
Enlive their pale trunks, that the present age
Joys in their joy and trembles at their rage:
Yet so to temper passion, that our ears
Take pleasure in their pain, and eyes in tears
Both weep and smile; fearful at plots so sad,
Then laughing at our fear; abus'd, and glad
To be abus'd; affected with that truth
Which we perceive is false, pleas'd in that ruth
At which we start, and, by elaborate play,
Tortur'd and tickl'd; by a crab-like way
Time past made pastime, and in ugly sort
Disgorging up his ravin for our sport:——
——While the plebeian imp, from lofty throne,
Creates and rules a world, and works upon
Mankind by secret engines; now to move
A chilling pity, then a rigorous love;
To strike up and stroke down, both joy and ire,
To steer the affections; and by heavenly fire
Mould us anew, stol'n from ourselves:——
This,—and much more, which cannot be express'd
But by himself, his tongue, and his own breast,—
Was Shakspeare's freehold; which his cunning brain
Improv'd by favour of the nine-fold train;—
The buskin'd muse, the comick queen, the grand
And louder tone of Clio, nimble hand
And nimbler foot of the melodious pair,
The silver-voic'd lady, the most fair
Calliope, she whose speaking silence daunts,
And she whose praise the heavenly body chants.
These jointly woo'd him, envying one another;
Obey'd by all as spouse, but lov'd as brother;—
And wrought a curious robe, of sable grave,
Fresh green, and pleasant yellow, red most brave,
And constant blue, rich purple, guiltless white,
The lowly russet, and the scarlet bright:
Branch'd and embroider'd like the painted spring;
Each leaf match'd with a flower, and each string
Of golden wire, each line of silk: there run
Italian works, whose thread the sisters spun;
And there did sing, or seem to sing, the choice
Birds of a foreign note and various voice;
Here hangs a mossy rock; there plays a fair
But chiding fountain, purled: not the air,
Nor clouds, nor thunder, but were living drawn;
Not out of common tiffany or lawn,
But fine materials, which the Muses know,
And only know the countries where they grow
Now, when they could no longer him enjoy,
In mortal garments pent,—Death may destroy,
They say, his body; but his verse shall live,
And more than nature takes our hands shall give:
In a less volume, but more strongly bound,
Shakspeare shall breathe and speak; with laurel crown'd,
Which never fades; fed with ambrosian meat,
In a well-lined vesture, rich and neat:—
So with this robe they clothe him, bid him wear it;
For time shall never stain, nor envy tear it.

The friendly admirer of his Endowments,

I. M. S.

These admirable verses were first prefixed to the second folio printed in 1632: they are here placed as a noble tribute from a contemporary to the genius of our immortal Poet. Conjecture has been vainly employed upon the initials I. M. S. affixed. I entirely subscribe to Mr. Boaden's opinion that they are from the pen of *George Chapman;* the structure of the verse and the phraseology bear marks of his hand, and the vein of poetry such as would do honour to his genius.

S. W. S

THE PREFACE OF THE PLAYERS.

Prefixed to the First Folio Edition published in 1623.

TO THE GREAT VARIETY OF READERS,

FROM the most able, to him that can but spell: there you are number'd. We had rather you were weigh'd. Especially, when the fate of all Bookes depends upon your capacities: and not of your heads alone, but of your purses. Well! it is now publique, and you wil stand for your priviledges wee know: to read, and censure. Do so, but buy it first. That doth best commend a Booke, the Stationer saies. Then, how odde soever your braines be, or your wisedomes, make your licence the same, and spare not. Judge your sixe-pen'orth, your shillings worth, your five shillings worth at a time, or higher, so you rise to the just rates, and welcome. But, whatever you do, Buy. Censure will not drive a Trade, or make the Jacke go. And though you be a Magistrate of wit, and sit on the Stage at Black-Friers, or the Cockpit, to arraigne Playes dailie, know, these Playes have had their triall alreadie, and stood out all Appeales; and do now come forth quitted rather by a Decree of Court, than any purchas'd Letters of commendation.

It had bene a thing, we confesse, worthie to have bene wished, that the Author himselfe had lived to have set forth, and overseen his owne writings; But since it hath bin ordain'd otherwise, and he by death departed from that right, we pray you, doe not envie his Friends, the office of their care and paine, to have collected and publish'd them; and so to have publish'd them, as where (before) you were abus'd with divers stolne, and surreptitious copies, maimed and deformed by the frauds and stealthes of injurious impostors, that expos'd them: even those are now offer'd to your view cur'd, and perfect of their limbes; and all the rest, absolute in their numbers, as he conceived thē: Who, as he was a happie imitator of Nature, was a most gentle expresser of it. His mind and hand went together: and what he thought, he uttered with that easinesse, that wee have scarse received from him a blot in his papers. But it is not our province, who only gather his works, and give them you, to praise him. It is yours that reade him. And there we hope, to your divers capacities, you will finde enough, both to draw, and hold you: for his wit can no more lie hid, then it could be lost. Reade him, therefore; and againe, and againe: And if then you doe not like him, surely you are in some manifest danger, not to understand him. And so we leave you to other of his Friends whom if you need, can bee your guides: if you neede them not, you can leade yourselves, and others. And such readers we wish him.

JOHN HEMINGE,
HENRIE CONDELL.

TEMPEST.

PRELIMINARY REMARKS.

"THE Tempest and the Midsummer Night's Dream (says Warburton) are the noblest efforts of that sublime and amazing imagination, peculiar to Shakspeare, which soars above the bounds of nature, without forsaking sense, or, more properly, carries nature along with him beyond her established limits."

No one has hitherto discovered the novel on which this play is founded; yet Collins the poet told Thomas Warton that the plot was taken from the romance of 'Aurelio and Isabella,' which was frequently printed during the sixteenth century, sometimes in three or four languages in the same volume. In the calamitous mental indisposition which visited poor Collins his memory failed him; and he most probably substituted the name of one novel for another; the fable of Aurelio and Isabella has no relation to the Tempest. Mr. Malone thought that no such tale or romance ever existed; yet a friend of the late Mr. James Boswell told him that he had some years ago actually perused an Italian novel which answered Collins' description; but his memory, unfortunately, did not enable him to recover it.

My friend, Mr. Douce, in his valuable 'Illustrations of Shakspeare,' published in 1807, had suggested that the outline of a considerable part of this play was borrowed from the account of Sir George Somers' voyage and shipwreck on the Bermudas in 1609; and had pointed out some passages which confirmed his suggestion. At the same time it appears that Mr. Malone was engaged in investigating the relations of this voyage: and he subsequently printed the results of his researches in a pamphlet, which he distributed among his friends; wherein he shows, that not only the title but many passages in the play were suggested to Shakspeare by the account of the tremendous *Tempest* which, in July, 1609, dispersed the fleet carrying supplies from England to the infant colony of Virginia, and wrecked the vessel in which Sir George Somers and the other principal commanders had sailed, on one of the Bermuda Islands.

Sir George Somers, Sir Thomas Gates, and Captain Newport, with nine ships and five hundred people, sailed from England in May, 1609, on board the Sea Venture, which was called *the Admiral's Ship;* and on the 25th of July she was parted from the rest by a *terrible tempest,* which lasted forty-eight hours and scattered the whole fleet, wherein some of them lost their masts and others were much distressed. Seven of the vessels, however, reached Virginia; and, after landing about three hundred and fifty persons, again set sail for England. Two of them were wrecked, in their way home, on the point of Ushant; the others returned safely to England, ship after ship, in 1610, bringing the news of the supposed loss of the Admiral's ship and her crew. During a great part of the year 1610 the fate of Somers and Gates was not known in England, but the latter, having been sent home by Lord Delaware, arrived in August or September. The Council of Virginia published a narrative of the disasters which had befallen the fleet, and of their miraculous escape. Previously however to its appearance, one Jourdan, who probably returned from Virginia in the same ship with Sir Thomas Gates, published a pamphlet entitled "A Discovery of the Bermudas, otherwise called *The Isle of Divels;* by Sir Thomas Gates, Sir George Somers, and Captain Newport, with divers others:" in which he relates the circumstances of the storm. "They were bound for Virginia, and at that time in 30° N. latitude. The whole crew, amounting to one hundred and fifty persons, weary with pumping, had given all for lost, and began to drink their strong waters, *and to take leave of each other,* intending to commit themselves to the mercy of the sea. Sir George Somers, who had sat three days and nights on the poop, with no food and little rest, at length descried land, and encouraged them (*many from weariness having fallen asleep*) to continue at the pumps. They complied, and fortunately the ship was driven and *jammed between two rocks,* fast lodged and locked for further budging." One hundred and fifty persons got on shore; and by means of their boat and skiff (for this was half a mile from land) they saved such part of their goods and provisions as the water had not spoiled, all the tackling and much of the iron of their ship, which was of great service to them in fitting out another vessel to carry them to Virginia.

"But our delivery," says Jourdan, "was not more strange in falling so opportunely and happily upon the land, as [than] our feeding and provision was, beyond our hopes, and all men's expectations, most admirable; for the Islands of the Bermudas, as every man knoweth that hath heard or read of them, were *never inhabited* by any Christian or Heathen people, but ever esteemed and reputed a most prodigious and *inchanted place,* affording nothing but gusts, storms, and foul weather; which made every navigator and mariner to avoid them as Scylla and Charybdis, or as they would shunne the Divell himself: and no man was ever heard to make for this place; but as, against their wils, they have, by storms and dangerounesse of the rocks lying seven leagues into the sea, suffered shipwracke. Yet did we finde there *the ayre so temperate* and the *country so aboundantly fruitfull* of all fit necessaries for the sustentation and preservation of man's life, that, most in a manner of all our provision of bread, beere, and victuall being quite spoiled in lying long drowned in salt water notwithstanding we were there for the space of nine months, we were not only well refreshed, comforted and with good satiety contented, but out of the aboundance thereof provided us some reasonable quantity and proportion of provision to carry us for Virginia, and to maintain ourselves and that company we found there:—wherefore my opinion sincerely of this island is, that whereas it hath beene, and is still, accounted the most dangerous, unfortunate, and forlorne place of the world, it is in truth the richest, healthfullest, and [most] pleasing land (the quantity and bignesse thereof considered,) and merely naturall, as ever man set foote upon."

The publication set forth by the Council of Virginia, entitled, "A true Declaration of the Estate of the Colony of Virginia, &c. 1610," relates the same facts and events in better language, and Shakspeare probably derived his first thought of working these adventures up into a dramatic form from an allusion to the drama in this piece.

"These islands of the Bermudas," says this narrative, "have ever been accounted as an *inchaunted* pile of rocks, and a *desert inhabitation for divells;* but all the *fairies* of the rocks were but flocks of birdes, and all the divels that haunted the woods were but herds of swine."—What is there in all this *Tragicall Comœdie* that should discourage us?

The covert allusions to several circumstances in the various narrations of this Voyage have been illustrated with great ingenuity by Mr. Malone; and many of them will no doubt have already struck the reader, but we must content ourselves with a reference to his more detailed account.

The plot of this play is very simple, independent of the magic; and Mr. Malone has pointed out two sources from whence he thinks Shakspeare derived suggestions for it. The one is a play by Robert Green, entitled "The Comical History of Alphonsus King of Arragon:" the other is the Sixth Metrical Tale of George Turberville,* formed on the fourth novel of the fourth day of the Decamerone of Boccaccio, to which he is probably indebted for the hint of the marriage of Claribel. The magic of the piece is unquestionably the creation of the great bard himself, suggested no doubt by the popular

* Tragical Tales, translated by Turberville in time of his troubles, out of sundrie Italians, &c. 8vo 1587

notions respecting the Bermudas. Mr. Malone confesses that the hints furnished by Green are so slight as not to detract from the merit of Shakspeare, and I have therefore not thought it necessary to follow him in his analysis. The late Dr. Vincent, the highly respected Dean of Westminster, pointed out a passage in Magellan's Voyage to the South Pole, which is to be found in "Eden's History of Travaile," printed in 1577, that may have furnished the first idea of Caliban, and as it is curious in itself, I shall venture to transcribe it. "Departyng from hence," says Eden, "they sayled to the 49 degre and a halfe under the pole antartike; where being wyntered, they were inforced to remayne there for the space of two monethes, all which tyme they saw no man: except that one day by chance they espyed a man of the stature of a gyant, who came to the haven *dauncing and singing*, and shortly after seemed to cast dust over his head. The captayne sent one of his men to the shore with the shippe boate, who made the lyke signe of peace. The which thyng the giant seeing, was out of feare, and came with the captayne's servant, to his presence, into a little islande. When he sawe the captayne with certayne of his company about him, he was greatly amazed; and made signes, *holding up his hande to heaven*, signifying thereby *that our men came from thence.* This giant was so byg that the head of one of our men of a meane stature came but to his waste. He was of good corporation and well made in all partes of his bodie, with a large visage painted with divers colours, but for the most parte yelow. Uppon his cheekes were paynted two hartes, and red circles about his eyes. The heare of his head was coloured whyte, and his apparell was the skynne of a beast sowed together. This beast (as seemed unto us) had a large head, and great eares lyke unto a mule, with the body of a cammell and tayle of a horse. The feet of the gyant were folded in the sayde skynne, after the manner of shooes. He had in his hande a bygge and shorte bowe; the sleyng whereof was made of a sinewe of that beaste. He had also a bundle of long arrowes made of reedes, feathered after the manner of ours, typte with sharp stones, in the stead of iron heades. The captayne caused him to eate and drinke, and gave him many thinges, and among other a great looking glasse, in the which as soon as he sawe his owne likeness, was sodaynly afrayde, and started backe with suche violence, that he overthrewe two that stood nearest about him. When the captayne had thus gyven him certayne haukes belles, with also a lookyng glasse, a combe, and a payre of beades of glasse, he sent him to lande with foure of his owne men well armed. Shortly after, they sawe another gyant of somewhat greater stature with his bowe and arrowes in his hande. As he drew nearer unto our men hee laide his hande on his head, and pointed up towards heaven, and our men did the lyke. The captayne sent his shippe boate to bring him to a little islande, beyng in the haven. This giant was very tractable and pleasaunt. He *soong and daunsed*, and in his daunsing left the print of his feete on the ground. After other xv. dayes were past, there came foure other giauntes without any weapons, but had hid their bowes and arrowes in certaine bushes. The captayne retayned two of these, which were youngest and best made. He tooke them by a deceite, in this manner; that giving them knyves, sheares, looking-glasses, belles, beades of chrystall, and such other trifles, he so fylled their handes, that they could holde no more; then caused two paire of shackels of iron to be putt on their legges, making signes that he would also give them those chaynes, which they liked very well because they were made of bright and shining metall. And whereas they could not carry them bycause theyr hands were full, the other giants would have carryed them, but the captayne would not suffer them. When they felt the shackels fast about theyr legges, they began to doubt; but the captayne did put them in comfort and bade them stand stille. In fine, when they sawe how they were deceived, they roared lyke bulles, and cryed upon theyr *great devill Setebos*, to help them. They say that when any of them dye, there appeare x or xi devils *leaping and daunsing* about the bodie of the dead, and seeme to have theyr bodies paynted with divers colours, and that among other there is one seene bigger than the residue, who maketh great mirth with rejoysing. This great devyll they call *Setebos*, and call the lesse Cheleule. One of these giantes which they tooke, declared by signes that he had seen devylles with two hornes above theyr heades, with *long heare downe to theyr feete*, and that they caste forth fyre at theyr throates both *before* and *behind*. The captayne named these people *Patagoni*. The moste parte of them weare the skynnes of such beastes whereof I have spoken before. They lyve of raw fleshe, and a certaine sweete roote which they call capar."

Caliban, as was long since observed by Dr. Farmer, is merely the metathesis of Cannibal. Of the Cannibals a long account is given by Eden, *ubi supra.*

"The Tempest," says the judicious Schlegel, "has little action and progressive movement; the union of Ferdinand and Miranda is fixed at their first meeting, and Prospero merely throws apparent obstacles in their way; the shipwrecked band go leisurely about the island; the attempts of Sebastian and Antonio on the life of the King of Naples, and of Caliban and his drunken companions against Prospero, are nothing but a feint, as we foresee that they will be completely frustrated by the magical skill of the latter; nothing remains therefore but the punishment of the guilty, by dreadful sights which harrow up their consciences, the discovery, and final reconciliation. Yet this want is so admirably concealed by the most varied display of the fascinations of poetry and the exhilaration of mirth; the details of the execution are so very attractive that it requires no small degree of attention to perceive that the denouement is, in some measure, already contained in the exposition. The history of the love of Ferdinand and Miranda, developed in a few short scenes, is enchantingly beautiful: an affecting union of chivalrous magnanimity on the one part, and, on the other, of the virgin openness of a heart which, brought up far from the world on an uninhabited island, has never learned to disguise its innocent movements. The wisdom of the princely hermit Prospero has a magical and mysterious air; the impression of the black falsehood of the two usurpers is mitigated by the honest gossiping of the old and faithful Gonzalo; Trinculo and Stephano, two good-for-nothing drunkards, find a worthy associate in Caliban; and Ariel hovers sweetly over the whole as the personified genius of the wonderful fable.

"Caliban has become a bye-word, as the strange creation of a poetical imagination. A mixture of the gnome and the savage, half demon, half brute; in his behaviour we perceive at once the traces of his native disposition, and the influence of Prosprero's education The latter could only unfold his understanding, without, in the slightest degree, taming his rooted malignity: it is as if the use of reason and human speech should be communicated to a stupid ape. Caliban is malicious, cowardly, false, and base in his inclinations; and yet he is essentially different from the vulgar knaves of a civilized world, as they are occasionally portrayed by Shakspeare. He is rude, but not vulgar; he never falls into the prosaical and low familiarity of his drunken associates, for he is a poetical being in his way; he always speaks too in verse.* He has picked up every thing dissonant and thorny in language, out of which he has composed his vocabulary, and of the whole variety of nature, the hateful, repulsive, and pettily deformed have alone been impressed on his imagination. The magical world of spirits, which the staff of Prospero has assembled on the island, casts merely a faint reflection into his mind, as a ray of light which falls into a dark cave, incapable of communicating to it either heat or illumination, merely serves to put in motion the poisonous vapours. The whole delineation of this monster is inconceivably consistent and profound, and notwithstanding its hatefulness, by no means hurtful to our feelings, as the honour of human nature is left untouched.

"In the zephyr-like Ariel the image of air is not to be mistaken, his name even bears an allusion to it; on the other hand, Caliban signifies the heavy element of earth. Yet they are neither of them allegorical personifications, but beings individually determined. In general we find, in the Midsummer Night's Dream, in the Tempest, in the magical part of Macbeth, and wherever Shakspeare avails himself of the popular belief in the invisible presence of spirits, and the possibility of coming in contact with them, a profound view of the inward life of Nature and her mysterious springs; which, it is true, ought never to be altogether unknown to the genuine poet, as poetry is altogether incompatible with mechanical physics, but which few have possessed in an equal degree with Dante and himself."†

It seems probable that this play was written in 1611 at all events between the years 1609 and 1614. It appears from the MSS. of Vertue that the Tempest was acted, by John Heminge and the rest of the King's Company, before Prince Charles, the Lady Elizabeth, and the Prince Palatine Elector, in the beginning of the year 1613

* Schlegel is not quite correct in asserting that Caliban "*always speaks in verse.*" Mr. Steevens, it is true, endeavoured to give a *metrical form* to some of his speeches, which were evidently intended for prose, and they are therefore in the present edition so printed. Shakspeare, throughout his plays, frequently introduces short prose speeches in the midst of blank verse.

† Lectures on Dramatic Literature by Aug. Will. Schlegel, translated by John Black, 1815. Vol. ii. p 178.

TEMPEST.

PERSONS REPRESENTED.[1]

ALONSO, *King of* Naples.
SEBASTIAN, *his Brother.*
PROSPERO, *the rightful Duke of* Milan.
ANTONIO, *his Brother, the usurping Duke of* Milan.
FERDINAND, *Son to the King of* Naples.
GONZALO, *an honest old Counsellor of* Naples.
ADRIAN, FRANCISCO, } *Lords.*
CALIBAN, *a savage and deformed Slave.*
TRINCULO, *a Jester.*
STEPHANO, *a drunken Butler.*
Master of a Ship, Boatswain, and Mariners.

MIRANDA, *Daughter to* Prospero.
ARIEL, *an airy Spirit.*
IRIS, CERES, JUNO, Nymphs, Reapers, } *Spirits.*

Other Spirits attending on Prospero.

SCENE, *the Sea, with a Ship; afterwards an uninhabited Island.*

ACT. I.

SCENE I.—*On a Ship at Sea. A Storm, with Thunder and Lightning. Enter a* Ship-master *and a* Boatswain.

Master.

BOATSWAIN,—

Boats. Here, master: what cheer?

Mast. Good: speak to the mariners: fall to't yarely,[2] or we run ourselves aground: bestir, bestir. [*Exit.*

Enter Mariners.

Boats. Heigh, my hearts; cheerly, cheerly, my hearts; yare, yare: Take in the top-sail; Tend to the master's whistle.—Blow till thou burst thy wind, if room enough!

Enter ALONSO, SEBASTIAN, ANTONIO, FERDINAND, GONZALO, *and others.*

Alon. Good Boatswain, have care. Where's the master? Play the men.[3]

Boats. I pray now, keep below.

Ant. Where is the master, boatswain?

Boats. Do you not hear him? You mar our labour! keep your cabins: you do assist the storm.

Gon. Nay, good, be patient.

Boats. When the sea is. Hence! What care these roarers for the name of king? To cabin: silence: trouble us not.

Gon. Good; yet remember whom thou hast aboard.

Boats. None that I more love than myself. You are a counsellor; if you can command these elements to silence, and work the peace of the present,[4] we will not hand a rope more; use your authority. If you cannot, give thanks you have lived so long, and make yourself ready in your cabin for the mischance of the hour, if it so hap.—Cheerly, good hearts.—Out of our way, I say. [*Exit.*

Gon. I have great comfort from this fellow: methinks, he hath no drowning mark upon him; his complexion is perfect gallows. Stand fast, good fate, to his hanging! make the rope of his destiny our cable, for our own doth little advantage! if he be not born to be hanged, our case is miserable. [*Exeunt.*

Re-enter Boatswain.

Boats. Down with the top-mast; yare; lower, lower; bring her to try with main course.[5] [*A cry within.*] A plague upon this howling! they are louder than the weather, or our office.—

Re-enter SEBASTIAN, ANTONIO, *and* GONZALO.

Yet again! what do you hear? Shall we give o'er, and drown? Have you a mind to sink?

Seb. A pox o' your throat! you bawling, blasphemous, uncharitable dog!

Boats. Work you, then.

Ant. Hang, cur, hang! you whoreson, insolent noise-maker, we are less afraid to be drowned than thou art.

Gon. I'll warrant him from drowning; though the ship were no stronger than a nut-shell, and as leaky as an unstanched[6] wench.

Boats. Lay her a-hold, a-hold; set her two courses;[7] off to sea again, lay her off.

Enter Mariners, *wet.*

Mar. All lost! to prayers, to prayers! all lost! [*Exeunt*

Boats. What, must our mouths be cold?

Gon. The king and prince at prayers! let us assist them,
For our case is as theirs.

Seb. I am out of patience.

Ant. We are merely[8] cheated of our lives by drunkards.—
This wide-chapped rascal;—'Would, thou might'st lie drowning,
The washing of ten tides!

Gon. He'll be hanged yet;
Though every drop of water swear against it,
And gape at wid'st to glut[9] him.

[*A confused noise within.*] Mercy on us!—We split, we split!—Farewell my wife and children!—Farewell, brother!—We split, we split, we split.—

Ant. Let's all sink with the king. [*Exit.*

Seb. Let's take leave of him. [*Exit.*

Gon. Now would I give a thousand furlongs of sea for an acre of barren ground; long[10] heath,

---

1 From the Folio Edition of 1623.

2 That is, readily, nimbly.

3 That is, act with spirit, behave like men. Thus Baret in his Alvearie: "*To play the man*, or to show himself a valiant man in any matter. Se virum præbere." P. 399.

"Viceroys and peers of Turkey *play the men.*"
Tamberlaine, 1590.

4 The *present instant.*

5 In Smith's Sea Grammar, 1627, 4to. under the article How to handle a Ship in a Storme:—"Let us lie as *Trie with our main course;* that is, to hale the tacke aboord, the sheet close aft, the boling set up, and the helm tied close aboord."

6 Mr. Steevens says *incontinent*, but the meaning is evident. In Beaumont and Fletcher's Mad Lover Chilas says to the frightened priestess:

——————— Down, you dog, then;
Be quiet and be *staunch* too, no *inundations.*

7 The *courses* are the main sail and fore sail. *To lay a ship a-hold*, is to bring her to lie as near the wind as she can, in order to keep clear of the land and get her out to sea.

8 *Merely*, absolutely, entirely; *Mere*, Lat.

9 To *englut*, to *swallow* him.

10 Instead of—*long* heath, *brown* furze, &c. Sir Thomas Hanmer reads—*ling*, heath, *broom*, furze, &c and I have no doubt rightly.

brown furze, any thing: The wills above be done! but I would fain die a dry death. [*Exit.*

SCENE II. *The Island: before the Cell of* Prospero. *Enter* PROSPERO *and* MIRANDA.

Mira. If by your art, my dearest father, you have
Put the wild waters in this roar, allay them:
The sky, it seems, would pour down stinking pitch,
But that the sea, mounting to the welkin's cheek,
Dashes the fire out. O, I have suffer'd
With those that I saw suffer! a brave vessel,
Who had no doubt some noble creature in her,
Dash'd all to pieces. O, the cry did knock
Against my very heart! Poor souls! they perish'd.
Had I been any god of power, I would
Have sunk the sea within the earth, or e'er[1]
It should the good ship so have swallowed, and
The freighting[2] souls within her.
Pro. Be collected:
No more amazement: tell your piteous heart,
There's no harm done.
Mira. O, woe the day!
Pro. No harm.
I have done nothing but in care of thee,
(Of thee, my dear one! thee, my daughter!) who
Art ignorant of what thou art, nought knowing
Of whence I am; nor that I am more better[3]
Than Prospero, master of a full poor cell,
And thy no greater father.
Mira. More to know
Did never meddle[4] with my thoughts.
Pro. 'Tis time
I should inform thee further. Lend thy hand,
And pluck my magick garment from me.—So:
[*Lays down his mantle.*
Lie there, my art.[5]—Wipe thou thine eyes; have comfort.
The direful spectacle of the wreck, which touch'd
The very virtue of compassion in thee,
I have with such provision in mine art
So safely order'd, that there is no soul—
No, not so much perdition as an hair,
Betid to any creature in the vessel
Which thou heard'st cry, which thou saw'st sink. Sit down;
For thou must now know further.
Mira. You have often
Begun to tell me what I am; but stopp'd
And left me to a bootless inquisition;
Concluding, *Stay, not yet.*—
Pro. The hour's now come;
The very minute bids thee ope thine ear;
Obey, and be attentive. Can'st thou remember
A time before we came unto this cell?
I do not think thou can'st; for then thou wast not
Out[6] three years old.
Mira. Certainly, sir, I can.
Pro. By what? by any other house, or person?
Of any thing the image tell me, that
Hath kept with thy remembrance.
Mira. 'Tis far off;
And rather like a dream than an assurance
That my remembrance warrants: Had I not
Four or five women once, that tended me?
Pro. Thou had'st, and more, Miranda: But how is it,
That this lives in thy mind? What seest thou else
In the dark backward and abysm[7] of time?
If thou remember'st aught, ere thou cam'st here,
How cam'st thou here, thou may'st.
Mira. But that I do not.
Pro. Twelve years since, Miranda, twelve years since,
Thy father was the duke of Milan, and
A prince of power.
Mira. Sir, are not you my father?
Pro. Thy mother was a piece of virtue, and
She said—thou wast my daughter; and thy father
Was duke of Milan; and his only heir
A princess;—no worse issued.
Mira. O, the heavens!
What foul play had we, that we came from thence?
Or blessed was't we did?
Pro. Both, both, my girl:
By foul play, as thou say'st, where we heav'd thence;
But blessedly holp hither.
Mira. O, my heart bleeds
To think o' the teen[8] that I have turned you to,
Which is from my remembrance! Please you further.
Pro. My brother, and thy uncle, call'd Antonio—
I pray thee, mark me,—that a brother should
Be so perfidious!—he whom, next thyself,
Of all the world I lov'd, and to him put
The manage of my state; as, at that time,
Through all the signiories it was the first,
And Prospero the prime duke; being so reputed
In dignity, and, for the liberal arts,
Without a parallel; those being all my study,
The government I cast upon my brother,
And to my state grew stranger, being transported,
And wrapped in secret studies. Thy false uncle—
Dost thou attend me?
Mira. Sir, most heedfully.
Pro. Being once perfected how to grant suits,
How to deny them; whom to advance, and whom
To trash[9] for overtopping; new created
The creatures that were mine; I say, or chang'd them,
Or else new form'd them: having both the key
Of officer and office, set all hearts i' th' state
To what tune pleas'd his ear; that now he was
The ivy, which had hid my princely trunk,
And suck'd my verdure out on't.—Thou attend'st not.
Mira. O good sir, I do.
Pro. I pray thee mark me.
I thus neglecting worldly ends, all dedicate
To closeness, and the bettering of my mind
With that, which, but by being so retir'd,
O'er-priz'd all popular rate, in my false brother
Awak'd an evil nature: and my trust,
Like a good parent,[10] did beget of him
A falsehood, in its contrary as great

---

1 i. e. or ever, ere ever; signifying, in modern English, *sooner than at any time.*

2 Instead of *freighting* the first folio reads *fraughting.*

3 The double superlative is in frequent use among our elder writers.

4 To *meddle*, is to *mix*, or to *interfere* with.

5 Lord Burleigh, when he put off his gown at night, used to say "Lie there, Lord Treasurer."—*Fuller's Holy State*, p. 257.

6 Out is used for *entirely, quite.* Thus in Act iv: "And be a boy right *out.*"

7 *Abysm* was the old mode of spelling *abyss;* from its French original *abisme.*

8 *Teen* is grief, sorrow.

9 *To trash* means to check the pace or progress of any one. The term is said to be still in use among sportsmen in the North, and signifies to correct a dog for misbehaviour in pursuing the game; or *overtopping* or outrunning the rest of the pack. *Trashes* are clogs strapped round the neck of a dog to prevent his over-speed.

Todd has given four instances from Hammond's works of the word in this sense. "Clog and *trash*"—"encumber and *trash*"—"to *trash* or overslow"—and "foreslowed and *trashed.*"

There was another word of the same kind used in Falconry (from whence Shakspeare very frequently draws his similies;) "*Trassing* is when a hawk raises aloft any fowl, and soaring with it, at length descends therewith to the ground."—*Dictionarium Rusticum*, 1704.

Probably this term is used by Chapman in his address to the reader prefixed to his translation of Homer

"That whosesoever muse dares use her wing,
When his muse flies she will be *trass't* by his,
And show as if a Bernacle should spring
Beneath an Eagle."

There is also a passage in the Bonduca of Beaumont and Fletcher, wherein Caratach says:

"I fled too,
But not so fast; your jewel had been lost then,
Young Hengo there, he *trasht* me, Nennius."

i. e. checked or stopped my flight.

I rather think it will be found that the Editors have been very precipitate in changing *trace* to *trash* in Othello, Act ii. Scene 1. See note on that passage.

10 Alluding to the observation that a father above the

As my trust was; which had, indeed, no limit,
A confidence sans bound. He being thus lorded,
Not only with what my revenue yielded,
But what my power might else exact,—like one,
Who having, unto truth, by telling of it,
Made such a sinner of his memory,
To credit his own lie,[1]—he did believe
He was indeed the duke; out of the substitution,
And executing the outward face of royalty,
With all prerogative:—Hence his ambition
Growing,—Dost hear?

Mira. Your tale, sir, would cure deafness.

Pro. To have no screen between this part he play'd
And him he play'd it for, he needs will be
Absolute Milan: Me, poor man!—my library
Was dukedom large enough; of temporal royalties
He thinks me now incapable: confederates
(So dry he was for sway) with the king of Naples,
To give him annual tribute, do him homage;
Subject his coronet to his crown, and bend
The dukedom, yet unbow'd, (alas, poor Milan!)
To most ignoble stooping.

Mira. O the heavens.

Pro. Mark his condition, and the event; then tell me,
If this might be a brother.

Mira. I should sin
To think but[2] nobly of my grandmother:
Good wombs have borne bad sons.

Pro. Now the condition.
This king of Naples, being an enemy
To me inveterate, hearkens my brother's suit;
Which was, that he in lieu[3] o' the premises,—
Of homage, and I know not how much tribute,—
Should presently extirpate me and mine
Out of the dukedom; and confer fair Milan,
With all the honours, on my brother: Whereon,
A treacherous army levied, one midnight
Fated to the purpose, did Antonio open
The gates of Milan; and, i' the dead of darkness,
The ministers for the purpose hurried thence
Me, and thy crying self.

Mira. Alack, for pity!
I, not rememb'ring how I cried out then,
Will cry it o'er again; it is a hint,[4]
That wrings mine eyes to't.

Pro. Hear a little further,
And then I'll bring thee to the present business
Which now's upon us; without the which, this story
Were most impertinent.

Mira. Wherefore did they not
That hour destroy us?

Pro. Well demanded, wench;
My tale provokes that question. Dear, they durst not;
(So dear the love my people bore me) nor set
A mark so bloody on the business; but
With colours fairer painted their foul ends.
In few, they hurried us aboard a bark;
Bore us some leagues to sea; where they prepar'd
A rotten carcass of a boat, not rigg'd,
Nor tackle, sail, nor mast; the very rats
Instinctively had quit[5] it; there they hoist us,
To cry to the sea that roar'd to us; to sigh
To the winds, whose pity, sighing back again,
Did us but loving wrong.

Mira. Alack! what trouble
Was I then to you!

Pro. O! a cherubim
Thou wast, that did preserve me! Thou didst smile,
Infuse with a fortitude from heaven,
When I have deck'd[6] the sea with drops full salt;
Under my burden groan'd; which rais'd in me
An undergoing stomach,[7] to bear up
Against what should ensue.

Mira. How came we ashore?

Pro. By Providence divine.
Some food we had, and some fresh water, that
A noble Neapolitan, Gonzalo,
Out of his charity, (who being then appointed
Master of this design,) did give us; with
Rich garments, linens, stuffs, and necessaries,
Which since have steaded much; so, of his gentleness,
Knowing I lov'd my books, he furnish'd me,
From my own library, with volumes that
I prize above my dukedom.

Mira. 'Would I might
But ever see that man!

Pro. Now I arise:—
Sit still, and hear the last of our sea-sorrow.
Here in this island we arriv'd; and here
Have I, thy school-master, made thee more profit
Than other princes can, that have more time
For vainer hours, and tutors not so careful.

Mira. Heavens thank you for't! And now I pray you, sir,
(For still 'tis beating in my mind,) your reason
For raising this sea-storm?

Pro. Know thus far forth.
By accident most strange, bountiful fortune,
Now my dear lady, hath mine enemies
Brought to this shore: and by my prescience
I find my zenith doth depend upon
A most auspicious star; whose influence
If now I court not, but omit, my fortunes,
Will ever after droop.—Here cease more questions;
Thou art inclin'd to sleep; 'tis a good dulness,
And give it way;—I know thou can'st not choose.—
[MIRANDA *sleeps.*
Come away, servant, come: I am ready now;
Approach, my Ariel; come.

Enter ARIEL.

Ari. All hail, great master! grave sir, hail! I come
To answer thy best pleasure; be't to fly,
To swim, to dive into the fire, to ride
On the curl'd clouds[8]: to thy strong bidding, task
Ariel, and all his quality[9].

Pro. Hast thou, spirit,
Perform'd to point[10] the tempest that I bade thee?

---

common rate of men has generally a son below it. *Heroum filii noxæ.*

1 "Who having made his memory such a sinner to truth as to credit his own lie by telling of it."

2 Tooke, in his Diversions of Purley, has clearly wn that we use one word, *But*, in modern English, or two words Bot and But, originally (in the Anglo Saxon) very different in signification, though (by repeated abbreviation and corruption) approaching in sound. Bot is the imperative of the A. S. *Botan*, to *boot*. But is the imperative of the A. S. *Be-utan*, *to be out*. By this means all the seemingly anomalous uses of *But* may be explained; I must however content myself with referring the reader to the Diversions of Purley, vol. i. p. 190. Merely remarking that *but* (as distinguished from *Bot*) and *be-out* have exactly the same meaning, viz. in modern English, *without*.

3 In *lieu* of the premises; that is, "in *consideration* of the premises,—&c." This seems to us a strange use of this French word, yet it was not then unusual.

"But takes their oaths *in lieu* of her assistance."
Beaumont and Fletcher's Prophetess

4 *Hint* is here for *cause* or *subject*. Thus in a future passage we have:—"Our *hint* of woe."

5 *Quit* was commonly used for *quitted*.

6 To *deck*, or *deg*, is still used in the northern counties for to *sprinkle*.

7 An *undergoing stomach* is a *stubborn resolution* a *temper* or *frame of mind* to bear.

8 This is imitated in Fletcher's Faithful Shepherdess,

"——tell me, sweetest,
What new service now is meetest
For the satyre; shall I stray
In the middle air, and stay
The sailing racke, or nimbly take
Hold by the moon, and gently make
Suit to the pale queen of night,
For a beame to give thee light?
Shall I dive into the sea,
And bring thee coral, making way
Through the rising waves, &c."

9 Ariel's *quality* is not his confederates, but the *powers of his nature* as a spirit, *his qualification in sprighting*

10 i. e. to the minutest article, literally from the French *a point*; so in the Chances,

"—— are you all fit?
To point, Sir"

Ari. To every article.
I boarded the king's ship; now on the beak[1],
Now in the waist, the deck, in every cabin,
I flam'd amazement: Sometimes, I'd divide,
And burn in many places; on the top-mast,
The yards, and bowsprit, would I flame distinctly,
Then meet, and join: Jove's lightnings, the precursors
O' the dreadful thunder-claps, more momentary
And sight-out running were not: The fire, and cracks
Of sulphurous roaring, the most mighty Neptune
Seem'd to besiege, and make his bold waves tremble,
Yea, his dread trident shake.
Pro. My brave spirit!
Who was so firm, so constant, that this coil[2]
Would not infect his reason?
Ari. Not a soul
But felt a fever of the mad[3], and play'd
Some tricks of desperation: All, but mariners,
Plung'd in the foaming brine, and quit the vessel,
Then all a-fire with me: the king's son, Ferdinand,
With hair up-staring (then like reeds, not hair,)
Was the first man that leap'd; cried, *Hell is empty,*
And all the devils are here.
Pro. Why, that's my spirit!
But was not this nigh shore?
Ari. Close by, my master.
Pro. But are they, Ariel, safe?
Ari. Not a hair perish'd;
On their sustaining garments not a blemish,
But fresher than before: and as thou bad'st me,
In troops I have dispers'd them 'bout the isle:
The king's son have I landed by himself;
Whom I left cooling of the air with sighs,
In an odd angle of the isle, and sitting,
His arms in this sad knot.
Pro. Of the king's ship,
The mariners, say, how thou hast dispos'd,
And all the rest o' the fleet?
Ari. Safely in harbour
Is the king's ship; in the deep nook, where once
Thou call'st me up at midnight to fetch dew
From the still-vex'd Bermoothes,[4] there she's hid:
The mariners all under hatches stow'd;
Whom, with a charm join'd to their suffer'd labour,
I have left asleep: and for the rest o' the fleet,
Which I dispers'd, they all have met again;
And are upon the Mediterranean flote,[5]
Bound sadly home for Naples;
Supposing that they saw the king's ship wreck'd,
And his great person perish.
Pro. Ariel, thy charge
Exactly is performed; but there's more work:
What is the time o' the day?
Ari. Past the mid season.
Pro. At least two glasses: the time 'twixt six and now
Must by us both be spent most preciously.
Ari. Is there more toil? since thou must give me pains,
Let me remember thee what thou hast promis'd,
Which is not yet perform'd me.
Pro. How now? moody?
What is't thou can'st demand?
Ari. My liberty.
Pro. Before the time be out? no more.
Ari. I pray thee
Remember, I have done thee worthy service;
Told thee no lies, made no mistakings, serv'd
Without or grudge or grumblings: thou didst promise
To bate me a full year.
Pro. Dost thou forget
From what a torment I did free thee?
Ari. No.
Pro. Thou dost; and think'st it much, to tread the ooze
Of the salt deep;—
To run upon the sharp wind of the north;
To do me business in the veins o' the earth,
When it is bak'd with frost.
Ari. I do not, sir.
Pro. Thou liest, malignant thing! Hast thou forgot
The foul witch, Sycorax, who, with age and envy
Was grown into a hoop? hast thou forgot her?
Ari. No, sir.
Pro. Thou hast: where was she born? speak; tell me.
Ari. Sir, in Argier.[6]
Pro. O, was she so? I must,
Once in a month, recount what thou hast been,
Which thou forget'st. This damn'd witch, Sycorax,
For mischiefs manifold, and sorceries terrible
To enter human hearing, from Argier,
Thou know'st, was banish'd; for one thing she did,
They would not take her life: Is not this true?
Ari. Ay, sir.
Pro. This blue-ey'd hag was hither brought with child,
And here was left by the sailors: Thou, my slave,
As thou report'st thyself, was then her servant:
And, for thou wast a spirit too delicate
To act her earthly and abhorr'd commands,
Refusing her grand hests,[7] she did confine thee,
By help of her more potent ministers,
And in her most unmitigable rage,
Into a cloven pine; within which rift
Imprison'd, thou didst painfully remain
A dozen years; within which space she died,
And left thee there; where thou didst vent thy groans,
As fast as mill-wheels strike: Then was this island,
(Save for the son that she did litter here,
A freckled whelp, hag-born) not honoured with
A human shape.
Ari. Yes; Caliban her son.
Pro. Dull thing, I say so; he, that Caliban,
Whom now I keep in service. Thou best know'st
What torment I did find thee in: thy groans
Did make wolves howl, and penetrate the breasts
Of ever-angry bears: it was a torment
To lay upon the damn'd, which Sycorax
Could not again undo; it was mine art,
When I arriv'd, and heard thee, that made gape
The pine, and let thee out.
Ari. I thank thee, master.
Pro. If thou more murmur'st, I will rend an oak,
And peg thee in his knotty entrails, till
Thou hast howl'd away twelve winters.
Ari. Pardon, master:
I will be correspondent to command,
And do my sprighting gently.
Pro. Do so; and after two days
I will discharge thee.
Ari. That's my noble master!
What shall I do? say what? what shall I do?
Pro. Go, make thyself like a nymph o' the sea: be subject
To no sight but thine and mine; invisible
To every eyeball else. Go, take this shape,
And hither come in't: go hence, with diligence.
[*Exit* Ariel.
Awake, dear heart, awake! thou hast slept well;
Awake!

1 The *beak* was a strong pointed body at the head of ancient galleys; it is used here for the forecastle or boltsprit. The *waist* is the part between the quarter-deck and the forecastle.
2 *Coil* is *bustle, tumult.*
3 That is such a fever as madmen feel when the frantic fits are on them.
4 The epithet here applied to the Bermudas will be best understood by those who have seen the chafing of the sea over the rugged rocks by which they are surrounded, and which renders access to them so difficult. It was then the current opinion that Bermudas was inhabited by *monsters* and *devils.* Setebos, the god of Caliban's dam, was an American devil, worshipped by the giants of Patagonia.
5 i. e. waves, or the sea. *Flot,* Fr.
6 The old English name of *Algiers*
7 *Behests, commands*

Mira. The strangeness of your story put
Heaviness in me.
Pro. Shake it off: Come on;
We'll visit Caliban, my slave, who never
Yields us kind answer.
Mira. 'Tis a villain, sir,
I do not love to look on.
Pro. But, as 'tis,
We cannot miss[1] him: he does make our fire,
Fetch in our wood; and serves in offices
That profit us. What ho! slave! Caliban!
Thou earth, thou! speak.
Cal. [*Within.*] There's wood enough within.
Pro. Come forth, I say; there's other business for thee:
Come forth, thou tortoise! when?[2]

Re-enter ARIEL, *like a Water-nymph.*

Fine apparition! My quaint[3] Ariel,
Hark in thine ear.
Ari. My lord, it shall be done. [*Exit.*
Pro. Thou poisonous slave, got by the devil himself
Upon thy wicked dam, come forth!

Enter CALIBAN.

Cal. As wicked dew as e'er my mother brush'd
With raven's feather from unwholesome fen,
Drop on you both! a south-west blow on ye,
And blister you all o'er!
Pro. For this, be sure, to-night thou shalt have cramps,
Side-stitches that shall pen thy breath up; urchins[4]
Shall, for that vast[5] of night that they may work
All exercise on thee: thou shalt be pinch'd
As thick as honey-combs, each pinch more stinging
Than bees that made them.
Cal. I must eat my dinner.
This island's mine, by Sycorax my mother,
Which thou tak'st from me. When thou camest first,
Thou strok'dst me, and mad'st much of me; would'st give me
Water with berries in't; and teach me how
To name the bigger light, and how the less,
That burn by day and night: and then I lov'd thee,
And shew'd thee all the qualities o' the isle,
The fresh springs, brine pits, barren place, and fertile;
Cursed be I that did so!—All the charms
Of Sycorax, toads, beetles, bats, light on you!
For I am all the subjects that you have,
Which first was mine own king: and here you sty me
In this hard rock, whiles you do keep from me
The rest of the island.
Pro. Thou most lying slave,
Whom stripes may move, not kindness: I have us'd thee,
Filth as thou art, with human care; and lodg'd thee
In mine own cell, till thou didst seek to violate
The honour of my child.
Cal. O ho, O ho!—'would it had been done!
Thou didst prevent me; I had peopled else
This isle with Calibans.
Pro. Abhorred slave,
Which any print of goodness will not take,
Being capable of all ill! I pitied thee,
Took pains to make thee speak, taught thee each hour
One thing or other; when thou didst not, savage,
Know thine own meaning, but wouldst gabble like
A thing most brutish, I endow'd thy purposes
With words that made them known: But thy vile race,
Though thou didst learn, had that in't which good natures
Could not abide to be with; therefore wast thou
Deservedly confin'd into this rock,
Who hadst deserv'd more than a prison.
Cal. You taught me language; and my profit on't
Is, I know how to curse: The red plague rid[6] you,
For learning me your language!
Pro. Hag-seed, hence!
Fetch us in fuel; and be quick, thou wert best,
To answer other business. Shrug'st thou, malice?
If thou neglect'st, or dost unwillingly
What I command, I'll rack thee with old cramps;
Fill all thy bones with aches:[7] make thee roar,
That beasts shall tremble at thy din!
Cal. No, 'pray thee!—
I must obey: his art is of such power, [*Aside*
It would control my dam's god, Setebos,[8]
And make a vassal of him.
Pro. So, slave; hence!
[*Exit* CALIBAN.

Re-enter ARIEL *invisible, playing and singing;*
FERDINAND *following him.*

ARIEL'S SONG.

Come unto these yellow sands,
And then take hands:
Court'sied when you have, and kiss'd,
(The wild waves whist[9])
Foot it featly here and there;
And, sweet sprites, the burden bear.
Hark, hark!
Bur. Bowgh, wowgh. [*dispersedly.*
The watch-dogs bark:
Bur. Bowgh, wowgh. [*dispersedly.*
Hark, hark! I hear
The strain of strutting chanticlere
Cry, Cock-a-doodle-doo.

Fer. Where should this musick be? i' the air, the earth?
It sounds no more;—and sure, it waits upon
Some god of the island. Sitting on a bank,
Weeping again the king my father's wreck,
This music crept by me upon the waters;
Allaying both their fury, and my passion,
With its sweet air: thence I have follow'd it,
Or it hath drawn me rather:—But 'tis gone.
No, it begins again.

---

1 i. e. we cannot *do without* him. The phrase is still common in the midland counties.

2 This is a common expression of impatience. Vide note on King Richard II. Act i. Scene 1.

3 *Quaint* here means brisk, spruce, dexterous, from the French *cointe.*

4 *Urchins* were fairies of a particular class. Hedgehogs were also called *urchins;* and it is probable that the sprites were so named, because they were of a mischievous kind, the *urchin* being anciently deemed a very noxious animal. Shakspeare again mentions these fairy beings in the Merry Wives of Windsor.
"Like urchins, ouphes, and fairies green and white."
In the phrase still current, "a little urchin," the idea of the fairy still remains.

5 That *vast* of night is that *space* of night. So, in Hamlet:
"In the dead *waste* and middle of the night," *nox vasta,* midnight, when all things are quiet and still, making the world appear one great uninhabited *waste.* In the pneumatology of ancient times visionary beings had different allotments of time suitable to the variety and nature of their agency.

6 Destroy.

7 The word *aches* is evidently a dissyllable here and in two passages of Timon of Athens. The reader will remember the senseless clamour that was raised against Kemble for his adherence to the text of Shakspeare in thus pronouncing it as the measure requires. "*Ake,*" says Baret in his Alvearie, "is the verb of this substantive *Ache,* ch being turned into k." And that ache was pronounced in the same way as the letter *h* is placed beyond doubt by the passage in Much Ado about Nothing, in which Margaret asks Beatrice for what she cries Heigh ho, and she answers for an *h.* i. e. *ache.* See the Epigram of Heywood adduced in illustration of that passage. This orthography and pronunciation continued even to the times of Butler and Swift. It would be easy to produce numerous instances.

8 "The giants when they found themselves fettered roared like bulls, and cried upon *Setebos* to help them" —*Eden's Hist. of Travayle,* 1577 p. 434

9 Still, silent

ARIEL sings.

Full fathom five thy father lies;
Of his bones are coral made;
Those are pearls that were his eyes:
Nothing of him that doth fade,
But doth suffer a sea-change
Into something rich and strange.
Sea-nymphs hourly ring his knell:
[*Burden*, ding-dong.
Hark! now I hear them,—ding-dong, bell.

Fer. The ditty does remember my drown'd father.—
This is no mortal business, nor no sound
That the earth owes:[1]—I hear it now above me.
Pro. The fringed curtains of thine eye advance,
And say, what thou seest yond'.
Mira. What is't? a spirit?
Lord, how it looks about! Believe me, sir,
It carries a brave form:—But 'tis a spirit.
Pro. No, wench; it eats and sleeps, and hath such senses
As we have, such: This gallant, which thou seest,
Was in the wreck; and but he's something stain'd
With grief, that's beauty's canker, thou might'st call him
A goodly person: he hath lost his fellows,
And strays about to find them.
Mira. I might call him
A thing divine; for nothing natural
I ever saw so noble.
Pro. It goes on, I see, [*Aside.*
As my soul prompts it:—Spirit, fine Spirit! I'll free thee
Within two days for this.
Fer. Most sure, the goddess
On whom these airs attend!—Vouchsafe, my prayer
May know, if you remain upon this island;
And that you will some good instruction give,
How I may bear me here; My prime request,
Which I do last pronounce, is, O you wonder!
If you be maid,[2] or no?
Mira. No wonder, sir;
But, certainly a maid.
Fer. My language! heavens!—
I am the best of them that speak this speech,
Were I but where 'tis spoken.
Pro. How! the best?
What wert thou, if the king of Naples heard thee?
Fer. A single thing, as I am now, that wonders
To hear thee speak of Naples: he does hear me;
And, that he does, I weep: myself am Naples;
Who with mine eyes, ne'er since at ebb, beheld
The king my father wreck'd.
Mira. Alack, for mercy!
Fer. Yes, faith, and all his lords; the duke of Milan,
And his brave son, being twain.
Pro. The duke of Milan,
And his more braver daughter, could control[3] thee,
If now 'twere fit to do't:—At the first sight [*Aside.*
They have chang'd eyes;—Delicate Ariel,
I'll set thee free for this!—A word, good sir;
I fear, you have done yourself some wrong:[4] a word.
Mira. Why speaks my father so ungently? This
Is the third man that e'er I saw; the first
That e'er I sighed for: pity move my father
To be inclin'd my way!
Fer. O, if a virgin,
And your affection not gone forth, I'll make you
The queen of Naples.
Pro. Soft, sir; one word more.—
They are both in either's powers: but this swift business
I must uneasy make, lest too light winning [*Aside.*
Make the prize light.—One word more; I charge thee,
That thou attend me: thou dost here usurp
The name thou ow'st not; and hast put thyself
Upon this island, as a spy, to win it
From me, the lord on't.
Fer. No, as I am a man.
Mira. There's nothing ill can dwell in such a temple:
If the ill spirit have so fair an house,
Good things will strive to dwell with 't.
Pro. Follow me.—[*To* FERD.
Speak not you for him; he's a traitor.—Come.
I'll manacle thy neck and feet together;
Sea-water shalt thou drink, thy food shall be
The fresh-brook muscles, wither'd roots, and husks
Wherein the acorn cradled: Follow.
Fer. No;
I will resist such entertainment, till
Mine enemy has more power. [*He draws.*
Mira. O dear father,
Make not too rash a trial of him, for
He's gentle, and not fearful.[5]
Pro. What, I say,
My foot my tutor!—Put thy sword up, traitor;
Who mak'st a show, but dar'st not strike, thy conscience
Is so possess'd with guilt: come from thy ward
For I can here disarm thee with this stick,
And make thy weapon drop.
Mira. Beseech you, father!
Pro. Hence; hang not on my garments.
Mira. Sir, have pity;
I'll be his surety.
Pro. Silence: one word more
Shall make me chide thee, if not hate thee. What!
An advocate for an impostor? hush!
Thou think'st there are no more such shapes as he,
Having seen but him and Caliban: Foolish wench!
To the most of men this is a Caliban,
And they to him are angels.
Mira. My affections
Are then most humble; I have no ambition
To see a goodlier man.
Pro. Come on; obey: [*To* FERD.
Thy nerves are in their infancy again,
And have no vigour in them.
Fer. So they are:
My spirits, as in a dream, are all bound up.
My father's loss, the weakness which I feel,
The wreck of all my friends, or this man's threats,
To whom I am subdued, are but light to me,
Might I but through my prison once a day
Behold this maid: all corners else o' the earth
Let liberty make use of; space enough
Have I in such a prison.
Pro. It works:—Come on.—
Thou hast done well, fine Ariel!—Follow me.—
[*To* FERD. *and* MIRA.
Hark, what thou else shalt do me. [*To* ARIEL.
Mira. Be of comfort:

---

1 i. e. *owns.* To *owe* was to *possess* or *appertain to*, in ancient language.

2 The folio of 1685 reads *made*, and many of the modern editors have laboured to persuade themselves that it was the true reading. It has been justly observed by M. Mason that the question is "whether our readers will adopt a natural and simple expression, which requires no comment, or one which the ingenuity of many commentators has but imperfectly supported."

3 To *control* here signifies to *confute*, to contradict unanswerably. The ancient meaning of *control* was to *check* or exhibit *a contrary account*, from the old French *contre-roller.*

4 "—— you have done yourself some wrong:" that is, *spoken a falsehood.* Thus in The Merry Wives of Windsor:
"This is not well, master Ford, this *wrongs you.*"

5 *Fearful* was sometimes used in the sense of *formidable, terrible, dreadful*, like the French *epouvantable*; as may be seen by consulting Cotgrave or any of our old dictionaries. Shakspeare almost always uses it in this sense. In K. Henry VI. Act iii. Scene 2, "A mighty and a *fearful* head they are." He has also *fearful* wars; *fearful* bravery; &c. &c. The verb to *fear* is most commonly used for to *fright*, to *terrify*, to *make afraid.* Mr. Gifford remarks, "as a proof how little our old dramatists were understood at the Restoration, that Dryden censures Jonson for an improper use of this word, the sense of which he altogether mistakes."

Brunche del.

TEMPEST.

Act II. Scene I.

My father's of a better nature, sir,
Than he appears by speech; this is unwonted,
Which now came from him.

Pro. Thou shalt be as free
As mountain winds: but then exactly do
All points of my command.

Ari. To the syllable.

Pro. Come, follow: speak not for him. [*Exeunt.*

ACT II.

SCENE I. *Another Part of the Island.* *Enter* ALONSO, SEBASTIAN, ANTONIO, GONZALO, ADRIAN, FRANCISCO, *and others.*

Gon. 'Beseech you, sir, be merry: you have cause
(So have we all) of joy; for our escape
Is much beyond our loss: our hint[1] of woe
Is common; every day, some sailor's wife,
The masters of some merchant,[2] and the merchant,
Have just our theme of woe: but for the miracle,
I mean our preservation, few in millions
Can speak like us: then wisely, good sir, weigh
Our sorrow with our comfort.

Alon. Pr'ythee, peace.

Seb. He receives comfort like cold porridge.

Ant. The visitor[3] will not give him o'er so.

Seb. Look, he's winding up the watch of his wit; by and by it will strike.

Gon. Sir,——

Seb. One:——Tell.

Gon. When every grief is entertain'd, that's offer'd,
Comes to the entertainer—

Seb. A dollar.

Gon. Dolour comes to him, indeed; you have spoken truer than you purposed.

Seb. You have taken it wiselier than I meant you should.

Gon. Therefore, my lord,—

Ant. Fie, what a spendthrift is he of his tongue!

Alon. I pr'ythee, spare.

Gon. Well, I have: But yet—

Seb. He will be talking.

Ant. Which of them, he, or Adrian, for a good wager, first begins to crow?

Seb. The old cock.

Ant. The cockrel.

Seb. Done: The wager?

Ant. A laughter.

Seb. A match.

Adr. Though this island seem to be desert,—

Seb. Ha, ha, ha!

Ant. So you've pay'd.

Adr. Uninhabitable, and almost inaccessible,—

Seb. Yet,—

Adr. Yet.

Ant. He could not miss it.

Adr. It must needs be of subtle, tender, and delicate temperance.[4]

Ant. Temperance was a delicate wench.

Seb. Ay, and a subtle; as he most learnedly delivered.

Adr. The air breathes upon us here most sweetly.

Seb. As if it had lungs, and rotten ones.

Ant. Or, as 'twere perfumed by a fen.

Gon. Here is every thing advantageous to life.

Ant. True; save means to live.

Seb. Of that there's none, or little.

Gon. How lush[5] and lusty the grass looks! how green!

Ant. The ground, indeed, is tawny.

Seb. With an eye[6] of green in't.

Ant. He misses not much.

Seb. No; he doth but mistake the truth totally.

Gon. But the rarity of it is (which is indeed almost beyond credit)—

Seb. As many vouch'd rarities are.

Gon. That our garments, being, as they were, drenched in the sea, hold, notwithstanding, their freshness, and glosses; being rather new dy'd than stain'd with salt water.

Ant. If but one of his pockets could speak, would it not say, he lies?

Seb. Ay, or very falsely pocket up his report.

Gon. Methinks, our garments are now as fresh as when we put them on first in Africk, at the marriage of the king's fair daughter Claribel to the king of Tunis.

Seb. 'Twas a sweet marriage, and we prosper well in our return.

Adr. Tunis was never graced before with such a paragon to their queen.

Gon. Not since widow Dido's time.

Ant. Widow? a pox o' that! How came that widow in? Widow Dido!

Seb. What if he had said widower Æneas too? good lord, how you take it!

Adr. Widow Dido, said you? you make me study of that: she was of Carthage, not of Tunis.

Gon. This Tunis, sir, was Carthage.

Adr. Carthage?

Gon. I assure you, Carthage.

Ant. His word is more than the miraculous harp.

Seb. He hath rais'd the wall, and houses too.

Ant. What impossible matter will he make easy next?

Seb. I think he will carry this island home in his pocket, and give it his son for an apple.

Ant. And sowing the kernels of it in the sea, bring forth more islands.

Gon. Ay?

Ant. Why, in good time.

Gon. Sir, we were talking that our garments seem now as fresh as when we were at Tunis at the marriage of your daughter, who is now queen.

Ant. And the rarest that e'er came there.

Seb. 'Bate, I beseech you, widow Dido.

Ant. O, widow Dido; ay, widow Dido.

Gon. Is not, sir, my doublet as fresh as the first day I wore it? I mean, in a sort.[8]

Ant. That sort was well fish'd for.

Gon. When I wore it at your daughter's marriage?

Alon. You cram these words into mine ears, against
The stomach of my sense: 'Would I had never
Married my daughter there! for, coming thence,
My son is lost; and, in my rate, she too,
Who is so far from Italy remov'd,
I ne'er again shall see her. O thou mine heir
Of Naples and of Milan, what strange fish
Hath made his meal on thee!

Fran. Sir, he may live,
I saw him beat the surges under him,
And ride upon their backs; he trod the water,
Whose enmity he flung aside, and breasted
The surge most swoln that met him: his bold head
'Bove the contentious waves he kept, and oar'd
Himself with his good arms in lusty stroke
To the shore, that o'er his wave-worn basis bow'd,
As stooping to relieve him: I not doubt,
He came alive to land.

Alon. No, no, he's gone.

Seb. Sir, you may thank yourself for this great loss;
That would not bless our Europe with your daughter,
But rather lose her to an African;

---

1 See note 14, p. 20.

2 It was usual to call a *merchant-vessel* a *merchant*, as we now say a *merchant-man.*

3 He calls Gonzalo the *visitor*, in allusion to the office of one who visits the sick to give advice and consolation.

4 Temperance is here used for *temperature*, or *temperateness*

5 *Lush* is *luxuriant*, in like manner *luscious* is used in A Midsummer Night's Dream:
"Quite over-canopied with *luscious* woodbine"

6 That is, with a *shade* or *small portion* of green.
"Red with an *eye* of blue makes a purple."—*Boyle.*

7 Alluding to the wonders of Amphion's music

8 That is, in a *manner* or *degree.*

Where she, at least, is banish'd from your eye,
Who has cause to wet the grief on't.

Alon. Pr'ythee, peace.

Seb. You were kneel'd to, and importun'd otherwise
By all of us; and the fair soul herself
Weigh'd,[1] between loathness and obedience, at
Which end o' the beam she'd bow. We have lost your son,
I fear, for ever; Milan and Naples have
More widows in them of this business' making,
Than we bring men to comfort them: the fault's
Your own.

Alon. So is the dearest[2] of the loss.

Gon. My lord Sebastian,
The truth you speak doth lack some gentleness,
And time to speak it in; you rub the sore,
When you should bring the plaster.

Seb. Very well.

Ant. And most chirurgeonly.

Gon. It is foul weather in us all, good sir,
When you are cloudy.

Seb. Foul weather?

Ant. Very foul.

Gon. Had I a plantation of this isle, my lord,—

Ant. He'd sow it with nettle-seed.

Seb. Or docks, or mallows.

Gon. And were the king of it, What would I do?

Seb. 'Scape getting drunk, for want of wine.

Gon. I' the commonwealth I would by contraries
Execute all things: for no kind of traffic[3]
Would I admit; no name of magistrate;
Letters should not be known; riches, poverty,
And use of service, none; contract, succession,
Bourn, bound of land, tilth, vineyard, none:
No use of metal, corn, or wine, or oil:
No occupation; all men idle, all;
And women too; but innocent and pure:
No sovereignty:—

Seb. And yet he would be king on't.

Ant. The latter end of his commmonwealth forgets the beginning.

Gon. All things in common nature should produce
Without sweat or endeavour: treason, felony,
Sword, pike, knife, gun, or need of any engine,[4]
Would I not have; but nature should bring forth,
Of its own kind, all foison,[5] all abundance,
To feed my innocent people.

Seb. No marrying among his subjects?

Ant. None, man; all idle; whores, and knaves.

Gon. I would with such perfection govern, sir,
To excel the golden age.[6]

Seb. 'Save his majesty!

Ant. Long live Gonzalo!

Gon. And, do you mark me, sir?—

Alon. Pr'ythee, no more: thou dost talk nothing to me.

Gon. I do well believe your highness; and did it to minister occasion to these gentlemen, who are of such sensible and nimble lungs, that they always use to laugh at nothing.

Ant. 'Twas you we laughed at.

Gon. Who, in this kind of merry fooling, am nothing to you; so you may continue, and laugh at nothing still.

Ant. What a blow was there given?

Seb. An it had not fallen flat-long.

Gon. You are gentlemen of brave mettle; you would lift the moon out of her sphere, if she would continue in it five weeks without changing.[7]

Enter ARIEL, *invisible, playing solemn music.*

Seb. We would so, and then go bat-fowling.

Ant. Nay, good my lord, be not angry.

Gon. No, I warrant you; I will not adventure my discretion so weakly. Will you laugh me asleep, for I am very heavy?

Ant. Go sleep, and hear us.

[*All sleep but* ALON. SEB. *and* ANT.

Alon. What, all so soon asleep! I wish mine eyes
Would, with themselves, shut up my thoughts: I find,
They are inclined to do so.

Seb. Please you, sir.
Do not omit the heavy offer of it:
It seldom visits sorrow; when it doth,
It is a comforter.

Ant. We two, my lord,
Will guard your person, while you take your rest,
And watch your safety.

Alon. Thank you: Wondrous heavy.

[ALONSO *sleeps.* *Exit* ARIEL.

Seb. What a strange drowsiness possesses them!

Ant. It is the quality o' the climate.

Seb. Why
Doth it not then our eye-lids sink? I find not
Myself dispos'd to sleep.

Ant. Nor I; my spirits are nimble.
They fell together all, as by consent;
They dropp'd, as by a thunder-stroke. What might
Worthy Sebastian?—O, what might?—No more;—
And yet, methinks, I see it in thy face,
What thou should'st be: the occasion speaks thee; and
My strong imagination sees a crown
Dropping upon thy head.

Seb. What, art thou waking?

Ant. Do you not hear me speak?

Seb. I do; and, surely,
It is a sleepy language; and thou speak'st
Out of thy sleep: What is it thou didst say?
This is a strange repose, to be asleep
With eyes wide open; standing, speaking, moving,
And yet so fast asleep.

Ant. Noble Sebastian,
Thou let'st thy fortune sleep—die rather; wink'st
Whiles thou art waking.

Seb. Thou dost snore distinctly;
There's meaning in thy snores.

Ant. I am more serious than my custom: you
Must be so too, if heed me; which to do,
Trebles thee o'er.[8]

Seb. Well; I am standing water.

Ant. I'll teach you how to flow.

Seb. Do so: to ebb,
Hereditary sloth instructs thee.

Ant. O,
If you but knew how you the purpose cherish,
Whiles thus you mock it! how, in stripping it,
You more invest it![9] Ebbing men, indeed,
Most often do so near the bottom run,
By their own fear, or sloth.

Seb. Pr'ythee, say on:
The setting of thine eye, and cheek, proclaim
A matter from thee; and a birth, indeed,
Which throes thee much to yield.

---

1 i. e. Deliberated, was in suspense.

2 See note on Twelfth Night, Act v. Sc. 1.

3 See Montaigne's Essays translated by John Florio, fol. 1603, Chap. "Of the Caniballes."

4 An *engine* was a term applied to any kind of *machine* in Shakspeare's age

5 *Foison* is only another word for *plenty* or *abundance* of provision, but chiefly of the fruits of the earth. In a subsequent scene we have—

"Earth's increase, and foison plenty."

6 See Montaigne as cited before.

7 Warburton remarks that "all this dialogue is a fine satire on the Utopian Treatise of Government, and the impracticable inconsistent schemes therein recommended."

8 Antonio apparently means to say, "You must be more serious than you usually are, if you would pay attention to my proposals; which attention, if you bestow it, will in the end make you *thrice what you are.*"

9 Sebastian introduces the simile of water. It is taken up by Antonio, who says he will teach his stagnant waters to flow. "It has already learned to ebb," says Sebastian. To which Antonio replies—"O, if you but knew how much even that metaphor, which you use in jest, encourages the design which I hint at; how, in stripping it of words of their common meaning, and using them figuratively, you adapt them to your own situation."—*Edinburgh Magazine Nov.* 1786

Ant. Thus, sir:
Although this lord of weak remembrance, this
(Who shall be of as little memory,
When he is earth'd,) hath here almost persuaded
(For he's a spirit of persuasion, only
Professes to persuade) the king, his son's alive;
'Tis as impossible that he's undrown'd,
As he that sleeps here, swims.
Seb. I have no hope
That he's undrown'd.
Ant. O, out of that no hope,
What great hope have you! no hope, that way, is
Another way so high in hope, that even
Ambition cannot pierce a wink beyond,[1]
But doubts discovery there. Will you grant, with me,
That Ferdinand is drown'd?
Seb. He's gone.
Ant. Then tell me,
Who's the next heir of Naples?
Seb. Claribel.
Ant. She that is queen of Tunis; she that dwells
Ten leagues beyond man's life; she that from Naples
Can have no note,[2] unless the sun were post,
(The man i' the moon's too slow,) till new-born chins
Be rough and razorable: she, from whom
We all were sea-swallow'd, though some cast again;
And, by that destiny, to perform an act,
Whereof what's past is prologue; what to come,
In your's and my discharge.[3]
Seb. What stuff is this?—How say you?
'Tis true, my brother's daughter's queen of Tunis;
So is she heir of Naples; 'twixt which regions
There is some space.
Ant. A space whose every cubit
Seems to cry out, *How shall that Claribel*
Measure us back to Naples?—Keep in Tunis,
And let Sebastian wake!—Say, this were death
That now hath seiz'd them; why they were no worse
Than now they are: There be, that can rule Naples,
As well as he that sleeps; lords, that can prate
As amply, and unnecessarily,
As this Gonzalo; I myself could make
A chough[4] of as deep chat. O, that you bore
The mind that I do! what a sleep were this
For your advancement! Do you understand me?
Seb. Methinks, I do.
Ant. And how does your content
Tender your own good fortune?
Seb. I remember,
You did supplant your brother Prospero.
Ant. True:
And, look, how well my garments sit upon me;
Much feater than before: My brother's servants
Were then my fellows, now they are my men.
Seb. But, for your conscience—
Ant. Ay, sir; where lies that? if it were a kybe,
'Twould put me to my slipper; but I feel not
This deity in my bosom: twenty consciences,
That stand 'twixt me and Milan, candied be they,
And melt, ere they molest! Here lies your brother,
No better than the earth he lies upon,
If he were that which now he's like, that's dead;
Whom I, with this obedient steel, three inches of it,
Can lay to bed for ever: whiles you, doing thus,
To the perpetual wink for aye might put
This ancient morsel, this sir Prudence, who
Should not upbraid our course. For all the rest,
They'll take suggestion,[5] as a cat laps milk;
They'll tell the clock to any business that
We say befits the hour.
Seb. Thy case, dear friend,
Shall be my precedent; as thou got'st Milan,
I'll come by Naples. Draw thy sword: one stroke
Shall free thee from the tribute which thou pay'st;
And I the king shall love thee.
Ant. Draw together:
And when I rear my hand, do you the like,
To fall it on Gonzalo.
Seb. O, but one word.
[*They converse apart*

Music. Re-enter ARIEL, *invisible.*

Ari. My master through his art foresees the danger
That you, his friend, are in; and sends me forth
For else his projects die,[6] to keep them living.
[*Sings in* GONZALO'*s ear.*

While you here do snoring lie,
Open-ey'd conspiracy
His time doth take:
If of life you keep a care,
Shake off slumber, and beware:
Awake! awake!

Ant. Then let us both be sudden.
Gon. Now, good angels, preserve the king
[*They wake.*
Alon. Why, how now, ho! awake! Why are you drawn?
Wherefore this ghastly looking?
Gon. What's the matter?
Seb. Whiles we stood here securing your repose,
Even now, we heard a hollow burst of bellowing
Like bulls, or rather lions; did it not wake you?
It struck mine ear most terribly.
Alon. I heard nothing.
Ant. O, 'twas a din to fright a monster's ear;
To make an earthquake; sure it was the roar
Of a whole herd of lions.
Alon. Heard you this, Gonzalo?
Gon. Upon mine honour, sir, I heard a humming,
And that a strange one too, which did awake me:
I shak'd you, sir, and cried; as mine eyes open'd,
I saw their weapons drawn:—there was a noise,
That's verity: 'Best stand upon our guard;
Or that we quit this place: let's draw our weapons.
Alon. Lead off this ground; and let's make further search
For my poor son.
Gon. Heavens keep him from these beasts!
For he is, sure, i' the island.
Alon. Lead away.
Ari. Prospero my lord shall know what I have done: [*Aside.*
So, king, go safely on to seek thy son. [*Exeunt.*

SCENE II. *Another part of the Island. Enter* CALIBAN, *with a burden of Wood. A noise of Thunder heard.*

Cal. All the infections that the sun sucks up
From bogs, fens, flats, on Prosper fall, and make him
By inch-meal a disease! His spirits hear me,
And yet I needs must curse. But they'll nor pinch
Fright me with urchin shows, pitch me i' the mire
Nor lead me, like a fire-brand, in the dark,

1 i. e. The utmost extent of the prospect of ambition, the point where the eye can pass no farther.

2 The commentators have treated this as a remarkable instance of Shakspeare's ignorance of geography; but though the real distance between Naples and Tunis is not so immeasurable, the intercourse in early times between the Neapolitans and the Tunisians was not so frequent as to make it popularly considered less than a formidable voyage; Shakspeare may however be countenanced in his poetical exaggeration, when we remember that Æschylus has placed the river Eridanus in Spain; and that Appolonius Rhodius describes the Rhone and the Po as meeting in one and discharging themselves into the Gulf of Venice.

3 What is past is the prologue to events which are to come; that depends on what you and I are to perform.

4 A *chough* is a bird of the jackdaw kind.

5 *Suggestion* is frequently used in the sense of *temptation*, or *seduction*, by Shakspeare and his contemporaries. The sense here is, that they will adopt and bear witness to any tale that may be dictated to them.

6 The old copies read "For else his *project dies.*" By the transposition of a letter, this passage, which has much puzzled the editors, is rendered more intelligible —"—to keep them living," relates to *projects*, and not to *Alonzo and Gonzalo*, as Steevens and Johnson erroneously supposed

Out of my way, unless he bid them; but
For every trifle are they set upon me:
Sometimes like apes, that moe[1] and chatter at me,
And after, bite me; then like hedge-hogs, which
Lie tumbling in my bare-foot way, and mount
Their pricks[2] at my foot-fall; sometime am I
All wound with adders, who, with cloven tongues,
Do hiss me into madness:—Lo! now! lo!

Enter TRINCULO.

Here comes a spirit of his; and to torment me,
For bringing wood in slowly: I'll fall flat;
Perchance he will not mind me.

Trin. Here's neither bush nor shrub, to bear off any weather at all, and another storm brewing: I hear it sing i' the wind: yond' same black cloud, yond' huge one, looks like a foul bumbard[3] that would shed his liquor. If it should thunder, as it did before, I know not where to hide my head: yond' same cloud cannot choose but fall by pailfuls.—What have we here? a man or a fish? Dead or alive? A fish: he smells like a fish; a very ancient and fish-like smell; a kind of, not of the newest, Poor-John. A strange fish! Were I in England now, (as once I was,) and had but this fish painted, not a holiday-fool there but would give a piece of silver: there would this monster make a man;[4] any strange beast there makes a man: when they will not give a doit to relieve a lame beggar, they will lay out ten to see a dead Indian. Legg'd like a man! and his fins like arms! Warm, o' my troth! I do now let loose my opinion, hold it no longer; this is no fish but an islander, that hath lately suffered by a thunderbolt. [*Thunder.*] Alas! the storm is come again: my best way is to creep under his garberdine;[5] there is no other shelter hereabout: Misery acquaints a man with strange bed-fellows. I will here shroud, till the dregs of the storm be past.

Enter STEPHANO, *singing; a bottle in his hand.*

Ste. *I shall no more to sea, to sea,*
Here shall I die ashore;—

This is a very scurvy tune to sing at a man's funeral:
Well, here's my comfort. [*Drinks.*

The master, the swabber, the boatswain, and I,
The gunner, and his mate,
Lov'd Mall, Megg, and Marian, and Margery,
But none of us cared for Kate:
For she had a tongue with a tang,
Would cry to a sailor, Go, hang:
She lov'd not the savour of tar nor of pitch,
Yet a tailor might scratch her where-e'er she did itch:
Then to sea boys, and let her go hang.

This is a scurvy tune too: But here's my comfort. [*Drinks.*

Cal. Do not torment me: O!

Ste. What's the matter? Have we devils here? Do you put tricks upon us with savages, and men of Inde? Ha! I have not scap'd drowning, to be afeard now of your four legs; for it hath been said, As proper a man as ever went on four legs, cannot make him give ground: and it shall be said so again, while Stephano breathes at nostrils.

Cal. The spirit torments me: O!

Ste. This is some monster of the isle, with four legs; who hath got, as I take it, an ague: Where the devil should he learn our language? I will give him some relief, if it be but for that: if I can recover him, and keep him tame, and get to Naples with him, he's a present for any emperor that ever trod on neat's-leather.

Cal. Do not torment me, pr'ythee;
I'll bring my wood home faster.

Ste. He's in his fit now; and does not talk after the wisest. He shall taste of my bottle: if he hath never drunk wine afore,[6] it will go near to remove his fit: if I can recover him, and keep him tame, I will not take too much[7] for him: he shall pay for him that hath him, and that soundly.

Cal. Thou dost me yet but little hurt; thou wilt
Anon, I know it by thy trembling:
Now Prosper works upon thee.

Ste. Come on your ways; open your mouth; here is that which will give language to you, cat; open your mouth: this will shake your shaking, I can tell you, and that soundly: you cannot tell who's your friend: open your chaps again.

Trin. I should know that voice: It should be—But he is drowned; and these are devils: O! defend me!—

Ste. Four legs, and two voices; a most delicate monster! His forward voice now is to speak well of his friend; his backward voice is to utter foul speeches, and to detract. If all the wine in my bottle will recover him, I will help his ague: Come,———Amen! I will pour some in thy other mouth.

Trin. Stephano,—

Ste. Doth thy other mouth call me? Mercy! mercy! This is a devil, and no monster: I will leave him; I have no long spoon.[8]

Trin. Stephano!—If thou beest Stephano, touch me, and speak to me; for I am Trinculo;—be not afeard,—thy good friend Trinculo.

Ste. If thou beest Trinculo, come forth; I'll pull thee by the lesser legs; If any be Trinculo's legs, these are they. Thou art very Trinculo, indeed: How cam'st thou to be the siege[9] of this moon-calf? Can he vent Trinculos?

Trin. I took him to be killed with a thunder-stroke:—But art thou not drowned, Stephano? I hope now, thou art not drowned. Is the storm overblown? I hid me under the dead moon-calf's[10] gaberdine, for fear of the storm: And art thou living, Stephano? O Stephano, two Neapolitans 'scap'd!

Ste. Pr'ythee, do not turn me about; my stomach is not constant.

Cal. These be fine things, an if they be not sprites.
That's a brave god, and bears celestial liquor:
I will kneel to him.

Ste. How did'st thou 'scape? How cam'st thou hither? swear by this bottle, how thou cam'st hither. I escaped upon a butt of sack, which the sailors heaved over-board, by this bottle! which I

---

1 To *moe* is to *make mouths.* "To make a moe like an ape. Distorquere os. Rictum deducere."—*Baret.*

2 *Pricks* is the ancient word for *prickles.*

3 A *bumbard* is a black jack of leather, to hold beer, &c.

4 i. e. *make a man's fortune.* Thus in A Midsummer Night's Dream—
"We are all *made men.*"
And in the old comedy of Ram Alley—
"She's a wench
Was born to *make us all.*"

5 A *gaberdine* was a coarse outer garment. "A shepherd's pelt, frock, or *gaberdine*, such a coarse long jacket as our porters wear over the rest of their garments," says Cotgrave. "A kind of rough cassock or frock like an Irish mantle," says Philips. It is from the low Latin *Galvardina*, whence the French *Galvardin* and *Gaban.* One would almost think Shakspeare had been acquainted with the following passage in Chapman's version of the fourth Book of the Odyssey:

"———The sea calves savour was
So passing sowre (they still being bred at seas)
It much afflicted us, for who can please
To *lie* by one of these same sea-bred whales"

6 No impertinent hint to those who indulge in the constant use of wine. When it is necessary for them as a medicine, it produces no effect.

7 Any sum, ever so much, an ironical expression implying that he would get as much as he could for him.

8 Shakspeare gives his characters appropriate language, "They belch forth proverbs in their drink," "Good liquor will *make a cat speak,*" and "he who eats with the devil had need of a *long spoon.*" The last is again used in The Comedy of Errors, Act iv. Sc. 2

9 *Siege* for *stool*, and in the dirtiest sense of the word.

10 The best account of the *moon calf* may be found in Drayton's poem with that title

made of the bark of a tree, with mine own hands, since I was cast a-shore.

Cal. I'll swear, upon that bottle, to be thy true subject; for the liquor is not earthly.

Ste. Here; swear then how thou escap'dst.

Trin. Swam a-shore, man, like a duck; I can swim like a duck, I'll be sworn.

Ste. Here, kiss the book: Though thou canst swim like a duck, thou art made like a goose.

Trin. O Stephano, hast any more of this?

Ste. The whole butt, man; my cellar is in a rock by the sea-side, where my wine is hid. How now, moon-calf? how does thine ague?

Cal. Hast thou not dropped from heaven?[1]

Ste. Out o' the moon, I do assure thee: I was the man in the moon,[2] when time was.

Cal. I have seen thee in her, and I do adore thee; my mistress shewed me thee, and thy dog, and thy bush.

Ste. Come, swear to that: kiss the book: I will furnish it anon with new contents: swear.

Trin. By this good light, this is a very shallow monster:—I afeard of him?—a very weak monster:—The man i' the moon?—a most poor credulous monster:—Well drawn, monster, in good sooth.

Cal. I'll shew thee every fertile inch o' the island;
And I will kiss thy foot: I pr'ythee, be my god.

Trin. By this light, a most perfidious and drunken monster; when his god's asleep, he'll rob his bottle.

Cal. I'll kiss thy foot: I'll swear myself thy subject.

Ste. Come on then; down, and swear.

Trin. I shall laugh myself to death at this puppy-headed monster: A most scurvy monster! I could find in my heart to beat him,—

Ste. Come, kiss.

Trin. —but that the poor monster's in drink: An abominable monster!

Cal. I'll shew thee the best springs; I'll pluck thee berries:
I'll fish for thee, and get thee wood enough.
A plague upon the tyrant that I serve!
I'll bear him no more sticks, but follow thee,
Thou wondrous man.

Trin. A most ridiculous monster; to make a wonder of a poor drunkard.

Cal. I pr'ythee, let me bring thee where crabs grow;
And I with my long nails will dig thee pig-nuts;
Shew thee a jay's nest, and instruct thee how
To snare the nimble marmozet; I'll bring thee
To clust'ring filberds, and sometimes I'll get thee
Young sea-mells[3] from the rock: Wilt thou go with me?

Ste. I pr'ythee now, lead the way, without any more talking.—Trinculo, the king and all our company else being drowned, we will inherit here.—Here; bear my bottle. Fellow Trinculo, we'll fill him by and by again.

Cal. *Farewell, master; farewell, farewell.* [*Sings drunkenly.*

Trin. A howling monster; a drunken monster.

Cal. *No more dams I'll make for fish;*
Nor fetch in firing
At requiring,
Nor scrape trenchering, nor wash dish;
'Ban 'Ban, Ca—Caliban,
Has a new master—Get a new man.
Freedom, hey-day! hey-day, freedom! hey-day, freedom!

Ste. O brave monster! lead the way. [*Exeunt.*

1 The Indians of the Island of S. Salvador asked by signs whether Columbus and his companions were *not come down from heaven.*

2 The reader may consult a curious note on this passage in Mr. Douce's very interesting Illustrations of Shakspeare; where it is observed that Dante makes *Cain* the *man in the moon* with his bundle of sticks; or in other words describes the moon by the periphrasis '*Caino e le spine*'

ACT III.

SCENE I.—*Before* Prospero's *Cell.* *Enter* FERDINAND, *bearing a Log.*

Fer. There be some sports are painful; and[4] their labour
Delight in them sets off:[5] some kinds of baseness
Are nobly undergone; and most poor matters
Point to rich ends. This my mean task
Would be as heavy to me, as odious; but
The mistress, which I serve, quickens what's dead,
And makes my labours pleasures: O, she is
Ten times more gentle than her father's crabbed;
And he's composed of harshness. I must remove
Some thousands of these logs, and pile them up,
Upon a sore injunction: My sweet mistress
Weeps when she sees me work; and says, such baseness
Had ne'er like executor. I forget:
But these sweet thoughts do even refresh my labours;
Most busy-less, when I do it.

Enter MIRANDA; *and* PROSPERO *at a distance.*

Mira. Alas, now! pray you,
Work not so hard: I would, the lightning had
Burnt up those logs, that you are enjoin'd to pile!
Pray, set it down, and rest you: when this burns,
'Twill weep for having wearied you: My father
Is hard at study; pray now, rest yourself;
He's safe for these three hours.

Fer. O most dear mistress,
The sun will set, before I shall discharge
What I must strive to do.

Mira. If you'll sit down,
I'll bear your logs the while: Pray, give me that;
I'll carry it to the pile.

Fer. No, precious creature;
I'd rather crack my sinews, break my back,
Than you should such dishonour undergo,
While I sit lazy by.

Mira. It would become me
As well as it does you: and I should do it
With much more ease; for my good will is to it,
And your's it is against.

Pro. Poor worm! thou art infected;
This visitation shews it.

Mira. You look wearily.

Fer. No, noble mistress; 'tis fresh morning with me,
When you are by at night.[6] I do beseech you,
(Chiefly that I might set it in my prayers,)
What is your name?

Mira. Miranda:—O my father,
I have broke your hest[7] to say so!

Fer. Admir'd Miranda!
Indeed, the top of admiration; worth
What's dearest to the world! Full many a lady
I have ey'd with best regard; and many a time
The harmony of their tongues hath into bondage
Brought my too diligent ear: for several virtues
Have I lik'd several women; never any
With so full soul, but some defect in her
Did quarrel with the noblest grace she ow'd,[8]
And put it to the foil: But you, O you,
So perfect, and so peerless, are created
Of every creature's best.[9]

3 A smaller species of sea-gulls.

4 Pope changed *and* to *but* here, without authority: we must read *and* in the sense of *and yet.*

5 *Molliter austerum studio fallente laborem.—Hor* Sat. ii. l. 2.

So, in Macbeth:

"The labour we delight in physics pain."

6 "Tu mihi curarum requies, tu nocte vel atra Lumen." *Tibull.* lib. iv. el. 13.

7 See Note 27, p. 26. 8 See Note 37, p. 31.

9 In the first book of Sidney's Arcadia, a lover says of his mistress:

"She is herself of *best things the collection.*"

In the third book there is a fable which may have been in Shakspeare's mind

Mira. I do not know
One of my sex; no woman's face remember,
Save, from my glass, mine own; nor have I seen
More that I may call men, than you, good friend,
And my dear father: how features are abroad,
I am skill-less of; but, by my modesty,
(The jewel in my dower,) I would not wish
Any companion in the world but you;
Nor can imagination form a shape,
Besides yourself, to like of: but I prattle
Something too wildly, and my father's precepts
I therein do forget.

Fer. I am, in my condition,
A prince, Miranda; I do think, a king;
(I would, not so!) and would no more endure
This wooden slavery, than to suffer
The flesh-fly blow my mouth.——Hear my soul speak;—
The very instant that I saw you, did
My heart fly to your service; there resides,
To make me slave to it; and, for your sake,
Am I this patient log-man.

Mira. Do you love me?

Fer. O heaven, O earth, bear witness to this sound,
And crown what I profess with kind event,
If I speak true; if hollowly, invert
What best is boded me to mischief! I,
Beyond all limit of what else[1] i' the world,
Do love, prize, honour you.

Mira. I am a fool,
To weep at what I am glad of.[2]

Pro. Fair encounter
Of two most rare affections! Heavens rain grace
On that which breeds between them!

Fer. Wherefore weep you?

Mira. At mine unworthiness, that dare not offer
What I desire to give; and much less take,
What I shall die to want: But this is trifling;
And all the more it seeks to hide itself,
The bigger bulk it shows. Hence, bashful cunning!
And prompt me, plain and holy innocence!
I am your wife, if you will marry me;
If not, I'll die your maid: to be your fellow[3]
You may deny me; but I'll be your servant,
Whether you will or no.

Fer. My mistress, dearest,
And I thus humble ever.

Mira. My husband then?

Fer. Ay, with a heart as willing
As bondage e'er of freedom: here's my hand.

Mira. And mine, with my heart in't: and now farewell,
Till half an hour hence.

Fer. A thousand! thousand!
[*Exeunt* FER. *and* MIR.

Pro. So glad of this as they, I cannot be,
Who are surpris'd with all; but my rejoicing
At nothing can be more. I'll to my book;
For yet, ere supper time, must I perform
Much business appertaining. [*Exit.*

SCENE II.—*Another part of the Island. Enter* STEPHANO *and* TRINCULO; CALIBAN *following with a Bottle.*

Ste. Tell not me;—when the butt is out, we will drink water; not a drop before: therefore bear up, and board 'em: Servant-monster, drink to me.

Trin. Servant-monster? the folly of this island! They say, there's but five upon this isle: we are three of them; if the other two be brained like us, the state totters.

Ste. Drink, servant-monster, when I bid thee; thy eyes are almost set in thy head.

Trin. Where should they be set else? he were a brave monster indeed, if they were set in his tail.

Ste. My man-monster hath drowned his tongue in sack: for my part, the sea cannot drown me: I swam, ere I could recover the shore, five-and-thirty leagues, off and on, by this light.—Thou shalt be my lieutenant, monster, or my standard.

Trin. Your lieutenant, if you list; he's no standard.

Ste. We'll not run, monsieur monster.

Trin. Nor go neither: but you'll lie, like dogs and yet say nothing neither.

Ste. Moon-calf, speak once in thy life, if thou beest a good moon-calf.

Cal. How does thy honour? Let me lick thy shoe: I'll not serve him, he is not valiant.

Trin. Thou liest, most ignorant monster; I am in case to justle a constable: Why, thou deboshed[4] fish thou, was there ever man a coward, that hath drunk so much sack as I to-day? Wilt thou tell a monstrous lie, being but half a fish, and half a monster?

Cal. Lo, how he mocks me! wilt thou let him, my lord?

Trin. Lord, quoth he!—that a monster should be such a natural!

Cal. Lo, lo, again! bite him to death, I pr'ythee.

Ste. Trinculo, keep a good tongue in your head; if you prove a mutineer, the next tree—The poor monster's my subject, and he shall not suffer indignity.

Cal. I thank my noble lord. Wilt thou be pleas'd to hearken once again to the suit I made thee?

Ste. Marry will I: kneel, and repeat it; I will stand, and so shall Trinculo.

Enter ARIEL, *invisible.*

Cal. As I told thee before, I am subject to a tyrant; a sorcerer, that by his cunning hath cheated me of this island.

Ari. Thou liest.

Cal. Thou liest, thou jesting monkey, thou!
I would, my valiant master would destroy thee:
I do not lie.

Ste. Trinculo, if you trouble him any more in his tale, by this hand, I will supplant some of your teeth.

Trin. Why, I said nothing.

Ste. Mum then, and no more.—[*To* CALIBAN.] Proceed.

Cal. I say, by sorcery he got this isle:
From me he got it. If thy greatness will
Revenge it on him—for, I know, thou dar'st;
But this thing dare not.

Ste. That's most certain.

Cal. Thou shalt be lord of it, and I'll serve thee.

Ste. How now shall this be compassed? Canst thou bring me to the party?

Cal. Yea, yea, my lord; I'll yield him thee asleep,
Where thou may'st knock a nail into his head.

Ari. Thou liest, thou canst not.

Cal. What a pied[5] ninny's this? Thou scurvy patch!—
I do beseech thy greatness, give him blows,
And take his bottle from him: when that's gone,
He shall drink nought but brine; for I'll not shew him
Where the quick freshes[6] are.

Ste. Trinculo, run into no further danger: in-

1 *What* else, for *whatsoever* else.

2 Steevens observes justly that this is one of those touches of nature which distinguish Shakspeare from all other writers. There is a kindred thought in Romeo and Juliet:

"Back, foolish tears, back to your native spring!
Your tributary drops belong to woe,
Which you mistaking offer up to joy."

3 i. e. your *companion.* Malone has cited a very apposite passage from Catullus; but, as Mr. Douce remarks, Shakspeare had more probably the pathetic old poem of The Nut Brown Maid in his recollection.

4 *Deboshed,* this is the old orthography of *debauched;* following the sound of the French original. In altering the spelling we have departed from the proper pronunciation of the word.

5 He calls him a *pied ninny,* alluding to Trinculo's party-coloured dress, he was a licensed fool or jester

6 *Quick freshes* are *living springs.*

terrupt the monster one word further, and, by this hand, I'll turn my mercy out of doors, and make a stock-fish of thee.

Trin. Why, what did I? I did nothing; I'll go further off.

Ste. Didst thou not say, he lied?

Ari. Thou liest.

Ste. Do I so? take thou that. [*Strikes him.*]
As you like this, give me the lie another time.

Trin. I did not give the lie:—Out o' your wits, and hearing too?——A pox o' your bottle! this can sack, and drinking do.—A murrain on your monster, and the devil take your fingers!

Cal. Ha, ha, ha!

Ste. Now, forward with your tale. Pr'ythee stand further off.

Cal. Beat him enough: after a little time,
I'll beat him too.

Ste. Stand further.—Come, proceed.

Cal. Why, as I told thee, 'tis a custom with him
I' the afternoon to sleep: there thou may'st brain him,
Having first seiz'd his books; or with a log
Batter his skull, or paunch him with a stake,
Or cut his wezand[1] with thy knife; Remember,
First to possess his books; for without them
He's but a sot, as I am, nor hath not
One spirit to command: They all do hate him,
As rootedly as I: Burn but his books;
He has brave utensils, (for so he calls them,)
Which, when he has a house, he'll deck withal.
And that most deeply to consider, is
The beauty of his daughter; he himself
Calls her a non-pareil: I never saw a woman,
But only Sycorax my dam, and she;
But she as far surpasseth Sycorax,
As great'st does least.

Ste. Is it so brave a lass?

Cal. Ay, my lord; she will become thy bed, I warrant,
And bring thee forth brave brood.

Ste. Monster, I will kill this man: his daughter and I will be king and queen: (save our graces!) and Trinculo and thyself shall be viceroys:—Dost thou like the plot, Trinculo?

Trin. Excellent.

Ste. Give me thy hand; I am sorry I beat thee: but, while thou livest, keep a good tongue in thy head.

Cal. Within this half hour will he be asleep;
Wilt thou destroy him then?

Ste. Ay, on mine honour.

Ari. This will I tell my master.

Cal. Thou mak'st me merry: I am full of pleasure;
Let us be jocund: Will you troll the catch
You taught me but while-ere?

Ste. At thy request, monster, I will do reason, any reason: Come on, Trinculo, let us sing. [*Sings.*

Flout 'em, and skout 'em; and skout 'em, and flout'em:
Thought is free.

Cal. That's not the tune.

[ARIEL *plays the tune on a tabor and pipe.*

Ste. What is this same?

Trin. This is the tune of our catch, played by the picture of No-body.[2]

Ste. If thou beest a man, shew thyself in thy likeness: if thou beest a devil, take't as thou list.

Trin. O, forgive me my sins!

Ste. He that dies, pays all debts: I defy thee.—Mercy upon us!

Cal. Art thou afeard?[3]

Ste. No, monster, not I.

Cal. Be not afeard; the isle is full of noises,
Sounds, and sweet airs, that give delight, and hurt not.
Sometimes a thousand twangling instruments
Will hum about mine ears; and sometimes voices,
That, if I then had wak'd after long sleep,
Will make me sleep again: and then, in dreaming,
The clouds, methought, would open, and shew riches
Ready to drop upon me; that, when I wak'd,
I cry'd to dream again.

Ste. This will prove a brave kingdom to me, where I shall have my music for nothing.

Cal. When Prospero is destroyed.

Ste. That shall be by and by: I remember the story.

Trin. The sound is going away: let's follow it, and after, do our work.

Ste. Lead, monster; we'll follow.—I would, I could see this taborer:[4] he lays it on.

Trin. Wilt come? I'll follow, Stephano. [*Exeunt*

SCENE III.—*Another part of the Island. Enter* ALONSO, SEBASTIAN, ANTONIO, GONZALO, ADRIAN, FRANCISCO, *and others.*

Gon. By'r lakin,[5] I can go no further, sir;
My old bones ache; here's a maze trod, indeed,
Through forth-rights, and meanders! by your patience,
I needs must rest me.

Alon. Old lord, I cannot blame thee,
Who am myself attach'd with weariness,
To the dulling of my spirits: sit down, and rest.
Even here I will put off my hope, and keep it
No longer for my flatterer: he is drown'd,
Whom thus we stray to find; and the sea mocks
Our frustrate search on land: Well, let him go.

Ant. I am right glad that he's so out of hope.
[*Aside to* SEBASTIAN
Do not, for one repulse, forego the purpose
That you resolv'd to effect.

Seb. The next advantage
Will we take thoroughly.

Ant. Let it be to-night:
For, now they are oppress'd with travel, they
Will not, nor cannot, use such vigilance,
As when they are fresh.

Seb. I say, to-night: no more.

Solemn and strange music; and PROSPERO *above, invisible. Enter several strange Shapes, bringing in a Banquet; they dance about it with gentle actions of salutation; and inviting the King, &c. to eat, they depart.*

Alon. What harmony is this? my good friends, hark!

Gon. Marvellous sweet music!

Alon. Give us kind keepers, heavens! What were these?

Seb. A living drollery:[6] Now I will believe
That there are unicorns; that, in Arabia
There is one tree, the phœnix' throne;[7] one phœnix
At this hour reigning there.

1 *Wezand*, i. e. throat or windpipe.

2 The picture of No-body was a common sign. There is also a wood cut prefixed to an old play of No-body and Some-body, which represents this notable person.

3 *To affear*, is an obsolete verb with the same meaning as *to affray, or make afraid.*

4 "You shall heare in the ayre the sound of *tabers and other instruments*, to put the trauellers in feare, &c. by evill spirites that make these soundes, and also do call diuerse of the trauellers by their names, &c."—*Trauels of Marcus Paulus, by John Frampton*, 4to. 1579. To some of these circumstances Milton also alludes:

"——calling shapes, and beckoning shadows dire;
And aery tongues that syllable men's names
On sands, and shores, and desert wildernesses."

5 *By'r lakin* is a contraction of *By our ladykin*, the diminutive of our lady.

6 Shows, called *Drolleries*, were in Shakspeare's time performed by puppets only. From these our modern *drolls*, exhibited at fairs, &c. took their name "A living drollery," is therefore a drollery not by wooden but by living personages.

7 "I myself have heard strange things of this kind of tree; namely, in regard of the Bird Phœnix, which is supposed to have taken that name of this date tree

Ant. I'll believe both;
And what does else want credit, come to me,
And I'll be sworn 'tis true: Travellers ne'er did lie,
Though fools at home condemn them.

Gon. If in Naples
I should report this now, would they believe me?
If I should say I saw such islanders,
(For, certes,[1] these are people of the island,)
Who, though they are of monstrous shape, yet note,
Their manners are more gentle, kind, than of
Our human generation you shall find
Many, nay, almost any.

Pro. Honest lord,
Thou hast said well; for some of you there present,
Are worse than devils. [*Aside.*

Alon. I cannot too much muse,[2]
Such shapes, such gesture, and such sound, expressing
(Although they want the use of tongue) a kind
Of excellent dumb discourse.

Pro. Praise in departing.[3] [*Aside.*

Fran. They vanish'd strangely.

Seb. No matter, since
They have left their viands behind; for we have stomachs.—
Will't please you taste of what is here?

Alon. Not I.

Gon. Faith, sir, you need not fear: When we were boys,
Who would believe that there were mountaineers,
Dew-lapp'd like bulls, whose throats had hanging at them
Wallets of flesh? or that there were such men,
Whose heads stood in their breasts? which now we find,
Each putter-out on five for one,[4] will bring us
Good warrant of.

Alon. I will stand too, and feed,
Although my last: no matter, since I feel
The best is past:—Brother, my lord the duke,
Stand too, and do as we.

Thunder and lightning. Enter ARIEL *like a Harpy; claps his wings upon the table, and, by quaint device, the Banquet vanishes.*

Ari. You are three men of sin, whom destiny,
(That hath to instrument this lower world,
And what is in't,) the never-surfeited sea
Hath caused to belch up; and on this island
Where man doth not inhabit; you 'mongst men
Being most unfit to live. I have made you mad:
[*Seeing* ALON. SEB. *&c. draw their swords.*
And even with such like valour, men hang and drown
Their proper selves. You fools! I and my fellows
Are ministers of fate; the elements
Of whom your swords are temper'd, may as well
Wound the loud winds, or with bemock'd-at stabs
Kill the still-closing waters, as diminish
One dowle[5] that's in my plume; my fellow ministers
Are like invulnerable: if you could hurt,
Your swords are now too massy for your strengths,
And will not be uplifted; But, remember,
(For that's my business to you,) that you three
From Milan did supplant good Prospero;
Expos'd unto the sea, which hath requit it,
Him, and his innocent child: for which foul deed
The powers, delaying, not forgetting, have
Incens'd the seas and shores, yea all the creatures,
Against your peace: Thee, of thy son, Alonso,
They have bereft; and do pronounce by me,
Lingering perdition (worse than any death
Can be at once,) shall step by step attend
You, and your ways; whose wraths to guard you from
(Which here, in this most desolate isle, else falls
Upon your heads,) is nothing, but heart's sorrow,
And a clear[6] life ensuing.

He vanishes in Thunder: then, to soft music, enter the Shapes again, and dance with mops and mowes, and carry out the table.

Pro. [*Aside.*] Bravely the figure of this harpy hast thou
Perform'd, my Ariel; a grace it had, devouring:
Of my instruction hast thou nothing 'bated,
In what thou hadst to say: so, with good life,[7]
And observation strange, my meaner ministers
Their several kinds have done: my high charms work,
And these, mine enemies, are all knit up
In their distractions: they now are in my power,
And in these fits I leave them, whilst I visit
Young Ferdinand, (whom they suppose is drown'd)
And his and my lov'd darling.
[*Exit* PROSPERO *from above.*

Gon. I' the name of something holy, sir why stand you
In this strange stare?

Alon. O, it is monstrous! monstrous
Methought, the billows spoke, and told me of it;
The winds did sing it to me; and the thunder,
That deep and dreadful organ-pipe, pronounc'd
The name of Prosper; it did bass my trespass.
Therefore my son i' the ooze is bedded; and
I'll seek him deeper than e'er plummet sounded,
And with him there lie mudded. [*Exit.*

Seb. But one fiend at a time,
I'll fight their legions o'er.

Ant. I'll be thy second.
[*Exeunt* SEB. *and* ANT.

Gon. All three of them are desperate; their great guilt,
Like poison given to work a great time after,[8]
Now 'gins to bite the spirits: I do beseech you
That are of suppler joints, follow them swiftly,
And hinder them from what this ectasy[9]
May now provoke them to.

Adr. Follow, I pray you.
Exeunt.

(called in Greek φοινιξ;) for it was assured unto me, that the said bird died with that tree, and revived of itselfe as the tree sprung againe."—*Holland's Translation of Pliny*, B. xiii. C. 4.

1 Certainly. 2 Wonder.

3 "*Praise in departing*," is a proverbial phrase signifying, Do not praise your entertainment too soon, lest you should have reason to retract your commendation.

4 "Each putter-out on five for one," i. e. each *traveller*; it appears to have been the custom to place out a sum of money upon going abroad to be returned with enormous interest if the party returned safe; a kind of insurance of a gambling nature.

5 Bailey, in his dictionary, says that *dowle* is a feather, or rather the single particles of the down. Coles, in his Latin Dictionary, 1679, interprets young *dowle* by *Lanugo*. And in a history of most Manual Arts, 1661, *wool* and *dowle* are treated as synonymous. Tooke contends that this word and others of the same form are nothing more than the past participle of *deal;* and Junius and Skinner both derive it from the same. I fully believe that Tooke is right; the provincial word *dool* is a *portion* of unploughed land left in a field; Coles, in his English Dictionary, 1701, has given *dowl* as a cant word, and interprets it *deal*. I must refer the reader to the Diversions of Purley for further proof.

6 A *clear* life; is a *pure*, *blameless*, life.

7 With good *life*, i. e. with the full bent and energy of mind. Mr. Henley says that the expression is still in use in the west of England.

8 The natives of Africa have been supposed to be possessed of the secret how to temper poisons with such art as not to operate till several years after they were administered. Their drugs were then as certain in their effect as subtle in their preparation.

9 Shakspeare uses *ecstasy* for any temporary alienation of mind, a fit, or madness. Minsheu's definition of this word will serve to explain its meaning wherever it occurs throughout the following pages. "Extasie or trance; *G.* extase; *Lat.* extasis, abstractio mentis. Est proprie mentis emotio, et quasi ex statione sua deturbatio seu furore, eu admiratione, seu timore, aliove casu decidat." *Guide to the Tongues*, 1617

ACT IV.

SCENE I.—*Before* Prospero's *Cell. Enter* PROSPERO, FERDINAND, *and* MIRANDA.

Pro. If I have too austerely punish'd you,
Your compensation makes amends; for I
Have given you here a thread of mine own life,
Or that for which I live; whom once again
I tender to thy hand: all thy vexations
Were but my trials of thy love, and thou
Hast strangely stood the test: here, afore Heaven,
I ratify this my rich gift. O Ferdinand,
Do not smile at me, that I boast her off,
For thou shalt find she will outstrip all praise,
And make it halt behind her.
Fer. I do believe it,
Against an oracle.
Pro. Then, as my gift, and thine own acquisition
Worthily purchas'd, take my daughter: But
If thou dost break her virgin knot[1] before
All sanctimonious ceremonies may
With full and holy rite be minister'd,
No sweet aspersion[2] shall the heavens let fall
To make this contract grow; but barren hate,
Sour-ey'd disdain, and discord, shall bestrew
The union of your bed with weeds so loathly,
That you shall hate it both: therefore, take heed,
As Hymen's lamps shall light you.
Fer. As I hope
For quiet days, fair issue, and long life,
With such love as 'tis now; the murkiest den,
The most opportune place, the strong'st suggestion[3]
Our worser Genius can, shall never melt
Mine honour into lust; to take away
The edge of that day's celebration,
When I shall think, or Phœbus' steeds are founder'd,
Or night kept chain'd below.
Pro. Fairly spoke;
Sit then, and talk with her, she is thine own.—
What, Ariel; my industrious servant Ariel!

Enter ARIEL.

Ari. What would my potent master? here I am.
Pro. Thou and thy meaner fellows your last service
Did worthily perform; and I must use you
In such another trick: go, bring the rabble,
O'er whom I give thee power, here, to this place:
Incite them to quick motion; for I must
Bestow upon the eyes of these young couple
Some vanity[4] of mine art; it is my promise,
And they expect it from me.
Ari. Presently?
Pro. Ay, with a twink.
Ari. Before you can say, *Come*, and *go*,
And breathe twice; and cry, *so, so;*
Each one, tripping on his toe,
Will be here with mop and mowe:
Do you love me, master? no.
Pro. Dearly, my delicate Ariel: Do not approach,
Till thou dost hear me call.
Ari. Well I conceive. [*Exit*
Pro. Look, thou be true; do not give dalliance
Too much the rein; the strongest oaths are straw
To the fire i' the blood: be more abstemious,
Or else, good night, your vow!
Fer. I warrant you, sir,
The white-cold virgin snow upon my heart
Abates the ardour of my liver.
Pro. Well.—
Now come, my Ariel; bring a corollary,[5]
Rather than want a spirit; appear, and pertly.—
No tongue; all eyes; be silent. [*Soft music.*

A Masque. Enter IRIS.

Iris. Ceres, most bounteous lady, thy rich leas
Of wheat, rye, barley, vetches, oats, and peas;
Thy turfy mountains, where live nibbling sheep,
And flat meads thatch'd with stover,[6] them to keep:
Thy banks with peonied and lilied brims,[7]
Which spongy April at thy hest betrims,
To make cold nymphs chaste crowns; and thy broom groves,
Whose shadow the dismissed bachelor loves,
Being lass-lorn;[8] thy pole-clipt vineyard;
And thy sea-marge, steril, and rocky-hard,
Where thou thyself dost air: The queen o' the sky
Whose watery arch, and messenger, am I,
Bids thee leave these; and with her sovereign grace,
Here on this grass-plot, in this very place,
To come and sport: her peacocks fly amain;
Approach, rich Ceres, her to entertain.

Enter CERES.

Cer. Hail, many-colour'd messenger, that ne'er
Dost disobey the wife of Jupiter;
Who, with thy saffron wings, upon my flowers
Diffusest honey-drops, refreshing showers:[9]
And with each end of thy blue bow dost crown
My bosky[10] acres, and my unshrubb'd down.
Rich scarf to my proud earth: Why hast thy queen
Summon'd me hither, to this short-grass'd green?
Iris. A contract of true love to celebrate;
And some donation freely to estate
On the bless'd lovers.
Cer. Tell me, heavenly bow,
If Venus, or her son, as thou dost know,
Do now attend the queen? since they did plot
The means, that dusky Dis my daughter got,
Her and her blind boy's scandal'd company
I have forsworn.

---

1 The same expression occurs in Pericles. Mr. Henley says that it is a manifest allusion to the zones of the ancients, which were worn as guardians of chastity before marriage.

2 *Aspersion* is here used in its primitive sense of *sprinkling*, at present it is used in its figurative sense of throwing out hints of calumny and detraction.

3 Suggestion here means *temptation* or wicked prompting.

4 "Some *vanity* of mine art" is some *illusion*. Thus in a passage, quoted by Warton, in his Dissertation on the Gesta Romanorum, from *Emare*, a metrical Romance.

"The emperor said on high
Sertes thys is a fayry
Or ellys a *vanite*."

5 That is, bring *more than are sufficient*. "*Corollary*, the addition or vantage above measure, an *overplus*, or *surplusage*."—*Blount*.

6 *Stover* is fodder for cattle, as hay, straw, and the like: *estovers* is the old law term, it is from *estouvier*, old French.

7 The old editions read *Pioned and Twilled brims*. In Ovid's Banquet of Sense, by Geo. Chapman, 1595, we meet with

"—Cuplike *twill-pants* strew'd in Bacchus bowers."

If *twill* be the name of any flower, the old reading may stand. Mr. Henley strongly contends for the old reading, and explains *pioned* to mean faced up with mire in the manner that ditchers trim the banks of ditches: *twilled* he derives from the French verb *touiller*, which Cotgrave interprets, "filthily to mix, to mingle, confound, or shuffle together." He objects to *peonied* and *lillied* because these flowers never blow in April. But Mr Boaden has pointed out a passage in Lord Bacon's Essay on Gardens which supports the reading in the text "In *April* follow the double white violet, the wall-flower, the stock-gilly-flower, the cowslip, flower-de-luces. and *lillies of all natures*; rose-mary flowers, the tulippe, the double *piony*, &c." Lyte, in his Herbal, says one kind of *peonie* is called by some, *maiden* or *virgin peonie*. And Pliny mentions the water-lilly as a preserver of chastity, B. xxvi. C. 10. Edward Fenton, in his "Secret Wonders of Nature," 1569, 4to. B. vi asserts that "the water-lilly mortifieth altogether the appetite of sensuality and defends from unchaste thoughts and dreams of venery." The passage certainly gains by the reading of Mr. Steevens, which I have, for these reasons, retained

8 That is, *forsaken by his lass*.

9 Mr. Douce remarks that this is an elegant expansion of the following lines in Phaer's Virgil Æneid, Lib. iv.

"Dame rainbow down therefore with saffron wings of drooping showres,
Whose face a thousand sundry hues against the sun devoures,
From heaven descending came."

10 *Bosky acres* are woody acres, fields intersected by luxuriant hedge-rows and copses.

Iris. Of her society
Be not afraid: I met a deity
Cutting the clouds towards Paphos; and her son
Dove-drawn with her: here thought they to have done
Some wanton charm upon this man and maid,
Whose vows are, that no bed-rite shall be paid
Till Hymen's torch be lighted: but in vain;
Mars' hot minion is returned again;
Her waspish-headed son has broke his arrows,
Swears he will shoot no more, but play with sparrows,
And be a boy right out.

Cer. Highest queen of state,
Great Juno comes; I know her by her gait.

Enter Juno.

Juno. How does my bounteous sister? Go with me,
To bless this twain, that they may prosperous be,
And honour'd in their issue.

SONG.

Jun. *Honour, riches, marriage-blessing,*
Long continuance, and increasing,
Hourly joys be still upon you!
Juno sings her blessings on you.

Cer. *Earth's increase, and foison[1] plenty;*
Barns and garners never empty;
Vines, with clust'ring bunches growing;
Plants, with goodly burden bowing;
Spring come to you, at the farthest,
In the very end of harvest!
Scarcity and want shall shun you;
Ceres' blessing so is on you.

Fer. This is a most majestic vision, and
Harmonious charmingly:[2] May I be bold
To think these spirits?

Pro. Spirits, which by mine art
I have from their confines call'd to enact
My present fancies.

Fer. Let me live here ever;
So rare a wonder'd[3] father, and a wife,
Make this place Paradise.

[Juno *and* Ceres *whisper, and send* Iris *on employment.*

Pro. Sweet now, silence:
Juno and Ceres whisper seriously;
There's something else to do: hush, and be mute,
Or else our spell is marr'd.

Iris. You nymphs, call'd Naiads, of the wand'ring brooks,
With your sedg'd crowns, and ever harmless looks,
Leave your crisp[4] channels, and on this green land
Answer your summons; Juno does command:
Come, temperate nymphs, and help to celebrate
A contract of true love; be not too late.

Enter certain Nymphs.

You sun-burn'd sicklemen, of August weary,
Come hither from the furrow, and be merry;
Make holy-day: your rye-straw hats put on,
And these fresh nymphs encounter every one
In country footing.

Enter certain Reapers, properly habited: they join with the Nymphs in a graceful dance; towards the end of which Prospero *starts suddenly, and speaks; after which, to a strange, hollow, and confused noise, they heavily vanish.*

Pro. [*Aside.*] I had forgot that foul conspiracy
Of the beast Caliban, and his confederates,
Against my life; the minute of their plot
Is almost come.—[*To the Spirits.*] Well done;—avoid;—no more.

Fer. This is strange: your father's in some passion
That works him strongly.

Mira. Never till this day,
Saw I him touch'd with anger so distemper'd.

Pro. You do look, my son, in a mov'd sort,
As if you were dismay'd: be cheerful, sir:
Our revels now are ended: these our actors,
As I foretold you, were all spirits, and
Are melted into air, into thin air:
And, like the baseless fabric of this vision,[5]
The cloud-capp'd towers, the gorgeous palaces,
The solemn temples, the great globe itself,
Yea, all which it inherit, shall dissolve;
And, like this insubstantial pageant faded,[6]
Leave not a rack[7] behind: We are such stuff
As dreams are made of, and our little life
Is rounded with a sleep.—Sir, I am vex'd;
Bear with my weakness; my old brain is troubled.
Be not disturb'd with my infirmity:
If you be pleas'd, retire into my cell,
And there repose; a turn or two I'll walk,
To still my beating mind.

Fer. Mira. We wish your peace. [*Exeunt.*

Pro. Come with a thought:—I thank you:—Ariel, come.

Enter Ariel.

Ari. Thy thoughts I cleave to: What's thy pleasure?

Pro. Spirit,
We must prepare to meet[8] with Caliban.

Ari. Ay, my commander: when I presented Ceres,
I thought to have told thee of it; but I fear'd,
Lest I might anger thee.

Pro. Say again, where didst thou leave these varlets?

Ari. I told you, sir, they were red-hot with drinking;
So full of valour, that they smote the air
For breathing in their faces; beat the ground
For kissing of their feet: yet always bending
Towards their project: then I beat my tabor,
At which, like unback'd colts, they prick'd their ears,

---

1 *Foison* is *abundance*, particularly of harvest corn.

2 For *charmingly harmonious.*

3 "So rare a wonder'd father," is a father able to produce such wonders.

4 *Crisp* channels; i. e. curled, from the curl raised by a breeze on the surface of the water. So in 1 K. Hen IV. Act i. Sc. 3.

"— Hid his *crisp* head in the hollow bank."

5 In the tragedy of Darius, by Lord Sterline, printed in 1603, is the following passage:

"Let greatness of her glassy sceptres vaunt
Not sceptres, no, but reeds, soon bruised soon broken;
And let this worldly pomp our wits enchant,
All fades, and scarcely leaves behind a token.
Those golden palaces, those gorgeous halls,
With furniture superfluously fair,
Those stately courts, those sky-encountering walls,
Evanish all like vapours in the air."

The preceding stanza also contains evidence of the same train of thought with Shakspeare.

"And when the eclipse comes of our glory's light,
Then what avails the adoring of a name?
A meer *illusion made to mock the sight,*
Whose best was but the shadow of a *dream.*"

It is evident that one poet imitated the other, and it seems probable that Shakspeare was the imitator. The exact period at which the Tempest was produced is not known, but it is thought not earlier than 1611. It was first printed in the folio of 1623. Lord Sterline also wrote a tragedy entitled Julius Cæsar, in which there are parallel passages to some in Shakspeare's play on the same subject, and Malone thinks the coincidence more than accidental.

6 *Faded*, i. e. *vanished*, from the Latin *vado.* The ancient English *pageants* were shows, on the reception of princes or other festive occasions; they were exhibited on stages in the open air. On these allegorical spectacles very costly ornaments were bestowed. See Warton's Hist. of Poetry, ii. 199, 202, Fabian, ii. 382 and above all Mr Gifford's Ben Jonson *passim.*

7 A *vapour* an *exhalation.* See Mr. Horne Tooke's admirable observation on this passage in the Diversions of Purley, Vol. ii. p. 388, 4to. ed.

8 To *counteract*, to play stratagem against stratagem.

"—— You may *meet*
With her abusive malice, and exempt
Yourself from the suspicion of revenge."
Cynthia's Revenge 1613.

Advanc'd their eye-lids, lifted up their noses,
As they smelt music; so I charm'd their ears,
That, calf-like, they my lowing follow'd, through
Tooth'd briers, sharp furzes, pricking goss, and thorns,
Which enter'd their frail shins: at last I left them
I' the filthy mantled pool beyond your cell,
There dancing up to the chins, that the foul lake
O'er-stunk their feet.

Pro. This was well done, my bird:
Thy shape invisible retain thou still:
The trumpery in my house, go, bring it hither,
For stale[1] to catch these thieves.

Ari. I go, I go. [*Exit.*

Pro. A devil, a born devil, on whose nature
Nurture[2] can never stick; on whom my pains,
Humanely taken, all, all lost, quite lost;
And as, with age, his body uglier grows,
So his mind cankers: I will plague them all,

Re-enter ARIEL *loaden with glistering apparel, &c.*

Even to roaring:—Come, hang them on this line.

PROSPERO *and* ARIEL *remain invisible. Enter* CALIBAN, STEPHANO, *and* TRINCULO; *all wet.*

Cal. Pray you, tread softly, that the blind mole may not
Hear a foot fall: we now are near his cell.

Ste. Monster, your fairy, which, you say, is a harmless fairy, has done little better than play'd the Jack[3] with us.

Trin. Monster, I do smell all horse-piss; at which my nose is in great indignation.

Ste. So is mine. Do you hear, monster? If I should take a displeasure against you; look you,—

Trin. Thou wert but a lost monster.

Cal. Good my lord, give me thy favour still:
Be patient, for the prize I'll bring thee to
Shall hood-wink this mischance; therefore, speak softly,
All's hush'd as midnight yet.

Trin. Ay, but to lose our bottles in the pool,—

Ste. There is not only disgrace and dishonour in that, monster, but an infinite loss.

Trin. That's more to me than my wetting: yet this is your harmless fairy, monster.

Ste. I will fetch off my bottle, though I be o'er ears for my labour.

Cal. Pr'ythee, my king, be quiet: Seest thou here,
This is the mouth of the cell: no noise, and enter:
Do that good mischief, which may make this island
Thine own for ever, and I, thy Caliban,
For aye thy foot-licker.

Ste. Give me thy hand: for I do begin to have bloody thoughts.

Trin. O king Stephano! O peer![4] O worthy Stephano! look, what a wardrobe here is for thee!

Cal. Let it alone, thou fool: it is but trash.

Trin. O, ho, monster; we know what belongs to a frippery:[5]—O king Stephano!

Ste. Put off that gown, Trinculo; by this hand, I'll have that gown.

Trin. Thy grace shall have it.

Cal. The dropsy drown this fool! what do you mean,
To doat thus on such luggage? Let it alone,[6]
And do the murder first: if he awake,
From toe to crown he'll fill our skins with pinches;
Make us strange stuff.

Ste. Be you quiet, monster.—Mistress line, is not this my jerkin? Now is the jerkin under the line: now, jerkin, you are like to lose your hair, and prove a bald jerkin.

Trin. Do, do: We steal by line and level, an't like your grace.

Ste. I thank thee for that jest; here's a garment for't: wit shall not go unrewarded, while I am king of this country: *Steal by line and level*, is an excellent pass of pate; there's another garment for't.

Trin. Monster, come, put some lime[7] upon your fingers, and away with the rest.

Cal. I will have none on't: we shall lose our time,
And all be turn'd to barnacles,[8] or to apes
With foreheads villanous low.

Ste. Monster, lay-to your fingers; help to bear this away, where my hogshead of wine is, or I'll turn you out of my kingdom: go to, carry this.

Trin. And this.

Ste. Ay, and this.

A noise of Hunters heard.[9] *Enter divers Spirits in shape of hounds, and hunt them about;* PROSPERO *and* ARIEL *setting them on.*

Pro. Hey, *Mountain*, hey!

Ari. *Silver!* there it goes, *Silver!*

Pro. *Fury! Fury!* there, *Tyrant*, there! hark, hark!

[CAL. STE. *and* TRIN. *are driven out.*

Go, charge my goblins that they grind their joints
With dry convulsions; shorten up their sinews
With aged cramps; and more pinch-spotted make them,
Than pard,[10] or cat o' mountain.

Ari. Hark, they roar

Pro. Let them be hunted soundly: At this hour
Lie at my mercy all mine enemies:
Shortly shall all my labours end, and thou
Shalt have the air at freedom: for a little,
Follow, and do me service. [*Exeunt.*

ACT V.

SCENE I.—*Before the Cell of* Prospero. *Enter* PROSPERO *in his magic robes, and* ARIEL.

Pro. Now does my project gather to a head:
My charms crack not; my spirits obey; and time
Goes upright with his carriage. How's the day?

Ari. On the sixth hour; at which time, my lord,
You said our work should cease.

Pro. I did say so,
When first I rais'd the tempest. Say, my spirit,
How fares the king and his followers?

Ari. Confin'd together
In the same fashion as you gave in charge;
Just as you left them, sir; all prisoners
In the lime grove which weather-fends[11] your cell:
They cannot budge, till you release.[12] The king,
His brother, and yours, abide all three distracted;
And the remainder mourning over them,
Brim-full of sorrow, and dismay; but chiefly
Him you term'd, sir, *The good old lord, Gonzalo;*
His tears run down his beard, like winter's drops
From eaves of reeds: your charm so strongly works them,
That if you now beheld them, your affections
Would become tender.

Pro. Dost thou think so, spirit?

Ari. Mine would, sir, were I human.

Pro. And mine shall.
Hast thou, which art but air, a touch,[13] a feeling
Of their afflictions? and shall not myself,
One of their kind, that relish all as sharply,
Passion as they, be kindlier mov'd than thou art?

---

1 *Stale*, in the art of fowling, signified a *bait* or *lure* to decoy birds.

2 *Nurture* is *Education*, in our old language.

3 To play the *Jack*, was to play the *Knave*.

4 This is a humorous allusion to the old ballad "King Stephen was a worthy peer," of which Iago sings a verse in Othello.

5 A shop for the sale of old clothes.—*Fripperie, Fr.*

6 The old copy reads—"Let's alone."

7 *Bird-lime.*

8 The *barnacle* is a kind of shell-fish, *lepas anatifera*, which ancient credulity believed to produce the barnacle-goose. Bishop Hall refers to it in the second Satire of his fourth Book—

"That Scottish *barnacle*, if I might choose,
That of a worm doth wax a winged goose."

Gerrard, in his Herbal, 1597, p. 1391, gives a full description of it; and the worthy Dr. Bullein treats those as ignorant and incredulous, who do not believe in the transformation.—*Bulwarke of Defence*, 1562. Caliban's Barnacle is the *clakis*, or tree-goose.

9 See Tyrwhitt's Chaucer, Note [illegible] 3441

10 Pard, i. e. Leopard.

11 *Defends it from the weather*

12 i. e. *Until you release them*

13 A *sensation.*

Though with their high wrongs I am struck to the quick,
Yet, with my nobler reason, 'gainst my fury,
Do I take part: the rarer action is
In virtue than in vengeance: they being penitent,
The sole drift of my purpose doth extend
Not a frown further: Go, release them, Ariel;
My charms I'll break, their senses I'll restore,
And they shall be themselves.

Ari. I'll fetch them, sir. [*Exit.*

Pro. Ye elves of hills, brooks, standing lakes, and groves[1];
And ye, that on the sands with printless foot
Do chase the ebbing Neptune, and do fly him
When he comes back; you demy-puppets, that
By moon-shine do the green-sour ringlets make,
Whereof the ewe not bites; and you, whose pastime
Is to make midnight-mushrooms; that rejoice
To hear the solemn curfew; by whose aid
(Weak masters though you be[2]) I have be-dimm'd
The noon-tide sun, call'd forth the mutinous winds,
And 'twixt the green sea and the azur'd vault
Set roaring war: to the dread rattling thunder
Have I given fire, and rifted Jove's stout oak
With his own bolt: the strong-bas'd promontory
Have I made shake; and by the spurs pluck'd up
The pine, and cedar: graves, at my command,
Have wak'd their sleepers; op'd and let them forth,
By my so potent art: But this rough magic
I here abjure: and, when I have requir'd
Some heavenly music, (which even now I do,)
To work mine end upon their senses, that
This airy charm is for, I'll break my staff,
Bury it certain fathoms in the earth,
And, deeper than did ever plummet sound,
I'll drown my book. [*Solemn music.*

Re-enter Ariel: *after him,* Alonso, *with a frantic gesture, attended by* Gonzalo; Sebastian *and* Antonio *in like manner, attended by* Adrian *and* Francisco: *They all enter the circle which* Prospero *had made, and there stand charmed; which* Prospero *observing, speaks.*

A solemn air, and the best comforter
To an unsettled fancy, cure thy brains,
Now useless, boil'd within thy skull[3]! There stand,
For you are spell-stopp'd.———
Holy Gonzalo, honourable man,
Mine eyes, even sociable to the shew of thine,
Fall fellowly drops.—The charm dissolves apace;
And as the morning steals upon the night,
Melting the darkness, so their rising senses
Begin to chase the ignorant fumes that mantle
Their clearer reason.—O my good Gonzalo,
My true preserver, and a loyal sir
To him thou follow'st; I will pay thy graces
Home, both in word and deed.—Most cruelly
Didst thou, Alonso, use me and my daughter:
Thy brother was a furtherer in the act;—
Thou'rt pinch'd for't now, Sebastian.—Flesh and blood,
You brother mine, that entertain'd ambition,
Expell'd remorse[4] and nature; who with Sebastian
(Whose inward pinches therefore are most strong,)
Would here have kill'd your king; I do forgive thee,
Unnatural though thou art!—Their understanding
Begins to swell; and the approaching tide
Will shortly fill the reasonable shores,
That now lie foul and muddy. Not one of them,
That yet looks on me, or would know me:—Ariel,
Fetch me the hat and rapier in my cell;
[*Exit* Ariel.
I will dis-case me, and myself present,
As I was sometime Milan:—quickly, spirit;
Thou shalt ere long be free.

Ariel *re-enters, singing, and helps to attire* Prospero.

Ari. *Where the bee sucks, there suck I;*
In a cowslip's bell I lie:
There I couch when owls do cry.
On the bat's back I do fly,
After summer, merrily:
Merrily, merrily, shall I live now,
Under the blossom that hangs on the bough[5].

Pro. Why, that's my dainty Ariel; I shall miss thee;
But yet thou shalt have freedom: so, so, so—
To the king's ship, invisible as thou art:
There shalt thou find the mariners asleep
Under the hatches; the master, and the boatswain,
Being awake, enforce them to this place;
And presently, I pr'ythee.

Ari. I drink the air before me and return
Or e'er your pulse twice beat. [*Exit* Ariel

Gon. All torment, trouble, wonder, and amazement
Inhabits here: Some heavenly power guide us
Out of this fearful country!

Pro. Behold, sir king,
The wronged duke of Milan, Prospero:
For more assurance that a living prince
Does now speak to thee, I embrace thy body,
And to thee and thy company, I bid
A hearty welcome.

Alon. Whe'r[6] thou beest he, or no
Or some enchanted trifle to abuse me,
As late I have been, I not know: thy pulse
Beats, as of flesh and blood; and, since I saw thee,
The affliction of my mind amends, with which,
I fear, a madness held me: this must crave
(An if this be at all) a most strange story.
Thy dukedom I resign; and do entreat
Thou pardon me my wrongs:—But how should Prospero
Be living, and be here?

Pro. First, noble friend,
Let me embrace thine age; whose honour cannot
Be measur'd, or confin'd.

Gon. Whether this be,
Or be not, I'll not swear.

Pro. You do yet taste
Some subtilties[7] o' the isle, that will not let you
Believe things certain:—Welcome, my friends all:
But you, my brace of lords, were I so minded,
[*Aside to* Seb. *and* Ant
I here could pluck his highness' frown upon you,
And justify you traitors: at this time
I'll tell no tales.

Seb. The devil speaks in him. [*Aside*

Pro. No:—
For you, most wicked sir, whom to call brother
Would even infect my mouth, I do forgive
Thy rankest fault; all of them; and require
My dukedom of thee, which, perforce, I know
Thou must restore.

Alon. If thou beest Prospero,
Give us particulars of thy preservation:
How thou hast met us here, who three hours since

1 This speech is in some measure borrowed from Medea's, in Ovid; the expressions are, many of them in the old translation by Golding. But the exquisite fairy imagery is Shakspeare's own.

2 That is; ye are powerful auxiliaries, but *weak* if left to yourselves Your employments are of the trivial nature before mentioned.

3 So in Mids. Night's Dream—
"Lovers and madmen have such *seething* brains."

4 *Remorse* is *pity, tenderness of heart; nature* is *natural affection.*

5 This was the received opinion so in Fairfax's Tasso, B iv St. 18.—
"The goblins, fairies, fiends, and furies mad,
Ranged in flowrie dales, and mountaines hore,
And under every trembling leaf they sit."

6 Whether.

7 *Subtilties* are quaint deceptive inventions; the word is common to ancient cookery, in which a disguised or ornamented dish is so termed.

8 The unity of time is most rigidly observed in this piece. The fable scarcely takes up a greater number of hours than are employed in the representation. Mr Steevens thinks that Shakspeare purposely designed to show the cavillers of the time, that he too could write a play within all the strictest laws of regularity

Were wreck'd upon this shore; where I have lost
(How sharp the point of this remembrance is!)
My dear son Ferdinand.
Pro. I am woe[1] for't, sir.
Alo. Irreparable is the loss; and Patience
Says, it is past her cure.
Pro. I rather think,
You have not sought her help; of whose soft grace,
For the like loss, I have her sovereign aid,
And rest myself content.
Alon. You the like loss?
Pro. As great to me, as late; and portable[2]
To make the dear loss, have I means much weaker
Than you may call to comfort you; for I
Have lost my daughter.
Alon. A daughter?
O heavens! that they were living both in Naples,
The king and queen there! that they were, I wish
Myself were mudded in that oozy bed
Where my son lies. When did you lose your daughter?
Pro. In this last tempest. I perceive, these lords
At this encounter do so much admire,
That they devour their reason; and scarce think
Their eyes do offices of truth, their words
Are natural breath: but, howsoe'er you have
Been justled from your senses, know for certain,
That I am Prospero, and that very duke
Which was thrust forth of Milan; who most strangely
Upon this shore, where you were wreck'd, was landed,
To be the lord on't. No more yet of this;
For 'tis a chronicle of day by day,
Not a relation for a breakfast, nor
Befitting this first meeting. Welcome, sir;
This cell's my court: here have I few attendants,
And subjects none abroad: pray you, look in.
My dukedom, since you have given me again,
I will requite you with as good a thing;
At least, bring forth a wonder, to content ye,
As much as me my dukedom.

The entrance of the Cell opens, and discovers FERDINAND *and* MIRANDA *playing at chess.*

Mira. Sweet lord, you play me false.
Fer. No, my dearest love,
I would not for the world.
Mira. Yes, for a score of kingdoms you should wrangle,[3]
And I would call it fair play.
Alon. If this prove
A vision of the island, one dear son
Shall I twice lose.
Seb. A most high miracle!
Fer. Though the seas threaten, they are merciful:
I have curs'd them without cause.
[FER. *kneels to* ALON.
Alon. Now all the blessings
Of a glad father compass thee about!
Arise, and say how thou cam'st here.
Mira. O! wonder!
How many goodly creatures are there here!
How beauteous mankind is! O brave new world,
That has such people in't!
Pro. 'Tis new to thee.
Alon. What is this maid, with whom thou wast at play?
Your eld'st acquaintance cannot be three hours:
Is she the goddess that hath sever'd us,
And brought us thus together?
Fer. Sir, she's mortal;
But, by immortal Providence, she's mine;
I chose her, when I could not ask my father
For his advice; nor thought I had one: she
Is daughter to this famous duke of Milan,
Of whom so often I have heard renown,
But never saw before; of whom I have
Received a second life, and second father
This lady makes him to me.
Alon. I am her's:
But O, how oddly will it sound, that I
Must ask my child forgiveness!
Pro. There, sir, stop:
Let us not burden our remembrances
With heaviness that's gone.
Gon. I have inly wept,
Or should have spoke ere this. Look down, you gods,
And on this couple drop a blessed crown;
For it is you, that have chalk'd forth the way
Which brought us hither!
Alon. I say, Amen, Gonzalo
Gon. Was Milan thrust from Milan, that his issue
Should become kings of Naples? O, rejoice
Beyond a common joy: and set it down
With gold on lasting pillars: In one voyage
Did Claribel her husband find at Tunis;
And Ferdinand, her brother, found a wife
Where he himself was lost; Prospero his dukedom,
In a poor isle; and all of us, ourselves,
When no man was his own.[4]
Alon. Give me your hands:
[*To* FER. *and* MIRA.
Let grief and sorrow still embrace his heart,
That doth not wish you joy!
Gon. Be't so! Amen!

Re-enter ARIEL, *with the* Master *and* Boatswain *amazedly following.*

O look, sir, look, sir; here are more of us!
I prophesied, if a gallows were on land,
This fellow could not drown:—Now, blasphemy,
That swear'st grace o'erboard, not an oath on shore?
Hast thou no mouth by land? What is the news?
Boats. The best news is, that we have safely found
Our king, and company: the next our ship,
Which, but three glasses since, we gave out split,—
Is tight and yare,[5] and bravely rigg'd, as when
We first put out to sea.
Ari. Sir, all this service
Have I done since I went. } [*Aside.*
Pro. My tricksy[6] spirit! }
Alon. These are not natural events; they strengthen,
From strange to stranger:—Say, how came you hither?
Boats. If I did think, sir, I were well awake,
I'd strive to tell you. We were dead of sleep,
And (how, we know not,) all clapp'd under hatches,
Where, but even now, with strange and several noises
Of roaring, shrieking, howling, gingling chains,
And more diversity of sounds, all horrible,
We were awak'd; straightway at liberty:
Where we, in all her trim, freshly beheld
Our royal, good, and gallant ship; our master
Cap'ring to eye her: On a trice, so please you,
Even in a dream, were we divided from them,
And were brought moping hither.

---

1 I am *sorry* for it. 2 *Bearable.*

3 Mr. Pye says, I conceive Shakspeare, who was no nice weigher of words, meant wrangling to be equivalent with playing false, or with unfair advantage. So in Henry V. the king, in allusion to the tennis balls, directs the ambassadors to tell the dauphin—

"He hath made a match with such a *wrangler*,
That all the courts of France shall be disturb'd
With chases."

Mr. Pye's explanation is correct; but his deduction that Shakspeare was "*no nice weigher of words*" is totally false. Shakspeare's words are always the most expressive and most appropriate. To *wrangle*, in the language of his time, was to *haft* or *overthwart*; to run back and yet not cease to contend.

4 When no man was *in his senses* or had *self-possession.*

5 See Note 2. Sc. 1.

6 *Neat, adroit.* Florio interprets "Pargoletta, quaint, pretty, nimble, *trixie*, tender, small." When we remember the tiny dimensions of Ariel, who could lie in the bell of a cowslip, the epithet, like all those of the great poet, will be found peculiarly appropriate

Ari. Was t well done? } [*Aside.*
Pro. Bravely, my diligence. Thou shalt be free. }
Alon. This is as strange a maze as e'er men trod:
And there is in this business more than nature
Was ever conduct[1] of: some oracle
Must rectify our knowledge.
Pro. Sir, my liege,
Do not infest your mind with beating on[2]
The strangeness of this business: at pick'd leisure,
Which shall be shortly, single I'll resolve you
(Which to you shall seem probable[3]) of every
These happen'd accidents: till when, be cheerful,
And think of each thing well.—Come hither, spirit; [*Aside.*
Set Caliban and his companions free:
Untie the spell. [*Exit* ARIEL.] How fares my gracious sir?
There are yet missing of your company
Some few odd lads, that you remember not.

Re-enter ARIEL, *driving in* CALIBAN, STEPHANO, *and* TRINCULO, *in their stolen apparel.*

Ste. Every man shift for all the rest, and let no man take care for himself; for all is but fortune:—Coragio, bully-monster, Coragio!

Trin. If these be true spies which I wear in my head, here's a goodly sight.

Cal. O Setebos, these be brave spirits, indeed!
How fine my master is! I am afraid
He will chastise me.
Seb. Ha, ha;
What things are these, my lord Antonio!
Will money buy them?
Ant. Very like; one of them
Is a plain fish, and, no doubt, marketable.
Pro. Mark but the badges of these men, my lords,
Then say, if they be true:[4]—This mis-shapen knave,
His mother was a witch; and one so strong
That could control the moon, make flows and ebbs,
And deal in her command, without her power:[5]
These three have robb'd me; and this demi-devil
(For he's a bastard one) had plotted with them
To take my life: two of these fellows you
Must know, and own; this thing of darkness I
Acknowledge mine.
Cal. I shall be pinch'd to death.
Alon. Is not this Stephano, my drunken butler?
Seb. He is drunk now: Where had he wine?
Alon. And Trinculo is reeling ripe: Where should they
Find this grand liquor that hath gilded them?[6]—
How cam'st thou in this pickle?

Trin. I have been in such a pickle, since I saw you last, that, I fear me, will never out of my bones: I shall not fear fly-blowing.

Seb. Why, how now, Stephano?
Ste. O, touch me not; I am not Stephano, but a cramp.
Pro. You'd be king of the isle, sirrah?
Ste. I should have been a sore one then.
Alon. This is as strange a thing as e'er I look'd on. [*Pointing to* CALIBAN.
Pro. He is as disproportion'd in his manners,
As in his shape:—Go, sirrah, to my cell;
Take with you your companions; as you look
To have my pardon, trim it handsomely.
Cal. Ay, that I will; and I'll be wise hereafter,
And seek for grace: What a thrice double ass
Was I, to take this drunkard for a god,
And worship this dull fool!
Pro. Go to; away!
Alon. Hence, and bestow your luggage where you found it.
Seb. Or stole it, rather.
[*Exeunt* CAL. STE. *and* TRIN.
Pro. Sir, I invite your highness, and your train
To my poor cell: where you shall take your rest
For this one night; which (part of it) I'll waste
With such discourse, as, I not doubt, shall make it
Go quick away: the story of my life,
And the particular accidents, gone by,
Since I came to this isle: And in the morn,
I'll bring you to your ship, and so to Naples,
Where I have hope to see the nuptial
Of these our dear-belov'd solemnized;
And thence retire me to my Milan, where
Every third thought shall be my grave.
Alon. I long
To hear the story of your life, which must
Take the ear strangely.
Pro. I'll deliver all;
And promise you calm seas, auspicious gales,
And sail so expeditious, that shall catch
Your royal fleet far off.—My Ariel,—chick,—
That is thy charge; then to the elements
Be free, and fare thou well!—[*Aside.*] Please you, draw near. [*Exeunt.*

EPILOGUE.

SPOKEN BY PROSPERO.

Now my charms are all o'erthrown,
And what strength I have's mine own,
Which is most faint: now, 'tis true,
I must be here confin'd by you,
Or sent to Naples: Let me not,
Since I have my dukedom got,
And pardon'd the deceiver, dwell
In this bare island, by your spell;
But release me from my bands,
With the help of your good hands,[7]
Gentle breath of yours my sails
Must fill, or else my project fails,
Which was to please: Now I want
Spirits to enforce, art to enchant;
And my ending is despair,
Unless I be reliev'd by prayer;
Which pierces so, that it assaults
Mercy itself, and frees all faults.
As you from crimes would pardon'd be,
Let your indulgence set me free.

[It is observed of *The Tempest*, that its plan is regular; this the author of *The Revisal* thinks, what I think too, an accidental effect of the story, not intended or regarded by our author. But whatever might be Shakspeare's intention in forming or adopting the plot, he has made it instrumental to the production of many characters, diversified with boundless invention, and preserved with profound skill in nature, extensive knowledge of opinions, and accurate observation of life. In a single drama are here exhibited princes, courtiers, and sailors, all speaking in their real characters. There is the agency of airy spirits, and of an earthly goblin. The operations of magic, the tumults of a storm, the adventures of a desert island, the native effusion of untaught affection, the punishment of guilt, and the final happiness of the pair for whom our passions and reason are equally interested.] JOHNSON.

1 *Conductor.*
2 There is a vulgar expression still in use, of similar import, "Still *hammering* at it."
3 This parenthetical passage seems to mean:—"When I have explained to you, then these strange events shall seem more probable than they do now."
4 *Honest.*
5 That is, work the same effects as the moon without her delegated authority.
6 The allusion is to the *elixir* of the Alchemists. The phrase of being *gilded* was a trite one for being *drunk*. Fletcher uses it in the Chances:—
Duke. Is she not drunk too?
Wh. A little *gilded* o'er, sir; old sack, old boys.
7 By your *applause*. *Noise* was supposed to dissolve a spell. Thus before in this play:—
"—— Hush! be mute;
Or else our *spell is marr'd*."

TWO GENTLEMEN OF VERONA

PRELIMINARY REMARKS.

THIS is one of Shakspeare's earliest if not his first play. It was not printed until 1623, but it is mentioned by Meres in his Wit's Treasury, printed in 1598. It bears strong internal marks of an early composition. Pope has observed, that "the style of this comedy is less figurative, and more natural and unaffected than the greater part of Shakspeare's, though supposed to be one of the first he wrote." Malone is inclined to consider this to be in consequence of that very circumstance, and that it is natural and unaffected because it was a youthful performance. "Though many young poets of ordinary talents are led by false taste to adopt inflated and figurative language, why should we suppose that such should have been the course pursued by this master genius? The figurative style of Othello, Lear, and Macbeth, written when he was an established and long practised dramatist, may be ascribed to the additional knowledge of men and things which he had acquired during a period of fifteen years; in consequence of which his mind teemed with images and illustrations, and thoughts crowded so fast upon him, that the construction, in these and some other plays of a still later period, is much more difficult and involved than in the productions of his youth."

Hanmer thought Shakspeare had no other hand in this play than the enlivening it with some speeches and lines, which, he thinks, are easily distinguished from the rest. Upton peremptorily asserts, "that if any proof can be drawn from manner and style, this play must be sent packing, and seek for its parent elsewhere." "How otherwise," says he, "do painters distinguish copies from originals, and have not authors their peculiar style and manner, from which a true critic can form as unerring judgment as a painter?" To this Johnson replies very satisfactorily: "I am afraid this illustration of a critic's science will not prove what is desired. A painter knows a copy from an original by rules somewhat resembling those by which critics know a translation, which, if it be literal, and literal it must be to resemble the copy of a picture, will be easily distinguished. Copies are known from originals, even when a painter copies his own picture; so if an author should literally translate his work, he would lose the manner of an original. Upton confounds the copy of a picture with the imitation of a painter's manner. Copies are easily known; but good imitations are not detected with equal certainty, and are, by the best judges, often mistaken. Nor is it true that the writer has always peculiarities equally distinguishable with those of the painter. The peculiar manner of each arises from the desire, natural to every performer, of facilitating his subsequent work by recurrence to his former ideas; this recurrence produces that repetition which is called habit. The painter, whose work is partly intellectual and partly manual, has habits of the mind, the eye, and the hand; the writer has only habits of the mind. Yet some painters have differed as much from themselves as from any other; and I have been told, that there is little resemblance between the first works of Raphael and the last. The same variation may be expected in writers; and, if it be true, as it seems, that they are less subject to habit, the difference between their works may be yet greater."

"But by the internal marks of composition we may discover the author with probability, though seldom with certainty. When I read this play, I cannot but think that I find both in the serious and ludicrous scenes, the language and sentiments of Shakspeare. It is not indeed one of his most powerful effusions; it has neither many diversities of character, nor striking delineation of life, but it abounds in γνομαι beyond most of his plays, and few have more lines or passages which, singly considered, are eminently beautiful. I am yet inclined to believe that it was not very successful, and suspect that it has escaped corruption, only because, being seldom played, it was less exposed to the hazards of transcription."

Pope has set what he calls a mark of reprobation upon the low and trifling conceits which are to be found in this play. It is true that the familiar scenes abound with quibbles and conceits; but the poet must not be condemned for adopting a mode of writing admired by his contemporaries; they were not considered low and trifling in Shakspeare's age, but on the contrary were very generally admired and allowed for pure and genuine wit. Yet some of these scenes have much farcical drollery and invention: that of Launce with his dog in the fourth act is an instance, and surely "Speed's mode of proving his master to be in love is neither deficient in wit or sense."

"The tender scenes in this play, though not so highly wrought as in some others, have often much sweetness of sentiment and expression." Schlegel says: "it is as if the world was obliged to accommodate itself to a transient youthful caprice, called love." Julia may be considered a light sketch of the lovely characters of Viola and Imogen. Her answer to Lucetta's advice against following her lover in disguise has been pointed out as a beautiful and highly poetical passage.

"That it should ever have been a question whether this comedy were the genuine and entire composition of Shakspeare appears to me very extraordinary," says Malone. "Hanmer and Upton never seem to have considered whether it were his first or one of his latest pieces:—is no allowance to be made for the first flights of a young poet? nothing for the imitation of a preceding celebrated dramatist,* which in some of the lower dialogues of this comedy (and these only) may, I think, be traced? But even these, as well as the other parts of the play, are perfectly Shakspearian (I do not say as finished and beautiful as any of his other pieces); and the same judgment must, I conceive, be pronounced concerning the Comedy of Errors and Love's Labour's Lost, by every person who is intimately acquainted with his manner of writing and thinking."

Sir William Blackstone observes, "that one of the great faults of the Two Gentlemen of Verona is the hastening too abruptly, and without preparation, to the *denouement*, which shows that it was one of Shakspeare's very early performances." Dr. Johnson in his concluding observations has remarked upon the geographical errors. They cannot be defended by attributing them to his youthful inexperience, for one of his later productions is also liable to the same objection. To which Malone replies: "The truth, I believe, is, that as he neglected to observe the rules of the drama with respect to the unities, though before he began to write they had been enforced by Sidney in a treatise which doubtless he had read; so he seems to have thought that the whole terraqueous globe was at his command; and as he brought in a child at the beginning of a play, who in the fourth act appears as a woman, so he seems to have set geography at defiance, and to have considered countries as inland or maritime just as it suited his fancy or convenience"

Some of the incidents in this play may be supposed to have been taken from The Arcadia, book I. ch. vi. where Pyrocles consents to head the Helots. The Arcadia was entered on the Stationers' books in 1588. The love adventure of Julia resembles that of Viola in Twelfth Night, and is indeed common to many of the ancient novels.

Mrs. Lennox informs us, that the story of Proteus and Julia might be taken from a similar one in "The Diana" of Montemayor. This pastoral romance was translated from the Spanish in Shakspeare's time, by Bartholomew Young, and published in 1598. It does not appear that it was previously published, though it was translated two or three years before by one Thomas Wilson, perhaps some parts of it may have been made public, or Shakspeare may have found the tale elsewhere. It has before been observed that Meres mentions the Two Gentlemen of Verona in his book, published in 1598. Malone conjectures that this play was the first that Shakspeare wrote, and places the date of its composition in the year 1591.

* Malone points at Lilly, whose comedies were performed with great success and admiration previous to Shakspeare's commencement of his dramatic career

TWO GENTLEMEN OF VERONA.

PERSONS REPRESENTED.

DUKE of MILAN, *Father to* Silvia.
VALENTINE, } *Gentlemen of Verona.*
PROTEUS, }
ANTONIO, *Father to* Pr.teus.
THURIO, *a foolish Rival to* Valentine.
EGLAMOUR, *Agent for* Silvia *in her escape.*
SPEED, *a clownish Servant to* Valentine.
LAUNCE, *Servant to* Proteus.
PANTHINO, *Servant to* Antonia.
Host, *where Julia lodges in Milan.*
Outlaws.

JULIA, *a Lady of Verona, beloved by* Proteus.
SILVIA, *the Duke's Daughter, beloved by* Valentine.
LUCETTA, *Waiting-woman to* Julia.

Servants, Musicians.

SCENE, *sometimes in* VERONA; *sometimes in* MILAN; *and on the frontiers of* MANTUA.

ACT I.

SCENE I.—*An open place in Verona. Enter* VALENTINE *and* PROTEUS.

Valentine.

CEASE to persuade, my loving Proteus;
Home-keeping youth have ever homely wits:[1]
Wer't not, affection chains thy tender days
To the sweet glances of thy honour'd love,
I rather would entreat thy company,
To see the wonders of the world abroad,
Than living dully sluggardiz'd at home,
Wear out thy youth with shapeless idleness.[2]
But, since thou lov'st, love still, and thrive therein,
Even as I would, when I to love begin.

Pro. Wilt thou begone? Sweet Valentine, adieu!
Think on thy Proteus, when thou, haply, seest
Some rare note-worthy object in thy travel:
Wish me partaker in thy happiness,
When thou dost meet good hap; and, in thy danger,
If ever danger do environ thee,
Commend thy grievance to my holy prayers,
For I will be thy bead's-man, Valentine.

Val. And on a love-book pray for my success.

Pro. Upon some book I love, I'll pray for thee.

Val. That's on some shallow story of deep love,
How young Leander cross'd the Hellespont.[3]

Pro. That's a deep story of a deeper love;
For he was more than over shoes in love.

Val. 'Tis true; for you are over boots in love,
And yet you never swam the Hellespont.

Pro. Over the boots? nay, give me not the boots.[4]

Val. No, I will not, for it boots thee not.

Pro. What?

Val. To be in love, where scorn is bought with groans;
Coy looks, with heart-sore sighs; one fading moment's mirth,
With twenty watchful, weary, tedious nights:
If haply won, perhaps a hapless gain;
If lost, why then a grievous labour won;
However, but a folly bought with wit,
Or else a wit by folly vanquished.

Pro. So by your circumstance, you call me fool.

Val. So, by your circumstance,[5] I fear, you'll prove.

Pro. 'Tis love you cavil at; I am not Love.

Val. Love is your master, for he masters you:
And he that is so yoked by a fool,
Methinks should not be chronicled for wise.

Pro. Yet writers say, As in the sweetest bud
The eating canker dwells, so eating love
Inhabits in the finest wits of all.

Val. And writers say, As the most forward bud
Is eaten by the canker ere it blow,
Even so by love the young and tender wit
Is turn'd to folly; blasting in the bud,
Losing his verdure even in the prime,
And all the fair effects of future hopes.
But wherefore waste I time to council thee,
That art a votary to fond desire?
Once more adieu: my father at the road
Expects my coming, there to see me shipp'd.

Pro. And thither will I bring thee, Valentine.

Val. Sweet Proteus, no; now let us take our leave.
To[6] Milan, let me hear from thee by letters,
Of thy success in love, and what news else
Betideth here in absence of thy friend;
And I likewise will visit thee with mine.

Pro. All happiness bechance to thee in Milan!

Val. As much to you at home! and so, farewell!
[*Exit* VALENTINE.

Pro. He after honour hunts, I after love.
He leaves his friends, to dignify them more;
I leave myself, my friends, and all for love.
Thou, Julia, thou hast metamorphos'd me;
Made me neglect my studies, lose my time,
War with good counsel, set the world at nought;
Made wit with musing weak, heart sick with thought.

Enter SPEED.

Speed. Sir Proteus, save you: Saw you my master?

Pro. But now he parted hence, to embark for Milan.

Speed. Twenty to one then he is shipp'd already;
And I have played the sheep,[7] in losing him.

Pro. Indeed a sheep doth very often stray,
An if the shepherd be awhile away.

Speed. You conclude that my master is a shepherd then, and I a sheep?

Pro. I do.

Speed. Why then, my horns are his horns, whether I wake or sleep.

Pro. A silly answer, and fitting well a sheep.

Speed. This proves me still a sheep.

Pro. True; and thy master a shepherd.

Speed. Nay, that I can deny by a circumstance.

---

1 Milton has the same play upon words in his Comus.
"It is for homely features to keep home,
They had their name thence."

2 The expression *shapeless idleness* is admirably expressive, as implying that idleness prevents the giving form or character to the manners.

3 The allusion is to Marlow's poem of Hero and Leander, which was entered on the Stationers' books in 1593, though not published till 1598. It was probably circulated in manuscript in the interim, as was the custom at that period. The poem seems to have made an impression on Shakspeare, who appears to have recently perused it, for he again alludes to it in the third act. And in As You Like It he has quoted a line from it.

4 A proverbial expression, now disused, signifying, 'Don't make a laughing-stock of me.' The French have a phrase *Bailler foin en corne:* which Cotgrave interprets, 'to give one the boots; to sell him a bargain.' Perhaps deduced from a humorous punishment at harvest home feasts in Warwickshire.

5 *Circumstance* is used equivocally. It here means *conduct;* in the preceding line, circumstantial deduction.

6 The construction of this passage, is, "Let me hear from thee by letters to Milan," i. e. addressed to Milan.

7 In Warwickshire, and some other counties, a *sheep* is pronounced a *ship.* Without this explanation the jest, such as it is, might escape the reader

Pro. It shall go hard, but I'll prove it by another.

Speed. The shepherd seeks the sheep, and not the sheep the shepherd; but I seek my master, and my master seeks not me: therefore I am no sheep.

Pro. The sheep for fodder follow the shepherd, the shepherd for food follows not the sheep; thou for wages followest thy master, thy master for wages follows not thee: therefore thou art a sheep.

Speed. Such another proof will make me cry baa.

Pro. But dost thou hear! gav'st thou my letter to Julia?

Speed. Ay, sir; I, a lost mutton, gave your letter to her, a laced mutton;[1] and she, a laced mutton, gave me, a lost mutton, nothing for my labour.

Pro. Here's too small a pasture for such a store of muttons.

Speed. If the ground be overcharged, you were best stick her.

Pro. Nay, in that you are astray; 'twere best pound you.

Speed. Nay, sir, less than a pound shall serve me for carrying your letter.

Pro. You mistake; I mean the pound, a pinfold.

Speed. From a pound to a pin? fold it over and over,
'Tis threefold too little for carrying a letter to your lover.

Pro. But what said she? did she nod?[2]

[SPEED *nods.*

Speed. I.

Pro. Nod, I! why, that's noddy.

Speed. You mistook, sir? I say she did nod: and you ask me, if she did nod; and I say, I.

Pro. And that set together is—noddy.

Speed. Now you have taken the pains to set it together, take it for your pains.

Pro. No, no, you shall have it for bearing the letter.

Speed. Well, I perceive I must be fain to bear with you.

Pro. Why, sir, how do you bear with me?

Speed. Marry, sir, the letter very orderly; having nothing but the word, noddy, for my pains.

Pro. Beshrew me, but you have a quick wit.

Speed. And yet it cannot overtake your slow purse.

Pro. Come, come, open the matter in brief: What said she?

Speed. Open your purse, that the money and the matter may be both at once delivered.

Pro. Well, sir, here is for your pains: What said she?

Speed. Truly, sir, I think you'll hardly win her.

Pro. Why? Could'st thou perceive so much from her?

Speed. Sir, I could perceive nothing at all from her; no, not so much as a ducat for delivering your letter: And being so hard to me that brought your mind, I fear she'll prove as hard to you in telling your mind. Give her no token but stones, for she's as hard as steel.

Pro. What, said she nothing?

Speed. No, not so much as—*take this for thy pains.* To testify your bounty, I thank you, you have testern'd[3] me; in requital whereof, henceforth carry your letters yourself: and so, sir, I'll commend you to my master.

Pro. Go, go, begone, to save your ship from wreck;
Which cannot perish, having thee aboard,
Being destined to a drier death on shore:—
I must go send some better messenger;
I fear my Julia would not deign my lines,
Receiving them from such a worthless post.

[*Exeunt.*

SCENE II. *The same. Garden of* Julia's *house.*
Enter JULIA *and* LUCETTA.

Jul. But say, Lucetta, now we are alone,
Would'st thou then counsel me to fall in love?

Luc. Ay, madam; so you stumble not unheedfully.

Jul. Of all the fair resort of gentlemen,
That every day with parle[4] encounter me,
In thy opinion, which is worthiest love?

Luc. Please you, repeat their names, I'll show my mind
According to my shallow simple skill.

Jul. What think'st thou of the fair Sir Eglamour?

Luc. As of a knight well-spoken, neat and fine;
But, were I you, he never should be mine.

Jul. What think'st thou of the rich Mercatio?

Luc. Well of his wealth; but of himself, so, so.

Jul. What think'st thou of the gentle Proteus?

Luc. Lord, lord! to see what folly reigns in us!

Jul. How now! what means this passion at his name?

Luc. Pardon, dear madam; 'tis a passing shame,
That I, unworthy body as I am,
Should censure[5] thus on lovely gentlemen.

Jul. Why not on Proteus, as of all the rest?

Luc. Then thus,——of many good I think him best.

Jul. Your reason?

Luc. I have no other but a woman's reason,
I think him so, because I think him so.

Jul. And would'st thou have me cast my love on him?

Luc. Ay, if you thought your love not cast away

Jul. Why, he of all the rest hath never mov'd me.

Luc. Yet he of all the rest, I think, best loves ye.

Jul. His little speaking shows his love but small.

Luc. Fire,[6] that's closest kept, burns most of all.

Jul. They do not love that do not show their love.

Luc. O, they love least, that let men know their love.

Jul. I would, I knew his mind.

Luc. Peruse this paper, madam.

Jul. *To Julia.*—Say, from whom?

Luc. That the contents will show.

Jul. Say, say; who gave it thee?

Luc. Sir Valentine's page; and sent, I think, from Proteus:
He would have given it you, but I, being in the way,
Did in your name receive it; pardon the fault, I pray.

Jul. Now, by my modesty, a goodly broker![7]
Dare you presume to harbour wanton lines?
To whisper and conspire against my youth?
Now, trust me, 'tis an office of great worth,
And you an officer fit for the place.
There, take the paper, see it be return'd;
Or else return no more into my sight.

Luc. To plead for love deserves more fee than hate.

---

1 Cotgrave explains *laced mutton*, une garce, putain, fille de joye. It was so established a term for a cortezan, that a lane in Clerkenwell, much frequented by loose women, is said to have been thence called Mutton Lane.

2 These words were supplied by Theobald to introduce what follows. In Speed's answer, the old spelling of the affirmative particle has been retained; otherwise the conceit would be unintelligible. *Noddy* was a game at cards.

3 *Testens*, or (as we now commonly call them, *testers*,) from a head that was upon them, were coined in 1542. Sir H. Spelman says they were a French coin of the value of 18d.; and he does not know but that they might have gone for as much in England. They were afterwards reduced to 12d 9d and finally, to *six pence.*

4 *Parle* is *talk.*

5 To *censure*, in Shakspeare's time, generally signified to give one's judgment or opinion. Thus in The Winter's Tale, Act. ii. Sc 1

"———How blest am I
In my just *censure?* in my true opinion?"

6 *Fire* is here pronounced as a dissyllable.

7 A matchmaker. It was sometimes used for a procuress.

Ju. Will you' be gone?

Luc. That you may ruminate. [*Exit.*

Jul. And yet, I would I had o'erlook'd the letter.
It were a shame to call her back again,
And pray her to a fault for which I chid her.
What fool is she, that knows I am a maid,
And would not force the letter to my view!
Since maids, in modesty, say *No*, to that
Which they would have the profferer construe, *Ay*.
Fie, fie, how wayward is this foolish love,
That, like a testy babe, will scratch the nurse,
And presently, all humbled, kiss the rod!
How churlishly I chid Lucetta hence,
When willingly I would have had her here!
How angerly I taught my brow to frown,
When inward joy enforc'd my heart to smile!
My penance is, to call Lucetta back,
And ask permission for my folly past:—
What ho! Lucetta!

Re-enter LUCETTA.

Luc. What would your ladyship?

Jul. Is it near dinner time?

Luc. I would it were:
That you might kill your stomach[2] on your meat,
And not upon your maid.

Jul. What is't you took up
So gingerly?

Luc. Nothing.

Jul. Why didst thou stoop then?

Luc. To take a paper up that I let fall.

Jul. And is that paper nothing?

Luc. Nothing concerning me.

Jul. Then let it lie for those that it concerns.

Luc. Madam, it will not lie where it concerns,
Unless it have a false interpreter.

Jul. Some love of your's hath writ to you in rhyme.

Luc. That I might sing it, madam, to a tune:
Give me a note: your ladyship can set.[3]

Jul. As little by such toys as may be possible:
Best sing it to the tune of *Light o' love.*

Luc. It is too heavy for so light a tune.

Jul. Heavy? belike it hath some burden then.

Luc. Ay; and melodious were it, would you sing it.

Jul. And why not you?

Luc. I cannot reach so high.

Jul. Let's see your song:—How now, minion?

Luc. Keep tune there still, so you will sing it out:
And yet, methinks, I do not like this tune.

Jul. You do not?

Luc. No, madam; it is too sharp.

Jul. You, minion, are too saucy.

Luc. Nay, now you are too flat,
And mar the concord with too harsh a descant:[4]
There wanteth but a mean to fill your song.

Jul. The mean is drown'd with your unruly base.

Luc. Indeed, I bid the base[5] for Proteus.

Jul. This babble shall not henceforth trouble me.
Here is a coil[6] with protestation!

[*Tears the letter.*

Go, get you gone; and let the papers lie:
You would be fingering them, to anger me.

Luc. She makes it strange; but she would be best pleas'd
To be so anger'd with another letter. [*Exit.*

Jul. Nay, would I were as anger'd with the same!
O hateful hands, to tear such loving words!
Injurious wasps! to feed on such sweet honey,
And kill the bees, that yield it, with your stings!
I'll kiss each several paper for amends.
And here is writ—*kind Julia*;—unkind Julia!
As in revenge of thy ingratitude,
I throw thy name against the bruising stones,
Trampling contemptuously on thy disdain.
Look, here is writ—*love-wounded Proteus*;—
Poor wounded name! my bosom, as a bed,
Shall lodge thee, till thy wound be thoroughly heal'd;
And thus I search it with a sovereign kiss.
But twice, or thrice, was Proteus written down:
Be calm, good wind, blow not a word away,
Till I have found each letter in the letter,
Except mine own name; that some whirlwind bear
Unto a rugged, fearful, hanging rock,
And throw it thence into the raging sea!
Lo, here in one line is his name twice writ,—
Poor forlorn Porteus, passionate Proteus,
To the sweet Julia;—that I'll tear away;
And yet I will not, sith[7] so prettily
He couples it to his complaining names:
Thus will I fold them one upon another;
Now kiss, embrace, contend, do what you will.

Re-enter LUCETTA.

Luc. Madam,
Dinner is ready, and your father stays.

Jul. Well, let us go.

Luc. What, shall these papers lie like tell-tales here?

Jul. If you respect them, best to take them up.

Luc. Nay, I was taken up for laying them down:
Yet here they shall not lie, for[8] catching cold.

Jul. I see you have a month's mind[9] to them.

Luc. Ay, madam, you may say what sights you see;
I see things too, although you judge I wink.

Jul. Come, come, will't please you go? [*Exeunt.*

SCENE III.—*The same. A Room in* Antonio' *House. Enter* ANTONIO *and* PANTHINC.

Ant. Tell me, Panthino, what sad[10] talk was that,
Wherewith my brother held you in the cloister?

Pant. 'Twas of his nephew Proteus, your son.

Ant. Why, what of him?

Pant. He wonder'd, that your lordship
Would suffer him to spend his youth at home;
While other men, of slender reputation,
Put forth their sons to seek preferment out:
Some, to the wars, to try their fortune there;
Some, to discover islands far away;
Some, to the studious universities.
For any, or for all these exercises,
He said, that Proteus, your son, was meet;
And did request me, to importune you,
To let him spend his time no more at home,
Which would be great impeachment[11] to his age,
In having known no travel in his youth.

Ant. Nor need'st thou much importune me to that
Whereon this month I have been hammering.
I have consider'd well his loss of time;
And how he cannot be a perfect man,
Not being try'd and tutor'd in the world:
Experience is by industry achiev'd,
And perfected by the swift course of time.
Then, tell me, whither were I best to send him?

---

1 First folio, *ye*.

2 *Stomach*, for passion or obstinacy.

3 *Set* is here used equivocally; in the preceding speech in the sense in which it is used by musicians, and in the present line in a quite different sense. To *set by* in old language signifies, to make account of, to estimate. See the first Book of Samuel, xviii. 30.

4 *Descant* signified formerly what we now call *variations*. It has been well defined to be musical paraphrase The *mean* is the tenor in music.

5 To *bid the base* means, to run fast, challenging another to pursue at the rustic game called Base, or Prisonbase. The allusion is somewhat obscure, but it appears to mean here, "to challenge to an encounter."

6 i. e. bustle, stir.

7 Since.

8 "*for* catching cold," i. e. lest they should catch cold, anciently a common form of expression. See Horne Tooke's explanation of this word in the first volume of "The Diversions of Purley."

9 *Month's mind, a longing*, probably from "the longing of women, which takes place (or commences, at least) in the first month of pregnancy." This is the ingenious conjecture of John Croft, Esq. of York. The commentators have endeavoured to refer this passage to the *month's minds*, or periodical celebrations in memory of dead persons, usual in times of popery;—but the phrase in this place can have no relation to them.

10 i. e. grave or serious.

11 *Impeachment* in this passage means *reproach* or *imputation*.

Pant. I think, your lordship is not ignorant,
How his companion, youthful Valentine,
Attends the emperor in his royal court.
Ant. I know it well.
Pant. 'Twere good, I think, your lordship sen him thither:
There shall he practise tilts and tou naments,
Hear sweet discourse, converse with noblemen;
And be in eye of every exercise,
Worthy his youth and nobleness of birth.
Ant. I like thy counsel: well hast thou advised:
And, that thou may'st perceive how well I like it,
The execution of it shall make known;
Even with the speediest expedition
I will despatch him to the emperor's court.
Pant. To-morrow, may it please you, Don Alphonso,
With other gentlemen of good esteem,
Are journeying to salute the emperor,
And to commend their service to his will.
Ant. Good company; with them shall Proteus go:
And, in good time,—now will we break with him.[1]

Enter PROTEUS.

Pro. Sweet love! sweet lines! sweet life!
Here is her hand, the agent of her heart:
Here is her oath for love, her honour's pawn:
O, that our fathers would applaud our loves,
To seal our happiness with their consents!
O heavenly Julia!
Ant. How now? what letter are you reading there?
Pro. May't please your lordship, 'tis a word or two
commendations sent from Valentine,
eliver'd by a friend that came from him.
Ant. Lend me the letter; let me see what news.
Pro. There is no news, my lord; but that he writes
How happily he lives, how well belov'd
And daily graced by the emperor;
Wishing me with him, partner of his fortune.
Ant. And how stand you affected to his wish?
Pro. As one relying on your lordship's will,
And not depending on his friendly wish.
Ant. My will is something sorted with his wish;
Muse[2] not that I thus suddenly proceed;
For what I will, I will, and there an end.
I am resolv'd, that thou shalt spend some time
With Valentinus in the emperor's court;
What maintenance he from his friends receives,
Like exhibition[3] thou shalt have from me.
To-morrow be in readiness to go:
Excuse it not, for I am peremptory.
Pro. My lord, I cannot be so soon provided;
Please you, deliberate a day or two.
Ant. Look, what thou want'st, shall be sent after thee:
No more of stay; to-morrow thou must go.—
Come on, Panthino; you shall be employed
To hasten on his expedition.
[*Exeunt* ANT. *and* PANT.
Pro. Thus have I shunn'd the fire, for fear of burning;
And drench'd me in the sea, where I am drown'd:
I fear'd to shew my father Julia's letter,
Lest he should take exceptions to my love;
And with the vantage of mine own excuse
Hath he excepted most against my love.
O, how this spring of love resembleth[4]
The uncertain glory of an April day;
Which now shows all the beauty of the sun,
And by and by a cloud takes all away!

Re-enter PANTHINO.

Pant. Sir Proteus, your father calls for you;
He is in haste, therefore, I pray you go.
Pro. Why, this it is! my heart accords thereto;
And yet a thousand times it answers, no. [*Exeunt.*

1 i. e. break the matter to him.
2 i. e. *wonder* not.
3 *Exhibition* is allowance of money; it is still used in the Universities for a stipend.

ACT II.

SCENE I. Milan. *A Room in the* Duke's *Palace. Enter* VALENTINE *and* SPEED.

Speed. Sir, your glove.
Val. Not mine; my gloves are on.
Speed. Why then this may be yours, for this is but one.[5]
Val. Ha! let me see: ay, give it me, it's mine:—
Sweet ornament that decks a thing divine!
Ah Silvia! Silvia!
Speed. Madam Silvia! madam Silvia!
Val. How now, sirrah?
Speed. She is not within hearing, sir.
Val. Why, sir, who bade you call her?
Speed. Your worship, sir; or else I mistook.
Val. Well, you'll still be too forward.
Speed. And yet I was last chidden for being too slow.
Val. Go to, sir; tell me, do you know madam Silvia?
Speed. She that your worship loves?
Val. Why, how know you that I am in love?
Speed. Marry, by these special marks: First, you have learned, like Sir Proteus, to wreath your arms like a male-content: to relish a love-song, like a robin-red-breast; to walk alone, like one that had the pestilence; to sigh, like a school-boy that had lost his A, B, C; to weep, like a young wench that had buried her grandam; to fast, like one that takes diet;[6] to watch, like one that fears robbing; to speak puling, like a beggar at Hollowmas.[7] You were wont, when you laugh'd, to crow like a cock; when you walked, to walk like one of the lions; when you fasted, it was presently after dinner; when you looked sadly, it was for want of money: and now you are metamorphosed with a mistress, that, when I look on you, I can hardly think you my master.
Val. Are all these things perceived in me?
Speed. They are all perceived without you.
Val. Without me? They cannot.
Speed. Without you! nay, that's certain, for, without you were so simple, none else would: but you are so without these follies, that these follies are within you, and shine through you like the water in an urinal; that not an eye, that sees you, but is a physician to comment on your malady.
Val. But, tell me, dost thou know my lady Silvia?
Speed. She that you gaze on so, as she sits at supper?
Val. Hast thou observed that? even she I mean.
Speed. Why, sir, I know her not.
Val. Dost thou know her by my gazing on her, and yet know'st her not?
Speed. Is she not hard-favour'd, sir?
Val. Not so fair, boy, as well favour'd.
Speed. Sir, I know that well enough.
Val. What dost thou know?
Speed. That she is not so fair, as (of you) well-favour'd.
Val. I mean, that her beauty is exquisite, but her favour infinite.
Speed. That's because the one is painted, and the other out of all count.
Val. How painted? and how out of count?
Speed. Marry, sir, so painted to make her fair, that no man counts of her beauty.

4 *Resembleth* is pronounced as if written *resembeleth*, which makes it a quadrisyllable.
5 *On* and *one* were anciently pronounced alike, and frequently written so.
6 To *take diet* is to be under a *regimen* for a disease.
7 The feast of All-hallows, or All Saints, at which time the poor in Staffordshire go from parish to parish *a souling*, as they call it; i. e. *begging and puling*, (or singing small, as Bailey's Dictionary explains *puling*,) for soul cakes, and singing what they call the souler's song. These terms point out the condition of this benevolence, which was, that the beggars should pray for the souls of the giver's departed friends

Val. How esteem'st thou me? I account of her beauty.

Speed. You never saw her since she was deformed.

Val. How long hath she been deform'd?

Speed. Ever since you loved her.

Val. I have loved her ever since I saw her; and still I see her beautiful.

Speed. If you love her, you cannot see her.

Val. Why?

Speed. Because love is blind. O, that you had mine eyes; or your own eyes had the lights they were wont to have, when you chid at Sir Proteus for going ungartered![1]

Val. What should I see then?

Speed. Your own present folly, and her passing deformity: for he, being in love, could not see to garter his hose; and you, being in love, cannot see to put on your hose.

Val. Belike, boy, then you are in love; for last morning you could not see to wipe my shoes.

Speed. True, sir; I was in love with my bed: I thank you, you swinged me for my love, which makes me the bolder to chide you for yours.

Val. In conclusion, I stand affected to her.

Speed. I would you were set,[2] so, your affection would cease.

Val. Last night she enjoined me to write some lines to one she loves.

Speed. And have you?

Val. I have.

Speed. Are they not lamely writ?

Val. No, boy, but as well as I can do them:—Peace, here she comes.

Enter SILVIA.

Speed. O excellent motion![3] O exceeding puppet! now will he interpret to her.

Val. Madam and mistress, a thousand good-morrows.

Speed. O, 'give you good even! here's a million of manners. [*Aside.*

Sil. Sir Valentine and servant, to you two thousand.

Speed. He should give her interest; and she gives it him.

Val. As you enjoin'd me, I have writ your letter,
Unto the secret nameless friend of yours;
Which I was much unwilling to proceed in,
But for my duty to your ladyship.

Sil. I thank you, gentle servant: 'tis very clerkly[4] done.

Val. Now trust me, madam, it came hardly off;
For, being ignorant to whom it goes,
I writ at random, very doubtfully.

Sil. Perchance you think too much of so much pains?

Val. No, madam, so it stead you, I will write,
Please you command, a thousand times as much:
And yet,—

Sil. A pretty period! Well, I guess the sequel;
And yet I will not name it:—and yet I care not;—
And yet take this again;—and yet I thank you;
Meaning henceforth to trouble you no more.

Speed. And yet you will; and yet another yet. [*Aside.*

Val. What means your ladyship? do you not like it?

Sil. Yes, yes; the lines are very quaintly writ:
But since unwillingly, take them again;
Nay, take them.

Val. Madam, they are for you.

Sil. Ay, ay; you writ them, sir, at my request;
But I will none of them; they are for you:
I would have had them writ more movingly.

Val. Please you, I'll write your ladyship another.

Sil. And, when it's writ, for my sake read it over:
And, if it please you, so; if not, why, so.

Val. If it please me, madam! what then?

Sil. Why if it please you take it for your labour,
And so good-morrow, servant. [*Exit* SILVIA.

Speed. O jest unseen, inscrutable, invisible,
As a nose on a man's face, or a weathercock on a steeple!
My master sues to her; and she hath taught her suitor,
He being her pupil, to become her tutor.
O excellent device! was there ever heard a better?
That my master, being scribe, to himself should write the letter?

Val. How now, sir? what are you reasoning with yourself?

Speed. Nay, I was rhyming; 'tis you that have the reason.

Val. To do what?

Speed. To be a spokesman from madam Silvia.

Val. To whom?

Speed. To yourself: why, she woos you by a figure.

Val. What figure?

Speed. By a letter, I should say.

Val. Why, she hath not writ to me?

Speed. What need she, when she hath made you write to yourself? Why, do you not perceive the jest?

Val. No, believe me.

Speed. No believing you indeed, sir: But did you perceive her earnest?

Val. She gave me none, except an angry word.

Speed. Why, she hath given you a letter.

Val. That's the letter I writ to her friend.

Speed. And that letter hath she deliver'd, and there an end.[5]

Val. I would, it were no worse.

Speed. I'll warrant you, 'tis as well:
For often have you writ to her; and she, in modesty,
Or else for want of idle time, could not again reply;
Or fearing else some messenger, that might her mind discover,
Herself hath taught her love himself to write unto her lover.
All this I speak in print;[6] for in print I found it.—
Why muse you, sir? 'tis dinner-time.

Val. I have dined.

Speed. Ay, but hearken, sir: though the cameleon Love can feed on the air, I am one that am nourished by my victuals, and would fain have meat: O, be not like your mistress; be moved, be moved. [*Exeunt.*

SCENE II. Verona. *A Room in* Julia's *House.*

Enter PROTEUS *and* JULIA.

Pro. Have patience, gentle Julia.

Jul. I must, where is no remedy.

Pro. When possibly I can, I will return.

Jul. If you turn not, you will return the sooner:
Keep this remembrance for thy Julia's sake. [*Giving a ring.*

Pro. Why then we'll make exchange; here, take you this.

Jul. And seal the bargain with a holy kiss.

Pro. Here is my hand for my true constancy;
And when that hour o'er-slips me in the day,
Wherein I sigh not, Julia, for thy sake,
The next ensuing hour some foul mischance
Torment me for my love's forgetfulness!
My father stays my coming: answer not
The tide is now: nay, not thy tide of tears,
That tide will stay me longer than I should; [*Exit* JULIA.

---

1 Going ungartered is enumerated by Rosalind as one of the undoubted marks of love. "Then your hose should be *ungartered*, your bonnet unbanded," &c. As You Like It, iii. 2.

2 *Set*, for seated, in opposition to stand in the preceding line. It appears, however, to be used metaphorically in the sense applied to the sun when it sinks below the horizon in the west. It is a miserable quibble hardly worth explanation.

3 Motion signified, in Shakspeare's time, a *puppet show* Speed means to say, what a fine puppet-show shall we have now? Here is the principal *puppet* to whom my master will be the interpreter. The show man was then frequently called the interpreter.

4 i. e. like a scholar.

5 There's the conclusion.

6 i. e. with exactness

ulia, farewell.—What! gone without a word!
Ay, so true love should do: it cannot speak;
For truth hath better deeds than words to grace it.

Enter PANTHINO.

Pant. Sir Proteus, you are staid for.
Pro. Go; I come, I come:—
Alas! this parting strikes poor lovers dumb.
[*Exeunt.*

SCENE III.—*The same. A Street Enter* LAUNCE, *leading a Dog.*

Laun. Nay, 'twill be this hour ere I have done weeping; all the kind[1] of the Launces have this very fault; I have received my proportion, like the prodigious son, and am going with Sir Proteus to the Imperial's court. I think, Crab my dog be the sourest-natured dog that lives: my mother weeping, my father wailing, my sister crying, our maid howling, our cat wringing her hands, and all our house in a great perplexity, yet did not this cruel-hearted cur shed one tear: he is a stone, a very pebble stone, and has no more pity in him than a dog: a Jew would have wept to have seen our parting; why, my grandam having no eyes, look you, wept herself blind at my parting. Nay, I'll show you the manner of it: This shoe is my father:—no, this left shoe is my father;—no, no, this left shoe is my mother;—nay, that cannot be so neither;—yes, it is so, it is so; it hath the worser sole; This shoe, with the hole in it, is my mother; and this my father: A vengeance on't! there 'tis: now, sir, this staff is my sister; for, look you, she is as white as a lily, and as small as a wand: this hat is Nan, our maid; I am the dog:—no, the dog is himself, and I am the dog;—oh, the dog is me, and I am myself: Ay, so, so. Now come I to my father; *Father, your blessing:* now should not the shoe speak a word for weeping; now should I kiss my father; well he weeps on:—now come I to my mother, (O, that she could speak now!) like a wood[2] woman;—well, I kiss her;—why there 'tis; here's my mother's breath up and down: now come I to my sister; mark the moan she makes: now the dog all this while sheds not a tear, nor speaks a word; but see how I lay the dust with my tears.

Enter PANTHINO.

Pan. Launce, away, away, aboard; thy master is shipped, and thou art to post after with oars. What's the matter? why weepest thou, man? Away, ass; you will lose the tide, if you tarry any longer.

Laun. It is no matter if the ty'd were lost; for it is the unkindest ty'd that ever any man ty'd.

Pan. What's the unkindest tide?

Laun. Why, he that's ty'd here; Crab, my dog.

Pan. Tut, man, I mean thou'lt lose the flood; and, in losing the flood, lose thy voyage; and, in losing thy voyage, lose thy master; and, in losing thy master, lose thy service; and in losing thy service,—Why dost thou stop my mouth?

Laun. For fear thou should'st lose thy tongue.

Pan. Where should I lose my tongue?

Laun. In thy tale.

Pan. In thy tail?

Laun. Lose the tide, and the voyage, and the master, and the service: And the tide!—Why, man, if the river were dry, I am able to fill it with my tears; if the wind were down, I could drive the boat with my sighs.

Pan. Come, come away, man; I was sent to call thee.

Laun. Sir, call me what thou darest.

Pan. Wilt thou go?

Laun. Well, I will go. [*Exeunt.*

SCENE IV.—Milan. *A Room in the* Duke's *Palace. Enter* VALENTINE, SILVIA, THURIO, *and* SPEED.

Sil. Servant—
Val. Mistress?
Speed. Master, Sir Thurio frowns on you.
Val. Ay, boy, it's for love.
Speed. Not of you.
Val. Of my mistress then.
Speed. 'Twere good you knocked him.
Sil. Servant, you are sad.[3]
Val. Indeed, madam, I seem so.
Thu. Seem you that you are not?
Val. Haply[4] I do.
Thu. So do counterfeits.
Val. So do you.
Thu. What seem I, that I am not?
Val. Wise.
Thu. What instance of the contrary?
Val. Your folly.
Thu. And how quote[5] you my folly?
Val. I quote it in your jerkin.
Thu. My jerkin is a doublet.
Val. Well, then, I'll double your folly.
Thu. How?

Sil. What, angry, Sir Thurio? do you change colour?

Val. Give him leave, madam; he is a kind of cameleon.

Thu. That hath more mind to feed on your blood, than live in your air.

Val. You have said, sir.

Thu. Ay, sir, and done too, for this time.

Val. I know it well, sir; you always end ere you begin.

Sil. A fine volley of words, gentlemen, and quickly shot off.

Val. 'Tis indeed, madam; we thank the giver.

Sil. Who is that, servant?

Val. Yourself, sweet lady; for you gave the fire. Sir Thurio borrows his wit from your ladyship's looks, and spends what he borrows, kindly in your company.

Thu. Sir, if you spend word for word with me, I shall make your wit bankrupt.

Val. I know it well, sir: you have an exchequer of words, and, I think, no other treasure to give your followers; for it appears by their bare liveries, that they live by your bare words.

Sil. No more, gentlemen, no more; here comes my father.

Enter DUKE.

Duke. Now, daughter Silvia, you are hard beset.
Sir Valentine, your father's in good health:
What say you to a letter from your friends
Of much good news?
Val. My lord, I will be thankful
To any happy messenger from thence.
Duke. Know you Don Antonio, your countryman?
Val. Ay, my good lord, I know the gentleman
To be of worth, and worthy estimation,
And not without desert so well reputed.
Duke. Hath he not a son?
Val. Ay, my good lord; a son, that well deserves
The honour and regard of such a father.
Duke. You know him well?
Val. I knew him as myself; for from our infancy
We have convers'd, and spent our hours together:
And though myself have been an idle truant,
Omitting the sweet benefit of time,
To clothe mine age with angel-like perfection;
Yet hath Sir Proteus, for that's his name,
Made use and fair advantage of his days;
His years but young, but his experience old;
His head unmellow'd, but his judgment ripe;
And, in a word, (for far behind his worth
Come all the praises that I now bestow,)
He is complete in feature,[6] and in mind,

---

1 *Kind*, is kindred. 2 Crazy, wild, distracted.
3 i. e. you are *serious*. 4 i. e. perhaps.

5 To *quote* is to mark, to observe, the old pronunciation was evidently *cote* from the French original

6 *Feature* in the poet's age was often used for form or person in general. Thus Baret: "The *feature* and facion, or the proportion and figure of the whole body. Conformatio quædam et figura totius oris et corporis." So in Ant. and Cleop. Act. ii. Sc. 5.

"Report the *feature* of Octavian."

Thus also Spenser:

"Which the fair *feature* of her limbs did hide"

With all good grace to grace a gentleman.
Duke. Beshrew[1] me, sir, but, if he make this good,
He is as worthy for an empress' love,
As meet to be an emperor's counsellor.
Well, sir; this gentleman is come to me,
With commendation from great potentates;
And here he means to spend his time a while:
I think, 'tis no unwelcome news to you.
Val. Should I have wish'd a thing, it had been he.
Duke. Welcome him then according to his worth.
Silvia, I speak to you; and you, Sir Thurio:—
For Valentine, I need not 'cite[2] him to it:
I'll send him hither to you presently. [*Exit* Duke.
Val. This is the gentleman, I told your ladyship,
Had come along with me, but that his mistress
Did hold his eyes lock'd in her crystal looks.
Sil. Belike, that now she hath enfranchis'd them
Upon some other pawn for fealty.
Val. Nay, sure, I think, she holds them prisoners still.
Sil. Nay, then he should be blind; and, being blind,
How could he see his way to seek out you?
Val. Why, lady, love hath twenty pair of eyes.
Thu. They say, that love hath not an eye at all.
Val. To see such lovers, Thurio, as yourself;
Upon a homely object love can wink.

Enter Proteus.

Sil. Have done, have done; here comes the gentleman.
Val. Welcome, dear Proteus!—Mistress, I beseech you,
Confirm his welcome with some special favour.
Sil. His worth is warrant for his welcome hither,
If this be he you oft have wish'd to hear from.
Val. Mistress, it is: sweet lady, entertain him
To be my fellow-servant to your ladyship.
Sil. Too low a mistress for so high a servant.
Pro. Not so, sweet lady; but too mean a servant
To have a look of such a worthy mistress.
Val. Leave off discourse of disability:—
Sweet lady, entertain him for your servant.
Pro. My duty will I boast of, nothing else.
Sil. And duty never yet did want his meed;
Servant you are welcome to a worthless mistress.
Pro. I'll die on him that says so, but yourself.
Sil. That you are welcome?
Pro. No; that you are worthless.

Enter Servant.

Ser. Madam, my lord your father would speak with you.
Sil. I'll wait upon his pleasure. [*Exit* Servant.
Come, Sir Thurio,
Go with me:—Once more, new servant, welcome:
I'll leave you to confer of home affairs;
When you have done, we look to hear from you.
Pro. We'll both attend upon your ladyship.
[*Exeunt* Silvia, Thurio, *and* Speed.
Val. Now, tell me, how do all from whence you came?
Pro. Your friends are well, and have them much commended.
Val. And how do yours?
Pro. I left them all in health.
Val. How does your lady? and how thrives your love?
Pro. My tales of love were wont to weary you;
I know you joy not in a love-discourse.
Val. Ay, Proteus, but that life is alter'd now:
I have done penance for contemning love;
Whose high imperious[3] thoughts have punish'd me
With bitter fasts, with penitential groans,
With nightly tears, and daily heart-sore sighs;
For, in revenge of my contempt of love,
Love hath chas'd sleep from my enthralled eyes,
And made them watchers of mine own heart's sorrow.
O, gentle Proteus, love's a mighty lord;
And hath so humbled me, as, I confess,
There is no woe[4] to his correction.
Nor, to his service, no such joy on earth!
Now, no discourse, except it be of love.
Now can I break my fast, dine, sup, and sleep,
Upon the very naked name of love.
Pro. Enough; I read your fortune in your eye
Was this the idol that you worship so?
Val. Even she; and is she not a heavenly saint?
Pro. No; but she's an earthly paragon.
Val. Call her divine.
Pro. I will not flatter her.
Val. O, flatter me; for love delights in praises.
Pro. When I was sick, you gave me bitter pills;
And I must minister the like to you.
Val. Then speak the truth by her; if not divine,
Yet let her be a principality,[5]
Sovereign to all the creatures on the earth.
Pro. Except my mistress.
Val. Sweet, except not any,
Except thou wilt except against thy love.
Pro. Have I not reason to prefer mine own?
Val. And I will help thee to prefer her too:
She shall be dignified with this high honour,—
To bear my lady's train; lest the base earth
Should from her vesture chance to steal a kiss,
And, of so great a favour growing proud,
Disdain to root the summer-swelling flower
And make rough winter everlastingly.
Pro. Why, Valentine, what braggardism is this?
Val. Pardon me, Proteus: all I can, is nothing
To her, whose worth makes other worthies nothing;
She is alone.
Pro. Then let her alone.
Val. Not for the world: why, man, she is mine own;
And I as rich in having such a jewel,
As twenty seas, if all their sand were pearl,
The water nectar, and the rocks pure gold.
Forgive me, that I do not dream on thee,
Because thou seest me dote upon my love
My foolish rival, that her father likes,
Only for his possessions are so huge,
Is gone with her along; and I must after,
For love, thou know'st, is full of jealousy
Pro. But she loves you?
Val. Ay, and we are betroth'd;
Nay, more, our marriage hour,
With all the cunning manner of our flight,
Determin'd of: how I must climb her window
The ladder made of cords: and all the means
Plotted; and 'greed on, for my happiness.
Good Proteus, go with me to my chamber,
In these affairs to aid me with thy counsel
Pro. Go on before; I shall inquire you forth
I must unto the road,[6] to disembark
Some necessaries that I needs must use;
And then I'll presently attend you.
Val. Will you make haste?
Pro. I will.— [*Exit* Val.
Even as one heat another heat expels,
Or as one nail by strength drives out another,
So the remembrance of my former love
Is by a newer object quite forgotten.
Is it her mien, or Valentinus' praise,
Her true perfection, or my false transgression,
That makes me, reasonless, to reason thus?
She's fair; and so is Julia, that I love;—
That I did love, for now my love is thaw'd·
Which, like a waxen image, 'gainst a fire,[7]
Bears no impression of the thing it was.
Methinks, my zeal to Valentine is cold;

1 A petty mode of adjuration equivalent to *ill betide me.*

2 *Cite*, for incite.

3 i. e. *imperial.* Thus in Hamlet:

"*Imperious* Cæsar dead and turn'd to clay."

4 *No woe*, no misery that can be compared to the punishment inflicted by love.

5 A *principality* is *an angel of the first order*

6 i. e. the *haven* where the ships lie at anchor.

7 Alluding to the figures made by witches as representatives of those they meant to destroy or torment V. *Macbeth* Act ii Sc. 3

And that I love him not, as I was wont:
O! but I love his lady, too, too much;
And that's the reason I love him so little.
How shall I dote on her with more advice,[1]
That thus without advice begin to love her?
'Tis but her picture[2] I have yet beheld,
And that hath dazzled[3] my reason's light;
But when I look on her perfections,
There is no reason but I shall be blind.
If I can check my erring love, I will;
If not, to compass her I'll use my skill. [*Exit.*

SCENE V.—*The same. A Street. Enter* SPEED *and* LAUNCE.

Speed. Launce! by mine honesty, welcome to Milan.

Laun. Forswear not thyself, sweet youth; for I am not welcome. I reckon this always—that a man is never undone, till he be hanged; nor never welcome to a place, till some certain shot be paid, and the hostess say, welcome.

Speed. Come on, you mad-cap, I'll to the alehouse with you presently; where, for one shot of five pence thou shalt have five thousand welcomes. But, sirrah, how did thy master part with madam Julia?

Laun. Marry, after they closed in earnest, they parted very fairly in jest.

Speed. But shall she marry him?

Laun. No.

Speed. How then? shall he marry her?

Laun. No, neither.

Speed. What, are they broken?

Laun. No, they are both as whole as a fish.

Speed. Why then, how stands the matter with them?

Laun. Marry, thus; when it stands well with him, it stands well with her.

Speed. What an ass art thou! I understand thee not.

Laun. What a block art thou, that thou canst not? My staff understands me.

Speed. What thou say'st?

Laun. Ay, and what I do too: look thee I'll but lean, and my staff understands me.

Speed. It stands under thee, indeed.

Laun. Why, stand under and understand is all one.

Speed. But tell me true, will't be a match?

Laun. Ask my dog: if he say, ay, it will; if he say, no, it will; if he shake his tail, and say nothing, it will.

Speed. The conclusion is then, that it will.

Laun. Thou shalt never get such a secret from me, but by a parable.

Speed. 'Tis well that I get it so. But, Launce, how say'st thou,[4] that my master is become a notable lover?

Laun. I never knew him otherwise.

Speed. Than how?

Laun. A notable lubber, as thou reportest him to be.

Speed. Why, thou whoreson ass, thou mistakest me.

Laun. Why, fool, I meant not thee; I meant thy master.

Speed. I tell thee, my master is become a hot lover.

Laun. Why, I tell thee, I care not though he burn himself in love. If thou wilt go with me to the ale-house, so; if not, thou art a Hebrew, a Jew, and not worth the name of a Christian.

Speed. Why?

Laun. Because thou hast not so much charity in thee, as to go to the ale with a Christian. Wilt thou go?

Speed. At thy service. [*Exeunt.*

1 i. e. on further knowledge, on better consideration.
2 Proteus means to say, that as yet he had only seen outward form, without having known her long enough to have any acquaintance with her mind.
3 *Dazzled* is used as a trisyllable.
4 i. e. what say'st thou to this circumstance

SCENE VI.—*The same. An Apartment in the Palace. Enter* PROTEUS.

Pro. To leave my Julia, shall I be forsworn;
To love fair Silvia, shall I be forsworn;
To wrong my friend, I shall be much forsworn;
And even that power, which gave me first my oath,
Provokes me to this threefold perjury.
Love bade me swear, and love bids me forswear:
O sweet suggesting[5] love, if thou hast sinn'd,
Teach me, thy tempted subject, to excuse it.
At first I did adore a twinkling star,
But now I worship a celestial sun.
Unheedful vows may heedfully be broken:
And he wants wit, that wants resolved will
To learn his wit to exchange the bad for better.—
Fie, fie, unreverend tongue! to call her bad,
Whose sovereignty so oft thou hast preferr'd
With twenty thousand soul-confirming oaths.
I cannot leave to love, and yet I do;
But there I leave to love, where I should love.
Julia I lose, and Valentine I lose:
If I keep them, I needs must lose myself;
If I lose them, thus find I by their loss,
For Valentine, myself; for Julia, Silvia.
I to myself am dearer than a friend;
For love is still most precious in itself:
And Silvia, witness heaven, that made her fair!
Shews Julia but a swarthy Ethiope.
I will forget that Julia is alive,
Rememb'ring that my love to her is dead;
And Valentine I'll hold an enemy,
Aiming at Silvia as a sweeter friend.
I cannot now prove constant to myself,
Without some treachery used to Valentine:—
This night, he meaneth with a corded ladder
To climb celestial Silvia's chamber-window;
Myself in counsel, his competitor:[6]
Now presently I'll give her father notice
Of their disguising, and pretended[7] flight;
Who all enrag'd, will banish Valentine;
For Thurio, he intends, shall wed his daughter:
But, Valentine being gone, I'll quickly cross,
By some sly trick, blunt Thurio's dull proceeding.
Love, lend me wings to make my purpose swift,
As thou hast lent me wit to plot this drift! [*Exit.*

SCENE VII.

Verona. *A Room in* Julia's *House. Enter* JULIA *and* LUCETTA.

Jul. Counsel, Lucetta; gentle girl, assist me!
And, e'en in kind love, I do conjure thee[8],—
Who art the table wherein all my thoughts
Are visibly character'd and engrav'd,—
To lesson me; and tell me some good mean,
How, with my honour, I may undertake
A journey to my loving Proteus.

Luc. Alas! the way is wearisome and long.

Jul. A true-devoted pilgrim is not weary
To measure kingdoms with his feeble steps;
Much less shall she, that hath love's wings to fly;
And when the flight is made to one so dear,
Of such divine perfection, as Sir Proteus.

Luc. Better forbear, till Proteus make return.

Jul. O, know'st thou not, his looks are my soul's food?
Pity the dearth that I have pined in,
By longing for that food so long a time.
Didst thou but know the inly touch of love,
Thou would'st as soon go kindle fire with snow,
As seek to quench the fire of love with words.

5 To *suggest*, in the language of our ancestors, was to *tempt*.
6 i. e. myself who am his *competitor* or *rival*, being admitted to his counsel. *Competitor* here means confederate, assistant, partner. Thus in Ant. Cleop. Act v Sc. 1.

That thou my brother, my *competitor*
In top of all design, my *mate* in empire,
Friend and *companion* in the front of war.

7 i. e. *proposed* or *intended* flight. The verb *pretendre* has the same signification in French.
8 The verb to *conjure*, or earnestly request, was then accented on the first syllable.

Luc. I do not seek to quench your love's hot fire;
But qualify the fire's[1] extreme rage,
Lest it should burn above the bounds of reason.
Jul. The more thou dam'st[2] it up, the more it burns;
The current, that with gentle murmur glides,
Thou know'st, being stopp'd, impatiently doth rage;
But, when his fair course is not hindered,
He makes sweet music with th' enamel'd stones,
Giving a gentle kiss to every sedge
He overtaketh in his pilgrimage;
And so by many winding nooks he strays,
With willing sport to the wild ocean.
Then let me go, and hinder not my course:
I'll be as patient as a gentle stream,
And make a pastime of each weary step,
Till the last step have brought me to my love;
And there I'll rest, as, after much turmoil,[3]
A blessed soul doth in Elysium.
Luc. But in what habit will you go along?
Jul. Not like a woman; for I would prevent
The loose encounters of lascivious men:
Gentle Lucetta, fit me with such weeds
As may beseem some well reputed page.
Luc. Why then your ladyship must cut your hair.
Jul. No, girl; I'll knit it up in silken strings,
With twenty odd-conceited true-love knots;
To be fantastic may become a youth
Of greater time than I shall show to be.
Luc. What fashion, madam, shall I make your breeches?
Jul. That fits as well, as—"tell me, good my lord,
"What compass will you wear your farthingale?"
Why, even what fashion thou best lik'st, Lucetta.
Luc. You must needs have them with a cod-piece,[4] madam.
Jul. Out, out, Lucetta; that will be ill favour'd.
Luc. A round hose, madam, now's not worth a pin,
Unless you have a cod-piece to stick pins on.
Jul. Lucetta, as thou lov'st me, let me have
What thou think'st meet, and is most mannerly:
But tell me, wench, how will the world repute me,
For undertaking so unstaid a journey?
I fear me, it will make me scandaliz'd.
Luc. If you think so, then stay at home, and go not.
Jul. Nay, that I will not.
Luc. Then never dream on infamy, but go.
If Proteus like your journey, when you come,
No matter who's displeas'd, when you are gone:
I fear me, he will scarce be pleas'd withal.
Jul. This is the least, Lucetta, of my fear:
A thousand oaths, an ocean of his tears,
And instances of infinite[5] of love,
Warrant me welcome to my Proteus.
Luc. All these are servants to deceitful men.
Jul. Base men, that use them to so base effect!
But truer stars did govern Proteus' birth:
His words are bonds, his oaths are oracles;
His love sincere, his thoughts immaculate;
His tears, pure messengers sent from his heart;
His heart as far from fraud, as heaven from earth.
Luc. Pray heaven, he prove so, when you come to him!
Jul. Now, as thou lov'st me, do him not that wrong,
To bear a hard opinion of his truth;
Only deserve my love, by loving him;
And presently go with me to my chamber,
To take a note of what I stand in need of.
To furnish me upon my longing[6] journey.
All that is mine I leave at thy dispose,
My goods, my lands, my reputation;
Only, in lieu thereof despatch me hence:
Come, answer not, but to it presently;
I am impatient of my tarriance. [*Exeunt*

ACT III.

SCENE I.—Milan. *An Anti-room in the* Duke's *Palace. Enter* DUKE, THURIO, *and* PROTEUS.

Duke. Sir Thurio, give us leave, I pray, awhile,
We have some secrets to confer about.
[*Exit* THURIO
Now, tell me, Proteus, what's your will with me?
Pro. My gracious lord, that which I would discover,
The law of friendship bids me to conceal:
But, when I call to mind your gracious favours
Done to me, undeserving as I am,
My duty pricks me on to utter that
Which else no worldly good should draw from me.
Know, worthy prince, Sir Valentine, my friend,
This night intends to steal away your daughter;
Myself am one made privy to the plot.
I know you have determin'd to bestow her
On Thurio, whom your gentle daughter hates;
And should she thus be stolen away from you,
It would be much vexation to your age.
Thus, for my duty's sake, I rather chose
To cross my friend in his intended drift,
Than, by concealing it, heap on your head
A pack of sorrows, which would press you down,
Being unprevented, to your timeless grave.
Duke. Proteus, I thank thee for thine honest care.
Which to requite, command me while I live.
This love of theirs myself have often seen,
Haply, when they have judged me fast asleep;
And oftentimes have purpos'd to forbid
Sir Valentine her company, and my court:
But, fearing lest my jealous aim[7] might err,
And so unworthily disgrace the man,
(A rashness that I ever yet have shunn'd,)
I gave him gentle looks; thereby to find
That which thyself hast now disclos'd to me.
And, that thou may'st perceive my fear of this,
Knowing that tender youth is soon suggested[8],
I nightly lodge her in an upper tower,
The key whereof myself have ever kept;
And thence she cannot be convey'd away.
Pro. Know, noble lord, they have devis'd a mean
How he her chamber-window will ascend,
And with a corded ladder fetch her down;
For which the youthful lover now is gone,
And this way comes he with it presently;
Where, if it please you, you may intercept him
But, good my lord, do it so cunningly,
That my discovery be not aimed at;
For love of you, not hate unto my friend,
Hath made me publisher of this pretence[9].
Duke. Upon mine honour, he shall never know
That I had any light from thee on this.
Pro. Adieu, my lord; Sir Valentine is coming.
[*Exit*

Enter VALENTINE.

Duke. Sir Valentine, whither away so fast?
Val. Please it your grace there is a messenger

---

1 *Fire* as a dissyllable, as if spelt *Fier.*
2 i. e. closest. 3 Trouble.
4 Whoever wishes to be acquainted with that singular appendage to dress, a *cod-piece*, may consult "Bulwer's Artificial Changeling." Ocular instruction may be had from the armour shown as John of Gaunt's in the Tower. However offensive this language may appear to modern ears, it certainly gave none to any of the spectators in Shakspeare's days. He only used the ordinary language of his contemporaries.
5 The second folio reads—"*as* infinite of love," Malone wished to read *of the* infinite of love, because he found "*the* infinite of thought" in Much Ado About Nothing. The text seems to me sufficiently intelligible, though we are not used to such construction. Malone has cited an instance of *infinite* used for *an infinity* from Lord Lonsdale's Memoirs, written in 1688.
6 By her *longing journey*, Julia means a journey which she shall pass in longing.
7 i. e. *guess*. In Romeo and Juliet we have
"I *aim'd* so near when I suppos'd you lov'd."
8 i. e. tempted. Vide Note on Act ii. Sc. 5, p. 136
9 i. e. *design*.

That stays to bear my letters to my friends,
And I am going to deliver them.
Duke. Be they of much import?
Val. The tenor of them doth but signify
My health, and happy being at your court.
Duke. Nay, then no matter; stay with me a while;
I am to break with thee of some affairs,
That touch me near, wherein thou must be secret.
'Tis not unknown to thee, that I have sought
To match my friend, Sir Thurio, to my daughter.
Val. I know it well, my lord; and, sure, the match
Were rich and honourable; besides, the gentleman
Is full of virtue, bounty, worth, and qualities
Beseeming such a wife as your fair daughter:
Cannot your grace win her to fancy him?
Duke. No, trust me; she is peevish, sullen, froward,
Proud, disobedient, stubborn, lacking duty;
Neither regarding that she is my child,
Nor fearing me as if I were her father:
And, may I say to thee, this pride of hers,
Upon advice, hath drawn my love from her;
And where[1] I thought the remnant of mine age
Should have been cherish'd by her childlike duty,
I now am full resolv'd to take a wife,
And turn her out to who will take her in:
Then let her beauty be her wedding-dower;
For me and my possessions she esteems not.
Val. What would your grace have me to do in this?
Duke. There is a lady, sir, in Milan, here,
Whom I affect; but she is nice, and coy,
And nought esteems my aged eloquence:
Now, therefore, would I have thee to my tutor,
(For long agone I have forgot to court:
Besides, the fashion of the time is chang'd;)
How, and which way, I may bestow myself,
To be regarded in her sun-bright eye.
Val. Win her with gifts, if she respect not words;
Dumb jewels often, in their silent kind,
More than quick words, do move a woman's mind.
Duke. But she did scorn a present that I sent her.
Val. A woman sometimes scorns what best contents her:
Send her another; never give her o'er;
For scorn at first makes after-love the more.
If she do frown, 'tis not in hate of you,
But rather to beget more love in you:
If she do chide, 'tis not to have you gone;
For why, the fools are mad, if left alone.
Take no repulse, whatever she doth say:
For, *get you gone*, she doth not mean, *away*:
Flatter, and praise, commend, extol their graces,
Though ne'er so black, say, they have angels' faces.
That man that hath a tongue, I say, is no man,
If with his tongue he cannot win a woman.
Duke. But she, I mean, is promis'd by her friends
Unto a youthful gentleman of worth;
And kept severely from resort of men,
That no man hath access by day to her.
Val. Why then I would resort to her by night.
Duke. Ay, but the doors be lock'd, and keys kept safe,
That no man hath recourse to her by night.
Val. What lets,[2] but one may enter at her window?
Duke. Her chamber is aloft, far from the ground;
And built so shelving that one cannot climb it
Without apparent hazard of his life.
Val. Why then, a ladder, quaintly made of cords,
To cast up with a pair of anchoring hooks,
Would serve to scale another Hero's tower,
So bold Leander would adventure it.
Duke. Now, as thou art a gentleman of blood,
Advise me where I may have such a ladder.
Val. When would you use it? pray, sir, tell me that.
Duke. This very night; for love is like a child,
That longs for every thing that he can come by.
Val. By seven o'clock I'll get you such a ladder.
Duke. But, hark thee; I will go to her alone;
How shall I best convey the ladder thither?
Val. It will be light, my lord, that you may bear it
Under a cloak that is of any length.
Duke. A cloak as long as thine will serve the turn?
Val. Ay, my good lord.
Duke. Then let me see thy cloak;
I'll get me one of such another length.
Val. Why, my cloak will serve the turn, my lord.
Duke. How shall I fashion me to wear a cloak?—
I pray thee, let me feel thy cloak upon me.—
What letter is this same? What's here? *To Silvia!*
And here an engine fit for my proceeding?
I'll be so bold to break the seal for once. [*reads.*

My thoughts do harbour with my Silvia nightly;
And slaves they are to me, that send them flying:
O, could their master come and go as lightly,
Himself would lodge where senseless they are lying.
My herald thoughts in thy pure bosom rest them;
While I, their king, that thither them importune,
Do curse the grace that with such grace hath bless'd them,
Because myself do want my servants' fortune:
I curse myself, for[3] *they are sent by me,*
That they should harbour where their lord should be.

What's here?
Silvia, this night I will enfranchise thee!
'Tis so; and here's the ladder for the purpose.—
Why, Phaeton (for thou art Merop's son,)
Wilt thou aspire to guide the heavenly car,
And with thy daring folly burn the world?
Wilt thou reach stars because they shine on thee?
Go, base intruder! over-weening slave!
Bestow thy fawning smiles on equal mates;
And think, my patience, more than thy desert,
Is privilege for thy departure hence:
Thank me for this, more than for all the favours
Which, all too much, I have bestow'd on thee.
But if thou linger in my territories
Longer than swiftest expedition
Will give thee time to leave our royal court,
By heaven, my wrath shall far exceed the love
I ever bore my daughter, or thyself.
Be gone, I will not hear thy vain excuse,
But, as thou lov'st thy life, make speed from hence.
[*Exit* DUKE.
Val. And why not death, rather than living torment?
To die, is to be banish'd from myself;
And Silvia is myself: banish'd from her,
Is self from self; a deadly banishment!
What light is light, if Silvia be not seen?
What joy is joy, if Silvia be not by?
Unless it be to think that she is by,
And feed upon the shadow of perfection,[4]
Except I be by Silvia in the night,
There is no music in the nightingale;
Unless I look on Silvia in the day,
There is no day for me to look upon:
She is my essence; and I leave to be,
If I be not by her fair influence
Foster'd, illumin'd, cherish'd, kept alive.
I fly not death, to fly his deadly doom;[5]
Tarry I here, I but attend on death;
But, fly I hence, I fly away from life.

Enter PROTEUS *and* LAUNCE.

Pro. Run, boy, run, run, and seek him out.
Laun. So-ho! so-ho!
Pro. What seest thou?
Laun. Him we go to find; there's not a hair[6] on's head, but 'tis a Valentine.

---

1 *Where* for *whereas*, often used by old writers.
2 i. e. hinders.
3 i. e. cause.
4 And feed upon the shadow of perfection.
Animum pictura pascit inani. *Virgil.*
5 i. e. *by flying*, or *in flying*. It is a Gallicism.
6 Launce is still quibbling, he is running down the *hare* he started when he first entered.

Pro. Valentine?
Val. No.
Pro. Who then? his spirit?
Val. Neither.
Pro. What then?
Val. Nothing.
Laun. Can nothing speak? master, shall I strike?
Pro. Whom would'st thou strike?
Laun. Nothing.
Pro. Villain, forbear.
Laun. Why, sir, I'll strike nothing: I pray you—
Pro. Sirrah, I say, forbear: Friend Valentine, a word.
Val. My ears are stopp'd, and cannot hear good news,
So much of bad already hath possess'd them.
Pro. Then in dumb silence will I bury mine,
For they are harsh, untunable, and bad.
Val. Is Silvia dead?
Pro. No, Valentine.
Val. No Valentine, indeed, for sacred Silvia!—
Hath she forsworn me?
Pro. No, Valentine.
Val. No Valentine, if Silvia have forsworn me!—
What is your news?
Laun. Sir, there's a proclamation that you are vanish'd.
Pro. That thou art banished, O, that's the news:
From hence, from Silvia, and from me, thy friend.
Val. O, I have fed upon this woe already,
And now excess of it will make me surfeit.
Doth Silvia know that I am banished?
Pro. Ay, ay; and she hath offer'd to the doom,
(Which, unrevers'd, stands in effectual force,)
A sea of melting pearl, which some call tears:
Those at her father's churlish feet she tender'd;
With them, upon her knees, her humble self;
Wringing her hands, whose whiteness so became them,
As if but now they waxed pale for woe:
But neither bended knees, pure hands held up,
Sad sighs, deep groans, nor silver-shedding tears,
Could penetrate her uncompassionate sire;
But Valentine, if he be ta'en, must die.
Besides, her intercession chaf'd him so
When she for thy repeal was suppliant,
That to close prison he commanded her,
With many bitter threats of 'biding there.
Val. No more; unless the next word that thou speak'st,
Have some malignant pow'r upon my life:
If so, I pray thee, breathe it in mine ear,
As ending anthem of my endless dolour.[1]
Pro. Cease to lament for that thou can'st not help,
And study help for that which thou lament'st.
Time is the nurse and breeder of all good.
Here if thou stay, thou canst not see thy love;
Besides, thy staying will abridge thy life.
Hope is a lover's staff; walk hence with that,
And manage it against despairing thoughts.
Thy letters may be here, though thou art hence;
Which, being writ to me, shall be deliver'd
Even in the milk-white bosom of thy love.[2]
The time now serves not to expostulate:
Come, I'll convey thee through the city gate;
And, ere I part with thee, confer at large
Of all that may concern thy love-affairs:
As thou lov'st Silvia, though not for thyself,
Regard thy danger, and along with me.
Val. I pray thee, Launce, an if thou seest my boy
Bid him make haste, and meet me at the north gate
Pro. Go, sirrah, find him out. Come, Valentine
Val. O my dear Silvia! hapless Valentine!
[*Exeunt* Valentine *and* Proteus

Laun. I am but a fool, look you; and yet I have the wit to think, my master is a kind of a knave: but that's all one, if he be but one knave. He lives not now, that knows me to be in love: yet I am in love; but a team of horse shall not pluck that from me; nor who 'tis I love, and yet 'tis a woman: but what woman, I will not tell myself: and yet 'tis a milk-maid: yet 'tis not a maid, for she hath had gossips[3]: yet 'tis a maid, for she is her master's maid, and serves for wages. She hath more qualities than a water-spaniel,—which is much in a bare[4] christian. Here is the cate-log [*Pulling out a paper*] of her condition.[5] Imprimis, *She can fetch and carry.* Why, a horse can do no more; nay, a horse cannot fetch, but only carry, therefore is she better than a jade. Item, *She can milk;* look you, a sweet virtue in a maid with clean hands.

Enter Speed.

Speed. How now, signior Launce? what news with your mastership?
Laun. With my master's ship? why it is at sea
Speed. Well, your old vice still, mistake the word
What news then in your paper?
Laun. The blackest news that ever thou heard'st
Speed. Why, man, how black?
Laun. Why, as black as ink.
Speed. Let me read them.
Laun. Fie on thee, jolt-head; thou canst not read.
Speed. Thou liest, I can.
Laun. I will try thee: Tell me this. Who begot thee?
Speed. Marry, the son of my grandfather.[6]
Laun. O illiterate loiterer! it was the son of thy grandmother: this proves that thou canst not read
Speed. Come, fool, come: try me in thy paper.
Laun. There: and saint Nicholas[7] be thy speed:
Speed. Imprimis, *She can milk.*
Laun. Ay, that she can.
Speed. Item, *She brews good ale.*
Laun. And therefore comes the proverb,—Blessing of your heart, you brew good ale.
Speed. Item, *She can sew.*
Laun. That's as much as to say, can she so?
Speed. Item, *She can knit.*
Laun. What need a man care for a stock with a wench, when she can knit him a stock.[8]
Speed. Item, *She can wash and scour.*

---

1 Grief.

2 So in Hamlet:
"These to her excellent white bosom."
To understand this mode of addressing letters, &c. it should be known that women anciently had a pocket in the forepart of their stays, in which they carried not only love letters and love tokens, but even their money, &c. In many parts of England rustic damsels still continue the practice. A very old lady informed Mr. Steevens, that when it was the fashion to wear very prominent stays it was the custom for stratagem or gallantry to drop its literary favours within the front of them.

3 *Gossips* not only signify those who answer for a child in baptism, but the tattling women who attend lyings-in. The quibble is evident.

4 *Bare*, has two senses, *mere* and *naked.* Launce, quibbling on, uses it in both senses, and opposes the naked female to the water-spaniel *covered with hairs of remarkable thickness.*

" *Condition*, honest behaviour or demeanour in living, a custume or facion. Mos. Moris, *facon de faire.*" *Baret.* The old copy reads *condition*, which was changed to *conditions* by *Rowe.*

6 It is undoubtedly true that the mother only knows the legitimacy of the child. Launce infers that if Speed could read, he must have read this well known observation.

7 *St. Nicholas* presided over scholars, who were therefore called St. Nicholas' clerks; either because the legend makes this saint to have been a bishop while yet a boy, or from his having restored three young scholars to life. By a quibble between *Nicholas* and *Old Nick* highwaymen are called Nicholas' clerks in Henry IV part 1. The *parish clerks* of London finding that *scholars*, more usually termed *clerks*, were under the patronage of this saint, conceived that *clerks* of any kind might have the same right, and accordingly took him as their patron, much in the same way as the woolcombers did St. Blaise, who was martyred with an instrument like a carding comb; the nailmakers St. *Clou*; and the booksellers St. John Port *Latin*

8 i. e. *stocking*

Laun. A special virtue; for then she need not be washed and scoured.

Speed. Item, *She can spin.*

Laun. Then may I set the world on wheels, when she can spin for her living.

Speed. Item, *She hath many nameless virtues.*

Laun. That's as much as to say, bastard virtues; that, indeed, know not their fathers, and therefore have no names.

Speed. *Here follow her vices.*

Laun. Close at the heels of her virtues.

Speed. Item, *She is not to be kissed fasting, in respect of her breath.*

Laun. Well, that fault may be mended with a breakfast: Read on.

Speed. Item, *She hath a sweet mouth.*[1]

Laun. That makes amends for her sour breath.

Speed. Item, *She doth talk in her sleep.*

Laun. It's no matter for that, so she sleep not in her talk.

Speed. Item, *She is slow in words.*

Laun. O villain, that set this down among her vices! To be slow in words, is a woman's only virtue: I pray thee, out with't; and place it for her chief virtue.

Speed. Item, *She is proud.*

Laun. Out with that too; it was Eve's legacy, and cannot be ta'en from her.

Speed. Item, *She hath no teeth.*

Laun. I care not for that neither, because I love crusts.

Speed. Item, *She is curst.*

Laun. Well, the best is, she hath no teeth to bite.

Speed. Item, *She will often praise her liquor.*

Laun. If her liquor be good, she shall: if she will not, I will; for good things should be praised.

Speed. Item, *She is too liberal.*[2]

Laun. Of her tongue she cannot; for that's writ down she is slow of: of her purse she shall not; for that I'll keep shut; now of another thing she may; and that cannot I help. Well, proceed.

Speed. Item, *She hath more hair than wit,*[3] *and more faults than hairs, and more wealth than faults.*

Laun. Stop there; I'll have her: she was mine, and not mine, twice or thrice in that last article: Rehearse that once more.

Speed. Item, *She hath more hair than wit.*—

Laun. More hair than wit,—it may be; I'll prove it: The cover of the salt hides the salt,[4] and therefore it is more than the salt; the hair that covers the wit, is more than the wit; for the greater hides the less. What's next?

Speed. *And more faults than hairs.*—

Laun. That's monstrous: O, that that were out!

Speed. *And more wealth than faults.*

Laun. Why, that word makes the faults gracious.[5] Well, I'll have her: and if it be a match, as nothing is impossible,—

Speed. What then?

Laun. Why, then will I tell thee, that thy master stays for thee at the north-gate.

Speed. For me?

Laun. For thee? ay; who art thou? he hath staid for a better man than thee.

Speed. And must I go to him?

Laun. Thou must run to him, for thou hast staid so long, that going will scarce serve the turn.

Speed. Why did'st not tell me sooner? 'pox of your love-letters! [*Exit.*

Laun. Now will he be swinged for reading my letter: An unmannerly slave, that will thrust himself into secrets! I'll after, to rejoice in the boy's correction.

SCENE II. *The same. A Room in the* Duke's *Palace. Enter* DUKE *and* THURIO; PROTEUS *behind.*

Duke. Sir Thurio, fear not, but that she will love you,
Now Valentine is banished from her sight.
Thu. Since his exile she has despis'd me most,
Forsworn my company, and rail'd at me,
That I am desperate of obtaining her.
Duke. This weak impress of love is as a figure
Trench'd[6] in ice; which with an hour's heat
Dissolves to water, and doth lose his form.
A little time will melt her frozen thoughts,
And worthless Valentine shall be forgot.—
How now, Sir Proteus? Is your countryman,
According to our proclamation, gone?
Pro. Gone, my good lord.
Duke. My daughter takes his going grievously.
Pro. A little time, my lord, will kill that grief.
Duke. So I believe; but Thurio thinks not so.—
Proteus, the good conceit I hold of thee,
(For thou hast shown some sign of good desert,)
Makes me the better to confer with thee.
Pro. Longer than I prove loyal to your grace,
Let me not live to look upon your grace.
Duke. Thou know'st, how willingly I would effect
The match between Sir Thurio and my daughter.
Pro. I do, my lord.
Duke. And also, I think, thou art not ignorant
How she opposes her against my will.
Pro. She did, my lord, when Valentine was here.
Duke. Ay, and perversely she persevers so.
What might we do, to make the girl forget
The love of Valentine, and love Sir Thurio?
Pro. The best way is to slander Valentine
With falsehood, cowardice, and poor descent;
Three things that women highly hold in hate.
Duke. Ay, but she'll think that it is spoke in hate.
Pro. Ay, if his enemy deliver it:
Therefore it must, with circumstance,[7] be spoken
By one, whom she esteemeth as his friend.
Duke. Then you must undertake to slander him.
Pro. And that, my lord, I shall be loth to do:
'Tis an ill office for a gentleman;
Especially against his very[8] friend.
Duke. Where your good word cannot advantage him,
Your slander never can endamage him;
Therefore the office is indifferent,
Being entreated to it by your friend.
Pro. You have prevail'd, my lord: if I can do it,
By aught that I can speak in his dispraise,
She shall not long continue love to him.
But say, this weed her love from Valentine,
It follows not that she will love Sir Thurio.
Thu. Therefore, as you unwind her love from him,
Lest it should ravel, and be good to none,
You must provide to bottom it on me:[9]
Which must be done, by praising me as much
As you in worth dispraise Sir Valentine.

---

1 Speed uses the term *a sweet mouth* in the sense of *a sweet tooth*; but Launce chooses to understand it in the literal and lauditory sense. Cotgrave renders "*Friand, A sweet-lips*, daintie-mouthed, sweet-toothed," &c.

2 *Liberal* is *licentious*, *free*, *frank*, beyond honesty or decency. Thus in Othello, Desdemonda says of Iago: "is he not a most profane and *liberal* counsellor."

3 This was an old familiar proverb, of which Steevens has given many examples. I will add one from Florio: "A tisty-tosty wag feather, *more haire than wit.*"

4 The ancient English *salt-cellar* was very different from the modern, being a large piece of plate, generally ornamented with a cover to keep the salt clean. There was but one on the dinner table, which was placed near the top, and those who sat below it were, for the most part, of inferior condition to those who sat above it.

5 *Gracious* was sometimes used for *favoured, countenanced*, like the Italian *Gratiato*, v. As you Like It, Act i. Sc. 2.

6 i. e. *cut*, *carved*; from the Fr *trancher*.

7 i. e. with the addition of such incidental particulars as may induce belief.

8 *Very*, that is, *true*; from the Lat. *verus*. Massinger calls one of his plays "A *Very* Woman."

9 As you unwind her love from him, make me the *bottom* on which you wind it. A bottom is the housewife's term for a ball of thread wound upon a central body

Duke. And, Proteus, we dare trust you in this kind;
Because we know, on Valentine's report,
You are already love's firm votary,
And cannot soon revolt and change your mind.
Upon this warrant shall you have access,
Where you with Silvia may confer at large;
For she is lumpish, heavy, melancholy,
And, for your friend's sake, will be glad of you;
Where you may temper her, by your persuasion,
To hate young Valentine, and love my friend.
Pro. As much as I can do, I will effect:—
But you, Sir Thurio, are not sharp enough;
You must lay lime,[1] to tangle her desires,
By wailful sonnets, whose composed rhymes,
Should be full fraught with serviceable vows.
Duke. Ay, much is the force of heaven-bred poesy.
Pro. Say, that upon the altar of her beauty
You sacrifice your tears, your sighs, your heart:
Write till your ink be dry; and with your tears
Moist it again; and frame some feeling line,
That may discover such integrity:[2]—
For Orpheus' lute was strung with poets' sinews;
Whose golden touch could soften steel and stones,
Make tigers tame, and huge leviathans
Forsake unsounded deeps to dance on sands.
After your dire-lamenting elegies,
Visit by night your lady's chamber window
With some sweet consort:[3] to their instruments
Tune a deploring dump;[4] the night's dead silence
Will well become such sweet complaining grievance.
This, or else nothing, will inherit her.[5]
Duke. This discipline shews thou hast been in love.
Thu. And thy advice this night I'll put in practice:
Therefore, sweet Proteus, my direction-giver,
Let us into the city presently
To sort[6] some gentlemen well skill'd in music:
I have a sonnet, that will serve the turn,
To give the onset to thy good advice.
Duke. About it, gentlemen.
Pro. We'll wait upon your grace till after supper:
And afterward determine our proceedings.
Duke. Even now about it; I will pardon you.
[*Exeunt.*

ACT IV.

SCENE I.—*A Forest, near* Mantua. *Enter certain* Out-laws.

1 *Out.* Fellows, stand fast; I see a passenger.
2 *Out.* If there be ten, shrink not, but down with'em.

Enter VALENTINE *and* SPEED.

3 *Out.* Stand, sir, and throw us that you have about you;
If not, we'll make you sit, and rifle you.
Speed. Sir, we are undone! these are the villains
That all the travellers do fear so much.
Val. My friends,—
1 *Out.* That's not so, sir; we are your enemies.
2 *Out.* Peace; we'll hear him.
3 *Out.* Ay, by my beard, will we; for he is a proper[7] man.
Val. Then know, that I have little wealth to lose;
A man I am, cross'd with adversity:
My riches are these poor habiliments,
Of which if you should here disfurnish me,
You take the sum and substance that I have.
2 *Out.* Whither travel you?
Val. To Verona.
1 *Out.* Whence came you?
Val. From Milan.
3 *Out.* Have you long sojourned there?
Val. Some sixteen months; and longer might have staid,
If crooked fortune had not thwarted me.
1 *Out.* What, were you banish'd thence?
Val. I was.
2 *Out.* For what offence?
Val. For that which now torments me to rehearse:
I kill'd a man, whose death I must repent;
But yet I slew him manfully in fight,
Without false vantage, or base treachery.
1 *Out.* Why ne'er repent it, if it were done so,
But were you banish'd for so small a fault?
Val. I was, and held me glad of such a doom.
1 *Out.* Have you the tongues?
Val. My youthful travel therein made me happy,
Or else I often had been miserable.
3 *Out.* By the bare scalp of Robin Hood's fat friar,[8]
This fellow were a king for our wild faction.
1 *Out.* We'll have him; sirs, a word.
Speed. Master, be one of them;
It is an honourable kind of thievery.
Val. Peace, villain!
2 *Out.* Tell us this: have you any thing to take to?
Val. Nothing but my fortune.
3 *Out.* Know, then, that some of us are gentlemen,
Such as the fury of ungovern'd youth
Thrust from the company of awful[9] men:
Myself was from Verona banish'd,
For practising to steal away a lady,
An heir, and near allied unto the duke.
2 *Out.* And I from Mantua, for a gentleman,
Whom, in my mood,[10] I stabbed unto the heart.
1 *Out.* And I, for such like petty crimes as these.
But to the purpose,—(for we cite our faults,
That they may hold excus'd our lawless lives,)
And, partly, seeing you are beautify'd
With goodly shape; and by your own report
A linguist, and a man of such perfection,
As we do in our quality[11] much want;—
2 *Out.* Indeed, because you are a banish'd man
Therefore, above the rest, we parley to you:
Are you content to be our general?
To make a virtue of necessity,
And live, as we do, in this wilderness?
3 *Out.* What say'st thou? wilt thou be of our consort?
Say ay, and be the captain of us all;
We'll do thee homage, and be rul'd by thee,
Love thee as our commander and our king.
1 *Out.* But if thou scorn our courtesy, thou diest
2 *Out.* Thou shalt not live to brag what we have offer'd.
Val. I take your offer, and will live with you;
Provided that you do no outrages
On silly women, or poor passengers.
3 *Out.* No, we detest such vile base practices.
Come, go with us, we'll bring thee to our crews,
And shew thee all the treasure we have got;
Which, with ourselves, all rest at thy dispose.
[*Exeunt*

1 i. e. *birdlime.*

2 i. e. sincerity, such as would be manifested by such impassioned writing. Malone suspects that a line following this has been lost.

3 The old copy has *consort*, which, according to Bullokar and Philips, signified "a set or company of musicians." If we print *concert*, as Malone would have it, the relative pronoun *their* has no correspondent word. It is true that Shakspeare frequently refers to words not expressed, but implied in the former part of a sentence. But the reference here is to *consort*, as appears by the subsequent words, "to *their* instruments."

4 *A dump* was the ancient term for a *mournful elegy*

5 To *inherit* is sometimes used by Shakspeare for *to obtain possession of*, without any idea of acquiring by inheritance. Milton in Comus has *disinherit* Chaos meaning only to *dispossess it.*

6 To *sort, to choose out.*

7 A *proper* man, was a comely, tall, or well proportioned man. *Uomo di bel taglio.*

8 Friar Tuck, one of the associates of Robin Hood.

9 *Awful* men, men full of awe and respect for the laws of society, and the duties of life

10 *Mood* is anger or resentment.

11 i. e. Condition, profession, occupation, v Hamlet Act ii. Sc. 2.

SCENE II.—Milan. *Court of the Palace.* *Enter* PROTEUS.

Pro. Already have I been false to Valentine,
And now I must be as unjust to Thurio.
Under the colour of commending him,
I have access my own love to prefer;
But Silvia is too fair, too true, too holy,
To be corrupted with my worthless gifts.
When I protest true loyalty to her,
She twits me with my falsehood to my friend;
When to her beauty I commend my vows,
She bids me think, how I have been forsworn
In breaking faith with Julia whom I lov'd:
And, notwithstanding all her sudden quips,[1]
The least whereof would quell a lover's hope,
Yet, spaniel-like, the more she spurns my love,
The more it grows and fawneth on her still.
But here comes Thurio; now must we to her window,
And give some evening music to her ear.

Enter THURIO, *and Musicians.*

Thu. How now, Sir Proteus? are you crept before us?
Pro. Ay, gentle Thurio; for, you know, that love
Will creep in service where it cannot go.
Thu. Ay, but, I hope, sir, that you love not here.
Pro. Sir, but I do; or else I would be hence.
Thu. Who? Silvia?
Pro. Ay, Silvia,—for your sake.
Thu. I thank you for your own. Now, gentlemen,
Let's tune, and to it lustily awhile.

Enter Host, *at a distance; and* JULIA *in boy's clothes.*

Host. Now, my young guest! methinks you're allycholly; I pray you, why is it?

Jul. Marry, mine host, because I cannot be merry.

Host. Come, we'll have you merry: I'll bring you where you shall hear music, and see the gentleman that you ask'd for.

Jul. But shall I hear him speak?
Host. Ay, that you shall.
Jul. That will be music. [*Music plays.*
Host. Hark! hark!
Jul. Is he among these?
Host. Ay: but peace, lets hear 'em.

SONG.

Who is Sylvia? What is she?
That all our swains commend her?
Holy, fair, and wise is she;
The heavens such grace did lend her,
That she might admired be.

Is she kind, as she is fair?
For beauty lives with kindness:
Love doth to her eyes repair,
To help him of his blindness;
And, being help'd, inhabits there.

Then to Silvia let us sing,
That Silvia is excelling;
She excels each mortal thing,
Upon the dull earth dwelling:
To her let us garlands bring.

Host. How now? are you sadder than you were before?
How do you, man? the music likes you not.
Jul. You mistake; the musician likes me not.
Host. Why, my pretty youth?
Jul. He plays false, father.
Host. How? out of tune on the strings?

Jul. Not so; but yet so false that he grieves my very heart-strings.

Host. You have a quick ear.

Jul. Ay, I would I were deaf! it makes me have a slow heart.

Host. I perceive, you delight not in music.
Jul. Not a whit, when it jars so.
Host. Hark, what fine change is in the music!
Jul. Ay; that change is the spite.

Host. You would have them always play but one thing?

Jul. I would always have one play but one thing. But, host, doth this Sir Proteus, that we talk on, often resort unto this gentlewoman?

Host. I tell you what Launce, his man, told me, he loved her out of all nick.[2]

Jul. Where is Launce?

Host. Gone to seek his dog; which, to-morrow, by his master's command, he must carry for a present to his lady.

Jul. Peace! stand aside! the company parts.
Pro. Sir Thurio, fear not you! I will so plead,
That you shall say, my cunning drift excels.
Thu. Where meet we?
Pro. At Saint Gregory's well.
Thu. Farewell. [*Exeunt* THU. *and Musicians.*

SILVIA *appears above, at her window.*

Pro. Madam, good even to your ladyship.
Sil. I thank you for your music, gentlemen:
Who is that, that spake?
Pro. One, lady, if you knew his pure heart's truth,
You'd quickly learn to know him by his voice.
Sil. Sir Proteus, as I take it.
Pro. Sir Proteus, gentle lady, and your servant.
Sil. What is your will?
Pro. That I may compass yours.
Sil. You have your wish; my will is even this,—
That presently you hie you home to bed.
Thou subtle, perjur'd, false, disloyal man!
Think'st thou, I am so shallow, so conceitless,
To be seduced by thy flattery,
That hast deceiv'd so many with thy vows
Return, return, and make thy love amends.
For me,—by this pale queen of night I swear
I am so far from granting thy request,
That I despise thee for thy wrongful suit;
And by and by intend to chide myself,
Even for this time I spend in talking to thee.
Pro. I grant, sweet love, that I did love a lady;
But she is dead.
Jul. 'Twere false, if I should speak it;
For, I am sure, she is not buried. [*Aside.*
Sil. Say, that she be; yet Valentine, thy friend,
Survives; to whom, thyself art witness,
I am betroth'd: And art thou not asham'd
To wrong him with thy importunacy?
Pro. I likewise hear, that Valentine is dead.
Sil. And so suppose am I; for in his grave,
Assure thyself, my love is buried.
Pro. Sweet lady, let me rake it from the earth.
Sil. Go to thy lady's grave, and call her's thence;
Or, at the least, in her's sepulchre thine.
Jul. He heard not that. [*Aside*
Pro. Madam, if your heart be so obdurate,
Vouchsafe me yet your picture for my love,
The picture that is hanging in your chamber;
To that I'll speak, to that I'll sigh and weep
For, since the substance of your perfect self
Is else devoted, I am but a shadow;
And to your shadow will I make true love.
Jul. If 'twere a substance, you would, sure, deceive it,
And make it but a shadow, as I am. [*Aside.*
Sil. I am very loth to be your idol, sir;
But, since your falsehood shall become you well
To worship shadows, and adore false shapes,
Send to me in the morning and I'll send it:
And so good rest.
Pro. As wretches have o'ernight,
That wait for execution in the morn.
[*Exeunt* PROTEUS; *and* SILVIA *from above.*
Jul. Host, will you go?
Host. By my halidom,[3] I was fast asleep.

1 *Sudden quips*, hasty, passionate reproaches.

2 i. e. Out of all reckoning or count; reckonings were kept upon nicked or notched sticks or tallies.

3 *Halidom*, (says Minsheu,) an old word, used by old countrywomen by manner of swearing.

Jul. Pray you, where lies Sir Proteus?
Host. Marry, at my house: Trust me, I think 'tis almost day.
Jul. Not so; but it hath been the longest night
That e'er I watch'd, and the most heaviest.[1]
[*Exeunt.*

SCENE III. *The same. Enter* EGLAMOUR.

Egl. This is the hour that madam Silvia
Entreated me to call and know her mind:
There's some great matter she'd employ me in.—
Madam, madam!

SILVIA *appears above, at her window.*

Sil. Who calls?
Egl. Your servant, and your friend;
One that attends your ladyship's command.
Sil. Sir Eglamour, a thousand times good-morrow.
Egl. As many, worthy lady, to yourself.
According to your ladyship's impose,[2]
I am thus early come, to know what service
It is your pleasure to command me in.
Sil. O Eglamour, thou art a gentleman,
(Think not, I flatter, for I swear, I do not,)
Valiant, wise, remorseful,[3] well accomplish'd.
Thou art not ignorant, what dear good-will
I bear unto the banish'd Valentine;
Nor how my father would enforce me marry
Vain Thurio, whom my very soul abhorr'd.
Thyself hast lov'd; and I have heard thee say,
No grief did ever come so near thy heart,
As when thy lady and thy true love died,
Upon whose grave thou vow'dst pure chastity.[4]
Sir Eglamour, I would to Valentine,
To Mantua, where, I hear, he makes abode;
And, for the ways are dangerous to pass,
I do desire thy worthy company,
Upon whose faith and honour I repose.
Urge not my father's anger, Eglamour,
But think upon my grief, a lady's grief;
And on the justice of my flying hence,
To keep me from a most unholy match,
Which heaven and fortune still reward with plagues.
I do desire thee, even from a heart
As full of sorrows as the sea of sands,
To bear me company, and go with me:
If not, to hide what I have said to thee,
That I may venture to depart alone.
Egl. Madam, I pity much your grievances;[5]
Which since I know they virtuously are placed,
I give consent to go along with you;
Recking[6] as little what betideth me,
As much I wish all good befortune you.
When will you go?
Sil. This evening coming.
Egl. Where shall I meet you?
Sil. At friar Patrick's cell,
Where I intend holy confession.
Egl. I will not fail your ladyship:
Good-morrow, gentle lady.
Sil. Good-morrow, kind Sir Eglamour.
[*Exeunt.*

SCENE IV. *The same. Enter* LAUNCE, *with his Dog.*

When a man's servant shall play the cur with him, look you, it goes hard: one that I brought up of a puppy; one that I saved from drowning, when three or four of his blind brothers and sisters went to it! I have taught him—even as one would say precisely, Thus I would teach a dog. I was sent to deliver him, as a present to mistress Silvia, from my master; and I came no sooner into the dining-chamber, but he steps me to her trencher, and steals her capon's leg. O, 'tis a foul thing, when a cur cannot keep[7] himself in all companies! I would have, as one should say, one that takes upon him to be a dog indeed, to be, as it were, a dog at all things. If I had not had more wit than he, to take a fault upon me that he did, I think verily he had been hanged for't: sure as I live, he had suffer'd for't: you shall judge. He thrusts me himself into the company of three or four gentleman-like dogs, under the duke's table: he had not been there (bless the mark) a pissing while; but all the chamber smelt him. *Out with the dog,* says one; *What cur is that?* says another; *Whip him out,* says the third; *Hang him up,* says the duke. I, having been acquainted with the smell before, knew it was Crab; and goes me to the fellow that whips the dogs: *Friend,* quoth I, *you mean to whip the dog? Ay, marry, do I,* quoth he. *You do him the more wrong,* quoth I; *'twas I did the thing you wot of.* He makes me no more ado, but whips me out of the chamber. How many masters would do this for their servant? Nay, I'll be sworn, I have sat in the stocks for puddings he hath stolen, otherwise he had been executed: I have stood on the pillory for geese he hath killed, otherwise he had suffered for't: thou think'st not of this now!—Nay, I remember the trick you served me, when I took my leave of madame Silvia: did not I bid thee still mark me, and do as I do? When didst thou see me heave up my leg, and make water against a gentlewoman's farthingale? didst thou ever see me do such a trick?

Enter PROTEUS *and* JULIA.

Pro. Sebastian is thy name? I like thee well,
And will employ thee in some service presently.
Jul. In what you please;—I will do what I can.
Pro. I hope, thou wilt.—How now, you whoreson peasant! [*To* LAUNCE.
Where have you been these two days loitering?
Laun. Marry, sir, I carried mistress Silvia the dog you bade me.
Pro. And what says she to my little jewel?
Laun. Marry, she says, your dog was a cur; and tells you, currish thanks is good enough for such a present.
Pro. But she received my dog?
Laun. No, indeed, did she not: here have I brought him back again.
Pro. What, didst thou offer her this from me?
Laun. Ay, sir; the other squirrel was stolen from me by the hangman's boys in the market-place: and then I offered her mine own; who is a dog as big as ten of yours, and therefore the gift the greater.
Pro. Go, get thee hence, and find my dog again
Or ne'er return again into my sight.
Away, I say: Stay'st thou to vex me here?
A slave, that, still an end[8] turns me to shame.
[*Exit* LAUNCE.
Sebastian, I have entertained thee,
Partly, that I have need of such a youth,
That can with some discretion do my business
For 'tis no trusting to yon foolish lowt;
But, chiefly for thy face and thy behaviour:
Which (if my augury deceive me not)

---

1 The double superlative is very often used by the writers of Shakspeare's time.

2 *Impose* is *injunction, command;* a task set at college in consequence of a fault is still called an *imposition.*

3 i. e. *pitiful.*

4 It was common in former ages for widowers and widows to make vows of chastity in honour of their deceased wives or husbands. Besides observing the vow, the widow was, for life, to wear a veil, and a mourning habit. The same distinction may have been made in respect of male votarists; this circumstance might inform the players how Sir Eglamour should be dressed; and will account for Silvia's having chosen him as a person in whom she could confide without injury to her character.

5 In Shakspeare's time *griefs* frequently signified grievances; and the present instance shows that in return *grievance* was sometimes used in the sense of *grief.*

6 *To reck* is *to care for.* So in Hamlet: "And *recks* not his own read."

7 i. e. *restrain.*

8 *Still an end,* and *most an end,* are vulgar expressions, and mean *perpetually, generally.* See *Gifford's Massinger,* iv. 282.

"Now help, good heaven! 'tis such an uncouth thing
To be a widow out of Term-time! I
Do feel such aguish qualms, and dumps, and fits,
And shakings *still an end.*" *The Ordinary.*

Witness good bringing up, fortune, and truth:
Therefore know thou, for this I entertain thee.
Go presently and take this ring with thee,
Deliver it to madam Silvia:
She loved me well deliver'd it to me.
Jul. It seems you loved her not, to leave her token:
She's dead, belike.
Pro. Not so; I think she lives.
Jul. Alas!
Pro. Why dost thou cry, alas?
Jul. I cannot choose but pity her.
Pro. Wherefore should'st thou pity her?
Jul. Because, methinks, that she lov'd you as well
As you do love your lady Silvia:
She dreams on him that has forgot her love;
You dote on her that cares not for your love.
'Tis pity, love should be so contrary:
And thinking on it makes me cry, alas!
Pro. Well, give her that ring, and therewithal
This letter;—that's her chamber.—Tell my lady,
I claim the promise for her heavenly picture.
Your message done, hie home unto my chamber,
Where thou shalt find me sad and solitary.
[*Exit* PROTEUS.
Jul. How many women would do such a message?
Alas, poor Proteus! thou hast entertained
A fox, to be the shepherd of thy lambs:
Alas, poor fool! why do I pity him
That with his very heart despiseth me?
Because he loves her, he despiseth me;
Because I love him, I must pity him.
This ring I gave him, when he parted from me,
To bind him to remember my good-will:
And now am I (unhappy messenger!)
To plead for that, which I would not obtain;
To carry that which I would have refus'd;
To praise his faith which I would have disprais'd.
I am my master's true confirmed love;
But cannot be true servant to my master,
Unless I prove false traitor to myself.
Yet I will woo for him: but yet so coldly,
As, heaven it knows, I would not have him speed.

Enter SILVIA, *attended.*

Gentlewoman, good day! I pray you be my mean
To bring me where to speak with madam Silvia.
Sil. What would you with her, if that I be she?
Jul. If you be she, I do entreat your patience
To hear me speak the message I am sent on.
Sil. From whom?
Jul. From my master, Sir Proteus, madam.
Sil. O!—he sends you for a picture?
Jul. Ay, madam.
Sil. Ursula, bring my picture there.
[*Picture brought.*
Go, give your master this: tell him from me,
One Julia, that his changing thoughts forget,
Would better fit his chamber than this shadow.
Jul. Madam, please you peruse this letter.—
Pardon me, madam; I have unadvis'd
Deliver'd you a paper that I should not;
This is the letter to your ladyship.
Sil. I pray thee let me look on that again.
Jul. It may not be; good madam, pardon me.
Sil. There, hold.
I will not look upon your master's lines.
I know they are stuff'd with protestations,
And full of new-found oaths; which he will break
As easily as I do tear his paper.
Jul. Madam, he sends your ladyship this ring.
Sil. The more shame for him that he sends it me;
For, I have heard him say a thousand times,
His Julia gave it him at his departure:
Though his false finger hath profan'd the ring,
Mine shall not do his Julia so much wrong.
Jul. She thanks you.
Sil. What say'st thou?
Jul. I thank you, madam, that you tender her
Poor gentlewoman! my master wrongs her much.
Sil. Dost thou know her?
Jul. Almost as well as I do know myself:
To think upon her woes, I do protest,
That I have wept a hundred several times.
Sil. Belike, she thinks that Proteus hath forsook her.
Jul. I think she doth, and that's her cause of sorrow.
Sil. Is she not passing fair?
Jul. She hath been fairer, madam, than she is.
When she did think my master lov'd her well,
She, in my judgment, was as fair as you;
But since she did neglect her looking-glass,
And threw her sun-expelling mask away,
The air hath starv'd the roses in her cheeks,
And pinch'd the lily-tincture of her face,
That now she is become as black as I.
Sil. How tall was she?
Jul. About my stature: for, at Pentecost,
When all our pageants of delight were play'd,
Our youth got me to play the woman's part,
And I was trimm'd in madam Julia's gown,
Which served me as fit, by all men's judgment,
As if the garment had been made for me;
Therefore, I know she is about my height.
And, at that time, I made her weep a good,[1]
For I did play a lamentable part:
Madam, 'twas Ariadne, passioning[2]
For Theseus' perjury, and unjust flight,
Which I so lively acted with my tears,
That my poor mistress, moved therewithal,
Wept bitterly; and, would I might be dead,
If I in thought felt not her very sorrow!
Sil. She is beholden to thee, gentle youth!—
Alas, poor lady! desolate and left!—
I weep myself, to think upon thy words.
Here, youth, there is my purse; I give thee this
For thy sweet mistress' sake, because thou lov'st her.
Farewell. [*Exit* SILVIA.
Jul. And she shall thank you for't, if e'er you know her.—
A virtuous gentlewoman, mild, and beautiful.
I hope my master's suit will be but cold,
Since she respects my mistress' love so much
Alas, how love can trifle with itself!
Here is her picture: Let me see; I think,
If I had such a tire, this face of mine
Were full as lovely as is this of hers:
And yet the painter flatter'd her a little,
Unless I flatter with myself too much.
Her hair is auburn, mine is perfect yellow
If that be all the difference in his love,
I'll get me such a colour'd periwig.[3]
Her eyes are grey as glass;[4] and so are mine
Ay, but her forehead's low, and mine's as high
What should it be, that he respects in her,
But I can make respective[6] in myself,
If this fond love were not a blinded god?
Come, shadow, come, and take this shadow up,
For 'tis thy rival. O thou senseless form,
Thou shalt be worshipp'd, kiss'd, lov'd, and ador'd;
And, were there sense in this idolatry,
My substance should be statue[7] in thy stead.

---

1 i. e. *in good earnest*, tout de bon.

2 To *passion* was used as a verb formerly.

3 False hair was worn by the ladies long before *wigs* were in fashion. So, in 'Northward Hoe,' 1607, "There is a new trade come up for cast gentlewomen of periwig making." *Perwickes* are mentioned by Churchyard in one of his earliest poems. And Barnabe Rich, in 'The Honestie of this Age,' 1615, has a philippic against this folly.

4 By *grey* eyes were meant what we now call *blue* eyes. Grey, when applied to the eyes is rendered by Coles, in his Dictionary, 1679, *Ceruleus*, *glaucus*

5 A high forehead was then accounted a feature eminently beautiful. Our author, in The Tempest, shows that low foreheads were in disesteem.
——— with foreheads *villanous low*.

6 *Respective*, i. e. *considerative*, *regardful*, v. Merchant of Venice, Act v. Sc. 1.

7 The word *statue* was formerly used to express a *portrait*, and sometimes a *statue* was called a *picture* Stowe says (speaking of Elizabeth's funeral,) that when the people beheld "her *statue* or *picture* lying upon the coffin, there was a general sighing." Thus in the 'City Madam,' by Massinger, Sir John Frugal de

I'll use thee kindly for thy mistress sake.
That us'd me so; or else by Jove I vow,
I should have scratch'd out your unseeing eyes,
To make my master out of love with thee. [*Exit.*

ACT V.

SCENE I.—*The same. An Abbey. Enter* EGLAMOUR.

Egl. The sun begins to gild the western sky;
And now it is about the very hour
That Silvia, at friar Patrick's cell, should meet me.
She will not fail; for lovers break not hours,
Unless it be to come before their time;
So much they spur their expedition.

Enter SILVIA.

See, where she comes; Lady, a happy evening!
Sil. Amen, amen! go on, good Eglamour!
Out at the postern by the abbey wall;
I fear I am attended by some spies.
Egl. Fear not: the forest is not three leagues off:
If we recover that, we are sure enough. [*Exeunt.*

SCENE II.—*The same. A Room in the* Duke's *Palace. Enter* THURIO, PROTEUS, *and* JULIA.

Thu. Sir Proteus, what says Silvia to my suit?
Pro. O, sir, I find her milder than she was;
And yet she takes exceptions at your person.
Thu. What, that my leg is too long?
Pro. No; that it is too little.
Thu. I'll wear a boot, to make it somewhat rounder.
Pro. But love will not be spurr'd to what it loaths.[1]
Thu. What says she to my face?
Pro. She says it is a fair one.
Thu. Nay, then the wanton lies; my face is black.
Pro. But pearls are fair; and the old saying is,
Black men are pearls in beauteous ladies' eyes.
Jul. 'Tis true; such pearls as put out ladies eyes;
For I had rather wink than look on them. [*Aside.*
Thu. How likes she my discourse?
Pro. Ill, when you talk of war.
Thu. But well, when I discourse of love and peace?
Jul. But better indeed, when you hold your peace. [*Aside.*
Thu. What says she to my valour?
Pro. O, sir, she makes no doubt of that.
Jul. She needs not, when she knows it cowardice. [*Aside.*
Thu. What says she to my birth?
Pro. That you are well deriv'd.
Jul. True, from a gentleman to a fool. [*Aside.*
Thu. Considers she my possessions?
Pro. O, ay; and pities them.
Thu. Wherefore?
Jul. That such an ass should owe[2] them. [*Aside.*
Pro. That they are out by lease.[3]
Jul. Here comes the Duke.

Enter DUKE.

Duke. How now, Sir Proteus? how now, Thurio?
Which of you saw Sir Eglamour of late?
Thu. Not I.
Pro. Nor I.
Duke. Saw you my daughter?
Pro. Neither.
Duke. Why, then she's fled unto that peasant Valentine;
And Eglamour is in her company.
'Tis true; for friar Laurence met them both,
As he in penance wander'd through the forest;
Him he knew well, and guess'd that it was she.
But, being mask'd, he was not sure of it:
Besides, she did intend confession
At Patrick's cell this even: and there she was not
These likelihoods confirm her flight from hence.
Therefore, I pray you, stand not to discourse,
But mount you presently; and meet with me
Upon the rising of the mountain foot
That leads towards Mantua, whither they are fled
Despatch, sweet gentlemen, and follow me. [*Exit.*
Thu. Why, this it is to be a peevish[4] girl,
That flies her fortune when it follows her:
I'll after; more to be reveng'd on Eglamour,
Than for the love of reckless[5] Silvia. [*Exu.*
Pro. And I will follow, more for Silvia's love,
Than hate of Eglamour that goes with her. [*Exit*
Jul. And I will follow more to cross that love,
Than hate for Silvia, that is gone for love. [*Exit*

SCENE III.—*Frontiers of* Mantua. *The Forest Enter* SILVIA, *and* Out-laws.

Out. Come, come;
Be patient, we must bring you to our captain.
Sil. A thousand more mischances than this one
Have learn'd me how to brook this patiently.
2 *Out.* Come, bring her away.
1 *Out.* Where is the gentleman that was with her?
3 *Out.* Being nimble-footed, he hath outrun us,
But Moyses and Valerius follow him.
Go thou with her to the west end of the wood,
There is our captain: we'll follow him that's fled:
The thicket is beset, he cannot 'scape.
1 *Out.* Come, I must bring you to our captain's cave:
Fear not; he bears an honorable mind,
And will not use a woman lawlessly.
Sil. O Valentine, this I endure for thee!
[*Exeunt*

SCENE IV. *Another part of the Forest Enter* VALENTINE.

Val. How use doth breed a habit in a man!
This shadowy desert, unfrequented woods,
I better brook than flourishing peopled towns·
Here can I sit alone, unseen of any,
And, to the nightingale's complaining notes,
Tune my distresses, and record[6] my woes.
O thou that dost inhabit in my breast,
Leave not the mansion so long tenantless;
Lest, growing ruinous, the building fall,
And leave no memory of what it was![7]
Repair me with thy presence, Silvia;
Thou gentle nymph, cherish thy forlorn swain!—
What halloing, and what stir, is this to-day?
These are my mates, that make their wills their law,
Have some unhappy passenger in chase:
They love me well; yet I have much to do
To keep them from uncivil outrages.
Withdraw thee, Valentine; who's this comes here?
[*Steps aside.*

Enter PROTEUS, SILVIA, *and* JULIA.

Pro. Madam, this service I have done for you,
(Though you respect not aught your servant doth)

---

sires that his daughters may take leave of their lovers' *statues*, though he had previously described them as pictures, which they evidently were.

1 Mr. Boswell thought that this line should be given to Julia, as well as a subsequent one, and that they were meant to be spoken aside. They are exactly in the style of her other sarcastic speeches; and Proteus, who is playing on Thurio's credulity, would hardly represent him as an object of *loathing* to Silvia.

2 i. e. possess them, *own them.*

3 By Thurio's *possessions* he himself understands his lands. But Proteus chooses to take the word likewise in a figurative sense, as signifying his *mental endowments*, and when he says they are *out by lease*, he means, that they are no longer enjoyed by their master (who is a fool,) but are leased out to another. *Edinburgh Magazine, Nov.* 1786.

4 *Peevish* in ancient language signified *foolish*

5 i. e. *careless, heedless.*

6 To *record*, anciently signified to *sing*. It is still used by bird fanciers to express the first essays of a bird to sing; and is evidently derived from the *recorder* or pipe with which they were formerly taught.

7 "O thou that dost inhabit in my breast,
Leave not the mansion so long tenantless;
Lest growing ruinous, the building fall,
And leave no memory of what it was."

It is hardly possible (says Steevens) to point out fou lines in Shakspeare more remarkable for ease and ele gance than the preceding

To hazard life, and rescue you from him
That would have forced your honour and your love.
Vouchsafe me, for my meed, but one fair look;
A smaller boon than this I cannot beg,
And less than this, I'm sure you cannot give.

Val. How like a dream is this I see and hear!
Love, lend me patience to forbear a while. [*Aside.*

Sil. O miserable, unhappy that I am!

Pro. Unhappy were you, madam, ere I came;
But, by my coming, I have made you happy.

Sil. By thy approach thou mak'st me most unhappy.

Jul. And me, when he approacheth to your presence. [*Aside.*

Sil. Had I been seized by a hungry lion,
I would have been a breakfast to the beast,
Rather than have false Proteus rescue me.
O, heaven be judge, how I love Valentine,
Whose life's as tender[1] to me as my soul;
And full as much (for more there cannot be)
I do detest false perjur'd Proteus:
Therefore begone, solicit me no more.

Pro. What dangerous action, stood it next to death,
Would I not undergo for one calm look?
O, 'tis the curse in love, and still approv'd,[2]
When women cannot love where they're belov'd.

Sil. When Proteus cannot love where he's belov'd.
Read over Julia's heart, thy first best love,
For whose dear sake thou didst then rend thy faith
Into a thousand oaths; and all those oaths
Descended into perjury, to love me.
Thou hast no faith left now,[3] unless thou hadst two,
And that's far worse than none; better have none
Than plural faith, which is too much by one:
Thou counterfeit to thy true friend!

Pro. In love,
Who respects friends?

Sil. All men but Proteus.

Pro. Nay, if the gentle spirit of moving words
Can no way change you to a milder form,
I'll woo you like a soldier, at arms' end;
And love you 'gainst the nature of love, force ye.

Sil. O heaven!

Pro. I'll force thee yield to my desire.

Val. Ruffian, let go that rude uncivil touch;
Thou friend of an ill fashion.

Pro. Valentine!

Val. Thou common friend, that's without faith or love,
(For such is a friend now,) treacherous man!
Thou hast beguil'd my hopes; nought but mine eye
Could have persuaded me: Now I dare not say
I have one friend alive; thou would'st disprove me.
Who should be trusted now, when one's right hand
Is perjur'd to the bosom? Proteus,
I am sorry I must never trust thee more,
But count the world a stranger for thy sake.
The private wound is deepest: O time most accurst!
'Mongst all foes, that a friend should be the worst!

Pro. My shame and guilt confound me.—
Forgive me, Valentine: if hearty sorrow
Be a sufficient ransom for offence,
I tender it here; I do as truly suffer,
As e'er I did commit.

Val. Then I am paid;
And once again I do receive thee honest:—
Who by repentance is not satisfied,
Is nor of heaven, nor earth; for these are pleas'd;
By penitence th' Eternal's wrath's appeas'd:—
And, that my love may appear plain and free,
All that was mine in Silvia, I give thee.

Jul. O me, unhappy! [*Faints.*

Pro. Look to the boy.

Val. Why, boy! why, wag! how now? what is the matter? Look up; speak.

Jul. O good sir, my master charg'd me to deliver a ring to Madam Silvia; which, out of my neglect was never done.

Pro. Where is that ring, boy?

Jul. Here 'tis: this is it. [*Gives a ring.*

Pro. How! let me see: why this is the ring I gave to Julia.

Jul. O, cry you mercy, sir, I have mistook; this is the ring you sent to Silvia. [*Shows another ring.*

Pro. But, how cam'st thou by this ring? at my depart, I gave this unto Julia.

Jul. And Julia herself did give it me:
And Julia herself hath brought it hither.

Pro. How! Julia!

Jul. Behold her that gave aim[4] to all thy oaths,
And entertain'd them deeply in her heart:
How oft hast thou with perjury cleft the root?[5]
O Proteus, let this habit make thee blush!
Be thou asham'd, that I have took upon me
Such an immodest raiment; if shame live
In a disguise of love:
It is the lesser blot modesty finds,
Women to change their shapes, than men their minds.

Pro. Than men their minds? 'tis true: O heaven! were man
But constant, he were perfect: that one error
Fills him with faults; makes him run through all the sins;
Inconstancy falls off, ere it begins:
What is in Silvia's face, but I may spy
More fresh in Julia's, with a constant eye?

Val. Come, come, a hand from either:
Let me be blest to make this happy close?
'Twere pity two such friends should be long foes.

Pro. Bear witness, heaven, I have my wish for ever.

Jul. And I mine.

Enter Out-laws, *with* DUKE *and* THURIO.

Out. A prize, a prize, a prize!

Val. Forbear, forbear, I say; it is my lord the duke.
Your grace is welcome to a man disgrac'd,
Banished Valentine.

Duke. Sir Valentine!

Thu. Yonder is Silvia; and Silvia's mine.

Val. Thurio, give back, or else embrace thy death;
Come not within the measure of my wrath:
Do not name Silvia thine: if once again,
Verona shall not hold thee.[6] Here she stands,
Take but possession of her with a touch;—
I dare thee but to breathe upon my love.

Thu. Sir Valentine, I care not for her, I;
I hold him but a fool, that will endanger
His body for a girl that loves him not:
I claim her not, and therefore she is thine.

Duke. The more degenerate and base art thou,
To make such means[7] for her as thou hast done,
And leave her on such slight conditions.—
Now, by the honour of my ancestry,
I do applaud thy spirit, Valentine,
And think thee worthy of an empress' love.
Know then, I here forget all former griefs,
Cancel all grudge, repeal thee home again.—
Plead a new state in thy unrivall'd merit,
To which I thus subscribe,—Sir Valentine,

---

1 i. e. as *dear.*

2 *approv'd* is *confirm'd by proof.*

3 The word *now* was supplied in the folio of 1632.

4 Steevens confounded the phrases of *to cry aim* Merry Wives of Windsor, Act iii. Sc. 2) and to *give aim*, both terms in archery. He who gave aim appears to have been called the *mark*, and was stationed near the butts, to inform the archers how near their arrows fell to the butt. We are indebted to Mr. Gifford for distinguishing the terms.—Vide *Massinger*, vol. ii. p. 27. Julia means to say that she was the *mark* that gave direction to his vows.

5 i. e. of her heart, the allusion to archery is continued, and to *cleaving the pin* in shooting at the butts.

6 "*Verona* shall not *hold* thee," is the reading of the only authentic copy. Theobald proposed the reading, "*Milan* shall not *behold* thee," which has been adopted by all subsequent editors, but there is no authority for the change. If the reading is erroneous, Shakspeare must be held accountable for this as well as some other errors in his early productions.

7 "*To make such means* for her," to make such *interest* for, to take such disingenuous pains about her

Thou art a gentleman, and well deriv'd;
Take thou thy Silvia, for thou hast deserv'd her.
Val. I thank your grace; the gift hath made me happy.
I now beseech you, for your daughter's sake,
To grant one boon that I shall ask of you.
Duke. I grant it for thine own, whate'er it be.
Val. These banish'd men, that I have kept withal,
Are men endued with worthy qualities;
Forgive them what they have committed here,
And let them be recall'd from their exile:
They are reformed, civil, full of good,
And fit for great employment, worthy lord.
Duke. Thou hast prevail'd: I pardon them, and thee;
Dispose of them, as thou know'st their deserts.
Come, let us go; we will include all jars[1]
With triumphs,[2] mirth, and rare solemnity.
Val. And, as we walk along, I dare be bold
With our discourse to make your grace to smile:
What think you of this page, my lord?
Duke. I think the boy hath grace in him; he blushes.
Val. I warrant you, my lord; more grace than boy.
Duke What mean you by that saying?
Val. Please you, I'll tell you as we pass along,
That you will wonder what hath fortuned.—
Come, Proteus; 'tis your penance, but to hear
The story of your loves discovered:
That done, one day of marriage shall be yours;
One feast, one house, one mutual happiness.
[*Exeunt.*

1 *Include* is here used for *conclude.* This is another of Shakspeare's Latinisms: "*includo*, to *include*, to shut in, to close in."—*Cooper.*

2 *Triumphs* are pageants, such as masks and shows.

[In this play there is a strange mixture of knowledge and ignorance, of care and negligence. The versification is often excellent, the allusions are learned and just, but the author conveys his heroes by sea from one inland town to another in the same country; he places the emperor at Milan, and sends his young men to attend him, but never mentions him more; he makes Proteus, after an interview with Silvia, say he has only seen her picture; and, if we may credit the old copies, he has, by mistaking places, left his scenery inextricable. The reason of all this confusion seems to be, that he took his story from a novel, which he sometimes followed, and sometimes forsook, sometimes remembered, and sometimes forgot.

That this play is rightly attributed to Shakspeare, I have little doubt. If it be taken from him, to whom shall it be given? This question may be asked of all the disputed plays, except *Titus Andronicus*; and it will be found more credible, that Shakspeare might sometimes sink below his highest flights, than that any other should rise up to his lowest. JOHNSON

Johnson's general remarks on this play are just, except that part in which he arraigns the conduct of the poet, for making Proteus say he had only seen the picture of Silvia, when it appears that he had had a personal interview with her. This however is not a blunder of Shakspeare's, but a mistake of Johnson's, who considers the passage alluded to in a more literal sense than the author intended it. Sir Proteus, it is true, had seen Silvia for a few moments; but though he could form from thence some idea of her person, he was still unacquainted with her temper, manners, and the qualities of her mind. He therefore considers himself as having seen her picture only.—The thought is just, and elegantly expressed.—So, in The Scornful Lady, the elder Loveless says to her:

I was mad once, when I loved *pictures;*
For what are shape and colours else, but *pictures*

M. MASON.]

MERRY WIVES OF WINDSOR

PRELIMINARY REMARKS.

A FEW of the incidents of this Comedy might have been taken from an old translation of *Il Pecorone* di *Giovanni Fiorentino.* The same story is to be met with in 'The Fortunate, the Deceived, and the Unfortunate Lovers, 1632.' A somewhat similar one occurs in the *Piacevoli Notti di Straparola. Notte* iv. *Favola* iv. The adventures of Falstaff seem to have been taken from the story of the lovers of Pisa in 'Tarleton's Newes out of Purgatorie,' *bl. l. no date*, but entered on the Stationers' books in 1590. The fishwife's tale, in 'Westward for Smelts,' a book from which Shakspeare borrowed part of the fable of Cymbeline, probably led him to lay the Scene at Windsor.

Mr Malone thinks that the following line in the earliest edition of this comedy, 'Sail like my pinnace to those golden shores,' shows that it was written after Sir Walter Raleigh's return from Guiana in 1596.

The first edition of the Merry Wives of Windsor was printed in 1602, and it was probably written in 1601, after the two parts of King Henry IV. being, as it is said, composed at the desire of Queen Elizabeth,* in order to exhibit Falstaff in love, when all the pleasantry which he could afford in any other situation was exhausted.

It may not be thought so clear that it was written after King Henry V. Nym and Bardolph are both hanged in that play, yet appear in Merry Wives of Windsor. Falstaff is disgraced in King Henry IV. Part ii. and dies in King Henry V. Yet in the Merry Wives of Windsor he talks as if he was still in favour at court. "If it should come to the ear of the court how I have been transformed," &c.: and Page discountenances Fenton's addresses to his daughter, *because he kept company with the wild Prince and with Poins.* These circumstances seem to favour the supposition that this play was written between the first and second parts of King Henry IV. But that it was not written then may be collected from the tradition above mentioned. The truth, probably is, that though it ought to be *read* (as Dr. Johnson observed,) between the second part of Henry IV. and Henry V. it was *written* after King Henry V. and after Shakspeare had killed Falstaff. In obedience to the royal commands, having revived him, he found it necessary at the same time to revive all those persons with whom he was wont to be exhibited; Nym, Bardolph, Pistol, and the Page: and disposed of them as he found it convenient without a strict regard to their situations or catastrophes in former plays.

Mr. Malone thinks that The Merry Wives of Windsor was revised and enlarged by the author after its first production. The old edition, in 1602, like that of Romeo and Juliet, he says, is apparently a rough draught and not a mutilated or imperfect copy.† The precise time when the alterations and additions were made has not been ascertained: some passages in the enlarged copy may assist conjecture on the subject, but nothing decisive can be concluded from such evidence.

This comedy was not printed in its present form till 1623, when it was published with the rest of Shakspeare's plays in folio. The imperfect copy of 1602 was again printed in 1619.

* This story seems to have been first mentioned by Dennis in the Dedication to his alteration of this play, under the title of 'The Comical Gallant.' 'This Comedy,' says he, 'was written at Queen Elizabeth's command, and by her direction, and she was so eager to see it acted that she commanded it to be finished in *fourteen days;* and was afterwards, as tradition tells us, very well pleased at the representation.' The information probably came originally from Dryden, who, from his intimacy with Sir W. Davenant, had opportunities of learning many particulars concerning Shakspeare.

† Mr. Boaden thinks that the chasms which occur in the story of the drama in this old copy afford evidence that it was imperfectly taken down during the representation.

The bustle and variety of the incidents, the rich assemblage of characters, and the skilful conduct of the plot of this delightful comedy, are unrivalled in any drama, ancient or modern.

Falstaff, the inimitable Falstaff, here again 'lards the lean earth'—' a butt and a wit, a humourist, and a man of humour, a touchstone and a laughing-stock, a jester and a jest—the most perfect comic character that ever was exhibited.' The jealous Ford, the uxorious Page, and their two joyous wives are admirably drawn.—Sir Hugh Evans and Doctor Caius no less so, and the duel scene between them irresistibly comic. The swaggering jolly Boniface mine host of the Garter; and last though not least, Master Slender and his cousin Shallow, are such a group as were never yet equalled by the pen or pencil of genius.

PERSONS REPRESENTED.

SIR JOHN FALSTAFF.
FENTON.
SHALLOW, *a country Justice.*
SLENDER, *Cousin to* Shallow.
MR. FORD, } *two gentlemen dwelling at* Windsor.
MR. PAGE, }
WILLIAM PAGE, *a Boy, Son to* Mr. Page.
SIR HUGH EVANS, *a Welsh Parson.*
DR. CAIUS, *a French Physician.*
Host of the Garter Inn.
BARDOLPH, }
PISTOL, } *Followers of* Falstaff.
NYM, }

ROBIN, *Page to* Falstaff.
SIMPLE, *Servant to* Slender.
RUGBY, *Servant to* Dr. Caius.

MRS. FORD.
MRS. PAGE.
MRS. ANNE PAGE, *her Daughter, in love with* Fenton.
MRS. QUICKLY, *Servant to* Dr. Caius.

Servants to Page, Ford, *&c.*

SCENE, Windsor, *and the Parts adjacent.*

ACT I.

SCENE I. Windsor. *Before* Page's *House.*
Enter JUSTICE SHALLOW, SLENDER, *and* SIR[1] HUGH EVANS.

Shal. Sir Hugh, persuade me not; I will make a Star-chamber matter of it: if he were twenty Sir John Falstaffs, he shall not abuse Robert Shallow, esquire.

Slen. In the county of Gloster, justice of peace, and *coram.*

Shal. Ay, cousin Slender, and *Cust-alorum.*[2]

Slen. Ay, and *ratolorum* too; and a gentleman born, master parson; who writes himself *armigero;* in any bill, warrant, quittance, or obligation, *armigero.*

Shal. Ay, that I do; and have done[3] any time these three hundred years.

Slen. All his successors, gone before him, have done't; and all his ancestors, that come after him, may: they may give the dozen white luces in their coat.

Shal. It is an old coat.

Eva. The dozen white louses do become an old coat well; it agrees well, passant: it is a familiar beast to man, and signifies—love.

Shal. The luce is the fresh fish; the salt fish is an old coat.[4]

Slen. I may quarter, coz?

Shal. You may, by marrying.

Eva. It is marrying indeed, if he quarter it.

Shal. Not a whit.

Eva. Yes, pe'r-lady; if he has a quarter of your coat, there is but three skirts for yourself, in my simple conjectures: but that is all one: If Sir John Falstaff have committed disparagements unto you, I am of the church, and will be glad to do my benevolence, to make atonements and compromises between you.

Shal. The Council[5] shall hear it; it is a riot.

Eva. It is not meet the Council hear a riot; there is no fear of Got in a riot: the Council, look you, shall desire to hear the fear of Got, and not to hear a riot; take your vizaments[6] in that.

Shal. Ha! o' my life, if I were young again, the sword should end it.

Eva. It is petter that friends is the sword, and end it: and there is also another device in my prain, which, peradventure, prings goot discretions with it: There is Anne Page, which is daughter to master George Page, which is pretty virginity.

Slen. Mistress Anne Page? She has brown hair, and speaks small[7] like a woman.

Eva. It is that fery person for all the 'orld, as just as you will desire; and seven hundred pounds of moneys, and gold, and silver, is her grandsire, upon his death's bed (Got deliver to a joyful resurrections!) give, when she is able to overtake seventeen years old: it were a goot motion, if we leave our pribbles and prabbles, and desire a marriage between master Abraham and mistress Anne Page.

Shal. Did her grandsire leave her seven hundred pounds?

Eva. Ay, and her father is make her a petter penny.

Shal. I know the young gentlewoman; she has good gifts.

Eva. Seven hundred pounds, and possibilities, is good gifts.

Shal. Well, let us see honest master Page: Is Falstaff there?

Eva. Shall I tell you a lie? I do despise a liar, as I do despise one that is false; or, as I despise one that is not true. The knight, Sir John, is there; and, I beseech you, be ruled by your well-willers. I will peat the door [*knocks*] for master Page What, hoa! Got pless your house here!

Enter PAGE.

Page. Who's there?

Eva. Here is Got's plessing, and your friend, and justice Shallow: and here young master Slender; that, peradventures, shall tell you another tale, if matters grow to your likings.

Page. I am glad to see your worships well: I thank you for my venison, master Shallow.

Shal. Master Page, I am glad to see you; Much

1 *Sir*, was a title formerly applied to priests and curates generally. *Dominus* being the academical title of a Bachelor (bas chevalier) of Arts, was usually rendered by *Sir* in English, and as most clerical persons had taken that degree, it became usual to style them *Sir.*

2 A corruption of *Custos Rotulorum.* It seems doubtful whether Shakspeare designed Shallow to make this mistake, for though he gives him folly enough, he makes him rather pedantic than illiterate. Unless we suppose, with Mr. Malone, that it might have been intended to ridicule the abbreviations used in writs, &c.

3 i. e. all the Shallows have done.

4 It seems that the latter part of this speech should be given to Sir Hugh. Shallow has just before said the coat is an old one; and now, that it is 'the luce, the fresh fish.' No, replies the parson, it cannot be old and fresh too—' the salt fish is an old coat.' Shakspeare is supposed to allude to the arms of Sir Thomas Lucy, who is said to have prosecuted him for a misdemeanor in his youth, and whom he now ridiculed under the character of Justice Shallow.

5 The Court of Star-chamber is meant

6 Advisement. 7 Soft.

good do it your good heart! I wished your venison better; it was ill kill'd:—How doth good mistress Page?—and I love[1] you always with my heart, la; with my heart.

Page. Sir, I thank you.

Shal. Sir, I thank you; by yea and no, I do.

Page. I am glad to see you, good master Slender.

Slen. How does your fallow greyhound, sir? I heard say, he was out-run on Cotsale.[2]

Page. It could not be judg'd, sir.

Slen. You'll not confess, you'll not confess.

Shal. That he will not;—'tis your fault, 'tis your fault:—'Tis a good dog.

Page. A cur, sir.

Shal. Sir, he's a good dog, and a fair dog; Can there be more said? he is good, and fair.—Is Sir John Falstaff here?

Page. Sir, he is within; and I would I could do a good office between you.

Eva. It is spoke as a christians ought to speak.

Shal. He hath wrong'd me, master Page.

Page. Sir, he doth in some sort confess it.

Shal. If it be confess'd, it is not redress'd; is not that so, master Page? He hath wrong'd me; indeed he hath;—at a word, he hath;—believe me;—Robert Shallow, esquire, saith he is wrong'd.

Page. Here comes Sir John.

Enter SIR JOHN FALSTAFF, BARDOLPH, NYM, *and* PISTOL.

Fal. Now, master Shallow; you'll complain of me to the king?

Shal. Knight, you have beaten my men, killed my deer, and broke open my lodge.

Fal. But not kiss'd your keeper's daughter?

Shal. Tut, a pin! this shall be answer'd.

Fal. I will answer it straight;—I have done all this:—That is now answer'd.

Shal. The Council shall know this.

Fal. 'Twere better for you, if it were known in counsel: you'll be laugh'd at.

Eva. *Pauca verba*, Sir John, good worts.

Fal. Good worts![3] good cabbage.—Slender, I broke your head; What matter have you against me?

Slen. Marry, sir, I have matter in my head against you; and against your coney-catching[4] rascals, Bardolph, Nym, and Pistol. They carried me to the tavern, and made me drunk, and afterwards picked my pocket.

Bar. You Banbury cheese![5]

Slen. Ay, it is no matter.

Pist. How now, Mephostophilus?[6]

Slen Ay, it is no matter.

Nym. Slice, I say! *pauca, pauca;*[7] slice! that's my humour.

Slen. Where's Simple, my man? can you tell, cousin?

Eva. Peace: I pray you! Now let us understand: There is three umpires in this matter, as I understand: that is—master Page, *fidelicet*, master Page; and there is myself, *fidelicet*, myself; and the three party is, lastly and finally, mine host of the Garter.

Page. We three, to hear it, and end it between them.

Eva. Fery goot: I will make a prief of it in my note-book; and we will afterwards 'ork upon the cause with as great discreetly as we can.

Fal. Pistol, ———

Pist. He hears with ears.

Eva. The tevil and his tam! what phrase is this, *He hears with ear?* Why, it is affectations.

Fal. Pistol, did you pick master Slender's purse?

Slen. Ay, by these gloves, did he (or I would I might never come in mine own great chamber again else,) of seven groats in mill-sixpences, and two Edward shovel-boards,[8] that cost me two shilling and twopence a-piece of Yead Miller, by these gloves.

Fal. Is this true, Pistol?

Eva. No; it is false, if it is a pick-purse.

Pist. Ha, thou mountain-foreigner!—Sir John, and master mine,
I combat challenge of this latten bilbo:[9]
Word of denial in thy labras[10] here;
Word of denial; froth and scum, thou liest.

Slen. By these gloves, then 'twas he.

Nym. Be avised, sir, and pass good humours: I will say, *marry, trap*, with you, if you run the nut-hook's[11] humour on me; that is the very note of it.

Slen. By this hat, then he in the red face had it: for though I cannot remember what I did when you made me drunk, yet I am not altogether an ass.

Fal. What say you, Scarlet and John?

Bard. Why, sir, for my part, I say, the gentleman had drunk himself out of his five sentences.

Eva. It is his five senses: fie, what the ignorance is!

Bard. And being fap,[12] sir, was, as they say, cashier'd; and so conclusions pass'd the careires.[13]

Slen. Ay, you spake in Latin then too; but 'tis no matter: I'll ne'er be drunk whilst I live again, but in honest, civil, godly company, for this trick: If I be drunk, I'll be drunk with those that have the fear of God, and not with drunken knaves.

Eva. So Got 'udge me, that is a virtuous mind.

Fal. You hear all these matters denied, gentlemen; you hear it.

Enter MISTRESS ANNE PAGE, *with wine;* MISTRESS FORD *and* MISTRESS PAGE *following.*

Page. Nay, daughter, carry the wine in; we'll drink within. [*Exit* ANNE PAGE.

Slen. O heaven! this is mistress Anne Page.

Page. How now, mistress Ford?

Fal. Mistress Ford, by my troth, you are very well met: by your leave, good mistress. [*kissing her.*

Page. Wife, bid these gentlemen welcome:—Come, we have a hot venison pasty to dinner; come, gentlemen, I hope we shall drink down all unkindness.

[*Exeunt all but* SHAL. SLENDER, *and* EVANS.

Slen. I had rather than forty shillings I had my book of Songs and Sonnets[14] here:—

Enter SIMPLE.

How now, Simple! where have you been? I must wait on myself, must I? You have not *The Book of Riddles* about you, have you?

---

1 First folio. *I thank.* The reading in the text is from the 4to. 1619.

2 The Cotswold Hills in Gloucestershire, famous for their fine turf, and therefore excellent for coursing.

3 Worts was the ancient term for all the cabbage kind.

4 A common name for cheats and sharpers in the time of Elizabeth. 'By a metaphor taken from those that rob warrens and *conie grounds*.'—*Minshew's Dict.*

5 Said in allusion to the thin carcass of Slender. So, in Jack Drum's Entertainment, 1601. "Put off your clothes, and you are like a *Banbury Cheese*, nothing but paring."

6 The name of a spirit, or familiar, in the old story book of Faustus: to whom there is another allusion Act ii. Sc. 2. It was a cant phrase, probably, for an ugly fellow.

7 Few words.

8 Mill sixpences were used as counters: and King Edward's shillings used in the game of shuffle-board.

9 *Latten*, from the Fr. Laiton, Brass. *Bilbo*, from Bilboa in Spain where fine sword blades were made. Pistol therefore calls Slender *a weak blade of base metal*, as one of brass would be.

10 *Lips.*

11 Metaphorically a bailiff or constable, who hooks or seizes debtors or malefactors with a staff or otherwise The meaning apparently is, 'if you try to bring me to justice.'

12 *Fap* was evidently a cant term for *Foolish.* It may have been derived from the Italian *Vappa*, which Florio explains "any wine that hath lost his force: used also for *a man or woman without wit or reason.*" In Hutton's Dict. 1583, one of the meanings of the Latin *Vappa* is a *Dissard or foolish man*, &c.

13 A military phrase for running the charge in a tournament or attack; here used metaphorically.

14 Slender means a popular book of Shakspeare's time, "*Songes and Sonnettes*, written by the Earle of Surrey and others," and published by Tottel in 1557

Sim. *Book of Riddles!* why, did you not lend it to Alice Shortcake upon Allhallowmas last, a fortnight afore Michaelmas?[1]

Shal. Come, coz; come, coz; we stay for you. A word with you, coz: marry this, coz: There is, as 'twere, a tender, a kind of tender, made afar off by Sir Hugh here;—Do you understand me?

Slen. Ay, sir, you shall find me reasonable; if it be so, I shall do that that is reason.

Shal. Nay, but understand me.

Slen. So I do, sir.

Eva. Give ear to his motions, master Slender: I will description the matter to you, if you be capacity of it.

Slen. Nay, I will do as my cousin Shallow says: I pray you, pardon me; he's a justice of peace in his country, simple though I stand here.

Eva. But this is not the question; the question is concerning your marriage.

Shal. Ay, there's the point, sir.

Eva. Marry, is it; the very point of it; to mistress Anne Page.

Slen. Why, if it be so, I will marry her upon any reasonable demands.

Eva. But can you affection the 'oman? Let us command to know that of your mouth, or of your lips; for divers philosophers hold that the lips is parcel[2] of the mouth;—Therefore, precisely, can you carry your good will to the maid?

Shal. Cousin Abraham Slender, can you love her?

Slen. I hope, sir,—I will do as it shall become one that would do reason.

Eva. Nay, Got's lords and his ladies, you must speak possitable, if you can carry her your desires towards her.

Shal. That you must: Will you, upon good dowry, marry her?

Slen. I will do a greater thing than that, upon your request, cousin, in any reason.

Shal. Nay, conceive me, conceive me, sweet coz; what I do is to pleasure you, coz: Can you love the maid?

Slen. I will marry her, sir, at your request; but if there be no great love in the beginning, yet heaven may decrease it upon better acquaintance, when we are married, and have more occasion to know one another: I hope upon familiarity will grow more contempt: but if you say, *marry her,* I will marry her, that I am freely dissolved, and dissolutely.

Eva. It is a fery discretion answer; save the faul' is in the 'ort dissolutely: the 'ort is, according to our meaning, resolutely;—his meaning is good.

Shal. Ay, I think my cousin meant well.

Slen. Ay, or else I would I might be hanged, la.

Re-enter ANNE PAGE.

Shal. Here comes fair mistress Anne:—Would I were young for your sake, mistress Anne!

Anne. The dinner is on the table; my father desires your worships' company.

Shal. I will wait on him, fair mistress Anne.

Eva. Od's plessed will! I will not be absence at the grace.

[*Exeunt* SHALLOW *and* SIR H. EVANS.

Anne. Will't please your worship to come in, sir?

Slen. No, I thank you, forsooth, heartily; I am very well.

Anne. The dinner attends you, sir.

Slen. I am not a-hungry, I thank you, forsooth: Go, sirrah, for all you are my man, go, wait upon my cousin Shallow[3] [*Exit* SIMPLE.] A justice of peace sometimes may be beholden to his friend for a man:—I keep but three men and a boy yet, till my mother be dead: But what though? yet I live like a poor gentleman born.

Anne. I may not go in without your worship. they will not sit till you come.

Slen. I'faith, I'll eat nothing; I thank you as much as though I did.

Anne. I pray you, sir, walk in.

Slen. I had rather walk here, I thank you: I bruised my shin the other day with playing at sword and dagger with a master of fence,[4] three veneys[5] for a dish of stewed prunes; and, by my troth, I cannot abide the smell of hot meat since. Why do your dogs bark so? be there bears i' the town?

Anne. I think there are, sir; I heard them talked of.

Slen. I love the sport well; but I shall as soon quarrel at it as any man in England:—You are afraid if you see the bear loose, are you not?

Anne. Ay, indeed, sir.

Slen. That's meat and drink to me now: I have seen Sackerson[6] loose twenty times; and have taken him by the chain: but, I warrant you, the women have so cried and shriek'd at it, that it pass'd:[7]—but women, indeed, cannot abide 'em; they are very ill-favour'd rough things.

Re-enter PAGE.

Page. Come, gentle master Slender, come; we stay for you.

Slen. I'll eat nothing; I thank you, sir.

Page. By cock and pye,[8] you shall not choose, sir: come, come.

Slen, Nay, pray you, lead the way.

Page. Come on, sir.

Slen. Mistress Anne, yourself shall go first.

Anne. Not I, sir; pray you, keep on.

Slen. Truly, I will not go first, truly, la: I will not do you that wrong.

Anne. I pray you, sir.

Slen. I'll rather be unmannerly than troublesome: you do yourself wrong, indeed, la. [*Exeunt.*

SCENE II. *The same.* *Enter* SIR HUGH EVANS *and* SIMPLE.

Eva. Go your ways, and ask of Doctor Caius' house, which is the way: and there dwells one mistress Quickly, which is in the manner of his nurse, or his dry nurse, or his cook, or his laundry,[9] his washer, and his wringer.

Simp. Well, sir.

Eva. Nay, it is petter yet:——give her this letter; for it is a 'oman that altogether's acquaintance with mistress Anne Page; and the letter is, to desire and require her to solicit your master's desires to mistress Anne Page: I pray you, be gone. I will make an end of my dinner; there's pippins and cheese to come. [*Exeunt.*

SCENE III. *A Room in the Garter Inn.* *Enter* FALSTAFF, HOST, BARDOLPH, NYM, PISTOL, *and* ROBIN.

Fal. Mine host of the Garter,—

Host. What says my bully-rook? Speak scholarly, and wisely.

Fal. Truly, mine host, I must turn away some of my followers.

1 This is an intended blunder. Theobald would in sober sadness have corrected it to Martlemas.

2 i. e. *part*, a law term, often used in conjunction with its synonyme.

3 It was formerly the custom in England for persons to be attended at dinner by their own servants wherever they dined.

4 *Master of fence* here signifies not merely a fencing-master, but a person who had taken his master's degree in the science. There were three degrees, a master's, a provost's, and a scholar's. For each of these a prize was played with various weapons, in some open place or square. Tarlton the player 'was allowed a master' on the 23d of October, 1587, 'he being ordinary grome of her majesty's chamber.' The unfortunate Robert Greene played his master's prize at Leadenhall with three weapons, &c. The MS. from which this information is derived is a Register belonging to some of the Schools of the noble Science of Defence, among the Sloane MSS.—*Brit. Mus. No.* 2530, xxvi. *D.*

5 Veney, or Venue, *Fr.* a touch or hit in the body at fencing, &c.

6 The name of a bear exhibited at Paris Garden in Southwark.

7 i. e. passed all expression.

8 By cock and pye was a popular adjuration See Note on Henry IV. P. 2, Act v Sc. 1.

9 i. e. *launder*, from the *Fr* *Lavandiere*

Host. Discard, bully Hercules; cashier; let them wag; trot, trot.

Fal. I sit at ten pounds a week.

Host. Thou'rt an emperor, Cæsar, Keisar,[1] and Pheezar, I will entertain Bardolph; he shall draw, he shall tap: said I well, bully Hector?

Fal. Do so, good mine host.

Host. I have spoke; let him follow: Let me see thee froth, and lime:[2] I am at a word; follow. [*Exit* Host.

Fal. Bardolph, follow him; a tapster is a good trade: an old cloak makes a new jerkin; a withered serving-man, a fresh tapster: Go; adieu.

Bard. It is a life that I have desired; I will thrive. [*Exit* BARD.

Pist. O base Gongarian wight! wilt thou the spigot wield?

Nym. He was gotten in drink: Is not the humour conceited? His mind is not heroic, and there's the humour of it.

Fal. I am glad I am so acquit of this tinder-box; his thefts were too open: his filching was like an unskilful singer, he kept not time.

Nym. The good humour is, to steal at a minute's rest.

Pist. Convey, the wise it call: Steal! foh; a fico[3] for the phrase!

Fal. Well, sirs, I am almost out at heels.

Pist. Why then let kibes ensue.

Fal. There is no remedy; I must coney-catch; I must shift.

Pist. Young ravens must have food.

Fal. Which of you know Ford of this town?

Pist. I ken the wight; he is of substance good.

Fal. My honest lads, I will tell you what I am about.

Pist. Two yards, and more.

Fal. No quips now, Pistol; indeed I am in the waist two yards about; but I am now about no waste; I am about thrift. Briefly, I do mean to make love to Ford's wife; I spy entertainment in her; she discourses, she carves,[4] she gives the leer of invitation: I can construe the action of her familiar style, and the hardest voice of her behaviour, to be English'd rightly, is, *I am Sir John Falstaff's.*

Pist. He hath studied her well, and translated her well; out of honesty into English.

Nym. The anchor is deep: will that humour pass?

Fal. Now, the report goes, she has all the rule of her husband's purse; she hath legions of angels.[5]

Pist. As many devils entertain; and, *To her, boy,* say I.

Nym. The humour rises; it is good; humour me the angels.

Fal. I have writ me here a letter to her: and here another to Page's wife; who even now gave me good eyes too, examined my parts with most judicious eyliads:[6] sometimes the beam of her view gilded my foot, sometimes my portly belly.

Pist. Then did the sun on dunghill shine.

Nym. I thank thee for that humour.[7]

Fal. O, she did so course o'er my exteriors with such a greedy intention,[8] that the appetite of her eye did seem to scorch me up like a burning glass! Here's another letter to her: she bears the purse too: she is a region in Guiana, all gold and bounty. I will be cheater[9] to them both, and they shall be exchequers to me; they shall be my East and West Indies, and I will trade to them both. Go, bear thou this letter to mistress Page; and thou this to mistress Ford: we will thrive, lads, we will thrive.

Pist. Shall I Sir Pandarus of Troy become,
And by my side wear steel? then, Lucifer take all!

Nym. I will run no base humour; here, take the humour-letter; I will keep the 'haviour of reputation.

Fal. Hold, sirrah [*to* ROB.,] bear you these letters tightly;[10]
Sail like my pinnace[11] to these golden shores.—
Rogues, hence avaunt! vanish like hailstones, go;
Trudge, plod, away, o' the hoof; seek shelter, pack!
Falstaff will learn the humour of this age,
French thrift, you rogues; myself, and skirted page.
[*Exeunt* FALSTAFF *and* ROBIN.

Pist. Let vultures gripe thy guts![12] for gourd and fullam[13] holds,
And high and low beguile the rich and poor:
Tester[14] I'll have in pouch, when thou shalt lack,
Base Phrygian Turk!

Nym. I have operations in my head, which be humours of revenge.

Pist. Wilt thou revenge?

Nym. By welkin, and her star!

Pist. With wit, or steel?

Nym. With both the humours, I:
I will discuss the humour of this love to Page.

Pist. And I to Ford shall eke unfold,
How Falstaff, varlet vile,
His dove will prove, his gold will hold,
And his soft couch defile.

Nym. My humour shall not cool: I will incense[15] Page to deal with poison; I will possess him with yellowness,[16] for the revolt of mien is dangerous: that is my true humour.

Pist. Thou art the Mars of malcontents: I second thee; troop on. [*Exeunt*

SCENE IV. *A Room in* Dr. Caius' *House. Enter* Mrs. QUICKLY, SIMPLE, *and* RUGBY.

Quick. What; John Rugby!—I pray thee, go to the casement, and see if you can see my master, master Doctor Caius, coming: if he do, i'faith, and find any body in the house, here will be an old abusing of God's patience, and the king's English.

Rug. I'll go watch. [*Exit* RUGBY.

Quick. Go; and we'll have a posset for't soon at night, in faith, at the latter end of a sea-coal fire.

1 *Keysar* old spelling for Cæsar, the general word for an emperor. Kings and Keysars is an old phrase in very common use, *Pheezar,* a made word from Pheeze, in the Induction to Taming of a Shrew.

2 To froth beer and to lime sack were tapster's tricks. Mr. Steevens says the first was done by putting soap in the bottom of the tankard; the other by mixing lime with the wine to make it sparkle in the glass.

3 'A *fico* for the phrase.' See K. Henry IV. Part 2. A. S.

4 It seems to have been a mark of kindness when a lady carved to a gentleman. So, in Vittoria Corombona: "Your husband is wondrous discontented. *Vit.* I did nothing to displease him, I *carved* to him at supper time."

5 Gold coin.

6 *Oeillades.* French. Ogles, wanton looks of the eyes. Cotgrave translates it, 'to cast a sheep's eye.'

7 What distinguishes the languages of Nym from that of the other attendants on Falstaff is the constant repetition of this phrase. In the time of Shakspeare such an affectation seems to have been sufficient to mark a character. Some modern dramatists have also thought so.

8 i. e. attention.

9 *Eschealour,* an officer in the Exchequer

10 Cleverly, adroitly.

11 A *pinnace* was a light vessel built for speed, and was also called a *Brigantine.* Under the words *Catascopium* and *Celox* in Hutton's Dictionary, 1583, we have 'a Brigantine or *Pinnace,* a light ship that goeth to espie.' Hence the word is used for a go-between. In Ben Jonson's Bartholomew Fair, Justice Overdo says of the pig-woman, "She has been before me, punk, *pinnace,* and bawd, any time these two and twenty years."

12 A burlesque on a passage in Tamburlaine. or the Scythian Shepherd

———"and now doth ghastly death
With greedy talons *gripe* my bleeding heart,
And like a harper tyers on my life."

Again, ibid,

"Griping our bowels with retorted thoughts."

13 In Decker's Bellman of London, 1640, among the false dice are enumerated 'a bale of fullams'—'a bale of gordes, with as many high men as low men, for passage.' The false dice were chiefly made at Fulham, hence the name. The manner in which they were made is described in The Complete Gamester, 1676 12mo.

14 Sixpence I'll have in pocket.

15 Instigate

16 Jealousy

An honest, willing, kind fellow, as ever servant shall come in house withal; and, I warrant you, no tell-tale, nor no breed-bate:[1] his worst fault is, that he is given to prayer; he is something peevish[2] that way: but nobody but has his fault;—but let that pass. Peter Simple, you say, your name is?

Sim. Ay, for a fault of a better.

Quick. And master Slender's your master?

Sim. Ay, forsooth.

Quick. Does he not wear a great round beard,[3] like a glover's paring knife?

Sim. No, forsooth: he hath but a little wee face, with a little yellow beard; a Cain-coloured beard.[4]

Quick. A softly-sprighted man, is he not?

Sim. Ay, forsooth: but he is as tall a man of his hands,[5] as any is between this and his head; he hath fought with a warrener.[6]

Quick. How say you?—O, I should remember him; Does he not hold up his head, as it were? and strut in his gait?

Sim. Yes, indeed, does he.

Quick. Well, heaven send Anne Page no worse fortune? Tell master parson Evans, I will do what I can for your master: Anne is a good girl, and I wish—

Re-enter RUGBY.

Rug. Out, alas! here comes my master.

Quick. We shall all be shent:[7] Run in here, good young man; go into this closet. [*Shuts* Simple *in the closet.*] He will not stay long.—What, John Rugby! John, what, John, I say!—Go, John, go inquire for my master; I doubt, he be not well, that he comes not home:—*and down, down, adown-a, &c.* [*Sings.*

Enter Doctor Caius.[8]

Caius. Vat is you sing? I do not like dese toys; Pray you, go and vetch me in my closet *un boitier verd;* a box, a green-a box; Do intend vat I speak? a-green-a box.

Quick. Ay, forsooth, I'll fetch it you. I am glad he went not in himself; if he had found the young man, he would have been horn-mad. [*Aside.*

Caius. Fe, fe, fe, fe! mai foi, il fait fort chaud. Je m'en vais a la Cour,—la grande affaire.

Quick. Is it this, sir?

Caius. Ouy; mette le au mon pocket; *Depeche,* quickly:—Vere is dat knave Rugby?

Quick. What, John Rugby! John!

Rug. Here, sir.

Caius. You are John Rugby, and you are Jack Rugby; Come, take-a your rapier, and come after my heel to de court.

Rug. 'Tis ready, sir, here in the porch.

Caius. By my trot, I tarry too long:—Od's me! *Qu'ay-j'oublie?* dere is some simples in my closet, dat I vill not for the varld I shall leave behind.

Quick. Ah me! he'll find the young man there, and be mad.

Caius. O diable, diable! vat is in my closet?—Villany? *larron!* [*Pulling* Simple *out.*] Rugby, my rapier.

Quick. Good master, be content.

Caius. Verefore shall I be content-a?

Quick. The young man is an honest man.

Caius. Vat shall de honest man do in my closet? dere is no honest man dat shall come in my closet.

Quick. I beseech you, be not so flegmatic; hear the truth of it: He came of an errand to me from parson Hugh.

Caius. Vell.

Sim. Ay, forsooth, to desire her to——

Quick. Peace, I pray you.

Caius. Peace-a your tongue:—Speak-a your tale.

Sim. To desire this honest gentlewoman, your maid, to speak a good word to mistress Anne Page for my master, in the way of marriage.

Quick. This is all, indeed, la; but I'll ne'er put my finger in the fire, and need not.

Caius. Sir Hugh send-a you?—Rugby, *baillez* me some paper:—Tarry you a little-awhile. [*Writes*

Quick. I am glad he is so quiet: if he had been thoroughly moved, you should have heard him so loud, and so melancholy;—But notwithstanding, man, I'll do your master what good I can: and the very yea and the no is, the French Doctor, my master,—I may call him my master, look you, for I keep his house; and I wash, wring, brew, bake, scour, dress meat and drink, make the beds, and do all myself;—

Sim. 'Tis a great charge, to come under one body's hand.

Quick. Are you avis'd o' that? you shall find it a great charge: and to be up early, and down late;—but notwithstanding (to tell you in your ear; I would have no words of it;) my master himself is in love with mistress Anne Page: but notwithstanding that,—I know Anne's mind,—that's neither here nor there.

Caius. You jack'nape; give-a dis letter to Sir Hugh; by gar, it is a shallenge: I vill cut his troat in de park; and I vill teach a scurvy jack-a-nape priest to meddle or make:—you may be gone; it is not good you tarry here:—by gar, I vill cut all his two stones; by gar, he shall not have a stone to trow at his dog. [*Exit* SIMPLE.

Quick. Alas, he speaks but for his friend.

Caius. It is no matter—a for dat:—do not you tell-a me dat I shall have Anne Page for myself?—by gar, I vill kill de Jack priest; and I have appointed mine host of *de Jarterre* to measure our weapon:—by gar, I vill myself have Anne Page.

Quick. Sir, the maid loves you, and all shall be well: we must give folks leave to prate: What, the good-jer![9]

Caius. Rugby, come to the court vid me;—By gar, if I have not Anne Page, I shall turn your head out of my door:—Follow my heels, Rugby.

[*Exeunt* CAIUS *and* RUGBY.

Quick. You shall have An fools-head of your own. No, I know Anne's mind for that: never a woman in Windsor knows more of Anne's mind

---

1 i. e. breeder of debate, maker of contention.

2 *Foolish.* Mrs. Quickly possibly blunders, and would say *precise.*

3 See a Note on K. Henry V. Act III. Sc. 6.

'And what a beard of the general's cut.'

4 It is said that Cain and Judas in old pictures and tapestry were constantly represented with yellow beards. In an age when but a small part of the nation could read, ideas were frequently borrowed from these representations. One of the copies reads a cane-coloured beard, i. e. of the colour of cane, and the reading of the 4to. a whey-coloured beard favours this reading.

5 This phrase has been very imperfectly explained by the commentators, though they have written 'about it, and about it.' Malone's quotation from Cotgrave was near the mark, but missed it: "*Haut a la main, Homme a la main, Homme de main. A man of his hands; a man of execution or valour; a striker,* like enough to lay about him; proud, surlie, sullen, stubborn." So says this truly valuable old dictionary: from which it is evident that *a tall man of his hands* was only a free version of the French *Homme haut a la main.* This equivocal use of the words *Haut* and *tall* will also explain the expression a *tall* fellow, or a *tall* man, wherever it occurs. Mercutio ridicules it as one of the affected phrases of the fantasticos of his age, 'a very good blade,' 'a very *tall* man!'—*Romeo and Juliet,* Act ii. Sc. 4.

6 The keeper of a warren.

7 Scolded, reprimanded.

8 It has been thought strange that Shakspeare should take the name of Caius for his Frenchman, as an eminent physician of that name, founder of Caius College, Oxford, flourished in Elizabeth's reign. But Shakspeare was little acquainted with literary history, and without doubt, from this unusual name, supposed him to have been some foreign quack. The character might however be drawn from the life, for in Jack Dover's Quest of Enquirie, 1604, a story called 'the Foole of Windsor,' turns upon a simple outlandish Doctor of Physicke.

9 The goujere, i. e. *morbus Gallicus.* The good-jer and good yeare were common corruptions of this phrase.

than I do; nor can do more than I do with her, I thank heaven.

Fent. [*Within.*] Who's within there, ho?

Quick. Who's there, I trow? Come near the house, I pray you.

Enter FENTON.

Fent. How now, good woman: how dost thou?

Quick. The better, that it pleases your good worship to ask.

Fent. What news? how does pretty Mistress Anne?

Quick. In truth, sir, and she is pretty, and honest, and gentle; and one that is your friend, I can tell you that by the way; I praise heaven for it.

Fent. Shall I do any good, thinkest thou? Shall I not lose your suit?

Quick. Troth, sir, all is in his hands above: but notwithstanding, master Fenton, I'll be sworn on a book, she loves you:—Have not your worship a wart above your eye?

Fent. Yes, marry, have I; what of that?

Quick. Well, thereby hangs a tale;—good faith, it is such another Nan:—but, I detest[1] an honest maid as ever broke bread:—We had an hour's talk of that wart:—I shall never laugh but in that maid's company!—But, indeed, she is given too much to allicholly[2] and musing: But for you—Well, go to.

Fent. Well, I shall see her to-day: Hold, there's money for thee; let me have thy voice in my behalf: if thou seest her before me, commend me—

Quick. Will I? i'faith, that we will: and I will tell your worship more of the wart, the next time we have confidence; and of other wooers.

Fent. Well, farewell; I am in great haste now. [*Exit.*

Quick. Farewell to your worship.—Truly, an honest gentleman; but Anne loves him not; for I know Anne's mind as well as another does: Out upon't! what have I forgot? [*Exit.*

ACT II.

SCENE I.—*Before* PAGE'S *House. Enter Mistress* PAGE, *with a letter.*

Mrs. Page. What! have I 'scaped love-letters in the holy-day time of my beauty, and am I now a subject for them? Let me see: [*Reads.*

Ask me no reason why I love you; for though love use reason for his precisian,[3] he admits him not for his counsellor: You are not young, no more am I; go to then, there's sympathy: you are merry, so am I; Ha! ha! then there's more sympathy: you love sack, and so do I; would you desire better sympathy? Let it suffice thee, mistress Page (at the least, if the love of a soldier can suffice,) that I love thee. I will not say, pity me, 'tis not a soldier-like phrase; but I say love me. By me,

Thine own true knight,
By day or night,
Or any kind of light,
With all his might
For thee to fight,
John Falstaff.

What a Herod of Jewry is this!—O wicked, wicked world!—one that is well nigh worn to pieces with age, to show himself a young gallant! What an unweighed behaviour hath this Flemish drunkard picked (with the devil's name) out of my conversation, that he dares in this manner assay me? Why, he hath not been thrice in my company!—What should I say to him?—I was then frugal of my mirth:—heaven forgive me!—Why, I'll exhibit a bill in the parliament for the putting down of fat men. How shall I be revenged on him? for revenged I will be, as sure as his guts are made of puddings.

Enter Mistress FORD.

Mrs. Ford. Mistress Page! trust me, I was going to your house.

Mrs. Page. And, trust me, I was coming to you. You look very ill.

Mrs. Ford. Nay, I'll ne'er believe that; I have to show to the contrary.

Mrs. Page. 'Faith, but you do, in my mind.

Mrs. Ford. Well, I do then; yet, I say, I could show you to the contrary: O, mistress Page, give me some counsel!

Mrs. Page. What's the matter, woman?

Mrs. Ford. O woman, if it were not for one trifling respect, I could come to such honour!

Mrs. Page. Hang the trifle, woman; take the honour: What is it?—dispense with trifles;—what is it?

Mrs. Ford. If I would but go to hell for an eternal moment, or so, I could be knighted.

Mrs. Page. What?—thou liest!—Sir Alice Ford!——These knights will hack;[4] and so thou should'st not alter the article of thy gentry.

Mrs. Ford. We burn day-light:[5] here, read, read;—perceive how I might be knighted.—I shall think the worse of fat men, as long as I have an eye to make difference of men's liking: And yet he would not swear; praised woman's modesty: and gave such orderly and well behaved reproof to all uncomeliness, that I would have sworn his disposition would have gone to the truth of his words: but they do no more adhere and keep place together, than the hundredth psalm to the tune of *Green sleeves.* What tempest, I trow, threw this whale, with so many tuns of oil in his belly, ashore at Windsor? How shall I be revenged on him? I think, the best way were to entertain him with hope, till the wicked fire of lust have melted him in his own grease.—Did you ever hear the like?

Mrs. Page. Letter for letter; but that the name of Page and Ford differs!—To thy great comfort in this mystery of ill opinions, here's the twin-brother of thy letter: but let thine inherit first; for, I protest, mine never shall. I warrant he hath a thousand of these letters, writ with blank space for different names, (sure more,) and these are of the second edition: He will print them out of doubt: for he cares not what he puts into the press,[6] when he would put us two. I had rather be a giantess, and lie under mount Pelion. Well, I will find you twenty lascivious turtles, ere one chaste man.

Mrs. Ford. Why, this is the very same; the very hand, the very words: What doth he think of us?

Mrs. Page. Nay, I know not: It makes me almost ready to wrangle with mine own honesty. I'll entertain myself like one that I am not acquainted withal; for, sure, unless he know some strain in me, that I know not myself, he would never have boarded me in his fury.

1 She means, I *protest.*

2 Melancholy.

3 The meaning of this passage is at present obscure. Dr. Johnson conjectured, with much probability, that Shakspeare wrote *Physician*, which would render the sense obvious.

4 *To hack* was the appropriate term for chopping off the spurs of a knight when he was to be degraded. The meaning therefore appears to be:—"these knights will degrade you for an unqualified pretender." Another explanation has been offered; supposing this to be a covert reflection upon the prodigal distribution of the honour of knighthood by King James "These knights will soon become so *hackneyed* that your honour will not be increased by becoming one."

5 A proverb applicable to superfluous actions in general.

6 Mrs. Page, who does not seem to have been intended in any degree for a learned lady, is here without the least regard to propriety made to talk like an author about the press and printing. The translations of the Classics, as Warton judiciously observes, soon inundated our poetry with pedantic allusions to ancient fable, often introduced as incongruously as the mention of Pelion here. The nautical allusions in the succeeding passages are not more appropriate. But Shakspeare does not often err in this way

Mrs. Ford. Boarding, call you it? I'll be sure to keep him above deck.

Mrs. Page. So will I; if he come under my hatches, I'll never to sea again. Let's be revenged on him: let's appoint him a meeting; give him a show of comfort in his suit; and lead him on with a fine-baited delay, till he hath pawn'd his horses to mine Host of the Garter.

Mrs. Ford. Nay, I will consent to act any villany against him, that may not sully the chariness[1] of our honesty. O, that my husband saw this letter! it would give eternal food to his jealousy.

Mrs. Page. Why, look, where he comes; and my good man too: he's as far from jealousy, as I am from giving him cause; and that, I hope, is an unmeasurable distance.

Mrs. Ford. You are the happier woman.

Mrs. Page. Let's consult together against this greasy knight: Come hither. [*They retire.*

Enter FORD, PISTOL, PAGE, *and* NYM.

Ford. Well, I hope it be not so.

Pist. Hope is a curtail[2] dog in some affairs: Sir John affects thy wife.

Ford. Why, sir, my wife is not young.

Pist. He woos both high and low, both rich and poor,
Both young and old, one with another, Ford:
He loves the gally-mawfry;[3] Ford, perpend.[4]

Ford. Love my wife?

Pist. With liver burning hot:[5] Prevent or go thou,
Like Sir Actæon he, with Ring-wood at thy heels:
O, odious is the name!

Ford. What name, sir?

Pist. The horn, I say: Farewell.
Take heed; have open eye; for thieves do foot by night:
Take heed, ere summer comes, or cuckoo-birds do sing.—
Away, Sir corporal Nym.——
Believe it, Page; he speaks sense. [*Exit* PISTOL.

Ford. I will be patient; I will find out this.

Nym. And this is true. [*To* PAGE.] I like not the humour of lying. He hath wronged me in some humours; I should have borne the humoured letter to her: but I have a sword, and it shall bite upon my necessity. He loves your wife; there's the short and the long. My name is corporal Nym; I speak, and I avouch. 'Tis true:—my name is Nym, and Falstaff loves your wife.—Adieu! I love not the humour of bread and cheese; and there's the humour of it. Adieu. [*Exit* NYM.

Page. *The humour of it,* quoth'a! here's a fellow frights humour[6] out of his wits.

Ford. I will seek out Falstaff.

Page. I never heard such a drawling, affecting rogue.

Ford. If I do find it, well.

Page. I will not believe such a Cataian,[7] though the priest of the town commended him for a true man.

Ford. 'Twas a good sensible fellow: Well.[8]

Page. How now, Meg?

Mrs. Page. Whither go you, George?—Hark you.

Mrs. Ford. How now, sweet Frank? why art thou melancholy?

Ford. I melancholy! I am not melancholy.—Get you home, go.

Mrs. Ford. 'Faith thou hast some crotchets in thy head now.—Will you go, mistress Page?

Mrs. Page. Have with you.—You'll come to dinner, George?—Look, who comes yonder: she shall be our messenger to this paltry knight. [*Aside to* MRS. FORD

Enter MISTRESS QUICKLY.

Mrs. Ford. Trust me, I thought on her: she'll fit it.

Mrs. Page. You are come to see my daughter Anne?

Quick. Ay, forsooth; And, I pray, how does good mistress Anne?

Mrs. Page. Go in with us, and see; we have an hour's talk with you.
[*Exeunt* MRS. PAGE, MRS. FORD, *and* MRS. QUICKLY.

Page. How now, master Ford?

Ford. You heard what this knave told me; did you not?

Page. Yes; and you heard what the other told me?

Ford. Do you think there is truth in them?

Page. Hang'em, slaves! I do not think the knight would offer it: but these that accuse him in his intent towards our wives, are a yoke of his discarded men; very rogues, now they be out of service.

Ford. Were they his men?

Page. Marry, were they.

Ford. I like it never the better for that.—Does he lie at the Garter?

Page. Ay, marry, does he. If he should intend this voyage towards my wife, I would turn her loose to him; and what he gets more of her than sharp words, let it lie on my head.

Ford. I do not misdoubt my wife; but I would be loath to turn them together: A man may be too confident: I would have nothing lie on my head; I cannot be thus satisfied.

Page. Look, where my ranting host of the Garter comes: there is either liquor in his pate, or money in his purse, when he looks so merrily.—How now, mine host?

Enter HOST *and* SHALLOW.

Host. How now, bully-rook? thou'rt a gentleman: cavalero-justice, I say.

Shal. I follow mine host, I follow.—Good even, and twenty, good master Page! Master Page, will you go with us? we have sport in hand.

Host. Tell him, cavalero-justice; tell him, bully-rook.

Shal. Sir, there is a fray to be fought, between Sir Hugh the Welsh priest, and Caius the French doctor.

Ford. Good mine host o' the Garter, a word with you.

Host. What say'st thou, bully-rook? [*They go aside.*

---

1 i. e. the caution which ought to attend on it.

2 A curtail dog was a common dog not meant for sport, part of the tails of such dogs being commonly cut off while they are puppies; it was a prevalent notion that the tail of a dog was necessary to him in running, hence a dog that missed his game was called a curtail, from which cur is probably derived.

3 A medley.

4 Consider.

5 The *liver* was anciently supposed to be the inspirer of amorous passions. Thus in an old Latin distich:
'Cor ardet, pulmo loquitur, fel commovet iras
Splen ridere facit, *cogit amare jecur.*'

6 The first folio reads—*English.* The abuse of this word *humour* by the coxcombs of the age had been admirably satirized by Ben Jonson. After a very pertinent disquisition on the real meaning and true application of the word, he concludes thus:

Asp. But that a rook by wearing a pied feather,
The cable hatband, or the three-piled ruff,
A yard of shoe-tie, or the Switzers knot
On his French garters, should affect a humour,
O 'tis worse than most ridiculous.
Cor. He speaks pure truth; and now if an idiot
Have but an apish or fantastic strain,
It is his *humour.*—
Induction to Every Man Out of his Humour

Steevens quotes an Epigram from Humours Ordinarie, 1607, to the same effect.

7 i. e. a Chinese, *Cataia, Cathay,* being the name given to China by the old travellers, some of whom have mentioned the dexterous thieving of the people there; hence a sharper or thief was sometimes called a *Cataian.*

8 This and the two preceding speeches are soliloquies of Ford, and have no connection with what Page says, who is also making comments on what had passed without attending to Ford

Shal. Will you [*to* PAGE] go with us to behold it? my merry host hath had the measuring of their weapons; and, I think he hath appointed them contrary places: for, believe me, I hear the parson is no jester. Hark, I will tell you what our sport shall be.

Host. Hast thou no suit against my knight, my guest-cavalier?

Ford. None, I protest: but I'll give you a pottle of burnt sack to give me recourse to him, and tell him, my name is Brook; only for a jest.

Host. My hand, bully: thou shalt have egress and regress; said I well? and thy name shall be Brook: It is a merry knight.—Will you go, Cavaliers?[1]

Shal. Have with you, mine host.

Page. I have heard, the Frenchman hath good skill in his rapier.

Shal. Tut, sir, I could have told you more: In these times you stand on distance, your passes, stoccadoes, and I know not what: 'tis the heart, master Page: 'tis here, 'tis here. I have seen the time, with my long sword,[2] I would have made you four tall fellows skip like rats.

Host. Here, boys, here, here! shall we wag?

Page. Have with you:—I had rather hear them scold than fight. [*Exeunt.* HOST, SHAL. *and* PAGE.

Ford. Though Page be a secure fool, and stands so firmly on his wife's frailty, yet I cannot put off my opinion so easily; She was in his company at Page's house; and, what they made[3] there, I know not. Well, I will look further into't: and I have a disguise to sound Falstaff: If I find her honest, I lose not my labour; if she be otherwise, 'tis labour well bestowed. [*Exit.*

SCENE II. *A Room in the Garter Inn. Enter* FALSTAFF *and* PISTOL.

Fal. I will not lend thee a penny.

Pist. Why, then the world's mine oyster,
Which I with sword will open.—
I will retort the sum in equipage.[4]

Fal. Not a penny. I have been content, sir, you should lay my countenance to pawn: I have grated upon my good friends for three reprieves for you and your coach-fellow[5] Nym; or else you had looked through the grate like a geminy of baboons. I am damned in hell, for swearing to gentlemen my friends, you were good soldiers, and tall fellows: and when mistress Bridget lost the handle of her fan,[6] I took't upon mine honour, thou hadst it not.

Pist. Didst thou not share? hadst thou not fifteen pence?

Fal. Reason, you rogue, reason: Think'st thou, I'll endanger my soul *gratis?* At a word, hang no more about me, I am no gibbet for you:—go.—A short knife and a throng;[7]—to your manor of Pickthatch,[8] go.—You'll not bear a letter for me, you rogue! you stand upon your honour!—Why, thou unconfinable baseness, it is as much as I can do to keep the terms of my honour precise. I, I, I myself sometimes, leaving the fear of heaven on the left hand, and hiding mine honour in my necessity, am fain to shuffle, to hedge, and to lurch; and yet, you, rogue, will ensconce[9] your rags, your cat-a-mountain looks, your red-lattice[10] phrases, and your bold-beating oaths, under the shelter of your honour! You will not do it, you?

Pist. I do relent; what would'st thou more of man?

Enter ROBIN.

Rob. Sir, here's a woman would speak with you.

Fal. Let her approach.

Enter MISTRESS QUICKLY

Quick. Give your worship good-morrow

Fal. Good-morrow, good wife.

Quick. Not so, an't please your worship

Fal. Good maid, then.

Quick. I'll be sworn; as my mother was, the first hour I was born.

Fal. I do believe the swearer: What with me?

Quick. Shall I vouchsafe your worship a word or two?

Fal. Two thousand, fair woman; and I'll vouchsafe thee the hearing.

Quick. There is one Mistress Ford, sir;—I pray, come a little nearer this ways:—I myself dwell with master doctor Caius.

Fal. Well, on: Mistress Ford, you say,——

Quick. Your worship says very true: I pray your worship, come a little nearer this ways.

Fal. I warrant thee, nobody hears;—mine own people, mine own people.

Quick. Are they so? Heaven bless them, and make them his servants!

Fal. Well: mistress Ford:—what of her?

Quick. Why, sir, she's a good creature. Lord, Lord! your worship's a wanton: Well, heaven forgive you, and all of us, I pray!

Fal. Mistress Ford:—come, mistress Ford,—

Quick. Marry, this is the short and the long of it; you have brought her into such a canaries[11] as 'tis wonderful. The best courtier of them all, when the court lay at Windsor, could never have brought her to such a canary. Yet there has been knights, and lords, and gentlemen, with their coaches; I warrant you, coach after coach, letter after letter, gift after gift; smelling so sweetly (all musk,) and so rushling, I warrant you, in silk and gold; and in such alligant terms; and in such wine and sugar of the best, and the fairest, that would have won any woman's heart; and, I warrant you, they could never get an eye-wink of her.—I had myself twenty angels given me this morning: but I defy all angels (in any such sort, as they say,) but in the way of honesty:—and, I warrant you, they could never get her so much as sip on a cup with the proudest of them all: and yet there has been earls, nay, which is more, pensioners;[12] but I warrant you, all is one with her.

1 The folio of 1623 reads *An-heires*, which is unintelligible; the word in the text, the conjecture of Mr. Boaden, Malone considered the best that had been offered. *Caualeires* would have been the orthography of the old copy, and the host has the term frequently in his mouth. Mr. Steevens substituted *on hearts*.

2 Before the introduction of rapiers the swords in use were of an enormous length and sometimes used with both hands. Shallow, with an old man's vanity, censures the innovation, and ridicules the terms and use of the rapier. See note on K. Henry IV. P. 1, Act ii. Sc. 4.

3 An obsolete phrase, signifying—'what they *did* there.' In Act iv. Sc. 2. of this play we have again, what *make* you here; for what *do* you here

4 *Equipage* appears to have been a cant term, which Warburton conjectured to mean stolen goods. Mr. Steevens thinks it means attendance; i. e. 'if you will lend me the money, I will pay you again in attendance,' but has failed to produce an example of the use of the word in that sense.

5 i. e. he who *draws* along with you, who is joined with you in all your knavery.

6 Fans were costly appendages of female dress in Shakspeare's time. They consisted of ostrich and other feathers, fixed into handles, some of which were made of gold, silver, or ivory of curious workmanship.

7 i. e. go and *cut purses in a crowd.* Purses being then worn hanging at the girdle.

8 *Pick't-hatch* was in Turnbull Street, Cow Cross, Clerkenwell, a haunt of the worst part of both sexes. The unseasonable and obstreperous irruptions of the swash-bucklers of that age rendered a *hatch* or half door with spikes upon it a necessary defence to a brothel, and hence the term became a cant phrase to denote a part of the town noted for brothels.

9 *A sconce* is a fortification; *to ensconce* is therefore to protect as with a fort.

10 *Alehouse language.* Red lattice windows formerly denoted an alehouse, as the chequers have done since

11 A mistake of Mrs. Quickly's for *quandaries. Canary* was, however, a quick and lively dance mentioned in All's Well that Ends well, Act ii. Sc. 1.

12 i. e. Gentlemen of the band of Pensioners. Their dress was remarkably splendid, and therefore likely to attract the notice of Mrs. Quickly. Hence, Shakspeare, in a Midsummer Night's Dream, has selected the gold en-coated cowslips to be *pensioners* to the Fairy Queen

Fal. But what says she to me? be brief, my good she Mercury.

Quick. Marry, she hath received your letter; for the which she thanks you a thousand times: and she gives you to notify, that her husband will be absence from his house between ten and eleven.

Fal. Ten and eleven?

Quick. Ay, forsooth; and then you may come and see the picture, she says, that you wot[1] of;—master Ford, her husband, will be from home. Alas! the sweet woman leads an ill life with him; he's a very jealousy man; she leads a very frampold[2] life with him, good heart.

Fal. Ten and eleven: Woman, commend me to her; I will not fail her.

Quick. Why, you say well: But I have another messenger to your worship: Mrs. Page hath her hearty commendations to you too;—and let me tell you in your ear, she's as fartuous a civil modest wife, and one (I tell you) that will not miss you morning nor evening prayer, as any is in Windsor, whoe'er be the other: and she bade me tell your worship, that her husband is seldom from home; but she hopes, there will come a time. I never knew a woman so dote upon a man; surely, I think you have charms, la; yes, in truth.

Fal. Not I, I assure thee; setting the attraction of my good parts aside, I have no other charms.

Quick. Blessing on your heart for't!

Fal. But, I pray thee, tell me this: has Ford's wife, and Page's wife, acquainted each other how they love me?

Quick. That were a jest, indeed!—they have not so little grace, I hope:—that were a trick, indeed! But mistress Page would desire you to send her your little page of all loves;[3] her husband has a marvellous infection to the little page; and, truly, master Page is an honest man. Never a wife in Windsor leads a better life than she does; do what she will, say what she will, take all, pay all, go to bed when she list, rise when she list, all is as she will; and, truly, she deserves it: for if there be a kind woman in Windsor, she is one. You must send her your page; no remedy.

Fal. Why, I will.

Quick. Nay, but do so then: and, look you, he may come and go between you both; and, in any case, have a nay word,[4] that you may know one another's mind, and the boy never need to understand any thing; for 'tis not good that children should know any wickedness; old folks, you know, have discretion, as they say, and know the world.

Fal. Fare thee well: commend me to them both: there's my purse; I am yet thy debtor.—Boy, go along with this woman.—This news distracts me!

[*Exeunt* QUICKLY *and* ROBIN.

Pist. This punk is one of Cupid's carriers:—
Clap on more sails; pursue, up with your fights;[5]
Give fire; she is my prize, or ocean whelm them all! [*Exit* PISTOL.

Fal. Say'st thou so, old Jack? go thy ways; I'll make more of thy old body than I have done. Will they yet look after thee? Wilt thou, after the expense of so much money, be now a gainer? Good body, I thank thee: Let them say, 'tis grossly done; so it be fairly done, no matter.

Enter BARDOLPH.

Bard. Sir John, there's one master Brook below would fain speak with you, and be acquainted with you: and hath sent your worship a morning's draught of sack.[6]

Fal. Brook is his name?

Bard. Ay, sir.

Fal. Call him in: [*Exit* BARDOLPH.] Such Brooks are welcome to me, that o'erflow such liquor. Ah! ha! mistress Ford and mistress Page, have I encompass'd you? go to; *via!*[7]

Re-enter BARDOLPH, *with* FORD *disguised.*

Ford. Bless you, sir.

Fal. And you, sir: Would you speak with me?

Ford. I make bold to press with so little preparation upon you.

Fal. You're welcome; What's your will? Give us leave, drawer. [*Exit* BARDOLPH.

Ford. Sir, I am a gentleman that have spent much; my name is Brook.

Fal. Good master Brook, I desire more acquaintance of you.

Ford. Good Sir John, I sue for yours: not to charge you; for I must let you understand, I think myself in better plight for a lender than you are: the which hath something embolden'd me to this unseason'd intrusion; for they say, if money go before, all ways do lie open.

Fal. Money is a good soldier, sir, and will on.

Ford. Troth, and I have a bag of money here troubles me: if you will help me to bear it, Sir John, take all, or half, for easing me of the carriage.

Fal. Sir, I know not how I may deserve to be your porter.

Ford. I will tell you, sir, if you will give me the hearing.

Fal. Speak, good master Brook; I shall be glad to be your servant.

Ford. Sir, I hear you are a scholar,—I will be brief with you;——and you have been a man long known to me, though I had never so good means, as desire, to make myself acquainted with you. shall discover a thing to you, wherein I must very much lay open mine own imperfection: but, good Sir John, as you have one eye upon my follies, as you hear them unfolded, turn another into the register of your own; that I may pass with a reproof the easier, sith[8] you yourself know, how easy it is to be such an offender.

Fal. Very well, sir; proceed.

Ford. There is a gentlewoman in this town, her husband's name is Ford.

Fal. Well, sir.

Ford. I have long loved her, and, I protest to you, bestowed much on her; followed her with a doting observance;[9] engrossed opportunities to meet her; fee'd every slight occasion, that could but niggardly give me sight of her; not only bought many presents to give her, but have given largely to many, to know what she would have given: briefly, I have pursued her, as love hath pursued me; which hath been on the wing of all occasions. But whatsoever I have merited, either in my mind or in my means, meed, I am sure, I have received none; unless experience be a jewel: that I have purchased

---

1 To *wot* is to *know*. So in K. Henry VIII. *wot* you what I found?

2 *Frampold* here means *fretful*, *peevish*, or *vexatious*. This obsolete word is of uncertain etymology.

3 *Of all loves*, is an adjuration only, and signifies no more than *by all means*, for the sake of all love. It is again used in Othello and in A Midsummer Night's Dream.

4 A *watchword*.

5 *Fights* are the waist cloths which hang round about the ship to hinder men from being seen in fight; or any place wherein men may cover themselves, and yet use their arms.—*Phillips' World of Words*.

6 It seems to have been a common custom in taverns in Shakspeare's time, to send presents of wine from one room to another either as a memorial of friendship, or (as in the present instance) by way of introduction to acquaintance. The practice was continued as late as the Restoration. In the Parliamentary History, vol. xxii. p. 114, we have the following passage from The Life of General Monk, by Dr. Price. "I came to the Three Tuns, before Guildhall, where the general had quartered two nights before I entered the tavern with a servant and portmanteau, and asked for a room, which I had scarce got into but *wine followed me as a present* from some citizens desiring leave to drink their morning's draught with me."

7 *Via*, an Italian word, which Florio explains:—"an adverb of encouragement, on away, go to, away forward, go on, despatch." It appears to have been a common exclamation in Shakspeare's time. Antonini renders it in Latin *eja, age.*

8 Since.

9 *Observance* is diligent heed, or attention.—*Bullokar.*

at an infinite rate; and that hath taught me to say this:

Love like a shadow flies, when substance love pursues;
Pursuing that that flies, and flying what pursues.

Fal. Have you received no promise of satisfaction at her hands?

Ford. Never.

Fal. Have you importuned her to such a purpose?

Ford. Never.

Fal. Of what quality was your love then?

Ford. Like a fair house, built upon another man's ground, so that I have lost my edifice, by mistaking the place where I erected it.

Fal. To what purpose have you unfolded this to me?

Ford. When I have told you that, I have told you all. Some say, that though she appear honest to me, yet, in other places, she enlargeth her mirth so far, that there is shrewd construction made of her. Now, Sir John, here is the heart of my purpose: You are a gentleman of excellent breeding, admirable discourse, of great admittance,[1] authentic in your place and person, generally allowed[2] for your many warlike, courtlike, and learned preparations.

Fal. O, sir!

Ford. Believe it, for you know it:—There is money; spend it, spend it, spend more; spend all I have; only give me so much of your time in exchange of it, as to lay an amiable siege to the honesty of this Ford's wife: use your art of wooing, win her consent to you; if any man may, you may as soon as any.

Fal. Would it apply well to the vehemency of your affection, that I should win what you would enjoy? Methinks you prescribe to yourself very preposterously.

Ford. O, understand my drift! she dwells so securely on the excellency of her honour, that the folly of my soul dares not present itself; she is too bright to be looked against. Now, could I come to her with any detection in my hand, my desires had instance and argument to commend themselves; I could drive her then from the ward[3] of her purity, her reputation, her marriage-vow, and a thousand other her defences, which now are too strongly embattled against me: What say you to't, Sir John?

Fal. Master Brook, I will first make bold with your money; next give me your hand; and last, as I am a gentleman, you shall, if you will, enjoy Ford's wife.

Ford. O good sir!

Fal. Master Brook, I say you shall.

Ford. Want no money, Sir John, you shall want none.

Fal. Want no mistress Ford, Master Brook, you shall want none. I shall be with her (I may tell you,) by her own appointment; even as you came in to me, her assistant, or go-between, parted from me: I say, I shall be with her between ten and eleven; for at that time the jealous rascally knave, her husband, will be forth. Come you to me at night; you shall know how I speed.

Ford. I am blest in your acquaintance. Do you know Ford, sir?

Fal. Hang him, poor cuckoldly knave! I know him not:—yet I wrong him to call him poor; they say, the jealous wittolly knave hath masses of money; for the which his wife seems to me well-favoured, I will use her as the key of the cuckoldly rogue's coffer; and there's my harvest-home.

Ford. I would you knew Ford, sir; that you might avoid him, if you saw him.

Fal. Hang him, mechanical salt-butter rogue! I will stare him out of his wits; I will awe him with my cudgel; it shall hang like a meteor o'er the cuckold's horns: master Brook, thou shalt know, I will predominate o'er the peasant, and thou shalt lie with his wife.—Come to me soon at night:—Ford's a knave, and I will aggravate his stile;[4] thou, master Brook, shalt know him for a knave and cuckold:—come to me soon at night. [*Exit.*

Ford. What a damned Epicurean rascal is this!—My heart is ready to crack with impatience.—Who says this is improvident jealousy?—My wife hath sent to him, the hour is fixed, the match is made. Would any man have thought this?—See the hell of having a false woman! my bed shall be abused, my coffers ransacked, my reputation gnawn at; and I shall not only receive this villanous wrong, but stand under the adoption of abominable terms, and by him that does me this wrong. Terms! names!——Amaimon sounds well; Lucifer, well; Barbason,[5] well; yet they are devils' additions, the names of fiends: but cuckold! wittol[6] cuckold! the devil himself hath not such a name. Page is an ass, a secure ass; he will trust his wife, he will not be jealous: I will rather trust a Fleming with my butter, parson Hugh the Welshman with my cheese, an Irishman with my aqua-vitæ[7] bottle, or a thief to walk my ambling gelding, than my wife with herself; then she plots, then she ruminates, then she devises: and what they think in their hearts they may effect, they will break their hearts but they will effect. Heaven be praised for my jealousy!—Eleven o'clock the hour—I will prevent this, detect my wife, be revenged on Falstaff, and laugh at Page. I will about it; better three hours too soon, than a minute too late. Fie, fie, fie! cuckold! cuckold! cuckold! [*Exit.*

SCENE III. *Windsor Park. Enter* CAIUS *and* RUGBY.

Caius. Jack Rugby.

Rug. Sir.

Caius. Vat is de clock, Jack?

Rug. 'Tis past the hour, sir, that Sir Hugh promised to meet.

Caius. By gar, he has save his soul, dat he is no come: he has pray his Pible vell, dat he is no come: by gar, Jack Rugby, he is dead already, if he be come.

Rug. He is wise, sir; he knew your worship would kill him, if he came.

Caius. By gar, de herring is no dead, so as I vill kill him. Take your rapier, Jack; I vill tell you how I vill kill him.

Rug. Alas, sir, I cannot fence.

Caius. Villany, take your rapier.

Rug. Forbear; here's company.

Enter HOST, SHALLOW, SLENDER, *and* PAGE.

Host. 'Bless thee, bully doctor.

Shal. Save you, master doctor Caius.

Page. Now, good master doctor!

Slen. Give you good-morrow, sir.

Caius. Vat be all you, one, too, tree, four, come for?

Host. To see thee fight, to see thee foin,[8] to see thee traverse, to see thee here, to see thee there: to see thee pass thy punto, thy stock, thy reverse, thy distance, thy montant.[9] Is he dead, my Ethiopian? is he dead, my Francisco? ha, bully

1 i. e. admitted into all, or the greatest companies.

2 *Allowed* is *approved*. So in King Lear:
——" if your sweet sway
Allow obedience," &c.

3 i. e. *defence.*

4 This is a phrase from the Herald's Office. Falstaff means that he will *add more titles to those Ford is already distinguished by.*

5 Reginald Scott, in his Discovery of Witchcraft, may be consulted concerning these demons. "*Amaimon,*" he says, "was King of the East, and *Barbatos* a great countie or earle." But Randle Holme, in his Academy of Armory, informs us that "*Amaymon* is the chief whose dominion is on the north part of the infernal gulf; and that *Barbatos* is like a Sagittarius, and has thirty legions under him."

6 A tame contented cuckold knowing himself to be one. From the Saxon *wittan*, to know.

7 Usquebaugh.

8 The ancient term for making a thrust in fencing.

9 Terms in fencing. The *stoccado*, the *reverso*, &c from the Italian.

What says my Æsculapius? my Galen? my heart of elder?[1] ha! is he dead, bully Stale?[2] is he dead?

Caius. By gar, he is de coward Jack priest of the vorld; he is not show his face.

Host. Thou art a Castilian, king-urinal! Hector of Greece, my boy!

Caius. I pray you, bear vitness that me have stay six or seven, two, tree hours for him, and he is no come.

Shal. He is the wiser man, master doctor: he is a curer of souls, and you a curer of bodies; if you should fight, you go against the hair of your professions: is it not true, master Page?

Page. Master Shallow, you have yourself been a great fighter, though now a man of peace.

Shal. Bodykins, master Page, though I now be old, and of the peace, if I see a sword out, my finger itches to make one: though we are justices, and doctors, and churchmen, master Page, we have some salt of our youth in us; we are the sons of women, master Page.

Page. 'Tis true, master Shallow.

Shal. It will be found so, master Page. Master doctor Caius, I am come to fetch you home. I am sworn of the peace; you have showed yourself a wise physician, and Sir Hugh hath shown himself a wise and patient churchman: you must go with me, master doctor.

Host. Pardon, guest justice:—A word, monsieur Muck-water.[3]

Caius. Muck-vater; vat is dat?

Host. Muck-water, in our English tongue, is valour, bully.

Caius. By gar, then I have as much muck-vater as de Englishman:—Scurvy jack-dog priest; by gar, me vil cut his ears.

Host. He will clapper-claw thee tightly, bully.

Caius. Clapper-de-claw! vat is dat?

Host. That is, he will make thee amends.

Caius. By gar, me do look, he shall clapper-de-law me; for, by gar, me vill have it.

Host. And I will provoke him to't, or let him wag.

Caius. Me tank you for dat.

Host. And moreover, bully,—But first, master guest, and master Page, and eke cavalero Slender, go you through the town to Frogmore. [*Aside to them.*

Page. Sir Hugh is there, is he?

Host. He is there: see what humour he is in; and I will bring the doctor about by the fields: will it do well?

Shal. We will do it.

Page, Shal. and Slen. Adieu, good master doctor. [*Exeunt* PAGE, SHALLOW, *and* SLENDER.

Caius. By gar, me vill kill de priest; for he speak for a jack-an-ape to Anne Page.

Host. Let him die: but, first, sheath thy impatience; throw cold water on thy choler: go about the fields with me through Frogmore; I will bring thee where Mrs. Anne Page is, at a farmhouse a feasting; and thou shalt woo her: Cry'd game,[4] said I well?

Caius. By gar, me tank you for dat: by gar, I love you; and I shall procure-a you de good guest, de earl, de knight, de lords, de gentlemen, my patients.

Host. For the which, I will be thy adversary towards Anne Page; said I well?

Caius. By gar, 'tis good; vell said.

Host. Let us wag then.

Caius. Come at my heels, Jack Rugby. [*Exeunt.*

ACT III.

SCENE I. *A Field near Frogmore.* *Enter* SIR HUGH EVANS *and* SIMPLE.

Eva. I pray you now, good master Slender's serving-man, and friend Simple by your name, which way have you looked for master Caius, that calls himself *Doctor of Physic?*

Sim. Marry, sir, the pittie-ward, the park-ward, every way; old Windsor way, and every way but the town way.

Eva. I most fehemently desire you, you will also look that way.

Sim. I will, sir.

Eva. 'Pless my soul! how full of cholers I am, and trempling of mind!—I shall be glad, if he have deceived me:—how melancholies I am!—I will knog his urinals about his knave's costard,[5] when I have good opportunities for the 'ork:—'pless my soul! [*Sings.*

To shallow rivers, to whose falls[6]
Melodious birds sing madrigals;
There will we make our peds of roses,
And a thousand fragrant posies.
To shallow———

'Mercy on me! I have a great dispositions to cry.

Melodious birds sing madrigals;—
When as I sat in Pabylon,[7]—
And a thousand vagram posies.
To shallow———

Sim. Yonder he is coming this way, Sir Hugh

Eva. He's welcome:——

To shallow rivers, to whose falls——

Heaven prosper the right!—What weapons is he?

Sim. No weapons, sir: There comes my master, master Shallow, and another gentleman from Frogmore, over the stile, this way.

Eva. Pray you, give me my gown; or else keep it in your arms.

Enter PAGE, SHALLOW, *and* SLENDER.

Shal. How now, master parson? Good morrow, good Sir Hugh. Keep a gamester from the dice,

---

1 *Heart of elder* The joke is that elder has a heart of *pith.*

2 *Bully-stale* and *king-urinal*, these epithets will be sufficiently obvious to those who recollect the prevalence of empirical water-doctors. *Castilian*, a cant word (like Cataian and Ethiopian,) appears to have been generally used as a term of reproach after the defeat of the Spanish Armada. The Host avails himself of the poor doctor's ignorance of English phraseology in applying to him these high-sounding opprobrious epithets; he here means to call him *coward.*

3 Drain of a dunghill.

4 Steevens tried to give some kind of meaning to this passage. "*Cry'd game,*" says he, "might mean in those days a professed buck, who was well known by the report of his gallantry as he could have been by proclamation." Warburton conjectures that we should read *Cry Aim*, that is, "Encourage me, do I not deserve it!" This suits the speaker and occasion, and is therefore very plausible. See the second scene of the third act of this play, where the phrase again occurs.

5 Head.

6 This is a part of a beautiful little pastoral, printed among Shakspeare's Sonnets in 1599: but in England's Helicon, 1600, it is attributed to Christopher Marlowe, and to it is subjoined an answer, called 'The Nymph's Reply,' signed *Ignoto*, which is thought to be the signature of Sir Walter Raleigh. Walton has inserted them both in his Complete Angler, under the character of that smooth song which was made by Kit Marlowe, now at least fifty years ago; and an *answer* to it, which was made by Sir Walter Raleigh in his younger days.—'Old fashioned poetry but choicely good.' Sir Hugh misrecites the lines in his panic. The reader will be pleased to find them at the end of the play.

7 This line is from the old version of the 137th Psalm:

"*When we did sit in Babylon,*
The *rivers* round about,
Then the remembrance of Sion,
The tears for grief burst out."

The word *rivers* in the second line was probably brought to Sir Hugh's thoughts by the line of the madrigal he had just repeated; and in his fright he blends the sacred and profane songs together. The old quarto has—'There lived a man in Babylon,' which was the first line of an old song mentioned in Twelfth Night; but the other line is more in character

and a good student from his book, and it is wonderful.

Slen. Ah, sweet Anne Page!

Page. Save you, good Sir Hugh!

Eva. 'Pless you from his mercy sake, all of you!

Shal. What! the sword and the word! do you study them both, master parson?

Page. And youthful still, in your doublet and hose, this raw rheumatic day?

Eva. There is reasons and causes for it.

Page. We are come to you, to do a good office, master parson.

Eva. Fery well: What is it?

Page. Yonder is a most reverend gentleman, who be like, having received wrong by some person, is at most odds with his own gravity and patience, that ever you saw.

Shal. I have lived fourscore years and upward; I never heard a man of his place, gravity, and learning, so wide of his own respect.

Eva. What is he?

Page. I think you know him; master doctor Caius, the renowned French physician.

Eva. Got's will, and his passion of my heart! I had as lief you would tell me of a mess of porridge.

Page. Why?

Eva. He has no more knowledge in Hibocrates and Galen,—and he is a knave besides; a cowardly knave, as you would desires to be acquainted withal.

Page. I warrant you, he's the man should fight with him.

Slen. O, sweet Anne Page!

Shal. It appears so, by his weapons:—Keep them asunder; here comes doctor Caius.

Enter Host, Caius, *and* Rugby.

Page. Nay, good master parson, keep in your weapon.

Shal. So do you, good master doctor.

Host. Disarm them, and let them question; let them keep their limbs whole, and hack our English.

Caius. I pray you, let-a me speak a word vit your ear: Verefore vill you not meet a-me?

Eva. Pray you, use your patience: In good time.

Caius. By gar, you are de coward, de Jack dog, John ape.

Eva. Pray you, let us not be laughing-stogs to other men's humours; I desire you in friendship, and I will one way or other make you amends:—I will knog your urinals about your knave's cogscomb, for missing your meetings and appointments.

Caius. *Diable!*—Jack Rugby,—mine *Host de Jarterre*, have I not stay for him, to kill him? have I not, at de place I did appoint?

Eva. As I am a Christians soul, now, look you, this is the place appointed; I'll be judgment by mine host of the Garter.

Host. Peace, I say Guallia and Gaul, French and Welsh; soul-curer and body-curer.

Caius. Ay, dat is very good! excellent!

Host. Peace, I say; hear mine host of the Garter. Am I politic? am I subtle? am I a Machiavel? Shall I lose my doctor? no; he gives me the potions, and the motions. Shall I lose my parson? my priest, my Sir Hugh? no; he gives me the proverbs and the no-verbs.—Give me thy hand, terrestial; so:—Give me thy hand, celestial; so. ——Boys of art, I have deceived you both; I have directed you to wrong places: your hearts are mighty, your skins are whole, and let burnt sack be the issue.—Come, lay their swords to pawn:—Follow me, lad of peace; follow, follow, follow.

Shal. Trust me, a mad host:—Follow, gentlemen, follow.

Slen. O, sweet Anne Page!

[*Exeunt* Shal. Slen. Page, *and* Host.

Caius. Ha! do I perceive dat? have you make-a de sot[1] of us? ha, ha!

Eva. This is well; he has made us his vlouting-stog.[2]—I desire you, that we may be friends; and let us knog our prains together, to be revenge on this same scall,[3] scurvy, cogging companion, the host of the Garter.

Caius. By gar, vit all my heart; he promise to bring me vere is Anne Page: by gar, he deceive me too.

Eva. Well, I will smite his noddles:—Pray you, follow. [*Exeunt*

SCENE II. *The street in Windsor.* *Enter* Mistress Page *and* Robin.

Mrs. Page. Nay, keep your way, little gallant; you were wont to be a follower, but now you are a leader: Whether had you rather lead mine eyes, or eye your master's heels?

Rob. I had rather, forsooth, go before you like a man, than follow him like a dwarf.

Mrs. Page. O you are a flattering boy; now, I see you'll be a courtier.

Enter Ford.

Ford. Well met, mistress Page: Whither go you?

Mrs. Page. Truly, sir, to see your wife; Is she at home?

Ford. Ay; and as idle as she may hang together, for want of company: I think, if your husbands were dead, you two would marry.

Mrs. Page. Be sure of that,—two other husbands.

Ford. Where had you this pretty weather-cock?

Mrs. Page. I cannot tell what the dickens his name is my husband had him of: What do you call your knight's name, sirrah?

Rob. Sir John Falstaff.

Ford. Sir John Falstaff!

Mrs. Page. He, he; I can never hit on's name. There is such a league between my good man and he!—Is your wife at home, indeed?

Ford. Indeed she is.

Mrs. Page. By your leave, sir;—I am sick, till I see her. [*Exeunt* Mrs. Page *and* Robin

Ford. Has Page any brains? hath he any eyes? hath he any thinking? Sure, they sleep; he hath no use of them. Why, this boy will carry a letter twenty miles, as easy as a cannon will shoot point blank twelve score. He pieces-out his wife's inclination; he gives her folly motion and advantage: and now she's going to my wife, and Falstaff's boy with her. A man may hear this shower sing in the wind!—and Falstaff's boy with her!—Good plots!—they are laid; and our revolted wives share damnation together. Well; I will take him; then torture my wife, pluck the borrowed veil of modesty from the so-seeming mistress Page, divulge Page himself for a secure and wilful Actæon; and to these violent proceedings all my neighbours shall cry aim.[4] [*Clock strikes.*] The clock gives me my cue, and my assurance bids me search; there I shall find Falstaff: I shall be rather praised for this, than mocked; for it is as positive as the earth is firm, that Falstaff is there: I will go.

Enter Page, Shallow, Slender, Host, Sir Hugh Evans, Caius, *and* Rugby

Shal. Page, &c. Well met, master Ford.

Ford. Trust me good knot: I have good cheer at home; and, I pray you all, go with me.

Shal. I must excuse myself, master Ford.

---

1 Fool.

2 Flouting-stock.

3 i. e. *scall'd-head*, a term of reproach. Chaucer imprecates on the scrivener who miswrites his verse—
"Under thy long locks mayest thou have the *scalle*"

4 To cry *aim*, in archery was *to encourage* the archers by crying out *aim* when they were about to shoot. Hence it came to be used for to applaud or encourage, in a general sense. It seems that the spectators in general cried *aim* occasionally, as a mere word of encouragement or applause Thus, in K. John Act ii. Sc. 1.
'It ill beseems this presence *to cry aim*
To these ill tuned repetitions'

Slen. And so must I, sir; we have appointed to dine with mistress Anne, and I would not break with her for more money than I'll speak of.

Shal. We have lingered about a match between Anne Page and my cousin Slender, and this day we shall have our answer.

Slen. I hope, I have your good will, father Page.

Page. You have, master Slender; I stand wholly for you:—but my wife, master doctor, is for you altogether.

Caius. Ay, by gar; and de maid is love-a me; my nursh-a Quickly tell me so mush.

Host. What say you to young master Fenton? he capers, he dances, he has eyes of youth, he writes verses, he speaks holyday,[1] he smells April and May: he will carry't, he will carry't; 'tis in his buttons;[2] he will carry't.

Page. Not by my consent, I promise you. The gentleman is of no having:[3] he kept company with the wild Prince and Poins; he is of too high a region, he knows too much. No, he shall not knit a knot in his fortunes with the finger of my substance: if he take her, let him take her simply; the wealth I have waits on my consent, and my consent goes not that way.

Ford. I beseech you, heartily, some of you go home with me to dinner: besides your cheer, you shall have sport; I will show you a monster.—— Master doctor, you shall go;—so shall you, master Page;—And you, Sir Hugh.

Shal. Well, fare you well:—we shall have the freer wooing at master Page's.

[*Exeunt* SHALLOW *and* SLENDER.

Caius. Go home, John Rugby; I come anon.

[*Exit* RUGBY.

Host. Farewell, my hearts: I will to my honest knight Falstaff, and drink canary with him.

[*Exit* Host.

Ford. [*Aside.*] I think, I shall drink in pipe-wine[4] first with him; I'll make him dance. Will you go, gentles?

All. Have with you, to see this monster.

[*Exeunt.*

SCENE III. *A Room in* Ford's *House.* *Enter* MRS. FORD *and* MRS. PAGE.

Mrs. Ford. What, John! what, Robert!

Mrs. Page. Quickly! quickly: Is the buck-basket—

Mrs. Ford. I warrant:—What, Robin, I say.

Enter Servants with a basket.

Mrs. Page. Come, come, come.

Mrs. Ford. Here, set it down.

Mrs Page. Give your men the charge; we must be brief.

Mrs. Ford. Marry, as I told you before, John and Robert, be ready here hard by in the brew-house; and when I suddenly call you, come forth, and (without any pause, or staggering) take this basket on your shoulders: that done, trudge with it in all haste, and carry it among the whitsters[5] in Datchet mead, and there empty it in the muddy ditch, close by the Thames' side.

Mrs. Page. You will do it?

Mrs. Ford. I have told them over and over, they lack no direction: Be gone, and come wher you are called. [*Exeunt* Servants

Mrs. Page. Here comes little Robin.

Enter ROBIN.

Mrs. Ford. How now, my eyas-musket?[6] wha news with you?

Rob. My master Sir John has come in at your back door, mistress Ford; and requests your company.

Mrs. Page. You little Jack-a-lent,[7] have you been true to us?

Rob. Ay, I'll be sworn: My master knows not of your being here; and hath threatened to put me into everlasting liberty, if I tell you of it; for, he swears, he'll turn me away.

Mrs. Page. Thou art a good boy; this secrecy of thine shall be a tailor to thee, and shall make thee a new doublet and hose.—I'll go hide me.

Mrs. Ford. Do so:—Go tell thy master, I am alone. Mistress Page, remember you your cue.

[*Exit* ROBIN.

Mrs. Page. I warrant thee; if I do not act it, hiss me. [*Exit* MRS. PAGE.

Mrs. Ford. Go to then: we'll use this unwholesome humidity, this gross watery pumpion;—we'll teach him to know turtles from jays.[8]

Enter FALSTAFF.

Fal. *Have I caught* thee, *my heavenly jewel?*[9] Why, now let me die, for I have lived long enough; this is the period of my ambition: O this blessed hour!

Mrs. Ford. O sweet Sir John!

Fal. Mistress Ford, I cannot cog, I cannot prate, mistress Ford. Now shall I sin in my wish: I would thy husband were dead: I'll speak it before the best lord, I would make thee my lady.

Mrs. Ford. I your lady, Sir John! alas, I should be a pitiful lady.

Fal. Let the court of France show me such another; I see how thine eye would emulate the diamond: Thou hast the right arched bent[10] of the brow, that becomes the ship-tire, the tire-valiant, or any tire of Venetian admittance.[11]

Mrs Ford. A plain kerchief, Sir John: my brows become nothing else; nor that well neither.

Fal. By the Lord, thou art a traitor to say so: thou would'st make an absolute courtier; and the firm fixture of thy foot would give an excellent motion to thy gait, in a semi-circled farthingale. I see what thou wert, if fortune thy foe[12] were not: nature is thy friend: Come, thou canst not hide it.

Mrs. Ford. Believe me, there's no such thing in me.

---

1 To speak out of the common style, superior to the vulgar, in allusion to the better dress worn on holidays. So in K. Henry IV. P. I.

"With many *holiday* and lady terms."

2 Alluding to an ancient custom among rustics, of trying whether they should succeed with their mistresses by carrying the flower called *bachelor's buttons* in their pockets. They judged of their good or bad success by their growing or not growing there. Hence, *to wear bachelor's buttons*, seems to have grown into a phrase for being unmarried.

3 i. e. Fortune or possessions. So, in Twelfth Night:

——'My *having* is not much;
I'll make division of my present with you:
Hold, there is half my coffer'

4 *Canary* is the name of a dance as well as of a wine. *Pipe-wine* is wine, not from the bottle but the pipe or cask. The jest consists in the ambiguity of the word, which signifies both a cask of wine and a musical instrument.—'I'll give him *pipe* wine, which will make him *dance*.'

5 Bleachers of linen.

6 *Young sparrow-hawk*, here used as a jocular term for a small child.

7 *A stuffed puppet* thrown at throughout lent, as cocks were at shrovetide. So, in 'The Weakest goes to the Wall,' 1600.

'A mere anotomy *a Jack of Lent*'

8 i. e. honest women from *loose ones*. The word *Putta* in Italian signifies both a *jay* and a loose woman. So, in Cymbeline:

————"some *jay* of Italy
Whose mother was her painting," &c.

9 This is the first line in the second song of Sidney's Astrophel and Stella.

10 First folio:—*beauty*.

11 That is, any fanciful head-dress worn by the celebrated beauties of Venice, or approved by them. In how much request the Venetian *tire* or head-dress was formerly held, appears from Burton's Anatomy of Melancholy, 1624. "Let her have the Spanish gait, the *Venetian tire*, Italian compliments and endowments."

12 *Fortune my Foe* is the beginning of a popular old ballad enumerating all the misfortunes that fall on mankind through the caprice of Fortune. The tune was the same with that of 'Death and the Lady,' to which the metrical lamentations of extraordinary criminals were chanted for two hundred years and more

Fal. What made me love thee? let that persuade thee, there's something extraordinary in thee. Come, I cannot cog, and say thou art this and that, like a many of these lisping hawthorn buds, that come like women in men's apparel, and smell like Bucklersbury[1] in simple-time; I cannot: but I love thee; none but thee; and thou deservest it.

Mrs. Ford. Do not betray me, sir; I fear you love mistress Page.

Fal. Thou might'st as well say, I love to walk by the Counter[2]-gate; which is as hateful to me as the reek of a lime-kiln.[3]

Mrs. Ford. Well, heaven knows how I love you; and you shall one day find it.

Fal. Keep in that mind; I'll deserve it.

Mrs. Ford. Nay, I must tell you, so you do; or else I could not be in that mind.

Rob. [*within.*] Mistress Ford, mistress Ford! here's mistress Page at the door, sweating and blowing, and looking wildly, and would needs speak with you presently.

Fal. She shall not see me; I will ensconce me behind the arras.[4]

Mrs. Ford. Pray you, do so; she's a very tattling woman.— [FALSTAFF *hides himself.*

Enter MISTRESS PAGE *and* ROBIN.

What's the matter? how now?

Mrs. Page. O mistress Ford, what have you done? You're ashamed, you are overthrown, you are undone for ever.

Mrs. Ford. What's the matter, good mistress Page?

Mrs. Page. O well-a-day, mistress Ford! having an honest man to your husband, to give him such cause of suspicion!

Mrs. Ford. What cause of suspicion?

Mrs. Page. What cause of suspicion?—Out upon you! how am I mistook in you!

Mrs. Ford. Why, alas! what's the matter?

Mrs. Page. Your husband's coming hither, woman, with all the officers in Windsor, to search for a gentleman, that, he says, is here now in the house, by your consent, to take an ill advantage of his absence: You are undone.

Mrs. Ford. Speak louder.—[*Aside.*]—'Tis not so, I hope.

Mrs. Page. Pray heaven it be not so, that you have such a man here; but 'tis most certain your husband's coming with half Windsor at his heels, to search for such a one. I come before to tell you: If you know yourself clear, why I am glad of it: but if you have a friend here, convey, convey him out. Be not amazed: call all your senses to you; defend your reputation, or bid farewell to your good life for ever.

Mrs. Ford. What shall I do?—There is a gentleman, my dear friend; and I fear not mine own shame, so much as his peril: I had rather than a thousand pound, he were out of the house.

Mrs. Page. For shame, never stand, *you had rather*, and *you had rather;* your husband's here at hand, bethink you of some conveyance: in the house you cannot hide him.—O, how have you deceived me!—Look, here is a basket; if he be of any reasonable stature, he may creep in here; and throw foul linen upon him, as if it were going to bucking: Or, it is whiting-time[5], send him by your two men to Datchet mead.

Mrs. Ford. He's too big to go in there: What shall I do?

Re-enter FALSTAFF.

Fal. Let me see't; let me see't! O let me see't! I'll in, I'll in;—follow your friend's counsel:—I'll in.

Mrs. Page. What! Sir John Falstaff! Are these your letters, knight?

Fal. I love thee, and none but thee;[6] help me away: let me creep in here; I'll never.

[*He goes into the basket; they cover him with foul linen.*

Mrs. Page. Help to cover your master, boy: Call your men, mistress Ford:—You dissembling knight!

Mrs. Ford. What, John, Robert, John! [*Exit* Robin; *Re-enter* Servants.] Go take up these clothes here, quickly; where's the cowl-staff?[7] look, how you drumble:[8] carry them to the laundress in Datchet mead;[9] quickly, come.

Enter FORD, PAGE, CAIUS, *and* SIR HUGH EVANS.

Ford. Pray you, come near: if I suspect without cause, why then make sport at me, then let me be your jest; I deserve it.—How now? whither bear you this?

Serv. To the laundress, forsooth.

Mrs. Ford. Why, what have you to do whither they bear it? You were best meddle with buck-washing.

Ford. Buck? I would I could wash myself of the buck! Buck! buck! buck? Ay, buck? I warrant you, buck; and of the season too, it shall appear. [*Exeunt* Servants *with the basket.*] Gentlemen, I have dreamed to-night; I'll tell you my dream. Here, here, here be my keys: ascend my chambers, search, seek, find out: I'll warrant we'll unkennel the fox:—Let me stop this way first;—So, now uncape.[10]

Page. Good master Ford, be contented: you wrong yourself too much.

Ford. True, master Page.—Up, gentlemen; you shall see sport anon: follow me, gentlemen. [*Exit.*

Eva. This is fery fantastical humours, and jealousies.

Caius. By gar, 'tis no de fashion of France: it is not jealous in France.

Page. Nay, follow him, gentlemen, see the issue of his search. [*Exeunt* EVANS, PAGE, *and* CAIUS.

Mrs. Page. Is there not a double excellency in this?

Mrs. Ford. I know not which pleases me better that my husband is deceived, or Sir John.

---

1 Formerly chiefly inhabited by druggists, who sold all kinds of herbs green as well as dry.

2 The *Counter* as a prison was odious to Falstaff.

3 So, in Coriolanus—

———' Whose breath *I hate*
As *reek* o' the rotten fens."

The name of this prison was a frequent subject of jocularity with our ancestors. Shakspeare has availed himself of it in the Comedy of Errors. My old acquaintance Baret records one pleasantly enough in his Alvearie, 1573.—" We saie merrily of him who hath been in the *Counter* or such like places of prison: He can sing his *counter-tenor* very well. And in anger we say, I will make you sing a counter-tenor for this geare: meaning imprisonment."

4 The spaces left between the walls and wooden frames on which the tapestry was hung, were not more commodious to our ancestors, than to the authors of ancient dramatic pieces.

5 Bleaching time.

6 These words, which are characteristic, and spoken to Mrs. Page aside, deserve to be restored from the old quarto. He had used the same words before to Mrs. Ford.

7 A staff used for carrying a *cowl* or tub with two handles to fetch water in. " *Bicollo*, a *cowle-staffe* to carie behind and before with, as they use in Italy to carie two buckets at once."—*Florio's Dictionary*, 1598

8 To *drumble* and *drone* meant *to move sluggishly* To *drumble*, in Devonshire, means to mutter in a sullen and inarticulate voice. A *drumble* drone, in the western dialect signifies a drone or humble-bee. That master genius of modern times, who knows so skilfully how to adapt his language to the characters and manners of the age in which his fable is laid, has adopted this word in 'The Fortunes of Nigel,' vol. ii. p. 298:—" Why how she *drumbles*—I warrant she stops to take a sip on the road."

9 Dennis observes that, 'it is not likely Falstaff would suffer himself to be carried to Datchet mead, which is half a mile from Windsor; and it is plain that they could not carry him, if he made any resistance.'

10 Hanmer proposed to read *uncouple;* but, perhaps, *uncape* had the same signification. It means, at any rate, to begin the hunt after him, when the holes for escape had been stopped

Mrs. Page. What a taking was he in, when your husband asked who[1] was in the basket!

Mrs. Page. I am half afraid he will have need of washing; so throwing him into the water will do him a benefit.

Mrs. Page. Hang him, dishonest rascal! I would all of the same strain were in the same distress.

Mrs. Ford. I think my husband hath some special suspicion of Falstaff's being here; for I never saw him so gross in his jealousy till now

Mrs. Page. I will lay a plot to try that And we will yet have more tricks with Falstaff: his dissolute disease will scarce obey this medicine.

Mrs. Ford. Shall we send that foolish carrion, mistress Quickly, to him, and excuse his throwing into the water; and give him another hope, to betray him to another punishment?

Mrs. Page. We'll do it; let him be sent for to-morrow eight o'clock to have amends.

Re-enter FORD, PAGE, CAIUS, *and* SIR HUGH EVANS.

Ford. I cannot find him: may be the knave bragged of that he could not compass.

Mrs. Page. Heard you that?

Mrs. Ford. Ay, ay, peace:—You use me well, master Ford, do you?

Ford. Ay, I do so.

Mrs. Ford. Heaven make you better than your thoughts?

Ford. Amen.

Mrs. Page. You do yourself mighty wrong, master Ford.

Ford. Ay, ay; I must bear it.

Eva. If there be any pody in the house, and in the chambers, and in the coffers, and in the presses, heaven forgive my sins at the day of judgment.

Caius. By gar, nor I too; dere is no bodies.

Page. Fie, fie, master Ford! are you not ashamed? What spirit, what devil suggests this imagination? I would not have your distemper in this kind for the wealth of Windsor Castle.

Ford. 'Tis my fault, master Page: I suffer for it.

Eva. You suffer for a pad conscience: your wife is as honest a 'omans as I will desires among five thousand, and five hundred too.

Caius. By gar, I see 'tis an honest woman.

Ford. Well;—I promised you a dinner:—Come, come, walk in the park: I pray you, pardon me; I will hereafter make known to you, why I have done this.—Come, wife;—Come, mistress Page; I pray you pardon me; pray heartily, pardon me.

Page. Let's go in, gentlemen; but, trust me, we'll mock him. I do invite you to-morrow morning to my house to breakfast; after, we'll a birding together; I have a fine hawk for the bush: Shall it be so?

Ford. Any thing.

Eva. If there is one, I shall make two in the company.

Caius. If there be one or two, I shall make-a de turd.

Eva. In your teeth: for shame.

Ford. Pray you go, master Page.

Eva. I pray you now remembrance to-morrow, on the lousy knave, mine host.

Caius. Dat is good; by gar, vit all my heart.

Eva. A lousy knave; to have his gibes, and his mockeries. [*Exeunt.*

SCENE IV. *A Room in Page's House. Enter* FENTON *and* MISTRESS ANNE PAGE.

Fent. I see, I cannot get thy father's love,
Therefore, no more turn me to him, sweet Nan
Anne. Alas! how then?
Fent. Why, thou must be thyself
He doth object, I am too great of birth;
And that, my state being gall'd with my expense,
I seek to heal it only by his wealth:
Besides these, other bars he lays before me —
My riots past, my wild societies;
And tells me, 'tis a thing impossible
I should love thee, but as a property.
Anne. May be, he tells you true.
Fent. No, heaven so speed me in my time to come!
Albeit, I will confess, thy father's wealth[2]
Was the first motive that I woo'd thee, Anne;
Yet, wooing thee, I found thee of more value
Than stamps in gold, or sums in sealed bags,
And 'tis the very riches of thyself
That now I aim at.
Anne. Gentle master Fenton,
Yet seek my father's love: still seek it, sir:
If opportunity and humblest suit
Cannot attain it, why then—Hark you hither.
[*They converse apart*

Enter SHALLOW, SLENDER, *and* MRS. QUICKLY.

Shal. Break their talk, mistress Quickly; my kinsman shall speak for himself.

Slen. I'll make a shaft or a bolt on't:[3] slid, tis but venturing.

Shal. Be not dismay'd.

Slen. No, she shall not dismay me: I care not for that,—but that I am afeard.

Quick. Hark ye; master Slender would speak a word with you.

Anne. I come to him.—This is my father's choice.
O, what a world of vile ill-favour'd faults
Looks handsome in three hundred pounds a year!
[*Aside.*

Quick. And how does good master Fenton? Pray you, a word with you.

Shal. She's coming; to her, coz. O boy, thou hadst a father!

Slen. I had a father, mistress Anne;—my uncle can tell you good jests of him:—Pray you, uncle, tell mistress Anne the jest, how my father stole two geese out of a pen, good uncle.

Shal. Mistress Anne, my cousin loves you.

Slen. Ay, that I do; as well as I love any woman in Gloucestershire.

Shal. He will maintain you like a gentlewoman.

Slen. Ay, that I will, come cut and long tail,[4] under the degree of a 'squire.

Shal. He will make you a hundred and fifty pounds jointure.

Anne. Good master Shallow, let him woo for himself.

Shal. Marry, I thank you for it; I thank you for that good comfort. She calls you, coz: I'll leave you.

Anne. Now, master Slender.

Slen. Now, good mistress Anne.

Anne. What is your will?

Slen. My will? od's heartlings, that's a pretty jest, indeed! I ne'er made my will yet, I thank heaven; I am not such a sickly creature, I give heaven praise.

Anne. I mean, master Slender, what would you with me?

---

1 Ritson thinks we should read *what*. This emendation is supported by a subsequent passage, where Falstaff says: "the jealous knave asked them once or twice *what* was in the basket." It is remarkable that Ford asked no such question.

2 Some light may be given to those who shall endeavour to calculate the increase of English wealth, by observing that Latymer, in the time of Edward VI. mentions it as a proof of his father's prosperity, "that though but a yeoman, he gave his daughters five pounds each for their portion." At the latter end of Elizabeth, seven hundred pounds were such a temptation to courtship, as made all other motives suspected. Congreve makes twelve thousand pounds more than counterbalance to the affection of Belinda. No poet will now fly his favourite character at less than fifty thousand. Below we have:

'O, what a world of vile ill favour'd faults
Looks handsome in three hundred pounds a year!'

3 A *shaft* was a long arrow, and a *bolt* a thick short one. The proverb probably means "I'll make something or other of it.—I will do it by some means or other."

4 The sense is obviously "Come who will to contend with me, under the degree of a squire." *Cut and long tail* means all kinds of curtail curs, and sporting dogs and all others. It is a phrase of frequent occurrence in writers of the period; every kind of dog being comprehended under *cut and longtail*, every rank of people the expression when metaphorically used

Slen. Truly, for mine own part, I would little or nothing with you: Your father, and my uncle, have made motions; if it be my luck, so: if not, happy man be his dole![1] They can tell you how things go, better than I can: You may ask your father; here he comes.

Enter PAGE *and* MISTRESS PAGE.

Page. Now, master Slender:—Love him, daughter Anne.—
Why, how now! what does master Fenton here?
You wrong me, sir, thus still to haunt my house:
I told you, sir, my daughter is dispos'd of.

Fent. Nay, master Page, be not impatient.

Mrs. Page. Good master Fenton, come not to my child.

Page. She is no match for you.

Fent. Sir, will you hear me?

Page. No, good master Fenton.
Come, master Shallow; come, son Slender; in:—
Knowing my mind, you wrong me, master Fenton.

[*Exeunt* PAGE, SHALLOW, *and* SLENDER.

Quick. Speak to mistress Page.

Fent. Good mistress Page, for that I love your daughter
In such a righteous fashion as I do,
Perforce, against all checks, rebukes, and manners,
I must advance the colours of my love,
And not retire: Let me have your good will.

Anne. Good mother, do not marry me to yond' fool.

Mrs. Page. I mean it not; I seek you a better husband.

Quick. That's my master, master doctor.

Anne. Alas, I had rather be set quick i' the earth,
And bowl'd to death with turnips.

Mrs. Page. Come, trouble not yourself: Good master Fenton,
I will not be your friend, nor enemy.
My daughter will I question how she loves you,
And as I find her, so am I affected;
'Till then, farewell, sir:—she must needs go in;
Her father will be angry.

[*Exeunt* MRS. PAGE *and* ANNE.

Fent. Farewell, gentle mistress; farewell, Nan.

Quick. This is my doing, now:—Nay, said I, will you cast away your child on a fool, and a physician? Look on master Fenton:—this is my doing.

Fent. I thank thee; and I pray thee, once[2] to-night
Give my sweet Nan this ring: There's for thy pains.

[*Exit.*

Quick. Now heaven send thee good fortune! A kind heart he hath: a woman would run through fire and water for such a kind heart. But yet, I would my master had mistress Anne; or I would master Slender had her; or, in sooth, I would master Fenton had her: I will do what I can for them all three; for so I have promised, and I'll be as good as my word; but speciously[3] for master Fenton. Well, I must of another errand to Sir John Falstaff from my two mistresses: What a beast am I to slack[4] it?

[*Exit.*

SCENE V. *A Room in the Garter Inn. Enter* FALSTAFF *and* BARDOLPH.

Fal. Bardolph, I say,—

Bard. Here, sir.

Fal. Go fetch me a quart of sack; put a toast in't. [*Exit* BARD.] Have I lived to be carried in a basket, like a barrow of butcher's offal; and to be thrown into the Thames? Well; if I be served such another trick, I'll have my brains ta'en out, and butter'd, and give them to a dog for a new year's gift. The rogues slighted me into the river with as little remorse,[5] as they would have drowned a bitch's blind puppies, fifteen i' the litter: and you may know by my size, that I have a kind of alacrity in sinking; if the bottom were as deep as hell, I should down. I had been drowned, but that the shore was shelvy and shallow; a death that I abhor; for the water swells a man; and what a thing should I have been, when I had been swelled! I should have been a mountain of mummy.

Re-enter BARDOLPH, *with the wine.*

Bard. Here's mistress Quickly, sir, to speak with you.

Fal. Come, let me pour in some sack to the Thames water; for my belly's as cold, as if I had swallowed snow-balls for pills to cool the reins. Call her in.

Bard. Come in, woman.

Enter MRS. QUICKLY.

Quick. By your leave; I cry you mercy: Give your worship good-morrow.

Fal. Take away these chalices:[6] Go brew me a pottle of sack finely.

Bar. With eggs, sir?

Fal. Simple of itself; I'll no pullet-sperm in my brewage.—[*Exit* BARDOLPH.]—How now?

Quick. Marry, sir, I come to your worship from mistress Ford.

Fal. Mistress Ford! I have had ford enough: I was thrown into the ford: I have my belly full of ford.

Quick. Alas the day! good heart, that was not her fault; she does so take on with her men; they mistook their erection.

Fal. So did I mine, to build upon a foolish woman's promise.

Quick. Well, she laments, sir, for it, that it would yearn your heart to see it. Her husband goes this morning a birding; she desires you once more to come to her between eight and nine: I must carry her word quickly: she'll make you amends, I warrant you.

Fal. Well, I will visit her: Tell her so; and bid her think what a man is: let her consider his frailty, and then judge of my merit.

Quick. I will tell her.

Fal. Do so. Between nine and ten say'st thou?

Quick. Eight and nine, sir.

Fal. Well, be gone: I will not miss her.

Quick. Peace be with you, sir! [*Exit.*

Fal. I marvel, I hear not of master Brook; he sent me word to stay within; I like his money well. O, here he comes.

Enter FORD.

Ford. Bless you, sir!

Fal. Now, master Brook? you come to know what hath passed between me and Ford's wife?

Ford. That, indeed, Sir John, is my business.

Fal. Master Brook, I will not lie to you; I was at her house the hour she appointed me.

Ford. And how sped you, sir?

Fal. Very ill-favouredly, master Brook.

Ford. How so, sir? Did she change her determination?

Fal. No, master Brook; but the peaking cornuto, her husband, master Brook, dwelling in a continual 'larum of jealousy, comes me in the instant of our encounter, after we had embraced, kissed, protested, and, as it were, spoke the prologue of our comedy; and at his heels a rabble of his companions, thither provoked and instigated by his distemper, and, forsooth, to search his house for his wife's love.

Ford. What, while you were there?

Fal. While I was there.

Ford. And did he search for you, and could not find you?

Fal. You shall hear. As good luck would have it, comes in one mistress Page; gives intelligence of Ford's approach; and, by her invention, and Ford's wife's distraction,[7] they conveyed me into a buck basket.

---

1 This is a proverbial expression of frequent occurrence. The apparent signification here is: 'Happiness be his portion who succeeds best,' but the general meaning of the phrase may be interpreted: 'Let his portion or lot be happy man.' *Dole* is the past participle and past tense of the A. S. verb *Dælan*, to deal, to divide, to distribute.

2 i. e. *some time* to-night. 3 Specially. 4 Neglect.

5 Pity. 6 Cups.

7 M. Mason proposes to read *direction*, but perhaps the change is not necessary

Ford. A buck-basket?

Fal. By the Lord, a buck-basket: rammed me in with foul shirts and smocks, socks, foul stockings, and greasy napkins; that, master Brook, there was the rankest compound of villanous smell, that ever offended nostril.

Ford. And how long lay you there?

Fal. Nay, you shall hear, master Brook, what I have suffered to bring this woman to evil for your good. Being thus crammed in a basket, a couple of Ford's knaves, his hinds, were called forth by their mistress, to carry me in the name of foul clothes to Datchet-lane: they took me on their shoulders; met the jealous knave their master in the door; who asked them once or twice what they had in their basket: I quaked for fear, lest the lunatic knave would have searched it; but Fate, ordaining he should be a cuckold, held his hand. Well; on went he for a search, and away went I for foul clothes. But mark the sequel, master Brook: I suffered the pangs of three several deaths; first, an intolerable fright, to be detected with[1] a jealous rotten bellwether: next, to be compassed like a good bilbo,[2] in the circumference of a peck, hilt to point, heel to head: and then, to be stopped in, like a strong distillation, with stinking clothes that fretted in their own grease: think of that,—a man of my kidney,—think of that; that am as subject to heat as butter; a man of continual dissolution and thaw; it was a miracle to 'scape suffocation. And in the height of this bath, when I was more than half stewed in grease, like a Dutch dish, to be thrown into the Thames, and cooled, glowing hot, in that surge, like a horse-shoe; think of that;—hissing hot,—think of that, master Brook.

Ford. In good sadness, sir, I am sorry that for my sake you have suffered all this. My suit then is desperate; you'll undertake her no more.

Fal. Master Brook, I will be thrown into Ætna, as I have been into Thames, ere I will leave her thus. Her husband is this morning gone a birding: I have received from her another embassy of meeting; 'twixt eight and nine is the hour, master Brook.

Ford. 'Tis past eight already, sir.

Fal. Is it? I will then address[3] me to my appointment. Come to me at your convenient leisure, and you shall know how I speed; and the conclusion shall be crowned with your enjoying her: Adieu. You shall have her, master Brook; master Brook, you shall cuckold Ford. [*Exit.*

Ford. Hum! ha! is this a vision? is this a dream? do I sleep? Master Ford, awake; awake, master Ford; there's a hole made in your best coat, master Ford. This 'tis to be married! this 'tis to have linen, and buck-baskets!—Well, I will proclaim myself what I am: I will now take the lecher; he is at my house: he cannot 'scape me; 'tis impossible he should; he cannot creep into a halfpenny purse, nor into a pepper-box: but, lest the devil that guides him should aid him, I will search impossible places. Though what I am I cannot avoid, yet to be what I would not, shall not make me tame: if I have horns to make one mad, let the proverb go with me, I'll be horn mad. [*Exit.*

ACT IV.

SCENE I.—*The Street.—Enter* MRS. PAGE, MRS. QUICKLY, *and* WILLIAM.

Mrs. Page. Is he at master Ford's already, think'st thou?

Quick. Sure, he is by this; or will be presently: but truly, he is very courageous[4] mad, about his throwing into the water. Mistress Ford desires you to come suddenly.

Mrs. Page. I'll be with her by and by; I'll but bring my young man here to school: Look, where his master comes; 'tis a playing-day, I see.

Enter SIR HUGH EVANS.

How now, Sir Hugh? no school to-day?

Eva. No; master Slender is let the boys leave to play.

Quick. Blessing of his heart!

Mrs. Page. Sir Hugh, my husband says, my son profits nothing in the world at his book; I pray you, ask him some questions in his accidence.

Eva. Come hither, William; hold up your head; come.

Mrs. Page. Come on, sirrah; hold up your head; answer your master, be not afraid.

Eva. William, how many numbers is in nouns?

Will. Two.

Quick. Truly, I thought there had been one number more; because they say, od's nouns.

Eva. Peace your tattlings. What is *fair*, William?

Will. *Pulcher.*

Quick. Poulcats! there are fairer things than poulcats, sure.

Eva. You are a very simplicity 'oman; I pray you peace. What is *lapis*, William?

Will. A stone.

Eva. And what is a stone, William?

Will. A pebble.

Eva. No, it is *lapis;* I pray you remember in your prain.

Will. *Lapis.*

Eva. That is good, William. What is he, William, that does lend articles?

Will. Articles are borrowed of the pronoun; and be thus declined, *Singulariter, nominativo, hic, hæc, hoc.*

Eva. *Nominativo, hig, hag, hog;* pray you, mark: *genetivo, hujus:* Well, what is your *accusative case?*

Will. *Accusativo, hinc.*

Eva. I pray you, have your remembrance, child; *Accusativo, hing, hang, hog.*

Quick. Hang hog is Latin for bacon, I warrant you.

Eva. Leave your prabbles, 'oman. What is the focative case, William?

Will. O—*vocativo*, O.

Eva. Remember, William; focative is *caret.*

Quick. And that's a good root.

Eva. 'Oman, forbear.

Mrs. Page. Peace.

Eva. What is your *genitive case plural*, William?

Will. *Genitive case?*

Eva. Ay.

Will. *Genetivo,—horum, harum, horum.*

Quick. 'Vengeance of *Jenny's* case! fie on her!—never name her, child, if she be a whore.

Eva. For shame, 'oman.

Quick. You do ill to teach the child such words: he teaches him to hick and to hack, which they'll do fast enough of themselves; and to call horum:—fie upon you!

Eva. 'Oman, art thou lunatics? hast thou no understandings for thy cases, and the numbers of the genders? Thou art as foolish christian creatures as I would desires.

Mrs. Page. Pr'ythee hold thy peace.

Eva. Show me now, William, some declensions of your pronouns.

Will. Forsooth, I have forgot.

Eva. It is *ki, kæ, cod;* if you forget your *kies*, your *kæs*, and your *cods*, you must be preeches.[5] Go your ways, and play, go.

1 *With, by*, and *of* were used indiscriminately with much licence by our ancestors. Thus in a subsequent passage of this play we have:—

'I sooner would suspect the sun *with* cold.

Detected appears to have been used in the sense of *suspected, impeached.* Cavendish, in his Metrical Visions, has this very phrase—*detected with*, for *impeached with*, or *held in suspicion by:*—

"What is he of our bloode that wold not be sory
To heare our names *with vile fame so detected.*"

Detected must have the same meaning here, for Falstaff was not *discovered*, but *suspected by* the jealous Ford. Some modern editors have unwarrantably substituted *by* for *with*.

2 A Bilbo is a Spanish blade remarkable for its temper and flexibility. The best were made at Bilboa, town in Biscay.

3 Make myself ready. 4 Outrageous.

5 Breeched, i. e flogged

Mrs. Page. He is a better scholar than I thought he was.

Eva. He is a good sprag[1] memory. Farewell, mistress Page.

Mrs. Page. Adieu, good Sir Hugh. [*Exit* SIR HUGH.] Get you home, boy.—Come we stay too long. [*Exeunt.*

SCENE II. *A Room in* Ford's *House. Enter* FALSTAFF *and* MRS. FORD.

Fal. Mistress Ford, your sorrow hath eaten up my sufferance: I see, you are obsequious[2] in your love, and I profess your requital to a hair's breadth; not only, mistress Ford, in the simple office of love, but in all the accoutrement, complement, and ceremony of it. But are you sure of your husband now?

Mrs. Ford. He's a birding, sweet Sir John.

Mrs. Page. [*within.*] What hoa, gossip Ford! what hoa!

Mrs. Ford. Step into the chamber, Sir John. [*Exit* FALSTAFF.

Enter MRS. PAGE.

Mrs. Page. How now, sweatheart? who's at home beside yourself?

Mrs. Ford. Why, none but mine own people.

Mrs. Page. Indeed?

Mrs. Ford. No, certainly;—speak louder. [*Aside.*

Mrs. Page. Truly, I am so glad you have nobody here.

Mrs. Ford. Why?

Mrs. Page. Why, woman, your husband is in his old lunes[3] again: he so takes on yonder with my husband; so rails against all married mankind; so curses all Eve's daughters, of what complexion soever; and so buffets himself on the forehead, crying, *Peer out, peer out!*[4] that any madness, I ever yet beheld, seemed but tameness, civility, and patience, to this his distemper he is in now: I am glad the fat knight is not here.

Mrs. Ford. Why, does he talk of him?

Mrs. Page. Of none but him; and swears, he was carried out, the last time he searched for him, in a basket: protests to my husband he is now here; and hath drawn him and the rest of their company from their sport, to make another experiment of his suspicion: but I am glad the knight is not here; now he shall see his own foolery.

Mrs. Ford. How near is he, mistress Page?

Mrs. Page. Hard by; at street end; he will be here anon.

Mrs. Ford. I am undone!—the knight is here.

Mrs. Page. Why, then you are utterly shamed, and he's but a dead man. What a woman are you?—Away with him, away with him, better shame than murder.

Mrs. Ford. Which way should he go? how should I bestow him? Shall I put him into the basket again?

Re-enter FALSTAFF.

Fal. No, I'll come no more i' the basket: May I not go out, ere he come?

Mrs. Page. Alas, three of master Ford's brothers watch the door with pistols,[5] that none shall issue out; otherwise you might slip away ere he came. But what make[6] you here?

Fal. What shall I do?—I'll creep up into the chimney.

Mrs. Ford. There they always used to discharge their birding-pieces: Creep into the kiln-hole.

Fal. Where is it?

Mrs. Ford. He will seek there on my word. Neither press, coffer, chest, trunk, well, vault, but he hath an abstract[7] for the remembrance of such places, and goes to them by his note: There is no hiding you in the house.

Fal. I'll go out then.

Mrs. Page. If you go out in your own semblance, you die, Sir John. Unless you go out disguised,—

Mrs. Ford. How might we disguise him?

Mrs. Page. Alas the day, I know not. There is no woman's gown big enough for him; otherwise, he might put on a hat, a muffler, and a kerchief, and so escape.

Fal. Good hearts, devise something: any extremity, rather than a mischief.

Mrs. Ford. My maid's aunt, the fat woman of Brentford,[8] has a gown above.

Mrs. Page. On my word, it will serve him; she's as big as he is: and there's her thrum'd hat,[9] and her muffler too: Run up, Sir John.

Mrs. Ford. Go, go, sweet Sir John: mistress Page and I will look some linen for your head.

Mrs. Page. Quick, quick; we'll come dress you straight: put on the gown the while. [*Exit* FALSTAFF.

Mrs. Ford. I would my husband would meet him in this shape: he cannot abide the old woman of Brentford; he swears, she's a witch; forbade her my house, and hath threatened to beat her.

Mrs. Page. Heaven guide him to thy husband's cudgel; and the devil guide his cudgel afterwards!

Mrs. Ford. But is my husband coming?

Mrs. Page. Ay, in good sadness, is he; and talks of the basket too, howsoever he hath had intelligence.

Mrs. Ford. We'll try that; for I'll appoint my men to carry the basket again, to meet him at the door with it, as they did last time.

Mrs. Page. Nay, but he'll be here presently: let's go dress him like the witch of Brentford.[10]

Mrs. Ford. I'll first direct my men, what they shall do with the basket. Go up, I'll bring linen for him straight. [*Exit.*

Mrs. Page. Hang him, dishonest varlet! we cannot misuse him enough.

We'll leave a proof, by that which we will do,
Wives may be merry, and yet honest too:
We do not act that often jest and laugh;
'Tis old but true, *Still swine eat all the draff.* [*Exit.*

Re-enter MRS. FORD, *with two* Servants.

Mrs. Ford. Go, sirs, take the basket again on your shoulders; your master is hard at door; if he bid you set it down, obey him, quickly despatch.

1 *Serv.* Come, come, take it up. [*Exit.*

2 *Serv.* Pray heaven, it be not full of the knight again.

1 *Serv.* I hope not; I had as lief bear so much lead.

Enter FORD, PAGE, SHALLOW, CAIUS, *and* SIR HUGH EVANS.

Ford. Ay, but if it prove true, master Page, have you any way then to unfool me again?—Set down the basket, villain:—Somebody call my wife:—You, youth in a basket, come out here!—O, you

1 Quick, alert. The word is *sprack.*

2 So, in Hamlet; 'To do *obsequious* sorrow.' The epithet *obsequious* refers, in both instances, to the seriousness with which *obsequies* are performed.

3 i. e. lunacy, frenzy.

4 Shakspeare refers to a sport of children, who thus call on a snail to push forth his horns:

" Peer out, peer out, peer out of your hole,
Or else I'll beat you as black as a coal."

5 This is one of Shakspeare's anachronisms: he has also introduced pistols in Pericles, in the reign of Antiochus, two hundred years before Christ.

6 This phrase has been already noticed. It occurs again in As You Like It, in the sense of *do:*

'Now, sir, what *make* you here?'

It also occurs in Hamlet, Othello, and Love's Labour's Lost.

7 i. e. a list, an inventory, or short note of.

8 In the early 4to. it is: "My maid's aunt *Gillian* of Brentford."

9 A hat composed of the weaver's tufts or *thrums,* or of very coarse cloth. A *muffler* was a part of female attire which only covered the lower part of the face.

10 This old witch Jyl or Gillian of Brentford seems to have been a character well known in popular story at the time. 'Jyl of Brentford's Testament' was printed by Copland long before, and Laneham enumerates it as in the collection of Capt. Cox, the mason, now well known to all, from the mention of him in the romance of Kenilworth.

panderly rascals! there's a knot, a ging,[1] a pack, a conspiracy against me: Now, shall the devil be shamed. What! wife, I say! come, come forth; behold what honest clothes you send forth to bleaching.

Page. Why, this passes![2] Master Ford, you are not to go loose any longer; you must be pinioned.

Eva. Why, this is lunatics! this is mad as a mad dog!

Shal. Indeed, master Ford, this is not well; indeed.

Enter Mrs. Ford.

Ford. So say I too, Sir.—Come hither, mistress Ford; mistress Ford, the honest woman, the modest wife, the virtuous creature, that hath the jealous fool to her husband!—I suspect without cause, mistress, do I?

Mrs. Ford. Heaven be my witness you do, if you suspect me in any dishonesty.

Ford. Well said, brazen-face; hold it out.—— Come forth, sirrah. [*Pulls the clothes out of the basket.*

Page. This passes!

Mrs. Ford. Are you not ashamed? let the clothes alone.

Ford. I shall find you anon.

Eva. 'Tis unreasonable! Will you take up your wife's clothes? Come away.

Ford. Empty the basket, I say.

Mrs. Ford. Why, man, why?

Ford. Master Page, as I am a man, there was one conveyed out of my house yesterday in this basket: Why may not he be there again? In my house I am sure he is: my intelligence is true; my jealousy is reasonable: Pluck me out all the linen.

Mrs. Ford. If you find a man there, he shall die a flea's death.

Page. Here's no man.

Shal. By my fidelity, this is not well, master Ford; this wrongs you.[3]

Eva. Master Ford, you must pray, and not follow the imaginations of your own heart: this is jealousies.

Ford. Well, he's not here I seek for.

Page. No, nor no where else, but in your brain.

Ford. Help to search my house this one time; if I find not what I seek, show no colour for my extremity, let me for ever be your table-sport; let them say of me, As jealous as Ford, that searched a hollow walnut for his wife's leman.[4] Satisfy me once more; once more search with me.

Mrs. Ford. What hoa, mistress Page! come you, and the old woman down; my husband will come into the chamber.

Ford. Old woman! What old woman is that?

Mrs. Ford. Why, it is my maid's aunt of Brentford.

Ford. A witch, a quean, an old cozening quean! Have I not forbid her my house? She comes of errands, does she? We are simple men; we do not know what's brought to pass under the profession of fortune-telling. She works by charms, by spells, by the figure, and such daubery[5] as this is; beyond our element; we know nothing.——Come down; you witch, you hag you; come down, I say.

Mrs. Ford. Nay, good, sweet husband;—good gentlemen, let him not strike the old woman.

Enter Falstaff *in women's clothes, led by* Mrs. Page.

Mrs. Page. Come, mother Pratt, come, give me your hand.

Ford. I'll *prat* her:——Out of my door, you witch! [*beats him*] you rag, you baggage, you polecat, you ronyon![6] out! out. I'll conjure you, I'll fortune-tell you. [*Exit* Falstaff.

Mrs. Page. Are you not ashamed? I think you have killed the poor woman.

Mrs. Ford. Nay, he will do it;—'Tis a goodly credit for you.

Ford. Hang her, witch!

Eva. By yea and no, I think, the 'oman is a witch indeed: I like not when a 'oman has a great peard; I spy a great peard under her muffler.

Ford. Will you follow, gentlemen? I beseech you, follow; see but the issue of my jealousy; if I cry out thus upon no trail,[7] never trust me when I open again.

Page. Let's obey his humour a little further: Come, gentlemen.

[*Exeunt* Page, Ford, Shallow, *and* Evans.

Mrs. Page. Trust me, he beat him most pitifully.

Mrs. Ford. Nay, by the mass that he did not; he beat him most unpitifully, methought.

Mrs. Page. I'll have the cudgel hallowed, and hang o'er the altar; it hath done meritorious service.

Mrs. Ford. What think you? May we, with the warrant of woman-hood, and the witness of a good conscience, pursue him with any further revenge?

Mrs. Page. The spirit of wantonness is, sure, scared out of him; if the devil have him not in fee-simple, with fine and recovery,[8] he will never, I think, in the way of waste,[9] attempt us again.

Mrs. Ford. Shall we tell our husbands how we have served him?

Mrs. Page. Yes, by all means; if it be but to scrape the figures out of your husband's brains. If they can find in their hearts, the poor unvirtuous fat knight shall be any further afflicted, we two will still be the ministers.

Mrs. Ford. I'll warrant they'll have him publicly shamed: and, methinks, there would be no period[10] to the jest, should he not be publicly shamed.

Mrs. Page. Come to the forge with it then, shape it: I would not have things cool. [*Exeunt.*

SCENE III. *A room in the Garter Inn. Enter* Host *and* Bardolph.

Bard. Sir, the Germans desire to have three of your horses: the duke himself will be to-morrow at court, and they are going to meet him.

Host. What duke should that be comes so secretly? I hear not of him in the court: Let me speak with the gentlemen; they speak English?

Bard. Ay, sir, I'll call them to you.

Host. They shall have my horses; but I'll make them pay, I'll sauce them: they have had my house a week at command; I have turned away my other guests: they must come off;[11] I'll sauce them; Come. [*Exeunt.*

SCENE IV. *A Room in* Ford's *House. Enter* Page, Ford, Mrs. Page, Mrs. Ford, *and* Sir Hugh Evans.

Eva. 'Tis one of the pest discretions of a 'oman as ever I did look upon.

Page. And did he send you both these letters at an instant?

Mrs. Page. Within a quarter of an hour.

Ford. Pardon me, wife: Henceforth do what thou wilt;
I rather will suspect the sun with cold,[12]
Than thee with wantonness: now doth thy honour stand,
In him that was of late an heretic,
As firm as faith.

---

1 Gang. 2 Surpasses, or goes beyond all bounds.
3 i. e. 'This is below your character, unworthy of you.'
4 Lover. 5 Falsehood, imposition.
6 Means much the same as *scall* or *scab*, from *Rogneuse, Fr.*
7 Expressions taken from the chase. *Trail* is the scent left by the passage of the game. *To cry out* is to *open*, or *bark*.
8 Ritson remarks that Shakspeare 'had been long enough in an attorney's office to know that *fee-simple* is the *largest estate*, and *fine and recovery* the *strongest assurance*, known to English Law.' How Mrs. Page acquired her knowledge of these terms he has not informed us.
9 This is another forensic expression. Mr. Steevens says that the meaning of the passage is, "he will not make further attempts to ruin us by corrupting our virtue and destroying our reputation."
10 i. e. *right period*, or *proper catastrophe*.
11 To *come off* is *to pay*, to *come down* (as we now say,) with a sum of money. It is a phrase of frequent occurrence in old plays.
12 The reading in the text was Mr. Rowe's. The old copies read 'I rather will suspect the sun with *gold*.'

Page. 'Tis well, 'tis well; no more.
Be not as extreme in submission,
As in offence;
But let our plot go forward: let our wives
Yet once again, to make us public sport,
Appoint a meeting with this old fat fellow,
Where we may take him, and disgrace him for it.

Ford. There is no better way than that they spoke of.

Page. How! to send him word they'll meet him in the park at midnight! fie, fie; he'll never come.

Eva. You say, he has been thrown into the rivers; and has been grievously peaten, as an old 'oman; methinks there should be terrors in him, that he should not come; methinks, his flesh is punished, he shall have no desires.

Page. So think I too.

Mrs. Ford. Devise but how you'll use him when he comes,
And let us two devise to bring him thither.

Mrs. Page. There is an old tale goes, that Herne the hunter,
Sometime a keeper here in Windsor forest,
Doth all the winter time, at still midnight,
Walk round about an oak, with great ragg'd horns;
And there he blasts the tree, and takes[1] the cattle;
And makes milch-kine yield blood, and shakes a chain
In a most hideous and dreadful manner:
You have heard of such a spirit; and well you know,
The supers tious idle-headed eld[2]
Received, and did deliver to our age,
This tale of Herne the hunter for a truth.

Page. Why, yet there want not many, that do fear
In deep of night to walk by this Herne's oak;[3]
But what of this?

Mrs. Ford. Marry, this is our device;
That Falstaff at that oak shall meet with us,
Disguised like Herne, with huge horns on his head.

Page. Well, let it not be doubted but he'll come,
And in this shape: When you have brought him thither,
What shall be done with him? what is your plot?

Mrs. Page. That likewise have we thought upon, and thus:
Nan Page my daughter, and my little son,
And three or four more of their growth, we'll dress
Like urchins, ouphes,[4] and fairies, green and white,
With rounds of waxen tapers on their heads,
And rattles in their hands; upon a sudden,
As Falstaff, she, and I, are newly met,
Let them from forth a saw-pit rush at once
With some diffused[5] song; upon their sight,
We two in great amazedness will fly:
Then let them all encircle him about,
And, fairy-like, to-pinch[6] the unclean knight;
And ask him, why, that hour of fairy revel,
In their so sacred paths he dares to tread,
In shape profane.

Mrs. Ford. And till he tell the truth,
Let the supposed fairies pinch him sound,[7]
And burn him with their tapers.

Mrs. Page. The truth being known,
We'll all present ourselves; dis-horn the spirit,
And mock him home to Windsor.

Ford. The children must
Be practised well to this, or they'll ne'er do't.

Eva. I will teach the children their behaviours, and I will be like a Jack-an-apes also, to burn the knight with my taber.

Ford. That will be excellent. I'll go buy them vizards.

Mrs. Page. My Nan shall be the queen of all the fairies,
Finely attired in a robe of white.

Page. That silk will I go buy;—and in that time
Shall master Slender steal my Nan away,
And marry her at Eton. [*Aside.*] Go, send to Falstaff straight.

Ford. Nay, I'll to him again in name of Brook
He'll tell me all his purpose: Sure, he'll come.

Mrs. Page. Fear not you that: Go, get us properties.[8]
And tricking for our fairies.

Eva. Let us about it: It is admirable pleasures, and fery honest knaveries.

[*Exeunt* PAGE, FORD, *and* EVANS.

Mrs. Page. Go, mistress Ford,
Send quickly to Sir John, to know his mind.

[*Exit* MRS. FORD.

I'll to the doctor; he hath my good will,
And none but he, to marry with Nan Page.
That Slender, though well landed, is an idiot;
And he my husband best of all affects:
The doctor is well money'd, and his friends
Potent at court; he, none but he, shall have her,
Though twenty thousand worthier come to crave her.

[*Exit.*

SCENE V. *A Room in the Garter Inn. Enter* HOST *and* SIMPLE.

Host. What would'st thou have, boor? what thick-skin? speak, breathe, discuss; brief, short, quick, snap.

Sim. Marry, sir, I come to speak with Sir John Falstaff from master Slender.

Host. There's his chamber, his house, his castle, his standing-bed, and truckle-bed;[9] 'tis painted about with the story of the prodigal, fresh and new: Go, knock and call; he'll speak like an *Anthropophaginian*[10] unto thee: Knock, I say.

Sim. There's an old woman, a fat woman, gone up into his chamber; I'll be so bold as stay, sir, till she come down: I come to speak with her, indeed.

Host. Ha! a fat woman! the knight may be robbed: I'll call.—Bully knight! Bully Sir John! speak from thy lungs military: Art thou there? it is thine host, thine Ephesian, calls.

Fal. [*above.*] How now, mine host?

Host. Here's a Bohemian-Tartar tarries the coming down of thy fat woman: Let her descend, bully, let her descend; my chambers are honourable: Fye! privacy? fye!

---

1 To *take* signifies *to seize* or *strike with a disease*, *to blast*. So, in Lear, Act ii. Sc. 4:
'Strike her young bones, ye *taking* airs, with lameness.'
And in Hamlet, Act. i. Sc. 1:
———"No planets strike,
No fairy *takes*, no witch has power to charm."
"Of a horse that is *taken*. A horse that is bereft of his feeling, moving, or stirring, is said to be *taken*, and in sooth so he is, in that he is arrested by so villanous a disease: yet some farriers, not well understanding the ground of the disease, conster the word taken to be stricken by some planet, or evil spirit, which is false."—C. vii. *Markham on Horses*, 1595. Thus also in Horman's Vulgaria, 1519. "He is *taken*, or benomed. Attonitus est."

2 Old age.

3 The tree which was by tradition shown as Herne's oak; being totally decayed, was cut down by his late majesty's order in 1795.

4 Elf, hobgoblin.

5 *Some diffused song*, appears to mean some *obscure strange* song. In Cavendish's Life of Wolsey the word occurs in this sense: "speak you Welsh to him: I doubt not but thy speech shall be more *diffuse* to him, than his French shall be to thee." Cotgrave explains *diffused* by the French *diffus*, *espars*, *obscure*, and in Cooper's Dictionary, 1584, I find *obscurum* interpreted 'obscure, difficult, *diffuse*, hard to understand.' Skelton uses *diffuse* several times for strange or obscure; for instance, in the Crown of Laurel:
"Perseus pressed forth with problems *diffuse*."

6 *To-pinch*: *to* has here an augmentative sense, like *be* has since had: *all* was generally prefixed, Spenser has all *to-torn*, all *to-rent*, &c. and Milton in Comus al: *to-ruffled*.

7 *Sound*, for *soundly*, the adjective used as an adverb

8 *Properties* are little incidental necessaries to a theatre: *tricking* is dress or ornament.

9 The usual furniture of chambers, at that time, was a *standing-bed*, under which was a *trochle*, *truckle*, or *running* bed: from *trochlea*, a low wheel or castor. In the standing bed lay the master, in the truckle the servant.

10 i. e. a cannibal: mine host uses these fustian words to astonish Simple.

Enter FALSTAFF.

Fal. There was, mine host, an old fat woman even now with me; but she's gone.

Sim. Pray you, sir, was't not the wise woman of Brentford?

Fal. Ay, marry, was it, muscle-shell;[1] What would you with her?

Sim. My master, sir, my master Slender, sent to her, seeing her go through the streets, to know, sir, whether one Nym, sir, that beguiled him of a chain, had the chain, or no.

Fal. I spake with the old woman about it.

Sim. And what says she, I pray, sir?

Fal. Marry, she says, that the very same man that beguiled master Slender of his chain, cozened him of it.

Sim. I would I could have spoken with the woman herself; I had other things to have spoken with her too, from him.

Fal. What are they? let us know.

Host. Ay, come; quick.

Sim. I may not conceal them, sir.

Fal. Conceal them, or thou diest.

Sim. Why, sir, they were nothing but about mistress Anne Page; to know if it were my master's fortune to have her, or no.

Fal. 'Tis, 'tis his fortune.

Sim. What, sir?

Fal. To have her,—or no: Go; say, the woman told me so.

Sim. May I be so bold to say so, sir?

Fal. Ay, Sir Tike; who more bold?

Sim. I thank your worship: I shall make my master glad with these tidings. [*Exit* SIMPLE.

Host. Thou art clerkly,[2] thou art clerkly, Sir John: Was there a wise woman with thee?

Fal. Ay, that there was, mine host; one that hath taught me more wit than ever I learned before in my life: and I paid nothing for it neither, but was paid[3] for my learning

Enter BARDOLPH.

Bard. Out, alas, sir! cozenage! mere cozenage!

Host. Where be my horses? speak well of them, varletto.

Bard. Run away with the cozeners: for so soon as I came beyond Eton, they threw me off, from behind one of them, in a slough of mire; and set spurs, and away, like three German devils, three Doctor Faustuses.

Host. They are gone but to meet the duke, villain: do not say, they be fled; Germans are honest men.

Enter SIR HUGH EVANS.

Eva. Where is mine host?

Host. What is the matter, sir?

Eva. Have a care of your entertainments: there is a friend of mine come to town, tells me, there is three cousin germans, that has cozened all the hosts of Readings, of Maidenhead, of Colebrook, of horses and money. I tell you for good-will, look you: you are wise, and full of gibes and vlouting-stogs; and it is not convenient you should be cozened: Fare you well. [*Exit.*

Enter DOCTOR CAIUS.

Caius. Vere is mine *Host de Jarterre.*

Host. Here, master doctor, in perplexity, and doubtful dilemma.

Caius. I cannot tell vat is dat: but it is tell-a me, dat you make grand preparations for a duke *de Jarmany:* by my trot, dere is no duke, dat the court is know to come; I tell you for good vill: adieu. [*Exit.*

Host. Hue and cry, villain, go:—assist me, knight; I am undone:—fly, run, hue and cry, villain! I am undone! [*Exeunt* HOST *and* BARDOLPH.

Fal. I would all the world might be cozened, for I have been cozen'd and beaten too. If it should come to the ear of the court, how I have been transformed, and how my transformation hath been washed and cudgeled, they would melt me out of my fat, drop by drop, and liquor fishermen's boots with me; I warrant they would whip me with their fine wits, till I were as crest-fallen as a dried pear. I never prospered since I forswore myself at *Primero.*[4] Well, if my wind were but long enough to say my prayers, I would repent.—

Enter MRS. QUICKLY.

Now! whence come you?

Quick. From the two parties, forsooth.

Fal. The devil take one party, and his dam the other, and so they shall be both bestowed! I have suffered more for their sakes, more than the villanous inconstancy of man's disposition is able to bear.

Quick. And have not they suffered? Yes, I warrant, speciously one of them; mistress Ford, good heart, is beaten black and blue, that you cannot see a white spot about her.

Fal. What tell'st thou me of black and blue! I was beaten myself into all the colours of the rainbow, and I was like to be apprehended for the witch of Brentford; but that my admirable dexterity of wit, my counterfeiting the action of an old woman deliver'd me, the knave constable had set me i' the stocks, i' the common stocks, for a witch.

Quick. Sir, let me speak with you in your chamber; you shall hear how things go; and, I warrant, to your content. Here is a letter will say somewhat. Good hearts, what ado here is to bring you together! Sure, one of you does not serve heaven well, that you are so crossed.

Fal. Come up into my chamber. [*Exeunt*

SCENE VI. *Another Room in the Garter Inn.*

Enter FENTON *and* HOST.

Host. Master Fenton, talk not to me; my mind is heavy, I will give over all.

Fent. Yet hear me speak: Assist me in my purpose,
And, as I am a gentleman, I'll give thee
A hundred pound in gold, more than your loss.

Host. I will hear you, master Fenton; and I will, at the least, keep your counsel.

Fent. From time to time I have acquainted you
With the dear love I bear to fair Anne Page
Who, mutually, hath answer'd my affection
(So far forth as herself might be her chooser,)
Even to my wish: I have a letter from her
Of such contents as you will wonder at;
The mirth whereof so larded with my matter,
That neither, singly, can be manifested,
Without the show of both;—wherein fat Falstaff
Hath a great scene: the image of the jest [*Showing the letter.*
I'll show you here at large. Hark, good mine host:
To-night at Herne's oak, just 'twixt twelve and one
Must my sweet Nan present the fairy queen;
The purpose why, is here;[5] in which disguise,
While other jests are something rank on foot,
Her father hath commanded her to slip
Away with Slender, and with him at Eton
Immediately to marry: she hath consented:
Now, sir,
Her mother, even strong against that match,
And firm for doctor Caius, hath appointed
That he shall likewise shuffle her away,
While other sports are tasking of their minds,
And at the deanery, where a priest attends,
Straight marry her: to this her mother's plot
She, seemingly obedient, likewise hath
Made promise to the doctor;—Now, thus it rests:
Her father means she shall be all in white;
And in that habit, when Slender sees his time

1 He calls poor Simple *muscle-shell,* because he stands with his mouth open.

2 i. e. Scholar-like.

3 *To pay,* in Shakspeare's time, signified *to beat;* in which sense it is still not uncommon in familiar language: 'Seven of the eleven I *paid,*' says Falstaff, in Henry IV. Part 1.

4 *Primero* was the fashionable *game at cards* in Shakspeare's time.

5 In the letter

To take her by the hand, and bid her go,
She shall go with him:—her mother hath intended,
The better to denote her to the doctor
(For they must all be mask'd and vizarded,)
That, quaint[1] in green she shall be loose enrob'd,
With ribands pendant, flaring 'bout her head;
And when the doctor spies his vantage ripe,
To pinch her by the hand, and, on that token,
The maid hath given consent to go with him.
Host. Which means she to deceive? father or mother?
Fent. Both, my good host, to go along with me:
And here it rests,—that you'll procure the vicar
To stay for me at church, 'twixt twelve and one,
And, in the lawful name of marrying,
To give our hearts united ceremony.
Host. Well, husband your device; I'll to the vicar:
Bring you the maid, you shall not lack a priest.
Fent. So shall I ever more be bound to thee;
Besides, I'll make a present recompense. [*Exeunt.*

ACT V.

SCENE I. *A Room in the Garter Inn.* *Enter* Falstaff *and* Mrs. Quickly.

Fal. Pr'ythee, no more prattling;—go.——I'll hold:[2] This is the third time; I hope, good luck lies in odd numbers. Away, go; they say, there is divinity in odd numbers, either in nativity, chance, or death.—Away.

Quick. I'll provide you a chain; and I'll do what I can to get you a pair of horns.

Fal. Away, I say; time wears: hold up your head and mince.[3] [*Exit* Mrs. Quickly.

Enter Ford.

How now, master Brook? Master Brook, the matter will be known to-night, or never. Be you in the Park about midnight, at Herne's oak, and you shall see wonders.

Ford. Went you not to her yesterday, sir, as you told me you had appointed?

Fal. I went to her, master Brook, as you see, like a poor old man: but I came from her, master Brook, like a poor old woman. That same knave, Ford, her husband, hath the finest mad devil of jealousy in him, master Brook, that ever governed frenzy. I will tell you.—He beat me grievously, in the shape of a woman; for in the shape of man, master Brook, I fear not Goliath with a weaver's beam; because I know also, life is a shuttle.[4] I am in haste; go along with me; I'll tell you all, master Brook. Since I plucked geese,[5] played truant, and whipped top, I knew not what it was to be beaten, till lately. Follow me: I'll tell you strange things of this knave Ford: on whom to-night I will be revenged, and I will deliver his wife into your hand.—Follow: Strange things in hand, master Brook! follow. [*Exeunt.*

SCENE II. *Windsor Park.* *Enter* Page, Shallow, *and* Slender.

Page. Come, come; we'll couch i'the castle-ditch, till we see the light of our fairies.—Remember, son Slender, my daughter.

Slen. Ay, forsooth; I have spoke with her, and we have a nay-word[6] how to know one another. I come to her in white, and cry, *mum;* she cries, *budget;* and by that we know one another.

Shal. That's good too: But what needs either your *mum*, or her *budget;* the white will decipher her well enough.—It hath struck ten o'clock.

Page. The night is dark; light and spirits will become it well. Heaven prosper our sport! No man means evil but the devil,[7] and we shall know him by his horns. Let's away; follow me. [*Exeunt.*

SCENE III. *The Street in Windsor.* *Enter* Mrs. Page, Mrs. Ford, *and* Dr. Caius.

Mrs. Page. Master doctor, my daughter is in green; when you see your time, take her by the hand, away with her to the deanery, and despatch it quickly: Go before into the park; we two must go together.

Caius. I know vat I have to do; Adieu.

Mrs. Page. Fare you well, sir. [*Exit* Caius.] My husband will not rejoice so much at the abuse of Falstaff, as he will chafe at the doctor's marrying my daughter: but 'tis no matter; better a little chiding, than a great deal of heart-break.

Mrs. Ford. Where is Nan now, and her troop of fairies? and the Welsh devil, Hugh?

Mrs. Page. They are all couched in a pit hard by Herne's oak, with obscured lights; which at the very instant of Falstaff's and our meeting, they will at once display to the night.

Mrs. Ford. That cannot choose but amaze him.

Mrs. Page. If he be not amazed, he will be mocked; if he be amazed, he will every way be mocked.

Mrs. Ford. We'll betray him finely.

Mrs. Page. Against such lewdsters, and their lechery,
Those that betray them do no treachery.

Mrs. Ford. The hour draws on; To the oak, to the oak! [*Exeunt.*

SCENE IV. *Windsor Park.* *Enter* Sir Hugh Evans *and* Fairies.

Eva. Trib, trib, fairies; come; and remember your parts: be pold, I pray you; follow me into the pit; and when I give the watch-'ords, do as I pid you; Come, come; trib, trib. [*Exeunt.*

SCENE V. *Another part of the Park.* *Enter* Falstaff *disguised, with a buck's head on.*

Fal. The Windsor bell hath struck twelve; the minute draws on: Now, the hot-blooded gods assist me:—Remember, Jove, thou wast a bull for thy Europa; love set on thy horns—O powerful love! that, in some respects, makes a beast a man; in some other, a man a beast.—You were also, Jupiter, a swan, for the love of Leda;—O, omnipotent love! how near the god drew to the complexion of a goose?—A fault done first in the form of a beast;—O Jove, a beastly fault! and then another fault in the semblance of a fowl; think on't, Jove; a foul fault.—When gods have hot backs, what shall poor men do? For me, I am here a Windsor stag; and the fattest, I think, i' the forest: send me a cool rut-time, Jove, or who can blame me to piss my tallow?[8] Who comes here? my doe?

Enter Mrs. Ford *and* Mrs. Page.

Mrs. Ford. Sir John? art thou there, my deer? my male deer?

Fal. My doe with the black scut?—Let the sky rain potatoes; let it thunder to the tune of *Green Sleeves;* hail kissing-comfits, and snow eringoes; let there come a tempest of provocation,[9] I will shelter me here. [*Embracing her.*

---

1 *Quaint*, here, may mean *neatly*, or *elegantly*, which were ancient acceptations of the word, and not *fantastically:* but either sense will suit.
2 Keep to the time.
3 i. e. *walk: to mince* signified to walk with affected delicacy.
4 An allusion to the Book of Job, c. vii. v. 6.
'My days are swifter than a weaver's *shuttle*.'
5 To strip a wild goose of its feathers was formerly an act of puerile barbarity.
6 Watchword

7 Page indirectly alludes to Falstaff, who was to have horns on his head.
8 This is technical. "During the time of their rut the harts live with small sustenance.—The red mushroome helpeth well to make them pysse their greace they are then in so vehement heat."—*Turberville's Book of Hunting*, 1575.
9 The sweet potato was used in England as a delicacy long before the introduction of the common potato by Sir Walter Raleigh in 1586. It was imported in considerable quantities from Spain and the Canaries and

Mrs. Ford. Mistress Page is come with me, sweetheart.

Fal. Divide me like a bride-buck,[1] each a haunch: I will keep my sides to myself, my shoulders for the fellow[2] of this walk, and my horns I bequeath your husbands. Am I a woodman?[3] ha! Speak I like Herne the hunter?—Why, now is Cupid a child of conscience; he makes restitution. As I am a true spirit, welcome! [*Noise within.*

Mrs. Page. Alas! What noise?

Mrs. Ford. Heaven forgive our sins!

Fal. What should this be?

Mrs. Ford. } *Mrs. Page.* } Away, away. [*They run off.*

Fal. I think, the devil will not have me damned, lest the oil that is in me should set hell on fire; he would never else cross me thus.

Enter SIR HUGH EVANS, *like a satyr;* MRS. QUICKLY, *and* PISTOL; ANNE PAGE, *as the Fairy Queen, attended by her brother and others, dressed like fairies, with waxen tapers on their heads.*

Quick. Fairies, black, grey, green, and white,
You moon-shine revellers, and shades of night,
You orphan-heirs[4] of fixed destiny,
Attend your office, and your quality.[5]———
Crier Hobgoblin, make the fairy o-yes.

Pist. Elves, list your names; silence, you airy toys.
Cricket, to Windsor chimneys shalt thou leap:
Where fires thou find'st unrak'd, and hearths unswept,
There pinch the maids as blue as bilberry:
Our radiant queen hates sluts, and sluttery.

Fal. They are fairies; he, that speaks to them, shall die:
I'll wink and couch: No man their works must eye. [*Lies down upon his face.*

Eva. Where's *Pede?*—Go you, and where you find a maid,
That, ere she sleep, has thrice her prayers said,
Raise up the organs of her fantasy,[6]
Sleep she as sound as careless infancy;
But those as sleep, and think not on their sins,
Pinch them, arms, legs, backs, shoulders, sides, and shins.

Quick. About, about;
Search Windsor castle, elves, within and out:
Strew good luck, ouphes, on every sacred room;
That it may stand till the perpetual doom,
In state as wholesome, as in state 'tis fit;
Worthy the owner, and the owner it.
The several chairs of order look you scour
With juice of balm, and every precious flower:[7]
Each fair instalment, coat, and several crest,
With loyal blazon, evermore be blest!
And nightly, meadow-fairies, look, you sing,
Like to the Garter's compass, in a ring:
The expressure that it bears, green let it be,
More fertile-fresh than all the field to see;
And, *Hony soit qui mal y pense*, write,
In emerald tufts, flowers purple, blue and white.
Like sapphire, pearl, and rich embroidery,
Buckled below fair knighthood's bending knee;
Fairies use flowers for their charactery.[8]
Away; disperse: But, 'till 'tis one o'clock,
Our dance of custom, round about the oak
Of Herne the hunter, let us not forget.

Eva. Pray you, lock hand in hand; yourselves in order set:
And twenty glow-worms shall our lanterns be,
To guide our measure round about the tree.
But, stay; I smell a man of middle earth.[9]

Fal. Heaven defend me from that Welsh fairy! lest he transform me to a piece of cheese!

Pist. Vile worm, thou wast o'erlook'd[10] even in thy birth.

Quick. With trial fire touch me his finger-end:
If he be chaste, the flame will back descend,
And turn him to no pain; but if he start,
It is the flesh of a corrupted heart.

Pist. A trial, come.

Eva. Come, will this wood take fire?
[*They burn him with their tapers.*

Fal. Oh, oh, oh!

Quick. Corrupt, corrupt, and tainted in desire!
About him fairies; sing a scornful rhyme:
And, as you trip, still pinch him to your time.

Eva. It is right; indeed he is full of lecheries and iniquity.

SONG.

Fye on sinful fantasy!
Fye on lust and luxury!
Lust is but a bloody fire,
Kindled with unchaste desire.
Fed in heart; whose flames aspire,
As thoughts do blow them, higher and higher
Pinch him, fairies, mutually;
Pinch him for his villany;
Pinch him, and burn him, and turn him about,
Till candles, and star-light, and moonshine be out.

During this song, the fairies pinch Falstaff. Doctor Caius *comes one way, and steals away a fairy in green;* Slender *another way, and takes off a fairy in white; and* Fenton *comes, and steals away* Mrs. Anne Page. *A noise of hunting is made within. All the fairies run away.* Falstaff *pulls off his buck's head, and rises.*

Enter PAGE, FORD, MRS. PAGE, *and* MRS. FORD. *They lay hold on him.*

Page. Nay, do not fly: I think, we have watch'd you now;
Will none but Herne the hunter serve your turn?

Mrs. Page. I pray you, come; hold up the jest no higher:—
Now, good Sir John, how like you Windsor wives?
See you these, husband? do not these fair yokes[11]
Become the forest better than the town?

---

was supposed to possess the power of restoring decayed vigour. The kissing-comfits were principally made of these and eringo roots, and were perfumed to make the breath sweet. Gerarde attributes the same virtues to the common potato which he distinguishes as the Virginian sort.

1 i. e. like a buck sent as a bribe.

2 The *keeper.* The shoulders of the buck were among his perquisites.

3 *The woodman* was an attendant on the forester. It is here however used in a wanton sense, for one who chooses female game for the object of his pursuit.

4 The old copy reads *orphan*-heirs. Warburton reads *ouphen*, and not without plausibility; *ouphes* being mentioned before and afterward. Malone thinks it means mortals by birth, but adopted by the fairies: *orphans* in respect of their real parents, and now only dependent on *destiny* herself.

5 Profession.

6 i. e. elevate her fancy, and amuse her tranquil mind with some delightful vision, *though* she sleep as soundly as an infant.

7 It was an article of ancient luxury to rub tables, &c. with aromatic herbs. So, in the Baucis and Philemon of Ovid, Met. viii.

———mensam—
aequatam *Mentha* abstersere virenti

Pliny informs us that the Romans did so to drive away evil spirits.

8 "*Charactery*, is a writing by characters, or by strange marks."—*Bullokar's English Expositor*, 12 mo. 1656.

9 By this term is merely meant a *mortal man*, in contradistinction to a *spirit* of the earth or of the air, such as a fairy or gnome. It was in use in the north of Scotland a century since, and appears borrowed from the Saxon *Middan Eard.*

10 By *o'er-looked* is here meant *bewitched* by an evil eye, the word is used in that sense in Glanvilli Saddu-cismi Triumphatus, p. 95. Steevens erroneously interprets it '*Slighted* as soon as born.' See note on the Merchant of Venice, Act iii. Sc. 2.

———"Beshrew your eyes,
They have *o'er-looked* me———"

11 The extremities of *yokes* for oxen, as still used in several counties of England, bent upwards, and rising very high, in shape resemble *horns.* In Cotgrave's Dictionary, *voce Jouelles*, we have '*Arched* or *yoked vines;* vines so under propped or fashioned that one may go under the middle of them.' See also Hutton's Latin, Greek, and English Lexicon, 1585, in *voce iu*

Ford. Now, sir, who's a cuckold now?—Master Brook, Falstaff's a knave, a cuckoldy knave; here are his horns, master Brook: And, master Brook, he hath enjoyed nothing of Ford's but his buck-basket, his cudgel, and twenty pounds of money, which must be paid to master Brook; his horses are arrested for it, master Brook.

Mrs. Ford. Sir John, we have had ill luck, we could never meet. I will never take you for my love again, but I will always count you my deer.

Fal. I do begin to perceive that I am made an ass.

Ford. Ay, and an ox too; both the proofs are extant.

Fal. And these are not fairies? I was three or four times in the thought, they were not fairies: and yet the guiltiness of my mind, the sudden surprise of my powers, drove the grossness of the foppery into a received belief, in despite of the teeth of all rhyme and reason, that they were fairies. See now, how wit may be made a Jack-a-lent, when 'tis upon ill employment!

Eva. Sir John Falstaff, serve Got, and leave your desires, and fairies will not pinse you.

Ford. Well said, fairy Hugh.

Eva. And leave you your jealousies too, I pray you.

Ford. I will never mistrust my wife again, till thou art able to woo her in good English.

Fal. Have I laid my brain in the sun, and dried it, that it wants matter to prevent so gross o'er-reaching as this? Am I ridden with a Welsh goat too? Shall I have a coxcomb of frize?[1] 'tis time I were choked with a piece of toasted cheese.

Eva. Seese is not good to give putter; your pelly is all putter.

Fal. Seese and putter! Have I lived to stand at the taunt of one that makes fritters of English? This is enough to be the decay of lust and late-walking through the realm.

Mrs. Page. Why, Sir John, do you think, though we would have thrust virtue out of our hearts by the head and shoulders, and have given ourselves without scruple to hell, that ever the devil could have made you our delight?

Ford. What, a hodge-pudding? a bag of flax?

Mrs. Page. A puffed man?

Page. Old, cold, withered, and of intolerable entrails?

Ford. And one that is as slanderous as Satan?

Page. And as poor as Job?

Ford. And as wicked as his wife?

Eva. And given to fornifications and to taverns, and sack and wine, and metheglins, and to drinkings, and swearings and starings, pribbles and prabbles?

Fal. Well, I am your theme; you have the start of me; I am dejected; I am not able to answer the Welsh flannel;[2] ignorance itself is a plummet o'er me:[3] use me as you will.

Ford. Marry, sir, we'll bring you to Windsor, to one master Brook, that you have cozened of money, to whom you should have been a pander: over and above that you have suffered, I think, to repay that money will be a biting affliction.

Mrs. Ford. Nay, husband, let that go to make amends;
Forgive that sum, and so we'll all be friends.

Ford. Well, here's my hand; all's forgiven at last.

Page. Yet be cheerful, knight: thou shalt eat a posset to-night at my house; where I will desire thee to laugh at my wife, that now laughs at thee:[4] Tell her, master Slender hath married her daughter.

Mrs. Page. Doctors doubt that: If Anne Page be my daughter, she is, by this, doctor Caius' wife. [*Aside.*

Enter SLENDER.

Slen. Whoo! ho! ho! father Page,

Page. Son! how now? how now, son? have you despatched?

Slen. Despatched!—I'll make the best in Gloucestershire know on't; would I were hanged, la, else.

Page. Of what, son?

Slen. I came yonder at Eton to marry mistress Anne Page, and she's a great lubberly boy. If it had not been i' the church, I would have swinged him, or he should have swinged me. If I did not think it had been Anne Page, would I might never stir, and 'tis a post-master's boy.

Page. Upon my life then you took the wrong.

Slen. What need you tell me that? I think so, when I took a boy for a girl: If I had been married to him, for all he was in woman's apparel, I would not have had him.

Page. Why this is your own folly. Did not I tell you, how you should know my daughter by her garments?

Slen. I went to her in white, and cry'd *mum*, and she cry'd *budget*, as Anne and I had appointed; and yet it was not Anne, but a post-master's boy.

Eva. Jeshu! Master Slender, cannot you see but marry boys?

Page. O, I am vexed at heart: What shall I do?

Mrs. Page. Good George, be not angry: I knew of your purpose; turned my daughter into green; and, indeed, she is now with the doctor at the deanery, and there married.

Enter CAIUS.

Caius. Vere is mistress Page? By gar, I am cozened: I ha' married *un garcon*, a boy; *un paisan*, by gar, a boy; it is not Anne Page: by gar, I am cozened.

Mrs. Page. Why, did you take her in green?

Caius. Ay, be gar, and 'tis a boy; be gar, I'll raise all Windsor. [*Exit* CAIUS.

Ford. This is strange! Who hath got the right Anne?

Page. My heart misgives me: Here comes master Fenton.

Enter FENTON *and* ANNE PAGE.

How now, master Fenton?

Anne. Pardon, good father! good my mother pardon!

Page. Now, mistress? how chance you went not with master Slender?

Mrs. Page. Why went you not with master doctor, maid?

Fent. You do amaze[5] her: Hear the truth of it.
You would have married her most shamefully,
Where there was no proportion held in love.
The truth is, she and I, long since contracted,
Are now so sure that nothing can dissolve us.
The offence is holy that she hath committed:
And this deceit loses the name of craft,
Of disobedience, or undutious title;
Since therein she doth evitate[6] and shun
A thousand irreligious cursed hours,
Which forced marriage would have brought upon her.

Ford. Stand not amaz'd: here is no remedy:—
In love, the heavens themselves do guide the state;
Money buys lands, and wives are sold by fate.

Fal. I am glad, though you have ta'en a special stand to strike at me, that your arrow hath glanced.

Page. Well, what remedy? Fenton, heaven give thee joy!
What cannot be eschew'd, must be embrac'd.

---

gum; 'a thing made with *forkes*, like a gallowes, a frame whereon vines are joyned.'

1 i. e. a fool's cap made out of Welsh materials. Wales was famous for this cloth.

2 The very word *flannel* is derived from a Welsh one, and it's almost unnecessary to add that it was originally the manufacture of Wales.

3 Ignorance itself weighs me down, and oppresses me

4 Dr. Johnson remarks, that the two plots are excellently connected, and the transition very artfully made in this speech.

5 Confound her by your questions.

6 Avoid

Fal. When night-dogs run, all sorts of deer are chas'd.[1]
Eva. I will dance and eat plums at your wedding.
Mrs. Page. Well, I will muse no further:—master Fenton,
Heaven give you many, many merry days!
Good husband, let us every one go home,
And laugh this sport o'er by a country fire;
Sir John and all.
Ford. Let it be so:—Sir John,
To master Brook you yet shall hold your word;
For he to-night shall lie with mistress Ford.
[*Exeunt.*

[Of this play there is a tradition preserved by Mr. Rowe, that it was written at the command of Queen Elizabeth, who was so delighted with the character of Falstaff, that she wished it to be diffused through more plays; but suspecting that it might pall by continued uniformity, directed the poet to diversify his manner, by showing him in love. No task is harder than that of writing to the ideas of another. Shakspeare knew what the queen, if the story be true, seems not to have known, that by any real passion of tenderness, the selfish craft, the careless jollity, and the lazy luxury of Falstaff must have suffered so much abatement, that little of his former cast would have remained. Falstaff could not love, but by ceasing to be Falstaff. He could only counterfeit love, and his professions could be prompted, not by the hope of pleasure, but of money. Thus the poet approached as near as he could to the work enjoined him; yet, having perhaps in the former plays completed his own idea, seems not to have been able to give Falstaff all his former power of entertainment.

This comedy is remarkable for the variety and number of the personages, who exhibit more characters, appropriated and discriminated, than perhaps can be found in any other play.

Whether Shakspeare was the first that produced upon the English stage the effect of language distorted and depraved by provincial or foreign pronunciation, I cannot certainly decide.[2] This mode of forming ridiculous characters can confer praise only on him who originally discovered it, for it requires not much of either wit or judgment; its success must be derived almost wholly from the player, but its power in a skilful mouth even he that dispises it is unable to resist.

The conduct of this drama is deficient; the action begins and ends often, before the conclusion, and the different parts might change places without inconvenience; but its general power, that power by which all works of genius shall finally be tried, is such, that perhaps it never yet had reader or spectator who did not think it too soon at the end. JOHNSON.]

THE PASTORAL BY CH. MARLOWE.

Referred to Act iii. *Sc.* 1, *of the foregoing Play*

Come, live with me, and be my love,
And we will all the pleasures prove,
That hills and valleys, dales and field,
And all the craggy mountains yield.
There will we sit upon the rocks,
And see the shepherds feed their flocks,
By shallow rivers, by whose falls
Melodious birds sing madrigals:
There will I make thee beds of roses
With a thousand fragrant posies,
A cap of flowers and a kirtle
Embroider'd all with leaves of myrtle;
A gown made of the finest wool,
Which from the pretty lambs we pull:
Fair lined slippers for the cold,
With buckles of the purest gold;
A belt of straw, and ivy buds,
With coral clasps and amber studs:
And if these pleasures may thee move,
Come, live with me, and be my love.
Thy silver dishes for thy meat,
As precious as the gods do eat,
Shall on thy ivory table be
Prepared each day for thee and me.
The shepherd swains shall dance and sing
For thy delight, each May morning:
If these delights thy mind may move,
Then live with me, and be my love.

---

1 Young and old, does as well as bucks. He alludes to Fenton's having *run down* Anne Page.

2 In The Three Ladies of London, 1584, is the character of an Italian Merchant very strongly marked by foreign pronunciation. Dr. Dodypoll, in the comedy of that name, is, like Caius, a French physician. This piece appeared at least a year before The Merry Wives of Windsor. The hero of it speaks such another jargo as the antagonist of Sir Hugh, and like him is cheated of his mistress. In several other pieces, more ancient than the earliest of Shakspeare's, provincial characters are introduced. In the old play of Henry V. French soldiers are introduced speaking broken English. STEEVENS

TWELFTH NIGHT; OR, WHAT YOU WILL.

PRELIMINARY REMARKS.

THE plot of this admirable Comedy appears to have been taken from the second tale in a collection by Barnabe Riche, entitled, "Rich his Farewell to the Militarie Profession," which was first printed in 1583. It is probably borrowed from *Les Histoires Tragiques de Belleforest*, vol. iv. Hist. viime. Belleforest, as usual, copied Bandello. In the fifth eglog of Barnaby Googe, published with his poems in 1563, an incident somewhat similar to that of the duke sending his page to plead his cause with the lady, and the lady falling in love with the page, may be found. But Rich's narration is the more probable source, and resembles the plot more completely. It is too long for insertion here, but may be found in the late edition of Malone's Shakspeare, by Mr. Boswell.

The comic scenes appear to have been entirely the creation of the poet, and they are worthy of his transcendent genius. It is indeed one of the most delightful of Shakspeare's comedies. Dr. Johnson thought the natural fatuity of Ague-cheek hardly fair game, but the good-nature with which his folly and his pretensions are brought forward for our amusement, by humouring his whims, are almost without a spice of satire. It is rather an attempt to give pleasure by exhibiting an exaggerated picture of his foibles, than a wish to give pain by exposing their absurdity. "How are his weaknesses nursed and dandled by Sir Toby into something 'high fantastical' when, on Sir Andrew's commendation of himself for dancing and fencing, Sir Toby answers—'Wherefore are these things hid? Wherefore have these gifts a curtain before them? Are they like to take dust like Mistress Mall's picture? Why dost thou not go to church in a galliard, and come home in a coranto. My very walk should be a jig! I would not so much as make water in a cinque-a pace. What dost thou mean. Is this a world to hide virtues in? I did think by the excellent constitution of thy leg, it was framed under the star of a galliard!' How Sir Toby, Sir Andrew, and the clown chirp over their cups; how they 'rouse the night-owl in a catch able to draw three souls out of one weaver!'—What can be better than Sir Toby's unanswerable answer to Malvolio: 'Dost thou think, because thou art virtuous, there shall be no more cakes and ale?'—We have a friendship for Sir Toby; we patronize Sir Andrew; we have an understanding with the clown, a sneaking kindness for Maria and her rogueries; we feel a regard for Malvolio, and sympathize with his gravity, his smiles, his cross-garters his yellow stockings, and imprisonment in the stocks But there is something that excites in us a stronger feeling than all this, it is Viola's confession of her love.

Duke. What's her history?
Viola. *A blank, my lord: She never told her love,*
But let concealment, like a worm i' the bud,
Feed on her damask cheek: she pin'd in thought;
And, with a green and yellow melancholy,
She sat like Patience on a monument,
Smiling at grief. *Was not this love, indeed?*
We men may say more, swear more; but, indeed,
Our shows are more than will; for still we prove
Much in our vows, but little in our love.
Duke. But died thy sister of her love, my boy?
Viola. I am all the daughters of my father's house,
And all the brothers too;—and yet I know not.

'Shakspeare alone could describe the effect of his own poetry:

"O, it came o'er my ear like the sweet south,
That breathes upon a bank of violets,
Stealing, and giving odour."

"What we so much admire here is not the image of Patience on a monument, which has been so generally quoted, but the lines before and after it, "They give a very echo to the seat where love is throned." How long ago it is since we first learnt to repeat them; and still they vibrate on the heart like the sounds which the passing wind draws from the trembling strings of a harp left on some desert shore! There are other passages of not less impassioned sweetness. Such is Olivia's address to Sebastian, whom she supposed to have already deceived her in a promise of marriage.

'*Blame not this haste of mine:——*
Plight me the full assurance of your faith,
That my most jealous and too doubtful soul
May live at peace.'

"One of the most beautiful of Shakspeare's Songs occurs in this play with a preface of his own to it.

'*Duke.* O fellow, come, the song we had last night.
Mark it, Cesario; it is old, and plain;
The spinsters and the knitters in the sun,
And the free maids that weave their thread with bones
Do use to chaunt it; it is silly sooth,
And dallies with the innocence of love,
Like the old age."

"After reading other parts of this play, and particularly the garden scene where Malvolio picks up the letter, if we were to say that Shakspeare's genius for comedy was less than his genius for tragedy, it would perhaps only prove that our own taste in such matters is more saturnine than mercurial."*

* Hazlitt's Characters of Shakspeare's Plays, p. 256

PERSONS REPRESENTED

ORSINO, *Duke of* Illyria.
SEBASTIAN, *a young Gentleman, Brother to* Viola.
ANTONIO, *a Sea Captain, Friend to* Sebastian.
A Sea Captain, *Friend to* Viola.
VALENTINE, CURIO, } *Gentlemen attending on the Duke.*
SIR TOBY BELCH, *Uncle of* Olivia.
SIR ANDREW AGUE-CHEEK.
MALVOLIO, *Steward to* Olivia.
FABIAN, Clown, } *Servants to* Olivia.
OLIVIA, *a rich Countess.*
VIOLA, *in love with the Duke.*
MARIA, Olivia's *Woman.*
Lords, Priests, Sailors, Officers, Musicians, and othe Attendants.

SCENE, *a City in* Illyria; *and the Sea Coast near it*

ACT I.

SCENE I. *An Apartment in the* Duke's *Palace.*

Enter DUKE, CURIO, Lords; *Musicians attending.*

Duke.

If music be the food of love, play on,
Give me excess of it; that, surfeiting,
The appetite may sicken, and so die.——
That strain again;—it hath a dying fall:
O, it came o'er my ear like the sweet south,[1]
That breathes upon a bank of violets,
Stealing, and giving odour.[2]—Enough; no more;
'Tis not so sweet now as it was before.
O spirit of love, how quick and fresh art thou!
That notwithstanding thy capacity
Receiveth as the sea, nought enters there,
Of what validity[3] and pitch soever,
But falls into abatement and low price,
Even in a minute! so full of shapes is fancy,
That it alone is high-fantastical.[4]

Cur. Will you go hunt, my lord?
Duke. What, Curio?
Cur. The hart
Duke. Why, so I do, the noblest that I have:
O, when mine eyes did see Olivia first,
Methought she purg'd the air of pestilence;
That instant was I turn'd into a hart;
And my desires, like fell and cruel hounds,
E'er since pursue me.[5]—How now? what news from her?

Enter VALENTINE.

Val. So please my lord, I might not be admitted,
But from her handmaid do return this answer:
The element itself, till seven years heat,[6]
Shall not behold her face at ample view;
But, like a cloistress, she will veiled walk,
And water once a day her chamber round
With eye-offending brine: all this, to season
A brother's dead love, which she would keep fresh,
And lasting, in her sad remembrance.
Duke. O, she, that hath a heart of that fine frame,
To pay this debt of love but to a brother,

1 The old copies read *sound,* the emendation is Pope's. Rowe had changed it to wind. In Sidney's Arcadia, 1590, we have—'more *sweet* than a gentle *south-west* wind which comes creeping over *flowery* fields.'

2 Milton has very successfully introduced the same image in Paradise Lost:

——'Now gentle gales,
Fanning their odoriferous wings, dispense
Native perfumes and whisper whence they stole
Those balmy spoils."

Shakspeare, in the Ninty-ninth Sonnet, has made the violet the thief.

'The forward violet thus did I chide:
Sweet thief, whence didst thou steal thy sweet that smells,
If not from my love's breath.'

Pope, in his Ode on St. Cecilia's Day; and Thomson, in his Spring have availed themselves of the epithet *a dying fall*

3 Value. 4 Fantastical to the height.

5 Shakspeare seems to think men cautioned against too great familiarity with forbidden beauty by the fable of Acteon, who saw Diana naked, and was torn to pieces by his hounds; as a man indulging his eyes or his imagination with a view of a woman he cannot gain, has his heart torn with incessant longing. An interpretation far more elegant and natural than Lord Bacon's, who, in his Wisdom of the Ancients, supposes this story to warn us against inquiring into the secrets of princes, by showing that those who know that which for reasons of state ought to be concealed will be detected and destroyed by their own servants. The thought may have been suggested by Daniel's Fifth Sonnet, in his Delia; or by Whitney's Emblems, 1586, p. 15; and a passage in the Dedication to Aldington's translation of 'The Golden Ass of Apuleius,' 1566, may have suggested these.

6 *Heat* for *heated*

How will she love, when the rich golden shaft
Hath kill'd the flock[1] of all affections else
That live in her! when liver, brain, and heart,[2]
These sovereign thrones, are all supplied, and fill'd
(Her sweet perfections) with one self[3] king!—
Away before me to sweet beds of flowers;
Love-thoughts lie rich, when canopied with bowers.
[*Exeunt.*

SCENE II. *The Sea Coast. Enter* VIOLA, Captain, *and* Sailors.

Vio. What country, friends, is this?
Cap. Illyria, lady.
Vio. And what should I do in Illyria?
My brother he is in Elysium.
Perchance he is not drown'd:—What think you, sailors?
Cap. It is perchance that you yourself were saved.
Vio. O my poor brother! and so, perchance, may he be.
Cap. True, madam: and, to comfort you with chance,
Assure yourself, after our ship did split,
When you, and that poor number saved with you,
Hung on our driving boat, I saw your brother,
Most provident in peril, bind himself
(Courage and hope both teaching him the practice)
To a strong mast, that lived upon the sea.
Where, like Arion on the dolphin's back,
I saw him hold acquaintance with the waves,
So long as I could see.
Vio. For saying so, there's gold:
Mine own escape unfoldeth to my hope,
Whereto thy speech serves for authority,
The like of him. Know'st thou this country?
Cap. Ay, madam, well; for I was bred and born
Not three hours travel from this very place.
Vio. Who governs here?
Cap. A noble duke, in nature,
As in his name?
Vio. What is his name?
Cap. Orsino.
Vio. Orsino! I have heard my father name him:
He was a bachelor then.
Cap. And so is now,
Or was so very late: for but a month
Ago I went from hence; and then 'twas fresh
In murmur (as you know, what great ones do,
The less will prattle of,) that he did seek
The love of fair Olivia.
Vio. What's she?
Cap. A virtuous maid, the daughter of a count
That died some twelvemonth since; then leaving her
In the protection of his son, her brother,
Who shortly also died: for whose dear love
They say she hath abjur'd the company
And sight of men.
Vio. O, that I serv'd that lady:
And might not be delivered to the world,
Till I had made mine own occasion mellow,
What my estate is.[4]
Cap. That were hard to compass;
Because she will admit no kind of suit,
No, not the duke's.
Vio. There is a fair behaviour in thee, captain;
And though that nature with a beauteous wall
Doth oft close in pollution, yet of thee
I will believe, thou hast a mind that suits
With this thy fair and outward character.
I pray thee, and I'll pay thee bounteously,
Conceal me what I am; and be my aid
For such disguise as, haply, shall become
The form of my intent. I'll serve this duke;
Thou shalt present me as an eunuch to him,[5]
It may be worth thy pains; for I can sing,
And speak to him in many sorts of music,
That will allow[6] me very worth his service.
What else may hap, to time I will commit;
Only shape thou thy silence to my wit.
Cap. Be you his eunuch, and your mute I'll be:
When my tongue blabs, then let mine eyes not see.
Vio. I thank thee: Lead me on. [*Exeunt.*

SCENE III. *A Room in* Olivia's *House. Enter* SIR TOBY BELCH *and* MARIA.

Sir To. What a plague means my niece, to take the death of her brother thus? I'm sure, care's an enemy to life.

Mar. By my troth, Sir Toby, you must come in earlier o'nights; your cousin, my lady, takes great exceptions to your ill hours.

Sir To. Why, let her except before excepted.[7]

Mar. Ay, but you must confine yourself within the modest limits of order.

Sir To. Confine? I'll confine myself no finer than I am: these clothes are good enough to drink in, and so be these boots too; an they be not, let them hang themselves in their own straps.

Mar. That quaffing and drinking will undo you: I heard my lady talk of it yesterday; and of a foolish knight, that you brought in one night here, to be her wooer.

Sir To. Who? Sir Andrew Ague-cheek?

Mar. Ay, he.

Sir To. He's as tall[8] a man as any's in Illyria.

Mar. What's that to the purpose?

Sir To. Why, he has three thousand ducats a year.

Mar. Ay, but he'll have but a year in all these ducats; he's a very fool and a prodigal.

Sir To. Fye, that you'll say so! he plays o' the viol-de-gambo, and speaks three or four languages word for word without book, and hath all the good gifts of nature.

Mar. He hath, indeed,—almost natural: for, besides that he's a fool, he's a great quarreller; and, but that he hath the gift of a coward to allay the gust he hath in quarrelling, 'tis thought among the prudent, he would quickly have the gift of a grave.

Sir To. By this hand they are scoundrels, and substracters, that say so of him. Who are they?

Mar. They that add moreover, he's drunk nightly in your company.

Sir To. With drinking healths to my niece; I'll drink to her, as long as there is a passage in my throat, and drink in Illyria: He's a coward, and a coystril,[9] that will not drink to my niece, till his brains turn o' the toe like a parish top.[10] What,

---

1 So, in Sidney's Arcadia—" the *flock* of unspeakable virtues."

2 The *liver, brain,* and *heart* were then considered the seats of *passion, judgment,* and *sentiments.* These are what Shakspeare calls *her sweet perfections,* though he has not very clearly expressed it.

3 *Self king* signifies *self same king*, i. e. one and the same king.

4 i. e. 'I wish I might not be *made public* to the world, with regard to the state of my birth and fortune, till I have gained a *ripe opportunity* for my design.' Johnson remarks that 'Viola seems to have formed a deep design with very little premeditation.' In the novel upon which the play is founded, the Duke being driven upon the isle of Cyprus, by a tempest, *Silla*, the daughter of the governor, falls in love with him, and on his departure goes in pursuit of him. All this Shakspeare knew, and probably intended to tell in some future scene, but afterwards forgot it. Viola, in Act ii. Sc. 4, plainly alludes to her having been secretly in love with the Duke, but it would have been inconsistent with her delicacy to have made an open confession of it to the Captain.

5 This plan of Viola's was not pursued, as it would have been inconsistent with the plot of the play. She was presented as a *page* not as an *eunuch.*

6 Approve.

7 A ludicrous use of a formal *law phrase.*

8 That is as *valiant* a man, as *tall* a man, is used here by Sir Toby with more than the usual licence of the word; he was pleased with the equivoque, and banters upon the diminutive stature of poor Sir Andrew and his utter want of courage.

9 A *coystril* is a low, mean, or worthless fellow.

10 A large top was formerly kept in every village, to be whipped in frosty weather, that the peasants might be kept warm by exercise, and out of mischief when they could not work. 'To sleep like a Town-top' is a proverbial expression.

wench! Castiliano volto;[1] for here comes Sir Andrew Ague-face.

Enter SIR ANDREW AGUE-CHEEK.

Sir And. Sir Toby Belch! how now, Sir Toby Belch.

Sir To. Sweet Sir Andrew!

Sir And. Bless you, fair shrew.

Mar. And you too, sir.

Sir To. Accost, Sir Andrew, accost.

Sir And. What's that?

Sir To. My niece's chamber-maid.

Sir And. Good mistress Accost, I desire better acquaintance.

Mar. My name is Mary, sir.

Sir And. Good mistress Mary Accost,——

Sir To. You mistake, knight: accost, is, front her, board her, woo her, assail her.

Sir And. By my troth, I would not undertake her in this company. Is that the meaning of accost?

Mar. Fare you well, gentlemen.

Sir To. An thou let part so, Sir Andrew, 'would thou might'st never draw sword again.

Sir And. An you part so, mistress, I would I might never draw sword again. Fair lady, do you think you have fools in hand?

Mar. Sir, I have not you by the hand.

Sir And. Marry, but you shall have; and here's my hand.

Mar. Now, sir, thought is free: I pray you, bring your hand to the buttery-bar, and let it drink.

Sir And. Wherefore, sweetheart? what's your metaphor?

Mar. It's dry, sir.

Sir And. Why, I think so; I am not such an ass, but I can keep my hand dry. But what's your jest?

Mar. A dry jest, sir.

Sir And. Are you full of them?

Mar. Ay, sir; I have them at my fingers' ends: marry, now I let go your hand, I am barren.

[*Exit* MARIA.

Sir To. O knight, thou lack'st a cup of canary: When did I see thee so put down?

Sir And. Never in your life, I think; unless you see canary put me down: Methinks, sometimes I have no more wit than a christian, or an ordinary man has: but I am a great eater of beef, and, I believe, that does harm to my wit.

Sir To. No question.

Sir And. An I thought that, I'd forswear it. I'll ride home to-morrow, Sir Toby.

Sir To. *Pourquoy*, my dear knight?

Sir And. What is *pourquoy?* do or not do? I would I had bestowed that time in the tongues, that I have in fencing, dancing, and bear-baiting: O, had I but followed the arts!

Sir To. Then hadst thou had an excellent head of hair.

Sir And. Why, would that have mended my hair?

Sir To. Past question; for thou seest it will not curl by nature.

Sir And. But it becomes me well enough, does't not?

Sir To. Excellent; it hangs like flax on a distaff: and I hope to see a housewife take thee between her legs and spin it off.

Sir And. 'Faith, I'll home to-morrow, Sir Toby: your niece will not be seen; or, if she be, it's four to one she'll none of me: the count himself, here hard by, woos her.

Sir To. She'll none o' the count; she'll not match above her degree, neither in estate, years, nor wit; I have heard her swear it. Tut, there's life in't, man

Sir And. I'll stay a month longer. I am a fellow o' the strangest mind i' the world; I delight in masques and revels sometimes altogether.

Sir To. Art thou good at these kickshaws, knight?

Sir And. As any man in Illyria, whatsoever he be, under the degree of my betters; and yet I will not compare with an old man.

Sir To. What is thy excellence in a galliard, knight?

Sir And. 'Faith, I can cut a caper.

Sir To. And I can cut the mutton to't.

Sir And. And, I think I have the back-trick, simply as strong as any man in Illyria.

Sir To. Wherefore are these things hid? wherefore have these gifts a curtain before them? are they like to take dust, like mistress Mall's picture?[2] why dost thou not go to church in a galliard, and come home in a coranto? My very walk should be a jig; I would not so much as make water, but in a sink-a-pace.[3] What dost thou mean? is it a world to hide virtues in? I did think, by the excellent constitution of thy leg, it was formed under the star of a galliard.

Sir And. Ay, 'tis strong, and it does indifferent well in a flame-coloured stock.[4] Shall we set about some revels?

Sir To. What shall we do else? were we not born under Taurus?

Sir And. Taurus? that's sides and heart.

Sir To. No, sir; it is legs and thighs.[5] Let me see thee caper: ha! higher: ha, ha!—excellent!

[*Exeunt.*

SCENE IV. *A Room in the* Duke's *palace.*

Enter VALENTINE, *and* VIOLA *in man's attire.*

Val. If the Duke continues these favours towards you, Cesario, you are like to be much advanced; he hath known you but three days, and already you are no stranger.

Vio. You either fear his humour, or my negligence, that you call in question the continuance of his love: Is he inconstant, sir, in his favours?

Val. No, believe me.

Enter DUKE, CURIO, *and* Attendants.

Vio. I thank you. Here comes the count.

Duke. Who saw Cesario, ho?

Vio. On your attendance, my lord; here.

Duke. Stand you awhile aloof.—Cesario,
Thou knowest no less but all; I have unclasp'd
To thee the book even of my secret soul:

---

1 The old copy reads Castiliano *vulgo*. Warburton proposed reading *Castiliano volto*. In English, put on your Castilian countenance, i. e. 'grave serious looks.' I have no doubt that Warburton was right, for that reading is required by the context, and Castiliano *vulgo* has no meaning. But I have met with a passage in Hall's Satires, B. iv. S. 2, which I think places it beyond a doubt:—

——'he can kiss hand in gree,
And with good grace bow it below the knee,
Or make a *Spanish face* with fawning cheer,
With th' hand congé like a cavalier,
And shake his head, and cringe his neck and side,' &c.

The Spaniards were in high estimation for courtesy, though the natural gravity of the national countenance was thought to be a cloak for villany. The *Castiliano volto* was in direct opposition to the *viso sciolto* which the noble Roman told Sir Henry Wootton would go safe over the world. Castiliano *vulgo*, besides its want of connexion or meaning in this place, could hardly have been a proverbial phrase, when we remember that Castile is the *noblest* part of Spain

2 i. e. Mall Cutpurse, whose real name was Mary Frith. She was at once an *hermaphrodite*, a bawd, a prostitute, a bully, a thief, and a receiver of stolen goods. A book called 'The Madde Prankes of Merry Mall of the Bankside, with her Walks in Man's Apparel, and to what purpose, by John Day,' was entered on the Stationers' books in 1610. Middleton and Decker wrote a Comedy, of which she is the heroine, and a life of her was published in 1662, with her portrait in male attire. As this extraordinary personage partook of both sexes, the *curtain* which Sir Toby mentions would not have been unnecessarily drawn before such a picture of her as might have been exhibited in an age of which neither too much delicacy nor too much decency was the characteristic.

3 *Cinque-pace*, the name of a dance, the measures whereof are regulated by the number 5, also called *a Galliard.*

4 Stocking.

5 Alluding to the medical astrology of the almanacks. Both the knights are wrong, but their ignorance is perhaps intentional. *Taurus* is made to govern the *neck and throat.*

Therefore, good youth, address thy gait[1] unto her;
Be not deny'd access, stand at her doors,
And tell them, there thy fixed foot shall grow,
Till thou have audience.

Vio. Sure, my noble lord,
If she be so abandon'd to her sorrow
As it is spoke, she never will admit me.

Duke. Be clamorous, and leap all civil bounds,
Rather than make unprofited return.

Vio. Say, I do speak with her, my lord; what then?

Duke. O, then unfold the passion of my love,
Surprise her with discourse of my dear faith:
It shall become thee well to act my woes;
She will attend it better in thy youth,
Than in a nuncio of more grave aspect.

Vio. I think not so, my lord.

Duke. Dear lad, believe it;
For they shall yet belie thy happy years
That say, thou art a man: Diana's lip
Is not more smooth and rubious; thy small pipe
Is as the maiden's organ, shrill and sound,
And all is semblative a woman's part.
I know thy constellation is right apt
For this affair:—Some four or five attend him;
All, if you will; for I myself am best,
When least in company:—Prosper well in this,
And thou shalt live as freely as thy lord,
To call his fortunes thine.

Vio. I'll do my best
To woo your lady: yet [*Aside,*] a barful[2] strife!
Whoe'er I woo, myself would be his wife. [*Exeunt.*

SCENE V. *A Room in* Olivia's *house. Enter* MARIA *and* Clown.[3]

Mar. Nay, either tell me where thou hast been, or I will not open my lips so wide as a bristle may enter, in way of thy excuse: my lady will hang thee for thy absence.

Clo. Let her hang me: he that is well hanged in his world needs to fear no colours.

Mar. Make that good.

Clo. He shall see none to fear.

Mar. A good lenten[4] answer: I can tell thee where that saying was born, of, I fear no colours.

Clo. Where, good mistress Mary!

Mar. In the wars; and that may you be bold to say in your foolery.

Clo. Well, God give them wisdom, that have it; and those that are fools, let them use their talents.

Mar. Yet you will be hanged for being so long absent: or, to be turned away, is not that as good as a hanging to you?

Clo. Many a good hanging prevents a bad marriage; and, for turning away, let summer bear it out.

Mar. You are resolute then?

Clo. Not so neither; but I am resolved on two points.

Mar. That, if one break,[5] the other will hold; or, if both break, your gaskins fall.

Clo. Apt, in good faith; very apt! Well, go thy way; if Sir Toby would leave drinking, thou wert as witty a piece of Eve's flesh as any in Illyria.

Mar. Peace, you rogue, no more o' that; here comes my lady: make your excuse wisely, you were best. [*Exit.*

Enter OLIVIA *and* MALVOLIO.

Clo. Wit, and't be thy will, put me into good fooling! Those wits, that think they have thee, do very oft prove fools; and I, that am sure I lack thee, may pass for a wise man: For what says Quinapalus? Better a witty fool, than a foolish wit. ———God bless thee, lady!

Oli. Take the fool away.

Clo. Do you not hear, fellows? Take away the lady.

Oli. Go to, you're a dry fool; I'll no more of you: besides you grow dishonest.

Clo. Two faults, madonna,[6] that drink and good counsel will amend: for give the dry fool drink, then is the fool not dry; bid the dishonest man mend himself; if he mend, he is no longer dishonest; if he cannot, let the botcher mend him: Any thing that's mended, is but patched: virtue, that transgresses, is but patched with sin: and sin, that amends, is but patched with virtue: If that this simple syllogism will serve, so; if it will not, what remedy? As there is no true cuckold but calamity, so beauty's a flower:—the lady bade take away the fool; therefore, I say again, take her away.

Oli. Sir, I bade them take away you.

Clo. Misprision in the highest degree!—Lady, *Cucullus non facit monachum;* that's as much as to say, I wear not motley in my brain. Good madonna, give me leave to prove you a fool.

Oli. Can you do it?

Clo. Dexterously, good madam.

Oli. Make your proof.

Clo. I must catechize you for it, madonna Good my mouse of virtue, answer me.

Oli. Well, sir, for want of other idleness, I'l. 'bide your proof.

Clo. Good madonna, why mourn'st thou?

Oli. Good fool, for my brother's death.

Clo. I think his soul is in hell, madonna.

Oli. I know his soul is in heaven, fool

Clo. The more fool you, madonna, to mourn for your brother's soul being in heaven.—Take away the fool, gentlemen.

Oli. What think you of this fool, Malvolio? doth he not mend?

Mal. Yes; and shall do, till the pangs of death shake him: Infirmity, that decays the wise, doth ever make the better fool.

Clo. God send you, sir, a speedy infirmity, for the better encreasing your folly! Sir Toby will be sworn that I am no fox; but he will not pass his word for twopence that you are no fool.

Oli. How say you to that, Malvolio?

Mal. I marvel your ladyship takes delight in such a barren rascal; I saw him put down the other day with an ordinary fool that has no more brain than a stone. Look you now, he's out of his guard already; unless you laugh and minister occasion to him, he is gagged. I protest I take these wise men, that crow so at these set of kind fools, no better than the fools' zanies.[7]

Oli. O, you are sick of self-love, Malvolio, and taste with a distempered appetite. To be generous, guiltless, and of free disposition, is to take those things for bird-bolts,[8] that you deem cannon-bullets: There is no slander in an allowed fool, though he do nothing but rail; nor no railing in a known discreet man, though he do nothing but reprove.

Clo. Now Mercury endure thee with leasing,[9] for thou speakest well of fools!

Re-enter MARIA.

Mar. Madam, there is at the gate a young gentleman, much desires to speak with you.

1 Go thy way.

2 A contest full of impediments.

3 The clown in this play is a domestic fool in the service of Olivia. He is specifically termed an *allowed* fool, and '*Feste*, the jester that the lady Olivia's father took much delight in.' Malvolio speaks of him as 'a *set* fool.' The dress of the domestic fool was of two sorts, described by Mr. Douce in his Essay on the Clowns and Fools of Shakspeare, to which we must refer the reader for full information. The dress sometimes appropriated to the character is thus described in Tarleton's Newes out of Purgatory: 'I saw one attired in russet, with a button'd cap upon his head, a bag by his side, and a strong bat in his hand; so artificially attired for a *clowne* as I began to call Tarleton's wonted shape to remembrance.'

4 Short and spare. 'Sparing, niggardly, insufficient, like the fare of old times in Lent. Metaphorically, *short, laconic.*' Says Steevens. I rather incline to Johnson's explanation, 'a good *dry* answer.' Steevens does not seem to have been aware that a dry fig was called a *lenten* fig. In fact, *lenten* fare was dry fare.

5 *Points* were laces which fastened the hose or breeches.

6 *Italian*, mistress, dame.

7 Fools' baubles.

8 *Bird-bolts* were short thick arrows with obtuse ends, used for shooting young rooks and other birds

9 Lying.

Oli. From the count Orsino, is it?

Mar. I know not, madam; 'tis a fair young man, and well attended,

Oli. Who of my people hold him in delay?

Mar. Sir Toby, madam, your kinsman.

Oli. Fetch him off, I pray you; he speaks nothing but madman: Fie on him! [*Exit* MARIA.] Go you, Malvolio; if it be a suit from the count, I am sick, or not at home; what you will to dismiss it. [*Exit* MALVOLIO.] Now you see, sir, how your fooling grows old, and people dislike it.

Clo. Thou hast spoke for us, madonna, as if thy eldest son should be a fool: whose skull Jove cram with brains, for here he comes, one of thy kin, has a most weak *pia mater*.[1]

Enter SIR TOBY BELCH.

Oli. By mine honour, half drunk.—What is he at the gate, cousin?

Sir To. A gentleman.

Oli. A gentleman! what gentleman?

Sir To. 'Tis a gentleman here—A plague o'these pickle-herrings!—How now, sot?

Clo. Good Sir Toby,——

Oli. Cousin, cousin, how have you come so early by this lethargy?

Sir To. Lechery! I defy lechery: There's one at the gate.

Oli. Ay, marry; what is he?

Sir To. Let him be the devil, an he will, I care not: give me faith, say I. Well, it's all one. [*Exit.*

Oli. What's a drunken man like, fool?

Clo. Like a drown'd man, a fool, and a madman: one draught above heat makes him a fool; the second mads him; and a third drowns him.

Oli. Go thou and seek the coroner, and let him sit o' my coz; for he's in the third degree of drink; he's drown'd; go, look after him.

Clo. He is but mad yet, madonna; and the fool shall look to the madman. [*Exit* Clown.

Re-enter MALVOLIO.

Mal. Madam, yond' young fellow swears he will speak to you. I told him you were sick; he takes on him to understand so much, and therefore comes to speak with you: I told him you were asleep; he seems to have a foreknowledge of that too, and therefore comes to speak with you. What is to be said to him, lady? he's fortified against any denial.

Oli. Tell him, he shall not speak with me.

Mal. He has been told so: and he says, he'll stand at your door like a sheriff's post,[2] and be the supporter of a bench, but he'll speak with you.

Oli. What kind of man is he?

Mal. Why, of man kind.

Oli. What manner of man?

Mal. Of very ill manner; he'll speak with you, will you or no.

Oli. Of what personage and years is he?

Mal. Not yet old enough for a man, nor young enough for a boy; as a squash is before 'tis a peascod, or a codling[3] when 'tis almost an apple: 'tis with him e'en standing water, between boy and man. He is very well favoured, and he speaks very shrewishly; one would think, his mother's milk were scarce out of him.

Oli. Let him approach: Call in my gentlewoman.

Mal. Gentlewoman, my lady calls. [*Exit.*

Re-enter MARIA.

Oli. Give me my veil; come, throw it o'er my face, We'll once more hear Orsino's embassy.

Enter VIOLA.

Vio. The honourable lady of the house, which is she?

Oli. Speak to me, I shall answer for her: Your will?

Vio. Most radiant, exquisite, and unmatchable beauty,—I pray you, tell me, if this be the lady of the house, for I never saw her: I would be loath to cast away my speech; for, besides that it is excellently well penn'd, I have taken great pains to con it. Good beauties, let me sustain no scorn; I am very comptible,[4] even to the least sinister usage.

Oli. Whence come you, sir?

Vio. I can say little more than I have studied, and that question's out of my part. Good gentle one, give me modest assurance, if you be the lady of the house, that I may proceed in my speech.

Oli. Are you a comedian?

Vio. No, my profound heart: and yet, by the very fangs of malice, I swear, I am not that I play. Are you the lady of the house?

Oli. If I do not usurp myself, I am.

Vio. Most certain, if you are she, you do usurp yourself; for what is yours to bestow, is not yours to reserve. But this is from my commission: I will on with my speech in your praise, and then shew you the heart of my message.

Oli. Come to what is important in't: I forgive you the praise.

Vio. Alas, I took great pains to study it, and 'tis poetical.

Oli. It is the more like to be feigned; I pray you, keep it in. I heard you were saucy at my gates; and allowed your approach, rather to wonder at you than to hear you. If you be not mad,[5] be gone; if you have reason, be brief: 'tis not that time of moon with me, to make one in so skipping[6] a dialogue.

Mar. Will you hoist sail, sir? here lies your way.

Vio. No, good swabber: I am to hull[7] here a little longer.—Some mollification for your giant,[8] sweet lady.

Oli. Tell me your mind.

Vio. I am a messenger.

Oli. Sure, you have some hideous matter to deliver, when the courtesy of it is so fearful. Speak your office.

Vio. It alone concerns your ear. I bring no overture of war, no taxation of homage; I hold the olive in my hand: my words are as full of peace as matter.

Oli. Yet you began rudely. What are you? what would you?

Vio. The rudeness, that hath appear'd in me have I learn'd from my entertainment. What I am, and what I would, are as secret as maidenhead: to your ears, divinity; to any other's, profanation.

Oli. Give us the place alone; we will hear this divinity. [*Exit* MARIA.] Now, sir, what is your text?

Vio. Most sweet lady,——

Oli. A comfortable doctrine, and much may be said of it. Where lies your text?

---

1 The membrane that covers the brain.

2 The sheriffs formerly had painted posts set up at their doors, on which proclamations, &c. were affixed.

3 *A codling* (according to Mr. Gifford,) means an *involucrum* or *kell*, and was used by our old writers for that early state of vegetation, when the fruit, after shaking off the blossom, began to assume a globular and determinate shape. Mr. Nares says, *a codling* was *a young raw apple*, fit for nothing without dressing, and that it is so named because it was chiefly eaten when *coddled* or scalded; codlings being particularly so used when unripe. Florio interprets 'Mele cotte, *quodlings*, boiled apples.'

4 Accountable.

5 The sense seems to require that we should read—'if you *be mad*, begone.' For the words *be mad* in the first part of the sentence are opposed to *reason* in the second.

6 i. e. wild, frolic, mad.

7 To *hull* means to drive to and fro upon the water without sails or rudder.

8 Ladies in romance are guarded by giants. Viola seeing the waiting-maid so eager to oppose her message, entreats Olivia to pacify her giant. There is also a pleasant allusion to the diminutive size of Maria, who is subsequently called *little villain*, *youngest wren of nine*, &c. It should be recollected that the female parts were played by *boys*

Vio. In Orsino's bosom?

Oli. In his bosom? In what chapter of his bosom?

Vio. To answer by the method, in the first of his heart.

Oli. O, I have read it; it is heresy. Have you no more to say?

Vio. Good madam, let me see your face.

Oli. Have you any commission from your lord to negotiate with my face? you are now out of your text: but we will draw the curtain, and shew you the picture. Look you, sir, such a one as I was, this presents:[1]—Is't not well done? [*Unveiling.*

Vio. Excellently done, if God did all.

Oli. 'Tis in grain, sir; 'twill endure wind and weather.

Vio. 'Tis beauty truly blent,[2] whose red and white
Nature's own sweet and cunning hand laid on:
Lady, you are the cruel'st she alive,
If you will lead these graces to the grave,
And leave the world no copy.[3]

Oli. O, sir, I will not be so hard-hearted; I will give out divers schedules of my beauty: It shall be inventoried; and every particle and utensil labelled to my will: as, item, two lips indifferent red; item, two gray eyes, with lids to them; item, one neck, one chin, and so forth. Were you sent hither to 'praise[4] me?

Vio. I see you what you are: you are too proud;
But, if you were the devil, you are fair.
My lord and master loves you; O, such love
Could be but recompens'd, though you were crown'd
The nonpareil of beauty!

Oli. How does he love me?

Vio. With adorations, with fertile tears,
With groans that thunder love, with sighs of fire.

Oli. Your lord does know my mind, I cannot love him:
Yet I suppose him virtuous, know him noble,
Of great estate, of fresh and stainless youth;
In voices well divulg'd,[5] free, learn'd, and valiant,
And, in dimension, and the shape of nature,
A gracious person: but yet I cannot love him;
He might have took his answer long ago.

Vio. If I did love you in my master's flame,
With such a suffering, such a deadly life,
In your denial I would find no sense,
I would not understand it.

Oli. Why, what would you?

Vio. Make me a willow cabin at your gate,
And call upon my soul within the house;
Write loyal cantons[6] of contemned love,
And sing them loud even in the dead of night;
Holla your name to the reverberate hills,
And make the babbling gossip of the air[7]
Cry out, Olivia! O, you should not rest
Between the elements of air and earth,
But you should pity me.

Oli. You might do much: What is your parentage?

Vio. Above my fortunes, yet my state is well:
I am a gentleman.

Oli. Get you to your lord;
I cannot love him: let him send no more;
Unless, perchance, you come to me again,
To tell me how he takes it. Fare you well:
I thank you for your pains: spend this for me.

Vio. I am no fee'd post,[8] lady; keep your purse;
My master, not myself, lacks recompense.
Love make his heart of flint, that you shall love;
And let your fervour, like my master's, be
Plac'd in contempt! Farewell, fair cruelty. [*Exit.*

Oli. What is your parentage?
Above my fortunes, yet my state is well:
I am a gentleman.—I'll be sworn thou art,
Thy tongue, thy face, thy limbs, actions, and spirit,
Do give thee five-fold blazon;[9]—Not too fast:—
soft! soft!
Unless the master were the man.—How now?
Even so quickly may one catch the plague?
Methinks, I feel this youth's perfections,
With an invisible and subtle stealth,
To creep in at mine eyes. Well, let it be.—
What, ho, Malvolio!—

Re-enter MALVOLIO.

Mal. Here, madam, at your service.

Oli. Run after that same peevish messenger,
The county's[10] man: he left this ring behind him,
Would I, or not; tell him, I'll none of it.
Desire him not to flatter with his lord,
Nor hold him up with hopes! I am not for him:
If that the youth will come this way to-morrow,
I'll give him reasons for't. Hie, thee, Malvolio.

Mal. Madam, I will. [*Exit.*

Oli. I do I know not what: and fear to find
Mine eye too great a flatterer for my mind.[11]
Fate, show thy force: ourselves we do not owe;[12]
What is decreed, must be; and be this so! [*Exit.*

ACT II.

SCENE I. *The Sea Coast. Enter* ANTONIO *and* SEBASTIAN.

Ant. Will you stay no longer? nor will you not that I go with you?

Seb. By your patience, no: my stars shine darkly over me; the malignancy of my fate might, perhaps, distemper yours; therefore I shall crave of you your leave, that I may bear my evils alone: It were a bad recompense for your love, to lay any of them on you.

Ant. Let me yet know of you, whither you are bound.

Seb. No, 'sooth, sir; my determinate voyage is mere extravagancy. But I perceive in you so excellent a touch of modesty, that you will not extort from me what I am willing to keep in; therefore it charges me in manners the rather to express[13] myself. You must know of me, then, Antonio, my name is Sebastian, which I called Rodorigo: my father was that Sebastian of Messaline,[14] whom, I know, you have heard of: he left behind him myself, and a sister, both born in an hour. If the heavens had been pleased, 'would we had so ended! but, you, sir, altered that; for, some hour before you took me from the breach of the sea, was my sister drowned.

Ant. Alas, the day!

Seb. A lady, sir, though it was said she much resembled me, was yet of many accounted beautiful: but, though I could not, with such estimable wonder,[15] overfar believe that, yet thus far I will boldly publish her, she bore a mind that envy could not but call fair: she is drowned already, sir, with salt water, though I seem to drown her remembrance again with more.[16]

1 The old copy reads, 'Look you, sir, such a one as I was this present.' M. Mason proposed to read 'Look you, sir, such *as once* I was, this *presents.*' The simple emendation in the text, which I have ventured upon, makes it intelligible. We may by the slight transposition of a word make it explain itself: 'Look you, sir, such a one I was, as this presents.'

2 Blended, mixed together.

3 Shakspeare has a similar thought repeated in his third, ninth, eleventh, and thirteenth sonnets.

4 i. e. appraise.

5 Well spoken of by the world.

6 Cantos, verses.

7 A most beautiful expression for an *echo.*

8 Messenger.

9 Proclamation of gentility.

10 Count.

11 i. e. she fears that her eyes had formed so flattering an idea of the supposed youth Cesario, that she should not have strength of mind sufficient to resist the impression.

12 i. e. we are not our own masters, we cannot govern ourselves; *owe* for *own, possess.*

13 Reveal.

14 Probably intended for *Metelin,* an island in the Archipelago.

15 i. e. esteeming wonder, or wonder and esteem.

16 There is a similar false thought in Hamlet:
'Too much of water hast thou, poor Ophelia,
And therefore I forbid my tears.'

Ant. Pardon me, sir, your bad entertainment.

Seb. O, good Antonio, forgive me your trouble.

Ant. If you will not murder me for my love, let me be your servant.

Seb. If you will not undo what you have done, that is, kill him whom you have recovered, desire it not. Fare ye well at once; my bosom is full of kindness; and I am yet so near the manners of my mother,[1] that upon the least occasion more, mine eyes will tell tales of me. I am bound to the count Orsino's court: farewell. [*Exit.*

Ant. The gentleness of all the gods go with thee!
I have many enemies in Orsino's court,
Else would I very shortly see thee there:
But, come what may, I do adore thee so,
That danger shall seem sport, and I will go. [*Exit.*

SCENE II. *A Street.* *Enter* Viola; Malvolio *following.*

Mal. Were not you even now with the countess Olivia?

Vio. Even now, sir; on a moderate pace I have since arrived but hither.

Mal. She returns this ring to you, sir; you might have saved me my pains, to have taken it away yourself. She adds moreover, that you should put your lord into a desperate assurance she will none of him: And one thing more; that you be never so hardy to come again in his affairs, unless it be to report your lord's taking of this. Receive it so.

Vio. She took the ring of me!—I'll none of it.

Mal. Come, sir, you peevishly threw it to her; and her will is, it should be so returned: if it be worth stooping for, there it lies in your eye; if not, be it his that finds it. [*Exit.*

Vio. I left no ring with her: What means this lady?
Fortune forbid my outside have not charm'd her!
She made good view of me; indeed so much,
That, sure methought her eyes had lost her tongue,[2]
For she did speak in starts distractedly.
She loves me, sure; the cunning of her passion
Invites me in this churlish messenger.
None of my lord's ring! why, he sent her none.
I am the man;—If it be so, (as 'tis,)
Poor lady, she were better love a dream.
Disguise, I see, thou art a wickedness,
Wherein the pregnant[3] enemy does much.
How easy is it for the proper-false[4]
In woman's waxen hearts to set their forms!
Alas, our frailty is the cause, not we;
For, such as we are made of, such we be.
How will this fadge?[5] My master loves her dearly:
And I, poor monster, fond as much on him;
And she, mistaken, seems to dote on me:
What will become of this! As I am man,
My state is desperate for my master's love;
As I am woman, now alas the day!
What thriftless sighs shall poor Olivia breathe?
O time, thou must untangle this, not I;
It is too hard a knot for me to untie. [*Exit.*

SCENE III.—*A Room in* Olivia's *House.* *Enter* Sir Toby Belch, *and* Sir Andrew Aguecheek.

Sir To. Approach, Sir Andrew: not to be a-bed after midnight, is to be up betimes; and *diluculo surgere*,[6] thou know'st.——

1 So, in Henry V. Act v. Sc. 6.
'And all my *mother* came into my eyes.'

2 i. e. the fixed and eager view she took of me perverted the use of her tongue, and made her talk distractedly.

3 Dexterous, ready fiend.

4 How easy is it for the proper (i. e. fair in their appearance,) and false (i. e. deceitful,) to make an impression on the easy hearts of women!

5 Suit, or fit.

6 *Diluculo surgere, saluberrimum est.* This adage is in Lilly's Grammar.

7 A ridicule of the medical theory of that time, which supposed health to consist in the just temperament of the *four elements* in the human frame. Homer agrees with Sir Andrew:
'——strength consists in spirits and in blood,
And those are ow'd to generous wine and food.'
Iliad ix.

Sir And. Nay, by my troth, I know not: but I know to be up late, is to be up late.

Sir To. A false conclusion; I hate it as an unfilled can: To be up after midnight, and to go to bed then, is early; so that to go to bed after midnight, is to go to bed betimes. Do not our lives consist of the four elements?

Sir And. 'Faith, so they say; but, I think, it rather consists of eating and drinking.[7]

Sir To. Thou art a scholar; let us therefore eat and drink.—Marian, I say!—a stoop of wine!

Enter Clown.

Sir And. Here comes the fool, i'faith.

Clo. How now, my hearts? Did you never see the picture of we three?[8]

Sir. To. Welcome, ass, now let's have a catch.

Sir And. By my troth, the fool has an excellent breast.[9] I had rather than forty shillings I had such a leg: and so sweet a breath to sing, as the fool has. In sooth, thou wast in very gracious fooling last night, when thou spokest of Pigrogromitus, of the Vapians passing the equinoctial of Queubus; 'twas very good, i'faith. I sent thee sixpence for thy leman:[10] Hadst it?

Clo. I did impeticos thy gratillity;[11] for Malvolio's nose is no whipstock: My lady has a white hand, and the Myrmidons are no bottle-ale houses.

Sir And. Excellent! Why, this is the best fooling, when all is done. Now a song.

Sir To. Come on; there is sixpence for you, let's have a song.

Sir And. There's a testril of me too: if one knight give a——

Clo. Would you have a love-song, or a song of good life?

Sir To. A love-song, a love-song.

Sir And. Ay, ay; I care not for good life.

SONG.

Clo. *O mistress mine, where are you roaming?*
O, stay and hear; your true love's coming,
That can sing both high and low:
Trip no further, pretty sweeting;
Journeys end in lovers' meeting,
Every wise man's son doth know.

Sir And. Excellent good, i'faith!

Sir To. Good, good.

Clo. *What is love? 'tis not hereafter;*
Present mirth hath present laughter;
What's to come is still unsure:
In delay there lies no plenty;
Then come kiss me, sweet-and-twenty,[12]
Youth's a stuff will not endure.

Sir And. A mellifluous voice, as I am true knight.

Sir To. A contagious breath.

Sir And. Very sweet and contagious, i'faith.

Sir To. To hear by the nose, it is dulcet in contagion. But shall we make the welkin dance[13] indeed? Shall we rouse the night-owl in a catch, that will draw three souls out of one weaver?[14] shall we do that?

8 Alluding to an old common sign representing *two* fools or loggerheads, under which was inscribed, 'We three loggerheads be.'

9 i. e. Voice. In Fiddes's Life of Wolsey, Append. p 128, 'Singing men *well breasted.*' The phrase is common to all writers of the poet's age.

10 i e. mistress.

11 The greater part of this scene, which the commentators have endeavoured to explain, is mere *gracious fooling*, and was hardly meant to be seriously understood. The Clown uses the same fantastic language before. By some the phrase has been thought to mean I did *impetticoat* or *impocket* thy *gratuity*.

12 *Sweet-and-twenty*, appears to have been an ancient term of endearment.

13 Drink till the sky seems to turn round.

14 Shakspeare represents weavers as much given to harmony in his time. The peripatetic philosophy then in vogue liberally gave every man three souls, the *vegetative* or *plastic*, the *animal*, and the *rational*. Thus, in Hutton's Dictionary, 1583, 'Plato feigned the soul to be *threefold*, whereof he placed reason in the head, anger in the breast, desire or lust under the heart, liver, lites, &c.' But it may be doubted whether any allusion

Sir And. An you love me, let's do't: I am dog at a catch.

Clo. By'r lady, sir, and some dogs will catch well.

Sir And. Most certain: let our catch be, *Thou knave.*

Clo. *Hold thy peace,* thou knave, knight? I shall be constrain'd in't, to call thee knave, knight.

Sir And. 'Tis not the first time I have constrain'd one to call me knave. Begin, fool: it begins, *Hold thy peace.*[1]

Clo. I shall never begin, if I hold my peace.

Sir And. Good, i'faith! Come, begin.

[*They sing a catch.*

Enter MARIA.

Mar. What a caterwauling do you keep here! If my lady have not called up her steward, Malvolio, and bid him turn you out of doors, never trust me.

Sir To. My lady's a Cataian,[2] we are politicians; Malvolio's a Peg-a-Ramsey,[3] and *Three merry men we be.* Am not I consanguineous? am I not of her blood? Tilley-valley,[4] lady! *There dwelt a man in Babylon, lady, lady!* [*Singing.*

Clo. Beshrew me, the knight's in admirable fooling.

Sir And. Ay, he does well enough, if he be disposed, and so do I too; he does it with a better grace, but I do it more natural.

Sir To. *O, the twelfth day of December,*[5]— [*Singing.*

Mar. For the love o' God, peace.

Enter MALVOLIO.

Mal. My masters, are you mad? or what are you! Have you no wit, manners, nor honesty, but to gabble like tinkers at this time of night? Do you make an alehouse of my lady's house, that ye squeak out your coziers'[6] catches without any mitigation or remorse of voice? Is there no respect of place, persons, nor time, in you?

Sir To. We did keep time, sir, in our catches. Sneck up![7]

Mal. Sir Toby, I must be round with you. My lady bade me tell you, that though she harbours you as her kinsman, she's nothing allied to your disorders. If you can separate yourself from your misdemeanors, you are welcome to the house; if not, an it would please you to take leave of her, she is very willing to bid you farewell.

Sir To. *Farewell, dear heart, since I must needs be gone.*

Mar. Nay, good Sir Toby.

Clo. *His eyes do show his days are almost done.*

Mal. Is't even so?

Sir To. *But I will never die.*

Clo. Sir Toby, there you lie.

Mal. This is much credit to you.

Sir To. *Shall I bid him go?* [*Singing.*

Clo. *What an if you do?*

Sir To. *Shall I bid him go, and spare not?*

Clo. *O no, no, no, no, you dare not.*

Sir To. Out o' time? sir, ye lie.—Art any more than a steward? Dost thou think, because thou art virtuous, there shall be no more cakes and ale?

Clo. Yes, by Saint Anne; and ginger shall be hot i'the mouth too.

Sir To. Thou'rt i'the right.—Go, sir, rub your chain[8] with crums.—A stoop of wine, Maria!

Mal. Mistress Mary, if you prized my lady's favour at any thing more than contempt, you would not give means for this uncivil rule;[9] she shall know of it, by this hand. [*Exit.*

Mar. Go shake your ears.

Sir And. 'Twere as good a deed as to drink when a man's a hungry, to challenge him to the field; and then to break promise with him, and make a fool of him.

Sir To. Do't knight; I'll write thee a challenge, or I'll deliver thy indignation to him by word of mouth.

Mar. Sweet Sir Toby, be patient for to-night, since the youth of the count's was to-day with my lady, she is much out of quiet. For monsieur Malvolio, let me alone with him: if I do not gull him into a nay-word,[10] and make him a common recreation, do not think I have wit enough to lie straight in my bed: I know I can do it.

Sir To. Possess us,[11] possess us; tell us some thing of him.

Mar. Marry, sir, sometimes he is a kind of Puritan.

Sir And. O, if I thought that, I'd beat him like a dog.

Sir To. What, for being a Puritan? thy exquisite reason, dear knight?

Sir And. I have no exquisite reason for't, but I have reason good enough.

Mar. The devil a Puritan that he is, or any thing constantly but a time pleaser; an affectioned[12] ass, that cons state without book, and utters it by great swarths:[13] the best persuaded of himself, so crammed, as he thinks, with excellencies, that it is his ground of faith, that all, that look on him, love him; and on that vice in him will my revenge find notable cause to work.

Sir To. What wilt thou do?

Mar. I will drop in his way some obscure epistles of love; wherein, by the colour of his beard, the shape of his leg, the manner of his gait, the expressure of his eye, forehead, and complexion, he shall find himself most feelingly personated: I can write very like my lady, your niece; on a forgotten matter we can hardly make distinction of our hands.

Sir To. Excellent! I smell a device.

Sir And. I have't in my nose too.

Sir To. He shall think, by the letters that thou wilt drop, that they come from my niece, and that she is in love with him.

Mar. My purpose is, indeed, a horse of that colour.

Sir And. And your horse now would make him an ass.

Mar. Ass, I doubt not.

Sir And. O, 'twill be admirable.

Mar. Sport royal, I warrant you: I know, my physic will work with him. I will plant you two, and let the fool make a third, where he shall find the letter; observe his construction of it. For this night, to bed; and dream on the event. Farewell. [*Exit.*

Sir To. Good night, Penthesilea.[14]

Sir And. Before me, she's a good wench.

Sir To. She's a beagle, true bred, and one that adores me; What o' that?

---

to this division of souls was intended. Sir Toby rather meant that the catch should be so harmonious that it would hale the soul out of a weaver *thrice over*, a rhodomontade way of expressing, that it would give this warm lover of song thrice more delight than it would give another man.

1 This catch is to be found in 'Pammelia, Musicke's Miscellanie, 1618.' The words and music are in the Variorum Shakspeare.

2 This word generally signified a sharper Sir Toby is too drunk for precision, and uses it merely as a term of reproach.

3 Name of an obscene old song.

4 An interjection of contempt equivalent to fiddle-faddle, possibly from the Latin *Titivillitium.*

5 Sir Toby, in his cups, is full of the fragments of old ballads: such as, 'There dwelt a man in Babylon' 'Three merry men are we,' &c. The latter was composed by W. Lawes, and may be found in Playford's Musical Companion, 1673.

6 *Cobblers*, or *botchers.* Dr. Johnson interprets it *tailors*, but erroneously.

7 An interjection of contempt, signifying, *go hang yourself*, or *go and be hanged.*

8 Stewards anciently wore a chain of silver or gold as a mark of superiority, as did other principal servants Wolsey's chief cook is described by Cavendish as wearing 'velvet or sattin with a chain of gold.' One of the methods used to clean gilt plate was *rubbing it with crums.*

9 Behaviour, or conduct. Hence gambols and frolicsome behaviour was called *mis-rule.*

10 By-word. 11 Inform us. 12 Affected.

13 i. e. by great parcels or heaps. *Swarths* are the rows of grass left by the scythe of the mower

14 Amazon.

Sir And. I was adored once too.

Sir To. Let's to bed, knight.—Thou hadst need send for more money.

Sir And. If I cannot recover your niece, I am a foul way out.

Sir To. Send for money, knight; if thou hast her not i' the end, call me Cut.[1]

Sir And. If I do not, never trust me, take it how you will.

Sir To. Come, come; I'll go burn some sack, 'tis too late to go to bed now: come, knight; come, knight. [*Exeunt.*

SCENE IV.—*A Room in the* Duke's *Palace.*

Enter DUKE, VIOLA, CURIO, *and others.*

Duke. Give me some music:—Now, good morrow, friends:—
Now, good Cesario, but that piece of song,
That old and antique song we heard last night;
Methought, it did relieve my passion much,
More than light airs and recollected terms,[2]
Of these most brisk and giddy-paced times:——
Come, but one verse.

Cur. He is not here, so please your lordship, that should sing it.

Duke. Who was it?

Cur. Feste, the jester, my lord: a fool, that the lady Olivia's father took much delight in: he is about the house.

Duke. Seek him out, and play the tune the while. [*Exit* CURIO.—*Music.*
Come hither, boy; if ever thou shalt love,
In the sweet pangs of it, remember me
For, such as I am, all true lovers are;
Unstaid and skittish in all motions else,
Save, in the constant image of the creature
That is belov'd.—How dost thou like this tune?

Vio. It gives a very echo to the seat
Where Love is thron'd.[3]

Duke. Thou dost speak masterly:
My life upon't, young though thou art, thine eye
Hath stay'd upon some favour that it loves;
Hath it not, boy?

Vio. A little, by your favour.[4]

Duke. What kind of woman is't?

Vio. Of your complexion.

Duke. She is not worth thee then. What years, i'faith?

Vio. About your years, my lord.

Duke. Too old, by heaven; Let still the woman take
An elder than herself; so wears she to him,
So sways she level in her husband's heart.
For, boy, however we do praise ourselves,
Our fancies are more giddy and unfirm,
More longing, wavering, sooner lost and worn,[5]
Than women's are.

Vio. I think it well, my lord.

Duke. Then let thy love be younger than thyself,
Or thy affection cannot hold the bent:
For women are as roses; whose fair flower,
Being once display'd, doth fall that very hour.

Vio. And so they are: alas, that they are so;
To die, even when they to perfection grow!

Re-enter CURIO *and* Clown.

Duke. O fellow, come, the song we had last night:—
Mark it, Cesario; it is old, and plain:
The spinsters and the knitters in the sun,
And the free[6] maids that weave their thread with bones,
Do use to chaunt it; it is silly sooth,[7]
And dallies with the innocence of love,
Like the old age.[8]

Clo. Are you ready, sir?

Duke. Ay; pr'ythee, sing. [*Music*

SONG.

Clo. *Come away, come away, death,*
And in sad cypress[9] *let me be laid;*
Fly away, fly away, breath;
I am slain by a fair cruel maid.
My shroud of white, stuck all with yew,
O, prepare it;
My part of death no one so true
Did share it.
Not a flower, not a flower sweet,
On my black coffin let there be strown,
Not a friend, not a friend greet
My poor corpse, where my bones shall be thrown
A thousand thousand sighs to save,
Lay me, O, where
Sad true-love never find my grave,
To weep there.

Duke. There's for thy pains.

Clo. No pains, sir; I take pleasure in singing, sir.

Duke. I'll pay thy pleasure then.

Clo. Truly, sir, and pleasure will be paid one time or another.

Duke. Give me now leave to leave thee.

Clo. Now, the melancholy god protect thee; and the tailor make thy doublet of changeable taffata, for thy mind is a very opal[10]—I would have men of such constancy put to sea, that their business might be every thing, and their intent every where; for that's it, that always makes a good voyage of nothing.—Farewell. [*Exit* Clown.

Duke. Let all the rest give place.—— [*Exeunt* CURIO *and Attendants.*
Once more, Cesario,
Get thee to yon' same sovereign cruelty:
Tell her, my love, more noble than the world,
Prizes not quantity of dirty lands;
The parts that fortune hath bestow'd upon her,
Tell her, I hold as giddily as fortune;
But 'tis that miracle, and queen of gems,
That nature pranks[11] her in, attracts my soul.

Vio. But, if she cannot love you, sir?

Duke. I cannot be so answer'd.

Vio. 'Sooth, but you must.
Say, that some lady, as, perhaps, there is,
Hath for your love as great a pang of heart
As you have for Olivia: you cannot love her;
You tell her so; Must she not then be answer'd?

Duke. There is no woman's sides
Can bide the beating of so strong a passion
As love doth give my heart: no woman's heart
So big, to hold so much; they lack retention.
Alas, their love may be call'd appetite,—

1 This term of contempt probably signified, call me *gelding* or horse. Falstaff, in Henry IV. Part I, says, 'Spit in my face, call me *horse*.' It is of common occurrence in old plays. *Cut* was a common contraction of *curtail*. One of the carriers' horses in the first part of Henry IV. is called *Cut*.

2 *Recalled, repeated* terms, alluding to the repetitions in songs.

3 i. e. to the heart.

4 The word *favour* is ambiguously used. In the preceding speech it signified *countenance*.

5 i. e. consumed, worn out.

6 i. e. *chaste* maids, employed in making lace. This passage has sadly puzzled the commentators; their conjectures are some of them highly amusing. Johnson says, '*free* is perhaps *vacant, unengaged, easy in mind*.' Steevens once thought it meant *unmarried*; then that it might mean *cheerful*: and at last concludes that 'its precise meaning cannot easily be pointed out.' Warton mentions, in his notes on L'Allegro of Milton, that it was a common attribute of woman, coupled mostly with *fair*, but he did not venture upon an explanation

7 *Silly sooth*, or rather *sely sooth*, is simple truth.

8 The *old age* is the *ages past*, times of simplicity.

9 It is not clear whether a shroud of the stuff now called crape, anciently called *cypress*, is here meant, or whether a coffin of cypress wood was intended. The cypress was used for funeral purposes; and the epithet *sad* is inconsistent with a *white* shroud. It is even possible that branches of cypress only may be meant. We see the shroud was *stuck all with yew*, and cypress may have been used in the same manner. In Quarles's Argalus and Parthenia, a knight is introduced, whose

——————'horse was black as jet,
His furniture was round about beset
With branches slipt from the *sad cypress tree*.'

10 The opal is a gem which varies its hues, as it is viewed in different lights.

11 That *beauty* which nature *decks* her in

No motion of the liver, but the palate,—
That suffer surfeit, cloyment, and revolt;
But mine is all as hungry as the sea,
And can digest as much: make no compare
Between that love a woman can bear me,
And that I owe Olivia.

Vio. Ay, but I know,—

Duke. What dost thou know?

Vio. Too well what love women to men may owe:
In faith, they are as true of heart as we.
My father had a daughter lov'd a man,
As it might be, perhaps, were I a woman,
I should your Lordship.

Duke. And what's her history?

Vio. A blank, my lord: She never told her love,
But let concealment, like a worm i'the bud,[1]
Feed on her damask cheek: she pin'd in thought;
And, with a green and yellow melancholy,
She sat like patience on a monument,
Smiling at grief.[2] Was not this love, indeed?
We men may say more, swear more: but, indeed,
Our shows are more than will; for still we prove
Much in our vows, but little in our love.

Duke. But died thy sister of her love, my boy?

Vio. I am all the daughters of my father's house,
And all the brothers too;—and yet I know not:—
Sir, shall I to this lady?

Duke. Ay, that's the theme.
To her in haste: give her this jewel; say,
My love can give no place, bide no denay.[3]

[*Exeunt.*

SCENE V.—Olivia's *Garden.* *Enter* SIR TOBY BELCH, SIR ANDREW AGUE-CHEEK, *and* FABIAN.

Sir To. Come thy ways, signior Fabian.

Fab. Nay, I'll come; if I lose a scruple of this sport, let me be boiled to death with melancholy.

Sir To. Would'st thou not be glad to have the niggardly rascally sheep-biter come by some notable shame?

Fab. I would exult, man; you know, he brought me out of favour with my lady, about a bear-baiting here.

Sir To. To anger him, we'll have the bear again; and we will fool him black and blue:—Shall we not, Sir Andrew?

Sir And. An we do not, it is pity of our lives.

Enter MARIA.

Sir To. Here comes the little villain:—How now, my nettle of India?[4]

Mar. Get ye all three into the box-tree: Malvolio's coming down this walk; he has been yonder i'the sun, practising behaviour to his own shadow, this half hour: observe him, for the love of mockery; for I know, this letter will make a contemplative idiot of him. Close, in the name of jesting! [*The men hide themselves.*] Lie thou there; [*throws down a letter*] for here comes the trout that must be caught with tickling. [*Exit* MARIA.

Enter MALVOLIO.

Mal. 'Tis but fortune; all is fortune. Maria once told me, she did affect me: and I have heard herself come thus near, that, should she fancy,[5] it should be one of my complexion. Besides, she uses me with a more exalted respect, than any one else that follows her. What should I think on't?

Sir To. Here's an overweening rogue!

Fab. O, peace! Contemplation makes a rare turkey-cock of him; how he jets[6] under his advanced plumes!

Sir And. 'Slight I could so beat the rogue

Sir To. Peace, I say.

Mal. To be count Malvolio;—

Sir To. Ah, rogue!

Sir And. Pistol him, pistol him.

Sir To. Peace, peace!

Mal. There is example for't; the lady of the Strachy[7] married the yeoman of the wardrobe

Sir And. Fie on him, Jezebel!

Fab. O, peace! now he's deeply in; look how imagination blows[8] him.

Mal. Having been three months married to her, sitting in my state,[9]—

Sir To. O, for a stone bow, to hit him in the eye!

Mal. Calling my officers about me, in my branched velvet gown; having come from a day bed,[10] where I left Olivia sleeping.

Sir To. Fire and brimstone!

Fab. O, peace, peace!

Mal. And then to have the humour of state: and after a demure travel of regard,—telling them I know my place, as I would they should do theirs—to ask for my kinsman Toby:

Sir To. Bolts and shackles!

Fab. O, peace, peace, peace! now, now.

Mal. Seven of my people, with an obedient start, make out for him: I frown the while; and, perchance, wind up my watch, or play with my some rich jewel. Toby approaches; court'sies[11] there to me:

Sir To. Shall this fellow live?

Fab. Though our silence be drawn from us with cars,[12] yet peace.

Mal. I extend my hand to him thus, quenching my familiar smile with an austere regard of control:[13]

---

1 So in the fifth Sonnet of Shakspeare:—

'Which like a *canker* in the fragrant rose
Doth spot the beauty of thy *budding* name.'

And in the Rape of Lucrece:—

'Why should the *worm* intrude the maiden *bud.*'

Again in Richard II.—

'But now will *canker* sorrow eat my *buds*,
And chase the native beauty from my *cheek.*'

2 So Middleton in *The Witch*, Act iv. Sc. 3:—

'She does not love me now, but painfully
Like one that's forc'd to smile upon a grief.'

The commentators have overlaid this exquisite passage with notes, and created difficulties where none existed. Mr. Boswell says, the meaning is obviously this:—'While she was smiling at grief, or in her grief, her placid resignation made her look like patience on a monument.'

3 Denial.

4 The first folio reads '*mettle* of India.' By the nettle of India is meant a zoophite, called *Urtica Marina*, abounding in the Indian seas. '*Quæ tacta totius corporis pruritum quendam excitat, unde nomen Urticæ est sortita.*'—*Franzii Hist. Animal.* 1665, p. 620. In Holland's translation of Pliny, Book ix. 'As for those nettles, &c. their qualities is to raise an itching smart.' So, Green in his 'Card of Fancie,' 'The flower of India, pleasant to be seen, but whoso smelleth to it feeleth present smart.' He refers to it again in his Mamilia, 1593. Maria has certainly excited a congenial sensation in Sir Toby. *Mettle* of India would signify my *girl of gold* my *precious girl*

5 Love.

6 To *jet* was to *strut.* 'To *jette* lordly through the streets that men may see them.' *Incedere magnifice per ora hominum.*' Baret. So, in Bussy D'Ambois:

'To *jet* in other's plumes so haughtily.'

7 Mr. R. P. Knight conjectures that this is a corruption of *Stratici*, a title anciently given to the Governors of Messina, and Illyria is not far from Messina. If so it will mean the *Governor's lady.* The word *Strachy* is printed with a capital and in Italics in the first folio

8 Puffs him up.

9 State chair.

10 Couch.

11 It is probable that this word was used to express acts of civility and reverence, by either men or women indiscriminately.

12 Thus in the Two Gentlemen of Verona, the clown says;—"who that is, *a team of horses* shall not *pluck from me.*"

13 It may be worthy of remark, that the leading ideas of Malvolio, in his *humour of state*, bear a strong resemblance to those of Alnaschar in 'The Arabian Nights.' Some of the expressions too are very similar Many Arabian fictions had found their way into obscure Latin and French books, and from thence into English ones, long before any version of 'The Arabian Nights' had appeared. In 'The Dialogues of Creatures Moralized,' *bl. l.* printed early in the sixteenth century, a story similar to that of Alnaschar is related. See Dial, c. p. 122, *reprint* of 1816

Sir To. And does not Toby take you a blow o' the lips then?

Mal. Saying, *Cousin Toby, my fortunes having cast me on your niece, give me this prerogative of speech:—*

Sir To. What, what?

Mal. You must amend your drunkenness.

Sir To. Out, scab!

Fab. Nay, patience, or we break the sinews of our plot.

Mal. Besides, you waste the treasure of your time with a foolish knight:

Sir And. That's me, I warrant you.

Mal. One Sir Andrew:

Sir And. I knew, 'twas I; for many do call me fool.

Mal. What employment have we here?

[*Taking up the letter.*

Fab. Now is the woodcock near the gin.

Sir To. O, peace! and the spirit of humours intimate reading aloud to him!

Mal. By my life, this is my lady's hand: these be her very *C*'s, her *U*'s, and her *T*'s; and thus makes she her great *P*'s. It is, in contempt of question, her hand.

Sir And. Her C's, her U's, and her T's: Why that?

Mal. [*reads*] *To the unknown beloved, this, and my good wishes:* her very phrases!—By your leave, wax.—Soft!—and the impressure her Lucrece, with which she uses to seal: 'tis my lady: To whom should this be?

Fab. This wins him, liver and all.

Mal. [*reads*] *Jove knows, I love:*
But who?
Lips do not move,
No man must know.

No man must know.—What follows? the numbers altered!—*No man must know:*—If this should be thee, Malvolio?

Sir To. Marry, hang thee, brock![1]

Mal. I may command, where I adore:
But silence, like a Lucrece knife,
With bloodless stroke my heart doth gore;
M, O, A, I, *doth sway my life.*

Fab. A fustian riddle!

Sir To. Excellent wench, say I.

Mal. M, O, A, I, *doth sway my life.*—Nay, but first, let me see,—let me see,—let me see.

Fab. What a dish of poison has she dressed him!

Sir To. And with what wing the stannyel[2] checks at it!

Mal. I may command where I adore. Why, she may command me; I serve her, she is my lady. Why, this is evident to any formal capacity.[3] There is no obstruction in this;—And the end,—What should that alphabetical position portend? if I could make that resemble something in me,—Softly!—*M, O, A, I.*—

Sir To. O, ay! make up that:—he is now at a cold scent.

Fab. Sowter[4] will cry upon't, for all this, though it be as rank as a fox.

Mal. M,—Malvolio;—*M,*—why, that begins my name.

Fab. Did not I say, he would work it out? the cur is excellent at faults.

Mal. M, But then there is no consonancy in the sequel; that suffers under probation: *A* should follow, but *O* does.

Fab. And *O* shall end, I hope.

Sir To. Ay, or I'll cudgel him, and make him cry, *O.*

Mal. And then *I* comes behind.

Fab. Ay, an you had any eye behind you, you might see more detraction at your heels, than fortunes before you.

Mal. M, O, A, I;—This simulation is not as the former:—and yet, to crush this a little, it would bow to me, for every one of these letters are in my name. Soft; here follows prose.—*If this fall into thy hand, revolve. In my stars I am above thee; but be not afraid of greatness: Some are born great, some achieve greatness, and some have greatness thrust upon them. Thy fates open their hands; let thy blood and spirit embrace them. And, to inure thyself to what thou art like to be, cast thy humble slough,[5] and appear fresh. Be opposite[6] with a kinsman, surly with servants: let thy tongue tang arguments of state; put thyself into the trick of singularity: She thus advises thee, that sighs for thee. Remember who commended thy yellow stockings; and wished to see thee ever cross-gartered:[7] I say, remember. Go to; thou art made, if thou desirest to be so; if not, let me see thee a steward still, the fellow of servants, and not worthy to touch fortune's fingers. Farewell. She that would alter services with thee,—The fortunate-unhappy.*

Day-light and champian[8] discovers not more: this is open. I will be proud, I will read politic authors, I will baffle Sir Toby, I will wash off gross acquaintance, I will be point-de-vice,[9] the very man. I do not now fool myself, to let imagination jade me; for every reason excites to this, that my lady loves me. She did commend my yellow stockings of late, she did praise my leg being cross-gartered; and in this she manifests herself to my love, and, with a kind of injunction, drives me to these habits of her liking. I thank my stars, I am happy. I will be strange, stout, in yellow stockings, and cross-gartered, even with the swiftness of putting on. Jove, and my stars be praised!—Here is yet a postscript. *Thou canst not choose but know who I am. If thou entertainest my love, let it appear in thy smiling; thy smiles become thee well: therefore in my presence still smile, dear my sweet, I pr'ythee.* Jove, I thank thee.—I will smile; I will do every thing that thou wilt have me. [*Exit.*

Fab. I will not give my part of this sport for a pension of thousands to be paid from the Sophy.[10]

Sir To. I could marry this wench for this device.

Sir And. So could I too.

Sir To. And ask no other dowry with her, but such another jest.

Enter MARIA.

Sir And. Nor I neither.

Fab. Here comes my noble gull-catcher.

Sir To. Wilt thou set thy foot o' my neck?

Sir And. Or o' mine either?

Sir To. Shall I play my freedom at tray-trip,[11] and become thy bond-slave?

Sir And. I'faith, or I either.

---

1 i. e. *badger*, a term of contempt. So in the Merry Conceited Jests of George Peele:—'This *self-conceited brock*.'

2 The common stone-hawk, which inhabits old buildings and rocks. *To check*, says Latham in his Book of Falconry, is, 'when crows, rooks, pies, or other birds coming in view of the hawk, she forsaketh her natural flight to fly at them.'

3 i. e. to any one *in his senses*, or whose *capacity* is not out of *form*.

4 *Sowter* is here used as the name of a hound. *Sowterly* is often employed as a term of abuse: a *Sowter* was a cobbler or botcher; quasi *Sutor*.

5 Skin of a snake.

6 i. e. adverse, hostile.

7 A fashion once prevailed for some time of wearing the garters *crossed* on the leg. It should be remembered that rich and expensive garters worn below the knee were then in use. Olivia's detestation of these fashions probably arose from thinking them coxcomical.

8 Open country.

9 i. e. *exactly* the same in every particular. The etymology of this phrase is very uncertain. The most probable seems the French *a point devise*. '*A poinct*,' says Nicot, 'adverbe. C'est en ordre et estat deu et convenable.' We have also *point blank*, for *direct* from the same source.

10 Alluding to Sir Robert Shirley, who was just returned in the character of ambassador from the Sophy. He boasted of the great rewards he had received, and lived in London with the utmost splendour.

11 An old game played with dice or tables. Thus in Machiavel's Dog. *Sig.* B. 4to. 1617.

'But leaving cards, let's go to dice awhile,
To passage *treitrippe*, hazard, or mumchance'

Sir To. Why, thou hast put him in such a dream, that, when the image of it leaves him, he must run mad.

Mar. Nay, but say true: does it work upon him?

Sir To. Like aqua-vitæ with a midwife.

Mar. If you will then see the fruits of the sport, mark his first approach before my lady: he will come to her in yellow stockings, and 'tis a colour he abhors; and cross-gartered, a fashion she detests; and he will smile upon her, which will now be so unsuitable to her disposition, being addicted to a melancholy as she is, that it cannot but turn him into a notable contempt: if you will see it, follow me.

Sir To. To the gates of Tartar, thou most excellent devil of wit!

Sir And. I'll make one too. [*Exeunt.*

ACT III.

SCENE I. Olivia's *Garden. Enter* VIOLA, *and* Clown *with a tabor.*

Vio. Save thee, friend, and thy music: Dost thou live by thy tabor?[1]

Clo. No, sir, I live by the church.

Vio. Art thou a churchman?

Clo. No such matter, sir; I do live by the church: for I do live at my house, and my house doth stand by the church.

Vio. So thou may'st say, the king lies by a beggar, if a beggar dwell near him: or, the church stands by thy tabor, if thy tabor stand by the church.

Clo. You have said, sir.—To see this age!—A sentence is but a cheveril[2] glove to a good wit; How quickly the wrong side may be turned outward!

Vio. Nay, that's certain; they, that dally nicely with words, may quickly make them wanton.

Clo. I would, therefore, my sister had had no name, sir.

Vio. Why, man?

Clo. Why, sir, her name's a word; and to dally with that word, might make my sister wanton: But, indeed, words are very rascals, since bonds disgraced them.

Vio. Thy reason, man?

Clo. Troth, sir, I can yield you none without words; and words are grown so false, I am loath to prove reason with them.

Vio. I warrant, thou art a merry fellow, and carest for nothing.

Clo. Not so, sir, I do care for something: but in my conscience, sir, I do not care for you; if that be to care for nothing, sir, I would it would make you invisible.

Vio. Art not thou the lady Olivia's fool?

Clo. No, indeed, sir; the lady Olivia has no folly: she will keep no fool, sir, till she be married; and fools are as like husbands, as pilchards are to herrings, the husband's the bigger; I am, indeed, not her fool, but her corrupter of words.

Vio. I saw thee late at the count Orsino's.

Clo. Foolery, sir, does walk about the orb, like the sun; it shines every where. I would be sorry, sir, but the fool should be as oft with your master, as with my mistress: I think I saw your wisdom there.

Vio. Nay, an thou pass upon me, I'll no more with thee. Hold, there's expenses for thee.

Clo. Now Jove, in his next commodity of hair send thee a beard!

Vio. By my troth, I'll tell thee; I am almost sick for one; though I would not have it grow on my chin. Is thy lady within?

Clo. Would not a pair of these have bred, sir?

Vio. Yes, being kept together, and put to use.

Clo. I would play lord Pandarus[3] of Phrygia, sir, to bring a Cressida to this Troilus.

Vio. I understand you, sir; 'tis well begg'd.

Clo. The matter, I hope, is not great, sir, begging but a beggar; Cressida was a beggar.[4] My lady is within, sir. I will construe to them whence you come; who you are, and what you would, are out of my welkin; I might say, element; but the word is over-worn. [*Exit.*

Vio. This fellow's wise enough to play the fool;
And, to do that well, craves a kind of wit:
He must observe their mood on whom he jests,
The quality of persons, and the time;
And, like the haggard,[5] check at every feather
That comes before his eye. This is a practice,
As full of labour as a wise man's art:
For folly, that he wisely shows, is fit;
But wise men, folly-fallen, quite taint their wit.

Enter SIR TOBY BELCH *and* SIR ANDREW AGUE-CHEEK.

Sir To. Save you, gentleman.

Vio. And you, sir.

Sir And. Dieu vous garde, monsieur.

Vio. Et vous aussi; votre serviteur.

Sir And. I hope, sir, you are; and I am yours.

Sir To. Will you encounter the house? my niece is desirous you should enter, if your trade be to her.

Vio. I am bound to your niece, sir: I mean, she is the list[6] of my voyage.

Sir To. Taste[7] your legs, sir, put them to motion.

Vio. My legs do better understand me, sir, than I understand what you mean by bidding me taste my legs.

Sir To. I mean, to go, sir, to enter.

Vio. I will answer you with gait and entrance: But we are prevented.[8]

Enter OLIVIA *and* MARIA.

Most excellent accomplished lady, the heavens rain odours on you!

Sir And. That youth's a rare courtier! *Rain odours!* well.

Vio. My matter hath no voice, lady, but to your own most pregnant[9] and vouchsafed ear.

Sir And. Odours, pregnant, and *vouchsafed*:—I'll get 'em all three ready.

Oli. Let the garden door be shut, and leave me to my hearing.

[*Exeunt* SIR TOBY, SIR ANDREW, *and* MARIA.

Give me your hand, sir.

Vio. My duty, madam, and most humble service.

Oli. What is your name?

Vio. Cesario is your servant's name, fair princess!

Oli. My servant, sir! 'Twas never merry world,
Since lowly feigning was call'd compliment;
You are a servant to the count Orsino, youth.

Vio. And he is yours, and his must needs be yours;
Your servant's servant is your servant, madam.

Oli. For him, I think not on him: for his thoughts,
'Would they were blanks, rather than fill'd with me!

Vio. Madam, I come to whet your gentle thoughts
On his behalf:—

Oli. O, by your leave, I pray you;
I bade you never speak again of him:
But, would you undertake another suit,

1 Tarleton, in a print before his Jests, 4to. 1611, is represented with a *Tabor*. But the instrument is found in the hands of fools, long before the time of Shakspeare.

2 Kid. Ray has a proverb 'He hath a conscience like a *cheverel's* skin.' See note on K. Henry VIII. Act ii. Sc. 4.

3 See the play of *Troilus and Cressida.*

4 In Henryson's Testament of Cresseid she is thus spoken of:—

——'great penurye
Thou shalt suffer, and as a *beggar* dye.'

And again,
'Thou shalt go begging from hous to hous,
With cuppe and clapper like a *Lazarous.*'

5 A *wild hawk*, or, hawk not well trained.

6 Bound, limit.

7 In the Frogs of Aristophanes a similar expression occurs, v. 462.

8 i. e. our purpose is anticipated. So in the 119th Psalm, 'Mine eyes *prevent* the night-watches.'

9 i. e. *ready, apprehensive; vouchsafed,* for *vouchsafing.*

I had rather hear you to solicit that,
Than music from the spheres.
Vio. Dear lady,——
Oli. Give me leave, 'beseech you: I did send,
After the last enchantment you did here,[1]
A ring in chase of you; so did I abuse
Myself, my servant, and, I fear me, you:
Under your hard construction must I sit,
To force that on you, in a shameful cunning,
Which you knew none of yours: What might you think?
Have you not set mine honour at the stake,
And baited it with all the unmuzzled thoughts
That tyrannous heart can think? To one of your receiving[2]
Enough is shown; a cyprus,[3] not a bosom,
Hides my heart: So let me hear you speak.
Vio. I pity you.
Oli. That's a degree to love.
Vio. No, not a grise;[4] for 'tis a vulgar[5] proof,
That very oft we pity enemies.
Oli. Why, then, methinks, 'tis time to smile again;
O world, how apt the poor are to be proud!
If one should be a prey, how much the better
To fall before the lion, than the wolf?
[*Clock strikes.*
The clock upbraids me with the waste of time.—
Be not afraid, good youth, I will not have you:
And yet, when wit and youth is come to harvest,
Your wife is like to reap a proper man:
There lies your way, due west.
Vio. Then westward-hoe:
Grace and good disposition 'tend your ladyship!
You'll nothing, madam, to my lord by me?
Oli. Stay:
I pr'ythee, tell me, what thou think'st of me.
Vio. That you do think, you are not what you are.
Oli. If I think so, I think the same of you.
Vio. Then think you right; I am not what I am.
Oli. I would you were as I would have you be!
Vio. Would it be better, madam, than I am,
I wish it might; for now I am your fool.
Oli. O, what a deal of scorn looks beautiful
In the contempt and anger of his lip!
A murd'rous guilt shows not itself more soon
Than love that would seem hid: love's night is noon.
Cesario, by the roses of the spring,
By maidhood, honour, truth, and every thing,
I love thee so, that, maugre[6] all thy pride,
Nor wit, nor reason, can my passion hide.
Do not extort thy reasons from this clause,
For, that I woo, thou therefore hast no cause:
But, rather, reason thus with reason fetter:
Love sought is good, but given unsought, is better.
Vio. By innocence I swear, and by my youth,
I have one heart, one bosom, and one truth,
And that no woman has; nor never none
Shall mistress be of it, save I alone.
And so adieu, good madam; never more
Will I my master's tears to you deplore.
Oli. Yet come again: for thou, perhaps, mays't move
That heart, which now abhors, to like his love.
[*Exeunt.*

SCENE II. *A Room in* Olivia's *House. Enter* Sir Toby Belch, Sir Andrew Ague-cheek, *and* Fabian.

Sir And. No, faith, I'll not stay a jot longer.

Sir To. Thy reason, dear venom, give thy reason.

Fab. You must needs yield your reason, Sir Andrew.

Sir And. Marry, I saw your niece do more favours to the count's serving man, than ever she bestowed upon me; I saw't i'the orchard.

Sir To. Did she see thee the while, old boy? tell me that.

Sir And. As plain as I see you now.

Fab. This was a great argument of love in her toward you.

Sir And. 'Slight! will you make an ass o'me?

Fab. I will prove it legitimate, sir, upon the oath of judgment and reason.

Sir To. And they have been grand jury-men, since before Noah was a sailor.

Fab. She did show favour to the youth in your sight, only to exasperate you, to awake your dormouse valour, to put fire in your heart, and brimstone in your liver: You should then have accosted her; and with some excellent jests, fire-new from the mint, you should have banged the youth into dumbness. This was looked for at your hand, and this was baulked: the double gilt of this opportunity you let time wash off, and you are now sailed into the north of my lady's opinion; where you will hang like an icicle on a Dutchman's beard, unless you do redeem it by some laudable attempt, either of valour, or policy.

Sir And. And't be any way, it must be with valour; for policy I hate: I had as lief be a Brownist[7] as a politician.

Sir To. Why then, build me thy fortunes upon the basis of valour. Challenge me the count's youth to fight with him; hurt him in eleven places; my niece shall take note of it: and assure thyself, there is no love-broker in the world can more prevail in man's commendation with woman, than report of valour.

Fab. There is no way but this, Sir Andrew.

Sir And. Will either of you bear me a challenge to him?

Sir To. Go, write it in a martial hand; be curst[8] and brief; it is no matter how witty, so it be eloquent, and full of invention: taunt him with the licence of ink: if thou *thou'st*[9] him some thrice, it shall not be amiss; and as many lies as will lie in thy sheet of paper, although the sheet were big enough for the bed of Ware[10] in England, set 'em down; go, about it. Let there be gall enough in thy ink; though thou write with a goose-pen, no matter: About it.

Sir And. Where shall I find you?

Sir To. We'll call thee at the *cubiculo*:[11] Go.
[*Exit* Sir Andrew.

Fab. This is a dear manakin to you, Sir Toby.

Sir To. I have been dear to him, lad; some two thousand strong, or so.

Fab. We shall have a rare letter from him: but you'll not deliver it.

Sir To. Never trust me then! and by all means stir on the youth to an answer. I think, oxen and wainropes[12] cannot hale them together. For Andrew, if he were opened, and you find so much blood in his liver as will clog the foot of a flea, I'll eat the rest of the anatomy.

Fab. And his opposite,[13] the youth, bears in his visage no great presage of cruelty.

Enter Maria.

Sir To. Look, where the youngest wren of nine[14] comes.

Mar. If you desire the spleen, and will laugh

---

1 i. e. after the enchantment your presence worked in my affections.
2 Ready apprehension.
3 i. e. a thin veil of crape or *cyprus*.
4 Step 5 Common.
6 *In spite of:* from the French *malgre.*
7 The *Brownists* were so called from Mr. Robert Browne, a noted separatist, in Queen Elizabeth's reign. They seem to have been the constant objects of popular satire.

8 'Be *curst* and brief.' *Curst* is *cross, froward, petulant.*
9 Shakspeare is thought to have had Lord Coke in his mind, whose virulent abuse of Sir Walter Raleigh on his trial was conveyed in a series of *thou's*. His resentment against the flagrant conduct of the attorney general on this occasion was probably heightened by the contemptuous manner in which he spoke of players in his charge at Norwich, and the severity he was always willing to exert against them.
10 This curious piece of furniture was a few years since still in being at one of the inns in that town. It was reported to be twelve feet square, and capable of holding twenty-four persons.
11 Chamber. 12 Wagon ropes. 13 i. e. adversary
14 The wren generally lays nine or ten eggs, and the

yourselves into stitches follow me: yon' gull Malvolio is turned heathen, a very renegado; for there is no Christian, that means to be saved by believing rightly, can ever believe such impossible passages of grossness. He's in yellow stockings.

Sir To. And cross-gartered?

Mar. Most villanously; like a pedant that keeps a school i'the church.—I have dogged him, like his murderer: He does obey every point of the letter that I dropped to betray him. He does smile his face into more lines, than are in the new map, with the augmentation of the Indies:[1] you have not seen such a thing as 'tis; I can hardly forbear hurling things at him. I know, my lady will strike him; if she do, he'll smile, and take't for a great favour.

Sir To. Come, bring us, bring us where he is. [*Exeunt.*

SCENE III. *A Street. Enter* ANTONIO *and* SEBASTIAN.

Seb. I would not, by my will, have troubled you;
But, since you make your pleasure of your pains,
I will no further chide you.

Ant. I could not stay behind you; my desire,
More sharp than filed steel, did spur me forth;
And not all love to see you (though so much
As might have drawn one to a longer voyage),
But jealousy what might befall your travel,
Being skilless in these parts: which, to a stranger,
Unguided and unfriended, often prove
Rough and unhospitable: My willing love,
The rather by these arguments of fear,
Set forth in your pursuit.

Seb. My kind Antonio,
I can no other answer make, but, thanks,
And thanks, and ever thanks: Often good turns
Are shuffled off with such uncurrent pay:
But, were my worth,[2] as is my conscience, firm,
You should find better dealing. What's to do?
Shall we go see the reliques of this town?

Ant. To-morrow, sir; best, first, go see your lodging.

Seb. I am not weary, and 'tis long to night;
I pray you, let us satisfy our eyes
With the memorials, and the things of fame,
That do renown this city.

Ant. 'Would you'd pardon me;
I do not without danger walk these streets:
Once, in a sea-fight, 'gainst the Count his galleys,
I did some service; of such note, indeed,
That, were I ta'en here, it would scarce be answer'd.

Seb. Belike, you slew great number of his people.

Ant. The offence is not of such a bloody nature;
Albeit the quality of the time, and quarrel,
Might well have given us bloody argument.
It might have since been answer'd in repaying
What we took from them; which, for traffic's sake,
Most of our city did: only myself stood out:
For which, if I be lapsed[3] in this place,
I shall pay dear.

Seb. Do not then walk too open.

Ant. It doth not fit me. Hold, sir, here's my purse:
In the south suburbs, at the Elephant,
Is best to lodge: I will bespeak our diet,
Whiles you beguile the time, and feed your knowledge,
With viewing of the town; there shall you have me.

Seb. Why I your purse?

Ant. Haply, your eye shall light upon some toy
You have desire to purchase; and your store,
I think, is not for idle markets, sir.

Seb. I'll be your purse-bearer, and leave you for
An hour.

Ant. To the Elephant.—

Seb. I do remember. [*Exeunt.*

SCENE IV. Olivia's *Garden. Enter* OLIVIA *and* MARIA.

Oli. I have sent after him: He says he'll come:
How shall I feast him? what bestow on him?
For youth is bought more oft, than begg'd, or borrow'd.
I speak too loud.——
Where is Malvolio?—he is sad, and civil,[4]
And suits well for a servant with my fortunes,
Where is Malvolio?

Mar. He's coming, madam; but in very strange manner. He is sure possessed, madam.

Oli. Why, what's the matter? does he rave?

Mar. No, madam, he does nothing but smile your ladyship were best to have some guard about you, if he come; for, sure, the man is tainted in his wits.

Oli. Go call him hither.—I'm as mad as he,
If sad and merry madness equal be.—

Enter MALVOLIO.

How now, Malvolio!

Mar. Sweet lady, ho, ho. [*Smiles fantastically.*

Oli. Smil'st thou?
I sent for thee upon a sad[5] occasion.

Mal. Sad, lady? I could be sad: This does make some obstruction in the blood, this cross-gartering: But what of that, if it please the eye of one, it is with me as the very true sonnet is: *Please one, and please all.*

Oli. Why, how dost thou, man? what is the matter with thee?

Mal. Not black in my mind, though yellow in my legs: It did come to his hands, and commands shall be executed. I think, we do know the sweet Roman hand.

Oli. Wilt thou go to bed, Malvolio?

Mal. To bed? ay, sweet-heart; and I'll come to thee.

Oli. God comfort thee! Why dost thou smile so, and kiss thy hand so oft?

Mar. How do you, Malvolio?

Mal. At your request? Yes; Nightingales answer daws.

Mar. Why appear you with this ridiculous boldness before my lady?

Mal. *Be not afraid of greatness:*—'Twas well writ.

Oli. What meanest thou by that, Malvolio?

Mal. *Some are born great,—*

Oli. Ha?

Mal. *Some achieve greatness,—*

Oli. What say'st thou?

Mal. *And some have greatness thrust upon them.*

Oli. Heaven restore thee!

Mal. *Remember, who commended thy yellow stockings;—*

Oli. Thy yellow stockings?

Mal. *And wished to see thee cross-gartered.*

Oli. Cross-gartered?

Mal. *Go to: thou art made, if thou desirest to be so;—*

Oli. Am I made?

Mal. *If not, let me see thee a servant still.*

Oli. Why, this is very midsummer madness.[6]

Enter Servant.

Ser. Madam, the young gentleman of the count Orsino's is returned; I could hardly entreat him back: he attends your ladyship's pleasure.

---

last hatched birds are usually the smallest of the brood. The *boy* who played Maria's part was probably of diminutive size.

1 Alluding to a Map engraved for the English translation of Linschoten's Voyage, published in 1598. This map is multilineal in the extreme, and is the first in which the *Eastern Islands* are included

2 Wealth, or fortune.

3 *Lapsed*, for *lapsing* or *transgressing*. See note on Hamlet, Act iii. Sc. 4.

4 '——he is *sad* and *civil*.' That is *serious* and *grave*, or *solemn*. Thus in Romeo and Juliet:—
'——Come, *civil* night,
Thou sober-suited matron, all in black.'

5 Grave.

6 ''Tis midsummer moon with you' was a proverbia phrase signifying you are mad. It was an ancient opinion that hot weather affected the brain

Oli. I'll come to him. [*Exit* Servant.] Good Maria, let this fellow be looked to. Where's my cousin Toby? Let some of my people have a special care of him; I would not have him miscarry for the half of my dowry.

[*Exeunt* Olivia *and* Maria.

Mal. Oh, ho! do you come near me now? no worse man than Sir Toby to look to me? This concurs directly with the letter: she sends him on purpose, that I may appear stubborn to him; for she incites me to that in the letter. *Cast thy humble slough*, says she; *be opposite with a kinsman, surly with servants,—let thy tongue tang with arguments of state,—put thyself into the trick of singularity;*—and, consequently, sets down the manner how; as, a sad face, a reverend carriage, a slow tongue, in the habit of some sir of note, and so forth. I have limed her;[1] but it is Jove's doing, and Jove make me thankful! And, when she went away now, *Let this fellow be looked to:* Fellow![2] not Malvolio, nor after my degree, but fellow. Why every thing adheres together; that no dram of a scruple, no scruple of a scruple, no obstacle, no incredulous or unsafe circumstance,—What can be said? Nothing that can be, can come between me and the full prospect of my hopes. Well, Jove, not I, is the doer of this, and he is to be thanked.

Re-enter Maria, *with* Sir Toby Belch *and* Fabian.

Sir To. Which way is he, in the name of sanctity? If all the devils in hell be drawn in little, and Legion himself possessed him, yet I'll speak to him.

Fab. Here he is, here he is:—How is't with you, sir? how is't with you, man?

Mal. Go off: I discard you; let me enjoy my private; go off.

Mar. Lo, how hollow the fiend speaks within him! did not I tell you?—Sir Toby, my lady prays you to have a care of him.

Mal. Ah, ha! does she so?

Sir To. Go to, go to; peace, peace, we must deal gently with him; let me alone. How do you, Malvolio? how is't with you? What man! defy the devil; consider, he's an enemy to mankind.

Mal. Do you know what you say?

Mar. La you, an you speak ill of the devil, how he takes it at heart! Pray God, he be not bewitched!

Fab. Carry his water to the wise woman.

Mar. Marry, and it shall be done to-morrow morning, if I live. My lady would not lose him for more than I'll say.

Mal. How now, mistress?

Mar. O lord!

Sir To. Pr'ythee, hold thy peace; this is not the way: Do you not see, you move him; let me alone with him.

Fab. No way but gentleness; gently, gently; the fiend is rough, and will not be roughly used.

Sir To. Why, how now, my bawcock?[3] how dost thou, chuck?

Mal. Sir?

Sir To. Ay, biddy, come with me. What, man! 'tis not for gravity to play at cherry-pit[4] with Satan: Hang him, foul collier![5]

Mar. Get him to say his prayers; good Sir Toby, get him to pray.

Mal. My prayers, minx?

Mar. No, I warrant you, he will not hear of godliness.

Mal. Go, hang yourselves all! you are idle shallow things: I am not of your element; you shall know more hereafter. [*Exit.*

Sir To. Is't possible?

Fab. If this were played upon a stage now, I could condemn it as an improbable fiction.

Sir To. His very genius hath taken the infection of the device, man.

Mar. Nay, pursue him now; lest the device take air, and taint.

Fab. Why, we shall make him mad, indeed.

Mar. The house will be the quieter.

Sir To. Come, we'll have him in a dark room,[6] and bound. My niece is already in the belief that he is mad; we may carry it thus, for our pleasure, and his penance, till our very pastime, tired out of breath, prompt us to have mercy on him: at which time, we will bring the device to the bar, and crown thee for a finder of madmen. But see, but see.

Enter Sir Andrew Ague-cheek.

Fab. More matter for a May morning.[7]

Sir And. Here's the challenge, read it; I warrant there's vinegar and pepper in't.

Fab. Is't so saucy?

Sir And. Ay is it, I warrant him; do but read.

Sir To. Give me. [*Reads.*] *Youth, whatsoever thou art, thou art but a scurvy fellow.*

Fab. Good, and valiant.

Sir To. *Wonder not, nor admire not in thy mind, why I do call thee so, for I will show thee no reason for't.*

Fab. A good note: that keeps you from the blow of the law.

Sir To. *Thou comest to the lady Olivia, and in my sight she uses thee kindly: but thou liest in thy throat, that is not the matter I challenge thee for.*

Fab. Very brief, and exceeding good sense-less.

Sir To. *I will way-lay thee going home; where if it be thy chance to kill me,—*

Fab. Good.

Sir To. *Thou killest me like a rogue and a villain.*

Fab. Still you keep o'the windy side of the law: Good.

Sir To. *Fare thee well: And God have mercy upon one of our souls! He may have mercy upon mine; but my hope is better, and so look to thyself. Thy friend, as thou usest him, and thy sworn enemy.*—Andrew Ague-cheek.

Sir To. If this letter move him not, his legs cannot: I'll give't him.

Mar. You may have very fit occasion for't; he is now in some commerce with my lady, and will by and by depart.

Sir To. Go, Sir Andrew; scout me for him at the corner of the orchard, like a bum-bailiff: so soon as ever thou seest him, draw; and, as thou drawest, swear horrible;[8] for it comes to pass oft, that a terrible oath, with a swaggering accent, sharply twanged off, gives manhood more approbation than ever proof itself would have earned him. Away.

Sir And. Nay, let me alone for swearing. [*Exit.*

Sir To. Now will I not deliver his letter: for the behaviour of the young gentleman gives him out to be of good capacity and breeding; his employment between his lord and my niece confirms no less; therefore this letter, being so excellently ignorant, will breed no terror in the youth, he will find it comes from a clodpole. But, sir, I will deliver his challenge by word of mouth; set upon Ague-cheek a notable report of valour; and drive the gentleman (as I know his youth will aptly receive it) into a most hideous opinion of his rage, skill, fury, and impetuosity. This will so fright them both, that they will kill one another by the look, like cockatrices.

---

1 Caught her as a bird with birdlime.

2 Malvolio takes the word in its old favourable sense of *companion*.

3 See Winter's Tale, Act i. Sc. 5.

4 A play among boys.

5 *Collier* was in Shakspeare's time a term of the highest reproach. The coal venders were in bad repute, not only from the blackness of their appearance, but that many of them were also great cheats. The devil is called collier for his blackness. Hence the proverb 'Like will to like, as the *devil* with the *collier*.'

6 The reason for putting him in a *dark room* was to make him believe he was *mad*, a *mad house* seems for merly to have been called a *dark house*.

7 It was usual on the First of May to exhibit metrical interludes of the comic kind, as well as other sports, such as the Morris Dance.

8 Adjectives are often used by Shakspeare and his cotemporaries adverbially.

Enter OLIVIA *and* VIOLA.

Fab. Here he comes with your niece: give them way, till he take leave, and presently after him.

Sir To. I will meditate the while upon some horrid message for a challenge.

[*Exeunt* SIR TOBY, FABIAN, *and* MARIA.

Oli. I have said too much unto a heart of stone,
And laid mine honour too unchary[1] out:
There's something in me, that reproves my fault;
But such a headstrong potent fault it is,
That it but mocks reproof.

Vio. With the same 'haviour that your passion bears,
Go on my master's griefs.

Oli. Here, wear this jewel[2] for me, 'tis my picture;
Refuse it not, it hath no tongue to vex you:
And, I beseech you, come again to-morrow,
What shall you ask of me that I'll deny,
That, honour sav'd, may upon asking give?

Vio. Nothing but this, your true love for my master.

Oli. How with mine honour may I give him that
Which I have given to you?

Vio. I will acquit you.

Oli. Well, come again to-morrow: Fare thee well;
A fiend, like thee, might bear my soul to hell. [*Exit.*

Re-enter SIR TOBY BELCH *and* FABIAN.

Sir To. Gentleman, God save thee.

Vio. And you, sir.

Sir To. That defence thou hast, betake thee to't: of what nature the wrongs are thou hast done him, I know not; but thy intercepter, full of despight, bloody as the hunter, attends thee at the orchard end: dismount thy tuck,[3] be yare[4] in thy preparation, for thy assailant is quick, skilful, and deadly.

Vio. You mistake, sir; I am sure no man hath any quarrel to me; my remembrance is very free and clear from any image of offence done to any man.

Sir To. You'll find it otherwise, I assure you: therefore, if you hold your life at any price, betake you to your guard; for your opposite hath in him what youth, strength, skill, and wrath, can furnish man withal.

Vio. I pray you, sir, what is he?

Sir To. He is knight, dubbed with unhatched rapier, and on carpet consideration;[5] but he is a devil in private brawl: souls and bodies hath he divorced three; and his incensement at this moment is so implacable, that satisfaction can be none but by pangs of death and sepulchre: hob, nob,[6] is his word; give't, or take't.

Vio. I will return again into the house, and desire some conduct of the lady. I am no fighter. I have heard of some kind of men, that put quarrels purposely on others, to taste their valour: belike, this is a man of that quirk.[7]

Sir To. Sir, no; his indignation derives itself out of a very competent injury; therefore, get you on, and give him his desire. Back you shall not to the house, unless you undertake that with me, which with as much safety you might answer him: therefore on, or strip your sword stark naked; for meddle you must, that's certain, or forswear to wear iron about you.

Vio. This is as uncivil as strange. I beseech you, do me this courteous office, as to know of the knight what my offence to him is; it is something of my negligence, nothing of my purpose.

Sir To. I will do so. Signior Fabian, stay you by this gentleman till my return. [*Exit* SIR TOBY.

Vio. Pray you, sir, do you know of this matter?

Fab. I know the knight is incensed against you, even to a mortal arbitrement;[8] but nothing of the circumstance more.

Vio. I beseech you, what manner of man is he?

Fab. Nothing of that wonderful promise, to read him by his form, as you are like to find him in the proof of his valour. He is, indeed, sir, the most skilful, bloody, and fatal opposite[9] that you could possibly have found in any part of Illyria: Will you walk towards him? I will make your peace with him, if I can.

Vio. I shall be much bound to you for't: I am one, that would rather go with sir priest, than sir knight: I care not who knows so much of my mettle. [*Exeunt.*

Re-enter SIR TOBY, *with* SIR ANDREW.

Sir To. Why, man, he's a very devil;[10] I have not seen such a firago.[11] I had a pass with him, rapier, scabbard, and all, and he gives me the stuck-in,[12] with such a mortal motion, that it is inevitable; and on the answer, he pays you[13] as surely as your feet hit the ground they step on: They say, he has been fencer to the Sophy.

Sir And. Pox on't, I'll not meddle with him.

Sir To. Ay, but he will not now be pacified; Fabian can scarce hold him yonder.

Sir And. Plague on't: an I thought he had been valiant and so cunning in fence, I'd have seen him damned ere I'd have challenged him. Let him let the matter slip, and I'll give him my horse, grey Capilet.

Sir To. I'll make the motion: stand here, make a good show on't; this shall end without the perdition of souls: Marry, I'll ride your horse as well as I ride you. [*Aside.*

Re-enter FABIAN *and* VIOLA.

I have his horse [*to* FAB.] to take up the quarrel; I have persuaded him, the youth's a devil.

Fab. He is as horribly conceited[14] of him; and pants, and looks pale, as if a bear were at his heels.

Sir To. There's no remedy, sir; he will fight with you for his oath's sake: marry, he hath better bethought him of his quarrel, and he finds that now scarce to be worth talking of: therefore draw, for the supportance of his vow; he protests, he will not hurt you.

Vio. Pray God defend me! A little thing would make me tell them how much I lack of a man. [*Aside.*

Fab. Give ground, if you see him furious.

Sir To. Come, Sir Andrew, there's no remedy; the gentleman will, for his honour's sake, have one bout with you; he cannot by the duello[15] avoid it; but he has promised me, as he is a gentleman and a soldier, he will not hurt you. Come on: to't.

Sir And. Pray God, he keep his oath! [*Draws.*

Enter ANTONIO.

Vio. I do assure you, 'tis against my will. [*Draws.*

Ant. Put up your sword;—If this young gentleman
Have done offence, I take the fault on me;
If you offend him, I for him defy you. [*Drawing*

Sir To. You, sir? why, what are you?

Ant. One sir, that for his love dares yet do more
Than you have heard him brag to you he will.

---

1 Uncautiously.

2 *Jewel* anciently signified any precious ornament of superfluity.

3 Rapier. 4 Ready, nimble.

5 i. e. he is a *carpet-knight* not dubbed in the field, but on some peaceable occasion; *unhatch'd* was probably used in the sense of *unhack'd*. But perhaps we should read *an hatch'd rapier*, i. e. a rapier the hilt of which was enriched with silver or gold.

6 A corruption most probably of *hab or nab:* have or have not, hit or miss at a venture. *Quasi, have,* or *n'ave*, i. e. have not, from the Saxon *habban* to have; *nabban*, not to have. So, in Holinshed's description of Ireland, 'The citizens in their rage shot *habbe or nabbe.*'

7 Sort. 8 Decision. 9 Adversary.

10 Shakspeare may have caught a hint for this scene from the behaviour of Sir John Dow and Sir A. La Foole in Jonson's Silent Woman, which was printed in 1609.

11 *Firago*, for virago. The meaning appears to be, I have never seen the most furious woman so obstreperous and violent as he is.

12 A corruption of *stoccata*, an Italian term in fencing

13 i. e. hits you.

14 He has a horrid conception of him

15 Laws of duel

Sir To. Nay, if you be an undertaker,[1] I am for you. [*Draws.*

Enter Two Officers.

Fab. O good Sir Toby, hold; here come the officers.

Sir To. I'll be with you anon. [*To* ANTONIO.

Vio. Pray, sir, put up your sword, if you please. [*To* SIR ANDREW.

Sir And. Marry, will I, sir;—and for that I promised you, I'll be as good as my word: He will bear you easily; and reins well.

1 *Off.* This is the man; do thy office.

2 *Off.* Antonio, I arrest thee at the suit
Of count Orsino.

Ant. You do mistake me, sir.

1 *Off.* No, sir, no jot; I know your favour well.
Though now you have no sea-cap on your head.—
Take him away; he knows, I know him well.

Ant. I must obey.—This comes with seeking you;
But there's no remedy; I shall answer it.
What will you do? Now my necessity
Makes me to ask you for my purse: It grieves me
Much more, for what I cannot do for you,
Than what befalls myself. You stand amaz'd;
But be of comfort.

2 *Off.* Come, sir, away.

Ant. I must entreat of you some of that money.

Vio. What money, sir?
For the fair kindness you have show'd me here,
And, part, being prompted by your present trouble,
Out of my lean and low ability
I'll lend you something: my having[2] is not much;
I'll make division of my present with you;
Hold, there is half my coffer.

Ant. Will you deny me now?
Is't possible, that my deserts to you
Can lack persuasion? Do not tempt my misery,
Lest that it make me so unsound a man,
As to upbraid you with those kindnesses
That I have done for you.

Vio. I know of none;
Nor know I you by voice, or any feature:
I hate ingratitude more in a man,
Than lying, vainness, babbling, drunkenness,
Or any taint of vice, whose strong corruption
Inhabits our frail blood.

Ant. O heavens themselves!

2 *Off.* Come, sir, I pray you go.

Ant. Let me speak a little. This youth that you see here,
I snatch'd one half out of the jaws of death;
Reliev'd him with such sanctity of love,——
And to his image, which, methought did promise
Most venerable worth, did I devotion.

1 *Off.* What's that to us? The time goes by; away.

Ant. But, O, how vile an idol proves this god!—
Thou hast, Sebastian, done good feature shame.—
In nature there's no blemish, but the mind;
None can be call'd deform'd, but the unkind:
Virtue is beauty; but the beauteous-evil
Are empty trunks, o'erflourished[3] by the devil.

1 *Off.* The man grows mad; away with him.
Come, come, sir.

Ant. Lead me on. [*Exeunt* Officers *with* ANT.

Vio. Methinks, his words do from such passion fly,
That he believes himself; so do not I.[4]
Prove true, imagination, O, prove true,
That I, dear brother, be now ta'en for you!

Sir To. Come hither, knight; come hither, Fabian; we'll whisper o'er a couplet or two of most sage saws.

Vio. He nam'd Sebastian; I my brother know
Yet living in my glass;[5] even such, and so,
In favour was my brother; and he went
Still in this fashion, colour, ornament,
For him I imitate; O, if it prove,
Tempests are kind, and salt waves fresh in love! [*Exit*

Sir To. A very dishonest paltry boy, and more a coward than a hare: his dishonesty appears, in leaving his friend here in necessity, and denying him; and for his cowardice, ask Fabian.

Fab. A coward, a most devout coward, religious in it.

Sir And. 'Slid, I'll after him again, and beat him.

Sir To. Do, cuff him soundly, but never draw thy sword.

Sir And. An I do not. [*Exit.*

Fab. Come, let's see the event.

Sir To. I dare lay any money, 'twill be nothing yet. [*Exeunt.*

ACT IV.—SCENE I. *The Street before* Olivia's *House. Enter* SEBASTIAN *and* Clown.

Clo. Will you make me believe that I am not sent for you?

Seb. Go to, go to, thou art a foolish fellow;
Let me be clear of thee.

Clo. Well held out, i'faith! No, I do not know you; nor am I not sent to you by my lady, to bid you come speak with her; nor your name is not master Cesario; nor this is not my nose neither.—Nothing, that is so, is so.

Seb. I pr'ythee, vent thy folly somewhere else;
Thou know'st not me.

Clo. Vent my folly! He has heard that word of some great man, and now applies it to a fool. Vent my folly! I am afraid this great lubber, the world, will prove a cockney.—I pr'ythee now, ungird thy strangeness, and tell me what I shall vent to my lady; Shall I vent to her, that thou art coming?

Seb. I pr'ythee, foolish Greek,[6] depart from me,
There's money for thee; if you tarry longer.
I shall give worse payment.

Clo. By my troth, thou hast an open hand:—These wise men that give fools money, get themselves a good report after fourteen years' purchase.[7]

Enter SIR ANDREW, SIR TOBY, *and* FABIAN.

Sir And. Now, sir, have I met you again? there's for you. [*Striking* SEBASTIAN.

Seb. Why, there's for thee, and there, and there:
Are all the people mad! [*Beating* SIR ANDREW.

Sir To. Hold, sir, or I'll throw your dagger o'er the house.

Clo. This will I tell my lady straight; I would not be in some of your coats for two-pence. [*Exit* Clown.

Sir To. Come on, sir; hold. [*Holding* SEBASTIAN.

Sir And. Nay, let him alone; I'll go another way to work with him; I'll have an action of battery against him, if there be any law in Illyria: though I struck him first, yet its no matter for that.

Seb. Let go thy hand.

Sir To. Come, sir, I will not let you go. Come, my young soldier, put up your iron: you are well fleshed; come on.

Seb. I will be free from thee. What wouldst thou now?
If thou dar'st tempt me further, draw thy sword. [*Draws.*

Sir To. What, what! Nay, then I must have an ounce or two of this malapert blood from you. [*Draws.*

---

1 i. e. one who takes up or *undertakes* the quarrel of another.

2 i. e. fortune, possessions.

3 Trunks, being then part of the furniture of apartments, were ornamented with scroll-work or *flourished* devices.

4 i. e. I do not yet believe myself, when from this accident, I gather hope of my brother's life.

5 His resemblance *survives* in the reflection of my own figure

6 *A merry Greek, or a foolish Greek* were ancient proverbial expressions applied to boon companions, good fellows, as they were called who spent their time in riotous mirth. Whether the Latin *pergræcari*, of the same import, furnished the phrase or not, it was in use in France and Italy as well as in England.

7 i. e. at a very extravagant price, *twelve* years' purchase being then the current price of estates.

Enter OLIVIA.

Oli. Hold, Toby; on thy life, I charge thee, hold.

Sir To. Madam!

Oli. Will it be ever thus? Ungracious wretch,
Fit for the mountains and the barbarous caves,
Where manners ne'er were preach'd! out of my sight!
Be not offended, dear Cesario?——
Rudesby,[1] be gone?—I pr'ythee, gentle friend,
[*Exeunt* SIR TOBY, SIR ANDREW, *and* FABIAN.
Let thy fair wisdom, not thy passion, sway
In this uncivil and unjust extent[2]
Against thy peace. Go with me to my house;
And hear thou there how many fruitless pranks
This ruffian hath botch'd up,[3] that thou thereby
May'st smile at this: thou shalt not choose but go;
Do not deny: Beshrew[4] his soul for me,
He started one poor heart[5] of mine in thee.

Seb. What relish is in this?[6] how runs the stream?
Or I am mad, or else this is a dream:—
Let fancy still my sense in Lethe steep;
If it be thus to dream, still let me sleep!

Oli. Nay, come, I pr'ythee: 'Would thou'dst be rul'd by me!

Seb. Madam, I will.

Oli. O, say so, and so be!
[*Exeunt.*

SCENE II. *A Room in* Olivia's *House. Enter* MARIA *and* Clown.

Mar. Nay, I pr'ythee, put on this gown, and this beard; make him believe, thou art Sir Topas the curate; do it quickly: I'll call Sir Toby the whilst.
[*Exit* MARIA.

Clo. Well, I'll put it on, and I will dissemble[7] myself in't; and I would I were the first that ever dissembled in such a gown. I am not tall[8] enough to become the function well; nor lean enough to be thought a good student: but to be said, an honest man, and a good housekeeper, goes as fairly as to say, a careful man, and a great scholar. The competitors[9] enter.

Enter SIR TOBY BELCH *and* MARIA.

Sir To. Jove bless thee, master parson.

Clo. *Bonos dies*, Sir Toby: for as the old hermit of Prague, that never saw pen and ink, very wittily said to a niece of king Gorboduc, *That, that is, is*: so I, being master parson, am master parson: For what is that, but that? and is, but is?[10]

Sir To. To him, Sir Topas.

Clo. What, hoa, I say;—Peace in this prison!

Sir To. The knave counterfeits well: a good knave.

Mal. [*in an inner chamber.*] Who calls there?

Clo. Sir Topas the curate, who comes to visit Malvolio the lunatic.

Mal. Sir Topas, Sir Topas, good Sir Topas, go to my lady.

Clo. Out, hyperbolical fiend! how vexest thou this man? talkest thou nothing but of ladies!

Sir To. Well said, master parson.

Mal. Sir Topas, never was man thus wronged: good Sir Topas, do not think I am mad: they have laid me here in hideous darkness.

Clo. Fye, thou dishonest Sathan! I call thee by the most modest terms; for I am one of those gentle ones, that will use the devil himself with courtesy: Say'st thou, that house is dark?

Mal. As hell, Sir Topas.

Clo. Why, it hath bay-windows[11] transparent as barricadoes, and the clear stories[12] towards the south-north are as lustrous as ebony; and yet complainest thou of obstruction?

Mal. I am not mad, Sir Topas: I say to you, this house is dark.

Clo. Madman, thou errest: I say, there is no darkness, but ignorance; in which thou art more puzzled than the Egyptians in their fog.

Mal. I say, this house is as dark as ignorance, though ignorance were as dark as hell; and I say, there was never man thus abused: I am no more mad than you are; make the trial of it in any constant question.[13]

Clo. What is the opinion of Pythagoras concerning wild-fowl?

Mal. That the soul of our grandam might haply inhabit a bird.

Clo. What thinkest thou of his opinion?

Mal. I think nobly of the soul, and no way approve his opinion.

Clo. Fare thee well: Remain thou still in darkness: thou shalt hold the opinion of Pythagoras, ere I will allow of thy wits; and fear to kill a woodcock,[14] lest thou dispossess the soul of thy grandam. Fare thee well.

Mal. Sir Topas, Sir Topas,—

Sir To. My most exquisite Sir Topas!

Clo. Nay, I am for all waters.[15]

Mar. Thou might'st have done this without thy beard and gown; he sees thee not.

Sir To. To him in thine own voice, and bring me word how thou findest him; I would, we were well rid of this knavery. If he may be conveniently delivered, I would he were; for I am now so far in offence with my niece, that I cannot pursue with any safety this sport to the upshot. Come by and by to my chamber. [*Exeunt* SIR TOBY *and* MARIA.

Clo. *Hey Robin, jolly Robin,*[16]
Tell me how thy lady does. [*Singing.*

---

1 Rude fellow. 2 Violence.
3 Made up. 4 Ill betide.

5 An equivoque is here intended between *hart* and *heart;* they were formerly written alike.

6 i. e. how does this taste? what judgment am I to make of it?

7 i. e. *disguise*. Shakespeare has here used a Latinism. '*Dissimulo*, to dissemble, to *cloak*, to hide, says Hutton's Dictionary, 1583. And Ovid, speaking of Achilles—
'Veste virum longa *dissimulatus* erat.'

8 The modern editors have changed this to *fat* without any apparent reason.

9 Confederates.

10 A humorous banter upon the language of the schools.

11 *Bay windows* were large projecting windows, probably so called because they occupied a whole *bay* or space between two cross beams in a building. Minshew says a bay-window, so called 'because it is builded in manner of a *bay* or road for ships, i. e. round.'

12 *Clear stories*, in Gothic Architecture, denote the row of windows running along the upper part of a lofty hall or of a church, over the arches of the nave: q. d. a *clear story*, a story without joists, rafters, or flooring. 'Over each side of the nave is a row of *clere story* windows.'—*Ormerod's Hist. of Cheshire*, i. 450. The first folio reads clear *stores*, the second folio clear *stones*, which was followed by all subsequent editors The emendation and explanation are Mr. Blakeway's. Randle Holme, however, in his Academy of Armory; says that '*clear story* windows are such windows that have no transum or cross-piece in the middle to break the same into two lights.'

13 Regular conversation.

14 The clown mentions a woodcock because it was proverbial as a foolish bird, and therefore a proper ancestor for a man out of his wits.

15 A proverbial phrase not yet satisfactorily explained. The meaning, however, appears to be 'I can turn my hand to any thing, or assume any character.' Florio in his translation of Montaigne, speaking of Aristotle, says 'he hath *an oar in every water*, and meddleth with all things.' And in his *Second Frutes*, there is an expression more resembling the import of that in the text. '*I am a knight for all saddles.*' Nash in his Lenten Stuffe, 1599, has almost the language of the clown.—'He is first broken to the sea in the Herring-man's skiffe or cock-boate, where having learned *to brooke all waters*, and drink as he can out of a tarrie can.' Mason's conjecture, that the allusion is to the *water* hue or colour of precious stones, is surely inadmissible.

16 This ballad may be found in Percy's Reliques of Ancient Poetry, Vol. i. p. 194, ed. 1794. Dr. Nott has also printed it among the poems of Sir Thomas Wiatt the elder, p. 188.

Mal. Fool,—

Clo. *My lady is unkind, perdy.*

Mal. Fool,—

Clo. *Alas, why is she so?*

Mal. Fool, I say;—

Clo. *She loves another*—Who calls, ha?

Mal. Good fool, as ever thou wilt deserve well at my hand, help me to a candle, and pen, ink, and paper; as I am a gentleman, I will live to be thankful to thee for't.

Clo. Master Malvolio!

Mal. Ay, good fool.

Clo. Alas, sir, how fell you besides your five wits?[1]

Mal. Fool, there was never man so notoriously abused: I am as well in my wits, fool, as thou art.

Clo. But as well? then you are mad, indeed, if you be no better in your wits than a fool.

Mal. They have here propertied me;[2] keep me in darkness, send ministers to me, asses, and do all they can to face me out of my wits.

Clo. Advise you what you say: the minister is here,—Malvolio, Malvolio, thy wits the heavens restore! endeavour thyself to sleep, and leave thy vain bibble babble.

Mal. Sir Topas,———

Clo. Maintain no words with him, good fellow.[3] —Who, I, sir? not I, sir. God b'wi'you, good Sir Topas.—Marry, amen.—I will, sir, I will.

Mal. Fool, fool, fool, I say.—

Clo. Alas, sir, be patient. What say you, sir? I am shent[4] for speaking to you.

Mal. Good fool, help me to some light, and some paper; I tell thee, I am as well in my wits as any man in Illyria.

Clo. Well-a-day,—that you were, sir!

Mal. By this hand, I am: Good fool, some ink, paper, and light, and convey what I will set down to my lady; it shall advantage thee more than ever the bearing of letter did.

Clo. I will help you to't. But tell me true, are you not mad, indeed? or do you but counterfeit?

Mal. Believe me, I am not; I tell thee true.

Clo. Nay, I'll ne'er believe a madman till I see his brains. I will fetch you light, and paper, and ink.

Mal. Fool, I'll requite it in the highest degree: pr'ythee, begone.

Clo. *I am gone, sir,*
And anon, sir,
I'll be with you again,
In a trice;
Like to the old vice,[5]
Your need to sustain;

Who with dagger of lath,
In his rage and his wrath,
Cries ah, ha! to the devil:
Like a mad lad,
Pare thy nails, dad,
Adieu, goodman devil. [*Exit.*

SCENE III. Olivia's *Garden. Enter* SEBASTIAN.

Seb. This is the air; that is the glorious sun;
This pearl she gave me, I do feel't and see't:
And though 'tis wonder that enwraps me thus,
Yet 'tis not madness. Where's Antonio then?
I could not find him at the Elephant:
Yet there he was; and there I found this credit,[6]
That he did range the town to seek me out.
His counsel now might do me golden service:
For though my soul disputes well with my sense,
That this may be some error, but no madness,
Yet doth this accident and flood of fortune
So far exceed all instance, all discourse,[7]
That I am ready to distrust mine eyes,
And wrangle with my reason, that persuades me
To any other trust, but that I am mad,
Or else the lady's mad; yet, if 'twere so,
She could not sway her house, command her followers,[8]
Take, and give back affairs, and their despatch,
With such a smooth, discreet, and stable bearing,
As, I perceive, she does: there's something in't,
That is deceivable.[9] But here the lady comes.

Enter OLIVIA *and a* Priest.

Oli. Blame not this haste of mine: If you mean well,
Now, go with me, and with this holy man,
Into the chantry[10] by: there, before him,
And underneath that consecrated roof,
Plight me the full assurance of your faith,
That my most jealous and too doubtful soul
May live at peace: He shall conceal it,
Whiles[11] you are willing it shall come to note,
What time we will our celebration keep
According to my birth. What do you say?

Seb. I'll follow this good man, and go with you,
And, having sworn truth,[12] ever will be true.

Oli. Then lead the way, good father:———And heavens so shine,
That they may fairly note this act of mine! [*Exeunt*

ACT V.

SCENE I. *The Street before* Olivia's *House*
Enter Clown *and* FABIAN.

Fab. Now, as thou lovest me, let me see his letter.

Clo. Good master Fabian, grant me another request.

Fab. Any thing.

Clo. Do not desire to see this letter.

Fab. That is, to give a dog, and, in recompense, desire my dog again.

Enter DUKE, VIOLA, *and* Attendants.

Duke. Belong you to the lady Olivia, friends?

Clo. Ay, sir; we are some of her trappings.

Duke. I know thee well: How dost thou, my good fellow?

Clo. Truly, sir, the better for my foes, and the worse for my friends.

Duke. Just the contrary; the better for thy friends.

Clo. No, sir, the worse.

Duke. How can that be?

Clo. Marry sir, they praise me, and make an ass

---

1 The *five wits*, in analogy to the five senses. It appears that the five wits were 'common wit, imagination, fantasy, estimation, memory.' *Wit* was then the general term for intellectual power.

2 Taken possession of.

3 The clown, in the dark, acts two persons, and counterfeits, by variation of voice, a dialogue between himself and Sir Topas.

4 Scolded, reprimanded.

5 The *vice* was the fool of the old moralities. He was grotesquely dressed in a cap with ass's ears, a long coat, and a dagger of lath. One of his chief employments was to make sport with the devil, leaping on his back and belabouring him with his dagger, till he made him roar. The devil, however, always carried him off in the end. The moral was, that sin, which has the courage to make very merry with the devil, and is allowed by him to take very great liberties, must finally become his prey. This used also to be the regular end of Punch in the puppet show (who was the legitimate successor of the old vice or iniquity,) until modern innovation, in these degenerate times, reversed the catastrophe. See Note on K. Henry V. Act. iv. Sc. 4.

6 i. e. *intelligence.* Mr. Steevens has referred to several passages which seem to imply that this word was used for *oral intelligence.* I find it thus in a letter from Elizabeth to Sir Nicholas Throckmorton among the Conway Papers. 'This beror came from you with great spede——We have heard his *credit* and fynd your carefulness and diligence very great.'

7 i. e. reason. 8 Servants. 9 i. e. deceptious.

10 '*Chantry*,' a little chapel, or particular altar in some cathedral or parochial church, endowed for the purpose of having masses sung therein for the souls of the founders

11 Until.

12 *Troth* or *fidelity.* It should be remarked that this was not an actual *marriage*, but a *betrothing*, affiancing, or solemn promise of future marriage; anciently distinguished by the name of *espousals.* This has been established by Mr. Douce in his very interesting Illustrations of Shakspeare, where the reader will find much curious matter on the subject, in a note on this passage

of me; now my foes tell me plainly I am an ass: so that by my foes, sir, I profit in the knowledge of myself; and by my friends I am abused: so that, conclusions to be as kisses, if your four negatives make your two affirmatives,[1] why, then the worse for my friends, and the better for my foes.

Duke. Why, this is excellent.

Clo. By my troth, sir, no; though it please you to be one of my friends.

Duke. Thou shalt not be the worse for me; there's gold.

Clo. But that it would be double-dealing, sir, I would you could make it another.

Duke. O, you give me ill counsel.

Clo. Put your grace in your pocket, sir, for this once, and let your flesh and blood obey it.

Duke. Well, I will be so much a sinner to be a double-dealer; there's another.

Clo. Primo, secundo, tertio, is a good play; and the old saying is, the third pays for all; the *triplex*, sir, is a good tripping measure; or the bells of St. Bennet, sir, may put you in mind; One, two, three.

Duke. You can fool no more money out of me at this throw: if you will let your lady know, I am here to speak with her, and bring her along with you, it may awake my bounty further.

Clo. Marry, sir, lullaby to your bounty, till I come again. I go, sir; but I would not have you to think, that my desire of having is the sin of covetousness; but, as you say, sir, let your bounty take a nap, I will awake it anon. [*Exit* Clown.

Enter ANTONIO *and* Officers.

Vio. Here comes the man, sir, that did rescue me.

Duke. That face of his I do remember well;
Yet, when I saw it last, it was besmear'd
As black as Vulcan, in the smoke of war:
A bawbling vessel was he captain of,
For shallow draught, and bulk, unprizable:
With which such scathful[2] grapple did he make
With the most noble bottom of our fleet,
That very envy, and the tongue of loss,
Cry'd fame and honour on him.—What's the matter?

1 Off. Orsino, this is that Antonio
That took the Phœnix and her fraught,[3] from Candy:
And this is he that did the Tiger board,
When your young nephew Titus lost his leg:
Here in the streets, desperate of shame and state,[4]
In private brabble did we apprehend him.

Vio. He did me kindness, sir; drew on my side;
But, in conclusion, put strange speech upon me,
I know not what 'twas, but distraction.

Duke. Notable pirate! thou salt-water thief!
What foolish boldness brought thee to their mercies,
Whom thou, in terms so bloody, and so dear,[5]
Hast made thine enemies?

Ant. Orsino, noble sir,
Be pleas'd that I shake off these names you give me;
Antonio never yet was thief, or pirate,
Though, I confess, on base and ground enough,
Orsino's enemy. A witchcraft drew me hither:
That most ingrateful boy there, by your side,
From the rude sea's enrag'd and foamy mouth
Did I redeem: a wreck past hope he was:
His life I gave him, and did thereto add
My love, without retention or restraint,
All his in dedication: for his sake,
Did I expose myself, pure for his love,
Into the danger of this adverse town,
Drew to defend him, when he was beset;
Where being apprehended, his false cunning
(Not meaning to partake with me in danger,)
Taught him to face me out of his acquaintance,
And grew a twenty-years-removed thing,
While one would wink; denied me mine own purse,
Which I had recommended to his use
Not half an hour before.

Vio. How can this be?

Duke. When came he to this town?

Ant. To-day, my lord; and for three months before
(No interim, not a minute's vacancy,)
Both day and night did we keep company.

Enter OLIVIA *and* Attendants.

Duke. Here comes the countess; now heaven walks on earth.——
But for thee, fellow, fellow, thy words are madness:
Three months this youth hath tended upon me;
But more of that anon.——Take him aside.

Oli. What would my lord, but that he may not have,
Wherein Olivia may seem serviceable?—
Cesario, you do not keep promise with me.

Vio. Madam?

Duke. Gracious Olivia,——

Oli. What do you say, Cesario?——Good my lord,——

Vio. My lord would speak, my duty hushes me.

Oli. If it be ought to the old tune, my lord,
It is as fat[6] and fulsome to mine ear,
As howling after music.

Duke. Still so cruel?

Oli. Still so constant, lord.

Duke. What! to perverseness? you uncivil lady,
To whose ingrate and unauspicious altars
My soul the faithfull'st offerings hath breath'd out,
That e'er devotion tender'd! What shall I do?

Oli. Even what it please my lord, that shall become him.

Duke. Why should I not, had I the heart to do it
Like the Egyptian thief,[7] at point of death,
Kill what I love; a savage jealousy,
That sometimes savours nobly?—But hear me this:
Since you to non-regardance cast my faith,
And that I partly know the instrument
That screws me from my true place in your favour,
Live you, the marble-breasted tyrant, still;
But this your minion, whom, I know, you love,
And whom, by heaven, I swear, I tender dearly,
Him will I tear out of that cruel eye,
Where he sits crowned in his master's spite.—
Come boy with me; my thoughts are ripe in mischief:
I'll sacrifice the lamb that I do love,
To spite a raven's heart within a dove. [*Going.*

Vio. And I, most jocund, apt, and willingly,
To do you rest, a thousand deaths would die.
[*Following.*

Oli. Where goes Cesario?

Vio. After him I love,
More than I love these eyes, more than my life,
More, by all mores, than e'er I shall love wife:
If I do feign, you witnesses above,
Punish my life for tainting of my love!

Oli. Ah me, detested! how am I beguil'd!

---

1 So, in Marlowe's Lust's Dominion:—
Come let's kisse.
Moor. Away, away.
Queen. No, no, says *I;* and *twice away* says *stay.*
Sir Philip Sidney has enlarged upon the thought in the Sixty-third Stanza of Astrophel and Stella.

2 Mischievous, destructive. 3 Freight.

4 Inattentive to his character or condition, like a desperate man.

5 Tooke has so admirably accounted for the application of the epithet *dear* by our ancient writers to any object which excites a sensation of *hurt, pain,* and consequently of *anxiety, solicitude, care, earnestness,* that I shall refer to it as the best comment upon the *apparently* opposite uses of the word in our great poet.

6 Dull, gross.

7 This *Egyptian Thief* was Thyamis. The story is related in the Aethiopics of Heliodorus. He was the chief of a band of robbers. Theogenes and Chariclea falling into their hands, Thyamis falls in love with Chariclea, and would have married her. But, being attacked by a stronger band of robbers, he was in such fear for his mistress that he causes her to be shut into a cave with his treasure. It was customary with those barbarians, when they despaired of their own safety, first to make away with those whom they held most dear, and desired for companions in the next life. Thyamis, therefore, benetted round with enemies, raging with love, jealousy, and anger, went to his cave, and calling aloud in the Egyptian tongue, so soon as he heard himself answered towards the cave's mouth by a Grecian making to the person by the direction of her voice, he caught her by the hair with his left hand, and (supposing her to be Chariclea) with his right hand plunged his sword into her breast

Vio. Who does beguile you? who does do you wrong?
Oli. Hast thou forgot thyself! Is it so long!—
Call forth the holy father. [*Exit an* Attendant.
Duke. Come away. [*To* VIOLA.
Oli. Whither, my lord?—Cesario, husband, stay.
Duke. Husband!
Oli. Ay, husband; Can he that deny?
Duke. Her husband, sirrah?
Vio. No, my lord, not I.
Oli. Alas, it is the baseness of thy fear,
That makes thee strangle thy propriety:[1]
Fear not, Cesario, take thy fortunes up;
Be that thou know'st thou art, and then thou art
As great as that thou fear'st.—O, welcome father!

Re-enter Attendant *and* Priest.

Father, I charge thee by thy reverence,
Here to unfold (though lately we intended
To keep in darkness, what occasion now
Reveals before 'tis ripe,) what thou dost know,
Hath newly past between this youth and me.
Priest. A contract of eternal bond of love.
Confirm'd by mutual joinder of your hands,
Attested by the holy close of lips,
Strengthen'd by interchangement of your rings;[2]
And all the ceremony of this compact
Seal'd in my function, by my testimony:
Since when, my watch hath told me, toward my grave
I have travell'd but two hours.
Duke. O, thou dissembling cub! what wilt thou be,
When time hath sow'd a grizzle on thy case?[3]
Or will not else thy craft so quickly grow,
That thine own trip shall be thine overthrow?
Farewell, and take her; but direct thy feet,
Where thou and I henceforth may never meet.
Vio. My lord, I do protest,—
Oli. O, do not swear;
Hold little faith, though thou hast too much fear.

Enter SIR ANDREW AGUE-CHEEK, *with his head broke.*

Sir And. For the love of God, a surgeon; send one presently to Sir Toby.
Oli. What's the matter?
Sir And. He has broke my head across, and has given Sir Toby a bloody coxcomb too: for the love of God, your help: I had rather than forty pound, I were at home.
Oli. Who has done this, Sir Andrew?
Sir And. The count's gentleman, one Cesario: we took him for a coward, but he's the very devil incardinate.
Duke. My gentleman, Cesario?
Sir And. Od's lifelings, here he is:—You broke my head for nothing; and that that I did, I was set on to do't by Sir Toby.
Vio. Why do you speak to me? I never hurt you:
You drew your sword upon me, without cause;
But I bespake you fair, and hurt you not.
Sir And. If a bloody coxcomb be a hurt, you have hurt me; I think you set nothing by a bloody coxcomb.

Enter SIR TOBY BELCH, *drunk, led by the* Clown.

Here comes Sir Toby halting, you shall hear more: but if he had not been in drink, he would have tickled you othergates[4] than he did.
Duke. How now, gentleman? how is't with you?
Sir To. That's all one; he has hurt me, and there's an end on't.—Sot, didst see Dick surgeon, sot?
Clo. O he's drunk, Sir Toby, an hour agone; his eyes were set at eight i'the morning.
Sir To. Then he's a rogue and a passy-measures pavin;[5] I hate a drunken rogue.
Oli. Away with him: Who hath made this havock with them?
Sir And. I'll help you, Sir Toby, because we'be dressed together.
Sir To. Will you help?—An ass-head, and a coxcomb, and a knave? a thin-faced knave, a gull?
Oli. Get him to bed and let his hurt be look'd to.
[*Exeunt* Clown, SIR TOBY, *and* SIR ANDREW.

Enter SEBASTIAN.

Seb. I am sorry, madam, I have hurt your kinsman;
But, had it been the brother of my blood,
I must have done no less, with wit and safety.
You throw a strange regard upon me, and
By that I do perceive it hath offended you;
Pardon me, sweet one, even for the vows
We made each other but so late ago.
Duke. One face, one voice one habit, and two persons;
A natural perspective,[6] that is, and is not.
Seb. Antonio! O, my dear Antonio,
How have the hours rack'd and tortur'd me,
Since I have lost thee.
Ant. Sebastian are you?
Seb. Fear'st thou that, Antonio?
Ant. How have you made division of yourself?—
An apple, cleft in two, is not more twin
Than these two creatures. Which is Sebastian?
Oli. Most wonderful!
Seb. Do I stand there? I never had a brother;
Nor can there be that deity in my nature,
Of here and every where. I had a sister,
Whom the blind waves and surges have devour'd:—
Of charity,[7] what kin are you to me? [*To* VIOLA.
What countryman? what name? what parentage?
Vio. Of Messaline: Sebastian was my father;
Such a Sebastian was my brother too,
So went he suited to his watery tomb:
If spirits can assume both form and suit,
You come to fright us.
Seb. A spirit I am, indeed;
But am in that dimension grossly clad,
Which from the womb I did participate.
Were you a woman, as the rest goes even,
I should my tears let fall upon your cheek,
And say—Thrice welcome, drowned Viola!
Vio. My father had a mole upon his brow.
Seb. And so had mine.

---

1 i. e. suppress, or disown thy property.
2 In ancient espousals the man received as well as gave a ring.
3 So, in Cary's Present State of England, 1626. Queen Elizabeth asked a knight named Young, how he liked a company of brave ladies? He answered, as I like my silver haired conies at home, the *cases* are far better than the bodies.'
4 Otherways.
5 The *pavin* was a grave Spanish dance. Sir John Hawkins derives it from *pavo* a *peacock*, and says that every *pavin* had its *galliard*, a lighter kind of air formed out of the former. Thus, in Middleton's More Dissemblers beside Women:
'I can dance nothing but ill favour'dly,
A strain or two of *passe measures galliard*.'
By which it appears that the *passe measure pavan*, and the *passe measure galliard* were only two different measures of one dance. Sir Toby therefore means by his quaint expression that the surgeon is a rogue and a *grave solemn coxcomb*. In the first act of the play he has shown himself well acquainted with the various kinds of dance. Shakspeare's characters are always consistent, and even in drunkenness preserve the traits of character which distinguished them when sober.
6 A *perspective* formerly meant a glass that assisted the sight in any way. The several kinds in use in Shakspeare's time are enumerated in Scot's Discoverie of Witchcraft, 1584, b. xiii. c. 19, where that alluded to by the Duke is thus described: 'There be glasses also wherein one man may see another man's image and not his own'—that optical illusion may be meant, which is called *anamorphosis*:—'where that which is, is not,' or appears, in a different position, another thing. This may also explain a passage in Henry V. Act v. Sc. 2: 'Yes, my lord, you see them *perspectively*, the cities turned into a maid.' Vide also K. Richard II. Act ii. Sc 1, and note there:
'Like *perspectives*, which rightly gazed upon
Show nothing, but confusion; ey'd awry
Distinguish form.'
7 Out of charity, tell me.

Vio. And died that day when Viola from her birth
Had number'd thirteen years.
Seb. O, that record is lively in my soul!
He finished, indeed, his mortal act,
That day that made my sister thirteen years.
Vio. If nothing lets[1] to make us happy both,
But this my masculine usurp'd attire,
Do not embrace me, till each circumstance
Of place, time, fortune, do cohere, and jump,
That I am Viola: which to confirm,
I'll bring you to a captain in this town,
Where lie my maiden weeds; by whose gentle help
I was preserv'd, to serve this noble count:
All the occurrence of my fortune since
Hath been between this lady, and this lord.
Seb. So comes it, lady, you have been mistook:
[*To* OLIVIA.
But nature to her bias drew in that.
You would have been contracted to a maid;
Nor are you therein, by my life, deceived,
You are betroth'd both to a maid and man.
Duke Be not amaz'd; right noble is his blood.—
If this be so, as yet the glass seems true,
I shall have share in this most happy wreck:
Boy, thou hast said to me a thousand times,
[*To* VIOLA.
Thou never shouldst love woman like to me.
Vio. And all those sayings will I over-swear;
And all those swearings keep as true in soul,
As doth that orbed continent the fire
That severs day from night.
Duke. Give me thy hand;
And let me see thee in thy woman's weeds.
Vio. The captain, that did bring me first on shore
Hath my maid's garments: he, upon some action,
Is now in durance, at Malvolio's suit,
A gentleman and follower of my lady's.
Oli. He shall enlarge him:—Fetch Malvolio hither:
And yet, alas, now I remember me,
They say, poor gentleman, he's much distract.

Re-enter Clown, *with a letter.*

A most extracting[2] frenzy of mine own
From my remembrance clearly banish'd his.—
How does he, sirrah?
Clo. Truly, madam, he holds Belzebub at the stave's end, as well as a man in his case may do; he has here writ a letter to you, I should have given it to you to-day morning; but as a madman's epistles are no gospels, so it skills not much when they are delivered.
Oli. Open it, and read it.
Clo. Look then to be well edified, when the fool delivers the madman:—*By the lord, Madam,*—
Oli. How now! art thou mad?
Clo. No, madam, I do but read madness: an hour ladyship will have it as it ought to be, you must allow *vox.*[3]
Oli. Pr'ythee, read i'thy right wits.
Clo. So I do, madonna; but to read his right wits, is to read thus: therefore perpend,[4] my princess, and give ear.
Oli. Read it you, sirrah. [*To* FABIAN.
Fab. [Reads] *By the Lord, madam, you wrong me, and the world shall know it: though you have put me into darkness, and given your drunken cousin rule over me, yet have I the benefit of my senses as well as your ladyship. I have your own letter that induced me to the semblance I put on; with the which I doubt not but to do myself much right, or you much shame. Think of me as you please. I leave my duty a little unthought of, and speak out of my injury.* *The madly-used* Malvolio.

Oli. Did he write this?
Clo. Ay, madam.
Duke. This savours not much of distraction.
Oli. See him delivered, Fabian; bring him hither. [*Exit* FABIAN.
My lord, so please you, these things further thought on,
To think me as well a sister as a wife,
One day shall crown the alliance on't, so please you,
Here at my house, and at my proper cost.
Duke. Madam, I am most apt to embrace your offer.—
Your master quits you [*To* VIOLA;] and, for your service done him,
So much against the mettle[5] of your sex,
So far beneath your soft and tender breeding,
And since you call'd me master for so long,
Here is my hand; you shall from this time be
Your master's mistress.
Oli. A sister?—you are she.

Re-enter FABIAN, *with* MALVOLIO.

Duke. Is this the madman?
Oli. Ay, my lord, this same
How now, Malvolio?
Mal. Madam, you have done me wrong,
Notorious wrong.
Oli. Have I, Malvolio? no.
Mal. Lady, you have. Pray you, peruse that letter:
You must not now deny it is your hand,
Write from it, if you can, in hand, or phrase,
Or say 'tis not your seal, nor your invention:
You can say none of this: Well, grant it then,
And tell me, in the modesty of honour,
Why you have given me such clear lights of favour,
Bade me come smiling, and cross-garter'd to you,
To put on yellow stockings, and to frown
Upon Sir Toby, and the lighter[6] people:
And, acting this in an obedient hope,
Why have you suffer'd me to be imprison'd,
Kept in a dark house, visited by the priest,
And made the most notorious geck,[7] and gull,
That e'er invention played on? tell me why.
Oli. Alas, Malvolio, this is not my writing,
Though, I confess, much like the character:
But, out of question, 'tis Maria's hand.
And now I do bethink me, it was she
First told me, thou wast mad: then cam'st[8] in smiling,
And in such forms which here were presuppos'd
Upon thee in the letter. Pr'ythee, be content:
This practice[9] hath most shrewdly pass'd upon thee,
But, when we know the grounds and authors of it
Thou shalt be both the plaintiff and the judge
Of thine own cause.
Fab. Good madam, hear me speak,
And let no quarrel, nor no brawl to come,
Taint the condition of this present hour,
Which I have wonder'd at. In hope it shall not,
Most freely I confess, myself, and Toby,
Set this device against Malvolio here,
Upon some stubborn and uncourteous parts
We had conceiv'd against him: Maria writ
The letter, at Sir Toby's great importance;[10]
In recompense whereof, he hath married her.
How with a sportful malice it was follow'd,
May rather pluck on laughter than revenge;
If that the injuries be justly weigh'd,
That have on both sides past.
Oli. Alas, poor fool! how have they baffled[11] thee!
Clo. Why, *some are born great, some achieve greatness, and some have greatness thrown upon them.* I

1 Hinders.
2 i. e. a frenzy that drew me away from every thing but its object.
3 This may be explained: 'If you would have the letter read in character, you must allow me to assume the *voice* or frantic tone of a madman.'
4 Consider.
5 Frame and constitution.
6 Inferior.
7 Fool.
8 *Thou* is here understood: 'then cam'st *thou* in smiling.'
9 *Practice* is a deceit, an insidious stratagem. So in the Induction to the Taming of the Shrew.
'Sirs, I will *practise* on this drunken man.'
10 Importunacy.
11 *Baffled* is cheated. See Note on the first Scene of K. Rich. II

was one, sir, in this interlude; one Sir Topas, sir; but that's all one:—*By the Lord, fool, I am not mad.*—But do you remember? *Madam, why laugh you at such a barren rascal? an you smile not, he's gagg'd:* And thus the whirligig of time brings in his revenges.

Mal. I'll be revenged on the whole pack of you. [*Exit.*

Oli. He hath been most notoriously abus'd.

Duke. Pursue him, and entreat him to a peace:—
He hath not told us of the captain yet;
When that is known and golden time convents,[1]
A solemn combination shall be made
Of our dear souls.—Mean time, sweet sister,
We will not part from hence—Cesario, come,
For so you shall be, while you are a man;
But, when in other habits you are seen,
Orsino's mistress, and his fancy's queen. [*Exeunt.*

SONG.

Clo. When that I was a little tiny boy,
With hey, ho, the wind and the rain,
A foolish thing was but a toy,
For the rain it raineth every day.

But when I came to man's estate,
With hey, ho, the wind and the rain,
'Gainst knaves and thieves men shut their gate,
For the rain it raineth every day.

But when I came, alas! to wive,
With hey, ho, the wind and the rain,
By swaggering could I never thrive,
For the rain it raineth every day,

But when I came unto my bed,
With hey, ho, the wind and the rain,
With toss-pots still had drunken head,
For the rain it raineth every day.

A great while ago the world begun,
With hey, ho, the wind and the rain,
But that's all one, our play is done,
And we'll strive to please you every day.
[*Exit*

1 i. e. Shall serve, agree, be convenient.

This play is in the graver part elegant and easy, and in some of the lighter scenes exquisitely humorous. Ague-cheek is drawn with great propriety, but his character is, in a great measure, that of natural fatuity, and is therefore not the proper prey of a satirist. The soliloquy of Malvolio is truly comic; he is betrayed to ridicule merely by his pride. The marriage of Olivia, and the succeeding perplexity, though well enough contrived to divert on the stage, wants credibility, and fails to produce the proper instruction required in the drama, as it exhibits no just picture of life. JOHNSON

MEASURE FOR MEASURE.

PRELIMINARY REMARKS.

SHAKSPEARE took the fable of this play from the Promos and Cassandra of George Whetstone, published, in 1578, of which this is 'The Argument.'

'In the city of Julio (sometimes under the dominion of Corvinus King of Hungary and Bohemia,) there was a law, that what man soever committed adultery should lose his head, and the woman offender should wear some disguised apparel, during her life, to make her infamously noted. This severe law, by the favour of some merciful magistrate, became little regarded, until the time of Lord Promos's authority; who convicting a young gentleman named Andrugio of incontinency, condemned both him and his minion to the execution of this statute. Andrugio had a very virtuous and beautiful gentlewoman to his sister, named Cassandra. Cassandra, to enlarge her brother's life, submitted an humble petition to the Lord Promos. Promos regarding her good behaviour, and fantasying her great beauty, was much delighted with the sweet order of her talk; and doing good, that evil might come thereof, for a time he reprieved her brother: but, wicked man, turning his liking into unlawful lust, he set down the spoil of her honour, ransom for her brother's life: chaste Cassandra, abhorring both him and his suit, by no persuasion would yield to this ransom. But in fine, won by the importunity of her brother (pleading for life,) upon these conditions she agreed to Promos: First, that he should pardon her brother, and after marry her. Promos, as fearless in promise, as careless in performance, with solemn vow signed her conditions; but worse than any infidel, his will satisfied, he performed neither the one nor the other: for to keep his authority unspotted with favour, and to prevent Cassandra's clamours, he commanded the jailer secretly to present Cassandra with her brother's head. The jailer [touched] with the outcries of Andrugio (abhorring Promos's lewdness,) by the providence of God provided thus for his safety. He presented Cassandra with a felon's head newly executed; who knew it not, being mangled, from her brother's (who was set at liberty by the jailer.) [She] was so aggrieved at this treachery, that, at the point to kill herself, she spared that stroke to be avenged of Promos: and devising a way, she concluded, to make her fortunes known to the king. She, executing this resolution, was so highly favoured of the king, that forthwith he hasted to do justice on Promos: whose judgment was to marry Cassandra, to repair her crased honour; which done, for his heinous offence, he should lose his head. This marriage solemnized, Cassandra tied in the greatest bonds of affection to her husband, became an earnest suitor for his life: the king tendering the general benefit of the commonweal before her special case, although he favoured her much, would not grant her suit. Andrugio (disguised among the company,) sorrowing the grief of his sister, bewrayed his safety, and craved pardon. The king to renown the virtues of Cassandra, pardoned both him and Promos. The circumstances of this rare history, in action lively followeth.'

Whetstone, however, has not afforded a very correct analysis of his play, which contains a mixture of comic scenes, between a bawd, a pimp, felons, &c. together with some serious situations which are not described. A hint, like a seed, is more or less prolific, according to the qualities of the soil on which it is thrown. This story, which in the hands of Whetstone produced little more than barren insipidity, under the culture of Shakspeare became fertile of entertainment. The curious reader may see the old play of Promos and Cassandra among 'Six old plays on which Shakspeare founded, &c.' published by Mr. Steevens, printed for S. Leacroft, Charing Cross. The piece exhibits an almost complete embryo of Measure for Measure; yet the hints on which it is formed are so slight, that it is nearly as impossible to detect them, as it is to point out in the acorn the future ramifications of the oak. The story originally came from the 'Hecatommithi' of Cinthio. Decad 8, novel 5, and is repeated in the Tragic Histories of Belleforest.

"This play," says Mr. Hazlitt, "is as full of genius as it is of wisdom. Yet there is an original sin in the nature of the subject, which prevents us from taking a cordial interest in it. 'The height of moral argument,' which the author has maintained in the intervals of passion, or blended with the more powerful impulses of nature, is hardly surpassed in any of his plays. But there is a general want of passion, the affections are at a stand; our sympathies are repulsed and defeated in all directions."

Isabella is a lovely example of female purity and vir

me; with mental energies of a very superior kind, she is placed in a situation to make trial of them all, and the firmness with which her virtue resists the appeal of natural affection has something in it heroically sublime. The passages in which she encourages her brother to meet death with firmness rather than dishonour, his burst of indignant passion on learning the price at which his life might be redeemed, and his subsequent clinging to life, and desire that she would make the sacrifice required, are among the finest dramatic passages of Shakspeare. What heightens the effect is that this scene follows the fine exhortation of the Duke in the character of the Friar about the little value of life, which had almost made Claudio 'resolved to die.' The comic parts of the play are lively and amusing, and the reckless Barnardine, 'fearless of what's past, present, and to come,' is in fine contrast to the sentimentality of the other characters. Shakspeare "was a moralist in the same sense in which nature is one. He taught what he had learnt from her. He showed the greatest knowledge of humanity with the greatest fellow feeling for it."*

Malone supposes this play to have been written about the close of the year 1603.

* Characters of Shakspeare's Plays, 2d ed. London. 1818, p. 120.

PERSONS REPRESENTED.

VINCENTIO, *Duke of* Vienna.
ANGELO, *Lord Deputy in the Duke's absence.*
ESCALUS, *an ancient Lord, joined with* Angelo *in the Deputation.*
CLAUDIO, *a young Gentleman.*
LUCIO, *a Fantastic.*
Two other like Gentlemen.
VARRIUS, *a Gentleman, Servant to the Duke.*
Provost.
THOMAS, PETER, } *Two Friars.*
A Justice.
ELBOW, *a simple Constable.*
FROTH, *a foolish Gentleman.*
Clown, *Servant to* Mrs. Over-done.
ABHORSON, *an Executioner.*
BARNARDINE, *a dissolute Prisoner.*

ISABELLA, *Sister to* Claudio.
MARIANA, *betrothed to* Angelo.
JULIET, *beloved by* Claudio.
FRANCISCA, *a Nun.*
MISTRESS OVER-DONE, *a Bawd.*

Lords, Gentlemen, Guards, Officers, and other Attendants.

SCENE, Vienna.

ACT I.

SCENE I. *An Apartment in the* Duke's *Palace.*

Enter DUKE, ESCALUS, Lords *and* Attendants.

Duke. Escalus,—
Escal. My lord.
Duke. Of government the properties to unfold,
Would seem in me to affect speech and discourse;
Since I am put to know,[1] that your own science
Exceeds, in that, the lists[2] of all advice
My strength can give you: Then no more remains
But that to your sufficiency,[3] as your worth is able,
And let them work. The nature of our people,
Our city's institutions, and the terms
For common justice, you are as pregnant[4] in,
As art and practice hath enriched any
That we remember: There is our commission,
From which we would not have you warp.—Call hither,
I say, bid come before us, Angelo.—
[*Exit an Attendant.*
What figure of us think you he will bear?
For you must know, we have with special soul
Elected him our absence to supply;
Lent him our terror, drest him with our love;
And given his deputation all the organs
Of our own power: What think you of it?
Escal. If any in Vienna be of worth
To undergo such ample grace and honour,
It is lord Angelo.

Enter ANGELO.

Duke. Look, where he comes.
Ang. Always obedient to your grace's will,
I come to know your pleasure.
Duke. Angelo,
There is a kind of character in thy life,
That, to the observer doth thy history
Fully unfold: Thyself and thy belongings
Are not thine own so proper,[5] as to waste
Thyself upon thy virtues, them on thee.
Heaven doth with us, as we with torches do;
Not light them for themselves: for if our virtues
Did not go forth of us, 'twere all alike
As if we had them not. Spirits are not finely touch'd,
But to fine issues:[6] nor nature never lends[7]
The smallest scruple of her excellence,
But like a thrifty goddess, she determines
Herself the glory of a creditor,
Both thanks and use.[8] But I do bend my speech
To one that can my part in him advertise;[9]
Hold therefore.—Angelo;
In our remove, be thou at full ourself;
Mortality and Mercy in Vienna
Live in thy tongue and heart:[10] Old Escalus,
Though first in question, is thy secondary:
Take thy commission.
Ang. Now, good my lord,
Let there be some more test made of my metal,
Before so noble and so great a figure
Be stamp'd upon it.
Duke. No more evasion:
We have with a leaven'd[11] and prepared choice
Proceeded to you; therefore take your honours.
Our haste from hence is of so quick condition,
That it prefers itself, and leaves unquestion'd
Matters of needful value. We shall write to you,

1 i. e. since I am *so placed as* to know. Mr. Stevens says it may mean, *I am compelled to acknowledge.* And ii stances from Henry VI. Pt. ii. Sc. 1.
——'had I first been *put* to speak my mind.'
2 *Lists* are bounds.
3 Some words seem to be lost here. The sense of which may have been
——— Then no more remains
But that to your sufficiency *you join*
A zeal as willing, as your worth is able,
And let them work.
Sufficiency is *skill* in government; *ability* to execute his office.
4 i. e. ready in.
5 So much thy own property. 6 i. e. high purposes.
7 Two negatives, not employed to make an affirmative, are common in Shakspeare's writings, so in Julius Cæsar:
'*Nor* to *no* Roman else.'
8 i. e. Nature *requires and allots* to *herself* the same advantages that creditors usually enjoy—*thanks* for the endowments she has bestowed, and extraordinary exertions in those whom she has favoured; by way of *us* (i. e. interest) for what she has lent.
9 i. e. to one who is already sufficiently conversant with the nature and duties of my office;—of that *office which I have now delegated to him.*
10 i. e. I delegate to thy tongue the power of pronouncing sentence of death, and to thy heart the privilege of exercising mercy.
11 A choice *mature, concocted, fermented;* i. e not hasty, but considerate.

As time and our concernings shall importune,
How it goes with us; and do look to know
What doth befall you here. So, fare you well;
To the hopeful execution do I leave you
Of your commissions.

Ang. Yet, give leave, my lord,
That we may bring you something on the way.

Duke. My haste may not admit it;
Nor need you on mine honour have to do
With any scruple: your scope[1] is as mine own;
So to enforce or qualify the laws,
As to your soul seems good. Give me your hand;
I'll privily away; I love the people,
But do not like to stage me to their eyes;
Though it do well, I do not relish well
Their loud applause, and *aves*[2] vehement;
Nor do I think the man of safe discretion,
That does affect it. Once more, fare you well.

Ang. The heavens give safety to your purposes!

Escal. Lead forth, and bring you back in happiness.

Duke. I thank you: Fare you well. [*Exit.*

Escal. I shall desire you, sir, to give me leave
To have free speech with you; and it concerns me
To look into the bottom of my place:
A power I have; but of what strength and nature
I am not yet instructed.

Ang. 'Tis so with me:—Let us withdraw together,
And we may soon our satisfaction have
Touching that point.

Escal. I'll wait upon your honour.
[*Exeunt.*

SCENE II. *A Street. Enter* Lucio *and two* Gentlemen.

Lucio. If the duke, with the other dukes, come not to composition with the king of Hungary, why, then all the dukes fall upon the king.

1 *Gent.* Heaven grant us its peace, but not the king of Hungary's!

2 *Gent.* Amen.

Lucio. Thou concludest like the sanctimonious pirate, that went to sea with the ten commandments, but scraped one out of the table.

2 *Gent.* Thou shalt not steal?

Lucio. Ay, that he razed.

1 *Gent.* Why, 'twas a commandment to command the captain and all the rest from their functions; they put forth to steal: There's not a soldier of us all, that, in the thanksgiving before meat, doth relish the petition well that prays for peace.

2 *Gent.* I never heard any soldier dislike it.

Lucio. I believe thee; for I think, thou never wast where grace was said.

2 *Gent.* No? a dozen times at least.

1 *Gent.* What? in metre?

Lucio. In any proportion,[3] or in any language.

1 *Gent.* I think, or in any religion.

Lucio. Ay! why not? Grace is grace, despite of all controversy: As for example; Thou thyself art a wicked villain, despite of all grace.

1 *Gent.* Well, there went but a pair of shears between us.[4]

Lucio. I grant; as there may between the lists and the velvet: Thou art the list.

1 *Gent.* And thou the velvet: thou art good velvet; thou art a three-pil'd piece, I warrant thee: I had as lief be a list of an English kersey, as be pil'd, as thou art pil'd, for a French velvet.[5] Do I speak feelingly now?

Lucio. I think thou dost; and, indeed, with most painful feeling of thy speech: I will, out of thine own confession, learn to begin thy health: but, whilst I live, forget to drink after thee.

1 *Gent.* I think, I have done myself wrong; have I not?

2 *Gent.* Yes, that thou hast; whether thou art tainted or free.

Lucio. Behold, behold, where madam Mitigation comes! I have purchased as many diseases under her roof, as come to—

2 *Gent.* To what, I pray?

1 *Gent.* Judge.

2 *Gent.* To three thousand dollars a-year

1 *Gent.* Ay, and more.

Lucio. A French crown more.

1 *Gent.* Thou art always figuring diseases in me; but thou art full of error; I am sound.

Lucio. Nay, not as one would say, healthy; but so sound, as things that are hollow; thy bones are hollow: impiety has made a feast of thee.

Enter Bawd.

1 *Gent.* How now? Which of your hips has the most profound sciatica?

Bawd. Well, well; there's one yonder arrested, and carried to prison, was worth five thousand of you all.

1 *Gent.* Who's that, I pray thee?

Bawd. Marry, sir, that's Claudio, signior Claudio.

1 *Gent.* Claudio to prison! 'tis not so.

Bawd. Nay, but I know, 'tis so; I saw him arrested; saw him carried away; and which is more, within these three days his head's to be chopped off.

Lucio. But, after all this fooling, I would not have it so: art thou sure of this?

Bawd. I am too sure of it: and it is for getting madam Julietta with child.

Lucio. Believe me, this may be: he promised to meet me two hours since; and he was ever precise in promise-keeping.

2 *Gent.* Besides, you know, it draws something near to the speech we had to such a purpose.

1 *Gent.* But most of all, agreeing with the proclamation.

Lucio. Away; let's go learn the truth of it.
[*Exeunt* Lucio *and* Gentlemen.

Bawd. Thus, what with the war, what with the sweat,[6] what with the gallows, and what with poverty, I am custom-shrunk. How now? what's the news with you?

Enter Clown.

Clo. Yonder man is carried to prison.

Bawd. Well; what has he done?

Clo. A woman.

Bawd. But what's his offence?

Clo. Groping for trouts in a peculiar river.

Bawd. What, is there a maid with child by him?

Clo. No; but there's a woman with maid by him: You have not heard of the proclamation, have you?

Bawd. What proclamation, man?

Clo. All houses in the suburbs of Vienna must be plucked down.

Bawd. And what shall become of those in the city?

Clo. They shall stand for seed: they had gone down too, but that a wise burgher put in for them.

Bawd. But shall all our houses of resort in the suburbs be pulled down?[7]

Clo. To the ground, mistress.

Bawd. Why, here's a change, indeed, in the commonwealth! What shall become of me?

---

1 *Scope* is extent of power. 2 *Aves* are hailings. 3 i. e. measure. 4 We are both of the same piece. 5 '*Pil'd*, for a French velvet.'—Velvet was esteemed according to the richness of the *pile*; three-pil'd was the richest. But *pil'd* also means *bald*. The jest alludes to the loss of hair in the French disease. Lucio, finding the Gentleman understands the distemper so well, and mentions it so *feelingly*, promises to remember to drink his *health*, but to forget *to drink after him*. In old times the cup of an infected person was thought to be contagious.

6 The *sweat;* the consequences of the curative process then used for a certain disease

7 In one of the Scotch Laws of James it is ordered, 'that *common women* be put at the utmost endes of townes, queire least peril of fire is.'—It is remarkable that the licensed *houses of resort* at Vienna, are at this time all in the suburbs, under the permission of the Committee of Chastity.

Clo. Come, fear not you; good counsellors lack no clients: though you change your place, you need not change your trade; I'll be your tapster still. Courage; there will be pity taken on you: you that have worn your eyes almost out in the service, you will be considered.

Bawd. What's to do here, Thomas Tapster? Let's withdraw.

Clo. Here comes signior Claudio, led by the provost to prison: and there's madam Juliet. [*Exeunt.*

SCENE III. *The same. Enter* Provost,[1] CLAUDIO, JULIET, *and* Officers; LUCIO *and two* Gentlemen.

Claud. Fellow, why dost thou show me thus to the world?
Bear me to prison where I am committed.
Prov. I do it not in evil disposition,
But from lord Angelo by special charge.
Claud. Thus can the demi-god, Authority,
Make us pay down for our offence by weight.—
The words of heaven;—on whom it will, it will;
On whom it will not, so; yet still 'tis just.[2]

Lucio. Why, how now, Claudio? whence comes this restraint?

Claud. From too much liberty, my Lucio, liberty;
As surfeit is the father of much fast,
So every scope by the immoderate use
Turns to restraint: Our natures do pursue,
(Like rats that ravin[3] down their proper bane)
A thirsty evil; and when we drink, we die.[4]

Lucio. If I could speak so wisely under an arrest, I would send for certain of my creditors: And yet, to say the truth, I had as lief have the foppery of freedom, as the morality of imprisonment.—What's thy offence, Claudio?

Claud. What, but to speak of, would offend again.
Lucio. What is it? murder?
Claud. No.
Lucio. Lechery?
Claud. Call it so.
Prov. Away, sir; you must go.
Claud. One word, good friend:—Lucio, a word with you. [*Takes him aside.*
Lucio. A hundred if they'll do you any good.—
Is lechery so look'd after?
Claud. Thus stands it with me:—Upon a true contract,
I got possession of Julietta's bed;[5]
You know the lady; she is fast my wife,
Save that we do the denunciation lack
Of outward order: this we came not to,
Only for propagation[6] of a dower
Remaining in the coffer of her friends;
From whom we thought it meet to hide our love,
Till time had made them for us. But it chances,
The stealth of our most mutual entertainment,
With character too gross, is writ on Juliet.
Lucio. With child, perhaps?
Claud. Unhappily, even so.
And the new deputy now for the duke,—
Whether it be the fault and glimpse of newness;
Or whether that the body public be
A horse whereon the governor doth ride,
Who, newly in the seat, that it may know
He can command, lets it straight feel the spur:
Whether the tyranny be in his place,
Or in his eminence that fills it up,
I stagger in:—But this new governor
Awakes me all the enrolled penalties,
Which have, like unscour'd armour, hung by the wall
So long, that nineteen zodiacks[7] have gone round,
And none of them been worn; and, for a name,
Now puts the drowsy and neglected act
Freshly on me:—'tis surely, for a name.

Lucio. I warrant, it is: and thy head stands so tickle[8] on thy shoulders, that a milk-maid, if she be in love, may sigh it off. Send after the duke, and appeal to him.

Claud. I have done so, but he's not to be found.
I pr'ythee, Lucio, do me this kind service:
This day my sister should the cloister enter,
And there receive her approbation:[9]
Acquaint her with the danger of my state;
Implore her, in my voice, that she make friends
To the strict deputy; bid herself assay him;
I have great hope in that: for in her youth
There is a prone[10] and speechless dialect,
Such as moves men; besides, she hath prosperous art
When she will play with reason and discourse,
And well she can persuade.

Lucio. I pray, she may: as well for the encouragement of the like, which else would stand under grievous imposition; as for the enjoying of thy life who I would be sorry should be thus foolishly lost at a game of tick-tack.[11] I'll to her.

Claud. I thank you, good friend Lucio.
Lucio. Within two hours,———
Claud. Come, officer, away. [*Exeunt.*

SCENE IV. *A Monastery. Enter* DUKE *and* Friar Thomas.

Duke. No; holy Father; throw away that thought;
Believe not that the dribbling dart of love
Can pierce a complete bosom:[12] why I desire thee
To give me secret harbour, hath a purpose
More grave and wrinkled than the aims and ends
Of burning youth.
Fri. May your grace speak of it?
Duke. My holy sir, none better knows than you
How I have ever lov'd the life remov'd;[13]
And held in idle price to haunt assemblies,
Where youth, and cost, and witless bravery keeps.[14]
I have delivered to lord Angelo
(A man of stricture[15] and firm abstinence,)
My absolute power and place here in Vienna,
And he supposes me travell'd to Poland;
For so I have strew'd it in the common ear,
And so it is receiv'd: Now, pious sir,
You will demand of me, why I do this?
Fri. Gladly, my lord.
Duke. We have strict statutes and most biting laws,
(The needful bits and curbs for headstrong steeds,)
Which for these fourteen years we have let sleep;
Even like an o'ergrown lion in a cave,
That goes not out to prey: Now, as fond fathers,
Having bound up the threat'ning twigs of birch,
Only to stick it in their children's sight,

---

1 i. e. gaoler.

2 Authority being absolute in Angelo, is finely styled by Claudio, *the demigod*, whose decrees are as little to be questioned as *the words of heaven*. The poet alludes to a passage in St. Paul's Epist. to the Romans, ch. ix. v. 15—18: 'I will have mercy on whom I will have mercy.'

3 To *ravin* is to voraciously devour.

4 So, in Chapman's Revenge for Honour:
'Like poison'd rats, which, when they've swallowed
The pleasing bane, rest not until they *drink*,
And can rest then much less, until they burst.

5 This speech is surely too indelicate to be spoken concerning Juliet before her face. Claudio may therefore be supposed to speak to Lucio apart.

6 This singular mode of expression has not been satisfactorily explained. The old sense of the word is 'promoting, inlarging, increasing, spreading.' It appears that Claudio would say: 'for the sake of *promoting* such a dower as her friends might heareafter bestow on her, when time had reconciled them to her clandestine marriage.' The verb is as obscurely used by Chapman in the Sixteenth book of the Odyssey:
———'to try if we
Alone may *propagate* to victory
Our bold encounters.'
Shakspeare uses 'To *propagate* their states,' for to *improve* or *promote* their conditions, in Timon of Athens, Act i. Sc. 1.

7 *Zodiacs*, yearly circles. 8 *Tickle*, for ticklish.

9 i. e. enter on her *noviciate* or *probation*.

10 *Prone*, is *prompt* or *ready*.

11 *Jouer au tric trac* is used in French in a wanton sense.

12 'A complete bosom' is a bosom completely armed.

13 i. e. retired.

14 *Bravery* is showy dress. *Keeps*, i. e. resides

15 Stricture; strictness.

For terror, not to use; in time the rod
Becomes more mock'd than fear'd: so our decrees,
Dead to infliction, to themselves are dead;
And liberty plucks justice by the nose;
The baby beats the nurse, and quite athwart
Goes all decorum.
Fri. It rested in your grace
To unloose this tied-up justice, when you pleas'd:
And it in you more dreadful would have seem'd,
Than in Lord Angelo.
Duke. I do fear, too dreadful:
Sith 'twas my fault to give the people scope,
'Twould be my tyranny to strike, and gall them
For what I bid them do: For we bid this be done,
When evil deeds have their permissive pass,
And not the punishment. Therefore, indeed, my father,
I have on Angelo impos'd the office;
Who may, in the ambush of my name, strike home,
And yet my nature never in the sight,
To do it slander: And to behold his sway,
I will, as 'twere a brother of your order,
Visit both prince and people: therefore, I pr'ythee,
Supply me with the habit, and instruct me
How I may formally in person bear me
Like a true friar. More reasons for this action,
At our more leisure shall I render you;
Only, this one:—Lord Angelo is precise;
Stands at a guard[1] with envy; scarce confesses
That his blood flows, or that his appetite
Is more to bread than stone: Hence shall we see,
If power change purpose, what our seemers be.
[*Exeunt.*

SCENE V. *A Nunnery. Enter* Isabella *and* Francisca.

Isab. And have you nuns no further privileges?
Fran. Are not these large enough?
Isab. Yes truly; I speak not as desiring more;
But rather wishing a more strict restraint
Upon the sisterhood, the votarists of Saint Clare.
Lucio. Ho! Peace be in this place? [*Within.*
Isab. Who's that which calls?
Fran. It is a man's voice: Gentle Isabella,
Turn you the key, and know his business of him;
You may, I may not; you are yet unsworn:
When you have vow'd, you must not speak with men,
But in the presence of the prioress:
Then, if you speak, you must not show your face;
Or, if you show your face, you must not speak.
He calls again; I pray you, answer him.
[*Exit* Francisca.
Isab. Peace and prosperity! Who is't that calls?

Enter Lucio.

Lucio. Hail, virgin, if you be; as those cheek-roses
Proclaim you are no less! Can you so stead me,
As bring me to the sight of Isabella,
A novice of this place, and the fair sister
To her unhappy brother Claudio?
Isab. Why her unhappy brother? let me ask;
The rather, for I now must make you know
I am that Isabella, and his sister.
Lucio. Gentle and fair, your brother kindly greets you:
Not to be weary with you, he's in prison.
Isab. Woe me! For what?
Lucio. For that, which, if myself might be his judge,
He should receive his punishment in thanks:
He hath got his friend with child.
Isab. Sir, mock me not:—your story.[2]
Lucio. 'Tis true, I would not,—though 'tis my familiar sin
With maids to seem the lapwing,[3] and to jest,
Tongue far from heart,—play with all virgins so:
I hold you as a thing ensky'd, and sainted;
By your renouncement, an immortal spirit;
And to be talked with in sincerity,
As with a saint.
Isab. You do blaspheme the good, in mocking me.
Lucio. Do not believe it. Fewness and truth,[4] 'tis thus:
Your brother and his lover[5] have embrac'd:
As those that feed grow full; as blossoming time,
That from the seedness the bare fallow brings
To teeming foison;[6] even so her plenteous womb
Expresseth his full tilth[7] and husbandry.
Isab. Some one with child by him?—My cousin Juliet?
Lucio. Is she your cousin?
Isab. Adoptedly; as school-maids change their names,
By vain though apt affection.
Lucio. She it is.
Isab. O let him marry her!
Lucio. This is the point.
The duke is very strangely gone from hence;
Bore many gentlemen, myself being one,
In hand, and hope of action: but we do learn
By those that know the very nerves of state,
His givings out were of an infinite distance
From his true-meant design. Upon his place,
And with full line[8] of his authority,
Governs Lord Angelo; a man, whose blood
Is very snow-broth; one who never feels
The wanton stings and motions of the sense;
But doth rebate[9] and blunt his natural edge
With profits of the mind, study and fast.
He (to give fear to use[10] and liberty,
Which have, for long, run by the hideous law,
As mice by lions,) hath pick'd out an act,
Under whose heavy sense your brother's life
Falls into forfeit: he arrests him on it;
And follows close the rigour of the statute,
To make him an example: all hope is gone,
Unless you have the grace[11] by your fair prayer
To soften Angelo: And that's my pith
Of business 'twixt you and your poor brother.
Isab. Doth he so seek his life?
Lucio. Has censur'd[12] him
Already; and, as I hear, the provost hath
A warrant for his execution.
Isab. Alas! what poor ability's in me
To do him good?
Lucio. Assay the power you have.
Isab. My power! Alas! I doubt,—
Lucio. Our doubts are traitors,
And make us lose the good we oft might win,
By fearing to attempt: Go to Lord Angelo,
And let him learn to know, when maidens sue,
Men give like gods; but when they weep and kneel,
All their petitions are as freely theirs
As they themselves would owe[13] them.
Isab. I'll see what I can do.
Lucio. But speedily.
Isab. I will about it straight;

---

1 i. e. on his defence.
2 The old copy reads:
'Sir, *make* me not your story.'
The emendation is Mr. Malone's.
3 This bird is said to draw pursuers from her nest by crying in other places. This was formerly the subject of a proverb, 'The lapwing cries most, farthest from her nest,' i. e. *tongue far from heart.* So, in The Comedy of Errors:
'*Adr.* Far from her nest the lapwing cries away;
My heart prays for him, though my tongue do curse.'
4 *Fewness and truth*, in few and true words.
5 i. e. his mistress.
6 *Teeming foison* is abundant produce.
7 *Tilth* is tillage. So in Shakspeare's third Sonnet:
'For who is she so fair, whose unrear'd *womb*
Disdains the *tillage* of thy husbandry?'
8 *Full line*, extent.
9 *To rebate* is *to make dull:* Aciem ferri hebetare *Baret.*
10 i. e. to intimidate *use*, or practices long countenanced by *custom.*
11 i. e. power of gaining favour.
12 To *censure* is to *judge.* This is the poet's general meaning for the word, but the editors have given him several others. Here they interpret it *censured, sentenced.* We have it again in the next scene:
'When I that *censure* him do so offend,
Let mine own judgment pattern out my death'
13 To *owe* is to *have*, to *possess.*

No longer staying but to give the mother[1]
Notice of my affair. I humbly thank you:
Commend me to my brother: soon at night
I'll send him certain word of my success.
Lucio. I take my leave of you.
Isab. Good sir, adieu.
[*Exeunt.*

ACT II.

SCENE I. *A Hall in* Angelo's *House. Enter* ANGELO, ESCALUS, *a* Justice, Provost,[2] Officers, *and other Attendants.*

Ang. We must not make a scare-crow of the law,
Setting it up to fear[3] the birds of prey,
And let it keep one shape, till custom make it
Their perch, and not their terror.
Escal. Ay, but yet
Let us be keen, and rather cut a little,
Than fall,[4] and bruise to death: Alas! this gentleman,
Whom I would save, had a most noble father.
Let but your honour know,[5]
(Whom I believe to be most strait in virtue,)
That, in the working of your own affections,
Had time coher'd[6] with place, or place with wishing,
Or that the resolute acting of your blood
Could have attain'd the effect of your own purpose,
Whether you had not sometime in your life
Err'd in this point which now you censure him,[7]
And pull'd the law upon you.
Ang. 'Tis one thing to be tempted, Escalus,
Another thing to fall. I not deny,
The jury, passing on the prisoner's life,
May, in the sworn twelve, have a thief or two
Guiltier than him they try: What's open made to justice,
That justice seizes. What know the laws,
That thieves do pass[8] on thieves? 'Tis very pregnant,[9]
The jewel that we find, we stoop and take it,
Because we see it; but what we do not see,
We tread upon, and never think of it.
You may not so extenuate his offence,
For[10] I have had such faults; but rather tell me,
When I, that censure him, do so offend,
Let mine own judgment pattern out my death,
And nothing come in partial. Sir, he must die.
Escal. Be it as your wisdom will.
Ang. Where is the provost?
Prov. Here, if it like your honour.
Ang. See that Claudio
Be executed by nine to-morrow morning:
Bring him his confessor, let him be prepared;
For that's the utmost of his pilgrimage.
[*Exit* Provost.
Escal. Well, heaven forgive him; and forgive us all!
Some rise by sin, and some by virtue fall:[11]
Some run from brakes[12] of vice, and answer none;
And some condemned for a fault alone.

Enter ELBOW, FROTH, Clown, Officers, *&c.*

Elb. Come, bring them away; if these be good people in a common-weal, that do nothing but use their abuses in common houses, I know no law, bring them away.

Ang. How now, sir! What's your name? and what's the matter?

Elb. If it please your honour, I am the poor duke's constable, and my name is Elbow; I do lean upon justice, sir, and do bring in here before your good honour two notorious benefactors.

Ang. Benefactors! Well; what benefactors are they? are they not malefactors?

Elb. If it please your honour, I know not well what they are: but precise villains they are, that I am sure of; and void of all profanation in the world, that good christians ought to have.

Escal. This comes off well;[13] here's a wise officer

Ang. Go to: What quality are they of? Elbow is your name? Why dost thou not speak, Elbow?

Clo. He cannot, sir; he's out at elbow.

Ang. What are you, sir?

Elb. He, sir? a tapster, sir; parcel-bawd; one that serves a bad woman; whose house, sir, was as they say, plucked down in the suburbs; and now she professes[14] a hot-house, which, I think, is a very ill house too.

Escal. How know you that?

Elb. My wife, sir, whom I detest[15] before heaven and your honour,—

Escal. How! thy wife?

Elb. Ay, sir; whom, I thank heaven, is an honest woman,—

Escal. Dost thou detest her therefore?

Elb. I say, sir, I will detest myself also, as well as she, that this house, if it be not a bawd's house, it is pity of her life, for it is a naughty house.

Escal. How dost thou know that constable?

Elb. Marry, sir, by my wife; who, if she had been a woman cardinally given, might have been accused in fornication, adultery, and all uncleanliness there.

Escal. By the woman's means?

Elb. Ay, sir, by mistress Over-done's means, but as she spit in his face, so she defied him.

Clo. Sir, if it please your honour, this is not so.

Elb. Prove it before these varlets here, thou honourable man, prove it.

Escal. Do you hear how he misplaces?
[*To* ANGELO.

Clo. Sir, she came in great with child; and longing (saving your honour's reverence,) for stew'd prunes:[16] sir, we had but two in the house, which at that very distant time stood, as it were, in a fruit-dish, a dish of some three pence; your honours have seen such dishes; they are not China dishes, but very good dishes.

Escal. Go to, go to: no matter for the dish, sir.

Clo. No indeed, sir, not of a pin; you are therein in the right: but to the point: As I say, this mistress Elbow, being, as I say, with child, and being great belly'd, and longing, as I said, for prunes; and having but two in a dish, as I said, master Froth here, this very man having eaten the rest, as I said, and, as I say, paying for them very honestly;—for, as you know, master Froth, I cou'd not give you three pence again.

Froth. No, indeed.

1 i. e. the *abbess.*

2 A kind of sheriff or jailer, so called in foreign countries.

3 To *fear* is to affright.

4 i. e. throw down; *to fall* a tree is still used for *to fell* it.

5 i. e. to examine. 6 i. e. suited.

7 To complete the sense of this line *for* seems to be required:—'which now you censure him *for.*' But Shakspeare frequently uses elliptical expressions.

8 An old forensic term, signifying *to pass judgment,* or *sentence.*

9 *Full of force or conviction,* or *full of proof in itself.* So, in Othello, Act ii. Sc. 1, 'As it is a most *pregnant* and unforc'd position.'

10 i. e. *cause* I have had such faults.

11 This line is printed in Italics as a quotation in the first folio.

12 The first folio here reads—'Some run from brakes of *ice.*' The correction was made by Rowe. *Brakes* most probably here signify *thorny perplexities;* but a *brake* was also used to signify a *trap* or *snare.* Thus in Skelton's Ellinour Rummin:

'It was a stale to take—the devil in *a brake.*'

And in Holland's Leaguer, a Comedy, by Sh. Marmion.

'——————her I'll make
A stale to catch this courtier in a *brake.*'

There can be no allusion to the instrument of torture mentioned by Steevens. A *brake* seems to have signified an engine or instrument in general.

13 i. e. *is well told.* The meaning of this phrase, when seriously applied to speech, is 'This is well delivered,' 'this story is well told.' But in the present instance it is used ironically.

14 *Professes a hot house,* i. e. keeps a bagnio.

15 *Detest,* for protest, or attest.

16 A favourite dish, anciently common in brothels

Clo. Very well: you being then, if you be remember'd, cracking the stones of the foresaid prunes.

Froth. Ay, so I did, indeed.

Clo. Why, very well: I telling you then, if you be remember'd, that such a one, and such a one, were past cure of the thing you wot of, unless they kept very good diet, as I told you.

Froth. All this is true.

Clo. Why, very well then.

Escal. Come, you are a tedious fool: to the purpose,—What was done to Elbow's wife, that he hath cause to complain of? Come me to what was done to her.

Clo. Sir, your honour cannot come to that yet.

Escal. No, sir, nor I mean it not.

Clo. Sir, but you shall come to it, by your honour's leave: And, I beseech you, look into master Froth here, sir; a man of fourscore pound a year; whose father died at Hallowmas:—Was't not at Hallowmas, master Froth?

Froth. All-holland[1] eve.

Clo. Why, very well; I hope here be truths: He, sir, sitting, as I say, in a lower[2] chair, sir;—'twas in the *Bunch of Grapes*, where, indeed, you have a delight to sit: Have you not?

Froth. I have so; because it is an open room, and good for winter.

Clo. Why, very well then:—I hope here be truths.

Ang. This will last out a night in Russia,
When nights are longest there: I'll take my leave,
And leave you to the hearing of the cause;
Hoping, you'll find good cause to whip them all.

Escal. I think no less; Good morrow to your lordship. [*Exit* ANGELO.
Now, sir, come on: What was done to Elbow's wife, once more?

Clo. Once, sir? there was nothing done to her once.

Elb. I beseech you, sir, ask him what this man did to my wife.

Clo. I beseech your honour, ask me.

Escal. Well, sir: What did this gentleman to her?

Clo. I beseech you, sir, look in this gentleman's face:—Good master Froth, look upon his honour; 'tis for a good purpose: Doth your honour mark his face?

Escal. Ay, sir, very well.

Clo. Nay, I beseech you, mark it well.

Escal. Well, I do so.

Clo. Doth your honour see any harm in his face?

Escal. Why, no.

Clo. I'll be supposed upon a book, his face is the worst thing about him: Good then; if his face be the worst thing about him, how could master Froth do the constable's wife any harm? I would know that of your honour.

Escal. He's in the right: Constable, what say you to it?

Elb. First, an it like you, the house is a respected house: next, this is a respected fellow; and his mistress is a respected woman.

Clo. By this hand, sir, his wife is a more respected person than any of us all.

Elb. Varlet, thou liest; thou liest, wicked varlet: the time is yet to come, that she was ever respected with man, woman, or child.

Clo. Sir, she was respected with him before he married with her.

Escal. Which is the wiser here? Justice, or Iniquity?[3] Is this true?

Elb. O thou caitiff! O thou varlet! O thou wicked Hannibal! I respected with her, before I was married to her? If ever I was respected with her, or she with me, let not your worship think me the poor duke's officer.—Prove this, thou wicked Hannibal, or I'll have mine action of battery on thee.

Escal. If he took you a box o' th' ear, you might have your action of slander too.

Elb. Marry, I thank your good worship for it: What is't your worship's pleasure I should do with this wicked caitiff?

Escal. Truly, officer, because he has some offences in him, that thou wouldst discover if thou couldst, let him continue in his courses till thou know'st what they are.

Elb. Marry, I thank your worship for it:—Thou see'st, thou wicked varlet now, what's come upon thee; thou art to continue now, thou varlet; thou art to continue.

Escal. Where were you born, friend? [*To* FROTH.

Froth. Here in Vienna, sir.

Escal. Are you of fourscore pounds a year?

Froth. Yes, and't please you, sir.

Escal. So.—What trade are you of, sir? [*To the* Clown.

Clo. A tapster; a poor widow's tapster.

Escal. Your mistress's name?

Clo. Mistress Over-done.

Escal. Hath she had any more than one husband?

Clo. Nine, sir; Over-done by the last.

Escal. Nine!—Come hither to me, master Froth. Master Froth, I would not have you acquainted with tapsters; they will draw you, master Froth, and you will hang them: Get you gone, and let me hear no more of you.

Froth. I thank your worship; for mine own part, I never come into any room in a taphouse, but I am drawn in.

Escal. Well, no more of it, master Froth: farewell. [*Exit* FROTH.]—Come you hither to me, master tapster; what's your name, master tapster?

Clo. Pompey.

Escal. What else?

Clo. Bum, sir.

Escal. 'Troth, and your bum is the greatest thing about you: so that, in the beastliest sense, you are Pompey the great. Pompey, you are partly a bawd, Pompey, howsoever you colour it in being a tapster. Are you not? come, tell me true; it shall be the better for you.

Clo. Truly, sir, I am a poor fellow, that would live.

Escal. How would you live, Pompey? by being a bawd? What do you think of the trade, Pompey? is it a lawful trade?

Clo. If the law would allow it, sir?

Escal. But the law will not allow it, Pompey; nor it shall not be allowed in Vienna.

Clo. Does your worship mean to geld and spay all the youth in the city?

Escal. No, Pompey.

Clo. Truly, sir, in my poor opinion, they will to't then: If your worship will take order[4] for the drabs and the knaves, you need not to fear the bawds.

Escal. There are pretty orders beginning, I can tell you: It is but heading and hanging.

Clo. If you head and hang all that offend that way but for ten year together, you'll be glad to give out a commission for more heads. If this law hold in Vienna ten year, I'll rent the fairest house in it, after three pence a bay:[5] if you live to see this come to pass, say, Pompey told you so.

Escal. Thank you, good Pompey; and, in requital of your prophecy, hark you,—I advise you, let me not find you before me again upon any complaint whatsoever, no, not for dwelling where you do; if I do Pompey, I shall beat you to your tent,

1 *All-holland Eve*, the Eve of All Saints' day.

2 Every house had formerly what was called a *low chair*, designed for the ease of sick people, and occasionally occupied by lazy ones.

3 i. e. constable or clown

4 To *take order* is to *take measures*, or precautions.

5 *A bay* is a principal division in building, as a *barn of three bays* is a barn twice crossed by beams. Coles in his Latin Dictionary defines 'a bay of building, *mensura 24 pedum*.' Houses appear to have been estimated by the number of bays.

and prove a shrewd Cæsar to you; in plain dealing, Pompey, I shall have you whipt: so for this time, Pompey, fare you well.

Clo. I thank your worship for your good counsel: but I shall follow it as the flesh and fortune shall better determine.
Whip me? No, no; let carman whip his jade;
The valiant heart's not whipt out of his trade. [*Exit.*

Escal. Come hither to me, master Elbow; come hither, master Constable. How long have you been in this place of constable?

Elb. Seven year and a half, sir.

Escal. I thought, by your readiness in the office, you had continued in it some time: You say, seven years together?

Elb. And a half, sir.

Escal. Alas! it hath been great pains to you! They do you wrong to put you so oft upon't: Are there not men in your ward sufficient to serve it?

Elb. Faith, sir, few of any wit in such matters: as they are chosen, they are glad to choose me for them: I do it for some piece of money, and go through with all.

Escal. Look you, bring me in the names of some six or seven, the most sufficient of your parish.

Elb. To your worship's house, sir?

Escal. To my house: Fare you well. [*Exit* ELBOW.] What's o'clock, think you?

Just. Eleven, sir.

Escal. I pray you home to dinner with me.

Just. I humbly thank you.

Escal. It grieves me for the death of Claudio;
But there's no remedy.

Just. Lord Angelo is severe.

Escal. It is but needful:
Mercy is not itself that oft looks so;
Pardon is still the nurse of second woe:
But yet,—Poor Claudio!—There's no remedy.
Come, sir. [*Exeunt.*

SCENE II. *Another Room in the same. Enter* Provost *and a* Servant.

Serv. He's hearing of a cause; he will come straight.
I'll tell him of you.

Prov. Pray you, do. [*Exit* Servant.] I'll know
His pleasure: may be, he will relent: Alas,
He hath but as offended in a dream!
All sects, all ages smack of this vice; and he
To die for it!—

Enter ANGELO.

Ang. Now, what's the matter, provost?

Prov. Is it your will Claudio shall die to-morrow?

Ang. Did I not tell thee, yea? hadst thou not order?
Why dost thou ask again?

Prov. Lest I might be too rash:
Under your good correction, I have seen,
When, after execution, judgment hath
Repented o'er his doom.

Ang. Go to; let that be mine:
Do you your office, or give up your place,
And you shall well be spar'd.

Prov. I crave your honour's pardon.—
What shall be done, sir, with the groaning Juliet?
She's very near her hour.

Ang. Dispose of her
To some more fitter place; and that with speed.

Re-enter Servant.

Serv. Here is the sister of the man condemn'd,
Desires access to you.

Ang. Hath he a sister?

Prov. Ay, my good lord; a very virtuous maid,
And to be shortly of a sisterhood,
If not already.

Ang. Well, let her be admitted.
[*Exit* Servant.

See you the fornicatress be remov'd;
Let her have needful, but not lavish, means;
There shall be order for it.

Enter LUCIO *and* ISABELLA.

Prov. Save your honour? [*Offering to retire*

Ang. Stay a little while.—[*To* ISAB.] You are welcome: What's your will?

Isa. I am a woful suitor to your honour,
Please but your honour hear me.

Ang. Well; what's your suit?

Isab. There is a vice, that most I do abhor,
And most desire should meet the blow of justice;
For which I would not plead, but that I must;
For which I must not plead, but that I am
At war, 'twixt will, and will not.

Ang. Well; the matter?

Isab. I have a brother is condemn'd to die:
I do beseech you, let it be his fault,
And not my brother.[1]

Prov. Heaven give thee moving graces

Ang. Condemn the fault, and not the actor of it!
Why, every fault's condemn'd, ere it be done:
Mine were the very cipher of a function,
To fine[2] the faults, whose fine stands in record,
And let go by the actor.

Isab. O just, but severe law!
I had a brother then.—Heaven keep your honour!
[*Retiring.*

Lucio. [*To* ISAB.] Give't not o'er so: to him again, intreat him:
Kneel down before him, hang upon his gown;
You are too cold; if you should need a pin,
You could not with more tame a tongue desire it
To him, I say.

Isab. Must he needs die?

Ang. Maiden, no remedy

Isab. Yes; I do think that you might pardon him,
And neither heaven, nor man, grieve at the mercy.

Ang. I will not do't.

Isab. But can you, if you would?

Ang. Look, what I will not, that I cannot do.

Isab. But might you do't, and do the world no wrong,
If so your heart were touch'd with that remorse
As mine is to him?

Ang. He's sentenc'd; 'tis too late.

Lucio. You are too cold. [*To* ISABELLA.

Isab. Too late? why, no; I, that do speak a word,
May call it back again: Well, believe[3] this,
No ceremony that to great ones 'longs,
Not the king's crown, nor the deputed sword,
The marshal's truncheon, nor the judge's robe,
Become them with one half so good a grace,
As mercy does. If he had been as you,
And you as he, you would have slipt like him;
But he, like you, would not have been so stern.

Ang. Pray you, begone.

Isab. I would to heaven I had your potency,
And you were Isabel! should it then be thus?
No; I would tell what 'twere to be a judge,
And what a prisoner.

Lucio. Ay, touch him: there's the vein. [*Aside*

Ang. Your brother is a forfeit of the law,
And you but waste your words.

Isab. Alas! alas!
Why, all the souls that were, were forfeit once;
And He that might the vantage best have took,
Found out the remedy: How would you be,
If he, which is the top of judgment, should
But judge you as you are? O, think on that
And mercy then will breathe within your lips,
Like man new made.[4]

Ang. Be you content, fair maid;
It is the law, not I, condemns your brother:
Were he my kinsman, brother, or my son,
It should be thus with him;—he must die to-morrow.

Isab. To-morrow? O, that's sudden! Spare him, spare him:

---

1 i. e. let my brother's fault die or be extirpated, but let not him suffer.

2 i. e. 'to pronounce the fine or sentence of the law upon the *crime*, and let the *delinquent* escape'

3 i. e. be assured of it.

4 'You will then be as tender-hearted and merciful as the first man was in his days of innocence'

He's not prepar'd for death! Even for our kitchens
We kill the fowl of season:[1] shall we serve heaven
With less respect than we do minister
To our gross selves? Good, good my lord, bethink you:
Who is it that hath died for this offence?
There's many have committed it.

Lucio. Ay, well said.

Ang. The law hath not been dead, though it hath slept:[2]
Those many had not dar'd to do that evil,
If the first man that did the edict infringe
Had answer'd for his deed: now, 'tis awake;
Takes note of what is done; and, like a prophet,
Looks in a glass,[3] that shows what future evils,
(Either now, or by remissness new-conceiv'd,
And so in progress to be hatch'd and born,)
Are now to have no successive degrees,
But, where they live, to end.

Isab. Yet show some pity.

Ang. I show it most of all, when I show justice;
For then I pity those I do not know,[4]
Which a dismiss'd offence would after gall;
And do him right, that, answering one foul wrong,
Lives not to act another. Be satisfied:
Your brother dies to-morrow: be content.

Isab. So you must be the first, that gives this sentence:
And he, that suffers: O, it is excellent
To have a giant's strength; but it is tyrannous
To use it like a giant.

Lucio. That's well said.

Isab. Could great men thunder
As Jove himself does, Jove would ne'er be quiet,
For every pelting,[5] petty officer,
Would use his heaven for thunder; nothing but thunder.——
Merciful heaven!
Thou rather, with thy sharp and sulphurous bolt,
Split'st the unwedgeable and gnarled[6] oak,
Than the soft myrtle:[7]—But man, proud man!
Drest in a little brief authority:
Most ignorant of what he's most assur'd,
His glassy essence,—like an angry ape,
Plays such fantastick tricks before high heaven,
As make the angels weep: who, with our spleens,
Would all themselves laugh mortal.[8]

Lucio. O, to him, to him, wench: he will relent;
He's coming, I perceive't.

Prov. Pray heaven, she win him!

Isab. We cannot weigh our brother with ourself:
Great men may jest with saints: 'tis wit in them!
But, in the less, foul profanation.

Lucio. Thou'rt in the right, girl; more o' that.

Isab. That in the captain's but a cholerick word,
Which in the soldier is flat blasphemy.

Lucio. Art advis'd o' that? more on't.

Ang. Why do you put these sayings upon me?

Isab. Because authority, though it err like others,
Hath yet a kind of medicine in itself,
That skins the vice o' the top:[9] Go to your bosom:
Knock there, and ask your heart, what it doth know
That's like my brother's fault: if it confess
A natural guiltiness, such as is his,
Let it not sound a thought upon your tongue
Against my brother's life.

Ang. She speaks, and 'tis
Such sense, that my sense breeds with it.[10]——
Fare you well.

Isab. Gentle my lord, turn back.

Ang. I will bethink me:—Come again to-morrow.

Isab. Hark, how I'll bribe you: Good my lord, turn back.

Ang. How! bribe me?

Isab. Ay, with such gifts, that heaven shall share with you.

Lucio. You had marr'd all else.

Isab. Not with fond[11] shekels of the tested[12] gold,
Or stones, whose rates are either rich, or poor,
As fancy values them: but with true prayers,
That shall be up at heaven, and enter there,
Ere sun-rise; prayers from preserved[13] souls,
From fasting maids, whose minds are dedicate
To nothing temporal.

Ang. Well: come to me
To-morrow.

Lucio. Go to; it is well away. [*Aside to* ISABEL

Isab. Heaven keep your honour safe!

Ang. Amen.[14]
For I am that way going to temptation, [*Aside*
Where prayers cross.[15]

Isab. At what hour to-morrow
Shall I attend your lordship?

Ang. At any time 'fore noon.

Isab. Save your honour!

[*Exeunt* LUCIO, ISABELLA, *and* Provost.

Ang. From thee; even from thy virtue.—
What's this? what's this? Is this her fault, or mine?
The tempter, or the tempted, who sins most? Ha!
Not she; nor doth she tempt: but it is I,
That lying by the violet, in the sun,
Do, as the carrion does, not as the flower,
Corrupt with virtuous season. Can it be,
That modesty may more betray our sense[16]
Than woman's lightness? Having waste ground enough,
Shall we desire to raze the sanctuary,
And pitch our evils there?[17] O, fy, fy, fy!
What dost thou? or, what art thou, Angelo?
Dost thou desire her foully, for those things
That make her good? O, let her brother live.
Thieves for their robbery have authority,
When judges steal themselves. What? do I love her,
That I desire to hear her speak again,
And feast upon her eyes? What is't I dream on?
O cunning enemy, that, to catch a saint,
With saints dost bait thy hook. Most dangerous

---

1 i. e. when in season.

2 '*Dormiunt aliquando leges, moriuntur nunquam*,' is a maxim of our law.

3 This alludes to the deceptions of the fortune-tellers, who pretended to see future events in a beryl, or crystal glass.

4 One of Judge Hale's 'Memorials' is of the same tendency:—'When I find myself swayed to mercy, let me remember that there is a mercy likewise due to the country.'

5 *Pelting* for paltry. 6 *Gnarled*, knotted.

7 Mr. Douce has remarked the close affinity between this passage and one in the second satire of Persius. Yet we have no translation of that poet of Shakspeare's age.

'Ignovisse putas, quia, cum tonat, ocyus ilex
Sulfure discutitur sacro, quam tuque domusque?'

8 The notion of angels weeping for the sins of men is rabbinical. By *spleens* Shakspeare meant that peculiar turn of the human mind, that always inclines it to a spiteful and unseasonable mirth. Had the angels *that*, they would laugh themselves out of their immortality, by indulging a passion unworthy of that prerogative

9 Shakspeare has used this indelicate metaphor again in Hamlet:—'It will but skin and film the ulcerous place.'

10 i. e. Such sense as breeds or *produces a consequence* in his mind. Malone thought that *sense* here meant *sensual desire*.

11 *Fond*, in its old signification sometimes meant *foolish*. In its modern sense it evidently implied a doting or extravagant affection; here it signifies *over-valued or prized by folly*.

12 i. e. *tried, refined*.

13 Preserved from the corruption of the world.

14 Isabella prays that his honour may be safe, meaning only to give him his title: his imagination is caught by the word *honour*, he feels that it is in danger, and therefore says amen to her benediction.

15 The petition of the Lord's Prayer, 'Lead us not into temptation,'—is here considered as *crossing* or intercepting the way in which Angelo was going: he was exposing himself to temptation by the appointment for the morrow's meeting.

16 *Sense* for sensual appetite.

17 No language could more forcibly express the aggravated profligacy of Angelo's passion, which the purity of Isabella but served the more to inflame. The desecration of edifices devoted to religion, by converting them to the most abject purposes of nature, was an eastern method of expressing contempt. See 2 Kings x. 27

Is that temptation, that doth goad us on
To sin in loving virtue: never could the strumpet,
With all her double vigour, art and nature,
Once stir my temper; but this virtuous maid
Subdues me quite;—Ever, till now,
When men were fond, I smil'd, and wonder'd how![1]
[*Exit.*

SCENE III. *A Room in a Prison.* *Enter* Duke, *habited like a Friar, and* Provost.

Duke. Hail to you, Provost! so, I think you are.
Prov. I am the provost: What's your will, good friar?
Duke. Bound by my charity, and my bless'd order,
I come to visit the afflicted spirits
Here in the prison: do me the common right
To let me see them; and to make me know
The nature of their crimes, that I may minister
To them accordingly.
Prov. I would do more than that, if more were needful.

Enter JULIET.

Look, here comes one; a gentlewoman of mine,
Who falling in the flames[2] of her own youth,
Hath blister'd her report: She is with child:
And he that got it, sentenc'd: a young man
More fit to do another such offence,
Than die for this.
Duke. When must he die?
Prov. As I do think, to-morrow.—
I have provided for you; stay a while, [*To* JULIET.
And you shall be conducted.
Duke. Repent you, fair one, of the sin you carry?
Juliet. I do; and bear the shame most patiently.
Duke. I'll teach you how you shall arraign your conscience,
And try your penitence, if it be sound,
Or hollowly put on.
Juliet. I'll gladly learn.
Duke. Love you the man that wrong'd you?
Juliet. Yes, as I love the woman that wrong'd him.
Duke. So then, it seems, your most offenceful act
Was mutually committed?
Juliet. Mutually.
Duke. Then was your sin of heavier kind than his.
Juliet. I do confess it, and repent it, father.
Duke. 'Tis meet so, daughter: But lest you do repent,
As that the sin hath brought you to this shame,—
Which sorrow is always towards ourselves, not heaven;
Showing, we'd not spare[3] heaven as we love it,
But as we stand in fear,—
Juliet. I do repent me, as it is an evil;
And take the shame with joy.
Duke. There rest.[4]
Your partner, as I hear, must die to-morrow,
And I am going with instruction to him.—
Grace go with you! *Benedicite!* [*Exit.*
Juliet. Must die to-morrow! O, injurious love[5],
That respites me a life, whose very comfort
Is still a dying horror!
Prov. 'Tis pity of him. [*Exeunt.*

SCENE IV. *A Room in* Angelo's *House.* *Enter* ANGELO.

Ang. When I would pray and think, I think and pray
To several subjects: heaven hath my empty words;
Whilst my invention,[6] hearing not my tongue,
Anchors on Isabel: Heaven in my mouth,
As if I did but only chew his name;
And in my heart, the strong and swelling evil
Of my conception: The state, whereon I studied,
Is like a good thing, being often read,
Grown fear'd and tedious; yea, my gravity,
Wherein (let no man hear me) I take pride,
Could I, with boot,[7] change for an idle plume,
Which the air beats for vain. O place! O form!
How often dost thou with thy case,[8] thy habit,
Wrench awe from fools, and tie the wiser souls
To thy false seeming?[9] Blood, thou still art blood!
Let's write good angel on the devil's horn,
'Tis not the devil's crest.[10]

Enter Servant.

How now, who's there?
Serv. One Isabel, a sister,
Desires access to you.
Ang. Teach her the way. [*Exit* Serv.
O heavens!
Why does my blood thus muster to my heart;
Making both it unable for itself,
And dispossessing all the other parts
Of necessary fitness?
So play the foolish throngs with one that swoons,
Come all to help him, and so stop the air
By which he should revive: and even so
The general,[11] subject to a well-wish'd king,
Quit their own part, and in obsequious fondness
Crowd to his presence, where their untaught love
Must needs appear offence.

Enter ISABELLA.

How now, fair maid?
Isab. I am come to know your pleasure.
Ang. That you might know it, would much better please me,
Than to demand what 'tis. Your brother cannot live.
Isab. Even so?—Heaven keep your honour! [*Retiring.*
Ang. Yet may he live awhile; and it may be,
As long as you, or I: Yet he must die.
Isab. Under your sentence?
Ang. Yea.
Isab. When, I beseech you? that in his reprieve,
Longer, or shorter, he may be so fitted,
That his soul sicken not.
Ang. Ha! Fye, these filthy vices! It were as good
To pardon him, that hath from nature stolen
A man already made,[12] as to remit
Their saucy sweetness,[13] that do coin heaven's image
In stamps that are forbid: 'tis all as easy
Falsely to take away a life true made,
As to put mettle in restrained means,
To make a false one.[14]

1 Dr. Johnson thinks the second act should end here.
2 The folio reads *flawes*.
3 i. e. not spare to offend heaven.
4 i. e. keep yourself in this frame of mind.
5 'O injurious *love*.' Sir Thomas Hanmer proposed to read *law* instead of *love*.
6 *Invention* for imagination. So, in Shakspeare's 103d Sonnet:

'—— a face, ——
That overgoes my blunt *invention* quite.'

And in King Henry V.

'O for a muse of fire, that would ascend
The brightest heaven of *invention*.'

7 *Boot* is profit. 8 i. e. outside.
9 Shakspeare judiciously distinguishes the different operations of high place upon different minds. Fools are frighted and wise men allured. Those who cannot judge but by the eye are easily awed by splendour; those who consider men as well as conditions, are easily persuaded to love the appearance of virtue dignified with power
10 'Though we should write *good angel* on the devil's horn, it will not change his nature, so as to give him a right to wear that *crest*.' This explanation of Malone's is confirmed by a passage in Lylys Midas, 'Melancholy! is melancholy a word for barber's mouth? Thou shouldst say heavy, dull, and doltish: melancholy is the *crest* of courtiers.'
11 i. e. the *people* or *multitude* subject to a king. So, in Hamlet: 'the play pleased not the million; 'twas caviare to the *general*.' It is supposed that Shakspeare, in this passage, and in one before (Act i. Sc. 2,) intended to flatter the unkingly weakness of James I. which made him so impatient of the crowds which flocked to see him, at his first coming, that he restrained them by a proclamation.
12 i. e. that hath killed a man.
13 *Sweetness* has here probably the sense of *lickerishness*.
14 The thought is simply, that murder is as easy as

Isab. 'Tis set down so in heaven, but not in earth.
Ang. Say you so? then I shall pose you quickly.
Which had you rather, That the most just law
Now took your brother's life; or, to redeem him,
Give up your body to such sweet uncleanness,
As she that he hath stain'd?
Isab. Sir, believe this,
I had rather give my body than my soul.[1]
Ang. I talk not of your soul: Our compell'd sins
Stand more for number than account.[2]
Isab. How say you?
Ang. Nay, I'll not warrant that; for I can speak
Against the thing I say. Answer to this;—
now the voice of the recorded law,
Pronounce a sentence on your brother's life:
Might there not be a charity in sin,
To save this brother's life?
Isab. Please you to do't,
I'll take it as a peril to my soul,
It is no sin at all, but charity.
Ang. Pleas'd you to do't, at peril of your soul,
Were equal poise of sin and charity.
Isab. That I do beg his life, if it be sin,
Heaven, let me bear it! you granting of my suit,
If that be sin, I'll make it my morn prayer
To have it added to the faults of mine,
And nothing of your answer.
Ang. Nay, but hear me:
Your sense pursues not mine: either you are ignorant,
Or seem so, craftily; and that's not good.
Isab. Let me be ignorant, and in nothing good,
But graciously to know I am no better.
Ang. Thus wisdom wishes to appear most bright,
When it doth tax itself: as these black masks[3]
Proclaim an enshield[4] beauty ten times louder
That beauty could displayed.—But mark me;
To be received plain, I'll speak more gross:
Your brother is to die.
Isab. So.
Ang. And his offence is so, as it appears
Accountant to the law upon that pain.[5]
Isab. True.
Ang. Admit no other way to save his life,
(As I subscribe[6] not that, nor any other,
But in the loss of question,[7]) that you, his sister,
Finding yourself desir'd of such a person,
Whose credit with the judge, or own great place,
Could fetch your brother from the manacles
Of the all-binding law; and that there were
No earthly mean to save him, but that either
You must lay down the treasures of your body
To this supposed, or else to let him suffer;
What would you do?
Isab. As much for my poor brother, as myself:
That is, were I under the terms of death,
The impression of keen whips I'd wear as rubies,
And strip myself to death, as to a bed
That longing I have been sick for, ere I'd yield
My body up to shame.
Ang. Then must your brother die.
Isab. And 'twere the cheaper way:
Better it were, a brother died at once,
Than that a sister, by redeeming him,
Should die for ever.
Ang. Were not you then as cruel as the sentence
That you have slander'd so?
Isab. Ignomy[8] in ransom, and free pardon,
Are of two houses: lawful mercy is
Nothing akin to foul redemption.
Ang. You seem'd of late to make the law a tyrant:
And rather prov'd the sliding of your brother
A merriment than a vice.
Isab. O pardon me, my lord; it oft falls out,
To have what we'd have, we speak not what we mean:
I something do excuse the thing I hate,
For his advantage that I dearly love.
Ang. We are all frail.
Isab. Else let my brother die,
If not a feodary, but only he,
Owe, and succeed by weakness.[9]
Ang. Nay, women are frail too,
Isab. Ay, as the glasses where they view themselves:
Which are as easy broke as they make forms.
Women!—Help heaven! men their creation mar
In profiting by them.[10] Nay, call us ten times frail;
For we are soft as our complexions are,
And credulous to false prints.[11]
Ang. I think it well:
And from this testimony of your own sex,
(Since, I suppose, we are made to be no stronger
Than faults may shake our frames) let me be bold;—
I do arrest your words; Be that you are,
That is, a woman; if you be more, you're none;
If you be one (as you are well express'd
By all external warrants,) show it now,
By putting on the destin'd livery.
Isab. I have no tongue but one: gentle my lord,
Let me entreat you speak the former language.
Ang. Plainly conceive, I love you.
Isab. My brother did love Juliet; and you tell me,
That he shall die for it.
Ang. He shall not, Isabel, if you give me love.
Isab. I know, your virtue hath a licence in't,
Which seems a little fouler than it is,
To pluck on others.[12]
Ang. Believe me, on mine honour,
My words express my purpose.
Isab. Ha! little honour to be much believ'd,
And most pernicious purpose!—seeming, seeming![13]—
I will proclaim thee, Angelo; look for't:
Sign me a present pardon for my brother,
Or, with an outstretch'd throat, I'll tell the world
Aloud, what man thou art.
Ang. Who will believe thee, Isabel?
My unsoil'd name, the austereness of my life,
My vouch[14] against you, and my place i' the state,
Will so your accusation overweigh,
That you shall stifle in your own report,
And smell of calumny.[15] I have begun;
And now I give my sensual race the rein:
Fit thy consent to my sharp appetite;
Lay by all nicety, and prolixious blushes,[16]
That banish what they sue for; redeem thy brother

fornication; and the inference which Angelo would draw is, that it is as improper to pardon the latter as the former.

1 Isabel appears to use the words 'give my body,' in a different sense to Angelo. Her meaning appears to be, 'I had rather *die* than forfeit my eternal happiness by the prostitution of my person.'

2 i. e. actions that we are compelled to, however numerous, are not imputed to us by heaven as crimes.

3 The masks worn by female spectators of the play are here probably meant; however improperly, a compliment to them is put into the mouth of Angelo: unless the demonstrative pronoun is put for the prepositive article? At the beginning of Romeo and Juliet, we have a passage of similar import:
'These happy *masks* that kiss fair ladies' brows,
Being *black*, put us in mind they hide the fair.'

4 i. e. enshielded, covered.

5 *Pain*, penalty 6 *Subscribe* agree to.

7 i. e. conversation that tends to nothing

8 *Ignomy*, Ignominy.

9 I adopt Mr. Nares' explanation of this difficult passage as the most satisfactory yet offered:—'If he is the only *feodary*, i. e. subject who holds by the common tenure of human frailty.' *Owes*, i. e. possesses and *succeeds by*, holds his right of succession by it. Warburton says that 'the allusion is so fine that it deserves to be explained.—The comparing mankind lying under the weight of original sin, to a feodary who owes *suit* and service to his lord, is not ill imagined.'

10 The meaning appears to be, that 'men debase their natures by taking advantage of women's weakness' She therefore calls on Heaven to assist them.

11 i. e. impressions.

12 i. e. 'your virtue assumes an air of *licentiousness*, which is not natural to you, on purpose to try me.'

13 *Seeming* is hypocrisy. 14 *Vouch*, assertion

15 A metaphor from a lamp or candle extinguished in its own grease.

16 *Prolixious blushes* mean what Milton has elegantly called—'Sweet reluctant *delay*.'

By yielding up thy body to my will;
Or else he must not only die the death,[1]
But thy unkindness shall his death draw out
To lingering sufferance: answer me to-morrow,
Or, by the affection that now guides me most,
I'll prove a tyrant to him: As for you,
Say what you can, my false o'erweighs your true.
[*Exit.*

Isab. To whom shall I complain? Did I tell this,
Who would believe me? O perilous mouths,
That bear in them one and the selfsame tongue,
Either of condemnation or approof!
Bidding the law make court'sy to their will;
Hooking both right and wrong to the appetite,
To follow as it draws! I'll to my brother:
Though he hath fallen by prompture[2] of the blood,
Yet hath he in him such a mind of honour,
That had he twenty heads to tender down
On twenty bloody blocks, he'd yield them up,
Before his sister should her body stoop
To such abhorr'd pollution.
Then Isabel, live chaste, and, brother, die:
More than our brother is our chastity.
I'll tell him yet of Angelo's request,
And fit his mind to death, for his soul's rest.
[*Exit.*

ACT III.

SCENE I. *A Room in the Prison. Enter* Duke, CLAUDIO, *and* Provost.

Duke. So, then you hope of pardon from lord Angelo?

Claud. The miserable have no other medicine,
But only hope:
I have hope to live, and am prepar'd to die.

Duke. Be absolute[3] for death; either death or life,
Shall thereby be the sweeter. Reason thus with life,—
If I do lose thee, I do lose a thing
That none but fools would keep:[4] a breath thou art,
(Servile to all the skiey influences,)
That dost this habitation, where thou keep'st,[5]
Hourly afflict: merely, thou art death's fool;
For him thou labour'st by thy flight to shun,
And yet runn'st toward him still: Thou art not noble;
For all the accommodations that thou bear'st,
Are nurs'd by baseness:[6] Thou art by no means valiant;
For thou dost fear the soft and tender fork
Of a poor worm:[7] Thy best of rest is sleep,
And that thou oft provok'st; yet grossly fear'st
Thy death, which is no more. Thou art not thyself;
For thou exist'st on many a thousand grains
That issue out of dust: Happy thou art not;
For what thou hast not, still thou striv'st to get;
And what thou hast, forget'st: Thou art not certain;
For thy complexion shifts to strange affects,[8]
After the moon: If thou art rich, thou art poor:
For, like an ass, whose back with ingots bows,
Thou bear'st thy heavy riches but a journey,
And death unloads thee: Friend, hast thou none;
For thine own bowels, which do call thee sire,
The mere effusion of thy proper loins,
Do curse the gout, serpigo,[9] and the rheum,
For ending thee no sooner: Thou hast nor youth, nor age;
But, as it were, an after-dinner's sleep,
Dreaming on both;[10] for all thy blessed youth
Becomes as aged, and doth beg the alms
Of palsied eld;[11] and when thou art old, and rich,
Thou hast neither heat, affection, limb, nor beauty,
To make thy riches pleasant. What's yet in this
That bears the name of life? Yet in this life
Lie hid more thousand deaths; yet death we fear,
That makes these odds all even.

Claud. I humbly thank you
To sue to live, I find, I seek to die:
And seeking death, find life: Let it come on.

Enter ISABELLA.

Isab. What, ho! Peace here; grace and good company!

Prov. Who's there? come in; the wish deserves a welcome.

Duke. Dear sir, ere long I'll visit you again

Claud. Most holy sir, I thank you.

Isab. My business is a word or two with Claudio.

Prov. And very welcome. Look, signior, here's your sister.

Duke. Provost, a word with you.

Prov. As many as you please.

Duke. Bring me to hear them speak, where I may be conceal'd,[12]
Yet hear them. [*Exeunt* Duke *and* Provost.

Claud. Now, sister, what's the comfort?

Isab. Why, as all comforts are, most good indeed:
Lord Angelo, having affairs to heaven,
Intends you for his swift embassador,
Where you shall be an everlasting leiger:[13]
Therefore your best appointment[14] make with speed;
To-morrow you set on.

Claud. Is there no remedy?

Isab. None, but such remedy, as to save a head,
To cleave a heart in twain.

Claud. But is there any?

Isab. Yes, brother, you may live;
There is a devilish mercy in the judge,
If you'll implore it, that will free your life,
But fetter you till death.

Claud. Perpetual durance?

Isab. Ay, just, perpetual durance; a restraint,
Though all the world's vastidity[15] you had,
To a determined scope.[16]

---

1 *The death.* This phrase seems originally to have been a mistaken translation of the French *La mort.* Chaucer uses it frequently, and it is common to all writers of Shakspeare's age.

2 i. e. temptation, instigation. 3 i. e. determined.

4 *Keep* here means *care for*, a common acceptation of the word in Chaucer and later writers.

5 i. e. dwellest. So, in Henry IV. Part i:
'Twas where the madcap duke his uncle *kept.*'

6 Shakspeare here meant to observe, that a minute analysis of life at once destroys that splendour which dazzles the imagination. Whatever grandeur can display, or luxury enjoy, is procured by *baseness*, by offices of which the mind shrinks from the contemplation. All the delicacies of the table may be traced back to the shambles and the dunghill, all magnificence of building was hewn from the quarry, and all the pomp of ornament from among the damps and darkness of the mine.

7 *Worm* is put for any creeping thing or *serpent.* Shakspeare adopts the vulgar error, that a serpent wounds with his tongue, and that his tongue is *forked.* In old tapestries and paintings the tongues of serpents and dragons always appear barbed like the point of an arrow.

8 The old copy reads *effects*. We should read *affects*, i. e. affections, passions of the mind. See Hamlet. Act iii. Sc 4.

9 *Serpigo*, is a leprous eruption.

10 This is exquisitely imagined. When we are young, we busy ourselves in forming schemes for succeeding time, and miss the gratifications that are before us; when we are old, we amuse the languor of age with the recollection of youthful pleasures or performances, so that our life, of which no part is filled with the business of the present time, resembles our dreams after dinner, when the events of the morning are mingled with the designs of the evening.

11 *Old age.* In youth, which is or ought to be the *happiest* time, man commonly wants means to obtain what he could enjoy, he is dependent on *palsied eld;* must beg alms from the coffers of hoary avarice; and being very niggardly supplied, *becomes as aged*, looks like an old man on happiness beyond his reach. And when he is *old and rich*, when he has wealth enough for the purchase of all that formerly excited his desires, he has no longer the powers of enjoyment.

12 The *first* folio reads, 'bring them to *hear me* speak, &c.' the *second* folio reads, 'bring them to speak.' The emendation is by Steevens.

13 A *leiger* is a resident.

14 i. e. preparation.

15 i. e. vastness of extent.

16 'To a determin'd scope.' A confinement of your

Claud. But in what nature?
Isab. In such a one as (you consenting to't)
Would bark your honour from that trunk you bear,
And leave you naked.[1]
Claud. Let me know the point.
Isab. O, I do fear thee, Claudio; and I quake,
Lest thou a feverous life should'st entertain,
And six or seven winters more respect
Than a perpetual honour. Dar'st thou die?
The sense of death is most in apprehension;
And the poor beetle, that we tread upon,
In corporal sufferance finds a pang as great
As when a giant dies.[2]
Claud. Why give you me this shame?
Think you I can a resolution fetch
From flowery tenderness? If I must die,
I will encounter darkness as a bride,
And hug it in mine arms.
Isab. There spake my brother; there my father's grave
Did utter forth a voice! Yes, thou must die:
Thou art too noble to conserve a life
In base appliances. This outward-sainted deputy,—
Whose settled visage and deliberate word
Nips youth i' the head, and follies doth enmew,[3]
As falcon doth the fowl,—is yet a devil;
His filth within being cast, he would appear
A pond as deep as hell.
Claud. The princely Angelo?
Isab. O, 'tis the cunning livery of hell,
The damned'st body to invest and cover
In princely guards![4] Dost thou think, Claudio,
If I would yield him my virginity,
Thou might'st be freed?
Claud. O, heavens! it cannot be.
Isab. Yes, he would give it thee, from this rank offence,
So to offend him still:[5] This night's the time
That I should do what I abhor to name,
Or else thou diest to-morrow.
Claud. Thou shalt not do't.
Isab. O, were it but my life,
I'd throw it down for your deliverance
As frankly[6] as a pin.
Claud. Thanks, my dear Isabel.
Isab. Be ready, Claudio, for your death to-morrow.
Claud. Yes.—Has he affections in him,
That thus can make him bite the law by the nose,
When he would force it?[7] Sure it is not sin;
Or of the deadly seven it is the least.
Isab. Which is the least?
Claud. If it were damnable, he, being so wise,
Why, would he for the momentary trick,
Be perdurably fin'd?—O Isabel!
Isab. What says my brother?
Claud. Death is a fearful thing.
Isab. And shamed life a hateful.
Claud. Ay, but to die, and go we know not where;
To lie in cold obstruction, and to rot
This sensible warm motion to become
A kneaded clod; and the delighted[8] spirit
To bathe in fiery floods, or to reside
In thrilling regions of thick-ribbed ice;[9]
To be imprison'd in the viewless[10] winds,
And blown with restless violence round about
The pendent world; or to be worse than worst
Of those, that lawless and incertain thoughts
Imagine howling!—'tis too horrible!
The weariest and most loathed worldly life,
That age, ach, penury, imprisonment
Can lay on nature, is a paradise
To what we fear of death.
Isab. Alas! alas!
Claud. Sweet sister, let me live.
What sin you do to save a brother's life,
Nature dispenses with the deed so far,
That it becomes a virtue.
Isab. O, you beast!
O, faithless coward! O, dishonest wretch!
Wilt thou be made a man out of my vice?
Is't not a kind of incest, to take life
From thine own sister's shame? What should I think?
Heaven shield, my mother play'd my father fair!
For such a warped slip of wilderness[11]
Ne'er issu'd from his blood. Take my defiance:[12]
Die; perish! might but my bending down
Reprieve thee from thy fate, it should proceed:
I'll pray a thousand prayers for thy death,
No word to save thee.
Claud. Nay, hear me, Isabel.
Isab. O, fye, fye, fye!
Thy sin's not accidental, but a trade:[13]
Mercy to thee would prove itself a bawd:
'Tis best that thou diest quickly. [*Going.*
Claud. O hear me, Isabella.

Re-enter Duke.

Duke. Vouchsafe a word, young sister, but one word.
Isab. What is your will?
Duke. Might you dispense with your leisure, I would by and by have some speech with you: the satisfaction I would require, is likewise your own benefit.

Isab. I have no superfluous leisure; my stay must be stolen out of other affairs; but I will attend you awhile.

Duke. [*To* Claudio, *aside.*] Son, I have overheard what hath passed between you and your sister. Angelo had never the purpose to corrupt her; only he hath made an essay of her virtue, to practise his judgment with the disposition of natures: she, having the truth of honour in her, hath made him that gracious denial which he is most glad to receive: I am confessor to Angelo, and I know this to be true; therefore prepare yourself to death:

---

mind to one painful idea: to ignominy, of which the remembrance can neither be suppressed nor escaped.

1 A metaphor, from stripping trees of their *bark*.

2 'And the poor beetle that we tread upon
In corporal sufferance finds a pang as great
As when a giant dies.'

This beautiful passage is in all our minds and memories, but it most frequently stands in quotation detached from the antecedent line:—'The sense of death is most in apprehension,' without which it is liable to an opposite construction. The meaning is:—'fear is the principal sensation in death, which has no pain; and the giant when he dies feels no greater pain than the beetle?'

3 'In whose presence the follies of youth are afraid to show themselves, as the fowl is afraid to flutter while the falcon hovers over it.' To *enmew* is a term in Falconry, signifying to restrain, to keep in a mew or cage either by force or terror.

4 *Guards* were trimmings, facings, or other ornaments applied upon a dress. It here stands, by synecdoche, for *dress*.

5 i. e. '*From the time* of my committing this offence, you might persist in sinning with safety.'

6 *Frankly*, freely.

7 'Has *he* passions that impel him to transgress the law at the very moment that he is enforcing it against others? Surely then it cannot be a sin so very heinous, since Angelo, who is so wise, will venture it?' Shakspeare shows his knowledge of human nature in the conduct of Claudio.

8 *Delighted*, is occasionally used by Shakspeare for *delightful*, or causing delight; delighted in. So, in Othello, Act ii. Sc. 3;

'If virtue no *delighted* beauty lack.'

And Cymbeline, Act v. Sc. 4:

'Whom best I love, I cross, to make my gift
The more delayed, *delighted*.

9 Jonson, in his Cataline, Act ii. Sc. 4, has a similar expression:—'We're spirits bound in *ribs of ice*.' Shakspeare returns to the various destinations of the disembodied Spirit, in that pathetic speech of Othello in the fifth Act. Milton seems to have had Shakspeare before him when he wrote the second book of Paradise Lost, v. 595—603.

10 *Viewless*, invisible, unseen.

11 *Wilderness*, for wildness.

12 i. e. my *refusal*.

13 *Trade*, an established habit, a custom, a practice.

Do not satisfy your resolution[1] with hopes that are fallible: to-morrow you must die; go to your knees, and make ready.

Claud. Let me ask my sister pardon. I am so out of love with life, that I will sue to be rid of it.

Duke.[2] Hold you there: Farewell.

[*Exit* CLAUDIO.

Re-enter Provost.

Provost, a word with you.

Prov. What's your will, father?

Duke. That now you are come, you will be gone: Leave me awhile with the maid; my mind promises with my habit, no loss shall touch her by my company.

Prov. In good time.[3] [*Exit* Provost.

Duke. The hand that hath made you fair, hath made you good: the goodness, that is cheap in beauty, makes beauty brief in goodness; but grace, being the soul of your complexion, should keep the body of it ever fair. The assault that Angelo hath made to you, fortune hath convey'd to my understanding; and, but that frailty hath examples for his falling, I should wonder at Angelo. How would you do to contend this substitute, and to save your brother?

Isab. I am now going to resolve him: I had rather my brother die by the law, than my son should be unlawfully born. But O, how much is the good duke deceived in Angelo! If ever he return, and I can speak to him, I will open my lips in vain, or discover his government.

Duke. That shall not be much amiss: Yet, as the matter now stands, he will avoid your accusation; he made trial of you only.—Therefore fasten your ear on my advisings; to the love I have in doing good, a remedy presents itself. I do make myself believe, that you may most uprighteously do a poor wronged lady a merited benefit; redeem your brother from the angry law; do no stain to your own gracious person; and much please the absent duke, if, peradventure, he shall ever return to have hearing of this business.

Isab. Let me hear you speak further; I have spirit to do any thing that appears not foul in the truth of my spirit.

Duke. Virtue is bold, and goodness never fearful. Have you not heard speak of Mariana the sister of Frederick, the great soldier, who miscarried at sea?

Isab. I have heard of the lady, and good words went with her name.

Duke. Her should this Angelo have married: was affianced to her by oath, and the nuptial appointed: between which time of the contract, and limit[4] of the solemnity, her brother Frederick was wrecked at sea, having in that perished vessel the dowry of his sister. But mark how heavily this befell to the poor gentlewoman: there she lost a noble and renowned brother, in his love toward her ever most kind and natural: with him the portion and sinew of her fortune, her marriage dowry; with both, her combinate[5] husband, this well-seeming Angelo.

Isab. Can this be so? Did Angelo so leave her?

Duke. Left her in her tears, and dry'd not one of them with his comfort; swallowed his vows whole pretending, in her, discoveries of dishonour: in few, bestowed[6] her on her own lamentation, which she yet wears for his sake; and he, a marble to her tears, is washed with them, but relents not.

Isab. What a merit were it in death, to take this poor maid from the world! What corruption in this life, that it will let this man live!—But how out of this can she avail?

Duke. It is a rupture that you may easily heal: and the cure of it not only saves your brother, but keeps you from dishonour in doing it.

Isab. Show me how, good father.

Duke. This forenamed maid hath yet in her the continuance of her first affection; his unjust unkindness, that in all reason should have quenched her love, hath, like an impediment in the current, made it more violent and unruly. Go you to Angelo: answer his requiring with a plausible obedience; agree with his demands to the point: only refer[7] yourself to this advantage,—first, that your stay with him may not be long; that the time may have all shadow and silence in it; and the place answer to convenience: this being granted in course, now follows all. We shall advise this wronged maid to stead up your appointment, go in your place; if the encounter acknowledge itself hereafter, it may compel him to her recompense: and here, by this, is your brother saved, your honour untainted, the poor Mariana advantaged, and the corrupt deputy scaled.[8] The maid will I frame, and make fit for his attempt. If you think well to carry this as you may, the doubleness of the benefit defends the deceit from reproof. What think you of it?

Isab. The image of it gives me content already; and, I trust, it will grow to a most prosperous perfection.

Duke. It lies much in your holding up: Haste you speedily to Angelo; if for this night he entreat you to his bed give him promise of satisfaction. I will presently to St. Luke's; there at the moated grange,[9] resides this dejected Mariana: At that place call upon me; and despatch with Angelo, that it may be quickly.

Isab. I thank you for this comfort: Fare you well, good father. [*Exeunt severally.*

SCENE II. *The street before the prison. Enter* Duke, *as a friar; to him* ELBOW, Clown, *and* Officers.

Elb. Nay, if there be no remedy for it, but that you will needs buy and sell men and women like beasts, we shall have all the world drink brown and white bastard.[10]

Duke. O, heavens! what stuff is here?

Clo. 'Twas never merry world, since, of two usuries, the merriest was put down, and the worser allow'd, by order of law, a furr'd gown to keep him warm; and furr'd with fox and lamb-skins[11] too, to signify, that craft, being richer than innocency, stands for the facing.

Elb. Come your way, sir;—Bless you, good father friar.

Duke. And you, good brother father:[12] What offence hath this man made you, sir?

Elb. Marry, sir, he hath offended the law; and,

1 *Do not satisfy your resolution,* appears to signify *do not quench or extinguish your resolution with fallible hopes. Satisfy* was used by old writers in the sense of to *stay, stop, quench,* or *stint:* as in the phrase 'Sorrow is *satisfied* with tears; Dolor *expletur* lachrymis.—To satisfy or *stint* hunger: Famem *explere.* To quench or satisfy thirst: Sitem *explere!*' A conjecture of the Hon. Charles Yorke's on this passage will be found in Warburton's Letters, p. 500, 8vo. ed.

2 *Hold you there:* continue in that resolution.

3 i. e. *a la bonne heure,* so be it, very well.

4 i. e. appointed time.

5 i. e. betrothed.

6 *Bestowed her on her own lamentation,* gave her up to her sorrows.

7 *Refer yourself,* have recourse to.

8 i. e. stripped of his covering or disguise, his affectation of virtue; *desquamatus.* A metaphor of a similar nature has before occurred in this play, taken from the barking, peeling, or stripping of trees. I cannot convince myself that it means *weighed,* unless we could imagine that *counterpoised* was intended.

9 *Grange,* a solitary farm-house.

10 *Bastard.* A sweet wine, Raisin wine, according to Minshew.

11 It is probable we should read 'fox *on* lambskins,' otherwise craft will not stand for the facing. Fox-skins and lamb-skins were both used as facings according to the statute of apparel, 24 Hen. 8. c. 13. So, in Characterismi, or Lenton's Leasures, &c. 1631:—'An usurer is an old fox clad in lamb-skin.'

12 The Duke humorously calls him *brother father,* because he had called him father friar, which is equivalent to *father brother,* friar being derived from *frere.* Fr.

sir, we take him to be a thief, too, sir; for we have found upon him, sir, a strange pick-lock,[1] which we have sent to the deputy.

Duke. Fye, sirrah, a bawd, a wicked bawd!
The evil that thou causest to be done,
That is thy means to live: Do thou but think
What 'tis to cram a maw, or clothe a back,
From such a filthy vice: say to thyself,—
From their abominable and beastly touches
I drink, I eat, array myself, and live.
Canst thou believe thy living is a life,
So stinkingly depending? Go, mend, go, mend.

Clo. Indeed, it does stink in some sort, sir; but yet, sir, I would prove——

Duke. Nay, if the devil have given thee proofs for sin,
Thou wilt prove his. Take him to prison, officer;
Correction and instruction must both work,
Ere this rude beast will profit.

Elb. He must before the deputy, sir; he has given him warning; the deputy cannot abide a whoremaster: if he be a whoremonger, and comes before him, he were as good go a mile on his errand.

Duke. That we were all, as some would seem to be
Free from our faults, as faults from seeming, free![2]

Enter Lucio.

Elb. His neck will come to your waist, a cord,[3] sir.

Clo. I spy comfort; I cry, bail: Here's a gentleman, and a friend of mine.

Lucio. How now, noble Pompey? What, at the heels of Cæsar? Art thou led in triumph? What, is there none of Pygmalion's images, newly made woman,[4] to be had now, for putting the hand in the pocket and extracting it clutch'd? What reply? Ha? What say'st thou to this tune, matter, and method? Is't not drown'd i'the last rain? Ha? What say'st thou, trot? Is the world as it was, man? Which is the way? Is it sad, and few words? Or how? The trick of it?

Duke. Still thus, and thus! still worse!

Lucio. How doth my dear morsel, thy mistress? Procures she still? Ha?

Clo. Troth, sir, she hath eaten up all her beef, and she is herself in the tub.[5]

Lucio. Why, 'tis good; it is the right of it; it must be so: Ever your fresh whore, and your powder'd bawd: An unshun'd[6] consequence; it must be so: Art going to prison, Pompey?

Clo. Yes, faith, sir.

Lucio. Why, 'tis not amiss, Pompey: Farewell: Go; say, I sent thee thither. For debt, Pompey? Or how?

Elb. For being a bawd, for being a bawd.

Lucio. Well, then imprison him: If imprisonment be the due of a bawd, why, 'tis his right: Bawd is he, doubtless, and of antiquity too; bawd-born. Farewell, good Pompey: Commend me to the prison, Pompey; You will turn good husband now, Pompey; you will keep the house.[7]

Clo. I hope, sir, your good worship will be my bail.

Lucio. No, indeed, will I not, Pompey; it is not the wear.[8] I will pray, Pompey, to increase your bondage: if you take it not patiently, why your mettle is the more: Adieu, trusty Pompey.—Bless you, friar.

Duke. And you.

Lucio. Does Bridget paint still, Pompey? Ha?

Elb. Come your ways, sir; come.

Clo. You will not bail me then, sir?

Lucio. Then, Pompey? nor now.—What news abroad, friar? What news?

Elb. Come your ways, sir; come.

Lucio. Go,—to kennel, Pompey, go;

[*Exeunt* Elbow, Clown, *and* Officers.

What news, friar, of the duke?

Duke. I know none: Can you tell me of any?

Lucio. Some say, he is with the emperor of Russia; other some, he is in Rome: But where is he, think you?

Duke. I know not where: But wheresoever, I wish him well.

Lucio. It was a mad fantastical trick of him, to steal from the state, and usurp the beggary he was never born to. Lord Angelo dukes it well in his absence; he puts transgression to't.

Duke. He does well in't.

Lucio. A little more lenity to lechery would do no harm in him: something too crabbed that way, friar.

Duke. It is too general a vice, and severity must cure it.

Lucio. Yes, in good sooth, the vice is of a great kindred; it is well ally'd: but it is impossible to extirp it quite, friar, till eating and drinking be put down. They say, this Angelo was not made by man and woman, after the downright way of creation: Is it true think you?

Duke. How should he be made then?

Lucio. Some report a sea-maid spawn'd him. Some that he was begot between two stock-fishes. —But it is certain, that when he makes water, his urine is congeal'd ice; that I know to be true: and he is a motion[9] ungenerative, that's infallible.

Duke. You are pleasant, sir; and speak apace.

Lucio. Why, what a ruthless thing is this in him, for the rebellion of a cod-piece, to take away the life of a man? Would the duke, that is absent, have done this? Ere he would have hang'd a man for the getting a hundred bastards, he would have paid for the nursing of a thousand: He had some feeling of the sport; he knew the service, and that instructed him to mercy.

Duke. I never heard the absent duke much detected[10] for women; he was not inclined that way.

Lucio. O, sir, you are deceived.

Duke. 'Tis not possible.

Lucio. Who? not the duke? yes, your beggar of fifty;—and his use was, to put a ducat in her clack-dish:[11] the duke had crotchets in him: He would be drunk too; and let me inform you.

Duke. You do him wrong, surely.

Lucio. Sir, I was an inward[12] of his: A shy fellow was the duke: and, I believe, I know the cause of his withdrawing.

Duke. What, I pr'ythee, might be the cause?

Lucio. No,—pardon;—'tis a secret must be lock'd within the teeth and the lips: but this I can let you understand,—The greater file[13] of the subject held the duke to be wise.

Duke. Wise? why, no question but he was.

---

1 It is not neccessary to take honest Pompey for a housebreaker, the locks he had occasion to pick were Spanish padlocks. In Jonson's Volpone, Corvino threatens to make his wife wear one of these strange contrivances.

2 i. e. 'As faults are free from or destitute of all comeliness or seeming.'

3 His neck will be tied, like your waist, with a cord. The friar wore a rope for a girdle.

4 i. e. Have you no new courtesans to recommend to your customers.

5 The method of cure for a certain disease was grossly called *the powdering tub.* See the notes on the tub fast and the diet, in Timon of Athens, Act iv. in the Variorum of Shakspeare.

6 i. e. inevitable.

7 i. e. stay at home, alluding to the etymology of *husband*.

8 i. e. fashion.

9 i. e. a puppet, or moving body, without the power of generation.

10 *Detected* for suspected.

11 A wooden dish with a moveable cover, formerly carried by beggars, which they *clacked* and clattered to show that it was empty. In this they received the alms. It was one mode of attracting attention. Lepers and other paupers deemed infectious, originally used it, that the sound might give warning not to approach too near, and alms be given without touching the object. The custom of *clacking* at Easter is not yet quite disused in some counties. Lucio's meaning is too evident, to want explanation.

12 i. e. intimate.

13 'The *greater file*,' the majority of his subjects

Lucio. A very superficial, ignorant, unweighing[1] fellow.

Duke. Either this is envy in you, folly, or mistaking; the very stream of his life, and the business he hath helmed,[2] must, upon a warranted need, give him a better proclamation. Let him be but testimonied in his own bringings forth, and he shall appear to the envious, a scholar, a statesman, and a soldier: Therefore, you speak unskilfully; or, if your knowledge be more, it is much darkened in your malice.

Lucio. Sir, I know him, and I love him.

Duke. Love talks with better knowledge, and knowledge with dearer love.

Lucio. Come, sir, I know what I know.

Duke. I can hardly believe that, since you know not what you speak. But, if ever the duke return (as our prayers are he may,) let me desire you to make your answer before him: If it be honest you have spoke, you have courage to maintain it: I am bound to call upon you; and, I pray you, your name?

Lucio. Sir, my name is Lucio; well known to the duke.

Duke. He shall know you better, sir, if I may live to report you.

Lucio. I fear you not.

Duke. O, you hope the duke will return no more; or you imagine me too unhurtful an opposite.[3] But, indeed, I can do you little harm; you'll forswear this again.

Lucio. I'll be hang'd first: thou art deceived in me, friar. But no more of this; Canst thou tell if Claudio die to-morrow, or no?

Duke. Why should he die, sir?

Lucio. Why? for filling a bottle with a tun-dish. I would, the duke, we talk of, were return'd again: this ungenitur'd[4] agent will unpeople the province with continency; sparrows must not build in his house-eaves, because they are lecherous. The duke yet would have dark deeds darkly answered; he would never bring them to light: would he were return'd! Marry, this Claudio is condemn'd for untrussing. Farewell, good friar; I pry'thee, pray for me. The duke, I say to thee again, would eat mutton[5] on Fridays. He's now past it; yet, and I say to thee, he would mouth with a beggar, though she smelt[6] brown bread and garlick: say, that I said so. Farewell. [*Exit.*

Duke. No might nor greatness in mortality
Can censure 'scape; back-wounding calumny
The whitest virtue strikes: What king so strong,
Can tie the gall up in the slanderous tongue?
But who comes here?

Enter ESCALUS, Provost, Bawd, *and* Officers.

Escal. Go, away with her to prison.

Bawd. Good my lord, be good to me; your honour is accounted a merciful man: good my lord.

Escal. Double and treble admonition, and still forfeit[7] in the same kind? This would make mercy swear, and play the tyrant.

Prov. A bawd of eleven years continuance, may it please your honour.

Bawd. My lord, this is one Lucio's information against me: mistress Kate Keep-down was with child by him in the duke's time, he promised her marriage; his child is a year and a quarter old, come Philip and Jacob: I have kept it myself; and see how he goes about to abuse me.

Escal. That fellow is a fellow of much licence:—let him be called before us.—Away with her to prison: Go to; no more words. [*Exeunt* Bawd *and* Officers.] Provost, my brother Angelo will not be alter'd, Claudio must die to-morrow: let him be furnished with divines, and have all charitable preparation: if my brother wrought by my pity, it should not be so with him.

Prov. So please you, this friar hath been with him, and advised him for the entertainment of death

Escal. Good even, good father.

Duke. Bliss and goodness on you!

Escal. Of whence are you?

Duke. Not of this country, though my chance is now
To use it for my time: I am a brother
Of gracious order, late come from the see,
In special business from his holiness.

Escal. What news abroad i' the world?

Duke. None, but that there is so great a fever on goodness, that the dissolution of it must cure it: novelty is only in request; and it is as dangerous to be aged in any kind of course, as it is virtuous to be constant in any undertaking. There is scarce truth enough alive, to make societies secure; but security enough, to make fellowships accurs'd:[8] much upon this riddle runs the wisdom of the world. This news is old enough, yet it is every day's news. I pray you, sir, of what disposition was the duke?

Escal. One, that, above all other strifes, contended especially to know himself.

Duke. What pleasure was he given to?

Escal. Rather rejoicing to see another merry, than merry at any thing which professed to make him rejoice: a gentleman of all temperance. But leave we him to his events, with a prayer they may prove prosperous; and let me desire to know how you find Claudio prepared. I am made to understand, that you have lent him visitation.

Duke. He professes to have received no sinister measure from his judge, but most willingly humbles himself to the determination of justice: yet had he framed to himself, by the instruction of his frailty, many deceiving promises of life; which I, by my good leisure, have discredited to him, and now is he resolved[9] to die.

Escal. You have paid the heavens your function, and the prisoner the very debt of your calling. I have labour'd for the poor gentleman, to the extremest shore of my modesty; but my brother justice have I found so severe, that he hath forced me to tell him, he is indeed—justice.[10]

Duke. If his own life answer the straitness of his proceeding, it shall become him well; wherein, if he chance to fail, he hath sentenced himself.

Escal. I am going to visit the prisoner: Fare you well.

Duke. Peace be with you!

[*Exeunt* ESCALUS *and* Provost.

He, who the sword of heaven will bear,
Should be as holy as severe;
Pattern in himself to know,
Grace to stand, and virtue go;[11]
More nor less to others paying,
Than by self-offences weighing.
Shame to him, whose cruel striking
Kills for faults of his own liking!
Twice treble shame on Angelo,

---

1 i. e. inconsiderate.

2 Guided, steered through, a metaphor from navigation.

3 *Opposite*, opponent.

4 *Ungenitur'd.* This word seems to be formed from *genitoirs*, a word which occurs several times in Holland's Pliny, vol. ii. p. 321, 560, 589, and comes from the French *genitoires.*

5 A wench was called a *laced mutton.* In Doctor Faustus, 1604, Lechery says, 'I am one that loves an inch of raw *mutton* better than an ell of stock-fish.'

6 Smelt, for smelt *of.*

7 *Forfeit*, transgress, offend, from *forfaire.* Fr.

8 The allusion is to those legal *securities* into which fellowship leads men to enter for each other. For this quibble Shakspeare has high authority, 'He that hateth *suretiship is sure.*' Prov. xi. 15.

9 i. e. satisfied; probably because conviction leads to decision or resolution.

10 *Summum jus, summa injuria.*

11 This passage is very obscure, nor can it be cleared without a more licentious paraphase than the reader may be willing to allow. 'He that bears the sword of heaven should be not less holy than severe; should be able to discover in himself a pattern of such grace as can avoid temptation, and such virtue as may go abroad into the world without danger of seduction.'

To weed my vice,[1] and let his grow!
O, what may man within him hide,
Though angel on the outward side!
How may likeness, made in crimes,
Mocking,[2] practice on the times,
To draw with idle spiders' stings
Most pond'rous and substantial things!
Craft against vice I must apply:
With Angelo to-night shall lie
His old betrothed, but despised;
So disguise shall, by the disguis'd,
Pay with falsehood false exacting,
And perform an old contracting. [Exit.

ACT IV.

SCENE I. *A Room in* Mariana's *House.* MARIANA *discovered sitting; a Boy singing.*

SONG.[3]

Take, oh take those lips away,
That so sweetly were forsworn;
And those eyes, the break of day,
Lights that do mislead the morn:
But my kisses bring again,
bring again,
Seals of love, but seal'd in vain,
seal'd in vain.

Mari. Break off thy song, and haste thee quick away;
Here comes a man of comfort, whose advice
Hath often still'd my brawling discontent.— [*Exit* Boy.

Enter DUKE.

I cry you mercy, sir; and well could wish
You had not found me here so musical;
Let me excuse me, and believe me so,—
My mirth is much displeas'd, but pleas'd my woe.[4]

Duke. 'Tis good: though music oft hath such a charm,
To make bad, good, and good provoke to harm.
I pray you, tell me, hath any body inquired for me here to-day? much upon this time have I promis'd here to meet.

Mari. You have not been inquired after. I have sat here all day.

Enter ISABELLA.

Duke. I do constantly believe you:—The time is come, even now. I shall crave your forbearance a little; may be, I will call upon you anon, for some advantage to yourself.

Mari. I am always bound to you. [*Exit.*

Duke. Very well met, and welcome.
What is the news from this good deputy?

Isab. He hath a garden circummur'd[5] with brick,
Whose western side is with a vineyard back'd;
And to that vineyard is a planched[6] gate,
That makes his opening with this bigger key:
This other doth command a little door,
Which from the vineyard to the garden leads;
There have I made my promise to call on him,
Upon the heavy middle of the night.

Duke. But shall you on your knowledge find this way?

Isab. I have ta'en a due and wary note upon't
With whispering and most guilty diligence,
In action all of precept, he did show me
The way twice o'er.

Duke. Are there no other tokens
Between you 'greed, concerning her observance?

Isab. No, none, but only a repair i'the dark;
And that I have possess'd[7] him, my most stay
Can be but brief; for I have made him know,
I have a servant comes with me along,
That stays[8] upon me; whose persuasion is,
I come about my brother.

Duke. 'Tis well born up.
I have not yet made known to Mariana
A word of this:—What, ho! within! come forth!

Re-enter MARIANA.

I pray you, be acquainted with this maid;
She comes to do you good.

Isab. I do desire the like.

Duke. Do you persuade yourself that I respect you?

Mari. Good friar, I know you do; and have found it.

Duke. Take then this your companion by the hand,
Who hath a story ready for your ear:
I shall attend your leisure; but make haste;
The vaporous night approaches.

Mari. Will't please you walk aside?
[*Exeunt* MARIANA *and* ISABELLA.

Duke. O place and greatness, millions of false eyes
Are stuck upon thee! volumes of report
Run with these false and most contrarious quests[9]
Upon thy doings! thousand 'scapes[10] of wit
Make thee the father of their idle dream,
And rack thee in their fancies!—Welcome!—How agreed?

Re-enter MARIANA *and* ISABELLA.

Isab. She'll take the enterprise upon her, father,
If you advise it.

Duke. It is not my consent,
But my entreaty too.

Isab. Little have you to say,
When you depart from him, but, soft and low,
Remember now my brother.

Mari. Fear me not.

Duke. Nor, gentle daughter, fear you not at all:
He is your husband on a pre-contract:
To bring you thus together, 'tis no sin;
Sith that the justice of your title to him
Doth flourish[11] the deceit. Come, let us go;
Our corn's to reap, for yet our tilth's[12] to sow.
[*Exeunt.*

SCENE II. *A Room in the Prison. Enter* Provost *and* Clown.

Prov. Come hither, sirrah: Can you cut off a man's head?

Clo. If the man be a bachelor, sir, I can: but if he be a married man, he is his wife's head, and I can never cut off a woman's head.

---

1 The duke's *vice* may be explained by what he says himself, Act. i. Sc. 4.

——' twas *my fault* to give the people scope.'

Angelo's vice requires no explanation.

2 ' How may *likeness*, made in crimes,
Mocking, practice on the times.'

The old copies read *making*. The emendation is Mr. Malone's. The sense of this obscure passage appears to be:—' How may persons assuming the *likeness* or semblance of virtue, while they are in fact guilty of the grossest crimes, impose with this counterfeit sanctity upon the world, in order to draw to themselves by the flimsiest pretensions the most solid advantages; such as pleasure, honour, reputation, &c.'

3 It does not appear certain to whom this beautiful little song rightly belongs. It is found with an additional stanza in Fletcher's Bloody Brother. Mr. Malone prints it as Shakspeare's, Mr. Boswell thinks Fletcher has the best claim to it: Mr. Webster that Shakspeare may have written the first stanza, and Fletcher the second. It may indeed be the property of some unknown or forgotten author. Be this as it may, the reader will be pleased to have the second stanza.

' Hide, oh hide those hills of snow
Which thy frozen bosom bears,
On whose tops the pinks that glow
Are of those that April wears.
But first set my poor heart free,
Bound in those icy chains by thee.'

4 Though the music soothed my sorrows, it had no tendency to produce light merriment.

5 *Circummur'd*, walled round.

6 *Planched*, planked, wooden.

7 i. e. *informed*. Thus Shylock says—
' I have *possess'd* your grace of what I purpose.'

8 *Stays*, waits. 9 *Quests*, inquisitions, inquiries.

10 *'Scapes*, sallies, sportive wiles.

11 i. e. *ornament*, embellish an action that would otherwise seem ugly.

12 *Tilth* here means land prepared for sowing. The old copy reads *tithe*; the emendation is Warburton's

Prov. Come, sir, leave me your snatches, and yield me a direct answer. To-morrow morning are to die Claudio and Barnardine: Here is in our prison a common executioner, who in his office lacks a helper: if you will take it on you to assist him, it shall redeem you from your gyves;[1] if not, you shall have your full time of imprisonment, and your deliverance with an unpitied[2] whipping; for you have been a notorious bawd.

Clo. Sir, I have been an unlawful bawd, time out f mind; but yet I will be content to be a lawful hangman. I would be glad to receive some instruction from my fellow partner.

Prov. What ho, Abhorson! Where's Abhorson, there?

Enter ABHORSON.

Abhor. Do you call, sir?

Prov. Sirrah, here's a fellow will help you to-morrow in your execution: If you think it meet, compound with him by the year, and let him abide here with you; if not, use him for the present, and dismiss him: He cannot plead his estimation with you; he hath been a bawd.

Abhor. A bawd, sir? Fye upon him, he will discredit our mystery.

Prov. Go to, sir; you weigh equally; a feather will turn the scale. [*Exit.*

Clo. Pray, sir, by your good favour (for, surely, sir, a good favour[3] you have, but that you have a hanging look,) do you call, sir, your occupation a mystery?

Abhor. Ay, sir, a mystery.

Clo. Painting, sir, I have heard say, is a mystery; and your whores, sir, being members of my occupation, using painting, do prove my occupation a mystery: but what mystery there should be in hanging, if I should be hang'd, I cannot imagine.

Abhor. Sir, it is a mystery.

Clo. Proof.

Abhor. Every true[4] man's apparel fits your thief: If it be too little for your thief, your true man thinks it big enough; if it be too big for your thief, your thief thinks it little enough: so every true man's apparel fits your thief.[5]

Re-enter Provost.

Prov. Are you agreed?

Clo. Sir, I will serve him; for I do find, your hangman is a more penitent trade than your bawd: he doth oftener ask forgiveness.

Prov. You, sirrah, provide your block and your axe, to-morrow four o'clock.

Abhor. Come on, bawd; I will instruct thee in my trade; follow.

Clo. I do desire to learn, sir; and, I hope, if you have occasion to use me for your own turn, you shall find me yare;[6] for, truly, sir, for your kindness, I owe you a good turn.

Prov. Call hither Barnardine and Claudio:
[*Exeunt* Clown *and* ABHORSON.
One has my pity; not a jot the other,
Being a murderer, though he were my brother.

Enter CLAUDIO.

Look, here's the warrant, Claudio, for thy death;
'Tis now dead midnight, and by eight to-morrow
Thou must be made immortal. Where's Barnardine?

Claud. As fast lock'd up in sleep, as guiltless labour
When it lies starkly[7] in the traveller's bones
He will not wake.

Prov. Who can do good on him?
Well, go, prepare yourself. But hark, what noise?
[*Knocking within.*
Heaven give your spirits comfort! [*Exit* CLAUDIO.
By and by:—
I hope it is some pardon, or reprieve,
For the most gentle Claudio.—Welcome, father.

Enter Duke.

Duke. The best and wholesome spirits of the night
Envelope you, good Provost! Who call'd here of late?

Prov. None, since the curfew rung.

Duke. Not Isabel?

Prov. No.

Duke. They will then, ere't be long.

Prov. What comfort is for Claudio?

Duke. There's some in hope.

Prov. It is a bitter deputy.

Duke. Not so, not so; his life is parallel'd
Even with the stroke[8] and line of his great justice,
He doth with holy abstinence subdue
That in himself, which he spurs on his power
To qualify[9] in others: were he meal'd[10]
With that which he corrects, then were he tyrannous,
But this being so, he's just.—Now are they come.—
[*Knocking within.*—Provost *goes out*
This is a gentle provost: Seldom when[11]
The steeled gaoler is the friend of men.—
How now? What noise? That spirit's possess'd with haste,
That wounds the unsisting[12] postern with these strokes.

Provost *returns, speaking to one at the door.*

Prov. There he must stay, until the officer
Arise to let him in; he is call'd up.

Duke. Have you no countermand for Claudio yet,
But he must die to-morrow?

Prov. None, sir, none.

Duke. As near the dawning, Provost, as it is,
You shall hear more ere morning.

Prov. Happily,[13]
You something know; yet, I believe, there comes
No countermand; no such example have we:
Besides, upon the very siege[14] of justice,
Lord Angelo hath to the public ear
Profess'd the contrary.

Enter a Messenger.

Duke. This is his lordship's man.

Prov. And here comes Claudio's pardon.

Mess. My lord hath sent you this note; and by me this further charge, that you swerve not from the smallest article of it, neither in time, matter, or other circumstance. Good-morrow; for, as I take it, it is almost day.

Prov. I shall obey him. [*Exit* Messenger.

Duke. This is his pardon; purchas'd by such sin.
[*Aside.*
For which the pardoner himself is in:
Hence hath offence his quick celerity,
When it is borne in high authority:
When vice makes mercy, mercy's so extended,

1 i. e. fetters.
2 i. e. a whipping that none shall pity.
3 *Favour* is countenance. 4 i. e. honest.
5 Warburton says, 'this proves the *thief's* trade a mystery, not the hangman's,' and therefore supposes that a speech in which the hangman proved his trade a mystery is lost, part of this last speech being in the old editions given to the clown. But Heath observes, 'The argument of the hangman is exactly similar to that of the clown. As the latter puts in his claim to the whores as members of his occupation, and in virtue of their painting would enroll his own fraternity in the mystery of painters so the former equally lays claim to the thieves as members of his occupation, and in their right endeavours to rank his brethren the hangmen under the mystery of fitters of apparel, or tailors.'
6 i. e. ready. 7 i. e. strongly.

8 *Stroke* is here put for the *stroke* of a pen, or a line.
9 To *qualify* is to temper, to moderate.
10 *Meal'd* appears to mean here sprinkled, o'erdusted, defiled; I cannot think that in this instance it has any relation to the verb *to mell*, meddle or mix with
11 This is absurdly printed Seldom, when, &c. in all the late editions. '*Seldom-when* (i. e. *rarely*, *not often*) is the steeled gaoler the friend of men.' Thus in old phraseology we have *seldom-time*, *any-when*, &c. The comma between seldom and when is not in the old copy, but an arbitrary addition of some editor.
12 The old copies read thus.—Monck Mason proposed, *unlisting*, i. e. unheeding, which is intelligible. But I prefer Sir W. Blackstone's suggestion, that *unsisting* may signify 'never at rest,' always opening.
13 *Hapily*, *haply*, perhaps the old orthography of the word.
14 i. e. seat.

That for the fault's love, is the offender friended.— Now, sir, what news?

Prov. I told you: Lord Angelo, be-like, thinking me remiss in mine office, awakens me with this unwonted putting on:[1] methinks, strangely; for he hath not used it before.

Duke. Pray you, let's hear.

Prov. [Reads.] *Whatever you may hear to the contrary, let Claudio be executed by four of the clock; and, in the afternoon, Barnardine; for my better satisfaction, let me have Claudio's head sent me by five. Let this be duly performed; with a thought, that more depends on it than we must yet deliver. Thus fail not to do your office, as you will answer it at your peril.* What say you to this, sir?

Duke. What is that Barnardine, who is to be executed in the afternoon?

Prov. A Bohemian born, but here nursed up and bred; one that is a prisoner nine years old.[2]

Duke. How came it that the absent duke had not either deliver'd him to his liberty, or executed him? I have heard, it was ever his manner to do so.

Prov. His friends still wrought reprieves for him: And, indeed, his fact, till now in the government of Lord Angelo, came not to an undoubtful proof.

Duke. Is it now apparent?

Prov. Most manifest, and not denied by himself.

Duke. Hath he borne himself penitently in prison? How seems he to be touched?

Prov. A man that apprehends death no more dreadfully, but as a drunken sleep: careless, reckless, and fearless of what's past, present, or to come; insensible of mortality, and desperately mortal.[3]

Duke. He wants advice.

Prov. He will hear none: he hath evermore had the liberty of the prison; give him leave to escape hence, he would not: drunk many times a day, if not many days entirely drunk. We have very often awaked him, as if to carry him to execution, and show'd him a seeming warrant for it: it hath not moved him at all.

Duke. More of him anon. There is written in your brow, Provost, honesty and constancy: if I read it not truly, my ancient skill beguiles me: but in the boldness of my cunning,[4] I will lay myself in hazard. Claudio, whom here you have a warrant to execute, is no greater forfeit to the law than Angelo who hath sentenced him: To make you understand this in a manifested effect, I crave but four days' respite; for the which you are to do me both a present and a dangerous courtesy.

Prov. Pray, sir, in what?

Duke. In the delaying death.

Prov. Alack! how may I do it? having the hour limited; and an express command, under penalty, to deliver his head in the view of Angelo? I may make my case as Claudio's, to cross this in the smallest.

Duke. By the vow of mine order, I warrant you, if my instructions may be your guide. Let this Barnardine be this morning executed, and his head borne to Angelo.

Prov. Angelo hath seen them both, and will discover the favour.[5]

Duke. O, death's a great disguiser: and you may add to it. Shave the head, and tie the beard; and say, it was the desire of the penitent to be so bared before his death: You know, the course is common.[6] If any thing fall to you upon this, more than thanks and good fortune, by the saint whom I profess, I will plead against it with my life.

Prov. Pardon me, good father; it is against my oath.

Duke. Were you sworn to the duke, or to the deputy?

Prov. To him, and to his substitutes.

Duke. You will think you have made no offence, if the duke avouch the justice of your dealing?

Prov. But what likelihood is in that?

Duke. Not a resemblance, but a certainty. Yet since I see you fearful, that neither my coat, integrity, nor my persuasion, can with ease attempt you, I will go further than I meant, to pluck all fears out of you. Look you, sir, here is the hand and seal of the duke. You know the character, I doubt not; and the signet is not strange to you.

Prov. I know them both.

Duke. The contents of this is the return of the duke; you shall anon overread it at your pleasure; where you shall find, within these two days he will be here. This is a thing that Angelo knows not: for he this very day receives letters of strange tenor; perchance, of the duke's death; perchance, entering into some monastery; but, by chance, nothing of what is writ.[7] Look, the unfolding star calls up the shepherd.[8] Put not yourself into amazement, how these things should be: all difficulties are but easy when they are known. Call your executioner, and off with Barnardine's head: I will give him a present shrift, and advise him for a better place. Yet you are amazed; but this shall absolutely resolve[9] you. Come away; it is almost clear dawn. [*Exeunt.*

SCENE III. *Another Room in the same. Enter* Clown.

Clo. I am as well acquainted here, as I was in our house of profession: one would think it were mistress Overdone's own house, for here be many of her old customers. First, here's young master Rash;[10] he's in for a commodity of brown paper and old ginger, ninescore and seventeen pounds; of which he made five marks, ready money:[11] marry, then, ginger was not much in request, for the old women were all dead. Then is there here one master Caper, at the suit of master Three-pile the mercer, for some four suits of peach-colour'd satin, which now peaches him a beggar. Then have we here young Dizy, and young master Deep-vow, and master Copper-spur, and master Starve-lackey the rapier and dagger man, and young Drop-heir that kill'd lusty Pudding, and master Forthright the tilter, and brave master Shoe-tie the great traveller, and wild Half-can that stabb'd Pots, and, I think, forty more; all great doers in our trade, and are now for the Lord's sake.[12]

Enter ABHORSON.

Abhor. Sirrah, bring Barnardine hither.

Clo. Master Barnardine! you must rise and be hang'd, master Barnardine!

---

1 *Putting on* is spur, incitement.

2 i. e. nine years in prison.

3 Perhaps we should read *mortally desperate.* As we have harmonious charmingly for charmingly harmonious, in the Tempest.

4 i. e. in *confidence* of my *sagacity.*

5 Countenance.

6 'Shave the head and tie the beard—the course is common.' This probably alludes to a practice among Roman Catholics of desiring to receive the *tonsure* of the monks before they died.

7 'What is writ;' we should read '*here* writ;' the Duke pointing to the letter in his hand.

8 So Milton in Comus:—
'The star that bids the shepherd fold
Now the top of heaven doth hold.'

9 i. e. convince you.

10 This enumeration of the inhabitants of the prison, affords a very striking view of the practices predominant in Shakspeare's age. Besides those whose follies are common to all times, we have four fighting men and a traveller. It is not unlikely that the originals of the pictures were then known. *Rash* was a silken stuff formerly worn in coats: all the names are characteristic

11 It was the practice of money lenders in Shakspeare's time, as well as more recently, to make advances partly in goods and partly in cash. The goods were to be resold generally at an enormous loss upon the cost price, and of these commodities it appears that *brown paper* and *ginger* often formed a part.

12 It appears from Davies's Epigrams, 1611, that this was the language in which prisoners who were confined for debt addressed passengers;—
'Good gentle writers, *for the Lord's sake, for the Lord's sake,*
Like *Ludgate prisoners*, lo, I, begging, make
My mone'

Abhor. What, ho, Barnardine!

Barnar. [*Within.*] A pox o' your throats! Who makes that noise there? What are you?

Clo. Your friends, sir; the hangman: You must be so good, sir, to rise and be put to death.

Barnar. [*Within.*] Away, you rogue, away; I am sleepy.

Abhor. Tell him, he must awake, and that quickly too.

Clo. Pray, master Barnardine, awake till you are executed, and sleep afterwards.

Abhor. Go in to him, and fetch him out.

Clo. He is coming, sir, he is coming; I hear his straw rustle.

Enter BARNARDINE.

Abhor. Is the axe upon the block, sirrah?

Clo. Very ready, sir.

Barnar. How now, Abhorson? what's the news with you?

Abhor. Truly, sir, I would desire you to clap into your prayers; for, look you, the warrant's come.

Barnar. You rogue, I have been drinking all night, I am not fitted for't.

Clo. O, the better, sir; for he that drinks all night, and is hanged betimes in the morning, may sleep the sounder all the next day.

Enter Duke.

Abhor. Look you, sir, here comes your ghostly father; Do we jest now, think you?

Duke. Sir, induced by my charity, and hearing how hastily you are to depart, I am come to advise you, comfort you, and pray with you.

Barnar. Friar, not I; I have been drinking hard all night, and I will have more time to prepare me, or they shall beat out my brains with billets: I will not consent to die this day, that's certain.

Duke. O, sir, you must: and therefore, I beseech you,
Look forward on the journey you shall go.

Barnar. I swear, I will not die to-day for any man's persuasion.

Duke. But hear you.——

Barnar. Not a word; if you have any thing to say to me, come to my ward; for thence will not I to-day. [*Exit.*

Enter Provost.

Duke. Unfit to live, or die: O, gravel heart!—
After him, fellows; bring him to the block.
[*Exeunt* ABHORSON *and* Clown.

Prov. Now, sir, how do you find the prisoner?

Duke. A creature unprepar'd, unmeet for death;
And, to transport[1] him in the mind he is,
Were damnable.

Prov. Here in the prison, father,
There died this morning of a cruel fever
One Ragozine, a most notorious pirate,
A man of Claudio's years; his beard and head,
Just of his colour: What if we do omit
This reprobate, till he were well inclined;
And satisfy the deputy with the visage
Of Ragozine, more like to Claudio?

Duke. O, 'tis an accident that heaven provides!
Despatch it presently; the hour draws on
Prefix'd by Angelo; See, this be done,
And sent according to command; whiles I
Persuade this rude wretch willingly to die.

Prov. This shall be done, good father, presently.
But Barnardine must die this afternoon:
And how shall we continue Claudio,
To save me from the danger that might come,
If he were known alive?

Duke. Let this be done:—Put them in secret holds,
Both Barnardine and Claudio; Ere twice
The sun hath made his journal greeting to
The under generation,[2] you shall find
Your safety manifested.

Prov. I am your free dependant.

Duke. Quick, despatch,
And send the head to Angelo. [*Exit* Provost.
Now will I write letters to Angelo,—
The provost he shall bear them,—whose contents
Shall witness to him I am near at home;
And that by great injunctions, I am bound
To enter publicly: him I'll desire
To meet me at the consecrated fount,
A league below the city; and from thence,
By cold gradation and weal-balanced form,
We shall proceed with Angelo.

Re-enter Provost.

Prov. Here is the head; I'll carry it myself.

Duke. Convenient is it: Make a swift return,
For I would commune with you of such things,
That want no ear but yours.

Prov. I'll make all speed.
[*Exit.*

Isab. [*Within*] Peace, ho, be here!

Duke. The tongue of Isabel;—She's come to know,
If yet her brother's pardon be come hither;
But I will keep her ignorant of her good,
To make her heavenly comforts of despair,
When it is least expected.

Enter ISABELLA.

Isab. Ho, by your leave.

Duke. Good morning to you fair and gracious daughter.

Isab. The better given me by so holy a man.
Hath yet the deputy sent my brother's pardon?

Duke. He hath releas'd him, Isabel, from the world;
His head is off, and sent to Angelo

Isab. Nay, but it is not so.

Duke. It is no other
Show your wisdom, daughter, in your close patience.

Isab. O, I will to him, and pluck out his eyes.

Duke. You shall not be admitted to his sight.

Isab. Unhappy Claudio! Wretched Isabel!
Injurious world! Most damned Angelo!

Duke. This nor hurts him, nor profits you a jot:
Forbear it therefore; give your cause to heaven.
Mark what I say, which you shall find
By every syllable a faithful verity:
The duke comes home to-morrow;—nay, dry your eyes;
One of our convent and his confessor,
Gives me this instance: Already he hath carried
Notice to Escalus and Angelo;
Who do prepare to meet him at the gates,
There to give up their power. If you can, pace your wisdom
In that good path that I would wish to go;
And you shall have your bosom[3] on this wretch,
Grace of the duke, revenges to your heart,
And general honour.

Isab. I am directed by you.

Duke. This letter then to friar Peter give;
'Tis that he sent me of the duke's return:
Say, by this token, I desire his company
At Mariana's house to-night. Her cause and yours,
I'll perfect him withal; and he shall bring you
Before the duke; and to the head of Angelo
Accuse him home, and home. For my poor self,
I am combined[4] by a sacred vow,
And shall be absent. Wend[5] you with this letter
Command these fretting waters from your eyes
With a light heart; trust not my holy order,
If I pervert your course.—Who's here?

Enter LUCIO.

Lucio. Good even
Friar, where is the Provost?

---

1 i. e. to remove him from one world to another. The French *trepas* affords a kindred sense.

2 The *under generation*, the antipodes.

3 Your *bosom*, is your heart's desire, your wish.

4 Shakspeare uses *combine* for *to bind by a pact or agreement*; so he calls Angelo the *combinate* husband of Mariana.

5 i. e. Go.

Duk. Not within, sir.

Lucio. O, pretty Isabella, I am pale at mine heart, to see thine eyes so red: thou must be patient: I am fain to dine and sup with water and bran; I dare not for my head fill my belly; one fruitful meal would set me to't: But they say the duke will be here to-morrow. By my troth, Isabel, I lov'd thy brother: if the old fantastical duke of dark corners had been at home, he had lived.

[*Exit* Isabella.

Duke. Sir, the duke is marvellous little beholden to your reports; but the best is he lives not in them.[1]

Lucio. Friar, thou knowest not the duke so well as I do: he's a better woodman[2] than thou takest him for.

Duke. Well, you'll answer this one day. Fare ye well.

Lucio. Nay, tarry; I'll go along with thee; I can tell thee pretty tales of the duke.

Duke. You have told me too many of him already, sir, if they be true; if not true, none were enough.

Lucio. I was once before him for getting a wench with child.

Duke. Did you such a thing?

Lucio. Yes, marry, did I; but was fain to forswear it; they would else have married me to the rotten meddlar.

Duke. Sir, your company is fairer than honest: Rest you well.

Lucio. By my troth, I'll go with thee to the lane's end: If bawdy talk offend you, we'll have very little of it: Nay, friar I am a kind of burr, I shall stick.

[*Exeunt.*

SCENE IV. *A Room in* Angelo's *House. Enter* Angelo *and* Escalus.

Escal. Every letter he hath writ hath disvouch'd[3] other.

Ang. In most uneven and distracted manner. His actions show much like to madness: pray heaven, his wisdom be not tainted! And why meet him at the gates, and redeliver our authorities there?

Escal. I guess not.

Ang. And why should we proclaim it in an hour before his entering, that, if any crave redress of injustice, they should exhibit their petitions in the street?

Escal. He shows his reason for that: to have a despatch of complaints; and to deliver us from devices hereafter, which shall then have no power to stand against us.

Ang. Well, I beseech you, let it be proclaim'd:
Betimes i' the morn, I'll call you at your house:
Give notice to such men of sort and suit,[4]
As are to meet him.

Escal. I shall, sir: fare you well.

[*Exit.*

Ang. Good night.—
This deed unshapes me quite, makes me unpregnant,[5]
And dull to all proceeding. A deflower'd maid!
And by an eminent body, that enforc'd
The law against it!—But that her tender shame
Will not proclaim against her maiden loss,
How might she tongue me? Yet reason dares[6] her?—no:
For my authority bears a credent[7] bulk,
That no particular[8] scandal once can touch,
But it confounds the breather.[9] He should have liv'd,
Save that his riotous youth, with dangerous sense
Might in the times to come, have ta'en revenge,
By so receiving a dishonour'd life,
With ransom of such shame. 'Would yet he had liv'd!
Alack, when once our grace we have forgot,
Nothing goes right; we would and we would not.

[*Exit.*[10]

SCENE V. *Fields without the Town. Enter* Duke *in his own habit, and Friar* Peter.

Duke. These letters at fit time deliver me.

[*Giving letters.*

The Provost knows our purpose, and our plot.
The matter being afoot, keep your instruction,
And hold you ever to our special drift;
Though sometimes you do blench[11] from this to that,
As cause doth minister. Go, call at Flavius' house,
And tell him where I stay: give the like notice
To Valentinus, Rowland, and to Crassus,
And bid them bring the trumpets to the gates;
But send me Flavius first.

F. Peter. It shall be speeded well.

[*Exit.* Friar

Enter Varrius.

Duke. I thank thee, Varrius; thou hast made good haste:
Come we will walk: There's other of our friends
Will greet us here anon, my gentle Varrius.

[*Exeunt.*

SCENE VI. *Street near the City Gate. Enter* Isabella *and* Mariana.

Isab. To speak so indirectly, I am loath;
I would say the truth; but to accuse him so,
That is your part: Yet I'm advis'd to do it;
He says, to 'vailful[12] purpose.

Mari. Be rul'd by him.

Isab. Besides, he tells me, that, if peradventure
He speak against me on the adverse side,
I should not think it strange; for 'tis a physic,
That's bitter to sweet end.

Mari. I would, friar Peter—

Isab. O, peace; the friar is come.

Enter Friar Peter.[13]

F. Peter. Come, I have found you out a stand most fit,
Where you may have such vantage on the duke,
He shall not pass you; Twice have the trumpets sounded;
The generous[14] and the gravest citizens,
Have hent[15] the gates, and very near upon
The Duke is ent'ring; therefore, hence, away.

[*Exeunt*

ACT V.

SCENE I. *A public Place near the City Gate.*

Mariana, (*veil'd,*) Isabella, *and* Peter, *at a distance. Enter at opposite doors,* Duke, Varrius, Lords; Angelo, Escalus, Lucio, Provost, Officers, *and* Citizens.

---

1 i. e. he depends not on them.

2 A *woodman* was an attendant on the forester; his great employment was hunting. It is here used in a wanton sense for a hunter of a different sort of game. So, Falstaff asks his mistresses in the Merry Wives of Windsor:—

——'Am I a woodman? Ha!'

3 *Disvouched* is contradicted.

4 Figure and rank.

5 Unready, unprepared; the contrary to *pregnant* in its sense of ready, apprehensive.

6 *To dare* has two significations; to *terrify*, as in The Maid's Tragedy;—

'——those mad mischiefs
Would *dare* a woman.'

And to *challenge* or *call forth*, as in K. Henry IV. p. 1.

'Unless a brother should a brother *dare*
To gentle exercise,' &c.

This passage will therefore bear two interpretations. between which the reader must choose.

7 *Credent*, creditable, not questionable.

8 *Particular* is *private*: a French sense of the word.

9 i. e. utterer.

10 Dr. Johnson thought the fourth Act should end here, 'for here is properly a cessation of action, a night intervenes, and the place is changed between the passages of this scene and those of the next. The fifth Act, beginning with the following scene, would proceed without any interruption of time or place.'

11 To *blench*, to start off, to fly off.

12 Availful.

13 He is called friar *Thomas* in the first Act.

14 *Generous*, for most noble, or those of rank. *Generosi*, Lat.

15 i. e. seized, laid hold on

Duke. My very worthy cousin, fairly met:—
Our old and faithful friend, we are glad to see you.
Ang. and Escal. Happy return be to your royal grace!
Duke. Many and hearty thankings to you both.
We have made inquiry of you; and we hear
Such goodness of your justice, that our soul
Cannot but yield you forth to public thanks,
Forerunning more requital.
Ang. You make my bonds still greater.
Duke. O, your desert speaks loud; and I should wrong it,
To lock it in the wards of covert bosom,
When it deserves of characters of brass
A forted residence, 'gainst the tooth of time,
And razure of oblivion: Give me your hand,
And let the subject see, to make them know
That outward courtesies would fain proclaim
Favours that keep within.—Come, Escalus;
You must walk by us on our other hand;—
And good supporters are you.

PETER *and* ISABELLA *come forward.*

F. Peter. Now is your time; speak loud, and kneel before him.
Isab. Justice, O royal duke! Vail[1] your regard,
Upon a wrong'd, I'd fain have said, a maid!
O worthy prince, dishonour not your eye
By throwing it on any other object,
Till you have heard me in my true complaint,
And given me, justice, justice, justice, justice!
Duke. Relate your wrongs: In what? by whom? Be brief:
Here is Lord Angelo shall give you justice!
Reveal yourself to him.
Isab. O, worthy duke,
You bid me seek redemption of the devil:
Hear me yourself; for that which I must speak
Must either punish me, not being believ'd,
Or wring redress from you; hear me, O, hear me, here.
Ang. My lord, her wits, I fear me, are not firm:
She hath been a suitor to me for her brother,
Cut off by course of justice.
Isab. By course of justice!
Ang. And she will speak most bitterly and strange.
Isab. Most strange, but yet most truly, will I [speak:
That Angelo's forsworn, is it not strange?
That Angelo's a murderer; is't not strange?
That Angelo is an adulterous thief,
An hypocrite, a virgin-violator;
Is it not strange, and strange?
Duke. Nay, ten times strange.
Isab. It is not truer he is Angelo,
Than this is all as true as it is strange:
Nay, it is ten times true; for truth is truth
To the end of reckoning.
Duke. Away with her:—Poor soul.
She speaks this in the infirmity of sense.
Isab. O prince, I conjure thee, as thou believ'st
There is another comfort than this world,
That thou neglect me not, with that opinion
That I am touch'd with madness: make not impossible
That which but seems unlike: 'tis not impossible
But one the wicked'st catiff on the ground,
May seem as shy, as grave, as just, as absolute,
As Angelo; even so may Angelo,
In all his dressings,[2] characts,[3] titles, forms,
Be an arch villain: believe it, royal prince,
If he be less, he's nothing; but he's more,
Had I more name for badness.
Duke. By mine honesty
If she be mad (as I believe no other,)
Her madness hath the oddest frame of sense,
Such a dependency of thing on thing,
As e'er I heard in madness.
Isab. O, gracious duke,
Harp not on that; nor do not banish reason
For inequality:[4] but let your reason serve
To make the truth appear, where it seems hid,
And hide the false, seems true.[5]
Duke. Many that are not mad,
Have, sure, more lack of reason.—What would you say?
Isab. I am the sister of one Claudio,
Condemn'd upon the act of fornication
To lose his head; condemn'd by Angelo:
I, in probation of a sisterhood,
Was sent to by my brother: One Lucio
As then the messenger;—
Lucio. That's I, an't like your grace
I came to her from Claudio, and desir'd her
To try her gracious fortune with Lord Angelo,
For her poor brother's pardon.
Isab. That's he, indeed
Duke. You were not bid to speak.
Lucio. No, my good lord;
Nor wish'd to hold my peace.
Duke. I wish you now then
Pray you, take note of it: and when you have
A business for yourself, pray heaven you then
Be perfect.
Lucio. I warrant your honour.
Duke. The warrant's for yourself; take heed to it.
Isab. This gentleman told somewhat of my tale.
Lucio. Right.
Duke. It may be right; but you are in the wrong
To speak before your time.—Proceed.
Isab. I went
To this pernicious caitiff deputy.
Duke. That's somewhat madly spoken.
Isab. Pardon it.
The phrase is to the matter.[6]
Duke. Mended again: the matter;—Proceed.
Isab. In brief,—to set the needless process by,
How I persuaded, how I pray'd, and kneel'd,
How he refell'd[7] me, and how I reply'd;
(For this was of much length,) the vile conclusion
I now begin with grief and shame to utter:
He would not, but by gift of my chaste body
To his concupiscible intemperate lust,
Release my brother; and, after much debatement,
My sisterly remorse[8] confutes mine honour,
And I did yield to him. But the next morn betimes.
His purpose surfeiting, he sends a warrant
For my poor brother's head.
Duke. This is most likely!
Isab. O, that it were as like as it is true![9]
Duke. By heaven, fond[10] wretch, thou know'st not what thou speak'st;
Or else thou art suborn'd against his honour,
In hateful practice:[11] First, his integrity
Stands without blemish:—next, it imports no reason
That with such vehemency he should pursue
Faults proper to himself: if he had so offended,
He would have weigh'd thy brother by himself,
And not have cut him off: Some one hath set you on,

1 To *vail* is to lower, to *let fall*, to cast down.
2 i. e. habiliments of office.
3 *Characts* are *distinctive marks* or characters. A statute of Edward VI. directs the seals of office of every bishop to have 'certain *characts* under the king's arms for the knowledge of the diocess.'
4 The meaning appears to be 'do not suppose me mad because I speak inconsistently or *unequally*.'
5 I must say with Mr. Steevens that 'I do not profess to understand these words.' Mr. Phelps proposes to read 'And *hid*, the false seems true.' i. e. 'The truth being hid, not discovered or made known, what is false seems true.'
6 i. e. *suited* to the matter; as in Hamlet: 'the phrase would be more german to the matter.'
7 *Refell'd* is refuted.
8 *Remorse* is pity.
9 The meaning appears to be 'O, that it had as much of the likeness or appearance, as it has of the reality of truth.'
10 i. e. foolish.
11 *Practice* was used by the old writers for any *insidious stratagem or treachery.*

Confess the truth, and say by whose advice
Thou cam'st here to complain.
Isab And is this all?
Then, oh, you blessed ministers above,
Keep me in patience; and, with ripen'd time,
Unfold the evil which is here wrapt up
In countenance![1]—Heaven shield your grace from woe,
As I, thus wrong'd, hence unbelieved go!
Duke. I know, you'd fain be gone:—An officer!
To prison with her:—Shall we thus permit
A blasting and a scandalous breath to fall
On him so near us? This needs must be a practice.
Who knew of your intent, and coming hither?
Isab. One that I would were here, friar Lodowick.
Duke. A ghostly father, belike:—Who knows that Lodowick?
Lucio. My lord, I know him; 'tis a meddling friar;
I do not like the man: had he been lay, my lord,
For certain words he spake against your grace
In your retirement, I had swing'd him soundly.
Duke. Words against me? This a good friar belike!
And to set on this wretched woman here
Against our substitute!—Let this friar be found.
Lucio. But yesternight, my lord, she and that friar
I saw them at the prison: a saucy friar,
A very scurvy fellow.
F. Peter. Blessed be your royal grace!
I have stood by, my lord, and I have heard
Your royal ear abus'd: First, hath this woman,
Most wrongfully accus'd your substitute;
Who is as free from touch or soil with her,
As she from one ungot.
Duke. We did believe no less.
Know you that friar Lodowick that she speaks of!
F. Peter. I know him for a man divine and holy;
Not scurvy nor a temporary meddler,[2]
As he's reported by this gentleman:
And, on my trust, a man that never yet
Did, as he vouches, misreport your grace.
Lucio. My lord, most villanously; believe it.
F. Peter. Well, he in time may come to clear himself;
But at this instant he is sick, my lord,
Of a strange fever: Upon his mere[3] request
(Being come to knowledge that there was complaint
Intended 'gainst lord Angelo) came I hither,
To speak, as from his mouth, what he doth know
Is true, and false; and what he with his oath,
And all probation, will make up full clear,
Whensoever he's convented.[4] First, for this woman
(To justify this worthy nobleman,
So vulgarly[5] and personally accused;)
Her shall you hear disproved to her eyes,
Till she herself confess it.
Duke. Good friar, let's hear it.
[ISABELLA *is carried off, guarded; and* MARIANA *comes forward.*
Do you not smile at this, lord Angelo!—
O heaven! the vanity of wretched fools!—
Give us some seats.—Come, cousin Angelo;
In this I'll be impartial;[6] be you judge
Of your own cause.—Is this the witness, friar?
First, let her show her face; and, after, speak.
Mari. Pardon, my lord; I will not show my face
Until my husband bid me.
Duke. What, are you married?
Mari. No, my lord.
Duke. Are you a maid?
Mari. No, my lord.
Duke. A widow then?
Mari. Neither, my lord?
Duke. Why, you
Are nothing then:—Neither maid, widow, nor wife?
Lucio. My lord, she may be a punk; for many of them are neither maid, widow, nor wife.
Duke. Silence that fellow; I would he had some cause
To prattle for himself.
Lucio. Well, my lord.
Mari. My lord, I do confess I ne'er was married,
And, I confess, besides, I am no maid:
I have known my husband; yet my husband knows not,
That ever he knew me.
Lucio. He was drunk then, my lord; it can be no better.
Duke. For the benefit of silence, 'would thou wert so too.
Lucio. Well, my lord.
Duke. This is no witness for lord Angelo.
Mari. Now I come to't, my lord:
She, that accuses him of fornication,
In selfsame manner doth accuse my husband;
And charges him, my lord, with such a time,
When I'll depose I had him in mine arms,
With all the effect of love.
Ang. Charges she more than me?
Mari. Not that I know.
Duke. No? you say, your husband.
Mari. Why, just, my lord, and that is Angelo,
Who thinks, he knows, that he ne'er knew my body,
But knows, he thinks, that he knew Isabel's.
Ang. This is a strange abuse:[7]—Let's see thy face.
Mari. My husband bids me; now I will unmask. [*Unveiling.*
This is that face, thou cruel Angelo,
Which, once thou swor'st, was worth the looking on:
This is the hand, which, with a vow'd contract,
Was fast belock'd in thine: this is the body
That took away the match from Isabel,
And did supply thee at thy garden-house,[8]
In her imagin'd person.
Duke. Know you this woman?
Lucio. Carnally, she says.
Duke. Sirrah, no more.
Lucio. Enough, my lord.
Ang. My lord, I must confess, I know this woman:
And, five years since, there was some speech of marriage
Betwixt myself and her; which was broke off,
Partly, for that her promised proportions
Came short of composition;[9] but, in chief,
For that her reputation was disvalued
In levity: since which time of five years,
I never spake with her, saw her, nor heard from her,
Upon my faith and honour.
Mari. Noble prince,
As there comes light from heaven, and words from breath,

---

1 i. e. false appearance.

2 It is hard to know what is meant by a *temporary meddler*, perhaps it was intended to signify '*one who introduced himself* as often as he could find opportunity *into other men's concerns.*'

3 *Mere* here means *absolute.*

4 *Convented*, cited, summoned. 5 i. e. publicly.

6 *Impartial* was used sometimes in the sense of *partial;* and that appears to be the sense here. In the language of the time, *im* was frequently used as an intensive or augmentative particle. *Un*partial was sometimes used in the modern sense of impartial. Yet Shakspeare uses the word in its proper sense in Richard II. Act i. Sc. 2.

'Mowbray, *impartial* are our eyes and ears,' &c.
'* * * *
Should nothing privilege him nor *partialize.*'

7 *Abuse* stands in this place for *deception* or *puzzle.* So in Macbeth:

'——My strange and self *abuse,*'

means this *strange deception* of myself.

8 *Garden houses* were formerly much in fashion, and often used as places of clandestine meeting and intrigue. They were chiefly such buildings as we should now call *summer houses*, standing in a walled or enclosed garden in the suburbs of London. See Stubb's Anatomie of Abuses, p. 57. 4to. 1597, or Reed's Old Plays, Vol. V. p. 84.

9 Her fortune which was promised *proportionate* to mine fell short of the *composition*, i. e. contract or bargain.

As there is sense in truth, and truth in virtue,
I am affianc'd this man's wife, as strongly
As words could make up vows: and, my good lord,
But Tuesday night last gone, in his garden-house,
He knew me as a wife: As this is true
Let me in safety raise me from my knees;
Or else for ever be confixed here,
A marble monument!

Ang. I did but smile till now;
Now, good my lord, give me the scope of justice;
My patience here is touch'd: I do perceive,
These poor informal[1] women are no more
But instruments of some more mightier member,
That sets them on: Let me have way, my lord,
To find this practice out.

Duke. Ay, with my heart;
And punish them unto your height of pleasure.—
Thou foolish friar; and thou pernicious woman,
Compact with her that's gone! think'st thou, thy oaths,
Though they would swear down each particular saint,
Were testimonies against his worth and credit,
That's seal'd in approbation?[2]—You, lord Escalus,
Sit with my cousin; lend him your kind pains
To find out this abuse, whence 'tis deriv'd.—
There is another friar that sets them on;
Let him be sent for.

F. Peter. Would he were here, my lord; for he, indeed,
Hath set the women on to this complaint:
Your provost knows the place where he abides,
And he may fetch him.

Duke. Go, do it instantly.— [*Exit* Provost.
And you, my noble and well-warranted cousin,
Whom it concerns to hear this matter forth,[3]
Do with your injuries as seems you best,
In any chastisement: I for a while
Will leave you; but stir not you, till you have well
Determined upon these slanderers.

Escal. My lord, we'll do it thoroughly.—[*Exit* Duke.] Signior Lucio, did not you say, you knew that friar Lodowick to be a dishonest person?

Lucio. *Cucullus non facit monachum:* honest in nothing, but in his clothes; and one that hath spoke most villanous speeches of the duke.

Escal. We shall entreat you to abide here till he come, and enforce them against him: we shall find this friar a notable fellow.

Lucio. As any in Vienna, on my word.

Escal. Call that same Isabel here once again; [*To an Attendant.*] I would speak with her: Pray you, my lord, give me leave to question; you shall see how I'll handle her.

Lucio. Not better than he, by her own report.

Escal. Say you?

Lucio. Marry, sir, I think, if you handled her privately, she would sooner confess; perchance, publicly, she'll be ashamed.

Re-enter Officers, *with* Isabella, *the* Duke, *in the Friar's habit, and* Provost.

Escal. I will go darkly to work with her.

Lucio. That's the way; for women are light[4] at midnight.

Escal. Come on, mistress: [*To* Isabella.] here's a gentlewoman denies all that you have said.

Lucio. My lord, here comes the rascal I spoke of: here with the provost.

Escal. In very good time:—speak not you to him, till we call upon you.

Lucio. Mum.

Escal. Come, sir: Did you set these women on to slander lord Angelo? they have confess'd you did.

Duke. 'Tis false.

Escal. How! know you where you are?

Duke. Respect to your great place! and let the devil
Be sometimes honour'd for his burning throne:—
Where is the duke? 'tis he should hear me speak.

Escal. The duke's in us; and he will hear you speak;
Look, you speak justly.

Duke. Boldly, at least:—But, O, poor souls,
Come you to seek the lamb here of the fox?
Good night to your redress. Is the duke gone?
Then is your cause gone too. The duke's unjust,
Thus to retort[5] your manifest appeal,
And put your trial in the villain's mouth,
Which here you come to accuse.

Lucio. This is the rascal: this is he I spoke of.

Escal. Why, thou unreverend and unhallow'd friar!
Is't not enough, thou hast suborn'd these women
To accuse this worthy man; but, in foul mouth,
And in the witness of his proper ear,
To call him villain?
And then to glance from him to the duke himself;
To tax him with injustice?—Take him hence;
To the rack with him:—We'll touze you joint by joint,
But we will know this purpose:—What! unjust?

Duke. Be not so hot; the duke
Dare no more stretch this finger of mine, than he
Dare rack his own; his subject am I not,
Nor here provincial:[6] My business in this state
Made me a looker-on here in Vienna,
Where I have seen corruption boil and bubble,
Till it o'errun the stew: laws, for all faults;
But faults so countenanc'd, that the strong statutes
Stand like the forfeits in a barber's shop,
As much in mock as mark.[7]

Escal. Slander to the state! Away with him to prison.

Ang. What can you vouch against him, signior Lucio?
Is this the man that you did tell us of?

Lucio. 'Tis he, my lord. Come hither, goodman bald-pate: Do you know me?

Duke. I remember, you, sir, by the sound of your voice: I met you at the prison in the absence of the duke.

Lucio. O, did you so? And do you remember what you said of the duke?

Duke. Most notedly, sir.

Lucio. Do you so, sir? And was the duke a flesh-monger, a fool, and a coward, as you then reported him to be?

Duke. You must, sir, change persons with me, ere you make that my report: you, indeed spoke so of him; and much more, much worse.

Lucio. O thou damnable fellow! Did not I pluck thee by the nose, for thy speeches?

Duke. I protest, I love the duke, as I love myself.

Ang. Hark! how the villain would close now, after his treasonable abuses.

Escal. Such a fellow is not to be talk'd withal:—
Away with him to prison:—Where is the provost?

---

1 *Informal* signifies *out of their senses.* So in the Comedy of Errors, Act. v. Sc. 1.

'To make of him a *formal* man again.'

The speaker had just before said that she would keep Antipholis of Syracuse, who is behaving like a madman, 'till she had brought him to his right wits again.

2 *Stamped* or *sealed*, as tried and *approved.*

3 i. e. out, to the end.

4 This is one of the words on which Shakspeare delights to quibble. Thus Portia, in the Merchant of Venice,

'Let me give *light*, but let me not be *light*'

5 To *retort* is to refer back.

6 'His subject am I not; nor here *provincial. Provincial* is pertaining to a province; most usually taken for the circuit of an ecclesiastical jurisdiction. The chief or head of any religious order in such a province was called the provincial, to whom alone the members of that order were accountable.

7 Barbers' shops were anciently places of great resort for passing away time in an idle manner. By way of enforcing some kind of regularity, and perhaps, at least as much to promote drinking, certain laws were usually hung up, the transgression of which was to be punished by specific *forfeits;* which were *as much in mock as mark,* because the barber had no authority of himself to enforce them, and also because they were of a ludicrous nature

—Away with him to prison; lay bolts enough upon him:—Let him speak no more:—Away with those giglots[1] too, and with the other confederate companion. [*The* Provost *lays hands on the Duke.*

Duke. Stay, sir; stay a while.

Ang. What! resists he? Help him, Lucio.

Lucio. Come, sir; come, sir; come, sir; foh, sir; Why, you bald-pated, lying rascal! you must be hooded, must you? Show your knave's visage, with a pox to you! show your sheep-biting face, and be hang'd an hour![2] Wilt not off?

[*Pulls off the Friar's hood, and discovers the* Duke.

Duke. Thou art the first knave that e'er made a duke.——
First, Provost, let me bail these gentle three:——
Sneak not away, sir; [*To* LUCIO.] for the friar and you
Must have a word anon:—lay hold on him.

Lucio. This may prove worse than hanging.

Duke. What you have spoke, I pardon; sit you down.—— [*To* ESCALUS.
We'll borrow place of him:—Sir, by your leave: [*To* ANGELO.
Hast thou or word, or wit, or impudence,
That yet can do thee office?[3] If thou hast,
Rely upon it till my tale be heard,
And hold no longer out.

Ang. O my dread lord,
I should be guiltier than my guiltiness,
To think I can be undiscernible,
When I perceive, your grace, like power divine,
Hath look'd upon my passes:[4] Then, good prince,
No longer session hold upon my shame,
But let my trial be mine own confession;
Immediate sentence then, and sequent death,
Is all the grace I beg.

Duke. Come hither, Mariana;—
Say, wast thou e'er contracted to this woman?

Ang. I was, my lord.

Duke. Go take her hence, and marry her instantly.—
Do you the office, friar; which consummate,
Return him here again:—Go with him, Provost.

[*Exeunt* ANGELO, MARIANA, PETER, *and* Provost.

Escal. My lord, I am more amaz'd at his dishonour,
Than at the strangeness of it.

Duke. Come hither, Isabel:
Your friar is now your prince: As I was then
Advertising, and holy[5] to your business,
Not changing heart with habit, I am still
Attorney'd at your service.

Isab. O, give me pardon,
That I, your vassal, have employed and pain'd
Your unknown sovereignty.

Duke. You are pardon'd, Isabel:
And now, dear maid, be you as free[6] to us.
Your brother's death, I know, sits at your heart;
And you may marvel, why I obscur'd myself,
Labouring to save his life; and would not rather
Make rash remonstrance of my hidden power,[7]
Than let him so be lost: O, most kind maid,
It was the swift celerity of his death,
Which I did think with slower foot came on,
That brain'd my purpose:[8] But, peace be with him!
That life is better life, past fearing death,
Than that which lives to fear: make it your comfort,
So happy is your brother.

Re-enter ANGELO, MARIANA, PETER, *and* Provost.

Isab. I do, my lord.

Duke. For this new-married man, approaching here,
Whose salt imagination yet hath wrong'd
Your well-defended honour, you must pardon
For Mariana's sake: but as he adjudg'd your brother
(Being criminal, in double violation
Of sacred chastity, and of promise-breach,[9]
Thereon dependent for your brother's life,)
The very mercy of the law cries out
Most audible, even from his proper[10] tongue,
An Angelo for Claudio, death for death,
Haste still pays haste, and leisure answers leisure;
Like doth quit like, and *Measure* still *for Measure*?[11]
Then, Angelo, thy fault's thus manifested;
Which though thou would'st deny, denies thee vantage:[12]
We do condemn thee to the very block
Where Claudio stoop'd to death, and with like haste;—
Away with him.

Mari. O, my most gracious lord,
I hope you will not mock me with a husband!

Duke. It is your husband mock'd you with a husband:
Consenting to the safeguard of your honour,
I thought your marriage fit; else imputation,
For that he knew you, might reproach your life,
And choke your good to come: for his possessions,
Although by confiscation they are ours,
We do instate and widow you withal,
To buy you a better husband.

Mari. O, my dear lord,
I crave no other, nor no better man.

Duke. Never crave him; we are definitive.

Mari. Gentle, my liege,— [*Kneeling.*

Duke. You do but lose your labour;
Away with him to death.—Now, sir, [*To* LUCIO.] to you.

Mari. O, my good lord!—Sweet Isabel, take my part;
Lend me your knees, and, all my life to come,
I'll lend you all my life to do you service.

Duke. Against all sense[13] you do importune her:
Should she kneel down, in mercy of this fact,
Her brother's ghost his paved bed would break,
And take her hence in horror.

Mari. Isabel,
Sweet Isabel, do yet but kneel by me;
Hold up your hands, say nothing, I'll speak all.
They say, best men are moulded out of faults;
And, for the most, become much more the better
For being a little bad: so may my husband.
O, Isabel! will you not lend a knee?

Duke. He dies for Claudio's death.

Isab. Most bounteous sir, [*Kneeling.*
Look, if it please you, on this man condemn'd,

---

1 *Giglots* are wantons.—
'——— young Talbot was not born
To be the pillage of a *giglot* wench.'
K. Henry VI. P. i.

2 Dr. Johnson goes seriously to work to prove that he did not understand this piece of vulgar humour; and Henley thinks the *collistrigium*, or original pillory, was alluded to! 'What Piper ho! be *hang'd awhile*,' is a line in an old madrigal. And in Ben Jonson's Bartholomew Fair, we have
'Leave the bottle behind you, *and be curst awhile.*'
In short, they are petty and familiar maledictions, rightly explained, 'a plague or a mischief on you.'

3 i. e. do thee *service*.

4 *Passes*, probably put for *trespasses;* or it may mean *courses*, from *passes*, Fr.

5 *Advertising and holy*, attentive and faithful.

6 i. e. *generous*;—pardon us as we have pardoned you.

7 *Rash remonstrance;* that is, a premature *display* of it, perhaps we should read *de*monstrance, but the word may be formed from *remonstrer*, French—*to show again.*

8 *That brain'd my purpose.* We still use in conversation a like phrase—'that knocked my design on the head.'

9 *Promise-breach.* It should be *promise*, breach is superfluous.

10 i. e. Angelo's own tongue.

11 *Measure* still *for measure.* This appears to have been a current expression for retributive justice. Equivalent to *like for like.* So, in the 3d part of Henry VI
'*Measure for measure* must be answered.'

12 i. e. 'to deny which will avail thee nothing.'

13 i. e. against *reason* and *affection*

As if my brother liv'd: I partly think,
A due sincerity govern'd his deeds,
Till he did look on me: since it is so,
Let him not die: My brother had but justice,
In that he did the thing for which he died:
For Angelo,
His act did not o'ertake his bad intent;
And must be buried but as an intent
That perish'd by the way:[1] thoughts are no subjects;
Intents but merely thoughts.

Mari. Merely, my lord.

Duke. Your suit's unprofitable; stand up, I say.—
I have bethought me of another fault:—
Provost, how came it Claudio was beheaded
At an unusual hour?

Prov. It was commanded so.

Duke. Had you a special warrant for the deed?

Prov. No, my good lord; it was by private message.

Duke. For which I do discharge you of your office:
Give up your keys.

Prov. Pardon me, noble lord:
I thought it was a fault, but knew it not;
Yet did repent me, after more advice:[2]
For testimony whereof, one in the prison
That should by private order else have died,
I have reserv'd alive.

Duke. What's he?

Prov. His name is Barnardine.

Duke. I would thou had'st done so by Claudio.
Go, fetch him hither; let me look upon him.
[*Exit* Provost.

Escal. I am sorry, one so learned and so wise
As you, lord Angelo, have still appear'd,
Should slip so grossly, both in the heat of blood,
And lack of temper'd judgment afterward.

Ang. I am sorry, that such sorrow I procure:
And so deep sticks it in my penitent heart,
That I crave death more willingly than mercy;
'Tis my deserving, and I do entreat it.

Re-enter Provost, BARNARDINE, CLAUDIO, *and* JULIET.

Duke. Which is that Barnardine?

Prov. This, my lord.

Duke. There was a friar told me of this man:—
Sirrah, thou art said to have a stubborn soul,
That apprehends no further than this world,
And squar'st thy life according. Thou'rt condemn'd;
But, for those earthly[3] faults, I quit them all;
And pray thee, take this mercy to provide
For better times to come:—Friar, advise him;
I leave him to your hand. What muffled fellow's that?

Prov. This is another prisoner, that I sav'd,
That should have died when Claudio lost his head;
As like almost to Claudio, as himself.
[*Unmuffles* CLAUDIO.

Duke. If he be like your brother, [*To* ISABELLA.] for his sake
Is he pardon'd; And, for your lovely sake,
Give me your hand, and say you will be mine,
He is my brother too: But fitter time for that.
By this, lord Angelo perceives he's safe;
Methinks, I see a quick'ning in his eye:—
Well, Angelo, your evil quits[4] you well:
Look that you love your wife; her worth, worth yours.[5]—
I find an apt remission in myself:
And yet here's one in place I cannot pardon;—
You, sirrah, [*To* LUCIO.] that knew me for a fool, a coward,
One all of luxury,[6] an ass, a madman;
Wherein have I so deserved of you,
That you extol me thus?

Lucio. 'Faith, my lord, I spoke it but according to the trick:[7] If you will hang me for it, you may, but I had rather it would please you, I might be whipp'd.

Duke. Whipp'd first, sir, and hang'd after.—
Proclaim it, provost, round about the city;
If any woman's wrong'd by this lewd fellow,
(As I have heard him swear himself, there's one
Whom he begot with child,) let her appear,
And he shall marry her: the nuptial finished,
Let him be whipp'd and hang'd.

Lucio. I beseech your highness, do not marry me to a whore! Your highness said even now, I made you a duke; good my lord, do not recompense me in making me a cuckold.

Duke. Upon mine honour thou shalt marry her.
Thy slanders I forgive: and therewithal
Remit thy other forfeits:[8]—Take him to prison:
And see our pleasure herein executed.

Lucio. Marrying a punk, my lord, is pressing to death, whipping, and hanging.

Duke. Sland'ring a prince deserves it.—
She, Claudio, that you wrong'd, look you restore.
Joy to you, Mariana!—love her, Angelo;
I have confess'd her, and I know her virtue.—
Thanks, good friend Escalus, for thy much goodness:
There's more behind, that is more gratulate.
Thanks, Provost, for thy care and secrecy;
We shall employ thee in a worthier place:—
Forgive him, Angelo, that brought you home
The head of Ragozine for Claudio's;
The offence pardons itself.—Dear Isabel,
I have a motion much imports your good;
Whereto if you'll a willing ear incline,
What's mine is yours, and what is yours is mine:
So, bring us to our palace; where we'll show
What's yet behind, that's meet you all should know.
[*Exeunt.*

[The novel of Giraldi Cinthio, from which Shakspeare is supposed to have borrowed this fable, may be read in *Shakspeare Illustrated*, elegantly translated, with remarks, which will assist the inquirer to discover how much absurdity Shakspeare has admitted or avoided.

I cannot but suspect that some other had new-modelled the novel of Cinthio, or written a story which in some particulars resembled it, and that Cinthio was not the author whom Shakspeare immediately followed. The Emperor in Cinthio is named Maximine: the Duke, in Shakspeare's enumeration of the persons of the drama, is called Vincentio. This appears a very slight remark; but since the Duke has no name in the play, nor is ever mentioned but by his title, why should he be called Vincentio among the *persons*, but because the name was copied from the story, and placed superfluously at the head of the list by the mere habit of transcription? It is therefore likely that there was then a story of Vincentio, Duke of Vienna, different from that of Maximine, Emperor of the Romans.

Of this play, the light or comick part is very natural and pleasing, but the grave scenes, if a few passages be excepted, have more labour than elegance. The plot is rather intricate than artful. The time of the action is indefinite; some time, we know not how much, must have elapsed between the recess of the Duke and the imprisonment of Claudio; for he must have learned the story of Mariana in his disguise, or he delegated his power to a man already known to be corrupted.* The unities of action and place are sufficiently preserved.]
Johnson

---

1 i. e. like the traveller, who dies on his journey, is obscurely interred, and thought of no more:
'Illum expirantem———
Obliti ignoto camporum in pulvere linquunt.'

2 i. e. *better consideration.* K. Henry V. Act ii. Sc. 2.

3 i. e. so far as they are punishable on *earth.*

4 Requites

5 'Her worth worth yours;' that is, 'her value is equal to yours, the match is not unworthy of you.'

6 Incontinence

7 Thoughtless practice

8 'Remit thy other *forfeits.*' Dr. Johnson says, *forfeits* mean *punishments*, but is it not more likely to signify *misdoings, transgressions*, from the French *forfait?* Steevens's Note affords instances of the word in this sense.

9 i. e. more *to be rejoiced in.* As Steevens rightly explained it.

* The Duke probably had learnt the story of Mariana in some of his former retirements, 'having ever loved the life removed.' And he had a suspicion that Angelo was but a *seemer*, and therefore stays to watch him.
Blackstone

MUCH ADO ABOUT NOTHING.

PRELIMINARY REMARKS.

It is said that the main plot of this play is derived from the story of Ariodante and Ginevra, in the fifth book of Ariosto's Orlando Furioso. Something similar may also be found in the fourth canto of the second book of Spenser's Faerie Queene; but a novel of Bandello's, copied by Belleforest in his Tragical Histories, seems to have furnished Shakspeare with the fable. It approaches nearer to the play in all particulars than any other performance hitherto discovered. No translation of it into English has, however, yet been met with.

The incidents of this play produce a striking effect on the stage, where it has ever been one of the most popular of Shakspeare's Comedies. The sprightly wit-encounters between Benedick and Beatrice, and the blundering simplicity of those inimitable men in office, Dogberry and Verges, relieve the serious parts of the play, which might otherwise have seemed too serious for comedy. There is a deep and touching interest excited for the innocent and much injured Hero, 'whose justification is brought about by one of those temporary consignments to the grave, of which, Shakspeare appears to have been fond.' In answer to Steevens's objection to the same artifice being made use of to entrap both the lovers, Schlegel observes that 'the drollery lies in the very symmetry of the deception. Their friends attribute the whole effect to themselves; but the exclusive direction of their raillery against each other is a proof of their growing inclination.'

This play is supposed to have been written in 1600, in which year it was first published.

PERSONS REPRESENTED.

Don Pedro, *Prince of* Arragon.
Don John, *his bastard Brother.*
Claudio, *a young Lord of* Florence, *favourite to* Don Pedro.
Benedick, *a young Lord of* Padua, *favourite likewise of* Don Pedro.
Leonato, *Governor of* Messina.
Antonio, *his Brother.*
Balthazar, *Servant to* Don Pedro.
Borachio, Conrade, } *Followers of* Don John.
Dogberry, Verges, } *Two foolish Officers.*
A Sexton.
A Friar.
A Boy.

Hero, *Daughter to* Leonato.
Beatrice, *Niece to* Leonato.
Margaret, Ursula, } *Gentlewomen attending on* Hero.

Messengers, Watch, and Attendants.

SCENE, Messina.

ACT I.

SCENE I.—*Before* Leonato's *House. Enter* Leonato, Hero, Beatrice, *and others, with a* Messenger.

Leonato.

I learn in this letter, that Don Pedro[1] of Arragon comes this night to Messina.

Mess. He is very near by this; he was not three leagues off when I left him.

Leon. How many gentlemen have you lost in this action?

Mess. But few of any sort, and none of name.

Leon. A victory is twice itself, when the achiever brings home full numbers. I find here, that Don Pedro hath bestowed much honour on a young Florentine called Claudio.

Mess. Much deserved on his part, and equally remembered by Don Pedro: He hath borne himself beyond the promise of his age; doing, in the figure of a lamb, the feats of a lion: he hath, indeed, better bettered expectation, than you must expect of me to tell you how.

Leon. He hath an uncle here in Messina will be very much glad of it.

Mess. I have already delivered him letters, and there appears much joy in him; even so much, that joy could not show itself modest enough, without a badge of bitterness.[2]

Leon. Did he break out into tears?

Mess. In great measure.[3]

Leon. A kind overflow of kindness: There are no faces truer than those that are so washed. How much better it is to weep at joy, than to joy at weeping!

Beat. I pray you, is signior Montanto[4] returned from the wars, or no?

Mess. I know none of that name, lady; there was none such in the army of any sort.[5]

Leon. What is he that you ask for, niece?

Hero. My cousin means signior Benedick of Padua.

Mess. O, he is returned; and as pleasant as ever he was.

Beat. He set up his bills[6] here in Messina, and challenged Cupid at the flight:[7] and my uncle's fool, reading the challenge, subscribed for Cupid, and challenged him at the bird-bolt. I pray you, how many hath he killed and eaten in these wars? But how many hath he killed? for, indeed, I promised to eat all of his killing.

Leon. Faith, niece, you tax signior Benedick too much; but he'll be meet[8] with you, I doubt it not.

---

1 The old copies read Don *Peter.*

2 Of all the transports of joy, that which is attended by tears is least offensive; because, carrying with it this mark of pain, it allays the envy that usually attends another's happiness. This is finely called a *modest* joy, such a one as did not insult the observer by an indication of happiness unmixed with pain. In Chapman's version of the 10th Odyssey, a somewhat similar expression occurs:

'——— our eyes wore
The same wet badge of weak humanity.'

This is an idea which Shakspeare seems to have delighted to introduce. It occurs again in Macbeth:

'——— my plenteous joys,
Wanton in fulness, seek to hide themselves
In drops of sorrow.'

3 i. e. in abundance.

4 *Montanto* was one of the ancient terms of the fencing school; a title humorously given to one whom she would represent as a bravado.

5 Rank.

6 This phrase was in common use for affixing a printed notice in some public place, long before Shakspeare's time, and long after. It is amply illustrated by Mr. Douce, in his 'Illustrations of Shakspeare.'

7 *Flights*, were long and light feathered arrows, that went directly to the mark.

8 Even.

Mess. He hath done good service, lady, in these wars.

Beat. You had musty victual, and he hath holp to eat it: he is a very valiant trencher-man, he hath an excellent stomach.

Mess. And a good soldier too, lady.

Beat. And a good soldier to a lady;—But what is he to a lord?

Mess. A lord to a lord, a man to a man; stuffed[1] with all honourable virtues.

Beat. It is so, indeed; he is no less than a stuffed man: but for the stuffing,—Well, we are all mortal.

Leon. You must not, sir, mistake my niece: there is a kind of merry war betwixt signior Benedick and her: they never meet, but there is a skirmish of wit between them.

Beat. Alas, he gets nothing by that. In our last conflict, four of his five wits[2] went halting off, and now is the whole man governed with one: so that if he have wit enough to keep himself warm, let him bear it for a difference[3] between himself and his horse: for it is all the wealth that he hath left, to be known a reasonable creature.—Who is his companion now? He hath every month a new sworn brother.

Mess. Is it possible?

Beat. Very easily possible: he wears his faith but as the fashion of his hat, it ever changes with the next block.[4]

Mess. I see, lady, the gentleman is not in your books.[5]

Beat. No: an he were, I would burn my study. But, I pray you, who is his companion? Is there no young squarer[6] now, that will make a voyage with him to the devil?

Mess. He is most in the company of the right noble Claudio.

Beat. O Lord! he will hang upon him like a disease: he is sooner caught than the pestilence, and the taker runs presently mad. God help the noble Claudio! if he have caught the Benedick, it will cost him a thousand pound ere he be cured.

Mess. I will hold friends with you, lady.

Beat. Do, good friend.

Leon. You will never run mad, niece.

Beat. No, not till a hot January.

Mess. Don Pedro is approached.

Enter DON PEDRO, *attended by* BALTHAZAR *and others*, DON JOHN, CLAUDIO, *and* BENEDICK.

D. Pedro. Good signior Leonato, you are come to meet your trouble: the fashion of the world is to avoid cost, and you encounter it.

Leon. Never came trouble to my house in the likeness of your grace: for trouble being gone, comfort should remain; but, when you depart from me, sorrow abides, and happiness takes his leave.

D. Pedro. You embrace your charge[7] too willingly.—I think, this is your daughter.

Leon. Her mother hath many times told me so.

Bene. Were you in doubt, sir, that you asked her?

Leon. Signior Benedick, no; for then were you a child.

D. Pedro. You have it full Benedick: we may guess by this what you are, being a man. Truly, the lady fathers herself:[8]—Be happy, lady! for you are like an honourable father.

Bene. If signior Leonato be her father, she would not have his head on her shoulders, for all Messina, as like him as she is.

Beat. I wonder, that you will still be talking, signior Benedick; no body marks you.

Bene. What, my dear lady Disdain! are you yet living?

Beat. Is it possible disdain should die, while she hath such meet food to feed it, as signior Benedick? Courtesy itself must convert to disdain, if you come in her presence.

Bene. Then is courtesy a turn-coat:—But it is certain, I am loved of all ladies, only you excepted: and I would I could find in my heart that I had not a hard heart; for, truly, I love none.

Beat. A dear happiness to women; they would else have been troubled with a pernicious suitor. I thank God, and my cold blood, I am of your humour for that; I had rather hear my dog bark at a crow, than a man swear he loves me.

Bene. God keep your ladyship still in that mind! so some gentleman or other shall 'scape a predestinate scratched face.

Beat. Scratching could not make it worse, an 'twere such a face as yours were.

Bene. Well, you are a rare parrot-teacher.

Beat. A bird of my tongue is better than a beast of yours.

Bene. I would my horse had the speed of your tongue; and so good a continuer: But keep your way o'God's name; I have done.

Beat. You always end with a jade's trick; I know you of old.

D. Pedro. This is the sum of all: Leonato,—signior Claudio, and signior Benedick,—my dear friend Leonato hath invited you all. I tell him, we shall stay here at the least a month; and he heartily prays, some occasion may detain us longer: I dare swear he is no hypocrite, but prays from his heart.

Leon. If you swear, my lord, you shall not be forsworn.—Let me bid you welcome, my lord, being reconciled to the prince your brother, I owe you all duty.

D. John. I thank you: I am not of many words, but I thank you.

Leon. Please it your grace lead on?

D. Pedro. Your hand, Leonato; we will go together. [*Exeunt all but* BENEDICK *and* CLAUDIO.

Claud. Benedick, didst thou note the daughter of signior Leonato?

Bene. I noted her not; but I looked on her.

Claud. Is she not a modest young lady?

Bene. Do you question me, as an honest man should do, for my simple true judgment; or would you have me speak after my custom, as being a professed tyrant to their sex?

Claud. No, I pray thee, speak in sober judgment.

Bene. Why, i'faith, methinks she is too low for a high praise, too brown for a fair praise, and too little for a great praise: only this commendation I can afford her; that were she other than she is, she were unhandsome; and being no other but as she is, I do not like her.

Claud. Thou thinkest, I am in sport; I pray thee, tell me truly how thou likest her.

Bene. Would you buy her, that you inquire after her.

---

1 *Stuffed*, in this first instance, has no ridiculous meaning. Mede, in his discourses on Scripture, quoted by Edwards, speaking of Adam, says, 'he whom God had *stuffed* with so many excellent qualities.' And in the Winter's Tale:

'Of *stuff'd* sufficiency.'

Beatrice starts an idea at the words *stuffed man*, and prudently checks herself in the pursuit of it. A stuffed man appears to have been one of the many cant phrases for a cuckold.

2 In Shakspeare's time *wit* was the general term for intellectual power. The *wits* seem to have been reckoned *five* by analogy to the five senses. So in Lear, Act iii. Sc. 4: 'Bless thy five wits.'

3 This is an heraldic term. So, in Hamlet, Ophelia says, 'You may wear your rue with a *difference*.'

4 The mould on which a hat is formed. It is here used for *shape* or *fashion*. See note on Lear, Act iv Sc. 6.

5 The origin of this phrase, which is still in common use, has not been clearly explained, though the sense of it is pretty generally understood. The most probable account derives it from the circumstance of servants and retainers being entered in the books of those to whom they were attached. *To be in one's books* was *to be in favour*. That this was the ancient sense of the phrase, and its origin, appears from Florio, in V.—'*Casso.* Cashier'd, crossed, cancelled, or put *out of booke* and checke roule.'

6 Quarreller.

7 Burthen, incumbrance.

8 This phrase is common in Dorsetshire. 'Jack fathers himself' is like his father

Claud. Can the world buy such a jewel?

Bene. Yea, and a case to put it into. But speak you this with a sad brow? or do you play the flouting Jack; to tell us Cupid is a good hare-finder, and Vulcan a rare carpenter?[1] Come, in what key shall a man take you to go in the song?[2]

Claud. In mine eye, she is the sweetest lady that ever I looked on.

Bene. I can see yet without spectacles, and I see no such matter: there's her cousin, an she were not possessed with a fury, exceeds her as much in beauty, as the first of May does the last of December. But I hope, you have no intent to turn husband; have you?

Claud. I would scarce trust myself, though I had sworn the contrary, if Hero would be my wife.

Bene. Is it come to this, i'faith? Hath not the world one man, but he will wear his cap with suspicion?[3] Shall I never see a bachelor of threescore again? Go to, i'faith; an thou wilt needs thrust thy neck into a yoke, wear the print of it, and sigh away Sundays.[4] Look, Don Pedro is returned to seek you.

Re-enter Don Pedro.

D. Pedro. What secret hath held you here, that you followed not to Leonato's?

Bene. I would, your grace would constrain me to tell.

D. Pedro. I charge thee on thy allegiance.

Bene. You hear, Count Claudio: I can be secret as a dumb man, I would have you think so; but on my allegiance,—mark you this, on my allegiance:—He is in love. With who?—now that is your grace's part.—Mark, how short his answer is:—With Hero, Leonato's short daughter.

Claud. If this were so, so were it uttered.

Bene. Like the old tale, my lord: it is not so, nor 'twas not so; but, indeed, God forbid it should be so.[5]

Claud. If my passion change not shortly, God forbid it should be otherwise.

D. Pedro. Amen, if you love her; for the lady is very well worthy.

Claud. You speak this to fetch me in, my lord.

D. Pedro. By my troth, I speak my thought.

Claud. And, in faith, my lord, I spoke mine.

Bene. And, by my two faiths and troths, my lord, I spoke mine.

Claud. That I love her, I feel.

D. Pedro. That she is worthy, I know.

Bene. That I neither feel how she should be loved, nor know how she should be worthy, is the opinion that fire cannot melt out of me; I will die in it at the stake.

D. Pedro. Thou wast ever an obstinate heretic in the despite of beauty.

Claud. And never could maintain his part, but in the force of his will.[6]

Bene. That a woman conceived me I thank her; that she brought me up, I likewise give her most humble thanks: but that I will have a recheat[7] winded in my forehead, or hang my bugle[8] in an invisible baldrick,[9] all women shall pardon me: Because I will not do them the wrong to mistrust any, I will do myself the right to trust none: and the fine[10] is, (for the which I may go the finer,) I will live a bachelor.

D. Pedro. I shall see thee, ere I die, look pale with love.

Bene. With anger, with sickness, or with hunger, my lord; not with love: prove, that ever I lose more blood with love, than I will get again with drinking, pick out mine eyes with a ballad-maker's pen, and hang me up at the door of a brothel-house, for the sign of blind Cupid.

D. Pedro. Well, if ever thou dost fall from this faith, thou wilt prove a notable argument.[11]

Bene. If I do, hang me in a bottle like a cat,[12] and shoot at me; and he that hits me, let him be clapped on the shoulder, and called Adam.[13]

D. Pedro. Well, as time shall try:
In time the savage bull doth bear the yoke.[14]

Bene. The savage bull may; but if ever the sensible Benedick bear it, pluck off the bull's horns, and set them in my forehead: and let me be vilely painted; and in such great letters as they write, *Here is good horse to hire*, let them signify under my sign—*Here you may see Benedick the married man.*

Claud. If this should ever happen, thou would'st be horn-mad.

D. Pedro. Nay, if Cupid have not spent all his quiver in Venice,[15] thou wilt quake for this shortly.

Bene. I look for an earthquake too then.

D. Pedro. Well, you will temporize with the hours. In the mean time, good signior Benedick, repair to Leonato's; commend me to him, and tell him, I will not fail him at supper; for, indeed, he hath made great preparation.

Bene. I have almost matter enough in me for such an embassage: and so I commit you—

Claud. To the tuition of God: From my house, (if I had it)—

D. Pedro. The sixth of July: Your loving friend, Benedick.

Bene. Nay, mock not, mock not: The body of your discourse is sometime guarded[16] with fragments, and the guards are but slightly basted on neither; ere you flout old ends any further, examine your conscience,[17] and so I leave you.

[*Exit* Benedick.

Claud. My liege, your highness now may do me good.

D. Pedro. My love is thine to teach; teach it but how,
And thou shalt see how apt it is to learn
Any hard lesson that may do thee good.

Claud. Hath Leonato any son, my lord!

D. Pedro. No child but Hero, she's his only heir;
Dost thou affect her, Claudio?

Claud. O my lord,
When you went onward on this ended action,
I look'd upon her with a soldier's eye,

1 Do you scoff and mock in telling us that Cupid, who is blind, is a good hare-finder; and that Vulcan, a blacksmith, is a good carpenter? Do you mean to amuse us with improbable stories?

2 i. e. to *join* in the song.

3 i. e. subject his head to the disquiet of jealousy.

4 i. e. become sad and serious. Alluding to the manner in which the Puritans usually spent the Sabbath, with sighs and gruntings, and other hypocritical marks of devotion.

5 The old tale, of which this is the burthen, has been traditionally preserved and recovered by Mr. Blakeway, and is perhaps one of the most happy illustrations of Shakspeare that has ever appeared.

6 Alluding to the definition of a heretic in the schools.

7 That is, *wear a horn on my forehead, which the huntsman may blow. A recheat* is the sound by which the dogs are called back.

8 i. e. *bugle-horn.*

9 *A belt.* The meaning seems to be 'or that I should be compelled to carry a horn on my forehead where there is nothing visible to support it.'

10 *The fine* is the conclusion.

11 A capital *subject* for satire.

12 It seems to have been one of the inhuman sports of the time, to enclose a cat in a wooden tub or bottle suspended aloft to be shot at.

13 i. e. Adam Bell, 'a passing good archer,' who, with Clym of the Cloughe and William of Cloudeslie, were outlaws as famous in the north of England, as Robin Hood and his fellows were in the midland counties

14 This line is from The Spanish Tragedy, or Hieronimo, &c.; and occurs, with a slight variation, in Watson's Sonnets, 1581.

15 Venice is represented in the same light as Cyprus among the ancients, and it is this character of the people that is here alluded to.

16 Trimmed ornamented.

17 'Examine if your sarcasms do not touch yourself.' *Old ends* probably means the conclusions of letters, which were frequently couched in the quaint forms used above

That lik'd, but had a rougher task in hand
Than to drive liking to the name of love:
But now I am return'd, and that war-thoughts
Have left their places vacant, in their rooms
Come thronging soft and delicate desires,
All prompting me how fair young Hero is,
Saying, I lik'd her ere I went to wars.

D. Pedro. Thou wilt be like a lover presently,
And tire the hearer with a book of words:
If thou dost love fair Hero, cherish it;
And I will break with her, and with her father,
And thou shalt have her: Was't not to this end,
That thou began'st to twist so fine a story?

Claud. How sweetly do you minister to love,
That know love's grief by his complexion!
But lest my liking might too sudden seem,
I would have salv'd it with a longer treatise.

D. Pedro. What need the bridge much broader than the flood?
The fairest grant is the necessity:[1]
Look, what will serve, is fit: 'tis once,[2] thou lov'st;
And I will fit thee with the remedy.
I know we shall have revelling to-night;
I will assume thy part in some disguise,
And tell fair Hero I am Claudio;
And in her bosom I'll unclasp my heart,
And take her hearing prisoner with the force
And strong encounter of my amorous tale:
Then, after, to her father, will I break;
And, the conclusion is, she shall be thine:
In practice let us put it presently. [*Exeunt.*

SCENE II. *A Room in* Leonato's *House. Enter* LEONATO *and* ANTONIO.

Leon. How now, brother? Where is my cousin, your son? Hath he provided this musick?

Ant. He is very busy about it. But, brother, I can tell you strange news that you yet dreamed not of.

Leon. Are they good?

Ant. As the event stamps them; but they have a good cover, they show well outward. The prince and Count Claudio, walking in a thick-pleached[3] alley in my orchard, were thus much overheard by a man of mine: The prince discovered to Claudio, that he loved my niece your daughter, and meant to acknowledge it this night in a dance; and, if he found her accordant, he meant to take the present time by the top, and instantly break with you of it.

Leon. Hath the fellow any wit, that told you this?

Ant. A good sharp fellow: I will send for him, and question him yourself.

Leon. No, no; we will hold it as a dream, till it appear itself:—but I will acquaint my daughter withal, that she may be the better prepared for an answer, if peradventure this be true. Go you, and tell her of it. [*Several persons cross the stage.*] Cousins,[4] you know what you have to do.—O, I cry you mercy, friend; you go with me, and I will use your skill:—Good cousins, have a care this busy time. [*Exeunt.*

SCENE III. *Another Room in* Leonato's *House. Enter* DON JOHN *and* CONRADE.

Con. What the good year,[5] my lord! why are you thus out of measure sad?

D. John. There is no measure in the occasion that breeds it, therefore the sadness is without limit.

Con. You should hear reason.

D. John. And when I have heard it, what blessing bringeth it?

Con. If not a present remedy, yet a patient sufferance.

D. John. I wonder, that thou being (as thou say'st thou art) born under Saturn, goest about to apply a moral medicine to a mortifying mischief. I cannot hide what I am:[6] I must be sad when I have cause, and smile at no man's jests; eat when I have stomach, and wait for no man's leisure; sleep when I am drowsy, and tend to no man's business; laugh when I am merry, and claw[7] no man in his humour.

Con. Yea, but you must not make the full show of this, till you may do it without controlment. You have of late stood out against your brother, and he hath ta'en you newly into his grace; where it is impossible you should take true root, but by the fair weather that you make yourself: it is needful that you frame the season for your own harvest.

D. John. I had rather be a canker[8] in a hedge, than a rose in his grace; and it better fits my blood to be disdained of all, than to fashion a carriage to rob love from any; in this, though I cannot be said to be a flattering honest man, it must not be denied that I am a plain-dealing villain. I am trusted with a muzzle, and enfranchised with a clog; therefore I have decreed not to sing in my cage: If I had my mouth, I would bite; if I had my liberty, I would do my liking: in the mean time, let me be that I am and seek not to alter me.

Con. Can you make no use of your discontent?

D. John. I make all use of it, for I use it only. Who comes here? What news, Borachio?

Enter BORACHIO.

Bora. I came yonder from a great supper; the prince, your brother, is royally entertained by Leonato; and I can give you intelligence of an intended marriage.

D. John. Will it serve for any model[10] to build mischief on? What is he for a fool, that betroths himself to unquietness?

Bora. Marry, it is your brother's right hand.

D. John. Who? the most exquisite Claudio?

Bora. Even he.

D. John. A proper squire! And who, and who? which way looks he?

Bora. Marry, on Hero, the daughter and heir of Leonato.

D. John. A very forward March chick! How came you to this?

Bora. Being entertained for a perfumer, as I was smoking a musty room,[11] comes me the prince and Claudio, hand in hand, in sad[12] conference: I whipt me behind the arras; and there heard it agreed upon, that the prince should woo Hero for himself, and having obtained her, give her to count Claudio.

D. John. Come, come, let us thither; this may prove food to my displeasure: that young start-up hath all the glory of my overthrow; if I can cross him any way, I bless myself every way: You are both sure,[13] and will assist me?

---

1 Mr. Hayley, with great acuteness, proposed to read 'The fairest grant is *to* necessity;' i. e. '*necessitas quod cogit defendit*.' The meaning may however be—'The fairest or most equitable concession is that which is needful only.'

2 i. e. once for all. So, in Coriolanus: '*Once* if he do require our voices, we ought not to deny him.' See Comedy of Errors, Act iii. Sc. 1.

3 Thickly interwoven.

4 *Cousins* were formerly enrolled among the dependants, if not the domestics of great families, such as that of Leonato.—Petruchio, while intent on the subjection of Katharine, calls out in terms imperative for his *cousin* Ferdinand.

5 The commentators say, that the original form of this exclamation was the *gougere*, i. e. *morbus gallicus*; which ultimately became obscure, and was corrupted into the *good year*, a very opposite form of expression.

6 This is one of Shakspeare's natural touches. An envious and unsocial mind, too proud to give pleasure, and too sullen to receive it, always endeavours to hide its malignity from the world and from itself, under the plainness of simple honesty, or the dignity of haughty independence.

7 Flatter.

8 *A canker* is the canker-rose, or dog-rose. 'I had rather be a neglected dog-rose in a hedge, than a garden-rose if it profited by his culture.'

9 i. e. 'for I make nothing else my counsellor.'

10 *Model* is here used in an unusual sense, but Bullokar explains it, '*Model*, the *platforme*, or form of any thing.'

11 The neglect of cleanliness among our ancestors rendered such precautions too often necessary.

12 Serious. 13 i. e. to be depended on.

Con. To the death, my lord.

D. John. Let us to the great supper; their cheer is the greater, that I am subdued: 'Would the cook were of my mind!—Shall we go prove what's to be done?

Bora. We'll wait upon your lordship. [*Exeunt.*

ACT II.

SCENE I. *A Hall in* Leonato's *House. Enter* LEONATO, ANTONIO, HERO, BEATRICE, *and others.*

Leon. Was not count John here at supper?

Ant. I saw him not.

Beat. How tartly that gentleman looks! I never can see him, but I am heart-burned an hour after.

Hero. He is of a very melancholy disposition.

Beat. He were an excellent man, that were made just in the mid-way between him and Benedick: the one is too like an image, and says nothing; and the other, too like my lady's eldest son, evermore tattling.

Leon. Then half signior Benedick's tongue in count John's mouth, and half count John's melancholy in signior Benedick's face,—

Beat. With a good leg, and a good foot, uncle, and money enough in his purse, such a man would win any woman in the world,—if he could get her good will.

Leon. By my troth, niece, thou wilt never get thee a husband, if thou be so shrewd of thy tongue.

Ant. In faith, she is too curst.

Beat. Too curst is more than curst: I shall lessen God's sending that way: for it is said, *God sends a curst cow short horns;* but to a cow too curst he sends none.

Leon. So, by being too curst, God will send you no horns.

Beat. Just, if he send me no husband: for the which blessing, I am at him upon my knees every morning and evening: Lord! I could not endure a husband with a beard on his face; I had rather lie in the woollen.

Leon. You may light upon a husband, that hath no beard.

Beat. What should I do with him? dress him in my apparel, and make him my waiting gentlewoman? He that hath a beard, is more than a youth; and he that hath no beard, is less than a man: and he that is more than a youth, is not for me; and he that is less than a man, I am not for him. Therefore I will even take sixpence in earnest of the bear-herd, and lead his apes into hell.

Leon. Well then, go you into hell?

Beat. No; but to the gate; and there will the devil meet me, like an old cuckold, with horns on his head, and say, *Get you to heaven, Beatrice, get you to heaven; here's no place for you maids:* so deliver I up my apes, and away to Saint Peter for the heavens; he shows me where the bachelors sit, and there live we as merry as the day is long.

Ant. Well, niece, [*To* HERO.] I trust, you will be ruled by your father.

Beat. Yes, faith; it is my cousin's duty to make courtesy, and say, *Father, as it please you:*— but yet for all that, cousin, let him be a handsome fellow, or else make another courtesy, and say, *Father, as it please me.*

Leon. Well, niece, I hope to see you one day fitted with a husband.

Beat. Not till God make men of some other metal than earth. Would it not grieve a woman to be over-mastered with a piece of valiant dust? to make an account of her life to a clod of wayward marl? No, uncle, I'll none: Adam's sons are my brethren; and truly, I hold it a sin to match in my kindred.

Leon. Daughter, remember what I told you; if the prince do solicit you in that kind, you know your answer.

Beat. The fault will be in the musick, cousin, if you be not woo'd in good time: if the prince be too important,[1] tell him, there is measure[2] in every thing, and so dance out the answer. For hear me, Hero; Wooing, wedding, and repenting, is as a Scotch jig, a measure, and a cinque-pace; the first suit is hot and hasty, like a Scotch jig, and full as fantastical; the wedding, mannerly-modest, as a measure full of state and ancientry; and then comes repentance, and, with his bad legs, falls into the cinque-pace faster and faster, till he sink into his grave.

Leon. Cousin, you apprehend passing shrewdly.

Beat. I have a good eye, uncle; I can see a church by day-light.

Leon. The revellers are entering; brother, make good room.

Enter DON PEDRO, CLAUDIO, BENEDICK, BALTHAZAR; DON JOHN, BORACHIO, MARGARET, URSULA, *and others, masked.*

D. Pedro. Lady, will you walk about with your friend?[3]

Hero. So you walk softly, and look sweetly, and say nothing, I am yours for the walk; and, especially, when I walk away.

D. Pedro. With me in your company?

Hero. I may say so, when I please.

D. Pedro. And when please you to say so?

Hero. When I like your favour; for God defend, the lute should be like the case![4]

D. Pedro. My visor is Philemon's roof; within the house is Jove.[5]

Hero. Why then your visor should be thatch'd.

D. Pedro. Speak low, if you speak love. [*Takes her aside.*

Bene. Well, I would you did like me.

Marg. So would not I, for your own sake; for I have many ill qualities.

Bene. Which is one?

Marg. I say my prayers aloud.

Bene. I love you the better; the hearers may cry, Amen.

Marg. God match me with a good dancer!

Balth. Amen.

Marg. And God keep him out of my sight, when the dance is done!—Answer, clerk.

Balth. No more words; the clerk is answered.

Urs. I know you well enough; you are signior Antonio.

Ant. At a word, I am not.

Urs. I know you by the waggling of your head.

Ant. To tell you true, I counterfeit him.

Urs. You could never do him so ill-well, unless you were the very man: Here's his dry hand up and down; you are he, you are he.

Ant. At a word I am not.

Urs. Come, come; do you think I do not know you by your excellent wit? Can virtue hide itself? Go to, mum, you are he; graces will appear, and there's an end.

Beat. Will you not tell me who told you so?

Bene. No, you shall pardon me.

Beat. Nor will you not tell me who you are?

Bene. Not now.

Beat. That I was disdainful,—and that I had my good wit out of the *Hundred merry Tales;*[6]—Well, this was signior Benedick that said so.

Bene. What's he?

Beat. I am sure, you know him well enough.

1 Importunate.

2 A *measure,* in old language, besides its ordinary meaning, signified also *a dance.*

3 Lover.

4 That is, 'God *forbid* that your face should be as homely and coarse as your mask.'

5 Alluding to the fable of Baucis and Philemon in Ovid, who describes the old couple as living in a thatched cottage.

'——*Stipulis et canna tecta palustri,*'

which Golding renders:

'The *roofe* thereof was *thatched* all with straw and fennish reede.'

6 This was the term for a *jest-book* in Shakspeare's time, from a popular collection of that name, about which the commentators were much puzzled, until a large frag

Bene. Not I, believe me.
Beat. Did he never make you laugh?
Bene. I pray you, what is he?
Beat. Why, he is the prince's jester; a very dull fool; only his gift is in devising impossible[1] slanders: none but libertines delight in him; and the commendation is not in his wit, but in his villany; for he both pleaseth men, and angers them, and then they laugh at him, and beat him: I am sure he is in the fleet: I would he had boarded[2] me.
Bene. When I know the gentleman, I'll tell him what you say.
Beat. Do, do: he'll but break a comparison or two on me; which, peradventure, not marked, or not laughed at, strikes him into melancholy; and then there's a partridge wing saved, for the fool will eat no supper that night. [*Music within.* We must follow the leaders.
Bene. In every good thing.
Beat. Nay, if they lead to any ill, I will leave them at the next turning.
[*Dance. Then exeunt all but* DON JOHN, BORACHIO, *and* CLAUDIO.
D. John. Sure my brother is amorous on Hero, and hath withdrawn her father to break with him about it: The ladies follow her, and but one visor remains.
Bora. And that is Claudio: I know him by his bearing.[3]
D. John. Are not you signior Benedick?
Claud. You know me well; I am he.
D. John. Signior, you are very near my brother in his love: he is enamoured on Hero; I pray you, dissuade him from her, she is no equal for his birth: you may do the part of an honest man in it.
Claud. How know you he loves her?
D. John. I heard him swear his affection.
Bora. So did I too; and he swore he would marry her to-night.
D. John. Come let us to the banquet.
[*Exeunt* DON JOHN, *and* BORACHIO.
Claud. Thus answer I in name of Benedick,
But hear these ill news with the ears of Claudio.—
'Tis certain so;—the prince woos for himself.
Friendship is constant in all other things,
Save in the office and affairs of love:
Therefore,[4] all hearts in love use their own tongues;
Let every eye negotiate for itself,
And trust no agent: for beauty is a witch,
Against whose charms faith melteth into blood.[5]
This is an accident of hourly proof,
Which I mistrusted not: Farewell, therefore, Hero!

Re-enter BENEDICK.

Bene. Count Claudio?
Claud. Yea, the same.
Bene. Come, will you go with me?
Claud. Whither?
Bene. Even to the next willow, about your own business, count. What fashion will you wear the garland of? About your neck, like an usurer's chain?[6] or under your arm, like a lieutenant's scarf? You must wear it one way, for the prince hath got your Hero.
Claud. I wish him joy of her.
Bene. Why, that's spoken like an honest drover; so they sell bullocks. But did you think the prince would have served you thus?
Claud. I pray you, leave me.
Bene. Ho! now you strike like the blind man. 'twas the boy that stole your meat, and you'll beat the post.
Claud. If it will not be, I'll leave you. [*Exit.*
Bene. Alas, poor hurt fowl! Now will he creep into sedges.——But, that my lady Beatrice should know me, and not know me! The Prince's fool!—Ha! it may be, I go under that title, because I am merry.—Yea; but so; I am apt to do myself wrong: I am not so reputed: it is the base, the bitter disposition of Beatrice, that puts the world into her person, and so gives me out.[7] Well, I'll be revenged as I may.

Re-enter DON PEDRO.

D. Pedro. Now, signior, where's the count. Did you see him?
Bene. Troth, my lord, I have play'd the part of lady Fame. I found him here as melancholy as a lodge in a warren;[8] I told him, and, I think, I told him true, that your grace had got the good will of this young lady; and I offered him my company to a willow tree, either to make him a garland, as being forsaken, or to bind him up a rod, as being worthy to be whipped.
D. Pedro. To be whipped! What's his fault?
Bene. The flat transgression of a schoolboy; who, being overjoyed with finding a bird's nest, shows it his companion, and he steals it.
D. Pedro. Wilt thou make a trust a transgression? The transgression is in the stealer.
Bene. Yet it had not been amiss, the rod had been made, and the garland too; for the garland he might have worn himself; and the rod he might have bestowed on you, who, as I take it, have stol'n his bird's nest.
D. Pedro. I will but teach them to sing, and restore them to the owner.
Bene. If their singing answer your saying, by my faith you say honestly.
D. Pedro. The lady Beatrice hath a quarrel to you; the gentleman, that danced with her, told her, she is much wronged by you.
Bene. O, she misused me past the endurance of a block; an oak, but with one green leaf on it, would have answered her; my very visor began to assume life, and scold with her:[9] She told me, not thinking I had been myself, that I was the prince's jester: that I was duller than a great thaw: hudling jest upon jest, with such impossible[10] convey-

ment was discovered in 1815, by my late lamented friend the Rev. J. Conybeare, Professor of Poetry in Oxford. I had the gratification of printing a few copies at the Chiswick press, under the title of 'Shakspeare's Jest Book.' It was printed by Rastell, and therefore must have been published previous to 1533. Another collection of the same kind, called, 'Tales and Quicke Answeres,' printed by Berthelette, and of nearly equal antiquity, was also reprinted at the same time; and it is remarkable that this collection is cited by Sir John Harrington under the title of 'the hundred merry tales.' It continued for a long period to be the popular name for collections of this sort, for in the London Chaunticlere, 1659, it is mentioned as being cried for sale by a ballad man.

1 Incredible, or inconceivable.

2 *Boarded,* besides its usual meaning, signified *accosted.*

3 Carriage, demeanour.

4 *Let,* which is found in the next line, is understood here.

5 *Blood* signifies *amorous heat* or *passion.* So, in All's Well that Ends Well, Act. iii. Sc. 7.

> 'Now his important *blood* will nought deny,
> That she'll demand.'

6 Chains of gold of considerable value were, in Shakspeare's time, worn by wealthy citizens, and others, in the same manner as they are now on public occasions by the aldermen of London. *Usury* was then a common topic of invective. So, in 'The Choice of Change,' 1598, 'Three sortes of people, in respect of necessity, may be accounted good:—*Merchants,* for they may play the *usurers,* instead of the Jews, &c.' Again, 'There is a scarcity of Jews, because Christians make an occupation of *usurie.*'

7 'It is the disposition of Beatrice, who takes upon herself to personate the world, and therefore represents the world as saying what she only says herself.'

8 A parallel thought occurs in Isaiah, c. i. where the prophet, in describing the desolation of Judah, says, 'The daughter of Zion is left as a cottage in a vineyard, as a *lodge* in a garden of cucumbers,' &c. It appears that these lonely buildings were necessary, as the cucumbers, &c. were obliged to be constantly watched and watered, and that as soon as the crop was gathered they were *forsaken.*

9 It is singular that a similar thought should be found in the tenth Thebaid of Statius, v. 658.

> '—— ipsa insanire videtur
> Sphynx galeæ custos.'

10 i. e. 'with a rapidity equal to that of jugglers

ance upon me, that I stood like a man at a mark, with a whole army shooting at me: She speaks poniards, and every word stabs: if her breath were as terrible as her terminations, there were no living near her, she would infect to the north star. I would not marry her, though she were endowed with all that Adam had left him before he transgressed; she would have made Hercules have turned spit; yea, and have cleft his club to make the fire too. Come, talk not of her; you shall find her the infernal Ate[1] in good apparel. I would to God, some scholar would conjure her; for, certainly, while she is here, a man may live as quiet in hell, as in a sanctuary; and people sin upon purpose, because they would go thither: so, indeed, all disquiet, horror, and perturbation follow her.

Re-enter CLAUDIO, BEATRICE, HERO, *and* LEONATO.

D. Pedro. Look, here she comes.

Bene. Will your grace command me any service to the world's end? I will go on the slightest errand now to the Antipodes, that you can devise to send me on; I will fetch you a toothpicker now from the farthest inch of Asia; bring you the length of Prester John's foot; fetch you a hair off the great Cham's beard: do you any embassage to the Pigmies, rather than hold three words conference with this harpy: You have no employment for me?

D. Pedro. None, but to desire your good company.

Bene. O God, sir, here's a dish I love not; I cannot endure my lady Tongue. [*Exit.*

D. Pedro. Come, lady, come; you have lost the heart of signior Benedick.

Beat. Indeed, my lord, he lent it me a while; and I give him use[2] for it, a double heart for his single one: marry, once before, he won it of me with false dice, therefore your grace may well say, I have lost it.

D. Pedro. You have put him down, lady, you have put him down.

Beat. So I would not he should do me, my lord, lest I should prove the mother of fools. I have brought count Claudio, whom you sent me to seek.

D. Pedro. Why, how now, count? wherefore are you sad?

Claud. Not sad, my lord.

D. Pedro. How then? Sick.

Claud. Neither, my lord.

Beat. The count is neither sad, nor sick, nor merry, nor well: but civil, count; civil as an orange, and something of that jealous complexion.

D. Pedro. I'faith, lady, I think your blazon to be true, though, I'll be sworn, if he be so, his conceit is false. Here, Claudio, I have wooed in thy name, and fair Hero is won; I have broke with her father, and his good will obtained: name the day of marriage, and God give thee joy!

Leon. Count, take of me my daughter, and with her my fortunes: his grace hath made the match, and all grace say Amen to it!

Beat. Speak, count, 'tis your cue.[3]

Claud. Silence is the perfectest herald of joy; I were but little happy, if I could say how much.—Lady, as you are mine, I am yours; I give away myself for you, and dote upon the exchange.

Beat. Speak, cousin, or, if you cannot, stop his mouth with a kiss, and let him not speak neither.

D. Pedro. In faith, lady, you have a merry heart.

Beat. Yea, my lord: I thank it, poor fool, it keeps on the windy side of care:—My cousin tells him in his ear, that he is in her heart.

Claud. And so she doth, cousin.

Beat. Good lord, for alliance!—Thus goes every one to the world but I,[4] and I am sun-burned; I may sit in the corner, and cry, heigh ho! for a husband.

D. Pedro. Lady Beatrice, I will get you one.

Beat. I would rather have one of your father's getting: Hath your grace ne'er a brother like you? Your father got excellent husbands, if a maid could come by them.

D. Pedro. Will you have me, lady?

Beat. No, my lord, unless I might have another for working-days; your grace is too costly to wear every day:—But, I beseech your grace, pardon me: I was born to speak all mirth, and no matter.

D. Pedro. Your silence most offends me, and to be merry best becomes you; for, out of question, you were born in a merry hour.

Beat. No, sure, my lord, my mother cri'd; but then there was a star danced, and under that was I born.—Cousins, God give you joy!

Leon. Niece, will you look to those things I told you of?

Beat. I cry you mercy, uncle.—By your grace's pardon. [*Exit* BEATRICE.

D. Pedro. By my troth, a pleasant-spirited lady.

Leon. There's little of the melancholy element in her, my lord: she is never sad, but when she sleeps; and not ever sad then; for I have heard my daughter say, she hath often dreamed of unhappiness,[5] and waked herself with laughing.

D. Pedro. She cannot endure to hear tell of a husband.

Leon. O, by no means; she mocks all her wooers out of suit.

D. Pedro. She were an excellent wife for Benedick.

Leon. O lord, my lord, if they were but a week married, they would talk themselves mad.

D. Pedro. Count Claudio, when mean you to go to church?

Claud. To-morrow, my lord: Time goes on crutches, till love have all his rites.

Leon. Not till Monday, my dear son, which is hence a just seven-night: and a time too brief too, to have all things answer my mind.

D. Pedro. Come, you shake the head at so long a breathing; but, I warrant thee, Claudio, the time shall not go dully by us; I will, in the interim, undertake one of Hercules' labours; which is, to bring signior Benedick and the lady Beatrice into a mountain of affection,[6] the one with the other. I would fain have it a match; and I doubt not but to fashion it, if you three will but minister such assistance as I shall give you direction.

Leon. My lord, I am for you, though it cost me ten nights' watching.

Claud. And I, my lord.

D. Pedro. And you, too, gentle Hero.

Hero. I will do any modest office, my lord, to help my cousin to a good husband.

D. Pedro. And Benedick is not the unhopefullest husband that I know: thus far can I praise him; he is of a noble strain,[7] of approved valour, and confirmed honesty. I will teach you how to humour your cousin, that she shall fall in love with Benedick:—and I, with your two helps, will so practice on Benedick, that, in despite of his quick wit and his queasy[8] stomach, he shall fall in love with Beatrice. If we can do this, Cupid is no longer an archer; his glory shall be ours, for we

---

whose *conveyances* or tricks appear *impossibilities. Impossible* may, however, be used in the sense of *incredible* or *inconceivable*, both here and in the beginning of the scene, where Beatrice speaks of '*impossible* slanders.'

1 The goddess of discord.

2 Interest.

3 i. e. your *part or turn*; a phrase among the players. V Note on Hamlet, Act ii. Sc. 2.

4 i. e. good lord, how many alliances are forming. Every one is likely to *be married* but I. I am *sun burned* means 'I have lost my beauty, and am consequently no longer an object to tempt a man to marry.'

5 i. e. mischief. *Unhappy* was often used for *mischievous*, as we now say an *unlucky* boy for a *mischievous* boy.

6 'A mountain of affection *with* one another' is, as Johnson observes, a strange expression; yet all that is meant appears to be '*a great deal* of affection.'

7 The same as *strene, descent, lineage*.

8 Squeamish

are the only love-gods. Go in with me, and I will tell you my drift. [*Exeunt.*

SCENE II. *Another Room in* Leonato's *House. Enter* DON JOHN *and* BORACHIO.

D. John. It is so: the count Claudio shall marry the daughter of Leonato.

Bora. Yea, my lord; but I can cross it.

D. John. Any bar, any cross, any impediment will be medicinable to me: I am sick in displeasure to him; and whatsoever comes athwart his affection, ranges evenly with mine. How canst thou cross this marriage?

Bora. Not honestly, my lord; but so covertly that no dishonesty shall appear in me.

D. John. Show me briefly how.

Bora. I think, I told your lordship, a year since, how much I am in the favour of Margaret, the waiting-gentlewoman to Hero.

D. John. I remember.

Bora. I can, at any unseasonable instant of the night, appoint her to look out at her lady's chamber-window.

D. John. What life is in that to be the death of this marriage?

Bora. The poison of that lies in you to temper. Go you to the prince, your brother; spare not to tell him, that he hath wronged his honour in marrying the renowned Claudio (whose estimation do you mightily hold up) to a contaminated stale,[1] such a one as Hero.

D. John. What proof shall I make of that?

Bora. Proof enough to misuse the prince, to vex Claudio, to undo Hero, and kill Leonato: Look you for any other issue?

D. John. Only to despite them, I will endeavour any thing.

Bora. Go then, find me a meet hour to draw Don Pedro and the count Claudio alone: tell them, that you know that Hero loves me; intend[2] a kind of zeal both to the prince and Claudio, as—in love of your brother's honour, who hath made this match; and his friend's reputation, who is thus like to be cozened with the semblance of a maid,—that you have discovered thus. They will scarcely believe this without trial: offer them instances; which shall bear no less likelihood, than to see me at her chamber-window; hear me call Margaret, Hero; hear Margaret term me Claudio;[3] and bring them to see this, the very night before the intended wedding; for, in the mean time I will so fashion the matter, that Hero shall be absent; and there shall appear such seeming truth of Hero's disloyalty, that jealousy shall be call'd assurance, and all the preparation overthrown.

D. John. Grow this to what adverse issue it can, I will put it in practice: Be cunning in the working this, and thy fee is a thousand ducats.

Bora. Be you constant in the accusation, and my cunning shall not shame me.

D. John. I will presently go learn their day of marriage. [*Exeunt.*

SCENE III. Leonato's *Garden. Enter* BENEDICK *and a* Boy.

Bene. Boy,—

Boy. Signior.

Bene. In my chamber-window lies a book; bring it hither to me in the orchard.[4]

Boy. I am here, already, sir.

Bene. I know that;—but I would have thee hence, and here again. [*Exit* Boy.]—I do much wonder, that one man, seeing how much another man is a fool when he dedicates his behaviours to love, will, after he hath laughed at such shallow follies in others, become the argument of his own scorn, by falling in love: And such a man is Claudio. I have known when there was no music with him but the drum and fife; and now had he rather hear the tabor and the pipe: I have known, when he would have walked ten mile afoot, to see a good armour; and now will he lie ten nights awake, carving the fashion of a new doublet.[5] He was wont to speak plain, and to the purpose, like an honest man, and a soldier; and now is he turn'd orthographer; his words are a very fantastical banquet, just so many strange dishes. May I be so converted, and see with these eyes? I cannot tell; I think not: I will not be sworn, but love may transform me to an oyster; but I'll take my oath on it, till he have made an oyster of me, he shall never make me such a fool. One woman is fair; yet I am well: another is wise; yet I am well: another virtuous; yet I am well: but till all the graces be in one woman, one woman shall not come in my grace. Rich she shall be, that's certain; wise, or I'll none; virtuous, or I'll never cheapen her; fair, or I'll never look on her; mild, or come not near me; noble, or not I for an angel; of good discourse, an excellent musician, and her hair shall be of what colour it please God.[6] Ha! the prince and monsieur Love! I will hide me in the arbour. [*Withdraws.*

Enter DON PEDRO, LEONATO, *and* CLAUDIO.

D. Pedro. Come, shall we hear this music?

Claud. Yea, my good lord:—How still the evening is,
As hush'd on purpose to grace harmony!

D. Pedro. See you where Benedick hath hid himself?

Claud. O, very well, my lord: the music ended
We'll fit the kid-fox[7] with a penny-worth.

Enter BALTHAZAR, *with music.*

D. Pedro. Come, Balthazar, we'll hear that song again.

Balth. O good my lord, tax not so bad a voice
To slander music any more than once.

D. Pedro. It is the witness still of excellency,
To put a strange face on his own perfection:—
I pray thee, sing, and let me woo no more.

Balth. Because you talk of wooing, I will sing:
Since many a wooer doth commence his suit
To her he thinks not worthy; yet he woos;
Yet will he swear, he loves.

D. Pedro. Nay, pray thee, come:
Or, if thou wilt hold longer argument,
Do it in notes.

Balth. Note this before my notes,
There's not a note of mine that's worth the noting.

D. Pedro. Why these are very crotchets that he speaks:
Note, notes, forsooth, and noting! [*Music.*

Bene. Now, *Divine air?* now is his soul ravished!

---

1 Shakspeare uses *stale* here, and in a subsequent scene, for *an abandoned woman.* A *stale* also meant a *decoy* or *lure*, but the two words had different origins. It is obvious why the term was applied to prostitutes.

2 Pretend.

3 The old copies read *Claudio* here. Theobald altered it to *Borachio;* yet if Claudio be wrong, it is most probably the poet's oversight. Claudio might conceive that the supposed Hero, called Borachio by the name of *Claudio* in consequence of a secret agreement between them, as a cover in case she were overheard; and *he* would know without a possibility of error that it was not Claudio with whom in fact she conversed. For the other arguments *pro* and *con* we must refer to the variorum Shakspeare.

4 *Orchard* in Shakspeare's time signified a *garden.* So in Romeo and Juliet:
'The orchard walls are high and hard to climb.'
This word was first written *hort-yard*, then by corruption *hort-chard*, and hence orchard.

5 This folly is the theme of all comic satire.

6 Benedick may allude to the fashion of dyeing the hair, very common in Shakspeare's time. Or to that of wearing false hair, which also then prevailed. So, in a subsequent scene: "I like the new tire within excellently, if the *hair* were a thought browner."

7 Kid-fox has been supposed to mean *discovered* or *detected* fox; *Kid* certainly meant known or discovered in Chaucer's time. It may have been a technical term in the game of *hide-fox;* old terms are sometimes longer preserved in jocular sports than in common usage. Some editors have printed it *hid-fox;* and others explained it *young* or *cub fox*

Is it not strange, that sheep's guts should hale souls out of men's bodies?—Well, a horn for my money, when all's done.

BALTHAZAR *sings.*

I.

Balth. *Sigh no more, ladies, sigh no more,*
Men were deceivers ever;
One foot in sea, and one on shore;
To one thing constant never:
Then sigh not so,
But let them go,
And be you blithe and bonny;
Converting all your sounds of woe
Into, Hey nonny, nonny.

II.

Sing no more ditties, sing no mo
Of dumps so dull and heavy;
The fraud of men was ever so,
Since summer first was leavy:
Then sigh not so, &c.

D. Pedro. By my troth, a good song.

Balth. And an ill singer, my lord.

D. Pedro. Ha? no; no, faith; thou singest well enough for a shift.

Bene. [*Aside.*] An he had been a dog, that should have howled thus, they would have hanged him; and, I pray God, his bad voice bode no mischief! I had as lief have heard the night-raven,[1] come what plague could have come after it.

D. Pedro. Yea, marry; [*To* CLAUDIO.]—Dost thou hear, Balthazar? I pray thee, get us some excellent music; for to-morrow night we would have it at the lady Hero's chamber window.

Balth. The best I can, my lord.

D. Pedro. Do so: farewell. [*Exeunt* BALTHAZAR *and music.*] Come hither, Leonato: What was it you told me of to-day? that your niece Beatrice was in love with signior Benedick?

Claud. O, ay:—Stalk on, stalk on; the fowl sits.[2] [*Aside to* PEDRO.] I did never think that lady would have loved any man.

Leon. No, nor I neither; but most wonderful, that she should so dote on signior Benedick, whom she hath in all outward behaviours seemed ever to abhor.

Bene. Is't possible? Sits the wind in that corner? [*Aside.*

Leon. By my troth, my lord, I cannot tell what to think of it; but that she loves him with an enraged affection,—it is past the infinite of thought.[3]

D. Pedro. May be, she doth but counterfeit.

Claud. Faith, like enough.

Leon. O God! counterfeit! There never was counterfeit of passion came so near the life of passion, as she discovers it.

D. Pedro. Why, what effects of passion shows she?

Claud. Bait the hook well; this fish will bite. [*Aside.*

Leon. What effects, my lord! She will sit you,—You heard my daughter tell you how.

Claud. She did, indeed.

D. Pedro. How, how, I pray you? You amaze me: I would have thought her spirit had been invincible against all assaults of affection.

Leon. I would have sworn it had, my lord; especially against Benedick.

Bene. [*Aside.*] I should think this a gull, but that the white-bearded fellow speaks it: knavery cannot, sure, hide itself in such reverence.

Claud. He hath ta'en the infection; hold it up. [*Aside.*

D. Pedro. Hath she made her affection known to Benedick?

Leon. No; and swears she never will: that's her torment.

Claud. 'Tis true, indeed; so your daughter says: *Shall I,* says she, *that have so oft encounter'd him with scorn, write to him that I love him!*

Leon. This says she now when she is beginning to write to him: for she'll be up twenty times a night: and there will she sit in her smock, till she have writ a sheet of paper:—my daughter tells us all.

Claud. Now you talk of a sheet of paper, I remember a pretty jest your daughter told us of.

Leon. O!—When she had writ it, and was reading it over, she found Benedick and Beatrice between the sheet!—

Claud. That.

Leon. O! she tore the letter into a thousand halfpence;[4] railed at herself, that she should be so immodest to write to one that she knew would flout her: *I measure him,* says she, *by my own spirit; for I should flout him, if he writ to me; yea, though I love him, I should.*

Claud. Then down upon her knees she falls, weeps, sobs, beats her heart, tears her hair, prays, curses:—*O sweet Benedick! God give me patience!*

Leon. She doth indeed; my daughter says so: and the ecstasy[5] hath so much overborne her, that my daughter is sometime afraid she will do a desperate outrage to herself: It is very true.

D. Pedro. It were good, that Benedick knew of it by some other, if she will not discover it.

Claud. To what end? He would but make a sport of it, and torment the poor lady worse.

D. Pedro. An he should, it were an alms to hang him: She's an excellent sweet lady; and, out of all suspicion, she is virtuous.

Claud. And she is exceeding wise.

D. Pedro. In every thing but in loving Benedick

Leon. O my lord, wisdom and blood[6] combating in so tender a body, we have ten proofs to one, that blood hath the victory. I am sorry for her, as I have just cause, being her uncle and her guardian.

D. Pedro. I would, she had bestow'd this dotage on me; I would have daff'd[7] all other respects, and made her half myself: I pray you, tell Benedick of it, and hear what he will say.

Leon. Were it good, think you?

Claud. Hero thinks surely, she will die: for she says, she will die if he love her not; and she will die ere she makes her love known; and she will die if he woo her, rather than she will 'bate one breath of her accustomed crossness.

D. Pedro. She doth well: if she should make tender of her love, 'tis very possible he'll scorn it; for the man, as you know all, hath a contemptible[8] spirit.

Claud. He is a very proper[9] man.

D. Pedro. He hath, indeed, a good outward happiness.

Claud. 'Fore God, and in my mind, very wise.

D. Pedro. He doth, indeed, show some sparks that are like wit.

Leon. And I take him to be valiant.

D. Pedro. As Hector, I assure you: and in the managing of quarrels you may say he is wise; for either he avoids them with great discretion, or undertakes them with a most christian-like fear.

Leon. If he do fear God, he must necessarily keep peace; if he break the peace, he ought to enter into a quarrel with fear and trembling.

D. Pedro. And so will he do; for the man doth fear God, howsoever it seems not in him by some large jests he will make. Well, I am sorry for your niece: Shall we go see Benedick, and tell him of her love?

---

1 i. e. the owl.

2 This is an allusion to the *stalking-horse;* a horse either real or factitious, by which the fowler anciently screened himself from the sight of the game.

3 i. e. 'but with what an enraged affection she loves him, it is beyond the infinite power of thought to conceive.'

4 i. e. into a thousand *small pieces;* it should be remembered that the *silver* halfpence, which were then current, were very minute pieces.

5 See the Tempest, Act iii. Sc. 1.

6 i. e. passion.

7 To *daff* is the same as to *do off,* to *doff,* to put aside.

8 That is, a spirit inclined to scorn and contempt [illegible] should be *contemptuous.*

9 Handsome.

MUCH ADO ABOUT NOTHING.

Act 3. Scene 1.

Claud. Never tell him, my lord; let her wear it out with good counsel.

Leon. Nay, that's impossible; she may wear her heart out first.

D. Pedro. Well, we'll hear further of it by your daughter; let it cool the while. I love Benedick well; and I could wish he would modestly examine himself, to see how much he is unworthy to have so good a lady.

Leon. My lord, will you walk? dinner is ready.

Claud. If he do not dote on her upon this, I will never trust my expectation. [*Aside.*

D. Pedro. Let there be the same net spread for her; and that must your daughter and her gentlewoman carry. The sport will be, when they hold one an opinion of another's dotage, and no such matter; that's the scene that I would see, which will be merely a dumb show. Let us send her to call him in to dinner. [*Aside.*

Exeunt DON PEDRO, CLAUDIO, *and* LEONATO.

BENEDICK *advances from the arbour.*

Bene. This can be no trick: The conference was sadly borne.[1]—They have the truth of this from Hero. They seem to pity the lady; it seems, her affections have their full bent.[2] Love me! why, it must be requited. I hear how I am censured: they say, I will bear myself proudly, if I perceive the love come from her; they say too, that she will rather die than give any sign of affection.—I did never think to marry:—I must not seem proud:—Happy are they that hear their detractions, and can put them to mending. They say the lady is fair; 'tis a truth, I can bear them witness: and virtuous; —'tis so, I cannot reprove it; and wise, but for loving me:—By my troth, it is no addition to her wit;—nor no great argument of her folly, for I will be horribly in love with her. I may chance have some odd quirks and remnants of wit broken on me, because I have railed so long against marriage:—But doth not the appetite alter? A man loves the meat in his youth that he cannot endure in his age: Shall quips, and sentences, and these paper bullets of the brain, awe a man from the career of his humour? No: The world must be peopled. When I said, I would die a bachelor, I did not think I should live till I were married.—Here comes Beatrice: By this day, she's a fair lady: I do spy some marks of love in her.

Enter BEATRICE.

Beat. Against my will I am sent to bid you come in to dinner.

Bene. Fair Beatrice, I thank you for your pains.

Beat. I took no more pains for those thanks than you take pains to thank me; if it had been painful, I would not have come.

Bene. You take pleasure then in the message?

Beat. Yea, just so much as you may take upon a knife's point, and choke a daw withal:—You have no stomach, signior; fare you well. [*Exit.*

Bene. Ha! *Against my will I am sent to bid you come to dinner*—there's a double meaning in that. *I took no more pains for those thanks than you took pains to thank me*—that's as much as to say, Any pains that I take for you is as easy as thanks:—If I do not take pity of her, I am a villain; if I do not love her, I am a Jew: I will go get her picture. [*Exit.*

ACT III.

SCENE I. Leonato's *Garden. Enter* HERO, MARGARET, *and* URSULA.

Hero. Good Margaret, run thee into the parlour;
There shalt thou find my cousin Beatrice
Proposing[3] with the Prince and Claudio:
Whisper her ear, and tell her, I and Ursula
Walk in the orchard, and our whole discourse
Is all of her; say, that thou overheard'st us;
And bid her steal into the pleached bower,
Where honey-suckles, ripen'd by the sun,
Forbid the sun to enter;—like favourites,
Made proud by princes, that advance their pride
Against that power that bred it:—there will she hide her,
To listen our propose:[4] This is thy office,
Bear thee well in it, and leave us alone.

Marg. I'll make her come, I warrant you, presently. [*Exit.*

Hero. Now, Ursula, when Beatrice doth come,
As we do trace this alley up and down,
Our talk must only be of Benedick:
When I do name him, let it be thy part
To praise him more than ever man did merit:
My talk to thee must be, how Benedick
Is sick in love with Beatrice: Of this matter
Is little Cupid's crafty arrow made,
That only wounds by hearsay. Now begin;

Enter BEATRICE, *behind.*

For look where Beatrice, like a lapwing, runs
Close by the ground, to hear our conference.

Urs. The pleasant'st angling is to see the fish
Cut with their golden oars the silver stream,
And greedily devour the treacherous bait:
So angle we for Beatrice; who even now
Is couched in the woodbine coverture:
Fear you not my part of the dialogue.—

Hero. Then go we near her, that her ear lose nothing
Of the false sweet bait, that we lay for it.—
[*They advance to the bower.*
No, truly, Ursula, she is too disdainful;
I know her spirits are as coy and wild
As haggards of the rock.[5]

Urs. But are you sure,
That Benedick loves Beatrice so entirely?

Hero. So says the prince, and my new-trothed lord.

Urs. And did they bid you tell her of it, madam?

Hero. They did entreat me to acquaint her of it;
But I persuaded them, if they lov'd Benedick,
To wish him[6] wrestle with affection,
And never to let Beatrice know of it.

Urs. Why did you so? Doth not the gentleman
Deserve as full,[7] as fortunate a bed,
As ever Beatrice shall couch upon?

Hero. O God of love! I know, he doth deserve
As much as may be yielded to a man:
But nature never fram'd a woman's heart
Of prouder stuff than that of Beatrice:
Disdain and scorn ride sparkling in her eyes,
Misprising[8] what they look on; and her wit
Values itself so highly, that to her
All matter else seems weak: she cannot love,
Nor take no shape nor project of affection,
She is so self-endear'd.

---

1 Seriously carried on.

2 Steevens and Malone assert that this is a metaphor from archery, saying that *the full bent* is the utmost extremity of exertion. Surely there is no ground for the assertion! It was one of the most common forms of expression in the language for *inclination, tendency*; and was used where it is impossible there could have been any allusion to the bending of a bow, as in these phrases, from a writer of Elizabeth's age: 'The day inclining or *bending* to the evening.—'*Bending* to a yellow colour.'

3 *Proposing* is conversing, from the French *Propos*, discourse, talk.

4 The folio reads *purpose.* The quarto *propose*, which appears to be right. See the preceding note. Though Mr. Reed has shown that purpose was sometimes used in the same sense.

5 A hawk not manned, or trained to obedience: a wild hawk. *Hagard*, Fr. Latham, in his Book of Falconry, says: 'Such is the greatness of her spirit, *she will not admit of any society* until such a time as nature worketh,' &c. So, in The Tragical History of Didaco and Violenta, 1576:

'Perchance she's not of haggard's kind,
Nor heart so hard to bend,' &c.

6 *Wish* him, that is, *recommend* or *desire* him. So in The Honest Whore, 1604:

'Go *wish* the surgeon to have great respect,' &c.

7 So, in Othello:

'What a *full* fortune does the thick lips owe.'

What Ursula means to say is, 'that he is as deserving of complete happiness as Beatrice herself.'

8 Undervaluing.

Urs. Sure, I think so;
And therefore, certainly, it were not good
She knew his love, lest she make sport at it.
Hero. Why, you speak truth: I never yet saw man,
How wise, how noble, young, how rarely featur'd,
But she would spell him backward:[1] if fair-faced,
She'd swear the gentleman should be her sister;
If black, why, nature, drawing of an antic,
Made a foul blot:[2] if tall, a lance ill-headed;
If low, an agate very vilely cut:[3]
If speaking, why a vane blown with all winds:
If silent, why a block moved with none.
So turns she every man the wrong side out;
And never gives to truth and virtue that
Which simpleness and merit purchaseth.
Urs. Sure, sure, such carping is not commendable.
Hero. No: nor to be so odd, and from all fashions,
As Beatrice is, cannot be commendable:
But who dare tell her so? If I should speak,
She'd mock me into air; O, she would laugh me
Out of myself, press me to death with wit.[4]
Therefore let Benedick, like cover'd fire,
Consume away in sighs, waste inwardly:
It were a better death than die with mocks;
Which is as bad as die with tickling.[5]
Urs. Yet tell her of it; hear what she will say.
Hero. No; rather I will go to Benedick,
And counsel him to fight against his passion:
And, truly, I'll devise some honest slanders
To stain my cousin with: One doth not know,
How much an ill word may empoison liking.
Urs. O, do not do your cousin such a wrong.
She cannot be so much without true judgment,
(Having so swift[6] and excellent a wit,
As she is priz'd to have,) as to refuse
So rare a gentleman as signior Benedick.
Hero. He is the only man of Italy,
Always excepted my dear Claudio.
Urs. I pray you, be not angry with me, madam,
Speaking my fancy; signior Benedick,
For shape, for bearing, argument,[7] and valour,
Goes foremost in report through Italy.
Hero. Indeed, he hath an excellent good name.
Urs. His excellency did earn it, ere he had it.—
When are you married, madam?
Hero. Why, every day;—to-morrow: Come, go in:
I'll show thee some attires; and have thy counsel,
Which is the best to furnish me to-morrow.
Urs. She's lim'd[8] I warrant you; we have caught her, madam.
Hero. If it prove so, then loving goes by haps:
Some Cupid kills with arrows, some with traps.
[*Exeunt* HERO *and* URSULA.

BEATRICE *advances.*

Beat. What fire is in mine ears?[9] Can this be true?
Stand I condemn'd for pride and scorn so much?
Contempt, farewell! and maiden pride, adieu!
No glory lives behind the back of such.
And, Benedick, love on, I will requite thee;
Taming my wild heart to thy loving hand;[10]
If thou dost love, my kindness shall incite thee
To bind our loves up in a holy band:
For others say, thou dost deserve; and I
Believe it better than reportingly. [*Exit*

SCENE II. *A Room in* Leonato's *House. Enter* DON PEDRO, CLAUDIO, BENEDICK, *and* LEONATO.

D. Pedro. I do but stay till your marriage be consummate, and then I go toward Arragon.

Claud. I'll bring you thither, my lord, if you'll vouchsafe me.

D. Pedro. Nay, that would be as great a soil in the new gloss of your marriage, as to show a child his new coat, and forbid him to wear it. I will only be bold with Benedick for his company: for, from the crown of his head to the sole of his foot, he is all mirth; he hath twice or thrice cut Cupid's bow-string, and the little hangman[11] dare not shoot at him: he hath a heart as sound as a bell, and his tongue is the clapper; for what his heart thinks, his tongue speaks.[12]

Bene. Gallants, I am not as I have been.

Leon. So say I; methinks you are sadder.

Claud. I hope, he be in love.

D. Pedro. Hang him, truant; there's no true drop of blood in him, to be truly touch'd with love: if he be sad, he wants money.

Bene. I have the tooth-ach.[13]

D. Pedro. Draw it.

Bene. Hang it!

Claud. You must hang it first, and draw it afterwards.

D. Pedro. What, sigh for the tooth-ach?

Leon. Where is but a humour, or a worm?

Bene. Well, every one can master a grief, but he that has it.

Claud. Yet say I, he is in love.

D. Pedro. There is no appearance of fancy[14] in him, unless it be a fancy that he hath to strange disguises; as, to be a Dutchman to-day; a Frenchman to-morrow; or in the shape of two countries at once;[15] as, a German from the waist downward, all slops;[16] and a Spaniard from the hip upward, no doublet: Unless he have a fancy to this foolery, as it appears he hath, he is no fool for fancy, as you would have it appear he is.

Claud. If he be not in love with some woman,

---

1 Alluding to the practice of witches in uttering prayers, i. e. misinterpret them. Several passages, containing a similar train of thought, are cited by Mr. Steevens from Lily's Euphues.

2 A *black* man here means a man with a dark or thick beard, which is the *blot* in nature's drawing.

3 An *agate* is often used metaphorically for a very diminutive person, in allusion to the figures cut in agate for rings, &c. Queen Mab is described, 'In shape no bigger than an *agate stone* on the forefinger of an alderman.' See note on K. Henry IV. Part 2.

4 The allusion is to an ancient punishment inflicted on those who refused to plead to an indictment. If they continued silent, they were pressed to death by heavy weights laid on their stomach. This species of torture is now abolished.

5 This word is intended to be pronounced as a trisyllable, it was sometimes written *tickeling.*

6 Quick, ready. 7 Conversation.

8 i. e. ensnared and entangled, as a sparrow with bird-lime.

9 Alluding to the proverbial saying, which is as old as Pliny's time: 'That when our *ears do glow and tingle*, some there be that in our absence do talke of us.' Holland's Translation, B. xxxiii. p. 297.

10 This image is taken from Falconry. She has been charged with being as wild as *haggards of the rock*; she therefore says, that wild as her heart is, she will *tame* it *to the hand.*

11 Dr. Farmer has illustrated this term by citing a passage from Sidney's Arcadia, B. II. C. xiv.; but it seems probable that no more is meant by *hangman* than *executioner*, slayer of hearts.

12 A covert allusion to the old proverb:
'As the fool thinketh
The bell clinketh.'

13 So, in The False One, by Beaumont and Fletcher
'O this sounds mangily,
Poorly and scurvily in a soldier's mouth,
You had best be troubled with the toothach too,
For lovers ever are.'

14 A play upon the word *fancy*, which Shakspeare uses for *love*, as well as for *humour, caprice*, or *affectation.*

15 So, in The Seven deadly Sinnes of London, by Decker, 1606, 'For an Englishman's sute is like a traitor's body that hath beene hanged, drawne, and quartered, and is set up in several places: his codpiece, in Denmarke; the collar of his dublet and the belly, in France; the wing and narrow sleeve, in Italy; the short waste hangs over a botcher's stall in Utrich; his huge sloppes speaks Spanish; Polonia gives him the bootes, &c.—and thus we mocke everie nation for keeping one fashion, yet steale patches from everie of them to piece out our pride; and are now laughing-stocks to them, because their cut so scurvily becomes us.'

16 Large loose breeches or trowsers. Hence a *slop seller* for one who furnishes seamen, &c. with clothes

there is no believing old signs: he brushes his hat o' mornings; What should that bode?

D. Pedro. Hath any man seen him at the barber's?

Claud. No, but the barber's man hath been seen with him; and the old ornament of his cheek hath already stuffed tennis-balls.

Leon. Indeed, he looks younger than he did, by the loss of a beard.

D. Pedro. Nay, he rubs himself with civet: Can you smell him out by that?

Claud. That's as much as to say, The sweet youth's in love.

D. Pedro. The greatest note of it is his melancholy.

Claud. And when was he wont to wash his face?

D. Pedro. Yea, or to paint himself? for the which, I hear what they say of him.

Claud. Nay, but his jesting spirit; which is now crept into a lutestring[1] and now governed by stops.

D. Pedro. Indeed, that tells a heavy tale for him: Conclude, conclude, he is in love.

Claud. Nay, but I know who loves him.

D. Pedro. That would I know too; I warrant, one that knows him not.

Claud. Yes, and his ill conditions; and, in despite of all, dies for him.

D. Pedro. She shall be buried with her face upwards.[2]

Bene. Yet is this no charm for the tooth-ach.—Old signior, walk aside with me: I have studied eight or nine wise words to speak to you, which these hobby-horses must not hear.

[*Exeunt* BENEDICK *and* LEONATO.

D. Pedro. For my life, to break with him about Beatrice.

Claud. 'Tis even so: Hero and Margaret have by this played their parts with Beatrice; and then the two bears will not bite one another when they meet.

Enter DON JOHN.

D. John. My lord and brother, God save you.

D. Pedro. Good den, brother.

D. John. If your leisure served, I would speak with you.

D. Pedro. In private?

D. John. If it please you:—yet Count Claudio may hear; for what I would speak of concerns him.

D. Pedro. What's the matter?

D. John. Means your lordship to be married tomorrow? [*To* CLAUDIO.

D. Pedro. You know, he does.

D. John. I know not that, when he knows what I know.

Claud. If there be any impediment, I pray you, discover it.

D. John. You may think, I love you not; let that appear hereafter, and aim better at me by that I now will manifest: For my brother, I think, he holds you well; and in dearness of heart hath holp to effect your ensuing marriage; surely, suit ill spent, and labour ill bestowed!

D. Pedro. Why, what's the matter?

D. John. I came hither to tell you; and, circumstances shortened, (for she hath been too long a talking of,) the lady is disloyal.

Claud. Who? Hero?

D. John. Even she; Leonato's Hero, your Hero, every man's Hero.

Claud. Disloyal?

D. John. The word is too good to paint out her wickedness; I could say, she were worse; think you of a worse title, and I will fit her to it. Wonder not till further warrant: go but with me to-night, you shall see her chamber-window entered; even the night before her wedding-day: if you love her then, to-morrow wed her: but it would better fit your honour to change your mind.

Claud. May this be so?

D. Pedro. I will not think it.

D. John. If you dare not trust that you see, confess not that you know: if you will follow me, I will show you enough; and when you have seen more, and heard more, proceed accordingly.

Claud. If I see any thing to-night why I should not marry her to-morrow; in the congregation, where I should wed, there will I shame her.

D. Pedro. And as I wooed for thee to obtain her, I will join with thee to disgrace her.

D. John. I will disparage her no farther, till you are my witnesses: bear it coldly but till midnight, and let the issue show itself.

D. Pedro. O day untowardly turned!

Claud. O mischief strangely thwarting!

D. John. O plague right well prevented!
So will you say, when you have seen the sequel.

[*Exeunt.*

SCENE III. *A Street. Enter* DOGBERRY *and* VERGES,[3] *with the* Watch.

Dogb. Are you good men and true?

Verg. Yea, or else it were pity but they should suffer salvation, body and soul.

Dogb. Nay, that were a punishment too good for them, if they should have any allegiance in them, being chosen for the prince's watch.

Verg. Well, give them their charge,[4] neighbour Dogberry.

Dogb. First, who think you the most desartless man to be constable?

1 *Watch.* Hugh Oatcake, sir, or George Seacoal; for they can write and read.

Dogb. Come hither, neighbour Seacoal. God hath blessed you with a good name: to be a well favoured man is the gift of fortune; but to write and read comes by nature.

2 *Watch.* Both which, master constable,——

Dogb. You have; I knew it would be your answer. Well, for your favour, sir, why, give God thanks, and make no boast of it; and for your writing and reading, let that appear when there is no need of such vanity. You are thought here to be the most senseless and fit man for the constable of the watch; therefore bear you the lantern: This is your charge: You shall comprehend all vagrom men: you are to bid any man stand, in the prince's name.

2 *Watch.* How if he will not stand?

Dogb. Why then, take no note of him, but let him go; and presently call the rest of the watch together, and thank God you are rid of a knave.

Verg. If he will not stand when he is bidden, he is none of the prince's subjects.

Dogb. True, and they are to meddle with none but the prince's subjects:—You shall also make no noise in the streets; for, for the watch to babble and talk, is most tolerable and not to be endured.

2 *Watch.* We will rather sleep than talk; we know what belongs to a watch.

Dogb. Why, you speak like an ancient and most quiet watchman; for I cannot see how sleeping should offend; only, have a care that your bills be not stolen:—Well, you are to call at all the alehouses, and bid those that are drunk get them to bed.

2 *Watch.* How if they will not?

Dogb. Why then, let them alone till they are sober; if they make you not then the better answer, you may say, they are not the men you took them for.

---

1 *Love-songs*, in Shakspeare's time, were sung to the lute. So, in Henry VI. Part I.
'As melancholy as an old lion or a *lover's lute*.'

2 i. e. 'in her lover's arms.' So in The Winter's Tale:
Flo. What? like a corse?
Per. No, like a bank for love to lie and play on;
Not like a corse:—or if,—not to be *buried*,
But quick and in my arms.'

3 The first of these worthies is named from the *Dog berry* or female cornel, a shrub that grows in every county in England. *Verges* is only the provincial pronunciation of *verjuice*.

4 To *charge* his fellows seems to have been a regular part of the duty of the constable.

2 *Watch.* Well, sir.

Dogb. If you meet a thief, you may suspect him, by virtue of your office, to be no true man: and, for such kind of men, the less you meddle or make with them, why, the more is for your honesty.

2 *Watch.* If we know him to be a thief, shall we not lay hands on him?

Dogb. Truly, by your office, you may; but I think, they that touch pitch will be defiled: the most peaceable way for you, if you do take a thief, is, to let him show himself what he is, and steal out of your company.

Verg. You have been always called a merciful man, partner.

Dogb. Truly, I would not hang a dog by my will; much more a man, who hath any honesty in him.

Verg. If you hear a child cry in the night, you must call to the nurse, and bid her still it.[1]

2 *Watch.* How if the nurse be asleep, and will not hear us?

Dogb. Why then, depart in peace, and let the child wake her with crying; for the ewe that will not hear her lamb when it baas, will never answer a calf when he bleats.

Verg. 'Tis very true.

Dogb. This is the end of the charge. You, constable, are to present the prince's own person; if you meet the prince in the night, you may stay him.

Verg. Nay, by'r lady, that, I think, he cannot.

Dogb. Five shillings to one on't, with any man that knows the statues, he may stay him: marry, not without the prince be willing; for, indeed, the watch ought to offend no man; and it is an offence to stay a man against his will.

Verg. By'r lady, I think, it be so.

Dogb. Ha, ha, ha! Well, masters, good night: an there be any matter of weight chances, call up me: keep your fellows' counsels and your own,[2] and good night.—Come, neighbour.

2 *Watch.* Well, masters, we hear our charge: let us go sit here upon the church-bench till two, and then all to bed.

Dogb. One word more, honest neighbours: I pray you, watch about signior Leonato's door; for the wedding being there to-morrow, there is a great coil to-night: Adieu, be vigitant, I beseech you.

[*Exeunt* Dogberry *and* Verges.

Enter Borachio *and* Conrade.

Bora. What! Conrade,—

Watch. Peace, stir not. [*Aside.*

Bora. Conrade, I say!

Con. Here, man, I am at thy elbow.

Bora. Mass, and my elbow itched; I thought there would a scab follow.

Con. I will owe thee an answer for that; and now forward with thy tale.

Bora. Stand thee close then under this pent-house, for it drizzles rain; and I will, like a true drunkard, utter all to thee.

Watch. [*Aside.*] Some treason, masters; yet stand close.

Bora. Therefore know, I have earned of Don John a thousand ducats.

Con. Is it possible that any villany should be so dear?

Bora. Thou shouldst rather ask, if it were possible any villany should be so rich; for when rich villains have need of poor ones, poor ones may make what price they will.

Con. I wonder at it.

Bora. That shows thou art unconfirmed:[3] Thou knowest, that the fashion of a doublet, or a hat, or a cloak, is nothing to a man.

Con. Yes, it is apparel.

Bora. I mean, the fashion.

Con. Yes, the fashion is the fashion.

Bora. Tush! I may as well say, the fool's the fool. But seest thou not what a deformed thief this fashion is?

Watch. I know that Deformed; he has been a vile thief this seven year; he goes up and down like a gentleman: I remember his name.

Bora. Didst thou not hear somebody?

Con. No; 'twas the vane on the house.

Bora. Seest thou not, I say, what a deformed thief this fashion is? how giddily he turns about all the hot bloods, between fourteen and five and thirty! sometime, fashioning them like Pharaoh's soldiers in the reechy[4] painting; sometime, like god Bel's priests in the old church window; sometime, like the shaven Hercules in the smirched[5] worm-eaten tapestry, where his cod-piece seems as massy as his club?

Con. All this I see; and see, that the fashion wears out more apparel than the man: But art not thou thyself giddy with the fashion too, that thou hast shifted out of thy tale into telling me of the fashion.

Bora. Not so neither: but know, that I have to-night wooed Margaret, the lady Hero's gentlewoman, by the name of Hero; she leans me out at her mistress' chamber-window, bids me a thousand times good night,—I tell this tale vilely:—I should first tell thee, how the Prince, Claudio, and my master, planted, and placed, and possessed by my master Don John, saw afar off in the orchard this amiable encounter.

Con. And thought they, Margaret was Hero?

Bora. Two of them did, the Prince and Claudio; but the devil my master knew she was Margaret; and partly by his oaths, which first possessed them, partly by the dark night, which did deceive them, but chiefly by my villany, which did confirm any slander that Don John had made, away went Claudio enraged; swore he would meet her as he was appointed, next morning at the temple, and there, before the whole congregation, shame her with what he saw over-night, and send her home again without a husband.

1 *Watch.* We charge you in the prince's name, stand.

2 *Watch.* Call up the right master constable: We have here recovered the most dangerous piece of lechery that ever was known in the commonwealth.

1 *Watch.* And one Deformed is one of them; I know him, he wears a lock.

Con. Masters, masters.

2 *Watch.* You'll be made bring Deformed forth, I warrant you.

Con. Masters,—

1 *Watch.* Never speak; we charge you, let us obey you to go with us.

Bora. We are like to prove a goodly commodity, being taken up of these men's bills.[6]

Con. A commodity in question,[7] I warrant you. Come, we'll obey you. [*Exeunt.*

SCENE IV. *A Room in* Leonato's *House. Enter* Hero, Margaret, *and* Ursula.

Hero. Good Ursula, wake my cousin Beatrice and desire her to rise.

Urs. I will, lady.

Hero. And bid her come hither.

Urs. Well. [*Exit* Ursula

Marg. Troth, I think, your other rabato[8] were better.

Hero. No, pray thee, good Meg, I'll wear this.

---

1 It is not impossible but that a part of this scene was intended as a burlesque upon 'The Statutes of the Streets, imprinted by Wolfe in 1595.'

2 This is part of the oath of a grand juryman, and is one of many proofs of Shakspeare's having been very conversant with legal proceedings and courts of justice at some period of his life.

3 Unpracticed in the ways of the world.

4 i. e. discoloured by smoke, *reeky* From *recan*, Saxon.

5 Soiled, sullied. Probably only another form of *smutched*. The word is peculiar to Shakspeare.

6 We have the same conceit in K. Henry VI. Part ii. 'My lord, when shall we go to Cheapside, and *take up commodities* upon our *bills*!'

7 i. e. in examination or trial.

8 A kind of ruff. *Rabat*, Fr. Menage says it comes from *rabattre*, to put back, being at first nothing but the collar of the shirt turned back toward the shoulders.

Marg. By my troth, it's not so good; and I warrant, your cousin will say so.

Hero. My cousin's a fool, and thou art another; I'll wear none but this.

Marg. I like the new tire[1] within excellently, if the hair were a thought browner: and your gown's a most rare fashion, i'faith. I saw the duchess of Milan's gown, that they praise so.

Hero. O, that exceeds, they say.

Marg. By my troth it's but a night-gown in respect of yours: Cloth of gold, and cuts, and laced with silver; set with pearls, down-sleeves, side-sleeves,[2] and skirts round, underborne with a blueish tinsel: but for a fine, quaint, graceful, and excellent fashion, yours is worth ten on't.

Hero. God give me joy to wear it, for my heart is exceeding heavy!

Marg. 'Twill be heavier soon by the weight of a man.

Hero. Fye upon thee! art not ashamed?

Marg. Of what, lady? of speaking honourably? Is not marriage honourable in a beggar? Is not your lord honourable without marriage? I think, you would have me say, saving your reverence,—*a husband:* an bad thinking do not wrest true speaking, I'll offend nobody: Is there any harm in—*the heavier for a husband?* None, I think, an it be the right husband, and the right wife; otherwise 'tis light, and not heavy: Ask my lady Beatrice else, here she comes.

Enter BEATRICE.

Hero. Good morrow, coz.

Beat. Good morrow, sweet Hero.

Hero. Why, how now! do you speak in the sick tune?

Beat. I am out of all other tune, methinks.

Marg. Clap us into—*Light o' love;* that goes without burden; do you sing it, and I'll dance it.

Beat. Yea, *Light o' love,*[3] with your heels?—then if your husband have stables enough, you'll see he shall lack no barns.[4]

Marg. O illegitimate construction! I scorn that with my heels.

Beat. 'Tis almost five o'clock, cousin; 'tis time you were ready. By my troth I am exceeding ill:—hey ho!

Marg. For a hawk, a horse, or a husband?

Beat. For the letter that begins them all, H.[5]

Marg. Well, an you be not turned Turk, there's no more sailing by the star.

Beat. What means the fool, trow?[6]

Marg. Nothing I; but God send every one their heart's desire!

Hero. These gloves the count sent me, they are an excellent perfume.

Beat. I am stuffed, cousin, I cannot smell.

Marg. A maid, and stuffed! there's goodly catching of cold.

Beat. O, God help me! God help me! how long have you profess'd apprehension?

Marg. Ever since you left it: doth not my wit become me rarely?

Beat. It is not seen enough, you should wear it in your cap.—By my troth, I am sick.

Marg. Get you some of this distilled Carduus Benedictus,[7] and lay it to your heart; it is the only thing for a qualm.

Hero. There thou prick'st her with a thistle.

Beat. Benedictus! why Benedictus? you have some moral[8] in this Benedictus.

Marg. Moral? no, by my troth, I have no moral meaning; I meant, plain holy-thistle. You may think, perchance, that I think you are in love: nay, by'r lady, I am not such a fool to think what I list; nor I list not to think what I can; nor, indeed, I cannot think, if I would think my heart out of thinking, that you are in love, or that you will be in love, or that you can be in love: yet Benedick was such another, and now is he become a man: he swore he would never marry; and yet now, in despite of his heart, he eats his meat without grudging:[9] and how you may be converted, I know not; but methinks, you look with your eyes as other women do.

Beat. What pace is this that thy tongue keeps?

Marg. Not a false gallop.

Re-enter URSULA.

Urs. Madam, withdraw; the prince, the count, signior Benedick, Don John, and all the gallants of the town, are come to fetch you to church.

Hero. Help to dress me, good coz, good Meg, good Ursula. [*Exeunt.*

SCENE V. *Another Room in* Leonato's *House.*

Enter LEONATO, *with* DOGBERRY *and* VERGES.

Leon. What would you with me, honest neighbour?

Dogb. Marry, sir, I would have some confidence with you, that decerns you nearly.

Leon. Brief, I pray you; for you see, 'tis a busy time with me.

Dogb. Marry, this it is, sir.

Verg. Yes, in truth it is, sir.

Leon. What is it, my good friends?

Dogb. Goodman Verges, sir, speaks a little off the matter: an old man, sir, and his wits are not so blunt, as, God help, I would desire they were; but in faith, honest as the skin between his brows.

Verg. Yes, I thank God, I am as honest as any man living, that is an old man and no honester than I.

Dogb. Comparisons are odorous: *palabras,*[10] neighbour Verges.

Leon. Neighbours, you are tedious.

Dogb. It pleases your worship to say so, but we are the poor[11] duke's officers; but, truly, for mine own part, if I were as tedious as a king, I could find in my heart to bestow it all of your worship.

Leon. All thy tediousness on me! ha!

1 Head-dress.

2 i. e. *long sleeves. Side* or *syde* in North Britain is used for *long* when applied to the garment. It has the same signification in Anglo-Saxon and Danish.

3 The name of a popular old dance tune, mentioned again in the Two Gentlemen of Verona, and in several of our old dramas. The notes are given in the Variorum Shakspeare.

4 A quibble between *barns* repositories for corn, and *bairns* children, formerly pronounced barns. So, in The Winter's Tale:

'Mercy on us, *a barn!* a very pretty *barn!*'

5 That is for an *ach* or pain, pronounced *aitch.* See note on Tempest, Act i. Sc. 2. Heywood has an epigram which best elucidates this:

'H is worst among letters in the cross-row,'
For if thou find him either in thine elbow,
In thine arm or leg, in any degree;
In thine head, or teeth, or toe, or knee;
Into what place soever H may pike him,
Wherever thou find him *ache* thou shalt not like him.'

6 So in The Merry Wives of Windsor:—'Who's there, *trow?*' This obsolete exclamation of inquiry is a contraction of *trow ye?* think you? believe you? Steevens was mistaken in saying, that To *trow* is to imagine, to conceive.

7 '*Carduus Benedictus*, or blessed thistle (says Cogan in his Haven of Health, 1595), so worthily named for the singular virtues that it hath.'—'This herbe may worthily be called *Benedictus*, or *Omnimorbia*, that it is a salve for every sore, not known to physitians of old time, but lately revealed by the speciall providence of Almighty God.'

8 'You have some *moral* in this Benedictus,' i. e. some *hidden meaning*, like the *moral* of a fable. Thus in the Rape of Lucrece:

'Nor could she *moralize* his wanton sight.'

And in the Taming of the Shrew, 'to expound the *meaning* or *moral* of his signs and tokens.'

9 i. e. '*feeds* on *love*, and likes his food.'

10 i. e. *words*, in Spanish. It seems to have been current here for a time, even among the vulgar; it was probably introduced by our sailors, as well as the corrupted form pala'ver. We have it again in the mouth of Sly the Tinker, 'Therefore *paucas pallabris:* let the world slide, Sessa.'

11 This stroke of pleasantry, arising from the transposition of the epithet *poor*, has already occurred in Measure for Measure. Elbow says; 'If it please your honour, I am the *poor duke's* constable.'

Dogb. Yea, and 'twere a thousand times more than 'tis; for I hear as good exclamation on your worship, as of any man in the city; and though I be but a poor man, I am glad to hear it.

Verg. And so am I.

Leon. I would fain know what you have to say.

Verg. Marry, sir, our watch to-night, excepting your worship's presence, have ta'en a couple of as arrant knaves as any in Messina.

Dogb. A good old man, sir; he will be talking; as they say, When the age is in, the wit is out; God help us! it is a world to see![1]—Well said, i'faith, neighbour Verges:—well, God's a good man; an two men ride of a horse, one must ride behind:—An honest soul, i'faith, sir: by my troth he is, as ever broke bread: but, God is to be worshipped: All men are not alike; alas! good neighbour!

Leon. Indeed, neighbour, he comes too short of you.

Dogb. Gifts, that God gives.

Leon. I must leave you.

Dogb. One word, sir: our watch, sir, have, indeed, comprehended two aspicious persons, and we would have them this morning examined before your worship.

Leon. Take their examination yourself, and bring it me; I am now in great haste, as it may appear unto you.

Dogb. It shall be suffigance.

Leon. Drink some wine ere you go; fare you well.

Enter a Messenger.

Mess. My lord, they stay for you to give your daughter to her husband.

Leon. I will wait upon them; I am ready.

[*Exeunt* Leonato *and* Messenger.

Dogb. Go, good partner, go, get you to Francis Seacoal, bid him bring his pen and inkhorn to the gaol; we are now to examination these men.

Verg. And we must do it wisely.

Dogb. We will spare for no wit, I warrant you; here's that, [*Touching his forehead,*] shall drive some of them to a *non com:* only get the learned writer to set down our excommunication, and meet me at the gaol. [*Exeunt.*

ACT IV.

SCENE I. *The Inside of a Church. Enter* Don Pedro, Don John, Leonato, Friar, Claudio, Benedick, Hero, *and* Beatrice, *&c.*

Leon. Come, Friar Francis, be brief; only to the plain form of marriage, and you shall recount their particular duties afterwards.

Friar. You come hither, my lord, to marry this lady?

Claud. No.

Leon. To be married to her, friar; you come to marry her.

Friar. Lady, you come hither to be married to this count.

Hero. I do.

Friar. If either of you know any inward impediment why you should not be conjoined, I charge you, on your souls, to utter it.[2]

Claud. Know you any, Hero?

Hero. None, my lord.

Friar. Know you any, count?

Leon. I dare make his answer, none.

Claud. O, what men dare do! what men may do! what men daily do! not knowing what they do!

Bene. How now! Interjections? Why, then some be of laughing, as, ha! ha! he!

Claud. Stand thee by, friar:—Father, by your leave!
Will you with free and unconstrained soul
Give me this maid, your daughter?

Leon. As freely, son, as God did give her me.

Claud. And what have I to give you back, whose worth
May counterpoise this rich and precious gift?

D. Pedro. Nothing, unless you render her again.

Claud. Sweet prince, you learn me noble thankfulness.—
There Leonato, take her back again.
Give not this rotten orange to your friend;
She's but the sign and semblance of her honour:—
Behold, how like a maid she blushes here:
O, what authority and show of truth
Can cunning sin cover itself withal!
Comes not that blood, as modest evidence,
To witness simple virtue? Would you not swear,
All you that see her that she were a maid,
By these exterior shows?—But she is none:
She knows the heat of a luxurious[3] bed:
Her blush is guiltiness, not modesty.

Leon. What do you mean, my lord?

Claud. Not to be married,
Not to knit my soul to an approved wanton.

Leon. Dear my lord, if you, in your own proof[4]
Have vanquish'd the resistance of her youth,
And made defeat of her virginity,——

Claud. I know what you would say; If I have known her,
You'll say she did embrace me as a husband,
And so extenuate the 'forehand sin:
No, Leonato,
I never tempted her with word too large;[5]
But, as a brother to his sister, show'd
Bashful sincerity, and comely love.

Hero. And seem'd I ever otherwise to you?

Claud. Out on thy seeming! I will write against it
You seem to me as Dian in her orb;
As chaste as is the bud ere it be blown;
But you are more intemperate in your blood
Than Venus or those pamper'd animals
That rage in savage sensuality.

Hero. Is my lord well, that he doth speak so wide?[6]

Leon. Sweet prince, why speak not you?

D. Pedro. What should I speak?
I stand dishonour'd, that have gone about
To link my dear friend to a common stale.

Leon. Are these things spoken? or do I but dream?

D. John. Sir, they are spoken, and these things are true.

Bene. This looks not like a nuptial.

Hero. True, O God.

Claud. Leonato stand I here?
Is this the prince? Is this the prince's brother?
Is this face Hero's? Are our eyes our own?

Leon. All this is so; but what of this my lord?

Claud. Let me but move one question to your daughter;
And by that fatherly and kindly power[7]
That you have in her, bid her answer truly.

Leon. I charge thee do so, as thou art my child.

Hero. O God, defend me! how am I beset!—
What kind of catechizing call you this?

Claud. To make you answer truly to your name.

Hero. Is it not Hero? Who can blot that name
With any just reproach?

Claud. Marry, that can Hero;
Hero itself can blot out Hero's virtue.
What man was he talk'd with you yesternight
Out at your window, betwixt twelve and one?
Now, if you are a maid, answer to this.

1 This was a common apostrophe of admiration equivalent to 'it is *wonderful*,' or 'it is admirable.'

2 This is borrowed from our marriage ceremony, which, (with a few changes in phraseology,) is the same as was used in Shakspeare's time.

3 Lascivious.

4 i. e. 'if in your own trial.'

5 Licentious.

6 i. e. 'So remotely from the present business.' 'You are *wide* of the matter,' is a familiar phrase still in use

7 i. e. 'natural power.' *Kind* is used for *nature* So in The Induction to The Taming of the Shrew—
'This do, and do it *kindly*, gentle sirs.'
which here also signifies *naturally*

Hero. I talk'd with no man at that hour, my lord.
D. Pedro. Why then are you no maiden.—Leonato,
I am sorry you must hear; upon my honour,
Myself, my brother, and this grieved count,
Did see her, hear her, at that hour last night,
Talk with a ruffian at her chamber-window;
Who hath, indeed, most like a liberal[1] villain,
Confess'd the vile encounters they have had
A thousand times in secret.
D. John. Fie, Fie! they are
Not to be nam'd, my lord, not to be spoke of;
There is not chastity enough in language,
Without offence to utter them: Thus, pretty lady,
I am sorry for thy much misgovernment.
Claud. O Hero! what a Hero hadst thou been,
If half thy outward graces had been placed
About thy thoughts, and counsels of thy heart!
But fare thee well, most foul, most fair! farewell,
Thou pure impiety, and impious purity!
For thee I'll lock up all the gates of love,
And on my eyelids shall conjecture hang,
To turn all beauty into thoughts of harm,
And never shall it more be gracious.[2]
Leon. Hath no man's dagger here a point for me?
[HERO *swoons.*
Beat. Why, how now, cousin? wherefore sink you down?
D. John. Come, let us go: these things, come thus to light,
Smother her spirits up.
[*Exeunt* DON PEDRO, DON JOHN, *and* CLAUDIO.
Bene. How doth the lady?
Beat. Dead, I think;—help, uncle;—
Hero! why, Hero!—Uncle!—Signior Benedict!—friar?
Leon. O fate take not away thy heavy hand!
Death is the fairest cover for her shame,
That may be wish'd for.
Beat. How now, cousin Hero?
Friar. Have comfort, lady.
Leon. Dost thou look up?
Friar. Yea; Wherefore should she not?
Leon. Wherefore? Why, doth not every earthly thing
Cry shame upon her? Could she here deny
The story that is printed in her blood?[3]—
Do not live, Hero; do not ope thine eyes:
For did I think thou wouldst not quickly die,
Thought I thy spirits were stronger than thy shames,
Myself would, on the rearward of reproaches,
Strike at thy life. Griev'd I, I had but one?
Chid I for that at frugal nature's frame?[4]
O, one too much by thee! Why had I one?
Why ever wast thou lovely in my eyes?
Why had I not with charitable hand,
Took up a beggar's issue at my gates;
Who smirched[5] thus, and mired with infamy,
I might have said, *No part of it is mine,*
This shame derives itself from unknown loins?
But mine, and mine I lov'd, and mine I prais'd,
And mine that I was proud on; mine so much,
That I myself was to myself not mine,
Valuing of her: why, she—O, she is fallen
Into a pit of ink! that the wide sea
Hath drops too few to wash her clean again;[6]
And salt too little, which may season give
To her foul tainted flesh!
Bene. Sir, sir, be patient:
For my part, I am so attir'd in wonder,
I know not what to say.
Beat. O, on my soul, my cousin is belied!
Bene. Lady, were you her bedfellow last night?
Beat. No, truly, not: although, until last night,
I have this twelvemonth been her bedfellow.
Leon. Confirm'd, confirm'd! O, that is stronger made,
Which was before barr'd up with ribs of iron!
Would the two princes lie? and Claudio lie?
Who lov'd her so, that, speaking of her foulness,
Wash'd it with tears? Hence from her; let her die.
Friar. Hear me a little;
For I have only been silent so long,
And given way unto this course of fortune,
By noting of the lady: I have mark'd
A thousand blushing apparitions start
Into her face; a thousand innocent shames
In angel whiteness bear away those blushes;
And in her eye there hath appear'd a fire,
To burn the errors that these princes hold
Against her maiden truth:—Call me a fool;
Trust not my reading nor my observations,
Which with experimental zeal doth warrant
The tenour of my book; trust not my age,
My reverence, calling, nor divinity,
If this sweet lady lie not guiltless here
Under some biting error.
Leon. Friar, it cannot be.
Thou seest, that all the grace that she hath left,
Is, that she will not add to her damnation
A sin of perjury; she not denies it;
Why seek'st thou then to cover with excuse
That which appears in proper nakedness?
Friar. Lady, what man is he you are accus'd of?
Hero. They know, that do accuse me; I know none:
If I know more of any man alive,
Than that which maiden modesty doth warrant,
Let all my sins lack mercy!—O my father,
Prove you that any man with me convers'd
At hours unmeet, or that I yesternight
Maintain'd the change of words with any creature,
Refuse me, hate me, torture me to death.
Friar. There is some strange misprision[7] in the princes.
Bene. Two of them have the very bent[8] of honour;
And if their wisdoms be misled in this,
The practice of it lives in John the bastard,
Whose spirits toil in frame of villanies.
Leon. I know not; If they speak but truth of her,
These hands shall tear her; if they wrong her honour,
The proudest of them shall well hear of it.
Time hath not yet so dried this blood of mine,
Nor age so eat up my invention,
Nor fortune made such havock of my means,
Nor my bad life reft me so much of friends,
But they shall find, awak'd in such a kind,
Both strength of limb, and policy of mind,
Ability in means, and choice of friends,
To quit me of them throughly.
Friar. Pause a while,
And let my counsel sway you in this case.
Your daughter here the princes left for dead;
Let her awhile be secretly kept in,
And publish it, that she is dead indeed:
Maintain a mourning ostentation;[9]
And on your family's old monument
Hang mournful epitaphs, and do all rites
That appertain unto a burial.
Leon. What shall become of this? What will this do?
Friar. Marry, this well carried, shall on her behalf
Change slander to remorse; that is some good.
But not for that, dream I on this strange course,
But on this travail look for greater birth.
She dying, as it must be so maintain'd,
Upon the instant that she was accus'd,
Shall be lamented, pitied and excus'd,
Of every hearer: For it so falls out,

1 *Liberal* here, as in many places of these plays, means *licentious beyond honesty or decency.* This sense of the word is not peculiar to Shakspeare.
2 i. e. graced, favoured, countenanced. See As You Like It, Act i. Sc. 2.
3 That is, 'which her *blushes* discovered to be true.'
4 *Frame* is order, contrivance, disposition of things.
5 See note 5, p. 160, ante.
6 The same thought is repeated in Macbeth:
'Will all great Neptune's *ocean wash* this blood
Clean from my hand.'
7 Misconception.
8 *Bent* is here used for the utmost degree of, or tendency to honourable conduct.
9 Show, appearance

That what we have we prize not to the worth,
Whiles we enjoy it; but being lack'd and lost,
Why, then we rack[1] the value; then we find
The virtue, that possession would not show us
Whiles it was ours:—So will it fare with Claudio:
When he shall hear she died upon[2] his words,
The idea of her life shall sweetly creep
Into his study of imagination;
And every lovely organ of her life
Shall come apparell'd in more precious habit,
More moving-delicate, and full of life,
Into the eye and prospect of his soul,
Than when she liv'd indeed:—then shall he mourn,
(If ever love had interest in his liver,[3])
And wish he had not so accused her;
No, though he thought his accusation true.
Let this be so, and doubt not but success
Will fashion the event in better shape
Than I can lay it down in likelihood.
But if all aim but this be levell'd false,
The supposition of the lady's death
Will quench the wonder of her infamy:
And, if it sort not well, you may conceal her
(As best befits her wounded reputation,)
In some reclusive and religious life,
Out of all eyes, tongues, minds, and injuries.

Bene. Signior Leonato, let the friar advise you:
And though, you know, my inwardness[4] and love
Is very much unto the prince and Claudio,
Yet, by mine honour, I will deal in this
As secretly, and justly, as your soul
Should with your body.

Leon. Being that I flow in grief,
The smallest twine may lead me.[5]

Friar. 'Tis well consented; presently away;
For to strange sores they strangely strain the cure.—
Come, lady, die to live: this wedding day,
Perhaps is but prolong'd; have patience, and endure.

[*Exeunt* Friar, HERO, *and* LEONATO.

Bene. Lady Beatrice, have you wept all this while?

Beat. Yea, and I will weep a while longer.

Bene. I will not desire that.

Beat. You have no reason, I do it freely.

Bene. Surely, I do believe your fair cousin is wrong'd.

Beat. Ah, how much might the man deserve of me, that would right her!

Bene. Is there any way to show such friendship?

Beat. A very even way, but no such friend.

Bene. May a man do it?

Beat. It is a man's office, but not yours.

Bene. I do love nothing in the world so well as you; is not that strange?

Beat. As strange as the thing I know not: It were as possible for me to say, I loved nothing so well as you: but believe me not; and yet I lie not; I confess nothing, nor I deny nothing:—I am sorry for my cousin.

Bene. By my sword, Beatrice, thou lovest me.

Beat. Do not swear by it, and eat it.

Bene. I will swear by it that you love me; and I will make him eat it, that says I love not you.

Beat. Will you not eat your word?

Bene. With no sauce that can be devised to it: I protest I love thee.

Beat. Why then, God forgive me!

Bene. What offence, sweet Beatrice?

Beat. You have staid me in a happy hour; I was about to protest, I loved you.

Bene. And do it with all thy heart.

Beat. I love you with so much of my heart, that none is left to protest.

Bene. Come, bid me do any thing for thee

Beat. Kill Claudio.

Bene. Ha! not for the wide world.

Beat. You kill me to deny it: Farewell

Bene. Tarry, sweet Beatrice.

Beat. I am gone, though I am here:[6]—There is no love in you:—Nay, I pray you, let me go.

Bene. Beatrice,—

Beat. In faith, I will go.

Bene. We'll be friends first.

Beat. You dare easier be friends with me, than fight with mine enemy.

Bene. Is Claudio thine enemy?

Beat. Is he not approved in the height a villain,[7] that hath slandered, scorned, dishonoured my kinswoman?—O, that I were a man!—What! bear her in hand[8] until they come to take hands; and then with public accusation, uncovered slander, unmitigated rancour,—O God, that I were a man! I would eat his heart in the market-place.

Bene. Hear me, Beatrice;—

Beat. Talk with a man out at a window?—a proper saying!

Bene. Nay but, Beatrice;—

Beat. Sweet Hero!—she is wronged, she is slandered, she is undone.

Bene. Beat—

Beat. Princes, and counties![9] Surely a princely testimony, a goodly count-confect;[10] a sweet gallant, surely! O that I were a man for his sake! or that I had any friend would be a man for my sake! But manhood is melted into courtesies,[11] valour into compliment, and men are only turned into tongue, and trim[12] ones too: he is now as valiant as Hercules, that only tells a lie, and swears it:—I cannot be a man with wishing, therefore I will die a woman with grieving.

Bene. Tarry, good Beatrice: By this hand I love thee.

Beat. Use it for my love some other way than swearing by it.

Bene. Think you in your soul the count Claudio hath wronged Hero?

Beat. Yea, as sure as I have a thought, or a soul.

Bene. Enough, I am engaged, I will challenge him; I will kiss your hand, and so leave you: By this hand Claudio shall render me a dear account: As you hear of me, so think of me. Go, comfort your cousin; I must say she is dead; and so farewell. [*Exeunt.*

SCENE II. *A Prison. Enter* DOGBERRY, VERGES,[13] *and* Sexton, *in gowns: and the* Watch, *with* CONRADE *and* BORACHIO.

Dogb. Is our whole dissembly appeared?

Verg. O, a stool and a cushion for the sexton!

Sexton. Which be the malefactors?

Dogb. Marry, that am I and my partner.

Verg. Nay, that's certain; we have the exhibition to examine.[14]

Sexton. But which are the offenders that are to be examined? let them come before master constable.

Dogb. Yea, marry, let them come before me.—What is your name, friend?

---

1 i. e. raise to the highest pitch.

2 Upon *the occasion* of his words she died: his words were the cause of her death.

3 The liver was anciently supposed to be the seat of love.

4 Intimacy.

5 This is one of Shakspeare's subtle observations upon life. Men, overpowered with distress, eagerly listen to the first offers of relief, close with every scheme, and believe every promise. He that has no longer any confidence in himself is glad to repose his trust in any other that will undertake to guide him.

6 i. e. 'I am in reality absent, *for my heart is gone from you,* I remain in person before you.'

7 So, in K. Henry VIII.: 'He's a traitor to the *height.*' *In præcipiti vitium stetit.*—JUV. i. 149

8 Delude her with false expectations.

9 *Countie* was the ancient term for a *count* or *earl.*

10 A specious nobleman made out of sugar.

11 Ceremonies.

12 *Trim* seems here to signify *apt, fair spoken. Tongue* used in the singular, and *trim ones* in the plural, is a mode of construction not uncommon in Shakspeare

13 Throughout this scene the names of *Kempe* and *Cowley,* two celebrated actors of the time, are put for *Dogberry* and *Verges* in the old editions.

14 This is a blunder of the constable's, for 'examination to exhibit.' In the last scene of the third act Leonato says: 'Take their examination yourself and bring it me.'

Bora. Borachio.

Dogb. Pray write down—Borachio.——Yours, sirrah?

Con. I am a gentleman, sir, and my name is Conrade.

Dogb. Write down—master gentleman Conrade.—Masters, do you serve God?

Con. Bora. Yea, sir, we hope.

Dogb. Write down—that they hope they serve God:—and write God first; for God defend but God should go before such villains!—Masters, it is proved already that you are little better than false knaves; and it will go near to be thought so shortly. How answer you for yourselves?

Con. Marry, sir, we say we are none.

Dogb. A marvellous witty fellow, I assure you; but I will go about with him.—Come you hither, sirrah; a word in your ear, sir; I say to you, it is thought you are false knaves.

Bora. Sir, I say to you, we are none.

Dogb. Well, stand aside.—'Fore God they are both in a tale: Have you writ down—that they are none?

Sexton. Master constable, you go not the way to examine; you must call forth the watch that are their accusers.

Dogb. Yea, marry, that's the eftest[1] way;—Let the watch come forth:—Masters, I charge you, in the prince's name, accuse these men.

1 *Watch.* This man said, sir, that Don John, the prince's brother, was a villain.

Dogb. Write down—prince John, a villain:—Why this is flat perjury, to call a prince's brother—villain.

Bora. Master constable,—

Dogb. Pray thee, fellow, peace; I do not like thy look, I promise thee.

Sexton. What heard you him say else?

2 *Watch.* Marry, that he had received a thousand ducats of Don John, for accusing the lady Hero wrongfully.

Dogb. Flat burglary, as ever was committed.

Verg. Yea, by the mass, that it is.

Sexton. What else, fellow?

1 *Watch.* And that count Claudio did mean, upon his words, to disgrace Hero before the whole assembly, and not marry her.

Dogb. O villain! thou wilt be condemned into everlasting redemption for this.

Sexton. What else?

2 *Watch.* This is all.

Sexton. And this is more, masters, than you can deny. Prince John is this morning secretly stolen away; Hero was in this manner accused, in this very manner refused, and upon the grief of this suddenly died.—Master constable, let these men be bound, and brought to Leonato's; I will go before, and show him their examination. [*Exit.*

Dogb. Come, let them be opinioned.

Verg. Let them be in the bands[2]—

Con. Off, coxcomb!

Dogb. God's my life! where's the sexton? let him write down—the prince's officer, coxcomb.—Come, bind them:——Thou naughty varlet.

Con. Away! you are an ass, you are an ass.

Dogb. Dost thou not suspect my place? Dost thou not suspect my years?—O that he were here to write me down—an ass!—but, masters, remember, that I am an ass; though it be not written down, yet forget not that I am an ass:—No, thou villain, thou art full of piety, as shall be proved upon thee by good witness. I am a wise fellow; and, which is more, an officer; and, which is more, a householder: and, which is more, as pretty a piece of flesh as any is in Messina; and one that knows the law, go to; and a rich fellow enough, go to; and a fellow that hath had losses; and one that hath two gowns, and every thing handsome about him:—Bring him away. O, that I had been writ down—an ass. [*Exeunt.*

ACT V.

SCENE I. *Before* Leonato's *House.* *Enter* LEONATO *and* ANTONIO.

Ant. If you go on thus, you will kill yourself;
And 'tis not wisdom, thus to second grief
Against yourself.

Leon. I pray thee, cease thy counsel
Which falls into mine ears as profitless
As water in a sieve: give not me counsel;
Nor let no comforter delight mine ear,
But such a one whose wrongs do suit with mine.
Bring me a father, that so lov'd his child,
Whose joy of her is overwhelm'd like mine,
And bid him speak of patience;
Measure his woe the length and breadth of mine,
And let it answer every strain for strain;
As thus for thus, and such a grief for such,
In every lineament, branch, shape, and form:
If such a one will smile, and stroke his beard:
Cry—sorrow, wag! and hem, when he should groan;[3]
Patch grief with proverbs; make misfortune drunk
With candle-wasters;[4] bring him yet to me,
And I of him will gather patience.
But there is no such man: For, brother, men
Can counsel, and speak comfort to that grief
Which they themselves not feel; but, tasting it,
Their counsel turns to passion, which before
Would give preceptial medicine to rage,
Fetter strong madness in a silken thread,
Charm ach with air, and agony with words:
No, no; 'tis all men's office to speak patience
To those that wring under the load of sorrow;
But no man's virtue, nor sufficiency,
To be so moral, when he shall endure
The like himself: therefore give me no counsel:
My griefs cry louder than advertisement.[5]

Ant. Therein do men from children nothing differ.

Leon. I pray thee, peace: I will be flesh and blood;
For there was never yet philosopher,
That could endure the tooth-ach patiently
However they have writ the style of gods,
And made a push[6] at chance and sufferance.

Ant. Yet bend not all the harm upon yourself;
Make those, that do offend you, suffer too.

Leon. There thou speak'st reason: nay, I will do so:
My soul doth tell me, Hero is belied,
And that shall Claudio know, so shall the prince
And all of them, that thus dishonour her.

Enter DON PEDRO *and* CLAUDIO.

Ant. Here comes the prince, and Claudio, hastily

D. Pedro. Good den, good den.

Claud. Good day to both of you.

Leon. Hear you, my lords,—

D. Pedro. We have some haste, Leonato.

Leon. Some haste, my lord!—well, fare you well, my lord:—
Are you so hasty now?—well, all is one.

D. Pedro. Nay, do not quarrel with us, good old man.

Ant. If he could right himself with quarreling,
Some of us would lie low.

Claud. Who wrongs him?

Leon. Marry, thou dost wrong me; thou dissembler, thou:—
Nay, never lay thy hand upon thy sword,
I fear thee not.

Claud. Marry, beshrew my hand,

---

1 i. e. the *quickest* way.

2 In the old copy this passage stands thus: '*Sexton.* Let them be in the hands of Coxcomb.'

3 The folio reads, 'And sorrow, wagge, cry hem,' &c.

4 *Candle wasters.* A contemptuous term for *book-worms* or *hard students* used by Ben Jonson in Cynthia's Revels, and others.

5 That is, 'than *admonition*, than *moral instruction*.'

6 *Push* is the reading of the old copy, which Pope altered to *pish* without any seeming necessity. To make a *push* at any thing is to contend against it or defy it

If it should give your age such cause of fear;
In faith, my hand meant nothing to my sword.

Leon. Tush, tush, man, never fleer and jest at me:
I speak not like a dotard, nor a fool;
As, under privilege of age, to brag
What I have done being young, or what would do,
Were I not old: Know, Claudio, to thy head,
Thou hast so wrong'd mine innocent child and me,
That I am forc'd to lay my reverence by;
And, with grey hairs, and bruise of many days,
Do challenge thee to trial of a man.
I say, thou hast belied mine innocent child;
Thy slander hath gone through and through her heart,
And she lies buried with her ancestors:
O! in a tomb where never scandal slept,
Save this of her's fram'd by thy villany.

Claud. My villany!

Leon. Thine, Claudio; thine I say,

D. Pedro. You say not right, old man.

Leon. My lord, my lord.
I'll prove it on his body, if he dare;
Despite his nice fence, and his active practice,[1]
His May of youth, and bloom of lustyhood.

Claud. Away, I will not have to do with you.

Leon. Canst thou so daff[2] me? Thou hast kill'd my child;
If thou kill'st me, boy, thou shalt kill a man.

Ant. He shall kill two of us, and men indeed:
But that's no matter; let him kill one first;—
Win me and wear me,—let him answer me,—
Come, follow me, boy; come, boy, follow me:[3]
Sir boy, I'll whip you from your foining[4] fence;
Nay, as I am a gentleman, I will.

Leon. Brother,—

Ant. Content yourself: God knows, I lov'd my niece;
And she is dead, slander'd to death by villains;
That dare as well answer a man, indeed,
As I dare take a serpent by the tongue;
Boys, apes, braggarts, jacks, milksops!—

Leon. Brother Antony,—

Ant. Hold you content; What, man! I know them, yea,
And what they weigh, even to the utmost scruple:
Scambling,[5] out-facing, fashion-mong'ring boys,
That lie, and cog, and flout, deprave and slander,
Go anticly, and show outward hideousness,[6]
And speak off half a dozen dangerous words,
How they might hurt their enemies, if they durst,
And this is all.

Leon. But, brother Antony,—

Ant. Come, 'tis no matter;
Do not you meddle, let me deal in this.

D. Pedro. Gentlemen both, we will not wake[7] your patience.
My heart is sorry for your daughter's death;
But, on my honour, she was charg'd with nothing
But what was true, and very full of proof.

Leon. My lord, my lord,—

D. Pedro. I will not hear you.

Leon. No?
Come, brother, away:—I will be heard;—

Ant. And shall,
Or some of us will smart for it.

[*Exeunt* LEONATO *and* ANTONIO.

Enter BENEDICK.

D. Pedro. See, see; here comes the man we went to seek.

Claud. Now, signior! what news?

Bene. Good day, my lord.

D. Pedro. Welcome, signior: You are almost come to part almost a fray.

Claud. We had like to have had our two noses snapped off with two old men without teeth.

D. Pedro. Leonato and his brother: What think'st thou? Had we fought, I doubt, we should have been too young for them.

Bene. In a false quarrel there is no true valour I came to seek you both.

Claud. We have been up and down to seek thee; for we are high-proof melancholy, and would fain have it beaten away: Wilt thou use thy wit?

Bene. It is in my scabbard; Shall I draw it?

D. Pedro. Dost thou wear thy wit by thy side?

Claud. Never any did so, though very many have been beside their wit.—I will bid thee draw, as we do the minstrels; draw, to pleasure us.[8]

D. Pedro. As I am an honest man, he looks pale:—Art thou sick, or angry?

Claud. What! courage, man! What though care killed a cat, thou hast mettle enough in thee to kill care.

Bene. Sir, I shall meet your wit in the career, an you charge it against me:—I pray you, choose another subject.

Claud. Nay, then give him another staff; this last was broke cross.[9]

D. Pedro. By this light, he changes more and more; I think, he be angry indeed.

Claud. If he be, he knows how to turn his girdle.[10]

Bene. Shall I speak a word in your ear?

Claud. God bless me from a challenge!

Bene. You are a villain;—I jest not;—I will make it good how you dare, with what you dare, and when you dare:—Do me right, or I will protest your cowardice. You have killed a sweet lady, and her death shall fall heavy on you: Let me hear from you.

Claud. Well, I will meet you, so I may have good cheer.

D. Pedro. What, a feast? a feast?

Claud. I'faith, I thank him; he hath bid[11] me to a calf's head and a capon; the which if I do not carve most curiously, say, my knife's naught.—Shall I not find a woodcock[12] too.

Bene. Sir, your wit ambles well; it goes easily.

D. Pedro. I'll tell thee how Beatrice praised thy wit the other day: I said thou hadst a fine wit: *True*, says she, *a fine little one*: *No*, said I, *a great wit*; *Right*, says she, *a great gross one*: *Nay*, said I, *a good wit*: *Just*; said she, *it hurts nobody*: *Nay*, said I, *the gentleman is wise*; *Certain*, said she, *a wise gentleman*:[13] *Nay*, said I, *he hath the tongues*: *That I believe*, said she, *for he swore a thing to me on Monday night, which he foreswore on Tuesday morning; there's a double tongue; there's two tongues.* Thus, did she, an hour together, transshape thy particular virtues; yet, at last, she concluded with a sigh, thou wast the properest man in Italy.

Claud. For the which she wept heartily, and said, she cared not.

D. Pedro. Yea, that she did; but yet, for all that, and if she did not hate him deadly, she would love him dearly: the old man's daughter told us all.

---

1 Skill in fencing.

2 This is only a corrupt form of *doff*, to *do off* or *put off*.

3 The folio reads:—
——Come, *sir* boy, come follow me.

4 Thrusting.

5 *Scambling* appears to have been much the same as *scrambling*; shifting or shuffling.

6 i. e. what in King Henry V. Act iii. Sc. 6, is called—
'—— *a horrid suit* of the camp.'

7 i. e. rouse, stir up, convert your patience into anger, by remaining longer in your presence.

8 'I will bid thee draw thy sword, as we bid the minstrels draw the bows of their fiddles, merely to please us.'

9 The allusion is to *tilting*. See note, As You Like It, Act iii. Sc. 4.

10 There is a proverbial phrase, 'If he be angry let him turn the buckle of his girdle.' Mr. Holt White says, 'Large belts were worn with the buckle before, but for wrestling the buckle was turned behind, to give the adversary a fairer grasp at the girdle. To turn the buckle behind was therefore a challenge.'

11 Invited.

12 A *woodcock*, being supposed to have no brains, was a common phrase for a foolish fellow. It means here one caught in a springe or trap, alluding to the plot against Benedick.

13 *Wise gentleman* was probably used ironically for a silly fellow; as we still say a *wise-acre*.

Claud. All, all; and moreover, *God saw him when he was hid in the garden.*

D. Pedro. But when shall we set the savage bull's horns on the sensible Benedick's head?

Claud. Yea, and text underneath, *Here dwells Benedick the married man?*

Bene. Fare you well, boy; you know my mind; I will leave you now to your gossip-like humour; you break jests as braggarts do their blades, which, God be thanked, hurt not.—My lord, for your many courtesies I thank you: I must discontinue your company: your brother, the bastard, is fled from Messina: you have, among you, killed a sweet and innocent lady: For my lord Lack-beard, there, he and I shall meet; and till then, peace be with him.
[*Exit* BENEDICK.

D. Pedro. He is in earnest.

Claud. In most profound earnest; And I'll warrant you, for the love of Beatrice.

D. Pedro. And hath challenged thee?

Claud. Most sincerely.

D. Pedro. What a pretty thing man is, when he goes in his doublet and hose, and leaves off his wit.[1]

Claud. He is then a giant to an ape; but then is an ape a doctor to such a man.

D. Pedro. But, soft you, let be;[2] pluck up my heart, and be sad![3] Did he not say, my brother was fled.

Enter DOGBERRY, VERGES, *and the* Watch, *with* CONRADE *and* BORACHIO.

Dogb. Come, you, sir; if justice cannot tame you, she shall ne'er weigh more reasons in her balance: nay, and you be a cursing hypocrite once, you must be looked to.

D. Pedro. How now, two of my brother's men bound! Borachio, one!

Claud. Hearken after their offence, my lord!

D. Pedro. Officers, what offence have these men done?

Dogb. Marry, sir, they have committed false report; moreover, they have spoken untruths; secondarily, they are slanders: sixth and lastly, they have belied a lady; thirdly, they have veried unjust things; and, to conclude, they are lying knaves.

D. Pedro. First, I ask thee what they have done; thirdly, I ask thee what's their offence; sixth and lastly, why they are committed; and, to conclude, what you lay to their charge?

Claud. Rightly reasoned, and in his own division; and, by my troth, there's one meaning well suited.[4]

D. Pedro. Whom have you offended, masters, that you are thus bound to your answer? this learned constable is too cunning to be understood: What's your offence?

Bora. Sweet prince, let me go no further to mine answer; do you hear me, and let this count kill me. I have deceived even your very eyes: what your wisdoms could not discover, these shallow fools have brought to light; who, in the night, overheard me confessing to this man, how Don John, your brother, incensed[5] me to slander the lady Hero; how you were brought into the orchard, and saw me court Margaret in Hero's garment; how you disgraced her, when you should marry her: my villany they have upon record; which I had rather seal with my death, than repeat over to my shame: the lady is dead upon mine and my master's false accusation; and, briefly, I desire nothing but the reward of a villain.

D. Pedro. Runs not this speech like iron through
your blood?

Claud. I have drunk poison, whiles he utter'd it.

D. Pedro. But did my brother set thee on to this?

Bora. Yea, and paid me richly for the practice of it.

D. Pedro. He is compos'd and fram'd of treachery:—
And fled he is upon this villany.

Claud. Sweet Hero! now thy image doth appear
In the rare semblance that I loved it first.

Dogb. Come, bring away the plaintiffs; by this time our Sexton hath reformed signior Leonato of the matter: And masters, do not forget to specify, when time and place shall serve, that I am an ass.

Verg. Here, here comes master signior Leonato, and the Sexton too.

Re-enter LEONATO *and* ANTONIO, *with the* Sexton.

Leon. Which is the villain? Let me see his eyes;
That when I note another man like him,
I may avoid him: Which of these is he?

Bora. If you would know your wronger, look on me.

Leon. Art thou the slave, that with thy breath hast kill'd
Mine innocent child?

Bora. Yea, even I alone.

Leon. No, not so, villain; thou bely'st thyself
Here stand a pair of honourable men,
A third is fled, that had a hand in it:—
I thank you, princes, for my daughter's death;
Record it with your high and worthy deeds;
'Twas bravely done, if you bethink you of it.

Claud. I know not how to pray your patience,
Yet I must speak: Choose your revenge yourself;
Impose[6] me to what penance your invention
Can lay upon my sin: yet sinn'd I not,
But in mistaking.

D. Pedro. By my soul, nor I;
And yet, to satisfy this good old man,
I would bend under any heavy weight
That he'll enjoin me to.

Leon. I cannot bid you bid my daughter live,
That were impossible; but, I pray you both,
Possess[7] the people in Messina here
How innocent she died: and, if your love
Can labour aught in sad invention,
Hang her an epitaph upon her tomb,[8]
And sing it to her bones; sing it to-night:—
To-morrow morning come you to my house;
And since you could not be my son-in-law,
Be yet my nephew: my brother hath a daughter
Almost the copy of my child that's dead,
And she alone is heir to both of us;[9]
Give her the right you should have given her cousin,
And so dies my revenge.

Claud. O, noble sir,
Your over-kindness doth wring tears from me!
I do embrace your offer; and dispose
For henceforth of poor Claudio.

Leon. To-morrow then I will expect your coming;
To-night I take my leave.—This naughty man
Shall face to face be brought to Margaret,
Who, I believe, was pack'd[10] in all this wrong,
Hir'd to it by your brother.

Bora. No, by my soul, she was not;
Nor knew not what she did, when she spoke to me;
But always hath been just and virtuous,
In any thing that I do know by her.

---

1 These words are probably meant to express what Rosaline, in As You Like It, calls the '*careless desolation*' of a lover.

2 The old copies read 'let *me* be,' the emendation is Malone's. *Let be* appears here to signify *hold, rest there.* It has the same signification in Saint Matthew, ch. xxvii. v. 49.

3 i. e. 'rouse thyself my heart and be prepared for serious consequences.'

4 That is, *one meaning put into many different dresses;* the Prince having asked the same question in four modes of speech.

5 Incited, instigated.

6 i. e. '*inflict* upon me whatever penance, &c.'

7 To *possess* anciently signified to *inform,* to *make acquainted with.* So in the Merchant of Venice:
'I have *possess'd* your grace of what I purpose.'

8 It was the custom among Catholics to attach, upon or near the tomb of celebrated persons, a written inscription either in prose or verse generally in praise of the deceased.

9 Yet Shakspeare makes Leonato say to Antonio, Act i. Sc. 5, 'How now, brother; where is my cousin your son,' &c.

10 i. e. combined: an accomplice.

Dogb. Moreover, sir (which, indeed, is not under white and black,) this plaintiff here, the offender, did call me ass: I beseech you, let it be remembered in his punishment: And also, the watch heard them talk of one Deformed: they say, he wears a key in his ear, and a lock hanging by it;[1] and borrows money in God's name; the which he hath used so long, and never paid, that now men grow hard-hearted, and will lend nothing for God's sake: Pray you, examine him upon that point.

Leon. I thank thee for thy care and honest pains.

Dogb. Your worship speaks like a most thankful and reverend youth: and I praise God for you.

Leon. There's for thy pains.

Dogb. God save the foundation.[2]

Leon. Go, I discharge thee of thy prisoner, and I thank thee.

Dogb. I leave an errant knave with your worship; which, I beseech your worship, to correct yourself, for the example of others. God keep your worship; I wish your worship well; God restore you to health: I humbly give you leave to depart; and if a merry meeting may be wished, God prohibit it.—Come, neighbour.

[*Exeunt* DOGBERRY, VERGES, *and* Watch.

Leon. Until to-morrow morning, lords, farewell.

Ant. Farewell, my lords; we look for you to-morrow.

D. Pedro. We will not fail.

Claud. To-night I'll mourn with Hero.

[*Exeunt* DON PEDRO *and* CLAUDIO.

Leon. Bring you these fellows on; we'll talk with Margaret,
How her acquaintance grew with this lewd[3] fellow.

[*Exeunt.*

SCENE II. Leonato's *Garden. Enter* BENEDICK *and* MARGARET, *meeting.*

Bene. Pray thee, sweet mistress Margaret, deserve well at my hands, by helping me to the speech of Beatrice.

Marg. Will you then write me a sonnet in praise of my beauty?

Bene. In so high a style, Margaret, that no man living shall come over it; for, in most comely truth, thou deservest it.

Marg. To have no man come over me? why, shall I always keep below stairs?[4]

Bene. Thy wit is as quick as the greyhound's mouth, it catches.

Marg. And your's as blunt as the fencer's foils, which hit, but hurt not.

Bene. A most manly wit, Margaret, it will not hurt a woman; and so, I pray thee, call Beatrice: I give thee the bucklers.[5]

Marg. Give us the swords, we have bucklers of our own.

Bene. If you use them, Margaret, you must put in the pickes with a vice; and they are dangerous weapons for maids.

Marg. Well, I will call Beatrice to you, who, I think hath legs. [*Exit* MARGARET.

Bene. And therefore will come.

The god of love, [Singing.
That sits above,
And knows me, and knows me,
How pitiful I deserve,—

I mean, in singing; but in loving,—Leander the good swimmer, Troilus the first employer of panders, and a whole book full of these quondam car pet mongers, whose names yet run smoothly in the even road of a blank verse, why, they were never so truly turned over and over as my poor self, in love: Marry, I cannot show it in rhyme; I have tried; I can find out no rhyme to *lady* but *baby*, an innocent rhyme; for *scarn, horn*, a hard rhyme; for *school, fool*, a babbling rhyme; very ominous endings: No, I was not born under a rhyming planet, nor I cannot woo in festival terms.[6]—

Enter BEATRICE.

Sweet Beatrice, would'st thou come when I called thee?

Beat. Yea, signior, and depart when you bid me

Bene. O, stay but till then!

Beat. *Then*, is spoken; fare you well now:—and yet, ere I go, let me go with that I came for, which is, with knowing what hath passed between you and Claudio.

Bene. Only foul words; and thereupon I will kiss thee.

Beat. Foul words is but foul wind, and foul wind is but foul breath, and foul breath is noisome; therefore I will depart unkissed.

Bene. Thou hast frighted the word out of his right sense, so forcible is thy wit: But, I must tell thee plainly, Claudio undergoes[7] my challenge; and either I must shortly hear from him, or I will subscribe him a coward. And, I pray thee now, tell me, for which of my bad parts didst thou first fall in love with me?

Beat. For them all together; which maintained so politic a state of evil, that they will not admit any good part to intermingle with them. But for which of my good parts did you first suffer love for me?

Bene. *Suffer love;* a good epithet! I do suffer love, indeed, for I love thee against my will.

Beat. In spite of your heart, I think; alas! poor heart! If you spite it for my sake, I will spite it for yours; for I will never love that which my friend hates.

Bene. Thou and I are too wise to woo peaceably.

Beat. It appears not in this confession: there's not one wise man among twenty that will praise himself.

Bene. An old, an old instance, Beatrice, that lived in the time of good neighbours:[8] if a man do not erect in this age his own tomb ere he dies, he shall live no longer in monument, than the bell rings, and the widow weeps.

Beat. And how long is that, think you?

Bene. Question![9]—Why, an hour in clamour, and a quarter in rheum: Therefore it is most expedient for the wise (if Don Worm, his conscience, find no impediments to the contrary,) to be the trumpet of his own virtues, as I am to myself: So much for praising myself, (who, I myself will bear witness, is praise-worthy,) and now tell me, How doth your cousin?

Beat. Very ill.

Bene. And how do you?

Beat. Very ill too.

Bene. Serve God, love me, and mend: there will I leave you too, for here comes one in haste

Enter URSULA.

Urs. Madam, you must come to your uncle;

1 It was one of the fantastic fashions of Shakspeare's time to wear a long hanging *lock of hair* dangling by the ear; it is often mentioned by cotemporary writers, and may be observed in some ancient portraits. The humour of this passage is in Dogberry's supposing the *lock* to have a key to it.

2 A phrase used by those who received alms at the gates of religious houses. Dogberry probably designed to say, 'God save the founder.'

3 Here *lewd* has not the common meaning; nor do I think it can be used in the more uncommon sense of *ignorant;* but rather means *knavish, ungracious, naughty*, which are the synonymes used with it in explaining the latin *pravus* in dictionaries of the sixteenth century.

4 Theobald proposed to read, *above* stairs; and the sense of the passage seems to require some such alteration: perhaps a word has been lost, and we may read 'why, shall I always keep *them* below stairs?' Of this passage Dr. Johnson says, 'I suppose every reader will find the meaning.'

5 i. e. 'I yield.'

6 i. e. '*in choice phraseology.*'

7 Is under challenge, or now stands challenged, by me.

8 i. e. 'when men were not envious, but every one gave another his due.'

9 This phrase appears to be equivalent to—'You ask a question indeed!'—or 'that is the question.'

yonder's old coil[1] at home: it is proved, my lady Hero hath been falsely accused, the Prince and Claudio mightily abused; and Don John is the author of all, who is fled and gone: Will you come presently?

Beat. Will you go hear this news, signior?

Bene. I will live in thy heart, die in thy lap, and be buried in thy eyes; and moreover, I will go with thee to thy uncle's. [*Exeunt.*

SCENE III. *The Inside of a Church. Enter* DON PEDRO, CLAUDIO, *and* Attendants, *with Music and Tapers.*

Claud. Is this the monument of Leonato?

Atten. It is, my lord.

Claud. [*Reads from a scrol*]

Done to death[2] *by slanderous tongues*
Was the Hero that here lies:
Death, in the guerdon[3] *of her wrongs,*
Gives her fame which never dies:
So the life, that died with shame,
Lives in death with glorious fame.

Hang thou there upon the tomb, [affixing it.
Praising her when I am dumb.—

Now, music, sound, and sing your solemn hymn.

SONG.

Pardon, Goddess of the night,
Those that slew thy virgin knight:[4]
For the which, with songs of woe,
Round about her tomb they go.
Midnight, assist our moan;
Help us to sigh and groan,
Heavily, heavily.
Graves yawn and yield your dead,
Till death be uttered,[5]
Heavily, heavily.

Claud. Now, unto thy bones good night!
Yearly will I do this rite.

D. Pedro. Good morrow, masters; put your torches out:
The wolves have prey'd; and look, the gentle day,
Before the wheels of Phœbus, round about
Dapples the drowsy east with spots of gray:
Thanks to you all, and leave us; fare you well.

Claud. Good morrow, masters; each his several way.

D. Pedro. Come, let us hence, and put on other weeds;
And then to Leonato's we will go.

Claud. And, Hymen, now with luckier issue speeds,
Than this, for whom we render'd up this woe!
[*Exeunt.*

SCENE IV. *A Room in* Leonato s *House. Enter* LEONATO, ANTONIO, BENEDICK, BEATRICE, URSULA, Friar, *and* HERO.

Friar. Did I not tell you she was innocent?

Leon. So are the prince and Claudio, who accused her
Upon the error that you heard debated:
But Margaret was in some fault for this;
Although against her will, as it appears
In the true course of all the question.

Ant. Well, I am glad that all things sort so well.

Bene. And so am I, being else by faith enforc'd
To call young Claudio to a reckoning for it.

Leon Well, daughter, and you gentlewoman all,
Withdraw into a chamber by yourselves;
And when I send for you come hither mask'd;
The prince and Claudio promis'd by this hour
To visit me:—You know your office, brother;
You must be father to your brother's daughter,
And give her to young Claudio. [*Exeunt Ladies.*

Ant. Which I will do with confirm'd countenance.

Bene. Friar, I must entreat your pains I think.

Friar. To do what, signior?

Bene. To bind me, or undo me, one of them.—
Signior Leonato, truth it is, good signior,
Your niece regards me with an eye of favour.

Leon. That eye my daughter lent her: 'Tis most true.

Bene. And I do with an eye of love requite her.

Leon. The sight whereof, I think, you had from me,
From Claudio, and the prince: But what's your will?

Bene. Your answer, sir, is enigmatical:
But, for my will, my will is, your good will
May stand with ours, this day to be conjoin'd
In the estate of honourable marriage;—
In which, good friar, I shall desire your help.

Leon. My heart is with your liking.

Friar And my help.
Here comes the prince, and Claudio.

Enter DON PEDRO *and* CLAUDIO, *with* Attendants.

D. Pedro. Good morrow to this fair assembly.

Leon. Good morrow, prince; good morrow, Claudio.
We here attend you; are you yet determin'd
To-day to marry with my brother's daughter?

Claud. I'll hold my mind, were she an Ethiope.

Leon. Call her forth, brother, here's the friar ready. [*Exit* ANTONIO.

D. Pedro. Good morrow, Benedick: Why, what's the matter.
That you have such a February face,
So full of frost, of storm, and cloudiness?

Claud. I think, he thinks upon the savage bull.[6]
Tush, fear not, man, we'll tip thy horns with gold.
And all Europa shall rejoice at thee;
As once Europa did at lusty Jove,
When he would play the noble beast in love.

Bene. Bull Jove, sir, had an amiable low:
And some such strange bull leap'd your father's cow,
And got a calf in that same noble feat,
Much like to you, for you have just his bleat.

Re-enter ANTONIO, *with the* Ladies *masked.*

Claud. For this I owe you: here comes other reckonings.
Which is the lady I must seize upon?

Ant. This same is she, and I do give you her.

Claud. Why, then she's mine: Sweet, let me see your face.

Leon. No, that you shall not till you take her hand
Before this friar; and swear to marry her.

Claud. Give me your hand before this holy friar;
I am your husband if you like of me.

Hero. And when I lived, I was your other wife:
[*Unmasking.*
And when you loved, you were my other husband.

Claud. Another Hero!

Hero. Nothing certainer:
One Hero died defil'd; but I do live,
And surely as I live I am a maid.

D. Pedro. The former Hero! Hero that is dead!

Leon. She died, my lord, but whiles her slander lived.

Friar. All this amazement can I qualify;
When, after that the holy rites are ended,
I'll tell you largely of fair Hero's death:
Mean time, let wonder seem familiar,
And to the chapel let us presently.

Bene. Soft and fair, Friar.—Which is Beatrice?

Beat. I answer to that name; [*Unmasking*]
What is your will?

Bene. Do not you love me?

Beat. Why, no, no more than reason.

Bene. Why, then your uncle, and the prince, and Claudio,

1 *Old coil* is *great* or *abundant bustle. Old* was a common augmentative in ancient familiar language.

2 This phrase occurs frequently in writers of Shakspeare's time, it appears to be derived from the French phrase, *faire mourir*. See note on K. Henry VI. Part III. Act ii. Sc. I.

3 Reward.

4 *Diana's* knight, or virgin knight, was the common poetical appellation of virgins in Shakspeare's time.

5 i. e. '*till death be spoken of.*'

6 Still alluding to the passage quoted from Hieronymo, or the Spanish Tragedy, in the first scene of the play.

Have been deceived; for they swore you did.

Beat. Do not you love me?

Bene. Troth, no, no more than reason.

Beat. Why, then my cousin, Margaret, and Ursula,
Are much deceiv'd; for they did swear you did.

Bene. They swore that you were almost sick for me.

Beat. They swore that you were well-nigh dead for me.

Bene. 'Tis no such matter:—Then you do not love me?

Beat. No, truly, but in friendly recompense.

Leon. Come, cousin, I am sure you love the gentleman.

Claud. And I'll be sworn upon't, that he loves her;
For here's a paper, written in his hand,
A halting sonnet of his own pure brain,
Fashion'd to Beatrice.

Hero And here's another,
Writ in my cousin's hand, stolen from her pocket,
Containing her affection unto Benedick.

Bene. A miracle! here's our own hands against our hearts!—Come, I will have thee; but, by this light, I take thee for pity.

Beat. I would not deny you; but, by this good day, I yield upon great persuasion; and, partly, to save your life, for I was told you were in a consumption.

Bene. Peace, I will stop your mouth. [*Kissing her.*

D. Pedro. How dost thou, Benedick the married man?

Bene. I'll tell thee what, prince; a college of wit-crackers cannot flout me out of my humour: Dost thou think, I care for a satire, or an epigram? No: if a man will be beaten with brains, he shall wear nothing handsome about him: In brief, since I do propose to marry, I will think nothing to any purpose that the world can say against it; and therefore never flout at me for what I have said against it; for man is a giddy thing, and this is my conclusion.—For thy part, Claudio, I did think to have beaten thee; but in that[1] thou art like to be my kinsman, live unbruised and love my cousin.

Claud. I had well hoped, thou wouldst have denied Beatrice, that I might have cudgelled thee out of thy single life, to make thee a double dealer; which, out of question, thou wilt be, if my cousin do not look exceeding narrowly to thee.

Bene. Come, come, we are friends:—let's have a dance ere we are married, that we may lighten our own hearts, and our wives' heels.

Leon. We'll have dancing afterwards.

Bene. First o'my word: therefore play, music— Prince, thou art sad; get thee a wife, get thee a wife: there is no staff more reverend than one tipped with horn.[2]

Enter a Messenger.

Mess. My lord, your brother John is ta'en in flight
And brought with armed men back to Messina.

Bene. Think not on him till to-morrow; I'll devise thee brave punishments for him.—Strike up, pipers. [*Dance. Exeunt.*

THIS play may be justly said to contain two of the most sprightly characters that Shakspeare ever drew. The wit, the humourist, the gentleman, and the soldier are combined in Benedick. It is to be lamented, indeed, that the first and most splendid of these distinctions is disgraced by unnecessary profaneness; for the goodness of his heart is hardly sufficient to atone for the licence of his tongue. The too sarcastic levity, which flashes out in the conversation of Beatrice, may be excused on account of the steadiness and friendship so apparent in her behaviour, when she urges her lover to risk his life by a challenge to Claudio. In the conduct of the fable, however, there is an imperfection similar to that which Dr. Johnson has pointed out in *The Merry Wives of Windsor*:—the second contrivance is less ingenious than the first:—or, to speak more plainly, the same incident is become stale by repetition. I wish some other method had been found to entrap Beatrice, than that very one which before had been successfully practised on Benedick.[3]

Much Ado about Nothing, (as I understand from one of Mr. Vertue's MSS.) formerly passed under the title of Benedick and Beatrix. Heming the player received, on the 20th of May, 1613, the sum of forty pounds, and twenty pounds more as his Majesty's gratuity, for exhibiting six plays at Hampton Court, among which was this comedy. STEEVENS.

1 Because.

2 Steevens, Malone, and Reed, conceive that there is an allusion here to the staff used in the ancient trial by wager of battle; but Mr. Douce thinks it is more probable the walking stick or staff of elderly persons was intended, such sticks were often *tipped* or headed with *horn*, sometimes *crosswise*, in imitation of the crutched sticks or *potences* of the friars, which were borrowed from the celebrated *tau* of St. Anthony.

3 Mr. Pye thus answers the objection of Steevens. 'The intention of the poet was to show that persons of either sex might be made in love with each other by supposing themselves beloved, though they were before enemies; and how he could have done this by any other means I do not know. He wanted to show the sexes were alike in this case, and to have employed different motives would have counteracted his own design.'

MIDSUMMER-NIGHT'S DREAM.

PRELIMINARY REMARKS.

WE may presume the plot of this play to have been the invention of Shakspeare, as the diligence of his commentators has failed to trace the sources from whence it is derived. Steevens says that the hint for it was probably received from Chaucer's Knight's Tale.

'In the Midsummer Night's Dream,' says Schlegel, 'there flows a luxuriant vein of the boldest and most fantastical invention; the most extraordinary combination of the most dissimilar ingredients seems to have arisen without effort by some ingenious and lucky accident, and the colours are of such clear transparency that we think that the whole of the variegated fabric may be blown away with a breath. The fairy world here described resembles those elegant pieces of Arabesque, where little Genii, with butterfly wings, rise half embodied above the flower cups. Twilight, moonshine, dew, and spring-perfumes are the element of these tender spirits; they assist nature in embroidering her carpet with green leaves, many coloured flowers, and dazzling insects; in the human world they merely sport in a childish and wayward manner with their beneficent or noxious influences. Their most violent rage dissolves in good-natured raillery; their passions, stripped of all earthly matter, are merely an ideal dream. To correspond with this, the loves of mortals are painted as a poetical enchantment, which, by a contrary enchantment, may be immediately suspended, and then renewed again. The different parts of the plot; the wedding of Theseus, the disagreement of Oberon and Titania, the flight of the two pair of lovers, and the theatrical operations of the mechanics, are so lightly and happily interwoven, that they seem necessary to each other for

MIDSUMMER NIGHT'S DREAM,

Act. I. Scene I.

the formation of a whole. Oberon is desirous of relieving the lovers from their perplexities, and greatly adds to them through the misapprehension of his servant, till he at last comes to the aid of their fruitless amorous pain, their inconstancy and jealousy, and restores fidelity to its old rights. The extremes of fanciful and vulgar are united when the enchanted Titania awakes and falls in love with a coarse mechanic with an ass's head, who represents, or rather disfigures the part of a tragical lover. The droll wonder of the transmutation of Bottom is merely the transmutation of a metaphor in its literal sense; but, in his behaviour during the tender homage of the Fairy Queen, we have a most amusing proof how much the consciousness of such a head-dress heightens the effect of his usual folly. Theseus and Hippolita are, as it were, a splendid frame for the picture; they take no part in the action, but appear with a stately pomp. The discourse of the hero and his Amazon, as they course through the forest with their noisy hunting train, works upon the imagination like the fresh breath of morning, before which the shapes of night disappear.'*

This is a production of the youthful and vigourous imagination of the poet. Malone places the date of its composition in 1594. There are two quarto editions, both printed in 1600: one by Thomas Fisher, the other by James Roberts.

* Lectures on Dramatic Literature, vol. ii. p. 176.

PERSONS REPRESENTED.

Theseus, *Duke of* Athens.
Egeus, *Father to* Hermia.
Lysander, } *in love with* Hermia.
Demetrius, }
Philostrate, *Master of the Revels to* Theseus.
Quince, *the Carpenter.*
Snug, *the Joiner.*
Bottom, *the Weaver.*
Flute *the Bellows-mender.*
Snout, *the Tinker.*
Starveling, *the Tailor.*

Hippolyta, *Queen of the* Amazons, *betrothed to* Theseus.
Hermia, *Daughter of* Egeus, *in love with* Lysander.
Helena, *in love with* Demetrius.

Oberon, *King of the Fairies.*
Titania, *Queen of the Fairies.*
Puck, or Robin-goodfellow, *a Fairy.*
Peas-blossom, }
Cobweb, } *Fairies.*
Moth, }
Mustard-seed, }
Pyramus, }
Thisbe, } *Characters in the Interlude performed by the Clowns.*
Wall, }
Moonshine. }
Lion. }

Other Fairies attending their King and Queen.
Attendants on Theseus *and* Hippolyta.

SCENE, Athens, *and a Wood not far from it.*

ACT I.

SCENE I. Athens. *A Room in the Palace of Theseus. Enter* Theseus, Hippolyta, Philostrate, *and* Attendants.

Theseus.

Now, fair Hippolyta, our nuptial hour
Draws on apace; four happy days bring in
Another moon: but, oh, methinks how slow
This old moon wanes! she lingers my desires,
Like to a step-dame, or a dowager,
Long withering out a young man's revenue.

Hip. Four days will quickly steep themselves in nights;
Four nights will quickly dream away the time;
And then the moon, like to a silver bow
Now bent in heaven, shall behold the night
Of our solemnities.

The. Go, Philostrate,
Stir up the Athenian youth to merriments;
Awake the pert and nimble spirit of mirth;
Turn melancholy forth to funerals,
The pale companion is not for our pomp.—
[*Exit* Philostrate.
Hippolyta, I woo'd thee with my sword,
And won thy love, doing thee injuries;
But I will wed thee in another key,
With pomp, with triumph,[1] and with revelling.

Enter Egeus, Hermia, Lysander, *and* Demetrius.

Ege. Happy be Theseus, our renowned duke![2]

The. Thanks, good Egeus: What's the news with thee?

Ege. Full of vexation come I, with complaint
Against my child, my daughter Hermia—
Stand forth, Demetrius;—My noble lord,
This man hath my consent to marry her:—
Stand forth, Lysander;—and, my gracious duke,
This hath bewitch'd[3] the bosom of my child:
Thou, thou, Lysander, thou hast given her rhymes
And interchang'd love tokens with my child:
Thou hast by moon-light at her window sung,
With feigning voice, verses of feigning love;
And stol'n the impression of her fantasy
With bracelets of thy hair, rings, gawds,[4] conceits,
Knacks, trifles, nosegays, sweet-meats; messengers
Of strong prevailment in unharden'd youth:
With cunning hast thou filch'd my daughter's heart;
Turn'd her obedience, which is due to me,
To stubborn harshness:—And, my gracious duke,
Be it so she will not here before your grace
Consent to marry with Demetrius,
I beg the ancient privilege of Athens;
As she is mine, I may dispose of her:
Which shall be either to this gentleman,
Or to her death; according to our law,
Immediately provided in that case.[5]

The. What say you, Hermia? be advis'd, fair maid:
To you your father should be as a god;
One that compos'd your beauties; yea, and one
To whom you are but as a form in wax,
By him imprinted, and within his power
To leave the figure, or disfigure it.
Demetrius is a worthy gentleman.

Her. So is Lysander.

The. In himself he is:
But, in this kind, wanting your father's voice,
The other must be held the worthier.

Her. I would my father look'd but with my eyes.

The. Rather your eyes must with his judgment look.

1 A *triumph* was a public show, such as a mask, pageant, procession, &c.

2 *Duke*, in our old language, was used for a leader or chief, as the Latin *Dux*.

3 The old copies read, 'This *man* hath bewitched.' The alteration was made in the second folio for the sake of the metre; but a redundant syllable at the commencement of a verse perpetually occurs in our old dramas.

4 Baubles, toys, trifles.

5 This line has a smack of legal common place. Shakspeare is supposed to have been placed while a boy in an attorney's office; at least he often displays that he was well acquainted with the phraseology of lawyers.

Her. I do entreat your grace to pardon me.
I know not by what power I am made bold;
Nor how it may concern my modesty,
In such a presence here, to plead my thoughts:
But I beseech your grace that I may know
The worst that may befall me in this case,
If I refuse to wed Demetrius.
The. Either to die the death, or to abjure
For ever the society of men.
Therefore, fair Hermia, question your desires,
Know of your youth, examine well your blood,
Whether, if you yield not to your father's choice,
You can endure the livery of a nun;
For aye[1] to be in shady cloister mew'd,
To live a barren sister all your life,
Chanting faint hymns to the cold fruitless moon.
Thrice blessed they, that master so their blood,
To undergo such maiden pilgrimage:
But earthlier happy[2] is the rose distill'd,
Than that, which, withering on the virgin thorn,
Grows, lives, and dies, in single blessedness.
Her. So will I grow, so live, so die, my lord,
Ere I will yield my virgin patent up
Unto his lordship, whose unwished yoke
My soul consents not to give sovereignty.
The. Take time to pause: and, by the next new moon,
(The sealing-day betwixt my love and me,
For everlasting bond of fellowship,)
Upon that day either prepare to die,
For disobedience to your father's will;
Or else to wed Demetrius, as he would:
Or on Diana's altar to protest,
For aye, austerity and single life.
Dem. Relent, sweet Hermia;—And, Lysander, yield
Thy crazed title to my certain right.
Lys. You have her father's love, Demetrius;
Let me have Hermia's: do you marry him.
Ege. Scornful Lysander! true, he hath my love,
And what is mine my love shall render him;
And she is mine; and all my right of her
I do estate unto Demetrius.
Lys. I am, my lord, as well deriv'd as he,
As well possess'd; my love is more than his;
My fortunes every way as fairly rank'd,
If not with vantage, as Demetrius';
And, which is more than all these boasts can be,
I am belov'd of beauteous Hermia:
Why should not I then prosecute my right?
Demetrius, I'll avouch it to his head,
Made love to Nedar's daughter, Helena,
And won her soul; and she, sweet lady, dotes,
Devoutly dotes, dotes in idolatry,
Upon this spotted[3] and inconstant man.
The. I must confess, that I have heard so much,
And with Demetrius thought to have spoke thereof;
But, being over-full of self-affairs,
My mind did lose it. But, Demetrius, come:
And come, Egeus; you shall go with me,
I have some private schooling for you both.—
For you, fair Hermia, look you arm yourself
To fit your fancies to your father's will;
Or else the law of Athens yields you up
(Which by no means we may extenuate)
To death, or to a vow of single life.—
Come, my Hippolyta: What cheer, my love?—
Demetrius, and Egeus, go along:
I must employ you in some business
Against our nuptial; and confer with you
Of something nearly that concerns yourselves.
Ege. With duty and desire we follow you.
[*Exeunt* THESEUS, HIPPOLYTA, EGEUS, DEMETRIUS, *and* Train.

Lys. How now, my love? Why is your cheek so pale?
How chance the roses there do fade so fast?
Her. Belike, for want of rain; which I could well
Beteem[4] them from the tempest of mine eyes.
Lys. Ah me! for aught that ever I could read,
Could ever hear by tale or history,
The course of true love never did run smooth:
But, either it was different in blood;
Her. O cross! too high to be enthrall'd to low!
Lys. Or else misgraffed, in respect of years;
Her. O spite! too old to be engaged to young!
Lys. Or else it stood upon the choice of friends:
Her. O hell! to choose love by another's eye!
Lys. Or, if there were a sympathy in choice,
War, death, or sickness did lay siege to it;
Making it momentany[5] as a sound,
Swift as a shadow, short as any dream;
Brief as the lightning in the collied[6] night,
That, in a spleen, unfolds both heaven and earth,
And ere a man hath power to say,—Behold!
The jaws of darkness do devour it up;
So quick bright things come to confusion.
Her. If then true lovers have been ever cross'd,
It stands as an edict in destiny:
Then let us teach our trial patience,
Because it is a customary cross,
As due to love, as thoughts, and dreams, and sighs,
Wishes, and tears, poor fancy's[7] followers.
Lys. A good persuasion; therefore, hear me, Hermia.
I have a widow aunt, a dowager
Of great revenue, and she hath no child:
From Athens is her house remote seven leagues;
And she respects me as her only son.
There, gentle Hermia, may I marry thee;
And to that place the sharp Athenian law
Cannot pursue us: If thou lov'st me then,
Steal forth thy father's house to-morrow night;
And in the wood, a league without the town
Where I did meet thee once with Helena,
To do observance to a morn of May,
There will I stay for thee
Her. My good Lysander!
I swear to thee, by Cupid's strongest bow;
By his best arrow with the golden head;
By the simplicity of Venus' doves;
By that which knitteth souls, and prospers loves;
And by that fire which burn'd the Carthage queen,[8]
When the false Trojan under sail was seen;
By all the vows that ever men have broke,
In number more than women ever spoke;—
In that same place thou hast appointed me,
To-morrow truly will I meet with thee.
Lys. Keep promise, love: Look, here comes Helena.

Enter HELENA.

Her. God speed fair Helena! Whither away?
Hel. Call you me fair? that fair again unsay.
Demetrius loves your fair:[9] O happy fair!
Your eyes are lode-stars;[10] and your tongue's sweet air
More tuneable than lark to shepherd's ear,
When wheat is green, when hawthorn buds appear.
Sickness is catching; O, were favour[11] so!
Yours would I catch, fair Hermia, ere I go;
My ear should catch your voice, my eye your eye,
My tongue should catch your tongue's sweet melody.
Were the world mine, Demetrius being bated,
The rest I'll give to be to you translated.[12]

1 Ever.
2 *Earthlier happy* for *earthly happier*, which Capel proposed to substitute.
3 As *spotless* is innocent, so *spotted* is wicked.
4 Bestow, give, *afford*, or *deign to allow*.
5 Momentary.
6 Blackened, as with smut, coal, &c.; figuratively, darkened. See Othello, Act ii. Sc. 3.
7 *Fancy* is *love*. So afterwards in this play:
'Fair Helena in *fancy* following me.'
8 Shakspeare forgot that Theseus performed his exploits before the Trojan war, and consequently long before the death of Dido.
9 *Fair* for fairness, beauty. Very common in writers of Shakspeare's age.
10 The *lode-star* is the leading or guiding star, that is the *polar star*. The magnet is for the same reason called the *lode*-stone.
11 Countenance, feature.
12 i e. changed, transformed

O, teach me how you look; and with what art
You sway the motion of Demetrius' heart.
Her. I frown upon him, yet he loves me still.
Hel. O, that your frowns would teach my smiles such skill!
Her. I give him curses, yet he gives me love,—
Hel. O, that my prayers could such affection move!
Her. The more I hate, the more he follows me.
Hel. The more I love, the more he hateth me.
Her. His folly, Helena, is no fault of mine.
Hel. None, but your beauty; 'Would that fault were mine!
Her. Take comfort; he no more shall see my face;
Lysander and myself will fly this place.—
Before the time I did Lysander see,
Seem'd Athens as a paradise to me:
O then, what graces in my love do dwell,
That he hath turn'd a heaven unto hell!
Lys. Helen, to you our minds we will unfold:
To-morrow night when Phœbe doth behold
Her silver visage in the wat'ry glass,
Decking with liquid pearl the bladed grass
(A time that lovers' flights doth still conceal,)
Through Athens' gates have we devis'd to steal.
Her. And in the wood, where often you and I
Upon faint primrose beds were wont to lie,
Emptying our bosoms of their counsel sweet,
There my Lysander and myself shall meet:
And thence, from Athens, turn away our eyes,
To seek new friends and stranger companies.
Farewell, sweet playfellow; pray thou for us,
And good luck grant thee thy Demetrius!
Keep word, Lysander: we must starve our sight
From lovers' food, till morrow deep midnight.
[*Exit* HERM.
Lys. I will, my Hermia.—Helena, adieu:
As you on him, Demetrius dote on you!
[*Exit* LYSANDER.
Hel. How happy some, o'er other some can be!
Through Athens I am thought as fair as she.
But what of that? Demetrius thinks not so;
He will not know what all but he do know.
And as he errs, doting on Hermia's eyes,
So I, admiring of his qualities.
Things base and vile, holding no quantity,
Love can transpose to form and dignity.
Love looks not with the eyes, but with the mind;
And therefore is winged Cupid painted blind;
Nor hath love's mind of any judgment taste;
Wings, and no eyes, figure unheedy haste:
And therefore is love said to be a child,
Because in choice he is so oft beguil'd.
As waggish boys in game[1] themselves forswear,
So the boy love is perjur'd every where:
For ere Demetrius look'd on Hermia's eyne,[2]
He hail'd down oaths, that he was only mine:
And when this hail some heat from Hermia felt,
So he dissolv'd, and showers of oaths did melt.
I will go tell him of fair Hermia's flight;
Then to the wood will he, to-morrow night,
Pursue her; and for this intelligence
If I have thanks, it is a dear expense:
But herein mean I to enrich my pain,
To have his sight thither and back again. [*Exit.*

SCENE II. *The same. A Room in a Cottage.—Enter* SNUG, BOTTOM, FLUTE, SNOUT, QUINCE, *and* STARVELING.[3]

Quin. Is all our company here?

Bot. You were best to call them generally, man by man, according to the scrip.

Quin. Here is the scroll of every man's name, which is thought fit, through all Athens, to play in our interlude before the duke and duchess, on his wedding-day at night.

Bot. First, good Peter Quince, say what the play treats on; then read the names of the actors; and so grow to a point.

Quin. Marry, our play is—The most lamentable comedy, and most cruel death of Pyramus and Thisby.[4]

Bot. A very good piece of work, I assure you, and a merry.—Now, good Peter Quince, call forth your actors by the scroll: Masters, spread yourselves.

Quin. Answer, as I call you.—Nick Bottom, the weaver.

Bot. Ready: Name what part I am for, and proceed.

Quin. You, Nick Bottom, are set down for Pyramus.

Bot. What is Pyramus? a lover, or a tyrant?

Quin. A lover, that kills himself most gallantly for love.

Bot. That will ask some tears in the true performing of it: If I do it, let the audience look to their eyes; I will move storms, I will condole in some measure. To the rest:—Yet my chief humour is for a tyrant: I could play Ercles rarely, or a part to tear a cat in, to make all split.

"The raging rocks,
With shivering shocks,
Shall break the locks
Of prison gates:
And Phibbus' car
Shall shine from far,
And make and mar
The foolish fates."

This was lofty!—Now name the rest of the players—This is Ercles' vein, a tyrant's vein; a lover is more condoling.

Quin. Francis Flute, the bellows-mender.

Flu. Here, Peter Quince.

Quin. You must take Thisby on you.

Flu. What is Thisby? a wandering knight?

Quin. It is the lady that Pyramus must love.

Flu. Nay, faith, let me not play a woman; I have a beard coming.

Quin. That's all one; you shall play it in a mask, and you may speak as small as you will.[5]

Bot. An I may hide my face, let me play Thisby too: I'll speak in a monstrous little voice;—*Thisne, Thisne—Ah, Pyramus, my lover dear; thy Thisby dear! and lady dear!*

Quin. No, no; you must play Pyramus; and, Flute, you Thisby.

Bot. Well, proceed.

Quin. Robin Starveling, the tailor.

Star. Here, Peter Quince.

Quin. Robin Starveling, you must play Thisby's mother.—Tom Snout, the tinker.

Snout. Here, Peter Quince.

Quin. You, Pyramus's father; myself, Thisby's father;—Snug, the joiner, you, the lion's part:—and, I hope, here is a play fitted.

Snug. Have you the lion's part written? pray you, if it be, give it me, for I am slow of study.

Quin. You may do it extempore, for it is nothing but roaring.

Bot. Let me play the lion too: I will roar, that I will do any man's heart good to hear me; I will

---

1 Sport. 2 Eyes.

3 In this scene Shakspeare takes advantage of his knowledge of the theatre, to ridicule the prejudices and competitions of the players. Bottom, who is generally acknowledged the principal actor, declares his inclination to be for a tyrant, for a part of fury, tumult, and noise, such as every young man pants to perform when he first appears upon the stage. The same Bottom, who seems bred in a tiring-room, has another histrionical passion. He is for engrossing every part, and would exclude his inferiors from all possibility of distinction He is therefore desirous to play Pyramus, Thisbe, and the Lion, at the same time.

4 Probably a burlesque upon the titles of some of our old Dramas.

5 This passage shows how the want of women on the old stage was supplied. If they had not a young man who could perform the part with a face that might pass for feminine, the character was acted in a mask, which was at that time a part of a lady's dress, and so much in use that it did not give any unusual appearance to the scene; and he that could modulate his voice to a female tone might play the woman very successfully

roar, that I will make the duke say, *Let him roar again, Let him roar again.*

Quin. An you should do it too terribly, you would fright the duchess and the ladies, that they would shriek; and that were enough to hang us all.

All. That would hang us every mother's son.

Bot. I grant you, friends, if that you should fright the ladies out of their wits, they would have no more discretion but to hang us: but I will aggravate my voice so, that I will roar you as gently as any sucking dove; I will roar you an[1] 'twere any nightingale.

Quin. You can play no part but Pyramus: for Pyramus is a sweet-faced man; a proper man, as one shall see in a summer's day; a most lovely, gentleman-like man; therefore you must needs play Pyramus.

Bot. Well, I will undertake it. What beard were I best to play it in?

Quin. Why, what you will.

Bot. I will discharge it in either your straw-coloured beard, your orange-tawny beard, your purple-in-grain beard, or your French-crown-colour beard, your perfect yellow.[2]

Quin. Some of your French crowns have no hair at all, and then you will play bare-faced.[3] But, masters, here are your parts: and I am to entreat you, request you, and desire you, to con them by to-morrow night; and meet me in the palace wood, a mile without the town, by moon-light; there will we rehearse: for if we meet in the city, we shall be dogg'd with company, and our devices known. In the mean time I will draw a bill of properties,[4] such as our play wants. I pray you, fail me not.

Bot. We will meet; and there we may rehearse more obscenely, and courageously. Take pains; be perfect, adieu.

Quin. At the duke's oak we meet.

Bot. Enough; Hold, or cut bow-strings.[5]

[*Exeunt.*

ACT II.

SCENE I. *A Wood near* Athens. *Enter a* Fairy *at one door; and* Puck *at another.*

Puck. How now, spirit! whither wander you?

Fai. Over hill, over dale,
 Thorough bush, thorough briar,[6]
Over park, over pale,
 Thorough flood, thorough fire.
I do wander every where,
Swifter than the moones sphere;
And I serve the fairy queen,
To dew her orbs[7] upon the green:
The cowslips tall her pensioners[8] be;
In their gold coats spots you see,
Those be rubies, fairy favours,
In those freckles live their savors:
I must go seek some dewdrops here,
And hang a pearl in every cowslip's ear.[9]
Farewell, thou lob[10] of spirits, I'll be gone;
Our queen and all her elves come here anon.

Puck. The king doth keep his revels here to-night;
Take heed the queen come not within his sight.
For Oberon is passing fell and wrath,
Because that she, as her attendant, hath
A lovely boy, stol'n from an Indian king;
She never had so sweet a changeling:[11]
And jealous Oberon would have the child
Knight of his train, to trace the forest wild.
But she, perforce, withholds the loved boy,
Crowns him with flowers, and makes him all her joy:
And now they never meet in grove, or green,
By fountain clear, or spangled star-light sheen,[12]
But they do square;[13] that all their elves, for fear,
Creep into acorn cups, and hide them there.

Fai. Either I mistake your shape and making quite,
Or else you are that shrewd and knavish sprite,
Call'd Robin Good-fellow: are you not he,
That fright the maidens of the villagery:
Skim milk; and sometimes labour in the quern,[14]
And bootless make the breathless housewife churn;
And sometime make the drink to bear no barm;[15]
Mislead night-wanderers, laughing at their harm?
Those that Hobgoblin call you, and sweet Puck,
You do their work;[16] and they shall have good luck.
Are not you he?

Puck. Thou speak'st aright;
I am that merry wanderer of the night.
I jest to Oberon, and make him smile,
When I a fat and bean-fed horse beguile,
Neighing in likeness of a filly foal:
And sometime lurk I in a gossip's bowl,
In very likeness of a roasted crab;[17]
And, when she drinks, against her lips I bob,
And on her wither'd dew-lap pour the ale.
The wisest aunt, telling the saddest tale,
Sometime for three-foot stool mistaketh me;
Then slip I from her bum, down topples she,
And *tailor* cries,[18] and falls into a cough;
And then the whole quire hold their hips, and loffe:
And yexen[19] in their mirth, and neeze, and swear
A merrier hour was never wasted there.—
But room, Faery, here comes Oberon.

Fai. And here my mistress:—'Would that he were gone!

1 As if.

2 It seems to have been a custom to stain or dye the beard.

3 This allusion to the *Corona Veneris*, or baldness attendant upon a particular stage of, what was then termed, the *French* disease, is too frequent in Shakspeare, and is here explained once for all.

4 Articles required in performing a play.

5 To meet *whether bowstrings hold or are cut* is to meet in all events. But the origin of the phrase has not been satisfactorily explained.

6 So Drayton, in his Nymphidia, or Court of Fairy:
'Thorough brake, thorough briar,
Thorough muck, thorough mire,
Thorough water, thorough fire.

7 The *orbs* here mentioned are those circles in the herbage commonly called fairy-rings, the cause of which is not yet certainly known.

8 The allusion is to Elizabeth's band of gentlemen *pensioners*, who were chosen from among the handsomest and tallest young men of family and fortune; they were dressed in habits richly garnished with *gold lace*.

9 In the old comedy of Doctor Dodypoll, 1600, an enchanter says,
'Twas I that led you through the painted meads
Where the light fairies danc'd upon the flowers,
Hanging on every leaf an orient pearl.'

10 Lubber or clown. *Lob*, lobcock, looby, and lubber, all denote inactivity of body and dulness of mind.

11 A *changeling* was a child changed by a fairy; it here means one stolen or got in exchange.

12 Shining.

13 Quarrel, For the probable cause of the use of *square* for *quarrel*, see Mr. Douce's Illustrations, vol. i p. 182

14 A *quern* was a handmill.

15 'And if that the bowle of curds and creame were not duly set out for Robin Goodfellow, the frier, and Sisse the dairy-maid, why then either the pottage was burnt next day in the pot, or the cheeses would not curdle, or the butter would not come, or the ale in the fat never would have good head. But if a Peeterpenny, or an housle-egg were behind, or a patch of tythe unpaid,—then ware of bull-beggars, spirits,' &c.

16 Milton refers to these traditions in L'Allegro.

17 Wild apple.

18 Dr. Johnson thought he remembered to have heard this ludicrous exclamation upon a person's seat slipping from under him. He that slips from his chair falls as a tailor squats upon his board. Hanmer thought the passage corrupt, and proposed to read '*rails* or cries.'

19 The old copy reads: 'And *waxen* in their mirth, &c.' Though a glimmering of sense may be extracted from this passage as it stands in the old copy, it seems most probable that we should read, as Dr. Farmer proposed, *yexen*. To *yex* is to hiccup, and is so explained in all the old dictionaries. The meaning of the passage will then be, that the objects of Puck's waggery laughed till their laughter ended in a *yex* or hiccup. Puck is speaking with an affectation of ancient phraseology.

SCENE II. *Enter* OBERON, *at one door, with his Train, and* TITANIA, *at another, with hers.*

Obe. Ill met by moon-light, proud Titania.
Tita. What, jealous Oberon? Fairy, skip hence;
I have forsworn his bed and company.
Obe. Tarry, rash wanton: Am not I thy lord?
Tita. Then I must be thy lady: But I know
When thou hast stol'n away from fairy land,
And in the shape of Corin sat all day,
Playing on pipes of corn;[1] and versing love
To amorous Phillida. Why art thou here,
Come from the farthest steep of India?
But that, forsooth, the bouncing Amazon,
Your buskin'd mistress, and your warrior love,
To Theseus must be wedded; and you come
To give their bed joy and prosperity.
Obe. How, canst thou thus, for shame, Titania,
Glance at my credit with Hippolyta,
Knowing I know thy love to Theseus?
Didst thou not lead him through the glimmering night
From Perigenia, whom he ravished?
And make him with fair Ægle break his faith,
With Ariadne, and Antiopa?[2]
Tita. These are the forgeries of jealousy:
And never, since the middle summer's spring,[3]
Met we on hill, in dale, forest, or mead,
By paved fountain, or by rushy brook,
Or on the beached margent of the sea,
To dance our ringlets to the whistling wind,
But with thy brawls thou hast disturb'd our sport.
Therefore the winds, piping to us in vain,
As in revenge, have suck'd up from the sea
Contagious fogs; which falling in the land,
Have every pelting[4] river made so proud,
That they have overborne their continents:[5]
The ox hath therefore stretch'd his yoke in vain,
The ploughman lost his sweat; and the green corn
Hath rotted, ere his youth attain'd a beard:
The fold stands empty in the drowned field,
And crows are fatted with the murrain flock;
The nine men's morris[6] is fill'd up with mud;
And the quaint mazes in the wanton green,
For lack of tread, are undistinguishable:
The human mortals[7] want their winter here;[8]
No night is now with hymn or carol blest:
Therefore the moon, the governess of floods,
Pale in her anger, washes all the air,
That rheumatic diseases do abound:
And thorough this distemperature, we see
The seasons alter: hoary-headed frosts
Fall in the fresh lap of the crimson rose;
And on old Hyems' chin, and icy crown,[9]
An odorous chaplet of sweet summer buds
Is, as in mockery, set: The spring, the summer,
The childing autumn,[10] angry winter, change[11]
Their wonted liveries; and the 'mazed world,
By their increase,[12] now knows not which is which
And this same progeny of evils comes
From our debate, from our dissension;
We are their parents and original.
Obe. Do you amend it then; it lies in you:
Why should Titania cross her Oberon?
I do but beg a little changeling boy,
To be my henchman.[13]
Tita. Set your heart at rest,
The fairy land buys not the child of me.
His mother was a vot'ress of my order:
And, in the spiced Indian air, by night,
Full often hath she gossip'd by my side
And sat with me on Neptune's yellow sands,
Marking the embarked traders on the flood;
When we have laugh'd to see the sails conceive,
And grow big bellied, with the wanton wind;
Which she, with pretty and with swimming gait
Following (her womb, then rich with my young squire,)
Would imitate; and sail upon the land,
To fetch me trifles, and return again,
As from a voyage, rich with merchandise.
But she, being mortal, of that boy did die;
And, for her sake, I do rear up her boy;
And, for her sake, I will not part with him.
Obe. How long within this wood intend you stay?
Tita. Perchance, till after Theseus' wedding-day.
If you will patiently dance in our round,
And see our moon-light revels, go with us;
If not, shun me, and I will spare your haunts.
Obe. Give me that boy, and I will go with thee.
Tita. Not for thy fairy kingdom.—Fairies, away
We shall chide down-right, if I longer stay.
[*Exeunt* TITANIA *and her* Train.
Obe. Well, go thy way: thou shalt not from this grove,
Till I torment thee for this injury.—
My gentle Puck, come hither: Thou remember'st
Since once I sat upon a promontory,
And heard a mermaid, on a dolphin's back,
Uttering such dulcet and harmonious breath,
That the rude sea grew civil at her song;
And certain stars shot madly from their spheres,
To hear the sea-maid's musick.
Puck. I remember.
Obe. That very time I saw (but thou could'st not,)
Flying between the cold moon and the earth,
Cupid all arm'd: a certain aim he took
At a fair vestal,[14] throned by the west;

---

1 The shepherd boys of Chaucer's time had
'Many a floite and litling horne
And *pipes made of grene corne.*'

2 See the Life of Theseus in North's Translation of Plutarch. Ægle, Ariadne, and Antiopa were all at different times mistresses to Theseus. The name of *Perigune* is translated by North *Perigouna.*

3 Spring seems to be here used for *beginning.* The *spring* of day is used for the dawn of day in K. Henry IV. Part II.

4 A very common epithet with our old writers, to signify paltry; *palting* appears to have been its original orthography

5 i. e. borne down the banks which contain them.

6 A rural game, played by making holes in the ground in the angles and sides of a square, and placing stones or other things upon them, according to certain rules. These figures are called *nine men's morris*, or *merrils*, because each party playing has nine men; they were generally cut upon turf, and were consequently choked up with mud in rainy seasons.

7 *Human mortals* is a mere pleonasm; and is neither put in opposition to *fairy mortals* nor to *human immortals*, according to Steevens and Ritson. It is simply the language of a fairy speaking of men. See Mr. Douce's Illustrations, vol. i. p. 185.

8 Theobald proposed to read '*their winter cheer.*'

9 This singular image was probably suggested to the poet by Golding's translation of Ovid, B. ii.:
'And lastly quaking for the colde, stoode *Winter* all forlorne,
With rugged head as white as dove, and garments all to-torne,
Forladen with the isycles, that dangled up and downe,
Upon his gray and *hourie beard,* and snowie *frozen crowne.*'

10 Autumn producing flowers unseasonably upon those of Summer.

11 The confusion of seasons here described is no more than a poetical account of the weather which happened in England about the time when the Midsummer-Night's Dream was written. The date of the piece may be determined by Churchyard's description of the same kind of weather in his 'Charitie,' 1595. Shakspeare fancifully ascribes this distemperature of seasons to a quarrel between the playful rulers of the fairy world; Churchyard, broken down by age and misfortunes, is seriously disposed to represent it as a judgment from the Almighty on the offences of mankind.

12 Produce. So in Shakspeare's 97th Sonnet;
'The *teeming Autumn*, big with rich *increase*,
Bearing the wanton burthen of the prime.'

13 Page of honour.

14 It is well known that a compliment to Queen Elizabeth was intended in this very beautiful passage. Warburton has attempted to show, that by the *mermaid* in the preceding lines, Mary Queen of Scots was intended. It is argued with his usual fanciful ingenuity, but will not bear the test of examination, and has been satisfactorily controverted. It appears to have been no uncommon practice to introduce a compliment to Elizabeth in the body of a play.

And loos'd his love-shaft smartly from his bow,
As it should pierce a hundred thousand hearts:
But I might see young Cupid's fiery shaft
Quench'd in the chaste beams of the wat'ry moon;
And the imperial vot'ress passed on,
In maiden meditation, fancy-free.[1]
Yet mark'd I where the bolt of Cupid fell:
It fell upon a little western flower,—
Before, milk-white; now purple with love's wound,
And maidens call it, love-in-idleness.[2]
Fetch me that flower: the herb I show'd thee once:
The juice of it on sleeping eye-lids laid,
Will make or man or woman madly dote
Upon the next live creature that it sees.
Fetch me this herb: and be thou here again,
Ere the leviathan can swim a league.

Puck. I'll put a girdle round about the earth
In forty minutes. [*Exit* Puck.

Obe. Having once this juice,
I'll watch Titania when she is asleep,
And drop the liquor of it in her eyes:
The next thing then she waking looks upon,
(Be it on lion, bear, or wolf, or bull,
On meddling monkey, or on busy ape,)
She shall pursue it with the soul of love.
And ere I take this charm off from her sight
(As I can take it with another herb,)
I'll make her render up her page to me.
But who comes here? I am invisible;
And I will overhear their conference.

Enter Demetrius, Helena *following him.*

Dem. I love thee not, therefore pursue me not.
Where is Lysander, and fair Hermia?
The one I'll slay, the other slayeth me.
Thou told'st me they were stol'n into this wood,
And here am I, and wood[3] within this wood,
Because I cannot meet with Hermia.
Hence, get thee gone, and follow me no more.

Hel. You draw me, you hard-hearted adamant;[4]
But yet you draw not iron, for my heart
Is true as steel; Leave you your power to draw,
And I shall have no power to follow you.

Dem. Do I entice you? Do I speak you fair?
Or, rather, do I not in plainest truth
Tell you—I do not, nor I cannot love you?

Hel. And even for that do I love you the more.
I am your spaniel; and, Demetrius,
The more you beat me, I will fawn on you:
Use me but as your spaniel, spurn me, strike me,
Neglect me, lose me; only give me leave,
Unworthy as I am, to follow you.
What worser place can I beg in your love,
(And yet a place of high respect with me,)
Than to be used as you do your dog?

Dem. Tempt not too much the hatred of my spirit;
For I am sick, when I do look on thee.

Hel. And I am sick, when I look not on you.

Dem. You do impeach[5] your modesty too much
To leave the city, and commit yourself
Into the hands of one that loves you not;
To trust the opportunity of night,
And the ill counsel of a desert place,
With the rich worth of your virginity.

Hel. Your virtue is my privilege for that.
It is not night when I do see your face,
Therefore I think I am not in the night:
Nor doth this wood lack worlds of company
For you, in my respect, are all the world:
Then how can it be said, I am alone,
When all the world is here to look on me?

Dem. I'll run from thee and hide me in the brakes,
And leave thee to the mercy of wild beasts.

Hel. The wildest hath not such a heart as you.
Run when you will, the story shall be chang'd;
Apollo flies, and Daphne holds the chase;
The dove pursues the griffin; the mild hind
Makes speed to catch the tiger. Bootless speed!
When cowardice pursues, and valour flies.

Dem. I will not stay thy questions; let me go:
Or, if thou follow me, do not believe
But I shall do thee mischief in the wood.

Hel. Ay, in the temple, in the town, the field,
You do me mischief. Fye, Demetrius!
Your wrongs do set a scandal on my sex
We cannot fight for love, as men may do
We should be woo'd, and were not made to woo.
I'll follow thee, and make a heaven of hell,
To die upon[6] the hand I love so well.
[*Exeunt* Dem. *and* Hel.

Obe. Fare thee well, nymph: ere he do leave this grove,
Thou shalt fly him, and he shall seek thy love.

Re-enter Puck.

Hast thou the flower there? Welcome, wanderer.

Puck. Ay, there it is.

Obe. I pray thee, give it me.
I know a bank whereon the wild thyme blows,
Where ox-lips[7] and the nodding violet grows;
Quite over-canopied with luscious woodbine,
With sweet musk-roses, and with eglantine:
There sleeps Titania, some time of the night,
Lull'd in these flowers with dances and delight;
And there the snake throws her enamel'd skin,
Weed wide enough to wrap a fairy in:
And with the juice of this I'll streak her eyes,
And make her full of hateful fantasies.
Take thou some of it, and seek through this grove
A sweet Athenian lady is in love
With a disdainful youth: anoint his eyes;
But do it, when the next thing he espies
May be the lady: Thou shalt know the man
By the Athenian garments he hath on.[8]
Effect it with some care, that he may prove
More fond on her, than she upon her love:
And look thou meet me ere the first cock crow.

Puck. Fear not, my lord, your servant shall do so.
[*Exeunt.*

SCENE III. *Another part of the Wood. Enter* Titania, *with her train.*

Tita. Come, now a roundel,[9] and a fairy song;
Then, for the third part of a minute, hence;
Some, to kill cankers in the musk-rose buds;
Some, war with rear-mice[10] for their leathern wings,
To make my small elves coats; and some, keep back
The clamorous owl, that nightly hoots, and wonders
At our quaint spirits:[11] Sing me now asleep
Then to your offices, and let me rest.

SONG.

1 Fai. *You spotted snakes, with double tongue,*
Thorny hedge-hogs, be not seen;
Newts,[12] *and blindworms,*[13] *do no wrong,*
Come not near our fairy queen:

1 Exempt from the power of love.

2 The tricolored violet, commonly called pansies, or heartsease, is here meant; one or two of its petals are of a purple colour. It has other fanciful and expressive names, such as—Cuddle me to you; Three faces under a hood; Herb trinity, &c.

3 Mad, raving.

4 'There is now a dayes a kind of *adamant* which draweth unto it fleshe, and the same so strongly, that it hath power to knit and tie together two mouthes of contrary persons, and draw the heart of a man out of his bodie without offending any part of him.' *Certaine Secrete Wonders of Nature, by Edward Fenton*, 1569.

5 i. e. bring it into question.

6 To *die upon*, &c. appears to have been used for 'to *die by* the hand.'

7 The greater cowslip.

8 Steevens thinks this rhyme of *man* and *on* a sufficient proof that the broad Scotch pronunciation once prevailed in England. But our ancient poets were not particular in making their rhymes correspond in sound, and I very much doubt a conclusion made upon such slender grounds.

9 The *roundel*, or round, as its name implies, was a dance of a circular kind.

10 Bats. 11 Sports 12 Efts

13 Slow-worms.

CHORUS. *Philomel, with melody,*
Sing in our sweet lullaby;
Lulla, lulla, lullaby; lulla, lulla, lullaby,
Never harm, nor spell nor charm,
Come our lovely lady nigh;
So, good night, with lullaby.

II.

2 Fai. *Weaving spiders, come not here;*
Hence, you long-legg'd spinners, hence:
Beetles black, approach not near;
Worm, nor snail, do no offence.

CHORUS. *Philomel, with melody, &c.*

1 Fai. Hence, away; now all is well;
One, aloof, stand sentinel.

[*Exeunt* Fairies. TITANIA *sleeps.*

Enter OBERON.

Obe. What thou seest when thou dost wake,
[*Squeezes the flower on* TITANIA'S *eyelids.*
Do it for thy true love take;
Love, and languish for his sake:
Be it ounce,[1] or cat, or bear,
Pard, or boar with bristled hair,
In thy eye that shall appear
When thou wak'st, it is thy dear;
Wake, when some vile thing is near. [*Exit.*

Enter LYSANDER *and* HERMIA.

Lys. Fair love, you faint with wandering in the wood;
And to speak troth, I have forgot our way;
We'll rest us, Hermia, if you think it good,
And tarry for the comfort of the day.

Her. Be it so, Lysander; find you out a bed,
For I upon this bank will rest my head.

Lys. One turf shall serve as pillow for us both;
One heart, one bed, two bosoms, and one troth.

Her. Nay, good Lysander; for my sake, my dear,
Lie further off yet, do not lie so near.

Lys. O, take the sense, sweet, of my innocence;[2]
Love takes the meaning, in love's conference.
I mean, that my heart unto yours is knit;
So that but one heart we can make of it:
Two bosoms interchained with an oath;
So then, two bosoms, and a single troth.
Then, by your side no bed-room me deny;
For, lying so, Hermia, I do not lie.

Her. Lysander riddles very prettily:—
Now much beshrew[3] my manners and my pride,
If Hermia meant to say, Lysander lied.
But, gentle friend, for love and courtesy
Lie further off; in human modesty
Such separation, as, may well be said,
Becomes a virtuous bachelor and a maid,
So far be distant; and good night, sweet friend:
Thy love ne'er alter, till thy sweet life end!

Lys. Amen, amen, to that fair prayer, say I;
And then end life, when I end loyalty!
Here is my bed: Sleep give thee all his rest!

Her. With half that wish the wisher's eyes be press'd! [*They sleep.*

Enter PUCK.

Puck. Through the forest have I gone,
But Athenian found I none,
On whose eyes I might approve
This flower's force in stirring love.
Night and silence! who is here?
Weeds of Athens he doth wear:
This is he, my master said,
Despised the Athenian maid;
And here the maiden, sleeping sound,
On the dank and dirty ground.
Pretty soul! she durst not lie
Near this lack-love, this kill-courtesy.
Churl, upon thy eyes I throw
All the power this charm doth owe:[4]
When thou wak'st, let love forbid
Sleep his seat on thy eye-lid.[5]
So awake, when I am gone;
For I must now to Oberon. [*Exit.*

Enter DEMETRIUS *and* HELENA, *running.*

Hel. Stay, though thou kill me, sweet Demetrius.

Dem. I charge thee, hence, and do not haunt me thus.

Hel. O, wilt thou darkling leave me? do not so

Dem. Stay, on thy peril; I alone will go.
[*Exit* DEMETRIUS.

Hel. O, I am out of breath in this fond chase!
The more my prayer, the lesser is my grace.[6]
Happy is Hermia, wheresoe'er she lies;
For she hath blessed and attractive eyes.
How came her eyes so bright? Not with salt tears:
If so, my eyes are oftener wash'd than hers.
No, no, I am as ugly as a bear;
For beasts that meet me, run away for fear:
Therefore, no marvel, though Demetrius
Do, as a monster, fly my presence thus.
What wicked and dissembling glass of mine
Made me compare with Hermia's sphery eyne!
But who is here?—Lysander! on the ground!
Dead? or asleep? I see no blood, no wound.
Lysander, if you live, good sir, awake.

Lys. And run through fire I will, for thy sweet sake. [*Waking.*
Transparent Helena; Nature shows her art,[7]
That through thy bosom makes me see thy heart.
Where is Demetrius? O, how fit a word
Is that vile name to perish on my sword!

Hel. Do not say so, Lysander; say not so.
What though he love your Hermia? Lord, what though?
Yet Hermia still loves you: then be content.

Lys. Content with Hermia? No: I do repent
The tedious minutes I with her have spent.
Not Hermia, but Helena I love:
Who will not change a raven for a dove?
The will of man is by his reason sway'd;
And reason says you are the worthier maid.
Things growing are not ripe until their season
So I, being young, till now ripe[8] not to reason;
And touching now the point of human skill,
Reason becomes the marshal to my will,
And leads me to your eyes; where I o'erlook
Love's stories written in love's richest book.

Hel. Wherefore was I to this keen mockery born?
When, at your hands, did I deserve this scorn?
Is't not enough, is't not enough, young man,
That I did never, no, nor never can,
Deserve a sweet look from Demetrius' eye,
But you must flout my insufficiency?
Good troth, you do me wrong, good sooth, you do
In such disdainful manner me to woo.
But fare you well: perforce I must confess,
I thought you lord of more true gentleness.
O, that a lady, of one man refus'd,
Should of another, therefore be abus'd! [*Exit.*

Lys. She sees not Hermia!—Hermia, sleep thou there;
And never mayst thou come Lysander near!
For, as a surfeit of the sweetest things
The deepest loathing to the stomach brings;
Or, as the heresies, that men do leave,
Are hated most of those they did deceive;

1 The small tiger, or tiger-cat.

2 i. e. 'understand *the meaning of my innocence*, or my *innocent meaning*. Let no suspicion of ill enter thy mind.' In the conversation of those who are assured of each other's kindness, not *suspicion* but *love takes the meaning*.

3 This word implies a sinister wish, and here means the same as if she had said, 'now *ill befall* my manners,' &c.

4 Possess.

5 So in Macbeth:
'Sleep shall neither night nor day
Hang upon his pent-house lid.'

6 i. e. the lesser my acceptableness, the favour I can gain.

7 The quartos have only—'Nature shews art.' The first folio—'Nature *her* shews art.' The second folio changes *her* to *here*. Malone thought we should read, 'Nature shews her art.'

8 i. e do not *ripen* to it

So thou, my surfeit, and my heresy,
Of all be hated; but the most of me!
And all my powers, address your love and might,
To honour Helen, and to be her knight! [*Exit.*

Her. [*starting.*] Help me, Lysander, help me! do thy best,
To pluck this crawling serpent from my breast!
Ah me, for pity!—what a dream was here?
Lysander, look, how I do quake with fear:
Methought a serpent eat my heart away,
And you sat smiling at his cruel prey:—
Lysander! what, remov'd? Lysander! lord!
What, out of hearing? gone? no sound, no word?
Alack, where are you? speak, an if you hear;
Speak, of all loves;[1] I swoon almost with fear.
No?—then I well perceive you are not nigh:
Either death, or you, I'll find immediately. [*Exit.*

ACT III.

SCENE I. *The same. The Queen of Fairies lying asleep. Enter* QUINCE, SNUG, BOTTOM, FLUTE, SNOUT, *and* STARVELING.

Bot. Are we all met?

Quin. Pat, pat; and here's a marvellous convenient place for our rehearsal: This green plot shall be our stage, this hawthorn brake out tyring house; and we will do it in action, as we will do it before the duke.

Bot. Peter Quince,—

Quin. What say'st thou, bully Bottom?

Bot. There are things in this comedy of *Pyramus and Thisby*, that will never please. First, Pyramus must draw a sword to kill himself; which the ladies cannot abide. How answer you that?

Snout. By'rlakin,[2] a parlous[3] fear.

Star. I believe, we must leave the killing out, when all is done.

Bot. Not a whit; I have a device to make all well. Write me a prologue: and let the prologue seem to say, we will do no harm with our swords; and that Pyramus is not killed indeed: and for the more better assurance, tell them, that I Pyramus am not Pyramus, but Bottom the weaver: This will put them out of fear.

Quin. Well, we will have such a prologue; and it shall be written in eight and six.[4]

Bot. No, make it two more; let it be written in eight and eight.

Snout. Will not the ladies be afeard of the lion?

Star. I fear it, I promise you.

Bot. Masters, you ought to consider with yourselves: to bring in, God shield us! a lion among ladies, is a most dreadful thing; for there is not a more fearful[5] wild-fowl than your lion, living; and we ought to look to it.

Snout. Therefore, another prologue must tell, he is not a lion.

Bot. Nay, you must name his name, and half his face must be seen through the lion's neck; and he himself must speak through, saying thus, or to the same defect,—Ladies, or fair ladies, I would wish you, or, I would request you, or, I would entreat you, not to fear, not to tremble: my life for yours. If you think I come hither as a lion, it were pity of my life: No, I am no such thing; I am a man as other men are:—and there, indeed, let him name his name; and tell them plainly he is Snug the joiner.[6]

Quin. Well, it shall be so. But there is two hard things; that is, to bring the moon-light into a chamber: for you know, Pyramus and Thisby meet by moon-light.

Snug. Doth the moon shine that night we play our play?

Bot. A calendar, a calendar! look in the almanack; find out moon-shine, find out moonshine.

Quin. Yes, it doth shine that night.

Bot. Why, then you may leave a casement of the great chamber window, where we play, open, and the moon may shine in at the casement.

Quin. Ay; or else one must come in with a bush of thorns and a lanthorn, and say, he comes to disfigure, or to present, the person of moon-shine. Then, there is another thing: we must have a wall in the great chamber; for Pyramus and Thisby, says the story, did talk through the chink of a wall.

Snug. You never can bring in a wall.—What say you, Bottom?

Bot. Some man or other must present wall: and let him have some plaster, or some loam, or some rough-cast about him, to signify wall; or let him hold his fingers thus, and through that cranny shall Pyramus and Thisby whisper.

Quin. If that may be, then all is well. Come, sit down, every mother's son, and rehearse your parts. Pyramus, you begin: when you have spoken your speech, enter into that brake,[7] and so every one according to his cue.

Enter PUCK *behind.*

Puck. What hempen home-spuns have we swaggering here,
So near the cradle of the fairy queen?
What, a play toward? I'll be an auditor;
An actor, too, perhaps, if I see cause.

Quin. Speak, Pyramus:—Thisby, stand forth.

Pyr. *Thisby, the flowers of odious savours sweet,—*

Quin. Odours, odours.

Pyr. ——*odours savours sweet:*
So hath thy breath, my dearest Thisby dear.—
But, hark, a voice! stay thou but here a while,
And by and by I will to thee appear. [*Exit.*

Puck. A stanger Pyramus than e'er play'd here! [*Aside.—Exit.*

This. Must I speak now?

Quin. Ay, marry, must you: for you must understand, he goes but to see a noise that he heard, and is to come again.

This. *Most radiant Pyramus, most lilly-white of hue,*
Of colour like the red rose on triumphant brier,
Most brisky Juvenal,[8] and eke most lovely Jew,
As true as truest horse, that yet would never tire,
I'll meet thee, Pyramus, at Ninny's tomb.

Quin. Ninus' tomb, man: Why you must not speak that yet; that you answer to Pyramus: you speak all your part at once, cues[9] and all.—Pyramus, enter; your cue is past; it is, *never tire.*

Re-enter PUCK, *and* BOTTOM *with an ass's head.*

This. O,—*As true as truest horse, that yet would never tire.*

Pyr. *If I were fair, Thisby, I were only thine.—*

Quin. O monstrous! O strange! we are haunted.
Pray, masters! fly, masters! help! [*Exeunt* Clowns.

Puck. I'll follow you, I'll lead you about a round,
Through bog, through bush, through brake, through brier;

---

1 By all that is dear.

2 i. e. by our ladykin or little lady, as ifakins, is a corruption of *by my faith.*

3 Corrupted from perilous; but used for *alarming, amazing.*

4 That is, in alternative verses of eight and six syllables.

5 Terrible.

6 Shakspeare may here allude to an incident said to have occurred in his time, which is recorded in a collection of anecdotes, stories, &c. entitled 'Mery Passages and Jeasts,' MS. Harl. 6395. 'There was a spectacle presented to Queen Elizabeth upon the water, and among others Harry Goldingham was to represent Arion upon the Dolphin's backe; but finding his voice to be verye hoarse and unpleasant when he came to perform it, he tears off his disguise, and swears he was none of Arion, not he, but even honest Harry Goldingham; which blunt discoverie pleased the queen better than if he had gone through in the right way:—yet he could order his voice to an instrument exceeding well.'

7 Thicket.

8 Young man.

9 The *cues* were the last words of the preceding speech, which serve as a hint to him who was to speak next; and generally written out with that which was to be learnt by rote.

Sometime a horse I'll be, sometime a hound,
A hog, a headless bear, sometime a fire;
And neigh, and bark, and grunt, and roar, and burn,
Like horse, hound, hog, bear, fire, at every turn.
[*Exit.*

Bot. Why do they run away? this is a knavery of them, to make me afeard.

Re-enter SNOUT.

Snout. O Bottom, thou art changed! what do I see on thee?

Bot. What do you see? you see an ass's head of your own; Do you?

Re-enter QUINCE.

Quin. Bless thee, Bottom! bless thee! thou art translated. [*Exit.*

Bot. I see their kavery! this is to make an ass of me; to fright me, if they could. But I will not stir from this place, do what they can: I will walk up and down here, and I will sing, that they shall hear I am not afraid. [*Sings.*

The ousel-cock, so black of hue,
With orange-tawney bill,
The throstle with his note so true,
The wren with little quill.

Tita. What angel wakes me from my flowery bed? [*Waking.*

Bot. *The finch, the sparrow, and the lark,*
The plain-song cuckoo[1] *gray,*
Whose note full many a man doth mark,
And dares not answer, nay;—

for, indeed, who would set his wit to so foolish a bird? who would give a bird the lie, though he cry, *cuckoo*, never so?

Tita. I pray thee, gentle mortal, sing again;
Mine ear is much enamour'd of thy note,
So is mine eye enthralled to thy shape;
And thy fair virtue's force perforce doth move me,
On the first view, to say, to swear, I love thee.

Bot. Methinks, mistress, you should have little reason for that: And yet, to say the truth, reason and love keep little company together nowadays: The more the pity, that some honest neighbours will not make them friends. Nay, I can gleek[2] upon occasion.

Tita. Thou art as wise as thou art beautiful.

Bot. Not so, neither; but if I had wit enough to get out of this wood, I have enough to serve mine own turn.

Tita. Out of this wood do not desire to go;
Thou shalt remain here, whether thou wilt or no.
I am a spirit of no common rate;
The summer still doth tend upon my state,
And I do love thee: therefore, go with me;
I'll give thee fairies to attend on thee;
And they shall fetch thee jewels from the deep:
And sing, while thou on pressed flowers dost sleep:
And I will purge thy mortal grossness so
That thou shalt like an airy spirit go.—
Peas-blossom! Cobweb! Moth! and Mustard-seed!

Enter four Fairies.

1 *Fai.* Ready.
2 *Fai.* And I.
3 *Fai.* And I.
4 *Fai.* And I.
All. Where shall we go?

Tita. Be kind and courteous to this gentleman;
Hop in his walks, and gambol in his eyes;
Feed him with apricocks and dewberries,[3]
With purple grapes, green figs, and mulberries;
The honey bags steal from the humble-bees,
And, for night tapers, crop their waxen thighs,
And light them at the fiery glow-worm's eyes,
To have my love to bed, and to arise;
And pluck the wings from painted butterflies,
To fan the moonbeams from his sleeping eyes:
Nod to him, elves, and do him courtesies.

1 *Fai.* Hail, mortal!
2 *Fai.* Hail!
3 *Fai.* Hail!
4 *Fai.* Hail!

Bot. I cry your worship's mercy, heartily.—I beseech, your worship's name?

Cob. Cobweb.

Bot. I shall desire you of more acquaintance,[4] good master Cobweb: If I cut my finger, I shall make bold with you.—Your name, honest gentleman?

Peas. Peas-blossom.

Bot. I pray you, commend me to mistress Squash,[5] your mother, and to master Peascod, your father. Good master Peas-blossom, I shall desire you of more acquaintance too.—Your name, I beseech you, sir?

Mus. Mustard-seed.

Bot. Good master Mustard-seed, I know your patience[6] well: that same cowardly, giant-like ox-beef hath devoured many a gentleman of your house: I promise you, your kindred hath made my eyes water ere now. I desire you more acquaintance, good master Mustard-seed.

Tita. Come, wait upon him; lead him to my bower.
The moon methinks looks with a watery eye;
And when she weeps, weeps every little flower,
Lamenting some enforced chastity.
Tie up my lover's tongue, bring him silently.
[*Exeunt.*

SCENE II *Another part of the Wood. Enter* OBERON.

Obe. I wonder if Titania be awak'd;
Then, what it was that next came in her eye,
Which she must dote on in extremity.

Enter PUCK.

Here comes my messenger.—How now, mad spirit?
What night-rule[7] now about this haunted grove?

Puck. My mistress with a monster is in love.
Near to her close and consecrated bower,
While she was in her dull and sleeping hour,
A crew of patches,[8] rude mechanicals,
That work for bread upon Athenian stalls,
Were met together to rehearse a play,
Intended for great Theseus' nuptial day.
The shallowest thick-skin of that barren sort,[9]
Who Pyramus presented, in their sport
Forsook his scene, and entered in a brake:
When I did him at this advantage take,
An ass's nowl[10] I fixed on his head;
Anon, his Thisbe must be answered,
And forth my mimic[11] comes: When they him spy,
As wild geese that the creeping fowler eye,
Or russet-pated choughs,[12] many in sort,[13]

1 The cuckoo, having no variety of note, sings in *plain song* (*plano cantu*), by which expression the uniform modulation or simplicity of the *chaunt* was anciently distinguished in opposition to *prick-song*, or variated music sung by note.

2 i. e. jest or scoff.

3 The fruit of a bramble called *Rubus cæsius*: sometimes called also the *blue-berry*.

4 'I shall desire *you of* more acquaintance.' This kind of phraseology was not uncommon.

5 A *squash* is an immature peascod. So in Twelfth Night, Act i. Sc. 5:
'As a *squash* is before 'tis a peascod.'

6 Mason proposes to read 'passing well,' which is plausible if change be necessary. The words are spoken ironically, as it was the prevailing opinion in Shakspeare's time, that mustard excited choler.

7 Revelry.

8 A *patch* sometimes means a *fool*, or *simpleton*; but it was a common contemptuous term, and may be either a corruption of the Italian *pazzo*, or derived from the *patch'd* clothes sometimes worn by persons of low condition. Tooke gives a different origin from the Saxon verb pæcan, to deceive by false appearances.

9 *Barren* is dull, unpregnant. *Sort* is company.

10 A *head*. The metamorphosis of Bottom might have been suggested by a similar trick played by Dr. Faustus. See his History, c. xliii.

11 Actor.

12 The *chough* is a bird of the daw kin

13 *Sort* is company, as abov .

Rising and cawing at the gun's report,
Sever themselves, and madly sweep the sky;
So, at his sight, away his fellows fly:
And, at our stamp, here o'er and o'er one falls;
He murder cries, and help from Athens calls.
Their sense, thus weak, lost with their fears, thus strong,
Made senseless things begin to do them wrong:
For briars and thorns at their apparel snatch;
Some, sleeves; some, hats; from yielders all things catch.
I led them on in this distracted fear,
And left sweet Pyramus translated there:
When in that moment (so it came to pass,)
Titania wak'd, and straightway lov'd an ass.

Obe. This falls out better than I could devise.
But hast thou yet latch'd[1] the Athenian's eyes
With the love-juice, as I did bid thee do?

Puck. I took him sleeping,—that is finish'd too,—
And the Athenian woman by his side;
That, when he wak'd, of force she must be ey'd.

Enter Demetrius *and* Hermia.

Obe. Stand close; this is the same Athenian.

Puck. This is the woman, but not this the man.

Dem. O, why rebuke you him that loves you so?
Lay breath so bitter on your bitter foe.

Her. Now I but chide, but I should use thee worse;
For thou, I fear, hast given me cause to curse.
If thou hast slain Lysander in his sleep,
Being o'er shoes in blood, plunge in the deep,
And kill me too.
The sun was not so true unto the day,
As he to me: Would he have stolen away
From sleeping Hermia? I'll believe as soon,
This whole earth may be bor'd; and that the moon
May through the centre creep, and so displease
Her brother's noon-tide with the Antipodes.
It cannot be, but thou hast murder'd him;
So should a murderer look; so dead, so grim.

Dem. So should the murder'd look; and so should I,
Pierc'd through the heart with your stern cruelty:
Yet you, the murderer, look as bright, as clear,
As yonder Venus in her glimmering sphere.

Her. What's this to my Lysander? Where is he?
Ah, good Demetrius, wilt thou give him me?

Dem. I had rather give his carcass to my hounds.

Her. Out, dog! out, cur! thou driv'st me past the bounds
Of maiden's patience. Hast thou slain him then?
Henceforth be never number'd among men!
O! once tell true, tell true, even for my sake;
Durst thou have look'd upon him, being awake,
And hast thou kill'd him sleeping? O brave touch![2]
Could not a worm, an adder, do so much?
An adder did it; for with doubler tongue
Than thine, thou serpent, never adder stung.

Dem. You spend your passion on a mispris'd[3] mood:
I am not guilty of Lysander's blood;
Nor is he dead, for aught that I can tell.

Her. I pray thee, tell me then that he is well.

Dem. An if I could, what should I get therefore?

Her. A privilege, never to see me more.—
And from thy hated presence part I so:
See me no more, whether he be dead or no. [*Exit.*

Dem. There is no following her in this fierce vein:
Here, therefore, for a while I will remain.
So sorrow's heaviness doth heavier grow
For debt that bankrupt sleep doth sorrow owe;
Which now, in some slight measure it will pay,
If for his tender here I make some stay.
[*Lies down.*

Obe. What hast thou done? thou hast mistaken quite,
And laid the love-juice on some true-love's sight:
Of thy misprision must perforce ensue
Some true-love turn'd, and not a false turn'd true.

Puck. Then fate o'er-rules; that, one man holding troth,
A million fail, confounding oath on oath.

Obe. About the wood go swifter than the wind,
And Helena of Athens look thou find:
All fancy-sick[4] she is, and pale of cheer[5]
With sighs of love, that cost the fresh blood dear[6]
By some illusion see thou bring her here;
I'll charm his eyes, against she do appear.

Puck. I go, I go; look, how I go:
Swifter than arrow from the Tartar's bow. [*Exit*

Obe. Flower of this purple die,
Hit with Cupid's archery,
Sink in apple of his eye!
When his love he doth espy,
Let her shine as gloriously
As the Venus of the sky.—
When thou wak'st, if she be by,
Beg of her for remedy.

Re-enter Puck.

Puck. Captain of our fairy band,
Helena is here at hand;
And the youth, mistook by me,
Pleading for a lover's fee;
Shall we their fond pageant see?
Lord, what fools these mortals be!

Obe. Stand aside: the noise they make,
Will cause Demetrius to awake.

Puck. Then will two at once woo one;
That must needs be sport alone;
And those things do best please me,
That befall preposterously.

Enter Lysander *and* Helena.

Lys. Why should you think, that I should woo in scorn?
Scorn and derision never come in tears:
Look, when I vow, I weep; and vows so born
In their nativity all truth appears.
How can these things in me seem scorn to you,
Bearing the badge of faith, to prove them true?

Hel. You do advance your cunning more and more
When truth kills truth, O devilish holy fray!
These vows are Hermia's; Will you give her o'er?
Weigh oath with oath, and you will nothing weigh.
Your vows, to her and me, put in two scales,
Will even weigh; and both as light as tales.

Lys. I had no judgment when to her I swore.

Hel. Nor none, in my mind, now you give her o'er

Lys. Demetrius loves her, and he loves not you

Dem. [*awaking.*] O Helen, goddess, nymph, perfect divine!
To what, my love, shall I compare thine eyne?
Crystal is muddy. O, how ripe in show
Thy lips, those kissing cherries, tempting grow!
That pure congealed white, high Taurus's snow,
Fann'd with the eastern wind, turns to a crow,
When thou hold'st up thy hand: O let me kiss
This princess of pure white, this seal[7] of bliss!

Hel. O spite! O hell! I see you all are bent
To set against me, for your merriment.
If you were civil, and knew courtesy,
You would not do me thus much injury.
Can you not hate me, as I know you do,
But you must join in souls,[8] to mock me too?
If you were men, as men you are in show,

1 *Latch'd* or *letch'd*, licked or smeared over.

2 A *touch* anciently signified a *trick*. Ascham has 'the shrewd *touches* of many curst boys.' And in the old story of Howleglas, 'for at all times he did some mad *touch*.'

3 '*On* a mispris'd mood,' i. e. *in* a mistaken manner. *On* was sometimes used licentiously for *in*.

4 Love-sick.

5 *Cheer* here signifies *countenance*, from cera, *Ital.* signifying 'the face, visage, sight, or *countenance*, *look* or *cheere* of a man or woman.' The old French *chere* had the same meaning.

6 So in K. Henry VI. we have 'blood-consuming, 'blood-drinking,' and 'blood-sucking sighs.' All alluding to the ancient supposition, that every sigh was indulged at the expense of a drop of blood.

7 So in Antony and Cleopatra:
'My playfellow, your *hand*; this kingly *seal*,
And plighter of high hearts.'

8 i. e. join heartily, unite in the same mind

You would not use a gentle lady so;
To vow, and swear, and superpraise my parts,
When, I am sure, you hate me with your hearts.
You both are rivals, and love Hermia;
And now both rivals to mock Helena:
A trim exploit, a manly enterprise,
To conjure tears up in a poor maid's eyes,
With your derision! none of noble sort[1]
Would so offend a virgin; and extort
A poor soul's patience, all to make you sport.

Lys. You are unkind, Demetrius; be not so;
For you love Hermia: this, you know, I know:
And here, with all good will, with all my heart,
In Hermia's love I yield you up my part;
And yours of Helena to me bequeath,
Whom I do love, and will do to my death.

Hel. Never did mockers waste more idle breath.

Dem. Lysander, keep thy Hermia; I will none:
If e'er I lov'd her, all that love is gone.
My heart with her but, as guest-wise, sojourn'd;
And now to Helen is it home return'd,
There to remain.

Lys. Helen, it is not so.

Dem. Disparage not the faith thou dost not know,
Lest, to thy peril, thou abide it dear.[2]—
Look where thy love comes; yonder is thy dear.

Enter HERMIA.

Her. Dark night, that from the eye his function takes,
The ear more quick of apprehension makes;
Wherein it doth impair the seeing sense,
It pays the hearing double recompense:—
Thou art not by mine eye, Lysander, found;
Mine ear I thank it, brought me to thy sound.
But why unkindly didst thou leave me so?

Lys. Why should he stay, whom love doth press to go?

Her. What love could press Lysander from my side?

Lys. Lysander's love, that would not let him bide.
Fair Helena, who more engilds the night
Than all you fiery oes[3] and eyes of light.
Why seek'st thou me? could not this make thee know,
The hate I bare thee made me leave thee so.

Her. You speak not as you think; it cannot be.

Hel. Lo, she is one of this confederacy!
Now I perceive they have conjoin'd all three,
To fashion this false sport in spite of me.
Injurious Hermia! most ungrateful maid!
Have you conspir'd, have you with these contriv'd
To bate me with this foul derision?
Is all the counsel that we two have shar'd,[4]
The sisters' vows, the hours that we have spent,
When we have chid the hasty-footed time
For parting us,—O, and is all forgot?
All school-days' friendship, childhood innocence?
We, Hermia, like two artificial[5] gods,
Have with our neelds[6] created both one flower,
Both on one sampler, sitting on one cushion,
Both warbling of one song, both in one key;
As if our hands, our sides, voices, and minds,
Had been incorporate. So we grew together,
Like to a double cherry, seeming parted;
But yet a union in partition,
Two lovely berries moulded on one stem:
So, with two seeming bodies, but one heart;
Two of the first,[7] like coats in heraldry,
Due but to one, and crowned with one crest.
And will you rent our ancient love asunder,
To join with men in scorning your poor friend?
It is not friendly, 'tis not maidenly:
Our sex, as well as I may chide you for it;
Though I alone do feel the injury.

Her. I am amazed at your passionate words:
I scorn you not; it seems that you scorn me.

Hel. Have you not set Lysander, as in scorn,
To follow me, and praise my eyes and face?
And made your other love, Demetrius,
(Who even but now did spurn me with his foot,)
To call me goddess, nymph, divine, and rare,
Precious, celestial? Wherefore speaks he this
To her he hates? and wherefore doth Lysander
Deny your love, so rich within his soul,
And tender me, forsooth, affection;
But by your setting on, by your consent?
What though I be not so in grace as you,
So hung upon with love, so fortunate;
But miserable most, to love unlov'd?
This you should pity, rather than despise.

Her. I understand not what you mean by this.

Hel. Ay, do, persever, counterfeit sad looks,
Make mows[8] upon me when I turn my back;
Wink at each other; hold the sweet jest up:
This sport, well carried, shall be chronicled.
If you have any pity, grace, or manners,
You would not make me such an argument.[9]
But, fare ye well: 'tis partly mine own fault;
Which death, or absence, soon shall remedy.

Lys. Stay, gentle Helena; hear my excuse;
My love, my life, my soul, fair Helena!

Hel. O excellent!

Her. Sweet, do not scorn her so.

Dem. If she cannot entreat, I can compel.

Lys. Thou canst compel no more than she entreat;
Thy threats have no more strength, than her weak prayers.—
Helen I love thee; by my life I do:
I swear by that which I will lose for thee,
To prove him false, that says I love thee not.

Dem. I say I love thee more than he can do.

Lys. If thou say so, withdraw and prove it too.

Dem. Quick, come,—

Her. Lysander, whereto tends all this?

Lys. Away, you Ethiop!

Dem. No, no, he'll—Sir,[10]
Seem to break loose; take on as you would follow;
But yet come not: You are a tame man, go!

Lys. Hang off, thou cat, thou burr: vile thing let loose;
Or I will shake thee from me like a serpent.

Her. Why are you grown so rude? what change is this,
Sweet love?

Lys. Thy love! out, tawny Tartar, out!
Out, loathed medicine! hated potion, hence!

Her. Do you not jest?

Hel. Yes, 'sooth: and so do you.

Lys. Demetrius, I will keep my word with thee.

Dem. I would, I had your bond; for, I perceive,
A weak bond holds you; I'll not trust your word.

Lys. What, should I hurt her, strike her, kill her dead?
Although I hate her, I'll not harm her so.

---

1 Degree, or quality.

2 Pay dearly for it, rue it.

3 i. e. circles.

4 'Is all the counsel that we two have shared,' &c. 'Gregory of Nazianzen's poem on his own life contains some beautiful lines (resembling these) which burst from the heart and speak the pangs of injured and lost friendship. Shakspeare had never read the poems of Gregory; he was ignorant of the Greek language; but his mother tongue, the language of nature, is the same in Cappadocia as in Britain.'—*Gibbon's Hist.* vol v p. 17, 8vo. ed.

5 i. e. ingenious, artful. *Artificiose*, Lat

6 i e. needles

7 Mr. Douce thus explains this passage: Helen says, 'we had two seeming bodies, but only one heart.' She then exemplifies the position by a simile—'we had *two of the first*, i. e. *bodies*, like the double coats in heraldry that belong to man and wife as *one person*, but which like our *single heart*, have but *one crest*.' Malone explains the heraldric allusion differently, but not so clearly nor satisfactorily.

8 Make mouths.

9 i. e. such a *subject* of light merriment.

10 This arrangement of the text is Malone's, who thus explains it. The words *he'll* are not in the folio, and *sir* is not in the quarto. Demetrius I suppose would say *no, no, he'll* not have the resolution to disengage himself from Hermia But turning to Lysander, he addresses him ironically: 'Sir, seem to break loose,' &c.

Her. What, can you do me greater harm than hate?
Hate me! wherefore? O me! what news, my love?
Am not I Hermia? Are not you Lysander?
I am as fair now as I was erewhile.
Since night you lov'd me; yet since night you left me:
Why, then you left me,—O, the gods forbid!—
In earnest shall I say?
Lys. Ay, by my life;
And never did desire to see thee more.
Therefore, be out of hope, of question, doubt,
Be certain nothing truer; 'tis no jest,
That I do hate thee, and love Helena.
Her. O me, you juggler! you canker-blossom![1]
You thief of love! what, have you come by night,
And stol'n my love's heart from him?
Hel. Fine, i'faith!
Have you no modesty, no maiden shame,
No touch of bashfulness? What, will you tear
Impatient answers from my gentle tongue?
Fie, fie! you counterfeit, you puppet you!
Her. Puppet! why so? Ay, that way goes the game.
Now I perceive that she hath made compare
Between our statures, she hath urg'd her height;
And with her personage, her tall personage,
Her height, forsooth, she hath prevail'd with him.—
And are you grown so high in his esteem,
Because I am so dwarfish, and so low?
How low am I, thou painted maypole? speak;
How low am I? I am not yet so low,
But that my nails can reach unto thine eyes.
Hel. I pray you, though you mock me, gentlemen,
Let her not hurt me: I was never curst;[2]
I have no gift at all in shrewishness;
I am a right maid for my cowardice;
Let her not strike me: You, perhaps, may think,
Because she's something lower than myself,
That I can match her.
Her. Lower! hark, again.
Hel. Good Hermia, do not be so bitter with me.
I evermore did love you, Hermia,
Did ever keep your counsels, never wrong'd you;
Save that, in love unto Demetrius,
I told him of your stealth unto this wood:
He follow'd you; for love, I follow'd him.
But he hath chid me hence: and threaten'd me
To strike me, spurn me, nay, to kill me too:
And now, so you will let me quiet go,
To Athens will I bear my folly back,
And follow you no further: Let me go:
You see how simple and how fond[3] I am.
Her. Why, get you gone: Who is't that hinders you?
Hel. A foolish heart that I leave here behind.
Her. What! with Lysander?
Hel. With Demetrius.
Lys. Be not afraid: she shall not harm thee, Helena.
Dem. No, sir; she shall not, though you take her part.
Hel. O, when she's angry, she is keen and shrewd:
She was a vixen, when she went to school;
And, though she be but little, she is fierce.
Her. Little again? nothing but low and little?—
Why will you suffer her to flout me thus?
Let me come to her.
Lys. Get you gone, you dwarf;
You minimus of hind'ring knot-grass[4] made;
You bead, you acorn.
Dem. You are too officious,
In her behalf that scorns your services:
Let her alone; speak not of Helena;
Take not her part: for if thou dost intend[5]
Never so little show of love to her,
Thou shalt aby it.[6]
Lys. Now she holds me not,
Now follow if thou dar'st, to try whose right,
Or thine, or mine, is most in Helena.
Dem. Follow? nay, I'll go with thee cheek by jole. [*Exeunt* Lys. *and* Dem.
Her. You, mistress, all this coil is 'long of you
Nay, go not back.
Hel. I will not trust you, I;
Nor longer stay in your curst company.
Your hands, than mine, are quicker for a fray;
My legs are longer though, to run away. [*Exit.*
Her. I am amaz'd, and know not what to say.
[*Exit, pursuing* Helena.
Obe. This is thy negligence: still thou mistak'st,
Or else committ'st thy knaveries wilfully.
Puck. Believe me, king of shadows, I mistook.
Did not you tell me, I should know the man
By the Athenian garments he had on?
And so far blameless proves my enterprise,
That I have 'nointed an Athenian's eyes:
And so far am I glad it so did sort,[7]
As this their jangling I esteem a sport.
Obe. Thou seest, these lovers seek a place to fight:
Hie, therefore, Robin, overcast the night;
The starry welkin cover thou anon
With drooping fog, as black as Acheron;
And lead these testy rivals so astray,
As one come not within another's way.
Like to Lysander sometime frame thy tongue,
Then stir Demetrius up with bitter wrong;
And sometime rail thou like Demetrius:
And from each other look thou lead them thus,
Till o'er their brows death-counterfeiting sleep
With leaden legs and batty wings doth creep:
Then crush this herb into Lysander's eye:
Whose liquor hath this virtuous property,
To take from thence all error with his might,
And make his eye-balls roll with wonted sight
When they next wake, all this derision
Shall seem a dream, and fruitless vision;
And back to Athens shall the lovers wend[8]
With league whose date till death shall never end.
Whiles I in this affair do thee employ,
I'll to my queen, and beg her Indian boy;
And then I will her charmed eye release
From monster's view, and all things shall be peace.
Puck. My fairy lord, this must be done with haste;
For night's swift dragons[9] cut the clouds full fast,
And yonder shines Aurora's harbinger;
At whose approach, ghosts, wandering here and there,
Troop home to church-yards: damned spirits all,
That in cross-ways and floods have burial,[10]
Already to their wormy beds[11] are gone;
For fear lest day should look their shames upon,
They wilfully themselves exile from light,
And must for aye consort with black-brow'd night.
Obe. But we are spirits of another sort:
I with the Morning's love[12] have oft made sport
And, like a forester, the groves may tread,
Even till the eastern gate, all fiery red,
Opening on Neptune with fair blessed beams,
Turns into yellow gold his salt-green streams.[13]
But, notwithstanding, haste; make no delay:
We may effect this business yet ere day.
[*Exit* Oberon.

1 A worm that preys on the leaves or buds of flowers, always beginning in the middle.
2 i. e. froward, cross, ill-conditioned, or ill-spoken.
3 Foolish.
4 Anciently knot-grass was believed to prevent the growth of children.
5 Pretend.
6 *Aby it*, for *abide* it, i. e. pay dearly for it, rue it.
7 Chance, fall out, from *sort*, French.
8 Go.
9 So in Cymbeline, Act ii. Sc. 11:
'Swift, swift, ye dragons of the night.'
See note on that passage.
10 The ghosts of self-murderers, who are buried in cross-roads; and of those who being drowned were condemned (according to the opinion of the ancients) to wander for a hundred years, as the rites of sepulchre had never been regularly bestowed on their bodies.
11 'Or that thy beauties lie in *wormy bed*.'—Milton's Ode on the Death of a fair Infant.
12 Cephalus, the mighty hunter, and paramour of Aurora, was here probably meant.
13 Oberon here boasts that he was not compelled, like meaner spirits, to vanish at the first dawn

Puck. Up and down, up and down,
I will lead them up and down:
I am fear'd in field and town;
Goblin, lead them up and down.
Here comes one.

Enter LYSANDER.

Lys. Where art thou, proud Demetrius? speak thou now.
Puck. Here, villain; drawn and ready. Where art thou?
Lys. I will be with thee straight.
Puck. Follow me then
To plainer ground. [*Exit* LYS. *as following the voice.*

Enter DEMETRIUS.

Dem. Lysander! speak again.
Thou runaway, thou coward, art thou fled?
Speak. In some bush? Where dost thou hide thy head?
Puck. Thou coward, art thou bragging to the stars,
Telling the bushes that thou look'st for wars,
And wilt not come? Come, recreant; come, thou child,
I'll whip thee with a rod: He is defil'd,
That draws a sword on thee.
Dem. Yea; art thou there?
Puck. Follow my voice; we'll try no manhood here. [*Exeunt.*

Re-enter LYSANDER.

Lys. He goes before me, and still dares me on;
When I come where he calls, then he is gone.
The villain is much lighter heel'd than I:
I follow'd fast, but faster he did fly;
That fallen am I in dark uneven way,
And here will rest me. Come, thou gentle day!
[*Lies down.*
For if but once thou show me thy gray light,
I'll find Demetrius, and revenge this spite. [*Sleeps.*

Re-enter PUCK *and* DEMETRIUS.

Puck. Ho, ho! ho, ho![1] Coward, why com'st thou not?
Dem. Abide me, if thou dar'st; for well I wot,
Thou runn'st before me, shifting every place;
And dar'st not stand, nor look me in the face.
Where art thou?
Puck. Come hither; I am here.
Dem. Nay, then thou mock'st me. Thou shalt buy this dear.[2]
If ever I thy face by day-light see:
Now, go thy way. Faintness constraineth me
To measure out my length on this cold bed.—
By day's approach look to be visited.
[*Lies down and sleeps.*

Enter HELENA.

Hel. O weary night, O long and tedious night,
Abate thy hours: shine, comforts from the east;
That I may back to Athens by day-light,
From these that my poor company detest:—
And, sleep, that sometimes shuts up sorrow's eye,
Steal me awhile from mine own company. [*Sleeps.*
Puck. Yet but three? Come one more;
Two of both kinds makes up four.
Here she comes, curst and sad:—
Cupid is a knavish lad,
Thus to make poor females mad.

Enter HERMIA.

Her. Never so weary, never so in woe,
Bedabbled with the dew, and torn with briars;
I can no further crawl, no further go;
My legs can keep no pace with my desires.
Here will I rest me, till the break of day,
Heaven shield Lysander, if they mean a fray.
[*Lies down*
Puck. On the ground
Sleep sound:
I'll apply
To your eye,
Gentle lover, remedy.
[*Squeezing the juice on* LYSANDER'S *eye*
When thou wak'st,
Thou tak'st
True delight
In the sight
Of thy former lady's eye
And the country proverb known,
That every man should take his own,
In your waking shall be shown:
Jack shall have Jill;
Nought shall go ill;
The man shall have his mare again, and all shall be well.[3]
[*Exit* PUCK.—DEM. HEL. *&c. sleep.*

ACT IV.

SCENE I. *The same. Enter* TITANIA *and* BOTTOM, *Fairies attending;* OBERON *behind unseen.*

Tita. Come, sit thee down upon this flowery bed,
While I thy amiable cheeks do coy,[4]
And stick musk-roses in thy sleek smooth head,
And kiss thy fair large ears, my gentle joy.
Bot. Where's Peas-blossom?
Peas. Ready.
Bot. Scratch my head, Peas-blossom.—Where's monsieur Cobweb?
Cob. Ready.
Bot. Monsieur Cobweb; good monsieur, get your weapons in your hand, and kill me a red-hipped humble-bee on the top of a thistle; and, good monsieur, bring me the honey-bag. Do not fret yourself too much in the action, monsieur; and, good monsieur, have a care the honey-bag break not; I would be loath to have you overflown with the honey-bag, signior. Where's monsieur Mustard-seed?
Must. Ready.
Bot. Give me your neif,[5] monsieur Mustard-seed. Pray you, leave your courtesy, good monsieur.
Must. What's your will?
Bot. Nothing, good monsieur, but to help cavalero Cobweb to scratch. I must to the barber's, monsieur; for, methinks, I am marvellous hairy about the face: and I am such a tender ass, if my hair do but tickle me, I must scratch.
Tita. What, wilt thou hear some music, my sweet love?
Bot. I have a reasonable good ear in music: let us have the tongs and the bones.[6]
Tita. Or say, sweet love, what thou desir'st to eat.
Bot. Truly, a peck of provender; I could munch your good dry oats. Methinks, I have a great desire to a bottle of hay: good hay, sweet hay, hath no fellow.
Tita. I have a venturous fairy that shall seek
The squirrel's hoard, and fetch thee new nuts.
Bot. I had rather have a handful, or two, of dried peas. But, I pray you, let none of your people stir me; I have an exposition of sleep come upon me.
Tita. Sleep thou, and I will wind thee in my arms
Fairies, be gone, and be all ways away.
So doth the woodbine, the sweet honeysuckle,
Gently entwist,—the female ivy so

1 This exclamation would have been uttered with more propriety by Puck, if he were not now playing an assumed character, which he seems to forget. In the old song printed by Percy, in which all his gambols are related, he concludes every stanza with ho! ho! ho! It was also the established dramatic exclamation given to the devil whenever he appeared on the stage, and attributed to him whenever he appeared in reality.

2 Johnson says, the poet perhaps wrote, 'thou shalt by this dear;' as in another place, 'thou shalt *aby* it.'

3 These three last lines are to be found in Haywood's Epigrams, or Three Hundred Proverbs. Steevens thinks we should read *still* instead of *well*, for the sake of the rhyme.

4 To *coy*, is to stroke or soothe with the hand. The behaviour of Titania on this occasion seems copied from that of the lady in Apuleius, lib. viii.

5 That is *fist*. So in K. Henry IV. Part II. Pistol says: 'Sweet knight, I kiss thy *neif*.'

6 The old rough rustic music of *the tongs*. The folio has this stage direction: 'Musicke Tongs, Rurall Music

Enrings the barky fingers of the elm.[1]
O, how I love thee! how I dote on thee!
[They sleep.

OBERON *advances.* *Enter* PUCK.

Obe. Welcome, good Robin. See'st thou this sweet sight?
Her dotage now I do begin to pity.
For meeting her of late behind the wood,
Seeking sweet savours for this hateful fool,
I did upbraid her, and fall out with her:
For she his hairy temples then had rounded
With coronet of fresh and fragrant flowers;
And that same dew, which sometime on the buds
Was wont to swell, like round and orient pearls,
Stood now within the pretty flourets' eyes,
Like tears, that did their own disgrace bewail.
When I had, at my pleasure, taunted her,
And she, in mild terms, begg'd my patience,
I then did ask of her her changeling child;
Which straight she gave me, and her fairy sent
To bear him to my bower in fairy land.
And now I have the boy, I will undo
This hateful imperfection of her eyes.
And, gentle Puck, take this transformed scalp
From off the head of this Athenian swain;
That he awaking when the other[2] do,
May all to Athens back again repair;
And think no more of this night's accidents,
But as the fierce vexation of a dream.
But first I will release the fairy queen.
Be, as thou wast wont to be.
[Touching her eyes with an herb.
See, as thou wast wont to see:
Dian's bud[3] o'er Cupid's flower
Hath such force and blessed power.
Now, my Titania; wake you, my sweet queen.

Tita. My Oberon! what visions have I seen!
Methought I was enamour'd of an ass.

Obe. There lies your love.

Tita. How came these things to pass?
O, how mine eyes do loathe his visage now!

Obe. Silence, awhile.—Robin, take off this head.—
Titania, music call; and strike more dead
Than common sleep, of all these five the sense.

Tita. Music, ho! music; such as charmeth sleep.

Puck. Now, when thou wak'st, with thine own fool's eyes peep.

Obe. Sound, music. *[Still music.]* Come, my queen, take hands with me,
And rock the ground whereon these sleepers be.
Now thou and I are new in amity;
And will, to-morrow midnight, solemnly,
Dance in Duke Theseus' house triumphantly,
And bless it to all fair posterity:
There shall the pairs of faithful lovers be
Wedded, with Theseus, all in jollity.

Puck. Fairy king, attend and mark;
I do hear the morning lark.

Obe. Then, my queen, in silence sad,[4]
Trip we after the night's shade:
We the globe can compass soon,
Swifter than the wand'ring moon.

Tita. Come, my lord; and in our flight,
Tell me how it came this night,
That I sleeping here was found,
With these mortals on the ground. *[Exeunt.*
[Horns sound within.

Enter THESEUS, HIPPOLYTA, EGEUS, *and Train.*

The. Go, one of you, find out the forester;—
For now our observation is perform'd:[5]
And since we have the vaward[6] of the day,
My love shall hear the music of my hounds.—
Uncouple in the western valley; go:
Despatch, I say, and find the forester.—
We will, fair queen, up to the mountain's top,
And mark the musical confusion
Of hounds and echo in conjunction.

Hip. I was with Hercules, and Cadmus, once,
When in a wood of Crete they bay'd the bear
With hounds of Sparta: never did I hear
Such gallant chiding;[7] for, besides the groves,
The skies, the fountains, every region near
Seem'd all one mutual cry: I never heard
So musical a discord, such sweet thunder.

The. My hounds are bred out of the Spartan kind,
So flew'd,[8] so sanded;[9] and their heads are hung
With ears that sweep away the morning dew;
Crook-knee'd, and dew-lapp'd like Thessalian bulls,
Slow in pursuit, but match'd in mouth like bells,
Each under each. A cry more tuneable
Was never holla'd to, nor cheer'd with horn,
In Crete, in Sparta, nor in Thessaly:
Judge, when you hear.—But, soft; what nymphs are these?

Ege. My lord, this is my daughter here asleep:
And this, Lysander; this Demetrius is;
This Helena, old Nedar's Helena:
I wonder of their being here together.

The. No doubt, they rose up early, to observe
The rite of May; and, hearing our intent,
Came here in grace of our solemnity.—
But, speak, Egeus; is not this the day
That Hermia should give answer of her choice?

Ege. It is, my lord.

The. Go, bid the huntsmen wake them with their horns.

Horns, and shout within. DEMETRIUS, LYSANDER, HERMIA, *and* HELENA, *wake and start up.*

The. Good-morrow, friends. Saint Valentine is past;
Begin these wood-birds but to couple now?

Lys. Pardon, my lord.
[He and the rest kneel to THESEUS

The. I pray you all, stand up
I know you are two rival enemies;
How comes this gentle concord in the world,
That hatred is so far from jealousy,
To sleep by hate, and fear no enmity?

Lys. My lord, I shall reply amazedly,
Half 'sleep, half waking: But as yet, I swear,
I cannot truly say how I came here:
But, as I think, (for truly would I speak,—
And now I do bethink me, so it is;)
I came with Hermia hither: our intent
Was to be gone from Athens, where we might be
Without the peril of the Athenian law.

Ege. Enough, enough, my lord; you have enough
I beg the law, the law, upon his head.—
They would have stol'n away, they would, Demetrius,
Thereby to have defeated you and me:
You, of your wife; and me, of my consent;
Of my consent that she should be your wife.

Dem. My lord, fair Helen told me of their stealth,
Of this their purpose hither, to this wood;
And I in fury hither followed them;
Fair Helena in fancy[10] following me.
But, my good lord, I wot not by what power
(But by some power it is), my love to Hermia,
Melted as doth the snow, seems to me now
As the remembrance of an idle gawd,[11]
Which in my childhood I did dote upon:

1 Steevens says, what Shakspeare seems to mean is this—So the woodbine, i. e. the sweet honeysuckle doth gently entwist the barky fingers of the elm, and so doth the female ivy enring the same fingers.

2 This was the phraseology of the time. So in K. Henry IV. Part I.—'and unbound the rest, and then came in the *other*.'

3 *Dian's bud* is the bud of the *Agnus Castus*, or *Chaste Tree*. 'The vertue of this hearbe is, that he will kepe man and woman *chaste*.'

4 *Sad* here signifies only *grave*, serious.

5 i. e. the honours due to the morning of *May*. So in a former scene—'to do *observance* to a morn of May.'

6 Forepart.

7 *Chiding* means here the *cry of hounds*. To *chide* is used sometimes for to sound, or make a noise, without any reference to scolding.

8 The *flews* are the large chaps of a deep-mouthed hound.

9 *Sanded* means of a sandy colour, which is one of the true denotements of a blood-hound.

10 *Fancy* is here *love* or *affection*, and is opposed to *fury*

11 Toy.

And all the faith, the virtue of my heart,
The object, and the pleasure of mine eye,
Is only Helena. To her, my lord,
Was I betroth'd ere I saw Hermia:
But, like in sickness, did I loathe this food:
But, as in health, come to my natural taste,
Now do I wish it, love it, long for it,
And will for evermore be true to it.

The. Fair lovers, you are fortunately met:
Of this discourse we more will hear anon.—
Egeus, I will overbear your will;
For in the temple, by and by with us,
These couples shall eternally be knit.
And, for the morning now is something worn,
Our purpos'd hunting shall be set aside.—
Away, with us, to Athens: Three and three,
We'll hold a feast in great solemnity.
Come, Hippolyta.

[*Exeunt* THE. HIP. EGE. *and Train.*

Dem. These things seem small and undistinguishable,
Like far-off mountains turned into clouds.

Her. Methinks, I see these things with parted eye,
When every thing seems double.

Hel. So methinks:
And I have found Demetrius like a jewel,
Mine own, and not mine own.[1]

Dem. Are you sure
That we are awake? It seems to me,
That yet we sleep, we dream.—Do not you think,
The duke was here, and bid us follow him?

Her. Yea; and my father.

Hel. And Hippolyta.

Lys. And he did bid us follow to the temple.

Dem. Why then, we are awake: let's follow him;
And, by the way, let us recount our dreams.

[*Exeunt.*

As they go out, BOTTOM *awakes.*

Bot. When my cue comes, call me, and I will answer:—my next is, *Most fair Pyramus.*—Hey, ho!—Peter Quince! Flute, the bellows-mender! Snout, the tinker! Starveling! God's my life! stolen hence, and left me asleep! I have had a most rare vision. I have had a dream,—past the wit of man to say what dream it was: Man is but an ass, if he go about to expound this dream. Methought I was —there is no man can tell what. Methought I was, and methought I had,—But man is but a patched fool, if he will offer to say what methought I had. The eye of man hath not heard, the ear of man hath not seen; man's hand is not able to taste, his tongue to conceive, nor his heart to report, what my dream was. I will get Peter Quince to write a ballad of this dream; it shall be called Bottom's Dream, because it hath no bottom; and I will sing it in the latter end of a play, before the duke: Peradventure, to make it the more gracious, I shall sing it at her death.[2] [*Exit.*

SCENE II. Athens. *A Room in* Quince's *House.* *Enter* QUINCE, FLUTE, SNOUT, *and* STARVELING.

Quin. Have you sent to Bottom's house? is he come home yet?

Star. He cannot be heard of. Out of doubt, he is transported.

Flu. If he come not, then the play is marred; It goes not forward, doth it?

Quin. It is not possible: you have not a man in all Athens able to discharge Pyramus but he.

Flu. No; he hath simply the best wit of any handicraft man in Athens.

Quin. Yea, and the best person too: and he is a very paramour, for a sweet voice.

Flu. You must say, paragon: a paramour is, God bless us, a thing of nought.

Enter SNUG.

Snug. Masters, the duke is coming from the temple, and there is two or three lords and ladies more married: if our sport had gone forward, we had all been made men.

Flu. O sweet bully Bottom! Thus hath he lost sixpence a-day during his life; he could not have 'scaped sixpence a-day: an the duke had not given him sixpence a-day for playing Pyramus, I'll be hang'd; he would have deserved it: sixpence a-day, in Pyramus, or nothing.[3]

Enter BOTTOM.

Bot. Where are these lads? where are these hearts?

Quin. Bottom!—O most courageous day! O most happy hour!

Bot. Masters, I am to discourse wonders: but ask me not what; for, if I tell you, I am no true Athenian. I will tell you every thing, right as it fell out.

Quin. Let us hear, sweet Bottom.

Bot. Not a word of me. All that I will tell you, is, that the Duke hath dined: Get your apparel together; good strings to your beards, new ribbons to your pumps; meet presently at the palace; every man look o'er his part; for, the short and the long is, our play is preferred. In any case, let Thisby have clean linen; and let not him, that plays the lion, pare his nails, for they shall hang out for the lion's claws. And, most dear actors, eat no onions, nor garlick, for we are to utter sweet breath; and I do not doubt, but to hear them say, it is a sweet comedy. No more words; away; go, away.

[*Exeunt.*

ACT V.

SCENE I. *The same. An Apartment in the Palace of* Theseus. *Enter* THESEUS, HIPPOLYTA, PHILOSTRATE, *Lords, and Attendants.*

Hip. 'Tis strange, my Theseus, that these lovers speak of.

The. More strange than true. I never may believe
These antique fables, nor these fairy toys.
Lovers, and madmen, have such seething brains,[4]
Such shaping fantasies, that apprehend
More than cool reason ever comprehends.
The lunatick, the lover, and the poet,
Are of imagination all compact:[5]
One sees more devils than vast hell can hold;
That is, the madman: the lover, all as frantick,
Sees Helen's beauty in a brow of Egypt:
The poet's eye, in a fine frenzy rolling,
Doth glance from heaven to earth, from earth to heaven;
And, as imagination bodies forth
The forms of things unknown, the poet's pen
Turns them to shapes, and gives to airy nothing
A local habitation, and a name.
Such tricks hath strong imagination;
That, if it would but apprehend some joy,
It comprehends some bringer of that joy;
Or, in the night, imagining some fear,
How easy is a bush suppos'd a bear?

Hip. But all the story of the night told over,
And all their minds transfigur'd so together,
More witnesseth than fancy's images,
And grows to something of great constancy;[6]
But, howsoever, strange and admirable.

1 Helena, perhaps, means to say, that having *found* Demetrius *unexpectedly*, she considered her property in him as insecure as that which a person has in a jewel that he has found by accident, which he knows not whether he shall retain, and which therefore may properly enough be called *his own and not his own.* Warburton proposed to read *gemell*, i. e. double; and it has also been proposed to read *gimmal*, which signifies a double ring.

2 Theobald conjectured, happily enough, that we should read '*after* death.'

3 Steevens says that Preston, the actor and author of Cambyses, was meant to be ridiculed here. The queen having bestowed a pension on him of twenty pounds a year for the pleasure she received from his acting in the play of Dido, at Cambridge, in 1564.

4 So in the Tempest:
'—— thy *brains*,
Now useless, *boil'd* within thy skull

5 i. e. are made of mere imagination.

6 i. e. consistency, stability, certainty

Enter LYSANDER, DEMETRIUS, HERMIA, *and* HELENA.

The. Here come the lovers, full of joy and mirth.—
Joy, gentle friends! joy, and fresh days of love,
Accompany your hearts!
Lys. More than to us
Wait on your royal walks, your board, your bed!
The. Come now; what masks, what dances shall we have,
To wear away this long age of three hours,
Between our after-supper, and bed time?
Where is our usual manager of mirth?
What revels are in hand? Is there no play,
To ease the anguish of a torturing hour?
Call Philostrate.
Philost. Here, mighty Theseus.
The. Say, what abridgment[1] have you for this evening?
What mask? what music? How shall we beguile
The lazy time, if not with some delight?
Philost. There is a brief,[2] how many sports are ripe;
Make choice of which your highness will see first.
[*Giving a paper.*
The. (*Reads.*) *The battle with the Centaurs, to be sung*
By an Athenian eunuch to the harp.
We'll none of that: that have I told my love,
In glory of my kinsman Hercules.
The riot of the tipsy Bacchanals,
Tearing the Thracian singer in their rage.
That is an old device; and it was play'd
When I from Thebes came last a conqueror.
The thrice three Muses mourning for the death
Of learning, late deceas'd in beggary.[3]
That is some satire, keen, and critical,
Not sorting with a nuptial ceremony.
A tedious brief scene of young Pyramus,
And his love Thisbe: very tragical mirth.
Merry and tragical! Tedious and brief!
That is, hot ice, and wonderous strange snow.
How shall we find the concord of this discord?
Philost. A play there is, my lord, some ten words long;
Which is as brief as I have known a play;
But by ten words, my lord, it is too long;
Which makes it tedious: for in all the play
There is not one word apt, one player fitted.
And tragical, my noble lord, it is;
For Pyramus therein doth kill himself.
Which, when I saw rehears'd, I must confess,
Made mine eyes water; but more merry tears
The passion of loud laughter never shed.
The. What are they that do play it?
Philost. Hard-handed men, that work in Athens here,[4]
Which never labour'd in their minds till now;
And now have toil'd their unbreath'd[5] memories
With this same play, against your nuptial.
The. And we will hear it.
Philost. No, my noble lord,
It is not for you: I have heard it over,
And it is nothing, nothing in the world:
Unless you can find sport in their intents,[6]
Extremely stretch'd, and conn'd with cruel pain,
To do you service.
The. I will hear that play;
For never any thing can be amiss,
When simpleness and duty tender it
Go, bring them in;—and take your places, ladies.
[*Exit* PHILOSTRATE.
Hip. I love not to see wretchedness o'ercharg'd,
And duty in his service perishing.
The. Why, gentle sweet, you shall see no such thing.
Hip. He says they can do nothing in this kind
The. The kinder we, to give them thanks for no thing.
Our sport shall be, to take what they mistake:
And what poor duty cannot do,
Noble respect takes it in might, not merit.[7]
Where I have come, great clerks have purposed
To greet me with premeditated welcomes;
Where I have seen them shiver and look pale,
Make periods in the midst of sentences,
Throttle their practis'd accent in their fears,
And, in conclusion, dumbly have broke off,
Not paying me a welcome: Trust me, sweet,
Out of this silence, yet, I pick'd a welcome;
And in the modesty of fearful duty
I read as much, as from the rattling tongue
Of saucy and audacious eloquence.
Love, therefore, and tongue-tied simplicity,
In least speak most, to my capacity.

Enter PHILOSTRATE.

Philost. So please your grace, the prologue is addrest.[8]
The. Let him approach. [*Flourish of trumpets*[9]

Enter Prologue.

Prol. *If we offend, it is with our good will.*
That you should think we come not to offend,
But with good-will. To shew our simple skill,
That is the true beginning of our end.
Consider then, we come but in despite.
We do not come as minding to content you,
Our true intent is. All for your delight,
We are not here. That you should here repent you.
The actors are at hand: and, by their show,
You shall know all, that you are like to know.
The. This fellow doth not stand upon points.
Lys. He hath rid his prologue, like a rough colt, he knows not the stop. A good moral, my lord: It is not enough to speak, but to speak true.
Hip. Indeed he hath played on this prologue like a child on a recorder;[10] a sound, but not in government.[11]
The. His speech was like a tangled chain; nothing impaired, but all disordered. Who is next?

Enter PYRAMUS *and* THISBE, Wall, Moonshine, *and* Lion, *as in dumb show.*

Prol. "Gentles, perchance, you wonder at this show;
"But wonder on, till truth make all things plain.
"This man is Pyramus, if you would know;
"This beauteous lady Thisby is, certain.
"This man, with lime and rough-cast doth present
"Wall, that vile wall which did these lovers sunder:
"And through wall's chink, poor souls, they are content
"To whisper; at the which let no man wonder.
"This man, with lantern, dog, and bush of thorn
"Presenteth moon-shine; for, if you will know,
"By moon-shine did these lovers think no scorn

1 Steevens thought, that by *abridgment* was meant a dramatic performance which crowds the events of years into a few hours. Surely the context seems to require a different explanation; an *abridgment* appears to mean some *pastime* to *shorten* the tedious evening.
2 Short account.
3 This may be an allusion to Spenser's poem: 'The Tears of the Muses on the Neglect and Contempt of Learning;' first printed in 1591.
4 It is thought that Shakspeare alludes here to 'certain good hearted men of Coventry,' who petitioned 'that they mought renew their old storial shew' before the Queen at Kenilworth: where the poet himself may have been present, as he was then twelve years old.
5 i. e. unexercised, unpractised.
6 *Intents* may be put for the object of their *attention* To *intend* and to *attend* were anciently synonymous.
7 The sense of this passage appears to be:—"What dutifulness tries to perform without ability, regardful generosity receives with complacency; estimating it, not by the actual *merit*, but according to the power or *might* of the humble but zealous performers.'
8 Ready.
9 Anciently the prologue entered after the third sounding of the trumpets, or, as we should now say, after the third music.
10 A kind of flageolet. To *record* anciently signified to *modulate*; perhaps the name arose from birds being taught to *record* by it.
11 i. e. not regularly, according to the time.

"To meet at Ninus' tomb, there, there to woo.
"This grisly beast, which by name lion hight,[1]
"The trusty Thisby, coming first by night,
"Did scare away, or rather did affright;
"And, as she fled, her mantle she did fall;
"Which lion vile with bloody mouth did stain:
"Anon comes Pyramus, swee youth, and tall,
"And finds his trusty Thisby's mantle slain:
"Whereat with blade, with bloody blameful blade,
"He bravely broach'd his boiling bloody breast;
"And, Thisby, tarrying in mulberry shade,
"His dagger drew, and died. For all the rest,
"Let lion, moon-shine, wall, and lovers twain,
"At large discourse, while here they do remain."

[*Exeunt* Prol. THISBE, Lion, *and* Moonshine.

The. I wonder, if the lion be to speak.

Dem. No wonder, my lord: one lion may, when many asses do.

Wall. "In this same interlude, it doth befall,
"That I, one Snout by name, present a wall:
"And such a wall, as I would have you think,
"That had in it a cranny'd hole, or chink,
"Through which the lovers, Pyramus and Thisby,
'Did whisper often very secretly.
"This loam, this rough-cast, and this stone, doth show
"That I am that same wall; the truth is so:
"And this the cranny is, right and sinister,
"Through which the fearful lovers are to whisper."

The. Would you desire lime and hair to speak better?

Dem. It is the wittiest partition that ever I heard discourse, my lord.

The. Pyramus draws near the wall: silence!

Enter PYRAMUS.

Pyr. "O grim-look'd night! O night with hue so black;
"O night, which ever art, when day is not!
"O night, O night, alack, alack, alack,
"I fear my Thisby's promise is forgot!—
"And thou, O wall, O sweet, O lovely wall,
"That stand'st between her father's ground and mine;
"Thou wall, O wall, O sweet, and lovely wall,
"Show me thy chink, to blink through with mine eyne. [Wall *holds up his Fingers.*
"Thanks, courteous wall: Jove shield thee well for this!
"But what see I? No Thisby do I see.
"O wicked wall, through whom I see no bliss:
"Curst be thy stones for thus deceiving me!"

The. The wall, methinks, being sensible, should curse again.

Pyr. No, in truth, sir, he should not. *Deceiving me,* is Thisby's cue: she is to enter now, and I am to spy her through the wall. You shall see, it will fall pat as I told you:—Yonder she comes.

Enter THISBE.

This. "O wall, full often hast thou heard my moans,
"For parting my fair Pyramus and me:
"My cherry lips have often kiss'd thy stones:
"Thy stones with lime and hair knit up in thee."

Pyr. "I see a voice: now will I to the chink,
"To spy an I can hear my Thisby's face.
"Thisby!"

This. "My love! thou art my love, I think."

Pyr. "Think what thou wilt, I am thy lover's grace;
"And like Limander[2] am I trusty still."

This. "And I like Helen, till the fates me kill."

Pyr. "Not Shafalus to Procrus was so true."

This. "As Shafalus to Procrus, I to you."

Pyr. "O, kiss me through the hole of this vile wall."

This. "I kiss the wall's hole, not your lips at all."

Pyr. "Wilt thou at Ninny's tomb meet me straightway?"

This. "Tide life, tide death, I come without delay."

Wall. "Thus have I, wall, my part discharged so;
"And, being done, thus wall away doth go."

[*Exeunt* Wall, PYRAMUS, *and* THISBE.

The. Now is the mural down between the two neighbours.

Dem. No remedy, my lord, when walls are so wilful to hear without warning.[3]

Hip. This is the silliest stuff that ever I heard.

The. The best in this kind are but shadows: and the worst are no worse, if imagination amend them

Hip. It must be your imagination then, and not theirs.

The. If we imagine no worse of them, than they of themselves, they may pass for excellent men. Here come two noble beasts in, a moon[4] and a lion.

Enter Lion and Moonshine.

Lion. "You, ladies, you, whose gentle hearts do fear
"The smallest monstrous mouse that creeps on floor,
"May now, perchance, both quake and tremble here,
"When lion rough in wildest rage doth roar.
"Then know, that I, one Snug the joiner, am
"No lion fell, nor else no lion's dam:
"For if I should as lion come in strife
"Into this place, 'twere pity on my life."

The. A very gentle beast, and of a good conscience

Dem. The very best at a beast, my lord, that e'er I saw.

Lys. This lion is a very fox for his valour.

The. True; and a goose for his discretion.

Dem. Not so, my lord: for his valour cannot carry his discretion; and the fox carries the goose.

The. His discretion, I am sure, cannot carry his valour; for the goose carries not the fox. It is well: leave it to his discretion, and let us listen to the moon.

Moon. "This lantern doth the horned moon present:"

Dem. He should have worn the horns on his head.

The. He is no crescent, and his horns are invisible within the circumference.

Moon. "This lantern doth the horned moon present:
"Myself the man i'the'moon do seem to be."

The. This is the greatest error of all the rest: the man should be put into the lantern: How is it else the man i'the moon?

Dem. He dares not come there for the candle; for, you see, it is already in snuff.[5]

Hip. I am aweary of this moon: Would he would change!

The. It appears, by his small light of discretion, that he is in the wane: but yet, in courtesy, in all reason, we must stay the time.

Lys. Proceed, moon.

Moon. All that I have to say, is, to tell you, that the lantern is the moon; I, the man in the moon; this thorn bush, my thorn bush; and this dog my dog.

Dem. Why, all these should be in the lantern; for they are in the moon. But silence; here comes Thisbe.

Enter THISBE.

This. "This is old Ninny's tomb: Where is my love?"

Lion. "Oh—."

[*The* Lion *roars.*—THISBE *runs off.*

---

1 Called.

2 *Limander* and *Helen,* blunderingly for Leander and Hero, as *Shafalus* and *Procrus* for Cephalus and Procris.

3 This alludes to the proverb, 'Walls have ears.' A *wall* between almost any *two neighbours* would soon be *down,* were it to exercise this faculty without previous *warning.*

4 The old copies read, a *man,* &c. The emendation is by Theobald.

5 An equivoque. *Snuff* signifies both the cinder of a candle and hasty anger.

Dem. Well roared, lion.

The. Well run, Thisbe.

Hip. Well shone moon.—Truly, the moon shines with a good grace.

The. Well moused,[1] lion.

[*The Lion tears* Thisbe's *Mantle, and exit.*

Dem. And so comes Pyramus.

Lys. And then the moon vanishes.

Enter Pyramus.

Pyr. "Sweet moon, I thank thee for thy sunny beams:
"I thank thee, moon, for shining now so bright.
"For, by thy gracious, golden, glittering streams,
"I trust to taste of truest Thisby's sight.
"But stay;—O spite!
"But mark;—Poor knight,
"What dreadful dole is here!
"Eyes do you see?
"How can it be?
"O dainty duck! O dear!
"Thy mantle good,
"What, stain'd with blood?
"Approach, ye furies fell!
"O fates! come, come;[2]
"Cut thread and thrum;[3]
"Quail, crush, conclude, and quell!"[4]

The. This passion, and the death of a dear friend, would go near to make a man look sad.

Hip. Beshrew my heart, but I pity the man.

Pyr. "O, wherefore, nature, didst thou lions frame?
"Since lion vile hath here deflour'd my dear:
"Which is—no, no—which was the fairest dame,
"That liv'd, that lov'd, that lik'd, that look'd with cheer.[5]
"Come, tears, confound:
"Out, sword, and wound
"The pap of Pyramus:
"Ay, that left pap,
"Where heart doth hop:
"Thus die I, thus, thus, thus.
"Now am I dead,
"Now am I fled;
"My soul is in the sky:
"Tongue, lose thy light!
"Moon take thy flight!
"Now die, die, die, die, die."

[*Dies.—Exit* Moonshine.

Dem. No die, but an ace, for him; for he is but one.

Lys. Less than an ace, man; for he is dead; he is nothing.

The. With the help of a surgeon, he might yet recover, and prove an ass.[6]

Hip. How chance moonshine is gone, before Thisbe comes back and finds her lover?

The. She will find him by star-light.—Here she comes; and her passion ends the play.

Enter Thisbe.

Hip. Methinks, she should not use a long one, for such a Pyramus: I hope, she will be brief.

Dem. A mote will turn the balance, which Pyramus, which Thisbe, is the better.

Lys. She hath spied him already with those sweet eyes.

Dem. And thus she moans,[7] *videlicet.*——

This. "Asleep, my love?
"What, dead, my dove?
"O Pyramus, arise,
"Speak, speak. Quite dumb?
"Dead, dead? A tomb
"Must cover thy sweet eyes.
"These lily brows,[8]
"This cherry nose,
"These yellow cowslip cheeks,
"Are gone, are gone:
"Lovers, make moan!
"His eyes were green as leeks.
"O sisters three,
"Come, come, to me,
"With hands as pale as milk;
"Lay them in gore,
"Since you have shore
"With shears his thread of silk.
"Tongue, not a word:—
"Come, trusty sword;
"Come, blade, my breast imbrue:
"And farewell, friends;—
"Thus Thisby ends:
"Adieu, adieu, adieu." [*Dies.*

The. Moonshine and lion are left to bury the dead.

Dem. Ay, and wall too.

Bot. No, I assure you; the wall is down that parted their fathers. Will it please you to see the epilogue, or to hear a Burgomask dance,[9] between two of our company?

The. No epilogue, I pray you: for your play needs no excuse. Never excuse; for when the players are all dead, there need none to be blamed. Marry, if he that writ it, had play'd Pyramus, and hanged himself with Thisbe's garter, it would have been a fine tragedy: and so it is, truly; and very notably discharged. But come, your Bergomask: let your epilogue alone. [*Here a dance of* Clowns.
The iron tongue of midnight hath told twelve:—
Lovers, to bed; 'tis almost fairy time.
I fear we shall outsleep the coming morn,
As much as we this night have overwatch'd.
This palpable-gross play hath well beguil'd
The heavy gait[10] of night.—Sweet friends, to bed.
A fortnight hold we this solemnity
In nightly revels, and new jollity. [*Exeunt.*

SCENE II. *Enter* Puck.

Puck. Now the hungry lion roars,
And the wolf behowls the moon;
Whilst the heavy ploughman snores,
All with weary task fordone.[11]
Now the wasted brands do glow,
Whilst the scritch-owl, scritching loud,
Puts the wretch that lies in woe,
In remembrance of a shroud.
Now it is the time of night,
That the graves all gaping wide,
Every one lets forth his sprite,
In the church-way paths to glide:
And we fairies, that do run,
By the triple Hecat's team,
From the presence of the sun,
Following darkness like a dream,
Now are frolic; not a mouse
Shall disturb this hallow'd house:

1 To *mouse*, according to Malone, signified to *mammock*, to tear in pieces, as a cat tears a mouse.

2 Dr. Farmer thought this was written in ridicule of a passage in Damon and Pythias, by Richard Edwards, 1582:

'Ye *furies*, all at once
On me your torments tire.
Gripe me, you greedy griefs
And present pangues of death;
You sisters three, with cruel hands,
With speed come stop my breath.'

3 *Thrum* is the end or extremity of a weaver's warp. It is used for any collection or tuft of short thread.

4 Destroy. 5 Countenance.

6 The character of Theseus throughout this play is more exalted in its humanity than in its greatness. Though some sensible observations on life and animated descriptions fall from him, as it is said of Iago, 'You shall taste him more as a soldier than as a wit,' which is a distinction he is here striving to deserve, though with little success; as in support of his pretensions he never rises higher than a *pun*, and frequently sinks as low as a *quibble*.

7 The old copies read *means*, which had anciently the same signification as *moans*. Theobald made the alteration.

8 The old copies read *lips* instead of *brows*. The alteration was made for the sake of the rhyme by Theobald.

9 A rustic dance framed in imitation of the people of *Bergamasco* (a province in the state of Venice,) who are ridiculed as being more clownish in their manners and dialect than any other people of Italy. The *lingua rustica* of the buffoons, in the old Italian comedies, is an imitation of their jargon.

10 i. e. slow passage, progress. 11 Overcome.

I am sent, with broom, before,
To sweep the dust behind the door.[1]

Enter OBERON *and* TITANIA, *with their Train.*

Obe. Through this house give glimmering light,[2]
By the dead and drowsy fire:
Every elf, and fairy sprite,
Hop as light as bird from brier;
And this ditty after me,
Sing and dance it trippingly.

Tita. First, rehearse this song by rote:
To each word a warbling note,
Hand in hand, with fairy grace,
Will we sing, and bless this place.

SONG AND DANCE.

Obe. Now, until the break of day,
Through this house each fairy stray.
To the best bride-bed will we,
Which by us shall blessed be;[3]
And the issue, there create,
Ever shall be fortunate.
So shall all the couples three
Ever true in loving be:
And the blots of nature's hand
Shall not in their issue stand;
Never mole, hare-lip, nor scar,
Nor mark prodigious,[4] such as are
Despised in nativity,
Shall upon their children be.—
With this field-dew consecrate,
Every fairy take his gate;[5]
And each several chamber bless,[6]
Through this palace with sweet peace:
E'er shall it in safety rest,
And the owner of it blest.
Trip away;
Make no stay;
Meet me all by break of day

[*Exeunt* OBERON, TITANIA, *and Train*

Puck. *If we shadows have offended,*
Think but this (and all is mended,)
That you have but slumber'd here,
While these visions did appear,
And this weak and idle theme,
No more yielding but a dream,
Gentles, do not reprehend:
If you pardon, we will mend.
And, as I'm an honest Puck,
If we have unearned luck,[7]
Now to 'scape the serpent's tongue,[8]
We will make amends, ere long:
Else the Puck a liar call.
So, good night unto you all.
Give me your hands,[9] *if we be friends,*
And Robin shall restore amends. [*Exit.*

WILD and fantastical as this play is, all the parts in their various modes are well written, and give the kind of pleasure which the author designed. Fairies in his time were much in fashion; common tradition had made them familiar, and Spenser's poem had made them great. JOHNSON.

JOHNSON'S concluding observations on this play are not conceived with his usual judgment. There is no analogy or resemblance between the Fairies of Spenser and those of Shakspeare. The Fairies of Spenser, as appears from his description of them in the second book of the Faerie Queene, canto x. were a race of mortals created by Prometheus, of the human size, shape, and affections, and subject to death. But those of Shakspeare, and of common tradition, as Johnson calls them, were a diminutive race of sportful beings, endowed with immortality and supernatural powers, totally different from those of Spenser. M. MASON.

1 Cleanliness is always necessary to invite the residence or favour of the Fairies.

2 Milton perhaps had this picture in his thoughts:
'And glowing embers through the room
Teach night to counterfeit a gloom.'

3 This ceremony was in old times used at all marriages. Mr. Douce has given the formula from the Manual for the use of Salisbury. We may observe on this strange ceremony, that the purity of modern times stands not in need of these holy aspersions to lull the senses and dissipate the illusions of the devil. The married couple would no doubt rejoice when the benediction was ended.

4 Portentous. 5 Way, course.

6 The same superstitious kind of benediction occurs in Chaucer's Millere's Tale, vol. i. p. 105, l. 22. Whittingham's Edit.

7 i. e. if we have better fortune than we have deserved

8 i. e. hisses.

9 Clap your hands, give us your applause

LOVE'S LABOUR'S LOST.

PRELIMINARY REMARKS.

THE novel upon which this comedy was founded has hitherto eluded the research of the commentators. Mr. Douce thinks it will prove to be of French extraction. 'The Dramatis Personæ in a great measure demonstrate this, as well as a palpable Gallicism in Act IV. Sc. 1: viz. the terming a *letter* a *capon.*'

This is one of Shakspeare's early plays, and the author's youth is certainly perceivable, not only in the style and manner of the versification, but in the lavish superfluity displayed in the execution: the uninterrupted succession of quibbles, equivoques, and sallies of every description. 'The sparks of wit fly about in such profusion that they form complete fireworks, and the dialogue for the most part resembles the bustling collision and banter of passing masks at a carnival.'* The scene in which the king and his companions detect each other's breach of their mutual vow, is capitally contrived. The discovery of Biron's love-letter while rallying his friends, and the manner in which he extricates himself, by ridiculing the folly of the vow, are admirable.

The grotesque characters, Don Adrian de Armado, Nathaniel the curate, and Holofernes, that prince of pedants, with the humours of Costard the clown, are well contrasted with the sprightly wit of the principal characters in the play. It has been observed that 'Biron and Rosaline suffer much in comparison with Benedick and Beatrice,' and it must be confessed that there is some justice in the observation. Yet Biron, 'that merry mad-cap Lord,' is not overrated in Rosaline's admirable character of him—

————'A merrier man,
Within the limit of becoming mirth,
I never spent an hour's talk withal:
His eye begets occasion for his wit;
For every object that the one doth catch,
The other turns to a mirth-moving jest;—
So sweet and voluble is his discourse.'

Shakspeare has only shown the inexhaustible powers of his mind in improving on the admirable originals of his own creation in a more mature age.

Malone placed the composition of this play first in 1591, afterwards in 1594. Dr. Drake thinks we may safely assign it to the earlier period. The first edition was printed in 1598.

* Schlegel.

PERSONS REPRESENTED.

FERDINAND, *King of* Navarre.
BIRON,[1] } *Lords, attending on the King.*
LONGAVILLE,
DUMAIN,
BOYET, } *Lords, attending on the Princess of* France.
MERCADE,
DON ADRIANO DE ARMADO, *a fantastical Spaniard.*
SIR NATHANIEL, *a Curate.*
HOLOFERNES, *a Schoolmaster.*
DULL, *a Constable.*
COSTARD, *a Clown.*
MOTH, *Page to* Armado.
A Forester.

Princess of France.
ROSALINE, } *Ladies, attending on the Princess.*
MARIA,
KATHARINE,
JAQUENETTA, *a country Wench.*

Officers and others, attendants on the King and Princess.

SCENE, Navarre.

This enumeration of Persons was made by Rowe

ACT I.

SCENE I. Navarre. *A Park with a Palace in it.*—*Enter the* King, BIRON, LONGAVILLE, *and* DUMAIN.

King.
Let fame, that all hunt after in their lives,
Live register'd upon our brazen tombs,
And then grace us in the disgrace of death;
When, spite of cormorant devouring time,
The endeavour of this present breath may buy
That honour, which shall bate his scythe's keen edge,
And make us heirs of all eternity.
Therefore, brave conquerors!—for so you are,
That war against your own affections,
And the huge army of the world's desires,—
Our late edict shall strongly stand in force:
Navarre shall be the wonder of the world;
Our court shall be a little Academe,
Still and contemplative in living art.
You three, Biron, Dumain, and Longaville,
Have sworn for three years' term to live with me,
My fellow-scholars, and to keep those statutes,
That are recorded in this schedule here:
Your oaths are past, and now subscribe your names;
That his own hand may strike his honour down,
That violates the smallest branch herein:
If you are arm'd to do, as sworn to do,
Subscribe to your deep oath, and keep it too.
Long. I am resolv'd: 'tis but a three years' fast;
The mind shall banquet, though the body pine:
Fat paunches have lean pates; and dainty bits
Make rich the ribs, but bank'rout quite the wits.
Dum. My loving lord, Dumain is mortified;
The grosser manner of these world's delights
He throws upon the gross world's baser slaves:
To love, to wealth, to pomp, I pine and die;
With all these[2] living in philosophy.
Biron. I can but say their protestation over,
So much, dear liege, I have already sworn,
That is, To live and study here three years.
But there are other strict observances:
As, not to see a woman in that term;
Which, I hope well, is not enrolled there:
And, one day in a week to touch no food;
And but one meal on every day beside;
The which, I hope, is not enrolled there:
And then, to sleep but three hours in the night,
And not be seen to wink of all the day;
(When I was wont to think no harm all night,
And make a dark night too of half the day;)
Which, I hope well, is not enrolled there:
O, these are barren tasks, too hard to keep;
Not to see ladies—study—fast—not sleep.
King. Your oath is pass'd to pass away from these.
Biron. Let me say no, my liege, an if you please,
I only swore, to study with your grace,
And stay here in your court for three years' space.
Long. You swore to that, Biron, and to the rest.
Biron. By yea and nay, sir, then I swore in jest.
What is the end of study? let me know.
King. Why, that to know, which else we should not know.
Biron. Things hid and barr'd, you mean, from common sense?
King. Ay, that is study's god-like recompense.
Biron. Come on then, I will swear to study so,
To know the thing I am forbid to know:
As thus—To study where I well may dine,
When I to feast expressly am forbid;
Or, study where to meet some mistress fine,
When mistresses from common sense are hid:
Or, having sworn too hard-a-keeping oath,
Study to break it, and not break my troth.
If study's gain be thus, and this be so,
Study knows that, which yet it doth not know.
Swear me to this, and I will ne'er say, no.
King. These be the stops that hinder study quite,
And train our intellects to vain delight.
Biron. Why, all delights are vain; but that most vain,
Which, with pain purchas'd, doth inherit pain:
As, painfully to pore upon a book,
To seek the light of truth: while truth the while
Doth falsely[3] blind the eyesight of his look:
Light, seeking light, doth light of light beguile:
So, ere you find where light in darkness lies,
Your light grows dark by losing of your eyes.[4]
Study me how to please the eye indeed,
By fixing it upon a fairer eye;
Who dazzling so, that eye shall be his heed,
And give him light that it was blinded by.[5]
Study is like the heaven's glorious sun,
That will not be deep-search'd with saucy looks,
Small have continual plodders ever won,
Save base authority from others' books.
These earthly godfathers of heaven's lights,
That give a name to every fixed star,
Have no more profit of their shining nights,
Than those that walk, and wot not what they are
Too much to know, is, to know nought but fame;
And every godfather can give a name.[6]
King. How well he's read, to reason against reading!
Dum. Proceeded well, to stop all good proceeding!

1 *Berowne* in all the old editions.
2 i. e. with all these companions. He may be supposed to point to the king, Biron, &c.
3 Dishonestly, treacherously.
4 The whole sense of this gingling declamation is only this, that a man by too close study may read himself blind.
5 The meaning is; that when he *dazzles*, that is, has his eye made weak, by fixing his eye upon a fairer eye, that *fairer eye* shall be his *heed* or guide, his *lode-star* and give him light that was blinded by it.
6 That is, too much knowledge gives no real solution of doubts, but merely *fame*, or a name, a thing which every godfather can give.

Long. He weeds the corn, and still lets grow the weeding.
Biron. The spring is near, when green geese are a breeding.
Dum. How follows that?
Biron. Fit in his place and time.
Dum. In reason nothing.
Biron. Something then in rhyme.
Long. Biron is like an envious sneaping[1] frost,
That bites the first-born infants of the spring.
Biron. Well, say I am; why should proud summer boast,
Before the birds have any cause to sing?
Why should I joy in an abortive birth?
At Christmas I no more desire a rose
Than wish a snow in May's new-fangled shows;[2]
But like of each thing that in season grows.
So you, to study now it is too late,
Climb o'er the house to unlock the little gate.
King. Well, sit you out: go home, Biron, adieu!
Biron. No, my good lord; I have sworn to stay with you:
And, though I have for barbarism spoke more,
Than for that angel knowledge you can say,
Yet confident I'll keep what I have swore,
And bide the penance of each three years' day.
Give me the paper, let me read the same;
And to the strict'st decrees I'll write my name.
King. How well this yielding rescues thee from shame!
Biron. [*Reads.*] Item, *That no woman shall come within a mile of my court.*—Hath this been proclaim'd?
Long. Four days ago.
Biron. Let's see the penalty. [*Reads.*] *On pain of losing her tongue.*—Who devis'd this penalty?
Long. Marry, that did I.
Biron. Sweet lord, and why?
Long. To fright them hence with that dread penalty.
Biron. A dangerous law against gentility.[3]
[*Reads.*] Item, *If any man be seen to talk with a woman within the term of three years, he shall endure such public shame as the rest of the court can possibly devise.*—
This article, my liege, yourself must break;
For, well you know, here comes in embassy
The French king's daughter, with yourself to speak,
A maid of grace, and complete majesty,—
About surrender-up of Aquitain
To her decrepit, sick, and bed-rid father:
Therefore this article is made in vain,
Or vainly comes the admired princess hither.
King. What say you, lords? why, this was quite forgot.
Biron. So study evermore is overshot;
While it doth study to have what it would,
It doth forget to do the thing it should:
And when it hath the thing it hunteth most,
'Tis won, as towns with fire; so won, so lost.
King. We must, of force, dispense with this decree;
She must lie[4] here on mere necessity.
Biron. Necessity will make us all forsworn
Three thousand times within this three years' space:
For every man with his affects is born;
Not by might master'd, but by special grace:
If I break faith, this word shall speak for me,
I am forsworn on mere necessity.—
So to the laws at large I write my name: [*Subscribes.*
And he, that breaks them in the least degree,
Stands in attainder of eternal shame;
Suggestions[5] are to others, as to me;
But, I believe, although I seem so loath,
I am the last that will last keep his oath.
But, is there no quick[6] recreation granted?
King. Ay, that there is: our court, you know, is haunted
With a refined traveller of Spain;
A man in all the world's new fashion planted,
That hath a mint of phrases in his brain:
One, whom the music of his own vain tongue
Doth ravish, like enchanting harmony;
A man of complements,[7] whom right and wrong
Have chose as umpire of their mutiny:
This child of fancy, that Armado hight,[8]
For interim to our studies, shall relate,
In high-born words, the worth of many a knight
From tawny Spain, lost in the world's debate.
How you delight, my lords, I know not, I;
But, I protest, I love to hear him lie,
And I will use him for my minstrelsy.[9]
Biron. Armado is a most illustrious wight,
A man of fire-new[10] words, fashion's own knight.
Long. Costard the swain, and he, shall be our sport;
And, so to study, three years is but short.

Enter DULL, *with a Letter, and* COSTARD.

Dull. Which is the duke's own person?
Biron. This, fellow; What would'st?
Dull. I myself reprehend his own person, for I am his grace's tharborough:[11] but I would see his own person in flesh and blood.
Biron. This is he.
Dull. Signior Arme—Arme—commends you. There's villany abroad; this letter will tell you more.
Cost. Sir, the contempts thereof are as touching me.
King. A letter from the magnificent Armado.
Biron. How low soever the matter, I hope in God for high words.
Long. A high hope for a low having: God grant us patience!
Biron. To hear? or forbear hearing?[12]
Long. To hear meekly, sir, and to laugh moderately; or to forbear both.
Biron. Well, sir, be it as the style[13] shall give us cause to climb in the merriness.
Cost. The matter is to me, sir, as concerning Jaquenetta. The manner of it is, I was taken with the manner.[14]
Biron. In what manner?
Cost. In manner and form following, sir; all those three: I was seen with her in the manor house, sitting with her upon the form, and taken following her into the park; which, put together, is, in manner and form following. Now, sir, for the manner,—it is the manner of a man to speak to a woman: for the form,—in some form.
Biron. For the following, sir?
Cost. As it shall follow in my correction; And God defend the right!
King. Will you hear this letter with attention?
Biron. As we would hear an oracle.

---

1 i. e. nipping.
2 By these *shows* the poet means *May-games*, at which a *snow* would be very unwelcome and unexpected. It is only a periphrasis for *May*.
3 The word *gentility* here does not signify that rank of people called *gentry;* but what the French express by *gentilesse*, i. e. *elegantia, urbanitas.*
4 That is, *reside* here. So in Sir Henry Wotton's equivocal definition: 'An ambassador is an honest man sent to *lie* (i. e. reside) abroad for the good of his country.'
5 Temptations. 6 Lively, sprightly.
7 *Complements* is here used in its ancient sense of *accomplishments.* Vide Note on K. Henry V. Act ii. Sc 2.
8 i. e. who is *called* Armado
9 I will make use of him instead of a *minstrel*, whose occupation was to relate fabulous stories.
10 i. e. new from the forge; we have still retained a similar mode of speech in the colloquial phrase *brand-new.*
11 i. e. third-borough, a peace-officer.
12 'To hear? or forbear *laughing?*' is possibly the true reading.
13 A quibble is here intended between a *stile* and *style.*
14 That is, *in the fact.* A thief is said to be taken with the manner (*mainour*) when he is taken with the thing stolen about him. The thing stolen was called *mainour manour*, or *meinour*, from the French *manier*, manu tractare.

Cost. Such is the simplicity of man to hearken after the flesh.

King. [*Reads.*] *Great deputy, the welkin's vicegerent, and sole dominator of Navarre, my soul's earth's God, and body's fostering patron.—*

Cost. Not a word of Costard yet.

King. *So it is,—*

Cost. It may be so: but if he say it is so, he is, in telling true, but so, so.

King. Peace.

Cost. —be to me, and every man that dares not fight!

King. No words.

Cost. —of other men's secrets, I beseech you.

King. *So it is, besieged with sable-coloured melancholy, I did commend the black-oppressing humour to the most wholesome physick of thy health-giving air; and, as I am a gentleman, betook myself to walk. The time when? About the sixth hour; when beasts most graze, birds best peck, and men sit down to that nourishment which is called supper. So much for the time when: Now for the ground which; which, I mean, I walked upon: it is ycleped thy park. Then for the place where; where, I mean, I did encounter that obscene and most preposterous event, that draweth from my snow-white pen the ebon-coloured ink, which here thou viewest, beholdest, surveyest, or seest: But to the place where,—It standeth north-north-east and by east from the west corner of thy curious-knotted garden.*[1] *There did I see that low-spirited swain, that base minnow of thy mirth,*[2]

Cost. Me.

King.—*that unletter'd small-knowing soul,*

Cost. Me.

King.—*that shallow vassal,*

Cost. Still me.

King.—*which, as I remember, hight Costard,*

Cost. O me!

King.—*sorted and consorted, contrary to thy established proclaimed edict and continent canon, with—with,—O with—but with this I passion to say wherewith,*

Cost. With a wench.

King.—*with a child of our grandmother Eve, a female; or, for thy more sweet understanding, a woman. Him I (as my ever-esteemed duty pricks me on) have sent to thee, to receive the meed of punishment, by thy sweet grace's officer, Antony Dull; a man of good repute, carriage, bearing, and estimation.*

Dull. Me, an't shall please you; I am Antony Dull.

King.—*For Jaquenetta, (so is the weaker vessel called, which I apprehended with the aforesaid swain,) I keep her as a vessel of thy law's fury; and shall, at the least of thy sweet notice, bring her to trial. Thine, in all compliments of devoted and heart-burning heat of duty.* Don Adriano de Armado.

Biron. This is not so well as I looked for, but the best that ever I heard.

King. Ay, the best for the worst. But, sirrah, what say you to this?

Cost. Sir, I confess the wench.

King. Did you hear the proclamation.

Cost. I do confess much of the hearing it, but little of the marking of it.

King. It was proclaimed a year's imprisonment, to be taken with a wench.

Cost. I was taken with none, sir; I was taken with a damosel.

King. Well, it was proclaimed damosel.

Cost. This was no damosel neither, sir; she was a virgin.

King. It is so varied too; for it was proclaimed, virgin.

Cost. If it were, I deny her virginity; I was taken with a maid.

King. This maid will not serve your turn, sir.

Cost. This maid will serve my turn, sir.

King. Sir, I will pronounce your sentence,
You shall fast a week with bran and water.

Cost. I had rather pray a month with mutton and porridge.

King. And Don Armado shall be your keeper.
—My lord Biron, see him deliver'd o'er.—
And go we, lords, to put in practice that
Which each to other hath so strongly sworn.

[*Exeunt* King, Longaville, *and* Dumain.

Biron. I'll lay my head to any good man's hat,
These oaths and laws will prove an idle scorn.—
Sirrah, come on.

Cost. I suffer for the truth, sir: for true it is, I was taken with Jaquenetta, and Jaquenetta is a true girl; and therefore, Welcome the sour cup of prosperity! Affliction may one day smile again, and till then, Sit thee down, sorrow! [*Exeunt.*

SCENE II. *Another part of the same.* Armado's *House. Enter* Armado *and* Moth.

Arm. Boy, what sign is it, when a man of great spirit grows melancholy?

Moth. A great sign, sir, that he will look sad.

Arm. Why, sadness is one and the self-same thing, dear imp.[3]

Moth. No, no; O lord, sir, no.

Arm. How canst thou part sadness and melancholy, my tender juvenal?[4]

Moth. By a familiar demonstration of the working, my tough senior.

Arm. Why tough senior? why tough senior?

Moth. Why, tender juvenal? why tender juvenal?

Arm. I spoke it, tender juvenal, as a congruent epitheton, appertaining to thy young days, which we may nominate tender.

Moth. And I, tough senior, as an appertinent title to your old time, which we may name tough.

Arm. Pretty, and apt.

Moth. How mean you, sir? I pretty, and my saying apt? or I apt, and my saying pretty?

Arm. Thou pretty, because little.

Moth. Little pretty, because little: Wherefore apt?

Arm. And therefore apt, because quick.

Moth. Speak you this in my praise, master?

Arm. In thy condign praise.

Moth. I will praise an eel with the same praise.

Arm. What? that an eel is ingenious?

Moth. That an eel is quick.

Arm. I do say, thou art quick in answers.
Thou heatest my blood.

Moth. I am answered, sir.

Arm. I love not to be crossed.

Moth. He speaks the mere contrary, crosses love not him. [*Aside.*

Arm. I have promised to study three years with the duke.

Moth. You may do it in an hour, sir.

Arm. Impossible.

Moth. How many is one thrice told?

Arm. I am ill at reckoning, it fitteth the spirit of a tapster.

Moth. You are a gentleman, and a gamester, sir.

Arm. I confess both; they are both the varnish of a complete man.

Moth. Then I am sure, you know how much the gross sum of deuce-ace amounts to.

Arm. It doth amount to one more than two.

Moth. Which the base vulgar do call three.

Arm. True.

---

1 Ancient gardens abounded with *knots* or figures, of which the lines intersected each other. In the old books of gardening are devices for them.

2 i. e. the contemptible little object that contributes to thy entertainment.

3 *Imp* literally means a graft, slip, scion, or sucker; and by metonymy is used for a child or boy. Cromwell, in his last letter to Henry VIII. prays for *the imp his son.* It was then perhaps growing obsolete. It is now used only to signify *young fiends;* as *the Devil and his imps.*

4 i. e. youth.

5 By *crosses* he means *money.* So in As You Like It: the Clown says to Celia 'If I *should bear you,* I should bear no *cross.*' Many coins were anciently marked with a *Cross* on one side

Moth. Why, sir, is this such a piece of study? Now here is three studied, ere you'll thrice wink: and how easy it is to put years to the word three, and study three years in two words, the dancing horse[1] will tell you.

Arm. A most fine figure!

Moth. To prove you a cypher. [*Aside.*

Arm. I will hereupon confess, I am in love: and, as it is base for a soldier to love, so am I in love with a base wench. If drawing my sword against the humour of affection would deliver me from the reprobate thought of it, I would take desire prisoner, and ransom him to any French courtier for a new devised courtesy. I think scorn to sigh; methinks, I should out-swear Cupid. Comfort me, boy: What great men have been in love?

Moth. Hercules, master.

Arm. Most sweet Hercules!—More authority, dear boy, name more; and, sweet my child, let them be men of good repute and carriage.

Moth. Samson, master: he was a man of good carriage, great carriage! for he carried the town-gates on his back, like a porter: and he was in love.

Arm. O well-knit Samson! strong-jointed Samson! I do excel thee in my rapier, as much as thou didst me in carrying gates. I am in love too,—Who was Samson's love, my dear Moth?

Moth. A woman, master.

Arm. Of what complexion?

Moth. Of all the four, or the three, or the two; or one of the four.

Arm. Tell me precisely of what complexion?

Moth. Of the sea-water green, sir.

Arm. Is that one of the four complexions?

Moth. As I have read, sir; and the best of them too.

Arm. Green, indeed, is the colour of lovers:[2] but to have a love of that colour, methinks, Samson had small reason for it. He, surely, affected her for her wit.

Moth. It was so, sir; for she had a green wit.

Arm. My love is most immaculate white and red.

Moth. Most maculate thoughts, master, are masked under such colours.

Arm. Define, define, well-educated infant.

Moth. My father's wit, and my mother's tongue, assist me!

Arm. Sweet invocation of a child; most pretty, and pathetical!

Moth. If she be made of white and red,
    Her faults will ne'er be known;
  For blushing cheeks by faults are bred,
    And fears by pale white shown:
  Then, if she fear, or be to blame,
    By this you shall not know;
  For still her cheeks possess the same,
    Which native she doth owe.[3]

A dangerous rhyme, master, against the reason of white and red.

Arm. Is there not a ballad, boy, of the King and the Beggar?[4]

Moth. The world was very guilty of such a ballad some three ages since: but, I think, now 'tis not to be found; or, if it were, it would neither serve for the writing, nor the tune.

Arm. I will have the subject newly writ o'er, that I may example my digression[5] by some mighty precedent. Boy, I do love that country girl, that I took in the park with the rational hind[6] Costard: she deserves well.

Moth. To be whipped; and yet a better love than my master. [*Aside.*

Arm. Sing, boy; my spirit grows heavy in love.

Moth. And that's great marvel, loving a light wench.

Arm. I say, sing.

Moth. Forbear till this company be past.

Enter DULL, COSTARD, *and* JAQUENETTA.

Dull. Sir, the duke's pleasure is, that you keep Costard safe: and you must let him take no delight, nor no penance; but a'must fast three days a-week: For this damsel, I must keep her at the park; she is allowed for the day-woman.[7] Fare you well.

Arm. I do betray myself with blushing.—Maid.

Jaq. Man.

Arm. I will visit thee at the lodge.

Jaq. That's hereby.[8]

Arm. I know where it is situate.

Jaq. Lord, how wise you are!

Arm. I will tell thee wonders.

Jaq. With that face?[9]

Arm. I love thee.

Jaq. So I heard you say.

Arm. And so farewell.

Jaq. Fair weather after you!

Dull. Come, Jaquenetta, away.

[*Exeunt* DULL *and* JAQUENETTA.

Arm. Villain, thou shalt fast for thy offences, ere thou be pardoned.

Cost. Well, sir, I hope, when I do it, I shall do it on a full stomach.

Arm. Thou shalt be heavily punished.

Cost. I am more bound to you, than your fellows, for they are but lightly rewarded.

Arm. Take away this villain; shut him up.

Moth. Come, you transgressing slave; away.

Cost. Let me not be pent up, sir; I will fast, being loose.

Moth. No, sir; that were fast and loose: thou shalt to prison.

Cost. Well, if ever I do see the merry days of desolation that I have seen, some shall see—

Moth. What shall some see?

Cost. Nay, nothing, master Moth, but what they look upon. It is not for prisoners to be too silent in their words; and, therefore, I will say nothing: I thank God, I have as little patience as another man; and, therefore, I can be quiet.

[*Exeunt* MOTH *and* COSTARD.

Arm. I do affect[10] the very ground, which is base, where her shoe, which is baser, guided by her foot, which is basest, doth tread. I shall be forsworn, (which is a great argument of falsehood,) if I love: And how can that be true love, which is falsely attempted? Love is a familiar: love is a devil: there is no evil angel but love. Yet Samson was so tempted: and he had an excellent strength: yet was Solomon so seduced; and he had a very good wit. Cupid's butt-shaft[11] is too hard for Hercules' club, and therefore too much odds for

1 This alludes to the celebrated bay horse Morocco, belonging to one Bankes, who exhibited his docile and sagacious animal through Europe. Many of his remarkable pranks are mentioned by cotemporary writers, and he is alluded to by numbers besides Shakspeare. The fate of man and horse is not known with certainty, but it has been asserted that they were both burnt at Rome, as magicians, by order of the Pope. The best account of Bankes and his horse is to be found in the notes to a French translation of Apuleius's Golden Ass, by Jean de Montlyard, 1602.

2 The allusion probably is to the *willow*, the supposed ornament of unsuccessful lovers.

3 Of which she is naturally possessed.

4 See Percy's Reliques of Antient Poetry, fourth edition, vol. i. p. 198.

5 *Digression* is here used for the act of going out of the right way, *transgression.*

6 Armado applies this epithet ironically to Costard.

7 *Taberna Casearia* is interpreted in the old Dictionaries a *daye* house, where cheese is made. A *day-woman* is therefore a *dairy-woman.* Johnson says *day* is an old word for milk. A dairy-maid is still called a *dey* or *day* in the northern parts of Scotland.

8 Jaquenetta and Armado are at cross-purposes. *Hereby* is used by her, (as among the common people of some counties,) in the sense of *as it may happen.* He takes it in the sense of *just by.*

9 This odd phrase was still in use in Fielding's time, who, putting it into the mouth of Beau Didapper, thinks it necessary to apologize (in a note) for its want of sense, by adding that it was taken verbatim from very polite conversation.

10 Love.

11 A kind of *arrow* used for shooting at butts with. The *butt* was the place on which the mark to be shot at was placed.

a Spaniard's rapier. The first and second cause will not serve my turn;[1] the passado he respects not, the duello he regards not: his disgrace is to be called boy; but his glory is to subdue men. Adieu, valour! rust, rapier! be still, drum! for your manager is in love; yea, he loveth. Assist me, some extemporal god of rhyme, for, I am sure, I shall turn sonneteer. Devise, wit; write, pen; for I am for whole volumes in folio. [*Exit.*

ACT II.

SCENE I. *Another part of the same. A Pavilion and Tents at a distance. Enter the* Princess *of* France, ROSALINE, MARIA, KATHARINE, BOYET, Lords, *and other* Attendants.

Boyet. Now, madam, summon up your dearest[2] spirits:
Consider who the king your father sends;
To whom he sends; and what's his embassy:
Yourself, held precious in the world's esteem;
To parley with the sole inheritor
Of all perfections that a man may owe,
Matchless Navarre; the plea of no less weight
Than Aquitain; a dowry for a queen.
Be now as prodigal of all dear grace,
As nature was in making graces dear,
When she did starve the general world beside,
And prodigally gave them all to you.
Prin. Good lord Boyet, my beauty, though but mean,
Needs not the painted flourish of your praise;
Beauty is bought by judgment of the eye,
Not utter'd by base sale of chapmen's tongues;
I am less proud to hear you tell my worth,
Than you much willing to be counted wise
In spending your wit in the praise of mine.
But now to task the tasker,—Good Boyet,
You are not ignorant, all-telling fame
Doth noise abroad, Navarre hath made a vow,
Till painful study shall out-wear three years,
No woman may approach his silent court:
Therefore to us seemeth it a needful course,
Before we enter his forbidden gates,
To know his pleasure; and in that behalf,
Bold[3] of your worthiness, we single you
As our best moving fair solicitor:
Tell him the daughter of the king of France,
On serious business, craving quick despatch,
Importunes personal conference with his grace.
Haste, signify so much; while we attend,
Like humbly-visag'd suitors, his high will.
Boyet. Proud of employment, willingly I go. [*Exit.*
Prin. All pride is willing pride, and yours is so,—
Who are the votaries, my loving lords,
That are vow-fellows with this virtuous duke?
1 *Lord.* Longaville is one.
Prin. Know you the man?
Mar. I know him madam; at a marriage feast,
Between lord Perigort and the beauteous heir
Of Jaques Falconbridge, solemnized
In Normandy, saw I this Longaville:
A man of sovereign parts he is esteem'd;
Well fitted[4] in the arts, glorious in arms:
Nothing becomes him ill, that he would well.
The only soil of his fair virtue's gloss
(If virtue's gloss will stain with any soil,)
Is a sharp wit match'd with too blunt a will;
Whose edge hath power to cut, whose will still wills
It should none spare that come within his power.
Prin. Some merry mocking lord, belike; is't so?
Mar. They say so most, that most his humours know.
Prin. Such short-liv'd wits do wither as they grow.
Who are the rest?
Kath. The young Dumain, a well accomplish'd youth,
Of all that virtue love for virtue lov'd;
Most power to do most harm, least knowing ill:
For he hath wit to make an ill shape good,
And shape to win grace though he had no wit.
I saw him at the duke Alençon's once:
And much too little of that good I saw,
Is my report, to his great worthiness.
Ros. Another of these students at that time
Was there with him: if I have heard a truth,
Biron they call him; but a merrier man,
Within the limit of becoming mirth,
I never spent an hour's talk withal:
His eye begets occasion for his wit;
For every object that the one doth catch,
The other turns to a mirth-moving jest;
Which his fair tongue (conceit's expositor,)
Delivers in such apt and gracious words,
That aged ears play truant at his tales,
And younger hearings are quite ravished:
So sweet and voluble is his discourse.
Prin. God bless my ladies; are they all in love
That every one her own hath garnish'd
With such bedecking ornaments of praise?
Mar. Here comes Boyet.

Re-enter BOYET.

Prin. Now, what admittance, lord?
Boyet. Navarre had notice of your fair approach;
And he, and his competitors[5] in oath,
Were all address'd[6] to meet you, gentle lady,
Before I came. Marry, thus much have I learnt,
He rather means to lodge you in the field
(Like one that comes here to besiege his court,)
Than seek a dispensation for his oath,
To let you enter his unpeopled house.
Here comes Navarre. [*The Ladies mask.*

Enter KING, LONGAVILLE, DUMAIN, BIRON, *and* Attendants.

King. Fair princess, welcome to the court of Navarre.
Prin. Fair, I give you back again: and, welcome I have not yet: the roof of this court is too high to be yours; and welcome to the wild fields too base to be mine.
King. You shall be welcome, madam, to my court.
Prin. I will be welcome then; conduct me thither.
King. Hear me, dear lady; I have sworn an oath.
Prin. Our lady help my lord! he'll be forsworn.
King. Not for the world, fair madam, by my will.
Prin. Why, will shall break it; will, and nothing else.
King. Your ladyship is ignorant what it is.
Prin. Where my lord so, his ignorance were wise
Where[7] now his knowledge must prove ignorance.
I hear your grace has sworn-out house-keeping:
'Tis deadly sin to keep that oath, my lord,
And sin to break it:
But pardon me, I am too sudden-bold;
To teach a teacher ill beseemeth me.
Vouchsafe to read the purpose of my coming,
And suddenly resolve me in my suit.
[*Gives a paper*
King. Madam, I will, if suddenly I may.
Prin. You will the sooner, that I were away;
For you'll prove perjur'd, if you make me stay.
Biron. Did not I dance with you in Brabant once?
Ros. Did not I dance with you in Brabant once?
Biron. I know you did.
Ros. How needless was it then
To ask the question!
Biron. You must not be so quick.
Ros. 'Tis 'long of you that spur me with such questions.
Biron. Your wit's too hot, it speeds too fast, 'twill tire.
Ros. Not till it leave the rider in the mire.
Biron. What time o' day?
Ros. The hour that fools should ask.
Biron. Now fair befall your mask!

---

1 See Notes on the last Act of As You Like It.
2 Best. 3 I.e. confident of it.
4 *Well fitted* is *well qualified*.
5 Confederates.
6 Prepared.
7 *Where* is here used for *whereas*.

Ros. Fair fall the face it covers!
Biron. And send you many lovers!
Ros. Amen, so you be none.
Biron. Nay, then will I be gone.
King. Madam, your father here doth intimate
The payment of a hundred thousand crowns;
Being but the one half of an entire sum,
Disbursed by my father in his wars.
But say, that he, or we (as neither have,)
Receiv'd that sum; yet there remains unpaid
A hundred thousand more; in surety of the which,
One part of Aquitain is bound to us,
Although not valued to the money's worth.
If then the king your father will restore
But that one half which is unsatisfied,
We will give up our right to Aquitain,
And hold fair friendship with his majesty.
But that, it seems, he little purposeth,
For here he doth demand to have repaid
A hundred thousand crowns; and not demands,
On payment of a hundred thousand crowns,
To have his title live in Aquitain;
Which we much rather had depart[1] withal,
And have the money by our father lent,
Than Aquitain so gelded[2] as it is.
Dear princess, were not his requests so far
From reason's yielding, your fair self should make
A yielding 'gainst some reason, in my breast,
And go well satisfied to France again.
Prin. You do the king my father too much wrong,
And wrong the reputation of your name,
In so unseeming to confess receipt
Of that which hath so faithfully been paid.
King. I do protest, I never heard of it;
And, if you prove it, I'll repay it back,
Or yield up Aquitain.
Prin. We arrest your word:—
Boyet, you can produce acquittances,
For such a sum, from special officers
Of Charles his father.
King. Satisfy me so.
Boyet. So please your grace, the packet is not come,
Where that and other specialties are bound;
To-morrow you shall have a sight of them.
King. It shall suffice me: at which interview,
All liberal reason I will yield unto.
Mean time, receive such welcome at my hand,
As honour, without breach of honour, may
Make tender of to thy true worthiness:
You may not come, fair princess, in my gates;
But here without you shall be so receiv'd,
As you shall deem yourself lodg'd in my heart,
Though so denied fair harbour in my house.
Your own good thoughts excuse me, and farewell:
To-morrow shall we visit you again.
Prin. Sweet health and fair desires consort your grace!
King. Thy own wish wish I thee in every place!
[*Exeunt* King *and his Train.*
Biron. Lady, I will commend you to my own heart.
Ros. 'Pray you, do my commendations; I would be glad to see it.
Biron. I would, you heard it groan.
Ros. Is the fool sick?
Biron. Sick at heart.
Ros. Alack, let it blood.
Biron. Would that do it good?
Ros. My Physick says, I.[3]
Biron. Will you prick't with your eye?
Ros. No *point*,[4] with my knife.
Biron. Now, God save thy life!
Ros. And yours from long living!
Biron. I cannot stay thanksgiving. [*Retiring.*
Dum. Sir, I pray you, a word: What lady is that same?
Boyet. The heir of Alençon, Rosaline her name.
Dum. A gallant lady! Monsieur, fare you well.
[*Exit.*
Long. I beseech you a word; What is she in the white?
Boyet. A woman sometimes, an you saw her in the light.
Long. Perchance, light in the light: I desire her name.
Boyet. She hath but one for herself; to desire that, were a shame.
Long. Pray you, sir, whose daughter?
Boyet. Her mother's, I have heard.
Long. God's blessing on your beard!
Boyet. Good sir, be not offended:
She is an heir of Falconbridge.
Long. Nay, my choler is ended.
She is a most sweet lady.
Boyet. Not unlike, sir; that may be.
[*Exit* LONG.
Biron. What's her name, in the cap?
Boyet. Katharine, by good hap.
Biron. Is she wedded, or no?
Boyet. To her will, sir, or so.
Biron. You are welcome, sir; adieu!
Boyet. Farewell to me, sir, and welcome to you.
[*Exit* BIRON.—*Ladies unmask.*
Mar. That last is Biron, the merry mad-cap lord;
Not a word with him but a jest.
Boyet. And every jest but a word.
Prin. It was well done of you to take him at his word.
Boyet. I was as willing to grapple, as he was to board.
Mar. Two hot sheeps, marry!
Boyet. And wherefore not ships?
No sheep, sweet lamb, unless we feed on your lips.
Mar. You sheep, and I pasture; Shall that finish the jest?
Boyet. So you grant pasture for me.
[*Offering to kiss her.*
Mar. Not so, gentle beast;
My lips are no common, though several[5] they be.
Boyet. Belonging to whom?
Mar. To my fortunes and me.
Prin. Good wits will be jangling; but, gentles, agree:
The civil war of wits were much better used
On Navarre and his book-men; for here 'tis abused.
Boyet. If my observation (which very seldom lies,)
By the heart's still rhetorick, disclosed with eyes,[6]
Deceive me not now. Navarre is infected.
Prin. With what?
Boyet. With that which we lovers entitle, affected.
Prin. Your reason?
Boyet. Why, all his behaviours did make their retire,
To the court of his eye, peeping thorough desire,
His heart, like an agate, with your print impressed,
Proud with his form, in his eye pride expressed:
His tongue, all impatient to speak and not see,[7]
Did stumble with haste in his eye-sight to be;
All senses to that sense did make their repair,
To feel only looking on fairest of fair;

1 *To depart* and *to part* were anciently synonymous.

2 This phrase appears to us unseemly to a princess, but it was a common metaphorical expression then much used. Perhaps it was no more considered offensive than it would be now to talk of the *castrations* of Holinshed. It was not peculiar to Shakspeare.

3 The old spelling of the affirmative particle *ay* is here retained for the sake of the rhyme.

4 *Point*, in French, is an adverb of negation, but, if properly spoken, is not sounded like the *point* of a knife. A quibble was however intended. Perhaps Shakspeare was not well acquainted with the pronunciation of French.

5 A quibble is here intended upon the word *several*, which besides its ordinary signification of separate, distinct, signified also an enclosed pasture, as opposed to an open field or common. Bacon and others used it in this sense.

6 So in Daniel's Complaint of Rosamond, 1594:
'Sweet *silent rhetoric* of persuading *eyes*.
Dumb eloquence.'

7 Although the expression in the text is extremely odd, yet the sense appears to be, that his tongue envied the quickness of his eyes, and strove to be as rapid in its utterance, as they in their perception

Methought all his senses were lock'd in his eye,
As jewels in crystal for some prince to buy;
Who tending their own worth, from where they were glass'd
Did point you to buy them along as you pass'd.
His face's own margent[1] did quote such amazes,
That all eyes saw his eyes enchanted with gazes;
I'll give you Aquitain, and all that is his,
An you give him for my sake but one loving kiss.

Prin. Come, to our pavilion: Boyet is dispos'd—

Boyet. But to speak that in words, which his eye hath disclos'd:
I only nave made a mouth of his eye,
By adding a tongue which I know will not lie.

Ros. Thou art an old love-monger, and speak'st skilfully.

Mar. He is Cupid's grandfather, and learns news of him.

Ros. Then was Venus like her mother; for her father is but grim.

Boyet. Do you hear, my mad wenches?

Mar. No.

Boyet. What then, do you see?

Ros. Ay, our way to be gone.

Boyet. You are too hard for me. [*Exeunt.*

ACT III.

SCENE I. *Another part of the same. Enter* Armado *and* Moth.

Arm. Marble, child, make passionate my sense of hearing.

Moth. *Concolinel*[2]—— [*Singing.*

Arm. Sweet air!—Go, tenderness of years; take this key, give enlargement to the swain, bring him festinately[3] hither; I must employ him in a letter to my love.

Moth. Master, will you win your love with a French brawl?[4]

Arm. How mean'st thou? brawling in French?

Moth. No, my complete master: but to jig off a tune at the tongue's end, canary[5] to it with your feet, humour it with turning up your eye-lids; sigh a note, and sing a note; sometime through the throat, as if you swallowed love with singing love; sometime through the nose, as if you snuffed up love by smelling love; with your hat penthouselike o'er the shop of your eyes; with your arms crossed on your thin belly-doublet, like a rabbit on a spit; or your hands in your pocket, like a man after the old painting; and keep not too long in one tune, but a snip and away. These are complements,[6] these are humours; these betray nice wenches—that would be betrayed without these; and make them men of note, (do you note, men?[7]) that most are affected to these.

Arm. How hast thou purchased this experience?

Moth. By my penny of observation.[8]

Arm. But O,—but O,—

Moth. —the hobby-horse is forgot.

Arm. Callest thou my love, hobby-horse?[9]

Moth. No, master; the hobby-horse is but a colt, and your love perhaps a hackney. But have you forgot your love?

Arm. Almost I had.

Moth. Negligent student? learn her by heart.

Arm. By heart, and in heart, boy.

Moth. And out of heart, master: all those three I will prove.

Arm. What wilt thou prove?

Moth. A man, if I live; and this, by, in, and without, upon the instant: By heart you love her, because your heart cannot come by her: in heart you love her, because your heart is in love with her; and out of heart you love her, being out of heart that you cannot enjoy her.

Arm. I am all these three.

Moth. And three times as much more, and yet nothing at all.

Arm. Fetch hither the swain; he must carry me a letter.

Moth. A message well sympathised; a horse to be an embassador for an ass!

Arm. Ha, ha! what sayest thou?

Moth. Marry, sir, you must send the ass upon the horse, for he is very slow-gaited: But I go.

Arm. The way is but short; away.

Moth. As swift as lead, sir,

Arm. Thy meaning, pretty ingenious?
Is not lead a metal heavy, dull, and slow?

Moth. *Minime*, honest master; or rather, master, no.

Arm. I say, lead is slow

Moth. You are too swift,[10] sir, to say so
Is that lead slow which is fir'd from a gun?

Arm. Sweet smoke of rhetoric!
He reputes me a cannon; and the bullet, that's he;-
I shoot thee at the swain.

Moth. Thump then, and I flee [*Exit*

Arm. A most acute juvenal: voluble and free c grace!
By thy favour, sweet welkin, I must sigh in thy face:
Most rude melancholy, valour gives thee place.
My herald is return'd.

Re-enter Moth *and* Costard.

Moth. A wonder, master; here's a Costard[11] broken in a shin.

Arm. Some enigma, some riddle;—come,—thy *l'envoy*;[12]—begin.

Cost. No egma, no riddle, no *l'envoy*: no salve in the mail,[13] sir: O, sir, plantain, a plain plantain; no *l'envoy*, no *l'envoy*, no salve, sir, but a plantain!

Arm. By virtue, thou enforcest laughter; thy silly thought, my spleen; the heaving of my lungs provokes me to ridiculous smiling; O, pardon me, my stars! Doth the inconsiderate take salve for *l'envoy*, and the word, *l'envoy*, for a salve?

Moth. Do the wise think them other? is not *l'envoy* a salve?

Arm. No, page; it is an epilogue or discourse, to make plain
Some obscure precedence that hath tofore been sain.
I will example it:
The fox, the ape, and the humble-bee,
Were still at odds, being but three.
There's the moral: Now the *l'envoy*.

1 In Shakspeare's time, notes, quotations, &c. were usually printed in the exterior margin of books.

2 A song is apparently lost here. In old comedies the songs are frequently omitted. On this occasion the stage direction is generally *Here they sing*—or *Cantant*

3 i. e. *hastily*.

4 A kind of dance; spelt *bransle* by some authors: being the French name for the same dance.

5 *Canary* was the name of a sprightly dance, sometimes accompanied by the castanets.

6 i. e. accomplishments.

7 One of the modern editors, with great plausibility, proposes to read 'do you note *me?*'

8 The allusion is probably to the old popular pamphlet, 'A Pennyworth of Wit.'

9 The *Hobby-horse* was a personage belonging to the ancient Morris dance, when complete. It was the figure of a horse fastened round the waist of a man, his own legs going through the body of the horse, and enabling him to walk, but concealed by a long footcloth: while false legs appeared where those of the man should be at the sides of the horse. Latterly the Hobby-horse was frequently omitted, which appears to have occasioned a popular ballad, in which was this line, or burden

10 Quick, ready.

11 i. e. a head; a name adopted from an apple shaped like a man's head. It must have been a common sort of apple, as it gave a name to the dealers in apples who were called *costar-mongers*.

12 An old French term for concluding verses, which served either to convey the moral, or to address the poem to some person.

13 A *mail* or *male* was a budget, wallet, or portmanteau. Costard, mistaking *enigma, riddle*, and *l'envoy* for names of salves, objects to the application of any *salve* in the budget, and cries out for a *plantain* leaf. There is a quibble upon *salve* and *salve*, a word with which it was not unusual to conclude epistles, &c and which therefore was a kind of *l'envoy*

Moth. I will add the *l'envoy*: Say the moral again.
Arm. The fox, the ape, and the humble-bee,
Were still at odds, being but three:
Moth. Until the goose came out of door,
And stay'd the odds by adding four.
Now will I begin your moral, and do you follow with my *l'envoy*.
The fox, the ape, and the humble-bee,
Were still at odds, being but three:
Arm. Until the goose came out of door,
Staying the odds by adding four.
Moth. A good *l'envoy*, ending in the goose,
Would you desire more?
Cost. The boy hath sold him a bargain, a goose; that's flat:—
Sir, your pennyworth is good, an your goose be fat.—
To sell a bargain well, is as cunning as fast and loose:
Let me see a fat *l'envoy*; ay, that's a fat goose.
Arm. Come hither, come hither: How did this argument begin?
Moth. By saying that a *Costard* was broken in a shin.
Then call'd you for the *l'envoy*.
Cost. True, and I for a plantain; Thus came your argument in;
Then the boy's fat *l'envoy*, the goose that you bought;
And he ended the market.[1]

Arm. But tell me; how was there a Costard[2] broken in a shin?

Moth. I will tell you sensibly.

Cost. Thou hast no feeling of it, Moth; I will speak that *l'envoy*.
I, Costard, running out, that was safely within,
Fell over the threshold, and broke my shin.

Arm. We will talk no more of this matter.

Cost. Till there be more matter in the shin.

Arm. Sirrah Costard, I will enfranchise thee.

Cost. O, marry me to one Frances:—I smell some *l'envoy*, some goose, in this.

Arm. By my sweet soul, I mean, setting thee at liberty, enfreedoming thy person; thou wert immured, restrained, captivated, bound.

Cost. True, true; and now you will be my purgation, and let me loose.

Arm. I give thee thy liberty, set thee from durance; and, in lieu thereof, impose on thee nothing but this: Bear this significant[3] to the country maid Jaquenetta: there is remuneration; [*Giving him money.*] for the best ward of mine honour, is, rewarding my dependants. Moth, follow. [*Exit.*

Moth. Like the sequel, I.—Signior Costard, adieu.

Cost. My sweet ounce of man's flesh! my incony[4] Jew!— [*Exit* MOTH.
Now will I look to this remuneration. Remuneration! O, that's the Latin word for three farthings: three farthings—remuneration.—*What's the price of this inkle? a penny:—No, I'll give you a remuneration:* why, it carries it.—Remuneration!—why, it is a fairer name than French crown. I will never buy and sell out of this word.

Enter BIRON.

Biron. O, my good knave Costard! exceedingly well met.

Cost. Pray you, sir, how much carnation ribbon may a man buy for a remuneration?

Biron. What is a remuneration?

Cost. Marry, sir, half-penny farthing.

Biron. O, why then, three-farthings-worth of silk.

Cost. I thank your worship: God be with you!

Biron. O, stay, slave; I must employ thee:
As thou wilt win my favour, good my knave,
Do one thing for me that I shall entreat.

Cost. When would you have it done, sir?

Biron. O, this afternoon.

Cost. Well, I will do it, sir: Fare you well.

Biron. O, thou knowest not what it is.

Cost. I shall know, sir, when I have done it.

Biron. Why, villain, thou must know first.

Cost. I will come to your worship to-morrow morning.

Biron. It must be done this afternoon. Hark, slave, it is but this;—
The princess comes to hunt here in the park,
And in her train there is a gentle lady;
When tongues speak sweetly, then they name her name,
And Rosaline they call her: ask for her;
And to her white hand see thou do commend
This seal'd-up counsel. There's thy guerdon;[5] go. [*Gives him money.*

Cost. Guerdon,—O sweet guerdon! better than remuneration; eleven-pence farthing better: Most sweet guerdon!—I will do it, sir, in print.[6]—Guerdon—remuneration. [*Exit.*

Biron. O!—And I, forsooth in love! I, that have been love's whip;
A very beadle to a humorous sigh;
A critic; nay, a knight-watch constable;
A domineering pedant o'er the boy,
Than whom no mortal so magnificent![7]
This wimpled,[8] whining, purblind, wayward boy;
This senior-junior, giant-dwarf, Dan Cupid;
Regent of love rhymes, lord of folded arms,
The anointed sovereign of sighs and groans,
Liege of all loiterers and malcontents,
Dread prince of plackets,[9] king of codpieces,
Sole imperator, and great general
Of trotting paritors[10]—O my little heart!—
And I to be a corporal of his field,[11]
And wear his colours[12] like a tumbler's hoop!
What? I! I love! I sue! I seek a wife!
A woman, that is like a German clock,[13]
Still a-repairing; ever out of frame;
And never going aright, being a watch,
But being watch'd that it may still go right?
Nay, to be perjur'd, which is worst of all;
And, among three, to love the worst of all;
A whitely wanton with a velvet brow,
With two pitch balls stuck in her face for eyes,
Ay, and, by heaven, one that will do the deed,
Though Argus were her eunuch and her guard:
And I to sigh for her! to watch for her!
To pray for her! Go to; it is a plague
That Cupid will impose for my neglect
Of his almighty dreadful little might.
Well, I will love, write, sigh, pray, sue, and groan,
Some men must love my lady, and some Joan.
[*Exit.*

---

1 Alluding to the proverb, 'Three women and a *goose* make a *market*.'

2 See p. 196, note 11.

3 Armado sustains his character well; he will not give any thing its vulgar name, he calls the *letter* he would send to Jaquenetta, a *significant*.

4 *Incony*. The meaning and etymology of this phrase is not clearly defined, though numerous instances of its use are adduced. *Sweet*, *pretty*, *delicate* seem to be some of its acceptations; and the best derivation seems to be from the northern word *canny* or *conny*, meaning *pretty*, the *in* will be intensive and equivalent to *very*.

5 *Guerdon*, Fr. is reward.

6 With the utmost nicety.

7 *Magnificent* here means glorying, boasting.

8 To *wimple* is to *veil*, from *guimple*, Fr. which Cotgrave explains, 'The crepine of a French hood,' i. e. the cloth going from the hood round the neck. Kersey explains it, 'The muffler or plaited linen cloth which nuns wear about their neck.' Shakspeare means no more than that Cupid was *hood-winked*.

9 *Plackets* were *stomachers*. See Note on Winter's Tale, Act iv. Sc. 3.

10 The officers of the spiritual courts who serve citations.

11 It appears from Lord Stafford's Letters, vol. ii. p. 199, that a *corporal of the field* was employed, as an aid-de-camp is now, 'in taking and carrying to and fro the directions of the general, or other higher officers of the field.'

12 It was once a mark of gallantry to wear a lady's colours. So in Cynthia's Revels by Jonson, 'despatches his lacquey to her chamber early, to know what her *colours* are for the day.' It appears that a tumbler's hoop was usually dressed out with coloured ribands.

13 Clocks, which were usually imported from Germany at this time, were intricate and clumsy pieces of mechanism, soon deranged, and frequently 'out of frame.'

ACT IV.

SCENE I. *Another part of the same. Enter the* Princess, Rosaline, Maria, Katharine, Boyet, *Lords, Attendants, and a Forester.*

Prin. Was that the king, that spurr'd the horse so hard
Against the steep uprising of the hill?
Boyet. I know not; but, I think, it was not he.
Prin. Whoe'er he was, he show'd a mounting mind.
Well, lords, to-day we shall have our despatch;
On Saturday we will return to France.—
Then, forester, my friend, where is the bush,
That we must stand and play the murderer in?
For. Here by, upon the edge of yonder coppice;
A stand, where you may make the fairest shoot.
Prin. I thank my beauty, I am fair that shoot,
And thereupon thou speak'st, the fairest shoot.
For. Pardon me, madam, for I meant not so.
Prin. What, what? first praise me, and again say, no?
O short-liv'd pride! Not fair? alack for woe!
For. Yes, madam, fair.
Prin. Nay, never paint me now;
Where fair is not, praise cannot mend the brow.
Here, good my glass,[1] take this for telling true;
[*Giving him money.*
Fair payment for foul words is more than due.
For. Nothing but fair is that which you inherit.
Prin. See, see, my beauty will be sav'd by merit.
O heresy in fair, fit for these days!
A giving hand, though foul, shall have fair praise.—
But come, the bow:—Now mercy goes to kill,
And shooting well is then accounted ill.
Thus will I save my credit in the shoot:
Not wounding, pity would not let me do't;
If wounding, then it was to shew my skill,
That more for praise, than purpose, meant to kill.
And, out of question, so it is sometimes;
Glory grows guilty of detested crimes;
When, for fame's sake, for praise, an outward part,
We bend to that the working of the heart:
As I, for praise alone, now seek to spill
The poor deer's blood, that my heart means no ill.
Boyet. Do not curst wives hold that self-sovereignty
Only for praise' sake, when they strive to be
Lords o'er their lords?
Prin. Only for praise: and praise we may afford
To any lady that subdues a lord.

Enter Costard.

Here comes a member of the commonwealth.[2]
Cost. God dig-you-den[3] all! Pray you, which is the head lady?
Prin. Thou shalt know her, fellow, by the rest that have no heads.
Cost. Which is the greatest lady, the highest?
Prin. The thickest, and the tallest.
Cost. The thickest, and the tallest! it is so; truth is truth.
An your waist, mistress, were as slender as my wit,
One of these maids' girdles for your waist should be fit.
Are not you the chief woman? you are the thickest here.
Prin. What's your will, sir? what's your will
Cost. I have a letter from monsieur Biron, to one lady Rosaline.
Prin. O, thy letter, thy letter; he's a good friend of mine:
Stand aside, good bearer.—Boyet, you can carve;
Break up this capon.[4]
Boyet. I am bound to serve.—
This letter is mistook, it importeth none here;
It is writ to Jaquenetta.
Prin. We will read it, I swear
Break the neck of the wax, and every one give ear.
Boyet. [Reads.] *By heaven, that thou art fair, is most infallible; true, that thou art beauteous: truth itself, that thou art lovely: More fairer than fair, beautiful than beauteous; truer than truth itself, have commiseration on thy heroical vassal! The magnanimous and most illustrate*[5] *king* Cophetua[6] *set eye upon the pernicious and indubitate beggar* Zenelophon; *and he it was that might rightly say,* veni, vidi, vici; *which to anatomize in the vulgar, (O base and obscure vulgar!)* videlicet, *he came, saw, and overcame: he came, one; saw, two; overcame, three. Who came? the king; Why did he come? to see; Why did he see? to overcome; To whom came he? to the beggar; What saw he? the beggar; Who overcame he? the beggar: The conclusion is victory; On whose side? the king's: the captive is enrich'd; On whose side? the beggar's; The catastrophe is a nuptial; On whose side? the king's? no, on both in one, or one in both. I am the king; for so stands the comparison: thou the beggar; for so witnesseth thy lowliness. Shall I command thy love? I may: Shall I enforce thy love? I could: Shall I entreat thy love? I will. What shalt thou exchange for rags? robes; For tittles, titles; For thyself, me. Thus, expecting thy reply, I profane my lips on thy foot, my eyes on thy picture, and my heart on thy every part.*
Thine, in the dearest design of industry,
Don Adriano de Armado.

Thus dost thou hear the Nemean lion roar
'Gainst thee, thou lamb, that standest as his prey;
Submissive fall his princely feet before,
And he from forage will incline to play:
But if thou strive, poor soul, what art thou then?
Food for his rage, repasture for his den.
Prin. What plume of feathers is he, that indited this letter?
What vane? what weathercock? did you ever hear better?
Boyet. I am much deceived, but I remember the style.
Prin. Else your memory is bad, going o'er it erewhile.[7]
Boyet. This Armado is a Spaniard, that keeps here in court;
A phantasm, a Monarcho,[8] and one that makes sport
To the prince, and his book-mates.
Prin. Thou, fellow, a word.
Who gave thee this letter?
Cost. I told you; my lord.
Prin. To whom shouldst thou give it?
Cost. From my lord to my lady.
Prin. From which lord, to which lady?
Cost. From my lord Biron, a good master of mine,
To a lady of France, that he call'd Rosaline.

---

1 Here Drs. Johnson and Farmer have each a note too long and too absurd to quote, to show it was the fashion for ladies to wear mirrors at their girdles. Steevens says justly (though he qualifies his assertion with *perhaps*) that Dr. Johnson is mistaken, and that the *forester* is the *mirror*. It is impossible for common sense to suppose otherwise.—*Pye.*

2 The princess calls Costard *a member of the commonwealth*, because he is one of the attendants on the king and his associates in their new modelled society

3 A corruption of God give you good even. See Romeo and Juliet, Act ii. Sc. 4.

4 i. e. open this letter. The poet uses this metaphor as the French do their *poulet*; which signifies both a young fowl and a love letter. To *break up* was a phrase for *to carve*.

5 Illustrious.

6 The ballad of King Cophetua and the Beggar Maid may be seen in the Reliques of Ancient Poetry, vol. i. The beggar's name was *Penelophon*. Shakspeare alludes to the ballad again in Romeo and Juliet; Henry IV. Part ii.; and in Richard II.

7 i. e. lately.
'I who *erewhile* the happy garden sung.'
Milton, Par. Reg
A pun is intended upon the word *stile*.

8 The allusion is to a fantastical character of the time 'Popular applause (says Meres in Wit's Treasurie, p 178,) doth nourish some, neither do they gape after any other thing but vaine praise and glorie,—as in our age Peter Shakerlye of Paules, and *Monarcho* that lived about the court'

Prin. Thou hast mistaken his letter. Come, lords, away.
Here, sweet, put up this; 'twill be thine another day.
[*Exit* Princess *and Train.*

Boyet. Who is the suitor? who is the suitor?[1]

Ros. Shall I teach you to know?

Boyet. Ay, my continent of beauty.

Ros. Why, she that bears the bow.
Finely put off!

Boyet. My lady goes to kill horns; but, if thou marry,
Hang me by the neck, if horns that year miscarry.
Finely put on!

Ros. Well then, I am the shooter.

Boyet. And who is your deer?

Ros. If we choose by the horns, yourself: come near.
Finely put on, indeed!

Mar. You still wrangle with her, Boyet, and she strikes at the brow.

Boyet. But she herself is hit lower: Have I hit her now?

Ros. Shall I come upon thee with an old saying, that was a man when king Pepin of France was a little boy, as touching the hit it?

Boyet. So I may answer thee with one as old, that was a woman when queen Guinever of Britain was a little wench, as touching the hit it.

Ros. *Thou canst not hit it, hit it, hit it,* [Singing.
Thou canst not hit it, my good man.

Boyet. *An I cannot, cannot, cannot,*
An I cannot, another can.
[*Exeunt* Ros. *and* Kath.

Cost. By my troth, most pleasant! how both did fit it!

Mar. A mark marvellous well shot! for they both did hit it.

Boyet. A mark! O, mark but that mark; A mark, says my lady!
Let the mark have a prick in't, to mete at, if it may be.

Mar. Wide o'the bow hand![2] I'faith your hand is out.

Cost. Indeed, a' must shoot nearer, or he'll ne'er hit the clout.

Boyet. An if my hand be out, then, belike your hand is in.

Cost. Then will she get the upshot by cleaving the pin.

Mar. Come, come, you talk greasily,[3] your lips grow foul.

Cost. She's too hard for you at pricks, sir; challenge her to bowl.

Boyet. I fear too much rubbing;[4] Good night, my good owl. [*Exeunt* Boyet *and* Maria.

Cost. By my soul, a swain! a most simple clown!
Lord, lord! how the ladies and I have put him down!
O' my troth, most sweet jests! most incony vulgar wit!
When it comes so smoothly off, so obscenely, as it were, so fit.
Armatho o' the one side,—O, a most dainty man!
To see him walk before a lady, and to bear her fan!
To see him kiss his hand! and how most sweetly a' will swear!—
And his page o' t' other side, that handful of wit!
Ah, heavens, it is a most pathetical[5] nit!
Sola, sola! [*Shouting within. Exit* Cost. *running*

SCENE II. *The same. Enter* Holofernes, Sir Nathaniel, *and* Dull.

Nath. Very reverent sport, truly; and done in the testimony of a good conscience.

Hol. The deer was, as you know, in *sanguis*,—blood; ripe as a pomewater,[6] who now hangeth like a jewel in the ear of *cœlo*, the sky, the welkin, the heaven; and anon falleth like a crab, on the face of *terra*,—the soil, the land, the earth.[7]

Nath. Truly, master Holofernes, the epithets are sweetly varied, like a scholar at the least; But, sir, I assure ye, it was a buck of the first head.[8]

Hol. Sir Nathaniel, *haud credo.*

Dull. 'Twas not a *haud credo*, 'twas a pricket.

Hol. Most barbarous intimation! yet a kind of insinuation, as it were, *in via*, in way, of explication; *facere*, as it were, replication, or, rather, *ostentare*, to show, as it were, his inclination,—after his undressed, unpolished, uneducated, unpruned, untrained, or rather unlettered, or, ratherest, unconfirmed fashion,—to insert again my *haud credo* for a deer.

Dull. I said, the deer was not a *haud credo;* 'twas a pricket.

Hol. Twice sod simplicity, *bis coctus!*—O thou monster, ignorance, how deformed dost thou look!

Nath. Sir, he hath never fed of the dainties that are bred in a book; he hath not eat paper, as it were; he hath not drunk ink; his intellect is not replenished; he is only an animal, only sensible in the duller parts;
And such barren plants are set before us, that we thankful should be
(Which we of taste and feeling are) for those parts that do fructify in us more than he.[9]
For as it would ill become me to be vain, indiscreet, or a fool,
So, were there a patch set on learning, to see him in a school:[10]
But, *omne bene*, say I; being of an old father's mind,
Many can brook the weather that love not the wind.

Dull. You two are book-men: Can you tell by your wit,
What was a month old at Cain's birth, that's not five weeks old as yet?

Hol. Dictynna, good man Dull; Dictynna,[11] good man Dull.

Dull. What is Dictynna?

Nath. A title to Phœbe, to Luna, to the moon.

Hol. The moon was a month old, when Adam was no more;
And raught[12] not to five weeks, when he came to fivescore.

---

1 An equivoque was here intended; it should appear that the words *shooter* and *suitor* were pronounced alike in Shakspeare's time.

2 This is a term in archery still in use, signifying 'a good deal to the left of the mark.' Of the other expressions, the *clout* was the white mark at which archers took aim. The *pin* was the wooden nail in the centre of it.

3 i. e. grossly. This scene, as Dr. Johnson justly remarks, 'deserves no care.'

4 To rub is a term at bowls.

5 *Pathetical* sometimes meant *passionate*, and sometimes *passion-moving*, in our old writers; but is here used by Costard as an idle expletive, as Rosalind's '*pathetical* break-promise,' in As You Like It.

6 *Pomewater*, a species of apple.

7 Warburton's conjecture that Florio, the author of the Italian Dictionary, was ridiculed under the name of Holofernes would derive some strength from the following definition: '*cielo, heaven*, the *skie*, firmament or *welkin. Terra*, the element called *earth*, anie ground, earth, countrie, *land, soile.*' But Florio's Dictionary was not published until 1598; and this play appears to have been written in 1594, though not printed until 1598.

8 In The Return from Parnassus, 1606, is the following account of the different appellations of deer at their different ages. '*Amoretto.* I caused the keeper to sever the *rascal deer* from the *bucks of the first head.* Now, sir, a *buck* is the *first* year, *a fawn;* the *second* year, a *pricket;* the *third* year, a *sorrel;* the *fourth* year, a *soare;* the fifth, a *buck of the first head;* the sixth year, a *complete buck.* Likewise your *hart*, is the *first* year, a *calfe;* the *second* year, a *brocket;* the *third* year, a *spade;* the *fourth* year, a *stag;* the sixth year, a *hart.* A *roe-buck* is the *first* year, a kid; the *second* year, a *gird;* the *third* year, a *hemuse;* and these are your special beasts for chase.'

9 The length of these lines was no novelty on the English stage. The Moralities afford whole scenes of the like measure.

10 The meaning is, to be in a school would as ill become a *patch*, or low fellow, as folly would become me.

11 Shakspeare might have found this uncommon title for Diana in the second book of Golding's translation of Ovid's Metamorphoses.

12 Reached

The allusion holds in the exchange.[1]

Dull. 'Tis true indeed; the collusion holds in the exchange.

Hol. God comfort thy capacity! I say, the allusion holds in the exchange.

Dull. And I say the pollution holds in the exchange; for the moon is never but a month old: and I say beside, that 'twas a pricket that the princess kill'd.

Hol. Sir Nathaniel, will you hear an extemporal epitaph on the death of the deer? and, to humour the ignorant, I have called the deer the princess kill'd, a pricket.

Nath. *Perge*, good master Holofernes, *perge;* so it shall please you to abrogate scurrility.

Hol. I will something affect the letter;[2] for it argues facility.

The praiseful princess pierc'd and prick'd a pretty pleasing pricket;
Some say, a sore; but not a sore, till now made sore with shooting.
The dogs did yell! put l to sore, then sorel jumps from thicket;
Or pricket, sore, or else sorel;[3] *the people fall a hooting.*
If sore be sore, then L to sore makes fifty sores: O sore L!
Of one sore I a hundred make, by adding but one more L.

Nath. A rare talent!

Dull. If a talent be a claw, look how he claws him with a talent.[4]

Hol. This is a gift that I have, simple, simple; a foolish extravagant spirit, full of forms, figures, shapes, objects, ideas, apprehensions, motions, revolutions: these are begot in the ventricle of memory, nourished in the womb of *pia mater;* and deliver'd upon the mellowing of occasion: But the gift is good in those in whom it is acute, and I am thankful for it.

Nath. Sir, I praise the Lord for you; and so may my parishioners; for their sons are well tutor'd by you, and their daughters profit very greatly under you: you are a good member of the commonwealth.

Hol. *Mehercle*, if their sons be ingenious, they shall want no instruction: if their daughters be capable, I will put it to them: But, *vir sapit, qui pauca loquitur:* a soul feminine saluteth us.

Enter JAQUENETTA *and* COSTARD.

Jaq. God give you good morrow, master person.

Hol. Master person,—*quasi* pers-on. And if one should be pierced, which is the one?

Cost. Marry, master schoolmaster, he that is likest to a hogshead.

Hol. Of piercing a hogshead! a good lustre of conceit in a turf of earth; fire enough for a flint, pearl enough for a swine: 'tis pretty; it is well.

Jaq. Good master parson, be so good as read me this letter; it was given me by Costard, and sent me from Don Armatho: I beseech you, read it.

Hol. *Fauste, precor gelida quando pecus omne sub umbra.*
Ruminat,—and so forth. Ah, good old Mantuan![5] I may speak of thee as the traveller doth of Venice:
——*Vinegia, Vinegia,*
Chi non te vede, ei non te pregia.[6]
Old Mantuan! old Mantuan! Who understandeth thee not, loves thee not.—*Ut, re, sol, la, mi, fa.*—[7] Under pardon, sir, what are the contents? or, rather as Horace says in his—What, my soul, verses?

Nath. Ay, sir, and very learned.

Hol. Let me hear a staff, a stanza, a verse *Lege, domine.*

Nath. If love make me forsworn, how shall swear to love?
Ah, never faith could hold, if not to beauty vowed!
Though to myself forsworn, to thee I'll faithful prove;
Those thoughts to me were oaks, to thee like osiers bowed.
Study his bias leaves, and makes his book thine eyes;
Where all those pleasures live that art would comprehend:
If knowledge be the mark, to know thee shall suffice;
Well learned is that tongue, that well can thee commend:
All ignorant that soul, that sees thee without wonder;
(Which is to me some praise, that I thy parts admire;)
Thy eye Jove's lightning bears, thy voice h. dreadful thunder,
Which, not to anger bent, is musick and sweet fire.
Celestial, as thou art, oh pardon, love, this wrong,
That sings heaven's praise with such an earthly tongue![8]

Hol. You find not the apostrophes, and so miss the accent; let me supervise the canzonet. Here are only numbers ratified; but, for the elegancy, facility, and golden cadence of poesy, *caret.* Ovidius Naso was the man: and why, indeed, Naso; but for smelling out the odoriferous flowers of fancy, the jerks of invention? *Imitari*, is nothing: so doth the hound his master, the ape his keeper, the tired horse[9] his rider. But damosella virgin, was this directed to you?

Jaq. Ay, sir, from one Monsieur Biron,[10] one of the strange queen's lords.

Hol. I will overglance the superscript. *To the snow white hand of the most beauteous lady Rosaline.* I will look again on the intellect of the letter, for the nomination of the party writing to the person written unto:

Your ladyship's in all desired employment, BIRON. Sir Nathaniel, this Biron is one of the votaries with the king; and here he hath framed a letter to a sequent of the stranger queen's, which, accidentally, or by the way of progression, hath miscarried.—Trip and go, my sweet; deliver this paper into the royal hand of the king; it may concern much: Stay not thy compliment; I forgive thy duty; adieu.

Jaq. Good Costard, go with me.—Sir, God save your life!

Cost. Have with thee, my girl.

[*Exeunt* COST. *and* JAQ.

Nath. Sir, you have done this in the fear of God, very religiously; and, as a certain father saith——

Hol. Sir, tell me not of the father, I do fear co-

1 i. e. the riddle is as good when I use the name of Adam, as when I use the name of Cain.

2 i. e. I will use or practise alliteration. To *affect* is thus used by Ben Jonson in his Discoveries: 'Spenser, in *affecting* the ancients, writ no language; yet I would have him read for his matter, but as Virgil read Ennius.'

3 For the explanation of the terms *pricket, sore* or *soar*, and *sorel* in this quibbling rhyme, the reader is prepared, by the extract from The Return from Parnassus, in a note at the beginning of the scene.

4 *Talon* was often written *talent* in Shakspeare's time. Honest Dull quibbles. One of the senses of to *claw* is to *flatter*.

5 The Eclogues of Mantuanus were translated before the time of Shakspeare, and the Latin printed on the opposite side of the page for the use of schools. In 1567 they were also versified by Tuberville.

6 This proverb occurs in Florio's Second Frutes, 1591, where it stands thus:
'Venetia, chi non ti vede non ti pretia
Ma chi ti vede, ben gli costa.'

7 He hums the notes of the gamut, as Edmund does in King Lear, Act i. Sc. 2.

8 These verses are printed, with some variations in The Passionate Pilgrim, 1599.

9 i. e. The horse adorned with ribands; Bankes's horse is here probably alluded to. Lyly, in his Mother Bombie, brings in a hackneyman and Mr. Halfpenny at cross-purposes with this word: 'Why didst thou bore the horse through the ears?'—'It was for *tiring.*'—'He would never *tire*,' replies the other.

10 Shakspeare forgot that Jaquenetta knew nothing of Biron, and had said just before that the letter had been 'sent to her from Don *Armatho*, and given to her by Costard'

lourable colours. But to return to the verses; Did they please you, sir Nathaniel?

Nath. Marvellous well for the pen.

Hol. I do dine to-day at the father's of a certain pupil of mine; where if, before repast, it shall please you to gratify the table with a grace, I will, on my privilege I have with the parents of the foresaid child or pupil, undertake your *ben venuto;* where I will prove those verses to be very unlearned, neither savouring of poetry, wit, nor invention: I beseech your society.

Nath. And thank you too: for society, (saith the text,) is the happiness of life.

Hol. And, certes,[2] the text most infallibly concludes it.—Sir, [*To* DULL.] I do invite you too; you shall not say me, nay: *pauca verba.* Away; the gentles are at their game, and we will to our recreation. [*Exeunt.*

SCENE III. *Another part of the same. Enter* BIRON, *with a Paper.*

Biron. The king he is hunting the deer: I am coursing myself: they have pitch'd a toil; I am toiling in a pitch;[3] pitch that defiles; defile! a foul word. Well, set thee down, sorrow! for so, they say, the fool said, and so say I, and I the fool. Well proved, wit! by the lord, this love is as mad as Ajax: it kills sheep; it kills me,[4] I a sheep: Well proved again on my side! I will not love: if I do, hang me; i'faith, I will not. O, but her eye,—by this light, but for her eye, I would not love her: yes, for her two eyes. Well, I do nothing in the world but lie, and lie in my throat. By heaven, I do love: and it hath taught me to rhyme, and to be melancholy; and here is part of my rhyme, and here my melancholy. Well, she hath one o'my sonnets already; the clown bore it, the fool sent it, and the lady hath it: sweet clown, sweeter fool, sweetest lady! By the world, I would not care a pin if the other three were in: Here comes one with a paper; God give him grace to groan!
[*Gets up into a tree.*

Enter the King, *with a Paper.*

King. Ah me!

Biron. [*Aside.*] Shot, by heaven!—Proceed, sweet Cupid; thou hast thump'd him with thy bird-bolt under the left pap:—I'faith, secrets.—

King. [Reads.] *So sweet a kiss the golden sun gives not*
To those fresh morning drops upon the rose,
As thy eye-beams, when their fresh rays have smote
The night of dew that on my cheeks down flows:
Nor shines the silver moon one half so bright
Through the transparent bosom of the deep,
As doth thy face through tears of mine give light;
Thou shin'st in every tear that I do weep:
No drop but as a coach doth carry thee,
So ridest thou triumphing in my woe;
Do but behold the tears that swell in me,
And they thy glory through thy grief will show:
But do not love thyself; then thou wilt keep,
My tears for glasses, and still make me weep.
O queen of queens, how far dost thou excel!
No thought can think, no tongue of mortal tell.—
How shall she know my griefs? I'll drop the paper;
Sweet leaves, shade folly. Who is he comes here?
[*Steps aside.*

Enter LONGAVILLE, *with a Paper.*

What, Longaville! and reading! listen ear.

Biron. Now, in thy likeness, one more fool, appear! [*Aside.*

Long. Ah me! I am forsworn.

Biron. Why, he comes in like a perjure,[5] wearing papers. [*Aside*

King. In love, I hope; Sweet fellowship in shame! [*Aside.*

Biron. One drunkard loves another of the name. [*Aside*

Long. Am I the first that have been perjur'd so?

Biron. [*Aside.*] I could put thee in comfort; not by two, that I know:
Thou mak'st the triumviry, the corner-cap of society,
The shape of love's Tyburn[6] that hangs up simplicity.

Long. I fear, these stubborn lines lack power to move;
O sweet Maria, empress of my love!
These numbers will I tear, and write in prose.

Biron. [*Aside.*] O, rhymes are guards on wanton Cupid's hose:
Disfigure not his slop.[7]

Long. This same shall go.—
[*He reads the Sonnet.*
Did not the heavenly rhetorick of thine eye
('Gainst whom the world cannot hold argument,)
Persuade my heart to this false perjury?
Vows for thee broke, deserve not punishment.
A woman I foreswore; but, I will prove,
Thou being a goddess, I fores ore not thee,
My vow was earthly, thou a heavenly love;
Thy grace being gain'd, cures all disgrace in me.
Vows are but breath, and breath a vapour is:
Then, thou, fair sun, which on my earth dost shine,
Exhal'st this vapour vow; in thee it is:
If broken then, it is no fault of mine;
If by me broke. What fool is not so wise,
To lose an oath to win a paradise?

Biron. [*Aside.*] This is the liver vein,[8] which makes flesh a deity;
A green goose, a goddess: pure, pure idolatry.
God amend us, God amend! we are much out o the way.

Enter DUMAIN, *with a Paper.*

Long. By whom shall I send this?—Company! stay. [*Stepping aside*

Biron. [*Aside.*] All hid, all hid, an old infant play
Like a demi-god here sit I in the sky,
And wretched fools' secrets heedfully o'er-eye.
More sacks to the mill! O heavens, I have my wish;
Dumain transform'd: four woodcocks[9] in a dish!

Dum. O most divine Kate!

Biron. O most profane coxcomb! [*Aside.*

Dum. By heaven, the wonder of a mortal eye!

Biron. By earth she is but corporal; there you lie. [*Aside.*

Dum. Her amber hairs for foul have amber coted.[10]

Biron. An amber-colour'd raven was well noted. [*Aside.*

Dum. As upright as the cedar.

Biron. Stoop, I say;
Her shoulder is with child. [*Aside.*

Dum. As fair as day.

Biron. Ay, as some days; but then no sun must shine. [*Aside.*

Dum. O that I had my wish!

Long. And I had mine! [*Aside.*

King. And I mine too, good Lord! [*Aside.*

Biron. Amen, so I had mine: Is not that a good word? [*Aside.*

Dum. I would forget her; but a fever she
Reigns in my blood, and will remember'd be.

---

1 That is, specious or fair seeming appearances.
2 Certainly, in truth.
3 Alluding to Rosaline's complexion, who is represented as a black beauty.
4 This is given as a proverb in Fuller's Gnomologia.
5 The ancient punishment of a perjured person was to wear on the breast a paper expressing the crime.
6 By *triumviry* and the *shape of love's Tyburn*, Shakspeare alludes to the gallows of the time, which was occasionally *triangular.*
7 *Slops* were wide kneed breeches, the garb in fashion in Shakspeare's time.
8 It has been already remarked that the *liver* was anciently supposed to be the seat of love.
9 A *woodcock* means a foolish fellow; that bird being supposed to have *no brains.*
10 *Coted* signifies *marked* or *noted.* The word is from the *coter* to *quote.* The construction of this passage will therefore be, 'her amber hairs have marked or shown that real amber is foul in comparison with themselves.'

Biron. A fever in your blood, why, then incision
Would let her out in saucers; Sweet misprision!
[*Aside.*

Dum. Once more I'll read the ode that I have writ

Biron. Once more I'll mark how love can vary wit. [*Aside.*

Dum *On a day, (alack the day!)*
Love, whose month is ever May,
Spied a blossom, passing fair,
Playing in the wanton air:
Through the velvet leaves the wind,
All unseen, 'gan passage find;
That the lover, sick to death,
Wish'd himself the heaven's breath,
Air, quoth he, *thy cheeks may blow;*
Air, would I might triumph so!
But alack, my hand is sworn,
Ne'er to pluck thee from thy thorn
Vow, alack, for youth unmeet;
Youth so apt to pluck a sweet.
Do not call it sin in me,
That I am forsworn for thee;—
Thee—for whom Jove would swear,[1]
Juno but an Ethiop were;
And deny himself for Jove,
Turning mortal for thy love.—

This will I send: and something else more plain,
That shall express my true love's fasting[2] pain.
O, would the King, Biron, and Longaville,
Were lovers too! Ill, to example ill,
Would from my forehead wipe a perjur'd note;
For none offend, where all alike do dote.

Long. Dumain, [*advancing.*] thy love is far from charity,
That in love's grief desir'st society:
You may look pale, but I should blush, I know,
To be o'erheard, and taken napping so.

King. Come, sir, [*advancing.*] you blush; as his your case is such;
You chide at him, offending twice as much:
You do not love Maria; Longaville
Did never sonnet for her sake compile;
Nor never lay his wreathed arms athwart
His loving bosom, to keep down his heart,
I have been closely shrouded in this bush,
And mark'd you both, and for you both did blush.
I heard your guilty rhymes, observ'd your fashion;
Saw sighs reek from you, noted well your passion:
Ah me! says one; O Jove! the other cries;
One, her hairs were gold, crystal the other's eyes:
You would for paradise break faith and troth;
[*To* Long.
And Jove, for your love, would infringe an oath.
[*To* Dumain.
What will Biron say, when that he shall hear
Faith infringed, which such zeal did swear?
How will he scorn? how will he spend his wit?
How will he triumph, leap, and laugh at it?
For all the wealth that ever I did see,
I would not have him know so much by me.

Biron. Now step I forth to whip hypocrisy.—
Ah, good my liege, I pray thee pardon me:
[*Descends from the Tree.*
Good heart, what grace hast thou, thus to reprove
These worms for loving, that art most in love?
Your eyes do make no coaches;[3] in your tears,
There is no certain princess that appears:
You'll not be perjur'd, 'tis a hateful thing;
Tush, none but minstrels like of sonneting.
But are you not asham'd? nay, are you not,
All three of you, to be thus much o'ershot?
You found his mote; the king your mote did see
But I a beam do find in each of three.
O, what a scene of foolery I have seen,
Of sighs, of groans, of sorrow, and of teen![4]
O me, with what strict patience have I sat,
To see a king transformed to a gnat![5]
To see great Hercules whipping a gigg,
And profound Solomon to tune a jigg,
And Nestor play at push-pin with the boys,
And critick[6] Timon laugh at idle toys?
Where lies thy grief, O tell me, good Dumain?
And gentle Longaville, where lies thy pain?
And where my liege's? all about the breast:
A caudle, ho!

King. Too bitter is thy jest.
Are we betray'd thus to thy over-view?

Biron. Not you by me, but I betray'd to you,
I, that am honest; I, that hold in sin
To break the vow I am engaged in;
I am betray'd, by keeping company
With moon-like men, of strange inconstancy.
When shall you see me write a thing in rhyme?
Or groan for Joan? or spend a minute's time
In pruning[7] me? When shall you hear that I
Will praise a hand, a foot, a face, an eye,
A gait, a state, a brow, a breast, a waist,
A leg, a limb?—

King. Soft; Whither away so fast?
A true man, or a thief, that gallops so?

Biron. I post from love: good lover, let me go.

Enter Jaquenetta *and* Costard.

Jaq. God bless the king!

King. What present hast thou there?

Cost. Some certain treason.

King. What makes treason here?[8]

Cost. Nay, it makes nothing, sir,

King. If it mar nothing neither,
The treason, and you, go in peace away together.

Jaq. I beseech your grace, let this letter be read;
Our parson misdoubts it; 'twas treason, he said.

Biron. Biron, read it over. [*Giving him the letter.*
Where hadst thou it?

Jaq. Of Costard.

King. Where hadst thou it?

Cost. Of Dun Adramadio, Dun Adramadio.

King. How now! what is in you? why dost thou tear it?

Biron. A toy, my liege, a toy; your grace needs not fear it.

Long. It did move him to passion, and therefore let's hear it.

Dum. It is Biron's writing, and here is his name.
[*Picks up the pieces.*

Biron. Ah, you whoreson loggerhead. [*To* Costard.] you were born to do me shame.—
Guilty, my lord, guilty; I confess, I confess.

King. What?

Biron. That you three fools lack'd me fool to make up the mess:
He, he, and you, my liege, and I,
Are pick-purses in love, and we deserve to die.
O, dismiss this audience, and I shall tell you more.

Dum. Now the number is even.

Biron. True, true; we are four:—
Will these turtles be gone?

King. Hence, sirs; away.

Cost. Walk aside the true folk, and let the traitors stay. [*Exeunt* Cost. *and* Jaq.

---

1 '*Thee*—for whom Jove would swear,
Juno but an Ethiop were.'
The old copy reads—
'*Thou* for whom Jove would swear.'
Pope thought this line defective, and altered it to—
'Thou for whom *even* Jove would swear.'

2 *Fasting* is longing, hungry, wanting.

3 Alluding to a passage in the King's Sonnet:
'No drop but as a *coach* doth carry thee.'

4 Grief.

5 *Gnat* is the reading of the old copy, and there seems no necessity for changing it to *knot* or any other word, as some of the editors have been desirous of doing. Neither do I think there is any allusion to the *singing* of the gnat, as others have supposed; but it is merely put as an insignificant insect, just as he calls the others *worms* above.

6 Cynic.

7 A bird is said to be *pruning* himself when he picks and sleeks his feathers.

8 That is—'what *does* treason here?' What *makest* thou there? or, what hast thou there to do? Quid istic tibi negotii est?—*Baret.* Shakspeare plays on this phrase in the same manner in As You Like It, Act i Sc. 1. and in King Richard III. Act i. Sc. 3.

Biron. Sweet lords, sweet lovers, O let us embrace!
As true we are as flesh and blood can be:
The sea will ebb and flow, heaven show his face;
Young blood will not obey an old decree:
We cannot cross the cause why we were born;
Therefore, of all hands,[1] must we be forsworn.
King. What, did these rent lines show some love of thine?
Biron. Did they, quoth you? Who sees the heavenly Rosaline,
That like a rude and savage man of Inde,
At the first opening of the gorgeous east,[2]
Bows not his vassal head; and, strucken blind,
Kisses the base ground with obedient breast?
What peremptory eagle-sighted eye
Dares look upon the heaven of her brow,
That is not blinded by her majesty?
King. What zeal, what fury hath inspir'd thee now?
My love, her mistress, is a gracious moon;
She, an attending star, scarce seen a light.
Biron. My eyes are then no eyes, nor I Biron:[3]
O, but for my love, day would turn to night!
Of all complexions the cull'd sovereignty
Do meet, as at a fair, in her fair cheek;
Where several worthies make one dignity;
Where nothing wants; that want itself doth seek.
Lend me the flourish of all gentle tongues,—
Fye, painted rhetorick! O, she needs it not:
To things of sale a seller's praise belongs;
She passes praise; then praise too short doth blot.
A wither'd hermit, five-score winters worn,
Might shake off fifty, looking in her eye:
Beauty doth varnish age, as if new-born,
And gives the crutch the cradle's infancy.
O, 'tis the sun, that maketh all things shine!
King. By heaven, thy love is black as ebony.
Biron. Is ebony like her? O wood divine!
A wife of such wood were felicity.
O, who can give an oath? where is a book?
That I may swear, beauty doth beauty lack,
If that she learn not of her eye to look:
No face is fair, that is not full so black.
King. O paradox! Black is the badge of hell,
The hue of dungeons, and the scowl of night;
And beauty's crest becomes the heavens well.[4]
Biron. Devils soonest tempt, resembling spirits of light.
O, if in black my lady's brows be deckt,
It mourns, that painting, and usurping hair,[5]
Should ravish doters with a false aspect:
And therefore is she born to make black fair.
Her favour turns the fashion of the days;
For native blood is counted painting now;
And therefore red, that would avoid dispraise,
Paints itself black, to imitate her brow.
Dum. To look like her, are chimney-sweepers black.
Long. And since her time, are colliers counted bright.
King. And Ethiops of their sweet complexion crack.
Dum. Dark needs no candles now, for dark is light.
Biron. Your mistresses dare never come in rain,
For fear their colours should be wash'd away.
King. 'Twere good, yours did; for, sir, to tell you plain,
I'll find a fairer face not wash'd to-day.
Biron. I'll prove her fair, or talk till doomsday here.
King. No devil will fright thee then so much as she.
Dum. I never knew man hold vile stuff so dear.
Long. Look, here's thy love: my foot and her face see. [*Shewing his Shoe.*
Biron. O, if the streets were paved with thine eyes,
Her feet were much too dainty for such tread!
Dum. O vile! then as she goes, what upward lies
The street should see as she walk'd over head.
King. But what of this? Are we not all in love?
Biron. O, nothing so sure? and thereby all forsworn.
King. Then leave this chat; and, good Biron, now prove
Our loving lawful, and our faith not torn.
Dum. Ay, marry, there;—some flattery for this evil.
Long. O, some authority how to proceed;
Some tricks, some quillets,[6] how to cheat the devil.
Dum. Some salve for perjury.
Biron. O, 'tis more than need!—
Have at you, then, affection's men at arms:
Consider what you first did swear unto;—
To fast,—to study,—and to see no woman;—
Flat treason 'gainst the kingly state of youth.
Say, can you fast? your stomachs are too young;
And abstinence engenders maladies.
And where that you have vow'd to study, lords,
In that each of you hath forsworn his book:
Can you still dream, and pore, and thereon look?
For when would you, my lord, or you, or you,
Have found the ground of study's excellence,
Without the beauty of a woman's face?
From woman's eyes this doctrine I derive:
They are the ground, the books, the academies,
From whence doth spring the true Promethean fire
Why, universal plodding prisons up
The nimble spirits in the arteries;
As motion, and long during action, tires
The sinewy vigour of the traveller.
Now, for not looking on a woman's face,
You have in that forsworn the use of eyes:
And study too, the causer of your vow:
For where is any author in the world,
Teaches such beauty as a woman's eye?
Learning is but an adjunct to ourself,
And where we are, our learning likewise is.
Then, when ourselves we see in ladies' eyes,
With ourselves,[7]
Do we not likewise see our learning there?
O, we have made a vow to study, lords:
And in that vow we have forsworn our books;
For when would you, my liege, or you, or you,
In leaden[9] contemplation, have found out
Such fiery numbers, as the prompting eyes
Of beauteous tutors have enrich'd you with?
Other slow arts entirely keep the brain;
And therefore finding barren practisers,
Scarce show a harvest of their heavy toil:
But love, first learned in a lady's eyes,
Lives not alone in mured in the brain;

---

1 i. e. at any rate, at all events.

2 Milton has transplanted this into the third line of the second book of Paradise Lost:
' Or where the *gorgeous east.*'

3 Here, and indeed throughout the play, the name of Biron is accented on the second syllable. In the first folio and quarto copies it is spelled *Berowne.* From the line before us it appears that it was pronounced *Biroon.*

4 *Crest* is here properly opposed to *badge. Black,* says the King, is the *badge of hell,* but that which graces heaven is the *crest of beauty. Black* darkens hell, and is therefore hateful: *white* adorns heaven, and is therefore lovely. *Crest,* is the very *top,* the *height* of beauty or utmost degree of fairness.

5 This alludes to the fashion prevalent among ladies in Shakspeare's time, of wearing false hair, or *periwigs* as they were then called, before that covering for the head had been adopted by men.

6 A *quillet* is a sly trick or turn in argument, or excuse. N. Bailey derives it, with much probability, from *quibblet,* as a diminutive of *quibble.*

7 This hemistich is omitted in all the modern editions except that by Mr. Boswell. It is found in the first quarto and first folio.

8 i. e. our true *books,* from which we derive most information; the *eyes* of woman.

9 So in Milton's Il Penseroso:
' With a sad *leaden,* downward cast
And in Gray's Hymn to Adversity:
' With *leaden* eye that loves the ground.

But, with the motion of all elements,
Courses as swift as thought in every power;
And gives to every power a double power
Above their functions and their offices.
It adds a precious seeing to the eye;
A lover's eyes will gaze an eagle blind;
A lover's ear will hear the lowest sound,
When the suspicious head of theft is stopp'd;
Love's feeling is more soft, and sensible,
Than are the tender horns of cockled snails;
Love's tongue proves dainty Bacchus gross in taste:
For valour, is not love a Hercules,
Still climbing trees in the Hesperides?[1]
Subtile as sphinx; as sweet, and musical,
As bright Apollo's lute, strung with his hair;
And, when love speaks, the voice of all the gods
Make heaven drowsy with the harmony.[2]
Never durst poet touch a pen to write,
Until his ink were temper'd with love's sighs;
O, then his lines would ravish savage ears,
And plant in tyrants mild humility.
From woman's eyes this doctrine I derive:
They sparkle still the right Promethean fire;
They are the books, the arts, the academes,
That show, contain, and nourish all the world;
Else, none at all in aught proves excellent:
Then fools you were these women to forswear;
Or, keeping what is sworn, you will prove fools.
For wisdom's sake, a word that all men love;
Or for love's sake, a word that loves all men;[3]
Or for men's sake, the authors of these women;
Or women's sake, by whom we men are men;
Let us once lose our oaths to find ourselves,
Or else we lose ourselves to keep our oaths:
It is religion to be thus forsworn:
For charity itself fulfills the law;
And who can sever love from charity?

King. Saint Cupid, then! and, soldiers, to the field!

Biron. Advance your standards, and upon them, lords;
Pell-mell, down with them! but be first advis'd,
In conflict that you get the sun of them.[4]

Long. Now to plain-dealing; lay these glozes by;
Shall we resolve to woo these girls of France?

King. And win them too: therefore let us devise
Some entertainment for them in their tents.

Biron. First, from the park let us conduct them thither;
Then, homeward, every man attach the hand
Of his fair mistress: in the afternoon
We will with some strange pastime solace them,
Such as the shortness of the time can shape;
For revels, dances, masks, and merry hours,
Fore-run fair Love,[5] strewing her way with flowers.

King. Away, away! no time shall be omitted,
That will be time, and may by us be fitted.

Biron. Allons! Allons!—Sow'd cockle reap'd no corn;
And justice always whirls in equal measure:
Light wenches may prove plagues to men forsworn,
If so, our copper buys no better treasure.
[*Exeunt.*

1 Shakspeare had read of 'the gardens of the *Hesperides*,' and thought the latter word was the name of the garden. Some of his contemporaries have made the same mistake.

2 Few passages have been more discussed than this. The most plausible interpretation of it is, 'Whenever love speaks, all the gods join their voices in harmonious concert.'

3 i. e. that is pleasing to all men. So in the language of the time:—*it likes me well*, for *it pleases me*. Shakspeare uses the word licentiously for the sake of the antithesis.

4 In the days of archery, it was of consequence to have the sun at the back of the bowmen, and in the face of the enemy. This circumstance was of great advantage to our Henry V. at the Battle of Agincourt. Shakspeare had, perhaps, an equivoque in his thoughts.

5 *Fair love* is *Venus*. So in Antony and Cleopatra: 'Now for the love of *love*, and *her* soft hours.'

6 i. e. enough's as good as a feast.

* 'I know not (says Johnson) what degree of respect Shakspeare intends to obtain for his vicar, but he has here put into his mouth a finished representation of colloquial excellence. It is very difficult to add any thing to his character of the school-master's table talk, and perhaps all the precepts of Castiglione will scarcely be found to comprehend a rule for conversation so justly delineated, so widely dilated, and so nicely limited.'

ACT V.

SCENE I. *Another part of the same. Enter* HOLOFERNES, SIR NATHANIEL, *and* DULL.

Hol. Satis quod sufficit.[6]

Nath. I praise God for you, sir: your reasons[7] at dinner have been sharp and sententious; pleasant without scurrility, witty without affection, audacious without impudency, learned without opinion, and strange without heresy. I did converse this *quondam* day with a companion of the king's, who is intituled, nominated, or called, Don Adriano de Armado.

Hol. Novi hominem tanquam te: His humour is lofty, his discourse peremptory, his tongue filed,[8] his eye ambitious, his gait majestical, and his general behaviour vain, ridiculous, and thrasonical.[9] He is too picked,[10] too spruce, too affected, too odd, as it were, too peregrinate, as I may call it.

Nath. A most singular and choice epithet.
[*Takes out his Table-book.*

Hol. He draweth out the thread of his verbosity finer than the staple of his argument. I abhor such fantastical phantasms, such insociable and point-devise[11] companions; such rackers of orthography, as to speak, doubt, fine, when he should say, doubt; det, when he should pronounce, debt: d, e, b, t; not d, e, t: he clepeth a calf, cauf; half, hauf; neighbour, *vocatur*, nebour, neigh, abbreviated, ne: This is abhominable, (which he would call abominable,) it insinuateth me of insanie; *Ne intelligis, domine?* to make frantic, lunatic.

Nath. *Laus deo, bone intelligo.*

Hol. *Bone?*——*bone*, for *bene*: *Priscian* a little scratch'd; 'twill serve.

Enter ARMADO, MOTH, *and* COSTARD.

Nath. *Videsne quis venit*

Hol. *Video, et gaudeo.*

Arm. Chirra! [*To* MOTH.

Hol. *Quare* Chirra, not sirrah?

Arm. Men of peace, well encounter'd.

Hol. Most military sir, salutation.

Moth. They have been at a great feast of languages, and stolen the scraps. [*To* COSTARD *aside.*

Cost. O, they have lived long in the alms-basket[12] of words! I marvel, thy master hath not eaten thee for a word: for thou art not so long by the head as *honorificabilitudinitatibus*:[13] thou art easier swallowed than a flap-dragon.[14]

Moth. Peace; the peal begins.

Arm. Monsieur, [*To* HOL.] are you not letter'd?

Moth. Yes, yes; he teaches boys the horn-book: What is a, b, spelt backward with a horn on his head?

Hol. Ba, *pueritia*, with a horn added.

Moth. Ba, most silly sheep, with a horn:—You hear his learning.

7 *Reason*, here signifies *discourse; audacious* is used in a good sense for *spirited, animated, confident; affection* is *affectation; opinion* is *obstinacy, opiniatrete.*

8 *Filed* is polished.

9 *Thrasonical* is vainglorious, boastful.

10 *Picked*, piked, or picket, neat, spruce, over nice, that is, *too nice in his dress*. The substantive is used by Ben Johnson in his Discoveries: *Pickedness* for *nicety in dress.*

11 A common expression for *exact, precise*, or *finical*

12 i. e. the refuse of words. The refuse meat of families was put into a *basket*, and given to the poor, in Shakspeare's time.

13 This word, whencesoever it comes, is often mentioned as the longest word known.

14 A *flap-dragon* was some small combustible body set on fire and put afloat in a glass of liquor. It was an act of dexterity in the toper to swallow it without burning his mouth

Hol. *Quis, quis*, thou consonant?

Moth. The third of the five vowels, if you repeat them; or the fifth, if I.

Hol. I will repeat them, a, e, i.—

Moth. The sheep: the other two concludes it; o, u.

Arm. No , by the salt wave of the Mediterraneum, a sweet touch, a quick venew[1] of wit: snip, snap, quick and home; it rejoiceth my intellect: true wit.

Moth. Offered by a child to an old man; which is wit-old.

Hol. What is the figure; what is the figure?

Moth. Horns.

Hol. Thou disputest like an infant: go, whip thy gig.

Moth. Lend me your horn to make one, and I will whip about your infamy *circum circa;* A gig of a cuckold's horn!

Cost. An I had but one penny in the world, thou shouldst have it to buy gingerbread: hold, there is the very remuneration I had of thy master, thou half-penny purse of wit, thou pigeon-egg of discretion. O, an the heavens were so pleased, that thou wert but my bastard! what a joyful father wouldst thou make me! Go to; thou hast it *ad dunghill*, at the fingers' ends, as they say.

Hol. O, I smell false Latin; dunghill for *unguem*.

Arm. Arts-man, *præambula;* we will be singled from the barbarous. Do you not educate youth at the charge-house[2] on the top of the mountain?

Hol. Or, *mons*, the hill.

Arm. At your sweet pleasure for the mountain.

Hol. I do, sans question.

Arm. Sir, it is the king's most sweet pleasure and affection, to congratulate the princess at her pavilion, in the posteriors of this day; which the rude multitude call, the afternoon.

Hol. The posterior of the day, most generous sir, is liable, congruent, and measureable for the afternoon: the word is well cull'd, chose; sweet and apt, I do assure you, sir, I do assure.

Arm. Sir, the king is a noble gentleman; and my familiar, I do assure you, very good friend:—For what is inward[3] between us, let it pass:—I do beseech thee, remember thy courtesy;[4]—I beseech thee, apparel thy head;—and among other importunate and most serious designs,—and of great import indeed, too;—but let that pass:—for I must tell thee, it will please his grace (by the world) sometime to lean upon my poor shoulder; and with his royal finger, thus, dally with my excrement,[5] with my mustachio: but, sweet heart, let that pass. By the world, I recount no fable; some certain special honours it pleaseth his greatness to impart to Armado, a soldier, a man of travel, that hath seen the world: but let that pass.—The very all of all is,—but, sweet heart, I do implore secrecy,—that the king would have me present the princess, sweet chuck, with some delightful ostentation, or show, or pageant, or antic, or firework. Now, understanding that the curate and your sweet self, are good at such eruptions, and sudden breaking out of mirth, as it were, I have acquainted you withal, to the end to crave your assistance.

Hol. Sir, you shall present before her the nine worthies.—Sir Nathaniel, as concerning some entertainment of time, some show in the posterior of this day, to be rendered by our assistance,—the king's command, and this most gallant, illustrate, and learned gentleman,—before the princess; I say, none so fit as to present the nine worthies.

Nath. Where will you find men worthy enough to present them?

Hol. Joshua, yourself; myself, or this gallant gentleman, Judas Maccabeus; this swain, because of his great limb or joint, shall pass[6] Pompey the great; the page, Hercules.

Arm. Pardon, sir, error: he is not quantity enough for that worthy's thumb: he is not so big as the end of his club.

Hol. Shall I have audience? He shall present Hercules in minority: his *enter* and *exit* shall be strangling a snake; and I will have an apology for that purpose.

Moth. An excellent device! so, if any of the audience hiss, you may cry: *well done Hercules! now thou crushest the snake!* that is the way to make an offence gracious;[7] though few have the grace to do it.

Arm. For the rest of the worthies?—

Hol. I will play three myself.

Moth. Thrice worthy gentleman!

Arm. Shall I tell you a thing

Hol. We attend.

Arm. We will have, if this fadge[8] not, an antic. I beseech you, follow.

Hol. *Via*,[9] goodman Dull! thou hast spoken no word all this while.

Dull. Nor understood none neither, sir.

Hol. *Allons!* we will employ thee.

Dull. I'll make one in a dance, or so; or I will play on the tabor to the worthies, and let them dance the hay.

Hol. Most dull, honest Dull, to our sport, away. [*Exeunt.*

SCENE II. *Another part of the same. Before the Princess's Pavilion. Enter the* Princess, Katharine, Rosaline, *and* Maria.

Prin. Sweet hearts, we shall be rich ere we depart,
If fairings thus come plentifully in;
A lady wall'd about with diamonds!—
Look you, what I have from the loving king

Ros. Madam, came nothing else along with that?

Prin. Nothing but this? yes, as much love in rhyme,
As would be cramm'd up in a sheet of paper,
Writ on both sides the leaf, margent and all;
That he was fain to seal on Cupid's name.

Ros. That was the way to make his god-head wax:[10]
For he hath been five thousand years a boy.

Kath. Ay, and a shrewd unhappy gallows too.

Ros. You'll ne'er be friends with him; he kill'd your sister.

Kath. He made her melancholy, sad, and heavy
And so she died: had she been light like you,
Of such a merry, nimble, stirring spirit,
She might have been a grandam ere she died:
And so may you; for a light heart lives long.

Ros. What's your dark meaning, mouse,[11] of this light word?

Kath. A light condition in a beauty dark.

Ros. We need more light to find your meaning out.

Kath. You'll mar the light by taking it in snuff;[12]
Therefore I'll darkly end the argument.

Ros. Look, what you do, you do it still i'the dark.

Kath. So do not you; for you are a light wench.

Ros. Indeed, I weigh not you; and therefore light.

Kath. You weigh me not,—O, that's you care not for me.

Ros. Great reason; for, Past cure is still past care.

Prin. Well bandied both: a set[13] of wit well play'd.

---

1 A hit. 2 Free-school. 3 Confidential.

4 By *remember thy courtesy*, Armado probably means 'remember that all this time thou art standing with thy hat off.' 'The putting off the hat at table is a kind of *courtesie* or ceremonie rather to be avoided than otherwise.'—*Florio's Second Frutes*, 1591.

5 The *beard* is called valour's *excrement* in the Merchant of Venice.

6 i. e. shall *march*, or walk in the procession for Pompey.

7 That is, convert our offence against yourselves into a dramatic propriety.

8 i. e. suit not, go not.

9 An Italian exclamation, signifying Courage! Come on!

10 Grow.

11 This was a term of endearment formerly.

12 *Snuff* is here used equivocally for *anger*, and the *snuff of a candle*. See King Henry IV. Act i. Sc. 3

13 A *set* is a term at tennis for a *game*

But Rosaline, you have a favour too:
Who sent it? and what is it?
Ros. I would, you knew:
And if my face were but as fair as yours,
My favour were as great: be witness this.
Nay, I have verses too, I thank Biron:
The numbers true: and, were the numb'ring too,
I were the fairest goddess on the ground:
I am compared to twenty thousand fairs.
O, he hath drawn my picture in his letter!
Prin. Any thing like?
Ros. Much, in the letters; nothing in the praise.
Prin. Beauteous as ink; a good conclusion.
Kath. Fair as a text B in a copy-book.
Ros. 'Ware pencils![1] How! let me not die your debtor,
My red dominical, my golden letter:
O, that your face were not so full of O's!
Kath. A pox[2] of that jest! and beshrew all shrows!
Prin. But what was sent to you from fair Dumain?
Kath. Madam, this glove.
Prin. Did he not send you twain.
Kath. Yes, madam; and moreover,
Some thousand verses of a faithful lover:
A huge translation of hypocrisy,
Vilely compil'd, profound simplicity.
Mar. This, and these pearls, to me sent Longaville;
The letter is too long by half a mile.
Prin. I think no less: Dost thou not wish in heart,
The chain were longer, and the letter short?
Mar. Ay, or I would these hands might never part.
Prin. We are wise girls, to mock our lovers so.
Ros. They are worse fools to purchase mocking so.
That same Biron I'll torture ere I go.
O, that I knew he were but in by the week![3]
How I would make him fawn, and beg and seek;
And wait the season, and observe the times,
And spend his prodigal wits in bootless rhymes;
And shape his service wholly to my behests;
And make him proud to make me proud that jests![4]
So potent-like[5] would I o'ersway his state,
That he should be my fool, and I his fate.
Prin. None are so surely caught, when they are catch'd,
As wit turn'd fool; folly, in wisdom hatch'd,
Hath wisdom's warrant, and the help of school;
And wit's own grace to grace a learned fool.[6]
Ros. The blood of youth burns not with such excess,
As gravity's revolt to wantonness.
Mar. Folly in fools bears not so strong a note,
As foolery in the wise, when wit doth dote;
Since all the power thereof it doth apply,
To prove, by wit, worth in simplicity.

Enter Boyet.

Prin. Here comes Boyet, and mirth is in his face.
Boyet. O, I am stabb'd with laughter! Where's her grace?
Prin. Thy news, Boyet?
Boyet. Prepare, madam, prepare!—
Arm, wenches, arm! encounters mounted are
Against your peace: Love doth approach disguis'd,
Armed in arguments; you'll be surpris'd:
Muster your wits; stand in your own defence;
Or hide your heads like cowards, and fly hence.
Prin. Saint Dennis to saint Cupid! What are they,
That charge their breath against us? say, scout, say.
Boyet. Under the cool shade of a sycamore,
I thought to close mine eyes some half an hour:
When lo! to interrupt my purpos'd rest,
Toward that shade I might behold addrest
The king and his companions: warily
I stole into a neighbour thicket by,
And overheard what you shall overhear,
That, by and by, disguis'd they will be here.
Their herald is a pretty knavish page,
That well by heart hath conn'd his embassage.
Action, and accent, did they teach him there;
Thus must thou speak, and thus thy body bear;
And ever and anon they made a doubt,
Presence majestical would put him out;
For, quoth the king, *an angel shalt thou see,*
Yet fear not thou, but speak audaciously.
The boy reply'd, *An angel is not evil;*
I should have fear'd her, had she been a devil.
With that all laugh'd, and clapp'd him on the shoulder;
Making the bold wag by their praises bolder.
One rubb'd his elbow, thus; and fleer'd, and swore,
A better speech was never spoke before:
Another, with his finger and his thumb,
Cry'd, *Via!*[7] *we will do't, come what will come:*
The third he caper'd, and cried, *All goes well:*
The fourth turn'd on the toe, and down he fell.
With that they all did tumble on the ground,
With such a zealous laughter, so profound,
That in the spleen ridiculous[8] appears,
To check their folly, passion's solemn tears.
Prin. But what, but what, come they to visit us?
Boyet. They do, they do; and are apparel'd thus,
Like Muscovites, or Russians:[9] as I guess,
The purpose is, to parle, to court, and dance:
And every one his love-feat will advance
Unto his several mistress; which they'll know
By favours several, which they did bestow.
Prin. And will they so? the gallants shall be task'd:
For, ladies, we will every one be mask'd;
And not a man of them shall have the grace,
Despite of suit, to see a lady's face.—
Hold, Rosaline, this favour thou shalt wear;
And then the king will court thee for his dear;
Hold, take thou this, my sweet, and give me thine;
So shall Biron take me for Rosaline.—
And change your favours too; so shall your loves
Woo contrary, deceiv'd by these removes.
Ros. Come on, then; wear the favours most in sight.
Kath. But, in this changing, what is your intent?
Prin. The effect of my intent is to cross theirs
They do it but in mocking merriment;
And mock for mock is only my intent.
Their several counsels they unbosom shall
To loves mistook; and so be mock'd withal,
Upon the next occasion that we meet,

1 She advises Katharine to *beware of drawing likenesses*, lest she should retaliate.

2 Theobald is scandalized at this language from a princess. But Dr. Farmer observes 'there need no alarm —the *small-pox* only is alluded to; with which it seems Katharine was pitted; or as it is quaintly expressed "her face was full of O's." Davison has a canzonet "on his lady's sicknesse of the *poxe*;" and Dr. Donne writes to his sister, "At my return from Kent, I found Pegge had the *poxe*."' Such a plague was the *small-pox* formerly, that its name might well be used as an imprecation.

3 This is an expression taken from the hiring of servants; meaning, 'I wish I knew that he was in love with me, or my *servant*,' as the phrase is.

4 The meaning of this obscure line seems to be,—I would make him proud to flatter me, who make a mock of his flattery.

5 The old copies read *pertaunt-like.* The modern editions read with Sir T Hanmer *portentlike;* of which Warburton has given an ingenious but unfounded explanation.

6 Johnson remarks that 'these are observations worthy of a man who has surveyed human nature with the closest attention.'

7 *Via.* See p. 83.

8 *Spleen ridiculous* is a ridiculous *fit* of laughter. The spleen was anciently supposed to be the cause of laughter.

9 In the first year of K. Henry VIII. at a banquet made for the foreign ambassadors in the parliament chamber at Westminster, 'came the Lorde Henry Earle of Wiltshire and the Lorde Fitzwater, in two long gownes of yellow satin traversed with white satin, and in every bend of white was a bend of crimosen sattin after the fashion of Russia or Ruslande, with furred hattes of grey on their hedes, either of them havyng an hatchet in their handes, and bootes with pykes turned up'—*Hall, Henry VIII. p.* 6.

With visages display'd, to talk and greet.
Ros. But shall we dance, if they desire us to't?
Prin. No; to the death, we will not move a foot:
Nor to their penn'd speech render we no grace;
But, while 'tis spoke, each turn away her face.
Boyet. Why, that contempt will kill the speaker's heart,
And quite divorce his memory from his part.
Prin. Therefore I do it: and, I make no doubt,
The rest will ne'er come in, if he be out.
There's no such sport, as sport by sport o'erthrown;
To make theirs ours, and ours none but our own:
So shall we stay, mocking intended game;
And they, well mock'd, depart away with shame.
[*Trumpets sound within.*
Boyet. The trumpet sounds; be mask'd, the maskers come. [*The Ladies mask.*

Enter the King, BIRON, LONGAVILLE, *and* DUMAIN, *in Russian habits, and masked;* MOTH, Musicians, *and* Attendants.

Moth. *All hail, the richest beauties on the earth!*
Boyet. Beauties no richer than rich taffata.[1]
Moth. *A holy parcel of the fairest dames,*
[The ladies turn their backs to him.
That ever turn'd their—backs—to mortal views!
Biron. *Their eyes*, villain, *their eyes.*
Moth. *That ever turn'd their eyes to mortal views! Out—*
Boyet. True; *out*, indeed.
Moth. *Out of your favours heavenly spirits, vouchsafe*
Not to behold—
Biron. *Once to behold*, rogue.
Moth. *Once to behold with your sun-beamed eyes.*
——with your sun-beamed eyes——
Boyet. They will not answer to that epithet;
You were best call it daughter-beamed eyes.
Moth. They do not mark me, and that brings me out.
Biron. Is this your perfectness? begone, you rogue.
Ros. What would these strangers? know their minds, Boyet:
If they do speak our language, 'tis our will
That some plain man recount their purposes:
Know what they would.
Boyet. What would you with the princess?
Biron. Nothing but peace and gentle visitation.
Ros. What would they, say they?
Boyet. Nothing but peace and gentle visitation.
Ros. Why, that they have; and bid them so be gone.
Boyet. She says, you have it, and you may be gone.
King. Say to her we have measur'd many miles,
To tread a measure with her on this grass.
Boyet. They say that they have measur'd many a mile,
To tread a measure[2] with you on this grass.
Ros. It is not so: ask them how many inches
Is in one mile: if they have measur'd many,
The measure then of one is easily told.
Boyet. If, to come hither you have measur'd miles,
And many miles, the princess bids you tell,
How many inches do fill up one mile.
Biron. Tell her we measure them by weary steps.
Boyet. She hears herself.
Ros. How many weary steps,
Of many weary miles you have o'ergone,
Are number'd in the travel of one mile?
Biron. We number nothing that we spend for you;
Our duty is so rich, so infinite,
That we may do it still without accompt.
Vouchsafe to show the sunshine of your face,
That we, like savages, may worship it.
Ros. My face is but a moon, and clouded too.
King. Blessed are clouds, to do as such clouds do!
Vouchsafe, bright moon, and these thy stars, to shine[3]
(Those clouds remov'd) upon our wat'ry eyne.
Ros. O vain petitioner! beg a greater matter;
Thou now request'st but moonshine in the water.
King. Then in our measure vouchsafe but one change;
Thou bid'st me beg; this begging is not strange.
Ros. Play, music, then: nay, you must do it soon. [*Music plays.*
Not yet:—no dance:—thus change I like the moon.
King. Will you not dance? How come you thus estrang'd?
Ros. You took the moon at full; but now she's chang'd.
King. Yet still she is the moon, and I the man.
The music plays; vouchsafe some motion to it.
Ros. Our ears vouchsafe it.
King. But your legs should do it.
Ros. Since you are strangers and come here by chance,
We'll not be nice: take hands;—We will not dance.
King. Why take we hands, then?
Ros. Only to part friends:—
Court'sy, sweet hearts; and so the measure ends.
King. More measure of this measure; be not nice.
Ros. We can afford no more at such a price.
King. Prize you yourselves; What buys your company?
Ros. Your absence only.
King. That can never be.
Ros. Then cannot we be bought: and so adieu;
Twice to your visor, and half once to you!
King. If you deny to dance, let's hold more chat.
Ros. In private then.
King. I am best pleas'd with that.
[*They converse apart.*
Biron. White-handed mistress, one sweet word with thee.
Prin. Honey, and milk, and sugar; there is three.
Biron. Nay then, two treys (an if you grow so nice,)
Metheglin, wort, and malmsey;—Well run, dice!
There's half a dozen sweets.
Prin. Seventh sweet, adieu!
Since you can cog,[4] I'll play no more with you.
Biron. One word in secret.
Prin. Let it not be sweet.
Biron. Thou griev'st my gall.
Prin. Gall? bitter.
Biron. Therefore meet.
[*They converse apart.*
Dum. Will you vouchsafe with me to change a word?
Mar. Name it.
Dum. Fair lady,—
Mar. Say you so? Fair lord,—
Take that for your fair lady.
Dum. Please it you,
As much in private, and I'll bid adieu.
[*They converse apart.*
Kath. What, was your visor made without a tongue?
Long. I know the reason, lady, why you ask.
Kath. O, for your reason! quickly, sir; I long
Long. You have a double tongue within your mask,
And would afford my speechless visor half.
Kath. Veal,[5] quoth the Dutchman;—Is not veal a calf?
Long. A calf, fair lady?
Kath. No, a fair lord calf.
Long. Let's part the word.

1 i. e. the taffata masks they wore.
2 A grave solemn dance, with slow and measured steps, like the minuet. As it was of so solemn a nature, it was performed at public entertainments in the Inns of Court; and it was not unusual, nor thought inconsistent, for the first characters in the law to bear a part in *treading a measure.* Sir Christopher Hatton was famous for it.
3 When Queen Elizabeth asked an ambassador how he liked her ladies?—'It is hard,' said he, 'to judge of stars in the presence of the sun.'
4 To *cog* is to lie or cheat. Hence, to cog the dice.
5 The same joke occurs in 'Dr. Dodypoll.' '*Doct* Hans, my very speciall friend; fait and trot me be right glad for see you *veale. Hans.* What, do you make a *calfe* of me, M. Doctor?'

Kath. No, I'll not be your half:
Take all, and wean it; it may prove an ox.
Long. Look how you butt yourself in these sharp mocks!
Will you give horns, chaste lady? do not so.
Kath. Then die a calf, before your horns do grow.
Long. One word in private with you, ere I die.
Kath. Bleat softly, then, the butcher hears you cry. [*They converse apart.*
Boyet. The tongues of mocking wenches are as keen
As is the razor's edge invisible,
Cutting a smaller hair than may be seen;
Above the sense of sense: so sensible
Seemeth their conference; their conceits have wings,
Fleeter than arrows, bullets, wind, thought, swifter things.
Ros. Not one word more, my maids; break off, break off.
Biron. By heaven, all dry-beaten with pure scoff!
King. Farewell, mad wenches; you have simple wits. [*Exeunt* King, Lords, MOTH, *Music, and* Attendants.
Prin. Twenty adieus, my frozen Muscovites.—
Are these the breed of wits so wonder'd at?
Boyet. Tapers they are, with your sweet breaths puff'd out.
Ros. Well-liking[1] wits they have; gross, gross; fat, fat.
Prin. O poverty in wit, kingly-poor flout!
Will they not, think you, hang themselves to-night?
Or ever, but in visors, show their faces?
This pert Biron was out of countenance quite.
Ros. O! they were all in lamentable cases!
The king was weeping-ripe for a good word.
Prin. Biron did swear himself out of all suit.
Mar. Dumain was at my service, and his sword:
No *point*,[2] quoth I; my servant straight was mute.
Kath. Lord Longaville said, I came o'er his heart,
And trow you what he call'd me?
Prin. Qualm, perhaps.
Kath. Yes, in good faith.
Prin. Go, sickness, as thou art!
Ros. Well, better wits have worn plain statute-caps.[3]
But will you hear? the king is my love sworn.
Prin. And quick Biron hath plighted faith to me.
Kath. And Longaville was for my service born.
Mar. Dumain is mine, as sure as bark on tree.
Boyet. Madam, and pretty mistresses, give ear:
Immediately they will again be here
In their own shapes; for it can never be,
They will digest this harsh indignity.
Prin. Will they return?
Boyet. They will, they will, God knows;
And leap for joy, though they are lame with blows:
Therefore, change favours;[4] and, when they repair,
Blow like sweet roses in this summer air.
Prin. How blow? how blow? speak to be understood.
Boyet. Fair ladies, mask'd, are roses in their bud:
Dismask'd, their damask sweet commixture shown,
Are angels vailing clouds,[5] or roses blown.
Prin. Avaunt, perplexity! What shall we do,
If they return in their own shapes to woo?
Ros. Good madam, if by me you'll be advis'd,
Let's mock them still, as well known, as disguis'd;
Let us complain to them what fools were here,
Disguis'd like Muscovites, in shapeless[6] gear;
And wonder, what they were; and to what end
Their shallow shows, and prologue vilely penn'd,
And their rough carriage so ridiculous,
Should be presented at our tent to us.
Boyet. Ladies, withdraw; the gallants are at hand.
Prin. Whip to our tents, as roes run over land.
[*Exeunt* Princess, Ros. KATH. *and* MARIA.

Enter the King, BIRON, LONGAVILLE, *and* DUMAIN, *in their proper habits.*

King. Fair sir, God save you! Where is the princess?
Boyet. Gone to her tent: Please it your majesty,
Command me any service to her thither?
King. That she vouchsafe me audience for one word.
Boyet. I will; and so will she, I know, my lord. [*Exit.*
Biron. This fellow pecks up wit, as pigeons peas;
And utters it again when Jove doth please:
He is wit's pedler: and retails his wares
At wakes and wassels,[7] meetings, markets, fairs:
And we that sell by gross, the Lord doth know,
Have not the grace to grace it with such show.
This gallant pins the wenches on his sleeve;
Had he been Adam, he had tempted Eve:
He can carve too, and lisp: Why this is he,
That kiss'd away his hand in courtesy;
This is the ape of form, monsieur the nice,
That, when he plays at tables, chides the dice
In honourable terms; nay, he can sing
A mean[8] most meanly; and, in ushering,
Mend him who can: the ladies call him, sweet,
The stairs, as he treads on them, kiss his feet:
This is the flower that smiles on every one,
To show his teeth as white as whales bone:[9]
And consciences, that will not die in debt,
Pay him the due of honey-tongued Boyet.
King. A blister on his sweet tongue with my heart,
That put Armado's page out of his part!

Enter the Princess, *usher'd by* BOYET; ROSALINE, MARIA, KATHARINE, *and Attendants.*

Biron. See where it comes!—Behaviour, what wert thou,
Till this man show'd thee? and what art thou now?
King. All hail, sweet madam, and fair time of day
Prin. Fair, in all hail, is foul, as I conceive.
King. Construe my speeches better, if you may.
Prin. Then wish me better, I will give you leave.
King. We came to visit you; and purpose now
To lead you to our court: vouchsafe it then.
Prin. This field shall hold me; and so hold your vow:
Nor God, nor I, delight in perjur'd men.
King. Rebuke me not for that which you provoke;
The virtue of your eye must break my oath.
Prin. You nick-name virtue: vice you should have spoke;
For virtue's office never breaks men's troth.
Now, by my maiden honour, yet as pure
As the unsullied lily, I protest,
A world of torments though I should endure,
I would not yield to be your house's guest:

---

1 *Well-liking* is the same as *well-conditioned*, fat. So in Job, xxxix. 4. Their young ones are in *good-liking*.

2 *No point.* A quibble on the French adverb of negation, as before, Act ii. Sc. 1.

3 An act was passed the 13th of Elizabeth (1571,) 'For the continuance of making and wearing woollen caps, in behalf of the trade of cappers, providing that all above the age of six years (except the nobility and some others,) should on Sabbath days and holidays, wear caps of wool, knit, thicked, and dressed in England, upon penalty of ten groats.'

The term *flat cap* for a citizen will now be familiar to most readers from the use made of it by the author of The Fortunes of Nigel. The meaning of this passage probably is, '*better wits may be found among citizens.*'

4 Features, countenances.

5 *Ladies unmask'd* are like *angels vailing clouds* or letting those clouds which obscured their brightness *sink* before them. So in The Merchant of Venice, Act i. Sc. 1.

'*Vailing* her high top lower than her ribs.'

6 Uncouth.

7 *Wassels.* Festive meetings, drinking-bouts: from the Saxon *was-hæl*, be in health, which was the form of drinking a health; the customary answer to which was *drinc-hæl*, I drink your health. The *wassel-cup*, *wassel-bowl*, *wassel-bread*, *wassel-candle*, were all aids or accompaniments to festivity.

8 The tenor in music.

9 *Whales* bone: the Saxon genitive case. It is a common comparison in the old poets. This bone was the tooth of the *Horse-whale*, morse, or walrus, now superseded by ivory.

So much I hate a breaking-cause to be
Of heavenly oaths, vow'd with integrity.
King. O, you have lived in desolation here,
Unseen, unvisited, much to our shame.
Prin. Not so, my lord; it is not so, I swear;
We have had pastimes here, and pleasant game;
A mess of Russians left us but of late.
King. How, madam? Russians?
Prin. Ay, in truth, my lord;
Trim gallants, full of courtship, and of state.
Ros. Madam, speak true:—It is not so, my lord;
My lady, (to the manner of the days,[1])
In courtesy, gives undeserving praise:
We four, indeed, confronted here with four
In Russian habit: here they stay'd an hour,
And talk'd apace; and in that hour, my lord,
They did not bless us with one happy word.
I dare not call them fools; but this I think,
When they are thirsty, fools would fain have drink.
Biron. This jest is dry to me.—Fair, gentle sweet,
Your wit makes wise things foolish; when we greet
With eyes best seeing heaven's fiery eye,
By light we lose light: Your capacity
Is of that nature, that to your huge store
Wise things seem foolish, and rich things but poor.
Ros. This proves you wise and rich; for in my eye,—
Biron. I am a fool, and full of poverty.
Ros. But that you take what doth to you belong,
It were a fault to snatch words from my tongue.
Biron. O, I am yours, and all that I possess.
Ros. All the fool mine?
Biron. I cannot give you less.
Ros. Which of the visors was it, that you wore?
Biron. Where? when? what visor? why demand you this?
Ros. There, then, that visor; that superfluous case,
That hid the worse, and show'd the better face.
King. We are descried; they'll mock us now downright.
Dum. Let us confess, and turn it to a jest.
Prin. Amaz'd, my lord? Why looks your highness sad?
Ros. Help, hold his brows! he'll swoon! Why look you pale?—
Sea-sick, I think, coming from Muscovy.
Biron. Thus pour the stars down plagues for perjury.
Can any face of brass hold longer out?—
Here stand I, lady; dart thy skill at me;
Bruise me with scorn, confound me with a flout;
Thrust thy sharp wit quite through my ignorance;
Cut me to pieces with thy keen conceit;
And I will wish thee never more to dance,
Nor never more in Russian habit wait.
O! never will I trust to speeches penn'd,
Nor to the motion of a schoolboy's tongue;
Nor never come in visor to my friend;[2]
Nor woo in rhyme, like a blind harper's song;
Taffata phrases, silken terms precise,
Three-pil'd[3] hyperboles, spruce affectation,
Figures pedantical; these summer-flies
Have blown me full of maggot ostentation:
I do forswear them, and I here protest,
By this white glove, (how white the hand, God knows!)
Henceforth my wooing mind shall be express'd
In russet yeas, and honest kersey noes:
And, to begin, wench,—so God help me, la!—
My love to thee is sound, sans crack or flaw.
Ros. *Sans* SANS, I pray you.[4]
Biron. Yet I have a trick
Of the old rage:—bear with me, I am sick;
I'll leave it by degrees. Soft, let us see;—
Write, *Lord have mercy on us*,[5] on those three;
They are infected, in their hearts it lies,
They have the plague, and caught it of your eyes:
These lords are visited; you are not free,
For the Lord's tokens on you do I see.
Prin. No, they are free, that gave these tokens to us.
Biron. Our states are forfeit, seek not to undo us.
Ros. It is not so; For how can this be true,
That you stand forfeit, being those that sue?[6]
Biron. Peace; for I will not have to do with you.
Ros. Nor shall not, if I do as I intend.
Biron. Speak for yourselves, my wit is at an end.
King. Teach us, sweet madam, for our rude transgression,
Some fair excuse.
Prin. The fairest is confession.
Were you not here, but even now, disguis'd?
King. Madam, I was.
Prin. And were you well advis'd?
King. I was, fair madam.
Prin. When you then were here,
What did you whisper in your lady's ear?
King. That more than all the world I did respect her.
Prin. When she shall challenge this, you will reject her.
King. Upon mine honour, no.
Prin. Peace, peace, forbear,
Your oath once broke, you force[7] not to forswear.
King. Despise me, when I break this oath of mine.
Prin. I will; and therefore keep it:—Rosaline,
What did the Russian whisper in your ear?
Ros. Madam, he swore, that he did hold me dear
As precious eye-sight; and did value me
Above this world: adding thereto, moreover,
That he would wed me, or else die my lover.
Prin. God give thee joy of him! the noble lord
Most honourably doth uphold his word.
King. What mean you, madam? by my life, my troth,
I never swore this lady such an oath.
Ros. By heaven, you did; and to confirm it plain,
You gave me this: but take it, sir, again.
King. My faith, and this, the princess I did give;
I knew her by this jewel on her sleeve.
Prin. Pardon, me, sir, this jewel did she wear;
And lord Biron, I thank him, is my dear:—
What; will you have me, or your pearl again?
Biron. Neither of either; I remit both twain.—
I see the trick on't:—Here was a consent,[8]
(Knowing aforehand of our merriment,)
To dash it like a Christmas comedy:
Some carry-tale, some please-man, some slight zany,[9]
Some mumble-news, some trencher-knight, some Dick,—
That smiles his cheek in jeers;[10] and knows the trick
To make my lady laugh, when she's dispos'd,—
Told our intents before; which once disclos'd,
The ladies did change favours; and then we,
Following the signs, woo'd but the sign of she.
Now, to our perjury to add more terror,
We are again forsworn; in will and error.[11]
Much upon this it is:—And might not you, [*To* Boyet.
Forestall our sport, to make us thus untrue?
Do not you know my lady's foot by the squire,[12]
And laugh upon the apple of her eye?

---

1 After the fashion of the times.
2 Mistress. 3 A metaphor from the *pile* of velvet.
4 i. e. without French words, I pray you.
5 This was the inscription put upon the doors of houses *infected* with the plague. The *tokens* of the plague were the first spots or discolorations of the skin.
6 That is, how can those be liable to forfeiture that begin the process? The quibble lies in the ambiguity of the word *sue*, which signifies *to proceed to law*, and *to petition*.
7 i. e. you *care* not, or do not *regard* forswearing
8 An agreement, a conspiracy. See as You Like It, Act ii. Sc. 2.
9 Buffoon.
10 The old copies read *yeeres*, the emendation is Theobald's.
11 i. e. first in *will*, and afterwards in *error*.
12 From *esquierre*, Fr. *rule*, or *square*. The sense is similar to the proverbial saying—*he has got the length of her foot.*

And stand between her back, sir, and the fire,
Holding a trencher, jesting merrily?
You put our page out: Go, you are allow'd;[1]
Die when you will, a smock shall be your shroud.
You leer upon me, do you? there's an eye,
Wounds like a leaden sword.

Boyet. Full merrily
Hath this brave manage, this career, been run.

Biron. Lo, he is tilting straight! Peace; I have done.

Enter COSTARD.

Welcome, pure wit! thou partest a fair fray.

Cost. O Lord, sir, they would know,
Whether the three worthies shall come in, or no.

Biron. What, are there but three?

Cost. No, sir; but it is vara fine,
For every one pursents three.

Biron. And three times thrice is nine.

Cost. Not so, sir; under correction, sir; I hope, it is not so:
You cannot beg us,[2] sir, I can assure you, sir; we know what we know:
I hope, sir, three times thrice, sir,—

Biron. Is not nine.

Cost. Under correction, sir, we know whereuntil it doth amount.

Biron. By Jove, I always took three threes for nine.

Cost. O lord, sir, it were pity you should get your living by reckoning, sir.

Biron. How much is it?

Cost. O Lord, sir, the parties themselves, the actors, sir, will show whereuntil it doth amount: for my own part, I am, as they say, but to parfect one man,—e'en one poor man; Pompion the great, sir.

Biron. Art thou one of the worthies?

Cost. It pleased them, to think me worthy of Pompion the great: for mine own part, I know not the degree of the worthy; but I am to stand for him.

Biron. Go, bid them prepare.

Cost. We will turn it finely off, sir; we will take some care. [*Exit* COSTARD.

King. Biron, they will shame us, let them not approach.

Biron. We are shame-proof, my lord: and 'tis some policy
To have one show worse than the king's and his company.

King. I say, they shall not come.

Prin. Nay, my good lord, let me o'errule you now;
That sport best pleases, that doth least know how:
Where zeal strives to content, and the contents
Die in the zeal of them which it presents,[3]
Their form confounded makes most form in mirth;
When great things labouring[4] perish in their birth.

Biron. A right description of our sport, my lord.

Enter ARMADO.

Arm. Anointed, I implore so much expense of thy royal sweet breath, as will utter a brace of words.

[ARMADO *converses with the* King, *and delivers him a paper.*]

Prin. Doth this man serve God?

Biron. Why ask you?

Prin. He speaks not like a man of God's making

Arm. That's all one, my fair, sweet, honey monarch: for, I protest, the schoolmaster is exceeding fantastical; too, too vain; too, too vain: But we will put it, as they say, to *fortuna della guerra.* I wish you the peace of mind, most royal couplement.[5] [*Exit* ARMADO.

King. Here is like to be a good presence of worthies: He presents Hector of Troy; the swain, Pompey the great; the parish curate, Alexander; Armado's page, Hercules; the pedant, Judas Machabæus.
And if these four worthies in their first show thrive,
These four will change habits, and present the other five.

Biron. There is five in the first show.

King. You are deceiv'd, 'tis not so.

Biron. The pedant, the braggart, the hedge-priest, the fool, and the boy:—
A bare throw at novum;[6] and the whole world again,
Cannot prick[7] out five such, take each one in his vein.

King. The ship is under sail, and here she comes amain.

[*Seats brought for the* King, Princess, &c.

Pageant of the Nine Worthies.

Enter COSTARD *arm'd, for* Pompey.

Cost. *I Pompey am,—*

Boyet. You lie, you are not he.

Cost. *I Pompey am,——*

Boyet. With libbard's head on knee.[8]

Biron Well said, old mocker; I must needs be friends with thee.

Cost. *I Pompey am, Pompey, surnam'd the big,—*

Dum. The great.

Cost. It is great, sir;—*Pompey surnam'd the great;*
That oft in field, with targe and shield, did make my foe to sweat:
And travelling along this coast, I here am come by chance;
And lay my arms before the legs of this sweet lass of France.
If your ladyship would say, *Thanks, Pompey,* I had done.

Prin. Great thanks, great Pompey.

Cost. 'Tis not so much worth; but, I hope, I was perfect: I made a little fault in, *great.*

Biron. My hat to a halfpenny, Pompey proves the best worthy.

Enter NATHANIEL *arm'd, for* Alexander.

Nath. *When in the world I liv'd, I was the world's commander;*
By east, west, north, and south, I spread my conquering might:
My 'scutcheon plain declares that I am Alisander.

Boyet. Your nose says, no, you are not; for it stands too right.[9]

Biron. Your nose smells, no, in this, most tender-smelling knight.[10]

Prin. The conqueror is dismay'd: Proceed, good Alexander.

---

1 That is, you are an *allowed* or a *licensed* fool or jester.

2 In the old common law was a writ *de idiota inquirendo*, under which if a man was legally proved an idiot, the profits of his lands, and the custody of his person, might be granted by the king to any subject. Such a person, when this grant was asked, was said *to be begged for a fool.* See Blackstone, b. 1. c. 8. § 18. One of the legal tests appears to have been to try whether the party could answer a simple arithmetical question.

3 The old copies read—

'Dies in the zeal of *that* which it presents.'

The emendation in the text is Malone's, and he thus endeavours to give this obscure passage a meaning. The word *it*, I believe, refers to *sport. That sport*, says the princess, pleases best, where the actors are least skilful; where zeal strives to please, and the contents, or *great things* attempted, perish in the very act of being produced, from the ardent zeal of those who present the sportive entertainment. *It*, however, may refer to *contents*, and that word may mean the most material part of the exhibition

4 *Labouring* here means in the act of parturition.

5 This word is used again by Shakspeare in his 21st Sonnet:

'Making a *couplement* of proud compare.'

6 A game at dice, properly called *novem quinque*, from the principal throws being *nine* and *five.* The first folio reads '*Abate* throw,' &c. The second folio, which reads 'A *bare* throw,' is evidently right.

7 Pick out.

8 This alludes to the old heroic habits, which, on the knees and shoulders, had sometimes by way of ornament the resemblance of a leopard's or lion's head. See Cotgrave's Dictionary, in v. *Masquine.*

9 It should be remembered, to relish this joke, that the head of Alexander was obliquely placed on his shoulders.

10 'His (Alexander's) body had so sweet a smell of itselfe that all the apparell he wore next unto his body, tooke thereof a passing delightful savour, as if it had been perfumed.' *North's Plutarch.*

Nath. *When in the world I liv'd, I was the world's commander;*—

Boyet. Most true, 'tis right; you were so, Alisander.

Biron. Pompey the great,——

Cost. Your servant, and Costard.

Biron. Take away the conqueror, take away Alisander.

Cost. O, sir, [*To* NATH.] you have overthrown Alisander the conqueror! You will be scraped out of the painted cloth for this: your lion, that holds his poll-ax sitting on a close-stool,[1] will be given to A-jax: he will be the ninth worthy. A conqueror, and afeard to speak! run away for shame, Alisander. [NATH. *retires.*] There, an't shall please you; a foolish mild man; an honest man, look you, and soon dash'd! He is a marvellous good neighbour, in sooth; and a very good bowler: but, for Alisander, alas, you see how 'tis;—a little o'erparted:—But there are worthies a coming will speak their mind in some other sort.

Prin. Stand aside, good Pompey.

Enter HOLOFERNES *arm'd, for* Judas, *and* MOTH *arm'd, for* Hercules.

Hol. *Great Hercules is presented by this imp,*
Whose club kill'd Cerberus, that three-headed canus,
And, when he was a babe, a child, a shrimp,
Thus did he strangle serpents in his manus:
Quoniam, *he seemeth in minority;*
Ergo, *I come with this apology.*—
Keep some state in thy *exit*, and vanish.

[*Exit* MOTH.

Hol. *Judas I am,*—

Dum. A Judas!

Hol. Not Iscariot, sir.—
Judas I am, ycleped Machabæus.

Dum. Judas Machabæus clipt, is plain Judas.

Biron. A kissing traitor:—How art thou prov'd Judas?

Hol. *Judas I am,*—

Dum. The more shame for you, Judas.

Hol. What mean you, sir?

Boyet. To make Judas hang himself.

Hol. Begin, sir; you are my elder.

Biron. Well follow'd: Judas was hang'd on an elder.

Hol. I will not be put out of countenance.

Biron. Because thou hast no face.

Hol. What is this?

Boyet. A cittern head.[2]

Dum. The head of a bodkin.

Biron. A death's face in a ring.

Long. The face of an old Roman coin, scarce seen.

Boyet. The pummel of Cæsar's faulchion.

Dum. The carv'd-bone face on a flask.[3]

Biron. St. George's half-cheek in a brooch.[4]

Dum. Ay, and in a brooch of lead.

Biron. Ay, and worn in the cap of a tooth-drawer:
And now, forward; for we have put thee in countenance.

Hol. You have put me out of countenance.

Biron. False; we have given thee faces.

Hol. But you have out-fac'd them all.

Biron. An thou wert a lion, we would do so.

Boyet. Therefore, as he is, an ass, let him go.
And so adieu, sweet Jude! nay, why dost thou stay?

Dum. For the latter end of his name.

Biron. For the ass to the Jude? give it him:—Jud-as, away.

Hol. This is not generous, not gentle, not humble.

Boyet. A light for monsieur Judas: it grows dark, he may stumble.

Prin. Alas, poor Machabæus, how hath he been baited!

Enter ARMADO *arm'd, for* Hector.

Biron. Hide thy head, Achilles; here comes Hector in arms.

Dum. Though my mocks come home by me, I will now be merry.

King. Hector was but a Trojan[5] in respect of this.

Boyet. But is this Hector?

Dum. I think, Hector was not so clean-timber'd.

Long. His leg is too big for Hector.

Dum. More calf, certain.

Boyet. No; he is best indued in the small.

Biron. This cannot be Hector.

Dum. He's a god or a painter; for he makes faces.

Arm. *The armipotent Mars, of lances*[6] *the almighty,*
Gave Hector a gift,—

Dum. A gilt nutmeg.

Biron. A lemon.

Long. Stuck with cloves.

Dum. No, cloven.

Arm. Peace.
The armipotent Mars, of lances the almighty,
Gave Hector a gift, the heir of Ilion;
A man so breath'd, that certain he would fight, yea
From morn till night, out of his pavilion.
I am that flower,—

Dum. That mint.

Long. That columbine.

Arm. Sweet lord Longaville, rein thy tongue.

Long. I must rather give it the rein; for it runs against Hector.

Dum. Ay, and Hector's a greyhound.

Arm. The sweet war-man is dead and rotten; sweet chucks, beat not the bones of the buried: when he breath'd, he was a man—But I will forward with my device: Sweet royalty, [*to the* Princess] bestow on me the sense of hearing.

[BIRON *whispers* COSTARD.

Prin. Speak, brave Hector; we are much delighted.

Arm. I do adore thy sweet grace's slipper.

Boyet. Loves her by the foot.

Dum. He may not by the yard.

Arm. *This Hector far surmounted Hannibal,*—

Cost. The party is gone, fellow Hector, she is gone; she is two months on her way.

Arm. What meanest thou?

Cost. Faith, unless you play the honest Trojan, the poor wench is cast away: she's quick; the child brags in her belly already; 'tis yours.

Arm. Dost thou infamonize me among potentates? thou shalt die.

Cost. Then shall Hector be whipp'd, for Jaquenetta that is quick by him; and hang'd, for Pompey that is dead by him.

Dum. Most rare Pompey!

Boyet. Renowned Pompey!

Biron. Greater than great, great, great, great Pompey! Pompey the huge!

Dum. Hector trembles.

Biron. Pompey is moved:—More Ates,[7] more Ates; stir them on! stir them on!

Dum. Hector will challenge him.

Biron. Ay, if he have no more man's blood in's belly than will sup a flea.

Arm. By the north pole, I do challenge thee.

Cost. I will not fight with a pole, like a northern man;[8] I'll slash; I'll do it by the sword:—I pray you, let me borrow my arms again.

---

1 This alludes to the arms given, in the old history of the Nine Worthies, to Alexander, 'the which did bear geules a lion or, seiante in a chayer, holding a battle-axe argent.'

2 The *cittern*, a musical instrument like a guitar, had usually a head grotesquely carved at the extremity of the neck and finger-board: hence these jests.

3 i. e. a soldier's powder-horn.

4 A *brooch* was an ornamental clasp for fastening hat-bands, girdles, mantles, &c. a *brooch of lead*, because of his pale and wan complexion, his leaden hue.

5 *Trojan* is supposed to have been a cant term for a thief. It was, however, a familiar name for any equal or inferior.

6 i. e. lance-men.

7 i. e. more instigation. Ate was the goddess of discord.

8 *Vir Borealis*, a clown. See 'An Optick Glasse of Humours, by T. W. 1663.' The reference may be, however, to the particular use of the quarter-staff in the northern counties.

Dum. Room for the incensed worthies.
Cost. I'll do it in my shirt.
Dum. Most resolute Pompey!
Moth. Master, let me take you a buttonhole lower. Do you not see, Pompey is uncasing for the combat? What mean you? you will lose your reputation.
Arm. Gentlemen, and soldiers, pardon me; I will not combat in my shirt.
Dum. You may not deny it; Pompey hath made the challenge.
Arm. Sweet bloods, I both may and will.
Biron. What reasons have you for't?
Arm. The naked truth of it is, I have no shirt; I go woolward[1] for penance.
Boyet. True, and it was enjoin'd him in Rome for want of linen: since when, I'll be sworn, he wore none, but a dish-clout of Jaquenetta's; and that a' wears next his heart for a favour.

Enter a Messenger MONSIEUR MERCADE.

Mer. God save you, Madam.
Prin. Welcome, Mercade;
But that thou interrupt'st our merriment.
Mer. I am sorry, madam; for the news I bring,
Is heavy in my tongue. The king your father—
Prin. Dead, for my life.
Mer. Even so; my tale is told.
Biron. Worthies, away; the scene begins to cloud.
Arm. For mine own part, I breathe free breath: I have seen the day of wrong through the little hole of discretion,[2] and I will right myself like a soldier. [*Exeunt Worthies.*
King. How fares your majesty?
Prin. Boyet, prepare; I will away to-night.
King. Madam, not so; I do beseech you, stay.
Prin. Prepare, I say.—I thank you, gracious lords,
For all your fair endeavours; and entreat,
Out of a new-sad soul, that you vouchsafe
In your rich wisdom, to excuse, or hide,
The liberal[3] opposition of our spirits:
If over-boldly we have borne ourselves
In the converse of breath, your gentleness
Was guilty of it.—Farewell, worthy lord!
A heavy heart bears not an humble[4] tongue:
Excuse me so, coming so short of thanks
For my great suit so easily obtain'd.
King. The extreme parts of time extremely form
All causes to the purpose of his speed;
And often, at his very loose,[5] decides
That which long process could not arbitrate:
And though the mourning brow of progeny
Forbid the smiling courtesy of love,
The holy suit which fain it would convince;[6]
Yet, since love's argument was first on foot,
Let not the cloud of sorrow justle it
From what it purpos'd; since, to wail friends lost,
Is not by much so wholesome, profitable,
As to rejoice at friends but newly found.
Prin. I understand you not; my griefs are double.
Biron. Honest plain words best pierce the ear of grief;
And by these badges understand the king.
For your fair sakes have we neglected time,
Play'd foul play with our oaths; your beauty, ladies,
Hath much deform'd us, fashioning our humours
Even to the opposed end of our intents;
And what in us hath seem'd ridiculous,—
As love is full of unbefitting strains;
All wanton as a child, skipping, and vain;
Form'd by the eye, and therefore, like the eye,
Full of strange shapes, of habits, and of forms,
Varying in subjects as the eye doth roll
To every varied object in his glance:
Which party-coated presence of loose love
Put on by us, if, in your heavenly eyes,
Have misbecom'd our oaths and gravities,
Those heavenly eyes, that look into these faults,
Suggested[7] us to make: Therefore, ladies,
Our love being yours, the error that love makes
Is likewise yours: we to ourselves prove false,
By being once false for ever to be true
To those that make us both,—fair ladies, you.
And even that falsehood, in itself a sin,
Thus purifies itself, and turns to grace.
Prin. We have receiv'd your letters, full of love;
Your favours, the embassadors of love;
And, in our maiden council, rated them
At courtship, pleasant jest, and courtesy,
As bombast,[8] and as lining to the time:
But more devout than this, in our respects,
Have we not been; and therefore met your loves
In their own fashion, like a merriment.
Dum. Our letters, madam, show'd much more than jest.
Long. So did our looks.
Ros. We did not quote[9] them so
King. Now, at the latest minute of the hour,
Grant us your loves.
Prin. A time, methinks, too short
To make a world-without-end bargain in:
No, no, my lord, your grace is perjur'd much,
Full of dear guiltiness; and, therefore this,—
If for my love (as there is no such cause)
You will do aught, this shall you do for me:
Your oath I will not trust; but go with speed
To some forlorn and naked hermitage,
Remote from all the pleasures of the world;
There stay, until the twelve celestial signs
Have brought about their annual reckoning:
If this austere insociable life
Change not your offer made in heat of blood;
If frosts, and fasts, hard lodging, and thin weeds,
Nip not the gaudy blossoms of your love,
But that it bear this trial, and last love;
Then at the expiration of the year,
Come challenge, challenge me by these deserts,
And, by this virgin palm, now kissing thine,
I will be thine; and, till that instant, shut
My woful self up in a mourning house;
Raining the tears of lamentation,
For the remembrance of my father's death.
If this thou do deny, let our hands part;
Neither intitled in the other's heart.
King. If this, or more than this, I would deny,
To flatter up these powers of mine with rest,
The sudden hand of death close up mine eye!
Hence ever then my heart is in thy breast.
Biron. And what to me, my love? and what to me?
Ros. You must be purged too, your sins are rank;
You are attaint with faults and perjury;
Therefore, if you my favour mean to get,
A twelvemonth shall you spend, and never rest,
But seek the weary beds of people sick.
Dum. But what to me, my love? but what to me?
Kath. A wife!—A beard, fair health, and honesty;
With three-fold love I wish you all these three.
Dum. O, shall I say, I thank you, gentle wife?
Kath. Not so, my lord:—a twelvemonth and a day
I'll mark no words that smooth-fac'd wooers say:
Come when the king doth to my lady come,
Then, if I have much love, I'll give you some.
Dum. I'll serve thee true and faithfully till then.
Kath. Yet swear not, lest you be forsworn again.
Long. What says Maria?
Mar. At the twelvemonth's end,
I'll change my black gown for a faithful friend.

1 That is, clothed in wool, and not in linen. A penance often enjoined in times of superstition.
2 Armado probably means to say in his affected style that 'he had discovered he was wronged.' 'One may see day at a little hole,' is a proverb.
3 Free, to excess.
4 By *humble* is here meant *obsequiously thankful.*
5 *Loose* may mean at the moment of his parting, i. e. of his *getting loose* or away from us.
6 i. e. which it fain would succeed in obtaining.
7 Tempted.
8 Thus in Decker's Satiromastix: 'You shall swear not to *bombast* out a new play with the old *linings* of jests.'
9 Regard.
10 Clothing

Long. I'll stay with patience: but the time is long.

Mar. The liker you; few taller are so young.

Biron. Studies my lady? mistress, look on me,
Behold the window of my heart, mine eye,
What humble suit attends thy answer there:
Impose some service on me for thy love.

Ros. Oft have I heard of you, my lord Biron,
Before I saw you; and the world's large tongue
Proclaims you for a man replete with mocks;
Full of comparisons and wounding flouts;
Which you on all estates will execute,
That lie within the mercy of your wit:
To weed this wormwood from your fruitful brain;
And, therewithal, to win me, if you please
(Without the which I am not to be won,)
You shall this twelvemonth term from day to day
Visit the speechless sick, and still converse
With groaning wretches; and your task shall be,
With all the fierce[1] endeavour of your wit,
To enforce the pained impotent to smile.

Biron. To move wild laughter in the throat of death?
It cannot be; it is impossible:
Mirth cannot move a soul in agony.

Ros. Why, that's the way to choke a gibing spirit,
Whose influence is begot of that loose grace,
Which shallow laughing hearers give to fools:
A jest's prosperity lies in the ear
Of him that hears it, never in the tongue
Of him that makes it: then, if sickly ears,
Deaf'd with the clamours of their own dear[2] groans,
Will hear your idle scorns, continue then,
And I will have you, and that fault withal;
But, if they will not, throw away that spirit,
And I shall find you empty of that fault,
Right joyful of your reformation.

Biron. A twelvemonth? well, befall what will befall,
I'll jest a twelvemonth in an hospital.

Prin. Ay, sweet my lord; and so I take my leave. [*To the* King.

King. No, madam; we will bring you on your way.

Biron. Our wooing doth not end like an old play;
Jack hath not Jill: these ladies' courtesy
Might well have made our sport a comedy.

King. Come, sir, it wants a twelvemonth and a day,
And then 'twill end.

Biron. That's too long for a play.

Enter ARMADO.

Arm. Sweet majesty, vouchsafe me,—

Prin. Was not that Hector?

Dum. The worthy knight of Troy.

Arm. I will kiss thy royal finger and take leave: I am a votary; I have vowed to Jaquenetta to hold the plough for her sweet love three years. But, most esteemed greatness, will you hear the dialogue that the two learned men have compiled, in praise of the owl and the cuckoo? it should have followed in the end of our show.

King. Call them forth quickly, we will do so.

Arm. Holla! approach.

Enter HOLOFERNES, NATHANIEL, MOTH, COSTARD, *and others.*

This side is Hiems, winter; this Ver, the spring; the one maintain'd by the owl, the other by the cuckoo. Ver, begin.

SONG.

I.

Spring. *When daisies pied, and violets blue,*
And lady-smocks all silver white,
And cuckoo-buds[3] *of yellow hue,*
Do paint the meadows with delight,
The cuckoo then, on every tree,
Mocks married men, for thus sings he,
Cuckoo;
Cuckoo, cuckoo,—O word of fear,
Unpleasing to a married ear!

II.

When shepherds pipe on oaten straws,
And merry larks are ploughmen's clocks,
When turtles tread, and rooks, and daws,
And maidens bleach their summer smocks,
The cuckoo, then, on every tree,
Mocks married men, for thus sings he,
Cuckoo;
Cuckoo, cuckoo,—O word of fear,
Unpleasing to a married ear!

III.

Winter. *When icicles hang by the wall,*
And Dick *the shepherd blows his nail,*
And Tom *bears logs into the hall,*
And milk comes frozen home in pail,
When blood is nipp'd, and ways be foul,
Then nightly sings the staring owl,
To-who;
To-whit, to-who, a merry note,
While greasy Joan *doth keel the pot.*

IV.

When all aloud the wind doth blow,
And coughing drowns the parson's saw,
And birds sit brooding in the snow,
And Marian's *nose looks red and raw,*
When roasted crabs[4] *hiss in the bowl,*
Then nightly sings the staring owl,
To-who;
To-whit, to-who, a merry note,
While greasy Joan *doth keel the pot.*[5]

Arm. The words of Mercury are harsh after the songs of Apollo. You that way; we, this way. [*Exeunt.*

IN this play, which all the editors have concurred to censure, and some have rejected as unworthy of our poet, it must be confessed that there are many passages mean, childish, and vulgar; and some which ought not to have been exhibited, as we are told they were, to a maiden queen. But there are scattered through the whole many sparks of genius; nor is there any play that has more evident marks of the hand of Shakspeare.
JOHNSON.

1 Vehement.

2 *Dear.* See note on Twelfth Night, Act. v. Sc. 1.

3 Gerarde in his Herbal, 1597, says, that the *flos cuculi cardamine,* &c. are called 'in English *cuckoo flowers,* in Norfolk, Canterbury bells, and at Namptwich, in Cheshire, *Ladie-smocks.*'

4 This wild English apple, roasted before the fire, and put into ale, was a very favorite indulgence in old times.

5 To *keel* or *kele,* is to *cool.*

MERCHANT OF VENICE.

PRELIMINARY REMARKS.

"THE Merchant of Venice," says Schlegel, "is one of Shakspeare's most perfect works: popular to an extraordinary degree, and calculated to produce the most powerful effect on the stage, and at the same time a wonder of ingenuity and art for the reflecting critic. Shylock, the Jew, is one of the inconceivable master-pieces of characterisation of which Shakspeare alone furnishes us with examples. It is easy for the poet and the player to exhibit a caricature of national sentiments, modes of speaking, and gestures. Shylock, however, is every thing but a common Jew; he possesses a very determinate and original individuality, and yet we perceive a slight touch of Judaism in every thing which he says or does. We imagine we hear a sprinkling of the Jewish pronunciation in the mere written words, as we sometimes still find it in the higher classes, notwithstanding their social refinement. In tranquil situations what is foreign to the European blood and Christian sentiments is less perceivable, but in passion the national stamp appears more strongly marked. All these inimitable niceties the finished art of a great actor can alone properly express. Shylock is a man of information, even a thinker in his own way; he has only not discovered the region where human feelings dwell: his morality is founded on the disbelief in goodness and magnanimity. The desire of revenging the oppressions and humiliations suffered by his nation is, after avarice, his principal spring of action. His hate is naturally directed chiefly against those Christians who possess truly Christian sentiments: the example of disinterested love of our neighbour seems to him the most unrelenting persecution of the Jews. The letter of the law is his idol; he refuses to lend an ear to the voice of mercy, which speaks to him from the mouth of Portia with heavenly eloquence: he insists on severe and inflexible justice, and it at last recoils on his own head. Here he becomes a symbol of the general history of his unfortunate nation. The melancholy and self-neglectful magnanimity of Antonio is affectingly sublime. Like a royal merchant, he is surrounded with a whole train of noble friends. The contrast which this forms to the selfish cruelty of the usurer Shylock, was necessary to redeem the honour of human nature. The judgment scene with which the fourth act is occupied is alone a perfect drama, concentrating in itself the interest of the whole. The knot is now untied, and according to the common idea the curtain might drop. But the poet was unwilling to dismiss his audience with the gloomy impressions which the delivery of Antonio, accomplished with so much difficulty, contrary to all expectation, and the punishment of Shylock, were calculated to leave behind: he has therefore added the fifth act by way of a musical after-piece in the play itself. The episode of Jessica, the fugitive daughter of the Jew, in whom Shakspeare has contrived to throw a disguise of sweetness over the national features, and the artifice by which Portia and her companion are enabled to rally their newly married husbands supply him with materials."

"The scene opens with the playful prattling of two lovers in a summer moonlight,

'When the sweet wind did gently kiss the trees.'

It is followed by soft music and a rapturous eulogy on this powerful disposer of the human mind and the world; the principal characters then make their appearance, and after an assumed dissension, which is elegantly carried on, the whole ends with the most exhilarating mirth."

Malone places the date of the composition of this play in 1598, Chalmers supposed it to have been written in 1597, and to this opinion Dr. Drake gives his sanction.

It appears, from a passage in Stephen Gosson's School of Abuse, &c. 1579, that a play comprehending the distinct plots of Shakpeare's Merchant of Venice had been exhibited long before he commenced writer. Gosson, making some exceptions to his condemnation of dramatic performances, mentions among others:—'*The Jew* shown at the Bull, representing the greediness of worldly choosers, and the bloody minds of usurers.—These plays,' continues he, 'are good and sweete plays.'

It cannot be doubted that Shakspeare, as in other instances, availed himself of this ancient piece. Mr. Douce observes, 'that the author of the old play of *The Jew*, and Shakspeare in his Merchant of Venice, have not confined themselves to one source only in the construction of their plot, but that the *Pecorone*, the *Gesta Romanorum*, and perhaps the old ballad of *Gernutus*, have been respectively resorted to.' It is however most probable that the original play was indebted chiefly, if not altogether, to the *Gesta Romanorum*, which contained both the main incidents; and that Shakspeare expanded and improved them, partly from his own genius, and partly as to the bond from the *Pecorone*, where the coincidences are too manifest to leave any doubt. Thus the scene being laid at Venice; the residence of the lady at Belmont; the introduction of the person bound for the principal; the double infraction of the bond, viz. the taking more or less than a pound of flesh, and the shedding of blood, together with the after incident of the ring, are common to the novel and the play. The whetting of the knife might perhaps be taken from the ballad of *Gernutus*. Shakspeare was likewise indebted to an authority that could not have occurred to the original author of the play in an English form; this was Silvayn's *Orator*, as translated by Munday. From that work Shylock's reasoning before the senate is evidently borrowed; but at the same time it has been most skilfully improved.*

There are two distinct collections under the title of *Gesta Romanorum*. The one has been frequently printed in *Latin*, but never in English; there is however a manuscript version, of the reign of Henry the Sixth, among the Harleian MSS. in the British Museum. This collection seems to have originally furnished the story of the *bond*. The other *Gesta* has never been printed in Latin, but a portion of it has been several times printed in *English*. The earliest edition referred to by Warton and Doctor Farmer, is by Wynken de Worde, without date, but of the beginning of the sixteenth century. It was long doubted whether this early edition existed, but it has recently been described in the Retrospective Review. The latter part of the thirty-second history in this collection may have furnished the incidents of the *caskets*.

But as many of the incidents in the *bond* story of the Merchant of Venice have a more striking resemblance to the first tale of the fourth day of the *Pecorone* of *Ser Giovanni*, this part of the plot was most probably taken immediately from thence. The story may have been extant in English in Shakspeare's time, though it has not hitherto been discovered.

The Pecorone was first printed in 1550 (not 1558, as erroneously stated by Mr. Steevens,) but was written almost two centuries before.

After all, unless we could recover the old play of The Jew mentioned by Gosson, it is idle to conjecture how far Shakspeare improved upon the plot of that piece The various materials which may have contributed to furnish the complicated plot of Shakspeare's play are to be found in the Variorum Editions, and in Mr. Douce's very interesting work.

---

* "The Orator, handling a hundred several Discourses, in form of Declamations, &c. written in French by Alexander Silvayn, and Englished by L. P. (Lazarus Pyol, i. e. Anthony Munday,) London, Printed by Adam Islip, 1596." Declamation 95. 'Of a Jew who would for his debt have a pound of flesh of a Christian

PERSONS REPRESENTED.[1]

DUKE of Venice.
Prince of Morocco, } *Suitors to* Portia.
Prince of Arragon, }
ANTONIO, *the Merchant of* Venice.
BASSANIO, *his Friend.*
SALANIO, }
SALARINO, } *Friends to* Antonio *and* Bassanio.
GRATIANO, }
LORENZO, *in love with* Jessica.
SHYLOCK, *a Jew.*
TUBAL, *a Jew, his Friend.*
LAUNCELOT GOBBO, *a Clown, Servant to* Shylock.
OLD GOBBO, *Father to* Launcelot.

SALERIO, *a Messenger from* Venice.
LEONARDO, *Servant to* Bassanio.
BALTHAZAR, } *Servants to* Portia.
STEPHANO, }

PORTIA, *a rich Heiress.*
NERISSA, *her Waiting-Maid.*
JESSICA, *Daughter to* Shylock.

Magnificoes of Venice, Officers *of the Court of Justice,* Jailer, Servants, *and other* Attendants.

SCENE, *partly at* Venice, *and partly at* Belmont, *the Seat of* Portia, *on the Continent.*

ACT I.

SCENE I. Venice. *A Street. Enter* ANTONIO, SALARINO, *and* SALANIO.

Antonio.

IN sooth, I know not why I am so sad;
It wearies me; you say, it wearies you;
But how I caught it, found it, or came by it,
What stuff 'tis made of, whereof it is born,
I am to learn;
And such a want-wit sadness makes of me,
That I have much ado to know myself.
Salar. Your mind is tossing on the ocean;
There, where your argosies[2] with portly sail,—
Like signiors and rich burghers on the flood,
Or, as it were the pageants of the sea,—
Do overpeer the petty traffickers,
That curt'sy to them, do them reverence,
As they fly by them with their woven wings.
Salan. Believe me, sir, had I such venture forth,
The better part of my affections would
Be with my hopes abroad. I should be still
Plucking the grass, to know where sits the wind;
Peering in maps, for ports, and piers, and roads;
And every object that might make me fear
Misfortune to my ventures, out of doubt,
Would make me sad.
Salar. My wind, cooling my broth,
Would blow me to an ague, when I thought,
What harm a wind too great might do at sea.
I should not see the sandy hour-glass run,
But I should think of shallows and of flats;
And see my wealthy Andrew dock'd in sand,
Vailing[3] her high-top lower than her ribs,
To kiss her burial. Should I go to church,
And see the holy edifice of stone,
And not bethink me straight of dangerous rocks;
Which touching but my gentle vessel's side,
Would scatter all her spices on the stream;
Enrobe the roaring waters with my silks;
And, in a word, but even now worth this,
And now worth nothing? Shall I have the thought
To think on this; and shall I lack the thought,
That such a thing, bechanc'd, would make me sad?
But, tell not me; I know, Antonio
Is sad to think upon his merchandise.
Ant. Believe me, no: I thank my fortune for it,
My ventures are not in one bottom trusted,
Nor to one place; nor is my whole estate
Upon the fortune of this present year:
Therefore, my merchandise makes me not sad.
Salan. Why, then you are in love.
Ant. Fye, fye!
Salan. Not in love neither? Then let's say, you are sad,
Because you are not merry: and 'twere as easy
For you, to laugh, and leap, and say, you are merry,
Because you are not sad. Now, by two-headed Janus,
Nature hath fram'd strange fellows in her time:
Some that will evermore peep through their eyes,
And laugh, like parrots, at a bag-piper;
And other of such vinegar aspect,
That they'll not show their teeth in way of smile,
Though Nestor swear the jest be laughable.

Enter BASSANIO, LORENZO, *and* GRATIANO.

Salan. Here comes Bassanio, your most noble kinsman,
Gratiano, and Lorenzo: Fare you well;
We leave you now with better company.
Salar. I would have staid till I had made you merry,
If worthier friends had not prevented me.
Ant. Your worth is very dear in my regard,
I take it, your own business calls on you,
And you embrace the occasion to depart.
Salar. Good morrow, my good lords.
Bass. Good signiors both, when shall we laugh? say, when?
You grow exceeding strange: Must it be so?
Salar. We'll make our leisures to attend on yours.
[*Exeunt* SALAR. *and* SALAN.
Lor. My lord Bassanio, since you have found Antonio,
We two will leave you: but, at dinner time,
I pray you, have in mind where we must meet.
Bass. I will not fail you.
Gra. You look not well, signior Antonio;
You have too much respect upon the world:
They lose it, that do buy it with much care.
Believe me, you are marvellously chang'd.
Ant. I hold the world but as the world, Gratiano;
A stage, where every man must play a part,
And mine a sad one.
Gra. Let me play the fool:
With mirth and laughter let old wrinkles come;
And let my liver rather heat with wine,
Than my heart cool with mortifying groans.
Why should a man, whose blood is warm within,
Sit like his grandsire cut in alabaster?
Sleep when he wakes? and creep into the jaundice
By being peevish? I tell thee what, Antonio,—
I love thee, and it is my love that speaks;—
There are a sort of men, whose visages
Do cream and mantle, like a standing pond;
And do a wilful[4] stillness entertain,
With purpose to be dress'd in an opinion
Of wisdom, gravity, profound conceit;
As who should say, *I am Sir Oracle,*

1 This enumeration of the Dramatis Personæ is by Mr. Rowe.
2 *Argosies* are large ships either for merchandise or war. The word has been supposed to be derived from the classical ship *Argo*, as a vessel eminently famous; and this seems the more probable from *Argis* being used for a ship in low Latin.
3 To *vail* is to *lower*, to *let fall*. From the French *avaler*.
4 i. e. an obstinate silence.

And, when I ope my lips, let no dog bark!
O, my Antonio, I do know of these,
That therefore only are reputed wise,
For saying nothing; who, I am very sure,
If they should speak, would almost damn those ears,
Which, hearing them, would call their brothers fools.
I'll tell thee more of this another time:
But fish not, with this melancholy bait,
For this fool's gudgeon, this opinion.—
Come, good Lorenzo:—Fare ye well, awhile;
I'll end my exhortation after dinner.

Lor. Well, we will leave you then till dinner-time:
I must be one of these same dumb wise men,
For Gratiano never lets me speak.

Gra. Well, keep me company but two years more,
Thou shalt not know the sound of thine own tongue.

Ant. Farewell: I'll grow a talker for this gear.[1]

Gra. Thanks, i'faith; for silence is only commendable
In a neat's tongue dried, and a maid not vendible.
[*Exeunt* GRA. *and* LOR.

Ant. Is that any thing now?

Bass. Gratiano speaks an infinite deal of nothing, more than any man in all Venice: His reasons are as two grains of wheat hid in two bushels of chaff; you shall seek all day ere you find them; and, when you have them, they are not worth the search.

Ant. Well; tell me now, what lady is this same
To whom you swore a secret pilgrimage,
That you to-day promis'd to tell me of?

Bass. 'Tis not unknown to you, Antonio,
How much I have disabled mine estate,
By something showing a more swelling port[2]
Than my faint means would grant continuance:
Nor do I now make moan to be abridg'd
From such a noble rate; but my chief care
Is, to come fairly off from the great debts,
Wherein my time, something too prodigal,
Hath left me gaged: To you, Antonio,
I owe the most in money, and in love;
And from your love I have a warranty
To unburthen all my plots, and purposes,
How to get clear of all the debts I owe.

Ant. I pray you, good Bassanio, let me know it;
And, if it stand, as you yourself still do,
Within the eye of honour, be assur'd,
My purse, my person, my extremest means,
Lie all unlock'd to your occasions.

Bass. In my school-days, when I had lost one shaft,
I shot his fellow of the selfsame flight[3]
The selfsame way, with more advised watch,
To find the other forth; and, by advent'ring both,
I oft found both: I urge this childhood proof,
Because what follows is pure innocence.
I owe you much: and, like a wilful youth,
That which I owe is lost: but if you please
To shoot another arrow that self way
Which you did shoot the first, I do not doubt,
As I will watch the aim, or to find both,
Or bring your latter hazard back again,
And thankfully rest debtor for the first.

Ant. You know me well; and herein spend but time,
To wind about my love with circumstance;
And out of doubt, you do me now more wrong,
In making question of my uttermost,
Than if you had made waste of all I have:
Then do but say to me what I should do,
That in your knowledge may by me be done,
And I am prest[4] unto it: therefore, speak.

Bass. In Belmont is a lady richly left,
And she is fair, and, fairer than that word,
Of wondrous virtues: sometimes[5] from her eyes
I did receive fair speechless messages:
Her name is Portia; nothing undervalued
To Cato's daughter, Brutus' Portia.
Nor is the wide world ignorant of her worth;
For the four winds blow in from every coast
Renowned suitors: and her sunny locks
Hang on her temples like a golden fleece;
Which makes her seat of Belmont, Colchos' strand
And many Jasons come in quest of her.
O my Antonio, had I but the means
To hold a rival place with one of them,
I have a mind presages me such thrift,
That I should questionless be fortunate.

Ant. Thou know'st, that all my fortunes are at sea;
Neither have I money, nor commodity
To raise a present sum: therefore go forth,
Try what my credit can in Venice do;
That shall be rack'd, even to the uttermost,
To furnish thee to Belmont, to fair Portia.
Go, presently inquire, and so will I,
Where money is; and I no question make,
To have it of my trust, or for my sake. [*Exeunt.*

SCENE II. Belmont. *A Room in* Portia's *House. Enter* PORTIA *and* NERISSA.

Por. By my troth, Nerissa, my little body is a-weary of this great world.

Ner. You would be, sweet madam, if your miseries were in the same abundance as your good fortunes are: And yet, for aught I see, they are as sick, that surfeit with too much, as they that starve with nothing: It is no mean happiness therefore, to be seated in the mean; superfluity comes sooner by white hairs,[6] but competency lives longer.

Por. Good sentences, and well pronounced.

Ner. They would be better if well followed.

Por. If to do were as easy as to know what were good to do, chapels had been churches, and poor men's cottages princes' palaces. It is a good divine that follows his own instructions: I can easier teach twenty what were good to be done, than be one of the twenty to follow mine own teaching. The brain may devise laws for the blood; but a hot temper leaps over a cold degree; such a hare is madness the youth, to skip o'er the meshes of good counsel the cripple. But this reasoning is not in the fashion to choose me a husband:—O me, the word choose! I may neither choose whom I would, nor refuse whom I dislike; so is the will of a living daughter curb'd by the will of a dead father: Is it not hard, Nerissa, that I cannot choose one, nor refuse none?

Ner. Your father was ever virtuous; and holy men, at their death, have good inspirations; therefore, the lottery, that he hath devised in these three chests, of gold, silver, and lead (whereof who chooses his meaning, chooses you,) will, no doubt, never be chosen by any rightly, but one who you shall rightly love. But what warmth is there in your affection towards any of these princely suitors that are already come?

Por. I pray thee over-name them; and as thou namest them, I will describe them; and, according to my description level at my affection.

Ner. First, there is the Neapolitan prince.[7]

Por. Ay, that's a colt,[8] indeed, for he doth nothing but talk of his horse; and he makes it a great appropriation to his own good parts, that he

1 *Gear* usually signifies *matter*, *subject*, or business in general. It is here, perhaps, a colloquial expression of no very determined import. It occurs again in this play, Act ii. Sc. 2: 'If Fortune be a woman, she's a good wench for *this gear.*'

2 *Port* is *state* or *equipage*. So in the Taming of a Shrew, Act i. Sc. 1.

'Thou shalt be master, Tranio, in my stead,
Keep house, and *port*, and servants, as I should.'

3 This method of finding a lost arrow is prescribed by P. Crescentius in his treatise De Agricultura, lib. x. c. xxviii. and is also mentioned in Howel's Letters, vol i. p. 183, edit. 1655, 12mo.

4 *Prest*, that is, *ready*; from the old French word of the same orthography, now *pret.*

5 Formerly.

6 i. e. superfluity sooner *acquires* white hairs; becomes old. We still say, how did he *come by* it?

7 The Neapolitans, in the time of Shakspeare, were eminently skilled in all that belongs to horsemanship.

8 *Colt* is used for a witless heady gay youngster whence the phrase used for an old man too juvenile that he still retains his *colt's tooth*

MERCHANT OF VENICE.

Act. I. Scene 3.

can shoe him himself: I am much afraid, my lady his mother played false with a smith.

Ner. Then, is there the county[1] Palatine.

Por. He doth nothing but frown; as who should say, *An if you will not have me, choose:* he hears merry tales, and smiles not: I fear, he will prove the weeping philosopher when he grows old, being so full of unmannerly sadness in his youth. I had rather be married to a death's head with a bone in his mouth, than to either of these. God defend me from these two!

Ner. How say you by the French lord, Monsieur Le Bon?

Por. God made him, and therefore let him pass for a man. In truth, I know it is a sin to be a mocker; But, he! why, he hath a horse better than the Neapolitan's; a better bad habit of frowning than the count Palatine: he is every man in no man: if a throstle[2] sing, he falls straight a capering; he will fence with his own shadow: If I should marry him, I should marry twenty husbands: if he would despise me, I would forgive him; for if he love me to madness, I shall never requite him.

Ner. What say you then to Faulconbridge, the young baron of England?

Por. You know, I say nothing to him; for he understands not me, nor I him: he hath neither Latin, French, nor Italian;[3] and you will come into the court and swear, that I have a poor penny-worth in the English. He is a proper man's[4] picture; But, alas! who can converse with a dumb show? How oddly he is suited! I think, he bought his doublet in Italy, his round hose in France, his bonnet in Germany, and his behaviour every where.

Ner. What think you of the Scottish lord, his neighbour?

Por. That he hath a neighbourly charity in him; for he borrowed a box of the ear of the Englishman, and swore he would pay him again, when he was able: I think, the Frenchman became his surety, and sealed under for another.

Ner. How like you the young German,[5] the Duke of Saxony's nephew?

Por. Very vilely in the morning, when he is sober; and most vilely in the afternoon, when he is drunk: when he is best, he is little worse than a man; and when he is worst, he is little better than a beast: and the worst fall that ever fell, I hope, I shall make shift to go without him.

Ner. If he should offer to choose, and choose the right casket, you should refuse to perform your father's will, if you should refuse to accept him.

Por. Therefore, for fear of the worst, I pray thee, set a deep glass of Rhenish wine on the contrary casket: for, if the devil be within, and that temptation without, I know he will choose it. I will do any thing, Nerissa, ere I will be married to a spunge.

Ner. You need not fear, lady, the having any of these lords; they have acquainted me with their determination: which is indeed, to return to their home, and to trouble you with no more suit; unless you may be won by some other sort than your father's imposition, depending on the caskets.

Por. If I live to be as old as Sibylla, I will die as chaste as Diana, unless I be obtained by the manner of my father's will; I am glad this parcel of wooers are so reasonable; for there is not one among them but I dote on his very absence, and I pray God grant them a fair departure.

Ner. Do you not remember, lady, in your father's time, a Venetian, a scholar, and a soldier, that came hither in company of the Marquis of Montferrat?

Por. Yes, yes, it was Bassanio; as I think, so was he called.

Ner. True, madam; he, of all the men that ever my foolish eyes looked upon, was the best deserving a fair lady.

Por. I remember him well; and I remember him worthy of thy praise.—How now! what news?

Enter a Servant.

Serv. The four strangers seek for you, madam, to take their leave: and there is a fore-runner come from a fifth, the Prince of Morocco; who brings word, the prince, his master, will be here to-night.

Por. If I could bid the fifth welcome with so good heart as I can bid the other four farewell, I should be glad of his approach: if he have the condition[6] of a saint, and the complexion of a devil, I had rather he should shrive me than wive me. Come, Nerissa.—Sirrah, go before.—Whiles we shut the gate upon one wooer, another knocks at the door. [*Exeunt.*

SCENE III. Venice. *A public Place.* *Enter* Bassanio *and* Shylock.

Shy. Three thousand ducats,—well.

Bass. Ay, sir, for three months.

Shy. For three months,—well.

Bass. For the which, as I told you, Antonio shall be bound.

Shy. Antonio shall become bound,—well.

Bass. May you stead me? Will you pleasure me? Shall I know your answer?

Shy. Three thousand ducats, for three months, and Antonio bound.

Bass. Your answer to that.

Shy. Antonio is a good man.

Bass. Have you heard any imputation to the contrary?

Shy. Ho, no, no, no, no;—my meaning, in saying he is a good man, is to have you understand me, that he is sufficient: yet his means are in supposition: he hath an argosy bound to Tripolis, another to the Indies; I understand moreover upon the Rialto, he hath a third at Mexico, a fourth for England,——and other ventures he hath, squander'd abroad: But ships are but boards, sailors but men: there be land-rats, and water-rats, water-thieves, and land-thieves; I mean, pirates; and then, there is the peril of waters, winds, and rocks: The man is, notwithstanding, sufficient;—three thousand ducats;—I think, I may take his bond.

Bass. Be assured you may.

Shy. I will be assured I may; and that I may be assured, I will bethink me: May I speak with Antonio?

Bass. If it please you to dine with us.

Shy. Yes, to smell pork; to eat of the habitation which your prophet, the Nazarite, conjured the devil into: I will buy with you, sell with you, talk with you, walk with you, and so following; but I will not eat with you, drink with you, nor pray with you. What news on the Rialto?—Who is he comes here?

Enter Antonio.

Bass. This is signior Antonio.

Shy. [*Aside.*] How like a fawning publican he looks!
I hate him for he is a Christian.
But more, for that, in low simplicity,
He lends out money gratis, and brings down
The rate of usance[7] here with us in Venice.

---

1 This is an allusion to the *Count* Albertus Alasco, a Polish Palatine, who was in London in 1583.

2 A *thrush;* properly the missel-thrush.

3 A satire on the ignorance of young English travellers in Shakspeare's time.

4 A *proper* man is a *handsome man.*

5 The Duke of Bavaria visited London, and was made a Knight of the Garter, in Shakspeare's time. Perhaps, in this enumeration of Portia's suitors, there may be some covert allusion to those of Queen Elizabeth.

6 i. e. the *nature, disposition.* So in Othello:
'—— and then of so gentle a *condition!*'

7 'It is almost incredible what gain the Venetians receive by the usury of the Jews, both privately and in common. For in every city the Jews keep open shops of usury, taking gages of ordinary for xv. in the hundred by the yeare; and if at the year's end the gage be not redeemed, it is forfeit, or at least done away to a

If I can catch him once upon the hip,[1]
I will feed fat the ancient grudge I bear him.
He hates our sacred nation; and he rails,
Even there where merchants most do congregate,
On me, my bargains, and my well-won thrift,
Which he calls interest: Cursed be my tribe,
If I forgive him.
Bass. Shylock, do you hear?
Shy. I am debating of my present store;
And, by the near guess of my memory,
I cannot instantly raise up the gross
Of full three thousand ducats: What of that?
Tubal, a wealthy Hebrew of my tribe,
Will furnish me: But soft; how many months
Do you desire?—Rest you fair, good signior; [*To* ANTONIO.
Your worship was the last man in our mouths.
Ant. Shylock, albeit I neither lend nor borrow,
By taking, nor by giving of excess,
Yet, to supply the ripe wants[2] of my friend,
I'll break a custom:—Is he yet possess'd,[3]
How much you would?
Shy. Ay, ay, three thousand ducats.
Ant. And for three months.
Shy. I had forgot,—three months, you told me so.
Well then, your bond; and, let me see,——But hear you;
Methought, you said, you neither lend nor borrow,
Upon advantage.
Ant. I do never use it.
Shy. When Jacob graz'd his uncle Laban's sheep,
This Jacob from our holy Abraham was
(As his wise mother wrought in his behalf,)
The third possessor; ay, he was the third.
Ant. And what of him? did he take interest?
Shy. No, not take interest; not, as you would say,
Directly interest: mark what Jacob did.
When Laban and himself were compromis'd,
That all the eanlings[4] which were streak'd, and pied,
Should fall as Jacob's hire; the ewes, being rank,
In the end of autumn turned to the rams:
And when the work of generation was
Between these woolly breeders in the act,
The skilful shepherd peel'd me certain wands,
And in the doing of the deed of kind,[5]
He stuck them up before the fulsome[6] ewes;
Who, then conceiving, did in eaning time
Fall party-colour'd lambs, and those were Jacob's.
This was a way to thrive, and he was blest;
And thrift is blessing, if men steal it not.
Ant. This was a venture, sir, that Jacob serv'd for;
A thing not in his power to bring to pass,
But sway'd, and fashion'd, by the hand of heaven.
Was this inserted to make interest good?
Or is your gold and silver, ewes and rams?
Shy. I cannot tell; I make it breed as fast:—
But note me, signior.
Ant. Mark you this, Bassanio,
The devil can cite scripture for his purpose.
An evil soul, producing holy witness,
Is like a villain with a smiling cheek;
A goodly apple rotten at the heart;
O, what a goodly outside falsehood[7] hath!
Shy. Three thousand ducats,—'tis a good round sum.
Three months from twelve, then let me see the rate.
Ant. Well, Shylock, shall we be beholden to you?
Shy. Signior Antonio, many a time and oft,
In the Rialto you have rated me
About my monies, and my usances:[8]
Still have I borne it with a patient shrug;
For sufferance is the badge of all our tribe:
You call me—misbeliever, cut-throat dog,
And spit upon my Jewish gaberdine,
And all for use of that which is mine own.
Well then, it now appears, you need my help.
Go to, then; you come to me, and you say,
Shylock, we would have monies; You say so;
You, that did void your rheum upon my beard,
And foot me, as you spurn a stranger cur
Over your threshold; monies is your suit
What shall I say to you? Should I not say,
Hath a dog money? is it possible,
A cur can lend three thousand ducats? or
Shall I bend low, and in a bondman's key
With 'bated breath, and whispering humbleness,
Say this,——
Fair sir, you spit on me on Wednesday last;
You spurn'd me such a day; another time
You call'd me—dog; and for these courtesies
I'll lend you thus much monies?
Ant. I am as like to call thee so again,
To spit on thee again, to spurn thee too.
If thou wilt lend this money, lend it not
As to thy friends; (for when did friendship take
A breed[9] for barren metal of his friend?)
But lend it rather to thine enemy;
Who, if he break, thou may'st with better face
Exact the penalty.
Shy. Why, look you, how you storm!
I would be friends with you, and have your love,
Forget the shames that you have stain'd me with,
Supply your present wants, and take no doit
Of usance for my monies, and you'll not hear me:
This is kind I offer.
Ant. This were kindness.
Shy. This kindness will I show:—
Go with me to a notary, seal me there
Your single bond; and, in a merry sport,
If you repay me not on such a day,
In such a place, such sum, or sums, as are
Express'd in the condition, let the forfeit
Be nominated for an equal pound
Of your fair flesh, to be cut off and taken
In what part of your body pleaseth me.
Ant. Content, in faith; I'll seal to such a bond,
And say, there is much kindness in the Jew.
Bass. You shall not seal to such a bond for me,
I'll rather dwell[10] in my necessity.
Ant. Why, fear not, man; I will not forfeit it;
Within these two months, that's a month before
This bond expires, I do expect return
Of thrice three times the value of this bond.
Shy. O father Abraham, what these Christians are;
Whose own hard dealings teaches them suspect
The thoughts of others! Pray you, tell me this;
If he should break his day, what should I gain
By the exaction of the forfeiture?
A pound of man's flesh, taken from a man,
Is not so estimable, profitable neither,
As flesh of muttons, beefs, or goats. I say,
To buy his favour, I extend this friendship:
If he will take it, so; if not, adieu;
And, for my love, I pray you wrong me not.
Ant. Yes, Shylock, I will seal unto this bond.

---

great disadvantage; by reason whereof the Jews are out of measure wealthy in those parts.'—*Thomas's Historye of Italye*, 1561, 4*to. f.* 77.

1 *To catch, or have, on the hip*, means *to have at an entire advantage.* The phrase seems to have originated from hunting, because, when the animal pursued is seized upon the hip, it is finally disabled from flight.

2 Wants *come to the height*, which admit no longer delay.

3 Informed.

4 Young lambs just dropt, or *ean'd.* This word is usually spelt *yean*, but the Saxon etymology demands *ean.* It is applied particularly to ewes.

5 i. e. of nature.

6 '*Fulsome*,' says Mr. Douce, 'has, doubtless, the same signification with the preceding epithet *rank.*' It is true that *rank* has sometimes the interpretation affixed to it of *rammish* in old Dictionaries, but there is also another meaning of the word which may be found in Baret's Alvearie, 1573, viz. *Fruitefull, ranck, battle*; Lat *fertilis.* This sense would also, I think, better accord with *fulsome*, if it could be shown to be a synonyme.

7 *Falsehood* here means knavery, treachery, as *truth* is sometimes used for honesty.

8 Interest.

9 i. e. *interest*, money *bred* from the principal.

10 i. e. *continue;* to *abide* has both the senses of *habitation* and *continuance.*

Shy. Then meet me forthwith at the notary's;
Give him direction for this merry bond,
And I will go and purse the ducats straight;
See to my house, left in the fearful[1] guard
Of an unthrifty knave; and presently
I will be with you. [*Exit.*

Ant. Hie thee, gentle Jew.
This Hebrew will turn Christian; he grows kind.

Bass. I like not fair terms, and a villain's mind.

Ant. Come on: in this there can be no dismay,
My ships come home a month before the day.
[*Exeunt.*

ACT II.

SCENE I. Belmont. *A Room in* Portia's *House.*

Flourish of Cornets.—Enter the Prince of Morocco, *and his Train;* PORTIA, NERISSA, *and other of her* Attendants.

Mor. Mislike me not for my complexion,
The shadow'd livery of the burnish'd sun,
To whom I am a neighbour, and near bred.
Bring me the fairest creature northward born,
Where Phœbus' fire scarce thaws the icicles,
And let us make incision[2] for your love,
To prove whose blood is reddest, his or mine.
I tell thee, lady, this aspect of mine
Hath fear'd[3] the valiant; by my love, I swear,
The best-regarded virgins of our clime
Have lov'd it too: I would not change this hue,
Except to steal your thoughts, my gentle queen.

Por. In terms of choice I am not solely led
By nice direction of a maiden's eyes:
Besides, the lottery of my destiny
Bars me the right of voluntary choosing:
But, if my father had not scanted me,
And hedg'd me by his wit, to yield myself
His wife, who wins me by that means I told you,
Yourself, renowned prince, then stood as fair,
As any comer I have looked on yet,
For my affection.

Mor. Even for that I thank you;
Therefore, I pray you, lead me to the caskets,
To try my fortune. By this scimitar,—
That slew the Sophy, and a Persian prince,
That won three fields of Sultan Solyman,—
I would out-stare the sternest eyes that look,
Out-brave the heart most daring on the earth,
Pluck the young suckling cubs from the she bear,
Yea, mock the lion when he roars for prey,
To win thee, lady: But, alas the while!
If Hercules, and Lichas, play at dice
Which is the better man, the greater throw
May turn by fortune from the weaker hand:
So is Alcides beaten by his page:
And so may I, blind fortune leading me,
Miss that which one unworthier may attain,
And die with grieving.

Por. You must take your chance;
And either not attempt to choose at all,
Or swear, before you choose,—if you choose wrong,
Never to speak to lady afterward
In way of marriage; therefore be advis'd.[4]

Mor. Nor will not; come, bring me unto my chance.

Por. First, forward to the temple; after dinner
Your hazard shall be made.

Mor. Good fortune then! [*Cornets.*
To make me blest, or cursed'st among men. [*Exeunt.*

SCENE II. Venice. *A Street.—Enter* LAUNCELOT GOBBO.[5]

Laun. Certainly my conscience will serve me to run from this Jew, my master: The fiend is at mine elbow; and tempts me, saying to me, *Gobbo, Launcelot Gobbo, good Launcelot, or good Gobbo, or good Launcelot Gobbo, use your legs, take the start, run away:* My conscience says,—*no; take heed, honest Launcelot; take heed, honest Gobbo; or,* as aforesaid, *honest Launcelot Gobbo; do not run; scorn running with thy heels:*[6] Well, the most courageous fiend bids me pack; *via!* says the fiend; *away!* says the fiend, *for the heavens;*[7] *rouse up a brave mind,* says the fiend, *and run.* Well, my conscience, hanging about the neck of my heart, says very wisely to me,—*my honest friend Launcelot, being an honest man's son,*—or rather an honest woman's son; for, indeed, my father did something smack, something grow to, he had a kind of taste;—well, my conscience says, *Launcelot, budge not; budge,* says the fiend; *budge not,* says my conscience: Conscience, say I, you counsel well; fiend, say I, you counsel well: to be ruled by my conscience, I should stay with the Jew my master, who, (God bless the mark!) is a kind of devil; and, to run away from the Jew, I should be ruled by the fiend, who, saving your reverence, is the devil himself: Certainly, the Jew is the very devil incarnation; and, in my conscience, my conscience is but a kind of hard conscience, to offer to counsel me to stay with the Jew: The fiend gives the more friendly counsel: I will run, fiend; my heels are at your commandment, I will run.

Enter old GOBBO,[8] *with a Basket.*

Gob. Master, young man, you, I pray you; which is the way to master Jew's?

Laun. [*Aside.*] O heavens, this is my true begotten father! who, being more than sand-blind,[9] high-gravel blind, knows me not:—I will try conclusions[10] with him.

Gob. Master young gentleman, I pray you, which is the way to master Jew's?

Laun. Turn up on your right hand, at the next turning, but, at the next turning of all, on your left; marry, at the very next turning, turn of no hand, but turn down indirectly to the Jew's house.

Gob. By God's sonties,[11] 'twill be a hard way to hit. Can you tell me whether one Launcelot, that dwells with him, dwell with him, or no?

Laun. Talk you of young master Launcelot?—Mark me now; [*aside.*] now will I raise the waters:—Talk you of young master Launcelot?

Gob. No master, sir, but a poor man's son: his father, though I say it, is an honest exceeding poor man, and, God be thanked, well to live.

Laun. Well, let his father be what he will, we talk of young master Launcelot.

Gob. Your worship's friend, and Launcelot, sir.

Laun. But I pray you *ergo,* old man, *ergo,* I beseech you; Talk you of young master Launcelot?

Gob. Of Launcelot, an't please your mastership.

---

1 *Fearful guard* is a guard that is not to be trusted, but gives cause of fear. To *fear* was anciently to *give* as well as *feel* terrors So in K. Henry IV. Part I.
'A mighty and a *fearful* head they are.'

2 To understand how the tawny prince, whose savage dignity is well supported, means to recommend himself by this challenge, it must be remembered that *red* blood is a traditionary sign of courage.

3 i. e. terrified.

4 i. e. *be considerate: advised* is the word opposite to rash.

5 The old copies read—*Enter the Clown alone;* and throughout the play this character is called the *Clown* at most of his entrances or exits.

6 'Scorn running with thy heels.' Mr. Steevens calls this *absurdity,* and introduces a brother critic, Sir Hugh Evans, to prove it. He inclines to the emendation of an arch-botcher of Shakspeare's text, who has proposed that we should read '*withe thy heels,*' i e. '*bind* them.' The poet's own authority ought to have taught Steevens better. In Much Ado about Nothing, we have 'O illegitimate construction! *I scorn that with my heels*'

7 *For the heavens* was merely a petty oath. To make the fiend conjure Launcelot to do a thing for *heaven's* sake is a specimen of that 'acute nonsense' which Barrow makes one of the species of wit, and which Shakspeare was sometimes very fond of.

8 It has been inferred from the name of Gobbo, that Shakspeare designed this character to be represented with a *hump-back.*

9 '*Sand-blind.* Having an imperfect sight, as if there was sand in the eye, *Myops.*'—*Holyoke's Dictionary.*

10 To try *conclusions,* was to put to the proof, in other words to try *experiments.*

11 God's *sonties* was probably a corruption of God's *saints,* in old language *sauntes: sante* and *sanctity*

Laun. *Ergo*, master Launcelot; talk not of master Launcelot, father; for the young gentleman (according to fates and destinies, and such odd sayings, the sisters three, and such branches of learning) is, indeed, deceased; or, as you would say, in plain terms, gone to heaven.

Gob. Marry, God forbid! the boy was the very staff of my age, my very prop.

Laun. Do I look like a cudgel, or a hovel-post, a staff, or a prop?—Do you know me, father?

Gob. Alack the day, I know you not, young gentleman: but, I pray you, tell me, is my boy (God rest his soul!) alive, or dead?

Laun. Do you not know me, father?

Gob. Alack, sir, I am sand-blind, I know you not.

Laun. Nay, indeed, if you had your eyes, you might fail of the knowing me: it is a wise father, that knows his own child. Well, old man, I will tell you news of your son: Give me your blessing: truth will come to light; murder cannot be hid long, a man's son may; but, in the end, truth will out.

Gob. Pray you, sir, stand up; I am sure, you are not Launcelot, my boy.

Laun. Pray you, let's have no more fooling about it, but give me your blessing; I am Launcelot, your boy that was, your son that is, your child that shall be.

Gob. I cannot think you are my son.

Laun. I know not what I shall think of that: but I am Launcelot, the Jew's man; and, I am sure, Margery, your wife, is my mother.

Gob. Her name is Margery, indeed: I'll be sworn, if thou be Launcelot, thou art mine own flesh and blood. Lord worship'd might he be! what a beard hast thou got! thou hast got more hair on thy chin, than Dobbin my thill-horse[1] has on his tail.

Laun. It should seem then, that Dobbin's tail grows backward; I am sure he had more hair on his tail, than I have on my face, when I last saw him.

Gob. Lord, how art thou changed! How dost thou and thy master agree? I have brought him a present; How 'gree you now?

Laun. Well, well; but, for mine own part, as I have set up my rest[2] to run away, so I will not rest till I have run some ground: my master's a very Jew: Give him a present! give him a halter: I am famish'd in his service; you may tell every finger I have with my ribs. Father, I am glad you are come; give me your present to one master Bassanio, who, indeed, gives rare new liveries; if I serve not him, I will run as far as God has any ground.—O rare fortune! here comes the man;—to him, father; for I am a Jew, if I serve the Jew any longer.

Enter BASSANIO, *with* LEONARDO, *and other Followers.*

Bass. You may do so;—but let it be so hasted, that supper be ready at the farthest by five of the clock: See these letters delivered; put the liveries to making; and desire Gratiano to come anon to my lodging. [*Exit a* Servant.

Laun. To him, father.

Gob. God bless your worship!

Bass. Gramercy; Would'st thou aught with me?

Gob. Here's my son, sir, a poor boy,———

Laun. Not a poor boy, sir, but the rich Jew's man; that would, sir, as my father shall specify,———

Gob. He hath a great infection, sir, as one would say, to serve———

Laun. Indeed, the short and the long is, I serve the Jew, and I have a desire, as my father shall specify,———

Gob. His master and he (saving your worship's reverence) are scarce cater-cousins:

Laun. To be brief, the very truth is, that the Jew having done me wrong, doth cause me, as my father, being I hope an old man, shall frutify unto you,———

Gob. I have here a dish of doves, that I would bestow upon your worship; and my suit is,———

Laun. In very brief, the suit is impertinent to myself, as your worship shall know by this honest old man; and, though I say it, though old man, yet poor man, my father.

Bass. One speak for both;—What would you?

Laun. Serve you, sir.

Gob. This is the very defect of the matter, sir.

Bass. I know thee well, thou hast obtain'd thy suit:

Shylock, thy master, spoke with me this day,
And hath preferr'd thee, if it be preferment,
To leave a rich Jew's service, to become
The follower of so poor a gentleman.

Laun. The old proverb is very well parted between my master Shylock and you, sir; you have the grace of God, sir, and he hath enough.

Bass. Thou speakest it well: Go, father, with thy son:—
Take leave of thy old master, and inquire
My lodging out:—Give him a livery,
[*To his Followers.*
More guarded[3] than his fellows: See it done.

Laun. Father, in:—I cannot get a service, no;—I have ne'er a tongue in my head.—Well; [*Looking on his palm.*] if any man in Italy have a fairer table;[4] which doth offer to swear upon a book, I shall have good fortune. Go to, here's a simple line of life! here's a small trifle of wives: Alas, fifteen wives is nothing; eleven widows, and nine maids, is a simple coming-in for one man: and then, to 'scape drowning thrice; and to be in peril of my life with the edge of a feather-bed:—here are simple 'scapes! Well, if fortune be a woman, she's a good wench for this gear.—Father, come; I'll take my leave of the Jew in the twinkling of an eye.
[*Exeunt* LAUNCELOT *and old* GOBBO.

Bass. I pray thee, good Leonardo, think on this;
These things being bought, and orderly bestow'd,
Return in haste, for I do feast to-night
My best esteem'd acquaintance; hie thee, go.

Leon. My best endeavours shall be done herein.

Enter GRATIANO.

Gra. Where is your master?

Leon. Yonder, sir, he walks.
[*Exit* LEONARDO.

Gra. Signior Bassanio,———

Bass. Gratiano!

Gra. I have a suit to you.

Bass. You have obtain'd it.

Gra. You must not deny me; I must go with you to Belmont.

Bass. Why, then you must;—But hear thee, Gratiano;
Thou art too wild, too rude, and bold of voice;—
Parts, that become thee happily enough,

have been proposed but apparently with less probability. Oaths of this kind are not unfrequent among our ancient writers. To avoid the crime of profane swearing, they sought to disguise the words by abbreviations, which ultimately lost even their similarity to the original phrase.

1 i. e. the *shaft*-horse, sometimes called the *thill*-horse.

2 'Set up my rest,' i. e. determined. See note on All's Well that Ends Well, Act ii. Sc. 2. Romeo and Juliet, Act iv. Sc. 5. Where it may be remarked that Shakspeare has again quibbled upon *rest*. 'The County Paris hath *set up his rest*, that you shall *rest* but little.'

3 i. e. ornamented. *Guards* were trimmings, facings, or other ornaments, such as gold and silver lace, applied upon a dress.

4 Mr. Tyrwhitt's explanation of this passage (which has much puzzled the commentators) seems the most plausible: Launcelot applauding himself for his success with Bassanio, and looking into the palm of his hand, which by fortune-tellers is called the *table*, breaks out into the following reflection:—'Well, if any man in Italy have a fairer table; which doth offer to swear upon a book, I shall have good fortune'—i. e. *a table* which doth *not only* promise *but* offer to swear upon a book *that* I shall have good fortune. He omits the conclusion of the sentence.

And in such eyes as ours appear not faults;
But where thou art not known, why, there they show
Something too liberal;[1]—pray thee, take pain
To allay with some cold drops of modesty[2]
Thy skipping spirit; lest, through thy wild behaviour,
I be misconstrued in the place I go to,
And lose my hopes.

Gra. Signior Bassanio, hear me:
If I do not put on a sober habit,
Talk with respect, and swear but now and then,
Wear prayer-books in my pocket, look demurely;
Nay more, while grace is saying, hood mine eyes
Thus with my hat,[3] and sigh, and say, amen;
Use all the observance of civility,
Like one well studied in a sad ostent[4]
To please his grandam, never trust me more.

Bass. Well, we shall see your bearing.[5]

Gra. Nay, but I bar to-night; you shall not gage me
By what we do to-night.

Bass. No, that were pity;
I would entreat you rather to put on
Your boldest suit of mirth, for we have friends
That purpose merriment: But fare you well,
I have some business.

Gra. And I must to Lorenzo, and the rest;
But we will visit you at supper-time. [*Exeunt.*

SCENE III. *The same. A Room in* Shylock's *House. Enter* JESSICA *and* LAUNCELOT.

Jess. I am sorry, thou wilt leave my father so;
Our house is hell, and thou, a merry devil,
Didst rob it of some taste of tediousness:
But fare thee well; there is a ducat for thee.
And, Launcelot, soon at supper shalt thou see
Lorenzo, who is thy new master's guest:
Give him this letter; do it secretly,
And so farewell; I would not have my father
See me talk with thee.

Laun. Adieu!—tears exhibit my tongue.—Most beautiful pagan,—most sweet Jew! If a Christian did not play the knave, and get thee, I am much deceived: But adieu! these foolish drops do somewhat drown my manly spirit; adieu! [*Exit.*

Jess. Farewell, good Launcelot.—
Alack, what heinous sin is it in me,
To be asham'd to be my father's child!
But though I am a daughter to his blood,
I am not to his manners: O Lorenzo,
If thou keep promise, I shall end this strife;
Become a Christian, and thy loving wife. [*Exit.*

SCENE IV. *The same. A Street. Enter* GRATIANO, LORENZO, SALARINO, *and* SALANIO.

Lor. Nay, we will slink away in supper-time;
Disguise us at my lodging, and return
All in an hour.

Gra. We have not made good preparation.

Salar. We have not spoke us yet of torch-bearers.

Salan. 'Tis vile, unless it may be quaintly order'd;
And better, in my mind, not undertook.

Lor. 'Tis now but four o'clock; we have two hours
To furnish us:—

Enter LAUNCELOT, *with a Letter.*

Friend Launcelot, what's the news?

Laun. An it shall please you to break up[6] this, it shall seem to signify.

Lor. I know the hand: in faith, 'tis a fair hand;
And whiter than the paper it writ on,
Is the fair hand that writ.

Gra. Love-news, in faith.

Laun. By your leave, sir.

Lor. Whither goest thou?

Laun. Marry, sir, to bid my old master the Jew to sup to-night with my new master the Christian.

Lor. Hold here, take this:—tell gentle Jessica,
I will not fail her;—speak it privately; go.—
Gentlemen, [*Exit* LAUNCELOT.
Will you prepare you for this masque to-night?
I am provided of a torch-bearer.

Salar. Ay, marry, I'll be gone about it straight.

Salan. And so will I.

Lor. Meet me, and Gratiano,
At Gratiano's lodging, some hour hence.

Salar. 'Tis good we do so.
[*Exeunt* SALAR. *and* SALAN.

Gra. Was not that letter from fair Jessica?

Lor. I must needs tell thee all: She hath directed,
How I shall take her from her father's house:
What gold, and jewels, she is furnish'd with;
What page's suit she hath in readiness.
If e'er the Jew her father come to heaven,
It will be for his gentle daughter's sake:
And never dare misfortune cross her foot,
Unless she do it under this excuse,—
That she is issue to a faithless Jew.
Come, go with me; peruse this, as thou goest
Fair Jessica shall be my torch-bearer. [*Exeunt.*

SCENE V. *The same. Before* Shylock's *House. Enter* SHYLOCK *and* LAUNCELOT.

Shy. Well, thou shalt see, thy eyes shall be thy judge,
The difference of old Shylock and Bassanio:—
What, Jessica!—thou shalt not gormandize,
As thou hast done with me;—What, Jessica!—
And sleep and snore, and rend apparel out;—
Why, Jessica, I say!

Laun. Why, Jessica!

Shy. Who bids thee call? I do not bid thee call.

Laun. Your worship was wont to tell me, I could do nothing without bidding.

Enter JESSICA.

Jes. Call you? What is your will?

Shy. I am bid[7] forth to supper, Jessica:
There are my keys:—But wherefore should I go?
I am not bid for love; they flatter me:
But yet I'll go in hate, to feed upon
The prodigal Christian.[8]—Jessica, my girl,
Look to my house: I am right loath to go:
There is some ill a brewing towards my rest,
For I did dream of money-bags to-night.

Laun. I beseech you, sir, go; my young master doth expect your reproach.

Shy. So do I his.

Laun. And they have conspired together.—I will not say, you shall see a masque; but if you do, then it was not for nothing that my nose fell a bleeding on Black-Monday[9] last at six o'clock i'the morning, falling out that year on Ash Wednesday was four year in the afternoon.

Shy. What! are there masques? Hear you me, Jessica:
Lock up my doors; and when you hear the drum,
And the vile squeaking of the wry-neck'd fife,
Clamber not you up to the casements then,
Nor thrust your head into the public street,
To gaze on Christian fools with varnish'd faces:
But stop my house's ears, I mean my casements:
Let not the sound of shallow foppery enter
My sober house.—By Jacob's staff, I swear,
I have no mind of feasting forth to-night;

1 Gross, licentious.

2 So in Hamlet:
'Upon the heat and flame of thy distemper
Sprinkle *cool* patience.'

3 It was anciently the custom to wear the hat on during the time of dinner.

4 i. e. grave appearance; *show* of staid and serious behaviour *Ostent* is a word very commonly used for *show* among old dramatic writers.

5 Carriage, deportment.

6 To break up was a term in carving.

7 Invited.

8 Shakspeare meant to heighten the malignity of Shylock's character by thus making him depart from his most settled resolve (that he will neither *eat, drink*, nor *pray* with Christians,) for the prosecution of his revenge

9 i. e. Easter-Monday. It was called Black-Monday from the severity of that day, April 4, 1360, which was so extraordinary that, of Edward the Third's soldiers, then before Paris, many died of the cold. Anciently a superstitious belief was annexed to the accident of *bleeding at the nose.*

But I will go.—Go you before me, sirrah;
Say, I will come.
Laun. I will go before, sir.—
Mistress, look out at window for all this;
There will come a Christian by,
Will be worth a Jewess' eye. [*Exit* Laun.
Shy. What says that fool of Hagar's offspring, ha?
Jes. His words were Farewell, mistress; nothing else.
Shy. The patch[1] is kind enough; but a huge feeder.
Snail-slow in profit, and he sleeps by day
More than the wild cat: drones hive not with me;
Therefore I part with him; and part with him
To one that I would have him help to waste
His borrow'd purse.—Well, Jessica, go in;
Perhaps I will return immediately;
Do, as I bid you,
Shut doors after you: fast bind, fast find;
A proverb never stale in thrifty mind. [*Exit.*
Jes. Farewell: and if my fortune be not crost,
I have a father, you a daughter, lost. [*Exit.*

SCENE VI. *The same. Enter* Gratiano *and* Salarino, *masqued.*

Gra. This is the pent-house, under which Lorenzo
Desir'd us to make stand.
Salar. His hour is almost past.
Gra. And it is marvel he out-dwells his hour,
For lovers ever run before the clock.
Salar. O, ten times faster Venus' pigeons[2] fly
To seal love's bonds new made, than they are wont,
To keep obliged faith unforfeited!
Gra. That ever holds: who riseth from a feast,
With that keen appetite that he sits down?
Where is the horse that doth untread again
His tedious measures with the unbated fire
That he did pace them first? All things that are,
Are with more spirit chased than enjoy'd.
How like a younker or a prodigal,
The scarfed[3] bark puts from her native bay,
Hugg'd and embraced by the strumpet wind![4]
How like the prodigal doth she return,
With over-weather'd ribs, and ragged sails,
Lean, rent, and beggar'd by the strumpet wind!

Enter Lorenzo.

Salar. Here comes Lorenzo;—more of this hereafter.
Lor. Sweet friends, your patience for my long abode;
Not I, but my affairs have made you wait;
When you shall please to play the thieves for wives,
I'll watch as long for you then.—Approach;
Here dwells my father Jew:—Ho! who's within?

Enter Jessica *above, in boy's clothes.*

Jes. Who are you! Tell me for more certainty,
Albeit I'll swear that I do know your tongue.
Lor. Lorenzo, and thy love.
Jes. Lorenzo, certain; and my love indeed;
For who love I so much? And now who knows,
But you, Lorenzo, whether I am yours?
Lor. Heaven, and thy thoughts are witness that thou art.
Jes. Here, catch this casket; it is worth the pains.
I am glad 'tis night, you do not look on me,
For I am much asham'd of my exchange;
But love is blind, and lovers cannot see
The pretty follies that themselves commit:
For if they could, Cupid himself would blush
To see me thus transformed to a boy.
Lor. Descend, for you must be my torch-bearer.
Jes. What, must I hold a candle to my shames?
They in themselves, good sooth, are too, too light.
Why, 'tis an office of discovery, love;
And I should be obscur'd.
Lor. So are you, sweet,
Even in the lovely garnish of a boy.
But come at once;
For the close night doth play the run-away,
And we are staid for at Bassanio's feast.
Jes. I will make fast the doors, and gild myself
With some more ducats, and be with you straight.
[*Exit from above.*
Gra. Now, by my hood, a gentile,[5] and no Jew.
Lor. Beshrew me, but I love her heartily:
For she is wise, if I can judge of her;
And fair she is, if that mine eyes be true;
And true she is, as she hath proved herself;
And therefore, like herself, wise, fair, and true,
Shall she be placed in my constant soul.

Enter Jessica, *below.*

What, art thou come?—On, gentlemen, away;
Our masquing mates by this time for us stay.
[*Exit with* Jessica *and* Salarino

Enter Antonio.

Ant. Who's there?
Gra. Signior Antonio?
Ant. Fye, fye, Gratiano! where are all the rest?
'Tis nine o'clock; our friends all stay for you:—
No masque to-night: the wind is come about,
Bassanio presently will go abroad:
I have sent twenty out to seek for you.
Gra. I am glad on't; I desire no more delight,
Than to be under sail and gone to-night. [*Exeunt.*

SCENE VII. Belmont. *A Room in* Portia's *House.—Flourish of Cornets. Enter* Portia, *with the* Prince of Morocco, *and both their Trains.*

Por. Go, draw aside the curtains, and discover
The several caskets to this noble prince:—
Now make your choice.
Mor. The first, of gold, who this inscription bears;—
Who chooseth me, shall gain what many men desire.
The second, silver, which this promise carries;—
Who chooseth me shall get as much as he deserves.
This third, dull lead, with warning all as blunt;
Who chooseth me, must give and hazard all he hath.
How shall I know if I do choose the right?
Por. The one of them contains my picture prince;
If you choose that, then I am yours withal.
Mor. Some god direct my judgment! Let me see,
I will survey the inscriptions back again:
What says this leaden casket?
Who chooseth me, must give and hazard all he hath.
Must give—For what? for lead? hazard for lead?
This casket threatens: Men, that hazard all,
Do it in hope of fair advantages:
A golden mind stoops not to shows of dross;
I'll then not give, nor hazard, aught for lead.
What says the silver, with her virgin hue?
Who chooseth me shall get as much as he deserves.
As much as he deserves?—Pause there, Morocco
And weigh thy value with an even hand:
If thou be'st rated by thy estimation,
Thou dost deserve enough; and yet enough
May not extend so far as to the lady;
And yet to be afeard of my deserving,
Were but a weak disabling of myself.
As much as I deserve!—Why, that's the lady:
I do in birth deserve her, and in fortunes,
In graces and in qualities of breeding;
But more than these, in love I do deserve.

---

1 i. e. fool or simpleton.

2 Johnson thought that lovers, who are sometimes called *turtles* or *doves* in poetry, were meant by Venus' *pigeons*. The allusion however, seems to be to the *doves* by which Venus's chariot is drawn: 'Venus drawn by *doves* is much more prompt to seal new bonds,' &c.

3 Gray evidently caught the imagery of this passage in his Bard, but dropt the allusion to the parable of the prodigal—
'Fair laughs the morn and soft the zephyr blows,
While proudly riding o'er the azure realm,
In gallant trim the gilded vessel goes;
Youth on the prow, and Pleasure at the helm;
Regardless of the sweeping whirlwind's sway,
That hush'd in grim repose expects his evening prey.'

4 So in Othello:
'The baudy wind, that kisses all it meets.'

5 A jest arising from the ambiguity of *Gentile*, which signifies both a *heathen* and *one well born*.

What if I stray'd no further, but chose here?—
Let's see once more this saying grav'd in gold:
Who chooseth me, shall gain what many men desire.
Why, that's the lady; all the world desires her.
From the four corners of the earth they come,
To kiss this shrine, this mortal breathing saint.
The Hyrcanian deserts, and the vasty wilds
Of wide Arabia, are as thorough-fares now,
For princes to come view fair Portia:
The watery kingdom, whose ambitious head
Spits in the face of heaven, is no bar
To stop the foreign spirits; but they come,
As o'er a brook, to see fair Portia.
One of these three contains her heavenly picture.
Is't like, that lead contains her? 'Twere damnation,
To think so base a thought; it were too gross
To rib[1] her cerecloth in the obscure grave.
Or shall I think, in silver, she's immur'd,
Being ten times undervalued[2] to try'd gold?
O sinful thought! Never so rich a gem
Was set in worse than gold. They have in England
A coin, that bears the figure of an angel
Stamped in gold; but that's insculp'd[3] upon;
But here an angel in a golden bed
Lies all within.—Deliver me the key;
Here do I choose, and thrive I as I may!

Por. There, take it, prince, and if my form lie there,
Then I am yours. [*He unlocks the golden casket.*

Mor. O hell! what have we here?
A carrion death, within whose empty eye
There is a written scroll: I'll read the writing.

All that glisters is not gold,
Often have you heard that told:
Many a man his life hath sold,
But my outside to behold:
Gilded tombs do worms infold.
Had you been as wise as bold,
Young in limbs, in judgment old,
Your answer had not been inscroll'd:[4]
Fare you well; your suit is cold.
Cold, indeed; and labour lost:
Then, farewell, heat; and welcome, frost.—
Portia, adieu! I have too griev'd a heart
To take a tedious leave: thus losers part. [*Exit.*

Por. A gentle riddance:——Draw the curtains, go;——
Let all of his complexion choose me so. [*Exeunt.*

SCENE VIII. Venice. *A Street. Enter* SALARINO *and* SALANIO.

Salar. Why, man, I saw Bassanio under sail;
With him is Gratiano gone along;
And in their ship, I am sure, Lorenzo is not.

Salan. The villain Jew with outcries rais'd the duke;
Who went with him to search Bassanio's ship.

Salar. He came too late, the ship was under sail;
But there the duke was given to understand,
That in a gondola were seen together
Lorenzo and his amorous Jessica:
Besides, Antonio certify'd the duke,
They were not with Bassanio in his ship.

Salan. I never heard a passion so confus'd,
So strange, outrageous, and so variable,
As the dog Jew did utter in the streets:
My daughter!—O my ducats!—O my daughter!
Fled with a Christian?—O my christian ducats!—
Justice! the law! my ducats, and my daughter!
A sealed bag, two sealed bags of ducats,
Of double ducats, stol'n from me by my daughter!
And jewels; two stones, two rich and precious stones,
Stol'n by my daughter! Justice! find the girl!
She hath the stones upon her, and the ducats!

Salar. Why, all the boys in Venice follow him,
Crying,—his stones, his daughter, and his ducats.

Salan. Let good Antonio look he keep his day,
Or he shall pay for this.

Salar. Marry, well remember'd
I reason'd[5] with a Frenchman yesterday;
Who told me,—in the narrow seas, that part
The French and English, there miscarried
A vessel of our country, richly fraught:
I thought upon Antonio, when he told me;
And wish'd in silence that it were not his.

Salan. You were best to tell Antonio what you hear;
Yet do not suddenly, for it may grieve him.

Salar. A kinder gentleman treads not the earth
I saw Bassanio and Antonio part:
Bassanio told him, he would make some speed
Of his return: he answer'd—*Do not so,*
Slubber[6] *not business for my sake, Bassanio,*
But stay the very riping of the time;
And for the Jew's bond, which he hath of me,
Let it not enter into your mind of love:
Be merry; and employ your chiefest thoughts
To courtship and such fair ostents[7] *of love*
As shall conveniently become you there:
And even there, his eye being big with tears,
Turning his face, he put his hand behind him,
And with affection wondrous sensible
He wrung Bassanio's hand, and so they parted.

Salan. I think, he only loves the world for him.
I pray thee, let us go, and find him out,
And quicken his embraced heaviness[8]
With some delight or other.

Salar. Do we so. [*Exeunt*

SCENE IX. Belmont. *A Room in* Portia's *House.*

Enter NERISSA, *with a* Servant.

Ner. Quick, quick, I pray thee, draw the curtain straight;
The prince of Arragon hath ta'en his oath,
And comes to his election presently.

Flourish of Cornets.

Enter the Prince of Arragon, PORTIA, *and their Trains.*

Por. Behold, there stand the caskets, noble prince:
If you choose that wherein I am contain'd,
Straight shall our nuptial rites be solemniz'd;
But if you fail, without more speech, my lord,
You must be gone from hence immediately.

Ar. I am enjoin'd by oath to observe three things:
First, never to unfold to any one
Which casket 'twas I chose; next, if I fail
Of the right casket, never in my life
To woo a maid in way of marriage; lastly,
If I do fail in fortune of my choice,
Immediately to leave you and be gone.

Por. To these injunctions every one doth swear,
That comes to hazard for my worthless self.

Ar. And so have I address'd[9] me: Fortune now
To my heart's hope!—Gold, silver, and base lead.
Who chooseth me, must give and hazard all he hath.
You shall look fairer, ere I give, or hazard.
What says the golden chest? ha! let me see:—
Who chooseth me, shall gain what many men desire.
What many men desire.—That many may be meant
By[10] the fool multitude, that choose by show,
Not learning more than the fond eye doth teach;
Which pries not to the interior, but, like the martlet,
Builds in the weather on the outward wall,
Even in the force[11] and road of casualty.
I will not choose what many men desire,
Because I will not jump[12] with common spirits,
And rank me with the barbarous multitudes.

---

1 Enclose.
2 i. e. if compared with tried gold. So before in Act i. Sc. 1.
'Her name is Portia, nothing *undervalued*
To Cato's daughter.'
3 Engraven.
4 i. e. *the answer you have got;* namely, '*Fare you well!*'
5 Conversed.
6 To slubber is to do a thing carelessly
7 Shows, tokens.
8 The heaviness he is fond of, or indulges.
9 Prepared.
10 *By* and *of* being synonymous, were used by our ancestors indifferently; Malone has adduced numerous instances of the use of *by*, in all of which, by substituting *of*, the sense is rendered clear to the modern reader.
11 Power.
12 To *jump* is to *agree* with

Why, then to thee, thou silver treasure-house;
Tell me once more what title thou dost bear:
Who chooseth me, shall get as much as he deserves;
And well said too: For who shall go about
To cozen fortune, and be honourable
Without the stamp of merit! Let none presume
To wear an undeserved dignity.
O, that estates, degrees, and offices,
Were not deriv'd corruptly! and that clear honour
Were purchased by the merit of the wearer!
How many then should cover, that stand bare?
How many be commanded, that command?
How much low peasantry would then be glean'd
From the true seed of honour! and how much honour
Pick'd from the chaff and ruin of the times,[1]
To be new varnish'd? Well, but to my choice:
Who chooseth me, shall get as much as he deserves;
I will assume desert;—Give me a key for this,
And instantly unlock my fortunes here.

Por. Too long a pause for that which you find there.

Ar. What's here? the portrait of a blinking idiot,
Presenting me a schedule. I will read it.
How much unlike art thou to Portia?
How much unlike my hopes, and my deservings?
Who chooseth me, shall have as much as he deserves.
Did I deserve no more than a fool's head?
Is that my prize? are my deserts no better?

Por. To offend, and judge, are distinct offices,
And of opposed natures.

Ar. What is here?

The fire seven times tried this;
Seven times tried that judgment is,
That did never choose amiss:
Some there be that shadows kiss;
Such have but a shadow's bliss:
There be fools alive, I wis,[2]
Silver'd o'er; and so was this.
Take what wife you will to bed,[3]
I will ever be your head:
So begone, sir, you are sped.
Still more fool I shall appear
By the time I linger here,
With one fool's head I came to woo,
But I go away with two.—
Sweet, adieu! I'll keep my oath,
Patiently to bear my wroath.[4]

[*Exeunt* Arragon, *and Train.*

Por. Thus hath the candle sing'd the moth.
O these deliberate fools! when they do choose,
They have the wisdom by their wit to lose.

Ner. The ancient saying is no heresy;—
Hanging and wiving goes by destiny.

Por. Come, draw the curtain, Nerissa.

Enter a Servant.

Serv. Where is my lady?

Por. Here; what would my lord?

Serv. Madam, there is alighted at your gate
A young Venetian, one that comes before
To signify the approaching of his lord:
From whom he bringeth sensible regreets;[5]
To wit, besides commends, and courteous breath,
Gifts of rich value; yet I have not seen
So likely an ambassador of love:
A day in April never came so sweet,
To show how costly summer was at hand.
As this fore-spurrer comes before his lord.

Por. No more, I pray thee; I am half afeard,
Thou wilt say anon, he is some kin to thee,
Thou spend'st such high-day[6] wit in praising him.—
Come, come, Nerissa; for I long to see
Quick Cupid's post, that comes so mannerly.

Ner. Bassanio, lord love, if thy will it be!

[*Exeunt.*

ACT III.

SCENE I. Venice. *A Street.* *Enter* Salanio *and* Salarino.

Salan. Now, what news on the Rialto?

Salar. Why, yet it lives there uncheck'd, that Antonio hath a ship of rich lading wreck'd on the narrow seas; the Goodwins, I think they call the place; a very dangerous flat, and fatal, where the carcasses of many a tall ship lie buried, as they say, if my gossip report be an honest woman of her word.

Salan. I would she were as lying a gossip in that, as ever knapp'd[7] ginger, or made her neighbours believe she wept for the death of a third husband. But it is true,—without any slips of prolixity, or crossing the plain highway of talk,—that the good Antonio, the honest Antonio,———O that I had a title good enough to keep his name company:—

Salar. Come, the full stop.

Salan. Ha,—what say'st thou?—Why the end is, he hath lost a ship.

Salar. I would it might prove the end of his losses!

Salan. Let me say amen betimes, lest the devil cross my prayer; for here he comes in the likeness of a Jew.—

Enter Shylock.

How now, Shylock? what news among the merchants?

Shy. You knew, none so well, none so well as you, of my daughter's flight.

Salar. That's certain; I, for my part, knew the tailor that made the wings she flew withal.

Salan. And Shylock, for his own part, knew the bird was fledg'd; and then it is the complexion of them all to leave the dam.

Shy. She is damn'd for it.

Salar. That's certain, if the devil may be her judge.

Shy. My own flesh and blood to rebel!

Salan. Out upon it, old carrion! rebels it at these years?

Shy. I say, my daughter is my flesh and blood.

Salar. There is more difference between thy flesh and hers, than between jet and ivory; more between your bloods, than there is between red wine and rhenish:—But tell us, do you hear whether Antonio have had any loss at sea or not?

Shy. There I have another bad match: a bankrupt, a prodigal, who dare scarce show his head on the Rialto;—a beggar, that used to come so smug upon the mart:—let him look to his bond: he was wont to call me usurer;—let him look to his bond: he was wont to lend money for a Christian courtesy:—let him look to his bond.

Salar. Why, I am sure, if he forfeit, thou wilt not take his flesh; What's that good for?

Shy. To bait fish withal: if it will feed nothing else, it will feed my revenge. He hath disgraced me, and hindered me of half a million; laughed at my losses, mocked at my gains, scorned my nation, thwarted my bargains, cooled my friends, heated mine enemies; and what's his reason? I am a Jew. Hath not a Jew eyes? hath not a Jew hands, organs, dimensions, senses, affections, passions? fed with the same food, hurt with the same weapons, subject to the same diseases, healed by the same means, warmed and cooled by the same winter and summer, as a Christian is? if you prick us, do we not bleed? if you tickle us, do we not laugh? if you poison us, do we not die? and if you wrong us, shall we not revenge? if we are like you in the rest, we will resemble you in that. If a Jew wrong a Christian, what is his humility: revenge; If a Christian wrong a Jew, what should his sufferance be by

1 The meaning is, how much meanness would be found among the great, and how much greatness among the mean.

2 Know.

3 The poet had forgotten that he who missed Portia was never to marry any other woman.

4 *Wroath* is used in some of the old writers for *misfortune* and is often spelt like *ruth* Caxton's Recuyell of the Historyes of Troye, 1471, has frequent instances of *wroth*.

5 Salutations.

6 So in the Merry wives of Windsor:
'——— He speaks holiday.'

7 To *knap* is to *break short*. The word occurs in the Common Prayer. 'He *knappeth* the spear in *sunder*. We still say '*snapp'd* short in two.'

Christian example? why, revenge. The villany you teach me, I will execute; and it shall go hard, but I will better the instruction.

Enter a Servant.

Serv. Gentlemen, my master Antonio is at his house, and desires to speak with you both.

Salar. We have been up and down to seek him.

Enter TUBAL.

Salan. Here comes another of the tribe; a third cannot be matched, unless the devil himself turn Jew. [*Exeunt* SALAN. SALAR. *and* Servant.

Shy. How now, Tubal, what news from Genoa? hast thou found my daughter?

Tub. I often came where I did hear of her, but cannot find her.

Shy. Why there, there, there, there! a diamond gone, cost me two thousand ducats in Frankfort! The curse never fell upon our nation till now; I never felt it till now:—two thousand ducats in that; and other precious, precious jewels.—I would, my daughter were dead at my foot, and the jewels in her ear! 'would she were hears'd at my foot, and the ducats in her coffin! No news of them?—Why, so:—and I know not what's spent in the search: Why, thou loss upon loss! the thief gone with so much, and so much to find the thief; and no satisfaction, no revenge: nor no ill luck stirring, but what lights o' my shoulders; no sighs, but o' my breathing; no tears, but o' my shedding.

Tub. Yes, other men have ill luck too; Antonio, as I heard in Genoa,—

Shy. What, what, what? ill luck, ill luck?

Tub. —hath an argosy cast away, coming from Tripolis.

Shy. I thank God, I thank God:—Is it true? is it true?

Tub. I spoke with some of the sailors that escaped the wreck.

Shy. I thank thee, good Tubal;—Good news, good news: ha! ha!—Where! in Genoa?

Tub. Your daughter spent in Genoa, as I heard, one night, fourscore ducats.

Shy. Thou stick'st a dagger in me:———I shall never see my gold again: Fourscore ducats at a sitting! fourscore ducats!

Tub. There came divers of Antonio's creditors in my company to Venice, that swear he cannot choose but break.

Shy. I am very glad of it; I'll plague him; I'll torture him; I am glad of it.

Tub. One of them showed me a ring, that he had of your daughter for a monkey.

Shy. Out upon her! Thou torturest me, Tubal: it was my turquoise;[1] I had it of Leah, when I was a bachelor: I would not have given it for a wilderness of monkeys.

Tub. But Antonio is certainly undone.

Shy. Nay, that's true, that's very true: Go, Tubal, fee me an officer, bespeak him a fortnight before: I will have the heart of him, if he forfeit; for were he out of Venice, I can make what merchandize I will: Go, go, Tubal, and meet me at our synagogue; go, good Tubal; at our synagogue, Tubal. [*Exeunt.*

SCENE II. Belmont. *A Room in* Portia's *House.*

Enter BASSANIO, PORTIA, GRATIANO, NERISSA, *and* Attendants. *The caskets are set out.*

Por. I pray you tarry; pause a day or two,
Before you hazard; for, in choosing wrong,
I lose your company; therefore, forbear a while:
There's something tells me, (but it is not love,)
I would not lose you: and you know yourself,
Hate counsels not in such a quality:
But lest you should not understand me well
(And yet a maiden hath no tongue but thought,)
I would detain you here some month or two,
Before you venture for me. I could teach you,
How to choose right, but then I am forsworn;
So will I never be: so may you miss me;
But if you do, you'll make me wish a sin,
That I had been forsworn. Beshrew your eyes,
They have o'erlook'd[2] me, and divided me;
One half of me is yours, the other half yours,——
Mine own, I would say; but if mine, then yours,
And so all yours: O! these naughty times
Put bars between the owners and their rights:
And so, though yours, not yours.—Prove it so,
Let fortune go to hell for it.—not I.
I speak too long; but 'tis to peize[3] the time;
To eke it, and to draw it out in length,
To stay you from election.

Bass. Let me choose:
For, as I am, I live upon the rack.

Por. Upon the rack, Bassanio? then confess
What treason there is mingled with your love.

Bass. None, but that ugly treason of mistrust,
Which makes me fear the enjoying of my love:
There may as well be amity and life
'Tween snow and fire, as treason and my love.

Por. Ay, but, I fear, you speak upon the rack,
Where men enforced do speak any thing.

Bass. Promise me life, and I'll confess the truth.

Por. Well then, confess, and live.

Bass. Confess, and love,
Had been the very sum of my confession:
O happy torment, when my torturer
Doth teach me answers for deliverance!
But let me to my fortune and the caskets.

Por. Away then: I'm lock'd in one of them;
If you do love me, you will find me out.—
Nerissa, and the rest, stand all aloof.—
Let music sound, while he doth make his choice;
Then, if he lose, he makes a swan-like end,[4]
Fading in music: that the comparison
May stand more proper, my eye shall be the stream,
And wat'ry death-bed for him: He may win;
And what is music then! then music is
Even as the flourish when true subjects bow
To a new-crowned monarch; such it is,
As are those dulcet sounds in break of day,
That creep into the dreaming bridegroom's ear,
And summon him to marriage. Now he goes,
With no less presence,[5] but with much more love,
Than young Alcides, when he did redeem
The virgin-tribute paid by howling Troy
To the sea-monster;[6] I stand for sacrifice
The rest aloof are the Dardanian wives,
With bleared visages, come forth to view
The issue of the exploit. Go, Hercules
Live thou, I live:—With much much more dismay
I view the fight, than thou that mak'st the fray.

Music, whilst BASSANIO *comments on the caskets to himself.*

SONG.

1. *Tell me, where is fancy*[7] *bred,*
Or in the heart, or in the head?
How begot, how nourished?
REPLY, REPLY.
2. *It is engender'd in the eyes,*
With gazing fed; and fancy dies
In the cradle where it lies;
Let us all ring fancy's knell;
I'll begin it,——Ding, dong, bell.
All. *Ding, dong, bell.*

1 The *Turquoise* is a well known precious stone found in the veins of the mountains on the confines of Persia to the east. In old times its value was much enhanced by the magic properties attributed to it in common with other precious stones, one of which was that it faded or brightened its hue as the health of the wearer increased or grew less.

2 To be *o'erlook'd*, forelooked, or eye-bitten, was a term for being *bewitched* by an *evil eye*

3 To *peize* is from *peser*, Fr. To *weigh* or *balance*

4 Alluding to the opinion which long prevailed, that the swan uttered a plaintive musical sound at the approach of death; there is something so touching in this ancient superstition that one feels loath to be undeceived

5 i. e. dignity of mien.

6 See Ovid. Metamorph. lib. xi. ver. 199. Malone says, Shakspeare had read the account of this adventure in the Old Legend of the Destruction of Troy

7 Love

Bass.—So may the outward shows be least themselves;
The world is still deceiv'd with ornament.[1]
In law, what plea so tainted and corrupt,
But, being season'd with a gracious[2] voice,
Obscures the show of evil? In religion,
What damned error, but some sober brow
Will bless it, and approve it[3] with a text,
Hiding the grossness with fair ornament?
There is no vice so simple, but assumes
Some mark of virtue on his outward parts.
How many cowards, whose hearts are all as false
As stairs of sand, wear yet upon their chins
The beards of Hercules, and frowning Mars;
Who, inward search'd, have livers white as milk?
And these assume but valour's excrement,[4]
To render them redoubted. Look on beauty,
And you shall see 'tis purchas'd by the weight;
Which therein works a miracle in nature,
Making them lightest that wear most of it:
So are those crisped snaky golden locks,
Which make such wanton gambols with the wind,
Upon supposed fairness, often known
To be the dowry of a second head,
The scull that bred them, in the sepulchre.[5]
Thus ornament is but the guiled[6] shore
To a most dangerous sea; the beauteous scarf
Veiling an Indian beauty; in a word,
The seeming truth which cunning times put on
To entrap the wisest. Therefore, thou gaudy gold,
Hard food for Midas, I will none of thee:
Nor none of thee, thou pale and common drudge[7]
'Tween man and man: but thou, thou meagre lead,
Which rather threat'nest, than dost promise aught,
Thy paleness[8] moves me more than eloquence,
And here choose I; Joy be the consequence!

Por. How all the other passions fleet to air,
As doubtful thoughts, and rash-embrac'd despair,
And shudd'ring fear and green-ey'd jealousy.
O love, be moderate, allay thy ecstacy,
In measure rain thy joy, scant this excess;
I feel too much thy blessing, make it less,
For fear I surfeit!

Bass. What find I here?
[*Opening the leaden casket.*
Fair Portia's counterfeit?[9] What demi-god
Hath come so near creation? Move these eyes?
Or whether, riding on the balls of mine,
Seem they in motion? Here are sever'd lips,
Parted with sugar breath; so sweet a bar
Should sunder such sweet friends: Here in her hairs
The painter plays the spider; and hath woven
A golden mesh to entrap the hearts of men,
Faster than gnats in cobwebs: But her eyes,—
How could he see to do them? having made one,
Methinks it should have power to steal both his,
And leave itself unfurnish'd:[10] Yet look, how far
The substance of my praise doth wrong this shadow
In underprizing it, so far this shadow
Doth limp behind the substance.—Here's the scroll,
The continent and summary of my fortune.

You that choose not by the view,
Chance as fair, and choose as true!
Since this fortune falls to you,
Be content and seek no new.
If you be well pleas'd with this,
And hold your fortune for your bliss,
Turn you where your lady is,
And claim her with a loving kiss.

A gentle scroll: Fair lady, by your leave:
[*Kissing her*
I come by note, to give, and to receive,
Like one of two contending in a prize,
That thinks he hath done well in people's eyes,
Hearing applause, and universal shout,
Giddy in spirit, still gazing, in a doubt
Whether those peals of praise be his or no,
So, thrice fair lady, stand I, even so;
As doubtful whether what I see be true,
Until confirm'd, sign'd, ratified by you.

Por. You see me, lord Bassanio, where I stand,
Such as I am: though, for myself alone,
I would not be ambitious in my wish,
To wish myself much better; yet, for you,
I would be trebled twenty times myself;
A thousand times more fair, ten thousand times
More rich;
That only to stand high on your account,
I might in virtues, beauties, livings, friends,
Exceed account: but the full sum of me
Is sum of something;[11] which, to term in gross,
Is an unlesson'd girl, unschool'd, unpractis'd:
Happy in this, she is not yet so old
But she may learn; happier than this,
She is not bred so dull but she can learn,
Happiest of all, is, that her gentle spirit
Commits itself to yours to be directed,
As from her lord, her governor, her king.
Myself, and what is mine, to you, and yours
Is now converted: but now I was the lord
Of this fair mansion, master of my servants,
Queen o'er myself; and even now, but now,
This house, these servants, and this same myself,
Are yours, my lord; I give them with this ring;
Which when you part from, lose, or give away,
Let it presage the ruin of your love,
And be my vantage to exclaim on you.

Bass. Madam, you have bereft me of all words,
Only my blood speaks to you in my veins:
And there is such confusion in my powers,
As, after some oration fairly spoke
By a beloved prince, there doth appear
Among the buzzing pleased multitude:
Where every something, being blent together,
Turns to a wild of nothing, save of joy,
Express'd, and not express'd: But when this ring
Parts from this finger, then parts life from hence;
O, then be bold to say, Bassanio's dead.

Ner. My lord and lady, it is now our time,
That have stood by, and seen our wishes prosper
To cry, good joy; Good joy, my lord, and lady!

Gra. My lord Bassanio, and my gentle lady,
I wish you all the joy that you can wish;
For, I am sure, you can wish none from me:[12]
And, when your honours mean to solemnize
The bargain of your faith, I do beseech you,
Even at that time I may be married too.

Bass. With all my heart, so thou canst get a wife.

Gra. I thank your lordship; you have got me one.
My eyes, my lord, can look as swift as yours:
You saw the mistress, I beheld the maid;
You lov'd, I lov'd; for intermission[13]
No more pertains to me, my lord, than you.
Your fortune stood upon the caskets there;
And so did mine too, as the matter falls
For wooing here, until I sweat again;
And swearing, till my very roof was dry
With oaths of love: at last,—if promise last,—
I got a promise of this fair one here,
To have her love, provided that your fortune

---

1 Bassanio begins abruptly, the first part of the argument has passed in his mind.

2 Pleasing; winning favour. 3 i. e. justify it.

4 That is, what a little higher is called the *beard* of Hercules. *Excrement*, from *excresco*, is used for every thing which appears to grow or vegetate upon the human body, as the hair, the beard, the nails.

5 Shakspeare has also satirized this fashion of false hair in Love's Labour's Lost.

6 *Guiled* for *guiling*, or *treacherous*.

7 I could wish to read
'—— thou *stale* and common drudge:'
for so I think the poet wrote.

8 In order to avoid the repetition of the epithet *pale* Warburton altered this to *plainness*, and he has been followed in the modern editions, but the reading of the old copy, which I have restored, is the true one.

9 *Counterfeit* anciently signified a *likeness*, a *resemblance*.

10 i. e. unfurnished with a companion or fellow.

11 The folio reads, 'Is sum of *nothing*,' which may probably be the true reading, as it is Portia's intention, in this speech, to undervalue herself.

12 That is, none *away from* me; none that I shall lose, if you gain it.

13 Pause delay

Achiev'd her mistress.
Por. Is this true, Nerissa?
Ner. Madam, it is, so you stand pleas'd withal.
Bass. And do you, Gratiano, mean good faith?
Gra. Yes, 'faith, my lord.
Bass. Our feast shall be much honour'd in your marriage.
Gra. We'll play with them, the first boy for a thousand ducats.
Ner. What, and stake down?
Gra. No; we shall ne'er win at that sport, and stake down.——
But who comes here? Lorenzo, and his infidel?
What, and my old Venetian friend, Salerio?

Enter LORENZO, JESSICA, *and* SALERIO.

Bass. Lorenzo, and Salerio, welcome hither?
If that the youth of my new interest here
Have power to bid you welcome:—By your leave,
I bid my very friends and countrymen,
Sweet Portia, welcome.
Por. So do I, my lord;
They are entirely welcome.
Lor. I thank your honour: For my part, my lord,
My purpose was not to have seen you here;
But meeting with Salerio by the way,
He did entreat me, past all saying nay,
To come with him along.
Sale. I did, my lord,
And I have reason for it. Signior Antonio
Commends him to you. [*Gives* BASSANIO *a letter.*
Bass. Ere I ope his letter,
I pray you, tell me how my good friend doth.
Sale. Not sick, my lord, unless it be in mind;
Nor well, unless in mind: his letter there
Will show you his estate.
Gra. Nerissa, cheer yon stranger; bid her welcome.
Your hand, Salerio; What's the news from Venice?
How doth that royal merchant, good Antonio?
I know, he will be glad of our success;
We are the Jasons, we have won the fleece.
Sale. 'Would you had won the fleece that he hath lost!
Por. There are some shrewd contents in yon' same paper,
That steal the colour from Bassanio's cheek:
Some dear friend dead: else nothing in the world
Could turn so much the constitution
Of any constant[1] man. What, worse and worse?—
With leave, Bassanio; I am half yourself,
And I must freely have the half of any thing
That this same paper brings you.
Bass. O, sweet Portia,
Here are a few of the unpleasant'st words
That ever blotted paper! Gentle lady,
When I did first impart my love to you,
I freely told you, all the wealth I had
Ran in my veins, I was a gentleman;
And then I told you true: and yet, dear lady,
Rating myself at nothing, you shall see
How much I was a braggart: When I told you
My state was nothing, I should then have told you
That I was worse than nothing; for, indeed,
I have engag'd myself to a dear friend,
Engag'd my friend to his mere enemy,
To feed my means. Here is a letter, lady
The paper as the body of my friend,
And every word in it a gaping wound,
Issuing life-blood—But is it true, Salerio?
Have all his ventures fail'd? What, not one hit?
From Tripolis, from Mexico, and England,
From Lisbon, Barbary, and India?
And not one vessel 'scape the dreadful touch
Of merchant-marring rocks?
Sale. Not one, my lord.
Besides, it should appear, that if he had
The present money to discharge the Jew,
He would not take it: Never did I know
A creature, that did bear the shape of man
So keen and greedy to confound a man:
He plies the duke at morning, and at night;
And doth impeach the freedom of the state,
If they deny him justice: twenty merchants,
The duke himself, and the magnificoes
Of greatest port, have all persuaded with him;
But none can drive him from the envious plea
Of forfeiture, of justice, and his bond.
Jes. When I was with him, I have heard him swear,
To Tubal, and to Chus, his countrymen,
That he would rather have Antonio's flesh,
Than twenty times the value of the sum
That he did owe him: and I know, my lord,
If law, authority, and power deny not,
It will go hard with poor Antonio.
Por. Is it your dear friend, that is thus in trouble?
Bass. The dearest friend to me, the kindest man
The best condition'd and unwearied spirit
In doing courtesies; and one in whom
The ancient Roman honour more appears,
Than any that draws breath in Italy.
Por. What sum owes he the Jew?
Bass. For me, three thousand ducats.
Por. What, no more?
Pay him six thousand, and deface the bond;
Double six thousand, and then treble that,
Before a friend of this description
Should lose a hair[2] through Bassanio's fault.
First, go with me to church, and call me wife:
And then away to Venice to your friend;
For never shall you lie by Portia's side
With an unquiet soul. You shall have gold
To pay the petty debt twenty times over;
When it is paid, bring your true friend along.
My maid Nerissa and myself, mean time,
Will live as maids and widows. Come, away;
For you shall hence upon your wedding-day:
Bid your friends welcome, show a merry cheer;[3]
Since you are dear bought, I will love you dear.—
But let me hear the letter of your friend.
Bass. [Reads.] *Sweet Bassanio, my ships have all miscarried, my creditors grow cruel, my estate is very low, my bond to the Jew is forfeit; and since, in paying it, it is impossible I should live, all debts are cleared between you and I, if I might but see you at my death: notwithstanding, use your pleasure: if your love do not persuade you to come, let not my letter.*
Por. O love, despatch all business, and be gone.
Bass. Since I have your good leave to go away,
I will make haste: but, till I come again,
No bed shall e'er be guilty of my stay,
Nor rest be interposer 'twixt us twain.
[*Exeunt.*

SCENE III. Venice. *A Street. Enter* SHYLOCK, SALANIO, ANTONIO, *and* Gaoler.

Shy. Gaoler, look to him;—Tell not me of mercy:—
This is the fool that lent out money gratis;—
Gaoler, look to him.
Ant. Hear me yet, good Shylock.
Shy. I'll have my bond; speak not against my bond;
I have sworn an oath, that I will have my bond:
Thou call'dst me dog, before thou hadst a cause:
But, since I am a dog, beware my fangs:
The duke shall grant me justice.—I do wonder,
Thou naughty gaoler, that thou art so fond[4]
To come abroad with him at his request.
Ant. I pray thee, hear me speak.
Shy. I'll have my bond; I will not hear thee speak;
I'll have my bond; and therefore speak no more.
I'll not be made a soft and dull-ey'd fool,
To shake the head, relent, and sigh, and yield
To christian intercessors. Follow not;
I'll have no speaking; I will have my bond.
[*Exit* SHYLOCK.

1 It should be remembered that *stedfast, sad, grave, sober,* were ancient synonymes of *constant.*

2 *Hair* is here used as a dissyllable.

3 i. e. air of countenance, look. 4 Foolish

Salan. It is the most impenetrable cur,
That ever kept with men.
Ant. Let him alone;
I'll follow him no more with bootless prayers.
He seeks my life; his reason well I know;
I oft deliver'd from his forfeitures
Many that have at times made moan to me;
Therefore he hates me.
Salan. I am sure, the duke
Will never grant this forfeiture to hold.
Ant. The duke cannot deny the course of law;
For the commodity that strangers have
With us in Venice, if it be denied,
Will much impeach the justice of the state;[1]
Since that the trade and profit of the city
Consisteth of all nations. Therefore, go:
These griefs and losses have so 'bated me,
That I shall hardly spare a pound of flesh
To-morrow to my bloody creditor.——
Well, gaoler, on:---Pray God, Bassanio come
To see me pay his debt, and then I care not!
[*Exeunt.*

SCENE IV. Belmont. *A Room in* Portia's *House. Enter* PORTIA, NERISSA, LORENZO, JESSICA, *and* BALTHAZAR.

Lor. Madam, although I speak it in your presence,
You have a noble and a true conceit
Of god-like amity; which appears most strongly
In bearing thus the absence of your lord.
But, if you knew to whom you show this honour,
How true a gentleman you send relief,
How dear a lover of my lord your husband,
I know, you would be prouder of the work,
Than customary bounty can enforce you.
Por. I never did repent for doing good,
Nor shall not now: for in companions
That do converse and waste the time together,
Whose souls do bear an equal yoke of love,
There must be needs a like proportion
Of lineaments,[2] of manners, and of spirit;
Which makes me think, that this Antonio,
Being the bosom lover[3] of my lord,
Must needs be like my lord: If it be so,
How little is the cost I have bestow'd,
In purchasing the semblance of my soul
From out the state of hellish cruelty?
This comes too near the praising of myself!
Therefore, no more of it: hear other things.
Lorenzo, I commit into your hands
The husbandry and manage of my house,
Until my lord's return; for mine own part
I have toward heaven breath'd a secret vow,
To live in prayer and contemplation,
Only attended by Nerissa here,
Until her husband and my lord's return:
There is a monastery two miles off,
And there we will abide. I do desire you,
Not to deny this imposition;
The which my love, and some necessity,
Now lays upon you.
Lor. Madam, with all my heart
I shall obey you in all fair commands.
Por. My people do already know my mind,
And will acknowledge you and Jessica,
In place of lord Bassanio and myself.
So fare you well, till we shall meet again.
Lor. Fair thoughts, and happy hours, attend on you.
Jes. I wish your ladyship all heart's content.
Por. I thank you for your wish, and am well pleas'd
To wish it back on you: fare you well, Jessica.---
[*Exeunt* JESSICA *and* LORENZO
Now, Balthazar,
As I have ever found thee honest, true,
So let me find thee still: Take this same letter,
And use thou all the endeavour of a man,
In speed to Padua; see thou render this
Into my cousin's hand, doctor Bellario;
And, look, what notes and garments he doth give thee,
Bring them, I pray thee, with imagin'd speed[4]
Unto the tranect,[5] to the common ferry
Which trades to Venice:—waste no time in words,
But get thee gone: I shall be there before thee.
Balth. Madam, I go with all convenient speed.
[*Exit.*
Por. Come on, Nerissa; I have work in hand,
That you yet know not of: we'll see our husbands,
Before they think of us.
Ner. Shall they see us?
Por. They shall, Nerissa; but in such a habit,
That they shall think we are accomplished
With what we lack. I'll hold thee any wager,
When we are both accouter'd like young men,
I'll prove the prettier fellow of the two,
And wear my dagger with the braver grace:
And speak, between the change of man and boy,
With a reed voice; and turn two mincing steps
Into a manly stride; and speak of frays,
Like a fine bragging youth: and tell quaint lies,
How honourable ladies sought my love,
Which I denying, they fell sick and died;
I could not do withal:[6]—then I'll repent,
And wish, for all that, that I had not kill'd them
And twenty of these puny lies I'll tell,
That men shall swear, I have discontinued school
Above a twelvemonth:—I have within my mind
A thousand raw tricks of these bragging Jacks,
Which I will practise.
Ner. Why, shall we turn to men?
Por. Fye; what a question's that,
If thou wert near a lewd interpreter?
But come, I'll tell thee all my whole device
When I am in my coach, which stays for us
At the park gate; and therefore haste away,
For we must measure twenty miles to-day.
[*Exeunt.*

SCENE V. *The same. A Garden. Enter* LAUNCELOT *and* JESSICA.

Laun. Yes, truly: for, look you, the sins of the father are to be laid upon the children; therefore, I promise you, I fear you.[7] I was always plain with you, and so now I speak my agitation of the matter: Therefore, be of good cheer; for, truly, I think, you are damn'd. There is but one hope in it that can do you any good; and that is but a kind of bastard hope neither.

Jes. And what hope is that, I pray thee?

Laun. Marry, you may partly hope that your father got you not, that you are not the Jew's daughter.

Jes. That were a kind of bastard hope, indeed, so the sins of my mother should be visited upon me.

Laun. Truly then I fear you are damn'd both by father and mother; thus when I shun Scylla, your

1 As this passage is a little perplexed in its construction, it may not be improper to explain it:—If, says Antonio, the duke stop the course of law, the denial of those rights to strangers, which render their abode at Venice so commodious and agreeable to them, will much impeach the justice of the state, &c.

2 The word *lineaments* was used with great laxity by our ancient writers.

3 This word was anciently applied to those of the same sex who had an esteem for each other. Ben Jonson concludes one of his letters to Dr. Donne, by telling him 'he is his *true lover*.'

4 i. e. with the celerity of imagination.

5 This word can only be illustrated at present by conjecture. It evidently implies the name of a place where the passage-boat set out, and is in some way derived from '*Tranare*, Ital. To pass or swim over:' perhaps, therefore, *Tranetto*, signified a little fording place or ferry, and hence the English word *Tranect*, but no other instance of its use has yet occurred.

6 Some of the commentators had strained this innocent phrase to a wanton meaning. Mr. Gifford, in a note on Jonson's Silent Woman, p. 470, has clearly shown, by ample illustration, that it signified nothing more than '*I could not help it*.'

7 So in K. Richard III.
'The king is sickly, weak, and melancholy,
And his physicians *fear* him mightily'

father, I fall into Charybdis, your mother:[1] well, you are gone both ways.

Jes. I shall be saved by my husband; he hath made me a Christian.

Laun. Truly, the more to blame he; we were Christians enough before; e'en as many as could well live, one by another: This making of Christians will raise the price of hogs; if we grow all to be pork-eaters, we shall not shortly have a rasher on the coals for money.

Enter LORENZO.

Jes. I'll tell my husband, Launcelot, what you say; here he comes.

Lor. I shall grow jealous of you shortly, Launcelot, if you thus get my wife into corners.

Jes. Nay, you need not fear us, Lorenzo; Launcelot and I are out: he tells me flatly, there is no mercy for me in heaven, because I am a Jew's daughter: and he says you are no good member of the commonwealth; for, in converting Jews to Christians, you raise the price of pork.

Lor. I shall answer that better to the commonwealth, than you can the getting up of the negro's belly: the Moor is with child by you, Launcelot.

Laun. It is much, that the Moor should be more[2] than reason: but if she be less than an honest woman, she is, indeed, more than I took her for.

Lor. How every fool can play upon the word! I think, the best grace of wit will shortly turn into silence; and discourse grow commendable in none only but parrots.—Go in, sirrah; bid them prepare for dinner.

Laun. That is done, sir; they have all stomachs.

Lor. Goodly lord, what a wit-snapper are you! then bid them prepare dinner.

Laun. That is done too, sir; only, cover is the word.

Lor. Will you cover then, sir?

Laun. Not so, sir, neither; I know my duty.

Lor. Yet more quarrelling with occasion! Wilt thou show the whole wealth of thy wit in an instant? I pray thee, understand a plain man in his plain meaning: go to thy fellows; bid them cover the table, serve in the meat, and we will come in to dinner.

Laun. For the table, sir, it shall be served in: for the meat, sir, it shall be covered; for your coming in to dinner, sir, why, let it be as humours and conceits shall govern. [*Exit* LAUNCELOT.

Lor. O dear discretion, how his words are suited![3]
The fool hath planted in his memory
An army of good words: And I do know
As many fools, that stand in better place,
Garnish'd like him, that for a tricksy word
Defy the matter. How cheer'st thou, Jessica!
And now, good sweet, say thy opinion,
How dost thou like the lord Bassanio's wife?

Jes. Past all expressing: It is very meet,
The lord Bassanio live an upright life;
For, having such a blessing in his lady,
He finds the joys of heaven here on earth;
And, if on earth he do not mean it, it
Is reason he should never come to heaven.
Why, if two gods should play some heavenly match,
And on the wager lay two earthly women,
And Portia one, there must be something else
Pawn'd with the other; for the poor rude world
Hath not her fellow.

Lor. Even such a husband
Hast thou of me, as she is for a wife.

Jes. Nay, but ask my opinion too of that.

Lor. I will anon; first let us go to dinner.

Jes. Nay, let me praise you, while I have a stomach.

Lor. No, pray thee let it serve for table-talk;
Then, howsoe'er thou speak'st, 'mong other things
I shall digest it.

Jes. Well, I'll set you forth. [*Exeunt.*

ACT IV.

SCENE I. Venice. *A Court of Justice. Enter the* Duke, *the Magnificoes;* ANTONIO, BASSANIO, GRATIANO, SALARINO, SALANIO, *and others*

Duke. What, is Antonio here?

Ant. Ready, so please your grace.

Duke. I am sorry for thee; thou art come to answer
A stony adversary, an inhuman wretch
Uncapable of pity, void and empty
From any dram of mercy.

Ant. I have heard,
Your grace hath ta'en great pains to qualify
His rigorous course; but since he stands obdurate
And that no lawful means can carry me
Out of his envy's[4] reach, I do oppose
My patience to his fury; and am arm'd
To suffer, with a quietness of spirit,
The very tyranny and rage of his.

Duke. Go one, and call the Jew into the court.

Salan. He's ready at the door: he comes, my lord

Enter SHYLOCK.

Duke. Make room, and let him stand before our face.—
Shylock, the world thinks, and I think so too,
That thou but lead'st this fashion of thy malice
To the last hour of act; and then, 'tis thought,
Thou'lt show thy mercy, and remorse,[5] more strange
Than is thy strange apparent[6] cruelty:
And where[7] thou now exact'st the penalty,
(Which is a pound of this poor merchant's flesh,)
Thou wilt not only lose the forfeiture,
But touch'd with human gentleness and love,
Forgive a moiety of the principal;
Glancing an eye of pity on his losses,
That have of late so huddled on his back;
Enough to press a royal[8] merchant down,
And pluck commiseration of his state
From brassy bosoms, and rough hearts of flint,
From stubborn Turks, and Tartars, never train'd
To offices of tender courtesy.
We all expect a gentle answer, Jew.

Shy. I have possess'd your grace of what I purpose;
And by our holy Sabbath have I sworn,
To have the due and forfeit of my bond:
If you deny it, let the danger light
Upon your charter, and your city's freedom.
You'll ask me, why I rather choose to have
A weight of carrion flesh, than to receive
Three thousand ducats: I'll not answer that:[9]
But, say, it is my humour;[10] Is it answer'd?

1 Alluding to the well known line.
'Incidis in Scyllam, cupiens vitare Charybdim.'
The author of which was unknown to Erasmus but was pointed out by Galeottus Martius. It is in the Alexandreis of Philip Gaultier, who flourished at the commencement of the 13th century. Nothing is more frequent than this proverb in our old English writers.

2 Milton's quibbling epigram has the same kind of humour to boast of—
'Galli ex concubitu gravidam te, *Pontia, Mori*,
Quis bene *moratam morigeram*que neget.'

3 i. e. suited or fitted to each other, arranged.

4 *Envy* in this place means *hatred* or *malice*.

5 *Remorse* in Shakspeare's time generally signified *pity, tenderness*.

6 i. e. seeming, not real.

7 Whereas.

8 *Royal* merchant is not merely a ranting epithet as applied to merchants, for such were to be found at Venice in the Sanudo's, the Giustiniani, the Grimaldi, &c. This epithet was striking and well understood in Shakspeare's time, when Gresham was dignified with the title of the *royal merchant*, both from his wealth, and because he constantly transacted the mercantile business of Queen Elizabeth.

9 The Jew being asked a question which the law does not require him to answer, stands upon his right and refuses; but afterwards gratifies his own malignity by such answers as he knows will aggravate the pain of the inquirer. I will not answer, says he, as to a legal question; but, since you want an answer, will this serve you!

10 The worthy Corporal Nym hath this apology usually at his finger's ends, and Shylock condescends to excuse his extravagant cruelty as a *humour*, or irresistible propensity of the mind. The word humour is not used in its modern signification, but for a peculiar quality which sways and masters the individual through all his actions

What if my house be troubled with a rat,
And I be pleas'd to give ten thousand ducats
To have it baned? What, are you answer'd yet?
Some men there are love not a gaping pig;[1]
Some, that are mad, if they behold a cat:
And others, when the bag-pipe sings i' the nose,
Cannot contain their urine; For affection,[2]
Master of passion, sways it to the mood
Of what it likes or loathes: Now, for your answer:
As there is no firm reason to be render'd,
Why he cannot abide a gaping pig:
Why he, a harmless necessary cat;
Why he, a woollen[3] bag-pipe; but of force
Must yield to such inevitable shame,
As to offend, himself being offended;
So can I give no reason, nor I will not,
More than a lodg'd hate, and a certain loathing
I bear Antonio, that I follow thus
A losing suit against him. Are you answer'd?

Bass. This is no answer, thou unfeeling man,
To excuse the current of thy cruelty.

Shy. I am not bound to please thee with my answer.

Bass. Do all men kill the things they do not love?

Shy. Hates any man the thing he would not kill?

Bass. Every offence is not a hate at first.

Shy. What, wouldst thou have a serpent sting thee twice?

Ant. I pray you, think you question[4] with the Jew:
You may as well go stand upon the beach,
And bid the main flood bate his usual height;
You may as well use question with the wolf,
Why he hath made the ewe bleat for the lamb;
You may as well forbid the mountain pines
To wag their high tops, and to make no noise,
When they are fretted with the gusts of heaven;[5]
You may as well do any thing most hard,
As seek to soften that (than which what's harder?)
His Jewish heart:—Therefore I do beseech you,
Make no more offers, use no further means,
But, with all brief and plain conveniency,
Let me have judgment, and the Jew his will.

Bass. For thy three thousand ducats here is six.

Shy. If every ducat in six thousand ducats
Were in six parts, and every part a ducat,
I would not draw them, I would have my bond.

Duke. How shalt thou hope for mercy, rend'ring none?

Shy. What judgment shall I dread, doing no wrong?
You have among you many a purchas'd slave,
Which, like your asses, and your dogs, and mules,
You use in abject and in slavish parts,
Because you bought them:—Shall I say to you,
Let them be free, marry them to your heirs?
Why sweat they under burdens? let their beds
Be made as soft as yours, and let their palates
Be season'd with such viands? You will answer,
The slaves are ours:—So do I answer you:
The pound of flesh, which I demand of him,
Is dearly bought, 'tis mine, and I will have it:
If you deny me, fye upon your law!
There is no force in the decrees of Venice:
I stand for judgment: answer; shall I have it?

Duke. Upon my power, I may dismiss this court,
Unless Bellario, a learned doctor,
Whom I have sent for to determine this,
Come here to-day.

Salar. My lord, here stays without
A messenger with letters from the doctor,
New come from Padua.

Duke. Bring us the letters; Call the messenger.

Bass. Good cheer, Antonio! What, man? courage yet!
The Jew shall have my flesh blood, bones, and all,
Ere thou shalt lose for me one drop of blood.

Ant. I am a tainted wether of the flock,
Meetest for death; the weakest kind of fruit
Drops earliest to the ground, and so let me:
You cannot better be employ'd, Bassanio,
Than to live still, and write mine epitaph.

Enter NERISSA, *dressed like a Lawyer's Clerk.*

Duke. Came you from Padua, from Bellario?

Ner. From both, my lord: Bellario greets your grace. [*Presents a Letter.*

Bass. Why dost thou whet thy knife so earnestly?

Shy. To cut the forfeiture from that bankrupt there.

Gra. Not on thy sole, but on thy soul,[6] harsh Jew,
Thou mak'st thy knife keen: but no metal can,
No, not the hangman's axe, bear half the keenness
Of thy sharp envy.[7] Can no prayers pierce thee?

Shy. No, none that thou hast wit enough to make.

Gra. O, be thou damn'd, inexorable dog!
And for thy life let justice be accus'd.
Thou almost mak'st me waver in my faith,
To hold opinion with Pythagoras,
That souls of animals infuse themselves
Into the trunks of men: thy currish spirit,
Govern'd a wolf, who, hang'd for human slaughter,
Even from the gallows did his fell soul fleet,
And, whilst thou lay'st in thy unhallow'd dam,
Infus'd itself in thee; for thy desires
Are wolfish, bloody, starv'd, and ravenous.

Shy. Till thou canst rail the seal from off my bond,
Thou but offend'st thy lungs to speak so loud:
Repair thy wit, good youth, or it will fall
To cureless ruin.—I stand here for law.

Duke. This letter from Bellario doth commend
A young and learned doctor to our court:—
Where is he?

Ner. He attendeth here hard by,
To know your answer, whether you'll admit him.

Duke. With all my heart: some three or four of you,
Go, give him courteous conduct to this place.—
Mean time, the court shall hear Bellario's letter.

[Clerk reads.] *Your grace shall understand, that, at the receipt of your letter, I am very sick: but in the instant that your messenger came, in loving visitation was with me a young doctor of Rome, his name is Balthasar: I acquainted him with the cause in controversy between the Jew and Antonio the merchant: we turned o'er many books together: he is furnish'd with my opinion: which, better'd with his own learning, (the greatness whereof I cannot enough commend,) comes with him, at my importunity, to fill up your grace's request in my stead. I beseech you, let his lack of years be no impediment to let him lack a reverend estimation; for I never knew so young a body with so old a head. I leave him to your gracious acceptance, whose trial shall better publish his commendation.*

Duke. You hear the learn'd Bellario, what he writes:
And here, I take it, is the doctor come.—

Enter PORTIA *dressed like a Doctor of Laws.*

Give me your hand: Came you from old Bellario?

Por. I did, my lord.

Duke. You are welcome: take your place
Are you acquainted with the difference
That holds this present question in the court?

Por. I am inform'd thoroughly of the cause.
Which is the merchant here, and which the Jew?

Duke. Antonio and old Shylock, both stand forth

1 A pig prepared for the table is most probably meant, for in that state is the epithet *gaping* most applicable to this animal.

2 *Affection* stands here for *tendency*, *disposition*; Appetitus animi.

3 It was usual to cover with *woollen cloth* the bag of this instrument. The old copies read *woollen*, the conjectural reading *swollen* was proposed by Sir J. Hawkins

4 Converse.

5 This image seems to have been caught from Golding's version of Ovid, 1587, book xv. p. 196:
'Such noise as pine-trees make, what time the heady easterne winde
Doth whizz amongst them.'

6 The conceit is that his *soul* was so hard that it might serve him for a whet-stone.

7 Malice

Por. Is your name Shylock?
Shy. Shylock is my name.
Por. Of a strange nature is the suit you follow;
Yet in such rule, that the Venetian law
Cannot impugn[1] you, as you do proceed —
You stand within his danger,[2] do you not?
[*To* ANTONIO.
Ant. Ay, so he says.
Por. Do you confess the bond?
Ant. I do.
Por. Then must the Jew be merciful.
Shy. On what compulsion must I? tell me that.
Por. The quality of mercy is not strain'd;[3]
It droppeth, as the gentle rain from heaven
Upon the place beneath: it is twice bless'd;
It blesseth him that gives, and him that takes:
'Tis mightiest in the mightiest; it becomes
The throned monarch better than his crown:
His sceptre shows the force of temporal power,
The attribute to awe and majesty,
Wherein doth sit the dread and fear of kings;
But mercy is above this sceptred sway,
It is enthroned in the hearts of kings,
It is an attribute to God himself:
And earthly power doth then show likest God's,
When mercy seasons justice.[4] Therefore, Jew,
Though justice be thy plea, consider this,—
That in the course of justice, none of us
Should see salvation; we do pray for mercy;
And that same prayer doth teach us all to render
The deeds of mercy.[5] I have spoke thus much,
To mitigate the justice of thy plea;
Which if thou follow, this strict court of Venice
Must needs give sentence 'gainst the merchant there.
Shy. My deeds upon my head! I crave the law,
The penalty and forfeit of my bond.
Por. Is he not able to discharge the money?
Bass. Yes, here I tender it for him in the court;
Yea, twice the sum: if that will not suffice,
I will be bound to pay it ten times o'er,
On forfeit of my hands, my head, my heart:
If this will not suffice, it must appear
That malice bears down truth.[6] And, I beseech you,
Wrest once the law to your authority:
To do a great right, do a little wrong;
And curb this cruel devil of his will.
Por. It must not be; there is no power in Venice
Can alter a decree established;
'Twill be recorded for a precedent;
And many an error, by the same example,
Will rush into the state: it cannot be.
Shy. A Daniel come to judgment! yea, a Daniel!—
O wise young judge, how do I honour thee!
Por. I pray you, let me look upon the bond.
Shy. Here 'tis, most reverend doctor, here it is.
Por. Shylock, there's thrice thy money offer'd thee.
Shy. An oath, an oath, I have an oath in heaven:
Shall I lay perjury upon my soul?
No, not for Venice.
Por. Why, this bond is forfeit;
And lawfully by this the Jew may claim
A pound of flesh, to be by him cut off
Nearest the merchant's heart:—Be merciful;
Take thrice thy money; bid me tear the bond.
Shy. When it is paid according to the tenour.—
It doth appear, you are a worthy judge;
You know the law, your exposition
Hath been most sound: I charge you by the law,
Whereof you are a well-deserving pillar,
Proceed to judgment: by my soul, I swear,
There is no power in the tongue of man
To alter me: I stay here on my bond.
Ant. Most heartily I do beseech the court
To give the judgment.
Por. Why then, thus it is.
You must prepare your bosom for his knife:
Shy. O noble judge! O excellent young man!
Por. For the intent and purpose of the law
Hath full relation to the penalty,
Which here appeareth due upon the bond.
Shy. 'Tis very true: O wise and upright judge!
How much more elder art thou than thy looks!
Por. Therefore lay bare your bosom.
Shy. Ay, his breast;
So says the bond;—Doth it not, noble judge?—
Nearest his heart, those are the very words.
Por. It is so. Are there balance here, to weigh
The flesh?
Shy. I have them ready.
Por. Have by some surgeon, Shylock, on your charge,
To stop his wounds, lest he do bleed to death.
Shy. Is it so nominated in the bond?
Por. It is not so express'd; But what of that?
'Twere good you do so much for charity.
Shy. I cannot find it; 'tis not in the bond.
Por. Come, merchant, have you any thing to say?
Ant. But little; I am arm'd, and well prepar'd.—
Give me your hand, Bassanio; fare you well!
Grieve not that I am fallen to this for you:
For herein fortune shows herself more kind
Than is her custom: it is still her use,
To let the wretched man out-live his wealth,
To view with hollow eye, and wrinkled brow,
An age of poverty; from which lingering penance
Of such misery doth she cut me off.
Commend me to your honourable wife:
Tell her the process of Antonio's end,
Say, how I lov'd you, speak me fair in death:
And, when the tale is told, bid her be judge,
Whether Bassanio had not once a love.
Repent not you that you shall lose your friend,
And he repents not that he pays your debt;
For, if the Jew do cut but deep enough,
I'll pay it instantly with all my heart.
Bass. Antonio, I am married to a wife,
Which is as dear to me as life itself:
But life itself, my wife, and all the world,
Are not with me esteem'd above thy life:
I would lose all, ay, sacrifice them all
Here to this devil, to deliver you.
Por. Your wife would give you little thanks for that,
If she were by, to hear you make the offer.
Gra. I have a wife, whom, I protest, I love,
I would she were in heaven, so she could
Entreat some power to change this currish Jew.
Ner. 'Tis well you offer it behind her back;
The wish would make else an unquiet house.
Shy. These be the christian husbands: I have a daughter:
'Would any of the stock of Barrabas[7]
Had been her husband, rather than a Christian!
[*Aside.*
We trifle time: I pray thee, pursue sentence.
Por. A pound of that same merchant's flesh is thine;
The court awards it, and the law doth give it.
Shy. Most rightful judge!
Por. And you must cut this flesh from off his breast;
The law allows it, and the court awards it.

---

1 To *impugn* is to oppose, to controvert.

2 i. e. within his reach or controul. The phrase is thought to be derived from a similar one in the monkish Latin of the middle age.

3 Shakspeare probably recollected the following verse of Ecclesiasticus, xxxv. 20, in composing these beautiful lines: 'Mercy is seasonable in the time of affliction, as clouds of rain in the time of drought.'

4 So in K. Edward III. a Tragedy, 1596:
'And Kings approach the nearest unto God,
By giving life and safety unto men.'

5 Portia referring the Jew to the Christian doctrine of Salvation, and the Lord's Prayer, is a little out of character.

6 i. e. malice oppressed *honesty*, a *true* man in old language is an *honest* man. We now call the jury good men and *true*.

7 Shakspeare seems to have followed the pronunciation usual to the theatre, *Barabbas* being sounded *Barabas* throughout Marlowe's Jew of Malta

Shy. Most learned judge!—A sentence: come, prepare.
Por. Tarry a little:—there is something else.—
This bond doth give thee here no jot of blood;
The words expressly are, a pound of flesh:
Take then thy bond, take thou thy pound of flesh;
But, in the cutting it, if thou dost shed
One drop of Christian blood, thy lands and goods
Are, by the laws of Venice, confiscate
Unto the state of Venice.
Gra. O upright judge!—Mark, Jew;—O learned judge!
Shy. Is that the law?
Por. Thyself shall see the act:
For, as thou urgest justice, be assur'd,
Thou shalt have justice, more than thou desir'st.
Gra. O learned judge!—Mark, Jew;—a learned judge!
Shy. I take this offer then;—pay the bond thrice,
And let the Christian go.
Bass. Here is the money.
Por. Soft;
The Jew shall have all justice:—soft!—no haste;—
He shall have nothing but the penalty.
Gra. O Jew! an upright judge, a learned judge!
Por. Therefore prepare thee to cut off the flesh,[1]
Shed thou no blood; nor cut thou less, nor more,
But just a pound of flesh: if thou tak'st more,
Or less, than a just pound,—be it but so much
As makes it light, or heavy, in the substance,
Or the division of the twentieth part
Of one poor scruple; nay, if the scale do turn
But in the estimation of a hair,—
Thou diest, and all thy goods are confiscate.
Gra. A second Daniel, a Daniel, Jew!
Now, infidel, I have thee on the hip.
Por. Why doth the Jew pause? take thy forfeiture.
Shy. Give me my principal, and let me go.
Bass. I have it ready for thee; here it is.
Por. He hath refus'd it in the open court;
He shall have merely justice, and his bond.
Gra. A Daniel, still say I; a second Daniel!—
I thank thee, Jew, for teaching me that word.
Shy. Shall I not have barely my principal?
Por. Thou shalt have nothing but the forfeiture,
To be so taken at thy peril, Jew.
Shy. Why then the devil give him good of it!
I'll stay no longer question.
Por. Tarry, Jew;
The law hath yet another hold on you.
It is enacted in the laws of Venice,—
If it be prov'd against an alien,
That by direct, or indirect attempts,
He seek the life of any citizen,
The party, 'gainst the which he doth contrive,
Shall seize one half his goods; the other half
Comes to the privy coffer of the state;
And the offender's life lies in the mercy
Of the duke only, 'gainst all other voice.
In which predicament, I say, thou stand'st:
For it appears by manifest proceeding,
That, indirectly, and directly too,
Thou hast contriv'd against the very life
Of the defendant: and thou hast incurr'd
The danger formerly by me rehears'd.
Down, therefore, and beg mercy of the duke.
Gra. Beg, that thou may'st have leave to hang thyself:
And yet, thy wealth being forfeit to the state,
Thou hast not left the value of a cord;
Therefore, thou must be hang'd at the state's charge.
Duke. That thou shalt see the difference of our spirit,
I pardon thee thy life before thou ask it:
For half thy wealth, it is Antonio's;
The other half comes to the general state,
Which humbleness may drive unto a fine.
Por. Ay, for the state; not for Antonio.
Shy. Nay, take my life and all, pardon not that:
You take my house, when you do take the prop
That doth sustain my house; you take my life,
When you do take the means whereby I live.
Por. What mercy can you render him, Antonio?
Gra. A halter gratis; nothing else, for God's sake.
Ant. So please my lord the duke and all the court,
To quit the fine for one half of his goods;
I am content, so he will let me have
The other half in use,[2]—to render it,
Upon his death, unto the gentleman
That lately stole his daughter:
Two things provided more.—That, for this favour,
He presently become a Christian;
The other, that he do record a gift,
Here in the court, of all he dies possess'd,
Unto his son Lorenzo, and his daughter.
Duke. He shall do this; or else I do recant
The pardon that I late pronounced here.
Por. Art thou contented, Jew, what dost thou say?
Shy. I am content.
Por. Clerk, draw a deed of gift.
Shy. I pray you, give me leave to go from hence:
I am not well; send the deed after me,
And I will sign it.
Duke. Get thee gone, but do it.
Gra. In christening thou shalt have two godfathers;
Had I been judge, thou shouldst have had ten more;[3]
To bring thee to the gallows, not to the font.
[*Exit* SHYLOCK.
Duke. Sir, I entreat you home with me to dinner.
Por. I humbly do desire your grace of pardon;
I must away this night toward Padua,
And it is meet I presently set forth.
Duke. I am sorry that your leisure serves you not.
Antonio, gratify this gentleman;
For, in my mind, you are much bound to him.
[*Exeunt* Duke, *Magnificoes, and Train.*
Bass. Most worthy gentleman, I and my friend
Have by your wisdom been this day acquitted
Of grievous penalties; in lieu whereof,
Three thousand ducats, due unto the Jew,
We freely cope your courteous pains withal.
Ant. And stand indebted, over and above,
In love and service to you evermore.
Por. He is well paid that is well satisfied;
And I, delivering you, am satisfied,
And therein do account myself well paid;
My mind was never yet more mercenary.
I pray you, know me, when we meet again;
I wish you well, and so I take my leave.
Bass. Dear sir, of force I must attempt you further;
Take some remembrance of us, as a tribute,
Not as a fee: grant me two things, I pray you,
Not to deny me, and to pardon me.
Por. You press me far, and therefore I will yield.
Give me your gloves, I'll wear them for your sake;
And, for your love, I'll take this ring from you:—
Do not draw back your hand; I'll take no more;
And you in love shall not deny me this.
Bass. This ring, good sir,—alas, it is a trifle;
I will not shame myself to give you this.
Por. I will have nothing else but only this;
And now, methinks, I have a mind to it.
Bass. There's more depends on this, than on the value.
The dearest ring in Venice will I give you,
And find it out by proclamation:
Only for this, I pray you, pardon me.
Por. I see, sir, you are liberal in offers:

1 Balthasar Gracian, the celebrated Spanish Jesuit, in his *Hero*, relates a similar judgment, which he attributes to the great Turk.

2 Antonio's offer has been variously explained. It appears to be 'that he will quit his share of the fine, as the duke has already done that portion due to the state, if Shylock will let him have it in *use* (i. e. at interest) during his life, to render it at his death to Lorenzo.'

3 i. e. a jury of *twelve* men to condemn him. This appears to have been an old joke.

You taught me first to beg: and now, methinks,
You teach me how a beggar should be answer'd.
Bass. Good sir, this ring was given me by my wife;
And when she put it on, she made me vow,
That I should neither sell, nor give, nor lose it.
Por. That 'scuse serves many men to save their gifts.
An if your wife be not a mad woman,
And know how well I have deserv'd this ring,
She would not hold out enemy for ever,
For giving it to me. Well, peace be with you!
[*Exeunt* PORTIA *and* NERISSA.
Ant. My lord Bassanio, let him have the ring;
Let his deservings, and my love withal,
Be valued 'gainst your wife's commandment.
Bass. Go, Gratiano, run and overtake him,
Give him the ring; and bring him, if thou canst,
Unto Antonio's house;—away, make haste.
[*Exit* GRATIANO.
Come, you and I will thither presently;
And in the morning early will we both
Fly toward Belmont: Come Antonio. [*Exeunt.*

SCENE II. *The same. A Street. Enter* PORTIA *and* NERISSA.

Por. Inquire the Jew's house out, give him this deed,
And let him sign it; we'll away to-night,
And be a day before our husbands home:
This deed will be well welcome to Lorenzo.

Enter GRATIANO.

Gra. Fair sir, you are well overtaken:
My lord Bassanio, upon more advice,[1]
Hath sent you here this ring; and doth entreat
Your company at dinner.
Por. That cannot be:
This ring I do accept most thankfully,
And so, I pray you, tell him: Furthermore,
I pray you, show my youth old Shylock's house.
Gra. That will I do.
Ner. Sir, I would speak with you:—
I'll see if I can get my husband's ring.
[*To* PORTIA.
Which I did make him swear to keep for ever.
Por. Thou may'st, I warrant: We shall have old[2] swearing,
That they did give the rings away to men;
But we'll outface them, and outswear them too.
Away, make haste; thou know'st where I will tarry.
Ner. Come, good sir, will you show me to this house? [*Exeunt.*

ACT V.

SCENE I. Belmont. *Avenue to* Portia's *House. Enter* LORENZO *and* JESSICA.

Lor. The moon shines bright:—In such a night as this,[3]
When the sweet wind did gently kiss the trees,
And they did make no noise: in such a night,
Troilus, methinks, mounted the Trojan walls,[4]
And sigh'd his soul toward the Grecian tents,
Where Cressid lay that night.
Jes. In such a night,
Did Thisbe fearfully o'ertrip the dew;
And saw the lion's shadow ere himself,
And ran dismay'd away.
Lor. In such a night,
Stood Dido, with a willow in her hand[5]
Upon the wild sea-banks, and wav'd her love
To come again to Carthage.
Jes. In such a night,
Medea gather'd the enchanted herbs
That did renew old Æson.[6]
Lor. In such a night,
Did Jessica steal from the wealthy Jew:
And with an unthrift love did run from Venice,
As far as Belmont.
Jes. In such a night,
Did young Lorenzo swear he lov'd her well;
Stealing her soul with many vows of faith,
And ne'er a true one.
Lor. In such a night,
Did pretty Jessica, like a little shrew,
Slander her love, and he forgave it her.
Jes. I would out-night you, did nobody come
But, hark, I hear the footing of a man.

Enter STEPHANO.

Lor. Who comes so fast in silence of the night?
Steph. A friend.
Lor. A friend? what friend? your name, I pray you, friend?
Steph. Stephano is my name; and I bring word,
My mistress will before the break of day
Be here at Belmont: she doth stray about
By holy crosses, where she kneels and prays
For happy wedlock hours.[7]
Lor. Who comes with her?
Steph. None, but a holy hermit, and her maid.
I pray you, is my master yet return'd?
Lor. He is not, nor we have not heard from him.—
But go we in, I pray thee, Jessica,
And ceremoniously let us prepare
Some welcome for the mistress of the house.

Enter LAUNCELOT.

Laun. Sola, sola, wo, ha, ho, sola, sola!
Lor. Who calls?
Laun. Sola! did you see master Lorenzo, and mistress Lorenzo? sola, sola!
Lor. Leave hollaing, man; here.
Laun. Sola! Where? where?
Lor. Here.
Laun. Tell him, there's a post come from my master, with his horn full of good news; my master will be here ere morning. [*Exit.*
Lor. Sweet soul, let's in, and there expect their coming.
And yet no matter;—Why should we go in?
My friend Stephano, signify, I pray you,
Within the house, your mistress is at hand;
And bring your music forth into the air.—
[*Exit* STEPHANO.
How sweet the moon-light sleeps upon this bank!
Here will we sit, and let the sounds of music
Creep in our ears;[8] soft stillness, and the night,
Become the touches of sweet harmony.
Sit, Jessica: Look, how the floor of heaven
Is thick inlaid with patines[9] of bright gold:
There's not the smallest orb, which thou behold'st,
But in his motion like an angel sings,
Still quiring to the young-ey'd cherubins;
Such harmony is in immortal souls;
But, whilst this muddy vesture of decay
Doth grossly close us in, we cannot hear it.—[10]

---

1 i. e. more reflection.

2 Of this once common augmentative in colloquial language there are various instances in the plays of Shakspeare, in the sense of *abundant, frequent.*

3 The several passages beginning with these words are imitated in the old comedy of Wily Beguiled, written before 1596. See the play in Hawkins's Origin of the Drama, vol. iii.

4 This image is from Chaucer's Troilus and Cresseide, b. v. v. 666, and 1142.

5 Steevens observes that this is one instance, among many, that might be brought to prove that Shakspeare was no reader of the classics.

6 Steevens refers to Gower's description of Medea in his Confessio Amantis

7 So in the Merry Devil of Edmonton:
'But there are *crosses*, wife: here's one in Waltham
Another at the abbey, and the third
At Ceston; and 'tis ominous to pass
Any of these without a Pater-noster.'
And this is a reason assigned for the delay of a wedding

8 So in Churchyard's Worthines of Wales, 1587:
'A *musicke* sweete that through *our eares shall creep*,
By secret arte, and lull a man asleep.'

9 A small flat dish or plate, used in the administration of the Eucharist; it was commonly of gold, or silver-gilt.

10 The folio editions, and the quarto printed by *Roberts*, read:
'Such harmony is in immortal souls;
But whilst this muddy vesture of decay
Doth grossly close *in it*, we cannot hear it.'

Enter Musicians.

Come, ho, and wake Diana with a hymn;
With sweetest touches pierce your mistress' ear,
And draw her home with music. [*Music.*

Jes. I am never merry, when I hear sweet music.

Lor. The reason is, your spirits are attentive:
For do but note a wild and wanton herd,
Or race of youthful and unhandled colts,[1]
Fetching mad bounds, bellowing, and neighing loud,
Which is the hot condition of their blood;
If they but hear perchance a trumpet sound,
Or any air of music touch their ears,
You shall perceive them make a mutual stand,
Their savage eyes turn'd to a modest gaze,
By the sweet power of music: Therefore, the poet
Did feign that Orpheus drew trees, stones, and floods;
Since nought so stockish, hard, and full of rage,
But music for the time doth change his nature:
The man that hath no music in himself,
Nor is not mov'd with concord of sweet sounds,
Is fit for treasons, stratagems, and spoils;[2]
The motions of his spirit are dull as night,
And his affections dark as Erebus:
Let no such man be trusted.—Mark the music.

Enter PORTIA *and* NERISSA *at a distance.*

Por. That light we see, is burning in my hall.
How far that little candle throws his beams!
So shines a good deed in a naughty world.

Ner. When the moon shone, we did not see the candle.

Por. So doth the greater glory dim the less:
A substitute shines brightly as a king,
Until a king be by; and then his state
Empties itself, as doth an inland brook
Into the main of waters. Music! hark!

Ner. It is your music, madam, of the house.

Por. Nothing is good, I see, without respect;[3]
Methinks, it sounds much sweeter than by day.

Ner. Silence bestows that virtue on it, madam.

Por. The crow doth sing as sweetly as the lark,
When neither is attended; and, I think,
The nightingale, if she should sing by day,
When every goose is cackling, would be thought
No better a musician than the wren.
How many things by season season'd are
To their right praise, and true perfection!—
Peace, hoa! the moon sleeps with Endymion,
And would not be awak'd! [*Music ceases.*

Lor. That is the voice,
Or I am much deceiv'd, of Portia.

Por. He knows me, as the blind man knows the cuckoo,
By the bad voice.

Lor. Dear lady, welcome home.

Por. We have been praying for our husbands' welfare,
Which speed, we hope, the better for our words.
Are they return'd?

Lor. Madam, they are not yet;
But there is come a messenger before,
To signify their coming.

Por. Go in, Nerissa,
Give order to my servants, that they take
No note at all of our being absent hence;—
Nor you, Lorenzo;—Jessica, nor you.
[*A tucket*[4] *sounds.*

Lor. Your husband is at hand, I hear his trumpet;
We are no tell-tales, madam; fear you not.

Por. This night, methinks, is but the daylight sick,
It looks a little paler; 'tis a day,
Such as a day is when the sun is hid.

Enter BASSANIO, ANTONIO, GRATIANO, *and their* Followers.

Bass. We should hold day with the Antipodes,
If you would walk in absence of the sun.

Por. Let me give light, but let me not be light;[5]
For a light wife doth make a heavy husband,
And never be Bassanio so for me;
But God sort all!—You are welcome home, my lord.

Bass. I thank you, madam: give welcome to my friend.—
This is the man, this is Antonio,
To whom I am so infinitely bound.

Por. You should in all sense be much bound to him
For, as I hear, he was much bound for you.

Ant. No more than I am well acquitted of.

Por. Sir, you are very welcome to our house.
It must appear in other ways than words,
Therefore, I scant this breathing courtesy.[6]
[GRATIANO *and* NERISSA *seem to talk apart.*

Gra. By yonder moon, I swear, you do me wrong;
In faith, I gave it to the judge's clerk:
Would he were gelt that had it, for my part,
Since you do take it, love, so much at heart.

Por. A quarrel, ho, already? what's the matter?

Gra. About a hoop of gold, a paltry ring
That she did give me; whose posy was
For all the world like cutler's poetry
Upon a knife,[7] *Love me, and leave me not.*

Ner. What talk you of the posy, or the value?
You swore to me, when I did give it you,
That you would wear it till your hour of death;
And that it should lie with you in your grave:
Though not for me, yet for your vehement oaths,
You should have been respective,[8] and have kept it
Gave it a judge's clerk!—but well I know,
The clerk will ne'er wear hair on his face that had it.

Gra. He will, an if he live to be a man

Ner. Ay, if a woman live to be a man.

Gra Now, by this hand, I gave it to a youth,—
A kind of boy; a little scrubbed boy,
No higher than thyself; the judge's clerk;
A prating boy, that begg'd it as a fee;
I could not for my heart deny it him.

Por. You were to blame, I must be plain with you,
To part so slightly with your wife's first gift;
A thing stuck on with oaths upon your finger,
And riveted so with faith unto your flesh.
I gave my love a ring, and made him swear
Never to part with it; and here he stands;
I dare be sworn for him, he would not leave it,
Nor pluck it from his finger, for the wealth
That the world masters. Now, in faith, Gratiano,
You give your wife too unkind a cause of grief;
An 'twere to me, I should be mad at it.

Bass. Why, I were best to cut my left hand off,
And swear I lost the ring defending it. [*Aside.*

Gra. My lord Bassanio gave his ring away
Unto the judge that begg'd it, and, indeed,
Deserv'd it too; and then the boy, his clerk,
That took some pains in writing, he begg'd mine;
And neither man, nor master, would take aught
But the two rings.

Por. What ring gave you, my lord?
Not that, I hope, which you receiv'd of me

Bass. If I could add a lie unto a fault,
I would deny it; but you see, my finger
Hath not the ring upon it; it is gone.

Por. Even so void is your false heart of truth.
By heaven, I will ne'er come in your bed
Until I see the ring.

---

1 We find the same thought in the Tempest:
———Then I beat my tabor,
At which, like *unback'd colts*, they pricked their ears,
Advanc'd their eyelids, lifted up their noses
As they smelt music.'

2 Steevens, in one of his splenetic moods, censures this passage as neither pregnant with physical and moral truth, nor poetically beautiful; and, with the assistance of Lord Chesterfield's tirade against music, levels a blow at the lovers and professors of it.

3 Not absolutely good, but relatively good, as it is modified by circumstances.

4 *Toccata*, Ital. a flourish on a trumpet.

5 Shakspeare delights to trifle with this word.

6 This verbal complimentary form, made up only of *breath*, i. e. words.

7 '———like cutler's poetry
Upon a knife.'
Knives were formerly inscribed, by means of *aqua fortis*, with short sentences in distich.

8 *Respective*, that is *considerative*, *regardful*; not respectful or respectable as Steevens supposed

Ner. Nor I in yours,
Till I again see mine.
Bass. Sweet Portia,
If you did know to whom I gave the ring,
If you did know for whom I gave the ring,
And would conceive for what I gave the ring,
And how unwillingly I left the ring,
When nought would be accepted but the ring,
You would abate the strength of your displeasure.
Por. If you had known the virtue of the ring,
Or half her worthiness that gave the ring,
Or your own honour to contain[1] the ring,
You would not then have parted with the ring.
What man is there so much unreasonable,
If you had pleas'd to have defended it
With any terms of zeal, wanted the modesty
To urge the thing held as a ceremony?[2]
Nerissa teaches me what to believe;
I'll die for't, but some woman had the ring.
Bass. No, by mine honour, madam, by my soul,
No woman had it, but a civil doctor,
Which did refuse three thousand ducats of me,
And begg'd the ring; the which I did deny him,
And suffer'd him to go displeas'd away;
Even he that had held up the very life
Of my dear friend. What should I say, sweet lady?
I was enforc'd to send it after him;
I was beset with shame and courtesy;
My honour would not let ingratitude
So much besmear it: Pardon me, good lady;
For, by these blessed candles[3] of the night,
Had you been there, I think, you would have begg'd
The ring of me to give the worthy doctor.
Por. Let not that doctor e'er come near my house:
Since he hath got the jewel that I lov'd,
And that which you did swear to keep for me,
I will become as liberal as you:
I'll not deny him any thing I have,
No, not my body, nor my husband's bed:
Know him I shall, I am well sure of it:
Lie not a night from home; watch me, like Argus:
If you do not, if I be left alone,
Now, by mine honour, which is yet my own,
I'll have that doctor for my bedfellow.
Ner. And I his clerk; therefore be well advis'd,
How you do leave me to mine own protection.
Gra. Well, do you so: let not me take him then;
For, if I do, I'll mar the young clerk's pen.
Ant. I am the unhappy subject of these quarrels.
Por. Sir, grieve not you; You are welcome notwithstanding.
Bass. Portia, forgive me this enforced wrong;
And, in the hearing of these many friends,
I swear to thee, even by thine own fair eyes,
Wherein I see myself,——
Por. Mark you but that!
In both my eyes he doubly sees himself:
In each eye, one:—swear by your double[4] self,
And there's an oath of credit.
Bass. Nay, but hear me:
Pardon this fault, and by my soul I swear,
I never more will break an oath with thee.
Ant. I once did lend my body for his wealth;[5]
Which, but for him that had your husband's ring,
[*To* PORTIA.
Had quite miscarried: I dare be bound again,
My soul upon the forfeit, that your lord
Will never more break faith advisedly.
Por. Then you shall be his surety: Give him this;
And bid him keep it better than the other.
Ant. Here, lord Bassanio; swear to keep this ring.
Bass. By heaven, it is the same I gave the doctor!
Por. I had it of him: pardon me, Bassanio:
For by this ring the doctor lay with me.
Ner. And pardon me, my gentle Gratiano;
For that same scrubbed boy, the doctor's clerk,
In lieu of this, last night did lie with me.
Gra. Why, this is like the mending of highways
In summer, where the ways are fair enough;
What! are we cuckolds, ere we have deserv'd it?
Por. Speak not so grossly.—You are all amaz'd:
Here is a letter, read it at your leisure;
It comes from Padua, from Bellario:
There you shall find, that Portia was the doctor;
Nerissa there, her clerk: Lorenzo here
Shall witness, I set forth as soon as you,
And but even now return'd: I have not yet
Enter'd my house.—Antonio, you are welcome;
And I have better news in store for you,
Than you expect: unseal this letter soon;
There you shall find, three of your argosies
Are richly come to harbour suddenly;
You shall not know by what strange accident
I chanced on this letter.
Ant. I am dumb.
Bass. Were you the doctor, and I knew you not?
Gra. Were you the clerk, that is to make me cuckold?
Ner. Ay; but the clerk that never means to do it;
Unless he live until he be a man.
Bass. Sweet doctor you shall be my bedfellow;
When I am absent, then lie with my wife.
Ant. Sweet lady, you have given me life, and living;
For here I read for certain, that my ships
Are safely come to road.
Por. How now, Lorenzo?
My clerk hath some good comforts too for you.
Ner. Ay, and I'll give them him without a fee.—
There do I give to you, and Jessica,
From the rich Jew, a special deed of gift,
After his death, of all he dies possess'd of.
Lor. Fair ladies, you drop manna in the way
Of starved people.
Por, It is almost morning,
And yet, I am sure, you are not satisfied
Of these events at full: Let us go in;
And charge us there upon inter'gatories,
And we will answer all things faithfully.
Gra. Let it be so: The first inter'gatory
That my Nerissa shall be sworn on, is,
Whether till the next night she had rather stay,
Or go to bed now, being two hours to day:
But were the day come, I should wish it dark,
That I were couching with the doctor's clerk.
Well, while I live, I'll fear no other thing
So sore, as keeping safe Nerissa's ring. [*Exeunt*

---

1 To *contain* had nearly the same meaning with to *retain*.

2 i. e. kept in a measure religiously, or superstitiously.

3 We have again the same expression in one of Shakspeare's Sonnets, in Macbeth, and in Romeo and Juliet.

4 *Double* is here used for *deceitful, full of duplicity*.

5 i. e. for his *advantage*; to obtain his happiness. *Wealth* was the term generally opposed to adversity or calamity

---

OF the *Merchant of Venice* the style is even and easy, with few peculiarities of diction, or anomalies of construction. The comic part raises laughter, and the serious fixes expectation. The probability of either one or the other story cannot be maintained. The union of two actions in one event is in this drama eminently happy. Dryden was much pleased with his own address in connecting the two plots of his *Spanish Friar*, which yet, I believe, the critic will find excelled by this play.

JOHNSON

AS YOU LIKE IT.

PRELIMINARY REMARKS.

DR. GREY and Mr. Upton asserted that this Play was *certainly borrowed* from the Coke's Tale of Gamelyn, printed in Urry's Chaucer, but it is hardly likely that Shakspeare saw that in manuscript, and there is a more obvious source from whence he derived his plot, viz. the pastoral romance of 'Rosalynde, or Euphues' Golden Legacy,' by Thomas Lodge, first printed in 1590. From this he has sketched his principal characters, and constructed his plot; but those admirable beings, the melancholy Jaques, the witty Touchstone, and his Audrey, are of the poet's own creation. Lodge's novel is one of those tiresome (I had almost said unnatural) pastoral romances, of which the Euphues of Lyly and the Arcadia of Sidney were also popular examples: it has, however, the redeeming merit of some very beautiful verses interspersed,* and the circumstance of its having led to the formation of this exquisite pastoral drama, is enough to make us withhold our assent to Steevens's splenetic censure of it as worthless'

'Touched by the magic wand of the enchanter, the dull and endless prosing of the novelist is transformed into an interesting and lively drama. The forest of Arden converted into a real Arcadia of the golden age. The highly sketched figures pass along in the most di versified succession: we see always the shady dark-green landscape in the back ground, and breathe in imagination the fresh air of the forest. The hours are here measured by no clocks, no regulated recurrence of duty or toil; they flow on unnumbered in voluntary occupation or fanciful idleness.—One throws himself down 'under the shade of melancholy boughs,' and indulges in reflection on the changes of fortune, the falsehood of the world, and the self-created torments of social life: others make the woods resound with social and festive songs, to the accompaniment of their horns. Selfishness, envy and ambition, have been left in the city behind them; of all the human passions, love alone has found an entrance into this silvan scene, where it dictates the same language to the simple shepherd, and the chivalrous youth, who hangs his love ditty to a tree?'†

> And this their life, exempt from public haunts,
> Finds tongues in trees, books in the running brooks,
> Sermons in stones, and good in every thing.

How exquisitely is the character of Rosalind conceiv ed, what liveliness and sportive gaiety, combined with the most natural and affectionate tenderness; the reader is as much in love with her as Orlando, and wonders not at Phebe's sudden passion for her when disguised as Ganymede; or Celia's constant friendship. Touchstone is indeed a 'rare fellow: he uses his folly as a stalking-horse, and under the presentation of that, he shoots his wit:' his courtship of Audrey, his lecture to Corin, his defence of cuckolds, and his burlesque upon the 'duello' of the age, are all most 'exquisite fooling.' It has been remarked, that there are few of Shakspeare's plays which contain so many passages that are quoted and remembered, and phrases that have become in a manner proverbial. To enumerate them would be to mention every scene in the play. And I must no longer detain the reader from this most delightful of Shakspeare's comedies.

Malone places the composition of this play in 1599 There is no edition known previous to that in the folic of 1623. But it appears among the miscellaneous entries of prohibited pieces in the Stationers' books, without any certain date.

* The following beautiful Stanzas are part of what is called 'Rosalynd's Madrigal,' and are not unworthy of a place even in a page devoted to Shakspeare:

> Love in my bosom like a bee
>   Doth suck his sweet:
> Now with his wings he plays with me,
>   Now with his feet.
> Within mine eyes he makes his nest,
> His bed amidst my tender breast,
> My kisses are his daily feast,
> And yet he robs me of my rest.
>   Ah, wanton, will ye?
>
> And if I sleep, then percheth he
>   With pretty flight;
> And makes a pillow of my knee
>   The livelong night.
> Strike I my lute, he tunes the string
> He music plays, if so I sing,
> He lends me every lovely thing;
> Yet cruel he my heart doth sting
>   Whist, wanton, still ye?

† Schlegel.

PERSONS REPRESENTED.

Duke, *living in exile.*
FREDERICK, *Brother to the* Duke, *and Usurper of his Dominions.*
AMIENS, } *Lords attending upon the* Duke *in his*
JAQUES, } *banishment.*
LE BEAU, *a Courtier attending upon* Frederick.
CHARLES, *his Wrestler.*
OLIVER, }
JAQUES, } *Sons of* Sir Rowland de Bois.
ORLANDO, }
ADAM, } *Servants to* Oliver.
DENNIS, }
TOUCHSTONE, *a Clown.*
SIR OLIVER MAR-TEXT, *a Vicar.*
CORIN, } *Shepherds.*
SYLVIUS, }
WILLIAM, *a country Fellow, in love with* Audrey.
A Person representing Hymen.
ROSALIND, *Daughter to the banished* Duke.
CELIA, *Daughter to* Frederick.
PHEBE, *a Shepherdess.*
AUDREY, *a country Wench.*
Lords belonging to the two Dukes; Pages, Foresters, *and other* Attendants.

The SCENE *lies, first, near* Oliver's *House; afterwards, partly in the* Usurper's *Court, and partly in the Forest of* Arden.

ACT I.

SCENE I. *An Orchard, near* Oliver's *House.*

Enter ORLANDO *and* ADAM.

Orlando.

As I remember, Adam, it was upon this fashion bequeathed me[1] by will: But a poor thousand crowns; and, as thou say'st, charged my brother, on his blessing, to breed me well: and there begins my sadness. My brother Jaques he keeps at school, and report speaks goldenly of his profit: for my part, he keeps me rustically at home, or, to speak more properly, stays[2] me here at home unkept: For call you that keeping for a gentleman of my birth, that differs not from the stalling of an ox?

1 Sir W. Blackstone proposed to read, '*He* bequeathed, &c.' Warburton proposed to read, '*My father* bequeathed, &c.' I have followed the old copy, which is sufficiently intelligible.

2 The old orthography *staies* was an easy corruption of *sties*: which Warburton thought the true reading.

His horses are bred better; for, besides that they are fair with their feeding, they are taught their manage, and to that end riders dearly hired: but I, his brother, gain nothing under him but growth: for the which his animals on his dunghills are as much bound to him as I. Besides this nothing that he so plentifully gives me, the something that nature gave me, his countenance seems to take from me: he lets me feed with his hinds, bars me the place of a brother, and, as much as in him lies, mines my gentility with my education. This is it, Adam, that grieves me; and the spirit of my father, which I think is within me, begins to mutiny against this servitude: I will no longer endure it, though yet I know no wise remedy how to a'oid it.

Enter OLIVER.

Adam. Yonder comes my master, your brother.

Orl. Go apart, Adam, and thou shalt hear how he will shake me up.

Oli. Now, sir! what make you here?[1]

Orl. Nothing: I am not taught to make any thing.

Oli. What mar you then, sir?

Orl. Marry, sir, I am helping you to mar that which God made, a poor unworthy brother of yours, with idleness.

Oli. Marry, sir, be better employed, and be naught awhile.[2]

Orl. Shall I keep your hogs, and eat husks with them? What prodigal portion have I spent, that I should come to such penury?

Oli. Know you where you are, sir?

Orl. O, sir, very well: here in your orchard.

Oli. Know you before whom, sir?

Orl. Ay, better than he[3] I am before knows me. I know you are my eldest brother; and, in the gentle condition of blood, you should so know me: The courtesy of nations allows you my better, in that you are the first-born; but the same tradition takes not away my blood, were there twenty brothers betwixt us: I have as much of my father in me, as you; albeit, I confess, your coming before me is nearer to his reverence.[4]

Oli. What, boy!

Orl. Come, come, elder brother, you are too young in this.

Oli. Wilt thou lay hands on me, villain.

Orl. I am no villain:[5] I am the youngest son of Sir Rowland de Bois; he was my father; and he is thrice a villain, that says, such a father begot villains: Wert thou not my brother, I would not take this hand from thy throat, till this other had pulled out thy tongue for saying so: thou hast railed on thyself.

Adam. Sweet masters, be patient; for your father's remembrance, be at accord.

Oli. Let me go, I say.

Orl. I will not, till I please: you shall hear me. My father charged you in his will to give me good education: you have trained me like a peasant, obscuring and hiding from me all gentleman-like qualities: the spirit of my father grows strong in me, and I will no longer endure it: therefore allow me such exercises as may become a gentleman, or give me the poor allottery my father left me by testament: with that I will go buy my fortunes.

Oli. And what wilt thou do? beg, when that is spent? Well, sir, get you in: I will not long be troubled with you: you shall have some part of your will: I pray you, leave me.

Orl. I will no further offend you than becomes me for my good.

Oli. Get you with him, you old dog.

Adam. Is old dog my reward? Most true, I have lost my teeth in your service.—God be with my old master! he would not have spoke such a word.

[*Exeunt* ORLANDO *and* ADAM.

Oli. Is it even so? begin you to grow upon me? I will physic your rankness, and yet give no thousand crowns neither. Hola, Dennis!

Enter DENNIS.

Den. Calls your worship?

Oli. Was not Charles, the Duke's wrestler, here to speak with me?

Den. So please you, he is here at the door, and importunes access to you.

Oli. Call him in. [*Exit* DENNIS.]—'Twill be good way; and to-morrow the wrestling is.

Enter CHARLES.

Cha. Good morrow to your worship.

Oli. Good monsieur Charles!—what's the new news at the new court!

Cha. There's no news at the court, sir, but the old news; that is, the old duke is banished by his younger brother the new duke; and three or four loving lords have put themselves into voluntary exile with him, whose lands and revenues enrich the new duke; therefore he gives them good leave[6] to wander.

Oli. Can you tell, if Rosalind, the duke's daughter,[7] be banished with her father.

Cha. O, no; for the duke's daughter,[8] her cousin, so loves her,—being ever from their cradles bred together,—that she would have followed her exile, or have died to stay behind her. She is at the court, and no less beloved of her uncle than his own daughter; and never two ladies loved as they do.

Oli. Where will the old duke live?

Cha. They say, he is already in the forest of Arden,[9] and a many merry men with him; and there they live like the old Robin Hood of England: they say, many young gentlemen flock to him every day; and fleet[10] the time carelessly, as they did in the golden world.

Oli. What, you wrestle to-morrow before the new duke?

Cha. Marry, do I, sir; and I came to acquaint you with a matter. I am given, sir, secretly to understand, that your younger brother, Orlando, hath a disposition to come in disguis'd against me to try a fall: To-morrow, sir, I wrestle for my credit; and he that escapes me without some broken limb, shall acquit him well. Your brother is but young, and tender; and, for your love, I would be loth to foil him, as I must, for my own honour, if he come in: therefore out of my love to you, I came hither to acquaint you withal; that either you might stay him from his intendment, or brook such disgrace well as he shall run into; in that it is a thing of his own search, and altogether against my will.

Oli. Charles, I thank thee for thy love to me, which thou shalt find I will most kindly requite. I had myself notice of my brother's purpose herein, and have by underhand means laboured to dissuade him from it; but he is resolute. I'll tell thee, Charles,—it is the stubbornest young fellow of France: full of ambition, an envious emulator of every man's good parts, a secret and villanous contriver against me his natural brother; therefore use thy discretion;

---

1 i. e. what *do* you here? See note in Love's Labour's Lost, Act iv. Sc. 3.

2 *Be naught awhile.* Warburton justly explained this phrase, which, he says, 'is only a north-country proverbial curse equivalent to *a mischief on you.*'

3 The first folio reads *him*, the second *he* more correctly.

4 Warburton proposed reading 'near his *revenue*,' which he explains, 'though you are no nearer in blood, yet it must be owned that you are nearer in estate.'

5 *Villain* is used in a double sense: by Oliver for a worthless fellow; and by Orlando, for a man of base extraction.

6 'He gives them *good leave*.' As often as this phrase occurs, it means a *ready assent.*

7 i. e. the *banished* duke's daughter.

8 i. e. the *usurping* duke's daughter; this may be sufficiently apparent by the words *her cousin*, yet it has been thought necessary to point out the ambiguity.

9 *Ardenne* is a forest of considerable extent in French Flanders, lying near the river Meuse, and between Charlemont and Rocroy.

10 *Fleet*, i. e. to *flitte*, to make to pass or flow.

I had as lief thou didst break his neck as his finger: and thou wert best look to't; for if thou dost him any slight disgrace, or if he do not mightily grace himself on thee, he will practice against thee by poison, entrap thee by some treacherous device, and never leave thee till he hath ta'en thy life by some indirect means or other: for, I assure thee, and almost with tears I speak it, there is not one so young and so villanous this day living. I speak but brotherly of him; but should I anatomize him to thee as he is, I must blush and weep, and thou must look pale and wonder.

Cha. I am heartily glad I came hither to you: If he come to-morrow, I'll give him his payment: If ever he go alone again, I'll never wrestle for prize more: And so, God keep your worship! [*Exit.*

Oli. Farewell, good Charles.—Now will I stir this gamester:[1] I hope, I shall see an end of him: for my soul, yet I know not why, hates nothing more than he. Yet he's gentle; never school'd, and yet learned; full of noble device; of all sorts[2] enchantingly beloved; and, indeed, so much in the heart of the world, and especially of my own people, who best know him, that I am altogether misprised; but it shall not be so long; this wrestler shall clear all: nothing remains, but that I kindle[3] the boy thither, which now I'll go about. [*Exit.*

SCENE II. *A Lawn before the* Duke's *Palace.*

Enter ROSALIND *and* CELIA.

Cel. I pray thee, Rosalind, sweet my coz, be merry.

Ros. Dear Celia, I show more mirth than I am mistress of; and would you yet I were merrier? Unless you could teach me to forget a banished father, you must not learn me how to remember any extraordinary pleasure.

Cel. Herein, I see, thou lovest me not with the full weight that I love thee: if my uncle, thy banished father, had banished thy uncle, the duke my father, so thou hadst been still with me, I could have taught my love to take thy father for mine; so wouldst thou, if the truth of thy love to me were so righteously temper'd as mine is to thee.

Ros. Well, I will forget the condition of my estate, to rejoice in yours.

Cel. You know, my father hath no child but I, nor none is like to have; and, truly, when he dies, thou shalt be his heir: for what he hath taken away from thy father perforce, I will render thee again in affection: by mine honour, I will; and when I break that oath, let me turn monster: therefore, my sweet Rose, my dear Rose, be merry.

Ros. From henceforth I will, coz, and deviso sports: let me see; What think you of falling in love?

Cel. Marry, I pr'ythee, do, to make sport withal: but love no man in good earnest; nor no further in sport neither, than with safety of a pure blush thou may'st in honour come off again.

Ros. What shall be our sport then?

Cel. Let us sit and mock the good housewife, Fortune, from her wheel, that her gifts may henceforth be bestowed equally.

Ros. I would, we could do so; for her benefits are mightily misplaced: and the bountiful blind woman doth most mistake in her gifts to women.

Cel. 'Tis true: for those, that she makes fair, she scarce makes honest; and those, that she makes honest, she makes very ill-favour'dly.

Ros. Nay, now thou goest from fortune's office to nature's: fortune reigns in gifts of the world, not in the lineaments of nature.

Enter TOUCHSTONE.

Cel. No? When nature hath made a fair creature, may she not by fortune fall into the fire?—Though nature hath given us wit to flout at fortune, hath not fortune sent in this fool to cut off the argument?

Ros. Indeed, there is fortune too hard for nature; when fortune makes nature's natural the cutter off of nature's wit.

Cel. Peradventure, this is not fortune's work neither, but nature's; who perceiving[4] our natural wits too dull to reason of such goddesses, hath sent this natural for our whetstone: for always the dulness of the fool is the whetstone of his wits.—How now, wit? whither wander you?

Touch. Mistress, you must come away to your father.

Cel. Were you made the messenger?

Touch. No, by mine honour; but I was bid to come for you.

Ros. Where learned you that oath, fool?

Touch. Of a certain knight, that swore by his honour they were good pancakes, and swore by his honour the mustard was naught; now, I'll stand to it, the pancakes were naught, and the mustard was good; and yet was not the knight forsworn.

Cel. How prove you that, in the great heap of your knowledge?

Ros. Ay, marry; now unmuzzle your wisdom.

Touch. Stand you both forth now: stroke your chins, and swear by your beards that I am a knave.

Cel. By our beards, if we had them, thou art.

Touch. By my knavery, if I had it, then I were: but if you swear by that that is not, you are not forsworn: no more was this knight, swearing by his honour, for he never had any; or if he had, he had sworn it away, before ever he saw those pancakes, or that mustard.

Cel. Pr'ythee, who is't that thou mean'st!

Touch. One that old Frederick, your father, loves

Cel.[5] My father's love is enough to honour him Enough! speak no more of him; you'll be whipp'd for taxation,[6] one of these days.

Touch. The more pity, that fools may not speak wisely, what wise men do foolishly.

Cel. By my troth, thou say'st true: for since the little wit, that fools have, was silenced, the little foolery, that wise men have, makes a great show Here comes Monsieur Le Beau.

Enter LE BEAU.

Ros. With his mouth full of news.

Cel. Which he will put on us, as pigeons feed their young.

Ros. Then shall we be news-cramm'd.

Cel. All the better; we shall be the more marketable. *Bon jour*, Monsieur Le Beau: What's the news?

Le Beau. Fair princess, you have lost much good sport.

Cel. Sport? Of what colour?

Le Beau. What colour, madam? how shall I answer you?

Ros. As wit and fortune will.

Touch. Or as the destinies decree.

Cel. Well said: that was laid on with a trowel.[7]

Touch. Nay, if I keep not my rank,——

Ros. Thou losest thy old smell.

Le Beau. You amaze me, ladies: I would have told you of good wrestling, which you have lost the sight of.

Ros. Yet tell us the manner of the wrestling.

Le Beau. I will tell you the beginning, and, if please your ladyships, you may see the end; for the best is yet to do; and here, where you are, they are coming to perform it.

---

1 i. e. frolicksome fellow.

2 i. e. of all *ranks*.

3 'But that I kindle the boy thither.' He means, 'that I excite the boy to it.'

4 The old copy reads *perceiveth*. The folio, 1632, reads *perceiving*.

5 This reply to the Clown, in the old copies, is given to Rosalind. *Frederick* was however the name of Celia's father, and it is therefore most probable the reply should be hers.

6 '— you'll be *whipp'd* for *taxation*.' This was the discipline usually inflicted upon fools.

7 'Laid on with a trowel.' This is a proverbial phrase not yet quite disused. It is, says Mason, to do any thing strongly, and without delicacy. If a man flatters grossly, it is a common expression to say, that he *lays it on with a trowel*.

Cel. Well,—the beginning, that is dead and buried.

Le Beau. There comes an old man, and his three sons,——

Cel. I could match this beginning with an old tale.

Le Beau. Three proper young men, of excellent growth and presence;——

Ros. With bills on their necks,—*Be it known unto all men by these presents,*[1]——

Le Beau. The eldest of the three wrestled with Charles, the duke's wrestler; which Charles in a moment threw him, and broke three of his ribs, that there is little hope of life in him: so he served the second, and so the third: Yonder they lie; the poor old man, their father, making such pitiful dole over them, that all the beholders take his part with weeping.

Ros. Alas!

Touch. But what is the sport, monsieur, that the ladies have lost?

Le Beau. Why, this that I speak of.

Touch. Thus men may grow wiser every day! it is the first time that ever I heard, breaking of ribs was sport for ladies.

Cel. Or I, I promise thee.

Ros. But is there any else longs to see this broken music in his sides? is there yet another dotes upon rib-breaking:—Shall we see this wrestling, cousin?

Le Beau. You must, if you stay here: for here is the place appointed for the wrestling, and they are ready to perform it.

Cel. Yonder, sure, they are coming: Let us now stay and see it.

Flourish. Enter DUKE FREDERICK, Lords, ORLANDO, CHARLES, *and* Attendants.

Duke F. Come on; since the youth will not be entreated, his own peril on his forwardness.

Ros. Is yonder the man?

Le Beau. Even he, madam.

Cel. Alas, he is too young: yet he looks successfully.

Duke F. How now, daughter and cousin? are you crept hither to see the wrestling?

Ros. Ay, my liege: so please you give us leave.

Duke F. You will take little delight in it, I can tell you, there is such odds in the men: In pity of the challenger's youth, I would fain dissuade him, but he will not be entreated: Speak to him, ladies; see if you can move him.

Cel. Call him hither, good Monsieur Le Beau.

Duke F. Do so; I'll not be by. [Duke *goes apart.*

Le Beau. Monsieur the challenger, the princesses call for you.

Orl. I attend them, with all respect and duty.

Ros. Young man, have you challenged Charles the wrestler?[2]

Orl. No, fair princess; he is the general challenger: I come but in, as others do, to try with him the strength of my youth.

Cel. Young gentleman, your spirits are too bold for your years: You have seen cruel proof of this man's strength: if you saw yourself with your eyes, or knew yourself with your judgment, the fear of your adventure would counsel you to a more equal enterprise. We pray you, for your own sake, to embrace your own safety, and give over this attempt.

Ros. Do, young sir; your reputation shall not therefore be misprised: we will make it our suit to the duke, that the wrestling might not go forward.

Orl. I beseech you, punish me not with your hard thoughts; wherein[3] I confess me much guilty, to deny so fair and excellent ladies any thing. But let your fair eyes and gentle wishes go with me to my trial: wherein, if I be foiled, there is but one shamed that was never gracious;[4] if killed, but one dead that is willing to be so; I shall do my friends no wrong, for I have none to lament me; the world no injury, for in it I have nothing, only in the world I fill up a place, which may be better supplied when I have made it empty.

Ros. The little strength that I have, I would it were with you.

Cel. And mine, to eke out hers.

Ros. Fare you well. Pray heaven, I be deceived in you!

Cel. Your heart's desires be with you.

Cha. Come, where is this young gallant, that is so desirous to lie with his mother earth?

Orl. Ready, sir; but his will hath in it a more modest working.

Duke F. You shall try but one fall.

Cha. No, I warrant your grace; you shall not entreat him to a second, that have so mightily persuaded him from a first.

Orl. You mean to mock me after; you should not have mocked me before: but come your ways.

Ros. Now, Hercules be thy speed, young man!

Cel. I would I were invisible, to catch the strong fellow by the leg. [CHA. *and* ORL. *wrestle*

Ros. O excellent young man!

Cel. If I had a thunderbolt in mine eye, I can tell who should down. [CHARLES *is thrown.* *Shout.*

Duke F. No more, no more.

Orl. Yes, I beseech your grace; I am not yet well breathed.

Duke F. How dost thou, Charles?

Le Beau. He cannot speak, my lord.

Duke F. Bear him away. [CHARLES *is borne out.*]
What is thy name, young man?

Orl. Orlando, my liege; the youngest son of Sir Rowland de Bois.

Duke F. I would, thou hadst been son to some man else.
The world esteem'd thy father honourable,
But I did find him still mine enemy:
Thou shouldst have better pleas'd me with this deed,
Hadst thou descended from another house.
But fare thee well; thou art a gallant youth;
I would, thou hadst told me of another father.
[*Exeunt* DUKE FRED. Train, *and* LE BEAU.

Cel. Were I my father, coz, would I do this?

Orl. I am more proud to be Sir Rowland's son,
His youngest son;[5]—and would not change that calling,[6]
To be adopted heir to Frederick.

Ros. My father lov'd Sir Rowland as his soul,
And all the world was of my father's mind:
Had I before known this young man his son,
I should have given him tears unto entreaties,
Ere he should thus have ventur'd.

Cel. Gentle cousin,
Let us go thank him, and encourage him:
My father's rough and envious disposition
Sticks me at heart.—Sir, you have well deserv'd:
If you do keep your promises in love
But justly, as you have exceeded all promise,
Your mistress shall be happy.

Ros. Gentleman,
[*Giving him a Chain from her neck.*
Wear this for me; one out of suits with fortune;[7]
That could give more, but that her hand lacks means.—
Shall we go, coz?

Cel. Ay:—Fare you well, fair gentleman.

---

1 Warburton thought the text should stand thus:
Ros. With bills on their necks,——
Touch. Be it known unto all men by these presents,—
The ladies and the fool being at *cross purposes*, Rosalind banteringly means *bills* or *halberds*. The Clown turns it jestingly to a *law instrument.*

2 This wrestling match is minutely described in Lodge's novel.

3 Johnson thought we should read '*therein.*' Mason proposed to read *herein.*

4 *Gracious* was anciently used in the sense of the Italian *gratiato*, i. e. *graced, favoured, countenanced;* as well as for graceful, comely, well favoured, in which sense Shakspeare uses it in other places.

5 The words 'than to be descended from any other house, however high,' must be understood.

6 *Calling* here means *appellation*, a very unusual if not unprecedented use of the word.

7 Out of *suits* appears here to signify out of *favour*, discarded by fortune. To *suit with* anciently signified *to agree with.*

Orl. Can I not say, I thank you? My better parts
Are all thrown down, and that which here stands up,
Is but a quintain,[1] a mere lifeless block.
Ros. He calls us back: my pride fell with my fortunes:
I'll ask him what he would:—Did you call, sir?—
Sir, you have wrestled well, and overthrown
More than your enemies.
Cel. Will you go, coz?
Ros. Have with you:—Fare you well.
[*Exeunt* Rosalind *and* Celia.
Orl. What passion hangs these weights upon my tongue?
I cannot speak to her, yet she urg'd conference.

Re-enter Le Beau.

O poor Orlando! thou art overthrown;
Or Charles, or something weaker, masters thee.
Le Beau. Good sir, I do in friendship counsel you
To leave this place: Albeit you have deserv'd
High commendation, true applause, and love;
Yet such is now the duke's condition,[2]
That he misconstrues all that you have done.
The duke is humourous; what he is, indeed,
More suits you to conceive, than me to speak of.
Orl. I thank you, sir: and, pray you, tell me this;
Which of the two was daughter of the duke,
That here was at the wrestling?
Le Beau. Neither his daughter, if we judge by manners;
But yet, indeed, the smaller[3] is his daughter:
The other is daughter to the banish'd duke,
And here detain'd by her usurping uncle,
To keep his daughter company; whose loves
Are dearer than the natural bond of sisters.
But I can tell you that of late this duke
Hath ta'en displeasure 'gainst his gentle niece;
Grounded upon no other argument,
But that the people praise her for her virtues,
And pity her for her good father's sake;
And on my life, his malice 'gainst the lady
Will suddenly break forth.—Sir, fare you well;
Hereafter in a better world than this,
I shall desire more love and knowledge of you.
Orl. I rest much bounden to you: fare you well!
[*Exit* Le Beau.
Thus must I from the smoke into the smother;
From tyrant duke, unto a tyrant brother:—
But heavenly Rosalind! [*Exit.*

SCENE III. *A Room in the Palace.* *Enter* Celia *and* Rosalind.

Cel. Why, cousin; why, Rosalind;—Cupid have mercy!—Not a word?

Ros. Not one to throw at a dog.

Cel. No, thy words are too precious to be cast away upon curs, throw some of them at me; come, lame me with reasons.

Ros. Then there were two cousins laid up; when the one should be lamed with reasons, and the other mad without any.

Cel. But is all this for your father?

Ros. No, some of it for my child's father.[4] O how full of briars is this working-day world!

Cel. They are but burs, cousin, thrown upon thee in holiday foolery; if we walk not in the trodden paths, our very petticoats will catch them.

Ros. I could shake them off my coat; these burs are in my heart.

Cel. Hem them away.

Ros. I would try: if I could cry hem, and have him.

Cel. Come, come, wrestle with thy affections.

Ros. O, they take the part of a better wrestler than myself.

Cel. O, a good wish upon you! you will try in time, in despite of a fall.—But turning these jests out of service, let us talk in good earnest: Is it possible, on such a sudden, you should fall into so strong a liking with old Sir Rowland's youngest son?

Ros. The duke my father lov'd his father dearly.

Cel. Doth it therefore ensue, that you should love his son dearly? By this kind of chase, I should hate him, for my father hated his father dearly;[5] yet I hate not Orlando.

Ros. No 'faith, hate him not, for my sake.

Cel. Why should I not? doth he not deserve well?[6]

Ros. Let me love him for that; and do you love him, because I do:—Look here comes the duke.

Cel. With his eyes full of anger.

Enter Duke Frederick, *with* Lords.

Duke F. Mistress, dispatch you with your safest haste,
And get you from our court.
Ros. Me, uncle?
Duke F. You, cousin;
Within these ten days if that thou be'st found
So near our public court as twenty miles,
Thou diest for it.
Ros. I do beseech your grace,
Let me the knowledge of my fault bear with me:
If with myself I hold intelligence,
Or have acquaintance with mine own desires;
If that I do not dream, or be not frantic,
(As I do trust I am not,) then dear uncle,
Never, so much as in a thought unborn,
Did I offend your highness.
Duke F. Thus do all traitors;
If their purgation did consist in words,
They are as innocent as grace itself:—
Let it suffice thee, that I trust thee not.
Ros. Yet your mistrust cannot make me a traitor.
Tell me, whereon the likelihood depends.
Duke F. Thou art thy father's daughter, there's enough.
Ros. So was I when your highness took his dukedom;
So was I when your highness banish'd him:
Treason is not inherited, my lord;
Or, if we did derive it from our friends,
What's that to me; my father was no traitor:
Then good, my liege, mistake me not so much,
To think my poverty is treacherous.
Cel. Dear sovereign hear me speak.
Duke F. Ay, Celia; we stay'd her for your sake,
Else had she with her father rang'd along.
Cel. I did not then entreat to have her stay,
It was your pleasure and your own remorse;[7]
I was too young that time to value her,
But now I know her; if she be a traitor,
Why so am I; we have still slept together,
Rose at an instant, learn'd, play'd, eat together,
And wheresoe'er we went, like Juno's swans,
Still we went coupled, and inseparable.
Duke F. She is too subtle for thee; and her smoothness,
Her very silence, and her patience,
Speak to the people, and they pity her.
Thou art a fool: she robs thee of thy name;
And thou wilt show more bright, and seem more virtuous,
When she is gone: then open not thy lips;
Firm and irrevocable is my doom
Which I have pass'd upon her; she is banish'd.

---

1 His *better parts*, i. e. his *spirits* or *senses*. *A quintain* was a figure set up for tilters to run at in mock resemblance of a tournament.

2 i. e. demeanour, temper, disposition. Antonio in the Merchant of Venice is called by his friend 'the best *condition'd* man.' *Humourous* is *capricious*.

3 The old copy reads *taller*, which is evidently wrong. Pope altered it to *shorter*. The present reading is Malone's

4 i. e. for him whom she hopes to marry and have children by. So Theobald explains this passage. Some of the modern editions read: 'my father's child.'

5 Shakspeare's apparent use of *dear* in a double sense has been already illustrated. See note on Twelfth Night, Act v. Sc. i.

6 Celia answers as if Rosalind had said '*love* him, for my sake,' which is the implied sense of her words.

7 i. e. compassion. So in Macbeth:
'Stop the access and passage to *remorse*'

Cel. Pronounce that sentence then on me, my liege:
cannot live out of her company.
Duke F. You are a fool:—You, niece, provide yourself;
If you out-stay the time, upon mine honour,
And in the greatness of my word, you die.
[*Exeunt* DUKE FREDERICK *and* Lords.
Cel. O my poor Rosalind! whither wilt thou go?
Wilt thou change fathers? I will give thee mine.
charge thee be not thou more griev'd than I am.
Ros. I have more cause.
Cel. Thou hast not, cousin;
Pr'ythee be cheerful: know'st thou not, the duke
Hath banish'd me his daughter?
Ros. That he hath not.
Cel. No? hath not? Rosalind lacks then the love
Which teacheth me that thou and I are one:
Shall we be sunder'd? shall we part, sweet girl?
No; let my father seek another heir.
Therefore devise with me, how we may fly,
Whither to go, and what to bear with us:
And do not seek to take your change[1] upon you,
To bear your griefs yourself, and leave me out;
For, by this heaven, now at our sorrows pale,
Say what thou canst, I'll go along with thee.
Ros. Why, whither shall we go?
Cel. To seek my uncle in the forest of Arden.
Ros. Alas what danger will it be to us,
Maids as we are, to travel forth so far?
Beauty provoketh thieves sooner than gold.
Cel. I'll put myself in poor and mean attire,
And with a kind of umber[2] smirch my face;
The like do you; so shall we pass along,
And never stir assailants.
Ros. Were it not better,
use that I am more than common tall,
That I did suit me all points like a man?
A gallant curtle-axe[3] upon my thigh,
A boar spear in my hand; and (in my heart
Lie there what hidden woman's fear there will,)
We'll have a swashing[4] and a martial outside;
As many other mannish cowards have,
That do outface it with their semblances.
Cel. What shall I call thee, when thou art a man?
Ros. I'll have no worse a name than Jove's own page,
And therefore, look you, call me Ganymede.
But what will you be call'd?
Cel. Something that hath a reference to my state;
No longer Celia, but Aliena.
Ros. But, cousin, what if we assay'd to steal
The clownish fool out of your father's court?
Would he not be a comfort to our travel?
Cel. He'll go along o'er the wide world with me;
Leave me alone to woo him: Let's away,
And get our jewels and our wealth together;
Devise the fittest time, and safest way
To hide us from pursuit that will be made
After my flight: Now go we in content,
To liberty, and not to banishment. [*Exeunt.*

1 The second folio reads *charge.* Malone explains it 'to take your *change* or reverse of fortune upon yourself, without any aid of participation.'

2 'A kind of *umber*,' a dusky yellow-coloured earth, brought from Umbria in Italy, well known to artists.

3 This was one of the old words for a *cutlass*, or short crooked sword, *coutelas*, French. It was variously spelled, *courtlas, courtlax, curtlax.*

4 i. e. as we now say, *dashing*; spirited and calculated to surprise.

5 The old copy reads '*not* the penalty.' Theobald proposed to read *but*, and has been followed by subsequent editors. 'Surely the old reading is right,' says Mr. Boswell; 'here we feel *not*, do not suffer, from the penalty of Adam; for when the winter's wind blows upon my body, I *smile* and say'—

6 It was currently believed in the time of Shakspeare that the toad had a stone contained in its head which was endued with singular virtues. This was called the *toad-stone.*

7 It *irks* me, i. e. it gives me pain. 'Mi rincresce, mi fa male.'—*Torriano's Dict.*

8 Barbed arrows.

ACT II.

SCENE I. *The forest of* Arden. *Enter* Duke *senior*, AMIENS, *and other* Lords, *in the dress of Foresters.*

Duke S. Now, my co-mates, and brothers in exile
Hath not old custom made this life more sweet
Than that of painted pomp? Are not these woods
More free from peril than the envious court?
Here feel we but[5] the penalty of Adam,
The seasons' difference; as, the icy fang,
And churlish chiding of the winter's wind,
Which when it bites and blows upon my body,
Even till I shrink with cold, I smile, and say,—
This is no flattery; these are counsellors
That feelingly persuade me what I am.
Sweet are the uses of adversity;
Which, like the toad, ugly and venomous,
Wears yet a precious jewel in his head;[6]
And this our life, exempt from public haunt,
Finds tongues in trees, books in the running brooks,
Sermons in stones, and good in every thing.
Ami. I would not change it: Happy is your grace,
That can translate the stubbornness of fortune
Into so quiet and so sweet a style.
Duke S. Come, shall we go and kill us venison?
And yet it irks[7] me, the poor dappled fools,—
Being native burghers of this desert city,—
Should in their own confines, with forked heads[8]
Have their round haunches gor'd.
1 *Lord.* Indeed, my lord,
The melancholy Jaques grieves at that;
And, in that kind, swears you do more usurp
Than doth your brother that hath banish'd you.
To-day, my lord of Amiens, and myself,
Did steal behind him as he lay along
Under an oak, whose antique root peeps out
Upon the brook that brawls along this wood:[9]
To the which place a poor sequester'd stag,
That from the hunter's aim had ta'en a hurt,
Did come to languish; and, indeed my lord,
The wretched animal heav'd forth such groans,
That their discharge did stretch his leathern coat
Almost to bursting; and the big round tears
Cours'd one another down his innocent nose[10]
In piteous chase; and thus the hairy fool,
Much marked of the melancholy Jaques,
Stood on the extremest verge of the swift brook,
Augmenting it with tears.
Duke S. But what said Jaques?
Did he not moralize this spectacle?
1 *Lord.* O yes, into a thousand similes.
First, for his weeping in the needless[11] stream;
Poor deer, quoth he, *thou mak'st a testament*
As worldlings do, giving thy sum of more
To that which had too much:[12] Then, being alone,
Left and abandon'd of his velvet friends;
'Tis right, quoth he; *this misery doth part*
The flux of company: Anon, a careless herd,
Full of the pasture, jumps along by him,
And never stays to greet him; *Ay*, quoth Jaques,
Sweep on, you fat and greasy citizens;
'Tis just the fashion: Wherefore do you look
Upon that poor and broken bankrupt there?
Thus most invectively he pierceth through
The body of country, city, court,

9 Gray, in his Elegy, has availed himself of this passage.:

'There at the foot of yonder nodding beech
That wreathes its old fantastic roots so high,
His listless length at noontide would he stretch,
And pore upon the brook that babbles by.'

10 'Saucius at quadrupes nota intra tecta refugit
Successitque gemens stabulis; questuque cruentus
Atque imploranti similis, tectum omne replevit.'
Virg.

11 i. e. the stream that *needed not* such a supply of moisture.

12 So in Shakspeare's Lover's Complaint:—

'——————in a river——
Upon whose weeping margin she was set
Like usury applying wet to wet'

Yea, and of this our life; swearing, that we
Are mere usurpers, tyrants, and what's worse,
To fright the animals, and to kill them up,
In their assign'd and native dwelling-place.

Duke S. And did you leave him in this contemplation?

2 Lord. We did, my lord, weeping and commenting
Upon the sobbing deer.

Duke S. Show me the place;
I love to cope[1] him in these sullen fits,
For then he's full of matter.

2 Lord. I'll bring you to him straight. [*Exeunt.*

SCENE II. *A Room in the Palace. Enter* Duke Frederick, Lords, *and* Attendants.

Duke F. Can it be possible that no man saw them?
It cannot be: some villains of my court
Are of consent and sufferance in this.

1 Lord. I cannot hear of any that did see her.
The ladies, her attendants of her chamber,
Saw her a-bed; and, in the morning early,
They found the bed untreasur'd of their mistress.

2 Lord. My lord, the roynish[2] clown, at whom so oft
Your grace was wont to laugh, is also missing.
Hesperia, the princess' gentlewoman,
Confesses, that she secretly o'er-heard
Your daughter and her cousin much commend
The parts and graces of the wrestler[3]
That did but lately foil the sinewy Charles;
And she believes, wherever they are gone,
That youth is surely in their company.

Duke F. Send to his brother; fetch that gallant hither;
If he be absent, bring his brother to me,
I'll make him find him: do this suddenly;
And let not search and inquisition quail[4]
To bring again these foolish run-aways. [*Exeunt.*

SCENE III. *Before* Oliver's *House. Enter* Orlando *and* Adam, *meeting.*

Orl. Who's there?

Adam. What! my young master?—O, my gentle master,
O, my sweet master, O you memory[5]
Of old Sir Rowland! why, what make you here?
Why are you virtuous? Why do people love you?
And wherefore are you gentle, strong, and valiant?
Why would you be so fond[6] to overcome
The bony priser[7] of the humorous duke?
Your praise is come too swiftly home before you.
Know you not, master, to some kind of men
Their graces serve them but as enemies?
No more do yours; your virtues, gentle master,
Are sanctified and holy traitors to you.
O, what a world is this, when what is comely
Envenoms him that bears it!

Orl. Why, what's the matter?

Adam. O unhappy youth,
Come not within these doors; within this roof
The enemy of all your graces lives:
Your brother—(no, no brother: yet the son—
Yet not the son;—I will not call him son
Of him I was about to call his father,)—
Hath heard your praises; and this night he means
To burn the lodging where you use to lie,
And you within it: if he fail of that,
He will have other means to cut you off:
I overheard him, and his practices.[8]
This is no place,[9] this house is but a butchery;
Abhor it, fear it, do not enter it.

Orl. Why, whither, Adam, wouldst thou have me go?

Adam. No matter whither, so you come not here

Orl. What, wouldst thou have me go and beg my food?
Or, with a base and boisterous sword, enforce
A thievish living on the common road?
This I must do, or know not what to do:
Yet this I will not do, do how I can;
I rather will subject me to the malice
Of a diverted blood,[10] and bloody brother.

Adam. But do not so: I have five hundred crowns
The thrifty hire I sav'd under your father,
Which I did store, to be my foster-nurse,
When service should in my old limbs lie lame,
And unregarded age in corners thrown;
Take that: and He that doth the ravens feed,
Yea, providently caters for the sparrow,[11]
Be comfort to my age! Here is the gold;
All this I give you: Let me be your servant,
Though I look old, yet I am strong and lusty:
For in my youth I never did apply
Hot and rebellious liquors in my blood;
Nor did not with unbashful forehead woo
The means of weakness and debility;
Therefore my age is as a lusty winter,
Frosty, but kindly: let me go with you,
I'll do the service of a younger man
In all your business and necessities.

Orl. O good old man; how well in thee app[ears]
The constant service of the antique world,
When service sweat for duty, not for meed!
Thou art not for the fashion of these times,
Where none will sweat, but for promotion;
And having that, do choke their service up
Even with the having:[12] it is not so with thee
But, poor old man, thou prun'st a rotten tree,
That cannot so much as a blossom yield,
In lieu of all thy pains and husbandry:
But come thy ways, we'll go along together,
And ere we have thy youthful wages spent,
We'll light upon some settled low content.

Adam. Master, go on, and I will follow thee,
To the last gasp, with truth and loyalty.—
From seventeen years till now almost fourscore
Here lived I, but now live here no more.
At seventeen years many their fortunes seek,
But at fourscore, it is too late a week:
Yet fortune cannot recompense me better,
Than to die well, and not my master's debtor.
[*Exeunt*

SCENE IV. *The Forest of* Arden. *Enter* Rosalind *in boy's clothes,* Celia *drest like a* Shepherdess, *and* Touchstone.

Ros. O Jupiter! how weary[13] are my spirits!

Touch. I care not for my spirits, if my legs were not weary.

Ros. I could find in my heart to disgrace my man's apparel, and to cry like a woman: but I must comfort the weaker vessel, as doublet and hose ought to show itself courageous to petticoat: therefore, courage, good Aliena.

Cel. I pray you, bear with me; I cannot go no further.

Touch. For my part, I had rather bear with you, than bear you; yet I should bear no cross,[14] if I did bear you; for, I think, you have no money in your purse.

---

1 i. e. to *encounter* him. Thus in K. Henry VIII. Act i. Sc. 2:
'——*cope* malicious censurers.'

2 'The *roynish* clown,' mangy or scurvy, from *roigneux*, French. The word is used by Chaucer.

3 *Wrestler* is here to be sounded as a trisyllable.

4 'To *quail*,' says Steevens, 'is to *faint*, to sink into dejection.' It may be so, but in neither of these senses is the word here used by Shakspeare.

5 Shakspeare uses *memory* for *memorial*.

6 I. e. rash, foolish.

7 I suspect that a *priser* was the term for a *wrestler*, a *prise* was a term in that sport for a grappling or hold taken

8 i. e. treacherous devices.

9 *Place* here signifies a *seat*, a *mansion*, a *residence*: it is not yet obsolete in this sense.

10 i. e. blood turned out of a course of nature. Affections alienated.

11 See St. Luke, xii. 6 and 24.

12 Even with the *promotion* gained by service is service extinguished.

13 The old copy reads *merry*; perhaps rightly. Rosalind's language as well as her dress may be intended to have an assumed character.

14 A *cross* was a piece of money stamped with a cross on this Shakspeare often quibbles.

Ros. Well, this is the forest of Arden.

Touch. Ay, now am I in Arden: the more fool I: when I was at home, I was in a better place; but travellers must be content.

Ros. Ay, be so, good Touchstone:—Look you, who comes here; a young man, and an old, in solemn talk.

Enter CORIN *and* SILVIUS.

Cor. That is the way to make her scorn you still.

Sil. O Corin, that thou knew'st how I do love her!

Cor. I partly guess; for I have lov'd ere now.

Sil. No, Corin, being old, thou canst not guess;
Though in thy youth thou wast as true a lover
As ever sigh'd upon a midnight pillow:
But if thy love were ever like to mine
(As sure I think did never man love so,)
How many actions most ridiculous
Hast thou been drawn to by thy fantasy?

Cor. Into a thousand that I have forgotten.

Sil. O, thou didst then ne'er love so heartily:
If thou remember'st not the slightest folly
That ever love did make thee run into,
Thou hast not lov'd:
Or if thou hast not sat as I do now,
Wearying thy hearer in thy mistress' praise,
Thou hast not lov'd:
Or if thou hast not broke from company,
Abruptly, as my passion now makes me,
Thou hast not lov'd: O Phebe, Phebe, Phebe!
[*Exit* SILVIUS.

Ros. Alas, poor shepherd! searching of thy wound,
I have by hard adventure found mine own.

Touch. And I mine: I remember, when I was in love, I broke my sword upon a stone, and bid him take that for coming anight to Jane Smile: and I remember the kissing of her batlet,[1] and the cow's dugs that her pretty chopp'd hands had milk'd: and I remember the wooing of a peascod[2] instead of her; from whom I took two cods, and, giving her them again, said, with weeping tears, *Wear these for my sake.* We, that are true lovers, run into strange capers: but as all is mortal in nature, so is all nature in love mortal[3] in folly.

Ros. Thou speak'st wiser than thou art 'ware of.

Touch. Nay, I shall ne'er be 'ware of mine own wit, till I break my shins against it.

Ros. Jove! Jove! this shepherd's passion
Is much upon my fashion.

Touch. And mine; but it grows something stale
with me.

Cel. I pray you, one of you question 'yond man,
If he for gold will give us any food;
I faint almost to death.

Touch. Holla; you, clown!

Ros. Peace, fool: he's not thy kinsman.

Cor. Who calls?

Touch. Your betters, sir.

Cor. Else are they very wretched.

Ros. Peace, I say:—
Good even to you, friend.

Cor. And to you, gentle sir, and to you all.

Ros. I pr'ythee, shepherd, if that love, or gold,
Can in this desert place buy entertainment,
Bring us where we may rest ourselves, and feed:
Here's a young maid with travel much oppress'd,
And faints for succour.

Cor. Fair sir, I pity her,
And wish for her sake, more than for mine own,
My fortunes were more able to relieve her:
But I am shepherd to another man,
And do not shear the fleeces that I graze;
My master is of churlish disposition,
And little recks[4] to find the way to heaven
By doing deeds of hospitality.
Besides, his cote,[5] his flocks, and bounds of feed,
Are now on sale, and at our sheepcote now,
By reason of his absence, there is nothing
That you will feed on: but what is, come see,
And in my voice[6] most welcome shall you be.

Ros. What is he that shall buy his flock and pasture?

Cor. That young swain that you saw here but
erewhile,
That little cares for buying any thing.

Ros. I pray thee, if it stand with honesty,
Buy thou the cottage, pasture, and the flock,
And thou shalt have to pay for it of us.

Cel. And we will mend thy wages: I like this
place,
And willingly could waste my time in it.

Cor. Assuredly, the thing is to be sold:
Go with me: if you like, upon report,
The soil, the profit, and this kind of life,
I will your very faithful feeder be,
And buy it with your gold right suddenly. [*Exeunt.*

SCENE V. *The same. Enter* AMIENS, JAQUES *and others.*

SONG.

Ami. *Under the greenwood tree,*
Who loves to lie with me,
And turn[7] *his merry note*
Unto the sweet bird's throat,
Come hither, come hither, come hither:
Here shall he see
No enemy,
But winter and rough weather.

Jaq. More, more, I pr'ythee, more.

Ami. It will make you melancholy, monsieur Jaques.

Jaq. I thank it. More, I pr'ythee, more. I can suck melancholy out of a song, as a weazel sucks eggs: More, I pr'ythee, more.

Ami. My voice is ragged;[8] I know, I cannot please you.

Jaq. I do not desire you to please me, I do desire you to sing: Come, more; another stanza: Call you them stanzas?

Ami. What you will, monsieur Jaques.

Jaq. Nay, I care not for their names; they owe me nothing: Will you sing?

Ami. More at your request, than to please myself.

Jaq. Well then, if ever I thank any man, I'll thank you: but that they call compliment, is like the encounter of two dog-apes; and when a man thanks me heartily methinks, I have given him a penny, and he renders me the beggarly thanks. Come, sing; and you that will not, hold your tongues.

Ami. Well, I'll end the song.—Sirs, cover the while: the duke will drink under this tree!—he hath been all this day to look you.

Jaq. And I have been all this day to avoid him. He is too disputable[9] for my company: I think of as many matters as he; but I give heaven thanks and make no boast of them. Come, warble, come.

SONG.

Who doth ambition shun, [All together here.
And loves to live i' the sun,
Seeking the food he eats,
And pleas'd with what he gets,
Come hither, come hither, come hither;
Here shall he see
No enemy,
But winter and rough weather.

1 *Batlet,* the instrument with which washers beat clothes.

2 A *peascod.* This was the ancient term for *peas* growing or gathered, the *cod* being what we now call the *pod.* It is evident why Shakspeare uses the former word.

3 In the middle counties, says Johnson, they use *mortal* as a particle of amplification, as *mortal* tall, *mortal* little. So the meaning here may be '*abounding* in folly.'

4 i. e. heeds, cares for. So in Hamlet:—' and *recks* not his own rede.'

5 i. e. *cot* or *cottage,* the word is still used in its compound form, as sheepcote in the next line.

6 *In my voice,* as far as I have a voice or vote, as far as I have the power to bid you welcome.

7 The old copy reads: ' And *turne* his merry note, which Pope altered unnecessarily to *tune,* the reading of all the modern editions.

8 *Ragged* and rugged had formerly the same meaning.

9 *Disputable,* i. e. disputatious

Jaq. I'll give you a verse to this note, that I made yesterday in despite of my invention.

Ami. And I'll sing it.

Jaq. Thus it goes:

If it do come to pass,
That any man turn ass,
Leaving his wealth and ease,
A stubborn will to please,
Ducdame, ducdame, ducdame;[1]
Here shall he see,
Gross fools as he,
An if he will come to me.

Ami. What's that *ducdame?*

Jaq. 'Tis a Greek invocation, to call fools into a circle. I'll go sleep if I can; if I cannot, I'll rail against all the first-born of Egypt.[2]

Ami. And I'll go seek the duke; his banquet is prepar'd. [*Exeunt severally.*

SCENE VI. *The same. Enter* ORLANDO *and* ADAM.

Adam. Dear master, I can go no further: O, I die for food! Here lie I down, and measure out my grave.[3] Farewell, kind master.

Orl. Why, how now, Adam! no greater heart in thee? Live a little; comfort a little; cheer thyself a little: if this uncouth forest yield any thing savage, I will either be food for it, or bring it for food to thee. Thy conceit is nearer death than thy powers. For my sake, be comfortable; hold death awhile at the arm's end: I will here be with thee presently; and if I bring thee not something to eat, I'll give thee leave to die: but if thou diest before I come, thou art a mocker of my labour. Well said! thou look'st cheerly: and I'll be with thee quickly.—Yet thou liest in the bleak air: Come, I will bear thee to some shelter; and thou shalt not die for lack of a dinner, if there live any thing in this desert. Cheerly, good Adam! [*Exeunt.*

SCENE VII. *The same. A Table set out. Enter* Duke *senior,* AMIENS, Lords, *and others.*

Duke S. I think he be transform'd into a beast;
For I can no where find him like a man.

1 Lord. My lord, he is but even now gone hence:
Here was he merry, hearing of a song.

Duke S. If he, compact of jars,[4] grow musical,
We shall have shortly discord in the spheres:—
Go, seek him; tell him, I would speak with him.

Enter JAQUES.

1 Lord. He saves my labour by his own approach.

Duke S. Why, how now, monsieur! What a life is this,
That your poor friends must woo your company?
What! you look merrily.

Jaq. A fool, a fool!—I met a fool i' the forest,
A motley fool;—a miserable world!
As I do live by food, I met a fool;
Who laid him down and bask'd him in the sun,
And rail'd on lady Fortune in good terms,
In good set terms,—and yet a motley fool.
Good-morrow, fool, quoth I: *No, sir,* quoth he,
Call me not fool, till heaven hath sent me fortune:[5]
And then he drew a dial from his poke;
And looking on it with lack-lustre eye,
Says, very wisely, *It is ten o'clock:*
Thus may we see, quoth he, *how the world wags:*
'Tis but an hour ago, since it was nine;
And after an hour more, 'twill be eleven;
And so, from hour to hour, we ripe and ripe,
And then, from hour to hour, we rot and rot,
And thereby hangs a tale. When I did hear
The motley fool thus moral on the time,
My lungs began to crow like chanticleer,
That fools should be so deep-contemplative,
And I did laugh, sans intermission,
An hour by his dial.—O noble fool!
A worthy fool! Motley's the only wear.[6]

Duke S. What fool is this?

Jaq. O worthy fool!—One that hath been a courtier;
And says, if ladies be but young, and fair,
They have the gift to know it: and in his brain,
Which is as dry as the remainder biscuit[7]
After a voyage,—he hath strange places cramm'd
With observation, the which he vents
In mangled forms:—O, that I were a fool!
I am ambitious for a motley coat.

Duke S. Thou shalt have one.

Jaq. It is my only suit;[8]
Provided, that you weed your better judgments
Of all opinion that grows rank in them,
That I am wise. I must have liberty
Withal, as large a charter as the wind,[9]
To blow on whom I please; for so fools have:
And they that are most galled with my folly,
They most must laugh: And why, sir, must they so?
The *why* is plain as way to parish church:
He, that a fool doth very wisely hit,
Doth very foolishly, although he smart,
[10]Not to seem senseless of the bob: if not,
The wise man's folly is anatomiz'd
Even by the squand'ring glances of the fool.
Invest me in my motley; give me leave
To speak my mind, and I will through and through
Cleanse the foul body of the infected world,[11]
If they will patiently receive my medicine.

Duke S. Fye on thee! I can tell what thou wouldst do.

Jaq. What, for a counter,[12] would I do, but good?

Duke S. Most mischievous foul sin, in chiding sin:
For thou thyself hast been a libertine,
As sensual as the brutish sting[13] itself;
And all the embossed sores, and headed evils,
That thou with licence of free foot hast caught,
Wouldst thou disgorge into the general world.

Jaq. Why, who cries out on pride,
That can therein tax any private party?
Doth it not flow as hugely as the sea,
Till that the very very means do ebb?[14]
What woman in the city do I name,
When that I say, The city-woman bears
The cost of princes on unworthy shoulders?
Who can come in, and say, that I mean her,
When such a one as she, such is her neighbour?
Or what is he of basest function,
That says, his bravery[15] is not on my cost,
(Thinking that I mean him,) but therein suits
His folly to the mettle of my speech?

---

1 Sir Thomas Hanmer reads *duc ad me*, i. e. bring him to me, which reading Johnson highly approves.

2 'The firstborn of Egypt,' a proverbial expression for *high-born* persons; it is derived from Exodus, xii. 29.

3 So in Romeo and Juliet:—
'—— fall upon the ground, as I do now,
Taking the measure of an unmade grave.'

4 i. e. made up of discords. In the Comedy of Errors we have '*compact* of credit,' for made up of credulity.

5 Alluding to the proverb, *Fortuna favet fatuis*, 'Fools have fortune.'

6 The fool was anciently dressed in a party-coloured coat.

7 So in Ben Jonson's Every Man out of his Humour:
'And now and then breaks a dry biscuit jest,
Which, that it may more easily be chew'd,
He steeps in his own laughter.'

8 'My only *suit*,' a quibble between *petition* and *dress* is here intended.

9 In Henry V. we have:—
'The *wind*, that *charter'd* libertine, is still.'

10 The old copies read only, *seem senseless*, &c. *not to* were supplied by Theobald.

11 So in Macbeth:—
'Cleanse the stuff'd bosom of that perilous stuff.'

12 About the time when this play was written, the French *counters* (i. e. pieces of false money used as a means of reckoning) were brought into use in England. They are again mentioned in Troilus and Cressida, and in the Winter's Tale.

13 So in Spenser's Faerie Queene, b. i. c. xii.:—
'A herd of bulls whom kindly rage doth *sting*'

14 The old copies read—
'Till that the *weary* very means do ebb,' &c.
The emendation is by Pope.

15 Finery.

There then; How then, what then?[1] Let me see wherein
My tongue hath wrong'd him: if it do him right,
Then he hath wrong'd himself; if he be free,
Why then, my taxing, like a wild goose flies,
Unclaim'd of any man.—But who comes here?

Enter ORLANDO, *with his Sword drawn.*

Orl. Forbear, and eat no more.
Jaq. Why, I have eat none yet.
Orl. Nor shalt not, till necessity be serv'd.
Jaq. Of what kind should this cock come of?
Duke S. Art thou thus bolden'd, man, by thy distress;
Or else a rude despiser of good manners,
That in civility thou seem'st so empty?
Orl. You touch'd my vein at first; the thorny point
Of bare distress hath ta'en[2] from me the show
Of smooth civility; yet I am inland bred,[3]
And know some nurture:[4] But forbear, I say;
He dies, that touches any of this fruit,
Till I and my affairs are answered.
Jaq. An you will not be answered with reason, I must die.
Duke S. What would you have? Your gentleness shall force,
More than your force move us to gentleness.
Orl. I almost die for food, and let me have it.
Duke S. Sit down and feed, and welcome to our table.
Orl. Speak you so gently? Pardon me, I pray you:
I thought, that all things had been savage here;
And therefore put I on the countenance
Of stern commandment: But, whate'er you are,
That in this desert inaccessible,[5]
Under the shade of melancholy boughs,
Lose and neglect the creeping hours of time,
If ever you have look'd on better days,
If ever been where bells have knoll'd to church;
If ever sat at any good man's feast;
If ever from your eye-lids wip'd a tear,
And know what 'tis to pity, and be pitied;
Let gentleness my strong enforcement be:
In the which hope, I blush, and hide my sword.
Duke S. True is it that we have seen better days;
And have with holy bell been knoll'd to church:
And sat at good men's feasts; and wip'd our eyes
Of drops that sacred pity hath engender'd:
And therefore sit you down in gentleness,
And take upon command[6] what help we have,
That to your wanting may be ministered.
Orl. Then, but forbear your food a little while,
Whiles, like a doe, I go to find my fawn,
And give it food.[7] There is an old poor man,
Who after me hath many a weary step
Limp'd in pure love: till he be first suffic'd,—
Oppress'd with two weak evils, age and hunger,—
I will not touch a bit.
Duke S. Go find him out,
And we will nothing waste till you return.
Orl. I thank ye; and be bless'd for your good comfort! [*Exit.*
Duke S. Thou seest, we are not all alone unhappy:
This wide and universal theatre
Presents more woful pageants than the scene
Wherein we play in.[8]
Jaq. All the world's a stage,
And all the men and women merely players:
They have their exits, and their entrances;
And one man in his time plays many parts,
His acts being seven ages.[9] At first, the infant,
Mewling and puking in the nurse's arms;
And then, the whining school-boy, with his satchel,
And shining morning face, creeping like snail
Unwillingly to school: and then, the lover;
Sighing like furnace,[10] with a woful ballad
Made to his mistress' eye-brow: Then, a soldier;
Full of strange oaths, and bearded like the pard,
Jealous in honour, sudden[11] and quick in quarrel,
Seeking the bubble reputation
Even in the cannon's mouth: And then, the justice;
In fair round belly, with good capon lin'd,
With eyes severe, and beard of formal cut,
Full of wise saws and modern[12] instances,
And so he plays his part: The sixth age shifts
Into the lean and slipper'd pantaloon;[13]
With spectacles on nose, and pouch on side,
His youthful hose well sav'd, a world too wide
For his shrunk shank; and his big manly voice,
Turning again toward childish treble, pipes
And whistles in his sound: Last scene of all,
That ends this strange eventful history,
Is second childishness, and mere oblivion;
Sans teeth, sans eyes, sans taste, sans every thing

Re-enter ORLANDO, *with* ADAM.

Duke S. Welcome: Set down your venerable burden,
And let him feed.
Orl. I thank you most for him.
Adam. So had you need;
I scarce can speak to thank you for myself.
Duke S. Welcome, fall to: I will not trouble you
As yet, to question you about your fortunes:—
Give us some music; and, good cousin, sing.

AMIENS *sings.*

SONG.

I.

Blow, blow, thou winter wind,
Thou art not so unkind[14]
As man's ingratitude;
Thy tooth is not so keen,
Because thou art not seen,[15]
Although thy breath be rude.
Heigh, ho! sing, heigh, ho! unto the green holly:
Most friendship is feigning, most loving mere folly:
Then, heigh, ho, the holly!
This life is most jolly.

II.

Freeze, freeze, thou bitter sky,
Thou dost not bite so nigh
As benefits forgot:

1 Malone thinks we should read, *where* then? in this redundant line.
2 'We might read *torn* with more elegance,' says Johnson, 'but elegance alone will not justify alteration.'
3 *Inland* here, and elsewhere in this play, is opposite to *outland*, or *upland*. Orlando means to say that he had not been *bred among clowns*.
4 *Nurture* is education, breeding, manners. 'It is a point of *nourtour* or *good manners* to salute them that you meete.'
5 'This desert inaccessible.' So in the Adventures of Simonides, by Barnabe Riche, 1580; '——and onely acquainted himselfe with this *unaccessible desert*.'
6 i. e. at your own command.
7 So in Venus and Adonis—
'Like a milch *doe*, whose swelling dugs do ake,
Hasting to *feede her fawn*.'

8 Pleonasms of this kind were by no means uncommon in the writers of Shakspeare's age; 'I was afeard to what end his talke would come *to*.' *Baret.*
9 In the old play of Damon and Pythias, we have—'Pythagoras said, that this world was like a stage whereon many play their parts.'
10 So in Cymbeline; 'He *furnaceth* the thick sighs from him.'
11 One of the ancient senses of *sudden* is *violent*
12 Trite, common, trivial.
13 The *pantaloon* was a character in the old Italian farces; it represented, as Warburton observes, a thin emaciated old man in *slippers*.
14 That is, thy action is not so contrary to thy *kind*, so *unnatural*, as the ingratitude of man.
15 Johnson thus explains this line, which some of the editors have thought corrupt or misprinted; 'Thou winter wind, says Amiens, thy rudeness gives the less pain, as *thou art not seen*, as thou art an enemy that dost not brave us with thy presence, and whose unkindness is therefore not aggravated by insult.'

Though thou the waters warp,[1]
Thy sting is not so sharp,
As friend remember'd not.[2]
Heigh, ho! sing, heigh, ho! &c.

Duke S. If that you were the good Sir Rowland's son,—
As you have whisper'd faithfully you were;
And as mine eye doth his effigies witness
Most truly limn'd, and living in your face,—
Be truly welcome hither: I am the duke,
That lov'd your father: The residue of your fortune,
Go to my cave and tell me.—Good old man,
Thou art right welcome as thy master is:
Support him by the arm.—Give me your hand,
And let me all your fortunes understand. [*Exeunt.*

ACT III.

SCENE I. *A Room in the Palace. Enter* Duke FREDERICK, OLIVER, Lords, *and* Attendants.

Duke F. Not see him since? Sir, sir, that cannot be:
But were I not the better part made mercy,
I should not seek an absent argument[3]
Of my revenge, thou present: But look to it;
Find out thy brother, wheresoe'er he is;
Seek him with candle: bring him dead or living,
Within this twelvemonth, or turn thou no more
To seek a living in our territory.
Thy lands, and all things that thou dost call thine,
Worth seizure, do we seize into our hands;
Till thou canst quit thee by thy brother's mouth,
Of what we think against thee.

Oli. O, that your highness knew my heart in this?
I never lov'd my brother in my life.

Duke F. More villain thou.—Well, push him out of doors;
And let my officers of such a nature
Make an extent[4] upon his house and lands:
Do this expediently,[5] and turn him going. [*Exeunt.*

SCENE II. *The Forest. Enter* ORLANDO, *with a Paper.*

Orl. Hang there, my verse, in witness of my love:
And thou, thrice-crowned queen of night,[6] survey
With thy chaste eye, from thy pale sphere above,
Thy huntress' name, that my full life doth sway.
O Rosalind! these trees shall be my books,
And in their barks my thoughts I'll character;
That every eye, which in this forest looks,
Shall see thy virtue witness'd every where.
Run, run, Orlando; carve, on every tree,
The fair, the chaste, and unexpressive[7] she. [*Exit.*

Enter CORIN *and* TOUCHSTONE.

Corin. And how like you this shepherd's life, master Touchstone?

Touch. Truly, shepherd, in respect of itself, it is a good life; but in respect that it is a shepherd's life, it is naught. In respect that it is solitary, I like it very well; but in respect that it is private, it is a very vile life. Now in respect it is in the fields, it pleaseth me well; but in respect it is not in the court, it is tedious. As it is a spare life, look you, it fits my humour well; but as there is no more plenty in it, it goes much against my stomach. Hast any philosophy in thee, shepherd?

Cor. No more, but that I know, the more one sickens, the worse at ease he is; and that he that wants money, means, and content, is without three good friends:—That the property of rain is to wet, and fire to burn: That good pasture makes fat sheep; and that a great cause of the night, is lack of the sun: That he that hath learned no wit by nature nor art, may complain of[8] good breeding, or comes of a very dull kindred.

Touch. Such a one is a natural[9] philosopher. Wast ever in court, shepherd?

Cor. No, truly.

Touch. Then thou art damn'd.

Cor. Nay, I hope,——

Touch. Truly, thou art damn'd; like an ill-roasted egg, all on one side.[10]

Cor. For not being at court? Your reason.

Touch. Why, if thou never wast at court, thou never saw'st good manners; if thou never saw'st good manners, then thy manners must be wicked; and wickedness is sin, and sin is damnation: Thou art in a parlous state, shepherd.

Cor. Not a whit, Touchstone: those, that are good manners at the court, are as ridiculous in the country, as the behaviour of the country is most mockable at the court. You told me, you salute not at the court, but you kiss your hands; that courtesy would be uncleanly, if courtiers were shepherds.

Touch. Instance, briefly; come, instance.

Cor. Why, we are still handling our ewes; and their fells, you know, are greasy.

Touch. Why, do not your courtier's hands sweat? and is not the grease of a mutton as wholesome as the sweat of a man? Shallow, shallow: A better instance, I say; come.

Cor. Besides, our hands are hard.

Touch. Your lips will feel them the sooner. Shallow, again: a more sounder instance, come.

Cor. And they are often tarr'd over with the surgery of our sheep; And would you have us kiss tar? The courtier's hands are perfumed with civet.

Touch. Most shallow man! Thou worms-meat, in respect of a good piece of flesh: Indeed!—Learn of the wise, and perpend: Civet is of a baser birth than tar; the very uncleanly flux of a cat. Mend the instance, shepherd.

Cor. You have too courtly a wit for me; I'll rest.

Touch. Wilt thou rest damn'd? God help thee, shallow man! God make incision[11] in thee! thou art raw.[12]

Cor. Sir, I am a true labourer; I earn that I eat, get that I wear; owe no man hate, envy no man's happiness; glad of other men's good, content with my harm: and the greatest of my pride is, to see my ewes graze, and my lambs suck.

---

1 'Though thou the *waters warp*.' Mr. Holt White has pointed out a Saxon adage in Hickes's Thesaurus, vol i. p. 221; *Winter shall warp water.* So that Shakspeare's expression was anciently proverbial. To *warp*, from the Gothic *Wairpan*, jacere, projicere, signified anciently to *weave*, as may be seen in Florio's Dict. v. *ordire;* or in Cotgrave v. *ourdir*. 'Though thou the waters *warp*,' may therefore be explained, as Mr. Nares suggests, 'Though thou *weave* the waters *into a firm texture*.'

2 *Remember'd* for remembering. So afterwards in Act iii. Sc. *ult.* 'And now I am *remember'd*,' i. e and now that I *bethink* me, &c.

3 The *argument* is used for the *contents* of a book; hence Shakspeare considered it as meaning the *subject*, and then used it for *subject* in another sense.

4 Seize by legal process.

5 i. e. *expeditiously*. Expedient is used by Shakspeare throughout his plays for *expeditious*.

6 This passage seems to evince a most intimate knowledge of ancient mythology, but Shakspeare was doubtless familiar with that fine racy old poet, Chapman's Hymns to Night and to Cynthia, which, though over-informed with learning, have many highly poetical passages.

7 i. e. *inexpressible*.

8 '*Of* good breeding,' &c. The anomalous use of this preposition has been remarked on many occasions in these plays.

9 A *natural* being a common term for a fool, Touchstone evidently intended to quibble on the word.

10 'Touchstone,' says Malone, 'I apprehend only means to say, that Corin is completely damned; as irretrievably destroyed as an egg that is spoiled in the roasting, by being done on one side only.' With Johnson I must say, that 'I do not fully comprehend the meaning of this jest.'

11 'God make incision in thee! thou art raw.' It has been ingeniously urged that *insition* or grafting is here meant, and that the phrase may be explained 'God put knowledge into thee,'—but we want instances to confirm this. Steevens thought the allusion here was to the common expression of *cutting for the simples;* and the subsequent speech of Touchstone, 'That is another *simple* sin in you,' gives colour to this conjecture.

12 i. e. ignorant, unexperienced.

Touch. That is another simple sin in you: to bring the ewes and rams together, and to offer to get your living by the copulation of cattle: to be bawd to a bell-wether; and to betray a she-lamb of a twelvemonth, to a crooked-pated, old, cuckoldy ram, out of all reasonable match. If thou be'st not damn'd for this, the devil himself will have no shepherds; I cannot see else how thou shouldst 'scape.

Cor. Here comes young master Ganymede, my new mistress's brother.

Enter ROSALIND, *reading a Paper.*

Ros. *From the east to western Ind,*
No jewel is like Rosalind,
Her worth, being mounted on the wind,
Through all the world bears Rosalind.
All the pictures, fairest lin'd,[1]
Are but black to Rosalind.
Let no face be kept in mind,
But the fair[2] *of Rosalind.*

Touch. I'll rhyme you so, eight years together; dinners, and suppers, and sleeping hours excepted; it is the right butter-woman's rank[3] to market.

Ros. Out, fool!

Touch. For a taste:—

If a hart do lack a hind,
Let him seek out Rosalind.
If the cat will after kind,
So, be sure, will Rosalind.
Winter-garments must be lin'd,
So must slender Rosalind.
They that reap, must sheaf and bind;
Then to cart with Rosalind.
Sweetest nut hath sourest rind,
Such a nut is Rosalind.
He that sweetest rose will find,
Must find love's prick, and Rosalind.

This is the very false gallop of verses: Why do you infect yourself with them?

Ros. Peace, you dull fool; I found them on a tree.

Touch. Truly, the tree yields bad fruit.

Ros. I'll graff it with you, and then I shall graff it with a medlar: then it will be the earliest fruit in the country: for you'll be rotten e'er you be half ripe, and that's the right virtue of the medlar.

Touch. You have said; but whether wisely or no, let the forest judge.

Enter CELIA, *reading a Paper.*

Ros. Peace!
Here comes my sister, reading; stand aside.

Cel. *Why should this desert silent*[4] *be?*
For it is unpeopled? No;
Tongues I'll hang on every tree,
That shall civil[5] *sayings show.*
Some, how brief the life of man
Runs his erring pilgrimage;
That the stretching of a span
Buckles in his sum of age.
Some, of violated vows
'Twixt the souls of friend and friend:
But upon the fairest boughs,
Or at every sentence' end,
Will I Rosalinda write;
Teaching all that read, to know
The quintessence of every sprite
Heaven would in little[6] *show.*
Therefore heaven nature charg'd[7]
That one body should be fill'd
With all graces wide enlarg'd:
Nature presently distill'd
Helen's cheek, but not her heart;
Cleopatra's majesty;
Atalanta's better part;[8]
Sad Lucretia's modesty.
Thus Rosalind of many parts
By heavenly synod was devis'd;
Of many faces, eyes, and hearts,
To have the touches dearest priz'd.
Heaven would that she these gifts should have,
And I to live and die her slave.

Ros. O most gentle Jupiter!—what tedious homily of love have you wearied your parishioners withal, and never cry'd, *Have patience, good people!*

Cel. How now! back friends;—Shepherd, go off a little:—Go with him, sirrah.

Touch. Come, shepherd, let us make an honourable retreat; though not with bag and baggage, yet with scrip and scrippage.

[*Exeunt* CORIN *and* TOUCHSTONE.

Cel. Didst thou hear these verses?

Ros. O, yes, I heard them all, and more too; for some of them had in them more feet than the verses would bear.

Cel. That's no matter; the feet might bear the verses.

Ros. Ay, but the feet were lame, and could not bear themselves without the verse, and therefore stood lamely in the verse.

Cel. But didst thou hear, without wondering, how thy name should be hanged and carv'd upon these trees?

Ros. I was seven of the nine days out of the wonder, before you come; for look here what I found on a palm-tree:[9] I never was so be-rhymed since Pythagoras' time, that I was an Irish rat,[10] which I can hardly remember.

Cel. Trow you, who hath done this?

Ros. Is it a man?

Cel. And a chain, that you once wore, about his neck: Change you colour?

Ros. I pr'ythee, who?

Cel. O, lord, lord! it is a hard matter for friends to meet; but mountains may be removed with earthquakes,[11] and so encounter.

Ros. Nay, but who is it?

Cel. Is it possible?

Ros. Nay, I pray thee now, with most petitionary vehemence, tell me who it is.

Cel. O wonderful, wonderful, and most wonderful wonderful, and yet again wonderful, and after that out of all whooping?[12]

Ros. Good my complexion![13] dost thou think, though I am caparison'd like a man, I have a

1 i. e. most fairly *delineated.*

2 *Fair* is beauty.

3 'The right butter-woman's *rank* to market' means the *jog-trot rate* (as it is vulgarly called) with which butter women *uniformly* travel *one after another* in their road to market. In its application to Orlando's poetry, it means a *set or string* of verses in the *same coarse cadence* and *vulgar uniformity of rhythm.*

4 The word *silent* is not in the old copy. Pope corrected the passage by reading
'Why should this *a* desert be?'
The present reading was proposed by Tyrwhitt, who observes that *the hanging of tongues on every tree* would not make it less a desert?

5 '*Civil*,' says Johnson, 'is here used in the same sense as when we say, *civil* wisdom and *civil* life, in opposition to a solitary state. This desert shall not appear *unpeopled*, for every tree shall teach the maxims or incidents of social life.'

6 i. e. in miniature. So in Hamlet. 'a hundred ducats a piece for his *picture in little.*'

7 The hint is probably taken from the Picture of Apelles, or the Pandora of the Ancients.

8 There is a great diversity of opinion among the commentators about what is meant by the *better part* of Atalanta, for which I must refer the reader, who is desirous of seeing this knotty point discussed, to the Variorum editions of Shakspeare.

9 A *palm tree* in the forest of Arden is as much out of its place as a lioness in a subsequent scene.

10 Johnson has called Rosalind a very learned lady for this trite allusion to the Pythagorean doctrine of the transmigration of souls. It was no less common than the other allusion of rhyming rats to death in Ireland. This fanciful idea probably arose from some metrical charm or incantation used there for ridding houses of rats

11 Alluding ironically to the proverb:
'Friends may meet, but mountains never greet'

12 To *whoop* or hoop is to cry out, to exclaim with astonishment.

13 'Good my complexion!' This singular phrase was probably only a little unmeaning exclamation si

doublet and hose in my disposition? One inch of delay more is a South sea of discovery.[1] I pr'ythee, tell me who is it? quickly, and speak apace: I would thou couldst stammer, that thou might'st pour this conceal'd man out of thy mouth, as wine comes out of a narrow-mouth'd bottle; either too much at once, or none at all. I pr'ythee take the cork out of thy mouth, that I may drink thy tidings.

Cel. So you may put a man in your belly.

Ros. Is he of God's making? What manner of man? Is his head worth a hat, or his chin worth a beard?

Cel. Nay, he hath but a little beard.

Ros. Why, God will send more if the man will be thankful: let me stay the growth of his beard, if thou delay me not the knowledge of his chin.

Cel. It is young Orlando; that tripp'd up the wrestler's heels, and your heart, both in an instant.

Ros. Nay, but the devil take mocking; speak sad brow, and true maid.[2]

Cel. I'faith, coz, 'tis he.

Ros. Orlando?

Cel. Orlando.

Ros. Alas the day! what shall I do with my doublet and hose?—What did he, when thou saw'st him? What said he? How looked he? Wherein went he?[3] What makes he here? Did he ask for me? Where remains he? How parted he with thee? and when shalt thou see him again? Answer me in one word.

Cel. You must borrow me Garagantua's[4] mouth first: 'tis a word too great for any mouth of this age's size: To say, ay, and no, to these particulars, is more than to answer in a catechism.

Ros. But doth he know that I am in this forest, and in man's apparel? Looks he as freshly as he did the day he wrestled?

Cel. It is as easy to count atomies,[5] as to resolve the propositions of a lover:—but take a taste of my finding him, and relish it with a good observance. I found him under a tree, like a dropp'd acorn.

Ros. It may well be call'd Jove's tree, when it drops forth such fruit.

Cel. Give me audience, good madam.

Ros. Proceed.

Cel. There lay he, stretch'd along, like a wounded knight.

Ros. Though it be pity to see such a sight, it well becomes the ground.

Cel. Cry, holla![6] to thy tongue, I pr'ythee; it curvets very unseasonably. He was furnish'd like a hunter.

Ros. O ominous! he comes to kill my heart.[7]

Cel. I would sing my song without a burden: thou bring'st me out of tune.

Ros. Do you not know I am a woman? when I think, I must speak. Sweet, say on.

Enter Orlando *and* Jaques.

Cel. You bring me out:—Soft! comes he not here?

Ros. 'Tis he; slink by, and note him.

[Celia *and* Rosalind *retire.*

Jaq. I thank you for your company; but, good faith, I had as lief have been myself alone.

Orl. And so had I; but yet, for fashion's sake, I thank you too for your society.

Jaq. God be with you; let's meet as little as we can.

Orl. I do desire we may be better strangers.

Jaq. I pray you, mar no more trees with writing love-songs in their barks.

Orl. I pray you, mar no more of my verses with reading them ill-favouredly.

Jaq. Rosalind is your love's name?

Orl. Yes, just.

Jaq. I do not like her name.

Orl. There was no thought of pleasing you, when she was christen'd.

Jaq. What stature is she of?

Orl. Just as high as my heart.

Jaq. You are full of pretty answers: Have you not been acquainted with goldsmiths' wives, and conn'd them out of rings?

Orl. Not so; but I answer you right painted cloth,[8] from whence you have studied your questions.

Jaq. You have a nimble wit; I think it was made of Atalanta's heels. Will you sit down with me? and we two will rail against our mistress the world, and all our misery.

Orl. I will chide no breather in the world, but myself; against whom I know most faults.

Jaq. The worst fault you have, is to be in love.

Orl. 'Tis a fault I will not change for your best virtue. I am weary of you.

Jaq. By my troth, I was seeking for a fool, when I found you.

Orl. He is drown'd in the brook; look but in and you shall see him.

Jaq. There shall I see mine own figure.

Orl. Which I take to be either a fool, or a cipher.

Jaq. I'll tarry no longer with you: farewell, good signior love.

Orl. I am glad of your departure; adieu, good monsieur melancholy.

[*Exit* Jaq.—Cel. *and* Ros. *come forward.*

Ros. I will speak to him like a saucy lacquey, and under that habit play the knave with him.—Do you hear, forester?

Orl. Very well; what would you?

Ros. I pray you, what is't o'clock?

Orl. You should ask me, what time o'day; there's no clock in the forest.

Ros. Then there is no true lover in the forest; else sighing every minute, and groaning every hour, would detect the lazy foot of time, as well as a clock.

Orl. And why not the swift foot of time? had not that been as proper?

Ros. By no means, sir: Time travels in divers paces with divers persons: I'll tell you who time ambles withal, who time trots withal, who time gallops withal, and who he stands still withal.

Orl. I pr'ythee, who doth he trot withal?

Ros. Marry, he trots hard with a young maid, between the contract of her marriage, and the day it is solemnized: if the interim be but a se'nnight, time's pace is so hard that it seems the length of seven years.

Orl. Who ambles time withal.

Ros. With a priest that lacks Latin, and a rich man that hath not the gout; for the one sleeps easily, because he cannot study; and the other lives merrily, because he feels no pain: the one lacking the burden of lean and wasteful learning; the other knowing no burden of heavy tedious penury: These time ambles withal.

Orl. Who doth he gallop withal

Ros. With a thief to the gallows: for though he

---

milar to Goodness me! many such have been current in familiar speech at all times.

1 '*A south sea of discovery*,' is not a discovery *as far off*, but as *comprehensive* as the South Sea, which being the largest in the world, affords the widest scope for exercising curiosity.

2 '*Speak sad brow, and true maid.*' Speak *seriously* and *honestly*; or in other words, 'speak with a *serious* countenance, and as *truly* as thou art a virgin.'

3 i. e. how was he dressed?

4 'Garagantua.' The giant of Rabelais, who swallowed five pilgrims, their staves and all, in a salad.

5 'An *atomie* is a mote flying in the sunne. Any thing so small that it cannot be made lesse' *Bullokar's English Expositor*, 1616.

6 *Holla!* This was a term of the manege, by which the rider restrained and *stopped* his horse.

7 A quibble between *hart* and *heart*, then spelt the same.

8 To answer *right painted cloth*, is to answer sententiously. We still say she talks *right* Billingsgate. *Painted cloth* was a species of hangings for the walls of rooms, which has generally been supposed and explained to mean *tapestry*; but was really *cloth* or canvass *painted* with various devices and mottos. The verses, mottos, and proverbial sentences on such cloths are often made the subject of allusion in our old writers.

go as softly as foot can fall, he thinks himself too soon there.

Orl. Who stays it withal?

Ros. With lawyers in the vacation: for they sleep between term and term, and then they perceive not how time moves.

Orl. Where dwell you, pretty youth?

Ros. With this shepherdess, my sister; here in the skirts of the forest, like fringe upon a petticoat.

Orl. Are you a native of this place?

Ros. As the coney that you see dwell where she is kindled.

Orl. Your accent is something finer than you could purchase in so removed[1] a dwelling.

Ros. I have been told so of many: but, indeed, an old religious uncle of mine taught me to speak, who was in his youth an inland[2] man; one that knew courtship[3] too well, for there he fell in love. I have heard him read many lectures against it; and I thank God, I am not a woman, to be touch'd with so many giddy offences as he hath generally tax'd their whole sex withal.

Orl. Can you remember any of the principal evils that he laid to the charge of women?

Ros. There were none principal; they were all like one another, as half-pence are; every one fault seeming monstrous, till his fellow fault came to match it.

Orl. I pr'ythee, recount some of them.

Ros. No; I will not cast away my physic, but on those that are sick. There is a man haunts the forest, that abuses our young plants with carving Rosalind on their barks; hangs odes upon hawthorns, and elegies on brambles; all forsooth, deifying the name of Rosalind: if I could meet that fancymonger, I would give him some good counsel, for he seems to have the quotidian of love upon him.

Orl. I am he that is so love-shaked; I pray you tell me your remedy.

Ros. There is none of my uncle's marks upon you: he taught me how to know a man in love; in which cage of rushes, I am sure, you are not prisoner.

Orl. What were his marks?

Ros. A lean cheek; which you have not: a blue eye,[4] and sunken; which you have not: an unquestionable spirit;[5] which you have not: a beard neglected; which you have not;—but I pardon you for that; for, simply, your having[6] in beard is a younger brother's revenue:—Then your hose should be ungarter'd, your bonnet unbanded, your sleeve unbuttoned, your shoe untied, and every thing about you demonstrating a careless desolation.[7] But you are no such man; you are rather point-device[8] in your accoutrements; as loving yourself, than seeming the lover of any other.

Orl. Fair youth, I would I could make thee believe I love.

Ros. Me believe it! you may as soon make her that you love believe it; which, I warrant, she is apter to do, than to confess she does: that is one of the points in which women still give the lie to their consciences. But, in good sooth, are you he that hangs the verses on the trees, wherein Rosalind is so admired?

Orl. I swear to thee, youth, by the white hand of Rosalind, I am that he, that unfortunate he.

Ros. But are you so much in love as your rhymes speak?

Orl. Neither rhyme nor reason can express how much.

Ros. Love is merely a madness; and I tell you, deserves as well a dark house and a whip, as madmen do: and the reason why they are not so punished and cured, is, that the lunacy is so ordinary, that the whippers are in love too: Yet I profess curing it by counsel.

Orl. Did you ever cure any so?

Ros. Yes, one; and in this manner. He was to imagine me his love, his mistress; and I set him every day to woo me: At which time would I, being but a moonish[9] youth, grieve, be effeminate, changeable, longing, and liking; proud, fantastical, apish, shallow, inconstant, full of tears, full of smiles; for every passion something, and for no passion truly any thing, as boys and women are for the most part cattle of this colour: would now like him, now loathe him; then entertain him, then forswear him; now weep for him, then spit at him; then I drave my suitor from his mad humour of love, to a living humour of madness;[10] which was to forswear the full stream of the world, and to live in a nook merely monastic: And thus I cured him; and this way will I take upon me to wash your liver as clean as a sound sheep's heart, that there shall not be one spot of love in't.

Orl. I would not be cured, youth.

Ros. I would cure you, if you would but call me Rosalind, and come every day to my cote, and woo me.

Orl. Now, by the faith of my love, I will: tell me where it is.

Ros. Go with me to it, and I'll show it you: and, by the way, you shall tell me where in the forest you live: Will you go?

Orl. With all my heart, good youth.

Ros. Nay, you must call me Rosalind:—Come, sister, will you go? [*Exeunt.*

SCENE III. *Enter* TOUCHSTONE *and* AUDREY;[11] JAQUES *at a distance, observing them.*

Touch. Come apace, good Audrey; I will fetch up your goats, Audrey: And how, Audrey? am I the man yet? Doth my simple feature content you?

Aud. Your features! Lord warrant us! what features?[12]

Touch. I am here with thee and thy goats, as the most capricious[13] poet, honest Ovid, was among the Goths.

Jaq. O knowledge ill-inhabited![14] worse than Jove in a thatch'd house! [*Aside.*

Touch. When a man's verses cannot be understood, nor a man's good wit seconded with the forward child, understanding, it strikes a man more dead than a great reckoning in a little room:[15]—Truly, I would the gods had made thee poetical.

Aud. I do not know what poetical is: Is it honest in deed, and word? Is it a true thing?

1 i. e. sequestered.

2 i. e. civilized. See note on Act ii. Sc. 7.

3 *Courtship* is here used for *courtly behaviour, courtiership.* See Romeo and Juliet, Act iii. Sc. 3. The context shows that this is the sense:—'for *there* he fell in love;' i. e. *at court.*

4 i. e. a blueness about the eyes, an evidence of anxiety and dejection.

5 i. e. *a spirit averse to conversation.* Shakspeare often uses *question* for discourse, conversation, as in the next scene: 'I met the duke yesterday, and had much *question* with him.'

6 *Having* is possession, estate.

7 These seem to have been the established and characteristical marks of a lover in Shakspeare's time.

8 i. e. *precise, exact;* drest with finical nicety.

9 *Moonish,* that is, as changeable as the moon.

10 'If,' says Johnson, 'this be the true reading, we must by *living* understand *lasting* or *permanent.*' But he suspected that this passage was corrupt; that originally some antithesis was intended, which is now lost.

11 *Audrey* is a corruption of *Etheldreda.* The saint of that name is so styled in ancient calendars.

12 'What features!' Mr. Nares's explanation of this passage appears to be the true one, it is that 'the word *feature* is too learned for the comprehension of Audrey,' and she reiterates it with simple wonder.

13 Shakspeare remembered that *caper* was Latin for a goat, and thence chose this epithet. There is also a poor quibble between *goats* and *goths.*

14 Ill-lodged.

15 'A great reckoning in a little room.' Warburton with his usual ingenuity, has found out a reference to the saying of Rabelais, that 'there was only one quarter of an hour in human life passed ill, and that was between the calling for a reckoning and the paying it.' Tavern jollity is interrupted by the coming in of a *great reckoning,* and there seems a sly insinuation that it could not be escaped from in a *little room.*

Touch. No, truly, for the truest poetry is the most feigning; and lovers are given to poetry; and what they swear in poetry, may be said, as lovers, they do feign.[1]

Aud. Do you wish, then, that the gods had made me poetical?

Touch. I do, truly: for thou swear'st to me thou art honest; now, if thou wert a poet, I might have some hope thou didst feign.

Aud. Would you not have me honest?

Touch. No truly, unless thou wert hard favour'd: for honesty coupled to beauty, is to have honey a sauce to sugar.

Jaq. A material fool![2] [*Aside.*

Aud. Well, I am not fair; and therefore I pray the gods make me honest!

Touch. Truly, and to cast away honesty upon a foul slut, were to put good meat into an unclean dish.

Aud. I am not a slut, though I thank the gods I am foul.[3]

Touch. Well, praised be the gods for thy foulness! sluttishness may come hereafter. But be it as it may be, I will marry thee: and to that end, I have been with Sir Oliver Mar-text, the vicar of the next village; who hath promised to meet me in this place of the forest, and to couple us.

Jaq. I would fain see this meeting. [*Aside.*

Aud. Well, the gods give us joy!

Touch. Amen. A man may if he were of a fearful heart, stagger in this attempt; for here we have no temple but the wood, no assembly but horn-beasts. But what though? Courage! As horns are odious, they are necessary. It is said,—Many a man knows no end of his goods: right; many a man has good horns, and knows no end of them. Well, that is the dowry of his wife; 'tis none of his own getting. Horns? Even so:———Poor men alone?—No, no; the noblest deer hath them as huge as the rascal.[4] Is the single man therefore blessed? No: as a wall'd town is more worthier than a village, so is the forehead of a married man more honourable than the bare brow of a bachelor: and by how much defence[5] is better than no skill, by so much is a horn more precious than to want.

Enter SIR[6] OLIVER MAR-TEXT.

Here comes Sir Oliver:—Sir Oliver Mar-text, you are well met: Will you dispatch us here under this tree, or shall we go with you to your chapel?

Sir Oli. Is there none here to give the woman?

Touch. I will not take her on gift of any man.

Sir Oli. Truly, she must be given, or the marriage is not lawful.

Jaq. [*Discovering himself.*] Proceed, proceed; I'll give her.

Touch. Good even, good master *What ye call't:* How do you, sir? You are very well met: God'ild you[7] for your last company: I am very glad to see you:—Even a toy in hand here, sir:—Nay; pray be cover'd.

Jaq. Will you be married, Motley?

Touch. As the ox hath his bow,[8] sir, the horse his curb, and the falcon her bells, so man hath his desires; and as pigeons bill, so wedlock would be nibbling.

Jaq. And will you, being a man of your breeding, be married under a bush, like a beggar? Get you to church, and have a good priest that can tell you what marriage is: this fellow will but join you together as they join wainscot; then one of you will prove a shrunk pannel, and, like green timber, warp, warp.

Touch. I am not in the mind but I were better to be married of him than of another: for he is not like to marry me well; and not being well married, it will be a good excuse for me hereafter to leave my wife. [*Aside.*

Jaq. Go thou with me, and let me counsel thee.

Touch. Come, sweet Audrey;
We must be married, or we must live in bawdry.
Farewell, good master Oliver!
Not—O sweet Oliver,
O brave Oliver,
Leave me not behind thee.
But—wind away,
Begone, I say,
I will not to wedding with thee.
[*Exeunt* JAQ. TOUCH. *and* AUDREY.

Sir Oli. 'Tis no matter; ne'er a fantastical knave of them all shall flout me out of my calling. [*Exit.*

SCENE IV. *The same. Before a Cottage. Enter* ROSALIND *and* CELIA.

Ros. Never talk to me, I will weep.

Cel. Do, I pr'ythee; but yet have the grace to consider, that tears do not become a man.

Ros. But have I not cause to weep?

Cel. As good cause as one would desire; therefore weep.

Ros. His very hair is of the dissembling colour.

Cel. Something browner than Judas's:[10] marry, his kisses are Judas's own children.

Ros. I'faith, his hair is of a good colour.

Cel. An excellent colour: your chestnut was ever the only colour.

Ros. And his kissing is as full of sanctity as the touch of holy bread.

Cel. He hath bought a pair of cast lips of Diana: a nun of winter's sisterhood kisses not more religiously; the very ice of chastity is in them.[11]

Ros. But why did he swear he would come this morning, and comes not?

Cel. Nay, certainly, there is no truth in him.

Ros. Do you think so?

Cel. Yes: I think he is not a pick-purse, nor a horse-stealer; but for his verity in love, I do think him as concave as a cover'd goblet, or a worm-eaten nut.

Ros. Not true in love?

Cel. Yes, when he is in; but, I think he is not in.

Ros. You have heard him swear downright, he was.

Cel. *Was* is not *is:* besides the oath of a lover is no stronger than the word of a tapster; they are both the confirmers of false reckonings: He attends here in the forest on the duke your father.

Ros. I met the duke yesterday, and had much question[12] with him. He asked me of what parentage I was; I told him, of as good as he; so he laugh'd, and let me go. But what talk we of fathers, when there is such a man as Orlando?

---

1 This should probably be read—'*it* may be said, as lovers they do feign.'

2 'A *material fool,*' is a fool with matter in him.

3 'I thank the gods I am foul.' The humour of this passage has, I think, been missed by the commentators. Audrey in the simplicity of her heart here 'thanks the gods amiss;' mistaking *foulness,* for some notable virtue, or commendable quality. But indeed *foul* was anciently used in opposition to *fair,* the one signifying *homely,* the other *handsome.*

4 Lean deer are called *rascal* deer.

5 i. e. the art of fencing.

6 '*Sir* Oliver.' This title, it has been already observed, was formerly applied to priests and curates in general. See notes on Merry Wives of Windsor, Act. i. Sc. 1.

7 i. e. God yield you, God reward you.

8 i. e. his *yoke,* which, in ancient time, resembled a bow or branching horns. See note on Merry Wives of Windsor, Act v Sc. 5.

9 The ballad of 'O sweete Olyver, leave me not behind thee,' and the answer to it, are entered on the Stationers' books in 1584 and 1586. Touchstone says I will sing—*not* that part of the ballad which says—'Leave me not behind thee;' *but* that which says—'Begone, I say,' probably part of the answer.

10 It has been already observed, in a note on The Merry Wives of Windsor, that Judas was constantly represented in old paintings and tapestry, with red *hair* and *beard.*

11 Surely this speech is sufficiently intelligible without the blundering of Theobald or the pedantic refinement of Warburton? There is humour in the expression *cast lips;* which Theobald rightly explained *left off,* as we still say *cast* clothes. Who would ever dream of taking this figurative passage in its literal meaning? The nun of *winter's* sisterhood, with the very *ice* of chastity in her lips, needs no explanation

12 *Question* is conversation.

Cel. O, that's a brave man! he writes brave verses, speaks brave words, swears brave oaths, and breaks them bravely, quite traverse, athwart[1] the heart of his lover;[2] as a puny tilter, that spurs his horse but on one side, breaks his staff like a noble goose:[3] but all's brave, that youth mounts, and folly guides:—Who comes here?

Enter CORIN.

Cor. Mistress, and master, you have oft inquired
After the shepherd that complain'd of love;
Who you saw sitting by me on the turf,
Praising the proud disdainful shepherdess
That was his mistress.

Cel. Well, and what of him?

Cor. If you will see a pageant truly play'd,
Between the pale complexion of true love
And the red glow of scorn and proud disdain,
Go hence a little, and I shall conduct you,
If you will mark it.

Ros. O, come, let us remove;
The sight of lovers feedeth those in love:—
Bring us unto this sight, and you shall say
I'll prove a busy actor in their play. [*Exeunt.*

SCENE V. *Another part of the Forest. Enter* SILVIUS *and* PHEBE.

Sil. Sweet Phebe, do not scorn me; do not, Phebe:
Say, that you love me not; but say not so
In bitterness. The common executioner,
Whose heart the accustom'd sight of death makes hard,
Falls not the axe upon the humbled neck,
But first begs pardon; Will you sterner be
Than he that dies and lives[4] by bloody drops?

Enter ROSALIND, CELIA, *and* CORIN, *at a distance.*

Phe. I would not be thy executioner:
I fly thee, for I would not injure thee.
Thou tell'st me, there is murder in mine eye:
'Tis pretty, sure, and very probable,
That eyes,—that are the frail'st and softest things,
Who shut their coward gates on atomies,—
Should be call'd tyrants, butchers, murderers!
Now I do frown on thee with all my heart;
And, if mine eyes can wound, now let them kill thee;
Now counterfeit to swoon; why now fall down;
Or, if thou canst not, O, for shame, for shame,
Lie not, to say mine eyes are murderers.
Now show the wound mine eye hath made in thee:
Scratch thee but with a pin, and there remains
Some scar of it; lean but upon a rush,
The cicatrice and palpable[5] impressure
Thy palm some moment keeps: but now mine eyes,
Which I have darted at thee, hurt thee not;
Nor, I am sure, there is no force in eyes
That can do hurt.

Sil. O dear Phebe,
If ever, (as that ever may be near,)
You meet in some fresh cheek the power of fancy,[6]
Then shall you know the wounds invisible
That love's keen arrows make.

Phe. But, till that time,
Come not thou near me: and, when that time comes,
Afflict me with thy mocks, pity me not;
As, till that time, I shall not pity thee.

Ros. And why, I pray you? [*Advancing.*] Who might be your mother,
That you insult, exult, and all at once,
Over the wretched? What though? you have no beauty,[7]
(As, by my faith, I see no more in you
Than without candle may go dark to bed,)
Must you be therefore proud and pitiless?
Why, what means this? Why do you look on me?
I see no more in you, than in the ordinary
Of nature's sale-work:—Od's my little life!
I think she means to tangle my eyes too:
No, 'faith, proud mistress, hope not after it;
'Tis not your inky brows, your black silk-hair,
Your bugle eye-balls, nor your cheek of cream,
That can entame my spirits to your worship,—
You foolish shepherd, wherefore do you follow her,
Like foggy south, puffing with wind and rain?
You are a thousand times a properer man,
Than she a woman: 'Tis such fools as you,
That make the world full of ill-favour'd children:
'Tis not her glass but you that flatters her;
And out of you she sees herself more proper,
Than any of her lineaments can show her.—
But mistress, know yourself; down on your knees
And thank heaven fasting, for a good man's love:
For I must tell you friendly in your ear,—
Sell when you can; you are not for all markets:
Cry the man mercy; love him; take his offer;
Foul is most foul, being foul to be a scoffer.[8]
So take her to thee, shepherd:—fare you well.

Phe. Sweet youth, I pray you chide a year together;
I had rather hear you chide than this man woo.

Ros. He's fallen in love with her foulness, and she'll fall in love with my anger: If it be so, as fast as she answers thee with frowning looks, I'll sauce her with bitter words.—Why look you so upon me?

Phe. For no ill will I bear you.

Ros. I pray you, do not fall in love with me,
For I am falser than vows made in wine:
Besides, I like you not: If you will know my house,
'Tis at the tuft of olives, here hard by:—
Will you go, sister?—Shepherd, ply her hard:—
Come, sister:—Shepherdess, look on him better,
And be not proud: though all the world could see,
None could be so abus'd in sight as he.[9]
Come, to our flock.

[*Exeunt* ROSALIND, CELIA, *and* CORIN.

Phe. Dead shepherd! now I find thy saw of might;
Who ever lov'd, that lov'd not at first sight?[10]

Sil. Sweet Phebe,—

Phe. Ha! what say'st thou, Silvius?

Sil. Sweet Phebe, pity me.

Phe. Why, I am sorry for thee, gentle Silvius.

Sil. Wherever sorrow is, relief would be;
If you do sorrow at my grief in love,
By giving love, your sorrow and my grief
Were both extermin'd.

Phe. Thou hast my love; is not that neighbourly?

Sil. I would have you.

Phe. Why, that were covetousness.
Silvius, the time was, that I hated thee;
And yet it is not, that I bear thee love;
But since that thou canst talk of love so well,
Thy company, which erst was irksome to me,
I will endure; and I'll employ thee too:

---

1 When the tilter, by unsteadiness or awkwardness, suffered his spear to be turned out of its direction, and to be *broken across* the body of his adversary, instead of by the push of the point, it was held very disgraceful.

2 i. e. *mistress.*

3 Sir Thomas Hanmer proposed to read '*nose-quilled* goose,' which has received some support from Farmer and Steevens.

4 i. e. he who to the very end of life, continues a common executioner. So in the second Scene of Act. v. of this play:—'*live* and *die* a shepherd.'

5 'The cicatrice and *palpable* impressure.' The old copy reads '*capable* impressure.' I think it is evident we should read *palpable.* For no one can surely be satisfied with the strained explanations offered by Johnson and Malone. *Cicatrice*, however improperly, is used for *skin mark*, which is in fact a *scar*, though not an indelible one.

6 Love.

7 'What though? you have *no* beauty.' This is the reading of the old copy, which Malone thought erroneous, and proposed to read *mo'* beauty; Steevens adopted his emendation, and reads *more.* This is certainly wrong; the whole of Rosalind's spirited address to Phebe tends to the disparagement of her beauty, and whoever reads it with attention will conclude with me that the old copy is right.

8 That is, says Johnson, 'The ugly seem most ugly, when, *though* ugly, they are scoffers.'

9 If all men could see you, none could be so *deceived* as to think you beautiful but he.

10 This line is from Marlowe's beautiful poem of Hero and Leander, left unfinished at his death in 1592, and first published in 1598, when it became very popular.

But do not look for further recompense,
Than thine own gladness that thou art employ'd.

Sil. So holy, and so perfect is my love,
And I in such a poverty of grace,
That I shall think it a most plenteous crop
To glean the broken ears after the man
That the main harvest reaps: loose now and then
A scatter'd smile, and that I'll live upon.

Phe. Know'st thou the youth that spoke to me erewhile?

Sil. Not very well, but I have met him oft.
And he hath bought the cottage, and the bounds,
That the old carlot[1] once was master of.

Phe. Think not I love him, though I ask for him;
'Tis but a peevish[2] boy:—yet he talks well;—
But what care I for words? yet words do well,
When he that speaks them pleases those that hear.
It is a pretty youth:—not very pretty:—
But, sure, he's proud; and yet his pride becomes him:
He'll make a proper man: The best thing in him
Is his complexion; and faster than his tongue
Did make offence, his eye did heal it up.
He is not very tall; yet for his years he's tall:
His leg is but so so; and yet 'tis well:
There was a pretty redness in his lip;
A little riper and more lusty red
Than that mix'd in his cheek; 'twas just the difference
Betwixt the constant red, and mingled damask.
There be some women, Silvius, had they mark'd him
In parcels as I did, would have gone near
To fall in love with him; but, for my part,
I love him not, nor hate him not; and yet
I have more cause to hate him than to love him:
For what had he to do to chide at me?
He said, mine eyes were black, and my hair black;
And, now I am remember'd, scorn'd at me:
I marvel, why I answer'd not again;
But that's all one; omittance is no quittance.
I'll write to him a very taunting letter,
And thou shalt bear it; Wilt thou, Silvius?

Sil. Phebe, with all my heart.

Phe. I'll write it straight;
The matter's in my head, and in my heart:
I will be bitter with him, and passing short:
Go with me, Silvius. [*Exeunt.*

ACT IV.

SCENE I. *The same.* *Enter* ROSALIND, CELIA *and* JAQUES.

Jaq. I pr'ythee, pretty youth, let me be better acquainted with thee.

Ros. They say, you are a melancholy fellow.

Jaq. I am so; I do love it better than laughing.

Ros. Those that are in extremity of either, are abominable fellows; and betray themselves to every modern[3] censure, worse than drunkards.

Jaq. Why, 'tis good to be sad and say nothing.

Ros. Why then, 'tis good to be a post.

Jaq. I have neither the scholar's melancholy, which is emulation; nor the musician's, which is fantastical; nor the courtier's, which is proud; nor the soldier's, which is ambitious; nor the lawyer's, which is politic; nor the lady's, which is nice;[4] nor the lover's, which is all these: but it is a melancholy of mine own, compounded of many simples, extracted from many objects; and, indeed, the sundry contemplation of my travels; which, by often rumination, wraps me in a most humorous sadness.[5]

Ros. A traveller! By my faith, you have great reason to be sad; I fear you have sold your own lands, to see other men's; then, to have seen much, and to have nothing, is to have rich eyes and poor hands.

Jaq. Yes, I have gained my experience.

Enter ORLANDO.

Ros. And your experience makes you sad: I had rather have a fool to make me merry, than experience to make me sad; and to travel for it too.

Orl. Good day, and happiness, dear Rosalind!

Jaq. Nay then, God be wi' you, an you talk in blank verse. [*Exit.*

Ros. Farewell, monsieur traveller: Look, you lisp, and wear strange suits: disable[6] all the benefits of your own country; be out of love with your nativity, and almost chide God for making you that countenance you are; or I will scarce think you have swam in a gondola.[7]—Why, how now, Orlando! where have you been all this while? You a lover?—An you serve me such another trick, never come in my sight more.

Orl. My fair Rosalind, I come within an hour of my promise.

Ros. Break an hour's promise in love? He that will divide a minute into a thousand parts, and break but a part of the thousandth part of a minute in the affairs of love, it may be said of him, that Cupid hath clapp'd him o' the shoulder, but I warrant him heart-whole.

Orl. Pardon me, dear Rosalind.

Ros. Nay, an you be so tardy, come no more in my sight: I had as lief be woo'd of a snail.

Orl. Of a snail?

Ros. Ay, of a snail; for though he comes slowly, he carries his house on his head: a better jointure, I think, than you can make a woman: Besides, he brings his destiny with him.

Orl. What's that?

Ros. Why, horns; which such as you are fain to be beholden to your wives for: but he comes armed in his fortune, and prevents the slander of his wife.

Orl. Virtue is no horn-maker; and my Rosalind is virtuous.

Ros. And I am your Rosalind.

Cel. It pleases him to call you so; but he hath a Rosalind of a better leer[8] than you.

Ros. Come, woo me, woo me; for now I am in a holiday humour, and like enough to consent: What would you say to me now, an I were your very very Rosalind?

Orl. I would kiss, before I spoke.

Ros. Nay, you were better speak first; and when you were gravelled for lack of matter, you might take occasion to kiss. Very good orators, when they are out, they will spit; and for lovers, lacking (God warn us!) matter, the cleanliest shift is to kiss.

Orl. How if the kiss be denied?

Ros. Then she puts you to entreaty, and there begins new matter.

Orl. Who could be out, being before his beloved mistress?

Ros. Marry, that should you, if I were your mistress; or I should think my honesty ranker than my wit.

Orl. What, of my suit?

Ros. Not out of your apparel, and yet out of your suit. Am not I your Rosalind?

Orl. I take some joy to say you are, because I would be talking of her.

Ros. Well, in her person, I say—I will not have you.

1 *Carlot.* This is printed in Italicks as a proper name in the old edition. It is however apparently formed from *carle* a peasant.

2 i. e. weak, silly.

3 i. e. *common, trifling.*

4 *Nice*, here means *tender, delicate*, and not *silly, trifling*, as Steevens supposed; though the word is occasionally used by Shakspeare in common with Chaucer, in the sense of the old French *nice niais.*

5 The old copy reads and points thus:—'and indeed the sundry contemplation of my travels, *in* which *by* often rumination, wraps me *in* a most humorous sadness.' The emendation is Malone's.

6 i. e. undervalue.

7 i. e. been at Venice; then the resort of all travellers, as Paris now. Shakspeare's cotemporaries also point their shafts at the corruption of our youth by travel. Bishop Hall wrote his little book *Quo Vadis?* to stem the fashion.

8 i. e. complexion colour

Orl. Then, in mine own person, I die.

Ros. No, faith, die by attorney. The poor world is almost six thousand years old, and in all this time there was not any man died in his own person, *videlicet*, in a love-cause. Troilus had his brains dashed out with a Grecian club; yet he did what he could to die before; and he is one of the patterns of love. Leander, he would have lived many a fair year, though Hero had turned nun, if it had not been for a hot midsummer night: for, good youth, he went but forth to wash him in the Hellespont, and, being taken with the cramp, was drowned; and the foolish chroniclers[1] of that age found it was—Hero of Sestos. But these are all lies; men have died from time to time, and worms have eaten them, but not for love

Orl. I would not have my right Rosalind of this mind; for, I protest, her frown might kill me.

Ros. By this hand, it will not kill a fly: But come, now I will be your Rosalind in a more coming-on disposition; and ask me what you will, I will grant it.

Orl. Then love me, Rosalind.

Ros. Yes, faith will I, Fridays, and Saturdays, and all.

Orl. And wilt thou have me?

Ros. Ay, and twenty such.

Orl. What say'st thou?

Ros. Are you not good?

Orl. I hope so.

Ros. Why, then, can one desire too much of a good thing?—Come, sister, you shall be the priest, and marry us.—Give me your hand, Orlando:—What do you say, sister?

Orl. Pray thee, marry us.

Cel. I cannot say the words.

Ros. You must begin,——*Will you, Orlando,*—

Cel. Go to:——Will you, Orlando, have to wife this Rosalind?

Orl. I will.

Ros. Ay, but when?

Orl. Why now; as fast as she can marry us.

Ros. Then you must say,—*I take thee, Rosalind, for wife.*

Orl. I take thee, Rosalind, for wife.

Ros. I might ask you for your commission; but —I do take thee, Orlando, for my husband: There a girl goes before the priest; and, certainly, a woman's thought runs before her actions.

Orl. So do all thoughts; they are winged.

Ros. Now tell me, how long you would have her after you have possessed her.

Orl. For ever and a day.

Ros. Say a day, without the ever: No, no, Orlando; men are April when they woo: December when they wed: maids are May when they are maids, but the sky changes when they are wives. I will be more jealous of thee than a barbary cock-pigeon over his hen; more clamorous than a parrot against rain; more new-fangled than an ape; more giddy in my desires than a monkey: I will weep for nothing, like Diana in the fountain;[2] and I will do that when you are disposed to be merry: I will laugh like a hyena,[3] and that when thou art inclined to sleep.

Orl. But will my Rosalind do so?

Ros. By my life, she will do as I do.

Orl. O, but she is wise.

Ros. Or else she could not have the wit to do this: the wiser, the waywarder: Make the doors[4] upon a woman's wit, and it will out at the casement; shut that, and 'twill out at the key-hole: stop that, 'twill fly with the smoke out at the chimney.

Orl. A man that had a wife with such a wit, he might say,—*Wit, whither wilt?*[5]

Ros. Nay, you might keep that check for it, till you met your wife's wit going to your neighbour's bed.

Orl. And what wit could wit have to excuse that?

Ros. Marry, to say,—she came to seek you there. You shall never take her without her answer,[6] unless you take her without her tongue. O, that woman that cannot make her fault her husband's occasion,[7] let her never nurse her child herself, for she will breed it like a fool.

Orl. For these two hours, Rosalind, I will leave thee.

Ros. Alas, dear love, I cannot lack thee two hours.

Orl. I must attend the duke at dinner; by two o'clock I will be with thee again.

Ros. Ay, go your ways, go your ways;—I knew what you would prove; my friends told me as much, and I thought no less:—that flattering tongue of yours won me:—'tis but one cast away, and so,—come, death.—Two o'clock is your hour?

Orl. Ay, sweet Rosalind.

Ros. By my troth, and in good earnest, and so God mend me, and by all pretty oaths that are not dangerous, if you break one jot of your promise, or come one minute behind your hour, I will think you the most pathetical[8] break-promise, and the most hollow lover, and the most unworthy of her you call Rosalind, that may be chosen out of the gross band of the unfaithful: therefore beware my censure, and keep your promise.

Orl. With no less religion, than if thou wert indeed my Rosalind: So, adieu.

Ros. Well, time is the old justice that examines all such offenders, and let time try: Adieu!

[*Exit* ORLANDO

Cel. You have simply misus'd our sex in your love prate: we must have your doublet and hose pluck'd over your head, and show the world what the bird hath done with her own nest.[9]

Ros. O coz, coz, coz, my pretty little coz, that thou didst know how many fathom deep I am in love! But it cannot be sounded; my affection hath an unknown bottom, like the bay of Portugal.

Cel. Or rather, bottomless; that as fast as you pour affection in, it runs out.

Ros. No, that same wicked bastard of Venus, that was begot of thought, conceived of spleen, and born of madness; that blind rascally boy, that abuses every one's eyes, because his own are out, let him be judge, how deep I am in love:—I'll tell thee, Aliena, I cannot be out of the sight of Orlando: I'll go find a shadow,[10] and sigh till he come.

Cel. And I'll sleep. [*Exeunt.*

SCENE II. *Another part of the Forest. Enter* JAQUES *and* Lords, *in the habit of Foresters*

Jaq. Which is he that kill'd the deer?

1 *Lord.* Sir, it was I.

Jaq. Let's present him to the duke, like a Roman conqueror; and it would do well to set the deer's

1 'The foolish *chroniclers.*' Sir Thomas Hanmer reads *coroners;* and it must be confessed the context seems to warrant the innovation, unless Shakspeare means to designate the *jury* impanneled on a coroner's inquest by the term *chroniclers.*

2 Figures, and particularly that of *Diana*, with water conveyed through them, were anciently a frequent ornament of fountains.

3 The bark of the hyena was thought to resemble a loud laugh.

4 i. e. *bar* the doors.

5 'Wit, whither wilt?' This was a kind of proverbial phrase, the origin of which has not been traced. It seems to be used chiefly to express a want of command over the fancy or inventive faculty. It occurs in many writers of Shakspeare's time.

6 This bit of satire is also to be found in Chaucer's Marchantes Tale, where Proserpine says of women on like occasion:

'For lacke of answere none of us shall dien.'

7 i. e. represent her fault as occasioned by her husband. Hanmer reads, her husband's *accusation.*

8 *Pathetical* and *passionate* were used in the same sense in Shakspeare's time. Whether Rosalind has any more meaning than Costard in the use of the word when he calls Armado's boy '*a most pathetical* nit.' I leave the reader to judge.

9 This is borrowed from Lodge's Rosalynd.

10 So in Macbeth:—

'Let us *seek* out some desolate *shade*, and there
Weep our sad bosoms empty.'

horns upon his head, for a branch of victory:—Have you no song, forester, for this purpose?

2 Lord. Yes, sir.

Jaq. Sing it; 'tis no matter how it be in tune, so it makes noise enough.

SONG.

1. *What shall he have that kill'd the deer?*
2. *His leather skin, and horns to wear.*
 1. *Then sing him home:*
Take thou no scorn, to wear the horn;
It was a crest ere thou wast born;
 1. *Thy father's father wore it;*
 2. *And thy father bore it:*
(The rest shall bear this burden.)
All. *The horn, the horn, the lusty horn,*
Is not a thing to laugh to scorn.[1] [Exeunt.

SCENE III. *The Forest. Enter* ROSALIND *and* CELIA.

Ros. How say you now? Is it not past two o'clock? and here much Orlando![2]

Cel. I warrant you, with pure love, and troubled brain, he hath ta'en his bow and arrows, and is gone forth—to sleep: Look, who comes here.

Enter SILVIUS.

Sil. My errand is to you, fair youth:—
My gentle Phebe, bid me give you this:
[*Giving a letter.*
I know not the contents; but as I guess,
By the stern brow, and waspish action
Which she did use as she was writing of it,
It bears an angry tenour: pardon me,
I am but as a guiltless messenger.

Ros. Patience herself would startle at this letter,
And play the swaggerer; bear this, bear all:
She says, I am not fair; that I lack manners;
She calls me proud; and, that she could not love me
Were man as rare as phœnix: Od's my will!
Her love is not the hare that I do hunt:
Why writes she so to me?—Well, shepherd, well,
This is a letter of your own device.

Sil. No, I protest, I know not the contents;
Phebe did write it.[3]

Ros. Come, come, you are a fool,
And turn'd into the extremity of love.
I saw her hand: she has a leathern hand,
A freestone-colour'd hand; I verily did think
That her old gloves were on, but 'twas her hands;
She has a huswife's hand: but that's no matter:
I say, she never did invent this letter;
This is a man's invention, and his hand.

Sil. Sure, it is hers.

Ros. Why, 'tis a boisterous and a cruel style,
A style for challengers: why, she defies me,
Like Turk to Christian: woman's gentle brain
Could not drop forth such giant-rude invention,
Such Ethiop words, blacker in their effect
Than in their countenance:—Will you hear the letter?

Sil. So please you, for I never heard it yet:
Yet heard too much of Phebe's cruelty.

Ros. She Phebes me: Mark how the tyrant writes.
Art thou god to shepherd turn'd, [Reads.
That a maiden's heart hath burn'd?
Can a woman rail thus?

Sil. Call you this railing?

Ros. *Why, thy godhead laid apart,*
Warr'st thou with a woman's heart?
Did you ever hear such railing?—
Whiles the eye of man did woo me,
That could do no vengeance[4] *to me*—
Meaning me, a beast.—
If the scorn of your bright eyne[5]
Have power to raise such love in mine,
Alack, in me what strange effect
Would they work in mild aspect?
Whiles you chid me, I did love;
How then might your prayers move?
He, that brings this love to thee,
Little knows this love in me:
And by him seal up thy mind;
Whether that thy youth and kind[6]
Will the faithful offer take
Of me, and all that I can make;
Or else by him my love deny,
And then I'll study how to die.

Sil. Call you this chiding?

Cel. Alas, poor shepherd!

Ros. Do you pity him? no, he deserves no pity.—Wilt thou love such a woman?—What, to make thee an instrument, and play false strains upon thee! not to be endured!—Well, go your way to her, (for I see, love hath made thee a tame snake,[7]) and say this to her;—That if she love me, I charge her to love thee: if she will not, I will never have her, unless thou entreat for her.—If you be a true lover, hence, and not a word; for here comes more company. [*Exit* SILVIUS

Enter OLIVER.

Oli. Good-morrow, fair ones: Pray you, if you know
Where, in the purlieus of this forest, stands
A sheep-cote, fenc'd about with olive-trees?

Cel. West of this place, down in the neighbour bottom,
The rank of osiers, by the murmuring stream,
Left on your right hand, brings you to the place:
But at this hour the house doth keep itself,
There's none within.

Oli. If that an eye may profit by a tongue,
Then I should know you by description;
Such garments, and such years: *The boy is fair,*
Of female favour, and bestows[8] *himself*
Like a ripe sister: but the woman low,
And browner than her brother. Are not you
The owner of the house I did inquire for?

Cel. It is no boast, being ask'd, to say, we are.

Oli. Orlando doth commend him to you both;
And to that youth he calls his Rosalind,
He sends this bloody napkin;[9] Are you he?

Ros. I am: What must we understand by this?

Oli. Some of my shame; if you will know of me
What man I am, and how, and why, and where
This handkerchief was stain'd.

Cel. I pray you, tell it.

Oli. When last the young Orlando parted from you,
He left a promise to return again
Within an hour; and, pacing through the forest,
Chewing the food of sweet and bitter fancy,[10]
Lo, what befell! he threw his eye aside,
And, mark, what object did present itself!
Under an oak,[11] whose boughs were moss'd with age
And high top bald with dry antiquity,
A wretched ragged man, o'ergrown with hair,
Lay sleeping on his back: about his neck
A green and gilded snake had wreath'd itself,

---

1 In Playford's Musical Companion, 1673, where this song is set to music by John Hilton, the words '*Then sing him home*' are omitted, and it should be remarked that in the old copy, these words, and those which have been regarded by the editors as a stage direction, are given in one line.

2 i. e. here is *no* Orlando. *Much* was a common ironical expression of doubt or suspicion, still used by the vulgar in the same sense; as, 'much of that!'

3 Mason thinks that part of Silvius's speech is lost, and that we should read—
'Phebe did write it *with her own fair hand.*'
and then Rosalind's reply follows more naturally.

4 i. e. mischief. 5 *Eyne* for eyes.

6 *Kind*, for *nature*, or *natural affections.*

7 A poor *snake* was a term of reproach equivalent to a wretch or poor creature. Hence also a *sneaking* or creeping fellow.

8 i. e. *acts*, or *behaves* like, &c.

9 A *napkin* and *handkerchief* were the same thing in Shakspeare's time, as we gather from the dictionaries of Baret and Hutton in their explanations of the word *Cæsitium* and *Sudarium.* Napkin, for handkerchief, is still in use in the north.

10 i. e. love, which is always thus described by our old poets as composed of contraries.

11 The ancient editions read, 'under an *old* oak which hurts the measure without improving the sense The correction was made by Steevens.

Who with her head, nimble in threats, approach'd
The opening of his mouth; but suddenly,
Seeing Orlando, it unlink'd itself,
And with indented glides did slip away
Into a bush: under which bush's shade
A lioness, with udders all drawn dry,
Lay couching, head on ground, with catlike watch,
When that the sleeping man should stir; for 'tis
The royal disposition of that beast,
To prey on nothing that doth seem as dead:
This seen, Orlando did approach the man,
And found it was his brother, his elder brother.

Cel. O, I have heard him speak of that same brother;
And he did render[1] him the most unnatural
That liv'd 'mongst men.

Oli. And well he might so do,
For well I know he was unnatural.

Ros. But, to Orlando;—Did he leave him there,
Food to the suck'd and hungry lioness?

Oli. Twice did he turn his back, and purpos'd so:
But kindness, nobler ever than revenge,
And nature, stronger than his just occasion,
Made him give battle to the lioness,
Who quickly fell before him; in which hurtling[2]
From miserable slumber I awak'd.

Cel. Are you his brother?

Ros. Was it you he rescu'd?

Cel. Was't you that did so oft contrive to kill him?

Oli. 'Twas I; but 'tis not I: I do not shame
To tell you what I was, since my conversion
So sweetly tastes, being the thing I am.

Ros. But, for the bloody napkin?—

Oli. By and by.
When from the first to last, betwixt us two,
Tears our recountments had most kindly bath'd;
As, how I came into that desert place;——
In brief he led me to the gentle duke,
Who gave me fresh array and entertainment,
Committing me unto my brother's love;
Who led me instantly unto his cave,
There stripp'd himself, and here upon his arm
The lioness had torn some flesh away,
Which all this while had bled; and now he fainted,
And cry'd, in fainting, upon Rosalind.
Brief, I recover'd him; bound up his wound;
And, after some small space, being strong at heart,
He sent me hither, stranger as I am,
To tell this story, that you might excuse
His broken promise, and to give this napkin,
Dy'd in his blood, unto the shepherd youth
That he in sport doth call his Rosalind.

Cel. Why, how now, Ganymede? sweet Ganymede? [ROSALIND *faints.*

Oli. Many will swoon when they do look on blood.

Cel. There is more in it:—Cousin—Ganymede!

Oli. Look, he recovers.

Ros. I would, I were at home.

Cel. We'll lead you thither:—
pray you, will you take him by the arm?

Oli. Be of good cheer, youth:—You a man?—
You lack a man's heart.

Ros. I do so, I confess it. Ah, sir, a body would think this was well counterfeited: I pray you, tell your brother how well I counterfeited.—Heigh ho!—

Oli. This was not counterfeit; there is too great testimony in your complexion, that it was a passion of earnest.

Ros. Counterfeit, I assure you.

Oli. Well then, take a good heart, and counterfeit to be a man.

Ros. So I do: but, i'faith, I should have been a woman by right.

Cel. Come, you look paler and paler; pray you, draw homewards:—Good sir, go with us.

Oli. That will I, for I must bear answer back
How you excuse my brother, Rosalind.

Ros. I shall devise something; But I pray you, commend my counterfeiting to him:—Will you go? [*Exeunt.*

ACT V.

SCENE I. *The same. Enter* TOUCHSTONE *and* AUDREY.

Touch. We shall find a time, Audrey; patience, gentle Audrey.

Aud. 'Faith, the priest was good enough, for all the old gentleman's saying.

Touch. A most wicked Sir Oliver, Audrey, a most vile Mar-text. But, Audrey, there is a youth here in the forest lays claim to you.

Aud. Ay, I know who 'tis; he hath no interest in me in the world: here comes the man you mean.

Enter WILLIAM.

Touch. It is meat and drink to me to see a clown: By my troth, we that have good wits, have much to answer for; we shall be flouting; we cannot hold.

Will. Good even, Audrey.

Aud. God ye good even, William.

Will. And good even to you, sir.

Touch. Good even, gentle friend: Cover thy head, cover thy head; nay, pry'thee, be covered. How old are you, friend?

Will. Five-and-twenty, sir.

Touch. A ripe age: Is thy name William?

Will. William, sir.

Touch. A fair name: Wast born i' the forest here?

Will. Ay, sir, I thank God.

Touch. *Thank God*;—a good answer: Art rich?

Will. 'Faith, sir, so, so.

Touch. *So, so*, is good, very good, very excellent good:—and yet it is not; it is but so so. Art thou wise?

Will. Ay, sir, I have a pretty wit.

Touch. Why, thou say'st well. I do now remember a saying; *The fool doth think he is wise, but the wise man knows himself to be a fool.* The heathen philosopher, when he had a desire to eat a grape, would open his lips when he put it into his mouth; meaning thereby, that grapes were made to eat, and lips to open.[3] You do love this maid?

Will. I do, sir.

Touch. Give me your hand: Art thou learned?

Will. No, sir.

Touch. Then learn this of me: To have, is to have: For it is a figure in rhetorick, that drink, being poured out of a cup into a glass, by filling the one doth empty the other: for all your writers do consent, that *ipse* is he; now you are not *ipse*, for I am he.

Will. Which he, sir?

Touch. He, sir, that must marry this woman: Therefore, you clown, abandon,—which is in the vulgar, leave,—the society,—which in the boorish is, company,—of this female,---which in the common is,---woman, which together is, abandon the society of this female; or, clown, thou perishest; or, to thy better understanding, diest; or, to wit, I kill thee, make thee away, translate thy life into death, thy liberty into bondage: I will deal in poison with thee, or in bastinado, or in steel; I will bandy with thee in faction; I will o'errun thee with policy; I will kill thee a hundred and fifty ways: therefore tremble, and depart.

Aud. Do, good William.

Will. God rest you, merry sir. [*Exit.*

Enter CORIN.

Cor. Our master and mistress seek you; come, away, away.

Touch. Trip, Audrey, trip, Audrey;---I attend, I attend. [*Exeunt.*

---

1 i. e. *represent* or *render* this account of him.
2 i. e. jostling or clashing, encounter.

3 Warburton thinks this a sneer at the insignificant sayings and actions recorded of the ancient philosophers by the writers of their lives

SCENE II. *The same. Enter* ORLANDO *and* OLIVER.

Orl. Is't possible, that on so little acquaintance you should like her? that but seeing, you should love her? and, loving, woo? and, wooing, she should grant? and will you persever to enjoy her?[1]

Oli. Neither call the giddiness of it in question, the poverty of her, the small acquaintance, my sudden wooing, nor her sudden consenting; but say with me, I love Aliena; say with her, that she loves me; consent with both, that we may enjoy each other: it shall be to your good: for my father's house, and all the revenue that was old Sir Rowland's, will I estate upon you, and here live and die a shepherd.

Enter ROSALIND.

Orl. You have my consent. Let your wedding be to-morrow: thither will I invite the duke, and all his contented followers: Go you, and prepare Aliena; for, look you, here comes my Rosalind.

Ros. God save you, brother.

Oli. And you, fair sister.[2]

Ros. O, my dear Orlando, how it grieves me to see thee wear thy heart in a scarf.

Orl. It is my arm.

Ros. I thought thy heart had been wounded with the claws of a lion.

Orl. Wounded it is, but with the eyes of a lady.

Ros. Did your brother tell you how I counterfeited to swoon, when he showed me your handkerchief?

Orl. Ay, and greater wonders than that.

Ros. O, I know where you are:---Nay, 'tis true: there never was any thing so sudden, but the fight of two rams, and Cæsar's thrasonical brag of---*I came, saw, and overcame:* For your brother and my sister no sooner met, but they looked; no sooner looked, but they loved; no sooner loved, but they sighed; no sooner sighed, but they asked one another the reason; no sooner knew the reason, but they sought the remedy: and in these degrees have they made a pair of stairs to marriage, which they will climb incontinent,[3] or else be incontinent before marriage: they are in the very wrath of love, and they will together; clubs cannot part them.[4]

Orl. They shall be married to-morrow; and I will bid the duke to the nuptial. But, O, how bitter a thing it is to look into happiness through another man's eyes! By so much the more shall I tomorrow be at the height of heart-heaviness, by how much I shall think my brother happy, in having what he wishes for.

Ros. Why then, to-morrow I cannot serve your turn for Rosalind?

Orl. I can live no longer by thinking.

Ros. I will weary you no longer then with idle talking. Know of me then, (for now I speak to some purpose,) that I know you are a gentleman of good conceit:[5] I speak not this, that you should bear a good opinion of my knowledge, insomuch, I say, I know you are; neither do I labour for a greater esteem than may in some little measure draw a belief from you, to do yourself good, and not to grace me. Believe then, if you please, that I can do strange things: I have, since I was three years old, conversed with a magician, most profound in this art, and yet not damnable. If you do love Rosalind so near the heart as your gesture cries it out, when your brother marries Aliena, shall you marry her: I know into what straits of fortune she is driven; and it is not impossible to me, if it appear not inconvenient to you, to set her before your eyes to-morrow; human as she is,[6] and without any danger.

Orl. Speakest thou in sober meanings?

Ros. By my life, I do; which I tender dearly, though I say I am a magician:[7] Therefore put you in your best array, bid[8] your friends; for if you will be married to-morrow, you shall; and to Rosalind, if you will.

Enter SILVIUS *and* PHEBE.

Look, here comes a lover of mine, and a lover of hers.

Phe. Youth, you have done me much ungentleness,
To show the letter that I writ to you.

Ros. I care not, if I have: it is my study,
To seem despiteful and ungentle to you:
You are there follow'd by a faithful shepherd;
Look upon him, love him; he worships you.

Phe. Good shepherd, tell this youth what 'tis to love.

Sil. It is to be all made of sighs and tears;—
And so am I for Phebe.

Phe. And I for Ganymede.

Orl. And I for Rosalind.

Ros. And I for no woman.

Sil. It is to be all made of faith and service;
And so am I for Phebe.

Phe. And I for Ganymede.

Orl. And I for Rosalind.

Ros. And I for no woman.

Sil. It is to be all made of fantasy,
All made of passion, and all made of wishes;
All adoration, duty, and observance,
All humbleness, all patience, and impatience,
All purity, all trial, all obeisance;[9]—
And so am I for Phebe.

Phe. And so am I for Ganymede.

Orl. And so am I for Rosalind.

Ros. And so am I for no woman.

Phe. If this be so, why blame you me to love you? [*To* ROSALIND.

Sil. If this be so, why blame you me to love you? [*To* PHEBE.

Orl. If this be so, why blame you me to love you?

Ros. Who do you speak to, *why blame you me to love you?*

Orl. To her, that is not here; nor doth not hear.

Ros. Pray you, no more of this; 'tis like the howling of Irish wolves against the moon.—I will help you, [*To* SILVIUS] if I can.—I would love you, [*To* PHEBE] if I could.—To-morrow meet me all together.—I will marry you, [*To* PHEBE] if ever I marry woman, and I'll be married to-morrow;— I will satisfy you, [*To* ORLANDO] if ever I satisfied man, and you shall be married to-morrow:—I will content you, [*To* SILVIUS] if what pleases you contents you, and you shall be married to-morrow.—As you [*To* ORLANDO] love Rosalind, meet;—as you [*To* SILVIUS] love Phebe,

1 Shakspeare, by putting this question into the mouth of Orlando, seems to have been aware of the improbability in his plot caused by deserting his original. In Lodge's novel the elder brother is instrumental in saving Aliena from a band of ruffians; without this circumstance the passion of Aliena appears to be very hasty indeed.

2 Oliver must be supposed to speak to her in the character she had assumed of a woman courted by his brother Orlando, for there is no evidence that he knew she was one.

3 *Incontinent* here signifies *immediately*, without any stay or delay, out of hand; so Baret explains it. But it had also its now usual signification, and Shakspeare delights in the equivoque

4 It was a common custom in Shakspeare's time, on the breaking out of a fray, to call out, 'clubs, clubs,' to part the combatants.

5 Conceit in the language of Shakspeare's age signified *wit;* or *conception*, and *imagination.*

6 'Human as she is,' that is, not a phantom, but the real Rosalind, without any of the danger generally conceived to attend upon the rites of incantation.

7 'I say I am a magician.' She alludes to the danger in which her avowal of practising magic, had it been a serious one, would have involved her. The poet refers to his own times, when it would have brought her life in danger.

8 i. e. invite.

9 '*Obeisance.*' The old copy reads *observance*, but it is very unlikely that word should have been set down by Shakspeare twice so close to each other. Ritson proposed the present emendation. *Observance* is *attention, deference.*

meet: And as I love no woman, I'll meet.—So fare you well; I have left you commands.

Sil. I'll not fail, if I live.

Phe. Nor I.

Orl. Nor I.

[*Exeunt.*

SCENE III. *The same. Enter* TOUCHSTONE *and* AUDREY.

Touch. To-morrow is the joyful day, Audrey; to-morrow will we be married.

Aud. I do desire it with all my heart; and I hope it is no dishonest desire, to desire to be a woman of the world.[1] Here comes two of the banish'd duke's pages.

Enter two Pages.

1 Page. Well met, honest gentleman.

Touch. By my troth, well met: Come, sit, sit, and a song.

2 Page. We are for you: sit i'the middle.

1 Page. Shall we clap into't roundly, without hawking, or spitting, or saying we are hoarse; which are the only prologues to a bad voice.

2 Page. I'faith, i'faith; and both in a tune, like two gipsies on a horse.

SONG.

I.

It was a lover, and his lass,
With a hey, and a ho, and a hey nonino,[2]
That o'er the green corn-field did pass,
In the spring time, the only pretty rank time,
When birds do sing, hey ding a ding, ding;
Sweet lovers love the spring.

II.

Between the acres of the rye,
With a hey, and a ho, and a hey nonino,
These pretty country folks would lie,
In spring time, &c.

III.

This carol they began that hour,
With a hey, and a ho, and a hey nonino,
How that life was but a flower
In spring time, &c.

IV.

And therefore take the present time,
With a hey, and ho, and a hey nonino;
For love is crowned with the prime
In spring time, &c.

Touch. Truly, young gentleman, though there was no greater matter in the ditty, yet the note was very untunable.

1 Page. You are deceived, sir; we kept time, we lost not our time.

Touch. By my troth, yes; I count it but time lost to hear such a foolish song. God be with you; and God mend your voices! Come, Audrey. [*Exeunt.*

SCENE IV. *Another part of the Forest. Enter* Duke *senior*, AMIENS, JAQUES, ORLANDO, OLIVER, *and* CELIA.

Duke S. Dost thou believe, Orlando, that the boy
Can do all this that he hath promised?

Orl. I sometimes do believe, and sometimes do not:
As those that fear they hope, and know they fear.[3]

Enter ROSALIND, SILVIUS, *and* PHEBE.

Ros. Patience once more, whiles our compact is urged;——
You say, if I bring in your Rosalind, [*To the* Duke.
You will bestow her on Orlando here?

Duke S. That would I, had I kingdoms to give with her.

Ros. And you say, you will have her, when I bring her? [*To* ORLANDO.

Orl. That would I, were I of all kingdoms king.

Ros. You say, you'll marry me, if I be willing? [*To* PHEBE.

Phe. That will I, should I die the hour after.

Ros. But if you do refuse to marry me,
You'll give yourself to this most faithful shepherd?

Phe. So is the bargain.

Ros. You say, that you'll have Phebe, if she will? [*To* SILVIUS.

Sil. Though to have her and death were both one thing.

Ros. I have promis'd to make all this matter even.
Keep you your word, O duke, to give your daughter;—
You yours, Orlando, to receive his daughter:—
Keep your word, Phebe, that you'll marry me;
Or else, refusing me, to wed this shepherd:—
Keep your word, Silvius, that you'll marry her,
If she refuse me:—and from hence I go,
To make these doubts all even.[4]

[*Exeunt* ROSALIND *and* CELIA.

Duke S. I do remember in this shepherd-boy
Some lively touches of my daughter's favour.

Orl. My lord, the first time that I ever saw him,
Methought he was a brother to your daughter:
But, my good lord, this boy is forest-born;
And hath been tutor'd in the rudiments
Of many desperate studies by his uncle,
Whom he reports to be a great magician,
Obscured in the circle of this forest.

Enter TOUCHSTONE *and* AUDREY.

Jaq. There is, sure, another flood toward, and these couples are coming to the ark! Here comes a pair of very strange beasts, which in all tongues are called fools.

Touch. Salutation and greeting to you all!

Jaq. Good, my lord, bid him welcome: This is the motley-minded gentleman, that I have so often met in the forest: he hath been a courtier, he swears.

Touch. If any man doubt that, let him put me to my purgation. I have trod a measure;[5] I have flattered a lady; I have been politic with my friend smooth with mine enemy; I have undone three tailors; I have had four quarrels, and like to have fought one.

Jaq. And how was that ta'en up?

Touch. 'Faith, we met, and found the quarrel was upon the seventh cause.

Jaq. How seventh cause?—Good my lord, like this fellow.

Duke S. I like him very well.

Touch. God'ild you, sir; I desire you of the like.[6] I press in here, sir, amongst the rest of the country copulatives, to swear, and to forswear; according as marriage binds, and blood breaks:[7]—A poor virgin, sir, an ill-favoured thing, sir, but mine own; a poor humour of mine, to take that that no man else will: Rich honesty dwells like a miser,

---

1 i. e. a married woman. So in Much Ado about Nothing, Beatrice says:—'Thus every one *goes to the world* but I.'

2 This burthen, which had a wanton sense, is common to many old songs. See Florio's Ital. Dict. Ed. 1611, sub voce *Fossa.*

3 This line is very obscure, and probably corrupt. Henley proposed to point it thus:

'As those that fear; they hope, and know they fear.'

And Malone explains it: '*As those who fear,—they,* even those very persons entertain *hopes*, that their fears will not be realized; *and* yet, at the same time, they well know there is reason for *their fears*.' Heath's appears to me the best emendation which has been proposed,

'As those that fear *their* hope, and know *their* fear.'

4 Thus in Measure for Measure;

'——— yet death we fear
That *makes these* odds *all even.*'

5 Touchstone, to prove that he has been a courtier, particularly mentions *a measure*, because it was a stately dance peculiar to the polished part of society, as the minuet in later times. Hence the phrase was *to tread a measure*, as we used to say *to walk a minuet.* See note on Much Ado about Nothing, Act ii. Sc. 1

6 'I desire you of the like.' This mode of expression occurs also in the Merchant of Venice, and in A Midsummer Night's Dream. It is frequent in Spenser:

'——— of pardon you I pray.'

7 By the marriage ceremony a man swears *that he will keep only to his wife*; but his *blood* or passion often makes him *break* his oath

sir, in a poor-house; as your pearl, in your foul oyster.

Duke S. By my faith, he is very swift and sententious.[1]

Touch. According to the fool's bolt, sir, and such dulcet diseases.[2]

Jaq. But, for the seventh cause; how did you find the quarrel on the seventh cause?

Touch. Upon a lie seven times removed:[3]—Bear your body more seeming,[4] Audrey, :—as thus, sir, I did dislike the cut of a certain courtier's beard; he sent me word, if I said his beard was not cut well, he was in the mind it was: This is called the *Retort courteous.* If I sent him word again, it was not well cut, he would send me word, he cut it to please himself: This is called the *Quip modest.* If again, it was not well cut, he disabled[5] my judgment: This is called the *Reply churlish.* If again, it was not well cut, he would answer, I spake not true: This is called the *Reproof valiant.* If again, it was not well cut, he would say, I lie: This is called the *Countercheck quarrelsome:* and so the *Lie circumstantial*, and the *Lie direct.*

Jaq. And how oft did you say,.his beard was not well cut?

Touch. I durst go no further than the *Lie circumstantial*, nor he durst not give me the *Lie direct;* and so we measured swords, and parted.

Jaq. Can you nominate in order now the degrees of the lie?

Touch. O, sir, we quarrel in print, by the book;[6] as you have books for good manners:[7] I will name you the degrees. The first, the Retort courteous; the second, the Quip modest; the third, the Reply churlish; the fourth, the Reproof valiant; the fifth, the Countercheck quarrelsome; the sixth, the Lie with circumstance; the seventh, the Lie direct. All these you may avoid, but the lie direct, and you may avoid that too, with an *If.* I knew when seven justices could not take up a quarrel; but when the parties were met themselves, one of them thought but of an *If*, as *If you said so, then I said so;* and they shook hands, and swore brothers. Your *If* is the only peace-maker; much virtue in *If.*

Jaq. Is not this a rare fellow, my lord? he's as good at any thing, and yet a fool.

Duke S. He uses his folly like a stalking-horse,[8] and under the presentation of that, he shoots his wit.

Enter HYMEN,[9] *leading* ROSALIND *in women's clothes; and* CELIA.

Still Music.

Hym. *Then is there mirth in heaven,*
When earthly things made even,
Atone[10] *together.*
Good duke, receive thy daughter,
Hymen from heaven brought her,
Yea, brought her hither;
That thou might'st join her hand with his
Whose heart within her bosom is.

Ros. To you I give myself, for I am yours:—
[*To* Duke S.
To you I give myself, for I am yours.
[*To* ORLANDO.

Duke S. If there be truth in sight, you are my daughter.

Orl. If there be truth in sight, you are my Rosalind.

Phe. If sight and shape be true,
Why then,—my love, adieu!

Ros. I'll have no father, if you be not he:—
[*To* Duke S.
I'll have no husband, if you be not he:—
[*To* ORLANDO.
Nor ne'er wed woman, if you be not she:—
[*To* PHEBE

Hym. Peace, ho! I bar confusion:
'Tis I must make conclusion,
Of these most strange events:
Here's eight that must take hands,
To join in Hymen's bands,
If truth holds true contents.[11]
You and you no cross shall part:
[*To* ORLANDO *and* ROSALIND
You and you are heart in heart:
[*To* OLIVER *and* CELIA
You [*To* PHEBE] to his love must accord,
Or have a woman to your lord:—
You and you are sure together,
[*To* TOUCHSTONE *and* AUDREY.
As the winter to foul weather.
Whiles a wedlock-hymn we sing,
Feed yourselves with questioning;[12]
That reason wonder may diminish,
How thus we met, and these things finisn

SONG.

Wedding is great Juno's crown;
O blessed bond of board and bed!
'Tis Hymen peoples every town;
High wedlock then be honoured:
Honour, high honour and renown,
To Hymen, god of every town!

Duke S. O my dear niece, welcome thou art to me;
Even daughter, welcome in no less degree.

Phe. I will not eat my word, now thou art mine;
Thy faith my fancy to thee doth combine.[13]
[*To* SILVIUS.

Enter JAQUES DE BOIS.

Jaq. de B. Let me have audience for a word or two;
I am the second son of old Sir Rowland,
That bring these tidings to this fair assembly:—
Duke Frederick, hearing how that every day
Men of great worth resorted to this forest,
Address'd[14] a mighty power! which were on foot,
In his own conduct, purposely to take
His brother here, and put him to the sword:
And to the skirts of this wild wood he came;
Where, meeting with an old religious man,
After some question with him, was converted
Both from his enterprize, and from the world:
His crown bequeathing to his banish'd brother,
And all their lands restor'd to them again
That were with him exil'd: This to be true,
I do engage my life.

Duke S. Welcome, young man;
Thou offer'st fairly to thy brothers' wedding:
To one, his lands withheld; and to the other,
A land itself at large, a potent dukedom.
First, in this forest, let us do those ends
That here were well begun, and well begot:

---

1 i. e. prompt and pithy

2 'Dulcet diseases.' Johnson thought we should read—'*discourses*:' but it is useless labour to endeavour to make the fantastic Touchstone orthodox in his meaning.

3 i. e. the lie removed seven times, counting backwards from the last and most aggravated species of lie, viz. the lie direct.

4 Seemly. 5 i. e. *impeached*, or *dispraised.*

6 The poet has, in this scene, rallied the mode of formal duelling, then so prevalent, with the highest humour and address. The book alluded to is entitled, 'Of Honour and Honourable Quarrels, by Vincentio Savioli,' 1594, 4to.

7 The Booke of Nurture; or, Schoole of Good Manners for Men, Servants, and Children, with *stans puer ad mensam*, 12mo. without date, in black letter, is most probably the work referred to. It was written by Hugh Rhodes, and first published in the reign of Edward VI.

8 'A stalking-horse.' See note on Much Ado about Nothing, Act ii. Sc. 3.

9 Rosalind is imagined by the rest of the company to be brought by enchantment, and is therefore introduced by a supposed aerial being in the character of Hymen.

10 i. e. *at one; accord*, or *agree* together. This is the old sense of the phrase, 'an *attonement*, a loving againe after a breach or falling out. Reditus in gratia cum aliquo.'—*Baret.*

11 i. e. unless truth fails of veracity; 'if there be *truth* in *truth.*

12 i. e. take your fill of *discourse.*

13 i. e. unite, attach. 14 i. e. prepared.

And after, every of this happy number,
That have endur'd shrewd days and nights with us,
Shall share the good of our returned fortune,
According to the measure of their states.
Meantime, forget this new-fall'n dignity,
And fall into our rustic revelry :—
Play, music ;—and you, brides and bridegrooms all,
With measure heap'd in joy, to the measures fall.

Jaq. Sir, by your patience : If I heard you rightly,
The duke hath put on a religious life,
And thrown into neglect the pompous court?

Jaq. de B. He hath.

Jaq. To him will I : out of these convertites
There is much matter to be heard and learn'd.—
You to your former honour I bequeath : [*To* Duke S.
Your patience and your virtue well deserve it :—
You [*To* ORLANDO] to a love that your true faith doth merit :—
You [*To* OLIVER] to your land and love, and great allies :—
You [*To* SYLVIUS] to a long and well deserved bed :—
And you [*To* TOUCHSTONE] to wrangling ; for thy loving voyage
Is but for two months victual'd :—So to your pleasures ;
I am for other than for dancing measures.

Duke S. Stay, Jaques, stay.

Jaq. To see no pastime, I :—what you would have
I'll stay to know at your abandon'd cave.[1] [*Exit.*

Duke S. Proceed, proceed : we will begin these rites,
And we do trust they'll end in true delights.
[*A dance.*

1 The reader feels some regret to take his leave of Jaques in this manner : and no less concern at not meeting with the faithful old Adam at the close. It is the more remarkable that Shakspeare should have forgotten him, because Lodge, in his novel, makes him captain of the king's guard.

2 It was formerly the general custom in England, as it is still in France and the Netherlands, to hang a *bush of ivy* at the door of a vintner: there was a classical propriety in this ; *ivy* being sacred to Bacchus.

3 *Furnished*, dressed.

EPILOGUE.

Ros. It is not the fashion to see the lady the epilogue ; but it is no more unhandsome, than to see the lord the prologue. If it be true, that *good wine needs no bush*,[2] 'tis true that a good play needs no epilogue : Yet to good wine they do use good bushes ; and good plays prove the better by the help of good epilogues. What a case am I in then, that am neither a good epilogue, nor cannot insinuate with you in the behalf of a good play? I am not furnished[3] like a beggar, therefore to beg will not become me : my way is, to conjure you ; and I'll begin with the women. I charge you, O women, for the love you bear to men, to like as much of this play as please you :[4] and I charge you, O men, for the love you bear to women (as I perceive, by your simpering, none of you hate them,) that between you and the women the play may please. If I were a woman,[5] I would kiss as many of you as had beards that pleased me, complexions that liked me,[6] and breaths that I defied not : and I am sure, as many as have good beards, or good faces, or sweet breaths, will, for my kind offer, when I make curt'sy, bid me farewell. [*Exeunt.*

OF this play the fable is wild and pleasing. I know not how the ladies will approve the facility with which both Rosalind and Celia give away their hearts. To Celia much may be forgiven for the heroism of her friendship. The character of Jaques is natural and well preserved. The comic dialogue is very sprightly, with less mixture of low buffoonery than in some other plays ; and the graver part is elegant and harmonious. By hastening to the end of this work, Shakspeare suppressed the dialogue between the usurper and the hermit, and lost an opportunity of exhibiting a moral lesson, in which he might have found matter worthy of his highest powers.
JOHNSON.

4 This is the reading of the old copy, which has been altered to 'as much of this play as please *them*,' but surely without necessity. It is only the omission of the *s* at the end of *please*, which gives it a quaint appearance, but it was the practice of the poet's age.

5 The parts of women were performed by men or boys in Shakspeare's time.

6 i. e. that I liked.

ALL'S WELL THAT ENDS WELL.

PRELIMINARY REMARKS.

THE fable of All's Well that Ends Well is derived from the story of Gilletta of Narbonne in the Decamerone of Boccaccio. It came to Shakspeare through the medium of Painter's Palace of Pleasure : and is to be found in the first volume, which was printed as early as 1566. The comic parts of the plot, and the characters of the Countess, Lafeu, &c. are of the poet's own creation, and in the conduct of the fable he has found it expedient to depart from his original more than it is his usual custom to do. The character of Helena is beautifully drawn, she is an heroic and patient sufferer of adverse fortune like Griselda, and placed in circumstances of almost equal difficulty. Her romantic passion for Bertram with whom she had been brought up as a sister ; her grief at his departure for the court, which she expresses in some exquisitely impassioned lines, and the retiring anxious modesty with which she confides her passion to the Countess, are in the poet's sweetest style of writing. Nor are the succeeding parts of her conduct touched with a less delicate and masterly hand. Placed in extraordinary and embarrassing circumstances, there is a propriety and delicacy in all her actions, which is consistent with the guileless innocence of her heart.

The King is properly made an instrument in the denouement of the plot of the play, and this a most striking and judicious deviation from the novel : his gratitude and esteem for Helen are consistent and honourable to him as a man and a monarch.

Johnson has expressed his dislike of the character of Bertram, and most fair readers have manifested their abhorrence of him, and have thought with Johnson that he ought not to have gone unpunished, for the sake not only of poetical but of *moral* justice. Schlegel has remarked that 'Shakspeare never attempts to mitigate the impression of his unfeeling pride and giddy dissipation. He intended merely to give us a military portrait ; and paints the true way of the world, according to which the injustice of men towards women is not considered in a very serious light, if they only maintain what is called the *honour* of the family.' The fact is, that the construction of his plot prevented him. Helen was to be rewarded for her heroic and persevering affection, and any more serious punishment than the temporary shame and remorse that awaits Bertram would have been inconsistent with comedy. It should also be remembered that he was constrained to marry Helen against his will. Shakspeare was a good-natured moralist ; and, like his own creation, old *Lafeu*, though he was delighted to strip off the mask of pretension, he thought that punishment might be carried too far. Who that has been diverted with the truly comic scenes in which Parolles is made to appear in his true character, could have wished him to have been otherwise dismissed ?—

'Though you are a fool and a knave, you shall eat.'

It has been remarked that 'the style of the whole play is more conspicuous for sententiousness than imagery :' and that 'the glowing colours of fancy could not have been introduced into such a subject.' May not the period of life at which it was produced have something to do with this? Malone places the date of its composition in 1606, and observes that a beautiful speech of the sick king has much the air of that moral and judicious reflection that accompanies an advanced period of life.

'——— let me not live
After my flame lacks oil, to be the snuff
Of younger spirits, whose apprehensive senses
All but new things disdain: whose judgments are
Mere fathers of their garments; whose constancies
Expire before their fashions.'

It appears probable that the original title of this play was 'Love's Labours Wonne:' at least a piece under that title is mentioned by Meres in his 'Wits Treasurie,' in 1598; but if this was the play referred to, what becomes of Malone's hypothesis relating to the date of its composition?

PERSONS REPRESENTED.

King of France.
Duke of Florence.
Bertram, Count of Rousillon.
Lafeu,[1] *an old Lord.*
Parolles,[1] *a follower of* Bertram.
Several young French Lords, *that serve with* Bertram *in the* Florentine *war.*
Steward, } *Servants to the* Countess of Rousillon.
Clown, }
A Page.

Countess of Rousillon, *Mother to* Bertram.
Helena, *a Gentlewoman protected by the Countess*
An old Widow of Florence.
Diana, *Daughter to the Widow.*
Violenta, } *Neighbours and Friends to the Widow.*
Mariana, }
Lords, *attending on the* King; Officers, Soldiers, &c. French *and* Florentine.
SCENE, *partly in* France, *and partly in* Tuscany

ACT I.

SCENE I. Rousillon. *A Room in the* Countess's *Palace. Enter* Bertram, *the* Countess of Rousillon, Helena, *and* Lafeu, *in mourning.*

Countess.

In delivering my son from me, I bury a second husband.

Ber. And I, in going, madam, weep o'er my father's death anew: but I must attend his majesty's command, to whom I am now in ward,[2] evermore in subjection.

Laf. You shall find of the king a husband, madam;—you, sir, a father: He that so generally is at all times good, must of necessity hold his virtue to you; whose worthiness would stir it up where it wanted, rather than lack it where there is such abundance.

Count. What hope is there of his majesty's amendment?

Laf. He hath abandoned his physicians, madam; under whose practices he hath persecuted time with hope; and finds no other advantage in the process but only the losing of hope by time.

Count. This young gentlewoman had a father (O, that *had!* how sad a passage[3] 'tis!) whose skill was almost as great as his honesty; had it stretched so far, would have made nature immortal, and death should have play for lack of work. 'Would, for the king's sake, he were living! I think, it would be the death of the king's disease.

Laf. How called you the man you speak of, madam?

Count. He was famous, sir, in his profession, and it was his great right to be so: Gerard de Narbon.

Laf. He was excellent, indeed, madam; the king very lately spoke of him, admiringly, and mourningly: he was skilful enough to have lived still, if knowledge could be set up against mortality.

Ber. What is it, my good lord, the king languishes of?

Laf. A fistula, my lord.

Ber. I heard not of it before.

Laf. I would, it were not notorious.—Was this gentlewoman the daughter of Gerard de Narbon?

Count. His sole child, my lord; and bequeathed to my overlooking. I have those hopes of her good, that her education promises: her dispositions she inherits, which make fair gifts fairer; for where an unclean mind carries virtuous qualities,[4] there commendations go with pity, they are virtues and traitors too; in her they are the better for their simpleness; she derives her honesty, and achieves her goodness.

Laf. Your commendations, madam, get from her tears.

Count. 'Tis the best brine a maiden can season[5] her praise in. The remembrance of her father never approaches her heart, but the tyranny of her sorrows takes all livelihood[6] from her cheek. No more of this, Helena, go to, no more; lest it be rather thought you affect a sorrow, than to have.[7]

Hel. I do affect a sorrow, indeed, but I have it too.[8]

Laf. Moderate lamentation is the right of the dead, excessive grief the enemy to the living.

Count. If the living be enemy to the grief, the excess makes it soon mortal.[9]

Ber. Madam, I desire your holy wishes.

Laf. How understand we that?

Count. Be thou blest, Bertram! and succeed thy father
In manners, as in shape! thy blood, and virtue,
Contend for empire in thee; and thy goodness
Share with thy birth-right! Love all, trust a few,
Do wrong to none: be able for thine enemy
Rather in power, than use; and keep thy friend
Under thy own life's key: be check'd for silence,
But never tax'd for speech. What heaven more will,
That thee may furnish,[10] and my prayers pluck down,
Fall on thy head! Farewell.—My lord,
'Tis an unseason'd courtier; good my lord,
Advise him.

1 Steevens says that we should write *Lefeu* and *Paroles.*

2 The heirs of great fortunes were formerly the king's *wards.* This prerogative was a branch of the feudal law.

3 In the Heautontimorumenos of Terence, which had been translated in Shakspeare's time, is the following passage:

'——— Filium unicum adolescentulum
Habeo. Ah quid dixi *Habere* me? imo
——— habui, Chreme,
Nunc habeam incertum est.'

4 We feel regret even in commending such qualities, joined with an evil disposition; they are *traitors,* because they give the possessors power over others; who, admiring such estimable qualities, are often betrayed by the malevolence of the possessors. Helena's virtues are the better because they are artless and open.

5 So in Chapman's version of the third Iliad:
'Season'd her tears her joys to see,' &c.

6 All appearance of life.

7 This kind of phraseology was not peculiar to Shakspeare, though it appears uncouth to us: it is plain that he meant—'lest it be rather thought you affect a sorrow than have *it.*'

8 Helena's *affected* sorrow was for the death of her father: her *real* grief related to Bertram and his departure.

9 That is, 'if the living do not indulge grief, grief destroys itself by its own excess.'

10 i. e. that may help thee with more and better qualifications

Laf. He cannot want the best
That shall attend his love.

Count. Heaven bless him!—Farewell, Bertram.
[*Exit* Countess.

Ber. The best wishes, that can be forged in your thoughts [*To* HELENA,] be servants to you![1] Be comfortable to my mother, your mistress, and make much of her.

Laf. Farewell, pretty lady: You must hold the credit of your father.
[*Exeunt* BERTRAM *and* LAFEU.

Hel. O, were that all!—I think not on my father,
And these great tears[2] grace his remembrance more
Than those I shed for him. What was he like?
I have forgot him: my imagination
Carries no favour in it, but Bertram's.
I am undone; there is no living, none,
If Bertram be away. It were all one,
That I should love a bright particular star,
And think to wed it, he is so above me:
In his bright radiance and collateral light
Must I be comforted, not in his sphere.
The ambition in my love thus plagues itself:
The hind, that would be mated by the lion,
Must die for love. 'Twas pretty, though a plague,
To see him every hour; to sit and draw
His arched brows, his hawking eye, his curls,
In our heart's table;[3] heart, too capable
Of every line and trick of his sweet favour:[4]
But now he's gone, and my idolatrous fancy
Must sanctify his relics. Who comes here?

Enter PAROLLES.

One that goes with him: I love him for his sake;
And yet I know him a notorious liar,
Think him a great way fool, solely[5] a coward;
Yet these fix'd evils sit so fit in him,
That they take place, when virtue's steely bones
Look bleak in the cold wind: withal, full oft we see
Cold wisdom waiting on superfluous folly.[6]

Par. Save you, fair queen.

Hel. And you, monarch.[7]

Par. No.

Hel. And no.

Par. Are you meditating on virginity?

Hel. Ay. You have some stain[8] of soldier in you: let me ask you a question: Man is enemy to virginity; how may we barricado it against him?

Par. Keep him out.

Hel. But he assails; and our virginity, though valiant in the defence, yet is weak: unfold to us some warlike resistance.

Par. There is none; man, sitting down before you, will undermine you, and blow you up.

Hel. Bless our poor virginity from underminers, and blowers up!—Is there no military policy, how virgins might blow up men?

Par. Virginity, being blown down, man will quicklier be blown up: marry, in blowing him down again, with the breach yourselves made, you lose your city. It is not politick in the commonwealth of nature, to preserve virginity. Loss of virginity is rational increase; and there was never virgin got, till virginity was first lost. That, you were made of, is metal to make virgins. Virginity, by being once lost, may be ten times found: by being ever kept, it is ever lost: 'tis too cold a companion; away with it.

Hel. I will stand for't a little, though therefore I die a virgin.

Par. There's little can be said in't; 'tis against the rule of nature. To speak on the part of virginity, is to accuse your mothers; which is most infallible disobedience. He, that hangs himself is a virgin: virginity murders itself;[9] and should be buried in highways, out of all sanctified limit, as a desperate offendress against nature. Virginity breeds mites, much like a cheese; consumes itself to the very paring, and so dies with feeding his own stomach. Besides, virginity is peevish, proud, idle, made of self-love, which is the most inhibited[10] sin in the canon. Keep it not: you cannot choose but lose by't: Out with't: within ten years it will make itself ten,[11] which is a goodly increase, and the principal itself not much the worse: Away with't.

Hel. How might one do, sir, to lose it to her own liking?

Par. Let me see: Marry, ill, to like him that ne'er it likes.[12] 'Tis a commodity will lose the gloss with lying; the longer kept, the less worth: off with't, while 'tis vendible: answer the time of request. Virginity, like an old courtier, wears her cap out of fashion; richly suited, but unsuitable: just like the brooch and toothpick, which wear[13] not now: Your date[14] is better in your pie and your porridge, than in your cheek: And your virginity, your old virginity, is like one of our French withered pears; it looks ill, it eats dryly; marry, 'tis a withered pear; it was formerly better; marry, yet, 'tis a withered pear: Will you any thing with it?

Hel. Not my virginity yet.[15]——
There shall your master have a thousand loves,
A mother, and a mistress, and a friend,
A phœnix, captain, and an enemy,
A guide, a goddess, and a sovereign,
A counsellor, a traitress, and a dear;
His humble ambition, proud humility,
His jarring concord, and his discord dulcet,
His faith, his sweet disaster: with a world
Of pretty, fond, adoptious christendoms,[16]
That blinking Cupid gossips. Now shall he—
I know not what he shall:—God send him well.—
The court's a learning-place:—and he is one——

Par. What one, i'faith?

Hel. That I wish well.—'Tis pity——

Par. What's pity?

Hel. That wishing well had not a body in't,
Which might be felt: that we, the poorer born,
Whose baser stars do shut us up in wishes,
Might with effects of them follow our friends,

---

1 i. e. may you be mistress of your wishes, and have power to bring them to effect.

2 That is, Helen's own tears, which were caused in reality by the departure of Bertram, though attributed by Lafeu and the Countess to the loss of her father, and which, from this misapprehension of theirs, *graced his memory more* than those she actually shed for him.

3 Helena considers her heart as the *tablet* on which his resemblance was portrayed.

4 i. e. every line and *trace* of his sweet countenance.

5 i. e. *altogether*, without any admixture of the opposite quality.

6 *Cold* for *naked*, as superfluous for overclothed. This makes the propriety of the antithesis.

7 Perhaps there is an allusion here to the fantastic Monarcho mentioned in a note on Love's Labour's Lost, Act i. Sc. 1.

8 That is, some *tincture*, some little of the hue or colour of a soldier; as much as to say, '*you that are a bit of a soldier*.'

9 He that hangs himself, and a virgin, are in this circumstance alike, they are both *self-destroyers*.

10 Forbidden.

1 The old copy reads, 'within ten years it will make itself *two*.' The emendation is Hanmer's. *Out with it* is used equivocally. Applied to virginity, it means, give it away; part with it: considered in another light, it signifies *put it out to interest*, it will produce you ten for one.

12 Parolles plays upon the word *liking*, and says, '*She must do ill for* virginity to be so lost, *must like him that likes not virginity*.'

13 The old copy reads *were*, Rowe corrected it. Shakspeare here, as in other places, uses the active for the passive.

14 A quibble on *date*, which means age, and a candied fruit then much used in pies.

15 I cannot but think, with Hanmer and Johnson, that some such clause as '*You're for the court*,' has been omitted. Unless we suppose, with Malone, that the omission is in Parolles's speech, and that he may have said, '*I am now bound for the court*.' Something of the kind is necessary to connect Helena's rhapsodical speech; she could not mean to say that she shall prove every thing to Bertram.

16 i. e. a number of pretty, fo[illegible], adopted appellations or *Christian names*, to which blind Cupid stands godfather. It is often used for *baptism* by old writers

And show what we alone must think;[1] which never
Returns us thanks.

Enter a Page.

Page. Monsieur Parolles, my lord calls for you. [*Exit* Page.

Par. Little Helen, farewell: if I can remember thee, I will think of thee at court.

Hel. Monsieur Parolles, you were born under a charitable star.

Par. Under Mars, I.

Hel. I especially think, under Mars.

Par. Why under Mars?

Hel. The wars have so kept you under, that you must needs be born under Mars.

Par. When he was predominant.

Hel. When he was retrograde, I think, rather.

Par. Why think you so?

Hel. You go so much backward, when you fight.

Par. That's for advantage.

Hel. So is running away, when fear proposes the safety; But the composition, that your valour and fear makes in you, is a virtue of a good wing,[2] and I like the wear well.

Par. I am so full of businesses, I cannot answer thee acutely: I will return perfect courtier; in the which, my instruction shall serve to naturalize thee, so thou wilt be capable[3] of a courtier's counsel, and understand what advice shall thrust upon thee; else thou diest in thine unthankfulness, and thine ignorance makes thee away: farewell. When thou hast leisure, say thy prayers; when thou hast none, remember thy friends: get thee a good husband, and use him as he uses thee: so farewell. [*Exit.*

Hel. Our remedies oft in ourselves do lie,
Which we ascribe to heaven: the fated sky
Gives us free scope; only, doth backward pull
Our slow designs, when we ourselves are dull.
What power is it which mounts my love so high;
That makes me see, and cannot feed mine eye?[4]
The mightiest space in fortune nature brings
To join like likes, and kiss like native things.[5]
Impossible be strange attempts, to those
That weigh their pains in sense; and do suppose,
What hath been cannot be: Who ever strove
To show her merit, that did miss her love?
The king's disease—my project may deceive me,
But my intents are fix'd, and will not leave me. [*Exit.*

SCENE II. Paris. *A Room in the* King's *Palace. Flourish of Cornets. Enter the* King of France, *with Letters; Lords and others attending.*

King. The Florentines and Senoys[6] are by the ears;
Have fought with equal fortune, and continue
A braving war.

1 Lord. So 'tis reported, sir.

King. Nay, 'tis most credible; we here receive it
A certainty, vouch'd from our cousin Austria,
With caution, that the Florentine will move us
For speedy aid; wherein our dearest friend
Prejudicates the business, and would seem
To have us make denial.

1 Lord. His love and wisdom,
Approv'd so to your majesty, may plead
For amplest credence.

King. He hath arm'd our answer
And Florence is denied before he comes:
Yet, for our gentlemen, that mean to see
The Tuscan service, freely have they leave
To stand on either part.

2 Lord. It may well serve
A nursery to our gentry, who are sick
For breathing and exploit.

King What's he comes here?

Enter Bertram, Lafeu, *and* Parolles.

1 Lord. It is the count Rousillon, my good lord,
Young Bertram.

King. Youth, thou bear'st thy father's face;
Frank nature, rather curious than in haste,
Hath well compos'd thee. Thy father's moral parts
May'st thou inherit too! Welcome to Paris.

Ber. My thanks and duty are your majesty's.

King. I would I had that corporal soundness now,
As when thy father, and myself, in friendship
First tried our soldiership! He did look far
Into the service of the time, and was
Discipled of the bravest: he lasted long;
But on us both did haggish age steal on,
And wore us out of act. It much repairs[7] me
To talk of your good father: In his youth
He had the wit, which I can well observe
To-day in our young lords; but they may jest,
Till their own scorn return to them unnoted,
Ere they can hide their levity in honour.[8]
So like a courtier, contempt nor bitterness
Were in his pride or sharpness: if they were,
His equal had awak'd them;[9] and his honour,
Clock to itself, knew the true minute when
Exception bid him speak, and, at this time,
His tongue obey'd his[10] hand: who were below him
He us'd as creatures of another place;
And bow'd his eminent top to their low ranks,
Making them proud of his humility,
In their poor praise he humbled: Such a man
Might be a copy to these younger times;
Which, follow'd well, would demonstrate them now
But goers backward.

Ber. His good remembrance, sir,
Lies richer in your thoughts, than on his tomb;
So in approof[11] lives not his epitaph,
As in your royal speech.

King. 'Would, I were with him! He would always say,
(Methinks I hear him now; his plausive words
He scatter'd not in ears, but grafted them,
To grow there, and to bear)—*Let him not live,*—
Thus his good melancholy oft began,
On the catastrophe and heel of pastime,
When it was out,—*let me not live,* quoth he
After my flame lacks oil, to be the snuff
Of younger spirits, whose apprehensive senses
All but new things disdain; whose judgments are

1 i. e. and show by realities what we now must only think.

2 This is a metaphor from Shakspeare's favorite source; Falconry. A bird of *good wing* was a bird of swift and strong flight. 'If your valour will suffer you to go backward for advantage, and your fear, for the same reason, will make you run away, the composition is a virtue that will fly far and swiftly.' Mason thinks we should read—'*is* like *to* wear well.'

3 *Capable* and *susceptible* were synonymous in Shakspeare's time, as appears by the dictionaries. Helen says before:

'heart too *capable*
Of every line and trick of his sweet favour.'

4 She means, 'why am I made to discern excellence, and left to long after it without the food of hope.'

5 *The mightiest space in fortune* is a licentious expression for persons *the most widely separated by fortune;* whom *nature* (i. e. natural affection) *brings to join like likes* (i. e. equals,) *and kiss like native things* (i. e. and unite like things formed by nature for each other.) Or in other words, 'Nature often unites those whom fortune or inequality of rank has separated.'

6 The citizens of the small republic of which Sienna is the capital. The *Sanesi,* as Boccaccio calls them. which Painter translates *Senois,* after the French method.

7 To *repair* in these plays generally signifies to *renovate.*

8 That is, 'cover petty faults with great merit:' *honour* does not stand for *dignity of rank or birth,* but *acquired reputation.* 'This is an excellent observation (says Johnson,) jocose follies, and slight offences, are only allowed by mankind in him that overpowers them by great qualities.'

9 *Nor* was sometimes used without reduplication. 'He was so like a courtier, that there was in his dignity of manner nothing contemptuous, and in his keenness of wit nothing bitter. If *bitterness* or contemptuousness ever appeared, they had been *awakened* by some injury, not of a man below him, but for his *equal.*'

10 *His* for *its.*

11 The *approbation* of his worth *lives not* so much *in his epitaph as in your royal speech.*

Mere fathers of their garments;[1] *whose constancies*
Expire before their fashions:——This he wish'd:
I, after him, do after him wish too,
Since I nor wax, nor honey, can bring home,
I quickly were dissolved from my hive,
To give some labourers room.
2 *Lord.* You are lov'd, sir;
They, that least lend it you, shall lack you first.
King. I fill a place, I know't.—How long is't, count,
Since the physician at your father's died?
He was much fam'd.
Ber. Some six months since, my lord.
King. If he were living, I would try him yet;—
Lend me an arm;—the rest have worn me out
With several applications:—nature and sickness
Debate it at their leisure.[2] Welcome, count;
My son's no dearer.
Ber. Thank your majesty.
[*Exeunt. Flourish.*

SCENE III. Rousillon. *A Room in the* Countess's *Palace. Enter* Countess, Steward, *and* Clown.[3]

Count. I will now hear; what say you of this gentlewoman?

Stew. Madam, the care I have had to even your content,[4] I wish might be found in the calendar of my past endeavours; for then we wound our modesty, and make foul the clearness of our deservings, when of ourselves we publish them.

Count. What does this knave here? Get you gone, sirrah: The complaints, I have heard of you, I do not all believe; 'tis my slowness, that I do not: for, I know, you lack not folly to commit them, and have ability enough to make such knaveries yours.

Clo. 'Tis not unknown to you, madam, I am a poor fellow.

Count. Well, sir.

Clo. No, madam, 'tis not so well, that I am poor; though many of the rich are damned: But, if I may have your ladyship's good will to go to the world,[5] Isabel the woman and I will do as we may.

Count. Wilt thou needs be a beggar?

Clo. I do beg your goodwill in this case.

Count. In what case?

Clo. In Isabel's case, and mine own. Service is no heritage: and, I think, I shall never have the blessing of God, till I have issue of my body: for, they say, bearns[6] are blessings.

Count. Tell me thy reason why thou wilt marry.

Clo. My poor body, madam, requires it: I am driven on by the flesh; and he must needs go, that the devil drives.

Count. Is this all your worship's reason?

Clo. Faith, madam, I have other holy reasons, such as they are.

Count. May the world know them?

Clo. I have been, madam, a wicked creature, as you and all flesh and blood are; and, indeed, I do marry, that I may repent.

Count. Thy marriage, sooner than thy wickedness.

Clo. I am out of friends, madam; and I hope to have friends for my wife's sake.

Count. Such friends are thine enemies, knave.

Clo. You are shallow, madam; e'en great friends; for the knaves come to do that for me, which I am a-weary of. He, that ears[7] my land, spares my team, and gives me leave to inn the crop: if I be his cuckold, he's my drudge: He that comforts my wife, is the nourisher of my flesh and blood; he, that cherishes my flesh and blood, loves my flesh and blood; he, that loves my flesh and blood, is my friend: *ergo*,[8] he that kisses my wife, is my friend. If men could be contented to be what they are, there were no fear in marriage: for young Charbon the puritan, and old Poysam[9] the papist, howsoe'er their hearts are severed in religion, their heads are both one, they may joll horns together, like any deer i'the herd.

Count. Wilt thou ever be a foul-mouthed and calumnious knave?

Clo. A prophet I, madam; and I speak the truth the next way:[10]

For I the ballad will repeat,
Which men full true shall find;
Your marriage comes by destiny,
Your cuckoo sings by kind.[11]

Count. Get you gone, sir; I'll talk with you more anon.

Stew. May it please you, madam, that he bid Helen come to you; of her I am to speak.

Count. Sirrah, tell my gentlewoman, I would speak with her; Helen I mean.

Clo. *Was this fair face the cause, quoth she,* [Singing.
Why the Grecians sacked Troy?
Fond done,[12] *done fond,*
Was this king Priam's joy.[13]
With that she sighed as she stood,
With that she sighed as she stood,
And gave this sentence then;
Among nine bad if one be good,
Among nine bad if one be good,
There's yet one good in ten.

Count. What, one good in ten; you corrupt the song, sirrah.

Clo. One good woman in ten, madam; which is a purifying o'the song: 'Would, God would serve the world so all the year! we'd find no fault with the tithe-woman, if I were the parson: One in ten, quoth a'! an we might have a good woman born, but on[14] every blazing star, or at an earthquake, 'twould mend the lottery well; a man may draw his heart out, ere he pluck one.

Count. You'll be gone, sir knave, and do as I command you?

Clo. That man should be at woman's command, and yet no hurt done!—Though honesty be no puritan, yet it will do no hurt; it will wear the surplice of humility over the black gown of a big heart.[15]—I am going, forsooth: the business is for Helen to come hither. [*Exit* Clown.

Count. Well, now.

Stew. I know, madam, you love your gentlewoman entirely.

Count. Faith, I do: her father bequeathed her to me; and she herself, without other advantage, may lawfully make title to as much love as she finds: there is more owing her, than is paid; and more shall be paid her, than she'll demand.

Stew. Madam, I was very late more near her than, I think, she wished me: alone she was, and did

1 Who have no other use of their faculties than to invent new modes of dress.
2 So in Macbeth:
'Death and nature do *contend* about them.'
3 The *Clown* in this comedy is a domestic fool of the same kind as Touchstone. Such fools were, in the poet's time, maintained in all great families, to keep up merriment in the house.
4 To act up to your desires. 5 To be married.
6 Children. 7 Ploughs. 8 Therefore.
9 Malone conjectures that we should read, '*Poisson* the papist,' alluding to the custom of eating fish on fast days: as *Charbon* the puritan alludes to the fiery zeal of that sect. It is much in Shakspeare's manner to use significant names.
10 The readiest way. 11 i. e. nature.
12 Foolishly done
13 The name of Helen brings to the Clown's memory this fragment of an old ballad; something has escaped him it appears, for *Paris* 'was king Priam's only joy, as Helen was Sir Paris's. According to two fragments quoted by the commentators.
14 The old copy reads *one*. Malone substituted *on*.
15 The clown answers, with the licentious petulance allowed to the character, that 'if a man does as a woman commands, it is likely he will do amiss;' that he does not amiss, he makes the effect not of his lady's goodness, but of his own *honesty*, which, though not very nice or *puritanical*, will do no hurt, but, unlike the *puritans*, will comply with the injunctions of superiors; and wear the 'surplice of humility over the black gown of a big heart;' will obey commands, though not much pleased with a state of subjection.

communicate to herself, her own words to her own ears; she thought, I dare vow for her, they touched not any stranger sense. Her matter was, she loved your son: Fortune, she said, was no goddess, that had put such difference betwixt their two estates; Love, no god, that would not extend his might, only where qualities were level; Diana,[1] no queen of virgins, that would suffer her poor knight to be surprised, without rescue, in the first assault, or ransom afterward: This she delivered in the most bitter touch of sorrow, that e'er I heard virgin exclaim in: which I held my duty, speedily to acquaint you withal; sithence,[2] in the loss that may happen, it concerns you something to know it.

Count. You have discharged this honestly; keep it to yourself: many likelihoods informed me of this before, which hung so tottering in the balance, that I could neither believe, nor misdoubt; Pray you, leave me: stall this in your bosom, and I thank you for your honest care: I will speak with you further anon. [*Exit* Steward.

Enter Helena.

Even so it was with me, when I was young:
If we[3] are nature's, these are ours; this thorn
Doth to our rose of youth rightly belong;
Our blood to us, this to our blood is born;
It is the show and seal of nature's truth,
Where love's strong passion is impress'd in youth:
By our remembrances[4] of days foregone,
Such were our faults;—or then we thought them none.
Her eyes are sick on't; I observe her now.

Hel. What is your pleasure, madam?

Count. You know, Helen,
I am a mother to you.

Hel. Mine honourable mistress.

Count. Nay, a mother;
Why not a mother? When I said, a mother,
Methought you saw a serpent: What's in mother,
That you start at it? I say I am your mother;
And put you in the catalogue of those
That were enwombed mine: 'Tis often seen,
Adoption strives with nature: and choice breeds
A native slip to us from foreign seeds:
You ne'er oppress'd me with a mother's groan,
Yet I express to you a mother's care:—
God's mercy, maiden! does it curd thy blood,
To say, I am thy mother? What's the matter,
That this distemper'd messenger of wet,
The many-colour'd Iris, rounds thine eye?[5]
Why?——that you are my daughter?

Hel. That I am not.

Count. I say, I am your mother.

Hel. Pardon, madam;
The count Rousillon cannot be my brother:
I am from humble, he from honour'd name;
No note upon my parents, his all noble:
My master, my dear lord he is; and I
His servant live, and will his vassal die:
He must not be my brother.

Count. Nor I your mother?

Hel. You are my mother, madam; 'Would, you were
(So that my lord, your son, were not my brother,)
Indeed, my mother!—or were you both our mothers,
I care no more for,[6] than I do for heaven,
So I were not his sister: Can't no other,[7]
But, I your daughter, he must be my brother?

Count. Yes, Helen, you might be my daughter-in-law;
God shield, you mean it not! daughter and mother,
So strive[8] upon your pulse: What, pale again?
My fear hath catch'd your fondness: Now I see
The mystery of your loneliness,[9] and find
Your salt tears' head.[10] Now to all sense 'tis gross,
You love my son; invention is asham'd,
Against the proclamation of thy passion,
To say, thou dost not: therefore tell me true.
But tell me then, 'tis so:—for, look, thy cheeks
Confess it, one to the other: and thine eyes
See it so grossly shown in thy behaviours,
That in their kind[11] they speak it: only sin
And hellish obstinacy tie thy tongue,
That truth should be suspected: Speak, is't so?
If it be so, you have wound a goodly clue;
If it be not, forswear't: howe'er, I charge thee,
As heaven shall work in me for thine avail,
To tell me truly.

Hel. Good madam, pardon me!

Count. Do you love my son?

Hel. Your pardon, noble mistress!

Count. Love you my son?

Hel. Do not you love him, madam?

Count. Go not about; my love hath in't a bond,
Whereof the world takes note: come, come, disclose
The state of your affection; for your passions
Have to the full appeach'd.

Hel. Then, I confess,
Here on my knee, before high heaven and you,
That before you, and next unto high heaven,
I love your son:—
My friends were poor, but honest: so's my love:
Be not offended; for it hurts not him,
That he is lov'd of me: I follow him not
By any token of presumptuous suit;
Nor would I have him, till I do deserve him;
Yet never know how that desert should be.
I know I love in vain, strive against hope;
Yet, in this captious[12] and intenible sieve,
I still pour in the waters of my love,
And lack not to lose still; thus, Indian-like,
Religious in mine error, I adore
The sun, that looks upon his worshipper,
But knows of him no more. My dearest madam,
Let not your hate encounter with my love,
For loving where you do: but, if yourself,
Whose aged honour cites a virtuous youth,[13]
Did ever, in so true a flame of liking,
Wish chastely, and love dearly, that your Dian
Was both herself and love;[14] O then give pity
To her, whose state is such, that cannot choose
But lend and give, where she is sure to lose;
That seeks not to find that her search implies,
But, riddle-like, lives sweetly where she dies.

Count. Had you not lately an intent, speak truly,
To go to Paris?

Hel. Madam, I had.

Count. Wherefore? tell true

Hel. I will tell truth; by grace itself, I swear,
You know, my father left me some prescriptions
Of rare and proved effects, such as his reading,
And manifest experience, had collected

1 The old copies omit *Diana*. Theobald inserted the word.

2 Since.

3 The old copy reads, 'if *ever* we are nature's.' The correction is Pope's

4 i. e. according to our recollection.

5 There is something exquisitely beautiful in this representation of that suffusion of colours which glimmers around the sight when eyelashes are wet with tears.

6 There is a designed ambiguity, i. e. I care as much for: I wish it equally.

7 i. e. 'can it *be* no other *way*, but *if* I *be* your daughter, he must be my brother?'

8 Contend.

9 The old copy reads *loveliness*. The emendation is Theobald's. It has been proposed to read *lowliness*.

10 The source, the cause of your grief.

11 In their language, according to their *nature*.

12 Johnson is perplexed about this word *captious* 'which (says he) I never found in this sense, yet I can not tell what to substitute, unless *carious* for rotten. Farmer supposes *captious* to be a contraction of *capacious!* Steevens believes that *captious* meant *recipient*, capable of receiving! and *intenible* incapable of holding or retaining:—he rightly explains the latter word, which is printed in the old copy *intemible* by mistake.

13 i. e. whose respectable conduct in age *proves* that you were no less virtuous when young.

14 Helena means to say—'If ever you wished that the deity who presides over chastity, and the queen of amorous rites, were one and the same person, or, in other words, if ever you wished for the honest and lawful completion of your chaste desires.' Malone thinks the line should be thus read:—
'Love dearly, and wish chastely, that your Dian,' &c

For general sovereignty; and that he will'd me
In heedfulest reservation to bestow them,
As notes, whose faculties inclusive were,
More than they were in note:[1] amongst the rest,
There is a remedy approv'd, set down,
To cure the desperate languishes, whereof
The king is render'd lost.

Count. This was your motive
For Paris, was it? speak.

Hel. My lord your son made me to think of this;
Else Paris, and the medicine, and the king,
Had, from the conversation of my thoughts,
Haply, been absent then.

Count. But think you, Helen,
If you should tender your supposed aid,
He would receive it? He and his physicians
Are of a mind; he, that they cannot help him;
They, that they cannot help: How shall they credit
A poor unlearned virgin, when the schools,
Embowell'd of their doctrine,[2] have left off
The danger to itself?

Hel. There's something hints,[3]
More than my father's skill, which was the greatest
Of his profession, that his good receipt
Shall, for my legacy, be sanctified
By the luckiest stars in heaven: and would your honour
But give me leave to try success, I'd venture
The well-lost life of mine on his grace's cure,
By such a day and hour.

Count. Dost thou believe't?

Hel. Ay, madam, knowingly.

Count. Why, Helen, thou shalt have my leave and love,
Means, and attendants, and my loving greetings
To those of mine in court; I'll stay at home,
And pray God's blessing into[4] thy attempt:
Be gone to-morrow; and be sure of this,
What I can help thee to, thou shalt not miss.
[*Exeunt.*

ACT II.

SCENE I. Paris. *A Room in the* King's *Palace. Flourish. Enter* King, *with young* Lords *taking leave for the* Florentine *war;* BERTRAM, PAROLLES, *and* Attendants.

King. Farewell, young lord,[5] these warlike principles
Do not throw from you:—and you, my lord, farewell:—
Share the advice betwixt you; if both gain all,
The gift doth stretch itself as 'tis receiv'd,
And is enough for both.

1 Lord. It is our hope, sir,
After well enter'd soldiers, to return
And find your grace in health.

King. No, no, it cannot be; and yet my heart
Will not confess he owes the malady
That doth my life besiege.[6] Farewell, young lords;
Whether I live or die, be you the sons
Of worthy Frenchmen: let higher Italy
(Those 'bated, that inherit but the fall
Of the last monarchy,)[7] see, that you come
Not to woo honour, but to wed it; when
The bravest questant[8] shrinks, find what you seek,
That fame may cry you loud: I say, farewell.

2 Lord. Health, at your bidding, serve your majesty!

King. Those girls of Italy, take heed of them,
They say, our French lack language to deny,
If they demand: beware of being captives,
Before you serve.[9]

Both. Our hearts receive your warnings.

King. Farewell.—Come hither to me.
[*The* King *retires to a Couch.*

1 Lord. O my sweet lord, that you will stay behind us!

Par. 'Tis not his fault; the spark——

2 Lord. O, 'tis brave wars!

Par. Most admirable: I have seen those wars.

Ber. I am commanded here, and kept a coil[10] with;
Too young, and *the next year*, and *'tis too early*.

Par. An thy mind stand to it, boy, steal away bravely.

Ber. I shall stay here the forehorse to a smock,
Creaking my shoes on the plain masonry,
Till honour be bought up and no sword worn,
But one to dance with![11] By heaven, I'll steal away.

1 Lord. There's honour in the theft.

Par. Commit it, count.

2 Lord. I am your accessary; and so farewell.

Ber. I grow to you, and our parting is a tortured body.[12]

1 Lord. Farewell, captain.

2 Lord. Sweet monsieur Parolles!

Par. Noble heroes, my sword and yours are kin. Good sparks and lustrous, a word, good metals:—You shall find in the regiment of the Spinii, one captain Spurio, with his cicatrice, an emblem of war, here on his sinister cheek; it was this very sword entrenched it: say to him, I live; and observe his reports for me.

2 Lord. We shall, noble captain.

Par. Mars dote on you for his novices! [*Exeunt* Lords.] What will you do?

Ber. Stay; the king—— [*Seeing him rise.*

Par. Use a more spacious ceremony to the noble lords: you have restrained yourself within the list of too cold an adieu: be more expressive to them; for they wear themselves in the cap of the time,[13] there do muster true gait;[14] eat, speak, and move under the influence of the most received star; and though the devil lead the measure,[15] such are to be followed: after them, and take a more dilated farewell.

Ber. And I will do so.

Par. Worthy fellows; and like to prove most sinewy sword-men.
[*Exeunt* BERTRAM *and* PAROLLES.

Enter LAFEU.

Laf. Pardon, my lord, [*Kneeling.*] for me and for my tidings.

King. I'll fee thee to stand up.

Laf. Then here's a man
Stands, that has brought his pardon. I would, you
Had kneel'd, my lord, to ask me mercy; and
That, at my bidding, you could so stand up.

---

1 Receipts in which greater virtues were enclosed than appeared to observation.

2 Exhausted of their skill.

3 The old copy reads—*in't.* The emendation is Hanmer's.

4 *Into* for *unto.* A common form of expression with old writers. See Troilus and Cressida, Act iii. Sc. 3. The third folio reads *unto.*

5 In this and the following instance the folio reads *lords.* The correction was suggested by Tyrwhitt.

6 i. e. as the common phrase runs, *I am still heart-whole;* my spirits, by not sinking under my distemper, do not acknowledge its influence.

7 I prefer Johnson's explanation of this obscure passage to any that has been offered:—'Let upper Italy, *where you are to exercise your valour*, see that you come to gain honour, to the *abatement*, that is to the *overthrow*, of those who inherit but the fall of the last monarchy or the remains of the Roman empire.' *Bated* and *abated* are used elsewhere by Shakspeare in a kindred sense.

8 Seeker, inquirer.

9 Be not captives before you are soldiers.

10 To be *kept a coil* is to be vexed or troubled with a *stir* or *noise.*

11 In Shakspeare's time it was usual for gentlemen to dance with swords on.

12 'I grow to you, and our parting is as it were to dissever or torture a body.'

13 They are the foremost in the fashion.

14 It seems to me that this passage has been wrongly pointed and improperly explained, *there do muster true gait;* if addressed to Bertram, it means *there exercise yourself in the gait of fashion;* eat, &c. But perhaps we should read *they* instead of *there*, or else insert *they* after *gait;* either of these slight emendations would render this obscure passage perfectly intelligible.

15 The dance.

King. I would, I had; so I had broke thy pate,
And ask'd thee mercy for't.
Laf. Goodfaith, across:[1]
But, my good lord, 'tis thus; Will you be cur'd
Of your infirmity?
King. No.
Laf. O, will you eat
No grapes, my royal fox? yes, but you will,
My noble grapes, an if my royal fox
Could reach them: I have seen a medicine,[2]
That's able to breathe life into a stone;
Quicken a rock, and make you dance canary,[3]
With spritely fire and motion; whose simple touch
Is powerful to araise king Pepin, nay,
To give great Charlemain a pen in his hand,
And write to her a love-line.[4]
King. What her is this?
Laf. Why, doctor she: My lord, there's one arriv'd,
If you will see her,—now, by my faith and honour,
If seriously I may convey my thoughts
In this my light deliverance, I have spoke
With one, that, in her sex, her years, profession,[5]
Wisdom, and constancy, hath amaz'd me more
Than I dare blame my weakness:[6] Will you see her,
(For that is her demand,) and know her business?
That done, laugh well at me.
King. Now, good Lafeu,
Bring in the admiration; that we with thee
May spend our wonder too, or take off thine,
By wond'ring how thou took'st it.
Laf. Nay, I'll fit you,
And not be all day neither. [*Exit* LAFEU.
King. Thus he his special nothing ever prologues.

Re-enter LAFEU, *with* HELENA.

Laf. Nay, come your ways.[7]
King. This haste hath wings indeed.
Laf. Nay, come your ways:
This is his majesty, say your mind to him:
A traitor you do look like; but such traitors
His majesty seldom fears: I am Cressid's uncle,[8]
That dare leave two together; fare you well. [*Exit.*
King. Now, fair one, does your business follow us?
Hel. Ay, my good lord. Gerard de Narbon was
My father; in what he did profess, well found.[9]
King. I knew him.
Hel. The rather will I spare my praises towards him;
Knowing him, is enough. On his bed of death
Many receipts he gave me; chiefly one,
Which, as the dearest issue of his practice,
And of his old experience the only darling,
He bade me store up, as a triple eye,[10]
Safer than mine own two, more dear; I have so:
And, hearing your high majesty is touch'd
With that malignant cause wherein the honour
Of my dear father's gift stands chief in power,
I come to tender it, and my appliance,
With all bound humbleness.
King. We thank you, maiden;
But may not be so credulous of cure,—
When our most learned doctors leave us; and
The congregated college have concluded
That labouring art can never ransom nature
From her inaidable estate,—I say we must not
So stain our judgment, or corrupt our hope,
To prostitute our past-cure malady
To empirics; or to dissever so
Our great self and our credit, to esteem
A senseless help, when help past sense we deem.
Hel. My duty then shall pay me for my pains:
I will no more enforce mine office on you;
Humbly entreating from your royal thoughts
A modest one to bear me back again.
King. I cannot give thee less, to be call'd grateful:
Thou thought'st to help me; and such thanks I give,
As one near death to those that wish him live;
But, what at full I know, thou know'st no part
I knowing all my peril, thou no art.
Hel. What I can do, can do no hurt to try,
Since you set up your rest[11] 'gainst remedy:
He that of greatest works is finisher,
Oft does them by the weakest minister:
So holy writ in babes hath judgment shown,
When judges have been babes.[12] Great floods have flown
From simple sources;[13] and great seas have dried,
When miracles have by the greatest been denied.[14]
Oft expectation fails, and most oft there
Where most it promises, and oft it hits,
Where hope is coldest, and despair most sits.
King. I must not hear thee; fare thee well, kind maid;
Thy pains, not us'd, must by thyself be paid
Proffers, not took, reap thanks for their reward
Hel. Inspired merit so by breath is barr'd:
It is not so with him that all things knows,
As 'tis with us that square our guess by shows.
But most it is presumption in us, when
The help of heaven we count the act of men.
Dear sir, to my endeavours give consent;
Of heaven, not me, make an experiment.
I am not an impostor, that proclaim
Myself against the level of mine aim;[15]
But know I think, and think I know most sure,
My art is not past power, nor you past cure.
King. Art thou so confident? Within what space
Hop'st thou my cure?
Hel. The greatest grace lending grace,[16]
Ere twice the horses of the sun shall bring
Their fiery torcher his diurnal ring;
Ere twice in murk and occidental damp
Moist Hesperus hath quench'd his sleepy lamp;
Or four and twenty times the pilot's glass
Hath told the thievish minutes how they pass;
What is infirm from your sound parts shall fly,
Health shall live free, and sickness freely die.
King. Upon thy certainty and confidence,
What dar'st thou venture?
Hel. Tax of impudence,—
A strumpet's boldness, a divulged shame,—
Traduc'd by odious ballads: my maiden's name
Sear'd otherwise; ne worse of worst extended,
With vilest torture let my life be ended.[17]
King. Methinks in thee some blessed spirit doth speak;
His powerful sound within an organ weak:
And what impossibility would slay
In common sense, sense saves another way.
Thy life is dear; for all, that life can rate

---

1 This word, which is taken from breaking a spear *across* in chivalric exercises, is used elsewhere by Shakspeare where a pass of wit miscarries. See As You Like It, Act iii. Sc. 4.

2 *Medicine* is here used by Lafeu ambiguously for *a female physician.*

3 It has been before observed that the canary was a kind of *lively dance.*

4 Malone thinks something has been omitted here: to complete the sense the line should read:—
'And *cause him* write to her a love line.'

5 By profession is meant her declaration of the object of her coming.

6 This is one of Shakspeare's perplexed expressions: 'To acknowledge how much she has astonished me would be to acknowledge more weakness that I am willing to do.'

7 Steevens has inconsiderately stigmatized this with the title of *vulgarism.* Malone has justly defended it as the phraseology of the poet's age, and adduces a similar mode of expression from our excellent old version of the Bible.

8 I am like Pandarus. See Troilus and Cressida.

9 Of known and acknowledged excellence.

10 A third eye.

11 i. e. '*Since you have determined* or *made up your mind* that there is no remedy.'

12 An allusion to Daniel judging the two Elders.

13 i. e. when Moses smote the rock in Horeb.

14 This must refer to the children of Israel passing the Red Sea, when miracles had been denied by Pharaoh.

15 I am not an impostor that proclaim one thing and design another, that proclaim a cure and aim at a fraud. I think what I speak.

16 i. e. the divine grace, lending me grace or power to accomplish it.

17 Let me be stigmatised as a strumpet, and, in addition (although that could not be worse, or a more ex

Worth name of life, in thee hath estimate:[1]
Youth, beauty, wisdom, courage, virtue, all
That happiness and prime[2] can happy call:
Thou this to hazard, needs must intimate
Skill infinite, or monstrous desperate.
Sweet practiser, thy physic I will try;
That ministers thine own death, if I die.

Hel. If I break time, or flinch in property[3]
Of what I spoke, unpitied let me die;
And well deserv'd: Not helping, death's my fee;
But, if I help, what do you promise me?

King. Make thy demand.

Hel. But will you make it even?

King. Ay, by my sceptre, and my hopes of heaven.[4]

Hel. Then shalt thou give me, with thy kingly hand,
What husband in thy power I will command:
Exempted be from me the arrogance
To choose from forth the royal blood of France;
My low and humble name to propagate
With any branch or impage of thy state:[5]
But such a one, thy vassal, whom I know
Is free for me to ask, thee to bestow.

King. Here is my hand; the premises observ'd,
Thy will by my performance shall be serv'd;
So make the choice of thy own time; for I,
Thy resolv'd patient, on thee still rely.
More should I question thee, and more I must;
Though, more to know, could not be more to trust;
From whence thou cam'st, how tended on,—But rest
Unquestion'd welcome, and undoubted blest.—
Give me some help here, ho!—If thou proceed
As high as word, my deed shall match thy deed.
[*Flourish. Exeunt.*

SCENE II. Rousillon. *A Room in the* Countess's *Palace. Enter* Countess *and* Clown.

Count. Come on, sir; I shall now put you to the height of your breeding.

Clo. I will show myself highly fed and lowly taught: I know my business is but to the court.

Count. To the court! why, what place make you special, when you put off that with such contempt? But to the court!

Clo. Truly, madam, if God have lent a man any manners, he may easily put it off at court: he that cannot make a leg, put off's cap, kiss his hand, and say nothing, has neither leg, hands, lip, nor cap; and, indeed, such a fellow, to say precisely, were not for the court: but, for me, I have an answer will serve all men.

Count. Marry, that's a bountiful answer, that fits all questions.

Clo. It is like a barber's chair, that fits all buttocks;[6] the pin-buttock, the quatch-buttock, the brawn buttock, or any buttock.

Count. Will your answer serve fit to all questions?

Clo. As fit as ten groats is for the hand of an attorney, as your French crown for your taffata punk, as Tib's rush for Tom's fore-finger,[7] as a pancake for Shrove-tuesday, a morris for May-day, as the nail to his hole, the cuckold to his horn, as a scolding quean to a wrangling knave, as the nun's lip to the friar's mouth; nay, as the pudding to his skin.

Count. Have you, I say, an answer of such fitness for all questions?

Clo. From below your duke, to beneath your constable, it will fit any question.

Count. It must be an answer of most monstrous size, that must fit all demands.

Clo. But a trifle neither, in good faith, if the learned should speak truth of it: here it is, and all that belongs to't: Ask me, if I am a courtier; it shall do you no harm to learn.

Count. To be young again, if we could: I will be a fool in question, hoping to be the wiser by your answer. I pray you, sir, are you a courtier?

Clo. O Lord, sir,[8] ——There's a simple putting off;—more, more, a hundred of them.

Count. Sir, I am a poor friend of yours, that loves you.

Clo. O Lord, sir,—Thick, thick, spare not me.

Count. I think, sir, you can eat none of this homely meat.

Clo. O Lord, sir,—Nay, put me to't, I warrant you.

Count. You were lately whipped, sir, as I think.

Clo. O Lord, sir,—Spare not me.

Count. Do you cry, *O Lord, sir*, at your whipping, and *spare not me?* Indeed, your *O Lord, sir*, is very sequent[9] to your whipping; you would answer very well to a whipping, if you were but bound to't.

Clo. I ne'er had worse luck in my life, in my—*O Lord, sir:* I see, things may serve long, but not serve ever.

Count. I play the noble housewife with the time, to entertain it so merrily with a fool.

Clo. O Lord, sir,—Why, there't serves well again.

Count. An end, sir, to your business: Give Helen this.
And urge her to a present answer back:
Commend me to my kinsmen, and my son;
This is not much.

Clo. Not much commendation to them.

Count. Not much employment for you: You understand me?

Clo. Most fruitfully; I am there before my legs

Count. Haste you again. [*Exeunt severally.*

SCENE III. Paris. *A Room in the* King's *Palace. Enter* BERTRAM, LAFEU, *and* PAROLLES.

Laf. They say, miracles are past; and we have our philosophical persons, to make modern[10] and familiar things, supernatural and causeless. Hence is it, that we make trifles of terrors; ensconcing[11] ourselves into seeming knowledge, when we should submit ourselves to an unknown fear.[12]

Par. Why, 'tis the rarest argument of wonder, that hath shot out in our latter times.

Ber. And so 'tis.

Laf. To be relinquish'd of the artists,——

Par. So I say; both of Galen and Paracelsus.

Laf. Of all the learned and authentic[13] fellows,—

Par. Right, so I say.

Laf. That gave him out incurable,—

Par. Why, there 'tis; so say I too.

Laf. Not to be helped,—

Par. Right: as 'twere, a man assured of an—

---

tended evil than what I have mentioned, the loss of my honour, which is the worst that could happen,) let me die with torture. *Ne* is *nor*.

1 i. e. may be *counted* among the gifts enjoyed by thee.

2 *Prime* here signifies that *sprightly vigour* which usually accompanies us in the prime of life; which old Montaigne calls, *cet estat plein de verdeur et de feste*, and which Florio translates, 'that state, full of lust, of *prime*, and mirth.'

3 *Property* seems to be used here for *performance* or *achievement*, singular as it may seem.

4 The old copy reads 'hopes of *help*.' The emendation is Thirlby's.

5 The old copy reads '*image* of thy state.' Warburton proposed *impage*, which Steevens rejects, saying unadvisedly 'there is no such word.' It is evident that Shakspeare formed it from 'an *impe*, a scion, or young slip of a tree.'

6 This is a common proverbial expression.

7 *Tom* and *Tibb* were apparently common names for a *lad and lass*, the *rush ring* seems to have been a kind of love token, for plighting of troth among rustic lovers.

8 A ridicule on this silly expletive of speech, then in vogue at court. Thus Clove and Orange, in Every Man in his Humour: 'You conceive me, sir?—O Lord, sir!'

9 Properly follows. 10 Common, ordinary.

11 *Sconce* being a term in fortification for a chief fortress. To *ensconce* literally signifies *to secure as in a fort.*

12 *Fear* means here an object of fear.

13 *Authentic* is *allowed, approved;* and seems to have been the proper epithet for a physician regularly bred or licensed. The diploma of a licentiate still has *authentice licentiatus*

Laf. Uncertain life, and sure death.

Par. Just, you say well; so would I have said.

Laf. I may truly say, it is a novelty to the world.

Par. It is, indeed: if you will have it in showing, you shall read it in——What do you call there?—

Laf. A showing of a heavenly effect in an earthly actor.

Par. That's it I would have said; the very same.

Laf. Why, your dolphin[1] is not lustier: 'fore me I speak in respect——

Par. Nay, 'tis strange, 'tis very strange, that is the brief and the tedious of it; and he is of a most facinorous[2] spirit, that will not acknowledge it to be the——

Laf. Very hand of heaven.

Par. Ay, so I say.

Laf. In a most weak——

Par. And debile minister, great power, great transcendence: which should, indeed, give us a further use to be made, than alone the recovery of the king, as to be[3]——

Laf. Generally thankful.

Enter King, Helena, *and* Attendants.

Par. I would have said it; you say well: Here comes the king.

Laf. Lustick,[4] as the Dutchman says: I'll like a maid the better, whilst I have a tooth in my head: Why, he's able to lead her a coranto.

Par. *Mort du Vinaigre!* Is not this Helen?

Laf. 'Fore God, I think so.

King. Go, call before me all the lords in court.—
[*Exit an* Attendant.
Sit, my preserver, by thy patient's side;
And with this healthful hand, whose banish'd sense
Thou hast repeal'd, a second time receive
The confirmation of my promis'd gift,
Which but attends thy naming.

Enter several Lords.

Fair maid, send forth thine eye: this youthful parcel
Of noble bachelors stand at my bestowing,
O'er whom both sovereign power and father's voice[5]
I have to use: thy frank election make;
Thou hast power to choose, and they none to forsake.

Hel. To each of you one fair and virtuous mistress
Fall, when love please!—marry, to each, but one![6]

Laf. I'd give bay Curtal,[7] and his furniture,
My mouth no more were broken than these boys',
And writ as little beard.

King. Peruse them well:
Not one of those, but had a noble father,

Hel. Gentlemen,
Heaven hath, through me, restor'd the king to health.

All. We understand it, and thank heaven for you.

Hel. I am a simple maid; and therein wealthiest,
That, I protest, I simply am a maid:——
Please it your majesty, I have done already:
The blushes in my cheeks thus whisper me,
We blush, that thou shouldst choose; but, be refus'd,
Let the white death sit on thy cheek for ever;
We'll ne'er come there again.[8]

King. Make choice; and, see,
Who shuns thy love, shuns all his love in me.

Hel. Now, Dian, from thy altar do I fly;
And to imperial Love, that god most high,
Do my sighs stream.—Sir, will you hear my suit?

1 *Lord.* And grant it.

Hel Thanks, sir, all the rest is mute.[9]

Laf. I had rather be in this choice than throw ames-ace[10] for my life.

Hel. The honour, sir, that flames in your fair eyes,
Before I speak, too threateningly replies:
Love make your fortunes twenty times above
Her that so wishes, and her humble love!

2 *Lord.* No better, if you please.

Hel. My wish receive,
Which great love grant! and so I take my leave.

Laf. Do all they deny her?[11] An they were sons of mine, I'd have them whipped; or I would send them to the Turk, to make eunuchs of.

Hel. Be not afraid [*To a* Lord] that I your hand should take;
I'll never do you wrong for your own sake:
Blessing upon your vows! and in your bed
Find fairer fortune, if you ever wed!

Laf. These boys are boys of ice, they'll none have her: sure, they are bastards to the English; the French ne'er got them.

Hel. You are too young, too happy, and too good,
To make yourself a son out of my blood.

4 *Lord.* Fair one, I think not so.

Laf. There's one grape yet,—I am sure thy father drank wine.—But if thou be'st not an ass, I am a youth of fourteen; I have known thee already.

Hel. I dare not say, I take you; [*To* Bertram] but I give
Me, and my service, ever whilst I live,
Into your guiding power.—This is the man.

King. Why then, young Bertram, take her, she's thy wife.

Ber. My wife, my liege? I shall beseech your highness,
In such a business give me leave to use
The help of mine own eyes.

King. Know'st thou not, Bertram,
What she has done for me?

Ber. Yes, my good lord;
But never hope to know why I should marry her.

King. Thou know'st she has raised me from my sickly bed.

Ber. But follows it, my lord, to bring me down
Must answer for your rising? I know her well;
She had her breeding at my father's charge:
A poor physician's daughter my wife!—disdain
Rather corrupt me ever!

King. 'Tis only title[12] thou disdain'st in her, the which
I can build up. Strange is it that our bloods,
Of colour, weight, and heat, pour'd all together,
Would quite confound distinction, yet stand off
In differences so mighty: If she be
All that is virtuous (save what thou dislik'st,
A poor physician's daughter), thou dislik'st
Of virtue for the name: but do not so:
From lowest place when virtuous things proceed,
The place is dignified by the doer's deed:
Where great additions[13] swell and virtue none,
It is a dropsied honour: good alone
Is good;—without a name, vileness is so:[14]

---

1 The *Dauphin* was formerly so written, but it is doubtful whether Lafeu means to allude to the *Prince* or the fish. The old orthography is therefore continued.

2 Wicked.

3 Dr. Johnson thought this and some preceding speeches in the scene were erroneously given to Parolles instead of to Lafeu. This seems very probable, for the humour of the scene consists in Parolles's pretensions to knowledge and sentiments which he has not.

4 *Lustigh* is the Dutch for active, pleasant, playful, sportive.

5 They were wards as well as subjects.

6 i. e. *except* one, meaning Bertram: *but* in the sense of *be-out.*

7 A *curtal* was the common phrase for a *horse;* i. e. I'd give my bay *horse,* &c. that my age were not greater than these boys:' a *broken mouth* is a mouth which has lost part of its teeth.

8 'My blushes (says Helen) thus whisper me—We blush that thou shouldst have the nomination of thy husband. However, choose him at thy peril; but if thou be refused, let thy cheeks be forever pale; we will never revisit them again.' *Be refused* means the same as 'thou being refused,' or, 'be thou refused.' The *white death* is the *paleness of death.*

9 i. e. 'I have no more to say to you.' So Hamlet, '*the rest is silence.*'

10 The lowest chance of the dice.

11 The scene must be so regulated that Lafeu and Parolles talk at a distance, where they may see what passes between Helena and the Lords, but not hear it, so that they know not by whom the refusal is made

12 i. e. the want of title.

13 Titles.

14 Good is good, independent of any worldly distinction: and so vileness would be ever vile, did not rank power, and fortune screen it from opprobrium.

The property by what it is should go,
Not by the title. She is young, wise, fair;
In these to nature she's immediate heir;
And these breed honour; that is honour's scorn,
Which challenges itself as honour's born,[1]
And is not like the sire: Honours best thrive,[2]
When rather from our acts we them derive
Than our fore-goers: the mere word's a slave,
Debauch'd on every tomb; on every grave,
A lying trophy, and as oft is dumb,
Where dust and damn'd oblivion is the tomb
Of honour'd bones indeed. What should be said?
If thou canst like this creature as a maid,
I can create the rest: virtue, and she,
Is her own dower; honour and wealth from me.

Ber. I cannot love her, nor will strive to do't.

King. Thou wrong'st thyself, if thou shouldst strive to choose.

Hel. That you are well restor'd, my lord, I am glad;
Let the rest go.

King. My honour's at the stake; which to defeat,[3]
I must produce my power: Here, take her hand,
Proud scornful boy, unworthy this good gift;
That dost in vile misprision shackle up
My love, and her desert; that canst not dream,
We, poising us in her defective scale,
Shall weigh thee to the beam: that wilt not know,
It is in us to plant thine honour, where
We please to have it grow: Check thy contempt:
Obey our will, which travails in thy good:
Believe not thy disdain, but presently
Do thine own fortunes that obedient right,
Which both thy duty owes, and our power claims;
Or I will throw thee from my care for ever,
Into the staggers[4] and the careless lapse
Of youth and ignorance; both my revenge and hate,
Loosing upon thee in the name of justice,
Without all terms of pity: Speak; thine answer.

Ber. Pardon, my gracious lord; for I submit
My fancy to your eyes: When I consider,
What great creation, and what dole[5] of honour,
Flies where you bid it, I find, that she, which late
Was in my nobler thoughts most base, is now
The praised of the king; who, so ennobled,
Is, as 'twere, born so.

King. Take her by the hand,
And tell her, she is thine: to whom I promise
A counterpoise; if not to thy estate,
A balance more replete.

Ber. I take her hand.

King. Good fortune, and the favour of the king,
Smile upon this contract: whose ceremony
Shall seem expedient on the now-born brief,
And be perform'd to-night:[6] the solemn feast
Shall more attend upon the coming space,
Expecting absent friends. As thou lov'st her,
Thy love's to me religious; else, does err.

[*Exeunt* King, BERTRAM, HELENA, Lords, *and* Attendants.

Laf. Do you hear, monsieur? a word with you.

Par. Your pleasure, sir?

Laf. Your lord and master did well to make his recantation.

Par. Recantation? My lord? my master?

Laf. Ay; Is it not a language, I speak?

Par. A most harsh one; and not to be understood without bloody succeeding. My master?

Laf. Are you companion to the count Rousillon?

Par. To any count; to all counts; to what is man.

Laf. To what is count's man: count's master is of another style.

Par. You are too old, sir; let it satisfy you, you are too old.

Laf. I must tell thee, sirrah, I write man; to which title age cannot bring thee.

Par. What I dare too well do, I dare not do.

Laf. I did think thee, for two ordinaries,[7] to be a pretty wise fellow; thou didst make tolerable vent of thy travel; it might pass: yet the scarfs, and the bannerets, about thee, did manifoldly dissuade me from believing thee a vessel of too great a burden. I have now found thee; when I lose thee again, I care not: yet art thou good for nothing but taking up;[8] and that thou art scarce worth.

Par. Hadst thou not the privilege of antiquity upon thee,——

Laf. Do not plunge thyself too far in anger, lest thou hasten thy trial; which if—Lord have mercy on thee for a hen! So, my good window of lattice, fare thee well; thy casement I need not open, for I look through thee. Give me thy hand.

Par. My lord, you give me most egregious indignity.

Laf. Ay, with all my heart; and thou art worthy of it.

Par. I have not, my lord, deserved it.

Laf. Yes, good faith, every dram of it; and I will not bate thee a scruple.

Par. Well, I shall be wiser.

Laf. E'en as soon as thou canst, for thou hast to pull at a smack o' the contrary. If ever thou be'st bound in thy scarf, and beaten, thou shalt find what it is to be proud of thy bondage. I have a desire to hold my acquaintance with thee, or rather my knowledge; that I may say, in the default,[9] he is a man I know.

Par. My lord, you do me most insupportable vexation.

Laf. I would it were hell-pains for thy sake, and my poor doing eternal: for doing I am past; as I will by thee, in what motion age will give me leave.[10] [*Exit.*

Par. Well, thou hast a son shall take this disgrace off me; scurvy, old, filthy, scurvy lord!—Well, I must be patient; there is no fettering of authority. I'll beat him by my life, if I can meet him with any convenience, an he were double and double a lord. I'll have no more pity of his age, than I would have of—I'll beat him, an if I could but meet him again.

Re-enter LAFEU.

Laf. Sirrah, your lord and master's married, there's news for you; you have a new mistress.

Par. I most unfeignedly beseech your lordship to make some reservation of your wrongs: He is my good lord: whom I serve above, is my master.

Laf. Who? God?

Par. Ay, sir.

Laf. The devil it is, that's thy master. Why dost thou garter up thy arms o' this fashion? dost make hose of thy sleeves? do other servants so? Thou wert best set thy lower part where thy nose stands By mine honour, if I were but two hours younger, I'd beat thee: methinks, thou art a general offence, and every man should beat thee. I think, thou wast created for men to breathe[11] themselves upon thee.

Par. This is hard and undeserved measure, my lord.

---

1 i. e. the child of honour.

2 The first folio omits *best;* the second folio supplies it.

3 The *implication* or *clause* of the sentence (as the grammarians say) here serves for the antecedent, 'which danger to defeat.'

4 The commentators here kindly inform us that *the staggers* is a violent disease in horses; but the word in the text has no relation, even *metaphorically* to it. *The reeling and unsteady course of a drunken or sick man is meant.*

5 i. e. portion.

6 Shakspeare uses *expedient* and *expediently* in the sense of *expeditiously:* and *brief* in the sense of a short note or intimation concerning any business, and sometimes without the idea of writing.

7 i. e. while I sate twice with thee at dinner.

8 To *take up* is to *contradict*, to *call to account;* as well as to *pick off the ground.*

9 i. e. at a need.

10 There is a poor conceit here hardly worth explaining, but that some of the commentators have misunderstood it:—'Doing I am *past*,' says Lafeu, 'as I will by thee, in what motion age will give me leave;' i. e. 'as I will *pass* by thee as fast as I am able' and he immediately goes out.

11 Exercise.

Laf. Go to, sir; you were beaten in Italy for picking a kernel out of a pomegranate; you are a vagabond, and no true traveller: you are more saucy with lords, and honourable personages, than the heraldry of your birth and virtue gives you commission. You are not worth another word, else I'd call you knave. I leave you. [*Exit.*

Enter BERTRAM.

Par. Good, very good; it is so then.—Good, very good; let it be concealed a while.

Ber. Undone, and forfeited to cares for ever!

Par. What is the matter, sweet heart?

Ber. Although before the solemn priest I have sworn,
I will not bed her.

Par. What? what, sweet heart?

Ber. O my Parolles, they have married me:—
I'll to the Tuscan wars, and never bed her.

Par. France is a dog-hole, and it no more merits
The tread of a man's foot: to the wars!

Ber. There's letters from my mother; what the import is,
I know not yet.

Par. Ay, that would be known: To the wars, my boy, to the wars!
He wears his honour in a box unseen,
That hugs his kicksy-wicksy[1] here at home;
Spending his manly marrow in her arms,
Which should sustain the bound and high curvet
Of Mars's fiery steed: To other regions!
France is a stable: we, that dwell in't, jades;
Therefore, to the war!

Ber. It shall be so; I'll send her to my house,
Acquaint my mother with my hate to her,
And wherefore I am fled; write to the king
That which I durst not speak: His present gift
Shall furnish me to those Italian fields,
Where noble fellows strike: War is no strife
To the dark house,[2] and the detested wife.

Par. Will this capricio hold in thee, art sure?

Ber. Go with me to my chamber, and advise me.
I'll send her straight away: To-morrow
I'll to the wars, she to her single sorrow.

Par. Why, these balls bound; there's noise in it.—'Tis hard;
A young man, married, is a man that's marr'd:
Therefore away, and leave her bravely; go:
The king has done you wrong; but, hush! 'tis so. [*Exeunt.*

SCENE IV. *The same. Another Room in the same. Enter* HELENA *and* Clown.

Hel. My mother greets me kindly; Is she well?

Clo. She is not well; but yet she has her health; she's very merry; but yet she is not well: but thanks be given, she's very well, and wants nothing i'the world; but yet she is not well.

Hel. If she be very well, what does she ail, that she's not very well?

Clo. Truly, she's very well, indeed, but for two things.

Hel. What two things?

Clo. One, that she's not in heaven, whither God send her quickly! the other, that she's in earth, from whence God send her quickly!

Enter PAROLLES.

Par. Bless you, my fortunate lady!

Hel. I hope, sir, I have your good-will to have mine own good fortunes.

Par. You had my prayers to lead them on: and to keep them on, have them still.—O, my knave! How does my old lady?

Clo. So that you had her wrinkles, and I her money, I would she did as you say.

Par. Why, I say nothing.

Clo. Marry, you are the wiser man; for many a man's tongue shakes out his master's undoing: To say nothing, to do nothing, to know nothing, and to have nothing, is to be a great part of your title; which is within a very little of nothing.

Par. Away, thou'rt a knave.

Clo. You should have said, sir, before a knave thou art a knave; that is, before me thou art a knave: this had been truth, sir.

Par. Go to, thou art a witty fool, I have found thee.

Clo. Did you find me in yourself, sir? or were you taught to find me? The search, sir, was profitable, and much fool may you find in you, even to the world's pleasure, and the increase of laughter.

Par. A good knave, i'faith, and well fed.[3]—
Madam, my lord, will go away to-night;
A very serious business calls on him.
The great prerogative and rite of love,
Which, as your due, time claims, he does acknowledge;
But puts it off by a[4] compell'd restraint;
Whose want, and whose delay, is strewed with sweets,
Which they distil now in the curbed time,
To make the coming hour o'erflow with joy,[5]
And pleasure drown the brim.

Hel. What's his will else?

Par. That you will take your instant leave o' the king.
And make this haste as your own good proceeding,
Strengthen'd with what apology you think
May make it probable need.[6]

Hel. What more commands he?

Par. That, having this obtain'd, you presently
Attend his further pleasure.

Hel. In every thing I wait upon his will.

Par. I shall report it so.

Hel. I pray you.—Come, sirrah. [*Exeunt.*

SCENE V. *Another Room in the same. Enter* LAFEU *and* BERTRAM.

Laf. But, I hope, your lordship thinks not him a soldier.

Ber. Yes, my lord, and of very valiant approof.

Laf. You have it from his own deliverance.

Ber. And by other warranted testimony.

Laf. Then my dial goes not true; I took this lark for a bunting.[7]

Ber. I do assure you, my lord, he is very great in knowledge, and accordingly valiant.

Laf. I have then sinned against his experience, and transgressed against his valour; and my state that way is dangerous, since I cannot yet find in my heart to repent. Here he comes; I pray you, make us friends, I will pursue the amity.

Enter PAROLLES.

Par. These things shall be done, sir. [*To* BERTRAM

Laf. Pray you, sir, who's his tailor?

Par. Sir?

Laf. O, I know him well: Ay, sir; he, sir, is a good workman, a very good tailor.

Ber. Is she gone to the king? [*Aside to* PAROLLES

Par. She is.

Ber. Will she away to-night?

Par. As you'll have her.

Ber. I have writ my letters, casketed my treasure
Given order for our horses, and to-night,
When I should take possession of the bride,—
And, ere I do begin,———

Laf. A good traveller is something at the latter end of a dinner; but one that lies three-thirds, and

1 A cant term for a wife.

2 The *dark house* is a house made gloomy by discontent.

3 Perhaps the old saying, 'better fed than taught,' is alluded to here as in a preceding scene, where the clown says, 'I will show myself *highly fed* and lowly taught.'

4 The old copy reads '*to* a compell'd restraint.'

5 The meaning appears to be, that the delay of the joys, and the expectation of them, would make them more delightful when they come. The *curbed time* means the time of restraint, *whose want* means *the want of which.*

6 A specious appearance of necessity.

7 The bunting nearly resembles the sky-lark; but has little or no song, which gives estimation to the sky lark.

uses a known truth to pass a thousand nothings with, should be once heard, and thrice beaten.—God save you, captain.

Ber. Is there any unkindness between my lord and you, monsieur?

Par. I know not how I have deserved to run into my lord's displeasure.

Laf. You have made shift to run into't, boots and spurs and all, like him that leaped into the custard;[1] and out of it you'll run again, rather than suffer question for your residence.

Ber. It may be, you have mistaken him, my lord.

Laf. And shall do so ever, though I took him at his prayers. Fare you well, my lord; and believe this of me, There can be no kernel in this light nut; the soul of this man is his clothes: trust him not in matter of heavy consequence; I have kept of them tame, and know their natures.—Farewell, monsieur: I have spoken better of you, than you have or will[2] deserve at my hand; but we must do good against evil. [*Exit.*

Par. An idle lord, I swear.

Ber. I think so.

Par. Why, do you not know him?

Ber. Yes, I do know him well; and common speech
Gives him a worthy pass. Here comes my clog.

Enter HELENA.

Hel. I have, sir, as I was commanded from you,
Spoke with the king, and have procur'd his leave
For present parting: only, he desires
Some private speech with you.

Ber. I shall obey his will.
You must not marvel, Helen, at my course,
Which holds not colour with the time, nor does
The ministration and required office
On my particular: prepar'd I was not
For such a business; therefore am I found
So much unsettled: This drives me to entreat you,
That presently you take your way for home;
And rather muse,[3] than ask, why I entreat you:
For my respects are better than they seem;
And my appointments have in them a need,
Greater than shows itself at the first view,
To you that know them not. This to my mother:
[*Giving a letter.*
'Twill be two days ere I shall see you; so
I leave you to your wisdom.

Hel. Sir, I can nothing say,
But that I am your most obedient servant.

Ber. Come, come, no more of that.

Hel. And ever shall
With true observance seek to eke out that,
Wherein toward me my homely stars have fail'd
To equal my great fortune.

Ber. Let that go:
My haste is very great: Farewell, hie home.

Hel. Pray, sir, your pardon.

Ber. Well, what would you say?

Hel. I am not worthy of the wealth I owe;[4]
Nor dare I say, 'tis mine; and yet it is;
But, like a timorous thief, most fain would steal
What law does vouch mine own.

Ber. What would you have?

Hel. Something; and scarce so much:—nothing, indeed.---
I would not tell you what I would: my lord---'faith, yes;---
Strangers and foes, do sunder, and not kiss.

Ber. I pray you stay not, but in haste to horse.

Hel. I shall not break your bidding, good my lord.

Ber. Where are my other men, monsieur?---Farewell. [*Exit* HELENA.
Go thou toward home; where I will never come,
Whilst I can shake my sword, or hear the drum:—
Away, and for our flight.

Par Bravely, coragio!
[*Exeunt.*

ACT III.

SCENE I. Florence. *A Room in the* Duke's *Palace. Flourish. Enter the* Duke *of* Florence, *attended; two* French Lords, *and others.*

Duke. So that, from point to point, now have you heard
The fundamental reasons of this war;
Whose great decision hath much blood let forth,
And more thirst after.

1 Lord. Holy seems the quarrel
Upon your grace's part; black and fearful
On the opposer.

Duke. Therefore we marvel much, our cousin France
Would, in so just a business, shut his bosom
Against our borrowing prayers.

2 Lord. Good my lord,
The reasons of our state I cannot yield,[5]
But like a common and an outward man,[6]
That the great figure of a council frames
By self-unable motion;[7] therefore dare not
Say what I think of it; since I have found
Myself in my uncertain grounds to fail
As often as I guess'd.

Duke. Be it his pleasure.

2 Lord. But I am sure, the younger of our nature,
That surfeit on their ease, will, day by day,
Come here for physic.

Duke. Welcome shall they be,
And all the honours, that can fly from us,
Shall on them settle. You know your places well;
When better fall, for your avails they fell:
To-morrow to the field. [*Flourish. Exeunt.*

SCENE II. Rousillon. *A Room in the* Countess's *Palace. Enter* Countess *and* Clown.

Count. It hath happened all as I would have had it, save, that he comes not along with her.

Clo. By my troth, I take my young lord to be a very melancholy man.

Count. By what observance, I pray you?

Clo. Why, he will look upon his boot, and sing, mend the ruff,[9] and sing; ask questions, and sing; pick his teeth, and sing; I know a man that had this trick of melancholy, sold a goodly manor for a song.

Count. Let me see what he writes, and when he means to come. [*Opening a Letter.*

Clo. I have no mind to Isbel, since I was at court; our old ling and our Isbels o' the country are nothing like your old ling and your Isbels o' the court: the brains of my Cupid's knocked out; and I begin to love, as an old man loves money, with no stomach.

Count. What have we here?

Clo. E'en that you have there. [*Exit.*

Count. [Reads.] *I have sent you a daughter-in-law: she hath recovered the king, and undone me. I have wedded her, not bedded her; and sworn to make the* not *eternal. You shall hear, I am run away; know it, before the report come. If there be breadth enough in the world, I will hold a long distance. My duty to you.*

Your unfortunate son,
BERTRAM

This is not well, rash and unbridled boy,
To fly the favours of so good a king;
To pluck his indignation on thy head,

---

1 It was a piece of foolery practised at city entertainments, when an allowed fool or jester was in fashion, for him to jump into a large deep custard set for the purpose, to cause laughter among the 'barren spectators.'

2 The first folio reads, 'than you have or will *to* deserve.'—Perhaps the word *wit* was omitted, the second folio omits *to*.

3 To *muse* is to *wonder*.

4 Possess, or own.

5 i. e. I cannot inform you of the reasons.

6 One not in the secret of affairs: so *inward* in contrary sense.

7 Warburton and Upton are of opinion that we should read, 'By self unable *notion*.'

8 As we say at present, our young fellows.

9 The tops of the boots in Shakspeare's time turned down, and hung loosely over the leg. The folding part or top was the *ruff*. It was of softer leather than the boot, and often fringed.

By the misprizing of a maid too virtuous
For the contempt of empire.

Re-enter Clown.

Clo. O madam, yonder is heavy news within, between two soldiers and my young lady.

Count. What is the mater?

Clo. Nay, there is some comfort in the news, some comfort; your son will not be killed so soon as I thought he would.

Count. Why should he be killed?

Clo. So say I, madam, if he run away, as I hear he does: the danger is in standing to't; that's the loss of men, though it be the getting of children. Here they come, will tell you more; for my part, I only hear, your son was run away. [*Exit* Clown.

Enter Helena *and two* Gentlemen.

1 *Gent.* Save you, good madam.
Hel. Madam, my lord is gone, for ever gone.
2 *Gent.* Do not say so.
Count. Think upon patience.—'Pray you, gentlemen,—
I have felt so many quirks of joy, and grief,
That the first face of neither, on the start,
Can woman[1] me unto't:—Where is my son, I pray you?
2 *Gent.* Madam, he's gone to serve the duke of Florence:
We met him thitherward; from thence we came,
And, after some despatch in hand at court,
Thither we bend again.
Hel. Look on his letter, madam; here's my passport.
[Reads.] *When thou canst get the ring upon my finger*[2] *which never shall come off, and show me a child begotten of thy body, that I am father to, then call me husband: but in such a* then *I write a* never.
This is a dreadful sentence!
Count. Brought you this letter, gentlemen?
1 *Gent.* Ay, madam;
And, for the contents' sake, are sorry for our pains.
Count. I pr'ythee, lady, have a better cheer;
If thou engrossest all the griefs are thine,[3]
Thou robb'st me of a moiety: He was my son;
But I do wash his name out of my blood,
And thou art all my child.—Towards Florence is he?
2 *Gent.* Ay, madam.
Count. And to be a soldier?
2 *Gent.* Such is his noble purpose: and, believe't,
The duke will lay upon him all the honour
That good convenience claims.
Count. Return you thither?
1 *Gent.* Ay, madam, with the swiftest wing of speed.
Hel. [Reads.] *Till I have no wife, I have nothing in France.*
'Tis bitter!
Count. Find you that there?
Hel. Ay, madam.
1 *Gent.* 'Tis but the boldness of his hand, haply, which
His heart was not consenting to.
Count. Nothing in France, until he have no wife!
There's nothing here, that is too good for him,
But only she; and she deserves a lord,
That twenty such rude boys might tend upon,
And call her hourly, mistress. Who was with him?
1 *Gent.* A servant only and a gentleman
Which I have some time known.
Count. Parolles, was't not.
1 *Gent.* Ay, my good lady, he.
Count. A very tainted fellow and full of wickedness.
My son corrupts a well-derived nature
With his inducement.
1 *Gent.* Indeed, good lady,
The fellow has a deal of that, too much,
Which holds him much to have.[4]
Count. You are welcome, gentlemen,
I will entreat you, when you see my son,
To tell him that his sword can never win
The honour that he loses: more I'll entreat you
Written to bear along.
2 *Gent.* We serve you, madam,
In that and all your worthiest affairs.
Count. Not so, but as we change our courtesies.[5]
Will you draw near?
[*Exeunt* Countess *and* Gentlemen.
Hel. *Till I have no wife, I have nothing in France.*
Nothing in France, until he has no wife!
Thou shalt have none, Rousillon, none in France,
Then hast thou all again. Poor lord! is't I
That chase thee from thy country, and expose
Those tender limbs of thine to the event
Of the none-sparing war? and is it I
That drive thee from the sportive court, where thou
Wast shot at with fair eyes, to be the mark
Of smoky muskets? O you leaden messengers,
That ride upon the violent speed of fire,
Fly with false aim; move the still-piecing[6] air,
That sings with piercing, do not touch my lord!
Whoever shoots at him, I set him there;
Whoever charges on his forward breast,
I am the caitiff, that do hold him to it;
And, though I kill him not, I am the cause
His death was so effected; better 'twere,
I met the ravin[7] lion when he roar'd
With sharp constraint of hunger; better 'twere
That all the miseries, which nature owes,
Were mine at once: No, come thou home, Rousillon,
Whence honour but of danger wins a scar,
As oft it loses all.[8] I will be gone:
My being here it is, that holds thee hence:
Shall I stay here to do't? no, no, although
The air of paradise did fan the house,
And angels offic'd all: I will be gone;
That pitiful rumour may report my flight,
To consolate thine ear. Come, night; end, day!
For, with the dark, poor thief, I'll steal away.
[*Exit.*

SCENE III. Florence. *Before the* Duke's *Palace.*

Flourish. Enter the Duke of Florence, Bertram, Lords, Officers, Soldiers, *and others.*

Duke. The general of our horse thou art; and we,
Great in our hope, lay our best love and credence
Upon thy promising fortune.
Ber. Sir, it is
A charge too heavy for my strength; but yet
We'll strive to bear it for your worthy sake,
To the extreme edge of hazard.[9]
Duke. Then go thou forth;
And fortune play upon thy prosperous helm,[10]
As thy auspicious mistress!
Ber. This very day,
Great Mars, I put myself into thy file:

1 i. e. affect me suddenly and deeply, as our sex are usually affected.

2 i. e. when you can get the ring which is on my finger into your possession.

3 If thou keepest all thy sorrows to thyself: an elliptical expression for 'all the griefs *that* are thine.'

4 This passage as it stands is very obscure; it appears to me that something is omitted after *much.* Warburton interprets it, 'That his vices stand him in stead of virtues.' And Heath thought the meaning was:—'This fellow hath a deal too much of *that* which alone can *hold* or judge that he has much in him;' i. e. folly and ignorance.

5 In reply to the gentleman's declaration that they are her servants, the countess answers—no otherwise than as she returns the same offices of civility.

6 The old copy reads, *still-peering.* The emendation was adopted by Steevens: *still-piecing* is still reuniting; *peecing* is the old orthography of the word. I must confess that I should give the preference to *still pacing*, i. e. *still-moving*, as more in the poet's manner.

7 That is the *ravenous* or ravening lion.

8 The sense is, 'From that place, where all the advantages that honour usually reaps from the danger it rushes upon, is only a scar in testimony of its bravery, as, on the other hand, it often is the cause of losing all even life itself.'

9 So in Shakspeare's 116th Sonnet:
'But bears it out, even to the *edge* of doom.'

10 In K Richard III. we have;
'*Fortune* and victory sit on thy *helm*

Make me out like my thoughts; and I shall prove
A lover of thy drum, hater of love. [*Exeunt.*

SCENE IV. Rousillon. *A Room in the* Countess's *Palace. Enter* Countess *and* Steward.

Count. Alas! and would you take the letter of her?
Might you not know, she would do as she has done,
By sending me a letter? Read it again.

Stew. *I am Saint Jaques'[1] pilgrim, thither gone;*
Ambitious love hath so in me offended,
That bare-foot plod I the cold ground upon,
With sainted vow my faults to have amended.
Write, write, that from the bloody course of war,
My dearest master, your dear son, may hie;
Bless him at home in peace, whilst I from far,
His name with zealous fervour sanctify:
His taken labours bid him me forgive;
I, his despiteful Juno,[2] sent him forth
From courtly friends, with camping foes to live,
Where death and danger dog the heels of worth:
He is too good and fair for death and me;
Whom I myself embrace, to set him free.

Count. Ah, what sharp stings are in her mildest words!——
Rinaldo, you did never lack advice[3] so much,
As letting her pass so; had I spoke with her,
I could have well diverted her intents,
Which thus she hath prevented.

Stew. Pardon me, madam:
If I had given you this at over-night,
She might have been o'erta'en; and yet she writes,
Pursuit would be in vain.

Count. What angel shall
Bless this unworthy husband? he cannot thrive,
Unless her prayers, whom heaven delights to hear,
And loves to grant, reprieve him from the wrath
Of greatest justice.—Write, write, Rinaldo,
To this unworthy husband of his wife;
Let every word weigh heavy of her worth,
That he does weigh[4] too light: my greatest grief,
Though little he do feel it, set down sharply.
Despatch the most convenient messenger:—
When, haply, he shall hear that she is gone,
He will return; and hope I may, that she,
Hearing so much, will speed her foot again,
Led hither by pure love: which of them both
Is dearest to me, I have no skill in sense
To make distinction:—Provide this messenger:—
My heart is heavy, and mine age is weak;
Grief would have tears, and sorrow bids me speak.
[*Exeunt.*

SCENE V. *Without the Walls of* Florence. *A Tucket afar off. Enter an old* Widow *of* Florence, DIANA, VIOLENTA, MARIANA, *and other Citizens.*

Wid. Nay, come; for if they do approach the city, we shall lose all the sight.

Dia. They say, the French count has done most honourable service.

Wid. It is reported that he has taken their greatest commander; and that with his own hand he slew the duke's brother. We have lost our labour; they are gone a contrary way: hark! you may know by their trumpets.

Mar. Come, let's return again, and suffice ourselves with the report of it. Well, Diana, take heed of this French earl: the honour of a maid is her name; and no legacy is so rich as honesty.

Wid. I have told my neighbour, how you have been solicited by a gentleman his companion.

Mar. I know that knave; hang him! one Parolles: a filthy officer he is in those suggestions[5] for the young earl.—Beware of them, Diana; their promises, enticements, oaths, tokens, and all these engines of lust, are not the things they go under:[6] many a maid hath been seduced by them; and the misery is, example, that so terrible shows in the wreck of maidenhead, cannot for all that dissuade succession, but that they are limed with the twigs that threaten them. I hope, I need not to advise you further; but, I hope, your own grace will keep you where you are, though there were no further danger known, but the modesty which is so lost.

Dia. You shall not need to fear me.

Enter HELENA, *in the dress of a Pilgrim.*

Wid. I hope so.——Look, here comes a pilgrim:
I know she will lie at my house: thither they send
one another: I'll question her.—
God save you, pilgrim! Whither are you bound?

Hel. To Saint Jaques le grand.
Where do the palmers[7] lodge, I do beseech you?

Wid. At the Saint Francis here, beside the port.

Hel. Is this the way?

Wid. Ay, marry, is it.—Hark you!
[*A march afar off.*
They come this way:—If you will tarry, holy pilgrim,
But till the troops come by,
I will conduct you where you shall be lodg'd;
The rather, for, I think, I know your hostess
As ample as myself.

Hel. Is it yourself?

Wid. If you shall please so, pilgrim.

Hel. I thank you, and will stay upon your leisure.

Wid. You came, I think, from France?

Hel. I did so.

Wid. Here you shall see a countryman of yours,
That has done worthy service.

Hel. His name, I pray you.

Dia. The count Rousillon; Know you such a one?

Hel. But by the ear, that hears most nobly of him,
His face I know not.

Dia. Whatsoe'er he is,
He's bravely taken here. He stole from France,
As 'tis reported, for[8] the king had married him
Against his liking: Think you it is so?

Hel. Ay, surely, mere the truth;[9] I know his lady.

Dia. There is a gentleman, that serves the count,
Reports but coarsely of her.

Hel. What's his name?

Dia. Monsieur Parolles.

Hel. O, I believe with him,
In argument of praise, or to the worth
Of the great count himself, she is too mean
To have her name repeated; all her deserving
Is a reserved honesty, and that
I have not heard examin'd.[10]

Dia. Alas, poor lady!
'Tis a hard bondage, to become the wife
Of a detesting lord.

Wid. Ay, right; good creature, wheresoe'er she is,[11]
Her heart weighs sadly: this young maid might do her
A shrewd turn, if she pleas'd.

Hel. How do you mean?
May be, the amorous count solicits her
In the unlawful purpose.

Wid. He does, indeed;
And brokes[12] with all that can in such a suit

---

1 At Orleans was a church dedicated to St. Jaques, to which pilgrims formerly used to resort, to adore a part of the cross pretended to be found there. See Heylin's France Painted to the Life, 1656, p. 270—6.

2 Alluding to the story of Hercules.

3 i. e. discretion or thought.

4 *Weigh* here means to value or esteem.

5 *Suggestions* are *temptations.*

6 They are not the things for which their names would make them pass. *To go under* the name of so and so is a common expression.

7 Pilgrims; so called from a staff or bough of palm they were wont to carry, especially such as had visited the holy places at Jerusalem. Johnson has given Stavely's account of the difference between *a palmer* and *a pilgrim* in his Dictionary.

8 *For*, here and in other places, signifies *cause*, which Tooke says is *always* its signification.

9 i. e. the mere truth, or merely the truth. *Mere* was used in the sense of simple, absolute, decided.

10 That is, *questioned, doubted.*

11 The old copy reads:

'*I write* good creature, wheresoe'er she is.'

Malone once deemed this an error, and proposed, '*A right* good creature,' which was admitted into the text, but he subsequently thought that the old reading was correct.

12 Deals with panders

Corrupt the tender honour of a maid:
But she is arm'd for him, and keeps her guard
In honestest defence.

Enter, with Drum and Colours, a party of the Florentine *Army*, BERTRAM, *and* PAROLLES.

Mar. The gods forbid else!
Wid. So, now they come:—
That is Antonio, the duke's eldest son;
That, Escalus.
Hel. Which is the Frenchman?
Dia. He;
That with the plume: 'tis a most gallant fellow;
I would, he lov'd his wife: if he were honester,
He were much goodlier:—Is't not a handsome gentleman?
Hel. I like him well.
Dia. 'Tis pity, he is not honest: Yond's that same knave,
That leads him to these places;[1] were I his lady,
I'd poison that vile rascal.
Hel. Which is he?
Dia. That jack-an-apes with scarfs: Why is he melancholy?
Hel. Perchance he's hurt i'the battle.
Par. Lose our drum! well.
Mar. He's shrewdly vexed at something: Look, he has spied us.
Wid. Marry, hang you!
Mar. And your courtesy, for a ring-carrier!
[*Exeunt* BERTRAM, PAROLLES, Officers, *and* Soldiers.
Wid. The troop is past: Come, pilgrim, I will bring you
Where you shall host: of enjoin'd penitents,
There's four or five, to great Saint Jaques bound,
Already at my house.
Hel. I humbly thank you:
Please it this matron, and this gentle maid,
To eat with us to-night, the charge, and thanking,
Shall be for me; and, to requite you further,
I will bestow some precepts on this virgin,
Worthy the note.
Both. We'll take your offer kindly. [*Exeunt.*

SCENE VI. *Camp before* Florence. *Enter* BERTRAM, *and the two* French Lords.

1 *Lord.* Nay, good my lord, put him to't: let him have his way.

2 *Lord.* If your lordship find him not a hilding,[2] hold me no more in your respect.

1 *Lord.* On my life, my lord, a bubble.

Ber. Do you think, I am so far deceived in him?

1 *Lord.* Believe it, my lord, in mine own direct knowledge, without any malice, but to speak of him, as my kinsman, he's a most notable coward, an infinite and endless liar, an hourly promise-breaker, the owner of no one good quality worthy your lordship's entertainment.

2 *Lord.* It were fit you knew him; lest, reposing too far in his virtue, which he hath not, he might, at some great and trusty business, in a main danger, fail you.

Ber. I would, I knew in what particular action to try him.

2 *Lord.* None better than to let him fetch off his drum, which you hear him so confidently undertake to do.

1 *Lord.* I, with a troop of Florentines, will suddenly surprise him; such I will have, whom, I am sure, he knows not from the enemy: we will bind and hoodwink him so, that he shall suppose no other but that he is carried into the leaguer[3] of the adversaries, when we bring him to our tents: Be but your lordship present at his examination; if he do not, for the promise of his life, and in the highest compulsion of base fear, offer to betray you, and deliver all the intelligence in his power against you, and that with the divine forfeit of his soul upon oath, never trust my judgment in any thing.

2 *Lord.* O, for the love of laughter, let him fetch his drum; he says, he has a stratagem for't: when your lordship sees the bottom of his success in't, and to what metal this counterfeit lump of ore[4] will be melted, if you give him not John Drum's entertainment,[5] your inclining cannot be removed. Here he comes.

Enter PAROLLES.

1 *Lord.* O, for the love of laughter, hinder not the humour of his design; let him fetch off his drum in any hand.[6]

Ber. How now, monsieur? this drum sticks sorely in your disposition.

2 *Lord.* A pox on't, let it go; 'tis but a drum.

Par. But a drum! Is't but a drum? A drum so lost!—There was an excellent command! to charge in with our horse upon our own wings, and to rend our own soldiers.

2 *Lord.* That was not to be blamed in the command of the service; it was a disaster of war that Cæsar himself could not have prevented, if he had been there to command.

Ber. Well, we cannot greatly condemn our success: some dishonour we had in the loss of that drum; but it is not to be recovered.

Par. It might have been recovered.

Ber. It might, but it is not now.

Par. It is to be recovered: but that the merit of service is seldom attributed to the true and exact performer, I would have that drum or another, or *hic jacet*.[7]

Ber. Why, if you have a stomach to't, monsieur, if you think your mystery in stratagem can bring this instrument of honour again into his native quarter, be magnanimous in the enterprise, and go on; I will grace the attempt for a worthy exploit: if you speed well in it, the duke shall both speak of it, and extend to you what further becomes his greatness, even to the utmost syllable of your worthiness.

Par. By the hand of a soldier, I will undertake it

Ber. But you must not now slumber in it.

Par. I'll about it this evening: and I will presently pen down my dilemmas,[8] encourage myself in my certainty, put myself into my mortal preparation, and, by midnight, look to hear further from me.

Ber. May I be bold to acquaint his grace, you are gone about it?

Par. I know not what the success will be, my lord; but the attempt I vow.

Ber. I know, thou art valiant; and, to the possibility of thy soldiership, will subscribe for thee.[9] Farewell.

Par. I love not many words. [*Exit.*

1 *Lord.* No more than a fish loves water.—Is not this a strange fellow, my lord? that so confidently seems to undertake this business, which he knows is not to be done; damns himself to do, and dares better be damned than to do't.

2 *Lord.* You do not know him, my lord, as we do: certain it is, that he will steal himself into a man's favour, and, for a week, escape a great deal

1 Theobald thought that we should read *paces;* but we may suppose the *places* alluded to be the houses of pimps and panders.

2 *A hilding* is a paltry fellow, a coward.

3 The *camp.* It seems to have been a new-fangled term at this time, introduced from the Low Countries.

4 The old copy reads *ours.* The emendation is Theobald's.

5 This was a common phrase for *ill treatment.*

6 A phrase for *at any rate.* Sometimes, '*at any hand.*'

7 I would recover the lost drum or another, or die in the attempt. An epitaph then usually began *hic jacet.*

8 The *dilemmas* of Parolles have nothing to do with those of the schoolmen, as the commentators imagined:—his *dilemmas* are the *difficulties* he was to encounter. Mr. Boswell argues that the penning down of these could not well encourage him in his *certainty:* but why are those distinct actions necessarily connected?

9 Steevens has mistaken this passage; Malone is right. Bertram's meaning is, that he will vouch for his doing all that it is possible for soldiership to effect. He was not yet certain of his cowardice.

of discoveries; but when you find him out, you have him ever after.

Ber. Why, do you think, he will make no deed at all of this, that so seriously he does address himself unto?

1 *Lord.* None in the world; but return with an invention, and clap upon you two or three probable lies: but we have almost embossed him,[1] you shall see his fall to-night; for, indeed, he is not for your lordship's respect.

2 *Lord.* We will make you some sport with the fox, ere we case him.[2] He was first smoked by the old lord Lafeu: when his disguise and he is parted, tell me what a sprat you shall find him; which you shall see this very night.

1 *Lord.* I must go look my twigs; he shall be caught.

Ber. Your brother, he shall go along with me.

1 *Lord.* As't please your lordship: I'll leave you. [*Exit.*

Ber. Now will I lead you to the house, and show you
The lass I spoke of.

2 *Lord.* But, you say, she's honest.

Ber. That's all the fault: I spoke with her but once,
And found her wondrous cold; but I sent to her,
By this same coxcomb that we have i'the wind,[3]
Tokens and letters which she did resend;
And this is all I have done: She's a fair creature:
Will you go see her?

2 *Lord.* With all my heart, my lord. [*Exeunt.*

SCENE VII. Florence. *A Room in the* Widow's *House. Enter* HELENA *and* Widow.

Hel. If you misdoubt me that I am not she,
I know not how I shall assure you further,
But I shall lose the grounds I work upon.[4]

Wid. Though my estate be fallen, I was well born,
Nothing acquainted with these businesses;
And would not put my reputation now
In any staining act.

Hel. Nor would I wish you.
First, give me trust, the count he is my husband;
And, what to your sworn counsel I have spoken,
Is so, from word to word; and then you cannot,
By the good aid that I of you shall borrow,
Err in bestowing it.

Wid. I should believe you;
For you have show'd me that, which well approves
You are great in fortune.

Hel. Take this purse of gold,
And let me buy your friendly help thus far,
Which I will overpay, and pay again,
When I have found it. The count he woos your daughter,
Lays down his wanton siege before her beauty,
Resolves to carry her; let her, in fine, consent,
As we'll direct her how 'tis best to bear it,
Now his important[5] blood will nought deny
That she'll demand: A ring the county[6] wears
That downward hath succeeded in his house,
From son to son, some four or five descents
Since the first father wore it: this ring he holds
In most rich choice; yet, in his idle fire,
To buy his will, it would not seem too dear,
Howe'er repented after.

Wid. Now I see
The bottom of your purpose.

Hel. You see it lawful then: It is no more,
But that your daughter, ere she seems as won,
Desires this ring; appoints him an encounter;
In fine, delivers me to fill the time,
Herself most chastely absent: after this,
To marry her, I'll add three thousand crowns
To what is past already.

Wid. I have yielded:
Instruct my daughter how she shall persever,
That time and place, with this deceit so lawful,
May prove coherent. Every night he comes
With musics of all sorts, and songs compos'd
To her unworthiness: It nothing steads us,
To chide him from our eaves:[7] for he persists,
As if his life lay on't.

Hel. Why then, to-night
Let us assay our plot; which, if it speed,
Is wicked meaning in a lawful deed,
And lawful meaning in a lawful act;
Where both not sin, and yet a sinful fact:[8]
But let's about it. [*Exeunt*

ACT IV.

SCENE I. *Without the* Florentine *Camp. Enter first* Lord, *with five or six* Soldiers *in ambush.*

1 *Lord.* He can come no other way but by this hedge' corner: When you sally upon him, speak what terrible language you will; though you understand it not yourselves, no matter: for we must not seem to understand him; unless some one among us, whom we must produce for an interpreter.

1 *Sold.* Good captain, let me be the interpreter.

1 *Lord.* Art not acquainted with him? knows he not thy voice?

1 *Sold.* No, sir, I warrant you.

1 *Lord.* But what linsy-woolsy hast thou to speak to us again?

1 *Sold.* Even such as you speak to me.

1 *Lord.* He must think us some band of strangers i'the adversary's entertainment.[9] Now he hath a smack of all neighbouring languages; therefore we must every one be a man of his own fancy, not to know what we speak one to another; so we seem to know, is to know straight our purpose:[10] chough's[11] language, gabble enough and good enough. As for you, interpreter, you must seem very politic. But couch, ho! here he comes; to beguile two hours in a sleep, and then to return and swear the lies he forges.

Enter PAROLLES.

Par. Ten o'clock: within these three hours 'twill be time enough to go home. What shall I say I have done? It must be a very plausible invention that carries it: They begin to smoke me; and disgraces have of late knocked too often at my door. I find my tongue is too fool-hardy; but my heart hath the fear of Mars before it, and of his creatures, not daring the reports of my tongue.

1 *Lord.* This is the first truth that e'er thine own tongue was guilty of. [*Aside.*

Par. What the devil should move me to undertake the recovery of this drum; being not ignorant of the impossibility, and knowing I had no such purpose? I must give myself some hurts, and say, I got them in exploit: Yet slight ones will not carry it: They will say, Came you off with so little? and great ones I dare not give. Wherefore?

1 That is, *almost run him down.* An *emboss'd* stag is one so hard chased that it foams at the mouth. *V.* note on The Induction to The Taming of the Shrew

2 Before we strip him naked, or unmask him.

3 This proverbial phrase is noted by Ray, p. 216, ed. 1737. It is thus explained by old Cotgrave: '*Estre sur vent,* To be in the wind, or to have the wind of. *To get the wind, advantage, upper hand of; to have a man under his lee.*'

4 i. e. by discovering herself to the Count.

5 *Important,* here and in other places, is used for *importunate.* Mr. Tyrwhitt says, that *important* may be from the French *emportant.*

6 i. e. the *Count.*

7 From under our windows.

8 This gingling *riddle* may be thus briefly explained. Bertram's is a *wicked* intention, though the act he commits is *lawful.* Helen's is both a *lawful* intention and a *lawful* deed. The *fact* as relates to Bertram was *sinful,* because he intended to commit adultery; yet neither he nor Helena *actually* sinned.

9 i. e. foreign troops in the enemy's pay.

10 The sense of this very obscure passage appears, from the context, to be: 'we must each fancy a jargon for himself, without aiming to be understood by each other; for, provided we appear to understand, that will be sufficient.' I suspect that a word or two is omitted

11 A bird of the jack-daw kind

what's the instance?[1] Tongue, I must put you into a butterwoman's mouth, and buy another of Bajazet's mute,[2] if you prattle me into these perils.

1 *Lord.* Is it possible, he should know what he is, and be that he is? [*Aside.*

Par. I would the cutting of my garments would serve the turn; or the breaking of my Spanish sword.

1 *Lord.* We cannot afford you so. [*Aside.*

Par. Or the baring[3] of my beard; and to say, it was in stratagem.

1 *Lord.* 'Twould not do. [*Aside.*

Par. Or to drown my clothes, and say, I was stripped.

1 *Lord.* Hardly serve. [*Aside.*

Par. Though I swore I leaped from the window of the citadel——

1 *Lord.* How deep? [*Aside.*

Par. Thirty fathom.

1 *Lord.* Three great oaths would scarce make that be believed. [*Aside.*

Par. I would, I had any drum of the enemy's; I would swear, I recovered it.

1 *Lord.* You shall hear one anon. [*Aside.*

Par. A drum now of the enemy's!

[*Alarum within.*

1 Lord. *Throca movousus, cargo, cargo, cargo.*

All. *Cargo, cargo, villianda par corbo, cargo.*

Par. O! ransom, ransom:—Do not hide mine eyes. [*They seize him and blindfold him.*

1 Sold. *Boskos thromuldo boskos.*

Par. I know you are the Muskos' regiment.
And I shall lose my life for want of language:
If there be here German, or Dane, low Dutch,
Italian, or French, let him speak to me,
I will discover that which shall undo
The Florentine.

1 Sold. *Boskos vauvado*:——
I understand thee, and can speak thy tongue:——
Kerelybonto:——Sir,
Betake thee to thy faith, for seventeen poniards
Are at thy bosom.

Par Oh!

1 *Sold.* O pray, pray, pray.——
Manka revania dulche.

1 Lord. *Oscorbi dulchos volivorca.*

1 *Sold.* The general is content to spare thee yet;
And, hoodwink'd as thou art, will lead thee on
To gather from thee: haply, thou may'st inform
Something to save thy life.

Par. O, let me live,
And all the secrets of our camp I'll show,
Their force, their purposes: nay, I'll speak that
Which you will wonder at.

1 *Sold.* But wilt thou faithfully?

Par. If I do not, damn me.

1 Sold. *Acordo linta.*——
Come on, thou art granted space.

[*Exit, with* PAROLLES *guarded.*

1 *Lord.* Go, tell the count Rousillon, and my brother,
We have caught the woodcock, and will keep him muffled,
Till we do hear from them.

2 *Sold.* Captain, I will.

1 *Lord.* He will betray us all unto ourselves;—
Inform 'em that.

2 *Sold.* So I will, sir.

1 *Lord.* Till then, I'll keep him dark, and safely lock'd. [*Exeunt.*

SCENE II. Florence. *A Room in the* Widow's *House.*

Enter BERTRAM *and* DIANA.

Ber. They told me, that your name was Fontibell.

Dia. No, my good lord, Diana.

Ber. Titled goddess;
And worth it, with addition! But, fair soul,
In your fine frame hath love no quality?
If the quick fire of youth light not your mind,
You are no maiden, but a monument:
When you are dead, you should be such a one
As you are now, for you are cold and stern;
And now you should be as your mother was,
When your sweet self was got.

Dia. She then was honest.

Ber. So should you be

Dia. No:
My mother did but duty; such, my lord,
As you owe to your wife.

Ber. No more of that!
I pr'ythee, do not strive against my vows:[4]
I was compell'd to her; but I love thee
By love's own sweet constraint, and will for ever
Do thee all rights of service.

Dia. Ay, so you serve us,
Till we serve you: but when you have our roses,
You barely leave our thorns to prick ourselves,
And mock us with our bareness.

Ber. How have I sworn?

Dia. 'Tis not the many oaths, that make the truth;
But the plain single vow, that is vow'd true.
What is not holy, that we swear not by,
But take the highest to witness:[5] Then, pray you, tell me,
If I should swear by Jove's great attributes,
I lov'd you dearly, would you believe my oaths,
When I did love you ill? this has no holding,
To swear by him whom I protest to love,
That I will work against him:[6] Therefore, your oaths
Are words, and poor conditions; but unseal'd;
At least, in my opinion.

Ber. Change it, change it;
Be not so holy-cruel: love is holy;
And my integrity ne'er knew the crafts
That you do charge men with: Stand no more off,
But give thyself unto my sick desires,
Who then recover: say, thou art mine, and ever
My love, as it begins, shall so persever.

Dia I see, that men make hopes, in such a war,[7]
That we'll forsake ourselves. Give me that ring.

Ber. I'll lend it thee, my dear, but have no power
To give it from me.

Dia. Will you not, my lord?

Ber. It is an honour 'longing to our house,
Bequeathed down from many ancestors;
Which were the greatest obloquy i'the world
In me to lose.

Dia. Mine honour's such a ring:
My chastity's the jewel of our house,
Bequeathed down from many ancestors;
Which were the greatest obloquy i'the world
In me to lose: Thus your own proper wisdom
Brings in the champion honour on my part,
Against your vain assault.

Ber. Here, take my ring:
My house, mine honour, yea, my life be thine,
And I'll be bid by thee.

---

1 The proof.

2 The old copy reads *mule.* The emendation was made by Warburton.

3 i. e. the *shaving* of my beard. To *bare* anciently signified to *shave.*

4 i. e. against his determined resolution never to cohabit with Helena.

5 The sense is—we never swear by what is not holy, but take to witness the Highest, the Divinity.

6 Heath's attempt at explanation of this very obscure passage does not satisfy me. It appears to be corrupt; and, after much attention to its probable meaning, and taken with the preceding and succeeding speeches, I feel persuaded that it should stand thus:

'If I should swear by *Love's* great attributes
I lov'd you dearly, would you believe my oaths,
When I did love you ill? this has no holding,
To swear by him, *when* I protest to love
That I will work against him.'

7 The old copy reads, 'make *ropes* in such a *scarre.* Rowe changed it to, 'make *hopes* in such *affairs*;' and Malone to, make *hopes* in such a *scene.* But *affairs* and *scene* have no literal resemblance to the old word *scarre*: *warre* is always so written in the old copy; the change is therefore less violent, more probable, and, I think, makes better sense.

Dia. When midnight comes, knock at my chamber window;
I'll order take, my mother shall not hear.
Now will I charge you in the band of truth,
When you have conquer'd my yet maiden bed,
Remain there but an hour, nor speak to me;
My reasons are most strong; and you shall know them,
When back again this ring shall be deliver'd:
And on your finger, in the night, I'll put
Another ring; that, what in time proceeds,
May token to the future our past deeds.
Adieu, till then; then, fail not: You have won
A wife of me, though there my hope be done.

Ber. A heaven on earth I have won, by wooing thee. [*Exit.*

Dia. For which live long to thank both heaven and me!
You may so in the end.——
My mother told me just how he would woo,
As if she sat in his heart; she says, all men
Have the like oaths: he had sworn to marry me,
When his wife's dead; therefore I'll lie with him,
When I am buried. Since Frenchmen are so braid,[1]
Marry that will, I'll live and die a maid:
Only in this disguise, I think't no sin,
To cozen him, that would unjustly win. [*Exit.*

SCENE III. *The* Florentine *Camp. Enter the two* French Lords, *and two or three* Soldiers.

1 *Lord.* You have not given him his mother's letter?

2 *Lord.* I have delivered it an hour since: there is something in't that stings his nature; for, on the reading it, he chang'd almost into another man.

1 *Lord.* He has much worthy blame laid upon him, for shaking off so good a wife, and so sweet a lady.

2 *Lord.* Especially he hath incurred the everlasting displeasure of the king, who had even tuned his bounty to sing happiness to him. I will tell you a thing, but you shall let it dwell darkly with you.

1 *Lord.* When you have spoken it 'tis dead, and I am the grave of it.

2 *Lord.* He hath perverted a young gentlewoman here in Florence, of a most chaste renown; and this night he fleshes his will in the spoil of her honour; he hath given her his monumental ring, and thinks himself made in the unchaste composition.

1 *Lord.* Now, God delay our rebellion; as we are ourselves, what things are we!

2 *Lord.* Merely our own traitors. And as in the common course of all treasons, we still see them reveal themselves, till they attain to their abhorred ends;[2] so he that in this action contrives against his own nobility, in his proper stream o'erflows himself.[3]

1 *Lord.* Is it not meant damnable[4] in us to be trumpeters of our unlawful intents? We shall not then have his company to-night.

2 *Lord.* Not till after midnight; for he is dieted to his hour.

1 *Lord.* That approaches apace; I would gladly have him see his company[5] anatomized; that he might take a measure of his own judgment,[6] wherein so curiously he had set this counterfeit.[7]

2 *Lord.* We will not meddle with him till he come; for his presence must be the whip of the other.

1 *Lord.* In the mean time, what hear you of these wars?

2 *Lord.* I hear, there is an overture of peace.

1 *Lord.* Nay, I assure you, a peace concluded.

2 *Lord.* What will count Rousillon do then? will he travel higher, or return again into France?

1 *Lord.* I perceive by this demand, you are not altogether of his council.

2 *Lord.* Let it be forbid, sir! so should I be a great deal of his act.

1 *Lord.* Sir, his wife, some two months since, fled from his house: her pretence is a pilgrimage to Saint Jaques le grand; which holy undertaking, with most austere sanctimony, she accomplished; and, there residing, the tenderness of her nature became as a prey to her grief; in fine, made a groan of her last breath, and now she sings in heaven.

2 *Lord.* How is this justified?

1 *Lord.* The stronger part of it by her own letters; which makes her story true, even to the point of her death: her death itself, which could not be her office to say, is come, was faithfully confirmed by the rector of the place.

2 *Lord.* Hath the count all this intelligence?

1 *Lord.* Ay, and the particular confirmations, point from point, to the full arming of the verity.

2 *Lord.* I am heartily sorry, that he'll be glad of this.

1 *Lord.* How mightily, sometimes, we make us comforts of our losses!

2 *Lord.* And how mightily, some other times, we drown our gain in tears! The great dignity, that his valour hath here acquired for him, shall at home be encountered with a shame as ample.

1 *Lord.* The web of our life is of a mingled yarn, good and ill together: our virtues would be proud, if our faults whipped them not; and our crimes would despair, if they were not cherish'd by our virtues.—

Enter a Servant.

How now? where's your master?

Serv. He met the duke in the street, sir, of whom he hath taken a solemn leave; his lordship will next morning for France. The duke hath offered him letters of commendations to the king.

2 *Lord.* They shall be no more than needful there, if they were more than they can commend.

Enter BERTRAM.

1 *Lord.* They cannot be too sweet for the king's tartness. Here's his lordship now. How now, my lord, is't not after midnight?

Ber. I have to-night despatched sixteen businesses, a month's length a-piece, by an abstract of success: I have conge'd with the duke, done my adieu with his nearest; buried a wife, mourned for her; writ to my lady mother, I am returning; entertained my convoy; and, between these main parcels of despatch, effected many nicer needs; the last was the greatest, but that I have not ended yet.

2 *Lord.* If the business be of any difficulty and this morning your departure hence, it requires haste of your lordship.

Ber. I mean, the business is not ended, as fearing to hear of it hereafter: But shall we have this dialogue between the fool and the soldier?—— Come, bring forth this counterfeit module;[8] he has deceived me, like a double-meaning prophesier.

2 *Lord.* Bring him forth: [*Exeunt* Soldiers.] he has sat in the stocks all night, poor gallant knave.

Ber. No matter; his heels have deserved it, in usurping his spurs[9] so long. How does he carry himself?

1 *Lord.* I have told your lordship already; the

---

1 i. e. *false, deceitful, tricking, beguiling.*

2 This may mean, 'they are perpetually talking about the mischief they intend to do, till they have obtained an opportunity of doing it.'

3 i. e. betrays his own secrets in his own talk.

4 *Damnable* for *damnably;* the adjective used adverbially.

5 *Company* for companion.

6 This is a very just and moral reason. Bertram, by finding how erroneously he has judged, will be less confident, and more easily moved by admonition.

7 *Counterfeit*, besides its ordinary signification of a person pretending to be what he is not, also meant a *picture*, the word *set* shows that the word is used in both senses here.

8 *Module* and *model* were synonymous. The meaning is, bring forth this counterfeit *representation* of a soldier.

9 An allusion to the degradation of a knight by hacking off his spurs.

stocks carry him. But, to answer you as you would be understood; he weeps like a wench that had shed her milk: he hath confessed himself to Morgan, whom he supposes to be a friar, from the time of his remembrance, to this very instant disaster of his setting i'the stocks: And what think you he hath confessed?

Ber. Nothing of me, has he?

2 *Lord.* His confession is taken, and it shall be read to his face: if your lordship be in't, as I believe you are, you must have the patience to hear it.

Re-enter Soldiers *with* PAROLLES.

Ber. A plague upon him! muffled! he can say nothing of me; hush! hush!

1 *Lord.* Hoodman[1] comes!—*Porto tartarossa.*

1 *Sold.* He calls for the tortures; What will you say without 'em?

Par. I will confess what I know without constraint; if ye pinch me like a pasty, I can say no more.

1 Sold. *Bosko chimurcho.*

2 Lord. *Boblibindo chicurmurco.*

1 *Sold.* You are a merciful general:—Our general bids you to answer to what I shall ask you out of a note.

Par. And truly, as I hope to live.

1 Sold. *First demand of him how many horse the duke is strong?* What say you to that?

Par. Five or six thousand; but very weak and unserviceable: the troops are all scattered, and the commanders very poor rogues, upon my reputation and credit, as I hope to live.

1 *Sold.* Shall I set down your answer so?

Par. Do; I'll take the sacrament on't, how and which way you will.

Ber. All's one to him. What a past-saving slave is this![2]

1 *Lord.* You are deceived, my lord; this is monsieur Parolles, the gallant militarist (that was his own phrase,) that had the whole theorick[3] of war in the knot of his scarf, and the practice in the chape[4] of his dagger.

2 *Lord.* I will never trust a man again for keeping his sword clean; nor believe he can have every thing in him, by wearing his apparel neatly.

1 *Sold.* Well, that's set down.

Par. Five or six thousand horse, I said,—I will say true, or thereabouts, set down, for I'll speak truth.

1 *Lord.* He's very near the truth in this.

Ber. But I con him no thanks[5] for't, in the nature he delivers it.

Par. Poor rogues, I pray you, say.

1 *Sold.* Well, that's set down.

Par. I humbly thank you, sir: a truth's a truth, the rogues are marvellous poor.

1 Sold. *Demand of him, of what strength they are a-foot.* What say you to that?

Par. By my troth, sir, if I were to live this present hour,[6] I will tell true. Let me see: Spurio a hundred and fifty, Sebastian so many, Corambus so many, Jaques so many; Guiltian, Cosmo, Lodowick, and Gratii, two hundred fifty each: mine own company, Chitopher, Vaumond, Bentii, two hundred and fifty each: so that the muster-file, rotten and sound, upon my life, amounts not to fifteen thousand poll; half of which dare not shake the snow from off their cassocks,[7] lest they shake themselves to pieces.

Ber. What shall be done to him?

1 *Lord.* Nothing, but let him have thanks. Demand of him my conditions,[8] and what credit I have with the duke.

1 *Sold.* Well, that's set down. *You shall demand of him, whether one captain Dumain be i'the camp, a Frenchman; what his reputation is with the duke, what his valour, honesty, and expertness in wars; or whether he thinks, it were not possible, with well-weighing sums of gold, to corrupt him to a revolt.* What say you to this? What do you know of it?

Par. I beseech you, let me answer to the particular of the intergatories:[9] Demand them singly.

1 *Sold.* Do you know this captain Dumain?

Par. I know him: he was a botcher's 'prentice in Paris, from whence he was whipped for getting the sheriff's fool[10] with child: a dumb innocent, that could not say him, nay.

[DUMAIN *lifts up his hand in anger.*

Ber. Nay, by your leave, hold your hands; though I know, his brains are forfeit to the next tile that falls.[11]

1 *Sold.* Well, is this captain in the duke of Florence's camp?

Par. Upon my knowledge, he is, and lousy.

1 *Lord.* Nay, look not so upon me; we shall hear of your lordship anon.

1 *Sold.* What is his reputation with the duke?

Par. The duke knows him for no other but a poor officer of mine; and writ to me this other day, to turn him out o'the band: I think, I have his letter in my pocket.

1 *Sold.* Marry, we'll search.

Par. In good sadness, I do not know; either it is there, or it is upon a file, with the duke's other letters, in my tent.

1 *Sold.* Here 'tis; here's a paper? Shall I read it to you?

Par. I do not know if it be it, or no.

Ber. Our interpreter does it well.

1 *Lord.* Excellently.

1 *Sold.* Dian. *The count's a fool, and full of gold,*—

Par. That is not the duke's letter, sir; that is an advertisement to a proper maid in Florence, one Diana, to take heed of the allurement of one count Rousillon, a foolish idle boy, but for all that, very ruttish: I pray you, sir, put it up again.

1 *Sold.* Nay, I'll read it first, by your favour.

Par. My meaning in't, I protest, was very honest in the behalf of the maid: for I knew the young count to be a dangerous and lascivious boy; who is a whale[12] to virginity, and devours up all the fry it finds.

Ber. Damnable, both sides rogue!

1 Sold. *When he swears oaths, bid him drop gold,*
and take it;
After he scores, he never pays the score:
Half won, is match well made; match, and well
make it:[13]
He ne'er pays after debts, take it before;
And say, a soldier, Dian, told thee this,
Men are to mell[14] *with, boys are not to kiss:*
For count of this, the count's a fool, I know it,
Who pays before, but not when he does owe it,
Thine, as he vow'd to thee in thine ear,
PAROLLES.

1 The game at blind man's buff was formerly called *Hoodman* blind.

2 In the old copy these words are given by mistake to Parolles.

3 Theory.

4 The *chape* is the catch or fastening of the sheath of his dagger.

5 i. e. I am not beholden to him for it, &c.

6 Perhaps we should read, 'if I were *but* to live this present hour;' unless the blunder is meant to show the fright of Parolles.

7 '*Cassocks.*' Soldiers' cloaks or upper garments.

8 i. e. disposition and character.

9 For interrogatories.

10 Female idiots, as well as male, though not so commonly, were retained in great families for diversion. It is not improbable that some real event of recent occurrence is alluded to.

11 In Whitney's Emblems there is a story of three women who threw dice to ascertain which of them should die first. She who lost affected to laugh at the decrees of fate, when a tile suddenly falling put an end to her existence. This book was certainly known to Shakspeare. The passages in Lucian and Plutarch are not so likely to have met the poet's eye.

12 There is probably an allusion here to the Story of Andromeda in old prints, where the monster is frequently represented as a *whale*.

13 i. e. a match well made is half won; make your match therefore, but make it well.

14 The meaning of the word *mell* from *meler*, French, is obvious. To *mell*, says Ruddiman, 'to fight, contend, meddle or *have to do with*.'

Ber. He shall be whipped through the army with this rhyme in his forehead.

2 *Lord.* This is your devoted friend, sir, the manifold linguist, and the armipotent soldier.

Ber. I could endure any thing before but a cat, and now he's a cat to me.

1 *Sold.* I perceive, sir, by the general's looks, we shall be fain to hang you.

Par. My life, sir, in any case: not that I am afraid to die; but that, my offences being many, I would repent out the remainder of nature; let me live, sir, in a dungeon, i'the stocks, or any where, so I may live.

1 *Sold.* We'll see what may be done, so you confess freely; therefore, once more to this captain Dumain: You have answered to his reputation with the duke, and to his valour: What is his honesty?

Par. He will steal, sir, an egg out of a cloister;[1] for rapes and ravishments he parallels Nessus.[2] He professes not keeping of oaths; in breaking them, he is stronger than Hercules. He will lie, sir, with such volubility, that you would think truth were a fool: drunkenness is his best virtue; for he will be swine-drunk; and in his sleep he does little harm, save to his bed-clothes about him; but they know his conditions, and lay him in straw. I have but little more to say, sir, of his honesty: he has every thing that an honest man should not have; what an honest man should have, he has nothing.

1 *Lord.* I begin to love him for this.

Ber. For this description of thine honesty? A pox upon him for me, he is more and more a cat.

1 *Sold.* What say you to his expertness in war?

Par. Faith, sir, he has led the drum before the English tragedians,—to belie him, I will not,—and more of his soldiership I know not; except in that country, he had the honour to be the officer at a place there call'd Mile End,[3] to instruct for the doubling of files: I would do the man what honour I can, but of this I am not certain.

1 *Lord.* He hath out-villained villainy so far, that the rarity redeems him.

Ber. A pox on him! he's a cat still.

1 *Sold.* His qualities being at this poor price, I need not ask you, if gold will corrupt him to revolt.

Par. Sir, for a *quart d'ecu*[4] he will sell the fee-simple of his salvation, the inheritance of it: and cut the entail from all remainders, and a perpetual succession for it perpetually.

1 *Sold.* What's his brother, the other captain Dumain?

2 *Lord.* Why does he ask him of me?

1 *Sold.* What's he?

Par. Ev'n a crow of the same nest; not altogether so great as the first in goodness, but greater a great deal in evil. He excels his brother for a coward, yet his brother is reputed one of the best that is: In a retreat he outruns any lackey; marry, in coming on he has the cramp.

1 *Sold.* If your life be sav'd, will you undertake to betray the Florentine?

Par. Ay, and the captain of his horse, count Rousillon.

1 *Sold.* I'll whisper with the general, and know his pleasure.

Par. I'll no more drumming; a plague of all drums! Only to seem to deserve well, and to beguile the supposition[5] of that lascivious young boy the count, have I run into this danger: Yet, who would have suspected an ambush where I was taken? [*Aside.*

1 *Sold.* There is no remedy, sir, but you must die: the general says, you, that have so traitorously discovered the secrets of your army, and made such pestiferous reports of men, very nobly held, can serve the world for no honest use; therefore you must die. Come, headsmen, off with his head.

Par. O Lord, sir; let me live, or let me see my death!

1 *Sold.* That shall you, and take your leave of all your friends. [*Unmuffling him*

So, look about you: Know you any here?

Ber. Good morrow, noble captain

2 *Lord.* God bless you, captain Parolles.

1 *Lord.* God save you, noble captain.

2 *Lord.* Captain, what greeting will you to my lord Lafeu? I am for France.

1 *Lord.* Good captain, will you give me a copy of the sonnet you writ to Diana in behalf of the count Rousillon? an I were not a very coward, I'd compel it of you; but fare you well.

[*Exeunt* BERTRAM, Lords, *&c.*

1 *Sold.* You are undone, captain: all but your scarf, that has a knot on't yet.

Par. Who cannot be crushed with a plot?

1 *Sold.* If you could find out a country where but women were that had received so much shame, you might begin an impudent nation. Fare you well, sir; I am for France too; we shall speak o you there. [*Exit.*

Par. Yet am I thankful: if my heart were great,
'Twould burst at this: Captain I'll be no more;
But I will eat and drink, and sleep as soft
As captain shall: simply the thing I am
Shall make me live. Who knows himself a braggart,
Let him fear this; for it will come to pass,
That every braggart shall be found an ass.
Rust, sword! cool, blushes! and, Parolles, live
Safest in shame! being fool'd, by foolery thrive!
There's place, and means, for every man alive.
I'll after them. [*Exit.*

SCENE IV. Florence. *A Room in the* Widow's *House. Enter* HELENA, Widow, *and* DIANA.

Hel. That you may well perceive I have not wrong'd you,
One of the greatest in the Christian world
Shall be my surety; 'fore whose throne, 'tis needful
Ere I can perfect mine intents, to kneel:
Time was, I did him a desired office,
Dear almost as his life; which gratitude
Through flinty Tartar's bosom would peep forth,
And answer, thanks: I duly am inform'd,
His grace is at Marseilles;[6] to which place
We have convenient convoy. You must know,
I am supposed dead: the army breaking,
My husband hies him home; where, heaven aiding,
And by the leave of my good lord the king,
We'll be, before our welcome.

Wid. Gentle madam,
You never had a servant, to whose trust
Your business was more welcome.

Hel. Nor you, mistress,
Ever a friend, whose thoughts more truly labour
To recompense your love: doubt not, but heaven
Hath brought me up to be your daughter's dower,
As it hath fated her to be my motive[7]
And helper to a husband. But, O strange men!
That can such sweet use make of what they hate,
When saucy[8] trusting of the cozen'd thoughts
Defiles the pitchy night! so lust doth play
With what it loathes, for that which is away:
But more of this hereafter:——You, Diana,
Under my poor instructions yet must suffer
Something in my behalf.

Dia. Let death and honesty
Go with your impositions, I am yours,[9]
Upon your will to suffer.

---

1 i. e. he will steal any thing, however trifling, from any place, however holy.

2 The Centaur killed by Hercules.

3 *Mile End Green* was the place for public sports and exercises. See K. Henry IV. P. II. Act iii. Sc. 2.

4 The fourth part of the smaller French crown, about eight-pence.

5 To deceive the opinion

6 It appears that Marseilles was pronounced as a word of three syllables. In the old copy it is written Marcellæ and Marcellus.

7 i. e. to be my mover.

8 *Saucy* was used in the sense of *wanton.* We have it with the same meaning in Measure for Measure.

9 i. e. let *death*, accompanied by *honesty*, go with *the task you impose*, *still* I am yours, &c.

Hel. Yet, I pray you,[1]——
But with the word, the time will bring on summer,
When briars shall have leaves as well as thorns,
And be as sweet as sharp. We must away;
Our waggon is prepar'd, and time revives us:
All's well that ends well: still the fine's the crown;[2]
Whate'er the course, the end is the renown.
[*Exeunt.*

SCENE V. Rousillon. *A Room in the* Countess's *Palace. Enter* Countess, LAFEU, *and* Clown.

Laf. No, no, no, your son was misled with a snipt-taffata fellow there; whose villainous saffron[3] would have made all the unbaked and doughy youth of a nation in his colour: your daughter-in-law had been alive at this hour; and your son here at home, more advanced by the king, than by that red-tailed humble-bee I speak of.

Count. I would, I had not known him! it was the death of the most virtuous gentlewoman, that ever nature had praise for creating: if she had partaken of my flesh, and cost me the dearest groans of a mother, I could not have owed her a more rooted love.

Laf. 'Twas a good lady, 'twas a good lady: we may pick a thousand salads, ere we light on such another herb.

Clo. Indeed, sir, she was the sweet-marjoram of the salad, or rather the herb of grace.[4]

Laf. They are not salad-herbs, you knave, they are nose-herbs.

Clo. I am no great Nebuchadnezzar, sir, I have not much skill in grass.[5]

Laf. Whether dost thou profess thyself; a knave, or a fool?

Clo. A fool, sir, at a woman's service, and a knave at a man's.

Laf. Your distinction?

Clo. I would cozen the man of his wife, and do his service.

Laf. So you were a knave at his service, indeed.

Clo. And I would give his wife my bauble,[6] sir, to do her service.

Laf. I will subscribe for thee; thou art both knave and fool.

Clo. At your service.

Laf. No, no, no.

Clo. Why, sir, if I cannot serve you, I can serve as great a prince as you are.

Laf. Who's that? a Frenchman?

Clo. Faith, sir, he has an English name;[7] but his phisnomy is more hotter[8] in France, than there.

Laf. What prince is that?

Clo. The black prince, sir, *alias*, the prince of darkness; *alias*, the devil.

Laf. Hold thee, there's my purse: I give thee not this to suggest thee from thy master thou talkest of; serve him still.

Clo. I am a woodland fellow, sir, that always loved a great fire; and the master I speak of, ever keeps a good fire. But, sure,[9] he is the prince of the world, let his nobility remain in his court. I am for the house with the narrow gate, which I take to be too little for pomp to enter: some, that humble themselves, may; but the many will be too chill and tender; and they'll be for the flowery way, that leads to the broad gate, and the great fire.

Laf. Go thy ways, I begin to be a-weary of thee; and I tell thee so before, because I would not fall out with thee. Go thy ways; let my horses be well looked to, without any tricks.

Clo. If I put any tricks upon 'em, sir, they shall be jades' tricks; which are their own right by the law of nature. [*Exit.*

Laf. A shrewd knave, and an unhappy.[10]

Count. So he is. My lord, that's gone, made himself much sport out of him: by his authority he remains here, which he thinks is a patent for his sauciness; and, indeed, he has no pace,[11] but runs where he will.

Laf. I like him well; 'tis not amiss: and I was about to tell you, since I heard of the good lady's death, and that my lord your son was upon his return home, I moved the king my master, to speak in the behalf of my daughter; which, in the minority of them both, his majesty, out of a self-gracious remembrance, did first propose: his highness hath promised me to do it: and, to stop up the displeasure he hath conceived against your son, there is no fitter matter. How does your ladyship like it?

Count. With very much content, my lord, and I wish it happily effected.

Laf. His highness comes post from Marseilles, of as able body as when he numbered thirty; he will be here to-morrow, or I am deceived by him that in such intelligence hath seldom failed.

Count. It rejoices me, that I hope I shall see him ere I die. I have letters that my son will be here to-night: I shall beseech your lordship, to remain with me till they meet together.

Laf. Madam, I was thinking, with what manners I might safely be admitted.

Count. You need but plead your honourable privilege.

Laf. Lady, of that I have made a bold charter; but, I thank my God, it holds yet.

Re-enter Clown.

Clo. O madam, yonder's my lord your son with a patch of velvet on's face: whether there be a scar under it, or no, the velvet knows; but 'tis a goodly patch of velvet: his left cheek is a cheek of two pile and a half, but his right cheek is worn bare.

Laf. A scar nobly got, or a noble scar, is a good livery of honour; so, belike, is that.

Clo. But it is your carbonadoed[12] face.

Laf. Let us go see your son, I pray you; I long to talk with the young noble soldier.

Clo. 'Faith, there's a dozen of 'em, with delicate fine hats, and most courteous feathers, which bow the head, and nod at every man. [*Exeunt.*

ACT V.

SCENE I. Marseilles. *A Street. Enter* HELENA, Widow, *and* DIANA, *with two* Attendants.

Hel. But this exceeding posting, day and night,
Must wear your spirits low: we cannot help it;

1 The reading proposed by Blackstone,
'Yet I 'fray you
But with the word: the time will bring, &c.'
seems required by the context, and makes the passage intelligible.

2 A translation of the common Latin proverb, *Finis coronat opus:* the origin of which has been pointed out by Mr. Douce, in his Illustrations, vol. i. p. 323.

3 It has been thought that there is an allusion here to the fashion of *yellow starch* for bands and ruffs, which was long prevalent: and also to the custom of colouring paste with saffron. The plain meaning seems to be—that Parolles's vices were of such a colourable quality as to be sufficient to corrupt the inexperienced youth of a nation, and make them take the same hue.

4 i. e. rue.

5 The old copy reads *grace.* The emendation is Rowe's: who also supplies the word *salad* in the preceding speech. The clown quibbles on *grass* and *grace.*

6 The fool's *bauble* was 'a short stick ornamented at the end with the figure of a fool's head, or sometimes with that of a doll or puppet. To this instrument there was frequently annexed an inflated bladder, with which the fool belaboured those who offended him, or with whom he was inclined to make sport. The French call a bauble, *marotte,* from *Marionette.*'

7 The old copy reads *maine.*

8 Warburton thought we should read, '*honour'd;*' but the Clown's allusion is double. To Edward *the black prince,* and to the *prince of darkness.* The presence of Edward was indeed *hot* in France: the other allusion is obvious.

9 Steevens thinks, with Sir T. Hanmer, that we should read *since.*

10 i. e. mischievously waggish, unlucky.

11 No *pace,* i. e. no prescribed course; he has the unbridled liberty of a fool.

12 *Carbonadoed* is 'slashed over the face in a manner that fetcheth the flesh with it,' metaphorically from a *carbonado* or collop of meat.

But, since you have made the days and nights as one,
To wear your gentle limbs in my affairs,
Be bold, you do so grow in my requital,
As nothing can unroot you. In happy time;——

Enter a gentle Astringer.[1]

This man may help me to his majesty's ear,
If he would spend his power.—God save you, sir.
Gent. And you.
Hel. Sir, I have seen you in the court of France.
Gent. I have been sometimes there.
Hel. I do presume, sir, that you are not fallen
From the report that goes upon your goodness;
And therefore, goaded with most sharp occasions,
Which lay nice manners by, I put you to
The use of your own virtues, for the which
I shall continue thankful.
Gent. What's your will?
Hel. That it will please you
To give this poor petition to the king;
And aid me with that store of power you have,
To come into his presence.
Gent. The king's not here.
Hel. Not here, sir?
Gent. Not, indeed:
He hence remov'd last night, and with more haste
Than is his use.
Wid. Lord, how we lose our pains!
Hel. *All's well that ends well*, yet;
Though time seem so adverse, and means unfit.—
I do beseech you, whither is he gone?
Gent. Marry, as I take it, to Rousillon;
Whither I am going.
Hel. I do beseech you, sir,
Since you are like to see the king before me,
Commend the paper to his gracious hand;
Which, I presume, shall render you no blame,
But rather make you thank your pains for it:
I will come after you, with what good speed
Our means will make us means.[2]
Gent. This I'll do for you.
Hel. And you shall find yourself to be well thank'd,
Whate'er falls more.——We must to horse again;—
Go, go, provide. [*Exeunt.*

SCENE II. Rousillon. *The inner Court of the* Countess's *Palace. Enter* Clown *and* PAROLLES.

Par. Good Monsieur Lavatch,[3] give my Lord Lafeu this letter: I have ere now, sir, been better known to you, when I have held familiarity with fresher clothes; but I am now, sir, muddied in fortune's mood,[4] and smell somewhat strong of her strong displeasure.

Clo. Truly, fortune's displeasure is but sluttish, if it smell so strong as thou speakest of: I will henceforth eat no fish of fortune's buttering. Pr'ythee, allow the wind.[5]

Par. Nay, you need not stop your nose, sir; I spake but by a metaphor.

Clo. Indeed, sir, if your metaphor stink,[6] I will stop my nose; or against any man's metaphor. Pr'ythee, get thee further.

Par. Pray you, sir, deliver me this paper.

Clo. Foh, pr'ythee, stand away; A paper from fortune's close-stool to give to a nobleman! Look, here he comes himself.

Enter LAFEU.

Here is a pur of fortune's, sir, or of fortune's cat, (but not a musk-cat,) that has fallen into the unclean fishpond of her displeasure, and, as he says, is muddied withal: Pray you, sir, use the carp as you may; for he looks like a poor, decayed, ingenious, foolish, rascally knave. I do pity his distress in my smiles[7] of comfort, and leave him to your lordship. [*Exit* Clown.

Par. My lord, I am a man whom fortune hath cruelly scratched.

Laf. And what would you have me to do? 'tis too late to pare her nails now. Wherein have you played the knave with fortune, that she should scratch you, who of herself is a good lady, and would not have knaves thrive long under her? There's a *quart d'ecu* for you: Let the justices make you and fortune friends; I am for other business.

Par. I beseech your honour, to hear me one single word.

Laf. You beg a single penny more: come, you shall ha't: save your word.

Par. My name, my good lord, is Parolles.

Laf. You beg more than one word then.[8]—Cox' my passion! give me your hand:—How does your drum?

Par. O my good lord, you were the first that found me.

Laf. Was I, in sooth? and I was the first that lost thee.

Par. It lies in you, my lord, to bring me in some grace, for you did bring me out.

Laf. Out upon thee, knave! dost thou put upon me at once both the office of God and the devil? one brings thee in grace, and the other brings thee out. [*Trumpets sound.*] The king's coming, I know by his trumpets.——Sirrah, inquire further after me: I had talk of you last night: though you are a fool and a knave, you shall eat; go to, follow.[9]

Par. I praise God for you. [*Exeunt.*

SCENE III. *The same. A Room in the* Countess's *Palace. Flourish. Enter* King, Countess, LAFEU, Lords, Gentlemen, Guards, &c.

King. We lost a jewel of her; and our esteem[10]
Was made much poorer by it: but your son,
As mad in folly, lack'd the sense to know
Her estimation home.[11]
Count. 'Tis past, my liège:
And I beseech your majesty to make it
Natural rebellion, done i' the blaze[12] of youth:
When oil and fire, too strong for reason's force,
O'erbears it, and burns on.
King. My honour'd lady,
I have forgiven and forgotten all;
Though my revenges were high bent upon him,
And watch'd the time to shoot.
Laf. This I must say,——
But first I beg my pardon,—The young lord
Did to his majesty, his mother, and his lady,
Offence of mighty note; but to himself
The greatest wrong of all: he lost a wife,
Whose beauty did astonish the survey

---

1 i. e. a gentleman falconer, called in Juliana Barnes' Book of Huntyng, &c. *Ostreger.* The term is applied particularly to those that keep goshawks.

2 i. e. 'they will follow with such speed as the means which they have will give them ability to exert.'

3 Perhaps a corruption of *La Vache.*

4 Warburton changed *mood*, the reading of the old copy, to *moat*, and was followed and defended by Steevens; but though the emendation was ingenious and well supported, it appears unnecessary. *Fortune's mood* is several times used by Shakspeare for the whimsical *caprice* of fortune.

5 i. e. stand to the leeward of me.

6 Warburton observes, 'that Shakspeare throughout his writings, if we except a passage in Hamlet, has scarce a metaphor that can offend the most squeamish reader'

7 Warburton says we should read, '*similes* of comfort,' such as calling him fortune's cat, carp, &c.

8 A quibble is intended on the word *Parolles*, which in French signifies *words*

9 Johnson justly observes that 'Parolles has many of the lineaments of Falstaff, and seems to be a character that Shakspeare delighted to draw, a fellow that had more wit than virtue. Though justice required that he should be detected and exposed, yet his vices sit so fit in him that he is not at last suffered to starve.'

10 i. e. in losing her we lost a large portion of our esteem, which she possessed.

11 Completely, in its full extent

12 The old copy reads *blade.* Theobald proposed the present reading.

Of richest eyes;[1] whose words all ears took captive;
Whose dear perfection, hearts that scorn'd to serve,
Humbly call'd mistress.

King. Praising what is lost,
Makes the remembrance dear.——Well, call him hither;——
We are reconcil'd, and the first view shall kill
All repetition:[2]—Let him not ask our pardon;
The nature of his great offence is dead,
And deeper than oblivion do we bury
The incensing relics of it: let him approach,
A stranger, no offender; and inform him,
So 'tis our will he should.

Gent. I shall, my liege.
[*Exit* Gentleman.

King. What says he to your daughter? have you spoke?——

Laf. All that he is hath reference to your highness.

King. Then shall we have a match. I have letters sent me,
That set him high in fame.

Enter Bertram.

Laf. He looks well on't.

King. I am not a day of season,[3]
For thou mayst see a sun-shine and a hail
In me at once: But to the brightest beams
Distracted clouds give way; so stand thou forth,
The time is fair again.

Ber. My high-repented blames,[4]
Dear sovereign, pardon to me.

King. All is whole;
Not one word more of the consumed time.
Let's take the instant by the forward top;
For we are old, and on our quick'st decrees
The inaudible and noiseless foot of time
Steals ere we can affect them: You remember
The daughter of this lord?

Ber. Admirably my liege: at first
I stuck my choice upon her, ere my heart
Durst make too bold a herald of my tongue:
Where the impression of mine eye infixing,
Contempt his scornful perspective did lend me,
Which warp'd the line of every other favour;
Scorn'd a fair colour, or express'd it stol'n;
Extended or contracted all proportions,
To a most hideous object: Thence it came,
That she, whom all men prais'd, and whom myself,
Since I have lost, have lov'd, was in mine eye
The dust that did offend it.

King. Well excus'd:
That thou didst love her, strikes some scores away
From the great compt: But love, that comes too late,
Like a remorseful pardon slowly carried,
To the great sender turns a sour offence,
Crying, that's good that's gone: our rash faults
Make trivial price of serious things we have,
Not knowing them, until we know their grave:
Oft our displeasures, to ourselves unjust,
Destroy our friends, and after weep their dust:
Our own love waking cries to see what's done,
While shameful hate sleeps out the afternoon.[5]
Be this sweet Helen's knell, and now forget her.
Send forth your amorous token for fair Maudlin:
The main consents are had; and here we'll stay
To see our widower's second marriage-day.

Count. Which better than the first, O dear heaven, bless!
Or, ere they meet, in me, O nature, cease!

Laf. Come on, my son, in whom my house's name
Must be digested, give a favour from you,
To sparkle in the spirits of my daughter,
That she may quickly come.—By my old beard,
And every hair that's on't, Helen, that's dead,
Was a sweet creature; such a ring as this,
The last that e'er I took her leave at court,[6]
I saw upon her finger.

Ber. Hers it was not.

King. Now, pray you, let me see it; for mine eye
While I was speaking, oft was fasten'd to't.—
This ring was mine: and, when I gave it Helen,
I bade her, if her fortune ever stood
Necessitied to help, that by this token[7]
I would relieve her: Had you that craft to reave her
Of what should stead her most?

Ber. My gracious sovereign,
Howe'er it pleases you to take it so,
The ring was never hers.

Count. Son, on my life,
I have seen her wear it; and she reckon'd it
At her life's rate.

Laf. I am sure, I saw her wear it.

Ber. You are deceiv'd, my lord, she never saw it:
In Florence was it from a casement thrown me[8]
Wrapp'd in a paper, which contain'd the name,
Of her that threw it: noble she was, and thought
I stood ingag'd:[9] but when I had subscrib'd[10]
To mine own fortune, and inform'd her fully,
I could not answer in that course of honour
And she had made the overture, she ceas'd,
In heavy satisfaction, and would never
Receive the ring again.

King. Plutus himself,
That knows the tinct and multiplying medicine,
Hath not in nature's mystery more science,
Than I have in this ring: 'twas mine, 'twas Helen's,
Whoever gave it you: Then if you know
That you are well acquainted with yourself,[12]
Confess 'twas hers, and by what rough enforcement
You got it from her: she call'd the saints to surety,
That she would never put it from her finger
Unless she gave it to yourself in bed,
(Where you have never come,) or sent it us
Upon her great disaster.

Ber. She never saw it.

King. Thou speak'st it falsely, as I love mine honour;
And mak'st conjectural fears to come into me,
Which I would fain shut out: If it should prove
That thou art so inhuman,—'twill not prove so;—
And yet I know not:—thou didst hate her deadly,
And she is dead; which nothing, but to close
Her eyes myself, could win me to believe,
More than to see this ring.—Take him away.—
[Guards *seize* Bertram
My fore-past proofs, howe'er the matter fall,
Shall tax my fears of little vanity,
Having vainly fear'd too little.[13]—Away with him;—
We'll sift this matter further.

---

1 So in As You Like It:—to have 'seen much and to have nothing, is to have *rich eyes* and poor hands.' Those who have seen the greatest number of fair women might be said to be the *richest* in ideas of beauty.

2 i. e. the first interview shall put an end to all recollection of the past.

3 i. e. a *seasonable day*; a mixture of sunshine and hail, of winter and summer, is *unseasonable*.

4 Faults repented of to the utmost.

5 This obscure couplet seems to mean that 'Our love awaking to the worth of the lost object too late laments: our shameful hate or dislike having slept out the period when our fault was remediable.'

6 'The last *time* that ever *I took leave of her* at court.'

7 Malone quarrels with the construction of this passage:—'I bade her, &c.—that by this token,' &c. but Shakspeare uses I *bade* her for I *told* her.

8 Johnson remarks that Bertram still continues to have too little virtue to deserve Helen. He did not know it was Helen's ring, but he knew that he had it not from a window.

9 Ingag'd, i. e. pledged to her, having received her pledge.

10 *Subscrib'd*, i. e. *submitted.* See Troilus and Cressida, Act ii. Sc. 3.

11 The philosopher's stone. Plutus, the great alchymist, who knows the secrets of the *elixir* and *philosopher's stone*, by which the alchymists pretended that base metals might be transmuted into gold.

12 Then if you have the proper consciousness of your own actions, confess, &c.

13 The *proofs which I have already had* are sufficient to show that my *fears* were not *vain* and irrational. I have unreasonably feared *too little*.

Ber. If you shall prove
This ring was ever hers, you shall as easy
Prove that I husbanded her bed in Florence,
Where yet she never was.
[*Exit* BERTRAM, *guarded.*

Enter a Gentleman.

King. I am wrapp'd in dismal thinkings.
Gent. Gracious sovereign,
Whether I have been to blame, or no, I know not;
Here's a petition from a Florentine,
Who hath, for four or five removes,[1] come short
To tender it herself. I undertook it,
Vanquish'd thereto by the fair grace and speech
Of the poor suppliant, who by this, I know,
Is here attending: her business looks in her
With an importing visage; and she told me,
In a sweet verbal brief, it did concern
Your highness with herself.

King. [Reads.] *Upon his many protestations to marry me, when his wife was dead, I blush to say it, he won me. Now is the Count Rousillon a widower; his vows are forfeited to me, and my honour's paid to him. He stole from Florence, taking no leave, and I follow him to his country for justice: Grant it me, O king; in you it best lies; otherwise a seducer flourishes, and a poor maid is undone.*
DIANA CAPULET.

Laf. I will buy me a son-in-law in a fair, and toll[2] for this; I'll none of him.
King. The heavens have thought well on thee, Lafeu,
To bring forth this discovery.—Seek these suitors:—
Go, speedily, and bring again the court.
[*Exeunt* Gentleman, *and some* Attendants.
I am afeard, the life of Helen, lady,
Was foully snatch'd.
Count. Now, justice on the doers!

Enter BERTRAM, *guarded.*

King. I wonder, sir, since wives are monsters to you,[3]
And that you fly them as you swear them lordship,
Yet you desire to marry.—What woman's that?

Re-enter Gentleman, *with* Widow, *and* DIANA.

Dia. I am, my lord, a wretched Florentine,
Deriv'd from the ancient Capulet:
My suit, as I do understand, you know,
And therefore know how far I may be pitied.
Wid. I am her mother, sir, whose age and honour
Both suffer under this complaint we bring,
And both shall cease,[4] without your remedy.
King. Come hither, count; Do you know these women?
Ber. My lord, I neither can, nor will deny
But that I know them: Do they charge me further?
Dia. Why do you look so strange upon your wife?
Ber. She's none of mine, my lord.
Dia. If you shall marry,
You give away this hand, and that is mine;
You give away heaven's vows, and those are mine;
You give away myself, which is known mine;
For I by vow am so embodied yours,
That she, which marries you, must marry me,
Either both or none.
Laf. Your reputation [*To* BERTRAM] comes too short for my daughter; you are no husband for her.
Ber. My lord, this is a fond and desperate creature,
Whom sometimes I have laugh'd with: let your highness
Lay a more noble thought upon mine honour,
Than for to think that I would sink it here.
King. Sir, for my thoughts, you have them ill to friend,
Till your deeds gain them: Fairer prove your honour,
Than in my thought it lies!
Dia. Good my lord,
Ask him upon his oath, if he does think
He had not my virginity.
King. What say'st thou to her?
Ber. She's impudent, my lord,
And was a common gamester to the camp.[5]
Dia. He does me wrong, my lord; if I were so,
He might have bought me at a common price:
Do not believe him: O, behold this ring,[6]
Whose high respect, and rich validity,
Did lack a parallel; yet, for all that,
He gave it to a commoner o' the camp,
If I be one.
Count. He blushes, and 'tis it:[7]
Of six preceding ancestors, that gem
Conferr'd by testament to the sequent issue,
Hath it been own'd and worn. This is his wife
That ring's a thousand proofs.
King. Methought, you said
You saw one here in court could witness it.
Dia. I did, my lord, but loath am to produce
So bad an instrument; his name's Parolles.
Laf. I saw the man to-day, if man he be.
King. Find him, and bring him hither.
Ber. What of him?
He's quoted[8] for a most perfidious slave,
With all the spots o' the world tax'd and debosh'd[9]
Whose nature sickens, but to speak a truth:
Am I or that, or this, for what he'll utter,
That will speak any thing?
King. She hath that ring of yours.
Ber. I think she has: certain it is, I lik'd her,
And boarded her i' the wanton way of youth:
She knew her distance, and did angle for me,
Maddening my eagerness with her restraint,
As all impediments in fancy's course
Are motives of more fancy; and, in fine,
Her insult coming with her modern grace,[10]
Subdued me to her rate: she got the ring;
And I had that, which any inferior might
At market-price have bought.
Dia. I must be patient;
You that turned off a first so noble wife,
May justly diet me. I pray you yet,
(Since you lack virtue, I will lose a husband),
Send for your ring, I will return it home,
And give me mine again.
Ber. I have it not.
King. What ring was yours, I pray you?
Dia. Sir, much like
The same upon your finger.
King. Know you this ring? this ring was his of late.
Dia. And this was it I gave him, being a-bed.
King. The story then goes false, you threw it him
Out of a casement.
Dia. I have spoke the truth.

1 *Removes* are *journeys* or *post stages*; she had not been able to overtake the king on the road.

2 The second folio reads:—'I will buy me a son-in-law in a fair, and toll for *him*: for this, I'll none of him.' I prefer the reading of the first folio, as in the text. The allusion is to the custom of paying *toll* for the liberty of selling in a fair, and means, 'I will buy me a son-in-law in a fair, and sell this one; pay *toll* for the liberty of selling him.'

3 The first folio reads:—
'I wonder, sir, *sir*; wives, &c.'
The emendation is Mr. Tyrwhitt's. *As* in the succeeding line means *as soon as*.

4 Decease, die.

5 The following passage from The False One of Beaumont and Fletcher will sufficiently elucidate this term when applied to a female:—
'—————— 'Tis a catalogue
Of all the *gamesters* in the court and city,
Which lord lies with that lady, and what gallant
Sports with that merchant's wife.'

6 i. e. value.

7 Malone remarks that the old copy reads, 'tis *hit* and that in many of our old chronicles he had found *hit* printed instead of *it*. It is not in our old chronicles alone, but in all our old writers that the word may be found in this form.

8 Noted. 9 Debauch'd.

10 'Every thing that obstructs *love* is an occasion by which *love* is heightened, and to conclude her *solicitation* concurring with her *common* or *ordinary* grace *she got the ring*.'

Enter PAROLLES.

Ber. My lord, I do confess the ring was hers.
King. You boggle shrewdly, every feather starts you.——
Is this the man you speak of?
Dia. Ay, my lord.
King. Tell me, sirrah, but tell me true, I charge you,
Not fearing the displeasure of your master
(Which, on your just proceeding, I'll keep off,)
By him, and by this woman here, what know you?

Par. So please your majesty, my master hath been an honourable gentleman; tricks he hath had in him, which gentlemen have.

King. Come, come, to the purpose: Did he love this woman?

Par. 'Faith, sir, he did love her; But how?

King. How, I pray you?

Par. He did love her, sir, as a gentleman loves a woman.

King. How is that?

Par. He loved her, sir, and loved her not.

King. As thou art a knave, and no knave:—
What an equivocal companion[1] is this?

Par. I am a poor man, and at your majesty's command.

Laf. He's a good drum, my lord, but a naughty orator.

Dia. Do you know, he promis'd me marriage?

Par. 'Faith, I know more than I'll speak.

King. But wilt thou not speak all thou know'st?

Par. Yes, so please your majesty: I did go between them, as I said; but more than that, he loved her,—for, indeed, he was mad for her, and talk'd of Satan, and of limbo, and of furies, and I know not what: yet I was in that credit with them at that time, that I knew of their going to bed; and of other motions, as promising her marriage, and things that would derive me ill will to speak of, therefore I will not speak what I know.

King. Thou hast spoken all already, unless thou canst say they are married: But thou art too fine[2] in thy evidence: therefore stand aside.—
This ring, you say, was yours?
Dia. Ay, my good lord.
King. Where did you buy it? or who gave it you?
Dia. It was not given me, nor I did not buy it.
King. Who lent it you?
Dia. It was not lent me neither.
King. Where did you find it then?
Dia. I found it not.
King. If it were yours by none of all these ways,
How could you give it him?
Dia I never gave it him.

Laf. This woman's an easy glove, my lord; she goes off and on at pleasure.

King. This ring was mine, I gave it his first wife.
Dia. It might be yours, or hers, for aught I know.
King. Take her away, I do not like her now;
To prison with her: and away with him.—
Unless thou tell'st me where thou hadst this ring,
Thou diest within this hour.
Dia. I'll never tell you.
King. Take her away.
Dia. I'll put in bail, my liege.
King. I think thee now some common customer.[3]
Dia. By Jove, if ever I knew man, 'twas you.
King Wherefore hast thou accused him all this while?
Dia. Because he's guilty, and he is not guilty;
He knows I am no maid, and he'll swear to't:
I'll swear I am a maid, and he knows not.
Great King, I am no strumpet, by my life;
I am either maid, or else this old man's wife.
[*Pointing to* LAFEU.
King. She does abuse our ears; to prison with her
Dia. Good mother, fetch my bail.—Stay, royal sir; [*Exit* Widow
The jeweller that owes[4] the ring is sent for
And he shall surety me. But for this lord,
Who hath abus'd me, as he knows himself,
Though yet he never harm'd me, here I quit him
He knows himself my bed he hath defil'd;
And at that time he got his wife with child:
Dead though she be, she feels her young one kick;
So there's my riddle, One, that's dead, is quick:
And now behold the meaning.

Re-enter Widow, *with* HELENA.

King. Is there no exorcist[5]
Beguiles the truer office of mine eyes?
Is't real that I see?
Hel. No, my good lord;
'Tis but the shadow of a wife you see,
The name, and not the thing.
Ber. Both, both: O, pardon!
Hel. O, my good lord, when I was like this maid,
I found you wondrous kind. There is your ring,
And, look you, here's your letter: This it says,
When from my finger you can get this ring,
And are by me with child, &c.—This is done:
Will you be mine, now you are doubly won?
Ber. If she, my liege, can make me know this clearly,
I'll love her dearly; ever, ever dearly.
Hel. If it appear not plain, and prove untrue,
Deadly divorce step between me and you!
O, my dear mother, do I see you living?

Laf. Mine eyes smell onions, I shall weep anon:—Good Tom Drum, [*To* PAROLLES,] lend me a handkerchief: So, I thank thee; wait on me home. I'll make sport with thee: Let thy courtesies alone, they are scurvy ones.

King. Let us from point to point this story know,
To make the even truth in pleasure flow:—
If thou be'st yet a fresh uncropped flower,
[*To* DIANA.
Choose thou thy husband, and I'll pay thy dower:
For I can guess, that, by thy honest aid,
Thou kept'st a wife herself, thyself a maid.—
Of that, and all the progress, more and less,
Resolvedly more leisure shall express;
All yet seems well; and if it end so meet,
The bitter past, more welcome is the sweet.
[*Flourish.*

Advancing.

The King's a beggar, now the play is done;
All is well ended, if this suit be won,
That you express content; which we will pay,
With strife to please you, day exceeding day:
Ours be your patience then, and yours our parts,[6]
Your gentle hands lend us, and take our hearts.
[Exeunt.

THIS play has many delightful scenes, though not sufficiently probable, and some happy characters, though not new, nor produced by any deep knowledge of human nature. Parolles is a boaster and a coward, such as has always been the sport of the stage, but perhaps never raised more laughter or contempt than in the hands of Shakspeare.

I cannot reconcile my heart to Bertram; a man noble without generosity, and young without truth; who marries Helen as a coward, and leaves her as a profligate: when she is dead by his unkindness, sneaks home to a second marriage, is accused by a woman he has wronged, defends himself by falsehood, and is dismissed to happiness.

The story of Bertram and Diana had been told before of Mariana and Angelo, and, to confess the truth, scarcely merited to be heard a second time. JOHNSON.

---

1 i. e. fellow.
2 In the French sense *trop fine.*
3 i. e. common woman, with whom any one may be *familiar.*
4 Owns.

5 Thus, in Julius Cæsar, Ligarius says:—
'Thou like an *exorcist* hast conjur'd up
My mortified spirit.'
Exorcist and *conjurer* were synonymous in Shakspeare's time.
6 i. e. hear us without interruption, and take our parts, i. e. support and defend us.

TAMING OF THE SHREW

PRELIMINARY REMARKS.

THERE is an old anonymous play extant with the same title, first printed in 1596, which (as in the case of King John and Henry V.) Shakspeare *rewrote*, 'adopting the order of the scenes, and inserting little more than a few lines which he thought worth preserving, or was in too much haste to alter.' Malone, with great probability, suspects the old play to have been the production of George Peele or Robert Greene.* Pope ascribed it to Shakspeare, and his opinion was current for many years, until a more exact examination of the original piece (which is of extreme rarity) undeceived those who were better versed in the literature of the time of Elizabeth than the poet. It is remarkable that the Induction, as it is called, has not been continued by Shakspeare so as to complete the story of Sly, or at least it has not come down to us; and Pope therefore supplied the deficiencies in this play from the elder performance; they have been degraded from their station in the text, as in some places incompatible with the fable and *Dramatis Personæ* of Shakspeare; the reader will, however, be pleased to find them subjoined to the notes. The origin of this amusing fiction may probably be traced to the sleeper awakened of the Arabian Nights: but similar stories are told of Philip the good Duke of Burgundy, and of the Emperor Charles the Fifth. Marco Polo relates something similar of the Ismaelian Prince Alo-eddin, or chief of the mountainous region, whom he calls, in common with other writers of his time, '*the old man of the mountain*.' Warton refers to a collection of short comic stories in prose, set forth by maister Richard Edwards, master of her majesties revels in 1570 (which he had seen in the collection of Collins the poet), for the immediate source of the fable of the old drama. The incidents related by Heuterus in his *Rerum Burgund.* lib. iv. is also to be found in Goulart's Admirable and Memorable Histories, translated by E. Grimeston, 4to. 1607. The story of Charles V. is related by Sir Richard Barckley, in A Discourse on the Felicitie of Man, printed in 1598; but the frolic, as Mr Holt White observes, seems better suited to the gaiety of the gallant Francis, or the revelry of our own boisterous Henry.

Of the story of the Taming of the Shrew no immediate English source has been pointed out. Mr. Douce has referred to a novel in the Piacevoli Notti of Straparola, notte 8, fav. 2, and to *El Conde Lucanor*, by Don Juan Manuel, Prince of Castile, who died in 1362, as containing similar stories. He observes that the character of Petruchio bears some resemblance to that of *Pisardo* in Straparola's novel, notte 8, fav. 7.

Schlegel remarks that this play 'has the air of an Italian comedy;' and indeed the love intrigue of Lucentio is derived from the Suppositi of Ariosto, through the translation of George Gascoigne. Johnson has observed the skilful combination of the two plots, by which such a variety and succession of comic incident is ensured without running into perplexity. Petruchio is a bold and happy sketch of a humorist, in which Schlegel thinks the character and peculiarities of an Englishman are visible. It affords another example of Shakspeare's deep insight into human character, that in the last scene the meek and mild Bianca shows she is not without a spice of self-will. The play inculcates a fine moral lesson, which is not always taken as it should be.

Every one, who has a true relish for genuine humour, must regret that we are deprived of Shakspeare's continuation of this Interlude of Sly,† 'who is indeed of kin to Sancho Panza.' We think with a late elegant writer, 'the character of Sly, and the remarks with which he accompanies the play, as good as the play itself.'

It appears to have been one of Shakspeare's earliest productions, and is supposed by Malone to have been produced in 1594.

* There was a second edition of the anonymous play in 1607; and the curious reader may consult it, in 'Six old Plays upon which Shakspeare founded, &c.' published by Steevens.

† Dr. Drake suggests that some of the passages in which Sly is introduced should be adopted from the old Drama, and connected with the text, so as to complete his story; making very slight alteration, and distinguishing the borrowed parts by some mark.

PERSONS REPRESENTED.*

A Lord.
CHRISTOPHER SLY, *a drunken Tinker.*
Hostess, Page, Players, Huntsmen, *and other* Servants *attending on the* Lord.
} *Persons in the Induction.*

BAPTISTA, *a rich Gentleman of* Padua.
VINCENTIO, *an old Gentleman of* Pisa.
LUCENTIO, *Son to* Vincentio, *in love with* Bianca.
PETRUCHIO, *a Gentleman of* Verona, *a Suitor to* Katharina.
GREMIO, HORTENSIO, } *Suitors to* Bianca.
TRANIO, BIONDELLO, } *Servants to* Lucentio.
GRUMIO, CURTIS, } *Servants to* Petruchio.
PEDANT, *an old fellow set up to personate* Vincentio

KATHARINA, *the Shrew,* BIANCA, *her Sister,* } *Daughters to* Baptista.
Widow.
Tailor, Haberdasher, *and* Servants *attending on* Baptista *and* Petruchio.

SCENE, *sometimes in* Padua; *and sometimes in* Petruchio's *House in the Country.*

* Characters in the Original Play of *The Taming of a Shrew*, entered on the Stationers' books in 1594, and printed in quarto in 1607.

A Lord, &c.
SLY.
A Tapster.
Page, Players, Huntsmen, &c.
} *Persons in the Induction.*

ALPHONSUS, *A Merchant of* Athens.
JEROBEL, Duke of Cestus.
AURELIUS, *his Son,* FERANDO, POLIDOR, } *Suitors to the Daughters of* Alphonsus
VALERIA, *Servant to* Aurelius.
SANDER, *Servant to* Ferando.
PHYLOTUS, *a Merchant who personates the* Duke.

KATE, EMELIA, PHYLEMA, } *Daughters to* Alphonsus.

Tailor, Haberdasher, *and* Servants *to* Ferando *and* Alphonsus.

SCENE, Athens; *and sometimes* Ferando's *Country House.*

INDUCTION.

SCENE I. *Before an Alehouse on a Heath.* *Enter* Hostess *and* SLY.

Sly.

I'LL pheese[1] you, in faith.

Host. A pair of stocks, you rogue!

Sly. Y'are a baggage; the Slies are no rogues: Look in the chronicles, we came in with Richard Conqueror. Therefore, *paucas pallabris;*[2] let the world slide: *Sessa!*[3]

Host. You will not pay for the glasses you have burst?[4]

Sly. No, not a denier: Go by, says Jeronimy;— Go to thy cold bed, and warm thee.[5]

Host. I know my remedy, I must go fetch the thirdborough.[6] [*Exit.*

Sly. Third, or fourth, or fifth borough, I'll answer him by law: I'll not budge an inch, boy; let him come, and kindly.

[*Lies down on the ground, and falls asleep.*

Wind Horns. Enter a Lord *from Hunting, with Huntsmen and Servants.*

Lord. Huntsman, I charge thee, tender well my hounds:
Brach Merriman,—the poor cur is emboss'd,[7]
And couple Clowder with the deep-mouth'd brach.[8]
Saw'st thou not, boy, how Silver made it good
At the hedge corner, in the coldest fault?
I would not lose the dog for twenty pound.

1 *Hunt.* Why, Belman is as good as he, my lord;
He cried upon it at the merest loss,
And twice to-day pick'd out the dullest scent:
Trust me, I take him for the better dog.

Lord. Thou art a fool; if Echo were as fleet,
I would esteem him worth a dozen such.
But sup them well, and look unto them all;
To-morrow I intend to hunt again.

1 *Hunt.* I will, my lord.

Lord. What's here? one dead, or drunk? See, doth he breathe?

2 *Hunt.* He breathes, my lord: Were he not warm'd with ale,
This were a bed but cold to sleep so soundly.

Lord. O monstrous beast! how like a swine he lies!
Grim death, how foul and loathsome is thine image!
Sirs, I will practise on this drunken man.———
What think you, if he were convey'd to bed,
Wrapp'd in sweet clothes, rings put upon his fingers,
A most delicious banquet by his bed,
And brave attendants near him when he wakes;
Would not the beggar then forget himself?

1 *Hunt.* Believe me, lord, I think he cannot choose.

2 *Hunt.* It would seem strange unto him when he wak'd.

Lord. Even as a flattering dream, or worthless fancy.
Then take him up, and manage well the jest:—
Carry him gently to my fairest chamber,
And hang it round with all my wanton pictures:
Balm his foul head with warm distilled waters,
And burn sweet wood to make the lodging sweet:
Procure me music ready when he wakes,
To make a dulcet and a heavenly sound:
And if he chance to speak, be ready straight,
And, with a low submissive reverence,
Say,—What is it your honour will command?
Let one attend him with a silver bason,
Full of rose-water, and bestrew'd with flowers,
Another bear the ewer, the third a diaper;
And say,—Will't please your Lordship cool your hands?
Some one be ready with a costly suit,
And ask him what apparel he will wear;
Another tell him of his hounds and horse,
And that his lady mourns at his disease:
Persuade him that he hath been lunatic.
And, when he says he is—, say that he dreams,
For he is nothing but a mighty lord.
This do, and do it kindly,[9] gentle sirs;
It will be pastime passing excellent,
If it be husbanded with modesty.[10]

1 *Hunt.* My lord, I warrant you, we'll play our part,
As he shall think, by our true diligence,
He is no less than what we say he is.

Lord. Take him up gently, and to bed with him:
And each one to his office when he wakes.—

[*Some bear out* SLY. *A trumpet sounds.*

Sirrah, go see what trumpet 'tis that sounds:---

[*Exit* Servant.

Belike, some noble gentleman; that means,
Travelling some journey, to repose him here.

Re-enter a Servant.

How now? who is it?

Serv. An it please your honour,
Players that offer service to your lordship.

Lord. Bid them come near:---

Enter Players.

Now, fellows, you are welcome

1 *Play.* We thank your honour.

Lord. Do you intend to stay with me to-night?

2 *Play.* So please your lordship to accept our duty?[11]

Lord. With all my heart.---This fellow I remember,
Since once he play'd a farmer's eldest son;---
'Twas where you woo'd the gentlewoman so well
I have forgot your name; but, sure, that part
Was aptly fitted, and naturally perform'd.

1 *Play.* I think 'twas Soto that your honour means.[12]

Lord. 'Tis very true;---thou didst it excellent.—
Well, you are come to me in happy time;
The rather for I have some sport in hand,
Wherein your cunning can assist me much.
There is a lord will hear you play to-night·
But I am doubtful of your modesties;
Lest, over-eying of his odd behaviour,
(For yet his honour never heard a play),
You break into some merry passion,
And so offend him? for I tell you, sirs,
If you should smile, he grows impatient.

1 *Play.* Fear not, my lord; we can contain ourselves,
Were he the veriest antick in the world.[13]

1 So again in Troilus and Cressida, Ajax says of Achilles:—'I'll pheese his pride.' And in Ben Jonson's Alchemist:
'Come, will you quarrel? I'll *feize* you, sirrah.'

2 Pocas palabras, *Span.* few words.

3 Cessa, *Ital.* be quiet.

4 Broke.

5 This line and the scrap of Spanish is used in burlesque from an old play called Hieronymo, or the Spanish Tragedy. The old copy reads: 'S. Jeronimy.' The emendation is Mason's.

6 An officer whose authority equals that of a constable.

7 '*Emboss'd,*' says Philips in his World of Words, 'is a term in hunting, *when a deer is so hard chased that she foams at the mouth;* it comes from the Spanish *Desembocar*, and is metaphorically used for any kind of *weariness.*'

8 *Brach* originally signified a particular species of dog used for the chace. It was a long eared dog, hunting by the scent.

9 Naturally.

10 Moderation.

11 It was in old times customary for players to travel in companies and offer their service at great houses.

12 The old copy prefixes the name of *Sincklo* to this line, who was an actor in the same company with Shakspeare. *Soto* is a character in Beaumont and Fletcher's Woman Pleased; he is *a farmer's eldest son*, but he does not *woo any gentlewoman.*

13 In the old play the dialogue is thus continued:
'*San.* [*To the other.*] Go get a dishclout to make cleyne your shooes, and Ile speak for the properties [*Exit* Player.] My lord, we must have a shoulder of mutton for a property, and a little vinegre to make our divell roar.'

Lord. Go, sirrah, take them to the buttery,[1]
And give them friendly welcome every one:
Let them want nothing that my house affords.---
[*Exeunt* Servants *and* Players.
Sirrah, go you to Bartholomew my page
[*To a* Servant.
And see him dress'd in all suits like a lady:
That done, conduct him to the drunkard's chamber,
And call him---Madam, do him obeisance,
Tell him from me (as he will win my love),
He bear himself with honourable action,
Such as he hath observ'd in noble ladies
Unto their lords, by them accomplish'd:
Such duty to the drunkard let him do,
With soft low tongue, and lowly courtesy:
And say,—What is't your honour will command,
Wherein your lady and your humble wife,
May show her duty, and make known her love?
And then—with kind embracements, tempting kisses,
And with declining head into his bosom,—
Bid him shed tears, as being overjoy'd
To see her noble lord restored to health,
Who, for twice[2] seven years, hath esteem'd him[3]
No better than a poor and loathsome beggar:
And if the boy have not a woman's gift,
To rain a shower of commanded tears,
An onion will do well for such a shift:
Which in a napkin being close convey'd,
Shall in despite enforce a watery eye.
See this despatch'd with all the haste thou canst;
Anon I'll give thee more instructions.——
[*Exit* Servant.
I know the boy will well usurp the grace,
Voice, gait, and action of a gentlewoman:
I long to hear him call the drunkard husband;
And how my men will stay themselves from laughter,
When they do homage to this simple peasant.
I'll in to counsel them: haply,[4] my presence
May well abate the over-merry spleen,
Which otherwise would grow into extremes.
[*Exeunt.*

SCENE II. *A Bedchamber in the* Lord's *House.* SLY *is discovered in a rich night gown, with Attendants; some with apparel, others with bason, ewer, and other appurtenances. Enter* Lord, *dressed like a Servant.*[5]

Sly. For God's sake, a pot of small ale.

1 *Serv.* Will't please your lordship drink a cup of sack?

2 *Serv.* Will't please your honour taste of these conserves?

3 *Serv.* What raiment will your honour wear to-day?

Sly. I am Christophero Sly; call not me—honour, nor lordship: I never drank sack in my life; and if you give me any conserves, give me conserves of beef. Ne'er ask me what raiment I'll wear: for I have no more doublets than backs, no more stockings than legs, nor no more shoes than feet; nay, sometimes, more feet than shoes, or such shoes as my toes look through the over leather.

Lord. Heaven cease this idle humour in your honour!
O, that a mighty man of such descent,
Of such possessions, and so high esteem,
Should be infused with so foul a spirit!

Sly. What, would you make me mad? Am not I Christopher Sly, old Sly's son of Burton-heath; by birth a pedler, by education a card-maker, by transmutation a bear-herd, and now by present profession a tinker? Ask Marian Hacket, the fat ale-wife of Wincot,[6] if she know me not: if she say I am not fourteen pence on the score for sheer ale,[7] score me up for the lyingest knave in Christendom. What, I am not bestraught:[8] Here's——

1 *Serv.* O, this it is that makes your lady mourn.

2 *Serv.* O, this it is that makes your servants droop.

Lord. Hence comes it that your kindred shun your house,
As beaten hence by your strange lunacy.
O, noble lord, bethink thee of thy birth;
Call home thy ancient thoughts from banishment,
And banish hence these abject lowly dreams:
Look how thy servants do attend on thee,
Each in his office ready at thy beck.
Wilt thou have music? hark! Apollo plays,
[*Music.*
And twenty caged nightingales do sing:
Or wilt thou sleep? we'll have thee to a couch,
Softer and sweeter than the lustful bed
On purpose trimm'd up for Semiramis.
Say, thou wilt walk; we will bestrew the ground.
Or wilt thou ride? thy horses shall be trapp'd,
Their harness studded all with gold and pearl.
Dost thou love hawking? thou hast hawks will soar
Above the morning lark: Or wilt thou hunt?
Thy hounds shall make the welkin answer them,
And fetch shrill echoes from the hollow earth.

1 *Serv.* Say, thou wilt course; thy greyhounds are as swift
As breathed stags, ay, fleeter than the roe.

2 *Serv.* Dost thou love pictures? we will fetch thee straight
Adonis, painted by a running brook;
And Cytherea all in sedges hid;
Which seem to move and wanton with her breath,
Even as the waving sedges play with wind.

Lord. We'll show thee Io, as she was a maid;
And how she was beguiled and surpris'd,
As lively painted as the deed was done.

3 *Serv.* Or Daphne roaming through a thorny wood:
Scratching her legs that one shall swear she bleeds:
And at that sight shall sad Apollo weep,
So workmanly the blood and tears are drawn.

Lord. Thou art a lord, and nothing but a lord:
Thou hast a lady far more beautiful
Than any woman in this waning age.

1 *Serv.* And, till the tears that she hath shed for thee,
Like envious floods, o'er-ran her lovely face,
She was the fairest creature in the world;
And yet she is inferior to none.

Sly. Am I a lord; and have I such a lady;
Or do I dream? or have I dream'd till now?
I do not sleep; I see, I hear, I speak;
I smell sweet savours, and I feel soft things:
Upon my life, I am a lord, indeed;
And not a tinker, nor Christophero Sly.—
Well, bring our lady hither to our sight;
And once again, a pot o'the smallest ale.

2 *Serv.* Will't please your mightiness to wash your hands;
[Servants *present a ewer, bason, and napkin.*

---

1 Pope remarks, in his preface to Shakspeare, that 'the top of the profession were then mere players, not gentlemen of the stage; they were led into the *buttery*, not placed at the lord's table, or the lady's toilette.'

2 The old copy reads *this*. The emendation is Theobald's.

3 *Him* is used for *himself*, as in Chapman's Banquet of Sense, 1595:
'The sense wherewith he feels *him* deified.'

4 Perhaps.

5 From the original stage direction in the first folio, it appears that Sly and the other persons mentioned in the Induction were intended to be exhibited here, and during the representation of the comedy, in a balcony above the stage.

6 *Wilnecotte*, says Warton, is a village in Warwickshire, with which Shakspeare was well acquainted, near Stratford. The house kept by our genial hostess still remains, but is at present a mill. There is a village also called *Barton on the heath* in Warwickshire.

7 *Sheer-ale* has puzzled the commentators; and as none of the conjectures offered appear to me satisfactory, I shall add one of my own. Maunday Thursday, the day preceding Good-Friday, was anciently called *Sheer*-Thursday, and as it was a day of great comfort to the poor from the doles or distribution of clothes, meat and drink, made by the rich; so *Sheer*-ale may have been ale which the Tinker had drunk on that day, at his own charge, or rather at that of his landlady, in addition to the portion he had received as alms. But after all, *sheer-ale* may mean nothing more than *ale unmixed, mere-ale*, or *pure ale*. The word *sheer* is still used for *mere, pure*.

8 i. e. distraught, distracted.

O, how we joy to see your wit restor'd!
O, that once more you knew but what you are!
These fifteen years you have been in a dream;
Or, when you wak'd, so wak'd as if you slept.
Sly. These fifteen years! by my fay,[1] a goodly nap.
But did I never speak of all that time?
1 *Serv*. O, yes, my lord; but very idle words:—
For though you lay here in this goodly chamber,
Yet would you say, ye were beaten out of door;
And rail upon the hostess of the house;
And say, you would present her at the leet,[2]
Because she brought stone jugs and no seal'd quarts:
Sometimes you would call out for Cicely Hacket.
Sly. Ay, the woman's maid of the house.
3 *Serv*. Why, sir, you know no house, nor no such maid,
Nor no such men as you have reckon'd up,—
As Stephen Sly, and old John Naps of Greece,[3]
And Peter Turf, and Henry Pimpernell;
And twenty more such names and men as these,
Which never were, nor no man ever saw.
Sly. Now, Lord be thanked for my good amends!
All. Amen.
Sly. I thank thee; thou shalt not lose by it.

Enter the Page, *as a Lady, with* Attendants.

Page. How fares my noble lord?
Sly. Marry, I fare well; for here is cheer enough.
Where is my wife?
Page. Here, noble lord; What is thy will with her?
Sly. Are you my wife, and will not call me—husband?
My men should call me—lord; I am your goodman.
Page. My husband and my lord, my lord and husband;
I am your wife in all obedience.
Sly. I know it well:—What must I call her?
Lord. Madam.
Sly. Al'ce madam, or Joan madam?
Lord. Madam, and nothing else: so lords call ladies.
Sly. Madam wife, they say that I have dream'd and slept
Above some fifteen year and more.
Page. Ay, and the time seems thirty unto me;
Being all this time abandon'd from your bed.
Sly. 'Tis much;——Servants, leave me and her alone.—
Madam, undress you, and come now to bed.
Page. Thrice noble lord, let me entreat of you
To pardon me yet for a night or two;
Or, if not so, until the sun be set:
For your physicians have expressly charg'd,
In peril to incur your former malady,
That I should yet absent me from your bed:
I hope this reason stands for my excuse.
Sly. Ay, it stands so, that I may hardly tarry so long. But I would be loath to fall into my dreams again; I will therefore tarry, in despite of the flesh and the blood.

Enter a Servant.

Serv. Your honour's players, hearing your amendment,
Are come to play a pleasant comedy,
For so your doctors hold it very meet;
Seeing too much sadness hath congeal'd your blood,
And melancholy is the nurse of frenzy,
Therefore they thought it good you hear a play,
And frame your mind to mirth and merriment,
Which bars a thousand harms, and lengthens life.
Sly. Marry, I will; let them play it: Is not a commonty[4] a Christmas gambol, or a tumbling trick?
Page. No, my good lord; it is more pleasing stuff.
Sly. What, household stuff?
Page. It is a kind of history.
Sly. Well, we'll see't: Come, madam wife, sit by my side, and let the world slip; we shall ne'er be younger. [*They sit down.*

ACT I.

SCENE I. Padua. *A public Place. Enter* LUCENTIO *and* TRANIO.

Luc. Tranio, since—for the great desire I had
To see fair Padua, nursery of arts,—
I am arriv'd for fruitful Lombardy,
The pleasant garden of great Italy;
And, by my father's love and leave, am arm'd
With his good will, and thy good company,
Most trusty servant, well approv'd in all;
Here let us breathe, and happily institute
A course of learning, and ingenious[5] studies.
Pisa, renowned for grave citizens,
Gave me my being, and my father first,
A merchant of great traffic through the world,
Vincentio, come of the Bentivolii.
Vincentio's son, brought up in Florence,
It shall become, to serve all hopes conceiv'd,[6]
To deck his fortune with his virtuous deeds:
And therefore, Tranio, for the time I study,
Virtue, and that part of philosophy
Will I apply,[7] that treats of happiness
By virtue 'specially to be achiev'd.
Tell me thy mind: for I have Pisa left,
And am to Padua come: as he that leaves
A shallow plash,[8] to plunge him in the deep,
And with satiety seeks to quench his thirst.
Tra. *Mi perdonate*,[9] gentle master mine,
I am in all affected as yourself.
Glad that you thus continue your resolve,
To suck the sweets of sweet philosophy.
Only, good master, while we do admire
This virtue, and this moral discipline,
Let's be no stoics, nor no stocks, I pray:
Or so devote to Aristotle's ethics,[10]
As Ovid be an outcast quite abjur'd:
Balke[11] logic with acquaintance that you have,
And practise rhetoric in your common talk:
Music and poesy use to quicken[12] you;
The mathematics, and the metaphysics,
Fall to them as you find your stomach serves you
No profit grows where is no pleasure ta'en:—
In brief, sir, study what you most affect.
Luc. Gramercies, Tranio, well dost thou advise
If, Biondello, thou wert come ashore,
We could at once put us in readiness;
And take a lodging fit to entertain
Such friends as time in Padua shall beget.
But stay awhile: What company is this?
Tra. Master, some show, to welcome us to town

Enter BAPTISTA, KATHARINA, BIANCA, GREMIO, *and* HORTENSIO. LUCENTIO *and* TRANIO *stand aside*.

Bap. Gentlemen, importune me no further,
For how I firmly am resolv'd you know;
That is—not to bestow my youngest daughter,

1 According to some old authorities, Sly here uses a very ladylike imprecation. 'Ecastor,' says Cooper, '*by my fay*, used only of women.' It is merely a contraction of *by my faith*.
2 That is at the *Court Leet*, where it was usual to present such matters, as appears from Kitchen on Courts: 'Also if tiplers sell by *cups* and dishes, *or measures sealed* or *not sealed*, is inquirable.'
3 Blackstone proposes to read, 'old John Naps o'the Green.' The addition seems to have been a common one.
4 For comedy.
5 *Ingenious* and *ingenuous* were very commonly confounded by old writers.
6 i. e. to fulfil the expectations of his friends.
7 *Apply* for *ply* is frequently used by old writers Thus Baret: 'with diligent endeavour to *applie* their studies.' And in Turberville's Tragic Tales: 'How she her wheele *applyde*.'
8 Small piece of water.
9 Pardon me.
10 The old copy reads Aristotle's *checks*. Blackstone suggests that we should read *ethics*, and the sense seems to require it; I have therefore admitted it into the text.
11 The modern editions read, '*Talk* logic, &c. The old copy reads *Balke*, which Mr. Boswell suggests may be right, although the meaning of the word is now lost
12 Animate.

Before I have a husband for the elder:
If either of you both love Katharina,
Because I know you well, and love you well,
Leave shall you have to court her at your pleasure.

Gre. To cart her rather: She's too rough for me:—
There, there, Hortensio, will you any wife?

Kath. I pray you, sir, [*To* BAP.] is it your will
To make a stale[1] of me amongst these mates?

Hor. Mates, maid! how mean you that? no mates for you,
Unless you were of gentler, milder mould.

Kath. I'faith, sir, you shall never need to fear;
I wis,[2] it is not half way to her heart:
But if it were, doubt not her care should be
To comb your noddle with a three-legg'd stool,
And paint your face, and use you like a fool.

Hor. From all such devils, good Lord, deliver us!

Gre. And me too, good Lord!

Tra. Hush, master! here is some good pastime toward;
That wench is stark mad, or wonderful froward.

Luc. But in the other's silence I do see
Maid's mild behaviour and sobriety.
Peace, Tranio.

Tra. Well said, master; mum! and gaze your fill.

Bap. Gentlemen, that I may soon make good
What I have said,—Bianca, get you in:
And let it not displease thee, good Bianca;
For I will love thee ne'er the less, my girl.

Kath. A pretty peat![3] 'tis best
Put finger in the eye,—an she knew why.

Bian. Sister, content you in my discontent.—
Sir, to your pleasure humbly I subscribe:
My books, and instruments, shall be my company;
On them to look, and practise by myself.

Luc. Hark, Tranio! thou may'st hear Minerva speak. [*Aside.*

Hor. Signior Baptista, will you be so strange?[4]
Sorry am I that our goodwill effects
Bianca's grief.

Gre. Why, will you mew[5] her up,
Signior Baptista, for this fiend of hell,
And make her bear the penance of her tongue?

Bap. Gentlemen, content ye; I am resolv'd:—
Go in, Bianca, [*Exit* BIANCA.
And for I know, she taketh most delight
In music, instruments, and poetry,
Schoolmasters will I keep within my house,
Fit to instruct her youth.—If you, Hortensio,
Or signior Gremio, you,—know any such,
Prefer[6] them hither; for to cunning[7] men
I will be very kind, and liberal
To mine own children in good bringing up;
And so farewell. Katharina, you may stay:
For I have more to commune with Bianca. [*Exit.*

Kath. Why, and I trust, I may go too: May I not?
What, shall I be appointed hours; as though, belike,
I knew not what to take and what to leave? Ha! [*Exit.*

Gre. You may go to the devil's dam: your gifts[8] are so good, here is none will hold you. Their[9] love is not so great, Hortensio, but we may blow our nails together, and fast it fairly out; our cake's dough on both sides. Farewell,—yet, for the love bear my sweet Bianca, if I can by any means light on a fit man to teach her that wherein she delights, I will wish[10] him to her father.

Hor. So will I, signior Gremio: but a word, I pray. Though the nature of our quarrel yet never brook'd parle, know now, upon advice,[11] it toucheth us both,—that we may yet again have access to our fair mistress, and be happy rivals in Bianca's love,—to labour and effect one thing 'specially.

Gre. What's that, I pray?

Hor. Marry, sir, to get a husband for her sister.

Gre. A husband! a devil.

Hor. I say, a husband.

Gre. I say, a devil: Think'st thou, Hortensio, though her father be very rich, any man is so very a fool to be married to hell?

Hor. Tush, Gremio, though it pass your patience and mine, to endure her loud alarums, why, man, there be good fellows in the world, an a man could light on them, would take her with all faults, and money enough.

Gre. I cannot tell; but I had as lief take her dowry with this condition,—to be whipped at the high-cross every morning.

Hor. 'Faith, as you say, there's small choice in rotten apples. But come; since this bar in law makes us friends, it shall be so far forth friendly maintained,—till by helping Baptista's eldest daughter to a husband, we set his youngest free for a husband, and then have to't afresh.—Sweet Bianca!—Happy man be his dole![12] He that runs fastest, gets the ring.[13] How say you, signior Gremio?

Gre. I am agreed: and 'would I had given him the best horse in Padua to begin his wooing, that would thoroughly woo her, wed her, and bed her, and rid the house of her. Come on.

[*Exeunt* GREMIO *and* HORTENSIO.

Tra. [*Advancing.*] I pray, sir, tell me,—Is it possible
That love should of a sudden take such hold?

Luc. O Tranio, till I found it to be true,
I never thought it possible, or likely;
But see! while idly I stood looking on,
I found the effect of love in idleness:
And now in plainness do confess to thee,—
That art to me as secret, and as dear,
As Anna to the queen of Carthage was,—
Tranio, I burn, I pine, I perish, Tranio,
If I achieve not this young modest girl:
Counsel me, Tranio for I know thou canst;
Assist me, Tranio, for I know thou wilt.

Tra. Master, it is no time to chide you now,
Affection is not rated[14] from the heart:
If love have touch'd you, nought remains but so,—
Redime te captum quam queas minimo.[15]

Luc. Gramercies, lad; go forward: this contents;
The rest will comfort, for thy counsel's sound.

Tra. Master, you look'd so longly[16] on the maid,
Perhaps you mark'd not what's the pith of all.

Luc. O yes, I saw sweet beauty in her face,
Such as the daughter[17] of Agenor had,
That made great Jove to humble him to her hand,
When with his knees he kiss'd the Cretan strand.

Tra. Saw you no more; mark'd you not, how her sister
Began to scold; and raise up such a storm,
That mortal ears might hardly endure the din?

Luc. Tranio, I saw her coral lips to move,
And with her breath she did perfume the air;
Sacred, and sweet, was all I saw in her.

---

1 She means 'do you intend to make a *strumpet* of me among these *companions?*' But the expression seems to have a quibbling allusion to the chess term of *stale-mate.*

2 Think.

3 Pet.

4 i. e. so odd, so different from others in your conduct.

5 To *mew* up, was to confine or shut up close, as it was the custom to confine hawks while they *mew'd* or moulted. *V.* note on K. Richard III. Act. i. Sc. 1.

6 Recommend.

7 *Cunning* has not yet lost its original signification of *knowing, learned* as may be observed in the translation of the Bible.

8 Endowments.

9 It seems that we should read—*Your* love. yr. in old writing stood for either *their* or *your.* If *their* love be right, it must mean—the goodwill of Baptista and Bianca towards us.

10 i. e. I will *recommend* him.

11 Consideration, or reflection

12 A proverbial expression. *Dole* is *lot, portion.* The phrase is of very common occurrence.

13 The allusion is probably to the sport of running at the *ring*, or some similar game.

14 Is not driven out by chiding.

15 This line is quoted as it appears in Lilly's Grammar, and not as it is in Terence. See Farmer's Essay on the Learning of Shakspeare.

16 Longingly.

17 Europa

Tra. Nay, then, 'tis time to stir him from his trance.
I pray, awake, sir; If you love the maid,
Bend thoughts and wits to achieve her. Thus it stands:
Her elder sister is so curst and shrewd,
That, till the father rids his hands of her,
Master, your love must live a maid at home:
And therefore has he closely mew'd her up,
Because she shall not be annoy'd with suitors.

Luc. Ah, Tranio, what a cruel father's he!
But art thou not advis'd, he took some care
To get her cunning schoolmasters to instruct her?

Tra. Ay, marry, am I, sir; and now 'tis plotted.

Luc. I have it, Tranio.

Tra. Master, for my hand,
Both our inventions meet and jump in one.

Luc. Tell me thine first.

Tra. You will be schoolmaster,
And undertake the teaching of the maid:
That's your device.

Luc. It is: May it be done?

Tra. Not possible: For who shall bear your part,
And be in Padua here Vincentio's son?
Keep house, and ply his book; welcome his friends;
Visit his countrymen, and banquet them?

Luc. Basta;[1] content thee, for I have it full.
We have not yet been seen in any house;
Nor can we be distinguish'd by our faces,
For man, or master: then it follows thus:—
Thou shalt be master, Tranio, in my stead,
Keep house, and port,[2] and servants, as I should:
I will some other be; some Florentine,
Some Neapolitan, or meaner man of Pisa.
'Tis hatch'd, and shall be so: Tranio, at once
Uncase thee; take my colour'd hat and cloak:
When Biondello comes, he waits on thee:
But I will charm him first to keep his tongue.

Tra. So had you need. [*They exchange habits.*
In brief then, sir, sith[3] it your pleasure is,
And I am tied to be obedient;
(For so your father charg'd me at our parting;
Be serviceable to my son, quoth he;
Although, I think, 'twas in another sense;)
I am content to be Lucentio,
Because so well I love Lucentio.

Luc. Tranio, be so, because Lucentio loves.
And let me be a slave, to achieve that maid
Whose sudden sight hath thrall'd my wounded eye.

Enter BIONDELLO.

Here comes the rogue.—Sirrah, where have you been?

Bion. Where have I been? Nay, how now, where are you?
Master, has my fellow Tranio stol'n your clothes?
Or you stol'n his? or both? pray what's the news?

Luc. Sirrah, come hither; 'tis no time to jest,
And therefore frame your manners to the time.
Your fellow Tranio here, to save my life,
Puts my apparel and my countenance on,
And I for my escape have put on his;
For in a quarrel, since I came ashore,
I kill'd a man, and fear I was descried:
Wait you on him, I charge you, as becomes,
While I make way from hence to save my life:
You understand me?

Bion. I, sir, ne'er a whit.

Luc. And not a jot of Tranio in your mouth;
Tranio is chang'd into Lucentio.

Bion. The better for him: 'Would, I were so too!

Tra. So would I, faith, boy, to have the next wish after,—
That Lucentio indeed had Baptista's youngest daughter.
But, sirrah,—not for my sake, but your master's—I advise
You use your manners discreetly in all kind of companies:
When I am alone, why then I am Tranio;
But in all places else, your master Lucentio.

Luc. Tranio, let's go:—
One thing more rests, that thyself execute.
To make one among these wooers: If thou ask me why,—
Sufficeth, my reasons are both good and weighty.
[*Exeunt.*[4]

1 Serv. *My lord, you nod; you do not mind the play.*

Sly. *Yes, by Saint Anne, do I. A good matter, surely: Comes there any more of it?*

Page. *My lord, 'tis but begun.*

Sly. *'Tis a very excellent piece of work, madam lady: 'Would, 'twere done!*

SCENE II. *The same. Before* Hortensio's *House*

Enter PETRUCHIO *and* GRUMIO.

Pet. Verona, for a while I take my leave,
To see my friends in Padua; but, of all,
My best beloved and approved friend,
Hortensio; and, I trow, this is his house:—
Here, sirrah Grumio; knock, I say.

Gru. Knock, sir! whom should I knock? is there any man has rebused your worship?

Pet. Villain, I say, knock me here soundly.

Gru. Knock you here, sir? why, sir, what am I, sir, that I should knock you here, sir?[5]

Pet. Villain, I say, knock me at this gate,
And rap me well, or I'll knock your knave's pate.

Gru. My master is grown quarrelsome: I should knock you first,
And then I know after who comes by the worst.

Pet. Will it not be?
'Faith, sirrah, an you'll not knock, I'll wring it;
I'll try how you can *sol, fa*, and sing it.
[*He wrings* GRUMIO *by the ears.*

Gru. Help, masters, help! my master is mad.

Pet. Now, knock when I bid you: sirrah! villain!

Enter HORTENSIO.

Hor. How now? what's the matter?—My old friend Grumio! and my good friend Petruchio!—
How do you all at Verona!

Pet. Signior Hortensio, come you to part the fray?
Con tutto il core bene trovato, may I say.

Hor. *Alla nostra casa bene venuto,*
Molto honorato, signor mio Petruchio.[6]
Rise, Grumio, rise; we will compound this quarrel.

Gru. Nay, 'tis no matter what he leges[7] in Latin.—If this be not a lawful cause for me to leave his service.—Look you, sir, he bid me knock him, and rap him soundly, sir: Well, was it fit for a servant to use his master so: being, perhaps, (for aught I see) two and thirty,—a pip out?[8]
Whom, 'would to God, I had well knock'd at first,
Then had not Grumio come by the worst.

Pet. A senseless villain—Good Hortensio,
I bade the rascal knock upon your gate,
And could not get him for my heart to do it.

Gru. Knock at the gate?—O heavens!
Spake you not these words plain,—*Sirrah, knock me here,*
Rap me here, knock me well, and knock me soundly?
And come you now with—knocking at the gate?

---

1 It is enough, *Ital.*

2 *Port* is figure, show, appearance.

3 Since.

4 Here in the old copy we have, 'The presenters above speak;' meaning Sly, &c. who were placed in a balcony raised at the back of the stage. After the words 'would it were done,' the marginal direction is, *They sit and mark.*

5 Malone remarks that Grumio's pretensions to wit have a strong resemblance to Dromio's, in The Comedy of Errors; and the two plays were probably written at no great distance of time from each other. I have elsewhere had occasion to observe that the idiom, 'Knock *me* here,' is familiar to the French language.

6 Gascoigne in his Supposes has spelt this name correctly *Petrucio*, but Shakspeare wrote it as it appears in the text, in order to teach the actors how to pronounce it

7 i. e. what he *alleges* in Latin. Grumio mistakes the *Italian* spoken for *Latin*. Tyrwhitt suggests that we should read—' Nay, 'tis no matter what *be leges* in Latin, if this be not a lawful cause for me to leave his service.' That is, ' 'Tis no matter what is *law* if this be not a lawful cause,' &c.

8 This passage has escaped the commentators, and yet it is more obscure than many they have explained

Pet. Sirrah, be gone, or talk not, I advise you.
Hor. Petruchio, patience; I am Grumio's pledge:
Why, this a heavy chance 'twixt him and you;
Your ancient, trusty, pleasant servant, Grumio.
And tell me now, sweet friend,—what happy gale
Blows you to Padua here, from old Verona?
Pet. Such wind as scatters young men through the world,
To seek their fortunes further than at home,
Where small experience grows. But, in a few,[1]
Signior Hortensio, thus it stands with me:—
Antonio, my father, is deceas'd;
And I have thrust myself into this maze,
Haply to wive, and thrive, as best I may:
Crowns in my purse I have, and goods at home,
And so am come abroad to see the world.
Hor. Petruchio, shall I then come roundly to thee,
And wish thee to a shrewd ill-favour'd wife?
Thou'dst thank me but a little for my counsel:
And yet I'll promise thee she shall be rich,
And very rich:—But thou'rt too much my friend,
And I'll not wish thee to her.
Pet. Signior Hortensio; 'twixt such friends as we
Few words suffice: and, therefore, if thou know
One rich enough to be Petruchio's wife,
(As wealth is burthen of my wooing dance,)
Be she as foul as was Florentius' love,[2]
As old as Sibyl, and as curst and shrewd
As Socrates' Xantippe, or a worse,
She moves me not, or not removes, at least,
Affection's edge in me; were she as rough
As are the swelling Adriatic seas;
I come to wive it wealthily in Padua;
If wealthily, then happily in Padua.
Gru. Nay, look you, sir, he tells you flatly what his mind is: Why, give him gold enough and marry him to a puppet, or an aglet-baby;[3] or an old trot with ne'er a tooth in her head, though she have as many diseases as two and fifty horses:[4] why, nothing comes amiss, so money comes withal.
Hor. Petruchio, since we have stepp'd thus far in,
I will continue that I broach'd in jest.
I can, Petruchio, help thee to a wife
With wealth enough, and young, and beauteous;
Brought up as best becomes a gentlewoman;
Her only fault (and that is faults enough,)
Is,—that she is intolerably curst,[5]
And shrewd, and froward; so beyond all measure,
That, were my state far worser than it is,
I would not wed her for a mine of gold.
Pet. Hortensio, peace; thou know'st not gold's effect:
Tell me her father's name, and 'tis enough;
For I will board her, though she chide as loud
As thunder, when the clouds in autumn crack.
Hor. Her father is Baptista Minola,
An affable and courteous gentleman:
Her name is Katharina Minola,
Renown'd in Padua for her scolding tongue.
Pet. I know her father, though I know not her;
And he knew my deceased father well:
I will not sleep, Hortensio, till I see her;
And therefore let me be thus bold with you,
To give you over at this first encounter,
Unless you will accompany me thither.
Gru. I pray you, sir, let him go while the humour lasts. O' my word, an she knew him as well as I do, she would think scolding would do little good upon him: She may, perhaps, call him half a score knaves or so: why, that's nothing; an he begin once, he'll rail in his rope-tricks.[6] I'll tell you what, sir,—an she stand[7] him but a little, he will throw a figure in her face, and so disfigure her with it, that she shall have no more eyes to see withal than a cat:[8] You know him not, sir.
Hor. Tarry, Petruchio, I must go with thee,
For in Baptista's keep[9] my treasure is:
He hath the jewel of my life in hold,
His youngest daughter, beautiful Bianca;
And her withholds from me, and other more
Suitors to her, and rivals in my love:
Supposing it a thing impossible,
(For those defects I have before rehears'd,)
That ever Katharina will be woo'd;
Therefore this order[10] hath Baptista ta'en;—
That none shall have access unto Bianca,
Till Katharine the curst have got a husband.
Gru. Katharine the curst!
A title for a maid, of all titles the worst.
Hor. Now shall my friend Petruchio do me grace,
And offer me, disguis'd in sober robes,
To old Baptista as a schoolmaster
Well seen[11] in musick, to instruct Bianca:
That so I may by this device, at least,
Have leave and leisure to make love to her,
And, unsuspected, court her by herself.

Enter GREMIO; *with him* LUCENTIO *disguised, with books under his arm.*

Gru. Here's knavery! See, to beguile the old folks, how the young folks lay their heads together! Master, master, look about you: Who goes there? ha!
Hor. Peace, Grumio: 'tis the rival of my love:—
Petruchio, stand by a while.
Gru. A proper stripling, and an amorous!
[*They retire.*
Gre. O, very well; I have perus'd the note.
Hark you, sir; I'll have them very fairly bound:
All books of love, see that at any hand;[12]
And see you read no other lectures to her:
You understand me;—Over and beside
Signior Baptista's liberality,
I'll mend it with a largess:[13] Take your papers too,
And let me have them very well perfum'd;
For she is sweeter than perfume itself,
To whom they go. What will you read to her?
Luc. Whate'er I read to her, I'll plead for you,
As for my patron, (stand you so assur'd,)
As firmly as yourself were still in place:
Yea, and (perhaps) with more successful words
Than you, unless you were a scholar, sir.
Gre. O this learning; what a thing it is!
Gru. O this woodcock! what an ass it is!
Pet. Peace, sirrah.
Hor. Grumio, mum!—God save you, signior Gremio!
Gre. And you're well met, signior Hortensio. Trow you,
Whither I am going?—To Baptista Minola.
I promis'd to enquire carefully
About a schoolmaster for fair Bianca:
And, by good fortune, I have lighted well

Perhaps it was passed over because it was not understood? The allusion is to the old game of *Bone-ace* or *one-and-thirty*. A *pip* is a spot upon a card. The old copy has it *peepe*.

1 *In a few*, means the same as *in short, in a few words*.

2 This allusion is to a story told by Gower in the first book of his Confessio Amantis. *Florent* is the name of a knight who bound himself to marry a deformed hag provided she taught him the solution of a riddle on which his life depended.

3 i. e. 'a diminutive being, not exceeding in size the *tag of a point*,' says Steevens; 'a small image or head cut on the tag of a point or lace,' says Malone. It was no such thing; an *aglet* was not only a *tag of a point*, but a *brooch* or '*jewel in one's cap*,' as Baret explains it. An *aglet-baby*, therefore was *a diminutive figure carved on an aglet or jewel*; such as Queen Mab is described:—

'In shape no bigger than an *agate stone*
On the fore-finger of an alderman.'

4 The *fifty diseases of a horse* seems to be proverbial, of which, probably, the text is only an exaggeration.

5 Cross, froward, petulant.

6 i. e. roguish tricks. *Ropery* is used by Shakspeare in Romeo and Juliet for roguery. A *rope-ripe* is one for whom the gallows groans, according to Cotgrave.

7 Withstand.

8 To endeavour to explain this would certainly be lost labour. Mr. Boswell justly remarks 'that nothing is more common in ludicrous or playful discourse than to use a comparison where no resemblance is intended.'

9 *Keep* here means *care*, keeping, custody.

10 To *take order* is to *take measures*.

11 To be *well seen* in any art was to be *well skilled* in it.

12 Rate. 13 Present.

On this young man; for learning and behaviour,
Fit for her turn; well read in poetry
And other books,—good ones, I warrant you.
Hor. 'Tis well: and I have met a gentleman,
Hath promis'd me to help me to another,
A fine musician to instruct our mistress;
So shall I no whit be behind in duty
To fair Bianca, so belov'd of me.
Gre. Belov'd of me,—and that my deeds shall prove.
Gru. And that his bags shall prove. [*Aside.*
Hor. Gremio, 'tis now no time to vent our love:
Listen to me, and if you speak me fair,
I'll tell you news indifferent good for either.
Here is a gentleman, whom by chance I met,
Upon agreement from us to his liking,
Will undertake to woo curst Katharine;
Yea, and to marry her, if her dowry please.
Gre. So said, so done, is well:
Hortensio, have you told him all her faults?
Pet. I know, she is an irksome brawling scold;
If that be all, masters, I hear no harm.
Gre. No! say'st me so, friend? What countryman?
Pet. Born in Verona, old Antonio's son:
My father dead, my fortune lives for me;
And I do hope good days, and long, to see.
Gre. O, sir, such a life, with such a wife, were strange:
But, if you have a stomach, to't o' God's name,
You shall have me assisting you in all.
But will you woo this wild cat?
Pet. Will I live?
Gru. Will he woo her? ay, or I'll hang her. [*Aside.*
Pet. Why came I hither, but to that intent?
Think you, a little din can daunt mine ears?
Have I not in my time heard lions roar?
Have I not heard the sea, puff'd up with winds,
Rage like an angry boar, chafed with sweat?
Have I not heard great ordnance in the field,
And heaven's artillery thunder in the skies?
Have I not in a pitched battle heard
Loud 'larums, neighing steeds, and trumpets' clang?
And do you tell me of a woman's tongue,
That gives not half so great a blow to the ear
As will a chestnut in a farmer's fire?
Tush! tush! fear boys with bugs.[1]
Gru. For he fears none. [*Aside.*
Gre. Hortensio, hark!
This gentleman is happily arriv'd,
My mind presumes, for his own good, and ours.
Hor. I promis'd, we would be contributors,
And bear his charge of wooing, whatsoe'er.
Gre. And so we will; provided that he win her.
Gru. I would, I were as sure of a good dinner. [*Aside.*

Enter TRANIO, *bravely apparell'd; and* BIONDELLO.

Tra. Gentlemen, God save you! If I may be bold,
Tell me, I beseech you, which is the readiest way
To the house of signior Baptista Minola?
Bion. He that has the two fair daughters:—is't
[*Aside to* TRANIO] he you mean?
Tra. Even he, Biondello.
Gre. Hark you, sir; You mean not her to——[2]
Tra. Perhaps him and her, sir; What have you to do?
Pet. Not her that chides, sir; at any hand, I pray.
Tra. I love no chiders, sir:—Biondello, let's away.
Luc. Well begun, Tranio. [*Aside.*
Hor. Sir, a word ere you go;—
Are you a suitor to the maid you talk of, yea or no?
Tra. An if I be, sir, is it any offence?
Gre. No; if without more words, you will get you hence.
Tra. Why, sir, I pray, are not the streets as free
For me as for you?
Gre. But so is not she.
Tra. For what reason, I beseech you?
Gre. For this reason, if you'll know,——
That she's the choice love of Signior Gremio.
Hor. That she's the chosen of Signior Hortensio.
Tra. Softly, my masters! if you be gentlemen,
Do me this right,—hear me with patience.
Baptista is a noble gentleman,
To whom my father is not all unknown;
And, were his daughter fairer than she is,
She may more suitors have, and me for one.
Fair Leda's daughter had a thousand wooers;
Then well one more may fair Bianca have:
And so she shall; Lucentio shall make one,
Though Paris came in hope to speed alone.
Gre. What! this gentleman will out-talk us all.
Luc. Sir, give him head; I know he'll prove a jade.
Pet. Hortensio, to what end are all these words?
Hor. Sir, let me be so bold as ask you,
Did you yet ever see Baptista's daughter?
Tra. No, sir; but hear I do that he hath two;
The one as famous for a scolding tongue,
As is the other for beauteous modesty.
Pet. Sir, sir, the first's for me; let her go by.
Gre. Yea, leave that labour to great Hercules;
And let it be more than Alcides' twelve.
Pet. Sir, understand you this of me, insooth;—
The youngest daughter, whom you hearken for,
Her father keeps from all access of suitors;
And will not promise her to any man,
Until the elder sister first be wed:
The younger then is free, and not before.
Tra. If it be so, sir, that you are the man
Must stead us all, and me among the rest;
An if you break the ice, and do this feat,—
Achieve the elder, set the younger free
For our access,—whose hap shall be to have her
Will not so graceless be, to be ingrate.[3]
Hor. Sir, you say well, and well you do conceiv
And since you do profess to be a suitor,
You must, as we do, gratify this gentleman,
To whom we all rest generally beholden.
Tra. Sir, I shall not be slack: in sign whereof,
Please ye we may contrive[4] this afternoon,
And quaff carouses to our mistress' health;
And do as adversaries[5] do in law,—
Strive mightily, but eat and drink as friends.
Gre. Bion. O excellent motion! Fellows,[6] let's begone.
Hor. The motion's good indeed, and be it so;—
Petruchio, I shall be your *ben venuto.* [*Exeunt.*

ACT II.

SCENE I. *The same. A Room in* Baptista's *House. Enter* KATHARINA *and* BIANCA.

Bian. Good sister, wrong me not, nor wrong yourself,
To make a bondmaid and a slave of me;
That I disdain: but for these other gawds,[7]
Unbind my hands, I'll put them off myself,
Yea, all my raiment, to my petticoat;
Or, what you will command me, will I do,
So well I know my duty to my elders.
Kath. Of all thy suitors, here I charge thee, tell
Whom thou lov'st best: see thou dissemble not.
Bian. Believe me, sister, of all the men alive
I never yet beheld that special face
Which I could fancy more than any other.
Kath. Minion, thou liest; Is't not Hortensio?
Bian. If you affect[8] him, sister, here I swear,
I'll plead for you myself, but you shall have him.

1 *Fright* boys with *bug-bears.*
2 This hiatus is in the old copy; it is most probable that an abrupt sentence was intended.
3 Ungrateful.
4 To *contrive* is to *wear out*, to *pass away*, from *contrivi*, the preterite of *contero*, one of the disused Latinisms
5 *Adversaries* most probably here signifies *contending barristers*, or counsellors; surely not their clients?
6 *Fellows* means *companions*, and not fellow-servants, as Malone supposed.
7 Toys, trifling ornaments
8 Love.

Kath. O then, belike, you fancy riches more;
You will have Gremio to keep you fair.
Bian. Is it for him you do envy me so?
Nay, then you jest; and now I well perceive,
You have but jested with me all this while:
I pr'ythee, sister Kate, untie my hands.
Kath. If that be jest, then all the rest was so.
[*Strikes her.*

Enter BAPTISTA.

Bap. Why, how now, dame! whence grows this insolence?——
Bianca, stand aside:—poor girl! she weeps:—
Go, ply thy needle; meddle not with her.—
For shame, thou hilding[1] of a devilish spirit,
Why dost thou wrong her that did ne'er wrong thee?
When did she cross thee with a bitter word?
Kath. Her silence flouts me, and I'll be reveng'd.
[*Flies after* BIANCA.
Bap. What, in my sight!—Bianca, get thee in.
[*Exit* BIANCA.
Kath. Will you not suffer me? Nay, now I see
She is your treasure, she must have a husband;
I must dance barefoot on her wedding-day,
And, for your love to her, lead apes in hell.[2]
Talk not to me; I will go sit and weep,
Till I can find occasion of revenge.
[*Exit* KATHARINA.
Bap. Was ever gentleman thus griev'd as I?
But who comes here?

Enter GREMIO, *with* LUCENTIO *in the habit of a mean man;* PETRUCHIO, *with* HORTENSIO, *as a Musician; and* TRANIO, *with* BIONDELLO *bearing a Lute and Books.*

Gre. Good-morrow, neighbour Baptista.
Bap. Good-morrow, neighbour Gremio: God save you, gentlemen!
Pet. And you, good sir! Pray, have you not a daughter
Call'd Katharina, fair and virtuous?
Bap. I have a daughter, sir, call'd Katharina.
Gre. You are too blunt, go to it orderly.
Pet. You wrong me, Signior Gremio: give me leave.—
I am a gentleman of Verona, sir,
That,—hearing of her beauty and her wit,
Her affability, and bashful modesty,
Her wondrous qualities, and mild behaviour,—
Am bold to show myself a forward guest
Within your house, to make mine eye the witness
Of that report which I so oft have heard,
And, for an entrance to my entertainment,
I do present you with a man of mine,
[*Presenting* HORTENSIO.
Cunning in music, and the mathematics,
To instruct her fully in those sciences,
Whereof, I know, she is not ignorant:
Accept of him, or else you do me wrong;
His name is Licio, born in Mantua.
Bap. You're welcome, sir; and he, for your good sake:
But for my daughter Katharine,—this I know,
She is not for your turn, the more my grief.
Pet. I see you do not mean to part with her;
Or else you like not of my company.
Bap. Mistake me not, I speak but as I find.
Whence are you, sir? what may I call your name?
Pet. Petruchio is my name; Antonio's son,
A man well known throughout all Italy.
Bap. I know him well: you are welcome for his sake.

Gre. Saving your tale, Petruchio, I pray,
Let us, that are poor petitioners, speak too:
Baccare![3] you are marvellous forward.
Pet. O, pardon me, Signior Gremio; I would fain be doing.
Gre. I doubt it not, sir; but you will curse your wooing.——
Neighbour, this is a gift very grateful, I am sure of it. To express the like kindness myself, that have been more kindly beholden to you than any, I freely give unto you this young scholar [*presenting* LUCENTIO,] that hath been long studying at Rheims; as cunning in Greek, Latin, and other languages, as the other in music and mathematics: his name is Cambio; pray, accept his service.
Bap. A thousand thanks, Signior Gremio: welcome, good Cambio.—But, gentle sir [*to* TRANIO,] methinks you walk like a stranger; May I be so bold to know the cause of your coming?
Tra. Pardon me, sir, the boldness is mine own,
That, being a stranger in this city here,
Do make myself a suitor to your daughter,
Unto Bianca, fair and virtuous.
Nor is your firm resolve unknown to me,
In the preferment of the eldest sister:
This liberty is all that I request,—
That, upon knowledge of my parentage,
I may have welcome 'mongst the rest that woo,
And free access and favour as the rest.
And toward the education of your daughters,
I here bestow a simple instrument,
And this small package of Greek and Latin books:[4]
If you accept them, then their worth is great.
Bap. Lucentio is your name? of whence, I pray?
Tra. Of Pisa, sir; son to Vincentio.
Bap. A mighty man of Pisa, by report
I know him well:[5] you are very welcome, sir.—
Take you [*to* HOR.] the lute, and you [*to* LUC.] the set of books,
You shall go see your pupils presently.
Holla, within!

Enter a Servant.

Sirrah, lead
These gentlemen to my daughters: and tell them both,
These are their tutors; bid them use them well.
[*Exit* Servant, *with* HORTENSIO, LUCENTIO *and* BIONDELLO.
We will go walk a little in the orchard,
And then to dinner: You are passing welcome,
And so I pray you all to think yourselves.
Pet. Signior Baptista, my business asketh haste
And every day I cannot come to woo.
You knew my father well; and in him, me,
Left solely heir to all his lands and goods,
Which I have better'd rather than decreas'd;
Then tell me, if I get your daughter's love,
What dowry shall I have with her to wife?
Bap. After my death, the one half of my lands:
And, in possession, twenty thousand crowns.
Pet. And for that dowry, I'll assure her of[6]
Her widowhood,—be it that she survive me,—
In all my lands and leases whatsoever:
Let specialties be therefore drawn between us,
That covenants may be kept on either hand.
Bap. Ay, when the special thing is well obtain'd
This is,—her love; for that is all in all.
Pet. Why, that is nothing: for I tell you, father,
I am as peremptory as she proud-minded;
And where two raging fires meet together,
They do consume the thing that feeds their fury:
Though little fire grows great with little wind,

1 A *hilding* signifies a *base low wretch:* it is applied to Katharina for the coarseness of her behaviour.

2 The origin of this very old proverbial phrase is not known. Steevens suggests that it might have been considered an act of posthumous retribution for women who refused to bear children, to be condemned to the care of apes in leading-strings after death.

3 A cant word meaning *go back*, in allusion to a proverbial saying, '*Backare*, quoth Mortimer to his sow.' Probably made in ridicule of some ignorant fellow who affected a knowledge of Latin without having it, and produced his *Latinized English* instead.

4 In the reign of Elizabeth the young ladies of quality were usually instructed in the learned languages, if any pains were bestowed upon their minds at all. The queen herself, Lady Jane Grey, and her sisters, &c. are trite instances.

5 This must be understood as meaning, *I know well who he is.*

6 Perhaps we should read '*on* her widowhood.' *On* and *of* are not unfrequently confounded by the printers of the old copy.

Yet extreme gusts will blow out fire and all:
So I to her, and so she yields to me;
For I am rough, and woo not like a babe.
Bap. Well may'st thou woo, and happy be thy speed!
But be thou arm'd for some unhappy words.
Pet. Ay, to the proof; as mountains are for winds,
That shake not, though they blow perpetually.

Re-enter HORTENSIO, *with his head broken.*

Bap. How now, my friend? why dost thou look so pale?
Hor. For fear, I promise you, if I look pale.
Bap. What, will my daughter prove a good musician?
Hor. I think, she'll sooner prove a soldier;
Iron may hold with her, but never lutes.
Bap. Why then thou canst not break her to the lute?
Hor. Why, no; for she hath broke the lute to me.
I did but tell her, she mistook her frets,[1]
And bow'd her hand to teach her fingering;
When, with a most impatient devilish spirit,
Frets, call you these? quoth she: *I'll fume with them:*
And, with that word, she struck me on the head,
And through the instrument my pate made way;
And there I stood amazed for a while,
As on a pillory, looking through the lute:
While she did call me,—rascal fiddler,
And—twangling Jack; with twenty such vile terms,
As she had studied to misuse me so.
Pet. Now, by the world, it is a lusty wench;
I love her ten times more than e'er I did:
O, how I long to have some chat with her!
Bap. Well, go with me, and be not so discomfited:
Proceed in practice with my younger daughter;
She's apt to learn, and thankful for good turns.—
Signior Petruchio, will you go with us;
Or, shall I send my daughter Kate to you?
Pet. I pray you, do; I will attend her here,—
[*Exeunt* BAPTISTA, GREMIO, TRANIO, *and* HORTENSIO.
And woo her with some spirit when she comes.
Say, that she rail; Why, then I'll tell her plain,
She sings as sweetly as a nightingale:
Say, that she frown; I'll say she looks as clear
As morning roses newly washed with dew:[2]
Say, she be mute, and will not speak a word;
Then I'll commend her volubility,
And say—she uttereth piercing eloquence:
If she do bid me pack, I'll give her thanks,
As though she bid me stay by her a week:
If she deny to wed, I'll crave the day
When I shall ask the banns, and when be married:
But here she comes; and now, Petruchio, speak.

Enter KATHARINA.

Good-morrow, Kate; for that's your name, I hear.
Kath. Well have you heard, but something hard[3] of hearing;
They call me—Katharine, that do talk of me.
Pet. You lie, in faith; for you are call'd plain Kate,
And bonny Kate, and sometimes Kate the curst;
But Kate, the prettiest Kate in Christendom,
Kate of Kate-Hall, my super-dainty Kate,
For dainties are all cates: and therefore, Kate,
Take this of me, Kate of my consolation;—
Hearing thy mildness prais'd in every town,
Thy virtues spoke of, and thy beauties sounded,
(Yet not so deeply as to thee belongs,)
Myself am mov'd to woo thee for my wife.
Kath. Mov'd! in good time: let him that mov'd you hither,
Remove you hence: I knew you at the first,
You were a moveable.
Pet. Why, what's a moveable?
Kath. A joint-stool.[4]
Pet. Thou hast hit it: come, sit on me.
Kath. Asses are made to bear, and so are you.
Pet. Women are made to bear, and so are you.
Kath. No such jade, sir, as you, if me you mean.
Pet. Alas, good Kate, I will not burden thee:
For knowing thee to be but young and light,—
Kath. Too light for such a swain as you to catch;
And yet as heavy as my weight should be.
Pet. Should be? should buz.
Kath. Well ta'en, and like a buzzard.
Pet. O, slow-wing'd turtle! shall a buzzard take thee?
Kath. Ay, for a turtle; as he takes a buzzard.[5]
Pet. Come, come, you wasp; i'faith, you are too angry.
Kath. If I be waspish, best beware my sting.
Pet. My remedy is then, to pluck it out.
Kath. Ay, if the fool could find it where it lies.
Pet. Who knows not where a wasp doth wear his sting?
In his tail.
Kath. In his tongue.
Pet. Whose tongue?
Kath. Yours, if you talk of tails: and so farewell.
Pet. What, with my tongue in your tail? nay, come again,
Good Kate; I am a gentleman.
Kath. That I'll try.
[*Striking him.*
Pet. I swear I'll cuff you, if you strike again.
Kath. So may you lose your arms:
If you strike me, you are no gentleman;
And if no gentleman, why, then no arms.
Pet. A herald, Kate? O, put me in thy books.
Kath. What is your crest? a coxcomb?
Pet. A combless cock, so Kate will be my hen.
Kath. No cock of mine, you crow too like a craven.[6]
Pet. Nay, come, Kate, come; you must not look so sour.
Kath. It is my fashion when I see a crab.
Pet. Why here's no crab; and therefore look not sour.
Kath. There is, there is.
Pet. Then show it me.
Kath. Had I a glass, I would.
Pet. What, you mean my face?
Kath. Well aim'd of[7] such a young one.
Pet. Now, by Saint George, I am too young for you.
Kath. Yet you are wither'd.
Pet. 'Tis with cares.
Kath. I care not.
Pet. Nay, hear you, Kate: in sooth you 'scape not so.
Kath. I chafe you, if I tarry; let me go.
Pet. No, not a whit; I find you passing gentle.
'Twas told me, you were rough, and coy, and sullen,
And now I find report a very liar;
For thou art pleasant, gamesome, passing courteous;
But slow in speech, yet sweet as spring-time flowers:
Thou canst not frown, thou canst not look askance,
Nor bite the lip as angry wenches will;
Nor hast thou pleasure to be cross in talk;
But thou with mildness entertain'st thy wooers,
With gentle conference, soft and affable.

---

1 *Frets* are the points at which a string is to be stopped, formerly marked on the neck of such instruments as the lute or guitar.

2 So Milton in L'Allegro:—
'There on beds of violets blue,
And fresh blown roses *wash'd in dew.*'
It is from the old play of the Taming of a Shrew:—
'As glorious as the morning *washt with dew.*'

3 This is a poor quibble upon *heard*, which was the pronounced *hard*.

4 A proverbial expression also used by the fool in King Lear: and in Lyly's Mother Bombie:—
'Cry your mercy; I took you for a *joint-stool.*'

5 This kind of expression seems also to have bee proverbial. So in The Three Lords of London, 1590:
'———— hast no more skill.
Than take a falcon for a buzzard'

6 A cowardly degenerate cock. 7 By.

Why does the world report, that Kate doth limp?
O slanderous world! Kate, like the hazle-twig,
Is straight and slender; and as brown in hue
As hazle-nuts, and sweeter than the kernels.
O, let me see thee walk: thou dost not halt.
Kath. Go, fool, and whom thou keep'st command.
Pet. Did ever Dian so become a grove,
As Kate this chamber with her princely gait?
O, be thou Dian, and let her be Kate;
And then let Kate be chaste, and Dian sportful!
Kath. Where did you study all this goodly speech?
Pet. It is extempore, from my mother-wit.
Kath. A witty-mother! witless else her son.
Pet. Am I not wise?
Kath. Yes; keep you warm.[1]
Pet. Marry, so I mean, sweet Katharine, in thy bed:
And therefore, setting all this chat aside,
Thus in plain terms:—Your father hath consented
That you shall be my wife; your dowry 'greed on;
And, will you, nill you, I will marry you.
Now, Kate, I am a husband for your turn;
For, by this light, whereby I see thy beauty,
(Thy beauty, that doth make me like thee well,)
Thou must be married to no man but me:
For I am he, am born to tame you, Kate:
And bring you from a wild Kate to a Kate[2]
Conformable, as other household Kates.
Here comes your father; never make denial,
I must and will have Katharine to my wife.

Re-enter BAPTISTA, GREMIO, *and* TRANIO.

Bap. Now,
Signior Petruchio: How speed you with
My daughter?
Pet. How but well, sir? how but well?
It were impossible I should speed amiss.
Bap. Why, how now, daughter Katharine; in your dumps?
Kath. Call you me, daughter? now I promise you,
You have show'd a tender fatherly regard,
To wish me wed to one half lunatic;
A mad-cap ruffian, and a swearing Jack,
That thinks with oaths to face the matter out.
Pet. Father, 'tis thus:—yourself and all the world,
That talk'd of her, have talk'd amiss of her;
If she be curst, it is for policy;
For she's not froward, but modest as the dove;
She is not hot, but temperate as the morn;
For patience she will prove a second Grissel;[3]
And Roman Lucrece for her chastity:
And to conclude,—we have 'greed so well together,
That upon Sunday is the wedding-day.
Kath. I'll see thee hang'd on Sunday first.
Gre. Hark, Petruchio! she says she'll see thee hang'd first.
Tra. Is this your speeding? nay, then, good night our part!
Pet. Be patient, gentlemen; I choose her for myself:
If she and I be pleas'd, what's that to you?
'Tis bargain'd 'twixt us twain, being alone,
That she shall still be curst in company.
I tell you, 'tis incredible to believe
How much she loves me: O, the kindest Kate!—
She hung about my neck; and kiss on kiss
She vied[4] so fast, protesting oath on oath,
That in a twink, she won me to her love.
O, you are novices! 'tis a world to see,[5]
How tame, when men and women are alone,
A meacock[6] wretch can make the curstest shrew.—
Give me thy hand, Kate: I will unto Venice,
To buy apparel 'gainst the wedding-day:—
Provide the feast, father, and bid the guests;
I will be sure, my Katharine shall be fine.
Bap. I know not what to say: but give me your hands;
God send you joy, Petruchio! 'tis a match.
Gre. Tra. Amen, say we; we will be witnesses.
Pet. Father, and wife, and gentlemen, adieu;
I will to Venice, Sunday comes apace:———
We will have rings, and things, and fine array;
And kiss me, Kate, we will be married o' Sunday.
[*Exeunt* PET. *and* KATH. *severally.*
Gre. Was ever match clapp'd up so suddenly?
Bap. Faith, gentlemen, now I play a merchant's part,
And venture madly on a desperate mart.
Tra. 'Twas a commodity lay fretting by you:
'Twill bring you gain, or perish on the seas.
Bap. The gain I seek is—quiet in the match.
Gre. No doubt, but he hath got a quiet catch.
But now, Baptista, to your younger daughter;—
Now is the day we long have looked for;
I am your neighbour, and was suitor first.
Tra. And I am one that love Bianca more
Than words can witness, or your thoughts can guess.
Gre. Youngling! thou canst not love so dear as I.
Tra. Grey-beard! thy love doth freeze.
Gre. But thine doth fry.
Skipper, stand back; 'tis age that nourisheth.
Tra. But youth, in ladies' eyes that flourisheth.
Bap. Content you, gentlemen; I'll compound this strife:
'Tis deeds must win the prize; and he, of both,
That can assure my daughter greatest dower,
Shall have Bianca's love—
Say, Signior Gremio, what can you assure her?
Gre. First, as you know, my house within the city
Is richly furnished with plate and gold;
Basons, and ewers, to lave her dainty hands;
My hangings all of Tyrian tapestry:
In ivory coffers I have stuff'd my crowns;
In cypress chests my arras, counterpoints,[7]
Costly apparel, tents,[8] and canopies.
Fine linen, Turkey cushions boss'd with pearl,
Valance of Venice gold in needle-work,
Pewter[9] and brass, and all things that belong
To house, or house-keeping: then, at my farm,
I have a hundred milch-kine to the pail,
Six score fat oxen standing in my stalls,
And all things answerable to this portion.
Myself am struck in years, I must confess;
And, if I die to-morrow, this is hers,
If, whilst I live, she will be only mine.
Tra. That only, came well in.———Sir, list to me
I am my father's heir, and only son:
If I may have your daughter to my wife,
I'll leave her houses three or four as good,
Within rich Pisa walls, as any one
Old Signior Gremio has in Padua;
Besides two thousand ducats by the year,
Of fruitful land, all which shall be her jointure.
What, have I pinch'd you, Signior Gremio?
Gre. Two thousand ducats by the year, of land!
My land amounts not to so much in all:
That she shall have; besides an argosy,[10]
That now is lying in Marseilles' road:——
What, have I chok'd you with an argosy?

---

1 This appears to allude to some proverb.
2 Thus the first folio. The second folio reads:—'a wild *Kat* to a Kate." The modern editors, 'a wild *cat.*'
3 The story of Griselda, so beautifully related by Chaucer, was taken by him from Boccaccio. It is thought to be older than the time of the Florentine, as it is to be found among the old *fabliaux.*
4 So in the old play:—
'*Redoubling kiss on kiss* upon my cheeks.'
To *vie* was a term in the old vocabulary of gaming, for *to wager* the goodness of one hand against another. There was also to *revie*, and other variations.
5 This phrase, which frequently occurs in old writers, is equivalent to, *it is a wonder, or a matter of admiration to see.*
6 *A tame dastardly creature*, particularly an over mild husband. 'A *mecocke* or pezzant, that hath his head under his wives girdle, or that lets his wife be his maist er.'—*Junius's Nomenclator, by Fleming*, 1585, p. 532
7 Coverings for beds; now called counter*panes.*
8 *Tents* were hangings, *tentes*, French, probably so named from the *tenters* upon which they were hung, *tenture de tapisserie* signified a *suit of hangings.*
9 *Pewter* was considered as such costly furniture, that we find in the Northumberland household book *vessels of pewter* were hired by the year.
10 A large vessel either for merchandize or war

Tra. Gremio, 'tis known, my father hath no less
Than three great argosies; besides two galliasses,[1]
And twelve tight galleys: these I will assure her,
And twice as much, whate'er thou offer'st next.

Gre. Nay, I have offer'd all, I have no more;
And she can have no more than all I have;—
If you like me, she shall have me and mine.

Tra. Why, then the maid is mine from all the world,
By your firm promise; Gremio is out-vied.[2]

Bap. I must confess, your offer is the best;
And, let your father make her the assurance,
She is your own; else, you must pardon me:
If you should die before him, where's her dower?

Tra. That's but a cavil; he is old, I young.

Gre. And may not young men die, as well as old?

Bap. Well, gentlemen,
I am thus resolv'd:—On Sunday next, you know,
My daughter Katharine is to be married:
Now, on the Sunday following, shall Bianca,
Be bride to you, if you make this assuarance;
If not, to Signior Gremio:
And so I take my leave, and thank you both. [*Exit.*

Gre. Adieu, good neighbour.—Now, I fear thee not;
Sirrah, young gamester, your father were a fool
To give thee all, and, in his waning age,
Set foot under thy table: Tut! a toy!
An old Italian fox is not so kind, my boy. [*Exit.*

Tra. A vengeance on your crafty wither'd hide!
Yet I have faced it with a card of ten.[3]
'Tis in my head to do my master good:—
I see no reason, but suppos'd Lucentio
Must get a father, call'd—suppos'd Vincentio;
And that's a wonder: fathers, commonly,
Do get their children; but, in this case of wooing,
A child shall get a sire, if I fail not of my cunning. [*Exit.*[4]

ACT III.

SCENE I. *A Room in* Baptista's *House.* *Enter* LUCENTIO, HORTENSIO, *and* BIANCA.

Luc. Fiddler, forbear; you grow too forward, sir:
Have you so soon forgot the entertainment
Her sister Katharine welcom'd you withal?

Hor. But, wrangling pedant, this is
The patroness of heavenly harmony:
Then give me leave to have prerogative;
And when in music we have spent an hour,
Your lecture shall have leisure for as much.

Luc. Preposterous ass! that never read so far
To know the cause why music was ordain'd!
Was it not to refresh the mind of man,
After his studies, or his usual pain?
Then give me leave to read philosophy,
And, while I pause, serve in your harmony.

Hor. Sirrah, I will not bear these braves of thine.

Bian. Why, gentlemen, you do me double wrong,
To strive for that which resteth in my choice:
I am no breeching scholar[5] in the schools;
I'll not be tied to hours, nor 'pointed times,
But learn my lessons as I please myself.
And, to cut off all strife, here sit we down:
Take you your instrument, play you the whiles,
His lecture will be done ere you have tun'd.

Hor. You'll leave his lecture when I am in tune?
[*To* BIANCA.—HORTENSIO *retires.*

Luc. That will be never!—tune your instrument.

Bian. Where left we last?

Luc. Here, madam:——
Hac ibat Simois; hic est Sigeia tellus;
Hic steterat Priami regia celsa senis.

Bian. Construe them.

Luc. *Hac ibat,* as I told you before,[6]—*Simois,* I am Lucentio,—*hic est,* son unto Vincentio of Pisa,—*Sigeia tellus,* disguised thus to get your love;—*Hic steterat,* and that Lucentio that comes a wooing, *Priami,* is my man Tranio,—*regia,* bearing my port,—*celsa senis,* that we might beguile the old pantaloon.

Hor. Madam, my instrument's in tune. [*Returning*

Bian. Let's hear.— [HORTENSIO *plays.*
O fye! the treble jars.

Luc. Spit in the hole, man, and tune again.

Bian. Now let me see if I can construe it: *Hac ibat Simois,* I know you not;—*hic est Sigeia tellus,* I trust you not;—*Hic steterat Priami,* take heed he hear us not;—*regia,* presume not;—*celsa senis,* despair not.

Hor. Madam, 'tis now in tune.

Luc. All but the base.

Hor. The base is right; 'tis the base knave that jars.
How fiery and forward our pedant is!
Now, for my life, the knave doth court my love:
Pedascule,[7] I'll watch you better yet.

Bian. In time I may believe, yet I mistrust.

Luc. Mistrust it not; for sure, Æacides
Was Ajax,[8]—call'd so from his grandfather.

Bian. I must believe my master; else, I promise you,
I should be arguing still upon that doubt:
But let it rest.—Now, Licio, to you:—
Good masters, take it not unkindly, pray,
That I have been thus pleasant with you both.

Hor. You may go walk [*to* LUCENTIO,] and give me leave awhile;
My lessons make no music in three parts.

Luc. Are you so formal, sir? well, I must wait,
And watch withal; for, but[9] I be deceiv'd,
Our fine musician groweth amorous. [*Aside*

Hor. Madam, before you touch the instrument,
To learn the order of my fingering,
I must begin with rudiments of art:
To teach you gamut in a briefer sort,
More pleasant, pithy, and effectual,
Than hath been taught by any of my trade:
And there it is in writing, fairly drawn.

Bian. Why, I am past my gamut long ago.

Hor. Yet read the gamut of Hortensio.

Bian. [*Reads.*] Gamut *I am, the ground of all accord.*

---

1 A *galiass, galeazza,* Ital. was a great or double galley. The masts were three, and the number of seats for rowers thirty-two.

2 The origin of this term is also from gaming. When one man *vied* upon another, he was said to be *outvied.*

3 This phrase, which often occurs in old writers, was most probably derived from some game at cards, wherein the standing boldly upon a *ten* was often successful. *To face it* meant, as it still does, to bully, to attack by impudence of face. Whether *a card of ten* was properly a *cooling card* has not yet been ascertained, but they are united in the following passage from Lyly's Euphues. 'And all lovers, he only excepted, are *cooled* with *a card of ten.*'

4 After this Mr. Pope introduced the following speeches of the *presenters* as they are called; from the old play:—

Slie. When will the fool come again?*

* This probably alludes to the custom of filling up the vacancy of the stage between the Acts by the appearance of a fool on the stage. Unless Sly meant *Sander* the servant to Ferando in the old piece, which seems likely from a subsequent passage.

Sim. Anon, my lord.

Slie. Give some more drink here; where's the tapster? Here, Sim, eat some of these things.

Sim. I do, my lord.

Slie. Here, Sim, I drink to thee.

5 No schoolboy, liable to be whipt.

6 This species of humour, in which Latin is translated into English of a perfectly different meaning, is to be found in two plays of Middleton, The Witch, and The Chaste Maid of Cheapside; and in other writers.

7 Pedant.

8 'This is only said to deceive Hortensio, who is supposed to be listening. The pedigree of Ajax, however, is properly made out, and might have been taken from Golding's Version of Ovid's Metamorphoses, book xiii.' or, it may be added, from any historical and poetical dictionary, such as is appended to Cooper's Latin Dictionary, and others of that time.

9 *But* is here used in its exceptive sense of *be-out,* without. Vide Note on the Tempest, Act iii. Sc. 1

A re, *to plead Hortensio's passion;*
B mi, *Bianca, take him for thy lord,*
C faut, *that loves with all affection,*
D sol re, *one cliff, two notes have I;*
E la mi, *show pity, or I die.*
Call you this—gamut? tut! I like it not:
Old fashions please me best; I am not so nice,[1]
To change true rules for odd inventions.

Enter a Servant.

Serv. Mistress, your father prays you leave your books,
And help to dress your sister's chamber up;
You know, to-morrow is the wedding-day.

Bian. Farewell, sweet masters both; I must be gone. [*Exeunt* BIANCA *and* Servant.

Luc. 'Faith, mistress, then I have no cause to stay. [*Exit.*

Hor. But I have cause to pry into this pedant;
Methinks, he looks as though he were in love:—
Yet if thy thoughts, Bianca, be so humble,
To cast thy wand'ring eyes on every stale,[2]
Seize thee that list: If once I find thee ranging,
Hortensio will be quit with thee by changing. [*Exit.*

SCENE II. *The same. Before* Baptista's *House.*

Enter BAPTISTA, GREMIO, TRANIO, KATHARINA, BIANCA, LUCENTIO, *and* Attendants.

Bap. Signior Lucentio, [*to* TRANIO,] this is the 'pointed day,
That Katharine and Petruchio should be married,
And yet we hear not of our son-in-law:
What will be said? what mockery will it be,
To want the bridegroom, when the priest attends
To speak the ceremonial rites of marriage?
What says Lucentio to this shame of ours?

Kath. No shame but mine: I must, forsooth, be forc'd
To give my hand, oppos'd against my heart,
Unto a mad-brain rudesby, full of spleen;[3]
Who woo'd in haste, and means to wed at leisure.
I told you, I, he was a frantic fool,
Hiding his bitter jests in blunt behaviour:
And, to be noted for a merry man,
He'll woo a thousand, 'point the day of marriage,
Make friends invite them, and proclaim the banns;[4]
Yet never means to wed where he hath woo'd.
Now must the world point at poor Katharine,
And say,—*Lo, there is mad Petruchio's wife,*
If it would please him come and marry her.

Tra. Patience, good Katharine, and Baptista too;
Upon my life, Petruchio means but well,
Whatever fortune stays him from his word:
Though he be blunt, I know him passing wise;
Though he be merry, yet withal he's honest.

Kath. 'Would, Katharine had never seen him though!

[*Exit, weeping, followed by* BIANCA *and others.*

Bap. Go, girl; I cannot blame thee now to weep;
For such an injury would vex a very saint,
Much more a shrew of thy impatient humour.

Enter BIONDELLO.

Bio. Master, master! news, old news,[5] and such news as you never heard of!

Bap. Is it new and old too? how may that be?

Bion. Why, is it not news to hear of Petruchio's coming?

Bap. Is he come?

Bion. Why, no, sir.

Bap. What then?

Bion. He is coming.

Bap. When will he be here?

Bion. When he stands where I am, and sees you there.

Tra. But, say, what:—To thine old news.

Bion. Why, Petruchio is coming, in a new hat and an old jerkin; a pair of old breeches, thrice turned; a pair of boots that have been candle-cases, one buckled, another laced; an old rusty sword ta'en out of the town armory, with a broken hilt and chapeless; with two broken points:[6] His horse hipped with an old mothy saddle, the stirrups of no kindred: besides, possessed with the glanders, and like to mose in the chine; troubled with the lampas, infected with the fashions,[7] full of windgalls, sped with spavins, raied with the yellows, past cure of the fives,[8] stark spoiled with the staggers, begnawn with the bots; swayed in the back, and shoulder-shotten; ne'er legged before; and with a half-checked bit, and a head-stall of sheep's leather; which, being restrained to keep him from stumbling, hath been often burst, and now repaired with knots: one girt six times pieced, and a woman's crupper of velure,[9] which hath two letters for her name, fairly set down in studs, and here and there pieced with packthread.

Bap. Who comes with him?

Bion. O sir, his lackey, for all the world caparisoned like the horse; with a linen stock[10] on one leg, and a kersey boot-hose on the other, gartered with a red and blue list: an old hat, and *The humour of forty fancies,*[11] pricked in't for a feather: a monster, a very monster in apparel; and not like a christian footboy, or a gentleman's lackey.

Tra. 'Tis some odd humour pricks him to this fashion!—
Yet oftentimes he goes but mean apparell'd.

Bap. I am glad he is come, howsoever he comes.

Bion. Why, sir, he comes not.

Bap. Didst thou not say, he comes?

Bion. Who? that Petruchio came?

Bap. Ay, that Petruchio came.

Bion. No, sir; I say, his horse comes with him on his back.

Bap. Why, that's all one.

Bion. Nay, by Saint Jamy, I hold you a penny,
A horse and a man is more than one, and yet not many.

Enter PETRUCHIO *and* GRUMIO.

Pet. Come, where be these gallants? who is at home?

Bap. You are welcome, sir.

Pet. And yet I come not well.

Bap. And yet you halt not.

Tra. Not so well apparell'd
As I wish you were.

Pet. Were it better, I should rush in thus.
But where is Kate? where is my lovely bride?—
How does my father?—Gentles, methinks you frown:
And wherefore gaze this goodly company,
As if they saw some wondrous monument,
Some comet, or unusual prodigy?

---

1 The equivocal use of the word *nice* by our ancestors has caused some confusion among the commentators; from Baret it appears to have been synonymous, with *tender, delicate, effeminate.*

2 A *stale* was a *decoy* or *bait;* originally the form of a bird was set up to allure a hawk or other bird of prey, and hence used for any object of allurement. *Stale* here may, however, only mean every *common* object, as *stale* was applied to *common* women.

3 Humour, caprice, inconstancy.

4 *Them* is not in the old copy, it was supplied by Malone: the second folio reads—*yes.*

5 *Old news.* These words were added by Rowe, and necessarily, as appears by the reply of Baptista. *Old,* in the sense of *abundant,* as '*old* turning the key,' &c. occurs elsewhere in Shakspeare.

6 Lest the reader should imagine that a sword *with two broken points* is here meant, he should know that *points* were tagged laces used in fastening different parts of the dress: two broken points would therefore add to the slovenly appearance of Petruchio.

7 i. e. the farcy, called fashions in the west of England.

8 Vives; a distemper in horses, little differing from the strangles.

9 Velvet.

10 Stocking.

11 Warburton's supposition, that Shakspeare ridicules some popular cheap book of this title, by making Petruchio prick it up in his footboy's hat instead of a feather, has been well supported by Steevens; he observes that 'a penny book, containing forty short poems, would, properly managed, furnish no unapt plume of feathers for the hat of a humourist's servant.'

Bap. Why sir, you know, this is your wedding-day:
First were we sad, fearing you would not come;
Now sadder, that you come so unprovided.
Fye! doff this habit, shame to your estate,
An eye-sore to our solemn festival.
Tra. And tell us, what occasion of import
Hath all so long detain'd you from your wife,
And sent you hither so unlike yourself?
Pet. Tedious it were to tell, and harsh to hear:
Sufficeth, I am come to keep my word,
Though in some part enforced to digress;[1]
Which, at more leisure, I will so excuse
As you shall well be satisfied withal.
But, where is Kate? I stay too long from her;
The morning wears, 'tis time we were at church.
Tra. See not your bride in these unreverent robes;
Go to my chamber, put on clothes of mine.
Pet. Not I, believe me; thus I'll visit her.
Bap. But thus, I trust, you will not marry her.
Pet. Good sooth, even thus; therefore have done with words;
To me she's married, not unto my clothes:
Could I repair what she will wear in me,
As I can change these poor accoutrements,
'Twere well for Kate, and better for myself.
But what a fool am I to chat with you,
When I should bid good-morrow to my bride,
And seal the title with a lovely kiss?
[*Exeunt* Pet. Gru. *and* Bion.
Tra. He hath some meaning in his mad attire:
We will persuade him, be it possible,
To put on better ere he go to church.
Bap. I'll after him, and see the event of this.
[*Exit.*
Tra. But, sir, to her[2] love concerneth us to add
Her father's liking; which to bring to pass,
As I before imparted to your worship,
I am to get a man,—whate'er he be,
It skills[3] not much; we'll fit him to our turn,—
And he shall be Vincentio of Pisa;
And make assurance, here in Padua,
Of greater sums than I have promised,
So shall you quietly enjoy your hope,
And marry sweet Bianca with consent.
Luc. Were it not that my fellow schoolmaster
Doth watch Bianca's steps so narrowly,
'Twere good, methinks, to steal our marriage;
Which once perform'd, let all the world say—no,
I'll keep mine own, despite of all the world.
Tra. That by degrees we mean to look into,
And watch our vantage in this business:
We'll overreach the greybeard, Gremio,
The narrow-prying father, Minola;
The quaint[4] musician, amorous Licio;
All for my master's sake, Lucentio.—

Re-enter Gremio.

Signior Gremio! came you from the church?
Gre. As willingly as e'er I came from school.
Tra. And is the bride and bridegroom coming home?
Gre. A bridegroom, say you? 'tis a groom, indeed,
A grumbling groom, and that the girl shall find.
Tra. Curster than she? why, 'tis impossible.
Gre. Why, he's a devil, a devil, a very fiend.
Tra. Why, she's a devil, a devil, the devil's dam.
Gre. Tut! she's a lamb, a dove, a fool to him.
I'll tell you, Sir Lucentio: When the priest
Should ask—if Katharine should be his wife,
Ay, by gogs-wouns, quoth he; and swore so loud,
That, all amaz'd, the priest let fall the book:
And, as he stoop'd again to take it up,
The mad-brain'd bridegroom took him such a cuff,
That down fell priest and book, and book and priest,
Now take them up, quoth he, *if any list.*
Tra. What said the wench, when he arose again?
Gre. Trembled and shook; for why, he stamp'd and swore,
As if the vicar meant to cozen him.
But after many ceremonies done,
He calls for wine:—*A health,* quoth he; as if
He had been aboard carousing to his mates
After a storm:—Quaff'd off the muscadel,[5]
And threw the sops all in the sexton's face;
Having no other reason,—
But that his beard grew thin and hungerly,
And seem'd to ask him sops as he was drinking.
This done, he took the bride about the neck;
And kiss'd her lips with such a clamourous smack,
That, at the parting, all the church did echo.
I, seeing this, came thence for very shame;
And after me, I know, the rout is coming:
Such a mad marriage never was before;
Hark, hark! I hear the minstrels play. [*Music.*

Enter Petruchio, Katharina, Bianca, Baptista, Hortensio, Grumio, *and Train.*

Pet. Gentlemen and friends, I thank you for your pains:
I know you think to dine with me to-day,
And have prepared great store of wedding cheer.
But so it is, my haste doth call me hence,
And therefore here I mean to take my leave.
Bap. Is't possible, you will away to-night?
Pet. I must away to-day, before night come.
Make it no wonder; if you knew my business,
You would entreat me rather go than stay.
And, honest company, I thank you all,
That have beheld me give away myself
To this most patient, sweet, and virtuous wife:
Dine with my father, drink a health to me;
For I must hence, and farewell to you all.
Tra. Let us entreat you stay till after dinner.
Pet. It may not be.
Gre. Let me entreat you.
Pet. It cannot be.
Kath. Let me entreat you.
Pet. I am content.
Kath. Are you content to stay?
Pet. I am content you shall entreat me stay,
But yet not stay, entreat me how you can.
Kath. Now, if you love me, stay.
Pet. Grumio, my horses.
Gru. Ay, sir, they be ready; the oats have eaten the horses.
Kath. Nay, then,
Do what thou canst, I will not go to-day;
No, nor to-morrow, nor till I please myself.
The door is open, sir, there lies your way,
You may be jogging whiles your boots are green;
For me, I'll not be gone, till I please myself;—
'Tis like you'll prove a jolly surly groom,
That take it on you at the first so roundly.
Pet. O, Kate, content thee; pr'ythee be not angry.
Kath. I will be angry; What hast thou to do?
Father, be quiet; he shall stay my leisure.
Gre. Ay, marry, sir; now it begins to work.
Kath. Gentlemen, forward to the bridal dinner:—
I see a woman may be made a fool,
If she had not a spirit to resist.
Pet. They shall go forward, Kate, at thy command:
Obey the bride, you that attend on her.
Go to the feast, revel and domineer,[6]
Carouse full measure to her maidenhead,
Be mad and merry,——or go hang yourselves,

1 i. e. to deviate from my promise.

2 The old copy reads, 'But, sir, love concerneth us to add, Her father's liking.' The emendation is Mr. Tyrwhitt's. The nominative case to the verb *concerneth* is here understood.

3 'It *matters* not much,' it is of no importance.

4 *Quaint* had formerly a more favorable meaning than *strange, awkward, fantastical,* and was used in commendation, as *neat, elegant, dainty, dexterous.*

5 The custom of having wine and sops distributed immediately after the marriage ceremony in the church is very ancient. It existed even among our Gothic ancestors, and is mentioned in the ordinances of the household of Henry VII. 'For the marriage of a Princess:'—'Then pottes of *Ipocrice* to be ready, and to bee put into cupps with *soppe,* and to be borne to the estates and to take a soppe and drinke.'

6 That is *bluster* or *swagger.*

But for my bonny Kate, she must with me.
Nay, look not big, nor stamp, nor stare, nor fret;
I will be master of what is mine own:
She is my goods, my chattels; she is my house,
My household-stuff, my field, my barn,
My horse, my ox, my ass, my any thing;
And here she stands, touch her whoever dare;
I'll bring my action on the proudest he
That stops my way in Padua.——Grumio,
Draw forth thy weapon, we're beset with thieves;
Rescue thy mistress, if thou be a man:—
Fear not, sweet wench, they shall not touch thee, Kate;
I'll buckler thee against a million.

[*Exeunt* PET. KATH. *and* GRU.

Bap. Nay, let them go, a couple of quiet ones!

Gre. Went they not quickly, I should die with laughing.

Tra. Of all mad matches, never was the like!

Luc. Mistress, what's your opinion of your sister?

Bian. That, being mad herself, she's madly mated.

Gre. I warrant him, Petruchio is Kated.

Bap. Neighbours and friends, though bride and bridegroom wants
For to supply the places at the table,
You know there wants no junkets[1] at the feast.—
Lucentio, you shall supply the bridegroom's place,
And let Bianca take her sister's room.

Tra. Shall sweet Bianca practise how to bride it?

Bap. She shall, Lucentio.—Come, gentlemen, let's go. [*Exeunt.*

ACT IV.

SCENE I. *A Hall in* Petruchio's *Country House.*

Enter GRUMIO.

Gru. Fye, fye on all tired jades! on all mad masters! and all foul ways! Was ever man so beaten? was ever man so rayed?[2] was ever man so weary? I am sent before to make a fire, and they are coming after to warm them. Now, were not I a little pot, and soon hot,[3] my very lips might freeze to my teeth, my tongue to the roof of my mouth, my heart in my belly, ere I should come by a fire to thaw me:—But I, with blowing the fire, shall warm myself; for, considering the weather, a taller man than I will take cold. Holla! hoa! Curtis!

Enter CURTIS.

Curt. Who is that, calls so coldly?

Gru. A piece of ice: If thou doubt it, thou may'st slide from my shoulder to my heel, with no greater run but my head and my neck. A fire, good Curtis.

Curt. Is my master and his wife coming, Grumio?

Gru. O, ay, Curtis, ay: and therefore fire, fire; cast on no water.[4]

Curt. Is she so hot a shrew as she's reported?

Gru. She was, good Curtis, before this frost: but thou know'st, winter tames man, woman, and beast: for it hath tamed my old master, and my new mistress, and myself,[5] fellow Curtis.

Curt. Away, thou three-inch fool! I am no beast.

Gru. Am I but three inches? why, thy horn is a foot; and so long am I,[6] at the least. But wilt thou make a fire, or shall I complain on thee to our mistress, whose hand (she being now at hand) thou shalt soon feel, to thy cold comfort, for being slow in thy hot office.

Curt. I pr'ythee, good Grumio, tell me, How goes the world?

Gru. A cold world, Curtis, in every office but thine; and, therefore, fire: Do thy duty, and have thy duty; for my master and mistress are almost frozen to death.

Curt. There's fire ready: And, therefore, good Grumio, the news?

Gru. Why, *Jack boy! ho boy!*[7] and as much news as thou wilt.

Curt. Come, you are so full of conycatching:—

Gru. Why, therefore, fire; for I have caught extreme cold. Where's the cook? is supper ready, the house trimmed, rushes strewed, cobwebs swept; the serving-men in their new fustian, their white stockings, and every officer his wedding garment on? Be the jacks fair within, the jills[8] fair without, the carpets laid,[9] and every thing in order?

Curt. All ready; and therefore I pray thee, news.

Gru. First, know, my horse is tired; my master and mistress fallen out.

Curt. How?

Gru. Out of their saddles into the dirt; and thereby hangs a tale.

Curt. Let's ha't good Grumio.

Gru. Lend thine ear.

Curt. Here.

Gru. There. [*Striking him*

Curt. This is to feel a tale, not to hear a tale.

Gru. And therefore 'tis called a sensible tale: and this cuff was but to knock at your ear, and beseech listening. Now I begin: *Imprimis*, we came down a foul hill, my master riding behind my mistress

Cur. Both on one horse?

Gru. What's that to thee?

Curt. Why, a horse.

Gru. Tell thou the tale:——But hadst thou not crossed me, thou shouldst have heard how her horse fell, and she under her horse; thou should'st have heard, in how miry a place: how she was bemoiled;[10] how he left her with the horse upon her; how he beat me because her horse stumbled; how she waded through the dirt to pluck him off me; how he swore; how she prayed—that never prayed before; how I cried; how the horses ran away, how her bridle was burst;[11] how I lost my crupper;—with many things of worthy memory; which now shall die in oblivion, and thou return unexperienced to thy grave.

Curt. By this reckoning, he is more shrew than she.[12]

Gru. Ay; and that thou and the proudest of you all shall find, when he comes home. But what talk I of this?—call forth Nathaniel, Joseph, Nicholas, Philip, Walter, Sugarsop, and the rest; let their heads be sleekly combed, their blue coats[13] brushed, and their garters of an indifferent[14] knit: let them curtsey with their left legs; and not presume to touch a hair of my master's horse-tail, till they kiss their hands. Are they all ready?

Curt. They are.

Gru. Call them forth.

Curt. Do you hear, ho! you must meet my master, to countenance my mistress.

Gru. Why, she hath a face of her own.

---

1 Delicacies. 2 Bewrayed, dirty.

3 *A little pot soon hot*, is a common proverb.

4 There is an old popular catch of three parts in these words:—

'Scotland burneth, Scotland burneth,
Fire, fire;——Fire, fire,
Cast on some more water.'

5 Grumio calls himself *a beast*, and Curtis one also by inference in calling him *fellow*: this would not have been noticed but that one of the commentators once thought it necessary to alter *myself* in Grumio's speech to *thyself*. Grumio's sentence is proverbial:
'Wedding, and ill-wintering tame both man and beast.'

6 Curtis contemptuously alludes to Grumio's diminutive size; and he in return calls Curtis a cuckold.

7 This is the beginning of an old round in three parts, the music is given in the Variorum Shakspeare.

8 It is probable that a quibble was intended. *Jack* and *jill* signify *two drinking vessels* as well as *men* and *maid-servants*.

9 The carpets were *laid* over the *tables*. The floors, as appears from the present passage and others, were strewed with rushes.

10 i. e. bedraggled, bemired.

11 Broken.

12 The term *shrew* was anciently applied to either sex as appears from Chaucer's Testam. of Love, fol. 300 Ed. Speght. 1598.

13 *Blue coats* were the usual habits of servants Hence a *blue-bottle* was sometimes used as a term of reproach for a servant.

14 Of an *indifferent knit* is *tolerably knit*, pretty good in quality. Hamlet says, 'I am myself *indifferent* honest,' i. e. *tolerably* honest. The reader, who will be at the pains to refer to the Variorum Shakspeare, may be amused with the discordant blunders of the most eminent commentators about this simple expression

Curt. Who knows not that?

Gru. Thou, it seems; that callest for company to countenance her.

Curt. I call them forth to credit her.

Gru. Why, she comes to borrow nothing of them.

Enter several Servants.

Nath. Welcome home, Grumio.

Phil. How now, Grumio?

Jos. What, Grumio!

Nich. Fellow Grumio!

Nath. How now, old lad?

Gru. Welcome, you;—how now, you; what, you;—fellow, you;—and thus much for greeting. Now, my spruce companions, is all ready, and all things neat?

Nath. All things is ready:[1] How near is our master?

Gru. E'en at hand, alighted by this; and therefore be not——Cock's passion, silence!——I hear my master.

Enter PETRUCHIO *and* KATHARINA.

Pet. Where be these knaves? What, no man at door,
To hold my stirrup, nor to take my horse!
Where is Nathaniel, Gregory, Philip?——

All Serv. Here, here, sir; here, sir.

Pet. Here, sir! here, sir! here, sir! here, sir!—
You logger-headed and unpolish'd grooms!
What, no attendance? no regard? no duty?
Where is the foolish knave I sent before?

Gru. Here, sir; as foolish as I was before.

Pet. You peasant swain! you whoreson, malt-horse drudge!
Did I not bid thee meet me in the park,
And bring along these rascal knaves with thee?

Gru. Nathaniel's coat, sir, was not fully made,
And Gabriel's pumps were all unpink'd i'the heel;
There was no link[2] to colour Peter's hat,
And Walter's dagger was not come from sheathing:
There were none fine, but Adam, Ralph, and Gregory;
The rest were ragged, old, and beggarly;
Yet, as they are, here are they come to meet you.

Pet. Go, rascals, go, and fetch my supper in.—
[*Exeunt some of the* Servants.
Where is the life that late I led?—[3] [Sings.
Where are those——Sit down, Kate, and welcome.
Soud, soud, soud, soud![4]

Re-enter Servants, *with supper.*

Why, when, I say?—Nay, good, sweet Kate, be merry.
Off with my boots, you rogues, you villains; When?

It was the friar of orders grey,[5] [Sings.
As he forth walked on his way:—

Out, out, you rogue! you pluck my foot awry:
Take that, and mend the plucking off the other.—
[*Strikes him.*
Be merry, Kate:—Some water, here; what, ho!
Where's my spaniel Troilus?—Sirrah, get you hence,
And bid my cousin Ferdinand come hither:—
[*Exit* Servant.
One, Kate, that you must kiss, and be acquainted with.—
Where are my slippers?—Shall I have some water?
[*A bason is presented to him.*
Come, Kate, and wash,[6] and welcome heartily.—
[Servant *lets the ewer fall.*
You whoreson villain! will you let it fall?
[*Strikes him.*

Kath. Patience, I pray you; 'twas a fault unwilling.

Pet. A whoreson, beetleheaded, flap-ear'd knave!
Come, Kate, sit down; I know you have a stomach.
Will you give thanks, sweet Kate; or else shall I?—
What is this? Mutton?

1 Serv. Ay.

Pet. Who brought it?

1 Serv. I.

Pet. 'Tis burnt; and so is all the meat:
What dogs are these!—Where is the rascal cook?
How durst you, villains, bring it from the dresser,
And serve it thus to me that love it not?
There, take it to you, trenchers, cups, and all.
[*Throws the meat, &c. about the stage.*
You heedless joltheads, and unmanner'd slaves!
What, do you grumble? I'll be with you straight.

Kath. I pray you, husband, be not so disquiet;
The meat was well, if you were so contented.

Pet. I tell thee, Kate, 'twas burnt and dried away;
And I expressly am forbid to touch it,
For it engenders choler, planteth anger;
And better 'twere that both of us did fast,—
Since, of ourselves, ourselves are choleric,—
Than feed it with such over-roasted flesh.
Be patient; to-morrow it shall be mended,
And, for this night, we'll fast for company:—
Come, I will bring thee to thy bridal chamber.
[*Exeunt* PET. KATH. *and* CURT.

Nath. [*Advancing.*] Peter, didst ever see the like?

Peter. He kills her in her own humour.

Re-enter CURTIS.

Gru. Where is he?

Curt. In her chamber,
Making a sermon of continency to her:
And rails, and swears, and rates; that she, poor soul,
Knows not which way to stand, to look, to speak;
And sits as one new-risen from a dream.
Away, away! for he is coming hither. [*Exeunt.*

Re-enter PETRUCHIO.

Pet. Thus have I politicly begun my reign,
And 'tis my hope to end successfully:
My falcon now is sharp, and passing empty;
And, till she stoop, she must not be full-gorged,
For then she never looks upon her lure.[8]
Another way I have to man my haggard,[9]
To make her come, and know her keeper's call,
That is,—to watch her, as we watch these kites
That bate,[10] and beat, and will not be obedient.
She eat no meat to-day, nor none shall eat;
Last night she slept not, nor to-night she shall not;
As with the meat, some undeserved fault
I'll find about the making of the bed;
And here I'll fling the pillow, there the bolster,
This way the coverlet, another way the sheets:—
Ay, and amid this hurly, I intend[11]
That all is done in reverend care of her;
And, in conclusion, she shall watch all night:
And, if she chance to nod, I'll rail and brawl,
And with the clamour keep her still awake.
This is a way to kill a wife with kindness;
And thus I'll curb her mad and headstrong humour.
He that knows better how to tame a shrew,
Now let him speak; 'tis charity to shew. [*Exit.*

---

1 The false concord here was no doubt intentional, it suits well with the character.

2 Green, in his Mihil Mumchance, says, 'This cozenage is used likewise in selling old hats found upon dunghills, instead of newe, blackt over with the *smoake of an olde link*.'

3 This ballad was well suited to Petruchio, as appears by the *answer* in A Handeful of Pleasant Delites, 1584; which is called 'Dame Beautie's replie to the lover late at libertie, and now complaineth him to be her captive,' entituled '*Where is the life that late I led?*'

4 A word coined by Shakspeare to express the noise made by a person heated and fatigued.

5 Dr. Percy has constructed his beautiful ballad, 'The Friar of Orders Gray,' from the various fragments and hints dispersed through Shakspeare's plays, with a few supplemental stanzas.

6 It was the custom in ancient times to wash the hands immediately before dinner and supper, and afterwards. As our ancestors eat with their fingers, we can not wonder at such repeated ablutions.

7 Shakspeare delights in allusions to Falconry; the following allegory comprises most of its terms. A hawk *full fed* was untractable, and refused the lure.

8 The lure was a thing stuffed to look like the game the hawk was to pursue; its use was to tempt him back after he had flown.

9 A *haggard* is a *wild hawk*, to *man* her is to tame her. To *watch* or *wake* a hawk was one part of the process of taming.

10 To *bate* is to flutter the wings as preparing for flight; *batter l'ale*, Italian.

11 *Intend* is used for *pretend*

SCENE II. Padua. *Before* Baptista's *House.*

Enter TRANIO *and* HORTENSIO.

Tra. Is't possible, friend Licio, that Bianca
Doth fancy any other but Lucentio?
I tell you, sir, she bears me fair in hand.
Hor. Sir, to satisfy you in what I have said,
Stand by, and mark the manner of his teaching.
[*They stand aside.*

Enter BIANCA *and* LUCENTIO.

Luc. Now, mistress, profit you in what you read?
Bian. What, master, read you? first resolve me that.
Luc. I read that I profess, the art of love.
Bian. And may you prove, sir, master of your art!
Luc. While you, sweet dear, prove mistress of my heart. [*They retire.*
Hor. Quick proceeders, marry! Now, tell me, I pray,
You that durst swear that your mistress Bianca
Lov'd none in the world so well as Lucentio.
Tra. O despiteful love! unconstant womankind!
I tell thee, Licio, this is wonderful.
Hor. Mistake no more: I am not Licio,
Nor a musician, as I seem to be;
But one that scorn to live in this disguise,
For such a one as leaves a gentleman,
And makes a god of such a cullion:[1]
Know, sir, that I am call'd—Hortensio.
Tra. Signior Hortensio, I have often heard
Of your entire affection to Bianca;
And since mine eyes are witness of her lightness,
I will with you,—if you be so contented,—
Forswear Bianca and her love for ever.
Hor. See, how they kiss and court!——Signior Lucentio,
Here is my hand, and here I firmly vow—
Never to woo her more; but do forswear her,
As one unworthy all the former favours
That I have fondly flatter'd her withal.
Tra. And here I take the like unfeigned oath,—
Ne'er to marry with her though she would entreat:
Fye on her! see, how beastly she doth court him.
Hor. 'Would, all the world, but he, had quite forsworn!
For me,—that I may surely keep mine oath,
I will be married to a wealthy widow,
Ere three days pass; which hath as long loved me,
As I have lov'd this proud disdainful haggard:
And so farewell, signior Lucentio.—
Kindness in women, not their beauteous looks,
Shall win my love:—and so I take my leave,
In resolution as I swore before.
[*Exit* HORTENSIO.—LUCENTIO *and* BIANCA *advance.*
Tra. Mistress Bianca, bless you with such grace
As 'longeth to a lover's blessed case!
Nay, I have ta'en you napping, gentle love;
And have forsworn you, with Hortensio.
Bian. Tranio, you jest; But have you both forsworn me?
Tra. Mistress, we have.
Luc. Then we are rid of Licio.
Tra. I'faith, he'll have a lusty widow now,
That shall be woo'd and wedded in a day
Bian. God give him joy!
Tra. Ay, and he'll tame her.
Bian. He says so, Tranio.
Tra. 'Faith he is gone unto the taming-school.
Bian. The taming-school! what, is there such a place?
Tra. Ay, mistress, and Petruchio is the master:
That teacheth tricks eleven and twenty long,—
To tame a shrew, and charm[2] her chattering tongue.

Enter BIONDELLO, *running.*

Bion. O master, master, I have watch'd so long
That I'm dog-weary; but at last I spied
An ancient angel[3] coming down the hill
Will serve the turn.
Tra. What is he, Biondello?
Bion. Master, a mercatante, or a pedant,[4]
I know not what; but formal in apparel,
In gait and countenance surely like a father.
Luc. And what of him, Tranio?
Tra. If he be credulous, and trust my tale,
I'll make him glad to seem Vincentio;
And give assurance to Baptista Minola,
As if he were the right Vincentio.
Take in your love, and then let me alone.
[*Exeunt* LUCENTIO *and* BIANCA.

Enter a Pedant.

Ped. God save you, sir!
Tra. And you, sir! you are welcome.
Travel you far on, or are you at the furthest?
Ped. Sir, at the furthest for a week or two:
But then up further; and as far as Rome;
And so to Tripoly, if God lend me life.
Tra. What countryman, I pray?
Ped. Of Mantua?
Tra. Of Mantua, sir?—marry, God forbid!
And come to Padua, careless of your life?
Ped. My life, sir! how, I pray? for that goes hard.
Tra. 'Tis death for any one in Mantua
To come to Padua: Know you not the cause?
Your ships are staid at Venice; and the duke
(For private quarrel 'twixt your duke and him)
Hath publish'd and proclaim'd it openly:
'Tis marvel; but that you're but newly come,
You might have heard it else proclaim'd about.
Ped. Alas, sir, it is worse for me than so;
For I have bills for money by exchange
From Florence, and must here deliver them.
Tra. Well, sir, to do you courtesy,
This will I do, and this will I advise you;—
First, tell me, have you ever been at Pisa
Ped. Ay, sir, in Pisa have I often been;
Pisa, renowned for grave citizens.
Tra. Among them, know you one Vincentio?
Ped. I know him not, but I have heard of him
A merchant of incomparable wealth.
Tra. He is my father, sir; and sooth to say,
In countenance somewhat doth resemble you.
Bion. As much as an apple doth an oyster, and all one. [*Aside.*
Tra. To save your life in this extremity,
This favour will I do you for his sake;
And think it not the worst of all your fortunes,
That you are like to Sir Vincentio.
His name and credit shall you undertake,
And in my house you shall be friendly lodged:
Look, that you take upon you as you should:
You understand me, sir;—so shall you stay
Till you have done your business in the city:
If this be courtesy, sir, accept of it.
Ped. O, sir, I do; and will repute you ever
The patron of my life and liberty.
Tra. Then go with me, to make the matter good.
This, by the way, I let you understand;—
My father is here look'd for every day,
To pass assurance[5] of a dower in marriage
'Twixt me and one Baptista's daughter here:
In all these circumstances I'll instruct you:
Go with me, sir, to clothe you as becomes you.
[*Exeunt.*

1 '*Coglione*, a *cuglion*, a gull, a meacock,' says Florio. It is equivalent to a great booby.

2 So in King Henry VI. Part 3.
'Peace, wilful boy, or I will charm your tongue.'
In Psalm lviii. we read of the *charmer* who *charms* wisely, in order to quell the fury of the adder.

3 For *angel*, Theobald, and after him Hanmer and Warburton, read *engle;* which Hanmer calls a *gull*, deriving it from *engluer*, French, to catch with birdlime: but without sufficient reason. Mr. Gifford, in a note on Jonson's Poetaster, is decidedly in favour of *enghle* with Hammer's explanation, and supports it by referring to Gascoigne's Supposes, from which Shakspeare took this part of his plot.

4 i. e. a merchant or a schoolmaster.

5 i. e. to agree upon a settlement of dower; Dotem firmare. Deeds are by law-writers called the common *assurances* of the realm, because thereby each man's property is *assured* to him. So in a subsequent scene: they are busied about a counterfeit *assurance*.

SCENE III. *A Room in* Petruchio's *House.*

Enter KATHARINA *and* GRUMIO.

Gru. No, no; forsooth; I dare not, for my life.

Kath. The more my wrong, the more his spite appears:
What, did he marry me to famish me?
Beggars that come unto my father's door,
Upon entreaty, have a present alms;
If not, elsewhere they meet with charity:
But I,—who never knew how to entreat,—
Am starv'd for meat, giddy for lack of sleep:
With oaths kept waking, and with brawling fed:
And that which spites me more than all these wants,
He does it under name of perfect love;
As who should say,—if I should sleep, or eat,
'Twere deadly sickness, or else present death.—
I pry'thee go, and get me some repast;
I care not what, so it be wholesome food.

Gru. What say you to a neat's foot?

Kath. 'Tis passing good; I pry'thee let me have it.

Gru. I fear it is too choleric a meat:—
How say you to a fat tripe, finely broil'd?

Kath. I like it well; good Grumio, fetch it me.

Gru. I cannot tell; I fear, 'tis choleric.
What say you to a piece of beef, and mustard?

Kath. A dish that I do love to feed upon.

Gru. Ay, but the mustard is too hot a little.[1]

Kath. Why, then the beef, and let the mustard rest.

Gru. Nay, then I will not; you shall have the mustard,
Or else you get no beef of Grumio.

Kath. Then both, or one, or any thing thou wilt.

Gru. Why, then the mustard without the beef.

Kath. Go, get thee gone, thou false deluding slave, [*Beats him.*
That feed'st me with the very name of meat:
Sorrow on thee, and all the pack of you,
That triumph thus upon my misery!
Go, get thee gone, I say.

Enter PETRUCHIO *with a dish of meat; and* HORTENSIO.

Pet. How fares my Kate? What, sweeting, all amort?[2]

Hor. Mistress, what cheer?

Kath. 'Faith, as cold as can be.

Pet. Pluck up thy spirits, look cheerfully upon me.
Here, love; thou see'st how diligent I am,
To dress thy meat myself, and bring it thee:
[*Sets the dish on a table.*
I am sure, sweet Kate, this kindness merits thanks.
What, not a word? Nay then, thou lov'st it not;
And all my pains is sorted to no 'proof:[3]——
Here, take away this dish.

Kath. Pray you, let it stand.

Pet. The poorest service is repaid with thanks;
And so shall mine, before you touch the meat.

Kath. I thank you, sir.

Hor. Signior Petruchio, fye! you are to blame!
Come, mistress Kate, I'll bear you company.

Pet. Eat it up all, Hortensio, if thou lov'st me.— [*Aside.*
Much good do it unto thy gentle heart!
Kate, eat apace:—And now, my honey love,
Will we return unto thy father's house;
And revel it as bravely as the best,
With silken coats, and caps, and golden rings,
With ruffs, and cuffs, and farthingales, and things;
With scarfs, and fans, and double change of bravery,[4]
With amber bracelets, beads, and all this knavery.
What, hast thou din'd? The tailor stays thy leisure,
To deck thy body with his ruffling[5] treasure.

Enter Tailor.

Come, tailor, let us see these ornaments;

Enter Haberdasher.

Lay forth the gown.—What news with you, sir?

Hab. Here is the cap your worship did bespeak

Pet. Why, this was moulded on a porringer!
A velvet dish;—fye, fye! 'tis lewd and filthy:
Why, 'tis a cockle, or a walnutshell,
A knack, a toy, a trick, a baby's cap;
Away with it; come, let me have a bigger.

Kath. I'll have no bigger; this doth fit the time,
And gentlewomen wear such caps as these.

Pet. When you are gentle, you shall have one too,
And not till then.

Hor. That will not be in haste. [*Aside*

Kath. Why, sir, I trust, I may have leave to speak;
And speak I will; I am no child, no babe:
Your betters have endur'd me say my mind;
And, if you cannot, best you stop your ears.
My tongue will tell the anger of my heart;
Or else my heart, concealing it, will break:
And, rather than it shall, I will be free
Even to the uttermost, as I please, in words.

Pet Why, thou say'st true; it is a paltry cap,
A custard-coffin,[6] a bauble, a silken pie:
I love thee well, in that thou lik'st it not.

Kath. Love me, or love me not, I like the cap,
And it I will have, or I will have none.

Pet. Thy gown? why, ay:—Come, tailor, let us see't.
O mercy, God! what masking stuff is here?
What's this? a sleeve! 'tis like a demi-cannon:
What! up and down, carv'd like an apple-tart?
Here's snip, and nip, and cut, and slish, and slash,
Like to a censer[7] in a barber's shop:—
Why, what, o'devil's name, tailor, call'st thou this?

Hor. I see, she's like to have neither cap nor gown. [*Aside.*

Tai. You bid me make it orderly and well,
According to the fashion, and the time.

Pet. Marry, and did; but if you be remember'd,
I did not bid you mar it to the time.
Go, hop me over every kennel home,
For you shall hop without my custom, sir:
I'll none of it; hence, make your best of it.

Kath. I never saw a better-fashion'd gown,
More quaint,[8] more pleasing, nor more commendable;
Belike, you mean to make a puppet of me.

Pet. Why, true; he means to make a puppet of thee.

Tai. She says, your worship means to make a puppet of her.

Pet. O monstrous arrogance! Thou liest, thou thread,
Thou thimble,

1 This is agreeable to the doctrine of the times. In The Glasse of Humours, no date, p. 60, it is said, 'But note here, that the first diet is not only in avoiding superfluity of meats, and surfeits of drinks, but also in eschewing such as are obnoxious, and least agreeable with our happy temperate state; as for a choleric man to abstain from all salt, *scorched*, *dry meats*, from *mustard*, and such like things as will aggravate his malignant humours.' Petruchio before objects to the over-roasted mutton.

2 That is, *all sunk* and *dispirited.* This gallicism is frequent in many of the old plays.

3 'And all *my* labour has ended in nothing, or *proved* nothing,' says Johnson. This can hardly be right. Mr. Douce's suggestion, that it means 'all my labour is *adapted* to no *approof*,' is much better; indeed there can be no doubt that we should read '*proof* with a mark of elision for *approof*; but *sort* is used in the sense of *sorter*, French, to issue, to terminate.' 'It *sorted* not' is frequently used by writers of that period for, It did not end so; or, It did not answer. Shakspeare uses *sort* for *lot*, *chance*, more than once.

4 Finery.

5 To *ruffle*, in Shakspeare's time, signified to *flaunt*, to *strut*, *to swagger*.

6 A coffin was the culinary term for the raised crust of a pie or custard.

7 These censers resembled our brasiers in shape, they had pierced convex covers.

8 *Quaint* was used as a term of commendation by our ancestors. It seems, when applied to dress, to have meant *spruce*, *trim*, *neat*, like the French *cointe*

Thou yard, three-quarters, half-yard, quarter, nail,
Thou flea, thou nit, thou winter cricket thou:—
Brav'd in mine own house with a skein of thread!
Away, thou rag, thou quantity, thou remnant;
Or I shall so be-mete[1] thee with thy yard,
As thou shalt think on prating whilst thou liv'st!
I tell thee, I, that thou hast marr'd her gown.

Tai. Your worship is deceiv'd; the gown is made
Just as my master had direction:
Grumio gave order how it should be done.

Gru. I gave him no order, I gave him the stuff.

Tai. But how did you desire it should be made?

Gru. Marry, sir, with needle and thread.

Tai. But did you not request to have it cut?

Gru. Thou hast faced many things.[2]

Tai. I have.

Gru. Face not me; thou hast brav'd[3] many men; brave not me; I will neither be fac'd nor brav'd. I say unto thee,—I bid thy master cut out the gown; but I did not bid him cut it to pieces:[4] *ergo*, thou liest.

Tai. Why, here is the note of the fashion to testify.

Pet. Read it.

Gru. The note lies in his throat, if he say I said so.

Tai. *Imprimis, a loose-bodied gown:*

Gru. Master, if ever I said loose-bodied gown,[5] sew me in the skirts of it, and beat me to death with a bottom of brown thread: I said, a gown.

Pet. Proceed.

Tai. *With a small compassed cape;*[6]

Gru. I confess the cape.

Tai. *With a trunk sleeve;——*

Gru. I confess two sleeves.

Tai. *The sleeves curiously cut.*

Pet. Ay, there's the villany.

Gru. Error i'the bill, sir; error i'the bill. I commanded the sleeves should be cut out, and sewed up again; and that I'll prove upon thee, though thy little finger be armed in a thimble.

Tai. This is true, that I say; an I had thee in place where, thou should'st know it.

Gru. I am for thee straight: take thou the bill,[7] give me thy mete-yard, and spare not me.

Hor. God-a-mercy, Grumio! then he shall have no odds.

Pet. Well, sir, in brief, the gown is not for me.

Gru. You are i'the right, sir; 'tis for my mistress.

Pet. Go, take it up unto thy master's use.

Gru. Villain, not for thy life: Take up my mistress' gown for thy master's use!

Pet. Why, sir, what's your conceit in that?

Gru. O, sir, the conceit is deeper than you think for:
Take up my mistress' gown to his master's use!
O, fye, fye, fye!

Pet. Hortensio, say thou wilt see the tailor paid:— [*Aside.*
Go take it hence; be gone, and say no more.

Hor. Tailor, I'll pay thee for thy gown to-morrow.
Take no unkindness of his hasty words:
Away, I say; commend me to thy master. [*Exit* Tailor.

Pet. Well, come, my Kate; we will unto your father's,
Even in these honest mean habiliments;
Our purses shall be proud, our garments poor;
For, 'tis the mind that makes the body rich;
And as the sun breaks through the darkest clouds
So honour peereth in the meanest habit.
What, is the jay more precious than the lark,
Because his feathers are more beautiful?
Or is the adder better than the eel,
Because his painted skin contents the eye?
O, no, good Kate; neither art thou the worse
For this poor furniture, and mean array.
If thou account'st it shame, lay it on me:
And therefore, frolic; we will hence forthwith,
To feast and sport us at thy father's house.—
Go, call my men, and let us straight to him;
And bring our horses unto Long-lane end,
There will we mount, and thither walk on foot.
Let's see; I think, 'tis now some seven o'clock,
And well we may come there by dinner time.

Kath. I dare assure you, sir, 'tis almost two;
And 'twill be supper time, ere you come there.

Pet. It shall be seven, ere I go to horse;
Look, what I speak, or do, or think to do,
You are still crossing it.—Sirs, let't alone:
I will not go to-day; and ere I do,
It shall be what o'clock I say it is.

Hor. Why, so! this gallant will command the sun [*Exeunt.*[8]

SCENE IV. Padua. *Before* Baptista's *House. Enter* TRANIO, *and the* Pedant *dressed like* VINCENTIO.

Tra. Sir, this is the house; Please it you, that I call?

Ped. Ay, what else? and, but[9] I be deceived,
Signior Baptista may remember me.
Near twenty years' ago, in Genoa, where
We were lodgers at the Pegasus.[10]

Tra. 'Tis well:
And hold your own, in any case, with such
Austerity as 'longeth to a father.

Enter BIONDELLO.

Ped. I warrant you: But, sir, here comes your boy;
'Twere good, he were school'd.

Tra. Fear you not him. Sirrah, Biondello,
Now do your duty throughly, I advise you;
Imagine 'twere the right Vincentio.

Bion. Tut! fear not me.

Tra. But hast thou done thy errand to Baptista?

Bion. I told him, that your father was at Venice?
And that you look'd for him this day in Padua.

Tra. Thou'rt a tall[11] fellow; hold thee that to drink.
Here comes Baptista:—set your countenance, sir.—

Enter BAPTISTA *and* LUCENTIO.

Signior Baptista, you are happily met.—
Sir, [*to the* Pedant.]
This is the gentleman I told you of;
I pray you, stand good father to me now,
Give me Bianca for my patrimony.

Ped. Soft, son!—
Sir, by your leave: having come to Padua
To gather in some debts, my son Lucentio
Made me acquainted with a weighty cause
Of love between your daughter and himself.
And,—for the good report I hear of you;
And for the love he beareth to your daughter,
And she to him,—to stay him not too long

1 Be-measure.

2 Turned up many garments with facings.

3 Grumio quibbles upon to *brave*, to *make fine*, as he does upon *facing*.

4 Mr. Douce remarks that this scene appears to have been originally borrowed from a story of Sir Philip Caulthrop and John Drakes, a silly shoemaker of Norwich, related in Camden's Remains and Leigh's Accedence of Armorie.

5 This being a very customary dress with women of abandoned character, was probably not much in repute.

6 A round cape.

7 A quibble is intended between the written *bill* and the *bill* or weapon of a foot soldier.

8 After this *exeunt* the characters before whom the play is supposed to be exhibited, were introduced, from the old play, by Mr. Pope in his edition.
'*Lord.* Who's within there! [*Enter Servants.*]
Asleep again! Go take him easily up, and put him in his own apparel again. But see you wake him not in any case.
Serv. It shall be done, my lord; come, help to bear him hence. [*They bear off* Sly'
Johnson thought the fifth act should begin here.

9 See the note on Act iii. Sc. 1.

10 Shakspeare has here taken a sign out of London, and hung it up in Padua. The *Pegasus* is the arms of the Middle Temple, and is a very popular sign.

11 i. e. a *high* fellow, a brave boy, as we now say, Vide note on Merry Wives of Windsor, Act i. Sc. 4.

I am content, in a good father's care,
To have him match'd; and,—if you please to like
No worse than I, sir,—upon some agreement,
Me shall you find most ready and most willing
With one consent to have her so bestow'd;
For curious[1] I cannot be with you,
Signior Baptista, of whom I hear so well.

Bap. Sir, pardon me in what I have to say:—
Your plainness, and your shortness, please me well.
Right true it is, your son Lucentio here
Doth love my daughter, and she loveth him,
Or both dissemble deeply their affections:
And, therefore, if you say no more than this,
That like a father you will deal with him,
And pass[2] my daughter a sufficient dower,
The match is made, and all is done:
Your son shall have my daughter with consent.

Tra. I thank you, sir. Where then do you know best,
We be affied;[3] and such assurance ta'en,
As shall with either part's agreement stand?

Bap. Not in my house, Lucentio; for you know,
Pitchers have ears, and I have many servants:
Besides, Old Gremio is hearkening still;
And, happily,[4] we might be interrupted.

Tra. Then at my lodging, an it like you, sir:
There doth my father lie; and there, this night
We'll pass the business privately and well:
Send for your daughter by your servant here,
My boy shall fetch the scrivener presently.
The worst is this,—that, at so slender warning,
You're like to have a thin and slender pittance.

Bap. It likes me well:—Cambio, hie you home,
And bid Bianca make her ready straight:
And, if you will, tell what hath happened:—
Lucentio's father is arrived in Padua,
And how she's like to be Lucentio's wife.

Luc. I pray the gods she may, with all my heart!

Tra. Dally not with the gods, but get thee gone.
Signior Baptista, shall I lead the way?
Welcome! one mess is like to be your cheer:
Come, sir: we'll better it in Pisa.

Bap. I follow you.

[*Exeunt* Tranio, Pedant, *and* Baptista.

Bion. Cambio.—

Luc. What say'st thou, Biondello?

Bion. You saw my master wink and laugh upon you?

Luc. Biondello, what of that?

Bion. 'Faith, nothing: but he has left me here behind, to expound the meaning or moral[5] of his signs and tokens.

Luc. I pray thee, moralize them.

Bion. Then thus. Baptista is safe, talking with the deceiving father of a deceitful son.

Luc. And what of him?

Bion. His daughter is to be brought by you to the supper.

Luc. And then?—

Bion. The old priest at St. Luke's church is at your command at all hours.

Luc. And what of all this?

Bion. I cannot tell; except[6] they are busied about a counterfeit assurance: Take you assurance of her, *cum privilegio ad imprimendum solum*[7] to the church;—take the priest, clerk, and some sufficient honest witnesses:
If this be not that you look for, I have no more to say,
But, bid Bianca farewell for ever and a day. [*Going.*

Luc. Hear'st thou, Biondello?

Bion. I cannot tarry: I knew a wench married in an afternoon as she went to the garden for parsley to stuff a rabbit; and so may you, sir; and so adieu, sir. My master hath appointed me to go to Saint Luke's, to bid the priest be ready to come against you come with your appendix. [*Exit.*

Luc. I may, and will, if she be so contented:
She will be pleas'd, then wherefore should I doubt?
Hap what hap may, I'll roundly go about her:
It shall go hard, if Cambio go without her. [*Exit*.[8]

SCENE V. *A public road. Enter* Petruchio, Katharina, *and* Hortensio.

Pet. Come on, o' God's name: once more toward our father's.
Good Lord, how bright and goodly shines the moon!

Kath. The moon! the sun; it is not moonlight now.

Pet. I say, it is the moon that shines so bright.

Kath. I know, it is the sun that shines so bright.

Pet. Now, by my mother's son, and that's myself,
It shall be moon or stars, or what I list,
Or ere I journey to your father's house:—
Go on, and fetch our horses back again.—
Evermore cross'd, and cross'd; nothing but cross'd.

Hor. Say as he says, or we shall never go.

Kath. Forward, I pray, since we have come so far,
And be it moon, or sun, or what you please:
And if you please to call it a rush candle,
Henceforth I vow it shall be so for me.

Pet. I say it is the moon.

Kath. I know, it is the moon.

Pet. Nay, then you lie; it is the blessed sun.

Kath. Then, God be bless'd, it is the blessed sun:—
But sun it is not, when you say it is not;
And the moon changes, even as your mind.
What you will have it nam'd, even that it is;
And so it shall be so,[9] for Katharine.

Hor. Petruchio, go thy ways; the field is won.

Pet. Well, forward, forward: thus the bowl should run,
And not unluckily against the bias.—
But soft; what company is coming here?

Enter Vincentio, *in a travelling dress.*

Good-morrow, gentle mistress: Where away? [*To* Vincentio.
Tell me, sweet Kate, and tell me truly too,[10]
Hast thou beheld a fresher gentlewoman?
Such war of white and red within her cheeks?
What stars do spangle heaven with such beauty,
As those two eyes become that heavenly face?
Fair lovely maid, once more good day to thee?
Sweet Kate, embrace her for her beauty's sake.

Hor. 'A will make the man mad, to make a woman of him.

Kath. Young budding virgin, fair, and fresh, and sweet,
Whither away: or where is thy abode?
Happy the parents of so fair a child;
Happier the man, whom favourable stars
Allot thee for his lovely bed-fellow![11]

---

1 i. e. scrupulous. 2 Assure, or convey; a law term.
3 Betrothed.
4 *Happily*, in Shakspeare's time, signified *peradventure*, as well as fortunately; we now write it *haply*.
5 i. e. the secret purpose.
6 The first folio reads *expect*.
7 These were the words of the old exclusive privilege for *imprinting* a book. A quibble is meant.
8 Here in the old play, the Tinker speaks again:—
'*Slie.* Sim, must they be married now?'
Lord. I, my lord.
Enter Ferando *and* Sander.
Slie. Look, Sim, the fool is come again now.'
9 We should probably read, 'and so it shall be *still*, for Katharine.'
10 In the first sketch of this play are two passages worth preserving, and which Pope thought to be from the hand of Shakspeare.
'Faire lovely maiden, young and affable,
More clear of hue, and far more beautiful
Than precious sardonyx or purple rocks
Of amethists, or glistering hyacinth—
—Sweete Kate, entertaine this lovely woman.
Kath. Fair lovely lady, bright and chrystalline
Beauteous and stately as the eye-train'd bird;
As glorious as the morning wash'd with dew,
Within whose eyes she takes her dawning beams,
And golden summer sleeps upon thy cheeks.
Wrap up thy radiations in some cloud,
Lest that thy beauty make this stately town
Inhabitable, like the burning zone,
With sweet reflections of thy lovely face.'
11 This is from the fourth book of Ovid's Metamorphoses, by Golding, 1586, p. 56. Ovid borrowed his ideas from the sixth book of the Odyssey, 154, &c

Pet. Why, how now, Kate! I hope thou art not mad;
This is a man, old, wrinkled, faded, wither'd;
And not a maiden, as thou say'st he is.
Kath Pardon, old father, my mistaking eyes,
That have been so bedazzled with the sun,
That every thing I look on seemeth green:[1]
Now I perceive thou art a reverend father;
Pardon, I pray thee, for my mad mistaking.
Pet. Do, good old grandsire; and, withal, make known
Which way thou travellest; if along with us,
We shall be joyful of thy company.
Vin. Fair sir,—and you, my merry mistress,—
That with your strange encounter much amaz'd me;
My name is call'd—Vincentio; my dwelling—Pisa;
And bound I am to Padua; there to visit
A son of mine, which long I have not seen.
Pet. What is his name?
Vin. Lucentio, gentle sir.
Pet. Happily met; the happier for thy son.
And now by law as well as reverend age,
I may entitle thee—my loving father;
The sister to my wife, this gentlewoman,
Thy son by this hath married: Wonder not,
Nor be not griev'd; she is of good esteem,
Her dowry wealthy, and of worthy birth;
Beside, so qualified as may beseem
The spouse of any noble gentleman.
Let me embrace with old Vincentio:
And wander we to see thy honest son,
Who will of thy arrival be full joyous.
Vin. But is this true? or is it else your pleasure,
Like pleasant travellers to break a jest
Upon the company you overtake?
Hor. I do assure thee, father, so it is.
Pet. Come, go along, and see the truth hereof;
For our first merriment hath made thee jealous.
[*Exeunt* PET. KATH. *and* VIN.
Hor. Well, Petruchio, this hath put me in heart.
Have to my widow; and if she be froward,
Then hast thou taught Hortensio to be untoward.
[*Exit.*

ACT V.

SCENE I. Padua. *Before* Lucentio's *House.*

Enter on one side BIONDELLO, LUCENTIO, *and* BIANCA; GREMIO *walking on the other side.*

Bion. Softly and swiftly, sir; for the priest is ready.

Luc. I fly, Biondello: but they may chance to need thee at home, therefore leave us.

Bion. Nay, faith, I'll see the church o'your back; and then come back to my master[2] as soon as I can.
[*Exeunt* LUC. BIAN. *and* BION.

Gre. I marvel Cambio comes not all this while.

Enter PETRUCHIO, KATHARINA, VINCENTIO, *and* Attendants.

Pet. Sir, here's the door, this is Lucentio's house,
My father's bears more toward the market-place;
Thither must I, and here I leave you, sir.
Vin. You shall not choose, but drink before you go;
I think, I shall command your welcome here,
And, by all likelihood, some cheer is toward.
[*Knocks.*

Gre. They're busy within, you were best knock louder.

Enter Pedant *above at a window.*

Ped. What's he, that knocks as he would beat down the gate?

Vin. Is Signior Lucentio within, sir?

Ped. He's within, sir, but not to be spoken withal.

Vin. What if a man bring him a hundred pound or two, to make merry withal?

Ped. Keep your hundred pounds to yourself; he shall need none, so long as I live.

Pet. Nay, I told you, your son was beloved in Padua.—Do you hear, sir?—to leave frivolous circumstances,—I pray you, tell Signior Lucentio, that his father is come from Pisa, and is here at the door to speak with him.

Ped. Thou liest: his father is come from Pisa,[3] and here looking out at the window.

Vin. Art thou his father?

Ped. Ay, sir; so his mother says, if I may believe her.

Pet. Why, how now, gentleman! [*To* VINCENT.] Why, this is flat knavery, to take upon you another man's name.

Ped. Lay hands on the villain; I believe 'a means to cozen somebody in this city under my countenance.

Re-enter BIONDELLO.

Bion. I have seen them in the church together. God send 'em good shipping!—But who is here? mine old master, Vincentio? now we are undone, and brought to nothing.

Vin Come hither, crack-hemp.
[*Seeing* BIONDELLO.

Bion. I hope, I may choose, sir.

Vin. Come hither, you rogue: What, have you forgot me?

Bion. Forgot you? no, sir: I could not forget you, for I never saw you before in all my life.

Vin. What, you notorious villain, didst thou never see thy master's father, Vincentio?

Bion. What, my old worshipful old master? yes, marry, sir; see where he looks out of the window.

Vin. Is't so, indeed? [*Beats* BIONDELLO.

Bion. Help, help, help! here's a madman will murder me. [*Exit.*

Ped. Help son! help, Signior Baptista!
[*Exit, from the window.*

Pet. Pr'ythee, Kate, let's stand aside, and see the end of this controversy. [*They retire.*

Re-enter Pedant *below;* BAPTISTA, TRANIO, *and* Servants.

Tra. Sir, what are you that offer to beat my servant?

Vin. What am I, sir? nay, what are you, sir?—O immortal gods! O fine villain! A silken doublet! a velvet hose! a scarlet cloak! and a copatain hat![4]—O, I am undone! I am undone! while I play the good husband at home, my son and my servant spend all at the university.

Tra. How now! what's the matter?

Bap. What, is the man lunatic?

Tra. Sir, you seem a sober ancient gentleman by your habit, but your words show you a madman: Why, sir, what concerns it you, if I wear pearl and gold? I thank my good father, I am able to maintain it.

Vin. Thy father? O, villain! he is a sail-maker in Bergamo.

Bap. You mistake, sir; you mistake, sir: Pray, what do you think is his name?

Vin. His name? as if I knew not his name; I have brought him up ever since he was three years old, and his name is—Tranio.

Ped. Away, away, mad ass! his name is Lucentio; and he is mine only son, and heir to the lands of me, Signior Vincentio.

Vin. Lucentio! O, he hath murdered his master!—Lay hold on him, I charge you, in the duke's name:—O, my son, my son!—tell me, thou villain, where is my son Lucentio?

Tra. Call forth an officer:[5] [*Enter one with an*

---

1 Another proof of Shakspeare's accurate observation of natural phænomena. When one has been long in the sunshine, the surrounding objects will often appear tinged with green. The reason is assigned by writers upon optics.

2 The old editions read *mistress.* The emendation is Theobald's, who rightly observes, that by *master*, Biondello means his pretended master, Tranio.

3 The old copy reads *Padua.*

4 A sugar-loaf hat, a *coppid-tanke hat;* galerus ac cuminatus.—*Junius Nomenclator*, 1585.

5 Here, in the original play, the Tinker speaks again·
'*Slie.* I say, weele have no sending to prison.
Lord. My lord, this is but the play; they're but in jest.
Slie. I tell thee, Sim, weele have no sending
To prison, that's flat; why, Sim, am I not Don Christo Vari?
Therefore, I say, they shall not goe to prison.

Officer.] Carry this mad knave to the gaol: -Father Baptista, I charge you see that he be forth coming.

Vin. Carry me to the gaol!

Gre. Stay, officer; he shall not go to prison.

Bap. Talk not, Signior Gremio; I say, he shall go to prison.

Gre. Take heed, Signior Baptista, lest you be coney-catched[1] in this business; I dare swear, this is the right Vincentio.

Ped. Swear, if thou darest.

Gre. Nay, I dare not swear it.

Tra. Then thou wert best say, that I am not Lucentio.

Gre. Yes, I know thee to be Signior Lucentio.

Bap. Away with the dotard; to the gaol with him.

Vin. Thus strangers may be haled and abused:---
O monstrous villain!

Re-enter BIONDELLO, *with* LUCENTIO, *and* BIANCA.

Bion. O, we are spoiled, and---Yonder he is; deny him, forswear him, or else we are all undone.

Luc. Pardon, sweet father. [*Kneeling.*

Vin. Lives my sweet son?

[BIONDELLO, TRANIO, *and* Pedant *run out.*

Bion. Pardon, dear father. [*Kneeling.*

Bap. How hast thou offended?
Where is Lucentio?

Luc. Here's Lucentio,
Right son unto the right Vincentio;
That have by marriage made thy daughter mine,
While counterfeit supposes blear'd thine eyne.[2]

Gre. Here's packing,[3] with a witness, to deceive us all!

Vin. Where is that damned villain, Tranio,
That fac'd and brav'd me in this matter so?

Bap. Why, tell me, is not this my Cambio?

Bian. Cambio is chang'd into Lucentio.

Luc. Love wrought these miracles. Bianca's love
Made me exchange my state with Tranio,
While he did bear my countenance in the town;
And happily I have arriv'd at last
Unto the wished haven of my bliss:—
What Tranio did, myself enforc'd him to;
Then pardon him, sweet father, for my sake.

Vin. I'll slit the villain's nose, that would have sent me to the gaol.

Bap. But do you hear, sir? [*To* LUCENTIO.] Have you married my daughter without asking my good-will?

Vin. Fear not, Baptista; we will content you, go to: But I will in, to be revenged for this villainy. [*Exit.*

Bap. And I, to sound the depth of this knavery. [*Exit.*

Luc. Look not pale, Bianca; thy father will not frown. [*Exeunt.* LUC. *and* BIAN.

Gre. My cake is dough:[4] But I'll in among the rest:
Out of hope of all,—but my share of the feast. [*Exit.*

PETRUCHIO *and* KATHARINA *advance.*

Kath. Husband, let's follow, to see the end of this ado.

Pet. First kiss me, Kate, and we will.

Kath. What, in the midst of the street?

Pet. What, art thou ashamed of me?

Kath. No, sir; God forbid:—but ashamed to kiss.

Pet. Why, then let's home again:—Come, sirrah, let's away.

Kath. Nay, I will give thee a kiss: now pray thee, love, stay.

Pet. Is not this well?—Come, my sweet Kate;
Better once than never, for never too late. [*Exeunt.*

SCENE II. *A Room in* Lucentio's *House. A Banquet set out. Enter* BAPTISTA, VINCENTIO, GREMIO, *the* Pedant, LUCENTIO, BIANCA, PETRUCHIO, KATHARINA, HORTENSIO, *and* Widow. TRANIO, BIONDELLO, GRUMIO, *and others. attending.*

Luc. At last, though long, our jarring notes agree
And time it is, when raging war is done,[5]
To smile at 'scapes and perils overblown.—
My fair Bianca, bid my father welcome,
While I with selfsame kindness welcome thine:-
Brother Petruchio,—sister Katharina,—
And thou, Hortensio, with thy loving widow,-
Feast with the best, and welcome to my house;
My banquet[6] is to close our stomachs up,
After our great good cheer: Pray you, sit down;
For now we sit to chat, as well as eat.
[*They sit at table*

Pet. Nothing but sit and sit, and eat and eat!

Bap. Padua affords this kindness, son Petruchio.

Pet. Padua affords nothing but what is kind.

Hor. For both our sakes, I would that word were true.

Pet. Now, for my life, Hortensio fears his widow.

Wid. Then never trust me if I be afeard.

Pet. You are sensible, and yet you miss my sense;
I mean, Hortensio is afeard of you.

Wid. He that is giddy, thinks the world turns round.

Pet. Roundly replied.

Kath. Mistress, how mean you that?

Wid. Thus I conceive by him.

Pet. Conceives by me!—How likes Hortensio that?

Hor. My widow says, thus she conceives her tale.

Pet. Very well mended: Kiss him for that, good widow.

Kath. He that is giddy, thinks the world turns round:———
I pray you, tell me what you meant by that.

Wid. Your husband, being troubled with a shrew,
Measures my husband's sorrow by his woe:[7]
And now you know my meaning.

Kath. A very mean meaning.

Wid. Right, I mean you.

Kath. And I am mean indeed, respecting you.

Pet. To her, Kate!

Hor. To her, widow!

Pet. A hundred marks, my Kate does put her down

Hor. That's my office.

Pet. Spoke like an officer:—Ha' to thee, lad.
[*Drinks to* HORTENSIO.

Bap. How likes Gremio these quick-witted folks?

Gre. Believe me, sir, they butt together well.

Bian. Head, and butt? a hasty-witted body
Would say, your head and butt were head and horn.

Vin. Ay, mistress bride, hath that awaken'd you?

Bian. Ay, but not frighted me; therefore I'll sleep again.

Pet. Nay, that you shall not; since you have begun,
Have at you for a bitter[8] jest or two.

Lord. No more they shall not, my lord:
They be runne away.
Slie. Are they run away, Sim? that's well:
Then gis some more drinke, and let them play againe.
Lord. Here, my lord.'

1 i. e. deceived, cheated.

2 This is probably an allusion to Gascoigne's comedy, entitled *Supposes*, from which several of the incidents are borrowed. Gascoigne's original was Ariosto's *I Suppositi.* The word *supposes* was often used as it is in the text, by Shakspeare's contemporaries; one instance, from Drayton's epistle of King John to Matilda, may suffice:—
' And tell me those are shadows and *supposes*.'

3 Plottings, underhand contrivances.

4 An obsolete proverb, repeated on the loss of hope or expectation. Its meaning is not easily explained. It has been suggested that a cake which comes out of the oven in a state of dough, is utterly spoiled.

5 The old copy reads *come;* the emendation is Rowe's.

6 The *banquet* here, as in other places of Shakspeare, was a refection similar to our modern *dessert*, consisting of cakes, sweetmeats, fruits, &c.

7 As this was meant for a rhyming couplet, it should be observed that *shrew* was pronounced *shrow.* See also the finale, where it rhymes to *so.*

8 The old copy reads *better.* The emendation is Capell's.

Bian. Am I your bird? I mean to shift my bush,
And then pursue me as you draw your bow:—
You are welcome all.
[*Exeunt* BIANCA, KATHARINA, *and* Widow.
Pet. She hath prevented me.—Here, Signior Tranio,
This bird you aim'd at, though you hit her not;
Therefore, a health to all that shot and miss'd.
Tra. O, sir, Lucentio slipp'd me like his grey-hound,
Which runs himself, and catches for his master.
Pet. A good swift[1] simile, but something currish.
Tra. 'Tis well, sir, that you hunted for yourself;
'Tis thought, your deer does hold you out a bay.
Bap. O ho, Petruchio, Tranio hits you now.
Luc. I thank thee for that gird,[2] good Tranio.
Hor. Confess, confess, hath he not hit you here?
Pet. 'A has a little gall'd me, I confess;
And, as the jest did glance away from me,
'Tis ten to one it maim'd you two outright.
Bap. Now, in good sadness, son Petruchio,
I think thou hast the veriest shrew of all.
Pet. Well, I say—no; and therefore, for assurance,
Let's each one send unto his wife;
And he, whose wife is most obedient
To come at first when he doth send for her,
Shall win the wager which we will propose.
Hor. Content:——What is the wager?
Luc. Twenty crowns.
Pet. Twenty crowns!
I'll venture so much on my hawk, or hound,
But twenty times so much upon my wife.
Luc. A hundred, then.
Hor. Content.
Pet. A match; 'tis done.
Hor. Who shall begin?
Luc. That will I. Go,
Biondello, bid your mistress come to me.
Bion. I go. [*Exit.*
Bap. Son, I will be your half, Bianca comes.
Luc. I'll have no halves; I'll bear it all myself.

Re-enter BIONDELLO.

How now! what news?
Bion. Sir, my mistress sends you word
That she is busy, and she cannot come.
Pet. How! she is busy, and she cannot come!
Is that an answer?
Gre. Ay, and a kind one too:
Pray God, sir, your wife send you not a worse.
Pet. I hope, better.
Hor. Sirrah, Biondello, go, and entreat my wife
To come to me forthwith. [*Exit* BIONDELLO.
Pet. O, ho! entreat her!
Nay, then she must needs come.
Hor. I am afraid, sir,
Do what you can, yours will not be entreated

Re-enter BIONDELLO.

Now where's my wife?
Bion. She says, you have some goodly jest in hand;
She will not come; she bids you come to her.
Pet. Worse and worse; she will not come! O vile,
Intolerable, not to be endur'd!
Sirrah, Grumio, go to your mistress;
Say, I command her come to me. [*Exit* GRUMIO.
Hor. I know her answer.
Pet. What?
Hor. She will not.
Pet. The fouler fortune mine, and there an end.

Enter KATHARINA.

Bap. Now, by my holidame, here comes Katharina!
Kath. What is your will, sir, that you send for me?
Pet. Where is your sister, and Hortensio's wife?
Kath. They sit conferring by the parlour fire.
Pet. Go fetch them hither; if they deny to come,
Swinge me them soundly forth unto their husbands:
Away, I say, and bring them hither straight.
[*Exit* KATHARINA.
Luc. Here is a wonder, if you talk of a wonder.
Hor. And so it is; I wonder what it bodes.
Pet. Marry, peace it bodes, and love, and quiet life,
An awful rule, and right supremacy;
And, to be short, what not, that's sweet and happy.
Bap. Now fair befall thee, good Petruchio!
The wager thou hast won; and I will add
Unto their losses twenty thousand crowns;
Another dowry to another daughter,
For she is chang'd, as she had never been.
Pet. Nay, I will win my wager better yet;
And show more sign of her obedience,
Her new-built virtue and obedience.

Re-enter KATHARINA, *with* BIANCA *and* Widow.

See, where she comes; and brings your froward wives
As prisoners to her womanly persuasion.—
Katharina, that cap of yours becomes you not;
Off with that bauble, throw it under foot.
[KATHARINA *pulls off her cap, and throws it down.*
Wid. Lord, let me never have a cause to sigh,
Till I be brought to such a silly pass!
Bian. Fye! what a foolish duty call you this?
Luc. I would, your duty were as foolish too:
The wisdom of your duty, fair Bianca,
Hath cost me a hundred crowns since supper-time.
Bian. The more fool you for laying on my duty.
Pet. Katharine, I charge thee, tell these head-strong women
What duty they do owe their lords and husbands.
Wid. Come, come, you're mocking; we will have no telling.
Pet. Come on, I say; and first begin with her.
Wid. She shall not.
Pet. I say, she shall;—and first begin with her.
Kath. Fye, fye! unknit that threat'ning unkind brow;
And dart not scornful glances from those eyes,
To wound thy lord, thy king, thy governor:
It blots thy beauty, as frosts do bite the meads;
Confounds thy fame, as whirlwinds shake fair buds,
And in no sense is meet or amiable.
A woman mov'd, is like a fountain troubled,
Muddy, ill seeming, thick, bereft of beauty;
And, while it is so, none so dry or thirsty
Will deign to sip, or touch one drop of it.
Thy husband is thy lord, thy life, thy keeper,
Thy head, thy sovereign; one that cares for thee,
And for thy maintenance: commits his body
To painful labour, both by sea and land;
To watch the night in storms, the day in cold,
While thou liest warm at home, secure and safe;
And craves no other tribute at thy hands,
But love, fair looks, and true obedience;—
Too little payment for so great a debt.
Such duty as the subject owes the prince,
Even such a woman oweth to her husband.
And, when she's froward, peevish, sullen, sour,
And, not obedient to his honest will,
What is she, but a foul contending rebel,
And graceless traitor to her loving lord?
I am asham'd, that women are so simple
To offer war, where they should kneel for peace,
Or seek for rule, supremacy, and sway,
When they are bound to serve, love, and obey.
Why are our bodies soft, and weak, and smooth,
Unapt to toil and trouble in the world;
But that our soft conditions[3] and our hearts,
Should well agree with our external parts?
Come, come, you froward and unable worms!
My mind hath been as big as one of yours,
My heart as great; my reason, haply, more,
To bandy word for word, and frown for frown
But now, I see, our lances are but straws;
Our strength as weak, our weakness past compare,—
That seeming to be most, which we least are.

1 Beside the original sense of speedy in motion, *swift* signified *witty, quick witted.*
2 A *gird* is a cut, a sarcasm, a stroke of satire.

3 That is, the gentle qualities of our minds

Then vail your stomachs,[1] for it is no boot;
And place your hands below your husband's foot:
In token of which duty, if he please,
My hand is ready, may it do him ease.

Pet. Why, there's a wench!—Come on, and kiss me, Kate.

Luc. Well, go thy ways, old lad; for thou shalt ha't.

Vin. 'Tis a good hearing, when children are toward.

Luc. But a harsh hearing when women are froward.

Pet. Come, Kate, we'll to bed:——
We three are married, but you two are sped.[2]
'Twas I won the wager, though you hit the white;[3]
[*To* LUCENTIO.
And, being a winner, God give you good night!
[*Exeunt* PETRUCHIO *and* KATH.

Hor. Now go thy ways, thou hast tam'd a curst shrew.

Luc. 'Tis a wonder, by your leave, she will be tam'd so. [*Exeunt.*[4]

OF this play the two plots are so well united that they can hardly be called two, without injury to the art with which they are interwoven. The attention is entertained with all the variety of a double plot, yet is not distracted by unconnected incidents.

The part between Katharina and Petruchio is eminently spritely and diverting. At the marriage of Bianca, the arrival of the real father, perhaps, produces more perplexity than pleasure. The whole play is very popular and diverting. JOHNSON.

---

1 '*Vail* your *stomachs*,' *abate* your *pride*, your *spirit*, *it is no boot*, i. e. it is profitless, it is no advantage.

2 i. e. the fate of you both is decided; for you both have wives who exhibit early proofs of disobedience.

3 The *white* was the central part of the mark or butt in archery. Here is also a play upon the name of *Bianca*, which is *white* in Italian.

4 The old play continues thus:—

Then enter two, bearing Slie *in his own apparel againe, and leaves him where they found him, and then goes out: then enters the* Tapster.

Tapster. Now that the darksome night is overpast,
And dawning day appeares in christall skie,
Now must I haste abroade: but softe! who's this?
What, Slie? O wondrous! hath he laine heere all night!
Ile wake him; I thinke he's starved by this,
But that his belly was so stufft with ale:
What now, Slie? awake for shame.

Slie. [Awaking.] Sim, give's more wine.—What all the players gone?—Am I not a lord?

Tap. A lord, with a murrain?—Come, art thou drunk still?

Slie. Who's this? Tapster!—Oh I have had the bravest dream that ever thou heard'st in all thy life.

Tap. Yea, marry, but thou hadst best get thee home, for your wife will curse you for dreaming here all night.

Slie. Will she? I know how to *tame a shrew*. I dreamt upon it all this night, and thou hast wak'd me out of the best dream that ever I had; but I'll to my wife, and tame her too, if she anger me'

WINTER'S TALE.

PRELIMINARY REMARKS.

THE story of this play is taken from The Pleasant History of Dorastus and Fawnia, by Robert Greene, which was first printed in 1588. The parts of Antigonus, Paulina, and Autolycus are of the poet's own creation; and many circumstances of the novel are omitted in the play.

'A booke entitled A Winter's Night's Pastime,' entered at Stationer's Hall, in 1594, but which has not come down to us, may have suggested the title, by which Shakspeare thought the romantic and extraordinary incidents of the play well characterised: he several times in the course of the last act makes one of his characters remark its similarity to *an old tale*. Schlegel has observed that 'The Winter's Tale is as appropriately named as the Midsummer Night's Dream. It is one of those tales which are peculiarly calculated to beguile the dreary leisure of a long winter evening, which are even attractive and intelligible to childhood, and which, animated by fervent truth in the delineation of character and passion, invested with the decoration of a poetry lowering itself, as it were, to the simplicity of the subject, transport even manhood back to the golden age of imagination. The calculation of probabilities has nothing to do with such wonderful and fleeting adventures, ending at last in general joy; and accordingly Shakspeare has here taken the greatest liberties with anachronisms and geographical errors: he opens a free navigation between Sicily and Bohemia, makes Julio Romano the contemporary of the Delphic Oracle, not to mention other incongruities.'

It is extraordinary that Pope should have thought only some single scenes of this play were from the hand of Shakspeare. It breathes his spirit throughout;—in the serious parts as well as in those of a lighter kind: and who but Shakspeare could have conceived that exquisite pastoral scene in which the loves of Florizel and Perdita are developed? It is indeed a pastoral of the golden age, and Perdita 'no Shepherdess, but Flora,
Peering in April's front,'
and breathing flowers, in the spring-tide of youth and beauty. How gracefully she distributes her emblematic favours! What language accompanies them! Well may Florizel exclaim:

'———— when you speak, sweet,
I'd have you do it ever!'

The reader reechoes the sentiment of the lover, and is sorry to come to the close. With what modest unconscious dignity are all her words and actions accompanied: even Polixenes, who looks on her with no favourable eye, says that there is

'———— nothing she does or says
But smacks of something greater than herself.'

The Shepherds and Shepherdesses, with whom she has been brought up, are such as ordinary life affords, and are judicious foils to this delightful couple of lovers.

The arch roguery and mirthful stratagems of Autolycus are very amusing, and his character admirably sustained. 'The jealousy of Leontes (says the judicious Schlegel) is not, like that of Othello, developed with all the causes, symptoms, and gradations; it is brought forward at once, and is portrayed as a distempered frenzy. It is a passion which does not produce the catastrophe, but merely ties the knot of the piece.' But it has the same intemperate course, is the same soul-goading passion which wrings a noble nature to acts of revengeful cruelty; at which, under happier stars, it would have shuddered, and which are no sooner committed than repented of.

The patient and affecting resignation of the wronged Hermione under circumstances of the deepest anguish; and the zealous and courageous remonstrances of the faithful Paulina, have the stamp of Shakspeare upon them. Indeed I know not what parts of this drama could be attributed to any even of the most skilful of his contemporaries. It was perhaps the discrepancies of the plot (which in fact almost divides it into two plays with an interval of sixteen years between,) and the anachronisms, which made Dryden* and Pope overlook the beauties of execution in this enchanting play.

---

* Dryden, in the Essay at the end of the second part of the Conquest of Grenada, speaking of the plays of Shakspeare and Fletcher, says:—'Witness the lameness of their plots; many of which, especially those which they wrote first (for even that age refined itself in some measure,) were made up of some ridiculous incoherent story, which in one play many times took up the business of an age. I suppose I need not name Pericles, nor the historical plays of Shakspeare; besides many of the rest, as *The Winter's Tale*, Love's Labour's Lost.

Malone places the composition of the Winter's Tale in 1611, because it was first licensed for representation by Sir George Bucke, Master of the Revels, who did not assume the functions of his office until August 1610. The mention of the '*Puritan* singing psalms to hornpipes' also points at this period, as does another passage, which is supposed to be a compliment to James on his escape from the Gowrie Conspiracy. These are conjectures, but probable ones; Malone had in former instances placed the date much earlier; first in 1594, and then in 1602. The supposition that Ben Jonson intended a sneer at this play in his induction to Bartholomew Fair has been satisfactorily answered by Mr Gifford.†

Horace Walpole in his Historic Doubts attempts to show that The Winter's Tale was intended (in compliment to Queen Elizabeth) as an indirect apology for her mother Ann Boleyn; but the ground for his conjecture is so slight as scarcely to deserve attention. Indeed it may be answered that the plot of the play is not the invention of Shakspeare, who therefore cannot be charged with this piece of flattery; if it was intended, it must be attributed to Greene, whose novel was published in 1588. I think with Mr. Boswell that these supposed allusions by Shakspeare to the history of his own time are very much to be doubted.

Measure for Measure, which were either grounded on impossibilities, or at least so meanly written, that the comedy neither caused your mirth, nor the serious parts your concernment.' Pope, in his Preface to Shakspeare, almost reechoes this: 'I should conjecture (says he) of some of the others, particularly Love's Labour's Lost, The Winter's Tale, Comedy of Errors, and Titus Andronicus, that only some characters or single scenes, or perhaps a few particular passages, are from the hand of Shakspeare.'

† Works of Ben Jonson, vol. iv. p. 371.

PERSONS REPRESENTED.

LEONTES, *King of* Sicilia.
MAMILLIUS, *his Son.*
CAMILLO, ANTIGONUS, CLEOMENES, DION, } Sicilian *Lords.*
Another Sicilian Lord.
ROGERO, *a* Sicilian *Gentleman.*
An Attendant *on the young* Prince Mamillius.
Officers *of a Court of Judicature.*
POLIXENES, *King of* Bohemia.
FLORIZEL, *his Son.*
ARCHIDAMUS *a* Bohemian *Lord*
A Mariner.
Gaoler.
An old Shepherd, *reputed Father of* Perdita.
Clown, *his Son.*
Servant *to the old Shepherd.*
AUTOLYCUS, *a Rogue.*
Time, *as Chorus.*

HERMIONE, *Queen to* Leontes.
PERDITA, *Daughter to* Leontes *and* Hermione.
PAULINA, *Wife to* Antigonus.
EMILIA, *a Lady,* Two other Ladies, } *attending the Queen.*
MOPSA, DORCAS, } *Shepherdesses.*

Lords, Ladies, *and* Attendants; Satyrs *for a Dance,* Shepherds, Shepherdesses, Guards, &c.

SCENE, *sometimes in* Sicilia, *sometimes in* Bohemia.

ACT I.

SCENE I. Sicilia. *An Antichamber in* Leontes' *Palace. Enter* CAMILLO *and* ARCHIDAMUS.

Archidamus.

IF you shall chance, Camillo, to visit Bohemia, on the like occasion whereon my services are now on foot, you shall see, as I have said, great difference betwixt our Bohemia, and your Sicilia.

Cam. I think, this coming summer, the King of Sicilia means to pay Bohemia the visitation which he justly owes him.

Arch. Wherein our entertainment shall shame us, we will be justified in our loves: for, indeed,—

Cam. Beseech you,———

Arch. Verily, I speak it in the freedom of my knowledge: we cannot with such magnificence—in so rare—I know not what to say.——We will give you sleepy drinks; that your senses, unintelligent of our insignificance, may, though they cannot praise us, as little accuse us.

Cam. You pay a great deal too dear for what's given freely.

Arch. Believe me, I speak as my understanding instructs me, and as mine honesty puts it to utterance.

Cam. Sicilia cannot show himself over-kind to Bohemia. They were trained together in their childhoods; and there rooted betwixt them then such an affection, which cannot choose but branch now. Since their more mature dignities, and royal necessities made separation of their society, their encounters, though not personal, have been royally attornied,[1] with interchange of gifts, letters, loving embassies; that they have seemed to be together, though absent; shook hands, as over a vast;[2] and embraced, as it were, from the ends of opposed winds. The heavens continue their loves!

Arch. I think, there is not in the world either malice, or matter, to alter it. You have an unspeakable comfort of your young prince Mamillius; it is a gentleman of the greatest promise, that ever came into my note.

Cam. I very well agree with you in the hopes of him: it is a gallant child; one that, indeed, physics the subject,[3] makes old hearts fresh: they, that went on crutches ere he was born, desire yet their life, to see him a man.

Arch. Would they else be content to die?

Cam. Yes; if there were no other excuse why they should desire to live.

Arch. If the king had no son, they would desire to live on crutches till he had one. [*Exeunt.*

SCENE II. *The same. A Room of State in the Palace. Enter* LEONTES, POLIXENES, HERMIONE, MAMILLIUS, CAMILLO, *and* Attendants.

Pol. Nine changes of the wat'ry star have been
The shepherd's note, since we have left our throne
Without a burden: time as long again
Would be fill'd up, my brother, with our thanks:
And yet we should, for perpetuity,
Go hence in debt: And therefore, like a cipher,
Yet standing in rich place, I multiply,
With one we-thank-you, many thousands more
That go before it.

Leon. Stay your thanks awhile;
And pay them when you part.

Pol. Sir, that's to-morrow.
I am question'd by my fears, of what may chance,
Or breed upon our absence: That[4] may blow
No sneaping[5] winds at home, to make us say,
This is put forth too truly![6] Besides, I have stay'd
To tire your royalty.

1 'Royally attornied.' Nobly supplied by substitution of embassies.

2 i. e. over a wide intervening space.

3 'Physics the subject.' Affords a cordial to the state, has the power of assuaging the sense of misery.

4 *That* for *Oh that!* is not uncommon in old writers.

5 *Sneaping*, nipping.

6 i. e. to make me say, I had too good reason for my fears concerning what may happen in my absence from home.

Leon. We are tougher, brother,
Than you can put us to't.
Pol. No longer stay.
Leon. One seven-night longer.
Pol. Very sooth, to-morrow.
Leon. We'll part the time between's then: and in that
I'll no gain-saying.
Pol. Press me not, 'beseech you, so:
There is no tongue that moves, none, none i'the world
So soon as yours, could win me: so it should now,
Were there necessity in your request, although
'Twere needful I denied it. My affairs
Do even drag me homeward: which to hinder
Were, in your love, a whip to me: my stay,
To you a charge and trouble: to save both,
Farewell, our brother.
Leon. Tongue-tied, our queen? speak you.
Her. I had thought, sir, to have held my peace, until
You had drawn oaths from him not to stay. You, sir,
Charge him too coldly: Tell him, you are sure,
All in Bohemia's well: this satisfaction
The by-gone day proclaim'd; say this to him,
He's beat from his best ward.
Leon. Well said, Hermione.
Her. To tell he longs to see his son, were strong:
But let him say so then, and let him go;
But let him swear so, and he shall not stay,
We'll thwack him hence with distaffs.—
Yet of your royal presence [*To* POL.] I'll adventure
The borrow of a week. When at Bohemia
You take my lord, I'll give him my commission,
To let him there a month, behind the gest[1]
Prefix'd for his parting: yet, good deed,[2] Leontes,
I love thee not a jar o' the clock behind
What lady she her lord.—You'll stay?
Pol. No, madam.
Her. Nay, but you will?
Pol. I may not, verily.
Her. Verily!
You put me off with limber vows: But I,
Though you would seek to unsphere the stars with oaths,
Should yet say, *Sir, no going.* Verily,
You shall not go; a lady's verily is
As potent as a lord's. Will you go yet?
Force me to keep you as a prisoner,
Not like a guest; so you shall pay your fees,
When you depart, and save your thanks. How say you?
My prisoner? or my guest? by your dread verily,
One of them you shall be.
Pol. Your guest, then, madam:
To be your prisoner, should import offending;
Which is for me less easy to commit,
Than you to punish.
Her. Not your gaoler, then,
But your kind hostess. Come, I'll question you
Of my lord's tricks, and yours, when you were boys,
You were pretty lordings[3] then.
Pol. We were, fair queen,
Two lads that thought there was no more behind,
But such a day to-morrow as to-day,
And to be boy eternal.
Her. Was not my lord the verier wag o' the two?
Pol. We were as twinn'd lambs, that did frisk i' the sun,
And bleat the one at the other: what we chang'd,
Was innocence for innocence; we knew not
The doctrine of ill doing, nor dream'd
That any did: Had we pursued that life,
And our weak spirits ne'er been higher rear'd
With stronger blood, we should have answer'd heaven
Boldly, *Not Guilty;* the imposition clear'd,[4]
Hereditary ours.
Her. By this we gather,
You have tripp'd since.
Pol. O, my most sacred lady,
Temptations have since then been born to us: for
In those unfledg'd days was my wife a girl;
Your precious self had then not cross'd the eyes
Of my young play-fellow.
Her. Grace to boot![5]
Of this make no conclusion; lest you say,
Your queen and I are devils: Yet, go on;
The offences we have made you do, we'll answer,
If you first sinn'd with us, and that with us
You did continue fault, and that you slipp'd not
With any but with us.
Leon. Is he won yet?
Her. He'll stay, my lord.
Leon. At my request he would not.
Hermione, my dearest, thou never spok'st
To better purpose.
Her. Never?
Leon. Never, but once.
Her. What? have I twice said well? when was't before?
I pr'ythee, tell me: Cram us with praise, and make us
As fat as tame things: One good deed, dying tongue-less,
Slaughters a thousand, waiting upon that.
Our praises are our wages: You may ride us,
With one soft kiss, a thousand furlongs, ere
With spur we heat an acre. But to the goal;—
My last good was, to entreat his stay;
What was my first? it has an elder sister,
Or I mistake you: O, 'would, her name were Grace!
But once before I spoke to the purpose: When?
Nay, let me hav't; I long.
Leon. Why that was when
Three crabbed months had sour'd themselves to death,
Ere I could make thee open thy white hand,
And clap[6] thyself my love; then didst thou utter,
I am yours for ever.
Her. It is grace, indeed.—
Why, lo you now, I have spoke to the purpose twice.
The one for ever earn'd a royal husband;
The other, for some while a friend.
[*Giving her hand to* POLIXENES
Leon. Too hot, too hot: [*Aside*
To mingle friendship far, is mingling bloods.
I have *tremor cordis* on me:—my heart dances;
But not for joy,—not joy.—This entertainment
May a free face put on; derive a liberty
From heartiness, from bounty, fertile bosom,[7]
And well become the agent: it may, I grant:
But to be paddling palms, and pinching fingers,
As now they are: and making practis'd smiles,
As in a looking-glass;—and then to sigh, as 'twere
The mort o' the deer;[8] O, that is entertainment
My bosom likes not, nor my brows.—Mamillius,
Art thou my boy?
Mam. Ay, my good lord.
Leon. I'fecks?
Why, that's my bawcock.[9] What, hast smutch'd thy nose?—

1 To *let* had for its synonymes to *stay* or *stop;* to *let him* there, is to stay him there. *Gests* were scrolls in which were marked the stages or places of rest in a progress or journey, especially a royal one.

2 i. e. *in*deed, in very deed, in troth. *Good deed* is used in the same sense by the Earl of Surrey, Sir John Hayward, and Gascoigne.

3 *Lordings*, a diminutive of lords, often used by Chaucer.

4 i. e. setting aside the original sin, bating the imposition from the offence of our first parents, we might have boldly protested our innocence.

5 'Grace to boot.' An exclamation equivalent to *give us grace.*

6 At entering into any contract, or plighting of troth, this clapping of hands together set the seal. Numerous instances of allusion to the custom have been adduced by the editors; one shall suffice, from the old play of Ram Alley: 'Come, *clap hands*, a match.' The custom is not yet disused in common life.

7 —— 'from bounty, fertile bosom,' I think with Malone that a letter has been omitted, and that we should read:—

'—— from bounty's fertile bosom.'

8 i. e. *the death of the deer.* The *mort* was also certain notes played on the horn at the death of the deer.

9 '*Bawcock*' A burlesque word of endearment sup

They say, it's a copy out of mine. Come, captain,
We must be neat; not neat, but cleanly, captain:
And yet the steer, the heifer, and the calf,
Are all call'd, neat.—Still virginalling[1]
[*Observing* POLIXENES *and* HERMIONE.
Upon his palm?—How now, you wanton calf?
Art thou my calf?
Mam. Yes, if you will, my lord.
Leon. Thou want'st a rough pash, and the shoots that I have,[2]
To be full[3] like me: yet, they say, we are
Almost as like as eggs; women say so,
That will say any thing: But were they false
As o'er-dyed blacks,[4] as wind, as waters; false
As dice are to be wish'd, by one that fixes
No bourn 'twixt his and mine; yet were it true
To say this boy were like me.—Come, sir page,
Look on me with your welkin[5] eye: Sweet villain!
Most dear'st! my collop![6]—Can thy dam?—may't be?
Affection! thy intention stabs the centre;[7]
Thou dost make possible, things not so held;
Communicat'st with dreams;—(How can this be?)
With what's unreal thou coactive art,
And fellow'st nothing: Then, 'tis very credent,[8]
Thou may'st conjoin with something; and thou dost;
(And that beyond commission, and I find it;)
And that to the infection of my brains,
And hardening of my brows.
Pol. What means Sicilia?
Her. He something seems unsettled.
Pol. How, my lord?
What cheer? how is't with you, best brother?
Her. You look,
As if you held a brow of much distraction:
Are you mov'd, my lord?
Leon. No, in good earnest.—
How sometimes nature will betray its folly,
Its tenderness, and make itself a pastime
To harder bosoms! Looking on the lines
Of my boy's face, methought I did recoil
Twenty-three years; and saw myself unbreech'd,
In my green velvet coat; my dagger muzzled,
Lest it should bite its master, and so prove,
As ornaments oft do, too dangerous.
How like, methought, I then was to this kernel,
This squash,[9] this gentleman:—Mine honest friend,
Will you take eggs for money?[10]
Mam. No, my lord, I'll fight.
Leon. You will? why, happy man be his dole![11]—my brother,
Are you so fond of your young prince, as we
Do seem to be of ours?
Pol. If at home, sir,
He's all my exercise, my mirth, my matter:
Now my sworn friend, and then mine enemy;
My parasite, my soldier, statesman, all;
He makes a July's day short as December;
And, with his varying childness, cures in me
Thoughts that would thick my blood.
Leon. So stands this squire
Offic'd with me: We two will walk, my lord,
And leave you to your graver steps.—Hermione,
How thou lov'st us, show in our brother's welcome;
Let what is dear in Sicily be cheap:
Next to thyself, and my young rover he's
Apparent[12] to my heart.
Her. If you would seek us,
We are yours i'the garden; Shall's attend you there.
Leon. To your own bents dispose you: you'll be found,
Be you beneath the sky:—I am angling now,
Though you perceive me not how I give line.
Go to, go to!
[*Aside. Observing* POLIXENES *and* HERMIONE.
How she holds up the neb,[13] the bill to him!
And arms her with the boldness of a wife
To her allowing[14] husband! Gone already!
Inch-thick, knee-deep, o'er head and ears a fork'd one[15]——
[*Exeunt* POL. HER. *and* Attendants.
Go, play, boy, play;—thy mother plays, and I
Play too; but so disgrac'd a part, whose issue
Will hiss me to my grave; contempt and clamour
Will be my knell.—Go, play, boy, play.—There have been,
Or I am much deceiv'd, cuckolds ere now;
And many a man there is, even at this present,
Now, while I speak this, holds his wife by the arm,
That little thinks, she has been sluic'd in his absence,
And his pond fish'd by his next neighbour, by
Sir Smile, his neighbour: nay, there's comfort in't,
Whiles other men have gates; and those gates open'd,
As mine, against their will: Should all despair,
That have revolted wives, the tenth of mankind
Would hang themselves. Physic for't there is none;
It is a bawdy planet, that will strike
Where 'tis predominant; and 'tis powerful, think it,
From east, west, north, and south: Be it concluded,
No barricado for a belly; know it;
It will let in and out the enemy,
With bag and baggage: many a thousand of us
Have the disease, and feel't not.—How now, boy?
Mam. I am like you, they say.
Leon. Why, that's some comfort.—
What! Camillo there?
Cam. Ay, my good lord.
Leon. Go play, Mamillius; thou'rt an honest man.— [*Exit* MAMILLIUS.
Camillo, this great sir will yet stay longer.
Cam. You had much ado to make his anchor hold;
When you cast out, it still came home.[16]
Leon. Didst note it?
Cam. He would not stay at your petitions; made
His business more material.[17]
Leon. Didst perceive it?—
They're here with me already:[18] whispering, rounding,[19]
Sicilia is a so-forth: 'Tis far gone,
When I shall gust[20] it last.—How came't, Camillo,
That he did stay?
Cam. At the good queen's entreaty.

---

posed to be derived from *beau-coq*, or boy-cock. It occurs again in Twelfth Night, and in King Henry V. and in both places is coupled with chuck or chick. It is said that *bra'cock* is still used in Scotland.

1 Still playing with her fingers as a girl playing on the virginals. Virginals were stringed instruments played with keys like a spinnet, which they resembled in all respects but in shape, spinnets being nearly triangular, and virginals of an oblong square shape like a small piano forte.

2 Thou wantest a rough *head*, and the budding horns that I have. A *pash* in some places denoting a young bull calf whose horns are springing; a *mad pash*, a mad-brained boy.

3 i. e. entirely.

4 i. e. old faded stuffs of other colours dyed black.

5 *Welkin* is *blue*, i. e. the colour of the welkin or sky.

6 In King Henry VI. Part I. we have—
'God knows thou art a *collop* of my flesh.'

7 *Affection* here means imagination. *Intention* is earnest consideration, eager attention. It is this vehemence of mind which affects Leontes, by making him conjure up unreal causes of disquiet; and thus, in the poet's language, 'stabs *him* to the centre.'

8 *Credent*, credible.

9 i. e. an immature pea-pod.

10 'Will you take eggs for money?' A proverbial phrase for 'will you suffer yourself to be cajoled or imposed upon?'

11 i. e. may happiness be his *portion!*

12 Heir apparent, next claimant.

13 i. e. mouth.

14 i. e. approving

15 i. e. a *horned* one, a *cuckold*.

16 'It still came home,' a nautical term, meaning 'the anchor would not take hold.'

17 The more you requested him to stay, the more urgent he represented that business to be which summoned him away.

18 Not Polixenes and Hermione, but casual observers.

19 To *round* in the ear was to tell secretly, to whisper

20 i. e. taste it:—
'ille domus sciet ultimus.'
Juv. Sat x.

Leon. At the queen's, be't: good, should be pertinent;
But so it is, it is not. Was this taken
By any understanding pate but thine?
For thy conceit is soaking, will draw in
More than the common blocks:—Not noted, is't,
But of the finer natures? by some severals,
Of head-piece extraordinary? lower messes,[1]
Perchance, are to this business purblind: say.
Cam. Business, my lord? I think, most understand
Bohemia stays here longer.
Leon. Ha?
Cam. Stays here longer.
Leon. Ay, but why?
Cam. To satisfy your highness, and the entreaties
Of our most gracious mistress.
Leon. Satisfy
The entreaties of your mistress?——satisfy?—
Let that suffice. I have trusted thee, Camillo,
With all the nearest things to my heart, as well
My chamber-councils: wherein, priestlike, thou
Hast cleans'd my bosom; I from thee departed
Thy penitent reform'd: but we have been
Deceiv'd in thy integrity, deceiv'd
In that which seems so.
Cam. Be it forbid, my lord!
Leon. To bide upon't:—Thou art not honest: or,
If thou inclin'st that way, thou art a coward;
Which hoxes[2] honesty behind, restraining
From course requir'd: Or else thou must be counted
A servant, grafted in my serious trust,
And therein negligent; or else a fool,
That see'st a game play'd home, the rich stake drawn,
And tak'st it all for jest.
Cam. My gracious lord,
I may be negligent, foolish, and fearful;
In every one of these no man is free,
But that his negligence, his folly, fear,
Amongst the infinite doings of the world,
Sometime puts forth: In your affairs, my lord,
If ever I were wilful-negligent,
It was my folly; if industriously
I play'd the fool, it was my negligence,
Not weighing well the end; if ever fearful
To do a thing, where I the issue doubted,
Whereof the execution did cry out
Against the non-performance,[3] 'twas a fear
Which oft affects the wisest: these, my lord,
Are such allow'd infirmities, that honesty
Is never free of. But, 'beseech your grace,
Be plainer with me; let me know my trespass
By its own visage: if I then deny it,
'Tis none of mine.
Leon. Have not you seen, Camillo,
(But that's past doubt: you have; or your eye-glass
Is thicker than a cuckold's horn;) or heard,
(For, to a vision so apparent, rumour
Cannot be mute,) or thought,—(for cogitation
Resides not in that man, that does not think,)[4]—
My wife is slippery? If thou wilt confess,
(Or else be impudently negative,
To have nor eyes, nor ears, nor thought,) then say
My wife's a hobby-horse; deserves a name
As rank as any flax-wench, that puts to
Before a troth-plight: say it, and justify it.
Cam. I would not be a stander-by, to hear
My sovereign mistress clouded so, without
My present vengeance taken: 'Shrew my heart
You never spoke what did become you less
Than this, which to reiterate, were sin
As deep as that, though true.[5]
Leon. Is whispering nothing?
Is leaning cheek to cheek? is meeting noses?
Kissing with inside lip? stopping the career
Of laughter with a sigh? (a note infallible
Of breaking honesty:) horsing foot on foot?
Skulking in corners? wishing clocks more swift?
Hours, minutes? noon, midnight? and all eyes blind
With the pin and web,[6] but theirs, theirs only,
That would unseen be wicked? is this nothing?
Why, then, the world, and all that's in't, is nothing,
The covering sky is nothing; Bohemia nothing;
My wife is nothing; nor nothing have these nothings,
If this be nothing.
Cam. Good my lord, be cur'd
Of this diseas'd opinion, and betimes;
For 'tis most dangerous.
Leon. Say, it be; 'tis true.
Cam. No, no, my lord.
Leon. It is: you lie, you lie:
I say, thou liest, Camillo, and I hate thee;
Pronounce thee a gross lout, a mindless slave;
Or else a hovering temporizer, that
Canst with thine eyes at once see good and evil,
Inclining to them both: Were my wife's liver
Infected as her life, she would not live
The running of one glass.[7]
Cam. Who does infect her?
Leon. Why he, that wears her like his medal,[8] hanging
About his neck, Bohemia: Who—if I
Had servants true about me: that bare eyes
To see alike mine honour as their profits,
Their own particular thrifts,—they would do that
Which should undo more doing: Ay, and thou,
His cup-bearer,—whom I from meaner form
Have bench'd, and rear'd to worship; who may'st see
Plainly, as heaven sees earth, and earth sees heaven,
How I am galled,—might'st bespice a cup,[9]
To give mine enemy a lasting wink;
Which draught to me were cordial.
Cam. Sir, my lord,
I could do this: and that with no rash[10] potion,
But with a ling'ring dram, that should not work
Maliciously like poison: But I cannot
Believe this crack to be in my dread mistress,
So sovereignly being honourable.
I have lov'd thee,——
Leon. Make't thy question, and go rot![11]

---

1 *Messes* is here put for *degrees, conditions.* The company at great tables were divided according to their rank into higher and lower messes. Those of lower condition sitting below the great standing salt in the centre of the table.

2 To *hox* is to hamstring, the proper word is to *hough.*

3 This is expressed obscurely, but seems to mean 'the execution of which (*when done*) cried out against the nonperformance *of it before;*' or, as Johnson laconically expresses it, was '*a thing necessary to be done,*' but which Camillo had delayed doing because he doubted the issue.

4 Theobald quoted this passage in defence of the well known line in his Double Falsehood, 'None but himself can be his parallel.'—'For who does not see at once,' says he, 'that he who does not think has no thought in him.' In the same light the subsequent editors view this passage, and read with Pope, 'that does not think *it.*' But the old reading is right, and the absurdity only in the misapprehension of it. Leontes means to say, 'Have you not thought that my wife is slippery (for cogitation resides not in the man that does not think *my wife is slippery.*') The four latter words, though disjoined from the word *think* by the necessity of a parenthesis, are evidently to be connected in construction with it.

5 To reiterate your accusation of her would be as great a sin as that, if committed, of which you accuse her.

6 The *pin and web* is the *cataract* in an early stage.

7 i. e. one hour.

8 The old copy reads '*her* medal.' The allusion is to the custom of wearing a medallion or jewel appended to a ribbon about the neck.

9 'Bespice a cup.' So in Chapman's Translation of the tenth book of the Odyssey:—

'——— with a festival
She'll first receive thee; but will *spice* thy bread
With flowery *poisons.*'

10 *Rash* is *hasty;* as in King Henry IV. Part II. '*rash* gunpowder.' *Maliciously* is *malignantly,* with effects *openly hurtful.*

11 Make that, i. e. Hermione's disloyalty, which is a clear point, a subject of doubt, and go rot! Dost think, I am such a fool as to torment myself, and bring disgrace on me and my child, without sufficient grounds?

Dost think, I am so muddy, so unsettled,
To appoint myself in this vexation? sully
The purity and whiteness of my sheets,
Which to preserve, is sleep; which being spotted,
Is goads, thorns, nettles, tails of wasps?[1]
Give scandal to the blood o' the prince my son,
Who, I do think is mine, and love as mine;
Without ripe moving to't? Would I do this?
Could man so blench?[2]

Cam. I must believe you, sir;
I do: and will fetch off Bohemia for't:
Provided, that when he's remov'd, your highness
Will take again your queen, as yours at first;
Even for your son's sake; and thereby, for sealing
The injury of tongues in courts and kingdoms
Known and allied to yours.

Leon. Thou dost advise me,
Even so as I mine own course have set down:
I'll give no blemish to her honour, none.

Cam. My lord,
Go then; and with a countenance as clear
As friendship wears at feasts, keep with Bohemia,
And with your queen: I am his cupbearer;
If from me he have wholesome beverage,
Account me not your servant.

Leon. This is all;
Do't, and thou hast the one half of my heart;
Do't not, thou split'st thine own.

Cam. I'll do't, my lord.

Leon. I will seem friendly, as thou hast advis'd me. [*Exit.*

Cam. O miserable lady!—But, for me,
What case stand I in? I must be the poisoner
Of good Polixenes: and my ground to do't
Is the obedience to a master; one,
Who, in rebellion with himself, will have
All that are his, so too.—To do this deed,
Promotion follows: If I could find example
Of thousands, that had struck anointed kings,
And flourish'd after, I'd not do't: but since
Nor brass, nor stone, nor parchment, bears not one,
Let villany itself forswear't. I must
Forsake the court: to do't, or no, is certain
To me a break-neck. Happy star, reign now!
Here comes Bohemia.

Enter POLIXENES.

Pol. This is strange! methinks,
My favour here begins to warp. Not speak?——
Good-day, Camillo.

Cam. Hail, most royal sir!

Pol. What is the news i'the court?

Cam. None rare, my lord.

Pol. The king hath on him such a countenance,
As he had lost some province, and a region,
Lov'd as he loves himself: even now I met him
With customary compliment; when he,
Wafting his eyes to the contrary, and falling
A lip of much contempt, speeds from me; and
So leaves me to consider what is breeding,
That changes thus his manners.

Cam. I dare not know, my lord.

Pol. How! dare not? do not. Do you know, and dare not
Be intelligent to me? 'Tis thereabouts;
For, to yourself, what you do know, you must,
And cannot say you dare not. Good Camillo,
Your chang'd complexions are to me a mirror,
Which shows me mine chang'd too: for I must be
A party in this alteration, finding
Myself thus alter'd with it.

Cam. There is a sickness
Which puts some of us in distemper; but
I cannot name the disease; and it is caught
Of you that yet are well.

Pol. How! caught of me?
Make me not sighted like the basilisk:
I have look'd on thousands, who have sped the better
By my regard, but kill'd none so. Camillo,——
As you are certainly a gentleman; thereto
Clerk-like, experienc'd, which no less adorns
Our gentry, than our parents' noble names,
In whose success we are gentle,[3]—I beseech you,
If you know aught which does behove my knowledge
Thereof to be inform'd, imprison it not
In ignorant concealment.

Cam. I may not answer.

Pol. A sickness caught of me, and yet I well!
I must be answer'd.—Dost thou hear, Camillo,
I conjure thee, by all the parts of man,
Which honour does acknowledge,—whereof the least
Is not this suit of mine,—that thou declare
What incidency thou dost guess of harm
Is creeping toward me; how far off, how near;
Which way to be prevented, if to be;
If not, how best to bear it.

Cam. Sir, I'll tell you,
Since I am charg'd in honour, and by him
That I think honourable: Therefore, mark my counsel;
Which must be even as swiftly follow'd, as
I mean to utter it; or both yourself and me
Cry, *lost*, and so good-night.

Pol. On, good Camillo.

Cam. I am appointed him to murder you.[4]

Pol. By whom, Camillo?

Cam. By the king.

Pol. For what?

Cam. He thinks, nay, with all confidence he swears,
As he had seen't, or been an instrument
To vice[5] you to't,—that you have touch'd his queen
Forbiddenly.

Pol. O, then my best blood turn
To an infected jelly; and my name
Be yoked with his, that did betray the best![6]
Turn then my freshest reputation to
A savour, that may strike the dullest nostril
Where I arrive; and my approach be shunn'd,
Nay, hated too, worse than the great'st infection
That e'er was heard, or read!

Cam. Swear his thought over[7]
By each particular star in heaven, and
By all their influences, you may as well
Forbid the sea for to obey the moon,
As, or by oath, remove, or counsel, shake
The fabric of his folly; whose foundation
Is pil'd upon his faith,[8] and will continue
The standing of his body.

Pol. How should this grow?

Cam. I know not: but, I am sure, 'tis safer to
Avoid what's grown, than question how 'tis born.
If therefore you dare trust my honesty,—
That lies enclosed in this trunk, which you
Shall bear along impawn'd,—away to-night.
Your followers I will whisper to the business;
And will, by twos, and threes, at several posterns,
Clear them o' the city: For myself, I'll put
My fortunes to your service, which are here
By this discovery lost. Be not uncertain:
For, by the honour of my parents, I
Have utter'd truth: which if you seek to prove,
I dare not stand by; nor shall you be safer

1 Something is necessary to complete the verse. Hanmer reads:—

'Is goads *and* thorns, nettles *and* tails of wasps.'

2 To blench is to *start off*, to shrink.

3 *Success*, for *succession*. *Gentle*, well born, was opposed to *simple*.

4 'I am appointed *him* to murder you,' I am the person appointed to murder you.

5 i. e. to screw or move you to it. A *vice* in Shakspeare's time meant any kind of winding screw. The *vice* of a clock was a common expression.

6 That is Judas. A clause in the sentence of excommunicated persons was: 'let them have part with Judas that betrayed Christ.'

7 'Swear his thought over.' The meaning apparently is '*over-swear* his thought by,' &c.

8 'Is pil'd upon his faith.' This folly which is erected on the foundation of settled *belief*.

Than one condemn'd by the king's own mouth, thereon
His execution sworn.

Pol. I do believe thee:
I saw his heart in his face.[1] Give me thy hand;
Be pilot to me, and thy places shall
Still neighbour mine;[2] My ships are ready, and
My people did expect my hence departure
Two days ago.—This jealousy
Is for a precious creature; as she's rare,
Must it be great; and, as his person's mighty,
Must it be violent; and as he does conceive,
He is dishonour'd by a man which ever
Profess'd to him, why, his revenges must
In that be made more bitter. Fear o'ershades me;
Good expedition be my friend, and comfort
The gracious queen, part of his theme, but nothing
Of his ill-ta'en suspicion![3] Come, Camillo;
I will respect thee as a father, if
Thou bear'st my life off hence: Let us avoid.

Cam. It is in mine authority, to command
The keys of all the posterns: Please your highness
To take the urgent hour: come, sir, away.
[*Exeunt.*

ACT II.

SCENE I. *The same. Enter* HERMIONE, MAMILLIUS, *and* Ladies.

Her. Take the boy to you: he so troubles me,
'Tis past enduring.

1 *Lady.* Come, my gracious lord,
Shall I be your playfellow?

Mam. No, I'll none of you.

1 *Lady.* Why, my sweet lord?

Mam. You'll kiss me hard; and speak to me as if I were a baby still.—I love you better.

2 *Lady.* And why so, my lord?

Mam. Not for because
Your brows are blacker; yet black brows, they say,
Become some women best; so that there be not
Too much hair there, but in a semicircle,
Or half-moon made with a pen.

2 *Lady.* Who taught you this?

Mam. I learn'd it out of women's faces.—Pray now
What colour are your eye-brows?

1 *Lady.* Blue, my lord.

Mam. Nay, that's a mock: I have seen a lady's nose
That has been blue, but not her eye-brows.

2 *Lady.* Hark ye:
The queen, your mother, rounds apace: we shall
Present our services to a fine new prince,
One of these days; and then you'd wanton with us,
If we would have you.

1 *Lady.* She is spread of late
Into a goodly bulk: Good time encounter her!

Her. What wisdom stirs amongst you? Come, sir, now
I am for you again: Pray you, sit by us,
And tell 's a tale.

Mam. Merry, or sad, shall't be?

Her. As merry as you will.

Mam. A sad tale's best for winter:
I have one of sprites and goblins.

Her. Let's have that, good sir.
Come on, sit down:—Come on, and do your best
To fright me with your sprites: you're powerful at it.

Mam. There was a man,——

Her. Nay, come, sit down; then on.

Mam. Dwelt by a church-yard;—I will tell it softly;
Yon crickets shall not hear it.

Her. Come on then,
And give't me in mine ear.

Enter LEONTES, ANTIGONUS, Lords, *and others.*

Leon. Was he met there? his train? Camillo with him?

1 *Lord.* Behind the tuft of pines I met them; never
Saw I men scour so on their way: I ey'd them
Even to their ships.

Leon. How bless'd am I
In my just censure?[4] in my true opinion?—
Alack, for lesser knowledge![5] How accurs'd,
In being so blest!—There may be in the cup
A spider[6] steep'd, and one may drink; depart,
And yet partake no venom; for his knowledge
Is not infected: but if one present
The abhorr'd ingredient to his eye; make known,
How he hath drunk, he cracks his gorge, his sides
With violent hefts:[7]—I have drunk, and seen the spider.
Camillo was his help in this, his pander:—
There is a plot against my life, my crown;
All's true that is mistrusted:—that false villain,
Whom I employ'd, was pre-employ'd by him:
He has discover'd my design, and I
Remain a pinch'd thing;[8] yea, a very trick
For them to play at will:—How came the posterns
So easily open?

1 *Lord.* By his great authority;
Which often hath no less prevail'd than so,
On your command.

Leon. I know't too well.——
Give me the boy; I am glad, you did not nurse him.
Though he does bear some signs of me, yet you
Have too much blood in him.

Her. What is this? sport?

Leon. Bear the boy hence, he shall not come about her;
Away with him:—and let her sport herself
With that she's big with; for 'tis Polixenes
Has made thee swell thus.

Her. But I'd say, he had not,
And, I'll be sworn, you would believe my saying,
Howe'er you lean to the nayward.

Leon. You, my lords,
Look on her, mark her well; be but about
To say, *she is a goodly lady*, and
The justice of your hearts will thereto add,
'Tis pity, she's not honest, honourable:
Praise her but for this her without-door form,
(Which, on my faith, deserves high speech) and straight
The shrug, the hum, or ha; these petty brands,
That calumny doth use:—O, I am out,
That mercy does; for calumny will sear[9]
Virtue itself:—these shrugs, these hums, and has,
When you have said, she's goodly, come between,
Ere you can say she's honest: But be it known,
From him that has most cause to grieve it should be,
She's an adultress.

Her. Should a villain say so,
The most replenish villain in the world,
He were as much more villain: you, my lord,
Do but mistake.

Leon. You have mistook, my lady,
Polixenes for Leontes: O thou thing,
Which I'll not call a creature of thy place,

---

1 'I saw his heart in his face.' In Macbeth we have;—
'To find the mind's construction in the face.'

2 i. e. I will *place* thee in elevated rank always near to my own in dignity, or near my person.

3 Johnson might well say, 'I can make nothing of the following words:'
'———— and comfort
The gracious queen, part of his theme, but nothing
Of his ill-ta'en suspicion.'
He suspected the line which connected them to the rest to have been lost. I have sometimes thought that we should read *not noting* instead of *but nothing*. Perhaps they will bear this construction: 'Good expedition be my friend, and *may my absence* bring comfort to the gracious queen who *is* part of his theme, but *who knows* nothing of his unjust suspicion.'

4 i. e. judgment.

5 'Alack, for lesser knowledge!' that is, O that my knowledge were less!

6 Spiders were esteemed poisonous in our author's time.

7 *Hefts*, heavings, things which are heaved up.

8 i. e. 'a thing *pinched* out of clouts, a puppet for them to move and actuate as they please.'

9 i. e. will *brand* it

Lest barbarism, making me the precedent,
Should a like language use to all degrees,
And mannerly distinguishment leave out
Betwixt the prince and beggar!---I have said,
She's an adultress; I have said with whom:
More, she's a traitor! and Camillo is
A federary[1] with her; and one that knows
What she should shame to know herself,
But[2] with her most vile principal, that she's
A bed-swerver, even as bad as those
That vulgars give bold'st titles; ay, and privy
To this their late escape.

Her. No, by my life,
Privy to none of this: How will this grieve you,
When you shall come to clearer knowledge, that
You thus have publish'd me? Gentle my lord,
You scarce can right me throughly then, to say
You did mistake.

Leon. No, no; if I mistake
In those foundations which I build upon,
The centre is not big enough to bear
A school-boy's top.[3]—Away with her to prison:
He, who shall speak for her, is afar off guilty,
But that he speaks.[4]

Her. There's some ill planet reigns:
I must be patient till the heavens look
With an aspect more favourable.—Good my lords,
I am not prone to weeping, as our sex
Commonly are; the want of which vain dew,
Perchance, shall dry your pities: but I have
That honourable grief lodg'd here, which burns
Worse than tears drown: 'Beseech you all, my lords,
With thoughts so qualified as your charities
Shall best instruct you, measure me;—and so
The king's will be perform'd!

Leon. Shall I be heard? [*To the Guards.*

Her. Who is't that goes with me?—'Beseech your highness,
My women may be with me; for, you see,
My plight requires it. Do not weep, good fools;
There is no cause: when you shall know your mistress
Has deserv'd prison, then abound in tears,
As I come out: this action, I now go on,[5]
Is for my better grace.—Adieu, my lord:
I never wish'd to see you sorry; now,
I trust, I shall.——My women, come; you have leave.

Leon. Go, do our bidding; hence.
[*Exeunt* Queen *and* Ladies.

1 *Lord.* 'Beseech your highness, call the queen again.

Ant. Be certain what you do, sir; lest your justice
Prove violence; in the which three great ones suffer,
Yourself, your queen, your son.

1 *Lord.* For her, my lord,—
I dare my life lay down, and will do't, sir,
Please you to accept it, that the queen is spotless
I'the eyes of heaven, and to you; I mean,
In this which you accuse her.

Ant. If it prove
She's otherwise, I'll keep my stables[6] where
I lodge my wife; I'll go in couples with her;
Then when I feel, and see her, no further trust her;
For every inch of woman in the world,
Ay, every dram of woman's flesh, is false,
If she be.

Leon. Hold your peaces.

1 *Lord.* Good my lord,—

Ant. It is for you we speak, not for ourselves.
You are abus'd, and by some putter-on,
That will be damn'd for't; 'would I knew the villain,
I would land-damn[7] him: Be she honour-flaw'd,—
I have three daughters; the eldest is eleven;
The second, and the third, nine, and some five;
If this prove true, they'll pay for't: by mine honour,
I'll geld them all: fourteen they shall not see,
To bring false generations; they are coheirs;
And I had rather glib[8] myself, than they
Should not produce fair issue.

Leon. Cease; no more.
You smell this business with a sense as cold
As is a dead man's nose: but I do see't and feel't,
As you feel doing thus; and see withal
The instruments that feel.[9]

Ant. If it be so,
We need no grave to bury honesty;
There's not a grain of it, the face to sweeten
Of the whole dungy earth.

Leon. What! lack I credit?

1 *Lord.* I had rather you did lack, than I, my lord,
Upon this ground: and more it would content me
To have her honour true, than your suspicion;
Be blam'd for't how you might.

Leon. Why, what need we
Commune with you of this? but rather follow
Our forceful instigation? Our prerogative
Calls not your counsels; but our natural goodness
Imparts this: which,—if you (or stupified,
Or seeming so in skill) cannot, or will not,
Relish as[10] truth, like us; inform yourselves,
We need no more of your advice: the matter,
The loss, the gain, the ordering on't, is all
Properly ours.

Ant. And I wish, my liege,
You had only in your silent judgment tried it,
Without more overture.

Leon. How could that be?
Either thou art most ignorant by age,
Or thou wert born a fool. Camillo's flight,
Added to their familiarity,
(Which was as gross as ever touch'd conjecture,
That lack'd sight only, nought for approbation,[11]
But only seeing, all other circumstances
Made up to the deed) doth push on this proceeding:
Yet, for a greater confirmation,
(For, in an act of this importance, 'twere
Most piteous to be wild) I have despatch'd in post,
To sacred Delphos, to Apollo's temple,
Cleomenes and Dion, whom you know
Of stuff'd sufficiency:[12] Now from the oracle
They will bring all; whose spiritual counsel had
Shall stop, or spur me. Have I done well?

1 *Lord.* Well done, my lord.

Leon. Though I am satisfied, and need no more
Than what I know, yet shall the oracle
Give rest to the minds of others; such as he,
Whose ignorant credulity will not
Come up to the truth: so have we thought it good,
From our free person she should be confined;
Lest that the treachery of the two fled hence,
Be left her to perform. Come, follow us;
We are to speak in public: for this business
Will raise us all.

Ant. [*Aside.*] To laughter, as I take it,
If the good truth were known. [*Exeunt.*

---

1 *Federary.* This word, which is probably of the poet's own invention, is used for *confederate, accomplice.*

2 One that knows what she should be ashamed to know herself, even if the knowledge of it was shared *but with* her paramour. It is the use of *but* for *be-out* (*only*, according to Malone) that obscures the sense.

3 i. e. no foundation can be trusted.

4 'He who shall speak for her is afar off guilty,
But that he speaks.'
He who shall speak for her is remotely guilty in merely speaking.

5 i. e. what I am now about to do.

6 Much has been said about this passage: one has thought it should be *stable-stand;* another that it means *station.* But it may be explained thus:—'If she prove false, I'll make my stables or kennel of my wife's chamber; I'll go in couples with her like a dog, and never leave her for a moment; trust her no further than I can feel and see her.'

7 'I would land-damn him.' Johnson interprets this: 'I will *damn* or condemn him to quit the land.'

8 *Glib* or *lib*, i. e. castrate.

9 I see and feel *my disgrace*, as you, Antigonus, *now* feel my doing this *to you*, and *as you now see* the instruments that feel, i. e. *my fingers.* Leontes must here be supposed to touch or lay hold of Antigonus.

10 The old copy reads *a* truth. Rowe made the correction.

11 i. e. proof.

12 i. e. of abilities more than sufficient.

SCENE II. *The same. The outer Room of a Prison. Enter* PAULINA *and* Attendants.

Paul. The keeper of the prison,—call to him;
[*Exit an* Attendant.
Let him have knowledge who I am,—Good lady!
No court in Europe is too good for thee,
What dost thou then in prison?—Now, good sir,

Re-enter Attendant, *with the* Keeper.

You know me, do you not?
Keeper. For a worthy lady,
And one whom I much honour.
Paul. Pray you, then,
Conduct me to the queen.
Keep. I may not, madam; to the contrary
I have express commandment.
Paul. Here's ado,
To lock up honesty and honour from
The access of gentle visitors!——Is it lawful,
Pray you, to see her women? any of them?
Emilia?
Keep. So please you, madam, to put
Apart these your attendants, I shall bring
Emilia forth.
Paul. I pray now, call her.
Withdraw yourselves. [*Exeunt* Attend.
Keep. And, madam,
I must be present at your conference.
Paul. Well, be it so, pr'ythee. [*Exit* Keeper.
Here's such ado to make no stain a stain,
As passes colouring.

Re-enter Keeper, *with* EMILIA.

Dear gentlewoman, how fares our gracious lady?
Emil. As well as one so great, and so forlorn,
May hold together: On her frights and griefs
(Which never tender lady hath borne greater),
She is, something before her time, deliver'd.
Paul. A boy?
Emil. A daughter; and a goodly babe,
Lusty, and like to live: the queen receives
Much comfort in't: says, *My poor prisoner,*
I am innocent as you.
Paul. I dare be sworn:
These dangerous unsafe lunes[1] o'the king! beshrew them!
He must be told on't, and he shall: the office
Becomes a woman best; I'll take't upon me:
If I prove honey-mouth'd, let my tongue blister;
And never to my red-look'd anger be
The trumpet any more:—Pray you, Emilia,
Commend my best obedience to the queen;
If she dares trust me with her little babe,
I'll show't the king, and undertake to be
Her advocate to th' loudest: We do not know
How he may soften at the sight o'the child;
The silence often of pure innocence
Persuades, when speaking fails.
Emil. Most worthy madam,
Your honour, and your goodness, is so evident,
That your free undertaking cannot miss
A thriving issue; there is no lady living,
So meet for this great errand: Please your ladyship
To visit the next room, I'll presently
Acquaint the queen of your most noble offer;
Who, but to-day, hammer'd of this design;
But durst not tempt a minister of honour,
Lest she should be denied.
Paul. Tell her, Emilia,
I'll use that tongue I have: if wit flow from it,
As boldness from my bosom, let it not be doubted
I shall do good.
Emil. Now be you blest for it!
I'll to the queen: Please you, come something nearer.
Keep. Madam, if't please the queen to send the babe,
I know not what I shall incur, to pass it,
Having no warrant.
Paul. You need not fear it, sir:
The child was prisoner to the womb; and is,
By law and process of great nature, thence
Freed and enfranchis'd: not a party to
The anger of the king; nor guilty of,
If any be, the trespass of the queen.
Keep. I do believe it.
Paul. Do not you fear: upon
Mine honour, I will stand 'twixt you and danger.
[*Exeunt.*

SCENE III. *The same. A Room in the Palace. Enter* LEONTES, ANTIGONUS, Lords, *and other* Attendants.

Leon. Nor night, nor day, no rest: It is but weakness
To bear the matter thus; mere weakness, if
The cause were not in being;—part o' the cause,
She, the adultress;—for the harlot king
Is quite beyond mine arm, out of the blank
And level[2] of my brain, plot-proof: but she
I can hook to me: Say, that she were gone,
Given to the fire, a moiety of my rest
Might come to me again.——Who's there?
1 *Attend.* My lord!
[*Advancing.*
Leon. How does the boy?
1 *Attend.* He took good rest to-night;
'Tis hop'd his sickness is discharg'd.
Leon. To see,
His nobleness!
Conceiving the dishonour of his mother,
He straight declin'd, droop'd, took it deeply;
Fasten'd and fix'd the shame on't in himself,
Threw off his spirit, his appetite, his sleep,
And downright languish'd.—Leave me solely:[3]—go,
See how he fares. [*Exit* Attend.]—Fye, fye! no thought of him;—
The very thought of my revenges that way
Recoil upon me: in himself too mighty;
And in his parties, his alliance,—Let him be,
Until a time may serve: for present vengeance,
Take it on her. Camillo and Polixenes
Laugh at me; make their pastime at my sorrow:
They should not laugh, if I could reach them; nor
Shall she, within my power.

Enter PAULINA, *with a Child.*

1 *Lord.* You must not enter.
Paul. Nay, rather, good my lords, be second to me
Fear you his tyrannous passion more, alas,
Than the queen's life? a gracious innocent soul;
More free, than he is jealous.
Ant. That's enough.
1 *Atten.* Madam, he hath not slept to night; commanded
None should come at him.
Paul. Not so hot, good sir;
I come to bring him sleep. 'Tis such as you,—
That creep like shadows by him, and do sigh
At each his needless heavings,—such as you
Nourish the cause of his awaking: I
Do come with words as med'cinal as true;
Honest, as either; to purge him of that humour,
That presses him from sleep.
Leon. What noise there, ho?
Paul. No noise, my lord; but needful conference
About some gossips for your highness.
Leon. How?——
Away with that audacious lady: Antigonus,
I charg'd thee, that she should not come about me;
I knew she would.
Ant. I told her so, my lord,
On your displeasure's peril, and on mine,
She should not visit you.
Leon. What, can'st not rule her
Paul. From all dishonesty, he can: in this,
(Unless he take the course that you have done,
Commit me, for committing honour) trust it,
He sha'l not rule me.

1 *Lunes.* This word has not been found in any other English writer; but it is used in old French for *frenzy, lunacy, folly.* A similar expression occurs in The Revenger's Tragedy, 1608.

2 *Blank* and *level* mean *mark* and *aim*, or *direction*. They are terms of gunnery.

3 i. e. leave me alone

Ant. Lo you now, you hear!
When she will take the rein, I let her run;
But she'll not stumble.

Paul. Good my liege, I come,—
And, I beseech you, hear me, who profess[1]
Myself your loyal servant, your physician,
Your most obedient counsellor; yet that dare
Less appear so, in comforting your evils,[2]
Than such as most seem yours:—I say, I come
From your good queen.

Leon. Good queen!

Paul. Good queen, my lord, good queen: I say, good queen;
And would by combat make her good, so were I
A man, the worst[3] about you.

Leon. Force her hence.

Paul. Let him, that makes but trifles of his eyes,
First hand me: on my own accord, I'll off;
But, first, I'll do my errand.—The good queen,
For she is good, hath brought you forth a daughter;
Here 'tis; commends it to your blessing.
[*Laying down the Child.*

Leon. Out!
A mankind[4] witch? Hence with her, out o' door:
A most intelligencing bawd!

Paul. Not so:
I am as ignorant in that, as you
In so entitling me: and no less honest
Than you are mad; which is enough, I'll warrant,
As this world goes, to pass for honest.

Leon. Traitors!
Will you not push her out? Give her the bastard:—
Thou dotard [*To* ANTIGONUS,] thou art woman-tir'd,[5] unroosted
By thy dame Partlet here:—take up the bastard;
Take't up, I say; give't to thy crone.[6]

Paul. For ever
Unvenerable be thy hands, if thou
Takest up the princess, by that forced[7] baseness
Which he has put upon't!

Leon. He dreads his wife.

Paul. So, I would, you did; then, 'twere past all doubt,
You'd call your children yours.

Leon. A nest of traitors!

Ant. I am none, by this good light.

Paul. Nor I; nor any,
But one, that's here; and that's himself: for he
The sacred honour of himself, his queen's,
His hopeful son's, his babe's, betrays to slander,
Whose sting is sharper than the sword's;[8] and will not
(For, as the case now stands, it is a curse
He cannot be compell'd to't,) once remove
The root of his opinion, which is rotten,
As ever oak, or stone, was sound.

Leon. A callat,[9]
Of boundless tongue; who late hath beat her husband,
And now baits me!—This brat is none of mine;
It is the issue of Polixenes:
Hence with it; and, together with the dam,
Commit them to the fire.

Paul. It is yours;
And, might we lay the old proverb to your charge,
So like you, 'tis the worse.—Behold, my lords,
Although the print be little, the whole matter
And copy of the father: eye, nose, lip,
The trick of his frown, his forehead; nay, the valley,
The pretty dimples of his chin, and cheek; his smiles;
The very mould and frame of hand, nail, finger:—
And, thou, good goddess nature, which hast made it
So like to him that got it, if thou hast
The ordering of the mind too, 'mongst all colours
No yellow[10] in't; lest she suspect, as he does,
Her children not her husband's!

Leon. A gross hag!—
And, lozel,[11] thou art worthy to be hang'd,
That wilt not stay her tongue.

Ant. Hang all the husbands
That cannot do that feat, you'll leave yourself
Hardly one subject.

Leon. Once more, take her hence.

Paul. A most unworthy and unnatural lord
Can do no more.

Leon. I'll have thee burn'd.

Paul. I care not.
It is a heretic that makes the fire,
Not she which burns in't. I'll not call you tyrant;
But this most cruel usage of your queen
(Not able to produce more accusation
Than your own weak-hing'd fancy) something savours
Of tyranny, and will ignoble make you,
Yea, scandalous to the world.

Leon. On your allegiance,
Out of the chamber with her. Were I a tyrant,
Where were her life? she durst not call me so,
If she did know me one. Away with her.

Paul. I pray you, do not push me; I'll be gone.
Look to your babe, my lord; 'tis yours: Jove send her
A better guiding spirit!—What need these hands?—
You, that are thus so tender o'er his follies,
Will never do him good, not one of you.
So, so:—Farewell; we are gone. [*Exit.*

Leon. Thou, traitor, hast set on thy wife to this.—
My child? away with't!—even thou, that hast
A heart so tender o'er it, take it hence,
And see it instantly consum'd with fire;
Even thou, and none but thou. Take it up straight:
Within this hour bring me word, 'tis done
(And by good testimony,) or I'll seize thy life,
With what thou else call'st thine: If thou refuse,
And wilt encounter with my wrath, say so;
The bastard brains with these my proper hands
Shall I dash out. Go, take it to the fire;
For thou sett'st on thy wife.

Ant. I did not, sir.
These lords, my noble fellows, if they please,
Can clear me in't.

1 *Lord* We can; my royal liege,
He is not guilty of her coming hither.

Leon. You are liars all.

1 *Lord.* 'Beseech your highness, give us better credit:
We have always truly serv'd you; and beseech
So to esteem of us; And on our knees we beg
(As recompense of our dear services,
Past, and to come) that you do change this purpose
Which, being so horrible, so bloody, must
Lead on to some foul issue: We all kneel.

Leon. I am a feather for each wind that blows;—
Shall I live on, to see this bastard kneel
And call me father? Better burn it now,
Than curse it then. But, be it; let it live:
It shall not neither.—You, sir, come you hither;
[*To* ANTIGONUS
You, that have been so tenderly officious
With lady Margery, your midwife, there,

1 The old copy has *professes.*

2 'In *comforting* your *evils.*' To *comfort*, in old language, is *to aid*, *to encourage*. *Evils* here mean *wicked courses.*

3 i. e. the *weakest*, or *least warlike*.

4 'A *mankind* witch.' In Junius's Nomenclator, by Abraham Fleming, 1585, *Virago* is interpreted 'A manly woman, or a *mankind* woman.' Johnson asserts that the phrase is still used in the midland counties for a woman violent, ferocious, and mischievous.

5 i. e. hen-pecked. To *tire* in Falconry is to *tear* with the beak. *Partlet* is the name of the hen in the old story of Reynard the Fox.

6 A *crone* was originally a toothless *old ewe*; and thence became a term of contempt for an *old woman*.

7 *Forced* is false; uttered with violence to truth *Baseness* for *bastardy*; we still say *base born.*

8 'Whose sting is sharper than the sword's.' So in Cymbeline:

'Slander,
Whose edge is sharper than the sword, whose tongue
Outvenoms all the worms of Nile.'

9 A *callat* is a *trull*.

10 'No *yellow*,' the colour of jealousy.

11 *Lozel*, a worthless fellow; one lost to all goodness From the Saxon *Losian*, to perish, to be lost. *Lorel losel*, *losliche*, are all of the same family.

To save this bastard's life:—for 'tis a bastard,
So sure as this beard's gray,[1]—what will you adventure
To save this brat's life?

Ant. Any thing, my lord,
That my ability may undergo,
And nobleness impose: at least, thus much;
I'll pawn the little blood which I have left,
To save the innocent: any thing possible.

Leon. It shall be possible: Swear by this sword,[2]
Thou wilt perform my bidding.

Ant. I will, my lord.

Leon. Mark, and perform it; (seest thou?) for the fail
Of any point in't shall not only be
Death to thyself, but to thy lewd-tongu'd wife;
Whom, for this time, we pardon. We enjoin thee,
As thou art liegeman to us, that thou carry
This female bastard hence; and that thou bear it
To some remote and desert place, quite out
Of our dominions; and that there thou leave it,
Without more mercy, to its own protection,
And favour of the climate. As by strange fortune
It came to us, I do in justice charge thee,—
On thy soul's peril, and thy body's torture,—
That thou commend it strangely to some place,[3]
Where chance may nurse, or end it: Take it up.

Ant. I swear to do this, though a present death
Had been more merciful.—Come on, poor babe:
Some powerful spirit instruct the kites and ravens,
To be thy nurses! Wolves, and bears, they say,
Casting their savageness aside, have done
Like offices of pity.—Sir, be prosperous
In more than this deed doth require! and blessing,[4]
Against this cruelty, fight on thy side,
Poor thing, condemn'd to loss![5]
[*Exit, with the Child.*

Leon. No, I'll not rear
Another's issue.

1 *Atten.* Please your highness, posts,
From those you sent to the oracle, are come
An hour since: Cleomenes and Dion,
Being well arrived from Delphos, are both landed,
Hasting to the court.

1 *Lord.* So please you, sir, their speed
Hath been beyond account.

Leon. Twenty-three days
They have been absent: 'Tis good speed; foretells,
The great Apollo suddenly will have
The truth of this appear. Prepare you, lords;
Summon a session, that we may arraign
Our most disloyal lady: for, as she hath
Been publicly accus'd, so shall she have
A just and open trial. While she lives,
My heart will be a burden to me. Leave me;
And think upon my bidding. [*Exeunt.*

ACT III.

SCENE I. *The same. A Street in some Town.* *Enter* Cleomenes *and* Dion.

Cleo. The climate's delicate; the air most sweet;
Fertile the isle;[6] the temple much surpassing
The common praise it bears.

Dion. I shall report,
For most it caught me, the celestial habits
(Methinks, I so should term them,) and the reverence
Of the grave wearers. O, the sacrifice!
How ceremonious, solemn, and unearthly
It was i'the offering!

Cleo. But, of all, the burst
And ear-deafening voice o'the oracle,
Kin to Jove's thunder, so surpris'd my sense,
That I was nothing.

Dion. If the event o' the journey
Prove as successful to the queen,—O, be't so!—
As it hath been to us, rare, pleasant, speedy,
The time is worth the use on't.[7]

Cleo. Great Apollo,
Turn all to the best! These proclamations,
So forcing faults upon Hermione,
I little like.

Dion. The violent carriage of it
Will clear, or end, the business: When the oracle,
(Thus by Apollo's great divine seal'd up)
Shall the contents discover, something rare,
Even then will rush to knowledge.——Go,—fresh horses;—
And gracious be the issue! [*Exeunt.*

SCENE II. *The same. A Court of Justice.* Leontes, Lords, *and* Officers, *appear properly seated.*

Leon. This sessions (to our great grief, we pronounce)
Even pushes 'gainst our heart: The party tried,
The daughter of a king; our wife; and one
Of us too much belov'd.—Let us be clear'd
Of being tyrannous, since we so openly
Proceed in justice; which shall have due course,
Even to the guilt, or the purgation.——
Produce the prisoner.

Offi. It is his highness' pleasure, that the queen
Appear in person here in court.—Silence!

Hermione *is brought in, guarded;* Paulina *and* Ladies, *attending.*

Leon. Read the indictment.

Offi. Hermione, *queen to the worthy* Leontes, *king of* Sicilia, *thou art here accused and arraigned of high treason, in committing adultery with* Polixenes, *king of* Bohemia; *and conspiring with* Camillo *to take away the life of our sovereign lord and king, thy royal husband; the pretence*[8] *whereof being by circumstances partly laid open, thou,* Hermione, *contrary to the faith and allegiance of a true subject, didst counsel and aid them, for their better safety, to fly away by night.*

Her. Since what I am to say, must be but that
Which contradicts my accusation; and
The testimony on my part, no other
But what comes from myself; it shall scarce boot me
To say, *Not guilty:* mine integrity,
Being counted falsehood,[9] shall, as I express it,
Be so receiv'd. But thus,—If powers divine
Behold our human actions (as they do,)
I doubt not then, but innocence shall make
False accusation blush, and tyranny
Tremble at patience.—You, my lord, best know
(Who least will seem to do so,) my past life
Hath been as continent, as chaste, as true,
As I am now unhappy; which[10] is more
Than history can pattern, though devis'd,
And play'd to take spectators: For behold me,—
A fellow of the royal bed, which owe[11]
A moiety of the throne, a great king's daughter,
The mother to a hopeful prince—here standing
To prate and talk for life, and honour, 'fore
Who please to come and hear. For life, I prize it
As I weigh grief, which I would spare:[12] for honour,

1 Leontes must mean the beard of Antigonus, which he may be supposed to touch. He himself tells us that twenty-three years ago he was unbreech'd, of course his age must be under thirty, and his own beard would hardly be gray.

2 It was anciently a practice to swear by the cross at the hilt of a sword.

3 i. e. *commit* it to some place as a stranger. To *commend* is to *commit*, according to the old dictionaries.

4 i. e. the favour of heaven.

5 i. e. to exposure, or to be lost or dropped.

6 Warburton has remarked that the temple of Apollo was at *Delphi*, which was not an island. But Shakspeare little regarded geographical accuracy. He followed Green's Dorastus and Fawnia, in which it is called the *isle* of Delphos. There was a temple of Apollo in the isle of *Delos.*

7 'The time is worth the use on't;' that is, the event of our journey will recompense us for the time we spent in it.

8 i. e. the *design.* Shakspeare often uses the word for *design* or *intention.*

9 i. e. my *virtue* being accounted *wickedness*, my assertion of it will pass but for a *lie.* Falsehood means both *treachery* and *lie.*

10 *Which*, that is, *which unhappiness.*

11 Own, possess.

12 I prize my life no more than I value grief, which I would willingly spare. This sentiment, which is pro

'Tis a derivative from me to mine,
And only that I stand for. I appeal
To your own conscience, sir, before Polixenes
Came to your court, how I was in your grace,
How merited to be so; since he came,
With what encounter so uncurrent I
Have strain'd, to appear thus:[1] if one jot beyond
The bound of honour; or, in act, or will,
That way inclining; harden'd be the hearts
Of all that hear me, and my near'st of kin
Cry, Fye upon my grave!

Leon. I ne'er heard yet,
That any of these bolder vices wanted
Less impudence to gainsay what they did,
Than to perform it first.[2]

Her. That's true enough;
Though 'tis a saying, sir, not due to me.

Leon. You will not own it.

Her. More than mistress of,
Which comes to me in name of fault, I must not
At all acknowledge. For Polixenes,
(With whom I am accus'd) I do confess,
I lov'd him, as in honour he requir'd;
With such a kind of love, as might become
A lady like me; with a love, even such,
So, and no other, as yourself commanded:
Which not to have done, I think, had been in me
Both disobedience and ingratitude,
To you, and toward your friend; whose love had spoke,
Even since it could speak, from an infant freely,
That it was yours. Now, for conspiracy,
I know not how it tastes; though it be dish'd
For me to try how: all I know of it,
Is, that Camillo was an honest man;
And, why he left your court, the gods themselves,
Wotting no more than I, are ignorant.

Leon. You knew of his departure, as you know
What you have underta'en to do in his absence.

Her. Sir,
You speak a language that I understand not:
My life stands in the level[3] of your dreams,
Which I'll lay down.

Leon. Your actions are my dreams;
You had a bastard by Polixenes,
And I but dream'd it:—As you were past all shame
(Those of your fact[4] are so,) so past all truth:
Which to deny, concerns more than avails:[5] for as
Thy brat hath been cast out, like to itself,
No father owning it (which is, indeed,
More criminal in thee, than it,) so thou
Shalt feel our justice; in whose easiest passage,
Look for no less than death.

Her. Sir, spare your threats;
The bug,[6] which you would fright me with, I seek.
To me can life be no commodity:
The crown and comfort of my life, your favour,
I do give lost; for I do feel it gone,
But know not how it went: My second joy,
And first-fruits of my body, from his presence
I am barr'd, like one infectious: My third comfort,
Starr'd most unluckily,[7] is from my breast,
The innocent milk in its most innocent mouth,
Haled out to murder: Myself on every post
Proclaim'd a strumpet; with immodest hatred,
The child-bed privilege denied, which 'longs
To women of all fashion:—Lastly, hurried
Here to this place, i'the open air, before
I have got strength of limit.[8] Now, my liege,
Tell me what blessings I have here alive,
That I should fear to die? Therefore, proceed.
But yet hear this; mistake me not;——No! life,
I prize it not a straw:—but for mine honour
(Which I would free,) if I shall be condemn'd
Upon surmises; all proofs sleeping else,
But what your jealousies awake; I tell you,
'Tis rigour, and not law.—Your honours all,
I do refer me to the oracle;
Apollo be my judge.

1 Lord. This your request
Is altogether just: therefore, bring forth,
And in Apollo's name, his oracle.

[*Exeunt certain* Officers.

Her. The emperor of Russia was my father:
O, that he were alive, and here beholding
His daughter's trial! that he did but see
The flatness[9] of my misery; yet with eyes
Of pity, not revenge!

Re-enter Officers with CLEOMENES *and* DION.

Offi. You here shall swear upon this sword of justice,
That you, Cleomenes and Dion, have
Been both at Delphos; and from thence have brought
This seal'd-up oracle, by the hand deliver'd
Of great Apollo's priest; and that, since then,
You have not dar'd to break the holy seal,
Nor read the secrets in't.

Cleo. Dion. All this we swear.

Leon. Break up the seals and read.

Offi. [*Reads.*] Hermione *is chaste,* Polixenes *blameless,* Camillo *a true subject,* Leontes *a jealous tyrant, his innocent babe truly begotten; and the king shall live without an heir, if that, which is lost, be not found.*[10]

Lords. Now blessed be the great Apollo!

Her. Praised!

Leon. Hast thou read truth?

Offi. Ay, my Lord; even so
As it is here set down.

Leon. There is no truth at all i'the oracle:
The sessions shall proceed; this is mere falsehood.

Enter a Servant, *hastily.*

Serv. My lord the king, the king!

Leon. What is the business?

Serv. O sir, I shall be hated to report it:
The prince your son, with mere conceit and fear
Of the queen's speed,[11] is gone.

Leon. How! gone?

Serv. Is dead.

Leon. Apollo's angry; and the heavens themselves
Do strike at my injustice. [HERMIONE *faints.*
How now there?

Paul. This news is mortal to the queen:—Look down,
And see what death is doing.

Leon. Take her hence;
Her heart is but o'ercharg'd; she will recover.—
I have too much believed mine own suspicion:—
'Beseech you, tenderly apply to her

---

bably derived from Ecclesiasticus, iii. 11, cannot be too often impressed on the female mind: 'The glory of a man is from the honour of his father; and *a mother in dishonour is a reproach to her children.*'

1 *Encounter so uncurrent* is *unallowed* or *unlawful meeting.—Strain'd* means *swerv'd* or gone astray from the line of duty.

2 It is to be observed that originally in our language, two negatives did not *affirm,* but only strengthen the negation. Examples of similar phraseology occur in several of our author's plays, and even in the first act of this very drama: in this passage, Johnson observes that, according to the present use of words, *less* should be *more,* or *wanted* should be *had.*

3 See note 2, p. 316. To stand within the *level* of a gun is to stand in a direct line with its mouth, and in danger of being hurt by its discharge. This expression often occurs in Shakspeare.

4 i. e. they who have done like you. Shakspeare had this from Dorastus and Fawnia, 'it was her part to *deny* such a monstrous crime, and to be impudent in forswearing the *fact,* since she had *passed all shame* in committing the fault.'

5 It is your *business* to deny this charge; but the mere denial will be useless, will prove nothing.

6 Bugbear.

7 'Starr'd most unluckily.' Ill-starred; born under an inauspicious planet.

8 *Strength of limit,* i. e. the degree of strength which it is customary to acquire before women are suffered to go abroad after child-bearing.

9 'The *flatness* of my misery,' that is *absoluteness,* the *completeness* of my misery.

10 This is almost literally from Greene's novel.

11 i. e. of the event of the queen's trial. We still say, he *sped* well or ill.

Some remedies for life.—Apollo, pardon
[*Exeunt* Paulina *and* Ladies, *with* Herm.
My great profaneness 'gainst thine oracle!—
I'll reconcile me to Polixenes;
New woo my queen; recall the good Camillo;
Whom I proclaim a man of truth, of mercy;
For, being transported by my jealousies
To bloody thoughts and to revenge, I chose
Camillo for the minister, to poison
My friend Polixenes: which had been done,
But that the good mind of Camillo tardied
My swift command, though I with death, and with
Reward, did threaten and encourage him,
Not doing it, and being done: he, most humane,
And fill'd with honour, to my kingly guest
Unclasp'd my practice; quit his fortunes here,
Which you knew great; and to the certain[1] hazard
Of all incertainties himself commended,[2]
No richer than his honour:—How he glisters
Thorough my rust! and how his piety
Does my deeds make the blacker![3]

Re-enter Paulina.

Paul. Woe the while!
O, cut my lace; lest my heart, cracking it,
Break too!
1 *Lord.* What fit is this, good lady?
Paul. What studied torments, tyrant, hast for me?
What wheels? racks? fires? What flaying? boiling
In leads or oils? what old, or newer torture
Must I receive; whose every word deserves
To taste of thy most worst? Thy tyranny
Together working with thy jealousies.—
Fancies too weak for boys, too green and idle
For girls of nine!—O, think, what they have done,
And then run mad, indeed; stark mad! for all
Thy by-gone fooleries were but spices of it.
That thou betray'dst Polixenes, 'twas nothing;
That did but show thee, of a fool, inconstant,[4]
And damnable[5] ungrateful: nor was't much,
Thou would'st have poison'd good Camillo's honour,[6]
To have him kill a king; poor trespasses,
More monstrous standing by: whereof I reckon
The casting forth to crows thy baby daughter,
To be or none, or little; though a devil
Would have shed water out of fire,[7] ere done't:
Nor is't directly laid to thee, the death
Of the young prince; whose honourable thoughts
(Thoughts high for one so tender) cleft the heart
That could conceive a gross and foolish sire
Blemish'd his gracious dam: this is not, no,
Laid to thy answer: But the last,—O, lords,
When I have said, cry, woe!—the queen, the queen,
The sweetest, dearest, creature's dead; and vengeance for't
Not dropp'd down yet.
1 *Lord.* The higher powers forbid!
Paul. I say, she's dead; I'll swear't: if word, nor oath,
Prevail not, go and see: if you can bring
Tincture, or lustre, in her lip, her eye,
Heat outwardly, or breath within, I'll serve you
As I would do the gods.—But, O thou tyrant!
Do not repent these things; for they are heavier
Than all thy woes can stir; therefore betake thee
To nothing but despair. A thousand knees
Ten thousand years together, naked, fasting,
Upon a barren mountain, and still winter
In storm perpetual, could not move the gods
To look that way thou wert.
Leon. Go on, go on:
Thou canst not speak too much; I have deserv'd
All tongues to talk their bitterest.
1 *Lord.* Say no more;
Howe'er the business goes, you have made fault
I'the boldness of your speech.
Paul. I am sorry for't;
All faults I make, when I shall come to know them,
I do repent: Alas, I have show'd too much
The rashness of a woman: he is touch'd
To the noble heart.—What's gone, and what's past help,
Should be past grief: Do not receive affliction
At my petition, I beseech you; rather
Let me be punish'd, that have minded you
Of what you should forget. Now, good my liege,
Sir, royal sir, forgive a foolish woman:
The love I bore your queen,—lo, fool again!—
I'll speak of her no more, nor of your children;
I'll not remember you of my own lord,
Who is lost too: Take your patience to you,
And I'll say nothing.
Leon. Thou didst speak but well,
When most the truth; which I receive much better
Than to be pitied of thee. Pr'ythee, bring me
To the dead bodies of my queen, and son;
One grave shall be for both; upon them shall
The causes of their death appear, unto
Our shame perpetual: Once a day I'll visit
The chapel where they lie: and tears, shed there,
Shall be my recreation: So long as
Nature will bear up with this exercise,
So long I daily vow to use it. Come,
And lead me to these sorrows. [*Exeunt*

SCENE III. Bohemia. *A desert Country near the Sea. Enter* Antigonus, *with the Child; and a* Mariner.

Ant. Thou art perfect[8] then, our ship hath touch'd upon
The deserts of Bohemia?
Mar. Ay, my lord; and fear
We have landed in ill time: the skies look grimly,
And threaten present blusters. In my conscience,
The heavens with that we have in hand are angry,
And frown upon us.
Ant. Their sacred wills be done!—Go, get aboard;
Look to thy bark; I'll not be long, before
I call upon thee.
Mar. Make your best haste; and go not
Too far i'the land; 'tis like to be loud weather,
Besides, this place is famous for the creatures
Of prey, that keep upon't.
Ant. Go thou away:
I'll follow instantly.
Mar. I am glad at heart
To be so rid o'the business. [*Exit.*
Ant. Come, poor babe:——
I have heard, (but not believ'd,) the spirits of the dead
May walk again: if such thing be, thy mother
Appear'd to me last night; for ne'er was dream
So like a waking. To me comes a creature,
Sometimes her head on one side, some another,
I never saw a vessel of like sorrow,
So fill'd, and so becoming: in pure white robes,
Like very sanctity, she did approach
My cabin where I lay: thrice bow'd before me
And, gasping to begin some speech, her eyes
Became two spouts: the fury spent, anon
Did this break from her: *Good* Antigonus,
Since fate, against thy better disposition,
Hath made thy person for the thrower-out
Of my poor babe, according to thine oath,—
Places remote enough are in Bohemia,
There weep, and leave it crying; and, for the babe

1 *Certain* is not in the first folio, it was supplied by the editor of the second.
2 See p. 318, note 3.
3 This vehement retractation of Leontes, accompanied with the confession of more crimes than he was suspected of, is agreeable to our daily experience, of the vicissitudes of violent tempers, and the eruptions of minds oppressed with guilt.
4 The same construction occurs in the second book of Phaer's version of the Æneid:
'When this the young men heard me speak, *of wild they waxed wood.*'
5 *Damnable* is used here adverbially.
6 The poet forgot that Paulina was absent during the king's self-accusation.
7 i. e. a devil would have shed tears of pity, ere he would have perpetrated such an action.
8 i. e. well assured.

Is counted lost for ever, Perdita,
I pr'ythee call't; for this ungentle business,
Put on thee by my lord, thou ne'er shalt see
Thy wife Paulina *more:* and so, with shrieks,
She melted into air. Affrighted much,
I did in time collect myself; and thought
This was so, and no slumber. Dreams are toys:
Yet, for this once, yea, superstitiously,
I will be squar'd by this. I do believe
Hermione hath suffer'd death; and that
Apollo would, this being indeed the issue
Of king Polixenes, it should here be laid,
Either for life or death, upon the earth
Of its right father.—Blossom, speed thee well!
[*Laying down the Child.*
There lie; and there thy character:[1] there these;
[*Laying down a Bundle.*
Which may, if fortune please, both breed thee, pretty,
And still rest thine.——The storm begins:—Poor wretch,
That, for thy mother's fault, art thus expos'd
To loss, and what may follow!—Weep I cannot,
But my heart bleeds; and most accurs'd am I,
To be by oath enjoin'd to this.—Farewell!
The day frowns more and more; thou art like to have
A lullaby too rough: I never saw
The heavens so dim by day. A savage clamour![2]—
Well may I get aboard!——This is the chase;
I am gone for ever. [*Exit, pursued by a Bear.*

Enter an old Shepherd.

Shep. I would, there were no age between ten and three-and-twenty; or that youth would sleep out the rest; for there is nothing in the between but getting wenches with child, wronging the ancientry, stealing, fighting.—Hark you now!——Would any but these boiled brains of nineteen and two-and-twenty, hunt this weather? They have scared away two of my best sheep; which, I fear, the wolf will sooner find than the master: if any where I have them, 'tis by the sea-side, browzing of ivy.[3] Good luck, an't be thy will! what have we here? [*Taking up the Child.*] Mercy on's, a barne; a very pretty barne! A boy, or a child[4], I wonder? A pretty one; a very pretty one: Sure some scape: though I am not bookish, yet I can read waiting-gentlewoman in the scape. This has been some stair-work, some trunk-work, some behind-door work: they were warmer that got this, than the poor thing is here. I'll take it up for pity: yet I'll tarry till my son come; he holla'd but even now. Whoa, ho, hoa!

Enter Clown.

Clo. Hilloa, loa!

Shep. What, art so near? If thou'lt see a thing to talk on when thou art dead and rotten, come hither. What ailst thou, man?

Clo. I have seen two such sights, by sea, and by land;—but I am not to say, it is a sea, for it is now the sky; betwixt the firmament and it, you cannot thrust a bodkin's point.

Shep. Why, boy, how is it?

Clo. I would, you did but see how it chafes, how it rages, how it takes up the shore! but that's not to the point: O, the most piteous cry of the poor souls! sometimes to see 'em, and not to see 'em: now the ship boring the moon with her main-mast; and anon swallowed with yest and froth, as you'd thrust a cork into a hogshead. And then for the land service,—To see how the bear tore out his shoulder-bone! how he cried to me for help, and said, his name was Antigonus, a nobleman:—But to make an end of the ship:—to see how the sea flap-dragoned[5] it; but, first, how the poor souls roared, and the sea mocked them;—and how the poor gentleman roared, and the bear mocked him, both roaring louder than the sea, or weather.

Shep. 'Name of mercy, when was this, boy?

Clo. Now, now; I have not winked since I saw these sights: the men are not yet cold under water, nor the bear half dined on the gentleman; he's at it now.

Shep. 'Would, I had been by, to have helped the old man![6]

Clo. I would you had been by the ship side, to have helped her; there your charity would have lacked footing. [*Aside.*

Shep. Heavy matters! heavy matters! but look thee here, boy. Now bless thyself; thou met'st with things dying, I with things new born. Here's a sight for thee; Look thee, a bearing-cloth[7] for a squire's child! Look thee here: take up, take up, boy; open't. So, let's see; It was told me, I should be rich, by the fairies: this is some changeling:[8]—open't: What's within, boy?

Clo. You're a made[9] old man; if the sins of your youth are forgiven you, you're well to live. Gold! all gold!

Shep. This is fairy gold, boy, and 'twill prove so: up with it, keep it close; home, home, the next[10] way. We are lucky, boy; and to be so still, requires nothing but secrecy,—Let my sheep go:—Come, good boy, the next way home.

Clo. Go you the next way with your findings; I'll go see if the bear be gone from the gentleman, and how much he hath eaten: they are never curst,[11] but when they are hungry: if there be any of him left, I'll bury it.

Shep. That's a good deed; If thou may'st discern by that which is left of him, what he is, fetch me to the sight of him.

Clo. Marry, will I: and you shall help to put him i' the ground.

Shep. 'Tis a lucky day, boy; and we'll do good deeds on't. [*Exeunt.*

ACT IV.

Enter Time, *as Chorus.*

Time. I,—that please some, try all; both joy and terror,
Of good and bad; that make, and unfold error,[12]
Now take upon me, in the name of Time,
To use my wings. Impute it not a crime,
To me, or my swift passage, that I slide
O'er sixteen years,[13] and leave the growth untried
Of that wide gap;[14] since it is in my power

1 i. e. *description.* The writing afterward discovered with Perdita.

2 'A savage clamour.' This clamour was the cry of the dogs and hunters; then seeing the bear, he cries *this is the chase*, i. e. the *animal pursued.*

3 This is from the novel. It is there said to be '*sea ivie*, on which they do greatly feed.'

4 A *barne.* This word is still in use in the northern dialects for a *child.* It is supposed to be derived from *born*, things born seeming to answer to the Latin *nati.* Steevens says that he had been told 'that in some of our inland countries a *child* signified a *female infant* in contradistinction to a male one;' but the assertion wants confirmation, and we may rather refer this use of it to the simplicity of the shepherd

5 i. e. *swallowed it*, as our ancient topers swallowed flap-dragons.

6 Shakspeare, who knew that he himself designed Antigonus for an *old* man, has inadvertently given this knowledge to the shepherd, who had never seen him.

7 A *bearing-cloth*, is the mantle of fine cloth, in which a child was carried to be baptized.

8 A *changeling.* Some child left behind by the fairies, in the room of one which they had stolen.

9 The old copies read *mad.* The emendation is Theobald's.

10 i. e. nearest.

11 *Curst* here signifies *mischievous.* The old adage says, '*Curst* cows have short horns.'

12 *Departed time* renders many facts obscure, and in that sense is the cause of error. *Time to come* brings discoveries with it.

13 It is certain that Shakspeare was well acquainted with the *laws* of the drama, as they are called, but disregarded, nay wilfully departed from them, and 'snatch'd a grace beyond the reach of art.' His productions are not therefore to be tried by such laws.

14 i. e. leave unexamined the progress of the intermediate time which filled up the gap in Perdita's story The reasoning of *Time* is not very clear; he seems to

To o'erthrow law, and in one self-born hour
To plant and o'erwhelm custom: Let me pass
The same I am, ere ancient'st order was,
Or what is now received: I witness to
The times that brought them in; so shall I do
To the freshest things now reigning: and make stale
The glistering of this present, as my tale
Now seems to it. Your patience this allowing,
I turn my glass; and give my scene such growing,
As you had slept between. Leontes leaving
The effects of his fond jealousies; so grieving,
That he shuts up himself; imagine me,[1]
Gentle spectators, that I now may be
In fair Bohemia; and remember well,
I mentioned a son o' the king's, which Florizel
I now name to you; and with speed so pace
To speak of Perdita, now grown in grace
Equal with wond'ring: What of her ensues,
I list not prophesy; but let Time's news
Be known, when 'tis brought forth:—a shepherd's daughter,
And what to her adheres, which follows after,
Is the argument[2] of time: Of this allow,[3]
If ever you have spent time worse ere now;
If never yet, that Time himself doth say,
He wishes earnestly you never may. [*Exit.*

SCENE I. *The same. A Room in the Palace of* Polixenes. *Enter* POLIXENES *and* CAMILLO.

Pol. I pray thee, good Camillo, be no more importunate: 'tis a sickness, denying thee any thing; a death, to grant this.

Cam. It is fifteen[4] years, since I saw my country: though I have, for the most part, been aired abroad, I desire to lay my bones there. Besides, the penitent king, my master, hath sent for me: to whose feeling sorrows I might be some allay, or I o'erween to think so; which is another spur to my departure.

Pol. As thou lovest me, Camillo, wipe not out the rest of thy services, by leaving me now: the need I have of thee, thine own goodness hath made; better not to have had thee, than thus to want thee: thou, having made me businesses, which none without thee can sufficiently manage, must either stay to execute them thyself, or take away with thee the very services thou hast done: which if I have not enough considered, (as too much I cannot,) to be more thankful to thee, shall be my study; and my profit therein, the heaping friendships.[5] Of that fatal country, Sicilia, pr'ythee speak no more: whose very naming punishes me with the remembrance of that penitent, as thou call'st him, and reconciled king, my brother: whose loss of his most precious queen and children, are even now to be afresh lamented. Say to me, when saw'st thou the prince Florizel, my son? Kings are no less unhappy, their issue not being gracious, than they are in losing them, when they have approved their virtues.

Cam. Sir, it is three days since I saw the prince: What his happier affairs may be, are to me unknown: but I have missingly noted,[6] he is of late much retired from court; and is less frequent to his princely exercises, than formerly he hath appeared.

Pol. I have considered so much, Camillo; and with some care; so far, that I have eyes under my service, which look upon his removedness: from whom I have this intelligence; That he is seldom from the house of a most homely shepherd; a man, they say, that from very nothing, and beyond the imagination of his neighbours, is grown into an unspeakable estate.

Cam. I have heard, sir, of such a man, who hath a daughter of most rare note: the report of her is extended more than can be thought to begin from such a cottage.

Pol. That's likewise part of my intelligence. But, I fear the angle[7] that plucks our son thither. Thou shalt accompany us to the place: where we will, not appearing what we are, have some question with the shepherd; from whose simplicity, I think it not uneasy to get the cause of my son's resort thither. Pr'ythee, be my present partner in this business, and lay aside the thoughts of Sicilia.

Cam. I willingly obey your command.

Pol. My best Camillo!—We must disguise our selves. [*Exeunt*

SCENE II. *The same. A Road near the* Shepherd's *Cottage. Enter* AUTOLYCUS,[8] *singing.*

When daffodils begin to peer,———
With heigh! the doxy over the dale,—
Why, then comes in the sweet o' the year;
For the red blood reigns in the winter's pale.[9]
The white sheet bleaching on the hedge,—
With hey! the sweet birds, O, how they sing!—
Doth set my pugging[10] *tooth on edge;*
For a quart of ale is a dish for a king.
The lark, that tirra-lirra chants,—
With, hey! with hey! the thrush and the jay:—
Are summer songs for me and my aunts,[11]
While we lie tumbling in the hay.

I have served Prince Florizel, and, in my time, wore three-pile;[12] but now I am out of service.

But shall I go mourn, for that my dear?
The pale moon shines by night:
And when I wander here and there,
I then do most go right.

If tinkers may have leave to live,
And bear the sow-skin budget;
Then my account I well may give,
And in the stocks avouch it.

My traffick is sheets; when the kite builds, look to lesser linen.[13] My father named me Autolycus; who, being, as I am, littered under Mercury, was likewise a snapper-up of unconsidered trifles: With die, and drab, I purchased this caparison; and my revenue is the silly cheat:[14] Gallows, and knock, are too powerful on the highway: beating, and hanging, are terrors to me; for the life to come, I sleep out the thought of it.—A prize! a prize!

Enter Clown.

Clo. Let me see;—Every 'leven wether—tods;[15] every tod yields—pound and odd shilling; fifteen hundred shorn,—What comes the wool to?

Aut. If the springe hold, the cock's mine. [*Aside.*

Clo. I cannot do it without counters.[16]—Let me see; what am I to buy for our sheep-shearing feast? *Three pound of sugar; five pound of currants: rice*

---

mean, that he who overthrows everything, and makes as well as overwhelms custom, may surely infringe the laws of custom as they are made by him.

1 i. e. imagine *with* me. It is a French idiom which Shakspeare has played upon in the Taming of the Shrew.

2 *Argument*, subject. 3 i. e. approve.

4 It should be *sixteen*, as Time has just stated, and future passages have it.

5 *Heaping friendships*, friendly offices.

6 *Missingly noted*, observed at intervals.

7 *Angle* is here used for the bait, or line and hook, that draws his son like a fish away.

8 Autolycus was the son of Mercury, and as famous for all the arts of fraud and thievery as his father.

9 i. e. 'the red, the *spring* blood now *reigns over* the *parts* lately under the *dominion of winter.*' A *pale* was a division, a place set apart from another, as the English *pale*, the *pale* of the church. The words *pale* and *red* were used for the sake of the antithesis. The *glow* of spring reigns over the *paleness* of winter.

10 A *puggard* was a cant name for some kind of thief

11 *Aunt* was a cant word for a *bawd* or *trull*.

12 i. e. rich velvet, so called.

13 Autolycus means that his practice was *to steal* sheets; leaving the smaller linen to be carried away by the kites, who will sometimes carry it off to line their nests.

14 The *silly cheat* is one of the slang terms belonging to *coney-catching* or *thievery*. It is supposed to have meant *picking of pockets*.

15 Every eleven sheep will produce a tod or twenty-eight pounds of wool. The price of a tod of wool was about 20 or 22*s*. in 1581.

16 *Counters* were circular pieces of base metal, anciently used by the illiterate to adjust their reckonings.

——What will this sister of mine do with rice? But my father hath made her mistress of the feast, and she lays it on. She hath made me four-and-twenty nosegays for the shearers: three-man song-men[1] all, and very good ones; but they are most of them means[2] and bases: but one Puritan amongst them, and he sings psalms to hornpipes. I must have *saffron*, to colour the warden pies;[3] *mace,—dates,*—none; that's out of my note: *nutmegs, seven; a race, or two, of ginger;* but that I may beg;—*four pound of prunes, and as many of raisins o' the sun.*

Aut. O, that ever I was born!

[*Grovelling on the ground.*

Clo. I' the name of me,—

Aut. O, help me, help me! pluck but off these rags; and then, death, death!

Clo. Alack, poor soul! thou hast need of more rags to lay on thee, rather than have these off.

Aut. O sir, the loathsomeness of them offends me more than the stripes I have received; which are mighty ones and millions.

Clo. Alas, poor man! a million of beating may come to a great matter.

Aut. I am robbed, sir, and beaten; my money and apparel ta'en from me, and these detestable things put upon me.

Clo. What, by a horse-man, or a foot-man?

Aut. A foot-man, sweet sir, a foot-man.

Clo. Indeed, he should be a foot-man, by the garments he hath left with thee; if this be a horseman's coat, it hath seen very hot service. Lend me thy hand, I'll help thee; come, lend me thy hand. [*Helping him up.*

Aut. O! good sir, tenderly, oh!

Clo. Alas, poor soul!

Aut. O, good sir, softly, good sir: I fear, sir, my shoulder-blade is out.

Clo. How now? canst stand?

Aut. Softly, dear sir; [*picks his pocket*] good sir, softly; you ha' done me a charitable office.

Clo. Dost lack any money? I have a little money for thee.

Aut. No, good sweet sir; no, I beseech you, sir; I have a kinsman not past three quarters of a mile hence, unto whom I was going; I shall there have money, or any thing I want: Offer me no money, I pray you: that kills my heart.[4]

Clo. What manner of fellow was he that robbed you?

Aut. A fellow, sir, that I have known to go about with trol-my dames:[5] I knew him once a servant of the prince; I cannot tell, good sir, for which of his virtues it was, but he was certainly whipped out of the court.

Clo. His vices, you would say; there's no virtue whipped out of the court: they cherish it, to make it stay there; and yet it will no more but abide.[6]

Aut. Vices I would say, sir. I know this man well: he hath been since an ape-bearer; then a process-server, a bailiff; then he compassed a motion[7] of the prodigal son, and married a tinker's wife within a mile where my land and living lies; and, having flown over many knavish professions, he settled only in rogue: some call him Autolycus.

Clo. Out upon him! Prig,[8] for my life, prig: he haunts wakes, fairs, and bear-batings.

Aut. Very true, sir, he sir, he; that's the rogue, that put me into this apparel.

Clo. Not a more cowardly rogue in all Bohemia, if you had but looked big, and spit at him, he'd have run.

Aut. I must confess to you sir, I am no fighter: I am false of heart that way; and that he knew, I warrant him.

Clo. How do you now?

Aut. Sweet sir, much better than I was; I can stand, and walk: I will even take my leave of you, and pace softly towards my kinsman's.

Clo. Shall I bring thee on the way?

Aut. No, good-faced sir: no, sweet sir.

Clo. Then fare thee well; I must go buy spices for our sheep-shearing.

Aut. Prosper you, sweet sir!—[*Exit* Clown.] Your purse is not hot enough to purchase your spice. I'll be with you at your sheep-shearing too: If I make not this cheat bring out another, and the shearers prove sheep, let me be unrolled,[9] and my name put in the book of virtue!

Jog on, jog on, the foot-path way,
And merrily hent[10] *the stile-a:*
A merry heart goes all the day,
Your sad tires in a mile-a. [*Exit.*

SCENE III. *The same. A* Shepherd's *Cottage.*
Enter FLORIZEL *and* PERDITA.

Flo. These your unusual weeds to each part of you
Do give a life; no shepherdess, but Flora,
Peering in April's front. This your sheep-shearing
Is as a meeting of the petty gods,
And you the queen on't.

Per. Sir, my gracious lord,
To chide at your extremes,[11] it not becomes me;
O, pardon, that I name them; your high self,
The gracious mark[12] o' the land, you have obscur'd
With a swain's wearing; and me, poor lowly maid,
Most goddess-like prank'd up: But that our feasts
In every mess have folly, and the feeders
Digest it with a custom, I should blush
To see you so attired; sworn, I think,
To show myself a glass.[13]

Flo. I bless the time,
When my good falcon made her flight across
Thy father's ground.

Per. Now Jove afford you cause
To me, the difference[14] forges dread; your greatness
Hath not been used to fear. Even now I tremble
To think, your father, by some accident,
Should pass this way, as you did: O, the fates!
How would he look, to see his work, so noble,
Vilely bound up?[15] What would he say? Or how
Should I, in these my borrow'd flaunts, behold
The sternness of his presence?

1 i. e. singers of catches in three parts.

2 *Means* are *tenors.*

3 *Wardens* are a large sort of pear, called in French *Poires de Garde*, because, being a late hard pear, they may be kept very long. It is said that their name is derived from the Anglo Saxon *wearden*, to preserve. They are now called *baking-pears*, and are generally coloured with *cochineal* instead of *saffron*, as of old.

4 Dame Quickly, speaking of Falstaff, says:—'the king hath *killed his heart.*'

5 '*Trol-my dames.*' The old English title of this game was *pigeon-holes;* as the arches in the board through which the balls are to be rolled resemble the cavities made for pigeons in a dove-house.

6 '*Abide,*' only sojourn, or dwell for a time.

7 'He compassed a motion,' &c.; he obtained a puppet-show, &c.

8 *Prig*, another cant phrase for the order of thieves. Harman in his Caveat for Cursetor, 1573, calls a horse-stealer 'a *prigger* of prancers; for to *prigge* in their language is to *steale.*'

9 i. e. dismissed from the society of rogues.

10 *To hent* the stile is to *take* the stile. It comes from the Saxon *hentan.*

11 i. e. the extravagance of his conduct in disguising himself in shepherd's clothes, while he pranked her up most gooddess-like.

12 *The gracious mark of the land* is *the object of all men's notice and expectation.*

13 'To show myself a glass.' She probably means that the prince, by the rustic habit he wears, seems as if he had sworn to show her as in a glass how she ought to be dressed, instead of being so goddess-like prank'd up. And were it not for the license and folly which custom had made familiar at such feasts, as that of sheep-shearing, when mimetic sports were allowable, she should blush to see him so attired.

14 Meaning the *difference* between his rank and hers.

15 'Vilely bound up.' This was a metaphor natural enough to a writer, though not exactly suitable in the mouth of Perdita. Shakspeare has repeated it more than once in Romeo and Juliet.

Flo. Apprehend
Nothing but jollity. The gods themselves,
Humbling their deities to love, have taken
The shapes of beasts upon them:[1] Jupiter
Became a bull, and bellow'd; the green Neptune
A ram, and bleated; and the fire-rob'd god,
Golden Apollo, a poor humble swain,
As I seem now: Their transformations
Were never for a piece of beauty rarer;
Nor in a way so chaste: since my desires
Run not before mine honour; nor my lusts
Burn hotter than my faith.
Per. O but dear[2] sir,
Your resolution cannot hold, when 'tis
Opposed, as it must be by the power o' the king:
One of these two must be necessities,
Which then will speak; that you must change this purpose,
Or I my life.
Flo. Thou dearest Perdita,
With these forc'd[3] thoughts, I pr'ythee, darken not
The mirth o' the feast: Or I'll be thine, my fair,
Or not my father's: for I cannot be
Mine own, nor anything to any, if
I be not thine: to this I am most constant,
Though destiny say, no. Be merry, gentle;
Strangle such thoughts as these, with any thing
That you behold the while. Your guests are coming:
Lift up your countenance; as it were the day
Of celebration of that nuptial, which
We two have sworn shall come.
Per. O lady fortune,
Stand you auspicious!

Enter Shepherd, *with* POLIXENES *and* CAMILLO, *disguised;* Clown, MOPSA, DORCAS, *and others.*

Flo. See, your guests approach:
Address yourself to entertain them sprightly,
And let's be red with mirth.
Shep. Fye, daughter! when my old wife liv'd, upon
This day, she was both pantler, butler, cook;
Both dame and servant: welcom'd all: serv'd all:
Would sing her song, and dance her turn: now here,
At upper end o' the table, now i' the middle;
On his shoulder, and his; her face o' fire
With labour; and the thing she took to quench it,
She would to each one sip: You are retired,
As if you were a feasted one, and not
The hostess of the meeting; Pray you, bid
These unknown friends to us welcome: for it is
A way to make us better friends, more known.
Come, quench your blushes; and present yourself
That which you are, mistress o'er the feast: Come on,
And bid us welcome to your sheep-shearing,
As your good flock shall prosper.
Per. Welcome, sir! [*To* POL.
It is is my father's will I should take on me
The hostesship o' the day:—Your're welcome, sir! [*To* CAMILLO.
Give me those flowers there, Dorcas.—Reverend sirs.
For you there's rosemary, and rue; these keep
Seeming, and savour,[4] all the winter long:
Grace, and remembrance, be to you both,
And welcome to our shearing!
Pol. Shepherdess,
(A fair one are you,) well you fit our ages
With flowers of winter.
Per. Sir, the year growing ancient,—
Not yet on summer's death, nor on the birth
Of trembling winter,—the fairest flowers o' the season
Are our carnations, and streak'd gilliflowers,
Which some call nature's bastards: of that kind
Our rustic garden's barren; and I care not
To get slips of them.
Pol. Wherefore, gentle maiden,
Do you neglect them?
Per. For[5] I have heard it said,
There is an art,[6] which, in their piedness, shares
With great creating nature.
Pol. Say, there be,
Yet nature is made better by no mean,
But nature makes that mean: so, o'er that art,
Which, you say, adds to nature, is an art
That nature makes. You see, sweet maid, we marry
A gentler scion to the wildest stock;
And make conceive a bark of baser kind
By bud of nobler race; This is an art
Which does mend nature,—change it rather: but
The art itself is nature.
Per. So it is.
Pol. Then make your garden rich in gilliflowers,[7]
And do not call them bastards.
Per. I'll not put
The dibble in earth to set one slip of them:
No more than, were I painted, I would wish
This youth should say, 'twere well: and only therefore
Desire to breed by me.—Here's flowers for you,
Hot lavender, mints, savory, marjoram;
The marigold, that goes to bed with the sun,
And with him rises weeping;[8] these are flowers
Of middle summer, and, I think, they are given
To men of middle age: You are very welcome.
Cam. I should leave grazing, were I of your flock,
And only live by gazing.
Per. Out, alas!
You'd be so lean, that blasts of January
Would blow you through and through.—Now, my fairest friend,
I would, I had some flowers o' the spring, that might
Become your time of day; and yours; and yours;
That wear upon your virgin branches yet
Your maidenheads growing:—O Proserpina,
For the flowers now, that, frighted, thou let'st fall
From Dis's[9] waggon! daffodils,
That come before the swallow dares, and take
The winds of March with beauty; violets, dim
But sweeter than the lids of Juno's eyes,[10]
Or Cytherea's breath; pale primroses,
That die unmarried,[11] ere they can behold

---

1 This speech is almost literally taken from the novel.

2 *Dear* is wanting in the oldest copy.

3 i. e. far-fetched, not arising from present objects.

4 i. e. appearance and smell. *Rue*, being used in exorcisms, was called *herb of grace*, and *rosemary* was supposed to strengthen the *memory*, it is prescribed for that purpose in the ancient herbals. Ophelia distributes the same plants with the same attributes.

5 *For* again in the sense of *cause*.

6 Surely there is no reference here to the impracticable pretence of producing flowers by art to rival those of nature, as Steevens supposed. The allusion is to the common practice of producing by art particular varieties of colours on flowers, especially on carnations.

7 In the folio edition it is spelt *Gillyvors*. Gelofer or gillofer was the old name for the whole class of carnations, pinks, and sweetwilliams; from the French *girofle*. There were also stock-gelofers, and wall-gelofers. The variegated gilliflowers or *carnations*, being considered as a produce of art, were properly called *nature's bastards*, and being streaked with white and red, Perdita considers them a proper emblem of a *painted* or immodest woman; and therefore declines to meddle with them. She connects the gardener's art of varying th colours of these flowers with the art of painting the face, a fashion very prevalent in Shakspeare's time. This is Mr. Douce's very ingenious solution of this riddle, which had embarrassed Mr. Steevens.

8 'Some call it *sponsus solis*, the spowse of the sunne, because it sleeps and is awakened with him.'—*Lupton's Notable Things*, book, vi.

9 See Ovid's Metam, b. v.—
'—— ut summa vestem laxavit ab ora
Collecti flores tunicis cecidere remissis;'
or the whole passage as translated by Golding, and given in the Variorum Shakspeare.

10 Johnson had not sufficient imagination to comprehend this exquisite passage, he thought that the poet had mistaken Juno for Pallas, and says, that 'sweeter than an eyelid is an odd image!' But the eyes of Juno were as remarkable as those of Pallas, and
'—— of a beauty never yet
Equalled in *height of tincture*.'
The beauties of Greece and other Asiatic nations tinged their eyelids of an obscure violet colour by means of some unguent, which was doubtless perfumed like those for the hair, &c. mentioned by Athenæus.

11 Perhaps the true explanation of this passage may be deduced from the subjoined verses in the original

Bright Phœbus in his strength, a malady
Most incident to maids; bold oxlips, and
The crown-imperial; lilies of all kinds,
The flower-de-luce being one! O, these I lack,
To make you garlands of; and, my sweet friend,
To strew him o'er and o'er.

Flo. What? like a corse?

Per. No, like a bank, for love to lie and play on;
Not like a corse: or if,—not to be buried,
But quick, and in mine arms. Come, take your flowers:
Methinks, I play as I have seen them do
In Whitsun' pastorals: sure, this robe of mine
Does change my disposition.

Flo. What you do,
Still betters what is done. When you speak, sweet,
I'd have you do it ever: when you sing,
I'd have you buy and sell so; so give alms;
Pray so; and for the ordering your affairs,
To sing them too: When you do dance, I wish you
A wave o' the sea, that you might ever do
Nothing but that; move still, still so, and own
No other function: Each your doing,
So singular in each particular,
Crowns what you are doing in the present deeds,
That all your acts are queens.

Per. O Doricles,
Your praises are too large: but that your youth,
And the true blood, which fairly peeps through it,[1]
Do plainly give you out an unstain'd shepherd,
With wisdom I might fear, my Doricles,
You woo'd me the false way.

Flo. I think, you have
As little skill to fear,[2] as I have purpose
To put you to't.—But, come, our dance, I pray:
Your hand, my Perdita: so turtles pair,
That never mean to part.

Per. I'll swear for 'em.[3]

Pol. This is the prettiest low-born lass, that ever
Ran on the green-sward: nothing she does, or seems,
But smacks of something greater than herself;
Too noble for this place.

Cam. He tells her something,
That makes her blood look out: Good sooth, she is
The queen of curds and cream.

Clo. Come on, strike up.

Dor. Mopsa must be your mistress: marry, garlic,
To mend her kissing with.

Mop. Now, in good time!

Clo. Not a word, a word; we stand upon our manners.[4]—
Come, strike up. [*Music.*

Here a dance of Shepherds *and* Shepherdesses.

Pol. Pray, good shepherd, what
Fair swain is this, which dances with your daughter?

Shep. They call him Doricles, and he boasts himself
To have a worthy feeding:[5] but I have it
Upon his own report, and I believe it;
He looks like sooth:[6] He says he loves my daughter;
I think so too; for never gaz'd the moon
Upon the water, as he'll stand, and read,
As 'twere, my daughter's eyes: and, to be plain,
I think, there is not half a kiss to choose,
Who loves another best.

Pol. She dances featly.[7]

Shep. So she does any thing; though I report it,
That should be silent; if young Doricles
Do light upon her, she shall bring him that
Which he not dreams of.

Enter a Servant.

Serv. O master, if you did but hear the pedler at the door, you would never dance again after a tabor and pipe; no, the bagpipe could not move you: he sings several tunes, faster than you'll tell money; he utters them as he had eaten ballads, and all men's ears grew to his tunes.

Clo. He could never come better; he shall come in: I love a ballad but even too well; if it be doleful matter, merrily set down, or a very pleasant thing indeed, and sung lamentably.

Serv. He hath songs, for man, or woman, of all sizes; no milliner can so fit his customers with gloves:[8] he has the prettiest love-songs for maids; so without bawdry, which is strange; with such delicate burdens of *dildos* and *fadings*;[9] *jump her and thump her*; and where some stretch-mouth'd rascal would, as it were, mean mischief, and break a foul gap into the matter, he makes the maid to answer, *Whoop, do me no harm, good man*; puts him off, slights him, with *Whoop, do me no harm, good man*.[10]

Pol. This is a brave fellow.

Clo. Believe me thou talkest of an admirable conceited fellow. Has he any unbraided wares?[11]

Serv. He hath ribbands of all the colours i' the rainbow; points,[12] more than all the lawyers in Bohemia can learnedly handle, though they come to him by the gross; inkles,[13] caddisses,[14] cambrics, lawns: why, he sings them over, as they were gods or goddesses; you would think, a smock were a she-angel; he so chants to the sleeve-hand,[15] and the work about the square on't.[16]

Clo. Pr'ythee, bring him in; and let him approach singing.

Per. Forewarn him, that he use no scurrilous words in his tunes.

Clo. You have of these pedlers, that have more in 'em than you'd think, sister.

Per. Ay, good brother, or go about to think.

Enter AUTOLYCUS, *singing.*

Lawn, as white as driven snow;
Cyprus, black as e'er was crow;
Gloves, as sweet as damask roses,
Masks for faces, and for noses;
Bugle-bracelet, necklace-amber,
Perfume for a lady's chamber;[17]
Golden quoifs, and stomachers,
For my lads to give their dears;
Pins, and poking-sticks of steel,[18]
What maids lack from head to heel:

---

edition of Milton's Lycidas, which he subsequently omitted, and altered the epithet *unwedded* to *forsaken* in the preceding line:

'Bring the rathe primrose that unwedded dies,
Colouring the pale cheek of unenjoy'd love.'

Every reader will see that the 'texture and sentiments' are derived from Shakspeare; and it serves as a beautiful illustration of his meaning.

1 Thus Marlow in his Hero and Leander;—
Through whose white skin softer than soundest sleep,
With damask eyes the ruby *blood doth peep*.'

2 i. e. you as little *know* how to fear that I am false, as, &c.

3 Johnson would transfer this speech to the king, and Ritson would read 'swear for *one*.' Mr. Douce has justly observed that no change is necessary. It is no more than a common phrase of acquiescence, like 'I'll *warrant* you.'

4 i. e. we are now on our good behaviour.

5 A valuable tract of pasturage. 6 Truth.

7 That is *dexterously, nimbly.*

8 The trade of a milliner was formerly carried on by men exclusively

9 'With a hie *dildo* dill, and a *dildo* dee,' is the burden of an old ballad or two. *Fading* is also another burden to a ballad found in Shirley's Bird in a Cage; and perhaps to others. It is also the name given to an Irish dance, probably from *fædan*, I whistle, as it was danced to the pipes.

10 This was also the burden of an old ballad.

11 i. e. *undamaged wares*, true and good. This word has sadly perplexed the commentators, who have all left the reader in the dark as to the *true* meaning. The quotation by Steevens from 'Any Thing for a Quiet Life' ought to have led to a right explanation:—'She says that you sent *ware* which is not warrantable, *braided ware*, and that you give not London measure.'

12 *Points*, upon which lies the quibble, were laces with tags.

13 A kind of tape.

14 A kind of ferret or worsted lace.

15 *Sleeve-hand*, the cuffs, or wristband.

16 The work about the bosom of it.

17 *Amber*, of which necklaces were made fit to perfume a lady's chamber.

18 These *poking-sticks* are described by Stubbes in his

Come, buy of me, come; come buy, come buy;
Buy, lads, or else your lasses cry;
Come buy, &c.

Clo. If I were not in love with Mopsa, thou shouldst take no money of me; but being enthrall'd as I am, it will also be the bondage of certain ribands and gloves.

Mop. I was promis'd them against the feast; but they come not too late now.

Dor. He hath promised you more than that, or there be liars.

Mop. He hath paid you all he promised you: may be, he has paid you more; which will shame you to give him again.

Clo. Is there no manners left among maids? will they wear their plackets, where they should bear their faces? Is there not milking-time, when you are going to bed, or kiln-hole,[1] to whistle off these secrets; but you must be tittle-tattling before all our guests? 'Tis well, they are whispering: Clamour your tongues,[2] and not a word more.

Mop. I have done. Come, you promised me a tawdry lace,[3] and a pair of sweet gloves.[4]

Clo. Have I not told thee, how I was cozened by the way, and lost all my money?

Aut. And, indeed, sir, there are cozeners abroad; therefore it behooves men to be wary.

Clo. Fear not thou man, thou shalt lose nothing here.

Aut. I hope so, sir; for I have about me many parcels of charge.

Clo. What hast here? ballads?

Mop. 'Pray now, buy some: I love a ballad in print, a'-life; for then we are sure they are true.

Aut. Here's one to a very doleful tune, How a usurer's wife was brought to bed of twenty money-bags at a burden; and how she longed to eat adders' heads, and toads carbonadoed.

Mop. Is it true think you?

Aut. Very true; and but a month old.

Dor. Bless me from marrying a usurer!

Aut. Here's the midwife's name to't, one mistress Taleporter; and five or six honest wives' that were present: Why should I carry lies abroad?

Mop. 'Pray you now, buy it.

Clo. Come on, lay it by: And let's first see more ballads; we'll buy the other things anon.

Aut. Here's another ballad, of a fish, that appeared upon the coast, on Wednesday the fourscore of April, forty thousand fathom above water, and sung this ballad against the hard hearts of maids; it was thought, she was a woman, and was turned into a cold fish, for she would not exchange flesh with one that loved her: The ballad is very pitiful and as true.[5]

Dor. Is it true, think you?

Aut. Five justices' hands at it; and witnesses, more than my pack will hold.

Clo. Lay it by too: another.

Aut. This is a merry ballad; but a very pretty one

Mop. Let's have some merry ones.

Aut. Why, this is a passing merry one; and goes to the tune of, *Two maids wooing a man*: there's scarce a maid westward, but she sings it; 'tis in request, I can tell you.

Mop. We can both sing it; if thou'lt bear a part thou shalt hear; 'tis in three parts.

Dor. We had the tune on't a month ago.

Aut. I can bear my part; you must know, 'tis my occupation: have at it with you.

SONG.

A. *Get you hence, for I must go;*
Where, it fits you not to know.
D. *Whither?* M. *O, whither?* D. *Whither?*
M. *It becomes thy oath full well,*
Thou to me thy secrets tell:
D. *Me too, let me go thither.*

M. *Or thou go'st to the grange, or mill:*
D. *If to either, thou dost ill.*
A. *Neither.* D. *What, neither?* A. *Neither?*
D. *Thou hast sworn my love to be:*
M. *Thou hast sworn it more to me:*
Then, whither go'st? say, whither.

Clo. We'll have this song out anon by ourselves: My father and the gentleman are in sad[6] talk, and we'll not trouble them: Come, bring away thy pack after me. Wenches, I'll buy for you both:—Pedler, let's have the first choice.—Follow me, girls.

Aut. And you shall pay well for 'em. [*Aside.*

Will you buy any tape,
Or lace for your cape,
My dainty duck, my dear-a?
Any silk, any thread,
Any toys for your head,
Of the new'st, and fin'st, fin'st wear-a?
Come to the pedler;
Money's a medler,
That doth utter[7] *all men's ware-a.*

[*Exeunt* Clown, AUT. DORC. *and* MOPSA.

Enter a Servant.

Serv. Master, there is three carters, three shepherds, three neat-herds, three swine-herds, that have made themselves all men of hair;[8] they call themselves saltiers:[9] and they have a dance which the wenches say is a gallimaufry of gambols, because they are not in't: but they themselves are o' the mind, (if it be not too rough for some, that know little but bowling,) it will please plentifully.

Shep. Away! we'll none on't; here has been too much homely foolery already:—I know, sir, we weary you.

Pol. You weary those that refresh us: Pray, let's see these four threes of herdsmen.

Serv. One three of them, by their own report, sir, hath danced before the king; and not the worst of

Anatomie of Abuses, Part ii:—'They be made of yron and steele, and some of brasse, kept as bright as silver, yea, some of silver itselfe; and it is well, if in processe of time, they grow not to be of gold. The fashion whereafter they be made, I cannot resemble to any thing so well as to a squirt or a little squibbe, which little children used to squirt water out withal; and when they come to starching and setting off their ruffes, then must this instrument be heated in the fire the better to stiffen the ruff.' Stowe informs us that 'about the sixteenth yeare of the queene (Elizabeth) began the making of *steele poking-sticks*, and until that time all lawndresses used setting sticks made of wood or bone.'

1 The kiln-hole generally means the fireplace for drying malt, still a noted gossiping place.

2 An expression taken from bell-ringing; now contracted to *clam.* The bells are said to be *clammed*, when, after a course of rounds or changes, they are all pulled off at once, and give a general clash or clam, by which the peal is concluded. As this *clam* is succeeded by a silence, it exactly suits the sense of the passage. —*Nares.*

3 A *tawdry lace* was a sort of necklace worn by country wenches; so named after St. Audrey (Ethelreda) who is said to have died of a swelling in her throat, which she considered as a particular judgment, for having been in her youth much addicted to wearing fine necklaces; or it probably implies that they were bought at the fair of St. Audrey, where gay toys of all sorts were sold. This fair was held in the Isle of Ely on the Saint's day, the 17th of October; Harpsfield, who tells the story of the saint, describes the necklace:—'Solent Angliæ nostræ mulieres torquem quendam, extenui et subtili serica confectum, collo gestare quam Ethelredæ torquem appellamus (tawdry lace) forsan in ejus quod diximus memoriam.'—*Hist. Eccles. Angl.* p. 86.

4 Sweet, or perfumed gloves, are often mentioned by Shakspeare; they were very much esteemed, and a frequent present in the poet's time.

5 All extraordinary events were then turned into ballads. In 1604 was entered on the stationers' books—'A strange report of a monstrous *fish* that appeared in the form of a woman from her waist upward.' To this it is highly probable that Shakspeare alludes.

6 i. e. serious.

7 'A sale or *utterance* of ware. Exactus.'—*Baret.*

8 It is most probable that they were dressed in goat skins. A dance of satyrs was no unusual entertainment in Shakspeare's time, or even at an earlier period. A very curious relation of a disguising or mummery of this kind, which had like to have proved fatal to some of the actors in it, is related by Froissart as occurring in the court of France in 1392.

9 Satyrs.

the three, but jumps twelve foot and a half by the squire.[1]

Shep. Leave your prating; since these good men are pleased, let them come in; but quickly now.

Serv. Why, they stay at door, sir. [*Exit.*

Re-enter Servant, *with twelve Rustics habited like Satyrs. They dance, and then exeunt.*

Pol. O, father, you'll know more of that hereafter.—[2]
Is it not too far gone?—'Tis time to part them.—
He's simple, and tells much. [*Aside.*]—How now, fair shepherd?
Your heart is full of something, that does take
Your mind from feasting. Sooth, when I was young,
And handed love, as you do, I was wont
To load my she with knacks: I would have ransack'd
The pedler's silken treasury, and have pour'd it
To her acceptance; you have let him go,
And nothing marted[3] with him: if your lass
Interpretation should abuse; and call this
Your lack of love or bounty; you were straited[4]
For a reply; at least, if you make a care
Of happy holding her.

Flo. Old sir, I know
She prizes not such trifles as these are:
The gifts she looks from me are pack'd and lock'd
Up in my heart; which I have given already,
But not deliver'd.—O, hear me breathe my life
Before this ancient sir, who, it should seem,
Hath sometime lov'd: I take thy hand; this hand,
As soft as dove's down, and as white as it;
Or Ethiopian's tooth, or the fann'd snow,
That's bolted[5] by the northern blasts twice o'er.

Pol. What follows this?
How prettily the young swain seems to wash
The hand, was fair before!—I have put you out:—
But to your protestation; let me hear
What you profess.

Flo. Do, and be witness to't.

Pol. And this my neighbour too?

Flo. And he, and more
Than he, and men; the earth, the heavens, and all;
That,—were I crown'd the most imperial monarch,
Thereof most worthy; were I the fairest youth
That ever made eye swerve; had force and knowledge,
More than was ever man's,—I would not prize them,
Without her love: for her employ them all;
Commend them, and condemn them, to her service,
Or to their own perdition.

Pol. Fairly offer'd.

Cam. This shows a sound affection.

Shep. But, my daughter,
Say you the like to him?

Per. I cannot speak
So well, nothing so well; no, nor mean better:
By the pattern of my own thoughts I cut out
The purity of his.

Shep. Take hands, a bargain;——
And, friends unknown, you shall bear witness to't:
I give my daughter to him, and will make
Her portion equal his.

Flo. O, that must be
I' the virtue of your daughter: one being dead,
I shall have more than you can dream of yet;
Enough then for your wonder: But, come on,
Contract us 'fore these witnesses.

Shep. Come, your hand;——
And, daughter, yours.

Pol. Soft, swain, a while, 'beseech you;
Have you a father?

Flo. I have: But what of him?

Pol. Knows he of this?

Flo. He neither does, nor shall.

Pol. Methinks, a father
Is, at the nuptial of his son, a guest
That best becomes the table. Pray you, once more
Is not your father grown incapable
Of reasonable affairs? is he not stupid
With age, and altering rheums? Can he speak? hear?
Know man from man? dispute his own estate?[6]
Lies he not bed-rid? and again does nothing,
But what he did being childish?

Flo. No, good sir;
He has his health, and ampler strength, indeed,
Than most have of his age.

Pol. By my white beard,
You offer him, if this be so, a wrong
Something unfilial: Reason, my son,
Should choose himself a wife; but as good reason
The father (all whose joy is nothing else
But fair posterity) should hold some counsel
In such a business.

Flo. I yield all this;
But, for some other reasons, my grave sir,
Which 'tis not fit, you know, I not acquaint
My father of this business.

Pol. Let him know't.

Flo. He shall not.

Pol. Pr'ythee, let him.

Flo. No, he must not.

Shep. Let him, my son; he shall not need to grieve
At knowing of thy choice.

Flo. Come, come, he must not:—
Mark our contract.

Pol. Mark your divorce, young sir,
[*Discovering himself.*
Whom son I dare not call; thou art too base
To be acknowledg'd: Thou a sceptre's heir,
That thus affect'st a sheep-hook!—Thou old traitor,
I am sorry that, by hanging thee, I can but
Shorten thy life one week.—And thou, fresh piece
Of excellent witchcraft; who, of force, must know
The royal fool thou cop'st with;——

Shep. O my heart

Pol. I'll have thy beauty scratch'd with briars, and made
More homely than thy state.—For thee, fond boy,—
If I may ever know, thou dost but sigh,
That thou no more shalt never see this knack, (as never
I mean thou shalt,) we'll bar thee from succession;
Not hold thee of our blood, no, not our kin.
Far[7] than Deucalion off:—Mark thou my words;
Follow us to the court.—Thou churl, for this time,
Though full of our displeasure, yet we free thee
From the dead blow of it.—And you, enchantment,—
Worthy enough a herdsman; yea, him too,
That makes himself, but for our honour therein,
Unworthy thee,—if ever, henceforth, thou
These rural latches to his entrance open,
Or hoop[8] his body more with thy embraces,
I will devise a death as cruel for thee,
As thou art tender to't. [*Exit*

Per. Even here undone!
I was not much afeard: for once, or twice,
I was about to speak;[9] and tell him plainly,
The selfsame sun, that shines upon his court,
Hides not his visage from our cottage, but
Looks on alike.[10]—Will't please you, sir, begone?
[*To* FLORIZEL.

1 Foot rule, *esquierre*, Fr.

2 This is an answer to something which the shepherd is supposed to have said to Polixenes during the dance.

3 Bought, trafficked.

4 *Straitened*, put to difficulties.

5 That is *sifted*.

6 i. e. 'converse about his own affairs.'

7 *Far*, in the old spelling *farre*, i. e. *farther*. The ancient comparative of *fer* was *ferrer*.

8 The old copy reads *hope*.

9 Warburton remarks that Perdita's character is here finely sustained. 'To have made her quite astonished at the king's discovery of himself had not become her birth; and to have given her presence of mind to have made this reply to the king, had not become her education.'

10 To *look on*, or *look upon*, without any substantive annexed, is a mode of expression which, though now unusual, appears to have been legitimate in Shakspeare's time.

I told you what would come of this: 'Beseech you,
Of your own state take care: this dream of mine,—
Being now awake, I'll queen it no inch further,
But milk my ewes, and weep.

Cam. Why, how now, father,
Speak, ere thou diest.

Shep. I cannot speak, nor think,
Nor dare to know that which I know.—O, sir,
[*To* Florizel.
You have undone a man of fourscore three,[1]
That thought to fill his grave in quiet: yea,
To die upon the bed my father died,
To lie close by his honest bones: but now
Some hangman must put on my shroud, and lay me
Where no priest shovels in dust.[2]—O cursed wretch!
[*To* Perdita.
That knew'st this was the prince, and wouldst adventure
To mingle faith with him.—Undone! undone!
If I might die within this hour, I have liv'd
To die when I desire. [*Exit.*

Flo. Why look you so upon me?
I am but sorry, not afeard! delay'd,
But nothing altered: What I was, I am:
More straining on, for plucking back; not following
My leash[3] unwillingly.

Cam. Gracious my lord,
You know your father's temper: at this time
He will allow no speech,—which, I do guess,
You do not purpose to him;—and as hardly
Will he endure your sight as yet, I fear:
Then, till the fury of his highness settle,
Come not before him.

Flo. I not purpose it.
I think, Camillo.

Cam. Even he, my lord.

Per. How often have I told you, 'twould be thus?
How often said, my dignity would last
But till 'twere known?

Flo. It cannot fail, but by
The violation of my faith; And then
Let nature crush the sides o' the earth together,
And mar the seeds within!—Lift up thy looks:—
From my succession wipe me, father! I
Am heir to my affection.

Cam. Be advis'd.

Flo. I am; and by my fancy:[4] if my reason
Will thereto be obedient, I have reason:
If not, my senses, better pleas'd with madness,
Do bid it welcome.

Cam. This is desperate, sir.

Flo. So call it; but it does fulfil my vow,
I needs must think it honesty. Camillo,
Not for Bohemia, nor the pomp that may
Be thereat glean'd; for all the sun sees, or
The close earth wombs, or the profound seas hide
In unknown fathoms, will I break my oath
To this my fair belov'd: Therefore, I pray you,
As you have ever been my father's honour'd friend,
When he shall miss me (as, in faith, I mean not
To see him any more), cast your good counsels
Upon his passion: Let myself and fortune
Tug for the time to come. This you may know,
And so deliver;—I am put to sea
With her, whom here I cannot hold on shore;
And most opportune to our[5] need, I have
A vessel rides fast by, but not prepar'd
For this design. What course I mean to hold
Shall nothing benefit your knowledge, nor
Concern me the reporting.

Cam. O, my lord,
I would your spirit were easier for advice
Or stronger for your need.

Flo. Hark, Perdita.——[*Takes her aside.*
I'll hear you by-and-by. [*To* Camillo.

Cam. He's irremoveable
Resolved for flight: Now were I happy, if
His going I could frame to serve my turn;
Save him from danger, do him love and honour,
Purchase the sight again of dear Sicilia,
And that unhappy king, my master, whom
I so much thirst to see.

Flo. Now, good Camillo,
I am so fraught with curious business, that
I leave out ceremony. [*Going.*

Cam. Sir, I think
You have heard of my poor services, i' the love
That I have borne your father?

Flo. Very nobly
Have you deserv'd: it is my father's music
To speak your deeds; not little of his care
To have them recompens'd as thought on.

Cam. Well, my lord,
If you may please to think I love the king;
And, through him, what is nearest to him, which is
Your gracious self; embrace but my direction,
(If your more ponderous and settled project
May suffer alteration,) on mine honour
I'll point you where you shall have such receiving
As shall become your highness; where you may
Enjoy your mistress (from the whom, I see,
There's no disjunction to be made, but by,
As heavens forefend! your ruin:) marry her;
And (with my best endeavours, in your absence)
Your discontenting[6] father strive to qualify,
And bring him up to liking.

Flo. How, Camillo,
May this, almost a miracle, be done?
That I may call thee something more than man,
And, after that, trust to thee.

Cam. Have you thought on
A place, whereto you'll go?

Flo. Not any yet:
But as the unthought-on accident[7] is guilty
To[8] what we wildly do; so we profess
Ourselves to be the slaves of chance, and flies
Of every wind that blows.

Cam. Then list to me:
This follows,—if you will not change your purpose,
But undergo this flight;—Make for Sicilia;
And there present yourself, and your fair princess
(For so, I see, she must be), 'fore Leontes;
She shall be habited as it becomes
The partner of your bed. Methinks, I see
Leontes, opening his free arms, and weeping
His welcomes forth: asks thee, the[9] son, forgiveness,
As 'twere i' the father's person: kisses the hands
Of your fresh princess: o'er and o'er divides him
'Twixt his unkindness and his kindness; the one
He chides to hell, and bids the other grow,
Faster than thought, or time.

Flo. Worthy Camillo,
What colour for my visitation shall I
Hold up before him?

Cam. Sent by the king your father
To greet him, and to give him comforts. Sir,
The manner of your bearing towards him, with
What you, as from your father shall deliver,
Things known betwixt us three, I'll write you down:
The which shall point you forth at every sitting,[10]
What you must say; that he shall not perceive

1 This speech of the old clown is admirably characteristic; his selfishness is seen by his concealing the adventure of Perdita, and here supported by the little regard he shows for his son or her: he is entirely taken up with himself, though *fourscore and three.*

2 Before the reform of the burial service by Edward VI. it was the custom for *the priest* to throw earth on the body in the form of a cross, and then sprinkle it with holy water.

3 *Leash*, a leading string.

4 *Fancy* here means *love*, as in other places already pointed out.

5 '*Our* need.' The old copy reads *her*. The emendation is Theobald's.

6 *Discontenting*, for discontented.

7 This *unthought-on accident* is the unexpected discovery made by Polixenes.

8 *Guilty to*, though it sound harsh to our ears, was the phraseology of Shakspeare.

9 The old copy reads, 'thee *there* son.' The correction was made in the third folio.

10 The council-days were called *sittings*, in Shakspeare's time.

But that you have your father's bosom there,
And speak his very heart.
Flo. I am bound to you:
There is some sap in this.
Cam. A course more promising
Than a wild dedication of yourselves
To unpath'd waters, undream'd shores; most certain,
To miseries enough: no hope to help you;
But as you shake off one, to take another:
Nothing so certain as your anchors: who
Do their best office, if they can but stay you
Where you'll be loath to be: Besides, you know,
Prosperity's the very bond of love;
Whose fresh complexion and whose heart together
Affliction alters.
Per. One of these is true:
I think affliction may subdue the cheek,
But not take in[1] the mind.
Cam. Yea, say you so?
There shall not, at your father's house, these seven years,
Be born another such.
Flo. My good Camillo,
She is as forward of her breeding, as
She is i' the rear our birth.
Cam. I cannot say, 'tis pity
She lacks instructions; for she seems a mistress
To most that teach.
Per. Your pardon, sir, for this;
I'll blush you thanks.
Flo. My prettiest Perdita.——
But, O, the thorns we stand upon!—Camillo,—
Preserver of my father, now of me;
The medicine of our house!—how shall we do?
We are not furnished like Bohemia's son;
Nor shall appear in Sicilia——
Cam. My lord,
Fear none of this: I think, you know, my fortunes
Do all lie there: it shall be so my care
To have you royally appointed, as if
The scene you play, were mine. For instance, sir,
That you may know, you shall not want,—one word.
[*They talk aside.*

Enter AUTOLYCUS.

Aut. Ha, ha! what a fool honesty is! and trust, his sworn brother, a very simple gentleman! I have sold all my trumpery; not a counterfeit stone, not a riband, glass, pomander,[2] brooch, table-book, ballad, knife, tape, glove, shoe-tie, bracelet, horn-ring, to keep my pack from fasting; they throng who should buy first; as if my trinkets had been hallowed,[3] and brought a benediction to the buyer: by which means, I saw whose purse was best in picture; and, what I saw, to my good use, I remembered. My clown (who wants but something to be a reasonable man) grew so in love with the wenches' song, that he would not stir his pettitoes, till he had both tune and words, which so drew the rest of the herd to me, that all their other senses stuck in ears: you might have pinch'd a placket,[4] it was senseless; 'twas nothing, to geld a codpiece of a purse; I would have filed keys off, that hung in chains: no hearing, no feeling, but my sir's song, and admiring the nothing of it. So that, in this time of lethargy, I picked and cut most of their festival purses; and had not the old man come in with a whoobub against his daughter and the king's son, and scared my choughs from the chaff, I had not left a purse alive in the whole army.

[CAMILLO, FLORIZEL, *and* PERDITA *come forward.*

Cam. Nay, but my letters by this means being there
So soon as you arrive, shall clear that doubt.
Flo. And those that you'll procure from king Leontes——
Cam. Shall satisfy your father.
Per. Happy be you!
All, that you speak, shows fair.
Cam. Who have we here?
[*Seeing* AUTOLYCUS.
We'll make an instrument of this; omit
Nothing, may give us aid.

Aut. If they have overheard me now,———why, hanging. [*Aside.*

Cam. How now, good fellow? Why shakest thou so? Fear not, man; here's no harm intended to thee.

Aut. I am a poor fellow, sir.

Cam. Why be so still; here's nobody will steal that from thee: Yet, for the outside of thy poverty, we must make an exchange: therefore, discase thee instantly, (thou must think, there's necessity in't,) and change garments with this gentleman: Though the pennyworth, on his side, be the worst, yet hold thee, there's some boot.[5]

Aut. I am a poor fellow, sir;—I know ye well enough. [*Aside.*

Cam. Nay, pr'ythee, despatch: the gentleman is half flayed[6] already.

Aut. Are you in earnest, sir?—I smell the trick of it. [*Aside.*

Flo. Despatch, I pr'ythee.

Aut. Indeed, I have had earnest; but I cannot with conscience take it.

Cam. Unbuckle, unbuckle.—
[FLO. *and* AUTOL. *exchange garments.*
Fortunate mistress,—let my prophecy
Come home to you!—you must retire yourself
Into some covert; take your sweetheart's hat,
And pluck it o'er your brows; muffle your face,
Dismantle you: and as you can, disliken
The truth of your own seeming; that you may
(For I do fear eyes over you) to shipboard
Get undescried.
Per. I see, the play so lies,
That I must bear a part.
Cam. No remedy.—
Have you done there?
Flo. Should I now meet my father,
He would not call me son.
Cam. Nay, you shall have
No hat:—Come, lady, come.—Farewell, my friend.
Aut. Adieu, sir.
Flo. O Perdita, what have we twain forgot?
Pray you, a word. [*They converse apart.*
Cam. What I do next, shall be to tell the king
[*Aside.*
Of this escape, and whither they are bound;
Wherein my hope is, I shall so prevail,
To force him after: in whose company
I shall review Sicilia; for whose sight
I have a woman's longing.

---

1 To *take in*, is *to conquer, to get the better of.*

2 *Pomanders* were little balls of perfumed paste, worn in the pocket, or hung about the neck, and even sometimes suspended to the wrist, according to Philips. They were used as amulets against the plague or other infections, as well as for mere articles of luxury. Various receipts for making them may be found in old books of housewifery, and even in one or two old plays. They have recently been revived and made into a variety of ornamental forms under the name of Amulets. Fumigating pastilles are another modification of the pomander. The name is derived from *pomme d'ambre*, I know not on what authority, for in all the old French dictionaries they are called *pommes de senteur.* Philips says *pomamber*, Dutch.

3 This alludes to the beads often sold by the Romanists, as made particularly efficacious by the touch of some relic.

4 Steevens has been very facetious about a *placket* and has explained it to be the opening in a woman's petticoat. It was no such thing, it was nothing more than a *stomacher*; as appears by Florio's Dictionary, under the word *Torace*: 'The breast or bulke of a man: also the middle space between the necke and the thighs: also a *placket*, a *stomacher*.' Thomas gives the same explanation of *Thorace*, except that he spells the word *placcard.*

5 *Boot* is advantage, profit. We now say *something to boot*, something besides the articles exchanged for each other.

6 Stripped.

Flo. Fortune speed us!—
Thus we set on, Camillo, to the sea-side.

Cam. The swifter speed, the better.

[*Exeunt* FLO. PER. *and* CAM.

Aut. I understand the business, I hear it: To have an open ear, a quick eye, and a nimble hand, is necessary for a cut-purse; a good nose is requisite also, to smell out work for the other senses. I see, this is the time that the unjust man doth thrive. What an exchange had this been, without boot? what a boot is here, with this exchange? Sure, the gods do this year connive at us, and we may do any thing *extempore*. The prince himself is about a pice of iniquity; stealing away from his father, with his clog at his heels: If I thought it were a piece of honesty to acquaint the king withal, I would not do't:[1] I hold it the more knavery to conceal it; and therein am I constant to my profession.

Enter Clown *and* Shepherd.

Aside, aside;—here is more matter for a hot brain: Every lane's end, every shop, church, session, hanging, yields a careful man work.

Clo. See, see; what a man you are now! there is no other way, but to tell the king she's a changeling, and none of your flesh and blood

Shep. Nay, but hear me.

Clo. Nay, but hear me.

Shep. Go to, then.

Clo. She being none of your flesh and blood, your flesh and blood has not offended the king: and, so, your flesh and blood is not to be punished by him. Show those things you found about her: those secret things, all but what she has with her: This being done, let the law go whistle; I warrant you.

Shep. I will tell the king all, every word, yea, and his son's pranks too: who, I may say, is no honest man neither to his father, nor to me, to go about to make me the king's brother-in-law.

Clo. Indeed, brother-in-law was the farthest off you could have been to him; and then your blood had been the dearer, by I know how[2] much an ounce.

Aut. Very wisely; puppies! [*Aside.*

Shep. Well; let us to the king; there is that in this fardel, will make him scratch his beard.

Aut. I know not what impediment this complaint may be to the flight of my master.

Clo. 'Pray heartily, he be at palace.

Aut. Though I am not naturally honest, I am so sometimes by chance:—Let me pocket up my pedler's excrement.[3] [*Takes off his false beard.*] How now, rustics? whither are you bound?

Shep. To the palace, an' it like your worship.

Aut. Your affairs there? what? with whom? the condition of that fardel,[4] the place of your dwelling, your names, your ages, of what having,[5] breeding, and any thing that is fitting to be known, discover.

Clo. We are but plain fellows, sir.

Aut. A lie; you are rough and hairy: Let me have no lying; it becomes none but tradesmen, and they often give us soldiers the lie: but we pay them for it with stamped coin, not stabbing steel: therefore they do not give us the lie.[6]

Clo. Your worship had like to have given us one, if you had not taken yourself with the manner.[7]

Shep. Are you a courtier, an't like you, sir?

Aut. Whether it like me, or no, I am a courtier. See'st thou not the air of the court, in these enfoldings? hath not my gait in it, the measure of the court,?[8] receives not thy nose court-odour from me? reflect I not on thy baseness, court-contempt? Think'st thou, for that I insinuate, or toze[9] from thee thy business, I am therefore no courtier? I am courtier, cap-a-pie; and one that will either push on, or pluck back thy business there: whereupon I command thee to open thy affair.

Shep. My business, sir, is to the king.

Aut. What advocate hast thou to him?

Shep. I know not, an't like you.

Clo. Advocate's the court word for a pheasant, say you have none.

Shep. None, sir; I have no pheasant, cock, nor hen.[10]

Aut. How bless'd are we, that are not simple men!
Yet nature might have made me as these are,
Therefore I'll not disdain.

Clo. This cannot but be a great courtier.

Shep. His garments are rich, but he wears them not handsomely.

Clo. He seems to be the more noble in being fantastical; a great man, I'll warrant; I know, by the picking on's teeth.

Aut. The fardel there? what's i' the fardel? Wherefore that box?

Shep. Sir, there lies such secrets in this fardel, and box, which none must know but the king; and which he shall know within this hour, if I may come to the speech of him.

Aut. Age, thou hast lost thy labour.

Shep. Why, sir?

Aut. The king is not at the palace; he is gone aboard a new ship to purge melancholy, and air himself: For, if thou be'st capable of things serious, thou must know, the king is full of grief.

Shep. So 'tis said, sir; about his son, that should have married a shepherd's daughter.

Aut. If that shepherd be not in hand-fast, let him fly; the curses he shall have, the tortures he shall feel, will break the back of man, the heart of monster.

Clo. Think you so, sir?

Aut. Not he alone shall suffer what wit can make heavy, and vengeance bitter; but those that are germane[11] to him, though removed fifty times, shall all come under the hangman: which though it be great pity, yet it is necessary. An old sheep-whistling rogue, a ram-tender, to offer to have his daughter come into grace! Some say he shall be stoned; but that death is too soft for him, say I: Draw our throne into a sheep-cote! all deaths are too few, the sharpest too easy.

Clo. Has the old man e'er a son, sir, do you hear, an't like you, sir?

Aut. He has a son, who shall be flayed alive; then, 'nointed over with honey, set on the head of a wasp's nest; then stand, till he be three quarters and a dram dead: then recovered again with acquavitæ, or some other hot infusion: then raw as he is, and in the hottest day prognostication proclaims,[12] shall he be set against a brick wall, the sun looking with a southward eye upon him; where he is to behold him, with flies blown to death. But

---

1 Steevens reads, 'If I thought it were *not* a piece of honesty to acquaint the king withal, I would do it.' The transposition of the word *not* was made by Hanmer; it does not render the passage more intelligible, and as we can extract a meaning out of the passage as it originally stood, I do not think so violent a transposition admissible.

2 We should probably read, 'by I know *not* how much an ounce.'

3 Thus in the Comedy of Errors: 'Why is time such a niggard of his hair, being as it is so plentiful an *excrement?*'

4 *Fardel* is a *bundle*, a *pack* or *burthen*. 'A pack that a man doth bear with him in the way,' says *Baret*.

5 i. e. estate, property.

6 The meaning is, they are *paid* for lying, therefore they do not *give* us the lie.

7 That is, *in the fact*. Vide Love's Labour's Lost, Act i. Sc. 1.

8 The *measure*, the stately tread of courtiers.

9 'Think'st thou *because I wind myself into*, or *draw* from thee thy business, I am therefore no courtier?' To *toze* is to pluck or draw out. As *to toze* or teize wool, *Carpere lanam*. See the old dictionaries.

10 Malone says, 'perhaps in the first of these speeches we should read, *a present*, which the old shepherd mistakes for a *pheasant*. The clowns perhaps thought courtiers as corruptible as some justices then were, of whom it is said, 'for half a dozen of chickens they would dispense with a whole dozen of penal statutes.'

11 *Germane*, related.

12 The hottest day foretold in the almanack

what talk we of these traitorly rascals, whose miseries are to be smiled at, their offences being so capital? Tell me (for you seem to be honest plain men) what you have to the king: being something gently considered,[1] I'll bring you where he is aboard, tender your persons to his presence, whisper him in your behalfs; and, if it be in man, besides the king, to effect your suits, here is man shall do it.

Clo. He seems to be of great authority: close with him, give him gold; and though authority be a stubborn bear, yet he is oft led by the nose with gold: show the inside of your purse to the outside of his hand, and no more ado: Remember stoned, and flayed alive.

Shep. An't please you, sir, to undertake the business for us, here is that gold I have: I'll make it as much more; and leave this young man in pawn, till I bring it you.

Aut. After I have done what I promised?

Shep. Ay, sir.

Aut. Well, give me the moiety:—Are you a party in this business?

Clo. In some sort, sir; but though my case be a pitiful one, I hope I shall not be flayed out of it.

Aut. O, that's the case of the shepherd's son:—Hang him, he'll be made an example.

Clo. Comfort, good comfort: we must to the king, and show our strange sights; he must know, 'tis none of your daughter nor my sister; we are gone else. Sir, I will give you as much as this old man does, when the business is performed; and remain, as he says, your pawn, till it be brought you.

Aut. I will trust you. Walk before toward the sea-side; go on the right hand; I will but look upon the hedge, and follow you.

Clo. We are blessed in this man, as I may say, even blessed.

Shep. Let's before, as he bids us; he was provided to do us good. [*Exeunt* Shepherd *and* Clown.

Aut. If I had a mind to be honest, I see, fortune would not suffer me; she drops booties in my mouth. I am courted now with a double occasion; gold, and a means to do the prince my master good; which, who knows how that may turn back to my advancement? I will bring these two moles, these blind ones, aboard him: if he think it fit to shore them again, and that the complaint they have to the king concerns him nothing, let him call me rogue, for being so far officious; for I am proof against that title, and what shame else belongs to't: To him I will present them; there may be matter in it. [*Exit.*

ACT V.

SCENE I. Sicilia. *A room in the Palace of* Leontes. *Enter* LEONTES, CLEOMENES, DION, PAULINA, *and others.*

Cleo. Sir, you have done enough, and have perform'd
A saintlike sorrow; no fault could you make,
Which you have not redeem'd; indeed, paid down
More penitence, than done trespass: at the last,
Do, as the heavens have done; forget your evil:
With them, forgive yourself.
Leon. Whilst I remember
Her and her virtues, I cannot forget
My blemishes in them; and so still think of
The wrong I did myself; which was so much,
That heirless it hath made my kingdom; and
Destroy'd the sweet'st companion that e'er man
Bred his hopes out of.
Paul. True, too true, my lord;
If, one by one, you wedded all the world,
Or, from the all that are, took something good,
To make a perfect woman; she, you kill'd,
Would be unparallel'd.
Leon. I think so. Kill'd!
She I kill'd? I did so: but thou strik'st me
Sorely, to say I did; it is as bitter
Upon thy tongue, as in my thought: Now, good now,
Say so but seldom.
Cleo. Not at all, good lady:
You might have spoken a thousand things that would
Have done the time more benefit, and grac'd
Your kindness better.
Paul. You are one of those,
Would have him wed again.
Dion. If you would not so
You pity not the state, nor the remembrance
Of his most sovereign dame; consider little,
What dangers, by his highness' fail of issue,
May drop upon his kingdom, and devour
Incertain lookers-on. What were more holy,
Than to rejoice, the former queen is well?[2]
What holier, than,—for royalty's repair,
For present comfort and for future good,—
To bless the bed of majesty again
With a sweet fellow to't?
Paul. There is none worthy
Respecting her that's gone. Besides, the gods,
Will have fulfill'd their secret purposes:
For has not the divine Apollo said,
Is't not the tenour of his oracle,
That king Leontes shall not have an heir,
Till his lost child be found? which, that it shall,
Is all as monstrous to our human reason,
As my Antigonus to break his grave,
And come again to me; who, on my life,
Did perish with the infant. 'Tis your counsel,
My lord should to the heavens be contrary,
Oppose against their wills.—Care not for issue; [*To* LEONTES
The crown will find an heir: Great Alexander
Left his to the worthiest; so his successor
Was like to be the best.
Leon. Good Paulina,—
Who hast the memory of Hermione,
I know, in honour,—O, that ever I
Had squar'd me to thy counsel!—then, even now,
I might have look'd upon my queen's full eyes;
Have taken treasure from her lips,——
Paul. And left them
More rich, for what they yielded.
Leon. Thou speak'st truth.
No more such wives; therefore no wife; one worse,
And better us'd, would make her sainted spirit
Again possess her corps; and, on this stage
(Where we offenders now appear,) soul-vex'd,
Begin, *And why to me?*[3]
Paul. Had she such power,
She had just cause.
Leon. She had; and would incense[4] me
To murder her I married.
Paul. I should so:
Were I the ghost that walk'd, I'd bid you mark
Her eye; and tell me, for what dull part in't
You chose her: then I'd shriek, that even your ears
Should rift[5] to hear me; and the words that follow'd
Should be, *Remember mine.*
Leon. Stars, stars,
And all eyes else dead coals!—fear thou no wife.
I'll have no wife, Paulina.
Paul. Will you swear
Never to marry, but by my free leave?
Leon. Never, Paulina; so be bless'd my spirit
Paul. Then, good my lords, bear witness to his oath.

1 i. e. being handsomely bribed: *to consider* often signified *to reward.*
2 i. e. at rest, dead.
3 The old copy reads, 'And begin, *why to me.*' The transposition of *and* was made by Steevens.
4 *Incense*, to *instigate* or *stimulate*, was the ancient sense of this word: it is rendered in the Latin dictionaries by *dare stimulo.*
5 i. e. split.

Cleo. You tempt him over-much.
Paul. Unless another,
As like Hermione as is her picture,
Affront[1] his eye.
Cleo. Good madam,—
Paul. I have done.
Yet, if my lord will marry,—if you will, sir,
No remedy, but you will: give me the office
To choose you a queen: she shall not be so young
As was your former; but she shall be such,
As, walk'd your first queen's ghost, it should take joy
To see her in your arms.
Leon. My true Paulina,
We shall not marry, till thou bidd'st us.
Paul. That
Shall be, when your first queen's again in breath;
Never till then.

Enter a Gentleman.

Gent. One that gives out himself prince Florizel,
Son of Polixenes, with his princess (she
The fairest I have yet beheld,) desires access
To your high presence.
Leon. What with him? he comes not
Like to his father's greatness: his approach,
So out of circumstance, and sudden, tells us,
'Tis not a visitation fram'd, but forc'd
By need, and accident. What train?
Gent. But few,
And those but mean.
Leon. His princess, say you, with him?
Gent. Ay; the most peerless piece of earth, I think,
That e'er the sun shone bright on.
Paul. O Hermione,
As every present time doth boast itself
Above a better, gone; so must thy grave[2]
Give way to what's seen now. Sir, you yourself
Have said, and writ so[3] (but your writing now
Is colder than that theme[4]) *She had not been*
Nor was not to be equall'd;—thus your verse
Flowed with her beauty once; 'tis shrewdly ebb'd,
To say, you have seen a better.
Gent. Pardon, madam:
The one I have almost forgot (your pardon;)
The other, when she has obtain'd your eye,
Will have your tongue too. This is a creature,
Would she begin a sect, might quench the zeal
Of all professors else: make proselytes
Of who she but bid follow.
Paul. How? not women?
Gent. Women will love her, that she is a woman
More worth than any man; men, that she is
The rarest of all women.
Leon. Go, Cleomenes;
Yourself, assisted with your honour'd friends,
Bring them to our embracement.—Still 'tis strange,
[*Exeunt* CLEOMENES, Lords, *and* Gentlemen.
He thus should steal upon us.
Paul. Had our prince
(Jewel of children) seen this hour, he had pair'd
Well with this lord; there was not full a month
Between their births.
Leon. Pr'ythee, no more; thou know'st,[5]
He dies to me again, when talk'd of: sure,
When I shall see this gentleman, thy speeches
Will bring me to consider that which may
Unfurnish me of reason.—They are come.——

Re-enter CLEOMENES, *with* FLORIZEL, PERDITA, *and* Attendants.

Your mother was most true to wedlock, prince;
For she did print your royal father off,
Conceiving you: Were I but twenty-one,
Your father's image is so hit in you,
His very air, that I should call you brother,
As I did him: and speak of something, wildly
By us perform'd before. Most dearly welcome!
And your fair princess, goddess!—O, alas!
I lost a couple, that 'twixt heaven and earth
Might thus have stood, begetting wonder, as
You, gracious couple, do! and then I lost
(All mine own folly) the society,
Amity too, of your brave father; whom,
Though bearing misery, I desire my life
Once more to look on him.[6]
Flo. By his command
Have I here touch'd Sicilia: and from him
Give you all greetings, that a king, at friend,[7]
Can send his brother: and, but infirmity
(Which waits upon worn times) hath something seiz'd
His wish'd ability, he had himself
The lands and waters 'twixt your throne and his
Measur'd, to look upon you; whom he loves
(He bade me say so) more than all the sceptres,
And those that bear them, living.
Leon. O, my brother,
(Good gentleman!) the wrongs I have done thee, stir
Afresh within me; and these thy offices,
So rarely kind, are as interpreters
Of my behind-hand slackness!—Welcome hither,
As is the spring to the earth. And hath he too
Expos'd this paragon to the fearful usage
(At least, ungentle) of the dreadful Neptune,
To greet a man, not worth her pains; much less
The adventure of her person?
Flo. Good my lord,
She came from Libya.
Leon. Where the warlike Smalus,
That noble honour'd lord, is fear'd, and lov'd?
Flo. Most royal sir, from thence; from him, whose daughter
His tears proclaim'd his, parting with her: thence
(A prosperous south-wind friendly) we have cross'd
To execute the charge my father gave me,
For visiting your highness: My best train
I have from your Sicilian shores dismiss'd;
Who for Bohemia bend, to signify
Not only my success in Libya, sir,
But my arrival, and my wife's, in safety,
Here, where we are.
Leon. The blessed gods
Purge all infection from our air, whilst you
Do climate here! You have a holy father,
A graceful[8] gentleman; against whose person,
So sacred as it is, I have done sin:
For which the heavens, taking angry note,
Have left me issueless; and your father's bless'd
(As he from heaven merits it) with you,
Worthy his goodness. What might I have been,
Might I a son and daughter now have looked on,
Such goodly things as you?

Enter a Lord.

Lord. Most noble sir,
That, which I shall report, will bear no credit,
Were not the proof so nigh. Please you, great sir,
Bohemia greets you from himself, by me:
Desires you to attach his son; who has
(His dignity and duty both cast off)
Fled from his father, from his hopes, and with
A shepherd's daughter.
Leon. Where's Bohemia? speak.
Lord. Here in the city; I now came from him.
I speak amazedly; and it becomes

---

1 i. e. meet his eye, or *encounter* it. *Affrontare*, Ital. Shakspeare uses this word with the same meaning again in Hamlet, Act iii. Sc. 1:
'That he, as 'twere by accident, may here
Affront Ophelia.'
i. e. thy beauties which are buried in the grave.
3 *So* relates not to what precedes, but to what follows: that she had not been *equall'd.*
4 i. e. than the corse of Hermione, the subject of your writing.
5 The old copy reads, ''Pr'ythee, no more; *cease;* thou know'st,' &c. Steevens made the omission of the redundant word, which he considers a mere marginal gloss or explanation of *no more.*
6 Steevens altered this to look *upon*, but there are many instances of similar construction in Shakspeare, incorrect as they may now appear.
7 i. e. *at amity*, as we now say. Malone, contrary to his usual custom, would here desert the old reading: and says he has met with *no example of similar phraseology!* He surely must have read very inattentively.
8 i. e. full of grace and virtue.

My marvel, and my message. To your court
Whiles he was hast'ning (in the chase, it seems,
Of this fair couple,) meets he on the way
The father of this seeming lady, and
Her brother, having both their country quitted
With this young prince.

Flo. Camillo has betrayed me;
Whose honour, and whose honesty, till now,
Endur'd all weathers.

Lord. Lay't so to his charge;
He's with the king your father.

Leon. Who? Camillo?

Lord. Camillo, sir; I spake with him: who now
Has these poor men in question.[1] Never saw I
Wretches so quake: they kneel, they kiss the earth;
Forswear themselves as often as they speak;
Bohemia stops his ears, and threatens them
With divers deaths in death.

Per. O, my poor father!—
The heavens sets spies upon us, will not have
Our contract celebrated.

Leon. You are married?

Flo. We are not, sir, nor are we like to be;
The stars, I see, will kiss the valleys first:—
The odds for high and low's alike.

Leon. My lord,
Is this the daughter of a king?

Flo. She is,
When once she is my wife.

Leon. That once, I see, by your good father's speed,
Will come on very slowly. I am sorry
Most sorry, you have broken from his liking,
Where you were tied in duty: and as sorry,
Your choice is not so rich in worth[2] as beauty,
That you might well enjoy her.

Flo. Dear, look up:
Though fortune, visible an enemy,
Should chase us with my father; power no jot
Hath she, to change our loves.—'Beseech you, sir,
Remember since you ow'd no more to time
Than I do now: with thought of such affections,
Step forth mine advocate; at your request,
My father will grant precious things, as trifles.

Leon. Would he do so, I'd beg your precious mistress,
Which he counts but a trifle.

Paul. Sir, my liege,
Your eye hath too much youth in't: not a month
'Fore your queen died, she was more worth such gazes
Than what you look on now.

Leon. I thought of her,
Even in these looks I made.—But your petition
[*To* FLORIZEL.
Is yet unanswer'd; I will to your father;
Your honour not o'erthrown by your desires,
I am a friend to them, and you: upon which errand
I now go toward him; therefore, follow me,
And mark what way I make: Come, good my lord.

SCENE II. *The same. Before the Palace. Enter* AUTOLYCUS *and a* Gentleman.

Aut. 'Beseech you, sir, were you present at this relation?

1 *Gent.* I was by at the opening of the fardel, heard the old shepherd deliver the manner how he found it; whereupon, after a little amazedness, we were all commanded out of the chamber; only this, methought, I heard the shepherd say, he found the child.

Aut. I would most gladly know the issue of it.

1 *Gent.* I make a broken delivery of the business;—But the changes I perceived in the king, and Camillo, were very notes of admiration; they seemed almost, with staring on one another, to tear the cases of their eyes; there was speech in their dumbness, language in their very gesture; they looked, as they had heard of a world ransomed, or one destroyed: A notable passion of wonder appeared in them: but the wisest beholder, that knew no more but seeing, could not say, if the importance[3] were joy, or sorrow: but in the extremity of the one, it must needs be.

Enter another Gentleman.

Here comes a gentleman, that, happily, knows more: The news, Rogero?

2 *Gent.* Nothing but bonfires: The oracle is fulfilled; the king's daughter is found: such a deal of wonder is broken out within this hour, that ballad-makers cannot be able to express it.

Enter a third Gentleman.

Here comes the lady Paulina's steward; he can deliver you more.—How goes it now, sir? this news, which is called true, is so like an old tale, that the verity of it is in strong suspicion: Has the king found his heir?

3 *Gent.* Most true; if ever truth were pregnant by circumstance: that, which you hear, you'll swear you see, there is such unity in the proofs. The mantle of queen Hermione:—her jewel about the neck of it: the letters of Antigonus, found with it, which they know to be his character:—the majesty of the creature, in resemblance of the mother;—the affection[4] of nobleness, which nature shows above her breeding,—and many other evidences, proclaim her, with all certainty, to be the king's daughter. Did you see the meeting of the two kings?

2 *Gent.* No.

3 *Gent.* Then have you lost a sight, which was to be seen, cannot be spoken of. There might you have beheld one joy crown another; so, and in such manner, that, it seemed, sorrow wept to take leave of them; for their joy waded in tears. There was casting up of eyes, holding up of hands; with countenance of such distraction, that they were to be known by garment, not by favour.[5] Our king being ready to leap out of himself for joy of his found daughter; as if that joy were now become a loss, cries, *O, thy mother, thy mother!* then asks Bohemia forgiveness; then embraces his son-in-law; then again worries he his daughter, with clipping[6] her; now he thanks the old shepherd, which stands by, like a weather-bitten conduit of many kings' reigns.[7] I never heard of such another encounter, which lames report to follow it, and undoes description to do it.

2 *Gent.* What, pray you, became of Antigonus, that carried hence the child?

3 *Gent.* Like an old tale still; which will have matter to rehearse, though credit be asleep, and not an ear open: He was torn to pieces with a bear: this avouches the shepherd's son; who has not only his innocence (which seems much) to justify him, but a handkerchief, and rings, of his, that Paulina knows.

1 *Gent.* What became of his bark, and his followers?

3 *Gent.* Wrecked the same instant of their master's death: and in the view of the shepherd: so that all the instruments which aided to expose the child, were even then lost, when it was found. But, O, the noble combat, that, 'twixt joy and sorrow, was fought in Paulina! She had one eye declined for the loss of her husband; another elevated that the oracle was fulfilled: She lifted the princess from the earth; and so locks her in embracing, as if she would pin her to her heart, that she might no more be in danger of losing.

1 *Gent.* The dignity of this act was worth the audience of kings and princes; for by such was it acted.

3. *Gent.* One of the prettiest touches of all, and

1 i. e. conversation.
2 *Worth* for descent or wealth.
3 i. e. *import*, the thing imported.
4 In Shakspeare's time, *to affect* a thing meant, to have a tendency or disposition to it. The *affections* were the *dispositions*, Appetitus animi.

5 *Favour* here stands for *mien*, *feature*.
6 i. e. embracing.
7 Conduits or fountains were frequently representations of the human figure. One of this kind has been already referred to in As You Like It, Act iv. Sc. 1.

that which angled for mine eyes (caught the water, though not the fish) was, when at the relation of the queen's death, with the manner how she came to it (bravely confessed, and lamented by the king,) how attentiveness wounded his daughter: till, from one sign of dolour to another, she did, with an *alas!* I would fain say, bleed tears; for, I am sure, my heart wept blood. Who was most marble there[1] changed colour; some swooned, all sorrowed: if all the world could have seen it, the woe had been universal.

1 *Gent.* Are they returned to the court?

3 *Gent.* No: the princess, hearing of her mother's statue, which is in the keeping of Paulina,—a piece many years in doing, and now newly performed by that rare Italian master, Julio Romano; who, had he himself eternity,[2] and could put breath into his work, would beguile nature of her custom, so perfectly he is her ape: he so near to Hermione hath done Hermione, that, they say, one would speak to her, and stand in hope of answer: thither with all greediness of affection, are they gone; and there they intend to sup.

2 *Gent.* I thought she had some great matter there in hand; for she hath privately, twice or thrice a day, ever since the death of Hermione, visited that removed[3] house. Shall we thither, and with our company piece the rejoicing?

1 *Gent.* Who would be thence, that has the benefit of access? every wink of an eye, some new grace will be born: our absence makes us unthrifty to our knowledge. Let's along. [*Exeunt* Gentlemen.

Aut. Now, had I not the dash of my former life in me, would preferment drop on my head. I brought the old man and his son aboard the prince; told him, I heard them talk of a fardel, and I know not what: but he at that time, over-fond of the shepherd's daughter (so he then took her to be,) who began to be much sea-sick, and himself little better, extremity of weather continuing, this mystery remained undiscovered. But 'tis all one to me: for had I been the finder-out of this secret, it would not have relished among my other discredits.

Enter Shepherd *and* Clown.

Here come those I have done good to against my will, and already appearing in the blossoms of their fortune.

Shep. Come, boy; I am past more children; but thy sons and daughters will be all gentlemen born.

Clo. You are well met, sir: You denied to fight with me this other day, because I was no gentleman born: See you these clothes? say, you see them not, and think me still no gentleman born: you were best say, these robes are not gentlemen born. Give me the lie; do; and try whether I am not now a gentleman born.

Aut. I know, you are now, sir, a gentleman born.

Clo. Ay, and have been so any time these four hours.

Shep. And so have I, boy.

Clo. So you have:—but I was a gentleman born before my father: for the king's son took me by the hand, and called me, brother; and then the two kings called my father, brother; and then the prince, my brother, and the princess, my sister, called my father, father; and so we wept: and there was the first gentlemanlike tears that ever we shed.

Shep. We may live, son, to shed many more.

Clo. Ay; or else 'twere hard luck, being in so preposterous estate as we are.

Aut. I humbly beseech you, sir, to pardon me all the faults I have committed to your worship, and to give me your good report to the prince my master.

Shep. 'Pr'ythee, son, do; for we must be gentle, now we are gentlemen.

Clo. Thou wilt amend thy life?

Aut. Ay, an it like your good worship.

Clo. Give me thy hand; I will swear to the prince, thou art as honest a true fellow as any is in Bohemia.

Shep. You may say it, but not swear it.

Clo. Not swear it, now I am a gentleman? Let boors and franklins[4] say it, I'll swear it.

Shep. How if it be false, son?

Clo. If it be ne'er so false, a true gentleman may swear it in the behalf of his friend:—And I'll swear to the prince thou art a tall[5] fellow of thy hands, and that thou wilt not be drunk; but I know thou art no tall fellow of thy hands, and that thou wilt be drunk; but I'll swear it: and I would, thou would'st be a tall fellow of thy hands.

Aut. I will prove so, sir, to my power.

Clo. Ay, by any means prove a tall fellow: If I do not wonder how thou darest venture to be drunk, not being a tall fellow, trust me not.—Hark! the kings and the princes, our kindred, are going to see the queen's picture. Come, follow us: we'll be thy good masters.[6] [*Exeunt.*

SCENE III. *The same. A Room in Paulina's House. Enter* LEONTES, POLIXENES, FLORIZEL, PERDITA, CAMILLO, PAULINA, Lords and Attendants.

Leon. O grave and good Paulina, the great comfort
That I have had of thee!

Paul. What, sovereign sir,
I did not well, I meant well: All my services,
You have paid home: but that you have vouchsaf'd
With your crown'd brother, and these your contracted
Heirs of your kingdoms, my poor house to visit,
It is a surplus of your grace, which never
My life may last to answer.

Leon. O Paulina,
We honour you with trouble: But we came
To see the statue of our queen: your gallery
Have we pass'd through, not without much content
In many singularities; but we saw no
That which my daughter came to look upon,
The statue of her mother.

Paul. As she liv'd peerless,
So her dead likeness, I do well believe,
Excels whatever yet you look'd upon,
Or hand of man hath done; therefore I keep it
Lonely,[7] apart: But here it is: prepare
To see the life as lively mock'd, as ever
Still sleep mock'd death: behold; and say, 'tis well.

[PAUL. *undraws a curtain and discovers a Statue.*

I like your silence, it the more shows off
Your wonder: But yet speak;—first, you, my liege,
Comes it not something near?

Leon. Her natural posture!—
Chide me, dear stone; that I may say, indeed,
Thou art Hermione: or, rather, thou art she,
In thy not chiding; for she was as tender
As infancy and grace.—But yet, Paulina,
Hermione was not so much wrinkled, nothing
So aged, as this seems.

Pol. O, not by much.

Paul. So much the more our carver's excellence;
Which lets go by some sixteen years, and makes her
As she liv'd now.

Leon. As now she might have done
So much to my good comfort, as it is
Now piercing to my soul. O, thus she stood,
Even with such life of majesty (warm life,
As now it coldly stands), when first I woo'd her!
I am asham'd: Does not the stone rebuke me,
For being more stone than it?—O, royal piece,
There's magic in thy majesty; which has
My evils conjured to remembrance; and
From thy admiring daughter took the spirits,
Standing like stone with thee:

1 'Who was most marble:' that is, those who had the hardest hearts.

2 However misplaced the praise, it is no small honour to Julio Romano to be thus mentioned by the poet. By *eternity* Shakspeare only means *immortality.*

3 i. e. remote

4 i. e. Yeomen.

5 i. e. a *bold, courageous* fellow.

6 *Good masters.* It was a common petitionary phrase to ask a superior to be *good lord* or *good master* to the supplicant.

7 The old copy reads *lovely*

Per. And give me leave;
And do not say, 'tis superstition, that
I kneel, and then implore her blessing.—Lady,
Dear queen, that ended when I but began,
Give me that hand of yours, to kiss.

Paul. O, patience;
The statue is but newly fix'd, the colour's
Not dry.

Cam. My lord, your sorrow was too sore laid on;
Which sixteen winters cannot blow away,
So many summers, dry; scarce any joy
Did ever so long live; no sorrow,
But kill'd itself much sooner.

Pol. Dear my brother,
Let him, that was the cause of this, have power
To take off so much grief from you, as he
Will piece up in himself.

Paul. Indeed, my lord,
If I had thought the sight of my poor image
Would thus have wrought[1] you (for the stone is mine,)
I'd not have show'd it.[2]

Leon. Do not draw the curtain.

Paul. No longer shall you gaze on't; lest your fancy
May think anon, it moves.

Leon. Let be, let be.
'Would, I were dead, but that, methinks, already[3]—
What was he that did make it?—See, my lord,
Would you not deem, it breathed? and that those veins
Did verily bear blood?

Pol. Masterly done:
The very life seems warm upon her lip.

Leon. The fixture of her eye has motion in't,[4]
As we are mock'd with art.[5]

Paul. I'll draw the curtain;
My lord's almost so far transported, that
He'll think anon it lives.

Leon. O sweet Paulina,
Make me to think so twenty years together;
No settled senses of the world can match
The pleasure of that madness. Let't alone.

Paul. I am sorry, sir, I have thus far stirr'd you; but
I could afflict you further.

Leon. Do, Paulina;
For this affliction has a taste as sweet
As any cordial comfort.—Still, methinks,
There is an air comes from her: What fine chisel
Could ever yet cut breath? Let no man mock me,
For I will kiss her.

Paul. Good my lord, forbear:
The ruddiness upon her lip is wet;
You'll mar it, if you kiss it; stain your own
With oily painting: Shall I draw the curtain?

Leon. No, not these twenty years.

Per. So long could I
Stand by, a looker on.

Paul. Either forbear,
Quit presently the chapel; or resolve you
For more amazement: If you can behold it,
I'll make the statue move indeed: descend,
And take you by the hand; but then you'll think
(Which I protest against,) I am assisted
By wicked powers.

Leon. What you can make her do,
I am content to look on: what to speak,
I am content to hear; for 'tis as easy
To make her speak, as move.

Paul. It is requir'd,
You do awake your faith: Then, all stand still;
Or those that think it is unlawful business
I am about, let them depart.

Leon. Proceed;
No foot shall stir.

Paul. Music; awake her: strike.— [*Music.*
'Tis time; descend; be stone no more: approach,
Strike all that look upon with marvel. Come;
I'll fill your grave up: stir; nay, come away;
Bequeath to death your numbness, for from him
Dear life redeems you.—You perceive she stirs:
[HERMIONE *comes down from the Pedestal.*
Start not: her actions shall be holy, as,
You hear, my spell is lawful: do not shun her,
Until you see her die again; for then
You kill her double: Nay, present your hand:
When she was young, you woo'd her; now, in age,
Is she become the suitor.

Leon. O, she's warm! [*Embracing her.*
If this be magic, let it be an art,
Lawful as eating.

Pol. She embraces him.

Cam. She hangs about his neck;
If she pertain to life, let her speak too.

Pol. Ay, and make't manifest where she has liv'd
Or, how stol'n from the dead?

Paul. That she is living,
Were it but told you, should be hooted at
Like an old tale; but it appears she lives,
Though yet she speak not. Mark a little while.—
Please you to interpose, fair madam; kneel,
And pray your mother's blessing.—Turn, good lady
Our Perdita is found.
[*Presenting* PER. *who kneels to* HER.

Her. You gods, look down,
And from your sacred vials pour your graces
Upon my daughter's head!—Tell me, mine own,
Where hast thou been preserved? where liv'd? how found
Thy father's court? for thou shalt hear, that I,—
Knowing by Paulina that the oracle
Gave hope, thou wast in being,—have preserv'd
Myself to see the issue.

Paul. There's time enough for that;
Lest they desire, upon this push to trouble
Your joys with like relation. Go together,
You precious winners[6] all; your exultation
Partake[7] to every one. I, an old turtle,
Will wing me to some wither'd bough; and there.
My mate, that's never to be found again,
Lament till I am lost.[8]

Leon. O peace, Paulina;
Thou should'st a husband take by my consent,
As I by thine, a wife: this is a match,
And made between's by vows. Thou hast found mine;
But how is it to be question'd: for I saw her,
As I thought, dead: and have in vain said many
A prayer upon her grave; I'll not seek far
(For him, I partly know his mind,) to find thee
An honourable husband:—Come, Camillo,
And take her by the hand: whose[9] worth, and honesty,
Is[10] richly noted; and here justified
By us, a pair of kings.—Let's from this place.—
What!—Look[11] upon, my brother:—both your pardons,

---

1 Worked, agitated.

2 The folio reads, '*I'd* not have show'd it.' In the late edition of Malone's Shakspeare it stands, '*I'll* not have show'd it.' But surely this is erroneous.

3 The sentence if completed would probably have been, 'but that, methinks, already *I converse with the dead.*'—His passion made him break off.

4 i. e. Though her eye be fixed, it seems to have motion in it.

5 *As* for *as if*. *With* has the force of *by*.

6 You who by this discovery have gained what you desired.

7 i. e. participate.

8 Thus in Lodge's Rosalynde, 1592:—

'A turtle sat upon a leavelesse tree
Mourning her absent pheere
With sad and sorry cheere:
And whilst her plumes she rents,
And for her love laments,' &c.

9 *Whose* relates to Camillo, though Paulina is the immediate antecedent. I have observed, in the loose construction of ancient phraseology, *whose* often used in this manner, where *his* would be more proper.

10 *It* is erroneously printed for *is* here in the late Variorum Shakspeare.

11 Look *upon* for look *on*. Thus in King Henry V Part III. Act ii. Sc. 3.

'And *look upon*, as if the tragedy,' &c

That e'er I put between your holy looks
My ill suspicion.—This your son-in-law,
And son unto the king (whom[1] heaven's directing,)
Is troth-plight to your daughter. Good Paulina,
Lead us from hence; where we may leisurely
Each one demand, and answer to his part
Perform'd in this wide gap of time, since first
We were dissever'd: Hastily lead away. [*Exeunt.*

THIS play, as Dr. Warburton justly observes, is, with all its absurdities, very entertaining. The character of Autolycus is naturally conceived, and strongly represented. JOHNSON.

*** This is not only a *frigid* note of approbation, but s unjustly attributed to Warburton, whose opinion is conveyed in more enthusiastic terms. He must in justice be allowed to speak for himself. 'This play throughout is written in the very spirit of its author And in telling this homely and simple, though agreeable, country tale,

"Our sweetest Shakspeare, Fancy's child,
Warbles his native wood-notes wild."

This was necessary to observe in mere justice to the play; as the meanness of the fable, and the extravagant conduct of it, had misled some of great name (i. e. Dryden and Pope) into a wrong judgment of its merit; which, as far as regards sentiment and character, is scarce inferior to any in the collection.'

1 *Whom* is here used where *him* would be now employed.

ADDITIONAL NOTE.

I will just take occasion to observe here, that at page 316, Sc. 3, of this play, Paulina says of Hermione, contrasting her with Leontes, that she is

'——— a gracious innocent soul;
More *free* than he is jealous.'

Where the epithet *free* evidently means *chaste*, *pure*. I regret that this instance did not occur to me when I wrote the note on Twelfth Night, p. 108, note 6.

COMEDY OF ERRORS.

PRELIMINARY REMARKS.

THE general idea of this play is taken from the *Menæchmi* of Plautus, but the plot is entirely recast, and rendered much more diverting by the variety and quick succession of the incidents. To the twin brothers of Plautus are added twin servants, and though this increases the improbability, yet, as Schlegel observes, 'when once we have lent ourselves to the first, which certainly borders on the incredible, we should not probably be disposed to cavil about the second; and if the spectator is to be entertained with mere perplexities, they cannot be too much varied.' The clumsy and inartificial mode of informing the spectator by a prologue of events, which it was necessary for him to be acquainted with in order to enter into the spirit of the piece, is well avoided, and shows the superior skill of the modern dramatist over his ancient prototype. With how much more propriety is it placed in the mouth of Ægeon, the father of the twin brothers, whose character is sketched with such skill as deeply to interest the reader in his griefs and misfortunes. Developement of character, however, was not to be expected in a piece which consists of an uninterrupted series of mistakes and laughter-moving situations. Steevens most resolutely maintained his opinion that this was a play only retouched by the hand of Shakspeare, but he has not given the grounds upon which his opinion was formed. We may suppose the doggerel verses of the dramas, and the want of distinct characterization in the dramatis personæ, together with the farcelike nature of some of the incidents made him draw this conclusion. Malone has given a satisfactory answer to the first objection, by adducing numerous examples of the same kind of long verse from the dramas of several of his contemporaries; and that Shakspeare was swayed by custom in introducing it into his early plays there can be no doubt; for it should be remembered that this kind of versification is to be found in Love's Labour's Lost, and in The Taming of the Shrew. His better judgment made him subsequently abandon it. The particular translation from Plautus which served as a model has not come down to us. There was a translation of the Menæchmi, by W. W. (Warner), published in 1595, which it is possible Shakspeare may have seen in manuscript: but from the circumstance of the brothers being, in the folio of 1623, occasionally styled Antipholus *Erotes* or *Errotis*. and Antipholus *Sereptus*, perhaps for *Surreptus* and *Erraticus*, while in Warner's translation the brothers are named Menæchmus *Sosicles* and Menæchmus *the traveller*, it is concluded that he was not the poet's authority. It is difficult to pronounce decidedly between the contending opinions of the critics, but the general impression upon my mind is that the whole of the play is from the hand of Shakspeare. Dr. Drake thinks it 'is visible throughout the entire play, as well in the broad exuberance of its mirth as in the cast of its more chastised parts, a combination of which may be found in the character of Pinch, who is sketched in his strongest and most marked style.' We may conclude with Schlegel's dictum, that 'this is the best of all written or possible Menæchmi; and if the piece is inferior in worth to other pieces of Shakspeare, it is merely because nothing more could be made of the materials.'

Malone first placed the date of this piece in 1593, or 1596, but lastly in 1592. Chalmers plainly showed that it should be ascribed to the early date of 1591. It was neither printed nor entered on the Stationers' books until it appeared in the folio of 1623.

PERSONS REPRESENTED

SOLINUS, Duke of Ephesus.
ÆGEON, *a Merchant of* Syracuse.
DROMIO *of* Ephesus, DROMIO *of* Syracuse, } *twin brothers, and* Attendants *on the two* Antipholuses.
ANTIPHOLUS *of* Ephesus, ANTIPHOLUS *of* Syracuse, } *twin brothers, and sons to* Ægeon *and* Æmilia, *but unknown to each other.*
BALTHAZAR, *a Merchant.*
ANGELO, *a Goldsmith.*
A Merchant, *friend to* Antipholus *of* Syracuse.
PINCH, *a Schoolmaster and a conjuror.*

ÆMILIA, *Wife to* Ægeon, *an Abbess at* Ephesus.
ADRIANA, *Wife to* Antipholus *of* Ephesus.
LUCIANA, *her sister.*
LUCE, *her servant.*
A Courtezan.

Gaoler, Officers, *and other* Attendants.

SCENE, Ephesus.

ACT I.

SCENE I. *A Hall in the* Duke's *Palace. Enter* Duke, Ægeon, Gaoler, Officer, *and other* Attendants.

Ægeon.

Proceed, Solinus, to procure my fall,
And, by the doom of death, end woes and all.
Duke. Merchant of Syracusa, plead no more;
I am not partial, to infringe our laws:
The enmity and discord, which of late
Sprung from the rancorous outrage of your duke
To merchants, our well-dealing countrymen,—
Who, wanting gilders[1] to redeem their lives,
Have seal'd his rigorous statutes with their bloods,
Excludes all pity from our threat'ning looks.
For, since the mortal and intestine jars
'Twixt thy seditious countrymen and us,
It hath in solemn synods been decreed,
Both by the Syracusans and ourselves,
To admit no traffic to our adverse towns:
Nay, more,
If any, born at Ephesus, be seen
At any Syracusan marts and fairs,
Again, If any, Syracusan born,
Come to the bay of Ephesus, he dies,
His goods confiscate to the duke's dispose;
Unless a thousand marks be levied,
To quit the penalty and to ransom him.
Thy substance, valued at the highest rate,
Cannot amount unto a hundred marks;
Therefore by law thou art condemn'd to die.
Æge. Yet this my comfort; when your words are done,
My woes end likewise with the evening sun.
Duke. Well, Syracusan, say, in brief, the cause
Why thou departedst from thy native home;
And for what cause thou cam'st to Ephesus?
Æge. A heavier task could not have been imposed,
Than I to speak my griefs unspeakable:
Yet, that the world may witness that my end
Was wrought by nature,[2] not by vile offence,
I'll utter what my sorrow gives me leave.
In Syracusa was I born: and wed
Unto a woman, happy but for me,
And by me too, had not our hap been bad.
With her I liv'd in joy; our wealth increas'd,
By prosperous voyages I often made
To Epidamnum, till my fatctor's death;
And the[3] great care of goods at random left,
Drew me from kind embracements of my spouse:
From whom my absence was not six months old,
Before herself (almost at fainting, under
The pleasing punishment that women bear)
Had made provision for her following me,
And soon, and safe, arrived where I was.
There she had not been long, but she became
A joyful mother of two goodly sons;
And, which was strange, the one so like the other,
As could not be distinguish'd but by names.
That very hour, and in the selfsame inn,
A poor[4] mean woman was delivered
Of such a burden, male twins, both alike:
Those, for their parents were exceeding poor,
I bought, and brought up to attend my sons.
My wife, not meanly proud of two such boys,
Made daily motions for our home return:
Unwilling I agreed; alas! too soon.
We came aboard:
A league from Epidamnum had we sail'd,
Before the always wind-obeying deep
Gave any tragic instance[5] of our harm:
But longer did we not retain much hope;
For what obscured light the heavens did grant
Did but convey unto our fearful minds
A doubtful warrant of immediate death;
Which, though myself would gladly have embrac'd,
Yet the incessant weepings of my wife,
Weeping before for what she saw must come,
And piteous plainings of the pretty babes,
That mourn'd for fashion, ignorant what to fear,
Forc'd me to seek delays for them and me.
And this it was,—for other means was none.—
The sailors sought for safety by our boat,
And left the ship, then sinking ripe, to us:
My wife, more careful for the latter-born,
Had fasten'd him unto a small spare mast,
Such as seafaring men provide for storms;
To him one of the other twins was bound,
Whilst I had been like heedful of the other.
The children thus dispos'd, my wife and I,
Fixing our eyes on whom our care was fix'd,
Fasten'd ourselves at either end the mast;
And floating straight, obedient to the stream,
Were carried towards Corinth, as we thought.
At length the sun, gazing upon the earth,
Dispers'd those vapours that offended us;
And, by the benefit of his wish'd light,
The seas wax'd calm, and we discovered
Two ships from far making amain to us,
Of Corinth that, of Epidaurus this:
But ere they came,—O, let me say no more!
Gather the sequel by that went before.
Duke. Nay, forward, old man, do not break off so;
For we may pity, though not pardon thee.
Æge. O, had the gods done so, I had not now
Worthily term'd them merciless to us!
For, ere the ships could meet by twice five leagues,
We were encounter'd by a mighty rock;
Which being violently borne upon,[6]
Our helpful ship was splitted in the midst.
So that, in this unjust divorce of us,
Fortune had left to both of us alike
What to delight in, what to sorrow for.
Her part, poor soul! seeming as burdened
With lesser weight, but not with lesser woe,
Was carried with more speed before the wind;
And in our sight they three were taken up
By fishermen of Corinth, as we thought.
At length, another ship had seiz'd on us;
And, knowing whom it was their hap to save,
Gave healthful[7] welcome to their shipwreck'd guests;
And would have reft the fisher's of their prey,
Had not their bark been very slow of sail,
And therefore homeward did they bend their course.—
Thus you have heard me sever'd from my bliss;
That by misfortunes was my life prolong'd,
To tell sad stories of my own mishaps.
Duke. And, for the sake of them thou sorrowest for,
Do me the favour to dilate at full
What hath befall'n of them, and thee, till now.
Æge. My youngest boy,[8] and yet my eldest care
At eighteen years became inquisitive
After his brother; and importun'd me,
That his attendant (for[9] his case was like,
Reft of his brother, but[10] retain'd his name)
Might bear him company in the quest of him:
Whom whilst I labour'd of a love to see,

1 A *gilder* was a coin valued from one shilling and sixpence to two shillings.
2 i. e. natural affection.
3 The old copy reads *he:* the emendation is Malone's. It is a happy restoration; for the manner in which Steevens pointed this passage gave to it a confused if not an absurd meaning.
4 The word *poor* was supplied by the editor of the second folio.
5 *Instance* appears to be used here for *symptom* or *prognostic.* Shakspeare uses this word with very great latitude.
6 The first folio reads 'borne *up*.'
7 The second folio altered this to '*helpful* welcome;' but change was unnecessary. A *healthful* welcome is a kind welcome, wishing health to their guests. It was not a *helpful* welcome, for the slowness of their bark prevented them from rendering assistance.
8 It appears, from what goes before, that it was the *eldest*, and not the *youngest*. He says, 'My wife, more careful of the latter-born,' &c.
9 The first folio reads *so:* the second *for.*
10 The personal pronoun *he* is suppressed: such phraseology is not unfrequent in the writings of that age

I hazarded the loss of whom I lov'd.
Five summers have I spent in furthest Greece,
Roaming clean through the bounds of Asia,
And, coasting homeward, came to Ephesus;
Hopeless to find, yet loath to leave unsought,
Or that, or any place that harbours men.
But here must end the story of my life;
And happy were I in my timely death,
Could all my travels warrant me they live.

Duke. Hapless Ægeon, whom the fates have mark'd
To bear the extremity of dire mishap!
Now, trust me, were it not against our laws,
Against my crown, my oath, my dignity,
Which princes, would they, may not disannul,
My soul should sue as advocate for thee.
But, though thou art adjudged to the death,
And passed sentence may not be recall'd,
But to our honour's great disparagement,
Yet will I favour thee in what I can:
Therefore, merchant, I'll limit thee this day,
To seek thy help by beneficial help:
Try all the friends thou hast in Ephesus;
Beg thou, or borrow, to make up the sum,
And live; if not,[1] then thou art doomed to die:—
Gaoler, take him to thy custody.

Gaol. I will, my lord.

Æge. Hopeless and helpless doth Ægeon wend,[2]
But to procrastinate his lifeless end. [*Exeunt.*

SCENE II. *A public Place. Enter* ANTIPHOLUS *and* DROMIO *of Syracuse, and a* Merchant.

Mer. Therefore, give out, you are of Epidamnum,
Lest that your goods too soon be confiscate.
This very day, a Syracusan merchant
Is apprehended for arrival here;
And, not being able to buy out his life,
According to the statute of the town,
Dies ere the weary sun set in the west.
There is your money that I had to keep.

Ant. S. Go bear it to the Centaur, where we host,
And stay there, Dromio, till I come to thee.
Within this hour it will be dinner-time:
Till that, I'll view the manners of the town,
Peruse the traders, gaze upon the buildings,
And then return, and sleep within mine inn;
For with long travel I am stiff and weary.
Get thee away.

Dro. S. Many a man would take you at your word,
And go indeed, having so good a mean. [*Exit* DRO. S.

Ant. S. A trusty villain,[3] sir; that very oft,
When I am dull with care and melancholy,
Lightens my humour with his merry jests.
What, will you walk with me about the town,
And then go to my inn, and dine with me?

Mer. I am invited, sir, to certain merchants,
Of whom I hope to make much benefit;
I crave your pardon. Soon, at five o'clock,
Please, you, I'll meet with you upon the mart:
And afterwards consort[4] you till bed-time;
My present business calls me from you now.

Ant. S. Farewell till then: I will go lose myself,
And wander up and down, to view the city.

Mer. Sir, I commend you to your own content. [*Exit* Merchant.

Ant. S. He that commends me to my own content,
Commends me to the thing I cannot get.
I to the world am like a drop of water,
That in the ocean seeks another drop;
Who falling there to find his fellow forth,
Unseen, inquisitive, confounds[5] himself:
So I, to find a mother, and a brother,
In quest of them, unhappy, lose myself.

Enter DROMIO *of* Ephesus.

Here comes the almanack of my true date,[6]—
What now? How chance, thou art return'd so soon?

Dro. E. Return'd so soon! rather approach'd too late:
The capon burns, the pig falls from the spit:
The clock hath strucken twelve upon the bell,
My mistress made it one upon my cheek:
She is so hot, because the meat is cold;
The meat is cold because you come not home;
You come not home, because you have no stomach;
You have no stomach, having broken your fast;
But we, that know what 'tis to fast and pray,
Are penitent for your default to-day.

Ant. S. Stop in your wind, sir; tell me this, I pray;
Where have you left the money that I gave you?

Dro. E. O,—sixpence, that I had o' Wednesday last,
To pay the saddler for my mistress' crupper;—
The saddler had it, sir, I kept it not.

Ant. S. I am not in a sportive humour now:
Tell me and dally not, where is the money?
We being strangers here, how dar'st thou trust
So great a charge from thine own custody?

Dro. E. I pray you, jest, sir, as you sit at dinner:
I from my mistress come to you in post;
If I return, I shall be post indeed;
For she will score your fault upon my pate.
Methinks, your maw, like mine, should be your clock,[7]
And strike you home without a messenger.

Ant. S. Come, Dromio, come, these jests are out of season;
Reserve them till a merrier hour than this:
Where is the gold I gave in charge to thee?

Dro. E. To me, sir? why you gave no gold to me.

Ant. S. Come on, sir knave, have done your foolishness,
And tell me, how thou hast dispos'd thy charge.

Dro. E. My charge was but to fetch you from the mart
Home to your house, the Phœnix, sir, to dinner;
My mistress, and her sister, stay for you.

Ant. S. Now, as I am a christian, answer me,
In what safe place you have bestow'd my money;
Or I shall break that merry sconce[8] of yours,
That stands on tricks when I am undispos'd:
Where is the thousand marks thou hadst of me?

Dro. E. I have some marks of yours upon my pate,
Some of my mistress' marks upon my shoulders,
But not a thousand marks between you both.—
If I should pay your worship those again,
Perchance you will not bear them patiently.

Ant. S. Thy mistress' marks! what mistress slave, hast thou?

Dro. E. Your worship's wife, my mistress at the Phœnix;
She that doth fast, till you come home to dinner,
And prays, that you will hie you home to dinner.

Ant. S. What, wilt thou flout me thus unto my face,
Being forbid? There, take you that, sir knave. [*Strikes him*

---

1 *No*, which is the reading of the first folio, was anciently often used for *not*. The second folio reads *not*.

2 Go.

3 That is, *a faithful slave*. It is the French sense of the word.

4 i. e. '*accompany you.*' In this line the emphasis must be laid on *time*, at the end of the line, to preserve the metre.

5 *Confounded*, here, does not signify *destroyed*, as Malone asserts, but *overwhelmed, mixed confusedly together, lost*.

6 They were both born in the same hour, and therefore the date of Dromio's birth ascertains that of his master.

7 The old copy reads *cook*. The emendation is Pope's

8 *Sconce* is *head*. So in Hamlet, Act v. Sc. 1:—'Why does he suffer this rude knave to knock him about the *sconce*.' A sconce signified a blockhouse, or strong fortification, 'for the most part round, in fashion of a head,' says *Blount*. I suppose that it was anciently used for a *lantern* also, on account of the round form of that [illegible]

Dro. E. What mean you, sir? for God's sake, hold your hands;
Nay, an you will not, sir, I'll take my heels.
[*Exit* DROMIO E.

Ant. S. Upon my life, by some device or other,
The villain is o'er-raught[1] of all my money.
They say, this town is full of cozenage:[2]
As, nimble jugglers, that deceive the eye;
Dark-working sorcerers, that change the mind;
Soul-killing witches, that deform the body;
Disguised cheaters, prating mountebanks,
And many such like liberties of sin:[3]
If it prove so, I will be gone the sooner.
I'll to the Centaur, to go seek this slave;
I greatly fear my money is not safe. [*Exit.*

ACT II.

SCENE I. *A Public Place. Enter* ADRIANA, *and* LUCIANA.

Adr. Neither my husband, nor the slave return'd,
That in such haste I sent to seek his master!
Sure, Luciana, it is two o'clock.

Luc. Perhaps, some merchant hath invited him,
And from the mart he's somewhere gone to dinner;
Good sister, let us dine, and never fret:
A man is master of his liberty;
Time is their master; and when they see time,
They'll go, or come: If so, be patient sister.

Adr. Why should their liberty than ours be more?

Luc. Because their business still lies out o'doors.

Adr. Look, when I serve him so, he takes it ill.

Luc. O, know, he is the bridle of your will.

Adr. There's none but asses, will be bridled so.

Luc. Why, headstrong liberty is lash'd with woe,[4]
There's nothing, situate under Heaven's eye,
But hath his bound, in earth, in sea, in sky:
The beasts, the fishes, and the winged fowls,
Are their males' subjects, and at their controuls:
Men, more divine, the masters of all these,
Lords of the wide world, and wild watry seas,
Indued with intellectual sense and souls,
Of more pre-eminence than fish and fowls,
Are masters to their females, and their lords:
Then let your will attend on their accords.

Adr. This servitude makes you to keep unwed.

Luc. Not this, but troubles of the marriage bed.

Adr. But, were you wedded, you would bear some sway.

Luc. Ere I learn love, I'll practise to obey.

Adr. How if your husband start some other where?[5]

Luc. Till he come home again, I would forbear.

Adr. Patience, unmov'd, no marvel though she pause;[6]
They can be meek, that have no other cause.[7]
A wretched soul, bruis'd with adversity,
We bid be quiet, when we hear it cry;
But were we burden'd with like weight of pain,
As much, or more, we should ourselves complain:
So thou, that hast no unkind mate to grieve thee,
With urging helpless patience[8] would'st relieve me:
But, if thou live to see like right bereft,
This fool-begg'd patience[9] in thee will be left.

Luc. Well, I will marry one day, but to try;—
Here comes your man, now is your husband nigh.

Enter DROMIO *of* Ephesus.

Adr. Say, is your tardy master now at hand?

Dro. E. Nay, he is at two hands with me, and that my two ears can witness.

Adr. Say, didst you speak with him? know'st thou his mind?

Dro. E. Ay, ay, he told his mind upon mine ear:
Beshrew his hand, I scarce could understand it.

Luc. Spake he so doubtfully, thou could'st not feel his meaning?

Dro. E. Nay, he struck so plainly, I could too well feel his blows; and withal so doubtfully, that I could scarce understand them.[10]

Adr. But say, I pr'ythee, is he coming home?
It seems he hath great care to please his wife.

Dro. E. Why, mistress, sure my master is horn-mad.

Adr. Horn-mad, thou villain?

Dro. E. I mean not cuckold-mad; but, sure he's stark-mad:
When I desir'd him to come home to dinner,
He ask'd me for a thousand marks in gold:
'*Tis dinner time*, quoth I; *My gold*, quoth he:
Your meat doth burn, quoth I; *My gold*, quoth he:
Will you come home?[11] quoth I; *My gold*, quoth he:
Where is the thousand marks I gave thee, villain?
The pig, quoth I, *is burn'd; My gold*, quoth he:
My mistress, sir, quoth I; *Hang up thy mistress;*
I know not thy mistress; out on thy mistress![12]

Luc. Quoth who?

Dro. E. Quoth my master:
I know, quoth he, *no house, no wife, no mistress*;—
So that my errand, due unto my tongue,
I thank him, I bear home upon my shoulders;
For, in conclusion, he did beat me there.

Adr. Go back again, thou slave, and fetch him home.

Dro. E. Go back again, and be new beaten home?
For God's sake, send some other messenger.

Adr. Back, slave, or I will break thy pate across.

Dro. E. And he will bless that cross with other beating:
Between you I shall have a holy head.

Adr. Hence, prating peasant; fetch thy master home.

Dro. E. Am I so round[13] with you, as you with me,
That like a football you do spurn me thus?
You spurn me hence, and he will spurn me hither:
If I last in this service, you must case me in leather.
[*Exit.*

Luc. Fie, how impatience loureth in your face!

Adr. His company must do his minions grace,
Whilst I at home starve for a merry look.[14]
Hath homely age the alluring beauty took
From my poor cheek? then he hath wasted it:
Are my discourses dull? barren my wit?
If voluble and sharp discourse be marr'd,
Unkindness blunts it, more than marble hard.
Do their gay vestments his affections bait?
That's not my fault, he's master of my state:
What ruins are in me, that can be found
By him not ruin'd? then is he the ground
Of my defeatures:[15] My decayed fair[16]

---

1 i. e. over-reached.

2 This was the character which the ancients gave of Ephesus.

3 That is, *licentious actions, sinful liberties.*

4 The meaning of this passage may be, that those who refuse the bridle must bear the lash, and that woe is the punishment of headstrong liberty.

5 'Elsewhere, *other where;* in another place, *alibi*,' says Baret. The sense is, 'How if your husband fly off in pursuit of some other woman?'

6 *To pause* is *to rest*, to be quiet.

7 i. e. *no cause* to be otherwise.

8 That is, by urging me to patience which affords no help.

9 '*Fool-begg'd* patience' is that *patience* which is so near to *idiotical simplicity*, that you might be represented to be a *fool*, and your guardianship *begg'd* accordingly.

10 i. e. scarce stand under them.

11 *Home* is not in the old copy: it was supplied to complete the verse by Capell.

12 We have an equally unmetrical line in the first Act:—
'Therefore, merchant, I'll limit thee this day.'

13 He plays upon the word *round*, which signifies spherical, as applied to himself; and *unrestrained*, or *free in speech* or *action*, as regards his mistress. The King in Hamlet desires the Queen to be *round* with her son.

14 So in Shakspeare's Sonnets, the forty-seventh and seventy-fifth:—
'When that mine eye is *famish'd for a look.*'
'Sometimes all full with feeding on his sight,
'And by and by clean *starved for a look.*'

15 *Defeat* and *defeature* were used for disfigurement or alteration of features. Cotgrave has 'Un visage desfaict: *Growne very leane, pale, wan,* or *decayed in feature and colour.*'

16 *Fair*, strictly speaking, is not used here for fair

A sunny look of his would soon repair:
But, too unruly deer, he breaks the pale,
And feeds from home; poor I am but his stale.[1]

Luc. Self-harming jealousy!—fie, beat it hence.

Adr. Unfeeling fools can with such wrongs dispense.
I know his eye doth homage otherwhere
Or else, what lets[2] it but he would be here?
Sister, you know, he promised me a chain;
'Would, that alone, alone he would detain,
So he would keep fair quarter with his bed!
I see, the jewel, best enamelled,
Will lose his beauty; and though gold 'bides still,
That others touch, yet often touching will
Wear gold: and no man, that hath a name,
But falsehood and corruption doth it shame.
Since that my beauty cannot please his eye,
I'll weep what's left away, and weeping die.

Luc. How many fond fools serve mad jealousy! [*Exeunt.*

SCENE II. *The same. Enter* ANTIPHOLUS *of* Syracuse.

Ant. S. The gold, I gave to Dromio, is laid up
Safe at the Centaur; and the heedful slave
Is wander'd forth, in care to seek me out.
By computation, and mine host's report,
I could not speak with Dromio, since at first
I sent him from the mart: See, here he comes.

Enter DROMIO *of* Syracuse.

How now, sir? is your merry humour alter'd?
As you love strokes, so jest with me again.
You know no Centaur? you received no gold?
Your mistress sent to have me home to dinner?
My house was at the Phœnix? Wast thou mad,
That thus so madly thou didst answer me?

Dro. S. What answer, sir? when spake I such a word?

Ant. S. Even now, even here, not half an hour since.

Dro. S. I did not see you since you sent me hence,
Home to the Centaur, with the gold you gave me.

Ant. S. Villain, thou didst deny the gold's receipt;
And told'st me of a mistress, and a dinner;
For which, I hope, thou felt'st I was displeas'd.

Dro. S. I am glad to see you in this merry vein:
What means this jest? I pray you, master, tell me.

Ant. S. Yea, dost thou jeer and flout me in the teeth?
Think'st thou, I jest? Hold, take thou that, and that. [*Beating him.*

Dro. S. Hold, sir, for God's sake: now your jest is earnest;
Upon what bargain do you give it me?

Ant. S. Because that I familiarly sometimes
Do use you for my fool, and chat with you,
Your sauciness will jest upon my love,
And make a common of my serious hours.[3]
When the sun shines, let foolish gnats make sport,
But creep in crannies, when he hides his beams
If you will jest with me, know my aspect,[4]
And fashion your demeanour to my looks,
Or I will beat this method in your sconce.

Dro. S. Sconce, call you it? so you would leave battering, I had rather have it a head: an you use these blows long, I must get a sconce for my head, and insconce[5] it too; or else I shall seek my wit in my shoulders. But, I pray, sir, why am I beaten?

Ant. S. Dost thou not know?

Dro. S. Nothing, sir; but that I am beaten.

Ant. S. Shall I tell you why?

Dro. S. Ay, sir, and wherefore; for, they say every why hath a wherefore.

Ant. S. Why, first,—for flouting me; and then wherefore,—
For urging it the second time to me.

Dro. S. Was there ever any man thus beaten out of season?
When, in the why, and the wherefore, is neither rhyme nor reason?—
Well, sir, I thank you.

Ant. S. Thank me, sir? for what?

Dro. S. Marry, sir, for this something that you gave me for nothing.

Ant. S. I'll make you amends next, to give you nothing for something. But say, sir, is it dinner-time?

Dro. S. No, sir; I think the meat wants that I have.

Ant. S. In good time, sir, what's that?

Dro. S. Basting.

Ant. S. Well, sir, then 'twill be dry.

Dro. S. If it be, sir, I pray you eat none of it.

Ant. S. Your reason?

Dro. S. Lest it make you choleric,[6] and purchase me another dry basting.

Ant. S. Well, sir, learn to jest in good time There's a time for all things.

Dro. S. I durst have denied that, before you were so choleric.

Ant. S. By what rule, sir?

Dro. S. Marry, sir, by a rule as plain as the plain bald pate of father Time himself.

Ant. S. Let's hear it.

Dro. S. There's no time for a man to recover his hair, that grows bald by nature.

Ant. S. May he not do it by fine and recovery?[7]

Dro. S. Yes, to pay a fine for a periwig, and recover the lost hair of another man.

Ant. S. Why is time such a niggard of hair, being, as it is, so plentiful an excrement?

Dro. S. Because it is a blessing that he bestows on beasts: and what he hath scanted men[8] in hair, he hath given them in wit.

Ant. S. Why, but there's many a man hath more hair than wit.[9]

Dro. S. Not a man of those, but he hath the wit to lose his hair.[10]

Ant. S. Why, thou didst conclude hairy men plain dealers without wit.

Dro. S. The plainer dealer, the sooner lost: Yet he loseth it in a kind of jollity.

Ant. S. For what reason?

Dro. S. For two; and sound ones too.

Ant. S. Nay, not sound, I pray you.

Dro. S. Sure ones, then.

Ant. S. Nay, not sure, in a thing falsing.[11]

---

ness, as Steevens supposed; but for *beauty*. Shakspeare has often employed it in this sense, without any relation to *whiteness of skin or complexion*. The use of the substantive instead of the adjective, in this instance, is not peculiar to him; but the common practice of his contemporaries.

1 Though Shakspeare sometimes uses *stale* for a decoy or bait, I do not think that he meant it here; or that Adriana can mean to call herself his *stalking-horse*. Probably she means she *is thrown aside, forgotten, cast off*, become *stale* to him. The dictionaries, in voce *Exoletus*, countenance this explanation.

2 Hinders.

3 i. e. intrude on them when you please.

4 Study my countenance.

5 *A sconce* was a fortification; to *insconce* was to *hide*, to protect as with a fort.

6 So in The Taming of the Shrew:—

'I tell thee, Kate, 'twas burnt and dried away,
And I expressly am forbid to touch it,
For it engenders *choler*, planteth anger.'

7 This is another instance of Shakspeare's acquaintance with technical law terms.

8 The old copy reads *them*: the emendation is Theobald's.

9 The following lines 'Upon [Suckling's] Aglaura printed in folio,' may serve to illustrate this proverbial sentence:—

'This great voluminous pamphlet may be said
To be like one that hath more hair than head;
More excrement than body:—trees which sprout
With broadest leaves have still the smallest fruit.'
Parnassus Biceps. 1656.

10 Shakspeare too frequently alludes to this loss of hair by a certain disease. It seems to have been a joke that pleased him, and probably tickled his auditors.

11 To *false*, as a verb, has been long obsolete: but it was current in Shakspeare's time.

Dro. S. Certain ones then.

Ant. S. Name them.

Dro. S. The one, to save the money that he spends in tiring; the other, that at dinner they should not drop in his porridge.

Ant. S. You would all this time have proved, there is no time for all things.

Dro. S. Marry, and did, sir; namely, e'en[1] no time to recover hair lost by nature.

Ant. S. But your reason was not substantial, why there is no time to recover.

Dro. S. Thus I mend it: Time himself is bald, and therefore, to the world's end, will have bald followers.

Ant. S. I knew 'twould be a bald conclusion:
But soft! who wafts[2] us yonder!

Enter ADRIANA *and* LUCIANA.

Adr. Ay, ay, Antipholus, look strange and frown;
Some other mistress hath thy sweet aspects,
I am not Adriana, nor thy wife.
The time was once, when thou unurg'd would'st vow,
That never words were music to thine ear,[3]
That never object pleasing in thine eye,
That never touch well welcome to thy hand,
That never meat sweet-savour'd in thy taste,
Unless I spake, look'd, touch'd, or carv'd to thee.
How comes it now, my husband, oh, how comes it,
That thou art then estranged from thyself?
Thyself I call it, being strange to me,
That, undividable, incorporate,
Am better than thy dear self's better part.
Ah, do not tear away thyself from me;
For know, my love, as easy may'st thou fall[4]
A drop of water in the breaking gulf,
And take unmingled thence that drop again,
Without addition, or diminishing,
As take from me thyself, and not me too.
How dearly would it touch thee to the quick,
Should'st thou but hear I were licentious?
And that this body, consecrate to thee,
By ruffian lust should be contaminate?
Would'st thou not spit at me, and spurn at me,
And hurl the name of husband in my face,
And tear the stain'd skin off my harlot brow,
And from my false hand cut the wedding ring,
And break it with a deep divorcing vow?
I know thou canst; and therefore, see, thou do it.
I am possess'd with an adulterate blot;
My blood is mingled with the crime of lust:
For, if we two be one, and thou play false,
I do digest the poison of thy flesh,
Being strumpeted[5] by thy contagion.
Keep then fair league and truce with thy true bed;
I live distain'd,[6] thou undishonoured.

Ant. S. Plead you to me, fair dame? I know you not:
In Ephesus I am but two hours old,
As strange unto your town, as to your talk;
Who, every word by all my wit being scann'd,
Want wit in all one word to understand.

Luc. Fie, brother! how the world is chang'd with you:
When were you wont to use my sister thus?
She sent for you by Dromio home to dinner.

Ant. S. By Dromio?

Dro. S. By me?

Adr. By thee: and this thou didst return from him,
That he did buffet thee, and, in his blows
Denied my house for his, me for his wife.

Ant. S. Did you converse, sir, with this gentlewoman?
What is the course and drift of your compact?

Dro. S. I, sir? I never saw her till this time.

Ant. S. Villain, thou liest; for even her very words
Didst thou deliver to me on the mart.

Dro. S. I never spake with her in all my life.

Ant. S. How can she thus then call us by our names,
Unless it be by inspiration?

Adr. How ill agrees it with your gravity,
To counterfeit thus grossly with your slave,
Abetting him to thwart me in my mood?
Be it my wrong, you are from me exempt,[7]
But wrong not that wrong with a more contempt
Come, I will fasten on this sleeve of thine
Thou art an elm, my husband, I a vine:[8]
Whose weakness, married to thy stronger state,
Makes me with thy strength to communicate:
If aught possess thee from me, it is dross,
Usurping ivy, briar, or idle[9] moss:
Who, all for want of pruning, with intrusion
Infect thy sap, and live on thy confusion.

Ant. S. To me she speaks; she moves me for her theme:
What, was I married to her in my dream?
Or sleep I now, and think I hear all this?
What error drives our eyes and ears amiss?
Until I know this sure uncertainty,
I'll entertain the offer'd[10] fallacy.

Luc. Dromio, go bid the servants spread for dinner.

Dro. S. O, for my beads! I cross me for a sinner.
This is the fairy land;—O, spite of spites!—
We talk with goblins, owls, and elvish sprites;[11]
If we obey them not, this will ensue,
They'll suck our breath, or pinch us black and blue.

Luc. Why prat'st thou to thyself, and answer'st not?
Dromio, thou drone,[12] thou snail, thou slug, thou sot

Dro. S. I am transformed, master, am not I?

Ant. S. I think, thou art, in mind, and so am I.

Dro. S. Nay, master, both in mind, and in my shape.

Ant. S. Thou hast thine own form.

Dro. S. No, I am an ape.

Luc. If thou art chang'd to aught, 'tis to an ass.

Dro. S. 'Tis true; she rides me, and I long for grass.
'Tis so, I am an ass; else it could never be,
But I should know her as well as she knows me.

Adr. Come, come, no longer will I be a fool,
To put the finger in the eye and weep,
Whilst man, and master, laugh my woes to scorn.—
Come sir, to dinner; Dromio, keep the gate:—
Husband, I'll dine above with you to day,
And shrive[13] you of a thousand idle pranks:
Sirrah, if any ask you for your master,
Say, he dines forth, and let no creature enter.—
Come, sister:—Dromio, play the porter well.

Ant. S. Am I in earth, in heaven, or in hell?
Sleeping or waking? mad, or well advis'd?
Known unto these, and to myself disguis'd!
I'll say as they say, and persevere so,
And in this mist at all adventures go.

Dro. S. Master, shall I be porter at the gate?

Adr. Ay; and let none enter, lest I break your pate.

Luc. Come, come, Antipholus, we dine too late.

[*Exeunt.*

---

1 The old copy, by mistake, has *in*.

2 i. e. *beckons* us.

3 Imitated by Pope in his Epistle from Sappho to Phaon:—
'My music then you could for ever hear,
And all my words were music to your ear.'

4 *Fall* is here a verb active.

5 Shakspeare is not singular in the use of this verb.

6 i. e. *unstain'd*.

7 i. e. *separated, parted.*

8 So Milton's Paradise Lost, b. v.:—
'——— They led the *vine*
To wed her *elm*. She spous'd about him twines
Her marriageable arms.'

9 i. e. *unfruitful.*

10 The old copy reads *freed*, which is evidently wrong, perhaps a corruption of *proffered* or *offer'd*.

11 Theobald changed *owls* to *ouphes* in this passage most unwarrantably. It was those, '*unlucking birds*, the striges or *screech-owls*, which are meant.

12 The old copy reads 'Dromio, thou *Dromio*.' The emendation is Theobald's.

13 i. e. call you to confession

ACT III.

SCENE I. *The same.* *Enter* ANTIPHOLUS *of* Ephesus, DROMIO *of* Ephesus, ANGELO, *and* BALTHAZAR.

Ant. E. Good signior Angelo, you must excuse us all:
My wife is shrewish when I keep not hours:
Say, that I linger'd with you at your shop,
To see the making of her carkanet,[1]
And that to-morrow you will bring it home.
But here's a villain, that would face me down,
He met me on the mart; and that I beat him,
And charg'd him with a thousand marks in gold;
And that I did deny my wife and house:—
Thou drunkard, thou, what didst thou mean by this?

Dro. E. Say what you will, sir, but I know what I know:
That you beat me at the mart, I have your hand to show:
If the skin were parchment, and the blows you gave were ink,
Your own handwriting would tell you what I think.

Ant. E. I think, thou art an ass.

Dro. E. Marry so it doth appear
By the wrongs I suffer, and the blows I bear.
I should kick, being kick'd; and, being at that pass,
You would keep from my heels, and beware of an ass.

Ant. E. You are sad, signior Balthazar: 'Pray God, our cheer
May answer my good will, and your good welcome here.

Bal. I hold your dainties cheap, sir, and your welcome dear.

Ant. E. O, signior Balthazar, either at flesh or fish,
A table full of welcome makes scarce one dainty dish.

Bal. Good meat, sir, is common; that every churl affords.

Ant. E. And welcome more common; for that's nothing but words.

Bal. Small cheer, and great welcome, makes a merry feast.

Ant. E. Ay, to a niggardly host, and more sparing guest;
But though my cates be mean, take them in good part;
Better cheer may you have, but not with better heart.
But, soft; my door is lock'd; Go bid them let us in.

Dro. E. Maud, Bridget, Marian, Cicely, Gillian, Jem'!

Dro. S. [*within.*] Mome,[2] malt-horse, capon, coxcomb, idiot, patch![3]
Either get thee from the door, or sit down at the hatch:
Dost thou conjure for wenches, that thou call'st for such store,
When one is one too many? Go, get thee from the door.

Dro. E. What patch is made our porter? My master stays in the street.

Dro. S. Let him walk from whence he came, lest he catch cold on's feet.

Ant. E. Who talks within there? ho, open the door.

Dro. S. Right, sir, I'll tell you when, an you'll tell me wherefore.

Ant. E. Wherefore? for my dinner; I have not din'd to-day.

Dro. S. Nor to-day here you must not; come again, when you may.

Ant. E. What art thou, that keep'st me out from the house I owe?[4]

Dro. S. The porter for this time, sir, and my name is Dromio.

Dro. E. O villain, thou hast stolen both mine office and my name;
The one ne'er got me credit, the other mickle blame.
If thou had'st been Dromio to-day in my place,
Thou would'st have chang'd thy face for a name, or thy name for an ass.

Luce. [*within.*] What a coil[5] is there? Dromio, who are those at the gate?

Dro. E. Let my master in, Luce.

Luce. 'Faith, no; he comes too late.
And so tell your master.

Dro. E. O Lord, I must laugh:—
Have at you with a proverb.—Shall I set in my staff?

Luce. Have at you with another: that's,—When? can you tell?

Dro. S. If thy name be call'd Luce, Luce, thou hast answer'd him well.

Ant. E. Do you hear, you minion? you'll let us in, I hope?[6]

Luce. I thought to have ask'd you.

Dro. S. And you said, no.

Dro. E. So, come, help; well struck; there was blow for blow.

Ant. E. Thou baggage, let me in.

Luce. Can you tell for whose sake?

Dro. E. Master knock the door hard.

Luce. Let him knock till it ake.

Ant. E. You'll cry for this, minion, if I beat the door down.

Luce. What needs all that, and a pair of stocks in the town?

Adr. [*within.*] Who is that at the door, that keeps all this noise?

Dro. S. By my troth, your town is troubled with unruly boys.

Ant. E. Are you there, wife? you might have come before.

Adr. Your wife, sir knave! go, get you from the door.

Dro. E. If you went in pain, master, this knave would go sore.

Ang. Here is neither cheer, sir, nor welcome; we would fain have either.

Bal. In debating which was best, we shall part[7] with neither.

Dro. E. They stand at the door, master; bid them welcome hither.

Ant. E. There is something in the wind, that we cannot get in.

Dro. E. You would say so, master, if your garments were thin.
Your cake here is warm within; you stand here in the cold:
It would make a man mad as a buck, to be so bought and sold.[8]

Ant. E. Go, fetch me something, I'll break ope the gate.

Dro. S. Break any breaking here, and I'll break your knave's pate.

Dro. E. A man may break a word with you, sir; and words are but wind;
Ay, and break it in your face, so he break it not behind.

Dro. S. It seems, thou wantest breaking; Out upon thee, hind!

Dro. E. Here is too much, out upon thee! I pray thee, let me in.

Dro. S. Ay, when fowls have no feathers, and fish have no fin.

---

1 A *carcanet* or chain for a lady's neck; a collar or chain of gold and precious stones: from the French *carcan.* It was sometimes spelled *karkanet* and *quarquenet.*

2 A *mome* was a *fool* or foolish jester. *Momar* is used by Plautus for a fool; whence the French *mommeur.*

3 *Patch* was a term of contempt often applied to persons of low condition, and sometimes applied to a *fool.*

4 I own, am owner of.

5 Bustle, tumult.

6 It seems probable that a line following this has been lost; in which Luce might be threatened with a *rope;* which would have furnished the rhyme now wanting. In a subsequent scene Dromio is ordered to go and buy a rope's end, for the purpose of using it on Adriana and her confederates.

7 Have part.

8 A proverbial phrase, meaning to be so over-reached by foul and secret practices

Ant. E. Well, I'll break in; Go borrow me a crow.
Dro. E. A crow without feather; master, mean you so?
For a fish without a fin, there's a fowl without a feather:
If a crow help us in, sirrah, we'll pluck a crow together.[1]
Ant. E. Go, get thee gone, fetch me an iron crow.
Bal. Have patience, sir: O, let it not be so:
Herein you war against your reputation,
And draw within the compass of suspect
The unviolated honour of your wife.
Once[2] this; your long experience of her wisdom,
Her sober virtue, years and modesty,
Plead on her part some cause to you unknown;
And doubt not, sir, but she will well excuse
Why at this time the doors are made[3] against you.
Be rul'd by me; depart in patience,
And let us to the Tiger all to dinner:
And, about evening, come yourself alone
To know the reason of this strange restraint.
If by strong hand you offer to break in,
Now in the stirring passage of the day,
A vulgar comment will be made of it;
And that supposed by the common rout
Against your yet ungalled estimation,
That may with foul intrusion enter in,
And dwell upon your grave when you are dead:
For slander lives upon succession;
For ever housed, where it gets possession.
Ant. E. You have prevail'd; I will depart in quiet,
And, in despite of mirth, mean to be merry.
I know a wench of excellent discourse,—
Pretty and witty; wild, and yet, too, gentle;
There will we dine: this woman that I mean,
My wife (but, I protest, without desert,)
Hath oftentimes upbraided me withal;
To her will we to dinner.—Get you home,
And fetch the chain; by this,[4] I know, 'tis made:
Bring it, I pray you, to the Porcupine;
For there's the house; that chain will I bestow
(Be it for nothing but to spite my wife)
Upon mine hostess there; good sir, make haste:
Since mine own doors refuse to entertain me,
I'll knock elsewhere, to see if they'll disdain me.
Ang. I'll meet you at that place, some hour hence.
Ant. E. Do so; this jest shall cost me some expense. [*Exeunt.*

SCENE II. *The same. Enter* LUCIANA, *and* ANTIPHOLUS *of* Syracuse.

Luc. And may it be that you have quite forgot
A husband's office? shall, Antipholus,
Even in the spring of love, thy love-strings rot?
Shall love, in building, grow so ruinous?[5]
If you did wed my sister for her wealth,
Then, for her wealth's sake, use her with more kindness:
Or, if you like elsewhere, do it by stealth;
Muffle your false love with some show of blindness:
Let not my sister read it in your eye;
Be not thy tongue thy own shame's orator,
Look sweet, speak fair, become disloyalty:
Apparel vice like virtue's harbinger:
Bear a fair presence, though your heart be tainted,
Teach sin the carriage of a holy saint:
Be secret-false; What need she be acquainted?
What simple thief brags of his own attaint?
'Tis double wrong, to truant with your bed,
And let her read it in thy looks at board:
Shame hath a bastard fame, well managed;
Ill deeds are doubled with an evil word.
Alas, poor women! make us but[6] believe,
Being compact of credit,[7] that you love us;
Though others have the arm, show us the sleeve;
We in your motion turn, and you may move us
Then, gentle brother, get you in again;
Comfort my sister, cheer her; call her wife:
'Tis holy sport, to be a little vain,[8]
When the sweet breath of flattery conquers strife.
Ant. S. Sweet mistress (what your name is else, I know not,
Nor by what wonder you do hit on mine,)
Less, in your knowledge and your grace, you show not,
Than our earth's wonder; more than earth divine.
Teach me, dear creature, how to think and speak;
Lay open to my earthly gross conceit,
Smother'd in errors, feeble, shallow, weak,
The folded meaning of your words' deceit.
Against my soul's pure truth why labour you,
To make it wander in an unknown field?
Are you a god? would you create me new?
Transform me, then, and to your power I'll yield.
But if that I am I, then well I know,
Your weeping sister is no wife of mine,
Nor to her bed no homage do I owe;
Far more, far more to you do I decline.[9]
O, train me not, sweet mermaid,[10] with thy note,
To drown me in thy sister's flood of tears;
Sing, siren, for thyself, and I will dote:
Spread o'er the silver waves thy golden hairs,[11]
And as a bed[12] I'll take thee, and there lie;
And, in that glorious supposition, think
He gains by death, that hath such means to die:—
Let love, being light, be drowned if she sink![13]
Luc. What, are you mad, that you do reason so?
Ant. S. Not mad, but mated;[14] how I do not know.
Luc. It is a fault that springeth from your eye.
Ant. S. For gazing on your beams, fair sun, being by.
Luc. Gaze where you should, and that will clear your sight.
Ant. S. As good to wink, sweet love, as look on night.
Luc. Why call you me love? call my sister so.
Ant. S. Thy sister's sister.
Luc. That's my sister.
Ant. S. No,
It is thyself, mine own self's better part;
Mine eye's clear eye, my dear heart's dearer heart;
My food, my fortune, and my sweet hope's aim;[15]
My sole earth's heaven, and my heaven's claim.
Luc. All this my sister is, or else should be.

---

1 The same quibble is to be found in one of the comedies of Plautus. Children of distinction among the Greeks and Romans had usually birds given them for their amusement. This custom Tyndarus, in The Captives, mentions, and says that, for his part, he had *tantum upupam. Upupa* signifies both a *lapwing* and a *mattock*, or some instrument with which stone was dug from the quarries.

2 *Once* this, here means *once for all; at once.*

3 i. e. made fast. The expression is still in use in some countries.

4 By this time.

5 In the old copy the first four lines stand thus:—
'And may it be that you have quite forgot
A husband's office? shall, Antipholus,
Even in the spring of love, thy love-springs rot?
Shall love in *buildings* grow so *ruinate*?'
The present emendation was proposed by Steevens, though he admitted Theobald's into his own text. *Love-springs* are the *buds of love*, or rather the young *shoots*. 'The *spring*, or young shoots that grow out of the stems or roots of trees.'—*Baret.*

6 Old copy, *not.*

7 i. e. being *made* altogether of credulity.

8 *Vain* is light of tongue.

9 'To *decline;* to turne or hang *toward* some place or thing.'—*Baret.*

10 Mermaid for siren.

11 So in Macbeth:—
'His *silver* skin laced with his *golden* blood'

12 The first folio reads:—
'And as a *bud* I'll take thee, and there lie;'
Which Malone thus explains:—'I, like an insect, will take thy bosom for a rose, or other flower,' and there
'"Involv'd in fragrance, burn and die."'

13 Malone says that by *love* here is meant the *queen of love.*

14 *Mated* means *matched with a wife*, and *confounded.* A quibble is intended.

15 i. e. all the happiness I wish for on earth, and all that I claim from heaven hereafter.

Ant. S. Call thyself sister, sweet, for I aim[1] thee:
Thee will I love, and with thee lead my life;
Thou hast no husband yet, nor I no wife:
Give me thy hand.

Luc. O, soft, sir, hold you still;
I'll fetch my sister, to get her good will. [*Exit* Luc.

Enter, from the House of Antipholus *of* Ephesus, Dromio *of* Syracuse.

Ant S. Why, how now, Dromio? where run'st thou so fast?

Dro. S. Do you know me, sir? am I Dromio? am I your man? am I myself?

Ant. S. Thou art Dromio, thou art my man, thou art thyself.

Dro. S. I am an ass, I am a woman's man, and besides myself.

Ant. S. What woman's man? and how besides thyself?

Dro S. Marry, sir, besides myself, I am due to a woman: one that claims me, one that haunts me, one that will have me.

Ant. S. What claim lays she to thee?

Dro. S. Marry, sir, such claim as you would lay to your horse; and she would have me as a beast; not that, I being a beast, she would have me; but that she, being a very beastly creature, lays claim to me.

Ant. S. What is she?

Dro. S. A very reverend body; ay, such a one as a man may not speak of, without he say, sir-reverence:[2] I have but lean luck in the match, and yet is she a wondrous fat marriage.

Ant. S. How dost thou mean, a fat marriage?

Dro. S. Marry, sir, she's the kitchen wench, and all grease; and I know not what use to put her to, but to make a lamp of her, and run from her by her own light. I warrant, her rags, and the tallow in them, will burn a Poland winter: if she lives till doomsday, she'll burn a week longer than the whole world.

Ant. S. What complexion is she of?

Dro. S. Swart,[3] like my shoe, but her face, nothing like so clean kept: For why? she sweats, a man may go over shoes in the grime of it.

Ant. S. That's a fault that water will mend.

Dro. S. No, sir, 'tis in grain: Noah's flood could not do it.

Ant. S. What's her name?

Dro. S. Nell, sir;—but her name and three quarters, that is, an ell and three quarters, will not measure her from hip to hip.[4]

Ant. S. Then she bears some breadth?

Dro. S. No longer from head to foot, than from hip to hip; she is spherical, like a globe; I could find out countries in her.

Ant. S. In what part of her body stands Ireland?

Dro. S. Marry, sir, in her buttocks; I found it out by the bogs.

Ant. S. Where Scotland?

Dro. S. I found it by the barrenness; hard, in the palm of the hand.[5]

Ant. S. Where France?

Dro. S. In her forehead; arm'd and reverted, making war against her heir.[6]

Ant. S. Where England?

Dro. S. I look'd for the chalky cliffs, but I could find no whiteness in them; but I guess it stood in her chin, by the salt rheum that run between France and it.

Ant. S. Where Spain?

Dro. S. 'Faith, I saw it not; but I felt it hot in her breath.

Ant. S. Where America, the Indies?

Dro. S. O, sir, upon her nose, all o'er embellish'd with rubies, carbuncles, sapphires, declining their rich aspect to the hot breath of Spain; who sent whole armadas of carracks[7] to be ballast at her nose.

Ant. S. Where stood Belgia, the Netherlands?

Dro. S. O, sir, I did not look so low. To conclude, this drudge, or diviner, laid claim to me; call'd me Dromio, swore I was assur'd[8] to her; told me what privy marks I had about me, as the mark on my shoulder, the mole in my neck, the great wart on my left arm, that I, amazed, ran from her as a witch: and, I think, if my breast had not been made of faith,[9] and my heart of steel, she had transform'd me to a curtail-dog, and made me turn i' the wheel.[10]

Ant. S. Go, hie thee presently, post to the road;
And if the wind blow any way from shore,
I will not harbour in this town to-night.
If any bark put forth, come to the mart,
Where I will walk, till thou return to me.
If every one knows us, and we know none,
'Tis time, I think, to trudge, pack, and be gone.

Dro. S. As from a bear a man would run for life,
So fly I from her that would be my wife. [*Exit.*

Ant. S. There's none but witches do inhabit here;
And therefore 'tis high time that I were hence.
She that doth call me husband, even my soul
Doth for a wife abhor; but her fair sister,
Possess'd with such gentle sovereign grace,
Of such enchanting presence and discourse,
Hath almost made me traitor to myself:
But, lest myself be guilty to[11] self-wrong,
I'll stop my ears against the mermaid's song.

Enter Angelo.

Ang. Master Antipholus?

Ant. S. Ay, that's my name.

Ang. I know it well, sir: Lo, here is the chain,
I thought to have ta'en you at the Porcupine:[12]
The chain unfinish'd made me stay thus long.

Ant. S. What is your will, that I shall do with this?

Ang. What, please yourself, sir: I have made it for you.

Ant. S. Made it for me, sir! I bespoke it not.

Ang. Not once nor twice, but twenty times you have:
Go home with it, and please your wife withal;
And soon at supper-time I'll visit you,
And then receive my money for the chain.

---

1 The old copy reads I *am* thee. The present reading is Steevens'. Others have proposed I *mean* thee; but *aim* for *aim at* was sometimes used.

2 This is a very old corruption of *save* reverence, *salva reverentia*. See Blount's Glossography, 1682.

3 *Swart*, or swarth, i. e. *dark, dusky*, infuscus.

4 This poor conundrum is borrowed by Massinger in The Old Law.

5 Had this play been revived after the accession of James, it is probable this passage would have been struck out; as was that relative to the Scotch lord in The Merchant of Venice, Act i. Sc. 1.

6 'An equivoque,' says Theobald, 'is intended. In 1589, Henry III. of France, being stabbed, was succeeded by Henry IV. of Navarre, whom he had appointed his successor; but whose claim the states of France resisted on account of his being a protestant. This I take to be what is meant by France making war against her heir Elizabeth had sent over the Earl of Essex with four thousand men to the assistance of Henry of Navarre, in 1591. This oblique sneer at France was therefore a compliment to the poet's royal mistress.' The other allusion is not of a nature to admit of explanation.

7 *Carracks*, large ships of burthen; *caraca*, Spanish *Ballast* is merely a contraction of *ballassed*; to *balass* being the old authography: as we write *drest* for *dressed*, *embost* for *embossed*, *&c.*

8 i. e. Affianced.

9 Alluding to the popular belief that a great share of *faith* was a protection from witchcraft.

10 A turnspit.

11 Pope, not understanding sufficiently the phraseology of Shakspeare, altered this to guilty *of* self-wrong. But guilty *to* was the construction of that age.

12 Porcupine throughout the old editions of these plays is written *porpentine*. I find it written *porpun* in an old phrase book, called Hormanni Vulgaria, 1519, thus: '*Porpyns* have longer prickles than Yrchins.'

Ant. S. I pray you, sir, receive the money now,
For fear you ne'er see chain, nor money, more.

Ang. You are a merry man, sir; fare you well. [*Exit.*

Ant. S. What I should think of this, I cannot tell;
But this I think, there's no man is so vain,
That would refuse so fair an offer'd chain.
I see, a man here needs not live by shifts,
When in the streets he meets such golden gifts.
I'll to the mart, and there for Dromio stay;
If any ship put out, then straight away. [*Exit.*

ACT IV.

SCENE I. *The same. Enter a* Merchant, ANGELO, *and an* Officer.

Mer. You know, since Pentecost the sum is due,
And since I have not much importun'd you;
Nor now I had not, but that I am bound
To Persia, and want gilders for my voyage:
Therefore make present satisfaction,
Or I'll attach you by this officer.

Ang. Even just the sum, that I do owe to you,
Is growing[1] to me by Antipholus:
And in the instant that I met with you,
He had of me a chain; at five o'clock,
I shall receive the money for the same:
Pleaseth you walk with me down to his house,
I will discharge my bond, and thank you too.

Enter ANTIPHOLUS *of* Ephesus, *and* DROMIO *of* Ephesus, *from the Courtezan's.*

Off. That labour may you save; see where he comes.

Ant. E. While I go to the goldsmith's house, go thou
And buy a rope's end; that will I bestow
Among my wife and her[2] confederates,
For locking me out of my doors by day.—
But soft, I see the goldsmith:—get thee gone:
Buy thou a rope, and bring it home to me.

Dro. E. I buy a thousand pound a year! I buy rope! [*Exit* DROMIO.

Ant. E. A man is well holp up, that trusts to you.
I promised your presence, and the chain;
But neither chain, nor goldsmith came to me:
Belike, you thought our love would last too long,
If it were chain'd together; and therefore came not.

Ang. Saving your merry humour, here's the note,
How much your chain weighs to the utmost carat;
The fineness of the gold, and chargeful fashion;
Which doth amount to three odd ducats more
Than I stand indebted to this gentleman;
I pray you, see him presently discharg'd,
For he is bound to sea, and stays but for it.

Ant. E. I am not furnish'd with the present money;
Besides, I have some business in the town:
Good signior, take the stranger to my house,
And with you take the chain, and bid my wife
Disburse the sum on the receipt thereof;
Perchance, I will[3] be there as soon as you.

Ang. Then you will bring the chain to her yourself?

Ant. E. No! bear it with you, lest I come not time enough.

Ang. Well, sir, I will: Have you the chain about you?

Ant. E. An if I have not, sir, I hope you have:
Or else you may return without your money.

Ang. Nay, come, I pray you, sir, give me the chain;
Both wind and tide stays for this gentleman,
And I, to blame, have held him here too long.

Ant. E. Good lord, you use this dalliance, to excuse
Your breach of promise to the Porcupine:
I should have chid you for not bringing it,
But, like a shrew, you first begin to brawl.

Mer. The hour steals on; I pray you, sir, despatch.

Ang. You hear how he importunes me; the chain—

Ant. E. Why, give it to my wife, and fetch your money.

Ang. Come, come, you know, I gave it you even now;
Either send the chain, or send by me some token.[4]

Ant. E. Fie! now you run this humour out of breath:
Come, where's the chain? I pray you let me see it.

Mer. My business cannot brook this dalliance;
Good sir, say, whe'r you'll answer me, or no;
If not, I'll leave him to the officer.

Ant. E. I answer you! What should I answer you?

Ang. The money, that you owe me for the chain.

Ant. E. I owe you none, till I receive the chain.

Ang. You know, I gave it you half an hour since.

Ant. E. You gave me none; you wrong me much to say so.

Ang. You wrong me more, sir, in denying it:
Consider, how it stands upon my credit.

Mer. Well, officer, arrest him at my suit.

Off. I do; and charge you in the duke's name to obey me.

Ang. This touches me in reputation:
Either consent to pay this sum for me,
Or I attach you by this officer.

Ant. E. Consent to pay thee that I never had!
Arrest me, foolish fellow, if thou dar'st.

Ang. Here is thy fee; arrest him, officer,
I would not spare my brother in this case,
If he should scorn me so apparently.

Off. I do arrest you, sir, you hear the suit.

Ant. E. I do obey thee, till I give thee bail:
But, sirrah, you shall buy this sport as dear
As all the metal in your shop will answer.

Ang. Sir, sir, I shall have law in Ephesus,
To your notorious shame, I doubt it not.

Enter DROMIO *of* Syracuse.

Dro. S. Master, there is a bark of Epidamnum,
That stays but till her owner comes aboard,
And then, sir, she bears away: our fraughtage,[5] sir,
I have convey'd aboard: and I have bought
The oil, the balsamum, and aqua-vitæ.
The ship is in her trim; the merry wind
Blows fair from land: they stay for naught at all,
But for their owner, master, and yourself.

Ant. E. How now! a madman! Why thou peevish[6] sheep,
What ship of Epidamnum stays for me?

Dro. S. A ship you sent me to, to hire waftage.[7]

Ant. E. Thou drunken slave, I sent thee for a rope,
And told thee to what purpose and what end.

Dro. S. You sent me for a rope's end as soon:
You sent me to the bay, sir, for a bark.

Ant. E. I will debate this matter at more leisure,
And teach your ears to list me with more heed.
To Adriana, villain, hie thee straight:
Give her this key, and tell her, in the desk,
That's cover'd o'er with Turkish tapestry,

---

1 i. e. accruing.

2 The old copy reads *their.*

3 *I will* for *I shall* is a Scotticism; but it is not unfrequent in old writers on this side of the Tweed.

4 Malone has a very long note on this passage, in which he says: 'it was not Angelo's meaning, that Antipholus of Ephesus should send a *jewel* or other token *by him*, but that Antipholus should send him with a verbal token to his wife, by which it might be ascertained that he came from Antipholus: and that she might safely pay the price of the chain [illegible] in the name of common sense, what does this prove?—Can it signify whether the token Angelo wishes Antipholus to send *by him* was to be *verbal* or *material? Tokens* were common in Shakspeare's time of many kinds; there were *tavern tokens*, which were counters of lead or leather. There were *written tokens* or *billes*, as they were then called, 'given to men by which they might receive a certain sum of money,' &c. Such a one Angelo probably requires.

5 Freight, cargo.

6 *Peevish* was used for *mad*, or *foolish.*

7 [illegible] e carriage: *hire* is here a dissyllable, and is spelt *hier* in the old copy.

There is a purse of ducats: let her send it;
Tell her I am arrested in the street,
And that shall bail me: hie thee, slave; be gone.
On, officer, to prison, till it come.
[*Exeunt* Mer. ANG. Officer, *and* ANT. E.

Dro. S. To Adriana! that is where we din'd,
Where Dowsabel did claim me for her husband:
She is too big, I hope, for me to compass.
Thither I must, although against my will,
For servants must their master's minds fulfil. [*Exit.*

SCENE II. *The same. Enter* ADRIANA, *and* LUCIANA.

Adr. Ah, Luciana, did he tempt thee so?
Might'st thou perceive austerely in his eye
That he did plead in earnest, yea or no?
Look'd he or red, or pale; or sad, or merrily?
What observation mad'st thou in this case,
Of his heart's meteors tilting in his face?[1]

Luc. First, he denied you had in him no right.[2]

Adr. He meant, he did me none; the more my spite.

Luc. Then swore he, that he was a stranger here.

Adr. And true he swore, though yet forsworn he were.

Luc. Then pleaded I for you.

Adr. And what said he?

Luc. That love I begg'd for you, he begg'd of me.

Adr. With what persuasion did he tempt thy love?

Luc. With words, that in an honest suit might move.
First, he did praise my beauty; then my speech.

Adr. Did'st speak him fair?

Luc. Have patience, I beseech.

Adr. I cannot, nor I will not, hold me still;
My tongue, though not my heart, shall have his will.
He is deformed, crooked, old, and sere,[3]
Ill-fac'd, worse-bodied, shapeless every where;
Vicious, ungentle, foolish, blunt, unkind;
Stigmatical in making,[4] worse in mind.

Luc. Who would be jealous then of such a one?
No evil lost is wail'd when it is gone.

Adr. Ah! but I think him better than I say,
And yet would herein others' eyes were worse:
Far from her nest the lapwing cries away;[5]
My heart prays for him, though my tongue do curse.

Enter DROMIO *of* Syracuse.

Dro. S. Here, go; the desk, the purse; sweet now, make haste.

Luc. How hast thou lost thy breath?

Dro. S. By running fast.

Adr. Where is thy master, Dromio? is he well?

Dro. S. No, he's in tartar-limbo, worse than hell:
A devil in an everlasting garment[6] hath him,
One, whose hard heart is button'd up with steel;
A fiend, a fairy,[7] pitiless and rough;
A wolf, nay worse, a fellow all in buff;
A back-friend, a shoulder-clapper, one that countermands
The passages of alleys, creeks, and narrow lands;[8]
A hound that runs counter, and yet draws dry-foot well;[9]
One that, before the judgment, carries poor souls to hell.[10]

Adr. Why man, what is the matter?

Dro. S. I do not know the matter: he is 'rested on the case.

Adr. What, is he arrested? tell me at whose suit?

Dro. S. I know not at whose suit he is arrested, well;
But is[11] in a suit of buff, which 'rested him, that can I tell:
Will you send him, mistress, redemption, the money in his desk?

Adr. Go fetch it, sister.—This I wonder at,
[*Exit* LUCIANA.
That he, unknown to me, should be in debt:
Tell me, was he arrested on a band?[12]

Dro. S. Not on a band, but on a stronger thing;
A chain, a chain; do you not hear it ring?

Adr. What, the chain?

Dro. S. No, no, the bell: 'tis time that I were gone
It was two ere I left him, and now the clock strikes one.

Adr. The hours come back! that did I never hear.

Dro. S. O yes: If any hour meet a sergeant, a' turns back for very fear.

Adr. As if time were in debt! how fondly dost thou reason?

Dro. S. Time is a very bankrupt, and owes more than he's worth to season.
Nay, he's a thief too: Have you not heard men say,
That time comes stealing on by night and day?
If he[13] be in debt, and theft, and a sergeant in the way,
Hath he not reason to turn back an hour in a day?

Enter LUCIANA.

Adr. Go, Dromio; there's the money, bear it straight;
And bring thy master home immediately.—
Come, sister: I am press'd down with conceit;[14]
Conceit, my comfort, and my injury. [*Exeunt.*

SCENE III. *The same. Enter* ANTIPHOLUS *of* Syracuse.

Ant. S. There's not a man I meet, but doth salute me
As if I were their well acquainted friend;[15]
And every one doth call me by my name.
Some tender money to me, some invite me,
Some other give me thanks for kindnesses;
Some offer me commodities to buy:
Even now a tailor call'd me in his shop,
And show'd me silks that he had bought for me,
And, therewithal, took measure of my body.
Sure, these are but imaginary wiles,
And Lapland sorcerers inhabit here.

Enter DROMIO *of* Syracuse.

Dro. S. Master, here's the gold you sent me for:
What, have you got the picture of old Adam new apparell'd?[16]

---

1 The allusion is to those meteors which have sometimes been thought to resemble armies meeting in the shock of battle. The following comparison in the second book of Paradise Lost best explains it:
'As when to warn proud cities, war appears
Wag'd in the troubled sky, and armies rush
To battle in the clouds, before each van
Prick forth the aery knights, and couch their spears,
Till thickest legions close; with feats of arms
From either end of heaven the welkin burns.'

2 This double negative had the force of a stronger asseveration in the phraseology of that age.

3 Dry, withered.

4 *Marked* or *stigmatized* by nature with deformity.

5 This expression, which appears to have been proverbial, is again alluded to in Measure for Measure, Act i. Sc. 5.

6 The *buff* or leather jerkin of the sergeant is called an *everlasting garment*, because it was so durable.

7 Theobald would read a *fury*; but a *fairy*, in Shakspeare's time, sometimes meant a *malevolent sprite*, and coupled as it is with pitiless and rough, the meaning is clear.

8 The first folio reads, *lans*. Shakspeare would have put *lanes* but for the sake of the rhyme.

9 'To hunt or run *counter*, signifies that the hounds or beagles hunt it by the heel,' i. e. run backward, mistaking the course of the game. To *draw dry foot* was to follow the scent or track of the game. There is a quibble upon *counter*, which points at the *prison* so called.

10 *Hell* was the cant term for prison. There was a place of this name under the Exchequer, where the king's debtors were confined.

11 Thus the old authentic copy. The omission of the personal pronoun was formerly very common: we should now write *he's*.

12 i. e. a *bond*. Shakspeare takes advantage of the old spelling to produce a quibble.

13 The old copy reads, 'If *I*,' &c.

14 Fanciful conception.

15 This actually happened to Sir H. Wotton when on his travels. See Reliquiæ Wottonianæ, 1685, p. 676.

16 Theobald reads, 'What, have you *got rid* of the picture of old Adam?' The emendation is approved and

Ant. S. What gold is this? what Adam dost thou mean?

Dro. S. Not that Adam, that kept the paradise, but that Adam that keeps the prison: he that goes in the calf's-skin that was kill'd for the prodigal: he that came behind you, sir, like an evil angel, and bid you forsake your liberty.

Ant. S. I understand thee not.

Dro. S. No? why, 'tis a plain case: he that went like a base-viol, in a case of leather; the man, sir, that, when gentlemen are tired, gives them a fob, and 'rests them; he, sir, that takes pity on decayed men, and gives them suits of durance; he that sets up his rest[1] to do more expolits with his mace than a morris-pike.[2]

Ant. S. What! thou mean'st an officer?

Dro. S. Ay, sir, the sergeant of the band; he, that brings any man to answer it, that breaks his band: one that thinks a man always going bed, and says, *God give you good rest.*

Ant. S. Well, sir, there rest in your foolery. Is there any ship puts forth to night? may we begone?

Dro. S. Why, sir, I brought you word an hour since, that the bark Expedition put forth to night; and then were you hindered by the sergeant, to tarry for the hoy Delay; Here are the angels that you sent for, to deliver you.

Ant. S. The fellow is distract, and so am I;
And here we wander in illusions;
Some blessed power deliver us from hence!

Enter a Courtezan.

Cour. Well met, well met, master Antipholus.
I see, sir, you have found the goldsmith now;
Is that the chain, you promis'd me to-day?

Ant. S. Satan, avoid! I charge thee tempt me not:

Dro. S. Master, is this mistress Satan?

Ant. S. It is the devil.

Dro. S. Nay, she is worse, she is the devil's dam; and here she comes in the habit of a light wench; and thereof comes, that the wenches say, *God damn me*, that's as much as to say, *God make me a light wench*. It is written, they appear to men like angels of light: light is an effect of fire, and fire will burn; *ergo*, light wenches will burn; Come not near her.

Cour. Your man and you are marvellous merry, sir.
Will you go with me? We'll mend our dinner here.[3]

Dro. S. Master, if you do, expect spoon-meat, or bespeak a long spoon.[4]

Ant. S. Why, Dromio?

Dro. S. Marry, he must have a long spoon, that must eat with the devil.

Ant. S. Avoid then, fiend! what tell'st thou me of supping?
Thou art, as you are all, a sorceress:
I conjure thee to leave me, and be gone.

Cour. Give me the ring of mine you had at dinner,
Or, for my diamond, the chain you promis'd;
And I'll be gone, sir, and not trouble you.

Dro. S. Some devil's ask but the parings of one's nail,
A rush, a hair, a drop of blood,[5] a pin,
A nut, a cherry-stone: but she, more covetous,
Would have a chain.
Master, be wise; an if you give it her,
The devil will shake her chain, and fright us with it.

Cour. I pray you, sir, my ring, or else the chain;
I hope you do not mean to cheat me so.

Ant. S. Avaunt, thou witch! Come, Dromio, let us go.

Dro. S. Fly, pride, says the peacock: Mistress that you know. [*Exeunt* ANT. *and* DRO.

Cour. Now out of doubt, Antipholus is mad,
Else would he never so demean himself:
A ring he hath of mine worth forty ducats,
And for the same he promis'd me a chain!
Both one, and other, he denies me now.
The reason that I gather he is mad
(Besides this present instance of his rage,)
Is a mad tale, he told to-day at dinner,
Of his own doors being shut against his entrance.
Belike, his wife, acquainted with his fits,
On purpose shut the doors against his way.
My way is now, to hie home to his house,
And tell his wife, that, being lunatic,
He rush'd into my house, and took perforce
My ring away: This course I fittest choose
For forty ducats is too much to lose. [*Exit.*

SCENE IV. *The same. Enter* ANTIPHOLUS *of* Ephesus, *and an* Officer.

Ant. E. Fear me not man, I will not break away,
I'll give thee, ere I leave thee, so much money
To warrant thee, as I am 'rested for.
My wife is in a wayward mood to-day;
And will not lightly trust the messenger,
That I should be attach'd in Ephesus:
I tell you, it will sound harshly in her ears.—

Enter DROMIO *of* Ephesus *with a rope's end.*

Here comes my man; I think, he brings the money.
How now, sir? have you that I sent you for?

Dro. E. Here's that, I warrant you, will pay them all.[6]

Ant. E. But where's the money?

Dro. E. Why, sir, I gave the money for the rope.

Ant. E. Five hundred ducats, villain, for a rope?

Dro. E. I'll serve you, sir, five hundred at the rate.

Ant. E. To what end did I bid thee hie thee home?

Dro. E. To a rope's end, sir: and to that end am I return'd.

Ant. E. And to that end, sir, I will welcome you. [*Beating him.*

Off. Good sir, be patient.

Dro. E. Nay, 'tis for me to be patient; I am in adversity.

Off. Good now, hold thy tongue.

Dro. E. Nay, rather persuade him to hold his hands.

Ant. E. Thou whoreson, senseless villain!

Dro. E. I would I were senseles, sir, that I might not feel your blows.

Ant. E. Thou art sensible in nothing but blows, and so is an ass.

Dro. E. I am an ass indeed; you may prove it by my long ears.[7] I have served him from the hour of my nativity to this instant, and have nothing at his hands for my service, but blows: when I am cold, he heats me with beating: when I am warm, he cools me with beating: I am waked with it, when I sleep; raised with it, when I sit; driven out of doors with it, when I go from home; welcomed home with it, when I return: nay, I bear it on my shoulders, as a beggar wont her brat; and, I think, when he hath lamed me, I shall beg with it from door to door.

Enter ADRIANA, LUCIANA, *and the* Courtezan, *with* PINCH[8] *and others.*

Ant. E. Come, go along; my wife is coming yonder.

adopted by Malone; but I think, with Johnson, that the text does not require interpolation.

1 This unfortunate phrase is again mistaken here by all the commentators. It has nothing to do with a *musket rest;* and the *rest of a pike* is a thing of the imagination. It is a metaphorical expression for being *determined, or resolutely bent to do a thing*, taken from the game of Primero.

2 A *morris pike* is a *moorish pike*, commonly used in the 16th century. It was not used in the morris dance, as Johnson erroneously supposed.

3 Probably by purchasing something additional in the adjoining market

4 This proverb is alluded to again in the Tempest, Act ii. Sc. 2, p. 50:—'He who eats with the devil had need of a long spoon.'

5 In the Witch, by Middleton, when a spirit descends, Hecate exclaims:

'There's one come down to fetch his dues,
A kisse, a coll, a sip of blood,' &c.

6 i. e. punish them all by corporal correction. Falstaff says, in King Henry IV. Part 1, 'I have pepper'd the rogues; two of them, I'm sure, I've *pay'd.*'

7 *Long* from frequent pulling.

8 In the old copy—'and a *schoolmaster* called

Dro. E. Mistress, *respice finem*,[1] respect your end; or rather the prophecy, like the parrot, *Beware the rope's end.*

Ant. E. Wilt thou still talk? [*Beats him.*

Cour. How say you now? is not your husband mad?

Adr. His incivility confirms no less.—
Good doctor Pinch, you are a conjuror;
Establish him in his true sense again,
And I will please you what you will demand.

Luc. Alas, how fiery and how sharp he looks!

Cour. Mark, how he trembles in his ecstacy![2]

Pinch. Give me your hand, and let me feel your pulse.

Ant. E. There is my hand and let it feel your ear.

Pinch. I charge thee, Satan, hous'd within this man,
To yield possession to my holy prayers,
And to thy state of darkness hie thee straight;
I conjure thee by all the saints in heaven.

Ant. E. Peace, doting wizard, peace; I am not mad.

Adr. O, that thou wert not, poor distressed soul!

Ant. E. You minion, you, are these your customers?[3]
Did this companion,[4] with a saffron face
Revel and feast it at my house to-day,
Whilst upon me the guilty doors were shut,
And I denied to enter in my house?

Adr. O, husband, God doth know you din'd at home,
Where 'would, you had remain'd until this time,
Free from these slanders, and this open shame!

Ant. E. Din'd at home! Thou villain, what say'st thou?

Dro. E. Sir, sooth to say, you did not dine at home.

Ant. E. Were not my doors lock'd up, and I shut out?

Dro. E. Perdy,[5] your doors were lock'd, and you shut out.

Ant. E. And did not she herself revile me there?

Dro. E. Sans fable, she herself revil'd you there.

Ant. E. Did not her kitchen maid rail, taunt, and scorn me?

Dro. E. Certes, she did; the kitchen-vestal scorn'd you.

Ant. E. And did not I in rage depart from thence?

Dro. E. In verity you did;—my bones bear witness,
That since have felt the vigour of his rage.

Adr. Is't good to sooth him in these contraries?

Pinch. It is no shame; the fellow finds his vein,
And, yielding to him, humours well his frenzy.

Ant. E. Thou hast suborn'd the goldsmith to arrest me.

Adr. Alas, I sent you money to redeem you,
By Dromio here, who came in haste for it.

Dro. E. Money by me? heart and good-will you might,
But, surely, master, not a rag of money.

Ant. E. Went'st not thou to her for a purse of ducats?

Adr. He came to me, and I deliver'd it.

Luc. And I am witness with her, that she did.

Dro. E. God and the rope-maker, bear me witness,
That I was sent for nothing but a rope!

Pinch. Mistress, both man and master is possess'd;
I know it by their pale and deadly looks:
They must be bound and laid in some dark room.

Ant. E. Say, wherefore didst thou lock me forth to-day,
And why dost thou deny the bag of gold?

Adr. I did not, gentle husband, lock thee forth.

Dro. E. And, gentle master, I receiv'd no gold
But I confess, sir, that we were lock'd out.

Adr. Dissembling villain, thou speak'st false in both.

Ant. E. Dissembling harlot, thou art false in all;
And art confederate with a damned pack,
To make a loathsome abject scorn of me:
But with these nails I'll pluck out these false eyes,
That would behold in me this shameful sport.

[Pinch *and his Assistants bind* Ant. *and* Dro.

Adr. O, bind him, bind him, let him not come near me.

Pinch. More company;—the fiend is strong within him.

Luc. Ah me, poor man, how pale and wan he looks!

Ant. E. What, will you murder me? Thou gaoler thou,
I am thy prisoner; wilt thou suffer them
To make a rescue?

Off. Masters, let him go;
He is my prisoner, and you shall not have him.

Pinch. Go, bind this man, for he is frantic too.

Adr. What wilt thou do, thou peevish[6] officer?
Hast thou delight to see a wretched man
Do outrage and displeasure to himself?

Off. He is my prisoner; if I let him go,
The debt he owes, will be requir'd of me.

Adr. I will discharge thee, ere I go from thee
Bear me forthwith unto his creditor,
And, knowing how the debt grows, I will pay it.
Good master doctor, see him safe convey'd
Home to my house.—O most unhappy day!

Ant. E. O most unhappy[7] strumpet!

Dro. E. Master, I am here enter'd in bond for you.

Ant. E. Out on thee, villain! wherefore dost thou mad me?

Dro. E. Will you be bound for nothing? be mad,
Good master; cry, the devil.—

Luc. God help, poor souls, how idly do they talk!

Adr. Go, bear him hence.—Sister, go you with me.—

[*Exeunt* Pinch *and Assistants with* Ant. *and* Dro.

Say now, whose suit is he arrested at?

Off. One Angelo, a goldsmith; Do you know him?

Adr. I know the man: What is the sum he owes?

Off. Two hundred ducats.

Adr. Say, how grows it due?

Off. Due for a chain, your husband had of him.

Adr. He did bespeak a chain for me, but had it not.

Cour. When as your husband, all in rage, to-day
Came to my house, and took away my ring
(The ring I saw upon his finger now,)
Straight after, did I meet him with a chain.

Adr. It may be so, but I did never see it:—
Come, gaoler, bring me where the goldsmith is,
I long to know the truth hereof at large.

Enter Antipholus *of* Syracuse, *with his rapier drawn, and* Dromio *of* Syracuse.

Luc. God, for thy mercy! they are loose again.

Adr. And come with naked swords; let's call more help,
To have them bound again.

Pinch.' As learning was necessary for an exorcist, the schoolmaster was often employed. Within a very few years, in country villages the pedagogue was still a reputed conjuror.

1 Buchanan wrote a pamphlet against the Lord of Liddington, which ends with these words: *respice finem, respice funem.* Shakspeare's quibble may be borrowed from this. The parrot's prophecy may be understood by means of the following lines in Hudibras:—

'Could tell what subtlest parrots mean,
That speak and think contrary clean;
What member 'tis of whom they talk,
When they cry *rope*, and *walk, knave, walk.*'

2 This *tremor* was anciently thought to be a sure indication of being possessed by the devil.

3 'A *customer*,' says Malone, 'is used in Othello for a common woman. Here it seems to signify one who visits such women.' It is surprising that a man like Malone, whose life had been devoted to the study and elucidation of Shakspeare, should so often seem ignorant of the language of the poet's time. 'A *customer* was a *familiar*, an *intimate*, a *customary haunter of any place*;' as any of the old dictionaries would have shown him under the word *consuetudo* or *custom.*

4 *Companion* is a word of contempt, anciently used as we now use *fellow.*

5 A corruption of the common French oath *par dieu*

6 Vide before, p. 345, note 6.

7 *Unhappy* for unlucky, i. e. mischievous.

Off. Away, they'll kill us.
[*Exeunt* Officer, ADR. *and* LUC.

Ant. S. I see these witches are afraid of swords.

Dro. S. She, that would be your wife, now ran from you.

Ant. S. Come to the Centaur; fetch our stuff[1] from thence:
I long, that we were safe and sound aboard.

Dro. S. Faith, stay here this night, they will surely do us no harm; you saw, they speak us fair, give us gold: methinks, they are such a gentle nation, that but for the mountain of mad flesh that claims marriage of me, I could find in my heart to stay here still, and turn witch.

Ant. S. I will not stay to-night for all the town;
Therefore away, to get our stuff aboard. [*Exeunt.*

ACT. V.

SCENE I. *The same.* *Enter* Merchant and ANGELO.

Ang. I am sorry, sir, that I have hinder'd you;
But, I protest, he had the chain of me,
Though most dishonestly he doth deny it.

Mer. How is the man esteem'd here in the city?

Ang. Of very reverend reputation, sir,
Of credit infinite, highly belov'd,
Second to none that lives here in the city;
His word might bear my wealth at any time.

Mer. Speak softly: yonder, as I think, he walks.

Enter ANTIPHOLUS *and* DROMIO *of* Syracuse.

Ang. Tis so; and that self chain about his neck,
Which he forswore, most monstrously, to have.
Good sir, draw near to me, I'll speak to him.
Signior Antipholus, I wonder much
That you would put me to this shame and trouble;
And not without some scandal to yourself,
With circumstance, and oaths, so to deny
This chain, which now you wear so openly:
Besides the charge, the shame, imprisonment,
You have done wrong to this my honest friend;
Who, but for staying on our controversy,
Had hoisted sail, and put to sea to-day:
This chain you had of me, can you deny it?

Ant. S. I think, I had; I never did deny it.

Mer. Yes, that you did, sir; and forswore it too.

Ant. S. Who heard me to deny it, or forswear it?

Mer. These ears of mine, thou knowest, did hear thee:
Fie on thee, wretch! 'tis a pity, that thou liv'st
To walk where any honest men resort.

Ant. S. Thou art a villain to impeach me thus:
I'll prove mine honour and mine honesty
Against thee presently, if thou dar'st stand.

Mer. I dare, and do defy thee for a villain.
[*They draw.*

Enter ADRIANA, LUCIANA, Courtezan, *and others.*

Adr. Hold, hurt him not, for God's sake; he is mad;—
Some get within him,[2] take his sword away:
Bind Dromio too, and bear them to my house.

Dro. S. Run, master, run; for God's sake take a house.[3]
This is some priory;—In, or we are spoil'd.
[*Exeunt* ANTIPH. *and* DRO. *to the Priory.*

Enter the Abbess.

Abb. Be quiet, people; Wherefore throng you hither?

Adr. To fetch my poor distracted husband, hence
Let us come in, that we may bind him fast,
And bear him home for his recovery.

Ang. I knew he was not in his perfect wits.

Mer. I am sorry now, that I did draw on him

Abb. How long hath this possession held the man?

Adr. This week he hath been heavy, sour, sad,
And much different from the man he was;
But, till this afternoon, his passion
Ne'er brake into extremity of rage.

Abb. Hath he not lost much wealth by wreck of sea?
Buried some dear friend? Hath not else his eye
Stray'd his affection in unlawful love?
A sin, prevailing much in youthful men,
Who give their eyes the liberty of gazing.
Which of these sorrows is he subject to?

Adr. To none of these, except it be the last,
Namely, some love, that drew him oft from home.

Abb. You should for that have reprehended him.

Adr. Why, so I did.

Abb. Ay, but not rough enough.

Adr. As roughly, as my modesty would let me.

Abb. Haply, in private.

Adr. And in assemblies too.

Abb. Ay, but not enough.

Adr. It was the copy[4] of our conference
In bed, he slept not for my urging it;
At board, he fed not for my urging it,
Alone, it was the subject of my theme;
In company, I often glanced it;
Still did I tell him it was vile and bad.

Abb. And therefore came it that the man was mad:
The venom clamours of a jealous woman
Poison more deadly than a mad dog's tooth.
It seems his sleeps were hinder'd by thy railing:
And therefore comes it that his head is light.
Thou say'st his meat was sauc'd with thy upbraidings:
Unquiet meals make ill digestions,
Thereof the raging fire of fever bred;
And what's a fever but a fit of madness?
Thou say'st his sports were hinder'd by thy brawls;
Sweet recreation barr'd, what doth ensue,
But moody and dull melancholy,
(Kinsman to grim and comfortless despair;)
And, at her heels, a huge infectious troop[5]
Of pale distemperatures and foes to life?
In food, in sport, and life-preserving rest
To be disturb'd, would mad or man or beast;
The consequence is then, thy jealous fits
Have scar'd thy husband from the use of wits.

Luc. She never reprehended him but mildly,
When he demean'd himself rough, rude, and wildly.
Why bear you these rebukes, and answer not?

Adr. She did betray me to my own reproof.—
Good people, enter, and lay hold on him.

Abb. No, not a creature enters in my house.

Adr. Then, let your servants bring my husband forth.

Abb. Neither: he took this place for sanctuary,
And it shall privilege him from your hands,
Till I have brought him to his wits again,
Or lose my labour in assaying it.

Adr. I will attend my husband, be his nurse,
Diet his sickness, for it is my office,

---

1 i. e. baggage. *Stuff* is the genuine old English word for all moveables.

2 i. e. close, grapple with him.

3 i. e. go into a house: we still say that a dog *takes* the water

4 'The *copy*,' says Steevens, 'that is the *theme*. We still talk of setting *copies* for boys!' Surely a boy's *copy* is not a *theme?* and that word occurs again in the fourth line of this speech. 'Our poet frequently uses *copy* for *pattern*,' says Malone. So in Twelfth Night: —'And leave the world no *copy*.' I believe Malone's *frequently* may be reduced to *two* other instances, one in Henry V. and another in a sonnet. I am persuaded that *copy* in the present instance neither means *theme* nor *pattern*, but *copie*, *plenty*, *copious source*, an old latinism, many times used by Ben Johnson. The word is spelt *copie* in the folio; and in King Henry V. where it means *pattern*, *example*, it is spelt *copy*. But the sense of the passage here will show that my interpretation is right.

5 I think that there is no doubt that this passage has suffered by incorrect printing; I am not satisfied with it, even with the parenthesis in which the third line is enclosed by Steevens. The second line evidently wants a word of two syllables, and I feel inclined to read the passage thus:—

'Sweet recreation barr'd, what doth ensue,
But moody [madness] and dull melancholy
Kinsmen to grim and comfortless despair;
And at *their* heels a huge infectious troop?'

Heath proposed a similar emendation, but placed *moping* where I have placed *madness*

And will have no attorney[1] but myself;
And therefore let me have him home with me.

Abb. Be patient; for I will not let him stir,
Till I have used the approv'd means I have,
With wholesome syrups, drugs, and holy prayers,
To make of him a formal man again:[2]
It is a branch and parcel of mine oath,
A charitable duty of my order;
Therefore depart, and leave him here with me.

Adr. I will not hence, and leave my husband here;
And ill it doth beseem your holiness,
To separate the husband and the wife.

Abb. Be quiet, and depart, thou shalt not have him. [*Exit* Abbess.

Luc. Complain unto the duke of this indignity.

Adr. Come, go; I will fall prostrate at his feet,
And never rise until my tears and prayers
Have won his grace to come in person hither,
And take perforce my husband from the abbess.

Mer. By this, I think, the dial points at five:
Anon, I am sure, the duke himself in person
Comes this way to the melancholy vale;
The place of death and sorry[3] execution,
Behind the ditches of the abbey here.

Ang. Upon what cause?

Mer. To see a reverend Syracusan merchant,
Who put unluckily into this bay
Against the laws and statutes of this town,
Beheaded publicly for his offence.

Ang. See, where they come; we will behold his death.

Luc. Kneel to the duke, before he pass the abbey.

Enter Duke *attended;* ÆGEON *bare-headed; with the Headsman and other* Officers.

Duke. Yet once again proclaim it publicly,
If any friend will pay the sum for him,
He shall not die, so much we tender him.

Adr. Justice, most sacred duke, against the abbess!

Duke. She is a virtuous and a reverend lady;
It cannot be, that she hath done thee wrong.

Adr. May it please your grace, Antipholus, my husband,—
Whom I made lord of me and all I had,
At your important[4] letters,—this ill day
A most outrageous fit of madness took him;
That desperately he hurried through the street
(With him his bondman, all as mad as he,)
Doing displeasure to the citizens
By rushing in their houses, bearing thence
Rings, jewels, any thing his rage did like.
Once did I get him bound, and sent him home,
Whilst to take order[5] for the wrongs I went,
That here and there his fury had committed.
Anon, I wot[6] not by what strong escape,
He broke from those that had the guard of him;
And with his mad attendant and himself,
Each one with ireful passion, with drawn swords,
Met us again, and madly bent on us,
Chas'd us away; till raising of more aid,
We came again to bind them: then they fled
Into this abbey, whither we pursued them:
And here the abbess shuts the gates on us,
And will not suffer us to fetch him out,
Nor send him forth, that we may bear him hence.
Therefore, most gracious duke, with thy command,
Let him be brought forth, and borne hence for help.

Duke. Long since, thy husband served me in my wars;
And I to thee engag'd a prince's word,
When thou didst make him master of thy bed,
To do him all the grace and good I could.—
Go, some of you, knock at the abbey-gate
And bid the lady abbess come to me;
I will determine this, before I stir.

Enter a Servant.

Serv. O mistress, mistress, shift and save yourself!
My master and his man[7] are both broke loose,
Beaten the maids a-row,[8] and bound the doctor,
Whose beard they have singed off with brands of fire;
And ever as it blaz'd they threw on him
Great pails of puddled mire to quench the hair:
My master preaches patience to him, and the while
His man with scissors nicks him[9] like a fool:
And, sure, unless you send some present help,
Between them they will kill the conjuror.

Adr. Peace, fool, thy master and his man are here;
And that is false, thou dost report to us.

Ser. Mistress, upon my life, I tell you true;
I have not breath'd almost, since I did see it.
He cries for you, and vows, if he can take you,
To scorch your face, and to disfigure you: [*Cry within.*
Hark, hark, I hear him, mistress; fly, begone.

Duke. Come, stand by me, fear nothing: Guard with halberds.

Adr. Ah me, it is my husband! Witness you,
That he is borne about invisible:
Even now we housed him in the abbey here;
And now he's there, past thought of human reason.

Enter ANTIPHOLUS *and* DROMIO *of* Ephesus.

Ant. E. Justice, most gracious duke, oh, grant me justice!
Even for the service that long since I did thee,
When I bestrid thee in the wars,[10] and took
Deep scars to save thy life; even for the blood
That then I lost for thee, now grant me justice.

Æge. Unless the fear of death doth make me dote,
I see my son Antipholus and Dromio.

Ant. E. Justice, sweet prince, against that woman there.
She whom thou gav'st to me to be my wife
That hath abused and dishonour'd me,
Even in the strength and height of injury!
Beyond imagination is the wrong,
That she this day hath shameless thrown on me.

Duke. Discover how, and thou shalt find me just.

Ant. E. This day, great duke, she shut the doors upon me,
While she with harlots[11] feasted in my house.

Duke. A grievous fault: say, woman, didst thou so?

Adr. No, my good lord;—myself, he, and my sister,
To-day did dine together: So befall my soul,
As this is false he burdens me withal!

Luc. Ne'er may I look on day, nor sleep on night,
But she tells to your highness simple truth!

Ang. O perjur'd woman! They are both forsworn.
In this the madman justly chargeth them.

Ant. E. My liege, I am advised[12] what I say:
Neither disturbed with the effect of wine,
Nor heady rash, provoked with raging ire,
Albeit my wrongs might make one wiser mad.
This woman lock'd me out this day from dinner,
That goldsmith there, were he not pack'd with her
Could witness it, for he was with me then;
Who parted with me to go fetch a chain,
Promising to bring it to the Porcupine,

---

1 i. e. substitute.

2 i. e. to bring him back to his senses, and the accustomed forms of sober behaviour. In Measure for Measure, '*informal* women' is used for just the contrary.

3 i. e. *dismal*:—' dismolde and sorrie, *atra funestus*.'

4 i. e. *importunate*.

5 i. e. to take measures.

6 To *wot* is to *know*. *Strong* escape is an escape effected by *strength* or violence.

7 *Are* is here inaccurately put for *have*.

8 i. e. successively, one after another.

9 The heads of fools were shaved, or their hair cut close, as appears by the following passage in The Choice of Change, 1598. 'Three things used by monks which provoke other men to laugh at their follies 1. They are *shaven* and *notched* on the head *like fooles*.' Florio explains, '*zuccone*, a shaven pate, a notted poll, a poll-pate, a gull, a *ninnie*.'

10 This act of friendship is frequently mentioned by Shakspeare.

11 *Harlot* was a term anciently applied to a rogue or base person among men, as well as to wantons among women. See Todd's Johnson.

12 'I speak with *consideration and circumspectly*, not *rashly and precipitately*.'

Where Balthazar and I did dine together.
Our dinner done, and he not coming thither,
I went to seek him: in the street I met him;
And in his company, that gentleman.
There did this perjur'd goldsmith swear me down,
That I this day of him receiv'd the chain,
Which, God he knows, I saw not: for the which,
He did arrest me with an officer.
I did obey; and sent my peasant home
For certain ducats: he with none return'd.
Then fairly I bespoke the officer,
To go in person with me to my house.
By the way we met
My wife, her sister, and a rabble more
Of vile confederates; along with them
They brought one Pinch; a hungry lean-fac'd villain,
A mere anatomy, a mountebank,
A thread-bare juggler, and a fortune-teller;
A needy, hollow-eyed, sharp-looking wretch,
A living dead man:[1] this pernicious slave,
Forsooth, took on him as a conjurer;
And, gazing in mine eyes, feeling my pulse,
And with no face, as 'twere, outfacing me,
Cries out I was possess'd: then altogether
They fell upon me, bound me, bore me thence,
And in a dark and dankish vault at home
There left me and my man, both bound together;
Till gnawing with my teeth my bonds in sunder,
I gain'd my freedom, and immediately
Ran hither to your grace; whom I beseech
To give me ample satisfaction
For these deep shames and great indignities.

Ang. My lord, in truth, thus far I witness with him;
That he din'd not at home, but was lock'd out.

Duke. But had he such a chain of thee, or no?

Ang. He had, my lord: and when he ran in here,
These people saw the chain about his neck.

Mer. Besides I will be sworn, these ears of mine
Heard you confess, you had the chain of him,
After you first forswore it on the mart,
And, thereupon I drew my sword on you;
And then you fled into this abbey here,
From whence, I think, you are come by miracle.

Ant. E. I never came within these abbey walls,
Nor ever didst thou draw thy sword on me:
I never saw the chain, so help me heaven!
And this is false, you burden me withal.

Duke. Why, what an intricate impeach is this!
I think you all have drunk of Circe's cup.
If here you hous'd him, here he would have been;
If he were mad, he would not plead so coldly:—
You say, he dined at home; the goldsmith here
Denies that saying:—Sirrah, what say you?

Dro. E. Sir, he din'd with her there, at the Porcupine.

Cour. He did; and from my finger snatch'd that ring.

Ant. E. 'Tis true, my liege, this ring I had of her.

Duke. Saw'st thou him enter at the abbey here?

Cour. As sure, my liege, as I do see your grace.

Duke. Why, this is strange:—Go, call the abbess hither;
I think, you are all mated,[2] or stark mad.
[*Exit an* Attendant.

Æge. Most mighty duke, vouchsafe me speak a word;
Haply I see a friend will save my life,
And pay the sum that may deliver me.

Duke. Speak freely, Syracusan, what thou wilt.

Æge. Is not your name, sir, call'd Antipholus?
And is not your bondman Dromio?

Dro. E. Within this hour, I was his bondman, sir,
But he, I thank him, gnaw'd in two my cords;
Now am I Dromio, and his man, unbound.

Æge. I am sure, you both of you remember me.

Dro. E. Ourselves, we do remember, sir, by you
For lately we were bound as you are now.
You are not Pinch's patient, are you, sir?

Æge. Why look you strange on me? you know me well.

Ant. E. I never saw you in my life, till now.

Æge. Oh! grief hath chang'd me, since you saw me last;
And careful hours, with Time's deformed[3] hand,
Have written strange defeatures[4] in my face:
But tell me yet, dost thou not know my voice?

Ant. E. Neither.

Æge. Dromio, nor thou?

Dro. E. No, trust me, sir, nor I.

Æge. I am sure, thou dost.

Dro. E. Ay, sir? but I am sure, I do not; and whatsoever a man denies, you are now bound to believe him.[5]

Æge. Not know my voice! O, time's extremity!
Hast thou so crack'd and splitted my poor tongue,
In seven short years, that here my only son
Knows not my feeble key of untun'd cares?[6]
Though now this grained[7] face of mine be hid
In sap-consuming winter's drizzled snow,
And all the conduits of my blood froze up;
Yet hath my night of life some memory,
My wasting lamp some fading glimmer left,
My dull deaf ears a little use to hear:
All these old witnesses[8] (I cannot err,)
Tell me, thou art my son Antipholus.

Ant. E. I never saw my father in my life.

Æge. But seven years since, in Syracusa, boy,
Thou know'st, we parted: but, perhaps, my son,
Thou sham'st to acknowledge me in misery.

Ant. E. The duke and all that know me in the city,
Can witness with me that it is not so;
I ne'er saw Syracusa in my life.

Duke. I tell thee, Syracusan, twenty years
Have I been patron to Antipholus,
During which time he ne'er saw Syracusa:
I see, thy age and dangers make thee dote.

Enter the Abbess, *with* ANTIPHOLUS Syracusan, *and* DROMIO Syracusan.

Abb. Most mighty duke, behold a man much wrong'd. [*All gather to see him.*

Adr. I see two husbands, or mine eyes deceive me.

Duke. One of these men is Genius to the other:
And so of these: Which is the natural man,
And which the spirit? Who deciphers them?

Dro. S. I, sir, am Dromio; command him away.

Dro. E. I, sir, am Dromio; pray, let me stay.

Ant. S. Ægeon, art thou not? or else his ghost?

Dro. S. O, my old master! who hath bound him here.

Abb. Whoever bound him, I will loose his bonds,
And gain a husband by his liberty:
Speak, old Ægeon, if thou be'st the man
That hadst a wife once call'd Æmilia,
That bore thee at a burden two fair sons:
O, if thou be'st the same Ægeon, speak,
And speak unto the same Æmilia!

Æge. If I dream not, thou art Æmilia:[9]
If thou art she, tell me, where is that son
That floated with thee on the fatal raft?

Abb. By men of Epidamnum, he, and I
And the twin Dromio, all were taken up;
But, by and by, rude fishermen of Corinth
By force took Dromio and my son from them,
And me they left with those of Epidamnum:

---

1 '——— but as a living death,
So *ded alive* of life he drew the breath.'
Sackville's Introduction to the Mirror of Magistrates.

2 *Mated* is *confounded.* See note on Macbeth, Act v. Sc. 1.

3 *Deformed* for *deforming.*

4 See note on Act ii. Sc. 1.

5 Dromio delights in a quibble, and the word *bound* has before been the subject of his mirth

6 i. e. the weak and discordant tone of my voice, which is changed by grief.

7 Furrowed, lined.

8 'But if my frosty signs and chaps of age,
Grave witnesses of true experience.'
Titus Adronicus, Sc. ult.

9 In the old copy this speech of Ægeon, and the subsequent one of the abbess follow the speech of the Duke. It is evident that they were transposed by mistake.

What then became of them, I cannot tell:
I, to this fortune that you see me in.
Duke. Why, here begins this morning story right;[1]
These two Antipholuses, these two so alike,
And these two Dromioes, one in semblance,—[2]
Besides her urging of her wreck at sea,—
These are the parents to these children,[3]
Which accidentally are met together.
Antipholus, thou cam'st from Corinth first.
Ant. S. No sir, not I; I came from Syracuse.
Duke. Stay, stand apart; I know not which is which.
Ant. E. I came from Corinth, my most gracious lord.
Dro. E. And I with him.
Ant. E. Brought to this town with that most famous warrior
Duke Menaphon, your most renowned uncle.
Adr. Which of you two did dine with me to-day?
Ant. S. I, gentle mistress.
Adr. And are not you my husband?
Ant. E. No, I say nay to that.
Ant. S. And so do I, yet did she call me so;
And this fair gentlewoman, her sister here,
Did call me brother:—What I told you then,
I hope, I shall have leisure to make good;
If this be not a dream I see and hear.
Ang. That is the chain, sir, which you had of me.
Ant. S. I think it be, sir; I deny it not.
Ant. E. And you, sir, for this chain arrested me.
Ang. I think I did, sir; I deny it not.
Adr. I sent you, money, sir, to be your bail,
By Dromio; but I think he brought it not.
Dro. E. No, none by me.
Ant. S. This purse of ducats I receiv'd from you,
And Dromio my man did bring them me:
I see, we still did meet each other's man,
And I was ta'en for him, and he for me,
And thereupon these Errors are arose.
Ant. E. These ducats pawn I for my father here.
Duke. It shall not need, thy father hath his life.
Cour. Sir, I must have that diamond from you.
Ant. E. There, take it; and much thanks for my good cheer.
Abb. Renowned duke, vouchsafe to take the pains
To go with us into the abbey here,
And hear at large discoursed all our fortunes:
And all that are assembled in this place,
That by this sympathized one day's error
Have suffer'd wrong, go, keep us company,
And we shall make full satisfaction.—
Twenty-five years have I but gone in travail
Of you, my sons, and till this present hour;—
My heavy burden here delivered.[4]
The duke, my husband, and my children both,
And you the calendars of their nativity,[5]
Go to a gossip's feast,[6] and go with me;
After so long grief, such nativity!
Duke. With all my heart, I'll gossip at this feast.
[*Exeunt* Duke, Abbess, ÆGEON, Courtezan, Merchant, ANGELO, *and* Attendants.
Dro S. Master, shall I fetch your stuff from shipboard?
Ant. E. Dromio, what stuff of mine hast thou embark'd?
Dro. S. Your goods, that lay at host, sir, in the Centaur.
Ant. S. He speaks to me; I am your master, Dromio;
Come, go with us: we'll look to that anon:
Embrace thy brother there, rejoice with him.
[*Exeunt* ANT. S. *and* ANT. E. ADR. *and* LUC.
Dro. S. There is a fat friend at your master's house,
That kitchen'd me for you to-day at dinner;
She now shall be my sister, not my wife.
Dro. E. Methinks you are my glass, and not my brother:
I see by you I am a sweet-faced youth.
Will you walk in to see their gossiping?
Dro. S. Not I, sir; you are my elder.
Dro. E. That's a question: how shall we try it:
Dro. S. We will draw cuts for the senior: till then, lead thou first.
Dro. E. Nay; then thus:
We came into the world, like brother and brother;
And now let's go hand in hand, not one before another. [*Exeunt.*

ON a careful revision of the foregoing scenes, I do not hesitate to pronounce them the composition of two very unequal writers. Shakspeare had undoubtedly a share in them; but that the entire play was no work of his, is an opinion which (as Benedict says) "fire can not melt out of me; I will die in it at the stake." Thus as we are informed by Aulus Gellius, Lib. III. Cap. 3, some plays were absolutely ascribed to Plautus, which in truth had only been (*retractatæ et expolitæ*) retouched and polished by him.

In this comedy we find more intricacy of plot than distinction of character; and our attention is less forcibly engaged, because we can guess in great measure how the denouement will be brought about. Yet the subject appears to have been reluctantly dismissed, even in this last and unnecessary scene, where the same mistakes are continued, till the power of affording entertainment is entirely lost. STEEVENS.

---

1 'The morning story' is what Ægeon tells the Duke in the first scene of this play.

2 *Semblance* is here a trisyllable. It appears probable that a line has been omitted here, the import of which may have been:

'*These* circumstances all concur to prove
These are the parents,' &c.

If it began with the word *these* as well as the succeeding one, the error would easily happen.

3 *Children* is here a trisyllable, it is often spelled as it was pronounced then, *childeren.*

4 The old copy reads, erroneously, thus:

'*Thirty-three* years have I but gone in travail
Of you, my sons; and till this present hour
My heavy burthen *are* delivered.

Theobald corrected it in the following manner:

Twenty-five years have I but gone in travail
Of you, my sons; *nor* till this present hour
My heavy *burdens are* delivered.'

Malone, after much argument, gives it thus.

Of you, my sons; *until* this present hour
My heavy burden *not* delivered.'

Thirty-three years are an evident error for *twenty-five*, this was corrected by Theobald. The reader will choose between the simple emendation which I have made in the text, and those made by Theobald and Malone.

5 i. e. the two Dromioes. Antipholus of Syracuse has already called one of them 'the almanack of my true date.' See note on Act 1, Sc. 2.

6 Heath thought that we should read, 'and joy with me.' Warburton proposed *gaud*, but the old reading is probably right.

MACBETH

PRELIMINARY REMARKS.

DR. JOHNSON thought it necessary to prefix to this play an apology for Shakspeare's magic;—in which he says, 'A poet who should now make the whole action of his tragedy depend upon enchantment, and produce the chief events by the assistance of supernatural agents, would be censured as transgressing the bounds of probability, be banished from the theatre to the nursery, and condemned to write fairy tales instead of tragedies.' He then proceeds to defend this transgression upon the ground of the credulity of the poet's age; when 'the scenes of enchantment, however they may be now ridiculed, were both by himself and his audience thought awful and affecting.' By whom, or when (always excepting *French* criticism,) these sublime conceptions were in danger of ridicule, he has not told us; and I sadly fear that this superfluous apology arose from the misgivings of the great critic's mind. Schlegel has justly remarked that, 'Whether the age of Shakspeare still believed in witchcraft and ghosts, is a matter of perfect indifference for the justification of the use which, in Hamlet and Macbeth, he has made of preexisting traditions. No superstition can ever be prevalent and widely diffused through ages and nations without having a foundation in human nature: on this foundation the poet builds; he calls up from their hidden abysses that dread of the unknown, that presage of a dark side of nature, and a world of spirits which philosophy now imagines it has altogether exploded. In this manner he is in some degree both the portrayer and the philosopher of a superstition; that is, not the philosopher who denies and turns into ridicule, but, which is still more difficult, who distinctly exhibits its origin to us in apparently irrational and yet natural opinions.'—In another place the same admirable critic says—'Since *The Furies* of Æschylus, nothing so grand and terrible has ever been composed: The Witches, it is true, are not divine Eumenides, and are not intended to be so; they are ignoble and vulgar instruments of hell. They discourse with one another like women of the very lowest class; for this was the class to which witches were supposed to belong. When, however, they address Macbeth, their tone assumes more elevation: their predictions have all the obscure brevity, the majestic solemnity, by which oracles have in all times contrived to inspire mortals with reverential awe. We here see that the witches are merely instruments; they are governed by an invisible spirit, or the operation of such great and dreadful events would be above their sphere.' Their agency was necessary; for natural motives alone would have seemed inadequate to effect such a change as takes place in the nature and dispositions of Macbeth. By this means the poet 'has exhibited a more sublime picture to us: an ambitious but noble hero, who yields to a deep laid hellish temptation: and all the crimes to which he is impelled by necessity, to secure the fruits of his first crime, cannot altogether eradicate in him the stamp of native heroism.' He has therefore given a threefold division to the guilt of that crime. The first idea comes from that being whose whole activity is guided by a lust of wickedness. The weird sisters surprise Macbeth in the moment of intoxication after his victory, when his love of glory has been gratified; they cheat his eyes by exhibiting to him as the work of fate what can only in reality be accomplished by his own deed, and gain credence for their words by the immediate fulfilment of the first prediction. The opportunity for murdering the king immediately offers itself; Lady Macbeth conjures him not to let it slip; she urges him on with a fiery eloquence, which has all those sophisms at command that serve to throw a false grandeur over crime. Little more than the mere execution falls to the share of Macbeth; he is driven to it as it were in a state of commotion, in which his mind is bewildered. Repentance immediately follows; nay, even precedes the deed; and the stings of his conscience leave him no rest either night or day. But he is now fairly entangled in the snares of hell; it is truly frightful to behold that Macbeth, who once as a warrior could spurn at death, now that he dreads the prospect of the life to come, clinging with growing anxiety to his earthly existence, the more miserable it becomes, and pitilessly removing out of his way whatever to his dark and suspicious mind seems to threaten danger. However much we may abhor his actions, we cannot altogether refuse to sympathize with the state of his mind; we lament the ruin of so many noble qualities; and, even in his last defence, we are compelled to admire in him the struggle of a brave will with a cowardly conscience.—The poet wishes to show that the conflict of good and evil in this world can only take place by the permission of Providence, which converts the curse that individual mortals draw down on their heads into a blessing to others. Lady Macbeth, who of all the human beings is the most guilty participator in the murder of the king, falls, through the horrors of her conscience, into a state of incurable bodily and mental disease; she dies, unlamented by her husband, with all the symptoms of reprobation. Macbeth is still found worthy of dying the death of a hero on the field of battle. Banquo atones for the ambitious curiosity which prompted him to wish to know his glorious descendants by an early death, as he thereby rouses Macbeth's jealousy; but he preserved his mind pure from the bubbles of the witches; his name is blessed in his race, destined to enjoy for a long succession of ages that royal dignity which Macbeth could only hold during his own life. In the progress of the action, this piece is altogether the reverse of Hamlet: it strides forward with amazing rapidity from the first catastrophe (for Duncan's murder may be called a catastrophe) to the last. Thought, and done! is the general motto; for, as Macbeth says,

> 'The flighty purpose never is o'ertook
> Unless the deed go with it.'

In every feature we see a vigorous heroic age in the hardy North, which steels every nerve. The precise duration of the action cannot be ascertained,—years, perhaps, according to the story; but we know that to the imagination the most crowded time appears always the shortest. Here we can hardly conceive how so very much can be compressed into so narrow a space; not merely external events—the very innermost recesses of the minds of the persons of the drama are laid open to us. It is as if the drags were taken from the wheels of time, and they rolled along without interruption in their descent. Nothing can equal the power of this picture in the excitation of horror. We need only allude to the circumstance attending the murder of Duncan, the dagger that hovers before the eyes of Macbeth, the vision of Banquo at the feast, the madness of Lady Macbeth; what can we possibly say on the subject that will not rather weaken the impression? Such scenes stand alone, and are to be found only in this poet; otherwise the tragic muse might exchange her mask for the head of Medusa.'*

Shakspeare followed the chronicle of Holinshed, and Holinshed borrowed his narration from the *chronicle of Scotland*, translated by John Bellenden, from the Latin of Hector Boethius, and first published at Edinburgh in 1541.

'Malcolm the Second, king of Scotland, had two daughters. The eldest was married to Crynin, the father of Duncan, Thane of the isles, and western parts of Scotland: and on the death of Malcolm without male issue Duncan succeeded to the throne. Malcolm's second daughter was married to Sinel, Thane of Glamis, the father of Macbeth. Duncan, who married the sister of Siward, Earl of Northumberland, was murdered by his cousin german Macbeth, in the castle of Inverness, about the year 1040 or 1045. Macbeth was himself slain by Macduff, according to Boethius in 1061, according to Buchanan in 1057, at which time Edward the Confessor reigned in England.

In the reign of Duncan, Banquo having been plundered by the people of Lochaber of some of the king's revenues, which he had collected, and being dangerously wounded in the affray, the persons concerned in this outrage were summoned to appear at a certain day But they slew the serjeant at arms who summoned them, and chose one Macdonwald as their captain. Macdonwald speedily collected a considerable body o

* Lectures on Dramatic Literature, by A. W Schlegel, translated by John Black, London, 1815, vol ii p. 200

forces from Ireland and the Western Isles, and in one action gained a victory over the king's army. In this battle Malcolm, a Scottish nobleman (who was lieutenant to Duncan in Lochaber) was slain. Afterwards Macbeth and Banquo were appointed to the command of the army; and Macdonwald, being obliged to take refuge in a castle in Lochaber, first slew his wife and children, and then himself. Macbeth, on entering the castle, finding his dead body, ordered his head to be cut off and carried to the king, at the castle of Bertha, and his body to be hung on a high tree.

At a subsequent period, in the last year of Duncan's reign, Sueno, king of Norway, landed a powerful army in Fife, for the purpose of invading Scotland. Duncan immediately assembled an army to oppose him, and gave the command of two divisions of it to Macbeth and Banquo, putting himself at the head of a third. Sueno was successful in one battle, but in a second was routed; and, after a great slaughter of his troops, he escaped with ten persons only, and fled back to Norway. Though there was an interval of time between the rebellion of Macdonwald and the invasion of Sueno, Shakspeare has woven these two actions together, and immediately after Sueno's defeat the present play commences.

It is remarkable that Buchanan has pointed out Macbeth's history as a subject for the stage. 'Multa hic fabuloso quidam nostrorum affingunt; sed quia *theatris* aut Milesiis fabulis sunt aptiora quam historiæ, ea omitto.'—*Rerum Scot. Hist. Lib.* vii.

Milton also enumerates the subject among those he considered well suited for tragedy, but it appears that he would have attempted to preserve the unity of time by placing the relation of the murder of Duncan in the mouth of his ghost.

Macbeth is one of the latest, and unquestionably one of the noblest efforts of Shakspeare's genius. Equally impressive in the closet and on the stage, where to witness its representation has been justly pronounced 'the first of all dramatic enjoyments.' Malone places the date of its composition in 1606, and it has been supposed to convey a dexterous and delicate compliment to James the first, who derived his lineage from Banquo, and first united the threefold sceptre of England, Scotland, and Ireland. At the same time the monarch's prejudices on the subject of demonology were flattered by the choice of the story.

It was once thought that Shakspeare derived some hints for his scenes of incantation from The Witch, a tragicomedy, by John Middleton, which, after lying long in manuscript, was published about thirty years since by Isaac Reed; but Malone* has with considerable ingenuity shown that Middleton's drama was most probably written subsequently to Macbeth.

* See the chronological order of the plays in the late Variorum Edition, by Mr. Boswell, vol. ii. p. 420.

PERSONS REPRESENTED.

DUNCAN, King *of* Scotland.
MALCOLM, DONALBAIN, } *his Sons.*
MACBETH, BANQUO, } *Generals of the King's Army.*
MACDUFF, LENOX, ROSSE, MENTEITH, ANGUS, CATHNESS, } *Noblemen of* Scotland.
FLEANCE, *Son to* Banquo.
SIWARD, Earl *of* Northumberland, *General of the English Forces.*
YOUNG SIWARD, *his Son.*
SEYTON, *an* Officer *attending on* Macbeth.
Son to Macduff.
An English Doctor. A Scotch Doctor.
A Soldier. A Porter. An old Man.
LADY MACBETH,[1]
LADY MACDUFF.
Gentlewoman *attending on* Lady Macbeth.
Hecate, and three Witches.[2]
Lords, Gentlemen, Officers, Soldiers, Murderers, Attendants, *and* Messengers.
The Ghost of Banquo, *and several other* Apparitions.

SCENE, *in the end of the Fourth Act, lies in* England; *through the rest of the play, in* Scotland; *and chiefly at* Macbeth's Castle.

ACT I.

SCENE I. *An open Place. Thunder and Lightning. Enter three* Witches.

1 *Witch.*

When shall we three meet again
In thunder, lightning, or in rain?
2 *Witch.* When the hurlyburly's[3] done,
When the battle's lost and won.
3 *Witch.* That will be ere set of sun.
1 *Witch.* Where the place?
2 *Witch.* Upon the heath:
3 *Witch.* There to meet with Macbeth.
1 *Witch.* I come, Graymalkin!
All. Paddock calls:—Anon.[4]
Fair is foul, and foul is fair:
Hover through the fog and filthy air.
[Witches *vanish.*

SCENE II. *A Camp near* Fores. *Alarum within. Enter King* DUNCAN, MALCOLM, DONALBAIN, LENOX, *with Attendants, meeting a bleeding Soldier.*[5]

Dun. What bloody man is that? He can report,
As seemeth by his plight, of the revolt
The newest state.
Mal. This is the sergeant,[6]
Who, like a good and hardy soldier, fought
'Gainst my captivity:—Hail, brave friend!
Say to the king the knowledge of the broil,
As thou didst leave it.

1 Lady Macbeth's name was Gruach filia Bodhe, according to Lord Hailes. Andrew of Wintown, in his Cronykil, informs us that she was the widow of Duncan; a circumstance with which Shakspeare was of course unacquainted.

2 As the play now stands, in Act iv. Sc. 1, three other witches make their appearance.

3 'When the hurlyburly's done.' In Adagia Scotica, or A Collection of Scotch Proverbs and Proverbial Phrases; collected by R. B.; very useful and delightful. *Lond.* 12mo. 1668:—

'Little kens the wife that sits by the fire
How the wind blows cold in *hurle burle swyre*.'

'i. e. in the *tempestuous* mountain-top,' says Mr. Todd, in a note on Spenser; to which Mr. Boswell gives his assent, and says, 'this sense seems agreeable to the witch's answer.' But Peacham, in his Garden of Eloquence, 1577, shows that this was not the ancient acceptation of the word among us: 'Onomatopeia, when we invent, devise, fayne, and make a name imitating the sound of that it signifyeth, as *hurlyburly*, for an *up rore* and *tumultuous stirre*.' So in Baret's Alvearie, 1573:—'But harke yonder: what *hurlyburly* or *noyse* is yonde: what *sturre ruffling* or *bruite* is that?'—The witches could not mean when the *storm* was done, but when the *tumult of the battle* was over; for they are to meet again in lightning, thunder, and rain: their element was a storm.

4 Upton observes, that, to understand this passage, we should suppose one familiar calling with the voice of a *cat*, and another with the croaking of a *toad*. A *paddock* most generally seems to have signified a *toad*, though it sometimes means a frog. What we now call a toadstool was anciently called a *paddock-stool*

5 The first folio reads *captain.*

6 *Sergeants*, in ancient times, were not the petty officers now distinguished by that title, but men performing one kind of feudal military service, in rank next to esquires

Sold. Doubtful it stood;
As two spent swimmers, that do cling together,
And choke their art. The merciless Macdonwald
(Worthy to be a rebel; for to that[1]
The multiplying villanies of nature
Do swarm upon him), from the western isles
Of Kernes and Gallowglasses is supplied;[2]
And fortune, on his damned quarry[3] smiling,
Show'd like a rebel's whore.[4] But all's too weak:
For brave Macbeth (well he deserves that name),
Disdaining fortune, with his brandish'd steel,
Which smok'd with bloody execution
Like valour's minion,
Carv'd out his passage, till he fac'd the slave;
And[5] ne'er shook hands, nor bade farewell to him,
Till he unseam'd him from the nave to the chaps,
And fix'd his head upon our battlements.
Dun. O, valiant cousin! worthy gentleman!
Sold. As whence the sun 'gins his reflection
Shipwrecking storms and direful thunders break;[6]
So from that spring, whence comfort seem'd to come,
Discomfort swells. Mark, king of Scotland, mark:
No sooner justice had, with valour arm'd,
Compell'd these skipping Kernes to trust their heels,
But the Norweyan lord, surveying vantage,
With furbish'd arms, and new supplies of men,
Began a fresh assault.
Dun. Dismay'd not this
Our captains, Macbeth and Banquo?
Sold. Yes;
As sparrows, eagles; or the hare, the lion.
If I say sooth,[7] I must report, they were
As cannons overcharg'd with double cracks;[8]
So they
Doubly redoubled strokes upon the foe:
Except they meant to bathe in reeking wounds,
Or memorize another Golgotha,[9]
I cannot tell:——
But I am faint, my gashes cry for help.
Dun. So well thy words become thee, as thy wounds;
They smack of honour both:—Go, get him surgeons. [*Exit* Soldier, *attended.*

Enter ROSSE.

Who comes here?
Mal. The worthy thane of Rosse.
Len. What a haste looks through his eyes! So should he look,
That seems to speak things strange.[10]
Rosse. God save the king!
Dun. Whence cam'st thou, worthy thane?
Rosse. From Fife, great king.
Where the Norweyan banners flout the sky,[11]
And fan our people cold.
Norway himself, with terrible numbers,
Assisted by that most disloyal traitor
The thane of Cawdor, 'gan a dismal conflict:
Till that Bellona's bridegroom,[12] lapp'd in proof
Confronted him with self-comparisons,[13]
Point against point rebellious, arm 'gainst arm,
Curbing his lavish spirit: And, to conclude,
The victory fell on us;——
Dun. Great happiness!
Rosse. That now
Sweno,[14] the Norways' king, craves composition,
Nor would we deign him burial of his men,
Till he disbursed, at Saint Colmes' Inch,[15]
Ten thousand dollars to our general use.
Dun. No more that thane of Cawdor shall deceive
Our bosom interest:—Go, pronounce his present death,
And with his former title greet Macbeth.
Rosse. I'll see it done.
Dun. What he hath lost, noble Macbeth hath won. [*Exeunt.*

SCENE III. *A Heath. Thunder. Enter the three* Witches.

1 *Witch.* Where hast thou been, sister?
2 *Witch.* Killing swine.
3 *Witch.* Sister, where thou?
1 *Witch.* A sailor's wife had chestnuts in her lap,
And mounch'd, and mounch'd, and mounch'd:—
Give me, quoth I:
Aroint thee,[16] *witch!* the rump-fed ronyon[17] cries.
Her husband's to Aleppo gone, master o' the Tiger:
But in a sieve I'll thither sail,[18]

---

1 Vide Tyrwhitt's Glossary to Chaucer, v. *for;* and Pegge's Anecdotes of the English Language, p. 205. *For to that* means no more than *for that*, or *cause that.* The late editions erroneously point this passage, and as erroneously explain it. I follow the punctuation of the first folio.

2 i. e. supplied *with* armed troops so named. *Of* and *with* are indiscriminately used by our ancient writers. *Gallowglasses* were heavy-armed foot-soldiers of Ireland and the western isles: *Kernes* were the lighter armed troops.

3 '*But* fortune on his damned *quarry* smiling.'—Thus the old copies. It was altered at Johnson's suggestion to *quarrel*, which is approved and defended by Steevens and Malone. But the old copy needs no alteration. *Quarry* means the *squadron*, escadre, or *square* body, into which Macdonwald's troops were formed, better to receive the charge; through which Macbeth 'carved out his passage till he faced the slave.'

4 The meaning is, that Fortune, while she smiled on him, deceived him.

5 The old copy reads *which.*

6 Sir W. D'Avenant's reading of this passage, in his alteration of the play, is a tolerable comment on it:—

'But then this daybreak of our victory
Serv'd but to light us into other dangers,
That spring from whence our hopes did seem to rise.'

Break is not in the first folio

7 Truth.

8 That is, *reports.*

9 i. e. make another Golgotha as memorable as the first.

10 'That seems *about* to speak strange things.'

11 So in King John:—

'*Mocking* the air with *colours* idly spread.'

12 By *Bellona's bridegroom* Shakspeare means Macbeth. *Lapp'd in proof* is defended by armour of proof.

13 Confronted him with self-comparisons.' By *him* is meant *Norway*, and by *self-comparisons* is meant that he gave him as good as he brought, showed that he was his equal.

14 It appears probable, as Steevens suggests, that *Sweno* was only a marginal reference, which has crept into the text by mistake, and that the line originally stood—

'That now the Norway's king craves composition.'

It was surely not necessary for Rosse to tell Duncan the name of his old enemy, the king of Norway.

15 *Colmes'* is here a dissyllable. *Colmes' Inch*, now called *Inchcomb*, is a small island, lying in the Firth of Edinburgh, with an abbey upon it dedicated to St. Columb. *Inch* or *inse*, in Erse, signifies an island.

16 The etymology of this imprecation is yet to seek *Rynt ye*, for *out with ye! stand off!* is still used in Cheshire, where there is also a proverbial saying, '*Rynt ye, witch*, quoth Besse Locket to her mother.' Tooke thought it was from *roynous*, and might signify 'a scab or scale on thee!' Others have derived it from the *rowan-tree*, or witch-hazle, the wood of which was believed to be a powerful charm against witchcraft; and every careful housewife had a churn-staff made of it. This superstition is as old as Pliny's time, who asserts that 'a serpent will rather creep into the fire than over a twig of *ash*.' The French have a phrase of somewhat similar sound and import—'*Arry-avant*, away there, ho!'—Mr. Douce thinks that '*aroint* thee' will be found to have a Saxon origin.

17 'Rump-fed ronyon,' a scabby or mangy woman, fed on offals; the *rumps* being formerly part of the emoluments or kitchen fees of the cooks in great houses

18 In The Discovery of Witchcraft, by Reginald Scott, 1584, he says it was believed that witches 'could sail in an egg-shell, a cockle, or muscle-shell, through and under the tempestuous seas.' And in another pamphlet, 'Declaring the damnable Life of Doctor Fian, a notable Sorcerer, who was buried at Edenborough in Januarie last, 1591,'—'All they together went to sea, each one in a riddle or cive, and went in the same very substantially, with flaggons of wine making merrie, and drinking by the way in the same riddles or cives,' &c.

Sir W. D'Avenant, in his Albovine, 1629, says

'He sits like a witch *sailing in a sieve.*'

It was the belief of the times, that though a witch could assume the form of any animal she pleased, the *tail* would still be wanting.

And, like a rat without a tail,
I'll do, I'll do, and I'll do.
2 *Witch.* I'll give thee a wind.[1]
1 *Witch.* Thou art kind.
3 *Witch.* And I another.
1 *Witch.* I myself have all the other;
And the very ports they blow,
All the quarters that they know
I' the shipman's card.[2]
I will drain him dry as hay:
Sleep shall, neither night nor day,
Hang upon his pent-house lid;
He shall live a man forbid:[3]
Weary sev'n-nights, nine times nine,
Shall he dwindle, peak, and pine:[4]
Though his bark cannot be lost,
Yet it shall be tempest-toss'd.[5]
Look what I have.
2 *Witch.* Show me, show me.
1 *Witch.* Here I have a pilot's thumb,
Wreck'd, as homeward he did come. [*Drum within.*
3 *Witch.* A drum, a drum;
Macbeth doth come.
All. The weird sisters,[6] hand in hand,
Posters of the sea and land,
Thus do go about, about;
Thrice to thine, and thrice to mine,
And thrice again, to make up nine:
Peace!—the charm's wound up.

Enter Macbeth *and* Banquo.

Macb. So foul and fair a day I have not seen.
Ban. How far is't call'd to Fores?—What are these,
So wither'd, and so wild in their attire;
That look not like the inhabitants o' the earth,
And yet are on't? Live you? or are you aught
That man may question? You seem to understand me,
By each at once her choppy finger laying
Upon her skinny lips:—You should be women,
And yet your beards forbid me to interpret
That you are so.
Macb. Speak, if you can;—What are you?
1 *Witch.* All hail, Macbeth! hail to thee, thane of Glamis![7]
2 *Witch.* All hail, Macbeth! hail to thee, thane of Cawdor!
3 *Witch.* All hail, Macbeth! that shalt be king hereafter.
Ban. Good sir, why do you start; and seem to fear
Things that do sound so fair?—I'the name of truth,
Are ye fantastical,[8] or that indeed
Which outwardly ye show? My noble partner
You greet with present grace, and great prediction
Of noble having,[9] and of royal hope,
That he seems rapt[10] withal; to me you speak not:
If you can look into the seeds of time,
And say, which grain will grow, and which will not:
Speak then to me, who neither beg, nor fear.
Your favours, nor your hate.
1 *Witch.* Hail!
2 *Witch.* Hail!
3 *Witch.* Hail!
1 *Witch.* Lesser than Macbeth, and greater.
2 *Witch.* Not so happy, yet much happier.
3 *Witch.* Thou shalt get kings, though thou be none:
So, all hail, Macbeth, and Banquo!
1 *Witch.* Banquo, and Macbeth, all hail!
Macb. Stay, you imperfect speakers, tell me more:
By Sinel's[11] death, I know, I am thane of Glamis;
But how of Cawdor? the thane of Cawdor lives,
A prosperous gentleman; and to be king
Stands not within the prospect of belief,
No more than to be Cawdor. Say, from whence
You owe this strange intelligence? or why
Upon this blasted heath you stop our way
With such prophetic greeting?—Speak, I charge you. [Witches *vanish.*
Ban. The earth hath bubbles, as the water has,
And these are of them:—Whither are they vanish'd?
Macb. Into the air: and what seem'd corporal, melted
As breath into the wind.—'Would, they had staid!
Ban. Were such things here, as we do speak about?
Or have we eaten of the insane root,[12]
That takes the reason prisoner?
Macb. Your children shall be kings.
Ban. You shall be king
Macb. And thane of Cawdor too; went it not so?
Ban. To the selfsame tune, and words. Who's here?

Enter Rosse *and* Angus.

Rosse. The king hath happily receiv'd, Macbeth,
The news of thy success: and when he reads
Thy personal venture in the rebels' fight,
His wonders and his praises do contend,
Which should be thine, or his: Silenc'd with that,[13]
In viewing o'er the rest o' the selfsame day,
He finds thee in the stout Norweyan ranks,
Nothing afeard of what thyself didst make,
Strange images of death. As thick as tale,[14]

1 This free gift of a wind is to be considered as an act of sisterly friendship; for witches were supposed to sell them.

2 i. e. the sailor's chart; *carte-marine.*

3 *Forbid,* i. e. forespoken, *unhappy,* charmed or bewitched. The explanation of Theobald and Johnson, '*interdicted* or under a curse,' is erroneous. A *forbodin* fellow, Scotice, still signifies an unhappy one.

4 This mischief was supposed to be put in execution by means of a waxen figure. Holinshed, speaking of the witchcraft practised to destroy King Duff, says that they found one of the witches roasting, upon a wooden broach, an image of wax at the fire, resembling in each feature the king's person, &c.—'for as the image did waste afore the fire, so did the bodie of the king break forth in sweat: and as for the words of the inchantment, they served to keepe him still waking *from sleepe.*' This may serve to explain the foregoing passage:—
'Sleep shall, neither night nor day,
Hang upon his pent-house lid.'

5 In the pamphlet about Dr. Fian, already quoted—'Againe it is confessed, that the said christened cat was the cause of the *Kinge's majestie's shippe, at his coming forth of Denmarke, had a contrarie winde to the rest of his shippes* then being in his companie.'—'And further the said witch declared, that his majestie had never come safely from the sea, if his faith had not prevailed above their intentions.' To this circumstance, perhaps, Shakspeare's allusion is sufficiently plain.

6 The old copy has *weyward,* evidently by mistake. *Weird,* from the Saxon, a *witch,* Shakspeare found in Holinshed. Gawin Douglas, in his translation of Virgil, renders the *parcæ* by *weird sisters.*

7 The thaneship of Glamis was the ancient inheritance of Macbeth's family. The castle where they lived is still standing, and was lately the magnificent residence of the earl of Strathmore. Gray has given a particular description of it in a Letter to Dr. Wharton.

8 i. e. creatures of fantasy or imagination.

9 Estate, fortune.

10 *Rapt* is rapturously affected; *extra se raptus.*

11 '*Sinel.*' The late Dr. Beattie conjectured that the real name of this family was *Sinane,* and that *Dunsinane,* or *the hill* of Sinane from thence derived its name.

12 The *insane root* was probably *henbane.* In Batman's Commentary on Bartholome de Propriet. Rerum, a book with which Shakspeare was familiar, is the following passage:—'Henbane is called *insana,* mad, for the use thereof is perillous; for if it be eate or dronke it breedeth madnesse, or slow lykenesse of sleepe. Therefore this hearb is called commonly mirilidium, for it taketh away wit and reason.'

13 i. e. admiration of your deeds, and a desire to do them justice by public commendation, contend in his mind for pre-eminence: he is *silenced with wonder.*

14 i. e. posts arrived as *fast* as they could be *counted.* '*Thicke* (says Baret,) that cometh often and *thicke* together: creber, frequens, *frequent, souvent venant.*' And again. 'Crebritas literarum, the often sending, or *thicke* coming of letters. *Thicke* breathing, anhelitus creber.' Shakspeare twice uses 'to speak *thick*' for 'to speak *quick.*' To *tale* or tell is to *score* or *number.* Rowe, not understanding this passage, altered it to 'as quick as *hail.*'

Came[1] post with post; and every one did bear
Thy praises in his kingdom's great defence,
And pour'd them down before him.

Ang. We are sent,
To give thee, from our royal master, thanks;
Only to herald thee into his sight, not pay thee.

Rosse. And, for an earnest of a greater honour,
He bade me, from him, call thee thane of Cawdor:
In which addition, hail, most worthy thane!
For it is thine.

Ban. What, can the devil speak true?

Macb. The thane of Cawdor lives? Why do you dress me
In borrow'd robes?

Ang. Who was the thane, lives yet;
But under heavy judgment bears that life
Which he deserves to lose. Whether he was combin'd
With those of Norway, or did line the rebel
With hidden help and vantage; or that with both
He labour'd in his country's wreck, I know not;
But treasons capital, confess'd, and prov'd,
Have overthrown him.

Macb. Glamis, and thane of Cawdor;
The greatest is behind.—Thanks for your pains.—
Do you not hope your children shall be kings,
When those that gave the thane of Cawdor to me,
Promis'd no less to them?

Ban. That, trusted home,[2]
Might yet enkindle[3] you unto the crown,
Besides the thane of Cawdor. But 'tis strange:
And oftentimes, to win us to our harm,
The instruments of darkness tell us truths;
Win us with honest trifles, to betray us
In deepest consequence.—
Cousins, a word, I pray you.

Macb. Two truths are told,
As happy prologues to the swelling act[4]
Of the imperial theme.—I thank you, gentlemen.—
This supernatural soliciting[5]
Cannot be ill; cannot be good:—If ill,
Why hath it given me earnest of success,
Commencing in a truth? I am thane of Cawdor:
If good, why do I yield to that suggestion[6]
Whose horrid image doth unfix my hair,
And make my seated[7] heart knock at my ribs,
Against the use of nature? Present fears
Are less than horrible imaginings:[8]
My thought, whose murder yet is but fantastical,
Shakes so my single[9] state of man, that function
Is smother'd in surmise;[10] and nothing is,
But what is not.[11]

Ban. Look, how our partner's rapt.

Macb. If chance will have me king, why, chance may crown me,
Without my stir.

Ban. New honours come upon him
Like our strange garments; cleave not to their mould,
But with the aid of use.

Macb. Come what come may;
Time and the hour runs through the roughest day.

Ban. Worthy Macbeth, we stay upon your leisure.

Macb. Give me your favour:[12]—my dull brain was wrought
With things forgotten. Kind gentlemen, your pains,
Are register'd where every day I turn
The leaf to read them.—Let us toward the king.—
Think upon what hath chanc'd: and, at more times,
The interim having weigh'd it,[13] let us speak
Our free hearts each to other.

Ban. Very gladly.

Macb. Till then, enough.—Come, friends.
[*Exeunt.*

SCENE IV. Fores. *A Room in the Palace.*

Flourish. Enter DUNCAN, MALCOLM, DONALBAIN, LENOX, *and* Attendants.

Dun. Is execution done on Cawdor? Are not
Those in commission yet return'd?

Mal. My liege,
They are not yet come back. But I have spoke
With one that saw him die: who did report,
That very frankly he confess'd his treasons;
Implor'd your highness' pardon; and set forth
A deep repentance: nothing in his life
Became him, like the leaving it; he died
As one that had been studied in his death,[14]
To throw away the dearest thing he ow'd,[15]
As 'twere a careless trifle.

Dun. There's no art,
To find the mind's construction in the face:[16]
He was a gentleman on whom I built
An absolute trust.—O worthiest cousin!

Enter MACBETH, BANQUO, ROSSE, *and* ANGUS.

The sin of my ingratitude even now
Was heavy on me: Thou art so far before,
That swiftest wing of recompense is slow
To overtake thee. 'Would, thou hadst less deserv'd;
That the proportion both of thanks and payment
Might have been mine! only I have left to say,
More is thy due than more than all can pay.[17]

Macb. The service and the loyalty I owe,
In doing it, pays itself. Your highness' part
Is to receive our duties: and our duties
Are to your throne and state, children, and servants;
Which do but what they should, by doing every thing
Safe toward your love and honour.[18]

---

1 '*Came post.*' The old copy reads *can.* Rowe made the emendation.

2 i. e. entirely, thoroughly relied on.

3 *Enkindle* means '*encourage* you to expect the crown.'

4 'As happy prologues to the swelling act.' So in the prologue to King Henry V.:—

'——— princes to act,
And monarchs to behold the *swelling* scene.'

5 i. e. *incitement.*

6 *Suggestion*, temptation.

7 *Seated*, firmly placed, fixed.

8 '——— Present fears
Are less than horrible imaginings.'

So in The Tragedie of Crœsus, by Lord Sterline, 1604:

'For as the shadow seems more monstrous still
Than doth the substance whence it hath the being,
So *th' apprehension of approaching ill
Seems greater than itself, whilst fears are lying.*'

9 By his *single state of man*, Macbeth means his *simple condition of human nature. Single soul*, for a simple or weak guileless person, was the phraseology of the poet's time. *Simplicity* and *singleness* were synonymous.

10 '——— that function
Is smother'd in surmise.'

The powers of action are oppressed by conjecture.

11 'But what is not.' Shakspeare has something like this sentiment in The Merchant of Venice:—

'Where every something, being blent together,
Turns to a wild of nothing.'

12 *Favour* is *countenance, good will*, and *not pardon*, as it has been here interpreted. Vide Hamlet, Act v. Sc. 2.

13 'The interim having weigh'd it.' *The interim* is probably here used adverbially—'You having weighed it *in* the interim.'

14 *Studied in his death* is well instructed in the art of dying. 'The behaviour of the thane of Cawdor corresponds in almost every circumstance with that of the unfortunate earl of Essex, as related by Stowe, p. 793 His asking the queen's forgiveness, his confession, repentance, and concern about behaving with propriety on the scaffold, are minutely described by that historian.' Steevens thinks that an allusion was intended 'to the severity of that justice which deprived the age of one of its greatest ornaments, and Southampton, Shakspeare's patron, of his dearest friend

15 *Ow'd*, owned, possessed.

16 We cannot construe the disposition of the mind by the lineaments of the face.

17 i. e. I owe thee more than all; nay, more than all which I can say or do will requite.

18 'Safe toward your love and honour.' Sir William Blackstone would read:—

Safe toward *you* love and honour

which he explains thus:—'Our duties are your children, and servants or vassals to your throne and state who do but what they should, by doing every thing with a saving of their love and honour toward you.' He says that it has reference to the old feudal *simple ho*

Dun. Welcome hither:
I have begun to plant thee, and will labour
To make thee full of growing.[1]—Noble Banquo,
That hast no less deserv'd, nor must be known
No less to have done so, let me enfold thee,
And hold thee to my heart.
Ban. There if I grow,
The harvest is your own.
Dun. My plenteous joys,
Wanton in fulness, seek to hide themselves
In drops of sorrow.[2]—Sons, kinsmen, thanes,
And you whose places are the nearest, know,
We will establish our estate upon
Our eldest, Malcolm; whom we name hereafter,
The prince of Cumberland:[3] which honour must
Not, unaccompanied, invest him only,
But signs of nobleness, like stars, shall shine
On all deservers.—From hence to Inverness,
And bind us further to you.
Macb. The rest is labour, which is not us'd for you:
I'll be myself the harbinger, and make joyful
The hearing of my wife with your approach;
So, humbly take my leave.
Dun. My worthy Cawdor!
Macb. The prince of Cumberland!—That is a step,
On which I must fall down, or else o'erleap, [*Aside.*
For in my way it lies. Stars, hide your fires!
Let not light see my black and deep desires:
The eye wink at the hand! yet let that be,
Which the eye fears, when it is done, to see. [*Exit.*
Dun. True, worthy Banquo; he is full so valiant;[4]
And in his commendations I am fed;
It is a banquet to me. Let us after him,
Whose care is gone before to bid us welcome:
It is a peerless kinsman. [*Flourish. Exeunt.*

SCENE V. Inverness. *A Room in* Macbeth's *Castle. Enter* Lady Macbeth, *reading a Letter.*

Lady M. *They met me in the day of success; and I have learned by the perfectest report,[5] they have more in them than mortal knowledge. When I burned in desire to question them further, they made themselves—air, into which they vanished. Whiles I stood rapt in the wonder of it, came missives[6] from the king, who all-hailed me,* Thane of Cawdor; *by which title, before, these weird sisters saluted me, and referred me to the coming on of time, with,* Hail, king that shalt be! *This have I thought good to deliver thee, my dearest partner of greatness; that thou mightest not lose the dues of rejoicing, by being ignorant of what greatness is promised thee. Lay it to thy heart, and farewell.*
Glamis thou art, and Cawdor; and shalt be
What thou art promis'd:—Yet do I fear thy nature.
It is too full o' the milk of human kindness,
To catch the nearest way: Thou would'st be great;
Art not without ambition; but without
The illness should attend it. What thou would'st highly,
That would'st thou holily; would'st not play false,
And yet would'st wrongly win; thou'dst have, great Glamis,
That which cries, *Thus thou must do, if thou have it:*
And that which rather thou dost fear to do,
Than wishest should be undone.[7] Hie thee hither
That I may pour my spirits in thine ear;[8]
And chastise with the valour of my tongue
All that impedes thee from the golden round,
Which fate and metaphysical[9] aid doth seem
To have thee crown'd withal.——What is your tidings?

Enter an Attendant.

Attend. The king comes here to-night.
Lady M. Thou'rt mad to say it:
Is not thy master with him? who, wer't so,
Would have inform'd for preparation.
Attend. So please you, it is true; our thane is coming:
One of my fellows had the speed of him;
Who, almost dead for breath, had scarcely more
Than would make up his message.
Lady M. Give him tending,
He brings great news. The raven himself is hoarse,
[*Exit* Attendant.
That croaks the fatal entrance of Duncan
Under my battlements. Come, come, you spirits
That tend on mortal[10] thoughts, unsex me here;
And fill me, from the crown to the toe, top-full
Of direst cruelty! make thick my blood,
Stop up the access and passage to remorse;
That no compunctious visitings of nature
Shake my fell purpose, nor keep peace between
The effect, and it![11] Come to my woman's breasts,

---

mage, which when done to a subject was always accompanied with a saving clause—'*saulf le foy que jeo doy a nostre seignor le roy;*' which he thinks suits well with the situation of Macbeth, now beginning to waver in his allegiance. Malone and Steevens seem to favour this explanation: but *safe* may merely mean *respectful, loyal;* like the old French word *sauf.* Shakspeare has used the old French phrase, *sauf votre honneur,* several times in King Henry V.

1 i. e. exuberant.

2 'In drops of sorrow.'
——lachrymas non sponte cadentes
ffudit, gemitusque expressit pectore læto;
on aliter manifesta potens abscondere mentis
Gaudia, quam lachrymis.' *Lucan*, lib. ix.

3 Holinshed says, 'Duncan having two sons, &c. he made the elder of them, called Malcolm, prince of Cumberland, as it was thereby to appoint him his successor in his kingdome immediatelie after his decease. Macbeth sorely troubled herewith, for that he saw by this means his hope sore hindered (where, by the old laws of the realme the ordinance was, that if he that should succeed were not of able age to take the charge upon himself, he that was next of blood unto him should be admitted,) he began to take counsel how he might usurpe the kingdome by force, having a just quarrel so to doe (as he tooke the matter) for that Duncane did what in him lay to defraud him of all manner of title and claime, which he might in time to come pretend, unto the crowne.'

4 'True, worthy Banquo,' &c. We must imagine that while Macbeth was uttering the six preceding lines, Duncan and Banquo had been conferring apart. Macbeth's conduct appears to have been their subject; and to some encomium supposed to have been bestowed on him by Banquo, the reply of Duncan refers.

5 *The perfectest report* is the best intelligence.

6 *Missives*, messengers.

7 Thou would'st have that [i. e. the crown] which cries unto thee, 'thou must do thus, if thou would'st have it, and *thou must do* that which rather,' &c. The difficulty of this passage in Italics seems to have arisen from its not having been considered as all uttered by the object of Macbeth's ambition. Malone is the author of this regulation, and furnished the explanation.

8 'That I may pour my spirits in thine ear.' So in Lord Sterline's Julius Cæsar, 1607:—
'Thou in my bosom used *to pour thy spright.*'

9 'Which fate and *metaphysical* aid,' &c.; i. e. *supernatural* aid. We find *metaphysics* explained '*things supernatural*' in the old dictionaries. 'To *have thee crown'd,*' is to *desire* that you should be crown'd.

10 'That tend on *mortal* thoughts.' *Mortal* and *deadly* were synonymous in Shakspeare's time. In another part of this play we have 'the *mortal* sword,' and '*mortal* murders.' We have '*mortal* war,' and '*mortal* hatred.' In Nashe's Pierce Pennilesse is a particular description of these spirits, and of their office. 'The second kind of devils, which he most employeth, are those northern *Martii*, called the *spirits of revenge*, and the authors of massacres, and seedsmen of mischief; for they have commission to incense men to rapines, sacrilege, theft, murder, wrath, fury, and all manner of cruelties: and they command certain of the southern spirits to wait upon them, as also great Arioch, that is termed *the spirit of revenge.*'

11 Lady Macbeth's purpose was to be effected by action. 'To keep peace between the effect and purpose,' means 'to delay the execution of her purpose, to prevent its proceeding to effect.' Sir Wm. Davenant's strange alteration of this play sometimes affords a reasonably good commentary upon it. Thus in the present instance:—
'————make thick
My blood, stop all passage to remorse,
That no relapses into mercy may

And take my milk for gall, you murd'ring ministers,
Wherever in your sightless substances
You wait on nature's mischief! Come, thick night,
And pall[1] thee in the dunnest smoke of hell!
That my keen knife see not the wound it makes;
Nor heaven peep through the blanket of the dark,[2]
To cry, *Hold, hold!*——Great Glamis! worthy Cawdor!

Enter MACBETH.

Greater than both, by the all-hail hereafter!
Thy letters have transported me beyond
This ignorant present,[3] and I feel now
The future in the instant.

Macb. My dearest love,
Duncan comes here to-night.

Lady M. And when goes hence?

Macb. To-morrow,—as he purposes.

Lady M. O, never
Shall sun that morrow see!
Your face, my thane, is as a book, where men
May read strange matters:—To beguile the time,
Look like the time; bear welcome in your eye,
Your hand, your tongue: look like the innocent flower,
But be the serpent under it. He that's coming
Must be provided for: and you shall put
This night's great business into my despatch;
Which shall to all our nights and days to come
Give solely sovereign sway and masterdom.

Macb. We will speak further.

Lady M. Only look up clear;
To alter favour[4] ever is to fear:
Leave all the rest to me. [*Exeunt.*

SCENE VI. *The same. Before the Castle. Hautboys. Servants of* Macbeth *attending. Enter* DUNCAN, MALCOLM, DONALBAIN, BANQUO, LENOX, MACDUFF, ROSSE, ANGUS, *and* Attendants.

Dun. This castle hath a pleasant seat:[5] the air
Nimbly and sweetly recommends itself
Unto our gentle senses.

Ban. This guest of summer,
The temple-haunting martlet, does approve,
By his lov'd mansionry, that the heaven's breath
Smells wooingly here: no jutty, frieze,
Buttress, nor coigne of vantage,[6] but this bird
Hath made his pendant bed, and procreant cradle:
Where they most breed and haunt, I have observ'd,
The air is delicate.[7]

Enter LADY MACBETH.

Dun. See, see! our honour'd hostess!
The love that follows us, sometime is our trouble,
Which still we thank as love. Herein I teach you
How you shall bid God yield[8] us for your pains,
And thank us for your trouble.

Lady M. All our service,
In every point twice done, and then done double,
Were poor and single business, to contend
Against those honours deep and broad, wherewith
Your majesty loads our house: For those of old,
And the late dignities heap'd up to them,
We rest your hermits.[9]

Dun. Where's the thane of Cawdor?
We cours'd him at the heels, and had a purpose
To be his purveyor: but he rides well:
And his great love, sharp as his spur, hath holp him
To his home before us: Fair and noble hostess,
We are your guest to-night.

Lady M. Your servants ever
Have theirs, themselves, and what is theirs, in compt,[10]
To make their audit at your highness' pleasure,
Still to return your own.

Dun. Give me your hand:
Conduct me to mine host; we love him highly,
And shall continue our graces towards him.
By your leave, hostess. [*Exeunt.*

SCENE VII. *The same. A Room in the Castle. Hautboys and Torches. Enter, and pass over the Stage, a Sewer,[11] and divers Servants with Dishes and Service. Then enter* MACBETH.

Macb. If it were done, when 'tis done, then 'twere well
It were done quickly: If the assassination
Could trammel up the consequence, and catch,
With his surcease, success; that but this blow
Might be the be-all and the end-all here,
But here, upon this bank and shoal of time,—
We'd jump the life to come.[12]—But, in these cases,
We still have judgment here; that we but teach
Bloody instructions, which, being taught, return
To plague the inventor: This even-handed justice

Shake my design, nor make it fall before
'Tis ripen'd to effect.'

1 To *pall*, from the Latin *pallio*, to wrap, to invest, to cover or hide as with a mantle or cloak.

2 Drayton, in his Mortimeriados, 1596, has an expression resembling this:—

'The sullen *night in mistie* RUGGE *is wrapp'd*.'

And in his Polyolbion, which was not published till 1612, we again find it:—

'Thick vapours that like *ruggs* still hang the troubled air.'

On this passage there is a long criticism in the Rambler, No. 168; to which Johnson in his notes refers the reader with much complacency.

3 i. e. beyond the present time, which is, according to the process of nature, ignorant of the future.

4 *Favour* is countenance.

5 i. e. situation. 6 i. e. convenient corner.

7 'This short dialogue,' says Sir Joshua Reynolds, 'has always appeared to me a striking instance of what in painting is termed *repose*. The conversation very naturally turns upon the beauty of the castle's situation, and the pleasantness of the air; and Banquo, observing the martlets' nests in every recess of the cornice, remarks, that where those birds most breed and haunt the air is delicate. The subject of this quiet and easy conversation gives that repose so necessary to the mind after the tumultuous bustle of the preceding scenes, and perfectly contrasts the scene of horror that immediately succeeds. It seems as if Shakspeare asked himself, What is a prince likely to say to his attendants on such an occasion? Whereas the modern writers seem, on the contrary, to be always searching for new thoughts, such as would never occur to men in the situation which is represented. This also is frequently the practice of Homer, who, from the midst of battles and horrors relieves and refreshes the mind of the reader, by introducing some quiet rural image or picture of familiar domestic life.'

8 The explanation by Steevens of this obscure passage seems the best which has been offered:—'Marks of respect importunately shown are sometimes troublesome, though we are still bound to be grateful for them, as indications of sincere attachment. If you pray for us on account of the trouble we create in your house, and thank us for the molestations we bring with us, it must be on such a principle. Herein I teach you, that the inconvenience you suffer is the result of our affection; and that you are therefore to pray for us, or thank us only as far as prayers and thanks can be deserved for kindnesses that fatigue, and honours that oppress. You are, in short, to make your acknowledgments for intended respect and love, however irksome our present mode of expressing them may have proved.'—To *bid* is here used in the Saxon sense of to *pray*. 'God *yield* us, is God *reward* us.

9 i. e. we as *hermits*, or *beadsmen*, shall ever pray for you.

10 *In compt*, subject to accompt.

11 A *sewer*, an officer so called from his placing the dishes on the table. *Asseour*, French; from *asseoir*, to *place*.

12 This passage has been variously explained. I have attempted briefly to express what I conceive to be its meaning:—'*Twere well it were done quickly, if, when 'tis done, it were done* (or at an *end*;) and that no sinister consequences would ensue. *If the assassination*, at the same time that it puts an end to Duncan's life, could make success certain, and that I might enjoy the crown unmolested, *we'd jump the life to come*, i.e. hazard or run the risk of what may happen in a future state. To *trammel* up was to *confine* or tie up. The legs of horses were *trammeled* to teach them to amble. There was also 'a *trammel*-net,' which was 'a long net to take great and small fowl with by night.' *Surcease* is *cessation*. 'To *surcease* or to *cease* from doing some thing: supersedeo, Lat.: *cesser*, Fr.'—*Baret*

Commend[1] the ingredients of our poison'd chalice
To our own lips. He's here in double trust:
First, as I am his kinsman and his subject,
Strong both against the deed; then, as his host,
Who should against his murderer shut the door,
Not bear the knife myself. Besides, this Duncan
Hath borne his faculties so meek, hath been
So clear in his great office, that his virtues
Will plead like angels, trumpet-tongued, against
The deep damnation of his taking off:
And pity, like a naked new-born babe,
Striding the blast, or heaven's cherubin, hors'd
Upon the sightless couriers[2] of the air,
Shall blow the horrid deed in every eye,
That tears shall drown the wind.—I have no spur
To prick the sides of my intent, but only
Vaulting ambition,[3] which o'erleaps itself,
And falls on the other—How now, what news?

Enter Lady Macbeth.

Lady M. He has almost supp'd: Why have you left the chamber?
Macb. Hath he ask'd for me?
Lady M. Know you not, he has?
Macb. We will proceed no further in this business:
He hath honour'd me of late; and I have bought
Golden opinions from all sorts of people,
Which would be worn now in their newest gloss,
Not cast aside so soon.
Lady M. Was the hope drunk,
Wherein you dress'd yourself? hath it slept since?
And wakes it now, to look so green and pale
At what it did so freely? From this time,
Such I account thy love. Art thou afeard
To be the same in thine own act and valour,
As thou art in desire? Would'st thou have that
Which thou esteem'st the ornament of life,
And live a coward in thine own esteem;
Letting I dare not wait upon I would,
Like the poor cat i' the adage?[4]
Macb. Pr'ythee, peace:
I dare do all that may become a man;
Who dares do more,[5] is none.
Lady M. What beast was't then,
That made you break this enterprise to me?
When you durst do it, then you were a man;
And, to be more than what you were, you would
Be so much more the man. Nor time, nor place,
Did then adhere,[6] and yet you would make both:
They have made themselves, and that their fitness now
Does unmake you. I have given suck; and know
How tender 'tis to love the babe that milks me:
I would, while it was smiling in my face,
Have pluck'd my nipple from his boneless gums,
And dash'd the brains out, had I so sworn, as you
Have done to this.
Macb. If we should fail,—
Lady M. We fail!
But screw your courage to the sticking-place,[7]
And we'll not fail. When Duncan is asleep
(Whereto the rather shall his day's hard journey
Soundly invite him,) his two chamberlains[8]
Will I with wine and wassel[9] so convince,[10]
That memory, the warder of the brain,
Shall be a fume, and the receipt of reason
A limbeck[11] only: When in swinish sleep
Their drenched[12] natures lie, as in a death,
What cannot you and I perform upon
The unguarded Duncan? what not put upon
His spongy officers; who shall bear the guilt
Of our great quell?[13]
Macb. Bring forth men-children only!
For thy undaunted mettle should compose
Nothing but males. Will it not be receiv'd,[14]
When we have mark'd with blood those sleepy two
Of his own chamber, and us'd their very daggers,
That they have don't?
Lady M. Who dares receive it other,
As we shall make our griefs and clamour roar
Upon his death?
Macb. I am settled, and bend up
Each corporal agent to this terrible feat.
Away, and mock the time with fairest show;
False face must hide what the false heart doth know.
[*Exeunt.*

ACT II.

SCENE I. *The same. Court within the Castle.*
Enter Banquo *and* Fleance, *and a* Servant, *with a Torch before them.*

Ban. How goes the night, boy?
Fle. The moon is down: I have not heard the clock.
Ban. And she goes down at twelve.
Fle. I take't, 'tis later, sir.
Ban. Hold, take my sword:—There's husbandry[15] in heaven,
Their candles are all out.—Take thee that too.
A heavy summons lies like lead upon me,
And yet I would not sleep: Merciful powers!
Restrain in me the cursed thoughts, that nature
Gives way to in repose:[16]—Give me my sword;—

Enter Macbeth, *and a* Servant *with a Torch.*

Who's there?

---

1 To *commend* was anciently used in the sense of the Latin *commendo*, to *commit*, to *address*, to *direct*, to *recommend*.

2 'The *sightless couriers of the air*' are what the poet elsewhere calls the *viewless winds*.

3 So in the tragedy of Cæsar and Pompey, 1607:—
'Why think you, lords, that 'tis *ambition's spur*
That *pricketh* Cæsar to these high attempts?'
Malone has observed that 'there are two distinct metaphors in this passage. I have no spur to prick the sides of my intent; I have nothing to *stimulate* me to the execution of my purpose but ambition, which is apt to overreach itself; this he expresses by the second image, of a person meaning to vault into his saddle, who, by taking too great a leap, will fall on the other side.'

4 This passage is perhaps sufficiently intelligible; but as Johnson and Steevens thought otherwise, I must offer a brief explanation.—'Would'st thou have *the crown*, that which thou esteem'st the ornament of life, and *yet* live a coward in thine own esteem,' &c. The adage of the cat is among Heywood's Proverbs, 1566:—
'The cat would eate fishe, and would not wet her feete.'

5 'Who dares *do* more is none.' The old copy, instead of '*do* more,' reads '*no* more:' the emendation is Rowe's.

6 *Adhere*, in the same sense as cohere.

7 'But screw your courage to the *sticking-place*.' Shakspeare seems to have taken his metaphor from the *screwing up* the chords of stringed instruments to their proper degree of tension, when the peg remains fast in its *sticking-place*; i. e. in the place from which it is not to recede, or go back.

8 The circumstance relative to Macbeth's slaughter of Duncan's chamberlains is copied from Holinshed's account of King Duffe's murder by Donwald.

9 *Wassel* is thus explained by Bullokar in his Expositor, 1616: '*Wassaile*, a term usual heretofore for *quaffing* and *carowsing*; but more especially signifying a merry cup (ritually composed, deckt and fill'd with country liquor) passing about amongst neighbours, meeting and entertaining one another on the vigil or eve of the new year, and commonly called the *wassail-bol*.'

10 To *convince* is to *overcome*.

11 A *limbeck* is a vessel through which distilled liquors pass into the recipient. So shall the *receipt* (i. e. receptacle) of reason be like this empty vessel.

12 i. e. drowned in drink.

13 *Quell* is *murder*; from the Saxon *quellan*, to kill

14 i. e. apprehended, understood.

15 *Husbandry* here means *thrift*, frugality.

16 It is apparent from what Banquo says afterwards, that he had been solicited in a dream to attempt something in consequence of the prophecy of the witches, that his waking senses were shocked at; and Shakspeare has here most exquisitely contrasted his character with that of Macbeth. Banquo is praying against being tempted to encourage thoughts of guilt even in his sleep; while Macbeth is hurrying into temptation, and revolving in his mind every scheme, however flagitious, that may assist him to complete his purpose. The one is unwilling to sleep, lest the same phantoms should assail his resolution again, while the other is depriving himself of rest through impatience to commit the murder.

Westall pi.k

LADY MACBETH.

Macbeth Act I Scene V

Macb. A friend.
Ban. What, sir, not yet at rest? The king's a-bed:
He hath been in unusual pleasure, and
Sent forth great largess[1] to your officers:[2]
This diamond he greets your wife withal,
By the name of most kind hostess; and shut up[3]
In measureless content.
Macb. Being unprepar'd,
Our will became the servant to defect;
Which else should free have wrought.[4]
Ban. All's well.
I dreamt last night of the three weird sisters:
To you they have show'd some truth.
Macb. I think not of them:
Yet, when we can entreat an hour to serve,
Would spend it in some words upon that business,
If you would grant the time.
Ban. At your kind'st leisure.
Macb. If you shall cleave to my consent,[5]—when 'tis,
It shall make honour for you.
Ban. So I lose none,
In seeking to augment it, but still keep
My bosom franchis'd, and allegiance clear,
I shall be counsel'd.
Macb. Good repose, the while!
Ban. Thanks, sir; The like to you! [*Exit* BAN.
Macb. Go, bid thy mistress, when my drink is ready,
She strike upon the bell. Get thee to bed.
[*Exit* Servant.
Is this a dagger, which I see before me,
The handle toward my hand? Come, let me clutch thee:——
I have thee not, and yet I see thee still.
Art thou not, fatal vision, sensible
To feeling, as to sight? or art thou but
A dagger of the mind: a false creation,
Proceeding from the heat-oppressed brain?
I see thee yet, in form as palpable
As this which now I draw.
Thou marshal'st me the way that I was going;
And such an instrument I was to use.
Mine eyes are made the fools o' the other senses,
Or else worth all the rest: I see thee still:
And on thy blade, and dudgeon,[6] gouts[7] of blood,
Which was not so before;—There's no such thing:
It is the bloody business, which informs
Thus to mine eyes.—Now o'er the one half world
Nature seems dead,[8] and wicked dreams abuse
The curtain'd sleeper;[9] witchcraft celebrates
Pale Hecate's offerings; and wither'd murder,
Alarum'd by his sentinel, the wolf,
Whose howl's his watch, thus with his stealthy pace,
With Tarquin's ravishing strides, towards his design
Moves like a ghost.[10]——Thou sure and firm-set earth,
Hear not my steps, which way they walk, for fear
Thy very stones prate of my where-about,
And take the present horror from the time,
Which now suits with it.[11]—Whiles I threat, he lives;
Words to the heat of deeds too cold breath gives.
[*A bell rings.*
I go, and it is done; the bell invites me.
Hear it not, Duncan; for it is a knell
That summons thee to heaven, or to hell. [*Exit.*

SCENE II. *The same.* *Enter* LADY MACBETH.

Lady M. That which hath made them drunk, hath made me bold:
What hath quench'd them, hath given me fire:—
Hark!—Peace!
It was the owl that shriek'd, the fatal bellman,
Which gives the stern'st good-night. He is about it:
The doors are open; and the surfeited grooms
Do mock their charge with snores: I have drugg'd their possets,

---

1 *Largess*, bounty.

2 The old copy reads *offices.* *Officers* of a household was the common term for servants in Shakspeare's time. He has before called the king's chamberlains 'his spongy *officers*.'

3 Steevens has rightly explained 'to *shut up*,' by 'to *conclude*,' and the examples he has adduced are satisfactory; but Mr. Boswell supposed that it meant *enclosed*, and quoted a passage from Barrow to support his opinion. The authorities of the poet's time are against Mr. Boswell's interpretation.

4 Being unprepared, our will (or desire to entertain the king honourably) became the servant to defect (i. e. was constrained by defective means,) which else should free have wrought (i. e. otherwise our zeal should have been manifest by more liberal entertainments.) *Which* relates not to the last antecedent, *defect*, but to *will.*

5 *Consent* is *accord*, *agreement*, a combination for a particular purpose. By 'if you shall cleave to my consent,' Macbeth means, 'if you shall adhere to me (i. e. agree or accord with my views,) when 'tis, (i. e. when events shall fall out as they are predicted,) it shall make honour for you.' Macbeth mentally refers to the crown which he expected to obtain in consequence of the murder that he was about to commit. *We* comprehend all that passes in his mind; but Banquo is still in ignorance of it. His reply is only that of a man who determines to combat every possible temptation to do ill; and therefore expresses a resolve that, in spite of future combinations of interest or struggles for power, he will attempt nothing that may obscure his present honours, alarm his conscience, or corrupt loyalty. Macbeth could never mean, while yet the success of his attack on the life of Duncan was uncertain, to afford Banquo the most dark or distant hint of his criminal designs on the crown. Had he acted thus incautiously, Banquo would naturally have become his accuser as soon as the murder had been discovered. Malone proposed to read *content* instead of *consent;* but his reasons are far from convincing, and there seems no necessity for change.

6 *Dudgeon* for *handle;* '*a dudgeon* dagger is a dagger whose handle is made of the root of box,' according to Bishop Wilkins in the dictionary subjoined to his *Real Character.* *Dudgeon* is the *root of box.* It has not been remarked that there is a peculiar propriety in giving the word to Macbeth, 'Pugnale alla scoccese, being a *Scotch* or *dudgeon haft* dagger,' according to *Torriano.*

7 *Gouts* drops; from the French *gouttes.*

8 Dryden's well known lines in the Conquest of Mexico are here transcribed, that the reader may observe the contrast between them and this passage of Shakspeare:—

'All things are hush'd as Nature's self lay dead.
The mountains seem to nod their drowsy head,
The little birds in dreams their songs repeat,
And sleeping flow'rs beneath the night dews sweat,
Even lust and envy sleep!'

In the second part of Marston's Antonio and Mellida, 1602, we have the following lines:—

''Tis yet the dead of night, yet all the earth is clutch'd
In the dull leaden hand of snoring sleep:
No breath disturbs the quiet of the air,
No spirit moves upon the breast of earth,
Save howling dogs, night-crows, and screeching owls,
Save meagre ghosts, Piero, and black thoughts
————I am great in blood,
Unequall'd in revenge:---you horrid scouts
That sentinel swart night, give loud applause
From your large palms.'

9 The old copy has *sleepe.* The emendation was proposed by Steevens, and is well worthy of a place in the text; the word *now* having been formerly admitted to complete the metre.

10 The old copy reads *sides:* Pope made the alteration. Johnson objects to the epithet *ravishing strides.* But Steevens has shown that a *stride* was not always an action of violence, impetuosity, or tumult. Thus in The Faerie Queene, b. iv. c. viii.

'With easy steps so soft as foot could *stride.*'

And in other places we have an *easy stride*, a *leisurable stride*, &c. Warburton observes, that the justness of the similitude is not very obvious. But a stanza in Shakspeare's Tarquin and Lucrece will explain it:—

'Now *stole upon the time in dead of night*,
When heavy sleep had clos'd up mortal eyes;
No comfortable *star did lend his light*,
No noise but owls' and *wolves' dead-boding cries;*
Now serves the season that they may surprise
The silly lambs. Pure thoughts are dead and still,
While lust *and* murder *wake to stain and kill.*'

11 Macbeth would have nothing break through the universal silence that added such horror to the night, as well suited with the bloody deed he was about to perform. Burke, in his Essay on the Sublime and Beautiful, observes, that 'all general privations are great because they are terrible.'

That death and nature do contend about them,
Whether they live or die.

Macb. [*Within.*] Who's there?—what, ho!

Lady M. Alack! I am afraid, they have awak'd,
And 'tis not done:—the attempt, and not the deed,
Confounds us:—Hark!—I laid their daggers ready,
He could not miss them.—Had he not resembled
My father as he slept, I had done't.—My husband?

Enter Macbeth.

Macb. I have done the deed:—Didst thou not hear a noise?

Lady M. I heard the owl scream, and the crickets cry.
Did not you speak?

Macb. When?

Lady M. Now.

Macb. As I descended?

Lady M. Ay.

Macb. Hark!—
Who lies i' the second chamber?

Lady M. Donalbain.

Macb. This is a sorry sight. [*Looking on his hands.*

Lady M. A foolish thought, to say a sorry sight.

Macb. There's one did laugh in his sleep, and one cried, *murder!*
That they did wake each other; I stood and heard them:
But they did say their prayers, and address'd them
Again to sleep.

Lady M. There are two lodg'd together.

Macb. One cried, *God bless us!* and, *Amen*, the other;
As[1] they had seen me, with these hangman's hands.
Listening their fear[2], I could not say, amen,
When they did say, God bless us.

Lady M. Consider it not so deeply.

Macb. But wherefore could not I pronounce, amen?
I had most need of blessing, and amen
Stuck in my throat.

Lady M. These deeds must not be thought
After these ways; so, it will make us mad.

Macb. Methought, I heard a voice cry, *Sleep no more!*
Macbeth does murder sleep, the innocent sleep;
Sleep, that knits up the ravell'd sleave[3] of care,
The death of each day's life, sore labour's bath,
Balm of hurt minds, great nature's second course,
Chief nourisher in life's feast;—

Lady M. What do you mean?

Macb. Still it cried, *Sleep no more!* to all the house:
Glamis hath murder'd sleep; and therefore Cawdor
Shall sleep no more. Macbeth shall sleep no more![4]

Lady M. Who was it that thus cried? Why, worthy thane,
You do unbend your noble strength, to think
So brainsickly of things:—Go, get some water,
And wash this filthy witness from your hand.—
Why did you bring these daggers from the place?
They must lie there: Go, carry them; and smear
The sleepy grooms with blood.

Macb. I'll go no more:
I am afraid to think what I have done;
Look on't again, I dare not.

Lady M. Infirm of purpose!
Give me the daggers: The sleeping, and the dead
Are but as pictures: 'tis the eye of childhood,
That fears a painted devil. If he do bleed,
I'll gild the faces of the grooms withal,
For it must seem their guilt.[5] [*Exit. Knocking within.*

Macb. Whence is that knocking?
How is't with me, when every noise appals me?
What hands are here! Ha! they pluck out mine eyes!
Will all great Neptune's ocean wash this blood[6]
Clean from my hand? No; this my hand will rather
The multitudinous seas incarnardine,[7]
Making the green—one red.[8]

Re-enter Lady Macbeth.

Lady M. My hands are of your colour; but I shame
To wear a heart so white. [*Knock.*] I hear a knocking
At the south entry:—retire we to our chamber:
A little water clears us of this deed:
How easy is it then? Your constancy
Hath left you unattended[9]—[*Knocking.*] Hark! more knocking:
Get on your nightgown, lest occasion call us,
And show us to be watchers:—Be not lost
So poorly in your thoughts.

Macb. To know my deed,—'twere best not know myself.[10] [*Knock.*
Wake Duncan with thy knocking! I would, thou could'st? [*Exeunt.*

SCENE III. *The same. Enter a* Porter.

[*Knocking within.*

Porter. Here's a knocking, indeed! If a man were porter of hell-gate, he should have old[11] turning the key. [*Knocking.*] Knock, knock, knock: Who's there, i' the name of Belzebub? Here's a farmer,[12] that hanged himself on the expectation of plenty: Come in time; have napkins[13] enough about you; here you'll sweat for't. [*Knocking.*] Knock, knock: Who's there i' the other devil's name? 'Faith, here's an equivocator,[14] that could swear in both the scales against either scale; who committed treason enough for God's sake, yet could not equivocate to heaven: O, come in, equivocator. [*Knocking.*] Knock, knock, knock; Who's there? 'Faith,

---

1 *As* for *as if.*

2 i. e. listening *to* their fear: the particle omitted.

3 *Sleave* is unwrought silk, sometimes also called *floss* silk. It appears to be the coarse ravelled part separated by passing through the slaie (reed comb) of the weaver's loom; and hence called *sleaved* or *sleided* silk. I suspect that *sleeveless*, which has puzzled the etymologists, is that which cannot be sleaved, sleided, or unravelled; and therefore useless: thus a *sleeveless* errand would be a *fruitless* one.

4 Steevens observes that this triple menace, accomodated to the different titles of Macbeth, is too quaint to be received as the natural ebullition of a guilty mind; but Mr. Boswell thinks that there is no ground for his objection. He thus explains the passage; *Glamis hath murder'd sleep;* and therefore my lately acquired dignity can afford no comfort to one who suffers the agony of remorse,—*Cawdor shall sleep no more;* nothing can restore me to that peace of mind which I enjoyed in a comparatively humble state; the once innocent *Macbeth shall sleep no more.*

5 This quibble too occurs frequently in old plays. Shakspeare has it in King Henry IV. Part II. Act iv. Sc. 4:—

'England shall double *gild* his treble *guilt.*'

6 Thus in The Insatiate Countess, by Marston, 1613:—

'Although the waves of all the northern sea
Should flow for ever through these guilty hands,
Yet the sanguinolent stain would extant be.'

7 To *incarnardine* is to stain of a red colour.

8 In the old copy the line stands thus:—

'Making the Green one, Red.'

The punctuation in the text was adopted by Stevens at the suggestion of Murphy. Malone prefers the old punctuation. Steevens has well defended the arrangement of his text, which seems to me to deserve the preference.

9 'Your constancy hath left you unattended.'—Vide note on King Henry V. Act v. Sc. 2.

10 This is an answer to Lady Macbeth's reproof 'While I have *the thoughts* of this deed, it were best not know, or *be lost* to myself.'

11 i. e. frequent

12 'Here's a farmer that hanged himself on the expectation of plenty.' So in Hall's Satires, b. iv sat. 6:—

'Each muckworme will be rich with lawless gaine,
Altho' he smother up mowes of seven yeares graine,
And hang'd himself when corne grows cheap againe.'

13 i. e. *handkerchiefs.* In the dictionaries of the time *sudarium* is rendered by '*napkin or handkerchief, wherewith we wipe away the sweat.*'

14 i. e. *a Jesuit.* That order were troublesome to the state, and held in odium in the reigns of Elizabeth and James. They were inventors of the execrable doctrine of *equivocation.*

here's an English tailor come hither, for stealing out of a French hose: Come in, tailor; here you may roast your goose. [*Knocking.*] Knock, knock: Never at quiet! What are you?—But this place is too cold for hell. I'll devil-porter it no further: I had thought to have let in some of all professions, that go the primrose way to the everlasting bonfire.[1] [*Knocking.*] Anon, anon; I pray you, remember the porter. [*Opens the gate.*

Enter MACDUFF *and* LENOX.

Macd. Was it so late, friend, ere you went to bed,
That you do lie so late?

Port. 'Faith, sir we were carousing till the second cock:[2] and drink, sir, is a great provoker of three things.

Macd. What three things does drink especially provoke?

Port. Marry, sir, nose-painting, sleep, and urine. Lechery, sir, it provokes, and unprovokes: it provokes the desire, but it takes away the performance: Therefore, much drink may be said to be an equivocator with lechery: it makes him, and it mars him; it sets him on, and it takes him off; it persuades him, and disheartens him; makes him stand to, and not stand to: in conclusion, equivocates him in[3] a sleep, and, giving him the lie, leaves him.

Macd. I believe, drink gave thee the lie, last night.

Port. That it did, sir, i' the very throat o' me: But I requited him for his lie: and, I think, being too strong for him, though he took up my legs sometime, yet I made a shift to cast him.

Macd. Is thy master stirring?—
Our knocking has awak'd him; here he comes.

Enter MACBETH.

Len. Good-morrow, noble sir!
Macb. Good-morrow, both!
Macd. Is the king stirring, worthy thane?
Macb. Not yet.
Macd. He did command me to call timely on him;
I have almost slipp'd the hour.
Macb. I'll bring you to him.
Macd. I know, this is a joyful trouble to you;
But yet, 'tis one.
Macb. The labour, we delight in, physics[4] pain.
This is the door.
Macd. I'll make so bold to call.
For 'tis my limited service.[5] [*Exit* MACDUFF.
Len. Goes the king hence to-day?
Macb. He does:—he did appoint it so.
Len. The night has been unruly; Where we lay,
Our chimneys were blown down: and, as they say,
Lamentings heard i' the air; strange screams of death;
And prophesying, with accents terrible,
Of dire combustion, and confus'd events,
New hatch'd to the woful time. The obscure bird
Clamour'd the livelong night: some say, the earth
Was feverous, and did shake.
Macb. 'Twas a rough night.
Len. My young remembrance cannot parallel
A fellow to it.

Re-enter MACDUFF.

Macd. O horror! horror! horror! Tongue, nor heart,
Cannot conceive, nor name thee![6]
Macb. Len. What's the matter?
Macd. Confusion now hath made his masterpiece!
Most sacrilegious murder hath broke ope
The Lord's anointed temple, and stole thence
The life o' the building.
Macb. What is't you say? the life?
Len. Mean you his majesty?
Macd. Approach the chamber, and destroy your sight
With a new Gorgon:—Do not bid me speak;
See and then speak yourselves.—Awake! awake!—
[*Exeunt* MACBETH *and* LENOX.
Ring the alarum-bell:—Murder! and treason!
Banquo, and Donalbain! Malcolm! awake!
Shake off this drowsy sleep, death's counterfeit,
And look on death itself!—up, up, and see
The great doom's image!——Malcolm! Banquo!
As from your graves rise up, and walk like sprights,
To countenance this horror! [*Bell rings*

Enter LADY MACBETH.

Lady M. What's the business,
That such a hideous trumpet calls to parley
The sleepers of the house? Speak, speak,——
Macd. O, gentle lady,
'Tis not for you to hear what I can speak:
The repetition, in a woman's ear,
Would murder as it fell.[7]——O Banquo! Banquo!

Enter BANQUO.

Our royal master's murder'd!
Lady M. Woe, alas!
What, in our house?
Ban. Too cruel, any where,——
Dear Duff, I pr'ythee, contradict thyself,
And say, it is not so.

Re-enter MACBETH *and* LENOX.

Macb. Had I but died an hour before this chance,
I had liv'd a blessed time; for, from this instant,
There's nothing serious in mortality:
All is but toys: renown, and grace, is dead;
The wine of life is drawn, and the mere lees
Is left this vault to brag of.

Enter MALCOLM *and* DONALBAIN.

Don. What is amiss?
Macb. You are, and do not know it:
The spring, the head, the fountain of your blood
Is stopp'd; the very source of it is stopp'd.
Macd. Your royal father's murder'd.
Mal. O, by whom?
Len. Those of his chamber, as it seem'd, had done't:
Their hands and faces were all badg'd with blood,
So were their daggers, which unwip'd, we found
Upon their pillows:
They star'd, and were distracted; no man's life
Was to be trusted with them.
Macb. O, yet, I do repent me of my fury,
That I did kill them.
Macd. Wherefore did you so?
Macb. Who can be wise, amaz'd, temperate, and furious,
Loyal and neutral, in a moment? No man:
The expedition of my violent love
Outran the pauser reason.—Here lay Duncan,
His silver skin lac'd with his golden blood;[8]
And his gash'd stabs look'd like a breach in nature,
For ruin's wasteful entrance: there, the murderers,
Steep'd in the colours of their trade, their daggers

---

1 So in Hamlet:—
'Himself the *primrose path* of dalliance treads.'
And in All's Well that Ends Well:—'The *flowery way* that leads to the great fire.'

2 i. e. till *three* o'clock. 3 *In* for *into*.

4 i. e. *alleviates it.* 5 i. e. *Appointed* service.

6 It has been already observed that Shakspeare uses two negatives, not to make an affirmative, but to deny more strongly.

7 'The repetition, in a woman's ear,
Would murder as it fell.'
So in Hamlet:—
'——He would drown the stage with tears,
And cleave the general ear with horrid speech.'
And in The Puritan, 1607:—'The punishments that shall follow you in this world would *with horrour kill the ear* should hear them related.'

8 'His silver skin lac'd with his golden blood.' To *gild* with blood is a very common phrase in old plays See also King John, Act ii. Sc. 2.—Johnson says, 'it is not improbable that Shakspeare put these forced and unnatural metaphors into the mouth of Macbeth, as a mark of artifice and dissimulation, to show the difference between the studied language of hypocrisy and the natural outcries of sudden passion. This whole speech, so considered, is a remarkable instance of judgment as consists of antithesis only.'

Unmannerly breech'd with gore:[1] Who could refrain,
That had a heart to love, and in that heart
Courage, to make his love known?
Lady M. Help me hence, ho!
Macd. Look to the lady.
Mal. Why do we hold our tongues,
That most may claim this argument for ours?
Don. What should be spoken,
Here, where our fate hid in an augre-hole,
May rush, and seize us? Let's away; our tears
Are not yet brew'd.
Mal. Nor our strong sorrow
Upon the foot of motion.
Ban. Look to the lady:—
[Lady Macbeth *is carried out.*
And when we have our naked frailties hid,[2]
That suffer in exposure, let us meet,
And question this most bloody piece of work,
To know it further. Fears and scruples shake us:
In the great hand of God I stand; and, thence,
Against the undivulg'd pretence[3] I fight
Of treasonous malice.
Macb. And so do I.
All. So all.
Macb. Let's briefly put on manly readiness,
And meet i' the hall together.
All. Well contented.
[*Exeunt all but* Mal. *and* Don.
Mal. What will you do? Let's not consort with them:
To show an unfelt sorrow, is an office
Which the false man does easy: I'll to England.
Don. To Ireland, I; our separated fortune
Shall keep us both the safer: where we are,
There's daggers in men's smiles: the near in blood,
The nearer bloody.[4]
Mal. This murderous shaft that's shot,
Hath not yet lighted;[5] and our safest way
Is, to avoid the aim. Therefore, to horse;
And let us not be dainty of leave-taking,
But shift away: There's warrant in that theft
Which steals itself, when there's no mercy left.
[*Exeunt.*

SCENE IV. *Without the Castle. Enter* Rosse *and an* Old Man.

Old M. Threescore and ten I can remember well:
Within the volume of which time, I have seen
Hours dreadful, and things strange; but this sore night
Hath trifled former knowings.
Rosse. Ah, good father,
Thou see'st, the heavens, as troubled with man's act,
Threaten his bloody stage: by the clock, 'tis day,
And yet dark night strangles the travelling lamp:
Is it night's predominance, or the day's shame,
That darkness does the face of earth entomb,
When living light should kiss it?[6]
Old M. 'Tis unnatural,
Even like the deed that's done. On Tuesday last,
A falcon, tow'ring in her pride of place,[7]
Was by a mousing owl hawk'd at, and kill'd.
Rosse. And Duncan's horses (a thing most strange and certain,)
Beauteous and swift, the minions of their race,
Turn'd wild in nature, broke their stalls, flung out,
Contending 'gainst obedience, as they would make
War with mankind.
Old M. 'Tis said, they ate each other.
Rosse. They did so; to the amazement of mine eyes,
That look'd upon't. Here comes the good Macduff:—

Enter Macduff.

How goes the world, sir, now?
Macd. Why, see you not?
Rosse. Is't known who did this more than bloody deed?
Macd. Those that Macbeth hath slain.
Rosse. Alas, the day!
What good could they pretend?[8]
Macd. They were suborn'd:
Malcolm and Donalbain, the king's two sons,
Are stol'n away and fled; which puts upon them
Suspicion of the deed.
Rosse. 'Gainst nature still.
Thriftless ambition, that will ravin up
Thine own life's means!—Then 'tis most like,
The sovereignty will fall upon Macbeth.[9]
Macd. He is already nam'd; and gone to Scone,
To be invested.
Rosse. Where is Duncan's body?
Macd. Carried to Colme-kill;[10]
The sacred storehouse of his predecessors,
And guardian of their bones.
Rosse. Will you to Scone?
Macd. No, cousin, I'll to Fife.
Rosse. Well, I will thither.
Macd. Well, may you see things well done there;—adieu!—
Lest our old robes sit easier than our new!
Rosse. Father, farewell.
Old M. God's benison go with you: and with those
That would make good of bad, and friends of foes!
[*Exeunt.*

---

1 '*Breech'd with gore*,' covered with blood to their hilts.

2 i. e. when we have clothed our half drest bodies, which may take cold from being exposed to the air. It is possible, as Steevens remarks, that in such a cloud of words, the meaning might escape the reader. The Porter had already said that this 'place is too *cold* for hell,' meaning the court-yard of the castle in which Banquo and the rest now are.

3 *Pretence* is here put for *design* or *intention*. It is so used again in the Winter's Tale:—' The *pretence* whereof being by circumstance partly laid open.' Thus again in this tragedy:—

'What good could they *pretend?*'

i. e. *intend* to themselves. Banquo's meaning is—' in our present state of doubt and uncertainty about this murder, I have nothing to do but to put myself under the direction of God; and, relying on his support, I here declare myself an eternal enemy to this treason, and to all its *further designs that have not yet come to light*.'

4 '——— the near in blood,
The nearer bloody.'

Meaning that he suspects Macbeth to be the murderer; for he was the nearest in blood to the two princes, being the cousin-german of Duncan.

5 The allusion of the *unlighted shaft* appears to be—the death of the king only could neither insure the crown to Macbeth, nor accomplish any other purpose, while his sons were yet living, who had therefore just reason to apprehend that they should be removed by the same means. Malcolm therefore means to say, 'The shaft has not yet done all its intended mischief: I and my brother are yet to be destroyed before it will light on the ground and do no more harm.'

6 'After the murder of King Duffe,' says Holinshed, 'for the space of six months togither there appeared no sunne by daye, nor moon by night in anie part of the realme; but still the sky was covered with continual clouds; and sometimes such outrageous winds arose, with lightenings and tempests, that the people were in great fear of present destruction.'—It is evident that Shakspeare had this passage in his thoughts. Most of the portents here mentioned are related by Holinshed, as accompanying King Duffe's death: 'there was a *sparhawk* strangled by an owl,' and 'horses of singular beauty and swiftness did eat their own flesh.'

7 'A falcon tow'ring in her *pride of place*,' a technical phrase in falconry for *soaring to the highest pitch*. Faulcon *haultain* was the French term for a towering or high flying hawk.

8 *Pretend*, in the sense of the Latin *prætendo*, to *design*, or '*lay for a thing before it come*,' as the old dictionaries explain it.

9 Macbeth, by his birth, stood next in succession to the crown, after the sons of Duncan. King Malcolm, Duncan's predecessor, had two daughters, the eldest of whom was the mother of Duncan, the younger the mother of Macbeth.—*Holinshed.*

10 *Colme-kill* is the famous *Iona*, one of the western isles mentioned by Holinshed, as the burial place of many ancient kings of Scotland. Colme-kill means the *cell* or chapel of St. Columbo

ACT III.

SCENE I. Fores. *A Room in the Palace. Enter* BANQUO.

Ban. Thou hast it now, King, Cawdor, Glamis, all,
As the weird women promis'd; and, I fear,
Thou play'dst most foully for't; yet it was said,
It should not stand in thy posterity:
But that myself should be the root and father
Of many kings. If there come truth from them
(As upon thee, Macbeth, their speeches shine,)
Why, by the verities on thee made good,
May they not be my oracles as well,
And set me up in hope? But, hush; no more.

Senet sounded. Enter MACBETH, *as King;* LADY MACBETH, *as Queen;* LENOX, ROSSE, Lords, Ladies, *and* Attendants.

Macb. Here's our chief guest.
Lady M. If he had been forgotten,
It had been as a gap in our great feast,
And all things unbecoming.
Macb. To-night we hold a solemn supper,[1] sir,
And I'll request your presence.
Ban. Let your highness
Command upon me; to the which, my duties
Are with a most indissoluble tie
For ever knit.
Macb. Ride you this afternoon?
Ban. Ay, my good lord.
Macb. We should have else desir'd your good advice
(Which still hath been both grave and prosperous,)
In this day's council; but we'll take to-morrow.
Is't far you ride?
Ban. As far, my lord, as will fill up the time
'Twixt this and supper: go not my horse the better,[2]
I must become a borrower of the night,
For a dark hour, or twain.
Macb. Fail not our feast.
Ban. My lord, I will not.
Macb. We hear, our bloody cousins are bestow'd
In England, and in Ireland; not confessing
Their cruel parricide, filling their hearers
With strange invention: But of that to-morrow:
When, therewithal, we shall have cause of state,
Craving us jointly. Hie you to horse: Adieu,
Till you return at night. Goes Fleance with you?
Ban. Ay, my good lord; our time does call upon us.
Macb. I wish your horses swift and sure of foot;
And so I do commend[3] you to their backs.
Farewell.—— [*Exit* BANQUO.
Let every man be master of his time
Till seven at night; to make society
The sweeter welcome, we will keep ourself
Till supper-time alone: while then, God be with you.
[*Exeunt* LADY MACBETH, Lords, Ladies, &c.
Sirrah, a word with you: attend those men
Our pleasure?
Atten. They are, my lord, without the palace-gate.
Macb. Bring them before us.—[*Exit* Atten.]
To be thus is nothing;
But to be safely thus:—Our fears in Banquo
Stick deep; and in his royalty[4] of nature
Reigns that, which would be fear'd: 'Tis much he dares;
And, to[5] that dauntless temper of his mind,
He hath a wisdom that doth guide his valour
To act in safety. There is none, but he
Whose being I do fear: and, under him,
My genius is rebuk'd; as, it is said,
Mark Antony's was by Cæsar. He chid the sisters
When first they put the name of King upon me,
And bade them speak to him; then, prophetlike,
They hail'd him father to a line of kings:
Upon my head they plac'd a fruitless crown,
And put a barren sceptre in my gripe,
Thence to be wrench'd with an unlineal hand,
No son of mine succeeding. If it be so,
For Banquo's issue have I fil'd[6] my mind;
For them the gracious Duncan have I murder'd;
Put rancours in the vessel of my peace
Only for them; and mine eternal jewel
Given to the common enemy of man,[7]
To make them kings; the seed of Banquo kings!
Rather than so, come, fate, into the list,
And champion me to the utterance![8]——Who's there?—

Re-enter Attendant, *with two* Murderers.

Now go to the door, and stay there till we call.
[*Exit* Attendant.
Was it not yesterday we spoke together?
1 Mur. It was, so please your highness.
Macb. Well then, now
Have you considered of my speeches? Know,
That it was he, in the times past, which held you
So under fortune; which, you thought, had been
Our innocent self: this I made good to you
In our last conference, pass'd in probation[9] with you,
How you were borne in hand;[10] how cross'd; the instruments;
Who wrought with them; and all things else, that might,
To half a soul, and to a notion craz'd,
Say, Thus did Banquo.
1 Mur. You made it known to us.
Macb. I did so; and went further, which is now
Our point of second meeting. Do you find
Your patience so predominant in your nature,
That you can let this go? Are you so gospell'd[11]
To pray for that good man, and for his issue,
Whose heavy hand has bow'd you to the grave,
And beggar'd yours for ever?
1 Mur. We are men, my liege.
Macb. Ay, in the catalogue ye go for men;
As hounds, and greyhounds, mongrels, spaniels, curs,
Shoughs,[12] water-rugs, and demi-wolves, are cleped[13]
All by the name of dogs: the valued file[14]
Distinguishes the swift, the slow, the subtle,
The house-keeper, the hunter, every one
According to the gift which bounteous nature
Hath in him clos'd; whereby he does receive
Particular addition,[15] from the bill
That writes them all alike: and so of men.

---

1 'A solemn supper.' This was the phrase of Shakspeare's time for a feast or banquet given on a particular occasion, to *solemnize* any event, as a birth, marriage, coronation, &c. Howel, in a letter to Sir T. Hawke, 1636, says, 'I was invited yesternight to a *solemne supper* by B. J. [Ben Jonson,] where you were deeply remembered.'

2 i. e. 'if my horse does not go *well*.' Shakspeare often uses the comparative for the *positive* and *superlative*.

3 i. e. *commit.*

4 Nobleness.

5 'And *to* that,' i. e. *in addition* to.

6 For defiled.

7 'The common enemy of man.' Shakspeare repeats the phrase in Twelfth Night, Act iii. Sc. 4:—'Defy the devil: consider, he's an *enemy to mankind*.' The phrase was common among his contemporaries; the word *fiend*, Johnson remarks, signifies *enemy*.

8 'To the utterance.' This phrase, which is found in writers who preceded Shakspeare, is borrowed from the French; *se battre a l'outrance*, to fight desperately or to extremity, even to death. The sense therefore is:—'Let fate, that has foredoomed the exaltation of Banquo's sons, enter the lists against me in defence of its own decrees, I will fight against it to the extremity, whatever be the consequence.'

9 i. e. 'passed in *proving to* you.'

10 To *bear in hand* is to delude by encouraging hope and holding out fair prospects, without any intention of performance.

11 i. e. 'are you so obedient to the precept of the gospel, which teaches us to pray for those who despitefully use us?'

12 *Shoughs* are probably what we now call *shocks*. Nashe, in his Lenten Stuffe, mentions them, 'a trundle tail tike or *shough* or two.'

13 *Cleped*, called.

14 The *valued file* is the *descriptive list* wherein their value and peculiar qualities are set down; such a list of dogs may be found in Junius's Nomenclator, by Fleming, and may have furnished Shakspeare with the idea.

15 *Particular addition*, title, description

Now, if you have a station in the file,
Not in the worst rank of manhood, say it;
And I will put that business in your bosoms,
Whose execution takes your enemy off;
Grapples you to the heart and love of us,
Who wear our health but sickly in his life,
Which in his death were perfect.
2 Mur. I am one, my liege,
Whom the vile blows and buffets of the world
Have so incens'd, that I am reckless what
I do, to spite the world.
1 Mur. And I another,
So weary with disasters, tugg'd with fortune
That I would set my life on any chance,
To mend it, or be rid on't.
Macb. Both of you
Know, Banquo was your enemy.
2 Mur. True, my lord.
Macb. So is he mine: and in such bloody distance,[1]
That every minute of his being thrusts
Against my near'st of life: And though I could
With bare-fac'd power sweep him from my sight,
And bid my will avouch it; yet I must not,
For certain friends that are both his and mine,
Whose loves I may not drop, but wail his fall
Whom I myself struck down: and thence it is,
That I to your assistance do make love;
Masking the business from the common eye,
For sundry weighty reasons.
2 Mur. We shall, my lord,
Perform what you command us.
1 Mur. Though our lives——
Macb. Your spirits shine through you. Within this hour at most,
I will advise you where to plant yourselves:
Acquaint you with the perfect spy o' the time,[2]
The moment on't: for't must be done to-night,
And something from the palace; always thought,
That I require a clearness:[3] And with him
(To leave no rubs, nor botches, in the work,)
Fleance his son, that keeps him company,
Whose absence is no less material to me
Than is his father's, must embrace the fate
Of that dark hour. Resolve yourselves apart;
I'll come to you anon.
2 Mur. We are resolv'd my lord.
Macb. I'll call upon you straight; abide within.
It is concluded:——Banquo, thy soul's flight,
If it find heaven, must find it out to-night. [*Exeunt.*

SCENE II. *The same. Another Room. Enter* Lady Macbeth, *and a* Servant.

Lady M. Is Banquo gone from court?
Serv. Ay, madam, but returns again to-night.
Lady M. Say to the king, I would attend his leisure
For a few words.
Serv. Madam, I will. [*Exit.*
Lady M. Nought's had, all's spent,
Where our desire is got without content:
'Tis safer to be that which we destroy,
Than, by destruction, dwell in doubtful joy.

Enter Macbeth.

How now, my lord? why do you keep alone,
Of sorriest[4] fancies your companions making?
Using those thoughts, which should indeed have died
With them they think on? Things without remedy
Should be without regard: what's done is done.
Macb. We have scotch'd the snake, not kill'd it;
She'll close, and be herself; whilst our poor malice
Remains in danger of her former tooth.
But let the frame of things disjoint,
Both the worlds suffer,
Ere we will eat our meal in fear, and sleep
In the affliction of these terrible dreams
That shake us nightly: Better be with the dead,
Whom we, to gain our place,[5] have sent to peace,
Than on the torture of the mind to lie
In restless ecstacy.[6] Duncan is in his grave;
After life's fitful fever, he sleeps well:
Treason has done his worst; nor steel, nor poison,
Malice domestic, foreign levy, nothing,
Can touch him further!
Lady M. Come on, gentle my lord;
Sleek o'er your rugged looks; be bright and jovial
Among your guests to-night.
Macb. So shall I, love;
And so, I pray, be you: let your remembrance[7]
Apply to Banquo: present him eminence,[8] both
With eye and tongue: unsafe, the while, that we
Must lave our honours in these flattering streams;
And make our faces vizards to our hearts,
Disguising what they are.[9]
Lady M. You must leave this.
Macb. O, full of scorpions is my mind, dear wife!
Thou know'st that Banquo, and his Fleance, lives.
Lady M. But in them nature's copy's[10] not eterne.
Macb. There's comfort yet; they are assailable:
Then be thou jocund: Ere the bat hath flown
His cloister'd flight; ere, to black Hecate's summons,
The shard-borne beetle,[11] with his drowsy hums,
Hath rung night's yawning peal, there shall be done
A deed of dreadful note.
Lady M. What's to be done?
Macb. Be innocent of the knowledge, dearest chuck,
Till thou applaud the deed. Come, seeling[12] night,
Skarf up the tender eye of pitiful day;
And, with thy bloody and invisible hand,
Cancel and tear to pieces that great bond
Which keeps me pale![13]—Light thickens; and the crow
Makes wing to the rooky wood:[14]

1 '*Bloody distance*' is mortal enmity.
2 i. e. the exact time when you may *look out* or lie in wait for him.
3 '———— always thought
That I require a clearness.'
'Always remembering that I must stand clear of suspicion.'
4 *Sorriest*, most melancholy.
5 The first folio reads *peace;* the second folio *place.*
6 *Ecstacy*, in its general sense, signifies any violent emotion or alienation of the mind. The old dictionaries render it *a trance, a dampe, a crampe.*
7 *Remembrance* is here employed as a quadrisyllable.
8 *Present him eminence*, do him the highest honour.
9 The sense of this passage (though clouded by metaphor, and perhaps by omission) appears to be as follows:—'It is a sign that our royalty is unsafe, when it must descend to flattery, and stoop to dissimulation.' The present arrangement of the text is by Malone.
10 Ritson has justly observed, that 'Nature's *copy*' alludes to *copyhold* tenure, in which the tenant holds an estate for *life*, having nothing but the *copy* of the rolls of his lord's court to show for it. A *life-hold* tenure may well be said to be not eternal. The subsequent speech of Macbeth, in which he says,
'Cancel and tear to pieces *that great bond.*'
confirms this explanation. Many of Shakspeare's allusions are to legal customs.
11 That is, the beetle *borne* along the air by its *shards* or *scaly* wings. Steevens had the merit of first showing that *shard* or *sherd* was the ancient word for a *scale* or outward covering, a case or sheath; as appears from the following passage cited by him from Gower's Confessio Amantis, b. vi. fol. 138:—
'She sigh, her thought a dragon tho,
Whose *sherdes* shynen as the sonne.'
And again in book v. speaking of a serpent:—
'He was so *sherded* all about,
It held all edge-tool without.'
12 i. e. blinding: to *seel* up the eyes of a hawk was to close them by sewing the eyelids together.
13 So in Cymbeline:—
'*Cancel his bond of life*, dear God, I pray.'
14 By the expression, *light thickens*, Shakspeare means that it is *growing dark*. Thus, in Fletcher's Faithful Shepherdess:—
'Fold your flocks up, for the air
'Gins to *thicken*, and the sun
Already his great course hath run.'
Spenser, in the Shepherd's Calendar, has:—
'———— the welkin *thicks* apace'
Notwithstanding Mr. Steevens's ingenious attempts to explain the *rooky* wood otherwise, it surely means no-

Good things of day begin to droop and drowse;
Whiles night's black agents to their preys do rouse.[1]
Thou marvell'st at my words; but hold thee still;
Things, bad begun, make strong themselves by ill:
So, pr'ythee, go with me. [*Exeunt.*

SCENE III. *The same. A Park or Lawn, with a Gate leading to the Palace. Enter three* Murderers.

1 *Mur.* But who did bid thee join with us?
3 *Mur.* Macbeth.
2 *Mur.* He needs not our mistrust; since he delivers
Our offices, and what we have to do,
To the direction just.
1 *Mur.* Then stand with us.
The west yet glimmers with some streaks of day:
Now spurs the lated traveller apace,
To gain the timely inn; and near approaches
The subject of our watch.
3 *Mur.* Hark! I hear horses.
Ban. [*within.*] Give us a light there, ho!
2 *Mur.* Then it is he; the rest
That are within the note of expectation,[2]
Already are i' the court.
1 *Mur.* His horses go about.
3 *Mur.* Almost a mile: but he does usually,
So all men do, from hence to the palace gate
Make it their walk.

Enter BANQUO *and* FLEANCE, *a Servant with a Torch preceding them.*

2 *Mur.* A light, a light!
3 *Mur.* 'Tis he.
1 *Mur.* Stand to't.
Ban. It will be rain to-night.
1 *Mur.* Let it come down.
[*Assaults* BANQUO.
Ban. O, treachery! Fly, good Fleance, fly, fly, fly;
Thou may'st revenge. O slave!
[*Dies.* Fleance *and* Servant *escape.*[3]
3 *Mur.* Who did strike out the light?
1 *Mur.* Was't not the way?
3 *Mur.* There's but one down: the son is fled.
2 *Mur.* We have lost best half of our affair.
1 *Mur.* Well, let's away, and say how much is done.

SCENE IV. *A Room of State in the Palace. A Banquet prepared. Enter* MACBETH, LADY MACBETH, ROSSE, LENOX, *Lords, and* Attendants.

Macb. You know your own degrees, sit down: at first[4]
And last, the hearty welcome.
Lords. Thanks to your majesty.
Macb. Ourself will mingle with society,
And play the humble host.
Our hostess keeps her state;[5] but, in best time,
We will require her welcome.
Lady M. Pronounce it for me, sir, to all our friends;
For my heart speaks, they are welcome.

Enter first Murderer, *to the door*

Macb. See, they encounter thee with their hearts' thanks:——
Both sides are even: Here I'll sit i' the midst:
Be large in mirth; anon, we'll drink a measure
The table round.—There's blood upon thy face.
Mur. 'Tis Banquo's, then.
Macb. 'Tis better thee without, than he within.[6]
Is he despatch'd?
Mur. My lord, his throat is cut; that I did for him.
Macb. Thou art the best o' the cut-throats: Yet he's good,
That did the like for Fleance: if thou didst it,
Thou art the nonpareil.
Mur. Most royal sir,
Fleance is 'scap'd.
Macb. Then comes my fit again: I had else been perfect;
Whole as the marble, founded as the rock;
As broad and general as the casing air:
But now, I am cabin'd, cribb'd, confin'd, bound in
To saucy doubts and fears. But Banquo's safe?
Mur. Ay, my good lord: safe in a ditch he bides,
With twenty trenched[7] gashes on his head;
The least a death to nature.
Macb. Thanks for that:——
There the grown serpent lies; the worm, that's fled,
Hath nature that in time will venom breed,
No teeth for the present.—Get thee gone; to-morrow
We'll hear ourselves again. [*Exit* Murderer.
Lady M. My royal lord,
You do not give the cheer: the feast is sold,
That is not often vouch'd while 'tis a making,
'Tis given with welcome: To feed were best at home;
From thence, the sauce to meat is ceremony;
Meeting were bare without it.
Macb. Sweet remembrancer!—
Now, good digestion wait on appetite,
And health on both!
Len. May it please your highness, sit?
[*The Ghost of* BANQUO *rises, and sits in* MACBETH'S *place.*
Macb. Here had we now our country's honour roof'd,
Were the grac'd person of our Banquo present,
Who may I rather challenge for unkindness,
Than pity for mischance![8]
Rosse. His absence, sir,
Lays blame upon his promise. Please it your highness
To grace us with your royal company?
Macb. The table's full.
Len. Here's a place reserv'd, sir!
Macb. Where?
Len. Here, my good lord. What is't that moves your highness?
Macb. Which of you have done this?
Lords. What, my good lord?
Macb. Thou canst not say, I did it: never shake
Thy gory locks at me.
Rosse. Gentlemen, rise; his highness is not well.
Lady M. Sit, worthy friends:—my lord is often thus,
And hath been from his youth: 'pray you, keep seat;
The fit is momentary; upon a thought[9]
He will again be well: If much you note him,

thing more than the wood inhabited by *rooks.* The poet has shown himself a close observer of nature, in marking the return of these birds to their nest-trees when the day is drawing to a close.

1 See note on King Richard III. Act iv. Sc. 1.

2 i. e. they who are set down in the list of guests, and expected to supper.

3 *Fleance*, after the assassination of his father, fled into Wales, where, by the daughter of the prince of that country, he had a son named Walter, who afterwards became Lord High Steward of Scotland, and from thence assumed the name of Sir Walter Steward. From him, in a direct line, King James I. was descended; in compliment to whom Shakspeare has chosen to describe Banquo, who was equally concerned with Macbeth in the murder of Duncan, as innocent of that crime.

4 'At first and last.' Johnson, with great plausibility, proposes to read, '*To* first and last.'

5 '*Keeps her state*,' continues in her chair of state A *state* was a royal chair with a canopy over it.

6 ''Tis better thee without than he within,' that is, am better pleased that the blood of Banquo should be o.. thy face than in his body. *He* is put for *him.*

7 'With twenty *trenched* gashes on his head.' From the French *trancher*, to cut.

8 Macbeth betrays himself by an overacted regard for Banquo, of whose absence from the feast he affects to complain, that he may not be suspected of knowing the cause, though at the same time he very unguardedly drops an allusion to that cause. *May I* seems to imply here a wish, not an assertion.

9 i. e. as speedily as *thought* can be exerted.

You shall offend him, and extend his passion;[1]
Feed, and regard him not.—Are you a man?
Macb. Ay, and a bold one, that dare look on that
Which might appal the devil.
Lady M. O proper stuff!
This is the very painting of your fear:
This is the air-drawn dagger, which, you said,
Led you to Duncan. O, these flaws[2] and starts
(Impostors to[3] true fear) would well become
A woman's story at a winter's fire,
Authoriz'd by her grandam. Shame itself!
Why do you make such faces? When all's done,
You look but on a stool.
Macb. Pr'ythee, see there! behold! look! lo! how say you?——
Why, what care I? If thou canst nod, speak too.—
If charnel-houses, and our graves, must send
Those that we bury,back, our monuments
Shall be the maws of kites.[4] [*Ghost disappears.*
Lady M. What! quite unmann'd in folly?
Macb. If I stand here, I saw him.
Lady M. Fye, for shame!
Macb. Blood hath been shed ere now, i' the olden time,
Ere human statute purg'd the general weal;
Ay, and since, too, murders have been perform'd
Too terrible for the ear: the times have been,
That, when the brains were out, the man would die,
And there an end: but now, they rise again,
With twenty mortal murders on their crowns,
And push us from our stools: This is more strange
Than such a murder is.
Lady M. My worthy lord,
Your noble friends do lack you.
Macb. I do forget:—
Do not muse[5] at me, my most worthy friends;
I have a strange infirmity, which is nothing
To those that know me. Come, love and health to all;
Then I'll sit down:——Give me some wine, fill full:
I'll drink to the general joy of the whole table,

Ghost rises.

And to our dear friend Banquo, whom we miss;
Would, he were here! to all, and him, we thirst,
And all to all.[6]
Lords. Our duties, and the pledge.
Macb. Avaunt! and quit my sight! Let the earth hide thee!
Thy bones are marrowless, thy blood is cold;
Thou hast no speculation[7] in those eyes
Which thou dost glare with!
Lady M. Think of this, good peers,
But as a thing of custom: 'tis no other;
Only it spoils the pleasure of the time.
Macb. What man dare, I dare:
Approach thou like the rugged Russian bear,
The arm'd rhinoceros, or the Hyrcan tiger,[8]
Take any shape but that, and my firm nerves
Shall never tremble: Or, be alive again,
And dare me to the desert with thy sword.
If trembling I inhabit[9] then, protest me
The baby of a girl. Hence, horrible shadow!
[*Ghost disappears.*
Unreal mockery, hence!—Why, so;—being gone,
I am a man again.—'Pray you, sit still.
Lady M. You have displac'd the mirth, broke the good meeting,
With most admir'd disorder.
Macb. Can such things be,
And overcome[10] us like a summer's cloud,
Without our special wonder? You make me strange
Even to the disposition that I owe,[11]
When now I think you can behold such sights,[12]
And keep the natural ruby of your cheeks,
When mine are blanch'd with fear.
Rosse. What sights, my lord?
Lady M. I pray you, speak not; he grows worse and worse;
Question enrages him: at once, good night:—
Stand not upon the order of your going,
But go at once.
Len. Good night, and better health
Attend his majesty!
Lady M. A kind good night to all!
[*Exeunt* Lords *and* Attendants.
Macb. It will have blood; they say, blood will have blood;
Stones have been known to move, and trees to speak;
Augures[13] and understood relations have,
By magot-pies, and choughs, and rooks, brought forth
The secret'st man of blood.—What is the night?
Lady M. Almost at odds with morning, which is which.
Macb. How say'st thou,[14] that Macduff denies his person,
At our great bidding?
Lady M. Did you send to him, sir?
Macb. I hear it by the way; but I will send:
There's not a one of them, but in his house
I keep a servant fee'd. I will, to-morrow,
(And betimes I will,) to the weird sisters:
More shall they speak; for now I am bent to know,
By the worst means, the worst: for mine own good,
All causes shall give way: I am in blood
Stept in so far, that, should I wade no more,
Returning were as tedious as go o'er:

---

1 i. e. prolong his suffering, make his fit longer.

2 *Flaws* are sudden gusts.

3 'Impostors *to* true fear.' Warburton's learning serves him not here; his explanation is erroneous. Malone idly suggests that *to* may be used for *of*. Mason has hit the meaning, though his way of accounting for it is wrong. It seems strange that none of the commentators should be aware that this was a form of *elliptic* expression, commonly used even at this day, in the phrase 'this is nothing *to* them,' i. e. *in comparison* to them.

4 The same thought occurs in Spenser's Faerie Queene, b. ii. c. viii.:—
'Be not entombed in the raven or the *kight*.'

5 Shakspeare uses to *muse* for to *wonder*, to be in *amaze*.

6 That is, 'we *desire to drink*' all good wishes to all.

7 'Thou hast no speculation in those eyes.' Bullokar, in his Expositor, 1616, explains '*Speculation*, the inward knowledge or *beholding* of a thing.' Thus, in the 115th Psalm:—'Eyes have they, but see not.'

8 *Hyrcan* for *Hyrcanian* was the mode of expression at that time.

9 Pope changed *inhabit*, the reading of the old copy, to *inhibit*, and Steevens altered *then* to *thee*, so that in the late editions this line runs:—
'If trembling I *inhibit thee*, protest me
The baby of a girl.'
To *inhibit* is to *forbid*, a meaning which will not suit with the context of the passage. The original text is sufficiently plain, and much in Shakspeare's manner. 'Dare me to the desert with thy sword; if then I do not meet thee there; if trembling I stay in my castle, or any *habitation*; if I then hide my head, or *dwell* in any place through fear, protest me the baby of a girl.' If it had not been for the meddling of Pope and others, this passage would have hardly required a note.

10 '*Overcome us*,' pass over us without wonder, as a casual summer's cloud passes unregarded.

11 i. e. possess.

12 'You strike me with amazement, make me scarce know myself, now when I think that you can behold such sights unmoved,' &c.

13 i. e. *auguries*, divinations; formerly spelt *augures*, as appears by Florio in voce *augurio*. By *understood relations*, probably, connected circumstances *relating* to the crime are meant. I am inclined to think that the passage should be pointed thus:—
'Stones have been known to move, and trees to speak
Augures; and understood relations have,
By magot-pies, and choughs, and rooks, brought forth
The secret'st man of blood.'
In all the modern editions we have it erroneously *augurs*. *Magot-pie* is the original name of the *magpie*: stories such as Shakspeare alludes to are to be found in Lupton's Thousand Notable Things, and in Goulart's Admirable Histories.

14 i. e. *what* say'st thou *to this circumstance?* Thus, in Macbeth's address to his wife, on the first appearance of Banquo's ghost!—
'—— behold! look! lo! *how say you*?'

Strange things I have in head, that will to hand;
Which must be acted, ere they may be scann'd.[1]

Lady M. You lack the season[2] of all natures, sleep.

Macb. Come, we'll to sleep: My strange and self abuse
Is the initiate fear, that wants hard use:—
We are yet but young in deed.[3] [*Exeunt.*

SCENE V. *The Heath. Thunder. Enter* HECATE,[4] *meeting the three* Witches.

1 *Witch.* Why, how now, Hecate? you look angerly.

Hec. Have I not reason, beldames, as you are,
Saucy, and overbold? How did you dare
To trade and traffic with Macbeth,
In riddles and affairs of death;
And I, the mistress of your charms,
The close contriver of all harms,
Was never call'd to bear my part,
Or show the glory of our art?
And, which is worse, all you have done
Hath been but for a wayward son,
Spiteful, and wrathful; who, as others do,
Loves for his own ends, not for you.
But make amends now: Get you gone,
And at the pit of Acheron
Meet me i' the morning; thither he
Will come to know his destiny.
Your vessels, and your spells, provide,
Your charms, and every thing beside;
I am for the air; this night I'll spend
Unto a dismal and a fatal end.
Great business must be wrought ere noon:
Upon the corner of the moon
There hangs a vaporous drop profound;[5]
I'll catch it ere it come to ground:
And that, distill'd by magic slights,[6]
Shall raise such artificial sprights,
As, by the strength of their illusion,
Shall draw him on to his confusion:
He shall spurn fate, scorn death, and bear
His hopes 'bove wisdom, grace, and fear:
And you all know, security
Is mortal's chiefest enemy.

Song. [*Within.*] *Come away, come away, &c.*[7]
Hark, I am call'd; my little spirit, see,
Sits in a foggy cloud, and stays for me. [*Exit.*

1 *Witch.* Come, let's make haste; she'll soon be back again. [*Exeunt.*

SCENE VI. Fores. *A Room in the Palace.* *Enter* LENOX *and another* Lord.

Len. My former speeches have but hit your thoughts,
Which can interpret further: only, I say,
Things have been strangely borne: The gracious Duncan
Was pitied of Macbeth:—marry, he was dead:—
And the right-valiant Banquo walk'd too late;
Whom you may say, if it please you, Fleance kill'd,
For Fleance fled. Men must not walk too late.
Who cannot[8] want the thought, how monstrous
It was for Malcolm, and Donalbain,
To kill their gracious father? damned fact!
How it did grieve Macbeth! did he not straight,
In pious rage, the two delinquents tear,
That were the slaves of drink, and thralls of sleep?
Was not that nobly done? Ay, and wisely too;
For, 'twould have anger'd any heart alive,
To hear the men deny it. So that, I say,
He has borne all things well: and I do think,
That, had he Duncan's sons under his key,
(As, an't please heaven, he shall not,) they should find
What 'twere to kill a father; so should Fleance.
But, peace!—for from broad words, and 'cause he fail'd
His presence at the tyrant's feast, I hear,
Macduff lives in disgrace: Sir, can you tell
Where he bestows himself?

Lord. The son of Duncan,
From whom this tyrant holds the due of birth,
Lives in the English court; and is receiv'd
Of the most pious Edward with such grace,
That the malevolence of fortune nothing
Takes from his high respect: Thither Macduff
Is gone to pray the holy king, upon his aid
To wake Northumberland, and warlike Siward:
That, by the help of these, (with Him above
To ratify the work,) we may again
Give to our tables meat, sleep to our nights;
Free from our feasts and banquets bloody knives;[9]
Do faithful homage, and receive free honours,[10]
All which we pine for now: And this report
Hath so exasperate[11] the king, that he
Prepares for some attempt of war.

Len. Sent he to Macduff?

Lord. He did: and with an absolute, *Sir, not I,*
The cloudy messenger turns me his back,
And hums; as who should say, *You'll rue the time*
That clogs me with this answer.

Len. And that well might
Advise him to a caution, to hold what distance
His wisdom can provide. Some holy angel
Fly to the court of England, and unfold
His message ere he come; that a swift blessing
May soon return to this our suffering country
Under a hand accurs'd![12]

Lord. I'll send my prayers with him! [*Exeunt.*

---

1 i. e. examined nicely.

2 'You lack the season of all natures, sleep.' Johnson explains this, '*You want sleep*, which *seasons* or gives the relish to *all natures*.' Indiget somni vitæ condimenti. So in All's Well that Ends Well: ''Tis the best brine a maiden can season her praise in.' It has, however, been suggested that the meaning is, 'You stand in need of the time or *season* of sleep which all natures require.' I incline to the last interpretation.

3 The editions previous to Theobald's read:—

'We're but young *indeed*.'

The *initiate fear* is the fear that always attends the first initiation into guilt, before the mind becomes callous and insensible by *hard use* or frequent repetition of it.

4 Shakspeare has been unjustly censured for introducing Hecate among the vulgar witches, and consequently for confounding ancient with modern superstitions. But the poet has elsewhere shown himself well acquainted with the classical connexion which this deity had with witchcraft. Reginald Scot, in his discovery, mentions it as the common opinion of all writers, that witches were supposed to have nightly 'meetings with Herodias and the Pagan gods,' and that 'in the night time they ride abroad with *Diana*, the goddess of the Pagans,' &c. Their dame or chief leader seems always to have been an old Pagan, as 'the Ladie Sibylla, Minerva, or Diana.'

5 Steevens remarks that Shakspeare's mythological knowledge on this occasion appears to have deserted him: for as *Hecate* is only one of the three names belonging to the same goddess, she could not properly be employed in one character to catch a drop that fell from her in another. In a Midsummer Night's Dream, however, the poet was sufficiently aware of her threefold capacity:—

'—— fairies, that do run
By the *triple* Hecat's team.'

The *vaporous drop profound* seems to have been meant for the same as the *virus lunare* of the ancients, being a foam which the moon was supposed to shed on particular herbs, or other objects, when strongly solicited by enchantment.

6 *Slights* are arts, subtle practices.

7 This song is to be found entire in The Witch, by Middleton.

8 'Who *cannot* want the thought;' &c. The sense requires 'who *can* want the thought;' but it is probably a lapse of the poet's pen.

9 'Free from our feasts and banquets bloody knives.' The construction is:—'Free our feasts and banquets from bloody knives.'

10 Johnson says, '*Free* may be either honours *freely bestowed*, not purchased by crimes; or honours *without slavery*, without dread of a tyrant.' I have shown in a note on Twelfth Night, Act ii. Sc. 4. that *free* meant *pure*, *chaste*, consequently *unspotted*, which may be its meaning here. *Free* also meant *noble*. See note on the Second Part of King Henry VI. Act iii. Sc. 1.

11 *Exasperate*, for exasperated.

12 The construction is, 'to this our country, suffering under a hand accursed.'

ACT IV.

SCENE I. *A dark Cave. In the middle, a Cauldron boiling. Thunder. Enter the three* Witches.[1]

1 *Witch.* Thrice the brinded cat hath mew'd.
2 *Witch.* Thrice; and once the hedge-pig whin'd.[2]
3 *Witch.* Harper cries:—'Tis time, 'tis time.
1 *Witch.* Round about the cauldron go;
In the poison'd entrails throw.——
Toad, that under coldest[3] stone,
Days and nights hast thirty-one
Swelter'd[4] venom, sleeping got,
Boil thou first i' the charmed pot!
All. Double, double toil and trouble;
Fire, burn; and, cauldron, bubble.
2 *Witch.* Fillet of a fenny snake,
In the cauldron boil and bake:
Eye of newt, and toe of frog,
Wool of bat, and tongue of dog,
Adder's fork, and blind-worm's[5] sting,
Lizard's leg, and owlet's wing,
For a charm of powerful trouble,
Like a hell-broth boil and bubble.
All. Double, double toil and trouble;
Fire, burn; and, cauldron bubble.
3 *Witch.* Scale of dragon, tooth of wolf;
Witch's mummy; maw and gulf[6]
Of the ravin'd[7] salt-sea shark;
Root of hemlock, digg'd i' the dark;
Liver of blaspheming Jew;
Gall of goat; and slips of yew,
Sliver'd[8] in the moon's eclipse;
Nose of Turk, and Tartar's lips;
Finger of birth-strangled babe,
Ditch-deliver'd by a drab,
Make the gruel thick and slab:
Add thereto a tiger's chaudron,[9]
For the ingredients of our cauldron.
All. Double, double toil and trouble;
Fire, burn; and, cauldron, bubble.
2 *Witch.* Cool it with a baboon's blood,
Then the charm is firm and good.

Enter Hecate, *and the other three* Witches.

Hec. O, well done! I commend your pains;
And every one shall share i' the gains.
And now about the cauldron sing,
Like elves and fairies in a ring,
Enchanting all that you put in.

SONG.[10]

Black spirits and white,
Red spirits and gray;
Mingle, mingle, mingle,
You that mingle may.

2 *Witch.* By the pricking of my thumbs,[11]
Something wicked this way comes:——
Open, locks, whoever knocks.

Enter Macbeth.

Macb. How now, you secret, black, and midnight hags?
What is't you do?
All. A deed without a name.
Macb. I conjure you, by that which you profess,
(Howe'er you come to know it,) answer me:
Though you untie the winds, and let them fight
Against the churches; though the yesty[12] waves
Confound and swallow navigation up;
Though bladed corn be lodg'd,[13] and trees blown down;
Though castles topple[14] on their warders' heads;
Though palaces, and pyramids, do slope
Their heads to their foundations; though the treasure
Of nature's germins[15] tumble all together,
Even till destruction sicken, answer me
To what I ask you.
1 *Witch.* Speak.
2 *Witch.* Demand.
3 *Witch.* We'll answer.
1 *Witch.* Say, if thou'dst rather hear it from our mouths,
Or from our masters'?
Macb. Call them, let me see them
1 *Witch.* Pour in sow's blood, that hath eaten
Her nine farrow;[16] grease, that's sweaten
From the murderer's gibbet, throw
Into the flame.
All. Come, high, or low,
Thyself, and office, deftly[17] show.

Thunder. An Apparition *of an armed Head rises.*

Macb. Tell me, thou unknown power,——
1 *Witch.* He knows thy thought,
Hear his speech, but say thou nought.[19]
App. Macbeth! Macbeth! Macbeth! beware Macduff;
Beware the thane of Fife.—Dismiss me:—Enough.[20] [*Descends.*
Macb. Whate'er thou art, for thy good caution, thanks;
Thou hast harp'd[21] my fear aright:—But one word more:—

---

1 '*Enter the three Witches.*' Dr. Johnson has called the reader's attention to the 'judgment with which Shakspeare has selected all the circumstances of his infernal ceremonies, and how exactly he has conformed to common opinions and traditions.'

2 'Thrice; and once the hedge-pig whin'd.' The urchin or hedgehog, like the toad, for its solitariness, the ugliness of its appearance, and from a popular belief that it sucked or poisoned the udders of cows, was adopted into the demonologic system; and its shape was sometimes supposed to be assumed by mischievous elves. Hence it was one of the plagues of Caliban in the Tempest.

3 'Coldest stone.' The old copy reads '*cold* stone;' the emendation is Steevens's. Mr. Boswell thinks that the alteration was unnecessary.

4 *Sweltered.* This word is employed to signify that the animal was moistened with its own cold exudations.

5 The *blind-worm* is the *slow-worm.*

6 *Gulf,* the throat.

7 To *ravin* according to Minshew is to *devour, to eat greedily. Ravin'd,* therefore, may be *glutted with prey.* Unless, with Malone, we suppose that Shakspeare used *ravin'd* for *ravenous,* the passive participle for the adjective. In Horman's Vulgaria, 1519, occurs 'Thou art a *ravenar* of delycatis.'

8 *Sliver* is a common word in the north, where it means *to cut a piece* or *slice.*

9 i. e. *entrails;* a word formerly in common use in books of cookery, in one of which, printed in 1597, is a receipt to make a pudding of a calf's *chaldron.*

10 'Black spirits and white.' The original edition of this play only contains the two first words of this song; the entire stanza is found in The Witch, by Middleton, and is there called 'A charme Song about a Vessel.'

11 'By the pricking of my thumbs.' It is a very ancient superstition, that all sudden pains of the body, and other sensations which could not naturally be accounted for, were presages of somewhat that was shortly to happen.

12 i. e. foaming, frothy.

13 i. e. laid flat by wind or rain.

14 *Topple,* tumble.

15 *Germens,* seeds which have begun to sprout or germinate.

16 'Pour in sow's blood, that hath eaten
Her nine farrow.'
Shakspeare probably caught this idea from the laws of Kenneth II. king of Scotland:—'If a sow *eate hir pigges,* let hyr be stoned to death and buried, that no man eate of hyr flesh.'—*Holinshed's History of Scotland, ed.* 1577, p. 181.

17 *Deftly* is adroitly, dexterously.

18 The armed head represents symbolically Macbeth's head cut off and brought to Malcolm by Macduff. The bloody child is Macduff, untimely ripped from his mother's womb. The child, with a crown on his head and a bough in his hand, is the royal Malcolm, who ordered his soldiers to hew them down a bough, and bear it before them to Dunsinane.

19 Silence was necessary during all incantations.

20 Spirits thus evoked were supposed to be impatient of being questioned.

21 *Harp'd,* touched on a passion as a harper touches a string.

1 *Witch.* He will not be commanded: Here's another,
More potent than the first.

Thunder. *An* Apparition *of a bloody Child rises.*

App. Macbeth! Macbeth! Macbeth!—
Macb. Had I three ears, I'd hear thee.[1]
App. Be bloody, bold,
And resolute: laugh to scorn the power of man,
For none of woman born shall harm Macbeth.[2]
[*Descends.*
Macb. Then live, Macduff; what need I fear of thee?
But yet I'll make assurance double sure,
And take a bond of fate: thou shalt not live;
That I may tell pale-hearted fear, it lies,
And sleep in spite of thunder.—What is this,

Thunder. *An* Apparition *of a Child crowned, with a Tree in his Hand, rises.*

That rises like the issue of a king;
And wears upon his baby brow the round
And top of sovereignty?[3]
All. Listen, but speak not to't.
App. Be lion-mettled, proud; and take no care
Who chafes, who frets, or where conspirers are;
Macbeth shall never vanquish'd be, until
Great Birnam wood to high Dunsinane hill[4]
Shall come against him. [*Descends.*
Macb. That will never be;
Who can impress the forest;[5] bid the tree
Unfix his earth-bound root? sweet bodements! good!
Rebellious head,[6] rise never, till the wood
Of Birnam rise, and our high-plac'd Macbeth
Shall live the lease of nature, pay his breath
To time, and mortal custom.—Yet my heart
Throbs to know one thing; Tell me, (if your art
Can tell so much,) shall Banquo's issue ever
Reign in this kingdom?
All. Seek to know no more.
Macb. I will be satisfied: deny me this,
And an eternal curse fall on you! Let me know:—
Why sinks that cauldron? and what noise[7] is this?
[*Hautboys.*
1 *Witch.* Show! 2 *Witch.* Show! 3 *Witch.* Show!
All. Show his eyes, and grieve his heart;[8]
Come like shadows, so depart.

Eight Kings appear, and pass over the Stage in order; the last with a Glass in his Hand; BANQUO *following.*

Macb. Thou art too like the spirit of Banquo; down!
Thy crown does sear mine eyeballs:—And thy hair,
Thou other gold-bound brow, is like the first:—
A third is like the former:—Filthy hags!
Why do you show me this?—A fourth?—Start, eyes!
What! will the line stretch out to the crack of doom?[9]
Another yet?—A seventh?—I'll see no more:—
And yet the eighth appears, who bears a glass,[10]
Which shows me many more; and some I see,
That twofold balls and treble sceptres carry;[11]
Horrible sight!—Now, I see, 'tis true;
For the blood-bolter'd[12] Banquo smiles upon me,
And points at them for his.—What, is this so?
1 *Witch.* Ay, sir, all this is so:—But why
Stands Macbeth thus amazedly?—
Come, sisters, cheer we up his sprights,[13]
And show the best of our delights;
I'll charm the air to give a sound,
While you perform your antique[14] round.
That this great king may kindly say,
Our duties did his welcome pay.
[*Music. The* Witches *dance, and vanish.*
Macb. Where are they? Gone?---Let this pernicious hour
Stand aye accursed in the calendar!—
Come in, without there!

Enter LENOX.

Len. What's your grace's will?
Macb. Saw you the weird sisters?
Len. No, my lord.
Macb. Came they not by you?
Len. No, indeed, my lord.
Macb. Infected be the air whereon they ride;
And damn'd all those that trust them!---I did hear
The galloping of horse: Who was't came by?
Len. 'Tis two or three, my lord, that bring you word,
Macduff is fled to England.
Macb. Fled to England?
Len. Ay, my good lord.
Macb. Time, thou anticipat'st[15] my dread exploits:
The flighty purpose never is o'ertook,
Unless the deed go with it: From this moment
The very firstlings of my heart shall be
The firstlings of my hand. And even now
To crown my thoughts with acts, be it thought and done:
The castle of Macduff I will surprise;
Seize upon Fife; give to the edge o' the sword
His wife, his babes, and all unfortunate souls
That trace[16] him in his line. No boasting like a fool:
This deed I'll do, before this purpose cool:

---

1 'Had I three ears, I'd hear thee.' This singular expression probably means no more than 'I will listen to thee with all attention.'

2 'For none of woman born shall harm Macbeth.' So Holinshed:—'And surely hereupon he had put Macduff to death, but that a certeine witch, whom he had in great trust, had told him, that he should never be slaine with man borne of anie woman, nor vanquished till the wood of Bernane came to the castle of Dunsinane. This prophecy put all fear out of his heart.'

3 The *round* is that part of a crown which encircles the head: the *top* is the ornament which rises above it.

4 The present accent of *Dunsinane* is right. In every subsequent instance the accent is misplaced.

5 i. e. command it to serve him like a soldier impressed.

6 'Rebellious *head.*' The old copy reads *dead;* the emendation is Theobald's.

7 *Noise* in our old poets is often literally synonymous for *music.*

8 'Show his eyes, and grieve his heart.' 'And the man of thine, whom I shall not cut off from mine altar, shall be to *consume thine eyes, and to grieve thine heart.*'—1 *Samuel*, ii. 33.

9 i. e. the dissolution of nature. *Crack* and *crash* were formerly synonymous.

10 This method of juggling prophecy is referred to in Measure for Measure, Act ii. Sc. 8:—

'——— and like a prophet
Looks in a *glass*, and shows me *future evils.*'

In an extract from the Penal Laws against witches, it is said 'they do answer either by voice, or else set before their eyes in *glasses*, chrystal stones, &c. the pictures or images of the persons or things sought for.'

11 'That twofold balls and treble sceptres carry.' This was intended as a compliment to James the First: he first united the two islands and the three kingdoms under one head, whose house too was said to be descended from Banquo, who is therefore represented not only as innocent, but as a noble character; whereas, according to history, he was confederate with Macbeth in the murder of Duncan.

12 In Warwickshire, when a horse, sheep, or other animal, perspires much, and any of the hair or wool, in consequence of such perspiration, or any redundant humour, becomes matted into tufts with grime and sweat, he is said to be *boltered;* and whenever the blood issues out and coagulates, forming the locks into hard clotted bunches, the beast is said to be *blood-boltered.* When a boy has a broken head, so that his hair is matted together with blood, his head is said to be *boltered* [pronounced *baltered.*] The word *baltereth* is used in this sense by Philemon Holland in his Translation of Pliny's Natural History, 1601, b. xii. c. xvii. p. 370. It is therefore applicable to Banquo, who had 'twenty trenched gashes on his head.'

13 i. e. *spirits.* It should seem that *spirits* was almost always pronounced *sprights* or *sprites* by Shakspeare's contemporaries.

14 *Antique* was the old spelling for *antic.*

15 i.e. preventest them, by taking away the opportunity.

16 i. e. follow, succeed in it.

But no more sights!---Where are these gentlemen?
Come, bring me where they are. [*Exeunt.*

SCENE II. Fife. *A Room in* Macduff's *Castle.*
Enter Lady Macduff, *her* Son, *and* Rosse.

L. Macd. What had he done, to make him fly the land?

Rosse. You must have patience, madam.

L. Macd. He had none;
His flight was madness: When our actions do not,
Our fears do make us traitors.[1]

Rosse. You know not,
Whether it was his wisdom, or his fear.

L. Macb. Wisdom! to leave his wife, to leave his babes,
His mansion, and his titles, in a place
From whence himself does fly? He loves us not;
He wants the natural touch[2]:—for the poor wren,
The most diminutive of birds, will fight,
Her young ones in her nest, against the owl.
All is the fear, and nothing is the love;
As little is the wisdom, where the flight
So runs against all reason.

Rosse. My dearest coz',
I pray you, school yourself: But, for your husband,
He is noble, wise, judicious, and best knows
The fits o' the season.[3] I dare not speak much further:
But cruel are the times, when we are traitors,
And do not know ourselves; when we hold rumour
From what we fear, yet know not what we fear;[4]
But float upon a wild and violent sea,
Each way, and move.---I take my leave of you:
Shall not be long but I'll be here again:
Things at the worst will cease, or else climb upward
To what they were before.---My pretty cousin,
Blessing upon you!

L. Macd. Father'd he is, and yet he's fatherless.

Rosse. I am so much a fool, should I stay longer,
It would be my disgrace, and your discomfort:
I take my leave at once. [*Exit* Rosse.

L. Macd. Sirrah,[5] your father's dead;
And what will you do now? How will you live?

Son. As birds do, mother.

L. Macd. What, with worms and flies?

Son. With what I get, I mean; and so do they.

L. Macd. Poor bird! thou'dst never fear the net, nor lime,
The pit-fall, nor the gin.

Son. Why should I, mother? Poor birds they are not set for.
My father is not dead, for all your saying.

L. Macd. Yes, he is dead; how wilt thou do for a father?

Son. Nay, how will you do for a husband?

L. Macd. Why, I can buy me twenty at any market.

Son. Then you'll buy 'em to sell again.

L. Macd. Thou speak'st with all thy wit; and yet i' faith,
With wit enough for thee.

Son. Was my father a traitor, mother?

L. Macd. Ay, that he was.

Son. What is a traitor?

L. Macd. Why, one that swears and lies.

Son. And be all traitors, that do so?

L. Macd. Every one that does so, is a traitor, and must be hanged.

Son. And must they all be hanged, that swear and lie?

L. Macd. Every one.

Son. Who must hang them?

L. Macd. Why, the honest men.

Son. Then the liars and swearers are fools: for there are liars and swearers enough to beat the honest men, and hang up them.

L. Macd. Now, God help thee, poor monkey!
But how wilt thou do for a father?

Son. If he were dead, you'd weep for him: if you would not, it were a good sign that I should quickly have a new father.

L. Macd. Poor prattler! how thou talk'st.

Enter a Messenger.

Mess. Bless you, fair dame! I am not to you known,
Though in your state of honour I am perfect.[6]
I doubt, some danger does approach you nearly.
If you will take a homely man's advice,
Be not found here; hence, with your little ones.
To fright you thus, methinks, I am too savage;
To do worse to you, were fell cruelty,
Which is too nigh your person. Heaven preserve you!
I dare abide no longer. [*Exit* Messenger.

L. Macd. Whither should I fly?
I have done no harm. But I remember now
I am in this earthly world; where, to do harm,
Is often laudable; to do good, sometime,
Accounted dangerous folly: Why then, alas!
Do I put up that womanly defence,
To say, I have done no harm?——What are these faces?

Enter Murderers.

Mur. Where is your husband?

L. Macd. I hope, in no place so unsanctified,
Where such as thou may'st find him.

Mur. He's a traitor.

Son. Thou ly'st, thou shag-ear'd[7] villain.

Mur. What, you egg! [*Stabbing him.*
Young fry of treachery!

Son. He has killed me, mother,
Run away, I pray you. [*Dies.*
[*Exit* Lady Macduff, *crying murder, and pursued by the* Murderers.

SCENE III. England. *A Room in the King's Palace. Enter* Malcolm *and* Macduff.[8]

Mal. Let us seek out some desolate shade, and there
Weep our sad bosoms empty.

Macd. Let us rather
Hold fast the mortal sword; and, like good men,
Bestride our downfall'n birthdom:[9] Each new morn,
New widows howl; new orphans cry; new sorrows
Strike heaven on the face, that it resounds
As if it felt with Scotland, and yell'd out
Like syllable of dolour.

Mal. What I believe, I'll wail;
What know, believe; and, what I can redress,
As I shall find the time to friend,[10] I will.
What you have spoke, it may be so, perchance.
This tyrant, whose sole name blisters our tongues,
Was once thought honest: you have lov'd him well;

---

1 'Our fears do make us traitors.' Our flight is considered as evidence of our treason.

2 *Natural touch*, natural affection.

3 *The fits o' the season* should appear to be the *violent disorders* of the season, its convulsions: as we still say figuratively *the temper of the times.*

4 'The best I can make of this passage is,' says Steevens:—'The times are cruel when our fears induce us to believe, or take for granted, what we hear rumoured or reported abroad; and yet at the same time, as we live under a tyrannical government, where *will* is substituted for *law*, we know not what we have to fear, because we know not when we offend.' Or, 'when we are led by our fears to believe every rumour of danger we hear, yet are not conscious to ourselves of any crime for which we should be disturbed with fears.'

5 *Sirrah* was not in our author's time a term of reproach, but sometimes used by masters to servants, parents to children, &c.

6 i. e. I am perfectly acquainted with your rank.

7 'Shag-ear'd villain.' It has been suggested that we should read *shag-hair'd*, an abusive epithet frequent in our old plays. *Hair* being formerly spelt *heare*, the corruption would easily arise.

8 This scene is almost literally taken from Holinshed's Chronicle, which is in this part an abridgment of the chronicle of Hector Boece, as translated by John Bellenden. From the recent reprints of both the Scottish and English chroniclers, quotations from them become the less necessary; they are now accessible to the reader curious in tracing the poet to his sources of information.

9 *Birthdom*, for the place of our birth, our native land

10 i. e. befriend.

He hath not touch'd you yet. I am young; but something
You may deserve[1] of him through me; and wisdom
To offer up a weak, poor, innocent lamb,
To appease an angry god.
Macd. I am not treacherous.
Mal. But Macbeth is.
A good and virtuous nature may recoil,
In an imperial charge.[2] But I shall crave your pardon;
That which you are, my thoughts cannot transpose:
Angels are bright still, though the brightest fell:
Though all things foul would wear the brows of grace,
Yet grace must still look so.[3]
Macd. I have lost my hopes.
Mal. Perchance, even there, where I did find my doubts.
Why in that rawness left you wife and child,
(Those precious motives, those strong knots of love,)
Without leave-taking?—I pray you,
Let not my jealousies be your dishonours,
But mine own safeties:—You may be rightly just,
Whatever I shall think.
Macd. Bleed, bleed, poor country!
Great tyranny, lay thou thy basis sure,
For goodness dares not check thee!—wear thou thy wrongs;—
The title is affeer'd![4]—Fare thee well, lord:
I would not be the villain that thou think'st
For the whole space that's in the tyrant's grasp,
And the rich East to boot.
Mal. Be not offended:
I speak not as in absolute fear of you.
I think our country sinks beneath the yoke:
It weeps, it bleeds; and each new day a gash
Is added to her wounds: I think, withal,
There would be hands uplifted in my right:
And here, from gracious England, have I offer
Of goodly thousands: But, for all this,
When I shall tread upon the tyrant's head,
Or wear it on my sword, yet my poor country
Shall have more vices than it had before;
More suffer, and more sundry ways than ever,
By him that shall succeed.
Macd. What should he be?
Mal. It is myself I mean: in whom I know
All the particulars of vice so grafted,
That, when they shall be open'd, black Macbeth
Will seem as pure as snow; and the poor state
Esteem him as a lamb, being compar'd
With my confineless harms.[5]
Macd. Not in the legions
Of horrid hell, can come a devil more damn'd
In evils, to top Macbeth.
Mal. I grant him bloody,
Luxurious,[6] avaricious, false, deceitful,
Sudden,[7] malicious, smacking of every sin
That has a name: But there's no bottom, none,
In my voluptuousness; your wives, your daughters,
Your matrons, and your maids, could not fill up
The cistern of my lust; and my desire
All continent impediments would o'erbear,
That did oppose my will: Better Macbeth
Than such a one to reign.
Macd. Boundless intemperance
In nature is a tyranny; it hath been
The untimely emptying of the happy throne,
And fall of many kings. But fear not yet
To take upon you what is yours: you may
Convey your pleasures in a spacious plenty,
And yet seem cold, the time you may so hood-wink.
We have willing dames enough: there cannot be
That vulture in you, to devour so many
As will to greatness dedicate themselves,
Finding it so inclin'd.
Mal. With this, there grows
In my most ill-compos'd affection, such
A staunchless avarice, that, were I king,
I should cut off the nobles for their lands;
Desire his jewels, and this other's house:
And my more-having would be as a sauce
To make me hunger more: that I should forge
Quarrels unjust against the good, and loyal
Destroying them for wealth.
Macd. This avarice
Sticks deeper; grows with more pernicious root
Than summer-seeming lust:[8] and it hath been
The sword of our slain kings: Yet do not fear;
Scotland hath foysons[9] to fill up your will,
Of your mere own: All these are portable,[10]
With other graces weigh'd.
Mal. But I have none: The king-becoming graces,
As justice, verity, temperance, stableness,
Bounty, perseverance, mercy, lowliness,
Devotion, patience, courage, fortitude,
I have no relish of them; but abound
In the division of each several crime,
Acting in many ways. Nay, had I power, I should
Pour the sweet milk of concord into hell
Uproar the universal peace, confound
All unity on earth.
Macd. O Scotland! Scotland!
Mal. If such a one be fit to govern, speak:
I am as I have spoken.
Macd. Fit to govern!
No, not to live.—O nation miserable,
With an untitled[11] tyrant bloody-sceptred,
When shalt thou see thy wholesome days again?
Since that the truest issue of thy throne
By his own interdiction stands accurs'd,
And does blaspheme his breed?—Thy royal father
Was a most sainted king; the queen, that bore thee,
Oftener upon her knees than on her feet,
Died every day she lived.[12] Fare thee well!
These evils, thou repeat'st upon thyself,
Have banish'd me from Scotland.—O, my breast,
Thy hope ends here!
Mal. Macduff, this noble passion,
Child of integrity, hath from my soul
Wip'd the black scruples, reconcil'd my thoughts

---

1 'You may *deserve* of him through me.' The old copy reads *discerne.* The emendation was made by Theobald. In the subsequent part of the line something is wanted to complete the sense. There is no verb to which *wisdom* can refer. Steevens conjectured that the line might originally have run thus:—

'——— but something
You may deserve through me; and wisdom *is it*
To offer,' &c.

2 'A good and virtuous nature may recoil
In an imperial charge.'

A good mind may recede from goodness in the execution of a royal commission.

3 This is not very clear. Johnson has thus attempted to explain it: 'My suspicions cannot injure you, if you be virtuous, by supposing that a traitor may put on your virtuous appearance. I do not say that your virtuous appearance proves you a traitor; for virtue must wear its proper form, though that form be counterfeited by villainy.'

4 To *affeer* is a law term, signifying to *assess* or *reduce to certainty.* The meaning therefore may be:—

'*The title is confirmed* to the usurper.'

My interpretation of the passage is this: 'Bleed, bleed, poor country! Great tyranny, lay thou thy basis sure, for goodness dares not check thee!' Then addressing Malcolm, Macduff says, 'Wear thou thy wrongs,—the title *to thy crown* is now confirmed—' *to the usurper*, he would probably have added, but that he interrupts himself with angry impatience, at being suspected of traitorous double-dealing.

5 i. e. immeasurable evils.

6 *Luxurious*, lascivious. 7 *Sudden*, passionate.

8 Sir W. Blackstone proposed to read *summer-seeding*, which was adopted by Steevens: but there appears no reason for change. The meaning of the epithet may be, 'lust *as hot as summer.*' In Donne's Poems, Malone has pointed out its opposite—*winter-seeming.*

9 *Foysons*, plenty.

10 *Portable* answers exactly to a phrase now in use. Such failings may be *borne with*, or are *bearable.*

11 'With an untitled tyrant.' Thus in Chaucer's Manciple's Tale:—

'Right so betwix a *titleles tiraunt*
And an outlawe.'

12 'Died every day she lived.' The expression is derived from the Sacred Writings:—'I protest by your rejoicing, which I have in Christ Jesus, *I die daily*'

To thy good truth and honour. Devilish Macbeth
By many of these trains hath sought to win me
Into his power; and modest wisdom plucks me
From over-credulous haste;[1] But God above
Deal between thee and me! for even now
I put myself to thy direction, and
Unspeak mine own detraction: here abjure
The taints and blames I laid upon myself,
For strangers to my nature. I am yet
Unknown to woman; never was forsworn;
Scarcely have coveted what was mine own;
At no time broke my faith; would not betray
The devil to his fellow; and delight
No less in truth, than life: my first false speaking
Was this upon myself: What I am truly,
Is thine, and my poor country's to command:
Whither, indeed, before thy here-approach,
Old Siward, with ten thousand warlike men,
All ready at a point, was setting forth:
Now we'll together; And the chance, of goodness,
Be like our warranted quarrel! Why are you silent?

Macd. Such welcome and unwelcome things at once,
'Tis hard to reconcile.

Enter a Doctor.

Mal. Well; more anon.—Comes the king forth, I pray you?

Doct. Ay, sir: there are a crew of wretched souls,
That stay his cure: their malady convinces[2]
The great assay of art; but at his touch,
Such sanctity hath heaven given his hand,
They presently amend.

Mal. I thank you, doctor. [*Exit.*

Macd. What's the disease he means?

Mal. 'Tis call'd the evil:
A most miraculous work in this good king;
Which often, since my here-remain in England,
I have seen him do. How he solicits heaven,
Himself best knows: but strangely visited people,
All swoln and ulcerous, pitiful to the eye,
The mere despair of surgery, he cures:
Hanging a golden stamp[3] about their necks,
Put on with holy prayers: and 'tis spoken,
To the succeeding royalty he leaves
The healing benediction. With this strange virtue,
He hath a heavenly gift of prophecy;
And sundry blessings hang about his throne,
To speak him full of grace.

Enter Rosse.

Macd. See, who comes here?

Mal. My countryman; but yet I know him not.

Macd. My ever-gentle cousin, welcome hither.

Mal. I know him now: Good God, betimes remove
The means that make us strangers!

Ross. Sir, Amen.

Macd. Stands Scotland where it did?

Rosse. Alas, poor country!
Almost afraid to know itself! It cannot
Be call'd our mother, but our grave: where nothing,
But who knows nothing, is once seen to smile;
Where sighs, and groans, and shrieks that rent[4] the air,
Are made, not mark'd; where violent sorrow seems
A modern ecstasy:[5] the dead man's knell
Is there scarce ask'd, for who; and good men's lives
Expire before the flowers in their caps,
Dying, or ere they sicken.

Macd. O, relation,
Too nice, and yet too true!

Mal. What is the newest grief?

Rosse. That of an hour's age doth hiss the speaker;
Each minute teems a new one.

Macd. How does my wife?

Rosse. Why, well.

Macd. And all my children?

Rosse. Well too.[6]

Macd. The tyrant has not batter'd at their peace?

Rosse. No; they were well at peace, when I did leave them.

Macd. Be not a niggard of your speech; How goes it?

Rosse. When I came hither to transport the tidings,
Which I have heavily borne, there ran a rumour
Of many worthy fellows that were out;
Which was to my belief witness'd the rather,
For that I saw the tyrant's power a-foot:
Now is the time of help! your eye in Scotland
Would create soldiers, make our women fight,
To doff[7] their dire distresses.

Mal. Be it their comfort,
We are coming thither: gracious England hath
Lent us good Siward, and ten thousand men;
An older, and a better soldier, none
That Christendom gives out.

Rosse. 'Would, I could answer
This comfort with the like! But I have words,
That would be howl'd out in the desert air,
Where hearing should not latch[8] them.

Macd. What concern they?
The general cause? or is it a fee-grief,[9]
Due to some single breast?

Rosse. No mind, that's honest,
But in it shares some woe; though the main part
Pertains to you alone.

Macd. If it be mine,
Keep it not from me, quickly let me have it.

Rosse. Let not your ears despise my tongue for ever,
Which shall possess them with the heaviest sound
That ever yet they heard.

Macd. Humph! I guess at it.

Rosse. Your castle is surpris'd; your wife, and babes,
Savagely slaughter'd: to relate the manner,
Were, on the quarry[10] of these murder'd deer,
To add the death of you.

Mal. Merciful heaven!—
What, man! ne'er pull your hat upon your brows,
Give sorrow words: the grief that does not speak,
Whispers the o'er fraught heart, and bids it break.[11]

---

1 *Credulous haste*, overhasty credulity.

2 i. e. *overcomes* it. We have before seen this word used in the same Latin sense, Act i. Sc. 7, of this play. 'To *convince* or convicte, to vanquish and overcome. *Evinco.*'—*Baret.*

3 *A golden stamp*, the coin called an angel; the value of which was ten shillings.

4 '*To rent* is an ancient verb, which has been long disused,' say the editors: in other words it is the old orthography of the verb to *rend.*

5 It has been before observed that Shakspeare uses *ecstasy* for every species of alienation of mind, whether proceeding from sorrow, joy, wonder, or any other exciting cause. *Modern* is generally used by him in the sense of *common.* *A modern ecstasy* is therefore *a common grief.*

6 Thus in Antony and Cleopatra:—

'———— We use
To say, *the dead are well.*'

7 To *doff* is to do off, to put off.

8 To *latch* (in the North) signifies the same as to *catch.* Thus also Golding, in his translation of the first book of Ovid's Metamorphoses:—

'As though he would, at everie stride, betweene his teeth hir *latch.*'

9 'Or is it a *fee-grief*,' a peculiar sorrow, a grief that hath but a single owner.

10 *Quarry*, the game after it is killed: it is a term used both in hunting and falconry. The old English tern *querre* is used for the *square* spot wherein the dead game was deposited. *Quarry* is also used for the game pursued.

11 '*Curæ leves loquuntur, ingentes stupent.*'

'Those are killing griefs which dare not speak.'
Vittoria Corombona.

'Light sorrows often speake,
When great, the heart in silence breake.'
Greene's Tragical History of Faire Bellora

'Striving to tell his woes, words would not come,
For light cares speak, when mighty griefs are dumbe.'
Daniel's Complaint of Rosamond

Macd. My children, too?
Rosse. Wife, children, servants, all
That could be found.
Macd. And I must be from thence!
My wife kill'd too?
Rosse. I have said.
Mal. Be comforted:
Let's make us med'cines of our great revenge,
To cure this deadly grief.
Macd. He has no children.—All my pretty ones?
Did you say, all?—O, hell-kite!—All?
What, all my pretty chickens, and their dam,
At one fell swoop?[1]
Mal. Dispute it like a man.[2]
Macd. I shall do so;
But I must also feel it as a man:
I cannot but remember such things were,
That were most precious to me.—Did heaven look on,
And would not take their part? Sinful Macduff,
They were all struck for thee! naught that I am,
Not for their own demerits, but for mine,
Fell slaughter on their souls: Heaven rest them now!
Mal. Be this the whetstone of your sword: let grief
Convert to anger; blunt not the heart, enrage it.
Macd. O, I could play the woman with mine eyes,
And braggart with my tongue!——But, gentle heavens,
Cut short all intermission:[3] front to front,
Bring thou this fiend of Scotland, and myself;
Within my sword's length set him; if he 'scape,
Heaven forgive him too!
Mal. This tune[4] goes manly.
Come, go we to the king: our power is ready;
Our lack is nothing but our leave: Macbeth
Is ripe for shaking, and the powers above
Put on their instruments.[5] Receive what cheer you may;
The night is long that never finds the day.
[*Exeunt.*

ACT V.

SCENE I. Dunsinane. *A Room in the Castle.*

Enter a Doctor *of Physic, and a Waiting* Gentlewoman.

Doct. I have two nights watched with you, but can perceive no truth in your report. When was it she last walked?

Gent. Since his majesty went into the field, I have seen her rise from her bed, throw her nightgown upon her, unlock her closet, take forth paper, fold it, write upon it, read it, afterwards seal it, and again return to bed; yet all this while in a most fast sleep.

Doct. A great perturbation in nature! to receive at once the benefit of sleep, and do the effects of watching.—In this slumbry agitation, besides her walking, and other actual performances, what, at any time, have you heard her say?

Gent. That, sir, which I will not report after her.

Doct. You may, to me; and 'tis most meet you should.

Gent. Neither to you, nor any one; having no witness to confirm my speech.

Enter LADY MACBETH, *with a Taper.*

Lo you, here she comes! This is her very guise; and, upon my life, fast asleep. Observe her; stand close.

Doct. How came she by that light?

Gent. Why, it stood by her: she has light by her continually; 'tis her command.

Doct. You see her eyes are open.

Gent. Ay, but their sense is shut.[6]

Doct. What is it she does now? Look, how she rubs her hands.

Gent. It is an accustomed action with her, to seem thus washing her hands; I have known her continue in this a quarter of an hour.

Lady M. Yet here's a spot.

Doct. Hark, she speaks: I will set down what comes from her, to satisfy my remembrance the more strongly.

Lady M. Out, damned spot! out, I say!—One: Two: Why, then 'tis time to do't:——Hell is murky![7]—Fye, my lord, fye! a soldier, and afeard? What need we fear who knows it, when none can call our power to account?—Yet who would have thought the old man to have had so much blood in him?

Doct. Do you mark that?

Lady M. The thane of Fife had a wife: Where is she now?——What, will these hands ne'er be clean?—No more o' that, my lord, no more o'that: you mar all with this starting.[8]

Doct. Go to, go to: you have known what you should not.

Gent. She has spoke what she should not, I am sure of that: Heaven knows what she has known.

Lady M. Here's the smell of the blood still: all the perfumes of Arabia will not sweeten this little hand. Oh! oh! oh!

Doct. What a sigh is there! The heart is sorely charged.

Gent. I would not have such a heart in my bosom, for all the dignity of the whole body.

Doct. Well, well, well,—

Gent. 'Pray God, it be, sir.

Doct. This disease is beyond my practice: Yet I have known those which have walked in their sleep, who have died holily in their beds.

Lady M. Wash your hands, put on your nightgown; look not so pale:—I tell you yet again, Banquo's buried; he cannot come out of his grave.

Doct. Even so?

Lady M. To bed, to bed; there's knocking at the gate. Come, come, come, come, give me your hand; What's done, cannot be undone: To bed, to bed, to bed. [*Exit* LADY MACBETH.

Doct. Will she go now to bed?
Gent. Directly.
Doct. Foul whisperings are abroad; Unnatural deeds
Do breed unnatural troubles: Infected minds
To their deaf pillows will discharge their secrets.
More needs she the divine, than the physician.—
God, God, forgive us all! Look after her;
Remove from her the means of all annoyance,
And still keep eyes upon her:—So, good night:
My mind she has mated,[9] and amaz'd my sight:
I think, but dare not speak.
Gent. Good night, good doctor.
[*Exeunt.*

---

1 'At one fell *swoop.*' *Swoop*, from the verb *to swoop* or *sweep*, is the descent of a bird of prey on his quarry

2 i. e. *contend* with your present sorrow like a man

3 *All intermission*, all pause, all intervening time.

4 The old copy reads *time.* The emendation is Rowe's

5 i. e encourage, thrust *us* their instruments forward against the tyrant.

6 'Ay, but their sense *is* shut.' The old copy reads 'Ay, but their sense *are* shut.' Malone has quoted other instances of the same inaccurate grammar, according to modern notions, from Julius Cæsar:—

'The posture of his blows *are* yet unknown.'

And from the hundred and twelfth Sonnet of Shakspeare:—

'In so profound abysm I throw all care
Of others' voices, that my adder's *sense*
To critick and to flatterer stopped *are.*'

7 Lady Macbeth, in her dream, imagines herself talking to her husband, who (she supposes) had just said *Hell is murky* (i. e. hell is a dismal place to go to in consequence of such a deed,) and repeats his words in contempt of his cowardice.—'Hell is murky!—Fye, my lord, fye! a soldier, and afeard?' This explanation is by Steevens, and appears to me very judicious.

8 'You mar all with this starting.' She is here again alluding to the terrors of Macbeth when the Ghost broke in on the festivity of the banquet.

9 'My mind she has *mated.*' *Mated*, or *amated*, from *matte*, old French, signified to *overcome, confound, dismay*, or *make afraid.*

SCENE II. *The Country near* Dunsinane. *Enter, with Drum and Colours,* MENTETH, CATHNESS, ANGUS, LENOX, *and* Soldiers.

Ment. The English power is near, led on by Malcolm,
His uncle Siward,[1] and the good Macduff.
Revenges burn in them: for their dear causes
Would, to the bleeding, and the grim alarm,
Excite the mortified man.[2]
Ang. Near Birnam wood
Shall we well meet them; that way are they coming.
Cath. Who knows, if Donalbain be with his brother?
Len. For certain, sir, he is not: I have a file
Of all the gentry; there is Siward's son,
And many unrough[3] youths, that even now
Protest their first of manhood.
Ment. What does the tyrant?
Cath. Great Dunsinane he strongly fortifies:
Some say, he's mad; others, that lesser hate him,
Do call it valiant fury: but, for certain,
He cannot buckle his distemper'd cause
Within the belt of rule.
Ang. Now does he feel
His secret murders sticking on his hands;
Now minutely revolts upbraid his faith-breach;
Those he commands, move only in command,
Nothing in love: now does he feel his title
Hang loose about him, like a giant's robe
Upon a dwarfish thief.
Ment. Who then shall blame
His pester'd senses to recoil, and start,
When all that is within him does condemn
Itself, for being there![4]
Cath. Well, march we on,
To give obedience where 'tis truly ow'd:
Meet we the medecin[5] of the sickly weal;
And with him pour we, in our country's purge,
Each drop of us.
Len. Or so much as it needs,
To dew the sovereign flower, and drown the weeds.
Make we our march towards Birnam.
[*Exeunt, marching.*

SCENE III. Dunsinane. *A Room in the Castle. Enter* MACBETH, Doctor, *and* Attendants.

Macb. Bring me no more reports; let them fly all;
Till Birnam wood remove to Dunsinane,
I cannot taint with fear. What's the boy Malcolm!
Was he not born of woman? The spirits that know
All mortal consequence, have pronounc'd me thus:
Fear not, Macbeth; no man, that's born of woman,
Shall e'er have power upon thee.——Then fly, false thanes,
And mingle with the English epicures:[6]
The mind I sway by, and the heart I bear,
Shall never sagg[7] with doubt, nor shake with fear.

Enter a Servant.

The devil damn thee black, thou cream-fac'd loon![8]
Where gott'st thou that goose look?
Serv. There is ten thousand——
Macb. Geese, villain?
Serv. Soldiers, sir.
Macb. Go, prick thy face, and over-red thy fear,
Thou lily-liver'd boy. What soldiers, patch?[9]
Death of thy soul! those linen cheeks of thine
Are counsellors to fear.[10] What soldiers, whey-face?
Serv. The English force, so please you.
Macb. Take thy face hence.—Seyton!—I am sick at heart,
When I behold—Seyton, I say!—This push
Will cheer me ever, or disseat me now.
I have liv'd long enough: my way of life
Is fall'n into the sear,[11] the yellow leaf:
And that which should accompany old age,
As honour, love, obedience, troops of friends,
I must not look to have; but, in their stead,
Curses, not loud, but deep, mouth-honour, breath,
Which the poor heart would fain deny, but dare not.
Seyton!——

Enter SEYTON.

Sey. What is your gracious pleasure?
Macb. What news more?
Sey. All is confirm'd my lord, which was reported.
Macb. I'll fight, till from my bones my flesh be hack'd.
Give me my armour.
Sey. 'Tis not needed yet.
Macb. I'll put it on.
Send out more horses, skirr[12] the country round;
Hang those that talk of fear.—Give me mine armour.
How does your patient, doctor?
Doct. Not so sick, my lord,
As she is troubled with thick-coming fancies,
That keep her from her rest.
Macb. Cure her of that:
Canst thou not minister to a mind diseas'd;[13]
Pluck from the memory a rooted sorrow;
Raze out the written troubles of the brain;
And, with some sweet oblivious antidote,
Cleanse the stuff'd bosom of that perilous stuff,
Which weighs upon the heart?
Doct. Therein the patient
Must minister to himself.
Macb. Throw physic to the dogs, I'll none of it:—
Come, put mine armour on; give me my staff:—
Seyton, send out.—Doctor, the thanes fly from me:
Come, sir, despatch:—If thou couldst, doctor, cast
The water of my land,[14] find her disease,

1 Duncan had two sons by his wife, who was the daughter of *Siward, Earl of Northumberland.—Holinshed.*

2 By *the mortified man* is meant a *religious man;* one who has mortified his passions, is dead to the world, has abandoned it, and all the affairs of it; an *ascetic.*

3 'And many unrough youths.' This odd expression means *smooth-faced, unbearded.*

4 i. e. when all the faculties of the mind are employed in self-condemnation.

5 *The medecin,* the physician. In the Winter's Tale, Camillo is called by Perdita 'the *medecin* of our house.'

6 Shakspeare derived this thought from Holinshed:—'The Scottish people before had no knowledge of nor understanding of fine fare or riotous surfeit; yet after they had once tasted the sweet poisoned bait thereof,' &c. 'those superfluities which came into the realme of Scotland with Englishmen.'—*Hist. of Scotland,* p. 179.

7 To *sag,* or *swag,* is to hang down by its own weight, or by an overload.

8 '——cream-fac'd *loon.*' This word, which signifies *a base abject fellow,* is now only used in Scotland; it was formerly common in England, but spelt *lown,* and is justly considered by Horne Tooke as the past participle of *to low* or abase. *Lowt* has the same origin.

9 *Patch,* an appellation of contempt, signifying *fool* or *low wretch.*

10 i. e. they infect others who see them with cowardice. In King Henry V. the King says to the conspirators, 'Your cheeks are paper.'

11 *Sear* is *dry, withered.* We have the same expression and sentiment in Spenser's Pastorals:—
'Also my lustful leaf is *drie* and *seare.*'
For '*way* of life' Johnston would read '*May* of life;' in which he was followed by Steevens and others. Warburton contended for the original reading, and was followed by Mason. At a subsequent period Steevens acquiesced in the propriety of the old reading, *way of life,* which he interprets, with his predecessors, *course* or *progress.* Malone followed the same tract. The fact is that these ingenious writers have mistaken the phrase, which is neither more nor less than a simple periphrasis for *life.*

12 i. e. *scour* the country round.

13 The following very remarkable passage in the Amadigi of Bernardo Tasso, which bears a striking resemblance to the words of Macbeth, was first pointed out in Mr. Weber's edition of Ford:—
'Ma chi puote con erbe, od argomenti
Guarir l'infermita del intelletto?'
Cant. xxxvi. *St.* 37

14 *To cast the water* was the empiric phrase for finding out disorders by the inspection of urine.

And purge it to a sound and pristine health,
I would applaud thee to the very echo,
That should applaud again.—Pull't off, I say.—
What rhubarb, senna,[1] or what purgative drug,
Would scour these English hence?—Hearest thou
of them?

Doct. Ay, my good lord; your royal preparation
Makes us hear something.

Macb. Bring it after me.——
I will not be afraid of death and bane,
Till Birnam forest come to Dunsinane. [*Exit.*

Doct. Were I from Dunsinane away and clear,
Profit again should hardly draw me here. [*Exit.*

SCENE IV. *Country near* Dunsinane: *A Wood in view. Enter, with Drum and Colours,* MALCOLM, *Old* SIWARD *and his* Son, MACDUFF, MENTETH, CATHNESS, ANGUS, LENOX, ROSSE, *and* Soldiers, *marching.*

Mal. Cousins, I hope the days are near at hand
That chambers will be safe.

Ment. We doubt it nothing.

Siw. What wood is this before us?

Ment. The wood of Birnam.

Mal. Let every soldier hew him down a bough,[2]
And bear't before him; thereby shall we shadow
The numbers of our host, and make discovery
Err in report of us.

Sold. It shall be done.

Siw. We learn no other, but the confident tyrant
Keeps still in Dunsinane, and will endure
Our setting down before't.

Mal. 'Tis his main hope:
For where there is advantage to be given,[3]
Both more and less[4] have given him the revolt;
And none serve with him but constrained things,
Whose hearts are absent too.

Macd. Let our just censures
Attend the true event, and put we on
Industrious soldiership.

Siw. The time approaches,
That will with due decision make us know
What we shall say we have, and what we owe.[5]
Thoughts speculative their unsure hopes relate;
But certain issue strokes must arbitrate:[6]
Towards which, advance the war.[7]
[*Exeunt, marching.*

SCENE V. Dunsinane. *Within the Castle. Enter, with Drums and Colours,* MACBETH, SEYTON, *and* Soldiers.

Macb. Hang out our banners on the outward walls;
The cry is still, *They come:* Our castle's strength
Will laugh a siege to scorn: here let them lie,
Till famine and the ague, eat them up:
Were they not forc'd with those that should be ours,
We might have met them dareful, beard to beard,
And beat them backward home. What is that
noise? [*A cry within, of women.*

Sey. It is the cry of women, my good lord.

Macb. I have almost forgot the taste of fears:
The time has been, my senses would have cool'd
To hear a night-shriek; and my fell[8] of hair
Would at a dismal treatise rouse, and stir
As life were in't: I have supp'd full with horrors;
Direness, familiar to my slaught'rous thoughts,
Cannot once start me.—Wherefore was that cry?

Sey. The queen, my lord, is dead.

Macb. She should have died hereafter;
There would have been a time for such a word.[9]
To-morrow, and to-morrow, and to-morrow,
Creeps in this petty pace from day to day,
To the last syllable of recorded time;[10]
And all our yesterdays have lighted fools
The way to dusty death. Out, out, brief candle!
Life's but a walking shadow; a poor player,
That struts and frets his hour upon the stage,
And then is heard no more: it is a tale
Told by an idiot, full of sound and fury,
Signifying nothing.——

Enter a Messenger.

Thou com'st to use thy tongue; thy story quickly

Mess. Gracious my lord,
I shall report that which I say I saw,
But know not how to do it.

Macb. Well, say, sir.

Mess. As I did stand my watch upon the hill,
I look'd toward Birnam, and anon, methought,
The wood began to move.

Macb. Liar and slave![11]

Mess. Let me endure your wrath, if't be not so:
Within this three mile may you see it coming;
I say, a moving grove.

Macb. If thou speak'st false,
Upon the next tree shalt thou hang alive,
Till famine cling[12] thee: if thy speech be sooth,
I care not if thou dost for me as much.—
I pall in resolution; and begin
To doubt the equivocation of the fiend,
That lies like truth: *Fear not, till Birnam wood
Do come to Dunsinane;*—and now a wood
Comes toward Dunsinane.—Arm, arm, and out!—
If this, which he avouches, does appear,
There is nor flying hence, nor tarrying here.
I 'gin to be a-weary of the sun,
And wish the estate o' the world were now undone.
Ring the alarum-bell:—Blow, wind! come, wrack!
At least we'll die with harness[13] on our back.
[*Exeunt.*

SCENE VI. *The same. A Plain before the Castle. Enter with Drums and Colours,* MALCOLM, *Old* SIWARD, MACDUFF, *&c. and their Army, with Boughs.*

Mal. Now near enough; your leavy screens
throw down,

1 'What rhubarb, senna.' The old copy reads *cyme.* The emendation is Rowe's.

2 A similar incident is recorded by Olaus Magnus, in his Northern History, lib. vii. cap. xx. De Strategemate Hachonis per Frondes.

3 'For where there is advantage to be given.' Dr. Johnson thought that we should read:—

'—— where there is *a vantage* to be *gone.*'

i. e. where there is an opportunity to be gone, all ranks desert him. We might perhaps read:—

'—— where there is advantage to be *gained;*'

and the sense would be nearly similar, with less violence to the text of the old copy.

4 i. e. Greater and less, or high and low, those of all ranks.

5 'What we shall say we have, and what we owe.' I think, with Mason, that Siward only means to say, in more pompous language, that the time approached which was to decide their fate.

6 *Arbitrate,* determine.

7 It has been understood that local rhymes were introduced in plays to afford an actor the advantage of a more pointed exit, or to close the scene with additional force. Yet, whatever might be Shakspeare's motive for continuing such a practice, he often seems immediately to repent of it; and in this tragedy, as in other places, has repeatedly counteracted it by hemistichs, which destroy the effect, and defeat the supposed purpose of the antecedent couplets.

8 '— my fell of hair,' my hairy part, my *capillitium. Fell* is skin, properly a sheep's skin with the wool on it.

9 'There would have been a time for such a word.' Macbeth might mean that there would have been a more convenient *time* for such a *word,* for such *intelligence.* By *a word* certainly more than a single one was meant.

10 '*The last syllable of recorded time*' seems to signify the utmost period fixed in the decrees of heaven for the period of life. The *record* of *futurity* is indeed no accurate expression; but as we only know transactions, past or present, the language of men affords no term for the volumes of prescience in which future events may be supposed to be written.

11 ['*Striking him*'] says the stage direction in the margin of all the modern editions: but this stage direction is not in the old copies: it was first interpolated by Rowe; and is now omitted on the suggestion of the late Mr. Kemble. See his Essay on Macbeth and King Richard III. Lond. 1817, p. 111.

12 To *cling,* in the northern counties, signifies to shrivel, wither, or dry up. *Clung-wood* is wood of which the sap is entirely dried or spent. The same idea is well expressed by Pope in his version of the nineteenth Iliad, 166:—

'*Clung with dry famine,* and with toils declin'd'

13 *Harness,* armour

And show like those you are:—You, worthy uncle,
Shall, with my cousin, your right noble son,
Lead our first battle: worthy Macduff, and we,
Shall take upon us[1] what else remains to do,
According to our order.

Siw. Fare you well.—
Do we but find the tyrant's power to-night,
Let us be beaten, if we cannot fight.

Macd. Make all our trumpets speak; give them all breath,
Those clamorous harbingers of blood and death.
[*Exeunt. Alarums continued.*

SCENE VII. *The same. Another part of the Plain. Enter* MACBETH.

Macb. They have tied me to a stake; I cannot fly,
But, bearlike, I must fight the course.[2]—What's he,
That was not born of woman? Such a one
Am I to fear, or none.

Enter Young SIWARD.

Yo. Siw. What is thy name?

Macb. Thou'lt be afraid to hear it.

Yo. Siw. No; though thou call'st thyself a hotter name
Than any is in hell.

Macb. My name's Macbeth.

Yo. Siw. The devil himself could not pronounce a title
More hateful to mine ear.

Macb. No, nor more fearful.

Yo. Siw. Thou liest, abhorred tyrant; with my sword
I'll prove the lie thou speak'st.
[*They fight, and Young* Siward *is slain.*

Macb. Thou wast born of woman.—
But swords I smile at, weapons laugh to scorn,
Brandish'd by man that's of a woman born. [*Exit.*

Alarums. Enter MACDUFF.

Macd. That way the noise is:—Tyrant show thy face:
If thou be'st slain, and with no stroke of mine,
My wife and children's ghosts will haunt me still.
I cannot strike at wretched kernes, whose arms
Are hir'd to bear their staves; either thou, Macbeth,
Or else my sword, with an unbatter'd edge,
I sheathe again undeeded. There thou should'st be;
By this great clatter, one of greatest note,
Seems bruited:[3] Let me find him, fortune!
And more I beg not. [*Exit. Alarum.*

Enter MALCOLM *and Old* SIWARD.

Siw. This way, my lord;—the castle's gently render'd:
The tyrant's people on both sides do fight;
The noble thanes do bravely in the war;
The day almost itself professes yours,
And little is to do.

Mal. We have met with foes
That strike beside us.

Siw. Enter, sir, the castle.
[*Exeunt. Alarum.*

Re-enter MACBETH.

Macb. Why should I play the Roman fool, and die[4]
On mine own sword? whiles I see lives the gashes
Do better upon them.

Re-enter MACDUFF

Macd. Turn, hell-hound, turn.

Macb. Of all men else I have avoided thee:
But get thee back, my soul is too much charg'd
With blood of thine already.

Macd. I have no words,
My voice is in my sword;[5] thou bloodier villain
Than terms can give thee out! [*They fight.*

Macb. Thou losest labour:
As easy mayst thou the intrenchant air[6]
With thy keen sword impress, as make me bleed:
Let fall thy blade on vulnerable crests;
I bear a charmed life,[7] which must not yield
To one of woman born.

Macd. Despair thy charm,
And let the angel, whom thou still hast serv'd,
Tell thee, Macduff was from his mother's womb
Untimely ripp'd.

Macb. Accursed be that tongue that tells me so,
For it hath cow'd my better part of man:
And be these juggling fiends no more believ'd,
That palter[8] with us in a double sense;
That keep the word of promise to our ear,
And break it to our hope.—I'll not fight with thee.

Macd. Then yield thee, coward,
And live to be the show and gaze o' the time.
We'll have thee, as our rarer monsters are,
Painted upon a pole; and underwrit,
Here may you see the tyrant.

Macb. I'll not yield
To kiss the ground before young Malcolm's feet,
And to be baited with the rabble's curse.
Though Birnam wood be come to Dunsinane,
And thou oppos'd, being of no woman born,
Yet I will try the last: Before my body
I throw my warlike shield; lay on, Macduff;
And damn'd be him that first cries, *Hold, enough.*[9]
[*Exeunt, fighting.*

Retreat. Flourish. Re-enter, with Drum and Colours, MALCOLM, *Old* SIWARD, ROSSE, LENOX, ANGUS, CATHNESS, MENTETH, *and* Soldiers.

Mal. I would, the friends we miss were safe arriv'd.

Siw. Some must go off: and yet, by these I see,
So great a day as this is cheaply bought.

Mal. Macduff is missing, and your noble son.

Rosse. Your son, my lord, has paid a soldier's debt;
He only liv'd but till he was a man:
The which no sooner had his prowess confirm'd
In the unshrinking station where he fought,
But like a man he died.

Siw. Then he is dead?

Rosse. Ay, and brought off the field: your cause of sorrow
Must not be measur'd by his worth, for then
It hath no end.

Siw. Had he his hurts before?

Rosse. Ay, on the front.

Siw. Why then, God's soldier be he!
Had I as many sons as I have hairs,
I would not wish them to a fairer death:[10]
And so his knell is knoll'd.

1 The first folio reads *upon's*.

2 'But, bearlike, I must fight the course.' This was a phrase at bear-baiting. 'Also you shall see two ten dog *courses* at the great bear.'—*Antipodes*, by Brome.

3 *Bruited* is *reported, noised* abroad; from *bruit*, Fr.

4 'Why should I play the Roman fool, and die.' Alluding probably to the suicide of Cato of Utica.

5 'My voice is in my sword.' Thus Casca, in Julius Cæsar:—
'Speak, hands, for me.'

6 '*The intrenchant air*,' the air which cannot be cut.

7 'I bear a charmed life.' In the days of chivalry, the champion's arms being ceremoniously blessed, each took an oath that he used no *charmed* weapons. Macbeth, in allusion to this custom, tells Macduff of the security he had in the prediction of the spirit.

8 'That palter with us in a double sense.' That *shuffle* with ambiguous expressions.

9 To cry *hold!* was the word of yielding (according to Carew's Survey of Cornwall, p. 74,) that is when one of the combatants cries so. To cry *hold!* when persons were fighting, was an authoritative way of separating them, according to the old military laws. This is shown by the following passage produced by Mr Tollet: it declares it to be a capital offence 'Whosoever shall strike stroke at his adversary, either in the heat or otherwise, if a third do cry *hold*, to the intent to part them.'—*Bellay's Instructions for the Wars*, 1599.

10 'When Siward, the martial Earl of Northumberland, understood that his son, whom he had sent against the Scotchmen, was slain, he demanded whether his wounds were in the fore part or hinder part of his body. When it was answered, "in the fore part;" he replied, "*I am right glad; neither wish I any other death to me or mine.*"—*Camden's Remaines*

Mal. He's worth more sorrow,
And that I'll spend for him.
Siw. He's worth no more;
They say, he parted well, and paid his score:
And so, God be with him!—Here comes newer comfort.

Re-enter MACDUFF, *with* MACBETH'S *Head on a Pole.*[1]

Macd. Hail, king! for so thou art; Behold, where stands
The usurper's cursed head: the time is free:
I see thee compass'd with thy kingdom's pearl,[2]
That speak my salutation in their minds;
Whose voices I desire aloud with mine,—
Hail, king of Scotland!
All. Hail, king of Scotland!
[*Flourish.*
Mal. We shall not spend a large expense[3] of time,
Before we reckon with your several loves,
And make us even with you. My thanes and kinsmen,
Henceforth be earls, the first that ever Scotland
In such an honour nam'd.[4] What's more to do,
Which would be planted newly with the time,
As calling home our exil'd friends abroad,
That fled the snares of watchful tyranny;
Producing forth the cruel ministers
Of this dead butcher, and his fiendlike queen;
Who, as 'tis thought, by self and violent hands
Took off her life;—this, and what needful else
That calls upon us, by the grace of Grace,
We will perform in measure, time, and place:
So thanks to all at once, and to each one,
Whom we invite to see us crown'd at Scone.
[*Flourish. Exeunt*

THIS play is deservedly celebrated for the propriety o its fictions, and solemnity, grandeur, and variety of its action; but it has no nice discriminations of character: the events are too great to admit the influence of particular dispositions, and the course of the action necessarily determines the conduct of the agents.

The danger of ambition is well described; and I know not whether it may not be said, in defence of some parts which now seem improbable, that in Shakspeare's time it was necessary to warn credulity against vain and illusive predictions.

The passions are directed to their true end. Lady Macbeth is merely detested; and though the courage of Macbeth preserves some esteem, yet every reader rejoices at his fall. JOHNSON.

1 These words, '*on a pole*,' Mr. Steevens added to the stage direction from the Chronicle. The stage directions of the players are often incorrect, and sometimes ludicrous.

2 '*Thy kingdom's pearl*,' thy kingdom's wealth or ornament. Rowe altered this to *peers*, without authority.

3 To *spend* an *expense* of time is, it is true, an awkward expression, yet it is probably correct; for, in the Comedy of Errors, Act iii. Sc. 1, Antipholus of Ephesus says 'This jest shall *cost* me some *expense*.'

4 'Malcolm, immediately after his coronation, called a parliament at Forfair; in the which he rewarded them with lands and livings that had assisted him against Macbeth. Manie of them that were before *thanes* were at this time made *earles*; as Fife, Menteith Atholl, Levenox, Murrey, Caithness, Rosse, and Angus.'—*Holinshed's History of Scotland*, p. 176

KING JOHN.

PRELIMINARY REMARKS.

THIS historical play was founded on a former drama, entitled 'The Troublesome Raigne of John, King of England, with the Discoverie of King Richard Cordelion's base Son, vulgarly named the Bastard Fawconbridge: also the Death of King John at Swinstead Abbey. As it was (sundry times) publikely acted by the Queenes Majesties Players in the honourable Cittie of London.' This piece, which was in two parts, was 'printed at London for Sampson Clarke, 1591,' without the author's name: was again republished in 1611, with the letters W. Sh. in the title-page; and afterwards, in 1622, with the name of William Shakspeare at length. It may be found by the curious reader among the 'Six Old Plays on which Shakspeare founded,' &c. published by Mr. Steevens and Mr. Nichols some years since.

Shakspeare has followed the old play in the conduct of its plot, and has even adopted some of its lines. The number of quotations from Horace, and similar scraps of learning scattered over this motley piece, ascertain it to have been the work of a scholar. It contains likewise a quantity of rhyming Latin and ballad metre; and, in a scene where the Bastard is represented as plundering a monastery, there are strokes of humour which, from their particular turn, were most evidently produced by another hand than that of Shakspeare. Pope attributes the old play to Shakspeare and Rowley conjointly; but we know not on what foundation. Dr. Farmer thinks there is no doubt that Rowley wrote the old play; and when Shakspeare's play was called for, and could not be procured from the players, a piratical bookseller reprinted the old one under his name.

Though, as Johnson observes, King John is not 'written with the utmost power of Shakspeare,' yet it has parts of preeminent pathos and beauty, and characters highly interesting drawn with great force and truth. The scene between John and Hubert is perhaps one of the most masterly and striking which our poet ever penned. The secret workings of the dark and turbulent soul of the usurper, ever shrinking from the full developement of his own bloody purpose, the artful expressions of grateful attachment by which he wins Hubert to do the deed, and the sententious brevity of the close, manifest that consummate skill and wonderful knowledge of human character which are to be found in Shakspeare alone. But what shall we say of that heart-rending scene between Hubert and Arthur? a scene so deeply affecting the soul with terror and pity, that even the sternest bosom must melt into tears; it would perhaps be too overpowering for the feelings, were it not for the 'alleviating influence of the innocence and artless eloquence of the poor child.' His death afterwards, when he throws himself from the prison walls, excites the deepest commiseration for his hapless fate. The maternal grief of Constance, moving the haughty unbending soul of a proud queen and affectionate mother to the very confines of the most hopeless despair, bordering on madness, is no less finely conceived, than sustained by language of the most impassioned and vehement eloquence. How exquisitely beautiful are the following lines:—

'Grief fills the room up of my absent child;
Lies in his bed; walks up and down with me;
Puts on his pretty looks, repeats his words,
Remembers me of all his gracious parts,
Stuffs out his vacant garments with his form;
Then have I reason to be fond of grief.'

Shakspeare has judiciously preserved the character of the Bastard Faulconbridge, which was furnished him by the old play, to alleviate by his comic humour the poignant grief excited by the too painful events of the tragic part of the play. Faulconbridge is a favourite with every one: he is not only a man of wit, but an heroic soldier; and we lean toward him from the first for the good humour he displays in his litigation with his brother respecting the succession to his supposed father:—

'He hath a trick of Cœur de Lion's face,
The very spirit of Plantagenet!'

This bespeaks our favour toward him: his courage, his wit, and his frankness secure it.

Schlegel has remarked that, in this play, 'the political and warlike events are dressed out with solemn pomp, for the very reason that they possess but little true grandeur. The falsehood and selfishness of the monarch are evident in the style of the manifesto; conventional dignity is most indispensable when personal dignity is wanting. Faulconbridge ridicules the secret springs of politics without disapproving them, but frankly confesses that he is endeavouring to make his fortune by similar means, and wishes rather to belong to the deceivers than the deceived.' Our commiseration is a little excited for the fallen and degraded monarch toward the close of the play. The death of the king and his previous suffering are not among the least impressive parts; they carry a pointed moral.

Malone places the date of the composition in 1596

PERSONS REPRESENTED.

KING JOHN:
PRINCE HENRY, *his Son; afterwards* King Henry III.
ARTHUR, Duke of Bretagne, *Son of* Geffrey, *late* Duke of Bretagne, *the elder Brother of* King John.
WILLIAM MARESHALL, Earl of Pembroke.
GEFFREY FITZ-PETER, Earl of Essex, *chief Justiciary of* England.
WILLIAM LONGSWORD, Earl of Salisbury.
ROBERT BIGOT, Earl of Norfolk.
HUBERT DE BURGH, *Chamberlain to the* King.
ROBERT FAULCONBRIDGE, *Son of* Sir Robert Faulconbridge:
PHILIP FAULCONBRIDGE, *his Half-brother, Bastard Son to* King Richard the First.
JAMES GURNEY, *Servant to* Lady Faulconbridge.
PETER *of* Pomfret, *a Prophet.*

PHILIP, King of France.
LEWIS, *the Dauphin.*
ARCHDUKE OF AUSTRIA
CARDINAL PANDULPH, *the Pope's Legate.*
MELUN, *a French Lord.*
CHATILLON, *Ambassador from* France to King John.

ELINOR, *the Widow of* King Henry II. *and Mother of* King John.
CONSTANCE, *Mother to* Arthur.
BLANCH, *Daughter to* Alphonso, King of Castile, *and Niece to* King John.
LADY FAULCONBRIDGE, *Mother to the Bastard and* Robert Faulconbridge.

Lords, Ladies, Citizens *of* Angiers, Sheriff, Heralds, Officers, Soldiers, Messengers, *and other* Attendants.

SCENE, *sometimes in* England, *and sometimes in* France.

ACT I.

SCENE I. Northampton. *A Room of State in the Palace. Enter* KING JOHN, QUEEN ELINOR, PEMBROKE, ESSEX, SALISBURY, *and others, with* CHATILLON.

King John.
Now, say, Chatillon, what would France with us?
Chat. Thus, after greeting, speaks the king of France,
In my behaviour,[1] to the majesty,
The borrow'd majesty of England here.
Eli. A strange beginning;—borrow'd majesty!
K. John. Silence, good mother; hear the embassy.
Chat. Philip of France, in right and true behalf
Of thy deceased brother Geffrey's son,
Arthur Plantagenet, lays most lawful claim
To this fair island, and the territories;
To Ireland, Poictiers, Anjou, Touraine, Maine:
Desiring thee to lay aside the sword,
Which sways usurpingly these several titles;
And put the same into young Arthur's hand,
Thy nephew, and right royal sovereign.
K. John. What follows, if we disallow of this?
Chat. The proud control[2] of fierce and bloody war,
To enforce these rights so forcibly withheld.
K. John. Here have we war for war, and blood for blood,
Controlment for controlment: so answer France.
Chat. Then take my king's defiance from my mouth,
The furthest limit of my embassy.
K. John. Bear mine to him, and so depart in peace:
Be thou as lightning in the eyes of France;
For ere thou canst report I will be there,
The thunder of my cannon shall be heard:
So, hence! Be thou the trumpet of our wrath,
And sullen[3] presage of your own decay.—
An honourable conduct let him have:—
Pembroke, look to't; Farewell, Chatillon.
[*Exeunt* CHATILLON *and* PEMBROKE.
Eli. What now, my son? have I not ever said,
How that ambitious Constance would not cease,
Till she had kindled France, and all the world,
Upon the right and party of her son?
This might have been prevented and made whole,
With very easy arguments of love!
Which now the manage[4] of two kingdoms must
With fearful bloody issue arbitrate.
K. John. Our strong possession, and our right for us.
Eli. Your strong possession, much more than your right;
Or else it must go wrong with you, and me:
So much my conscience whispers in your ear;
Which none but heaven, and you, and I, shall hear

Enter the Sheriff *of* Northamptonshire, *who whispers* ESSEX.

Essex. My liege, here is the strangest controversy,
Come from the country to be judg'd by you,
That e'er I heard: Shall I produce the men?
K. John. Let them approach.— [*Exit* Sheriff.
Our abbies, and our priories, shall pay

Re-enter Sheriff, *with* ROBERT FAULCONBRIDGE, *and* PHILIP, *his bastard Brother.*[5]

This expedition's charge.—What men are you?
Bast. Your faithful subject, I, a gentleman,
Born in Northamptonshire; and eldest son,
As I suppose, to Robert Faulconbridge;
A soldier, by the honour-giving hand
Of Cœur-de-lion knighted in the field.
K. John. What art thou?

---

1 *In my behaviour* probably means 'In the words and action I am now going to use.'
2 *Control* here means *constraint* or *compulsion.*
3 i. e. gloomy, dismal.
4 i. e. conduct, administration.
5 Shakspeare in adopting the character of Philip Faulconbridge from the old play, proceeded on the following slight hint:—
'Next them a bastard of the king's deceas'd,
A hardie wild-head, rough and venturous.'
The character is compounded of two distinct personages. 'Sub illius temporis curriculo *Falcasius de Brente*, Neusteriensis, et spurius ex parte matris, atque Bastardus, qui in vili jumento manticato ad Regis paulo ante clientelam descenderat.' *Mathew Paris.*—Holinshed says that 'Richard I. had a natural son named Philip, who, in the year following, killed the Viscount de Limoges to revenge the death of his father.' Perhaps the name of Faulconbridge was suggested by the following passage in the continuation of Harding's Chronicle, 1543, fol. 24, 6:—'One *Faulconbridge*, th' erle of Kent his *bastarde*, a stoute-hearted man.'

Rob. The son and heir to that same Faulconbridge.

K. John. Is that the elder, and art thou the heir?
You came not of one mother then, it seems.

Bast. Most certain of one mother, mighty king,
That is well known; and, as I think, one father:
But, for the certain knowledge of that truth,
I put you o'er to heaven, and to my mother;
Of that I doubt, as all men's children may.

Eli. Out on thee, rude man! thou dost shame thy mother,
And wound her honour with this diffidence.

Bast. I, madam? no, I have no reason for it;
That is my brother's plea, and none of mine;
The which if he can prove, 'a pops me out
At least from fair five hundred pound a year;
Heaven guard my mother's honour, and my land!

K. John. A good blunt fellow:—Why, being younger born,
Doth he lay claim to thine inheritance?

Bast. I know not why, except to get the land.
But once he slander'd me with bastardy:
But whe'r[1] I be as true begot, or no,
That still I lay upon my mother's head;
But, that I am as well begot, my liege,
(Fair fall the bones that took the pains for me!)
Compare our faces, and be judge yourself.
If old Sir Robert did beget us both,
And were our father, and this son like him;—
O old Sir Robert, father, on my knee
I give heaven thanks, I was not like to thee.

K. John. Why, what a madcap hath heaven lent us here!

Eli. He hath a trick[2] of Cœur-de-lion's face,
The accent of his tongue affecteth him:
Do you not read some tokens of my son
In the large composition of this man?

K. John. Mine eye hath well examined his parts,
And finds them perfect Richard.——Sirrah, speak,
What doth move you to claim your brother's land?

Bast. Because he hath a half-face, like my father;
With that half face would he have all my land:
A half-faced groat[3] five hundred pound a year!

Rob. My gracious liege, when that my father liv'd,
Your brother did employ my father much;—

Bast. Well, sir, by this you cannot get my land;
Your tale must be how he employ'd my mother.

Rob. And once despatch'd him in an embassy
To Germany, there, with the emperor,
To treat of high affairs touching that time:
The advantage of his absence took the king,
And in the mean time sojourn'd at my father's;
Where how he did prevail, I shame to speak:
But truth is truth; large lengths of seas and shores[4]
Between my father and my mother lay
(As I have heard my father speak himself,)
When this same lusty gentleman was got.
Upon his death-bed he by will bequeath'd
His lands to me; and took it, on his death,
That this my mother's son was none of his;
And, if he were, he came into the world
Full fourteen weeks before the course of time.
Then, good my liege, let me have what is mine,
My father's land, as was my father's will.

K. John. Sirrah, your brother in legitimate,
Your father's wife did after wedlock bear him:
And, if she did play false, the fault was hers;
Which fault lies on the hazards of all husbands
That marry wives. Tell me, how if my brother,
Who, as you say, took pains to get this son,
Had of your father claim'd this son for his?
In sooth, good friend, your father might have kept
This calf, bred from his cow, from all the world;
In sooth, he might: then, if he were my brother's,
My brother might not claim him; nor your father,
Being none of his, refuse him: This concludes,[5]—
My mother's son did get your father's heir;
Your father's heir must have your father's land.

Rob. Shall then my father's will be of no force,
To dispossess that child which is not his?

Bast. Of no more force to dispossess me, sir,
Than was his will to get me, as I think.

Eli. Whether hadst thou rather,—be a Faulconbridge,
And like thy brother, to enjoy thy land;
Or the reputed son of Cœur-de-lion,
Lord of thy presence,[6] and no land beside?

Bast. Madam, an if my brother had my shape,
And I had his, Sir Robert his,[7] like him:
And if my legs were too such riding-rods,
My arms such eel-skins stuff'd; my face so thin,
That in mine ear I durst not stick a rose,
Lest men should say, Look, where three-farthings[8] goes!
And, to[9] his shape, were heir to all this land,
'Would, I might never stir from off this place,
I'd give it every foot to have this face;
I would not be sir Nob[10] in any case.

Eli. I like thee well; Wilt thou forsake thy fortune,
Bequeath thy land to him, and follow me?
I am a soldier, and now bound to France.

Bast. Brother, take you my land, I'll take my chance:
Your face hath got five hundred pounds a year;
Yet sell your face for five pence, and 'tis dear.—
Madam, I'll follow you unto the death.

Eli. Nay, I would have you go before me thither.

Bast. Our country manners give our betters way.

K. John. What is thy name?

Bast. Philip, my liege; so is my name begun;
Philip, good old Sir Robert's wife's eldest son.

K. John. From henceforth bear his name whose form thou bear'st:
Kneel thou down, Philip, but arise[11] more great.
Arise, Sir Richard, and Plantagenet.[12]

Bast. Brother, by the mother's side, give me your hand;
My father gave me honour, yours gave land:
Now blessed be the hour by night or day,
When I was got, Sir Robert was away.

Eli. The very spirit of Plantagenet!—
I am thy grandame, Richard; call me so.

Bast. Madam, by chance, but not by truth What though?
Something about, a little from the right,
In at the window, or else o'er the hatch:[13]
Who dares not stir by day, must walk by night;
And have is have, however men do catch:
Near or far off, well won is still well shot;
And I am I, howe'er I was begot.

---

1 Whether.

2 Shakspeare uses the word *trick* generally in the sense of 'a peculiar air or cast of countenance or feature.'

3 The poet makes Faulconbridge allude to the silver groats of Henry VII. and Henry VIII. which had on them a *half-face* or profile. In the reign of John there were no groats at all, the first being coined in the reign of Edward III.

4 This is Homeric, and is thus rendered by Chapman in the first Iliad:—

'—— hills enow, and farre-resounding seas
Powre out their shades and deepes betweene.'

5 i. e. 'this is a decisive argument.'

6 *Lord of thy presence* means *possessor of thy own dignified and manly appearance,* resembling thy great progenitor.

7 *Sir Robert his* for 'Sir Robert's;' *his,* according to a mistaken notion formerly received, being the sign of the genitive case.

8 Queen Elizabeth coined threepenny, threehalfpenny, and threefarthing pieces; these pieces all had her head on the obverse, and some of them a *rose* on the reverse. Being of silver, they were extremely *thin;* and hence the allusion. The *roses* stuck in the ear, or in a lock near it, were generally of ribbon; but Burton says that it was once the fashion to stick real flowers in the ear. Some gallants had their ears bored and wore their mistresses' silken shoestrings in them.

9 *To* his shape, i. e. *in addition* to it.

10 Robert

11 The old copy reads *rise.*

12 *Plantagenet* was not a family name, but a nick name, by which a grandson of Geoffrey, the first Earl of Anjou, was distinguished, from his wearing a *broom-stalk* in his bonnet.

13 These expressions were common in the time of Shakspeare for being born out of wedlock.

K John. Go, Faulconbridge; now hast thou thy desire,
A landless knight makes thee a landed squire.—
Come, madam, and come, Richard; we must speed
For France, for France; for it is more than need.
Bast. Brother, adieu; Good fortune come to thee!
For thou wast got i' the way of honesty.
[*Exeunt all but the* Bastard.
A foot of honour better than I was;
But many a many foot of land the worse.
Well, now can I make any Joan a lady:——
Good den,[1] *Sir Richard,—God-a-mercy, fellow;*—
And if his name be George, I'll call him Peter:
For new-made honour doth forget men's names;
'Tis too respective,[2] and too sociable,
For your conversion.[3] Now your traveller,[4]—
He and his toothpick at my worship's mess;[5]
And when my knightly stomach is suffic'd,
Why then I suck my teeth, and catechise
My picked man of countries:[6]——*My dear sir*
(Thus, leaning on my elbow, I begin,)
I shall beseech you—That is question now;
And then comes answer like an A B C-book:—[7]
O sir, says answer, *at your best command;*
At your employment; at your service, sir:——
No, sir, says question, *I, sweet sir, at yours;*
And, so, ere answer knows what question would
(Saving in dialogue of compliment;
And talking of the Alps, and Apennines,
The Pyrenean, and the river Po,)
It draws towards supper in conclusion so.
But this is worshipful society,
And fits the mounting spirit, like myself:
For he is but a bastard to the time,
That doth not smack of observation:[8]
(And so am I, whether I smack, or no;)
And not alone in habit and device,
Exterior form, outward accoutrement;
But from the inward motion to deliver
Sweet, sweet, sweet poison for the age's tooth:
Which, though I will not practise to deceive,
Yet, to avoid deceit, I mean to learn;
For it shall strew the footsteps of my rising.—
But who comes in such haste, in riding robes?
What woman-post is this? hath she no husband,
That will take pains to blow a horn before her?[9]

Enter Lady Faulconbridge *and* James Gurney.

O me! it is my mother;—How now, good lady?
What brings you here to court so hastily?
Lady F. Where is that slave, thy brother? where is he,
That holds in chase mine honour up and down?
Bast. My brother Robert? old Sir Robert's son?
Colbrand the giant,[10] that same mighty man?
Is it Sir Robert's son, that you seek so?
Lady F. Sir Robert's son! Ay, thou unreverend boy,
Sir Robert's son! Why scorn'st thou at Sir Robert?
He is Sir Robert's son; and so art thou.
Bast. James Gurney, wilt thou give us leave awhile!
Gur. Good leave, good Philip.
Bast. Philip?—sparrow![11]—James,
There's toys abroad;[12] anon I'll tell thee more.
[*Exit* Gurney
Madam, I was not old Sir Robert's son;
Sir Robert might have eat his part in me
Upon Good Friday, and ne'er broke his fast:
Sir Robert could do well; Marry, (to confess!)
Could he get me? Sir Robert could not do it;
We know his handy-work:—Therefore, good mother,
To whom am I beholden for these limbs?
Sir Robert never holp to make this leg.
Lady F. Hast thou conspired with thy brother too
That for thine own gain should'st defend mine honour?
What means this scorn, thou most untoward knave?
Bast. Knight, knight, good mother,—Basilisco like:[13]
What! I am dubb'd; I have it on my shoulder
But, mother, I am not Sir Robert's son;
I have disclaim'd Sir Robert, and my land;
Legitimation, name, and all is gone:
Then, good my mother, let me know my father,
Some proper man, I hope; Who was it, mother?
Lady F. Hast thou denied thyself a Faulconbridge?
Bast. As faithfully as I deny the devil.
Lady F. King Richard Cœur-de-lion was thy father;
By long and vehement suit I was seduc'd
To make room for him in my husband's bed:——
Heaven, lay not my transgression to my charge!
Thou art the issue of my dear offence,
Which was so strongly urg'd, past my defence.
Bast. Now, by this light, were I to get again,
Madam, I would not wish a better father.
Some sins do bear their privilege on earth,
And so doth yours; your fault was not your folly:
Needs must you lay your heart at his dispose,—
Subjected tribute to commanding love,—
Against whose fury and unmatched force
The awless lion could not wage the fight,
Nor keep his princely heart from Richard's hand.
He, that perforce robs lions of their hearts,[14]
May easily win a woman's. Ay, my mother,
With all my heart I thank thee for my father!

---

1 Good evening.

2 *Respective* does not here mean *respectful*, as the commentators have explained it, but *considerative, regardful.*

3 Change of condition.

4 It is said, in All's Well that Ends Well, that 'a traveller is a good thing after dinner.' In that age of newly excited curiosity, one of the entertainments at great tables seems to have been the discourse of a traveller. To use a toothpick seems to have been one of the characteristics of a travelled man who affected foreign fashions.

5 'At my worship's mess' means at that part of the table where I, as a *knight*, shall be placed. See note on All's Well that Ends Well, Act i. Sc. 2.—'Your *worship*' was the regular address to a knight or esquire, in Shakspeare's time, as 'your *honour*' was to a lord.

6 *My picked man of countries* may be equivalent to *my travelled fop: picked* generally signified affected, over nice, or curious in dress. *Conquisite* is explained in the dictionaries *exquisitely, pikedly:* so that our modern *exquisites* and *dandies* are of the same race.

7 An ABC or *absey-book*, as it was then called, is a *catechism.*

8 i. e. he is accounted but a mean man, in the present age, who does not show by his dress, deportment, and talk, that he has travelled and made observations in foreign countries.

9 Shakspeare probably meant to insinuate that a woman who travels about like *a post* was likely to *horn* her husband.

10 Colbrand was a Danish giant, whom Guy of Warwick discomfited in the presence of King Athelstan. The History of Guy was a popular book in the poet's age Drayton has described the combat very pompously in his Polyolbion.

11 The Bastard means '*Philip!* Do you take me for a *sparrow?*' The sparrow was called *Philip* from its note, which was supposed to have some resemblance to that word, '*phip phip* the sparrows as they fly.'—*Lyly's Mother Bombie.*

12 i. e. rumours, idle reports.

13 This is a piece of satire on the stupid old drama of Soliman and Perseda, printed in 1599, which had probably become the butt for stage sarcasm. In this piece there is a bragging cowardly knight called Basilisco. His pretension to valour is so blown and seen through that Piston, a buffoon servant in the play, jumps upon his back, and will not disengage him till he makes Basilisco swear upon his dagger to the contents, and in the terms he dictates; thus:—

Bas. O, I swear, I swear.
Pist. By the contents of this blade,—
Bas. By the contents of this blade,—
Pist. I, the aforesaid Basilico—
Bas. I, the aforesaid Basilico,—*knight,* good fellow *knight.*
Pist. *Knave,* good fellow, *knave.*

14 Shakspeare alludes to the fabulous history of King Richard I. which says that he derived his appellation of *Cœur de Lion* from having plucked out a lion's heart to whose fury he had been exposed by the Duke of Austria for having slain his son with a blow of his fist The story is related in several of the old chronicles, as well as in the old metrical romance

Who lives and dares but say, thou didst not well
When I was got, I'll send his soul to hell.
Come, lady, I will show thee to my kin;
And they shall say, when Richard me begot,
If thou hadst said him nay, it had been sin:
Who says it was, he lies; I say, 'twas not.
[*Exeunt.*

ACT II.

SCENE I. France. *Before the Walls of* Angiers.

Enter, on one side, the Archduke *of* Austria,[1] *and Forces; on the other*, PHILIP, King *of* France, *and Forces;* LEWIS, CONSTANCE, ARTHUR, *and* Attendants.

Lew. Before Angiers well met, brave Austria.—
Arthur, that great forerunner of thy blood,
Richard, that robb'd the lion of his heart,
And fought the holy wars in Palestine,
By this brave duke came early to his grave:
And, for amends to his posterity,
At our importance,[2] hither is he come,
To spread his colours, boy, in thy behalf;
And to rebuke the usurpation
Of thy unnatural uncle, English John:
Embrace him, love him, give him welcome hither.
Arth. God shall forgive you Cœur-de-lion's death,
The rather, that you give his offspring life,
Shadowing their right under your wings of war
I give you welcome with a powerless hand,
But with a heart full of unstained love:
Welcome before the gates of Angiers, duke.
Lew. A noble boy! Who would not do thee right?
Aust. Upon thy cheek lay I this zealous kiss,
As seal to this indenture of my love;
That to my home I will no more return,
Till Angiers, and the right thou hast in France,
Together with that pale, that white-fac'd shore,
Whose foot spurns back the ocean's roaring tides,
And coops from other lands her islanders,
Even till that England, hedg'd in with the main,
That water-walled bulwark, still secure
And confident from foreign purposes,
Even till that utmost corner of the west
Salute thee for her king: till then, fair boy,
Will I not think of home, but follow arms.
Const. O, take his mother's thanks, a widow's thanks,
Till your strong hand shall help to give him strength,
To make a more[3] requital to your love.
Aust. The peace of heaven is theirs, that lift their swords
In such a just and charitable war.
K. Phi. Well then, to work; our cannon shall be bent
Against the brows of this resisting town.——
Call for our chiefest men of discipline,
To cull the plots of best advantages:[4]—
We'll lay before this town our royal bones,
Wade to the market-place in Frenchmen's blood,
But we will make it subject to this boy.
Const. Stay for an answer to your embassy,
Lest unadvis'd you stain your swords with blood:
My lord Chatillon may from England bring
That right in peace, which here we urge in war:
And then we shall repent each drop of blood,
That hot rash haste so indirectly shed.

Enter CHATILLON.

K. Phi. A wonder, lady!—lo, upon thy wish,
Our messenger Chatillon is arriv'd.—
What England says, say briefly, gentle lord,
We coldly pause for thee; Chatillon, speak.
Chat. Then turn your forces from this paltry siege,
And stir them up against a mightier task.
England, impatient of your just demands,
Hath put himself in arms; the adverse winds,
Whose leisure I have staid, have given him time
To land his legions all as soon as I:
His marches are expedient[5] to this town,
His forces strong, his soldiers confident.
With him along is come the mother-queen,
An Ate,[6] stirring him to blood and strife:
With her her niece, the Lady Blanch of Spain,
With them a bastard of the king's deceas'd:
And all the unsettled humours of the land,—
Rash, inconsiderate, fiery voluntaries,
With ladies' faces, and fierce dragons' spleens,—
Have sold their fortunes at their native homes,
Bearing their birthrights proudly on their backs,
To make a hazard of new fortunes here.
In brief, a braver choice of dauntless spirits,
Than now, the English bottoms have waft[7] o'er,
Did never float upon the swelling tide,
To do offence and scath[8] in Christendom.
The interruption of their churlish drums
[*Drums beat.*
Cuts off more circumstance; they are at hand,
To parley, or to fight; therefore, prepare.
K. Phi. How much unlook'd for is this expedition!
Aust. By how much unexpected, by so much
We must awake endeavour for defence;
For courage mounteth with occasion:
Let them be welcome then, we are prepar'd.

Enter KING JOHN, ELINOR, BLANCH, *the* Bastard, PEMBROKE, *and Forces.*

K. John. Peace be to France: if France in peace permit
Our just and lineal entrance to our own!
If not, bleed France, and peace ascend to heaven!
Whiles we, God's wrathful agent, do correct
Their proud contempt that beat his peace to heaven
K. Phi. Peace be to England; if that war return
From France to England, there to live in peace!
England we love; and, for that England's sake,
With burden of our armour here we sweat:
This toil of ours should be a work of thine;
But thou from loving England art so far,
That thou hast under-wrought[9] his lawful king,
Cut off the sequence[10] of posterity,
Outfaced infant state, and done a rape
Upon the maiden virtue of the crown.
Look here upon thy brother Geffrey's face:—
These eyes, these brows, were moulded out of his.
This little abstract doth contain that large,
Which died in Geffrey; and the hand of time
Shall draw this brief[11] into as huge a volume.
That Geffrey was thy elder brother born,
And this his son; England was Geffrey's right,
And this is Geffrey's: In the name of God,
How comes it then, that thou art call'd a king,
When living blood doth in these temples beat,
Which owe the crown that thou o'ermasterest?
K. John. From whom hast thou this great commission, France,
To draw my answer from thy articles?
K. Phi. From that supernal[12] judge, that stirs good thoughts
In any breast of strong authority,
To look into the blots and stains of right.
That judge hath made me guardian to this boy.
Under whose warrant, I impeach thy wrong;
And, by whose help, I mean to chastise it.
K. John. Alack, thou dost usurp authority.
K. Phi. Excuse; it is to beat usurping down.
Eli. Who is it, thou dost call usurper, France?
Const. Let me make answer;—thy usurping son.

1 Leopold Duke of Austria, by whom Richard had been thrown into prison in 1193, died in consequence of a fall from his horse, in 1195, some years before the date of the events upon which this play turns. The cause of the enmity between Richard and the Duke of Austria is variously related by the old chroniclers. Shakspeare has been led into this anachronism by the old play of King John.

2 Importunity.
3 i. e. *greater.*
4 To mark the best stations to overawe the town.
5 Immediate, expeditious.
6 The Goddess of Revenge.
7 *Waft* for *wafted.*
8 Damage, harm, hurt.
9 Undermined.
10 Succession.
11 A short writing, abstract, or description
12 Celestial.

Eli. Out, insolent, thy bastard shall be king;
That thou mayst be a queen, and check the world![1]
Const. My bed was ever to thy son as true,
As thine was to thy husband; and this boy
Liker in feature to his father Geffrey,
Than thou and John in manners; being as like,
As rain to water, or devil to his dam.
My boy a bastard! By my soul, I think,
His father never was so true begot;
It cannot be, an if thou wert his mother.[2]
Eli. There's a good mother, boy, that blots thy father.
Const. There's a good grandam, boy, that would blot thee.
Aust. Peace!
Bast. Hear the crier.[3]
Aust. What the devil art thou?
Bast. One that will play the devil, sir, with you,
An 'a may catch your hide and you alone.[4]
You are the hare of whom the proverb goes,
Whose valour plucks dead lions by the beard;[5]
I'll smoke your skin-coat, an I catch you right;
Sirrah, look to't; i' faith, I will, i' faith.
Blanch. O, well did he become that lion's robe,
That did disrobe the lion of that robe!
Bast. It lies as sightly on the back of him,
As great Alcides' shoes[6] upon an ass:—
But, ass, I'll take that burden from your back;
Or lay on that shall make your shoulders crack.
Aust. What cracker is this same, that deafs our ears
With this abundance of superfluous breath?
K. Phi. Lewis, determine what we shall do straight.
Lew. Women and fools, break off your conference.—
King John, this is the very sum of all,—
England, and Ireland, Anjou, Touraine, Maine,
In right of Arthur do I claim of thee:
Wilt thou resign them, and lay down thy arms?
K. John. My life as soon:—I do defy thee, France.
Arthur of Bretagne, yield thee to my hand;
And, out of my dear love, I'll give thee more
Than e'er the coward hand of France can win:
Submit thee, boy.
Eli. Come to thy grandam, child.
Const. Do, child, go to it' grandam, child;
Give grandam kingdom, and it' grandam will
Give it a plum, a cherry, and a fig:
There's a good grandam.
Arth. Good my mother, peace!
I would, that I were low laid in my grave;
I am not worth this coil[7] that's made for me.
Eli. His mother shames him so, poor boy, he weeps.
Const. Now shame upon you, whe'r[8] she does or no!
His grandam's wrongs, and not his mother's shames,
Draw those heaven-moving pearls from his poor eyes,
Which heaven shall take in nature of a fee;
Ay, with these crystal beads heaven shall be brib'd
To do him justice, and revenge on you.
Eli. Thou monstrous slanderer of heaven and earth!
Const. Thou monstrous injurer of heaven and earth;
Call not me slanderer; thou, and thine, usurp
The dominations, royalties, and rights,
Of this oppressed boy: This is thy eldest son's son,
Infortunate in nothing but in thee;
Thy sins are visited in this poor child;
The canon of the law is laid on him,
Being but the second generation
Removed from thy sin-conceiving womb.
K. John. Bedlam, have done.
Const. I have but this to say,—
That he's not only plagued for her sin,
But God hath made her sin and her the plague
On this removed issue, plagu'd for her,
And with her plague, her sin; his injury
Her injury, the beadle to her sin;[9]
All punish'd in the person of this child,
And all for her; a plague upon her!
Eli. Thou unadvised scold, I can produce
A will, that bars the title of thy son.
Const. Ay, who doubts that? a will! a wicked will;
A woman's will; a canker'd grandam's will!
K. Phi. Peace, lady; pause, or be more temperate:
It ill beseems this presence, to cry aim[10]
To these ill-tuned repetitions.—
Some trumpet summon hither to the walls
These men of Angiers; let us hear them speak,
Whose title they admit, Arthur's or John's.

Trumpets sound. Enter Citizens *upon the Walls.*

1 Cit. Who is it that hath warn'd us to the walls?
K. Phi. 'Tis France, for England.
K. John. England, for itself:
You men of Angiers, and my loving subjects,—
K. Phi. You loving men of Angiers, Arthur's subjects,
Our trumpet call'd you to this gentle parle.[11]
K. John. For our advantage;—Therefore, hear us first.——
These flags of France, that are advanced here
Before the eye and prospect of your town,
Have hither march'd to your endamagement:
The cannons have their bowels full of wrath;
And ready mounted are they, to spit forth
Their iron indignation 'gainst your walls:
All preparation for a bloody siege,
And merciless proceeding by these French,
Confront your city's eyes, your winking gates;
And, but for our approach, those sleeping stones,
That as a waist do girdle you about,
By the compulsion of their ordnance
By this time from their fixed beds of lime
Had been dishabited, and wide havoc made
For bloody power to rush upon your peace.

---

1 'Surely (says Holinshed,) Queen Eleanor, the king's mother, was sore against her nephew Arthur, rather moved thereto by envye conceyved against his mother, than upon any just occasion, given in behalfe of the childe; for that she saw, if he were king, *how his mother Constance would looke to beare the most rule within the realme of Englande*, till her son should come of lawful age to governe of himselfe. So hard a thing it is to bring women to agree in one minde, their natures commonly being so contrary.'

2 Constance alludes to Elinor's infidelity to her husband, Louis the VIIth, when they were in the Holy Land; on account of which he was divorced from her. She afterwards, in 1151, married our King Henry II.

3 Alluding to the usual proclamation for *silence* made by criers in the courts of justice, beginning *Oyez*, corruptly pronounced *O-yes*. Austria had just said *Peace!*

4 Austria, who had killed King Richard Cœur-de-lion, wore, as the spoil of that prince, a lion's *hide*, which had belonged to him. This was the ground of the Bastard's quarrel.

5 The proverb alluded to is 'Mortuo leoni et lepores insultant.'—*Erasmi Adagia.*

6 Theobald thought that we should read *Alcides' shows*: but Malone has shown that the shoes of Hercules were very frequently introduced in the old comedies on much the same occasions. Theobald supposed that the shoes must be placed on the *back* of the ass, instead of upon his *hoofs*, and therefore proposed his alteration.

7 Bustle. 8 Whether.

9 The key to this obscure passage is contained in the last speech of Constance, where she alludes to the denunciation of the *second commandment* of 'visiting the iniquities of the parents upon the children unto the *third* and *fourth* generation.' Young Arthur is here represented as not only suffering *from* the guilt of his grandmother, but also by *her* in person, she being made the very instrument of his sufferings. So that he is *plagued on her account*, and *with her plague*, which is *her sin*, i.e. (taking by a common figure the cause for the consequence) the *penalty entailed upon it.* *His* injury, or the evil *he* suffers, *her* sin brings upon him, and *her* injury or the evils *she* inflicts he suffers from *her*, as the beadle to her sin, or executioner of the punishment annexed to it.

10 i. e. to encourage. It is a term taken from archery See note on the Merry Wives of Windsor, Act iii. Sc 2

11 Conference

But, on the sight of us, your lawful king,——
Who painfully, with much expedient march,
Have brought a countercheck before your gates,
To save unscratch'd your city's threaten'd cheeks,—
Behold, the French, amaz'd, vouchsafe a parle:
And now, instead of bullets wrapp'd in fire,
To make a shaking fever in your walls,
They shoot but calm words, folded up in smoke,
To make a faithless error in your ears:
Which trust accordingly, kind citizens,
And let us in, your king; whose labour'd spirits,
Forewearied[1] in this action of swift speed,
Crave harbourage within your city walls.

K. Phi. When I have said, make answer to us both.
Lo, in this right hand, whose protection
Is most divinely vow'd upon the right
Of him it holds, stands young Plantagenet;
Son to the elder brother of this man,
And king o'er him, and all that he enjoys:
For this down-trodden equity, we tread
In warlike march these greens before your town,
Being no further enemy to you,
Than the constraint of hospitable zeal,
In the relief of this oppressed child,
Religiously provokes. Be pleased then
To pay that duty, which you truly owe,
To him that owes[2] it; namely, this young prince:
And then our arms, like to a muzzled bear,
Save in aspect, have all offence seal'd up;
Our cannons' malice vainly shall be spent
Against the invulnerable clouds of heaven;
And, with a blessed and unvex'd retire,
With unhack'd swords, and helmets all unbruis'd,
We will bear home that lusty blood again,
Which here we came to spout against your town,
And leave your children, wives, and you, in peace.
But if you fondly pass our proffer'd offer,
'Tis not the roundure[3] of your old-fac'd walls
Can hide you from our messengers of war;
Though all these English, and their discipline,
Were harbour'd in their rude circumference.
Then, tell us, shall your city call us lord,
In that behalf which we have challeng'd it?
Or shall we give the signal to our rage,
And stalk in blood to our possession?

1 Cit. In brief, we are the king of England's subjects;
For him, and in his right, we hold this town.

K. John. Acknowledge then the king, and let me in.

1 Cit. That can we not: but he that proves the king,
To him will we prove loyal; till that time,
Have we ramm'd up our gates against the world.

K. John. Doth not the crown of England prove the king?
And, if not that, I bring you witnesses,
Twice fifteen thousand hearts of England's breed,—

Bast. Bastards, and else.

K. John. To verify our title with their lives.

K. Phi. As many, and as well born bloods as those,——

Bast. Some bastards too.

K. Phi. Stand in his face, to contradict his claim.

1 Cit. Till you compound whose right is worthiest,
We, for the worthiest, hold the right from both.

K. John. Then God forgive the sin of all those souls,
That to their everlasting residence,
Before the dew of evening fall, shall fleet,
In dreadful trial of our kingdom's king!

K. Phi. Amen, Amen!—Mount, chevaliers! to arms!

Bast. St. George,—that swing'd the dragon, and e'er since,
Sits on his horseback at mine hostess' door,
Teach us some fence;—Sirrah, were I at home,
At your den, sirrah [*To* Austria], with your lioness,
I'd set an ox-head to your lion's hide,[4]
And make a monster of you.

Aust. Peace; no more.

Bast. O, tremble; for you hear the lion roar.

K. John. Up higher to the plain; where we'll set forth,
In best appointment, all our regiments.

Bast. Speed then, to take advantage of the field.

K. Phi. It shall be so;—[*To* LEWIS] and at the other hill
Command the rest to stand.—God, and our right!

[*Exeunt.*

SCENE II. *The same. Alarums and Excursions; then a Retreat. Enter a* French Herald, *with trumpets to the gates.*

F. Her. [5]You men of Angiers, open wide your gates,
And let young Arthur, Duke of Bretagne, in;
Who, by the hand of France, this day hath made
Much work for tears in many an English mother,
Whose sons lie scattered on the bleeding ground:
Many a widow's husband grovelling lies,
Coldly embracing the discolour'd earth;
And victory, with little loss, doth play
Upon the dancing banners of the French;
Who are at hand, triumphantly display'd,
To enter conquerors, and to proclaim
Arthur of Bretagne, England's king, and yours.

Enter an English Herald, *with trumpets.*

E. Her. Rejoice, you men of Angiers, ring your bells;
King John, your king and England's doth approach,
Commander of this hot malicious day!
Their armours, that march'd hence so silver-bright,
Hither return all gilt with Frenchmen's blood;[6]
There stuck no plume in any English crest,
That is removed by a staff of France;
Our colours do return in those same hands
That did display them when we first march'd forth;
And, like a jolly troop of huntsmen,[7] come
Our lusty English, all with purpled hands,
Dyed in the dying slaughter of their foes:
Open your gates, and give the victors way.

Cit. Heralds, from off our towers we might behold,
From first to last, the onset and retire
Of both your armies; whose equality
By our best eyes cannot be censured:[8]
Blood hath bought blood, and blows have answer'd blows;
Strength match'd with strength, and power confronted power:
Both are alike; and both alike we like.
One must prove greatest; while they weigh so even,
We hold our town for neither; yet for both.

Enter, at one side, KING JOHN, *with his Power;* ELINOR, BLANCH, *and the* Bastard, *at the other,* KING PHILIP, LEWIS, AUSTRIA, *and Forces.*

K. John. France, hast thou yet more blood to cast away?
Say, shall the current of our right run[9] on?
Whose passage, vex'd with thy impediment,
Shall leave his native channel, and o'erswell
With course disturb'd even thy confining shores;
Unless thou let his silver water keep
A peaceful progress to the ocean.

---

1 Worn out. 2 Owns.

3 *Roundure*, from *rondare*, Fr.; circle.

4 So in the old play of King John:—
'But let the frolic Frenchman take no scorn
If Philip fronts him with an English horn.'

5 Johnson observes 'This speech is very poetical and smooth, and, except the conceit of the *widow's husband* embracing *the earth*, is just and beautiful.'

6 Shakspeare has used this image in Macbeth, Act. ii. Sc 3:—
'—— Here lay Duncan,
His *silver skin* laced with his *golden blood.*'

7 It was anciently one of the savage practices of the chase for all to stain their hands in the blood of the deer as a trophy.

8 Estimated, judged, determined. Shakspeare should have written, 'whose *superiority*, or whose *inequality* cannot be censured.'

9 The first folio reads *roam*: the change was made in the second folio.

K. Phi. England, thou hast not sav'd one drop of blood,
In this hot trial, more than we of France;
Rather, lost more: And by this hand I swear,
That sways the earth this climate overlooks,—
Before we will lay down our just-borne arms,
We'll put thee down, 'gainst whom these arms we bear,
Or add a royal number to the dead;
Gracing the scroll, that tells of this war's loss,
With slaughter coupled to the name of kings.

Bast. Ha, majesty! how high thy glory towers,
When the rich blood of kings is set on fire!
O, now doth death line his dead chaps with steel;
The swords of soldiers are his teeth, his fangs;
And now he feasts, mousing[1] the flesh of men,
In undetermin'd differences of kings.—
Why stand these royal fronts amazed thus?
Cry, havock, kings! back to the stained field,
You equal potents,[2] fiery-kindled spirits!
Then let confusion of one part confirm
The other's peace; till then, blows, blood, and death!

K. John. Whose party do the townsmen yet admit?

K. Phi. Speak, citizens, for England; who's your king?

1 Cit. The king of England, when we know the king.

K. Phi. Know him in us, that here hold up his right.

K. John. In us, that are our own great deputy,
And bear possession of our person here;
Lord of our presence, Angiers, and of you.

1 Cit. A greater power than we, denies all this;
And, till it be undoubted, we do lock
Our former scruple in our strong-barr'd gates:
King'd of our fears;[3] until our fears, resolv'd,
Be by some certain king purg'd and depos'd.

Bast. By heaven, these scroyles[4] of Angiers flout you, kings;
And stand securely on their battlements,
As in a theatre, whence they gape and point
At your industrious scenes and acts of death.
Your royal presences be rul'd by me;
Do like the mutines[5] of Jerusalem,
Be friends a while, and both conjointly bend
Your sharpest deeds of malice on this town:
By east and west let France and England mount
Their battering cannon, charged to the mouths;
Till their soul-fearing[6] clamours have brawl'd down
The flinty ribs of this contemptuous city:
I'd play incessantly upon these jades,
Even till unfenced desolation
Leave them as naked as the vulgar air.
That done, dissever your united strength,
And part your mingled colours once again;
Turn face to face, and bloody point to point:
Then, in a moment, fortune shall cull forth
Out of one side her happy minion;
To whom in favour she shall give the day,
And kiss him with a glorious victory.
How like you this wild counsel, mighty states?
Smacks it not something of the policy?

K. John. Now, by the sky that hangs above our heads,
I like it well;—France, shall we knit our powers,
And lay this Angiers even with the ground;
Then, after, fight who shall be king of it?

Bast. An if thou hast the mettle of a king—
Being wrong'd, as we are, by this peevish town,—
Turn thou the mouth of thy artillery,
As we will ours, against these saucy walls:
And when that we have dash'd them to the ground,
Why, then defy each other; and, pell-mell,
Make work upon ourselves, for heaven, or hell.

K. Phi. Let it be so:—Say, where will you assault?

K. John. We from the west will send destruction
Into this city's bosom.

Aust. I from the north.

K. Phi. Our thunder from the south,
Shall rain their drift of bullets on this town.

Bast. O prudent discipline! From north to south,
Austria and France shoot in each other's mouth:[7] [*Aside.*
I'll stir them to't:—Come, away, away!

1 Cit. Hear us, great kings! vouchsafe a while to stay,
And I shall show you peace, and fair-fac'd league;
Win you this city without stroke or wound;
Rescue those breathing lives to die in beds,
That here come sacrifices for the field;
Persever not, but hear me, mighty kings.

K. John. Speak on, with favour; we are bent to hear.

1 Cit. That daughter there of Spain, the lady Blanch,[8]
Is near to England; Look upon the years
Of Lewis the Dauphin, and that lovely maid:
If lusty love should go in quest of beauty,
Where should he find it fairer than in Blanch?
If zealous[9] love should go in search of virtue,
Where should he find it purer than in Blanch?
If love ambitious sought a match of birth,
Whose veins bound richer blood than Lady Blanch?
Such as she is, in beauty, virtue, birth,
Is the young Dauphin every way complete:
If not complete, O say, he is not she;
And she again wants nothing, to name want,
If want it be not, that she is not he:
He is the half part of a blessed man,
Left to be finished by such a she;
And she a fair divided excellence,
Whose fullness of perfection lies in him.
O, two such silver currents, when they join,
Do glorify the banks that bound them in:
And two such shores to two such streams made one,
Two such controlling bounds shall you be, kings,
To these two princes, if you marry them.
This union shall do more than battery can,
To our fast-closed gates: for, at this match,
With swifter spleen[10] than powder can enforce,
The mouth of passage shall we fling wide ope,
And give you entrance; but, without this match
The sea enraged is not half so deaf,
Lions more confident, mountains and rocks
More free from motion; no, not death himself
In mortal fury half so peremptory,
As we to keep this city.

Bast. Here's a stay,[11]
That shakes the rotten carcass of old death

---

1 Mr. Pope changed this to *mouthing*, and was followed by subsequent editors. '*Mousing*,' says Malone, 'is mammocking and devouring eagerly, as a cat devours a mouse.' 'Whilst Troy was swilling sack and sugar, and *mousing* fat venison, the mad Greekes made bonfires of their houses.'—*The Wonderful Year*, by Decker, 1603.—Shakspeare often uses familiar terms in his most serious speeches; and Malone has adduced other instances in this play: but in this very speech 'his dead *chaps*' is surely not more elevated than *mousing*.

2 Potentates.

3 The old copy reads '*Kings* of our fear, &c.' The emendation is Mr. Tyrwhitt's. '*King'd* of our fears,' i. e. our fears being our kings or rulers. It is manifest that the reading of the old copy is corrupt, and that it must have been so worded, that their fears should be styled their *kings* or masters, and not they kings or masters of their fears, because in the next line mention is made of these *fears* being *deposed*.

4 *Escrouelles*, Fr. scabby fellows.

5 The *mutines* are the mutineers, the seditious.

6 i. e. *soul-appalling*; from the verb to *fear*, to make afraid.

7 The poet has made Faulconbridge forget that he had made a similar mistake.

8 The Lady *Blanch* was daughter to Alphonso, the ninth king of Castile, and was niece to King John by his sister Eleanor.

9 *Zealous* for *pious*.

10 *Spleen* is used by Shakspeare for any violent hurry or tumultuous speed. In a Midsummer Night's Dream he applies *spleen* to the *lightning*.

11 A *stay* here seems to mean *a supporter of a cause*. 'Here's an extraordinary partisan or maintainer that shakes,' &c. Baret translates *columen vel firmamen*

Out of his rags! Here's a large mouth, indeed,
That spits forth death, and mountains, rocks, and seas;
Talks as familiarly of roaring lions
As maids of thirteen do of puppy-dogs!
What cannoneer begot this lusty blood?
He speaks plain cannon, fire, and smoke, and bounce:
He gives the bastinado with his tongue;
Our ears are cudgel'd; not a word of his,
But buffets better than a fist of France:
Zounds! I was never so bethump'd with words,
Since I first call'd my brother's father, dad.

Eli. Son, list to this conjunction, make this match;
Give with our niece a dowry large enough:
For by this knot thou shalt so surely tie
Thy now unsur'd assurance to the crown,
That yon green boy shall have no sun to ripe
The bloom that promiseth a mighty fruit.
I see a yielding in the looks of France;
Mark, how they whisper: urge them, while their souls
Are capable of this ambition:
Lest zeal, now melted by the windy breath
Of soft petitions, pity, and remorse,
Cool and congeal again to what it was.

1 *Cit.* Why answer not the double majesties
This friendly treaty of our threaten'd town?

K. Phi. Speak England first, that hath been forward first
To speak unto this city: What say you?

K. John. If that the Dauphin there, thy princely son,
Can in this book of beauty read,[1] I love,
Her dowry shall weigh equal with a queen:
For Anjou, and fair Touraine, Maine, Poictiers,
And all that we upon this side the sea
(Except this city now by us besieg'd)
Find liable to our crown and dignity,
Shall gild her bridal bed; and make her rich
In titles, honours, and promotions,
As she in beauty, education, blood,
Holds hand with any princess of the world.

K. Phi. What say'st thou, boy? look in the lady's face.

Lew. I do, my lord, and in her eye I find
A wonder, or a wondrous miracle,
The shadow of myself form'd in her eye;
Which, being but the shadow of your son,
Becomes a sun, and makes your son a shadow;
I do protest, I never lov'd myself,
Till now infixed I beheld myself
Drawn in the flattering table[2] of her eye.
[*Whispers with* BLANCH.

Bast. Drawn in the flattering table of her eye!—
Hang'd in the frowning wrinkle of her brow!—
And quarter'd in her heart?—he doth espy
Himself love's traitor: This is pity now,
That hang'd, and drawn, and quarter'd, there should be,
In such a love, so vile a lout as he.

Blanch. My uncle's will, in this respect, is mine:
If he see aught in you, that makes him like,
That any thing he sees, which moves his liking,
I can with ease translate it to my will;
Or, if you will, (to speak more properly,)
I will enforce it easily to my love.
Further I will not flatter you, my lord,
That all I see in you is worthy love,
Than this,—that nothing do I see in you,
(Though churlish thoughts themselves should be your judge,)
That I can find should merit any hate.

K. John. What say these young ones? What say you, my niece?

Blanch. That she is bound in honour still to do
What you in wisdom shall vouchsafe to say.

K. John. Speak, then, prince Dauphin; can you love this lady?

Lew. Nay, ask me if I can refrain from love;
For I do love her most unfeignedly.

K. John. Then do I give Volquessen,[3] Touraine, Maine,
Poictiers, and Anjou, these five provinces,
With her to thee; and this addition more,
Full thirty thousand marks of English coin.—
Philip of France, if thou be pleas'd withal,
Command thy son and daughter to join hands.

K. Phi. It likes us well;—Young princes, close your hands.[4]

Aust. And your lips, too; for I am well assur'd
That I did so, when I was first assur'd.[5]

K. Phi. Now, citizens of Angiers, ope your gates,
Let in that amity which you have made;
For, at Saint Mary's chapel, presently,
The rites of marriage shall be solemniz'd.—
Is not the Lady Constance in this troop?—
I know, she is not; for this match, made up,
Her presence would have interrupted much:—
Where is she and her son? tell me, who knows.

Lew. She is sad and passionate[6] at your highness' tent.

K. Phi. And, by my faith, this league, that we have made,
Will give her sadness very little cure.—
Brother of England, how may we content
This widow lady? In her right we came;
Which we, God knows, have turn'd another way,
To our own vantage.[7]

K. John. We will heal up all;
For we'll create young Arthur duke of Bretagne,
And earl of Richmond; and this rich fair town
We make him lord of.—Call the Lady Constance,
Some speedy messenger bid her repair
To our solemnity:—I trust we shall,
If not fill up the measure of her will,
Yet in some measure satisfy her so,
That we shall stop her exclamation.
Go we, as well as haste will suffer us,
To this unlook'd for, unprepared pomp.
[*Exeunt all but the* Bastard.—*The* Citizens *retire from the Walls.*

Bast. Mad world! mad kings! mad composition!
John, to stop Arthur's title in the whole,
Hath willingly departed[8] with a part:
And France (whose armour conscience buckled on;
Whom zeal and charity brought to the field,
As God's own soldier,) rounded[9] in the ear
With that same purpose-changer, that sly devil;
That broker, that still breaks the pate of faith;
That daily break-vow; he that wins of all,

---

tum reipublicæ by 'the *stay*, the chiefe mainteyner and succour of,' &c. It has been proposed to read, 'Here's a *say*,' i. e. a speech; and it must be confessed that it would agree well with the tenor of the subsequent part of Faulconbridge's speech.

1 So in Pericles:—
'Her *face the book* of praises,' &c.

2 The *table* is the plain surface on which any thing is depicted or written. *Tablette*, Fr. Our ancestors called their memorandum-books a pair of writing *tables*. Vide Baret's Alvearie, 1575, Letter T. No. 2.

3 This is the ancient name for the country now called the *Vexin*, in Latin Pagus Velocassinus. That part of it called the *Norman Vexin* was in dispute between Philip and John. This and the subsequent line (except the words 'do I give') are taken from the old play.

4 See Winter's Tale, Act i. Sc 2

5 Affianced, contracted.

6 *Passionate* here means *agitated*, *perturbed*, a prey to mournful sensations, not moved or disposed to anger Thus in the old play, entitled, The true Tragedie of Richard Duke of York, 1600:—
'——— Tell me, good madam,
Why is your grace so *passionate* of late?'

7 Advantage.

8 To *part* and *depart* were formerly synonymous. So in Cooper's Dictionary, v. 'communico, to communicate or *departe* a thing I have with another.'

9 To *round* or *rown* in the ear is to *whisper*; from the Saxon *runian*, susurrare. The word and its etymology is fully illustrated by Casaubon, in his Treatise de Ling. Saxonica, and in a Letter by Sir H. Spelman, published in Wormius, Literatura Runica Hafniæ, 1651, p. 4

Of kings, of beggars, old men, young men, maids,—
Who having no external thing to lose
But the word maid,—cheats the poor maid of that;
That smooth-faced gentleman, tickling commodity;[1]—
Commodity, the bias of the world;
The world, who of itself is peised well,
Made to run even, upon even ground;
Till this advantage, this vile drawing bias,
This sway of motion, this commodity,
Makes it take head from all indifferency,
From all direction, purpose, course, intent:
And this same bias, this commodity,
This bawd, this broker, this all-changing word,
Clapp'd on the outward eye of fickle France,
Hath drawn him from his own determin'd aid,
From a resolv'd and honourable war,
To a most base and vile-concluded peace.—
And why rail I on this commodity?
But for because he hath not woo'd me yet:
Not that I have the power to clutch[2] my hand,
When his fair angels[3] would salute my palm:
But for[4] my hand, as unattempted yet,
Like a poor beggar, raileth on the rich.
Well, whiles I am a beggar, I will rail,
And say,—there is no sin, but to be rich;
And being rich, my virtue then shall be,
To say,—there is no vice, but beggary:
Since kings break faith upon commodity,
Gain, be my lord! for I will worship thee!
[*Exit.*[5]

ACT III.

SCENE I. *The same. The* French King's *Tent.*
Enter CONSTANCE, ARTHUR, *and* SALISBURY.

Const. Gone to be married! gone to swear a peace!
False blood to false blood join'd! Gone to be friends!
Shall Lewis have Blanch? and Blanch those provinces?
It is not so; thou hast misspoke, misheard;
Be well advis'd, tell o'er thy tale again:
It cannot be; thou dost but say, 'tis so:
I trust, I may not trust thee; for thy word
Is but the vain breath of a common man;
Believe me, I do not believe thee, man;
I have a king's oath to the contrary.
Thou shalt be punish'd for thus frighting me,
For I am sick, and capable[6] of fears.
Oppress'd with wrongs, and therefore full of fears;
A widow, husbandless, subject to fears;
A woman, naturally born to fears;
And though thou now confess, thou didst but jest,
With my vex'd spirits I cannot take a truce,
But they will quake and tremble all this day.
What dost thou mean by shaking of thy head?
Why dost thou look so sadly on my son?
What means that hand upon that breast of thine?
Why holds thine eye that lamentable rheum,
Like a proud river peering[7] o'er his bounds?
Be these sad signs confirmers of thy words?
Then speak again; not all thy former tale,
But this one word, whether thy tale be true.

Sal. As true, as, I believe, you think them false,
That give you cause to prove my saying true.

Const. O, if thou teach me to believe this sorrow,
Teach thou this sorrow how to make me die;
And let belief and life encounter so,
As doth the fury of two desperate men,
Which, in the very meeting, fall, and die.—
Lewis marry Blanch! O, boy, then where art thou?
France friend with England! what becomes of me?—
Fellow, be gone; I cannot brook thy sight;
This news hath made thee a most ugly man.

Sal. What other harm have I, good lady, done,
But spoke the harm that is by others done?

Const. Which harm within itself so heinous is,
As it makes harmful all that speak of it.

Arth. I do beseech you, madam, be content.

Const. If thou, that bidd'st me be content, wert grim,
Ugly, and sland'rous to thy mother's womb,
Full of unpleasing blots, and sightless[8] stains,
Lame, foolish, crooked, swart,[9] prodigious,
Patch'd with foul moles, and eye-offending marks,
I would not care, I then would be content;
For then I should not love thee; no, nor thou
Become thy great birth, nor deserve a crown.
But thou art fair; and at thy birth, dear boy!
Nature and fortune join'd to make thee great:
Of nature's gifts thou may'st with lilies boast,
And with the half-blown rose: but fortune, O!
She is corrupted, chang'd, and won from thee;
She adulterates hourly with thine uncle John;
And with her golden hand hath pluck'd on France
To tread down fair respect of sovereignty,
And made his majesty the bawd to theirs.
France is a bawd to fortune, and King John;
That strumpet fortune, that usurping John:—
Tell me, thou fellow, is not France forsworn?
Envenom him with words; or get thee gone,
And leave those woes alone, which I alone
Am bound to under-bear.

Sal. Pardon me, madam,
I may not go without you to the kings.

Const. Thou may'st, thou shalt, I will not go with thee:
I will instruct my sorrows to be proud;
For grief is proud, and makes his owner stout.[10]
To me, and to the state of my great grief,
Let kings assemble; for my grief's so great,
That no supporter but the huge firm earth
Can hold it up: here I and sorrow sit;
Here is my throne, bid kings come bow to it.
[*She throws herself on the ground.*

Enter KING JOHN, KING PHILIP, LEWIS, BLANCH, ELINOR, Bastard, AUSTRIA, *and* Attendants.

K. Phi. 'Tis true, fair daughter; and this blessed day,
Ever in France shall be kept festival:
To solemnize this day, the glorious sun
Stays in his course, and plays the alchemist;
Turning, with splendour of his precious eye,
The meagre cloddy earth to glittering gold:
The yearly course, that brings this day about,
Shall never see it but a holyday.

Const. A wicked day, and not a holyday!— [*Rising*
What hath this day deserv'd? what hath it done;
That it in golden letters should be set
Among the high tides,[11] in the calendar?
Nay, rather, turn this day out of the week;[12]
This day of shame, oppression, perjury:

1 *Commodity* is *interest, advantage.* So Baret:—'What fruite or *commoditie* had he by this his friendship?' *Alvearie*, Letter C. 867. The construction of this passage, though harsh to modern ears, is—'*Commodity*, he that wins of all,—*he that* cheats the poor maid of that only external thing she has to lose, namely the word maid, i. e. her chastity.'

Henderson has adduced a passage from Cupid's Whirligig, 1607, which happily illustrates the word *bias* in this passage:—

'O, the world is like a *byas* bowle, and it runs
All on the rich men's sides.'

2 Clasp. 3 Coin. 4 i. e. but *cause.*

5 In the old copy, the Second Act extends to the end of the speech of Lady Constance, in the next scene, at the conclusion of which she throws herself on the ground. The present division, which was made by Theobald, is certainly right.

6 *Capable* is *susceptible.*

7 This seems to have been imitated by Marston, in his Insatiate Countess, 1603:—
'Then how much more in me, whose youthful veins,
Like a proud river, overflow their bounds.'

8 Unsightly.

9 *Swart* is *dark*, dusky. *Prodigious* is *portentous*, so deformed as to be taken for a *foretoken of evil.*

10 The old copy reads, 'makes *its* owner *stoop.*' The emendation is Sir T. Hanmer's.

11 Solemn seasons, times to be observed above others

12 In allusion to Job iii. 3.—'Let the day perish,' &c.; and v. 6, 'Let it not be joined to the days of the year, let it not come into the number of the months.'

Or, if it must stand still, let wives with child
Pray, that their burdens may not fall this day,
Lest that their hopes prodigiously be cross'd;[1]
But[2] on this day, let seamen fear no wreck;
No bargains break, that are not this day made:
This day, all things begun come to ill end;
Yea, faith itself to hollow falsehood change!

K. Phi. By heaven, lady, you shall have no cause
To curse the fair proceedings of this day:
Have I not pawn'd to you my majesty?

Const. You have beguil'd me with a counterfeit,[3]
Resembling majesty; which, being touch'd, and tried,
Proves valueless: You are forsworn, forsworn;
You came in arms to spill mine enemies' blood,
But now in arms you strengthen it with yours:
The grappling vigour and rough frown of war
Is cold in amity and painted peace,
And our oppression hath made up this league:—
Arm, arm, you heavens, against these perjur'd kings!
A widow cries; be husband to me, heavens!
Let not the hours of this ungodly day
Wear out the day in peace; but, ere sunset,
Set armed discord 'twixt these perjur'd kings!
Hear me, O, hear me!

Aust. Lady Constance, peace.

Const. War! war! no peace! peace is to me a war.
O Lymoges! O Austria![4] thou dost shame
That bloody spoil: Thou slave, thou wretch, thou coward,
Thou little valiant, great in villany!
Thou ever strong upon the stronger side!
Thou fortune's champion, that dost never fight
But when her humorous ladyship is by
To teach thee safety! thou art perjur'd, too,
And sooth'st up greatness. What a fool art thou,
A ramping fool; to brag, and stamp, and swear,
Upon my party! thou cold-blooded slave,
Hast thou not spoke like thunder on my side?
Been sworn my soldier? bidding me depend
Upon thy stars, thy fortune, and thy strength?
And dost thou now fall over to my foes?
Thou wear a lion's hide! doff it for shame,
And hang a calf's-skin on those recreant limbs.[5]

Aust. O, that a man should speak those words to me!

Bast. And hang a calf's-skin on those recreant limbs.

Aust. Thou dar'st not say so, villain, for thy life.

Bast. And hang a calf's-skin on those recreant limbs.[6]

K. John. We like not this; thou dost forget thyself.

Enter PANDULPH.

K. Phi. Here comes the holy legate of the pope.

Pand. Hail, you anointed deputies of heaven!—
To thee, King John, my holy errand is
I Pandulph, of fair Milan cardinal,
And from Pope Innocent the legate here,
Do, in his name, religiously demand,
Why thou against the church, our holy mother,
So wilfully dost spurn; and, force perforce,
Keep Stephen Langton, chosen archbishop
Of Canterbury, from that holy see?
This, in our 'foresaid holy father's name,
Pope Innocent, I do demand of thee.

K. John. What earthly name to interrogatories,[7]
Can task the free breath of a sacred king?
Thou canst not, cardinal, devise a name
So slight, unworthy, and ridiculous,
To charge me to an answer, as the pope.
Tell him this tale; and from the mouth of England,
Add thus much more,—That no Italian priest
Shall tithe or toll in our dominions;
But as we under heaven are supreme head,
So under him, that great supremacy,
Where we do reign, we will alone uphold,
Without the assistance of a mortal hand:
So tell the pope: all reverence set apart,
To him and his usurp'd authority.

K. Phi. Brother of England, you blaspheme in this.

K. John. Though you, and all the kings of Christendom,
Are led so grossly by this meddling priest,
Dreading the curse that money may buy out.
And, by the merit of vile gold, dross, dust,
Purchase corrupted pardon of a man,
Who, in that sale, sells pardon from himself:
Though you, and all the rest, so grossly led,
This juggling witchcraft with revenue cherish;
Yet I, alone, alone do me oppose
Against the pope, and count his friends my foes.

Pand. Then, by the lawful power that I have,
Thou shalt stand curs'd, and excommunicate:
And blessed shall he be, that doth revolt
From his allegiance to an heretic;
And meritorious shall that hand be call'd,
Canonized, and worship'd as a saint,
That takes away by any secret course
Thy hateful life.

Const. O, lawful let it be,
That I have room with Rome to curse a while!
Good father cardinal, cry thou, amen,
To my keen curses; for, without my wrong,
There is no tongue hath power to curse him right.

Pand. There's law and warrant, lady, for my curse.

Const. And for mine too; when law can do no right,
Let it be lawful, that law bar no wrong:
Law cannot give my child his kingdom here;
For he that holds his kingdom, holds the law:
Therefore, since law itself is perfect wrong,

1 i. e. be disappointed by the production of a prodigy, a monster.

2 *But* for *unless;* its exceptive sense of *be out.* In the ancient almanacs the days supposed to be favourable or unfavourable to bargains are distinguished, among a number of particulars of the like importance.

3 i. e. a false coin; a representation of the king being usually impressed on his coin. A *counterfeit* formerly signified also a *portrait.* The word seems to be here used equivocally.

4 Shakspeare, in the person of Austria, has conjoined the two well known enemies of Richard Cœur-de-lion. Leopold, duke of Austria, threw him into prison in a former expedition (in 1193); but the castle of Chaluz, before which he fell (in 1199), belonged to Vidomar, viscount of Limoges. The archer who pierced his shoulder with an arrow (of which wound he died) was Bertrand de Gourdon. Austria in the old play is called Lymoges, the Austrich duke. Holinshed says, 'The same year Philip, bastard sonne to King Richard, to whom his father had given the castell and honour of Coniacke, killed the viscount of Lymoges in revenge of his father's death,' &c.

5 Sir John Hawkins thought that there was here a sarcastic intention of calling Austria *a fool;* he says that a calf-skin coat was anciently the dress of a fool. It is more probable, as Ritson observes, that she means to call him a coward; she tells him that a calf's-skin would suit his recreant limbs better than a lion's. A *calf-hearted fellow* is still used for a dastardly person.

6 Pope inserted the following lines from the old play here, which he thought necessary 'to explain the ground of the Bastard's quarrel with Austria:'—

'*Aust.* Methinks that Richard's pride, and Richard's fall,
Should be a precedent to fright you all.
Faulc. What words are these? How do my sinews shake!
My father's foe clad in my father's spoil;
How doth Alecto whisper in my ears,
Delay not, Richard, kill the villain straight;
Disrobe him of the matchless monument,
Thy father's triumph o'er the savages!—
Now by his soul I swear, my father's soul,
Twice will I not review the morning's rise,
Till I have torn that trophy from thy back,
And split thy heart for wearing it so long.'

7 What earthly name *subjoined* to interrogatories, can force a king to *speak* and answer them? The old copy reads *earthy.* The emendation was Pope's. It has also *tash* instead of *task* in the next line, which was substituted by Theobald. Johnson observes that this must have been a very captivating scene at the time of our struggles with popery

How can the law forbid my tongue to curse?
Pand. Philip of France, on peril of a curse,
Let go the hand of that arch-heretic;
And raise the power of France upon his head,
Unless he do submit himself to Rome.
Eli. Look'st thou pale, France? do not let go thy hand.
Const. Look to that, devil! lest that France repent,
And, by disjoining hands, hell lose a soul.
Aust. King Philip, listen to the cardinal.
Bast. And hang a calf's-skin on his recreant limbs.
Aust. Well, ruffian, I must pocket up these wrongs,
Because——
Bast. Your breeches best may carry them.[1]
K. John. Philip, what say'st thou to the cardinal?
Const. What should he say, but as the cardinal?
Lew. Bethink you, father; for the difference
Is, purchase of a heavy curse from Rome,
Or the light loss of England for a friend:
Forgo the easier.
Blanch. That's the curse of Rome.
Const. O Lewis, stand fast; the devil tempts thee here,
In likeness of a new untrimmed[2] bride.
Blanch. The Lady Constance speaks not from her faith,
But from her need.
Const. O, if thou grant my need,
Which only lives but by the death of faith,
That need must needs infer this principle,——
That faith would live again by death of need;
O, then, tread down my need, and faith mounts up;
Keep my need up, and faith is trodden down.
K. John. The king is mov'd, and answers not to this.
Const. O, be remov'd from him, and answer well.
Aust. Do so, King Philip; hang no more in doubt.
Bast. Hang nothing but a calf's-skin, most sweet lout.
K. Phi. I am perplex'd, and know not what to say.
Pand. What canst thou say, but will perplex thee more,
If thou stand excommunicate, and curs'd?
K. Phi. Good reverend father, make my person yours,
And tell me how you would bestow yourself.
This royal hand and mine are newly knit;
And the conjunction of our inward souls
Married in league, coupled and link'd together
With all religious strength and sacred vows;
The latest breath that gave the sound of words,
Was deep-sworn faith, peace, amity, true love,
Between our kingdoms, and our royal selves;
And even before this truce, but new before,—
No longer than we well could wash our hands,
To clap this royal bargain up of peace,
Heaven knows, they were besmear'd and overstain'd
With slaughter's pencil; where revenge did paint
The fearful difference of incensed kings:—
And shall these hands, so lately purg'd of blood,
So newly join'd in love, so strong in both,[3]
Unyoke this seizure, and this kind regreet?[4]
Play fast and loose with faith? so jest with heaven,
Make such unconstant children of ourselves,
As now again to snatch our palm from palm:
Unswear faith sworn; and on the marriage bed
Of smiling peace to march a bloody host,
And make a riot on the gentle brow
Of true sincerity? O holy sir,
My reverend father, let it not be so:
Out of your grace, devise, ordain, impose
Some gentle order; and then we shall be bless'd
To do your pleasure, and continue friends.
Pand. All form is formless, order orderless,
Save what is opposite to England's love.
Therefore, to arms! be champion of our church!
Or let the church, our mother, breathe her curse,
A mother's curse, on her revolting son.
France, thou may'st hold a serpent by the tongue
A cased[5] lion by the mortal paw,
A fasting tiger safer by the tooth,
Than keep in peace that hand which thou dost hold.
K. Phi. I may disjoin my hand, but not my faith.
Pand. So mak'st thou faith an enemy to faith;
And, like a civil war, sett'st oath to oath,
Thy tongue against thy tongue. O, let thy vow
First made to heaven, first be to heaven perform'd;
That is to be the champion of our church!
What since thou swor'st, is sworn against thyself,
And may not be performed by thyself:
For that, which thou hast sworn to do amiss,
Is not amiss when it is truly done;[6]
And being not done, where doing tends to ill,
The truth is then most done not doing it:
The better act of purposes mistook
Is, to mistake again: though indirect,
Yet indirection thereby grows direct,
And falsehood falsehood cures; as fire cools fire,
Within the scorched veins of one new burn'd.
It is religion, that doth make vows kept;
But thou hast sworn against religion;
By what thou swear'st, against the thing thou swear'st;
And mak'st an oath the surety for thy truth
Against an oath: The truth thou art unsure
To swear, swear only not to be forsworn;[7]
Else, what a mockery should it be to swear?
But thou dost swear only to be forsworn;
And most forsworn, to keep what thou dost swear
Therefore, thy latter vows, against thy first:
Is in thyself rebellion to thyself:
And better conquest never canst thou make,
Than arm thy constant and thy nobler parts
Against those giddy loose suggestions:
Upon which better part our prayers come in,
If thou vouchsafe them: but, if not, then know,
The peril of our curses light on thee;
So heavy, as thou shalt not shake them off,
But, in despair, die under their black weight.
Aust. Rebellion, flat rebellion!
Bast. Will't not be?
Will not a calf-skin stop that mouth of thine?
Lew. Father, to arms!
Blanch. Upon thy wedding day!
Against the blood that thou hast married?
What, shall our feast be kept with slaughter'd men?
Shall braying trumpets, and loud churlish drums,—
Clamours of hell,—be measures to our pomp?
O husband, hear me!—ah, alack! how new
Is husband in my mouth? even for that name,
Which till this time my tongue did ne'er pronounce,
Upon my knee I beg, go not to arms
Against mine uncle.
Const. O, upon my knee,
Made hard with kneeling, I do pray to thee,
Thou virtuous Dauphin, alter not the doom
Forethought by heaven.
Blanch. Now shall I see thy love; What motive may
Be stronger with thee than the name of wife?
Const. That which upholdeth him that thee upholds,
His honour: O, thine honour, Lewis, thine honour!

---

1 This may be a proverbial sarcasm; but the allusion is now lost.

2 *Trim* is dress. *Comptus virgineus* is explained by the dictionaries, 'The attyre of maydens, or maidenly *trimming*.' An *untrimmed* bride may therefore mean a bride *undressed* or disencumbered of the forbidding forms of dress.

3 i. e. so strong both in *hatred* and *love*; in deeds of *amity* or deeds of *blood*.

4 A *regreet* is an exchange of salutation.

5 *A cased lion* is a lion irritated by confinement.

6 'Where doing tends to ill,' where an intended act is criminal, the *truth* is *most done* by *not doing* the act. The criminal act therefore, which thou hast sworn to do, *is not amiss*, will not be imputed to you as a crime, if it be done *truly*, in the sense I have now affixed to *truth*: that is, if you do *not* do it.

7 *By what thou swear'st*, &c. 'In swearing by religion against religion, thou hast sworn *by what thou swear'st*; i. e. in that which thou hast sworn, *against the thing thou swearest by*; i. e. religion

Lew. I muse, your majesty doth seem so cold,
When such profound respects do pull you on.

Pand. I will denounce a curse upon his head.

K. Phi. Thou shalt not need:—England, I'll fall from thee.

Const. O fair return of banish'd majesty!

Eli. O foul revolt of French inconstancy!

K. John. France, thou shalt rue this hour within this hour.

Bast. Old time the clock-setter, that bald sexton time,
Is it as he will? well, then, France shall rue.

Blanch. The sun's o'ercast with blood: Fair day, adieu!
Which is the side that I must go withal?
I am with both: each army hath a hand;
And in their rage, I having hold of both,
They whirl asunder, and dismember me.
Husband, I cannot pray that thou may'st win;
Uncle, I needs must pray that thou may'st lose;
Father, I may now wish the fortune thine;
Grandam, I will not wish thy wishes thrive:
Whoever wins, on that side shall I lose;
Assured loss, before the match be play'd.

Lew. Lady, with me; with me thy fortune lies.

Blanch. There where my fortune lives, there my life dies.

K. John. Cousin, go draw our puissance together,— [*Exit* Bastard.
France, I am burn'd up with inflaming wrath;
A rage, whose heat hath this condition,
That nothing can allay, nothing but blood,
The blood, and dearest valued blood, of France.

K. Phi. Thy rage shall burn thee up, and thou shalt turn
To ashes, ere our blood shall quench that fire:
Look to thyself, thou art in jeopardy.

K. John. No more than he that threats.—To arms let's hie! [*Exeunt.*

SCENE II. *The same. Plains near* Angiers.

Alarums; Excursions. Enter the Bastard, *with* AUSTRIA'S *Head.*

Bast. Now, by my life, this day grows wondrous hot;
Some airy devil[1] hovers in the sky,
And pours down mischief. Austria's head, lie there,
While Philip breathes.

Enter KING JOHN, ARTHUR, *and* HUBERT.

K.John. Hubert, keep this boy:—Philip,[2] make up:
My mother is assailed in our tent,
And ta'en, I fear.

Bast. My lord, I rescu'd her;
Her highness is in safety, fear you not:
But on, my liege: for very little pains
Will bring this labour to a happy end. [*Exeunt.*

SCENE III. *The same. Alarums; Excursions; Retreat. Enter* KING JOHN, ELINOR, ARTHUR, *the* Bastard, HUBERT, *and* LORDS.

K. John. So shall it be; your grace shall stay behind, [*To* ELINOR.
So strongly guarded.—Cousin, look not sad: [*To* ARTHUR.
Thy grandam loves thee, and thy uncle will
As dear be to thee as thy father was.

Arth. O, this will make my mother die with grief.

K. John. Cousin, [*To the* Bastard,] away for England; haste before:
And, ere our coming, see thou shake the bags
Of hoarding abbots: angels[3] imprisoned
Set thou at liberty; the fat ribs of peace
Must by the hungry now be fed upon:
Use our commission in his utmost force.

Bast. Bell, book, and candle[4] shall not drive me back;
When gold and silver becks me to come on.
I leave your highness:—Grandam, I will pray
(If ever I remember to be holy)
For your fair safety: so I kiss your hand.

Eli. Farewell, my gentle cousin.

K. John. Coz, farewell. [*Exit* Bastard.

Eli. Come hither, little kinsman; hark, a word. [*She takes* ARTHUR *aside.*

K. John. Come hither, Hubert. O my gentle Hubert,
We owe thee much; within this wall of flesh
There is a soul counts thee her creditor,
And with advantage means to pay thy love:
And, my good friend, thy voluntary oath
Lives in this bosom, dearly cherished.
Give me thy hand. I had a thing to say,—
But I will fit it with some better time.
By heaven, Hubert, I am almost asham'd
To say what good respect I have of thee.

Hub. I am much bounden to your majesty.

K. John. Good friend, thou hast no cause to say so yet:
But thou shalt have; and creep time ne'er so slow,
Yet it shall come, for me to do thee good.
I had a thing to say,—But let it go:
The sun is in the heaven, and the proud day,
Attended with the pleasures of the world,
Is all too wanton, and too full of gawds,[5]
To give me audience:—If the midnight bell
Did, with his iron tongue and brazen mouth,
Sound one unto[6] the drowsy race of night;
If this same were a churchyard where we stand,
And thou possessed with a thousand wrongs;
Or if that surly spirit, melancholy,
Had bak'd thy blood, and made it heavy, thick,
(Which, else, runs tickling up and down the veins,
Making that idiot, laughter, keep men's eyes,
And strain their cheeks to idle merriment,
A passion hateful to my purposes;)
Or if that thou could'st see me without eyes,
Hear me without thine ears, and make reply
Without a tongue, using conceit[7] alone,
Without eyes, ears, and harmful sound of words;
Then, in despite of brooded[8] watchful day,
I would into thy bosom pour my thoughts:
But ah, I will not:—Yet, I love thee well;
And, by my troth, I think, thou lov'st me well.

Hub. So well, that what you bid me undertake,
Though that my death were adjunct to my act,
By heaven, I'd do't.

---

1 There is a minute description of numerous devils or spirits, and their different functions, in Nash's Pierce Pennilesse his Supplication, 1592, where we find the following passage:—'The spirits of the *aire* will mixe themselves with thunder and lightning, and so infect the clyme where they raise any tempest, that sodainely great mortalitie shall ensue to the inhabitants. The spirits of *fire* have their mansions under the regions of the moone.'

2 Here the king, who had knighted him by the name of *Sir Richard*, calls him by his former name. Shakspeare has followed the old plays, and the best authenticated history. The queen mother, whom King John had made regent in Anjou, was in possession of the town of Mirabeau, in that province. On the approach of the French army, with Arthur at their head, she sent letters to King John to come to her relief, which he immediately did. As he advanced to the town he encountered the army that lay before it, routed them, and took Arthur prisoner. The queen in the mean while remained in perfect security in the castle of Mirabeau

3 Gold coin of that name.

4 It appears from Johnson's Ecclesiastical Laws, that sentence of excommunication was to be 'explained in order in English, with *bells tolling* and *candles lighted* that it may cause the greater dread; for laymen have greater regard to this solemnity than to the effect of such sentences.'

5 Showy ornaments.

6 The old copy reads *into*, the emendation is Theobald's.

7 Conception.

8 Pope proposed to read *broad-eyed*, instead of *brooded*. The alteration, it must be confessed, is elegant, but unnecessary. The allusion is to the vigilance of animals while brooding, or with a brood of young ones under their protection. *Brooded* may be used for *brooding*, as *delighted* for *delighting*, and *discontented* for *discontenting*, in other places of these plays. To sit *on brood*, or *abrood*, is the old term applied to birds during the period of incubation. All the metaphorical uses of the verb to *brood* are common to the Latin *incubo*

K. John. Do not I know, thou would'st?
Good Hubert, Hubert, Hubert, throw thine eye
On yon young boy: I'll tell thee what, my friend,
He is a very serpent in my way;
And, wheresoe'er this foot of mine doth tread,
He lies before me: Dost thou understand me?
Thou art his keeper.
Hub. And I will keep him so,
That he shall not offend your majesty.
K. John. Death.
Hub. My lord?
K. John. A grave.
Hub. He shall not live.
K. John. Enough.
I could be merry now: Hubert, I love thee;
Well, I'll not say what I intend for thee;
Remember.——Madam, fare you well:
I'll send those powers o'er to your majesty.
Eli. My blessing go with thee!
K. John. For England, cousin:
Hubert shall be your man, attend on you
With all true duty.—On toward Calais, ho![1]
[*Exeunt.*

SCENE IV. *The same. The* French King's *Tent.*
Enter King Philip, Lewis, Pandulph, *and* Attendants.

K. Phi. So, by a roaring tempest on the flood,
A whole armado[2] of convicted[3] sail
Is scatter'd and disjoin'd from fellowship.
Pand. Courage and comfort! all shall yet go well.
K. Phi. What can go well, when we have run so ill?
Are we not beaten? Is not Angiers lost?
Arthur ta'en prisoner? divers dear friends slain?
And bloody England into England gone,
O'erbearing interruption, spite of France?
Lew. What he hath won, that hath he fortified:
So hot a speed with such advice dispos'd,
Such temperate order in so fierce a cause,[4]
Doth want example; Who hath read, or heard,
Of any kindred action like to this?
K. Phi. Well could I bear that England had this praise,
So we could find some pattern of our shame.

Enter Constance.

Look, who comes here! a grave unto a soul;
Holding the eternal spirit, against her will,
In the vile prison of afflicted breath:—[5]
I pr'ythee, lady, go away with me.
Const. Lo, now! now see the issue of your peace!
K. Phi. Patience, good lady! comfort, gentle Constance!
Const. No, I defy[6] all counsel, all redress,
But that which ends all counsel, true redress,
Death, death:—O amiable lovely death!
Thou odoriferous stench! sound rottenness!
Arise forth from the couch of lasting night,
Thou hate and terror to prosperity,
And I will kiss thy detestable bones;
And put my eyeballs in thy vaulty brows;
And ring these fingers with thy household worms;
And stop this gap of breath[7] with fulsome dust,
And be a carrion monster like thyself:
Come, grin on me; and I will think thou smil'st,
And buss thee as thy wife! Misery's love,
O, come to me!
K. Phi. O fair affliction, peace.
Const. No, no, I will not, having breath to cry:—
O, that my tongue were in the thunder's mouth
Then with a passion would I shake the world;
And rouse from sleep that fell anatomy,
Which cannot hear a lady's feeble voice,
Which scorns a modern[8] invocation.
Pand. Lady, you utter madness, and not sorrow.
Const. Thou art not holy to belie me so;
I am not mad: this hair I tear is mine;
My name is Constance: I was Geffrey's wife;
Young Arthur is my son, and he is lost:
I am not mad:—I would to heaven, I were!
For then, 'tis like I should forget myself:
O, if I could, what grief should I forget!—
Preach some philosophy to make me mad,
And thou shalt be canoniz'd, cardinal;
For, being not mad, but sensible of grief,
My reasonable part produces reason
How I may be deliver'd of these woes,
And teaches me to kill or hang myself:
If I were mad, I should forget my son;
Or madly think, a babe of clouts were he
I am not mad; too well, too well I feel
The different plague of each calamity.
K. Phi. Bind up those tresses; O, what love I note
In the fair multitude of those her hairs!
Where but by chance a silver drop hath fallen,
Even to that drop ten thousand wiry friends
Do glew themselves in sociable grief;
Like true, inseparable, faithful loves,
Sticking together in calamity.
Const. To England, if you will.[9]
K. Phi. Bind up your hairs.
Const. Yes, that I will; and wherefore will I do it?
I tore them from their bonds; and cried aloud,
O that these hands could so redeem my son
As they have given these hairs their liberty!
But now I envy at their liberty,
And will again commit them to their bonds,
Because my poor child is a prisoner.——
And, father cardinal, I have heard you say,
That we shall see and know our friends in heaven:
If that be true, I shall see my boy again;
For, since the birth of Cain, the first male child,
To him that did but yesterday suspire,[10]
There was not such a gracious[11] creature born,
But now will canker sorrow eat my bud,
And chase the native beauty from his cheek,
And he will look as hollow as a ghost;
As dim and meagre as an ague's fit;
And so he'll die; and, rising so again,
When I shall meet him in the court of heaven
I shall not know him: therefore never, never
Must I behold my pretty Arthur more.
Pand. You hold too heinous a respect of grief.
Const. He talks to me, that never had a son.[12]
K. Phi. You are as fond of grief, as of your child.
Const. Grief fills the room up of my absent child,[13]

---

1 King John, after he had taken Arthur prisoner, sent him to the town of Falaise, in Normandy, under the care of Hubert, his chamberlain, from whence he was afterwards removed to Rouen, and delivered to the custody of Robert de Veypont. Here he was secretly put to death. 'This is one of those scenes (says Steevens) to which may be promised a lasting commendation. Art could add little to its perfection; no change in dramatic taste can injure it; and time itself can subtract nothing from its beauties.'

2 *Armado* is a fleet of war; the word is adopted from the Spanish, and the recent defeat of the *Spanish armado* had made it familiar.

3 *Convicted* is vanquished, overcome. To *convince* and *convict* were synonymous.

4 A *fierce cause* is a cause conducted with precipitation. *Fierce* wretchedness in Timon of Athens is *hasty, sudden* misery.

5 '—— the vile prison of afflicted breath' is *the body*; the same vile prison in which the breath is confined

6 To *defy* formerly signified to *refuse*, to *reject*. 'I do *defy* thy commiseration.'—*Romeo and Juliet.*

7 i. e. this mouth.

8 i. e. common.

9 Probably Constance in despair means to apostrophize the absent King John:—'Take my son to England if you will.'

10 To *suspire* Shakspeare uses for to *breathe.*

11 *Gracious* is used by Shakspeare often in the sense of *beautiful, comely, graceful.* Florio, in his Italian Dictionary, shows that this was no uncommon signification; he explains *gratioso*, graceful, *gracious*, also *comely, fine, well-favoured, gentle.*

12 To the same purpose Macduff observes:—
'He has no children.——'

13 'Perfruitur lachrymis, et amat pro conjuge luctum
Lucan, l ix

Lies in his bed, walks up and down with me;
Puts on his pretty looks, repeats his words,
Remembers me of all his gracious parts,
Stuffs out his vacant garments with his form;
Then, have I reason to be fond of grief.
Fare you well: had you such a loss as I,
I could give better comfort than you do.—
I will not keep this form upon my head,
[*Tearing off her head-dress.*
When there is such disorder in my wit.
O lord, my boy, my Arthur, my fair son!
My life, my joy, my food, my all the world!
My widow-comfort, and my sorrow's cure! [*Exit.*

K. Phi. I fear some outrage, and I'll follow her. [*Exit.*

Lew. There's nothing in this world can make me joy;
Life is as tedious as a twice-told tale,[1]
Vexing the dull ear of a drowsy man;
And bitter shame hath spoil'd the sweet world's[2] taste,
That it yields nought, but shame, and bitterness.

Pand. Before the curing of a strong disease,
Even in the instant of repair and health,
The fit is strongest; evils, that take leave,
On their departure most of all show evil:
What have you lost by losing of this day?

Lew. All days of glory, joy, and happiness.

Pand. If you had won it, certainly, you had.
No, no: when fortune means to men most good,
She looks upon them with a threatening eye.
'Tis strange, to think how much King John hath lost
In this which he accounts so clearly won:
Are not you griev'd, that Arthur is his prisoner?

Lew. As heartily, as he is glad he hath him.

Pand. Your mind is all as youthful as your blood.
Now hear me speak, with a prophetic spirit;
For even the breath of what I mean to speak
Shall blow each dust, each straw, each little rub,
Out of the path which shall directly lead
Thy foot to England's throne; and, therefore, mark.
John hath seiz'd Arthur; and it cannot be,
That, whiles warm life plays in that infant's veins,
The misplac'd John should entertain an hour,
One minute, nay, one quiet breath of rest:
A sceptre, snatch'd with an unruly hand,
Must be as boisterously maintain'd as gain'd:
And he, that stands upon a slippery place,
Makes nice of no vile hold to stay him up:
That John may stand, then Arthur needs must fall;
So be it, for it cannot be but so.

Lew. But what shall I gain by young Arthur's fall?

Pand. You, in the right of Lady Blanch your wife,
May then make all the claim that Arthur did.

Lew. And lose it, life and all, as Arthur did.

Pand. How green are you, and fresh in this old world!
John lays you plots;[3] the time conspires with you:
For he, that steeps his safety in true blood,
Shall find but bloody safety, and untrue.
This act, so evilly born, shall cool the hearts
Of all his people, and freeze up their zeal;
That none so small advantage shall step forth,
To check his reign, but they will cherish it:
No natural exhalation in the sky,
No scape[4] of nature, no distemper'd day,
No common wind, no custom'd event,
But they will pluck away his natural cause,
And call them meteors, prodigies, and signs,
Abortives, presages, and tongues of heaven,
Plainly denouncing vengeance upon John.

Lew. May be, he will not touch young Arthur's life,
But hold himself safe in his prisonment.

Pand. O, sir, when he shall hear of your approach,
If that young Arthur be not gone already,
Even at that news he dies: and then the hearts
Of all his people shall revolt from him,
And kiss the lips of unacquainted change;
And pick strong matter of revolt, and wrath,
Out of the bloody fingers' ends of John.
Methinks, I see this hurly[5] all on foot;
And, O, what better matter breeds for you,
Than I have nam'd!—The bastard Faulconbridge
Is now in England, ransacking the church,
Offending charity: If but a dozen French
Were there in arms, they would be as a call[6]
To train ten thousand English to their side;
Or, as a little snow,[7] tumbled about,
Anon becomes a mountain. O noble Dauphin,
Go with me to the king: 'Tis wonderful,
What may be wrought out of their discontent·
Now that their souls are topfull of offence,
For England go; I will whet on the king.

Lew. Strong reasons make strong[8] actions: Let us go;
If you say, ay, the king will not say, no. [*Exeunt*

ACT IV.

SCENE I. Northampton.[9] *A Room in the Castle.*

Enter HUBERT *and two* Attendants.

Hub. Heat me these irons hot: and, look thou stand
Within the arras:[10] when I strike my foot
Upon the bosom of the ground, rush forth:
And bind the boy, which you shall find with me,
Fast to the chair: be heedful: hence, and watch.

1 *Attendant.* I hope, your warrant will bear out the deed.

Hub. Uncleanly scruples! Fear not you: look to't.— [*Exeunt* Attendants.
Young lad, come forth; I have to say with you.

Enter ARTHUR.

Arth. Good morrow, Hubert.

Hub. Good morrow, little prince.

Arth. As little prince (having so great a title
To be more prince,) as may be.—You are sad.

Hub. Indeed, I have been merrier.

Arth. Mercy on me!
Methinks nobody should be sad but I:
Yet, I remember, when I was in France,
Young gentlemen would be as sad as night,
Only for wantonness.[11] By my christendom,[12]

---

1 'For when thou art angry, all our days are gone, we bring *our years to an end, as it were a tale that is told.*' Psalm xc.

2 The old copy reads *word's*. The alteration was made by Pope. Malone thinks that it is unnecessary; and that by the *sweet word, life* is meant. Steevens prefers Pope's emendation, which is countenanced by Hamlet's

'How weary, *stale, flat*, and unprofitable
Seem to me all the uses of this world!'

3 'John lays *you* plots.' A similar phrase occurs in the First Part of King Henry VI.:—

'He writes *me* here.'

4 The old copy reads *scope*. The emendation is Pope's. Shakspeare finely calls a monstrous birth an *escape of nature*, as if it were produced while she was busy elsewhere, or intent upon some other thing.

5 *Hurly* is *tumult*.

6 The image is taken from the manner in which birds are sometimes caught; one being placed for the purpose of drawing others to the net by his note or call.

7 Bacon, in his History of Henry VII. speaking of Simnel's march, observes that their *snowball* did not gather as it went.

8 The first folio reads *strange;* the second folio *strong*.

9 There is no circumstance, either in the original play or in this of Shakspeare, to point out the particular castle in which Arthur is supposed to be confined. The castle of Northampton has been mentioned merely because, in the first act, King John seems to have been in that town. It has already been stated that Arthur was in fact confined at Falaise, and afterwards at Rouen, where he was put to death.

10 Tapestry.

11 This is a satirical glance at the fashionable affectation of his time by Shakspeare: which Lyly also ridicules in his Midas:—'Now every base companion, being in his *muble-fubles*, says he is *melancholy*.' Again · '*Melancholy* is the crest of courtiers, and now every base companion says he is *melancholy*.'

12 i. e. by my *baptism*. The use of this word for

So I were out of prison, and kept sheep,
I should be as merry as the day is long;
And so I would be here, but that I doubt
My uncle practises more harm to me:
He is afraid of me, and I of him:
Is it my fault that I was Geffrey's son?
No, indeed, is't not; And I would to heaven,
I were your son, so you would love me, Hubert.
Hub. If I talk to him, with his innocent prate
He will awake my mercy, which lies dead:
Therefore I will be sudden, and despatch. [*Aside.*
Arth. Are you sick, Hubert? you look pale to-day:
In sooth, I would you were a little sick;
That I might sit all night, and watch with you:
I warrant, I love you more than you do me.
Hub. His words do take possession of my bosom.——
Read here, young Arthur. [*Showing a paper.*]
How now, foolish rheum! [*Aside.*
Turning dispiteous torture out of door!
I must be brief, lest resolution drop
Out at mine eyes, in tender womanish tears.——
Can you not read it? is it not fair writ?
Arth. Too fairly, Hubert, for so foul effect:
Must you with hot irons burn out both mine eyes?
Hub. Young boy, I must.
Arth. And will you?
Hub. And I will.
Arth. Have you the heart? When your head did but ake,
I knit my handkerchief about your brows
(The best I had, a princess wrought it me,)
And I did never ask it you again:
And with my hand at midnight held your head;
And, like the watchful minutes to the hour,
Still and anon cheer'd up the heavy time;
Saying, What lack you? and, Where lies your grief?
Or, What good love may I perform for you?
Many a poor man's son would have lain still,
And ne'er have spoke a loving word to you;
But you at your sick service had a prince.
Nay, you may think my love was crafty love,
And call it cunning; Do, an if you will:
If heaven be pleas'd that you must use me ill,
Why, then you must.—Will you put out mine eyes?
These eyes, that never did, nor never shall,
So much as frown on you?
Hub. I have sworn to do it;
And with hot irons must I burn them out.
Arth. Ah, none, but in this iron age, would do it!
The iron of itself, though heat[1] red-hot,
Approaching near these eyes, would drink my tears,
And quench his fiery indignation
Even in the matter of mine innocence:
Nay, after that, consume away in rust,
But for containing fire to harm mine eye.
Are you more stubborn-hard than hammer'd iron?
An if an angel should have come to me,
And told me, Hubert should put out mine eyes,
I would not have believ'd him; no tongue, but Hubert's.
Hub. Come forth. [*Stamps.*

Re-enter Attendants, *with Cords, Irons, &c.*

Do as I bid you do.
Arth. O, save me, Hubert, save me; my eyes are out,
Even with the fierce looks of these bloody men.
Hub. Give me the iron I say, and bind him here.
Arth. Alas! what need you be so boist'rous-rough?
I will not struggle, I will stand stone-still.
For heaven's sake, Hubert, let me not be bound!
Nay, hear me, Hubert! drive these men away,
And I will sit as quiet as a lamb:
I will not stir, nor wince, nor speak a word;
Nor look upon the iron angerly:
Thrust but these men away, and I'll forgive you,
Whatever torment you do put me to.
Hub. Go, stand within; let me alone with him.
1 *Attendant.* I am best pleas'd to be from such a deed. [*Exeunt* Attendants.
Arth. Alas! I then have chid away my friend;
He hath a stern look, but a gentle heart;—
Let him come back, that his compassion may
Give life to yours.
Hub. Come, boy, prepare yourself.
Arth. Is there no remedy?
Hub. None, but to lose your eyes.
Arth. O heaven!—that there were but a mote in yours,
A grain, a dust, a gnat, a wand'ring hair,
Any annoyance in that precious sense!
Then, feeling what small things are boist'rous there,
Your vile intent must needs seem horrible.
Hub. Is this your promise? go to, hold your tongue.
Arth. Hubert, the utterance of a brace of tongues
Must needs want pleading for a pair of eyes;
Let me not hold my tongue; let me not, Hubert!
Or, Hubert, if you will, cut out my tongue,[2]
So I may keep mine eyes: O, spare mine eyes,
Though to no use, but still to look on you!
Lo, by my troth, the instrument is cold,
And would not harm me.
Hub. I can heat it, boy.
Arth. No, in good sooth; the fire is dead with grief,
Being create for comfort, to be us'd
In undeserv'd extremes:[3] See else yourself;
There is no malice in this burning coal;
The breath of heaven hath blown his spirit out,
And strew'd repentant ashes on his head.
Hub. But with my breath I can revive it, boy.
Arth. And if you do, you will but make it blush,
And glow with shame of your proceedings, Hubert:
Nay, it, perchance, will sparkle in your eyes;
And, like a dog that is compell'd to fight,
Snatch at his master that doth tarre[4] him on.
All things, that you should use to do me wrong,
Deny their office: only you do lack
That mercy, which fierce fire, and iron, extends,
Creatures of note for mercy-lacking uses.
Hub. Well, see to live; I will not touch thine eyes
For all the treasure that thine uncle owes:[5]
Yet am I sworn, and I did purpose, boy,
With this same very iron to burn them out.
Arth. O, now you look like Hubert! all this while
You were disguis'd.
Hub. Peace: no more. Adieu:
Your uncle must not know but you are dead:
I'll fill these dogged spies with false reports.
And, pretty child, sleep doubtless, and secure,
That Hubert, for the wealth of all the world,
Will not offend thee.
Arth. O heaven!—I thank you, Hubert.
Hub. Silence; no more: Go closely[6] in with me;
Much danger do I undergo for thee. [*Exeunt.*

SCENE II. *The same. A Room of State in the Palace. Enter* King John, *crowned;* Pembroke, Salisbury, *and other* Lords. *The* King *takes his State.*

K. John. Here once again we sit, once again crown'd,
And look'd upon, I hope, with cheerful eyes.

---

christening or baptism is not peculiar to Shakspeare; it was common in his time. Hearne has published a *Prone* from a MS. of Henry the Seventh's time, in the glossary to Robert of Gloucester in a note on the word midewinter, by which it appears that it was the ancient orthography. 'The childer ryzt schape & *chrystyndome.*' It is also used by Lyly, Fanshaw, Harington, and Fairfaxe.

1 The participle *heat*, though now obsolete, was in use in Shakspeare's time. 'He commanded that they should heat the furnace one seven times more than it was wont to be *heat.*'—*Daniel*, iii. 19.

2 'This is according to nature,' says Johnson. 'We imagine no evil so great as that which is near us.'

3 'The fire being *created*, not to hurt, but *to comfort is dead with grief* for finding itself used in acts of cruelty, which, being innocent, I have *not deserved.*'

4 i. e. *stimulate, set him on.*

5 Owns.

6 i. e. secretly privately.

Pem. This once again, but that your highness pleas'd,
Was once superfluous:[1] you were crown'd before,
And that high royalty was ne'er pluck'd off;
The faiths of men ne'er stained with revolt;
Fresh expectation troubled not the land,
With any long'd-for change, or better state.
Sal. Therefore, to be possess'd with double pomp,
To guard[2] a title that was rich before,
To gild refined gold, to paint the lily,
To throw a perfume on the violet,
To smooth the ice, or add another hue
Unto the rainbow, or with taper-light
To seek the beauteous eye of heaven to garnish,
Is wasteful, and ridiculous excess.
Pem. But that your royal pleasure must be done,
This act is as an ancient tale new told;[3]
And, in the last repeating, troublesome,
Being urged at a time unseasonable.
Sal. In this, the antique and well-noted face
Of plain old form is much disfigured:
And, like a shifted wind unto a sail,
It makes the course of thoughts to fetch about:
Startles and frights consideration;
Makes sound opinion sick, and truth suspected,
For putting on so new a fashion'd robe.
Pem. When workmen strive to do better than well,
They do confound their skill in covetousness:[4]
And, oftentimes, excusing of a fault,
Doth make the fault the worse by the excuse;
As patches, set upon a little breach,
Discredit more in hiding of the fault,[5]
Than did the fault before it was so patch'd.
Sal. To this effect, before you were new-crown'd,
We breath'd our counsel: but it pleas'd your highness
To overbear it; and we are all well pleas'd;
Since all and every part of what we would,[6]
Doth make a stand at what your highness will.
K. John. Some reasons of this double coronation
I have possess'd you with, and think them strong;
And more, more strong (when lesser is my fear,)
I shall indue you with: Mean time, but ask
What you would have reform'd, that is not well;
And well shall you perceive, how willingly
I will both hear and grant you your requests.
Pem. Then I (as one that am the tongue of these,
To sound[7] the purposes of all their hearts,)
Both for myself and them (but, chief of all,
Your safety, for the which myself and them
Bend their best studies), heartily request
The enfranchisement[8] of Arthur; whose restraint
Doth move the murmuring lips of discontent
To break into this dangerous argument,—
If, what in rest you have, in right you hold,
Why then your fears (which, as they say, attend
The steps of wrong), should move you to mew up[9]
Your tender kinsman, and to choke his days
With barbarous ignorance, and deny his youth
The rich advantage of good exercise?[10]
That the time's enemies may not have this
To grace occasions, let it be our suit,
That you have bid us ask his liberty;
Which for our goods we do no further ask,
Than whereupon our weal, on you depending,
Counts it your weal, he have his liberty.
K. John. Let it be so; I do commit his youth

Enter HUBERT.

To your direction.—Hubert, what news with you?
Pem. This is the man should do the bloody deed;
He show'd his warrant to a friend of mine:
The image of a wicked heinous fault
Lives in his eye, that close aspect of his
Does show the mood of a much troubled breast;
And I do fearfully believe, 'tis done,
What we so fear'd he had a charge to do.
Sal. The colour of the king doth come and go,
Between his purpose and his conscience,[11]
Like heralds 'twixt two dreadful battles set:
His passion is so ripe it needs must break.
Pem. And when it breaks, I fear, will issue thence
The foul corruption of a sweet child's death.
K. John. We cannot hold mortality's strong hand:—
Good lords, although my will to give is living,
The suit which you demand is gone and dead:
He tells us, Arthur is deceas'd to-night.
Sal. Indeed, we fear'd his sickness was past cure.
Pem. Indeed, we heard how near his death he was,
Before the child himself felt he was sick:
This must be answer'd, either here, or hence.
K. John. Why do you bend such solemn brows on me?
Think you, I bear the shears of destiny?
Have I commandment on the pulse of life?
Sal. It is apparent foul-play; and 'tis shame,
That greatness should so grossly offer it:
So thrive it in your game! and so farewell.
Pem. Stay yet, Lord Salisbury; I'll go with thee
And find the inheritance of this poor child,
His little kingdom of a forced grave.
That blood, which ow'd[12] the breadth of all this isle,
Three foot of it doth hold; Bad world the while!
This must not be thus borne: this will break out
To all our sorrows, and ere long, I doubt.
[*Exeunt* Lords.
K. John. They burn in indignation; I repent
There is no sure foundation set on blood;
No certain life achiev'd by others' death—

Enter a Messenger.

A fearful eye thou hast; Where is that blood,
That I have seen inhabit in those cheeks?
So foul a sky clears not without a storm:
Pour down thy weather:—How goes all in France?
Mess. From France to England.[13]—Never such a power
For any foreign preparation,
Was levied in the body of a land!
The copy of your speed is learn'd by them;
For, when you should be told they do prepare,
The tidings come that they are all arriv'd.
K. John. O, where hath our intelligence been drunk?
Where hath it slept?[14] Where is my mother's care?
That such an army could be drawn in France,
And she not hear of it?
Mess. My liege, her ear
Is stopp'd with dust; the first of April, died

1 i. e. this one time more, was one time more than enough. It should be remembered that King John was now crowned for the *fourth time.*

2 To *guard* is to *ornament.*

3 Shakspeare has here repeated an idea which he had first put into the mouth of the Dauphin:—
'Life is as tedious as a twice-told tale,
Vexing the dull ear of a drowsy man.'

4 i. e. not by their avarice, but in an eager desire of excelling.

5 *Fault* means *blemish.*

6 Since the whole and each particular part of our wishes, &c.

7 To *declare,* to publish the purposes of all, &c

8 Releasement.

9 The construction of this passage is 'If you have a good title to what you have now in *rest* (i. e. *quiet*), why then *is it* that your fears should move you?' &c.

10 In the middle ages, the whole education of princes and noble youths consisted in martial exercises, &c. Mental improvement might have been had in a prison as well as any where else.

11 The *purpose* of the king, to which Salisbury alludes, is that of putting Arthur to death, which he considers as not yet accomplished, and therefore supposes that there might be still a conflict in the king's mind—
'Between his *purpose* and his *conscience.*'

12 i. e. '*own'd* the *breadth* of all this isle.' The two last variorum editions erroneously read '*breath* for *breadth,*' which is found in the old copy.

13 The king asks *how all goes in France;* the messenger catches the word *goes,* and answers, that whatever is in France *goes* now *into* England.

14 So in Macbeth:—
'———— Was the hope *drunk*
Wherein you drest yourself? hath it *slept* since?'

Your noble mother; And, as I hear, my lord,
The Lady Constance in a frenzy died
Three days before: but this from rumour's tongue
I idly heard; if true, or false, I know not.

K. John. Withhold thy speed, dreadful occasion!
O, make a league with me, till I have pleas'd
My discontented peers!—What! mother dead?
How wildly then walks my estate in France![1]—
Under whose conduct came those powers of France,
That thou for truth giv'st out, are landed here?

Mess. Under the Dauphin.

Enter the Bastard *and* PETER *of* POMFRET.

K. John. Thou hast made me giddy
With these ill tidings.—Now, what says the world
To your proceedings? do not seek to stuff
My head with more ill news, for it is full.

Bast. But if you be afeard to hear the worst,
Then let the worst, unheard, fall on your head.

K. John. Bear with me, cousin; for I was amaz'd[2]
Under the tide; but now I breathe again
Aloft the flood; and can give audience
To any tongue, speak it of what it will.

Bast. How I have sped among the clergymen,
The sums I have collected shall express.
But, as I travelled hither through the land,
I find the people strangely fantasied;
Possess'd with rumours, full of idle dreams;
Not knowing what they fear, but full of fear:
And here's a prophet,[3] that I brought with me
From forth the streets of Pomfret, whom I found
With many hundreds treading on his heels;
To whom he sung, in rude harsh sounding rhymes,
That, ere the next Ascension-day at noon,
Your highness should deliver up your crown.

K. John. Thou idle dreamer, wherefore didst thou so?

Peter. Foreknowing that the truth will fall out so.

K. John. Hubert, away with him; imprison him;
And on that day at noon, whereon, he says,
I shall yield up my crown, let him be hang'd:
Deliver him to safety,[4] and return,
For I must use thee.—O my gentle cousin,
[*Exit* HUBERT, *with* PETER.
Hear'st thou the news abroad, who are arriv'd?

Bast. The French, my lord; men's mouths are full of it:
Besides, I met Lord Bigot, and Lord Salisbury
(With eyes as red as new-enkindled fire),
And others more, going to seek the grave
Of Arthur, who, they say, is kill'd to-night
On your suggestion.

K. John. Gentle kinsman, go,
And thrust thyself into their companies:
I have a way to win their loves again;
Bring them before me.

Bast. I will seek them out.

K. John. Nay, but make haste; the better foot before.——
O, let me have no subject enemies,
When adverse foreigners affright my towns
With dreadful pomp of stout invasion!—
Be Mercury, set feathers to thy heels;
And fly, like thought, from them to me again.

Bast. The spirit of the time shall teach me speed.
[*Exit.*

K. John. Spoke like a sprightful noble gentleman.—
Go after him; for he, perhaps, shall need
Some messenger betwixt me and the peers;
And be thou he.

Mess. With all my heart, my liege.
[*Exit.*

K. John. My mother dead!

Re-enter HUBERT.

Hub. My lord, they say, five moons were seen to-night:
Four fixed; and the fifth did whirl about
The other four, in wondrous motion.

K. John. Five moons?

Hub. Old men, and beldams, in the streets
Do prophesy upon it dangerously:
Young Arthur's death is common in their mouths;
And when they talk of him, they shake their heads,
And whisper one another in the ear;
And he, that speaks, doth gripe the hearer's wrist;
Whilst he, that hears, makes fearful action,
With wrinkled brows, with nods, with rolling eyes,[5]
I saw a smith stand with his hammer, thus,
The whilst his iron did on the anvil cool,
With open mouth swallowing a tailor's news;
Who, with his shears and measure in his hand,
Standing on slippers (which his nimble haste
Had falsely thrust upon contrary feet),[6]
Told of a thousand warlike French,
That were embattailed and rank'd in Kent:
Another lean unwash'd artificer
Cuts off his tale, and talks of Arthur's death.

K. John. Why seek'st thou to possess me with these fears?
Why urgest thou so oft young Arthur's death?
Thy hand hath murder'd him; I had a mighty cause
To wish him dead, but thou hadst none to kill him.

Hub. Had none, my lord! why, did you not provoke me?

K. John. It is the curse of kings to be attended
By slaves, that take their humours for a warrant
To break within the bloody house of life:
And, on the winking of authority,
To understand a law; to know the meaning
Of dangerous majesty, when, perchance, it frowns
More upon humour than advis'd respect.[7]

Hub. Here is your hand and seal for what I did.

K. John. O, when the last account 'twixt heaven and earth
Is to be made, then shall this hand and seal
Witness against us to damnation!
How oft the sight of means to do ill deeds,
Make deeds ill done! Hadest not thou been by,
A fellow by the hand of nature mark'd,
Quoted,[8] and sign'd, to do a deed of shame,
This murder had not come into my mind:
But, taking note of thy abhorr'd aspect,
Finding thee fit for bloody villany,
Apt, liable, to be employ'd in danger,
I faintly broke with thee of Arthur's death;
And thou, to be endeared to a king,
Made it no conscience to destroy a prince.

Hub. My lord,——

K. John. Hadst thou but shook thy head, or made a pause,[9]

---

1 i. e. how ill my affairs *go* in France.

2 Astonied, stunned, confounded, are the ancient synonymes of *amazed*, obstupesco.

3 This man was a hermit in great repute with the common people. Notwithstanding the event is said to have fallen out as he prophesied, the poor fellow was inhumanly dragged at horses' tails through the streets of Warham, and, together with his son, who appears to have been even more innocent than his father, hanged afterwards upon a gibbet. *Holinshed*, in anno 1213.—Speed says that Peter the hermit was suborned by the pope's legate, the French king, and the barons for this purpose.

4 i. e. to safe custody.

5 This may be compared with a spirited passage in Edward III. Capel's Prolusions, p. 75:—

'Our men, with open mouths and staring eyes,
Look on each other, as they did attend
Each other's words, and yet no creature speaks;
A tongue-tied fear hath made a midnight hour,
And speeches sleep through all the waking region.'

6 This passage, which called forth the antiquarian knowledge of so many learned commentators, is now, from the return of the fashion of *right and left shoes*, become intelligible without a note.

7 Deliberate consideration.

8 To *quote* is to note or mark.

9 There are many touches of nature in this conference of John with Hubert. A man engaged in wickedness would keep the profit to himself, and tranfer the guilt to his accomplice. These reproaches vented against Hubert are not words of art or policy, but the eruptions of a mind swelling with consciousness of a crime, and desirous of discharging its misery on another. This account of the timidity of guilt is drawn, *ab ipsis recessibus mentis*, from the intimate knowledge of mankind; particularly that line in which he says, that *to have bid*

When I spake darkly what I purposed;
Or turn'd an eye of doubt upon my face,
And[1] bid me tell my tale in express words;
Deep shame had struck me dumb, made me break off,
And those thy fears might have wrought fears in me:
But thou didst understand me by my signs,
And didst in signs again parley with sin;
Yea, without stop, didst let thy heart consent,
And, consequently, thy rude hand to act
The deed, which both our tongues held vile to name.—
Out of my sight, and never see me more!
My nobles leave me; and my state is brav'd,
Even at my gates, with ranks of foreign powers;
Nay, in the body of this fleshly land,
This kingdom, this confine of blood and breath,
Hostility and civil tumult reigns
Between my conscience, and my cousin's death.

Hub. Arm you against your other enemies,
I'll make a peace between your soul and you.
Young Arthur is alive: This hand of mine
Is yet a maiden and an innocent hand,
Not painted with the crimson spots of blood.
Within this bosom never enter'd yet
The dreadful motion of a murd'rous thought,
And you have slander'd nature in my form;
Which, howsoever rude exteriorly,
Is yet the cover of a fairer mind
Than to be butcher of an innocent child.

K. John. Doth Arthur live? O, haste thee to the peers,
Throw this report on their incensed rage,
And make them tame to their obedience!
Forgive the comment that my passion made
Upon thy feature; for my rage was blind,
And foul imaginary eyes of blood
Presented thee more hideous than thou art.
O, answer not; but to my closet bring
The angry lords, with all expedient[2] haste:
I conjure thee but slowly; run more fast.[3]

SCENE III. *The same. Before the Castle. Enter* ARTHUR, *on the Walls.*

Arth. The wall is high; and yet will I leap down:[4]—
Good ground, be pitiful, and hurt me not!—
There's few, or none, do know me; if they did,
This ship-boy's semblance hath disguis'd me quite.
I am afraid; and yet I'll venture it.
If I get down, and do not break my limbs,
I'll find a thousand shifts to get away:
As good to die, and go, as die, and stay.
[*Leaps down.*
O me! my uncle's spirit is in these stones——
Heaven take my soul, and England keep my bones!
[*Dies.*

Enter PEMBROKE, SALISBURY, *and* BIGOT.

Sal. Lords, I will meet him at Saint Edmund's Bury;
It is our safety, and we must embrace
This gentle offer of the perilous time.

Pem. Who brought that letter from the cardinal?

Sal. The Count Melun, a noble lord of France
Whose private with me,[5] of the Dauphin's love,
Is much more general than these lines import.

Big. To-morrow morning let us meet him then.

Sal. Or, rather then set forward: for 'twill be
Two long days' journey, lords, or e'er[6] we meet.

Enter the Bastard.

Bast. Once more to-day well met, distemper'd[7] lords!
The king, by me, requests your presence straight.

Sal. The king hath dispossess'd himself of us;
We will not line his thin bestained cloak
With our pure honours, nor attend the foot
That leaves the print of blood where'er it walks
Return, and tell him so; we know the worst.

Bast. Whate'er you think, good words, I think were best.

Sal. Our griefs, and not our manners, reason[8] now.

Bast. But there is little reason in your grief;
Therefore, 'twere reason, you had manners now.

Pem. Sir, sir, impatience hath its privilege.

Bast. 'Tis true: to hurt his master, no man else.

Sal. This is the prison: What is he lies here?
[*Seeing* ARTHUR

Pem. O death, made proud with pure and princely beauty!
The earth had not a hole to hide this deed.

Sal. Murder, as hating what himself hath done,
Doth lay it open, to urge on revenge.

Big. Or, when he doom'd this beauty to a grave,
Found it too precious-princely for a grave.

Sal. Sir Richard, what think you? Have you beheld,
Or have you read, or heard? or could you think?
Or do you almost think, although you see,
That you do see? could thought, without this object,
Form such another? This is the very top,
The height, the crest, or crest unto the crest,
Of murder's arms: this is the bloodiest shame,
The wildest savag'ry, the vilest stroke,
That ever wall-ey'd wrath, or staring rage,
Presented to the tears of soft remorse.[9]

Pem. All murders past do stand excus'd in this:
And this, so sole, and so unmatchable,
Shall give a holiness, a purity,
To the yet unbegotten sins of time,[10]
And prove a deadly bloodshed but a jest,
Exampled by this heinous spectacle.

Bast. It is a damned and a bloody work,
The graceless action of a heavy hand,
If that it be the work of any hand.

Sal. If that it be the work of any hand?—
We had a kind of light, what would ensue:
It is the shameful work of Hubert's hand;
The practice, and the purpose, of the king:—
From whose obedience I forbid my soul,
Kneeling before this ruin of sweet life,
And breathing to his breathless excellence
The incense of a vow, a holy vow;
Never to taste the pleasures of the world,
Never to be infected with delight,
Nor conversant with ease and idleness,

---

him tell his tale in *express* words would have *struck him dumb*: nothing is more certain than that bad men use all the arts of fallacy upon themselves, palliate their actions to their own minds by gentle terms, and hide themselves from their own detection in ambiguities and subterfuges.—*Johnson.*

1 The old copy reads '*As* bid me,' &c. Malone made the correction, in which I concur; though *as* frequently is used for *that, which.* See Julius Cæsar, Act. i. Sc. 2.

2 Expeditious.

3 The old play of The Troublesome Raigne of King John is divided into two parts; the first of which concludes with the king's despatch of Hubert on this message; the second begins with *Enter Arthur*, &c. as in the following scene.

4 Shakspeare has followed the old play. In what manner Arthur was deprived of his life is not ascertained. Matthew Paris relating the event, uses the word *evanuit;* and it appears to have been conducted with impenetrable secrecy. The French historians say that John, coming in a boat during the night to the castle of Rouen, where the young prince was confined, stabbed him while supplicating for mercy, fastened a stone to the body, and threw it into the Seine, in order to give some colour to a report, which he caused to be spread, that the prince, attempting to escape out of a window, fell into the river, and was drowned.

5 Private account.

6 The use of *or* for *ere, before*, is at least as old as Chaucer's time. *Ere ever, or ever, or ere,* is, in modern English, *sooner than at any time; before ever:* and this is the sense in which Shakspeare and our elder writers constantly use the phrase.

7 i. e. ruffled, out of humour.

8 To *reason,* in Shakspeare, is not so often to *argue* as to *talk.*

9 Pity.

10 The old copy reads '*in of times.*' The emendation is Pope's.

'Till I have set a glory to this head,[1]
By giving it the worship of revenge.
Pem. Big. Our souls religiously confirm thy words.

Enter HUBERT.

Hub. Lords, I am hot with haste in seeking you:
Arthur doth live; the king hath sent for you.
Sal. O, he is bold, and blushes not at death:—
Avaunt, thou hateful villain, get thee gone!
Hub. I am no villain.
Sal. Must I rob the law?
[*Drawing his sword.*
Bast. Your sword is bright, sir; put it up again.[2]
Sal. Not till I sheath it in a murderer's skin.
Hub. Stand back, Lord Salisbury, stand back, I say;
By heaven, I think my sword's as sharp as yours:
I would not have you, lord, forget yourself,
Nor tempt the danger of my true[3] defence;
Lest I, by marking of your rage, forget
Your worth, your greatness, and nobility.
Big. Out, dunghill! dar'st thou brave a nobleman?
Hub. Not for my life: but yet I dare defend
My innocent life against an emperor.
Sal. Thou art a murderer.
Hub. Do not prove me so;[4]
Yet I am none: Whose tongue soe'er speaks false,
Not truly speaks; who speaks not truly, lies.
Pem. Cut him to pieces.
Bast. Keep the peace, I say.
Sal. Stand by, or I shall gall you, Faulconbridge.
Bast. Thou wert better gall the devil, Salisbury:
If thou but frown on me, or stir thy foot,
Or teach thy hasty spleen to do me shame,
I'll strike thee dead. Put up thy sword betime;
Or I'll so maul you and your toasting-iron,
That you shall think the devil is come from hell.
Big. What wilt thou do, renowned Faulconbridge?
Second a villain, and a murderer?
Hub. Lord Bigot, I am none.
Big. Who kill'd this prince?
Hub. 'Tis not an hour since I left him well:
I honour'd him, I lov'd him; and will weep
My date of life out, for his sweet life's loss.
Sal. Trust not those cunning waters of his eyes,
For villany is not without such rheum;
And he, long traded in it, makes it seem
Like rivers of remorse[5] and innocency.
Away, with me, all you, whose souls abhor
The uncleanly savours of a slaughter-house,
For I am stifled with this smell of sin.
Big. Away, toward Bury, to the Dauphin there!
Pem. There, tell the king, he may inquire us out.
[*Exeunt* Lords.
Bast. Here's a good world!—Knew you of this fair work?
Beyond the infinite and boundless reach
Of mercy, if thou didst this deed of death,
Art thou damn'd, Hubert.
Hub. Do but hear me, sir.
Bast. Ha! I'll tell thee what;
Thou art damn'd as black—nay, nothing is so black;
Thou art more deep damn'd than prince Lucifer:[6]
There is not yet so ugly a fiend of hell
As thou shalt be, if thou didst kill this child.
Hub. Upon my soul,———
Bast. If thou didst but consent
To this most cruel act, do but despair,
And, if thou want'st a cord, the smallest thread
That ever spider twisted from her womb,
Will serve to strangle thee; a rush will be
A beam to hang thee on; or would'st thou drown thyself,
Put but a little water in a spoon,
And it shall be as all the ocean,
Enough to stifle such a villain up.———
I do suspect thee very grievously.
Hub. If I in act, consent, or sin of thought
Be guilty of the stealing that sweet breath
Which was embounded in this beauteous clay,
Let hell want pains enough to torture me!
I left him well.
Bast. Go, bear him in thine arms.-
I am amaz'd,[7] methinks; and lose my way
Among the thorns and dangers of this world.—
How easy dost thou take all England up!
From forth this morsel of dead royalty,
The life, the right, and truth of all this realm
Is fled to heaven: and England now is left
To tug and scamble, and to part by the teeth
The unowed interest[8] of proud-swelling state.
Now, for the bare-pick'd bone of majesty,
Doth dogged war bristle his angry crest,
And snarleth in the gentle eyes of peace:
Now powers from home, and discontents at home
Meet in one line; and vast confusion waits
(As doth a raven on a sick-fall'n beast,)
The imminent decay of wrested pomp.
Now happy he, whose cloak and cincture[9] can
Hold out this tempest. Bear away that child,
And follow me with speed; I'll to the king:
A thousand businesses are brief in hand,
And heaven itself doth frown upon the land.
[*Exeunt.*

ACT V.

SCENE I. *The same. A Room in the Palace.*
Enter KING JOHN, PANDULPH, *with the Crown, and* Attendants.

K. John. Thus have I yielded up into your hand
The circle of my glory.
Pand. Take again
[*Giving* JOHN *the Crown*
From this my hand, as holding of the pope,
Your sovereign greatness and authority.
K. John. Now keep your holy word: go meet the French;
And from his holiness use all your power
To stop their marches, 'fore we are inflam'd.
Our discontented counties[10] do revolt;
Our people quarrel with obedience;
Swearing allegiance, and the love of soul,
To stranger blood, to foreign royalty.

---

1 The old copy reads, "'Till I have set a glory to this *hand.*' This is a copy of the vows made in the ages of superstition and chivalry. Pope thought that we should read 'a glory to this *head,*' pointing to the head of the dead prince, and using *worship* in its common acceptation. A *glory* is a circle of rays, such as is represented surrounding the heads of saints and other holy persons. The solemn confirmation of the other lords seems to require this sense. Gray, the poet (says Dr. Farmer,) was much pleased with this correction. The old reading has been explained, 'till I have famed and renowned my own hand by giving it the honour of revenge for so foul a deed.'

2 So in Othello:—'Keep up your bright swords; for the dew will rust them.' Both Faulconbridge and Othello speak contemptuously. 'You have shown that your sword is bright, and now you may put it up again; you shall not use it.'

3 *Honest* defence, defence in a *good cause.*

4 Dr Johnson has, I think, mistaken the sense of this passage, which he explains—'Do not make me a murderer, by compelling me to kill you; I am hitherto not a murderer.' By 'Do not *prove* me so,' Hubert means 'do not *provoke me,* or *try my patience* so.' This was a common acceptation of the word. 'To assay, to *prove,* to try, to tempt one to do evil.' *Baret,* in v. Prove.

5 Pity.

6 So in the old play:—
'Hell, Hubert, trust me, all the plagues of hell
Hangs on performance of this damned deed;
This seal, the warrant of the body's bliss,
Ensureth Satan chieftain of thy soul.'

7 i. e. *confounded.*

8 i. e. the interest which is not at this moment legally *possessed* by any one. On the death of Arthur, the *right* to the crown devolved to his sister Eleanor.

9 Girdle.

10 *Counties* here most probably mean, not the divisions of the kingdom, but the *lords* and *nobility* in general.

This inundation of mistemper'd humour
Rests by you only to be qualified.
Then pause not; for the present time's so sick,
That present medicine must be minister'd,
Or overthrow incurable ensues.

Pand. It was my breath that blew this tempest up,
Upon your stubborn usage of the pope:
But, since you are a gentle convertite,[1]
My tongue shall hush again this storm of war,
And make fair weather in your blustering land.
On this Ascension-day, remember well,
Upon your oath of service to the pope,
Go I to make the French lay down their arms.
[*Exit.*

K. John. Is this Ascension-day? Did not the prophet
Say, that, before Ascension-day at noon,
My crown I should give off? Even so I have:
I did suppose, it should be on constraint;
But, heaven be thank'd, it is but voluntary.

Enter the Bastard.

Bast. All Kent hath yielded; nothing there holds out,
But Dover castle: London hath receiv'd,
Like a kind host, the Dauphin and his powers:
Your nobles will not hear you, but are gone
To offer service to your enemy;
And wild amazement hurries up and down
The little number of your doubtful friends.

K. John. Would not my lords return to me again,
After they heard young Arthur was alive?

Bast. They found him dead, and cast into the streets;
An empty casket, where the jewel of life,[2]
By some damn'd hand was robb'd and ta'en away.

K. John. That villain Hubert told me, he did live.

Bast. So, on my soul, he did, for aught he knew.
But wherefore do you droop? why look you sad?
Be great in act, as you have been in thought;
Let not the world see fear, and sad distrust,
Govern the motion of a kingly eye:
Be stirring as the time; be fire with fire;
Threaten the threat'ner, and outface the brow
Of bragging horror: so shall inferior eyes,
That borrow their behaviours from the great,
Grow great by your example, and put on
The dauntless spirit of resolution.[3]
Away; and glister like the god of war,
When he intendeth to become the field:[4]
Show boldness, and aspiring confidence.
What, shall they seek the lion in his den,
And fright him there? and make him tremble there?
O, let it not be said!—Forage,[5] and run
To meet displeasure further from the doors;
And grapple with him, ere he come so nigh.

K. John. The legate of the pope hath been with me,
And I have made a happy peace with him;
And he hath promised to dismiss the powers
Led by the Dauphin.

Bast. O inglorious league!
Shall we, upon the footing of our land,
Send fair-play orders, and make compromise,
Insinuation, parley, and base truce,
To arms invasive? shall a beardless boy,
A cocker'd silken wanton brave our fields,
And flesh his spirit in a warlike soil,
Mocking the air with colours idly spread,[6]
And find no check? Let us, my liege, to arms
Perchance, the cardinal cannot make your peace;
Or if he do, let it at least be said,
They saw we had a purpose of defence.

K. John. Have thou the ordering of this presen time.

Bast. Away then, with good courage; yet, I know,
Our party may well meet a prouder foe.[7] [*Exeunt.*

SCENE II. *A Plain, near* St. Edmund's-Bury.
Enter, in arms, LEWIS, SALISBURY, MELUN, PEMBROKE, BIGOT, *and* Soldiers.

Lew. My Lord Melun, let this be copied out,
And keep it safe for our remembrance:
Return the precedent[8] to these lords again;
That having our fair order written down,
Both they, and we, perusing o'er these notes,
May know wherefore we took the sacrament,
And keep our faiths firm and inviolable.

Sal. Upon our sides it never shall be broken
And, noble Dauphin, albeit we swear
A voluntary zeal, and unurg'd faith,
To your proceedings; yet, believe me, prince,
I am not glad that such a sore of time
Should seek a plaster by contemn'd revolt,
And heal the inveterate canker of one wound,
By making many: O, it grieves my soul,
That I must draw this metal from my side
To be a widow-maker; O and there,
Where honourable rescue and defence,
Cries out upon the name of Salisbury:
But such is the infection of the time,
That, for the health and physic of our right,
We cannot deal but with the very hand
Of stern injustice and confused wrong.—
And is't not pity, O my grieved friends!
That we, the sons and children of this isle,
Were born to see so sad an hour as this;
Wherein we step after a stranger[9] march
Upon her gentle bosom, and fill up
Her enemies' ranks (I must withdraw and weep
Upon the spot[10] of this enforced cause,)
To grace the gentry of a land remote,
And follow unacquainted colours here?
What, here?—O nation, that thou could'st remove!
That Neptune's arms, who clippeth[11] thee about,
Would bear thee from the knowledge of thyself,
And grapple[12] thee unto a Pagan shore;
Where these two Christian armies might combine
The blood of malice in a vein of league,
And not to-spend it[13] so unneighbourly!

---

1 Convert.

2 Dryden has transferred this image to a speech of Antony, in All for Love:—
'An *empty circle*, since the *jewel's* gone.'
So in King Richard II:—
'A *jewel* in a ten times barr'd up chest,
Is a bold spirit in a loyal breast.'

3 So in Macbeth:—
'Let's briefly *put on manly readiness*,
And meet i' the hall together.'

4 Thus in Hamlet:—
——— such a sight as this
Becomes the field.'

5 *Forage* here seems to mean to *range abroad*; which Dr. Johnson says is its original sense: but *fourrage*, the French source of it, is formed from the low Latin *foderagium*, food: the sense of ranging therefore appears to be secondary.

6 We have the same image in Macbeth:—
'Where the Norweyan banners flout the sky,
And fan our people cold.'
From these two passages Gray formed the first lines of his 'Bard.'

7 i e. I know that our party is able to cope with one yet prouder, and more confident of its strength than theirs.

8 i. e. the *rough draught* of the original treaty. In King Richard II. the scrivener employed to engross the indictment of Lord Hastings says, 'It took him eleven hours to write it, and that the *precedent* was full as long a doing.'

9 Shakspeare often uses *stranger* as an adjective See the last scene:—
'Swearing allegiance and the love of soul
To *stranger* blood, to foreign royalty.'

10 i. e. the *stain.*

11 To *clip* is to *embrace;* not yet obsolete in the northern counties.

12 The old copy reads *cripple.* The emendation was made by Pope. The poet alludes to the wars carried on by the Christian princes in the Holy Land against the Saracens, where the united armies of France and England might have laid their animosities aside and fought in the cause of Christ, instead of fighting against brethren and countrymen.

13 Shakspeare here employs a phraseology used before in the Merry Wives of Windsor:—
'And, fairy-like, *to*-pinch the unclean knight.'

Lew. A noble temper dost thou show in this;
And great affections, wrestling in thy bosom,
Do make an earthquake of nobility.
O, what a noble combat hast thou fought,
Between compulsion and a brave respect![1]
Let me wipe off this honourable dew,
That silvery doth progress on thy cheeks:
My heart hath melted at a lady's tears,
Being an ordinary inundation;
But this effusion of such manly drops,
This shower, blown up by tempest of the soul,[2]
Startles mine eyes, and makes me more amaz'd
Than had I seen the vaulty top of heaven
Figur'd quite o'er with burning meteors.
Lift up thy brow, renowned Salisbury,
And with a great heart heave away this storm:
Commend these waters to those baby eyes,
That never saw the giant world enrag'd;
Nor met with fortune other than at feasts,
Full warm of blood, of mirth, of gossiping.
Come, come; for thou shalt thrust thy hand as deep
Into the purse of rich prosperity,
As Lewis himself:—so, nobles, shall you all,
That knit your sinews to the strength of mine.

Enter PANDULPH, *attended.*

And even there, methinks, an angel spake:[3]
Look, where the holy legate comes apace,
To give us warrant from the hand of heaven;
And on our actions set the name of right,
With holy breath.

Pand. Hail, noble prince of France!
The next is this,—King John hath reconcil'd
Himself to Rome; his spirit is come in,
That so stood out against the holy church,
The great metropolis and see of Rome:
Therefore thy threat'ning colours now wind up,
And tame the savage spirit of wild war;
That, like a lion foster'd up at hand,
It may lie gently at the foot of peace,
And be no further harmful than in show.

Lew. Your grace shall pardon me, I will not back;
I am too high-born to be propertied,[4]
To be a secondary at control,
Or useful serving-man, and instrument,
To any sovereign state throughout the world.
Your breath first kindled the dead coal of wars,
Between this chastis'd kingdom and myself,
And brought in matter that should feed this fire;
And now 'tis far too huge to be blown out
With that same weak wind which enkindled it.
You taught me how to know the face of right,
Acquainted me with interest to[5] this land,
Yea, thrust this enterprise into my heart;
And come you now to tell me, John hath made
His peace with Rome? What is that peace to me?
I, by the honour of my marriage-bed,
After young Arthur, claim this land for mine;
And, now it is half-conquer'd, must I back,
Because that John hath made his peace with Rome?
Am I Rome's slave? What penny hath Rome borne,
What men provided, what munition sent,
To underprop this action? is't not I,
That undergo this charge? who else but I,
And such as to my claim are liable,
Sweat in this business, and maintain this war?
Have I not heard these islanders shout out,
Vive le roy! as I have bank'd their towns?[6]
Have I not here the best cards for the game,
To win this easy match play'd for a crown?
And shall I now give o'er the yielded set?
No, no, on my soul, it never shall be said.

Pand. You look but on the outside of this work.

Lew. Outside or inside, I will not return
Till my attempt so much be glorified
As to my ample hope was promised
Before I drew this gallant head of war,[7]
And cull'd these fiery spirits from the world,
To outlook[8] conquest, and to win renown
Even in the jaws of danger and of death.— [*Trumpet sounds.*
What lusty trumpet thus doth summon us?

Enter the Bastard, *attended.*

Bast. According to the fair play of the world,
Let me have audience; I am sent to speak;—
My holy lord of Milan, from the king
I come to learn how you have dealt for him;
And, as you answer, I do know the scope
And warrant limited unto my tongue.

Pand. The Dauphin is too wilful-opposite,
And will not temporize with my entreaties;
He flatly says, he'll not lay down his arms.

Bast. By all the blood that ever fury breath'd,
The youth says well:—Now hear our English king;
For thus his royalty doth speak in me.
He is prepar'd; and reason too, he should:
This apish and unmannerly approach,
This harness'd masque, and unadvised revel,
This unhair'd[9] sauciness, and boyish troops,
The king doth smile at; and is well prepar'd
To whip this dwarfish war, these pigmy arms,
From out the circle of his territories.
That hand, which had the strength, even at your door
To cudgel you, and make you take the hatch;[10]
To dive, like buckets, in concealed wells;
To crouch in litter of your stable planks;
To lie, like pawns, lock'd up in chests and trunks
To hug with swine; to seek sweet safety out
In vaults and prisons; and to thrill, and shake,
Even at the crying of your nation's crow,[11]
Thinking his voice an armed Englishman;—
Shall that victorious hand be feebled here,
That in your chambers gave you chastisement?
No: Know, the gallant monarch is in arms;
And like an eagle o'er his aiery[12] towers,
To souse annoyance that comes near his nest.—
And you degenerate, you ingrate revolts,
You bloody Neroes, ripping up the wound
Of your dear mother England, blush for shame:
For your own ladies, and pale-visag'd maids,
Like Amazons, come tripping after drums;
Their thimbles into armed gauntlets change,
Their neelds[13] to lances, and their gentle hearts
To fierce and bloody inclination.

Lew. There end thy brave,[14] and turn thy face in peace:
We grant, thou canst outscold us: fare thee well:
We hold our time too precious to be spent
With such a brabbler.

Pand. Give me leave to speak.

Bast. No, I will speak.

---

1 This *compulsion* was the necessity of a reformation in the state; which according to Salisbury's opinion (who in his preceding speech calls it an *enforced cause*) could only be procured by foreign arms; and the *brave respect* was the love of country.

2 'This windy *tempest* till it *blow up rain*
Held back his sorrow's tide.'—*Rape of Lucrece.*

3 *In what I have now said* an angel spake: for see, the holy legate approaches to give a warrant from *heaven*, and the name of *right*, to our cause.

4 Appropriated.

5 This was the phraseology of the time:—
'He hath more worthy interest *to* the state,
Than thou the shadow of succession.'
King Henry IV. Part ii.

6 i. e. passed along the banks of the river. Thus in the old play:—
'—— from the hollow holes of Thamesis
Echo apace replied, *Vive le roi!*
From thence along the wanton rolling glade
To Troynovant, your fair metropolis.'
We still say to *coast* and to *flank;* and to *bank* has no less propriety, though not reconciled to us by modern usage.

7 i. e. *assembled it*, drew it out of the field.

8 Face down, bear down by a show of magnanimity So before:— '—— *outface* the brow
Of bragging horror.'

9 The old copies read *unheard:* the emendation is Theobald's. It should be remarked that *hair* was often spelt *hear*.

10 To *take*, for to *leap*. Hunters still say to *take* a hedge or gate, meaning to *leap* over them. Baret has '*to take* horse, to leap on horseback.'

11 i. e. the crowing of a cock; *Gallus* being both a *cock* and a *Frenchman*.

12 Nest 13 Needles. 14 Boast

Lew. We will attend to neither:—
Strike up the drums; and let the tongue of war
Plead for our interest; and our being here.

Bast. Indeed, your drums, being beaten, will cry out;
And so shall you, being beaten: Do but start
An echo with the clamour of thy drum,
And even at hand a drum is ready brac'd,
That shall reverberate all as loud as thine;
Sound but another, and another shall,
As loud as thine, rattle the welkin's ear,
And mock the deep-mouth'd thunder: for at hand
(Not trusting to this halting legate here,
Whom he hath us'd rather for sport than need,)
Is warlike John; and in his forehead sits
A bare-ribb'd death, whose office is this day
To feast upon whole thousands of the French.

Lew. Strike up our drums, to find this danger out.

Bast. And thou shalt find it, Dauphin, do not doubt. [*Exeunt.*

SCENE III. *The same. A Field of Battle.*

Alarums. Enter KING JOHN *and* HUBERT.

K. John. How goes the day with us? O, tell me, Hubert.

Hub. Badly, I fear: How fares your majesty?

K. John. This fever, that hath troubled me so long,
Lies heavy on me: O, my heart is sick!

Enter a Messenger.

Mess. My lord, your valiant kinsman, Faulconbridge,
Desires your majesty to leave the field;
And send him word by me, which way you go.

K. John. Tell him, toward Swinstead, to the abbey there.

Mess. Be of good comfort; for the great supply,[1]
That was expected by the Dauphin here,
Are wreck'd three nights ago on Goodwin Sands.
This news was brought to Richard[2] but even now:
The French fight coldly, and retire themselves.

K. John. Ah me! this tyrant fever burns me up,
And will not let me welcome this good news.——
Set on toward Swinstead: to my litter straight;
Weakness possesseth me, and I am faint. [*Exeunt.*

SCENE IV. *The same. Another part of the same.*

Enter SALISBURY, PEMBROKE, BIGOT, *and others.*

Sal. I did not think the king so stor'd with friends.

Pem. Up once again; put spirit in the French;
If they miscarry, we miscarry too.

Sal. That misbegotten devil, Faulconbridge,
In spite of spite, alone upholds the day.

Pem. They say, King John, sore sick, hath left the field.

Enter MELUN *wounded, and led by Soldiers.*

Mel. Lead me to the revolts of England here.

Sal. When we were happy, we had other names.

Pem. It is the Count Melun.

Sal. Wounded to death.

Mel. Fly, noble English, you are bought and sold;[3]
Unthread the rude eye of rebellion,
And welcome home again discarded faith.
Seek out King John, and fall before his feet:
For, if the French be lords of this loud day,
He[4] means to recompense the pains you take,
By cutting off your heads: Thus hath he sworn,
And I with him, and many more with me,
Upon the altar of Saint Edmund's Bury;
Even on that altar, where we swore to you
Dear amity and everlasting love.

Sal. May this be possible? may this be true?

Mel. Have I not hideous death within my view,
Retaining but a quantity of life;
Which bleeds away, even as a form of wax
Resolveth[5] from his figure 'gainst the fire?
What in the world should make me now deceive,
Since I must lose the use of all deceit?
Why should I then be false; since it is true
That I must die here, and live hence by truth?
I say again, if Lewis do win the day,
He is forsworn, if e'er those eyes of yours
Behold another day break in the east:
But even this night,—whose black contagious breath
Already smokes about the burning crest
Of the old, feeble, and day-wearied sun,—
Even this ill night, your breathing shall expire,
Paying the fine of rated treachery,
Even with a treacherous fine of all your lives,
If Lewis by your assistance win the day.
Commend me to one Hubert, with your king;
The love of him,—and this respect besides,
For that my grandsire was an Englishman,
Awakes my conscience to confess all this.
In lieu whereof, I pray you, bear me hence
From forth the noise and rumour of the field,
Where I may think the remnant of my thoughts
In peace, and part this body and my soul
With contemplation and devout desires.

Sal. We do believe thee,—And beshrew my soul
But I do love the favour and the form
Of this most fair occasion, by the which
We will untread the steps of damned flight;
And, like a bated and retired flood,
Leaving our rankness[6] and irregular course,
Stoop low within those bounds we have o'erlook'd,
And calmly run on in obedience,
Even to our ocean, to our great King John.——
My arm shall give thee help to bear thee hence;
For I do see the cruel pangs of death
Right[7] in thine eye.—Away, my friends! New flight!
And happy newness,[8] that intends old right.
[*Exeunt, leading off* MELUN.

SCENE V. *The same. The* French Camp. *Enter* LEWIS *and his Train.*

Lew. The sun of heaven, methought, was loath to set;
But stay'd, and made the western welkin blush,
When the English measur'd backward their own ground,
In faint retire: O, bravely came we off,
When with a volley of our needless shot,
After such bloody toil, we bid good night;
And wound our tott'ring[9] colours clearly up,
Last in the field, and almost lords of it!

Enter a Messenger.

Mess. Where is my prince, the Dauphin?

Lew. Here:—What news?

Mess. The Count Melun is slain; the English lords,
By his persuasion, are again fallen off:
And your supply, which you have wish'd so long,
Are cast away, and sunk, on Goodwin Sands.

Lew. Ah, foul shrewd news!—Beshrew thy very heart!
I did not think to be so sad to-night,
As this hath made me.—Who was he, that said,
King John did fly, an hour or two before
The stumbling night did part our weary powers?

---

1 *Supply* is here used as a noun of multitude, as it is again in scene v.

2 The king had not long since called him by his original name of *Philip*, but the messenger could not take the same liberty.

3 A proverbial expression intimating treachery.

4 The Frenchman, i. e. Lewis means, &c.

5 i. e. *dissolveth.*

6 *Rankness*, as applied to a river, here signifies *exuberant, ready to overflow;* as applied to the actions of the speaker and his party it signifies *wanton wildness.* Petulantia.
'Rain added to a *river* that is *rank*
Perforce will force it overflow the bank.'

7 Immediate.

8 Innovation.

9 *Tott'ring* colours is the reading of the old copy, which was unnecessarily altered to *tatter'd* by Johnson, who is followed by the subsequent editors. To *totter* in old language, was to *waver*, to *shake* with a tremulous motion as colours would do in the wind. It is obvious that *tatter'd* cannot be the right word, for how could their *tatter'd* colours be *clearly wound up?* 'To *tottre* (says Baret,) nutare, vaccilare, see shake and wagge.' The colours were *waving* in the wind during the battle, and were wound up at the close of it.

Mess. Whoever spoke it, it is true, my lord.

Lew. Well; keep good quarter,[1] and good care to-night;
The day shall not be up so soon as I,
To try the fair adventure of to-morrow. [*Exeunt.*

SCENE VI. *An open Place in the neighbourhood of* Swinstead-Abbey. *Enter the* Bastard *and* HUBERT, *meeting.*

Hub. Who's there? speak, ho! speak quickly, or I shoot.

Bast. A friend:—What art thou?

Hub. Of the part of England.

Bast. Whither dost thou go?

Hub. What's that to thee? Why may not I demand
Of thine affairs, as well as thou of mine?

Bast. Hubert, I think.

Hub. Thou hast a perfect[2] thought:
I will, upon all hazards, well believe,
Thou art my friend, that know'st my tongue so well:
Who art thou?

Bast. Who thou wilt: an if thou please,
Thou may'st befriend me so much, as to think
I come one way of the Plantagenets.

Hub. Unkind remembrance! thou, and eyeless night,[3]
Have done me shame:—Brave soldier, pardon me,
That any accent, breaking from thy tongue,
Should 'scape the true acquaintance of mine ear.

Bast. Come, come; sans compliment, what news abroad?

Hub. Why, here walk I, in the black brow of night,
To find you out.

Bast. Brief, then; and what's the news?

Hub. O, my sweet sir, news fitting to the night,
Black, fearful, comfortless, and horrible.

Bast. Show me the very wound of this ill news;
I am no woman, I'll not swoon at it.

Hub. The king, I fear, is poison'd by a monk:[4]
I left him almost speechless, and broke out
To acquaint you with this evil; that you might
The better arm you to the sudden time,
Than if you had at leisure[5] known of this.

Bast. How did he take it? who did taste to him?

Hub. A monk, I tell you; a resolved villain,
Whose bowels suddenly burst out: the king
Yet speaks, and, peradventure, may recover.

Bast. Who didst thou leave to tend his majesty?

Hub. Why, know you not? the lords are all come back,
And brought prince Henry in their company;
At whose request the king hath pardon'd them,
And they are all about his majesty.

Bast. Withhold thine indignation, mighty heaven,
And tempt us not to bear above our power!——
I'll tell thee, Hubert, half my power this night,
Passing these flats, are taken by the tide,
These Lincoln washes have devoured them;
Myself, well mounted, hardly have escap'd.
Away, before! conduct me to the king;
I doubt, he will be dead, or ere I come. [*Exeunt.*

SCENE VII. *The Orchard of* Swinstead-Abbey. *Enter* PRINCE HENRY,[6] SALISBURY, *and* BIGOT.

P. Hen. It is too late; the life of all his blood
Is touch'd corruptibly; and his pure brain
(Which some suppose the soul's frail dwelling-house,)
Doth, by the idle comments that it makes,
Foretell the ending of mortality.

Enter PEMBROKE.

Pem. His highness yet doth speak: and holds belief,
That, being brought into the open air,
It would allay the burning quality
Of that fell poison which assaileth him.

P. Hen. Let him be brought into the orchard here.
Doth he still rage? [*Exit* BIGOT.

Pem. He is more patient
Than when you left him; even now he sung.

P. Hen. O vanity of sickness! fierce extremes,
In their continuance,[7] will not feel themselves.
Death, having prey'd upon the outward parts,
Leaves them insensible;[8] and his siege is now
Against the mind, the which he pricks and wound
With many legions of strange fantasies;
Which, in their throng and press to that last hold,
Confound themselves. 'Tis strange, that death should sing.——
I am the cygnet to this pale faint swan,
Who chants a doleful hymn to his own death;
And, from the organ-pipe of frailty, sings
His soul and body to their lasting rest.

Sal. Be of good comfort, prince; for you are born
To set a form upon that indigest
Which he hath left so shapeless and so rude.[9]

Re-enter BIGOT *and Attendants, who bring in* KING JOHN *in a Chair.*

K. John. Ay, marry, now, my soul hath elbow room;
It would not out at windows, nor at doors.
There is so hot a summer in my bosom,
That all my bowels crumble up to dust:
I am a scribbled form, drawn with a pen
Upon a parchment; and against this fire
Do I shrink up.

P. Hen. How fares your majesty?

K. John. Poison'd,—ill fare;—dead, forsook cast off;
And none of you will bid the winter come,
To thrust his icy fingers in my maw;[10]
Nor let my kingdom's rivers take their course
Through my burn'd bosom; nor entreat the north
To make his bleak winds kiss my parched lips,
And comfort me with cold:—I do not ask you much,

---

1 i. e. keep in your allotted posts or stations.

2 i. e. a *well informed* one.

3 The old copy reads '*endless* night.' The emendation was made by Theobald.

4 Not one of the historians who wrote within sixty years of the event mentions this improbable story. The tale is, that a monk, to revenge himself on the king for a saying at which he took offence, poisoned a cup of ale, and having brought it to his majesty, drank some of it himself, to induce the king to taste it, and soon afterwards expired. Thomas Wylkes is the first who mentions it in his Chronicle as a *report.* According to the best accounts John died at Newark, of a fever.

5 i. e. less speedy, after some delay.

6 Prince Henry was only nine years old when his father died.

7 *Continuance* here means *continuity.* Bacon uses it in that sense also. So Baret, 'If the disease be of any *continuance*, if it be an old and settled disease.' I should not have thought this passage needed elucidation, had not Malone proposed to read 'in *thy* continuance.'

8 The old copy reads *invisible.* Sir T. Hanmer proposed the reading admitted into the text. Malone has endeavoured to elaborate a meaning out of the old reading but without success. I must refer the reader to the variorum editions for his argument, and Steevens's vein of pleasant irony upon it.

9 A description of Chaos, almost in the very words of Ovid:—

Quem dixere Chaos rudis indigestæque moles.—*Met.* i.

Which Chaos hight a huge *rude* heap:—
No sunne as yet with lightsome beames the *shapeless* world did view. *Golding's Translation.*

10 This scene has been imitated by Beaumont and Fletcher, in A Wife for a Month, Act iv. Decker, in the Gull's Hornbook, has the same thought:—'the morning waxing cold thrust his frosty fingers into thy bosome.' Perhaps Shakspeare was acquainted with the following passages in two of Marlowe's plays, which must both have been written previous to King John, for Marlowe died in 1593:—

'O I am dull, and the cold hand of sleep
Hath thrust his icy fingers in my breast,
And made a frost within me.'—*Lust's Dominion.*

'O poor Zabina, O my queen, my queen,
Fetch me some *water* for my *burning breast,*
To *cool* and *comfort* me with longer date.'
Tamburlaine, 1591

The corresponding passage in the old play runs thus
'Philip, some drink. O for the frozen Alps
To tumble on, and cool this inward heat
That rageth as a furnace seven-fold.'

I beg cold comfort: and you are so strait,[1]
And so ingrateful, you deny me that.
P. Hen. O, that there were some virtue in my tears,
That might relieve you!
K. John. The salt in them is hot.—
Within me is a hell; and there the poison
Is, as a fiend, confin'd to tyrannize
On unreprievable condemned blood.

Enter the Bastard.

Bast. O, I am scalded with my violent emotion,
And spleen of speed to see your majesty.
K. John. O cousin, thou art come to set mine eye:
The tackle of my heart is crack'd and burn'd;
And all the shrouds, wherewith my life should sail,
Are turned to one thread, one little hair:
My heart hath one poor string to stay it by,
Which holds but till thy news be uttered:
And then all this thou seest, is but a clod,
And module[2] of confounded royalty.
Bast. The Dauphin is preparing hitherward:
Where, heaven he knows, how we shall answer him:
For, in a night, the best part of my power,
As I upon advantage did remove,
Were in the washes, all unwarily,
Devoured by the unexpected flood.[3] [*The King dies.*
Sal. You breathe these dead news in as dead an ear.—
My liege! my lord!—But now a king,—now thus.
P. Hen. Even so must I run on, and even so stop.
What surety of the world, what hope, what stay,
When this was now a king, and now is clay!
Bast. Art thou gone so? I do but stay behind,
To do the office for thee of revenge;
And then my soul shall wait on thee to heaven,
As it on earth hath been thy servant still.——
Now, now, you stars, that move in your right spheres,
Where be your powers? Show now your mended faiths;
And instantly return with me again,
To push destruction and perpetual shame
Out of the weak door of our fainting land:
Straight let us seek, or straight we shall be sought;
The Dauphin rages at our very heels.
Sal. It seems, you know not then so much as we:
The cardinal Pandulph is within at rest,
Who half an hour since came from the dauphin;
And brings from him such offers of our peace
As we with honour and respect may take,
With purpose presently to leave this war.
Bast. He will the rather do it, when he sees
Ourselves well sinewed to our defence.
Sal. Nay, it is in a manner done already;
For many carriages he hath despatch'd
To the seaside, and put his cause and quarrel
To the disposing of the cardinal:
With whom yourself, myself, and other lords,
If you think meet, this afternoon will post
To consummate this business happily.
Bast. Let it be so:—And you, my noble prince,
With other princes that may best be spared,
Shall wait upon your father's funeral.
P. Hen. At Worcester must his body be interr'd;[4]
For so he will'd it.
Bast. Thither shall it then.
And happily may your sweet self put on
The lineal state and glory of the land!
To whom, with all submission, on my knee,
I do bequeath my faithful services
And true subjection everlastingly.
Sal. And the like tender of our love we make,
To rest without a spot for evermore.
P. Hen. I have a kind soul, that would give you thanks,
And knows not how to do it, but with tears.
Bast. O, let us pay the time but needful woe,
Since it hath been beforehand with our griefs.—[5]
This England never did (nor never shall)
Lie at the proud foot of a conqueror,
But when it first did help to wound itself.
Now these her princes are come home again,
Come the three corners of the world in arms,
And we shall shock them: Nought shall make us rue
If England to itself do rest but true.[6] [*Exeunt.*

THE tragedy of King John, though not written with the utmost power of Shakspeare, is varied with a very pleasing interchange of incidents and characters. The lady's grief is very affecting; and the character of the Bastard contains that mixture of greatness and levity which this author delighted to exhibit. JOHNSON

---

1 Narrow, avaricious.

2 *Module* and model were only different modes of spelling the same word. Model signified not an archetype, after which something was to be formed, but the thing formed after an archetype, a *copy*. Bullokar, in his Expositor, 1616, explains '*model*, the platform, or form of any thing.'

3 This untoward accident really happened to King John himself. As he passed from Lynn to Lincolnshire he lost by an inundation all his treasure, carriages, baggage, and regalia.

4 In crastino S. Lucæ Johannes Rex Angliæ in castro de Newark obiit, et sepultus est in ecclesia Wigorniensi inter corpora S. Oswaldi et sancti [Wolstani] Chronic. sive Annal. Prioratus de Dunstable, edit. a T. Hearne, t. i. p. 173. A stone coffin, containing the body of King John, was discovered in the cathedral church of Worcester, July 17, 1797.

5 'As previously we have found sufficient cause for lamentation, let us not waste the time in superfluous sorrow.'

6 This sentiment may have been borrowed from the following passage in the old play:—
'Let England live but true within herself,
And all the world can never wrong her state.'

THE LIFE AND DEATH OF

KING RICHARD THE SECOND.

PRELIMINARY REMARKS.

IN the construction of this play Shakspeare has followed Holinshed, his usual historical authority, some passages of the Chronicle he has transplanted into the drama with very little alteration.

It has been suspected that there was an old play on the subject of King Richard II. which the poet might have seen. Sir Gillie Merrick, who was concerned in the harebrained business of the Earl of Essex, is accused of having procured to be played before the conspirators 'the play of the deposing of Richard the Second; when it was told him by one of the players that the play was *old*, and they should have loss in playing it, because few would come to it, there was forty shillings extraordinary given to play, and so thereupon played it was!' It seems probable, from a passage in the State Trials, quoted by Mr. Tyrwhitt, that this old play bore the title of King Henry IV, and not King Richard II, and it could not be Shakspeare's King Henry IV, as that commences a year after the death of King Richard. 'It may seem strange (says Malone) that this old play should have been represented after Shakspeare's drama on the same subject had been printed: the reason undoubtedly was, that in the old play the deposing of King Richard II. made a part of the exhibition: but in the first edition of Shakspeare's play, one hundred and fifty-four lines, describing a kind of trial of the king, and his actual deposition in parliament, were omitted: nor was it probably represented on the stage. Merrick, Cuffe, and the rest of Essex's train, naturally preferred the play in which his *deposition* was represented, their plot not aiming at the life of the queen. It is, I know, commonly thought that the parliament scene, as it is called, which was first printed in the 4to of 1608, was an addition made by Shakspeare to this play after its first representation: but it seems to me more probable that it was written with the rest, and suppressed in the printed copy of 1597, from the fear of offending Elizabeth; against whom the Pope had published a bull in the preceding year, exhorting her subjects to take up arms against her. In 1599 Hayward published his History of the first year of King Henry IV. which is in fact nothing more than a history of the deposing of King Richard II. The displeasure which that book excited at court sufficiently accounts for the omitted lines not being inserted in the copy of this play, which was published in 1602.* Hayward was heavily censured in the Star Chamber, and committed to prison. In 1608, when James was quietly and firmly settled on the throne, and the fear of internal commotion, or foreign invasion, no longer subsisted, neither the author, the managers of the theatre, nor the bookseller, could entertain any apprehension of giving offence to the sovereign; the rejected scene was therefore restored without scruple, and from some playhouse copy probably found its way to the press.'†

Malone places the date of its composition in 1593; Mr. Chalmers in 1596. The play was first entered on the stationers' books by Andrew Wise, August 29, 1597; and there were four quarto editions published during the life of Shakspeare, viz. in 1597, 1598, 1608, and 1615.

This play may be considered the first link in the chain of Shakspeare's historical dramas, which Schlegel thinks the poet designed to form one great whole, 'as it were an historical heroic poem, of which the separate plays constitute the rhapsodies.'

'In King Richard the Second the poet exhibits to us a noble kingly nature, at first obscured by levity and the errors of unbridled youth, and afterwards purified by misfortune, and rendered more highly splendid and illustrious. When he has lost the love and reverence of his subjects, and is on the point of losing also his throne, he then feels with painful inspiration the elevated vocation of the kingly dignity, and its prerogatives over personal merit and changeable institutions. When the earthly crown has fallen from off his head, he first appears as a king whose innate nobility no humiliation can annihilate. This is felt by a poor groom: he is shocked that his master's favourite horse should have carried the proud Bolingbroke at his coronation; he visits the captive king in his prison, and shames the desertion of the great. The political history of the deposition is represented with extraordinary knowledge of the world;—the ebb of fortune on the one hand, and the swelling tide on the other, which carries every thing along with it; while Bolingbroke acts as a king, and his adherents behave towards him as if he really were so, he still continues to give out that he comes with an armed band, merely for the sake of demanding his birthright and the removal of abuses. The usurpation has been long completed before the word is pronounced, and the thing publicly avowed. John of Gaunt is a model of chivalrous truth: he stands there like a pillar of the olden time which he had outlived.'‡

This drama abounds in passages of eminent poetical beauty; among which every reader will recollect the pathetic description of Richard's entrance into London with Bolingbroke, of which Dryden said that 'he knew nothing comparable to it in any other language;' John of Gaunt's praise of England,

'Dear for her reputation through the world;'

and Mowbray's complaint at being banished for life.

* This is a mistake of Mr. Malone's, there is no quarto copy of the date of 1602, he probably meant the edition of 1598.

† Malone's Chronology of Shakspeare's plays.

‡ Schlegel's Lectures on Dramatic Literature, vol ii p. 224.

PERSONS REPRESENTED.

King Richard the Second.
Edmund *of* Langley, Duke *of* York, } *Uncles to the King.*
John *of* Gaunt, Duke *of* Lancaster, }
Henry, *surnamed* Bolingbroke, Duke *of* Hereford, *Son to* John *of* Gaunt; *afterwards* King Henry IV.
Duke *of* Aumerle, *Son to the* Duke *of* York.
Mowbray, Duke *of* Norfolk.
Duke *of* Surrey.
Earl *of* Salisbury. Earl Berkley.
Bushy, }
Bagot, } *Creatures to* King Richard.
Green, }
Earl *of* Northumberland.
Henry Percy, *his Son.*
Lord Ross. Lord Willoughby. Lord Fitzwater.
Bishop *of* Carlisle. Abbot *of* Westminster.
Lord Marshal; *and another Lord.*
Sir Pierce *of* Exton. Sir Stephen Scroop
Captain of a Band of Welshmen.

Queen *to* King Richard.
Duchess *of* Gloster.
Duchess *of* York.
Lady attending on the Queen.

Lords, Heralds, Officers, Soldiers, two Gardeners, Keeper, Messenger, Groom, *and other* Attendants.

SCENE, *dispersedly in* England *and* Wales.

ACT I.

SCENE I. London. *A Room in the Palace. Enter* King Richard, *attended;* John *of* Gaunt, *and other Nobles with him.*

King Richard.

Old[1] John of Gaunt, time-honour'd Lancaster,
Hast thou, according to thy oath and band,[2]
Brought hither Henry Hereford[3] thy bold son;
Here to make good the boisterous late appeal,
Which then our leisure would not let us hear,
Against the Duke of Norfolk, Thomas Mowbray?

Gaunt. I have, my liege.

K. Rich. Tell me, moreover, hast thou sounded him,
If he appeal the duke on ancient malice;
Or worthily as a good subject should,
On some known ground of treachery in him?

Gaunt. As near as I could sift him on that argument,—
On some apparent danger seen in him,
Aim'd at your highness; no inveterate malice.

1 '*Old* John of Gaunt, *time-honour'd* Lancaster.' Our ancestors, in their estimate of old age, appear to have reckoned somewhat differently from us, and to have considered men as *old* whom we should now esteem as *middle-aged.* With them, every man that had passed fifty seems to have been accounted an old man. John of Gaunt, at the period when the commencement of this play is laid (1398), was only fifty-eight years old: he died in 1399, aged fifty-nine. This may have arisen from its being customary in former times to enter life at an earlier period than we do now. Those who married at fifteen, had at fifty been masters of a house and family for thirty-five years.

2 When these public challenges were accepted, each combatant found a pledge for his appearance at the time and place appointed. *Band* and *bond* were formerly synonymous.

3 In the old play, and in Harding's Chronicle, Bolingbroke's title is written *Herford* and *Harford.* This was the pronunciation of our poet's time, and he therefore uses this word as a dissyllable

K. Rich. Then call them to our presence, face to face,
And frowning brow to brow, ourselves will hear
The accuser, and the accused, freely speak:—
[*Exeunt some* Attendants.
High stomach'd are they both, and full of ire,
In rage deaf as the sea, hasty as fire.

Re-enter Attendants, *with* BOLINGBROKE[1] *and* NORFOLK.

Boling. May many years of happy days befall
My gracious sovereign, my most loving liege!
Nor. Each day still better other's happiness;
Until the heavens, envying earth's good hap,
Add an immortal title to your crown!
K. Rich. We thank you both: yet one but flatters us,
As well appeareth by the cause you come:[2]
Namely, to appeal each other of high treason.—
Cousin of Hereford, what dost thou object
Against the Duke of Norfolk, Thomas Mowbray?
Boling. First, (heaven be the record of my speech!)
In the devotion of a subject's love,
Tendering the precious safety of my prince,
And free from other misbegotten hate,
Come I appellant to this princely presence.—
Now, Thomas Mowbray, do I turn to thee,
And mark my greeting well; for what I speak,
My body shall make good upon this earth,
Or my divine soul answer it in heaven.
Thou art a traitor, and a miscreant;
Too good to be so, and too bad to live:
Since, the more fair and crystal is the sky,
The uglier seem the clouds that in it fly.
Once more, the more to aggravate the note,
With a foul traitor's name stuff I thy throat;
And wish (so please my sovereign), ere I move,
What my tongue speaks, my right-drawn sword[3] may prove.
Nor. Let not my cold words here accuse my zeal:
'Tis not the trial of a woman's war,
The bitter clamour of two eager tongues,
Can arbitrate this cause betwixt us twain:
The blood is hot that must be cool'd for this:
Yet can I not of such tame patience boast,
As to be hush'd, and nought at all to say:
First, the fair reverence of your highness curbs me
From giving reins and spurs to my free speech;
Which else would post, until it had return'd
These terms of treason doubled down his throat.
Setting aside his high blood's royalty,
And let him be no kinsman to my liege,
I do defy him, and I spit at him;
Call him—a slanderous coward, and a villain:
Which to maintain, I would allow him odds;
And meet him, were I tied to run a-foot
Even to the frozen ridges of the Alps,
Or any other ground inhabitable[4]
Where ever Englishman durst set his foot.
Mean time, let this defend my loyalty,—
By all my hopes, most falsely doth he lie.
Boling. Pale trembling coward, there I throw my gage,
Disclaiming here the kindred of the king;
And lay aside my high blood's royalty,
Which fear, not reverence, makes thee to except:
If guilty dread hath left thee so much strength,
As to take up mine honour's pawn, then stoop;
By that, and all the rites of knighthood else,
Will I make good against thee, arm to arm,
What I have spoke, or thou canst worst devise.
Nor. I take it up; and, by that sword I swear,
Which gently lay'd my knighthood on my shoulder,
I'll answer thee in any fair degree,
Or chivalrous design of knightly trial;
And, when I mount, alive may I not light,
If I be a traitor, or unjustly fight!
K. Rich. What doth our cousin lay to Mowbray' charge?
It must be great, that can inherit[5] us
So much as of a thought of ill in him.
Boling. Look, what I speak my life shall prove it true;—
That Mowbray hath receiv'd eight thousand nobles
In name of lendings for your highness' soldiers;
The which he hath detain'd for lewd[6] employments
Like a false traitor, and injurious villain.
Besides I say, and will in battle prove,—
Or here, or elsewhere, to the furthest verge
That ever was survey'd by English eye,—
That all the treasons for these eighteen years
Complotted and contrived in this land,
Fetch from false Mowbray their first head and spring.
Further I say,—and further will maintain
Upon his bad life, to make all this good,—
That he did plot the Duke of Gloster's death;[7]
Suggest[8] his soon-believing adversaries;
And, consequently, like a traitor coward,
Sluic'd out his innocent soul through streams of blood:
Which blood, like sacrificing Abel's, cries,
Even from the tongueless caverns of the earth,
To me for justice, and rough chastisement;
And by the glorious worth of my descent,
This arm shall do it, or this life be spent.
K. Rich. How high a pitch his resolution soars:—
Thomas of Norfolk, what say'st thou to this?
Nor. O, let my sovereign turn away his face,
And bid his ears a little while be deaf,
Till I have told this slander of his blood,[9]
How God, and good men, hate so foul a liar.
K. Rich. Mowbray, impartial are our eyes, and ears:
Were he my brother, nay, my kingdom's heir
(As he is but my father's brother's son,)
Now by my sceptre's awe I make a vow,
Such neighbour nearness to our sacred blood
Should nothing privilege him, nor partialize
The unstooping firmness of my upright soul;
He is our subject, Mowbray, so art thou;
Free speech, and fearless, I to thee allow.
Nor. Then, Bolingbroke, as low as to thy heart,
Through the false passage of thy throat, thou liest!
Three parts of that receipt I had for Calais,
Disburs'd I duly to his highness' soldiers:
The other part reserv'd I by consent;
For that my sovereign liege was in my debt,
Upon remainder of a dear account,
Since last I went to France to fetch his queen:[10]
Now swallow down that lie.——For Gloster's death,——
I slew him not; but to my own disgrace,
Neglected my sworn duty in that case.—

1 Drayton asserts that Henry Plantagenet, the eldest son of John of Gaunt, was not distinguished by the name of Bolingbroke till after he had assumed the crown. He is called earl of Hereford by the old historians, and was surnamed Bolingbroke from having been born at the town of that name in Lincolnshire, about 1366.

2 i. e. 'by the cause you come *on*.' The suppression of the preposition has been shown to have been frequent with Shakspeare.

3 My *right-drawn* sword is my sword drawn in a right or just cause.

4 i. e. uninhabitable.

5 To inherit, in the language of Shakspeare, is to *possess*.

6 *Lewd* formerly signified *knavish*, *ungracious*, *naughty*, *idle*, beside its now general acceptation.

7 Thomas of Woodstock, the youngest son of Edward III. who was murdered at Calais in 1397. See Froissart, chap ccxxvi.

8 i. e. *prompt* them, set them on by injurious hints.

9 Reproach to his ancestry.

10 The duke of Norfolk was joined in commission with Edward Earl of Rutland (the Aumerle of this play) to go to France in the year 1395, to demand in marriage Isabel, eldest daughter of Charles VI. then between seven and eight years of age. Richard was married to his young consort in November 1396, at Calais; his first wife, Anne, daughter of Charles IV. emperor of Germany, died at Shene on Whit Sunday, 1394. His marriage with Isabella was merely political, it was accompanied with an agreement for a truce between France and England for thirty years.

For you, my noble lord of Lancaster,
The honourable father to my foe,
Once did I lay an ambush for your life,
A trespass that doth vex my grieved soul:
But, ere I last receiv'd the sacrament,
I did confess it: and exactly begg'd
Your grace's pardon, and, I hope, I had it.
This is my fault: As for the rest appeal'd,[1]
It issues from the rancour of a villain,
A recreant and most degenerate traitor:
Which in myself I boldly will defend;
And interchangeably hurl down my gage
Upon this overweening[2] traitor's foot,
To prove myself a loyal gentleman
Even in the best blood chamber'd in his bosom:
In haste whereof, most heartily I pray
Your highness to assign our trial day.

K. Rich. Wrath-kindled gentlemen, be rul'd by me:
Let's purge this choler without letting blood:
This we prescribe, though no physician;[3]
Deep malice makes too deep incision:
Forget, forgive; conclude, and be agreed;
Our doctors say, this is no time to bleed.—
Good uncle, let this end where it begun:
We'll calm the duke of Norfolk, you your son.

Gaunt. To be a make-peace shall become my age:
Throw down, my son, the duke of Norfolk's gage.

K. Rich. And, Norfolk, throw down his.

Gaunt. When, Harry? when?[4]
Obedience bids, I should not bid again.

K. Rich. Norfolk, throw down; we bid; there is no boot.[5]

Nor. Myself I throw, dread sovereign, at thy foot:
My life thou shalt command, but not my shame:
The one my duty owes; but my fair name
(Despite of death, that lives upon my grave,)[6]
To dark dishonour's use thou shalt not have.
I am disgrac'd, impeach'd, and baffled[7] here;
Pierc'd to the soul with slander's venom'd spear;
The which no balm can cure, but his heart-blood
Which breath'd this poison.

K. Rich. Rage must be withstood:
Give me his gage:—Lions make leopards[8] tame.

Nor. Yea, but not change their[9] spots: take but my shame,
And I resign my gage. My dear, dear lord,
The purest treasure mortal times afford,
Is—spotless reputation; that away,
Men are but gilded loam, or painted clay.
A jewel in a ten times barr'd up chest
Is—a bold spirit in a loyal breast.
Mine honour is my life; both grow in one;
Take honour from me, and my life is done:
Then, dear my liege, mine honour let me try;
In that I live, and for that will I die.

K. Rich. Cousin, throw down your gage; do you begin.

Boling. O, God defend my soul from such foul sin!
Shall I seem crest-fallen in my father's sight?
Or with pale beggar-fear impeach my height
Before this out-dar'd dastard Ere my tongue
Shall wound mine honour with such feeble wrong,
Or sound so base a parle, my teeth shall tear
The slavish motive of recanting fear;
And spit it bleeding in his high disgrace,
Where shame doth harbour, even in Mowbray's face. [*Exit* GAUNT

K. Rich. We were not born to sue, but to command:
Which since we cannot do to make you friends,
Be ready, as your lives shall answer it,
At Coventry, upon Saint Lambert's day;
There shall your swords and lances arbitrate
The swelling difference of your settled hate;
Since we cannot atone[10] you, we shall see
Justice design[11] the victor's chivalry.—
Lord Marshal, command our officers at arms
Be ready to direct these home alarms. [*Exeunt.*

SCENE II. *The same. A Room in the Duke of Lancaster's Palace. Enter* GAUNT, *and Duchess of* Gloster.[12]

Gaunt. Alas! the part[13] I had in Gloster's blood
Doth more solicit me, than your exclaims,
To stir against the butchers of his life.
But since correction lieth in those hands,
Which made the fault that we cannot correct,
Put we our quarrel to the will of heaven;
Who when he sees[14] the hours ripe on earth,
Will rain hot vengeance on offenders' heads.

Duch. Finds brotherhood in thee no sharper spur?
Hath love in thy old blood no living fire?
Edward's seven sons, whereof thyself art one,
Were as seven phials of his sacred blood,
Or seven fair branches springing from one root:
Some of those seven are dried by nature's course,
Some of those branches by the destinies cut:
But Thomas, my dear lord, my life, my Gloster,—
One phial full of Edward's sacred blood,
One flourishing branch of his most royal root,—
Is crack'd, and all the precious liquor spilt;
Is hack'd down, and his summer leaves all faded,
By envy's hand, and murder's bloody axe.
Ah, Gaunt! his blood was thine; that bed, that womb,
That mettle, that self-mould, that fashion'd thee,
Made him a man; and though thou liv'st, and breath'st,
Yet art thou slain in him: thou dost consent[15]
In some large measure to thy father's death,
In that thou seest thy wretched brother die,
Who was the model of thy father's life.
Call it not patience, Gaunt, it is despair:
In suffering thus thy brother to be slaughter'd,
Thou show'st the naked pathway to thy life,
Teaching stern murder how to butcher thee:
That which in mean men we entitle—patience,
Is pale cold cowardice in noble breasts.
What shall I say? to safeguard thine own life,
The best way is—to 'venge my Gloster's death.

Gaunt. Heaven's is the quarrel; for heaven's substitute,
His deputy anointed in his sight,
Hath caus'd his death; the which if wrongfully,
Let heaven revenge; for I may never lift
An angry arm against his minister.

---

1 Charged. 2 Arrogant.

3 Pope thought that some of the rhyming verses in this play were not from the hand of Shakspeare.

4 This abrupt elliptical exclamation of impatience is again used in the Taming of a Shrew:—'Why *when*, I say! Nay, good sweet Kate, be merry.' It appears to be equivalent to 'when will such a thing be done?'

5 'There is no *boot*,' or it *booteth* not, is as much as to say 'there is no *help*,' resistance would be vain, or *profitless*.

6 i. e. my name that lives on my grave in despite of death.

7 *Baffled* in this place signifies 'abused, reviled, reproached in base terms;' which was the ancient signification of the word, as well as to deceive or circumvent.

8 There is an allusion here to the crest of Norfolk, which was a *golden leopard*.

9 The old copies have '*his* spots.' The alteration was made by Pope

10 i. e. make them friends, 'to make agreement or *atonement*, to reconcile them to each other.'

11 To *design* is to *mark out*, to *show* by a token. It is the sense of the Latin *designo*. I may here take occasion to remark that Shakspeare's learning appears to me to have been underrated; it is almost always evident in his choice of expressive terms derived from the Latin, and used in their original sense. The propriety of this expression here will be obvious, when we recollect that *designator* was '*a marshal*, a master of the play or prize, who appointed every one his place, and adjudged the victory.'

12 The duchess of Gloster was Eleanor Bohun, widow of Duke Thomas, son of Edward III.

13 i. e. my relationship of consanguinity to Gloster.

14 The old copy erroneously reads 'who when *they see*.'

15 i. e. assent; *consent* is often used by the poet for *accord agreement*

Duch. Where then, alas! may I complain myself?[1]

Gaunt. To heaven, the widow's champion and defence.

Duch. Why then, I will. Farewell, old Gaunt.
Thou go'st to Coventry, there to behold
Our cousin Hereford and fell Mowbray fight:
O, sit my husband's wrongs on Hereford's spear,
That it may enter butcher Mowbray's breast!
Or, if misfortune miss the first career,
Be Mowbray's sins so heavy in his bosom,
That they may break his foaming courser's back,
And throw the rider headlong in the lists,
A caitiff recreant to my cousin Hereford!
Farewell, old Gaunt; thy sometime brother's wife,
With her companion grief must end her life.

Gaunt. Sister, farewell: I must to Coventry:
As much good stay with thee, as go with me!

Duch. Yet one word more;—Grief boundeth where it falls,
Not with the empty hollowness, but weight:
I take my leave before I have begun;
For sorrow ends not when it seemeth done.
Commend me to my brother, Edmund York,
Lo, this is all:—Nay, yet depart not so:
Though this be all, do not so quickly go;
I shall remember more. Bid him—O, what?—
With all good speed at Plashy[2] visit me.
Alack, and what shall good old York there see,
But empty lodgings and unfurnish'd walls,[3]
Unpeopled offices, untrodden stones?
And what cheer there for welcome, but my groans?
Therefore commend me; let him not come there,
To seek out sorrow that dwells every where:
Desolate, desolate, will I hence, and die;
The last leave of thee takes my weeping eye.
[*Exeunt.*

SCENE III. Gosford Green, *near* Coventry. *Lists set out, and a Throne.* Heralds, *&c. attending. Enter the* Lord Marshal, *and* AUMERLE.[4]

Mar. My lord Aumerle, is Harry Hereford arm'd?

Aum. Yea, at all points: and longs to enter in.

Mar. The duke of Norfolk, sprightfully and bold,
Stays but the summons of the appellant's trumpet.

Aum. Why then, the champions are prepar'd, and stay
For nothing but his majesty's approach.

Flourish of Trumpets. Enter KING RICHARD, *who takes his seat on his Throne;* GAUNT, *and several* Noblemen, *who take their places. A Trumpet is sounded, and answered by another Trumpet within. Then enter* NORFOLK *in armour, preceded by a* Herald.

K. Rich. Marshal, demand of yonder champion
The cause of his arrival here in arms:
Ask him his name; and orderly proceed
To swear him in the justice of his cause.

Mar. In God's name, and the king's, say who thou art,
And why thou com'st, thus knightly clad in arms?
Against what man thou com'st, and what thy quarrel?
Speak truly, on thy knighthood, and thy oath;
As so defend thee heaven, and thy valour!

Nor. My name is Thomas Mowbray, duke of Norfolk;[5]
Who hither come engaged by my oath,
(Which heaven defend a knight should violate!)
Both to defend my loyalty and truth,
To God, my king, and my[6] succeeding issue,
Against the duke of Hereford that appeals me;
And, by the grace of God, and this mine arm,
To prove him, in defending of myself,
A traitor to my God, my king, and me:
And, as I truly fight, defend me heaven
[*He takes his seat.*

Trumpet sounds. Enter BOLINGBROKE, *in armour; preceded by a* Herald.

K. Rich. Marshal, ask yonder knight in arms,
Both who he is, and why he cometh hither
Thus plated in habiliments of war;
And formally according to our law
Depose him in the justice of his cause.

Mar. What is thy name? and wherefore com'st thou hither,
Before king Richard, in his royal lists?
Against whom comest thou; and what's thy quarrel?
Speak like a true knight, so defend thee heaven!

Boling. Harry of Hereford, Lancaster, and Derby,
Am I; who ready here do stand in arms,
To prove, by heaven's grace, and my body's valour,
In lists, on Thomas Mowbray, duke of Norfolk,
That he's a traitor, foul and dangerous,
To God of heaven, King Richard, and to me;
And, as I truly fight, defend me heaven!

Mar. On pain of death, no person be so bold,
Or daring-hardy, as to touch the lists;
Except the marshal, and such officers
Appointed to direct these fair designs.

Boling. Lord marshal, let me kiss my sovereign's hand,
And bow my knee before his majesty:
For Mowbray, and myself, are like two men
That vow a long and weary pilgrimage;
Then let us take a ceremonious leave,
And loving farewell, of our several friends.

Mar. The appellant in all duty greets your highness,
And craves to kiss your hand and take his leave.

K. Rich. We will descend, and fold him in our arms.
Cousin of Hereford, as thy cause is right,
So be thy fortune in this royal fight!
Farewell, my blood; which if to-day thou shed
Lament we may, but not revenge thee dead.

Boling. O, let no noble eye profane a tear
For me, if I be gored with Mowbray's spear;
As confident, as is the falcon's flight
Against a bird, do I with Mowbray fight.——
My loving lord [*To* Lord Marshal,] I take my leave of you;—
Of you, my noble cousin, Lord Aumerle;—
Not sick, although I have to do with death;

1 To *complain* is commonly a verb neuter; but it is here used as a verb active. It is a literal translation of the old French phrase, *me complaindre;* and is not peculiar to Shakspeare.

2 Her house in Essex.

3 In our ancient castles the naked stone walls were only covered with tapestry or arras, hung upon tenter-hooks, from which it was easily taken down on every removal of the family. (See the Preface to the Northumberland Household Book, by Dr. Percy.) The *offices* of our old English mansions were the rooms designed for keeping the various stores of provisions, bread, wine, ale, &c. and for culinary purposes. They were always situate within the house, on the ground-floor (for there were no subterraneous rooms till about the middle of the reign of Charles I.), and nearly adjoining each other. When dinner had been set on the board by the sewers, the proper officers attended in each of these offices. Sometimes, on occasions of great festivity, these offices were all thrown open, and unlimited licence given to all comers to eat and drink at their pleasure. The duchess therefore laments that, in consequence of the murder of her husband, all the hospitality of plenty is at an end; 'the walls are unfurnished, the lodging rooms empty, and the *offices* unpeopled. All is solitude and silence; her groans are the only cheer that her guests can expect.'

4 The Duke of Norfolk was Earl Marshal of England; but being himself one of the combatants, the Duke of Surry, (Thomas Holland) officiated. Shakspeare has made a slight mistake by introducing that nobleman as a distinct person from the marshal in the present drama. Edward duke of *Aumerle* (so created by his cousin-german Richard II. in 1397, was the eldest son of Edward duke of York, fifth son of Edward III.) officiated as high constable at the lists of Coventry. He was killed at the battle of Agincourt, in 1415.

5 The duke of Hereford, being the appellant, entered the lists first, according to the historians.

6 '*His* succeeding issue' is the reading of the first folio: the quartos all read *my.*

But lusty, young, and cheerly drawing breath.——
Lo, as at English feasts, so I regreet
The daintiest last, to make the end most sweet:
O thou, the earthly author of my blood,— [*To* GAUNT.
Whose youthful spirit, in me regenerate,
Doth with a twofold vigour lift me up
To reach at victory above my head,—
Add proof unto mine armour with thy prayers;
And with thy blessings steel my lance's point,
That it may enter Mowbray's waxen coat,
And furbish new the name of John of Gaunt,
Even in the lusty 'haviour of his son.

Gaunt. Heaven in thy good cause make thee prosperous!
Be swift like lightning in the execution;
And let thy blows, doubly redoubled,
Fall like amazing thunder on the casque
Of thy adverse pernicious enemy:
Rouse up thy youthful blood, be valiant and live.

Boling. Mine innocency, and Saint George to thrive! [*He takes his seat.*

Nor. [*Rising.*] However heaven, or fortune, cast my lot,
There lives or dies, true to King Richard's throne,
A loyal, just, and upright gentleman:
Never did captive with a freer heart
Cast off his chains of bondage, and embrace
His golden uncontroll'd enfranchisement,
More than my dancing soul doth celebrate
This feast of battle with mine adversary.—
Most mighty liege,—and my companion peers,—
Take from my mouth the wish of happy years:
As gentle and as jocund as to jest,[1]
Go I to fight; Truth hath a quiet breast.

K. Rich. Farewell, my lord: securely I espy
Virtue with valour couched in thine eye.——
Order the trial, marshal, and begin.
[*The* King *and the* Lords *return to their seats.*

Mar. Harry of Hereford, Lancaster, and Derby,
Receive thy lance; and God defend the right!

Boling. [*Rising.*] Strong as a tower in hope, I cry—amen.

Mar. Go bear this lance [*To an* Officer] to Thomas duke of Norfolk.

1 *Her.* Harry of Hereford, Lancaster, and Derby,
Stands here for God, his sovereign, and himself,
On pain to be found false and recreant,
To prove the duke of Norfolk, Thomas Mowbray,
A traitor to his God, his king, and him,
And dares him to set forward to the fight.

2 *Her.* Here standeth Thomas Mowbray, duke of Norfolk,
On pain to be found false and recreant,
Both to defend himself, and to approve
Henry of Hereford, Lancaster, and Derby,
To God, his sovereign, and to him, disloyal;
Courageously, and with a free desire,
Attending but the signal to begin.

Mar. Sound, trumpets; and set forward, combatants. [*A Charge sounded.*
Stay, the king hath thrown his warder[2] down.

K. Rich. Let them lay by their helmets and their spears,
And both return back to their chairs again:
Withdraw with us:—and let the trumpets sound,
While we return these dukes what we decree.— [*A long Flourish.*
Draw near, [*To the Combatants.*
And list, what with our council we have done.
For that our kingdom's earth should not be soil'd
With that dear blood which it hath fostered;
And for our eyes do hate the dire aspect
Of civil[3] wounds plough'd up with neighbours' swords;
[And for we think the eagle-winged pride
Of sky-aspiring and ambitious thoughts,
With rival-hating envy, set you on
To wake our peace, which in our country's cradle
Draws the sweet infant breath of gentle sleep;[4]]
Which so rous'd up with boisterous untun'd drums,
With harsh resounding trumpets' dreadful bray,
And grating shock of wrathful iron arms,
Might from our quiet confines fright fair peace,
And make us wade even in our kindred's blood;—
Therefore, we banish you our territories:——
You, cousin Hereford, upon pain of death,
Till twice five summers have enrich'd our fields,
Shall not regreet our fair dominions,
But tread the stranger paths of banishment.

Boling. Your will be done: This must my comfort be,——
That sun, that warms you here, shall shine on me;
And those his golden beams, to you here lent,
Shall point on me, and gild my banishment.

K. Rich. Norfolk, for thee remains a heavier doom,
Which I with some unwillingness pronounce:
The fly-slow[5] hours shall not determinate
The dateless limit of thy dear exile;—
The hopeless word[6] of—never to return
Breathe I against thee, upon pain of life.

Nor. A heavy sentence, my most sovereign liege,
And all unlook'd for from your highness' mouth:
A dearer merit;[7] not so deep a maim
As to be cast forth in the common air,
Have I deserved at your highness' hand.
The language I have learn'd these forty years,
My native English, now I must forego:
And now my tongue's use is to me no more,
Than an unstringed viol or a harp:
Or like a cunning instrument cas'd up,
Or, being open, put into his hands
That knows no touch to tune the harmony.
Within my mouth you have engaol'd my tongue,
Doubly portcullis'd, with my teeth, and lips:
And dull, unfeeling, barren ignorance
Is made my gaoler to attend on me.
I am too old to fawn upon a nurse,
Too far in years to be a pupil now;
What is thy sentence then, but speechless death,
Which robs my tongue from breathing native breath?

K. Rich. It boots thee not to be compassionate;[8]
After our sentence plaining comes too late.

Nor. Then thus I turn me from my country's light,
To dwell in solemn shades of endless night. [*Retiring.*

---

1 To *jest* in old language sometimes signified *to play a part in a masque.*

2 A *warder* was a kind of truncheon or staff carried by persons who presided at these single combats; the throwing down of which seems to have been a solemn act of prohibition to stay proceedings. A different movement of the warder had an opposite effect. In Drayton's Battle of Agincourt, Erpingham is represented throwing it up as a signal for a charge.

3 Capel's copy of the quarto edition of this play reads 'Of *cruel* wounds,' &c. Malone's copy of the same edition, and all the other editions, read 'Of *civil* wounds,' &c.

4 The five lines in brackets are omitted in the folio.

5 The old copies read '*sly-slow* hours.' Pope reads '*fly-slow* hours,' which has been admitted into the text, and conveys an image highly beautiful and just. It is however remarkable that Pope, in the fourth book of his Essay on Man, v 226, has employed the epithet which, in the present instance, he has rejected:—
'All *sly-slow* things with circumspective eyes.'

6 *Word,* for *sentence;* any short phrase was called a *word.* Thus Ascham, in a Letter to Queen Elizabeth, 'Saving that one unpleasaunte *word* in that Patent, called "*Duringe pleasure,*" turned me after to great displeasure.'—*Conway Papers.*

7 As Shakspeare used *merit,* in this place, in the sense of *reward,* he frequently uses the word *meed,* which properly signifies *reward,* to express *merit.*

8 *Compassionate* is apparently here used in the sense of *complaining, plaintive;* but no other instance of the word in this sense has occurred to the commentators. May it not be an error of the press, for '*so passionate?*' which would give the required meaning to the passage; *passionate* being frequently used for *to express passion* or *grief, to complain.* 'Now leave we this amorous hermit *to passionate* and *playne* his mis fortune.'—*Palace of Pleasure,* vol. ii. Ll. 5.

K. Rich. Return again, and take an oath with thee.
Lay on our royal sword your banish'd hands;
Swear by the duty that you owe to heaven
(Our part therein we banish with yourselves,)
To keep the oath that we administer:—
You never shall (so help you truth and heaven!)
Embrace each other's love in banishment;
Nor never look upon each other's face;
Nor never write, regreet, nor reconcile
This lowering tempest of your home-bred hate;
Nor never by advised[1] purpose meet,
To plot, contrive, or complot any ill,
'Gainst us, our state, our subjects, or our land.
Boling. I swear.
Nor. And I, to keep all this.
Boling. Norfolk, so far as to mine enemy;[2]—
By this time, had the king permitted us,
One of our souls had wander'd in the air,
Banish'd this frail sepulchre of our flesh,
As now our flesh is banish'd from this land:
Confess thy treasons, ere thou fly the realm;
Since thou hast far to go, bear not along
The clogging burden of a guilty soul.
Nor. No, Bolingbroke; if ever I were traitor,
My name be blotted from the book of life,
And I from heaven banish'd, as from hence!
But what thou art, heaven, thou, and I do know;
And all too soon, I fear, the king shall rue.—
Farewell, my liege:—Now no way can I stray;
Save back to England, all the world's my way.
[*Exit.*[3]
K. Rich. Uncle, even in the glasses of thine eyes
I see thy grieved heart: thy sad aspect
Hath from the number of his banish'd years
Pluck'd four away;—Six frozen winters spent,
Return [*To* BOLING.] with welcome home from banishment.
Boling. How long a time lies in one little word!
Four lagging winters, and four wanton springs,
End in a word; Such is the breath of kings.
Gaunt. I thank my liege, that, in regard of me,
He shortens four years of my son's exile:
But little vantage shall I reap thereby;
For, ere the six years, that he hath to spend,
Can change their moons, and bring their times about,
My oil-dried lamp, and time-bewasted light,
Shall be extinct with age, and endless night;
My inch of taper will be burnt and done,
And blindfold death not let me see my son.
K. Rich. Why, uncle, thou hast many years to live.
Gaunt. But not a minute, king, that thou canst give:
Shorten my days thou canst with sullen sorrow,
And pluck nights from me, but not lend a morrow:[4]
Thou canst help time to furrow me with age,
But stop no wrinkle in his pilgrimage;
Thy word is current with him for my death;
But, dead, thy kingdom cannot buy my breath.
K. Rich. Thy son is banish'd upon good advice,[5]
Whereto thy tongue a party[6] verdict gave;
Why at our justice seem'st thou then to lower?
Gaunt. Things sweet to taste, prove in digestion sour.
You urg'd me as a judge; but I had rather,
You would have bid me argue like a father:—
O, had it been a stranger, not my child,
To smooth his fault I should have been more mild:[7]
A partial slander[8] sought I to avoid,
And in the sentence my own life destroy'd.
Alas, I look'd, when some of you should say
I was too strict, to make mine own away;
But you gave leave to my unwilling tongue,
Against my will, to do myself this wrong.
K. Rich. Cousin, farewell;—and, uncle, bid him so;
Six years we banish him, and he shall go.
[*Flourish. Exeunt* K. RICH. *and Train.*
Aum. Cousin, farewell; what presence must not know,
From where you do remain, let paper show.
Mar. My lord, no leave take I: for I will ride,
As far as land will let me, by your side.
Gaunt. O, to what purpose dost thou hoard thy words,
That thou return'st no greeting to thy friends?
Boling. I have too few to take my leave of you,
When the tongue's office should be prodigal
To breathe the abundant dolour of the heart.
Gaunt. Thy grief is but thy absence for a time.
Boling. Joy absent, grief is present for that time.
Gaunt. What is six winters? they are quickly gone.
Boling. To men in joy; but grief makes one hour ten.
Gaunt. Call it a travel that thou tak'st for pleasure.
Boling. My heart will sigh, when I miscall it so.
Which finds it an enforced pilgrimage.
Gaunt. The sullen passage of thy weary steps
Esteem a foil, wherein thou art to set
The precious jewel of thy home-return.
Boling. Nay, rather, every tedious stride make[9]
Will but remember me, what a deal of world
I wander from the jewels that I love.
Must I not serve a long apprenticehood
To foreign passages; and in the end,
Having my freedom, boast of nothing else,
But that I was a journeyman to grief?
Gaunt. All places that the eye of heaven[10] visits
Are to a wise man ports and happy havens
Teach thy necessity to reason thus;
There is no virtue like necessity.
Think not the king did banish thee;
But thou the king:[11] Woe doth the heavier sit,
Where it perceives it is but faintly borne.
Go, say—I sent thee forth to purchase honour
And not—the king exil'd thee: or suppose,
Devouring pestilence hangs in our air,
And thou art flying to a fresher clime.
Look, what thy soul holds dear, imagine it
To lie that way thou go'st, not whence thou com'st:
Suppose the singing birds, musicians;
The grass whereon thou tread'st, the presence strew'd;[12]
The flowers, fair ladies; and thy steps, no more
Than a delightful measure, or a dance:
For gnarling sorrow hath less power to bite
The man that mocks at it, and sets it light.

---

1 Premeditated, deliberated.

2 The first folio reads 'So *fare*.' This line seems to be addressed by way of caution to Mowbray, lest he should think that Bolingbroke was about to conciliate him.

3 The duke of Norfolk went to Venice, 'where for thought and melancholy he deceased.'—*Holinshed.*

4 It is a matter of very melancholy consideration, that all human advantages confer more power of doing evil than good.

5 Consideration.

6 Had a part or share in it.

7 This couplet is wanting in the folio.

8 i. e. the reproach of partiality.

9 This speech and that which follows are not in the folio.

10 i. e. the sun

11 Shakspeare probably remembered Euphues' exhortation to Botonio to take his exile patiently. 'Nature hath given to man a country no more than she hath a house, or lands, or livings. Socrates would neither call himself an Athenian, neither a Grecian, but a citizen of the world. Plato would never accompt him banished, that had the sunne, fire, ayre, water, and earth, that he had before; where he felt the winter's blast, and the summer's blaze; where the same sunne and same moone shined; whereby he noted that *every place was a country to a wise man, and all parts a palace to a quiet mind.*—When it was cast in Diogenes' teeth, that the Sinoponetes had banished him from Pontus; Yea, said he, I them of Diogenes.'

12 We have other allusions to the practice of strewing rushes over the floor of the *presence chamber* in Shakspeare.

Boling. O, who can hold a fire in his hand,[1]
By thinking on the frosty Caucasus?
Or cloy the hungry edge of appetite,
By bare imagination of a feast?
Or wallow naked in December snow,
By thinking on fantastic summer's heat?
O, no! the apprehension of the good,
Gives but the greater feeling to the worse:
Fell sorrow's tooth doth never rankle more,
Than when it bites, but lanceth not the sore.
Gaunt. Come, come, my son, I'll bring thee on thy way:
Had I thy youth, and cause, I would not stay.
Boling. Then, England's ground, farewell; sweet soil, adieu;
My mother, and my nurse, that bears me yet!
Where'er I wander, boast of this I can,——
Though banish'd, yet a trueborn Englishman.[2]
[*Exeunt.*

SCENE IV. *The same. A Room in the* King's *Castle. Enter* KING RICHARD, BAGOT, *and* GREEN; AUMERLE *following.*

K. Rich. We did observe.[3]—Cousin Aumerle,
How far brought you high Hereford on his way?
Aum. I brought high Hereford, if you call him so,
But to the next highway, and there I left him.
K. Rich. And, say, what store of parting tears were shed?
Aum. 'Faith, none by[4] me: except the north-east wind,
Which then blew bitterly against our faces,
Awak'd the sleeping rheum; and so, by chance,
Did grace our hollow parting with a tear.
K. Rich. What said our cousin, when you parted with him?
Aum. Farewell:
And, for my heart disdained that my tongue
Should so profane the word, that taught me craft
To counterfeit oppression of such grief,
That words seemed buried in my sorrow's grave.
Marry, would the word farewell have lengthen'd hours,
And added years to his short banishment,
He should have had a volume of farewells;
But, since it would not, he had none of me.
K. Rich. He is our cousin, cousin; but 'tis doubt,
When time shall call him home from banishment,
Whether our kinsman come to see his friends.
Ourself, and Bushy,[5] Bagot here, and Green,
Observ'd his courtship to the common people:—
How he did seem to dive into their hearts,
With humble and familiar courtesy;
What reverence he did throw away on slaves;
Wooing poor craftsmen, with the craft of smiles,
And patient underbearing of his fortune,
As 'twere, to banish their affects with him.
Off goes his bonnet to an oyster-wench;
A brace of draymen bid—God speed him well,
And had the tribute of his supple knee,[6]
With—*Thanks, my countrymen, my loving friends;*
As were our England in reversion his,
And he our subjects' next degree in hope.[7]
Green. Well, he is gone; and with him go these thoughts.
Now for the rebels, which stand out in Ireland
Expedient[8] manage must be made, my liege,
Ere further leisure yield them further means
For their advantage, and your highness' loss.
K. Rich. We will ourself in person to this war
And, for[9] our coffers—with too great a court,
And liberal largess—are grown somewhat light,
We are enforc'd to farm our royal realm;
The revenue whereof shall furnish us
For our affairs in hand: If that come short,
Our substitutes at home shall have blank charters;
Whereto, when they shall know what men are rich,
They shall subscribe them for large sums of gold,
And send them after to supply our wants;
For we will make for Ireland presently.

Enter BUSHY.

Bushy, what news?
Bushy. Old John of Gaunt is grievous sick, my lord;
Suddenly taken; and hath sent post-haste,
To entreat your majesty to visit him.
K. Rich. Where lies he?
Bushy. At Ely-house.
K. Rich. Now put it, heaven, in his physician's mind,
To help him to his grave immediately!
The lining of his coffers shall make coats
To deck our soldiers for these Irish wars.—
Come, gentlemen, let's all go visit him:
'Pray God, we may make haste, and come too late.
[*Exeunt.*

ACT II.

SCENE I. London. *A Room in Ely-house.* GAUNT *on a Couch; the* DUKE OF YORK,[10] *and others standing by him.*

Gaunt. Will the king come? that I may breathe my last
In wholesome counsel to his unstaied youth.
York. Vex not yourself, nor strive not with your breath;
For all in vain comes counsel to his ear.
Gaunt. O, but they say, the tongues of dying men
Enforce attention, like deep harmony:
Where words are scarce, they are seldom spent in vain.
For they breathe truth, that breathe their words in pain.
He, that no more must say, is listen'd more
Than they whom youth and ease have taught to glose;[11]
More are men's ends mark'd, than their lives before:
The setting sun, and music at the close,[12]
As the last taste of sweets, is sweetest last;
Writ in remembrance, more than things long past:

1 There is a passage resembling this in the fifth book of Cicero's Tusculan Questions, which were translated and published by John Dolman, in 1561. There is also something which might serve for a hint in Euphues.

2 Dr. Johnson thought that the First Act should end here.

3 The king here addressed Green and Bagot, who, we may suppose, had been talking to him of Bolingbroke's 'courtship to the common people,' at the time of his departure. 'Yes,' says Richard, 'we did observe it.'

4 The first folio and the quarto of 1597 read ''Faith, none *for* me.' The emendation was made in the folio, 1632.

5 The earlier quarto copies read, 'Ourself and Bushy,' and no more. The folio:
'Ourself, and Bushy here, Bagot, and Greene.'
In the quarto, the stage-direction says, 'Enter the King, with *Bushie*,' &c.; but in the folio, 'Enter the King, Aumerle,' &c. because it was observed that Bushy comes in afterward. On this account we have adopted a transposition made in the quarto of 1634.

6 To illustrate this, it should be remembered that *courtesying* (the act of reverence now confined to women) was anciently practised by men.

7 'Spes altera Romæ.'—*Virg.*

8 Shakspeare often uses *expedient* for *expeditious*, but here its ordinary signification of *fit, proper*, will suit the context equally well.

9 i. e. cause.

10 Edmond duke of York was the fifth son of Edward III. and was born, in 1441, at Langley, near St. Albans, Herts; from whence he had his surname. 'He was of an indolent disposition, a lover of pleasure, and averse to business; easily prevailed upon to lie still and consult his own quiet, and never acting with spirit upon any occasion.'—*Lowth's William of Wykeham*, p. 205.

11 To insinuate, to lie, to flatter.

12 'This I suppose to be a musical term,' says Steevens So in Lingua, 1607:—
'I dare engage my ears the *close* will jar.'
Surely this is a supererogatory conclusion. Shakspeare evidently means no more than that music is sweetest in its close, or when the last sweet sounds rest on the de

Though Richard my life's counsel would not hear,
My death's sad tale may yet undeaf his ear.

York. No; it is stopp'd with other flattering sounds,
As, praises of his state: then, there are found
Lascivious metres; to whose venom sound
The open ear of youth doth always listen:
Report of fashions in proud Italy;[1]
Whose manners still our tardy apish nation
Limps after, in base imitation,
Where doth the world thrust forth a vanity,
(So it be new, there's no respect how vile,)
That is not quickly buzz'd into his ears?
Then all too late comes counsel to be heard,
Where will doth mutiny with wit's regard.[2]
Direct not him, whose way himself will choose;
'Tis breath thou lack'st, and that breath wilt thou lose.

Gaunt. Methinks, I am a prophet new inspir'd;
And thus, expiring, do foretell of him:
His rash[3] fierce blaze of riot cannot last;
For violent fires soon burn out themselves:
Small showers last long, but sudden storms are short;
He tires betimes, that spurs too fast betimes;
With eager feeding, food doth choke the feeder:
Light vanity, insatiate cormorant,
Consuming means, soon preys upon itself.
This royal throne of kings, this sceptred isle,
This earth of majesty, this seat of Mars,
This other Eden, demi-paradise;
This fortress, built by nature for herself,
Against infection,[4] and the hand of war;
This happy breed of men, this little world;
This precious stone set in the silver sea,
Which serves it in the office of a wall,
Or as a moat defensive to a house,
Against the envy of less happier lands;
This blessed plot, this earth, this realm, this England,
This nurse, this teeming womb of royal kings,
Fear'd by their breed,[5] and famous by their birth,
Renowned for their deeds as far from home,
(For Christian service, and true chivalry,)
As is the sepulchre in stubborn Jewry,
Of the world's ransom, blessed Mary's son:
This land of such dear souls, this dear dear land,
Dear for her reputation through the world,
Is now leas'd out, (I die pronouncing it,)
Like to a tenement, or pelting[6] farm:
England, bound in with the triumphant sea,
Whose rocky shore beats back the envious siege
Of watery Neptune, is now bound in with shame,
With inky blots, and rotten parchment bonds;
That England, that was wont to conquer others,
Hath made a shameful conquest of itself:
O, would the scandal vanish with my life,
How happy then were my ensuing death!

Enter KING RICHARD, *and* Queen;[7] AUMERLE, BUSHY, GREEN, BAGOT, ROSS,[8] *and* WILLOUGHBY.[9]

York. The king is come: deal mildly with his youth;
For young hot colts, being rag'd,[10] do rage the more.

Queen. How fares our noble uncle, Lancaster?

K. Rich. What comfort, man? How is't with aged Gaunt?

Gaunt. O, how that name befits my composition!
Old Gaunt, indeed; and gaunt[11] in being old:
Within me grief hath kept a tedious fast;
And who abstains from meat, that is not gaunt?
For sleeping England long time have I watch'd;
Watching breeds leanness, leanness is all gaunt:
The pleasure, that some fathers feed upon,
Is my strict fast, I mean—my children's looks;
And, therein fasting, hast thou made me gaunt
Gaunt am I for the grave, gaunt as a grave,
Whose hollow womb inhabits nought but bones.

K. Rich. Can sick men play so nicely with their names?

Gaunt. No, misery makes sport to mock itself.
Since thou dost seek to kill my name in me,
I mock my name, great king, to flatter thee.

K. Rich. Should dying men flatter with those that live?

Gaunt. No, no; men living flatter those that die

K. Rich. Thou, now a dying, say'st—thou flatter'st me.

Gaunt. O, no; thou diest, though I the sicker be

K. Rich. I am in health, I breathe, and see thee ill.

Gaunt. Now, He that made me, knows I see thee ill;
Ill in myself to see, and in thee seeing ill.
Thy deathbed is no lesser than thy land,
Wherein thou liest in reputation sick:
And thou, too careless patient as thou art,
Committ'st thy anointed body to the cure
Of those physicians that first wounded thee:
A thousand flatterers sit within thy crown,
Whose compass is no bigger than thy head;
And yet, incaged in so small a verge,
The waste is no whit lesser than thy land;
O, had thy grandsire, with a prophet's eye,
Seen how his son's son should destroy his sons,
From forth thy reach he would have laid thy shame,
Deposing thee before thou wert possess'd,
Which art possess'd[12] now to depose thyself.
Why, cousin, wert thou regent of the world,
It were a shame to let this land by lease:
But, for thy world, enjoying but this land,
Is it not more than shame, to shame it so!
Landlord of England art thou now, not king
Thy state of law is bondslave to the law;[13]
And thou——

K. Rich. ——a lunatic lean-witted fool,
Presuming on an ague's privilege,

---

lighted ear. But Steevens's soul, like that of his great coadjutor, does not seem to have been attuned to harmony. The context might, however, have shown him how superfluous his supposition was; and I have to apologize for diverting the attention of the reader from this beautiful passage for a moment.

1 The poet has charged the times of King Richard II. with a folly not perhaps known then, but very frequent in his own time, and much lamented by the wisest of our ancestors.

2 Where the will rebels against the notices of the understanding.

3 i. e hasty, violent.

4 Johnson raised a doubt whether we should not read *invasion* here. Farmer and Malone, upon the authority of a misprint in Allot's England's Parnassus, where this passage is quoted, 'Against *intestion*,' &c. propose to read *infestion*, a word of their own coinage. Malone's long note proves nothing: he thinks that we could receive no other *infection* from abroad than the *plague*, but it is evident that the poet may allude to the *infection* of vicious manners and customs. It is true that *infestation* was in use for 'a troubling, molesting, or disturbing:' but as all the old copies read *infection*, there seems to be no sufficient reason for disturbing the text.

5 i. e. by *reason of* their breed. The quarto of 1598 reads thus:—

'Fear'd by their breed, and famous *for* their birth.'

6 'In this 22d yeare of King Richard, the common fame ranne that the king had *letten to farme* the realme unto Sir William Scrope, earle of Wiltshire, and then treasurer of England, to Syr John Bushey, Sir John Bagot, and Sir Henry Greene, Knightes.'—*Fabian.* *Pelting* is paltry, pitiful, petty.

7 Shakspeare has deviated from historical truth in the introduction of Richard's queen as a woman; for Anne, his first wife, was dead before the period at which the commencement of the play is laid; and Isabella, his second wife, was a child at the time of his death.

8 i. e. William Lord Ross, of Hamlake, afterwards lord treasurer to Henry IV.

9 William Lord Willoughby, of Eresby.

10 Ritson proposes to read:—

'—— being *rein'd*, do rage the more.'

11 Meagre, thin. 12 Mad.

13 'Thy legal state, that rank in the state and these large desmesnes, which the constitution allotted thee, are now bondslave to the law; being subject to the same legal restrictions as every ordinary pelting farm that has been let on lease.'

Dar'st with thy frozen admonition
Make pale our cheek; chasing the royal blood,
With fury, from his native residence.
Now by my seat's right royal majesty,
Wert thou not brother to great Edward's son,
This tongue that runs so roundly in thy head,
Should run thy head from thy unreverent shoulders.
Gaunt. O, spare me not, my brother Edward's son,
For that I was his father Edward's son;
That blood already, like the pelican,
Hast thou tapp'd out, and drunkenly carous'd:
My brother Gloster, plain well-meaning soul,
(Whom fair befall in heaven 'mongst happy souls!)
May be a precedent and witness good,
That thou respect'st not spilling Edward's blood:
Join with the present sickness that I have,
And thy unkindness be like crooked age,
To crop at once a too-long wither'd flower.
Live in thy shame, but die not shame with thee!—
These words hereafter thy tormentors be—
Convey me to my bed, then to my grave:
Love they[1] to live, that love and honour have.
[*Exit, borne out by his* Attendants.
K. Rich. And let them die, that age and sullens have;
For both hast thou, and both become the grave.
York. 'Beseech your majesty, impute his words
To wayward sickliness and age in him:
He loves you, on my life, and holds you dear
As Harry duke of Hereford, were he here.
K. Rich. Right; you say true: as Hereford's love, so his:
As theirs, so mine; and all be as it is.
Enter NORTHUMBERLAND.
North. My liege, old Gaunt commends him to your majesty.
K. Rich. What says he?
North. Nay, nothing; all is said:
His tongue is now a stringless instrument;
Words, life, and all, old Lancaster hath spent.
York. Be York the next that must be bankrupt so!
Though death be poor, it ends a mortal woe.
K. Rich. The ripest fruit first falls, and so doth he;
His time is spent, our pilgrimage must be:[2]
So much for that.——Now for our Irish wars:
We must supplant those rough rug-headed kernes;[3]
Which live like venom, where no venom else,
But only they, hath privilege to live.[4]
And for these great affairs do ask some charge,
Towards our assistance, we do seize to us
The plate, coin, revenues, and moveables,
Whereof our uncle Gaunt did stand possess'd.
York. How long shall I be patient? Ah, how long
Shall tender duty make me suffer wrong?
Not Gloster's death, nor Hereford's banishment,
Not Gaunt's rebukes, nor England's private wrongs,
Nor the prevention of poor Bolingbroke
About his marriage,[5] nor my own disgrace,
Have ever made me sour my patient cheek,
Or bend one wrinkle on my sovereign's face.—
I am the last of noble Edward's sons,
Of whom thy father, prince of Wales, was first;
In war, was never lion rag'd more fierce,
In peace was never gentle lamb more mild,
Than was that young and princely gentleman:
His face thou hast, for even so look'd he,
Accomplish'd with the number of thy hours;[6]
But, when he frown'd, it was against the French,
And not against his friends: his noble hand
Did win what he did spend, and spent not that
Which his triumphant father's hand had won:
His hands were guilty of no kindred's blood,
But bloody with the enemies of his kin.
O, Richard! York is too far gone with grief,
Or else he never would compare between.
K. Rich. Why, uncle, what's the matter?
York. O, my liege
Pardon me, if you please; if not, I, pleas'd
Not to be pardon'd, am content withal.
Seek you to seize, and gripe into your hands,
The royalties and rights of banish'd Hereford?
Is not Gaunt dead? and doth not Hereford live?
Was not Gaunt just? and is not Harry true?
Did not the one deserve to have an heir?
Is not his heir a well-deserving son?
Take Hereford's rights away, and take from time
His charters, and his customary rights;
Let not to-morrow then ensue to-day;
Be not thyself, for how art thou a king,
But by fair sequence and succession?
Now, afore God (God forbid, I say true!)
If you do wrongfully seize Hereford's rights,
Call in the letters patents that he hath
By his attornies-general to sue
His livery,[7] and deny his offer'd homage,
You pluck a thousand dangers on your head,
You lose a thousand well-disposed hearts,
And prick my tender patience to those thoughts
Which honour and allegiance cannot think.
K. Rich. Think what you will; we seize into our hands
His plate, his goods, his money, and his lands.
York. I'll not be by the while: My liege, farewell:
What will ensue hereof, there's none can tell;
But by bad courses may be understood,
That their events can never fall out good. [*Exit.*
K. Rich. Go, Bushy, to the earl of Wiltshire straight;
Bid him repair to us to Ely-house,
To see this business: To-morrow next
We will for Ireland; and 'tis time, I trow;
And we create, in absence of ourself,
Our uncle York lord governor of England,
For he is just, and always lov'd us well.—
Come on, our queen: to-morrow must we part
Be merry, for our time of stay is short. [*Flourish*
[*Exeunt,* King, Queen, BUSHY, AUMERLE GREEN, *and* BAGOT.
North. Well, lords, the duke of Lancaster is dead
Ross. And living too; for now his son is duke.
Willo. Barely in title, not in revenue.
North. Richly in both, if justice had her right.
Ross. My heart is great; but it must break with silence,
Ere't be disburden'd with a liberal[8] tongue.
North. Nay, speak thy mind; and let him ne'er speak more,
That speaks thy words again, to do thee harm!
Willo. Tends that thou would'st speak, to the duke of Hereford?
If it be so, out with it boldly, man;
Quick is mine ear to hear of good towards him
Ross. No good at all, that I can do for him;
Unless you call it good to pity him,
Bereft and gelded of his patrimony.
North. Now, afore heaven, 'tis shame, such wrongs are borne,
In him a royal prince, and many more
Of noble blood in this declining land.
The king is not himself, but basely led

1 i. e. *let them love* to live, &c.

2 That is, 'our pilgrimage *is yet to come.*'

3 *Kernes* were Irish peasantry, serving as light-armed foot soldiers. Shakspeare makes York say, in the second part of King Henry VI. that Cade, when in Ireland, used to disguise himself as a *shag-haired crafty kerne.* The kerne is an ordinary foot soldier, according to Stanihurst; kerne (*kigheyren*) signifieth *a shower of hell*, because they are taken for no better than *rake-hells*, or the devil's *black-garde.*'---*Description of Ireland*, ch. 8, fol. 28.

4 Alluding to the idea that no venomous reptiles live in Ireland.

5 When the duke of Hereford went into France after his banishment, he was honourably entertained at that court, and would have obtained in marriage the only daughter of the duke of Berry, uncle to the French king had not Richard prevented the match.

6 i. e. when he was of thy age.

7 On the death of every person who held by knight's service, his heir, if under age, became a ward of the king's; but if of age, he had a right to sue out a writ of *ouster le main*, i. e. *livery*, that the king's hand might be taken off, and the land *delivered* to him. To '*deny his offer'd homage*' was to refuse to admit the homage by which he was to hold his lands.

8 Free.

By flatterers; and what they will inform,
Merely in hate 'gainst any of us all,
That will the king severely prosecute
'Gainst us, our lives, our children, and our heirs.
Ross. The commons hath he pill'd[1] with grievous taxes,
And quite lost their hearts: the nobles hath he fin'd
For ancient quarrels, and quite lost their hearts.
Willo. And daily new exactions are devis'd;
As blanks,[2] benevolences, and I wot not what:
But what, o' God's name, doth become of this?
North. Wars have not wasted it, for warr'd he hath not,
But basely yielded upon compromise
That which his ancestors achiev'd with blows:
More hath he spent in peace, than they in wars.
Ross. The earl of Wiltshire hath the realm in farm.
Willo. The king's grown bankrupt, like a broken man.
North. Reproach, and dissolution, hangeth over him.
Ross. He hath not money for these Irish wars,
His burdenous taxations notwithstanding,
But by the robbing of the banish'd duke.
North. His noble kinsman; most degenerate king!
But, lords, we hear this fearful tempest sing,[3]
Yet seek no shelter to avoid the storm:
We see the wind sit sore upon our sails,
And yet we strike not, but securely perish.[4]
Ross. We see the very wreck that we must suffer;
And unavoided is the danger now,
For suffering so the causes of our wreck.
North. Not so; even through the hollow eyes of death,
I spy life peering; but I dare not say
How near the tidings of our comfort is.
Willo. Nay, let us share thy thoughts, as thou dost ours.
Ross. Be confident to speak, Northumberland:
We three are but thyself; and, speaking so,
Thy words are but as thoughts; therefore, be bold.
North. Then thus:—I have from Port le Blanc, a bay
In Brittany, receiv'd intelligence,
That Harry Hereford, Reignold Lord Cobham,
[The son of Richard earl of Arundel,][5]
That late broke from the duke of Exeter,
His brother, archbishop late of Canterbury,
Sir Thomas Erpingham, Sir John Ramston,
Sir John Norbery, Sir Robert Waterton, and Francis Quoint,—
All these well furnish'd by the duke of Bretagne,
With eight tall[6] ships, three thousand men of war,
Are making hither with all due expedience,[7]
And shortly mean to touch our northern shore:
Perhaps, they had ere this; but that they stay
The first departing of the king for Ireland.
If then we shall shake off our slavish yoke,
Imp[8] out our drooping country's broken wing,
Redeem from broking pawn the blemish'd crown,
Wipe off the dust that hides our sceptre's gilt,[9]
And make high majesty look like itself,
Away, with me, in post to Ravenspurg:
But if you faint, as fearing to do so,
Stay, and be secret, and myself will go.
Ross. To horse, to horse! urge doubts to them that fear.
Willo. Hold out my horse, and I will first be there. [*Exeunt.*

SCENE II. *The same. A Room in the Palace.*

Enter QUEEN, BUSHY, *and* BAGOT.

Bushy. Madam, your majesty is too much sad:
You promis'd, when you parted with the king,
To lay aside life-harming heaviness,
And entertain a cheerful disposition.
Queen. To please the king, I did; to please myself,
I cannot do it; yet I know no cause
Why I should welcome such a guest as grief,
Save bidding farewell to so sweet a guest
As my sweet Richard: Yet, again, methinks,
Some unborn sorrow, ripe in fortune's womb,
Is coming towards me; and my inward soul
With nothing trembles: at something it grieves,
More than with parting from my lord the king.
Bushy. Each substance of a grief hath twenty shadows,
Which show like grief itself, but are not so:
For sorrow's eye, glazed with blinding tears,
Divides one thing entire to many objects;
Like perspectives,[10] which, rightly gaz'd upon,
Show nothing but confusion; ey'd awry,
Distinguish form: so your sweet majesty
Looking awry upon your lord's departure,
Finds shapes of grief, more than himself, to wail;
Which, look'd on as it is, is nought but shadows
Of what it is not. Then, thrice-gracious queen,
More than your lord's departure weep not; more's not seen:
Or if it be, 'tis with false sorrow's eye,
Which, for things true, weeps things imaginary.
Queen. It may be so; but yet my inward soul
Persuades me, it is otherwise: Howe'er it be,
I cannot but be sad; so heavy sad,
As,—though, in thinking, on no thought I think,[11]—
Makes me with heavy nothing faint and shrink.
Bushy. 'Tis nothing but conceit,[12] my gracious lady.
Queen. 'Tis nothing less: conceit is still deriv'd
From some fore-father grief; mine is not so;
For nothing hath begot my something grief;
Or something hath the nothing that I grieve:
'Tis in reversion that I do possess;
But what it is, that is not yet known; what
I cannot name; 'tis nameless woe, I wot.

---

1 Pillaged.

2 Stow records that Richard II. 'compelled all the religious, gentlemen, and commons, to set their seales to *blankes*, to the end he might, if it pleased him, oppress them severally, or all at once; some of the commons paid him 1000 marks, some 1000 pounds,' &c.

3 So in the Tempest:—
'——— another *storm* brewing, I *hear it sing* in the wind.'

4 'And yet we strike not *our sails*, but perish by *too great confidence in our security*:' this is another Latinism. *Securely* is used in the sense of *securus*.

5 The line in brackets, which was necessary to complete the sense, has been supplied upon the authority of Holinshed. Something of a similar import must have been omitted by accident in the old copies.

6 Stout. 7 Expedition.

8 When the wing feathers of a hawk were dropped or forced out by any accident, it was usual to supply as many as were deficient. This operation was called 'to *imp* a hawk.' It is often used metaphorically, as in this instance. The word is said to come from the Saxon *impan*, to graft, or inoculate.

9 Gilding.

10 It has been shown in a former note that *perspective* meant optical glasses, to assist the sight in any way. Mr. Henley says that 'the perspectives here mentioned were round crystal glasses, the convex surface of which was cut into faces like those of the rose-diamond: the concave left uniformly smooth; which if placed as here represented, would exhibit the different appearances described by the poet.' But it may have reference to that kind of optical delusion called *anamorphosis*, which is a *perspective* projection of a picture, so that at one point of view it shall appear a confused mass, or different to what it really is, in another, an exact and regular representation. Sometimes it is made to appear confused to the naked eye, and regular when viewed in a *glass or mirror* of a certain form. 'A picture of a chancellor of France, presented to the common beholder a multitude of little faces; but if one did look at it through a *perspective*, there appeared only the single pourtraiture of the chancellor.'—*Humane Industry*, 1651.

11 The old copies have '*on* thinking,' which is an evident error: we should read, 'As though *in* thinking;' i. e. 'though musing, I have no idea of calamity.' The involuntary and unaccountable depression of the mind which every one has sometimes felt, is here very forcibly described.

12 Fanciful conception.

Enter GREEN.

Green. God save your majesty!—and well met, gentlemen:—
I hope, the king is not yet shipp'd for Ireland.
Queen. Why hop'st thou so? 'tis better hope, he is;
For his designs crave haste, his haste good hope;
Then wherefore dost thou hope, he is not shipp'd?
Green. That he, our hope, might have retir'd his power,[1]
And driven into despair an enemy's hope,
Who strongly hath set footing in this land:
The banish'd Bolingbroke repeals himself,
And with uplifted arms is safe arriv'd
At Ravenspurg.
Queen. Now, God in heaven forbid!
Green. O, madam, 'tis too true: and that is worse,—
The Lord Northumberland, his young son Henry Percy,
The lords of Ross, Beaumond, and Willoughby,
With all their powerful friends, are fled to him.
Bushy. Why have you not proclaim'd Northumberland,
And all the rest of the revolted faction, traitors?[2]
Green. We have: whereon the earl of Worcester
Hath broke his staff, resign'd his stewardship,
And all the household servants fled with him
To Bolingbroke.
Queen. So, Green, thou art the midwife to my woe,
And Bolingbroke my sorrow's dismal heir:[3]
Now hath my soul brought forth her prodigy;
And I, a gasping new-deliver'd mother,
Have woe to woe, sorrow to sorrow join'd.
Bushy. Despair not, madam.
Queen. Who shall hinder me?
I will despair, and be at enmity
With cozening hope; he is a flatterer,
A parasite, a keeper-back of death,
Who gently would dissolve the bands of life,
Which false hope lingers in extremity.

Enter YORK.

Green. Here comes the duke of York.
Queen. With signs of war about his aged neck;
O, full of careful business are his looks!——
Uncle,
For heaven's sake, speak comfortable words.
York. Should I do so, I should belie my thoughts:
Comfort's in heaven; and we are on the earth,
Where nothing lives but crosses, care, and grief.
Your husband he is gone to save far off,
Whilst others come to make him lose at home:
Here am I left to underprop his land;
Who, weak with age, cannot support myself:——
Now comes the sick hour that his surfeit made;
Now shall he try his friends that flatter'd him.

Enter a Servant.

Serv. My lord, your son was gone before I came.
York. He was?—Why, so!—go all which way it will!—
The nobles they are fled, the commons they are cold,
And will, I fear, revolt on Hereford's side.——
Sirrah, get thee to Plashy, to my sister Gloster;
Bid her send me presently a thousand pound:—
Hold, take my ring.
Serv. My lord, I had forgot to tell your lordship:
To-day, as I came by, I called there;
But I shall grieve you to report the rest.
York. What is it, knave?
Serv. An hour before I came, the duchess died.
York. God for his mercy! what a tide of woes
Comes rushing on this woeful land at once!
I know not what to do:—I would to God
(So my untruth[4] had not provok'd him to it,)
The king had cut off my head with my brother's.[5]—
What, are there no posts despatch'd for Ireland?—
How shall we do for money for these wars?—
Come, sister,[6]—cousin, I would say: pray, pardon me.—
Go, fellow [*To the* Servant.] get thee home, provide some carts,
And bring away the armour that is there.—
[*Exit* Servant.
Gentlemen, will you go muster men? if I know
How, or which way, to order these affairs,
Thus disorderly thrust into my hands,
Never believe me. Both are my kinsmen;
The one's my sovereign, whom both my oath
And duty bids defend; the other again,
Is my kinsman, whom the king hath wrong'd;
Whom conscience and my kindred bids to right.
Well, somewhat we must do.—Come, cousin, I'll
Dispose of you:—Gentlemen, go, muster up your men,
And meet me presently at Berkley-castle.
I should to Plashy too;——
But time will not permit:—All is uneven,
And every thing is left at six and seven.
[*Exeunt* YORK *and* Queen.
Bushy. The wind sits fair for news to go to Ireland,
But none returns. For us to levy power,
Proportionable to the enemy,
Is all impossible.
Green. Besides, our nearness to the king in love,
Is near the hate of those love not the king.
Bagot. And that's the wavering commons: for their love
Lies in their purses; and whoso empties them,
By so much fills their hearts with deadly hate.
Bushy. Wherein the king stands generally condemn'd.
Bagot. If judgment lie in them, then so do we,
Because we ever have been near the king.
Green. Well, I'll for refuge straight to Bristol Castle;
The earl of Wiltshire is already there.
Bushy. Thither will I with you: for little office
Will the hateful commons perform for us;
Except like curs to tear us all to pieces.—
Will you go along with us?
Bagot. No; I'll to Ireland to his majesty.
Farewell: if heart's presages be not vain,
We three here part, that ne'er shall meet again.
Bushy. That's as York thrives to beat back Bolingbroke.
Green. Alas, poor duke! the task he undertakes
Is—numb'ring sands, and drinking oceans dry;
Where one on his side fights, thousands will fly.
Bushy. Farewell at once; for once, for all, and ever.
Green. Well, we may meet again.
Bagot. I fear me, never.
[*Exeunt.*

SCENE III. *The Wilds in* Glostershire. *Enter* BOLINGBROKE *and* NORTHUMBERLAND, *with Forces.*

Boling. How far is it, my lord, to Berkley now?
North. Believe me, noble lord,
I am a stranger here in Glostershire.
These high wild hills, and rough uneven ways,

1 *Retir'd*, i. e. drawn it back; a French sense.
2 The first quarto, 1597, reads:—
'And all the rest of the revolted faction, traitors?'
The folio, and the quarto of 1598 and 1608:—
'And the rest *of the revolting* faction, traitors?'
3 The queen had said before, that 'some unborn sorrow, ripe in fortune's womb, was coming toward her.' She talks afterward of her unknown griefs 'being begotten;' she calls Green 'the midwife of her woe;' and then means to say in the same metaphorical style, that the arrival of Bolingbroke was the dismal offspring that her foreboding sorrow was big of; which she expresses by calling him her 'sorrow's dismal heir,' and explains more fully in the following line:—
'Now hath my soul brought forth her prodigy.'
4 Disloyalty, treachery.
5 Not one of York's brothers had his head cut off, either by the king or any one else. Gloster, to whose death he probably alludes, was smothered between two beds at Calais.
6 This is one of Shakspeare's touches of nature. York is talking to the queen, his cousin, but the recent death of his sister is uppermost in his mind.

Draw out our miles, and make them wearisome:
And yet your fair discourse hath been as sugar,
Making the hard way sweet and delectable.
But, I bethink me, what a weary way
From Ravenspurg to Cotswold, will be found
In Ross and Willoughby, wanting your company:
Which, I protest, hath very much beguil'd
The tediousness and process of my travel:
But theirs is sweeten'd with the hope to have
The present benefit which I possess:
And hope to joy,[1] is little less in joy,
Than hope enjoy'd: by this the weary lords
Shall make their way seem short; as mine hath done
By sight of what I have, your noble company.
Boling. Of much less value is my company,
Than your good words. But who comes here?

Enter HARRY PERCY.

North. It is my son, young Harry Percy,
Sent from my brother Worcester, whencesoever.—
Harry, how fares your uncle?
Percy. I had thought, my lord, to have learn'd his health of you.
North. Why, is he not with the queen?
Percy. No, my good lord; he hath forsook the court,
Broken his staff of office, and dispers'd
The household of the king.
North. What was his reason?
He was not so resolv'd, when last we spake together.
Percy. Because your lordship was proclaimed traitor.
But he, my lord, is gone to Ravenspurg,
To offer service to the duke of Hereford;
And sent me o'er by Berkley, to discover
What power the duke of York had levied there;
Then with direction to repair to Ravenspurg.
North. Have you forgot the duke of Hereford, boy?
Percy. No, my good lord; for that is not forgot,
Which ne'er I did remember: to my knowledge,
I never in my life did look on him.
North. Then learn to know him now; this is the duke.
Percy. My gracious lord, I tender you my service,
Such as it is, being tender, raw, and young;
Which elder days shall ripen and confirm
To more approved service and desert.
Boling. I thank thee, gentle Percy; and be sure,
I count myself in nothing else so happy,
As in a soul rememb'ring my good friends;
And, as my fortune ripens with thy love,
It shall be still thy true love's recompense:
My heart this covenant makes, my hand thus seals it.
North. How far is it to Berkley? And what stir
Keeps good old York there, with his men of war?
Percy. There stands the castle, by yon tuft of trees,
Mann'd with three hundred men, as I have heard:
And in it are the lords of York, Berkley, and Seymour;
None else of name, and noble estimate.

Enter ROSS *and* WILLOUGHBY.

North. Here come the lords of Ross and Willoughby,
Bloody with spurring, fiery-red with haste.
Boling. Welcome, my lords: I wot your love pursues
A banish'd traitor: all my treasury
Is yet but unfelt thanks, which, more enrich'd,
Shall be your love and labour's recompense.
Ross. Your presence makes us rich, most noble lord.
Willo. And far surmounts our labour to attain it.
Boling. Evermore thanks, the exchequer of the poor;
Which, till my infant fortune comes to years,
Stands for my bounty. But who comes here?

Enter BERKLEY.

North. It is my lord of Berkley, as I guess.
Berk. My lord of Hereford, my message is to you
Boling. My lord, my answer is—to Lancaster;[2]
And I am come to seek that name in England:
And I must find that title in your tongue,
Before I make reply to aught you say.
Berk. Mistake me not, my lord; 'tis not my meaning,
To raze one title of your honour out:[3]—
To you, my lord, I come (what lord you will,)
From the most gracious regent of this land,
The duke of York; to know, what pricks you on
To take advantage of the absent time,[4]
And fright our native peace with self-born arms.

Enter YORK, *attended.*

Boling. I shall not need transport my words by you;
Here comes his grace in person.—My noble uncle! [*Kneels.*
York. Show me thy humble heart, and not thy knee,
Whose duty is deceivable and false.
Boling. My gracious uncle!—
York. Tut, tut!
Grace me no grace, nor uncle me no uncle:[5]
I am no traitor's uncle; and that word—grace,
In an ungracious mouth, is but profane.
Why have those banish'd and forbidden legs
Dar'd once to touch a dust of England's ground?
But then more why;——Why have they dar'd to march
So many miles upon her peaceful bosom;
Frighting her pale-fac'd villages with war,
And ostentation of despised[6] arms?
Com'st thou because the anointed king is hence?
Why, foolish boy, the king is left behind,
And in my loyal bosom lies his power.
Were I but now the lord of such hot youth,
As when brave Gaunt, thy father, and myself,
Rescued the Black Prince, that young Mars of men,
From forth the ranks of many thousand French;
O, then, how quickly should this arm of mine,
Now prisoner to the palsy, chastise thee,
And minister correction to thy fault!
Boling. My gracious uncle, let me know my fault;
On what condition stands it, and wherein?
York. Even in condition of the worst degree,—
In gross rebellion, and detested treason:
Thou art a banish'd man, and here art come,
Before the expiration of thy time,
In braving arms against thy sovereign.
Boling. As I was banish'd, I was banish'd Hereford;
But as I come, I come for Lancaster,

---

1 To *joy* is here used as a verb; it is equivalent with *to rejoice*. '*To joy*, to clap hands, to rejoyce.' *Baret.* Shakspeare very frequently uses it in this sense.

2 'Your message, you say, is to my lord of *Hereford.* My answer is, It is not to him, it is to the *Duke of Lancaster.*'

3 'How the names of them which for capital crimes against majestie were *erased out* of the publicke records, tables, and registers, or forbidden to be borne by their posteritie, when their memory was damned, I could show at large.'—*Camden's Remaines*, 1605, p. 136.

4 Time of the king's absence.

5 In Romeo and Juliet we have the same kind of phraseology:—
'Thank me no thankings, nor proud me no prouds.'

6 Perhaps Shakspeare here uses *despised* for *hated* or *hateful* arms? Sir Thomas Hanmer changed it to *despiteful*, but the old copies all agree in reading *despised*. Shakspeare uses the word again in a singular sense in Othello, Act i. Sc. 1, where Brabantio exclaims upon the loss of his daughter:—
'——— what's to come of my *despised* time
Is nought but bitterness.'
It has been suggested that '*despised* is used to denote the general contempt in which the British held the French forces. The duke of Bretagne furnished Bolingbroke with three thousand French soldiers.'

And, noble uncle, I beseech your grace,
Look on my wrongs with an indifferent[1] eye:
You are my father, for, methinks, in you
I see old Gaunt alive; O, then, my father!
Will you permit that I shall stand condemn'd
A wand'ring vagabond; my rights and royalties
Pluck'd from my arms perforce, and given away
To upstart unthrifts? Wherefore was I born?
If that my cousin king be king of England,
It must be granted, I am duke of Lancaster.
You have a son, Aumerle, my noble kinsman;
Had you first died, and he been thus trod down,
He should have found his uncle Gaunt a father,
To rouse his wrongs,[2] and chase them to the bay.
I am denied to sue my livery[3] here,
And yet my letters patent give me leave:
My father's goods are all distrain'd, and sold;
And these, and all, are all amiss employ'd.
What would you have me do? I am a subject,
And challenge law: Attornies are denied me;
And therefore personally I lay my claim
To my inheritance of free descent.

North. The noble duke hath been too much abus'd.

Ross. It stands your grace upon[4] to do him right.

Willo. Base men by his endowments are made great.

York. My lords of England, let me tell you this,—
I have had feeling of my cousin's wrongs,
And labour'd all I could to do him right:
But in this kind to come, in braving arms,
Be his own carver, and cut out his way,
To find out right with wrong,—it may not be;
And you, that do abet him in this kind,
Cherish rebellion, and are rebels all.

North. The noble duke hath sworn, his coming is
But for his own: and, for the right of that,
We all have strongly sworn to give him aid;
And let him ne'er see joy, that breaks that oath.

York. Well, well, I see the issue of these arms;
I cannot mend it, I must needs confess,
Because my power is weak, and all ill left:
But, if I could,—by him that gave me life!—
I would attach you all, and make you stoop
Unto the sovereign mercy of the king;
But, since I cannot, be it known to you,
I do remain as neuter. So, fare you well;—
Unless you please to enter in the castle,
And there repose you for this night.

Boling. An offer, uncle, that we will accept.
But we must win your grace, to go with us
To Bristol Castle; which, they say, is held
By Bushy, Bagot, and their complices,
The caterpillars of the commonwealth,
Which I have sworn to weed, and pluck away.

York. It may be, I will go with you:—but yet I'll pause;
For I am loath to break our country's laws.
Nor friends, nor foes, to me welcome you are:
Things past redress, are now with me past care.[5]
[*Exeunt.*

SCENE IV.[6] *A Camp in* Wales. *Enter* Salisbury,[7] *and a* Captain.

Cap. My lord of Salisbury, we have staid ten days,
And hardly kept our countrymen together,
And yet we hear no tidings from the king;
Therefore we will disperse ourselves: farewell.

Sal. Stay yet another day, thou trusty Welshman:
The king reposeth all his confidence
In thee.

Cap. 'Tis thought, the king is dead: we will not stay.
The bay-trees in our country are all wither'd,[8]
And meteors fright the fixed stars of heaven;
The pale-fac'd moon looks bloody on the earth,
And lean-look'd prophets whisper fearful change;
Rich men look sad, and ruffians dance and leap,—
The one in fear to lose what they enjoy,
The other, to enjoy by rage and war:
These signs forerun the death or fall of kings.—
Farewell; our countrymen are gone and fled,
As well assur'd, Richard their king is dead. [*Exit.*

Sal. Ah, Richard! with the eyes of heavy mind,
I see thy glory, like a shooting star,
Fall to the base earth from the firmament!
Thy sun sets weeping in the lowly west,
Witnessing storms to come, woe, and unrest:
Thy friends are fled, to wait upon thy foes:
And crossly to thy good all fortune goes. [*Exit.*

ACT III.

SCENE I. Bolingbroke's *Camp at* Bristol. *Enter* Bolingbroke, York, Northumberland, Percy, Willoughby, Ross: *Officers behind with* Bushy *and* Green, *prisoners.*

Boling. Bring forth these men.—
Bushy and Green, I will not vex your souls
(Since presently your souls must part your bodies,)
With too much urging your pernicious lives,
For 'twere no charity: yet, to wash your blood
From off my hands, here, in the view of men,
I will unfold some causes of your deaths.
You have misled a prince, a royal king,
A happy gentleman in blood and lineaments,
By you unhappied and disfigur'd clean.[9]
You have, in manner, with your sinful hours,
Made a divorce betwixt his queen and him;
Broke the possession of a royal bed,[10]
And stain'd the beauty of a fair queen's cheeks
With tears drawn from her eyes by your foul wrongs.
Myself—a prince, by fortune of my birth,
Near to the king in blood; and near in love,
Till you did make him misinterpret me,——
Have stoop'd my neck under your injuries,
And sigh'd my English breath in foreign clouds,
Eating the bitter bread of banishment:
Whilst you have fed upon my signories,
Dispark'd[11] my parks, and fell'd my forest woods;
From my own windows torn my household coat,
Raz'd out my impress,[12] leaving me no sign,—

1 *Indifferent* is *impartial.* The instances of this use of the word among the poet's contemporaries are very numerous.

2 *Wrongs* is probably here used for *wrongers.*

3 See the former scene, p. 412, n. 7.

4 Steevens explains the phrase, '*It stands your grace upon,*' to mean, 'it is your interest; it is matter of consequence to you.' But hear Baret, 'The heyre is bound; the heyre ought, or it is the heyre's part to defend; *it standeth him upon;* or is in his charge. *Incumbit defensio mortis hæredi.*' The phrase is therefore equivalent to *it is incumbent upon your grace.*

5 '——— Things without remedy
Should be without regard.' *Macbeth.*

6 Johnson thought this scene had been by some accident transposed, and that it should stand as the *second* scene in the *third* act.

7 John Montacute, earl of Salisbury.

8 This enumeration of prodigies is in the highest degree poetical and striking. The poet received the hint from Holinshed: 'In this yeare, in a manner through out all the realme of Englande, old *baie trees* withered &c.' This, as it appears from T. Lupton's Syxt Booke of Notable Things, bl. 4to. was esteemed a bad omen. 'Neyther falling sicknes, neyther devyll, wyll infest or hurt one in that place whereas a *bay tree* is. The Romaynes call it the plant of the good angel, &c.' See also Evelyn's Sylva, 4to. 1776, p. 396.

9 i. e. quite, completely

10 There seems to be no authority for this. Isabel Richard's second queen, was but nine years old at this period; his first queen, Anne, died in 1392, and he was very fond of her.

11 To *dispark* signifies to divest a park of its name and character, by destroying the enclosures, and the vert (or whatever bears green leaves, whether wood or underwood,) and the beasts of the chase therein; laying it open.

12 The *impress* was a device, or motto. Ferne, in his Blazon of Gentry, 1588, observes that 'the arms, &c. of traitors and rebels may be defaced and removed wheresoever they are fixed or set.' For the punishment of a base knight see Spenser's Faerie Queen b. v. c. iii. st. 37.

Save men's opinions, and my living blood,—
To show the world I am a gentleman,
This, and much more, much more than twice all this,
Condemns you to the death:—See them deliver'd over
To execution and the hand of death.

Bushy. More welcome is the stroke of death to me,
Than Bolingbroke to England.—Lords, farewell.

Green. My comfort is,—that heaven will take our souls,
And plague injustice with the pains of hell.

Boling. My Lord Northumberland, see them despatch'd.

[*Exeunt* NORTHUMBERLAND, *and others, with Prisoners.*

Uncle, you say, the queen is at your house;
For heaven's sake, fairly let her be entreated:
Tell her, I send to her my kind commends,[1]
Take special care my greetings be deliver'd.

York. A gentleman of mine I have despatch'd
With letters of your love to her at large.

Boling. Thanks, gentle uncle.—Come, lords, away:
To fight with Glendower and his complices;
Awhile to work, and, after, holiday. [*Exeunt.*[2]

SCENE II. *The Coast of Wales. A Castle in view. Flourish: Drums and Trumpets. Enter* KING RICHARD, *Bishop of* Carlisle, AUMERLE, *and Soldiers.*

K. Rich. Barkloughly Castle call you[3] this at hand?

Aum. Yea, my lord: How brooks your grace the air,
After your late tossing on the breaking seas?

K. Rich. Needs must I like it well; I weep for joy,
To stand upon my kingdom once again.——
Dear earth, I do salute thee with my hand,
Though rebels wound thee with their horses' hoofs:
As a long parted mother with her child
Plays fondly with her tears, and smiles, in meeting;
So, weeping, smiling, greet I thee, my earth,
And do thee favour with my royal hands.
Feed not thy sovereign's foe, my gentle earth,
Nor with thy sweets comfort his ravenous sense:
But let thy spiders, that suck up thy venom,
And heavy-gaited toads, lie in their way;
Doing annoyance to the treacherous feet,
Which with usurping steps do trample thee.
Yield stinging nettles to mine enemies:
And when they from thy bosom pluck a flower,
Guard it, I pray thee, with a lurking adder;
Whose double tongue may with a mortal touch
Throw death upon thy sovereign's enemies.—
Mock not my senseless conjuration, lords;
This earth shall have a feeling, and these stones
Prove armed soldiers, ere her native king
Shall falter under foul rebellious arms.

Bishop. Fear not, my lord; that Power, that made you king,
Hath power to keep you king, in spite of all.
The means that heaven yields must be embrac'd,
And not neglected; else, if heaven would,
And we will not, heaven's offer we refuse;
The proffer'd means of succour and redress.

Aum. He means, my lord, that we are too remiss;
Whilst Bolingbroke, through our security,
Grows strong and great, in substance, and in friends.

K. Rich. Discomfortable cousin! know'st thou not,
That when the searching eye of heaven is hid
Behind the globe, and[4] lights the lower world,
Then thieves and robbers range abroad unseen,
In murders, and in outrage, bloody here;
But when, from under this terrestrial ball,
He fires the proud tops of the eastern pines,[5]
And darts his light through every guilty hole,
Then murders, treasons, and detested sins,
The cloak of night being pluck'd from off their backs
Stand bare and naked, trembling at themselves?
So when this thief, this traitor, Bolingbroke,—
Who all this while hath revell'd in the night,
Whilst we were wand'ring with the antipodes,
Shall see us rising in our throne the east,
His treasons will sit blushing in his face,
Not able to endure the sight of day;
But, self-affrighted, tremble at his sin.
Not all the water in the rough rude sea
Can wash the balm from an anointed king
The breath of worldly men cannot depose
The deputy elected by the Lord:[6]
For every man that Bolingbroke hath press'd,
To lift shrewd steel against our golden crown,
God for his Richard hath in heavenly pay
A glorious angel: then, if angels fight,
Weak men must fall; for heaven still guards the right.

Enter SALISBURY.

Welcome, my lord; How far off lies your power?[7]

Sal. Nor near, nor further off, my gracious lord,
Than this weak arm: Discomfort guides my tongue,
And bids me speak of nothing but despair.
One day too late, I fear, my noble lord,
Hath clouded all thy happy days on earth:
O, call back yesterday, bid time return,
And thou shalt have twelve thousand fighting men!
To-day, to-day, unhappy day, too late,
O'erthrows thy joys, friends, fortune, and thy state;
For all the Welshmen, hearing thou wert dead,
Are gone to Bolingbroke, dispers'd, and fled.

Aum. Comfort, my liege: why looks your grace so pale?

K. Rich. But now, the blood of twenty thousand men
Did triumph in my face, and they are fled;
And, till so much blood thither come again,
Have I not reason to look pale and dead?
All souls that will be safe, fly from my side;
For time hath set a blot upon my pride.

Aum. Comfort, my liege: remember who you are.

K. Rich. I had forgot myself: Am I not king?
Awake thou sluggard[8] majesty! thou sleep'st.
Is not the king's name forty thousand names?[9]
Arm, arm, my name! a puny subject strikes
At thy great glory.—Look not to the ground,
Ye favourites of a king; Are we not high?
High be our thoughts: I know, my uncle York
Hath power enough to serve our turn. But who
Comes here?

Enter SCROOP.

Scroop. More health and happiness betide my liege,
Than can my care-tun'd tongue deliver him.

K. Rich. Mine ear is open, and my heart prepar'd:[10]

---

1 Commendations.

2 Johnson says, 'here may be properly inserted the last scene of the second act.'

3 The quarto of 1597 reads *they.*

4 The old copies read '*that* lights,' &c. The alteration was made by Johnson.

5 'It is not easy (says Steevens) to point out an image more striking and beautiful than this, in any poet, ancient or modern.'

6 Here is the doctrine of the divine right of kings, and of the passive obedience of subjects, expressed in the strongest terms. Johnson observes that it has been the fashion to impute the original of every tenet which we have been taught to think false or foolish to the reign of King James I. But this doctrine was never carried further in any country, than in this island, while the house of Tudor sat on the throne.

7 Force.

8 The first quarto reads '*coward* majesty.'

9 So in King Richard III.:—
'Besides, the king's name is a tower of strength.'

10 'It seems to be the design of the poet to raise Richard to esteem in his fall, and consequently to interest the reader in his favour. He gives him only passive fortitude, the virtue of a confessor, rather than of a king In his prosperity we saw him imperious and oppressive; but in his distress he is wise, patient, and pious' *Johnson*

The worst is worldly loss, thou canst unfold.
Say, is my kingdom lost? why, 'twas my care!
And what loss is it, to be rid of care?
Strives Bolingbroke to be as great as we?
Greater he shall not be; if he serve God,
We'll serve him too, and be his fellow so:
Revolt our subjects? that we cannot mend;
They break their faith to God, as well as us:
Cry woe, destruction, ruin, loss, decay:
The worst is—death, and death will have his day.

Scroop. Glad am I, that your highness is so arm'd
To bear the tidings of calamity
Like an unseasonable stormy day,
Which makes the silver rivers drown their shores,
As if the world were all dissolv'd to tears;
So high above his limits swells the rage
Of Bolingbroke, covering your fearful land
With hard bright steel, and hearts harder than steel.
White-beards have arm'd their thin and hairless scalps
Against the majesty; and boys, with women's voices,
Strive to speak big, and clap their female joints
In stiff unwieldy arms against thy crown:
The very beadsmen learn to bend their bows
Of double-fatal yew[1] against thy state;
Yea, distaff-women manage rusty bills
Against thy seat: both young and old rebel,
And all goes worse than I have power to tell.

K. Rich. Too well, too well, thou tell'st a tale so ill:
Where is the earl of Wiltshire? where is Bagot?[2]
What is become of Bushy? where is Green?
That they have let the dangerous enemy
Measure our confines with such peaceful steps?
If we prevail, their heads shall pay for it.
I warrant, they have made peace with Bolingbroke.

Scroop. Peace have they made with him, indeed, my lord.

K. Rich. O villains, vipers, damn'd without redemption!
Dogs, easily won to fawn on any man!
Snakes, in my heart-blood warm'd, that sting my heart!
Three Judases, each one thrice worse than Judas!
Would they make peace? terrible hell make war
Upon their spotted souls for this offence!

Scroop. Sweet love, I see, changing his property,
Turns to the sourest and most deadly hate;—
Again uncurse their souls; their peace is made
With heads, and not with hands: those whom you curse,
Have felt the worst of death's destroying wound,
And lie full low, grav'd[3] in the hollow ground.

Aum. Is Bushy, Green, and the earl of Wiltshire dead?

Scroop. Yea, all of them at Bristol lost their heads.

Aum. Where is the duke, my father, with his power?

K. Rich. No matter where; of comfort no man speak:
Let's talk of graves, of worms, and epitaphs;
Make dust our paper, and with rainy eyes
Write sorrow on the bosom of the earth.
Let's choose executors, and talk of wills:
And yet not so,—for what can we bequeath,
Save our deposed bodies to the ground?
Our lands, our lives, and all are Bolingbroke's,
And nothing can we call our own, but death;
And that small model[4] of the barren earth,
Which serves as paste and cover to our bones.
For heaven's sake, let us sit upon the ground,
And tell sad stories of the death of kings:—
How some have been depos'd, some slain in war;
Some haunted by the ghosts they have depos'd;
Some poison'd by their wives, some sleeping kill'd;
All murder'd:—For within the hollow crown,
That rounds the mortal temples of a king,
Keeps death his court: and there the antick sits,[5]
Scoffing his state, and grinning at his pomp;
Allowing him a breath, a little scene
To monarchise, be fear'd, and kill with looks;
Infusing him with self and vain conceit,—
As if this flesh, which walls about our life,
Were brass impregnable; and humour'd thus,
Comes at the last, and with a little pin
Bores through his castle wall, and—farewell, king!
Cover your heads, and mock not flesh and blood
With solemn reverence; throw away respect,
Tradition,[6] form, and ceremonious duty,
For you have but mistook me all this while.
I live with bread like you, feel want, taste grief,
Need friends:—Subjected thus,
How can you say to me—I am a king?

Car. My lord, wise men ne'er wail their present woes,
But presently prevent the ways to wail.
To fear the foe, since fear oppresseth strength,
Gives, in your weakness, strength unto your foe.
And so your follies fight against yourself.
Fear, and be slain; no worse can come, to fight:
And fight and die, is death destroying death;[7]
Where fearing dying, pays death servile breath.

Aum. My father hath a power, inquire of him;
And learn to make a body of a limb.

K. Rich. Thou chid'st me well:—Proud Bolingbroke, I come
To change blows with thee for our day of doom.
This ague-fit of fear is over-blown;
An easy task it is, to win our own.——
Say, Scroop, where lies our uncle with his power?
Speak sweetly, man, although thy looks be sour.

Scroop. Men judge by the complexion of the sky
The state and inclination of the day:
So may you by my dull and heavy eye,
My tongue hath but a heavier tale to say.
I play the torturer, by small and small,
To lengthen out the worst that must be spoken:—
Your uncle York hath join'd with Bolingbroke;
And all your northern castles yielded up,
And all your southern gentlemen in arms
Upon his party.

K. Rich. Thou hast said enough.——
Beshrew thee, cousin, which didst lead me forth [*To* Aumerle.
Of that sweet way I was in to despair!
What say you now? What comfort have we now?
By heaven, I'll hate him everlastingly,
That bids me be of comfort any more.[8]
Go, to Flint Castle; there I'll pine away;

1 *Yew* is called *double-fatal*, because of the poisonous quality of the leaves, and on account of the wood being used for instruments of death. From some ancient statutes it appears that every Englishman, while archery was practised, was obliged to keep in his house either a bow of *yew* or some other wood. It has been supposed that *yews* were anciently planted in church-yards not only to defend the church from the wind, but on account of their use in making *bows;* while their poisonous quality was kept from doing mischief to the cattle, in that sacred enclosure.

2 The mention of Bagot here is a lapse of the poet or the king; but perhaps it may have been intended to mark more strongly the perturbation of the king's mind, by making him inquire at first for Bagot, whose loyalty, on further recollection, might show him the impropriety of the question.

3 i. e. *buried* The verb is not peculiar to Shakspeare.

4 A *small model*, or *module*, for they were the same in Shakspeare's time, seems to mean in this place a *small portion* or *quantity*. It is a Latinism, from '*modulus*, the *measure* or *quantity* of a thing.'

5 It is not impossible that Shakspeare borrowed this idea from that most exquisite emblematic book of engravings on wood, the Dance of Death, or Imagines Mortis, attributed to Holbein. See the seventh print.

6 *Tradition* here seems to mean *traditional practices*, i. e. *established* or *customary homage*.

7 That is, to *die fighting* is to return the evil that we suffer, to destroy the destroyers.

8 This sentiment is drawn from nature. Nothing is more offensive to a mind convinced that its distress is without remedy, and preparing to submit quietly to irresistible calamity, than these petty and conjectured comforts, which unskilful officiousness thinks it virtue to administer.

A king, woe's slave, shall kingly woe obey.
That power I have, discharge; and let them go
To ear[1] the land that hath some hope to grow,
For I have none:—Let no man speak again
To alter this, for counsel is but vain.

Aum. My liege, one word.

K. Rich. He does me double wrong,
That wounds me with the flatteries of his tongue.
Discharge my followers, let them hence:—Away,
From Richard's night, to Bolingbroke's fair day.
[*Exeunt.*

SCENE III. Wales. *A Plain before* Flint *Castle. Enter, with Drum and Colours,* BOLINGBROKE *and Forces;* YORK, NORTHUMBERLAND, *and others.*

Boling. So that by this intelligence we learn,
The Welshmen are dispers'd; and Salisbury
Is gone to meet the king, who lately landed,
With some few private friends, upon this coast.

North. The news is very fair and good, my lord;
Richard not far from hence, hath hid his head.

York. It would beseem the lord Northumberland,
To say—King Richard:—Alack the heavy day,
When such a sacred king should hide his head!

North. Your grace mistakes me;[2] only to be brief,
Left I his title out.

York. The time hath been,
Would you have been so brief with him, he would
Have been so brief with you, to shorten you
For taking so the head, your whole head's length.

Boling. Mistake not, uncle, further than you should.

York. Take not, good cousin, further than you should,
Lest you mis-take: The heavens are o'er your head.

Boling. I know it, uncle; and oppose not
Myself against their will.—But who comes here?

Enter PERCY.

Well,[3] Harry; what, will not this castle yield?

Percy. The castle royally is mann'd, my lord,
Against thy entrance.

Boling. Royally!
Why, it contains no king?

Percy. Yes, my good lord,
It doth contain a king: King Richard lies
Within the limits of yon lime and stone:
And with him are the Lord Aumerle, Lord Salisbury,
Sir Stephen Scroop; besides a clergyman
Of holy reverence; who, I cannot learn.

North. Belike, it is the bishop of Carlisle.

Boling. Noble lord,[4] [*To* NORTH.
Go to the rude ribs of that ancient castle;
Through brazen trumpet send the breath of parle
Into his ruin'd ears, and thus deliver:
Harry Bolingbroke
On both his knees doth kiss King Richard's hand;
And sends allegiance, and true faith of heart,
To his most royal person: hither come
Even at his feet to lay my arms and power;
Provided that, my banishment repeal'd,
And lands restor'd again, be freely granted:
If not, I'll use the advantage of my power,
And lay the summer's dust with showers of blood,
Rain'd from the wounds of slaughter'd Englishmen:
The which, how far off from the mind of Bolingbroke
It is, such crimson tempest should bedrench
The fresh green lap of fair King Richard's land,
My stooping duty tenderly shall show.
Go, signify as much; while here we march
Upon the grassy carpet of this plain.—
[NORTHUMBERLAND *advances to the Castle, with a Trumpet.*
Let's march without the noise of threat'ning drum,
That from the castle's totter'd[5] battlements
Our fair appointments may be well perus'd.
Methinks, King Richard and myself should meet
With no less terror than the elements
Of fire and water, when their thund'ring shock
At meeting tears the cloudy cheeks of heaven.
Be he the fire, I'll be the yielding water:
The rage be his, while on the earth I rain
My waters; on the earth, and not on him.
March on, and mark King Richard how he looks.

A Parley sounded, and answered by another Trumpet within. Flourish. Enter on the walls KING RICHARD, *the* Bishop *of* Carlisle, AUMERLE, SCROOP, *and* SALISBURY.

York. See, see, King Richard doth himself appear,[6]
As doth the blushing discontented sun
From out the fiery portal of the east;
When he perceives the envious clouds are bent
To dim his glory, and to stain the track
Of his bright passage to the occident.
Yet looks he like a king; behold, his eye,
As bright as is the eagle's, lightens forth
Controlling majesty; Alack, alack, for woe,
That any harm should stain so fair a show!

K. Rich. We are amaz'd; and thus long have we stood
To watch the fearful bending of thy knee,
[*To* NORTHUMBERLAND.
Because we thought ourself thy lawful king:
And if we be, how dare thy joints forget
To pay their awful duty to our presence?
If we be not, show us the hand of God
That hath dismiss'd us from our stewardship;
For well we know, no hand of blood and bone
Can gripe the sacred handle of our sceptre,
Unless he do profane, steal, or usurp.
And though you think, that all, as you have done,
Have torn their souls, by turning them from us,
And we are barren, and bereft of friends;—
Yet know,—my master, God omnipotent,
Is must'ring in his clouds, on our behalf,
Armies of pestilence; and they shall strike
Your children yet unborn, and unbegot,
That lift your vassal hands against my head,
And threat the glory of my precious crown.
Tell Bolingbroke (for yond', methinks, he is,)
That every stride he makes upon my land,
Is dangerous treason: He is come to ope
The purple testament[7] of bleeding war;
But ere the crown he looks for live in peace,
Ten thousand bloody crowns of mothers' sons
Shall ill become the flower of England's face;[8]
Change the complexion of her maid-pale peace
To scarlet indignation, and bedew
Her pastures' grass with faithful English blood.

North. The king of heaven forbid, our lord the king
Should so with civil and uncivil arms
Be rush'd upon! Thy thrice-noble cousin,
Harry Bolingbroke, doth humbly kiss thy hand
And by the honourable tomb he swears,
That stands upon thy royal grandsire's bones;
And by the royalties of both your bloods,
Currents that spring from one most gracious head;
And by the buried hand of warlike Gaunt;
And by the worth and honour of himself,

1 To *ear* the land is to *till* it, to *plough* it.

2 The word *me*, which is wanting in the old copies, was supplied by Hanmer.

3 The old copy reads, '*Welcome,* Harry:' the emendation is Hanmer's.

4 Shakspeare frequently, in his addresses to persons, begins with an hemistich; and sometimes blends short prosaic sentences with his metrical dialogues.

5 *Totter'd,* the reading of the two first quartos, is here probably used for *tottering*, according to the frequent usage of our poet. The other copies read *tatter'd*

6 The six first lines of this speech are erroneously given to Bolingbroke in the old copies.

7 Shakspeare uses the word *testament* in its legal sense. Bolingbroke is come to open the testament of war, that he may peruse what is decreed there in his favour. *Purple* is an epithet referring to the future effusion of blood.

8 i. e. England's flowery face, the flowery surface of England's soil.

Comprising all that may be sworn or said,—
His coming hither hath no further scope,
Than for his lineal royalties, and to beg
Enfranchisement immediate on his knees:
Which on the royal party granted once,
His glittering arms he will commend[1] to rust,
His barbed steeds to stables, and his heart
To faithful service of your majesty.
This swears he, as he is a prince, is just;
And, as I am a gentleman, I credit him.

K. Rich. Northumberland, say,—thus the king returns;
His noble cousin is right welcome hither;
And all the number of his fair demands
Shall be accomplish'd without contradiction:
With all the gracious utterance thou hast,
Speak to his gentle hearing kind commends.—
We do debase ourself, cousin, do we not, [*To* AUMERLE.
To look so poorly, and to speak so fair?
Shall we call back Northumberland, and send
Defiance to the traitor, and so die?

Aum. No, good my lord; let's fight with gentle words,
Till time lend friends, and friends their helpful swords.

K. Rich. O God! O God! that e'er this tongue of mine,
That laid the sentence of dread banishment
On yon proud man, should take it off again
With words of sooth![2] O, that I were as great
As is my grief, or lesser than my name!
Or that I could forget what I have been!
Or not remember what I must be now!
Swell'st thou, proud heart? I'll give thee scope to beat,
Since foes have scope to beat both thee and me.

Aum. Northumberland comes back from Bolingbroke.

K. Rich. What must the king do now? Must he submit?
The king shall do it. Must he be depos'd?
The king shall be contented: Must he lose
The name of king? o'God's name, let it go;
I'll give my jewels, for a set of beads;
My gorgeous palace, for a hermitage;
My gay apparel,[3] for an alms-man's gown;
My figur'd goblets, for a dish of wood;
My sceptre, for a palmer's walking-staff;
My subjects, for a pair of carved saints;
And my large kingdom for a little grave,
A little, little grave, an obscure grave:—
Or I'll be buried in the king's highway,
Some way of common trade,[4] where subjects' feet
May hourly trample on their sovereign's head:
For on my heart they tread, now whilst I live;
And, buried once, why not upon my head?——
Aumerle, thou weep'st; My tender-hearted cousin!—
We'll make foul weather with despised tears;
Our sighs, and they, shall lodge the summer corn,
And make a dearth in this revolting land.
Or shall we play the wantons with our woes,
And make some pretty match with shedding tears?
As thus:—To drop them still upon one place,
Till they have fretted us a pair of graves
Within the earth; and, therein laid,—*There lies*
Two kinsmen, digg'd their graves with weeping eyes?
Would not this ill do well?—Well, well, I see
I talk but idly, and you mock at me.—
Most mighty prince, my Lord Northumberland,
What says King Bolingbroke? will his majesty
Give Richard leave to live till Richard die?
You make a leg,[5] and Bolingbroke says—ay.[6]

North. My lord, in the base[7] court he doth attend
To speak with you; may't please you to come down?

K. Rich. Down, down, I come; like glistering Phaeton,
Wanting the manage of unruly jades.
[NORTH. *retires to* BOLING.
In the base court? Base court,[8] where kings grow base,
To come at traitors' calls, and do them grace.
In the base court? Come down? Down, court, down, king!
For night-owls shriek, where mounting larks should sing. [*Exeunt from above.*

Boling. What says his majesty?

North. Sorrow and grief of heart
Makes him speak fondly,[9] like a frantic man:
Yet he is come.

Enter KING RICHARD, *and his* Attendants, *below.*

Boling. Stand all apart,
And show fair duty to his majesty.——
My gracious lord,— [*Kneeling.*

K. Rich. Fair cousin, you debase your princely knee,
To make the base earth proud with kissing it:
Me rather had, my heart might feel your love,
Than my unpleas'd eye see your courtesy.
Up, cousin, up; your heart is up, I know,
Thus high at least [*touching his own head,*] although your knee be low.

Boling. My gracious lord, I come but for mine own.

K. Rich. Your own is yours, and I am yours, and all.

Boling. So far be mine, my most redoubted lord,
As my true service shall deserve your love.

K. Rich. Well you deserve:—They well deserve to have,
That know the strong'st and surest way to get.—
Uncle, give me your hand: nay, dry your eyes;
Tears show their love, but want their remedies.—
Cousin, I am too young to be your father,
Though you are old enough to be my heir
What you will have, I'll give, and willing too;
For do we must, what force will have us do.—
Set on towards London:—Cousin, is it so?

Boling. Yea, my good lord.

K. Rich. Then I must not say, no.[10]
[*Flourish. Exeunt.*

SCENE IV. Langley. Duke *of* York's *Garden.*

Enter the Queen, *and two* Ladies.

Queen. What sport shall we devise here in this garden,
To drive away the heavy thought of care?

1 Lady. Madam, we'll play at bowls.

Queen. 'Twill make me think,
The world is full of rubs, and that my fortune
Runs 'gainst the bias.[11]

1 Lady. Madam, we will dance.

---

1 *Commend* for *commit.*

2 *Sooth* is *sweet*, as well as *true*. In this place *sooth* means *sweetness* or *softness*. Thus to *soothe* still means to calm and sweeten the mind.

3 Richard's expense in regard to dress was very extraordinary. 'He had one coate which he caused to be made for him of gold and stone, valued at 3000 marks.' —*Holinshed.*

4 'Some way of common *trade*' is some way of frequent resort, a common course; as, at present, 'a road of much traffic,' i. e. frequent resort.

5 A bow.

6 It should be remembered that the affirmative particle *ay* was formerly written and sounded *I*, which rhymed well with *die*.

7 Lower

8 That is the *lower court* of the castle; *basse cour*, Fr. Thus in Cavendish's Life of Wolsey:—'My lord being advertised that the duke was coming, even at hand, he caused all his gentlemen to wait upon him down through the hall into the *base court*.'—Edition 1825, p. 211.

9 Foolishly.

10 'The duke, with a sharpe high voyce bade bring forth the king's horses; and then two little nagges, not worth forty franks, were brought forth: the king was set on one, and the earle of Salisburie on the other; and thus the duke brought the king from Flint to Chester, where he was delivered to the duke of Gloucester's sonne (that loved him but little, for he had put their father to death,) who led him straight to the castle.'—Stowe (p. 521. edit. 1605,) from a manuscript account written by a person who was present.

11 *The bias* was a weight inserted in one side of a bowl, which gave it a particular inclination in bowling

Queen. My legs can keep no measure in delight,
When my poor heart no measure keeps in grief;
Therefore, no dancing, girl; some other sport.
1 *Lady.* Madam, we'll tell tales.
Queen. Of sorrow, or of joy?[1]
1 *Lady.* Of either, madam.
Queen. Of neither, girl:
For if of joy, being altogether wanting,
It doth remember me the more of sorrow;
Or if of grief, being altogether had,
It adds more sorrow to my want of joy:
For what I have, I need not to repeat;
And what I want, it boots[2] not to complain.[3]
1 *Lady.* Madam, I'll sing.
Queen. 'Tis well, that thou hast cause;
But thou should'st please me better, would'st thou weep.
1 *Lady.* I could weep, madam, would it do you good.
Queen. And I could weep,[4] would weeping do me good,
And never borrow any tear of thee.
But stay, here come the gardeners:
Let's step into the shadow of these trees.—

Enter a Gardener, *and two* Servants.

My wretchedness unto a row of pins,
They'll talk of state; for every one doth so
Against a change: Woe is forerun with woe.[5]
[Queen *and* Ladies *retire.*
Gard. Go, bind thou up yon' dangling apricocks,
Which, like unruly children, make their sire
Stoop with oppression of their prodigal weight:
Give some supportance to the bending twigs.—
Go thou, and, like an executioner,
Cut off the heads of too fast growing sprays,
That look too lofty in our commonwealth:
All must be even in our government.——
You thus employ'd, I will go root away
The noisome weeds, that without profit suck
The soil's fertility from wholesome flowers.
1 *Serv.* Why should we, in the compass of a pale,
Keep law, and form, and due proportion,
Showing, as in a model, our firm estate?
When our sea-walled garden, the whole land,
Is full of weeds; her fairest flowers chok'd up,
Her fruit-trees all unprun'd, her hedges ruin'd,
Her knots[6] disorder'd, and her wholesome herbs
Swarming with caterpillars?
Gard. Hold thy peace:—
He that hath suffer'd this disorder'd spring,
Hath now himself met with the fall of leaf:
The weeds, that his broad-spreading leaves did shelter,
That seem'd in eating him to hold him up,
Are pluck'd up, root and all, by Bolingbroke;
I mean, the earl of Wiltshire, Bushy, Green.
1 *Serv.* What, are they dead?
Gard. They are; and Bolingbroke
Hath seiz'd the wasteful king.—Oh! what pity is it,
That he had not so trimm'd and dress'd his land,
As we this garden! We[7] at time of year
Do wound the bark, the skin of our fruit trees;
Lest, being over-proud with sap and blood,
With too much riches it confound itself:
Had he done so to great and growing men,
They might have liv'd to bear, and he to taste
Their fruits of duty. All superfluous branches
We lop away, that bearing boughs may live:
Had he done so, himself had borne the crown,
Which waste of idle hours hath quite thrown down.
1 *Serv.* What, think you then, the king shall be depos'd?
Gard. Depress'd he is already; and depos'd,
'Tis doubt,[8] he will be: Letters came last night
To a dear friend of the good duke of York's,
That tell black tidings.
Queen. O, I am press'd to death,
Through want of speaking!—Thou, old Adam's likeness, [*Coming from her concealment.*
Set to dress this garden, how dares
Thy harsh rude tongue sound this unpleasing news?
What Eve, what serpent hath suggested thee
To make a second fall of cursed man?
Why dost thou say, King Richard is depos'd?
Dar'st thou, thou little better thing than earth,
Divine his downfal? Say, where, when, and how,
Cam'st thou by these ill tidings? speak, thou wretch.
Gard. Pardon me, madam: little joy have I,
To breathe this news; yet, what I say is true.
King Richard, he is in the mighty hold
Of Bolingbroke: their fortunes both are weigh'd:
In your lord's scale is nothing but himself,
And some few vanities that make him light;
But in the balance of great Bolingbroke,
Besides himself, are all the English peers,
And with that odds he weighs King Richard down.
Post you to London, and you'll find it so;
I speak no more than every one doth know.
Queen. Nimble mischance, that art so light of foot,
Doth not thy embassage belong to me,
And am I last that knows it? O, thou think'st
To serve me last, that I may longest keep
Thy sorrow in my breast.—Come, ladies, go,
To meet at London London's king in woe.—
What, was I born to this! that my sad look
Should grace the triumph of great Bolingbroke?—
Gardener, for telling me this news of woe,
I would, the plants thou graft'st, may never grow.
[*Exeunt* Queen *and* Ladies.
Gard. Poor queen! so that thy state might be no worse,
I would, my skill were subject to thy curse.—
Here did she drop[9] a tear; here, in this place,
I'll set a bank of rue, sour herb of grace:
Rue, even for ruth, here shortly shall be seen,
In the remembrance of a weeping queen. [*Exeun.*

ACT IV.

SCENE I. London. Westminster Hall.[10] *The* Lords *spiritual on the right side of the Throne; the* Lords *temporal on the left; the* Commons *below. Enter* BOLINGBROKE, AUMERLE, SURREY,[11] NORTHUMBERLAND, PERCY, FITZWATER, *another* Lord, Bishop *of* Carlisle, Abbot *of* Westminster, *and* Attendants. Officers *behind, with* BAGOT.

Boling. Call forth Bagot:——
Now, Bagot, freely speak thy mind;
What thou dost know of noble Gloster's death;
Who wrought it with the king, and who perform'd
The bloody office of his timeless[12] end.
Bagot. Then set before my face the Lord Aumerle.
Boling. Cousin, stand forth, and look upon that man.
Bagot. My Lord Aumerle, I know, your daring tongue

1 All the old copies read 'of sorrow or of grief.' Pope made the necessary alteration.

2 Profits. 3 See note on Act i. Sc. 2.

4 The old copies read 'and I could *sing*.' The emendation is Pope's.

5 The poet, according to the common doctrine of prognostication, supposes dejection to forerun calamity, and a kingdom to be filled with rumours of sorrow when any great disaster is impending.

6 *Knots* are figures planted in box, the lines of which frequently intersected each other in the old fashion of gardening.

7 *We* is not in the old copy. It was added by Malone.

8 This uncommon phraseology has already occurred in the present play:—
'He is our cousin, cousin; but 'tis *doubt*
When time shall call him home,' &c.

9 The quarto of 1597 reads *fall*. The quarto of 1598 and the folio read *drop*.

10 The rebuilding of Westminster Hall, which Richard had begun in 1397, being finished in 1399, the first meeting of parliament in the new edifice was for the purpose of deposing him.

11 Thomas Holland, earl of Kent, brother to John Holland, earl of Exeter, was created duke of Surrey in 1597. He was half brother to the king, by his mother Joan, who married Edward the Black Prince after the death of her second husband Thomas Lord Holland.

12 i. e. untimely

Scorns to unsay what once it hath deliver'd.
In that dead time when Gloster's death was plotted,
I heard you say,—*Is not my arm of length,*
That reacheth from the restful English court
As far as Calais, to my uncle's head?
Amongst much other talk, that very time,
I heard you say, that you had rather refuse
The offer of a hundred thousand crowns,
Than Bolingbroke's return to England;
Adding withal, how blest this land would be,
In this your cousin's death.
Aum. Princes, and noble lords,
What answer shall I make to this base man?
Shall I so much dishonour my fair stars,[1]
On equal terms to give him chastisement?
Either I must, or have mine honour soil'd
With the attainder of his sland'rous lips.——
There is my gage, the manual seal of death,
That marks thee out for hell; I say, thou liest,
And will maintain, what thou hast said, is false,
In thy heart-blood, though being all too base,
To stain the temper of my knightly sword.
Boling. Bagot, forbear, thou shalt not take it up.
Aum. Excepting one, I would he were the best
In all this presence, that hath mov'd me so.
Fitz. If that thy valour stand on sympathies,[2]
There is my gage, Aumerle, in gage to thine:
By that fair sun that shows me where thou stand'st,
I heard thee say, and vauntingly thou spak'st it,
That thou wert cause of noble Gloster's death.
If thou deny'st it, twenty times thou liest;
And I will turn thy falsehood to thy heart,
Where it was forged, with my rapier's point.
Aum. Thou dar'st not, coward, live to see that day.
Fitz. Now, by my soul, I would it were this hour.
Aum. Fitzwater, thou art damn'd to hell for this.
Percy. Aumerle, thou liest; his honour is as true,
In this appeal, as thou art all unjust:
And, that thou art so, there I throw my gage,
To prove it on thee to the extremest point
Of mortal breathing; seize it, if thou dar'st.
Aum. And if I do not, may my hands rot off,
And never brandish more revengeful steel
Over the glittering helmet of my foe!
Lord. I task the earth to the like, forsworn Aumerle;
And spur thee on with full as many lies
As may be holla'd in thy treacherous ear
From sun to sun:[3] there is my honour's pawn;
Engage it to the trial, if thou dar'st.
Aum. Who sets me else? by heaven, I'll throw at all:
I have a thousand spirits in one breast,[4]
To answer twenty thousand such as you.
Surrey. My Lord Fitzwater, I do remember well
The very time Aumerle and you did talk.
Fitz. 'Tis very true: you were in presence then;
And you can witness with me, this is true.
Surrey. As false, by heaven, as heaven itself is true.
Fitz. Surrey, thou liest.
Surrey. Dishonourable boy!
That lie shall lie so heavy on my sword,
That it shall render vengeance and revenge
Till thou the lie-giver, and that lie, do lie
In earth as quiet as thy father's scull.
In proof whereof, there is my honour's pawn,
Engage it to the trial, if thou dar'st.
Fitz. How fondly dost thou spur a forward horse!
If I dare eat, or drink, or breathe, or live,
I dare meet Surrey in a wilderness,[5]
And spit upon him, whilst I say, he lies,
And lies, and lies: there is my bond of faith,
To tie thee to my strong correction.—
As I intend to thrive in this new world,[6]
Aumerle is guilty of my true appeal:
Besides, I heard the banish'd Norfolk say,
That thou, Aumerle, didst send two of thy men
To execute the noble duke at Calais.
Aum. Some honest Christian trust me with a gage,
That Norfolk lies: here do I throw down this,[7]
If he may be repeal'd to try his honour.
Boling. These differences shall all rest under gage,
Till Norfolk be repeal'd: repeal'd he shall be,
And, though mine enemy, restor'd again
To all his land and signories; when he's return'd,
Against Aumerle we will enforce his trial.
Car. That honourable day shall ne'er be seen.—
Many a time hath banish'd Norfolk fought
For Jesu Christ; in glorious Christian field
Streaming the ensign of the Christian cross,
Against black pagans, Turks, and Saracens:
And, toil'd with works of war, retir'd himself
To Italy; and there, at Venice, gave
His body to that pleasant country's earth,[8]
And his pure soul unto his captain Christ,
Under whose colours he had fought so long.
Boling. Why, bishop, is Norfolk dead?
Car. As sure as I live, my lord.
Boling. Sweet peace conduct his sweet soul to the bosom
Of good old Abraham!—Lords appellants,
Your differences shall all rest under gage,
Till we assign you to your days of trial.

Enter YORK, *attended.*

York. Great duke of Lancaster, I come to thee
From plume-pluck'd Richard; who with willing soul
Adopts thee heir, and his high sceptre yields
To the possession of thy royal hand:
Ascend his throne, descending now from him,—
And long live Henry, of that name the fourth!
Boling. In God's name, I'll ascend the regal throne.[9]
Car. Marry, God forbid!—
Worst in this royal presence, may I speak,
Yet best beseeming me to speak the truth.
'Would God, that any in this noble presence
Were enough noble to be upright judge
Of noble Richard; then true nobless[10] would
Learn him forbearance from so foul a wrong.
What subject can give sentence on his king?
And who sits here, that is not Richard's subject?
Thieves are not judg'd, but they are by to hear,
Although apparent guilt be seen in them:
And shall the figure of God's majesty,[11]

1 The *birth* is supposed to be influenced by *stars*; therefore the poet, with his allowed licence, takes *stars* for birth. We learn from Pliny's Nat. Hist. that the vulgar error assigned the brightest and fairest stars to the rich and great:—'Sidera singulis attributa nobis, et clara divitibus, minora pauperibus,' &c. lib. i. c. viii.

2 This is a translated sense much harsher than that of stars, explained in the preceding note. Fitzwater throws down his gage as a pledge of battle, and tells Aumerle that if he stands upon sympathies, that is upon equality of blood, the combat is now offered him by a man of rank not inferior to his own. *Sympathy* is an affection incident at once to two subjects. This community of affection implies a likeness or equality of nature; and hence the poet transferred the term to equality of blood.

3 i. e. from sunrise to sunset.

4 'A thousand hearts are great within my bosom.'
King Richard III.

5 I dare meet him where no help can be had by me against him

6 i. e. in this world, where I have just begun to be an actor. Surrey has just called him *boy*.

7 Holinshed says that on this occasion he threw down a hood that he had borrowed.

8 This is not historically true. The duke of Norfolk's death did not take place till after Richard's murder.

9 Hume gives the words that Henry actually spoke on this occasion, which he copied from Knyghton, and accompanies them by a very ingenious commentary.— *Hist. of Eng.* 4to ed. vol. ix. p. 50.

10 i. e. *nobleness*; a word now obsolete, but common in Shakspeare's time.

11 This speech, which contains in the most express sive terms the doctrine of passive obedience, is founded upon Holinshed's account. The sentiments would not in the reign of Elizabeth or James have been regarded as novel or unconstitutional. It is observable that usurpers are as ready to avail themselves of *divine right* as lawful sovereigns; to dwell upon the sacredness of their persons, and the sanctity of their charac-

His captain, steward, deputy elect,
Anointed, crowned, planted many years,
Be judg'd by subject and inferior breath,
And he himself not present? O, forbid[1] it, God,
That, in a Christian climate, souls refin'd
Should show so heinous, black, obscene a deed!
I speak to subjects, and a subject speaks,
Stirr'd up by heaven, thus boldly for his king.
My lord of Hereford here, whom you call king,
Is a foul traitor to proud Hereford's king:
And if you crown him, let me prophecy,—
The blood of English shall manure the ground,
And future ages groan for this foul act;
Peace shall go sleep with Turks and infidels,
And, in this seat of peace, tumultuous wars
Shall kin with kin, and kind with kind confound:
Disorder, horror, fear, and mutiny
Shall here inhabit, and this land be call'd
The field of Golgotha, and dead men's sculls.
O, if you rear[2] this house against this house,
It will the wofullest division prove,
That ever fell upon this cursed earth:
Prevent, resist it, let it not be so,
Lest child's child's children[3] cry against you—woe!

North. Well have you argu'd, sir; and, for your pains,
Of capital treason we arrest you here:—
My lord of Westminster, be it your charge
To keep him safely till his day of trial.—
May't please you, lords, to grant the commons' suit.[4]

Boling. Fetch hither Richard, that in common view
He may surrender; so we shall proceed
Without suspicion.

York. I will be his conduct.[5] [*Exit.*

Boling. Lords, you that are here under our arrest,
Procure your sureties for your days of answer:—
Little are we beholden to your love, [*To* CAR.
And little look'd for at your helping hands.

Re-enter YORK, *with* KING RICHARD, and Officers *bearing the Crown, &c.*

K. Rich. Alack, why am I sent for to a king,
Before I have shook off the regal thoughts
Wherewith I reign'd? I hardly yet have learn'd
To insinuate, flatter, bow, and bend my knee:[6]—
Give sorrow leave a while to tutor me
To this submission. Yet I well remember
The favours[7] of these men: Were they not mine?
Did they not sometime cry, all hail! to me?
So Judas did to Christ: but he, in twelve,
Found truth in all but one; I, in twelve thousand, none.
God save the king!—Will no man say, amen?
Am I both priest and clerk? well then, amen.
God save the king! although I be not he:
And yet, amen, if heaven do think him me.—
To do what service am I sent for hither?

York. To do that office, of thine own good will,
Which tired majesty did make thee offer,——
The resignation of thy state and crown
To Henry Bolingbroke.

K. Rich. Give me the crown,—Here, cousin, seize the crown;
On this side, my hand; and on that side, yours.
Now is this golden crown like a deep well,
That owes[8] two buckets filling one another,
The emptier ever dancing in the air,
The other down, unseen, and full of water:
That bucket down, and full of tears am I,
Drinking my griefs, whilst you mount up on high.

Boling. I thought, you had been willing to resign.

K. Rich. My crown, I am; but still my griefs are mine:
You may my glories and my state depose,
But not my griefs; still am I king of those.

Boling. Part of your cares you give me with your crown.

K. Rich. Your cares set up, do not pluck my cares down.
My care is—loss of care, by old care done;[9]
Your care is—gain of care, by new care won:
The cares I give, I have, though given away;
They tend[10] the crown, yet still with me they stay.

Boling. Are you contented to resign the crown?

K. Rich. Ay, no;—no, ay;—for I must nothing be;
Therefore no no, for I resign to thee.
Now mark me how I will undo myself:—
I give this heavy weight from off my head,
And this unwieldy sceptre from my hand,
The pride of kingly sway from out my heart,
With mine own tears I wash away my balm,[11]
With mine own hands I give away my crown,
With mine own tongue deny my sacred state,
With mine own breath release all duteous oaths:[12]
All pomp and majesty I do forswear;
My manors, rents, revenues, I forego;
My acts, decrees, and statutes, I deny:
God pardon all oaths, that are broke to me!
God keep all vows unbroke, are made[13] to thee!
Make me, that nothing have, with nothing griev'd;
And thou with all pleas'd, that hast all achiev'd!
Long mayst thou live in Richard's seat to sit,
And soon lie Richard in an earthly pit!
God save King Henry, unking'd Richard says,
And send him many years of sunshine days!—
What more remains?

North. No more, but that you read [*Offering a Paper.*
These accusations, and these grievous crimes,
Committed by your person, and your followers,
Against the state and profit of this land;
That, by confessing them, the souls of men
May deem that you are worthily depos'd.

K. Rich. Must I do so? and must I ravel ou
My weav'd up follies? Gentle Northumberland
If thy offences were upon record,
Would it not shame thee in so fair a troop,
To read a lecture of them? If thou would'st,[14]
There should'st thou find one heinous article,—
Containing the deposing of a king,
And cracking the strong warrant of an oath,—
Mark'd with a blot, damn'd in the book of heaven:-
Nay, all of you, that stand and look upon me,
Whilst that my wretchedness doth bait myself,—
Though some of you, with Pilate, wash your hands,
Showing an outward pity; yet you Pilates
Have here deliver'd me to my sour cross,
And water cannot wash away your sin.

North. My lord, despatch; read o'er these articles.

K. Rich. Mine eyes are full of tears, I cannot see:
And yet salt water blinds them not so much,

---

ter. Even that 'cut-purse of the empire,' Claudius, in Hamlet, affects to believe that—

'—— such divinity doth hedge a king.'

1 The quarto reads *forfend.*

2 The quarto reads *raise.*

3 i. e. grandchildren. Pope altered it to 'children's children,' and was followed by others. The old copies read, 'Lest child, childs children.'

4 What follows, almost to the end of the act, is not found in the first two quartos. The addition was made in the quarto of 1608. In the quarto, 1597, after the words 'his day of trial,' the scene thus closes:—

'*Bol.* Let it be so: and lo! on Wednesday next
We solemnly proclaim our coronation.
Lords be ready all.'

5 i. e. conductor.

6 The quarto reads *limbs.*

7 Countenances, features.

8 Owns.

9 Shakspeare often obscures his meaning by playing with sounds. Richard seems to say here that 'his cares are not made less by the increase of Bolingbroke's cares;'—'his grief is, that his regal cares are at an end, by the cessation of care to which he had been accustomed.'

10 Attend.

11 Oil of consecration.

12 The first quarto reads *duty's rites.*

13 Thus the folio. The quarto reads *that swear.*

14 That is, if thou would'st read over a list of thy own deeds.

But they can see a sort[1] of traitors here.
Nay, if I turn mine eyes upon myself,
I find myself a traitor with the rest:
For I have given here my soul's consent,
To undeck the pompous body of a king;
Make glory base; and sovereignty, a slave;
Proud majesty, a subject; state, a peasant.
North. My lord,——
K. Rich. No lord of thine, thou haught,[2] insulting man,
Nor no man's lord; I have no name, no title,—
No, not that name was given me at the font,—
But 'tis usurp'd:—Alack the heavy day,
That I have worn so many winters out,
And know not now what name to call myself!
O, that I were a mockery king of snow,
Standing before the sun of Bolingbroke,
To melt myself away in water-drops!—
Good king,—great king,—(and yet not greatly good,)
An if my word be sterling yet in England,
Let it command a mirror hither straight;
That it may show me what a face I have,
Since it is bankrupt of his[3] majesty.
Boling. Go some of you, and fetch a looking-glass. [*Exit an* Attendant.
North. Read o'er this paper, while the glass doth come.
K. Rich. Fiend! thou torment'st me ere I come to hell.
Boling. Urge it no more, my Lord Northumberland.
North. The commons will not then be satisfied.
K. Rich. They shall be satisfied: I'll read enough,
When I do see the very book indeed
Where all my sins are writ, and that's—myself.

Re-enter Attendant, *with a Glass.*

Give me that glass, and therein will I read.—
No deeper wrinkles yet? Hath sorrow struck
So many blows upon this face of mine,
And made no deeper wounds?—O, flattering glass,
Like to my followers in prosperity,
Thou dost beguile me! Was this face the face,
That every day under his household roof
Did keep ten thousand men?[4] Was this the face,
That, like the sun, did make beholders wink:[5]
Was this the face, that fac'd so many follies,
And was at last out-fac'd by Bolingbroke?
A brittle glory shineth in this face:
As brittle as the glory is the face;
[*Dashes the Glass against the ground.*
For there it is, crack'd in a hundred shivers.—
Mark, silent king, the moral of this sport,—
How soon my sorrow hath destroy'd my face.
Boling. The shadow of your sorrow hath destroy'd
The shadow of your face.
K. Rich. Say that again.
The shadow of my sorrow? Ha! let's see:—
'Tis very true, my grief lies all within;[6]
And these external manners of lament
Are merely shadows to the unseen grief,
That swells with silence in the tortur'd soul;
There lies the substance: and I thank thee, king,
For thy great bounty, that not only giv'st
Me cause to wail, but teachest me the way
How to lament the cause. I'll beg one boon,
And then be gone, and trouble you no more.
Shall I obtain it?
Boling. Name it, fair cousin.
K. Rich. Fair cousin! I am greater than a king:
For, when I was a king, my flatterers
Were then but subjects: being now a subject,
I have a king here to my flatterer.
Being so great, I have no need to beg
Boling. Yet ask.
K. Rich. And shall I have?
Boling. You shall.
K. Rich. Then give me leave to go.
Boling. Whither?
K. Rich. Whither you will, so I were from your sights.
Boling. Go, some of you, convey him to the Tower.
K. Rich. O, good! Convey?—Conveyers[7] are you all,
That rise thus nimbly by a true king's fall.[8]
[*Exeunt* K. Rich. *some* Lords, *and a* Guard.
Boling. On Wednesday next we solemnly set down
Our coronation: lords, prepare yourselves.
[*Exeunt all but the* Abbot, Bishop *of* Carlisle, *and* Aumerle.
Abbot. A woful pageant have we here beheld.
Car. The woe's to come: the children yet unborn
Shall feel this day as sharp to them as thorn.
Aum. You holy clergymen, is there no plot
To rid the realm of this pernicious blot?
Abbot. Before I freely speak my mind herein,
You shall not only take the sacrament
To bury mine intents, but also to effect
Whatever I shall happen to devise:—
I see your brows are full of discontent,
Your hearts of sorrow, and your eyes of tears;
Come home with me to supper; I will lay
A plot, shall show us all a merry day. [*Exeunt*

ACT V.

SCENE I. London. *A Street leading to the Tower.*

Enter Queen, *and* Ladies.

Queen. This way the king will come; this is the way
To Julius Cæsar's ill-erected tower,[9]
To whose flint bosom my condemned lord
Is doom'd a prisoner, by proud Bolingbroke:
Here let us rest, if this rebellious earth
Have any resting for her true king's queen.

Enter King Richard, *and* Guards.

But soft, but see, or rather do not see,
My fair rose wither: Yet look up; behold;
That you in pity may dissolve to dew,
And wash him fresh again with true-love tears.—
Ah, thou, the model where old Troy did stand;
Thou map[10] of honour; thou King Richard's tomb,
And not King Richard; thou most beauteous inn,[11]
Why should hard-favour'd grief be lodg'd in thee,
When triumph is become an ale-house guest?
K. Rich. Join not with grief, fair woman, do not so,
To make my end too sudden: learn, good soul
To think our former state a happy dream;
From which awak'd, the truth of what we are
Shows us but this; I am sworn brother,[12] sweet,

1 A *sort* is a *set* or *company*.
2 i. e. *haughty*.
3 *His* for *its*. It was common in the poet's time to use the personal for the neutral pronoun.
4 'To his household came every day to meate ten thousand men.'—*Chronicle History*.
5 The quarto omits this line and the four preceding words.
6 'But I have that within which passeth show.' These but the trappings and the suits of woe.'—*Hamlet*.
7 To *convey* was formerly often used in an ill sense. Pistol says of stealing, '*convey* the wise it call;' and 'to convey' is the word for slight of hand or juggling. Richard means that it is a term of contempt, '*jugglers* are you all.'
8 This is the last of the additional lines first printed in the quarto of 1608. In the first editions there is no personal appearance of King Richard.
9 By *ill-erected* is probably meant *erected for evil purposes*.
10 *Model* anciently signified, according to the dictionaries, 'the *platform* or form of any thing.' And *map* is used for *picture* resemblance. In the Rape of Lucrece Shakspeare calls sleep 'the *map* of death.'
11 *Inn* does not probably here mean a house of public entertainment, but a *dwelling* or *lodging* generally. In which sense the word was anciently used
12 *Sworn brother* alludes to the *fratres jurati*, who in the age of adventure, bound themselves by mutual oaths to share fortunes together.

RICHARD & BOLINGBROKE.

King Richard II Act V Scene II.

To grim necessity; and he and I
Will keep a league till death. Hie thee to France,
And cloister there in some religious house:
Our holy lives must win a new world's crown,
Which our profane hours here have stricken down.

Queen. What, is my Richard both in shape and mind
Transform'd and weakened? Hath Bolingbroke
Depos'd thine intellect? hath he been in thy heart?
The lion, dying, thrusteth forth his paw,
And wounds the earth, if nothing else, with rage
To be o'erpower'd; and wilt thou, pupil-like,
Take thy correction mildly? kiss the rod,
And fawn on rage with base humility,
Which art a lion, and a king of beasts?

K. Rich. A king of beasts, indeed: if aught but beasts,
I had been still a happy king of men.
Good sometime queen, prepare thee hence for France:
Think, I am dead; and that even here thou tak'st,
As from my death-bed, my last living leave.
In winter's tedious nights, sit by the fire
With good old folks, and let them tell thee tales
Of woful ages, long ago betid:[1]
And, ere thou bid good night, to quit[2] their grief,
Tell them the lamentable fall[3] of me,
And send the hearers weeping to their beds.
For why, the senseless brands will sympathize
The heavy accent of thy moving tongue,
And, in compassion, weep the fire out:
And some will mourn in ashes, some coal-black,
For the deposing of a rightful king.

Enter NORTHUMBERLAND, *attended.*

North. My lord, the mind of Bolingbroke is chang'd;
You must to Pomfret, not unto the Tower.——
And, madam, there is order ta'en for you:[4]
With all swift speed you must away to France.

K. Rich. Northumberland, thou ladder wherewithal
The mounting Bolingbroke ascends my throne,—
The time shall not be many hours of age
More than it is, ere foul sin, gathering head,
Shall break into corruption: thou shalt think,
Though he divide the realm, and give thee half,
It is too little, helping him to all;
And he shall think, that thou, which know'st the way
To plant unrightful kings, wilt know again,
Being ne'er so little urg'd, another way
To pluck him headlong from the usurped throne.
The love of wicked friends converts to fear;
That fear, to hate; and hate turns one, or both,
To worthy danger, and deserved death.

North. My guilt be on my head, and there an end.
Take leave, and part; for you must part forthwith.

K. Rich. Doubly divorc'd?—Bad men, ye violate
A twofold marriage; 'twixt my crown and me;
And then, betwixt me and my married wife.—
Let me unkiss the oath 'twixt thee and me;
And yet not so, for with a kiss 'twas made.[5]—
Part us, Northumberland: I towards the north,
Where shivering cold and sickness pines the clime;
My wife to France; from whence, set forth in pomp,
She came adorned hither like sweet May,
Sent back like Hallowmas,[6] or short'st of day.

Queen. And must we be divided? must we part?

K. Rich. Ay, hand from hand, my love, and heart from heart.

Queen. Banish us both, and send the king with me.

North. [7]That were some love, but little policy.

Queen. Then whither he goes, thither let me go?

K. Rich. So two, together weeping, make one woe.
Weep thou for me in France, I for thee here;
Better far off, than—near, be ne'er the near'.[8]
Go, count thy way with sighs; I, mine with groans.

Queen. So longest way shall have the longest moans.

K. Rich. Twice for one step I'll groan, the way being short,
And piece the way out with a heavy heart.
Come, come, in wooing sorrow let's be brief.
Since, wedding it, there is such length in grief.
One kiss shall stop our mouths, and dumbly part.
Thus give I mine, and thus I take thy heart.
[*They kiss.*

Queen. Give me mine own again; 'twere no good part,
To take on me to keep, and kill thy heart.[9]
[*Kiss again.*
So now I have mine own again, begone,
That I may strive to kill it with a groan.

K. Rich. We make woe wanton with this fond delay:
Once more, adieu; the rest let sorrow say. [*Exeunt.*

SCENE II. *The same. A Room in the* Duke of York's *Palace. Enter* YORK, *and his* Duchess.[10]

Duch. My lord, you told me, you would tell the rest,
When weeping made you break the story off
Of our two cousins coming into London.

York. Where did I leave?

Duch. At that sad stop, my lord,
Where rude misgovern'd hands, from windows' tops,
Threw dust and rubbish on King Richard's head.

York. Then, as I said, the duke, great Bolingbroke,—
Mounted upon a hot and fiery steed,
Which his aspiring rider seem'd to know,—
With slow, but stately pace, kept on his course,
While all tongues cried—God save thee, Bolingbroke!
You would have thought the very windows spake,
So many greedy looks of young and old
Through casements darted their desiring eyes
Upon his visage; and that all the walls,
With painted imag'ry, had said at once,—
Jesu preserve thee! welcome, Bolingbroke!
Whilst he, from one side to the other turning,
Bare-headed, lower than his proud steed's neck
Bespake them thus,—I thank you, countrymen:
And thus still doing, thus he pass'd along.

Duch. Alas, poor Richard! where rides he the while?

York. As in a theatre, the eyes of men,[11]
After a well-grac'd actor leaves the stage,
Are idly bent on him that enters next,
Thinking his prattle to be tedious:
Even so, or with much more contempt, men's eyes
Did scowl on Richard; no man cried, God save him;

1 Passed.
2 To *requite* their mournful stories.
3 The quarto of 1597 reads *tale.*
4 Thus in Othello:—
'Honest Iago hath *ta'en order* for it.'
5 A *kiss* appears to have been an established circumstance in our ancient marriage ceremonies.
6 All Hallows, i. e. All Saints, Nov. 1.
7 The quartos give this speech to the king.
8 Never the nigher, i. e. 'it is better to be at a great distance than being near each other, to find that we are yet not likely to be peaceably and happily united.'
9 So in King Henry V Act ii. Sc. 2:—
'— the king hath *kill'd* his *heart.*'

10 The first wife of Edward duke of York was Isabella, daughter of Peter the Cruel, king of Castile and Leon. He married her in 1372, and had by her the duke of Aumerle, and all his other children. In introducing her the poet has departed widely from history; for she died in 1394, four or five years before the events related in the present play. After her death York married Joan, daughter of John Holland, earl of Kent, who survived him about thirty-four years, and had three other husbands.
11 'The painting of this description is so lively, and the words so moving, that I have scarce read any thing comparable to it in any other language.'—*Dryden: Pref. to Troilus and Cressida.*

No joyful tongue gave him his welcome home:
But dust was thrown upon his sacred head;
Which with such gentle sorrow he shook off,—
His face still combating with tears and smiles,
The badges of his grief and patience,—
That had not God, for some strong purpose, steel'd
The hearts of men, they must perforce have melted,
And barbarism itself have pitied him.
But heaven hath a hand in these events;
To whose high will we bound our calm contents.
To Bolingbroke are we sworn subjects now,
Whose state and honour I for aye allow.

Enter Aumerle.

Duch. Here comes my son Aumerle.
York. Aumerle that was;
But that is lost, for being Richard's friend;
And, madam, you must call him Rutland[1] now:
I am in parliament pledge for his truth,
And lasting fealty to the new-made king.
Duch. Welcome, my son: Who are the violets now,
That strew the green lap of the new-come spring?[2]
Aum. Madam, I know not, nor I greatly care not;
God knows, I had as lief be none as one.
York. Well, bear you well in this new spring of time,
Lest you be cropp'd before you come to prime.
What news from Oxford? hold those justs and triumphs?
Aum. For aught I know, my lord, they do.
York. You will be there, I know.
Aum. If God prevent it not; I purpose so.
York. What seal is that, that hangs without thy bosom?[3]
Yea, look'st thou pale? let me see the writing.
Aum. My lord, 'tis nothing.
York. No matter then who sees it;
I will be satisfied, let me see the writing.
Aum. I do beseech your grace to pardon me;
It is a matter of small consequence,
Which for some reasons I would not have seen.
York. Which for some reasons, sir, I mean to see.
I fear, I fear,——
Duch. What should you fear?
'Tis nothing but some bond that he is enter'd into
For gay apparel, 'gainst the triumph day.
York. Bound to himself? what doth he with a bond
That he is bound to? Wife, thou art a fool.—
Boy, let me see the writing.
Aum. I do beseech you, pardon me; I may not show it.
York. I will be satisfied; let me see it, I say.
[*Snatches it, and reads.*
Treason! foul treason!—villain! traitor! slave!
Duch. What is the matter, my lord?
York. Ho! who is within there? [*Enter a* Servant.] Saddle my horse.
God for his mercy! what treachery is here!
Duch. Why, what is it, my lord?
York. Give me my boots, I say; saddle my horse:—
Now by mine honour, by my life, my troth,
I will appeach the villain. [*Exit* Servant.
Duch. What's the matter?
York. Peace, foolish woman.
Duch. I will not peace:—What is the matter, son?
Aum. Good mother, be content; it is no more
Than my poor life must answer.
Duch. Thy life answer?

Re-enter Servant, *with Boots.*

York. Bring me my boots, I will unto the king.
Duch. Strike him, Aumerle.—Poor boy, thou art amaz'd:
Hence, villain; never more come in my sight.—
[*To the* Servant.
York. Give me my boots, I say.
Duch. Why, York, what wilt thou do?
Wilt thou not hide the trespass of thine own?
Have we more sons? or are we like to have?
Is not my teeming date drunk up with time?
And wilt thou pluck my fair son from mine age,
And rob me of a happy mother's name?
Is he not like thee? is he not thine own?
York. Thou fond mad woman,
Wilt thou conceal this dark conspiracy?
A dozen of them here have ta'en the sacrament,
And interchangeably set down their hands,
To kill the king at Oxford.
Duch. He shall be none;
We'll keep him here: Then what is that to him?
York. Away,
Fond woman! were he twenty times my son,
I would appeach him.
Duch. Hadst thou groan'd for him,
As I have done, thou'dst be more pitiful.
But now I know thy mind; thou dost suspect,
That I have been disloyal to thy bed,
And that he is a bastard, not thy son:
Sweet York, sweet husband, be not of that mind:
He is as like thee as a man may be,
Not like to me, or any of my kin,
And yet I love him.
York. Make way, unruly woman.
[*Exit.*
Duch. After, Aumerle; mount thee upon his horse;
Spur, post; and get before him to the king,
And beg thy pardon ere he do accuse thee.
I'll not be long behind; though I be old,
I doubt not but to ride as fast as York:
And never will I rise up from the ground,
Till Bolingbroke have pardon'd thee: Away;
Begone. [*Exeunt.*

SCENE III. Windsor. *A Room in the Castle.*

Enter Bolingbroke *as King;* Percy, *and other* Lords.

Boling. Can no man tell of my unthrifty son?
'Tis full three months since I did see him last:—
If any plague hang over us, 'tis he.
I would to God, my lords, he might be found:
Inquire at London, 'mongst the taverns there,
For there, they say, he daily doth frequent,
With unrestrained loose companions;
Even such, they say, as stand in narrow lanes,
And beat our watch, and rob our passengers;
While he, young, wanton, and effeminate boy,
Takes on the point of honour, to support
So dissolute a crew.[4]
Percy. My lord, some two days since I saw the prince;
And told him of these triumphs held at Oxford.
Boling. And what said the gallant?
Percy. His answer was,—he would unto the stews;
And from the commonest creature pluck a glove,
And wear it as a favour; and with that
He would unhorse the lustiest challenger.
Boling. As dissolute, as desperate: yet, through both
I see some sparkles[5] of a better hope,
Which elder days may happily bring forth.
But who comes here?

Enter Aumerle, *hastily.*

Aum. Where is the king?

---

1 'The dukes of Aumerle, Surrey, and Exeter were deprived of their dukedoms by an act of Henry's first parliament, but were allowed to retain the earldoms of *Rutland*, Kent, and Huntingdon.'—*Holinshed.*

2 So in Milton's Song on May Morning:—
'—— who from her *green lap* throws
The yellow cowslip and the pale primrose.'

3 The seals of deeds were formerly impressed on slips or labels of parchment appendant to them.

4 This is a very proper introduction to the future character of King Henry V. to his debaucheries in his youth, and his greatness in his manhood, as the poet has described them. But it has been ably contended by Mr. Luders that the whole story of his dissipation was a fiction. At this period (i. e. 1400) he was but twelve years old, being born in 1388.

5 The folio reads *sparks*

Boling. What means
Our cousin, that he stares and looks so wildly?
Aum. God save your grace. I do beseech your majesty,
To have some conference with your grace alone.
Boling. Withdraw yourselves, and leave us here alone.— [*Exeunt* PERCY *and* Lords.
What is the matter with our cousin now?
Aum. For ever may my knees grow to the earth, [*Kneels.*
My tongue cleave to my roof within my mouth,
Unless a pardon, ere I rise, or speak.
Boling. Intended, or committed, was this fault?
If but[1] the first, how heinous e'er it be,
To win thy after-love, I pardon thee.
Aum. Then give me leave that I may turn the key,
That no man enter till my tale be done.
Boling. Have thy desire. [AUM. *locks the door.*
York. [*Within.*] My liege, beware; look to thyself;
Thou hast a traitor in thy presence there.
Boling. Villain, I'll make thee safe. [*Drawing.*
Aum. Stay thy revengeful hand;
Thou hast no cause to fear.
York. [*Within.*] Open the door, secure, foolhardy king:
Shall I, for love, speak treason to thy face?
Open the door, or I will break it open.
[BOLINGBROKE *opens the door.*

Enter YORK.

Boling. What is the matter, uncle? speak;
Recover breath; tell us how near is danger,
That we may arm us to encounter it.
York. Peruse this writing here, and thou shalt know
The treason that my haste forbids me show.
Aum. Remember, as thou read'st, thy promise past:
I do repent me; read not my name there,
My heart is not confederate with my hand.
York. 'Twas, villain, ere thy hand did set it down.
I tore it from the traitor's bosom, king:
Fear, and not love, begets his penitence:
Forget to pity him, lest thy pity prove
A serpent that will sting thee to the heart.
Boling. O heinous, strong, and bold conspiracy!
O loyal father of a treacherous son!
Thou sheer,[2] immaculate, and silver fountain,
From whence this stream through muddy passages,
Hath held his current, and defil'd himself!
Thy overflow of good converts to bad;
And thy abundant goodness shall excuse
This deadly blot in thy digressing[3] son.
York. So shall my virtue be his vice's bawd;
And he shall spend mine honour with his shame,
As thriftless sons their scraping fathers' gold.
Mine honour lives when his dishonour dies,
Or my sham'd life in his dishonour lies:
Thou kill'st me in his life; giving him breath,
The traitor lives, the true man's put to death.
Duch. [*Within.*] What ho, my liege! for God's sake let me in.
Boling. What shrill-voic'd suppliant makes this eager cry?
Duch. A woman, and thine aunt, great king; 'tis I.
Speak with me, pity me, open the door;
A beggar begs, that never begg'd before.
Boling. Our scene is alter'd,—from a serious thing,
And now chang'd to *The Beggar and the King*.—
My dangerous cousin, let your mother in;
I know, she's come to pray for your foul sin.
York. If thou do pardon, whosoever pray,
More sins, for his forgiveness, prosper may.
This fester'd joint cut off, the rest rests sound,
This let alone, will all the rest confound.

Enter Duchess.

Duch. O king, believe not this hard-hearted man;
Love, loving not itself, none other can.
York. Thou frantic woman, what dost thou make[5] here?
Shall thy old dugs once more a traitor rear?
Duch. Sweet York, be patient: Hear me, gentle liege. [*Kneels.*
Boling. Rise up, good aunt.
Duch. Not yet, I thee beseech.
For ever will I kneel[6] upon my knees,
And never see day that the happy sees,
Till thou give joy; until thou bid me joy,
By pardoning Rutland, my transgressing boy.
Aum. Unto my mother's prayers, I bend my knee. [*Kneels.*
York. Against them both, my true joints bended be. [*Kneels.*
Ill may'st thou thrive, if thou grant any grace![7]
Duch. Pleads he in earnest? look upon his face;
His eyes do drop no tears, his prayers are in jest;
His words come from his mouth, ours from our breast;
He prays but faintly, and would be denied;
We pray with heart, and soul, and all beside.
His weary joints would gladly rise, I know;
Our knees shall kneel till to the ground they grow:
His prayers are full of false hypocrisy;
Ours, of true zeal and deep integrity.
Our prayers do out-pray his; then let them have
That mercy, which true prayers ought to have.
Boling. Good aunt, stand up.
Duch. Nay, do not say—stand up,
But, pardon, first; and afterwards, stand up.
An if I were thy nurse, thy tongue to teach,
Pardon—should be the first word of thy speech.
I never long'd to hear a word till now;
Say—pardon, king; let pity teach thee how:
The word is short, but not so short as sweet;
No word like pardon, for kings' mouths so meet.
York. Speak it in French, king; say, *pardonnez moy.*[8]
Duch. Dost thou teach pardon pardon to destroy?
Ah, my sour husband, my hard-hearted lord,
That sett'st the word itself against the word!—
Speak, pardon, as 'tis current in our land:
The chopping[9] French we do not understand.
Thine eye begins to speak, set thy tongue there,
Or, in thy piteous heart plant thou thine ear;
That, hearing how our plaints and prayers do pierce,
Pity may move thee, pardon to rehearse.
Boling. Good aunt, stand up.
Duch. I do not sue to stand,
Pardon is all the suit I have in hand.
Boling. I pardon him, as God shall pardon me.
Duch. O happy vantage of a kneeling knee!
Yet am I sick for fear: speak it again;
Twice saying pardon, doth not pardon twain,
But makes one pardon strong.
Boling. With all my heart
I pardon him.[10]
Duch. A god on earth thou art.

---

1 The old copies read 'If *on*,' &c Pope made the alteration.

2 *Sheer* is *pellucid, transparent.*

3 Thus in Romeo and Juliet:—

'*Digressing* from the valour of a man.'

To digress is to deviate from what is right or regular.

4 It is probable that the old ballad of 'King Cophetua and the Beggar Maid' is here alluded to. The reader will find it in the first volume of Dr. Percy's Reliques of Ancient Poetry. There may have been a popular Interlude on the subject, for the story is alluded to by other cotemporaries of the poet.

5 i. e. 'what dost thou *do* here?'

6 Thus the folio The quarto copies read *walk*

7 This line is not in the folio.

8 The French *moy* being made to rhime with *destroy* would seem to imply that the poet was not well acquainted with the true pronunciation of that language: perhaps it was imperfectly understood in his time by those who had not visited France.

9 The *chopping* French, i. e. the *changing* or changeable French. Thus '*chopping* churches' is *changing* one church for another; and *chopping* logic is discoursing or *interchanging* logic with another. To *chop* and change is still a common idiom.

10 The old copies read 'I pardon him with all my heart' The transposition was made by Pope

Boling. But for our trusty brother-in-law,[1]—and the abbot,[2]
With all the rest of that consorted crew,—
Destruction straight shall dog them at the heels.—[3]
Good uncle, help to order several powers
To Oxford, or where'er these traitors are:
They shall not live within this world, I swear,
But I will have them, if I once know where.
Uncle, farewell,—and cousin too,[4] adieu:
Your mother well hath pray'd, and prove you true.
Duch. Come, my old son;—I pray God make thee new. [*Exeunt.*

SCENE IV. *Enter* Exton, *and a* Servant.

Exton. Didst thou not mark the king, what words he spake?
Have I no friend will rid me of this living fear?
Was it not so?
Serv. Those were his very words.
Exton. Have I no friend? quoth he; he spake it twice,
And urg'd it twice together; did he not?
Serv. He did.
Exton. And, speaking it, he wistfully look'd on me;
As who should say,—I would, thou wert the man
That would divorce this terror from my heart;
Meaning, the king at Pomfret. Come, let's go;
I am the king's friend, and will rid[5] his foe. [*Exeunt.*

SCENE V. Pomfret. *The Dungeon of the Castle.* *Enter* King Richard.

K. Rich. I have been studying how I may compare
This prison, where I live, unto the world:
And, for because the world is populous,
And here is not a creature but myself,
I cannot do it;—Yet I'll hammer it out.
My brain I'll prove the female to my soul;
My soul, the father: and these two beget
A generation of still-breeding thoughts,
And these same thoughts people this little world;[6]
In humours, like the people of this world,
For no thought is contented. The better sort,—
As thoughts of things divine,—are intermix'd
With scruples, and do set the word itself
Against the word:[7]
As thus, *Come, little ones*; and then again,—
It is as hard to come, as for a camel
To thread the postern of a needle's eye.
Thoughts tending to ambition, they do plot
Unlikely wonders: how these vain weak nails
May tear a passage through the flinty ribs
Of this hard world, my ragged prison walls;
And, for they cannot, die in their own pride.
Thoughts tending to content, flatter themselves,—
That they are not the first of fortune's slaves,
Nor shall not be the last; like silly beggars,
Who, sitting in the stocks, refuge their shame,—
That many have, and others must sit there:
And in this thought they find a kind of ease,
Bearing their own misfortune on the back
Of such as have before endur'd the like:
Thus play I, in one person, many people,[8]
And none contented: Sometimes am I king:
Then treason makes me wish myself a beggar,
And so I am: Then crushing penury
Persuades me, I was better when a king;
Then am I king'd again: and, by-and-by,
Think that I am unking'd by Bolingbroke,
And straight am nothing:—But, whate'er I am,
Nor I, nor any man, that but man is,
With nothing shall be pleas'd, till he be eas'd
With being nothing.—Music do I hear? [*Music.*
Ha, ha! keep time:—How sour sweet music is,
When time is broke, and no proportion kept!
So is it in the music of men's lives.
And here have I the daintiness of ear
To check[9] time broke in a disorder'd string;
But for the concord of my state and time,
Had not an ear to hear my true time broke.
I wasted time, and now doth time waste me.
For now hath time made me his numb'ring clock:
My thoughts are minutes; and, with sighs, they jar[10]
Their watches on to mine eyes, the outward watch,[11]
Whereto my finger, like a dial's point,
Is pointing still, in cleansing them from tears.
Now, sir, the sound, that tells what hour it is,[12]
Are clamorous groans, that strike upon my heart,
Which is the bell: So sighs, and tears, and groans,
Show minutes, times, and hours:—but my time
Runs posting on in Bolingbroke's proud joy,
While I stand fooling here, his Jack o' the clock.[13]
This music mads me, let it sound no more;
For, though it have holp madmen to their wits,[14]
In me, it seems, it will make wise men mad;
Yet blessing on his heart that gives it me!
For 'tis a sign of love; and love to Richard
Is a strange brooch[15] in this all hating world.

Enter Groom.

Groom. Hail, royal prince!
K. Rich. Thanks, noble peer;
The cheapest of us is ten groats too dear.
What art thou? and how comest thou hither,
Where no man never comes, but that sad dog
That brings me food, to make misfortune live?
Groom. I was a poor groom of thy stable, king,
When thou wert king; who, travelling towards York,
With much ado, at length have gotten leave
To look upon my sometimes[16] master's face.
O, how it yearn'd my heart, when I beheld,
In London streets, that coronation day,
When Bolingbroke rode on roan Barbary!
That horse, that thou so often hast bestrid;
That horse, that I so carefully have dress'd!
K. Rich. Rode he on Barbary? Tell me, gentle friend,
How went he under him?

---

1 The brother-in-law meant was John duke of Exeter and earl of Huntingdon (own brother to Edward II.) who had married the Lady Elizabeth, Bolingbroke's sister.

2 i. e. the abbot of Westminster.

3 'Death and destruction dog thee at the heels.' *King Richard III.*

4 *Too*, which is not in the old copies, was added by Theobald for the sake of the metre.

5 To *rid* and to *dispatch* were formerly synonymous, as may be seen in the old Dictionaries, 'To *ridde* or *dispatche* himself of any man.'—'To *dispatche* or *ridde* one quickly.' Vide Baret's Alvearie, 1576, in Ridde and Dispatche.

6 i. e. his own body.

7 By the *word* is meant the Holy Scriptures. The folio reads the *faith* itself against the *faith*.

8 This is the reading of the quarto, 1597; alluding, perhaps, to the custom of our early theatres. The title pages of some of our Moralities show that three or four characters were frequently represented by *one person*. The folio, and other copies, read 'in one *prison*.'

9 The folio reads 'to *hear*.' 10 Tick.

11 It should be recollected that there are three ways in which a clock notices the progress of time, viz. by the vibration of the pendulum, the index on the dial, and the striking of the hour. To these the king, in his comparison, severally alludes; his sighs corresponding to the *jarring* or ticking of the pendulum, which, at the same time that it watches or numbers the seconds, marks also their progress in minutes on the dial-plate, or *outward watch*, to which the king compares his eyes; and their want of figures is supplied by a succession of tears (or minute drops, to use an expression of Milton,) his finger, by as regularly wiping these away, performs the office of the *dial's point*: his clamorous groans are the sounds that tell the hour.

12 Should we not read:—
'Now, sir, the *sounds* that *tell* what hour it is
Are clamorous groans?' &c.

13 That is, *I strike for him*. One of these automatons is alluded to in King Richard III. Act. iv. Sc. 2:—
'Because that, like a *Jack*, thou keep'st the stroke
Between thy begging and my meditation.'

14 See Burton's Anatomy of Melancholy, part ii. sec. 2

15 *Brooch*, an ornamented buckle, and also a jewel in general, here figuratively used for *jewel*.

16 *Sometimes* was used for *former*, as well as *sometime*. Aliquando.

Groom. So proudly, as if he disdain'd the ground.[1]
K. Rich. So proud that Bolingbroke was on his back!
That jade hath eat bread from my royal hand;
This hand hath made him proud with clapping him.
Would he not stumble? Would he not fall down
(Since pride must have a fall), and break the neck
Of that proud man that did usurp his back?
Forgiveness, horse! why do I rail on thee,
Since thou, created to be awed by man,
Wast born to bear? I was not made a horse;
And yet I bear a burden like an ass,
Spur-gall'd, and tir'd by jauncing[2] Bolingbroke.

Enter Keeper, *with a Dish.*

Keep. Fellow, give place; here is no longer stay. [*To the* Groom.
K. Rich. If thou love me, 'tis time thou wert away.
Groom. What my tongue dares not, that my heart shall say. [*Exit.*
Keep. My lord, will't please you to fall to?
K. Rich. Taste of it first, as thou art wont to do.
Keep. My lord, I dare not; Sir Pierce of Exton, who
Lately came from the king, commands the contrary.
K. Rich. The devil take Henry of Lancaster, and thee!
Patience is stale, and I am weary of it. [*Beats the* Keeper.
Keep. Help, help, help!

Enter EXTON, *and* Servants, *armed.*

K. Rich. How now? what means death in this rude assault?
Villain, thy own hand yields thy death's instrument.
[*Snatching a weapon and killing one.*
Go thou, and fill another room in hell.
[*He kills another, and then* EXTON *strikes him down.*[3]
That hand shall burn in never-quenching fire,
That staggers thus my person.—Exton, thy fierce hand
Hath with the king's blood stain'd the king's own land.
Mount, mount, my soul! thy seat is up on high,
Whilst my gross flesh sinks downward, here to die. [*Dies.*[4]
Exton. As full of valour, as of royal blood:
Both have I spilt! O, 'would the deed were good!
For now the devil, that told me—I did well,
Says, that this deed is chronicled in hell.
This dead king to the living king I'll bear;—
Take hence the rest, and give them burial here. [*Exeunt.*

SCENE VI. Windsor. *A Room in the Castle.*

Flourish. Enter BOLINGBROKE, *and* YORK, *with* Lords *and* Attendants.

Boling. Kind uncle York, the latest news we hear
Is—that the rebels have consum'd with fire
Our town of Cicester in Glocestershire;
But whether they be ta'en, or slain, we hear not.

Enter NORTHUMBERLAND.

Welcome, my lord: What is the news?
North. First, to thy sacred state wish I all happiness.
The next news is,—I have to London sent
The heads of Salisbury, Spencer, Blunt, and Kent:[5]
The manner of their taking may appear
At large discoursed in this paper here. [*Presenting a paper*
Boling. We thank thee, gentle Percy, for thy pains;
And to thy worth will add right worthy gains.

Enter FITZWATER.

Fitz. My lord, I have from Oxford sent to London
The heads of Brocas and Sir Bennet Seely;
Two of the dangerous consorted traitors,
That sought at Oxford thy dire overthrow.
Boling. Thy pains, Fitzwater, shall not be forgot;
Right noble is thy merit, well I wot.

Enter PERCY, *with the Bishop of* Carlisle.

Percy. The grand conspirator, abbot of Westminster,[6]
With clog of conscience, and sour melancholy,
Hath yielded up his body to the grave:
But here is Carlisle living to abide
Thy kingly doom, and sentence of his pride.
Boling. Carlisle, this is your doom:—[7]
Choose out some secret place, some reverend room,
More than thou hast, and with it 'joy thy life;
So, as thou liv'st in peace, die free from strife:
For though mine enemy thou hast ever been,
High sparks of honour in thee have I seen.

Enter EXTON, *with* Attendants *bearing a Coffin.*

Exton. Great king, within this coffin I present
Thy buried fear: herein all breathless lies
The mightiest of thy greatest enemies,
Richard of Bourdeaux, by me hither brought.
Boling. Exton, I thank thee not; for thou hast wrought
A deed of slander, with thy fatal hand,
Upon my head, and all this famous land.
Exton. From your own mouth, my lord, did I this deed.
Boling. They love not poison that do poison need,
Nor do I thee; though I did wish him dead,
I hate the murderer, love him murdered.
The guilt of conscience take thou for thy labour,
But neither my good word nor princely favour:
With Cain go wander through the shade of night,
And never show thy head by day nor light.——
Lords, I protest, my soul is full of woe,
That blood should sprinkle me, to make me grow:
Come, mourn with me for what I do lament,
And put on sullen black incontinent:[8]
I'll make a voyage to the Holy Land,
To wash this blood off from my guilty hand:—
March sadly after; grace my mournings here,
In weeping after this untimely bier. [*Exeunt*

THIS play is one of those which Shakspeare has apparently revised; but as success in works of invention is not always proportionate to labour, it is not finished at last with the happy force of some other of his tragedies, nor can it be said much to affect the passions, or enlarge the understanding. JOHNSON.

---

1 Froissart relates a yet more silly tale of a greyhound of King Richard's, 'who was wont to leape upon the king, but left the king and came to the erle of Derby, duke of Lancastre, and made to him the same friendly countenance and chere as he was wont to do to the king.' —*Froissart, by Berners*, v. ii. fo. cccxxx.

2 *Jancing* is *hard riding*, from the old French word *iancer*, which Cotgrave explains 'To stir a horse in the stable till he sweat withal; or (as our) to jaunt.'

3 These stage directions are not in the old copies.

4 The representation here given of the king's death is perfectly agreeable to Hall and Holinshed (who copied from Fabian, with whom the story of Exton is thought to have its origin.) But the fact was otherwise. He refused food for several days, and died of abstinence and a broken heart. See Walsingham, Otterburne, the monk of Evesham, the Continuator of the History of Croyland, and the Godstow Chronicle. His body, after being submitted to public inspection in the church of Pomfret, was brought to London, and exposed in Cheapside for two hours, 'his heade on a black cushion, and his visage open,' when it was viewed, says Froissart, by twenty thousand persons, and finally in St. Paul's Cathedral. Stowe seems to have had before him a manuscript history of the latter part of King Richard's life, written by a person who was with him in Wales. He says 'he was imprisoned in Pomfrait Castle, where xv dayes and nightes they vexed him with continual hunger, thirst, and cold, and finally bereft him of his life with such a kind of death as never before that time was knowen in England.'

5 So the folio. The quarto reads of *Oxford, Salisbury*, Blunt, and Kent. The folio is right according to the histories.

6 This abbot of Westminster was William de Colchester. The relation, which is taken from Holinshed is untrue, as he survived the king many years; and though called 'the grand conspirator,' it is very doubtful whether he had any concern in the conspiracy; at least nothing was proved against him.

7 The bishop of Carlisle was committed to the Tower but on the intercession of his friends obtained leave to change his prison for Westminster Abbey. In order to deprive him of his see, the pope, at the king's instance, translated him to a bishopric *in partibus infidelium*, and the only preferment he could ever after obtain was a rectory in Gloucestershire.

8 Immediately.

FIRST PART OF

KING HENRY THE FOURTH.

PRELIMINARY REMARKS.

'SHAKSPEARE has apparently designed a regular connection of these dramatic histories, from Richard the Second to Henry the Fifth. King Henry, at the end of Richard the Second, declares his purpose to visit the Holy Land, which he resumes in the first speech of this play. The complaint made by King Henry, in the last act of King Richard the Second, of the wildness of his son, prepares the reader for the frolics which are here to be recounted, and the characters to be exhibited.' —*Johnson.*

The historical dramas of Shakspeare have indeed become the popular history. Vain attempts have been made by Walpole to vindicate the character of King Richard III. and in later times by Mr. Luders, to prove that the youthful dissipation ascribed to King Henry V. is without foundation. The arguments are probable, and ingeniously urged, but we still cling to our early notions of 'that mad-cap—that same sword and buckler Prince of Wales.' No plays were ever more read, nor does the inimitable, all-powerful genius of the poet ever shine out more than in the two parts of King Henry IV. which may be considered as one long drama divided.

It has been said that 'Falstaff is the summit of Shakspeare's comic invention,' and we may consequently add, the most inimitable comic character ever delineated; for who could invent like Shakspeare? Falstaff is now to us hardly a creature of the imagination, he is so definitely and distinctly drawn, that the mere reader of these dramas has the complete impression of a personal acquaintance. He is surrounded by a group of comic personages from time to time, each of which would have been sufficient to throw any ordinary creation into the shade; but they only serve to make the supereminent humour of the knight doubly conspicuous. What can come nigher to truth and real individual nature than those admirable delineations, Shallow and Silence? How irresistibly comic are all the scenes in which Falstaff is made to humour the fatuity and vanity of this precious pair.

The historic characters are delineated with a felicity and individuality not inferior in any respect. Harry Percy is a creation of the first order; and our favourite harebrained Prince of Wales, in whom mirthful pleasantry and midnight dissipation are mixed up with heroic dignity and generous feeling, is a rival worthy of him. Owen Glendower is another personification, managed with the most consummate skill; and the graver characters are sustained and opposed to each other in a manner peculiar to our great poet alone.

The transactions contained in the First Part of King Henry IV. are comprised within the period of about ten months; for the action commences with the news brought of Hotspur having defeated the Scots under Archibald earl of Douglas, at Holmedon (or Halidown Hill,) which battle was fought on Holyrood-day (the 14th of September,) 1402; and it closes with the battle of Shrewsbury, on Saturday, the 21st of July, 1403.

Malone places the date of the composition of this play in 1597; Dr. Drake in 1596. It was first entered at Stationers' Hall, February 25, 1597. There are no less than five quarto editions published during the author's life, viz. in 1598, 1599, 1604, 1608, 1613. For the piece which is supposed to have been its original the reader is referred to the 'Six Old Plays on which Shakspeare founded,' &c. published by Steevens and Nichols

PERSONS REPRESENTED.

KING HENRY THE FOURTH.
HENRY, Prince *of* Wales, } *Sons to the King.*
Prince JOHN *of* Lancaster, }
Earl *of* Westmoreland, } *Friends to the King.*
SIR WALTER BLUNT, }
THOMAS PERCY, Earl *of* Worcester.
HENRY PERCY, Earl *of* Northumberland.
HENRY PERCY, *surnamed* Hotspur, *his son.*
EDWARD MORTIMER, Earl *of* March.
SCROOP, Archbishop *of* York.
ARCHIBALD, Earl *of* Douglas.
OWEN GLENDOWER.
SIR RICHARD VERNON.
SIR JOHN FALSTAFF.
POINS. GADSHILL.
PETO. BARDOLPH.

LADY PERCY, *Wife to* Hotspur, *and Sister to* Mortimer.
LADY MORTIMER, *Daughter to* Glendower, *and Wife to* Mortimer.
MRS. QUICKLY, *Hostess of a Tavern in Eastcheap.*
Lords, Officers, Sheriff, Vintner, Chamberlain, Drawers, two Carriers, Travellers *and* Attendants.

SCENE, England.

ACT I.

SCENE I. London. *A Room in the Palace.*

Enter KING HENRY, WESTMORELAND, SIR WALTER BLUNT, *and others.*

King Henry.

So shaken as we are, so wan with care,
Find we a time for frighted peace to pant,
And breathe short-winded accents of new broils
To be commenc'd in stronds[1] afar remote.
No more the thirsty entrance of this soil[2]
Shall daub her lips with her own children's blood;
No more shall trenching war channel her fields,
Nor bruise her flowrets with the armed hoofs
Of hostile paces: those opposed eyes,
Which,—like the meteors of a troubled heaven,
All of one nature, of one substance bred,—

1 Strands, banks of the sea.

2 Upon this passage the reader is favoured with three pages of notes in the Variorum Shakspeare. Steevens adopted Monk Mason's bold conjectural emendation, and reads—

'No more the thirsty *Erinnys* of this soil;'

which, in my opinion, does not make the passage clearer, to say nothing of the improbability of such a corruption as *entrance* for *Erinnys.* Mr. Douce proposed to read *entrails* instead of *entrance;* and Steevens once thought that we should read *entrants.* I am satisfied with the following explanation of the text, modified

Did lately meet in the intestine shock
And furious close of civil butchery,
Shall now, in mutual, well-beseeming ranks,
March all one way; and be no more oppos'd
Against acquaintance, kindred, and allies:
The edge of war, like an ill-sheathed knife,
No more shall cut his master. Therefore, friends,
As far as to the sepulchre of Christ,
(Whose soldier now, under whose blessed cross
We are impressed and engag'd to fight,)
Forthwith a power of English shall we levy,[1]
Whose arms were moulded in their mother's womb,
To chase these pagans, in those holy fields,
Over whose acres walk'd those blessed feet,
Which, fourteen hundred years ago, were nail'd
For our advantage, on the bitter cross.
But this our purpose is a twelvemonth old,
And bootless 'tis to tell you—we will go;
Therefore we meet not now:—Then let me hear
Of you, my gentle cousin Westmoreland,
What yesternight our council did decree,
In forwarding this dear expedience.[2]

West. My liege, this haste was hot in question,
And many limits[3] of the charge set down
But yesternight: when, all athwart, there came
A post from Wales, loaden with heavy news;
Whose worst was,—that the noble Mortimer,
Leading the men of Herefordshire to fight
Against the irregular and wild Glendower,
Was by the rude hands of that Welshman taken,
And a thousand of his people butchered:
Upon whose dead corpse there was such misuse,
Such beastly, shameless transformation,
By those Welshwomen[4] done, as may not be,
Without much shame, retold or spoken of.

K. Hen. It seems, then, that the tidings of this broil
Brake off our business for the Holy Land.

West. This, match'd with other, did, my gracious lord;
For more uneven and unwelcome news
Came from the north, and thus it did import.
On Holyrood-day,[5] the gallant Hotspur there,
Young Harry Percy,[6] and brave Archibald,[7]
That ever-valiant and approved Scot,
At Holmedon met,
Where they did spend a sad and bloody hour;
As by discharge of their artillery,
And shape of likelihood, the news was told;
For he that brought them, in the very heat
And pride of their contention did take horse,
Uncertain of the issue any way.

K. Hen. Here is a dear and true-industrious friend,
Sir Walter Blunt, new lighted from his horse,
Stain'd[8] with the variation of each soil
Betwixt that Holmedon and this seat of ours;
And he hath brought us smooth and welcome news.
The earl of Douglas is discomfited;
Ten thousand bold Scots, two-and-twenty knights,
Balk'd[9] in their own blood, did Sir Walter see
On Holmedon's plains: Of prisoners, Hotspur took
Mordake earl of Fife, and eldest son
To beaten Douglas,[10] and the earls of Athol,
Of Murray, Angus, and Menteith.[11]
And is not this an honourable spoil?
A gallant prize? ha, cousin, is it not?

West. In faith,
It is a conquest for a prince to boast of.

K. Hen. Yea, there thou mak'st me sad, and mak'st me sin
In envy that my lord Northumberland
Should be the father of so blest a son:
A son, who is the theme of honour's tongue;
Amongst a grove, the very straightest plant;
Who is sweet fortune's minion, and her pride:
Whilst I, by looking on the praise of him,
See riot and dishonour stain the brow
Of my young Harry. O, that it could be prov'd,
That some night-tripping fairy had exchang'd
In cradle-clothes our children where they lay,
And call'd mine—Percy, his—Plantagenet!
Then would I have his Harry, and he mine.
But let him from my thoughts:—What think you, coz,
Of this young Percy's pride? the prisoners,[12]
Which he in this adventure hath surpris'd,
To his own use he keeps; and sends me word,
I shall have none but Mordake earl of Fife.

West. That is his uncle's teaching, this is Worcester,
Malevolent to you in all aspects;[13]
Which makes him prune[14] himself, and bristle up
The crest of youth against your dignity.

K. Hen. But I have sent for him to answer this;
And, for this cause, awhile we must neglect
Our holy purpose to Jerusalem.
Cousin, on Wednesday next our council we
Will hold at Windsor; so inform the lords:
But come yourself with speed to us again;
For more is to be said, and to be done,
Than out of anger can be uttered.[15]

West. I will, my liege. [*Exeunt.*

SCENE II. *The same. Another Room in the Palace. Enter* HENRY, *Prince of* Wales, *and* FALSTAFF.

Fal. Now, Hal, what time of day is it, lad?

---

from that of Malone:—'No more shall this soil *have* the lips of her thirsty entrance (i. e. surface) daubed with the blood of her own children.' The soil is personified, and called the *mother* of those who live upon her surface; as in the following passage of King Richard II.:—

'——— sweet *soil*, adieu,
My *mother* and my nurse, that bears me yet.'

1 To levy a power *to* a place has been shown by Mr. Gifford to be neither unexampled nor corrupt, but good authorized English. 'Scipio, before he *levied* his force *to* the walls of Carthage, gave his soldiers the print of the city on a cake to be devoured.'—*Gosson's School of Abuse*, 1587, E. 4.

2 Expedition.

3 *Limits* here seem to mean *appointments* or *determinations.*

4 See Thomas of Walsingham, p. 557, or Holinshed, p. 528.

5 i. e. September 14th.

6 'This *Harry Percy* was surnamed, for his often pricking, *Henry Hotspur*, as one that seldom times rested, if there were anie service to be done abroad.'—*Holinshed's Hist. of Scotland*, p. 240.

7 *Archibald* Douglas, Earl Douglas.

8 No circumstance could have been better chosen to mark the expedition of Sir Walter. It is used by Falstaff in a similar manner,—'to stand *stained with travel*,' &c.

9 *Balk'd* in their own blood, is *heaped*, or *laid on heaps*, in their own blood. A *balk* was a ridge or bank of earth standing up between two furrows and to *balk* was to throw up the earth so as to form those heaps or banks. It was sometimes used in the sense of *monceau*. Fr. for a heap or hill.

10 Mordake, earl of Fife, who was son to the duke of Albany, regent of Scotland, is here called the son of Earl Douglas, through a mistake, into which the poet was led by the omission of a comma in the passage from whence he took this account of the Scottish prisoners.

11 This is a mistake of Holinshed in his English History, for in that of Scotland, pp. 259, 262, 419, he speaks of the earl of Fife and Menteith as one and the same person.

12 Percy had an exclusive right to these prisoners, except the earl of Fife. By the law of arms, every man who had taken any captive, whose redemption did not exceed ten thousand crowns, had him clearly to himself to acquit or ransom at his pleasure. But Percy could not refuse the earl of Fife to the king; for, being a prince of the royal blood, (son to the duke of Albany, brother to King Robert III.) Henry might justly claim him, by his acknowledged military prerogative.

13 An astrological allusion. Worcester is represented as a malignant star, that influenced the conduct of Hotspur.

14 The metaphor is borrowed from falconry. A hawk is said to *prune* herself when she picks off the loose feathers and smooths the rest: it is applied to other birds, and is perhaps so familiar as hardly to require a note.

15 That is, more is to be said than anger will suffer me to say; more than can issue from a mind disturbed like mine

P. Hen. Thou art so fat-witted, with drinking of old sack, and unbuttoning thee after supper, and sleeping upon benches after noon, that thou hast forgotten to demand that truly which thou would'st truly know. What the devil hast thou to do with the time of the day? unless hours were cups of sack, and minutes capons, and clocks the tongues of bawds, and dials the signs of leaping-houses, and the blessed sun himself a fair hot wench in flame-coloured taffata, I see no reason why thou should'st be so superfluous to demand the time of the day.

Fal. Indeed, you come near me now, Hal; for we, that take purses, go by the moon and seven stars; and not by Phœbus,—he, *that wandering knight so fair.*[1] And, I pray thee, sweet wag, when thou art king,—as, God save thy grace—(majesty, I should say; for grace thou wilt have none,)——

P. Hen. What, none?

Fal. No, by my troth; not so much as will serve to be prologue to an egg and butter.

P. Hen. Well, how then? come, roundly, roundly.

Fal. Marry, then, sweet wag, when thou art king, let not us, that are squires of the night's body, be called thieves of the day's beauty;[2] let us be—Diana's foresters,[3] gentlemen of the shade, minions of the moon: And let men say, we be men of good government: being governed as the sea is, by our noble and chaste mistress the moon, under whose countenance we—steal.

P. Hen. Thou say'st well; and it holds well too; for the fortune of us, that are the moon's men, doth ebb and flow like the sea; being governed as the sea is, by the moon. As, for proof, now: A purse of gold most resolutely snatched on Monday night, and most dissolutely spent on Tuesday morning; got with swearing—lay by;[4] and spent with crying—bring in:[5] now, in as low an ebb as the foot of the ladder; and, by and by, in as high a flow as the ridge of the gallows.

Fal. By the Lord, thou say'st true, lad. And is not my hostess of the tavern a most sweet wench?

P. Hen. As the honey of Hybla, my old lad of the castle.[6] And is not a buff jerkin, a most sweet robe of durance?[7]

Fal. How now, how now, mad wag? what, in thy quips, and thy quiddities? what a plague have I to do with a buff jerkin?

P. Hen. Why, what a pox have I to do with my hostess of the tavern?

Fal. Well, thou hast called her to a reckoning, many a time and oft.

P. Hen. Did I ever call for thee to pay thy part?

Fal. No; I'll give thee thy due, thou hast paid all there.

P. Hen. Yea, and elsewhere, so far as my coin would stretch; and where it would not, I have used my credit.

Fal. Yea, and so used it, that were it not here apparent that thou art heir apparent,—But, I pr'ythee, sweet wag, shall there be gallows standing in England when thou art king? and resolution thus fobbed as it is, with the rusty curb of old father antic the law? Do not thou, when thou art king, hang a thief.

P. Hen. No; thou shalt.

Fal. Shall I? O rare! By the Lord, I'll be a brave judge.

P. Hen. Thou judgest false already; I mean, thou shalt have the hanging of the thieves, and so become a rare hangman.

Fal. Well, Hal, well; and in some sort it jumps with my humour, as well as waiting in the court, I can tell you.

P. Hen. For obtaining of suits?

Fal. Yea, for obtaining of suits: whereof the hangman hath no lean wardrobe. 'Sblood, I am as melancholy as a gib[8] cat, or a lugged bear.

P. Hen. Or an old lion; or a lover's lute.

Fal. Yea, or the drone of a Lincolnshire bagpipe.[9]

P. Hen. What sayest thou to a hare,[10] or the melancholy of Moor-ditch?[11]

Fal. Thou hast the most unsavoury similes: and art, indeed, the most comparative,[12] rascalliest,—sweet young prince,—But, Hal, I pr'ythee, trouble me no more with vanity. I would to God, thou and I knew where a commodity of good names were to be bought: An old lord of the council rated me the other day in the street about you, sir; but I marked him not: and yet he talk'd very wisely; but I regarded him not: and yet he talk'd wisely, and in the street too.

P. Hen. Thou did'st well; for wisdom cries out in the streets, and no man regards it.[13]

---

1 Falstaff, with great propriety, according to vulgar astronomy, calls the sun a *wandering knight*, and by this expression evidently alludes to some knight of romance; perhaps 'The Knight of the Sun;' el Cavallero del Febo, a popular book in his time. The words may be part of some forgtoten ballad.

2 'Let not us who are body squires to the night (i. e. adorn the night) be called a disgrace to the day.' To take away the beauty of the day may probably mean to disgrace it. A 'squire of the body' originally signified the attendant of a knight. It became afterwards the cant term for *a pimp*. Falstaff puns on the words *knight* and *beauty*, quasi *booty*.

3 'Exile and slander are justly me awarded,
My wife and heire lacke lands and lawful right;
And me their lord made dame *Diana's knight.*'

This is the lament of Thomas Mowbray, duke of Norfolk, in The Mirror for Magistrates. Hall, in his Chronicles, says that certain persons who appeared as *foresters* in a pageant exhibited in the reign of King Henry VIII. were called *Diana's knights*.

4 To *lay by* is to *be still*. It occurs again in King Henry VIII.:—

'Even the billows of the sea
Hung their heads, and then *lay by.*'

Steevens says that it is a term adopted from navigation.

5 i. e. 'bring in more wine.'

6 Old lad of the castle. This passage has been supposed to have a reference to the name of Sir John *Oldcastle*. Rowe says that there was a tradition that the part of Falstaff was originally written by Shakspeare under that name. Fuller, in his Church History, book iv. p. 168, mentions this change in the following manner:—'Stage poets have themselves been very bold with, and others very merry at, the memory of Sir John Oldcastle, whom they have fancied a boon companion, a jovial royster, and a coward to boot. The best is, Sir John Falstaff hath relieved the memory of Sir John Oldcastle, and of late is substituted buffoon in his place.' In confirmation of this, it may be remarked that one of Falstaff's speeches in the first edition has *Old.* instead of *Falst.* prefixed to it: and in the epilogue to the Second Part of King Henry IV. the poet makes a kind of retractation for having made too free with Sir John Oldcastle's name—'Where, for any thing I know, *Falstaff* shall die of a sweat, unless he be killed with your hard opinions; for *Oldcastle* died a martyr, and *this is not the man.*'

7 The *buff*, or leather jerkin, was the common habit of a serjeant, or sheriff's officer, and is called a robe of *durance* on that account, as well as for its durability: an equivoque is intended. In the Comedy of Errors, Act iv. Sc. 2, it is called an *everlasting garment*. *Durance* might also have signified some lasting kind of stuff, such as is at present called *everlasting*.

8 A *gib* cat is a *male* cat, from Gilbert, the northern name for a he cat. *Tom* cat is now the usual term.

9 'Lincolnshire bagpipes' is a proverbial saying; the allusion is as yet unexplained. Perhaps it was a favourite instrument in that county, as well as in the north.

10 The *hare* was esteemed a melancholy animal, from her solitary sitting in her form; and, according to the physic of the times, the flesh of it was supposed to generate melancholy.

11 *Moor-ditch*, a part of the ditch surrounding the city of London, between Bishopsgate and Cripplegate, opened to an unwholesome, impassable morass, and was consequently not frequented by the citizens, like other suburbial fields, and therefore had an air of melancholy. Thus in Taylor's Pennylesse Pilgrimage, 1618:—'my body being tired with travel, and my mind attired with moody muddy, *Moore-ditch melancholy.*'

12 *Comparative;* this epithet, which is used here for *one who is fond of making comparisons*, occurs again in Act iii. Sc. 2, of this play.

13 This is a scriptural expression See Proverbs, i 20 and 24

Fal. O thou hast damnable iteration;[1] and art, indeed, able to corrupt a saint. Thou hast done much harm upon me, Hal,—God forgive thee for it! Before I knew thee, Hal, I knew nothing; and now am I, if a man should speak truly, little better than one of the wicked. I must give over this life, and I will give it over; by the Lord, an I do not, I am a villain; I'll be damned for never a king's son in Christendom.

P. Hen. Where shall we take a purse to-morrow, Jack?

Fal. Where thou wilt, lad, I'll make one; an I do not, call me villain, and baffle[2] me.

P. Hen. I see a good amendment of life in thee: from praying, to purse-taking.

Enter Poins, *at a distance.*

Fal. Why, Hal, 'tis my vocation, Hal; 'tis no sin for a man to labour in his vocation. Poins!—Now shall we know if Gadshill have set a match.[3] O, if men were to be saved by merit, what hole in hell were hot enough for him? This is the most omnipotent villain, that ever cried, Stand, to a true[4] man.

P. Hen. Good morrow, Ned.

Poins. Good morrow, sweet Hal.—What says monsieur Remorse? What says Sir John Sack-and-Sugar?[5] Jack, how agrees the devil and thee about thy soul, that thou soldest him on Good-friday last, for a cup of Madeira, and a cold capon's leg?

P. Hen. Sir John stands to his word, the devil shall have his bargain; for he was never yet a breaker of proverbs, he will give the devil his due.

Poins. Then art thou damned for keeping thy word with the devil.

P. Hen. Else he had been damned for cozening the devil.

Poins. But, my lads, my lads, to-morrow morning, by four o'clock, early at Gadshill: There are pilgrims going to Canterbury with rich offerings, and traders riding to London with fat purses: I have visors[6] for you all, you have horses for yourselves; Gadshill lies to-night in Rochester; I have bespoke supper to-morrow night in Eastcheap; we may do it as secure as sleep: If you will go, I will stuff your purses full of crowns; If you will not, tarry at home, and be hanged.

Fal. Hear me, Yedward; if I tarry at home, and go not, I'll hang you for going.

Poins. You will, chops?

Fal. Hal, wilt thou make one?

P. Hen. Who, I rob? I a thief? not I, by my faith.

Fal. There's neither honesty, manhood, nor good fellowship in thee, nor thou camest not of the blood royal, if thou darest not stand for ten shillings.[7]

P. Hen. Well, then once in my days I'll be a mad-cap.

Fal. Why, that's well said.

P. Hen. Well, come what will, I'll tarry at home.

Fal. By the Lord, I'll be a traitor then, when thou art king.

P. Hen. I care not.

Poins. Sir John, I pr'ythee, leave the prince and me alone; I will lay him down such reasons for this adventure, that he shall go.

Fal. Well, may'st thou have the spirit of persuasion, and he the ears of profiting, that what thou speakest may move, and what he hears may be believed, that the true prince may (for recreation sake) prove a false thief; for the poor abuses of the time want countenance. Farewell: you shall find me in Eastcheap.

P. Hen. Farewell, thou latter spring! Farewell All-hallown summer![8] [*Exit* Falstaff.

Poins. Now, my good sweet honey lord, ride with us to-morrow; I have a jest to execute, that I cannot manage alone. Falstaff, Bardolph, Peto, and Gadshill,[9] shall rob those men that we have already way-laid; yourself, and I, will not be there: and when they have the booty, if you and I do not rob them, cut this head from my shoulders.

P. Hen. But how shall we part with them in setting forth?

Poins. Why, we will set forth before or after them, and appoint them a place of meeting, wherein it is at our pleasure to fail; and then will they adventure upon the exploit themselves; which they shall have no sooner achieved, but we'll set upon them.

P. Hen. Ay, but, 'tis like, that they will know us, by our horses, by our habits, and by every other appointment, to be ourselves.

Poins. Tut! our horses they shall not see; I'll tie them in the wood; our visors we will change, after we leave them; and sirrah, I have cases of buckram for the nonce,[10] to immask our noted outward garments.

P. Hen. But, I doubt, they will be too hard for us.

Poins. Well, for two of them, I know them to be as true-bred cowards as ever turned back; and for the third, if he fight longer than he sees reason, I'll forswear arms. The virtue of this jest will be, the incomprehensible lies that this same fat rogue will tell us, when we meet at supper: how thirty, at least, he fought with; what wards, what blows, what extremities he endured; and, in the reproof[11] of this, lies the jest.

P. Hen. Well, I'll go with thee: provide us all things necessary, and meet me to-morrow night[12] in Eastcheap; there I'll sup. Farewell.

Poins. Farewell, my lord. [*Exit* Poins.

---

1 i. e. thou hast a *wicked trick of repetition*, and (*by the misapplication of holy texts*) art indeed able to corrupt a saint.

2 *To baffle* is to use contemptuously, or treat with ignominy; to unknight. It was originally a punishment of infamy inflicted on recreant knights, one part of which was *hanging them up by the heels*. Hall, in his Chronicle, p. 40, mentions it as still practised in Scotland. Something of the same kind is implied in a subsequent scene, where Falstaff says: '*hang me up by the heels* for a rabbit sucker, or a poulterer's hare.' See King Richard II. Act i. Sc. 1.

3 *To set a match* is to make an appointment. So in Ben Jonson's Bartholomew Fair, 'Peace, sir, they'll be angry if they hear you eaves-dropping, now they are *setting their match*.' The folio reads set a *watch*; *match* is the reading of the quarto.

4 Honest.

5 After all the discussion about Falstaff's favourite beverage, here mentioned for the first time, it appears to have been the Spanish wine which we now call *sherry*. Falstaff expressly calls it *sherris-sack*, that is *sack* from *Xeres*. '*Sherry* sack, so called from *Xeres*, a sea town of Corduba, in Spain, where that kind of *sack* is made.'—*Blount's Glossographia.* It derives its name of *sack* probably from being a *dry* wine, *vin sec.* And it was anciently written *seck*. 'Your best *sacke*,' says Gervase Markham, 'are of *Seres* in Spaine.'—*Engl. Housewife.* The difficulty about it has arisen from the later importation of sweet wines from Malaga, the Canaries, &c. which were at first called Malaga, or Canary *sacks*; sack being by that time considered as a name applicable to all white wines.

6 Masks.

7 Falstaff is quibbling on the word *royal*. The *real* or *royal* was of the value of *ten shillings*.

8 i. e. late summer. *All hallown* tide meaning All-saints, which festival is the first of November.

9 The old copy reads Falstaff, *Harvey, Rossil*, and Gadshill. Theobald thinks that Harvey and Rossil might be the names of the actors who played the parts of *Bardolph* and *Peto*.

10 For the *nonce* signified for the *purpose*, for the *occasion*, for the *once*. Junius and Tooke, in their Etymology of *Anon*, led the way; and Mr. Gifford has since clearly explained its meaning. The editor of the new edition of Warton's History of English Poetry (vol ii. p. 496,) has shown that it is nothing more than a slight variation of the A. S. 'for then anes'—'for then anis,'—'for then ones, or once.' Similar inattention to this form of the prepositive article has produced the phrases 'at the nale,' 'at the nend;' which have been transformed from 'at than ale,' 'at than end.'

11 *Reproof* is *confutation*. To refute, to refell, to disallow, were ancient synonymes of *to reprove*.

12 We should read *to-night*, for the robbery was to be committed, according to Poins, 'to-morrow morning by four o'clock.' Shakspeare had forgotten what he had written at the beginning of this scene

P. Hen. I know you all, and will a while uphold
The unyok'd humour of your idleness:
Yet herein will I imitate the sun;
Who doth permit the base contagious clouds[1]
To smother up his beauty from the world,
That, when he please again to be himself,
Being wanted, he may be more wonderd at,
By breaking through the foul and ugly mists
Of vapours, that did seem to strangle[2] him.
If all the year were playing holidays,
To sport would be as tedious as to work;
But, when they seldom come, they wish'd-for come,
And nothing pleaseth but rare accidents.
So, when this loose behaviour I throw off,
And pay the debt I never promised,
By how much better than my word I am,
By so much shall I falsify men's hopes;[3]
And, like bright metal on a sullen[4] ground,
My reformation, glittering o'er my fault,
Shall show more goodly, and attract more eyes,
Than that which hath no foil to set it off.
I'll so offend, to make offence a skill;
Redeeming time, when men think least I will.
[*Exit.*

SCENE III. *The same. Another Room in the Palace. Enter* KING HENRY, NORTHUMBERLAND, WORCESTER, HOTSPUR, SIR WALTER BLUNT, *and others.*

K. Hen. My blood hath been too cold and temperate,
Unapt to stir at these indignities,
And you have found me; for, accordingly,
You tread upon my patience: but, be sure,
I will from henceforth rather be myself,
Mighty, and to be fear'd, than my condition,[5]
Which hath been smooth as oil, soft as young down,
And therefore lost that title of respect,
Which the proud soul ne'er pays, but to the proud.
Wor. Our house, my sovereign liege, little deserves
The scourge of greatness to be used on it;
And that same greatness too which our own hands
Have holp to make so portly.
North. My lord,——
K. Hen. Worcester, get thee gone, for I do see
Danger and disobedience in thine eye:
O, sir, your presence is too bold and peremptory,
And majesty might never yet endure
The moody frontier[6] of a servant brow.
You have good leave to leave us; when we need
Your use and counsel, we shall send for you.—
[*Exit* WORCESTER.
You were about to speak. [*To* NORTH.
North. Yea, my good lord.
Those prisoners in your highness' name demanded,
Which Harry Percy here at Holmedon took,
Were, as he says, not with such strength denied
As is deliver'd to your majesty:
Either envy, therefore, or misprision
Is guilty of this fault, and not my son.
Hot. My liege, I did deny no prisoners,
But, I remember, when the fight was done,
When I was dry with rage, and extreme toil,
Breathless and faint, leaning upon my sword,
Came there a certain lord, neat, trimly dress'd,
Fresh as a bridegroom; and his chin, new reap'd,
Show'd like a stubble-land at harvest home;[7]
He was perfumed like a milliner:
And 'twixt his finger and his thumb he held
A pouncet-box,[8] which ever and anon
He gave his nose, and took't away again;—
Who, therewith angry, when it next came there,
Took it in snuff:[9]—and still he smil'd, and talk'd;
And, as the soldiers bore dead bodies by,
He call'd them—untaught knaves, unmannerly,
To bring a slovenly unhandsome corse
Betwixt the wind and his nobility.
With many holiday and lady terms
He question'd me; among the rest demanded
My prisoners, in your majesty's behalf.
I then, all smarting, with my wounds being cold,
To be so pester'd with a popinjay,[10]
Out of my grief[11] and my impatience,
Answer'd neglectingly, I know not what;
He should, or he should not;—for he made me mad,
To see him shine so brisk, and smell so sweet,
And talk so like a waiting-gentlewoman,
Of guns, and drums, and wounds (God save the mark!)
And telling me the sovereign'st thing on earth
Was parmaceti, for an inward bruise;[12]
And that it was great pity, so it was,
That villanous salt-petre should be digg'd
Out of the bowels of the harmless earth
Which many a good tall fellow had destroy'd
So cowardly; and, but for these vile guns,
He would himself have been a soldier.
This bald unjointed, chat of his, my lord,
I answer'd indirectly as I said;
And, I beseech you, let not his report
Come current for an accusation,
Betwixt my love and your high majesty.
Blunt. The circumstance consider'd, good my lord,
Whatever Harry Percy then had said,
To such a person, and in such a place,
At such a time, with all the rest re-told,
May reasonably die, and never rise
To do him wrong, or any way impeach
What then he said, so he unsay it now.
K. Hen. Why, yet he doth deny his prisoners;
But with proviso, and exception,—
That we, at our own charge, shall ransom straight
His brother-in-law, the foolish Mortimer;[13]

'Full many a glorious morning have I seen,
Flatter the mountain tops with sovereign eye,—
Anon *permit* the *basest clouds* to ride
With *ugly* rack on his celestial face.'
Shakspeare's 33d Sonnet.

2 Thus in Macbeth:—
'And yet dark night *strangles* the travelling lamp.'

3 *Hopes* is used simply for *expectations*, no uncommon use of the word even at the present day.

4 So in King Richard II.:—
'The *sullen* passage of thy weary steps
Esteem a *foil*, wherein thou art to set
The precious jewel of thy home return.'

5 *Condition* is used for *nature, disposition*, as well as *estate* or fortune. It is so interpreted by Philips, in his World of Words. And we find it most frequently used in this sense by Shakspeare and his contemporaries.

6 *Frontier* is said anciently to have meant *forehead*, to prove which the following quotation has been adduced from *Stubbe's Anatomy of Abuses*: 'Then on the edges of their bolster'd hair, which standeth ousted round their *frontiers*, and hangeth over their brow.' Mr. Nares has justly observed, that 'this does not seem to explain the above passage, "The moody *forehead* of a servant brow," is not sense.' Surely it may be better interpreted 'the moody or threatening *outwork*:' in which sense *frontier* is used in Act ii. Sc

7 To completely understand this simile the reader should bear in mind that the courtier's beard, according to the fashion in the poet's time, would not be closely shaved, but *shorn* or *trimmed*, and would therefore show like a stubble land new reap'd.

8 A box perforated with small holes, for carrying perfumes; quasi *pounced-box*.

9 *Took it in snuff* means no more than *snuffed it up*, but there is a quibble on the phrase, which was equivalent to *taking huff at it*, in familiar modern speech; to be angry, to take offence; '*To take in snuffe*, Pigliar ombra, Pigliar in mala parte.'—*Torriano.*

10 A *popinjay* or *popingay* is a *parrot*.

11 i. e. *pain, dolor ventris* is rendered *belly-grief* in the old dictionaries.

12 So in Sir T. Overburie's Characters, 1616 [An Ordinarie Fencer,] 'his wounds are seldom skin-deepe; for an *inward-bruise* lambstones and sweete breads are his only *spermaceti*.'

13 Shakspeare has fallen into some contradictions with regard to this Lord Mortimer. Before he makes his personal appearance in the play, he is repeatedly spoken of as Hotspur's *brother-in-law*. In Act II. Lady Percy expressly calls him *her brother* Mortimer. And yet when he enters in the third Act, he calls Lady Percy *his aunt*, which in fact she was and not his sister.

Who, on my soul, hath wilfully betray'd
The lives of those that he did lead to fight
Against the great magician, damn'd Glendower;
Whose daughter, as we hear, the earl of March
Hath lately married. Shall our coffers then
Be emptied, to redeem a traitor home?
Shall we buy treason? and indent[1] with fears,
When they have lost and forfeited themselves?
No, on the barren mountains let him starve;
For I shall never hold that man my friend,
Whose tongue shall ask me for one penny cost
To ransom home revolted Mortimer.

Hot. Revolted Mortimer!
He never did fall off, my sovereign liege,
But by the chance of war;—To prove that true,
Needs no more but one tongue for all those wounds,
Those mouthed wounds, which valiantly he took,
When on the gentle Severn's sedgy bank,
In single opposition, hand to hand,
He did confound[2] the best part of an hour
In changing hardiment with great Glendower:
Three times they breath'd, and three times did they drink,
Upon agreement, of swift Severn's flood;
Who, then affrighted with their bloody looks,
Ran fearfully among the trembling reeds,
And hid his crisp[3] head in the hollow bank,
Blood-stained with these valiant combatants.
Never did bare[4] and rotten policy
Colour her working with such deadly wounds;
Nor never could the noble Mortimer
Receive so many, and all willingly:
Then let him not be slander'd with revolt.

K. Hen. Thou dost belie him, Percy, thou dost belie him;
He never did encounter with Glendower;
I tell thee,
He durst as well have met the devil alone,
As Owen Glendower for an enemy.
Art thou not asham'd? But, sirrah, henceforth
Let me not hear you speak of Mortimer:
Send me your prisoners with the speediest means,
Or you shall hear in such a kind from me
As will displease you.—My Lord Northumberland,
We license your departure with your son:—
Send us your prisoners, or you'll hear of it.
[*Exeunt* KING HENRY, BLUNT, *and Train.*

Hot. And if the devil come and roar for them,
I will not send them;—I will after straight,
And tell him so; for I will ease my heart,
Although it be with hazard of my head.

North. What, drunk with choler? stay, and pause awhile;
Here comes your uncle.

Re-enter WORCESTER.

Hot. Speak of Mortimer?
'Zounds, I will speak of him; and let my soul
Want mercy, if I do not join with him:
Yea, on his part, I'll empty all these veins,
And shed my dear blood drop by drop i' the dust,
But I will lift the down-trod Mortimer
As high i' the air as this unthankful king,
As this ingrate and canker'd Bolingbroke.

North. Brother, the king hath made your nephew mad. [*To* WORCESTER.

Wor. Who struck this heat up, after I was gone?

Hot. He will, forsooth, have all my prisoners;
And when I urg'd the ransom once again
Of my wife's brother, then his cheek look'd pale;
And on my face he turn'd an eye of death,
Trembling even at the name of Mortimer.

Wor. I cannot blame him: Was he not proclaim'd,
By Richard that dead is, the next of blood?[5]

North. He was; I heard the proclamation:
And then it was, when the unhappy king
(Whose wrongs in us God pardon!) did set forth
Upon his Irish expedition;
From whence he, intercepted, did return
To be depos'd, and shortly, murdered.

Wor. And for whose death, we in the world's wide mouth
Live scandaliz'd, and foully spoken of.

Hot. But, soft, I pray you; Did King Richard then
Proclaim my brother Edmund Mortimer
Heir to the crown?

North. He did; myself did hear it.

Hot. Nay, then I cannot blame his cousin king,
That wish'd him on the barren mountains starv'd.
But shall it be, that you,—that set the crown
Upon the head of this forgetful man;
And, for his sake, wear the detested blot
Of murd'rous subornation,—shall it be,
That you a world of curses undergo;
Being the agents, or base second means,
The cords, the ladder, or the hangman rather?—
O, pardon me, that I descend so low,
To show the line, and the predicament,
Wherein you range under this subtle king.
Shall it, for shame, be spoken in these days,
Or fill up chronicles in time to come,
That men of your nobility and power,
Did gage them both in an unjust behalf,—
As both of you, God pardon it! have done,-
To put down Richard, that sweet lovely rose,
And plant this thorn, this canker,[6] Bolingbroke?
And shall it, in more shame, be further spoken,
That you are fool'd, discarded, and shook off
By him, for whom these shames ye underwent?
No; yet time serves, wherein you may redeem
Your banish'd honours, and restore yourselves
Into the good thoughts of the world again:
Revenge the jeering, and disdain'd[7] contempt,
Of this proud king; who studies, day and night,
To answer all the debt he owes to you,
Even with the bloody payment of your deaths.
Therefore, I say,——

Wor. Peace, cousin, say no more
And now I will unclasp a secret book,
And to your quick-conceiving discontents
I'll read you matter deep and dangerous;
As full of peril, and advent'rous spirit,
As to o'erwalk a current, roaring loud,
On the unsteadfast footing of a spear.

This inconsistency may be accounted for as follows; it appears from Dugdale and Sandford's account of the Mortimer family, that there were two of them taken prisoners at different times by Glendower, each of them bearing the name of *Edmund;* one being *Edmund, earl of March,* nephew to *Lady Percy,* and the proper Mortimer of this play; the other Sir Edmund Mortimer, uncle to the former, and *brother* to *Lady Percy.* The poet has confounded the two persons.

1 To *indent with fears* is *to enter into compact with cowards.* 'To make a covenant or *to indent* with one. Paciscor.'—*Baret.*

2 Shakspeare uses *confound* for *spending* or losing time.

3 *Crisp* is *curled.* Thus in Kyd's Cornelia, 1595:—
'O beauteous Tyber, with thine easy streams
That glide as smoothly as a Parthian shaft,
Turn not thy *crispy* tides, like silver curls,
Back to thy grass-green banks to welcome us.'

4 Some of the quarto copies read *base*

5 Roger Mortimer, earl of March, was declared heir apparent to the crown in 1385: but he was killed in Ireland in 1398. The person who was proclaimed heir apparent by Richard II. previous to his last voyage to Ireland, was *Edmund* Mortimer, son of Roger, who was then but seven years old: he was not Lady Percy's brother, but her nephew. He was the undoubted heir to the crown after the death of Richard. Thomas Walsingham asserts that he married a daughter of Owen Glendower, and the subsequent historians copied him. Sandford says that he married Anne Stafford, daughter of Edmund earl of Stafford. Glendower's daughter was married to his antagonist Lord Grey of Ruthven. Holinshed led Shakspeare into the error. This Edmund, who is the Mortimer of the present play, was born in 1392, and consequently, at the time when this play is supposed to commence, was little more than ten years old. The prince of Wales was not fifteen.

6 The *canker-rose* is the dog-rose, the *flower of the Cynosbaton.* So in Much Ado about Nothing:—'I had rather be a *canker* in a hedge, than a rose in his grace.'

7 i. e. disdainful.

Hot. If he fall in, good night:—or sink or swim;
Send danger from the east unto the west,
So honour cross it from the north to south,
And let them grapple:—O! the blood more stirs,
To rouse a lion, than to start a hare.
North. Imagination of some great exploit
Drives him beyond the bounds of patience.
Hot. By heaven, methinks, it were an easy leap,
To pluck bright honour from the pale-fac'd moon;
Or dive into the bottom of the deep,[1]
Where fathom-line could never touch the ground,
And pluck up drowned honour by the locks;
So he, that doth redeem her thence, might wear,
Without corrival, all her dignities:
But out upon this half-fac'd fellowship![2]
Wor. He apprehends a world of figures[3] here,
But not the form of what he should attend.—
Good cousin, give me audience for a while.
Hot. I cry you mercy.
Wor. Those same noble Scots,
That are your prisoners,——
Hot. I'll keep them all;
By heaven, he shall not have a Scot of them:
No, if a Scot would save his soul, he shall not:
I'll keep them, by this hand.
Wor. You start away,
And lend no ear unto my purposes.—
Those prisoners you shall keep.
Hot. Nay, I will; that's flat:—
He said, he would not ransom Mortimer;
Forbad my tongue to speak of Mortimer;
But I will find him when he lies asleep,
And in his ear I'll holla—Mortimer!
Nay,
I'll have a starling shall be taught to speak
Nothing but Mortimer, and give it him,
To keep his anger still in motion.
Wor. Hear you,
Cousin; a word.
Hot. All studies here I solemnly defy,[4]
Save how to gall and pinch this Bolingbroke:
And that same sword-and-buckler[5] prince of Wales,—
But that I think his father loves him not,
And would be glad he met with some mischance,
I'd have him poison'd with a pot of ale.[6]
Wor. Farewell, kinsman! I will talk to you,
When you are better temper'd to attend.
North. Why, what a wasp-tongue[7] and impatient fool
Art thou, to break into this woman's mood;
Tying thine ear to no tongue but thine own?
Hot. Why, look you, I am whipp'd and scourg'd with rods,
Nettled, and stung with pismires, when I hear
Of this vile politician, Bolingbroke.
In Richard's time,—What do you call the place?—
A plague upon't!—it is in Gloucestershire;—
'Twas where the mad-cap duke his uncle kept:
His uncle York;—where I first bow'd my knee
Unto this king of smiles, this Bolingbroke,
When you and he came back from Ravenspurg.
North. At Berkley castle.
Hot. You say true:——
Why, what a candy[8] deal of courtesy
This fawning greyhound then did proffer me!
Look,—*when his infant fortune came to age,*
And—*gentle Harry Percy,*—and, *kind cousin,*—
O, the devil take such cozeners!———God forgive me!——
Good uncle, tell your tale, for I have done.
Wor. Nay, if you have not, to't again;
We'll stay your leisure.
Hot. I have done, i'faith.
Wor. Then once more to your Scottish prisoners.
Deliver them up without their ransom straight,
And make the Douglas' son your only mean
For powers in Scotland; which, for divers reasons,
Which I shall send you written,—be assur'd,
Will easily be granted.—You, my lord,—
[*To* NORTHUMBERLAND.
Your son in Scotland being thus employed,-
Shall secretly into the bosom creep
Of that same noble prelate, well belov'd,
The archbishop.
Hot. Of York, is't not?
Wor. True; who bears hard
His brother's death at Bristol, the Lord Scroop.
I speak not this in estimation,[9]
As what I think might be, but what I know
Is ruminated, plotted, and set down;
And only stays but to behold the face
Of that occasion that shall bring it on.
Hot. I smell it; upon my life, it will do well.
North. Before the game's a-foot, thou still let'st slip.[10]
Hot. Why, it cannot choose but be a noble plot:-
And then the power of Scotland, and of York,—
To join with Mortimer, ha?
Wor. And so they shall.
Hot. In faith, it is exceedingly well aim'd.
Wor. And 'tis no little reason bids us speed,
To save our heads by raising of a head;[11]
For, bear ourselves as even as we can,
The king will always think him in our debt;[12]
And think we think ourselves unsatisfied,
Till he hath found a time to pay us home.

1 Warburton observes that Euripides has put the same sentiment into the mouth of Eteocles:—'I will not, madam, disguise my thoughts; I would scale heaven, I would descend to the very entrails of the earth, if so be that by that price I could obtain a kingdom.' Johnson says, 'Though I am far from condemning this speech, with Gildon and Theobald, as absolute madness, yet I cannot find in it that profundity of reflection, and beauty of allegory, which Warburton endeavoured to display. This sally of Hotspur may be, I think, soberly and rationally vindicated as the violent eruption of a mind inflated with ambition and fired with resentment; as the boasted clamour of a man able to do much, and eager to do more; as the dark expression of indetermined thoughts. The passage from Euripides is surely not allegorical; yet it is produced, and properly, as parallel.'—In the Knight of the Burning Pestle, Beaumont and Fletcher have put this rant into the mouth of Ralph the apprentice, who, like Bottom, appears to be fond of acting parts *to tear a cat in.*

2 *Half-faced*, which has puzzled the commentators, seems here meant to convey a contemptuous idea of something imperfect. As in Nashe's Apology of Pierce Pennilesse:—'With all other ends of your *half-faced* English.'

3 Shapes created by his imagination.

4 To *defy* was sometimes used in the sense of to *renounce, reject, refuse*, by Shakspeare and his cotemporaries.

5 '*Sword and buckler prince*' is here used as a term of contempt. The following extracts will help us to the precise meaning of the epithet:—'This field, commonly called West Smithfield, was for many years called Ruffian's Hall, by reason it was the usual place for frayes and common fighting, during the time that sword and bucklers were in use; when every *serving man*, from the base to the best, carried a *buckler* at his back, which hung by the hilt or pomel of his *sword*.'—*Stowe's Survey of London.*

6 This is said in allusion to low pot-house company, with which the prince associated.

7 The first quarto, 1598, reads *wasp-stung*, which Steevens thought the true reading. The quarto of 1599 reads *wasp-tongue*, which Malone strenuously contends for; and I think with Mr. Nares that he is right. 'He who is stung by wasps has a real cause for impatience: but *waspish*, which is often used by Shakspeare, is petulant from temper; and *wasp-tongue* therefore very naturally means *petulant-tongue*, which was exactly the accusation meant to be urged.' The folio altered it unnecessarily to *wasp-tongued.*

8 i. e. 'what a deal of candy courtesy.

9 Conjecture.

10 This phrase is taken from hunting. To *let slip* is to *loose* a greyhound.

11 A body of forces.

12 This is a natural description of the state of mind between those that have conferred, and those that have received obligations too great to be satisfied. That this would be the event of Northumberland's disloyalty was predicted by King Richard in the former play.

And see already, how he doth begin
To make us strangers to his looks of love.

Hot. He does, he does; we'll be reveng'd on him.

Wor. Cousin,[1] farewell:—No further go in this,
Than I by letters shall direct your course.
When time is ripe (which will be suddenly,)
I'll steal to Glendower, and Lord Mortimer;
Where you and Douglas, and our powers at once
(As I will fashion it,) shall happily meet,
To bear our fortunes in our own strong arms,
Which now we hold at much uncertainty.

North. Farewell, good brother:—we shall thrive, I trust.

Hot. Uncle, adieu:—O, let the hours be short,
Till fields, and blows, and groans applaud our sport! [*Exeunt.*

ACT II.

SCENE I. Rochester. *An Inn Yard. Enter a* Carrier, *with a lantern in his hand.*

1 *Car.* Heigh ho! An't be not four by the day, I'll be hanged: Charles' wain[2] is over the new chimney, and yet our horse not packed. What, ostler!

Ost. [*Within.*] Anon, anon.

1 *Car.* I pr'ythee, Tom, beat Cut's saddle, put a few flocks in the point: the poor jade is wrung in the withers out of all cess.[3]

Enter another Carrier.

2 *Car.* Pease and beans are as dank[4] here as a dog, and that is the next way to give poor jades the bots:[5] this house is turned upside down, since Robin ostler died.

1 *Car.* Poor fellow! never joyed since the price of oats rose; it was the death of him.

2 *Car.* I think, this be the most villainous house in all London road for fleas: I am stung like a tench.[6]

1 *Car.* Like a tench? by the mass, there is ne'er a king in Christendom could be better bit than I have been since the first cock.

2 *Car.* Why, they will allow us ne'er a jorden, and then we leak in your chimney; and your chamber-lie breeds fleas like a loach.[7]

1 *Car.* What, ostler! come away and be hanged, come away.

2 *Car.* I have a gammon of bacon, and two razes[8] of ginger, to be delivered as far as Charing Cross.

1 *Car.* 'Odsbody! the turkeys in my pannier are quite starved.[9]—What, ostler!—A plague on thee! hast thou never an eye in thy head? canst not hear? An 'twere not as good a deed as drink, to break the pate of thee, I am a very villain.—Come, and be hang'd:—Hast no faith in thee?

Enter GADSHILL.[10]

Gads. Good morrow, carriers. What's o'clock?

1 *Car.* I think it be two o'clock.

Gads. I pr'ythee, lend me thy lantern, to see my gelding in the stable.

1 *Car.* Nay, soft, I pray ye; I know a tric worth two of that, i'faith.

Gads. I pr'ythee, lend me thine.

2 *Car.* Ay, when? canst tell?—Lend me thy lantern, quoth a?—marry, I'll see thee hanged first.

Gads. Sirrah carrier, what time do you mean to come to London?

2 *Car.* Time enough to go to bed with a candle, I warrant thee.—Come, neighbour Mugs, we'll call up the gentlemen; they will along with company, for they have great charge. [*Exeunt* Carriers.

Gads. What, ho! chamberlain!

Cham. [*Within.*] At hand, quoth pick-purse.[11]

Gads. That's even as fair as—at hand, quoth the chamberlain: for thou variest no more from picking of purses, than giving direction doth from labouring; thou lay'st the plot how.[12]

Enter Chamberlain.

Cham. Good morrow, master Gadshill. It holds current, that I told you yesternight: There's a franklin[13] in the wild of Kent, hath brought three hundred marks with him in gold: I heard him tell it to one of his company, last night at supper; a kind of auditor; one that hath abundance of charge too, God knows what. They are up already, and call for eggs and butter: They will away presently.

Gads. Sirrah, if they meet not with Saint Nicholas' clerks,[14] I'll give thee this neck.

Cham. No, I'll none of it: I pr'ythee, keep that for the hangman; for, I know, thou worship'st Saint Nicholas as truly as a man of falsehood may.

Gads. What talkest thou to me of the hangman? if I hang, I'll make a fat pair of gallows: for, if I hang, old Sir John hangs with me; and, thou knowest, he's no starveling. Tut! there are other Trojans that thou dreamest not of, the which, for sport sake, are content to do the profession some grace; that would, if matters should be looked into, for their own credit sake, make all whole. I am joined with no foot land-rakers,[15] no long-staff, sixpenny strikers;[16] none of these mad, mustachio, purple-

---

1 This was a common address in Shakspeare's time to nephews, nieces, and grand-children. See Holinshed, *passim.* Hotspur was Worcester's nephew.

2 Charles' wain was the vulgar name for the constellation called the *great bear.* It is a corruption of *Chorles* or *Churl's* wain. *Chorl* is frequently used for a *countryman* in old books, from the Saxon *ceorl.*

3 '*Out of all cess*' is 'out of all measure.' Excessively, *prœter modum.* To *cess,* or assess, was to number, muster, value, *measure,* or appraise.

4 *Dank* is moist, wet, and consequently *mouldy.*

5 *Bots* are *worms;* a disease to which horses are very subject.

6 Dr. Farmer thought *tench* a mistake for *trout;* probably alluding to the red spots with which the trout is covered, having some resemblance to the spots on the skin of a flea-bitten person.

7 It appears from a passage in Holland's translation of Pliny's Nat. Hist. b. ix. c. xlvii. that anciently fishes were supposed to be infested with fleas. 'Last of all some fishes there be which of themselves are given to breed *fleas* and lice; among which the chalcis, a kind of turgot, is one.' Mason suggests that 'breeds fleas as fast as a loach breeds loaches,' may be the meaning of the passage; the loach being reckoned a peculiarly prolific fish.

8 The commentators have puzzled themselves and their readers about this word *razes:* Theobald asserts that a *raze* is the Indian term for a *bale.* I have somewhere seen the word used for a *fraile,* or little rush basket, such as figs, raisins, &c. are usually packed in; but I cannot now recall the book to memory in which it occurred. Such a package was much more likely to be meant than a bale. The poet perhaps intended to mark the *petty importance* of the carrier's business.

9 This is one of the poet's anachronisms. Turkeys were not brought into England until the reign of Henry VIII.

10 Gadshill has his name from a place on the Kentish Road, where robberies were very frequent. A curious narrative of a gang, who appear to have infested that neighbourhood in 1590, is printed from a MS. paper of Sir Roger Manwood's in Boswell's Shakspeare, vol xvi. p. 431.

11 This is a proverbial phrase, frequently used in old plays.

12 Thus in the life and death of Gamaliel Ratsey, 1605:—'———he dealt with the *chamberlaine* of the house, to learn which way they went in the morning, which the *chamberlaine* performed accordingly, and that with great care and diligence, for he knew he should partake of their fortunes if they sped.'

13 A freeholder or yeoman, a man above a vassal or villain, but not a gentleman. This was the *Franklin* of the age of Elizabeth. In earlier times he was a person of much more dignity. See Canterbury Tales, v. 333, and Mr. Tyrwhitt's note upon it.

14 In a note on The Two Gentlemen of Verona, Act iii. Sc. 1, is an account of the origin of this expression as applied to scholars; and as Nicholas or old Nick is a cant name for the devil, so thieves are equivocally called *Saint Nicholas' clerks.*

15 Footpads.

16 A *striker* was a *thief.*

hued malt-worms: but with nobility, and tranquillity; burgomasters, and great oneyers;[1] such as can hold in; such as will strike sooner than speak, and speak sooner than drink, and drink sooner than pray: And yet I lie; for they pray continually to their saint, the commonwealth; or, rather, not pray to her, but prey on her; for they ride up and down on her, and make her their boots.[2]

Cham. What, the commonwealth their boots? will she hold out water in foul way?

Gads. She will, she will; justice hath liquored her.[3] We steal as in a castle,[4] cock-sure; we have the receipt of fern-seed, we walk invisible.

Cham. Nay, by my faith, I think you are more beholden to the night, than to fern-seed,[5] for your walking invisible.

Gads. Give me thy hand: thou shalt have a share of our purchase,[6] as I am a true man.

Cham. Nay, rather let me have it, as you are a false thief.

Gads. Go to; *Homo* is a common name to all men. Bid the ostler bring my gelding out of the stable. Farewell, you muddy knave. [*Exeunt.*

SCENE II. *The Road by* Gadshill. *Enter* PRINCE HENRY, *and* POINS; BARDOLPH *and* PETO, *at some distance.*

Poins. Come, shelter, shelter: I have removed Falstaff's horse, and he frets like a gummed velvet.[7]

P. Hen. Stand close.

Enter FALSTAFF.

Fal. Poins! Poins, and be hanged! Poins!

P. Hen. Peace, ye fat-kidneyed rascal; What a brawling dost thou keep?

Fal. Where's Poins, Hal?

P. Hen. He is walked up to the top of the hill, I'll go seek him. [*Pretends to seek* POINS.

Fal. I am accursed to rob in that thief's company: the rascal hath removed my horse, and tied him I know not where. If I travel but four foot by the squire[8] further afoot, I shall break my wind. Well, I doubt not but to die a fair death for all this, if I 'scape hanging for killing that rogue. I have forsworn his company hourly, any time this two-and-twenty years, and yet I am bewitched with the rogue's company. If the rascal have not given me medicines[9] to make me love him, I'll be hang'd; it could not be else; I have drunk medicines.—Poins!—Hal!—a plague upon you both!—Bardolph!—Peto!—I'll starve, ere I'll rob a foot further. An 'twere not as good a deed as drink, to turn true man, and leave these rogues, I am the veriest varlet that ever chewed with a tooth. Eight yards of uneven ground, is threescore and ten miles afoot with me; and the stony-hearted villains know it well enough: A plague upon't, when thieves cannot be true to one another! [*They whistle.*] Whew! —A plague upon you all! Give me my horse, you rogues; give me my horse, and be hang'd.

P. Hen. Peace, ye fat-guts! lie down; lay thine ear close to the ground, and list if thou canst hear the tread of travellers.

Fal. Have you any levers to lift me up again, being down? 'Sblood, I'll not bear mine own flesh so far afoot again, for all the coin in thy father's exchequer. What a plague mean ye to colt[10] me thus?

P. Hen. Thou liest, thou art not colted, thou art uncolted.

Fal. I pr'ythee, good Prince Hal, help me to my horse: good king's son.

P. Hen. Out, you rogue! shall I be your ostler!

Fal. Go, hang thyself in thy own heir-apparent garters! If I be ta'en, I'll peach for this. An I have not ballads made on you all, and sung to filthy tunes, let a cup of sack be my poison: When a jest is so forward, and afoot too,—I hate it.

Enter GADSHILL.

Gads. Stand.

Fal. So I do, against my will.

Poins. O, 'tis our setter: I know his voice.

Enter BARDOLPH.

Bard. What news?

Gads. Case ye, case ye; on with your visors; there's money of the king's coming down the hill; 'tis going to the king's exchequer.

Fal. You lie, you rogue; 'tis going to the king's tavern.

Gads. There's enough to make us all.

Fal. To be hanged.

P. Hen. Sirs, you four shall front them in the narrow lane; Ned Poins and I will walk lower: if they 'scape from your encounter, they light on us

Peto. How many be there of them?

Gads. Some eight, or ten.

Fal. Zounds! will they not rob us?

P. Hen. What, a coward, Sir John Paunch?

Fal. Indeed, I am not John of Gaunt, your grandfather; but yet no coward, Hal.

P. Hen. Well, we leave that to the proof.

Poins. Sirrah Jack, thy horse stands behind the hedge; when thou needest him, there thou shalt find him. Farewell, and stand fast.

Fal. Now cannot I strike him, if I should be hanged.

P. Hen. Ned, where are our disguises?

Poins. Here, hard by; stand close. [*Exeunt* P. HEN. *and* POINS.

Fal. Now, my masters, happy man be his dole,[11] say I; every man to his business.

Enter Travellers.

1 *Trav.* Come, neighbour; the boy shall lead our horses down the hill: we'll walk afoot a while, and ease our legs.

Thieves. Stand.

Trav. Jesu bless us!

Fal. Strike; down with them; cut the villains' throats: Ah! whoreson caterpillars! bacon-fed

1 Some of the commentators have been at great pains to conjecture what class of persons were meant by *great oneyers*. One proposed to read *moneyers*; another *mynheers*; and Malone coins a word, *onyers*, which he says may mean a *public accountant*, from the term *o-ni*, used in the exchequer. The ludicrous nature of the appellations which Gadshill bestows upon his associates might have sufficiently shown them that such attempts must be futile; 'nobility and *tranquillity*, burgomasters and *great oneyers*.' Johnson has judiciously explained it. 'Gadshill tells the chamberlain that he is joined with no mean wretches, but with "burgomasters and great ones," or, as he terms them in merriment by a cant termination, great *one-y-ers*, or great *one-eers*, as we say *privateer*, auctioneer, *circuiteer*.'

2 A quibble upon *boots* and *booty*. *Boot* is *profit, advantage*.

3 Alluding to *boots* in the preceding passage. In the Merry Wives of Windsor, Falstaff says:—'They would melt me out of my fat drop by drop, and *liquor* fishermen's boots with me.'

4 *As in a castle* was a proverbial phrase for security. Stevens has adduced several examples of its use in cotemporary writers

5 *Fern-seed* was supposed to have the power of rendering persons invisible: the seed of fern is itself invisible; therefore to find it was a magic operation, and in the use it was supposed to communicate its own property.

6 *Purchase* was anciently understood in the sense of *gain, profit*, whether legally or illegally obtained. The commentators are wrong in saying that it meant stolen goods.

7 This allusion we often meet with in the old comedies. Thus in The Malecontent, 1604:—'I'll come among you, like *gum* into taffata, to *fret, fret*.' Velvet and taffata were sometimes stiffened with gum; but the consequence was, that the stuff being thus hardened, quickly rubbed and fretted itself out.

8 i. e. the *square* or measure. A carpenter's rule was called a *square*; from *esquierre*, Fr.

9 Alluding to the vulgar notion of *love-powders*.

10 To *colt* is to *trick, fool*, or *deceive*; perhaps from the wild tricks of a colt.

11 i. e. be his lot or portion happiness. This proverbial phrase has been already explained in the notes on The Merry Wives of Windsor, The Taming of the Shrew, and Winter's Tale

knaves! they hate us youth: down with them; fleece them.

1 *Trav.* O, we are undone, both we and ours, for ever.

Fal. Hang ye, gorbellied[1] knaves; Are ye undone? No, ye fat chuffs;[2] I would, your store were here! On, bacons, on! What, ye knaves? young men must live: You are grand-jurors are ye? We'll jure ye, i'faith.

[*Exeunt* FAL. *&c. driving the* Travellers *out.*

Re-enter PRINCE HENRY *and* POINS.

P. Hen. The thieves have bound the true[3] men: Now could thou and I rob the thieves, and go merrily to London, it would be argument[4] for a week, laughter for a month, and a good jest for ever.

Poins. Stand close, I hear them coming.

Re-enter Thieves.

Fal. Come, my masters, let us share, and then to horse before day. An the prince and Poins be not two arrant cowards, there's no equity stirring: there's no more valour in that Poins, than in a wild duck.

P. Hen. Your money. [*Rushing out upon them.*

Poins. Villains.

As they are sharing, the Prince *and* POINS *set upon them.* FALSTAFF, *after a blow or two, and the rest, run away, leaving the booty behind them.*

P. Hen. Got with much ease. Now merrily to horse:
The thieves are scatter'd, and possess'd with fear
So strongly, that they dare not meet each other;
Each takes his fellow for an officer.
Away, good Ned. Falstaff sweats to death,
And lards the lean earth as he walks along:
Wer't not for laughing, I should pity him.

Poins. How the rogue roar'd! [*Exeunt.*

SCENE III. Warkworth. *A Room in the Castle.*

Enter HOTSPUR, *reading a Letter.*[5]

——*But, for my own part, my lord, I could be well contented to be there, in respect of the love I bear your house.*—He could be contented,—Why is he not, then? In respect of the love he bears our house:—he shows in this, he loves his own barn better than he loves our house. Let me see some more. *The purpose you undertake is dangerous;*—Why, that's certain; 'tis dangerous to take a cold, to sleep, to drink! but I tell you, my lord fool, out of this nettle, danger, we pluck this flower, safety. *The purpose you undertake is dangerous; the friends you have named, uncertain; the time itself unsorted; and your whole plot too light, for the counterpoise of so great an opposition.*—Say you so, say you so? I say unto you again, you are a shallow, cowardly hind, and you lie. What a lack-brain is this? By the Lord, our plot is a good plot as ever was laid; our friends true and constant: a good plot, good friends, and full of expectation: an excellent plot, very good friends. What a frosty-spirited rogue is this? Why, my lord of York[6] commends the plot, and the general course of the action. 'Zounds, an I were now by this rascal, I could brain him with his lady's fan.[7] Is there not my father, my uncle, and myself? Lord Edmund Mortimer, my lord of York, and Owen Glendower? Is there not, besides, the Douglas? Have I not all their letters, to meet me in arms by the ninth of the next month; and are they not, some of them, set forward already? What a pagan rascal is this? an infidel? Ha! you shall see now, in very sincerity of fear and cold heart, will he to the king, and lay open all our proceedings. O, I could divide myself, and go to buffets, for moving such a dish of skimmed milk with so honourable an action! Hang him! let him tell the king: We are prepared: I will set forward to-night.

Enter LADY PERCY.

How now, Kate?[8] I must leave you within these two hours.

Lady. O my good lord, why are you thus alone?
For what offence have I, this fortnight, been
A banish'd woman from my Harry's bed?
Tell me, sweet lord, what is't that takes from thee
Thy stomach, pleasure, and thy golden sleep?[9]
Why dost thou bend thine eyes upon the earth;
And start so often when thou sit'st alone?
Why hast thou lost the fresh blood in thy cheeks;
And given my treasures, and my rights of thee,
To thick-ey'd musing, and curs'd melancholy?
In thy faint slumbers, I by thee have watch'd,
And heard thee murmur tales of iron wars:
Speak terms of manage to the bounding steed,
Cry, *Courage!—to the field!* And thou hast talk'd
Of sallies, and retires;[10] of trenches, tents,
Of palisadoes, frontiers,[11] parapets;
Of basilisks,[12] of cannon, culverin;
Of prisoners' ransom, and of soldiers slain,
And all the 'currents[13] of a heady fight.
Thy spirit within thee hath been so at war,
And thus hath so bestirr'd thee in thy sleep,
That beads of sweat have stood upon thy brow,
Like bubbles in a late-disturbed stream:
And in thy face strange motions have appear'd,
Such as we see when men restrain their breath
On some great sudden haste. O, what portents are these?
Some heavy business hath my lord in hand,
And I must know it, else he loves me not.

Hot. What, ho! is Gilliams with the packet gone?

Enter Servant.

Serv. He is, my lord, an hour ago.

Hot. Hath Butler brought those horses from the sheriff?

Serv. One horse, my lord, he brought even now.

Hot. What horse? a roan, a crop-ear, is it not?

Serv. It is, my lord.

Hot. That roan shall be my throne.
Well, I will back him straight: O *esperance!*—[14]
Bid Butler lead him forth into the park.

[*Exit* Servant.

Lady. But hear you, my lord.

Hot. What say'st thou, my lady?

Lady. What is it carries you away?

Hot. Why, my horse, my love, my horse.

Lady. Out, you mad-headed ape!
A weasel hath not such a deal of spleen,[15]
As you are toss'd with. In faith,
I'll know your business, Harry, that I will.
I fear, my brother Mortimer doth stir

---

1 *Gorbellied* is *big-paunched*, corpulent.

2 A term of reproach usually applied to avaricious old citizens. It is of uncertain derivation. Cotgrave interprets '*Un gros marroufle*, a big cat; also an ouglie luske or clusterfist; also a rich churl or *fat chuffe*.'

3 *True* for *honest*: thus opposing the *true* men to the *thieves.*

4 *Argument* is subject matter for conversation.

5 This letter was from George Dunbar, Earl of March, in Scotland.

6 Richard Scroop, archbishop of York.

7 See note on the Merry Wives of Windsor, Act ii. Sc. 3.

8 Shakspeare either mistook the name of Hotspur's wife (which was not *Katherine*, but *Elizabeth*), or else designedly changed it, out of the remarkable fondness he seems to have had for the name of *Kate*. Hall and Holinshed call her erroneously *Elinor.*

9 In King Richard III. we have '*leaden* slumber' In Virgil '*ferreus* somnus.' Homer terms sleep *brazen*, or, more strictly, *copper.*

10 *Retires* are retreats.

11 *Frontiers* formerly meant not only the bounds of different territories, but also the *forts* built along or near those limits. Thus in Ives's Practice of Fortification, 1589:—'A forte not placed where it were needful, might skantly be accounted for *frontier.*' Florio interprets 'frontiera, a *frontire* or bounding place: also *a skonce, a bastion, a defence, a trench, or block-house*, upon or about confines or borders.'

12 *Basilisks* are a species of ordnance, probably so named from the imaginary serpent or dragon, with figures of which it was ordinary to ornament great guns

13 Occurrences.

14 The motto of the Percy family.

15 So in Cymbeline we have:—
'As *quarrellous* as the weasel'

About his title; and hath sent for you,
To line[1] his enterprise: But if you go——

Hot. So far afoot, I shall be weary, love.

Lady. Come, come, you paraquito, answer me
Directly to this question that I ask.
In faith, I'll break thy little finger, Harry,
An if thou wilt not tell me all things true.

Hot. Away,
Away, you trifler!—Love? I love thee not,
I care not for thee, Kate: this is no world,
To play with mammets,[2] and to tilt with lips:
We must have bloody noses, and crack'd crowns,
And pass them current too.—Gods me, my horse!—
What say'st thou, Kate? what would'st thou have with me?

Lady. Do you not love me? do you not indeed?
Well, do not then; for since you love me not,
I will not love myself. Do you not love me?
Nay, tell me, if you speak in jest, or no?

Hot. Come, wilt thou see me ride?
And when I am o' horseback, I will swear
I love thee infinitely. But hark you, Kate;
I must not have you henceforth question me
Whither I go, nor reason whereabout:
Whither I must, I must; and, to conclude,
This evening must I leave you, gentle Kate.
I know you wise; but yet no further wise,
Than Harry Percy's wife: constant you are;
But yet a woman: and for secrecy,
No lady closer; for I well believe,
Thou wilt not utter what thou dost not know;
And so far will I trust thee, gentle Kate!

Lady. How! so far?

Hot. Not an inch further. But hark you, Kate?
Whither I go, thither shall you go too;
To-day will I set forth, to-morrow you.—
Will this content you, Kate?

Lady. It must, of force.

SCENE IV. Eastcheap.[3] *A Room in the* Boar's Head *Tavern. Enter* PRINCE HENRY *and* POINS.

P. Hen. Ned, pr'ythee, come out of that fat room, and lend me thy hand to laugh a little.

Poins. Where hast been, Hal?

P. Hen. With three or four loggerheads, amongst three or four score hogsheads. I have sounded the very base string of humility. Sirrah, I am sworn brother to a leash of drawers; and can call them all by their Christian names, as—Tom, Dick, and Francis. They take it already upon their salvation, that, though I be but prince of Wales, yet I am the king of courtesy; and tell me flatly I am no proud Jack, like Falstaff; but a Corinthian,[4] a lad of mettle, a good boy,—by the Lord, so they call me; and when I am king of England, I shall command all the good lads in Eastcheap. They call—drinking deep, dying scarlet: and when you breathe in your watering, they cry—hem! and bid you play it off.[5]—To conclude, I am so good a proficient in one quarter of an hour, that I can drink with any tinker in his own language during my life. I tell thee, Ned, thou hast lost much honour, that thou wert not with me in this action. But, sweet Ned,—to sweeten which name of Ned, I give thee this penny-worth of sugar,[6] clapped even now in my hand by an under-skinker;[7] one that never spake other English in his life, than—*Eight shillings and sixpence*, and—*You are welcome;* with this shrill addition,—*Anon, anon, sir! Score a pint of bastard in the Half-moon*, or so. But, Ned, to drive away the time till Falstaff come, I pr'ythee, do thou stand in some by-room, while I question my puny drawer, to what end he gave me the sugar; and do thou never leave calling—Francis, that his tale to me may be nothing but—anon. Step aside, and I'll show thee a precedent.

Poins. Francis!

P. Hen. Thou art perfect.

Poins. Francis! [*Exit* POINS.

Enter FRANCIS.

Fran. Anon, anon, sir. Look down into the Pomegranate, Ralph.

P. Hen. Come hither, Francis.

Fran. My lord.

P. Hen. How long hast thou to serve, Francis?

Fran. Forsooth, five year, and as much as to—

Poins. [*Within.*] Francis!

Fran. Anon, anon, sir!

P. Hen. Five years! by'rlady, a long lease for the clinking of pewter. But, Francis, darest thou be so valiant, as to play the coward with thy indenture, and to show it a fair pair of heels, and run from it?

Fran. O lord, sir! I'll be sworn upon all the books in England, I could find in my heart-

Poins. [*Within.*] Francis!

Fran. Anon, anon, sir.

P. Hen. How old art thou, Francis?

Fran. Let me see,—About Michaelmas next I shall be—

Poins. [*Within.*] Francis!

Fran. Anon, sir.—Pray you, stay a little, my lord

P. Hen. Nay, but hark you, Francis: For the sugar thou gavest me,—'twas a pennyworth, was't not?

Fran. O lord, sir! I would it had been two.

P. Hen. I will give thee for it a thousand pound: ask me when thou wilt, and thou shalt have it.

Poins. [*Within.*] Francis!

Fran. Anon, anon.

P. Hen. Anon, Francis? No, Francis: but to-morrow, Francis; or, Francis, on Thursday; or, indeed, Francis, when thou wilt. But, Francis,—

Fran. My lord?

P. Hen. Wilt thou rob this leathern-jerkin,[8] crystal-button, nott-pated,[9] agate-ring, puke-stocking,[10] caddis-garter,[11] smooth-tongue, Spanish-pouch,—

---

1 i. e. to *strengthen.*

2 *Mammets* were *puppets* or *dolls*, here used by Shakspeare for a *female plaything;* a diminutive of *mam.* 'Quasi dicat parvam matrem, seu matronulam.' — 'Icunculæ, *mammets* or puppets that goe by devises of wyer or strings, as though they had life and moving.' *Junius's Nomenclator, by Fleming*, 1585.—Mr. Gifford has thrown out a conjecture about the meaning of *mammets* from the Italian *mammetta*, which signified *a bosom* as well as a *young wench.* See Ben Jonson's Works, vol. v. p. 66. I have not found the word used in *English* in that sense; but *mammet*, for a puppet or dressed up *living doll*, is common enough.

3 *Eastcheap* is selected with propriety for the scene of the prince's merry meetings, as it was near his own residence: a mansion called Cold Harbour (near All Hallows Church, Upper Thames Street), was granted to Henry Prince of Wales. 11 Henry IV. 1410. Rymer, vol. viii. p. 628. In the old anonymous play of King Henry V *Eastcheap* is the place where Henry and his companions meet:—'*Hen. V.* You know the old tavern in Eastcheap; there is good wine.' Shakspeare has hung up a sign for them that he saw daily; for the Boar's Head tavern was very near Blackfriars' Playhouse.—*Stowe's Survey.*

Sir John Falstaff was in his lifetime a considerable benefactor to Magdalen College, Oxford; and though the College cannot give the particulars at large, the *Boar's Head* in *Southwark*, and Caldecot Manor in Suffolk were part of the lands, &c. he bestowed.

4 A *Corinthian* was a *wencher* a *debauchee.* The fame of *Corinth*, as a place of resort for loose women, was not yet extinct.

5 Mr. Gifford has shown that there is no ground for the filthy interpretation of this passage which Steevens chose to give. '*To breathe in your watering*,' is 'to stop and take breath when you are drinking.'

6 It appears from two passages cited by Steevens that the drawers kept *sugar* folded up in paper, ready to be delivered to those who called for sack.

7 An *under-skinker* is a tapster, an *under-drawer. Skink* is *drink, liquor;* from *scenc*, drink, Saxon.

8 The prince intends to ask the drawer whether he will rob his master, whom he denotes by these contemptuous distinctions.

9 *Nott-pated* is *shorn-pated*, or *cropped;* having the hair cut close.

10 *Puke-stockings* are *dark-coloured stockings. Puke* is a colour between russet and black; *pullus*, Lat. according to the dictionaries. By the receipt for dyeing it, it appears to have been a *dark gray* or *slate colour.*

11 *Caddis* was probably a kind of *ferret* or *worsted lace.* A slight kind of serge still bears the name of *cadis* in France. In Glapthorne's Wit in a Constable, we are told of 'footmen in *cuddis*.' *Garters* being formerly worn in sight were often of rich materials; to wear a coarse cheap sort was therefore reproachful.

Fran. O lord, sir, who do you mean?

P. Hen. Why then, your brown bastard[1] is your only drink: for, look you, Francis, your white canvass doublet will sully: in Barbary, sir, it cannot come to so much.

Fran. What, sir?

Poins. [*Within.*] Francis!

P. Hen. Away, you rogue; Dost thou not hear them call?

[*Here they both call him; the Drawer stands amazed, not knowing which way to go.*

Enter Vintner.

Vint. What! stand'st thou still, and hear'st such a calling? Look to the guests within. [*Exit* FRAN.] My lord, old Sir John, with half a dozen more, are at the door; Shall I let them in?

P. Hen. Let them alone awhile, and then open the door. [*Exit* Vintner.] Poins!

Re-enter POINS.

Poins. Anon, anon, sir.

P. Hen. Sirrah, Falstaff and the rest of the thieves are at the door; Shall we be merry?

Poins. As merry as crickets, my lad. But hark ye; What cunning match have you made with this jest of the drawer? come, what's the issue?

P. Hen. I am now of all humours, that have show'd themselves humours, since the old days of good man Adam, to the pupil age of this present twelve o'clock at midnight. [*Re-enter* FRANCIS *with wine.*] What's o'clock, Francis?

Fran. Anon, anon, sir.

P. Hen. That ever this fellow should have fewer words than a parrot, and yet the son of a woman!—His industry is—up-stairs, and down-stairs; his eloquence, the parcel of a reckoning. I am not yet of Percy's mind, the Hotspur of the north: he that kills me some six or seven dozen of Scots at a breakfast, washes his hands, and says to his wife,—*Fye upon this quiet life! I want work. O my sweet Harry*, says she, *how many hast thou killed to-day? Give my roan horse a drench*, says he; and answers, *Some fourteen*, an hour after; *a trifle, a trifle.* I pr'ythee, call in Falstaff; I'll play Percy, and that damned brawn shall play dame Mortimer his wife. *Rivo*,[2] says the drunkard. Call in ribs, call in tallow.

Enter FALSTAFF, GADSHILL, BARDOLPH, *and* PETO.

Poins. Welcome, Jack. Where hast thou been?

Fal. A plague of all cowards, I say, and a vengeance too! marry, and amen!—Give me a cup of sack, boy.—Ere I lead this life long, I'll sew netherstocks,[3] and mend them, and foot them too. A plague of all cowards!—Give me a cup of sack, rogue.—Is there no virtue extant? [*He drinks.*

P. Hen. Didst thou never see Titan kiss a dish of butter? pitiful-hearted butter, that melted at the sweet tale of the sun![4] if thou didst, then behold that compound.

Fal. You rogue, here's lime[5] in this sack too: There is nothing but roguery to be found in villainous man: Yet a coward is worse than a cup of sack with lime in it; a villainous coward.—Go thy ways, old Jack; die when thou wilt, if manhood, good manhood, be not forgot upon the face of the earth, then am I a shotten herring. There lives not three good men unhanged in England; and one of them is fat, and grows old: God help the while! a bad world, I say! I would, I were a weaver; I could sing psalms or any thing:[6] A plague of all cowards, I say still.

P. Hen. How now, wool-sack? what mutter you?

Fal. A king's son! If I do not beat thee out of thy kingdom with a dagger of lath,[7] and drive all thy subjects afore thee like a flock of wild geese, I'll never wear hair on my face more. You prince of Wales!

P. Hen. Why, you whoreson round man! what's the matter?

Fal. Are you not a coward? answer me to that; and Poins there?

Poins. 'Zounds, ye fat paunch, an ye call me coward, I'll stab thee.

Fal. I call thee coward! I'll see thee damned ere I call thee coward: but I would give a thousand pound, I could run as fast as thou canst. You are straight enough in the shoulders, you care not who sees your back: Call you that backing of your friends? A plague upon such backing! give me them that will face me.—Give me a cup of sack:—I am a rogue, if I drunk to-day.

P. Hen. O villain, thy lips are scarce wiped since thou drunk'st last.

Fal. All's one for that. A plague of all cowards, still say I. [*He drinks.*

P. Hen. What's the matter?

Fal. What's the matter? there be four of us here have ta'en a thousand pound this morning.

P. Hen. Where is it, Jack? where is it?

Fal. Where is it? taken from us it is: a hundred upon poor four of us.

P. Hen. What, a hundred, man?

Fal. I am a rogue, if I were not at half-sword with a dozen of them two hours together. I have 'scap'd by miracle. I am eight times thrust through the doublet; four, through the hose; my buckler cut through and through;[8] my sword hacked like a hand-saw, *ecce signum.* I never dealt better since I was a man: all would not do. A plague of all cowards!—Let them speak; if they speak more or

---

1 A kind of sweet Spanish wine, of which there were two sorts, brown and white. Baret says that '*bastarde* is *muscadel, sweete wine*, mulsum.' *Bastard wines* are said to be *Spanish wines* in general, by Olaus Magnus. He speaks of them with almost as much enthusiasm as Falstaff does of sack, and concludes by saying, 'Nullum vinum majoris pretii est, quam *bastardum*, ob dulcedinis nobilitatem.'—*De Gent. Septent.* p. 521.

2 Of this exclamation, which was frequently used in Bacchanalian revelry, the origin or derivation has not been discovered.

3 Stockings.

4 'Didst thou never see Titan kiss a dish of butter?' alludes to Falstaff's entering in a great heat, *melting* with the motion, like butter with the heat of the sun. '*Pitiful-hearted*' is used in the sense which Cotgrave gives to '*misericordieux*, merciful, *pitiful, compassionate, tender*.' Theobald reads 'pitiful-hearted *butter*,' which is countenanced by none of the old copies, but affords a clear sense. Malone and Steevens have each given a reading, founded upon the quarto of 1598, which has '—— at the sweet tale of the *sonnes*:' but they differ in their explanations of the passage. Their arguments are too long for this place, and are the less necessary as I do not adopt the readings upon which they are founded. Bishop Earle, in his Microcosmography, giving the character of a pot poet, says, 'His frequentest works go out in single sheets, and are chaunted from market to market to a vile tune and a worse throat; whilst the poor country wench *melts like butter* to hear them.'

5 Eliot, in his Orthoepia, 1593, speaking of *sack* and *rhenish*, says, 'The vintners of London put in lime; thence proceed infinite maladies, specially the goutes.'

6 This is the reading of the first quarto, 1598. The folio reads 'I could sing all manner of songs.' The passage was probably altered to avoid the penalty of the statute, 3 Jac. I. cxxi. Weavers are mentioned as lovers of music in the Twelfth Night. The protestants who fled from the persecutions of the duke of Alva were mostly *weavers*, and, being Calvinists, were distinguished for their love of psalmody. Weavers were supposed to be generally good singers: their trade being sedentary, they had an opportunity of practising, and sometimes in parts, while they were at work.

7 A *dagger of lath* is the weapon given to the Vice in the Old Moralities. In the second part of this play Falstaff calls Shallow a *Vice's dagger*.

8 It appears from the old comedy of The Two Angry Women of Abingdon, (1599) that this method of defence and fight was then going out of fashion:—'I see by this dearth of good swords that *sword and buckler fight* begins to grow out. I am sorry for it; I shall never see good manhood again. If it be once gone, this poking fight of rapier and dagger will come up then: then a tall man and a good sword-and-buckler-man will be spitted like a cat or a coney: then a boy will be as good as a man,' &c.

less than truth, they are villains, and the sons of darkness.

P. Hen. Speak, sirs; how was it?

Gads. We four set upon some dozen,——

Fal. Sixteen, at least, my lord.

Gads. And bound them.

Peto. No, no, they were not bound.

Fal. You rogue, they were bound, every man of them; or I am a Jew else, an Ebrew Jew.[1]

Gads. As we were sharing, some six or seven fresh men set upon us,——

Fal. And unbound the rest, and then come in the other.

P. Hen. What, fought you with them all?

Fal. All? I know not what ye call, all; but if I fought not with fifty of them, I am a bunch of radish: if there were not two or three and fifty upon poor old Jack, then I am no two-legged creature.

Poins. 'Pray God, you have not murdered some of them.

Fal. Nay, that's past praying for: for I have peppered two of them: two, I am sure, I have paid; two rogues in buckram suits. I tell thee what, Hal,—if I tell thee a lie, spit in my face, call me horse. Thou knowest my old ward;—here I lay, and thus I bore my point. Four rogues in buckram let drive at me,——

P. Hen. What, four? thou saidst but two, even now.

Fal. Four, Hal; I told thee four.

Poins. Ay, ay, he said four.

Fal. These four came all a-front, and mainly thrust at me. I made me no more ado, but took all their seven points in my target thus.

P. Hen. Seven? why, there were but four, even now.

Fal. In buckram.

Poins. Ay, four, in buckram suits.

Fal. Seven, by these hilts, or I am a villain else.

P. Hen. Pr'ythee, let him alone; we shall have more anon.

Fal. Dost thou hear me, Hal?

P. Hen. Ay, and mark thee too, Jack.

Fal. Do so, for it is worth the listening to. These nine in buckram, that I told thee of,——

P. Hen. So, two more already.

Fal. Their points being broken,——

Poins. Down fell their hose.[2]

Fal. Began to give me ground: But I followed me close, came in foot and hand; and, with a thought, seven of the eleven I paid.

P. Hen. O monstrous! eleven buckram men grown out of two!

Fal. But, as the devil would have it, three misbegotten knaves, in Kendal[3] green, came at my back, and let drive at me;—for it was so dark, Hal, that thou could'st not see thy hand.

P. Hen. These lies are like the father that begets them; gross as a mountain, open, palpable. Why, thou clay-brained guts; thou knotty-pated fool; thou whoreson, obscene, greasy tallow-keech[4]——

Fal. What, art thou mad? art thou mad? is not the truth, the truth?

P. Hen. Why, how could'st thou know these men in Kendal green, when it was so dark thou could'st not see thy hand? come tell us your reason; What sayest thou to this?

Poins. Come, your reason, Jack, your reason.

Fal. What, upon compulsion? No; were I at the strappado,[5] or all the racks in the world, I would not tell you on compulsion. Give you a reason on compulsion! if reasons were as plenty as blackberries, I would give no man a reason upon compulsion, I.

P. Hen. I'll be no longer guilty of this sin: this sanguine coward, this bed-presser, this horse-back-breaker, this huge hill of flesh;——

Fal. Away, you starveling, you elf-skin,[6] you dried neats-tongue, bull's pizzle, you stock-fish,—O, for breath to utter what is like thee!—you tailor's yard, you sheath, you bow-case, you vile standing tuck;——

P. Hen. Well, breathe awhile, and then to it again: and when thou hast tired thyself in base comparisons, hear me speak but this.

Poins. Mark, Jack.

P. Hen. We two saw you four set on four; you bound them, and were masters of their wealth.——Mark now, how plain a tale shall put you down.—Then did we two set on you four: and, with a word out-faced you from your prize, and have it; yea, and can show it you here in the house:—and, Falstaff, you carried your guts away as nimbly, with as quick dexterity, and roared for mercy, and still ran and roared, as ever I heard bull-calf. What a slave art thou, to hack thy sword as thou hast done; and then say, it was in fight? What trick, what device, what starting-hole, canst thou now find out to hide thee from this open and apparent shame?

Poins. Come let's hear, Jack; What trick hast thou now?

Fal. By the Lord, I knew ye, as well as he that made ye. Why, hear ye, my masters: Was it for me to kill the heir apparent? Should I turn upon the true prince? Why, thou knowest, I am as valiant as Hercules: but beware instinct; the lion will not touch the true prince. Instinct is a great matter; I was a coward on instinct. I shall think the better of myself and thee, during my life; I, for a valiant lion, and thou for a true prince. But, by the Lord, lads, I am glad you have the money.——Hostess, clap to the doors; watch to-night, pray to-morrow.—Gallants, lads, boys, hearts of gold, all the titles of good fellowship come to you! What, shall we be merry? shall we have a play extempore?

P. Hen. Content;—and the argument shall be, thy running away.

Fal. Ah! no more of that, Hal, an thou lovest me.

Enter Hostess.

Host. My lord the prince,——

P. Hen. How now, my lady the hostess? what say'st thou to me?

Host. Marry, my lord, there is a nobleman of the court at door, would speak with you: he says, he comes from your father.

P. Hen. Give him as much as will make him a royal man,[7] and send him back again to my mother.

---

1 So in The Two Gentlemen of Verona:—'Thou art an *Hebrew*, a *Jew*, and not worth the name of a Christian.'

2 The same jest has already occurred in Twelfth Night, Act i. Sc. 5. To understand it, the double meaning of *point* must be remembered, which signifies a *tagged lace* used by our ancestors to fasten their garments, as well as *the sharp end of a weapon.* So in Sir Giles Goosecap, a comedy, 1606:—'Help me to truss my *points.*'—'I had rather see your hose about your heels than I would help you to truss a point.'

3 *Kendal Green* was the livery of Robert earl of Huntingdon and his followers, when in a state of outlawry, under the name of Robin Hood and his men. The colour took its name from *Kendal*, in Westmoreland, formerly celebrated for its cloth manufacture. *Green* still continues the colour of woodmen and gamekeepers.

4 A *keech* is a round lump of fat, rolled up by the butcher in order to be carried to the chandler, and in its form resembles the rotundity of a fat man's belly. The old editions read *catch.*

5 The *strappado* was a dreadful punishment inflicted on soldiers and criminals, by drawing them up on high with their arms tied backward. Randle Holme says that they were suddenly let fall half way with a jerk, which not only broke the arms but shook all the joints out of joint. He adds, 'which punishment it is better to be hanged than for a man to undergo.' *Academy of Arms and Blazon*, b. iii. p. 310.

6 It has been proposed to read *eel-skin*, with great plausibility. Shakspeare had historical authority for the *leanness* of the prince. Stowe speaking of him, says 'He exceeded the mean stature of men, his neck long, body *slender* and *lean*, and his bones small,' &c.

7 This is a kind of a joke upon *noble* and *royal*, two coins, one of the value of 6*s*. 8*d*. the other 10*s*. 'Mr

Fal. What manner of man is he?

Host. An old man.

Fal. What doth gravity out of his bed at midnight?—Shall I give him his answer?

P. Hen. 'Pr'ythee, do, Jack.

Fal. 'Faith, and I'll send him packing. [*Exit.*

P. Hen. Now, sirs; by'r lady, you fought fair;—so did you, Peto;—so did you, Bardolph: you are lions too, you ran away upon instinct, you will not touch the true prince, no,—fye!

Bard. 'Faith, I ran when I saw others run.

P. Hen. Tell me now in earnest, How came Falstaff's sword so hacked?

Peto. Why, he hacked it with his dagger; and said, he would swear truth out of England, but he would make you believe it was done in fight; and persuaded us to do the like.

Bard. Yea, and to tickle our noses with speargrass, to make them bleed; and then to beslubber our garments with it, and to swear it was the blood of true men. I did that I did not this seven year before, I blushed to hear his monstrous devices.

P. Hen. O villain, thou stolest a cup of sack eighteen years ago, and wert taken with the manner,[1] and ever since thou hast blushed extempore: Thou hast fire[2] and sword on thy side, and yet thou ran'st away; What instinct hast thou for it?

Bard. My lord, do you see these meteors? do you behold these exhalations?

P. Hen. I do.

Bard. What think you they portend?

P. Hen. Hot livers and cold purses.[3]

Bard. Choler, my lord, if rightly taken.

P. Hen. No, if rightly taken, halter.

Re-enter FALSTAFF.

Here comes lean Jack, here comes bare-bone. How now, my sweet creature of bombast?[4] How long is't ago, Jack, since thou sawest thine own knee?

Fal. My own knee? when I was about thy years, Hal, I was not an eagle's talon in the waist; I could have crept into any alderman's thumb-ring:[5] A plague of sighing and grief! it blows a man up like a bladder. There's villainous news abroad: here was Sir John Bracy from your father; you must to the court in the morning. That same mad fellow of the north, Percy; and he of Wales, that gave Amaimon[6] the bastinado, and made Lucifer cuckold, and swore the devil his true liegeman upon the cross of a Welsh hook[7]—What, a plague, call you him?——

Poins. O, Glendower.

Fal. Owen, Owen; the same;—and his son-in-law, Mortimer; and old Northumberland; and that sprightly Scot of Scots, Douglas, that runs o'horseback up a hill perpendicular.

P. Hen. He that rides at high speed, and with his pistol[8] kills a sparrow flying.

Fal. You have hit it.

P. Hen. So did he never the sparrow.

Fal. Well, that rascal hath good metal in him; he will not run.

P. Hen. Why, what a rascal art thou then, to praise him so for running?

Fal. O'horseback, ye cuckoo! but, afoot, he will not budge a foot.

P. Hen. Yes, Jack, upon instinct.

Fal. I grant ye, upon instinct. Well, he is there too, and one Mordake, and a thousand blue-caps[9] more: Worcester is stolen away to-night; thy father's beard is turned white with the news; you may buy land now as cheap as stinking mackarel.

P. Hen. Why then, 'tis like, if there come a hot June, and this civil buffeting hold, we should buy maidenheads as they buy hob-nails, by the hundreds.

Fal. By the mass, lad, thou sayest true; it is like, we shall have good trading that way.—But, tell me, Hal, art thou not horribly afeard? thou being heir apparent, could the world pick thee out three such enemies again, as that fiend Douglas, that spirit Percy, and that devil Glendower? Art thou not horribly afraid? doth not thy blood thrill at it?

P. Hen. Not a whit, i'faith; I lack some of thy instinct.

Fal. Well, thou wilt be horribly chid to-morrow, when thou comest to thy father: if thou love me, practise an answer.

P. Hen. Do thou stand for my father, and examine me upon the particulars of my life.

Fal. Shall I? content:—This chair shall be my state,[10] this dagger my sceptre, and this cushion my crown.

P. Hen. Thy state is taken for a joint-stool, thy golden sceptre for a leaden dagger, and thy precious rich crown, for a pitiful bald crown!

Fal. Well, an the fire of grace be not quite out of thee, now shalt thou be moved.—Give me a cup of sack, to make mine eyes look red, that it may be thought I have wept; for I must speak in passion, and I will do it in King Cambyses'[11] vein.

P. Hen. Well, here is my leg.[12]

Fal. And here is my speech:—Stand aside, nobility.

Host. This is excellent sport, i'faith.

Fal. Weep not, sweet queen, for trickling tears
are vain.

Host. O, the father, how he holds his countenance!

Fal. For God's sake, lords, convey my tristful
queen,
For tears do stop the flood-gates of her eyes.[13]

Host. O rare! he doth it as like one of these harlotry players, as I ever see.

Fal. Peace, good pint-pot; peace, good ticklebrain.—Harry, I do not only marvel where thou

---

John Blower, in a sermon before her majesty, first said:—'My *royal* queen,' and a little after, 'My *noble* queen.' Upon which says the queen, 'What, am I *ten groats* worse than I was?'—*Hearne's Discourse of some Antiquities between Windsor and Oxford.*

1 i. e. *taken in the fact.* See Love's Labour's Lost, Act i. Sc. 1.

2 The *fire* in Bardolph's face.

3 i. e. drunkenness and poverty.

4 i. e. 'my sweet *stuffed* creature.' *Bombast* is *cotton.* Gerard calls the cotton plant the *bombast* tree. It is here used for the *stuffing of clothes.* See a note on Love's Labour's Lost, Act v. Sc. 2.

5 The custom of wearing a ring upon the thumb is very ancient. The rider of the brazen horse in Chaucer's Squiers Tale:—

'———upon his *thombe* he had a ring of gold.'

Grave personages, citizens, and aldermen wore a plain broad gold ring upon the thumb, which often had a motto engraved in the inside of it. An alderman's thumb-ring, and its motto, is mentioned in The Antipodes, by Brome.

6 A demon; who is described as one of the four kings who rule over all the demons in the world.

7 The *Welsh hook* was a kind of hedging bill made with a hook at the end, and a long handle like the partisan or halbert. 'The Welsh glaive,' (which appears to be the same thing,) Grose says, 'is a kind of bill sometimes reckoned among the pole-axes.'

8 Pistols were not in use in the age of Henry IV They are said to have been much used by the Scotch in Shakspeare's time.

9 *Scotsmen*, on account of their blue bonnets.

10 In the old anonymous play of King Henry V. the same strain of humour is discoverable:—'Thou shalt be my lord chief justice, and shalt sit in this chair; and I'll be the young prince, and hit thee a box of the ear, &c. A *state* is a chair with a canopy over it.

11 The banter is here upon the play called A Lamentable Tragedie mixed full of pleasant Mirthe, containing the Life of Cambises, King of Persia, by Thomas Preston [1570.] There is a marginal direction in this play, 'At this tale tolde, let the queen weep,' which is probably alluded to, though the measure in the parody is not the same with that of the original.

12 i. e. *my obeisance.*

13 Thus in Cambyses:—

'*Queen.* These words to hear makes stilling tears
issue from chrystall eyes.'

Ritson thinks that the following passage in Soliman and Perseda is glanced at:—

'How can mine eyes dart forth a pleasant look,
When they are *stopp'd with floods of flowing tears*?'

spendest thy time, but also how thou art accompanied: for though the camomile, the more it is trodden on, the faster it grows, yet youth, the more it is wasted, the sooner it wears. That thou art my son, I have partly thy mother's word, partly my own opinion; but chiefly, a villainous trick of thine eye, and a foolish hanging of thy nether lip, that doth warrant me. If then thou be son to me, here lies the point;—Why, being son to me, art thou so pointed at? Shall the blessed sun of heaven prove a micher,[1] and eat blackberries? a question not to be asked. Shall the son of England prove a thief, and take purses? a question to be asked. There is a thing, Harry, which thou hast often heard of, and it is known to many in our land by the name of pitch: this pitch, as ancient writers do report, doth defile; so doth the company thou keepest: for, Harry, now I do not speak to thee in drink, but in tears; not in pleasure, but in passion; not in words only, but in woes also:—And yet there is a virtuous man, whom I have often noted in thy company, but I know not his name.

P. Hen. What manner of man, an it like your majesty?

Fal. A good portly man, i'faith, and a corpulent; of a cheerful look, a pleasing eye, and a most noble carriage; and, as I think, his age some fifty, or by'r-lady, inclining to threescore; And now I remember me, his name is Falstaff: if that man should be lewdly given, he deceiveth me; for, Harry, I see virtue in his looks. If then the tree may be known by the fruit, as the fruit by the tree, then, peremptorily I speak it, there is virtue in that Falstaff: him keep with, the rest banish. And tell me now, thou naughty varlet, tell me, where hast thou been this month?

P. Hen. Dost thou speak like a king? Do thou stand for me, and I'll play my father.

Fal. Depose me? if thou dost it half so gravely, so majestically, both in word and matter, hang me up by the heels for a rabbet-sucker,[2] or a poulter's hare.

P. Hen. Well, here I am set.

Fal. And here I stand:—judge, my masters.

P. Hen. Now, Harry? whence come you?

Fal. My noble lord, from Eastcheap.

P. Hen. The complaints I hear of thee are grievous.

Fal. 'Sblood, my lord, they are false:—nay, I'll tickle ye for a young prince, i'faith.

P. Hen. Swear'st thou, ungracious boy? henceforth ne'er look on me. Thou art violently carried away from grace: there is a devil haunts thee, in the likeness of a fat old man: a tun of man is thy companion. Why dost thou converse with that trunk of humours, that bolting-hutch[3] of beastliness, that swoln parcel of dropsies, that huge bombard[4] of sack, that stuffed cloak-bag of guts, that roasted Manningtree[5] ox with the pudding in his belly, that reverend vice, that gray iniquity, that father ruffian, that vanity in years? Wherein is he good, but to taste sack and drink it? wherein neat and cleanly, but to carve a capon and eat it? wherein cunning, but in craft? wherein crafty, but in villainy? wherein villainous, but in all things? wherein worthy, but in nothing?

Fal. I would, your grace would take me with you;[6] Whom means your grace?

P. Hen. That villainous abominable misleader of youth, Falstaff, that old white-bearded Satan.

Fal. My lord, the man I know.

P. Hen. I know, thou dost.

Fal. But to say, I know more harm in him than in myself, were to say more than I know. That he is old (the more the pity,) his white hairs do witness it: but that he is (saving your reverence) a whore-master, that I utterly deny. If sack and sugar be a fault, God help the wicked! If to be old and merry be a sin, then many an old host that I know, is damned: if to be fat be to be hated, then Pharaoh's lean kine are to be loved. No, my good lord; banish Peto, banish Bardolph, banish Poins; but for sweet Jack Falstaff, kind Jack Falstaff, true Jack Falstaff, valiant Jack Falstaff, and therefore more valiant, being as he is, old Jack Falstaff, banish not him thy Harry's company; banish plump Jack, and banish all the world.

P. Hen. I do, I will. [*A knocking heard.*

[*Exeunt* Hostess, FRANCIS, *and* BARDOLPH.

Re-enter BARDOLPH, *running.*

Bard. O, my lord, my lord; the sheriff, with a most monstrous watch, is at the door.

Fal. Out, you rogue! play out the play; I have much to say in the behalf of that Falstaff.

Re-enter Hostess, *hastily.*

Host. O Jesu, my lord! my lord!——

Fal. Heigh, heigh! the devil rides upon a fiddle-stick: What's the matter?

Host. The sheriff and all the watch are at the door: they are come to search the house: Shall I let them in?

Fal. Dost thou hear, Hal? never call a true piece of gold, a counterfeit: thou art essentially mad, without seeming so.

P. Hen. And thou a natural coward, without instinct.

Fal. I deny your *major:* if you will deny the sheriff, so; if not, let him enter: if I become not a cart as well as another man, a plague on my bringing up! I hope, I shall as soon be strangled with a halter as another.

P. Hen. Go, hide thee behind the arras;[7]—the rest walk up above. Now, my masters, for a true face, and good conscience.

Fal. Both which I have had: but their date is out, and therefore I'll hide me.

[*Exeunt all but the* Prince *and* POINS.

P. Hen. Call in the sheriff.——

Enter Sheriff *and* Carrier.

Now, master Sheriff; what's your will with me?

Sher. First, pardon me, my lord. A hue and cry
Hath follow'd certain men unto this house.

P. Hen. What men?

Sher. One of them is well known, my gracious lord,
A gross fat man.

Car. As fat as butter.

P. Hen. The man, I do assure you, is not here;
For I myself at this time have employ'd him.
And, Sheriff, I will engage my word to thee,
That I will, by to-morrow dinner time,
Send him to answer thee, or any man,
For any thing he shall be charg'd withal:
And so let me entreat you leave the house.

---

1 A *micher* here signifies a *truant.* So in an old phrase book, Hormanni Vulgaria, 1509:—'He is a *mychar;* vagus est non discolus.' To *mich* was to skulk, to hide; and hence the word sometimes also signified *a skulking thief,* and sometimes *a miser.* In Lyly's Mother Bombie, 1594, we have: 'How like a *micher* he stands, as if he had *truanted* from honesty.'

2 A young rabbit.

3 The machine which separates flour from bran.

4 A *bombard* was a very large leathern vessel to hold drink, perhaps so called from its similarity to a sort of cannon of the same name. That it was not a barrel, as some have supposed, is evident from the following passage:—

'His boots as wide as the black jacks,
Or *bombards* toss'd by the king's guards.'
Shirley's Martyr'd Soldier.

5 Manningtree, in Essex, formerly enjoyed the privilege of fairs, by exhibiting a certain number of stage plays yearly. It appears from other intimations that there were great festivities there, and much good eating at Whitsun ales, &c.

6 i. e. go no faster than I can follow.

7 When arras was first brought into England, it was suspended on small hooks driven into the walls of houses and castles; but this practice was soon discontinued After the damp of the stone and brickwork had been found to rot the tapestry, it was fixed on frames of wood at such distance from the wall as prevented the damp from being injurious; large spaces were thus left between the arras and the walls, sufficient to contain even one of Falstaff's bulk. Our old dramatists avail themselves of this convenient hiding place upon all occasions

Sher. I wil., my .ord: There are two gentlemen
Have in this robbery lost three hundred marks.
P. Hen. It may be so: if he have robb'd these men,
He shall be answerable; and so, farewell.
Sher. Good night, my noble lord.
P. Hen. I think it is good morrow: Is it not?
Sher. Indeed, my lord, I think it be two o'clock.
[*Exeunt* Sheriff *and* Carrier.

P. Hen. This oily rascal is known as well as Paul's.[1] Go call him forth.

Poins. Falstaff!—fast asleep behind the arras, and snorting like a horse.

P. Hen. Hark, how hard he fetches breath: Search his pockets. [POINS *searches.*] What hast thou found?

Poins. Nothing but papers, my lord.

P. Hen. Let's see what they be: read them.

Poins. Item, A capon, 2*s.* 2*d.*
Item, Sauce, 4*d.*
Item, Sack, two gallons, 5*s.* 8*d.*[2]
Item, Anchovies, and sack after supper, 2*s.* 6*d.*
Item, Bread, a halfpenny.

P. Hen. O monstrous! but one halfpenny-worth of bread to this intolerable deal of sack!—What there is else, keep close; we'll read it at more advantage: there let him sleep till day. I'll to the court in the morning; we must all to the wars, and thy place shall be honourable. I'll procure this fat rogue a charge of foot; and, I know, his death will be a mark of twelve-score.[3] The money shall be paid back again with advantage. Be with me betimes in the morning; and so good morrow, Poins.

Poins. Good morrow, good my lord. [*Exeunt.*

ACT III.

SCENE I. Bangor. *A Room in the* Archdeacon's *House. Enter* HOTSPUR, WORCESTER, MORTIMER, *and* GLENDOWER.

Mort. These promises are fair, the parties sure,
And our induction[4] full of prosperous hope.
Hot. Lord Mortimer,—and cousin Glendower,—
Will you sit down?—
And, uncle Worcester:—A plague upon it!
I have forgot the map.
Glend. No, here it is.
Sit, cousin Percy; sit, good cousin Hotspur,
For by that name as oft as Lancaster
Doth speak of you, his cheek looks pale; and, with
A rising sigh, he wisheth you in heaven.
Hot. And you in hell, as often as he hears
Owen Glendower spoke of.
Glend. I cannot blame him: at my nativity,
The front of heaven was full of fiery shapes,[5]
Of burning cressets;[6] and, at my birth,
The frame and huge foundation of the earth,
Shak'd like a coward.
Hot. Why, so it would have done
At the same season, if your mother's cat had
But kitten'd, though yourself had ne'er been born.
Glend. I say, the earth did shake when I was born.
Hot. And I say, the earth was not of my mind,
If you suppose, as fearing you it shook.
Glend. The heavens were all on fire, the earth did tremble.
Hot. O, then the earth shook to see the heavens on fire,
And not in fear of your nativity.
Diseased nature oftentimes breaks forth
In strange eruptions: oft the teeming earth
Is with a kind of colick pinch'd and vex'd
By the imprisoning of unruly wind
Within her womb; which, for enlargement striving,
Shakes the old beldame[7] earth, and topples[8] down
Steeples, and moss-grown towers. At your birth
Our grandam earth, having this distemperature,
In passion shook.
Glend. Cousin, of many men
I do not bear these crossings. Give me leave
To tell you once again,—that, at my birth,
The front of heaven was full of fiery shapes;
The goats ran from the mountains, and the herds
Were strangely clamorous to the frighted fields.
These signs have mark'd me extraordinary;
And all the courses of my life do show,
I am not in the roll of common men.
Where is he living,—clipp'd in with the sea
That chides the banks of England, Scotland, Wales,—
Which calls me pupil, or hath read to me?
And bring him out, that is but woman's son,
Can trace me in the tedious ways of art,
And hold me pace in deep experiments.
Hot. I think, there is no man speaks better Welsh:—
I'll to dinner.
Mort. Peace, cousin Percy; you will make him mad.
Glend. I can call spirits from the vasty deep.
Hot. Why, so can I; or so can any man:
But will they come, when you do call for them?
Glend. Why, I can teach you, cousin, to command
The devil.
Hot. And I can teach thee, coz, to shame the devil,
By telling truth; Tell truth, and shame the devil.—
If thou have power to raise him, bring him hither,
And I'll be sworn, I have power to shame him hence.
O, while you live, tell truth, and shame the devil.
Mort. Come, come,
No more of this unprofitable chat.
Glend. Three times hath Henry Bolingbroke made head
Against my power: thrice from the banks of Wye,
And sandy-bottom'd Severn, have I sent him,
Bootless[9] home, and weather-beaten back.
Hot. Home without boots, and in foul weather too
How 'scapes he agues, in the devil's name?
Glend. Come, here's the map: Shall we divide our right,
According to our three-fold order ta'en?
Mort. The archdeacon hath divided it
Into three limits, very equally:

1 St. Paul's Cathedral.

2 In a very curious letter from Thomas Rainolds, vice chancellor of Oxford, in 1566, to Cardinal Pole, among the Conway Papers, he entreats the suppression of some of the wine taverns in Oxford, and states as one of his reasons that they sell Gascony wine at 16*d.* a gallon, *sacke* at 2*s.* 4*d.* per gallon, and Malvoisie at 2*s.* 6*d.* to the utter ruin of the poor students.' In Florio's First Frutes, 1578:—'Claret wine, red and white, is sold for fivepence the quarte, and *sacke* for sixpence; muscadel and malmsey for eight.' Twenty years afterwards sack had probably risen to eightpence or eightpence halfpenny a quart, which would make the computation of five shillings and eightpence for two gallons correct. To the note on *sack*, at p. 433, we may add that *sack* is called *Vinum Hispanicum* by Coles, and *Vin d'Espagne* by Sherwood. In Florio's Second Frutes it is *Vino de Spagna.*

3 A *score*, in the language Toxopholites, was *twenty yards.* A mark of *twelve score* meant a mark at a distance of *two hundred and forty yards.*

4 *Induction* is used by Shakspeare for *commencement, beginning.* The introductory part of a play or poem was called the *induction.* Such is the prelude of the Tinker to the Taming of the Shrew. Sackville's *induction* to the Mirror for Magistrates is another instance

5 Shakspeare has amplified the hint of Holinshed, who says, 'Strange wonders happened at the nativity of this man; for the same night that he was born, all his father's horses in the stable were found to stand in blood up to their bellies.' The poet had probably also heard that, in 1402, a blazing star appeared, which the Welsh bards represented as portending good fortune to Owen Glendower.

6 *Cressets* were open lamps, exhibited on a beacon, carried upon a pole or otherwise suspended. Cotgrave thus describes them under the word *falot*, 'a cresset light (such as they use in playhouses,) made of ropes wreathed, pitched, and put into small open cages of iron.'

7 *Beldame*, and *belsire*, formerly signified *grand mother* and *grandfather.*

8 To *topple*, in its active sense, is to *throw down*

9 Shakspeare has already, in Act ii. Sc. 1, quibbled upon *boots* and *boot*, profit.

England, from Trent and Severn hitherto,[1]
By south and east, is to my part assign'd:
All westward, Wales beyond the Severn shore,
And all the fertile land within that bound,
To Owen Glendower: and, dear coz, to you
The remnant northward, lying off from Trent.
And our indentures tripartite are drawn:
Which being sealed interchangeably,
(A business that this night may execute,)
To-morrow, cousin Percy, you, and I,
And my good lord of Worcester, will set forth,
To meet your father, and the Scottish power,
As is appointed us, at Shrewsbury.
My father Glendower is not ready yet,
Nor shall we need his help these fourteen days:—
Within that space [*To* GLEND.] you may have drawn together
Your tenants, friends, and neighbouring gentlemen.

Glend. A shorter time shall send me to you, lords,
And in my conduct shall your ladies come:
From whom you now must steal, and take no leave;
For there will be a world of water shed,
Upon the parting of your wives and you.

Hot. Methinks, my moiety,[2] north from Burton here,
In quantity equals not one of yours:
See, how this river comes me cranking[3] in,
And cuts me from the best of all my land,
A huge half moon, and monstrous cantle[4] out.
I'll have the current in this place damm'd up;
And here the smug and silver Trent shall run,
In a new channel, fair and evenly:
It shall not wind with such a deep indent,
To rob me of so rich a bottom here.

Glend. Not wind? it shall, it must; you see, it doth.

Mort. Yea,
But mark, how he bears his course, and runs me up
With like advantage on the other side;
Gelding the opposed continent as much,
As on the other side it takes from you.

Wor. Yea, but a little charge will trench him here,
And on this north side win this cape of land;
And then he runs straight and even.

Hot. I'll have it so; a little charge will do it.

Glend. I will not have it alter'd.

Hot. Will not you?

Glend. No, nor you shall not.

Hot. Who shall say me nay?

Glend. Why, that will I.

Hot. Let me not understand you then,
Speak it in Welsh.

Glend. I can speak English, lord, as well as you;
For I was train'd up in the English court;[5]
Where, being but young, I framed to the harp
Many an English ditty, lovely well,
And gave the tongue a helpful ornament;[6]
A virtue that was never seen in you.

Hot. Marry, and I'm glad of it with all my heart;
I had rather be a kitten, and cry—mew,
Than one of these same metre ballad-mongers:
I had rather hear a brazen canstick[7] turn'd,
Or a dry wheel grate on an axle-tree;
And that would set my teeth nothing on edge,
Nothing so much as mincing poetry;
'Tis like the forc'd gait of a shuffling nag.

Glend. Come, you shall have Trent turn'd.

Hot. I do not care: I'll give thrice so much land
To any well-deserving friend;
But, in the way of bargain, mark ye me,
I'll cavil on the ninth part of a hair.
Are the indentures drawn? shall we be gone

Glend. The moon shines fair, you may away by night:
I'll in and haste the writer,[8] and, withal,
Break with your wives of your departure hence:
I am afraid, my daughter will run mad,
So much she doteth on her Mortimer. [*Exit.*

Mort. Fye, cousin Percy! how you cross my father!

Hot. I cannot choose: sometimes he angers me,
With telling me of the moldwarp[9] and the ant,
Of the dreamer Merlin and his prophecies;
And of a dragon and a finless fish,
A clip-wing'd griffin, and a moulten raven,
A couching lion, and a ramping cat,
And such a deal of skimble-skamble stuff
As puts me from my faith. I tell you what,—
He held me, last night, at least nine hours,
In reckoning up the several devils' names,
That were his lackeys: I cried, humph,—and well,—go to,—
But mark'd him not a word. O, he's as tedious
As is a tired horse, a railing wife;
Worse than a smoky house;—I had rather live
With cheese and garlick, in a windmill, far,
Than feed on cates, and have him talk to me,
In any summer-house in christendom.

Mort. In faith, he is a worthy gentleman;
Exceedingly well read, and profited
In strange concealments;[10] valiant as a lion,
And wondrous affable: and as bountiful
As mines of India. Shall I tell you, cousin?
He holds your temper in a high respect,
And curbs himself even of his natural scope,
When you do cross his humour; 'faith, he does:
I warrant you, that man is not alive,
Might so have tempted him as you have done,
Without the taste of danger and reproof;
But do not use it oft, let me entreat you.

Wor. In faith, my lord, you are too wilful-blame;[11]
And since your coming hither, have done enough
To put him quite beside his patience.
You must needs learn, lord, to amend this fault.
Though sometimes it show greatness, courage, blood,
(And that's the dearest grace it renders you,)
Yet oftentimes it doth present harsh rage,
Defect of manners, want of government,
Pride, haughtiness, opinion,[12] and disdain:
The least of which, haunting a nobleman,
Loseth men's hearts; and leaves behind a stain
Upon the beauty of all parts besides,
Beguiling them of commendation.

Hot. Well, I am school'd; good manners be your speed!
Here come our wives, and let us take our leave.

Re-enter GLENDOWER, *with the* Ladies.

Mort. This is the deadly spite that angers me,—
My wife can speak no English, I no Welsh.

---

1 i. e. to this spot (pointing to the map.)

2 A *moiety* was frequently used by the writers of Shakspeare's age as a portion of any thing, though not divided into equal parts.

3 To *crank* is to crook, to turn in and out. *Crankling* is used by Drayton in the same sense: speaking of a river, he says that Meander
'Hath not so many turns and *crankling* nooks as she.'

4 A *cantle* is a *portion*, a *part*, a *corner* or *fragment* of any thing. The French had *chanteau* and *chantel*, and the Italians *canto* and *cantone* in the same sense.

5 Owen Glendower's real name was Owen ap-Gryffyth Vaughan. He took the name of Glendower from the lordship of which he was the owner.

6 This disputed passage seems to me to mean that he gave to the language the helpful ornament of *verse.* Hotspur's answer shows that he took it in that sense.

7 A very common contraction of *candlestick*. The noise to which Hotspur alludes is mentioned in A New Trick to cheat the Devil, 1636:—

'As if you were to lodge in Lothbury,
Where they *turn brazen candlesticks.*'

8 i. e. the writer of the articles. The old copy reads 'I'll haste the writer, &c.' The two necessary words (*in and*) were suggested by Steevens.

9 The *moldwarp* is the *mole*, A. S. *molde* and *weorpan*; because it warps or renders the surface of the earth uneven by its hillocks.

10 Skilled in wonderful secrets.

11 Shakspeare has several compounds in which the first adjective has the power of an adverb. In King Richard III. we meet with *childish*-foolish, *senseless* obstinate, and *mortal*-staring.

12 i. e. self-opinion or conceit

Glend. My daughter weeps; she will not part with you,
She'll be a soldier too, she'll to the wars.
Mort. Good father, tell her,—that she, and my aunt Percy,
Shall follow in your conduct[1] speedily.
[GLEND. *speaks to his daughter in* Welsh, *and she answers him in the same.*
Glend. She's desperate here; a peevish self-will'd harlotry,[2]
One that no persuasion can do good upon.
[LADY M. *speaks to* MORTIMER *in* Welsh.
Mort. I understand thy looks: that pretty Welsh
Which thou pourest down from these swelling heavens,[3]
I am too perfect in; and, but for shame,
In such a parley would I answer thee.
[LADY M. *speaks.*
I understand thy kisses, and thou mine,
And that's a feeling disputation:
But I will never be a truant, love,
Till I have learn'd thy language; for thy tongue
Makes Welsh as sweet as ditties highly penn'd,
Sung by a fair queen in a summer's bower,
With ravishing division, to her lute.[4]
Glend. Nay, if you melt, then will she run mad.
[LADY M. *speaks again.*
Mort. O, I am ignorance itself in this.
Glend. She bids you on the wanton rushes lay you down,[5]
And rest your gentle head upon her lap,
And she will sing the song that pleaseth you,
And on your eyelids crown the god of sleep,[6]
Charming your blood with pleasing heaviness;
Making such difference 'twixt wake and sleep,
As is the difference betwixt day and night,
The hour before the heavenly-harness'd team
Begins his golden progress in the east.
Mort. With all my heart I'll sit, and hear her sing:
By that time will our book,[7] I think, be drawn.
Glend. Do so;
And those musicians that shall play to you,
Hang in the air a thousand leagues from hence;
And straight they shall be here: sit, and attend.
Hot. Come, Kate, thou art perfect in lying down: Come, quick, quick; that I may lay my head in thy lap.
Lady P. Go, ye giddy goose.
[GLENDOWER *speaks some* Welsh *words, and then the Music plays.*
Hot. Now I perceive the devil understands Welsh;
And 'tis no marvel, he's so humorous.
By'r-lady, he's a good musician.
Lady P. Then should you be nothing but musical; for you are altogether governed by humours. Lie still, ye thief, and hear the lady sing in Welsh.
Hot. I had rather hear *Lady*, my brach,[8] howl in Irish.
Lady P. Would'st thou have thy head broken?
Hot. No.
Lady P. Then be still.
Hot. Neither; 'tis a woman's fault.[9]
Lady P. Now God help thee!
Hot. To the Welsh lady's bed.
Lady P. What's that?
Hot. Peace! she sings.
[*A* Welsh *song sung by* LADY M.
Hot. Come, Kate, I'll have your song too.
Lady P. Not mine, in good sooth.
Hot. Not yours, in good sooth! 'Heart, you swear like a comfit-maker's wife! Not you, in good sooth: and, As true as I live; and, As God shall mend me; and, As sure as day:
And giv'st such sarcenet surety for thy oaths,
As if thou never walk'st further than Finsbury.[10]
Swear me, Kate, like a lady, as thou art,
A good mouth-filling oath; and leave in sooth,
And such protest of pepper-gingerbread,
To velvet-guards,[11] and Sunday-citizens.
Come, sing.
Lady P. I will not sing.
Hot. 'Tis the next way to turn tailor, or be red-breast teacher.[12] An the indentures be drawn, I'll away within these two hours; and so come in when ye will. [*Exit.*
Glend. Come, come, Lord Mortimer; you are as slow,
As hot lord Percy is on fire to go.
By this our book's drawn; we'll but seal, and then
To horse immediately.
Mort. With all my heart. [*Exeunt.*

SCENE II. London. *A Room in the Palace.*

Enter KING HENRY, Prince *of* Wales, *and* Lords.

K. Hen. Lords, give us leave: the Prince of Wales and I
Must have some private conference: But be near at hand,
For we shall presently have need of you.
[*Exeunt* Lords
I know not whether God will have it so,
For some displeasing service[13] I have done,
That in his secret doom, out of my blood
He'll breed revengement and a scourge for me;
But thou dost, in thy passages of life,
Make me believe,—that thou art only mark'd
For the hot vengeance and the rod of heaven,
To punish my mistreadings. Tell me else,
Could such inordinate, and low desires,
Such poor, such bare, such lewd, such mean attempts,[14]
Such barren pleasures, rude society,
As thou art match'd withal, and grafted to,

1 Guard, escort.

2 Capulet, in Romeo and Juliet, reproaches his daughter in the same words:—
'*A peevish self-will'd harlotry* it is.'

3 It seems extraordinary that Steevens could for a moment conceive that Mortimer meant his *lady's two prominent lips!* It is obvious, as Mr. Douce has remarked, that *her eyes swollen with tears* are meant, whose language he is too perfect in, and could answer with the like if it were not for shame.

4 A compliment to Queen Elizabeth was perhaps here intended, who was a performer on the lute and virginals. See Melvil's Memoirs, folio, p. 50. *Divisions*, which were then uncommon in vocal music, are *variations of melody upon some given fundamental harmony.*

5 It has been already remarked, that it was long the custom in this country to strew the floors with rushes, as we now cover them with carpets.

6 So in Beaumont and Fletcher's Philaster:—
——— who shall take his lute,
And touch it till he *crown a silent sleep*
Upon my eyelid.'
The God of Sleep is not only to sit on Mortimer's eyelids, but to *sit crowned*, that is, with sovereign dominion.

7 It was usual to call any manuscript of bulk a *book* in ancient times, such as patents, grants, articles, covenants, &c.—In a MS. letter from Sir Richard Sackville, in 1560, to Lady Throckmorton, announcing *a grant* of some land to her husband Sir Nicholas, he says, 'It hath pleased the queen's majesty to sign Mr. Frogmorton's *book*.'—*Conway Papers.*

8 Hound.

9 That this is spoken ironically is sufficiently obvious, as Mr. Pye has observed; but the strange attempts to *misunderstand* the passage made by some commentators, make the observation in some measure necessary.

10 *Finsbury*, being then open walks and fields, was the common resort of the citizens, as appears from many old plays.

11 *Velvet-guards*, or *trimmings of velvet*, being the city fashion in Shakspeare's time, the term was used metaphorically to designate such persons.

12 Tailors, like weavers, have ever been remarkable for their vocal skill. Percy is jocular in his mode of persuading his wife to sing, and this is a humorous turn which he gives to his argument, 'Come, sing.'—'I will not sing.'—''Tis the next (i. e. readiest, nearest) way to turn tailor or redbreast teacher.' The meaning is, '*to sing* is to put yourself upon a level with tailors and teachers of birds.'

13 *Service*, for *action.*

14 *Mean attempts* are *mean, unworthy undertakings* *Lewd*, in this place, has its original signification of *idle, ungracious, naughty*

Accompany the greatness of thy blood,
And hold their level with thy princely heart?

P. Hen. So please your majesty, I would I could
Quit all offences with as clear excuse,
As well as, I am doubtless, I can purge
Myself of many I am charg'd withal:
Yet such extenuation let me beg,[1]
As, in reproof of many tales devis'd,—
Which oft the ear of greatness needs must hear,—
By smiling pickthanks[2] and base newsmongers,
I may, for some things true, wherein my youth
Hath faulty wander'd and irregular,
Find pardon on my true submission.

K. Hen. God pardon thee!—yet let me wonder, Harry,
At thy affections, which do hold a wing
Quite from the flight of all thy ancestors.
Thy place in council thou hast rudely lost,[3]
Which by thy younger brother is supplied;
And art almost an alien to the hearts
Of all the court and princes of my blood:
The hope and expectation of thy time
Is ruin'd; and the soul of every man
Prophetically does forethink thy fall.
Had I so lavish of my presence been,
So common-hackney'd in the eyes of men,
So stale and cheap to vulgar company;
Opinion, that did help me to the crown,
Had still kept loyal to possession;[4]
And left me in reputeless banishment,
A fellow of no mark, nor likelihood.
By being seldom seen, I could not stir,
But, like a comet, I was wonder'd at:
That men would tell their children, *This is he;*
Others would say,—*Where? which is Bolingbroke?*
And then I stole all courtesy from heaven,[5]
And dress'd myself in such humility,
That I did pluck allegiance from men's hearts,
Loud shouts and salutations from their mouths,
Even in the presence of the crowned king.
Thus did I keep my person fresh, and new;
My presence, like a robe pontifical,
Ne'er seen, but wonder'd at: and so my state,
Seldom, but sumptuous, showed like a feast;
And won, by rareness, such solemnity.
The skipping king, he ambled up and down
With shallow jesters, and rash bavin[6] wits,
Soon kindled, and soon burn'd: carded[7] his state;
Mingled his royalty with carping[8] fools;
Had his great name profaned with their scorns;
And gave his countenance, against his name,
To laugh at gibing boys, and stand the push
Of every beardless vain comparative:[9]
Grew a companion to the common streets,
Enfeoff'd[10] himself to popularity:
That being daily swallow'd by men's eyes,
They surfeited with honey; and began
To loathe the taste of sweetness, whereof a little
More than a little is by much too much.
So, when he had occasion to be seen,
He was but as the cuckoo is in June,
Heard, not regarded; seen, but with such eyes,
As, sick and blunted with community,
Afford no extraordinary gaze,
Such as is bent on sunlike majesty,
When it shines seldom in admiring eyes:
But rather drowz'd, and hung their eyelids down,
Slept in his face, and render'd such aspect
As cloudy men use to their adversaries;
Being with his presence glutted, gorg'd, and full.
And in that very line, Harry, standest thou:
For thou hast lost thy princely privilege,
With vile participation; not an eye
But is a-weary of thy common sight,
Save mine, which hath desir'd to see thee more;
Which now doth that I would not have it do,
Make blind itself with foolish tenderness.

P. Hen. I shall hereafter, my thrice-gracious lord,
Be more myself.

K. Hen. For all the world,
As thou art to this hour, was Richard then
When I from France set foot at Ravenspurg;
And even as I was then, is Percy now.
Now by my sceptre, and my soul to boot,
He hath more worthy interest to the state,[11]
Than thou, the shadow of succession:
For, of no right, nor colour like to right,
He doth fill fields with harness in the realm;
Turns head against the lion's armed jaws;
And, being no more in debt to years than thou,
Leads ancient lords and reverend bishops on,
To bloody battles, and to bruising arms.
What never-dying honour hath he got
Against renowned Douglas; whose high deeds,
Whose hot incursions, and great name in arms,
Holds from all soldiers chief majority,
And military title capital,
Through all the kingdoms that acknowledge Christ?
Thrice hath this Hotspur Mars in swathing clothes,
This infant warrior, in his enterprises
Discomfited great Douglas; ta'en him once,
Enlarged him, and made a friend of him,
To fill the mouth of deep defiance up,
And shake the peace and safety of our throne.
And what say you to this? Percy, Northumberland,
The archbishop's grace of York, Douglas, Mortimer,
Capitulate[12] against us, and are up.
But wherefore do I tell these news to thee?

---

1 The construction of this passage is somewhat obscure. Johnson thus explains it:—'Let me beg so much extenuation, that *upon confutation of many false charges, I may be pardoned some which are true.*' *Reproof* means *disproof.*

2 A sycophant, a flatterer, one who is studious to gain favour, or to *pick* occasions for obtaining *thanks.*

3 This appears to be an anachronism. The prince's removal from council, in consequence of his striking the Lord Chief Justice Gascoigne, was some years after the battle of Shrewsbury, (1403.) His brother the duke of Clarence was appointed president in his room, and he was not created a duke till 1411.

4 True to him that had then possession of the crown.

5 Massinger, in The Great Duke of Florence, has adopted this expression:—

'———— Giovanni,
A prince in expectation, when he lived here
Stole courtesy from heaven; and would not to
The meanest servant in my father's house
Have kept such distance.'

Mr. Gifford, in the following note on this passage, gives the best explanation of the phrase, which the commentators have altogether mistaken:—'The plain meaning of the phrase is, that the affability and sweetness of Giovanni were of a heavenly kind, i. e. more perfect than was usually found among men, resembling that divine condescension which excludes none from its regard, and, therefore, immediately derived or *stolen* from heaven, from whence all good proceeds. The word *stolen* here means little else than *to win by imperceptible progression, by gentle violence.*'

6 *Bavins* are brushwood, or small fagots used for lighting fires.

7 To *card* is to mix, or debase by mixing. The metaphor is probably taken from mingling *coarse* wool with *fine*, and *carding* them together, thereby diminishing the value of the latter. The phrase is used by other writers for to mingle or mix.

8 The quarto, 1598, reads *capring.* The quarto, 1599, and subsequent old copies, read *carping*, which I am inclined to think from the context is the word which Shakspeare wrote. 'A carping momus,' and 'a carping fool,' were very common expressions in that age.

9 i. e. every beardless vain young fellow who affected wit, or was *a dealer in comparisons.* Vide Act i. Sc. 2.

10 i. e. *gave himself up*, absolutely and entirely, *to popularity.* *To enfeoff* is a law term, signifying *to give* or grant any thing to another in fee simple.

11 'Interest *to* the state.' We should now write *in* the state; but this was the phraseology of the poet's time. So in The Winter's Tale, 'he is less frequent *to* his princely exercises than formerly.' 'Thou hast but the shadow of succession, compared with the more worthy interest in the state (i. e. great popularity) which he possesses.'

12 To *capitulate*, according to the old dictionaries, formerly signified *to make articles of agreement.* The nobles enumerated had entered into such articles, or *confederated* against the king.

Why, Harry, do I tell thee of my foes,
Which art my near'st and dearest[1] enemy?
Thou that art like enough,—through vassal fear,
Base inclination, and the start of spleen——
To fight against me under Percy's pay,
To dog his heels, and court'sy at his frowns,
To show how much degenerate thou art.

P. Hen. Do not think so, you shall not find it so;
And God forgive them, that have so much sway'd
Your majesty's good thoughts away from me!
I will redeem all this on Percy's head,
And, in the closing of some glorious day,
Be bold to tell you, that I am your son;
When I will wear a garment all of blood,
And stain my favours[2] in a bloody mask,
Which, wash'd away, shall scour my shame with it.
And that shall be the day, whene'er it lights,
That this same child of honour and renown,
This gallant Hotspur, this all-praised knight,
And your unthought-of Harry, chance to meet:
For every honour sitting on his helm,
'Would they were multitudes; and on my head
My shames redoubled! for the time will come,
That I shall make this northern youth exchange
His glorious deeds for my indignities.
Percy is but my factor, good my lord,
To engross up glorious deeds on my behalf;
And I will call him to so strict account,
That he shall render every glory up,
Yea, even the slightest worship of his time,
Or I will tear the reckoning from his heart.
This, in the name of God, I promise here:
The which if he be pleas'd I shall perform,
I do beseech your majesty, may salve
The long-grown wounds of my intemperance:
If not, the end of life cancels all bands;[3]
And I will die a hundred thousand deaths,
Ere break the smallest parcel[4] of this vow.

K. Hen. A hundred thousand rebels die in this:—
Thou shalt have charge, and sovereign trust, herein.

Enter BLUNT.

How now, good Blunt? thy looks are full of speed.

Blunt. So hath the business that I come to speak of.
Lord Mortimer of Scotland[5] hath sent word,—
That Douglas, and the English rebels, met,
The eleventh of this month, at Shrewsbury:
A mighty and a fearful head they are,
If promises be kept on every hand,
As ever offer'd foul play in a state.

K. Hen. The earl of Westmoreland set forth to-day;
With him my son, Lord John of Lancaster;
For this advertisement[6] is five days old:—
On Wednesday next, Harry, you shall set
Forward; on Thursday, we ourselves will march:
Our meeting is Bridgnorth: and, Harry, you
Shall march through Glostershire; by which account,
Our business valued, some twelve days hence
Our general forces at Bridgnorth shall meet.
Our hands are full of business: let's away;
Advantage feeds him[7] fat, while men delay.
[*Exeunt.*

SCENE III. Eastcheap. *A Room in the Boar's Head Tavern.* *Enter* FALSTAFF *and* BARDOLPH.

Fal. Bardolph, am I not fallen away vilely since this last action? do I not bate? do I not dwindle? Why, my skin hangs about me like an old lady's loose gown; I am wither'd like an old apple-John. Well, I'll repent, and that suddenly, while I am in some liking;[8] I shall be out of heart shortly, and then I shall have no strength to repent. An I have not forgotten what the inside of a church is made of, I am a pepper-corn, a brewer's horse:[9] the inside of a church! Company, villanous company, hath been the spoil of me.

Bard. Sir John, you are so fretful, you cannot live long.

Fal. Why, there is it:—come, sing me a bawdy song; make me merry. I was as virtuously given, as a gentleman need to be; virtuous enough: swore little; diced, not above seven times a week; went to a bawdy-house, not above once in a quarter—of an hour; paid money that I borrowed, three or four times; lived well, and in good compass: and now I live out of all order, out of all compass.

Bard. Why, you are so fat, Sir John, that you must needs be out of all compass; out of all reasonable compass, Sir John.

Fal. Do thou amend thy face, and I'll amend my life: Thou art our admiral,[10] thou bearest the lantern in the poop,—but 'tis in the nose of thee: thou art the knight of the burning lamp.

Bard. Why, Sir John, my face does you no harm.

Fal. No, I'll be sworn; I make as good use of it as many a man doth of a death's head, or a *memento mori:* I never see thy face, but I think upon hell-fire, and Dives that lived in purple; for there he is in his robes, burning, burning. If thou wert any way given to virtue, I would swear by thy face; my oath should be, By this fire: but thou art altogether given over; and wert indeed, but for the light in thy face, the son of utter darkness. When thou ran'st up Gads-hill in the night to catch my horse, if I did not think thou hadst been an *ignis fatuus*, or a ball of wildfire, there's no purchase in money. O, thou art a perpetual triumph, an everlasting bonfire-light! Thou hast saved me a thousand marks in links and torches, walking with thee in the night betwixt tavern and tavern:[11] but the sack that thou hast drunk me, would have bought me lights as good cheap,[12] at the dearest chandler's in

1 See p. 119, note 5.

2 *Favours* is probably here used for *colours*; the *scarf* by which a knight of rank was distinguished.

3 Bonds. 4 Part.

5 There was no such person as *Lord Mortimer of Scotland;* but there was a Lord March of Scotland, (George Dunbar,) who having quitted his own country in disgust, attached himself so warmly to the English, and did them such signal services in their wars with Scotland, that the parliament petitioned the king to bestow some reward on him. He fought on the side of King Henry in this rebellion, and was the means of saving his life at the battle of Shrewsbury. The poet recollected that there was a Scottish lord on the king's side, who bore the same title with the English family on the rebels' side, (one being *earl of March* in England, the other *earl of March* in Scotland,) but his memory deceived him as to the particular name which was common to both. He took it to be *Mortimer* instead of *March*.

6 Intelligence. 7 Feeds *himself* fat.

8 *Liking* is *condition, plight of body.* 'If one be in better plight of body, or better *liking*.'

9 That Falstaff was unlike a *brewer's horse* may be collected from a conundrum in The Devil's Cabinet Opened:—'What is the difference between a drunkard and a *brewer's horse*?—Because one carries all his liquor on his back, and the other in his belly.' *Malt horse*, which is the same thing, was a common term of reproach, and is used elsewhere by Shakspeare, and by Ben Jonson.

10 So Decker, in his Wonderful Year, 1605:—'An antiquary might have pickt rare matter out of his *nose*.—The Hamburghers offered I know not how many dollars for his company in an East Indian voyage, to have stood a nights *in the poope of their admiral, only to save the charges of candles*.' That it was an old joke appears from a passage in Bullein's Dialogue against the Fever Pestilence, 1578, cited by Malone.

11 Steevens has taken occasion here to mention that *candles and lanterns to let* were then cried about London, the streets not being then lighted.

12 '*Cheap* being derived from KAVPON, Gothic, is the past participle of cypan, Sax. to traffic, to bargain, to buy and sell. *Good cheap* was therefore a *good bargain*.' Our ancestors not only used *good cheap*, but *better cheap*, in the sense which we now use *cheap* and *cheaper*. Tooke thinks that *bad-cheap* was also used, but has adduced no example. Baret translates the *ova vilia* of Horace by *good cheap eggs*; and the *minoris vendere aliquid*, of Plautus, by *to sell better-cheap*. *Cheap* and *cheaping* therefore came to signify *a market*, which led Johnson to suppose that good-cheap was derived from *a bon marche* All the northern dialects

Europe. I have maintained that salamander of yours with fire, any time this two and thirty years; Heaven reward me for it!

Bard. 'Sblood, I would my face were in your belly!

Fal. God-a-mercy! so should I be sure to be heart-burned.

Enter Hostess.

How now, dame Partlet the hen? have you inquired yet, who picked my pocket?

Host. Why, Sir John! what do you think, Sir John? Do you think I keep thieves in my house? I have searched, I have inquired, so has my husband, man by man, boy by boy, servant by servant: the tithe of a hair was never lost in my house before.

Fal. You lie, hostess; Bardolph was shaved and lost many a hair: and I'll be sworn, my pocket was picked: Go to, you are a woman, go.

Host. Who I? I defy thee: I was never called so in mine own house before.

Fal. Go to, I know you well enough.

Host. No, Sir John; you do not know me, Sir John: I know you, Sir John: you owe me money, Sir John, and now you pick a quarrel to beguile me of it: I bought you a dozen of shirts to your back.

Fal. Dowlas, filthy dowlas: I have given them away to bakers' wives, and they have made bolters of them.

Host. Now, as I am a true woman, holland of eight shillings an ell.[1] You owe money here besides, Sir John, for your diet, and by-drinkings, and money lent you, four and twenty pound.

Fal. He had his part of it; let him pay.

Host. He? alas, he is poor; he hath nothing.

Fal. How! poor? look upon his face; What call you rich? let them coin his nose, let them coin his cheeks; I'll not pay a denier. What, will you make a younker[2] of me? shall I not take mine ease in mine inn,[3] but I shall have my pocket picked? I have lost a seal-ring of my grandfather's worth forty mark.

Host. O Jesu! I have heard the prince tell him, I know not how oft, that that ring was copper.

Fal. How! the prince is a Jack, a sneak-cup; and, if he were here, I would cudgel him like a dog, if he would say so.

Enter PRINCE HENRY *and* POINS, *marching.* FALSTAFF *meets the* Prince, *playing on his truncheon like a fife.*

Fal. How now, lad? is the wind in that door, i'faith? must we all march?

Bard. Yea, two and two, Newgate-fashion?

Host. My lord, I pray you, hear me.

P. Hen. What sayest thou, mistress Quickly? How does thy husband? I love him well, he is an honest man.

Host. Good my lord, hear me.

Fal. Pr'ythee, let her alone, and list to me.

P. Hen. What sayest thou, Jack?

Fal. The other night I fell asleep here behind the arras, and had my pocket picked: this house is turned bawdy-house, they pick pockets.

P. Hen. What didst thou lose, Jack?

Fal. Wilt thou believe me, Hal? three or four bonds of forty pound a-piece, and a seal-ring of my grandfather's.

P. Hen. A trifle, some eight-penny matter.

Host. So I told him, my lord; and I said I heard your grace say so: And, my lord, he speaks most vilely of you, like a foul-mouthed man as he is; and said, he would cudgel you.

P. Hen. What! he did not?

Host. There's neither faith, truth, nor womanhood in me else.

Fal. There's no more faith in thee than in a stewed prune;[4] nor no more truth in thee, than in a drawn fox; and for womanhood, maid Marian[5] may be the deputy's wife of the ward to thee. Go, you thing, go.

Host. Say, what thing? what thing?

Fal. What thing? why a thing to thank God on.

Host. I am no thing to thank God on, I would thou should'st know it; I am an honest man's wife and, setting thy knighthood aside, thou art a knave to call me so.

Fal. Setting thy womanhood aside, thou art a beast to say otherwise.

Host. Say, what beast, thou knave thou?

Fal. What beast? why an otter.

P. Hen. An otter, Sir John! why an otter?

Fal. Why? she's neither fish, nor flesh; a man knows not where to have her.

Host. Thou art an unjust man in saying so; thou or any man knows where to have me, thou knave thou.

P. Hen. Thou sayest true, hostess; and he slanders thee most grossly.

Host. So he doth you, my lord; and said this other day, you ought him a thousand pound.

P. Hen. Sirrah, do I owe you a thousand pound

Fal. A thousand pound, Hal? a million: thy love is worth a million; thou owest me thy love.

Host. Nay, my lord, he called you Jack, and said, he would cudgel you.

Fal. Did I, Bardolph?

Bard. Indeed, Sir John, you said so.

Fal. Yea; if he said, my ring was copper.

P. Hen. I say, 'tis copper: Darest thou be as good as thy word now?

Fal. Why, Hal, thou knowest, as thou art but man, I dare: but, as thou art prince, I fear thee, as I fear the roaring of the lion's whelp.

P. Hen. And why not, as the lion?

Fal. The king himself is to be feared as the lion: Dost thou think, I'll fear thee as I fear thy father? nay, an I do, I pray God, my girdle break?[6]

P. Hen. O, if it should, how would thy guts fall about thy knees! But, sirrah, there's no room for faith, truth, nor honesty, in this bosom of thine; it is filled up with guts, and midriff. Charge an honest woman with picking thy pocket! Why, thou whore-

---

have the same form of speech that our ancestors used; thus *godt-kop*, *betre kop*, in Swedish; *got kiob*, *better kiob*, in Danish, &c. Florio has 'buon-mercato, *good-cheape*, a good bargaine.'

1 *Eight shillings an ell*, for holland linen, appears a high price for the time, but hear Stubbes in his Anatomie of Abuses:—'In so much as I have heard of shirtes that have cost some ten shillinges, some twentie, some fortie, some five pound, some twentie nobles, and (which is horrible to heare) some ten pound a peece, yea the meanest shirte that commonly is worn of any doest cost a crowne or a noble at the least; and yet that is scarsely thought fine enough for the simplest person.'

2 *Younker* is here used for a novice, a dupe, or a person thoughtless through inexperience.

3 This was a common phrase for *enjoying one's self in quiet, as if at home*; not very different in its application from that maxim, *Every man's house is his castle. Inne* originally signified a house or habitation. When the word began to change its meaning, and to be used for a house of public entertainment, the proverb still continuing in force, was applied in the latter sense. Falstaff puns upon the word *inn* in order to represent the wrong done him the more strongly. Old Heywood has one or two epigrams which turn upon this phrase.

4 Steevens has been too abundantly copious on the subject of *stewed prunes*. They were a refection particularly common in brothels in Shakspeare's time, perhaps from mistaken notions of their antisyphilitic properties. It is not easy to understand Falstaff's similes, perhaps he means as faithless as a *strumpet* or a *bawd*. *A drawn fox* is surely neither an *exenterated fox!* nor a fox drawn over the grounds to exercise the hounds; but a *hunted fox*, a fox *drawn* from his cover, whose cunning in doubling and deceiving the hounds makes the simile perfectly appropriate.

5 One of the characters in the ancient morris dance, generally a man dressed like a woman, sometimes a strumpet; and therefore forms an allusion to describe women of a masculine character. A curious tract entitled 'Old Meg of Herefordshire for a *Mayd Marian* and Hereford Town for a Morris-dance, 1609,' was reprinted by Mr. Triphook in 1816.

6 This *imprecation* is supposed to have reference to the old adage, '*Ungirt, unblest.*' It appears to have been also proverbial.

son, impudent, embossed[1] rascal, if there were any thing in thy pocket but tavern-reckonings, memorandums of bawdy-houses, and one poor penny-worth of sugar-candy to make thee long-winded; if thy pocket were enriched with any other injuries but these, I am a villain. And yet you will stand to it; you will not pocket up wrong; Art thou not ashamed?

Fal. Dost thou hear, Hal? thou knowest, in the state of innocency, Adam fell; and what should poor Jack Falstaff do, in the days of villany? Thou seest I have more flesh than another man; and therefore more frailty.——You confess then, you picked my pocket?

P. Hen. It appears so by the story.

Fal. Hostess, I forgive thee: Go, make ready breakfast; love thy husband, look to thy servants, cherish thy guests: thou shalt find me tractable to any honest reason: thou seest, I am pacified.—Still?—Nay, pr'ythee, be gone. [*Exit* Hostess.] Now, Hal, to the news at court: for the robbery, lad,—How is that answered?

P. Hen. O, my sweet beef, I must still be good angel to thee:—The money is paid back again.

Fal. O, I do not like that paying back, 'tis a double labour.

P. Hen. I am good friends with my father, and may do any thing.

Fal. Rob me the exchequer the first thing thou doest, and do it with unwashed hands too.

Bard. Do, my lord.

P. Hen. I have procured thee, Jack, a charge of foot.

Fal. I would, it had been of horse. Where shall I find one that can steal well? O for a fine thief, of the age of two and twenty, or thereabouts! I am heinously unprovided. Well, God be thanked for these rebels, they offend none but the virtuous; I laud them, I praise them.

P. Hen. Bardolph——

Bard. My lord.

P. Hen. Go bear this letter to Lord John of Lancaster,—my brother John;—this to my lord of Westmoreland.—Go, Poins, to horse, to horse; for thou, and I, have thirty miles to ride yet ere dinner time.——Jack, meet me to-morrow i'the Temple-hall at two o'clock i'the afternoon: there shalt thou know thy charge; and there receive money, and order for their furniture.[2]
The land is burning; Percy stands on high;
And either they, or we, must lower lie.

[*Exeunt* Prince, POINS, *and* BARDOLPH.

Fal. Rare words! brave world!——Hostess, my breakfast; come:—
O, I could wish, this tavern were my drum. [*Exit.*

ACT IV.

SCENE I. *The rebel Camp near* Shrewsbury.

Enter HOTSPUR, WORCESTER, *and* DOUGLAS.

Hot. Well said, my noble Scot: If speaking truth,
In this fine age, were not thought flattery,
Such attribution should the Douglas have,[3]
As not a soldier of this season's stamp
Should go so general current through the world.
By heaven, I cannot flatter; I defy[4]
The tongues of soothers; but a braver place
In my heart's love, hath no man than yourself;
Nay, task me to the word; approve me, lord.

Doug. Thou art the king of honour:
No man so potent breathes upon the ground,
But I will beard[5] him.

Hot. Do so, and 'tis well:—

Enter a Messenger, *with Letters.*

What letters hast thou there?—I can but thank you.

Mess. These letters come from your father,—

Hot. Letters from him! why comes he not himself?

Mess. He cannot come, my lord; he's grievous sick.

Hot. 'Zounds! how has he the leisure to be sick,[6]
In such a justling time? Who leads his power?
Under whose government come they along?

Mess. His letters bear his mind, not I, my lord.[7]

Wor. I pr'ythee, tell me, doth he keep his bed?

Mess. He did, my lord, four days ere I set forth?
And at the time of my departure thence,
He was much fear'd by his physicians.

Wor. I would, the state of time had first been whole,
Ere he by sickness had been visited;
His health was never better worth than now.

Hot. Sick now! droop now! this sickness doth infect
The very life-blood of our enterprise;
'Tis catching hither, even to our camp.——
He writes me here,—that inward sickness—
And that his friends by deputation could not
So soon be drawn; nor did he think it meet,
To lay so dangerous and dear a trust
On any soul remov'd,[8] but on his own.
Yet doth he give us bold advertisement,—
That with our small conjunction, we should on,
To see how fortune is dispos'd to us:
For, as he writes, there is no quailing[9] now;
Because the king is certainly possess'd[10]
Of all our purposes. What say you to it?

Wor. Your father's sickness is a maim to us.

Hot. A perilous gash, a very limb lopp'd off:—
And yet, in faith, 'tis not; his present want
Seems more than we shall find it:—Were it good
To set the exact wealth of all our states
All at one cast? to set so rich a main
On the nice hazard of one doubtful hour?
It were not good; for therein should we read
The very bottom and the soul of hope:
The very list, the very utmost bound
Of all our fortunes.

Doug. 'Faith, and so we should;
Where[11] now remains a sweet reversion;
We may boldly spend upon the hope of what
Is to come in:
A comfort of retirement[12] lives in this.

Hot. A rendezvous, a home to fly unto,
If that the devil and mischance look big
Upon the maidenhead of our affairs.

Wor. But yet, I would your father had been here.
The quality and hair[13] of our attempt
Brooks no division: It will be thought
By some, that know not why he is away,
That wisdom, loyalty, and mere dislike
Of our proceedings, kept the earl from hence,
And think, how such an apprehension
May turn the tide of fearful faction,
And breed a kind of question in our cause:

---

1 Swoln, puffy, blown up.

2 I have followed Mr. Douce's suggestion in printing thus much of this speech in prose. No correct ear will ever receive it as blank verse, notwithstanding the efforts by omission, &c. to convert it into metre.

3 This expression is frequent in Holinshed, and is applied by way of preeminence to the head of *the* Douglas family.

4 Disdain.

5 To *beard* is to *oppose face to face*, in a daring and hostile manner, to threaten even to his *beard.*

6 Epaminondas being told, on the evening before the battle of Leuctra, that an officer of distinction had died in his tent, exclaimed, 'Good gods! how could any body find time to die in such a conjuncture.'—*Xenophon Hellenic*, l. vi.

7 The folio reads 'not I his mind.' The quarto, 1598, 'not I my mind.' The emendation is Capell's.

8 That is, on any *less near* to himself, or whose interest is *remote.*

9 *Quailing* is fainting, slackening, flagging; or failing in vigour or resolution; going back. Cotgrave renders it by *alachissement.*

10 Informed.

11 *Where*, for *whereas.*

12 i. e. 'a support to which we may have recourse.'

13 '*Hair* was anciently used metaphorically for the *colour*, *complexion*, or *nature* of a thing. *Pelo* (in Italian) is used for the *colour* of a horse, also for the *countenance* of a man:' and *poil*, in French, has the same significations, *esser d'un pelo*, *estre d'un poil* To be of the same *hair*, quality, or condition.

For, well you know, we of the offering[1] side
Must keep aloof from strict arbitrement;
And stop all sight-holes, every loop, from whence
The eye of reason may pry in upon us:
This absence of your father's draws a curtain,[2]
That shows the ignorant a kind of fear
Before not dreamt of.

Hot. You strain too far.
I, rather, of his absence make this use;—
It lends a lustre, and more great opinion,
A larger dare to our great enterprise,
Than if the earl were here: for men must think,
If we, without his help, can make a head,
To push against the kingdom; with his help,
We shall o'erturn it topsy-turvy down.—
Yet all goes well, yet all our joints are whole.

Doug. As heart can think: there is not such a word
Spoke of in Scotland, as this term[3] of fear.

Enter SIR RICHARD VERNON.

Hot. My cousin Vernon! welcome, by my soul.

Ver. 'Pray God, my news be worth a welcome, lord.
The earl of Westmorland, seven thousand strong,
Is marching hitherwards; with him, Prince John.

Hot. No harm: What more?

Ver. And further, I have learn'd,
The king himself in person is set forth,
Or hitherwards intended speedily,
With strong and mighty preparation.

Hot. He shall be welcome too. Where is his son,
The nimble-footed[4] mad-cap prince of Wales,
And his comrades, that daff'd the world aside,
And bid it pass?

Ver. All furnish'd, all in arms,
All plum'd: like estridges that with the wind
Bated, like eagles having lately bath'd;[5]
Glittering in golden coats, like images;
As full of spirit as the month of May,
And gorgeous as the sun at midsummer;
Wanton as youthful goats, wild as young bulls.
I saw young Harry,—with his beaver[6] on,
His cuisses[7] on his thighs, gallantly arm'd,—
Rise from the ground like feather'd Mercury,
And vaulted with such ease into his seat,
As if an angel dropp'd down from the clouds,
To turn and wind a fiery Pegasus,
And witch the world with noble horsemanship.

Hot. No more, no more; worse than the sun in March,
This praise doth nourish agues. Let them come;
They come like sacrifices in their trim,
And to the fire-ey'd maid of smoky war,
All hot, and bleeding, will we offer them:
The mailed Mars shall on his altar sit,
Up to the ears in blood. I am on fire,
To hear this rich reprisal is so nigh,
And yet not ours:—Come, let me take[8] my horse
Who is to bear me, like a thunderbolt,
Against the bosom of the prince of Wales:
Harry to Harry shall, hot horse to horse,
Meet, and ne'er part, till one drop down a corse.—
O, that Glendower were come!

Ver. There is more news.
I learn'd in Worcester, as I rode along,
He cannot draw his power this fourteen days.

Doug. That's the worst tidings that I hear of yet.

Wor. Ay, by my faith, that bears a frosty sound.

Hot. What may the king's whole battle reach unto?

Ver. To thirty thousand.

Hot. Forty let it be;
My father and Glendower being both away,
The powers of us may serve so great a day.
Come, let us make a muster speedily:
Doomsday is near; die all, die merrily.

Doug. Talk not of dying; I am out of fear
Of death, or death's hand, for this one half year.
[*Exeunt.*

SCENE II. *A Public Road near* Coventry. *Enter* FALSTAFF *and* BARDOLPH.

Fal. Bardolph, get thee before to Coventry; fill me a bottle of sack; our soldiers shall march through; we'll to Sutton-Colfield to-night.

Bard. Will you give me money, captain?

Fal. Lay out, lay out.

Bard. This bottle makes an angel.

Fal. And if it do, take it for thy labour; and if it make twenty, take them all, I'll answer the coinage. Bid my lieutenant Peto meet me at the town's end

Bard. I will, captain: farewell. [*Exit.*

Fal. If I be not ashamed of my soldiers, I am a soused gurnet.[9] I have misused the king's press damnably. I have got, in exchange of a hundred and fifty soldiers, three hundred and odd pounds. I press me none but good householders, yeomen's sons: inquire me out contracted bachelors, such as had been asked twice on the bans; such a commo-

1 The *offering* side is the *assailing* side. Baret renders '*Attentare* pudicitiam puellæ, to *assaile* a maydens chastitie: to *offer*.'

2 To *draw* a curtain had anciently the same meaning as to *undraw* one at present. Thus in the Second Part of King Henry VI. quarto, 1600:—'Then the *curtaines* being *drawne*, Duke Humphrey is *discovered* in his bed.'

3 The folio reads '*dream* of fear.'

4 Shakspeare rarely bestows his epithets at random. Stowe says of the prince:—'He was passing swift in running, insomuch that he, with two other of his lords, without hounds, bow, or other engine, would take a wilde bucke, or doe, in a large parke.'

5 This is the reading of all the old copies, which Hanmer not understanding, altered to—

'All plum'd like estridges, *and* with the wind
Bating like eagles, &c.'

Then came Johnson, who supposed that there must be necessity for emendation, as it had already been attempted: he changed it thus:—

'All plum'd like estridges, that *wing* the wind;
Bated like eagles, &c.'

This reading has been adopted by Malone, and by Steevens, with a voluminous commentary to show its necessity. But surely, if a clear sense can be deduced from the passage as it stands, no conjectural alteration of the text should be admitted. The meaning of the passage is obviously this:—'The prince and his comrades were all furnish'd, all in arms, all plumed: like estridges (ostriches) that bated (i. e. flutter or beat) the wind *with their wings*; like eagles having lately bathed.' Johnson's reading is exceptionable, if it was not an unwarrantable innovation, because *to wing the wind* and *to bate* are the same thing; and the difficulties of an elliptical construction are not avoided by it. Malone's notion, that a line had been omitted, has not my concurrence. Nor do I think with Mr. Douce, that by *estridges, estridge* falcons are here meant, though the word may be used in that sense in Antony and Cleopatra. The ostridge's plumage would be more likely to occur to the poet, from the circumstance of its being the cognizance of the prince of Wales. So in Drayton's Polyolbion, Song 22:—

'Prince Edward all in gold, as he great Jove had been,
The Mountford's *all in plumes like estridges* were seen

Bating, or to *bate*, in falconry, is the unquiet fluttering of a hawk. *To beat the wing, batter l' ale*, Ital. All birds *bate*, i. e. flutter, beat, or flap their wings to dry their feathers after bathing; and the mode in which the ostrich uses its wings, to assist itself in running with the wind, is of this character; it is a fluttering or a flapping, not a flight. The fluttering motion and flapping of the plumed crests of the prince and his associates naturally excited these images. *Bated* refers both to the flapping of the plumes, and of the wings of the ostrich; the plumage of that bird is displayed to more advantage when its wings are in motion, than when at rest; and hence the propriety of representing the feathers of the helmets flouting the air to the plumage of the ostrich when its wings were in motion, or when it 'bated the air, like eagles lately bathed.'

6 The *beaver* of a helmet was a moveable piece, which lifted up or down to enable the wearer to drink or take breath more freely. It is frequently, though improperly, used to express *the helmet* itself.

7 Armour for the thighs.

8 The quartos of 1598 and 1599 read *taste*.

9 The *gurnet*, or gurnard, was a fish of the piper kind. It was probably deemed a vulgar dish when soused or pickled, hence *soused gurnet* was a common term of reproach.

dity of warm slaves, as had as lief hear the devil as a drum; such as fear the report of a caliver,[1] worse than a struck fowl, or a hurt wild-duck. I pressed me none but such toasts and butter,[2] with hearts in their bellies no bigger than pins' heads, and they have bought out their services; and now my whole charge consists of ancients, corporals, lieutenants, gentlemen of companies, slaves as ragged as Lazarus in the painted cloth, where the glutton's dogs licked his sores: and such as, indeed, were never soldiers; but discarded unjust serving-men, younger sons to younger brothers, revolted tapsters, and ostlers trade-fallen; the cankers of a calm world, and a long peace; ten times more dishonourable ragged than an old faced ancient:[3] and such have I, to fill up the rooms of them that have bought out their services, that you would think, that I had a hundred and fifty tattered prodigals, lately come from swine keeping, from eating draff and husks. A mad fellow met me on the way, and told me, I had unloaded all the gibbets, and pressed the dead bodies. No eye hath seen such scare-crows. I'll not march through Coventry with them, that's flat:—Nay, and the villains march wide betwixt the legs, as if they had gives[4] on; for indeed, I had the most of them out of prison. There's but a shirt and a half in all my company: and the half-shirt is two napkins, tacked together, and thrown over the shoulders like a herald's coat without sleeves; and the shirt, to say the truth, stolen from my host at Saint Albans, or the red-nose inn-keeper of Daintry.[5] But that's all one; they'll find linen enough on every hedge.

Enter PRINCE HENRY *and* WESTMORELAND.

P. Hen. How now, blown Jack? how now, quilt?

Fal. What, Hal? How now, mad wag? what a devil dost thou in Warwickshire?—My good lord of Westmoreland, I cry you mercy; I thought, your honour had already been at Shrewsbury.

West. 'Faith, Sir John, 'tis more than time that I were there, and you too; but my powers are there already: The king, I can tell you, looks for us all: we must away all night.

Fal. Tut, never fear me; I am as vigilant as a cat to steal cream.

P. Hen. I think, to steal cream indeed; for thy theft hath already made thee butter. But tell me, Jack; Whose fellows are these that come after?

Fal. Mine, Hal, mine.

P. Hen. I did never see such pitiful rascals.

Fal. Tut, tut; good enough to toss; food for powder, food for powder; they'll fill a pit, as well as better: tush, man, mortal men, mortal men.

West. Ay, but, Sir John, methinks they are exceeding poor and bare; too beggarly.

Fal. 'Faith, for their poverty,—I know not where they had that: and for their bareness,—I am sure, they never learned that of me.

P. Hen. No, I'll be sworn; unless you call three fingers on the ribs, bare. But, sirrah, make haste; Percy is already in the field.

Fal. What, is the king encamped?

West. He is, Sir John; I fear, we shall stay too long.

Fal. Well,
To the latter end of a fray, and the beginning of a feast,
Fits a dull fighter, and a keen guest. [*Exeunt.*

SCENE III. *The Rebel Camp near* Shrewsbury.

Enter HOTSPUR, WORCESTER, DOUGLAS, *and* VERNON.

Hot. We'll fight with him to-night.
Wor. It may not be
Doug. You give him then advantage.
Ver. Not a whit.
Hot. Why say you so? looks he not for supply?
Ver. So do we.
Hot. His is certain, ours is doubtful.
Wor. Good cousin, be advis'd; stir not to-night.
Ver. Do not, my lord.
Doug. You do not counsel well:
You speak it out of fear, and cold heart.
Ver. Do me no slander, Douglas: by my life
(And I dare well maintain it with my life,)
If well-respected honour bid me on,
I hold as little counsel with weak fear,
As you, my lord, or any Scot that lives:[6]—
Let it be seen to-morrow in the battle,
Which of us fears.
Doug. Yea, or to-night.
Ver. Content.
Hot. To-night, say I.
Ver. Come, come, it may not be.
I wonder much, being men of such great leading,[7]
That you foresee not what impediments
Drag back our expedition: Certain horse
Of my cousin Vernon's are not yet come up:
Your uncle Worcester's horse came but to-day;
And now their pride and mettle is asleep,
Their courage with hard labour tame and dull,
That not a horse is half the half of himself.
Hot. So are the horses of the enemy
In general, journey-bated, and brought low;
The better part of ours is full of rest.
Wor. The number of the king exceedeth ours:
For God's sake, cousin, stay till all come in.
[*The trumpet sounds a parley.*

Enter SIR WALTER BLUNT.

Blunt. I come with gracious offers from the king,
If you vouchsafe me hearing, and respect.
Hot. Welcome, Sir Walter Blunt; And 'would to God,
You were of our determination!
Some of us love you well: and even those some
Envy your great deserving, and good name;
Because you are not of our quality,[8]
But stand against us like an enemy.
Blunt. And God defend, but still I should stand so,
So long as, out of limit, and true rule,
You stand against anointed majesty!
But, to my charge.—The king hath sent to know
The nature of your griefs;[9] and whereupon
You conjure from the breast of civil peace
Such bold hostility, teaching his duteous land
Audacious cruelty: If that the king
Have any way your good deserts forgot,—
Which he confesseth to be manifold,—
He bids you name your griefs; and, with all speed,
You shall have your desires, with interest;
And pardon absolute for yourself, and these,
Herein misled by your suggestion.
Hot. The king is kind; and, well we know, the king
Knows at what time to promise, when to pay.
My father, and my uncle, and myself,
Did give him that same royalty he wears:
And,—when he was not six and twenty strong,
Sick in the world's regard, wretched and low,
A poor unminded outlaw sneaking home,
My father gave him welcome to the shore:
And,—when he heard him swear, and vow to God,

1 A gun.

2 'Londoners, and all within the sound of Bow bell, are in reproach called cockneys, and *eaters of buttered toasts*.'—*Moryson's Itin.* 1617.

3 'An old *faced ancient*' is an old *patched standard*. To *face* a garment was to *line* or *trim* it. Thus in the present play:—
'To *face* the garment of rebellion
With some fine colour.'

4 Fetters. 5 Daventry.

6 The old copies read 'that *this day* lives;' but the words, as Mason observes, weaken the sense and destroy the measure.

7 *Leading* is experience in the *conduct of armies*. The old copies have 'such leading *as you are*;' but the superfluous words serve only to destroy the metre.

8 *Quality*, in its general sense, anciently signified *profession, occupation*. Shakspeare here gives it metaphorically for one of the same *fraternity* or *fellowship*.

9 Grievances.

He came but to be duke of Lancaster,
To sue his livery,[1] and beg his peace;
With tears of innocency, and terms of zeal,—
My father, in kind heart and pity mov'd,
Swore him assistance, and perform'd it too.
Now, when the lords, and barons of the realm
Perceiv'd Northumberland did lean to him,
The more and less[2] came in with cap and knee;
Met him in boroughs, cities, villages;
Attended him on bridges, stood in lanes,
Laid gifts before him, proffer'd him their oaths,
Gave him their heirs as pages; follow'd him,
Even at the heels, in golden multitudes.
He presently,—as greatness knows itself,—
Steps me a little higher than his vow
Made to my father, while his blood was poor,
Upon the naked shore at Ravenspurg:[3]
And now, forsooth, takes on him to reform
Some certain edicts, and some strait decrees,
That lie too heavy on the commonwealth:
Cries out upon abuses, seems to weep
Over his country's wrongs; and, by this face,
This seeming brow of justice, did he win
The hearts of all that he did angle for.
Proceeded further; cut me off the heads
Of all the favourites, that the absent king
In deputation left behind him here,
When he was personal in the Irish war.

Blunt. Tut, I came not to hear this.

Hot. Then, to the point.——
In short time after, he depos'd the king;
Soon after that, depriv'd him of his life;
And, in the neck of that,[4] task'd the whole state:
To make that worse, suffer'd his kinsman March
(Who is, if every owner were well plac'd,
Indeed his king) to be engag'd[5] in Wales,
There without ransom to lie forfeited:
Disgrac'd me in my happy victories;
Sought to entrap me by intelligence:
Rated my uncle from the council-board;
In rage dismiss'd my father from the court;
Broke oath on oath, committed wrong on wrong:
And, in conclusion, drove us to seek out
This head of safety; and, withal, to pry
Into his title, the which we find
Too indirect for long continuance.

Blunt. Shall I return this answer to the king?

Hot. Not so, Sir Walter; we'll withdraw awhile.
Go to the king; and let there be impawn'd
Some surety for a safe return again,
And in the morning early shall mine uncle
Bring him our purposes: and so farewell.

Blunt. I would, you would accept of grace and love.

Hot. And, may be, so we shall.

Blunt. 'Pray heaven, you do!
[*Exeunt.*

SCENE IV. *A Room in the Archbishop's House.*

Enter the Archbishop of York, *and a* Gentleman.

Arch. Hie, good Sir Michael; bear this sealed brief,[6]
With winged haste, to the lord marshal;[7]
This to my cousin Scroop; and all the rest
To whom they are directed: if you knew
How much they do import, you would make haste.

Gent. My good lord,
I guess their tenor.

Arch. Like enough, you do.
To-morrow, good Sir Michael, is a day,
Wherein the fortune of ten thousand men
Must 'bide the touch: For, sir, at Shrewsbury,
As I am truly given to understand,
The king, with mighty and quick-raised power,
Meets with Lord Harry: and I fear, Sir Michael,
What with the sickness of Northumberland
(Whose power was in the first proportion,)
And what with Owen Glendower's absence thence,
(Who with them was a rated sinew too,[8]
And comes not in, o'er-ruled by prophecies,)—
I fear, the power of Percy is too weak
To wage an instant trial with the king.

Gent. Why, good my lord, you need not fear there's Douglas,
And Lord Mortimer.

Arch. No, Mortimer's not there.

Gent. But there is Mordake, Vernon, Lord Harry Percy,
And there's my lord of Worcester; and a head
Of gallant warriors, noble gentlemen.

Arch. And so there is: but yet the king hath drawn
The special head of all the land together:—
The prince of Wales, Lord John of Lancaster,
The noble Westmoreland, and warlike Blunt;
And many more cor-rivals, and dear men
Of estimation and command in arms.

Gent. Doubt not, my lord, they shall be well oppos'd.

Arch. I hope no less, yet needful 'tis to fear;
And, to prevent the worst, Sir Michael, speed:
For, if Lord Percy thrive not, ere the king
Dismiss his power, he means to visit us,—
For he hath heard of our confederacy.——
And 'tis but wisdom to make strong against him;
Therefore, make haste: I must go write again
To other friends; and so farewell, Sir Michael.
[*Exeunt severally.*

ACT V.

SCENE I. *The King's Camp near* Shrewsbury.

Enter KING HENRY, PRINCE HENRY, PRINCE JOHN *of* Lancaster, SIR WALTER BLUNT, *and* SIR JOHN FALSTAFF.

K. Hen. How bloodily the sun begins to peer
Above yon busky[9] hill! the day looks pale
At his distemperature.

P. Hen. The southern wind
Doth play the trumpet to his purposes:
And, by his hollow whistling in the leaves,
Foretells a tempest, and a blustering day.

K. Hen. Then with the losers let it sympathize;
For nothing can seem foul to those that win.—

Trumpet. Enter WORCESTER *and* VERNON.

How now, my lord of Worcester? 'tis not well,
That you and I should meet upon such terms
As now we meet: You have deceiv'd our trust;
And made us doff our easy robes of peace,
To crush our old limbs[10] in ungentle steel;

---

1 That is, to sue out the delivery or possession of his lands. This law term has been already explained in King Richard II. Act ii. Sc. 1.

2 The greater and the less.

3 The whole of this speech alludes to passages in King Richard II.

4 So in Painter's Palace of Pleasure: 'Great mischiefes succedyng *one in another's necke.*' *Task'd* is here used for *taxed:* it was common to use these words indiscriminately, says Steevens. *Taskes* were tributes or subsidies, and should not be confounded with *taxes*, which are carefully distinguished by Baret. He interprets '*telonium*, the place where *tasks* or *tributes* are paied.' Philips, in his World of Words, says, '*Tasck* is an old British word, signifying *tribute*, from whence haply cometh our word *task*, which is a duty or labour *imposed* upon any one.'

5 The old copies read *engag'd*, which Theobald altered to *incag'd*, without reason: to be engaged is to be pledged as an hostage.

6 A *brief* is any short writing, as a *letter*, &c.

7 Thomas Lord Mowbray.

8 A strength on which we reckoned, a help of which we made account.

9 'I do not know (says Mr. Blakeway) whether Shakspeare ever surveyed the ground of Battlefield, but he has described the sun's rising over Haughmound Hill from that spot as accurately as if he had. It still merits the name of a *busky* hill.' Milton writes the word, perhaps more properly, *bosky*, it is from the French *boscageux*, woody.

10 Shakspeare forgot that he was not at this time *old*, it was only four years since the deposition of King Richard

This is not well, my lord, this is not well.
What say you to't? will you again unknit
This churlish knot of all-abhorred war?
And move in that obedient orb again,
Where you did give a fair and natural light:
And be no more an exhal'd meteor,
A prodigy of fear, and a portent
Of broached mischief to the unborn times?

Wor. Hear me, my liege;
For mine own part, I could be well content
To entertain the lag-end of my life
With quiet hours; for, I do protest,
I have not sought the day of this dislike.

K. Hen. You have not sought for it! how comes it then?

Fal. Rebellion lay in his way, and he found it.

P. Hen. Peace, chewet,[1] peace.

Wor. It pleas'd your majesty, to turn your looks
Of favour, from myself, and all our house;
And yet I must remember you, my lord,
We were the first and dearest of your friends.
For you, my staff of office did I break
In Richard's time; and posted day and night
To meet you on the way, and kiss your hand,
When yet you were in place and in account
Nothing so strong and fortunate as I.
It was myself, my brother, and his son,
That brought you home, and boldly did outdare
The dangers of the time: You swore to us,—
And you did swear that oath at Doncaster,—
That you did nothing purpose 'gainst the state;
Nor claim no further than your new-fall'n right,
The seat of Gaunt, dukedom of Lancaster:
To this we swore our aid. But, in short space,
It rain'd down fortune showering on your head;
And such a flood of greatness fell on you,—
What with our help: what with the absent king!
What with the injuries of a wanton time;
The seeming sufferances that you had borne;
And the contrarious winds, that held the king
So long in his unlucky Irish wars,
That all in England did repute him dead,—
And, from this swarm of fair advantages,
You took occasion to be quickly woo'd
To gripe the general sway into your hand:
Forgot your oath to us at Doncaster;
And, being fed by us, you us'd us so
As that ungentle gull, the cuckoo's bird,[2]
Useth the sparrow: did oppress our nest;
Grew by our feeding to so great a bulk,
That even our love durst not come near your sight,
For fear of swallowing: but with nimble wing
We were enforc'd, for safety sake, to fly
Out of your sight, and raise this present head:
Whereby we stand opposed[3] by such means
As you yourself have forg'd against yourself;
By unkind usage, dangerous countenance,
And violation of all faith and troth
Sworn to us in your younger enterprise.

K. Hen. These things, indeed, you have articulated,[4]
Proclaim'd at market-crosses, read in churches;
To face the garment of rebellion
With some fine colour, that may please the eye
Of fickle changelings, and poor discontents,
Which gape, and rub the elbow, at the news
Of hurlyburly innovation:
And never yet did insurrection want
Such water colours, to unpaint his cause;
Nor moody beggars, starving[5] for a time
Of pellmell havoc and confusion.

P. Hen. In both our armies, there is many a soul
Shall pay full dearly for this encounter,
If once they join in trial. Tell your nephew,
The Prince of Wales doth join with all the world
In praise of Henry Percy: By my hopes,—
This present enterprise set off his head,—[6]
I do not think, a braver gentleman,
More active-valiant, or more valiant-young,
More daring, or more bold, is now alive,
To grace this latter age with noble deeds.
For my part, I may speak it to my shame,
I have a truant been to chivalry;
And so, I hear, he doth account me too.
Yet this before my father's majesty,—
I am content, that he shall take the odds
Of his great name and estimation;
And will, to save the blood on either side,
Try fortune with him in a single fight.

K. Hen. And, prince of Wales, so dare we venture thee,
Albeit, considerations infinite
Do make against it:—No, good Worcester, no,[7]
We love our people well: even those we love,
That are misled upon your cousin's part:
And, will they take the offer of our grace,
Both he, and they, and you, yea, every man
Shall be my friend again, and I'll be his:
So tell your cousin, and bring me word
What he will do:—But if he will not yield,
Rebuke and dread correction wait on us,
And they shall do their office. So, be gone;
We will not now be troubled with reply:
We offer fair, take it advisedly.

[*Exeunt* WORCESTER *and* VERNON.

P. Hen. It will not be accepted, on my life
The Douglas and the Hotspur both together
Are confident against the world in arms.

K. Hen. Hence, therefore, every leader to his charge;
For, on their answer, will we set on them:
And God befriend us, as our cause is just!

[*Exeunt* KING, BLUNT, *and* PRINCE JOHN.

Fal. Hal, if thou see me down in the battle, and bestride me,[8] so; 'tis a point of friendship.

P. Hen. Nothing but a colossus can do thee that friendship. Say thy prayers, and farewell.

Fal. I would it were bed-time, Hal, and all well.

P. Hen. Why, thou owest God a death. [*Exit.*

Fal. 'Tis not due yet; I would be loath to pay him before his day. What need I be so forward with him that calls not on me? Well, 'tis no matter; Honour pricks me on. Yea, but how if honour prick me off when I come on? how then? Can honour set to a leg? No. Or an arm? No. Or take away the grief of a wound? No. Honour hath no skill in surgery then? No. What is honour? A word. What is in that word, honour? What is that honour? Air. A trim reckoning!—Who hath it? He that died o'Wednesday. Doth he feel it? No. Doth he hear it? No. Is it insensible then? Yea, to the dead. But will it not live with the living? No. Why? Detraction will not suffer it:—therefore I'll none of it: Honour is a mere scutcheon, and so ends my catechism. [*Exit.*

---

1 A *chewet* was (as Theobald justly observes) a noisy chattering bird, a *pie* or jackdaw; called also in French *chouette*. This simple and satisfactory explanation would not do for Steevens and Malone, who finding that *chewets* were also little round *pies* made of minced meat, thought that the prince compared Falstaff, for his unseasonable chattering, to a minced pie! The word is a diminutive of *chough*, pronounced *chouh*, from the Saxon *ceo*. Graculus Monedula. *Belon*, in his *History of Birds*, describes the *chouette* as the smallest kind of chough or crow, and this will account for the diminutive termination of its name.

2 'The Titling, therefore, that sitteth, being thus deceived, hatcheth the egge, and bringeth up the chicke of another bird:—and this she doth so long, untill the young cuckow being once fledge and readie to flie abroad, is so bold as to seize upon the old titling, and eat up her that hatched her.'—*Pliny's Nat. Hist. by Holland*, b. x. ch. 9.

3 i. e. we stand in opposition to you.

4 The quartos read *articulate*. To *articulate* is to set down in *articles*.

5 i. e. anxiously expecting a time.

6 That is, *taken from his account*

7 Mason suggests that we should read '*know* good Worcester, know, &c.'

8 In the battle of Agincourt, Henry, when king, did this *act of friendship* for his brother the duke of Gloucester.

SCENE II. *The Rebel Camp. Enter* WORCESTER *and* VERNON.

Wor. O, no, my nephew must not know, Sir Richard,
The liberal kind offer of the king.
Ver. 'Twere best, he did.
Wor. Then we are all undone.
It is not possible, it cannot be,
The king should keep his word in loving us;
He will suspect us still, and find a time
To punish this offence in other faults:
Suspicion all our lives shall be stuck full of eyes:
For treason is but trusted like the fox;
Who, ne'er so tame, so cherish'd, and lock'd up,
Will have a wild trick of his ancestors.
Look how we can, or sad, or merrily,
Interpretation will misquote our looks;
And we shall feed like oxen at a stall,
The better cherish'd, still the nearer death.
My nephew's trespass may be well forgot.
It hath the excuse of youth, and heat of blood;
And an adopted name of privilege,—
A hare-brain'd Hotspur, govern'd by a spleen:
All his offences live upon my head,
And on his father's;—we did train him on;
And, his corruption being ta'en from us,
We, as the spring of all, shall pay for all.
Therefore, good cousin, let not Harry know,
In any case, the offer of the king.
Ver. Deliver what you will, I'll say, 'tis so.
Here comes your cousin.

Enter HOTSPUR *and* DOUGLAS; *and Officers and Soldiers, behind.*

Hot. My uncle is return'd:—Deliver up
My lord of Westmoreland.[1]—Uncle, what news?
Wor. The king will bid you battle presently.
Doug. Defy him by the lord of Westmoreland.
Hot. Lord Douglas, go you and tell him so.
Doug. Marry, and shall, and very willingly. [*Exit.*
Wor. There is no seeming mercy in the king.
Hot. Did you beg any? God forbid!
Wor. I told him gently of our grievances,
Of his oath-breaking; which he mended thus,—
By now forswearing that he is forsworn:
He calls us rebels, traitors; and will scourge
With haughty arms this hateful name in us.

Re-enter DOUGLAS.

Doug. Arm, gentlemen; to arms! for I have thrown
A brave defiance in King Henry's teeth,
And Westmoreland, that was engag'd, did bear it;
Which cannot choose but bring him quickly on.
Wor. The prince of Wales stepp'd forth before the king,
And, nephew, challeng'd you to single fight.
Hot. O, 'would the quarrel lay upon our heads;
And that no man might draw short breath to-day,
But I, and Harry Monmouth! Tell me, tell me,
How show'd his tasking?[2] seem'd it in contempt?
Ver. No, by my soul; I never in my life
Did hear a challenge urg'd more modestly,
Unless a brother should a brother dare
To gentle exercise and proof of arms.
He gave you all the duties of a man;
Trimm'd up your praises with a princely tongue;
Spoke your deservings like a chronicle;
Making you ever better than his praise,
By still dispraising praise, valued with you:
And, which became him like a prince indeed,
He made a blushing cital[3] of himself;
And chid his truant youth with such a grace,
As if he master'd[4] there a double spirit,
Of teaching, and of learning, instantly.
There did he pause: But let me tell the world
If he outlive the envy of this day,
England did never owe[5] so sweet a hope,
So much misconstrued in his wantonness.
Hot. Cousin, I think thou art enamoured
Upon his follies; never did I hear
Of any prince, so wild at liberty:[6]
But, be he as he will, yet once ere night
I will embrace him with a soldier's arm,
That he shall shrink under my courtesy.—
Arm, arm, with speed:——And, fellows, soldiers, friends,
Better consider what you have to do,
Than I, that have not well the gift of tongue,
Can lift your blood up with persuasion.

Enter a Messenger.

Mess. My lord, here are letters for you.
Hot. I cannot read them now.—
O gentlemen, the time of life is short;
To spend that shortness basely, were too long,
If life did ride upon a dial's point,
Still ending at the arrival of an hour.
An if we live, we live to tread on kings;
If die, brave death, when princes die with us!
Now for our consciences,—the arms are fair,
When the intent of bearing them is just.

Enter another Messenger.

Mess. My lord, prepare: the king comes on apace.
Hot. I thank him, that he cuts me from my tale,
For I profess not talking; Only this—
Let each man do his best: and here draw I
A sword, whose temper I intend to stain
With the best blood that I can meet withal
In the adventure of this perilous day.
Now,—Esperance![7]—Percy!—and set on.—
Sound all the lofty instruments of war,
And by that music let us all embrace:
For, heaven to earth, some of us never shall
A second time do such a courtesy.
[*The Trumpets sound. They embrace, and exeunt*

SCENE III. *Plain near* Shrewsbury. *Excursions, and Parties fighting. Alarum to the Battle. Then enter* DOUGLAS *and* BLUNT, *meeting.*

Blunt. What is thy name, that in the battle thus
Thou crossest me? what honour dost thou seek
Upon my head?
Doug. Know then, my name is Douglas;
And I do haunt thee in the battle thus,
Because some tell me that thou art a king.
Blunt. They tell thee true.
Doug. The lord of Stafford dear to-day hath bought
Thy likeness: for, instead of thee, King Harry,
This sword hath ended him: so shall it thee,
Unless thou yield thee as my prisoner.
Blunt. I was not born a yielder, thou proud Scot;[8]
And thou shalt find a king that will revenge
Lord Stafford's death.
[*They fight, and* BLUNT *is slain*

Enter HOTSPUR.

Hot. O Douglas, hadst thou fought at Holmedon thus,
I never had triumph'd upon a Scot.
Doug. All's done, all's won; here breathless lies the king.
Hot. Where?

---

1 Westmoreland was impawned as a surety for the safe return of Worcester. See Act iv. Sc. 3.

2 *Tasking* as well as *taxing* was used for *reproof*. We still say 'he took him to *task*.'

3 i. e. '*mention* of himself.' To *cite* is to quote, allege, or mention any passage or incident. The mistakes of Pope and others have induced me to give an explanation of this word, which I should otherwise have thought sufficiently intelligible.

4 That is, *was master of*.

5 Own.

6 *So wild at liberty* may mean so wild and licentious, or loose in his conduct. Johnson misunderstood and wrong pointed this passage. The quarto copies most of them read 'so wild *a libertie*.' Steevens suggests that perhaps the author wrote 'so wild *a libertine*;' to which reading I very much incline.

7 *Esperance*, or *Esperanza*, has always been the motto of the Percy family. Shakspeare uses *esperance* as a word of four syllables, the e final having the same power as in French verse

8 The folio reads:—
'I was not born to yield thou haughty Scot.'

Doug. Here.

Hot. This, Douglas? no, I know this face full well:
A gallant knight he was, his name was Blunt;
Semblably[1] furnish'd like the king himself.

Doug. A fool go with thy soul, whither[2] it goes!
A borrow'd title hast thou bought too dear.
Why didst thou tell me that thou wert a king?

Hot. The king hath many marching in his coats.

Doug. Now, by my sword, I will kill all his coats.
I'll murder all his wardrobe, piece by piece,
Until I meet the king.

Hot. Up, and away;
Our soldiers stand full fairly for the day. [*Exeunt.*

Other Alarums. Enter FALSTAFF.

Fal. Though I could 'scape shot-free at London, I fear the shot here; here's no scoring, but upon the pate.—Soft! who art thou? Sir Walter Blunt;—there's honour for you: Here's no vanity![3]—I am as hot as molten lead, and as heavy too: God keep lead out of me! I need no more weight than mine own bowels.—I have led my raggamuffins where they are peppered: there's but three of my hundred and fifty left alive; and they are for the town's end, to beg during life. But who comes here!

Enter PRINCE HENRY.

P. Hen. What, stand'st thou idle here? lend me thy sword:
Many a nobleman lies stark and stiff
Under the hoofs of vaunting enemies,
Whose deaths are unreveng'd: Pr'ythee, lend me thy sword.

Fal. O Hal, I pr'ythee give me leave to breathe a while.—Turk Gregory[4] never did such deeds in arms, as I have done this day. I have paid Percy, I have made him sure.

P. Hen. He is, indeed; and living to kill thee. I pr'ythee, lend me thy sword.

Fal. Nay, before God, Hal, if Percy be alive, thou get'st not my sword; but take my pistol, if thou wilt.

P. Hen. Give it me: What, is it in the case?

Fal. Ay, Hal: 'tis hot, 'tis hot; there's that will sack a city. [*The* Prince *draws out a bottle of sack.*

P. Hen. What, is't a time to jest and dally now?
[*Throws it at him, and exit.*

Fal. Well, if Percy be alive, I'll pierce him.[5] If he do come in my way, so: if he do not, if I come in his, willingly, let him make a carbonado[6] of me. I like not such grinning honour as Sir Walter hath: Give me life: which if I can save, so; if not, honour comes unlooked for, and there's an end. [*Exit.*

SCENE IV. *Another Part of the Field. Alarums: Excursions. Enter the* KING, PRINCE HENRY, PRINCE JOHN, *and* WESTMORELAND.

K. Hen. I pr'ythee,
Harry, withdraw thyself; thou bleed'st too much:[7]—
Lord John of Lancaster, go you with him.

P. John. Not I, my lord, unless I did bleed too.

P. Hen. I beseech your majesty, make up,
Lest your retirement do amaze your friends.

K. Hen. I will do so:
My lord of Westmoreland, lead him to his tent.

West. Come, my lord, I'll lead you to your tent.

P. Hen. Lead me, my lord? I do not need your help:
And heaven forbid, a shallow scratch should drive
The prince of Wales from such a field as this;
Where stain'd nobility lies trodden on,
And rebels' arms triumph in massacres!

P. John. We breathe too long:—Come, cousin Westmoreland,
Our duty this way lies; for God's sake, come.
[*Exeunt* P. JOHN *and* WESTMORELAND.

P. Hen. By heaven, thou hast deceiv'd me, Lancaster,
I did not think thee lord of such a spirit;
Before, I lov'd thee as a brother, John;
But now, I do respect thee as my soul.

K. Hen. I saw him hold Lord Percy at the point,
With lustier maintenance than I did look for
Of such an ungrown warrior.[8]

P. Hen. O, this boy
Lends mettle to us all! [*Exit.*

Alarums. Enter DOUGLAS.

Doug. Another king! they grow like Hydra's heads:
I am the Douglas, fatal to all those
That wear those colours on them.—What art thou,
That counterfeit'st the person of a king?

K. Hen. The king himself; who, Douglas, grieves at heart,
So many of his shadows thou hast met,
And not the very king. I have two boys,
Seek Percy, and thyself, about the field:
But, seeing thou fall'st on me so luckily,
I will assay thee; so defend thyself.

Doug. I fear, thou art another counterfeit,
And yet, in faith, thou bear'st thee like a king:
But mine, I am sure, thou art, whoe'er thou be,
And thus I win thee.
[*They fight; the King being in danger, enter* PRINCE HENRY.

P. Hen. Hold up thy head, vile Scot, or thou art like
Never to hold it up again! the spirits
Of valiant Shirley, Stafford, Blunt, are in my arms:
It is the prince of Wales, that threatens thee;
Who never promiseth, but he means to pay.—
[*They fight;* DOUGLAS *flies*
Cheerly, my lord: How fares your grace?—
Sir Nicholas Gawsey hath for succour sent,
And so hath Clifton; I'll to Clifton straight.

K. Hen. Stay, and breathe a while:—
Thou hast redeem'd thy lost opinion;[9]
And show'd thou mak'st some tender of my life,
In this fair rescue thou hast brought to me.

P. Hen. O heaven! they did me too much injury,
That ever said, I hearken'd for your death.
If it were so, I might have let alone
The insulting hand of Douglas over you;
Which would have been as speedy in your end,
As all the poisonous potions in the world,
And sav'd the treacherous labour of your son.

K. Hen. Make up to Clifton, I'll to Sir Nicholas Gawsey. [*Exit* KING HENRY.

Enter HOTSPUR.

Hot. If I mistake not, thou art Harry Monmouth.

P. Hen. Thou speak'st as if I would deny my name.

1 That is *in seeming* or *outward appearance.*

2 *Whither* for *whithersoever.* Thus Baret, '*Whether*, or *to what place you will.* Quovis.' *Any-whether* also signified to *any place.* In the last scene of the second act, Hotspur says to his wife:—

'*Whither* I go, thither shalt thou go too.'

3 'Here's *no* vanity,' the negative is here used ironically, to designate the excess of a thing.

4 '*Turk* Gregory' means Gregory the Seventh, called Hildebrand This furious friar surmounted almost invincible obstacles to deprive the emperor of his right of investiture of bishops, which his predecessors had long attempted in vain. Fox, in his Martyrology, has made Gregory so odious that the Protestants would be well pleased to hear him thus characterized, as uniting the attributes of their two great enemies, the Turk and the Pope, in one. There was an old tragedy on the subject of Hildebrand, but not even the title of it has come down to us.

5 'Well, if Percy be alive, I'll pierce him,' is addressed to the prince as he goes out; the rest of the speech is a soliloquy. Shakspeare was not aware that he ridiculed the serious etymology of the Scottish historian:—'*Piercy a penetrando* oculum Regis Scotorum ut fabulatur Boetius.'—*Skinner.*

6 A rasher or collop of meat cut crosswise for the gridiron.

7 History says that the prince was wounded in the face by an arrow.

8 '— the earle of Richmond withstood his violence, and *kept him at the sword's point*, without advantage, longer than his companions either thought or judged.'—*Holinshed*, p. 759.

9 *Opinion* for *estimation, reputation,* the opinion of the world. The word was then used in that sense

Hot. My name is Harry Percy.

P. Hen. Why, then I see
A very valiant rebel of the name.
I am the prince of Wales; and think not, Percy,
To share with me in glory any more:
Two stars keep not their motion in one sphere;
Nor can one England brook a double reign,
Of Harry Percy, and the prince of Wales.

Hot. Nor shall it, Harry, for the hour is come
To end the one of us; And 'would to God,
Thy name in arms were now as great as mine!

P. Hen. I'll make it greater, ere I part from thee;
And all the budding honours on thy crest
I'll crop, to make a garland for my head.

Hot. I can no longer brook thy vanities.

[*They fight.*

Enter FALSTAFF.

Fal. Well said, Hal! to it, Hal!—Nay, you shall find no boy's play here, I can tell you.

Enter DOUGLAS; *he fights with* FALSTAFF, *who falls down as if he were dead, and exit* DOUGLAS. HOTSPUR *is wounded, and falls.*[1]

Hot. O, Harry, thou hast robb'd me of my youth:
I better brook the loss of brittle life,
Than those proud titles thou hast won of me;
They wound my thoughts, worse than thy sword my flesh:——
But thought's the slave of life, and life time's fool;
And time, that takes survey of all the world,
Must have a stop.[2] O, I could prophesy,
But that the earthy and cold hand of death
Lies on my tongue:—No, Percy, thou art dust,
And food for—— [*Dies.*

P. Hen. For worms, brave Percy: Fare thee well, great heart!—
Ill-weav'd ambition, how much art thou shrunk!
When that this body did contain a spirit,
A kingdom for it was too small a bound;[3]
But now, two paces of the vilest earth
Is room enough:—This earth, that bears thee dead,
Bears not alive so stout a gentleman.
If thou wert sensible of courtesy,
I should not make so dear a show of zeal:—
But let my favours[4] hide thy mangled face;
And, even in thy behalf, I'll thank myself
For doing these fair rites of tenderness.
Adieu, and take thy praise with thee to heaven!
Thy ignomy[5] sleep with thee in the grave,
But not remember'd in thy epitaph!—

[*He sees* FALSTAFF *on the ground.*

What! old acquaintance! could not all this flesh
Keep in a little life? Poor Jack, farewell!
I could have better spar'd a better man.
O, I should have a heavy miss of thee,
If I were much in love with vanity.
Death hath not struck so fat a deer to-day,
Though many dearer, in this bloody fray:—
Embowell'd[6] will I see thee by and by;
Till then, in blood by noble Percy lie. [*Exit.*

Fal. [*Rising slowly.*] Embowelled! if thou embowel me to-day, I'll give you leave to powder[7] me, and eat me too, to-morrow. 'Sblood, 'twas time to counterfeit, or that hot termagant Scot had paid me scot and lot too. Counterfeit? I lie, I am no counterfeit: To die, is to be a counterfeit; for he is but the counterfeit of a man who hath not the life of a man: but to counterfeit dying, when a man thereby liveth, is to be no counterfeit, but the true and perfect image of life indeed. The better part of valour is—discretion; in the which better part, I have saved my life. 'Zounds, I am afraid of this gunpowder Percy, though he be dead: How, if he should counterfeit too, and rise? I am afraid, he would prove the better counterfeit. Therefore I'll make him sure: yea, and I'll swear I killed him. Why may not he rise as well as I? Nothing confutes me but eyes, and nobody sees me. Therefore, sirrah [*stabbing him,*] with a new wound in your thigh, come you along with me.

[*Takes* HOTSPUR *on his back.*

Re-enter PRINCE HENRY *and* PRINCE JOHN.

P. Hen. Come, brother John, full bravely hast thou flesh'd
Thy maiden sword.

P. John. But, soft! whom have we here?
Did you not tell me, this fat man was dead?

P. Hen. I did; I saw him dead, breathless and bleeding
On the ground.——
Art thou alive? or is it phantasy
That plays upon our eyesight? I pr'ythee, speak;
We will not trust our eyes, without our ears:—
Thou art not what thou seem'st.

Fal. No, that's certain; I am not a double man: but if I be not Jack Falstaff, then am I a Jack. There is Percy [*throwing the body down:*] if your father will do me any honour, so; if not, let him kill the next Percy himself. I look to be either earl or duke, I can assure you.

P. Hen. Why, Percy I killed myself, and saw thee dea

Fal. Didst thou?—Lord, lord, how this world is given to lying!—I grant you, I was down, and out of breath; and so was he: but we rose both in an instant, and fought a long hour by Shrewsbury clock. If I may be believed, so; if not, let them, that should reward valour, bear the sin upon their own heads. I'll take it upon my death, I gave him this wound in the thigh: if the man were alive, and would deny it, I would make him eat a piece of my sword.

P. John. This is the strangest tale that e'er I heard.

P. Hen. This is the strangest fellow, brother John.—
Come, bring your luggage nobly on your back:
For my part, if a lie may do thee grace,
I'll gild it with the happiest terms I have.

[*A Retreat is sounded.*

The trumpet sounds retreat, the day is ours.
Come, brother, let's to the highest of the field,
To see what friends are living, who are dead.

[*Exeunt* P. HEN. *and* P. JOHN

Fal. I'll follow, as they say, for reward. He that rewards me, God reward him! If I do grow great, I'll grow less; for I'll purge, and leave sack, and live cleanly, as a nobleman should do.

[*Exit bearing off the Body.*

SCENE V. *Another Part of the Field. The Trumpets sound. Enter* KING HENRY, PRINCE HENRY, PRINCE JOHN, WESTMORELAND, *and others, with* WORCESTER, *and* VERNON, *prisoners.*

K. Hen. Thus ever did rebellion find rebuke.—
Ill-spirited Worcester! did we not send grace,
Pardon, and terms of love to all of you?
And would'st thou turn our offers contrary?

---

1 Shakspeare had no authority for making Hotspur fall by the hand of the prince. Holinshed says, 'The king slew that day with his own hand six and thirty persons of his enemies. The other of his party, encouraged by his doings, fought valiantly, and slew the Lord Percy, called Henry Hotspur.' Speed says that Percy was killed by an unknown hand.

2 Hotspur, in his last moments endeavours to console himself. The glory of the prince wounds his thoughts, but *thought*, being dependent on *life*, must cease with it, and will soon be at an end. *Life*, on which *thought* depends, is itself of no great value, being the fool and sport of *time;* of time which, with all its dominion over sublunary things, *must* itself at last be stopped *Johnson.*

3 'Carminibus confide bonis—jacet ecce Tibullus,
Vix manet e toto parva quod urna capit.'—*Ovid*

4 His *scarf*, with which he covers Percy's face.

5 Thus the folio. The quartos read *ignominy.*

6 To *imbowell* was the old term for *embalming* the body, as was usually done by those of persons of rank. Thus in Aulicus Coquinariæ, 1650:—'The next day was solemnly appointed for *imbowelling* the corps, in the presence of some of the counsell, all the physicians, chirurgions, apothecaries, and the Palsgrave's physician.'

7 Salt

Misuse the tenor o' thy kinsman's trust?
Three knights upon our party slain to day,
A noble earl, and many a creature else,
Had been alive this hour,
If, like a christian, thou hadst truly borne
Betwixt our armies true intelligence.

Wor. What I have done, my safety urged me to;
And I embrace this fortune patiently,
Since not to be avoided it falls on me.

K. Hen. Bear Worcester to the death, and Vernon too:
Other offenders we will pause upon.—

[*Exeunt* WOR. *and* VERNON, *guarded.*

How goes the field?

P. Hen. The noble Scot, Lord Douglas, when he saw
The fortune of the day quite turn'd from him,
The noble Percy slain, and all his men
Upon the foot of fear, fled with the rest;
And, falling from a hill, he was so bruis'd,
That the pursuer took him. At my tent
The Douglas is; and I beseech your grace,
I may dispose of him.

K. Hen. With all my heart.

P. Hen. Then, brother John of Lancaster, to you
This honourable bounty shall belong:
Go to the Douglas, and deliver him
Up to his pleasure, ransomless, and free:
His valour, shown upon our crests to-day,
Hath taught[1] us how to cherish such high deeds,
Even in the bosom of our adversaries.

Lan. I thank your grace for this high courtesy,
Which I shall give away immediately.

K. Hen. Then this remains,—that we divide our power.—
You, son John, and my cousin Westmoreland,
Towards York shall bend you, with your dearest speed,
To meet Northumberland, and the prelate Scroop,
Who, as we hear, are busily in arms:
Myself,—and you, son Harry, will towards Wales
To fight with Glendower, and the earl of March.
Rebellion in this land shall lose his sway,
Meeting the check of such another day:
And since this business so fair is done,
Let us not leave till all our own be won. [*Exeunt.*

1 The quarto of 1598 reads *shown.*

SECOND PART OF

KING HENRY THE FOURTH.

PRELIMINARY REMARKS.

THE transactions comprised in this play take up about nine years. The action commences with the account of Hotspur's being defeated and killed [1403;] and closes with the death of King Henry IV. and the coronation of King Henry V. [1412-13.] 'Upton thinks these two plays improperly called The First and Second Parts of Henry the Fourth. "The first play ends (he says) with the peaceful settlement of Henry in the kingdom by the defeats of the rebels." This is hardly true for the rebels are not yet finally suppressed. The second, he tells us, shows Henry the Fifth in the various lights of a good-natured rake, till, on his father's death, he assumes a more manly character. This is true; but this representation gives us no idea of a dramatic action These two plays will appear to every reader, who shall peruse them without ambition of critical discoveries, to be so connected, that the second is merely a sequel to the first; to be two only to be one.'—JOHNSON.

This play was entered at Stationers' Hall, August 23, 1600. There are two copies, in quarto, printed in that year; but it is doubtful whether they are different editions, or the one only a corrected impression of the other.

Malone supposes it to have been composed in 1598.

PERSONS REPRESENTED.

KING HENRY THE FOURTH:
HENRY, Prince *of* Wales, *afterwards* King Henry V.; — *his Sons.*
THOMAS, Duke *of* Clarence; — *his Sons.*
PRINCE JOHN *of* Lancaster, *afterwards* (2 Henry V.) Duke *of* Bedford; — *his Sons.*
PRINCE HUMPHREY *of* Gloster, *afterwards* (2 Henry V.) Duke *of* Gloster; — *his Sons.*
Earl *of* Warwick; — *of the* King's *Party.*
Earl *of* Westmoreland; — *of the* King's *Party.*
GOWER; HARCOURT; — *of the* King's *Party.*
Lord Chief Justice of the King's Bench.
A Gentleman attending on the Chief Justice.
Earl *of* Northumberland; — *Enemies to the King.*
SCROOP, Archbishop *of* York; — *Enemies to the King.*
LORD MOWBRAY; LORD HASTINGS; — *Enemies to the King.*
LORD BARDOLPH; SIR JOHN COLEVILE. — *Enemies to the King.*
TRAVERS *and* MORTON, *Domestics of* Northumberland.
FALSTAFF, BARDOLPH, PISTOL, *and* Page.
POINS *and* PETO, *Attendants on* Prince Henry.
SHALLOW *and* SILENCE, *Country Justices.*
DAVY, *Servant to* Shallow.
MOULDY, SHADOW, WART, FEEBLE, *and* BULL-CALF, *Recruits.*
FANG *and* SNARE, *Sheriff's Officers.*
RUMOUR. A Porter.
A Dancer, *Speaker of the Epilogue.*

LADY NORTHUMBERLAND. LADY PERCY
Hostess QUICKLY. DOLL TEAR-SHEET.

Lords *and other* Attendants; Officers, Soldiers, Messenger, Drawers, Beadles, Grooms, *&c.*

SCENE, England.

INDUCTION.

Warkworth. *Before* Northumberland's *Castle.*
Enter RUMOUR *painted full of Tongues.*[1]

Rum. Open your ears; For which of you will stop
The vent of hearing when loud Rumour speaks?
I, from the orient to the drooping[2] west,
Making the wind my post-horse, still unfold
The acts commenced on this ball of earth:
Upon my tongues continual slanders ride;
The which in every language I pronounce,
Stuffing the ears of men with false reports.
I speak of peace while covert enmity,
Under the smile of safety, wounds the world:
And who but Rumour, who but only I,
Make fearful musters, and prepar'd defence;
Whilst the big ear, swoln with some other grief,
Is thought with child by the stern tyrant war,
And no such matter? Rumour is a pipe
Blown by surmises, jealousies, conjectures;
And of so easy and so plain a stop,[3]
That the blunt monster with uncounted heads,
The still-discordant wavering multitude,
Can play upon it. But what need I thus
My well-known body to anatomize
Among my household? Why is rumour here?
I run before King Harry's victory;
Who, in a bloody field by Shrewsbury,
Hath beaten down young Hotspur, and his troops
Quenching the flame of bold rebellion
Even with the rebels' blood. But what mean I
To speak so true at first? my office is
To noise abroad,—that Harry Monmouth fell
Under the wrath of noble Hotspur's sword;
And that the king before the Douglas' rage
Stoop'd his anointed head as low as death.
This have I rumour'd through the peasant towns
Between that royal field of Shrewsbury
And this worm-eaten hold of ragged stone,[4]
Where Hotspur's father, old Northumberland,
Lies crafty-sick: the posts come tiring on,
And not a man of them brings other news
Than they have learn'd of me; from Rumour's tongues
They bring smooth comforts false, worse than true wrongs. [*Exit.*

1 This was the common way of representing this personage, no unfrequent character in the masques of the poet's time. In a masque on St. Stephen's Night, 1614, by Thomas Campion, *Rumour* comes on in a skin coat *full of winged tongues.* Several other instances are cited in the Variorum Shakspeare.

2 The force of this epithet will be best explained by the following passage in Macbeth:—
'Good things of day begin to *droop* and drowse,
And night's black agents to their preys do rouse.'

3 The *stops* are the holes in a flute or pipe.

4 Northumberland's castle.

ACT I.

SCENE I. *The same. The* Porter *before the Gate.*
Enter LORD BARDOLPH.

Bardolph.
WHO keeps the gate here, ho?—Where is the earl?
Port. What shall I say you are?
Bard. Tell thou the earl,
That the Lord Bardolph doth attend him here.
Port. His lordship is walk'd forth into the orchard;
Please it your honour, knock but at the gate,
And he himself will answer.

Enter NORTHUMBERLAND.

Bard. Here comes the earl.
North. What news, Lord Bardolph? every minute now
Should be the father of some stratagem;
The times are wild; contention, like a horse
Full of high feeding, madly hath broke loose,
And bears down all before him.
Bard. Noble earl,
I bring you certain news from Shrewsbury.
North. Good, an heaven will!
Bard. As good as heart can wish:—
The king is almost wounded to the death;
And, in the fortune of my lord your son,
Prince Harry slain outright; and both the Blunts
Kill'd by the hand of Douglas: young prince John,
And Westmoreland, and Stafford, fled the field;
And Harry Monmouth's brawn, the hulk Sir John,
Is prisoner to your son: O, such a day,
So fought, so follow'd, and so fairly won,
Came not, till now, to dignify the times,
Since Cæsar's fortunes!
North. How is this deriv'd?
Saw you the field? came you from Shrewsbury?
Bard. I spake with one, my lord, that came from thence;
A gentleman well bred, and of good name,
That freely render'd me these news for true.
North. Here comes my servant, Travers, whom I sent
On Tuesday last to listen after news.
Bard. My lord, I over-rode him on the way;
And he is furnish'd with no certainties,
More than he haply may retail from me.

Enter TRAVERS.

North. Now, Travers, what good tidings come with you?
Tra. My lord, Sir John Umfrevile turn'd me back
With joyful tidings; and, being better hors'd,
Outrode me. After him, came, spurring hard,
A gentleman almost forspent[1] with speed,
That stopp'd by me to breathe his bloodied horse:
He ask'd the way to Chester; and of him
I did demand, what news from Shrewsbury.
He told me, that rebellion had bad luck,
And that young Harry Percy's spur was cold:
With that he gave his able horse the head,
And, bending forward, struck his armed heels
Against the panting sides of his poor jade[2]
Up to the rowel-head; and, starting so,
He seem'd in running to devour the way,[3]
Staying no longer question.
North. Ha!——Again.
Said he, young Harry Percy's spur was cold?
Of Hotspur,[4] coldspur? that rebellion
Had met ill luck!
Bard. My lord, I'll tell you what;
If my young lord your son have not the day,
Upon mine honour, for a silken point[5]
I'll give my barony: never talk of it.

1 Exhausted.

2 *Jade* is not used by Shakspeare as a *term* of contempt; for King Richard II. gives this appellation to his favourite horse Roan Barbary, which Henry IV. rode at his coronation:—
'That *jade* hath eat bread from my royal hand.'
The commentators suppose that a *jade* meant a horse kept for drudgery, a hackney; but this is not the fact It was only another name for a horse, as *nag* since.

3 So in the book of Job, ch. xxxix:—'He *swalloweth the ground* in fierceness and rage.'

4 Hotspur seems to have been a very common term for a man of vehemence and precipitation.

5 A *silken point* is a *tagged lace.*

North. Why should the gentleman, that rode by Travers,
Give then such instances of loss?

Bard. Who, he?
He was some hilding[1] fellow, that had stol'n
The horse he rode on; and, upon my life,
Spoke at a venture. Look, here comes more news.

Enter MORTON.

North. Yea, this man's brow, like to a title-leaf,
Foretells the nature of a tragic volume:
So looks the strond, whereon the imperious flood
Hath left a witness'd usurpation.[2]——
Say, Morton, didst thou come from Shrewsbury?

Mor. I ran from Shrewsbury, my noble lord;
Where hateful death put on his ugliest mask,
To fright our party.

North. How doth my son, and brother?
Thou tremblest: and the whiteness in thy cheek
Is apter than thy tongue to tell thy errand.
Even such a man, so faint, so spiritless,
So dull, so dead in look, so woe-begone,[3]
Drew Priam's curtain in the dead of night,
And would have told him, half his Troy was burn'd:
But Priam found the fire, ere he his tongue,
And I my Percy's death, ere thou report'st it.
This thou would'st say,—Your son did thus, and thus;
Your brother, thus; so fought the noble Douglas;
Stopping my greedy ear with their bold deeds:
But in the end, to stop mine ear indeed,
Thou hast to sigh to blow away this praise,
Ending with—brother, son, and all are dead.

Mor. Douglas is living, and your brother, yet:
But, for my lord your son,——

North. Why, he is dead.
See, what a ready tongue suspicion hath!
He, that but fears the thing he would not know,
Hath, by instinct, knowledge from others' eyes,
That what he fear'd is chanc'd. Yet speak, Morton;
Tell thou thy earl, his divination lies;
And I will take it as a sweet disgrace,
And make thee rich for doing me such wrong.

Mor. You are too great to be by me gainsaid:
Your spirit is too true, your fears too certain.

North. Yet, for all this, say not that Percy's dead.
I see a strange confession in thine eye:
Thou shak'st thy head, and hold'st it fear or sin,
To speak a truth. If he be slain, say so:
The tongue offends not, that reports his death:
And he doth sin, that doth belie the dead;
Not he, which says the dead is not alive.
Yet the first bringer of unwelcome news
Hath but a losing office; and his tongue
Sounds ever after as a sullen bell,
Remember'd knolling a departing friend.[4]

Bard. I cannot think, my lord, your son is dead.

Mor. I am sorry, I should force you to believe
That, which I would to heaven I had not seen:
But these mine eyes saw him in bloody state,
Rend'ring faint quittance,[5] wearied and out-breath'd,
To Harry Monmouth: whose swift wrath beat down
The never-daunted Percy to the earth,
From whence with life he never more sprung up.
In few, his death (whose spirit lent a fire
Even to the dullest peasant in his camp,)
Being bruited[6] once, took fire and heat away
From the best temper'd courage in his troops:
For from his metal was his party steel'd;
Which once in him abated, all the rest
Turn'd on themselves, like dull and heavy lead.
And as the thing that's heavy in itself,
Upon enforcement, flies with greatest speed;
So did our men, heavy in Hotspur's loss,
Lend to this weight such lightness with their fear,
That arrows fled not swifter toward their aim,
Than did our soldiers, aiming at their safety,
Fly from the field: Then was that noble Worcester
Too soon ta'en prisoner: and that furious Scot,
The bloody Douglas, whose well-labouring sword
Had three times slain the appearance of the king,
'Gan vail[7] his stomach, and did grace the shame
Of those that turn'd their backs; and, in his flight,
Stumbling in fear, was took. The sum of all
Is,—that the king hath won; and hath sent out
A speedy power to encounter you, my lord,
Under the conduct of young Lancaster,
And Westmoreland: this is the news at full.

North. For this I shall have time enough to mourn.
In poison there is physic; and these news,
Having been well, that would have made me sick,
Being sick, have in some measure made me well:
And as the wretch, whose fever-weaken'd joints,
Like strengthless hinges, buckle under life,
Impatient of his fit, breaks like a fire
Out of his keeper's arms; even so my limbs,
Weaken'd with grief, being now enrag'd with grief,[8]
Are thrice themselves: hence therefore, thou nice[9] crutch;
A scaly gauntlet now, with joints of steel,
Must glove this hand: and hence, thou sickly quoif;
Thou art a guard too wanton for the head,
Which princes, flesh'd with conquest, aim to hit.
Now bind my brows with iron; and approach
The ragged'st hour that time and spite dare bring,
To frown upon the enrag'd Northumberland!
Let heaven kiss earth! Now let not nature's hand
Keep the wild flood confin'd! let order die!
And let this world no longer be a stage,
To feed contention in a lingering act;
But let one spirit of the first-born Cain
Reign in all bosoms, that, each heart being set
On bloody courses, the rude scene may end,
And darkness be the burier of the dead![10]

Tra. This strained passion doth you wrong, my lord.[11]

Bard. Sweet earl, divorce not wisdom from you honour.

Mor. The lives of all your loving complices
Lean on your health; the which, if you give o'er
To stormy passion, must perforce decay.

---

1 i. e. *Hilderling*, base, low fellow.

2 An attestation of its ravage.

3 Dr. Bently is said to have thought this passage corrupt; and therefore (with a greater degree of gravity than the reader will probably express) proposed the following emendation:—

'So dead, so dull in look *Ucalegon*,
Drew Priam's curtain,' &c.

The name of *Ucalegon* occurs in the third Iliad, and in the Æneid.

4 So in Shakspeare's seventy-first Sonnet:—

'——You shall hear the surly *sullen* bell
Give warning to the world that I am fled.'

Milton has adopted this expressive epithet:—

'I hear the far-off curfew sound
Over some wide-water'd shore,
Swinging slow with *sullen* roar.'

The *bell* anciently was rung before the dying person had expired, and thence was called the *passing* bell. Mr. Douce thinks it probable that this bell might have been originally used to drive away demons, who were supposed to watch for the parting soul

5 By *faint quittance* a *faint return* of blows is meant.

6 i. e. reported, noised abroad.

7 i. e. began to fall his courage, to let his spirits sink under his fortunes. *To vail* is to *lower*, to cast down.

8 *Grief*, in the latter part of this line, is used, in its present sense, for *sorrow*; in the former part for *bodily pain.*

9 Steevens explains *nice* here by *trifling*; but Shakspeare, like his contemporaries, uses it in the sense of *effeminate, delicate, tender*.

10 'The conclusion of this noble speech (says Johnson) is extremely striking. There is no need to suppose it exactly philosophical; *darkness*, in poetry, may be *absence of eyes*, as well as privation of light. Yet we may remark that, by an ancient opinion, it has been held that if the human race, for whom the world was made, were extirpated, the whole system of sublunary nature would cease at once.'

11 This line in the quarto is by mistake given to *Umfreville*, who is spoken of in this very scene as absent. It is given to *Travers* at Steevens's suggestion.

You cast the event of war, my noble lord,[1]
And summ'd the account of chance, before you said,—
Let us make head. It was your presurmise,
That in the dole[2] of blows your son might drop:
You knew, he walk'd o'er perils, on an edge,
More likely to fall in, than to get o'er;[3]
You were advis'd,[4] his flesh was capable
Of wounds, and scars; and that his forward spirit
Would lift him where most trade of danger rang'd;
Yet did you say,—Go forth; and none of this,
Though strongly apprehended, could restrain
The stiff-borne action: What hath then befallen,
Or what hath this bold enterprise brought forth,
More than that being which was like to be?

Bard. We all, that are engaged to this loss,[5]
Knew that we ventur'd on such dangerous seas,
That, if we wrought out life, 'twas ten to one:
And yet we ventur'd, for the gain propos'd
Chok'd the respect of likely peril fear'd;
And, since we are o'erset, venture again.
Come, we will all put forth; body, and goods.

Mor. 'Tis more than time: And, my most noble lord,
I hear for certain, and do speak the truth,——
The gentle archbishop of York is up,[6]
With well-appointed powers; he is a man,
Who with a double surety binds his followers.
My lord your son had only but the corps,
But shadows, and the shows of men, to fight:
For that same word, rebellion, did divide
The action of their bodies from their souls;
And they did fight with queasiness,[7] constrain'd,
As men drink potions; that their weapons only
Seem'd on our side, but, for their spirits and souls,
This word, rebellion, it had froze them up,
As fish are in a pond: But now the bishop
Turns insurrection to religion:
Suppos'd sincere and holy in his thoughts,
He's follow'd both with body and with mind;
And doth enlarge his rising with the blood
Of fair King Richard, scrap'd from Pomfret stones:
Derives from heaven his quarrel, and his cause;
Tells them, he doth bestride a bleeding land,[8]
Gasping for life under great Bolingbroke;
And more[9] and less do flock to follow him.

North. I knew of this before; but, to speak truth,
This present grief had wip'd it from my mind.
Go in with me; and counsel every man
The aptest way for safety, and revenge:
Get posts, and letters, and make friends with speed;
Never so few, and never yet more need. [*Exeunt.*

SCENE II. London. *A Street. Enter* SIR JOHN FALSTAFF, *with his* Page *bearing his Sword and Buckler.*

Fal. Sirrah, you giant, what says the doctor to my water?[10]

Page. He said, sir, the water itself was a good healthy water: but for the party that owed[11] it, he might have more diseases than he knew for.

Fal. Men of all sorts take a pride to gird[12] at me: The brain of this foolish-compounded clay, man, is not able to vent any thing that tends to laughter, more than I invent, or is invented on me: I am not only witty in myself, but the cause that wit is in other men. I do here walk before thee, like a sow, that hath overwhelmed all her litter but one. If the prince put thee into my service for any other reason than to set me off, why then I have no judgment. Thou whoreson mandrake,[13] thou art fitter to be worn in my cap, than to wait at my heels I was never manned with an agate[14] till now: but I will set you neither in gold nor silver, but in vile apparel, and send you back again to your master, for a jewel; the juvenal,[15] the prince your master, whose chin is not yet fledged. I will sooner have a beard grow in the palm of my hand, than he shall get one on his cheek; and yet he will not stick to say, his face is a face-royal: God may finish it when he will, it is not a hair amiss yet: he may keep it still as a face-royal,[16] for a barber shall never earn sixpence out of it; and yet he will be crowing, as if he had writ man ever since his father was a bachelor. He may keep his own grace, but he is almost out of mine, I can assure him.———What said master Dumbleton about the satin for my short cloak, and slops?

Page. He said, sir, you should procure him better assurance than Bardolph: he would not take his bond and yours; he liked not the security.

Fal. Let him be damned like the glutton! may his tongue be hotter![17]—A whoreson Achitophel! a rascally yea-forsooth knave! to bear a gentleman in hand,[18] and then stand upon security!—The whoreson smooth-pates do now wear nothing but high shoes, and bunches of keys at their girdles; and if a man is thorough[19] with them in honest taking up, then they must stand upon—security. I had as lief they would put ratsbane in my mouth, as offer to stop it with security. I looked he should have sent me two and twenty yards of satin, as I am a true knight, and he sends me security. Well, he may sleep in security; for he hath the horn of abundance, and the lightness of his wife shines through it; and yet cannot he see, though he have

---

1 The fourteen following lines, and a number of others in this play, were not in the quarto edition.

2 Dealing, or distribution.

3 So in King Henry IV. Part I:—
'As full of peril and adventurous spirit,
As to o'erwalk a current roaring loud,
On the unsteadfast footing of a spear.'

4 That is, you were *warned* or *aware*.

5 This mode of expression has before been noticed.

6 This and the following twenty lines are not found in the quarto.

7 Against their stomachs.

8 That is, 'stand over his country, as she lies bleeding and prostrate, to protect her.' It was the office of a friend to protect his fallen comrade in battle in this manner. Shakspeare has alluded to it in other places.

9 i. e. great and small, *all ranks*.

10 This quackery was once so much in fashion that Linacre, the founder of the College of Physicians, formed a statute to restrain apothecaries from carrying the *water* of their patients to a doctor, and afterwards giving medicines in consequence of the opinions pronounced concerning it. This statute was followed by another, which forbade the doctors themselves to pronounce on any disorder from such an uncertain diagnostic. But this did not extinguish the practice, which has even its dupes in these enlightened times.

11 Owned.

12 '*Gird* (Mr. Gifford says) is a mere metathesis of *gride*, and means a thrust, a blow; the metaphorical use of the word for a smart stroke of wit, taunt, reproachful retort, &c. is justified by a similar application of kindred terms in all languages

13 A root supposed to have the shape of a man. Quacks and impostors counterfeited, with the root briony, figures resembling parts of the human body, which were sold to the credulous as endued with specific virtues. See Sir Thomas Brown's Vulgar Errors, p. 72, edit. 1686, for some very curious particulars.

14 An *agate* is used metaphorically for a very diminutive person, in allusion to the small figures cut in agate for rings and broaches. Thus Florio explains 'Formaglio: ouches, broaches, or tablets and jewels, that yet some old men wear in their hats, with *agath-stones*, cut and graven with some formes and images on them, namely, of famous men's heads.'

15 *Juvenal* occurs in A Midsummer Night's Dream, and in Love's Labour's Lost. It is also used in many places by Chaucer for a *young man*.

16 Johnson says that, by a *face-royal*, Falstaff means a face exempt from the touch of vulgar hands. As a *stag-royal* is not to be hunted, a *mine-royal* is not to be dug. Steevens imagines that there may be a quibble intended on the coin called a real, or *royal*; that a barber can no more earn sixpence by his face, than by the face stamped on the coin, the one requiring as little shaving as the other. Mason thinks that Falstaff's conceit is, 'If nothing be taken out of a *royal*, it will remain a *royal* still, as it was.' The reader will decide for himself. I have nothing better in the way of conjecture to offer.

17 An allusion to the fate of the rich man, who had fared sumptuously every day, when he requested a drop of water to cool his tongue, being tormented with flames

18 To *bear in hand* is *to keep in expectation by false promises.*

19 i. e. in their debt, by *taking up* goods on credit.

his own lantern to light him.———Where's Bardolph?

Page. He's gone into Smithfield, to buy your worship a horse.

Fal. I bought him in Paul's,[1] and he'll buy me a horse in Smithfield: an I could get me but a wife in the stews, I were manned, horsed, and wived.

Enter the Lord Chief Justice,[2] *and an* Attendant.

Page. Sir, here comes the nobleman that committed the prince for striking him about Bardolph.

Fal. Wait close, I will not see him.

Ch. Just. What's he that goes there?

Atten. Falstaff, an't please your lordship.

Ch. Just. He that was in question for the robbery?

Atten. He, my lord: but he hath since done good service at Shrewsbury; and, as I hear, is now going with some charge to the lord John of Lancaster.

Ch. Just. What, to York? Call him back again.

Atten. Sir John Falstaff!

Fal. Boy, tell him, I am deaf.

Page. You must speak louder, my master is deaf.

Ch. Just. I am sure he is, to the hearing of any thing good.—Go, pluck him by the elbow: I must speak with him.

Atten. Sir John,——

Fal. What! a young knave, and beg! Is there not wars? is there not employment? Doth not the king lack subjects? do not the rebels need soldiers? Though it be a shame to be on any side but one, it is worse shame to beg than to be on the worst side, were it worse than the name of rebellion can tell how to make it.

Atten. You mistake me, sir.

Fal. Why, sir, did I say you were an honest man? setting my knighthood and my soldiership aside, I had lied in my throat if I had said so.

Atten. I pray you, sir, then set your knighthood and your soldiership aside; and give me leave to tell you, you lie in your throat, if you say I am any other than an honest man.

Fal. I give thee leave to tell me so! I lay aside that which grows to me! If thou get'st any leave of me, hang me; if thou takest leave, thou wert better be hanged; You hunt counter,[3] hence! avaunt!

Atten. Sir, my lord would speak with you.

Ch. Just. Sir John Falstaff, a word with you.

Fal. My good lord!—God give your lordship good time of day. I am glad to see your lordship abroad: I heard say, your lordship was sick: I hope, your lordship goes abroad by advice. Your lordship, though not clean past your youth, hath yet some smack of age in you, some relish of the saltness of time; and I most humbly beseech your lordship, to have a reverend care of your health.

Ch. Just. Sir John, I sent for you before your expedition to Shrewsbury.

Fal. An't please your lordship, I hear, his majesty is returned with some discomfort from Wales.

Ch. Just. I talk not of his majesty:—You would not come when I sent for you.

Fal. And I hear moreover, his highness is fallen into this same whoreson apoplexy.

Ch. Just. Well, heaven mend him! I pray, let me speak with you.

Fal. This apoplexy is, as I take it, a kind of lethargy, an't please your lordship; a kind of sleeping in the blood, a whoreson tingling.

Ch. Just. What tell you me of it? be it as it is.

Fal. It hath its original from much grief; from study, and perturbation of the brain: I have read the cause of its effects in Galen; it is a kind of deafness.

Ch. Just. I think, you are fallen into the disease, for you hear not what I say to you.

Fal.[4] Very well, my lord, very well: rather, an't please you, it is the disease of not listening, the malady of not marking, that I am troubled withal.

Ch. Just. To punish you by the heels would amend the attention of your ears; and I care not, if I do become your physician.

Fal. I am as poor as Job, my lord; but not so patient: your lordship may minister the potion of imprisonment to me, in respect to poverty; but how I should be your patient to follow your prescriptions, the wise may make some dram of a scruple, or, indeed, a scruple itself.

Ch. Just. I sent for you, when there were matters against you for your life, to come speak with me.

Fal. As I was then advised by my learned counsel in the laws of this land-service, I did not come.

Ch. Just. Well, the truth is, Sir John, you live in great infamy.

Fal. He that buckles him in my belt, cannot live in less.

Ch. Just. Your means are very slender, and your waste is great.

Fal. I would it were otherwise; I would my means were greater, and my waist slenderer.

Ch. Just. You have misled the youthful prince.

Fal. The young prince hath misled me: I am the fellow with the great belly, and he my dog.

Ch. Just. Well, I am loath to gall a new-heal'd wound; your day's service at Shrewsbury hath a little gilded over your night's exploit on Gad's-hill you may thank the unquiet time for your quiet o'erposting that action.

Fal. My lord?

Ch. Just. But since all is well, keep it so: wake not a sleeping wolf.

Fal. To wake a wolf, is as bad as to smell a fox.

Ch. Just. What! you are as a candle, the better part burnt out.

Fal. A wassel candle,[5] my lord; all tallow: if I did say of wax, my growth would approve the truth.

Ch. Just. There is not a white hair on your face, but should have his effect of gravity.

Fal. His effect of gravy, gravy, gravy.

Ch. Just. You follow the young prince up and down, like his ill angel.

Fal. Not so, my lord; your ill angel is light;[6] but, I hope, he that looks upon me, will take me without weighing: and yet, in some respects, I grant, I cannot go, I cannot tell:[7] Virtue is of so

1 The body of old *St. Paul's* Church, in London, was a constant place of resort for business and amusement, and consequently frequented by idle people of all descriptions. Advertisements were fixed-up there, bargains made, servants hired, &c.

2 This judge was Sir Wm. Gascoigne, chief justice of the King's Bench. He died Dec. 17, 1413, and was buried in Harewood Church, in Yorkshire. His effigy is on his monument, and may be seen in Gough's Sepulchral Monuments, vol. ii.

3 To *hunt counter* was to hunt the wrong way, to trace the scent backwards; to *hunt it by the heel* is the technical phrase. Falstaff means to tell the man that he is on a wrong scent. The folio and the modern editions print *hunt-counter* with a hyphen, so as to make it appear like a name; but in the quartos the words are disjoined—*hunt counter.* Cotgrave explains '*contre-pied*, that which we call *counter* in *hunting*;' and '*tenir contrepied*, to set or hold his foot against another man's, whereby to stop him from going any further; to cross or impeach the designes or enterprises of another.' There does not seem to be any allusion to the Counter prison here; though such allusions were very common in the poet's age.

4 In the quarto edition this speech stands thus:

'*Old.* Very well, my lord, very well.'

This is a strong corroboration of the tradition that Falstaff was first called *Oldcastle.*

5 A *wassel candle* is a large candle lighted up at a feast. There is a poor quibble upon the word *wax*, which signifies increase as well as the matter of the honeycomb.

6 'As light as a clipt angel' is a comparison frequent in the old comedies.

7 *I cannot tell*, Johnson explains, 'I cannot be taken in a reckoning, I cannot pass current.' Mr. Gifford objects to this explanation, and says that it merely means 'I cannot tell what to think of it.' The phrase with that signification, was certainly common (says Mr Boswell); but as it will also bear the sense which Dr. Johnson assigned to it, his interpretation appears to me to suit the context better Let the reader judge.

little regard in these coster-monger times,[1] that true valour is turned bear-herd: Pregnancy[2] is made a tapster, and hath his quick wit wasted in giving reckonings: all the other gifts appertinent to man, as the malice of this age shapes them, are not worth a gooseberry. You, that are old, consider not the capacities of us that are young: you measure the heat of our livers with the bitterness of your galls: and we that are in the vaward of our youth, I must confess, are wags too.

Ch. Just. Do you set down your name in the scroll of youth, that are written down old with all the characters of age? Have you not a moist eye? a dry hand? a yellow cheek? a white beard? a decreasing leg? an increasing belly? Is not your voice broken? your wind short? your chin double? your wit single?[3] and every part about you blasted with antiquity? and will you yet call yourself young? Fye, fye, fye, Sir John!

Fal. My lord, I was born about three of the clock in the afternoon, with a white head, and something a round belly. For my voice,—I have lost it with hollaing, and singing of anthems. To approve my youth further, I will not: the truth is, I am only old in judgment and understanding: and he that will caper with me for a thousand marks, let him lend me the money, and have at him. For the box o' the ear that the prince gave you,—he gave it like a rude prince, and you took it like a sensible lord. I have checked him for it; and the young lion repents; marry, not in ashes, and sackcloth; but in new silk and old sack.

Ch. Just. Well, heaven send the prince a better companion!

Fal. Heaven send the companion a better prince! I cannot rid my hands of him.

Ch. Just. Well, the king hath severed you and Prince Harry: I hear, you are going with Lord John of Lancaster, against the archbishop, and the earl of Northumberland.

Fal. Yea; I thank your pretty sweet wit for it. But look you pray, all you that kiss my lady peace at home, that our armies join not in a hot day! for, by the Lord, I take but two shirts out with me, and I mean not to sweat extraordinarily: if it be a hot day, an I brandish any thing but my bottle, I would I might never spit white again. There is not a dangerous action can peep out his head, but I am thrust upon it: Well, I cannot last ever:[4] But it was always yet the trick of our English nation, if they have a good thing, to make it too common. If you will needs say, I am an old man, you should give me rest. I would to God, my name were not so terrible to the enemy as it is. I were better to be eaten to death with rust, than to be scoured to nothing with perpetual motion.

Ch. Just. Well, be honest, be honest; and God bless your expedition!

Fal. Will your lordship lend me a thousand pounds, to furnish me forth?

Ch. Just. Not a penny, not a penny; you are too impatient to bear crosses.[5] Fare you well: Commend me to my cousin Westmoreland.

[*Exeunt* Chief Justice *and* Attendant.

Fal. If I do, fillip me with a three-man beetle.[6]—A man can no more separate age and covetousness, than he can part young limbs and lechery: but the gout galls the one, and the pox pinches the other; and so both the degrees prevent[7] my curses—Boy!——

Page. Sir?

Fal. What money is in my purse?

Page. Seven groats and two-pence.

Fal. I can get no remedy against this consumption of the purse: borrowing only lingers and lingers it out, but the disease is incurable.—Go bear this letter to my lord of Lancaster; this to the prince; this to the earl of Westmoreland; and this to old mistress Ursula, whom I have weekly sworn to marry since I perceived the first white hair on my chin: About it; you know where to find me. [*Exit* Page.] A pox of this gout! or, a gout of this pox! for the one, or the other, plays the rogue with my great toe. It is no matter, if I do halt; I have the wars for my colour, and my pension shall seem the more reasonable: A good wit will make use of any thing; I will turn diseases to commodity.[8] [*Exit.*

SCENE III. York. *A Room in the* Archbishop's *Palace. Enter the* Archbishop *of* York; *the* LORDS HASTINGS, MOWBRAY, *and* BARDOLPH.

Arch. Thus have you heard our cause, and known our means;
And, my most noble friends, I pray you all,
Speak plainly your opinions of our hopes:—
And first, lord marshal, what say you to it?
Mowb. I well allow the occasion of our arms,
But gladly would be better satisfied,
How, in our means, we should advance ourselves
To look with forehead bold and big enough
Upon the power and puissance of the king.
Hast. Our present musters grow upon the file
To five and twenty thousand men of choice;
And our supplies live largely in the hope
Of great Northumberland, whose bosom burns
With an incensed fire of injuries.
Bard. The question then, Lord Hastings, standeth thus:—
Whether our present five and twenty thousand
May hold up head without Northumberland.
Hast. With him, we may.
Bard. Ay, marry, there's the point:
But if without him we be thought too feeble,
My judgment is, we should not step too far
Till we had his assistance by the hand:
For, in a theme so bloody-fac'd as this,
Conjecture, expectation, and surmise
Of aids uncertain, should not be admitted.
Arch. 'Tis very true, Lord Bardolph; for, indeed
It was young Hotspur's case at Shrewsbury.
Bard. It was, my lord; who lin'd himself with hope
Eating the air on promise of supply,
Flattering himself with project of a power
Much smaller than the smallest of his thoughts
And so, with great imagination,
Proper to madmen, led his powers to death,
And, winking, leap'd into destruction.
Hast. But, by your leave, it never yet did hurt,
To lay down likelihoods, and forms of hope.
Bard. Yes, in this present quality of war;—
Indeed the instant action,[10] (a cause on foot),

1 *Coster-monger times* are *petty peddling times;* when the prevalence of trade has produced that meanness that rates the merit of every thing by money.

2 *Pregnancy* is *readiness.*

3 *Single* is *simple, silly.* How much has been written about this phrase, and to how little purpose! *Single-witted* and *single-soul'd* were common epithets with our ancestors, to designate *simple persons.*

4 The rest of this speech, which is not in the folio, is restored from the quarto copy.

5 A quibble is here intended between crosses, contraryings, and the sort of money so called.

6 This alludes to a common but cruel diversion of boys, called *fillipping* the toad. They lay a board, two or three feet long, at right angles, over a transverse piece, two or three inches thick; then placing the toad at one end of the board, the other end is struck by a bat or large stick, which throws the poor toad forty or fifty feet perpendicular from the earth: and the fall generally kills it. A *three-man beetle* is a heavy beetle, with three handles, used in driving piles, &c.

7 To *prevent* is to anticipate.
'Mine eyes *prevent* the night watches.'—*Ps.* cxix.
One of our old translators renders the 'Noctem quæ instabat interpræcapere; to *prevent* the night that was at hand.'

8 *Commodity* is *profit, interest.*

9 That is, *which turned out to be much smaller than.* &c.

10 The first twenty lines of this speech were first inserted in the folio, 1623. This passage has perplexed the editors. The old copies read:

'Yes, *if* this present quality of war,
Indeed the instant action: a cause on foot
Lives so in hope: As in,' &c.

It has been proposed to read:—

'Yes, *if* this present quality of war;—

Lives so in hope, as in an early spring
We see the appearing buds; which, to prove fruit,
Hope gives not so much warrant, as despair,
That frosts will bite them. When we mean to build,
We first survey the plot, then draw the model;
And when we see the figure of the house,
Then must we rate the cost of the erection:
Which if we find outweighs ability,
What do we then, but draw anew the model
In fewer offices; or, at least, desist
To build at all? Much more, in this great work,
(Which is, almost, to pluck a kingdom down,
And set another up,) should we survey
The plot of situation, and the model;
Consent[1] upon a sure foundation;
Question surveyors; know our own estate,
How able such a work to undergo,
To weigh against his opposite; or else,
We fortify in paper, and in figures,
Using the names of men instead of men:
Like one, that draws the model of a house
Beyond his power to build it; who, half through,
Gives o'er, and leaves his part-created cost
A naked subject to the weeping clouds,
And waste for churlish winter's tyranny.

Hast. Grant, that our hopes (yet likely of fair birth,)
Should be still-born, and that we now possess'd
The utmost man of expectation;
I think, we are a body strong enough,
Even as we are, to equal with the king.

Bard. What! is the king but five and twenty thousand?

Hast. To us, no more; nay, not so much, Lord Bardolph.
For his divisions, as the times do brawl,
Are in three heads: one power against the French,[2]
And one against Glendower; perforce, a third
Must take up us: So is the unfirm king
In three divided; and his coffers sound
With hollow poverty and emptiness.

Arch. That he should draw his several strengths together,
And come against us in full puissance,
Need not be dreaded.

Hast. If he should do so,
He leaves his back unarm'd, the French and Welsh
Baying him at the heels: never fear that.

Bard. Who, is it like, should lead his forces hither?

Hast. The duke of Lancaster,[3] and Westmoreland:
Against the Welsh, himself, and Harry Monmouth:
But who is substituted 'gainst the French,
I have no certain notice.

Arch. Let us on;[4]
And publish the occasion of our arms.
The commonwealth is sick of their own choice,
Their over-greedy love hath surfeited:—
An habitation giddy and unsure
Hath he, that buildeth on the vulgar heart.
O thou fond many![5] with what loud applause
Didst thou beat heaven with blessing Bolingbroke,
Before he was what thou would'st have him be?
And being now trimm'd[6] in thine own desires,
Thou, beastly feeder, art so full of him,
That thou provok'st thyself to cast him up.
So, so, thou common dog, didst thou disgorge
Thy glutton bosom of the royal Richard;
And now thou would'st eat thy dead vomit up,
And howl'st to find it. What trust is in these times?
They that, when Richard liv'd, would have him die,
Are now become enamour'd on his grave:
Thou, that threw'st dust upon his goodly head,
When through proud London he came sighing on
After the admired heels of Bolingbroke,
Cry'st now, *O earth, yield us that king again,*
And take thou this! O thoughts of men accurst!
Past, and to come, seem best; things present, worst.

Mowb. Shall we go draw our numbers, and set on?

Hast. We are time's subjects, and time bids be gone. [*Exeunt.*

ACT II.

SCENE I. London. *A Street. Enter* Hostess; FANG, *and his Boy, with her; and* SNARE *following.*

Host. Master Fang, have you entered the action?

Fang. It is entered.

Host. Where is your yeoman?[7] Is it a lusty yeoman? will a' stand to't?

Fang. Sirrah, where's Snare?

Host. O lord, ay: good master Snare.

Snare. Here, here.

Fang. Snare, we must arrest Sir John Falstaff.

Host. Yea, good master Snare; I have entered him and all.

Snare. It may chance cost some of us our lives, for he will stab.

Host. Alas the day! take heed of him; he stabbed me in mine own house, and that most beastly: in good faith, a' cares not what mischief he doth, if his weapon be out: he will foin[8] like any devil; he will spare neither man, woman, nor child.

Fang. If I can close with him, I care not for his thrust.

Host. No, nor I neither: I'll be at your elbow.

Fang. An I but fist him once; an a' come but within my vice;[9]—

Host. I am undone by his going; I warrant you, he's an infinitive thing upon my score:—Good master Fang, hold him sure;—good master Snare, let him not 'scape. He comes continually to Pie-corner (saving your manhoods,) to buy a saddle; and he's indited to dinner to the lubbar's head in Lumbert-street, to master Smooth's the silkman: I pray ye, since my exion is entered, and my case so openly known to the world, let him be brought in to his answer. A hundred mark is a long loan[10] for a poor lone woman to bear: and I have borne, and borne, and borne; and have been fubbed off, and fubbed off, and fubbed off, from this day to that day, that it is a shame to be thought on. There is no honesty in such dealing; unless a woman should be made an ass, and a beast, to bear every knave's wrong.——

Induc'd the instant action: a cause on foot
Lives so in hope, as in,' &c.

The reading adopted by Steevens and Malone, from Johnson's suggestion, is that which I have given; it affords a clear sense, and agrees with the whole tenor of Bardolph's argument; at the same time little violence is done to the text, two letters only being changed.

1 Agree.

2 During this rebellion of Northumberland and the Archbishop a French army of twelve thousand men landed at Milford Haven in aid of Owen Glendower. See Holinshed, p. 531.

3 This is an anachronism. Prince John of Lancaster was not created a duke till the second year of the reign of his brother, King Henry V. At this time Prince Henry was actually duke of Lancaster. Shakspeare was misled by Stowe, who, speaking of the first parliament of King Henry IV. says, 'Then the king rose, and made his eldest sonne prince of Wales, &c.: his *second sonne* was there made duke of Lancaster.' Annales, 1631.—He seems to have consulted Stowe (p. 323) between the times of finishing the last play and beginning of the present.

4 This speech first appeared in the folio.

5 *Many* or *meyny;* from the French *mesnie*, a *multitude.*

6 Dressed.

7 A bailiff's follower was formerly called a serjeant's *yeoman.*

8 Thrust.

9 The quarto reads *view.* *Vice* is used for *grasp* or clutch. The *fist* is vulgarly called the *vice* in the west of England.

10 The old copies read 'long *one;*' which Theobald supposed was a corruption of *lone* or *loan.* Mr. Douce thinks the alteration unnecessary; and that the hostess means to say that a hundred *mark* is a long *score*, or *reckoning*, for her to bear

Enter SIR JOHN FALSTAFF, Page, *and* BARDOLPH.

Yonder he comes; and that arrant malmsey-nose knave, Bardolph, with him. Do your offices, do your offices, master Fang, and master Snare; do me, do me, do me your offices.

Fal. How now? whose mare's dead? what's the matter?

Fang. Sir John, I arrest you at the suit of Mistress Quickly.

Fal. Away, varlets!—Draw, Bardolph; cut me off the villain's head; throw the quean in the channel.

Host. Throw me in the channel? I'll throw thee in the channel. Wilt thou? wilt thou? thou bastardly rogue!—Murder, murder! O thou honey-suckle[1] villain! wilt thou kill God's officers, and the king's? O thou honey-seed[1] rogue! thou art a honey-seed; a man-queller,[2] and a woman-queller.

Fal. Keep them off, Bardolph.

Fang. A rescue! a rescue!

Host. Good people, bring a rescue or two.—Thou wo't, wo't thou? thou wo't, wo't thou? do, do, thou rogue! do, thou hemp-seed!

Fal. Away, you scullion! you rampallian! you fustilarian! I'll tickle your catastrophe.

Enter the Lord Chief Justice, *attended.*

Ch. Just. What's the matter? keep the peace here, ho!

Host. Good my lord, be good to me! I beseech you, stand to me!

Ch. Just. How now, Sir John? what, are you brawling here?
Doth this become your place, your time, and business?
You should have been well on your way to York—
Stand from him, fellow; wherefore hang'st thou on him?

Host. O my most worshipful lord, an't please your grace, I am a poor widow of Eastcheap, and he is arrested at my suit.

Ch. Just. For what sum?

Host. It is more than for some, my lord: it is for all, all I have: he hath eaten me out of house and home; he hath put all my substance into that fat belly of his;—but I will have some of it out again, or I'll ride thee o' nights, like the mare.

Fal. I think I am as like to ride the mare, if I have any vantage of ground to get up.

Ch. Just. How comes this, Sir John? Fye! what man of good temper would endure this tempest of exclamation? Are you not ashamed to enforce a poor widow to so rough a course to come by her own?

Fal. What is the gross sum that I owe thee?

Host. Marry, if thou wert an honest man, thyself, and the money too. Thou didst swear to me upon a parcel-gilt[3] goblet, sitting in my Dolphin-chamber, at the round table, by a sea-coal fire, upon Wednesday in Wheeson-week,[4] when the prince broke thy head for liking his father[5] to a singing-man of Windsor; thou didst swear to me then, as I was washing thy wound, to marry me, and make me my lady thy wife. Canst thou deny it? Did not goodwife Keech, the butcher's wife, come in then, and call me gossip Quickly? coming in to borrow a mess of vinegar; telling us, she had a good dish of prawns; whereby thou didst desire to eat some; whereby I told thee, they were ill for a green wound? And didst thou not, when she was gone down stairs, desire me to be no more so familiarity with such poor people; saying that ere long they should call me madam? And didst thou not kiss me, and bid me fetch thee thirty shillings? I put thee now to thy book-oath; deny it if thou canst.

Fal. My lord, this is a poor mad soul; and she says, up and down the town, that her eldest son is like you: she hath been in good case, and, the truth is, poverty hath distracted her. But for these foolish officers, I beseech you, I may have redress against them.

Ch. Just. Sir John, Sir John, I am well acquainted with your manner of wrenching the true cause the false way. It is not a confident brow, nor the throng of words that come with such more than impudent sauciness from you, can thrust me from a level consideration: you have, as it appears to me, practised upon the easy-yielding spirit of this woman, and made her serve your uses both in purse and person.

Host. Yea, in troth, my lord.

Ch. Just. 'Pr'ythee, peace:—Pay her the debt you owe her, and unpay the villany you have done with her; the one you may do with sterling money, and the other with current repentance.

Fal. My lord, I will not undergo this sneap[6] without reply. You call honourable boldness, impudent sauciness: if a man will make court'sy, and say nothing, he is virtuous: No, my lord, my humble duty remembered, I will not be your suitor; I say to you, I do desire deliverance from these officers, being upon hasty employment in the king's affairs.

Ch. Just. You speak as having power to do wrong: but answer in the effect of your reputation,[7] and satisfy the poor woman.

Fal. Come hither, hostess. [*Taking her aside*

Enter GOWER.

Ch. Just. Now, master Gower; what news?

Gow. The king, my lord, and Harry prince of Wales,
Are near at hand: the rest the paper tells.

Fal. As I am a gentleman:——

Host. Nay, you said so before.

Fal. As I am a gentleman;——Come, no more words of it.

Host. By this heavenly ground I tread on, I must be fain to pawn both my plate, and the tapestry of my dining-chambers.

Fal. Glasses, glasses, is the only drinking: and for thy walls,—a pretty slight drollery, or the story of the prodigal, or the German hunting in water-work,[8] is worth a thousand of these bed-hangings, and these fly-bitten tapestries. Let it be ten pound, if thou canst. Come, and it were not for thy humours, there is not a better wench in England. Go wash thy face, and 'draw[9] thy action: Come, thou must not be in this humour with me! dost not know me? Come, come, I know thou wast set on to this?

Host. 'Pray thee, Sir John, let it be but twenty nobles; i'faith I am loath to pawn my plate, in good earnest, la.

---

1 It is scarce necessary to remark that *honey-suckle* and *honey-seed* are Dame Quickly's corruptions of *homicidal* and *homicide*.

2 To *quell* was anciently used for to *kill*. '*A man-queller, a manslayer*, or *murderer; homicida*.'—*Junius's Nomenclator*, 1585.

3 *Parcel-gilt* is partly gilt, or gilt only in parts. Laneham, in his Letter from Kenilworth, describing a bride-cup, says, 'It was formed of a sweet sucket barrel, a faire turn'd foot set to it, all seemly be-sylvered and *parcel gilt*.' The expression is too common in old writers to need further illustration.

4 The folio reads *Whitsun-week*: but the corruption is in the hostess's manner.

5 The folio has '*for likening him to*,' &c.

6 *Sneap* is *reproof, rebuke*. Thus in Brome's Antipodes:—

'Do you *sneap* me, my lord?'

And again:—

'No need to come hither to be *sneap'd*'
'——— even as now I was not,
When you *sneap'd* me, my lord.'

Snip, snib, sneb, and snub, are different forms of the same word. To *sneap* was originally to *check* or pinch by frost. Shakspeare has *sneaping* frost and *sneaping* winds in other places.

7 Suitably to your character.

8 *Water work* is *water colour paintings* or *hangings*. The painted cloth was generally oil colour; but a cheaper sort, probably resembling in their execution some modern paper-hangings, was brought from Holland or Germany, executed in water colour, or distemper. The German hunting, or wild boar hunt, would consequently be a prevalent subject.

9 Withdraw.

Fal. Let it alone; I'll make other shift: you'll be a fool still.

Host. Well, you shall have it, though I pawn my gown. I hope you'll come to supper; you'll pay me altogether.

Fal. Will I live?—Go, with her, with her; [*To* BARDOLPH.] hook on, hook on.

Host. Will you have Doll Tear-sheet meet you at supper?

Fal. No more words; let's have her.

[*Exeunt* Hostess, BARDOLPH, *Officers, and Page.*

Ch. Just. I have heard better news.

Fal. What's the news, my good lord?

Ch. Just. Where lay the king last night?

Gow. At Basingstoke, my lord.

Fal. I hope, my lord, all's well: What's the news, my lord?

Ch. Just. Come all his forces back?

Gow. No; fifteen hundred foot, five hundred horse,
Are march'd up to my lord of Lancaster,
Against Northumberland and the archbishop.

Fal. Comes the king back from Wales, my noble lord?

Ch. Just. You shall have letters of me presently:
Come, go along with me, good master Gower.

Fal. My lord!

Ch. Just. What's the matter?

Fal. Master Gower, shall I entreat you with me to dinner?

Gow. I must wait upon my good lord here: I thank you, good Sir John.

Ch. Just. Sir John, you loiter here too long, being you are to take soldiers up in counties as you go.

Fal. Will you sup with me, master Gower?

Ch. Just. What foolish master taught you these manners, Sir John?

Fal. Master Gower, if they become me not, he was a fool that taught them me.—This is the right fencing grace, my lord; tap for tap, and so part fair.

Ch. Just. Now the lord lighten thee! thou art a great fool. [*Exeunt.*

SCENE II. *The same. Another Street. Enter* PRINCE HENRY *and* POINS.

P. Hen. Trust me, I am exceeding weary.

Poins. Is it come to that? I had thought, weariness durst not have attached one of so high blood.

P. Hen. 'Faith, it does me; though it discolours the complexion of my greatness to acknowledge it. Doth it not show vilely in me to desire small beer?

Poins. Why, a prince should not be so loosely studied, as to remember so weak a composition.

P. Hen. Belike then, my appetite was not princely got; for, by my troth, I do now remember the poor creature, small beer. But, indeed, these humble considerations make me out of love with my greatness. What a disgrace is it to me, to remember thy name? or to know thy face to-morrow? or to take note how many pair of silk stockings thou hast; *viz.* these and those that were the peach-colour'd ones? or to bear the inventory of thy shirts; as, one for superfluity, and one other for use?—but that the tennis-court keeper knows better than I; for it is a low ebb of linen with thee, when thou keepest not racket there; as thou hast not done a great while, because the rest of thy low-countries have made a shift to eat up thy holland: and God knows, whether those that bawl out the ruins of thy linen,[1] shall inherit his kingdom: but the midwives say, the children are not in the fault; whereupon the world increases, and kindreds are mightily strengthened.

Poins. How ill it follows, after you have laboured so hard, you should talk so idly? Tell me, how many good young princes would do so, their fathers being so sick as yours at this time is?

P. Hen. Shall I tell thee one thing, Poins?

Poins. Yes; and let it be an excellent good thing.

P. Hen. It shall serve among wits of no higher breeding than thine.

Poins. Go to; I stand the push of your one thing that you will tell.

P. Hen. Why, I tell thee,—it is not meet that I should be sad, now my father is sick: albeit I could tell to thee (as to one it pleases me, for fault of a better, to call my friend,) I could be sad, and sad indeed too.

Poins. Very hardly, upon such a subject.

P. Hen. By this hand, thou think'st me as far in the devil's book, as thou, and Falstaff, for obduracy and persistency: Let the end try the man. But I tell thee,—my heart bleeds inwardly, that my father is so sick: and keeping such vile company as thou art, hath in reason taken from me all ostentation[2] of sorrow.

Poins. The reason?

P. Hen. What would'st thou think of me, if I should weep?

Poins. I would think thee a most princely hypocrite.

P. Hen. It would be every man's thought: and thou art a blessed fellow, to think as every man thinks; never a man's thoughts in the world keeps the road-way better than thine: every man would think me a hypocrite indeed. And what accites your most worshipful thought to think so?

Poins. Why, because you have been so lewd, and so much engrafted to Falstaff.

P. Hen. And to thee.

Poins. By this light, I am well spoken of, I can hear it with mine own ears: the worst that they can say of me is, that I am a second brother, and that I am a proper fellow of my hands;[3] and those two things, I confess, I cannot help. By the mass, here comes Bardolph.

P. Hen. And the boy that I gave Falstaff: he had him from me christian; and look, if the fat villain have not transformed him ape.

Enter BARDOLPH *and* Page.

Bard. 'Save your grace!

P. Hen. And yours, most noble Bardolph!

Bard. Come, you virtuous ass [*To the Page,*] you bashful fool, must you be blushing? wherefore blush you now? What a maidenly man at arms are you become! Is it such a matter, to get a pottlepot's maidenhead?

Page. He called me even now, my lord, through a red-lattice,[4] and I could discern no part of his face from the window: at last, I spied his eyes; and, methought, he had made two holes in the ale-wife's new petticoat, and peeped through.

P. Hen. Hath not the boy profited?

Bard. Away, you whoreson upright rabbit, away!

Page. Away, you rascally Althea's dream, away!

P. Hen. Instruct us, boy: What dream, boy?

Page. Marry, my lord, Althea dreamed she was delivered of a firebrand; and therefore I call him her dream.

P. Hen. A crown's worth of good interpretation.—There it is, boy. [*Gives him money.*

Poins. O, that this good blossom could be kept from cankers!—Well, there is sixpence to preserve thee.

---

1 His *bastard children*, wrapt up in his old shirts. The ellipsis *out* for *out of*, Steevens says, is sometimes used.

2 *Ostentation* is not here used for *boastful* show, but for mere *outward show*:—

'Like one well studied in a sad *ostent*
To please his grandam.'—*Merchant of Venice.*

3 *A proper fellow of my hands* is the same as *a tall fellow of his hands*, which has been already explained in a note on The Merry Wives of Windsor, Act i. Sc. 4. That *a tall* or *a proper fellow* was sometimes used in an equivocal sense for *a thief*, there can be no doubt. Cotgrave has a proverb, 'Les beaux hommes au gibet. The gibbet makes an end of *proper men.*' A *striker* is one of its meanings, according to Cotgrave, 'who taking a *proper* youth to be his apprentice, to teach him the order of *striking* and foisting.'—*Greene's Art of Cony Catching.*

4 An alehouse window.

Bard. An you do not make him be hanged among you, the gallows shall have wrong.

P. Hen. And how doth thy master, Bardolph?

Bard. Well, my lord. He heard of your grace's coming to town; there's a letter for you.

Poins. Delivered with good respect.—And how doth the martlemas,[1] your master?

Bard. In bodily health, sir.

Poins. Marry, the immortal part needs a physician; but that moves not him; though that be sick, it dies not.

P. Hen. I do allow this wen[2] to be as familiar with me as my dog: and he holds his place; for, look you, how he writes.

Poins. [*Reads.*] John Falstaff, *knight*,——Every man must know that, as oft as he has occasion to name himself. Even like those that are kin to the king; for they never prick their finger, but they say, *There is some of the king's blood spilt: How comes that?* says he that takes upon him not to conceive: the answer is as ready as a borrower's[3] cap; *I am the king's poor cousin, sir.*

P. Hen. Nay, they will be kin to us, or they will fetch it from Japhet. But the letter:—

Poins. *Sir* John Falstaff, *knight, to the son of the king, nearest his father, Harry, Prince of Wales, greeting.*—Why, this is a certificate.

P. Hen. Peace!

Poins. *I will imitate the honourable Roman*[4] *in brevity:*—he sure means brevity in breath; short-winded.—*I commend me to thee, I commend thee, and I leave thee. Be not too familiar with* Poins: *for he misuses thy favours so much, that he swears, thou art to marry his sister* Nell. *Repent at idle times as thou may'st, and so farewell.*

> *Thine, by yea and no (which is as much as to say, as thou usest him,)*
> Jack Falstaff, *with my familiars;*
> John *with my brothers and sisters;*
> *and Sir* John, *with all Europe.*

My lord, I will steep this letter in sack, and make him eat it.

P. Hen. That's to make him eat twenty of his words. But do you use me thus, Ned? must I marry your sister?

Poins. May the wench have no worse fortune! but I never said so.

P. Hen. Well, thus we play the fools with the time: and the spirits of the wise sit in the clouds, and mock us.—Is your master here in London?

Bard. Yes, my lord.

P. Hen. Where sups he? doth the old boar feed in the old frank?[5]

Bard. At the old place, my lord; in Eastcheap.

P. Hen. What company?

Page. Ephesians, my lord; of the old church.[6]

P. Hen. Sup any women with him?

Page. None, my lord, but old mistress Quickly, and mistress Doll Tear-sheet.

P. Hen. What pagan[7] may that be?

Page. A proper gentlewoman, sir, and a kinswoman of my master's.

P. Hen. Even such kin as the parish heifers are to the town bull. Shall we steal upon them, Ned, at supper?

Poins. I am your shadow, my lord; I'll follow you.

P. Hen. Sirrah, you boy,—and Bardolph;—no word to your master, that I am yet come to town: There's for your silence.

Bard. I have no tongue, sir.

Page. And for mine, sir,—I will govern it.

P. Hen. Fare ye well; go. [*Exeunt* BARDOLPH *and* PAGE.]—This Doll Tear-sheet should be some road.

Poins. I warrant you, as common as the way between Saint Albans and London.

P. Hen. How might we see Falstaff bestow[8] himself to-night in his true colours, and not ourselves be seen?

Poins. Put on two leather jerkins, and aprons, and wait upon him at his table as drawers.

P. Hen. From a god to a bull? a heavy descension![9] it was Jove's case. From a prince to a prentice? a low transformation! that shall be mine: for, in every thing, the purpose must weigh with the folly. Follow me, Ned. [*Exeunt.*

SCENE III. Warkworth. *Before the Castle.*

Enter NORTHUMBERLAND, LADY NORTHUMBERLAND, *and* LADY PERCY.

North. I pray thee, loving wife, and gentle daughter,
Give even way unto my rough affairs;
Put not you on the visage of the times,
And be, like them, to Percy troublesome.

Lady N. I have given over, I will speak no more.
Do what you will; your wisdom be your guide.

North. Alas, sweet wife, my honour is at pawn;
And, but my going, nothing can redeem it.

Lady P. O, yet, for God's sake, go not to these wars!
The time was, father, that you broke your word,
When you were more endear'd to it than now;
When your own Percy, when my heart's dear Harry
Threw many a northward look, to see his father
Bring up his powers: but he did long in vain.
Who then persuaded you to stay at home?
There were two honours lost; yours, and your son's.
For yours,—may heavenly glory brighten it!
For his,—it stuck upon him, as the sun
In the grey vault of heaven: and, by his light,
Did all the chivalry of England move
To do brave acts; he was, indeed, the glass
Wherein the noble youth did dress themselves.
He had no legs, that practis'd not his gait:[10]
And speaking thick,[11] which nature made his blemish,
Became the accents of the valiant:
For those that could speak low, and tardily,
Would turn their own perfection to abuse,
To seem like him: So that, in speech, in gait,
In diet, in affections of delight,
In military rules, humours of blood,
He was the mark and glass, copy and book,[12]
That fashion'd others. And him,—O wondrous him
O miracle of men!—him did you leave
(Second to none, unseconded by you,)
To look upon the hideous god of war
In disadvantage; to abide a field,
Where nothing but the sound of Hotspur's name
Did seem defensible:[13]—so you left him:

---

1 Falstaff is before called 'thou *latter spring, all-hallown summer*,' and Poins now calls him *martlemas*, a corruption of *martinmas*, which means the same thing. The feast of St. Martin being considered the latter end of autumn. *Este de St. Martin* is a French proverb for a *late summer*. It means therefore an old fellow with juvenile passions.

2 Swoln excrescence.

3 The old copy reads a *borrowed* cap. The emendation is Warburton's.

4 That is *Julius Cæsar*. Falstaff alludes to the *veni, vidi, &c.*, which he afterwards quotes.

5 A sty: a place to fatten a boar in.

6 A cant phrase probably signifying *topers*, or *jolly companions of the old sort.*

7 Massinger, in The City Madam, has used this phrase for a *wench*:—

> '——— in all these places
> I've had my several *pagans* billeted.'

8 i. e. *act*. In a MS. letter from Secretary Conway to Buckingham, at the Isle of Ree, 'also what the lords have advanced for the expedition towards you, since Saturday that they returned from Windsor with charge to *bestowe themselves* seriously in it.'—*Conway Papers*

9 The folio reads *declension*.

10 The twenty-two following lines were first given in the folio.

11 Speaking *thick* is speaking *quick*, rapidity of utterance. Baret translates the *anhilitus creber* of Virgil *thicke-breathing*.

12 Thus in the Rape of Lucrece:—

> 'For princes are the *glass*, the school, the *book*
> Where subjects' eyes do learn, do read, do look.'

13 *Defensible* does not in this place mean *capable of defence*, but *bearing strength, furnishing the means of defence*: the passive for the active participle.

Never, O never, do his ghost the wrong,
To hold your honour more precise and nice
With others, than with him; let them alone;
The marshal, and the archbishop, are strong:
Had my sweet Harry had but half their numbers,
To-day might I, hanging on Hotspur's neck,
Have talk'd of Monmouth's grave.

North. Beshrew[1] your heart,
Fair daughter! you do draw my spirits from me,
With new lamenting ancient oversights.
But I must go, and meet with danger there;
Or it will seek me in another place,
And find me worse provided.

Lady N. O, fly to Scotland,
Till that the nobles, and the armed commons,
Have of their puissance made a little taste.

Lady P. If they get ground and vantage of the king,
Then join you with them, like a rib of steel,
To make strength stronger; but, for all our loves,
First let them try themselves: So did your son;
He was so suffer'd; so came I a widow;
And never shall have length of life enough,
To rain upon remembrance[2] with mine eyes,
That it may grow and sprout as high as heaven,
For recordation to my noble husband.

North. Come, come, go in with me: 'tis with my mind,
As with the tide swell'd up unto its height,
That makes a still-stand, running neither way.
Fain would I go to meet the archbishop,
But many thousand reasons hold me back:——
I will resolve for Scotland; there am I,
Till time and vantage crave my company. [*Exeunt.*

SCENE IV. London. *A Room in the* Boar's Head *Tavern in* Eastcheap. *Enter Two* Drawers.

1 *Draw.* What the devil hast thou brought there? apple-Johns? thou know'st, Sir John cannot endure an apple-John.[3]

2 *Draw.* Mass, thou sayest true: The prince once set a dish of apple-Johns before him, and told him, there were five more Sir Johns: and, putting off his hat, said, *I will now take my leave of these six dry, round, old, withered knights.* It angered him to the heart; but he hath forgot that.

1 *Draw.* Why then, cover, and set them down: And see if thou canst find out Sneak's noise;[4] mistress Tear-sheet would fain hear some music. Despatch:—The room where they supped is too hot; they'll come in straight.

2 *Draw.* Sirrah, here will be the prince, and master Poins anon: and they will put on two of our jerkins, and aprons; and Sir John must not know of it: Bardolph hath brought word.

1 *Draw.* By the mass, here will be old utis:[5] It will be an excellent stratagem.

2 *Draw.* I'll see if I can find out Sneak. [*Exit.*

Enter Hostess *and* DOLL TEAR-SHEET.

Host. I'faith, sweet heart, methinks now you are in an excellent good temperality: your pulsidge beats as extraordinarily as heart would desire; and your colour, I warrant you, is as red as any rose: But, i'faith, you have drunk too much canaries; and that's a marvellous searching wine, and it perfumes the blood ere one can say,—What's this? How do you now?

Dol. Better than I was. Hem.

Host. Why, that's well said; a good heart's worth gold. Look, here comes Sir John.

Enter FALSTAFF, *singing.*

Fal. *When Arthur first in court.*[6]—Empty the jordan.—*And was a worthy king:* [*Exit* Drawer.] How now, mistress Doll?

Host. Sick of a calm: yea, good sooth.

Fal. So is all her sect;[7] an they be once in a calm, they are sick.

Dol. You muddy rascal, is that all the comfort you give me?

Fal. You make fat rascals,[8] mistress Doll.

Dol. I make them! gluttony and diseases make them; I make them not.

Fal. If the cook help to make the gluttony, you help to make the diseases, Doll: we catch of you, Doll, we catch of you; grant that, my poor virtue, grant that.

Dol. Ay, marry; our chains, and our jewels.

Fal. *Your brooches, pearls, and owches;*[9]—for to serve bravely, is to come halting off, you know: To come off the breach with his pike bent bravely, and to surgery bravely; to venture upon the charged chambers[10] bravely:——

Dol. Hang yourself, you muddy conger, hang yourself!

Host. By my troth, this is the old fashion; you two never meet, but you fall to some discord: you are both, in good truth, as rheumatic[11] as two dry toasts; you cannot one bear with another's confirmities. What the good-year! one must bear, and that must be you: [*To* DOLL.] you are the weaker vessel, as they say, the emptier vessel.

Dol. Can a weak empty vessel bear such a huge full hogshead? there's a whole merchant's venture of Bordeaux stuff in him: you have not seen a hulk better stuffed in the hold.—Come, I'll be friends with thee, Jack: thou art going to the wars; and whether I shall ever see thee again, or no, there is nobody cares.

Re-enter Drawer.

Draw. Sir, ancient[12] Pistol's below, and would speak with you.

Dol. Hang him, swaggering rascal! let him not come hither: it is the foul-mouth'dst rogue in England.

Host. If he swagger, let him not come here; no, by my faith; I must live amongst my neighbours;

---

1 Ill-betide.

2 Alluding to the plant *rosemary*, so called because it was the symbol of *remembrance*, and therefore used at weddings and funerals.

3 This apple, which was said to keep two years, is well described by Philips:—

'Nor *John-apple*, whose wither'd rind entrench'd
By many a furrow, aptly represents
Decrepid age.'

Falstaff has already said of himself, 'I am withered like an old *apple-John.*'

4 A *noise*, or a *consort*, was used for *a set or company of musicians.* Sneak was a street minstrel, and therefore the drawer goes out to listen for his band. Falstaff addresses them as a company in another scene. In the old play of King Henry IV. 'There came the young prince, and two or three more of his companions, and called for wine good store, and then sent for a *noyse of musitians,*' &c.

5 *Old utis* is *old festivity*, or *merry doings. Utis*, or *utas*, being the *eighth* day after any festival; any day between the feast and the eighth day was said to be within the *utas.* So Sir Thomas More, in the last letter he wrote to his daughter the day before his execution desires to die on the morrow, 'For it is Saint Thomas' even, and the *utas* of Saint Peter.'

6 The entire ballad is in the first volume of Dr. Percy's Reliques of Ancient Poetry.

7 Steevens is right in his assertion that *sect* and *sex* were anciently synonymous; the instances of the use of the one for the other are too numerous for it to have been a mere vulgar corruption.

8 Falstaff alludes to a phrase of the forest. '*Rascall* (says Puttenham, p. 150) is properly the hunting term given to young deer *leane* and out of season, and not to people.'

9 Falstaff gives these splendid names to something very different from gems and ornaments, as we still use *carbuncle.* The passage, as Johnson observed, is not deserving of further illustration.

10 To understand this quibble it is necessary to remember that a chamber signifies not only an apartment, but *a small piece of ordnance.*

11 Mrs. Quickly means *splenetic.* It should be remarked, however, that *rheum* seems to have been a cant word for *spleen.*

12 That is, 'he that carrieth the colours to a company of foot soldiers, an ensign bearer.'—*Philips.* Falstaff was captain, Peto lieutenant, and Pistol *ensign.* I have met with the word in old MSS written *ansine*

I'll no swaggerers: I am in good name and fame with the very best:—Shut the door;—there comes no swaggerers here: I have not lived all this while to have swaggering now:—shut the door, I pray you.

Fal. Dost thou hear, hostess?

Host. 'Pray you, pacify yourself, Sir John; there comes no swaggerers here.

Fal. Dost thou hear? it is mine ancient.

Host. Tilly-fally, Sir John, never tell me; your ancient swaggerer comes not in my doors. I was before master Tisick,[1] the deputy, the other day; and, as he said to me,—it was no longer ago than Wednesday last,—*Neighbour Quickly*, says he;—master Dumb, our minister, was by then;—*Neighbour Quickly*, says he, *receive those that are civil; for*, saith he, *you are in an ill name*;—now he said so, I can tell whereupon; *for*, says he, *you are an honest woman, and well thought on; therefore take heed what guests you receive: Receive*, says he, *no swaggering companions.*——There comes none here;——you would bless you to hear what he said:—no, I'll no swaggerers.

Fal. He's no swaggerer, hostess; a tame cheater,[2] he, you may stroke him as gently as a puppy greyhound: he will not swagger with a Barbary hen, if her feathers turn back in any show of resistance.—Call him up, drawer.

Host. Cheater, call you him? I will bar no honest man my house, nor no cheater:[3] But I do not love swaggering; by my troth, I am the worse, when one says—swagger: feel, masters, how I shake; look you, I warrant you.

Dol. So you do, hostess.

Host. Do I? yea, in very truth, do I, an 'twere an aspen leaf: I cannot abide swaggerers.

Enter Pistol, Bardolph, *and* Page.

Pist. 'Save you, Sir John!

Fal. Welcome, ancient Pistol. Here, Pistol, I charge you with a cup of sack: do you discharge upon mine hostess.

Pist. I will discharge upon her, Sir John, with two bullets.

Fal. She is pistol-proof, sir; you shall hardly offend her.

Host. Come, I'll drink no proofs, nor no bullets: I'll drink no more than will do me good, for no man's pleasure, I.

Pist. Then to you, mistress Dorothy; I will charge you.

Dol. Charge me? I scorn you, scurvy companion. What! you poor, base, rascally, cheating, lack-linen mate! Away, you mouldy rogue; away! I am meat for your master.

Pist. I know you, mistress Dorothy.

Dol. Away, you cut-purse rascal! you filthy bung,[4] away! by this wine, I'll thrust my knife in your mouldy chaps, an you play the saucy cuttle with me. Away, you bottle-ale rascal! you basket-hilt stale juggler, you!—Since when, I pray you, sir?—What, with two points[5] on your shoulder? much![6]

Pist. I will murder your ruff for this.

Fal. No more, Pistol; I would not have you go off here: discharge yourself of our company, Pistol.

Host. No, good captain Pistol; not here, sweet captain.

Dol. Captain! thou abominable damned cheater, art thou not ashamed to be called—captain? If captains were of my mind, they would truncheon you out, for taking their names upon you before you have earned them. You a captain, you slave! for what? for tearing a poor whore's ruff in a bawdy-house?—He a captain! Hang him, rogue! He lives upon mouldy stewed prunes, and dried cakes.[7] A captain! these villains will make the word captain as odious as the word occupy;[8] which was an excellent good word before it was ill-sorted; therefore captains had need look to it.

Bard. 'Pray thee, go down, good ancient.

Fal. Hark thee hither, mistress Doll.

Pist. Not I: tell thee what, corporal Bardolph;—I could tear her:—I'll be revenged on her.

Page. 'Pray thee, go down.

Pist. I'll see her damned first;—to Pluto's damned lake, to the infernal deep, with Erebus and tortures vile also. Hold hook and line, say I. Down! down, dogs! down, faitors![9] Have we not Hiren here?[10]

Host. Good captain Peesel, be quiet; it is very late, i'faith: I beseek you now, aggravate your choler.

Pist. These be good humours, indeed! Shall packhorses,
And hollow pamper'd jades of Asia,
Which cannot go but thirty miles a day,[11]
Compare with Cæsars, and with Cannibals,[12]
And Trojan Greeks? nay, rather damn them with
King Cerberus; and let the welkin roar.
Shall we fall foul for toys?

Host. By my troth, captain, these are very bitter words.

---

1 The names of Master *Tisick* and Master *Dumb* are ludicrously intended to denote that the deputy was pursy and short-winded; the minister one of those who preached only the homilies set forth by authority. The puritans nicknamed them Dumb-dogs, and the opprobrious epithet continued in use as late as the reign of King Charles II. See *Burnet's Own Times*, vol. i. p. 395.

2 A *cheater* sometimes meant an *unfair gamester.* But *tame cheater* seems to have meant a *rogue* in general.

3 The humour consists in Mrs. Quickly's mistaking a *cheater* for an *escheator*, or officer of the exchequer. Greene, in his Mihil Munchaunce, has the following passage, which gives the origin of the phrase:—'They call their art by a new found name as *cheating*, themselves *cheators*, and the dice cheters: borrowing the term from among our lawyers, with whom all such casuals as fall to the lord, at the holding of his leets, as waifes, straies, and such like, be called *chetes*, and are accustomably to be *escheated* to the lord's use.' Lord Coke, in his Charge at Norwich, 1607, puns upon the equivoque:—'But if you will be content to let the *escheator* alone, and not look into his actions, he will be contented by deceiving you to change his name, taking unto himself the two last syllables only, with the *es* left out, and so turn *cheater*.'

4 To *nip a bung*, in the cant of thievery, was to *cut a purse.* '*Bung* is now used for a *pocket*, heretofore for a *purse*.'—*Belman of London*, 1610. Doll means to call him *pick-pocket*. *Cuttle*, and *cuttle-bung*, were also cant terms for the knife used by cutpurses. These terms are therefore used by metonymy for a thief.

5 Laces, marks of his commission.

6 An expression of disdain.

7 There is a personage of the same stamp with Pistol in A Woman's a Weathercock, by Nat. Field, 1612 who is thus described:—

'Thou unspeakable rascal, thou a soldier!
That with thy slops and cat-a-mountain face,
Thy blather-chaps, and thy robustious words,
Fright'st the poor whore, and terribly dost exact
A weekly subsidy, twelve pence a piece,
Whereon thou livest; and on my conscience
Thou snap'st besides with cheats and cutpurses.'

'*Mouldy stewed prunes and dried cakes*' are put for the refuse of brothels.

8 This word had been perverted to an obscene meaning. An *occupant* was also a term for a woman of the town, and an *occupier* meant a *wencher*. Ben Jonson, in his Discoveries, says:—'Many, out of their own obscene apprehensions, refuse proper and fit words, as *occupy*, nature,' &c.

9 Traitors, rascals.

10 Shakspeare has put into the mouth of Pistol a tissue of absurd and fustian passages from many ridiculous old plays. Part of this speech is parodied from The Battle of Alcazar, 1594. *Have we not Hiren here*, is probably a line from a play of George Peele's, called The Turkish Mahomet and Hiren the fair Greek. It is often used ludicrously by subsequent dramatists. *Hiren*, from its resemblance to siren, was used for a seducing woman, and consequently for a courtesan. Pistol, in his rants, twice brings in the same words, but apparently meaning to give his sword the name of *Hiren*. Mrs. Quickly, with admirable simplicity, supposes him to ask for a woman.

11 This is a parody of the lines addressed by Tamberlane to the captive princes who draw his chariot, in Marlowe's Tamberlaine, 1590

12 A blunder for Hannibal

Bard. Be gone good ancient: this will grow to a brawl anon.

Pist. Die men, like dogs; give crowns like pins; Have we not Hiren here?

Host. O' my word, captain, there's none such here. What the good-year! do you think, I would deny her? for God's sake, be quiet.

Pist. Then feed and be fat, my fair Calipolis:[1]
Come, give's some sack.
Si fortuna me tormenta, sperato me contenta.[2]—
Fear we broadsides? no, let the fiend give fire:
Give me some sack;—and, sweetheart, lie thou there. [*Laying down his sword.*
Come we to full points here; and are *et ceteras* nothing?[3]

Fal. Pistol, I would be quiet.

Pist. Sweet knight, I kiss thy neif![4] What! we have seen the seven stars.

Dol. Thrust him down stairs; I cannot endure such a fustian rascal.

Pist. Thrust him down stairs! know we not Galloway nags?[5]

Fal. Quoit[6] him down, Bardolph, like a shove-groat shilling: nay, if he do nothing but speak nothing, he shall be nothing here.

Bard. Come, get you down stairs.

Pist. What! shall we have incision? shall we imbrue?—— [*Snatching up his sword.*
Then death rock me asleep, abridge my doleful days!
Why, then, let grievous, ghastly, gaping wounds
Untwine the sisters three! Come, Atropos, I say![7]

Host. Here's goodly stuff toward!

Fal. Give me my rapier, boy.

Dol. I pray thee, Jack, I pray thee, do not draw.

Fal. Get you down stairs.

[*Drawing, and driving* PISTOL *out.*

Host. Here's a goodly tumult! I'll forswear keeping house, afore I'll be in these tirrits and frights. So; murder, I warrant you.——Alas, alas! put up your naked weapons, put up your naked weapons.

[*Exeunt* PISTOL *and* BARDOLPH.

Dol. I pray thee, Jack, be quiet; the rascal is gone. Ah, you whoreson little valiant villain, you.

Host. Are you not hurt i'the groin? methought, he made a shrewd thrust at your belly.

Re-enter BARDOLPH.

Fal. Have you turned him out of doors?

Bard. Yes, sir. The rascal's drunk: you have hurt him, sir, in the shoulder.

Fal. A rascal! to brave me!

Dol. Ah, you sweet little rogue, you! Alas, poor ape, how thou sweat'st! Come, let me wipe thy face;—come on, you whoreson chops:—Ah, rogue! i'faith, I love thee. Thou art as valorous as Hector of Troy, worth five of Agamemnon, and ten times better than the nine worthies. Ah, villain!

Fal. A rascally slave! I will toss the rogue in a blanket.

Dol. Do, if thou darest for thy heart: if thou dost, I'll canvass thee between a pair of sheets.

Enter Music.

Page. The music is come, sir.

Fal. Let them play;—Play, sirs;—Sit on my knee, Doll. A rascally bragging slave! the rogue fled from me like quicksilver.

Dol. I'faith, and thou followedst him like a church. Thou whoreson little tidy Bartholomew boar-pig,[8] when wilt thou leave fighting o' days, and foining o' nights, and begin to patch up thine old body for heaven?

Enter behind PRINCE HENRY *and* POINS, *disguised like Drawers.*

Fal. Peace, good Doll! do not speak like a death's head: do not bid me remember mine end.

Dol. Sirrah, what humour is the prince of?

Fal. A good shallow young fellow: he would have made a good pantler, he would have chipped bread well.

Dol. They say, Poins has a good wit.

Fal. He a good wit? hang him, baboon! his wit is as thick as Tewksbury mustard; there is no more conceit in him, than in a mallet.

Dol. Why does the prince love him so then?

Fal. Because their legs are both of a bigness; and he plays at quoits well; and eats conger and fennel;[9] and drinks off candles' ends for flap-dragons:[10] and rides the wild mare with the boys;[11] and jumps upon joint-stools; and swears with a good grace; and wears his boot very smooth, like unto the sign of the leg: and breeds no bate with telling of discreet stories;[12] and such other gambol faculties he hath, that show a weak mind and an able body, for the which the prince admits him: for the prince himself is such another; the weight of a hair will turn the scales between their avoirdupois.

P. Hen. Would not this nave of a wheel[13] have his ears cut off?

Poins. Let's beat him before his whore.

P. Hen. Look, if the withered elder hath not his poll clawed like a parrot.

Poins. Is it not strange, that desire should so many years outlive performance?

Fal. Kiss me, Doll.

P. Hen. Saturn and Venus this year in conjunction![14] what says the almanack to that?

---

1 This is again a burlesque upon a line in The Battle of Alcazar, in which Muley Mahomet enters to his wife with lion's flesh on his sword:—
'Feed then and faint not, my faire Callypolis.'

2 Pistol is supposed to read this motto on his sword; by singular chance Mr. Douce picked up an old rapier with the same motto in French:—
Si fortuno me tourmento, l'esperance me contente.
A representation is given of it in his Illustrations, vol. i. p. 453.

3 That is, Shall we stop here, and have no further entertainment?

4 *Neif* is used by Shakspeare for *fist.* It is a north country word, to be found in Ray's Collection.

4 Common hackneys.

5 i. e. *pitch* him down. The *shove-groat shillings* were such broad shillings of King Edward VI. as Slender calls *Edward shovel-boards,* in The Merry Wives of Windsor, Act i. Sc. 1.

7 Pistol makes use of fragments of old ballads as well as old plays:—
'O death, rock me on slepe,
Bring me on quiet rest,'
is an ancient song, attributed to Anne Boleyn. There is another in the Gorgeous Gallery of Gallant Inventions, 1578, which has furnished him with some of his rhodomontade:—
'I hate this loathsome life,
O Atropos, draw nie
Untwist the thread of mortall strife,
Send death, and let me die.'

8 Doll says this in coaxing playful ridicule of Falstaff's enormous bulk. Roasted pigs were formerly among the chief attractions of Bartholomew fair; they were sold, piping hot, in booths and on stalls, and were ostentatiously displayed to excite the appetite of passengers. It was a common subject of allusion.

9 *Fennel* was generally esteemed an inflammatory herb, and therefore to eat *conger and fennel* was to eat two high and hot things together. *Fennel* was also regarded as an emblem of *flattery.*

10 The *flap-dragon* was some small combustible material swallowed alight in a glass of liquor: a *candle's end* formed a very formidable and disagreeable flap-dragon, and to swallow it was consequently among the gallants considered an act of merit, or of gallantry, when done in honour of the toper's mistress.

11 *Riding the wild mare* is another name for the childish sport of see-saw, or what the French call *bascule* and *balançoire.*

12 Mr Douce thinks Falstaff's meaning to be that Poins excites no censure by telling his companions *modest* stories, or, in plain English, that he tells them nothing but *immodest* ones.

13 Falstaff is humourously called *nave of a wheel,* from his rotundity of figure. The equivoque between *nave* and *knave* is obvious.

14 This was indeed a prodigy. The astrologers, says Ficinus, remark that *Saturn and Venus* are never conjoined.

Poins. And, look, whether the fiery Trigon,[1] his man, be not lisping to his master's old tables, his note-book, his counsel-keeper.

Fal. Thou dost give me flattering busses.

Dol. Nay, truly: I kiss thee with a most constant heart.

Fal. I am old, I am old.

Dol. I love thee better than I love e'er a scurvy young boy of them all.

Fal. What stuff wilt have a kirtle[2] of? I shall receive money on Thursday: thou shalt have a cap to-morrow. A merry song, come: it grows late, we'll to bed. Thou'lt forget me, when I am gone.

Dol. By my troth thou'lt set me a weeping, an thou sayest so: prove that ever I dress myself handsome till thy return.——Well, hearken the end.

Fal. Some sack, Francis.

P. Hen. Poins. Anon, anon, sir. [*Advancing.*

Fal. Ha! a bastard son of the king's?—And art not thou Poins his brother?

P. Hen. Why, thou globe of sinful continents, what a life dost thou lead?

Fal. A better than thou; I am a gentleman, thou art a drawer.

P. Hen. Very true, sir: and I come to draw you out by the ears.

Host. O, the Lord preserve thy good grace! by my troth, welcome to London.—Now the Lord bless that sweet face of thine! O Jesu, are you come from Wales?

Fal. Thou whoreson mad compound of majesty,—by this light flesh and corrupt blood, thou art welcome. [*Leaning his hand upon* DOLL.

Dol. How! you fat fool, I scorn you.

Poins. My lord, he will drive you out of your revenge, and turn all to a merriment, if you take not the heat.

P. Hen. You whoreson candle-mine, you, how vilely did you speak of me even now, before this honest, virtuous, civil gentlewoman?

Host. 'Blessing o' your good heart! and so she is, by my troth.

Fal. Didst thou hear me?

P. Hen. Yes; and you knew me, as you did when you ran away by Gads-hill: you knew, I was at your back; and spoke it on purpose, to try my patience.

Fal. No, no, no; not so; I did not think thou wast within hearing.

P. Hen. I shall drive thee then to confess the wilful abuse; and then I know how to handle you.

Fal. No abuse, Hal, on mine honour; no abuse.

P. Hen. Not! to dispraise me; and call me—pantler, and bread-chipper, and I know not what?

Fal. No abuse, Hal.

Poins. No abuse!

Fal. No abuse, Ned, in the world; honest Ned, none. I dispraised him before the wicked, that the wicked might not fall in love with him:—in which doing, I have done the part of a careful friend, and a true subject, and thy father is to give me thanks for it. No abuse, Hal;—none, Ned, none;—no, boys, none.

P. Hen. See now, whether pure fear, and entire cowardice, doth not make thee wrong this virtuous gentlewoman to close with us? Is she of the wicked? Is thine hostess here of the wicked? Or is the boy of the wicked? Or honest Bardolph, whose zeal burns in his nose, of the wicked?

Poins. Answer, thou dead elm, answer.

Fal. The fiend hath pricked down Bardolph irrecoverable; and his face is Lucifer's privy-kitchen, where he doth nothing but roast malt-worms. For the boy,—there is a good angel about him; but the devil outbids him too.[3]

P. Hen. For the women,——

Fal. For one of them,—she is in hell already, and burns, poor soul! For the other,—I owe her money; and whether she be damned for that, I know not.

Host. No, I warrant you.

Fal. No, I think thou art not; I think, thou art quit for that: Marry, there is another indictment upon thee, for suffering flesh to be eaten in thy house, contrary to the law;[4] for the which, I think, thou wilt howl.

Host. All victuallers do so: What's a joint of mutton or two in a whole Lent?

P. Hen. You, gentlewoman,——

Dol. What says your grace?

Fal. His grace says that which his flesh rebels against.

Host. Who knocks so loud at door? look to the door there, Francis.

Enter PETO.

P. Hen. Peto, how now? what news

Peto. The king your father is at Westminster:
And there are twenty weak and wearied posts,
Come from the north: and, as I came along,
I met, and overtook, a dozen captains,
Bare-headed, sweating, knocking at the taverns,
And asking every one for Sir John Falstaff.

P. Hen. By heaven, Poins, I feel me much to blame,
So idly to profane the precious time;
When tempest of commotion, like the south
Borne with black vapour, doth begin to melt,
And drop upon our bare unarmed heads.
Give me my sword, and cloak:—Falstaff, good night.

[*Exeunt* PRINCE HENRY, POINS, PETO, *and* BARDOLPH.

Fal. Now comes in the sweetest morsel of the night, and we must hence, and leave it unpick'd. [*Knocking heard.*] More knocking at the door?

Re-enter BARDOLPH.

How now? what's the matter?

Bard. You must away to court, sir, presently; a dozen captains stay at door for you.

Fal. Pay the musicians, sirrah. [*To the* Page.]—Farewell, hostess;—farewell, Doll.—You see, my good wenches, how men of merit are sought after: the undeserver may sleep, when the man of action is called on. Farewell, good wenches: If I be not sent away post, I will see you again ere I go.

Dol. I cannot speak;—if my heart be not ready to burst;—Well, sweet Jack, have a care of thyself.

Fal. Farewell, farewell.

[*Exeunt* FALSTAFF *and* BARDOLPH.

Host. Well, fare thee well: I have known thee these twenty-nine years, come peascod-time; but an honester, and truer-hearted man,—Well, fare thee well.

Bard. [*Within.*] Mistress Tear-sheet,——

Host. What's the matter?

Bard. [*Within.*] Bid mistress Tear-sheet come to my master.

Host. O run, Doll, run; run, good Doll.

[*Exeunt.*

ACT III.

SCENE I. *A Room in the Palace. Enter* KING HENRY *in his Nightgown, with a* Page.

K. Hen. Go, call the earls of Surrey and of Warwick;
But ere they come, bid them o'er-read these letters,

1 *Trigon* or triangle, a term in the old judicial astrology. They called it a *fiery trigon* when the three upper planets met in a fiery sign; which was thought to denote rage and contention.

2 Few words, as Mr. Gifford observes, have occasioned such controversy among the commentators as *kirtle.* These familiar terms frequently are the most baffling to the antiquary, for being in general use they were clearly understood by our ancestors, and are not therefore accurately defined in the dictionaries. A *kirtle* was undoubtedly *a petticoat*, which sometimes had a body without sleeves attached to it.

3 The quarto reads 'and the devil *blinds* him too.'

4 Baret defines, a '*victualling house*, a tavern where

And well consider of them: Make good speed.——
[*Exit* Page.
How many thousand of my poorest subjects
Are at this hour asleep!—O sleep, O gentle sleep,
Nature's soft nurse, how have I frighted thee,
That thou no more wilt weigh my eyelids down,
And steep my senses in forgetfulness?
Why rather, sleep, liest thou in smoky cribs,
Upon uneasy pallets stretching thee,
And hush'd with buzzing night-flies to thy slumber;
Than in the perfum'd chambers of the great,
Under the canopies of costly state,
And lull'd with sounds of sweetest melody?
O thou dull god, why liest thou with the vile,
In loathsome beds; and leav'st the kingly couch,
A watch-case,[1] or a common 'larum bell?
Wilt thou upon the high and giddy mast
Seal up the ship-boy's eyes, and rock his brains
In cradle of the rude imperious surge;
And in the visitation of the winds,
Who take the ruffian billows by the top,
Curling their monstrous heads, and hanging them
With deaf'ning clamours in the slippery clouds,[2]
That, with the hurly,[3] death itself awakes?
Canst thou, O partial sleep! give thy repose
To the wet sea-boy in an hour so rude;
And, in the calmest and most stillest night,
With all appliances and means to boot,
Deny it to a king? Then, happy low,[4] lie down!
Uneasy lies the head that wears a crown.

Enter WARWICK *and* SURREY.

War. Many good morrows to your majesty!
K. Hen. Is it good morrow, lords?
War. 'Tis one o'clock, and past.
K. Hen. Why then, good morrow[5] to you all, my lords,
Have you read o'er the letters that I sent you?
War. We have, my liege.
K. Hen. Then you perceive, the body of our kingdom
How foul it is; what rank diseases grow,
And with what danger, near the heart of it.
War. It is but as a body, yet, distemper'd.[6]
Which to his former strength may be restor'd,
With good advice, and little medicine:——
My Lord Northumberland will soon be cool'd.
K. Hen. O heaven! that one might read the book of fate;
And see the revolution of the times
Make mountains level, and the continent
(Weary of solid firmness) melt itself
Into the sea! and, other times, to see
The beachy girdle of the ocean
Too wide for Neptune's hips;[7] how chances mock,
And changes fill the cup of alteration
With divers liquors! O, if this were seen,[8]
The happiest youth,—viewing his progress through,
What perils past, what crosses to ensue,—
Would shut the book, and sit him down and die.
'Tis not ten years gone,
Since Richard, and Northumberland, great friends,
Did feast together, and, in two years after,
Were they at wars: It is but eight years since
This Percy was the man nearest my soul;
Who like a brother toil'd in my affairs,
And laid his love and life under my foot;
Yea, for my sake, even to the eyes of Richard,
Gave him defiance. But which of you was by,[9]
(You, cousin Nevil,[10] as I may remember,)
[*To* WARWICK.
When Richard,—with his eyes brimfull of tears,
Then check'd and rated by Northumberland,—
Did speak these words, now prov'd a prophecy?
Northumberland, thou ladder, by the which
My cousin Bolingbroke ascends my throne;—
Though then, heaven knows, I had no such intent;
But that necessity so bow'd the state,
That I and greatness were compell'd to kiss:——
The time shall come, thus did he follow it,
The time will come, that foul sin, gathering head,
Shall break into corruption:—so went on,
Foretelling this same time's condition,
And the division of our amity.
War. There is a history in all men's lives,
Figuring the nature of the time's deceas'd:
The which observ'd, a man may prophesy,
With a near aim, of the main chance of things
As yet not come to life; which in their seeds,
And weak beginnings, lie intreasured.
Such things become the hatch and brood of time;
And, by the necessary form of this,
King Richard might create a perfect guess,
That great Northumberland, then false to him,
Would, of that seed, grow to a greater falseness;
Which should not find a ground to root upon,
Unless on you.
K. Hen. Are these things then necessities
Then let us meet them like necessities:—
And that same word even now cries out on us;
They say, the bishop and Northumberland
Are fifty thousand strong.
War. It cannot be, my lord
Rumour doth double, like the voice and echo,
The numbers of the fear'd;—Please it your grace
To go to bed; upon my life, my lord,
The powers that you already have sent forth,
Shall bring this prize in very easily.
To comfort you the more, I have receiv'd
A certain instance, that Glendower is dead.[11]
Your majesty hath been this fortnight ill;

---

meate is eaten *out of due season.*' By several statutes made in the reigns of Queen Elizabeth and King James I. for the regulation and observance of fish days, victuallers were expressly forbidden to utter *flesh in Lent.* The brothels were formerly screened under the pretence of being victualling-houses and taverns.

1 A *watch case* here may mean the case of a watch-light; but the following article, cited by Strutt in his Manners and Customs. vol. iii. p. 70, from an old inventory, may throw some light upon it:—'Item, a laume (*larum*) or *watche* of iron, *in an iron case*, with two leaden plumets.'

2 Some of the officious modern editors altered *clouds* to *shrowds*, meaning the rope ladders of a ship, thus marring the poet's noble image. Steevens judiciously opposed himself to this alteration, but was wrong in asserting that '*shrowds* had anciently the same meaning as *clouds*.' *Shrowdes* were *covertures, hiding places* of any kind, aerial or otherwise. This will be found the meaning of the word in all the passages cited by Steevens. That *clouds* was the poet's word there can be no doubt.

3 *Hurly* is a *noise* or *tumult*. As hurly-burly in the first scene of Macbeth. See note there.

4 Warburton's conjecture, that this is a corrupt reading for *happy lowly clown*, deserves attention

5 This mode of phraseology, where only two persons are addressed, is not very correct; but Shakspeare has used it again in King Henry VI. Part 2. where York addresses his two friends Salisbury and Warwick.

6 *Distempered* means *disordered, sick*; being only in that state which foreruns or produces diseases.

7 'When I have seen the hungry ocean gain
Advantage on the kingdom of the shore,
And the firm soil win of the wat'ry main,
Increasing store with loss, and loss with store,
When I have seen such interchange of state,' &c.
Shakspeare's sixty-fourth Sonnet

8 This and the three following lines are from the quarto copy. Johnson having misunderstood the line:—
'What perils past, what crosses to ensue;'
it may be necessary to remark that the perils are spoken of prospectively, as seen by the youth in the book of fate. The construction is, 'What perils *having been* past, what crosses *are* to ensue.'

9 The reference is to King Richard II. Act iv. Sc. 2: but neither Warwick nor the king were present at that conversation. Henry had then ascended the throne; either the king's or the poet's memory failed him.

10 The earldom of Warwick was at this time in the family of *Beauchamp*, and did not come into that of the *Nevils* till many years after: when Anne, the daughter of this earl, married *Richard Nevil*, son of the earl of Salisbury, who makes a conspicuous figure in the Third Part of King Henry VI. under the title of *Earl of Warwick*.

11 Glendower did not die till after King Henry IV Shakspeare was led into this error by Holinshed. Vide note on the First Part of King Henry IV. Act iii. Sc. 1.

And these unseason'd hours, perforce, must add
Unto your sickness.

K. Hen. I will take your counsel:
And, were these inward wars once out of hand,
We would, dear lords, unto the Holy Land.

[*Exeunt.*

SCENE II. *Court before Justice* Shallow's *House in* Gloucestershire. *Enter* SHALLOW *and* SILENCE, *meeting;* MOULDY, SHADOW, WART, FEEBLE, BULL-CALF, *and Servants, behind.*

Shal. Come on, come on, come on; give me your hand, sir, give me your hand, sir: an early stirrer, by the rood.[1] And how doth my good cousin Silence?

Sil. Good morrow, good cousin Shallow.

Shal. And how doth my cousin, your bedfellow? and your fairest daughter, and mine, my god-daughter Ellen?

Sil. Alas, a black ouzel, cousin Shallow.

Shal. By yea and nay, sir, I dare say, my cousin William is become a good scholar: He is at Oxford, still, is he not?

Sil. Indeed, sir; to my cost.

Shal. He must then to the inns of court shortly: I was once of Clement's inn, where, I think, they will talk of mad Shallow yet.

Sil. You were called—lusty Shallow, then, cousin.

Shal. By the mass, I was called any thing; and I would have done any thing, indeed, and roundly too. There was I, and little John Doit of Staffordshire, and black George Bare, and Francis Pickbone, and Will Squele a Cotswold man,[2]—you had not four such swinge-bucklers[3] in all the inns of court again: and, I may say to you, we knew where the bona-robas[4] were; and had the best of them all at commandment. Then was Jack Falstaff, now Sir John, a boy: and page to Thomas Mowbray, duke of Norfolk.

Sil. This Sir John, cousin, that comes hither anon about soldiers?

Shal. The same Sir John, the very same. I saw him break Skogan's[5] head at the court gate, when he was a crack,[6] not thus high: and the very same day did I fight with one Sampson Stockfish, a fruiterer, behind Gray's Inn. O, the mad days that I have spent! and to see how many of mine old acquaintance are dead!

Sil. We shall all follow, cousin.

Shal. Certain, 'tis certain; very sure, very sure: death, as the Psalmist saith, is certain to all: all shall die. How a good yoke of bullocks at Stamford fair?

Sil. Truly, cousin, I was not there.

Shal. Death is certain.—Is old Double of your town living yet?

Sil. Dead, sir.

Shal. Dead!—See, see!—he drew a good bow;—And dead!—he shot a fine shoot:—John of Gaunt loved him well, and betted much money on his head. Dead!—he would have clapped i'the clout at twelve score;[7] and carried you a forehand shaft a fourteen and fourteen and a half, that it would have done a man's heart good to see.——How a score of ewes now?

Sil. Thereafter as they be: a score of good ewes may be worth ten pounds.

Shal. And is old Double dead!

Enter BARDOLPH, *and one with him.*

Sil. Here come two of Sir John Falstaff's men, as I think.

Bard. Good morrow, honest gentlemen: I beseech you, which is Justice Shallow?

Shal. I am Robert Shallow, sir; a poor esquire of this county, and one of the king's justices of the peace: What is your good pleasure with me?

Bard. My captain, sir, commends him to you; my captain, Sir John Falstaff; a tall gentleman, by heaven, and a most gallant leader.

Shal. He greets me well, sir; I knew him a good backsword-man: How doth the good knight? may I ask, how my lady his wife doth?

Bard. Sir, pardon; a soldier is better accommodated, than with a wife.

Shal. It is well said, in faith, sir; and it is well said indeed too. Better accommodated!—it is good: yea, indeed, it is: good phrases are surely, and ever were, very commendable. Accommodated!—it comes from *accommodo:* very good; a good phrase.[8]

Bard. Pardon me, sir; I have heard the word. Phrase, call you it? By this good day, I know not the phrase; but I will maintain the word with my sword, to be a soldierlike word, and a word of exceeding good command. Accommodated: That is, when a man is, as they say, accommodated; or when a man is,—being,—whereby,—he may be thought to be accommodated; which is an excellent thing.

Enter FALSTAFF.

Shal. It is very just:—Look, here comes good Sir John.—Give me your good hand, give me your worship's good hand: By my troth, you look well, and bear your years very well: welcome, good Sir John.

Fal. I am glad to see you well, good master Robert Shallow:—Master Sure-card, as I think.

Shal. No, Sir John; it is my cousin Silence, in commission with me.

Fal. Good master Silence, it well befits you should be of the peace.

Sil. Your good worship is welcome.

Fal. Fye! this is hot weather.—Gentlemen, have you provided me here half a dozen sufficient men?

Shal. Marry, have we, sir. Will you sit?

Fal. Let me see them, I beseech you.

Shal. Where's the roll? where's the roll? where's the roll?—Let me see, let me see. So, so, so, so: Yea, marry, sir:—Ralph Mouldy:—let them appear as I call; let them do so, let them do so.——Let me see; Where is Mouldy?

---

1 The *rood* is the *cross* or *crucifix.* *Rode,* Sax.

2 The Cotswold Hills in Gloucestershire were famous for rural sports of all kinds; by distinguishing Will Squele as a Cotswold man, Shallow meant to have it understood that he was well versed in manly exercises, and consequently of a daring spirit and athletic constitution.

3 *Swinge-bucklers* and *swash-bucklers* were terms implying *rakes* and *rioters* in the time of Shakspeare. See a note on sword and buckler men in the First Part of King Henry IV. Act i. Sc. 3.

4 '*Buona-roba* as we say, good stuff; a good wholesome plump-cheeked wench.' *Florio.*

5 There has been a doughty dispute between Messieurs Ritson and Malone whether there were two Scogans, *Henry* and *John,* or only one. Shakspeare probably got his idea of Scogan from his jests, which were published by Andrew Borde in the reign of King Henry VIII. Holinshed, speaking of the distinguished persons of King Edward the Fourth's time, mentions '*Scogan,* a learned gentleman, and student for a time in Oxford, of a pleasaunte witte, and bent to mery devises, in respecte whereof he was called into the courte, where giving himself to his natural inclination of mirthe and pleasaunt pastime, he plaied many sporting parts, althoughe not in such uncivil manner as hath bene of hym reported.' The uncivil reports have relation to the above jests. Ben Jonson introduces Scogan with Skelton in his Masque of The Fortunate Isles, and describes him thus:—

'—— *Skogan,* what was he?
O, a fine gentleman, and master of arts
Of Henry the Fourth's time, that made disguises
For the king's sons, and writ in ballad royal
Daintily well.——
In rhyme, fine tinkling rhyme, and flowing verse,
With now and then some sense! and he was paid for't,
Regarded, and rewarded; which few poets
Are nowadays.'

6 A *crack* is a *boy.*

7 Hit the white mark at twelve score yards. By the statute 33 Hen. VIII. c. 9, every person turned of seventeen years of age, who shoots at a less distance than twelve score, is to forfeit six shillings and eight pence.

8 It appears that it was fashionable in the poet's time to introduce this word *accommodate* upon all occasions. Ben Jonson, in his Discoveries, calls it one of the perfumed terms of the time. The indefinite use of it is well ridiculed by Bardolph's vain attempt to define it

Moul. Here, an't please you.

Shal. What think you, Sir John? a good limbed fellow: young, strong, and of good friends.

Fal. Is thy name Mouldy?

Moul. Yea, an't please you.

Fal. 'Tis the more time thou wert used.

Shal. Ha, ha, ha! most excellent, i'faith! things, that are mouldy, lack use: Very singular good!—In faith, well said, Sir John; very well said.

Fal. Prick him. [*To* SHALLOW.

Moul. I was pricked well enough before, an you could have let me alone: my old dame will be undone now, for one to do her husbandry, and her drudgery: you need not to have pricked me; there are other men fitter to go out than I.

Fal. Go to; peace, Mouldy, you shall go, Mouldy, it is time you were spent.

Moul. Spent!

Shal. Peace, fellow, peace; stand aside; Know you where you are?—For the other, Sir John:—let me see;—Simon Shadow!

Fal. Ay marry, let me have him to sit under: he's like to be a cold soldier.

Shal. Where's Shadow?

Shad. Here, sir.

Fal. Shadow, whose son art thou?

Shad. My mother's son, sir?

Fal. Thy mother's son! like enough; and thy father's shadow: so the son of the female is the shadow of the male: It is often so, indeed; but not much of the father's substance.

Shal. Do you like him, Sir John?

Fal. Shadow will serve for summer,—prick him;—for we have a number of shadows to fill up the muster book.

Shal. Thomas Wart!

Fal. Where's he?

Wart. Here, sir.

Fal. Is thy name Wart?

Wart. Yea, sir.

Fal. Thou art a very ragged wart.

Shal. Shall I prick him, Sir John?

Fal. It were superfluous; for his apparel is built upon his back, and the whole frame stands upon pins: prick him no more.

Shal. Ha, ha, ha!—you can do it, sir; you can do it: I commend you well.—Francis Feeble!

Fee. Here, sir.

Fal. What trade art thou, Feeble?

Fee. A woman's tailor, sir.

Shal. Shall I prick him ,sir?

Fal. You may: but if he had been a man's tailor, he would have pricked you.—Wilt thou make as many holes in an enemy's battle, as thou hast done in a woman's petticoat?

Fee. I will do my good will, sir; you can have no more.

Fal. Well said, good woman's tailor! well said, courageous Feeble! Thou wilt be as valiant as the wrathful dove, or most magnanimous mouse.—Prick the woman's tailor well, master Shallow; deep, master Shallow.

Fee. I would, Wart might have gone, sir.

Fal. I would, thou wert a man's tailor; that thou might'st mend him, and make him fit to go. I cannot put him to a private soldier, that is the leader of so many thousands: Let that suffice, most forcible Feeble.

Fee. It shall suffice, sir.

Fal. I am bound to thee, reverend Feeble.—Who is next?

Shal. Peter Bull-calf of the green!

Fal. Yea, marry, let us see Bull-calf.

Bull. Here, sir.

Fal. 'Fore God, a likely fellow!—Come, prick me Bull-calf till he roar again.

Bull. O lord! good my lord captain,—

Fal. What, dost thou roar before thou art pricked?

Bull. O lord, sir! I am a diseased man.

Fal. What disease hast thou?

Bull. A whoreson cold, sir; a cough, sir; which I caught with ringing in the king's affairs, upon his coronation-day, sir.

Fal. Come, thou shalt go to the wars in a gown; we will have away thy cold; and I will take such order, that thy friends shall ring for thee.—Is here all?

Shal. Here is two[1] more called than your number; you must have but four here, sir;—and so, I pray you, go in with me to dinner.

Fal. Come, I will go drink with you, but I cannot tarry dinner. I am glad to see you, in good troth, master Shallow.

Shal. O, Sir John, do you remember since we lay all night in the windmill in Saint George's Fields.

Fal. No more of that, good master Shallow, no more of that.

Shal. Ha, it was a merry night. And is Jane Night-work alive?

Fal. She lives, master Shallow.

Shal. She never could away with me.[2]

Fal. Never, never: she would always say, she could not abide master Shallow.

Shal. By the mass, I could anger her to the heart. She was then a bona-roba. Doth she hold her own well?

Fal. Old, old, master Shallow.

Shal. Nay, she must be old; she cannot choose but be old; certain, she's old; and had Robin Night-work by old Night-work, before I came to Clement's Inn.

Sil. That's fifty-five years ago.

Shal. Ha, cousin Silence, that thou hadst seen that that this knight and I have seen!—Ha, Sir John, said I well?

Fal. We have heard the chimes at midnight, master Shallow.

Shal. That we have, that we have, that we have; in faith, Sir John, we have; our watch-word was, *Hem, boys!*—Come, let's to dinner; come, let's to dinner:—O, the days that we have seen!—Come, come. [*Exeunt* FAL. SHAL. *and* SILENCE.

Bull. Good master corporate Bardolph, stand my friend; and here is four Harry ten shillings[3] in French crowns for you. In very truth, sir, I had as lief be hanged, sir, as go: and yet, for mine own part, sir, I do not care; but rather, because I am unwilling, and, for mine own part, have a desire to stay with my friends; else, sir, I did not care, for mine own part, so much.

Bard. Go to; stand aside.

Moul. And, good master corporal captain, for my old dame's sake, stand my friend: she has nobody to do any thing about her, when I am gone: and she is old, and cannot help herself: you shall have forty, sir.

Bard. Go to; stand aside.

Fee. By my troth, I care not;—a man can die but once;—we owe God a death,—I'll ne'er bear a base mind:—an't be my destiny, so; an't be not, so: No man's too good to serve his prince; and let it go which way it will, he that dies this year is quit for the next.

Bard. Well said; thou'rt a good fellow.

Fee. 'Faith, I'll bear no base mind.

Re-enter FALSTAFF, *and* Justices.

Fal. Come, sir, which men shall I have?

---

1 There is in fact but *one* more called than Falstaff required, perhaps we might with Mr. Capel omit the word *two*.

2 This was a common expression of dislike; which is even used at a later period by Locke in his Conduct of the Understanding. It is of some antiquity also; for I find it frequently in Horman's Vulgaria, 1519: 'He *cannot away* to marry Thetis, or to lie with her: Thetidis connubia vitat. I *cannot away* to be guilty of dissembling: Non sustineo esse conscius mihi dissimulanti.'

3 There were no coins of ten shillings value in Henry the Fourth's time. Shakspeare's *Harry ten shillings* were those of Henry VII. or VIII. He thought that these might do for any other Henry.

Shal. Four, of which you please.

Bard. Sir, a word with you:—I have three pound[1] to free Mouldy and Bull-calf.

Fal. Go to; well.

Shal. Come, Sir John, which four will you have?

Fal. Do you choose for me.

Shal. Marry then, Mouldy, Bull-calf, Feeble, and Shadow

Fal. Mouldy, and Bull-calf:—For you, Mouldy, stay at home till you are past service:—and, for your part, Bull-calf,—grow till you come unto it; I will none of you.

Shal. Sir John, Sir John, do not yourself wrong: they are your likeliest men, and I would have you served with the best.

Fal. Will you tell me, master Shallow, how to choose a man? Care I for the limb, the thewes,[2] the stature, bulk, and big assemblance of a man! Give me the spirit, master Shallow.—Here's Wart;—you see what a ragged appearance it is: he shall charge you, and discharge you, with the motion of a pewterer's hammer; come off, and on, swifter than he that gibbets-on the brewer's bucket. And this same half-fac'd fellow, Shadow,—give me this man; he presents no mark to the enemy: the foeman may with as great aim level at the edge of a penknife: And, for a retreat,—how swiftly will this Feeble, the woman's tailor, run off? O, give me the spare men, and spare me the great ones.—Put me a caliver[3] into Wart's hand, Bardolph.

Bard. Hold, Wart, traverse:[4] thus, thus, thus.

Fal. Come, manage me your caliver. So:—very well:—go to:—very good:—exceeding good.—O, give me always a little, lean, old, chapped, bald shot.[5]—Well said, i' faith Wart; thou'rt a good scab: hold, there's a tester for thee.

Shal. He is not his craft's-master, he doth not do it right. I remember at Mile-end green[6] (when I lay at Clement's Inn,—I was then Sir Dagonet in Arthur's show,)[7] there was a little quiver[8] fellow, and 'a would manage you his piece thus: and 'a would about, and about, and come you in, and come you in: *rah, tah, tah*, would 'a say; *bounce*, would 'a say; and away again would 'a go, and again would 'a come:—I shall never see such a fellow.

Fal. These fellows will do well, master Shallow—God keep you, master Silence; I will not use many words with you:—Fare you well, gentlemen both: I thank you: I must a dozen mile to-night.—Bardolph, give the soldiers coats.

Shal. Sir John, heaven bless you, and prosper your affairs, and send us peace! As you return, visit my house; let our old acquaintance be renewed: peradventure, I will with you to the court.

Fal. I would you would, master Shallow.

Shal. Go to; I have spoke, at a word. Fare you well. [*Exeunt* SHALLOW *and* SILENCE.

Fal. Fare you well, gentle gentlemen. On, Bardolph; lead the men away. [*Exeunt* BARDOLPH, Recruits, *&c.*] As I return, I will fetch off these justices: I do see the bottom of Justice Shallow. Lord, lord, how subject we old men are to this vice of lying! This same starved justice hath done nothing but prate to me of the wildness of his youth, and the feats he had done about Turnbull Street![9] and every third word a lie, duer paid to the hearer than the Turk's tribute. I do remember him at Clement's Inn, like a man made after supper of a cheese-paring: when he was naked, he was, for all the world like a forked radish, with a head fantastically carved upon it with a knife: he was so forlorn, that his dimensions to any thick sight were invincible:[10] he was the very Genius of famine; yet lecherous as a monkey, and the whores called him mandrake:[11] he came ever in the rear-ward of the fashion; and sung those tunes to the over-scutched[12] huswives that he heard the carmen whistle, and swear—they were his fancies, or his good-nights.[13] And now is this Vice's dagger[14] become a squire; and talks as familiarly of John of Gaunt, as if he had been sworn brother to him: and I'll be sworn he never saw him but once in the Tilt-yard; and then he burst[15] his head, for crowding among the marshal's men. I saw it; and told John of Gaunt, he beat his own name;[16] for you might have truss'd him, and all his apparel, into an eel skin; the case of a treble haut-boy was a mansion for him, a court; and now has he land and beeves Well; I will be acquainted with him, if I return: and it shall go hard, but I will make him a philosopher's two stones[17] to me: If the young dace be

---

1 Bardolph was to have *four* pound: perhaps he means to conceal part of his profit.

2 Shakspeare uses *thewes* in a sense almost peculiar to himself, for *muscular strength* or *sinews*.

3 A *caliver* was less and lighter than a musket; and was fired without a rest. Falstaff's meaning is that though Wart is unfit for a musqueteer, yet, if armed with a lighter piece, he may do good service.

4 *Traverse* was an ancient military term for *march!*

5 *Shot*, for *shooter*.

6 *Mile End Green* was the place for public sports and exercises. Stowe mentions that, in 1585, 4000 citizens were trained and exercised there. And again, that 30,000 citizens *shewed* on the 27th August, 1599, on the *Miles-end*; where they *trained* all that day and other dayes under their captaines (also citizens) until the 4th of September. The pupils of this military school were thought but slightly of. Shakspeare has already referred to *Mile End* and its military exercises rather contemptuously in All's Well that Ends Well, Act iv. Sc. 3.

7 *Arthur's show* was not, as some have supposed, a *masque or pageant*, in which an exact representation of Arthur and his knights was made, but an exhibition of Toxopholites, styling themselves 'The Auncient Order, Society, and Unitie laudable of Prince Arthure and his Knightly Armory of the Round Table.' The associates of which were fifty-eight in number, taking the names of the knights in the romantic history of that chivalric worthy. According to their historian and poet, Richard Robinson, this Society was established by charter under King Henry the Eighth, who, 'when he [illegible] good archer indeede, he chose him and ordain-[illegible] a knight of this order.' Robinson's [illegible] in 1583, and in a MS. list of his own [illegible], now in the British Museum, he says, 'Mr. Thomas Smith her majestie's customer, representing [illegible] Prince Arthure, gave me for his booke vs. His 58 knightes [illegible] every one for his xviijd. and every [illegible] for his booke viijd. when they shott under the same [illegible] Arthure at *Myles end green*.' Shakspeare has admirably heightened the ridicule of Shallow's vanity and folly, by making him boast in this parenthesis that he was *Sir Dagonet*, who, though one of the knights, is also represented in the romance as King Arthur's *fool* This society is also noticed by Richard Mulcaster (who was a member) in his book Concerning the Training up of Children, 1581, in a passage communicated to Malone by the Rev. Mr. Bowle.

8 *Quiver* is *nimble, active*.

9 *Turnbull-street*, or *Turnball-street*, is a corruption of *Turnmill-street*, near Clerkenwell; anciently the resort of bullies, rogues, and other dissolute persons The reader will remember its vicinity to *Ruffians' Hall*, now Smithfield Market. Pickt Hatch, a celebrated brothelry, is supposed to have been situate in or near Turnbull-street.

10 Steevens has adopted Rowe's alteration of this word *invincible* to *invisible*, without necessity. The word is metaphorically used for *not to be mastered* or *taken in*

11 See Sir Thomas Brown's Vulgar Errors, 1686, p 72; and note on Act i. Sc. 2, of this play.

12 i. e. *whipped*, *carted*, says Pope; and notwithstanding Johnson's doubts, Pope is right. A *scutcher* was a whip or riding rod, according to *Cotgrave*. And for a further illustration of this passage the reader, curious in such matters, may turn to Torriano's Italian Dictionary, 1659, in v. Trentuno.

13 Titles of little poems.

14 For some account of the *Vice* and his *dagger of lath* the reader may see Twelfth Night, Act iv. Sc. 2 There is something excessively ludicrous in the comparison of Shallow to this powerless weapon of that droll personage the Old Vice or fool.

15 *Burst*, *brast* and *broken*, were formerly synonymous; as may be seen under the words *break* and *broken*, in Baret.

16 *Gaunt* is thin, slender.

17 This is only a humorous exaggerative way of expressing 'He shall be more than the philosopher's stone to me, or *twice* as good. I will make gold out of him.'

a bait for the old pike, I see no reason, in the law of nature, but I may snap at him. Let time shape, and there an end. [*Exit.*

ACT IV.

SCENE I. *A Forest in* Yorkshire. *Enter the* Archbishop *of* York, MOWBRAY, HASTINGS, *and others.*

Arch. What is this forest called?
Hast. 'Tis Gualtree forest, an't shall please your grace.
Arch. Here stand, my lords; and send discoveries forth,
To know the numbers of our enemies.
Hast. We have sent forth already.
Arch. 'Tis well done.
My friends, and brethren in these great affairs,
I must acquaint you that I have receiv'd
New-dated letters from Northumberland;
Their cold intent, tenour, and substance, thus:—
Here doth he wish his person, with such powers
As might hold sortance[1] with his quality,
The which he could not levy; whereupon
He is retir'd, to ripe his growing fortunes,
To Scotland: and concludes in hearty prayers,
That your attempts may overlive the hazard,
And fearful meeting of their opposite.
Mowb. Thus do the hopes we have in him touch ground,
And dash themselves to pieces.

Enter a Messenger.

Hast. Now, what news?
Mess. West of this forest, scarcely off a mile,
In goodly form comes on the enemy:
And, by the ground they hide, I judge their number
Upon, or near, the rate of thirty thousand.
Mowb. The just proportion that we gave them out.
Let us sway[2] on, and face them in the field.

Enter WESTMORELAND.

Arch. What well-appointed[3] leader fronts us here?
Mowb. I think, it is my lord of Westmoreland.
West. Health and fair greeting from our general,
The prince, Lord John and duke of Lancaster.
Arch. Say on, my lord of Westmoreland, in peace;
What doth concern your coming?
West. Then, my lord,
Unto your grace do I in chief address
The substance of my speech. If that rebellion
Came like itself, in base and abject routs,
Led on by bloody[4] youth, guarded[5] with rage,
And countenanc'd by boys, and beggary;
I say, if damn'd commotion so appear'd
In his true, native, and most proper shape,
You, reverend father, and these noble lords
Had not been here, to dress the ugly form
Of base and bloody insurrection
With your fair honours. You, lord archbishop,—
Whose see is by a civil peace maintain'd;
Whose beard the silver hand of peace hath touch'd;
Whose learning and good letters peace hath tutor'd,
Whose white investments[6] figure innocence,
The dove and very blessed spirit of peace,—
Wherefore do you so ill translate yourself,
Out of the speech of peace, that bears such grace,
Into the harsh and boist'rous tongue of war?
Turning your books to graves,[7] your ink to blood,
Your pens to lances; and your tongue divine
To a loud trumpet, and a point of war?
Arch. Wherefore do I this?—so the question stands.
Briefly to this end:—We are all diseas'd;
And, with our surfeiting, and wanton hours,
Have brought ourselves into a burning fever,
And we must bleed for it: of which disease
Our late king, Richard, being infected, died.
But, my most noble lord of Westmoreland,
I take not on me here as a physician;
Nor do I, as an enemy to peace,
Troop in the throngs of military men:
But, rather, show a while like fearful war,
To diet rank minds, sick of happiness;
And purge the obstructions, which begin to stop
Our very veins of life. Hear me more plainly.
I have in equal balance justly weigh'd
What wrongs our arms may do, what wrongs we suffer.
And find our griefs[8] heavier than our offences.
We see which way the stream of time doth run,
And are enforc'd from our most quiet sphere[9]
By the rough torrent of occasion:
And have the summary of all our griefs,
When time shall serve, to show in articles,
Which, long ere this, we offer'd to the king,
And might by no suit gain our audience:
When we are wrong'd, and would unfold our griefs
We are denied access unto his person[10]
Even by those men that most have done us wrong
The dangers of the days but newly gone,
(Whose memory is written on the earth
With yet-appearing blood,) and the examples
Of every minute's instance[11] (present now,)
Have put us in these ill-beseeming arms:
Not to break peace, or any branch of it;
But to establish here a peace indeed,
Concurring both in name and quality.
West. When ever yet was your appeal denied?
Wherein have you been galled by the king?
What peer hath been suborn'd to grate on you?
That you should seal this lawless bloody book,
Of forg'd rebellion with a seal divine,
And consecrate commotion's bitter edge?[12]
Arch. My brother general, the commonwealth,
To brother born an household cruelty,
I make my quarrel in particular.[13]

---

1 Be suitable.
2 That is, *let us pass on with our armament.* To *sway* was sometimes used for a rushing hasty movement.
3 Completely accoutred.
4 Baret carefully distinguishes between *bloody*, full of blood, *sanguineous*, and *bloody*, desirous of blood, *sanguinarius*. In this speech Shakspeare uses the word in both senses.
5 *Guarded* is a metaphor taken from dress; *to guard* being to ornament with guards or facings.
6 'Formerly all bishops wore white, even when they travelled.'—*Hody's History of Convocations*, p. 141. This white investment was the episcopal rochet.
7 Warburton very plausibly reads *glaives*; Steevens proposed *greaves*; and this emendation has my full concurrence. It should be remarked that *greaves*, or leg-armour, is sometimes spelt *graves*.
8 Grievances.
9 The old copies read 'from our most quiet *there*.' Warburton made the alteration; I am not quite persuaded that it was necessary.
10 In Holinshed the Archbishop says, 'Where he and his companie were in armes, it was for feare of the king, to whom he could have no free accesse, by reason of such a multitude of flatterers as were about him.'
11 'Examples of every minute's instance,' are 'Examples which every minute *instances* or supplies.' Which even the present minute presses on their notice.
12 Commotion's *bitter edge?* that is, the *edge* of bitter strife and *commotion*; the sword of rebellion. This line is omitted in the folio.
13 The second line of this very obscure speech is omitted in the folio. As the passage stands I can make nothing of it; nor do any of the explanations which have been offered appear to me satisfactory. I think with Malone that a line has been lost, though I do not agree with him in the sense he would give to it. It is with all proper humility I offer the following reading:—

> 'My *quarrel* general, the commonwealth,
> *Whose wrongs do loudly call out for redress*;
> To brother born an household cruelty,
> I make my quarrel in particular.'

i. e. my *general* cause of discontent is public wrongs, my *particular* cause the death of my own brother, who was beheaded by the king's order. This circumstance is referred to in the first part of this play:—

> 'The archbishop—who bears hard
> His brother's death at Bristol, the Lord Scroop.'

The answer of Westmoreland makes it obvious that

West. There is no need of any such redress;
Or, if there were, it not belongs to you.
Mowb. Why not to him, in part; and to us all,
That feel the bruises of the days before;
And suffer the condition of these times
To lay a heavy and unequal hand
Upon our honours?
West. O my good lord Mowbray,[1]
Construe the times to their necessities,
And you shall say indeed,—it is the time,
And not the king, that doth you injuries.
Yet, for your part, it not appears to me,
Either from the king, or in the present time,
That you should have an inch of any ground
To build a grief on: Were you not restor'd
To all the duke of Norfolk's signiories,
Your noble and right well remember'd father's?
Mowb. What thing in honour had my father lost,
That need to be reviv'd and breath'd in me?
The king, that lov'd him, as the state stood then,
Was, force perforce, compell'd to banish him:
And then, when Harry Bolingbroke, and he,—
Being mounted, and both roused in their seats,
Their neighing coursers daring of the spur,
Their armed staves[2] in charge, their beavers[3] down,
Their eyes of fire sparkling through sights[4] of steel,
And the loud trumpet blowing them together;
Then, then, when there was nothing could have staid
My father from the breast of Bolingbroke,
O, when the king did throw his warder[5] down,
His own life hung upon the staff he threw:
Then threw he down himself; and all their lives,
That by indictment, and by dint of sword,
Have since miscarried under Bolingbroke.
West. You speak, Lord Mowbray, now you know not what:
The earl of Hereford[6] was reputed then
In England the most valiant gentleman;
Who knows, on whom fortune would then have smil'd?
But, if your father had been victor there,
He ne'er had borne it out of Coventry:
For all the country, in a general voice,
Cried hate upon him; and all their prayers, and love,
Were set on Hereford, whom they doted on,
And bless'd, and grac'd indeed, more than the king.
But this is mere digression from my purpose.—
Here come I from our princely general,
To know your griefs; to tell you from his grace,
That he will give you audience: and wherein
It shall appear that your demands are just,
You shall enjoy them; every thing set off,
That might so much as think you enemies.
Mowb. But he hath forc'd us to compel this offer;
And it proceeds from policy, not love.
West. Mowbray, you overween, to take it so;
This offer comes from mercy, not from fear;
For, lo! within a ken our army lies;
Upon mine honour, all too confident
To give admittance to a thought of fear.
Our battle is more full of names than yours,
Our men more perfect in the use of arms,
Our armour all as strong, our cause the best;
Then reason wills, our hearts should be as good:—
Say you not then, our offer is compell'd.
Mowb. Well, by my will, we shall admit no parley.
West. That argues but the shame of your offence:
A rotten case abides no handling.
Hast. Hath the Prince John a full commission,
In very ample virtue of his father,
To hear, and absolutely to determine
Of what conditions we shall stand upon?
West. That is intended[7] in the general's name.
I muse, you make so slight a question.
Arch. Then take, my lord of Westmoreland, this schedule;
For this contains our general grievances;—
Each several article herein redress'd;
All members of our cause, both here and hence,
That are insinew'd to this action,
Acquitted by a true substantial form;
And present execution of our wills
To us, and to our purposes, consign'd;[8]
We come within our awful[9] banks again,
And knit our powers to the arm of peace.
West. This will I show the general. Please you, lords,
In sight of both our battles we may meet:
And either end in peace, which heaven so frame;
Or to the place of difference call the swords
Which must decide it.
Arch. My lord, we will do so.
[*Exit* WEST.
Mowb. There is a thing within my bosom, tells me,
That no conditions of our peace can stand.
Hast. Fear you not that: if we can make our peace
Upon such large terms, and so absolute,
As our conditions shall consist[10] upon,
Our peace shall stand as firm as rocky mountains.
Mowb. Ay, but our valuation shall be such,
That every slight and false-derived cause,
Yea, every idle, nice,[11] and wanton reason,
Shall, to the king, taste of this action:
That, were our royal faiths[12] martyrs in love,
We shall be winnow'd with so rough a wind,
That even our corn shall seem as light as chaff,
And good from bad find no partition.
Arch. No, no, my lord; Note this, the king is weary
Of dainty and such picking[13] grievances:
For he hath found,—to end one doubt by death,
Revives two greater in the heirs of life.
And therefore will he wipe his tables[14] clean;
And keep no tell-tale to his memory,
That may repeat and history his loss
To new-remembrance: For full well he knows
He cannot so precisely weed this land,
As his misdoubts present occasion:
His foes are so enrooted with his friends,
That, plucking to unfix an enemy,
He doth unfasten so, and shake a friend.
So that this land, like an offensive wife,
That hath enrag'd him on to offer strokes;
As he is striking, holds his infant up,
And hangs resolv'd correction in the arm
That was uprear'd to execution.
Hast. Besides, the king hath wasted all his rods
On late offenders, that he now doth lack

---

something about *redress* of public wrongs should have fallen from the archbishop. Johnson proposed to read *quarrel* instead of *brother* in the first line, and explained the passage much as I have done. I have merely superadded the line, which seems to me necessary to complete the sense, and make Westmoreland's reply intelligible.

1 The thirty-seven following lines are not in the quarto.

2 i. e. their *lances* fixed in the rest for the encounter.

3 It has been already observed that the *beaver* was a moveable piece of the helmet, which lifted up or down, to enable the bearer to drink or breathe more freely.

4 The perforated part of the helmets, through which they could see to direct their aim. *Visiere*, Fr.

5 Truncheon.

6 This is a mistake: he was *duke* of Hereford.

7 *Intended* is *understood*, i. e. meant without expressing it. *Entendu*, Fr.; *subauditur*, Lat.

8 The old copy reads *confin'd.* Johnson proposed to read *consign'd;* which must be understood in the Latin sense, *consignatus*, *signed*, *sealed*, *ratified*, *confirmed;* which was indeed the old meaning according to the dictionaries. Shakspeare uses *consign* and *consigning* in other places in this sense.

9 *Awful* for *lawful;* or under the due awe of authority.

10 To *consist*, to *rest;* consisto.—*Baret*

11 Trivial.

12 The faith due to a king. So in King Henry VIII. —'The citizens have shown at full their *royal* minds,' i. e. their minds well affected to the king.

13 Piddling, insignificant.

14 Alluding to the table books of slate, ivory, &c. used by our ancestors.

The very instruments of chastisement:
So that his power, like to a fangless lion,
May offer, but not hold.

Arch. 'Tis very true;—
And therefore be assur'd, my good lord marshal,
If we do now make our atonement well,
Our peace will, like a broken limb united,
Grow stronger for the breaking.

Mowb. Be it so.
Here is return'd my lord of Westmoreland.

Re-enter WESTMORELAND.

West. The prince is here at hand: Pleaseth your lordship,
To meet his grace just distance 'tween our armies?

Mowb. Your grace of York, in God's name then set forward.

Arch. Before, and greet his grace: my lord, we come. [*Exeunt.*

SCENE II. *Another Part of the Forest. Enter, from one side,* MOWBRAY, *the* Archbishop, HASTINGS, *and others: from the other side,* PRINCE JOHN *of* Lancaster, WESTMORELAND, Officers, *and* Attendants.

P. John. You are well encounter'd here, my cousin Mowbray:—
Good day to you, gentle lord archbishop;—
And so to you, Lord Hastings,—and to all.—
My lord of York, it better show'd with you,
When that your flock, assembled by the bell,
Encircled you, to hear with reverence
Your exposition on the holy text;
Than now to see you here an iron man,[1]
Cheering a rout of rebels with your drum,
Turning the word to sword, and life to death.
That man that sits within a monarch's heart,
And ripens in the sunshine of his favour,
Would he abuse the countenance of the king,
Alack, what mischiefs might he set abroach,
In shadow of such greatness! With you, lord bishop,
It is even so:—Who hath not heard it spoken,
How deep you were within the books of God?
To us, the speaker in his parliament:
To us, the imagin'd voice of God himself:
The very opener, and intelligencer,
Between the grace, the sanctities[2] of heaven,
And our dull workings:[3] O, who shall believe,
But you misuse the reverence of your place;
Employ the countenance and grace of heaven,
As a false favourite doth his prince's name,
In deeds dishonourable? You have taken up;[4]
Under the counterfeited zeal of God,
The subjects of the substitute, my father;
And, both against the peace of heaven and him,
Have here up-swarm'd them.

Arch. Good, my lord of Lancaster,
I am not here against your father's peace:
But, as I told my lord of Westmoreland,
The time misorder'd doth, in common sense,[5]
Crowd us, and crush us, to this monstrous form,
To hold our safety up. I sent your grace
The parcels and particulars of our grief;
The which hath been with scorn shov'd from the court,
Whereon this Hydra son of war is born:
Whose dangerous eyes may well be charm'd asleep,[6]
With grant of our most just and right desires:
And true obedience of this madness cur'd,
Stoop tamely to the foot of majesty.

Mowb. If not, we ready are to try our fortunes
To the last man.

Hast. And though we here fall down
We have supplies to second our attempt;
If they miscarry, theirs shall second them:
And so, success[7] of mischief shall be born;
And heir from heir shall hold this quarrel up,
Whiles England shall have generation.

P. John. You are too shallow, Hastings, much too shallow,
To sound the bottom of the after-times.

West. Pleaseth your grace to answer them directly,
How far-forth do you like their articles?

P. John. I like them all, and do allow[8] them well.
And swear here by the honour of my blood,
My father's purposes have been mistook;
And some about him have too lavishly
Wrested his meaning, and authority.—
My lord, these griefs shall be with speed redress'd;
Upon my soul, they shall. If this may please you,
Discharge your powers[9] unto their several counties,
As we will ours: and here, between the armies,
Let's drink together friendly, and embrace;
That all their eyes may bear those tokens home,
Of our restored love and amity.

Arch. I take your princely word for these redresses.

P. John. I give it you, and will maintain my word;
And thereupon I drink unto your grace.

Hast. Go, captain [*To an* Officer,] and deliver to the army
This news of peace; let them have pay, and part;
I know, it will well please them; Hie thee, captain. [*Exit* Officer

Arch. To you, my noble lord of Westmoreland.

West. I pledge your grace: And, if you knew what pains
I have bestow'd to breed this present peace,
You would drink freely: but my love to you
Shall show itself more openly hereafter.

Arch. I do not doubt you.

West. I am glad of it.—
Health to my lord, and gentle cousin, Mowbray.

Mowb. You wish me health in very happy season;
For I am, on the sudden, something ill.

Arch Against ill chances, men are ever merry,
But heaviness foreruns the good event.

West. Therefore be merry, coz: since sudden sorrow
Serves to say thus,—Some good thing, comes tomorrow.

Arch. Believe me, I am passing light in spirit.

Mowb. So much the worse, if your own rule be true. [*Shouts within.*

P. John. The word of peace is render'd; Hark, how they shout!

Mowb. This had been cheerful, after victory.

Arch. A peace is of the nature of a conquest;
For then both parties nobly are subdued,
And neither party loser.

P. John. Go, my lord,
And let our army be discharged too.— [*Exit* WESTMORELAND.
And, good my lord, so please you, let our trains
March by us; that we may peruse the men
We should have cop'd withal.

Arch. Go, good Lord Hastings,
And, ere they be dismiss'd, let them march by. [*Exit* HASTINGS.

P. John. I trust, my lords, we shall lie to-night together.—

---

1 Holinshed says of the Archbishop, that, 'coming foorth amongst them *clad in armour*, he encouraged and pricked them foorth to take the enterprize in hand.'

2 This expression has been adopted by Milton:—
'Around him all the *sanctities of heaven*
Stood thick as stars.'

3 *Dull workings* are *labours of thought.*

4 Raised up in arms.

5 *Common sense* is *the general sense of general danger.*

6 Alluding to the dragon charmed to rest by the spells of Medea.

7 Succession.

8 Approve.

9 It was Westmoreland who made this deceitful proposal, as appears from Holinshed:—'The earl of Westmoreland, using more policie than the rest, said, whereas our people have been long in armour, let them depart home to their woonted trades: In the mean time let us drink togither in signe of agreement, that the people on both sides may see it, and know that it is true, that we be light at a point.'

Re-enter WESTMORELAND.

Now, cousin, [illegible] stands our army still?
West. The [illegible], having charge from you to stand,
[illegible] until they hear you speak.
[illegible] They know their duties.

Re-enter HASTINGS.

Hast. My lord, our army is dispers'd already:
Like youthful steers unyok'd, they take their courses
East, west, north, south; or, like a school broke up,
Each hurries toward his home, and sporting-place.
West. Good tidings, my Lord Hastings; for the which
I do arrest thee, traitor, of high treason:—
And you, lord archbishop,—and you, Lord Mowbray,
Of capital treason I attach you both.
Mowb. Is this proceeding just and honourable?
West. Is your assembly so?
Arch. Will you thus break your faith?
P. John. I pawn'd thee none:
I promis'd you redress of these same grievances,
Whereof you did complain; which, by mine honour,
I will perform with a most christian care.
But, for you, rebels,—look to taste the due
Meet for rebellion, and such acts as yours.
Most shallowly did you these arms commence,
Fondly[1] brought here, and foolishly sent hence.—
Strike up our drums, pursue the scatter'd stray;
Heaven, and not we, have safely fought to-day.—
Some guard these traitors to the block of death;
Treason's true bed, and yielder up of breath.
[*Exeunt.*[2]

SCENE III. *Another Part of the Forest. Alarums: Excursions. Enter* FALSTAFF *and* COLEVILE, *meeting.*

Fal. What's your name, sir? of what condition are you: and of what place, I pray?

Cole. I am a knight, sir; and my name is—Colevile of the dale.

Fal. Well then, Colevile is your name; a knight is your degree; and your place, the dale: Colevile shall still be your name; a traitor your degree; and the dungeon your place,—a place deep enough: so shall you still be Colevile of the dale.

Cole. Are not you Sir John Falstaff?

Fal. As good a man as he, sir, whoe'er I am. Do ye yield, sir? or shall I sweat for you? If I do sweat, they are drops of thy lovers, and they weep for thy death: therefore rouse up fear and trembling, and do observance to my mercy.

Cole. I think, you are Sir John Falstaff; and in that thought, yield me.

Fal. I have a whole school of tongues in this belly of mine; and not a tongue of them all speaks any other word but my name. An I had but a belly of any indifferency, I were simply the most active fellow in Europe: My womb, my womb, my womb undoes me.—Here comes our general.

Enter PRINCE JOHN *of* Lancaster, WESTMORELAND, *and others.*

P. John. The heat is past, follow no further now;—
Call in the powers, good cousin Westmoreland.—
[*Exit* WEST.
Now, Falstaff, where have you been all this while?
When every thing is ended, then you come:
These tardy tricks of yours will, on my life,
One time or other break some gallows' back.

Fal. I would be sorry, my lord, but it should be thus; I never knew yet, but rebuke and check was the reward of valour. Do you think me a swallow, an arrow, or a bullet? have I, in my poor and old motion, the expedition of thought? I have speeded hither with the very extremest inch of possibility; I have foundered nine score and odd posts: and here, travel-tainted as I am, have, in my pure and immaculate valour, taken Sir John Colevile of the dale, a most furious knight, and valorous enemy: But what of that? he saw me, and yielded; that I may justly say with the hook-nosed fellow of Rome,[3] —— I came, saw, and overcame.

P. John. It was more of his courtesy than your deserving.

Fal. I know not; here he is, and here I yield him: and I beseech your grace, let it be booked with the rest of this day's deeds; or, by the Lord, I will have it in a particular ballad else, with mine own picture on the top of it, Coleville kissing my foot: To the which course, if I be enforced, if you do not all show like gilt two-pences to me; and I, in the clear sky of fame, o'ershine you as much as the full moon doth the cinders of the element,[4] which show like pins' heads to her; believe not the word of the noble: Therefore let me have right, and let desert mount.

P. John. Thine's too heavy to mount.

Fal. Let it shine then.

P. John. Thine's too thick to shine.

Fal. Let it do something, my good lord, that may do me good, and call it what you will.

P. John. Is thy name Colevile?[5]
Cole. It is, my lord.
P. John. A famous rebel art thou, Colevile.
Fal. And a famous true subject took him.
Cole. I am, my lord, but as my betters are,
That led me hither: had they been rul'd by me,
You should have won them dearer than you have.

Fal. I know not how they sold themselves: but thou, like a kind fellow, gavest thyself away; and I thank thee for thee.

Re-enter WESTMORELAND.

P. John. Now, have you left pursuit?
West. Retreat is made, and execution stay'd.
P. John. Send Colevile, with his confederates,
To York, to present execution:[6]—
Blunt, lead him hence; and see you guard him sure.
[*Exeunt some with* COLEVILE.
And now despatch we toward the court, my lords;
I hear, the king my father is sore sick:
Our news shall go before us to his majesty,—
Which, cousin, you shall bear,—to comfort him;
And we with sober speed will follow you.

Fal. My lord, I beseech you, give me leave to go through Glostershire: and, when you come to court, stand my good lord,[7] 'pray, in your good report.

---

1 i. e. foolishly.

2 'It cannot but raise some indignation to find this horrid violation of faith passed over thus slightly by the poet without any note of censure or detestation.'—*Johnson.* That Shakspeare followed the historians is no excuse; for it is the duty of a poet always to take the side of virtue.—I had some doubt whether I should retain this reflection upon the poetical justice of Shakspeare; but I have been determined to do so by the hope that it may lead to the discussion of the passage. I would not willingly believe that the poet approved this abominable piece of treachery.

3 Cæsar. 4 A ludicrous term for the *stars.*

5 It appears that Colevile was designed to be pronounced as a trisyllable; it is often spelt *Colleville* in the old copies.

6 'At the king's coming to Durham the Lord Hastings, *Sir John Colevile of the dale,* &c. being convicted of the conspiracy, were there beheaded.'—*Holinshed,* p. 530. It is to be observed that there are two accounts of the termination of the archbishop of York's conspiracy, *both* of which are given by Holinshed. He states that on the archbishop and earl marshal submitting to the king and to his son Prince John, there present, 'their troopes skaled and fledde their wayes; but being pursued, many were taken, many slain, &c.; the archbishop and earl marshall were brought to Pomfret to the king, who from thence went *to Yorke, whyther the prisoners were also brought, and there beheaded.*' It is this last account that Shakspeare has followed, but with some variation; for the names of Colevile and Hastings are not mentioned among those who were beheaded at York.

7 Johnson was so much unacquainted with ancient phraseology as to make difficulties about this phrase, which is one of the most common petitionary forms of our ancestors. *Stand my good lord* or *be my good*

P. John. Fare you well, Falstaff: I, in my condition,[1]
Shall better speak of you than you deserve. [*Exit.*

Fal. I would you had but the wit; 'twere better than your dukedom.—Good faith, this same young sober-blooded boy doth not love me: nor a man cannot make him laugh;—but that's no marvel, he drinks no wine. There's never any of these demure boys come to any proof: for thin drink doth so over-cool their blood, and making many fish-meals, that they fall into a kind of male green-sickness; and then, when they marry, they get wenches: they are generally fools and cowards;—which some of us should be too, but for inflammation. A good sherris sack[2] hath a two-fold operation in it. It ascends me into the brain; dries me there all the foolish and dull, and crudy vapours which environ it: makes it apprehensive, quick, forgetive,[3] full of nimble, fiery, and delectable shapes; which delivered o'er to the voice (the tongue,) which is the birth, becomes excellent wit. The second property of your excellent sherris is,—the warming of the blood; which, before cold and settled, left the liver white and pale, which is the badge of pusillanimity and cowardice: but the sherris warms it, and makes it course from the inwards to the parts extreme. It illumineth the face: which, as a beacon, gives warning to all the rest of this little kingdom, man, to arm: and then the vital commoners, and inland petty spirits, muster me all to their captain, the heart; who, great, and puffed up with this retinue, doth any deed of courage; and this valour comes of sherris: So that skill in the weapon is nothing, without sack; for that sets it a-work; and learning, a mere hoard of gold kept by a devil;[4] till sack commences it,[5] and sets it in act and use. Hereof comes it, that Prince Harry is valiant: for the cold blood he did naturally inherit of his father, he hath, like lean, steril, and bare land, manured, husbanded, and tilled, with excellent endeavour of drinking good, and good store of fertile sherris; that he is become very hot, and valiant. If I had a thousand sons, the first human principle I would teach them, should be,—to forswear thin potations, and addict themselves to sack.

Enter BARDOLPH.

How now, Bardolph?

Bard. The army is discharged all, and gone.

Fal. Let them go. I'll through Glostershire; and there will I visit master Robert Shallow, esquire: I have him already tempering[6] between my finger and my thumb, and shortly will I seal with him. Come away. [*Exeunt.*

SCENE IV. Westminster. *A Room in the Palace. Enter* KING HENRY, CLARENCE, PRINCE HUMPHREY, WARWICK, *and others.*

K. Hen. Now, lords, if heaven doth give successful end
To this debate that bleedeth at our doors,
We will our youth lead on to higher fields,
And draw no swords but what are sanctified.
Our navy is address'd,[7] our power collected,
Our substitutes in absence well invested,
And every thing lies level to our wish:
Only, we want a little personal strength;
And pause us, till those rebels, now afoot,
Come underneath the yoke of government.

War. Both which, we doubt not but your majesty
Shall soon enjoy.

K. Hen. Humphrey, my son of Gloster,
Where is the prince your brother?

P. Humph. I think, he's gone to hunt, my lord, at Windsor.

K. Hen. And how accompanied?

P. Humph. I do not know, my lord.

K. Hen. Is not his brother, Thomas of Clarence, with him?

P. Humph. No, my good lord; he is in presence here.

Cla. What would my lord and father?

K. Hen. Nothing but well to thee, Thomas of Clarence.
How chance, thou art not with the prince thy brother?
He loves thee, and thou dost neglect him, Thomas;
Thou hast a better place in his affection,
Than all thy brothers: cherish it, my boy;
And noble offices thou may'st effect
Of mediation, after I am dead,
Between his greatness and thy other brethren:—
Therefore, omit him not: blunt not his love:
Nor lose the good advantage of his grace,
By seeming cold or careless of his will.
For he is gracious, if he be observ'd;[8]
He hath a tear for pity, and a hand
Open as day for melting charity:
Yet, notwithstanding, being incens'd, he's flint,
As humorous[9] as winter, and as sudden
As flaws congealed in the spring of day.[10]
His temper, therefore, must be well observ'd:
Chide him for faults, and do it reverently,
When you perceive his blood inclin'd to mirth;
But, being moody, give him line and scope;
Till that his passions, like a whale on ground,
Confound themselves with working. Learn this, Thomas,
And thou shalt prove a shelter to thy friends;
A hoop of gold, to bind thy brothers in;
That the united vessel of their blood,
Mingled with venom of suggestion,[11]
(As, force perforce, the age will pour it in,)
Shall never leak, though it do work as strong
As aconitum,[12] or rash gunpowder.

Cla. I shall observe him with all care and love.

K. Hen. Why art thou not at Windsor with him, Thomas?

Cla. He is not there to-day; he dines in London.

K. Hen. And how accompanied? canst thou tell that?

Cla. With Poins, and other his continual followers.

---

lord, means *stand my friend, be my patron or benefactor*, report well of me.

1 *Condition* is most frequently used by Shakspeare for *nature, disposition.* The prince may therefore mean, 'I shall in my good nature speak better of you than you deserve.'

2 Vide note on King Henry IV. Part 1. Act. i. Sc. ii.

3 Inventive, imaginative.

4 It was anciently supposed that all the mines of gold, &c. were guarded by evil spirits. See the Secret Wonders of Nature and Art, by Edw. Fenton, 1569, p. 91.

5 *Commences it*, that is *brings it into action.* Tyrwhitt thinks it is probable that there is an allusion to the *commencement* and *act* of the universities, which give to students a complete authority *to use* those *hoards of learning* which have entitled them to their degrees. As the dictionaries of the poet's time explain this matter, the conjecture seems probable.

6 A pleasant allusion to the old use of *soft wax* for sealing.

7 Ready, prepared.
'To-morrow for our march are we *address'd.*'
King Henry V.

8 i. e. if he has *respectful attention shown him*

9 'His qualities were beauteous as his form,
For maiden-tongu'd he was, and therefore free;
Yet *if men mov'd him*, was he such a *storm*
As oft 'twixt May and April is to see,
When winds breathe sweet, unruly though they be
Shakspeare's Lover's Complaint.

Humorous was used for *capricious*, as *humoursome* now is.

10 A *flaw* is a sudden gust of violent wind; alluding to the opinion of some philosophers, that the vapours being congealed in the air by cold (which is the most intense in the morning,) and being afterwards rarefied and let loose by the warmth of the sun, occasion those sudden and impetuous gusts of wind which are called *flaws.* Shakspeare uses the word again in King Henry VI. and in his Venus and Adonis.

11 Though their blood be inflamed by the *temptations* to which youth is peculiarly subject.

12 *Aconitum*, or aconite, *wolfs-bane*, a poisonous herb. *Rash* is sudden, hasty, violent.

K. Hen. Most subject is the fattest soil to weeds;
And he, the noble image of my youth,
Is overspread with them: Therefore my grief
Stretches itself beyond the hour of death:
The blood weeps from my heart, when I do shape,
In forms imaginary, the unguided days,
And rotten times, that you shall look upon,
When I am sleeping with my ancestors.
For when his headstrong riot hath no curb,
When rage and hot blood are his counsellors,
When means and lavish manners meet together,
O, with what wings shall his affections[1] fly
Towards fronting peril and oppos'd decay!

War. My gracious lord, you look beyond him quite:
The prince but studies his companions,
Like a strange tongue: wherein, to gain the language,
'Tis needful, that the most immodest word
Be look'd upon, and learn'd: which once attain'd,
Your highness knows, comes to no further use,
But to be known, and hated.[2] So, like gross terms,
The prince will, in the perfectness of time,
Cast off his followers: and their memory
Shall as a pattern or a measure live,
By which his grace must mete the lives of others;
Turning past evils to advantages.

K. Hen. 'Tis seldom—when the bee doth leave her comb
In the dead carrion.[3]—Who's here? Westmoreland?

Enter WESTMORELAND.

West. Health to my sovereign! and new happiness
Added to that that I am to deliver!
Prince John, your son, doth kiss your grace's hand:
Mowbray, the bishop Scroop, Hastings, and all,
Are brought to the correction of your law;
There is not now a rebel's sword unsheath'd,
But peace puts forth her olive every where.
The manner how this action hath been borne,
Here at more leisure may your highness read;
With every course, in his particular.[4]

K. Hen. O Westmoreland, thou art a summer bird,
Which ever in the haunch of winter sings
The lifting up of day. Look! here's more news.

Enter HARCOURT.

Har. From enemies heaven keep your majesty;
And, when they stand against you, may they fall
As those that I am come to tell you of!
The Earl Northumberland, and the Lord Bardolph,
With a great power of English, and of Scots,
Are by the sheriff of Yorkshire overthrown:
The manner and true order of the fight,
This packet, please it you, contains at large.

K. Hen. And wherefore should these good news make me sick?
Will fortune never come with both hands full,
But write her fair words still in foulest letters?
She either gives a stomach, and no food,—
Such are the poor, in health; or else a feast,
And takes away the stomach,—such are the rich,
That have abundance, and enjoy it not.
I should rejoice now at this happy news;
And now my sight fails, and my brain is giddy:
O me! come near me, now I am much ill. [*Swoons.*

P. Humph. Comfort, your majesty!

Cla. O my royal father!

West. My sovereign lord, cheer up yourself, look up!

War. Be patient, princes; you do know, these fits
Are with his highness very ordinary.
Stand from him, give him air; he'll straight be well.

Cla. No, no; he cannot long hold out these pangs;
The incessant care and labour of his mind
Hath wrought the mure,[5] that should confine it in,
So thin, that life looks through, and will break out.

P. Humph. The people fear me;[6] for they do observe
Unfather'd heirs,[7] and loathly birds of nature:
The seasons change their manners, as the year[8]
Had found some months asleep, and leap'd them over.

Cla. The river hath thrice flow'd, no ebb between:[9]
And the old folk, time's doting chronicles,
Say, it did so, a little time before
That our great grandsire, Edward, sick'd and died.

War. Speak lower, princes, for the king recovers.

P. Humph. This apoplex will, certain, be his end.

K. Hen. I pray you, take me up, and bear me hence
Into some other chamber: softly, 'pray.
[*They convey the* King *into an inner part of the Room, and place him on a Bed.*
Let there be no noise made, my gentle friends;
Unless some dull[10] and favourable hand
Will whisper music to my weary spirit.

War. Call for the music in the other room.

K. Hen. Set me the crown upon my pillow here.

Cla. His eye is hollow, and he changes much

War. Less noise, less noise.

Enter PRINCE HENRY.

P. Hen. Who saw the Duke of Clarence?

Cla. I am here, brother, full of heaviness.

P. Hen. How now! rain within doors, and none abroad!
How doth the king?

P. Humph. Exceeding ill.

P. Hen. Heard he the good news yet?
Tell it him.

---

1 *Affections*, in the language of Shakspeare's time, are *passions*, *desires*. Appetitus animi.

2 A parallel passage occurs in Terence:—
' ——— quo modo adolescentulus
Meretricum ingenia et mores posset noscere
Mature ut cum cognovit, perpetuo oderit.'

3 As the bee, having once placed her comb in a carcass, stays by her honey, so he that has once taken pleasure in bad company will continue to associate with those that have the art of pleasing him.

4 The detail contained in Prince John's letter.

5 *Mure* for *wall* is another of Shakspeare's Latinisms. It was not in frequent use by his cotemporaries. *Wrought it thin* is *made it thin by gradual detriment*: *wrought* being the preterite of *work*.

6 To *fear* anciently signified to *make afraid*, as well as to *dread*. 'A vengeance light on thee that so doth *feare me*, or makest me so *feared*.'—*Baret*.

7 That is, equivocal births, monsters.

8 i. e. as *if* the year.

9 An historical fact. On Oct. 12, 1411, this happened.

10 Johnson asserts that *dull* here signifies 'melancholy, gentle, soothing.' Malone says that it means 'producing dullness or heaviness.' The fact is that *dull* and *slow* were synonymous. '*Dullness*, slowness; tarditas, tardivete. Somewhat *dull* or *slowe*; tardiusculus, tardelet;' says *Baret*. But Shakspeare uses *dulness* for *drowsiness* in the Tempest. And Baret has also this sense:—' Slow, *dull*, asleepe, drousie, astonied, heavie; *torpidus*.' It has always been thought that *slow* music induces sleep. Ariel enters playing *solemn music* to produce this effect, in the Tempest. The notion is not peculiar to our great poet, as the following exquisite lines, almost worthy of his hand, may witness:—

'Oh, lull me, lull me, charming air,
My senses rock'd with wonder sweet;
Like snow on wool thy fallings are,
Soft like a spirit are thy feet.
Grief who need fear
That hath an ear?
Down let him lie,
And slumbering die,
And change his soul for harmony.'

(*From Wit Restored*, 1658.) They are attributed to Dr. Strode, who died in 1644

P. Humph. He alter'd much upon the hearing it.
P. Hen. If he be sick
With joy, he will recover without physic.
War. Not so much noise, my lords;—sweet prince, speak low;
The king your father is dispos'd to sleep.
Cla. Let us withdraw into the other room.
War. Will't please your grace to go along with us?
P. Hen. No; I will sit and watch here by the king.[1] [*Exeunt all but* P. HENRY.
Why doth the crown lie there upon his pillow,
Being so troublesome a bedfellow?
O polish'd perturbation! golden care!
That keeps the ports[2] of slumber open wide
To many a watchful night!—sleep with it now!
Yet not so sound, and half so deeply sweet,
As he, whose brow, with homely biggin[3] bound,
Snores out the watch of night. O majesty!
When thou dost pinch thy bearer, thou dost sit
Like a rich armour worn in heat of day,
That scalds with safety. By his gates of breath
There lies a downy feather, that stirs not:
Did he suspire, that light and weightless down
Perforce must move.—My gracious lord!—my father!—
This sleep is sound indeed; this is a sleep,
That from this golden rigol[4] hath divorc'd
So many English kings. Thy due, from me,
Is tears, and heavy sorrows of the blood;
Which nature, love, and filial tenderness,
Shall, O dear father, pay thee plenteously:
My due, from thee, is this imperial crown;
Which, as immediate from thy place and blood,
Derives itself to me. Lo, here it sits,— [*Putting it on his head.*
Which heaven shall guard: And put the world's whole strength
Into one giant arm, it shall not force
This lineal honour from me: This from thee
Will I to mine leave, as 'tis left to me. [*Exit.*
K. Hen. Warwick! Gloster! Clarence!

Re-enter WARWICK, *and the rest.*

Cla. Doth the king call!
War. What would your majesty? How fares your grace?
K. Hen. Why did you leave me here alone, my lords?
Cla. We left the prince my brother here, my liege,
Who undertook to sit and watch by you.
K. Hen. The prince of Wales? Where is he? let me see him:
He is not here.
War. This door is open; he is gone this way.
P. Humph. He came not through the chamber where we stay'd.
K. Hen. Where is the crown? who took it from my pillow?
War. When we withdrew, my liege, we left it here.
K. Hen. The prince hath ta'en it hence:—go, seek him out;
Is he so hasty, that he doth suppose
My sleep my death?
Find him, my lord of Warwick; chide him hither. [*Exit* WARWICK.
This part of his conjoins with my disease,
And helps to end me.—See, sons, what things you are!
How quickly nature falls into revolt,
When gold becomes her object!
For this the foolish over-careful fathers
Have broke their sleep with thoughts, their brains with care,
Their bones with industry;
For this they have engrossed and pil'd up
The canker'd heaps of strange-achieved gold;
For this they have been thoughtful to invest
Their sons with arts, and martial exercises:
When, like the bee, tolling[5] from every flower
The virtuous sweets;
Our thighs pack'd with wax, our mouths with honey,
We bring it to the hive; and, like the bees,
Are murder'd for our pains. This bitter taste
Yields his engrossments[6] to the ending father.

Re-enter WARWICK.

Now, where is he that will not stay so long
Till his friend sickness hath determin'd[7] me?
War. My lord, I found the prince in the next room,
Washing with kindly tears his gentle cheeks,
With such a deep demeanor in great sorrow,
That tyranny, which never quaff'd but blood,
Would, by beholding him, have wash'd his knife
With gentle eye-drops. He is coming hither.
K. Hen. But wherefore did he take away the crown?

Re-enter PRINCE HENRY.

Lo, where he comes.—Come hither to me, Harry.
Depart the chamber, leave us here alone.
[*Exeunt* CLARENCE, PRINCE HUMPHREY, Lords, *&c.*
P. Hen. I never thought to hear you speak again.
K. Hen. Thy wish was father, Harry, to that thought:
I stay too long by thee, I weary thee.
Dost thou so hunger for my empty chair,
That thou wilt needs invest thee with mine honours
Before thy hour be ripe? O foolish youth!
Thou seek'st the greatness that will overwhelm thee.
Stay but a little; for my cloud of dignity
Is held from falling with so weak a wind,
That it will quickly drop: my day is dim.
Thou hast stol'n that, which, after some few hours,
Were thine without offence; and, at my death,
Thou hast seal'd up my expectation:[8]
Thy life did manifest, thou lov'dst me not,
And thou wilt have me die assured of it.
Thou hid'st a thousand daggers in thy thoughts;
Which thou hast whetted on thy stony heart,
To stab at half an hour[9] of my life.
What! canst thou not forbear me half an hour?
Then get thee gone, and dig my grave thyself;
And bid the merry bells ring to thine ear,
That thou art crowned, not that I am dead.
Let all the tears that should bedew my hearse,
Be drops of balm, to sanctify thy head:
Only compound me with forgotten dust;
Give that, which gave thee life, unto the worms.
Pluck down my officers, break my decrees;
For now a time is come to mock at form,
Harry the fifth is crown'd;—Up, vanity!
Down, royal state! all you sage counsellors, hence!
And to the English court assemble now,
From every region, apes of idleness!
Now, neighbour confines, purge you of your scum.
Have you a ruffian, that will swear, drink, dance,
Revel the night; rob, murder, and commit
The oldest sins the newest kind of ways?
Be happy, he will trouble you no more:
England shall double gild his treble guilt;[10]

---

1 The hint only of this beautiful scene is taken from Holinshed, p. 541. The poet has wrought up the bare bald narration of the chronicler in the most pathetic and poetical manner.

2 Gates.

3 A *biggin* was a *head band* of coarse cloth; so called because such a forehead-cloth was worn by the Begunes, an order of nuns. 'Upon his head he wore a filthy coarse *biggin*, and next it a garnish of night-caps.' Nash, speaking of a miser in his *Pierce Penniless*.

4 i. e. *circle*; probably from the old Italian *rigolo*, a small wheel.

5 Taking toll. 6 Accumulations

7 i. e. *ended.* It is still used in that sense in legal conveyances.

8 i. e. confirmed my opinion.

9 *Hour*, anciently written *hower*, is used sometimes as a dissyllable, as well by Shakspeare as others.

10 This playing upon words seems to have been highly admired in the age of Shakspeare

England shall give him office, honour, might:
For the fifth Harry, from curb'd licence plucks
The muzzle of restraint, and the wild dog
Shall flesh his tooth in every innocent.
O my poor kingdom, sick with civil blows!
When that my care could not withhold thy riots,
What wilt thou do, when riot is thy care?
O, thou wilt be a wilderness again,
Peopled with wolves, thy old inhabitants!
P. Hen. O, pardon me, my liege! but for my tears, [*Kneeling.*
The moist impediments unto my speech,
I had forestall'd this dear and deep rebuke,
Ere you with grief had spoke, and I had heard
The course of it so far. There is your crown;
And he that wears the crown immortally,
Long guard it yours! If I affect it more,
Than as your honour, and as your renown,
Let me no more from this obedience rise,
Which my most true and inward-duteous spirit
Teacheth this prostrate and exterior bending![1]
Heaven witness with me, when I here came in,
And found no course of breath within your majesty,
How cold it struck my heart! If I do feign,
O, let me in my present wildness die;
And never live to show the incredulous world
The noble change that I have purposed!
Coming to look on you, thinking you dead
(And dead almost, my liege, to think you were,)
I spake unto the crown as having sense,
And thus upbraided it: *The care on thee depending,*
Hath fed upon the body of my father;
Therefore, thou, best of gold, art worst of gold.
Other, less fine in carat, is more precious,
Preserving life in med'cine potable:[2]
But thou, most fine, most honour'd, most renown'd,
Hast eat thy bearer up. Thus, my most royal liege,
Accusing it, I put it on my head;
To try with it,—as with an enemy,
That had before my face murder'd my father,—
The quarrel of a true inheritor.
But if it did infect my blood with joy,
Or swell my thoughts to any strain of pride;
If any rebel or vain spirit of mine
Did, with the least affection of a welcome,
Give entertainment to the might of it,
Let God for ever keep it from my head!
And make me as the poorest vassal is,
That doth with awe and terror kneel to it!
K. Hen. O my son!
Heaven put it in thy mind, to take it hence,
That thou might'st win the more thy father's love,
Pleading so wisely in excuse of it.
Come hither, Harry, sit thou by my bed;
And hear, I think, the very latest counsel
That ever I shall breathe. Heaven knows, my son,
By what by-paths, and indirect crook'd ways,
I met this crown; and I myself know well,
How troublesome it sat upon my head:
To thee it shall descend with better quiet,
Better opinion, better confirmation;
For all the soil[3] of the achievement goes
With me into the earth. It seem'd in me,
But as an honour snatch'd with boisterous hand;
And I had many living, to upbraid
My gain of it by their assistances;
Which daily grew to quarrel and to bloodshed,
Wounding supposed peace:[4] all these bold fears,[5]
Thou see'st with peril I have answered:
For all my reign hath been but as a scene
Acting that argument; and now my death
Changes the mode:[6] for what in me was purchas'd,[7]
Falls upon thee in a more fairer sort;
So thou the garland wear'st successively.[8]
Yet, though thou stand'st more sure than I could do,
Thou art not firm enough, since griefs are green:
And all thy friends, which thou must make thy friends,
Have but their stings and teeth newly ta'en out;
By whose fell working I was first advanc'd,
And by whose power I well might lodge a fear
To be again displac'd: which to avoid,
I cut them[9] off; and had a purpose now
To lead out many to the Holy Land;
Lest rest, and lying still, might make them look
Too near unto my state. Therefore, my Harry,
Be it thy course, to busy giddy minds
With foreign quarrels; that action, hence borne out,
May waste the memory of the former days.
More would I, but my lungs are wasted so,
That strength of speech is utterly denied me.
How I came by the crown, O God, forgive![10]
And grant it may with thee in true peace live!
P. Hen. My gracious liege,
You won it, wore it, kept it, gave it me;
Then plain, and right, must my possession be:
Which I, with more than with a common pain,
'Gainst all the world will rightfully maintain.

Enter PRINCE JOHN *of* Lancaster, WARWICK, Lords, *and others.*

K. Hen. Look, look, here comes my John of Lancaster.
P. John. Health, peace, and happiness, to my royal father!
K. Hen. Thou bring'st me happiness, and peace son John;
But health, alack, with youthful wings is flown
From this bare, wither'd trunk: upon thy sight,
My worldly business makes a period.——
Where is my lord of Warwick?
P. Hen. My lord of Warwick
K. Hen. Doth any name particular belong
Unto the lodging where I first did swoon?
War. 'Tis call'd Jerusalem, my noble lord.
K. Hen. Laud be to God!—even there my life must end.[11]

---

1 The Variorum Shakspeare reads:—
'Let me no more from this obedience rise
(Which my most true and inward duteous spirit
Teacheth.) this prostrate and exterior bending!'
Johnson and others have considered this passage as obscure in the construction; but it was only made so by their wrong pointing. The obvious sense is, 'Let me no more rise from this *obeisance*, which my most *loyal* and inwardly duteous spirit teacheth this prostrate and exterior bending.' *Obeisance* and *obedience* were formerly used indiscriminately the one for the other. *Truth* is always used for *loyalty*.

2 It was long a prevailing opinion that a solution of gold had great medicinal virtues; and that the incorruptibility of the metal might be communicated to the body impregnated with it. *Potable gold* was one of the panacea of ancient quacks.

3 *Soil* is *stain, spot, blemish.*

4 *Supposed peace* is *imagined* peace, counterfeit, not real.

5 *Fears* are *objects of fear;* terrors.

6 The *mode* is the *state* or *form* of things.

7 *Purchas'd* here signifies *obtained by eager pursuit.* It is from the French *pourchas*, and was sometimes so spelled when used to signify the obtaining of lands or honours by any other means than by title or descent. See Spelman's Glossary, in *purchacia;* and Minshew's Guide to the Tongues, in *pourchas.*

8 i. e. *by order of succession.* Johnson observes that 'every usurper snatches a claim of hereditary right as soon as he can.' So did Richard Cromwell in his first speech to parliament:—'For my own part being, by the providence of God, and the disposition of the law, my father's *successor*, and bearing the place in the government that I do,' &c.—*Harleian Miscellany*, vol i. p. 21.

9 Mason proposes to read 'I cut *some off*,' which seems indeed necessary. The sense would then be, '*Some* I have cut off, and many I intended to lead to the Holy Land.'

10 This is a true picture of a mind divided between heaven and earth. He prays for the prosperity of guilt, while he deprecates its punishment.

11 'At length he recovered his speech and understanding, and perceiving himselfe in a strange place, which he knew not, he willed to know if the chamber had anie particular name, whereunto answer was made, that it was called *Jerusalem.* Then said the king, Lauds be given to the Father of Heaven, for now I know that I shall die here in this chamber, according to the prophesie.

It hath been prophesied to me many years,
I should not die but in Jerusalem;
Which vainly I supposed, the Holy Land—
But, bear me to that chamber; there I'll lie;
In that Jerusalem shall Harry die. [*Exeunt.*

ACT V.

SCENE I. Glostershire. *A Hall in* Shallow's *House. Enter* SHALLOW, FALSTAFF, BARDOLPH, *and* Page.

Shal. By cock and pye,[1] sir, you shall not away to-night.——What, Davy, I say!

Fal. You must excuse me, master Robert Shallow.

Shal. I will not excuse you; you shall not be excused; excuses shall not be admitted; there is no excuse shall serve; you shall not be excused.—Why, Davy!

Enter DAVY.

Davy. Here, sir.

Shal. Davy, Davy, Davy,—let me see, Davy; let me see:—yea, marry, William cook, bid him come hither.—Sir John, you shall not be excused.

Davy. Marry, sir, thus;—those precepts[2] cannot be served: and, again, sir,—Shall we sow the head-land with wheat?

Shal. With red wheat, Davy. But for William cook:——Are there no young pigeons?

Davy. Yes, sir.——Here is now the smith's note, for shoeing, and plough-irons.

Shal. Let it be cast,[3] and paid:—Sir John, you shall not be excused.

Davy. Now, sir, a new link to the bucket must needs be had;—And, sir, do you mean to stop any of William's wages, about the sack he lost the other day at Hinckley fair?

Shal. He shall answer it:——Some pigeons, Davy; a couple of short-legged hens; a joint of mutton; and any pretty little tiny kickshaws, tell William cook.

Davy. Doth the man of war stay all night, sir?

Shal. Yes, Davy. I will use him well; A friend i' the court is better than a penny in purse.[4] Use his men well, Davy; for they are arrant knaves, and will backbite.

Davy. No worse than they are back-bitten, sir; for they have marvellous foul linen.

Shal. Well conceited, Davy. About thy business, Davy.

Davy. I beseech you, sir, to countenance William Visor of Wincot[5] against Clement Perkes of the hill.

Shal. There are many complaints, Davy, against that Visor; that Visor is an arrant knave on my knowledge.

Davy. I grant your worship, that he is a knave, sir: but yet, God forbid, sir, but a knave should have some countenance at his friend's request. An honest man, sir, is able to speak for himself, when a knave is not. I have served your worship truly, sir, this eight years; and if I cannot once or twice in a quarter bear out a knave against an honest man, I have but a very little credit with your worship.[6] The knave is mine honest friend, sir; therefore, I beseech your worship, let him be countenanced.

Shal. Go to; I say, he shall have no wrong. Look about, Davy. [*Exit* DAVY.] Where are you, Sir John? Come, off with your boots.—Give me your hand, master Bardolph.

Bard. I am glad to see your worship.

Shal. I thank thee with all my heart, kind master Bardolph:—and welcome, my tall fellow. [*To the* Page.] Come, Sir John. [*Exit* SHALLOW.

Fal. I'll follow you, good master Robert Shallow. Bardolph, look to our horses. [*Exeunt* BARDOLPH *and* Page.] If I were sawed into quantities, I should make four dozen of such bearded hermit's-staves as master Shallow. It is a wonderful thing, to see the semblable coherence of his men's spirits and his: They, by observing him, do bear themselves like foolish justices; he, by conversing with them, is turned into a justicelike serving-man; their spirits are so married in conjunction with the participation of society, that they flock together in consent,[7] like so many wild geese. If I had a suit to master Shallow, I would humour his men, with the imputation of being near their master:[8] if to his men, I would curry with master Shallow, that no man could better command his servants. It is certain, that either wise bearing, or ignorant carriage, is caught, as men take diseases, one of another: therefore, let men take heed of their company. I will devise matter enough out of this Shallow, to keep Prince Harry in continual laughter, the wearing-out of six fashions (which is four terms, or two actions,[9]) and he shall laugh without *intervallums.* O, it is much, that a lie, with a slight oath, and a jest, with a sad brow,[10] will do with a fellow that never had the ache in his shoulders! O, you shall see him laugh, till his face be like a wet cloak ill laid up.

Shal. [*Within.*] Sir John!

Fal. I come, master Shallow; I come, master Shallow. [*Exit* FALSTAFF.

SCENE II. Westminster. *A Room in the Palace. Enter* WARWICK *and the* Lord Chief Justice.

War. How now, my lord chief justice? whither away?

Ch. Just. How doth the king?

---

of me declared, that I should depart this life in Jerusalem.'—*Holinshed*, p. 541.

The late Dr. Vincent pointed out a remarkable coincidence in a passage of Anna Comnena (Alexias, lib. vi. p. 162, ed. Paris, 1658,) relating to the death of Robert Guiscard, king of Sicily, in a place called Jerusalem, at Cephalonia. In Lodge's Devils Conjured is a similar story of Pope Sylvester; but the Pope outwitted the Devil. And Fuller, in his Church History, b. v. p. 178, relates something of the same kind about Cardinal Wolsey, of whom it had been predicted *that he should have his end at Kingston.* Which was thought to be fulfilled by his dying in the custody of Sir William Kingston.

1 This adjuration, which seems to have been a popular substitute for profane swearing, occurs in several old plays. *By cock* is supposed to be a corruption or disguise of the name of God in favour of pious ears: but the addition of *pie* has not yet been satisfactorily accounted for. It has been conjectured that it may be only a ludicrous oath by the common sign of an alehouse, *The Cock and Magpie*, or *Cock and Pie*, being a most ancient and favourite sign. It should appear from the following passage, in A Catechisme containing the Summe of Religion, by George Giffard, 1583, that it was not considered as a corruption of the sacred name. 'Men suppose that they do not offende when they do not sweare falsely; and because they will not take the name of God to abuse it, they sware by *small things*; as *by cock and pie*, by the mousefoot, and many such like.'

2 *Precepts* are *warrants.* Davy has almost as many employments as Scrub in the Beaux Stratagem.

3 i. e. cast up, computed.

4 'A friend in court is worth a penny in purse,' is one of Camden's proverbial sentences. See his Remaines, 4to. 1605.

5 *Wilnecote* or *Wincot*, is a village in Warwickshire, near Stratford. The old copies read *Woncot*

6 This is no exaggerated picture of the course of justice in Shakspeare's time. Sir Nicholas Bacon, in a speech to parliament, 1559, says, 'Is it not a monstrous disguising to have a justice a maintainer, acquitting some for gain, enditing others for malice, bearing with him as his servant, overthrowing the other as his enemy.' *D'Ewes*, p. 34. He repeats the same words again in 1571. *Ib.* 153. A member of the house of commons, in 1601, says, 'A justice of peace is a living creature, that for half a dozen chickens will dispense with a dozen of penal statutes,' &c.

7 *Consent* is *accord*, agreement; a combination for any particular purpose. Baret renders '*secta*, a divers *consente* in sundry wilful opinions.'

8 i.e. admitted to their master's confidence.

9 There is something humorous in making a spendthrift compute time by the operation of an action for debt.

10 i. e. a *serious* face.

War. Exceeding well; his cares are now all ended.
Ch. Just. I hope, not dead.
War. He's walk'd the way of nature;
And, to our purposes, he lives no more.
Ch. Just. I would, his majesty had call'd me with him:
The service that I truly did his life,
Hath left me open to all injuries.
War. Indeed, I think, the young king loves you not.
Ch. Just. I know, he doth not; and do arm myself,
To welcome the condition of the time;
Which cannot look more hideously upon me
Than I have drawn it in my fantasy.

Enter PRINCE JOHN, PRINCE HUMPHREY, CLARENCE, WESTMORELAND, *and others.*

War. Here come the heavy issue of dead Harry:
O, that the living Harry had the temper
Of him, the worst of these three gentlemen!
How many nobles then should hold their places,
That must strike sail to spirits of vile sort!
Ch. Just. Alas! I fear, all will be overturn'd.
P. John. Good morrow, cousin Warwick.
P. Humph. Cla. Good morrow, cousin.
P. John. We meet like men that had forgot to speak.
War. We do remember; but our argument
Is all too heavy to admit much talk.
P. John. Well, peace be with him that hath made us heavy!
Ch. Just. Peace be with us, lest we be heavier!
P. Humph. O, good my lord, you have lost a friend, indeed:
And I dare swear, you borrow not that face
Of seeming sorrow; it is, sure, your own.
P. John. Though no man be assur'd what grace to find,
You stand in coldest expectation:
I am the sorrier; 'would, 'twere otherwise.
Cla. Well, you must now speak Sir John Falstaff fair;
Which swims against your stream of quality.
Ch. Just. Sweet princes, what I did, I did in honour,
Led by the impartial conduct of my soul;
And never shall you see, that I will beg
A ragged and forestall'd remission.—[1]
If truth and upright innocency fail me,
I'll to the king my master that is dead,
And tell him who hath sent me after him.
War. Here comes the prince.

Enter KING HENRY V.

Ch. Just. Good morrow; and heaven save your majesty!
King. This new and gorgeous garment, majesty,
Sits not so easy on me as you think.—
Brothers, you mix your sadness with some fear;
This is the English, not the Turkish court;
Not Amurath an Amurath[2] succeeds,
But Harry Harry: Yet be sad, good brothers,
For, to speak truth, it very well becomes you;
Sorrow so royally in you appears,
That I will deeply put the fashion on,
And wear it in my heart. Why then, be sad:
But entertain no more of it, good brothers,
Than a joint burden laid upon us all.
For me, by heaven, I bid you be assur'd,
I'll be your father and your brother too;
Let me but bear your love, I'll bear your cares.
Yet weep, that Harry's dead; and so will I:
But Harry lives, that shall convert those tears,
By number, into hours of happiness.
P. John, &c. We hope no other from your majesty.
King. You all look strangely on me;—and you most; [*To the* Chief Justice.
You are, I think, assur'd I love you not.
Ch. Just. I am assur'd, if I be measur'd rightly,
Your majesty hath no just cause to hate me.
King. No!
How might a prince of my great hopes forget
So great indignities you laid upon me?
What! rate, rebuke, and roughly send to prison
The immediate heir of England? Was this easy?[3]
May this be wash'd in Lethe, and forgotten?
Ch. Just. I then did use the person of your father;
The image of his power lay then in me:
And, in the administration of his law,
Whiles I was busy for the commonwealth,
Your highness pleased to forget my place,
The majesty and power of law and justice,
The image of the king whom I presented,
And struck me in my very seat of judgment;[4]
Whereon, as an offender to your father,
I gave bold way to my authority,
And did commit you. If the deed were ill,
Be you contented, wearing now the garland,
To have a son set your decrees at nought;
To pluck down justice from your awful bench;
To trip the course of law, and blunt the sword
That guards the peace and safety of your person,
Nay, more; to spurn at your most royal image,
And mock your workings in a second body.[5]
Question your royal thoughts, make the case yours;
Be now the father, and propose a son:[6]
Hear your own dignity so much profan'd,
See your most dreadful laws so loosely slighted,
Behold yourself so by a son disdain'd;
And then imagine me taking your part,
And, in your power, soft silencing your son.
After this cold considerance, sentence me;
And, as you are a king, speak in your state,[7]
What I have done, that misbecame my place,
My person, or my liege's sovereignty.
King. You are right, justice, and you weigh this well;
Therefore still bear the balance and the sword:
And I do wish your honours may increase,
Till you do live to see a son of mine
Offend you, and obey you, as I did.
So shall I live to speak my father's words;
Happy am I, that have a man so bold,
That dares do justice on my proper son:
And not less happy, having such a son,
That would deliver up his greatness so
Into the hands of justice.—You did commit me:
For which, I do commit into your hand
The unstain'd sword that you have us'd to bear,
With this remembrance,[8]—That you use the same
With the like bold, just, and impartial spirit,

1 'A ragged and forestalled remission' is a remission or pardon obtained by beggarly supplication. *Forestalling* is *prevention.* In a former scene the prince says to his father:—

'But for my tears, &c.
I had *forestall'd* this dear and deep rebuke.'

2 Amurath IV. emperor of the Turks, died in 1596; his second son, Amurath, who succeeded him, had all his brothers strangled at a feast, to which he invited them, while yet ignorant of their father's death. It is highly probable that Shakspeare alludes to this transaction. The play may have been written while the fact was still recent.

3 *Was this easy?* was this a *light offence?*

4 It has already been remarked that Sir William Gascoigne, the chief justice in this play, died in the reign of Henry IV.; and consequently this scene has no foundation in fact. Shakspeare was misled by Stowe, or probably was careless about the matter While Gascoigne was at the bar, Henry of Bolingbroke was his client, who appointed him his attorney to sue out his livery in the Court of Wards: but Richard II. defeated his purpose. When Bolingbroke became Henry IV. he appointed Gascoigne chief justice. In that station he acquired the character of a learned, upright, wise, and intrepid judge. The story of his committing the prince is told by Sir Thomas Elyot, in his book entitled The Governor; but Shakspeare followed the Chronicles.

5 Treat with contempt your acts executed by a representative.

6 i.e. image to yourself that you have a son.

7 In your regal character and office.

8 *Remembrance;* that is *admonition* or *warning*

As you have done 'gainst me. There is my hand;
You shall be as a father to my youth:
My voice shall sound as you do prompt mine ear;
And I will stoop and humble my intents
To your well practis'd, wise directions.——
And, princes all, believe me, I beseech you;—
My father is gone wild into his grave,[1]
For in his tomb lie my affections;
And with his spirit sadly[2] I survive,
To mock the expectation of the world;
To frustrate prophecies; and to raze out
Rotten opinion, who hath writ me down
After my seeming. The tide of blood in me
Hath proudly flow'd in vanity, till now:
Now doth it turn, and ebb back to the sea;
Where it shall mingle with the state[3] of floods,
And flow henceforth in formal majesty.
Now call we our high court of parliament:
And let us choose such limbs of noble counsel,
That the great body of our state may go
In equal rank with the best govern'd nation;
That war, or peace, or both at once, may be
As things acquainted and familiar to us;——
In which you, father, shall have foremost hand.—
[*To the* Lord Chief Justice.
Our coronation done, we will accite,[4]
As I before remember'd, all our state:
And (God consigning to my good intents,)
No prince, nor peer, shall have just cause to say,
Heaven shorten Harry's happy life one day.
[*Exeunt.*

SCENE III. Glostershire. *The Garden of* Shallow's *House. Enter* FALSTAFF, SHALLOW, SILENCE, BARDOLPH, *the* Page, *and* DAVY.

Shal. Nay, you shall see mine orchard: where, in an arbour, we will eat a last year's pippin of my own graffing, with a dish of carraways,[5] and so forth;—come, cousin Silence;—and then to bed.

Fal. 'Fore God, you have here a goodly dwelling, and a rich.

Shal. Barren, barren, barren; beggars all, beggars all, Sir John:—marry, good air.—Spread, Davy; spread, Davy; well said, Davy.

Fal. This Davy serves you for good uses; he is your serving-man, and your husbandman.

Shal. A good varlet, a good varlet, a very good varlet, Sir John.—By the mass, I have drunk too much sack at supper:——a good varlet. Now sit down, now sit down:—come, cousin.

Sil. Ah, sirrah! quoth-a,—we shall
Do nothing but eat, and make good cheer,
[Singing.
And praise heaven for the merry year;
When flesh is cheap, and females dear,[6]
And lusty lads roam here and there,
So merrily,
And ever among so merrily.

Fal. There's a merry heart!—Good master Silence, I'll give you a health for that anon.

Shal. Give master Bardolph some wine, Davy.

Davy. Sweet sir, sit; [*Seating* BARDOLPH *and the* Page *at another table.*] I'll be with you anon:—most sweet sir, sit.——Master page, good master page, sit: proface![7] What you want in meat, we'll have in drink. But you must bear; The heart's all.
[*Exit.*

Shal. Be merry, master Bardolph;—and my little soldier there, be merry.

Sil. *Be merry, be merry, my wife has all;*
[Singing.
For women are shrews, both short and tall:
'Tis merry in hall, when beards wag all,[8]
And welcome merry shrove-tide.[9]
Be merry, be merry, &c.

Fal. I did not think, master Silence had been a man of this mettle.

Sil. Who I? I have been merry twice and once, ere now.

Re-enter DAVY.

Davy. There is a dish of leather-coats[10] for you.
[*Setting them before* BARDOLPH.

Shal. Davy,—

Davy. Your worship?—I'll be with you straight. [*To* BARD.]—A cup of wine, sir?

Sil. *A cup of wine, that's brisk and fine,*
And drink unto the leman mine; [Singing.
And a merry heart lives long-a.

Fal. Well said, master Silence.

Sil. And we shall be merry;—now comes in the sweet of the night.

Fal. Health and long life to you, master Silence.

Sil. *Fill the cup, and let it come;*
I'll pledge you a mile to the bottom.

Shal. Honest Bardolph, welcome: if thou wantest any thing, and wilt not call, beshrew thy heart.—Welcome, my little tiny thief; [*To the* Page.] and welcome, indeed, too.—I'll drink to master Bardolph, and to all the cavaleroes about London.

Davy. I hope to see London once ere I die.

Bard. An I might see you there, Davy,—

Shal. By the mass, you'll crack a quart together. Ha! will you not, master Bardolph?

Bard. Yes, sir, in a pottle pot.

Shal. I thank thee:—The knave will stick by thee, I can assure thee that: he will not out; he is true bred.

Bard. And I'll stick by him, sir.

Shal. Why, there spoke a king. Lack nothing: be merry. [*Knocking hard.*] Look who's at door there: Ho! who knocks? [*Exit* DAVY.

Fal. Why, now you have done me right.
[*To* SILENCE, *who drinks a bumper.*

Sil. *Do me right,*[11] [Singing.

---

1 The meaning is, My *wild* dispositions having ceased on my father's death, and being now as it were buried in his tomb, he and wildness are interred in the same grave.

2 *Sadly* is soberly, seriously; *sad* is opposed to *wild.*

3 That is, with the *majestic dignity* of the ocean, the chief of floods.

4 Summons.

5 This passage, which was long a subject of dispute, some pertinaciously maintaining that *carraways* meant *apples* of that name, has been at length properly explained by the following quotations from Cogan's Haven of Health, 1599:—'For the same purpose *careway seeds* are used to be made in comfits, *and to be eaten with apples*, and surely very good for that purpose, for all such things as breed wind, would be eaten with other things that breake wind.' Again:—'Howbeit we are wont to eate *carrawaies*, or *biskets*, or some other kind of comfits or seedes, together with apples, thereby to breake winde ingendred by them; and surely this is a verie good way for students.' The truth is, that apples and carraways were formerly always eaten together; and it is said that they are still served up on particular days at Trinity College, Cambridge.

6 The character of Silence is admirably sustained; he would scarcely speak a word before, and now there is no end to his garrulity. He has a catch for every occasion:—

'When flesh is *cheap* and females *dear.*'

Here the double sense of *dear* must be remembered.

7 An expression of welcome equivalent to *Much good may it do you!*

8 This proverbial rhyme is of great antiquity; it is found in Adam Davie's Life of Alexander:—

'Merrie swithe it is in hall
When the berdes waveth alle.'

9 *Shrovetide* was the ancient *carnival*; 'In most places where the Romish religion is generally professed, it is a time wherein more than ordinary liberty is tolerated, as it were in recompense of the abstinence (penance which is to be undergone for a time) for the future; whence by a metaphor it may be taken for any time of rioting or licence.'—*Philips's World of Words.* T. Warton does not seem to have known that *shrovetide* and *carnival* were the same, or that *carniscapium* and *carnisprivium* were the low Latin terms for the latter. *Shrovetide* was a season of such mirth that *shroving*, or to *shrove*, signified to be merry.

10 Apples commonly called russetines.

11 To *do a man right* and to *do him reason* were formerly the usual expressions in pledging healths; he who drank a bumper expected that a bumper should be drunk to his toast. To this Bishop Hall alludes in his Quo Vadis:—'Those *formes of ceremonious quaffing*, in which men have learned to make gods of others and

And dub me knight:
Samingo.[2]
Is't not so?

Fal. 'Tis so.

Sil. Is't so? Why, then say, an old man can do somewhat.

Re-enter DAVY.

Davy. An it please your worship, there's one Pistol come from the court with news.

Fal. From the court, let him come in.—

Enter PISTOL.

Fal. How now, Pistol?

Pist. God save you, Sir John!

Fal. What wind blew you hither, Pistol?

Pist. Not the ill wind which blows no man to good.[3]—Sweet knight, thou art now one of the greatest men in the realm.

Sil. By'r lady, I think 'a be; but goodman Puff of Barson.[4]

Pist. Puff?
Puff in thy teeth, most recreant coward base!—
Sir John, I am thy Pistol, and thy friend,
And helter-skelter have I rode to thee;
And tidings do I bring, and lucky joys,
And golden times, and happy news of price.

Fal. I pr'ythee now, deliver them like a man of this world.

Pist. A foutra for the world, and worldlings base!
I speak of Africa, and golden joys.

Fal. O base Assyrian knight, what is thy news?
Let king Cophetua know the truth thereof.

Sil. *And Robin Hood, Scarlet, and John.* [Sings.

Pist. Shall dunghill curs confront the Helicons?
And shall good news be baffled?
Then, Pistol, lay thy head in Furies' lap.

Shal. Honest gentleman, I know not your breeding.

Pist. Why then, lament therefore.

Shal. Give me pardon, sir:—If, sir, you come with news from the court, I take it, there is but two ways; either to utter them, or to conceal them. I am, sir, under the king, in some authority.

Pist. Under which king, Bezonian?[5] speak, or die.

Shal. Under King Harry.

Pist. Harry the Fourth? or Fifth?

Shal. Harry the Fourth.

Pist. A foutra for thine office!—
Sir John, thy tender lambkin now is king;
Harry the Fifth's the man. I speak the truth:
When Pistol lies, do this; and fig me,[6] like
The bragging Spaniard.

Fal. What! is the old king dead?

Pist. As nail in door:[7] The things I speak, are just.

Fal. Away, Bardolph; saddle my horse.—Master Robert Shallow, choose what office thou wilt in the land, 'tis thine.—Pistol, I will double-charge thee with dignities.

Bard. O joyful day!—I would not take a knighthood for my fortune.

Pist. What? I do bring good news?

Fal. Carry master Silence to bed.—Master Shallow, my Lord Shallow, be what thou wilt, I am fortune's steward. Get on thy boots; we'll ride all night:—O, sweet Pistol:—Away, Bardolph. [*Exit* BARD.]—Come, Pistol, utter more to me; and, withal, devise something to do thyself good.—Boot, boot, master Shallow; I know, the young king is sick for me. Let us take any man's horses; the laws of England are at my commandment. Happy are they which have been my friends; and woe to my lord chief justice!

Pist. Let vultures vile seize on his lungs also!
Where is the life that late I led, say they:
Why, here it is; Welcome these pleasant days.
[*Exeunt.*

SCENE IV. London. *A Street. Enter* Beadles, *dragging in Hostess* QUICKLY, *and* DOLL TEARSHEET.[8]

Host. No, thou arrant knave; I would I might die, that I might have thee hanged: thou hast drawn my shoulder out of joint.

1 *Bead.* The constables have delivered her over to me; and she shall have whipping-cheer enough, I warrant her: There hath been a man or two lately killed about her.

Dol. Nut-hook, nut-hook,[9] you lie. Come on; I'll tell thee what, thou damned tripe-visaged rascal; an the child I now go with do miscarry, thou hadst better thou hadst struck thy mother, thou paper-faced villain.

Host. O the Lord, that Sir John were come, he would make this a bloody day to somebody. But I pray God, the fruit of her womb miscarry!

1 *Bead.* If it do, you shall have a dozen of cushions[10] again; you have but eleven now. Come, I charge you both go with me; for the man is dead, that you and Pistol beat among you.

Doll. I'll tell thee what, thou thin man in a censer![11] I will have you as soundly swinged for this,

---

beasts of themselves: and lose their reason, whiles they pretend to *do reason*.'

1 He who drank a bumper on his knees to the health of his mistress, was dubbed a knight for the evening.

2 In Nashe's play called Summer's Last Will and Testament, 1600, Bacchus sings the following catch:—

'Monsieur *Mingo* for quaffing doth surpass
In cup, or can, or glass;
God Bacchus, do me right,
And dub me knight,
Domingo.'

In Rowland's Epigrams, 1600, Monsieur *Domingo* is celebrated as a toper. It has been supposed that the introduction of Domingo as a burthen to a drinking song was intended as a satire on the luxury of the Dominicans; but whether the change to *Samingo* was a blunder of Silence in his cups, or was a real contraction of San Domingo, is uncertain. Why Saint Dominick should be the patron of topers does not appear.

3 So in Bulleine's Dialogue of the Fever Pestilence, 1564:—

'No winde but it doth turn some man to good.'

4 *Barston* is a village in Warwickshire, lying between Coventry and Solyhull.

5 *Bezonian*, according to Florio a *bisogno*, is '*a new levied souldier, such as comes needy to the wars*.' Cotgrave, in *bisongne*, says 'a filthie knave, or clowne, a raskall, a *bisonian*, base humoured scoundrel.' Its original sense is a beggar, a needy person; it is often met with very differently spelt in the old comedies.

6 An expression of contempt or insult by putting the thumb between the fore and middle finger, and forming a coarse representation of a disease to which the name of *ficus* has always been given. The custom has been regarded as originally Spanish, but without foundation, they most probably had it from the Romans. Pistol seems to accompany the phrase with an appropriate gesticulation. In explaining the *higas dar* of the Spaniards, Minshew says, after describing it, 'a manner as they use in England *to bore the nose with the finger, as in disgrace*.' The phrase is amply explained in Mr. Douce's Illustrations of Shakspeare, vol. i. p. 492.

7 Steevens remarks that this proverbial expression is oftener used than understood. The *door nail* is the nail in ancient doors on which the knocker strikes. It is therefore used as a comparison for one irrecoverably dead, one who has fallen (as Virgil says) *multa morte*, i. e. with abundant death, such as reiterated strokes on the head would produce.

8 In the quarto, 1600, we have 'Enter *Sincklo*, and three or four officers.' And the name of *Sincklo* is prefixed to the Beadle's speeches. Sincklo is also introduced in The Taming of the Shrew, he was an actor in the same company with Shakspeare.

9 It has already been observed (Merry Wives of Windsor, Act i. Sc. 1) that *nut-hook* was a term of reproach for a bailiff or constable. Cleveland says of a committee-man:—'He is the devil's *nut-hook*, the sign with him is always in the clutches.'

10 That is to stuff her out, that she might counterfeit pregnancy. In Greene's Dispute between a He Conycatcher, &c. 1592—'to wear a *cushion* under her own kirtle, and to faine herself with child.'

11 Doll humorously compares the beadle's spare figure to the embossed figures in the middle of the pierced convex lid of a censer made of thin metal. The sluttery of rush-strewed chambers rendered censers or fire pans in which coarse perfumes were burnt most necessary utensils. In Much Ado About Nothing, Borachio says that he had been entertained for a perfumer to smoke a *musty room* at Leonato's.

you blue-bottle rogue![1] you filthy famished correctioner! if you be not swinged, I'll forswear half-kirtles.[2]

1 *Bead.* Come, come, you she knight-errant, come.

Host. O, that right should thus overcome might! Well; of sufferance comes ease.

Dol. Come, you rogue, come; bring me to a justice.

Host. Ay; come, you starved blood-hound.

Dol. Goodman death! goodman bones!

Host. Thou atomy[3] thou!

Dol. Come, you thin thing; come, you rascal!

1 *Bead.* Very well. [*Exeunt.*

SCENE V. *A public Place near* Westminster Abbey. *Enter Two* Grooms, *strewing Rushes.*

1 *Groom.* More rushes, more rushes.

2 *Groom.* The trumpets have sounded twice.

1 *Groom.* It will be two o'clock ere they come from the coronation: Despatch, despatch.

[*Exeunt* Grooms.

Enter FALSTAFF, SHALLOW, PISTOL, BARDOLPH, *and the* Page.

Fal. Stand here by me, master Robert Shallow; I will make the king do you grace: I will leer upon him, as 'a comes by; and do but mark the countenance that he will give me.

Pist. God bless thy lungs, good knight.

Fal. Come here, Pistol; stand behind me.—O, if I had had time to have made new liveries, I would have bestowed the thousand pound I borrowed of you. [*To* SHALLOW.] But 'tis no matter; this poor show doth better: this doth infer the zeal I had to see him.

Shal. It doth so.

Fal. It shows my earnestness of affection.

Shal. It doth so.

Fal. My devotion.

Shal. It doth, it doth, it doth.

Fal. As it were, to ride day and night; and not to deliberate, not to remember, not to have patience to shift me.

Shal. It is most certain.

Fal. But to stand stained with travel, and sweating with desire to see him: thinking of nothing else; putting all affairs else in oblivion; as if there were nothing else to be done, but to see him.

Pist. 'Tis *semper idem*, for *absque hoc nihil est:* 'Tis all in every part.[4]

Shal. 'Tis so, indeed.

Pist. My knight, I will inflame thy noble liver,
And make thee rage.
Thy Doll, and Helen of thy noble thoughts,
Is in base durance, and contagious prison;
Haul'd thither
By most mechanical and dirty hand:—
Rouse up revenge from ebon den with fell Alecto's snake,
For Doll is in; Pistol speaks nought but truth.

Fal. I will deliver her.

[*Shouts within, and the Trumpets sound.*

Pist. There roar'd the sea, and trumpet clangor sounds.

Enter the King *and his Train, the* Chief Justice *among them.*

Fal. God save thy grace, King Hal! my royal Hal![5]

Pist. The heavens thee guard and keep, most royal imp[6] of fame!

Fal. God save thee, my sweet boy!

King. My lord chief justice, speak to that vain man.

Ch. Just. Have you your wits? know you what 'tis you speak?

Fal. My king! my Jove! I speak to thee, my heart!

King. I know thee not, old man: Fall to thy prayers;
How ill white hairs become a fool, and jester!
I have long dream'd of such a kind of man,
So surfeit-swell'd, so old, and so profane;[7]
But, being awake, I do despise my dream.
Make less thy body hence,[8] and more thy grace,
Leave gormandizing; know, the grave doth gape
For thee thrice wider than for other men:—
Reply not to me with a fool-born jest;
Presume not, that I am the thing I was:
For heaven doth know, so shall the world perceive,
That I have turn'd away my former self;
So will I those that kept me company.
When thou dost hear I am as I have been,
Approach me; and thou shalt be as thou wast,
The tutor and the feeder of my riots:
Till then, I banish thee, on pain of death,—
As I have done the rest of my misleaders,—
Not to come near our person by ten mile.
For competence of life, I will allow you,
That lack of means enforce you not to evil:
And, as we hear you do reform yourselves,
We will,—according to your strength, and qualities,—
Give you advancement.[9]—Be it your charge, my lord,
To see perform'd the tenor of our word.
Set on. [*Exeunt* King, *and his Train.*

Fal. Master Shallow, I owe you a thousand pound.

Shal. Ay, marry, Sir John; which I beseech you to let me have home with me.

Fal. That can hardly be, master Shallow. Do not you grieve at this; I shall be sent for in private to him: look you, he must seem thus to the world. Fear not your advancement; I will be the man yet, that shall make you great.

Shal. I cannot perceive how; unless you give me your doublet, and stuff me out with straw. I beseech you, good Sir John, let me have five hundred of my thousand.

Fal. Sir, I will be as good as my word: this that you heard, was but a colour.

Shal. A colour, I fear, that you will die in, Sir John.

Fal. Fear no colours; go with me to dinner. Come, lieutenant Pistol;—come, Bardolph:—I shall be sent for soon at night.

Re-enter PRINCE JOHN, *the* Chief Justice, Officers, *&c.*

Ch. Just. Go, carry Sir John Falstaff to the Fleet;[10]
Take all his company along with him.

Fal. My lord, my lord,—

Ch. Just. I cannot now speak: I will hear you soon. Take them away.

---

1 Beadles usually wore a blue livery.

2 A *half kirtle* was a kind of *apron* or *fore part* of the dress of a woman. It could not be a cloak, as Malone supposed; nor a short bedgown, as Steevens imagined.

3 The hostess's corruption of *anatomy.*

4 Warburton thought that we should read:—
'"Tis *all in all and* all in every part.'

5 A similar scene occurs in the anonymous old play of King Henry V. Falstaff and his companions address the king in the same manner, and are dismissed as in this play.

6 Child, offspring.

7 *Profane* (says Johnson) in our author often signifies *love of talk.*

8 Henceforward.

9 This circumstance Shakspeare may have derived from the old play of King Henry V. But Hall, Holinshed, and Stowe give nearly the same account of the dismissal of Henry's loose companions. Every reader regrets to see Falstaff so hardly used, and Johnson's vindication of the king does not diminish that feeling. Poins, Johnson thinks, ought to have figured in the conclusion of the play, but I do not believe that any one had ever been sensible of the poet's neglect of him until Johnson pointed it out.

10 Johnson confesses that he does not see 'why Falstaff is carried to the Fleet; he has committed no new fault, and therefore incurred no punishment; but the different agitations of fear, anger, and surprise in him and his company, made a good scene to the eye; and our author, who wanted them no longer on the stage, was glad to find this method of sweeping them away.'

Pist. *Si fortuna me tormenta, spero me contenta.*
[*Exeunt* Fal. Shal. Pist. Bard. Page, *and* Officers.

P. John. I like this fair proceeding of the king's:
He hath intent, his wonted followers
Shall all be very well provided for;
But all are banish'd, till their conversations
Appear more wise and modest to the world.

Ch. Just. And so they are.

P. John. The king hath call'd his parliament, my lord.

Ch. Just. He hath.

P. John. I will lay odds,—that, ere this year expire,
We bear our civil swords, and native fire,
As far as France: I heard a bird so sing,
Whose music, to my thinking, pleas'd the king.
Come, will you hence? [*Exeunt.*

EPILOGUE.

Spoken by a Dancer.

First, my fear; then, my court'sy; last, my speech. My fear is, your displeasure; my court'sy, my duty; and my speech, to beg your pardons. If you look for a good speech now, you undo me: for what I have to say, is of mine own making; and what, indeed, I should say, will, I doubt, prove mine own marring. But to the purpose, and so to the venture.—Be it known to you (as it is very well,) I was lately here in the end of a displeasing play, to pray your patience for it, and to promise you a better. I did mean, indeed, to pay you with this: which, if, like an ill venture, it come unluckily home, I break, and you, my gentle creditors, lose. Here, I promised you, I would be, and here I commit my body to your mercies: bate me some, and I will pay you some, and, as most debtors do, promise you infinitely.

If my tongue cannot entreat you to acquit me, will you command me to use my legs? and yet that were but light payment,—to dance out of your debt. But a good conscience will make any possible satisfaction, and so will I. All the gentlewomen here have forgiven me; if the gentlemen will not, then the gentlemen do not agree with the gentlewomen, which was never seen before in such an assembly.

One word more, I beseech you. If you be not too much cloyed with fat meat, our humble author will continue the story, with Sir John in it, and make you merry with fair Katharine of France: where, for any thing I know, Falstaff shall die of a sweat, unless already he be killed with your hard opinions; for Oldcastle died a martyr, and this is not the man. My tongue is weary; when my legs are too, I will bid you good night: and so kneel down before you;—but, indeed, to pray for the queen.[1]

I fancy every reader, when he ends this play, cries out with Desdemona, 'O most lame and impotent conclusion!' As this play was not, to our knowledge, divided into acts by the author, I could be content to conclude it with the death of Henry the Fourth:—

'In that Jerusalem shall Harry die.'

These scenes, which now make the fifth act of *Henry the Fourth*, might then be the first of *Henry the Fifth*; but the truth is, that they do not unite very commodiously to either play. When these plays were represented, I believe they ended as they are now ended in the books; but Shakspeare seems to have designed that the whole series of action, from the beginning of *Richard the Second* to the end of *Henry the Fifth*, should be considered by the reader as one work upon one plan, only broken into parts by the necessity of exhibition.

None of Shakspeare's plays are more read than the *First and Second Parts of Henry the Fourth.* Perhaps no author has ever, in two plays, afforded so much delight. The great events are interesting, for the fate of kingdoms depends upon them; the slighter occurrences are diverting, and, except one or two, sufficiently probable; the incidents are multiplied with wonderful fertility of invention, and the characters diversified with the utmost nicety of discernment, and the profoundest skill in the nature of man.

The prince, who is the hero both of the comic and tragic part, is a young man of great abilities and violent passions, whose sentiments are right, though his actions are wrong; whose virtues are obscured by negligence, and whose understanding is dissipated by levity. In his idle hours he is rather loose than wicked; and when the occasion forces out his latent qualities, he is great without effort, and brave without tumult. The trifler is roused into a hero, and the hero again reposes in the trifler. The character is great, original, and just.

Percy is a rugged soldier, choleric and quarrelsome, and has only the soldier's virtues, generosity and courage.

But Falstaff, unimitated, unimitable Falstaff, how shall I describe thee? thou compound of sense and vice: of sense which may be admired, but not esteemed; of vice which may be despised, but hardly detested. Falstaff is a character loaded with faults, and with those faults which naturally produce contempt. He is a thief and a glutton, a coward and a boaster, always ready to cheat the weak, and prey upon the poor; to terrify the timorous, and insult the defenceless. At once obsequious and malignant, he satirizes in their absence those whom he lives by flattering. He is familiar with the prince only as an agent of vice, but of this familiarity he is so proud, as not only to be supercilious and haughty with common men, but to think his interest of importance to the Duke of Lancaster. Yet the man thus corrupt, thus despicable, makes himself necessary to the prince that despises him, by the most pleasing of all qualities, perpetual gaiety; by an unfailing power of exciting laughter; which is more frequently indulged, as his wit is not of the splendid or ambitious kind, but consists in easy scapes and sallies of levity, which make sport, but raise no envy. It must be observed, that he is stained with no enormous or sanguinary crimes, so that his licentiousness is not so offensive but that it may be borne for his mirth.

The moral to be drawn from this representation is, that no man is more dangerous than he that with a will to corrupt, hath the power to please; and that neither wit nor honesty ought to think themselves safe with such a companion, when they see Henry seduced by Falstaff.

Mr. Upton thinks these two plays improperly called the *First and Second Parts of Henry the Fourth.* The first play ends, he says, with the peaceful settlement of Henry in the kingdom by the defeat of the rebels. This is hardly true; for the rebels are not yet finally suppressed. The second, he tells us, shows *Henry the Fifth* in the various lights of a good-natured rake, till, on his father's death, he assumes a more manly character. This is true; but this representation gives us no idea of a dramatic action. These two plays will appear to every reader, who shall peruse them without ambition of critical discoveries, to be so connected, that the second is merely a sequel to the first; to be two only because they are too long to be one. JOHNSON.

---

1 Most of the ancient interludes conclude with a prayer for the king or queen. Hence perhaps, the *Vivant Rex et Regina*, at the bottom of our modern play bills.

KING HENRY THE FIFTH.

PRELIMINARY REMARKS.

THE transactions comprised in this play commence about the latter end of the first, and terminate in the eighth year of this king's reign: when he married Katharine, princess of France, and closed up the differences betwixt England and that crown.

This play, in the quarto edition of 1608, is styled *The Chronicle History of Henry*, &c. which seems to have been the title appropriated to all Shakspeare's historical dramas. Thus in *The Antipodes*, a comedy by R. Brome:—

'These lads can act the emperors' lives all over,
And Shakspeare's *Chronicled Histories* to boot.'

The players, likewise, in the folio of 1623, rank these pieces under the title of *Histories*

It is evident that a play on this subject had been performed before the year 1592. Nash, in his *Pierce Penniless*, dated in that year, says, 'What a glorious thing it is to have *Henry the Fift* represented on the stage, leading the French king prisoner, and forcing both him and the Dolphin to sweare fealtie.' Perhaps this same play was thus entered on the books of the Stationers' Company:—'Thomas Strode] May 2. 1594. A booke entituled The famous Victories of Henry the Fift, containing the honourable Battle of Agincourt.' There are two more entries of a play of King Henry V. viz. between 1596 and 1615, and one August 14, 1600. Malone had an edition printed in 1598, and Steevens had two copies of this play, one without date, and the other dated 1617, both printed by Bernard Alsop; from one of these it was reprinted in 1778, among six old plays on which Shakspeare founded, &c. published by Mr. Nichols. It is thought that this piece is prior to Shakspeare's King Henry V. and that it is the very 'displeasing play' alluded to in the epilogue to the Second Part of King Henry IV. 'for Oldcastle died a martyr, &c.' Oldcastle is the Falstaff of the piece, which is despicable, and full of ribaldry and impiety. Shakspeare seems to have taken not a few hints from it; for it comprehends, in some measure, the story of the two parts of King Henry IV. as well as of King Henry V. and no ignorance could debase the gold of Shakspeare into such dross, though no chemistry, but that of Shakspeare, could exalt such base metal into gold. This piece must have been performed before the year 1588, Tarlton, the comedian, who played both the parts of the Chief Justice and the Clown in it, having died in that year.

This anonymous play of King Henry V. is neither divided into acts or scenes, is uncommonly short, and has all the appearance of having been imperfectly taken down during the representation.

There is a play called Sir John Oldcastle, published in 1600, with the name of William Shakspeare prefixed to it. The prologue of which serves to show that a former piece, in which the character of Oldcastle was introduced, had given great offence:—

'The doubtful title (gentlemen) prefixt
Upon the argument we have in hand,
May breed suspense, and wrongfully disturbe
The peaceful quiet of your settled thoughts.
To stop which scruple, let this breefe suffice:
It is no *pamper'd glutton* we present,
Nor *aged councellour to youthful sinne*;
But one whose vertue shone above the rest,
A valiant martyr and a vertuous peere;
In whose true faith and loyalty exprest
Unto his sovereigne, and his countries weale,
We strive to pay that tribute of our love
Your favours merit: let faire truth be grac'd,
Since forg'd invention former time defac'd.'

Shakspeare's play, according to Malone, seems to have been written in the middle of the year 1599. There are three quarto editions in the poet's lifetime, 1600, 1602, and 1608. In all of them the choruses are omitted, and the play commences with the fourth speech of the second scene.

'King Henry the Fifth is visibly the favourite hero of Shakspeare in English history: he portrays him endowed with every chivalrous and kingly virtue; open, sincere, affable, yet still disposed to innocent raillery, as a sort of reminiscence of his youth, in the intervals between his dangerous and renowned achievements To bring his life after his ascent to the crown on the stage was, however, attended with great difficulty. The conquests in France were the only distinguished event of his reign: and war is much more an epic than a dramatic object.—If we would have dramatic interest war must only be the means by which something else is accomplished, and not the last aim and substance of the whole.' In King Henry the Fifth, no opportunity was afforded Shakspeare of rendering the issue of the war dramatic; but he has availed himself of other circumstances attending it with peculiar care. 'Before the battle of Agincourt he paints in the most lively colours the light-minded impatience of the French leaders for the moment of battle, which to them seemed infallibly the moment of victory; on the other hand, he paints the uneasiness of the English king and his army, from their desperate situation, coupled with the firm determination, if they are to fall, at least to fall with honour. He applies this as a general contrast between the French and English national characters; a contrast which betrays a partiality for his own nation, certainly excusable in a poet, especially when he is backed with such a glorious document as that of the memorable battle in question. He has surrounded the general events of the war with a fulness of individual characteristic, and even sometimes comic features. A heavy Scotchman, a hot Irishman, a well-meaning, honourable, pedantic Welshman, all speaking in their peculiar dialects. But all this variety still seemed to the poet insufficient to animate a play of which the object was a conquest, and no thing but a conquest. He has therefore tacked a prologue (in the technical language of that day, a chorus) to the beginning of each act. These prologues, which unite epic pomp and solemnity with lyrical sublimity, and among which the description of the two camps before the battle of Agincourt forms a most admirable night piece, are intended to keep the spectators constantly in mind that the peculiar grandeur of the actions there described cannot be developed on a narrow stage; and that they must supply the deficiencies of the representation from their own imaginations. As the subject was not properly dramatic, in the form also Shakspeare chose rather to wander beyond the bounds of the species, and to sing as a poetic herald, what he could not represent to the eye, than to cripple the progress of the action by putting long speeches in the mouths of the persons of the drama.

'However much Shakspeare celebrates the French conquest of King Henry, still he has not omitted to hint to us, after his way, the secret springs of this undertaking. Henry was in want of foreign wars to secure himself on the throne; the clergy also wished to keep him employed abroad, and made an offer of rich contributions to prevent the passing of a law which would have deprived them of the half of their revenues. His learned bishops are consequently as ready to prove to him his undisputed right to the crown of France, as he is to allow his conscience to be tranquillized by them. They prove that the Salic law is not, and never was, applicable to France; and the matter is treated in a more succinct and convincing manner than such subjects usually are in manifestoes. After his renowned battles Henry wished to secure his conquests by marriage with a French princess; all that has reference to this is intended for irony in the play. The fruit of this union, from which two nations promised to themselves such happiness in future, was that very feeble Henry the Sixth, under whom every thing was so miserably lost. It must not, therefore, be imagined that it was without the knowledge and will of the poet that an heroic drama turns out a comedy in his hands, and ends, in the manner of comedy, with a marriage of convenience.'*

* Schlegel

PERSONS REPRESENTED

King Henry the Fifth.
Duke *of* Gloster, } *Brothers to the* King.
Duke *of* Bedford, }
Duke *of* Exeter *Uncle to the* King.
Duke of York, *Cousin to the* King.
Earl *of* Salisbury,
Earl *of* Westmoreland,
Earl *of* Warwick.
Archbishop *of* Canterbury.
Bishop *of* Ely.
Earl *of* Cambridge, } *Conspirators against the* King.
Lord Scroop, }
Sir Thomas Grey, }
Sir Thomas Erpingham, } *Officers in* King Henry's *Army.*
Gower, }
Fluellen, }
Macmorris, }
Jamy, }
Bates, } *Soldiers in the same.*
Court, }
Williams, }
Nym, } *Formerly Servants to* Falstaff, *now Soldiers in the same.*
Bardolph }
Pistol, }
Boy, *Servant to them.*
A Herald. Chorus.

Charles the Sixth, *King of* France.
Lewis, *the Dauphin.*
Dukes of Burgundy, Orleans, *and* Bourbon.
The Constable of France.
Rambures, } *French Lords*
Grandpree, }
Governor of Harfleur.
Montjoy, *a French Herald.*
Ambassadors *to the* King of England.

Isabel, *Queen of* France.
Katharine, *Daughter of* Charles *and* Isabel.
Alice, *a Lady attending on the Princess* Katharine.
Quickly, Pistol's *Wife, an Hostess.*

Lords, Ladies, Officers, French *and* English Soldiers, Messengers, *and* Attendants.

The SCENE, *at the beginning of the Play, lies in* England; *but afterwards wholly in* France.

Enter Chorus.

O, for a muse of fire, that would ascend
The brightest heaven of invention!
A kingdom for a stage, princes to act,
And monarchs to behold the swelling scene!
Then should the warlike Harry, like himself,
Assume the port of Mars: and, at his heels,
Leash'd in like hounds, should famine, sword, and fire,
Crouch for employment. But pardon, gentles all,
The flat unraised spirit, that hath dar'd,
On this unworthy scaffold, to bring forth
So great an object: Can this cockpit hold
The vasty fields of France? or may we cram
Within this wooden O, the very casques,[1]
That did affright the air at Agincourt?
O, pardon! since a crooked figure may
Attest, in little place, a million;
And let us, ciphers to this great accompt,
On your imaginary forces[2] work:
Suppose, within the girdle of these walls
Are now confin'd two mighty monarchies,
Whose high upreared and abutting fronts
The perilous, narrow ocean parts asunder.
Piece out our imperfections with your thoughts;
Into a thousand parts divide one man,
And make imaginary puissance:
Think, when we talk of horses, that you see them
Printing their proud hoofs i' the receiving earth:
For 'tis your thoughts that now must deck our kings,
Carry them here and there; jumping o'er times;
Turning the accomplishment of many years
Into an hour-glass; For the which supply,
Admit me chorus to this history;
Who, prologue like, your humble patience pray
Gently to hear, kindly to judge, our play.

ACT I.

SCENE I. London.[3] *An Antechamber in the King's Palace. Enter the* Archbishop *of* Canterbury, *and* Bishop *of* Ely.[4]

Canterbury.

My lord, I'll tell you,—that self bill is urg'd,
Which in the eleventh year o' the last king's reign
Was like, and had indeed against us pass'd,
But that the scambling[5] and unquiet time
Did push it out of further question.[6]
Eli. But how, my lord, shall we resist it now?
Cant. It must be thought on. If it pass against us,
We lose the better half of our possession:
For all the temporal lands, which men devout
By testament have given to the church,
Would they strip from us: being valued thus,—
As much as would maintain, to the king's honour,
Full fifteen earls, and fifteen hundred knights:
Six thousand and two hundred good esquires;
And, to relief of lazars, and weak age,
Of indigent faint souls, past corporal toil,
A hundred alms-houses, right well supplied;
And to the coffers of the king beside,
A thousand pounds by the year: Thus runs the bill.
Ely. This would drink deep.
Cant. 'Twould drink the cup and all
Ely. But what prevention?
Cant. The king is full of grace, and fair regard.
Ely. And a true lover of the holy church.
Cant. The courses of his youth promis'd it not
The breath no sooner left his father's body,
But that his wildness, mortified in him,
Seem'd to die too:[7] yea, at that very moment,
Consideration like an angel came,
And whipp'd the offending Adam out of him
Leaving his body as a paradise,
To envelop and contain celestial spirits.
Never was such a sudden scholar made:
Never came reformation in a flood,
With such a heady current, scouring faults;
Nor never hydra-headed wilfulness
So soon did lose his seat, and all at once,
As in this king.
Ely. We are blessed in the change.
Cant. Hear him but reason in divinity
And, all admiring, with an inward wish

---

1 O for circle, alluding to the circular form of the heatre. The *very* casques does not mean the identical casques, but the casques alone, or merely the casques.

2 '*Imaginary* forces:' Imaginary for imaginative, or *your powers of fancy.* The active and passive are often confounded by old writers.

3 This first scene was added in the folio, together with the choruses, and other amplifications. It appears from Hall and Holinshed that the events passed at Leicester, where King Henry V. held a parliament in the second year of his reign. But the chorus at the beginning of the second act shows that the poet intended to make London the place of his first scene.

4 'Cantc bury and Ely.' Henry Chicheley, a Carthusian monk, recently promoted to the see of Canterbury. John Fordham, bishop of Ely, consecrated 1388, died 1426.

5 i. e. *scrambling.*

6 *Question* is debate.

7 The same thought occurs in the preceding play where King Henry V. says:—

'My father is gone wild into his grave,
For in his tomb lie my affections.'

You would desire, the king were made a prelate:
Hear him debate of commonwealth affairs,
You would say,—it hath been all in all his study:
List his discourse of war, and you shall hear
A fearful battle render'd you in music:
Turn him to any cause of policy,
The Gordian knot of it he will unloose,
Familiar as his garter; that, when he speaks,
The air, a charter'd libertine, is still,[1]
And the mute wonder lurketh in men's ears,
To steal his sweet and honey'd sentences;
So that the art and practic part of life
Must be the mistress to his theoric:[2]
Which is a wonder, how his grace should glean it,
Since his addiction was to courses vain:
His companies[3] unletter'd, rude, and shallow;
His hours fill'd up with riots, banquets, sports;
And never noted in him any study,
Any retirement, any sequestration
From open haunts and popularity.[4]

Ely. The strawberry grows underneath the nettle,
And wholesome berries thrive and ripen best,
Neighbour'd by fruit of baser quality:
And so the prince obscur'd his contemplation
Under the veil of wildness; which, no doubt,
Grew like the summer grass, fastest by night,
Unseen, yet crescive[5] in his faculty.

Cant. It must be so: for miracles are ceased;
And therefore we must needs admit the means,
How things are perfected.

Ely. But, my good lord,
How now for mitigation of this bill
Urg'd by the commons? Doth his majesty
Incline to it, or no?

Cant. He seems indifferent;
Or, rather, swaying more upon our part,
Than cherishing the exhibiters against us;
For I have made an offer to his majesty,—
Upon our spiritual convocation:
And in regard of causes now in hand,
Which I have open'd to his grace at large,
As touching France,—to give a greater sum
Than ever at one time the clergy yet
Did to his predecessors part withal.

Ely. How did this offer seem receiv'd, my lord?

Cant. With good acceptance of his majesty;
Save, that there was not time enough to hear
(As, I perceiv'd, his grace would fain have done)
The severals, and unhidden passages[6]
Of his true titles to some certain dukedoms;
And, generally, to the crown and seat of France,
Deriv'd from Edward his great grandfather.

Ely. What was the impediment that broke this off?

Cant. The French ambassador upon that instant
Crav'd audience: and the hour I think is come,
To give him hearing: Is it four o'clock?

Ely. It is.

Cant. Then go we in, to know his embassy;
Which I could, with a ready guess, declare,
Before the Frenchman speak a word of it.

Ely. I'll wait upon you; and I long to hear it.
[*Exeunt.*

SCENE II. *The same. A Room of State in the same. Enter* KING HENRY, GLOSTER, BEDFORD, EXETER, WARWICK, WESTMORELAND, *and Attendants.*

K. Hen. Where is my gracious lord of Canterbury?

Exe. Not here in presence.

K. Hen. Send for him, good uncle.[7]

West. Shall we call in the ambassador my liege?

K. Hen. Not yet, my cousin; we would be resolv'd,
Before we hear of him, of some things of weight,
That task our thoughts,[8] concerning us and France.

Enter the Archbishop *of* Canterbury, *and* Bishop *of* Ely.

Cant. God, and his angels, guard your sacred throne,
And make you long become it!

K. Hen. Sure, we thank you.
My learned lord, we pray you to proceed;
And justly and religiously unfold,
Why the law Salique, that they have in France,
Or should, or should not, bar us in our claim.
And God forbid, my dear and faithful lord,
That you should fashion, wrest, or bow your reading,
Or nicely charge your understanding soul
With opening titles miscreate,[9] whose right
Suits not in native colours with the truth;
For God doth know, how many, now in health,
Shall drop their blood in approbation[10]
Of what your reverence shall incite us to:
Therefore take heed how you impawn our person,[11]
How you awake the sleeping sword of war;
We charge you in the name of God, take heed:
For never two such kingdoms did contend,
Without much fall of blood; whose guiltless drops
Are every one a woe, a sore complaint,
'Gainst him, whose wrongs give edge unto the swords
That make such waste in brief mortality.
Under this conjuration, speak, my lord:
And we will hear, note, and believe in heart,
That what you speak is in your conscience wash'd
As pure as sin with baptism.

Cant. Then hear me, gracious sovereign,—and you peers,
That owe your lives, your faith, and services,
To this imperial throne:—There is no bar[12]
To make against your highness' claim to France,
But this, which they produce from Pharamond,—
In terram Salicam mulieres ne succedant,
No woman shall succeed in Salique land;
Which Salique land the French unjustly gloze,
To be the realm of France, and Pharamond
The founder of this law and female bar.
Yet their own authors faithfully affirm,
That the land Salique lies in Germany,
Between the floods of Sala and of Elbe:
Where Charles the Great, having subdued the Saxons,
There left behind and settled certain French;
Who, holding in disdain the German women,

1 Johnson has noticed the exquisite beauty of this line.

2 'So that the *art and practic* part of life
Must be the mistress to his *theoric.*'
He discourses with so much skill on all subjects, 'that his *theory* must have been taught by *art* and *practice,*' which is strange, since he could see little of the true art or practice among his loose companions, nor ever refused to digest his practice into theory. *Practic* and *theoric*, or rather *practique* and *theorique*, was the old orthography of *practice* and *theory*.

3 *Companies*, for companions.

4 *Popularity* meant *familiarity with the common people*, as well as popular favour or applause.

5 This expressive word is used by Drant, in his Translation of Horace's Art of Poetry, 1567.

6 'The *severals*, and *unhidden passages*.' The *particulars* and *clear unconcealed circumstances* of his true titles, &c.

7 'Send for him, good uncle.' The person here addressed was Thomas Beaufort, half brother to King Henry IV being one of the sons of John of Gaunt by Katharine Swynford. He was not made duke of Exeter till the year after the battle of Agincourt, 1416. He was properly now only earl of Dorset. Shakspeare may have confounded this character with John Holland duke of Exeter, who married Elizabeth, the king's aunt He was executed at Plashey, in 1400. The old play began with the next speech.

8 i. e. keep our thoughts busied.

9 Or burthen your knowing or conscious soul with displaying false titles in a specious manner or opening pretensions, which, if shown in their native colours, would appear to be false.

10 'Shall drop their blood in *approbation*.' *Approbation* is used by Shakspeare for *proving* or establishing by proof.

11 'Therefore take heed how you *impawn our person*.' To *impawn* was to *engage or pledge*.

12 'There is no bar,' &c. The whole speech is taken from Holinshed.

13 To *gloze* is to expound or explain and sometimes to comment upon.

For some dishonest manners of their life,
Establish'd there this law,—to wit, no female
Should be inheritrix in Salique land;
Which Salique, as I said, 'twixt Elbe and Sala,
Is at this day in Germany call'd—Meisen.
Thus doth it well appear, the Salique law
Was not devised for the realm of France:
Nor did the French possess the Salique land
Until four hundred one and twenty years
After defunction of king Pharamond,
Idly suppos'd the founder of this law;
Who died within the year of our redemption
Four hundred twenty-six; and Charles the Great
Subdued the Saxons, and did seat the French
Beyond the river Sala, in the year
Eight hundred five. Besides, their writers say,
King Pepin, which deposed Childerick,
Did, as their general, being descended
Of Blithild, which was daughter to King Clothair,
Make claim and title to the crown of France.
Hugh Capet also,—that usurp'd the crown
Of Charles the duke of Lorain, sole heir male
Of the true line and stock of Charles the Great,—
To fine[1] his title with some show of truth,
(Though, in pure truth, it was corrupt and naught,)
Convey'd[2] himself as heir to the Lady Lingare,
Daughter to Charlemain, who was the son
To Lewis the emperor, and Lewis the son
Of Charles the Great. Also King Lewis the Tenth,[3]
Who was sole heir to the usurper Capet,
Could not keep quiet in his conscience,
Wearing the crown of France, till satisfied
That fair Queen Isabel, his grandmother,
Was lineal of the Lady Ermengare,
Daughter to Charles the foresaid duke of Lorain:
By the which marriage, the line of Charles the Great
Was reunited to the crown of France.
So that, as clear as is the summer's sun,
King Pepin's title, and Hugh Capet's claim,
King Lewis his satisfaction, all appear
To hold in right and title of the female:
So do the kings of France unto this day;
Howbeit they would hold up this Salique law,
To bar your highness claiming from the female;
And rather choose to hide them in a net,
Than amply to imbare[4] their crooked titles
Usurp'd from you and your progenitors.

K. Hen. May I, with right and conscience, make this claim?

Cant. The sin upon my head, dread sovereign!
For in the book of Numbers is it writ,—
When the son dies, let the inheritance
Descend unto the daughter. Gracious lord,
Stand for your own; unwind your bloody flag;
Look back unto your mighty ancestors;
Go, my dread lord, to your great grandsire's tomb,
From whom you claim: invoke his warlike spirit,
And your great uncle's, Edward the Black Prince;
Who on the French ground play'd a tragedy,
Making defeat on the full power of France;
Whiles his most mighty father on a hill
Stood smiling; to behold his lion's whelp
Forage in blood of French nobility.[5]
O noble English, that could entertain
With half their forces the full pride of France;
And let another half stand laughing by,
All out of work, and cold for action![6]

Ely. Awake remembrance of those valiant dead,
And with your puissant arm renew their feats:
You are their heir, you sit upon their throne;
The blood and courage that renowned them,
Runs in your veins; and my thrice-puissant liege
Is in the very May-morn of his youth,
Ripe for exploits and mighty enterprises.

Exe. Your brother kings and monarchs of the earth,
Do all expect that you should rouse yourself,
As did the former lions of your blood.

West. They know, your grace hath cause, and means, and might;
So hath your highness;[7] never king of England
Had nobles richer, and more loyal subjects;
Whose hearts have left their bodies here in England,
And lie pavilion'd in the fields of France.

Cant. O, let their bodies follow, my dear liege,
With blood, and sword, and fire, to win your right:
In aid whereof, we of the spirituality
Will raise your highness such a mighty sum,
As never did the clergy at one time
Bring in to any of your ancestors.

K. Hen. We must not only arm to invade the French;
But lay down our proportions to defend
Against the Scot, who will make road upon us
With all advantages.

Cant. They of those marches,[8] gracious sovereign,
Shall be a wall sufficient to defend
Our inland from the pilfering borderers.

K. Hen. We do not mean the coursing snatchers only,
But fear the main intendment[9] of the Scot,
Who hath been still a giddy neighbour to us;
For you shall read, that my great grandfather
Never went with his forces into France,
But that the Scot on his unfurnish'd kingdom
Came pouring, like the tide into a breach,
With ample and brimfulness of his force;
Galling the gleaned land with hot essays;
Girding with grievous siege, castles and towns;
That England, being empty of defence,
Hath shook and trembled at the ill neighbourhood.[10]

Cant. She hath been then more fear'd[11] than harm'd, my liege:
For hear her but exampled by herself,—
When all her chivalry hath been in France,
And she a mourning widow of her nobles,
She hath herself not only well defended,
But taken, and impounded as a stray,
The king of Scots; whom she did send to France,
To fill King Edward's fame with prisoner kings;
And make your chronicle as rich with praise,
As is the ooze and bottom of the sea
With sunken wreck and sumless treasuries

West. But there's a saying, very old and true,—
If that you will France win,
Then with Scotland first begin:
For once the eagle England being in prey,
To her unguarded nest the weasel Scot
Comes sneaking, and so sucks her princely eggs:
Playing the mouse, in absence of the cat,
To spoil and havoc more than she can eat.

Exe. It follows, then, the cat must stay at home:
Yet that is but a crush'd necessity;[12]

---

1 'To *fine* his title with some show of truth.' To *fine* is to embellish, to trim, to make showy or specious: Limare.

2 '*Convey'd* himself as heir to the *Lady Lingare.*' Shakspeare found this expression in Holinshed; and, though it sounds odd to modern ears, it is classical.

3 'Lewis the *Tenth.*' This should be Lewis the Ninth, as it stands in Hall's Chronicle. Shakspeare has been led into the error by Holinshed, whose Chronicle he followed.

4 'Than amply to *imbare* their crooked titles.' The folio reads *imbarre*; the quarto *imbace*. As there is no other example of such a word, I cannot but think that this is an error of the press for *unbare*.

5 This alludes to the battle of Cressy; as described by Holinshed, vol. ii. p. 372

6 'Cold *for* action,' want of action being the cause of their being cold.

7 i. e. your highness hath indeed what they think and know you have.

8 'They of those *marches.*' The marches are the *borders*.

9 'But fear the main intendment of the Scot,
Who hath been still a giddy neighbour to us.'
The *main intendment* is the *principal purpose*, that he will *bend his whole force* against us: the Bellum in aliquem *intendere*, of Livy. A *giddy* neighbour is an *unstable, inconstant* one.

10 The quarto reads 'at the bruit thereof.'

11 *Fear'd* here means *frightened*

12 'Yet that is but a *crush'd* necessity.' This is the reading of the folio. The editors of late editions have adopted the reading of the quarto copy, 'curs'd neces

Since we have locks to safeguard necessaries,
And pretty traps to catch the petty thieves.
While that the armed hand doth fight abroad,
The advised head defends itself at home:
For government, though high, and low, and lower,
Put into parts, doth keep in one concent;[1]
Congreeing in a full and natural close,
Like music.
Cant. True: therefore doth heaven divide
The state of man in divers functions,
Setting endeavour in continual motion;
To which is fixed, as an aim or butt,
Obedience: for so work the honey bees;
Creatures, that, by a rule in nature, teach
The act[2] of order to a peopled kingdom.
They have a king, and officers of sorts:[3]
Where some, like magistrates, correct at home;
Others, like merchants, venture trade abroad;
Others, like soldiers, armed in their stings,
Make boot upon the summer's velvet buds;
Which pillage they with merry march bring home
To the tent-royal of their emperor:
Who, busied in his majesty, surveys
The singing masons building roofs of gold;
The civil[4] citizens kneading up the honey;
The poor mechanic porters crowding in
Their heavy burdens at his narrow gate;
The sad-ey'd justice, with his surly hum,
Delivering o'er to executors[5] pale
The lazy yawning drone. I this infer,—
That many things, having full reference
To one concent, may work contrariously;
As many arrows, loosed several ways,
Fly to one mark;
As many several ways meet in one town;
As many fresh streams run in one self-sea;
As many lines close in the dial's centre;
So may a thousand actions, once afoot,
End in one purpose, and be all well borne
Without defeat.[6] Therefore to France, my liege.
Divide your happy England into four;
Whereof take you one quarter into France,
And you withal shall make all Gallia shake.
If we, with thrice that power left at home,
Cannot defend our own door from the dog,
Let us be worried; and our nation lose
The name of hardiness, and policy.
K. Hen. Call in the messengers sent from the Dauphin.
[*Exit an* Attendant. *The* King *ascends his Throne.*
Now are we well resolv'd: and by God's help;
And yours, the noble sinews of our power,—
France being ours, we'll bend it to our awe,
Or break it all to pieces: Or there we'll sit,
Ruling, in large and ample empery,[7]
O'er France, and all her almost kingly dukedoms;
Or lay these bones in an unworthy urn,
Tombless, with no remembrance over them:
Either our history shall, with full mouth,
Speak freely of our acts; or else our grave,
Like Turkish mute, shall have a tongueless mouth,
Not worship'd with a waxen epitaph.[8]

Enter Ambassadors *of* France.

Now are we well prepar'd to know the pleasure
Of our fair cousin Dauphin; for, we hear,
Your greeting is from him, not from the king.
Amb. May it please your majesty, to give us leave
Freely to render what we have in charge;
Or shall we sparingly show you far off
The Dauphin's meaning, and our embassy?
K. Hen. We are no tyrant, but a Christian king,
Unto whose grace our passion is as subject,
As are our wretches fetter'd in our prisons:
Therefore, with frank and with uncurbed plainness,
Tell us the Dauphin's mind.
Amb. Thus then, in few
Your highness, lately sending into France,
Did claim some certain dukedoms, in the right
Of your great predecessor, King Edward the Third.
In answer of which claim, the prince our master
Says,—that you savour too much of your youth;
And bids you be advis'd, there's nought in France,
That can be with a nimble galliard[9] won;
You cannot revel into dukedoms there:
He therefore sends you, meeter for your spirit,
This tun of treasure: and, in lieu of this,
Desires you, let the dukedoms, that you claim,
Hear no more of you. This the Dauphin speaks.
K. Hen. What treasure, uncle?
Exe. Tennis-balls, my liege.[10]
K. Hen. We are glad the Dauphin is so pleasant with us;
His present, and your pains, we thank you for:
When we have match'd our rackets to these balls,
We will, in France, by God's grace, play a set,
Shall strike his father's crown into the hazard:[11]
Tell him, he hath made a match with such a wrangler,
That all the courts of France will be disturb'd
With chaces.[12] And we understand him well,
How he comes o'er us with our wilder days,
Not measuring what use we made of them.
We never valu'd this poor seat[13] of England;
And therefore, living hence,[14] did give ourself
To barbarous license; As 'tis ever common,
That men are merriest when they are from home.
But tell the Dauphin,—I will keep my state;
Be like a king, and show my sail of greatness,
When I do rouse me in my throne of France:
For that I have laid by my majesty,[15]
And plodded like a man for working-days,
But I will rise there with so full a glory,
That I will dazzle all the eyes of France,
Yea, strike the Dauphin blind to look on us.

---

sity,' and by so doing have certainly not rendered the passage more intelligible; indeed none of the attempts at explanation are satisfactory.

1 *Concent* is connected harmony in general, and not confined to any specific consonance. *Concentio* and *concentus* are both used by Cicero for the union of voices or instruments, in what we should now call a *chorus* or *concert*.

2 'The *act* of order' is the *statute* or *law* of order; as appears from the reading of the quarto. 'Creatures that by awe *ordain* an *act* of order to a peopled kingdom.'

3 i. e. of different degrees: if it be not an error of the press for *sort*, i. e. *rank*.

4 'The *civil* citizens kneading up the honey.' *Civil* is *grave*. See Twelfth Night, Act iii. Sc. 4. Johnson observes, to *knead* the honey is not physically true. The bees do, in fact, knead the wax more than the honey.

5 '*Executors*' for executioners. Thus also Burton, in his Anatomy of Melancholy, p. 38, ed. 1632:—'Tremble at an *executor*, and yet not feare hell-fire.'

6 'Without defeat.' The quartos read, 'Without *defect*.'

7 '*Empery*.' This word, which signifies *dominion*, is now obsolete, though once in general use.

8 'Not worship'd with a *waxen* epitaph.' The quartos read '— with a *paper* epitaph.' Either a *paper* or a *waxen* epitaph is an epitaph easily destroyed; one that can confer no lasting honour on the dead. Steevens thinks that the allusion is to *waxen tablets*, as any thing written upon them was easily effaced. Mr. Gifford says that a *waxen epitaph* was an epitaph affixed to the hearse or grave with wax. But it appears to me that the expression may be merely metaphorical, and not allusive to either.

9 A *galliard* was an ancient spritely dance, as its name implies.

10 In the old play of King Henry V. this present consists of a *gilded tun of tennis balls*, and a carpet.

11 The *hazard* is a place in the tennis-court, into which the ball is sometimes struck.

12 A *chace* at tennis is that spot where a ball falls, beyond which the adversary must strike his ball to gain a point or *chace*. At long tennis it is the spot where the ball leaves off rolling. We see therefore why the king has called himself a *wrangler*.

13 i. e. the throne.

14 'And therefore living *hence*;' that is *from hence*, away from this seat or throne.

15 'For that I have laid by my majesty.' To qualify myself for this undertaking, I have descended from my station, and studied the arts of life in a lower character.

And tell the pleasant prince,—this mock of his
Hath turn'd his balls to gun-stones;[1] and his soul
Shall stand sore charged for the wasteful vengeance
That shall fly with them: for many a thousand widows
Shall this his mock mock out of their dear husbands;
Mock mothers from their sons, mock castles down;
And some are yet ungotten, and unborn,
That shall have cause to curse the Dauphin's scorn.
But this lies all within the will of God,
To whom I do appeal; and in whose name,
Tell you the Dauphin, I am coming on,
To venge me as I may, and to put forth
My rightful hand in a well hallow'd cause.
So, get you hence in peace; and tell the Dauphin,
His jest will savour but of shallow wit,
When thousands weep, more than did laugh at it.—
Convey them with safe conduct.—Fare you well.
[*Exeunt* Ambassadors.

Exe. This was a merry message.

K. Hen. We hope to make the sender blush at it.
[*Descends from his Throne.*
Therefore, my lords, omit no happy hour,
That may give furtherance to our expedition:
For we have now no thought in us but France;
Save those to God, that run before our business.
Therefore, let our proportions for these wars
Be soon collected; and all things thought upon,
That may, with reasonable swiftness, add
More feathers to our wings; for, God before,
We'll chide this Dauphin at his father's door.
Therefore, let every man now task his thought,[2]
That this fair action may on foot be brought.
[*Exeunt.*

ACT II.

Enter CHORUS.

Cho. Now all the youth of England are on fire,
And silken dalliance in the wardrobe lies;
Now thrive the armourers, and honour's thought
Reigns solely in the breast of every man:
They sell the pasture now, to buy the horse;
Following the mirror of all Christian kings,
With winged heels, as English Mercuries.
For now sits Expectation in the air;
And hides a sword, from hilt unto the point,
With crowns imperial, crowns, and coronets,[3]
Promis'd to Harry, and his followers.
The French, advis'd by good intelligence
Of this most dreadful preparation,
Shake in their fear; and with pale policy
Seek to divert the English purposes.
O England!—model to thy inward greatness,
Like little body with a mighty heart,—
What might'st thou do, that honour would thee do,
Were all thy children kind and natural!
But see thy fault! France hath in thee found out
A nest of hollow bosoms, which he fills
With treacherous crowns: and three corrupted men,—
One, Richard earl of Cambridge;[4] and the second
Henry Lord Scroop[5] of Masham; and the third,
Sir Thomas Grey, knight of Northumberland,—
Have, for the gilt[6] of France, (O guilt, indeed!)
Confirm'd conspiracy with fearful France;
And by their hands this grace of kings must die
(If hell and treason hold their promises,)
Ere he take ship for France, and in Southampton.
Linger your patience on; and well digest
The abuse of distance, while we force a play.[7]
The sum is paid; the traitors are agreed;
The king is set from London; and the scene
Is now transported, gentles, to Southampton:
There is the playhouse now, there must you sit:
And thence to France shall we convey you safe,
And bring you back, charming the narrow seas
To give you gentle pass; for, if we may,
We'll not offend one stomach with our play.
But, till the king come forth, and but till then,
Unto Southampton do we shift our scene.[8] [*Exit*

SCENE I. *The same.* Eastcheap. *Enter* NYM *and* BARDOLPH.

Bard. Well met, Corporal Nym.

Nym. Good morrow, Lieutenant Bardolph.[9]

Bard. What, are ancient Pistol and you friends yet?

Nym. For my part, I care not: I say little: but when time shall serve, there shall be smiles;[10]—but that shall be as it may. I dare not fight; but I will wink, and hold out mine iron: It is a simple one: but what though? it will toast cheese; and it will endure cold as another man's sword will: and there's the humour of it.

Bard. I will bestow a breakfast, to make you friends; and we'll be all three sworn brothers[11] to France; let it be so, good Corporal Nym.

Nym. 'Faith, I will live so long as I may, that's the certain of it; and when I cannot live any longer, I will do as I may: that is my rest,[12] that is the rendezvous of it.

Bard. It is certain, corporal, that he is married to Nell Quickly: and, certainly, she did you wrong; for you were troth-plight to her.

Nym. I cannot tell; things must be as they may: men may sleep, and they may have their throats about them at that time; and, some say, knives have edges. It must be as it may: though patience be a tired mare, yet she will plod. There must be conclusions. Well, I cannot tell.[13]

---

1 'Hath turn'd his balls to *gun-stones*.' When ordnance was first used they discharged balls not of iron but of stone.

2 'Task his thought.' We have this phrase before.

3 Expectation is also personified by Milton:—
—— while *Expectation* stood
In horror.'—
In ancient representations of trophies, &c. it is common to see swords encircled with crowns. Shakspeare's image is supposed to be taken from a wood cut in the first edition of Holinshed.

4 'Richard earl of Cambridge' was Richard de Conisbury, younger son of Edmund Langley, duke of York. He was father of Richard duke of York, and grandfather of Edward the Fourth.

5 'Henry Lord Scroop' was a third husband of Joan, duchess of York, mother in law of Richard earl of Cambridge.

6 Gilt for golden money.

7 The old copy reads:—
'Linger your patience on, and *we'll* digest
The abuse of distance; force a play.'
The alteration was made by Pope.

8 'But till the king come forth, and *but* till then,
Unto Southampton do we shift our scene.'
The old copy reads:—
'But till the king come forth, and *not* till then.'
The emendation was proposed by Mr. Roderick, and deserves admission into the text. Malone has plainly shown that it is a common typographical error. The objection is, that a scene in London intervenes; but this may be obviated by transposing that scene to the end of the first act. The division into acts and scenes, it should be recollected, is the arbitrary work of Mr. Rowe and the subsequent editors; and the first act of this play, as it is now divided, is unusually short. This chorus has slipped out of its place.

9 At this scene begins the connexion of this play with the latter part of King Henry IV. The characters would be indistinct and the incidents unintelligible without the knowledge of what passed in the two former plays.

10 'When time shall serve, there shall be *smiles*.' Dr. Farmer thought that this was an error of the press for *smites*, i. e. *blows*, a word used in the poet's age, and still provincially current. The passage, as it stands, has been explained:—'I care not whether we are friends at present; however, when time shall serve, *we shall be in good humour with each other*: but be it as it may.'

11 'Sworn brothers.' In the times of adventure it was usual for two or more chiefs to bind themselves to share in each other's fortunes, and divide their acquisitions between them. They were called *fratres jurati*. These cut-purses set out for France as if they were going to make a conquest of the kingdom.

12 'That is my *rest*;' that is my *determination*.

13 i. e. I know not what to say or think of it. See this phrase amply illustrated in Mr. Gifford's Ben Jonson, vol. i. p. 125. No phrase is more common in our

Enter PISTOL *and* MRS. QUICKLY.

Bard. Here comes ancient Pistol, and his wife: good corporal, be patient here.—How now, mine host Pistol?

Pist. Base tike,[1] call'st thou me—host?
Now, by this hand I swear, I scorn the term;
Nor shall my Nell keep lodgers.

Quick. No, by my troth, not long: for we cannot lodge and board a dozen or fourteen gentlewomen, that live honestly by the prick of their needles, but it will be thought we keep a bawdy-house straight. [NYM *draws his sword.*] O well-i-day, Lady, if he be not drawn now![2] we shall see wilful adultery and murder committed. Good Lieutenant Bardolph,—good corporal, offer nothing here.

Nym. Pish!

Pist. Pish for thee, Iceland dog![3] thou prick-eared cur of Iceland!

Quick. Good Corporal Nym, show the valour of a man, and put up thy sword.

Nym. Will you shog off? I would have you *solus*. [*Sheathing his sword.*

Pist. Solus, egregious dog? O viper vile!
The *solus* in thy most marvellous face;
The *solus* in thy teeth, and in thy throat,
And in thy hateful lungs, yea, in thy maw, perdy;
And, which is worse, within thy nasty mouth!
I do retort the *solus* in thy bowels:
For I can take,[4] and Pistol's cock is up,
And flashing fire will follow.

Nym. I am not Barbason;[5] you cannot conjure me, I have a humour to knock you indifferently well: If you grow foul with me, Pistol, I will scour you with my rapier, as I may, in fair terms: if you would walk off, I would prick your guts a little, in good terms, as I may; and that's the humour of it.

Pist. O braggard vile, and damned furious wight!
The grave doth gape, and doting death is near;
Therefore exhale.[6] [PISTOL *and* NYM *draw.*

Bard. Hear me, hear me what I say:—he that strikes the first stroke, I'll run him up to the hilts, as I am a soldier. [*Draws.*

Pist. An oath of mickle might; and fury shall abate.
Give me thy fist, thy fore-foot to me give;
Thy spirits are most tall.

Nym. I will cut thy throat, one time or other, in fair terms; that is the humour of it.

Pist. Coupe le gorge, that's the word?—I thee defy again.
O hound of Crete, think'st thou my spouse to get?
No; to the spital go,
And from the powdering-tub of infamy
Fetch forth the lazar kite of Cressid's kind,[7]
Doll Tear-sheet she by name, and her espouse:
I have, and I will hold, the *quondam*[8] Quickly
For the only she; and—*Pauca*, there's enough.

Enter the Boy.

Boy. Mine host Pistol, you must come to my master,—and you, hostess;—he is very sick, and would to bed.—Good Bardolph, put thy nose between his sheets, and do the office of a warming-pan: 'faith, he's very ill.

Bard. Away, you rogue.

Quick. By my troth, he'll yield the crow a pudding one of these days: the king has killed his heart.—Good husband, come home presently. [*Exeunt* MRS. QUICKLY *and* BOY.

Bard. Come, shall I make you two friends? We must to France together; Why, the devil, should we keep knives to cut one another's throats?

Pist. Let floods o'erswell, and fiends for food howl on!

Nym. You'll pay me the eight shillings I won of you at betting?

Pist. Base is the slave that pays.

Nym. That now I will have; that's the humour of it.

Pist. As manhood shall compound; Push home.

Bard. By this sword, he that makes the first thrust, I'll kill him; by this sword, I will.

Pist. Sword is an oath, and oaths must have their course.

Bard. Corporal Nym, an thou wilt be friends, be friends: an thou wilt not, why then be enemies with me too. Pr'ythee, put up.

Nym. I shall have my eight shillings, I won of you at betting?

Pist. A noble[9] shalt thou have, and present pay
And liquor likewise will I give to thee,
And friendship shall combine, and brotherhood,
I'll live by Nym, and Nym shall live by me;—
Is not this just?—for I shall sutler be
Unto the camp, and profits will accrue.
Give me thy hand.

Nym. I shall have my noble?

Pist. In cash most justly paid.

Nym. Well then, that's the humour of it.

Re-enter MRS. QUICKLY.

Quick. As ever you came of women, come in quickly to Sir John: Ah, poor heart! he is so shaked of a burning quotidian tertian, that it is most lamentable to behold. Sweet men, come to him.

Nym. The king hath run bad humours on the knight, that's the even of it.

Pist. Nym, thou hast spoke the right;
His heart is fracted and corroborate.

Nym. The king is a good king: but it must be as it may; he passes some humours, and careers.

Pist. Let us condole the knight; for, lambkins, we will live. [*Exeunt.*

SCENE II. Southampton. *A Council Chamber.*

Enter EXETER, BEDFORD, *and* WESTMORELAND.

Bed. 'Fore God, his grace is bold, to trust these traitors.

Exe. They shall be apprehended by and by.

West. How smooth and even they do bear themselves!
As if allegiance in their bosoms sat,
Crowned with faith, and constant loyalty.

Bed. The king hath note of all that they intend,
By interception which they dream not of.

Exe. Nay, but the man that was his bedfellow,[10]

---

old dramatic writers; yet it had escaped the commentators on Shakspeare.

1 i. e. base fellow. Still used in the north; where a *tike* is also a dog of a large common breed; as a mastiff, or shepherd's dog.

2 'O well-i-day, Lady, if he be not drawn now!' The folio has 'O well-a-day, Lady, if he be not *hewn* now;' an evident error of the press. The quarto reads 'O Lord! here's Corporal Nym's—now,' &c.

3 '*Iceland dogges*, curled and rough all over, which, by reason of the length of their heare, make show neither of face nor of body. And yet thes curres, forsoothe, because they are so strange, are greatly set by, esteemed, taken up, and made of, many times instead of the spaniell gentle or comforter.'—Abraham Fleming's translation of Caius de Canibus, 1576, *Of English Dogges. Island cur* is again used as a term of contempt in 'Epigrams served out in Fifty-two several Dishes;' *no date*:—

'He wears a gown lac'd round, laid down with furre,
Or, miser-like, a pouch where never man
Could thrust his finger, but this *island curre*.'

4 'For I can *take*.' Malone would change this, without necessity, to 'I can *talk*.' Pistol only means, 'I can *understand*, or *comprehend* you.' It is still common in the plebeian phrase: 'Do you *take* me?' for Do you know my meaning?

5 *Barbason* is the name of a demon mentioned in The Merry Wives of Windsor. The unmeaning tumour of Pistol's speech very naturally reminds Nym of the sounding nonsense uttered by conjurers.

6 By *exhale*, Pistol, in his fantastic language, probably means *die* or *breathe your last*. Malone suggests that he may only mean '*draw, haul*, or lug out.'

7 '*The lazar kite of Cressid's kind*.' Of Cressida's nature, see the play of Troilus and Cressida.

8 Formerly.

9 The *noble* was worth six shillings and eight-pence.

10 'That was his *bedfellow*.' Thus Holinshed:—'The said Lord Scroop was in such favour with the king, that he admitted him sometimes to be his *bedfellow*.' This familiar appellation of *bedfellow* was common among the ancient nobility. This custom, which now appears so strange and unseemly to us, continued to

Whom he hath cloy'd[1] and grac'd with princely favours,—
That he should, for a foreign purse, so sell
His sovereign's life to death and treachery!

Trumpet sounds. Enter KING HENRY, SCROOP, CAMBRIDGE, GREY, Lords, *and* Attendants.

K. Hen. Now sits the wind fair, and we will aboard.
My lord of Cambridge,—and my kind lord of Masham,—
And you, my gentle knight,——give me your thoughts;
Think you not, that the powers we bear with us,
Will cut their passage through the force of France;
Doing the execution, and the act,
For which we have in head[2] assembled them?
Scroop. No doubt, my liege, if each man do his best.
K. Hen. I doubt not that: since we are well persuaded,
We carry not a heart with us from hence,
That grows not in a fair consent[3] with ours;
Nor leave not one behind, that doth not wish
Success and conquest to attend on us.
Cam. Never was monarch better fear'd, and lov'd,
Than is your majesty; there's not, I think, a subject,
That sits in heart-grief and uneasiness
Under the sweet shade of your government.
Grey. Even those that were your father's enemies,
Have steep'd their galls in honey; and do serve you
With hearts create[4] of duty and of zeal.
K. Hen. We therefore have great cause of thankfulness;
And shall forget the office of our hand,
Sooner than quittance of desert and merit,
According to the weight and worthiness.
Scroop. So service shall with steeled sinews toil;
And labour shall refresh itself with hope,
To do your grace incessant services.
K. Hen. We judge no less.—Uncle of Exeter,
Enlarge the man committed yesterday,
That rail'd against our person: we consider,
It was excess of wine that set him on;
And, on his more advice,[5] we pardon him.
Scroop. That's mercy, but too much security:
Let him be punish'd, sovereign; lest example
Breed, by his sufferance, more of such a kind.
K. Hen. O, let us yet be merciful.
Cam. So may your highness, and yet punish too.
Grey. Sir, you show great mercy, if you give him life,
After the taste of much correction.
K. Hen. Alas, your too much love and care of me
Are heavy orisons 'gainst this poor wretch.
If little faults, proceeding on distemper,[6]
Shall not be wink'd at, how shall we stretch our eye,
When capital crimes, chew'd, swallow'd, and digested,
Appear before us?—We'll yet enlarge that man,
Though Cambridge, Scroop, and Grey,—in their dear care,
And tender preservation of our person,—
Would have him punish'd. And now to our French causes;
Who are the late[7] commissioners?
Cam. I one, my lord;
Your highness bade me ask for it to-day.
Scroop. So did you me, my liege.
Grey. And me, my royal sovereign.
K. Hen. Then, Richard, earl of Cambridge, there is yours;—
There yours, Lord Scroop of Masham;—and, sir knight,
Grey of Northumberland, this same is yours:—
Read them; and know, I know your worthiness.—
My lord of Westmoreland,—and uncle Exeter,—
We will aboard to-night.—Why, how now, gentlemen?
What see you in those papers, that you lose
So much complexion?—look ye, how they change!
Their cheeks are paper.—Why, what read you there,
That hath so cowarded and chased your blood
Out of appearance?
Cam. I do confess my fault;
And do submit me to your highness' mercy.
Grey. Scroop. To which we all appeal.
K. Hen. The mercy, that was quick[8] in us but late,
By your own counsel is suppress'd and kill'd:
You must not dare, for shame, to talk of mercy;
For your own reasons turn into your bosoms,
As dogs upon their masters, worrying them.—
See you, my princes, and my noble peers,
These English monsters! My lord of Cambridge here,—
You know, how apt our love was, to accord
To furnish him with all appertinents
Belonging to his honour; and this man
Hath, for a few light crowns, lightly conspir'd,
And sworn unto the practices of France,
To kill us here in Hampton: to the which,
This knight, no less for bounty bound to us
Than Cambridge is,—hath likewise sworn—But O!
What shall I say to thee, Lord Scroop; thou cruel,
Ingrateful, savage, and inhuman creature!
Thou, that didst bear the key of all my counsels,
That knew'st the very bottom of my soul,
That almost might'st have coin'd me into gold,
Would'st thou have practis'd on me for thy use?
May it be possible, that foreign hire
Could out of thee extract one spark of evil
That might annoy my finger? 'tis so strange,
That, though the truth of it stands off as gross
As black from white,[9] my eye will scarcely see it.
Treason and murder, ever kept together,
As two yoke-devils swore to either's purpose,
Working so grossly[10] in a natural cause,
That admiration did not whoop at them:[11]
But thou, 'gainst all proportion, didst bring in
Wonder, to wait on treason, and on murder:
And whatsoever cunning fiend it was,
That wrought upon thee so preposterously,
H'ath got the voice in hell for excellence:
And other devils, that suggest by treasons,
Do botch and bungle up damnation
With patches, colours, and with forms being fetch'd
From glistering semblances of piety;
But he, that temper'd thee,[12] bade thee stand up,
Gave thee no instance why thou should'st do treason,
Unless to dub thee with the name of traitor.
If that same demon, that hath gull'd thee thus,
Should with his lion gait walk the whole world,
He might return to vasty Tartar[13] back,
And tell the legions—I can never win
A soul so easy as that Englishman's.
O, how hast thou with jealousy infected

---

the middle of the seventeenth century, if not later. Cromwell obtained much of his intelligence during the civil wars from the mean men with whom he slept.

1 'Whom he hath *cloy'd* and grac'd.' The quarto reads '*dull'd* and cloy'd.'

2 'For which we have *in head* assembled them.' In *head* seems equivalent to the modern millitary term *in force.*

3 '*Consent*' is accord, agreement.

4 'i. e. hearts compounded or made up of duty and zeal.'

5 i. e. his better consideration, or more circumspect behaviour.

6 '*Distemper*' here put for *intemperance*, or *riotous excess*

7 i. e. those lately appointed.

8 i. e. living.

9 'Though the truth of it stands off as gross
As black from white.'

Though the truth be as apparent and visible as black and white contiguous to each other. To *stand off* is to be *prominent.*

10 i. e. plainly, evidently.

11 'Did not *whoop* at them.' That they excited no exclamation of surprise.

12 'He that *temper'd* thee.' That is, he that ruled thee. '*Temperator*, he that *tempereth*, or moderateth; he that knoweth how to rule and order.'—*Cooper.*

13 i. e. Tartarus, the fabled place of future punishment.

The sweetness of affiance![1] Show men dutiful?
Why, so didst thou: Seem they grave and learned?
Why, so didst thou: Come they of noble family?
Why, so didst thou: Seem they religious?
Why, so didst thou: Or are they spare in diet;
Free from gross passion, or of mirth, or anger;
Constant in spirit, not swerving with the blood;
Garnish'd and deck'd in modest complement;[2]
Not working with the eye, without the ear,
And, but in purged judgment, trusting neither?
Such, and so finely bolted,[3] didst thou seem:
And thus thy fall hath left a kind of blot,
To mark the full-fraught man, and best indued,[4]
With some suspicion. I will weep for thee;
For this revolt of thine, methinks, is like
Another fall of man.—Their faults are open,
Arrest them to the answer of the law;—
And God acquit them of their practices!

Exe. I arrest thee of high treason, by the name of Richard earl of Cambridge.

I arrest thee of high treason, by the name of Henry Lord Scroop of Masham.

I arrest thee of high treason, by the name of Thomas Grey, knight of Northumberland.

Scroop. Our purposes God justly hath discover'd;
And I repent my fault more than my death;
Which I beseech your highness to forgive,
Although my body pay the price of it.

Cam. For me,—the gold of France did not seduce;[5]
Although I did admit it as a motive,
The sooner to effect what I intended:
But God be thanked for prevention;
Which I in sufferance heartily will rejoice,[6]
Beseeching God and you to pardon me.

Grey. Never did faithful subject more rejoice
At the discovery of most dangerous treason,
Than I do at this hour joy o'er myself,
Prevented from a damned enterprise:
My fault, but not my body, pardon, sovereign.

K. Hen. God quit you in his mercy! Hear your sentence.
You have conspir'd against our royal person,
Join'd with an enemy proclaim'd, and from his coffers
Receiv'd the golden earnest of our death;
Wherein you would have sold your king to slaughter,
His princes and his peers to servitude,
His subjects to oppression and contempt,
And his whole kingdom into desolation.
Touching our person, seek we no revenge;
But we our kingdom's safety must so tender,
Whose ruin you three sought, that to her laws
We do deliver you. Get you therefore hence,
Poor miserable wretches, to your death:
The taste whereof, God, of his mercy, give you
Patience to endure, and true repentance
Of all your dear offences!—Bear them hence.
[*Exeunt Conspirators, guarded.*

Now, lords, for France; the enterprise whereof
Shall be to you, as us, like glorious
We doubt not of a fair and lucky war:
Since God so graciously hath brought to light
This dangerous treason, lurking in our way,
To hinder our beginnings, we doubt not now,
But every rub is smoothed on our way.
Then, forth, dear countrymen; let us deliver
Our puissance into the hand of God,
Putting it straight in expedition.
Cheerly to sea; the signs of war advance:[7]
No king of England, if not king of France.
[*Exeunt.*

SCENE III. London. Mrs. Quickly's *House in* Eastcheap. *Enter* PISTOL, MRS. QUICKLY, NYM, BARDOLPH, *and* BOY.

Quick. Pr'ythee, honey-sweet husband, let me bring[8] thee to Staines.

Pist. No; for my manly heart doth yearn.—
Bardolph, be blithe;—Nym, rouse thy vaunting veins.
Boy, bristle thy courage up: for Falstaff he is dead,
And we must yearn therefore.

Bard. 'Would, I were with him, wheresome'er he is, either in heaven, or hell!

Quick. Nay, sure, he's not in hell; he's in Arthur's bosom, if ever man went to Arthur's bosom. 'A made a finer end, and went away, an it had been any christom[9] child; 'a parted even just between twelve and one, e'en at turning o' the tide;[10] for after I saw him fumble with the sheets, and play with flowers, and smile upon his fingers' ends, I knew there was but one way; for his nose was as sharp as a pen, and 'a babbled of green fields.[11] How now, Sir John? quoth I: what, man! be of good cheer. So 'a cried out—God, God, God! three or four times: now I, to comfort him, bid him, 'a should not think of God; I hoped, there was no need to trouble himself with any such thoughts yet: So 'a bade me lay more clothes on his feet: I put my hand into the bed, and felt them, and they were as cold as any stone; then I felt to his knees, and so upward, and upward, and all was as cold as any stone.

Nym. They say, he cried out of sack.

Quick. Ay, that 'a did.

Bard. And of women.

Quick. Nay, that 'a did not.

Boy. Yes, that 'a did; and said, they were devils incarnate.

Quick. 'A could never abide carnation; 'twas a colour he never liked.

Boy. 'A said once, the devil would have him about women.

Quick. 'A did in some sort, indeed, handle women: but then he was rheumatic;[12] and talked of the whore of Babylon.

---

1 'The sweetness of affiance!' Shakspeare uses this aggravation of the guilt of treachery with great judgment. One of the worst consequences of breach of trust is the diminution of that confidence which makes the happiness of life, and the dissemination of suspicion, which is the poison of society.—*Johnson.*

2 '*Complement*' has here the same meaning as in Love's Labour's Lost, Act i. Sc. 1. Bullokar defines it, '*Court ship*, [i. e. courtiership] fulness, perfection, *fine behaviour*.' The gradual change of this word, to its meaning of *ceremonious words*, may be traced in Blount's Glossography.

3 *Bolted* is the same as *sifted*, and has consequently the meaning of *refined*.

4 i. e. endowed, or gifted.

5 'For me, the gold of France did not seduce.' '—— diverse write that Richard earle of Cambridge did not conspire with the Lord Scroope, &c. for the murthering of King Henrie, to please the French king withall, but onlie to the intent to exalt the crowne to his brother-in-law Edmund earle of Marche, as heir to Lionel duke of Clarence, who being for diverse secret impediments not able to have issue, the earl of Cambridge was sure that the crowne should come to him by his wife, and to his children of her begotten. And therefore (as was thought) he rather confessed himselfe for neede of money to be corrupted by the French king, lest the earl of Marche should have tasted of the same cuppe that he had drunken, and what should have come to his own children he much doubted,' &c.—*Holinshed.*

6 i. e. 'at which prevention, in suffering, I will heartily rejoice.'

7 'The *signs of war* advance.' Phaer, in rendering the first line of the eighth Æneid, 'Ut belle signum, &c. has

'When *signe of war* from Laurent townes, &c

8 i. e. let me *accompany thee*.

9 i. e. *chrisom* child: which was one that died within the month of birth, because during that time they wore the *chrisom cloth*, a white cloth put upon a child newly christened, wherewith women used to shroud the child if dying within the month; otherwise it was brought to church at the day of purification.

10 'Even at the turning o' the tide.' It has been a very old opinion, which Mead, *De Imperio Solis* quotes, as if he believed it, that nobody dies but in the time of ebb.

11 'And 'a babbled of green fields.' The first folio reads 'For his nose was as sharp as a pen, and a Table of green fields.' Theobald gave the present reading of the text, which, though entirely conjectural, is better than any thing which has been offered in the idle babble of the numerous notes on this passage.

12 *Rheumatic.* Mrs. Quickly means lunatic.

Boy. Do you not remember, 'a saw a flea stick upon Bardolph's nose; and 'a said, it was a black soul burning in hell-fire?

Bard. Well, the fuel is gone, that maintained that fire; that's all the riches I got in his service.

Nym. Shall we shog off? the king will be gone from Southampton.

Pist. Come, let's away.—My love, give me thy lips.
Look to my chattels, and my moveables:
Let senses rule; the word is, *Pitch and Pay;*
Trust none;
For oaths are straws, men's faiths are wafer-cakes,
And hold-fast is the only dog, my duck;[1]
Therefore, *caveto* be thy counsellor.
Go, clear thy crystals.[2]—Yoke-fellows in arms,
Let us to France! like horse-leeches, my boys;
To suck, to suck, the very blood to suck!

Boy. And that is but unwholesome food, they say.

Pist. Touch her soft mouth, and march.

Bard. Farewell, hostess. [*Kissing her.*

Nym. I cannot kiss, that is the humour of it; but adieu.

Pist. Let housewifery appear; keep close,[3] I thee command.

Quick. Farewell; adieu. [*Exeunt.*

SCENE IV. France. *A Room in the* French King's *Palace. Enter the* French King *attended:* the Dauphin, *the* DUKE *of* BURGUNDY, *the* Constable, *and others.*

Fr. King. Thus come the English with full power upon us;
And more than carefully it us concerns,
To answer royally in our defences.
Therefore the dukes of Berry and of Bretagne,
Of Brabant, and of Orleans, shall make forth,—
And you, Prince Dauphin, with all swift despatch,
To line, and new repair, our towns of war,
With men of courage, and with means defendant:
For England his approaches makes as fierce,
As waters to the sucking of a gulf.
It fits us then, to be as provident
As fear may teach us, out of late examples
Left by the fatal and neglected English
Upon our fields.

Dau. My most redoubted father,
It is most meet we arm us 'gainst the foe:
For peace itself should not so dull[4] a kingdom
(Though war, nor no known quarrel, were in question,)
But that defences, musters, preparations,
Should be maintain'd, assembled, and collected,
As were a war in expectation.
Therefore, I say, 'tis meet we all go forth,
To view the sick and feeble parts of France:
And let us do it with no show of fear:
No, with no more, than if we heard that England
Were busied with a Whitsun morris-dance:
For, my good liege, she is so idly king'd,
Her sceptre so fantastically borne
By a vain, giddy, shallow, humorous youth,
That fear attends her not.

Con. O peace, Prince Dauphin!
You are too much mistaken in this king:
Question your grace the late ambassadors,—
With what great state he heard their embassy,
How well supplied with noble counsellors,
How modest in exception,[5] and, withal,
How terrible in constant resolution,—
And you shall find, his vanities fore-spent
Were but the outside of the Roman Brutus,[6]
Covering discretion with a coat of folly;
As gardeners do with ordure hide those roots
That shall first spring, and be most delicate.

Dau. Well, 'tis not so, my lord high constable,
But though we think it so, it is no matter:
In cases of defence, 'tis best to weigh
The enemy more mighty than he seems,
So the proportions of defence are fill'd;
Which, of a weak and niggardly projection,[7]
Doth, like a miser, spoil his coat, with scanting
A little cloth.

Fr. King. Think we King Harry strong;
And, princes, look, you strongly arm to meet him
The kindred of him hath been flesh'd upon us;
And he is bred out of that bloody strain,[8]
That haunted us in our familiar paths:
Witness our too much memorable shame,
When Cressy battle fatally was struck,
And all our princes captiv'd, by the hand
Of that black name, Edward, Black Prince of Wales;
Whiles that his mountain sire,—on mountain standing,
Up in the air, crown'd with the golden sun,—[9]
Saw his heroical seed, and smil'd to see him
Mangle the work of nature, and deface
The patterns that by God and by French fathers
Had twenty years been made. This is a stem
Of that victorious stock: and let us fear
The native mightiness and fate of him.[10]

Enter a Messenger.

Mess. Ambassadors from Henry king of England
Do crave admittance to your majesty.

Fr. King. We'll give them present audience. Go, and bring them.
[*Exeunt* Mess. *and certain* Lords.
You see, this chase is hotly follow'd, friends.

Dau. Turn head, and stop pursuit; for coward dogs
Most spend their mouths,[11] when what they seem to threaten,
Runs far before them. Good my sovereign,
Take up the English short; and let them know
Of what a monarchy you are the head;
Self-love, my liege, is not so vile a sin
As self-neglecting.

Re-enter Lords, *with* EXETER *and Train.*

Fr. King. From our brother England?

Exe. From him; and thus he greets your majesty.

---

1 Pistol puts forth a string of proverbs. '*Pitch and pay, and go your way,*' is one in Florio's Collection; 'Brag is a good dog, and *Holdfast* a better,' is one of the others to which he alludes.

2 i. e. dry thine eyes.

3 The quartos read 'Keep fast thy buggle boe.' The meaning of which may be gathered from the following passage in Shirley's Gentleman of Venice:—

'———— the courtisans of Venice
Shall keep their bugle bowes for thee, dear uncle.'

4 'For peace itself should not so *dull* a kingdom.' To *dull* is to render torpid, insensible, or inactive; to dispirit. 'In idleness to wax *dull* and without spirit: Torpescere.'—*Baret.*

5 'How modest in exception.' How diffident and decent in making objections.

6 '—— the outside of the Roman Brutus.' Warburton has a strained explanation of this passage. Shakspeare's meaning is explained by the following lines in The Rape of Lucrece:—

'Brutus who pluck'd the knife from Lucrece' side,
Seeing such emulation in their woe,
Began to *clothe his wit* in state and pride,
Burying in Lucrece' wound his *folly's show.*
———— he throws that *shallow habit by.*'

7 'Which, of a weak and niggardly projection.' The construction of this passage is perplexed, and the grammatical concord not according to our present notions; but its meaning appears to be, 'So the proportions of defence are filled; which, *to make* of a weak and niggardly projection (i. e. *contrivance*,) *is to do* like a miser who spoils his coat with scanting a little cloth.

8 *Strain* is lineage.

9 'Whiles that his mountain sire,—on mountain standing,
Up in the air, crown'd with the golden sun.
There is much childish misunderstanding of this passage in the notes. Steevens is right when he says that, divested of its poetical finery, it means that the king stood upon a hill, with the sun shining over his head, to see the battle; as before described in the first scene of the play.

10 i. e. what is allotted him by destiny.

11 i. e. *bark;* the sportsman's term.

He wills you, in the name of God Almighty,
That you divest yourself, and lay apart
The borrow'd glories, that, by gift of heaven,
By law of nature, and of nations, 'long
To him, and to his heirs: namely, the crown,
And all wide-stretched honours that pertain,
By custom and the ordinance of times,
Unto the crown of France. That you may know,
'Tis no sinister, nor no awkward claim,
Pick'd from the worm-holes of long varnish'd days,
Nor from the dust of old oblivion rak'd,
He sends you this most memorable line,[1]
[*Gives a Paper.*
In every branch truly demonstrative:
Willing you, overlook this pedigree:
And, when you find him evenly derived
From his most fam'd of famous ancestors,
Edward the Third, he bids you then resign
Your crown and kingdom, indirectly held
From him the native and true challenger.

Fr. King. Or else what follows?

Exe. Bloody constraint; for it you hide the crown
Even in your hearts, there will he rake for it;
And therefore in fierce tempest is he coming,
In thunder, and in earthquake, like a Jove:
(That, if requiring fail, he will compel:)
And bids you, in the bowels of the Lord,
Deliver up the crown; and to take mercy
On the poor souls, for whom this hungry war
Opens his vasty jaws: and on your head
Turns he the widows' tears, the orphans' cries,
The dead men's blood, the pining maidens' groans,
For husbands, fathers, and betrothed lovers,
That shall be swallow'd in this controversy.
This is his claim, his threat'ning, and my message:
Unless the Dauphin be in presence here,
To whom expressly I bring greeting too.

Fr. King. For us, we will consider of this further:
To-morrow shall you bear our full intent
Back to our brother England.

Dau. For the Dauphin,
I stand here for him; What to him from England?

Exe. Scorn, and defiance; slight regard, contempt,
And any thing that may not misbecome
The mighty sender, doth he prize you at.
Thus says my king: and, if your father's highness
Do not, in grant of all demands at large,
Sweeten the bitter mock you sent his majesty,
He'll call you to so hot an answer for it,
That caves and womby vaultages of France
Shall chide[2] your trespass, and return your mock
In second accent of his ordnance.

Dau. Say, if my father render fair reply,
It is against my will: for I desire
Nothing but odds with England; to that end,
As matching to his youth and vanity,
I did present him with those Paris balls.

Exe. He'll make your Paris Louvre shake for it,
Were it the mistress court of mighty Europe:
And, be assur'd, you'll find a difference
(As we, his subjects, have in wonder found,)
Between the promise of his greener days,
And these he masters now; now he weighs time,
Even to the utmost grain; which you shall read
In your own losses, if he stay in France.

Fr. King. To-morrow shall you know our mind at full.

Exe. Despatch us with all speed, lest that our king
Come here himself to question our delay;
For he is footed in this land already.

Fr. King. You shall be soon despatch'd, with fair conditions:
A night is but smal breath, and little pause,
To answer matters of this consequence. [*Exeunt.*

ACT III.

Enter CHORUS.

Chor. Thus with imagin'd wing our swift scene flies,
In motion of no less celerity
Than that of thought. Suppose, that you have seen
The well-appointed king at Hampton pier[3]
Embark his royalty; and his brave fleet
With silken streamers the young Phœbus fanning.
Play with your fancies; and in them behold,
Upon the hempen tackle, ship-boys climbing:
Hear the shrill whistle, which doth order give
To sounds confus'd: behold the threaden sails,
Borne with the invisible and creeping wind,
Draw the huge bottoms through the furrow'd sea,
Breasting the lofty surge: O, do but think,
You stand upon the rivage,[4] and behold
A city on the inconstant billows dancing;
For so appears this fleet majestical,
Holding due course to Harfleur. Follow, follow!
Grapple your minds to sternage of this navy;[5]
And leave your England, as dead midnight, still,
Guarded with grandsires, babies, and old women,
Either past or not arrived to, pith and puissance:
For who is he, whose chin is but enrich'd
With one appearing hair, that will not follow
These cull'd and choice-drawn cavaliers to France?
Work, work, your thoughts, and therein see a siege:
Behold the ordnance on their carriages,
With fatal mouths gaping on girded Harfleur
Suppose the ambassador from the French come back;
Tells Harry—that the king doth offer him
Katharine his daughter; and with her, to dowry
Some petty and unprofitable dukedoms.
The offer likes not: and the nimble gunner
With linstock[6] now the devilish cannon touches,
[*Alarum; and Chambers*[7] *go off.*
And down goes all before them. Still be kind,
And eke out our performance with your mind.
[*Exit.*

SCENE I. *The same. Before* Harfleur. *Alarums. Enter* KING HENRY, EXETER, BEDFORD, GLOSTER, *and* Soldiers, *with Scaling Ladders.*

K. Hen. Once more unto the breach, dear friends, once more;
Or close the wall up with our English dead!
In peace, there's nothing so becomes a man,
As modest stillness and humility:
But when the blast of war blows in our ears,
Then imitate the action of the tiger;
Stiffen the sinews, summon up the blood,
Disguise fair nature with hard-favour'd rage:
Then lend the eye a terrible aspect;
Let it pry through the portage of the head,[8]
Like the brass cannon: let the brow o'erwhelm it,
As fearfully, as doth a galled rock

---

1 'Memorable line;' this genealogy, this deduction of his *lineage.*

2 'Shall *chide* your trespass.' To *chide* is to resound, to echo.

3 'The *well-appointed* king at *Hampton* pier.' '*Well-appointed,*' that is, well furnished with all necessaries of war. The old copies read '*Dover* pier:' but the poet himself, and all accounts, and even the Chronicles which he followed, say that the king embarked at Southampton. A minute account still exists among the records of the town; and it is remarkable that a low level plain where the army encamped is now covered by the sea, and called *Westport.*

4 *Rivage,* the bank, or shore; *rivage,* Fr.

5 'To *sternage* of this navy.' The *stern,* or *sternage,* being the hinder part of the ship. The meaning of this passage is, 'Let your minds follow this navy.' The *stern* was anciently synonymous to *rudder.* 'The *sterne* of a ship, *gubernaculum.*'—*Baret.*

6 '*Linstock*' is here put for a *match;* but it was strictly speaking, the staff to which the match for firing ordnance was fixed.

7 '*Chambers,*' small pieces of ordnance.

8 'The *portage* of the head.' Shakspeare uses *portage* for loop-holes or port-holes.

O'erhang and jutty[1] his confounded base,
Swill'd with the wild and wasteful ocean.
Now set the teeth, and stretch the nostril wide;
Hold hard the breath, and bend up every spirit
To his full height!—On, on, you noble English,[2]
Whose blood is fet[3] from fathers of war-proof!
Fathers, that, like so many Alexanders,
Have, in these parts, from morn till even fought,
And sheath'd their swords for lack of argument;[4]
Dishonour not your mothers; now attest,
That those, whom you call'd fathers, did beget you!
Be copy now to men of grosser blood,
And teach them how to war!—And you, good yeomen,
Whose limbs were made in England, show us here
The mettle of your pasture; let us swear
That you are worth your breeding: which I doubt not;
For there is none of you so mean and base,
That hath not noble lustre in your eyes.
I see you stand like greyhounds in the slips,[5]
Straining upon the start. The game's afoot;
Follow your spirit: and, upon this charge,
Cry—God for Harry! England! and Saint George!
[*Exeunt. Alarum, and Chambers go off.*

SCENE II. *The same. Forces pass over; then enter* Nym, Bardolph, Pistol, *and* Boy.

Bard. On, on, on, on, on! to the breach! to the breach!

Nym. 'Pray thee, corporal,[6] stay; the knocks are too hot; and, for mine own part, I have not a case of lives:[7] the humour of it is too hot, that is the very plain-song of it.

Pist. The plain-song is most just; for humours do abound;
Knocks go and come; God's vassals drop and die;
And sword and shield,
In bloody field,
Doth win immortal fame.

Boy. 'Would I were in an alehouse in London! I would give all my fame for a pot of ale, and safety.

Pist. And I:
If wishes would prevail with me,
My purpose should not fail with me,
But thither would I hie.

Boy. As duly, but not as truly,
As bird doth sing on bough.

Enter Fluellen.[8]

Flu. Got's plood!—Up to the preaches, you rascals! will you not up to the preaches?
[*Driving them forward.*

Pist. Be merciful, great duke, to men of mould![9]
Abate thy rage, abate thy manly rage!
Abate thy rage, great duke!
Good bawcock, bate thy rage! use lenity, sweet chuck!

Nym. These be good humours!—your honour wins bad humours.
[*Exeunt* Nym, Pistol, *and* Bardolph, *followed by* Fluellen.

Boy. As young as I am, I have observed these three swashers. I am boy to them all three: but all they three, though they would serve me, could not be man to me: for, indeed, three such antics do not amount to a man. For Bardolph,—he is white-liver'd, and red-fac'd; by the means whereof, 'a faces it out, but fights not. For Pistol,—he hath a killing tongue, and a quiet sword; by the means whereof 'a breaks words, and keeps whole weapons. For Nym,—he hath heard, that men of few words are the best men:[10] and therefore he scorns to say his prayers, lest 'a should be thought a coward: but his few bad words are match'd with as few good deeds; for 'a never broke any man's head but his own; and that was against a post when he was drunk. They will steal any thing, and call it,—purchase.[11] Bardolph stole a lute case: bore it twelve leagues, and sold it for three half-pence. Nym, and Bardolph, are sworn brothers in filching; and in Calais they stole a fire-shovel: I knew, by that piece of service the men would carry coals.[12] They would have me as familiar with men's pockets as their gloves or their handkerchiefs; which makes much against my manhood, if I should take from another's pocket to put into mine; for it is plain pocketing up of wrongs. I must leave them and seek some better service: their villany goes against my weak stomach, and therefore I must cast it up.
[*Exit* Boy.

Re-enter Fluellen, Gower *following.*

Gow. Captain Fluellen, you must come presently to the mines; the duke of Gloster would speak with you.

Flu. To the mines! tell you the duke, it is not so good to come to the mines: For, look you, the mines is not according to the disciplines of the war; the concavities of it is not sufficient; for, look you, th' adversary (you may discuss unto the duke, look you,) is dight himself four yards under the countermines:[13] by Cheshu, I think, 'a will plow up all, if there is not better directions.

Gow. The duke of Gloster, to whom the order of the siege is given, is altogether directed by an Irishman; a very valiant gentleman, i'faith.

Flu. It is captain Macmorris, is it not?

Gow. I think it be.

Flu. By Chesu, he is an ass, as in the 'orld: I will verify as much in his peard: he has no more directions in the true disciplines of the wars, look you, of the Roman disciplines, than is a puppy dog.

Enter Macmorris *and* Jamy, *at a distance.*

Gow. Here 'a comes; and the Scots captain, Captain Jamy, with him.

Flu. Captain Jamy is a marvellous falorous gentleman, that is certain: and of great expedition, and knowledge, in the ancient wars, upon my particular knowledge of his directions: by Cheshu, he will maintain his argument as well as any military man in the 'orld, in the disciplines of the pristine wars of the Romans.

Jamy. I say, gud-day, Captain Fluellen.

Flu. God-den to your worship, goot Captain Jamy.

---

1 'O'erhang and *jutty* his *confounded* base,
Swill'd with the wild and wasteful ocean.'
To *jutty* is to project; jutties, or jetties, are projecting moles to break the force of the waves. *Confounded* is neither worn, or wasted, as Johnson tells us; nor destroyed, as Malone infers; but *vexed*, or *troubled*. *Swill'd* anciently was used for '*washed much, or long*, drowned, surrounded by water: *Prolutus*.'

2 'You *noble* English.' The folio reads *noblish*, by mistake; the compositor having taken twice the final syllable *ish*. Steevens reads *noblest*. This speech is not in the quartos.

3 'Whose blood is *fet* from fathers of war-proof.' Mr. Pope took the liberty of altering this word to *fetch'd*. The sacred writings afford us many instances of its use. '*Asciita* et accepta a Græcis, *Fet* and taken out of Greece.' It is often coupled with far, as in the expressions '*far-fet* and dear bought,' 'affectated and *far-fet*.'

4 *Argument* is matter, subject.

5 *Slips* are contrivances of leather to start two dogs at the same time.

6 '*Corporal*.' Bardolph is called *lieutenant* in a former scene; so that there is a lapse of memory in the poet in one or other of these instances.

7 'A *case* of lives;' that is, a '*pair* of lives:' as a '*case* of pistols,' a '*case* of poniards,' 'a *case* of masks.'

8 *Fluellen* is merely the Welsh pronunciation of *Lluellyn*, as *Floyd* is of *Lloyd*.

9 i. e. 'be merciful, great *commander*, to men of *earth*, to poor mortal men.' *Duke* is only a translation of the Roman *dux*. Sylvester, in his Du Bartas, calls Moses 'a great duke.'

10 'The *best* men;' that is, *bravest*. So, in the next line, *good deeds* are *brave actions*.

11 *Purchase*, which anciently signified *gain*, *profit*, was the cant term used for any thing obtained by cheating; as appears by *Green's Art of Coneycatching*.

12 '*Carry coals*.' See note on the first scene of Romeo and Juliet.

13 'Is *dight* himself;' that is, the enemy had digged four yards under the countermines.

Gow. How now, Captain Macmorris? have you quit the mines? have the pioneers given o'er?

Mac. By Chrish la, tish ill done: the work ish give over, the trumpet sound the retreat. By my hand, I swear, and by my father's soul, the work ish ill done; it ish give over: I would have blowed up the town, so Chrish save me, la, in an hour. O, tish ill done, tish ill done; by my hand, tish ill done!

Flu. Captain Macmorris, I peseech you now, will you vouchsafe me, look you, a few disputations with you, as partly touching or concerning the disciplines of the war, the Roman wars, in the way of argument, look you, and friendly communication; partly, to satisfy my opinion, and partly, for the satisfaction, look you, of my mind, as touching the direction of the military discipline; that is the point.

Jamy. It sall be very gud, gud feith, gud captains bath: and I sall quit[1] you with gud leve, as I may pick occasion; that sall I, marry.

Mac. It is no time to discourse, so Chrish save me, the day is hot, and the weather, and the wars, and the king, and the dukes; it is no time to discourse. The town is beseeched, and the trumpet calls us to the breach; and we talk, and, by Chrish, do nothing; 'tis shame for us all: so God sa' me, 'tis shame to stand still; it is shame, by my hand: and there is throats to be cut, and works to be done: and there ish nothing done, so Chrish sa' me, la.

Jamy. By the mess, ere theise eyes of mine take themselves to slumber, aile do gude service, or aile ligge i' the grund for it; ay, or go to death: and aile pay it as valorously as I may, that sall I surely do, that is the breff and the long: Mary, I wad full fain heard some question 'tween you 'tway.

Flu. Captain Macmorris, I think, look you, under your correction, there is not many of your nation——

Mac. Of my nation? What ish my nation? ish a villain, and a bastard, and a knave, and a rascal? What ish my nation? Who talks of my nation?

Flu. Look you, if you take the matter otherwise than is meant, Captain Macmorris, peradventure, I shall think you do not use me with that affability as in discretion you ought to use me, look you; being as goot a man as yourself, both in the disciplines of wars, and in the derivation of my birth, and in other particularities.

Mac. I do not know you so good a man as myself: so Chrish save me, I will cut off your head.

Gow. Gentlemen both, you will mistake each other.

Jamy. Au! that's a foul fault.

[*A Parley sounded.*

Gow. The town sounds a parley.

Flu. Captain Macmorris, when there is more better opportunity to be required, look you, I will be so bold as to tell you, I know the disciplines of war; and there is an end. [*Exeunt.*

SCENE III. *The same. Before the Gates of* Harfleur. *The* Governor *and some* Citizens *on the Walls; the* English *Forces below. Enter* King Henry *and his Train.*

K. Hen. How yet resolves the governor of the town?
This is the latest parle we will admit:
Therefore, to our best mercy give yourselves;
Or, like to men proud of destruction,
Defy us to our worst; for, as I am a soldier
(A name, that, in my thoughts, becomes me best,)
If I begin the battery once again,
I will not leave the half-achieved Harfleur
Till in her ashes she lie buried.
The gates of mercy shall be all shut up;[2]
And the flesh'd soldier,—rough and hard of heart,
In liberty of bloody hand, shall range
With conscience wide as hell; mowing like grass
Your fresh-fair virgins, and your flowering infants.
What is it then to me, if impious war,—
Array'd in flames, like to the prince of fiends,—
Do, with his smirch'd complexion, all fell feats
Enlink'd to waste and desolation?
What is't to me, when you yourselves are cause,
If your pure maidens fall into the hand
Of hot and forcing violation?
What rein can hold licentious wickedness,
When down the hill he holds his fierce career?
We may as bootless spend our vain command
Upon the enraged soldiers in their spoil,
As send precepts to the Leviathan
To come ashore. Therefore, you men of Harfleur,
Take pity of your town, and of your people,
Whiles yet my soldiers are in my command;
Whiles yet the cool and temperate wind of grace
O'erblows the filthy and contagious clouds[3]
Of deadly murder, spoil, and villany.
If not, why, in a moment, look to see
The blind and bloody soldier with foul hand
Defile the locks of your shrill-shrieking daughters,
Your fathers taken by the silver beards,
And their most reverend heads dash'd to the walls,
Your naked infants spitted upon pikes;
Whiles the mad mothers with their howls confus'd
Do break the clouds, as did the wives of Jewry
At Herod's bloody-hunting slaughtermen.
What say you? will you yield, and this avoid?
Or, guilty in defence, be thus destroy'd?

Gov. Our expectation hath this day an end.
The Dauphin, whom of succour we entreated,[4]
Returns us—that his powers are not yet ready
To raise so great a siege. Therefore, dread king,
We yield our town, and lives, to thy soft mercy:
Enter our gates; dispose of us, and ours;
For we no longer are defensible.

K. Henry. Open your gates.—Come, uncle Exeter,
Go you and enter Harfleur; there remain,
And fortify it strongly 'gainst the French:
Use mercy to them all. For us, dear uncle,—
The winter coming on, and sickness growing
Upon our soldiers,—we'll retire to Calais.
To-night in Harfleur will we be your guest;
To-morrow for the march are we addrest.[5]

[*Flourish. The* King, *&c. enter the Town.*

SCENE IV.[6] Rouen. *A Room in the Palace.* *Enter* Katharine *and* Alice.

Kath. *Alice, tu as esté en Angleterre, et tu parles bien le langage.*

Alice. *Un peu, madame.*

Kath. *Je te prie, m'enseignez; il faut que j'apprenne à parler. Comment appellez vous la main, en Anglois?*

Alice. *La main? elle est appellée,* de hand.

Kath. De hand. *Et les doigts?*

Alice. *Les doigts? ma foy, j' oublie les doigts,*

---

1 'I shall quit you;' that is, I shall, with your permission, *requite you;* that is, *answer you*, or *interpose with my arguments*, as I shall find opportunity.

2 'The gates of mercy shall be all shut up.' Gray has borrowed this thought in his Elegy:—

'And shut the gates of mercy on mankind.'

3 'Whiles yet the cool and temperate wind of grace
O'erblows the filthy and contagious clouds.'

To *overblow* is to *drive away*, to *keep off*. Johnson observes that this is a very harsh metaphor.

4 'Whom *of* succour we entreated.' See A Midsummer Night's Dream, Act iii. Sc. 1, in a note on the passage:—'I shall desire you *of* more acquaintance.'

5 i. e. prepared

6 Every one must wish with Warburton and Farmer to believe that this scene is an interpolation. Yet as Johnson remarks, the grimaces of the two Frenchwomen, and the odd accent with which they uttered the English, might divert an audience more refined than could be found in the poet's time. There is in it not only the French language, but the French spirit. Alice compliments the princess upon the knowledge of four words, and tells her that she pronounces like the English themselves. The princess suspects no deficiency in her instructress, nor the instructress in herself. The extraordinary circumstance of introducing a character speaking French in an English drama was no novelty to our early stage.

mais je me souviendray. Les doigts? je pense, qu'ils sont appellé de fingres; *ouy*, de fingres.

Kath. *La main*, de hand; *les doigts*, de fingres. *Je pense, que je suis le bon escolier. J'ay gagné deux mots d'Anglois vistement. Comment appellez vous les ongles?*

Alice. *Les ongles? les appellons*, de nails.

Kath. De nails. *Escoutez; dites moy, si je parle bien:* de hand, de fingres, de nails.

Alice. *C'est bien dit, madame; il est fort bon Anglois.*

Kath. *Dites moy en Anglois, le bras.*

Alice. De arm, *madame.*

Kath. *Et le coude.*

Alice. De elbow.

Kath. De elbow. *Je m'en faitz la répétition de tous les mots, que vous m'avez appris dès à present.*

Alice. *Il est trop difficile, madame, comme je pense.*

Kath. *Excusez moy, Alice; escoutez:* De hand, de fingre, de nails, de arm, de bilbow.

Alice. De elbow, *madame.*

Kath. *O Seigneur Dieu! je m'en oublie;* De elbow. *Comment appellez vous le col?*

Alice. De neck, *madame.*

Kath. De neck: *Et le menton?*

Alice. De chin.

Kath. De sin. *Le col*, de neck: *le menton*, de sin.

Alice. *Ouy. Sauf vostre honneur; en vérité, vous prononcez les mots aussi droict que les natifs d'Angleterre.*

Kath. *Je ne doute point d'apprendre par la grace de Dieu; et en peu de temps.*

Alice. *N'avez vous pas déjà oublié ce que je vous ay enseigné?*

Kath. *Non, je réciteray à vous promptement.* De hand, de fingre, de mails,—

Alice. De nails, *madame.*

Kath. De nails, de arme, de ilbow.

Alice. *Sauf vostre honneur*, de elbow.

Kath. *Ainsi dis je;* de elbow, de neck, *et* de sin; *Comment appellez vous le pieds et la robe?*

Alice. De foot, *madame; et* de con.

Kath. De foot *et* de con? *O Seigneur Dieu! ces sont mots de son mauvais, corruptible, grosse, et impudique, et non pour les dames d'honneur d'user; Je ne voudrois prononcer ces mots devant les Seigneurs de France, pour tout le monde. Il faut* de foot, *et* de con, *neant-moins. Je reciterai une autre fois ma leçon ensemble:* De hand, de fingre, de nails, de arm, de elbow, de neck, de sin, de foot, de con.

Alice. *Excellent, madame!*

Kath. *C'est assez pour une fois; allons nous à disner.* [Exeunt.

SCENE V. *The same. Another Room in the same. Enter the* French King, *the* Dauphin, Duke *of* Bourbon, *the* Constable *of* France, *and others.*

Fr. King. 'Tis certain, he hath pass'd the river
Some.

Con. And if he be not fought withal, my lord,
Let us not live in France; let us quit all,
And give our vineyards to a barbarous people.

Dau. *O Dieu vivant!* shall a few sprays of us,
The emptying of our fathers' luxury,[1]
Our scions, put in wild and savage stock,
Spirt up so suddenly into the clouds,
And overlook their grafters?

Bour. Normans, but bastard Normans, Norman bastards!
Mort de ma vie! if they march along
Unfought withal, but I will sell my dukedom,
To buy a slobbery and a dirty farm
In that nook-shotten[2] isle of Albion.

Con. *Dieu de battailes!* where have they this mettle?
Is not their climate foggy, raw, and dull?
On whom, as in despite, the sun looks pale,
Killing their fruit with frowns? Can sodden water,
A drench for sur-rein'd[3] jades, their barley broth,
Decoct their cold blood to such valiant heat?
And shall our quick blood, spirited with wine,
Seem frosty? O, for honour of our land,
Let us not hang like roping icicles
Upon our houses' thatch, whiles a more frosty people
Sweat drops of gallant youth in our rich fields;
Poor—we may call them, in their native lords.

Dau. By faith and honour,
Our madams mock at us; and plainly say,
Our mettle is bred out; and they will give
Their bodies to the lust of English youth,
To new-store France with bastard warriors.

Bour. They bid us—to the English dancing schools,
And teach lavoltas[4] high, and swift corantos,
Saying, our grace is only in our heels,
And that we are most lofty runaways.

Fr. King. Where is Montjoy, the herald? speed him hence;
Let him greet England with our sharp defiance.
Up, princes; and, with spirit of honour edg'd,
More sharper than your swords, hie to the field:
Charles De-la-bret,[5] high constable of France;
You dukes of Orleans, Bourbon, and of Berry,
Alençon, Brabant, Bar, and Burgundy:
Jaques Chatillion, Rambures, Vaudemont,
Beaumont, Grandpre, Roussi, and Fauconberg,
Foix, Lestrale, Bouciqualt, and Charolois;
High dukes, great princes, barons, lords, and knights,
For your great seats, now quit you of great shames.
Bar Harry England, that sweeps through our land
With pennons[6] painted in the blood of Harfleur!
Rush on his host, as doth the melted snow
Upon the valleys; whose low vassal seat
The Alps doth spit and void his rheum upon:
Go down upon him,—you have power enough,—
And in a captive chariot, into Rouen
Bring him our prisoner.

Con. This becomes the great.
Sorry am I, his numbers are so few,
His soldiers sick, and famish'd in their march;
For, I am sure, when he shall see our army,
He'll drop his heart into the sink of fear,
And, for achievement, offer us his ransom.[7]

Fr. King. Therefore, lord constable, haste on Montjoy:
And let him say to England, that we send

---

1 *Luxury* for lust.
'To't, Luxury, pellmell, for I lack soldiers.'—*Lear.*

2 '*Nook-shotten* isle.' *Shotten* signifies any thing projected: so *nook-shotten isle* is an isle that shoots out into capes, promontories, and necks of land, the very figure of Great Britain. Randle Holme, in his Accedence of Armory, p. 358, has '*Querke*, a *nook-shotten* pane' [of glass.]

3 'A drench for sur-rein'd jades.' *Sur-rein'd* is probably over-ridden or over-strained. Steevens observes that it is common to give horses, over-ridden or feverish, ground malt and hot water mixed, which is called a mash. To this the Constable alludes.

4 'Lavoltas high.' The *lavolta*, or volta, 'a kind of turning French dance,' says Florio; in which the man turns the woman round several times, and then assists her in making a high spring or cabriole. The reader will find a very curious and amusing article on the subject in Mr. Douce's Illustrations of Shakspeare, vol. i. p. 489.

5 This should be Charles D'Albret; but the metre would not admit of the change. Shakspeare followed Holinshed, who calls him *Delabreth*. The other French names have been corrected.

6 *Pennons* were flags or streamers, upon which the arms, device, and motto of a knight were painted. 'A *penon* must be tow yardes and a halfe long, made round att the end, and conteyneth the armes of the owner, and serveth for the conduct of fifty men.'—*MSS. Harl.* No. 2413. A banneret was created by cutting off the point of the pennon, and making it a banner, which was peculiar to the nobility.

7 'And for achievement offer us his ransom.' That is, instead of achieving a victory over us, make a proposal to pay us a sum as ransom.

To know what willing ransom he will give.—
Prince Dauphin, you shall stay with us in Roüen.[1]

Dau. Not so, I do beseech your majesty.

Fr. King. Be patient, for you shall remain with us.—
Now, forth, lord constable, and princes all;
And quickly bring us word of England's fall.

[*Exeunt.*

SCENE VI. *The* English *Camp in* Picardy.

Enter GOWER *and* FLUELLEN.

Gow. How now, Captain Fluellen, come you from the bridge?

Flu. I assure you, there is very excellent service committed at the pridge.

Gow. Is the duke of Exeter safe?

Flu. The duke of Exeter is as magnanimous as Agamemnon; and a man that I love and honour with my soul, and my heart, and my duty, and my life, and my livings, and my uttermost powers: he is not (God be praised, and plessed!) any hurt in the 'orld; but keeps the pridge most valiantly,[2] with excellent discipline. There is an ensign there at the pridge,—I think, in my very conscience, he is as valiant as Mark Antony; and he is a man of no estimation in the 'orld: but I did see him do gallant service.

Gow. What do you call him?

Flu. He is called—ancient Pistol.

Gow. I know him not.

Enter PISTOL.

Flu. Do you not know him? Here comes the man.

Pist. Captain, I thee beseech to do me favours:
The duke of Exeter doth love thee well.

Flu. Ay, I praise Got; and I have merited some love at his hands.

Pist. Bardolph, a soldier, firm and sound of heart,
Of buxom valour,[3] hath,—by cruel fate,
And giddy fortune's furious fickle wheel,
That goddess blind,
That stands upon the rolling restless stone,—

Flu. By your patience, ancient Pistol. Fortune is painted plind, with a muffler[4] before her eyes, to signify to you that fortune is plind: And she is painted also with a wheel; to signify to you, which is the moral of it, that she is turning, and inconstant, and variations, and mutabilities: and her foot, look you, is fixed upon a spherical stone, which rolls, and rolls, and rolls;—In good truth, the poet is make a most excellent description of fortune: fortune, look you, is an excellent moral.

Pist. Fortune is Bardolph's foe, and frowns on him;
For he hath stolen a *pix*,[5] and hanged must 'a be.
A damned death!
Let gallows gape for dog, let man go free,
And let not hemp his windpipe suffocate:
But Exeter hath given the doom of death,
For *pix* of little price.
Therefore, go speak, the duke will hear thy voice;
And let not Bardolph's vital thread be cut
With edge of penny cord, and vile reproach:
Speak, captain, for his life, and I will thee requite.

Flu. Ancient Pistol, I do partly understand your meaning.

Pist. Why then rejoice therefore.

Flu. Certainly, ancient, it is not a thing to rejoice at; for if, look you, he were my brother, I would desire the duke to use his goot pleasure, and put him to executions; for disciplines ought to be used.

Pist. Die and be damn'd; and *figo*[6] for thy friendship!

Flu. It is well.

Pist. The fig of Spain! [*Exit* PISTOL.

Flu. Very good.[7]

Gow. Why, this is an arrant counterfeit rascal; I remember him now; a bawd; a cutpurse.

Flu. I'll assure you, 'a utter'd as prave 'ords at the pridge, as you shall see in a summer's day: But it is very well; what he has spoke to me, that is well, I warrant you, when time is serve.

Gow. Why, 'tis a gull, a fool, a rogue; that now and then goes to the wars, to grace himself, at his return into London, under the form of a soldier. And such fellows are perfect in great commanders' names: and they will learn you by rote, where services were done:—at such and such a sconce,[8] at such a breach, at such a convoy; who came off bravely, who was shot, who disgraced, what terms the enemy stood on; and this they con perfectly in the phrase of war, which they trick up with new-tuned oaths: And what a beard of the general's cut,[9] and a horrid suit of the camp, will do among foaming bottles, and ale-washed wits, is wonderful to be thought on! but you must learn to know such slanders of the age,[10] or else you may be marvellous mistook.

Flu. I tell you what, Captain Gower;—I do perceive, he is not the man that he would gladly make show to the 'orld he is; if I find a hole in his coat, I will tell him my mind. [*Drum heard.*] Hark

1 *Rouen* is spelt *Roan* in the old copy. It was pronounced as a monosyllable.

2 'But keeps the pridge most valiantly.' After Henry had passed the Some, the French endeavoured to intercept him in his passage to Calais; and for that purpose attempted to break down the only bridge that there was over the small river of Ternois, at Blangi, over which it was necessary for Henry to pass. But Henry having notice of their design, sent a part of his troops before him, who attacking and putting the French to flight, preserved the bridge till the whole English army arrived and passed over it.

3 '*Buxom* valour.' It is true that, in the Saxon and our elder English, *buxom* meant *pliant, yielding, obedient;* and in this sense Spenser uses it: but as we know it was also used for *lusty, rampant*, however mistakenly, it was surely very absurd to give the older meaning to it here, as Steevens did. Pistol would be much more likely to take the popular sense, than one founded on etymology. Blount, after giving the old legitimate meaning of *buxomeness*, says, 'It is now mistaken for *lustiness* or *rampancy*.'

4 A *muffler* was a fold of linen used for concealing the face of a woman.

5 'A *pix*.' The folio reads *pax:* but Holinshed, whom Shakspeare followed, says, 'A foolish soldier stole a *pixe* out of a church, for which cause he was apprehended, and the king would not once more remove till the *box* was restored, and the offender strangled.' It was the box in which the consecrated wafers were kept, originally so named from being made of *box;* but in later times it was made of gold, silver, and other costly materials.

6 'And *figo* for thy friendship.' See note on King Henry IV. Part 2. The *Spanish fig* probably alludes to the custom of giving poisoned figs to those who were the objects of either Spanish or Italian revenge; to which custom there are numerous allusions in our old dramas. In the quarto copies of this play we have:—
'The fig of Spain within thy jaw.' And afterwards:—
'The fig of Spain within thy bowels and thy dirty maw.'

7 'Very good.' In the quartos, instead of these two words, we have:—
'Captain Gower, cannot you hear it lighten and thunder?'

8 'Such and such a *sconce*.' Steevens has erroneously explained this, 'a hasty, rude, inconsiderable kind of fortification.' The quotation from Sir Thomas Smythe only described some particularly imperfect sconces. A *sconce* was a block-house or *chief-fortress*, for the most part round in fashion of a head; hence the head is ludicrously called a sconce: a lantern was also called a sconce, because of its round form.

9 'A beard of the general's cut.' Our ancestors were very curious in the fashion of their beards; a certain cut was appropriated to certain professions and ranks They are some of them humourously described in a ballad in The Prince D'Amour, 1660. The *spade* beard and the *stiletto* beard appear to have been appropriated to the soldier.

10 'Such slanders of the age.' Nothing was more common than such huffcap pretending braggarts as Pistol in the poet's age: they are the continual subject of satire to his contemporaries. To the reader who has any acquaintance with our early writers it would be superfluous to cite instances. Steevens mentions Basilico, in Solyman and Perseda, as likely to have given the hint of Pistol's character to Shakspeare.

you, the king is coming; and I must speak with him from the pridge.[1]

Enter KING HENRY, GLOSTER, *and* Soldiers.

Flu. Got pless your majesty!

K. Hen. How now, Fluellen? camest thou from the bridge?

Flu. Ay, so please your majesty. The duke of Exeter has very gallantly maintained the pridge: the French is gone off, look you; and there is gallant and most prave passages: Marry, th'athversary was have possession of the pridge; but he is enforced to retire, and the duke of Exeter is master of the pridge; I can tell your majesty, the duke is a prave man.

K. Hen. What men have you lost, Fluellen?

Flu. The perdition of th'athversary hath been very great, very reasonable great: marry, for my part, I think the duke hath lost never a man, but one that is like to be executed for robbing a church, one Bardolph, if your majesty know the man: his face is all bubukles, and whelks,[2] and knobs, and flames of fire; and his lips plows at his nose, and it is like a coal of fire, sometimes plue, and sometimes red; but his nose is executed, and his fire's out.

K. Hen. We would have all such offenders so cut off:—and we give express charge, that in our marches through the country, there be nothing compelled from the villages, nothing taken but paid for; none of the French upbraided, or abused in disdainful language; For when lenity and cruelty play for a kingdom, the gentler gamester is the soonest winner.

Tucket sounds. Enter MONTJOY.

Mont. You know me by my habit.[3]

K. Hen. Well then, I know thee; What shall I know of thee?

Mont. My master's mind.

K. Hen. Unfold it.

Mont. Thus says my king:—Say thou to Harry of England, Though we seemed dead, we did but sleep; Advantage is a better soldier than rashness. Tell him, we could have rebuked him at Harfleur; but that we thought not good to bruise an injury, till it were full ripe:—now we speak upon our cue,[4] and our voice is imperial! England shall repent his folly, see his weakness, and admire our sufferance. Bid him, therefore, consider of his ransom; which must proportion the losses we have borne, the subjects we have lost, the disgrace we have digested; which, in weight to re-answer, his pettiness would bow under. For our losses, his exchequer is too poor; for the effusion of our blood, the master of his kingdom too faint a number; and for our disgrace, his own person, kneeling at our feet, but a weak and worthless satisfaction. To this add—defiance: and tell him, for conclusion, he hath betrayed his followers, whose condemnation is pronounced. So far my king and master; so much my office.

K. Hen. What is thy name? I know thy quality.

Mont. Montjoy.

K. Hen. Thou dost thy office fairly. Turn thee back,
And tell thy king,—I do not seek him now;
But could be willing to march on to Calais
Without impeachment:[5] for, to say the sooth,
(Though 'tis no wisdom to confess so much
Unto an enemy of craft and vantage,)
My people are with sickness much enfeebled,
My numbers lessen'd; and those few I have,
Almost no better than so many French;
Who, when they were in health, I tell thee, herald,
I thought, upon one pair of English legs
Did march three Frenchmen.—Yet, forgive me, God,
That I do brag thus!—this your air of France
Hath blown that vice in me; I must repent.
Go, therefore, tell thy master, here I am;
My ransom, is this frail and worthless trunk;
My army, but a weak and sickly guard;
Yet, God before,[6] tell him we will come on,
Though France himself, and such another neighbour,
Stand in our way. There's for thy labour, Montjoy.
Go, bid thy master well advise himself:
If we may pass, we will; if we be hinder'd,
We shall your tawny ground with your red blood
Discolour:[7] and so, Montjoy, fare you well.
The sum of all our answer is but this:
We would not seek a battle, as we are;
Nor, as we are, we say, we will not shun it;
So tell your master.

Mont. I shall deliver so. Thanks to your highness. [*Exit* MONTJOY.

Glo. I hope they will not come upon us now.

K. Hen. We are in God's hand, brother, not in theirs.
March to the bridge; it now draws toward night:—
Beyond the river we'll encamp ourselves;
And on to-morrow bid them march away. [*Exeunt.*

SCENE VII. *The* French *Camp, near* Agincourt.

Enter the Constable *of* France, *the* LORD RAMBURES, *the* DUKE *of* ORLEANS, Dauphin, *and others.*

Con. Tut! I have the best armour of the world.—'Would, it were day!

Orl. You have an excellent armour; but let my horse have his due.

Con. It is the best horse of Europe.

Orl. Will it never be morning?

Dau. My lord of Orleans, and my lord high constable, you talk of horse and armour,—

Orl. You are as well provided of both, as any prince in the world.

Dau. What a long night is this!——I will not change my horse with any that treads but on four pasterns. *Ca, ha!* He bounds from the earth, as if his entrails were hairs;[8] *le cheval volant*, the Pegasus, *qui a les narines de feu!* When I bestride him, I soar, I am a hawk: he trots the air; the

---

1 'From the pridge.' These words are not in the quarto. If not a mistake of the compositor, who may have caught them from the king's speech, they must mean *about* the bridge, or *concerning* it.

2 'His face is all bubukles, and *whelks*, and knobs.' *Whelks* are not stripes, as Mr. Nares interprets the word; but pimples, or blotches: *Papulæ*. 'A pimple, a *whelke*; Bourion ou bubbe qui vient en face.' Mr. Steevens remarks that Chaucer's Sompnour may have afforded Shakspeare a hint for Bardolph's face. He also had

'A fire red cherubimes face,'

with '*welkes* white,' and 'knobbes sitting on his cheekes.'—*Cant. Tales*, v. 628.

3 'You know me by my habit.' That is, by his herald's coat. The person of a herald being inviolable was distinguished by a richly emblazoned dress. *Montjoie* is the title of the first king at arms in France, as *Garter* is in this country

4 i. e. in our turn. This theatrical phrase has been already noticed.

5 i. e. without *impediment*. Empechement, Fr. See Cotgrave's Dictionary

6 *God before* was then used for *God being my guide*.

7 'We shall your tawny ground with your red blood Discolour.'

This is from Holinshed. 'My desire is, that none of you be *so unadvised* as to be the occasion that I in my defence shall *colour* and make *red your tawny* ground with the effusion of Christian blood. When he had thus answered the herauld he gave him a great rewarde, and licenced him to depart.' It was always customary to give a reward, or largess, to the herald, whether he brought a message of defiance or congratulation. I will just observe by the way, that the heralds do not appear to have been held in the highest esteem formerly; I find them, in a very curious passage of Robert Rolle's *Speculum Vitæ*, classed with all the other infamous itinerant professions, as courtezans, jugglers, minstrels, thieves, and hangmen.

8 'He bounds from the earth, as if his entrails were hairs.' Alluding to the bounding of tennis-balls, which were stuffed with hair.

earth sings when he touches it; the basest horn of his hoof is more musical than the pipe of Hermes.

Orl. He's of the colour of the nutmeg.

Dau. And of the heat of the ginger. It is a beast for Perseus: he is pure air and fire;[1] and the dull elements of earth and water never appear in him, but only in patient stillness, while his rider mounts him: he is, indeed, a horse; and all other jades you may call—beasts.[2]

Con. Indeed, my lord, it is a most absolute and excellent horse.

Dau. It is the prince of palfreys; his neigh is like the bidding of a monarch, and his countenance enforces homage.

Orl. No more, cousin.

Dau. Nay, the man hath no wit, that cannot, from the rising of the lark to the lodging of the lamb, vary deserved praise on my palfrey: it is a theme as fluent as the sea; turn the sands into eloquent tongues, and my horse is argument for them all: 'tis a subject for a sovereign to reason on, and for a sovereign's sovereign to ride on; and for the world (familiar to us, and unknown,) to lay apart their particular functions, and wonder at him. I once wrote a sonnet in his praise, and began thus: *Wonder of nature,—*

Orl. I have heard a sonnet begin so to one's mistress.

Dau. Then did they imitate that which I composed to my courser; for my horse is my mistress.

Orl. Your mistress bears well.

Dau. Me well; which is the prescript praise and perfection of a good and particular mistress.

Con. *Ma foy!* the other day, methought, your mistress shrewdly shook your back.

Dau. So, perhaps, did yours.

Con. Mine was not bridled.

Dau. O! then, belike, she was old and gentle; and you rode like a Kerne of Ireland, your French hose off, and in your strait trossers.[3]

Con. You have good judgment in horsemanship.

Dau. Be warned by me then: they that ride so, and ride not warily, fall into foul bogs; I had rather have my horse to my mistress.

Con. I had as lief have my mistress a jade.

Dau. I tell thee, constable, my mistress wears her own hair.

Con. I could make as true a boast as that, if I had a sow to my mistress.

Dau. *Le chien est retourné à son propre vomissement, et la truie lavée au bourbier:*[4] thou makest use of any thing.

Con. Yet do I not use my horse for my mistress; or any such proverb, so little kin to the purpose.

Ram. My lord constable, the armour, that I saw in your tent to-night, are those stars, or suns, upon it?

Con. Stars, my lord.

Dau. Some of them will fall to-morrow, I hope.

Con. And yet my sky shall not want.

Dau. That may be, for you bear a many superfluously! and 'twere more honour, some were away.

Con. Even as your horse bears your praises; who would trot as well, were some of your brags dismounted.

Dau. 'Would, I were able to load him with his desert! Will it never be day? I will trot to-morrow a mile, and my way shall be paved with English faces.

Con. I will not say so, for fear I should be faced out of my way: But I would it were morning, for I would fain be about the ears of the English.

Ram. Who will go to hazard with me for twenty English prisoners?

Con. You must first go yourself to hazard, ere you have them.

Dau. 'Tis midnight, I'll go arm myself. [*Exit.*

Orl. The Dauphin longs for morning.

Ram. He longs to eat the English.

Con. I think, he will eat all he kills.

Orl. By the white hand of my lady, he's a gallant prince.

Con. Swear by her foot, that she may tread out the oath.

Orl. He is, simply, the most active gentleman of France.

Con. Doing is activity: and he will still be doing.

Orl. He never did harm, that I heard of.

Con. Nor will do none to-morrow; he will keep that good name still.

Orl. I know him to be valiant.

Con. I was told that, by one that knows him better than you.

Orl. What's he?

Con. Marry, he told me so himself; and he said, he cared not who knew it.

Orl. He needs not, it is no hidden virtue in him.

Con. By my faith, sir, but it is; never any body saw it, but his lackey: 'tis a hooded valour; and, when it appears, it will bate.[5]

Orl. Ill will never said well.

Con. I will cap that proverb with—There is flattery in friendship.

Orl. And I will take up that with—Give the devil his due.

Con. Well placed; there stands your friend for the devil: have at the very eye of that proverb, with—a pox of the devil.

Orl. You are the better at proverbs, by how much—a fool's bolt is soon shot.

Con. You have shot over.

Orl. 'Tis not the first time you were overshot.

Enter a Messenger.

Mess. My lord high constable, the English lie within fifteen hundred paces of your tent.

Con. Who hath measured the ground?

Mess. The Lord Grandpre.

Con. A valiant and most expert gentleman.—'Would, it were day![6]—Alas, poor Harry of England!—He longs not for the dawning, as we do.

---

1 'He is pure air and fire.' Thus Cleopatra, speaking of herself:—

'I am *air* and *fire*; my other elements
I give to baser life.'

2 'He is, indeed, a *horse*; and all other *jades* you may call—*beasts*.' There has been much foolish contention about this passage; the sense of which is plain enough. I have elsewhere observed that *jade* is not always used for a tired or contemptible horse. The Dauphin means 'that his charger is indeed a *horse*, and alone worthy of that name; all others may be called *beasts* in comparison of him.' Beast is here used in the sense of the Latin *jumentum*, contemptuously to signify an animal only fit for the cart or packsaddle.

3 'Like a Kerne of Ireland, your French hose off, and in your *strait trossers*.' This expression is here merely figurative, as Theobald long since observed, for *femoribus denudatis*. But it is certain that the Irish *trossers*, or trowsers, were anciently the direct contrary to the modern garments of that name. 'Their *trowses*, commonly spelt *trossers*, were long pantaloons *exactly fitted to the shape*.' Bulwer, in his Pedigree of the English Gallant, 1653, says, 'Now our hose are made so close to our breeches that, like the *Irish trossers*, they too manifestly discover the dimensions of every part.'—I will add that Spenser says Chaucer's description of Sir Thopas gives 'the very manner and fashion of the Irish horseman,—in his *long hose*, his riding shoes of costly cordwaine, his hacqueton, and his habergeon,' &c.—*State of Ireland*, p. 115; Ed. Dublin, 1809.

4 It has been remarked that Shakspeare was habitually conversant with his bible: we have here a strong presumptive proof that he read it, at least occasionally, in French. This passage will be found almost literally in the Geneva Bible, 1588. 2 Peter ii. 22.

5 ''Tis a hooded valour; and, when it appears, it will bate.' This poor pun depends upon the equivocal use of *bate*. When a hawk is unhooded, her first action is to bate (i. e. beat her wings, or flutter.) The hawk wants no courage, but invariably bates upon the removal of her hood. The Constable would insinuate by his double entendre that the Dauphin's courage, when it appears (i. e. when he prepares for encounter,) will *bate*; i. e. soon diminish or evaporate.

6 Instead of this and the succeeding speeches, the quartos conclude this scene with a couplet:—

'——— Come, come away;
The sun is high, and we wear out the day.'

Orl. What a wretched and peevish[1] fellow is this king of England, to mope with his fat-brained followers so far out of his knowledge!

Con. If the English had any apprehension, they would run away.

Orl. That they lack; for if their heads had any intellectual armour, they could never wear such heavy head-pieces.

Ram. That island of England breeds very valiant creatures; their mastiffs are of unmatchable courage.

Orl. Foolish curs! that run winking into the mouth of a Russian bear, and have their heads crushed like rotten apples: You may as well say,—that's a valiant flea, that dare eat his breakfast on the lip of a lion.

Con. Just, just; and the men do sympathise with the mastiffs, in robustious and rough coming on, leaving their wits with their wives; and then give them great meals of beef, and iron and steel, they will eat like wolves, and fight like devils.

Orl. Ay, but these English are shrewdly out of beef.

Con. Then we shall find to-morrow—they have only stomachs to eat, and none to fight. Now is it time to arm: Come, shall we about it?

Orl. It is now two o'clock: but, let me see,—by ten,
We shall have each a hundred Englishmen.
[*Exeunt.*

ACT IV.

Enter CHORUS.

Chor. Now entertain conjecture of a time,
When creeping murmur, and the poring dark,
Fills the wide vessel of the universe,[2]
From camp to camp, through the foul womb of night,
The hum of either army stilly sounds,[3]
That the fix'd sentinels almost receive
The secret whispers of each other's watch:[4]
Fire answers fire; and through their paly flames
Each battle sees the other's umber'd[5] face:
Steed threatens steed in high and boastful neighs,
Piercing the night's dull ear; and from the tents,
The armourers, accomplishing the knights,
With busy hammers closing rivets up,[6]
Give dreadful note of preparation.
The country cocks do crow, the clocks do toll,
And the third hour of drowsy morning name.
Proud of their numbers, and secure in soul,
The confident and over-lusty[7] French
Do the low-rated English play at dice;
And chide the cripple tardy-gaited night,
Who, like a foul and ugly witch, doth limp
So tediously away. The poor condemned English,
Like sacrifices, by their watchful fires
Sit patiently, and inly ruminate
The morning's danger; and their gestures sad,
Investing lank-lean cheeks,[8] and war-worn coats,
Presenteth them unto the gazing moon
So many horrid ghosts. O, now, who will behold
The royal captain of this ruin'd band,
Walking from watch to watch, from tent to tent,
Let him cry—Praise and glory on his head!
For forth he goes, and visits all his host;
Bids them good morrow, with a modest smile;
And calls them—brothers, friends, and countrymen.
Upon his royal face there is no note,
How dread an army hath enrounded him:
Nor doth he dedicate one jot of colour
Unto the weary and all-watched night;
But freshly looks, and over-bears attaint,
With cheerful semblance, and sweet majesty,
That every wretch, pining and pale before,
Beholding him, plucks comfort from his looks
A largess universal, like the sun,
His liberal eye doth give to every one,
Thawing cold fear. Then, mean and gentle all,
Behold, as may unworthiness define,
A little touch of Harry in the night:
And so our scene must to the battle fly:
Where (O for pity!) we shall much disgrace—
With four or five most vile and ragged foils,
Right ill-dispos'd, in brawl ridiculous,—
The name of Agincourt: Yet, sit and see;
Minding[9] true things, by what their mockeries be.
[*Exit.*

SCENE I. *The* English *Camp at* Agincourt.

Enter KING HENRY, BEDFORD, *and* GLOSTER.

K. Hen. Gloster, 'tis true, that we are in great danger;
The greater therefore should our courage be.—
Good morrow, brother Bedford.—God Almighty!
There is some soul of goodness in things evil,
Would men observingly distil it out;
For our bad neighbour makes us early stirrers,
Which is both healthful, and good husbandry:
Besides, they are our outward consciences,
And preachers to us all; admonishing,
That we should dress us fairly for our end.[10]

---

1 *Peevish*, i. e. foolish.

2 'Fills the wide vessel of the universe.' Warburton says *universe* for *horizon*. Upon which Johnson remarks:—'The universe, in its original sense, no more means this globe singly than the circuit of the horizon; but however large in its philosophical sense, it may be poetically used for as much of the world as falls under observation.'

3 'The hum of either army *stilly* sounds.' This expression applied to sound is not peculiar to Shakspeare; we have 'a *still* small voice' in the sacred writings, and Florio's Dictionary in the word *sussura*, has 'a buzzing, a murmuring, a charming, a humming, a soft, gentle, *still noise*, as of running water falling with a gentle stream, or as trees make with the wind, &c.' It is the 'murmure tacito' of Ovid.

4 'The secret whispers of each other's watch.' Holinshed says that the distance between the two armies was but two hundred and fifty paces: and again, 'at their coming into the village, fires were made (by the English) to give light on every side, as there were likewise by the French hoste.'

5 It has been said that the distant visages of the soldiers would appear of an *umber* colour when beheld through the light of midnight fires. I suspect that nothing more is meant than '*shadow'd* face.' The epithet '*paly* flames' is against the other interpretation. *Umbre* for *shadow* is common in our elder writers.

6 'The armourers, accomplishing the knights,
With busy hammers closing rivets up.'
This does not solely refer to the riveting the plate armour before it was put on, out as to part when it was on. The top of the cuirass had a little projecting bit of iron that passed through a hole pierced through the bottom of the casque. When both were put on, the smith or armourer presented himself, with his rivetting hammer, *to close the rivet up;* so that the party's head should remain steady, notwithstanding the force of any blow that might be given on the cuirass or helmet. This custom prevailed more particularly in tournaments. See Varietes Historiques, 1752, 12mo. tom. ii. p. 73 *Douce.*

7 'The confident and over-lusty French
Do the low-rated English play at dice.'
Over-lusty, i. e. *over-saucy*. Thus in North's Plutarch:—'Cassius's soldiers did shewe themselves verie stubborn and lustie in the camp.' This is Steevens's explanation; the word *lusty*, however, was synonymous with lively. 'To be *lively* or *lustie*, to be in his force or strength, Vigeo.' It is also meant 'in good plight, jolly.' By 'Do the low-rated English play at dice;' is meant 'do play them away, or play for them at dice' The circumstance is from Holinshed.

8 '——— their gestures sad,
Investing lank-lean cheeks.'
Thus Sidney, in Astrophel, song 2, has:—
'Anger *invests* the face with a lovely grace.'

9 '*Minding* true things.' To *mind* is the same as to call to remembrance. Thus Baret:—'I *minde* this matter, and thinke still that it is before my eyes; in oculis animoque versatur mihi hæc res.'

10 'That we should dress us fairly for our end.' Malone took this for an abbreviation of *address* us, and printed it thus, 'dress us. Steevens very reasonably doubted the propriety of the elision, but would take *dress* in its ordinary acceptation. 'To *dress* is to *make ready* to *prepare*. Paro, Lat.'

Thus may we gather honey from the weed,
And make a moral of the devil himself.

Enter ERPINGHAM.[1]

Good morrow, old Sir Thomas Erpingham:
A good soft pillow for that good white head
Were better than a churlish turf of France.

Erp. Not so, my liege; this lodging likes me better,
Since I may say—now lie I like a king.

K. Hen. 'Tis good for men to love their present pains,
Upon example; so the spirit is eased;
And, when the mind is quicken'd, out of doubt,
The organs, though defunct and dead before,
Break up their drowsy grave, and newly move
With casted slough and fresh legerity.[2]
Lend me thy cloak, Sir Thomas.—Brothers both,
Commend me to the princes in our camp;
Do my good morrow to them; and, anon,
Desire them all to my pavilion.

Glo. We shall, my liege.

[*Exeunt* GLOSTER *and* BEDFORD.

Erp. Shall I attend your grace?

K. Hen. No, my good knight;
Go with my brothers to my lords of England:
I and my bosom must debate awhile,
And then I would no other company.

Erp. The Lord in heaven bless thee, noble Harry!

[*Exit* ERPINGHAM.

K. Hen. God-a-mercy, old heart! thou speakest cheerfully.

Enter PISTOL.

Pist. *Qui va la?*

K. Hen. A friend.

Pist. Discuss unto me; Art thou officer;
Or art thou base, common, and popular?

K. Hen. I am a gentleman of a company.

Pist. Trailest thou the puissant pike?

K. Hen. Even so: What are you?

Pist. As good a gentleman as the emperor.

K. Hen. Then you are a better than the king.

Pist. The king's a bawcock, and a heart of gold,
A lad of life, an imp[3] of fame;
Of parents good, of fist most valiant:
I kiss his dirty shoe, and from my heart-strings
I love the lovely bully. What's thy name?

K. Hen. Harry *le Roy*.

Pist. *Le Roy!* a Cornish name: art thou of Cornish crew?

K. Hen. No, I am a Welshman.

Pist. Knowest thou Fluellen.

K. Hen. Yes.

Pist. Tell him, I'll knock his leek about his pate,
Upon Saint Davy's day.

K. Hen Do not you wear your dagger in your cap that day, lest he knock that about yours.

Pist. Art thou his friend?

K. Hen. And his kinsman too.

Pist. The *figo* for thee then!

K. Hen. I thank you: God be with you!

Pist. My name is Pistol called. [*Exit.*

K. Hen. It sorts[4] well with your fierceness.

Enter FLUELLEN *and* GOWER, *severally.*

Gow. Captain Fluellen!

Flu. So! in the name of Cheshu Christ, speak lower. It is the greatest admiration in the universal orld, when the true and auncient prerogatifes and laws of the wars is not kept: if you would take the pains but to examine the wars of Pompey the Great, you shall find, I warrant you, that there is no tiddle taddle, or piddle paddle, in Pompey's camp; I warrant you, you shall find the ceremonies of the wars, and the cares of it, and the forms of it, and the sobriety of it, and the modesty of it, to be otherwise.

Gow. Why, the enemy is loud; you heard him all night.

Flu. If the enemy is an ass, and a fool, and a prating coxcomb, is it meet, think you, that we should also, look you, be an ass, and a fool, and a prating coxcomb; in your own conscience now?

Gow. I will speak lower.

Flu. I pray you, and beseech you, that you will.

[*Exeunt* GOWER *and* FLUELLEN.

K. Hen. Though it appear a little out of fashion,
There is much care and valour in this Welshman.

Enter BATES, COURT, *and* WILLIAMS.

Court. Brother John Bates, is not that the morning which breaks yonder?

Bates. I think it be: but we have no great cause to desire the approach of day.

Will. We see yonder the beginning of the day. but, I think, we shall never see the end of it.—Who goes there?

K. Hen. A friend.

Will. Under what captain serve you?

K. Hen. Under Sir Thomas Erpingham.

Will. A good old commander, and a most kind gentleman: I pray you, what thinks he of our estate?

K. Hen. Even as men wrecked upon a sand, that look to be washed off the next tide.

Bates. He hath not told his thought to the king?

K. Hen. No; nor it is not meet he should. For, though I speak it to you, I think, the king is but a man, as I am: the violet smells to him, as it doth to me; the element shows to him, as it doth to me; all his senses have but human conditions:[5] his ceremonies laid by, in his nakedness he appears but a man; and though his affections are higher mounted than ours, yet, when they stoop, they stoop with the like wing;[6] therefore when he sees reason of fears, as we do, his fears, out of doubt, be of the same relish as ours are: Yet, in reason, no man should possess him with any appearance of fear, lest he, by showing it, should dishearten his army.

Bates. He may show what outward courage he will: but, I believe, as cold a night as 'tis, he could wish himself in the Thames up to the neck; and so I would he were, and I by him, at all adventures, so we were quit here.

K. Hen. By my troth, I will speak my conscience of the king; I think, he would not wish himself any where but where he is.

Bates. Then, would he were here alone; so should he be sure to be ransomed, and a many poor men's lives saved.

K. Hen. I dare say, you love him not so ill, to wish him here alone; howsoever you speak this, to feel other men's minds: Methinks, I could not die any where so contented, as in the king's company; his cause being just, and his quarrel honourable.

Will. That's more than we know.

Bates. Ay, or more than we should seek after; for we know enough, if we know we are the king's subjects; if his cause be wrong, our obedience to the king wipes the crime of it out of us.

Will. But, if the cause be not good, the king himself hath a heavy reckoning to make; when all those legs, and arms, and heads, chopped off in a battle, shall join together at the latter day, and cry all—We died at such a place; some, swearing; some, crying for a surgeon; some, upon their wives left poor behind them; some, upon the debts they

---

1 *Sir Thomas Erpingham* came over with Bolingbroke from Bretagne, and was one of the commissioners to receive King Richard's abdication. He was at this time warden of Dover Castle, and his arms are still visible on the side of the Roman Pharos.

2 'With casted *slough* and fresh *legerity*.' The allusion is to the casting of the slough or skin of the snake annually, by which act he is supposed to regain new vigour and fresh youth. *Legerity* is lightness, nimbleness.

3 'An imp of fame.' See Second Part of King Henry IV. Act v. Sc. 5.

4 i. e. agrees, accords.

5 i. e. but human *qualities*.

6 '—though his affections are higher *mounted* than ours, when they *stoop*, they stoop with like wing.' This passage alludes to the ancient sport of falconry. When the hawk, after soaring aloft, or *mounting* high, descended in its flight, it was said to *stoop*

owe; some, upon their children rawly[1] left. I am afeard there are few die well, that die in battle; for how can they charitably dispose of any thing, when blood is their argument? Now, if these men do not die well, it will be a black matter for the king that led them to it; whom to disobey were against all proportion of subjection.

K. Hen. So, if a son, that is by his father sent about merchandise, do sinfully miscarry upon the sea, the imputation of his wickedness, by your rule, should be imposed upon his father that sent him: or if a servant, under his master's command, transporting a sum of money, be assailed by robbers, and die in many irreconciled iniquities, you may call the business of the master the author of the servant's damnation:—But this is not so: the king is not bound to answer the particular endings of his soldiers, the father of his son, nor the master of his servant; for they purpose not their death, when they purpose their services. Besides, there is no king, be his cause never so spotless, if it come to the arbitrement of swords, can try it out with all unspotted soldiers. Some, peradventure, have on them the guilt of premeditated and contrived murder; some, of beguiling virgins with the broken seals of perjury;[2] some, making the wars their bulwark, that have before gored the gentle bosom of peace with pillage and robbery. Now, if these men have defeated the law, and outrun native punishment,[3] though they can outstrip men, they have no wings to fly from God: war is his beadle, war is his vengeance; so that here men are punished, for before-breach of the king's laws, in now the king's quarrel: where they feared the death, they have borne life away; and where they would be safe, they perish: Then if they die unprovided, no more is the king guilty of their damnation, than he was before guilty of those impieties for the which they are now visited. Every subject's duty is the king's;[4] but every subject's soul is his own. Therefore should every soldier in the wars do as every sick man in his bed, wash every mote out of his conscience: and dying so, death is to him advantage; or not dying, the time was blessedly lost, wherein such preparation was gained: and, in him that escapes, it were not sin to think, that making God so free an offer, he let him outlive that day to see his greatness, and to teach others how they should prepare.

Will. 'Tis certain, every man that dies ill, the ill is upon his own head, the king is not to answer for it.

Bates. I do not desire he should answer for me; and yet I determine to fight lustily for him.

K. Hen. I myself heard the king say, he would not be ransomed.

Will. Ay, he said so, to make us fight cheerfully: but, when our throats are cut, he may be ransomed, and we ne'er the wiser.

K. Hen. If I live to see it, I will never trust his word after.

Will. 'Mass, you'll pay[5] him then! That's a perilous shot out of an elder gun,[6] that a poor and private displeasure can do against a monarch! you may as well go about to turn the sun to ice, with fanning in his face with a peacock's feather. You'll never trust his word after! come, 'tis a foolish saying.

K. Hen. Your reproof is something too round:[7] I should be angry with you, if the time were convenient.

Will. Let it be a quarrel between us, if you live.

K. Hen. I embrace it.

Will. How shall I know thee again?

K. Hen. Give me any gage of thine, and I will wear it in my bonnet: then, if ever thou darest acknowledge it, I will make it my quarrel.

Will. Here's my glove, give me another of thine.

K. Hen. There.

Will. This will I also wear in my cap: if ever thou come to me and say, after to-morrow, *This is my glove*, by this hand, I will take thee a box on the ear.

K. Hen. If ever I live to see it, I will challenge it.

Will. Thou darest as well be hanged.

K. Hen. Well, I will do it, though I take thee in the king's company.

Will. Keep thy word: fare thee well.

Bates. Be friends, you English fools, be friends; we have French quarrels enough, if you could tell how to reckon.

K. Hen. Indeed, the French may lay twenty French crowns to one, they will beat us; for they bear them on their shoulders: But it is no English treason to cut French crowns; and, to-morrow, the king himself will be a clipper. [*Exeunt* Soldiers.

Upon the king![8] let us our lives, our souls,
Our debts, our careful wives, our children, and
Our sins, lay on the king;—we must bear all.
O hard condition! twin-born with greatness,
Subjected to the breath of every fool,
Whose sense no more can feel but his own wringing!
What infinite heart's ease must kings neglect,
That private men enjoy?
And what have kings, that privates have not too
Save ceremony, save general ceremony?
And what art thou, thou idol ceremony?
What kind of god art thou, that suffer'st more
Of mortal griefs, than do thy worshippers?
What are thy rents? what are thy comings in?
O ceremony, show me but thy worth!
What is thy soul of adoration?[9]
Art thou aught else but place, degree, and form,
Creating awe and fear in other men?
Wherein thou art less happy, being fear'd,
Than they in fearing.
What drink'st thou oft, instead of homage sweet,
But poison'd flattery? O, be sick, great greatness
And bid thy ceremony give thee cure!
Think'st thou, the fiery fever will go out
With titles blown from adulation?
Will it give place to flexure and low bending?
Canst thou, when thou command'st the beggar's knee,
Command the health of it? No, thou proud dream,
That play'st so subtly with a king's repose:
I am a king, that find thee; and I know,
'Tis not the balm, the sceptre, and the ball,
The sword, the mace, the crown imperial,
The inter-tissued robe of gold and pearl,
The farced[10] title running 'fore the king,
The throne he sits on, nor the tide of pomp
That beats upon the high shore of this world,

---

1 i. e. their children left *immaturely*, left young and helpless.

2 '— beguiling virgins with the broken seals of perjury.' Thus in the song at the beginning of the fourth act of Measure for Measure:—

> 'That so sweetly were forsworn—
> Seals of love, but seal'd in vain.'

3 i. e. the punishment they are born to.

4 'Every subject's duty is the king's.' This is a very just distinction, and the whole argument is well followed and properly concluded.—*Johnson.*

5 *To pay* here signifies to bring to account, to punish.

6 'That's a perilous shot out of an elder gun.' In the quarto the thought is more opened—*It is a great displeasure that an elder gun can do against a cannon*, or a subject against a monarch.

7 'Too *round*' is too rough, too unceremonious

8 'Upon the king.' There is something very striking and solemn in the soliloquy into which the king breaks immediately as soon as he is left alone. Something like this every breast has felt. Reflection and seriousness rush upon the mind upon the separation of gay company and especially after forced and unwilling merriment.—*Johnson.* This beautiful speech was added after the first edition.

9 'What is *thy* soul of adoration?' This is the reading of the old copy, which Malone changed to:—

> 'What is *the* soul of adoration?'

I think erroneously. The present reading is sufficiently intelligible, 'O ceremony, show me what value thou art of? What is thy soul or essence of external worship or adoration? *Art thou*,' &c. If Malone's reading is adopted, it would be necessary to read '*Are they*,' &c. because ceremony and adoration are then both personified

10 *Farced* is stuffed. The tumid puffy titles with which a king's name is introduced.

No, not all these, thrice-gorgeous ceremony,
Not all these, laid in bed majestical,
Can sleep so soundly as the wretched slave;
Who, with a body fill'd, and vacant mind,
Gets him to rest, cramm'd with distressful bread;[1]
Never sees horrid night, the child of hell;
But, like a lackey, from the rise to set,
Sweats in the eye of Phœbus, and all night
Sleeps in Elysium; next day, after dawn,
Doth rise, and help Hyperion[2] to his horse;
And follows so the ever-running year
With profitable labour, to his grave:
And, but for ceremony, such a wretch,
Winding up days with toil, and nights with sleep,
Had the fore-hand and vantage of a king.
The slave, a member of the country's peace,
Enjoys it; but in gross brain little wots,
What watch the king keeps to maintain the peace,
Whose hours the peasant best advantages.[3]

Enter ERPINGHAM.

Erp. My lord, your nobles, jealous of your absence,
Seek through your camp to find you.
K. Hen. Good old knight,
Collect them all together at my tent:
I'll be before thee.
Erp. I shall do't, my lord. [*Exit.*
K. Hen. O God of battles! steel my soldiers' hearts!
Possess them not with fear: take from them now[4]
The sense of reckoning of the opposed numbers:
Pluck their hearts from them not to-day, O Lord!
O not to-day! Think not upon the fault
My father made in compassing the crown!
I Richard's body have interred new;
And on it have bestow'd more contrite tears,
Than from it issued forced drops of blood.
Five hundred poor I have in yearly pay,
Who twice a day their wither'd hands hold up
Toward heaven, to pardon blood; and I have built
Two chantries,[5] where the sad and solemn priests
Sing still for Richard's soul. More will I do:
Though all that I can do, is nothing worth;
Since that my penitence comes after all,
Imploring pardon.

Enter GLOSTER.

Glo. My liege!
K. Hen. My brother Gloster's voice?—Ay;
I know thy errand, I will go with thee:—
The day, my friends, and all things stay for me.
[*Exeunt.*

SCENE II. *The* French *Camp.* *Enter* Dauphin, ORLEANS, RAMBURES, *and others.*

Orl. The sun doth gild our armour; up, my lords.
Dau. *Montez a cheval:*—My hors[illegible] lacquey? ha!
Orl. O brave spirit!
Dau. *Via!*[6]*—les eaux et la terre*——
Orl. *Rien puis? l'air et le feu*——
Dau. *Ciel!* cousin Orleans.——

Enter Constable.

Now, my lord Constable.
Con. Hark, how our steeds for present service neigh.
Dau. Mount them, and make incision in their hides;
That their hot blood may spin in English eyes,
And doubt[7] them with superfluous courage: Ha!
Ram. What, will you have them weep our horses' blood?
How shall we then behold their natural tears?

Enter a Messenger.

Mess. The English are embattled, you French peers.
Con. To horse, you gallant princes! straight to horse!
Do but behold yon poor and starved band,
And your fair show shall suck away their souls,
Leaving them but the shales and husks of men.
There is not work enough for all our hands;
Scarce blood enough in all their sickly veins,
To give each naked curtle-ax a stain,
That our French gallants shall to-day draw out,
And sheath for lack of sport: let us but blow on them,
The vapour of our valour will o'erturn them.
'Tis positive 'gainst all exceptions, lords,
That our superfluous lackeys, and our peasants,—
Who in unnecessary action swarm
About our squares of battle,[8]—were enough
To purge this field of such a hilding[9] foe;
Though we, upon this mountain's basis by
Took stand for idle speculation:
But that our honours must not. What's to say?
A very little little let us do,
And all is done. Then let the trumpets sound
The tucket-sonuance,[10] and the note to mount:
For our approach shall so much dare the field,
That England shall couch down in fear, and yield.

Enter GRANDPRE.

Grand. Why do you stay so long, my lords of France?
Yon island carrions,[11] desperate of their bones,
Ill-favour'dly become the morning field:
Their ragged curtains[12] poorly are let loose,
And our air shakes them passing scornfully.
Big Mars seems bankrupt in their beggar'd host,
And faintly through a rusty beaver peeps.

---

1 '— cramm'd with distressful bread.' However oddly this may sound to modern ears, it was sufficiently intelligible to our ancestors. *Distressful bread* is the bread or food of poverty; Mensa angusta. Johnson observes that these lines are exquisitely pleasing. 'To sweat in the eye of Phœbus,' and 'to sleep in Elysium,' are expressions very poetical.

2 Apollo. See Hamlet, Act i. Sc. 2.

3 He little knows at the expense of how much royal vigilance that peace, which brings most advantage to the peasant, is maintained. To *advantage* is a verb used by Shakspeare in other places. It was formerly in general use.

4 The late editions exhibit the passage thus:—
'——— take from them now
The sense of reckoning, if the opposed numbers
Pluck their hearts from them!—Not to-day, O Lord,
O not to-day, think not upon,' &c.

5 'Two chantries.' One of these was for Carthusian monks, and was called *Bethlehem;* the other was for religious men and women of the order of Saint Bridget, and was named *Sion.* They were on opposite sides of the Thames, and adjoined the royal manor of Sheen, now called Richmond.

6 *Via,* an exclamation of encouragement, *on, away;* of Italian origin.

7 'That their hot blood may spin in English eyes,
And *doubt* them with superfluous courage.'
This is the reading of the folio which Malone has altered to *dout,* i. e. *do out* in provincial language. It appears to me that there is no reason for the substitution.

8 'About our *squares* of battle.' Thus in Antony and Cleopatra:—
'——— no practice had
In the brave *squares* of battle.'

9 'A *hilding* foe' is a paltry, cowardly, base foe. Thus in All's Well that Ends Well, the French lords call Bertram '*a hilding*.'

10 'The tucket sonuance,' &c. He uses the terms of the field as if they were going out only to chase for sport. To *dare* the field is a phrase in falconry. Birds are dared when by the falcon in the air they are terrified from rising so as to be taken by hand. Such an easy capture the lords expected to make of the English. The *tucket-sonuance* was a flourish on the trumpet as a signal to prepare to march. The phrase is derived from the Italian *toccata,* a prelude or flourish, and *suonanza,* a sound, a resounding. Thus in the Devil's Law Case, 1623, two *tuckets* by two several trumpets.

11 'Yon island carrions.' The description of the English is founded on Holinshed's melancholy account, speaking of the march from Harfleur to Agincourt:—'The Englishmen were brought into great misery in this journey; their victual was in a manner all spent, and now could they get none:—rest none could they take, for their enemies were ever at hand to give them allarmes: daily it rained, and nightly it freezed; of fewel there was great scarcity, but of fluxes great plenty, money they had enough, but wares to bestow it upon for their releife or comforte, had they little or none.'

12 Their ragged *curtains* are their *colours*

Their horsemen sit like fixed candlesticks,[1]
With torch-staves in their hand: and their poor jades
Lob down their heads, dropping the hides and hips;
The gum down-roping from their pale-dead eyes;
And in their pale dull mouths the gimmal[2] bit
Lies foul with chew'd grass, still and motionless;
And their executors, the knavish crows,
Fly o'er them all, impatient for their hour.
Description cannot suit itself in words,
To demonstrate the life of such a battle.
In life so lifeless as it shows itself.

Con. They have said their prayers, and they stay for death.

Dau. Shall we go send them dinners, and fresh suits,
And give their fasting horses provender,
And after fight with them?

Con. I stay but for my guard;[3] On, to the field:
I will the banner from a trumpet take,
And use it for my haste. Come, come, away!
The sun is high, and we outwear the day. [*Exeunt.*

SCENE III. *The* English *Camp. Enter the* English *Host;* GLOSTER, BEDFORD, EXETER, SALISBURY, *and* WESTMORELAND.

Glo. Where is the king?

Bed. The king himself is rode to view their battle.

West. Of fighting men they have full threescore thousand.

Exe. There's five to one; besides, they all are fresh.

Sal. God's arm strike with us! 'tis a fearful odds.
God be with you, princes all; I'll to my charge;
If we no more meet, till we meet in heaven,
Then, joyfully,—my noble lord of Bedford,—
My dear lord Gloster,—and my good lord Exeter,
And my kind kinsman,[4]—warriors all, adieu!

Bed. Farewell, good Salisbury; and good luck go with thee!

Exe. Farewell, kind lord; fight valiantly to-day:
And yet I do thee wrong, to mind thee of it,
For thou art fram'd of the firm truth of valour.
[*Exit* SALISBURY.

Bed. He is as full of valour, as of kindness;
Princely in both.

West. O that we now had here

Enter KING HENRY.

But one ten thousand of those men in England,
That do no work to-day!

K. Hen. What's he, that wishes so?
My cousin Westmoreland?[5]—No, my fair cousin:
If we are mark'd to die, we are enough
To do our country loss; and if to live,
The fewer men, the greater share of honour.
God's will! I pray thee, wish not one man more.
By Jove, I am not covetous for gold;
Nor care I, who doth feed upon my cost;
It yearns[6] me not, if men my garments wear;
Such outward things dwell not in my desires:
But, if it be a sin to covet honour,
I am the most offending soul alive.
No, 'faith, my coz, wish not a man from England:
God's peace! I would not lose so great an honour,
As one man more, methinks, would share from me,
For the best hope I have. O, do not wish one more.
Rather proclaim it, Westmoreland, through my host,
That he, which hath no stomach to this fight,
Let him depart; his passport shall be made,
And crowns for convoy put into his purse:
We would not die in that man's company
That fears his fellowship to die with us.
This day is call'd—the feast of Crispian:[7]
He, that outlives this day, and comes safe home,
Will stand a tip-toe when this day is nam'd,
And rouse him at the name of Crispian.
He, that shall live this day, and see old age,
Will yearly on the vigil feast his friends,
And say—to morrow is Saint Crispian:
Then will he strip his sleeve, and show his scars,
And say, these wounds I had on Crispin's day.
Old men forget; yet all shall be forgot,
But he'll remember, with advantages,[8]
What feats he did that day; Then shall our names,
Familiar in their mouths as household words—
Harry the King, Bedford and Exeter,
Warwick and Talbot, Salisbury and Gloster,
Be in their flowing cups freshly remember'd:
This story shall the good man teach his son;
And Crispin Crispian shall ne'er go by,
From this day to the ending of the world,[9]
But we in it shall be remembered:
We few, we happy few, we band of brothers,
For he, to-day that sheds his blood with me,
Shall be my brother; be he ne'er so vile
This day shall gentle his condition:[10]
And gentlemen in England, now a bed,
Shall think themselves accurs'd, they were not here:
And hold their manhoods cheap, while any speaks,
That fought with us upon Saint Crispin's day.

Enter SALISBURY.

Sal. My sovereign lord, bestow yourself with speed;
The French are bravely[11] in their battles set,
And will with all expedience[12] charge on us.

K. Hen. All things are ready, if our minds be so.

West. Perish the man, whose mind is backward now!

K. Hen. Thou dost not wish more help from England, cousin?

West. God's will, my liege, 'would you and I alone,
Without more help, might fight this battle out!

K. Hen. Why, now thou hast unwish'd five thousand men;[13]

---

1 Ancient candlesticks were often in the form of human figures, holding the socket for the lights, in their extended hands.

2 The *gimmal bit* was probably a bit in which two parts or links were united, as in the *gimmal* ring, so called because they were double linked, from *gemellus*, Lat.

3 'I stay but for my *guard.*' Dr. Johnson and Mr. Steevens were of opinion that *guard* here means rather something of ornament, than an attendant or attendants.

4 'And my kind kinsman.' This is addressed to Westmoreland by the speaker, who was *Thomas Montacute*, earl of Salisbury: he was not in point of fact related to Westmoreland, there was only a kind of connection by marriage between their families.

5 In the quarto this speech is addressed to Warwick. The incongruity of praying like a Christian and swearing like a heathen, which Johnson objects against, arose from the necessary conformation to the statute 3 James I. c xxi. against introducing the sacred name on the stage. The players omitted it where they could, and where the metre would not allow of the omission they substituted some other word in its place.

6 To *yearn* is to grieve or vex.

7 'The feast of Crispian.' The battle of Agincourt was fought upon the 25th of October, 1415

8 'With advantages.' Old men, notwithstanding the natural forgetfulness of old age, shall remember their feats of this day, and remember to tell them with advantage. Age is commonly boastful, and inclined to magnify past acts and past times.

9 'From this day to the ending,' &c Johnson has a note on this passage, which concludes by saying that 'the civil wars have left in the nation scarcely any tradition of more ancient history.'

10 i. e. shall advance him to the rank of a gentleman King Henry V. inhibited any person but such as had a right by inheritance or grant, from bearing coats of arms, except those who fought with him at the battle of Agincourt; and these last were allowed the chief seats at all feasts and public meetings.

11 i. e. in a braving manner. 'To go *bravely* is to look aloft; and to go gaily, desiring to have the pre-eminence: Speciose ingredi; *faire le brave.*'

12 i. e. expedition.

13 '—thou hast unwished five thousand men' By wishing only thyself and me, thou hast wished five thousand men away. The poet, inattentive to numbers, puts *five thousand*, but in the last scene the French are said to be full *three score thousand*, which Exeter declares to be five to one; the numbers of the English are variously stated: Holinshed makes them fifteen thousand, others but nine thousand.

BATTLE OF AGINCOURT.

Henry V. Act IV. Scene IV.

Which likes me better, than to wish us one.—
You know your places: God be with you all!

Tucket. Enter MONTJOY.

Mont. Once more I come to know of thee, King Harry,
If for thy ransom thou wilt now compound,
Before thy most assured overthrow:
For, certainly, thou art so near the gulf,
Thou needs must be englutted. Besides, in mercy,
The Constable desires thee—thou wilt mind[1]
Thy followers of repentance; that their souls
May make a peaceful and a sweet retire
From off these fields, where (wretches) their poor bodies
Must lie and fester.

K. Hen. Who hath sent thee now?

Mont. The Constable of France.

K. Hen. I pray thee, bear my former answer back;
Bid them achieve me, and then sell my bones.
Good God! why should they mock poor fellows thus?
The man, that once did sell the lion's skin
While the beast liv'd, was kill'd with hunting him.
A many of our bodies shall, no doubt,
Find native graves; upon the which, I trust,
Shall witness live in brass[2] of this day's work:
And those that leave their valiant bones in France,
Dying like men, though buried in your dunghills,
They shall be fam'd; for there the sun shall greet them,
And draw their honours reeking up to heaven;
Leaving their earthly parts to choke your clime,
The smell whereof shall breed a plague in France.
Mark then abounding valour in our English;[3]
That, being dead, like to the bullet's grazing,
Break out into a second course of mischief,
Killing in relapse of mortality.
Let me speak proudly;—Tell the Constable,
We are but warriors for the working-day:
Our gayness, and our gilt,[4] are all besmirch'd
With rainy marching in the painful field;
There's not a piece of feather in our host,
(Good argument, I hope, we shall not fly,)
And time hath worn us into slovenry:
But, by the mass, our hearts are in the trim:
And my poor soldiers tell me—yet ere night
They'll be in fresher robes; or they will pluck
The gay new coats o'er the French soldiers' heads,
And turn them out of service. If they do this
(As, if God please, they shall,) my ransom then
Will soon be levied. Herald, save thou thy labour;
Come thou no more for ransom, gentle herald;
They shall have none, I swear, but these my joints;
Which if they have, as I will leave 'em to them,
Shall yield them little, tell the Constable.

Mont. I shall, King Harry. And so fare thee well:
Thou never shalt hear herald any more. [*Exit.*

K. Hen. I fear, thou'lt once more come again for ransom.

Enter the Duke of York.[5]

York. My lord, most humbly on my knee I beg
The leading of the vaward.[6]

K. Hen. Take it, brave York.—Now, soldiers, march away:—
And how thou pleasest, God, dispose the day!
[*Exeunt.*

SCENE IV. *The Field of Battle. Alarums: Excursions. Enter* French Soldier, PISTOL, *and* Boy.

Pist. Yield, cur.

Fr. Sol. *Je pense, que vous estes le gentilhomme de bonne qualité.*

Pist. Quality? Callino, castore me![7] art thou a gentleman? What is thy name? discuss.

Fr. Sol. *O seigneur Dieu!*

Pist. O, signieur Dew should be a gentleman:—
Perpend my words, O signieur Dew, and mark;—
O signieur Dew, thou diest on point of fox,[8]
Except, O signieur, thou do give to me
Egregious ransom.

Fr. Sol. *O, prennez misericorde! ayez pitié de moy!*

Pist. Moy shall not serve, I will have forty moys;
For I will fetch thy rim[9] out at throat,
In drops of crimson blood.

Fr. Sol. *Est-il impossible d' eschapper la force de ton bras?*

Pist. Brass, cur!
Thou damned and luxurious mountain goat,
Offer'st me brass?

Fr. Sol. *O pardonnez moy!*

Pist. Say'st thou me so? is that a ton of moys?[10]
Come hither, boy; Ask me this slave, in French,
What is his name.

Boy. *Escoutez; Comment estes-vous appellé?*

Fr. Sol. *Monsieur le Fer.*

Boy. He says, his name is—master Fer.

Pist. Master Fer! I'll fer him, and firk[11] him, and ferret him:—discuss the same in French unto him.

Boy. I do not know the French for fer, and ferret, and firk.

Pist. Bid him prepare, for I will cut his throat.

Fr. Sol. *Que dit-il, monsieur?*

Boy. *Il me commande de vous dire que vous faites*

---

1 i. e. remind.

2 i. e. in brazen plates, anciently let into tombstones.

3 'Mark then *abounding* valour in our English;
That being dead, like to the bullet's grazing,
Break out into a second course of mischief,
Killing in relapse of mortality.'
Theobald, with over busy zeal for emendation, changed *abounding* into *a bounding*, and found the allusion exceedingly beautiful, comparing the revival of the English valour to the rebounding of a cannon ball. There is, as usual, an idle controversy between Malone and Steevens, the one preferring the old reading; and the other, from a spirit of opposition to his rival, which ever guided him, supporting Theobald's alteration.

4 i. e. golden show, superficial gilding.

5 'The *Duke of York.*' This *Edward* duke of York has already appeared in King Richard II. under the title of *duke of Aumerle.* He was the son of Edmond Langley, the duke of York of the same play, who was the fifth son of King Edward III. Richard, earl of Cambridge, who appears in the second act of this play, was younger brother to this Edward duke of York.

6 The *vaward* is the vanguard.

7 'Callino, castore me!' The jargon of the old copies where these words are printed *Qualitie calmie custure me*—was changed by former editors into 'Quality, call you me? construe me.' Malone found *Calen o custure me*, mentioned as the burthen of a song in 'A Handful of Plesant Delites,' 1584 And Mr. Boswell discovered that it was an old Irish song, which is printed in Playford's Musical Companion, 1667 or 1673:—
'Callino, Callino, Callino, castore me,
Eva ee, eva ee, loo, loo, loo lee.'
The words are said to mean 'Little girl of my heart for ever and ever.' 'They have, it is true (says Mr. Boswell,) no great connection with the poor Frenchman's supplications, nor were they meant to have any; Pistol, instead of attending to him, contemptuously hums a tune.'

8 '—thou diest on point of *fox.*' *Fox* is an old cant word for a *sword.* Generally *old fox;* it was applied to the old English broadsword.

9 'For I will fetch thy *rim* out at thy throat.' Pistol is not very scrupulous in the nicety of his language, he uses rim (rynme) for the intestines generally. It is not very clear what our ancestors meant by it; Bishop Wilkins defines it 'the membrane of the belly;' Florio makes it the omentum, 'a fat pannicle, caule, sewet, *rim*, or kell, wherein the bowels are lapt.' Holmes, in his Acad. of Armory, calls the *peritonæum* 'the paunch or *rim* of the belly.' Which is defined by others to be the '*inner rine* of the belly.' It was not therefore the diaphragm or midriff, as Steevens supposed.

10 Pistol's *moy* is probably a vulgar corruption of *moydore* (itself a corruption of *moeda d'oro*,) at least we have no better solution to offer. The moydore was current in England for about 27s

11 To *firk* is to beat or scourge; *fouetter*, to *yerk* and to *jerk* are words of the same import.

vous prest; car ce soldat icy est disposé tout à cette heure de couper vostre gorge.

Pist. Ouy, couper gorge, par ma foy, pesant,
Unless thou give me crowns, brave crowns;
Or mangled shalt thou be by this my sword.

Fr. Sol. *O, je vous supplie pour l'amour de Dieu, me pardonner! Je suis gentilhomme de bonne maison: gardez ma vie, et je vous donneray deux cents escus.*

Pist. What are his words?

Boy. He prays you to save his life: he is a gentleman of a good house; and, for his ransom, he will give you two hundred crowns.

Pist. Tell him—my fury shall abate, and I
The crowns will take.

Fr. Sol. *Petit monsieur, que dit-il?*

Boy. *Encore qu'il est contre son jurement, de pardonner aucun prisonnier; neantmoins, pour les escus que vous l'avez promis, il est content de vous donner la liberté, le franchisement.*

Fr. Sol. *Sur mes genoux, je vous donne mille remerciemens: et je m'estime heureux que je suis tombé entre les mains d'un chevalier, je pense, le plus brave, valiant, et très distingué seigneur d'Angleterre.*

Pist. Expound unto me, boy.

Boy. He gives you, upon his knees, a thousand thanks: and he esteems himself happy that he hath fallen into the hands of (as he thinks) the most brave, valorous, and thrice worthy signieur of England.

Pist. As I suck blood, I will some mercy show.—
Follow me, cur. [*Exit* PISTOL.

Boy. *Suivez-vous le grand capitaine.*
[*Exit* French Soldier.

I did never know so full a voice issue from so empty a heart: but the saying is true,—The empty vessel makes the greatest sound. Bardolph, and Nym, had ten times more valour than this roaring devil i' the old play, that every one may pare his nails with a wooden dagger;[1] and they are both hanged; and so would this be, if he durst steal any thing adventurously. I must stay with the lackeys, with the luggage of our camp: the French might have a good prey of us, if he knew of it; for there is none to guard it but boys. [*Exit.*

SCENE V. *Another Part of the Field of Battle.*

Alarums. Enter Dauphin, ORLEANS, BOURBON, Constable, RAMBURES, *and others.*

Con. *O diable!*

Orl. *O seigneur!—le jour est perdu, tout est perdu!*

Dau. *Mort de ma vie!* all is confounded, all!
Reproach and everlasting shame
Sits mocking in our plumes.—*O meschante fortune!*—
Do not run away. [*A short Alarum.*

Con. Why, all our ranks are broke.

Dau. O perdurable shame!—let's stab ourselves.
Be these the wretches that we play'd at dice for?

Orl. Is this the king we sent to for his ransom?

Bour. Shame, and eternal shame, nothing but shame!
Let us die in fight:[2] Once more back again;
And he that will not follow Bourbon now,
Let him go hence, and with his cap in hand,
Like a base pander, hold the chamber-door,
Whilst by a slave, no gentler than my dog,[3]
His fairest daughter is contaminate.

Con. Disorder, that hath spoil'd us, friend us now!
Let us, in heaps, go offer up our lives
Unto these English, or else die with fame.[4]

Orl. We are enough, yet living in the field,
To smother up the English in our throngs,
If any order might be thought upon.

Bour. The devil take order now! I'll to the throng;
Let life be short; else, shame will be too long.
[*Exeunt.*

SCENE VI. *Another Part of the Field. Alarums.*

Enter KING HENRY *and Forces;* EXETER, *and others.*

K. Hen. Well have we done, thrice-valiant countrymen:
But all's not done, yet keep the French the field.

Exe. The duke of York commends him to your majesty.

K. Hen. Lives he, good uncle? thrice, within this hour,
I saw him down; thrice up again, and fighting;
From helmet to the spur, all blood he was.

Exe. In which array (brave soldier) doth he lie,
Larding the plain: and by his bloody side,
(Yoke-fellow to his honour-owing wounds)
The noble earl of Suffolk also lies.
Suffolk first died, and York, all haggled over,
Comes to him, where in gore he lay insteep'd,
And takes him by the beard; kisses the gashes,
That bloodily did yawn upon his face;
And cries aloud,—*Tarry, dear cousin Suffolk!
My soul shall thine keep company to heaven:
Tarry, sweet soul, for mine, then fly abreast;
As, in this glorious and well-foughten field,
We kept together in our chivalry!*
Upon these words I came, and cheer'd him up.
He smil'd me in the face, raught[5] me his hand,
And, with a feeble gripe, says,—*Dear my lord,
Commend my service to my sovereign.*
So did he turn, and over Suffolk's neck
He threw his wounded arm, and kiss'd his lips.
And so, espous'd to death, with blood he seal'd
A testament of noble-ending love.
The pretty and sweet manner of it forc'd
Those waters from me, which I would have stopp'd.
But I had not so much of man in me,
But[6] all my mother came into mine eyes,
And gave me up to tears.

K. Hen. I blame you not;
For, hearing this, I must perforce compound
With mistful eyes, or they will issue too.—
[*Alarum*
But, hark! what new alarum is this same?—
The French have reinforc'd their scatter'd men:
Then every soldier kill his prisoners;
Give the word through. [*Exeunt*

SCENE VII. *Another Part of the Field. Alarums. Enter* FLUELLEN *and* GOWER.

Flu. Kill the poys and the luggage! 'tis expressly against the law of arms: 'tis as arrant a piece of knavery, mark you now, as can be offered in the 'orld: In your conscience now, is it not?

Gow. 'Tis certain, there's not a boy left alive; and the cowardly rascals, that ran from the battle, have done this slaughter: besides, they have burned and carried away all that was in the king's tent; wherefore the king, most worthily, hath caused every soldier to cut his prisoner's throat.[7] O, 'tis a gallant king!

Flu. Ay, he was porn at Monmouth, captain Gower: What call you the town's name, where Alexander the pig was born?

---

1 '—this roaring devil i' the old play, that every one may pare his nails with a wooden dagger.' See note on Twelfth Night, Act iv. Sc. 2. In the old play of The Taming of a Shrew, one of the players says, 'My lord, we must have a little vinegar to make our *devil roar.*' Ho! ho! and Ah! ha! seem to have been the exclamations constantly given to the devil, who is, in the old mysteries, as turbulent and vainglorious as Pistol. The Vice or fool, among other indignities, used to threaten to pare his nails with his dagger of lath; the devil being supposed from choice to keep his claws long and sharp.

2 The old copy wants the word *fight*, which was supplied by Malone. Theobald proposed "let us die *in stant*,' which Stevens adopted

3 i. e. who has no more gentility.

4 This line is from the quartos.

5 i. e. reached.

6 '*But* all my mother came into my eyes,
And gave me up to tears.'
Thus the quarto. The folio reads '*And* all,' &c. *But* has here the force of but *that*.

7 'Caused every soldier to cut his prisoner's throat. The king killed his prisoners (says Johnson) because he expected another battle, and he had not sufficient men to guard one army and fight another. Gower's reason is, as we see, different. Shakspeare followed Holinshed, who gives *both* reasons for Henry's conduct, but has chosen to make the king mention one of them and Gower the other.

Gow. Alexander the great.

Flu. Why, I pray you, is not pig, great? The pig, or the great, or the mighty, or the huge, or the magnanimous, are all one reckonings, save the phrase is a little variations.

Gow. I think, Alexander the great was born in Macedon; his father was called—Philip of Macedon, as I take it.

Flu. I think, it is in Macedon, where Alexander is porn. I tell you, captain,—If you look in the maps of the 'orld, I warrant, you shall find, in the comparisons between Macedon and Monmouth, that the situations, look you, is both alike. There is a river in Macedon; and there is also moreover a river at Monmouth: it is called Wye, at Monmouth: but it is out of my prains, what is the name of the other river; but 'tis all one, 'tis so like as my fingers is to my fingers, and there is salmons in both. If you mark Alexander's life well, Harry of Monmouth's life is come after it indifferent well; for there is figures in all things. Alexander (God knows, and you know,) in his rages, and his furies, and his wraths, and his cholers, and his moods, and his displeasures, and his indignations, and also being a little intoxicates in his prains, did, in his ales and his angers, look you, kill his pest friend, Clytus.

Gow. Our king is not like him in that; he never killed any of his friends.

Flu. It is not well done, mark you now, to take tales out of my mouth, ere it is made an end and finished. I speak but in the figures and comparisons of it: As Alexander[1] is kill his friend Clytus, being in his ales and his cups; so also Harry Monmouth, being in his right wits and his goot judgments, is turn away the fat knight with the great pelly-doublet: he was full of jests, and gipes, and knaveries, and mocks; I am forgot his name.[2]

Gow. Sir John Falstaff.

Flu. That is he: I can tell you, there is goot men porn at Monmouth.

Gow. Here comes his majesty.

Alarum. Enter KING HENRY, *with a Part of the* English *Forces;* WARWICK,[3] GLOSTER, EXETER, *and others.*

K. Hen. I was not angry since I came to France
Until this instant.—Take a trumpet, herald;
Ride thou unto the horsemen on yon hill;
If they will fight with us, bid them come down,
Or void the field; they do offend our sight:
If they'll do neither, we will come to them;
And make them skirr[4] away, as swift as stones
Enforced from the old Assyrian slings:
Besides, we'll cut the throats of those we have;[5]
And not a man of them, that we shall take,
Shall taste our mercy:—Go, and tell them so.

Enter MONTJOY.

Exe. Here comes the herald of the French, my liege.

Glo. His eyes are humbler than they us'd to be.

K. Hen. How now, what means this, herald? know'st thou not,
That I have fin'd these bones of mine for ransom?
Com'st thou again for ransom?

Mont. No, great king:
I come to thee for charitable licence,
That we may wander o'er this bloody field,
To book our dead, and then to bury them;
To sort our nobles from our common men;
For many of our princes (woe the while!)
Lie drown'd and soak'd in mercenary blood
(So do our vulgar drench their peasant limbs
In blood of princes;) and their wounded steeds
Fret fetlock deep in gore, and, with wild rage,
Yerk out their armed heels at their dead masters,
Killing them twice. O, give us leave, great king,
To view the field in safety, and dispose
Of their dead bodies.

K. Hen. I tell thee truly, herald,
I know not, if the day be ours, or no;
For yet a many of your horsemen peer,
And gallop o'er the field.

Mont. The day is yours.

K. Hen. Praised be God, and not our strength, for it!—
What is this castle call'd, that stands hard by?

Mont. They call it—Agincourt.

K. Hen. Then call we this—the field of Agincourt,
Fought on the day of Crispin Crispianus.

Flu. Your grandfather of famous memory, an't please your majesty, and your great-uncle Edward the plack prince of Wales, as I have read in the chronicles, fought a most prave pattle here in France.

K. Hen. They did, Fluellen.

Flu. Your majesty says very true: If your majesties is remember'd of it, the Welshmen did goot service in a garden where leeks did grow, wearing leeks in their Monmouth caps;[6] which, your majesty knows, to this hour is an honourable padge of the service; and, I do believe, your majesty takes no scorn to wear the leek upon Saint Tavy's day.

K. Hen. I wear it for a memorable honour:
For I am Welsh, you know, good countryman.

Flu. All the water in Wye cannot wash your

---

1 'As Alexander,' &c. Steevens thinks that Shakspeare here ridicules the *parallels* of Plutarch: he appears to have been well read in Sir Thomas North's Translation.

2 Johnson observes, that this is the last time *Falstaff* can make sport. The poet was loath to part with him, and has continued his memory as long as he could.

3 Richard Beauchamp, earl of Warwick. He did not, however, obtain that title till 1417, two years after the era of this play.

4 i. e. *scour* away. To run swiftly in various directions. It has the same meaning in Macbeth, Act v. Sc. iii. '*Skirr* the country round.'

5 'Besides, we'll cut the throats of those we have.' Johnson accuses the poet of having made the king cut the throats of his prisoners twice over. Malone replies that the incongruity, if it be one, is Holinshed's, for thus the matter is stated by him: While the battle was yet going on, about six hundred horsemen, who were the first that fled, hearing that the English tents were a good way distant from the army, without a sufficient guard, entered and pillaged the king's camp. 'When the outcry of the *lackies and boys which run away for fear of the Frenchmen*, thus spoiling the camp, came to the king's ears, he doubting lest his enemies should gather together again and begin a new fielde, and mistrusting further that the *prisoners* would either be an aide to his enemies, or very enemies to their takers indeed, if they were suffered to live, contrary to his accustomed gentleness, commanded by sounde of trumpet that *every man upon pain of death should incontinently slea his prisoner.*' This was the first transaction. Holinshed proceeds, 'When this lamentable slaughter was ended, the Englishmen disposed themselves in order of battayle, ready to abide a new fielde, and also to invade and newly set on their enemies.—Some write, that the king *perceiving his enemies in one parte to assemble together*, as though they meant to give a new battle for preservation of the prisoners, *sent to them a herault, commanding them either to depart out of his sight, or else to come forward at once and give battaile; promising herewith, that, if they did offer to fight agayne, not only those prisoners which his people already had taken, but also so many of them as in this new conflicte, which they thus attempted, should fall into his hands, should die the death without redemption.*' The fact is, that notwithstanding the first order concerning the prisoners, they were not all put to death, as appears from a subsequent passage, and the concurrent testimony of various historians, upon whose authority Hume says that Henry, on discovering that his danger was not so great as he at first apprehended from the attack on his camp, 'stopped the slaughter, and was still able *to save a great number.*' It was policy in Henry to intimidate the French by threatening to kill his prisoners, and occasioned them, in fact, to lay down their arms.

6 Monmouth, according to Fuller, was celebrated for its caps, which were particularly worn by soldiers. The best caps were formerly made at Monmouth, where the *capper's* chapel still remains. He adds, 'If at this day the phrase of *wearing a Monmouth cap* be taken in a bad acception, I hope the inhabitants of that town will endeavour to disprove the occasion.' *Worthies of England*, 1660, p. 50.

majesty's Welsh plood out of your pody, I can tell you that: Got pless it and preserve it, as long as it pleases his grace, and his majesty too!

K. Hen. Thanks, good my countryman.

Flu. By Chesu, I am your majesty's countryman, I care not who know it; I will confess it to all the 'orld: I need not to be ashamed of your majesty, praised be Got, so long as your majesty is an honest man.

K. Hen. God keep me so!—Our heralds go with him;
Bring me just notice of the numbers dead
On both our parts.—Call yonder fellow hither.
[*Points to* WILLIAMS. *Exeunt* MONTJOY *and others.*

Exe. Soldier, you must come to the king.

K. Hen. Soldier, why wear'st thou that glove in thy cap?

Will. An't please your majesty, 'tis the gage of one that I should fight withal, if he be alive.

K. Hen. An Englishman?

Will. An't please your majesty, a rascal, that swagger'd with me last night: who, if 'a live, and ever dare to challenge this glove, I have sworn to take him a box o' the ear: or, if I can see my glove in his cap (which he swore, as he was a soldier, he would wear, if alive,) I will strike it out soundly.

K. Hen. What think you, captain Fluellen? is it fit this soldier keep his oath?

Flu. He is a craven[1] and a villain else, an't please your majesty, in my conscience.

K. Hen. It may be his enemy is a gentleman of great sort, quite from the answer of his degree.[2]

Flu. Though he be as goot a gentleman as the tevil is, as Lucifer and Belzebub himself, it is necessary, look your grace, that he keep his vow and his oath: if he be perjured, see you now, his reputation is as arrant a villain, and a Jack-sauce,[3] as ever his plack shoe trod upon Got's ground and his earth, in my conscience, la.

K. Hen. Then keep thy vow, sirrah, when thou meet'st the fellow.

Will. So I will, my liege, as I live.

K. Hen. Who servest thou under?

Will. Under captain Gower, my liege.

Flu. Gower is a goot captain; and is goot knowledge and literature in the wars.

K. Hen. Call him hither to me, soldier.

Will. I will, my liege. [*Exit.*

K. Hen. Here, Fluellen: wear thou this favour for me, and stick it in thy cap: When Alençon and myself were down together,[4] I plucked this glove from his helm: if any man challenge this, he is a friend to Alençon and an enemy to our person; if thou encounter any such, apprehend him, an thou dost love me.

Flu. Your grace does me as great honours, as can be desired in the hearts of his subjects: I would fain see the man, that has but two legs, that shall find himself aggriefed at this glove, that is all; but I would fain see it once; an please Got of his grace, that I might see it.

K. Hen. Knowest thou Gower?

Flu. He is my dear friend, an please you.

K. Hen. Pray thee, go seek him, and bring him to my tent.

Flu. I will fetch him. [*Exit.*

K. Hen. My lord of Warwick,—and my brother Gloster,
Follow Fluellen closely at the heels:
The glove, which I have given him for a favour,
May, haply, purchase him a box o'the ear;
It is the soldier's; I, by bargain, should
Wear it myself. Follow, good cousin, Warwick:
If that soldier strike him (as, I judge
By his blunt bearing, he will keep his word,)
Some sudden mischief may arise of it;
For I do know Fluellen valiant,
And, touch'd with choler, hot as gunpowder,
And quickly will return an injury:
Follow, and see there be no harm between them.
Go you with me, uncle of Exeter. [*Exeun.*

SCENE VIII. *Before* King Henry's *Pavilion.*

Enter GOWER *and* WILLIAMS.

Will. I warrant it is to knight you, captain.

Enter FLUELLEN.

Flu. Got's will and his pleasure, captain, I peseech you now, come apace to the king: there is more goot toward you, peradventure, than is in your knowledge to dream of.

Will. Sir, know you this glove?

Flu. Know the glove? I know, the glove is a glove.

Will. I know this; and thus I challenge it. [*Strikes him.*

Flu. 'Sblud, an arrant traitor, as any's in the universal 'orld, or in France, or in England.

Gow. How now, sir? you villain!

Will. Do you think I'll be forsworn?

Flu. Stand away, captain Gower; I will give treason his payment into plows,[5] I warrant you.

Will. I am no traitor.

Flu. That's a lie in thy throat.—I charge you in his majesty's name, apprehend him; he's a friend of the duke Alençon's.

Enter WARWICK *and* GLOSTER.

War. How now, how now! what's the matter?

Flu. My lord of Warwick, here is (praised be Got for it!) a most contagious treason come to light, look you, as you shall desire in a summer's day. Here is his majesty.

Enter KING HENRY *and* EXETER.

K. Hen. How now! what's the matter?

Flu. My liege, here is a villain, and a traitor, that, look your grace, has struck the glove which your majesty is take out of the helmet of Alençon.

Will. My liege, this was my glove; here is the fellow of it: and he, that I gave it to in change, promised to wear it in his cap; I promised to strike him, if he did: I met this man with my glove in his cap, and I have been as good as my word.

Flu. Your majesty hear now (saving your majesty's manhood,) what an arrant, rascally, beggarly, lowsy knave it is: I hope, your majesty is pear me testimony, and witness, and avouchments, that this is the glove of Alençon, that your majesty is give me, in your conscience now.

K. Hen. Give me thy glove,[6] soldier; look, here is the fellow of it. 'Twas I, indeed, thou promised'st to strike; and thou hast given me most bitter terms.

Flu. An please your majesty let his neck answer for it, if there is any martial law in the 'orld.

K. Hen. How canst thou make me satisfaction?

Will. All offences, my liege, come from the heart: never came any from mine, that might offend your majesty.

K. Hen. It was ourself thou didst abuse.

Will. Your majesty came not like yourself: you appeared to me but as a common man; witness the night, your garments, your lowliness; and what your highness suffered under that shape, I beseech you, take it for your own fault, and not

1 *Craven.* See Hamlet, Act iv. Sc. 4.

2 'Of great sort, quite from the answer of his degree.' *Great sort* is high rank. A man of such rank is not bound to *answer* to the challenge from one of the soldier's *low degree.*

3 Jack-sauce for saucy Jack.

4 Henry was felled to the ground by the duke of Alençon, but recovered and slew two of the duke's attendants. Alençon was afterwards killed by the king's *guard*, contrary to Henry's intention, who wished to have saved him.

5 '*Into* plows.' It has been suggested that we should read '*in* plows,' but it was not intended that Fluellen should speak very correctly, and *into* for *in* is still used in Scotland.

6 i. e. the glove that thou hast now in thy cap; it was the king's glove, which he had given to Williams

mine; for had you been as I took you for, I made no offence; therefore, I beseech your highness, pardon me.

K. Hen. Here, uncle Exeter, fill this glove with crowns,
And give it to this fellow.—Keep it, fellow;
And wear it for an honour in thy cap,
Till I do challenge it.—Give him the crowns:—
And, captain, you must needs be friends with him.

Flu. By this day and this light, the fellow has mettle enough in his pelly;—Hold, there is twelve pence for you, and I pray you to serve Got, and keep you out of prawls, and prabbles, and quarrels, and dissensions, and, I warrant you, it is the petter for you.

Will. I will none of your money.

Flu. It is with a goot will; I can tell you, it will serve you to mend your shoes: Come, wherefore should you be so pashful? your shoes is not so goot: 'tis a goot silling, I warrant you, or I will change it.

Enter an English Herald.

K. Hen. Now, Herald: are the dead numbered?

Her. Here is the number of the slaughter'd French. [*Delivers a Paper.*

K. Hen. What prisoners of good sort are taken, uncle?

Exe. Charles duke of Orleans, nephew to the king;
John duke of Bourbon, and Lord Bouciqualt:
Of other lords, and barons, knights, and 'squires,
Full fifteen hundred, besides common men.

K. Hen. This note doth tell me of ten thousand French,
That in the field lie slain: of princes, in this number,
And nobles bearing banners, there lie dead
One hundred twenty-six: added to these,
Of knights, esquires, and gallant gentlemen,
Eight thousand and four hundred; of the which,
Five hundred were but yesterday dubb'd knights:[1]
So that, in these ten thousand they have lost,
There are but sixteen hundred mercenaries;
The rest are—princes, barons, lords, knights, squires,
And gentlemen of blood and quality.
The names of those their nobles that lie dead,—
Charles De-la-bret, high constable of France;
Jaques of Chatillon, admiral of France;
The master of the cross-bows, lord Rambures;
Great-master of France, the brave Sir Guischard Dauphin;
John duke of Alençon; Antony duke of Brabant,
The brother to the duke of Burgundy;
And Edward duke of Bar: of lusty earls,
Grandpre, and Roussi, Fauconberg, and Foix,
Beaumont, and Marle, Vaudemont, and Lestrale.
Here was a royal fellowship of death!——
Where is the number of our English dead?
[Herald *presents another Paper.*
Edward the duke of York, the earl of Suffolk,
Sir Richard Ketley, Davy Gam, esquire:[2]
None else of name; and, of all other men,
But five and twenty. O God, thy arm was here,
And not to us, but to thy arm alone
Ascribe we all.—When, without stratagem,
But in plain shock, and even play of battle,
Was ever known so great and little loss,
On one part and on the other?—Take it, God,
For it is only thine!

Exe. 'Tis wonderful!

K. Hen. Come, go we in procession to the village:
And be it death proclaimed through our host,
To boast of this, or take that praise from God
Which is his only.

Flu. Is it not lawful, an please your majesty, to tell how many is killed?

K. Hen. Yes, captain; but with this acknowledgment,
That God fought for us.

Flu. Yes, my conscience, he did us great goot.

K. Hen. Do we all holy rites;[3]
Let there be sung *Non nobis*, and *Te Deum.*
The dead with charity enclos'd in clay,
We'll then to Calais; and to England then;
Where ne'er from France arriv'd more happy men.
[*Exeunt.*

ACT V.

Enter CHORUS.

Cho. Vouchsafe to those that have not read the story,
That I may prompt them: and of such as have,
I humbly pray them to admit the excuse
Of time, of numbers, and due course of things,
Which cannot in their huge and proper life
Be here presented. Now we bear the king
Toward Calais: grant him there; there seen,
Heave him away upon your winged thoughts,
Athwart the sea: Behold, the English beach
Pales in the flood with men, with wives, and boys,
Whose shouts and claps outvoice the deep-mouth'd sea,
Which, like a mighty whiffler[5] 'fore the king,
Seems to prepare his way: so let him land;
And, solemnly, see him set on to London.
So swift a pace hath thought, that even now
You may imagine him upon Blackheath:
Where that his lords desire him, to have borne
His bruised helmet, and his bended sword,
Before him, through the city: he forbids it,
Being free from vainness and self-glorious pride;
Giving full trophy, signal, and ostent,
Quite from himself, to God.[6] But now behold,
In the quick forge and workinghouse of thought,
How London doth pour out her citizens!
The mayor, and all his brethren, in best sort,—
Like to the senators of the antique Rome,
With the plebeians swarming at their heels,—
Go forth, and fetch their conquering Cæsar in:
As, by a lower, but by loving likelihood,[7]
Were now the general of our gracious empress[8]

1 'Five hundred were but yesterday dubb'd knights.' In ancient times the distribution of this honour appears to have been customary on the eve of a battle.

2 'Davy Gam, esquire.' This gentleman being sent out by Henry, before the battle, to reconnoitre the enemy, and to find out their strength, made this report:—'May it please you, my liege, there are enough to be killed, enough to be taken prisoners, and enough to run away.' He saved the king's life in the field. Had the poet been apprized of this circumstance, the brave Welshman would probably have been more particularly noticed, and not have been merely a name in a muster roll.—See Drayton's Battaile of Agincourt, 1627, p. 50 and 54; and Dunster's Edition of Philips's Cyder, a poem, p. 74.

3 'Do we all holy rites.' 'The king, when he saw no appearance of enemies, caused the retreate to be blowen; and, gathering his army together, gave thanks to Almighty God for so happy a victorie, causing his prelates and chapeleins to sing this psalme—*In exitu Israel de Egypto;* and commaunding every man to kneele down on the grounde at this verse—*Non nobis, Domine, non nobis sed nomini tuo da gloriam;* which done, he caused *Te Deum* and certain anthems to be sung, giving laud and praise to God, and not boasting of his own force or any humaine power.'—*Holinshed.*

4 'Toward Calais: grant him there; there seen.' Steevens proposes, in order to complete the metre, that we should read:—
'Toward Calais: grant him there; there seen *awhile.*'

5 'Which, like a mighty *whiffler* 'fore the king,
Seems to prepare his way.'
Whifflers were persons going before a great personage or procession, furnished with staves or wands to clear the way. The junior liverymen of the city companies, who walk first in processions, are still called *whifflers*, from the circumstance of their going before.

6 'i. e. transferring all the honours of conquest from himself to God.'

7 i. e. similitude.

8 i. e. the earl of Essex. Shakspeare grounded his anticipation of such a reception for Essex on his return from Ireland, upon what had already occurred at his setting forth, when he was accompanied by an immense

(As, in good time, he may,) from Ireland coming,
Bringing rebellion broached[1] on his sword,
How many would the peaceful city quit,
To welcome him? much more, and much more cause,
Did they this Harry. Now in London place him;
(As yet the lamentation of the French
Invites the king of England's stay at home:)
The emperor's coming[2] in behalf of France,
To order peace between them, we omit,
And all the occurrences, whatever chanc'd,
Till Harry's back-return again to France;
There must we bring him; and myself have play'd
The interim, by remembering you—'tis past.
Then brook abridgement; and your eyes advance
After your thoughts, straight back again to France. [*Exit.*

SCENE I. France. *An* English *Court of Guard.*

Enter FLUELLEN *and* GOWER.

Gow. Nay, that's right; but why wear you your leek to-day? Saint Davy's day is past.

Flu. There is occasions and causes why and wherefore in all things: I will tell you, as my friend, Captain Gower; The rascally, scald, beggarly, lowsy, pragging knave, Pistol,—which you and yourself, and all the 'orld, know to be no petter than a fellow, look you now, of no merits,—he is come to me, and prings me pread and salt yesterday, look you, and bid me eat my leek: it was in a place where I could not breed no contentions with him; but I will be so pold as to wear it in my cap till I see him once again, and then I will tell him a little piece of my desires.

Enter PISTOL.

Gow. Why, here he comes, swelling like a turkey-cock.

Flu. 'Tis no matter for his swellings, nor his turkey-cocks.—Got pless you, ancient Pistol! you scurvy, lowsy knave, Got pless you!

Pist. Ha! art thou Bedlam? dost thou thirst, base Trojan,
To have me fold up Parca's fatal web?[3]
Hence! I am qualmish at the smell of leek.

Flu. I peseech you heartily, scurvy lowsy knave, at my desires, and my requests, and my petitions, to eat, look you, this leek; because, look you, you do not love it, nor your affections, and your appetites, and your digestions, does not agree with it, I would desire you to eat it.

Pist. Not for Cadwallader, and all his goats.

Flu. There is one goat for you. [*Strikes him.*] Will you be so good, scald knave, as eat it?

Pist. Base Trojan, thou shalt die.

Flu. You say very true, scald knave, when Got's will is: I will desire you to live in the mean time, and eat your victuals; come, there is sauce for it. [*Strikes him again.*] You called me yesterday mountain-squire; but I will make you to-day a squire of low degree. I pray you, fall to; if you can mock a leek, you can eat a leek.

Gow. Enough, captain; you have astonish'd[4] him.

Flu. I say, I will make him eat some part of my leek, or I will peat his pate four days:—Pite, I pray you; it is goot for your green wound, and your ploody coxcomb.

Pist. Must I bite?

Flu. Yes, certainly; and out of doubt, and out of questions too, and ambiguities.

Pist. By this leek, I will most horribly revenge, I eat, and eke I swear.[5]—

Flu. Eat, I pray you: Will you have some more sauce to your leek? there is not enough leek to swear by.

Pist. Quiet thy cudgel; thou dost see, I eat.

Flu. Much goot do you, scald knave, heartily. Nay, 'pray you, throw none away; the skin is goot for your proken coxcomb. When you take occasions to see leeks hereafter, I pray you, mock at them! that is all.

Pist. Good.

Flu. Ay, leeks is goot:—Hold you, there is a groat to heal your pate.

Pist. Me a groat?

Flu. Yes, verily, and in truth, you shall take it; or I have another leek in my pocket, which you shall eat.

Pist. I take thy groat, in earnest of revenge.

Flu. If I owe you any thing, I will pay you in cudgels; you shall be a woodmonger, and buy nothing of me but cudgels. God be wi' you, and keep you, and heal your pate. [*Exit.*

Pist. All hell shall stir for this.

Gow. Go, go; you are a counterfeit cowardly knave. Will you mock at an ancient tradition,—begun upon an honourable respect, and worn as a memorable trophy of predeceased valour,—and dare not avouch in your deeds any of your words? I have seen you gleeking[6] and galling at this gentleman twice or thrice. You thought, because he could not speak English in the native garb, he could not therefore handle an English cudgel: you find it otherwise; and, henceforth, let a Welsh correction teach you a good English condition.[7] Fare you well. [*Exit.*

Pist. Doth fortune play the huswife[8] with me now?
News have I, that my Nell is dead i' the spital
Of malady of France;
And there my rendezvous is quite cut off.
Old I do wax; and from my weary limbs
Honour is cudgel'd. Well, bawd will I turn,
And something lean to cut-purse of quick hand,
To England will I steal, and there I'll steal:
And patches will I get unto these scars,
And swear, I got them in the Gallia wars. [*Exit.*

SCENE II. Troyes *in* Champagne. *An Apartment in the* French King's *Palace. Enter, at one Door,* KING HENRY, BEDFORD, GLOSTER, EXETER, WARWICK, WESTMORELAND, *and other* Lords; *at another the* French King, QUEEN ISABEL, *the* PRINCESS KATHARINE, Lords, Ladies, *&c. the* DUKE *of* BURGUNDY, *and his Train.*

K. Hen. Peace to this meeting, wherefore we are met![9][10]

---

concourse of all ranks, showering blessings upon his head. The continuator of Stowe's Chronicle gives us a long account of it. But how unfortunately different his return was from what the poet predicted, may be seen in the Sydney Papers, vol. ii. p. 127.

1 *Broached* is spitted, transfixed.

2 'The emperor's coming.' The Emperor Sigismund, who was married to Henry's second cousin. This passage stands in the following embarrassed and obscure manner in the folio:—

'———— Now in London place him.
As yet the lamentation of the French
Invites the king of England's stay at home:
The emperor's coming in behalf of France,
To order peace between them: and omit
All the occurrences,' &c.

The liberty I have taken is to transpose the word *and*, and substitute *we* in its place.

3 'To have me fold up Parca's fatal web?' 'Dost thou desire to have me put thee to death?'

4 Stunned.

5 'I eat, and *eke* I swear.' The folio has '*eat I* swear.'

6 *Gleeking* is scoffing, sneering.

7 i. e. disposition.

8 *Huswife*, for jilt, or hussy, as we have it still in vulgar speech.

9 [*Exit.*] 'The comic scenes of these plays are now at an end, and all the comic personages are now dismissed. Falstaff and Mrs. Quickly are dead: Nym and Bardolph are hanged; Gadshill was lost immediately after the robbery; Poins and Peto have vanished since, one knows not how; and Pistol is now beaten into obscurity. I believe every reader regrets their departure.'—*Johnson.*

10 'Peace to this meeting, wherefore we are met!' Peace, for which we are here met, be to this meeting. Here, Johnson thought, that the chorus should have been prefixed, and the fifth act begun.

Unto our brother France,—and to our sister,
Health and fair time of day:—joy and good wishes
To our most fair and princely cousin Katharine;
And (as a branch and member of this royalty,
By whom this great assembly is contriv'd,)
We do salute you, Duke of Burgundy;—
And, princes French, and peers, health to you all!
Fr. King. Right joyous are we to behold your face,
Most worthy brother England; fairly met:—
So are you, princes English, every one.
Q. Isa. So happy be the issue, brother England,
Of this good day, and of this gracious meeting,
As we are now glad to behold your eyes;
Your eyes, which hitherto have borne in them
Against the French, that met them in their bent,
The fatal balls of murdering basilisks:[1]
The venom of such looks, we fairly hope,
Have lost their quality; and that this day
Shall change all griefs, and quarrels, into love.
K. Hen. To cry amen to that, thus we appear.
Q. Isa. You English princes all, I do salute you.
Bur. My duty to you both, on equal love,
Great kings of France and England! That I have labour'd
With all my wits, my pains, and strong endeavours,
To bring your most imperial majesties
Unto this bar[2] and royal interview,
Your mightiness on both parts best can witness.
Since then my office hath so far prevail'd,
That, face to face, and royal eye to eye,
You have congreeted; let it not disgrace me,
If I demand, before this royal view,
What rub, or what impediment, there is,
Why that the naked, poor, and mangled peace,
Dear nurse of arts, plenties, and joyful births,
Should not, in this best garden of the world,
Our fertile France, put up her lovely visage?
Alas! she hath from France too long been chas'd;
And all her husbandry doth lie on heaps,
Corrupting in its own fertility.
Her vine, the merry cheerer of the heart,
Unpruned dies: her hedges even-pleached,—
Like prisoners wildly overgrown with hair,
Put forth disorder'd twigs: her fallow leas
The darnel, hemlock, and rank fumitory,
Doth root upon; while that the coulter rusts,
That should deracinate[3] such savagery:
The even mead, that erst brought sweetly forth
The freckled cowslip, burnet, and green clover,
Wanting the scythe, all uncorrected, rank,
Conceives by idleness; and nothing teems,
But hateful docks, rough thistles, kecksies, burs,
Losing both beauty and utility.
And as our vineyards, fallows, meads, and hedges,
Defective in their natures,[4] grow to wildness;
Even so our houses, and ourselves, and children,
Have lost, or do not learn, for want of time,
The sciences that should become our country;
But grow, like savages,—as soldiers will,
That nothing do but meditate on blood,—
To swearing and stern looks, diffus'd[5] attire,
And every thing that seems unnatural.
Which to reduce into our former favour,[6]
You are assembled: and my speech entreats,
That I may know the let, why gentle peace
Should not expel these inconveniences,
And bless us with her former qualities.
K. Hen. If, duke of Burgundy, you would the peace,
Whose want gives growth to the imperfections
Which you have cited, you must buy that peace
With full accord to all our just demands;
Whose tenours and particular effects
You have, enschedul'd briefly, in your hands.
Bur. The king hath heard them; to the which, as yet,
There is no answer made.
K. Hen. Well then, the peace,
Which you before so urg'd, lies in his answer.
Fr. King. I have but with a cursorary eye
O'erglanc'd the articles: pleaseth your grace
To appoint some of your council presently
To sit with us once more, with better heed
To resurvey them, we will, suddenly,
Pass our accept, and peremptory answer.[7]
K. Hen. Brother, we shall.—Go, uncle Exeter,
And brother Clarence,—and you, brother Gloster,
Warwick—and Huntingdon,[8]—go with the king:
And take with you free power, to ratify,
Augment, or alter, as your wisdoms best
Shall see advantageable for our dignity,
Any thing in, or out of, our demands;
And we'll consign thereto.—Will you, fair sister,
Go with the princes, or stay here with us?
Q. Isa. Our gracious brother, I will go with them;
Haply, a woman's voice may do some good,
When articles, too nicely urg'd, be stood on.
K. Hen. Yet leave our cousin Katharine here with us;
She is our capital demand, compris'd
Within the fore-rank of our articles.
Q. Isa. She hath good leave.
[*Exeunt all but* HENRY, KATHARINE, *and her Gentlewoman.*
K. Hen. Fair Katharine, and most fair!
Will you vouchsafe to teach a soldier terms,
Such as will enter at a lady's ear,
And plead his lovesuit to her gentle heart?
Kath. Your majesty shall mock at me; I cannot speak your England.

K. Hen. O fair Katharine, if you will love me soundly with your French heart, I will be glad to hear you confess it brokenly with your English tongue. Do you like me, Kate?

Kath. *Pardonnez moy*, I cannot tell vat is—like me.

K. Hen. An angel is like you, Kate; and you are like an angel.

Kath. *Que dit il? que je suis semblable à les anges.*

Alice. *Ouy, vrayment, (sauf vostre grace,) ainsi dit il.*

K. Hen. I said so, dear Katharine; and I must not blush to affirm it.

Kath. *O bon Dieu! les langues des hommes sont pleines de tromperies.*

K. Hen. What says she, fair one? that the tongues of men are full of deceits?

Alice. *Ouy;* dat de tongues of de mans is be full of deceits: dat is de princess.

K. Hen. The princess is the better Englishwo-

1 The *basilisk* was a *serpent* which, it was anciently supposed, could destroy the object of his vengeance by merely looking at it.

2 'This bar;' that is, this barrier, this place of congress. The Chronicles represent a former interview in a field near Melun, with a *barre* or barrier of separation between the pavilions of the French and English; but the treaty was then broken off. It was now renewed at Troyes, but the scene of conference was St. Peter's church in that town, a place inconvenient for Shakspeare's action; his editors have therefore laid it in a palace.

3 To *deracinate* is to force up by the roots

4 'Defective in their *natures*.' It has been proposed to read *nurtures*, i. e. culture, as I think, very plausibly. But Steevens concurs in Upton's opinion, that change is unnecessary. '*Sua deficiunt natura:* They were not defective in their *crescive* nature, for they grew to wildness; but they were defective in their proper and favourable nature, which was to bring forth food for man.'

5 '*Diffused attire.*' I have observed, in a note on The Merry Wives of Windsor, Act iv. Sc. 4, that *diffuse* was used for *obscure, confused.* I find, from Florio's Dictionary, that *diffused*, or *defused*, were used for *confused. Diffused attire* is therefore *disordered* or *dishevelled attire.*

6 *Favour* here means comeliness of appearance. We still say well or ill *favoured* for well or ill *looking.*

7 '*Pass our accept*, and peremptory answer.' To *pass* here signifies 'to finish, end, or agree upon the acceptance which we shall give them, and return our peremptory answer.'

8 '*Huntingdon.*' John Holland, earl of Huntingdon, who afterwards married the widow of Edmund Mortimer, earl of March. Neither Huntingdon nor Clarence are in the list of Dramatis Personæ, as neither of them speak a word.

man. I'faith, Kate, my wooing is fit for thy understanding: I am glad, thou canst speak no better English; for if thou could'st, thou would'st find me such a plain king, that thou would'st think, I had sold my farm to buy my crown.[1] I know no ways to mince it in love, but directly to say—I love you: then, if you urge me further than to say—Do you in faith? I wear out my suit. Give me your answer; i'faith, do; and so clap hands and a bargain: How say you, lady?

Kath. *Sauf vostre honneur*, me understand well.

K. Hen. Marry, if you would put me to verses, or to dance for your sake, Kate, why you undid me: for the one, I have neither words nor measure; and for the other, I have no strength in measure,[2] yet a reasonable measure in strength. If I could win a lady at leap-frog, or by vaulting into my saddle with my armour on my back, under the correction of bragging be it spoken, I should quickly leap into a wife. Or, if I might buffet for my love, or bound my horse for her favours, I could lay on like a butcher, and sit like a jack-an-apes, never off: but, before God, I cannot look greenly,[3] nor gasp out my eloquence, nor I have no cunning in protestation; only downright oaths, which I never use till urged, nor never break for urging. If thou canst love a fellow of this temper, Kate, whose face is not worth sun-burning, that never looks in his glass for love of any thing he sees there, let thine eye be thy cook. I speak to thee plain soldier: If thou canst love me for this, take me: if not, to say to thee—that I shall die, is true: but—for thy love, by the Lord, no; yet I love thee too. And while thou livest, dear Kate, take a fellow of plain and uncoined[4] constancy; for he perforce must do thee right, because he hath not the gift to woo in other places: for these fellows of infinite tongue, that can rhyme themselves into ladies' favours,—they do always reason themselves out again. What! a speaker is but a prater; a rhyme is but a ballad. A good leg will fall;[5] a straight back will stoop; a black beard will turn white; a curled pate will grow bald; fair face will wither; a full eye will wax hollow: but a good heart, Kate, is the sun and moon; or, rather, the sun, and not the moon; for it shines bright, and never changes, but keeps his course truly. If thou would have such a one, take me: And take me, take a soldier; take a soldier, take a king: And what sayest thou then to my love? speak, my fair, and fairly, I pray thee.

Kath. Is it possible dat I should love de enemy of France?

K. Hen. No; it is not possible you should love the enemy of France, Kate: but, in loving me, you should love the friend of France; for I love France so well, that I will not part with a village of it; I will have it all mine: and, Kate, when France is mine, and I am yours, then yours is France, and you are mine.

Kath. I cannot tell vat is dat.

K. Hen. No, Kate? I will tell thee in French; which, I am sure, will hang upon my tongue like a new-married wife about her husband's neck, hardly to be shook off. *Quand j'ay la possession de France, et quand vous avez le possèssion de moi* (let me see, what then? Saint Dennis be my speed!)—*donc vostre est France, et vous estes mienne.* It is as easy for me, Kate, to conquer the kingdom, as to speak so much more French: I shall never move thee in French, unless it be to laugh at me.

Kath. *Sauf vostre honneur, le François que vous parlez est meilleur que l' Anglois lequel je parle.*

K. Hen. No, 'faith, is't not, Kate: but thy speaking of my tongue, and I thine, most truly falsely, must needs be granted to me much at one. But, Kate, dost thou understand thus much English? Canst thou love me?

Kath. I cannot tell.

K. Hen. Can any of your neighbours tell, Kate? I'll ask them. Come, I know, thou lovest me: and at night when you come into your closet, you'll question this gentlewoman about me; and I know, Kate, you will, to her, dispraise those parts in me, that you love with your heart; but, good Kate, mock me mercifully; the rather, gentle princess, because I love thee cruelly. If ever thou be'st mine, Kate, (as I have a saving faith within me, tells me,—thou shalt,) I get thee with scambling, and thou must therefore needs prove a good soldier-breeder: Shall not thou and I, between Saint Dennis and Saint George, compound a boy, half French half English, that shall go to Constantinople, and take the Turk by the beard?[6] shall we not? what sayest thou, my fair flower-de-luce?

Kath. I do not know dat.

K. Hen. No; 'tis hereafter to know, but now to promise: do but now promise, Kate, you will endeavour for your French part of such a boy; and, for my English moiety, take the word of a king and a bachelor. How answer you, *la plus belle Katharine du monde, mon très chere et divine déesse?*

Kath. Your *majesté* 'ave *fausse* French enough to deceive the most *sage damoiselle* dat is *en France.*

K. Hen. Now, fye upon my false French! By mine honour, in true English, I love thee, Kate: by which honour I dare not swear, thou lovest me; yet my blood begins to flatter me that thou dost, notwithstanding the poor and untempering effect of my visage.[7] Now beshrew my father's ambition! he was thinking of civil wars when he got me; therefore was I created with a stubborn outside, with an aspect of iron, that, when I come to woo ladies, I fright them. But, in faith, Kate, the elder I wax, the better I shall appear: my comfort is, that old age, that ill layer-up of beauty, can do no more spoil upon my face; thou hast me, if thou hast me, at the worst; and thou shalt wear me, it thou wear me, better and better; And therefore tell me, most fair Katharine, will you have me? Put off your maiden blushes; avouch the thoughts of your heart with the looks of an empress; take me by the hand, and say,—Harry of England, I am thine: which word thou shalt no sooner bless mine ear withal, but I will tell thee aloud—England is thine, Ireland is thine, France is thine, and Henry Plantagenet is thine; who, though I speak it before his face, if he be not fellow with the best king, thou shalt find the best king of good fellows. Come, your answer in broken music; for thy voice is music, and thy English broken: therefore, queen of all, Katharine, break thy mind to me in broken English,—Wilt thou have me?

Kath. Dat is, as it shall please de *roy mon pere*

---

1 'That thou would'st think I had sold my farm to buy my crown.' Johnson thinks this blunt honest kind of English wooing is inconsistent with the previous character of the king; and quotes the Dauphin's *opinion* of him, 'that he was fitter for a ball-room than the field.' This opinion however was erroneous. Shakspeare only meant to characterise English downright sincerity; and surely the previous habits of Henry, as represented in former scenes, do not make us expect great refinement or polish in him upon this occasion, especially as fine speeches would be lost upon the princess from her imperfect comprehension of his language.

2 i. e. in *dancing.*

3 i. e. like a young lover, awkwardly.

4 'A fellow of plain and *uncoined constancy.*' This passage has been sadly misunderstood. The prince evidently means to say, 'Take a fellow of blunt *unadorned courage* or *purpose*, because he hath not the gift to woo in other places like these fellows of infinite tongue.' Constancy is most frequently used for courage, or resolution, by Shakspeare.

5 i. e. shrink, fall away.

6 'Take the Turk by the beard.' This is one of the poet's anachronisms. The Turks had not possession of Constantinople until the year 1453; when Henry had been dead thirty-one years.

7 'The poor and *untempering* effect of my visage.' *Untempering* is *unsoftening, unmitigating.* I am surprised that Steevens should not have objected to this word as he did to *seasoning.* It is of the same forma tion. 'To *temper* or mitigate sorrow with mirth. *Condire* per translationem, ut condire tristitiam hilaritate. Cicero.'—*Baret.*

K. Hen. Nay, it will please him well, Kate; it shall please him, Kate.

Kath. Den it shall also content me.

K. Hen. Upon that I will kiss your hand, and I call you—my queen.

Kath. *Laissez, mon seigneur, laissez, laissez: ma foy, je ne veux point que vous abaissez vostre grandeur, en baisant la main d'une vostre indigne serviteure; excusez moy, je vous supplie, mon très puissant seigneur.*

K. Hen. Then I will kiss your lips, Kate.

Kath. *Les dames, et damoiselles, pour estre baisées devant leur nopces, il n'est pas le coûtume de France.*

K. Hen. Madam, my interpreter, what says she?

Alice. Dat it is not de fashion *pour les* ladies of France,—I cannot tell what is, *baiser, en* English.

K. Hen. To kiss.

Alice. Your majesty *entendre* bettre *que moy.*

K. Hen. It is not the fashion for the maids in France to kiss before they are married, would she say?

Alice. *Ouy, vrayment.*

K. Hen. O Kate, nice customs curt'sy to great kings. Dear Kate, you and I cannot be confined within the weak list[1] of a country's fashion: we are the makers of manners, Kate; and the liberty that follows our places, stops the mouths of all find-faults; as I will do yours, for upholding the nice fashion of your country, in denying me a kiss: therefore, patiently, and yielding. [*Kissing her.*] You have witchcraft in your lips, Kate; there is more eloquence in a sugar touch of them, than in the tongues of the French council; and they should sooner persuade Harry of England, than a general petition of monarchs. Here comes your father.

Enter the French King *and* Queen, BURGUNDY, BEDFORD, GLOSTER, EXETER, WESTMORELAND, *and other* French *and* English Lords.

Bur. God save your majesty! my royal cousin, teach you our princess English?

K. Hen. I would have her learn, my fair cousin, how perfectly I love her; and that is good English.

Bur. Is she not apt?

K. Hen. Our tongue is rough, coz; and my condition is not smooth: so that, having neither the voice nor the heart of flattery about me, I cannot so conjure up the spirit of love in her, that he will appear in his true likeness.

Bur. Pardon the frankness of my mirth, if I answer you for that. If you would conjure in her, you must make a circle: if conjure up love in her in his true likeness, he must appear naked, and blind; Can you blame her then, being a maid yet rosed over with the virgin crimson of modesty, if she deny the appearance of a naked blind boy in her naked seeing self? It were, my lord, a hard condition for a maid to consign to.

K. Hen. Yet they do wink, and yield; as love is blind, and enforces.

Bur. They are then excused, my lord, when they see not what they do.

K. Hen. Then, good my lord, teach your cousin to consent to winking.

Bur. I will wink on her to consent, my lord, if you will teach her to know my meaning: for maids, well summered and warm kept, are like flies at Bartholomew-tide, blind, though they have their eyes; and then they will endure handling, which before would not abide looking on.

K. Hen. This moral[2] ties me over to time, and a hot summer; and so I will catch the fly, your cousin, in the latter end, and she must be blind too.

Bur. As love is, my lord, before it loves.

K. Hen. It is so: and you may, some of you, thank love for my blindness; who cannot see many a fair French city, for one fair French maid that stands in my way.

Fr. King. Yes, my lord, you see them perspectively, the cities turned into a maid;[3] for they are all girdled with maiden walls, that war hath never entered.

K. Hen. Shall Kate be my wife?

Fr. King. So please you.

K. Hen. I am content; so the maiden cities you talk of, may wait on her: so the maid, that stood in the way of my wish, shall show me the way to my will.

Fr. King. We have consented to all terms of reason.

K. Hen. Is't so, my lords of England?

West. The king hath granted every article:
His daughter, first; and then, in sequel, all,
According to their firm proposed natures.

Exe. Only, he hath not yet subscribed this:—Where your majesty demands,—That the king of France, having any occasion to write for matter of grant, shall name your highness in this form, and with this addition, in French,—*Notre très cher filz Henry roy d'Angleterre, héritier de France;* and thus in Latin,—*Præclarissimus*[4] *filius noster Henricus rex Angliæ, et hæres Franciæ.*

Fr. King. Nor this I have not, brother, so denied,
But your request shall make me let it pass.

K. Hen. I pray you then, in love and dear alliance,
Let that one article rank with the rest:
And, thereupon, give me your daughter.

Fr. King. Take her, fair son; and from her blood raise up
Issue to me: that the contending kingdoms
Of France and England, whose very shores look pale
With envy of each other's happiness,
May cease their hatred: and this dear conjunction
Plant neighbourhood and christianlike accord
In their sweet bosoms, that never war advance
His bleeding sword 'twixt England and fair France

All. Amen!

K. Hen. Now welcome, Kate:—and bear me witness all,
That here I kiss her as my sovereign queen. [*Flourish.*

Q. Isa. God, the best maker of all marriages,
Combine your hearts in one, your realms in one!
As man and wife, being two, are one in love,
So be there 'twixt your kingdoms such a spousal,
That never may ill office, or fell jealousy,
Which troubles oft the bed of blessed marriage,
Thrust in between the paction of these kingdoms,
To make divorce of their incorporate league;
That English may as French, French Englishmen
Receive each other!—God speak this Amen!

All. Amen!

K. Hen. Prepare we for our marriage:—on which day,
My lord of Burgundy, we'll take your oath,
And all the peers', for surety of our leagues.—
Then shall I swear to Kate, and you to me;
And may our oaths well kept and prosp'rous be! [*Exeunt.*

Enter CHORUS.

Thus far, with rough, and all unable pen,
Our bending[5] author hath pursu'd the story;

1 The slight barrier.

2 A *moral* is the *meaning* or application of a fable.

3 'Yes, my lord, you see them perspectively, the cities turned into a maid.' See note on Twelfth Night, Act v Sc. 1.

4 *Præclarissimus* for *Præcarissimus*. Shakspeare followed Holinshed, in whose Chronicle it stands thus. Indeed all the old historians have the same blunder. In the original treaty of Troyes, printed in Rymer, it is *præcarissimus.*

5 'Our *bending author.*' That is, unequal to the weight of his subject, and *bending* beneath it. Thus Milton, in his Apology for Smectymnus, speaking of Bishop Hall:—'In a strain as pitiful—manifested a presumptuous undertaking with *weak and unexamined shoulders.*'

In little room confining mighty men,
Mangling by starts the full course of their glory.[1]
Small time, but, in that small, most greatly liv'd
This star of England; fortune made his sword;
By which the world's best garden[2] he achiev'd,
And of it left his son imperial lord.
Henry the Sixth, in infant bands crown'd king
Of France and England, did this king succeed;
Whose state so many had the managing,
That they lost France, and made his England bleed:
Which oft our stage hath shown; and, for their sake,
In your fair minds let this acceptance take. [*Exit.*

1 'Mangling by starts the full course of their glory.' That is, by touching only on select parts.

THIS play has many scenes of high dignity, and many of easy merriment. The character of the king is well supported, except in his courtship, where he has neither the vivacity of Hal, nor the grandeur of Henry The humour of Pistol is very happily continued: his character has perhaps been the model of all the bullies that have yet appeared on the English stage.

The lines given to the Chorus have many admirers; but the truth is, that in them a little may be praised, and much must be forgiven; nor can it be easily discovered why the intelligence given by the Chorus is more necessary in this play than in many others where it is omitted. The great defect of this play is the emptiness and narrowness of the last act, which a very little diligence might have easily avoided. JOHNSON.

2 i.e. France. A similar distinction is bestowed on Lombardy in The Taming of The Shrew:—
'The pleasant garden of great Italy?

END OF VOL. I.

www.ingramcontent.com/pod-product-compliance
Lightning Source LLC
LaVergne TN
LVHW021300110826
845150LV00003B/445

* 9 7 8 1 4 2 5 5 6 0 1 1 9 *